OXFORD COMMENTARIES ON INTERNATIONAL LAW

General Editors: Professor Philip Alston Professor of International Law
at New York University, and Professor Laurence Boisson de Chazournes
Professor of International Law at the University of Geneva

The UN Sustainable Development Goals

The UN Sustainable Development Goals

A Commentary

Edited by
ILIAS BANTEKAS
FRANCESCO SEATZU

Assistant Editor
KATERINA AKESTORIDI

OXFORD
UNIVERSITY PRESS

Great Clarendon Street, Oxford, OX2 6DP,
United Kingdom

Oxford University Press is a department of the University of Oxford.
It furthers the University's objective of excellence in research, scholarship,
and education by publishing worldwide. Oxford is a registered trade mark of
Oxford University Press in the UK and in certain other countries

© Ilias Bantekas and Francesco Seatzu 2023

The moral rights of the authors have been asserted

First Edition published in 2023

All rights reserved. No part of this publication may be reproduced, stored in
a retrieval system, or transmitted, in any form or by any means, without the
prior permission in writing of Oxford University Press, or as expressly permitted
by law, by licence or under terms agreed with the appropriate reprographics
rights organization. Enquiries concerning reproduction outside the scope of the
above should be sent to the Rights Department, Oxford University Press, at the
address above

You must not circulate this work in any other form
and you must impose this same condition on any acquirer

Public sector information reproduced under Open Government Licence v3.0
(http://www.nationalarchives.gov.uk/doc/open-government-licence/open-government-licence.htm)

Published in the United States of America by Oxford University Press
198 Madison Avenue, New York, NY 10016, United States of America

British Library Cataloguing in Publication Data

Data available

Library of Congress Control Number: 2023934002

ISBN 978–0–19–288517–3

DOI: 10.1093/law/9780192885173.001.0001

Printed and bound by
CPI Group (UK) Ltd, Croydon, CR0 4YY

Links to third party websites are provided by Oxford in good faith and
for information only. Oxford disclaims any responsibility for the materials
contained in any third party website referenced in this work.

Preface

Although heavily discussed and detailed in countless international legal papers, the individual Sustainable Development Goals (SDGs) have not until now been the object of any international legal commentary. There are several reasons behind this absence, none of which are, however, connected with the existence of a common perception of their irrelevance (or little relevance) in the international legal order. On the contrary, there are more than a few international legal authors who acknowledge and insist on the tremendous importance of the SDGs as a tool for rethinking public international law. Yet in this line of acknowledgment and reasoning it has also been observed that enquiring into the role of public international law for the SDGs brings to the forefront crucial questions such as the capacity of international law to support specific objectives of the SDGs and their correlated targets.

Having said that, it is true that the adoption of the SDGs by the UN General Assembly in September 2015 ranged from jubilation on the part of many to criticism on the part of a few. Citizens, both individually and more often organized in various forms of association, had mounted an unprecedented campaign in favour of a set of global development goals to address challenges currently facing humanity. They obtained very strong support from governments and the United Nations, and had been able to organize themselves into some highly effective groups and coalitions. Individuals and civil society groups and coalitions had significantly contributed to the new global development goals at an early stage. However, as the set of development goals and related 169 targets took more concrete shape, they lost domination of the adoption process in favour of the governments.

For most, the SDGs and related targets and indicators seemed a huge achievement, and one that had been reached in the face of noteworthy obstacles. The key representatives of civil society had mounted a major rear-guard action as the project of replacing the Millennium Development Goals (MDGs; the predecessors of SDGs) appeared to reach fruition with the adoption of the Johannesburg Plan of Implementation (JPOI), a 'blueprint' for implementation of the Rio Declaration and Agenda 21, in early 2002. Gradually, a shared awareness arose in the representatives of civil society and the independent experts that the way the global development goals were framed in the JPOI substantially restated the MDGs, making one wonder what the added value of the JPOI was in development policy apart from the detailed inclusion of environmental issues. This awareness significantly contributed to the prompt restart of the negotiations for a new set of global development goals and to the adoption of the seventeen SDGs in 2015. To most, the outcome of the SDGs retained the essence of the project and contained an array of advanced and meaningful issues. To some, nevertheless, the compromises that had to be reached for their adoption were largely unsuccessful, undermining the concept of sustainable development and the prospects for its realization. This related in particular to the alleged inconsistency and limited enforceability of most of the goals as reflected in the final text of the seventeen SDGs and related targets.

This major commentary analyses the substance of this 'compromise'. It offers an authoritative interpretation of the global development goals that are expressed in the SDGs, set against their drafting history and implementation practice. More than that, it seeks to assess and evaluate the end result in great detail, trying to identify to what extent the seventeen SDGs and their related targets and indexes manage to reflect or set standards relating to sustainable development that are respectful of the needs of all people including and especially of the people living in extreme poverty, while being sufficiently realistic to foster actual enforcement by governments.

Additionally, this commentary seeks to identify the relationship between public international law and the SDGs. To what extent do the SDGs and related targets reflect, or advance, public international law in the current area of sustainable development? As no general, legally binding instrument has yet emerged in this area, the question is whether the SDGs have fostered or developed customary international law. The fact that there is much overlap between the SDGs and human rights and between the SDGs and the Paris Agreement, is quite encouraging in this respect. Still, exploring the existence or otherwise of an international custom in this sector is a distraught task. And, in fact much depends on national implementation practice.

This commentary indicates that the SDGs and their provisions and targets have played an important role in reshaping internal legislation since their adoption. Some of the language of the targets has been replicated directly in domestic legal instruments. In other cases, the more aspirational provisions and targets of the SDGs have at least been a useful campaigning instrument for civil society movements and for individual experts in their interactions with governments. Nevertheless, it is not always evident if this practice reflects an emerging sense of legal duty that might be translated into *opinio iuris ac necessitatis* at the international level or a political compromise. In addition to the national level, at the international level, UN human rights mechanisms have made frequent references to the SDGs and correlated targets.

International courts have also, though more slowly, started to make explicit reference to the SDGs and their targets. At the regional level, this extends in particular to the European Court of Human Rights (ECtHR) and the European Court of Justice (ECJ). At the universal level, some specific issue areas such as climate change, land use, productivity to help end hunger, and the protection of life below water have already been addressed on some occasions, offering a developing jurisprudence on areas of great concern at global level.

The authors would like to express their gratitude to all contributors. This is a gigantic treatise in the mould of encyclopaedias of past times that amassed vast amounts of knowledge. This task would have been unachievable had it not been for the dedication and professionalism of all those who worked tirelessly to bring this book to print. The editors would like to also pay tribute to our original commissioning editors, namely Jack McNichol and Merel Alstein, as well as the series editors of OUP's Treaty

Commentaries series for believing in the value of this project and ultimately rendering it possible. Many of our contributors have received financial and other assistance from their employers to enable them to work in this project. This assistance is acknowledged more specifically elsewhere. The editors on their part would like to thank their respective institutions also for financial and other assistance in the course of this project. Our appreciation goes out to Hamad bin Khalifa University and Qatar Foundation, as well as the University of Cagliari.

The contents of the book are accurate as of 1 January 2022. The editors are happy to receive comments and suggestions from readers.

Contents

List of Contributors	xliii
Table of Cases	li
Table of Legislation	lv
List of Abbreviations	lxxi

Sustainable Development Goals: Their Political and Legal Nature under International Law	1
Ilias Bantekas and Katerina Akestoridi	
I. Introduction	1
II. The Millennium Development Goals	1
A. The Historical and Political Undercurrents of the MDGs	3
B. Neoliberalism and the MDGs	5
C. The Early Role of International Organizations in Development Finance	7
D. The Implications of the MDGs Process for the Development Paradigm	13
III. The Sustainable Development Goals	18
A. A Political History of the SDGs	21
B. The SDGs' Transformative Dimension	27
C. The Legal Nature of the SDGs under International Law	31

1	**SDG 1 'End Poverty in All Its Forms Everywhere'**	37
	Krista Nadakavukaren Schefer	
	I. Introduction	37
	II. *Travaux Préparatoires*	39
	A. Prioritizing Poverty	39
	B. Agenda 2030	42
	III. Commentary on the Goal	43
	A. Why is Poverty Eradication the Primary Sustainable Development Goal?	43
	B. Poverty Reduction as an International Action Item: A Brief History	44
	1. From MDG 1 to SDG 1	48
	2. Setting the Post-2015 Agenda	49
	3. Alterations from MDG 1	50
	4. Agenda 2030	54
	C. Multi-variant Nature of Poverty Reduction	54
	D. Critique of SDG 1	55
	1. A Place for Law	55
	2. Will We Reach the Goal?	59
	IV. Commentaries of Targets	60
	A. Target 1.1 Eradicate Extreme Poverty	60
	1. SDG Indicator 1.1.1	61
	a) Eradicate extreme poverty	61
	2. Sources of Target	61
	3. Statistical/Empirical Analysis	61
	4. COVID-19 Effects	63

5.	Implementation Efforts at the Domestic and International Levels	64
6.	Critique	67

B. Target 1.2 Reduce Poverty by At Least 50 per cent — 69
1. SDG Indicator 1.2.1 — 69
   a) Halve population below national poverty line — 69
2. SDG Indicator 1.2.2 — 69
   a) Population in poverty according to national definitions — 69
3. Sources of Target — 69
4. Statistical/Empirical Analysis — 70
5. Implementation Efforts at the Domestic and International Levels — 72
6. Critique — 74
   a) Proportion — 74
   b) Use of national poverty lines — 75

C. Target 1.3 Implement Nationally Appropriate Social Protection Systems and Measures for All, Including Floors, and by 2030 Achieve Substantial Coverage of the Poor and the Vulnerable — 76
1. SDG Indicator 1.3.1 — 76
   a) Population covered by social protection floors/systems — 76
2. Sources of Target — 77
3. Statistical/Empirical Analysis — 78
4. Implementation Efforts at the Domestic and International Levels — 79
   a) ILO — 80
   b) IMF — 81
   c) UN Addis Ababa Action Agenda — 81
   d) Other actions — 82
5. Critique — 83

D. Target 1.4 Equal Rights to Ownership, Basic Services, Technology, and Economic Resources — 86
1. SDG Indicator 1.4.1 — 86
   a) Access to basic services — 86
2. Indicator 1.4.2 — 86
   a) Secure tenure rights to land — 86
3. Sources of Target — 87
4. Statistical/Empirical Analysis — 89
5. Implementation Efforts at the Domestic and International Levels — 91
6. Critique — 94

E. Target 1.5 Build Resilience to Environmental, Economic, and Social Disasters — 96
1. SDG Indicator 1.5.1 — 96
   a) Deaths and affected persons from natural disasters — 96
2. Indicator 1.5.2 — 96
   a) Direct economic loss from natural disasters — 96
3. Indicator 1.5.3 — 97
   a) Disaster risk reduction strategies — 97
4. Indicator 1.5.4 — 97
   a) Local disaster risk reduction — 97
5. Sources of Target — 97
6. Statistical/Empirical Analysis — 99
7. Implementation Efforts at the Domestic and International Levels — 101
8. Critique — 104

CONTENTS xi

F.	Target 1.a Mobilization of resources to end poverty	105
	1. SDG Indicator 1.a.1	106
	a) Domestic resources to poverty reduction programmes	106
	2. Indicator 1.a.2	106
	a) Government spending on essential services	106
	3. Indicator 1.a.3	106
	a) Inflows directly allocated to poverty reduction programmes	106
	4. Sources of Target	106
	5. Statistical/Empirical Analysis	108
	6. Implementation Efforts at the Domestic and International Levels	110
	7. Critique	112
G.	Target 1.b Create Sound Policy Frameworks at the National, Regional, and International Levels, Based on Pro-Poor and Gender-Sensitive Development Strategies, to Support Accelerated Investment in Poverty Eradication Actions	115
	1. SDG Indicator 1.b.1	115
	a) Proportion of government recurrent and capital spending to sectors that disproportionately benefit women, the poor and vulnerable groups	115
	2. Sources of Target	115
	3. Statistical/Empirical Analysis	116
	4. Implementation Efforts at the Domestic and International Levels	117
	5. Critique	119

2 SDG 2 'End Hunger, Achieve Food Security and Improved Nutrition and Promote Sustainable Agriculture ("Zero Hunger")' 121
Elif Askin

I.	Introduction	121
II.	Framing SDG 2: Development and Definition of Terms and Core Issues	126
III.	*Travaux Préparatoires*	133
	A. OWG: Stocktaking Phase	135
	1. Food Security and Nutrition	136
	2. Sustainable Agriculture	138
	B. OWG: Negotiations and Drafting of the Proposed Sustainable Development Goal 2	140
IV.	Commentary on SDG 2	148
	A. Interlinkages with Other SDGs	148
	B. The Nexus between SDG 2 and International Law	152
	1. SDG 2 and International Human Rights Law, in particular the Right to Food	153
	2. SDG 2 and International Economic Law, in particular Trade and Investment Law	158
	C. The Importance of a Rights-Based Approach to SDG 2: Human Rights Mainstreaming	161
V.	Commentary on the Targets	165
	A. General Remarks	165
	B. SDG 2 Targets and Indicators	168
	1. Target 2.1 By 2030, End hunger and ensure access by all people, in particular the poor and people in vulnerable situations, including infants, to safe, nutritious and sufficient food all year round	168

xii CONTENTS

	a) Source of target	168
	b) Empirical analysis: domestic and international efforts of implementation	169
	c) Critique	171
2.	Target 2.2 By 2030, End all forms of malnutrition, including achieving, by 2025, the internationally agreed targets on stunting and wasting in children under 5 years of age, and address the nutritional needs of adolescent girls, pregnant and lactating women and older persons	172
	a) Source of target	172
	b) Empirical analysis: domestic and international efforts of implementation	172
	c) Critique	174
3.	Target 2.3 By 2030, Double the agricultural productivity and incomes of small-scale food producers, in particular women, indigenous peoples, family farmers, pastoralists and fishers, including through secure and equal access to land, other productive resources and inputs, knowledge, financial services, markets and opportunities for value addition and non-farm employment	175
	a) Source	175
	b) Empirical analysis: domestic and international efforts of implementation	175
	c) Critique	176
4.	Target 2.4 By 2030, Ensure sustainable food production systems and implement resilient agricultural practices that increase productivity and production, that help maintain ecosystems, that strengthen capacity for adaptation to climate change, extreme weather, drought, flooding and other disasters and that progressively improve land and soil quality	177
	a) Source of target	177
	b) Empirical analysis: domestic and international efforts of implementation	177
	c) Critique	179
5.	Target 2.5 By 2020, Maintain the genetic diversity of seeds, cultivated plants and farmed and domesticated animals and their related wild species, including through soundly managed and diversified seed and plant banks at the national, regional and international levels, and promote access to and fair and equitable sharing of benefits arising from the utilization of genetic resources and associated traditional knowledge, as internationally agreed	180
	a) Source of target	180
	b) Empirical analysis: domestic and international efforts of implementation	181
	c) Critique	181
6.	Target 2.a Increase investment, including through enhanced international cooperation, in rural infrastructure, agricultural research and extension services, technology development and plant and livestock gene banks in order to enhance agricultural productive capacity in developing countries, in particular least developed countries	182
	a) Source of target	182

b) Empirical analysis: domestic and international efforts of implementation	182
c) Critique	183
7. Target 2.b Correct and prevent trade restrictions and distortions in world agricultural markets, including through the parallel elimination of all forms of agricultural export subsidies and all export measures with equivalent effect, in accordance with the mandate of the Doha Development Round	184
a) Source of target	184
b) Empirical analysis: domestic and international efforts of implementation	184
c) Critique	185
8. Target 2.c Adopt measures to ensure the proper functioning of food commodity markets and their derivatives and facilitate timely access to market information, including on food reserves, in order to help limit extreme food price volatility	186
a) Source of target	186
b) Empirical analysis: domestic and international efforts of implementation	186
c) Critique	186
VI. Conclusion	187

3 SDG 3 'Good Health and Well-Being—Ensure Healthy Lives and Promote Well-Being for All at All Ages' — 189

Jane A Hofbauer and Christina Binder

I. Introduction	189
II. *Travaux Préparatoires*	193
A. Background	193
B. The OWG Sessions and the Adoption Phase	199
1. The Stocktaking Phase—OWG-4 (17–19 June 2013)	199
2. The Negotiation Phase—OWGs-9–13 (March–July 2014)	204
3. The Intergovernmental Negotiations—Fine-Tuning and Adoption (January–August 2015)	207
III. 'Good Health and Well-Being' in SDG 3	209
A. The Role of the World Health Organization as the Lead Agency in the Achievement of 'Good Health and Well-Being'	209
B. Global Health—A Development Perspective and Human Rights Critique	213
C. Assessment and General Critique	222
IV. Targets and Indicators of Goal 3	224
A. Overview	224
B. Commentary and Critique to Individual Targets	230
1. Target 3.1 By 2030, reduce the global maternal mortality ratio to less than 70 per 100,000 live births	230
a) Sources of target	230
b) Empirical analysis and efforts of international/domestic implementation	231
c) Critique	232
2. Target 3.2 By 2030, end preventable deaths of newborns and children under 5 years of age, with all countries aiming to reduce neonatal	

xiv CONTENTS

mortality to at least as low as 12 per 1,000 live births and under-5
mortality to at least as low as 25 per 1,000 live births — 233
  a) Sources of target — 233
  b) Empirical analysis and efforts of international/domestic
     implementation — 234
  c) Critique — 236
3. Target 3.3 By 2030, end the epidemics of AIDS, tuberculosis, malaria
   and neglected tropical diseases and combat hepatitis, water-borne
   diseases and other communicable diseases — 236
  a) Sources of target — 236
  b) Empirical analysis and efforts of international/domestic
     implementation — 239
  c) Critique — 240
4. Target 3.4 By 2030, reduce by one-third premature mortality from
   non-communicable diseases through prevention and treatment and
   promote mental health and well-being — 241
  a) Sources of target — 241
  b) Empirical analysis and efforts of international/domestic
     implementation — 242
5. Target 3.5 Strengthen the prevention and treatment of substance
   abuse, including narcotic drug abuse and harmful use of alcohol — 244
  a) Sources of target — 244
  b) Empirical analysis — 245
  c) Critique and efforts of international/domestic implementation — 245
6. Target 3.6 By 2020, halve the number of global deaths and injuries
   from road traffic accidents — 246
  a) Sources of target — 246
  b) Empirical analysis — 246
  c) Critique and efforts of international/domestic implementation — 246
7. Target 3.7 By 2030, ensure universal access to sexual and reproductive
   health-care services, including for family planning, information and
   education, and the integration of reproductive health into national
   strategies and programmes — 247
  a) Sources of target — 247
  b) Empirical analysis and efforts of international/domestic
     implementation — 248
  c) Critique — 249
8. Target 3.8 Achieve universal health coverage, including financial
   risk protection, access to quality essential health-care services and
   access to safe, effective, quality and affordable essential medicines and
   vaccines for all — 250
  a) Sources of target — 250
  b) Empirical analysis and efforts of international/domestic
     implementation — 251
  c) Critique — 253
9. Target 3.9 By 2030, substantially reduce the number of deaths and
   illnesses from hazardous chemicals and air, water and soil pollution
   and contamination — 254
  a) Sources of target — 254

b) Empirical analysis and efforts of international/domestic implementation	255
c) Critique	256
10. Target 3.a Strengthen the implementation of the WHO Framework Convention on Tobacco Control in all countries, as appropriate	256
a) Sources of target	256
b) Empirical analysis and efforts of international/domestic implementation	257
c) Critique	258
11. Target 3.b Support the research and development of vaccines and medicines for the communicable and non-communicable diseases that primarily affect developing countries, provide access to affordable essential medicines and vaccines, in accordance with the Doha Declaration on the TRIPS Agreement and Public Health, which affirms the right of developing countries to use to the full the provisions in the agreement on trade related aspects of intellectual property rights regarding flexibilities to protect public health, and, in particular, provide access to medicines for all	258
a) Sources of target	258
b) Empirical analysis	259
c) Critique	261
12. Target 3.c Substantially increase health financing and the recruitment, development, training and retention of the health workforce in developing countries, especially in least developed countries and small island developing states	262
a) Sources of target	262
b) Empirical analysis and efforts of international/domestic implementation	262
c) Critique	263
13. Target 3.d Strengthen the capacity of all countries, in particular developing countries, for early warning, risk reduction and management of national and global health risks	263
a) Sources of target	263
b) Empirical analysis and efforts of international/domestic implementation	263
c) Critique	264
V. Conclusion	265

4 SDG 4 'Ensure Inclusive and Equitable Quality Education and Promote Lifelong Learning Opportunities for All'	267
Jane Kotzmann, Morgan Stonebridge, and John R Morss	
I. Introduction	267
II. *Travaux Préparatoires*	268
A. Background	268
B. The OWG Sessions	271
III. Commentary on Goal	276
A. Inclusive and Equitable Education in SDG 4	276
B. Sources and Linkages with Human Rights	278
1. UDHR	279
2. Core International Human Rights Treaties	281

xvi CONTENTS

	3. Other Core International Human Rights Instruments	282
C.	Development	283
D.	Empirical Evidence	285
E.	Best Practices	290
F.	General Critique	294

IV. Targets and Indicators of Goal 4 — 297
  A. Background — 297
  B. Analysis and Critique of Each Target — 298
    1. Target 4.1 By 2030, ensure that all girls and boys complete free, equitable and quality primary and secondary education leading to relevant and effective learning outcomes — 298
      a) Sources of target — 298
      b) Statistical/empirical analysis — 300
      c) Efforts taken at domestic and international level — 302
      d) Critique — 304
    2. Target 4.2 By 2030, ensure that all girls and boys have access to quality early childhood development, care and pre-primary education so that they are ready for primary education — 305
      a) Sources of target — 305
      b) Statistical/empirical analysis — 307
      c) Efforts taken at a domestic and international level — 310
      d) Critique — 311
    3. Target 4.3 By 2030, ensure equal access for all women and men to affordable and quality technical, vocational and tertiary education, including university — 313
      a) Sources of target — 313
      b) Statistical/empirical analysis — 314
      c) Efforts taken at domestic and international level — 317
      d) Critique — 319
    4. Target 4.4 By 2030, substantially increase the number of youth and adults who have relevant skills, including technical and vocational skills, for employment, decent jobs and entrepreneurship — 321
      a) Sources of target — 321
      b) Statistical/empirical analysis — 322
      c) Efforts taken at domestic and international level — 324
      d) Critique — 326
    5. Target 4.5 By 2030, eliminate gender disparities in education and ensure equal access to all levels of education and vocational training for the vulnerable, including persons with disabilities, Indigenous peoples and children in vulnerable situations — 327
      a) Sources of target — 327
      b) Statistical/empirical analysis — 329
      c) Efforts taken at domestic and international level — 331
      d) Critique — 334
    6. Target 4.6 By 2030, ensure that all youth and a substantial proportion of adults, both men and women, achieve literacy and numeracy — 336
      a) Sources of target — 336
      b) Statistical/empirical analysis — 337
      c) Efforts taken at domestic and international level — 339
      d) Critique — 341

7. Target 4.7 By 2030, ensure that all learners acquire the knowledge and skills needed to promote sustainable development, including, among others, through education for sustainable development and sustainable lifestyles, human rights, gender equality, promotion of a culture of peace and non-violence, global citizenship and appreciation of cultural diversity and of culture's contribution to sustainable development ... 343
    a) Sources of target ... 343
    b) Statistical/empirical analysis ... 344
    c) Efforts taken at domestic and international level ... 347
    d) Critique ... 350
8. Target 4.a Build and upgrade education facilities that are child, disability and gender sensitive and provide safe, non-violent, inclusive and effective learning environments for all ... 352
    a) Source of target ... 352
    b) Statistical/empirical analysis ... 353
    c) Efforts taken at domestic and international level ... 356
    d) Critique ... 357
9. Target 4.b By 2020, substantially expand globally the number of scholarships available to developing countries, in particular least developed countries, small island developing States and African countries, for enrolment in higher education, including vocational training and information and communications technology, technical, engineering and scientific programmes, in developed countries and other developing countries ... 358
    a) Source of target ... 358
    b) Statistical/empirical analysis ... 360
    c) Efforts taken at domestic and international level ... 361
    d) Critique ... 362
10. Target 4.c By 2030, substantially increase the supply of qualified teachers, including through international cooperation for teacher training in developing countries, especially least-developed countries and small island developing States ... 364
    a) Sources of target ... 364
    b) Statistical/empirical analysis ... 365
    c) Efforts taken at domestic and international level ... 366
    d) Critique ... 367

5   SDG 5 'Achieve Gender Equality and Empower All Women and Girls' ... 371
Rangita de Silva de Alwis

  I. Introduction ... 371
  II. *Travaux Préparatoires* ... 372
  III. Commentary on the Goal ... 375
    A. Comparison with MDG ... 375
    B. A Goal-based Approach ... 377
    C. A Mainstream Growth-oriented Approach Rather than Tackling Structural Challenges ... 378
    D. Neglect of a Structural Lens ... 378
    E. Human Rights ... 379
  IV. Targets and Indicators of Goal 5 ... 380

xviii CONTENTS

A. Overview		380
B. Analysis and Critique of Each Target		381
1. Target 5.1 End all forms of discrimination against all women and girls everywhere		381
a) Sources of the target		381
b) Empirical analysis		381
c) Efforts taken at international and national level		385
i) What more needs to be done: some case studies		388
Polygamy		388
Guardianship		389
Husband obedience		389
Bank accounts		390
Customary laws		390
Nationality laws		390
d) Critique		391
2. Target 5.2 Eliminate all forms of violence against all women and girls in the public and private spheres, including trafficking and sexual and other types of exploitation		392
a) Sources of the target		392
b) Empirical analysis		392
c) Efforts taken at international and national level		395
i) A structural response to gender-based violence: the importance of prevention of violence through education		400
d) Critique		402
3. Target 5.3 Eliminate all harmful practices, such as child, early, and forced marriage and female genital mutilation		413
a) Sources of the target		413
b) Empirical analysis		414
c) Efforts taken at international and national level		416
i) What more needs to be done: some case studies		419
d) Critique		420
4. Target 5.4 Recognise and value unpaid care and domestic work through the provision of public services, infrastructure and social protection policies and the promotion of shared responsibility within the household and the family as nationally appropriate		420
a) Sources of the target and empirical analysis		420
b) Efforts taken at international and domestic level		422
i) What more needs to be done: some cases		422
c) Critique		424
5. Target 5.5 Ensure women's full and effective participation and equal opportunities for leadership at all levels of decision-making in political, economic and public life		425
a) Sources of the target		425
b) Empirical analysis		425
i) COVID-19 impact		427
c) Critique		427
i) Political participation		427
6. Target 5.6 Ensure universal access to sexual and reproductive health and reproductive rights as agreed in accordance with the Programme of Action of the International Conference on Population and Development and the Beijing Platform for Action and the outcome documents of their review conferences		428

a) Sources of the target		428
b) Empirical analysis		429

7. Target 5.a Undertake reforms to give women equal rights to economic resources, as well as access to ownership and control over land and other forms of property, financial services, inheritance and natural resources, in accordance with national laws — 431

    a) Sources of the target — 431
    b) Empirical analysis — 431

8. Target 5.b Enhance the use of enabling technology, in particular information and communications technology, to promote the empowerment of women — 434

    a) Sources of the target — 434
    b) Empirical analysis — 434
    c) Critique — 436

9. Target 5.c Adopt and strengthen sound policies and enforceable legislation for the promotion of gender equality and the empowerment of all women and girls at all levels — 436

    a) Sources of the target — 436
    b) Empirical analysis — 436
    c) Critique — 437

Annex/Postscript — 437

Law Reform on Women's Economic Participation — 439

6 SDG 6 'Ensure Availability and Sustainable Management of Water and Sanitation for All' — 441

Owen McIntyre

  I. Introduction — 441

  II. Background — 447

    A. *Travaux Préparatoires* — 449

  III. Targets and Indicators of Goal 6 — 453

    A. Overview — 453

    B. Analysis and Critique of Each Target — 453

      1. Target 6.1 By 2030, achieve universal and equitable access to safe and affordable drinking water for all — 453

      2. Target 6.2 By 2030, achieve access to adequate equitable sanitation and hygiene for all and end open defecation, paying special attention to the needs of women and girls and those in vulnerable situations — 462

      3. Target 6.3 By 2030, improve water quality by reducing pollution, eliminating dumping and minimizing release of hazardous chemicals and materials, halving the proportion of untreated wastewater and substantially increasing recycling and safe use globally — 469

      4. Target 6.4 By 2030, substantially increase water-use efficiency across all sectors and ensure sustainable withdrawals and supply of freshwater to address water scarcity and substantially reduce the number of people suffering from water scarcity — 472

        a) Water efficiency — 472
        b) Water scarcity — 475

      5. Target 6.5 By 2030, implement integrated water resources management at all levels, including through transboundary cooperation as appropriate — 478

xx CONTENTS

	a) Integrated water resources management	478
	b) Transboundary cooperation	482
6.	Target 6.6 By 2020, protect and restore water-related ecosystems, including mountains, forests, wetlands, rivers, aquifers and lakes	486
7.	Target 6.a By 2030, expand international cooperation and capacity-building support to developing countries in water- and sanitation-related activities and programmes, including water harvesting, desalination, water efficiency, wastewater treatment, recycling and reuse technologies	492
8.	Target 6.b Support and strengthen the participation of local communities in improving water and sanitation management	495

IV. Monitoring and Implementation — 502
V. Conclusion — 507

7 SDG 7 'Ensure Access to Affordable, Reliable, Sustainable and Modern Energy for All' — 509
Francesco Seatzu and Katerina Akestoridi

I. Introduction — 509
II. *Travaux Préparatoires* — 510
  A. A Stand-alone or a Cross-cutting Target? — 512
III. Commentary on the Goal — 517
  A. 'Sustainable' Interpretation and Application of the Guiding Principles of International Energy Law and Policy — 518
  B. The Further Development of a Human Rights Approach to International Energy Law and Policy — 522
  C. The Increase of Energy-Efficient Technologies in the Management of Clean Energy — 523
IV. Commentary on Targets — 525
  A. Target 7.1 By 2030, ensure universal access to affordable, reliable and modern energy for all — 525
    1. Sources of the Target — 525
    2. Empirical Analysis — 527
      a) Indicator 7.1.1: Proportion of population with electricity access — 527
      b) Indicator 7.1.2: Proportion of population with primary reliance on clean fuels and technology — 529
    3. Implementation Efforts at International/Domestic Level — 530
    4. Critique — 531
  B. Target 7.2 By 2030, increase substantially the share of renewable energy in the global energy mix — 533
    1. Sources of the Target — 533
    2. Empirical Analysis — 535
    3. Implementation Efforts at International/Domestic Level — 536
    4. Critique — 538
  C. Target 7.3 Double the global rate of improvement in energy efficiency by 2030 — 539
    1. Sources of Target — 539
    2. Empirical Analysis and Implementation Efforts at International/Domestic Level — 540
    3. Critique — 541

D. Target 7.a By 2030, enhance international cooperation to facilitate access to clean energy research and technology, including renewable energy, energy efficiency and advanced and cleaner fossil-fuel technology, and promote investments in energy infrastructure and clean energy technology 541
   1. Sources of Target 541
   2. Empirical Analysis and Implementation Efforts at the International/Domestic Level 542
   3. Critique 543
E. Target 7.b By 2030, expand infrastructure and upgrade technology for supplying modern and sustainable energy services for all in developing countries, in particular least developed countries, small island developing States and landlocked developing countries, in accordance with their respective programmes of support 543
   1. Source of Target 543
   2. Empirical Analysis and Implementation Efforts at the International/Domestic Level 544
   3. Critique 544

8 SDG 8 'Promote Sustained, Inclusive and Sustainable Economic Growth, Full and Productive Employment and Decent Work for All' 545
Francesco Seatzu and Katerina Akestoridi

  I. Introduction 545
  II. *Travaux Préparatoires* 548
   A. Background 548
   B. The OWG Sessions 552
    1. The Stocktaking Phase 552
     a) OWG-4 (17–19 June 2013) 555
     b) OWG-5 (25–27 November 2013) 559
    2. The Negotiation Phase 562
     a) OWGs-9–13 (March–July 2014) 562
  III. Goal Commentary 569
   A. Inclusive and Sustainable Economic Growth in SDG 8 569
    1. The Neoliberal Connotation of Growth and Its Contradiction with Human Development and Environmental Sustainability 569
   B. The Role of the World Bank in the Achievement of SDG 8 573
   C. Full and Productive Employment and Decent Work for All 574
    1. The Human Right to Decent Work 575
    2. The ILO's Decent Work Agenda 579
  IV. Targets and Indicators of Goal 8 582
   A. Overview 582
   B. Analysis and Critique of Each Target 584
    1. Target 8.1 Sustain per capita economic growth in accordance with national circumstances and, in particular, at least 7 per cent gross domestic product growth per annum in the least developed countries 584
     a) Sources of the target and empirical analysis 584
     b) Implementation efforts at the international/domestic level 585
     c) Critique 585
    2. Target 8.2 Achieve higher levels of economic productivity through diversification, technological upgrading and innovation, including through a focus on high-value added and labour-intensive sectors 585

a) Sources of the target and its critique	585
b) Empirical analysis	587
c) Implementation efforts at the international and domestic level	587

3. Target 8.3 Promote development-oriented policies that support productive activities, decent job creation, entrepreneurship, creativity and innovation, and encourage the formalization and growth of micro-, small- and medium-sized enterprises, including through access to financial services — 587

a) Sources of the target and its critique	587
b) Empirical analysis	588
c) Implementation efforts at the international and domestic levels	588

4. Target 8.4 Improve progressively, through 2030, global resource efficiency in consumption and production and endeavour to decouple economic growth from environmental degradation, in accordance with the 10-Year Framework of Programmes on Sustainable Consumption and Production, with developed countries taking the lead — 588

a) Sources of the target and its critique	588
b) Empirical analysis and implementation efforts at the international and domestic levels	589

5. Target 8.5 By 2030, achieve full and productive employment and decent work for all women and men, including for young people and persons with disabilities, and equal pay for work of equal value — 590

a) Sources of the target	590
b) Empirical analysis and a critique of the effectiveness of indicators	591
c) Implementation efforts at the international and domestic levels	595
d) Critique	597

6. Target 8.6 By 2020, substantially reduce the proportion of youth not in employment, education or training — 598

a) Sources of the target and empirical analysis	598
b) Implementation efforts at the international and domestic levels	599
c) Critique	600

7. Target 8.7 Take immediate and effective measures to eradicate forced labour, end modern slavery and human trafficking and secure the prohibition and elimination of the worst forms of child labour, including recruitment and use of child soldiers, and by 2025 end child labour in all its forms — 600

a) Sources of the target	600
i) Slavery, servitude, forced and compulsory labour as grave forms of exploitation	601
ii) Economic exploitation of children	605
iii) Child labour at the intersection of labour and human rights law	606
b) Empirical analysis, countries' implementation efforts, and critique	609

8. Target 8.8 Protect labour rights and promote safe and secure working environments for all workers, including migrant workers, in particular women migrants, and those in precarious employment — 611

a) Sources of the target and empirical analysis	611
i) Indicator 8.8.1	611
Indicator 8.8.1: implementation efforts at the international and domestic levels	613

ii) Indicator 8.8.2 614
b) Critique 616
9. Target 8.9 By 2030, devise and implement policies to promote sustainable tourism that creates jobs and promotes local culture and products 616
a) Sources of the target 616
b) Empirical analysis and implementation efforts at international and domestic levels 622
c) Critique 625
10. Target 8.10 Strengthen the capacity of domestic financial institutions to encourage and expand access to banking, insurance and financial services for all 626
a) Sources of the target and its critique 626
b) Empirical analysis and implementation efforts at the international and domestic levels 627
11. Target 8.a Increase Aid for Trade support for developing countries, in particular least developed countries, including through the Enhanced Integrated Framework for Trade related Technical Assistance to Least Developed Countries 627
a) Sources of the target, empirical analysis, and critique 627
12. Target 8.b By 2020, develop and operationalize a global strategy for youth employment and implement the Global Jobs Pact of the International Labour Organization 628
a) Sources of the target 628
b) Empirical analysis and implementation efforts at the international and domestic levels 630
c) Critique 631
V. Conclusion 631

9 SDG 9 'Build Resilient Infrastructure, Promote Inclusive and Sustainable Industrialization, and Foster Innovation' 633
P Sean Morris
I. Introduction 633
II. Goal Commentary: Framing and Negotiating Industry, Innovation and Infrastructure 639
A. Towards a Revitalized Vision of Global Sustainable Development 640
B. State-led Actors and the Open Working Group (OWG) Sessions 643
C. Non-state Actors or 'Major Groups' 658
1. International Non-governmental Organizations (INGOs) and Intergovernmental Organizations (IGOs) 664
2. Transnational Corporations 667
3. Civil Society (NGOs) 671
4. Actors and Narratives—An Assessment 673
III. Target Commentary: Targets and Indicators of Industry, Innovation, and Infrastructure 676
A. Introducing SDG 9: Industry, Innovation, and Infrastructure 676
B. A Long-term View of Individual Targets 678
C. Custodians and Tier Classifications 679
D. Assessment of Individual Targets 681
E. The Individual Targets and Their Legal Characteristics 683

xxiv CONTENTS

1. Target 9.1 Develop quality, reliable, sustainable and resilient infrastructure, including regional and trans-border infrastructure, to support economic development and human well-being, with a focus on affordable and equitable access for all ... 685
2. Target 9.2 Promote inclusive and sustainable industrialization, and by 2030 raise significantly industry's share of employment and GDP in line with national circumstances, and double its share in the LDCs ... 687
3. Target 9.3 Increase the access of small-scale industrial and other enterprises, particularly in developing countries, to financial services including affordable credit and their integration into value chains and markets ... 690
4. Target 9.4 By 2030, upgrade infrastructure and retrofit industries to make them sustainable, with increased resource use efficiency and greater adoption of clean and environmentally sound technologies and industrial processes, all countries taking in accordance with their respective capabilities ... 691
5. Target 9.5 Enhance scientific research, upgrade the technological capabilities of industrial sectors in all countries, particularly developing countries, including by 2030 encouraging innovation and increasing the number of R&D workers per one million people by x% and public and private R&D spending ... 693
6. Target 9.a Facilitate sustainable and resilient infrastructure development in developing countries through enhanced financial, technological and technical support to African countries, LDCs, LLDCs and SIDS ... 695
7. Target 9.b Support domestic technology development, research and innovation in developing countries including ensuring a conducive policy environment for inter alia industrial diversification and value addition to commodities ... 697
8. Target 9.c Significantly increase access to ICT and strive to provide universal and affordable access to internet in LDCs by 2020 ... 698
9. SDG 9 Legal Relations ... 700
   IV. Empirical Results: Sample Study on Vaccines and Technological Innovation: Law, Intellectual Property, and Sustainable Development ... 702
   V. Critique, Findings, and Outlook ... 705

10 SDG 10 'Reduce Inequality Within and Among Countries' ... 711
   Johanna Aleria P Lorenzo
   I. Introduction ... 711
   A. Cognate Concepts ... 713
   B. Inequality of Opportunities versus Inequality of Outcomes ... 715
   C. Horizontal versus Vertical Inequalities ... 717
   D. Intersecting Dimensions ... 718
   E. Intrinsic and Instrumental Values ... 719
   II. *Travaux Préparatoires* ... 720
   A. OWG: Stocktaking Phase ... 720
   B. OWG: Negotiations and Drafting of Proposed Sustainable Development Goals ... 723
   C. HLP Report ... 727
   III. Commentary on the Goal ... 729

A. Inequality and International Law	734
B. Human Rights and Labour Rights	737
C. Trade, Investment, Aid	740
D. Inequality, Interlinkages, and Sustainable Development	742
IV. Commentary on the Targets	743
A. Omitted Targets	744
B. Duplicated Targets	744
C. Transferred Targets	745
D. The Current Targets	746
1. Target 10.1 By 2030, progressively achieve and sustain income growth of the bottom 40% of the population at a rate higher than the national average	746
a) Source of target	746
b) Empirical analysis: domestic and international efforts	748
c) Critique	750
2. Target 10.2 By 2030, empower and promote the social, economic and political inclusion of all, irrespective of age, sex, disability, race, ethnicity, origin, religion or economic or other status	753
a) Source of target	753
b) Empirical analysis: domestic and international efforts	754
c) Critique	755
3. Target 10.3 Ensure equal opportunity and reduce inequalities of outcome, including by eliminating discriminatory laws, policies and practices and promoting appropriate legislation, policies and actions in this regard	757
a) Source of target	757
b) Empirical analysis: domestic and international efforts	757
c) Critique	759
4. Target 10.4 Adopt policies, especially fiscal, wage and social protection policies, and progressively achieve greater equality	761
a) Source of target	761
b) Empirical analysis: domestic and international efforts	762
c) Critique	764
5. Target 10.5 Improve the regulation and monitoring of global financial markets and institutions and strengthen the implementation of such regulations	767
a) Source of target	767
b) Empirical analysis: domestic and international efforts	768
c) Critique	769
6. Target 10.6 Ensure enhanced representation and voice for developing countries in decision-making in global international economic and financial institutions in order to deliver more effective, credible, accountable and legitimate institutions	771
a) Source of target	771
b) Empirical analysis: domestic and international efforts	771
c) Critique	773
7. Target 10.7 Facilitate orderly, safe, regular and responsible migration and mobility of people, including through the implementation of planned and well-managed migration policies	775
a) Source of target	775
b) Empirical analysis: domestic and international efforts	775

xxvi CONTENTS

c) Critique	776
8. Target 10.a Implement the principle of special and differential treatment for developing countries, in particular least developed countries, in accordance with World Trade Organization agreements	779
a) Source of target	779
b) Empirical analysis: domestic and international efforts	780
c) Critique	781
9. Target 10.b Encourage official development assistance and financial flows, including foreign direct investment, to States where the need is greatest, in particular least developed countries, African countries, small island developing States and landlocked developing countries, in accordance with their national plans and programmes	785
a) Source of target	785
b) Empirical analysis: domestic and international efforts	786
c) Critique	787
10. Target 10.c By 2030, reduce to less than 3 per cent the transaction costs of migrant remittances and eliminate remittance corridors with costs higher than 5 per cent	791
a) Source of target	791
b) Empirical analysis: domestic and international efforts	792
c) Critique	793
E. Final Observations on Targets, Indicators, and Data	794
V. Conclusion	795

11 SDG 11 'Make Cities and Human Settlements Inclusive, Safe, Resilient, and Sustainable'
Hannah Birkenkötter

	799
I. Introduction	799
II. *Travaux Préparatoires*	801
A. The UN-Habitat Agenda: From Vancouver to Istanbul and Beyond	802
B. SDG 11 in the Negotiations of the 2030 Agenda for Sustainable Development	807
III. Commentary on the Goal	809
A. Cities and Urbanization in the 2030 Agenda and the New Urban Agenda and Linkages to Other SDGs	811
B. Cities as Subjects of International Law and Their Relationship with International Organizations	814
C. SDG 11 and International Human Rights	818
D. SDG 11 and Other International Instruments: UNESCO, Sendai Framework, and Environmental Standards, Including Climate Change	820
IV. Commentaries on Targets and Indicators	823
A. Target 11.1 By 2030, ensure access for all to adequate, safe and affordable housing and basic services and upgrade slums	824
1. Sources of Target	824
2. Empirical Analysis	826
3. Implementation Efforts Taken at Domestic and International Level	827
4. Critique	828
B. Target 11.2 By 2030, provide access to safe, affordable, accessible and sustainable transport systems for all, improving road safety, notably by expanding public transport, with special attention to the needs of those	

CONTENTS xxvii

in vulnerable situations, women, children, persons with disabilities and
older persons ... 829
1. Sources of Target ... 829
2. Empirical Analysis ... 831
3. Implementation Efforts Taken at Domestic and International Level ... 831
4. Critique ... 833
C. Target 11.3 By 2030, enhance inclusive and sustainable urbanization and
capacity for participatory, integrated and sustainable human settlement
planning and management in all countries ... 834
1. Sources of Target ... 834
2. Empirical Analysis ... 835
3. Implementation Efforts Taken at Domestic and International Level ... 836
4. Critique ... 836
D. Target 11.4 Strengthen efforts to protect and safeguard the world's
cultural and natural heritage ... 837
1. Sources of Target ... 837
2. Empirical Analysis ... 838
3. Implementation Efforts Taken at Domestic and International Level ... 839
4. Critique ... 839
E. Target 11.5 By 2030, significantly reduce the number of deaths and the
number of people affected and substantially decrease the direct economic
losses relative to global gross domestic product caused by disasters,
including water-related disasters, with a focus on protecting the poor and
people in vulnerable situations ... 840
1. Sources of Target ... 840
2. Empirical Analysis ... 842
3. Implementation Efforts Taken at Domestic and International Level ... 843
4. Critique ... 844
F. Target 11.6 By 2030, reduce the adverse per capita environmental impact
of cities, including by paying special attention to air quality and municipal
and other waste management ... 844
1. Sources of Target ... 844
2. Empirical Analysis ... 846
3. Implementation Efforts Taken at Domestic and International Level ... 846
4. Critique ... 848
G. Target 11.7 By 2030, provide universal access to safe, inclusive and
accessible, green and public spaces, in particular for women and children,
older persons and persons with disabilities ... 848
1. Sources of Target ... 848
2. Empirical Analysis ... 850
3. Implementation Efforts Taken at Domestic and International Level ... 850
4. Critique ... 851
H. Target 11.a Support positive economic, social and environmental links
between urban, peri-urban and rural areas by strengthening national and
regional development planning ... 852
1. Sources of Target ... 852
2. Empirical Analysis ... 852
3. Implementation Efforts Taken at Domestic and International Level ... 853
4. Critique ... 853

xxviii CONTENTS

I. Target 11.b By 2020, substantially increase the number of cities and human settlements adopting and implementing integrated policies and plans towards inclusion, resource efficiency, mitigation and adaptation to climate change, resilience to disasters, and develop and implement, in line with the Sendai Framework for Disaster Risk Reduction 2015–2030, holistic disaster risk management at all levels — 854
    1. Sources of Target — 854
    2. Empirical Analysis — 854
    3. Implementation Efforts Taken at Domestic and International Level — 855
    4. Critique — 855

J. Target 11.c Support least developed countries, including through financial and technical assistance, in building sustainable and resilient buildings utilizing local materials — 856
    1. Sources of Target — 856
    2. Empirical Analysis — 856
    3. Implementation Efforts Taken at Domestic and International Level — 856
    4. Critique — 856

12 SDG 12 'Ensure Sustainable Consumption and Production Patterns' — 859
Kateřina Mitkidis and Adriana Šefčíková

I. Introduction — 859
II. *Travaux Préparatoires* — 861
  A. Contested Issues During the Negotiations — 861
    1. A Stand-alone versus an Integrated Goal — 861
    2. The CBDR Principle — 863
III. Commentary — 864
  A. Content, Structure, and Language of SDG 12 — 864
  B. SDG 12 and International Law — 865
  C. Challenges to Effective Regulation: Variety of Stakeholders and Covered Topics — 868
  D. Regional Differences — 870
  E. Critique — 871
  F. Commentary to Individual Targets — 872
    1. Target 12.1 Implement the 10-year framework of programmes on sustainable consumption and production, all countries taking action, with developed countries taking the lead, taking into account the development and capabilities of developing countries — 872
      a) Sources of target — 872
      b) Empirical analysis — 873
      c) Implementation efforts at domestic/international level — 874
      d) Critique — 876
    2. Target 12.2 By 2030, achieve the sustainable management and efficient use of natural resources — 877
      a) Sources of target — 877
      b) Empirical analysis — 878
      c) Implementation efforts at domestic/international level — 879
      d) Critique — 882
    3. Target 12.3 By the end of 2030, halve per capita global food waste at the retail and consumer levels and reduce food losses along production and supply chains, including post-harvest losses — 883

	a) Sources of target	883
	b) Empirical analysis	885
	c) Implementation efforts at domestic/international level	886
	d) Critique	890
4.	Target 12.4 By 2020, achieve the environmentally sound management of chemicals and all wastes throughout their life cycle, in accordance with agreed international frameworks, and significantly reduce their release to air, water and soil in order to minimize their adverse impacts on human health and the environment	891
	a) Sources of target and empirical analysis	891
	b) Implementation efforts at domestic/international level	892
	c) Critique	897
5.	Target 12.5 By 2030, substantially reduce waste generation through prevention, reduction, recycling and reuse	899
	a) Sources of target	899
	b) Empirical analysis	902
	c) Implementation efforts at domestic/international level	903
	d) Critique	905
6.	Target 12.6 Encourage companies, especially large and transnational companies, to adopt sustainable practices and to integrate sustainability information into their reporting cycle	905
	a) Sources of target	905
	b) Empirical analysis	908
	c) Implementation efforts at domestic/international level	909
	d) Critique	911
7.	Target 12.7 Promote public procurement practices that are sustainable, in accordance with national policies and priorities	912
	a) Sources of target	912
	b) Empirical analysis	914
	c) Implementation efforts at domestic/international level	916
	d) Critique	920
8.	Target 12.8 By 2030, ensure that people everywhere have the relevant information and awareness for sustainable development and lifestyles in harmony with nature	921
	a) Sources of target	921
	b) Empirical analysis	923
	c) Implementation efforts at domestic/international level	925
	d) Critique	927
9.	Target 12.a Support developing countries to strengthen their scientific and technological capacity to move towards more sustainable patterns of consumption and production	928
	a) Sources of target	928
	b) Empirical analysis	930
	c) Implementation efforts at domestic/international level	932
	d) Critique	932
10.	Target 12.b Develop and implement tools to monitor sustainable development impacts for sustainable tourism that creates jobs and promotes local culture and products	933
	a) Sources of target	933
	b) Empirical analysis	936

c) Implementation efforts at domestic/international level	937
d) Critique	940

11. Target 12.c Rationalize inefficient fossil-fuel subsidies that encourage wasteful consumption by removing market distortions, in accordance with national circumstances, including by restructuring taxation and phasing out those harmful subsidies, where they exist, to reflect their environmental impacts, taking fully into account the specific needs and conditions of developing countries and minimizing the possible adverse impacts on their development in a manner that protects the poor and the affected communities — 940

a) Sources of target	940
b) Empirical analysis	942
c) Implementation efforts at domestic/international level	944
d) Critique	946

13 SDG 13 'Take Urgent Action to Combat Climate Change and Its Impacts' 949
Francesca Romanin Jacur

I. Introduction	949
II. *Travaux Préparatoires*	950
A. Background	950
B. OWG-7	951
C. OWG-10	954
D. OWG-11	955
E. OWG-13	955
III. Principles of International Law and Climate Change	958
A. Equity and Differentiation: The Principle of Common but Differentiated Responsibilities and Respective Capabilities (CBDR-RC)	959
IV. The Multilateral Climate Change Regime	961
A. The UN Framework Convention on Climate Change (UNFCCC)	961
B. The Kyoto Protocol	962
C. The Paris Agreement	966
D. The Implementation of the Paris Agreement by the Subsequent Conferences of the Parties: From Katowice to Glasgow	968
V. Tackling Climate Change Across Other Fields of International Law	970
A. Climate Change and Human Rights	970
1. The Inter-American Court of Human Rights	971
B. International Trade Law and Climate Change: Conflicts and Synergies	972
1. Cap and Trade Schemes	976
2. Carbon Taxes	979
C. International Investment Law and Climate Change: Towards Convergence	982
D. Climate Change in the Jurisprudence of International and National Courts	988
1. The International Court of Justice	988
2. The East African Court of Justice	989
VI. Targets and Indicators of Goal 13	989
A. Overview	989
B. Target 13.1 Strengthen resilience and adaptive capacity to climate-related hazards and natural disasters in all countries	990
1. Sources of the Target	990
2. Implementation Efforts and Critique	991
3. Empirical Analysis	992

C. Target 13.2 Integrate climate change measures into national policies,
strategies and planning 994
  1. Sources of the Target and Implementation Efforts 994
    a) Environmental and climate impact assessment 994
    b) Good regulatory practices 998
  2. Empirical Analysis 999
  3. Critique 1000
D. Target 13.3 Improve education, awareness-raising and human and
institutional capacity on climate change mitigation, adaptation, impact
reduction and early warning 1000
  1. Sources of the Target and Implementation Efforts 1000
    a) Climate litigation before domestic courts 1002
  2. Empirical Analysis 1005
  3. Critique 1005
E. Target 13.a Implement the commitment undertaken by developed-
country parties to the United Nations Framework Convention on Climate
Change to a goal of mobilizing jointly $100 billion annually by 2020 from
all sources to address the needs of developing countries in the context of
meaningful mitigation actions and transparency on implementation and
fully operationalize the Green Climate Fund through its capitalization as
soon as possible 1006
  1. Sources of the Target and Implementation Efforts 1006
  2. Empirical Analysis 1010
    a) 13.a.1 Amounts provided and mobilized in United States
dollars per year in relation to the continued existing collective
mobilization goal of the $100 billion commitment through to 2025 1010
  3. Critique 1010
F. Target 13.b Promote mechanisms for raising capacity for effective climate
change-related planning and management in least developed countries
and small island developing States, including focusing on women, youth
and local and marginalized communities 1011
  1. Sources of the Target and Implementation Efforts 1011
  2. Empirical Analysis 1013
  3. Critique 1013
VII. Final Remarks 1013

14 SDG 14 'Conserve and Sustainably Use the Oceans, Seas, and Marine Resources for Sustainable Development' 1015
Eirini-Erasmia Fasia and Christos Kypraios
I. Introduction 1015
II. *Travaux Préparatoires* 1019
  A. Background 1019
  B. The Open Working Group Sessions (OWG) 1020
    1. The Stocktaking Phase (March 2013–February 2014) 1020
    2. The Negotiation Phase (March 2014–July 2014) 1023
III. Goal Commentary 1026
  A. Conservation and Sustainable Use in SDG 14 1026
  B. Balancing between Conservation and Use 1027
  C. Framework Governing the Oceans 1029
    1. Law of the Sea and Sustainability: An Overview 1030

2.	Functional Approach and Cooperation in Ocean Governance	1034
3.	Conservation and Management of Marine Living Resources	1038
	a) Territorial Sea and EEZ	1038
	b) High seas	1039
4.	Protection and Preservation of the Marine Environment	1041
5.	Monitoring and Enforcement Challenges	1042

IV. Human Rights and Goal 14 — 1046
V. Targets and Indicators of Goal 14 — 1048
   A. Overview — 1048
   B. Analysis and Critique of Each Target — 1050

1. Target 14.1 By 2025, prevent and significantly reduce marine pollution of all kinds, in particular from land-based activities, including marine debris and nutrient pollution — 1050
   a) Source of target — 1050
   b) Empirical analysis — 1051
   c) Implementation efforts at domestic/international level — 1052
   d) Critique — 1052

2. Target 14.2 By 2020, sustainably manage and protect marine and coastal ecosystems to avoid significant adverse impacts, including by strengthening their resilience, and take action for their restoration in order to achieve healthy and productive oceans — 1053
   a) Source of target — 1053
   b) Empirical analysis — 1055
   c) Critique — 1055

3. Target 14.3 Minimize and address the impacts of ocean acidification, including through enhanced scientific cooperation at all levels. — 1057
   a) Source of target — 1057
   b) Empirical analysis — 1057
   c) Implementation efforts at international/domestic level — 1058
   d) Critique — 1058

4. Target 14.4 By 2020, effectively regulate harvesting and end overfishing, illegal, unreported and unregulated fishing and destructive fishing practices and implement science-based management plans, in order to restore fish stocks in the shortest time feasible, at least to levels that can produce maximum sustainable yield as determined by their biological characteristics — 1059
   a) Sources of target — 1059
   b) Empirical analysis — 1059
   c) Implementation efforts at domestic/international level — 1059
   d) Critique — 1061

5. Target 14.5 By 2020, conserve at least 10 per cent of coastal and marine areas, consistent with national and international law and based on the best available scientific information — 1062
   a) Sources of target — 1062
   b) Empirical analysis — 1062
   c) Implementation efforts at domestic/international level — 1062
   d) Critique — 1063

6. Target 14.6 By 2020, prohibit certain forms of fisheries subsidies which contribute to overcapacity and overfishing, eliminate subsidies that contribute to illegal, unreported and unregulated fishing and refrain from introducing new such subsidies, recognizing that

appropriate and effective special and differential treatment for
developing and least developed countries should be an integral part of
the World Trade Organization fisheries subsidies negotiation 1063
a) Sources of target 1063
b) Empirical analysis 1064
c) Implementation efforts at domestic/international level 1064
d) Critique 1070
7. Target 14.7 By 2030, increase the economic benefits to Small Island
developing States and least developed countries from the sustainable
use of marine resources, including through sustainable management
of fisheries, aquaculture and tourism 1071
a) Sources of target 1071
b) Empirical analysis 1071
c) Implementation efforts at domestic/international level 1071
d) Critique 1071
8. Target 14.a Increase scientific knowledge, develop research
capacity and transfer marine technology, taking into account
the Intergovernmental Oceanographic Commission Criteria
and Guidelines on the Transfer of Marine Technology, in order
to improve ocean health and to enhance the contribution of
marine biodiversity to the development of developing countries,
in particular small island developing States and least developed
countries 1072
a) Sources of target 1072
b) Empirical analysis 1072
c) Implementation efforts at domestic/international level 1072
d) Critique 1073
9. Target 14.b Provide access for small-scale artisanal fishers to marine
resources and markets 1073
a) Sources of target 1073
b) Empirical analysis 1074
c) Critique 1074
10. Target 14.c Enhance the conservation and sustainable use of oceans
and their resources by implementing international law as reflected in
UNCLOS, which provides the legal framework for the conservation
and sustainable use of oceans and their resources, as recalled in
paragraph 158 of The Future We Want 1074
a) Sources of target 1074
b) Empirical analysis 1074
c) Critique 1074

15 SDG 15 'Protect, Restore and Promote Sustainable Use of Terrestrial
Ecosystems, Sustainably Manage Forests, Combat Desertification,
and Halt and Reverse Land Degradation and Halt Biodiversity Loss' 1077
Frederic Perron-Welch, Jorge Cabrera Medaglia, Dario Piselli,
Alexandra Goodman, and Aleksandra Spasevski
I. *Travaux Préparatoires* 1077
A. The OECD International Development Targets 1077
B. The UN Millennium Declaration, Millennium Development Goals, and
2010 Biodiversity Target 1078
C. The 2005 UN World Summit 1079

xxxiv CONTENTS

D. The Global Objectives on Forests and Non-Legally Binding Instrument
on All Types of Forests 1080
E. The Strategic Plan for Biodiversity 2011–2020 and UN Decade on
Biodiversity 1081
F. The UN Conference on Sustainable Development (Rio + 20) and Group
of 20 (G20) Los Cabos Summit 1081
G. Development of the Post-2015 UN Development Framework 1083
H. Negotiation of SDG Goal 15 1083

II. Commentary on Goal 15 1085
A. Sources 1085
B. Developmental Analysis 1089
C. Best Practices 1092
D. Critique 1094

III. Commentaries on Targets 1098
A. Target 15.1 By 2020, ensure the conservation, restoration and sustainable
use of terrestrial and inland freshwater ecosystems and their services,
in particular forests, wetlands, mountains and drylands, in line with
obligations under international agreements 1098
1. Source of Target 1098
2. Empirical Analysis 1100
3. Efforts at the International and Domestic Levels 1102
4. Critique 1105
B. Target 15.a Mobilize and significantly increase financial resources from
all sources to conserve and sustainably use biodiversity and ecosystems 1107
C. Target 15.2 By 2020, promote the implementation of sustainable
management of all types of forests, halt deforestation, restore degraded
forests and substantially increase afforestation and reforestation globally 1109
1. Sources of Target 1109
2. Empirical Analysis 1110
3. Efforts at the Domestic and International Levels 1111
4. Critique 1111
D. Target 15.b Mobilize significant resources from all sources and at all
levels to finance sustainable forest management and provide adequate
incentives to developing countries to advance such management,
including for conservation and reforestation 1113
E. Target 15.3 By 2030, combat desertification, restore degraded land and
soil, including land affected by desertification, drought and floods, and
strive to achieve a land degradation-neutral world 1113
1. Sources of Target 1113
2. Empirical Analysis 1115
3. Efforts at the Domestic and International Levels 1116
4. Critique 1117
F. Target 15.4 By 2030, ensure the conservation of mountain ecosystems,
including their biodiversity, in order to enhance their capacity to provide
benefits that are essential for sustainable development 1118
1. Sources of Target 1118
2. Empirical Analysis 1119
3. Efforts at the Domestic and International Levels 1121
4. Critique 1122

G. Target 15.5 Take urgent and significant action to reduce the degradation of natural habitats, halt the loss of biodiversity and, by 2020, protect and prevent the extinction of threatened species 1124
1. Sources of Target 1124
2. Empirical Analysis 1125
3. Efforts at the Domestic and International Levels 1127
4. Critique 1129
H. Target 15.6 Promote fair and equitable sharing of the benefits arising from the utilization of genetic resources and promote appropriate access to such resources, as internationally agreed 1130
1. Sources of Target 1131
2. Empirical Analysis 1137
3. Efforts at the Domestic and International Levels 1138
4. Critique 1141
I. Target 15.7 Take urgent action to end poaching and trafficking of protected species of flora and fauna and address both demand and supply of illegal wildlife products 1142
1. Sources of Target 1142
2. Empirical Analysis 1143
3. Efforts at the Domestic and International Levels 1144
4. Critique 1145
J. Target 15.8 By 2020, introduce measures to prevent the introduction and significantly reduce the impact of invasive alien species on land and water ecosystems and control or eradicate the priority species 1146
1. Sources of Target 1147
2. Empirical Analysis 1147
3. Efforts at the Domestic and International Levels 1148
4. Critique 1149
K. Target 15.9 By 2020, integrate ecosystem and biodiversity values into national and local planning, development processes, poverty reduction strategies and accounts 1149
1. Sources of Target 1150
2. Empirical Analysis 1151
3. Efforts at the Domestic and International Levels 1152
4. Critique 1154

16 SDG 16 'Promote Peaceful and Inclusive Societies for Sustainable Development, Provide Access to Justice for All and Build Effective, Accountable, and Inclusive Institutions at All Levels' 1157
Tom Kabau
I. Introduction 1157
II. *Travaux Préparatoires* 1158
A. An Overview of the Preparatory Initiatives 1158
B. Formulating SDG 16 Targets: Conceptual and Thematic Considerations 1159
1. Deliberation on the Rule of Law and Interdependent Concepts 1159
2. Discussions Regarding the Role of Institutions and their Structuring 1161
3. Perspectives Regarding Conflict Resolution and Post-Conflict Peace-Building 1161
4. Discourse on Inclusiveness and Broad Participation for Social Equity 1163
5. Reflections on Access to Justice 1163

xxxvi CONTENTS

6. Focus on Reduction of Corruption and Bribery   1164
7. Perspectives Regarding Elimination of Violence against Children   1164
8. Deliberations on the Conceptual Interlinkages and Interdependence of Thematic Concepts   1164
9. Opinions Regarding Improvements to Indicators in the Post-MDGs Period   1165

III. Goal Commentary   1166
  A. Legal Foundations and Some Thematic Concerns   1167
    1. International Legal Obligations as the Source for SDG 16 Targets   1167
      a) Sustainable development as a legal principle   1170
        i) Meaning and scope of sustainable development   1170
        ii) Legal aspects of sustainable development   1171
      b) Relevance of the right to development   1172
    2. Thematic Considerations in the Conceptualization of SDG 16   1174
      a) Conflict resolution and peace as a sustainable development concern   1174
      b) Corruption and bribery as a sustainable development concern   1175
      c) The rule of law as a sustainable development concern   1177
      d) Inclusivity and broad participation as a sustainable development concern   1178

IV. Theoretical Perspectives Relevant to SDG 16   1180
  A. Third World Approaches to International Law   1181
  B. Institutionalism   1182
  C. John Rawls' Theory of Justice   1184

V. Commentary on SDG 16 Targets   1187
  A. Evaluating SDG 16 Targets through Indicators   1187
    1. Nature and Context of SDG 16 Indicators   1190
    2. Limitations of Indicators in Measuring SDG 16 Targets' Progress   1190
    3. Improving the Credibility and Accuracy of Indicators   1192
  B. Realization and Evaluation of SDG 16 Targets   1198
    1. Target 16.1 Significantly reduce all forms of violence and related death rates everywhere   1199
      a) Indicator 16.1.1 Number of victims of intentional homicide per 100,000 population, by sex and age   1199
        i) Empirical analysis   1200
        ii) Implementation efforts   1201
      b) Indicator 16.1.2 Conflict-related deaths per 100,000 population, by sex, age, and cause   1202
        i) Empirical analysis   1202
        ii) Implementation efforts   1204
        iii) Critique   1204
      c) Indicator 16.1.3 Proportion of population subjected to (a) physical violence, (b) psychological violence and (c) sexual violence in the previous 12 months   1205
        i) Empirical analysis and implementation efforts   1205
      d) Indicator 16.1.4 Proportion of population that feel safe walking alone around the area they live   1206
        i) Empirical analysis and implementation efforts   1207
        ii) Critique of Target 16.1 Indicators   1208
    2. Target 16.2 End abuse, exploitation, trafficking and all forms of violence against and torture of children   1208

a) Indicator 16.2.1 Proportion of children aged 1–17 years who experienced any physical punishment and/or psychological aggression by caregivers in the past month 1209
   i) Empirical analysis 1209
   ii) Implementation efforts 1209
b) Indicator 16.2.2 Number of victims of human trafficking per 100,000 population, by sex, age and form of exploitation 1210
   i) Empirical analysis 1210
   ii) Implementation efforts 1211
c) Indicator 16.2.3 Proportion of young women and men aged 18–29 years who experienced sexual violence by age 18 1213
   i) Empirical analysis and implementation efforts 1213

3. Target 16.3 Promote the rule of law at the national and international levels and ensure equal access to justice for all 1213
a) Indicator 16.3.2 Unsentenced detainees as a proportion of overall prison population 1214
   i) Empirical analysis 1214
   ii) Implementation efforts 1215
b) Indicator 16.3.3 Proportion of the population who have experienced a dispute in the past two years and who accessed a formal or informal dispute resolution mechanism, by type of mechanism 1215
   i) Empirical evaluation methodology 1215
   ii) Implementation efforts 1216

4. Target 16.4 By 2030, significantly reduce illicit financial and arms flows, strengthen the recovery and return of stolen assets and combat all forms of organized crime 1219
a) Indicator 16.4.1 Total value of inward and outward illicit financial flows (in current United States dollars) 1219
   i) Empirical statistics and implementation 1219
b) Indicator 16.4.2 Proportion of seized, found or surrendered arms whose illicit origin or context has been traced or established by a competent authority in line with international instruments 1220
   i) Empirical analysis and implementation 1220
   ii) Critique of target 16.4 indicators 1221

5. Target 16.5 Substantially reduce corruption and bribery in all their forms 1221
a) Indicator 16.5.1 Proportion of persons who had at least one contact with a public official and who paid a bribe to a public official, or were asked for a bribe by those public officials, during the previous 12 months 1221
b) Indicator 16.5.2 Proportion of businesses that had at least one contact with a public official and that paid a bribe to a public official, or were asked for a bribe by those public officials during the previous 12 months 1222
   i) Empirical analysis 1222
   ii) Indicators 16.5.1 and 16.5.2 implementation efforts 1223

6. Target 16.6 Develop effective, accountable and transparent institutions at all levels 1226

xxxviii CONTENTS

a) Indicator 16.6.1 Primary government expenditures as a
proportion of original approved budget, by sector (or by budget
codes or similar) — 1226
   i) Empirical analysis — 1226
b) Indicator 16.6.2 Proportion of population satisfied with their last
experience of public services — 1227
   i) Empirical evaluation methodology — 1227
   ii) Implementation efforts — 1227
7. Target 16.7 Ensure responsive, inclusive, participatory and
representative decision-making at all levels — 1228
a) Indicator 16.7.1 Proportions of positions in national and local
institutions, including (a) the legislatures; (b) the public service;
and (c) the judiciary, compared to national distributions, by sex,
age, persons with disabilities and population groups — 1228
   i) Empirical analysis — 1228
   ii) Implementation efforts — 1229
b) Indicator 16.7.2 Proportion of population who believe decision-
making is inclusive and responsive, by sex, age, disability and
population group — 1230
   i) Implementation efforts — 1230
   ii) Critique of target 16.7 indicators — 1230
8. Target 16.8 Broaden and strengthen the participation of developing
countries in the institutions of global governance — 1232
a) Indicator 16.8.1 Proportion of members and voting rights of
developing countries in international organizations — 1232
   i) Empirical analysis and implementation efforts — 1232
   ii) Critique — 1233
9. Target 16.9 By 2030, provide legal identity for all, including birth
registration — 1235
a) Indicator 16.9.1 Proportion of children under 5 years of age whose
births have been registered with a civil authority, by age — 1235
   i) Empirical analysis — 1235
   ii) Implementation efforts and critique — 1236
10. Target 16.10 Ensure public access to information and protect
fundamental freedoms, in accordance with national legislation and
international agreements — 1237
a) Indicator 16.10.1 Number of verified cases of killing, kidnapping,
enforced disappearance, arbitrary detention and torture of
journalists, associated media personnel, trade unionists and
human rights advocates in the previous 12 months — 1237
   i) Empirical analysis — 1238
b) Indicator 16.10.2 Number of countries that adopt and implement
constitutional, statutory and/or policy guarantees for public
access to information — 1239
   i) Empirical analysis — 1239
   ii) Implementation efforts — 1239
11. Target 16.a Strengthen relevant national institutions, including
through international cooperation, for building capacity at all levels,
in particular in developing countries, to prevent violence and combat
terrorism and crime — 1240

a) Indicator 16.a.1 Existence of independent national human rights institutions in compliance with the Paris Principles — 1241
    i) Empirical analysis and implementation — 1241
    ii) Critique — 1242
12. Target 16.b Promote and enforce non-discriminatory laws and policies for sustainable development — 1243
a) Indicator 16.b.1 Proportion of population reporting having personally felt discriminated against or harassed in the previous 12 months on the basis of a ground of discrimination prohibited under international human rights law — 1243
    i) Empirical evaluation methodology — 1243
    ii) Implementation efforts — 1244
VI. Conclusion — 1244

17 SDG 17 'Strengthen the Means of Implementation and Revitalize the Global Partnership for Sustainable Development' — 1247
Andreas Rechkemmer and Damilola Olawuyi

I. Introduction — 1247
II. *Travaux Préparatoires* — 1249
III. Commentary on SDG 17 — 1258
  A. Background: SDG 17 in the Context of Globalization and Global Governance — 1258
  B. Governance Modes and Modalities for Implementation of SDG 17 — 1261
IV. Commentary on Targets and Indicators of Goal 17 — 1269
  A. Overview — 1269
  B. Analysis and Critique of Each Target — 1271
    1. Economic and Financial Targets — 1271
      a) Target 17.1: Strengthen domestic resource mobilization, including through international support to developing countries, to improve domestic capacity for tax and other revenue collection — 1272
      b) Target 17.2 Developed Countries to implement fully their official development assistance commitments, including the commitment by many developed countries to achieve the target of 0.7 per cent of gross national income for official development assistance (ODA/GNI) to developing countries and 0.15 to 0.20 per cent of ODA/GNI to least developed countries; ODA providers are encouraged to consider setting a target to provide at least 0.20 per cent of ODA/GNI to least developed counties — 1278
      c) Targets 17.3 and 17.5 Mobilise additional financial resources for developing countries from multiple sources; Adopt and implement investment promotion regimes for least developed countries — 1281
      d) Target 17.4 Assist developing countries in attaining long-term debt sustainability through coordinated policies aimed at fostering debt financing, debt relief and debt restructuring, as appropriate and address the external debt of highly indebted poor countries to reduce debt distress — 1284
    2. Trade and Market-related Targets — 1286
      a) Target 17.10 Promote universal, rules-based, open, non-discriminatory and equitable multilateral trading system under

xl CONTENTS

the World Trade Organization, including through the conclusion
of negotiations under its Doha Development Agenda   1289
  b) Targets 17.11 and 17.12: Significantly increase the exports of
developing countries, in particular with a view to doubling the
least developed countries' shares of global exports by 2020; Realise
timely implementation of duty-free and quota-free market access
on a lasting basis for all least developed countries, consistent
with World Trade Organization decisions, including by ensuring
that preferential rules of origin applicable to imports from least
developed countries are transparent and simple, and contribute to
facilitating market access   1293
3. Knowledge, Technology Transfer, and Capacity-building-related
Targets   1295
  a) Target 17.6 Enhance North–South, South–South and triangular
regional and international cooperation on and access to science,
technology and innovation and enhance knowledge sharing on
mutually agreed terms, including through improved coordination
among existing mechanisms, in particular at the United Nations
level, and through a global technology; Target 17.7 Promote
the development, transfer, dissemination and diffusion of
environmentally sound technologies to developing countries
on favourable terms, including on concessional and preferential
terms, as mutually agreed; Target 17.8 Fully operationalize
the technology bank and science, technology and innovation
capacity-building mechanism for least developed countries by
2017 and enhance the use of enabling technology, in particular
information and communications technology   1296
  b) Target 17.9 Enhance international support for implementing
effective and targeted capacity-building in developing countries
to support national plans to implement all the Sustainable
Development Goals, including through North-South, South-
South and triangular cooperation; Target 17.18 By 2020, enhance
capacity-building support to developing countries, including for
least developed countries and small island developing States, to
increase significantly the availability of high-quality, timely and
reliable data disaggregated by income, gender, age, race, ethnicity,
migratory status, disability, geographic location and other
characteristics relevant in national contexts; Target 17.19 By 2030,
build on existing initiatives to develop measurements of progress
on sustainable development that complement gross domestic
product, and support statistical capacity-building   1306
4. Partnership, Stakeholder, Policy, and Governance-related Targets   1313
  a) Target 17.13 Enhance global macroeconomic stability, including
through policy coordination and policy coherence; Target 17.14
Enhance policy coherence for sustainable development; Target
17.15 Respect each country's policy space and leadership to
establish and implement policies for poverty eradication and
sustainable development   1313
  b) Target 17.16 Enhance the Global Partnership for Sustainable
Development, complemented by multi-stakeholder partnerships

that mobilize and share knowledge, expertise, technology and financial resources, to support the achievement of the Sustainable Development Goals in all countries, in particular developing countries; Target 17.17 Encourage and promote effective public, public-private and civil society partnerships, building on the experience and resourcing strategies of partnerships   1315

    V. Conclusion   1322

Index   1325

List of Contributors

Principal Editors

Ilias Bantekas LLB (Athens), LLM, PhD (Liverpool), BA/Dip Theology (Cambridge), FCIArb, is Professor of Transnational Law at Hamad bin Khalifa University (Qatar Foundation), Adjunct Professor of international law at Georgetown University, Edmund A Walsh School of Foreign Service, and Senior Associate Fellow at the Institute of Advanced Legal Studies (IALS) University of London. He has advised private clients, charities, governments, and inter-governmental organizations (UN, UNDP, EU, Council of Europe, and others) in most fields of international law and transnational contracts. In addition he regularly serves as arbitrator in international commercial disputes. He has written more than 180 peer-reviewed articles in leading journals such as the American Journal of International Law, British Yearbook of International Law, European Journal of International Law, Arbitration International, American Review of International Arbitration, Journal of International Dispute Settlement, Berkeley Journal of International Law, and others. He has authored thirteen books, including: *Introduction to International Arbitration* (CUP 2015); *Commentary to the UNCITRAL Model Law on International Arbitration* (CUP 2020), with P Ortolani and others); *International Law* (5th edn, OUP 2021, with E Papastavridis); *International Human Rights Law and Practice* (3rd edn, CUP 2020, with L Oette); *Sovereign Debt and Human Rights* (OUP 2018, with C Lumina); *Islamic Contract Law* (OUP 2022, with J Ercanbrack et al); *The Contract Law of Qatar* (CUP 2023).

Francesco Seatzu read law at the University of Cagliari, receiving a JD (first class with distinction), before completing his studies for a PhD at the University of Nottingham. He has been Visiting Scholar and Professor in several universities, including the University Complutense of Madrid (2001), the University of Nottingham (2003), the University of Glasgow (2006), the University of Bordeaux IV (2010), the University of Sevilla (2015), the University 'Carlos III' of Madrid (2015), the University of Valencia (2016, 2017, 2018, and 2019), the University of Alcalà (2017), the University of Huelva (2017), the University of Murcia (2018), and the University of Donostia-San Sebastian (2019). Professor Francesco Seatzu is a Member of the Doctoral School of International and EU Law of the State University of Milano since 2007, of the CIDOIE (Centro Interuniversitario sul Diritto delle Organizzazioni Internazionali Economiche) of the Italian Society of International Law. He is a member of the Board of Editors of Revue des Droits de l'Homme, Journal du Droit International (Clunet), Diritto del Commercio Internazionale, Anuario de los Cursos de Derechos Humanos de Donostia-San Sebastián, Cuadernos de Derecho Transnacional, Anuario de derecho internacional, Revista Electrónica, Iberoamericana, and Diritto Pubblico Comparato e Europeo. Moreover, he has also been a member of the Board of Editors of the Journal of Private International Law. His current research interests include the law of international organizations, with a particular focus on the law of international development banks and of the sub-regional economic organizations in Latin America, as well as international investment law and policy, international human rights law, and general international law. Such a variety of interests is mirrored in his publishing record which counts three monographs (one co-authored with Marco Odello), eight edited books, and more than 100 articles, published in international and national journals and renowned edited volumes.

Assistant Editor

Katerina Akestoridi read law at the Democritus University of Thrace (LL.B (hons)), the University College London (LL.M (merit) and the Institute of Advanced Legal Studies, University of London (PhD). Katerina was a Teaching Associate at Université Catholique de Lille during the first semester of the academic year 2021–2022. She previously held a Fellowship at the Faculties of Law and Political Sciences of the University of Cagliari, Italy, and has worked as a research assistant at University College London and the University of Zurich. She has taught extensively at postgraduate level in the subjects of human rights law, environmental protection, and international development, including the role of international financial institutions, businesses, and charities in the realization of the Sustainable Development Goals, and has served as deputy editor of the IALS Student Law Review (open-access journal). Katerina has also practised law in Athens, Greece and consulted in the non-governmental organization sector, having interned at the Human Rights Institute of the International Bar Association (IBAHRI) and the European Human Rights Advocacy Centre (EHRAC), where she worked on projects pertaining to the rule of law, democracy, and human rights, including the implementation of ECHR judgments. Her general research interests pertain to human rights law, environmental and climate change law, and international development, while her current research focuses on the accountability of international financial institutions for sustainable development, their role as lawmakers in international sustainable development law and the nexus between the Sustainable Development Goals and International Law. Recent publications include: 'Enhancing the Transformative Potential of the Sustainable Development Goals' (Global Jurist 2020, with F Seatzu); 'The Role of Business in International Development and the Attainment of the Sustainable Development Goals' in I Bantekas and M Stein (eds), *The Cambridge Companion to Business and Human Rights Law* (CUP 2021).

Contributors' Biographies

SDG 1:

Krista Nadakavukaren Scheffer is a Vice Director of the Swiss Institute of Comparative Law. She is also on the faculty of the World Trade Institute in Bern and is an adjunct instructor at the Universities of Basel and Bern. Long interested in the intersection of international economic law and other areas of international law, Dr Nadakavukaren's research has looked at poverty, corruption, human rights, and vulnerability on their own as well as in connection with the more traditional topics of trade and investment law. Professor Nadakavukaren is a native of the United States. She received her *juris doctor* from Georgetown University Law School, and her doctorate and Habilitation from the University of Bern.

SDG 2:

Dr Elif Askin, MLaw, is a Senior Researcher and Lecturer at the Faculty of Law of the University of Zurich, Switzerland, and a Senior Research Affiliate at the Max Planck Institute for Comparative Public Law and International Law in Heidelberg, Germany. She is also a Lecturer at the Europa-Institut of the Saarland University in Germany. Prior to joining the University of Zurich, Dr Askin was a Research Fellow and a Senior Research Fellow at the Max Planck Institute for Comparative Public Law and International Law in Heidelberg. She was a Visiting Fellow at the Institute for International and Comparative Law in Africa at the University of Pretoria in South Africa. Her main fields of research are public international law and international human rights law, with a particular emphasis on economic, social, and cultural rights and their extraterritorial application.

SDG 3:

Dr Christina Binder, E.MA, has held the Chair for International Law and International Human Rights Law at the University of the Bundeswehr Munich since April 2017. Prior to this, she was University Professor of International Law at the Department of European, International and Comparative Law at the University of Vienna and Deputy Director of the interdisciplinary Research Centre 'Human Rights'. She is member of the ILA Committee on Human Rights in Times of Emergency. Christina is member of the Executive Board and former Vice-President of the European Society of International Law (ESIL), was member of the Executive Board of the European Inter-University Center for Human Rights and Democratization (EIUC) (2016–2019) and is member of the Council of the Global Campus of Human Rights since 2019. Her research focuses on a number of public international law issues, including human rights, the law of treaties, and international investment law as well as international environmental law. She is co-editor of the *Zeitschrift für Menschenrechte,* the *European Yearbook of International Economic Law* and of the *Hungarian Yearbook of International and European Law* and has widely published, in edited volumes and in peer-reviewed journals.

Jane Hofbauer, LL.M., is a postdoctoral researcher and lecturer at the University of the Bundeswehr Munich. Previously she worked at the University of Vienna and the Boltzmann Institute for Human Rights. Her research focuses particularly on international dispute settlement, international environmental and human rights law. She is co-editor of the Austrian Review of International and European Law (ARIEL) and the Zeitschrift für das Recht der nachhaltigen Entwicklung (Journal on Sustainable Development Law). She is a member of the ILA Committee on Sustainable Development and the Green Economy in International Trade Law.

SDG 4:

Dr Jane Kotzmann is an Alfred Deakin Postdoctoral Research Fellow at Deakin Law School, where she researches in human rights, particularly the right to education, and animal law. Dr Kotzmann holds degrees in Law (Hons) and Commerce from Deakin University and a Postgraduate Diploma in Teaching (Teach for Australia) from the University of Melbourne. Her PhD in Law from Deakin University explored the application of human rights norms to higher education policy and culminated in her published monograph, *The Human Rights-Based Approach to Higher Education* (OUP 2018).

Dr John R Morss is Senior Lecturer in International Law at Deakin Law School. With a PhD in early childhood cognitive development from the University of Edinburgh, he was formerly Lecturer in Psychology at the Ulster University and Senior Lecturer in Education at the University of Otago. His publications include three sole authored monographs and three co-edited collections and his current research interests are self-determination, and the challenge of foreign state immunity for those seeking justice in relation to conduct attributable to the Holy See.

Morgan Stonebridge is a research assistant and PhD candidate at Deakin Law School, where she researches the law as it relates to animals. Her doctoral thesis explores the connection between empathy and animal rights. Morgan holds a degree in Law (Hons) from Deakin University. Her publications include four co-authored articles, and her Honours paper has been published by the University of Queensland Law Journal.

SDG 5:

Rangita de Silva de Alwis is a globally recognized international women's human rights scholar. She serves as Associate Dean of International Affairs at the University of Pennsylvania Law School where she teaches International Women's Human Rights, Women, Law and Leadership and the Policy Lab on

xlvi   LIST OF CONTRIBUTORS

AI and Bias. She was also appointed the Hillary Rodham Clinton Distinguished Fellow at Georgetown Institute for Women, Peace, and Security and Senior Fellow at the Center for the Legal Profession at Harvard Law School. She was also a Fellow with the Harvard Human Rights Program. She was Nonresident Leader in Practice at Harvard Kennedy School's Women and Public Policy Program (2019–2021). She served as Senior Advisor to the SDG Fund, where she helped co- author papers on SDG Goal 16. As the Distinguished Adviser to Under Secretary General Phumzile Mlambo Ngcuka, the Head of UN Women (2013–2021), she conducted a study on Redefining the Role of Leadership in the Age of the SDG's at Harvard Law School's Center for the Legal Profession. She has published widely on the intersections of the Convention on the Elimination of Discrimination against Women with other human rights treaties, the Women Peace and Security Agenda and the SDGs. She has a LLM and SJD from Harvard Law School.

SDG 6:

Owen McIntyre is a Professor at the School of Law, University College Cork (National University of Ireland), Director of the LL.M. (Environmental & Natural Resources Law) Programme: <https://www.ucc.ie/en/ckl48/> and Co-Director of the Centre for Law & Environment: <https://www.ucc.ie/en/lawenvironment/>. His principal research interests lie in the field of International Water Law. He is General Editor of the Journal of Water Law and has served as the inaugural Chair of the IUCN World Commission on Environmental Law Specialist Group on Water and Wetlands, as a panel member of the Project Complaints Mechanism of the European Bank for Reconstruction and Development (EBRD), and as a member of the Scientific Committee of the European Environment Agency. He holds visiting positions at the University of Dundee, Charles University Prague, Xiamen University, and Wuhan University. He consults widely in the fields of International Water and Environmental Law for such organizations as the World Bank, Asian Development Bank, United Nations Development Programme, and the European Union, and also advises river basin commissions (RBOs) around the world on transboundary water cooperation.

SDG 7 and SDG 8: Francesco Seatzu and Katerina Akestoridi (see editors' biographies)

SDG 9:

P Sean Morris is a Non-Stipendiary Fellow ('Grant-Funded Researcher') in the Faculty of Law, University of Helsinki and an Affiliated Fellow at the Erik Castren Institute of International Law and Human Rights, University of Helsinki. Sean previously convened and taught International Economic Law, at the University of Helsinki. Sean is a generalist international lawyer and works closely on matters in relation to international legal history, the history of international intellectual property rights, law of the sea and sustainability, state responsibility, and international tribunals. Sean has written a number of articles in these areas and has edited the following books: *Intellectual Property and the Law of Nations, 1860—1920* (Brill 2022); *The League of Nations and the Development of International Law: A New Intellectual History of the Advisory Committee of Jurists* (Routledge 2021); *Transforming the Politics of International Law: The Advisory Committee of Jurists and the Formation of the World Court in the League of Nations* (Routledge 2021).

SDG 10:

Dr Johanna Aleria P Lorenzo is an Assistant Professor at the University of Amsterdam Law School and the Amsterdam Center for International Law (ACIL). Her teaching includes Masters courses on general international law and international trade law. She specializes in international law and development, international trade law, and the legal aspects of international financial institutions (IFIs). Dr Lorenzo's research and publications concentrate on sustainability, development, and global governance issues arising from the intersections of international economic law, international environmental law, and international human rights law. Her doctoral dissertation, which was awarded by Yale Law School the Ambrose Gherini Prize for best paper in international law, scrutinized the multilateral development banks' environmental and social policies and their independent accountability mechanisms, to explain how IFIs and other non-state actors participate in the international law-making process concerning sustainable development.

SDG 11:

Hannah Birkenkötter is an assistant professor at the Law Department of Instituto Tecnológico Autónomo de México (ITAM), and an associated researcher at the Chair of Public Law and Jurisprudence, Humboldt University Berlin. Her research focuses on topics of general international law, international institutional law, especially the United Nations, and international legal theory. Her work has been published in venues such as Global Constitutionalism, the International Journal of Constitutional Law, and the German Yearbook of International Law. She was awarded the 2021 Dissertation Award of the Academic Council on the UN System.

SDG 12:

Kateřina Mitkidis is associate professor at the Department of Law, Aarhus University, Denmark. Kateřina is interested in the ways law and legal tools are designed and used to steer behaviour in socially and environmentally sound and responsible directions. Her research particularly focuses on the intersection of European environmental and pharmaceutical law, and on the practice of using typically private law tools, such as contracts, to advance public interests. She has published a book on this topic titled *Sustainability Clauses in International Business Contracts* (Eleven International Publishing 2015). She was a visiting scholar at Duke University, USA (2016) and Vanderbilt University, USA (2012). Before joining academia, Kateřina worked as legal trainee for Baker&McKenzie Prague office and as junior lawyer in Hájek&Zrzavecký, Czech Republic.

Adriana Šefčíková is a former Research Assistant at the Department of Law, Aarhus University, where she provided assistance with researching a broad range of sustainability-related topics. Adriana is particularly interested in how different legal disciplines can support a sustainable green transition. Her Master's thesis defended in 2020 at the Faculty of Law of Charles University inspired an article titled 'Climate Change Litigation with a Human Face' published in the Nordic Environmental Law Journal in 2021. Furthermore, she participated in a number of academic student competitions and achieved excellent results, such as being awarded the Zdeněk Madar Award for the best paper in the section of Environmental Law, and second place in the Czech Envi Thesis competition. Before embarking on an academic career, Adriana worked as a student legal assistant for Fialová Law Firm in Prague and provided legal consulting for the public at a student legal clinic.

SDG 13:

Francesca Romanin Jakur is Senior Researcher in International Law at the University of Brescia. She is also Adjunct Professor of 'International Climate Change and Energy Law' at the University of Milan. Previously, she served as Legal Advisor to the Italian Ministry of the Environment, providing assistance in international environmental and climate change law. Francesca holds a PhD in International Law from the University of Milano and a *Diplôme des Haute Etudes Supérieurs* (DESUP) in EU Law from the Paris University (Université Paris I Panthéon-Sorbonne/Collège des Hautes Etudes Européennes Miguel Servet). She is the author of several publications in Italian, in English, and in French in international law matters. She teaches international law in Italian universities and abroad and held capacity-building workshops in Northern Africa (Morocco, Tunisia) and in the Balkans (Former Republic of Macedonia, Albania) on international environmental and climate change law.

SDG 14:

Dr Christos Kypraios is the Research and Programmes Manager of the Bonavero Institute of Human Rights at the Faculty of Law, University of Oxford, and a Senior Common Room member at Mansfield College, University of Oxford. Before joining the Bonavero Institute, Christos

xlviii   LIST OF CONTRIBUTORS

worked for six years as Research Fellow and Senior Research Fellow at the Max Planck Institute for Comparative Public Law and International Law in Heidelberg, Germany, currently being one of its Senior Research Affiliates. Christos is a Greek-qualified lawyer and studied law at the National and Kapodistrian University of Athens (LL.B (hons)), the University of Nottingham (LL.M (dist) in International Law), and the University of Basel (Dr iur), as well as international relations (MA (dis)) and history (MA (dis)) at Istanbul Bilgi University and Sciences Po Paris. His general research interests relate to human rights law, economic law, law of the sea, and space law, while his current research in Oxford focuses on the application of human rights in the context of space activities and technologies.

Eirini E Fasia is a DPhil candidate and Law tutor at the University of Oxford. Her research focuses on the international law of the sea, environmental law, and state responsibility. Eirini is also a researcher at the Oxford Martin Programme on Sustainable Oceans, a Graduate Teaching Assistant in the Law Faculty of the University of Oxford, and International Law tutor in the Diplomatic Studies Programme at the Department of Continuing Education of the University of Oxford. Eirini has studied law at the Democritus University of Thrace (LL.B (dist)), the University of Athens (LL.M (dist)) and the University of Oxford (Mjur (dist) and MPhil). Eirini has worked as a lawyer in Athens and is admitted to practise law in Greece (member of the Athens Bar). She has also worked as an intern at the Max Planck Institute for Comparative Public Law and International Law in Heidelberg.

SDG 15:

Jorge Cabrera Medaglia DCL LLM MBA BCL (University of Costa Rica) is Professor of Environmental Law in the Postgraduate Programme on Environmental, Agricultural, and Biodiversity Law at the University of Costa Rica, and Lead Counsel for Biodiversity and Biosafety Law at the Centre for International Sustainable Development Law (CISDL). He was Head of Delegation for Costa Rica at the first meeting of the Conference of the Parties (COP) to the Convention on Biological Diversity (CBD), and a member of the Costa Rican National Biodiversity Commission (1995–1998). Professor Cabrera Medaglia also served as a member of the Costa Rican delegation to the CBD from 2000–2010, as a Co-Chair of the CBD Expert Panel on Access and Benefit Sharing (ABS) and co-chaired the negotiations on Traditional Knowledge for the Nagoya Protocol on ABS at COP 10 in 2010.

Frederic Perron-Welch MA (Toronto) JD Environmental Law (Dalhousie) is a Doctoral Fellow at the Grotius Centre for International Legal Studies at Leiden Law School and Visiting Fellow at the United Nations Research Institute for Social Development (UNRISD). He was a Legal Research Fellow in the Biodiversity and Biosafety Law Programme of the CISDL from 2010 to 2022, also serving as Programme Coordinator from 2011 to 2016. Mr Perron-Welch has written extensively on international biodiversity law and policy, and worked with national governments, the United Nations, intergovernmental organizations, the private sector, university researchers, and civil society organizations to advance understanding and implementation of the CBD over the past decade. He was called to the Bar of Ontario in 2011.

Aleksandra Spasevski BS (Guelph) MES (Waterloo) has been recognized as one of Canada's Top 25 Environmentalists under 25 based on her work as a youth and biodiversity activist in Canada and role as co-founder of Canadian Youth Biodiversity Network, a group that advocates for youth participation in biodiversity policymaking at national and international levels. She works as the Sustainability Engagement Coordinator at University of Waterloo and is a board member of the Ontario Environment Network (OEN) and Protect Our Water and Environmental Resources (POWER). Through her work at the university and with various charities, she looks to support young people and Indigenous communities through research, projects, and consultations.

Dario Piselli is an affiliated researcher with the Centre for International Environmental Studies of the Graduate of International and Development Studies (IHEID), in Geneva, Switzerland. He previously held a number of research positions at the Centre for International Environmental Studies (2018–2020) and the Global Health Centre (2016–2018) of the IHEID, and he also worked as an independent consultant. Dario holds a PhD in International Law from the IHEID, an MSc in Environment and Development from the London School of Economics and Political Science, and a JD from the University of Siena. His main research interests include international and European biodiversity law, global health governance, and science and technology policy interfaces in health and environment. He is currently working as an Expert in Environment, Human Health and Well-being at the European Environment Agency (EEA) in Copenhagen, Denmark.

Alexandra Goodman is the Senior Law Fellow at the International Council of Environmental Law. Holding law degrees from New York (Brooklyn Law) and France (Jean Moulin III), she has worked for the United Nations, Global Pact Coalition, Global Network for Study of Human Rights and Environment (GNHRE), Natural Resources Defense Council, and Open Society Foundations. Alexandra's publications include academic articles, blogs, UN Security Council's Repertoire, and a legal textbook. Alexandra's field work spans more than twenty-five Global South countries.

SDG 16:

Tom Kabau is a Senior Lecturer at the School of Law, Jomo Kenyatta University of Agriculture and Technology, an Advocate of the High Court of Kenya, and has previously provided research and consultancy services to various organizations. He also serves as an African Area Advisor for the Oxford Bibliographies in International Law. Kabau holds a Doctor of Philosophy (PhD) degree in Public International Law from the University of Hong Kong, and Master of Laws (LLM) and Bachelor of Laws (LLB) degrees from the University of Nairobi. He has also been a Research Fellow at Utrecht University, and was a 2015 Transnational Law Summer Institute Fellow at King's College London.

SDG 17:

Dr Andreas Rechkemmer is a Senior Professor at Hamad Bin Khalifa University's College of Public Policy (CPP) and coordinates the College's Master of Public Policy (MPP) program. Prior to joining HBKU, he was a tenured full professor and held the American Humane Endowed Chair at the University of Denver. Being an internationally recognized expert on global sustainable development, Dr Rechkemmer has held senior positions with the United Nations, including that of Executive Director of the International Human Dimensions Programme on Global Environmental Change at the United Nations University. He also served as Chief Science and Policy Advisor of the Global Risk Forum in Davos, Switzerland. His previous academic appointments and affiliations include the University of Cologne, Free University of Berlin, Beijing Normal University, Colorado State University, and the United Nations University. He has been principal investigator of various funded projects and managed grants from major science funders, including the US National Science Foundation, the Research Council of Norway, and the Federal Government of Germany. Dr Rechkemmer has authored, co-authored, and edited several books as well as numerous articles and chapters. He is one of the editors of the forthcoming *Oxford Handbook on Complex Disaster Risks and Resilience* and the editor of the book *UNEO—Towards an International Environment Organization* (Nomos Publishers 2005). He is the chief editor of the new book series, *Sustainable Development in the 21st Century* (published by Nomos).

Damilola S Olawuyi, SAN, FCIArb. is an associate professor of energy and environmental law at Hamad Bin Khalifa University (HBKU) College of Law, Doha, Qatar. He is also Chancellor's Fellow and Director of the Institute for Oil, Gas, Energy, Environment and Sustainable Development (OGEES Institute), Afe Babalola University, Ado Ekiti, Nigeria. Professor Olawuyi holds a doctorate in energy and environmental law from the University of Oxford; a master of laws (LL.M) from Harvard University, and another LL.M from the University of Calgary. He is an Independent Expert of the African Union's Working Group on Extractive Industries, Environment, and Human Rights

l LIST OF CONTRIBUTORS

Violations in Africa; Vice Chair of the International Law Association; and Chair of the Association of Environmental Law Lecturers in Middle East and North African Universities (ASSELLMU). A prolific and highly regarded scholar, his most recent book publications include: *Environmental Law in Arab States* (OUP 2022), *Local Content and Sustainable Development in Global Energy Markets* (CUP 2021), *The Human Rights Based Approach to Carbon Finance* (CUP 2018), and *Climate Change Law and Policy in the Middle East and North Africa Region* (Routledge 2021).

SDG 1: Krista Nadakavukaren Schefer k.nadakavukaren@unibas.ch

SDG 2: Askin Elif askin@mpil.de

SDG 3: Binder Christina c.binder@unibw.de

Jane Hofbauer jane.hofbauer@unibw.de

SDG 4: Jane Kotzmann j.kotzmann@deakin.edu.au

John Morss john.morss@deakin.edu.au

Elaine Unterhalter e.unterhalter@ucl.ac.uk

SDG 5: Rangita de Silva de Alwis rdesilva@law.upenn.edu

SDG 6: McIntyre Owen o.mcintyre@ucc.ie

SDG 7: Francesco Seatzu seatzu@hotmail.com

Katerina Akestoridi kakestoridi@gmail.com

SDG 8: Francesco Seatzu seatzu@hotmail.com

Katerina Akestoridi kakestoridi@gmail.com

SDG 9: P Sean MORRIS sean.morris@helsinki.fi

SDG 10: Johanna Aleria Lorenzo japlorenzo@aya.yale.edu/ johanna.lorenzo@kfg-intlaw.de

SDG 11: Hannah Birkenkötter hannah.birkenkoetter@rewi.hu-berlin.de

SDG 12: Adriana Šefčíková adriana.sefcikova@gmail.com

Katerina Mitkidis katpe@law.au.dk

SDG 13: Francesca Romanin Jacur francesca.romanin@unimi.it

SDG 14: Christos Kypraios c.c.kypraios@gmail.com and

Irini Fasia: irinifasia@gmail.com

SDG 15: Frederic Perron-Welch f.perron-welch@umail.leidenuniv.nl

Jorge Cabrera jorgecmedaglia@hotmail.com,

Dario Piselli dario.piselli@graduateinstitute.ch

Alexandra Goodman alex.sophia.goodman@gmail.com

Aleksandra Spasevski aspasevski@uwaterloo.ca

SDG 16: Tom Kabau tomkabau@gmail.com

SDG 17: Dr Andreas Rechkemmer ARechkemmer@hbku.edu.qa

Dr Damilola S Olawuyi dolawuyi@hbku.edu.qa

Table of Cases

AFRICAN COMMISSION ON HUMAN AND PEOPLE'S RIGHTS

African Commission on Human and Peoples' Rights v Republic of Kenya [2017] African
  Court on Human and Peoples' Rights, Application No. 006/2012 (Judgment) 1172–73
Centre for Minority Rights Development (Kenya) and Minority Rights Group International
  on Behalf of Endorois Welfare Council v Kenya [2010] African Commission on
  Human and Peoples' Rights, Application No. 276/2003 1172–73
Social and Economic Rights Action Center and the Center for Social and Economic
  Rights v Nigeria, African Commission on Human and Peoples' Rights, Communication
  No. 155/96, 30th Ordinary Session (13–27 October 2001)..............................497

ARBITRATION AWARDS

Arbitration between Barbados and the Republic of Trinidad and Tobago, relating to
  the delimitation of the exclusive economic zone and the continental shelf between
  them, decision of 11 April 2006 1031–32
Iron Rhine Arbitration (Belgium/Netherlands), 27 RIAA 1067
South China Sea Arbitration (The Republic of the Philippines v the People's Republic
  of China) PCA Case No. 2013-19 (Award) 12 July 2016 1041–42

CONVENTION ON THE RIGHTS OF THE CHILD COMMITTEE (CRCC)

Sacchi and others, v Argentina et al., Communication No. 107/2019 (23 Sep 2019) and
  CRC Decision CRC/C/88/D/107/2019 (8 October 2021)..............................1012

DOMESTIC CASE LAW

Beja and Others v Premier of the Western Cape and Others (21332/10)
  [2011] ZAWCHC 97; [2011] 3 All SA 401 (WCC); 2011 (10) BCLR 1077
  (WCC) (29 April 2011) (South Africa) 467–68
Bundesverwaltungsgericht (W109 2000179-1/291E) (2 February) (Germany).................986
Colorado v New Mexico 459 US 176 (1982) (United States)..............................474–75
Constitutional Court (Verfassungsgerichtshof), E 875/2017 and E 886/2017
  (2 August 2017) (Germany) 996
Nokotyana and Others v Ekurhuleni Metropolitan Municipality and Others
  CCT 31/09 [2009] ZACC 33 (19 November 2009) (South Africa).....................467–68
Samsung Electronics Co., Ltd., et al v Apple Inc., 137 S. Ct. 429 (2016) (United States) 636–37
Suomen perustuslaki (1999) SDK 731/1999 (Finland) 317–18
Urgenda Foundation v The State of the Netherlands, Supreme Court of the Netherlands,
  Number 19/00135 (20 December 2019) (Netherlands)............... 986, 1002–04, 1040–41

EAST AFRICAN COURT OF JUSTICE (EACJ)

Center for Food and Adequate Living Rights et al. v Tanzania and Uganda,
  6 November 2020 (pending)..989

EUROPEAN COMMISSION ON HUMAN RIGHTS

Van Droogenbroeck v Belgium (Commission's report, 9 July 1980) Series B, No. 44............604

lii TABLE OF CASES

EUROPEAN COMMITTEE OF SOCIAL RIGHTS

International Federation for Human Rights (FIDH) and Inclusion Europe v
  Belgium (No. 141/2017) [2021] 277
Mental Disability Advocacy Centre (MDAC) v Belgium (2018) 66 EHRR SE13 277

EUROPEAN COURT OF HUMAN RIGHTS (ECTHR)

Chowdury and Others v Greece, App No. 21884/15 (ECtHR, 30 March 2017)............... 603–4
Guerra and Others v Italy (1998) 26 European Human Rights Reports 357 497
Leyla Şahin v Turkey [2005] No. 44774/98 ECtHR 134 317
Mürsel Eren v Turkey [2006] No. 60856/00 ECtHR 41 317
Rantsev v Cyprus and Russia, App No. 25965/04 (ECtHR, judgment 10 January 2010) 603–4
Siliadin v France App No. 7331/01 (ECtHR, 26 July 2005) 602–4
Tarantino. v Italy (2013) No. 25851/09 ECtHR 43 317
Zander v Sweden, 18 European Human Rights Reports 175 (1993)........................... 497

EUROPEAN UNION, COURT OF JUSTICE OF THE EU (CJEU)

Armando Ferrão Carvalho and Others v The European Parliament and the Council
  (Case C-565/19 P) ECLI:EU:C:2021:252... 970–71
Commission v Kingdom of the Netherlands (Case C-368/10) [2012] ECR I-284 920–21
Concordia Bus (Case C-513/99) [2002] ECR I-7213 920–21
EVN and Wienstrom (Case C-448/01) [2003] ECR I-14527............................... 920–21
Gut Springenheide GmbH v Oberkreisdirektor des Kreises Steinfurt (Case C-216/96)
  [1998] ECR I-4657 927–28

HUMAN RIGHTS COMMITTEE (HRC)

Ioane Teitiota v New Zealand, Communication No. 2728/2016,
  UN Doc CCPR/C/127/D/2728/2016... 841

INTER-AMERICAN COMMISSION OF HUMAN RIGHTS

Yanomami case, (Case 7615 Brazil), Inter-American Commission on Human Rights,
  1984–1985 Annual Report 24, OEA/Ser.L/V/II.66, doc 10, rev 1 (1985) 497

INTER-AMERICAN COURT OF HUMAN RIGHTS (IACTHR)

Advisory Opinion OC-23/17 of 15 November 2017 Requested by the Republic of Colombia,
  'A Request for an Advisory Opinion from the Inter-American Court of Human Rights
  Concerning the Interpretation of Article 1(1), 4(1) and 5(1) of the American
  Convention on Human Rights'... 971–72
Awas Tingni Mayagna (Sumo) Indigenous Community v Nicaragua, Judgment of
  31 August 2001, Inter-American Court of Human Rights (Ser. C), No. 79 (2001).......... 497
Juridical Condition and Rights of the Undocumented Migrants, Advisory Opinion
  OC-18, Inter-American Court of Human Rights Series A No. 18 (17 September 2003)...... 577

INTERNATIONAL CENTRE FOR THE SETTLEMENT OF INVESTMENT DISPUTE RESOLUTION (ICSID)

9REN Holding S.a.r.l v Kingdom of Spain, ICSID Case No. ARB/15/15 986
Eskosol S.p.A. in liquidazione v Italian Republic, ICSID Case No. ARB/15/50 986
Fisheries Jurisdiction (Spain v Canada) (Jurisdiction of the Court) [1998] ICJ Rep 432......... 1039
Fisheries Jurisdiction (United Kingdom v Iceland) (Merits) [1974] ICJ Rep 3..............1039–40
Helnan International Hotels v Egypt ICSID Case No. ARB/05/19 (17 October 2006)
  Decision of the Tribunal on Objection to Jurisdiction...............................789–90

TABLE OF CASES   liii

ICSID Award of 8 Dec 2016, Urbaser S.A. and Consorcio de Aguas Bilbao Bizkaia, Bilbao
    Biskaia Ur Partzuergoa v The Argentine Republic, ICSID Case No ARB/07/26............160
Joy Mining v Egypt ICSID Case No. ARB/03/11 (6 August 2004) Award on Jurisdiction......789–90
LESI-Dipenta v Algeria ICSID Case No. ARB/03/8 (10 January 2005) Award..............789–90
Quiborax S.A. et al v Plurinational State of Bolivia ICSID Case No. ARB/06/2
    (27 September 2012) Decision on Jurisdiction.....................................789–90
Rockhopper v Italy, ECT, ICSID Case No. ARB/17/14, Pending 986
Salini et al v Morocco ICSID Case No. ARB/00/4 (23 July 2001) Decision on Jurisdiction.....789–90
Strabag and others v Germany, Energy Charter Treaty, 2019, ICSID Case
    No. ARB/19/29, Pending..986
Tecnicas Medioambientales Tecmed S.A. v United Mexican States (29 May 2003)
    ICSID Case No. ARB(AF)/00/2 867–68
Uniper v Netherlands, 2021, ICSID Case No. ARB/21/22..................................986
Westmoreland v Canada, 2019, ICSID Case No. UNCT/20/3 985–86

INTERNATIONAL COURT OF JUSTICE (ICJ)

Case Concerning Pulp Mills on the River Uruguay (Argentina v Uruguay), judgment
    of 20 April 2010...162
Certain Activities Carried out by Nicaragua in the Border Area (Costa Rica v Nicaragua)
    and Construction of A Road in Costa Rica along the San Juan River (Nicaragua v
    Costa Rica) [2015] ICJ Rep 665 ....995, 1092–94
Certain Activities Carried Out by Nicaragua in the Border Area (Costa Rica v Nicaragua)
    (Compensation) [2018] ICJ Reports 15........................... 988–89, 1092–94, 1153
Fisheries Jurisdiction (Spain v Canada) (Jurisdiction of the Court) [1998] ICJ Rep 432.........1039
Gabcikovo-Nagymaros Project (Hungary v Slovakia) (Judgment)
    1997 ICJ Reports 7 ....604, 633, 701, 702, 783, 1004, 1028–29, 1033–34, 1101
ICJ 8 July 1996, Advisory Opinion on the Legality of the Threat or Use of
    Nuclear Weapons [1996] ICJ Rep. 226..517–18
North Sea Continental Shelf (Federal Republic of Germany v Denmark; Federal Republic
    of Germany v Netherlands) (Judgment) [1969] ICJ Rep 3 1171
Pulp Mills on the River Uruguay (Argentina v Uruguay) (Judgment)
    [2010] ICJ Rep 14.....................162, 485–86, 500, 545–46, 783, 995, 1016–17, 1028–29
Whaling in the Antarctic (Australia v Japan, New Zealand intervening) [2014] ICJ Rep 226 783

INTERNATIONAL CRIMINAL COURT (ICC)

Prosecutor, The v Dominic Ongwen (2021) ICC Trial Chamber IX 296

INTERNATIONAL TRIBUNAL OF THE LAW OF THE SEA (ITLOS)

Case by Singapore In and Around the Straits of Johor (Malaysia v Singapore)
    (Provisional Measures), Order of 8 October 2003, International Tribunal for the
    Law of the Sea (ITLOS) 1037–38
Delimitation of the Maritime Boundary in the Bay of Bengal (Bangladesh/Myanmar)
    (Judgment) [2012] ITLOS Rep...1031–32
ITLOS Advisory Opinion 2015...1041–42
Land Reclamation Case by Singapore In and Around the Straits of Johor
    (Malaysia v Singapore) (Provisional Measures), Order of 8 October 2003.............1037–38
M/V 'Norstar' Case (Panama v Italy) (Judgment) [2019] 1044
M/V 'Saiga' (No. 2) (Saint Vincent and the Grenadines v Guinea) (Judgment)
    [1999] ITLOS Rep 10...1044
M/V 'Virginia G' (Panama/Guinea-Bissau) (Judgment) [2014] ITLOS Rep 4 1044
MOX Plant case (Ireland v United Kingdom) (Provisional Measures), Order of
    3 December 2001 (2002) 41 ILM 405...1037–38
MOX Plant case (Request for provisional measures), [2002] ITLOS Rep 110 1037

liv TABLE OF CASES

Responsibilities and obligations of States sponsoring Persons and Entities with respect
to activities in the Area, Case No. 17, Advisory Opinion (ITLOS Seabed Disputes
Chamber, 1 February 2011) (2011) 50 ILM 458 ....995, 1092–94
Southern Bluefin Tuna (New Zealand v Japan; Australia v Japan) (Order for
Provisional Measures) [1999] ITLOS Rep 280 .... 1031–32, 1041–42

PERMANENT COURT OF ARBITRATION (PCA)

Guyana v Suriname ICGJ 370 (PCA 2007) 1037–38
Permanent Court of Arbitration, Indus Waters Kishenganga Arbitration
(Pakistan v India), Partial Award, 18 February 2013 487–89
South China Sea Arbitration (The Republic of the Philippines v the People's Republic
of China) PCA Case No. 2013-19 (Award) 12 July 2016 1041–42

WTO APPELLATE BODY

Dominican Republic—Measures Affecting the Importation and Internal Sale of
Cigarettes WT/DS302/AB/R (adopted 19 May 2005) 980–81
European Communities—Conditions for the Granting of Tariff Preferences to Developing
Countries—Appellate Body Report (7 April 2004) WT/DS246/AB/R 782
United States—Import Prohibition of Certain Shrimp and Shrimp Products—Appellate
Body Report (12 October 1998) WT/DS58/AB/R (Shrimp/Turtle case) 783, 867, 868,
975, 976, 979
United States—Measures Concerning the Importation, Marketing and Sale of Tuna and
Tuna Products (Short title: US—Tuna II (Mexico) WT/DS381/49/Rev1
(17 January 2019) 867
United States—Shrimp, Decision of AB from 21 November 2001 867
United States—Standards for Reformulated and Conventional Gasoline, WT/DS2/R,
adopted on 20 May 1996 974
United States—Tuna/Dolphin I, GATT DS21/R 867
United States—Tuna/Dolphin II, GATT DS29/R.......................................867
United States—Tuna/Dolphin II, GATT DS29/R.......................................976

Table of Legislation

INTERNATIONAL INSTRUMENTS

Aarhus Convention *see* UNECE
Convention on Access to Information,
Public Participation in Decision-
Making and Access to Justice in
Environmental Matters 1998
Additional Protocol to the 1969 American
Convention on Human Rights in the
Area of Economic, Social and Cultural
Rights 1988 (Protocol of San Salvador)
Art 6 575–76
Art 7(d) 466–67
Art 10 215–16
Art 11 . . . . 497, 1047–48
Art 11(1) 466–67, 990
Art 11(2) 990
Art 12(2)(a) 186
Art 13 317
African Charter on Human and Peoples'
Rights 1981 (Banjul Charter) 1011–12
Art 4 990
Art 14 215–16
Art 15 575–76
Art 16 1047–48
Art 17 317
Art 22(2) 1172–73, 1175–76
Art 24 . . . . 177, 497, 620–21, 990, 1047–48
Art 25 1002
African Charter on the Rights and
Welfare of the Child 1990
Art 11(3)(c) 317
Art 14 215–16
African Convention on the Conservation
of Nature and Natural Resources
1968 (1968 Algiers Convention) 1087
African Convention on the Conservation
of Nature and Natural Resources 2003
(2003 Maputo Convention) 1088–89
African Union Convention on Preventing
and Combating Corruption 2003
Preamble 1168–69
Art 3(1) 1168–69
Art 3(3) 1274–76
Agreement Between Canada and the
United States of America on Great
Lakes Water Quality 2012 1099
Agreement between the European Union
and Japan for an Economic Partnership
2018 (EU-Japan FTA), Art 4(4) 983

Agreement concerning the Adoption of
Uniform Conditions for Periodical
Technical Inspections of Wheeled
Vehicles and the Reciprocal
Recognition of Such
Inspections 1997 246–47
Agreement Creating the Organisation for
the Management and Development
of the Kagera Basin 1977
Art 2 489–90
Agreement on Conservation of
Polar Bears 1973 1127–28
Agreement on Cooperation for
Sustainable Development of the
Mekong River Basin 1995
(Mekong Agreement) 489–90
Agreement on Environmental Cooperation
(AEC) among the Governments of the
United States of America, the United
Mexican States, and Canada 2018
Art 10(2)(y) 1290–91
Agreement on Environmental Cooperation
between Canada and Chile 1997
Art 8 1291–92
Agreement on Government Procurement
2012 (GPA) *see* WTO Agreement on
Government Procurement 2012
Agreement on Port State Measures to
Prevent, Deter and Eliminate Illegal,
Unreported and Unregulated
Fishing 2009 (PSMA) 1064–70
Preamble 1068
Art 9 1068–69
Art 10 1068–69
Art 11 1069
Art 11(2) 1068–69
Art 12 1069
Art 15 1069
Art 18 1069
Art 20 1069–70
Art 21 1069–70
Annex A 1068–69
Agreement on Subsidies and Countervailing
Measures 1994 (ASCM) *see* WTO
Agreement on Subsidies and
Countervailing Measures 1994
Agreement on the Establishment of the
Zambezi Water Commission 2004
(ZAMCOM Agreement)
Art 16(8) 499

lvi TABLE OF LEGISLATION

Agreement on Trade-Related Aspects
of Intellectual Property Rights
1994 (TRIPs Agreement) *see* WTO
Agreement on Trade-Related Aspects
of Intellectual Property Rights 1994
Agreement on Trade Related Investment
Measures (TRIMs) 1994 *see* WTO
Agreement on Trade Related
Investment Measures (TRIMs) 1994
Agreement Relating to the Implementation
of Part XI of the 1982 United Nations
Convention on the Law of the Sea 1994 ... 1037
Agreements on the Protection of the
Meuse and Scheldt 1994
Art 3 489–90
Algiers Convention 1968 *see* African
Convention on the Conservation of
Nature and Natural Resources 1968
Alpine Convention 1991 *see* Convention
Concerning the Protection of the
Alps 1991
American Convention on Human Rights
1969 (ACHR; Pact of San José)
Art 4(1) 990
American Declaration on the Rights and
Duties of Man 1948 (Bogotá Declaration)
Art XI 214–15, 1047–48
Art XII 317
Art XXII. 175
Antigua Convention 2002 *see* Convention
for Cooperation in the Sustainable
Development of the Marine and Coastal
Environment of the Northeast Pacific 2002
Apia Convention 1976 *see* Convention
on Conservation of Nature in the
South Pacific 1976
Arab Charter on Human Rights 2004
Art 39 215–16
Association of South-East Asian Nations
(ASEAN) Agreement on the Conservation
of Nature and Natural Resources
1985 (1985 ASEAN Convention) 1088
Art 3(a) 1127–28
Art 5(c). 1127–28
Art 7(b) 1127–28
Art 10(a) 1127–28
Art 13 1127–28
Art 19 1127–28
Art 20(4) 1127–28
Banjul Charter *see* African Charter on
Human and Peoples' Rights 1981
Basel Convention on the Control of
Transboundary Movements of
Hazardous Wastes and their
Disposal 1989 .... 471, 1250–51
Preamble 892–93
Art 4(2) 892–93

Bern Convention 1979 *see* Convention
on the Conservation of European
Wildlife and Natural Habitats 1979
Bogotá Declaration *see* American
Declaration on the Rights and
Duties of Man 1948 317
Carpathian Convention 2003 *see*
Framework Convention on
the Protection and Sustainable
Development of the Carpathians 2003
Cartagena Protocol on Biosafety to the UN
1992 UN Convention on Biological
Diversity 2000 549–50
Charter of Fundamental Rights of
2000
Art 35 215–16
Charter of the United Nations 1945
(UN Charter). 8–9, 19–20, 26–27, 32–33,
53–54, 152–53, 296, 815,
1167, 1248, 1249–50, 1255
Art 27(3) 1234
Arts 55 and 56 .... 783, 788
Art 71 666–67
Chapter VII 1205
Colorado Treaty *see* Treaty between the
United States of America and Mexico
Respecting Utilization of Waters of
the Colorado and Tijuana Rivers and
of the Rio Grande 1944 490–91
Comprehensive and Progressive
Agreement for Trans-Pacific
Partnership 2018 (CPTPP) 1290–91
Comprehensive Economic and Trade
Agreement 2016 (CETA)
Chapter 24 1290–91
Constitution of the World Health
Organization 1946 .... 209–10, 214–15
Preamble 209, 218
Art 1 209–10
Art 2 209–10
Art 21(1) 264
Art 21(a) 264
Arts 44*ff* 209–10
Convention Concerning the Protection
of the Alps 1991 (1991 Alpine
Convention) 1088, 1099, 1121
Preamble 1127–28
Art 2 1127–28
Convention Concerning the Protection
of the World Cultural and Natural
Heritage 1972 (World Heritage
Convention) 837–39, 1087–88,
1109, 1118, 1125, 1143
Art 2 .... 837–38, 1127–28
Art 3 837–38
Convention Creating the Niger
Basin Authority 1980 489–90

TABLE OF LEGISLATION lvii

Convention Designed to Ensure the
Conservation of Various Species of
Wild Animals in Africa, Which Are
Useful to Man or Inoffensive 1900
(1900 London Convention) . . . 1085–86, 1090
Convention Establishing an International
Relief Union 1927 93
Convention for Cooperation in the
Sustainable Development of the
Marine and Coastal Environment of
the Northeast Pacific 2002 (Antigua
Convention)
Art 3(1)(a) 684
Convention for the Prevention of Marine
Pollution by Dumping from Ships
and Aircraft 1972 (1972 London
Convention) 1058
Convention for the Protection of Birds
Useful to Agriculture 1902
(1902 Paris Convention) 1085–86, 1087
Convention for the Protection of
the Marine Environment of the
North-East Atlantic 1992 (OSPAR
Convention) 1030–31
Convention for the Suppression of
Unlawful Acts against the Safety of
Maritime Navigation 2005 1030–31
Convention on Biological Diversity 1992
see UN Convention on Biological
Diversity 1992
Convention on Conservation of Nature
in the South Pacific 1976 (1976 Apia
Convention) 1088
Preamble 1127–28
Art 1(b) 1127–28
Convention on Cooperation for the
Protection and Sustainable Use of the
Danube River 1994
Art 1(c). 489–90
Art 2 489–90
Art 14 499
Convention on Elimination of all forms of
Discrimination against Women 1979
(CEDAW) 8–9, 230–31, 268–69,
330–31, 336, 353, 371–74, 379, 392,
420, 713, 819–20, 848–49
Art 1 . . . . 381, 388, 737, 755
Art 2 . . . . 381, 388, 759, 760–61
Art 3 . . . . 737, 750–51
Art 7 . . . . 425, 1167–68
Art 7(c). 755–56
Art 8 1167–68
Art 9 390–91
Art 10 . . . . . . 215–16, 273, 289, 313, 328, 401–2
Art 10(b) 352–53
Art 10(c) 402
Art 10(e) 336–37

Art 10(h) 217t
Art 11 . . . . 217t, 420, 575–76
Art 11(1)(e) 85
Art 11(1)(f) 215–16
Art 11(e) 557
Art 12 . . . . 216–17, 217t, 230–31,
575–76, 848–49
Art 12(1) 215–16, 217t
Art 12(2) 172
Art 14 . . . . 289, 328
Art 14(2)(h). 522
Art 14(2) 467–68, 824–25
Art 14(2)(a) 755–56
Art 14(2)(b). 215–16
Art 14(2)(c) 85
Art 14(2)(d). 336–37
Art 14(c) 557
Art 15(2) 431
Art 16 420
Art 16(1)(h). 431
Convention on Environmental Impact
Assessment in a Transboundary Context
1991 see UNECE Convention on
Environmental Impact Assessment in a
Transboundary Context 1991
Convention on International Trade in
Endangered Species of Wild Fauna
and Flora 1973 (CITES). 701, 1087–88,
1109, 1125, 1129, 1142–46,
1250–51, 1291–92
Art VIII(1). 1145
Appendix I. 1145–46
Appendix II 1145–46
Convention on long-range transboundary
air pollution 1979 822–23
Convention on Nature Protection and
Wild Life Preservation in the Western
Hemisphere 1940 (1940
Pan-American Convention) 1086–87
Preamble 1127–28
Convention on Road Signs and
Signals 1968. 246–47
Convention on Road Traffic 1968 246–47
Convention on Sustainable Management
of Lake Tanganyika 2003
(Lake Tanganyika Convention)
Art 5(2)(d). 499
Art 15(c) 500
Art 17 499
Convention on the Conservation and
Management of Highly Migratory
Fish Stocks in the Western and
Central Pacific Ocean 2000 1030–31
Convention on the Conservation of European
Wildlife and Natural Habitats 1979 (1979
Bern Convention). 1088, 1099
Art 1(1) 1127–28

lviii TABLE OF LEGISLATION

Art 3(1) 1127–28
Art 3(3) 1127–28
Art 4(1) 1127–28
Art 4(4) 1127–28
Art 12..........................1127–28
Convention on the Conservation of
  Migratory Species of Wild Animals
  1979 (CMS).... 1087–88, 1125, 1129, 1143
Art III(4)(a) to (c)....................1127
Arts IV and V 1127
Convention on the Law of the
  Non-Navigational Uses of
  International Watercourses 1997 1099
Convention on the Protection of the
  Rhine 1999 1099
Art 2............................489–90
Art 3............................489–90
Art 5............................489–90
Art 14.............................499
Convention on the Protection of
  the Underwater Cultural
  Heritage 2001 1030–31
Convention on the Rights of Persons with
  Disabilities 2006 (CRPD).... 268–69, 330–31,
    713, 819, 830–33, 848–49, 1167–68
Art 2.............................356
Art 4(1) 737
Art 4(1)(b)........................760–61
Art 5(e)(iv) 217t
Art 9............. 352–53, 830–33, 848–49
Art 9(1) 830
Art 9(2) 832
Art 11...........................1011–12
Art 20............................830–33
Art 22.............................353
Art 24............................299, 328
Art 24(1) 282, 289, 352–53
Art 25............................215–16
Art 28............................168–69
Art 28(2) 85, 750–51, 765
Convention on the Rights of the Child
  1989 (CRC) see UN Convention on
  the Rights of the Child 1989
Convention on Wetlands of International
  Importance especially as Waterfowl
  Habitat 1971 (as amended in
  1982 and 1987) (1971 Ramsar
  Convention) 487–89, 1036–37,
    1087–88, 1101, 1109, 1125, 1143
Art 3(1) 1098–99
Art 4..............................1127
Convention Relating to the Status of
  Refugees 1951 (Refugee Convention)
Art 22............................289
Art 22(1) and (2)...................282–83
Convention relating to the Status of
  the River Gambia 1978
Art 4............................489–90

Convention relating to the Statute of the
  Senegal River 1964
Art 2............................489–90
Art 4............................489–90
Convention Relative to the Preservation
  of Fauna and Flora in their
  Natural State 1933 (1933 London
  Convention) 1086–87, 1090
Convention to Suppress the Slave Trade
  and Slavery 1926
Art 1............................603–4
Council of Europe Convention on
  Preventing and Combating Violence
  Against Women and Domestic
  Violence 2011 (CETS-No. 210)
  (Istanbul Convention) 398
Declaration on the Principles of Forest
  Management 1992 46–47
Declaration on the Right to
  Development
Art 1(1) 522
Arts 3 and 4.......................217t
Declaration on the Right to Development
  1986 32–33
Energy Charter Treaty 1994 (ECT)..... 518–21,
    985–86
Preamble 985
Art 2.............................520
Art 4.............................521
Art 7.............................521
Art 8.............................519–20
Art 18............................520–21
Art 19............................520–21
Art 24(2) 521
Escazú Agreement 2018 see Regional
  Agreement on Access to Information,
  Public Participation and Justice in
  Environmental Matters in Latin
  America and the Caribbean 2018
EU-Canada Comprehensive
  Economic and Trade Agreement
  2016 (CETA)...................998–99
Art 4(4) 998–99
Art 21(3) 998–99
Art 21(3) and (4)...................998–99
European Convention on Human
  Rights 1950
Art 2............................1003–04
Art 4............................601, 602–4
Art 8............................1003–04
Protocol No 1, Art 2 317
European Social Charter 1961
Arts 5 and 6 614–15
Art 11............................215–16
Art 13............................215–16
FAO Agreement Relating to the
  Implementation of Part XI of the
  1982 United Nations Convention

TABLE OF LEGISLATION lix

on the Law of the Sea 1994 (FAO
Compliance Agreement)....1030, 1064–65
Art III...............................1064–70
Art III(8) 1065
Art IV..............................1064–65
Art V(2)..............................1065
FAO Agreement to Promote Compliance
with International Conservation and
Management Measures by Fishing
Vessels on the High Seas 1993 (FAO
Compliance Agreement)............1043
Framework Agreement on the Sava River
Basin 2002
Art 3.............................489–90
Framework Convention on the Protection
and Sustainable Development of the
Carpathians 2003 (2003 Carpathian
Convention) 1088–89, 1099, 1121
General Agreement on Tariffs and
Trade 1947 (1947 GATT) 129
General Agreement on Tariffs and
Trade 1994 (1994 GATT) 973–74
Part IV.............................782
Art I 974, 978, 980–81
Art III... 974, 977, 978, 979, 980–81, 1287–89
Art XI.............................1287–89
Art XX 974, 976, 977, 978, 979, 980–81
Art XXXVII.........................782
Art XXXVIII, para 3(b) 782
Great Lakes Water Quality
Agreement 1978.................489–90
Helsinki Convention 1992 *see* UNECE
Convention on the Protection and Use
of Transboundary Watercourses and
International Lakes 1992
ILO Asbestos Convention 1986 (No 162)....897–99
ILO Chemical Convention 1990
(No 170).......................897–99
ILO Convention concerning Indigenous
and Tribal peoples in Independent
Countries 1989 (No 169).............498
ILO Convention concerning the Protection
and Integration of Indigenous and Other
Tribal and Semi-Tribal Populations in
Independent Countries 1957 (No 107)....498
ILO Conventions relating to Decent Work
and to Social Justice 579–81
ILO Discrimination in Respect of
Employment and Occupation
Convention 1958 (No 111) ...714–15, 755–56
ILO Employment Injury Benefits Convention
1964 (No 121).........................80
ILO Equal Remuneration Convention
1951 (No 100)...................755–56
ILO Equality of Treatment (Social Security)
Convention 1962 (No 118) 80
Art 3(1) 765–66
Art 4..............................765–66

ILO Forced Labour Convention
1932 (No 29)
Art 2(1) 604
ILO Freedom of Association and
Protection of the Right to Organise
Convention 1948 (No 87) 614–15
ILO Invalidity, Old-Age and Survivors'
Benefits Convention 1967 (No 128).....80
ILO Maintenance of Social Security Rights
Convention 1982 (No 157) 80, 765–66
ILO Maternity Protection Convention
2000 (No 183).......................80
ILO Medical Care and Sickness Benefits
Convention 1969 (No 130) 80
ILO Migrant Workers (Supplementary
Provisions) Convention 1975
(No 143)...........................777
Art 3................................777
Art 4................................777
Art 5................................777
ILO Migration for Employment
Convention (Revised) 1949 (No 97)
Art 9..............................793–94
ILO Minimum Age Convention
1973 (No 138)....................605–6
Art 2...............................606
Art 3(1) 606
ILO Minimum Wage Fixing Convention
1970 (No 131)...................755–56
ILO Night Work of Young Persons
(Industry) Convention 1919
(No 6)...........................605–6
ILO Prevention of Major Industrial
Accidents Convention 1993
(No 174).........................897–99
ILO Protection of Wages Convention
1949 (No 95) 755–56
ILO Right to Organise and Collective
Bargaining Convention 1949
(No 98)..........................614–15
ILO Safety and Health in Agriculture
Convention 2001 (No 184) 897–99
ILO Social Security (Minimum Standards)
Convention 1952 (No. 102)..... 80, 85–86,
557, 765–66
Art 9(b) 85
Art 9(c)..............................85
Art 15(b) 85
Art 15(c) 85
Art 21(b) 85
Art 27(b) 85
Art 27(c) 85
Art 41(b) 85
Art 41(c) 85
Art 48(b) 85
Art 55(b) 85
Art 55(c) 85
Art 61(c) 85

lx TABLE OF LEGISLATION

ILO Violence and Harassment Convention
2019 (No. 190)....................399
ILO Worst forms of Labour Convention
1999 (No 182)..............605–6, 607–8
Art 3(d) 606, 607
Inter-American Convention on
Protecting the Human Rights of
Older Persons 2015
Art 19...........................215–16
International Convention for the Control
and Management of Ship's Ballast
Water and Sediments 2004 .....1147, 1149
International Convention for the Prevention
of Pollution from Ships 1973
(MARPOL) 1035–36, 1058, 1250–51
International Convention for the
Protection of Birds 1950 1087
International Convention for the Safety
of Life at Sea 1974 (SOLAS)
Arts IV and V 1068–69
International Convention on the Elimination
of All Forms of Racial Discrimination
1965 (ICERD)................. 268–69, 713
Art 1(1) 737, 755
Art 2...............................737
Art 2(1)(c) 759
Art 2(2).............................750–51
Art 5(c)..............................755–56
Art 5(e)(i) 755–56
Art 5(e)(iii) 824–25
Art 5(v) 281–82, 289
Art 28(1)(c).........................281–82
International Convention on the
Protection of the Rights of All
Migrant Workers and Members of
Their Families 1990 (ICRMW).........777
Preamble 612–13
Art 5(e)(i) 575–76
Art 7...............................737
Art 10..............................282
Art 11(1) 776–77
Art 11(2)...........................776–77
Art 13.........................289, 298–99
Art 14(d) 282
Art 25(3)...........................612–13
Art 26..............................614–15
Art 27...............................85
Art 27(1) 765–66
Art 28......... 215–16, 612–13, 1047–48
Art 30.............................282, 289
Art 43.....................215–16, 282, 289
Art 45...........................215–16
International Covenant on Civil and
Political Rights 1966 (ICCPR) ... 8–9, 713, 841
Art 1(2) 866, 1047–48
Art 2...............................759
Art 2(1) 737

Art 6................... 217t, 819, 841
Art 6(1) 776–77, 990
Art 7.............................776–77
Art 8..............................601
Art 8(1) and (2)..................776–77
Art 8(3)(a) 776–77
Art 8(3)(c) 575–76
Art 9(1) 776–77
Art 12......................841, 844–45
Art 19.............................1167
Art 21.............................614–15
Art 22.....................575–76, 614–15
Art 25 .... 755–56, 1167–68
Art 26(1) 759
International Covenant on Economic,
Social and Cultural Rights 1966
(ICESCR)......8–9, 17–18, 200–1, 268–69,
300, 330–31, 339, 431, 453–54,
483–84, 493–95, 714–15, 766
Art 1(1) 773–74
Art 1(2) 866
Art 2(1) 156–57, 182, 183, 217t,
738, 750–51, 793–94
Art 2(2) 737, 738, 750–51, 759, 794–95
Art 3..............................737
Art 3(1)(c) 322
Art 4.............................759–60
Art 6 .... 321–22, 575–76
Art 6(1) 321–22
Art 6(2) 321–22
Art 7.............................576–77
Art 7(a)(i) 755–56
Art 7(b) 611–12
Art 8.............................576–77
Art 9 ....85, 557, 576–77, 765
Art 10 .... 85, 217t
Art 10(2) 85
Art 11 ....154–55, 164, 174, 183, 443–44,
483, 522, 576–77, 800, 819, 824–25, 866
Art 11(1) 152–53, 168–69, 172,
182, 755–56, 824–25
Art 11(2) 154–55, 172
Art 11(2)(a).................175, 177, 182
Art 11(2)(b)..............156–57, 184, 186
Art 12........... 215–16, 217t, 219, 443–44,
483, 522, 866, 1047–48
Art 12(1) 218
Art 12(2) 217t
Art 12(2)(a)........... 216–17, 428–29, 889
Art 12(2)(b) to (c)..................611–12
Art 13.........17–18, 273, 281–82, 305, 306,
319–20, 327–28, 336, 344
Art 13(1) 313–14
Art 13(2) 313–14
Art 13(2)(c).......................313, 321
Art 13(2)(e).............. 313–14, 319–20
Art 14................. 281–82, 305, 327–28

TABLE OF LEGISLATION lxi

Art 15 620–21
Art 15(1)(b) 182, 217*t*, 929–30
Art 17 825
Art 23(3) 281–82
Art 28 281–82
Art 28(1) 281–82
Art 29 281–82
Art 116 1047–48
International Plant Protection
  Convention 1991 (IPPC) 1147
International Treaty on Plant Genetic
  Resources for Food and
  Agriculture 2001
Art 1.1 180
Art 6 181
Art 9 181
Art 17 181
Art 18 181
International Treaty on Plant Genetic
  Resources for Food and Agriculture
  2001 (ITPGRFA) 1131, 1135–37
Preamble 1136
Art 1.1 ....180, 1135
Art 6 ....181, 1136
Art 9.2(a) and (b) 1137
Art 10 1136
Art 12.4 1136
Art 13 1136
Art 13.2 1136
Annex I 1136
International Tropical Timber Agreement
  2006 (ITTA) 1109, 1110
Art 1 1111
Kiev PRTR Protocol 2003 *see* UNECE
  Protocol on Pollutant Release and
  Transfer Registers 2003
Kiev SEA Protocol 2003 *see* UNECE
  Protocol on Strategic Environmental
  Assessment to The 1991 Convention
  on Environmental Impact Assessment
  in a Transboundary Context 2003
Kyoto Protocol to the United Nations
  Framework Convention on Climate
  Change 1997 .... 534, 962–66, 968, 984,
               1078–79, 1253–54, 1258–59
Art 3(1) 930, 962–63
Art 4 ....963, 976–77
Art 6 963–64
Art 12 963–64
Art 17 .... 963–64, 976–77
Annex I 962–63, 976–77, 1309–10
Lake Tanganyika Convention 2003
  see Convention on Sustainable
  Management of Lake Tanganyika 2003
London Convention 1900 *see* Convention
  Designed to Ensure the Conservation
  of Various Species of Wild Animals in

Africa, Which Are Useful to Man
  or Inoffensive 1900
London Convention 1933 *see* Convention
  Relative to the Preservation of Fauna
  and Flora in their Natural State 1933
London Convention 1972 *see* Convention for
  the Prevention of Marine Pollution by
  Dumping from Ships and Aircraft 1972
Maputo Convention 2003 *see* African
  Convention on the Conservation of
  Nature and Natural Resources 2003
MARPOL *see* International Convention
  for the Prevention of Pollution from
  Ships 1973
Marrakech Agreement Establishing the
  World Trade Organization 1994
Preamble 633
Annex 1C (TRIPs Agreement) *see*
  Agreement on Trade-Related Aspects
  of Intellectual Property Rights 1994
Mekong Agreement *see* Agreement
  on Cooperation for Sustainable
  Development of the Mekong
  River Basin 1995 489–90
Minamata Convention on Mercury 2013
Art 1 892–93
Montreal Protocol on Substances that
  Deplete the Ozone Layer 1987 892–93,
                                 1250–51
Nagoya Protocol on Access to Genetic
  Resources and the Fair and Equitable
  Sharing of Benefits Resulting from
  their Utilization 2010 .... 1073, 1131,
                          1136, 1137–42
Preamble 1133
Art 1 1133
Annex 1135
North American Agreement on
  Environmental Cooperation
Art 10(2)(i) 1127–28
Art 45(2)(a)(iii) 1127–28
North American Agreement on
  Environmental Cooperation
  1994 (NAAEC) 1291–92
North American Free Trade Agreement
  (NAFTA) 1994
Art 1102 985–86
Art 1105 985–86
Optional Protocol to the 1989 UN
  Convention on the Rights of the Child
  on the Involvement of Children in
  Armed Conflicts 2002 (OPAC)......607–8
Optional Protocol to the 1989 UN
  Convention on the Rights of the
  Child on the Sale of Children, Child
  Prostitution and Child Pornography
  2000 (OPSC) 607–8

lxii TABLE OF LEGISLATION

Organization of American States Inter-
American Democratic Charter 2001
Art 1 834–35
OSPAR Convention *see* Convention for the
Protection of the Marine Environment
of the North-East Atlantic 1992
Pact of San José *see* American Convention
on Human Rights 1969
Pan-American Convention 1940 *see*
Convention on Nature Protection and
Wild Life Preservation in the Western
Hemisphere 1940
Paris Agreement 2015 . . . . 534, 545–46, 701,
810, 888–89, 966–70, 984, 1004, 1058,
1096, 1253–54, 1258–59, 1295–96, 1297
Arts 1 to 4 540
Art 2(2) 966
Art 4(2) 967
Art 4(4) 540
Art 7(2) 177
Art 9(3) 967, 1009
Art 9(9) 1009
Art 10(4) 930
Art 12 925
Art 13(9) 1009–10
Art 14 968
Paris Convention 1902 *see* Convention
for the Protection of Birds Useful to
Agriculture 1902
Protocol Against the Smuggling of Migrants
by Land, Sea, and Air, Supplementing
the 2000 United Nations Convention
Against Transnational Organized
Crime 2000
Part II 777
Arts 5 and 6 777
Art 10 777
Protocol for Sustainable Development of
Lake Victoria Basin 2003 1099
Protocol of San Salvador *see* Additional
Protocol to the 1969 American
Convention on Human Rights in
the Area of Economic, Social and
Cultural Rights 1988
Protocol on Energy Efficiency and Related
Environmental Aspects
1994 (PEEREA) 521, 985
Art 7 524
Protocol on Shared Watercourse Systems
in the Southern African Development
Community (SADC) 1995, Art 2 . . . 489–90
Protocol on Strategic Environmental
Assessment to the 1991 Convention
on Environmental Impact Assessment
in a Transboundary Context 2003 498
Protocol on Water and Health to the 1992
UNECE (Helsinki) Convention on the

Protection and Use of Transboundary
Watercourses and International Lakes
1999 (UNECE Protocol on Water
and Health) 453–54, 463–64, 504–5
Art 9(2) 485–86
Protocol to Prevent, Suppress and Punish
Trafficking in Persons, Especially
Women and Children to the 2000 UN
Convention Against Transnational
Organized Crime 2000
Art 3 602
Protocol to the 1972 London Convention
on the Prevention of Marine Pollution
by Dumping of Wastes and Other
Matter 1996 1058
Protocol to the 2003 African Charter on
Human and Peoples' Rights on the
Rights of Women in Africa 2003
(2003 Maputo Protocol) 1088–89
Art 14 215–16
Art 14(2) 172
Art 15 172
Art 18 . . . . 467–68, 1047–48
Refugee Convention *see* Convention
Relating to the Status of Refugees 1951
Regional Agreement on Access to
Information, Public Participation
and Justice in Environmental Matters
in Latin America and the Caribbean
2018 (Escazú Agreement) 502
Art 1 1047–48
Arts 4 to 7 1047–48
Art 6(1) 1002
Art 6(3)(g) 1002
Art 9 1047–48
Art 11(2) 182
Rotterdam Convention on the Prior
Informed Consent Procedure for
Certain Hazardous Chemicals and
Pesticides in International Trade 1998. . 471
Art 1 892–93
Art 15(2) 925
Social Charter of the Americas 2012, Art 22 991
SOLAS *see* International Convention for
the Safety of Life at Sea 1974
Southern African Development Community
(SADC) Protocol on Shared
Watercourses 2000
Art 2 479–80
Southern African Development
Community (SADC) Protocol against
Corruption 2001, Preamble 1168–69
Statute of the Uruguay River 1975
Art 36 489–90
Stockholm Convention on Persistent
Organic Pollutants 2001
Art 1 892–93

TABLE OF LEGISLATION lxiii

Art 10(2) 925
Annexes D to F 471
Treaty between the United States of
America and Mexico Respecting
Utilization of Waters of the Colorado
and Tijuana Rivers and of the Rio
Grande 1944 (Colorado Treaty) 490–91
Treaty for Amazonian Cooperation 1978
Art I 489–90
Art VII 489–90
Treaty of the River Plate Basin 1969
Art I 489–90
Treaty on European Union
(EU treaty-TEU)..................522–23
Protocol on Energy Efficiency and
Related Environmental Aspects
1995, Art 7.....................523–24
UN Agreement for the Implementation of
the Provisions of the United Nations
Convention on the Law of the Sea
of 10 December 1982 relating to the
Conservation and Management of
Straddling Fish Stocks and Highly
Migratory Fish Stocks 1995 (UN Fish
Stocks Agreement - UNFSA) 1030,
1037, 1041, 1043, 1059, 1060, 1064
Art 2 1030
Arts 2 and 3 1065
Art 5 1030
Art 6 1065
Art 8(4) 1065
Art 18 1065–66
Art 19 1066
Art 20 1066
Art 21 1066
Art 23 1068–69
UN Charter *see* Charter of the
United Nations 1945
UN Convention against Corruption 2003
(UNCAC) 1143
Chapter III.......................1168–69
UN Convention against Transnational
Organized Crime 2000 (UNTOC)....1143
UN Convention on Biological Diversity
1992 (CBD)........46–47, 200–1, 487–89,
500, 549–50, 620–21, 888–89, 1033,
1073, 1078–80, 1085, 1088–89,
1099–101, 1102–19, 1122, 1124–26,
1127–39, 1141, 1143, 1144, 1148–49,
1150, 1151, 1152–53, 1252, 1253–54
Preamble 1133
Art 1 .... 491, 1099–100, 1124, 1132
Art 2 .... 1028–29, 1099, 1126, 1133
Art 3 ....1047–48, 1133
Art 4 1100
Art 4(a) and (b)......................1132
Art 6 1047–48

Arts 6 to 10 180
Art 6(b) 1150
Art 8 1124
Art 8(d) 1099–100
Art 8(f)...................491, 1099–100
Art 8(h) 1147, 1148–49
Art 8(j)............................1134
Art 10 1047–48
Art 10(a) 1150
Art 10(c) 1134
Art 11 ....1150, 1152–53
Art 13 922
Art 14 ....1047–48, 1150
Art 15 ....180, 1132, 1133, 1134
Art 16 1134
Art 19 1134
Art 20 1102–8
Art 20(2) 1108
UN Convention on Conditions for
Registration of Ships 1986..........1044
UN Convention on Consent to Marriage,
Minimum Age for Marriage and
Registration of Marriages 1964.....413–14
UN Convention on the Law of the Non-
Navigational Uses of International
Watercourses 1997 (UN Watercourses
Convention) 471, 489–90, 491, 500, 1147
Part III 499
Part IV 469, 487–89
Art 5(2) 495
Art 6(1) 456, 492
Art 7 492
Art 7(2) 456
Art 10(1) 454–55
Art 10(2) 442–43, 454–56
Arts 11 to 19 499
Art 20 ....486, 1100
Art 21 469–70
Art 21(2) 469, 470
Art 21(3) 469–70
Art 22 486
Art 23(3) 486
Arts 20 to 23 469
UN Convention on the Law of the Sea 1982
(UNCLOS) 620–21, 1030–48, 1059,
1073, 1074–75, 1250–51
Preamble 1032, 1035–36
Part VII 1041–42
Part XI 1034–35
Part XII 1030–31, 1037–38, 1041–42
Art 2 1068
Art 8 1068
Art 17(1) 1055–56
Art 25(2) 1068
Art 61 1038
Art 62(2) 1038
Arts 63 and 64 1040–41

lxiv TABLE OF LEGISLATION

Arts 63 to 65 1039–40
Art 87.............................1039
Art 91.............................1044
Art 92(1).........................1043
Art 94.............................1043
Art 116..................... 1039, 1067–68
Art 117............. 1039, 1043, 1067–68
Art 118........... 1030–31, 1039–40, 1041
Art 119............................1040
Art 120............................1039
Art 123............................1037
Art 140(1)......................1055–56
Art 153(2) to (4)................1055–56
Art 192..........................1041–42
Art 194............................1052
Art 194(5).........................1042
Art 197...................... 1037, 1041
Art 198............................1037
Art 201............................1058
Art 207............................1058
Art 207(1) and (2)..................1052
Art 207(4) and (5)..................1037
Art 208............................1058
Art 208(5).........................1037
Art 209............................1058
Art 210(4).........................1037
Art 211............................1058
Art 211(1).........................1037
Art 212............................1058
Art 212(3).........................1037
Art 231............................1052
Art 237.........................1030–31
Arts 243 and 244...................1072
Art 256............................1072
Art 257............................1072
Art 266(2) and (3).................1072
Art 311.........................1030–31
Arts 63 to 65 1031
Annex III.......................1055–56

UN Convention on the Political Rights
of Women 1952..................... 425

UN Convention on the Rights of the Child
1989 (CRC).....8–9, 268–69, 295–96, 300,
309, 336, 415, 819, 824–25, 848–49,
897–99, 1169, 1209–10, 1213, 1235
Preamble 235
Arts 1 to 7..........................235
Art 2(1) 737
Art 4......................... 217t, 750–51
Art 6......................... 217t, 305–6
Art 6(1) 990
Art 7(1) 1169
Art 17..............................235
Art 19..............................235
Arts 23 to 25 235
Art 23(3) 268–69
Art 24................... 215–16, 217t, 235

Art 24(1) 172
Art 24(2) 467–68
Art 24(2)(c)...................168–69, 172
Art 26............................... 85
Art 27..............................235
Art 27(3) 824–25
Art 28........ 268–69, 289, 298–99, 305, 306
Art 28(1) 299
Art 28(3) 299, 336–37
Art 28(e) 327–28
Art 29.........................235, 268–69
Art 29(1) 344
Arts 31 to 33 235
Art 24..........................1047–48
Art 32.........................575–76, 606
Arts 33 to 36 607–8
Art 41..............................313
Art 44..............................309

UN Convention to Combat Desertification
in those Countries Experiencing
Serious Drought and/or
Desertification, Particularly in
Africa 1994 (UNCCD)...... 991, 1078–80,
1088–89, 1097, 1099, 1101, 1109,
1113–19, 1125, 1252, 1253–54
Art 1(a) 1116
Art 1(b) 1113–14, 1115
Art 1(f).........................1113–14
Art 2.........................1115, 1116
Arts 2 and 3........................1116
Art 2(2).........................1109–10
Art 6..............................1116
Art 8..............................922
Art 10(2)(a).........................991
Art 19..............................922

UN Declaration on the Rights of
Indigenous Peoples 2007
(UNDRIP).......................335–36
Art 14(2) 282–83, 328
Art 18..........................1011–12
Art 26(1) and (2)....................175
Art 31(2) 180

UN Framework Convention on Climate
Change 1992 (UNFCCC) 46–47, 542,
549–50, 620–21, 666, 701, 733–34,
821–22, 888–89, 945, 949, 952, 953,
955, 958, 961–62, 968, 984, 988, 989, 994,
999, 1001, 1010, 1013, 1033, 1082, 1085,
1097, 1109, 1111, 1113–16, 1118, 1119,
1122, 1125, 1252, 1253–54, 1258–59,
1291–92, 1295–96, 1308, 1311
Preamble 959–60, 990
Art 2.........................962, 1114
Art 2(1)(a)..........................534
Art 3..............................958
Art 3(1) 959–60
Art 3(5) 981

TABLE OF LEGISLATION   lxv

Art 4 962
Art 4(1)(c) 534
Art 4(1)(d) 1114
Art 4(3) 1006
Art 4(4) 1007
Art 4(8) 990
Art 4.1(f) 995
Art 5 . . . . 962, 1000–01
Art 6 922
Art 12 962
Art 12(1) 1006–07
Arts 7 to 11 962
Annex B 534
Annex I 1000
Annex II 1006–07
UN Watercourses Convention *see*
   UN Convention on the Law of
   the Non-Navigational Uses of
   International Watercourses 1997
UNECE Convention on Access to
   Information, Public Participation
   in Decision-Making and Access to
   Justice in Environmental Matters
   1998 (Aarhus Convention) 498, 502,
                                       925, 1001–02
   Art 4 930
UNECE Convention on Environmental
   Impact Assessment in a
   Transboundary Context 1991
   (Espoo Convention) 881, 995
   Art 2 498
   Art 3(8) 498
   Art 4(2) 498
   Appendix I 500
UNECE Convention on Long-range
   Transboundary Air Pollution
   Art 1 845–46
UNECE Convention on the Protection and
   Use of Transboundary Watercourses
   and International Lakes 1992
   (UNECE Water Convention;
   Helsinki Convention) . . . 489–90, 1099, 1101
   Art 1(2) 489–90
   Art 2(2) 489–90
   Art 2(2)(d) 1100
   Art 3(1)(i) 489–90
   Art 5(2) 485–86
   Art 9 485–86
   Art 16 499
   Art 21 485–86
   Art 24 485–86
   Art 33(2) 485–86
UNECE Protocol on Pollutant Release
   and Transfer Registers 2003
   (Kiev PRTR Protocol) 994
UNECE Protocol on Strategic Environmental
   Assessment to The 1991 Convention on

Environmental Impact Assessment
   in a Transboundary Context 2003
   (Kiev SEA Protocol) 881, 925, 995
UNECE Protocol on Water and Health
   see Protocol on Water and Health
   to the 1992 UNECE (Helsinki)
   Convention on the Protection and
   Use of Transboundary Watercourses
   and International Lakes 1999 . . . . . 469, 471
   Art 3 469
   Art 4(2)(b) 466
UNESCO Convention Against
   Discrimination in Education 1960
   (CADE) 300, 305, 330–31, 339, 714–15
   Preamble 299
   Art 4 . . . . 298–99, 336
   Art 4(a) 313, 327–28
   Arts 3 and 4 282–83
UNESCO Convention on Technical and
   Vocational Education 1989 (CTVE)
   Art 3(1)(c) 322
United States-Mexico-Canada Agreement
   2018 (USMCA) 1290–91
   Art 11(7) 998–99
   Art 28 998–99
Universal Declaration of Human Rights
   1948 (UDHR) 19–20, 26–27, 32–33,
            152–53, 268–69, 279–81, 294–95, 298–99,
                431, 517–18, 578, 738, 803, 1167
   Art 2 737
   Art 3 . . . . 217t, 990
   Art 4 601
   Art 12 866
   Art 19 1167
   Art 20 614–15
   Art 21 834–35
   Art 21(1) 834–35
   Art 22 . . . . 84, 557, 620–21
   Art 23 575–76
   Art 25 . . . . 2, 84, 154–55, 214–15, 218–20,
                              415, 522, 575–76
   Art 25(1) 866, 1047–48
   Art 26 . . . . 273, 279, 298–99, 305,
                              313–14, 321, 344
   Art 26(1) 280, 327–28
   Art 26(2) 279
   Art 27 . . . . 217t, 620–21
   Art 27(1) 280
   Art 28 . . . . 217t, 773–74
Vienna Convention for the Protection
   of the Ozone Layer 1985 1250–51
   Preamble 930
   Art 2(2) 874–75
Vienna Convention on the Law of
   Treaties 1969 517–18
   Art 2(1)(a) 815
   Art 31(3)(c) 984

lxvi TABLE OF LEGISLATION

WHO Framework Convention on
Tobacco Control 2003 . . . . .242, 256–58
World Heritage Convention *see* Convention
Concerning the Protection of the World
Cultural and Natural Heritage 1972
WTO Agreement on Government
Procurement 2012 (GPA) 917–18
WTO Agreement on Subsidies and
Countervailing Measures 1994
(ASCM). 977–78
WTO Agreement on Trade-Related Aspects
of Intellectual Property Rights 1994
(TRIPs Agreement) 637–38, 661
Art 27(1) 704
Art 31(b) 700–1
Art 66(1) 258–59
WTO Agreement on Trade Related
Investment Measures (TRIMs) 1994 1292
Art 2.1 1287–89
Annex. 1287–89
ZAMCOM Agreement *see* Agreement
on the Establishment of the Zambezi
Water Commission 2004

NATIONAL AND REGIONAL LEGISLATION

Algeria

Family Code
Art 8 388–89
Art 11 389
Art 30 389
Art 39 389–90

Andorra

Law on the Eradication of Gender
Violence and Domestic Violence
2015, Art 6 403–06

Argentina

Law on the Comprehensive Protection of
Women 2009
Art 7 407–08
Art 10 407–08

Austria

University Organisation and Studies Act 2002
s 2 332–33
s 3 332–33
s 20a 332–33

Benin

Law on the Prevention and Repression
of Violence against Women
2012, Art 5 403–06

Bolivia

Comprehensive Law to Guarantee
Women a Life Free of Violence
2013, Art 17. .409–11

Canada

Corruption, Drug Trafficking and Other
Serious Crimes Act 1992 1226
Indian Act 1876. 391
Prevention of Corruption Act 2018 1226

Chile

Civil Procedure Code,
Arts 829 to 832. 389–90

China

Anti-food Waste Law of the People's
Republic of China, Order No 78
of the President of the People's
Republic of China
(29 April 2021) 887–88

Colombia

Law 1257 (on the Awareness, Prevention
and Sanctioning of Discrimination and
Violence Against Women) 2008
Art 14. 409–11
Art 20 409–11

Comoros

Penal Code, Art 331 390

Czech Republic

Act no 110/1997 Coll. on Foodstuffs
and Tobacco Products and on
Amendments to Some
Related Acts. .886–87

Denmark

Danish Financial Statements Act (as
amended by Law No 1403 of
27 December 2008), s 99a 907

Ecuador

Law to Prevent and Eradicate Violence
Against Women 2018
Art 9. 409–11
Art 25. 403–06
Art 31 403–06

Egypt

Criminal Procedural Code 397
Penal Code, Art 242 386–87

European Union

Regulation (EC) No 1907/2006 concerning the Registration, Evaluation, Authorisation and Restriction of Chemicals (REACH), establishing a European Chemicals Agency, amending Directive 1999/45/EC and repealing Council Regulation (EEC) No 793/93 and Commission Regulation (EC) No 1488/94 as well as Directive 76/769/EEC and Commission Directives 91/155/EEC, 93/67/EEC, 93/105/EC and 2000/ 21/EC [2006] OJ L136/3 (REACH Regulation) 881
recital 69.........................894–95
recital 70.........................894–95
Art 5 894–95
Art 6 (1) 894–95
Art 7 894–95
Art 29 894–95
Art 55 894–95
Art 60(4) 894–95
Art 68 894–95
Arts 5 and 6 894–95
Regulation (EU) 2019/631 setting CO2 Emission Performance Standards for new Passenger Cars and for New Light Commercial Vehicles, and repealing Regulation (EC) No 443/ 2009 and (EU) No 510/2011 [2019] OJ L 111/13 704
Regulation (EU) 2021/1119 establishing the framework for achieving climate neutrality and amending Regulations (EC) No 401/2009 and (EU) 2018/ 1999 (European Climate Law), recital 13 978
Directive 76/464/EEC on Pollution Caused by Certain Dangerous Substances Discharged into the Aquatic Environment [1976] OJ L129/23 471
Directive 76/769/EEC on the Approximation of the Laws, Regulations and administrative Provisions of the Member States Relating to Restrictions on the Marketing and Use of Certain Dangerous Substances and Preparations [1976] OJ L 262/201 894–95
Directive 82/176/EEC concerning the Discharge of Mercury by the Chlor-Alkali Electrolysis Industry [1982] OJ L81 471
Directive 83/513/EEC concerning the Discharge of Cadmium [1983] OJ L291/1 471
Directive 84/156/EEC concerning the Discharge of Mercury by the

Chlor-Alkali Electrolysis Industry [1984] OJ L74 471
Directive 84/491/EEC on Limit Values and Quality Objectives for Discharges of Hexachlorocyclohexane [1984] OJ L274/11 471
Directive 86/280/EEC on Limit Values and Quality Objectives for Discharges of Certain Dangerous Substances Included in List I of the Annex to Directive 76/464/EEC, including Carbon Tetrachloride, DDT and Pentachlorophenol, [1986] OJ L181/16 ... 471
Directive 88/347/EEC on Limit Values and Quality Objectives relating to Aldrin, Dieldrin, Endrin, Isodrin, Hexachlorobenzene, Hexachlorobutadine, and Chloroform (1988) OJ L158/35 471
Directive 94/62/EC on packaging and packaging waste [1994] OJ L 365/10 ... 903
Directive 1999/31/EC on the landfill of waste [1999] OJ L 182/1............. 903
Directive 2000/53/EC on end-of life vehicles- Commission Statements [2000] OJ L 269/34.................. 903
Directive 2000/60/EC establishing a framework for Community action in the field of water policy [2000] OJ L327/1 (Water Framework Directive -WFD) 471, 476–77
Art 5 479–80
Art 11 479–80
Annex VII 477
Directive 2003/87/EC establishing a scheme for GHG emission allowance trading within the Community, that defines 'allowance' as: 'an allowance to emit 1 tonne of carbon dioxide equivalent during a specified period valid only for the purposes of meeting the requirements of the Directive and which is transferable in accordance with the provisions of this Directive (ETS Directive)' 977, 984
Directive 2006/66/EC on batteries and accumulators and waste batteries and accumulators and repealing Directive 91/157/EEC [2006] OJ L 266/1........ 903
Directive 2008/98/EC on waste and repealing certain Directives OJ L 312/3 (Waste Framework Directive), Art 4 903
Directive 2009/29/EC amending Directive 2003/87/EC so as to improve and extend the greenhouse gas emission allowance trading scheme of the Community [2009] OJ L 140/63....... 978

lxviii   TABLE OF LEGISLATION

Directive 2011/36/EU on preventing and
combating trafficking in human
beings and protecting victims that
replaced Council Framework decision
2002/629/JHA [2011] OJ L101/1 602–3
Directive 2012/19/EU on waste electrical
and electronic equipment (WEEE)
[2012] OJ L 197/38 903
Directive 2012/27/EU on energy efficiency,
amending Directives 2009/125/
EC and 2010/30/EU and repealing
Directives 2004/8/EC and 2006/32/
EC (Energy Efficiency Directive)
[2012] OJ L 315/1 539–40
Directive 2013/34/EU on the annual
financial statements, consolidated
financial statements and related
reports of certain types of
undertakings, amending Directive
2006/43/EC and repealing Council
Directives 78/660/EEC and 83/349/
EEC [2013] OJ L 182/19, as amended
by Directive 2014/95/EU..........908–9
Art 19a...........................909–10
Directive 2014/24/EU on public
procurement and repealing Directive
2004/18/EC [2014] OJ L 94/65 (Public
Procurement Directive)
Art 18...........................918–19
Art 67...........................917–18
Directive 2014/95/EU amending
Directive 2013/34/EU as regards
disclosure of non-financial and
diversity information by certain large
undertakings and groups [2014] OJ L
330/1 909–10
Directive 2019/633 on unfair trading
practices in business-to-business
relationships in the agricultural and
food supply chain [2019]
OJ L 111/59 889–90

Finland

Constitution 1919 (2000 draft), s 16.....317–18

France

Act no 2016-138 on Fight against the Food
Waste (Loi n° 2016-138 du 11 février
2016 relative à la lutte contre le gaspillage
alimentaire) (11 February 2016)....886–87
Law No 2001-420 dated 15 May 2001, on
New Economic Regulations, Art 116 907

Gabon

Civil Code, Art 257....................389–90
Family Law, Arts 177 and 178 388–89

Germany

Bundesteilhabegesetz (Federal
Participation Act) 2016 758

Guinea Bissau

Domestic Violence Law 2014,
Art 10........................403–06

India

Black Money (Undisclosed Foreign
Income and Assets) and Imposition
of Tax Act 2015 1225
Fugitive Economic Offenders Act 2018 1225
Prevention of Corruption Act 2018 1225
Prevention of Money Laundering Act 1225
Right to Information Act 2005 1240
Whistle blowers Protection Act 2014......1225

Ireland

Water Services Act 2007 (as amended) ...505–6

Italy

Act no 166 Coll. concerning the donation
and distribution of food and
pharmaceutical products for pur-ì
sociale e per la limitazione degli
sprechi) (19 August 2016) 886–87
Law No 119/2013 (converting into law, with
amendments, Law Decree No 39/2013
containing urgent provisions, inter
alia, on the fight against gender-based
violence) 2013, Art 5 403–06,
                                    407–08
Lombardy Regional Law, Act n. 27 (Legge
Regionale 1 ottobre 2015, No 27
Politiche regionali in materia di
turismo e attrattività del territorio
lombardo (October 2015), Art 75(2) ... 939

Jamaica

Deoxyribonucleic Acid (DNA) Evidence
Act 2016.........................1202
Law Reform (Zones of Special Operations)
(Special Security and Community
Development Measures) Act 2017 1202
Proceeds of Crime Act 2007 1220–21

Japan

Act on Promotion of Resource Circulation
for Plastics 2021 904–5
Basic Act for Establishing a Sound
Material-Cycle Society (Act
No 110 of 2000)....................904–5
Basic Act on Education 2006, Art 2(3)......348

TABLE OF LEGISLATION   lxix

Law for Promotion of Effective
    Utilisation of Resources............904–5

Kenya
Constitution, Art 27.....................1244

Korea
Act on Promotion of Purchase of Green
    Products........................919–20

Kyrgyzstan
Law on Safeguarding and Protection
    from Domestic Violence 2017,
    Art 13.........................403–06

Laos
Law on Preventing and Combatting
    Violence against Women and
    Children 2014
    Art 18..........................403–06
    Art 27..........................407–08

Lebanon
Law no 293 on domestic violence,
    Art 522...........................390
Penal Code
    Art 522...........................390
    Art 562...........................390

Liberia
Domestic Relations Law 1973, s 2.2.....419–20

Malaysia
Anti-Trafficking in Persons and
    Anti-Smuggling of Migrants
    Act 2007.........................1212
Constitution, Art 5(3) 1217

Mexico
General Act on the Rights of Children
    and Adolescents in respect of the
    minimum age for marriage...........418
General Law on Women's Access to a Life
    Free of Violence 2007
    Art 40..........................409–11
    Art 45..........................403–06

Namibia
Flexible Land Tenure Act 4 of
    2012, Art 2.........................93
Recognition of Marriages Act 1991,
    Art 10.33 420

Nicaragua
Integral Law on Violence against Women
    and to Reform Law No 641 'Penal
    Code' 2012, Art 19 403–06,
                           407–08

Nigeria
Child Rights Act 2003 1209–10

Norway
Act on Public Procurement of 17 June 2016,
    No 73 (LOV-2016-06-17-73) 919–20

Panama
Law to Criminalize Femicide and
    Violence Against Women 2013,
    Art 24..........................409–11

Peru
Act to Prevent, Punish and Eradicate
    Violence Against Women and
    Members of the Family Group 2015
    Art 27..........................407–08
    Art 41..........................409–11
    Art 45..........................409–11

Philippines
Republic Act No 10524, 'An Act Expanding
    the Positions Reserved for Persons With
    Disability, Amending for the purpose
    Republic Act No 7277 (as amended)'....758

Portugal
Law for the prevention of domestic violence,
    protection and the assistance of victims
    2009, Arts 77 and 78..............403–06

Russian Federation
Regulation No 162 422–23

Senegal
Loi No 2003-14 du 4 juin 2004 relative
    aux Mutuelles de santé, art 8 (non-
    discrimination in access to healthcare)....439

Sierra Leone
Anti-Corruption Act 2008 (as amended) 1223
Anti-Corruption Right to Access
    Information Law 2013..............1240
Child Rights Act 2007, s 34 419–20
Citizenship Act 1973 390–91
Citizenship Act 2017 390–91

South Africa

Bill of Rights 390
Children's Act
  s 12(5)............................... 390
  s 17 390
Constitution 390
Promotion of Access to Information
    Act 2000.......................... 1240

Spain

Law on Comprehensive Protection
    Measures against Gender Violence
    2004, Art 6.....................403–06

Sudan

Anti-Trafficking Act 2014 1211

Tanzania

Marriage Act, s 10(1) 388–89

United Kingdom

Equality Act 2006 423
Procurement Reform (Scotland) Act
    2014 (asp 12), s 9.................919–20
Waste (Scotland) Regulations 2012 886–87

United States

Endangered Species Act 1973 867
Family Violence Prevention and Services
    Act, s 311 409–11
New York State Excess Food Act........886–87
Violence Against Women Act 1994
    (as amended)...................407–08
  Title IV, Chapter 9..................409–11
Violence Against Women Reauthorization
    Act, 2013—An Act To reauthorize
    the Violence Against Women Act
    of 1994, s 1301..................409–11

Venezuela

Civil Code 420

Vietnam

Inclusive Education Guidelines for Persons
    with Disabilities 2006................ 291
National Law on Persons with
    Disabilities 2012.................... 291

Zimbabwe

Public Finance Management
    Act 2009.......................... 1224

List of Abbreviations

3Rs	reduce, reuse, and recycle
10YFP	10 Year Framework of Programmes
AAAA	Addis Ababa Action Agenda
AAAQ	Availability, Accessibility, Acceptability, and Quality
AAL	annual average loss
AAU	Assignment Amount Units
ABMS	Anti-Bribery Management System
ABNJ	areas beyond national jurisdiction
ABS	access and benefit-sharing
ACERWC	African Committee of Experts on the Rights and Welfare of the Child
ACHR	American Convention on Human Rights
ACHPR	African Charter on Human and Peoples' Rights
ACORN	Anti-Corruption in Nigeria (UK)
ACRWC	African Charter on the Rights and Welfare of the Child
ADB	Asian Development Bank
ADFD	Abu Dhabi Fund for Development
AEDC	Australian Early Development Census
AfCETA	African Continental Free Trade Area
AfDB	African Development Bank
AFT	Aid for Trade
AIMM	Anticipated Impact Measurement and Monitoring
ALE	adult learning and education
ALMA	African Leaders Malaria Alliance
AMCOW	African Ministers Council on Water
AMR	common but differentiated responsibilities
AoA	Agreement on Agriculture
APEIs	Areas of Particular Environmental Interest
ARENA	Australian Renewable Energy Agency
AROPE	at risk of poverty or social exclusion
ASCM	Agreement on Subsidies and Countervailing Measures
ASEAN	Association of Southeast Asian Nations
ASPNet	Associated Schools Network
ASSELLAU	Association of Environmental Law Lecturers in African Universities
ASSELLMU	Association of Environmental Law Lecturers in Middle East and North African Universities
ATI	Alternative Tourism Initiative (Greece)
ATM	automated teller machine
B2B	business-to-business
B2C	business-to-consumer
BBBEE	Broad-Based Black Economic Empowerment (South Africa)
BBNJ	Biodiversity beyond National Jurisdiction

lxxii LIST OF ABBREVIATIONS

BCG	Bio-Circular Green (Thailand)
BHR	business and human rights
BIREC	Beijing International Renewable Energy Conference
BIT	Bilateral Investment Treaty
BEST	Battery-Energy Storage Technologies
BpFA	Beijing Platform for Action
BRC	biodiversity-related conventions
BRI	Belt and Road Initiative (China)
BRIC	Brazil, Russia, India, and China
BTAs	Border Tax Adjustments
BURs	Biennial Update Reports
CADE	Convention against Discrimination in Education
CARICOM	Caribbean Community
CARMMA	Campaign on Accelerated Reduction of Maternal Mortality in Africa
CBD	Convention on Biological Diversity
CBDR	common but differentiated responsibility
CBDR-RC	Common but differentiated responsibilities and respective capabilities
CBOs	community-based organizations
CCAMLR	Commission for the Conservation of Antarctic Marine Living Resources
CCBSP	Commission for the Conservation and Management of Pollock Resources in the Central Bering Sea
CCPCJ	Commission on Crime Prevention and Criminal Justice
CCSBT	Convention on the Conservation of the Southern Bluefin Tuna
CDM	Clean Development Mechanism
CE	circular economy
CEAP	Circular Economy Action Plan
CEB	Chief Executives Board for Coordination
CECSCR	Committee on Economic, Social and Cultural Rights
CEDAW	Convention on the Elimination of All Forms of Discrimination against Women
CEPS	Centre for European Policy Studies
CER	Certified Emission Reductions
CESCR	Committee on Economic, Social and Cultural Rights
CET	clean energy technology
CETA	EU-Canada Comprehensive Economic and Trade Agreement
CIDA	Canadian International Development Agency
CITES	Convention on International Trade in Endangered Species of Wild Fauna and Flora
CMA	Conference of the Parties serving as the meeting of the Parties to the Paris Agreement
CMM	conservation and management measures
CMP	Conference of the Parties serving as the meeting of the Parties to the Kyoto Protocol
CMS	Convention on Migratory Species
CMW	Convention on the Rights of All Migrant Workers and Members of their families
CommICSCR	Committee on the International Covenant on Economic, Social and Cultural Rights

COP	Conference of the Parties
COVAX	COVID-19 Vaccine Global Access Facility
CPTPP	Comprehensive and Progressive Agreement for Trans-Pacific Partnership
CRBP	Children's Rights and Business Principles
CRC	Convention on the Rights of the Child
CRPD	Convention on the Rights of Persons with Disabilities
CRS	Creditor Reporting System
CSD	Commission on Sustainable Development
CSE	comprehensive sexuality education
CSO	civil society organization
CSRD	Corporate Sustainability Reporting Directive
CTD	Committee on Trade and Development
CTE	Committee on Trade and Environment
CTVE	Convention on Technical and Vocational Education
CUP	Cambridge University Press
DAC	Development and Assistance Committee
DCF	UN Development Cooperation Forum
DESA	UN Department of Economic and Social Affairs
DESD	Decade of Education for Sustainable Development
DEVAW	Declaration on the Elimination of Violence against Women
DFI	domestic financial institution
DfID	Department for International Development (UK)
DMC	domestic material consumption
DNA	Designated National Authority
DRC	Democratic Republic of Congo
DRM	domestic resource mobilization
DRR	Disaster Risk Reduction
DSI	digital sequence information
DSSI	Debt Service Suspension Initiative
DTCs	Developing and Transition countries
EC	European Communities
ECA	Economic Commission for Africa
ECCE	early childhood care or education
ECDI	Early Childhood Development Index
ECHA	European Chemicals Agency in Helsinki
ECHR	European Convention on Human Rights
ECLAC	Economic Commission for Latin America and the Caribbean
ECOSOC	UN Economic and Social Council
ECT	Energy Charter Treaty
ECtHR	European Court of Human Rights
EEZ	exclusive economic zone
EFA	Education For All
EFR	environmental flow requirements
EIA	environmental impact assessment
ENAP	Every Newborn Action Plan
EPA	Environmental Protection Agency ((United States)
EPG	Eminent Persons Group
EPMM	Ending Preventable Maternal Mortality

lxxiv LIST OF ABBREVIATIONS

EPO	European Patent Office
ERP	Enterprise Resource Planning
ERUs	Emission Reduction Units
ES	Ecosystem Services
ESA	Eastern and Southern Africa
ESC	economic, social, and cultural
ESD	Education for Sustainable Development
ESTs	environmentally sound technologies
ETS	Emission Trading Schemes
EU	European Union
EXIM	Export-Import Bank of China
FACB	freedom of association and collective bargaining
FACTI	High Level Panel on International Financial Accountability, Transparency and Integrity for Achieving the 2030 Agenda
FAO	Food and Agriculture Organization
FCTC	Framework Convention on Tobacco Control
FDES	Framework for the Development of Environmental Statistics
FDI	foreign direct investment
FET	fair and equitable treatment
FFD	Financing for Development
FFDO	Financing for Development Office
FFFSR	Friends of Fossil Fuel Subsidy Reform
FFS	fossil fuel subsidies
FFSR	Fossil Fuel Subsidy Reform
FFST	Fossil Fuel Subsidies Tracker
FGM	female genital mutilation
FIES	Food Insecurity Experience Scale
FIT	Feed-in-tariffs
FLI	food loss index
FSB	Financial Stability Board
FTA	Free Trade Agreement
FWI	food waste index
FWL	food waste and food loss
G7	Group of Seven
G20	Group of Twenty
GA	General Assembly
GAP	Global Action Programme
GARs	Global Assessment Reports
GATS	General Agreement on Trade in Services
GATT	General Agreement on Tariffs and Trade
GBF	Global Biodiversity Framework
GBO	Global Biodiversity Outlook
GBV	gender-based violence
GCC	Gulf Cooperation Council
GCED	Global Citizenship Education
GCET	Global Code of Ethics for Tourism
GCF	Green Climate Fund
GDP	gross domestic product

GEF	Global Environmental Facility
GEF	Global Environmental Fund
GEFI	Global Education First Initiative
GEMR	Global Education Monitoring Report
GEO BON	Group on Earth Observations' Biodiversity Observation Network
GESAMP	Group of Experts on the Scientific Aspects of Marine Environmental Protection
GEWE	gender equality and women's empowerment
GFCM	General Fisheries Commission for the Mediterranean
GFF	Global Financing Facility for Women, Children and Adolescents
GGBV	global gender-based violence
GHG	green-house gas
GIF	Global Indicator Framework
GiZ	German Cooperation Agency
GLASS	Global Antimicrobial Resistance and Use Surveillance System
GLTN	Global Land Tool Network
GNI	gross national income
GNP	gross national product
GOF	global objectives on forests
GoF47	Group of Friends of Paragraph 47
GPA	Agreement on Governmental Procurement
GPEDC	Global Partnership for Effective Development Cooperation
GPI	Gender Parity Index
GPIS	Green Procurement Information System (South Korea)
GPP	Gross Primary Productivity
GR	genetic resources
GRI	Global Reporting Initiative
GSP	Generalised System of Preferences
GSP	High-level Panel on Global Sustainability
GTPI	Global Tourism Plastics Initiative
GVA	gross value added
GWP	Global Water Partnership
HALE	health-adjusted life expectancy
HBM	Health Belief Model
HDI	human development index
HIPC	Heavily Indebted Poor Countries Initiative
HLP	High Level Panel
HLPE	High-Level Panel of Experts on Food Security and Nutrition
HLPF	High-Level Political Forum
HLPFSD	High Level Political Forum on Sustainable Development
HOSDGCLA	Heads of State Declaration for Greater Climate Ambition
HPV	human papilloma virus
HRC	Human Rights Council
HSE	health, safety, and environmental
HSS	health systems strengthening
IAASTD	International Assessment of Agricultural Knowledge, Science and Technology for Development
IAEG-SDGs	Inter-agency and Expert Group on SDG Indicators

LIST OF ABBREVIATIONS

IAIA	International Association for Impact Assessment
IAS	invasive alien species
IATP	Institute for Agriculture and Trade Policy
IATT	Interagency Task Team on Science, Technology and Innovation
IATTC	Inter-American Tropical Tuna Commission
IBRD	International Bank for Reconstruction and Development
ICAO	International Civil Aviation Organization
ICC	International Criminal Court
ICC	Indigenous Cultural Consultant
ICCA	Indigenous and community conserved areas
ICCAR	International Coalition of Inclusive and Sustainable Cities
ICCAT	International Commission for the Conservation of Atlantic Tunas
ICCM	International Conference for Chemicals Management
ICCPR	International Covenant on Civil and Political Rights
ICCS	International Classification of Crime for Statistical Purposes
ICCWC	International Consortium on Combating Wildlife Crime
ICERD	International Convention on the Elimination of All Forms of Racial Discrimination
ICESCR	International Covenant on Economic, Social and Cultural Rights
ICESDF	Intergovernmental Committee of Experts on Financing for Sustainable Development
ICIMOD	International Centre for Integrated Mountain Development
ICJ	International Court of Justice
ICLEI	International Council for Local Environment Initiatives
ICPD	International Conference on Population and Development
ICPDR	International Commission for the Protection of the Danube River
ICRMW	International Convention on the Protection of the Rights of All Migrant Workers and Members of Their Families
ICSID	International Centre for Settlement of Investment Disputes
ICT	information and communications technology
IDA	International Development Association
IDG	International Development Goal
IDEA	Institute for Democracy and Electoral Assistance
IDM	Individual Deprivation Measure
IDP	internally displaced person
IDTs	International Development Targets
IEA	International Energy Agency
IEc	Industrial Economics
IET	international emission trading scheme
IFAD	International Fund for Agricultural Development
IFF	illicit financial flows
IFI	international financial institution
IFMSA	International Federal of Medical Students' Association
IGC	intergovernmental conference
IGG	Inclusive Green Growth
IGME	Inter-Agency Group for Child Mortality Estimation
IGO	International Governmental Organization

LIST OF ABBREVIATIONS lxxvii

IHDP-IT	International Human Dimensions Program on Global Environmental Change—Industrial Transformation Project
IHP	International Hydrological Programme
IHR	International Health Regulations
IIA	international investment agreement
IIED	International Institute for Environment and Development
IISD	International Institute for Sustainable Development
ILA	International Law Association
ILC	Indigenous and local communities
ILC	International Law Commission
ILO	International Labour Organization
ILUA	Indigenous Land Use Agreement (Australia)
IMF	International Monetary Fund
INCD	Intergovernmental Negotiating Committee on Desertification
INFF	integrated national financing framework
INGO	international non-governmental organization
INRC	Independent National Commission on Human Rights (Liberia)
IOC	Intergovernmental Oceanographic Commission
IOE	International Organization of Employers
IOM	International Organization for Migration
IOTC	Indian Ocean Tuna Commission
IP	intellectual property
IPBES	Intergovernmental Panel on Biodiversity and Ecosystem Services
WHO	Independent Police Complains Commission (Mauritius)
IPCC	Intergovernmental Panel on Climate Change
IPEC	International Programme on the Elimination of Child Labour
IPEN	International Persistent Organic Pollutants Elimination Network
IPLC	Indigenous peoples and local communities
IPOA-IUU	International Plan of Action to prevent, deter, and eliminate IUU fishing
IPPC	International Plant Protection Convention
IPU	Inter-Parliamentary Union
IPV	intimate partner violence
IRC	International Red Cross
IREA	International Renewable Energy Agency
IRENA	International Renewable Energy Agency
ITPGRFA	International Treaty on Plant Genetic Resources for Agriculture
ISA	International Seabed Authority
ISAR	International Standards of Accounting and Reporting
ISDS	investor-state dispute settlement
ISCO	International Standard Classification of Occupations
ISO	International Organization for Standardization
ISWA	International Solid Waste Association
ITF	International Transport Forum
ITLOS	International Treaty on the Law of the Seas
ITPGRFA	International Treaty on Plant Genetic Resources for Food and Agriculture
ITTA	International Tropical Timber Agreement
ITU	International Telecommunication Union
ITUC	International Trade Union Confederation

lxxviii LIST OF ABBREVIATIONS

IUCN	International Union for the Conservation of Nature and Natural Resources
IUU	illegal, unreported, and unregulated
IWI	Inclusive Wealth Index
IWRM	integrated water resources management
JI	Joint Implementation
JICA	Japan International Cooperation Agency
JPOI	Johannesburg Plan of Implementation
KAPPGP	Korean Act on Promotion of Purchase of Green Products
KBA	key biodiversity areas
KEITI	Korea Environmental Industry and Technology Committee
KNCHR	Kenya National Commission on Human Rights
KONEPS	Korean Online E-Procurement System
KPI	key performance indicator
L2SM	link to the subject matter
LBO	Local Biodiversity Outlook
LCRs	local content requirements
LDCs	least developed countries
LDN	Land Degradation Neutral
LEAP	Livelihood Empowerment Against Poverty (Ghana)
LED	light-emitting diode
LERN	Liberia Early Warning and Response Network
LGBT	lesbian, gay, bisexual and transexual
LGBTIQ	lesbian, gay, bisexual, transgender, intersex, and queer or questioning
LGMA	Local Governments and Municipal Authorities
LINC	Leadership for Inclusion (Ireland)
LLDCs	Landlocked Developing Countries
LMICs	low- to middle-income countries
LOSC	Law of the Sea Convention
LPG	liquefied petroleum gas
LTC	Legal and Technical Commission
LT-LEDS	long-term low greenhouse gas emission development strategies
LULUCF	land use, land-use change, and forestry
MA	Millennium Ecosystem Assessment
MADS	Local Authorities Digital System (Zimbabwe)
MAM	Meilleurs Artisans du Monde (Cameroon)
MARPOL	International Convention for the Prevention of Pollution from Ships
MAT	mutually agreed terms
MCS	monitoring, control, surveillance
MDB	multilateral development bank
MCR2030	Making Cities Resilient 2030
MDG	Millennium Development Goal
MEA	Multinational Environmental Agreement
MEAT	Most Economically Advantageous Tenders
MENA	Middle East and North Africa
MEXT	Ministry of Education, Culture, Sports, Science and Technology (Japan)
MF	material footprint
MFN	Most Favoured Nation

MGCI	Mountain Green Cover Index
MGoS	Major Groups and other Stakeholders
MHI	median household income
MHTI	medium- and high-tech industry
MIC	Middle-income Country
MICS	Multiple Indicator Cluster Survey
MiGOF	Migration Governance Framework
MIKE	Monitoring the Illegal Killing of Elephants
MLS	multilateral system
MMR	maternal mortality ratio
MNCs	multinational corporations
MOCA	Major Organised Crime and Anti-Corruption Agency (Kenya)
MOI	means of implementation
MOOC	Massive Online Open Course
MPA	Marine protected area
MPOWER	(i) *Monitoring* tobacco consumption and the effectiveness of preventive measures; (ii) *Protect* people from tobacco smoke; (iii) *Offer* help to quit tobacco use; (iv) *Warn* about the dangers of tobacco; (v) *Enforce* bans on tobacco advertising, promotion and sponsorship; and (vi) *Raise* taxes on tobacco
MSMEs	micro-, small, and medium-sized enterprises
MSP	Marine Spatial Planning
MST	Measuring the Sustainability of Tourism
MTF	Marrakech Task Force
MVA	manufacturing value added
NAAEC	North American Agreement on Environmental Cooperation
NAFO	Northwest Atlantic Fisheries Organization
NAFTA	North American Free Trade Agreement
NAMAs	Nationally Appropriate Mitigation Actions
NAMA	Non-Agricultural Market Access
NAMMCO	North Atlantic Marine Mammal Commission
NAPs	National Adaptation Plans/Programmes
NAPA	National Academy of Public Administration (United States)
NAPESD	National Action Plan on Education for Sustainable Development (Germany)
NASCO	North Atlantic Salmon Conservation Organization
NBSAP	National Biodiversity Strategy and Action Plan
NC	National Communications
NCDs	non-communicable diseases
NCP	Nature's Contributions to People
NCW	Nation Council Women (Egypt)
NDC	nationally determined contribution
NEAFC	North-East Atlantic Fisheries Commission
NEET	not in employment, education, or training
NESP	National Education Sector Plan (Kenya)
NGO	non-governmental organization
NHRI	national human rights institution
NIEO	New International Economic Order

lxxx LIST OF ABBREVIATIONS

NIMBY	Not-In-My-Back-Yard
NIRs	National Inventory Reports
NLBI	Non-Legally Binding Instrument
NOAA	National Oceanic and Atmospheric Administration
NPAFC	North Pacific Anadromous Fish Commission
NPFC	North Pacific Fisheries Commission
NRR	national recycling rate
NSSD	national strategy for sustainable development
NSO	national statistical offices
NSVAW	National Strategy for Combating Violence Against Women (Egypt)
NTDs	neglected tropical diseases
OAS	Organization of American States
OCHA	Office for the Coordination of Humanitarian Affairs
ODA	official development assistance
ODI	Overseas Development Institute
OECD	Organisation for Economic Co-operation and Development
OECD-MAPs	OECD's Methodology for Assessing Procurement Systems
OECM	other effective area-based conservation measures
OHCHR	Office of the United Nations Commissioner on Human Rights
OIHP	*Office International d'Hygiene Public*
OPAC	Optional Protocol to the Convention on the Rights of the Child on the Involvement of Children in Armed Conflicts
OPEC	Organization of Petroleum Exporting Countries
OPSC	Optional Protocol to the Convention on the Rights of the Child on the Sale of Children, Child Prostitution and Child Pornography
OUP	Oxford University Press
OWG	Open Working Group
P3	public–private partnerships
PACD	Plan of Action to Combat Desertification
PBSO	Peacebuilding Support Office
PCA	Permanent Court of Arbitration
PEEREA	Protocol on Energy Efficiency and Related Environmental Aspects
PES	payments for ecosystem services
PGRFA	plant genetic resources for food and agriculture
PIC	prior informed consent
PILNA	Pacific Islands Literacy and Numeracy Assessment
PISA	Programme for International Student Assessment
PLGS	Policy, Legislation and Governance Section
PML	probable maximum loss
POPs	persistent organic pollutants
POPIN	UN Population Information Network
PoU	prevalence of undernourishment
PP	public procurement
PPM	process and production method
PPP	public–private partnership
PRI	Peace Research Institute (Sudan)
PRME	Principles for Responsible Management Education
PRSP	Poverty Reduction Strategy Paper

LIST OF ABBREVIATIONS lxxxi

PRSPs	poverty reduction strategy plans
PRTR	Protocol on Pollutant Release and Transfer Registers
PSMA	Agreement on Port State Measures
PWDs	persons with disabilities
QFC	Qatar Financial Center
R&D	research and development
RACE	Reaching All Children with Education (Lebanon)
RBM	results-based management
RBMP	River Basin Management Plan
RBO	river basin organization
REDD +	Reducing Emissions from Deforestation and Degradation
REMP	regional environmental management plan
RFBs	Regional Fisheries Bodies
RFMA	regional fisheries management arrangement
RFMO	regional fisheries management organization
RTD	right to development
S&D	special and differential
S&T	science and technology
SAICM	Strategic Approach to International Chemicals Management
SBI	Subsidiary Body for Implementation
SBSTA	Subsidiary Body for Scientific and Technical Advice
SBSTTA	Subsidiary Body on Scientific, Technical and Technological Advice
SCI	service coverage index
SCP	sustainable consumption and production
SCYCLE	Sustainable Cycles
SD	sustainable development
SDG	Sustainable Development Goal
SDSN	Sustainable Development Solutions Network
SDT	special and differential treatment
SE4ALL	Sustainable Energy for All
SEA	Strategic Environmental Assessment
SEAFO	South East Atlantic Fisheries Organization
SEARCCT	Southeast Asia Regional Centre for Counter Terrorism (Malaysia)
SEEA	System of Environmental-Economic Accounting
SEEA-EA	System of Environmental-Economic Accounting—Ecosystem Accounting
SFM	sustainable forest management
SGBV	sexual and gender-based violence
SIByS	Sistema de Identificación de Bienes y Servicios (Argentina)
SIDC	small island developing countries
SIDS	small island developing states
SIOFA	Southern Indian Ocean Fisheries Agreement
SloCat	Partnership on Sustainable, Low Carbon Transport
SMART	specific, measurable, agreed, realistic, and time-bound
SMEs	small and medium-size enterprises
SMM	spatial management measures
SMTA	standard material transfer agreement
SOLAS	International Convention for the Safety of Life at Sea
SPAR	State Party Self-Assessment Annual Reporting

lxxxii LIST OF ABBREVIATIONS

SPP	sustainable public procurement
SPRFMO	South Pacific Regional Fisheries Management Organization
SRFC	Sub-regional Fisheries Commission
SRMNCAH	sexual, reproductive, maternal, newborn, child and adolescent health
SRP	Student Refugee Program (Canada)
STEM	science, technology, engineering, and mathematics
STI	science, technology, and innovation
STI	sexually transmitted infection
SUHAKAM	Human Rights Commission of Malaysia
SWB	subjective well-being
TAC	total allowable catch
TAP	transparency, accountability, and participation
TAR	Third Assessment Report
TB	tuberculosis
TBT Agreement	Technical Barriers to Trade Agreement
TERA	The Energy and Resources Institute
TFEC	total final energy consumption
TFM	Technology Facilitation Mechanism
TKIP	traditional knowledge, innovations, and practices
TNCs	transnational corporations
TOSSD	total official support for sustainable development
TPES	total primary energy supply
TST	Technical Support Team
TRIMs	Trade Related Investment Measures
TRIPS	Agreement on Trade-Related Aspects of Intellectual Property Rights
TSA	Tourism Satellite Account
TWAIL	Third World approaches to international law
TWW	total water withdrawal
UCCN	UNESCO Creative Cities Network
UCLG	United Cities and Local Governments
UDHR	Universal Declaration of Human Rights
UHC	universal health coverage
UIS	UNESCO Institute for Statistics
UN	United Nations
UNAIDS	Joint United Nations Programme on HIV/AIDS
UNCAC	United Nations Convention against Corruption
UNCCD	United Nations Convention to Combat Desertification
UNCED	United Nations Conference on Environment and Development
UNCHE	United Nations Conference on the Human Environment
UNCLOS	United Nations Convention on the Law of the Sea
UNCRD	United Nations Centre for Regional Development
UNCTAD	United Nations Conference on Trade and Development
UNCTOC	United Nations Convention against Transnational Organized Crime
UNDESA	United Nations Department of Economic and Social Affairs
UNDG	United Nations Development Group
UNDOC	United Nations Office on Drugs and Crime
UNDP	United Nations Development Programme
UNDRIP	United Nations Declaration on the Rights of Indigenous Peoples

UNDRO	United Nations Office of the Disaster Relief Co-ordinator
UNDRR	United Nations Office for Disaster Risk Reduction
UNECE	United Nations Economic Commission for Europe
UNECLAC	United Nations Economic Commission for Latin America and the Caribbean
UNEP	United Nations Environment Programme
UNESCO	United Nations Educational, Scientific and Cultural Organisation
UNEWEC	United Nations Every Woman, Every Child
UNFCCC	United Nations Framework Convention of Climate Change
UNFF	United Nations Forum on Forests
UNFPA	United Nations Population Fund
UNFSA	United Nations Fish Stocks Agreement
UNGPs	United Nations Guiding Principles on Business and Human Rights
UNHCR	United Nations High Commissioner for Refugees
UNHHSF	United Nations Habitat and Human Settlements Foundation
UNHRP	United Nations Housing Rights Programme
UNIATF	United Nations Inter-Agency Task Force on the Prevention and Control of Non-Communicable Diseases
UNICEF	United Nations International Children's Emergency Fund
UNIDO	United Nations Industrial Development Organisation
UNISDR	United Nations International Strategy for Disaster Reduction Secretariat
UNITAR	United Nations Institute for Training and Research
UNODC	United Nations Office on Drugs and Crime
UNOPS	United Nations Office for Project Services
UNRAA	United Nations Relief and Rehabilitation Administration
UNSC	United Nations Security Council
UNSC	United Nations Statistical Commission
UNSCCUR	United Nations Scientific Conference on Conservation and Utilization of Resources
UNSD	United Nations Statistics Division
UNSDSN	United Nations Sustainable Development Solution Network
UNSGAB	United Nations Secretary-General's Advisory Board on Water and Sanitation
USP2030	Universal Social Protection to Achieve the Sustainable Development Goals
UNTC	United Nations Treaty Collection
UNTT	United Nations Task Team
UNU	United Nations University
UNWTO	United Nations World Tourism Organization
USMCA	U.S.–Mexico–Canada Agreement
VAT	value-added tax
VMS	vessel monitoring system
VNR	Voluntary National Review
WASH	water supply, sanitation, and hygiene
WCED	World Commission on Environment and Development
WCPFC	Western and Central Pacific Fisheries Commission
WDPA	World Database on Protected Areas
WEF	World Economic Forum

lxxxiv LIST OF ABBREVIATIONS

WEHAB   Water, Energy, Health, Agriculture, and Biodiversity
WEOG   Western European and Others Group
WFD   Water Framework Directive
WFP   World Food Programme
WHA   World Health Assembly
WHO   World Health Organization
WHOQOL   World Health Organization Quality of Life
WINS   Water Information Network System
WMG   Women's Major Group
WMO   World Meteorological Organization
WSPDB   World Social Protection Database
WSSD   World Summit for Sustainable Development
WUSC   World University Service of Canada
WTO   World Trade Organization
WWF   World Wildlife Fund

Sustainable Development Goals

Their Political and Legal Nature under International Law

Ilias Bantekas and Katerina Akestoridi

I. Introduction

This book contains an exhaustive analysis of the journey, as well as the sources, progress, and tools of the complex phenomenon that is constituted by the Sustainable Development Goals (SDGs). This introductory chapter is meant to shed some light on the historical and political realities underpinning the development movement that began in the 1980s and which ultimately culminated in the first coordinated effort towards global development objectives, first in the form of the Millennium Development Goals (MDGs) as currently transformed into the SDGs. We call this a political effort because the key financing stakeholders were keen to avoid the insertion of any language that could be interpreted as giving rise to any obligations. The rationale behind this is obvious, as are also the benevolent features underlying development finance. Even so, the SDGs have taken on a life of their own and in the process, their legal nature has followed a path that straddles politics and law, and most importantly, international human rights law. This chapter attempts to show how this process began and where we now stand in terms of both the legal and political context.

II. The Millennium Development Goals

The beginning of the new millennium marked a pivotal momentum in the process of international development as leaders of all Member States to the United Nations (UN) adopted with one accord a set of international development objectives that would permeate the organization's policy agenda for the coming fifteen years. The MDGs, as they were called, encompassed eight aims and twenty-one further targets through which the development challenges of the century would be tackled in a collective endeavour to improve people's lives and set the foundations for a better future. Eradication of extreme poverty and hunger (MDG 1), universal primary education (MDG 2), gender equality and the empowerment of women (MDG 3), reduction in child mortality (MDG 4), improvement of maternal health (MDG 5), confrontation of chronic and infectious diseases (MDG 6), and environmental sustainability (MDG 7) comprised the

2 POLITICAL AND LEGAL NATURE OF SGDS UNDER INTERNATIONAL LAW

list of the specific priorities set, fulfilled through a global partnership for development (MDG 8).[1]

The MDGs echo the international community's noble call for the creation of a global environment in which the person is situated at the centre of concerns for social progress.[2] Upon this premise, development is measured against the values of freedom, dignity, fairness, solidarity, and tolerance to ensure not only socio-economic security, but also the circumstances for equal opportunities by which to thrive and live a life of value. In this respect, the MDGs explicitly draw upon the foundational principles of the Universal Declaration of Human Rights[3] for a peaceful, just, and prosperous world, which were reaffirmed later in the Millennium Declaration,[4] the MDGs' immediate harbinger. It is along these lines that a strong quest for cooperation between rich and poor developed with the aim of promoting and advancing these aims. This shared responsibility[5] attaches a bold character to a political commitment towards the MDGs and asserts that the latter entrench an unparalleled international consensus on a strategic vision for development.

The direct reference to a joint pledge to achieve the MDGs also denotes a major swing in the way international society is conceived and supports further the claims that the MDGs imparted new impetus to development thinking. For what is now being prioritized is a purposive understanding of the international community, whereby the agreed common ends are the driving force in the interplay of state relations. This lies in contrast to an earlier 'procedural conception' of international society in which alliance resembles a 'level playing field' where despite a common respect for the norms governing state affairs, states still strive to advance their own distinct interests.[6] Under the new paradigm, the focus is shifted to shared outcomes and international relations become, thus, critically instrumental in a 'cooperative venture'[7] to pursue them. Since individual state gains are expected to defer to mutual purposes, development practices tend to move away from targeting national economies *per se* to capturing the needs of people within nation states in as optimal a way as possible. Consequently, they are not merely intended to bridge the inequality gap between developed and developing countries. Rather, they point towards particular groups of the population, aspiring

---

[1] United Nations Statistics Division, 'Official List of MDGs and Indicators for Monitoring Progress 2008' <http://unstats.un.org/unsd/mdg/Host.aspx?Content=Indicators/OfficialList.htm> accessed 29 November 2022.

[2] KA Annan, '"We the Peoples", The Role of the United Nations in the 21st Century' (United Nations—Department of Public Information 2000) <https://digitallibrary.un.org/record/413745?ln=en> accessed 29 November 2022.

[3] United Nations General Assembly, *Universal Declaration of Human Rights* (10 December 1948) 217/A (III), Art 25. 'Everyone has the right to a standard of living adequate for the health and well-being of himself and of his family, including food, clothing, housing and medical care and necessary social services ...'

[4] UNGA Resolution 55/2 (8 September 2000) (*Millennium Declaration*).

[5] ibid, Values and Principles paras 2 and 6.

[6] C Gore, 'The Global Development Cycle, MDGs and the Future of Poverty Reduction' (presentation at the 12th EADI General Conference in Geneva, June 2008), available from the Development Studies Association <http://www.devstud.org.uk/downloads/4b9e9da140e21_Gore_PAPER.pdf> accessed 12 March 2016.

[7] ibid. Also, ME Salomon, *Global Responsibility for Human Rights: World Poverty and the Development of International Law* (OUP 2007) 64.

to guarantee minimum subsistence levels,[8] and create the circumstances that will enable them to climb the welfare ladder. The MDGs' policy agenda seems to embrace this individual-oriented approach to development, introducing for the first time clear, concise, and time-bound goals.

Yet, reflections of the MDGs' novelty are not solely confined to the changes brought in the way the international community understood development. Evidence of their dynamic nature that is capable of global transformation is furthermore found in the international community's response to the challenge of on-ground implementation. Broad coalitions and capacity building of key national and international constituencies evolved under the aegis of the UN Millennium Campaign[9] and the UN Millennium Project,[10] which were exclusively commissioned to support the implementation of the MDGs. These specialized mechanisms opened the floor for concerted discussions among a great network of development practitioners, over the course of which governmental policy-makers, representatives of international financial institutions, UN agencies, and the private sector provided an action plan that embodied practical investment strategies to achieve the MDGs' initiative and an operational outline to monitor its progress.[11] The MDGs movement became, thus, institutionalized and development planning was reshaped too. Indeed, the conversion of global goals into sensible outcomes for natural persons and the launch of a core package of wide-ranging interventions to accomplish them contributed to the setup of an intensively coordinated and results-oriented model for international development, which until then the international community lacked.[12] The new-fangled 'institutional apparatus'[13] featured now concrete outputs and informed decision-making by countries and supervisory bodies, favouring at the same time political accountability and social feedback. Consequently, it constituted a robust operational platform at the service of the MDGs agenda.

A. The Historical and Political Undercurrents of the MDGs

Nevertheless, criticism of the MDGs framework has not eclipsed, bringing to the forefront the flip side of their abovementioned positive aspects. To appreciate the origins of the more restrained voices that were raised as an offset against the enthusiasm for the MDGs avant-garde, it is crucial to have a detailed look at the political and historical context and the ideological underpinnings that nurtured their inception. For it would

---

[8] Referred to in the literature as 'basic needs'. The concept emerged in the framework of research during the International Labour Organisation's World Employment Program. Richard Jolly, 'The World Employment Conference: The Enthronement of Basic Needs' (1976) A9 Development Policy Review 31.

[9] *United Nations Millennium Campaign*, <http://www.millenniumcampaign.org/> accessed 17 March 2016.

[10] *United Nations Millennium Project*, <http://www.unmillenniumproject.org/> accessed 17 March 2016.

[11] ibid.

[12] C Dunning and M Elgin-Cossart, 'Can the SDGs Really 'Leave No One Behind'?' (*Centre for Global Development*, 7 January 2015) <http://www.cgdev.org/blog/can-sdgs-really-leave-no-one-behind> accessed 21 March 2016.

[13] P Alston, 'Ships Passing in the Night: The Current State of the Human Rights and Development Debate Seen through the Lens of the Millennium Development Goals' (2005) 27(3) Human Rights Quarterly 755.

be over-simplistic to argue that a single UN summit in the year 2000 led to the agreement on the MDGs. Quite the reverse, the final outcome unfolded following multiple, complex, and long-winded phases during which socio-political ideas and the interests of international institutions and financially powerful countries exercised great influence in the shaping of mechanisms for achieving global development goals. That said, the chronological benchmark for the emergence of development initiatives aiming at the elimination of poverty and human deprivation could be traced back to the development decades that followed the 'Golden Epoch' of fiscal growth for most nations in the mid-twentieth century.[14] A retrospect of that period reveals that the synthesis of the development policy landscape was strongly associated with the substantive meaning attached to the notion of prosperity which, due to the unprecedented financial growth, was unavoidably interpreted in terms of economic progress. Consequentially, poverty reduction strategies were delineated in the wake of the economic models deployed over this timespan in order to realize economic progress. Two main schools of thought dominated the debate about the best practice for countries to develop and eradicate destitution: at first, national developmentalism, and subsequently, with the progressive pre-eminence of neoliberalism in the political realm, global integration.[15]

National developmentalism emerged at the decay of the colonial era as a development theory whose implementation would reverse the negative impact of the economic practices effectuated by the Europeans in their colonies. Arguably, the said historical period was symbolic of the exploitation of resources of the non-European world by its conquerors. Yet, behind such an attitude lied the rationale that active interference in the economic affairs of the colonies constituted part of a 'civilizing devoir' that was believed to enhance global affluence levels. The presumption was that the colonies lacked the technical capacity or willingness to harness their natural assets in a resourceful way and join the rest of the world that was moving to an industrialized stage of development. The Europeans therefore perceived their intervention a necessity for triggering the modernization of their colonies, although in practice their stance led to the net transfer of wealth from the colonized to them and left the former suffering economic, political, and moral ruin. Notwithstanding the ethical matters concerning the colonizers' behaviour, the embedded logic was that those nations could only be developed under their influence.[16]

Evidently, development was bestowed a national character which hereafter became the only source from which development strategies derived legitimacy. Just like developed states designed their post-war development programmes according to their own standards so as to maximize their national gains,[17] so too the countries of the South should have (and had) the potential to develop themselves, provided they implemented

---

[14] KKS Dadzie, 'National and International Policies for Development' in South Centre (ed), *Facing the Challenge; Responses to the Report of the South Commission* (Zed Books 1993) 203–36.

[15] Gore (n 6) 4.

[16] I Wallerstein, 'After Developmentalism and Globalization, What?' (2005) 83(3) Social Forces 1263.

[17] To the extent, thus, that developmentalism signifies a national programme of action for development, it is a term that can be used to describe the policy for economic advancement applied by developed countries too.

appropriate policies. This affirmation stemmed by and large from the empowerment received as a result of the colonized peoples' battles for freedom, which left little scope for the sovereign powers of the North to continue with their externally imposed policies. Hence, while wealth accumulation and the creation of a steady environment that would foster the sustenance of economic growth and citizens' welfare continued to be the most important elements of development strategies, the latter became an issue of domestic affairs for those countries and the involvement of the West was restricted to providing technical and advisory support (aid) to developing nations, as opposed to being in actual control of all actions that would mobilize the evolution of the developing world.[18]

The heyday of national developmentalism came to its end amidst the global economic crisis in the 1970s that sprung from the increase in oil prices and affected the North and the South alike, albeit not equally. Persistently high inflation, combined with big unemployment rates and stagnant demand were the dominant traits in the economy of countries in the North. The countries of the South suffered disequilibrium in their balance of payments given that their export value declined dramatically, whereas the cost of imports was set higher due to the doldrums the economy had entered worldwide.[19] For the North, which had already achieved its industrialization and could present a surplus in capital, an effective response to the crisis was in sight. By contrast, the South fared poorly. The scarcity in liquid assets resulted in excessive borrowing from developed states, which culminated in a serious and unsustainable debt crisis as industrialization in these countries slowed down, their currencies depreciated, and interest rates rose, making debt service impossible.[20] This crack in the international economy paved the way for a polemic against developmentalism as an ultimately dysfunctional system for development. The national identity embedded in it was now considered mere protectionism, which trapped states in economic policies that eventually neither gave them a competitive advantage in the markets nor proved to have equipped them with effective mechanisms to deal with the crisis that had emerged.

B. Neoliberalism and the MDGs

This attack against the presiding development model was backed by the expansion of neoliberalism, which was promoted as the ideological corrective against the concept of 'nation' upon which developmentalism was premised.[21] Although globalization is generally viewed as a complex, unavoidable,[22] and multi-layered phenomenon, in reality

---

[18] Wallerstein (n 16).

[19] ibid 1264.

[20] ibid. See also I Bantekas and C Lumina (eds), *Sovereign Debt and Human Rights* (OUP 2018).

[21] S George, 'A Short History of Neoliberalism: Twenty Years of Elite Economics and Emerging Opportunities for Structural Change' (Conference on Economic Sovereignty in a Globalising World, Bangkok, 24–26 March 1999), *Global Exchange* <http://www.globalexchange.org/resources/econ101/neoliberalismhist> accessed 2 May 2017.

[22] R Howard-Hassmann, 'The Second Great Transformation: Human Rights Leapfrogging in the Era of Globalisation' (2005) 27 Human Rights Quarterly 1.

6 POLITICAL AND LEGAL NATURE OF SGDS UNDER INTERNATIONAL LAW

it is neither complex, global, nor a phenomenon. It is a wholly artificial construct that was purposely engineered by a handful of states in order to pursue a particular economic agenda.[23] Its theoretical underpinning is neoliberal theory and particularly the so-called Washington Consensus which posits that free, unregulated markets and trade liberalization are the only way to spur financial growth. As a result, any governmental interference with market forces constitutes an impediment to growth and by extension to the potential for human well-being. This theory is largely discredited, not because increased trade and investment are inimical to human progress—quite the contrary; rather, it has been aptly demonstrated that economic and financial growth does not necessarily translate into human well-being, nor is there any direct correlation between the two.[24] Neoliberalism assumes that because the competitive forces inherent in markets drive competition and innovation to produce better and cheaper products and services, citing as examples the progress of industrialized nations, this model should be encouraged worldwide, particularly in developing nations. No doubt, inefficient and corrupt governments in the developing world have failed to make any tangible gains from the nationalization of their natural resources and other industries and have instead accumulated significant debts. It was natural therefore for neoliberal advocates to maintain that besides trade and financial liberalization, states should accept deregulation, privatization, unhindered foreign direct investment (FDI), and competitive exchange rates in order to attract foreign capital. They also maintained that since the public sector generally tends to expand and become inefficient, governments should be flexible and downsized and subject to strict fiscal discipline.[25]

There are several deficiencies to this otherwise laudable agenda. It suffices to note that none of the pursuits of neoliberalism was directly geared towards alleviating poverty, joblessness, universal healthcare, or other social goals. Privatization, one of the mantras of neoliberalism, is a good example. By way of illustration, although the privatization of the health and water sectors may render the provision of these public goods cost-effective and efficient, private operators naturally deny them to those unable to afford them; yet the right to health and water are fundamental rights whose provision is incumbent on the state. As a result, privatization that is unregulated and not subject to any social controls will be inclined towards deprivation and discrimination between the vulnerable and the wealthy.[26]

A comparison of the two economic theories demonstrates that they share a common ground to the extent that both associate development with fiscal returns and assume that an end to hardship will stem from the economy's growth as a natural consequence. However, there is a stark contrast between them which is apparent: national developmentalism was empowered by the intention to improve the conditions that

---

[23] See particularly the forceful argument of P O'Connell, 'On Reconciling Irreconcilables: Neo-liberal Globalisation and Human Rights' (2007) 7 Human Rights Law Review 483, 489.

[24] UN Secretary-General Report, 'Globalisation and its Impact on the Full Enjoyment of All Human Rights', UN Doc. A/55/342 (31 August 2000), para 13.

[25] WK Tabb, *Economic Governance in the Age of Globalisation* (Columbia University Press 2005) 3.

[26] UN Commission on Human Rights (OHCHR), 'Report on Economic, Social and Cultural Rights: Liberalisation of Trade in Services and Human Rights', UN Doc E/CN.4/Sub.2/2002/9 (25 June 2002), paras 44–45.

affected people's lives through the rebuilding of nations after the end of the Second World War, whereas neoliberalism and its upshot, globalization, propagated growth having put on the side-lines the question of who the beneficiaries should be. In this context *growth* became the key political pursuit for states. Therefore, development has been typically associated with the overall wealth of states and is often linked to indicators such as 'growth', 'per capita income', and 'balance of payments', among others. The particular indicators of this type of development are intended to measure the overall wealth of states, not the well-being of their citizens. By way of illustration, whereas a country's gross domestic product (GDP), which represents the market value of its products and services, may be high, the standard of living of its people can still remain relatively low. This is because GDP is not a measure of personal income, nor does it take into account the disparity in the distribution of wealth or the enjoyment of essential services and goods such as healthcare, education, water, and food. The measurement of human well-being is a relatively new phenomenon in the economics and human rights literature. In 1990 the United Nations (UN) Development Programme (UNDP) published its first *Human Development Report* with the aim of demonstrating how economic growth translates into human development.[27]

C. The Early Role of International Organizations in Development Finance

In the frame of the described changeover from one economic policy to the other, the influence of international organizations was pivotal in bringing the issue of poverty and inequality from the shadows to the light. The landmark year for the resurgence of interest in the topic was 1990 with the publication of the World Bank's first *World Development Report* that emphasized the staggering dimensions of poverty worldwide and the importance of a two-part strategy for development, namely the implementation of macroeconomic adjustment so that the least developed countries would be enabled to accede to the new economic order, in conjunction with social policies enhancing living standards.[28] On a parallel course, the idea that people must be at the centre of development emerged in clear language in the UN's inaugural *Human Development Report*. In a robust tone it was articulated that the purpose of development is to offer people options in life that are not limited to the acquisition of material things but capture a wider spectrum that encompasses increased life expectancy, education, political stability and freedom, personal security, community participation, productivity, involvement in social and cultural affairs, and the safeguarding of human rights.[29] It became therefore recognizable that development as a process goes beyond the attainment

[27] UNDP, *Human Development Report* (OUP 1990) 9.
[28] The World Bank, *World Development Report 1990—Poverty* (OUP 1990). Also available online <https://openknowledge.worldbank.org/bitstream/handle/10986/5973/WDR%201990%20-%20English.pdf?sequence=5> accessed 19 May 2017.
[29] UNDP, *Human Development Report 1990* (n 27) 10.

of income, which helps formulate human choices and therefore is a *means* rather than the *end* of development. The distinction between means and ends is key to the human development approach and differentiates the latter from the wealth-based approach to development.[30] Sen and Anand explain that the two approaches to development, namely wealth maximization and human development, differ in two respects: (i) their ultimate objectives, and (ii) the effectiveness of distinct instruments. With regard to ultimate objectives, the human development approach affords intrinsic value to the quality of life people can lead (end) and only instrumental relevance to other elements such as income and wealth that are important only to reach the goal of human well-being (means). In particular, in recognizing the importance of economic growth as a means for human development they argue that the contingent nature of its effectiveness as means (how it is used to promote human development) should be considered. This is also true of its non-uniqueness as means, although others are important too, such as social organization.[31]

The call for reorientation of development strategies found fertile ground within UN bodies which, in a series of summits,[32] broadened the concept of poverty as being multidimensional and started to shape a practical proposal for an alternative model of development that would not be preoccupied by economic growth. Having as a roadmap the human development hypothesis, the attention of country delegates was predominately drawn to income poverty, employment, infant and maternal mortality, access to inclusive primary education, decrease in malnutrition, clean water, the environment, social integration, and gender equality in light of discussions about reproductive health and women's empowerment. The necessity for a multi-sectoral approach to poverty reduction was embedded in respective declarations, confirming the mounting commitment of national leaders for a target-driven global policy agenda on development. For the UN, freedom from poverty constituted an 'ethical, social, political and economic imperative of humankind'[33] that was validated by the principles of human dignity, equality, democracy, peace, and mutual responsibility, as enshrined in the UN Charter and the respective human rights conventions concluded until then.[34] Upon this basis, the urge for coordinated efforts amongst national governments, the UN, development

[30] I Bantekas, 'Wealth and Growth-based Policies have Augmented Global Poverty and Eroded Human Rights: A Return to Human-Centred Thinking' (2012) 1 International Human Rights Law Review 30.

[31] S Anand and A Sen, *Sustainable Human Development: Concepts and Priorities* (UNDP Office of Development Studies 1996).

[32] Among many, the most important were (i) UNICEF's 'Children's Summit' in New York in 1990; (ii) the World Summit for Social Development in Copenhagen and the UN Fourth World Conference in Beijing (both in 1995); and (iii) the UN Conference on the Environment and Development (Earth Summit) in 2001 in Rio. For an exhaustive reference to these summits, see D Hulme, 'The Millennium Development Goals (MDGs): A Short History of the World's Biggest Promise' (September 2009) University of Manchester Brooks World Poverty Institute, Working Paper 100.

[33] United Nations, *Report of the World Summit for Social Development, Copenhagen 6-12 March 1995*, A/CONF.166/9 (1996).

[34] These were the International Covenant on Civil and Political Rights (adopted 16 December 1966, entered into force 23 March 1976) 999 *UNTS* 171; the International Covenant on Economic, Social and Cultural Rights (adopted 16 December 1966, entered into force 3 January 1976) 993 *UNTS* 3; the Convention on Elimination of all forms of Discrimination against Women (adopted 18 December 1979, entered into force 3 September 1981) 1249 *UNTS* 13; and the Convention on the Rights of the Child (adopted 20 November 1989, entered into force 2 September 1990) 1577 *UNTS* 3.

banks, and civil society to achieve these targets did not emanate merely from solidarity among nations. Rather, its thrust derived from a human rights approach and imperative.[35]

Even so, as discussions intensified, the more evident it became that politics was inevitably interwoven in the formation of large-scale programmes intended to be transformative. To begin with, the magnitude of the proclaimed transformation caused the concern of most conservative voices for which market-based growth was the source of welfare. Without doubt, the dynamic of the rights-based approach advocated in UN summits was inspiring and motivating but the discussions still took place in the circumference of the economic climate established by neoliberalism. Under the influence of this parameter, the most conservative voices speaking for the North argued that poverty predicated on the reduction of income took precedence over the broader facets of the phenomenon,[36] supposedly because the principal denominator for a better quality of life and for people to have power over their future was economic well-being. Consequently, they remained intransigent in their view that a new development framework should not deviate from fostering economic growth by placing social development higher in the hierarchy of development goals. Development should be pursued within the new global context, that being the single global economic system. This was to be achieved by developing countries' accession to this system. In addition, the emulation of the market structures of the industrialized world should implicitly be something that the new synergy of states ought to promote.[37] In this light, rich donor countries regarded the increase of affluence in the developing world as an opportunity to expand their investments and find new target audiences for their goods and services.[38] There was, thus, a guided self-interest[39] on their behalf that underlay the formation of the new action plan, although existing data about people living in conditions of extreme poverty had a moderating effect on it.[40] Accordingly, their support for the agenda through foreign aid would instead assist the process of modernization and industrialization.[41]

[35] Notably the UNDP restructured its program and made poverty eradication its overriding priority, acquiring the title of the UN's principal 'antipoverty arm'. See, UNDP, *Human Development Report 1997* (OUP 1997) foreword and Ch 6, 106.

[36] Hulme, 'The Millennium Development Goals' (n 32) 14.

[37] This was largely the approach taken by the Development Assistance Committee (DAC) of the Organisation of Economic Cooperation and Development (OECD) which in its 1977 'Statement on Development Co-operation and Economic Growth' stipulates that: 'meeting basic human needs is not a substitute for, but an essential component of, more economic growth which involves modernisation, provision of infrastructure and industrialisation ... a basic needs approach is not primarily welfare or charity but productivity-oriented, aiming at increasing the productive income of the poor and strengthening the basis for long-term self-generating development', cited in H Führer, 'The Story of Official Development Assistance: A History of the Development Assistance Committee and the Development Cooperation Directorate in Dates, Names and Figures'(1996) 94(67) OECD/GD 30.

[38] Development Assistance Committee (DAC), *Shaping the 21st Century: The Contribution of Development Cooperation* (OECD 1996) 6.

[39] ibid.

[40] Ingvar Carlsson and others, *Our Global Neighbourhood: The Report of the Commission on Global Governance* (OUP 1995) 139.

[41] This persistence on growth can be traced back to the 1970s. See D. Williams, *International Development and Global Politics—History, Theory and Practice* (Routledge 2012), Ch 2 in which he explains that development policy was shaped in the years up to the 1970s by 'development economics' and the 'modernisation theory'. Even in the decades of structural adjustment that followed the financial and debt crisis of the 1980s, lending towards developing states by the World Bank and the International Monetary Fund (IMF) aimed at economic liberalization and governance reforms so that they could participate in the global economic system of free trade and achieve

10 POLITICAL AND LEGAL NATURE OF SGDS UNDER INTERNATIONAL LAW

While politicians strove to keep the debate about development initiatives within the spectrum of economic liberalization, aid agencies' economic and organizational issues were equally influential in channelling the deliberations towards a specific direction. At the time of the meetings, there was a dramatic decline in the budgets of official development assistance (ODA) and a general unwillingness by governments to fund development projects, leaving aid agencies both with a shortfall in funds and without a mandate.[42] Trends in aid flows had largely been determined by governments' political and economic ambitions over the decades.[43] At first, it was the pursuit of European states to keep a foot in the economic and political life of the former colonies that had led to great sums of aid being disbursed. Similarly, aid provision constituted a catalytic component of the US international relations after the Second World War. Having the intent to guarantee its own economic and security interests, it allocated aid in developing countries for their economic advancement and political stability. ODA provision reached its peak during the years of the Cold War in an attempt by the United States to find allies against the ideological influence of the Soviet Union. At this point aid for the economic transformation of the South was used for political domination in the fight against communism and the economic system it introduced. Yet, the termination of the Cold War and the prevalence of economic liberalism radically modified the geopolitical circumstances that had influenced international relations until that moment, weakening thereby the indirect causes served through aid supply.[44] As a result, allocations of ODA drifted significantly and donor institutions found themselves being marginalized. The dialogue for a new development agenda was a prolific occasion for them to redefine and justify their purpose. Just like politicians who, for reasons of mutual gains, focused their attention on the economic aspects of the strategy in formation, members of the donor club laid emphasis on those parts that would boost their organizational performance. For this they needed a set of specific, measurable, agreed, realistic, and time-bound goals (SMART)[45] that would mobilize again action for development projects and defend aid provision by demonstrating its effective contribution to fixed objectives. Clearly, their outcome-based standpoint brought to the forefront a managerial approach to the agenda that resembled a results-oriented public policy reform much more than a model at the service of a broad-based vision for development.[46]

---

macroeconomic stability. The influence of social goals in poverty alleviation didn't seem to be significant in practice, although the new development strategies were gradually proclaimed in a language of 'participation', 'partnership', and 'ownership' in an effort to include governments from both industrialized and developing countries and civil society in the process. See D Williams, 'The History of International Development Aid' in M Moschella and C Weaver (eds), *Handbook of Global Economic Governance—Players, Power and Paradigms* (Routledge 2014).

[42] OECD, 'Official Development Assistance Trends 1960–2016', <http://www2.compareyourcountry.org/oda?cr=20001&cr1=oecd&lg=en&page=1> accessed 30 May 2017.

[43] J-M Severino and O Ray, 'The End of ODA: Death and Rebirth of a Global Public Policy' (March 2009) Centre for Global Development, Working Paper No 167, 2–3.

[44] ibid.

[45] D Hulme, 'Lessons from the Making of the Millennium Development Goals: Human Development meets Results-based Management in an Unfair World' (2010) 41(1) Institute of Development Studies Bulletin 15, 16.

[46] A Binnebdijk, *Results-based Management in the Development Cooperation Agencies: A Review of Experience*, DAC Working Party on Aid Evaluation (OECD 2001) 3–4.

It is therefore not surprising that the concept of tied aid emerged, whose political dimension overrode all other considerations.[47]

Be that as it may, consultations regarding development metamorphosed into a balancing assessment of the donors' challenges, the politics of economic growth and the UN promulgations for a human-centred development. The culmination of this agenda-setting exercise was a list of seven International Development Goals (IDGs) that aspired to render the idea of human development practical and effective without undermining the premise that economic growth is central to development.[48] Simultaneously, the donor agencies' importunity for recording progress encouraged the prioritization of goals that were measurable and easy to quantify.

To regain its title as prime mover in the development initiatives the Secretariat reconfigured the poverty discourse at its Millennium Summit. This time the discussions drew keenly upon its plan to revise the UN's institutional role in the twenty-first century and re-establish the broad vision for development which, from its perspective, had been compromised by political priorities and aid agencies' interests. Declaring that men and women should be freed from '*abject and dehumanizing poverty*',[49] the organization put forward a framework of poverty eradication aims that differed from the IDGs' listing both in scope and substance. Growth obviously remained the stepping-stone to poverty reduction and the most promising route to engage globalization. Nonetheless, the outline was more expansive since it included technology as a means of development for transition for the economies of the developing world and specified rich countries' duties towards the less fortunate as far as debt relief, trade, and official development assistance were concerned. Conversely, it touched upon matters of gender equality, women's reproductive health, and child mortality vaguely,[50] tempering the human development crux that was present in the IDGs. Finally, the aims were presented in a rather descriptive way that was lacking the thinking behind the results-based management (RBM) approach that donors preferred.[51]

---

[47] In a 2006 report the OECD estimated that approximately 58 per cent of bilateral aid was tied. Tied aid refers to aid granted under condition that the recipient purchase goods and services from the donor. See OECD, *Development Cooperation Report 2005: Efforts and Policies of the Members of the Development Assistance Committee* (OECD 2006) 31. By 2010 tied aid had fallen to less than 20 per cent. There is no consensus on the ethical or legal perspectives of this practice under international law, although states are generally keen to hide so-called aid for trade as was the case in the early 1990s where the United Kingdom financed the construction of the Pergau dam in Malaysia, which in turn proceeded to buy £1 billion worth of British arms. In *R v Secretary of State for Foreign Affairs ex parte World Development Movement* (UK) (1995), the High Court ruled that the project was not of any economic or humanitarian benefit to the Malaysian people. It should also be noted that the drafters of the Paris Declaration on Aid Effectiveness have pledged to minimize tied aid and the Development Assistance Committee (DAC) of the OECD issued a (revised) Recommendation on Untying ODA to LDCs and HIPCs, DCD/DAC (2014) 37 Final (12 August 2014), by which it recommends the lifting of all tied aid.

[48] DAC, *Shaping the 21st Century* (n 38); Hulme, 'Lessons from the Making' (n 45) 17–18 who describes the stance of developing countries and financial institutions such as the World Bank and the International Monetary Fund to the IDGs.

[49] Annan (n 2) 77.

[50] Hulme, 'The Millennium Development Goals' (n 32) 26.

[51] RBM is a managerial strategy to development programmes and implementation that lays emphasis on performance by setting and measuring specific outcomes. Notwithstanding the value that lies in such a strategy, its prevalence in design of the MDGs narrowed down the agenda to quantifiable targets and indicators that didn't capture the quantitative elements of human development and the scope of objectives in the Millennium Declaration. Ultimately, given the overly narrow focus on producing results, the MDGs became a minimalist agenda that

12   POLITICAL AND LEGAL NATURE OF SGDS UNDER INTERNATIONAL LAW

Those variations signalled the risk of a disagreement on what should finally comprise a plan for development and of the establishment of a dual process in the formation of development policies: a UN-led poverty reduction strategy and one that developed detached from the influence of the donor community.[52] To avoid the application of double standards, the floor opened for an additional round of deliberations, this time collectively, with all major players of the development sector collaborating to design a single framework of development goals that would guide their programmes and assess their effectiveness.[53] The product of the negotiations was enunciated in the Millennium Declaration,[54] which constituted a merge of the aforesaid competing poverty reduction agendas. A global consensus was achieved, first and foremost, on the elimination of extreme material poverty, uttered as lack of income, food, and clean water. Universal primary education, infant, child, and maternal mortality, the extinction of serious and life-threatening diseases, and rich countries' contribution and accountability regarding the realization of the new frame constituted the other themes that gained universal political endorsement and upon which an agreement on collaboration was reached. These thematic subjects were imprinted as the MDGs in the first UN Millennium Summit follow-up report,[55] subsequent to consultations with international public servants and technical advisors from all multilateral organizations who defined the individual targets and indicators.[56] The roadmap for a global mechanism on poverty reduction was finalized and efforts henceforward would focus on its implementation.[57]

reflected a narrow understanding of the goals and gave rise to non-inclusive and structurally non-reformist development policies. Hulme, 'Lessons from the Making' (n 45) and Binnebdijk (n 46).

[52] Hulme uses the term 'twin-track process' to pinpoint that the goal-setting exercise had been proceeding in parallel tracks. See Hulme, 'The Millennium Development Goals' (n 32), 31.

[53] The intention of all development institutions to coordinate their efforts was expressed in the common report compiled by the IMF, the OECD, the UN, and the World Bank Group (WBG), which was published in 2000. In this document, all four institutions agreed that poverty eradication is the crucial challenge of development and that the most effective way to tackle the issue is by setting quantitative goals against which performance would be measured. See IMF, OECD, UN, WBG, *2000 A Better World for All: Progress towards the International Development Goals* <https://www.imf.org/external/pubs/ft/jointpub/world/2000/eng/bwae.pdf> accessed 19 May 2017.

[54] UNGA, *Millennium Declaration* (n 4).

[55] UNGA, 'Report of the Secretary-General: Road Map towards the implementation of the United Nations Millennium Declaration' (September 2001) UN Doc A/56/326.

[56] Consultations took place in the framework of World Bank meeting on 19–21 March 2001 at Washington DC entitled 'From Consensus to Action: A Seminar on the International Development Goals', Transcript of proceedings <http://documents.worldbank.org/curated/en/141081468335951810/pdf/662710v20TRANS065765B0ma rch02002001.pdf> accessed 29 November 2022. Decent work (MDG 1, target 1b) and reproductive health (MDG 5, target 5b) were finally added in 2005. See UNGA Res A/RES/60/1 (16 September 2005) 11 and 16 respectively.

[57] After the adoption of the MDGs, cooperation on development was established further at the first International Conference on Financing for Development that took place in Monterrey in 2002. The principles of a holistic and integrated approach to the multifaceted challenges of development were expressed in the 'Monterrey Consensus', which also introduced the Financing for Development follow-up meetings that continue to date. See, *UN Report of the International Conference on Financing for Development, Monterrey-Mexico, 18–22 March 2002,* A/CONF.197/ 11; and Financing for Development, *Monterrey Consensus of the International Conference on Financing for Development—Final Texts and Agreements Adopted at the Conference on Financing for Development, Monterrey-Mexico, 18–22 March 2002* (UN Publications 2003). Also, UN *Department of Economic and Social Affairs, Financing for Development* website <http://www.un.org/esa/ffd/overview/monterrey-conference.html> accessed 29 November 2022.

D. The Implications of the MDGs Process for the Development Paradigm

As much as the MDGs depict a universal agreement to encounter a set of global social and environmental challenges, their adoption constituted anything but a simple and straightforward process. The primitive stage for their conceptualization can be found in reflections on poverty and income inequality, which developed on the margins of the process of national economies' evolution and transformation towards global integration and the harmonization of living standards worldwide. The idea of human development was blended with a managerial tactic to form a policy narrative that captured a spectrum of the multidimensional problem of poverty but widely offered the probability of tangible results—an important element of the agenda, whereby the world's leaders could maintain a political advantage, aid organizations could regain their purpose, and civil society could be comforted by reporting on the progress towards a kind of development that aspired to dissolve the uneven spread of prosperity in the world.[58] Over the long haul, the MDGs arose from the fermentation of ideas about development, state politics, and the objectives of each one of the development organizations in an open-ended process of formatting global public policy. The interaction of these parameters, while being the motive force for a consensus on their content, caused simultaneously the fragmentation of their formulation that challenged the goals' success at four different tiers: (i) their conceptualization; (ii) their execution; (iii) ownership; and (iv) equity.[59]

Results-based management had a much more direct impact on the making of the Goals and triumphed over its ideational counterpart. Its 'common-sense nature and linearity'[60] were the tenets that in effect specified the goals and narrowed the scope of the development agenda to quantifiable proposals that were built around targets and indicators. Based on this premise, an aspired-to-be inclusive action plan for development was converted into a minimalist or incomplete agenda that did not capture the breadth of the objectives enclosed in the Millennium Declaration nor did it empower the links between aims in the same or different development field.[61] For all the value that can be found in measuring and monitoring performance through indicators, the focus on the latter undermines the complexity of the targets themselves and the quantitative nature of the development progress overall, not least since—as the word implies—they are meant to be indicative of progress and not divert efforts towards their fulfilment in their own right. As a result, the execution of such a results-oriented system of the goals is overly reliant on the precision, accuracy and relevance of the targets and indicators

---

[58] Hulme, 'The Millennium Development Goals' (n 32), 43–48.

[59] J Waage and others, 'The Millennium Development Goals: A Cross-Sectoral Analysis and Principles for Goal Setting after 2015' (2010) 376 The Lancet 991, 1000.

[60] D Hulme, 'Governing Global Poverty: Global Ambivalence and the Millennium Development Goals' in J Clapp and R Wilkinson (eds), *Global Governance, Poverty and Inequality* (Routledge 2010) 135–61.

[61] ibid.

and becomes susceptible to their weaknesses: quite often data, based on which indicators are defined, are either not available or of poor quality. In turn, indicators cannot be measured systematically, thereby causing complications at the target level, mainly due to the targets' vagueness and lack of implementation mechanisms. Ultimately, this leads to a very narrow understanding of a respective goal, thus to non-inclusive and small-scale policies that give piecemeal solutions.[62]

To illustrate the argument with an example, a critical study[63] of MDG 1 (halve global poverty and hunger) revealed the operational weaknesses that MDGs bear: Target 1A prompted the world community to collaborate on halving by 2015 the proportion of people whose income was below US$1/day (henceforth, throughout the book, all monetary values will be in US dollars, uncles otherwise specified). At the outset one can acknowledge the statistical notation of the goal and the corollary it has on the conceptualization of poverty, which was conceived too narrowly as income-based destitution, contrary to the broad understanding of the concept based on the theory of human development.[64] Furthermore, the choice of the $1-a-day poverty threshold is doubtful concerning how accurately it can reflect estimates of poverty incidence. It has been criticized as arbitrary in its construction and as one that is calculated on consumption and purchasing power parity, excluding other facets of human well-being like health or education.[65] In addition, the inconsistencies between household survey data and national statistics on growth have further raised questions about an existing bias in determining poverty levels. The problems with the Goal are aggregated at the indicator level by the fact that they lacked reference to the exact intervention actions or required resources so that the target could be achieved.[66] Quantification of the proportion of the population below $1/day, the poverty gap ratio, and the share of the poorest in national consumption[67] serves its role in achieving a result-based outcome, namely to reduce poverty by 50 per cent, but is of no avail towards outputs in terms of policy practices. Within this framework, effective execution of the Goal seems less promising.

Questions around the ownership of the Goals emanated from an *ex-post* evaluation of their actual impact on national development strategies and donors' practices in their effort to substantiate their promise for partnership. Regarding the former, the crux of the matter lay primarily in the relevance of MDG priorities and targets found in the so-called Poverty Reduction Strategy Papers (PRSPs), namely developing countries' national planning framework for development and, therefore, their perception as national

---

[62] Waage and others (n 59) 997.

[63] ibid. Supplementary Web appendix, p.1 available <http://www.thelancet.com/cms/attachment/2001011584/2003798891/mmc1.pdf> accessed 19 May 2017.

[64] Defined as a situation of sustained or chronic deprivation of the resources, capabilities, choices, security, and power for the enjoyment of an adequate standard of living and other political, socioeconomic and cultural entitlements; Committee on Economic, Social and Cultural Rights, 'Substantive Issues Arising in the Implementation of the International Covenant on Economic, Social and Cultural Rights: Poverty and the International Covenant on Economic, Social and Cultural Rights', UN Doc E/C.12/2001/10, 10 May 2001, para 8.

[65] SG Reddy and TW Pogge, 'How Not to Count the Poor' (29 October 2005) in S Anand and others (eds), *Debates on the Measurement of Global Poverty* (OUP 2010). See, however, M Ravallion, 'How Not to Count the Poor? A Reply to Reddy and Pogge' in ibid.

[66] Waage and others (n 59) Table 1, p. 998.

[67] United Nations Statistics Division (n 1).

targets. One would logically expect that given the universal political consensus on the Goals, PRSPs would include the whole spectrum of the MDGs and reflect an individual country's strong commitment to their implementation. Contrary to these expectations, not only were the Goals picked upon selectively by policy-makers but a discrepancy concerning the degree of implementation was also noted, even among those Goals that constituted priority areas.[68] There is a twofold explanation for this: first, the fact that developing countries' involvement in the development of the MDGs framework was actually limited (lack of participation); and secondly, the misapprehension that the MDGs, which were targets set at the global level, could be transposed effectively into domestic jurisdictions unchanged and successfully bring about the desired outcomes at a global scale. However, without taking into consideration local circumstances and the differences of technical and financial potentiality among countries, the Goals were stripped of country-specific pragmatism.[69] As a consequence, there was a mismatch with the particular development situation of countries and preoccupation with the goals was either downgraded to a typical mention in the reporting process of monitoring progress on the MDGs or the Goals were instrumentalized by countries to attract donor resources for governmental aims that were simply easier to achieve;[70] a tactic that casts doubts as to whether the MDGs were translated from 'consensus objectives' to 'planning targets' that would actually encourage development in line with national priorities.[71]

The problematics of ownership by the international community are directly linked to the process that led to the formulation of the MDGs as described in the previous section. The involvement of so many organizations in the identification of the Goals and targets crafted a complex institutional structure that comprised of UN agencies, funds, multilateral and bilateral donor organizations,[72] each of which asserted competence either on the whole of a Goal or on its specific targets. Compartmentalization of key responsibilities was an unavoidable consequence of this complexity and rendered the coordination of activities difficult, in particular because of ambiguity as to which

[68] For a comprehensive analysis, see S Fukuda-Parr, 'Are the MDGs Priority in Development Strategies and Aid Programmes? Only Few Are!' (2008) International Poverty Centre, UNDP Brasilia, Working Paper No 48.

[69] J Vandermoortele, 'The MDGs: 'M' for Misunderstood?' (*UNU-WIDER* 2007) <https://www.wider.unu.edu/publication/mdgs-'m'-misunderstood> accessed 29 November 2022. As the author states: 'the global MDG targets must be tailored to make them context-sensitive—which is essential for generating a sense of national ownership. Global targets are meant to encourage countries to strive for accelerated progress. Their applicability, however, can only be tested and judged against what is realistically achievable under country-specific circumstances. To be meaningful, national targets require adaptation; not a mindless adoption of global targets....'

[70] For example, targets concerned with the empowerment of the most vulnerable groups such as gender violence or women's empowerment and political representation were neglected. See S Fukuda-Parr, 'Reducing Inequality— The Missing MDG: A Content Review of PRSPs and Bilateral Donor Policy Statements' (2010) 41(1) Institute of Development Studies Bulletin 26.

[71] Fukuda-Parr, 'Are the MDGs Priority' (n 68), Section 2.2. 'The Instrumentality of the MDGs', 3. The author distinguishes between three functional uses of global goals: as consensus objectives, monitoring benchmarks, and as planning targets.

[72] For a list of the UN's Fund, programmes, and specialized agencies see *UN* <http://www.un.org/en/sections/about-un/funds-programmes-specialized-agencies-and-others/> accessed 29 November 2022; for an indicative list of bilateral donors see *Canadian Trade Commissioner Service* <http://tradecommissioner.gc.ca/development-developpement/bilateral-agencies-organismes-bilateraux.aspx?lang=eng> accessed 29 November 2022.

should assume leadership in the implementation of the respective Goal.[73] The accomplishment of the MDGs was constrained by the absence of a clear action plan with defined duties and obligations for every actor. Lack of leadership resulted in lack of accountability[74] of the institutions charged with the realization of the MDG agenda and also weakened the relationships with civil society organizations and other public and private entities that agreed to work together on the Goals and the development process in general.[75] Against this background, the international community's ambition to bolster global partnership in the identified key sectors for development was threatened by fragmentation as policy coherence was hindered by the *ad hoc* nature of the cooperation between stakeholders and their focus mostly on short-term issues rather than the promotion of systemic change.[76]

The challenge to the MDGs' success at the fourth tier, equity, is a corollary to the problems at the level of conceptualization, which led to a very narrow understanding of the Goals and delinked them from the core objectives of the Millennium Declaration and the UN's development agenda. What comprised the essence of the latter were human development and a wider share of the benefits of economic globalization between and within countries. Although the ideology of neoliberalism remained untangled, the content and character of the agenda was permeated by the values of human freedom, dignity, solidarity, and tolerance. A fundamental concern for equity and equality of all persons was also present.[77]

Equity stems from the idea of 'moral equality', namely the principle that people in a society should be treated as equals because they share a common humanity or human dignity. It is a normative concept and is concerned with equality, fairness, and social justice.[78] In the context of development it finds application in three areas: (i) equal life chances; (ii) equal concern for people's needs, and; (iii) meritocracy in order to 'level the playing field' for everyone. Equality, on the other hand, is concerned with the distribution of goods or outcomes, requiring that people receive equal amounts or subject to equal treatment.[79] It aims to promote fairness so long as everyone starts from the same

---

[73] Look at example of MDG 4 and MDG 5 (Reduce child mortality and improve maternal health), mentioned in Waage and others (n 59), 1002–03.

[74] OHCHR, *Who Will Be Accountable? Human Rights and the Post-2015 Development Agenda* (OHCHR 2013); W Van Ginneken, 'Social Protection, the Millennium Development Goals and Human Rights' (2011) 42(6) Institute of Development Studies Bulletin 111.

[75] UNGA Res A/RES/60/215, 'Towards Global Partnerships' (29 March 2006), points 2 and 3, 3.

[76] Global partnership for development constituted also MDG 8 and included targets on aid, trade, debt relief, and improved access to essential medicines and new technologies. After the Monterrey Consensus (n 57) and the Johannesburg Plan of Implementation States incorporated resource mobilization, global governance, and policy coherence: UN, *Johannesburg Declaration on Sustainable Development and Plan of Implementation of the World Summit on Sustainable Development: The Final Text of Agreements Negotiated by Governments at the World Summit on Sustainable Development, 26 August–4 September 2002* (United Nations Department of Public Information 2003). Also UN System Task Team on the Post-2015 UN Development Agenda, 'A Renewed Global Partnership for Development—Frequently Asked Questions' <http://www.un.org/en/development/desa/policy/untaskteam_undf/faqs.pdf> accessed 29 November 2022.

[77] JA Ocampo, *The United Nations Development Agenda: Development for All* (UN Publications 2007) iii.

[78] H Jones, 'Equity in Development—Why It Is Important and How to Achieve It' (2009) Overseas Development Institute, London, Working Paper No 311, 3–7.

[79] ibid 9.

place and is offered the same aid.[80] However, both concepts have built in the notion of universality, which presupposes that the benefits of a policy reach out to all people, not just particular groups, or a proportion of certain groups. The well-being of a society as a whole should be maximized. This element was absent in the formulation of the MDGs, given that the targets were framed in a way that optimized the living conditions for some, by and large in poor countries, rather than ameliorating the gap between wealthy and poor people within and between countries.[81] Hence, they were not relevant to rich countries, which supported the process through finance and technology transfer only. But their implementation in developing countries was problematic too. The Goals' minimalistic approach—with the focus on the attainment of *minimum* levels of economic and social goods for the respective target groups—did not redress unfair social constructions beyond the line of minimum adequacy. That meant that hardship would be sustained, albeit at lower levels, and one could plausibly argue that it could also be deemed acceptable since 'basic needs' as an absolute minimum of goods would be enjoyed. However, equity is concerned with relative distribution in society of things that are not only 'needed' for people but constitute a prerequisite for their full participation in society.[82] As the MDGs were constructed, concentrating on improving poverty levels on average and to a minimum standard, they did not take account of the particularities of certain groups (such as the worst off amongst the poor) nor did they give everyone the means to become agents of their own development.[83] Reducing inequity was the MDGs' 'missing target'.[84]

The exclusion of equity and equality from the agenda stressed yet another dimension of the MDGs' critique that validated even more the argument that the Goals moved away from the spirit of the Millennium Declaration and the human development approach: the neglect of human rights standards.[85] As lofty and important as the MDGs were, they risked denigrating the very values they seek to exalt and protect. First and foremost, the rights language entrenched in the Millennium Declaration was not iterated in the MDGs for fear that somehow the goals might be transformed into justiciable entitlements. One might naturally think that although unfortunate, lack of justiciability was a small price to pay for securing the much-needed aid to the world's poor; after all, the goals and their indicators are strikingly similar to the rights found in the

---

[80] C Solomon-Pryce, 'Is Equity the same as Equality?' (*LSE Equity, Diversity and Inclusion Taskforce*, 9 December 2015) <http://blogs.lse.ac.uk/equityDiversityInclusion/2015/12/is-equity-the-same-as-equality/> accessed 19 May 2017.

[81] Waage and others (n 59), 1005–07.

[82] Jones (n 78), 6 incl. footnote 6.

[83] That's why the MDGs framework was critiqued as not taking a pro-poor approach. See J. Vandermoortele, 'The MDGs and Pro-Poor Policies: Related but not Synonymous' (November 2004) United Nations Development Program, International Poverty Centre, Working Paper No 3. On the criticism that some population groups were left out of the MDGs framework see Section 2 and citations therein in M Fehling and others, 'Limitations of the Millennium Development Goals: A literature Review' (2013) 8(10) Global Public Health 1109 and online <https://www.ncbi.nlm.nih.gov/pmc/articles/PMC3877943/> accessed 19 May 2017.

[84] Fukuda-Parr, 'Reducing Inequality' (n 70).

[85] UN System Task Team on the Post-2015 UN Development Agenda, 'Review of the Contributions of the MDG Agenda to foster development: Lessons for the Post-2015 UN Development Agenda', Discussion Note, March 2012, 12 <https://sustainabledevelopment.un.org/content/documents/843taskteam.pdf> accessed 19 May 2017.

International Bill of Human Rights.[86] Sadly, this is not the case. True, there are many similarities between the goals and economic, social, and cultural (ESC) rights. However, whereas these rights, as proclaimed in the International Covenant on Economic, Social and Cultural Rights (ICESCR), are meant to apply to all persons without any discrimination, thus reaching the poorest of the poor, the MDGs on many occasions only require states to halve certain poverty indicators. Given the absence of an obligation to disaggregate results in the MDGs, it is tempting for target states to focus on the relatively well-off among the poor and make no special provision for vulnerable groups.[87] As a result, the element of universality of the relevant right is lost. Moreover, some Goals were clearly inconsistent with human rights. By way of illustration, Goal 2 called for universal primary education, ignoring the requirement of free and high-quality education as enshrined in article 13 of ICESCR. More worrying was the technocratic trend set in the MDGs with an emphasis on the mobilization of financial resources over and above the transformation of power relations that play a large part in the creation of poverty and under-development. The MDGs therefore ignored the fundamental role of civil and political rights in the achievement of ESC rights.[88]

All things considered, one can infer that a rights language would give a forceful impetus to the MDGs, converting the socioeconomic issues they address into rights with a clearly defined scope and content that raise specific commitments on behalf of states which should be fulfilled at least to a minimum core.[89] Unfortunately, as much as the human rights dogma underlined UN proclamations about the purpose of development, it faded away during deliberations on the MDGs initiative. As a result, the two paradigms pointed to different directions in terms of strategy and design, despite their shared concern to advance the dignity, well-being, and freedom of individuals in general. The potential to supplement each other fruitfully and facilitate in practical ways their shared concern was real, but could only be realized though their integration.[90] Nevertheless, such a synergy was not contemplated.

III. The Sustainable Development Goals

The quest for comprehensiveness in the design and implementation of development policies became the centrepiece of the SDGs that were adopted in the framework of Agenda 2030 for Sustainable Development. Considering economic, social,

[86] See Alston (n 8) 759 and 762 for a human rights critique on the MDGs. For further criticism, see ibid.
[87] OHCHR (n 26) 4. Fukuda-Parr, 'Reducing Inequality' (n 70).
[88] HRC, 'Consolidation of Findings of the High-level Task Force on the Implementation of the Right to Development', UN Doc A/HRC/15/WG.2/TF/2/Add.1 (25 March 2010), paras 65–66.
[89] UN Committee on Economic, Social and Cultural Rights (CESCR), 'General Comment No 3: The Nature of States Parties' Obligations (Art. 2, Para. 1 of the Covenant)', UN Doc E/1991/23 (14 December 1990) 10.
[90] UNDP, *Human Development Report 2000*, 19 <http://hdr.undp.org/sites/default/files/reports/261/hdr_2000_en.pdf> accessed 19 May 2017. Alston (n 8) offers a critical analysis on the MDGs/human-rights divide, arguing that the lip service paid to one another was reciprocal since reference to the MDGs within the human rights system was also not systematic (p 761) and 'the human rights community has itself shown a significant degree of obstinacy when it comes to making the necessary outreach to endure that its own agenda is effectively promoted within the context of the international community's development agenda' (p 827).

and environmental issues as components and overarching objectives of development and combining them with a broader spectrum of topics such as prosperity, the planet, peace, security, and justice, the SDGs present an action plan that is more transformative in scope and responds to existing and new development challenges for developing and developed states in the current century. The new set of global goals consists of: (i) No Poverty (SDG 1); (ii) Zero Hunger (SDG 2); (iii) Good Health and Well-being (SDG 3); (iv) Quality Education (SDG4); (v) Gender Equality (SDG 5); (vi) Clean Water and Sanitation (SDG 6); (vii) Affordable and Clean Energy (SDG 7); (viii) Decent Work and Economic Growth (SDG 8); (ix) Industry Innovation and Infrastructure (SDG 9); (x) Reduced Inequalities (SDG 10); (xi) Sustainable Cities and Communities (SDG 11); (xii) Responsible Consumption and Production (SDG 12); (xiii) Climate Action (SDG 13); (xiv) Life below Water (SDG 14); (xv) Life on Land (SDG 15); (xvi) Peace, Justice and Strong Institutions (SDG 16); (xvii) Partnerships for the Goals (SDG 17).

Much like the MDGs, the SDGs are set against targets and indicators focused on measurable outcomes, yet their holistic approach to development is evident at a glance. To illustrate this point suffices to consider the wording of the SDGs. To name a few, SDG 1 is concerned with the eradication of poverty in its multidimensional nature and the exclusion of individuals from the economic and other means (such as services) necessary for human well-being wherever it occurs. This makes the goal relevant not only to poor countries but also to developed regions where poverty in relative terms is also recorded; targets on education, to refer back to our earlier example, are not limited to universal primary education but include secondary, tertiary, and lifelong learning (SDG 4); The SDGs thus constitute a broader framework of development goals that aspire to become relevant to all individuals not solely by completing the MDGs' unfinished business but by expanding the mandate of the systemic framework for development to include the interplay between poverty, inequalities, environmental degradation, and institutional impediments to development, namely lack of the rule of law in domestic orders, transparency and accountability of public and private entities, and weak regulations to tackle corruption and organized crime.[91]

Indeed, alongside the interdependence and indivisibility of the SDGs, states declared that the agenda is applicable to everyone on the basis of full respect for human dignity and the principles of equity, equality, and non-discrimination as expressed in the UN Charter, the Universal Declaration of Human Rights (UDHR), and other human rights treaties and declarations, such as the Millennium Declaration. In fact, in the third preambular paragraph of Agenda 2030 it is stated that the SDGs seek to realize the human rights of all. Within this framework, the right to development (RTD) holds a prominent status and its importance for the realization of the goals is explicitly recognized.[92] In light of this, human rights seem to have been embedded in the new financing for development framework as well, set at the third International conference on Financing

---

[91] The SDGs reflect in their content the outcomes of previous UN summits and conferences. See UNGA, Transforming Our World: The 2030 Agenda for Sustainable Development (21 October 2015), UN Doc A/RES/70/1, para 11.
[92] ibid paras 10 and 35.

for Development in Addis Ababa. Respect for all human rights underlines states' commitments under the Addis Ababa Action Agenda (AAAA),[93] which pledges to provide a social protection floor for everyone[94] and lays emphasis on development actors' accountability in relation to their financing promises that are subject to review for the first time.[95] Besides the equitable distribution of resources so that all persons have their most basic needs met, human rights are a key objective for the AAAAs[96] which in this regard aim to establish an international development financing system that is just, cooperative, transparent, and premised on human rights standards.[97] Most importantly, the AAAA constitutes an integral part of Agenda 2030,[98] meaning that the human rights principles applicable to the realization of the socioeconomic and environmental SDGs apply to the means-of-implementation targets too, not least since the latter are of equal importance to the rest of the Goals.[99]

Notwithstanding the direct bearing on human rights in the making of the goals, the SDG agenda has been criticized for failing to conform to both human rights and the normative standards of the concept of sustainable development. The cornerstone of the critique is found in the predominant role of economic growth as the means to eradicate poverty and in the favouritism towards mainstream development that reinvigorates the poor–rich divide. SDG 8 not only requires that per capita economic growth is sustained but sets a specific threshold of 7 per cent of GDP per year, albeit for developing countries mainly. It also advocates for an expanded access to financial services for the accumulation of assets and increase in investments with a view to stimulate the economy. While growth cannot be deemed to be devoid of value for the eradication of poverty, at least in its material sense, there is considerable evidence demonstrating that even though the average annual growth rate of real GDP per capita worldwide is increasing year on year, moderate poverty (less than \$2.50/day) still exists, income disparities are widening while all the more wealth is concentrated on a small portion of the world's population.[100] Obviously, aggregate economic growth does not have the anticipated

[93] UNGA Res 69/313 (27 July 2015).

[94] ibid para 12.

[95] ibid paras 130–134.

[96] That human rights considerations should permeate development finance programmes was raised by the OHCHR during the third international conference on financing for development and the negotiations of the Addis Ababa Action Agenda (AAAA), its outcome document. It was emphasized that the objective of financing development should be the equitable distribution of resources so that all persons have their most basic needs met and human rights are made a reality for all; see OHCHR, *Key Messages on Financing for Development and Human Rights*, <https://www.ohchr.org/Documents/Issues/Development/KeyMessageHRFinancingDevelopment.pdf>accessed 29 November 2022.

[97] Civil society denies that this holds true. On the same note, civil society expressed scepticism about the new financing framework to achieve Agenda 2030 for sustainable development, stating that although the AAAA promulgates the realignment of financial flows with public goals, the agenda does not tackle the structural injustices in the current economic system and that development finance is not people-centred. See Global Policy Watch, 'Third FfD Failing to Finance Development—Civil Society Response to the Addis Ababa Action Agenda on Financing for Development' 16 July 2015 (Blog) <https://www.globalpolicywatch.org/blog/2015/07/16/civil-society-response-agenda-financing-development/> accessed 29 November 2022.

[98] Agenda 2030 (n 91), paras 40 and 62.

[99] ibid para 61.

[100] The World Bank Group, 'Statistical Appendix in Global Economic Prospects: Broad-based Up-turn but for How Long?' (January 2018) 233 <http://www.worldbank.org/en/publication/global-economic-prospects#data> accessed 19 March 2018; C Lakner and C Sanchez, 'The 2017 Global Poverty Update from the WB' (*Let's Talk*

impact.[101] To be sure, a restructuring of the world's wealth-extracting mechanism is necessary, meaning that the rules on trade, taxation, and debt should be changed. Yet, the SDGs do not take the bold step to address these issues adequately. The language of the respective Goals is vague and no concrete measures to tackle them are mentioned.[102] What this signals then is a risk that the transformative nature of the SDGs is compromised.

A. A Political History of the SDGs

Just like the MDGs, the SDGs have their genesis in a number of UN summits and consultations among development institutions that took place alongside those that laid the basis for the MDGs. The central theme of this series of talks constituted the relationship of humans with the natural environment as a constituent element of the world system within which development is pursued. Indeed, the heavy economic exploitation of natural resources upon which the post-war vision of development for growth maximization had much been grounded had raised concerns about the detrimental impact of development practices on the environment[103] and the ability of nature to replenish its reserves at such a pace that continuous and unlimited economic progress would be feasible in the long run.[104] The environment's role in development was underscored for the first time at the UN Scientific Conference on Conservation and Utilization of Resources (UNSCCUR) in 1949,[105] but it was not until the 1970s that environmental and economic sustainability was crystallized in the international community as an urgent matter.[106]

At the 1972 Conference on the Human Environment states declared 'man has the fundamental right to freedom, equality and adequate conditions of life in an

---

Development, 16 October 2017) <http://blogs.worldbank.org/developmenttalk/2017-global-poverty-update-world-bank> accessed 19 March 2018.

[101] JY Kim, 'Ending Poverty requires more than Growth', WBG Press Release No 2014/434/DEC, 10 April 2014 <https://ourworldindata.org/poverty> accessed 29 November 2022.

[102] T Pogge and M Sengupta, 'The Sustainable Development Goals as Drafted: Nice Idea, Poor Execution' (2015) 24 Washington International Law Journal 571, 575 and footnotes 14 and 15. For another critical review see IT Winkler and C Williams, 'The Sustainable Development Goals and Human Rights: A Critical Early Review' (2017) 21 The International Journal of Human Rights 1023.

[103] See eg UNDP, *Human Development Reports* <http://hdr.undp.org/> accessed 29 November 2022.

[104] Preoccupation with the issue of availability of natural resources can be documented in eighteenth-century German laws regulating the forestry industry, according to which the extent a forest could be harvested was dependent upon the capacity of the forest to regenerate each year. This is also when 'sustainable development' as a term is first documented. See, *Lexikon der Nachhaltigkeit* <https://www.nachhaltigkeit.info/artikel/definition en_1382.htm?> accessed 18 November 2017. Similarly D Ricardo admits that economic growth will be hindered due to the scarcity of natural resources and points to the necessity for effective conservations measures if human survival is to be ensured: D Ricardo, *The Principles of Political Economy and Taxation* (Dent 1965) as cited by M-C Gordonier Segger, 'Sustainable Development in International Law' in HC Bugge and C Voigt, *Sustainable Development in International and National Law—What Did the Brundtland Report Do to Legal Thinking and Legal Development, and Where Can We Go from Here?* (Europa Law Publishing 2008) 93.

[105] UN Economic and Social Council (ECOSOC) Res. 32(IV) (28 March 1947), Yearbook of the UN, 1946–47, 492.

[106] DH Meadows and others, *The Limits to Growth: A Report for the Club of Rome's Project on the Predicament of Mankind* (Universe Books 1972).

environment of a quality that permits a life of dignity and wellbeing.[107] In this statement countries acknowledge that the environment gives people physical sustenance and affords them the opportunity to progress in the social, economic, and scientific level, setting the foundations for a direct link between development and environmental sustainability. Development as a collective process of change should aim at 'sustainable living,[108] namely the improvement of the quality of human life while living within the carrying capacity of supporting ecosystems.

The new quest was explicated a decade later by the World Commission on Environment and Development (WCED or Brundtland Commission).[109] The Brundtland Report addressed development within the broader context of uneven economic growth and the unbalanced distribution of its benefits and costs among rich and poor countries, as well as inappropriate technology that puts the resource base at risk. It also highlighted the lack of informed decision-making that merges environment, economics, and human needs in development planning. The Brundtland report[110] stated that the major objective of development is the satisfaction of everyone's human needs and aspirations for an improved quality of life in perpetuity. Conditions of poverty and inequity are associated with ecological and other crises that hinder the realization of this objective, hence there is a need for a development path that deals with these issues in a comprehensive and integrated manner. The Commission introduced in the development discourse the concept of sustainable development, defined as 'development that meets the needs of the present without compromising the ability of the future generations to meet their own needs'.

Significantly, the Commission reinstated the centrality of human beings in the development process and by making clear that everyone should have their needs met, whether in the present or the future, it sets explicitly universalism as the ethical value that should guide development. Furthermore, there is a direct appeal to social justice because the claim for fulfilment of each generation's needs implies in essence a claim of fair and just relations between individuals and the institutions. This is also true in respect of economic and social arrangements that affect generations' ability to meet those needs. Such fairness is founded on the axiom that humans are fundamentally equal and is manifested in the fair distribution of income and wealth as well as in society's organizational set-up that gives individuals the same opportunity to participate in democratic processes and decision-making.[111] The combination of the two leads to an understanding of human needs *lato sensu* that includes the freedom to achieve dignity and respect of the person through active involvement in society's organizational system in addition to

---

[107] UN Conference on the Human Environment, 'Stockholm Declaration on the Human Environment' (16 June 1972) UN Doc A/CONF.48/14/Rev.1, Principle 1.

[108] IUCN, UNEP, WWF, *Caring for the Earth: A Strategy for Sustainable Living* (Routledge 2013); UNGA Res 37/7 (28 October 1982) 'World Charter for Nature'.

[109] UNGA Res A/38/161 (19 December 1983) 'Process of Preparation of the Environmental Perspective to the Year 2000 and Beyond'.

[110] World Commission on Environment and Development (WCED), *Our Common Future* (OUP 1987).

[111] This is a reflection of Rawls' two principles of justice, namely: (i) equal liberty and (ii) difference and fair equality of opportunity. See J Rawls, *A Theory of Justice* (Harvard University Press 1999) 266.

the enjoyment of material goods. Therefore, the objective of sustainable development is current and future societies where people have the opportunity to lead meaningful lives, defined by the achievement of adequate standards of living and the empowerment to actively choose and decide upon the full range of factors that determine the quality of their lives. That said, the Commission pointed towards a wider spectrum of well-being, therefore embracing the concept of human development as one that informs the content of sustainable development. By extension, the responsibility to guarantee this outcome for present and future generations does not merely reflect the just allocation and utilization of specific resources in terms of total stock of natural, physical, and human capital. It should instead be construed as a general duty to afford generations the entitlement of access to the same opportunity to fulfil their legitimate aspirations for a better life in dignity.[112] This involves sharing a generalized capacity to create well-being based upon distributional equity that applies to individuals within the same generation (intra-generational equity) and between those in the future (inter-generational equity). On the account of this freedom-based understanding of sustainable development, the concept can be defined as 'development that prompts the capabilities of present people without compromising the capabilities of future generations'.[113]

To the extent thus that sustainable development represents a shared claim of all to the capability to lead worthwhile lives, it could be argued that the purpose of development is to create the enabling environment in which all people can expand their capabilities, and opportunities can be enlarged for both present and future generations.[114] This is a broader interpretation of the approach taken in the first UN *Human Development Report*, which identified the elements of human well-being. Due to the parameter of sustainability that requires equal attention be paid to the lives of people between periods of time, the objective of development can be depicted in the pursuance of *sustainable human well-being*.[115] Just like human development professes development outcomes beyond the economic outputs of growth, so too sustainable human development purports to a wider net of results in the economic, social, and environmental field since sustainable human well-being is contingent upon the elimination of constraints in all three systems. Indeed, since the introduction of the Brundtland definition of sustainable development, it has been embedded in the international development discourse that sustainable development aims at eradicating poverty, protecting natural resources, and changing unsustainable production and consumption patterns. Hence, it is a multidimensional undertaking aiming to achieve a higher quality of life

---

[112] This has been defined as *sustainability* by Anand and Sen (n 31) 19–21, 27–28. When considered solely as an obligation to maintain resources, a further distinction is made between weak and strong sustainability; see, A Chandani, 'Distributive Justice and Sustainability as a Viable Foundation for the Future Climate Regime' (2007) 2 Carbon Climate Law Review 152, 160. However, it is more appropriate to define it from a normative perspective as an exemplification of the commitments to equity inherent in the morals of social justice and universalism which are the normative foundation of the concept of sustainable development.

[113] A Sen, 'The Ends and Means of Sustainability' (2013) 14 Journal of Human Development and Capabilities 6, 11.

[114] UNDP, *Human Development Report 1994* (OUP 1994) 13.

[115] AB Zampetti, 'Entrenching Sustainable Human Development in the Design of the Global Agenda after 2015' (2015) 43 Denver Journal of International Law and Policy 277, 298.

24 POLITICAL AND LEGAL NATURE OF SGDS UNDER INTERNATIONAL LAW

for all people that encompasses economic, social, and environmental components that are interdependent and mutually reinforcing.[116] The so-called three pillars of sustainable development are hierarchically equal and it is assumed that the realization of their constituent elements simultaneously and to the same degree, brings about a holistic human-centred approach to development. Sustainable human well-being, it therefore follows, stems from the balanced integration of its aforementioned three dimensions that should be premised upon the principles of dignity, equity, justice, participation, and good governance, and conform to states' obligations under the UN Charter and human rights treaties.[117] However, this balancing cannot mean same-degree satisfaction because the three pillars are not qualitatively equal due to the incompatibility of their determinative characteristics and their divergent functioning (eg material well-being versus protection of ecosystems). Hence, while all three are necessary for sustainable development, sustainable human well-being requires that a choice be made regarding the degree of satisfaction of each tenet. The question to ask is what determines how this choice is made, particularly since policy choices in the context of development are not detached from moral and political theses regarding the relationship between the three components of development. This may give rise to different conceptions of sustainable development which is rendered a blanket term and legitimizes policies that may adhere to its tripartite framework but do not foster (sustainable) human well-being. This has been a reason why sustainable development is considered a contested and 'vague' concept. The three-pillar model does not address the point so it is of little avail to look for an answer to the question in it.[118]

Let us now move a few years later to the 2002 World Summit for Sustainable Development (WSSD) in Johannesburg, which produced the first specific and time-bound targets that emphasized the practical side of the Brundtland definition of sustainable development. These were exemplified in the Johannesburg Plan of Implementation (JPOI), a 'blueprint' for implementation of the Rio Declaration and Agenda 21. More

---

[116] There is no one single definition of sustainable development. For a sample variety of formulations, see UNGA Res 51/240 (15 October 1997) 'UN Agenda for Development' 1; World Summit on Sustainable Development (26 August–4 September 2002), Johannesburg Declaration on Sustainable Development, UN Doc A/CONF.199/20 (4 September 2002): 'poverty eradication, changing unsustainable patterns of production and consumption and protecting and managing the natural resource base of economic and social development are overarching objectives of, and essential requirements for, sustainable development'. ILA New Delhi Declaration of Principles of International Law Relating to Sustainable Development (2 April 2002), reproduced in (2002) 2 Politics, Law & Economics 211, 212: 'The objective of sustainable development involves a comprehensive and integrated approach to economic, social and political processes, which aims at the sustainable use of natural resources of the Earth and the protection of the environment on which nature and human life as well as social and economic development depend and which seeks to realize the right of all human beings to an adequate living standard on the basis of their active, free and meaningful participation in development and in the fair distribution of benefits resulting therefrom, with due regard to the needs and interests of future generations.'

[117] UNGA Resolution 66/288, 'The Future We Want' (11 September 2012). UN Doc A/RES/66/288.

[118] M Lehtonen, 'The Environmental-Social Interface of Sustainable Development: Capabilities, Social Capital, Institutions' (2009) 49 Ecological Economics 199, 201; S Connelly, 'Mapping Sustainable Development as a Contested Concept' (2007) 12 Local Environment 259. Recourse to the normative foundation of sustainable development (ie universality, human dignity, equity, and justice) offers clarification for its foundational principles that are uncontested in the international human rights and development discourse. They can serve as the objective criteria by which to determine the degree of satisfaction of sustainable development components, as well as provide necessary clarity. Consequently, it could be said that the balancing of the pillars is achieved through their prioritization on the basis of normative standards.

specifically, in its substantive chapters the JPOI elaborated, among others, the issue of poverty eradication, setting the year 2015 as the deadline to halve the proportion of people who live on less than $1/day, suffer from hunger, and do not have access to safe drinking water and basic sanitation.[119] A number of actions were proposed to defeat the causes of ill health and their impact on development, especially for the most vulnerable groups of society (women, children, disabled),[120] while priority was also given to matters such as the suspension of the adverse effects of chemicals on human health and the environment,[121] the protection of ecosystems[122] and biodiversity,[123] and energy production and efficiency.[124]

For the most part, the way the goals were framed restated the MDGs, making one wonder about the added value of the JPOI in development policy apart from the detailed inclusion of environmental issues. Yet, reference to environmental protection and development concerns in a document that sets priorities for action in the field of development cannot but attest to the fact that these issues were not considered as being merely interrelated. They were the subject of a global consensus that economic, social, and environmental issues constituted components and overarching objectives of (sustainable) development and should be dealt with in a balanced manner.[125] To this end, the JPOI took a step forward to cure the observed fragmentation in the institutional architecture for development, which had been underlined as one of the major drawbacks to the MDG success. It linked all the relevant bodies and organizations in the development sector at the international, regional/sub-regional, and national level, making the UN Economic and Social Council (ECOSOC) the focal point for supervision of the UN's inter-agency activities in the framework of sustainable development and for the promotion of their collaboration with affiliated institutions such as international financial institutions (IFIs) and the World Trade Organization (WTO). At the same time the mandates of each UN body (economic, social, and environmental) were defined more clearly, being tailored to address on-the-ground challenges in all three development sectors through particular mechanisms, specific operation measures, and detailed review processes.[126]

Attention to the praxis of sustainable development continued to be high on the international community's agenda. Ten years after the WSSD, at a new UN Conference for sustainable development held again in Rio,[127] world leaders issued a political outcome document that contained clear and practical measures for implementing sustainable development. In the 'Future We Want',[128] governments and civil society

---

[119] JPOI (n 76), section II 'Poverty Eradication' 7(a), 8, 25, 26.
[120] ibid section VI 'Health and Sustainable Development'.
[121] ibid section III 'Sustainable Consumption and Production', 23.
[122] ibid 30(d), 31, 32(c).
[123] ibid 44.
[124] ibid section II 9; section III 15 and 20; section IV 25, 38, and 44.
[125] ibid Preamble 2.
[126] Cordonier Segger (n 104) 107–13.
[127] UN Conference for Sustainable Development, *Report of the Conference on Sustainable Development (20–22 June 2012) UN Doc A/CONF.216/16* <http://www.un.org/ga/search/view_doc.asp?symbol=A/CONF.216/16&Lang=E> accessed 19 May 2017.
[128] 'The Future We Want' (n 117).

declared their determination to realize their commitments in the social, economic, and environmental fields undertaken in all preceding UN summits and conferences and bridge the gaps in promoting inclusive economic growth, social development, and environmental protection that would benefit all people.[129] They took enlightened decisions on the thematic areas of the WSSD and JPOI and others such as food security, cities, and clean oceans, agreed on the importance of a strategy to finance projects in these areas[130] and established a high-level political forum for follow-up and review of progress.[131]

Within this context, it was recognized that focused and coherent action on sustainable development could be pursued more effectively with the development of goals as the drivers of implementation and mainstreaming of sustainable development in the post-2015 UN agenda.[132] These goals should be action-oriented, concise, limited in number but global in nature, and universally applicable to all countries without prejudice to the development particularities and capabilities of each country. In terms of content, they should reflect Agenda 21, the JPOI and the Rio Principles, addressing the three-dimensional nature of development and the interlinkages of its three pillars.[133]

The mandate to form a new set of goals was assigned to an Open Working Group (OWG) under the auspices of the UN Secretary-General and in open consultation with governments, civil society, the scientific community, representatives from the business sector, and the UN system in general.[134] The OWG's proposal comprised seventeen SDGs and 169 targets,[135] which would be 'further elaborated through indicators focused on measurable outcomes'.[136] Relying on the MDGs archetype, the new scheme of goals appeared to be more comprehensive and responsive to the new development challenges that had been previously identified. In addition, their content was largely influenced by broader topics such as the connection between peaceful societies, good governance, human rights, the rule of law, and development, the importance of which had been highlighted by several studies on the post-2015 development agenda.[137] Of

[129] ibid 5 and 6.

[130] *Sustainable Development Knowledge Platform* <https://sustainabledevelopment.un.org/rio20> accessed 19 March 2018.

[131] High-level Political Forum in Sustainable Development <https://sustainabledevelopment.un.org/index.php?menu=1556> accessed 19 March 2018.

[132] 'The Future We Want' (n 117) 245–46.

[133] ibid 246–47.

[134] ibid 248–49 and UN Secretary-General, 'A Life of Dignity for All: Accelerating Progress towards the Millennium Development Goals and Advancing the UN Development Agenda beyond 2015', UN Doc A/68/202 (26 July 2013), 37(b)–(g).

[135] OWG Proposal for Sustainable Development Goals, <https://sustainabledevelopment.un.org/content/documents/1579SDGs per cent20Proposal.pdf> accessed 19 March 2018; for the full report see Report of the Open Working Group of the General Assembly on Sustainable Development Goals (OWG Report), UN Doc A/68/970 <http://undocs.org/A/68/970> accessed 19 March 2018.

[136] OWG Report 18.

[137] UN Secretary-General, *A Life of Dignity for All* (n 134); Sustainable Development Solution Networks, *An Action Agenda for Sustainable Development: Report for the UN Secretary-General*, June 2013 <https://unstats.un.org/unsd/broaderprogress/pdf/130613-SDSN-An-Action-Agenda-for-Sustainable-Development-FINAL.pdf> accessed 19 March 2018; High Level Panel on Eminent Persons on a Post-2015 Development Agenda, *A New Global Partnership: Eradicate Poverty and Transform Economies through Sustainable Development*, May 2013 <https://sustainabledevelopment.un.org/content/documents/8932013-05%20-%20HLP%20Report%20-%20A%20New%20Global%20Partnership.pdf> accessed 19 March 2018; E Solheim, *Development Cooperation*

course, the principles of equity, equality, non-discrimination, and inclusion that had been missing from the MDGs continued to be highlighted as a key prerequisite for a people-centred development agenda[138] in accordance with the UN Charter, the UDHR, and other human rights treaties that seemed to be the direct source of the Goals' legitimacy.[139] Hence, the Goals were organized around the rudiments of human dignity, economic prosperity, the planet, peace, security, and justice. As with the MDGs, global partnership would play a catalytic role for the realization of the Goals.

B. The SDGs' Transformative Dimension

A first reading of the goals confirms manifestly the bold character of this new action plan for the people and the planet. Not only do the SDGs address issues that the MDGs did not touch on but even those that are repeated portray a more holistic approach. An obvious example is SDG 1 that is not limited to eradicating extreme poverty, which is most likely to be observed in poor countries. Instead, all forms of deprivation and exclusion from the economic and other resources that contribute to an improved living standard are promoted, wherever they occur.[140] By the same token, SDG 5 which advocates gender equality and the empowerment of women/girls, calls for an end in all forms of discrimination and exploitation against them (including trafficking, child marriage, and female genital mutilation)—concerns that MDG 3 target did not explicitly consider.[141] SDG 3 sets more precise targets for reducing maternal and child mortality and tackles health issues expansively (eg family planning, universal health coverage, support of research for medicines and vaccines for diseases)[142] compared to MDGs 4 to 6. Last but not least, SDG 4 includes secondary and tertiary education and lifelong learning in contrast to MDG 2, which focused on universal primary education only. In this way, the SDGs pledge to complete the MDGs' unfinished business and seek to reflect universality, a quality feature that differentiates them from the MDGs, which constituted goals designed by development policy officials for a specific category of people. The SDGs are concerned with global well-being and capture its multi-dimensional nature, thanks to the participatory and transparent process that preceded their adoption.[143] The SDGs therefore are indeed transformative in scope and possess

---

Report 2013: Ending Poverty, OECD Publishing 2013 <http://www.oecd-ilibrary.org/docserver/download/43131 11e.pdf?expires=1521481533&id=id&accname=guest&checksum=4DADD8F66F295E40D12A3344AA8A9 53C> accessed 19 March 2018.

[138] UN Secretary-General, *The Road to Dignity by 2030: Ending Poverty, Transforming All Lives and Protecting the Planet*, UN Doc A/69/70 (4 December 2014) and 'The Future We Want' (n 117) 8.

[139] 'The Future We Want' (n 117) at 5–9.

[140] ibid SDG 1 all Targets.

[141] ibid SDG 5, Targets 5.1 to 5.3.

[142] ibid SDG 3, Targets 3.1 and 3.2, 3.7, 3.8, 3.9b.

[143] VP Nanda, 'The Journey from the Millennium Development Goals to the Sustainable Development Goals' (2016) 44(3) Denver Journal of International Law and Policy 389, 406.

a great potential to guide development efforts post-2015 for sustainable improvements in human well-being.

Nonetheless, scepticism overshadowed their dynamic for reasons that are more profound than the complexity of the Goals and the difficulty to communicate them to stakeholders or the public in general.[144] The critique contends that the SDGs represent nothing less than a 'development as usual' model. That is to say that the acclaimed change they aim towards is not grounded on a radical restructuring of the world economic system and its wealth-extracting mechanisms that have constantly been blamed for perpetuating global poverty and inequality.[145] In fact, the status quo and the power relationships between countries in crafting the world's poor–rich divide are sustained. The main argument in support of this thesis rests in the prevalence of economic growth within the SDGs' framework as the tool to eradicate poverty. SDG 8 speaks lucidly about the promotion of economic growth in terms of GDP and the invigoration of national financial institutions to expand access to financial services for all. On the face of it, the correlation between economic growth and poverty reduction results from a logical inductive reasoning: if poverty exists due to lack of financial resources, then the production of more money by an annual GDP increase of a specific percentage means greater share in consumption, thus less poverty and hunger. This logic begs the question about the effectiveness of aggregate economic growth. As the most recent data by the World Bank indicate, global growth has been climaxing year after year reaching 3.0 per cent GDP in 2017 with growth in emerging markets and developing economies scaling up to 4.3 per cent.[146] However, there is also evidence showing that the increasing trend in global income has not profited all people throughout the years. The 2017 global poverty update from the World Bank demonstrates that the total number of poor for the reference year 2013 was 2.5 million more than the initial estimate, leaving the share of the population that is classified as extremely poor to unchanged levels (10.7 per cent).[147] Interestingly enough, the number of extremely poor people rose to 830 million in 2015[148] and it is estimated presently that 50 per cent of the global population still lives on moderate poverty levels (less than $2.50/day).[149] Moreover, an estimated of 80 per cent of the world's population lives in countries where income differentials are widening whilst 75 per cent of global wealth is concentrated in just 20 per cent of the world's population.[150]

Clearly, the data point to the fact that only a fraction of the global wealth generated benefits the poor. That is not to infer that the value of growth is void altogether.

---

[144] J Kuosmanen, 'SDGs—A Beacon of Light or another Stumble in Global Governance?' (*Oxford Human Rights Hub*, 26 September 2015) <http://ohrh.law.ox.ac.uk/sustainable-development-goals-a-beacon-of-light-or-anot her-stumble-in-global-governance/> accessed 19 March 2018.

[145] See I Bantekas, 'The Linkages between Business & Human Rights & their Underlying Causes' (2021) 43 Human Rights Quarterly 118.

[146] The World Bank Group, Statistical Appendix (n 100).

[147] Lakner and Sanchez (n 100).

[148] UN Conference on Trade and Development (UNCTAD), *Development and Globalisation: Facts and Figures 2016*, 3 <http://stats.unctad.org/Dgff2016/DGFF2016.pdf> accessed 19 March 2018.

[149] *Statistic Brain*, World Poverty Statistics (24 March 2017) <https://www.statisticbrain.com/world-poverty-sta tistics/> accessed 19 March 2018.

[150] ibid.

Yet, if growth doesn't 'trickle down' to the poorest, poverty is not prone to reduction even if all countries grew at speeding rates.[151] For poverty to reach zero levels by 2030, systemic changes to the arrangements of the wealth generating sources are necessary, putting issues such as the current trading practice, illicit financial flows, tax collection, and sovereign debt under scrutiny for being the causes behind the exacerbation of poverty. Unfortunately, the SDGs lack precise language when it comes to addressing such thorny questions. For instance, SDG 16 and SDG 17 call only in general terms for a significant reduction in illicit financial and arms flows and cooperation on building up developing countries' capacity for mobilizing domestic resources for development, in particular by tax and other revenue collection.[152] There is an obvious omission to name specific measures in light of these matters, for example to harmonize anti-laundering regulation internationally, subject governments' fiscal policy-making to public participation, legislate in favour of criminal and other sanctions against agents (government officials, banks, corporations) for facilitating illicit financial flows, to name a few.[153]

Likewise, the targets on trade are pursued under the regulatory framework of the WTO despite the declaration to endorse a universal, open, and non-discriminatory multilateral trading system.[154] This means that orthodox positions on trade liberalization, including free trade agreements between individual governments and some countries, the removal of tariffs for imported goods, deregulation of the economy, and concentration of trading power to multinational corporations maintain prominence, affording developing countries no latitude in regulating their national economies according to their development needs. Therefore, developing countries are caught in a cycle of unfair competition that reduces state revenue and dismantles the societal net by giving rise to unemployment and lower income, hence deepening the impoverishment of their people.[155] The same is to be said about the pressure inflicted on poor countries because of their unsustainable debt stock. Target 17.4 captures the problem providing for debt financing, debt relief, and debt restructuring. Yet, all three options constitute ways to manage existing debt and make its repayment viable; they do not lead to debt cancellation, which remains developing countries' request, especially for illegitimate debts.[156] Consequently, large amounts of domestic finances are diverted away from public spending on national economies and the welfare state since lenders' demands

---

[151] Kim (n 101).

[152] Target 16.4: 'By 2030, significantly reduce illicit financial and arms flows, strengthen the recovery and return of stolen assets and combat all forms of organised crime'; Target 17.1: 'Strengthen domestic resource mobilisation, including through international support to developing countries' in Agenda 2030 (n 91).

[153] Pogge and Sengupta, 'The Sustainable Development Goals as Drafted: Nice Idea, Poor Execution' (n 102) 571, 575 and footnotes 14 and 15.

[154] Target 17.10.

[155] For an excellent overview of trade liberalization and its impact on developing countries see Share the World's Resources, '10 Policies to Finance the Global Sharing Economy' in *Financing the Global Sharing Economy* (October 2012) 158 <https://www.sharing.org/information-centre/reports/financing-global-sharing-economy> accessed 19 March 2018.

[156] Share the World's Resources, *Beyond the Sustainable Development Goals: Uncovering the Truth about Global Poverty and Demanding the Universal Realisation of Article 25* (29 September 2015) <https://www.sharing.org/information-centre/reports/beyond-sustainable-development-goals-uncovering-truth-about-global>accessed 19 March 2018.

acquire priority. Surprisingly, developing countries pay over $1.4 billion per day in debt service and return over 400 per cent in repayments compared to the sums of ODA they receive.[157] Had this money been put into strengthening the development capacity of states, they would definitely be a step forward in realizing their people's needs.

The SDGs' shortcomings are not simply technicalities on the policy level. They have noticeable ramifications for the agenda's theoretical underpinning that brings into the spotlight the second critique: whether development goals are founded on a specific theory of development, and if so, which. The question is debatable, not least since it is difficult to ignore the fact that development issues are complex and most of the times politically sensitive. It falls beyond the scope of this book to provide a deep analysis of this, suffice though to say that irrespective of the choice on a theory of development, development goals definitely portray an ideology, a normative assessment, of aspired political, social, and economic changes in a society. The SDGs are no exception to that. They stemmed from the concept of sustainable development which ought to provide a more holistic approach to development, indicating the gaps the pre-existing development thinking demonstrated in capturing the whole spectrum of development matters. The SDGs then should have been a projection of the normative standards the concept entails, namely 'human development' and the virtues of justice and equity that lie at the core of the concept and should be applied in the economic, social, and environmental context—exactly as the Resolution on Sustainable Development proclaimed. Along these lines, the SDGs should drive a dynamic process of change that permits the full realization of human potential, offering the enhanced freedom to individuals to choose and lead the life they esteem, and fostering for everyone within present and future generations the accumulation of an 'inclusive wealth'[158]—physical capital (ie infrastructure), human capital (skills, knowledge), and natural capital (environmental supplies).

This pursuit points to a broader conceptualization of development and poverty from which the SDGs agenda in practice moves away. Given the emphasis on economic growth and the way it is sought, development is still viewed through the lens of neoliberalism and becomes synonymous with the former. Equally, quality of life is equated with fiscal gains and levels of consumption, a correlation that treats the accumulation of wealth as an end in itself. Based on this logic global poverty is predominantly configured as material deprivation and the monetary trait of it is prioritized. In turn, considerations of well-being and happiness hinge solely on the availability of commodities and are not decoupled from GDP per capita. This logic runs contrary to the meaning of well-being in the light of sustainable development, which encompasses also subjective contemplations by virtue of the fact that individuals exercise their own judgment on

---

[157] ibid 146.

[158] P Dasgupta, 'Measuring Sustainable Development: Theory and Application' (2007) 24 Asian Development Review 1 as cited in V Spaiser and others, 'The Sustainable Development Oxymoron: Quantifying and Modelling the Incompatibility of Sustainable Development Goals' (2016) 24(6) International Journal of Sustainable Development and World Ecology 457, 464. Accordingly, the Inclusive Wealth Index (IWI) was developed to measure sustainability. For information see, <http://sdg.iisd.org/news/unu-unep-launch-inclusive-wealth-index-for-measuring-sustainability/> and <https://us2.campaign-archive.com/?u=33cf89da7ade3a85156c5eda4&id=2326160347&e=69fb50bd2f> accessed 19 March 2018.

the significance of the material, psychological, social, and environmental resources, in other words on each element of wealth, based on their personal system of values and perception of good life. It furthermore contradicts the interpretation of human needs, which in the framework of sustainable development again include but are not limited to those objectively required for minimalist subsistence. Hence, the concept of sustainable development requires a specific balancing exercise to manage the quantity and quality of accomplishment of the economic, social, and environmental pillar respectively in order to meet people's needs. By implication, some of the SDGs and their targets shall be prioritized over the others and not all of them can be satisfied to the same degree. This is particularly true for those concerned with material production and consumption for which sufficiency rather than maximal attainment should be satisfactory.[159] Accordingly, constant economic growth ceases being an ultimate good in itself that is supposed to result in increased individual wealth for the greatest number of people. Rather it acquires a more purposive character, being the medium to satisfying the conditions that allow people to develop to their fullest potential as free and equal persons. In this respect, one could argue that a proportionality test should be applied to growth, keeping its attainment to the levels necessary for the realization of the other goals. In the SDGs agenda, however, growth is undifferentiated and represents the sole measure of progress. Ultimately, human and environmental development becomes a secondary feature of the agenda.

C. The Legal Nature of the SDGs under International Law

The foregoing sections demonstrated that the notion of development is determined by the historical and social context in a said period of time. How its theoretical underpinnings are shaped and are translated into practical outcomes rests in a normative judgment about the most preferable way to remedy real-life problems of socioeconomic and environmental nature and realize human well-being. Predominantly, such process takes place at a high political level due to the complexity of the issues and their sensitivity for stakeholders' vested interests, be they governments, international financial institutions, non-governmental organizations, etc. Thereafter, development talks transpire in the midst of diverse concerns by international actors. As the latter exercise power in global policy-making, they affect the mechanisms, processes, and institutions through which common development affairs are managed; conflicting interests are accommodated and cooperative action is taken in order to administer the economic and financial, human, and natural resources for sustainable development in the best way possible. The effective response to development challenges is thus a matter of (economic, social, and environmental) governance.[160]

---

[159] Waage and others (n 59) 1009.

[160] TG Weiss and R Thakur, *The UN and Global Governance: An Idea and its Prospects* (Indiana University Press 2006); Carlsson and others (n 40) ch 1, 2.

In this respect, the international community has employed goal-setting as an efficacious tool for sustainable development governance. Indeed, global goals and their targets are deemed a unique intellectual achievement of the UN[161] because they specify policy priorities, help steer action, mobilize resources, and offer a structure for benchmarking stakeholders' performance towards the achievement of common development aims.[162] As a result, the content of UN declarations and resolutions in which development agendas are framed as normative prescriptions is clarified. Moreover, it becomes possible to hold stakeholders accountable for their conduct since goals are 'prescriptive norms that define what "ought to be done" and are intended to lead to behavior change'.[163] Perceived in this sense, goal-setting simulates rule-making which also purports to prompt individual or collective behaviour of key actors towards desired outcomes. Yet, there is an intrinsic difference between goal-setting and rule-making as means of governance. Rules govern actors' conduct by virtue of binding laws or regulations and their enforcement is induced through compliance mechanisms whereas goals articulate aspirations for a specific time frame and their compliance pull derives from the enthusiasm, support, and stimulus for the delineated outcomes that was generated from the process of their making. Even the High-level Political Forum (HLPF) that is tasked with monitoring progress on the SDGs lacks legally binding decision-making powers and enforcement capability. The SDGs build on the political rhetoric for an inclusive international society by which the international community sought to inspire and rally its members to cooperate for a sustainable world. In the very words of the Declaration in Agenda 2030: 'The SDGs and targets are integrated and indivisible, global in nature and universally applicable ... Targets are defined as aspirational and global, with each Government setting its own national targets guided by the global level of ambition but taking into account national circumstances.'[164] Because of this tone of inspiration and ambition, it has been argued that the SDGs and their targets cannot be converted into legally binding obligations but encompass purely an exhortation towards international actors to respond ambitiously to the global aspiration of sustainability.[165] By implication, Agenda 2030 is a political declaration of intent and the Goals politically and morally binding at best. Against this background, the status of the SDGs in international law has been controversial.

Nonetheless, the SDGs declaration does not cease to reiterate the relevance of international law to the SDGs. Agenda 2030 is guided by the purposes and principles of the Charter of the United Nations, it is grounded in the Universal Declaration of Human

---

[161] R Jolly and others, *UN Ideas that Changed the World* (Indiana University Press 2009).

[162] N Kanie and F Biermann (eds), *Governing through Goals: Sustainable Development Goals as Governance Innovation* (MIT Press 2017), particularly O. Young, 'Conceptualisation: Goal settings as a Strategy for Earth System Governance' in ibid 31–34.

[163] S Fukuda-Parr, 'Global Goals as a Policy Tool: Intended and Unintended Consequences' (2014) 15(2–3) Journal of Human Development and Capabilities 118, 120.

[164] Agenda 2030 (n 91) para 55.

[165] D French, 'The Global Goals: Formalism forgone, Contested Legality and Re-Imaginings of International Law' in Z Yihdego and others (eds), *2016 Ethiopian Yearbook of International Law* (Springer 2016)151–78.

Rights, human rights treaties, the Millennium Declaration, and is informed by the Declaration on the Right to Development. Besides, the landmark soft-law documents that have laid the foundation for sustainable development and compose the body of international environmental law are cited as key sources of the Agenda. Beyond the named legal instruments, however, the Agenda is to be implemented in a manner that is consistent with the rights and obligations of states under international law in general.[166] It appears therefore that there is full respect for international law and seemingly the intention to join goals and the law together for maximum compliance with the Agenda. Within this framework, the goals can be seen to represent to a great extent existing international commitments and can be assigned to corresponding legal frameworks.[167] Truly, for some it is easier to identify the international agreements in which they are embedded. To name a few, the environmental goals (climate change and biodiversity) or the goals on education, gender equality, decent work, water, and sanitation reflect clearly the substance and underlying norms of environmental and human rights law respectively. It follows that the Goals can be read as norms further defining the rights and obligations that states assume in international agreements and even extend them to other actors.[168] In this capacity, they could also serve as a 'coordinating and synthesizing framework for existing legal obligations functioning also as a remedy to the fragmentation of international law'.[169] Undoubtedly, the SDGs have not been inserted into a normative vacuum nor have they emerged without law existing at the background. A nexus between the SDGs and international law exists.

The interplay between law and the SDGs is corollary to the normative status of Agenda 2030. UNGA resolutions adopt recommendations and not decisions that create legal effects in international law *per se*. However, they do contain soft-law norms with normative credence for the interpretation and application of the law. Agenda 2030, while soft, possesses such legal authority to the extent that it was carefully negotiated, debated, drafted, and universally endorsed as an effective formula to set the grounds for an internationally agreed regulatory framework and policy strategy on sustainable development. In this regard, the statements made therein intended to establish certain standards for state practice and decision-making, creating in turn the legitimate expectation that actors will commit to and observe the agreed in good faith, and streamline their conduct consistency with sustainable development's economic, social, and environmental objectives.[170] Having said that, Agenda 2030 as well as the Stockholm, the Rio, and the Johannesburg Declarations unavoidably influence the interpretation and application of existing rules of international law in the respective fields

---

[166] Agenda 2030 (n 91) paras 10 and 11.

[167] RE Kim, 'The Nexus between International Law and the Sustainable Development Goals' (2016) 25(1) Review of European Community and International Environmental Law 15, 16.

[168] MMTA Brus, 'Soft Law in Public International Law: A Pragmatic or Principled Choice?' Comparing the Sustainable Development Goals and the Paris Agreement' (22 March 2017) 11 <https://ssrn.com/abstract=2945 942> accessed 29 November 2022.

[169] Kim (n 167) 16 and 17.

[170] FAC Castañeda, 'A Call for Rethinking the Sources of International Law: Soft Law and the Other Side of the Coin' (2013) XIII Annuario Mexicano de Derecho International 335, 369.

by the articulation of specific principles relating to sustainable development. On these grounds, their legal effects are not negligible and nothing precludes that the enshrined norms transform into binding rules.[171]

In the light of the above, the case that the SDGs are endowed with the same status can be made plausibly. They do not create binding obligations, yet their observance is not entirely optional either, given their universal acceptance and legitimacy. Consequently, the Goals may contribute to the development of the legal discipline when attached to the norms of respective legal fields.[172] Scholars have already defended this proposition, for instance, in the context of the use and conservation of water crossing international boundaries and how water resources can be managed in a way that fulfils the human right to safe drinking water and sanitation. Relevant international instruments may be interpreted in the light of SDG 6. Hence, the Goal may infuse the practice of this area of law with the theory and practice of socioeconomic and participatory human rights as well as new perspectives to water management stemming from the environmental dimension of sustainable development.[173] Similarly, the targets of goals comprising the environmental cluster of the SDGs (eg climate change, oceans conservation, air pollution, etc) can be linked to specific international law provisions. Thereafter, SDGs 13 to 15 may not only reinforce current international law but also contribute to the integration of the different international agreements within the cluster in those instances where their targets overlap.[174]

It follows that the SDGs do have normative consequences for the progressive development of international law by clarifying the meaning of already established legal frameworks in the various fields of international law or by shaping the content and paving the way for the formulation of new norms that may comprise a more consolidated perspective on international development law that is currently missing. This holds true even for those goals that could not be easily matched with existing conventions or customary rules of international law. A teleological interpretation of Agenda 2030 and consideration of the linkages between the Goals through their targets could also apply to the underpinning legal frameworks and mainstream into them dimensions that so far have not been anchored in law. The principle of sustainable development is crucial in this manner, being the signpost for this assimilation. Hence, all goals will obtain a normative underpinning and new entries for the development of the economic, social, and environmental legal regimes will be created. Ultimately, the fact that the Goals fall outside the ambit of classical law-making in international law (its formal sources included) and are not formulated in an unequivocal legal form and content does not lessen their legal weight. They are legitimate because they mirror the

---

[171] Zampetti (n 115) 287–88, who notes also the transformation of some of the Millennium Declaration commitments into customary international law.

[172] W Scholtz and M Barnard, 'The Environment and the Sustainable Development Goals: "We Are on a Road to Nowhere"' in D French and L Kotzé (eds), *Sustainable Development Goals: Law, Theory and Implementation* (Edward Elgar 2018)227.

[173] O McIntyre, 'International Water Law and SDG6: Mutually Reinforcing Paradigms' in ibid 173.

[174] Scholtz and Barnard (n 172); also N Sánchez Castillo-Winckels, 'How the Sustainable Development Goals Promote a New Conception of Ocean Commons Governance' in French and Kotzé (eds) (n 172) 121–24.

shared values and interests of the members of the international community, who have the authority to decide on their making and accept them as appropriate. *Ergo*, the intent to regulate, even in the absence of well-embedded law, is present. Accordingly, there seems no reason to deny their transformative potential not only in policy but in law as well, recognizing their impact on the progressive development of 'hard' law on sustainable development.[175]

---

[175] Brus (n 168).

SDG 1

'End Poverty in All Its Forms Everywhere'

Krista Nadakavukaren Schefer

I. Introduction

When the world's leaders endorsed the outcome document of the United Nations (UN) Conference on Sustainable Development (Rio+20 Conference), they accepted as their own the report titled 'The Future We Want'.[1] The future, according to that 2012 document, was to be 'economically, socially, and environmentally sustainable', as well as people-centred.[2] Underlying each of these hopes was the dream of no poverty—a dream seemingly as elusive as it was long-standing.[3]

Although the Rio+20 Conference had originally foreseen a work programme on the green economy (in the context of poverty and sustainable development), and even though the origins of the Conference lay firmly in environmental concerns, the 2012 Conference document was explicitly oriented toward sustainability in the interest of persons rather than the environment for its own sake.[4] 'The Future We Want' report emerging from Rio+20 makes clear that sustainable development, in the view of the UN members, is about improving human lives. More specifically, it is about ensuring that individuals have the entire range of resources available to them that are necessary to living a life of fulfilment now and in the future. In their own words, the UN members promised to 'renew [their] commitment to sustainable development and to ensuring the promotion of an economically, socially and environmentally sustainable future for our planet and for present and future generations'.[5]

Significantly, while 'The Future We Want' downplayed references to the green economy, it maintained its focus on poverty reduction, calling it 'the greatest global

---

[1] UNGA Resolution 66/288, 'The Future We Want', A/RES/66/288 (11 September 2012) (endorsing the outcome document of the Rio+20 Conference, 'The Future We Want'; the document is annexed to the resolution) ('The Future We Want').

[2] ibid para 1.

[3] M Kamau and others, *Transforming Multilateral Diplomacy: The Inside Story of the Sustainable Development Goals* (Routledge 2018) 7. For a discussion of the history of poverty studies, see A O'Connor, 'Poverty Knowledge and the History of Poverty Research' in D Brady and LM Burton (eds), *The Oxford Handbook of the Social Science of Poverty* (OUP 2016); for an account of the development literature addressing poverty differences among global regions, see S Bhattacharyya, 'The Historical Origin of Poverty in Developing Countries' in Brady and Burton (eds) ibid.

[4] J Schleicher and others, 'Will the Sustainable Development Goals Address the Links between Poverty and the Natural Environment?' (2018) 34 Current Opinion in Environmental Sustainability 43, 44.

[5] 'The Future We Want' (n 1) para 1.

38   SDG 1

challenge facing the world'.[6] The report then emphasized the circular nature of poverty and environmental degradation:

> 3. Poverty eradication, changing unsustainable and promoting sustainable patterns of consumption and production and protecting and managing the natural resource base of economic and social development are the overarching objectives of and essential requirements for sustainable development.

In setting out poverty as an issue to be addressed, 'The Future We Want' points out to the unevenness of the success of the Millennium Development Goals (MDG) in reducing poverty levels[7] and calls for poverty reduction to receive the 'highest priority' in setting the development agenda.[8] The report also considered the issue of social security programmes worthy of discussion when considering poverty.[9] Concerns of poverty's relation to other global concerns were highlighted throughout the report, including direct references to poverty in the sections on food security and agricultural development,[10] water and sanitation,[11] energy services,[12] sustainable tourism,[13] sustainable housing and settlements,[14] health,[15] decent work and employment opportunities,[16] oceans,[17] disaster risk reduction,[18] sharing of genetic resources,[19] land management and desertification,[20] mountain social and ecosystems,[21] and education.[22]

The call to develop sustainable development goals was the report's main feature. Proposed essentially as a way of generating support for the overall programme of action,[23] the use of discrete targets and indicators was seen to be promisingly motivational and politically astute. The Sustainable Development Goals (SDGs) were to be similar in format to the MDGs, but broader and universal. Moreover, the process by which the goals should be determined was to be state-led rather than Secretariat-led in order to ensure acceptance in the General Assembly (GA).[24] 'The Future We Want'

---

[6] ibid para 2.
[7] ibid para 105.
[8] ibid para 106.
[9] ibid para 107.
[10] ibid para 109.
[11] ibid para 120.
[12] ibid paras 125–126.
[13] ibid para 131.
[14] ibid paras 134–135.
[15] ibid para 138.
[16] ibid paras 147–148, 151,
[17] ibid para 158.
[18] ibid para 186.
[19] ibid para 199.
[20] ibid paras 205, 207.
[21] ibid paras 211–212.
[22] ibid para 229.
[23] See the description of the political/diplomatic background of the Rio+20 Conference and outcome document in Kamau and others (n 3) 28–43 (emphasizing the effects of the 2009 Copenhagen Climate Conference failure on the Rio+20 Conference preparations and results).
[24] ibid.

therefore established the basis for the Open Working Group (OWG) to draft a limited number of SDGs and put them forth for adoption. It was the OWG that then conceived the individual goals, targets, and indicators.

II. *Travaux Préparatoires*

The OWG began its task by considering the UN members' perceived 'priority areas'.[25] Gleaned from a questionnaire sent to all members in September 2012,[26] those areas did not, in fact, include poverty reduction as one of the top three most important areas.[27] However, the Conclusions stated:

> 77. Member States generally agreed that poverty eradication must remain the highest priority, completing the unfinished business of Goal 1, and that to realize this goal sustained, inclusive and equitable economic growth in developing countries is a necessary requirement.[28]

This ensured a prominent role for poverty eradication in the SDGs.

A. Prioritizing Poverty

In 2013, the UNGA again put forth its own views in support of the steps being taken to pull together a post-2015 work agenda.[29] Acknowledging a continued commitment to the MDGs, the leaders also declared their intention to pursue a more ambitious set of interests, even while permitting national differences in how those interests would be approached. Interest in poverty eradication followed this intention, broadening and deepening MDG 1, but simultaneously leaving room for country differences.

> 19. We are resolved that the post-2015 development agenda should reinforce the international community's commitment to poverty eradication and

---

[25] ibid 78.

[26] Questionnaire related to the development of Sustainable Development Goals (28 September 2012) (<https://sustainabledevelopment.un.org/content/documents/14421360Questionnaire%20SDGs_final_2809-1.pdf>). See also summary of results of the questionnaire: UNGA, Initial Input of the Secretary-General to the Open Working Group on Sustainable Development Goals, A/67/634 (17 December 2012).

[27] See 'Initial Input of the Secretary-General to the Open Working Group on Sustainable Development Goals' (n 26) 5 (chart indicating frequency of priorities showing food security as the most mentioned issue, followed by water and sanitation, energy, and education; poverty eradication followed in fifth place, apparently tied with health).

[28] ibid para 77.

[29] UNGA, 'Outcome document of the special event to follow up efforts made towards achieving the Millennium Development Goals', A/68/L.4 (1 October 2013).

sustainable development. We underline the central imperative of poverty eradication .... Recognizing the intrinsic interlinkage between poverty eradication and the promotion of sustainable development, we underline the need for a coherent approach that integrates in a balanced manner the three dimensions of sustainable development. This coherent approach involves working towards a single framework and set of goals, universal in nature and applicable to all countries, while taking account of differing national circumstances and respecting national policies and priorities.[30]

Given the political acceptability of maintaining attention to the problem of poverty, discussion in the OWG was about how to place poverty reduction within the panoply of the other goals. By the end of the OWG's second session, co-chair Kamau was able to express his feeling that there was 'an emerging consensus to place poverty eradication as the overarching goal of the SDGs [and] suggested that [it] could be seen as the starting point of the post-2015 agenda'.[31]

Kamau's intuitions proved correct. When the draft SDGs were released to the preconference delegations, poverty eradication had its proposed place as Sustainable Development Goal 1 (SDG 1). While the contours of SDG 1 remained somewhat in flux throughout the OWG process, the fact that the fight against poverty would be the core of SDG 1 was never challenged.

The OWG's co-chairs' Focus Area document of March 2014 suggested a framing of poverty eradication with a description that is strikingly similar to the final Goal and its targets. The February 2014 'Focus Area 1' was poverty eradication:

> Eradication of poverty in all its forms remains the overriding priority and a necessary condition for sustainable development. The pursuit of this would provide a strong nexus to the realization of the unfinished business of the MDGs. Some areas that could be considered include: eradicating absolute poverty; reducing relative poverty; addressing inequalities at both national and international levels; access to property and productive assets, finance and markets for all women and men; providing social protection to reduce vulnerabilities of the poor, including children, youth, unemployed, persons with disabilities, indigenous people and local communities and older persons. Since poverty is multidimensional, progress is linked to action in all other focus areas.

In March 2014, the responses to the Focus Area document—labelled 'Encyclopedia Groupinica'—indicated an extremely high level of agreement on a number of the elements and substantial agreement on almost all of them. Views on the eradication of poverty by 2030, for example, varied only by the terms used to define the type of poverty

---

[30] ibid para 19.
[31] 'Summary—Second Session of the OWG on SDGs', 17–19 April 2013, p 14.

intended ('extreme poverty', 'extreme income poverty', 'absolute poverty', 'people living below 1.25 USD a day', 'extreme poverty and living on less than $2.50 a day') and how to describe the target ('eradicate', 'eliminate', 'reduce to zero'). There was one suggestion for attending to the 'intensity of poverty' and one called for looking at vulnerability to poverty.[32]

The question of relative poverty and inequality excited more varied responses. Numerous suggestions referred to the need to reduce 'multidimensional' poverty and called to 'end extreme economic inequality within and between countries', to 'reduce relative poverty and address inequalities at both national and international levels', and to minimize 'income and wealth disparities at all level[s]'.[33]

Social protection, natural disaster resilience, access to property and productive assets, and ensuring international development financing were all readily supported even in the early negotiations.[34] Topics that did not make it into the later negotiations on SDG 1 included numerous other aspects that are closely related to poverty but which were placed elsewhere in the Goals: nutrition, hunger, employment, special requirements of rural populations, culture, family policies, and governance.[35]

By May, the co-chairs' new draft was substantially streamlined, even if the final structure and language was far from complete. The Working Document for the May OWG included the following text:

Focus Area 1. Poverty eradication, building shared prosperity and promoting equality
End poverty in all its forms everywhere
a) eradicate extreme poverty by 2030
b) reduce the proportion of people living below national poverty lines by 2030
c) by 2030 implement nationally appropriate social protection measures including floors, with focus on coverage of the most marginalized
d) build resilience of the poor and reduce by x% deaths and economic losses related to disasters
e) achieve full and productive employment for all, including women and young people
f) ensure equality of economic opportunity for all women and men, including secure rights to own land, property and other productive assets and access to financial services for all women and men

Interesting is the lack of unity, even at that point, on the implementation measures. Whereas the co-chairs were able to record numerous adherents to most of the

---

[32] The suggestion for looking at intensity is attributed to Pakistan, while Australia/the Netherlands/United Kingdom suggested vulnerability to falling below a $2.50/day level. Encyclopedia Groupinica 2, footnotes 8 and 10 and accompanying text.
[33] ibid 3–4.
[34] ibid 5–9.
[35] ibid 5–9.

42   SDG 1

individual goals,[36] just how to pay for the goals' implementation clearly remained contentious.

B. Agenda 2030

Agenda 2030, which sets out the SDGs in their finalized form, explains the context and the aspirations of the UN members for the post-2015 world.[37] The new Agenda, says the Preamble, 'is a plan of action for people, planet and prosperity. It also seeks to strengthen universal peace in larger freedom'.[38] Using the catch-phrase 'People–Planet–Prosperity–Peace–Partnership', the world's leaders wanted to emphasize their broad-based vision of a good future for the world's inhabitants. Not only were people to live in dignity and fulfilment of their bodily, social, and intellectual needs, the planet's natural resources were to be protected and societies were to be peaceful. Cooperation among countries and peoples was going to help ensure that the financial and knowledge resources were available to those who needed assistance.[39]

The enormity of Agenda 2030 did not escape its drafters—they write of the 'bold and transformative steps'[40] that will be necessary to achieve goals and promise that 'lives of all will be profoundly improved'[41] if the world community succeeds in its attempt. The Declaration itself continues in the same vein, calling it 'an Agenda of unprecedented scope and significance'[42] and a reflection of 'a supremely ambitious and transformational vision'.[43]

Yet, for all the lofty language, the Agenda is dedicated to an overriding goal: lasting poverty elimination. 'We are committed to ending poverty in all its forms and dimensions, including by eradicating extreme poverty by 2030.'[44] To be sure, the men and women that drafted and approved Agenda 2030 realized that lasting poverty eradication requires a broad-based programme of action—one that will require an environmental consciousness as well as attention to social factors and geopolitical relations. The best tool to spur action in this direction, they determined, was to set it forth clearly and prominently.

---

[36] Working Document for OWG 11, p 1, footnotes 1–8 (each footnote except footnote 4 appears to record the explicit supporters of the point).
[37] UNGA, 'Transforming Our World: The 2030 Agenda for Sustainable Development', A/RES/70/1 (21 October 2015).
[38] ibid Preamble 1.
[39] ibid 2.
[40] ibid 1.
[41] ibid 2.
[42] ibid para 5.
[43] ibid para 7.
[44] ibid para 24.

III. Commentary on the Goal

A. Why is Poverty Eradication the Primary Sustainable Development Goal?

That poverty reduction will remain the poster-child of the United Nations and a first goal among equals in the international community's programme for pursuing a sustainable future seems justified. Poverty, after all, is the ultimate unfreedom[45] and a life of poverty is one of unimaginable potential wasted.[46] Fighting poverty is therefore rightly called a 'moral imperative'; it is 'simply not acceptable'.[47]

The international answer to poverty eradication has, since at least the post-Second World War era,[48] been one of economic growth, or the concept of 'development', as a means of generating resources and employment that can lift populations out of poverty.[49] Yet development, as the world has learned, cannot be sustainable where the environment and communities are ignored. The SDGs—including SDG 1—are as much reflections of lessons learned from past mistakes as they are 'visionary'. Just as millions are being raised out of poverty, millions more are being born into poverty of a dangerously stubborn nature. The problems of wealth inequality across states but also across communities within states are worsening. Climate change and ecosystem degradation are pushing prosperity further and further out of reach for the most vulnerable and increasing their vulnerability. Peace itself is fragile where poverty is left unaddressed, whether that be because of dissatisfaction among the disadvantaged or because the impoverished have little to risk when offered a chance to fight. The Agenda 2030 commitment to ending poverty is therefore one against which little can be said on the conceptual level.

Judging by the words used, poverty elimination is the overriding goal of the international community today. As such, it is fitting that the first of the SDGs is 'End poverty in all its forms everywhere'. The call is to ensure that every individual may live a lifetime

---

[45] The idea of 'unfreedoms' is most readily attributed to Amartya Sen. See A Sen, *Development as Freedom* (OUP 2001).

[46] A study on innovators in the United States generated the term 'Lost Einsteins' (and 'Lost Marie Curies') to describe the poverty (and gendered) effects on a child's (un-)likelihood to put his/her talents to full use in adulthood. A Bell and others, 'Who Becomes an Inventor in America? The Importance of Exposure to Innovation' (2019) 134(2) Quarterly Journal of Economics 647–713, 708.

[47] M Bachelet, 'Opening Note' in MF Davis and others (eds), *Research Handbook on Human Rights and Poverty* (Edward Elgar 2021) xviii.

[48] Koponen notes that the idea of development being 'invented' in 1949 is highly contested, with some looking to the post-First World War mandate system as the beginning and many historians looking at European colonialism as the real starting point. J Koponen, 'Development: History and Power of the Concept' (2020) 47(1) Forum for Development Studies 1, 2–3.

[49] Koponen describes the meaning of the concept as one connecting three ideas: '(1) a desired goal, an ideal state of affairs to strive for; (2) a transformative process or, rather, a set of processes towards that goal; and (3) intentional human action based on the belief that a well-meant intervention will trigger processes leading to what we ideally regard as development'. ibid 5. He stresses that it is the action-toward-a-goal aspect that distinguishes 'development' from related concepts such as 'progress' and that it is based on the assumption that there is an 'embryonic present form' upon which the action will lead to the future, ideal form. ibid 6–7.

without experiencing deprivations on account of a lack of resources or access to services and without facing the fear of falling into poverty.

The fight against poverty is not only a part of achieving sustainable development, it is a prerequisite to it. The words of Agenda 2030 are clear: 'eradicating poverty in all its forms and dimensions, including extreme poverty, is the greatest global challenge and an indispensable requirement for sustainable development'.[50]

Setting the eradication of poverty at the centre of an agenda to protect the planet and its population is critical not only because of poverty's impacts on the physical environment and the long-term capacity of economies to provide for their people, but because poverty must be eliminated if the international community aspires to secure a future of dignity and optimism for its citizens and peace for all. Before the world is rid of poverty, neither peace nor justice—the international community's dual goals—will be achievable.

Whether the international community is ready to accept the challenge posed by SDG 1 remains to be seen. Governments were eager to put their voices behind the Goal, but policy decisions will have to be taken and measures implemented that have a real impact on the lives of those suffering from poverty for progress to happen. These will require determination and a readiness to prioritize resource use.[51]

B. Poverty Reduction as an International Action Item: A Brief History

At the time of the SDG agenda-setting discussions, the international community was still convinced of the centrality of poverty eradication to the overall goal of sustainable development. The Rio+20 Conference's outcome document, 'The Future We Want', set out the 'common vision' of the leaders of the world's states as one of committing to working toward sustainable economic, social, and environmental conditions for all generations everywhere.[52] The paragraphs following this overall vision underline the central role of eliminating poverty in this vision. Paragraph 2 is absolutely clear on this:

> Poverty eradication is the greatest global challenge facing the world today and an indispensable requirement for sustainable development. In this regard, we are committed to freeing humanity from poverty and hunger as a matter of urgency.[53]

---

[50] G.A. Res. 70/1, 'Transforming our World: The 2030 Agenda for Sustainable Development', para 2 (25 September 2015).

[51] Jeffrey Sachs wrote in the early 2000s that the international community would need to spend $175 billion per year for twenty years to eliminate poverty, a sum that would be more than covered if each state committed to spending 0.7 per cent of its gross domestic product (GDP) actually did so. J Sachs, *The End of Poverty: Economic Possibilities for Our Time* (Penguin Press 2005). With the exception of Denmark, Luxembourg, the Netherlands, Norway, Sweden, and Turkey, however, governmental spending remains below this level. OECD (2021), 'Net ODA' (ODA indicators for the year 2019) <https://doi.org/10.1787/33346549-en> accessed on 17 January 2021.

[52] 'The Future We Want' (n 1), Annex para 1.

[53] ibid para 2.

It is important to keep in mind, however, that 'The Future We Want' was not the original basis for approaching poverty reduction as a global aim. Poverty as a central concern of the international community has had a long history, but SDG 1 can most clearly be tied to the evolution of thinking about poverty in the context of sustainable development.[54]

The 2012 discussions, therefore, have their early roots in the 1972 UN Conference on the Human Environment which took place in Stockholm.[55] That Conference essentially 'invented' the field of international environmental law,[56] but it was environmental law in the service of humankind. The Stockholm Declaration leaves no doubt that natural resources must be managed and maintained for all generations in order to ensure the 'fundamental right to freedom, equality and adequate conditions of life, in an environment of a quality that permits a life of dignity and well-being' of all persons.[57] The human-centric nature of the Declaration was critical to its acceptance by the representatives of the developing countries.[58]

The fifteen-year anniversary of Stockholm witnessed the beginning of the era of sustainable development in the United Nations. The World Commission on Environment and Development set forth the widely accepted definition of sustainable development as development that 'meets the needs of the present without compromising the ability of future generations to meet their own needs'.[59] While this definition aims to ensure that 'development' was understood to be a function of environment, economy, and society, the problem of poverty was at its core. Found in the same paragraph as the definition of sustainable development is the Commission's warning about failing to address poverty. On the one hand, the inability to meet basic needs is 'an evil in itself'; on the other, poverty stands as a constant threat to the environment: '[a] world in which poverty is endemic will always be prone to ecological and other catastrophes'.[60] Commission Chairperson Brundtland wrote, therefore, of the need for economic growth in order to reduce poverty, even as she recognized that future growth must take 'environment [as] an ally, not a victim'.[61]

At the beginning of the 1990s, global attention to poverty took a turn. This happened both in the UN and in the World Bank. As Hulme explains, the World Bank's 'World Development Report 1990' indicated that the World Bank was putting poverty reduction back at the centre of its activities, having been somewhat sidelined in the

---

[54] See D Hulme, 'The Millennium Development Goals (MDGs): A Short History of the World's Biggest Promise' (September 2009) BWPI Working Paper 100, 7–12 (recounting the various policy steps from Franklin Roosevelt's Four Freedoms Speech in 1944 to the Millennium Declaration).

[55] For an account of the motivations and procedures leading to the Stockholm Conference, see LB Sohn, 'The Stockholm Declaration on the Human Environment' (1973) 14(3) Harvard International Law Journal 423.

[56] See ibid 431, footnote 38 and accompanying text (quoting Canadian representative to the Stockholm conference, JA Beesley, as calling the Declaration 'a first step toward the development of international environmental law').

[57] Declaration of the United Nations Conference on the Human Environment, Principle 1 (June 1972).

[58] Sohn (n 55) 432, footnote 43 and accompanying text (noting Ghana's representative's suggestion that the connection between environmental interests and development made the Declaration important to developing countries).

[59] 'Report of the World Commission on Environment and Development: Our Common Future' (1987), para 27.

[60] ibid.

[61] GH Brundtland, 'Our Common Future—Call for Action' (1987) 14(4) Environmental Conservation, 291, 292.

46 SDG 1

Bretton Woods Institutions' policies in the 1980s.[62] The Report, titled 'Poverty', begins by expressing that the 'enormous economic progress' of the previous decades had led to rapid advancements in development and yet there were still more than one billion people living in extreme poverty. This, the report writes, is 'staggering—and all the more shameful'.[63] The Report continues by recognizing the uneven burden of poverty on certain populations, emphasizing the discrepancies within countries as well as the fact that global poverty is concentrated in certain geographic regions. While the World Bank emphasized the need for foreign aid to countries with large populations living in poverty,[64] it also acknowledged the difficulties in effecting improvements where governments lack robust development policies[65] and encouraged domestic social programmes involving both transfers and social service provision.[66]

In the same year, the UN Development Programme (UNDP) released its first 'Human Development Report'.[67] The latter is noteworthy for the very broad view of development that it took and the characterization of poverty: human development, it stated, 'is a process of enlarging people's choices'.[68] Taking the 'capabilities approach' to human development, the authors of the report reveal that human development choices are related to income, but are not solely defined by income—the human development index thus takes 'decent living standards' or 'command over resources needed for a decent living' into consideration, but also looks at longevity and knowledge.[69] The philosophy of human development is repeated in the SDGs.

Twenty years after Stockholm, the international community met in Rio de Janiero for a new summit dedicated to the environmental aspects of sustainable development.[70] The 1992 Rio Conference, or 'Earth Summit', resulted in the Rio Declaration and three multilateral environmental agreements[71] as well as a work programme. The latter, Agenda 21,[72] built on the Stockholm Conference's warnings about economic growth without regard to the environment. Agenda 21 became the first modern global action plan on sustainable development and its level of ambition left the international environmental policy community feeling optimistic about the shift in attitude toward how the global system needed to respond to future challenges.[73] For the present chapter,

---

[62] Hulme (n 54) 8.

[63] World Bank, 'World Development Report: Poverty' (1990) 1 (Overview).

[64] ibid 4, 127–37.

[65] ibid 4.

[66] ibid 90–102.

[67] ibid. See UNDP, *Human Development Report 1990: Concept and Measurement of Human Development* (New York 1990) (available at <http://www.hdr.undp.org/en/reports/global/hdr1990>).

[68] 'Human Development Report 1990' 10.

[69] ibid 12.

[70] UN Conference on Environment & Development, Rio de Janerio, Brazil, 3–14 June 1992.

[71] The UN Framework Convention on Climate Change 1771 UNTS 107 (adopted 9 May 1992, entered into force 21 March 1994); the Convention on Biological Diversity, 1760 UNTS 69 (adopted 5 June 1992, entered into force 29 December 1993); the Declaration on the Principles of Forest Management (1992).

[72] United Nations Conference on Environment & Development, Agenda 21 (1992).

[73] See J Sachs, *A Brief History of the SDGs* (SDG Academy, 20 August 2019) (<https://sdgacademylibrary.med iaspace.kaltura.com/media/A+Brief+History+of+the+SDGs/1_7kkjfmxx/123650921>, accessed 11 March 2023). Sachs comments, however, that the optimism quickly died as a result of governments' subsequent refusal to advance the climate change agenda. ibid.

COMMENTARY ON THE GOAL   47

Agenda 21 was significant for its Chapter 3, which made poverty a 'programme area'. Recognizing poverty as a 'complex multidimensional problem', Agenda 21 called explicitly for the 'eradication of poverty and hunger, greater equity in income distribution and human resource development'.[74] Labelling these 'major challenges', the Agenda pressed for national policies and international support to address ending poverty.[75]

In 1995, the World Summit on Social Development gathered a record 117 leaders in Copenhagen to discuss poverty reduction.[76] It was here that poverty eradication became a firm political goal of the international community. While providing no binding obligations and allowing each country to determine its own deadline for achieving a state of no poverty, the Summit led not only to 1996 being declared the International Year for the Eradication of Poverty but even more important was that 'it clearly had a profound impact on multilateral and some bilateral programmes, which increasingly began to define their developmental role as poverty eradication or reduction'.[77]

Overlapping the Copenhagen Summit was a discussion in the Organisation for Economic Co-operation and Development's (OECD) Development and Assistance Committee (DAC). The DAC, representing the world's largest donor economies, appears to be the origin of the Goals-approach to global work programme creation. Where the UN conferences were releasing high-level declarations about agendas to improve sustainable development for all, the DAC was much more targeted. In May 1996, it released a list of seven 'International Development Goals' approved by all OECD members.[78] The format of having poverty reduction efforts channelled into targets appealed to the philosophy of new public management that was embraced at the time.[79] The International Development Goals therefore became important forerunners to the MDGs,[80] even while their approach to poverty (focused on income poverty) was much narrower than what would emerge from the UN.

The Rio+5 meetings again pointed to poverty—generally recognizing its importance but also noting the lack of progress in improvements under Agenda 21. In the opening plenary, the main focus was on the environmental aspects of sustainable development, but poverty remained a topic. Leaders from Africa were the most pointedly critical, commenting on the continuation of deep poverty and the growing inequalities;[81] but European leaders, too, decried the lack of progress on poverty elimination, tying the need to reduce poverty to environmental progress.[82]

---

[74] Agenda 21 (n 86) 3.1.
[75] ibid.
[76] Hulme (n 54) 11.
[77] ibid (suggesting MG Schechter, *United Nations Global Conferences* (Routledge 2005) 141).
[78] OECD, 'Shaping the 21st Century: The Contribution of Development Cooperation' (6–7 May 1996).
[79] ibid 20.
[80] ibid 40 (stating that 'the IDGs became the basis for the MDGs').
[81] See comments of President Mugabe (Zimbabwe) and Mkapa (Tanzania) from 23 June 1997 (<https://documents-dds-ny.un.org/doc/UNDOC/GEN/N97/857/17/PDF/N9785717.pdf?OpenElement>).
[82] For example, ibid 18 (President Anzár (Spain)); ibid 19 (comments of Prime Minister Blair (United Kingdom)); ibid 20 (Chancellor Kohl (Germany)).

48   SDG 1

As the end of the twentieth century approached, global attention shifted again toward the human dimension of sustainable development. Research by social scientists in academia and research institutions was adding to the further study of poverty reduction policies and deepening the understanding of the effects of poverty on individuals and groups at this time.[83] The World Bank's *Voices of the Poor* project, involving interviews and case studies of over 100,000 poor persons expounding on their frustrations, hopes, and fears, offered invaluable insights into the reality of poverty's multidimensionality.[84]

In 2000, then-Secretary General Kofi Annan put out his report 'We the Peoples: The Role of the United Nations in the 21st Century', calling for a 'freedom from want' and prioritizing poverty reduction as a matter of human dignity. Release of 'We the Peoples' spurred further negotiations prior to the September Millennium Conference. The Declaration finally adopted by the world leaders[85] looked to ensure a 'peaceful, prosperous and just' world.[86]

The Millennium Declaration redirected the attention of the international community to the human impacts of poverty, stressing the need to 'free our fellow men, women and children from the abject and dehumanizing conditions of extreme poverty'.[87] Although couched within a framework of peace and security goals, the MDGs were, according to Secretary-General Ban Ki-Moon, essentially a programme in which poverty reduction was not *just* a main element, it was the main element of the new millennium project.

> The global mobilization behind the Millennium Development Goals has produced the most successful anti-poverty movement in history. The landmark commitment entered into by world leaders in the year 2000—to 'spare no effort to free our fellow men, women and children from the abject and dehumanizing conditions of extreme poverty'—was translated into an inspiring framework of eight goals and, then, into wide-ranging practical steps that have enabled people across the world to improve their lives and their future prospects.[88]

1. From MDG 1 to SDG 1

When the September 2000 UN Millennium Development Goals Declaration set out the international community's aims for the next fifteen years, ending extreme poverty and hunger was Goal 1.[89] Defining the goal with three targets (to '[h]alve, between 1990 and 2015, the proportion of people whose income is less than $1 a day'; to '[a]chieve

---

[83] Brady and Destro note that the 1990s were also times of substantial scholarly attention to poverty in the United States. D Brady and LM Destro, 'Poverty' in Béland and others (eds), *The Oxford Handbook of U.S. Social Policy* (OUP 2015) 589.

[84] See D Narayan, 1 *Voices of the Poor: Can Anyone Hear Us?* (World Bank 2000); D. Narayan and others, 2 *Voices of the Poor: Crying Out for Change* (World Bank 2000); D Narayan and P Petesch (eds), 3 *Voices of the Poor: From Many Lands* (World Bank 2002).

[85] UN Millennium Declaration, General Assembly resolution 55/2 of 8 September 2000.

[86] ibid para 1

[87] ibid para 11.

[88] B Ki-Moon, 'Foreword', *The Millennium Development Goals Report 2015* (United Nations 2015).

[89] United Nations, Millennium Development Goals, Goal 1: Eradicate Extreme Poverty & Hunger.

full and productive employment and decent work for all, including women and young people';[90] and to '[h]alve, between 1990 and 2015, the proportion of people who suffer from hunger'), the MDGs were looking at more than simply raising the incomes of the world's poorest, incorporating some multidimensionality to the programme.

In May 2001, just eight months after the Millennium Declaration had set the goal of eradication of extreme poverty, the Committee on Economic, Social and Cultural Rights (CESCR) defined poverty as 'a human condition characterized by the sustained or chronic deprivation of the resources, capabilities, choices, security and power necessary for the enjoyment of an adequate standard of living and other civil, cultural, economic, political and social rights'.[91] With this definition, the CESCR made the connection between poverty and all human rights explicit without needing to proclaim a 'right to not be impoverished'.

Fighting poverty thus became more than an ethical quest—it became an essential part of the United Nations' programme to secure the full enjoyment of human rights for all. The *Voices of the Poor* project and Amartya Sen's *Development as Freedom* had already shed light on the complexities of poverty's impacts on individuals, but a legal anchoring in human rights lagged behind.

The 2002 Johannesburg Declaration[92] reinforced the goal of reducing poverty by at least half.[93] It even considered the establishment of a 'world solidarity fund' financed by the private sector and individuals to help developing countries move people out of poverty.[94]

2. Setting the Post-2015 Agenda

As the post-2015 Agenda began being discussed, the centrality of poverty to a sustainable international system never shifted. In the multiple resolutions and documents emerging from the pre-Rio+20 Conference meetings, in 'The Future We Want' report, and throughout the pre-Agenda 2030 conference preparations and OWG meetings, there was a clear determination that poverty would need attention. Poverty eradication, in fact, was mentioned not only repeatedly, but repeatedly as one of the two main reasons (if not the main reason) for the project.[95]

---

[90] The decent work target was added in 2007 and, given its absence from the Agenda, was not given the attention that the poverty and hunger targets were. See DF Frey and G MacNaughton (2016) 'A Human Rights Lens on Full Employment and Decent Work in the 2030 Sustainable Development Agenda' SAGE Open (doi: 10.1177/2158244016649580; accessed 17 January 2021).

[91] CESCR, 'Substantive Issues Arising in the Implementation of the International Covenant on Economic, Social and Cultural Rights: Poverty and the International Covenant on Economic, Social and Cultural Rights', E/C.12/2001/10, para 8 (10 May 2001).

[92] Johannesburg Declaration, paras 11–12.

[93] See 'Draft plan of implementation of the World Summit on Sustainable Development, Note by the Secretariat', A/Conf.199/L1, proposed para 6(b) (26 June 2002).

[94] See ibid.

[95] Not only did 'The Future We Want' discuss poverty eradication as an overriding issue for sustainable development, the Open Working Group meetings took up poverty as the first topic for discussion, placed poverty as first on its list of topics to address in more detail, and gave 'nearly unanimous support' to having poverty eradication as 'Focus Area 1'. 'The Future We Want' (n 1); Co-chairs' Summary Bullet Points from OWG-2 (19 April 2013) (noting that 'Poverty eradication remains the overriding objective of the international community'); Kamau and

50   SDG 1

When the OWG of the General Assembly on Sustainable Development Goals released its Report to the UN in August 2014, it highlighted the centrality of poverty to achieving the United Nations' agendas. 'Poverty eradication', as 'the greatest global challenge facing the world',[96] was to be one of three 'overarching objectives and essential requirements for sustainable development'.[97]

The importance of poverty elimination revealed in the OWG's Report reflected the discussions that had taken place since the first of their thirteen sessions. The first session, describing states' concerns and proposals for shaping the SDGs, touched on the myriad interconnections among the social, environmental, and economic aspects of the issues to be addressed in the new agenda. While social concerns were most frequently mentioned as priority areas in a questionnaire completed by members,[98] the elimination of poverty remained a primary goal, given its relevance to reaching any other goal. 'Member States generally agreed that poverty eradication must remain the highest priority', the meeting concluded, and 'sustained, inclusive and equitable economic growth in developing countries' is a requirement for achieving it.[99]

3. Alterations from MDG 1

The MDGs had made no claim to promoting a 'right to not live in poverty'. Moreover, whether the MDG approach to poverty was compatible with the existing human rights framework was debated, with prominent voices from the human rights community split on the question.[100] Clearly, however, there was a recognition that as a political tool, a global political platform to encourage actions focused on improving the economic security of those deprived of the means to subsist could lead to positive changes. MDG 1 made the fight against extreme poverty a recognized tool of the state in respecting, protecting, and pursuing other human rights.

Thus, as the world community began to think about the post-MDG work programme, poverty reduction remained a central concern. By openly pledging that the world leaders 'are committed to freeing humanity from poverty and hunger as a matter of urgency',[101] the GA set the stage for securing the place of poverty reduction in their work programme.

others (n 3) 134–35 (Box 6.1, setting out the February 2014 list of the OWG Co-Chair's Focus Areas, with 'Poverty eradication' as number one); IISD, 32(9) Earth Negotiations Bulletin 12 (8 March 2014) (reporting on the Ninth session of the OWG); OWG, Working Document for 5–9 May Session of Open Working Group (<https://sustain abledevelopment.un.org/content/documents/3686WorkingDoc_0205_additionalsupporters.pdf>) (with 'very broad consensus' noted for the target 'Eradicate extreme poverty by 2030').

[96] UNGA, 'Report of the Working Group of the General Assembly on Sustainable Development Goals', A/68/970, p 6, IV.2 (12 August 2014).
[97] ibid IV.3.
[98] 'Initial Input of the Secretary-General to the Open Working Group on Sustainable Development Goals', A/67/634, para 16 (on page 5) (17 December 2012).
[99] ibid para 77.
[100] See, eg, M Langford, 'A Poverty of Rights: Six Ways to Fix the MDGs' (2010) 41(1) Institute of Development Studies Bulletin 83–91.
[101] 'Resolution adopted by the General Assembly on 27 July 2012', A/RES/66/288, Annex para 2 (11 September 2012).

COMMENTARY ON THE GOAL 51

When the OWG began its investigation into how to shape the post-2015 agenda shortly afterwards, it unsurprisingly put poverty at the head of the list of topics to address. The OWG Secretary-General's 'Initial inputs' report opened the Conclusions with the following paragraphs:

77. Member States generally agreed that poverty eradication must remain the highest priority, completing the unfinished business of [Millennium Development] Goal 1, and that to realize this goal sustained, inclusive and equitable economic growth in developing countries is a necessary requirement.

78. Beyond this, there was broad recognition of the need to ensure that all humanity has access to basic goods and services for a decent life, productive employment, health and education. Many stressed the need to address inequalities of different kinds in the post-2015 development agenda.

The OWG's first substantive session, in mid-April 2013, accordingly took up the poverty question, maintaining MDG 1 as a 'point of departure'.[102] While it was clear that poverty reduction would be one of the SDGs, the fundamental question of how to feature the aim of poverty reduction within the structural framework of SDGs was not yet clear. While some delegates urged the maintenance of a separate goal for poverty eradication,[103] other delegations stressed the need for 'holistic' approaches to reducing poverty as a cross-cutting theme, suggesting that questions of poverty be built into all the other goals.[104]

The contours of 'poverty' were also open to discussion. While the MDGs focused on 'extreme' poverty, the post-2015 agenda appeared to be convinced early on of the need to look at deprivation more generally. This conviction arose out of the burgeoning literature investigating poverty that was emerging from academia and development institutions during the first decade and a half of the 2000s. Experts, including Sabina Alkire and Abhijit Banerjee, were heard and allowed to present the concepts of the multidimensional poverty index, the distribution of deprivation, and aspects of inequality.[105] Discussed in the early OWG session, these ideas fostered further thought to be given to the considerations of how to create measurable goals when the available data were non-existent.[106]

The OWG discussions on the contours of the goal, as expressed through its targets, are discussed further below. One item is worthy of a brief mention here: the role of inequality within the poverty goal. As already stated, the overriding importance of poverty eradication to the SDGs was never in doubt. Neither, in fact, was the importance of

---

[102] See Co-Chairs' Summary Bullet Points from OWG-2 (https://sdgs.un.org/sites/default/files/documents/1826bullet2.pdf). The OWG's Second Session took place 17–19 April 2013, and addressed the general format of the proposed SDGs and the topic of poverty eradication.

[103] For example, India's position (<https://sdgs.un.org/sites/default/files/statements/3542India.pdf> accessed 11 March 2023).

[104] For example, the position of the Pacific Small Island Developing States (<https://sdgs.un.org/statements/pacific-small-island-developing-states-psids-10939> accessed 11 March 2023).

[105] See generally, discussion papers and presentations from the second OWG session (<https://sdgs.un.org/events/second-session-open-working-group-sustainable-development-goals-6971> accessed 11 March 2023).

[106] ibid.

52   SDG 1

increasing equality. What was less clear was whether or how to combine them. When the OWG co-chairs produced their 'Focus Areas' draft in February 2014, the first on the list was 'Poverty eradication'. The March meetings to discuss this list, however, made clear that a number of delegates saw inequality as the indivisible partner to eliminating poverty. The draft circulated prior to the April OWG (OWG-10) thus indicated 'Poverty eradication, building shared prosperity and promoting equality' as a Focus Area, although it retained 'End poverty in all its forms everywhere' as the draft heading for the Goal.[107]

With the demand for attention to equality as strong as it was, the co-chairs added a separate equality goal at the end of the May OWG. The 'zero draft', containing seventeen goals, therefore maintained the title of Goal 1.[108] Interestingly, however, for the OWG-12 (June 2014), the co-chairs' revised 'zero draft' of fifteen goals included 'End poverty and reduce inequality in all their dimensions everywhere'. The deletion of inequality from the final version therefore happened between June and July of 2014.

By the time Agenda 2030 was presented to the international community, global poverty reduction statistics were lending credibility to the idea of global goal-setting. Achieving the numerical target for extreme poverty five years ahead of schedule, the success of MDG 1 was widely praised as spectacular. As noted in the 2016 'Lessons from Practice' report, the world more than met MDG 1's target, reducing the number of persons living in extreme poverty from 47 per cent to 14 per cent between 1990[109] and 2015.[110] Global attention had clearly pushed the agenda and had allowed willing governments to act more forcefully than they perhaps would have been able to without the international mandate to act.[111]

The success of MDG 1 notwithstanding, critics had pointed out a number of weaknesses. Many of the critics pointed out the lack of relevant data for examining the success of MDGs. The World Bank itself noted that there was no way of accurately assessing progress in poverty reduction in many countries around the world during the years following 2000 because the data had never before been systematically collected by

---

[107] Kamau and others (n 3) 138.

[108] Interestingly, the Sustainable Development Solutions Network, directed by Jeffrey Sachs, produced a draft of ten SDGs at the same time, with the first 'End extreme poverty including hunger'. Sustainable Development Solutions Network, 'An Action Agenda for Sustainable Development: Report for the UN Secretary-General' (5 May 2014).

[109] The MDGs used 1990 as the benchmark year. J Mayer, 'Achieving the Millennium Development Goals' (<https://www.iied.org/achieving-millennium-development-goals>; accessed 2 January 2021).

[110] United Nations Development Programme, 'From the MDGs to Sustainable Development for All' (November 2016) 13.

[111] Note, however, that caution is advisable when looking at causation (rather than correlation) between the MDGs and progress on poverty reduction. C Kenny and A Sumner, 'More Money or More Development: What Have the MDGs Achieved?' (2011) Center for Global Development Working Paper 278, 23–24 ('The causal chain from international agreement to policy change to development outcomes is a long one with many confounding influences. Given that, it is impossible to say with any certainty what was the impact of the MDGs. Having said that, the evidence available fits a story which suggests that the MDGs may well have played a role in increasing aid flows in the new Millennium, and that aid may have had some role in improving outcomes. At the same time, the weak available evidence suggests they may have had only a limited impact on policies in developing countries and on the course of global broad-based poverty reduction'.)

COMMENTARY ON THE GOAL   53

governments.[112] The question of setting out targets for which there are measurable data remains a concern in the SDGs. While it is a concern on which there has been substantial attention given since the beginning, SDG 1's more broad-based approach to poverty (looking, for example, at causes as well as effects) both exacerbates the lack of data and sharpens the difficulties in creating quality datasets.

Related to this question of data was the dissatisfaction over the lack of disaggregation of the MDG results. The UN Statistics Division pointed out the failure of the declaration of the success of MDG 1 to consider the 'variability in poverty levels ... across and within regions and countries, as well as between different population groups'.[113] The Division also indicated a need for knowing intra-household consumption patterns to fully understand the results of household surveys on poverty.[114]

Another critique of MDG 1 addressed by the SDG drafters was that of the goal's sole focus on extreme poverty. This was problematic in two ways. On the one hand, looking only at relieving extreme poverty, defined to focus on populations living on less than $1.25 a day masked the difficulties of the large number of 'vulnerable' persons that were living with less than $2 a day. The success of MDG 1 lay largely in achieving incomes of more than $1.25 a day for large numbers of people. The newly non-extreme poor, however, were largely still very poor, with most living with incomes between $1.25 and $2 per day. Significantly, these populations are extremely vulnerable: they are able to remain out of extreme poverty only so long as they experience no adverse occurrences, even of a short-term nature. The SDG drafters would need to take a broader view of poverty to ensure that those living precariously close to the extreme poverty line remained of concern to governments.

A separate problem with the focus on extreme poverty was that the MDG's income-based definition of $1.25 a day pointed almost solely at the 'global South'. In the TST Issues Brief on Poverty Eradication prepared for the SDG discussions, there was not even a mention of Europe, North America, or Australia.[115] By ignoring the difficult living circumstances engendered by economic inequality in higher income countries, the MDG 1 permitted the 'global North' to escape scrutiny of government failures to address deprived portions of their own populations.

Finally, objections to the MDG approach came from those raising objections to the lack of explicit reference to human rights.[116] The 'development goals' language suggests a programme of step-by-step improvements in global living standards, achievable through a methodical process of growth. What it lacked was any sense of moral

---

[112] World Bank/IBRD, *Global Monitoring Report 2011: Improving the Odds of Achieving the MDGs* (World Bank 2011) 4. See also Kenny and Sumner (n 111) 24 ('much of the confusion around progress related to the current set of MDGs may derive from choices made to include indicators for which data was very weak (not least maternal mortality), base target levels on politics not realistic assessment of potential progress and to translate global goals into country goals without recognizing how much higher this was raising the bar on rates of global progress').

[113] United Nations Statistics Division, 'Compendium of Statistical Notes for the Open Working Group on Sustainable Development Goals (OWG)' (March 2014) para 2.1.

[114] ibid para 2.12.

[115] TST Issues Brief: Poverty Eradication, p 1.

[116] Langford (n 100); G Sen and A Mukherjee, 'No Empowerment without Rights, No Rights without Politics: Gender Equality, MDGs and the post 2015 Development Agenda' (2014) 15 Journal of Human Development & Capabilities 188.

obligation to afford to all persons—as soon as possible—a guarantee of a life of dignity. As the content of the MDGs added nothing to the rights already universally acknowledged in the United Nations Charter, the international covenants, and the individual human rights treaties, the unambitious language of 'goals' and 'targets'—not to mention the lack of any enforcement mechanisms—revealed to the human rights community a cynical glossing over of an underlying lack of ambition on the part of world leaders to effect potentially painful changes to existing power structures.

In considering the post-2015 agenda, the MDGs were thus both starting point and counterpoint. The dedication to further poverty reduction was to continue but broaden to incorporate the criticisms of unequal burdens. The effectiveness of a 'goals listing' approach for awareness-raising was to be kept, but the number of goals expanded. The use of targets was to be maintained, but data collection would need to be improved.

4. Agenda 2030

In 2015, the new Agenda 2030 put forth a significantly more ambitious programme of SDGs than had its predecessor. Where the Millennium Declaration aimed to achieve eight targets in its fifteen year existence, Agenda 2030 put out seventeen interlinked targets intended to 'transform the world to better meet human needs and the requirements of economic transformation, while protecting the environment, ensuring peace and realizing human rights'.[117] The explicitness with which the interconnectedness of the different targets was indicated opens countless possibilities in the way governments, institutions, and even individuals can attempt to move the international community toward its goals. It also mandates that all actors involved in pursuing the SDGs recognize that the progress made on one goal will have impacts—positive or negative—on the achievement of other goals. The inherently multi-variant nature of poverty's causes and effects makes the interconnections with economic development, environmental protection, and peace as essential to SDG 1's understanding as the human rights dimensions are. The interconnectedness itself, however, also risks blurring the boundaries of the goals, making measurement more difficult and more open to challenge.

C. Multi-variant Nature of Poverty Reduction

Neither sustainable development nor poverty reduction can be adequately pursued without a multifaceted, all-society approach. Agenda 2030 recognizes this with its exhortation to '[a]ll countries and all stakeholders, acting in collaborative partnership' as those who are called upon to 'implement this plan'.[118] More detail on how society addresses poverty is left open, as the SDGs are meant to 'respect national policy space' and the 'importance of regional and subregional dimensions' is acknowledged.

---

[117] W Hongbo, 'Overview' in United Nations, *The Millennium Development Goals Report 2015* (United Nations 2015) 9.

[118] Resolution adopted by the General Assembly, 'Transforming Our World: The 2030 Agenda for Sustainable Development', A/RES/70/1, Preamble (21 October 2015).

Governments are therefore largely free to create their own poverty reduction pathways. Given deep divisions among experts on how to best pursue poverty reduction, the openness of SDG 1 is simultaneously its greatest strength and most vulnerable element. Whatever a state does to pursue the goal can be challenged as inappropriate or insufficient or lauded as incremental and contextually necessary.

D. Critique of SDG 1

Scepticism surrounding the 'world's largest advertising campaign' (as the SDG conference was labelled) came from multiple sources—from *The Economist* and the Gates Foundation to prominent philosophers and human rights lawyers.[119] The difficulties in achieving both economic growth and environmental sustainability and ensuring social harmony was a point of attack that could have been expected, as the UN's use of the contested concept of 'sustainable development' did not engage in the debates surrounding the inherent contradictions of the 'triple bottom line' approach.[120]

Equally open to critics was the choice and scope of the targets. While widely acclaimed on the political level, the SDGs are open to easy challenge as simultaneously hopelessly unattainable or as too little, too late. The goal of eliminating poverty, in particular, can be criticized by either of these: whereas the target year of 2030 appears unlikely to be met, for individuals living today without sufficient necessities, a promise of solutions in even the near future cannot be of much comfort.

The difficulties in achieving all the goals led to further fears that a call for the eradication of poverty in all its forms is susceptible to manipulation by governments for political gains. This potential is reinforced by the lack of universal standards for classifying and collecting the data that exist as well as from the absence of data that is a feature of many states.[121]

1. A Place for Law

With the acknowledgement that unequal distributions of the gains from economic growth making clear that sustainable poverty reduction requires attention to the flow of economic gains from growth and that just as clearly, the environmental and labour aspects of the sources of economic gains cannot be ignored, the international community has taken a large step forward in seeing the path out of poverty as one requiring simultaneous, multidisciplinary efforts. We also know that attention to social and cultural norms is necessary—that changing the role of women in the community and in the household can change trajectories. The international community recognizes that

---

[119] J Hickel, 'Five reasons to think twice about the UN's Sustainable Development Goals' Africa at LSE and South Asia at LSE Cross Blog Series (23 September 2015) (<https://blogs.lse.ac.uk/southasia/2015/09/23/five-reasons-to-think-twice-about-the-uns-sustainable-development-goals/> accessed 11 March 2023).

[120] See, eg, N Eisenmenger and others, 'The Sustainable Development Goals Prioritize Economic Growth over Sustainable Resource Use: A Critical Reflection on the SDGs from a Socio-Ecological Perspective' (2020) 15 Sustainability Science 1101 (<https://doi.org/10.1007/s11625-020-00813-x> accessed 11 March 2023).

[121] Criticisms of the individual targets will be set forth in the respective sections.

discrimination, physical violence, crime, lack of education, and poor health are all both causes and effects of poverty, and poverty's harms will not be eradicated until these norms can be changed.

Laws alone cannot change entrenched social and cultural norms. Yet, it is still important to recognize the role of the law in ending (or perpetuating) poverty. Legal, as well as social and economic measures, must be put into place to support those living in poverty to realize their human rights and freedoms and to ensure that everyone has access to them to move out of poverty.

While legal changes were not at the heart of discussions surrounding SDG 1, the targets give plenty for lawyers to consider. One of the main legal changes called for is that of strengthening systems of property ownership to give impoverished communities and individuals security in their possessions. Land rights, for example, are said to foster investments leading to higher productivity as well as higher regard for sustainability. Adjusting regulatory structures to permit under-resourced families and individuals access to financing is another area of consideration. Under the label 'inclusive financing', programmes are being set up to allow for cybercurrencies to change the way capital is accessed and leveraged. Changing the rules on land use and construction standards are further areas in which legal frameworks will need to be reconsidered if SDG 1 is to be fully met.

At the same time, where the targets and indicators of SDG 1 spell out a number of the measurable aspects of advances to which law must contribute, some observers were frustrated that indications of governmental commitment to poverty reduction failed to go beyond easy promises to attempt to reach good numbers. Fundamental shifts, underlain by legal obligations, remained distanced from SDG 1 and its targets. The lack of explicit incorporation of existing human rights obligations into SDG 1 may be the most jarring aspect of the post-2015 global agenda on poverty eradication.

The Special Rapporteur on Extreme Poverty and Human Rights harshly criticized the global message of progress on the poverty issue in his February 2020 Report on the Parlous State of Poverty Eradication. Special Rapporteur Alston praised the very real improvements in quality of life for billions of people that have emerged over the past 200 years, but lambasted the 'mainstream pre-pandemic triumphalist narrative' that trumpets success while masking the reality that continues to face far too many people—one of 'few opportunities, countless indignities, unnecessary hunger, and preventable death, and [remaining] too poor to enjoy basic human rights'.[122]

While the Special Rapporteur's comments can be read as a problem with the Goals' reliance on inherently unreliable (because manipulable) statistics, underlying Alston's critique is the more fundamental problem of using development goals as the international tool of choice to address the current and future conditions of life facing individuals. The SDGs—including, and perhaps most starkly, SDG 1—continue the MDGs' 'development goal' approach to eliminating severe impairments to human dignity, despite having tweaked it since the 2000s. This approach, explained above, sets forth a target wish toward which governments are encouraged to orient their policies and to

---

[122] A/HRC/44/40 (2 July 2020).

improve upon the results of their past behaviours. It does not engage with past failures of the development agenda. Rather, it 'lock[s] in ... for the next 15 years ... a failing economic model that requires urgent and deep structural changes, and ... kick[s] the hard challenge of real transformation down the road'.[123] The concern that the SDG was less transformational than business as usual supported the distrust of the Agenda.

There were more fundamental criticisms, too. The first was a very practical one: with neither a defined responsible agent nor any mechanism to hold anyone accountable for failure to reach the goal, critics view the SDG ideal as a dangerous deception. The vehicle of 'goals' permits governments and the international community as a whole to mask their/its failure to live up to their legally binding human rights obligations with high-profile reports of advancement. SDG 1—not despite its individual targets but indeed because of its individual targets—is unable to inspire, much less demand, the international community effectively to ensure that no individual will suffer the material and social deprivations that make a life of dignity impossible. Thomas Pogge and Mitu Sengupta are among the critics of the SDGs, even while they acknowledge some improvements over the MDGs. They note with approval that the SDGs place a generalized responsibility on the international community to achieve the targets set out, but say this is not enough for real advancement:

> It is not enough to specify, however exactly, what needs to be done; governments must also agree, for each specific task, who is responsible for ensuring that it actually will get done. If no such division of labor is agreed upon, then all we have is a long list of Sustainable Development Wishes along with the pious hope that economic growth and charitable activities will move things far enough in the right direction.[124]

Sharper disagreement with the SDGs arises from the failure to take seriously the human rights implicated in the SDGs. Here, SDG 1 is particularly vulnerable. Like Alston, Pogge and Sengupta are adamant that a 'goals' approach to the needs of the poor is fundamentally misguided. They vividly illustrate the problem of the Goal's approach to poverty reduction with analogies to past human rights abuses:

> The development goals discourse invites a diachronic, incremental approach: we have a certain distance to traverse, and so we set off toward our destination and approach it step-by-step. This image is wholly out of place when rights are at issue. When we recognize a human right not to be enslaved, then we must not make a 25-year plan aiming to halve the number of slaves or aiming to reduce floggings by half. When we recognize a human right not to be exterminated, then we must not make a 25-year plan to halve the killing rate at Nazi concentration camps. When we recognize a human right

---

[123] Hickel (n 133).

[124] T Pogge and M Sengupta, 'A Critique of the Sustainable Development Goals' Potential to Realize the Human Rights of All: Why Being Better than the MDGs is Not Good Enough' (2016) 32(2) Journal of International and Comparative Social Policy 83.

58   SDG 1

not to be subjected to economic institutions under which many millions foreseeably and avoidably cannot meet their basic needs, then we must not make a 25-year plan to halve these severe deprivations but must at once initiate the necessary institutional reforms.[125]

Ending poverty in all its forms is a goal that is as ambitious as it is necessary to ensuring that every individual has the opportunity to live a life of dignity. As attention to the growth in wealth inequality grows, so too does the recognition that combatting poverty is not solely a matter for low-income countries where the majority of those who struggle to feed and shelter themselves live, but that high-income countries also must address the conditions facing those within their own communities who are unable to realize their potential due to a lack of income, opportunities, or social connection. The SDG 1's main contribution is in heightening awareness that the problem of poverty one that is truly global.[126]

At the same time, Goal 1 challenges head on the idea that poverty will always exist. The so-called fallacy of intractability is an idea that has a particularly strong hold in the United States,[127] but given the oversized role that country's views play in international policy-making, such a belief can have an influence much beyond its borders.

None of the problems taken up by the individual SDGs was first realized in 2015, and this is plainly true of Goal 1. Attention to extreme poverty has existed for millennia as a matter of ethical concern, with exhortations to assist the poor found in the holy books of all the major world religions and charitable practices honoured by governments since ancient times.

Laws providing for systems of governmental assistance of those who were unable to provide for themselves, however, only became widespread with the rise of the Industrial Revolution and its concomitant creation of a large group of the working poor.

Significantly, much of the history of anti-poverty policies was focused on relief. Heeded by the religious and the wealthy, ethically based alms-giving could provide immediate sustenance to the poor, but the programmes did not aim to eliminate poverty as such. Reduction of poverty requires more than immediate offers of food or money. It requires more, even, than a fostering of primary education and perhaps basic

---

[125] ibid 5–6.

[126] It is not only politicians and development institutions that have largely failed to address the comprehensive, global nature of poverty, so has most of poverty research. Brady and Burton introduce their 2016 volume collecting differing views on poverty with the following:

'For far too long, the social science of poverty has been fractured and fragmented. There is a rich tradition of research on urban poverty ... however this literature rarely engages with research on rural poverty even within [the same country]. Poverty research on the United States broadly neglects the study of poverty in other rich democracies [citation omitted]. The literature on poverty across rich democracies rarely engages with the study of poverty in developing countries. At the same time, scholars of poverty in developing countries seem to exist as a separate community from scholars studying poverty in the United States or Europe.' D Brady and LM Burton, 'Introduction' in Brady and Burton (eds) (n 3).

[127] Brady and Destro describe the 'fallacy of intractability' as a presumption that poverty levels will always be high and that social policy is of little effectiveness in reducing poverty based on the fact that poverty has consistently been high. Described as a belief among US social scientists, Brady and Destro point to the detrimental effects on the literature, which often fails to take account of political sources of the ineffectiveness of policy reduction efforts and instead blames weaknesses in the policy. Brady and Destro (n 83) 597.

COMMENTARY ON THE GOAL   59

healthcare—although those are also necessary. Lasting poverty reduction requires investments in entire groups of persons, attention to institutional structures, and a resource base that is both quantitatively abundant and qualitatively diverse enough to ensure that future needs can be sourced from it without endangering the quality of life of any. In short, to eliminate poverty, governments must channel resources sustainably to those persons and communities that are suffering as well as to and from those persons and communities that have the capacity to help improve the lives of all. SDG 1 makes the latter a global aim.

2. Will We Reach the Goal?

Currently, reaching Goal 1 by 2030 appears unlikely. The United Nations indicated in 2020 that the world is not on course for achieving the target even before the COVID-19 pandemic,[128] and noted that with the global economic downturn caused by the COVID-19 pandemic, an estimated 71 million persons were pushed into extreme poverty in 2020, leading to the first worsening of poverty levels since 1998.[129]

The United Nations is neither alone in its pessimism nor the most pessimistic of concerned observers. The World Bank has warned that progress on reducing extreme poverty has been slowing since 2015 on account of armed conflict and the effects of climate change.[130] With the added effects of COVID-19, the quarter century of success was even more distinctly reversed, with an estimated 88 million people moving into extreme poverty as a result.[131] Significantly, the demographics of those moving into poverty as a result of the economic contractions following the COVID-19 pandemic are different than those most impacted by conflict or climate change. Whereas the latter factors are particularly damaging to the poorest portions of society—preventing their escape from extreme poverty—COVID-19 resulted in a set of newly impoverished individuals and families. Those first affected most heavily by restrictions in economic activities were often living in urban areas, had a formal education, and had been working in service sectors.[132] This realization is important as the instruments to combat poverty will need to take into account the differences.

Similar messages emerge from governmental and academic studies of poverty. The World Data Lab's[133] 'World Poverty Clock' indicates a 1.4 person per second 'gap' in the poverty escape rate—meaning, that while 2.4 persons would need to move out of

---

[128] UN, *The Sustainable Development Goals Report 2020* (United Nations 2020) 6 (<https://unstats.un.org/sdgs/report/2020/The-Sustainable-Development-Goals-Report-2020.pdf> accessed 4 January 2021).

[129] ibid 24.

[130] World Bank, *Poverty and Shared Prosperity 2020: Reversals of Fortune* (The World Bank 2020) (available at <https://openknowledge.worldbank.org/bitstream/handle/10986/34496/9781464816024.pdf> accessed 16 January 2021).

[131] ibid 5.

[132] OECD, 'The COVID-19 Crisis in Urban and Rural Areas' (<https://www.oecd-ilibrary.org/sites/c734c0fe-en/index.html?itemId=/content/component/c734c0fe-en#> accessed 4 July 2021). The OECD notes that this was particularly true in the first half of 2020. ibid.

[133] The World Data Lab is a cooperative project funded by the International Fund for Agricultural Development and the German Federal Ministry for Economic Cooperation and Development. See https://worldpoverty.io/about accessed 16 January 2021.

poverty every second to achieve the SDG 1 by 2030, currently only one person per second is doing so.[134]

The Clock also highlights that poverty levels are changing unevenly. While most of Asia and South America is 'on track' to eliminate extreme poverty, much of Africa is not.[135] Indeed, not only is progress stalling (ie they are 'off track' for reaching SDG 1) for many African countries, extreme poverty levels are rising in nineteen[136] of them (as well as in six[137] other countries). The authors of the World in Data entry on Global Extreme Poverty explain that 'it is the fact that still almost every tenth person lives in extreme poverty and the slowing progress against extreme poverty that motivate this entry',[138] and go on to warn of the 'stagnation of the world's poorest' and the expectation that in 2030 there will still be 500 million people living on less than $1.90 per day.[139]

Beyond the bad news in the fight to eliminate extreme poverty, the aims of SDG 1 with regard to the other forms of poverty seem to be slipping out of reach. Inequality even in middle- and high-income economies is far from levels considered sustainable.[140] Like extreme poverty, the world was not on track to meet the SDG 1 target for relative poverty prior to 2020 and the numbers appear to have become worse in the wake of the COVID-19 recession.[141]

There is much public support for the goal, however, and this alone is positive. Such support mutually encourages governments and non-state actors to take up discussions that would otherwise encounter too much political opposition.

IV. Commentaries of Targets

A. Target 1.1 Eradicate Extreme Poverty

UN definition: By 2030, eradicate extreme poverty for all people everywhere, currently measured as people living on less than $1.90 a day.

---

[134] <https://worldpoverty.io/headline> accessed 16 January 2021.

[135] ibid.

[136] Angola, Burundi, Chad, Central African Republic, Democratic Republic of Congo, Republic of the Congo, Equatorial Guinea, Eritrea, Eswatini, Madagascar, Malawi, Namibia, Nigeria, Somalia, South Africa, South Sudan, Sudan, Zambia, and Zimbabwe. ibid.

[137] Afghanistan, Belize, Haiti, Papua New Guinea, Venezuela, and Yemen. ibid.

[138] M Roser and E Ortiz-Ospina, 'Global Extreme Poverty' (*OurWorldInData.org*, 2013) <https://ourworldindata.org/extreme-poverty>.

[139] ibid.

[140] United Nations, *Inequality—Bridging the Divide* (<https://www.un.org/en/un75/inequality-bridging-divide> 4 July 2021). ('Today, 71 percent of the world's population live in countries where inequality has grown. This is especially important because inequalities within countries are the inequalities people feel day to day, month to month, year to year. This is how people stack up and compare themselves with their neighbours, family members, and society. Since 1990, income inequality has increased in most developed countries and in some middle-income countries, including China and India.')

[141] FHG Ferreira, 'Inequality in the Time of COVID-19' (Summer 2021) Finance Development 20, 22.

1. SDG Indicator 1.1.1

a) Eradicate extreme poverty

Definition: Indicator 1.1.1 is the proportion of population below the international poverty line, by sex, age, employment status, and geographical location (urban/rural).

2. Sources of Target

The early realization that the MDG's focus on extreme poverty would not be sufficient did not mean that the plight of the very poorest was no longer felt to be itself a worthy cause for action. Thus, the first target of SDG 1 extends the MDG 1 call to eliminate poverty by calling for the ending of extreme poverty by 2030. Unlike MDG 1, target 1 for SDG 1 does not soften the meaning of 'eradicate' by giving the international community room merely to reduce the numbers of persons living in extreme poverty—the target and its indicator, each silent about what 'eradicate' might otherwise mean, underscore that the word 'eradicate' must be read true to its definition: 'to remove entirely; to extirpate; to get rid of'.[142] Thus, the target is clarified to apply to 'all people everywhere'. This scope was not challenged by the OWG members.

That said, the target did generate some discussion. In particular, the co-chairs' summary of the April 2013 OWG discussions describe a difference among members on which definition of poverty should be used in the SDGs. There were two lines of disagreement: one discussion concerned the correct level of daily income to use as a baseline; the second took on the more fundamental question of whether the Goal should look solely to income measurements or to the multidimensionality of poverty. The former question was resolved by agreeing to apply the then-current $1.25 a day measurement established as the international poverty line in 2008 (based on 2005 purchasing-power parity). That figure was updated for the SDGs to the $1.90 a day measurement used as of 2015. This target will need to take into account the new figure of $2.15 a day that the World Bank adopted as of September 2022.

Interesting is the level of disaggregation requested by indicator 1.1.1. The United Nations Statistical Commission's March 2015 draft technical report on the indicator framework contains a proposal for looking at the proportion of the population below the international poverty line 'disaggregated by sex and age group'.[143] While this was ranked as 'easily feasible', there was no recorded assessment of the feasibility of assessing the relevant proportions based on employment status or geography.

3. Statistical/Empirical Analysis

All contemporary evidence points toward a disappointing result for target 1.1. According to the World Bank, from the 2015 global level of extreme poverty of 10.1 per cent of the world population, the level declined to 8.4 per cent in 2019 but rose again in

---

[142] *Oxford English Dictionary*, 'eradicate, v.' (<https://www.oed.com/search?searchType=dictionary&q=eradic ate&_searchBtn=Search> accessed 11 March 2023).

[143] Technical report by the Bureau of the United Nations Statistical Commission (UNSC) on the process of the development of an indicator framework for the goals and targets of the post-2015 development agenda, Working draft, Annex 5 (March 2015).

2020 to over 9 per cent in the wake of the COVID-19 pandemic.[144] The pandemic, combined with the effects of conflict and climate change, are seriously threatening to derail progress on SDG 1.

In the years preceding 2020, the figures on global extreme poverty were underscoring a disturbing bifurcation of progress on reducing extreme poverty. While extreme poverty remains exceptional in Australia, Europe, and North America, it seems to be stubbornly persistent and even growing in Africa. Concentrated in Sub-Saharan Africa, extreme poverty has proven the exception in the global success story on extreme poverty. The World Bank points out that even though many of the economies have small populations, the poverty rates in many have hardly dropped since 1990, half remaining over 35 per cent.[145] The deep poverty in this region has been difficult to counter for decades, causing concern among the development community and spurring a large literature on 'poverty traps' and how to break them,[146] the effects of foreign aid on poverty levels,[147] and the importance of governance.[148] Yet, despite the intensive study of the causes and effects and the multiple attempts by multiple agencies (international, governmental, and non-governmental), lasting improvements remain stubbornly absent and even those who have moved out of extreme poverty remain vulnerable to falling back.[149]

Recent extreme poverty figures indicate a more pessimistic view of likely developments in the near future. Not only are the numbers of persons living on less than $2.15 a day rising in Sub-Saharan Africa, they are stagnating or rising in North Africa and the Middle East. Moreover, there continues to be a lack of data from India, where no official poverty count has taken place since 2011.[150] With such a large population, reliance on

[144] World Bank (n 130) 34 (see figure 1.4 and accompanying text.
[145] ibid 46.
[146] The idea of a poverty trap is that of a 'self-reinforcing mechanism whereby countries start poor and remain poor ... so that current poverty is a direct cause of poverty in the future'. A Kraay and D McKenzie, 'Do Poverty Traps Exist? Assessing the Evidence' (2014) 28(3) Journal of Economic Perspectives 127, 127. The notion of poverty traps suggests that external assistance is needed to move out of poverty. ibid 127–28. See also S Bowles and others (eds), *Poverty Traps* (Princeton University Press 2006); JD Sachs and others, 'Ending Africa's Poverty Trap' (2004) Brookings Papers on Economic Activity, 117. Coates and MacMillan describe the use of 'graduation' as a way to break ultra-poor poverty traps at the household level in their discussion of 'the science of hope'. L Coates and S MacMillan, 'Breaking Out of the Poverty Trap' in H Kharas and others (eds), *Leave No One Behind: Time for Specifics on the Sustainable Development Goals* (Brookings Institution Press 2019).
[147] Compare, eg, Sachs and others (n 146) with K Kalu, *Foreign Aid and the Future of Africa* (Palgrave MacMillan 2018) (arguing that foreign aid has alleviated some of the worst symptoms of poverty in Africa, but that it cannot eliminate poverty because poverty in Africa is not caused by a lack of financial resources).
[148] P Collier, *The Bottom Billion: Why the Poorest Countries are Falling and What Can Be Done About It* (OUP 2008); C Burnside and D Dollar, 'Aid, Policies, and Growth' (2000) 90(4) American Economics Review 847 (arguing that foreign aid can help economies grow if there are good policies in place).
[149] World Bank (n 130 144) 3.
[150] The Indian government has not had an official count of its poor since 2011. World Bank, *Poverty & Equity Brief: India* (April 2020); Asian Development Bank, *Basic Statistics 2021* (April 2021) (indicating 'no data' for portion of population below the $1.90/day poverty line for India). In that year, the Indian National Sample Survey Office changed its estimation methodologies to use different reference periods to calculate consumption rather than using a uniform period of thirty days. 'India's Poverty Rate at 12.4% in 2011–12', Business Standard, 6 October 2015 (<https://www.business-standard.com/article/economy-policy/india-s-poverty-rate-at-12-4-in-2011-12-115100600073_1.html> accessed 30 June 2021).

estimates from India necessarily makes global poverty figures uncertain and claims of improvement suspect.[151]

4. COVID-19 Effects

The international community has witnessed the global spread of COVID-19 not only stopping progress on the reduction of extreme poverty but as a large step backwards in the efforts to lift people from the edge of subsistence. The *Sustainable Development Goals Report 2020* estimated that 'tens of millions of people will be pushed back into poverty, undoing years of steady improvement'[152] and the World Bank's *Reversals of Fortune* report estimates that between 110 and 150 million persons will move into extreme poverty in 2020–21 due to the combined effects of the pandemic, climate change, and armed conflict (and this report appeared prior to the Russian war in Ukraine, which has contributed further to growth in extreme poverty).[153] The economic slowdown combined with the health impacts were the main factors in lowering income levels and wealth around the world, and jeopardizing the commitment to 'leaving no one behind'.

Country level reports are equally sobering. A UN/China study on the effects of COVID in China revealed that in the five counties examined, two-thirds of the households faced a 32 per cent decrease in their income, mainly due to employment losses,[154] and as many as 5 million people risk falling back into poverty.[155] Particularly worrying is that this pandemic-related poverty may be 'more severe than before', given the reduced availability of government aid and the potentially long-lasting reduction in employment opportunities.[156]

The effect of the pandemic on Asia's other population giant is also striking. The Pew Research Center's analysis of World Bank data estimates that between 2020 and 2021, the number of Indians living in extreme poverty has leapt from 60 million to 134 million.[157] This is the first rise in poverty levels in that country since the 1970s.[158]

Beyond the numbers of people living in extreme poverty, the composition of the global extreme poor is likely to shift due to the COVID-19 pandemic. The gendered effects of the 2020–21 pandemic were widely reported. As in other economic crises, women are impacted more than men because of their over-representation in informal and precarious employment, but the pandemic added to the differential impacts

---

[151] R Kochhar, 'The Pandemic Stalls Growth in the Global Middle Class, Pushes Poverty Up Sharply' (18 March 2021) Pew Research Center, 15.

[152] United Nations, 'Goal 1: End poverty in all its forms everywhere' in *The Sustainable Development Goals Report 2020* (n 128).

[153] World Bank, *Reversals of Fortune* (n 144).

[154] China International Center for Economic and Technical Exchanges, United Nations Development Program, United Nations Children's Fund, United Nations Population Fund, and United Nations Resident Coordinator Office, 'Socioeconomic Impact Assessment of the COVID-19 Pandemic in Five Poverty Counties in China' (January 2021) 69.

[155] ibid 8.

[156] ibid.

[157] R Mahapatra, 'Mass Poverty is Back in India' DownToEarth, 7 April 2021 (<https://www.downtoearth.org.in/blog/governance/mass-poverty-is-back-in-india-76348> accessed 30 June 2021) (citing Pew Research Center data).

[158] ibid.

by augmenting the burden of care work and simultaneous rise in levels of domestic violence.[159]

Less apparent than the effects of the pandemic on poor women is the geographically differentiated poverty impact: urban dwellers were more likely to experience significantly increased economic disadvantages than persons in rural communities. Crowded living conditions and inadequate sanitation made social distancing impossible, and the lockdown measures eliminated many jobs in the informal sector.[160]

5. Implementation Efforts at the Domestic and International Levels

When the MDGs called for a halving of poverty, the main approach to achieving this goal was still a mixture of charitable giving and 'growing out' of poverty.[161] Given the continued emphasis on unidimensional measures of poverty well into the 2000s, achieving the goal would require increasing incomes—little else.[162] Thus, governments, with the help of the multilateral and regional development banks and the IMF, committed to liberalizing trade, stimulating investment, and attending to domestic productivity to generate jobs and stimulate consumption. International institutions and non-governmental organizations would relieve the suffering of the extreme poor with direct assistance. In short, reaching MDG 1 seemed to call for 'simply increasing financial resources'.[163]

The SDGs are aimed at continuing the MDG efforts to reduce extreme poverty but intensifying the commitment to ensuring that the worst off benefit from such efforts. Thus, rather than implementing fundamentally new programmes, the measures taken within the framework of target 1.1 are mainly outgrowths of earlier programmes.

One such step is the awareness-raising declaration of a United Nations 'Decade' aimed at keeping poverty on the international political agenda and to promote action.[164] As it did in 1997 and again in 2008, the UN General Assembly declared 2018–2027 the Third United Nations Decade for the Eradication of Poverty.[165] This time the UN called for efforts to stimulate capital flows to developing and least-developed countries in hopes of stimulating economic development through investment,[166] it 'recognized' the positive role of increased trade flows on fostering growth,[167] and reiterated the need for official development assistance[168] and other 'voluntary contributions'[169]

---

[159] JP Bohoslavsky, 'Covid-19, the Economy and Human Rights' (2020) 30 Sur International Journal of Human Rights 85, 90.
[160] B Boza-Kiss and others, 'How has the COVID-19 pandemic affected the urban poor?' (20 May 2021) (<https://iiasa.ac.at/blog/may-2021/how-has-covid-19-pandemic-affected-urban-poor> accessed 11 March 2023).
[161] Kalu (n 147) 3.
[162] P De Muro and others, 'Composite Indices of Development and Poverty: An Application to MDGs' (2011) 104 Social Indicators Research 1–18.
[163] M Fehling and others, 'Limitations of the Millennium Development Goals: A Literature Review' (2013) 8(10) Global Public Health 1109, 1115.
[164] See United Nations, 'International Decades' (<https://www.un.org/en/observances/international-decades> accessed 7 June 2021).
[165] UNGA, 'Implementation of the Third United Nations Decade for the Eradication of Poverty (2018–2027)', A/C.2/73/L.9 (18 October 2018).
[166] ibid para 26.
[167] ibid Preamble, p 4.
[168] ibid para 34.
[169] ibid para 36.

to go to low-income countries to ensure that they can provide public services to their populations.

Despite its continuation of older approaches, the post-2015 Agenda has witnessed a slight shift in priorities from what they were at the beginning of the 2000s. Thus, efforts are also shifting. One aspect that is obvious in the current efforts to combat extreme poverty is the weight given to addressing the social structures and environmental conditions that keep certain populations in dire economic straits. There is, first of all, a recognition that globally, geographic 'pockets' of extreme poverty persist despite the advances made against extreme poverty in many economies.[170] Thus, many projects target Sub-Saharan Africa and South Asia, where 80 per cent of the world's extreme poor live.[171] These projects include academic research[172], studies by multilateral and regional development institutions,[173] efforts by non-governmental organizations to improve education, health, or access to financing,[174] as well as national and subnational government action to improve productive infrastructure, to increase cash-like transfers, and to implement or broaden social protection.

Second, the geography of extreme poverty within countries indicates a prevalence of poverty among rural populations, in communities facing or just emerging from violent conflict, and among certain 'vulnerable' population groups, including racial or ethnic minorities, persons with disabilities, and women. These findings have long informed many of the efforts of multilateral and regional institutions as well as national governments' and civil society organizations' poverty-reduction programmes.[175] More nuanced research is now looking at 'poverty hotspots' inside countries and points to the 'subnational dualism' as a characteristic of both rich and poor countries.[176] The findings suggest that geographic areas that are hostile for agriculture, are prone to natural

[170] See Ministerial declaration of the 2017 high-level political forum for sustainable development, E/HLS/2017/1, para 14 (31 July 2017).

[171] See UNDP and Oslo Governance Centre, 'Goal 1: No poverty' ('Facts and figures' section on the people living on less than $2.15 per day) (<https://www.undp.org/sustainable-development-goals/no-poverty> accessed 11 March 2023).

[172] There are hundreds of articles and books on poverty reduction in Sub-Saharan Africa. While economic literature is often about measurement of the dimensions of poverty or modelling results of policy interventions, the legal literature is often focused on questions tying poverty to legal rights to land, human rights, or international economic regulations.

[173] The World Bank's Sahel Adaptive Social Protection Program, for example, sponsors research and programming on social protection in six Sahel countries. See, Sahel Adaptive Social Protection Program (ASPP), Documentation <(https://www.worldbank.org/en/programs/sahel-adaptive-social-protection-program-trust-fund#5> accessed 7 June 2021). Besides project financing, the African Development Bank has an active blog on Economic Growth, Human and Social Development as well as programmes on poverty-related questions of gender equality and climate change. <https://blogs.afdb.org/economic-growth-human-and-social-development>.

[174] The Gates Foundation alone has three regional headquarters in Africa and in 2016 pledged to invest $5 billion in five years for health and anti-poverty programmes on the continent. 'Gates Foundation to Invest $5 Billion in Africa over Five Years', Philanthropy News Digest, 19 July 2016 (<https://philanthropynewsdigest.org/news/gates-foundation-to-invest-5-billion-in-africa-over-five-years> accessed 7 June 2021).

[175] For example, IMF, *Somalia: Poverty Reduction Strategy Paper—Joint Staff Advisory Note* (International Monetary Fund March 2020) paras 40–41 (setting forth Somalia's plans for reducing poverty, including measures of 'human development' that emphasizes the problems of violent conflict and displaced persons, as well as the gendered cultural practices that need to be restrained). But see L Qian-Qian and others, 'Poverty Reduction within the Framework of SDGs and Post-2015 Development Agenda' (2015) 6 Advances in Climate Change Research 67, 72 (warning that although the assumption of the SDGs is that most of those living in extreme poverty are rural populations, an increasing proportion of the world's extreme poor is living in cities).

[176] JL Cohen and others, 'Spatial Targeting of Poverty Hotspots' in Kharas and others (eds) (n 146) 209–37.

disasters, where the population suffers from communicable disease, and which are removed from the economic opportunities of urban centres are likely to remain burdened with poverty beyond 2030.[177] The research supports the idea that in order to 'leave no one behind', 'spatial targeting'—increased aid measures taken to relieve the poverty factors in a particular context—will be necessary.[178]

More striking even than the heightened contextualization of poverty eradication efforts is the increased attention to the interconnectedness of extreme poverty with decision-making and governance in all areas. The 2017 High-Level Political Forum for Sustainable Development devoted its 2017 session to 'Eradicating poverty in all its forms and dimensions through promoting sustainable development, expanding opportunities and addressing related challenges'. The outcome document indicated the very broad approach to the international community's poverty eradication efforts.[179] The activities of stakeholders such as the United Nations Development Programme accordingly span the spectrum from education and microfinance projects to empower women and girls, to offering educational training to persons displaced by violent conflict, and to giving vocational support to victims of civil war.[180] In particular, there is a renewed discussion over universal versus targeted poverty reduction efforts.[181] While targeted programmes seem to lend themselves best to reducing poverty of particular groups, they may be more expensive and less politically acceptable than universal coverage programmes.[182] Thus, India was one of the first developing countries to seriously begin considering the introduction of a system of cash/income transfer payments to all but the wealthiest 25 per cent in hopes of eliminating poverty while simultaneously limiting financial waste.[183]

Finally, poverty eradication efforts in the SDGs attend to the challenges that global changes pose to the poorest. While climate change was the natural focus of the 'resilience'-enhancing efforts of the years immediately following the appearance of Agenda 2030, since 2020 the focus on resilience has expanded to include resilience to communicable disease. At the time of writing, in fact, most commentary and programming dedicated to extreme poverty is tied to attempts to ensure relief from COVID-19's impacts on poor populations in the form of heightened vaccine availability or from the pandemic's economic effects.

[177] ibid 214, 216–18.
[178] ibid 212.
[179] Ministerial declaration of the 2017 high-level political forum on sustainable development, convened under the auspices of the Economic and Social Council, on the theme 'Eradicating poverty and promoting prosperity in a changing world', E/HLS/2017/1 (31 July 2017).
[180] UNDP and Oslo Governance Centre, 'Goal 1: No poverty' ('Goals in Action') (<https://www.undp.org/sustainable-development-goals/no-poverty> accessed 11 March 2023).
[181] RM Desai, 'Rethinking the Universalism Versus Targeting Debate, Brookings Future Development' *Brookings Future Development blog*, 31 May 2021 (<https://www.brookings.edu/blog/future-development/2017/05/31/rethinking-the-universalism-versus-targeting-debate/> accessed 7 June 2021).
[182] ibid.
[183] Government of India, 'Universal Basic Income: A Conversation with and Within the Mahatma' in *Economic Survey 2016–2017* (Government of India 2017) 172–212 (<https://www.indiabudget.gov.in/budget2017-2018/es2016-17/echap09.pdf> accessed 7 June 2021); S Khosla, 'India's Universal Basic Income: Bedeviled by the Details' (2018) Carnegie India: Brief (February 2018) (<https://carnegieendowment.org/files/CEIP_Khosla_Report_Brief.pdf> accessed 7 June 2021).

6. Critique

While SDG 1 takes a broad view of 'poverty', with its reference to 'in all its forms', the first target is much more pointed, aiming to eliminate, or 'eradicate', extreme poverty around the world. Target 1.1 reflects a continuation of the MDG goal targeting absolute poverty and underlines the literal, short-term unsustainability of life faced by those without the means to secure adequate food, water, or shelter. While couched in a broader goal, the first target fails to improve on several of the most objectionable aspects of the MDG poverty goal.

By focusing the target on the international poverty line, the indicators use a universal standard of measurement rather than relying on the development of local quantifications. The figure of $1.90 reflected the then-current standard of minimum income necessary to cover subsistence costs, up from the MDGs $1 a day, which was criticized as too low.[184]

The main criticism of target 1.1 is based on its use of a measure of poverty that is itself highly contested. Target 1.1 indicates that the definition of its own term 'extreme poverty' is a measurement of '$1.90 a day'. This indicates that target 1.1 uses (i) a basic needs approach to poverty that (ii) is considered by many to be too low and too rigid. The basic needs measurement of poverty is a method of viewing poverty from a viewpoint of having an income that is insufficient to cover subsistence costs. The discrete figure is calculated by taking the mean of the poverty lines of the fifteen poorest economies and universalizing this by means of a hypothetical exchange rate called the 'purchasing power parity'.[185] As explained by UN Stats:

> When measuring international poverty of a country, the international poverty line at PPP is converted to local currencies in 2011 price and is then converted to the prices prevailing at the time of the relevant household survey using the best available Consumer Price Index (CPI). (Equivalently, the survey data on household consumption or income for the survey year are expressed in the prices of the ICP base year, and then converted to PPP $s.) Then the poverty rate is calculated from that survey.[186]

Thus, the absolute poverty approach is an objective, quantitative, single-dimension, income- and expenditure-based, absolute approach to the measurement of poverty.[187] Widely used by the World Bank, this measure is easily available for reporting purposes (statistics are widely available for more than 100 countries)[188] and can be updated to reflect inflation. Indeed, as mentioned above, in September 2022 the figure was updated to reflect increased costs. It is now $2.15 a day, calculated in 2017 dollars.

---

[184] Professor at Harvard's Kennedy School of Government and former World Bank economist Lant Pritchett called the World Bank's poverty line 'absurdly low', 'completely arbitrary', and 'extremist'. L Pritchett, 'Extreme Poverty is Too Extreme' (2013) *Center for Global Development blog*, 7 October 2013 (<https://www.cgdev.org/blog/extreme-poverty-too-extreme> accessed 4 July 2021).

[185] The UN Statistics Office explains the measure as 'a common standard in measuring extreme poverty, anchored to what poverty means in the world's poorest countries'. UN Stats, 'Target 1.1' (September 2020).

[186] ibid.

[187] See TM Smeeding, 'Poverty Measurement' in Brady and Burton (eds) (n 3) 23 (figure 2.1 sets out an organigram of poverty measurement concepts).

[188] ibid 24.

68   SDG 1

Nevertheless, there are a number of methodological weaknesses in using such an absolute measure for extreme poverty. First, despite the wide availability of the statistics on poverty, the accuracy of such statistics remains subject to varying levels of data. For the least developed economies and the poorest communities, gathering the relevant information may be challenging and subject to error.[189] Second, any measurement of poverty that relies on income estimation is going to be suspect in economies with large informal employment sectors, such as many of the least developed countries (LDCs) (where a large number of the extreme poor live), and consumption measures are sometimes estimates extrapolated from national accounts rather than survey-based.

Besides the numerous methodological concerns with the $1.90/day ruler, even if the measurements were accurate, many would challenge target 1.1 on a conceptual level as 'very crude'.[190] First, focusing on a single figure invites—and may in some cases justify—the scepticism of the SDGs as a marketing tool. Where computational adjustments can make the difference between 'achieving' a target or not, there is a danger that apparent reductions in poverty are due to different ways of calculating the number of persons in poverty rather than to real improvements in living standards.

Relatedly, the fixation with a single figure, under which a person is poor but over which she is not, may lead to reaching the Goal by raising incomes to, at the extreme, $1.91/day (or $2.16/day). Such 'progress' is neither economically sustainable (because these persons remain highly vulnerable to slipping back into poverty) nor morally sustainable (because their life has not been made noticeably better).

One can also object to the global poverty line indicator as incompatible with Goal 1's multidimensional view of poverty. Target 1.1 employs a single-dimensional approach to poverty, looking at extreme poverty as a matter of income or consumption. This leaves aside the interconnectedness of difficulties facing those in extreme poverty. Where long-term eradication of poverty is a goal, the idea of moving populations beyond incomes of $1.90/2.15 a day seems woefully inadequate. As several observers have pointed out, a life of minimal survival is far from a life of full capabilities.

Finally, the continued reliance on poverty reduction strategy plans (PRSPs) as agenda setters for low-income countries is problematic. Although prized as a way of ensuring 'ownership' of and national 'buy-in' to poverty reduction plans, critics accuse such instruments as being not only little more than 'the best ideological shell of neoliberalism today', but (perhaps more worryingly) a 'narrow, politically naïve approach to governance'.[191] PRSPs entail a 're-framing of poverty, via the combination of poverty assessments, macro-planning and budgeting with debt relief, plurally funded poverty alleviation approaches and decentralized governance [that] is now a fact of life in the bulk of poor countries, especially in sub-Saharan Africa. In general, ... PRSP frames

---

[189] UN Stats, 'Target 1.1' (n 185).

[190] A Sen, 'Poverty: An Ordinal Approach to Measurement' (1976) 44(2) Econometrica 219, 219 (describing the approach of counting the persons below the poverty line and taking that as a proportion of the total population the 'head-count ration', which, he states is 'obviously a very crude index').

[191] D Craig and D Porter, 'Poverty Reduction Strategy Papers: A New Convergence' (2003) 31(1) World Development 53 (citing Perry Anderson, 'Renewals' (2000) 11(1) New Left Rev. 11).

poverty in a number of ways which are naïvely technical, but by no means neutral.'[192] Where countries must adhere to PRSPs to remain eligible for debt relief or Official Development Assistance (ODA), the experienced hardships of persons living in extreme poverty may not be addressed in ways that would empower them.

B. Target 1.2 Reduce Poverty by At Least 50 per cent

UN definition: By 2030, reduce at least by half the proportion of men, women and children of all ages living in poverty in all its dimensions according to national definitions.

1. SDG Indicator 1.2.1
a) Halve population below national poverty line
Definition: Indicator 1.2.1 is the proportion of population living below the national poverty line.

2. SDG Indicator 1.2.2
a) Population in poverty according to national definitions
Definition: Indicator 1.2.2 is the proportion of men, women, and children of all ages living in poverty in all its dimensions according to national definitions.

3. Sources of Target
The limitations of the MDG 1 included its narrow focus—looking at extreme poverty and aiming to reduce (by half) the proportion of persons living on the edge of subsistence. So conceived, MDG 1 not only largely excluded industrialized states from scrutiny, it also encouraged those states within its scope to move their populations on the edges of poverty out of poverty—leaving the poorest poor. The SDG's emphasis on multi-dimensional poverty—poverty 'in all its forms'—remedied the first weakness, requiring that industrialized states, too, take steps to reduce the number of poor within their borders.

As the OWG began its work, the delegates took up the discussion of how to ensure that progress on SDG 1 would reflect an actual improvement in the livelihoods of populations around the globe. The February 2014 Focus Area document noted that within the area of poverty reduction, 'areas that could be considered include: ... reducing relative poverty; addressing inequalities at both national and international levels'.[193] The Encyclopedia Groupinica comments showed strong support for addressing the proportion of people living under national poverty lines.[194] Throughout the OWG sessions,

---

[192] ibid 60.

[193] Focus Area Document, 'Focus Area 1. Poverty eradication' (February 2014) 1.

[194] Pakistan, China/Indonesia/Kazakhstan, Australia/Netherlands/United Kingdom, United States/Canada/Israel were explicit about attending to persons living under poverty as nationally defined. Encyclopedia Groupinica 2–3.

China emphasized the use of national poverty lines to define relative poverty.[195] Other groups stressed particularly wealth disparities and inequalities as aspects SDG 1 should take up.[196]

As completed, target 1.2 looks at the income-poor and the vulnerable found in all societies, aiming for a reduction in the percentage of the population living below the national poverty line.[197] By ensuring that the impoverished sectors of the population in middle- and high-income countries are accounted for, the idea of universality of the SDGs is apparent.

Beyond this, the target incorporates the 'leave no-one behind' concept mainly by asking for disaggregated statistics on those below the national poverty line. This takes on the interest in ensuring that the most vulnerable are beneficiaries of the halving of poverty.

4. Statistical/Empirical Analysis

According to the OECD, relative poverty—measured as those living with less than 50 per cent of the median income—averaged 11.7 per cent in OECD members in 2016 (the latest figures). This average disguises significant differences among OECD economies, where the United States witnesses nearly 18 per cent poverty (close to the corresponding figure in India and higher than in Russia) and Iceland only about 5 per cent.[198]

On a regional and country level, statistics on relative poverty vary and are difficult to compare, as different countries use different factors and even different concepts of measurement.[199] That said, none looks likely to achieve the halving of their numbers by 2030. In fact, the effects of the 2020–2021 pandemic appear to be reversing the already slow downward trends of poverty figures in major economies.

COVID-19's impact on SDG target 1.2 was severe on both an objective and subjective measure of poverty. Objectively, the number of households suffering net income losses in 2020–2021 increased, with job losses and health costs pushing many into poverty or vulnerability. Additionally, the restrictions put into place by governments to slow the spread of disease caused many individuals to face (or to face heightened levels of) other dimensions of poverty: social exclusion, lack of access to public services, ill health, insufficient food, unstable employment, stress, and lack of self-esteem.

The European Union measures persons living in poverty as those living on less than 60 per cent of the median income level. Under this scale, the European statistical authority (Eurostat) indicated 2016 poverty levels as encompassing 23.5 per cent of the

[195] M Sengupta, 'Transformational Change or Tenuous Wish List? A Critique of SDG 1 ('End Poverty in All Its Forms Everywhere')' (2018) 37(1) Social Alternatives 10, 14. See also IISD, 32(10) Earth Negotiations Bulletin (7 April 2014) 4.

[196] Ethiopia and France/Germany/Switzerland made such interventions, the latter stressing the interconnectedness of relative poverty and inequalities and tying them to ending discrimination. Encyclopedia Groupinica 3.

[197] The reduction 'at least by half' seems to have been agreed to in the informal discussions between June and July 2014. See IISD, 32(13) Earth Negotiations Bulletin (22 July 2014) 5.

[198] OECD, Society at a Glance 2019: OECD Social Indicators (OECD 2019) 100–01 (section on 'Poverty').

[199] Although dated, the papers submitted for the ECLAC Poverty Statistics seminar highlight the numerous differences among government methodologies for determining poverty levels. Economic Commission for Latin America and the Caribbean, 'Poverty Statistics', LC/R.1814 (17 April 1998).

EU 28 population.[200] The European Commission also defines poverty multidimensionally, counting persons 'at risk of poverty or social exclusion' (AROPE). AROPE combines a low net disposable income, an inability to purchase goods normally expected within society ('serious material deprivation'), and employment levels in a household. The 2019 AROPE level for the EU 27 was 20.9 per cent of the population, down from 21.6 in 2018.[201] The effects of the 2020 pandemic, however, are harming the living conditions of the poor and vulnerable and increasing inequalities.[202] In the EU, estimates are for a 4.8 per cent increase in AROPE figures.[203]

The Economic Commission for Latin America and the Caribbean (ECLAC) reports similar trends.[204] According to the estimates, income poverty affected 187 million people (30.5 per cent of the population) in 2019—a slight increase over the previous years after 2015 (when 29.1 per cent of the population lived in poverty).[205] While the ECLAC figures were creeping upwards until 2019,[206] the projected effects of the COVID are for a large jump in numbers of persons in poverty. Even taking into account emergency cash transfer programmes, in 2020 209 million persons were living in poverty in the region—3.2 per cent more than in the year before.[207] In addition, the Commission estimates that 'between 2019 and 2020, the vulnerable population living on incomes up to three times the poverty line increased by 3.3 percentage points'.[208] Also similar to the European context, the Latin American increases in poverty and income loss disproportionately burdened the lower income and vulnerable groups. Women, the youngest, but also older persons and those with less education have seen greater unemployment,[209] as did those working in domestic service.[210] Moreover, those persons of indigenous or African descent also seemed to face both a disproportionate share of job losses and inability to telework.[211]

Asian countries have witnessed tremendous reductions in poverty since 1990 and were on a track of continued drops in the number of persons living below the poverty line until 2020, when COVID-19 began to effect economies there.[212] The Asian Development Bank estimates that in 2020 896 million people lived on less than $3.20 per day—over 160 million more than would have without the pandemic's economic

---

[200] See Eurostat, 'People at risk of poverty or social exclusion by age and sex' ILC_PEPS01 (last update 1 July 2021) (EU 28 figures are used for 2013–20). Extreme poverty is defined as living on 40 per cent of the median standard of living. EAPN France, *National Poverty Watch Report* (EAPN 2020) 4 (noting that the European average is 6.4 per cent of the population living in extreme poverty).

[201] Eurostat, 'People at risk of poverty or social exclusion by age and sex' (n 200).

[202] European Anti Poverty Network, 'Supercharging Poverty?' (November 2020) (<https://www.eapn.eu/wp-content/uploads/2021/01/EAPN-EU-Poverty-Watch-2020-final-version-4937.pdf> accessed 12 June 2021).

[203] ibid 15 (citing AROPE Europe 2020 indicators and EC, 2020 Strategic Foresight Report).

[204] See ECLAC, *Social Panorama of Latin America 2020* (United Nations 2021).

[205] ibid 49.

[206] ibid.

[207] ibid 73.

[208] ibid.

[209] ibid 100–03 (note that the report states that Dominican Republic is an exception to the differential impacts based on educational attainment).

[210] ibid 104–05.

[211] ibid 106.

[212] A Martinez and others, 'How much has COVID-19 turned back Asia's poverty clock?' *Asian Development Blog*, 3 November 2020 (<https://blogs.adb.org/blog/how-much-has-covid-19-turned-back-asia-s-poverty-clock> accessed 19 June 2021).

impact.[213] In Asia, as elsewhere, the pandemic's effects impacted the already vulnerable most severely. The vulnerable in Asia include not only women and persons with disabilities but also the many earning their livelihood in the informal economy. Workers in the informal economy and those in micro-, small, and medium enterprises were particularly affected by the pandemic as governments mandated restrictions on movements that either eliminated their ability to work or prevented their potential customers to access their services.[214] Migrant workers were similarly left jobless, reducing not only their living standards but also those of the families reliant on remittances.[215]

5. Implementation Efforts at the Domestic and International Levels

Poverty reduction on a national level has been a concern of governments since long before the 2015 declaration of Agenda 2030. National poverty lines, too, have been in use for decades. Thus, most progress on target 1.2 will not be progress *because of* the SDGs. That said, the SDGs are incentivizing governments to tailor measures so as to demonstrate and highlight progress in the areas they target. Thus, while efforts to increase the incomes of those below the national poverty line (indicator 1.2.1) are unlikely to have witnessed dramatic differences since 2015, states that had not been considering multidimensional poverty (indicator 1.2.2), may be considering new approaches to poverty reduction. Finally, on the international level, SDG-specific efforts are being made to address the area of improving data collection and to developing the tools to analyse data relevant to assessing progress.

Countries around the world have made numerous efforts to adjust their national poverty reduction programmes to focus on multidimensional poverty as well as to reduce relative poverty. The EU, as one of the leaders in the fight against poverty in all its forms, had taken steps to lower poverty levels already in 2010, with the Europe 2020 strategy to stimulate 'smart, sustainable and inclusive growth'.[216] The programme approached poverty reduction as a main feature, and significantly emphasized reducing the risk of income poverty and improvement in the levels of material deprivation as well as the reduction of the number of persons who were underemployed.[217]

Although the Europe 2020 programme to reduce vulnerability to poverty to 20 million by 2020 failed to achieve its aim,[218] there have been a number of efforts taken by the EU to address the multidimensionality of poverty. One step was the adoption of

[213] ibid.

[214] B Malay and P Baisakh, 'Impact of COVID-19 Pandemic on Inequalities in Asia' (November 2020) 14 (<https://gcap.global/wp-content/uploads/2020/11/Impact-of-COVID-19-on-Inequalities-in-Asia-GCAP-11-Nov.pdf> accessed 19 June 2021).

[215] ibid (pointing particularly to Nepal, which generates 30 per cent of its GDP from remittances).

[216] European Commission, Europe 2020: A Strategy for Smart, Sustainable and Inclusive Growth, COM(2010) 2020 final (3 March 2010). See particularly ibid 11.

[217] ibid 10–11; Eurostat, 'Europe 2020 indicators—poverty and social exclusion' (16 July 2018) (available at <https://ec.europa.eu/eurostat/statistics-explained/index.php?title=Archive:Europe_2020_indicators_-_poverty_and_social_exclusion&oldid=394836> accessed 1 July 2021).

[218] As of 2020, the Commission reported that there were 96.5 million persons at risk of poverty and social exclusion. European Commission, 'Poverty and Social Exclusion' (<https://ec.europa.eu/eurostat/web/products-eurostat-news/-/edn-20211015-1> accessed 11 March 2023).

the European Pillar of Social Rights in 2017 by member states and its inclusion in the European Council's 2019–2024 strategic agenda. The Pillar of Social Rights sets out twenty principles reflecting a 'Social Europe' and its 'social rulebook'.[219] Emphasizing a skilled and flexible labour force alongside social protections, the Pillar Principles are heavily weighted toward securing employment and protecting the employee's participation in an equal opportunity labour market. That said, the Action Plan of 2021 maintains a target on poverty numbers: 'The number of people at risk of poverty or social exclusion should be reduced by at least 15 million by 2030' and of those, at least 5 million should be children.[220] To track implementation, the European Commission implemented (and in 2021 revised) a 'Social Scoreboard' to look at how well the European Pillar of Social Rights is being fulfilled.[221] The Scoreboard is explicitly tied to the SDGs, with SDG 1 among the goals the measures target.

An action plan for poverty reduction was also recently concluded by Canada. Its first such programme, the Canadian Poverty Reduction Strategy ('Opportunity for All') plans to halve (based on 2015 figures) poverty by 2030—clearly a goal tied to target 1.2.[222] The Strategy foresees the establishment of a National Advisory Council on Poverty and legislation to give the programme a legal basis.[223] The Canadian government is also introducing a national poverty line for the first time.[224] The line will be calculated using region-specific costs of goods and services necessary for a person to 'participate in society today and going forward'.[225] In accordance with recent literature on poverty, the Canadian plan looks directly at the poverty gap, addressing 'deep income poverty' and those in the lowest income levels and considers asset resilience as one of the elements in protecting from vulnerabilities.[226]

Further efforts to make progress on target 1.2 include academic efforts to develop multidimensional poverty measurement tools. One such project, developed by an interdisciplinary team funded by the Australian Research Council between 2010 and 2014, promulgated the so-called Individual Deprivation Measure (IDM) to assess gender disparities in poverty.[227] Designed to measure poverty inclusively—taking into account specifically gender bias in measurements—the researchers of the IDM highlighted numerous problems with conventional poverty lines beyond their gender agnosticism.[228] Described further below, the IDM suggests alternatives for governments

---

[219] <https://op.europa.eu/webpub/empl/european-pillar-of-social-rights/en/> accessed 11 March 2023.

[220] European Commission, 'The European Pillar of Social Rights Action Plan' COM(2021) 102 final, p 7 (4 March 2021).

[221] <https://ec.europa.eu/eurostat/web/european-pillar-of-social-rights/indicators/social-scoreboard-indicators> accessed 11 March 2023.

[222] <https://www.canada.ca/en/employment-social-development/programs/results/poverty-reduction.html> accessed 11 March 2023.

[223] ibid.

[224] ibid.

[225] ibid.

[226] ibid.

[227] See T Pogge and S Wisor, 'Measuring Poverty: A Proposal' in M Adler and M Fleurbaey (eds), *Oxford Handbook of Well-Being and Public Policy* (OUP 2016); S Wisor and others, *The Individual Deprivation Measure: A Gender-Sensitive Approach to Poverty Measurement, Individual Deprivation Measure* (IDM 2016).

[228] ibid.

74 SDG 1

to take into consideration when designing policies to leave no one behind when reducing poverty in all its forms.

6. Critique

Whereas the large majority of those living in extreme poverty are found in low-income countries, the idea of reducing poverty 'in all its forms' requires high-income states to address the poverty found within their own populations as well. Target 1.2, however, suffers from two main flaws, both similar to those of MDG 1. The first flaw is target 1.2's failure to ensure that no-one will be living in poverty in 2030. The target's use of 'proportions of the population' as its measure of success violates the 'leave no-one behind' principle of the SDGs. The second flaw is the target's failure to ensure all persons will be living lives of dignity in 2030. The reason for this rests with the use of national poverty lines.

a) Proportion

Target 1.2 strikingly walks back SDG 1's overall claim of aiming to 'eradicate' poverty in all its forms, requiring a mere halving of the proportion of persons living in poverty, even if all the individuals are suffering severe deprivations. In this way, the fundamental framework of target 1.2 collides with the human rights-based approach that exists in international law.[229]

Target 1.2 exists because even with an income above the global minimum, not everyone has the means to live in dignity. Even in high-income countries, persons in poverty may not enjoy the human right to an adequate standard of living (and are often also unable to realize their civil rights fully) and frequently face discrimination in access to public services. The international law of human rights demands that states—even with low GDP—secure 'the satisfaction of, at the very least, minimum essential levels of' (for example) nutrition, shelter, and basic healthcare, as well as not treating anyone discriminatorily to the extent financially possible.[230] A poverty target that does not underline the state's obligation to provide prompt relief from deprivations of these minimum rights for *each* individual is worse than unambitious: it is an egregious moral failure and a breach of international law. Nor can the fact that even a large number of persons are made better off make leaving the other half in deep poverty acceptable.[231]

Moreover, the halving figure leaves the possibility that states achieve the target such that 'the worst affected human populations are no better off' than now.[232] Bringing

---

[229] See generally E Pribytkova, 'Global Obligations for Sustainable Development: Harmonizing the 2030 Agenda for Sustainable Development and International Human Rights Law' (2020) 41(4) University of Pennsylvania Journal of International Law 1031, 1050–56 (setting forth the differences between the human rights framework and the SDG framework for sustainable development).

[230] Committee on Economic, Social and Cultural Rights, CESCR General Comment No 3: The Nature of States Parties' Obligations (art 2, para 1, of the Covenant), E/1991/23 (1991) para 10 (explaining the 'minimum core obligation'); see KG Young, 'The Minimum Core of Economic and Social Rights: A Concept in Search of Content' (2008) 33 Yale Journal of International Law 113.

[231] See T Pogge, 'Fighting Global Poverty' (2017) 13 International Journal of Law in Context 512, 516.

[232] NK Poku and J Whitman, 'The Millennium Development Goals and Development After 2015' (2011) 32(1) Third World Quarterly 181, 185.

those just under the poverty line to just above it may reduce the overall proportion of persons in 'poverty', but it would leave the most deprived in as bad a condition as before. This avoids the concerns about inequality and of leaving no-one behind and demands significantly less than what states are already responsible for under international human rights law.

b) Use of national poverty lines

Aside from the lack of a human rights approach, target 1.2 moves SDG 1 away from a universal approach to poverty reduction. The push to use national poverty lines ('poverty ... according to national definitions') as the measure of who is living in 'poverty' is understandable from a political perspective,[233] but their use hinders valid comparison of country efforts across states.[234]

More fundamentally, any reliance on poverty lines gives a misleading view of the incidence of poverty—its extent, its depth, and its duration.[235] Poverty lines rely on two sets of numbers: the first are those indicating how much income or consumption each unit of study (often the household) enjoys within a given time period; the second is the line below which the household (or individual) is considered to be living in poverty.[236] When either of these numbers is inaccurate, the use of the poverty line will not correctly reflect poverty in the society being assessed. The problem is that measuring each is fraught with imprecision.

The income/consumption measure is unsound largely because it relies on self-reported data. Where the measure is income, not only is it likely that the interviewee only mentions legal earnings, but official definitions omit some forms of income and do not account for some forms of costs associated with income.[237] Poverty statistics calculated using consumption measures (such as those of most low-income countries) are broadly considered better at reflecting multidimensional poverty (by accounting for material deprivation), but they too are often defective.[238] Interviewees may forget having made purchases, particularly when the time period for which the investigation is set stretches back for several months.[239] Where spending is recorded, analysts cannot determine the reason for it—and thus cannot determine whether low expenditures

---

[233] But see Sengupta (n 195) 14 ('It feels wrong that Agenda 2030 re-commits states to realising their international human rights obligations on the one hand, while suggesting, on the other, that they need to meet only national benchmarks while striving for these goals').

[234] A study that looks at the different results emerging from income-based and consumption-based poverty lines highlights the impact that different methodologies have even within a single country. A Cutillo and others, 'Income-Based and Consumption-Based Measurement of Absolute Poverty: Insights from Italy, Social Indicators Research' (May 2020) (<https://doi.org/10.1007/s11205-020-02386-9> accessed 11 March 2023).

[235] Commentators are convinced that none of the main types of poverty lines are adequate for assessing multidimensional poverty. RL O'Brien and DS Pedulla, *Beyond the Poverty Line* (SSIR 2010) (citing JE Foster, 'Absolute Versus Relative Poverty' (1988) 88(2) American Economics Review 335).

[236] R Haveman, 'Changing the Poverty Measure: Pitfalls and Potential Gains' (1993) Focus 24 (text available at <https://www.irp.wisc.edu/publications/focus/pdfs/foc143e.pdf> accessed 2 July 2021).

[237] See ibid 25.

[238] The World Bank uses a 'modified mixed reference period', subjecting consumption of food items to a weekly recording period rather than the monthly or yearly period of recording for other goods and services.

[239] Haveman (n 236).

are really an indication of deprivation (poverty) or merely one of voluntary savings (thrift).[240]

The other element of a poverty line is the line under which the household is considered poor (the 'cutoff'). Even more so than the income/consumption figures, this figure can lead to a distorted view of poverty and cannot capture the multidimensional aspects of poverty. For one thing, '[t]here is no consensus on what is to be counted in determining how well off people are'.[241] Not only is the basket of goods and services open to challenge but national poverty lines may or may not take into consideration regional differences in cost of living, they may or may not include costs of social belonging, and they may or may not consider the impact of varying household compositions. Further, no poverty line can assess the depth or duration of poverty—elements that are essential for policy-makers adequately to approach their task of reducing poverty.[242]

Finally, research establishes that the line itself is gendered (largely ignoring the different preference sets of women) and aged (agnostic as to the specific aspects of child poverty).[243] Yet, despite decades of research in improving the methods of poverty measurement, change is avoided because in practice poverty lines are highly susceptible to politicization: any 'official poverty statistic is ... a symbol with far-reaching ideological and political implications'.[244] Thus, changes to poverty lines are difficult for governments to agree to because either they will make the administration look bad (if poverty numbers are thereby increased) or they can spur accusations of opportunistic manipulation (if poverty numbers decrease).[245]

C. Target 1.3 Implement Nationally Appropriate Social Protection Systems and Measures for All, Including Floors, and by 2030 Achieve Substantial Coverage of the Poor and the Vulnerable

1. SDG Indicator 1.3.1
a) Population covered by social protection floors/systems
Definition: Indicator 1.3.1 is the proportion of population covered by social protection floors/systems, by sex, distinguishing children, unemployed persons, older persons,

---

[240] See BD Meyer and JX Sullivan, 'Identifying the Disadvantaged: Official Poverty, Consumption Poverty, and the New Supplemental Poverty Measure' (2012) 26(3) Journal of Economic Perspectives 111, 116–18 (illustrating the problem of high out-of-pocket healthcare expenditures as being either because of poor health or because of valuing healthcare more than other possible expenditures).

[241] Haveman (n 236) 24.

[242] O'Brien and Pedulla (n 235).

[243] See the work on the Individual Deprivation Measure, led by Thomas Pogge and Allison Jaggar, <https://globaljustice.yale.edu/individual-deprivation-measure> accessed 12 March 2023

[244] R Haveman, 'Who Are the Nation's 'Truly Poor'? Problems and Pitfalls in (Re)defining and Measuring Poverty' (1993) 11(1) Brookings Review 24, 24 ('Revising the official measure will be controversial).

[245] O'Brien and Pedulla (n 235) footnote 3 and accompanying text.

persons with disabilities, pregnant women, newborns, work-injury victims, and the poor and the vulnerable.

2. Sources of Target

The SDG 1 target of achieving 'nationally appropriate social protection systems and measures for all' and 'substantial coverage of the poor and vulnerable' by 2030 adds an important thickness to the overall goal of eliminating poverty. Assuming that among the most important tools to protect human dignity—even in the face of no (or low) earned income—are those subsumed under the term 'social protection',[246] the target's call for social protection visibly ties international human rights guarantees with international labour law principles, forging an expansive community to oversee and, critically, to guide the international community as it strives to move toward the goal. As the International Labour Organization (ILO) says, social protection systems 'are fundamental not only in reducing poverty, but also in preventing that people fall (back) into poverty across the life cycle ... This is one critical element of any policy framework aiming at leaving no one behind (SDG target 1.3).'[247]

Whereas the characteristic of poverty used by the MDGs was that of low income, it is widely recognized that governmental programmes to supplement earned income or to offer benefits to low-income groups can relieve some of the disadvantages of poverty. In the years leading to the SDGs, there were strong calls to include social protection in the new framework, with experts noting that 'their absence constitutes a potentially serious threat to efforts to end poverty'.[248]

The SDG drafters included target 1.3 to encourage governments to offer protection to income-deprived members of society on the basis of need ('social assistance'),[249] as an entitlement ('social security'),[250] and/or as active measures to stimulate access to the labour market. These programmes should ensure that each person may live a life of dignity even when suffering from old-age, ill-health, disability, unemployment, pregnancy, or other conditions.[251] The target particularly requests states to report on governmental programmes that offer social protection 'floors' to those below a certain income level as well as to present a breakdown of the coverage of such programmes for specific population groups (women, the elderly, rural populations) and in terms of the type of protection (unemployment, health, disability, old age, children, maternity, etc).[252]

---

[246] But see M Elkins and others, 'Did Social Protection Assist with Progress Towards the Millennium Development Goals?' in SA Churchill (ed), *Moving from the Millennium to Sustainable Development Goals* (Palgrave Macmillan 2020) 228 (highlighting that the arguments about social protection's beneficial effects on poverty and, in particular, development, are debatable).

[247] International Labour Organization, *World Social Protection Report 2017–2019: Universal Social Protection to Achieve the Sustainable Development Goals* (ILO 2017) 2.

[248] A Fiszbein and others, 'Social Protection and Poverty Reduction: Global Patterns and Some Targets' (2014) 61 World Development 167, 175.

[249] A Charbord, 'The Right to Social Security Including Pensions' (2010) 41 Studies in Transnational Legal Policy 469, 470.

[250] ibid.

[251] ibid 469.

[252] See United Nations, 'Indicator: 4. Percentage of Eligible Population Covered by National Social Protection Programs' (<https://indicators.report/indicators/i-4/> accessed 15 February 2021).

3. Statistical/Empirical Analysis

One of the difficulties in measuring poverty and attempting to quantify the impacts of poverty on the lives of those affected by it is the difference between earned income, all income, and access to free (or subsidized) goods and services.[253] Moreover, even when assessing the extent of social protection in the form of cash or in-kind transfers, the statistics may not reflect all programmes that act to protect the poor.[254] Recent improvements in the amount of data reported and available allow current figures to reflect the protections available more accurately, but make comparisons across time potentially inaccurate.[255]

Independent of the exact definition, the availability of social protection varies greatly across the globe and even within states. In 2019, G7 members issued a statement together with the ILO stating that 55 per cent of the world's people had no social protection[256] and the ILO says that only 27 per cent have 'adequate' coverage.[257] For most of the developing world, the figures are much lower (from 29.1 per cent coverage in Morocco to 1.9 per cent in Nigeria).[258] Within the United States, social protection regimes are much less protective of the income-poor and those at risk of poverty than are the programmes of other industrialized countries, and they address inequality only slightly.[259] Indeed, studies have shown that the post-tax effects of the US welfare system actually worsen inequality for persons of colour (particularly Black and Hispanic households) and for single mothers.[260]

In response to the COVID-19 pandemic, global coverage of social protection has changed dramatically. A World Bank study reported an increase in social protection measures of almost 148 per cent between December 2020 and mid-May 2021.[261] The increase included not only a greater number of social protection measures on offer but also measures that were more generous and that lasted longer than pre-pandemic measures. Cash transfers, for example, which account for an average of 52 per cent of the monthly GDP per capita in Sub-Saharan Africa, increased by an average of more than 90 per cent from Spring 2020 to Spring 2021.[262] The national programmes reached more than 100 million persons in some cases:

---

[253] L Lein and others, 'Social Policy, Transfers, Programs, and Assistance' in Brady and Burton (eds) (n 3) 733–34 (explaining the wide variety of programme types and coverage across nations).

[254] For example, Brady and Destro suggest that studies on US welfare often disregard or undervalue certain programmes that in practice offer substantial protection to low-income individuals but that are offered in the form of insurance rather than as targeted assistance. Brady and Destro (n 83) 588.

[255] U Gentilini and others, 'Social Protection and Jobs Responses to COVID-19: A Real-Time Review of Country Measures' ('Living paper' version 15, 14 May 2021) 4 (World Bank study on social protection responses).

[256] G7-ILO, 'Towards Universal Social Protection and achieving SDG 1.3: Social Protection—A Global Priority' (<http://www.ilo.org/wcmsp5/groups/public/---dgreports/---cabinet/documents/briefingnote/wcms_732720.pdf> accessed 15 Feb. 2021).

[257] ILO, 'Social Protection' (<https://www.ilo.org/global/topics/social-security/lang--en/index.htm> accessed 28 June 2021).

[258] M Rutkowski, 'The Road to Social Protection, Beyond Jobs' Hindustan Times, 20 February 2019 (table listing figures from 2010s; Tunisia, Brazil, Turkey, Chile, Egypt, and Argentina were all over or just below the 55 per cent average) (<https://www.hindustantimes.com/india-news/the-road-to-social-protection-beyond-jobs/story-yTqh28lQA0rhKATtvRV6PO.html> accessed 15 February 2021).

[259] S Moller and J Misra, 'Inequality' in Béland and others (eds) (n 83) 609–12.

[260] ibid 609.

[261] Gentilini (n 255) 4.

[262] ibid 6–7.

COMMENTARIES OF TARGETS   79

With over 206 million individuals covered, India's Pradhan Mantri Jan Dhan Yojana (PMJDY) program is the largest Covid-related cash transfer scheme worldwide. Such program is followed by three cash transfer interventions all reaching over a hundred million people, namely the US first stimulus check (160 million), Japan's one-off universal program reaching about (116.5) [sic], and Pakistan's Ehsaas (100.9).[263]

Moreover, while the composition of social protection remains heavily oriented toward social assistance programmes (including cash transfers and in-kind food voucher programmes),[264] the COVID response measures included a disproportionate increase in active labour market assistance programmes.[265] Measures on wage subsidies and training, labour regulation, and shorter working times increased by 330 per cent in comparison to pre-COVID times.[266]

Despite the rise in social protection, it is unclear whether the pandemic-spurred increases are sustainable. Nearly one-third of the cash transfer programmes, for example, were specific to COVID and are not foreseen to continue.[267] More worryingly, the cash transfers underscored global inequalities even while supporting many vulnerable persons during the worst months of the pandemic-related economic downturn. This is clear from different views on the figures spent. Higher-income countries generally gave not only much more per capita ($847) than low-income countries did ($4), they also spent a higher percentage of their GDP on their social protection programmes than lower income countries did. Whereas Sweden spends 16 per cent of its GDP and the United States spends 9 per cent of its GDP on social protection, Afghanistan's 3 per cent GDP spending on social protection is particularly high for low-income countries.[268] In addition, the percentage of the population reached with cash transfers was significantly higher in high-income countries (26.7 per cent) than in low-income countries (4.5 per cent).[269]

4. Implementation Efforts at the Domestic and International Levels
Placing social security as a target in the SDGs provides stakeholders an additional reason to call for fuller implementation of the calls for comprehensive social protection systems that the global community has issued in different fora. Two main centres of SDG-related efforts relating to social protection are the ILO and the International Monetary Fund (IMF). The UN's Addis Ababa Action Agenda as well as states and other governmental and non-governmental organizations' programmes are also actively pursuing the social protection target.

---

[263] ibid 10.
[264] ibid (noting that 55 per cent of global social protection programmes are in the form of social assistance, and that this is particularly prevalent in low-income countries).
[265] ibid 4, 6, Table 3 (measures on wage subsidies and training, labour regulation, and shorter working times increased by 330 per cent).
[266] ibid.
[267] ibid 7.
[268] ibid 16.
[269] ibid 13.

80 SDG 1

a) ILO

Concluded long before the SDGs, the ILO's main convention on social security is the 1952 Social Security (Minimum Standards) Convention (No 102). That Convention, currently ratified by fifty-nine ILO members, sets out the basic principle that states are responsible for ensuring that residents in their territory enjoy at least the protections set forth in the Convention to at least the degree specified. Parties must select a minimum of three of nine areas of social protection (medical care, sickness benefits, unemployment benefits, old-age benefits, worker injury compensation, family benefits, invalidity benefits, or survivors' benefits) to which they oblige themselves and ensure the financing and administration of such programmes. The Parties may determine whether the benefits are to be provided in the form of social assistance, social insurance, or universal benefits, or some combination of the three.[270]

Building on Convention 102, the Social Protection Floors Recommendation of 2012 set out that members should establish 'social protection floors', defined as 'sets of basic social security guarantees which secure protection aimed at preventing or alleviating poverty, vulnerability and social exclusion'.[271] This Recommendation, in turn, forms the basis for the Organization's 2016 'Global Flagship Programme: Building Social Protection Floors for All'.[272]

Established in the wake of the SDGs, the Social Protection Floors programme calls attention to human rights as well as to economic rationales to support states' development of four specific 'floors': 'essential health care for all residents'; 'social protection for all children'; 'support to all people of working age in cases of unemployment, maternity, disability and work injury'; and 'pensions for all older persons'.[273] There are numerous projects actively pursued by the ILO within the framework of this agenda, many looking to reform national legal systems for social assistance. In addition, since July 2015, eight states have ratified Convention 102, accepting thereby new international legal obligations to improve social protection coverage in at least three areas.[274]

---

[270] Further Conventions and Recommendations create more rigorous standards of protection for different groups of beneficiaries, but have been less widely ratified. See Equality of Treatment (Social Security) Convention, 1962 (No 118) (thirty-eight ratifications); Employment Injury Benefits Convention, 1964 (No 121) (twenty-four ratifications); Invalidity, Old-Age and Survivors' Benefits Convention, 1967 (No 128) (seventeen ratifications); Medical Care and Sickness Benefits Convention, 1969 (No 130) (sixteen ratifications); Maintenance of Social Security Rights Convention, 1982 (No 157) (four ratifications); Employment Promotion and Protection against Unemployment Convention, 1988 (No 168) (eight ratifications); Maternity Protection Convention, 2000 (No 183) (thirty-nine ratifications). The Recommendations include Medical Care and Sickness Benefits Recommendation, 1969 (No 134); Employment Promotion and Protection against Unemployment Recommendation, 1988 (No 176); Invalidity, Old-Age and Survivors' Benefits Recommendation, 1967 (No 131); Employment Injury Benefits Recommendation, 1964 (No 121); Maternity Protection Recommendation, 2000 (No 191); Maintenance of Social Security Rights Recommendation, 1983 (No 167); Social Protection Floors Recommendation, 2012 (No 202).

[271] ILO, 'R202—Social Protection Floors Recommendation, 2012 (No 202)', paras 2, 4.

[272] ILO, 'Building Social Protection Floors for All: Global Flagship Programme', 8 (<https://www.social-protect ion.org/gimi/RessourcePDF.action?id=51737> accessed 28 June 2021).

[273] ibid.

[274] See Ratifications of C102—Social Security (Minimum Standards) Convention, 1952 (entry into force 27 April 1955) (Argentina ratified 27 July 2016, Benin ratified 14 June 2019, Cabo Verde ratified 10 January 2020, Dominican Republic ratified 11 July 2016, Morocco ratified 14 June 2019, Russia ratified 26 February 2019, St. Vincent and the Grenadines ratified 25 November 2015, Ukraine ratified 6 June 2016).

Perhaps the most important development related to the SDGs is the data compilation on target 1.3 in the ILO's World Social Protection Database (WSPDB). Begun in the late 1950s, the WSPDB is now receiving data not only from government administrations but also from 'other agencies'[275] and has a dedicated webpage on which global and country-level statistics are available on the disaggregated levels of social protection coverage.[276]

b) IMF

In May 2018, the Special Rapporteur on Extreme Poverty and Human Rights reported that '[n]o international institution exerts greater influence than IMF over issues such as ... social protection.'[277] Not unanimously welcomed, this role reflects both the IMF's early position as guardian of governmental fiscal rigor and its post-SDG strategy of promoting social protection as a part of its mandate to promote sustainable economic growth.[278] Already attending to social protection spending of its client governments since the 2000s (increasingly after the global financial crisis of 2007–08), the IMF only began to address the 'macro-criticality of social protection' in the recent past.[279]

In 2019, the Fund's Executive Board adopted the 'Strategy for IMF Engagement on Social Spending'.[280] The Strategy is intended to further the SDGs by providing a framework for analysing social spending in a context of financial sustainability and with an aim of reducing inequality while increasing inclusive growth. Given the IMF's approach to governmental spending, the Strategy is the subject of significant scepticism and many have criticized its implementation.[281]

c) UN Addis Ababa Action Agenda

The 2015 United Nations Addis Ababa Action Agenda (AAAA) on financing for development set out the UN members' commitment to establishing 'a new social compact' to eliminate poverty through social protection systems. Paragraph 12 of the AAAA states:

> To end poverty in all its forms everywhere and finish the unfinished business of the Millennium Development Goals, we commit to a new social compact. In this effort, we will provide fiscally sustainable and nationally appropriate social protection systems and measures for all, including floors, with a focus on those furthest below the poverty line and the vulnerable, persons with disabilities, indigenous persons, children,

---

[275] See, eg, sources for the report on Cabo Verde (https://www.social-protection.org/gimi/WSPDB.action?id=19> accessed 29 June 2021) (listing as source of data ILOSTAT, ISSA/SSA, ECLAC, IMF, WHO, World Bank, UNDP, UNICEF, and Cabo Verde itself).

[276] See World Social Protection Data Dashboards <https://www.social-protection.org/gimi/WSPDB.action?id=32> accessed 11 March 2023.

[277] Special Rapporteur on extreme poverty and human rights, 'Report on the International Monetary Fund and its Impact on Social Protection', UN Doc A/HRC/38/33, para 3 (8 May 2018).

[278] See V Engstrom, 'Unpacking the Debate on Social Protection Floors' (2019) 9 Goettingen Journal of International Law 571, 580–83 (describing the IMF's history of support for social protection measures).

[279] A/HRC/38/33, paras 31–54.

[280] IMF, 'A Strategy for IMF Engagement on Social Spending', IMF Policy Paper, 14 June 2019.

[281] See generally Engstrom (n 278).

youth and older persons. We also encourage countries to consider setting nationally appropriate spending targets for quality investments in essential public services for all, including health, education, energy, water and sanitation, consistent with national sustainable development strategies.

Tying in with SDG 1's means of implementation (MOI), the AAAA is a cornerstone for making progress on target 1.3. The 2019 meeting in Ethiopia to discuss social protection systems examined, in particular, best practices for countries with substantial numbers of persons in informal employment.

d) Other actions

Other international groupings and institutions are also urging action on target 1.3. The Global Partnership for Universal Social Protection to Achieve the Sustainable Development Goals (USP2030), a collaboration of regional, governmental, and non-governmental agencies, put out a five-point action plan in February 2019, with 'core principles' for governments to implement.[282] The OECD is working on social protection largely through its Development Centre, co-organizing high-level conferences, analysing data, and performing research and reviews.[283] The European Union's EU Social Protection Systems Programme, supported by the OECD and the Finnish government, aims to improve policies and develop capacities for implementing poverty-alleviating social protection programmes in developing countries.[284]

On the national and local level, movements to reduce the vulnerability of persons in or at risk of poverty through social assistance are highly political and subject to vigorous debate. The role of government in social protection regimes can and does vary according to the political philosophy of the community, with more socialist states taking on all or most of the offering of benefits and more liberal regimes involving private actors in their efforts to serve the target public.[285] Cultural differences also exist, with East Asian states only recently offering governmental social protections and Latin American states typically being more forthcoming in transfers to income-poor families.[286]

One of the most notable national level movements in recent years has been the rise in the idea of offering a basic income to all, independent of employment status. As set out by two of its most renowned promoters, a project of providing an unconditional basic income to a population would require cash (not in-kind) payments to all legal (fiscal) residents.[287] More than just social assistance, however, Van Parijs and Vanderborght emphasize that the income must be 'unconditional' in the 'strong' sense:

---

[282] See Global Partnership for Universal Social Protection to Achieve the Sustainable Development Goals, Together to Achieve Universal Social Protection by 2030: A Call to Action (5 February 2019) (<https://www.oecd.org/dev/inclusivesocietiesanddevelopment/USP2030_Call_to_action.pdf>).

[283] See <https://www.oecd.org/dev/> accessed 11 March 2023.

[284] See <https://www.oecd.org/dev/inclusive-societies-development/social-protection.htm> accessed 11 March 2023

[285] ibid 5–6.

[286] See generally C-S Lee and I-H Koo, 'The Welfare States and Poverty' in Brady and Burton (eds) (n 3) 723–25.

[287] P van Parijs and Y Vanderborght, *Basic Income: A Radical Proposal for a Free Society and a Sane Economy* (Harvard University Press 2017).

It is strictly an individual entitlement, as opposed to linked to the household situation; it is what is commonly called universal, as opposed to subjected to an income or means test; and it is obligation free, as opposed to tied to an obligation to work or prove willingness to work.[288]

One analysis of basic income projects in Finland, Utrecht, and Barcelona points out that these trials, while not being 'universal', hold hope for the further trials planned in developing countries, where the reduction of bureaucratic hurdles to social protection may be more significant.[289]

Facing significant scepticism in the past, the potential benefits of basic income became more discussed as robot technologies improved and the possibility of massive unemployment for workers whose tasks could be carried out by a robot increased.[290] The impact of the COVID-pandemic on swaths of workers—leaving them without an income because their place of employment could not be open—heightened interest in the idea of ensuring that each person have a right to a minimum income, independent of notions of 'deservingness'.

Beyond governments, other stakeholder's activities in social protection are varied and potentially fruitful. One of the areas closely tied to the SDGs that is generating academic and civil society interest is that of adaptive social protection.[291] This term refers to flexible systems of social protection that allow households to become more resilient to climate change and disaster risks.[292] With a focus on insurance measures and cash transfers, adaptive social protection combines risk assessments from different sectors to link government spending to at-risk individuals or households, in the expectation that the most vulnerable can be the main beneficiaries.[293]

5. Critique

Regimes of social protections are of three basic types.[294] The first, and that with the longest history, is social assistance.[295] Social assistance regimes support individuals in need by giving them cash or in-kind transfers. Being need-based, social assistance

---

[288] ibid 9.

[289] J Coll, 'Wise Cities & the Universal Basic Income: Facing the Challenges of Inequality, the 4th Industrial Revolution and the New Socioeconomic Paradigm' (2017) 183 Notes internacionals CIDOB (<https://www.cidob.org/publicaciones/serie_de_publicacion/notes_internacionals/n1_183/wise_cities_the_universal_basic_income_facing_the_challenges_of_inequality_the_4th_industrial_revolution_and_the_new_socioeconomic_paradigm> accessed 29 June 2021).

[290] Van Parijs and Vanderborght (n 287) 5; D Arthur, 'Basic Income: A Radical Idea Enters the Mainstream' Parliamentary Library Research Paper Series, 2016–17 (18 November 2016) Parliament of Australia, 13–18.

[291] For example, Adaptive Social Protection in the Development Agenda, European Development Days, 16 June 2021 (<http://socieux.eu/knowledge_cpt/adaptive-social-protection-in-the-development-agenda/> accessed 11 March 2023).

[292] See M Davies and others, ' "Adaptive Social Protection": Synergies for Poverty Reduction' (2008) 39(4) Institute for Development Studies Bulletin 105.

[293] United Nations University, 'Five Facts on Adaptive Social Protection (ASP)' (18 May 2020) (<https://ehs.unu.edu/news/news/five-facts-on-adaptive-social-protection-asp.html> accessed 28 June 2021).

[294] D Béland and others, 'The Fragmented American Welfare State: Putting the Pieces Together' in Béland and others (n 83) 5. Note that this typology does not include a separate category of labour market interventions, which others describe as one of the three basic forms (next to social assistance and social insurance).

[295] ibid.

programmes limit their recipients according to a particular criteria or set of criterion (often income, health status, status as a mother, or age). A second type of social regime is social insurance.[296] While also providing cash or in-kind transfers, the eligible recipients are those who have contributed to the fund from which the assistance is financed. While benefits might prevent vulnerable individuals from falling into poverty, many recipients are neither vulnerable nor at risk of poverty. Finally, social protection may be offered in the form of universal benefits.[297] As the name indicates, universal benefits are transfers that each citizen or resident receives, independent of either need or earlier contributions.

Any of the three types of social protection regime can be considered within the term 'social security' as set forth in SDG 1. With the additional wording of 'nationally appropriate' qualifying the protections to be secured to all, the target is distinctly diffuse. The aim to ensure 'floors' below which no individual must survive, rather than clarifying the scope, makes it more ambiguous.[298] That said, the language of 'floors' fits easily with that of the human-rights concept of minimum core obligations—allowing for target 1.3 to be seen as linked to existing human rights dialogues.[299]

The main critique of target 1.3 from a legal point of view, then, must be that it adds nothing substantive to the existing obligation of states in respect of social protection. The Universal Declaration on Human Rights (UDHR), as customary law, already binds each state to fulfil its obligations in the dimensions foreseen by the SDGs. Article 22 of the UDHR states:

> Everyone, as a member of society, has the right to social security and is entitled to realization, through national effort and international co-operation and in accordance with the organization and resources of each State, of the economic, social and cultural rights indispensable for his dignity and the free development of his personality.

Relatedly, Article 25 UDHR is categorical on the universality and the breadth of the right to an adequate standard of living:

> Everyone has the right to a standard of living adequate for the health and well-being of himself and of his family, including food, clothing, housing and medical care and necessary social services, and the right to security in the event of unemployment, sickness, disability, widowhood, old age or other lack of livelihood in circumstances beyond his control.

Together these provisions set out a clear human right to both social assistance and social security for all. As with every human right, the right to social protection places a

[296] ibid.
[297] ibid.
[298] Engstrom (n 278) 573.
[299] ibid 577.

three-pronged obligation on the state: to respect, protect, and fulfil it.[300] Thus, social protection can be demanded by each individual, the state must ensure social protection on a non-discriminatory basis, and every effort must be made by the state to increase the breadth and depth of its coverage.

Numerous human rights treaties call for the right to social security as well.[301] The International Covenant on Economic, Social and Cultural Rights (ICESCR) a prominent source of such obligations, with 171 states parties to the ICESCR and a further four having signed.[302] Article 9 ICESCR, for example, specifically declares 'the right of everyone to social security, including social insurance'. The right of working mothers 'to adequate social security benefits' is found in Article 10.[303] The CESCR's General Comment No 19, moreover, highlights not only the breadth of the term 'social security'[304] but underlines the state's minimum core obligation of providing 'access to a social security scheme that provides a minimum essential level of benefits to all individuals and families that will enable them to acquire at least essential health care, basic shelter and housing, water and sanitation, foodstuffs, and the most basic forms of education'.[305]

The International Labour Organization's Convention 102,[306] discussed above, sets out in more detail what has been expected of states in the area of social protection for seventy years. The protections called for by the ILO extend to classes of persons that are not necessarily workers. While employees (and sometimes their families) are mentioned in every type of benefit, some also indicate the protected class as being that of 'economically active'[307] persons or 'residents'.[308]

Finally, many state constitutions refer to a right to social security.[309] While these vary in their detail and may limit the right to protection to what the state can afford, these provisions 'are an important tool' to promote social protection.[310]

---

[300] The three-part framework was set out in the 1997 Maastricht Guidelines on Violations of Economic, Social and Cultural Rights and repeated in the CESCR's General Comment 12 on the right to food. See International Commission of Jurists and others, 'The Maastricht Guidelines on Violations of Economic, Social and Cultural Rights' (1998) 20(3) Human Rights Quarterly 691; United Nations Committee on Economic, *Social and Cultural Rights, General Comment 12* (The Right to Adequate Food), E/C.12/1999/5, 20th session (United Nations 1999). But see DJ Karp, 'What is the Responsibility to Respect Human Rights? Reconsidering the "Respect, Protect, and Fulfill" Framework' (2020) 12 International Theory 83.

[301] International Covenant on Economic, Social and Cultural Rights, 993 UNTS 3 (adopted 16 December 1966; entry into force 3 January 1976). See also Convention on the Elimination of All Forms of Discrimination against Women, art 11(1)(e) and art 14(2)(c); Convention on the Rights of the Child, art 26; International Convention on the Protection of the Rights of All Migrant Workers and Members of Their Families, art 27; Convention on the Rights of Persons with Disabilities, art 28(2).

[302] Status of Ratification Interactive Dashboard, International Covenant on Economic, Social and Cultural Rights (<https://indicators.ohchr.org/> accessed 4 July 2021).

[303] art 10(2) ICESCR.

[304] Committee on Economic, Social and Cultural Rights (CESCR), General Comment No 19 (The Right to Social Security, article 9), E/C.12/GC/19 (2008).

[305] CESCR, General Comment 19, para 59(a).

[306] ILO, Social Security (Minimum Standards) Convention, 1952. See also ILO, Declaration of Philadelphia, art III(f)–(i) (1944) (giving the ILO the task to help members ensure the availability of social protection to all).

[307] For example, ILO Convention 102, art 9(b), arts 15(b), 27(b), 41(b), 48(b), 55(b), 61(b).

[308] For example, ILO Convention 102, arts 9(c), 15(c), 21(b), 27(c), 41(c), 55(c), 61(c).

[309] M Kaltenborn, 'Overcoming Extreme Poverty by Social Protection Floors Approaches to Closing the Right to Social Security Gap' (2017) 10(2) Law and Development Review 237, 243–44, footnote 23 and accompanying text.

[310] ibid 244.

86 SDG 1

Importantly, the legal basis of social protection programmes is seen as particularly important for sustainable achievements in poverty reduction, as persons must be able to rely on enforceable claims to protection if the systems are to be robust and durable.[311] Target 1.3 encourages and perhaps implies establishing legally binding social protection floors, but it does not specify the promulgation of legislation. In keeping with the SDGs as instruments of awareness-raising and of marking of political emphasis, target 1.3 is not a step toward expanding obligations on states.[312] To achieve lasting poverty reduction will therefore take more: more attention put on states' institutional capacity to provide adequate social protection; more attention to accountability mechanisms;[313] and more attention to capacity building and financing assistance for developing country governments.[314]

D. Target 1.4 Equal Rights to Ownership, Basic Services, Technology, and Economic Resources

UN definition: By 2030, ensure that all men and women, in particular the poor and the vulnerable, have equal rights to economic resources, as well as access to basic services, ownership and control over land and other forms of property, inheritance, natural resources, appropriate new technology and financial services, including microfinance.

1. SDG Indicator 1.4.1
a) Access to basic services
Definition: Indicator 1.4.1 is the proportion of population living in households with access to basic services.

2. Indicator 1.4.2
a) Secure tenure rights to land
Definition: Indicator 1.4.2 is the proportion of total adult population with secure tenure rights to land, (i) with legally recognized documentation, and (ii) who perceive their rights to land as secure, by sex and type of tenure.

---

[311] ibid 254–55 (citing M Sepulveda and C Nyst, *The Human Rights Approach to Social Protection* (Ministry for Foreign Affairs of Finland 2012) 26).

[312] Indeed, while several states have ratified the Convention since the SDGs, it is not clear that there was causality between the SDGs and these ratifications. Moreover, adherence to the Convention does not appear to be particularly rigorous: the 2020 report of the ILO Committee of Experts on the Application of Conventions and Recommendations indicated that there were direct requests given to twenty-three ratifying countries regarding problems in implementation of C102. ILO, Application of International Labour Standards 2020, International Labour Conference 109th Session, 2020.

[313] Kaltenborn (n 309) 253.

[314] ibid 263–65.

3. Sources of Target

The motivation for target 1.4 is firmly based on a need for persons to have protected claims on the means for maintaining a life of dignity and productivity. 'The Future We Want' had already set forth the General Assembly's call for 'people-centred' development with social protections,[315] sustainable cities with basic services available to all,[316] equal opportunities for women and men,[317] and increased distribution of technology,[318] so the content of target 1.4 as a whole had clear resonance from the beginning.

As the vision of SDG 1 was that of including the multidimensionality of poverty rather than solely the financial aspects of poverty, a focus on personal and social well-being was necessary within the Goal. Together with strong concerns about the inequality of treatment of impoverished individuals, these interests came together in target 1.4. The development of the target beyond the general directions of the poverty eradication goal in general, however, is open to some level of conjecture.

The OWG co-chairs' initial Focus Area document, discussed in the March 2014 session, had already suggested including property rights and financial inclusion with its target of:

> access to property and productive assets, finance and markets for all women and men; providing social protection to reduce vulnerabilities of the poor, including children, youth, unemployed, persons with disabilities, indigenous people and local communities and older persons.[319]

This received mainly praise by the negotiation participants, although numerous groups wished for additions, only some of which appear in the final version. The Indigenous Peoples Major Group's request, for example, for access to natural resources to be considered, has reflection in target 1.4, but the numerous calls for a reference to 'rights' remained largely unsatisfied.[320]

Innovatively, the target pushes forward an idea of rights to access to the Internet and to financial services. This acknowledges the ever-growing reliance of society's 'knowledge economy'[321] on the use of the Internet for communication and economic growth and the central role that banking and insurance play in the lives even of the very poor. With Mexico and Peru specifically mentioning access to the Internet,[322] and the United

---

[315] 'The Future We Want' (n 1) para 6.

[316] For example, ibid paras 134–35.

[317] For example, ibid paras 238, 240–41.

[318] For example, ibid para 44.

[319] Open Working Group Co-Chairs, 'Focus Area Document' (24 February 2014).

[320] See Compilation Major Groups Statements and Focus Areas Responses for OWG-9 (prepared for 3–5 March 2014) (<https://sdgs.un.org/sites/default/files/documents/3362Compilation%2520Major%2520Groups%2520Statements%2520and%2520Focus%2520Areas%2520Responses_March%252025_final.pdf> accessed 11 March 2023).

[321] Barrera argues for economic rights in the 'knowledge', or 'learning' economy based on the heightened need for human capital development in systems where human capital is the basis for value creation. A Barrera, 'Economic Rights in the Knowledge Economy' in S Hertel and L Minkler (eds), *Economic Rights: Conceptual, Measurement, and Policy Issues* (CUP 2007).

[322] IISD, 32(10) Earth Negotiations Bulletin 5 (7 April 2014).

States, Canada, and Israel's simultaneous call for attention to connecting the poor to markets,[323] the reality of the power of new technology to help reduce poverty was given recognition.

The maturing field of financial inclusion aims to promote the availability of banking (and to a lesser extent, insurance) services to poor households in order to increase their productive possibilities. Bangladesh (home to Muhammad Yunus, winner of the Nobel Peace Prize for his founding of the Grameen Bank) brought up the need for financial inclusion early in the negotiating process,[324] and Nigeria's call for addressing the role of banks and stock exchanges supported this.[325]

The accounts of the May 2014 session of the OWG indicate that India[326] and Bangladesh[327] both preferred a reference to 'productive resources' than to land and 'property and productive assets'. Egypt (for Algeria, Morocco, and Tunisia), on the other hand, did not like the 'rights' language at all, preferring a reference simply to 'access to' such resources.[328] Romania (for Poland)[329] and Sweden[330] suggested adding 'inheritance' to the list of resources.

The co-chair's 'zero draft' of 2 June 2014 was closer to the final wording, but still varied substantially from the current text:

> [B]y 2030 ensure development opportunities for all men and women, including secure rights to own land, property and other productive resources, and access to financial services, with particular focus on the poor, the most marginalized and people in vulnerable situations.[331]

Difficult discussions in the final OWG session in July led to the current language. Given the 'informal-informal' form of negotiations, it is impossible to know the details of why the language is as it is, but the International Institute for Sustainable Development (IISD) report gives insights as to a few of the crucial differences:

> Target 1.4 (equal rights to economic resources) was the most difficult target to resolve under this goal, largely because of references in the zero draft to the right to own land and property. Delegations were divided over this concept, with some arguing that property ownership was essential to ending poverty. Others called for ensuring equal 'access to' rather than 'rights to' such resources. One delegation called for including reference to inheritance. Several delegations said that, if the target retains the formulation

---

[323] ibid 3.
[324] ibid 4.
[325] ibid 6.
[326] IISD, 32(11) Earth Negotiations Bulletin 4 (12 May 2014).
[327] ibid 5.
[328] ibid.
[329] ibid 4.
[330] ibid 5.
[331] Co-chairs of the OWG, Introduction and Proposed Goals and Targets on Sustainable Development for the Post 2015 Development Agenda (2 June 2014) (target 1.5 in the draft).

with "equal rights," they would oppose reference to inheritance. Eventually, the 'right to' own land or property was removed and replaced by 'control over.'[332]

The end result is a target that is broadly supportive of persons having the opportunity to acquire the resources they need to be economically productive, but that omits any hints of a human rights approach.

4. Statistical/Empirical Analysis

Target 1.4's ambitions are starkly reduced through its very limited indicators. Indicator 1.4.1 asks for the proportion of the population, disaggregated by sex and age, with access to basic services. Indicator 1.4.2 requests numbers on the proportion of adults, again disaggregated by sex and age, with either recognized or perceived security of tenure. The indicators are closely related to the extent that many living in conditions of insecure tenure are also deprived of basic services.

For both indicators, that latest statistics give grounds for concern. UN-Habitat estimates that 1.8 billion people cannot access adequate housing.[333] These findings are particularly true of impoverished urban dwellers, most of whom have no security of land tenure, many of whom live in slums with no access to basic services, and who have been particularly vulnerable to the risks of COVID-19.[334]

At the end of 2019 (prior to the wide onset of COVID-19), the Special Rapporteur on adequate housing indicated even worse figures:

> More than 1.8 billion people worldwide lack adequate housing, and the number of people living in informal settlements has now surpassed 1 billion. It is estimated that 15 million people are forcibly evicted every year and that approximately 150 million people are homeless.[335]

Homelessness data are more difficult to estimate. Official UN global figures from 2005, when the United Nations last made a global survey, shows 100 million persons as without homes.[336] The OECD recently reports under 1 per cent homelessness in industrialized countries, but notes that in some of these (including Israel, England, and the United States), rates have increased significantly between 2018 and 2020.[337]

Perhaps more disturbing than the numbers alone is the explanation the Special Rapporteur has for the downward trend. Inadequate housing (and with it, the

---

[332] IISD, 32(13) Earth Negotiations Bulletin (22 July 2014) 5.

[333] <https://unhabitat.org/programme/housing-rights> accessed 11 March 2023.

[334] *The Sustainable Development Goals Report 2020* (n 128) 46.

[335] 'Guidelines for the Implementation of the Right to Adequate Housing: Report of the Special Rapporteur on adequate housing as a component of the right to an adequate standard of living, and on the right to non-discrimination in this context', A/HRC/43/43, para 2 (26 December 2019) (citations omitted).

[336] Homelessness World Cup Foundation, 'Global Homelessness Statistics' (<https://homelessworldcup.org/homelessness-statistics/> accessed 5 July 2021).

[337] OECD, 'HC3.1. Homeless Population' 27 May 2021, 3–4 (https://www.oecd.org/els/family/HC3-1-Homeless-population.pdf> accessed 11 March 2023).

availability of basic services) is affecting larger numbers of people, he wrote, because of economic growth—not in spite of it. The economic system that has pushed rising inequality is driving investments in the housing markets that raise prices for those who do not own property or land, making it increasingly difficult for them to afford land or housing.[338] The system itself is making the problem more severe, meaning that improvements can only come from a change in how the market works. Quick fixes will never be enough.

In the area of access to new technologies the statistics look more promising. In January 2021 there were an estimated 4.66 billion Internet users, indicating a growth of over 7 per cent since January 2020 and a global 'Internet penetration rate' of 59.5 per cent.[339] While the highest rates of Internet users regionally is Northern Europe, it is not only the industrialized economies that have large numbers of users.[340] Similar growth is demonstrated in the use of mobile phones: from approximately 3.7 billion phone users in 2015, there are now an estimated 5.2 billion users.

Beyond usage, the idea of Internet rights is gaining traction both as an outgrowth of international human rights guarantees of free speech and the right to information[341] and within national constitutional law.[342] Target 1.4's emphasis on access to new 'technology' sidesteps the still-challenged idea of unrestricted access to Internet *content* while promoting governmental action to provide for the necessary *infrastructure* penetration in their territories.

Access to financial services and access to microfinance are related, with both focused on overcoming financial exclusion and, in turn, income inequality and poverty.[343] Financial exclusion, an involuntary lack of access to financial services, may be market-driven (because the individuals or enterprises have very little capital or income, making them financially uninteresting for the service providers) or socio-cultural.[344] It may be due to discrimination, a lack of available information, a lack of financial education/awareness, or a mismatch between the services demanded and those offered.[345] The result, presumably, is the inability of the poor to be economically productive and to 'grow out' of their poverty.

---

[338] A/HRC/43/43 (n 335) para 4.

[339] J Johnson, 'Global digital population as of January 2021' (7 April 2021) (<https://datareportal.com/reports/digital-2021-global-overview-report> accessed 11 March 2023.

[340] ibid (reporting that China has 854 million users—the largest number of any country—and India has 550 million Internet users).

[341] Conceding that there was no identifiable right to the Internet, Special Rapporteur on the Right to Freedom of Expression, Frank La Rue, set out the positive and negative aspects of any 'right to the Internet', forming the basis for much of the consequent discussions of such a right. Special Rapporteur on the Promotion and Protection of the Right to Freedom of Opinion and Expression, Human Rights Council, U.N. Doc A/HRC/17/27 (16 May 2011) 3.

[342] K Chawla, 'Right to Internet Access—A Constitutional Argument' (2017) 7 Indian Journal of Constitutional Law 57, 65–75. But see L Huawen and Y Yan, 'Interpretation of the Concept of the Right to Internet Access from the Perspective of International Law' (2016) 15 Journal of Human Rights 140, 15053 (arguing that there is no international right to the Internet and that to say there is would damage the authoritative value of international law).

[343] A Manji, 'Eliminating Poverty—Financial Inclusion, Access to Land, and Gender Equality in International Development' (2010) 73 Modern Law Review 985, 992–93.

[344] Johnson (n 339).

[345] ibid.

COMMENTARIES OF TARGETS   91

One of the main sources of global data on use[346] of financial services is the World Bank's 'Global Findex' project. According to Global Findex, 2 billion adults were 'unbanked' in 2014. By 2017, accounts were created by over 500 million adults, raising the percentage of adults with a bank account to 69 per cent—a 7 per cent increase in just three years.[347] While industrialized economies still have significantly greater financial inclusion figures overall, the spread of mobile money accounts in the developing economies (particularly in Sub-Saharan Africa) has led to clear gains in access to low-cost, secure payments.[348] There are still inequalities, however. Wealth[349] and gender[350] gaps in account ownership have not narrowed significantly, and younger adults,[351] 'out of labour force' persons,[352] and those with low levels of education[353] are also disproportionately unbanked, particularly in countries where overall levels of banking are high.[354]

5. Implementation Efforts at the Domestic and International Levels

Efforts to achieving target 1.4 are largely coordinated by UN-Habitat and the World Bank, whose basic tasks are closely related to the target's aims. Progress on the issues of land tenure on the official level is slow (only seven countries submitted information about land targets in the 2020 National Voluntary Reports),[355] but there are numerous programmes and projects ongoing. Such efforts are both on the level of project work in countries and on the conceptual level, where internationally applicable methodologies are being developed to support reporting on the indicators.

Much work on target 1.4 is centred on improving the conditions of urban poverty. In 2016, the Habitat III Conference concluded a document called the New Urban Agenda,[356] in which the Member States committed themselves to working to achieve the spectrum of issues contained in target 1.4. The Agenda's 'shared vision' for urban areas ('cities and human settlements') is particularly notable for its human rights perspective, even promoting a 'right to the city':

---

[346] The World Bank explains that use of financial services is easier to track than is access, but that policy-makers are generally not concerned with those non-users who have access to services. World Bank, Financial Access (<https://www.worldbank.org/en/publication/gfdr/gfdr-2016/background/financial-access> accessed 11 March 2023).

[347] A Demirgüç-Kunt and others, *The Global Findex Database 2017: Measuring Financial Inclusion and the Fintech Revolution* (World Bank Group 2018) 2.

[348] ibid.

[349] Half of the world's unbanked adults are in the poorest 40 per cent of the population, with 27 per cent living in the poorest 20 per cent. ibid 36.

[350] Women compose 56 per cent of the global unbanked adult population. ibid.

[351] Thirty per cent of the unbanked are 15–24 year-olds. ibid 38.

[352] Persons without a job and who are not looking for work make up 47 per cent of the unbanked, although they are only 37 per cent of the adult population in developing countries. ibid.

[353] Sixty-two per cent of the unbanked have only a primary education. ibid.

[354] ibid 4.

[355] Land Portal Foundation reported that the Inter-agency Expert Group on Sustainable Development Goal Indicators attempted to drop target 1.4 in October 2015, but the Global Donor Working Group on Land convinced them to maintain it. In 2017, target indicator 1.4.2 was moved from Tier III to Tier II. Nevertheless, there were no mention of the aims of target 1.4 in the Secretary General's 2020 SDG Progress Report. UN Economic and Social Council, Progress towards the Sustainable Development Goals: Report of the Secretary-General, E/2020/57 (28 April 2020) paras 9–13

[356] Habitat III, *New Urban Agenda: Quito Declaration on Sustainable Cities and Human Settlements for All* (United Nations 2017) para 11.

92   SDG 1

11. We share a vision of cities for all, referring to the equal use and enjoyment of cities and human settlements, seeking to promote inclusivity and ensure that all inhabitants, of present and future generations, without discrimination of any kind, are able to inhabit and produce just, safe, healthy, accessible, affordable, resilient and sustainable cities and human settlements to foster prosperity and quality of life for all. We note the efforts of some national and local governments to enshrine this vision, referred to as 'right to the city', in their legislation, political declarations and charters.

12. We aim to achieve cities and human settlements where all persons are able to enjoy equal rights and opportunities, as well as their fundamental freedoms, guided by the purposes and principles of the Charter of the United Nations, including full respect for international law. In this regard, the New Urban Agenda is grounded in the Universal Declaration of Human Rights [and] international human rights treaties ....[357]

The Agenda also includes principles that tailor closely to the SDGs and target 1.4 in particular:

14. To achieve our vision, we resolve to adopt a New Urban Agenda guided by the following interlinked principles:

(a) Leave no one behind, by ending poverty in all its forms and dimensions, including the eradication of extreme poverty, by ensuring equal rights and opportunities ... by promoting safety and eliminating discrimination ... and by providing equal access for all to physical and social infrastructure and basic services, as well as adequate and affordable housing;

(b) Ensure sustainable and inclusive urban economies by ... promoting secure land tenure ....[358]

Most importantly, the members take 'commitments' reflecting the content of the poverty reduction target, but set out from a human right perspective:

26. We commit ourselves to urban and rural development that is people-centred, protects the planet, and is age- and gender-responsive and to the realization of all human rights and fundamental freedoms, ...

27. We reaffirm our pledge that no one will be left behind and commit ourselves to promoting equally the shared opportunities and benefits that urbanization can offer ....

34. We commit ourselves to promoting equitable and affordable access to sustainable basic physical and social infrastructure for all, without discrimination, including affordable serviced land, housing, modern and renewable energy, safe drinking water and sanitation, safe, nutritious and adequate food, waste disposal, sustainable mobility,

---

[357] ibid paras 11–12.
[358] ibid para 14.

COMMENTARIES OF TARGETS   93

health care and family planning, education, culture, and information and communications technologies. We further commit ourselves to ensuring that these services are responsive to the rights and needs of women, children and youth, older persons and persons with disabilities, migrants, indigenous peoples and local communities, as appropriate, and to those of others in vulnerable situations.[359]

Another major focus of efforts to achieve target 1.4 is on developing legal or quasi-legal security of tenure. This is occurring conceptually[360] and experientially, through the development of tools to ease registration and enforcement of land rights. For the latter, UN-Habitat has developed a Global Land Tool Network (GLTN) with a number of types of tools that encompass legal measures but also administrative practices, planning, and financing.[361] The GLTN's Access to Land and Tenure Security tool illustrates the network's aim to be flexible and adaptable. It emphasizes the 'spectrum' of possible arrangements that can increase the security of tenure. Where formally documented registration is one possibility, customary tenure, collective land use rights, or rights to access natural resource on a territory are all alternative possibilities that may provide equal benefits for the individuals.[362]

One GLTN-sponsored project[363] was Namibia's Flexible Land Tenure Act, which creates 'starter title rights' to be 'alternative forms of land title that are simpler and cheaper to administer than existing forms' so as 'to provide security of title for persons who live in informal settlements or who are provided with low income housing' and thereby 'empower the persons concerned economically'.[364] Other projects include the development of a blockchain platform for land registration in informal urban settlements in Afghanistan[365] and collaboration on a guidance tool for monitoring and analysing data relating to women's land rights.[366]

Beyond the New Urban Agenda, UN-Habitat sponsors country programmes focused on sustainable urban development and urban resilience, particularly in connection

---

[359] ibid paras 26–27, 34.

[360] ibid para 35. As progressive as the Agenda appears, it is notable that for land tenure in particular, its 'promotion' wording is less ambitious than its 1996 predecessor, in which the states committed to 'providing legal security of tenure and equal access to land to all people, including women and those living in poverty.' United Nations Conference on Human Settlements (Habitat II), 'Istanbul Declaration on Human Settlements', A/CONF.165/14, Annex I, para 40(b) (7 August 1996). See A Layard, 'Researching Urban Law' (2020) 21 German Law Journal 1446, 1459. An interesting aspect of the Agenda is its placement of implementation responsibility on local governments. K Gomes da Silva, 'The New Urban Agenda and Human Rights Cities: Interconnections between the Global and the Local' (2018) 36(4) Netherlands Human Rights Quarterly 290 (2018).

[361] UN-Habitat, Land Tools (<https://unhabitat.org/topic/land>; 3 July 2021).

[362] <http://gltn.net/access-to-land-and-tenure-security/> accessed 11 March 2023.

[363] ibid.

[364] Namibia, Flexible Land Tenure Act 4 of 2012, art 2. See also Regulations Made in Terms of Flexible Land Tenure Act 4 of 2012 (2018).

[365] <https://unhabitat.org/news/02-dec-2020/un-habitat-oict-and-lto-network-release-first-open-source-urban-land-registry> accessed 11 March 2023.

[366] GLTN, UN-Habitat, and UNWOMEN, Getting It Right From Planning to Reporting: A Guidance Tool for Women's Land Rights Data and Statistics (May 2021) (<https://gltn.net/download/getting-it-right-from-planning-to-reporting-a-guidance-tool-for-womens-land-rights-data-and-statistics/?wpdmdl=17165&refresh=60e02d77492931625304439> accessed 11 March 2023).

with climate change.[367] Within its five flagship programmes, for example, social inclusion, improved access to basic services, digital transformation, climate resiliency, and (significantly) performance assessment are highlighted.[368]

Financial inclusion is another area of rapid development. Microfinance—both in banking and insurance, has been joined by digital finance as programme areas for a wide variety of actors, both public and private.[369]

6. Critique

As a profile-raising tool, target 1.4 is hugely important. If acted upon, it promises to improve the lives of hundreds of millions of poor and vulnerable people, urban and rural, living in industrialized as well as developing and least-developed economies. The indicator's relevance to development can hardly be questioned. Land tenure and property rights have been studied for decades in the context of pro-poor policy-making, both in rural and more recently in urban settings.[370] The importance of groups such as indigenous peoples to have access to natural resources is essential for their ability to remain out of poverty and to continue living with their culture intact. The importance of access to services and technology has also been solidly confirmed, as has the potentially life-changing character of accessible financing for low-income individuals and households.

Moreover, general human rights principles are detectable in the text of target 1.4.[371] Its call for ensuring basic services caters to the values of dignity, agency, and autonomy; the call for equal rights of access to such services and to property rights underscores the principle of non-discrimination. The target could even strengthen the development of new rights—rights to access to the Internet and a right to payment services,[372] for example—which could assist in sustaining the income potential of low-income individuals. Recognition of rights to access natural resources, too, may be particularly beneficial for indigenous peoples, many of whom fall under national poverty lines in the states in which they reside.

---

[367] See UN-Habitat, SDG Project Assessment Tool Vol. 1: General Framework, Bibliography (September 2020).

[368] See UN-Habitat, 'Five flagship programmes for a decade of action on the sustainable development goals' (<https://unhabitat.org/programmes> accessed 12 July 2021) (providing links to the programmes: Inclusive, Vibrant Neighbourhoods and Communities; People-Centered Smart Cities; RISE-UP: Resilient Settlements for the Urban Poor; Inclusive cities: Enhancing the positive impacts of urban migration; Sustainable Development Goals Cities).

[369] The Global Partnership for Financial Inclusion, for example, is a collaborative effort between G-20 countries, 'interested non-G20 countries' and a number of partners, such as the World Bank, the International Finance Corporation, the Consultative Group to Assist the Poor, Better than Cash Alliance, and the International Fund for Agricultural Development. GPFI. About GPFI (<https://www.gpfi.org/about-gpfi> accessed 11 March 2023).

[370] G Payne and others, 'Land Tenure and Property Rights: An Introduction' (2004) 28 Habitat International 167.

[371] See UNOCHR, *Guiding Principles on Extreme Poverty and Human Rights* (United Nations 2012) 5–11 (defining 'foundational principles' of human rights).

[372] The European Union grants a right to payment services for all legal residents. Directive 2014/92/EU of the European Parliament and of the Council of 23 July 2014 on the comparability of fees related to payment accounts, payment account switching and access to payment accounts with basic features Text with EEA relevance (23 July 2014). Switzerland's Supreme Court has also declared that the federal postal service has an obligation (with few limitations) to conclude a contract for payment services with every resident. Decision 4A_417/2009 (26 March 2010).

COMMENTARIES OF TARGETS 95

That said, target 1.4 not only avoids the language of rights; it undercuts some basic existing human rights obligations. An egregious example is that the non-discriminatory aspect of access to economic resources does not apply to access to basic services. This is particularly disturbing given the clearly politically motivated refusal to extend equal inheritance rights to women.[373]

Another weakness is that the target addresses such a multitude of loosely related issues that it appears to be more a desperate political compromise than the product of systematic analysis. That the accepted legal status of the issues mentioned is not comparable[374] opens the door to dismissing all the issues as wishes. At the same time, like the World Bank, whose interests are directly reflected, target 1.4 fails to add language to protect against the potential dangers of financialization—questions of how to deal with indebtedness and forfeiture, for example, are simply omitted.[375]

On the other hand, target 1.4 is also largely duplicative of the other goals' targets. This is true, *inter alia*, for secure rural land tenure and financial services (target 2.3); ensuring access to basic healthcare (target 3.8); ensuring access to primary education (target 4.1); ensure non-discrimination of women (SDG 5 as a whole); securing access to drinking water and sanitation, including special attention to women and girls (targets 6.1, 6.2); ensuring access to energy (target 7.1); ensure access to financial resources and credit (target 9.3); increase access to the Internet (target 9.c); and ensuring equal opportunities and non-discrimination (targets 10.2 and 10.3). The target, therefore, serves solely to highlight that these questions are poverty-relevant, but given that the SDGs are a poverty-motivated agenda, this arguably offers no real added value.

Even the combination of above-mentioned items would not detract from its existence if those were target 1.4's only weaknesses. The target, however, has other flaws. One is that 1.4 is far too ambitious to be an 'action-oriented and measurable' target as the OWG delegates wanted.[376] This is not just about the 2030 deadline—which, for such a wide-ranging target that will require numerous changes of national laws as well as implicating infrastructure projects, was foreseeably impossible even in 2014. Equally serious is that just the measurability of progress on the target will also require 'strong effort' by governments who must consider what specific data to collect and how to do so.[377]

Most problematic is that target 1.4 focuses solely on 'access'. Such a limited demand fails to recognize that for access to resources and services to be valuable, it must be access to resources and services of *quality*.[378] The OWG recognized this early on, writing:

---

[373] See IISD, 32(13) Earth Negotiations Bulletin (22 July 2014) 5.

[374] For example, the legally accepted status of access to basic education is far more established than that of access to the Internet or to microfinance.

[375] Manji (n 343) 994.

[376] See IISD, Summary of the Twelfth Session of the UN General Assembly Open Working Group on Sustainable Development Goals: 16–20 June 2014, 32(12) Earth Negotiations Bulletin 19 (23 June 2014).

[377] UNSC, Technical report by the Bureau of the United Nations Statistical Commission on the process of the development of an indicator framework for the goals and targets of the post-2015 development agenda: Working draft, Annex 5 (March 2015).

[378] See A/HRC/43/43 (n 335) para 15 ('the right to adequate housing [is not] a right to mere physical shelter or to housing conceived as a commodity. Rather the right to housing must be understood in relation to the inherent dignity of the human person').

96   SDG 1

The poor suffer not only from lack of access to basic services but also very often from the poor quality of the services provided. [...] Thus, both access and quality of services available to the poor need to be addressed going forward.[379]

To define the quality of resources the government must ensure, a reasonable starting point would be 'adequacy', as required in human rights law. Extrapolating from the CESCR's General Comment 4 on the right to adequate housing,[380] one can extrapolate that rights to basic services, infrastructure, and financial inclusion would only be fulfilled if such services or infrastructure are *affordable*, even to the poorest individuals; that they are *accessible*, even to those who have limited means of traveling across a city, those who cannot take time during normal working hours to pursue financing possibilities, or those who cannot read or hear; that the resources are *appropriate* to the age, sex, and religion or belief system of the person seeking them; and that there is at least some *legal structure of protection* of property rights. Each of the elements of the Committee's test are of utmost relevance to target 1.4's benefits for the poor, for access to inadequate or inappropriate resources and services will not lead to lasting poverty eradication.

E. Target 1.5 Build Resilience to Environmental, Economic, and Social Disasters

UN definition: By 2030, build the resilience of the poor and those in vulnerable situations and reduce their exposure and vulnerability to climate-related extreme events and other economic, social and environmental shocks and disasters.

1. SDG Indicator 1.5.1
a) Deaths and affected persons from natural disasters
Definition: Indicator 1.5.1 is the number of deaths, missing persons, and directly affected persons attributed to disasters.

2. Indicator 1.5.2
a) Direct economic loss from natural disasters
Definition: Indicator 1.5.2 is the direct economic loss attributed to disasters in relation to global gross domestic product (GDP).

---

[379] OWG, Interim Report, 12-42396, para 40 (late 2013; undated document received from governmental contact). It continued in the next paragraph to call for better governance: 'With respect to provision of universal access, many stressed the importance of strengthening institutional capacities at all levels to deliver better targeted and higher quality services. This was frequently formulated in terms of the need to address weaknesses in governance.' ibid para 41.
[380] CESCR, General Comment No 4: the right to adequate housing (art 11(1) of the Covenant) (1991) para 8 (the Committee also includes location in its determination of adequacy).

3. Indicator 1.5.3
a) Disaster risk reduction strategies
Definition: Indicator 1.5.3 is the number of countries that adopt and implement national disaster risk reduction strategies in line with the *Sendai Framework* for Disaster Risk Reduction 2015–2030.

4. Indicator 1.5.4
a) Local disaster risk reduction
Definition: Indicator 1.5.4 is the proportion of local governments that adopt and implement local disaster risk reduction strategies in line with national disaster risk reduction strategies.

5. Sources of Target
Though not specified in the main text of the target, SDG target 1.5 is intended to ensure that UN members make progress on implementing the Sendai Framework for Disaster Risk Reduction as adopted by them in March 2015. The substantive overlap of the two programmes extends to the reporting, as each member's SDG reports for target 1.5 are to be submitted by its Sendai Framework Focal Point through the Framework's own Monitoring System.[381]

The need to address natural hazards and resilience in the SDGs was highlighted from the beginning of the discussions about how the post-2015 development programme should be conceptualized.[382] In 2012, the UN System Task Team produced a report, 'Disaster Risk and Resilience',[383] which urged the international community to give disaster risk reduction prominence in the new development goals. The System Task Team emphasized that the lack of a clear 'causal link' between disaster preparedness and economic development had prevented sufficient attention to be given to this dimension of development in the past,[384] but that actions taken by regions and individual states in the recent past had shown the connections,[385] and that the new discussions for global development goals should not ignore this critical issue.[386]

The work of experts strengthened the call for including environmental catastrophes and disasters in the post-2015 Agenda. A paper by the Overseas Development Institute's Tom Mitchell evaluated a number of concrete proposals for targets and indicators.[387] Mitchell's paper pointed out a number of considerations for framing the

---

[381] UN Statistics Wiki, Indicator 1.5.3 in E-Handbook on SDG Indicators (13 September 2018).
[382] The TST Issues Brief submitted to delegations prior to the beginning of the OWG sessions in 2013 proposed consideration of the environmental aspects of development in the form of negative goals (including the prevention of natural hazards) and positive goals (including the promotion of resilience). TST Issues Brief: Conceptual Issues (2013).
[383] UN System Task Team on post-2015 UN Development Agenda, Disaster Risk and Resilience (2012).
[384] ibid 7.
[385] ibid 8.
[386] ibid 3, 7–8.
[387] T Mitchell, Options for including disaster resilience in post-2015 development goals (September 2012) (<https://www.aecid.es/Centro-Documentacion/Documentos/Divulgaci%C3%B3n/Otros%20documentos. pdf#search=Mitchell%20options%20for%20including%20disaster%20relief> accessed 11 March 2023).

98   SDG 1

disaster/resilience goal, emphasizing that its connection with the overall values of the Agenda would be important. Thus, if poverty reduction were to be central, the indicators relevant to disaster prevention would be different than if sustainable development were the overriding goal.[388]

Soon after, the UN Technical Support Team (TST) published its Issues Brief on Climate Change and Natural Disasters.[389] That paper, written to inform the OWG directly of the contours of the problem, begins with a forceful call to take the matter of disaster seriously: 'Climate change and disaster risk are fundamental threats to sustainable development and the eradication of poverty.'[390]

In response to the OWG Co-Chairs' March 2014 Focus Area list, a number of members supported bringing a reference to natural disasters into the poverty eradication goal. Along with Australia, Canada, France, Germany, Israel, the Netherlands, Switzerland, the United Kingdom, and the United States, Ethiopia, Mexico, Montenegro, Peru, and Slovenia called for SDG 1 to ask countries to 'build resilience', some adding words about reducing economic loss, some about reducing deaths.[391] The United States (with Canada and Israel) called for the inclusion of 'man-made disasters'.[392]

The OWG sessions do not detail the discussions of the wording of target 1.5, although several delegations of differing economic status brought up the interwoven relationship between poverty and natural disasters as a central concern. Mexico and Peru, Costa Rica, and France (for Germany and Switzerland) all called again for natural disaster risk management or resilience in the OWG's April 2014 meeting.[393] In May 2014, several delegations repeated their call, joined, too, by Vietnam (for Bhutan and Thailand), which suggested broadening the focus to financial and social disasters.[394] India, on the other hand, reportedly called for disasters to be taken up under a different goal.[395] Discussions prior to the finalization of the text reportedly included references to even further issues—civil conflict and pollution were mentioned.[396] The final draft allowed the broad range of 'shocks and disasters', both natural and man-made.

The indicators on the Sendai Framework implementation arose through the work of the open-ended intergovernmental expert working group dedicated to this task.[397]

---

[388] ibid 2–3.

[389] TST Issues Brief: Climate Change and Natural Disasters (2013).

[390] ibid 1.

[391] See Encyclopedia Groupinica, p 6, footnotes 52–61 and accompanying text (2014).

[392] ibid.

[393] IISD, Summary of the tenth session of the UN General Assembly Open Working Group on Sustainable Development Goals: 31 March–4 April 2014, 32(10) Earth Negotiations Bulletin 4–5 (7 April 2014).

[394] IISD, Summary of the eleventh session of the UN General Assembly Open Working Group on Sustainable Development Goals: 5–9 May 2014, 32(11) Earth Negotiations Bulletin 4 (12 May 2014).

[395] ibid.

[396] IISD, Summary of the thirteenth session of the UN General Assembly Open Working Group on Sustainable Development Goals: 14–19 July 2014, 32(13) Earth Negotiations Bulletin 5 (22 July 2014).

[397] See A/RES/69/284 (establishing the working group).

COMMENTARIES OF TARGETS 99

These indicators were added only after the working group concluded its discussions, in 2016.[398]

Using the Sendai Framework's definition of 'disaster',[399] the working group's suggested targets were substantially pared down for target 1.5. Of particular note is the omission of disaggregation of data. This was recommended by the working group due to the realization that, while such data would be valuable in assessing risk reduction proposals, most countries do not have disaggregated information.[400]

6. Statistical/Empirical Analysis

Progress on target 1.5 is tracked by UNSTATS largely on the basis of the Sendai Framework for Disaster Risk Reduction 2015–2030. The Sendai Framework, described below, asks for data from member countries on seven of its own targets: (A) a substantial reduction of mortality due to disasters; (B) a substantial reduction in the number of persons affected by disasters; (C) a reduction in the economic loss from disasters, as measured by GDP; (D) a substantial reduction in damage to critical infrastructures and service supply; (E) an increase in the number of national and local governments with disaster risk reduction strategies; (F) a substantial increase in support to developing countries for implementation of the Sendai Framework; and (G) an increase in both early warning systems and information about disaster risks.[401] The direct connections between the Sendai Framework and SDG 1.5 are found in the targets A, B, C, and E,[402] the monitoring of which is complementary.

According to the latest (2018) Sendai Framework report, there was noticeable progress on a number of the targets, although reporting is not complete. The UNSTATS reports the following results on its SDG 1 information page:

> Based on the latest reporting under the Sendai Framework monitoring process from 80 countries in 2018, 23,458 deaths and 2,164 persons missing were attributed to disasters. Direct economic losses of $23.6 billion were reported by 63 countries, of

---

[398] United Nations General Assembly, 'Note by the Secretary-General: Report of the open-ended intergovernmental expert working group on indicators and terminology relating to disaster risk reduction', A/71/644 (1 December 2016). See also United Nations Statistical Commission, 'Update on the work to finalize the proposals for the global indicators for the Sustainable Development Goals: Prepared by the Inter-agency and Expert Group on Sustainable Development Goal Indicators', para 7 (February 2016).

[399] The Sendai Framework defines a disaster as '[a] serious disruption of the functioning of a community or a society at any scale due to hazardous events interacting with conditions of exposure, vulnerability and capacity, leading to one or more of the following: human, material, economic and environmental losses and impacts'. On the terminology of natural hazards, disasters, and extreme events see S Banholzer and others, 'The Impact of Climate Change on Natural Disasters' in Z Zommers and A Singh (eds), *Reducing Disaster: Early Warning Systems for Climate Change* (Springer Science + Business Media, 2014) 26–27 (<https://www.ssec.wisc.edu/~kossin/articles/Chapter_2.pdf>).

[400] A/71/644, para 23. See also Technical report by the Bureau of the United Nations Statistical Commission, Annex 5 (rating a proposed indicator of 'Number of persons affected by hazardous events by sex' as CBB—the 'C' indicating that feasibility would be 'difficult, even with strong effort').

[401] See Sendai Framework for Disaster Risk Reduction 2015–2030 (adopted 18 March 2015) (<https://www.preventionweb.net/files/43291_sendaiframeworkfordrren.pdf> accessed 11 March 2023).

[402] UNDRR, The Sendai Framework and the SDGs (<https://www.undrr.org/implementing-sendai-framework/sf-and-sdgs> accessed 28 March 2021).

which 73 per cent ($17.1 billion) were recorded in the agricultural sector and 16 per cent ($3.8 billion) in the housing sector.[403]

The reported numbers on Sendai Framework Target A (global disaster mortality) indicated that the 2018 figure was significantly lower than the number in 2017, although this varied by region.[404] Other sources[405] indicate an increase in deaths in each of the years from 2017 to 2019. While the variation between the sets of numbers may be due to different definitions of 'disaster', the gross numbers are not overly important. Differences in the number of events make large differences in the total number of deaths, so the focus of disaster mortality reduction efforts is better set on multi-year trends.

That said, measuring progress on risk reduction does need a basis in data. A sombre note is revealed by the findings of the Snapshot of Reporting for 2018.[406] This document, focusing on the reporting by states, rather than on the figures in the reports, admits that Member States are challenged to collect and submit the data requested by the Framework and its targets. The 'data architecture', the introduction notes,

> includes clearly articulated methods, well-defined processes for data management and quality control, a designated custodian for each indicator or sub-indicator, well-established channels of communication across different government ministries and institutions and an agreed-on timeline for data collection, reporting and aggregation. Not all Member States have the entirety of the necessary architecture in place for collecting disaster-related data.[407]

The existing difficulties in data collection lead to an incomplete dataset on the individual targets of the Sendai Framework.

Equally serious is that the Snapshot of Reporting shows a drop in the number of reporting states between 2017 and 2018. This drop is both in the number of states that started reporting on the targets (from forty-seven in 2017 to twenty-five in 2018) and in those that had validated the results of the targets (from nineteen members validating all targets in 2017 to fourteen having validated all targets in 2018). Moreover, with two exceptions, there were fewer states reporting on each of the sub-indicators in 2018 than in the previous year.[408]

The absence of reports from certain groups of states is particularly problematic from the viewpoint of poverty reduction. A bare 51 per cent of LDCs reported on their disaster risk reduction targets and only 21 per cent of the small island developing states

---

[403] <https://unstats.un.org/sdgs/report/2020/goal-01/> accessed 28 March 2021.

[404] See UNDRR, 'Monitoring the Implementation of Sendai Framework for Disaster Risk Reduction 2015–2030: A Snapshot of Reporting for 2018' (UN 2020) Figure 7, p 13 (the figure, in the form of a bar graph, does not give exact numbers).

[405] Our World in Data is one such source of information. See H Ritchie and M Roser, 'Natural Disasters' (2014, updated 2019). Published online at OurWorldInData.org. <https://ourworldindata.org/natural-disasters> accessed 28 March 2021.

[406] 'Snapshot of Reporting for 2018' (n 404).

[407] ibid 7.

[408] The two exceptions were on targets D5 and E2.

did so.[409] With particularly vulnerable populations (the LDCs because of the low level of resources available and the small island developing states (SIDS) because of their high level of risk due to climate change), these countries' data would be of great importance to accurate measurement of progress in risk reduction on a global scale.

Gaps in the datasets of the Sendai Framework include those in the relevant statistics for progress on SDG 1.5.[410] As a result, it is hard to know precisely what the status of target 1.5 is.

What the UN data reveal is that LDCs continue to suffer the most from natural disasters. The losses of life in LDCs are disproportionate to such losses reported by industrialized states: per million persons living in disaster-affected areas, in low-income countries 130 people died, while in high-income countries only 18 died.[411] The economic losses measured by GDP, on the other hand, were heavily counted in high-income countries, although losses as a percentage of GDP again tilts the disadvantages to low-income countries.[412] The global inequality in disaster impacts remains disfavourable to LDCs even though World Bank data on, for example, displacement of persons due to disaster for high income countries increased by 20 per cent from 2015 to 2017 while it dropped by 31 per cent for LDCs over the same time period.[413]

More promising is the relatively high level of reports submitted on the adoption and implementation of national and local risk reduction strategies. In terms of national risk reduction strategies, between 2015 and 2019, eighty countries (41 per cent) reported having a strategy in place that is aligned with the Sendai Framework's requirements to at least some extent, and eight of them reported full alignment.[414] The number of countries reporting on at least some alignment of local disaster strategies with the Sendai Framework was forty-three.[415]

7. Implementation Efforts at the Domestic and International Levels

Although natural resource destruction and depletion are both effects of and drivers of poverty,[416] the MDGs had not addressed the topic of disasters; this, despite the fact that disaster relief and disaster prevention had long been a matter of international concern.

Extreme events and natural disasters have been a topic for the international community for over a century.[417] Early international attention to disasters formed in the

---

[409] 'Snapshot of Reporting for 2018' (n 404) 9.

[410] Of the three target 1.5 indicators, only 1.5.1 is a Tier I indicator, indicating that for 1.5.2 and 1.5.3, there is a lack of reported data. That said, the Secretary-General's 2021 report only indicated submitted reports for indicator 1.5.3. High-level political forum on sustainable development, 'Progress towards the Sustainable Development Goals: Report of the Secretary General, Supplementary Information' E/2021/58 11.

[411] Centre for Research on the Epidemiology of Disasters and United Nations Office for Disaster Risk Reduction, *Economic Losses, Poverty & Disasters 1998–2017* (2018) 20.

[412] ibid 17, 22.

[413] See Our World in Data (<https://ourworldindata.org/grapher/internally-displaced-persons-from-disasters?tab=table> accessed 11 March 2023).

[414] 'Snapshot of Reporting for 2018' (n 404) 23.

[415] ibid.

[416] See OWA, 'Summary—Second Session of the OWG on SDGs, 1719 April 2013', p 12 (describing discussion of the panel moderated by E Jesperson).

[417] See generally, A de Urioste, 'When Will Help Be on the Way—The Status of International Disaster Response Law' (2006) 15 Tulane Journal of International and Comparative Law 181, 183–86.

102 SDG 1

nineteenth century, when the Second Conference of the International Red Cross (IRC) (1869) called for an expansion of its humanitarian work to any 'public calamity which, like war, demands immediate and organized assistance'.[418] Shortly afterwards, the Third IRC Conference (1884) added natural disasters to its programme of relief efforts.[419] The Red Cross continued to be the main international actor in disaster relief coordination throughout the early twentieth century, including leading the move to conclude the Convention for the Establishment of an International Relief Union.[420] Yet, despite some valuable research, the International Relief Union did not contribute substantially to the advancement of coordinated disaster relief.

Following a number of severe earthquakes, the international community took its first main step forward in disaster relief coordination.[421] In 1971, UN General Assembly Resolution 2816 (XXIV) created the Office of the Disaster Relief Co-ordinator (UNDRO).[422] The Co-ordinator was to report directly to the Secretary-General and was delegated the authority to create cooperative arrangements and to coordinate with other UN organizations, the Red Cross Societies, and relevant governments in the area of disaster assistance and relief work.[423] The Office itself was mainly established to coordinate the international response to natural disasters, but also worked to improve pre-disaster planning.[424] UN Member State governments were encouraged (the Resolution 'invites' Member States) to establish contingency plans to ensure the necessary legislation and procedures, emergency stockpiles, and training programmes would be in place in case of disaster.[425] No less important, the Resolution encouraged governments to improve warning systems.[426] Finally, Resolution 2816 called on potential donors to inform the Office of the extent of their willingness to contribute to relief efforts.[427]

The work of UNDRO was valuable but limited due to its reliance on governments to request its help.[428] Further efforts were needed to highlight the importance of disaster relief and prevention.

---

[418] ibid 183 (citing International Federation of Red Cross and Red Crescent Societies, *World Disasters Report 2000* (IFRC 2000) 149).

[419] ibid.

[420] ibid 184. See Convention Establishing an International Relief Union, 12 July 1927.

[421] Four earthquakes with high fatalities (Morocco—13,100; Chile—3,000; Yugoslavia—1,000; and Peru—67,000) as well as a cyclone in Bangladesh (300,000) occurred between 1960 and 1970, as did numerous less fatal but high loss storms in the United States, Japan, and Germany. See G Berz, 'List of Major Natural Disasters, 1960–1987' (1988) 1 Natural Hazards 97–99.

[422] UN General Assembly Resolution 2816 (XXVI) of 14 December 1971, Assistance in cases of natural disasters and other disaster situations.

[423] ibid para 1.

[424] I Lütem, 'The United Nations Disaster Relief Coordinator (UNDRO)' (1985) 1 Journal of the World Association for Emergency and Disaster Medicine supplement 1, 301–03, 301 (<https://core.ac.uk/download/pdf/85213757.pdf; 28 March 2021).

[425] UN General Assembly Resolution 2816 (XXVI) (n 422) para 8.

[426] ibid para 8(f).

[427] ibid para 9.

[428] For example, S Jiang, 'International Disaster Response Law and Policy in China: Evolution, Problem and Resolution' (2013) 12 Chinese Journal of International Law 455 (explaining the reluctance of the Chinese governments to accept foreign assistance in the face of natural disasters from 1949 through 1986); Lütem (n 424) 302–03 (noting the 'reluctance' of some governments in requesting assistance from the UNDRO).

COMMENTARIES OF TARGETS   103

The result of a concentrated move to generate attention was the United Nations' designation of the 1990s as the International Decade for Natural Disaster Reduction.[429] The objective of the designation was clearly oriented toward reducing damage through coordinated international action:

> The objective of the International Decade for Natural Disaster Reduction is to reduce through concentrated international action, especially in developing countries, the loss of life, property damage and social and economic disruption caused by natural disasters such as earthquakes, windstorms, tsunamis, floods, landslides, volcanic eruptions, wildfires, grasshopper and locust infestations, drought and desertification and other calamities of natural origin.[430]

Attention was to be particularly paid to generating and spreading information on disaster preparedness and prevention and damage mitigation.[431]

Then, in 1991, the General Assembly passed Resolution 46/182, creating a 'blueprint' for a unified humanitarian system in the UN.[432] Called a 'pivotal revolution' by the United Nations itself,[433] this resolution ultimately led to the creation of the Office for the Coordination of Humanitarian Affairs (OCHA) and its incorporation of UNDRO.[434] A notable aspect of the Annex to Resolution 46/182 is its explicit discussion of sustainable development. In paragraph 10, the Annex puts forth as a General Principle, the following:

> Economic growth and sustainable development are essential for prevention of and preparedness against natural disasters and other emergencies. Many emergencies reflect the underlying crisis in development facing developing countries.[435]

Prior to the MDGs, the problematic effects of natural disasters on global stability was emphasized in a United Nations World Conference on Natural Disaster Reduction held in Yokohama, Japan. The 1994 Conference resulted in the Yokohama Strategy for a Safer World: Guidelines for Natural Disaster Prevention, Preparedness and Mitigation. The Yokohama Strategy was not directly addressed in the MDGs, but parallel to them international disaster response management was being solidified.

A decade later, the World Conference on Disaster Reduction in Hyogo, Japan took a first step toward a reorientation in the thinking about disasters. The resulting Hyogo Framework for Action 2005–2015: Building the Resilience of Nations and Communities

---

[429] See General Assembly Resolution 44/236 from December 1989.
[430] ibid Annex, para 1.
[431] ibid Annex, para 3.
[432] United Nations General Assembly Resolution 46/182, 'Strengthening of the coordination of humanitarian emergency assistance of the United Nations' (19 December 1991).
[433] OCHA, 'Resolution 46/182, which created the humanitarian system, turns twenty-five' (10 December 2016) (<https://www.unocha.org/story/resolution-46182-which-created-humanitarian-system-turns-twenty-five> accessed 28 March 2021).
[434] de Urioste (n 417) 186.
[435] UNGA Res. 46/182 (n 432), Annex.

104 SDG 1

to Disaster, as its full title reveals, emphasized the need for increased resilience to disasters rather than disaster relief. As defined by the United Nations, 'resilience' means the 'ability of a system, community or society exposed to hazards to resist, absorb, accommodate and recover from the effects of a hazard in a timely and efficient manner, including through the preservation and restoration of its essential basic structures and functions'.[436] Resilient communities, the Hyogo Framework suggests, attend to risk assessment and risk management, governance, and education, technology transfer, and capacity building, but also to cultural diversity and community participation.[437]

Having the capacity to withstand disaster became recognized and formed the basis for the Sendai Framework of 2015. The UN members adopted the Sendai Framework at the same time as they adopted the SDGs, all considered a part of the 2030 Agenda.[438] This allowed for a cohesive approach to poverty elimination and climate change resilience from the beginning. Members' subsequent actions within either framework are therefore aligned.[439]

8. Critique

Among the SDG 1 targets, target 1.5 is the one leaving the least room for fundamental objection. Indeed, with the text specifically pointing to reducing the impacts of climate change on the poor and vulnerable, target 1.5 has a clearer and more focused framework than the other targets—and one that had already been thoroughly discussed in another multistakeholder forum and then applied to the poverty focus of SDG 1.

Critiques of target 1.5, then, largely track those of the Sendai Framework. One analysis of weaknesses in the Sendai Framework points to its confusing conglomeration of goals (preventing or reducing risk) and outcomes (reducing vulnerability and strengthening resilience); to its weak integration of the specific problems of disaster risk in conflict/low-security contexts; to the failure to address the problems of weak governance and fragile states; and the low level of accountability.[440] The measurement of disasters also undervalues small-scale disasters, which reportedly cause nearly 70 per cent of the economic losses, a large portion of which are born by vulnerable households.[441] Like the rest of the targets, the Sendai Framework (and therefore target 1.5) also omits a firm tie-in with the framework of human rights.[442]

Moreover, when looking at target 1.5 indicators—which were largely taken from the Sendai Framework—one could dispute the focus of the indicators on poverty reduction. While lives lost, lives affected, and economic losses are each factors that certainly can affect the poor, they do not only affect the poor. In fact, the use of economic losses

---

[436] UNSIDR, *Terminology on Disaster Risk Reduction* (United Nations 2009) 20.

[437] L Zhou and others, 'The Implication of Hyogo Framework for Action for Disaster Resilience Education' (2014) 18 Oricedua Economics and Finance 576, 578.

[438] UNDRR, 'What is the Sendai Framework for Disaster Risk Reduction?' (<https://www.undrr.org/implementing-sendai-framework/what-sendai-framework> accessed 11 March 2023).

[439] ibid.

[440] M Oxley, *Review of the Sendai Framework for Disaster Risk Reduction 2015–2030* (GNDR 2015).

[441] PreventionWeb, Disaster Losses and Statistics (2021) (<https://www.preventionweb.net/disaster-risk/disaster-losses> accessed 4 July 2021).

[442] Oxley (n 440).

as an indicator could be seen as devaluing low-income regions affected by disasters, as economic losses of industrialized countries tend to vastly exceed those of developing countries in the event of a disaster.[443]

An overriding assessment of target 1.5, however, is that it is offers a welcome and valuable reminder of how climate change threatens the most vulnerable. With the effects of climate change most dramatically demonstrated by the increasing intensity and frequency of extreme temperatures and high-precipitation events, shifts in the patterns of hurricanes, fires, droughts, and floods regionally, and uncertainties in weather predictions,[444] calling attention to the costs of disaster may be the most effective way to channel action on it.

As the international community can expect more extreme natural events as the climate continues to warm,[445] responding to climate change needs to be a motivating force behind the SDGs. The link between Earth's changing physical conditions to the goal of poverty reduction is integral to overall sustainable development and the effects of climate change, 'superimposed on existing vulnerabilities',[446] are going to make achieving the eradication of poverty more difficult. Target 1.5 is therefore a critical element of the larger climate change-sustainable development matrix. It is directed at both establishing a foundational data pool and at moving governments toward proactively responding to the challenges climate change poses to both eliminating poverty and to keeping impoverished communities at the centre of sustainable development efforts.

Of course, climate change does not only threaten ecosystem health and neither are 'natural' catastrophes the only focus of target 1.5. The broad definition of 'disaster' relied upon in the Sendai Framework makes this clear, and it is in light of epidemics and pandemics that the value states place on implementing measures under target 1.5 will become apparent in the near future.

F. Target 1.a Mobilization of resources to end poverty

UN definition: Ensure significant mobilization of resources from a variety of sources, including through enhanced development cooperation, in order to provide adequate and predictable means for developing countries, in particular least developed countries, to implement programmes and policies to end poverty in all its dimensions.

---

[443] See PreventionWeb, 'Disaster Losses and Statistics' (2021) (<https://www.preventionweb.net/disaster-risk/disaster-losses>); UNDRR, UCLouvain, CRED, and USAID, *2020: The Non-COVID Year in Disasters* (2020) (Executive Summary and Figure 7).

[444] The 2012 report by the Intergovernmental Panel on Climate Change drew the causal link between climate change and extreme climatic events. IPCC, 'Summary for Policymakers' in CB Field and others (eds), *Managing the Risks of Extreme Events and Disasters to Advance Climate Change Adaptation: A Special Report of Working Groups I and II of the Intergovernmental Panel on Climate Change (IPCC)* (CUP 2012) 3–21.

[445] ibid.

[446] L Qian-Qian and others, 'Poverty Reduction within the Framework of SDGs and Post-2015 Development Agenda' (2015) 6 Advances in Climate Change Research i 67, 68 (referring to both the IPCC and the OECD).

106 SDG 1

1. SDG Indicator 1.a.1

a) Domestic resources to poverty reduction programmes

Definition: Indicator 1.a.1 is the proportion of domestically generated resources allocated by the government directly to poverty reduction programmes (PROPOSED FOR DELETION).

2. Indicator 1.a.2

a) Government spending on essential services

Definition: Indicator 1.a.2 is the proportion of total government spending on essential services (education, health and social protection).

3. Indicator 1.a.3

a) Inflows directly allocated to poverty reduction programmes

Definition: Indicator 1.a.3 is the sum of total grants and non-debt-creating inflows directly allocated to poverty reduction programmes as a proportion of GDP.

4. Sources of Target

The amount of funding dedicated to poverty reduction attracted a great deal of attention during the OWG sessions. The first of the 'means of implementation' (MOI) targets for SDG 1, target 1.a. tackles the obvious problem of the need for finances to end poverty and the particular problem of developing and least developed countries' inability to rely on their own funds to achieve the hoped-for eradication of poverty. Using the language of 'a variety of sources', the target takes up the developing/least developed countries' calls in the OWG for poverty eradication to be mainly financed by wealth transfers from high-income to low-income countries while also accepting the views that called for national governments to bear the responsibility for prioritizing poverty reduction through their public spending programmes.

Following on from long-standing debates over the role of foreign aid in combatting extreme poverty, the OWG debates on target 1.a reflected two separate questions. One was the general issue of whether MOIs should be included in each SDG.[447] This was a matter discussed throughout the OWG sessions and across goals up until the July 2014 meeting.[448]

The second was a division between those who wanted the SDGs to demand that high-income states dedicate more of their wealth to helping raise standards of living in the developing and least-developed economies and those who felt that governments should be held more accountable to spending resources on ensuring a domestic

---

[447] The European Union, for example, objected to dividing discussion of the MOI into each separate goal. See IISD, 32(10) Newsletter summary 3 (April 2014). Others were reportedly convinced that MOIs need to be listed for the individual goals, as the experience of MDG 8 showed that a single goal for financing was ineffective. IISD, 32(12) Newsletter summary 15 (June 2014).

[448] For example, 32(13) Newsletter summary 5 (July 2014) (reporting that '[m]any [delegates] called for moving the two MOI targets 1.a (development cooperation) and 1.b (sound policy frameworks) to Goal 17 (MOI)').

COMMENTARIES OF TARGETS   107

framework that pointedly focusses on poverty relief and poverty reduction. For SDG 1, the implications of this second issue were more important.

The March 2014 OWG session set the stage for the target 1.a discussions. On the second day of the session, a joint meeting with the Intergovernmental Committee of Experts on Financing for Sustainable Development (ICESDF) gave delegates the opportunity to hear what experts considered necessary for the implementation of the SDGs.[449] The ICESDF representatives indicated a desire to move away from looking at poverty reduction as mainly one of increased levels of ODA, defined generally as governmental flows of grants and concessional loans to promote the welfare of the recipient country,[450] and toward one of looking for multiple sources of financing overseen by the OECD's Development Assistance Committee (DAC). As set out in a report of the meeting, one ICESDF expert said that '[a]ll options for financing must be explored, as every option has a role'.[451] This includes ODA but also 'domestic resource mobilization' and private funds.[452]

Not all OWG members agreed. Bolivia, speaking on behalf of the Group of 77, and Benin, voicing the concerns of the LDCs, led the push to ensure that the SDG idea of 'universality' did not come at the cost of preferential treatment for those countries that needed more assistance. Their reactions to the post-OWG 9 Focus Area document heavily emphasized the MOI aspects of poverty eradication, calling for increased levels of predictable development assistance, a 'renewed and strengthened global partnership for development',[453] and debt relief.[454] Calls also included ones for reform of the international development banks and financial institutions to enhance the voice of developing countries within them and to ensure access to necessary finances, as well as a wish to improve the effective regulation of financial markets.[455] Tunisia made a special call for relaxing restrictions of migration to provide persons to move across borders 'regardless of their qualification'.[456] None of these made it into the target.

The final targets on SDG 1 need to be read in view of the United Nations' Addis Ababa Financing for Development (FFD) conference results from July 2015. While target 1.a (and target 1.b) leaves out much detail, the details are found in the AAAA. That document sets out the UN members' goals of pursuing 'sustainable development in the spirit of global partnership and solidarity', including a goal of ending poverty.[457] The AAAA then emphasizes domestic spending for sustainable development[458] before

---

[449] IISD, 32(9) Summary 8 (9 March 2014) (describing meeting of).

[450] See OECD, 'Official Development Assistance (ODA): What is ODA?' (April 2021) (<https://www.oecd.org/dac/financing-sustainable-development/development-finance-standards/What-is-ODA.pdf> accessed 11 March 2023).

[451] ibid 9 (reporting on the comments of R Ray).

[452] ibid.

[453] Encyclopedia Groupinica, p 10, footnote 109 and accompanying text.

[454] ibid footnote 111 and accompanying text.

[455] ibid footnotes 110 and 112 and accompanying text.

[456] ibid 11 footnote 117 and accompanying text.

[457] UNGA, Addis Ababa Action Agenda of the Third International Conference on Financing for Development (Addis Ababa Action Agenda), A/RES/69/313, Annex para 1 (adopted 27 July 2015).

[458] The AAAA lists five 'action areas'. Action area A is 'Domestic public resources'. A/RES/69/313, Annex paras 20–34.

108 SDG 1

discussing financial partnerships with the private sector.[459] The question of ODA and other foreign aid is third.[460]

5. Statistical/Empirical Analysis

The agencies responsible for compiling the data on target 1.a are the Institute for Statistics (UIS) of the United Nations Educational, Scientific and Cultural Organization (UNESCO) and the OECD. While the UIS focusses on Indicator 1.a.2's call for domestic resources dedicated to essential services (defined as education, health, and social protection), the OECD collects statistics on foreign development assistance.[461]

For domestic spending data, the UIS partners with the World Bank, the World Health Organization (WHO), and the ILO. The World Bank puts together consolidated data on education expenditures, while the WHO tracks health spending by governments, and the ILO has data on social spending excluding health.[462]

Research indicates varying amounts spent by governments on essential services but no significant increases per sector overall. Global averages in the health sector have remained quite constant over time (6 per cent GDP spent on health each year since 2001),[463] and in education, while the average is more variable, post-2015 figures indicate a drop in spending as a percentage of GDP (4.02 per cent in 2001, 4.66 per cent in 2009, 4.2 per cent in 2012, 4.62 per cent in 2015, and 4.53 in 2017).[464]

Overall, spending tends to increase with the economic strength of the economy.[465] Country-specific spending, however, is highly individualized and generalizations can give a distorted view. First, spending by some developing countries on education is much higher than the average (Cuba with 12.8 and Sierra Leone with 7.7, for example, far outspend the United States' 5.0 in education as a percentage of GDP).[466] Second, spending progressions are not always linear, varying from year to year. The WHO's Global Health Expenditure Database (latest figures are from 2018) reveals, for example, that Afghanistan's governmental health spending dropped by 0.7 per cent between 2015 (10.11 per cent) and 2018 (9.4 per cent), with a peak of 11.78 per cent in 2017, while that of the Bahamas increased over 1.5 per cent between 2015 (5.21 per cent)

---

[459] AAAA Action area B is 'Domestic and international private business and finance' (paras 35–49).

[460] AAAA Action area C is 'International development cooperation' (paras 50–78). Further action area subjects include trade (D), debt (E), systemic issues (F), and science, technology, and capacity building (G). ibid paras 79–124.

[461] Indicator 1.a.1 is proposed for deletion. E/CN.3/2020/2, Annex II, D.

[462] H Kharas and J McArthur, 'Building the SDG Economy: Needs, spending, and financing for universal achievement of the Sustainable Development Goals', Global Economy and Development at Brookings Working Paper 131 (Brookings Institution, October 2019) 6.

[463] WHO, Global Health Expenditure Database, Visualizations: Table of regional averages for key indicators <https://apps.who.int/nha/database/Regional_Averages/Index/en> accessed 23 May 2021.

[464] World Bank, Government expenditure on education, total (per cent of GDP) <https://data.worldbank.org/indicator/SE.XPD.TOTL.GD.ZS> accessed 11 March 2023 (using UIS statistics data from September 2020).

[465] Kharas and McArthur (n 462) 6 ('The most striking part of the figure is the tight linkage between SDG spending and per capita income.... The slope of the trend line is approximately 1.13, meaning that for every 10 percent higher per capita income, countries show an 11.3 percent higher level of average SDG spending.') (footnote omitted).

[466] World Bank, Government expenditure on education, All Countries and Economies, <https://data.worldbank.org/indicator/SE.XPD.TOTL.GD.ZS> accessed 11 March 2023 (using UIS statistics data from September 2020).

and 2017 (6.83 per cent) before dropping somewhat in 2018 (6.25 per cent); and that of Bolivia rose significantly from 2015 (6.55 per cent) to 2016 (6.83 per cent), but fell to below-2015 levels by 2018 (6.3 per cent).[467]

The OECD, through its DAC, is the main institution tracking flows of development assistance from Member States. Its most recent data indicate that in 2020, of its thirty members, six have given 0.7 per cent or more of gross national income (GNI), and eleven have given 0.4 per cent or more.[468] While the United States is the largest donor in absolute amounts, it gives less than 0.2 per cent of its income for ODA.

Significantly, the OECD has adjusted the official definition of ODA subsequent to Agenda 2030. In 2016, for example, the 'developmental role that military actors sometimes play' was acknowledged by the DAC's revisions of its rules for assessing how much military expenditures can count to a donor's ODA account.[469] In 2017, such rule clarifications for in-country refugee-care meant that such expenditures were allowed to be counted to ODA.[470] In 2018, the definition of ODA changed to include more specific rules on the grant portion of financial flows,[471] and in 2019, the DAC made the 'grant equivalent' measure of ODA data standard.[472]

The OECD also has encouraged progress on the SDGs by developing an additional measure of development assistance aimed specifically at measuring resource flows that

---

[467] WHO, Global Health Expenditure Database, Visualizations: Country Profiles (<https://apps.who.int/nha/database/country_profile/Index/en> accessed 23 May 2021).

[468] OECD, 'Official Development Assistance (ODA): What is ODA?' 1 (with table).

[469] ibid 3.

[470] ibid 2.

[471] Until 2017, the OECD defined ODA as 'those flows to countries and territories on the DAC List of ODA Recipients and to multilateral institutions which are:

    i   provided by official agencies, including state and local governments, or by their executive agencies; and

    ii each transaction of which:

        o is administered with the promotion of the economic development and welfare of developing countries as its main objective; and

        o is concessional in character and conveys a grant element of at least 25 per cent (calculated at a rate of discount of 10 per cent).'

OECD, Official Development Assistance—Definition and Coverage: ODA (<https://www.oecd.org/dac/financing-sustainable-development/development-finance-standards/officialdevelopmentassistancedefinitionandcoverage.htm> accessed 22 May 2021).

As of 2018, the definition is:

'those flows to countries and territories on the DAC List of ODA Recipients and to multilateral development institutions which are:

    i   provided by official agencies, including state and local governments, or by their executive agencies; and

    ii each transaction of which:

        o is administered with the promotion of the economic development and welfare of developing countries as its main objective; and

        o is concessional in character. In DAC statistics, this implies a grant element of at least

          ■ **45 per cent** in the case of bilateral loans to the official sector of LDCs and other LICs (calculated at a rate of discount of 9 per cent).

          ■ **15 per cent** in the case of bilateral loans to the official sector of LMICs (calculated at a rate of discount of 7 per cent).

          ■ **10 per cent** in the case of bilateral loans to the official sector of UMICs (calculated at a rate of discount of 6 per cent).

          ■ **10 per cent** in the case of loans to multilateral institutions (calculated at a rate of discount of 5 per cent for global institutions and multilateral development banks, and 6 per cent for other organisations, including sub-regional organisations).'

ibid (references and notes omitted).

[472] ibid 2.

are intended to support sustainable development. The new measure is called 'total official support for sustainable development', or TOSSD.[473] The TOSSD counts sustainable development-oriented ODA (strictly defined), but also governmental flows from non-OECD states (including, importantly, China), resources to support international public goods, and officially supported private financial flows.[474] Categorized in Pillar I (ODA and other government to government flows), Pillar II (expenditures for international public goods), and 'Mobilization' (private financial flows 'mobilized by official interventions'),[475] the TOSSD 'visualization tool' presents the data collected according to pillar, sector, recipient, and SDG targeted.[476] According to the TOSSD's newly published data,[477] in 2019, approximately $226.37 million Pillar I funds were distributed, nearly $70 million Pillar II funds were given, and just over $47 million private funds were mobilized for the SDGs.[478] A large majority of all types of funding went to 'Developing countries, unspecified', while the single largest individual recipient of Pillar I funds was India.[479]

The flows of mobilized private funds in 2019 went mainly to Argentina, India, and the region 'Far East Asia'.[480] Of the total, 6 per cent of the TOSSD resources were specifically allocated to SDG 1—significantly more than for any other single SDG.[481] Within SDG 1, the greatest percentage of specified funds (nearly 35 per cent) went to target 1.5 (disaster prevention and resilience).[482] That said, target 1.a received over 20 per cent of the targeted resources.

6. Implementation Efforts at the Domestic and International Levels

There are innumerable efforts being taken around the world, globally, regionally, nationally, and locally, most not directly stemming from SDG obligations but many of which refer to them. That said, resources for combating poverty are often channelled through institutions providing financing for development. These are located in multiple arenas and the landscape is becoming an increasingly dense network of governmental and non-governmental actors, multi-stakeholder platforms, and 'partnerships'. The international context for development assistance has separate centres.

One of the main actors helping to coordinate these efforts is the OECD's DAC, described above. Not only does the DAC monitor OECD members' foreign assistance budgets (ODA) and the overall flows of sustainable development related funding from all sources (through its TOSSD), it has been fostering work on aid effectiveness by providing best practice guidelines for donors.

---

[473] ibid 7.

[474] ibid.

[475] <https://tossd.online/about> (setting out the content of the individual pillars as well as pointing to the data providers and indicating the degree of availability of data).

[476] <https://tossd.online/< (the year will also be a filter; at time of writing, the data is only available for 2019).

[477] The first data collection was released by the TOSSD in March 2021. TOSSD, What are the key milestones? <https://tossd.org/what-is-tossd/> accessed 23 May 2021.

[478] <https://tossd.online/> accessed 23 May 2021 (by Pillar).

[479] <https://tossd.online/> accessed 23 May 2021 (by Recipient).

[480] <https://tossd.online/> accessed 23 May 2021 (by Recipient).

[481] <https://tossd.online/> accessed 23 May 2021 (by SDG).

[482] <https://tossd.online/> accessed 23 May 2021 (by SDG).

Together, the OECD and the UNDP are developing and promoting good practices in the giving of aid. The four OECD High-Level Fora on Aid Effectiveness (2002 in Rome, 2005 in Paris, 2008 in Accra, and 2011 in Busan)[483] professed to establish a 'global partnership for development' by addressing donor accountability and realizing a more active role for recipient government involvement.[484] These non-binding statements attempt to set forth a 'consensus' view on how various sources of development-oriented resource flows should be governed. Whereas the Paris and Accra meetings specifically looked to deepen the 'ownership' of development cooperation by aid recipients, the 2011 Busan Partnership for Effective Development Cooperation (referred to as the Global Partnership for Effective Development Cooperation, or GPEDC) expanded the donor focus to include non-traditional stakeholders such as private funds and civil society.[485] Post-2015, the GPEDC began to specifically look at the SDGs, including targets 1.a and 1.b.[486] The latest report includes valuable information on the numerous 'development partners'' actions with a specific emphasis on how the funding fits within national development programmes[487] and on the predictability of the donor's actions.[488]

For its part, the United Nations has continued on AAAA with further programmes and policy fora. One, the Inter-agency Task Force on Financing for Development, has a dual mandate: 'to monitor progress on the Addis Agenda and advise governments on Financing for Sustainable Development'.[489] The Task Force is composed of more than fifty UN agencies, offices, and commissions, as well as the Bretton Woods institutions and the World Trade Organization (WTO). It is coordinated by the UN Department of Economic and Social Affairs (DESA) and is dedicated to assisting governments plan for SDG expenditures. The Task Force developed guidance materials on implementing an 'integrated national financing framework', or INFF, for example, and has helped develop an online tool to help governments create and use such frameworks. Publications, such as their annual reports, also make analyses of data more accessible.[490]

DESA also hosts the intergovernmental ECOSOC Financing for Development Forum.[491] The Forum's April 2021 document on agreed conclusions and

---

[483] See OECD, 'The High Level Fora on Aid Effectiveness: A History' (<https://www.oecd.org/dac/effectiveness/thehighlevelforaonaideffectivenessahistory.htm> accessed 11 March 2023).

[484] See generally R Bissio, 'The Paris Declaration on Aid Effectiveness' in OHCHR, *Realizing the Right to Development* (OHCHR 2013) 233–47 (<https://www.ohchr.org/Documents/Issues/Development/RTDBook/PartIIIChapter17.pdf> accessed 23 May 2021). Bissio notes, however, that the 'new level of supranational economic governance' created by the Paris Declaration threatens to increase the imbalance between donors and recipients that had already existed. ibid 235.

[485] ibid 235, footnote 9 and accompanying text.

[486] See OECD/UNDP, *Making Development Co-Operation More Effective: 2016 Progress Report* (OECD 2016) 44–54.

[487] For example, ibid 154 (Table B.1a).

[488] ibid 157 (Table B.5a).

[489] United Nations, 'Inter-agency Task Force on Financing for Development: Our Mandate' (<https://developmentfinance.un.org/> accessed 24 May 2021).

[490] The 2021 Annual Report focuses on the effects of COVID on financing, emphasizing the impact of the pandemic on domestic spending, ODA, and the flows of private resources. Inter-agency Task Force on Financing for Development, *Financing for Sustainable Development Report 2021* (UN 2021) (available at <https://developmentfinance.un.org/sites/developmentfinance.un.org/files/FSDR_2021.pdf> accessed 24 May 2021).

[491] See UN Department of Economimc and Social Affairs, Financing: What We Do, <https://www.un.org/development/desa/financing/what-we-do/ECOSOC/financing-development-forum/FFD-forum-home> accessed 11 March 2023.

112   SDG 1

recommendations, following the AAAA's structure.[492] It highlighted the Forum's concerns about the COVID-19 pandemic's negative effects on inequality within and across governments and its impacts on governments' varying abilities to provide health services to their populations.[493]

The Development Cooperation Forum (DCF) is yet another UN-based grouping. This is a multi-stakeholder forum dedicated to bringing together a wide spectrum of development actors to exchange information and best practices in order to further effective development cooperation. The DCF puts out a periodic survey to examine, in its own words, 'key enablers' of development cooperation: 'national development cooperation policies, country results frameworks, development cooperation information systems and national development cooperation forums, with capacity support as cross-cutting.'[494] It also holds conferences in the form of 'high-level meetings', at which expert panels discuss current issues.[495]

7. Critique

Although both the causes and the effects of poverty can be seen as political, societal, ecological, psychological, historical, medical, and educational—just to list some of the factors—the financial component of poverty reduction efforts is still important. MDG 8 had called for official foreign development aid levels of high-income countries of at least 0.7 per cent of gross domestic income. With only five countries achieving these levels of aid during the 2000s, there was a strong desire on the part of many UN members to reinforce the obligation of global partnership in the SDGs negotiations.[496] Others, however, felt that funding must be more broadly based, including in particular contributions by private enterprise.[497]

The question of the sourcing of the necessary financing is one that plagued the SDGs, and the result of this fundamental debate is target 1.a's open language on the need for 'resources from a variety of sources'. Explicitly including an acknowledgement of the importance of ODA, target 1.a maintains the SDG commitment to common but differentiated responsibilities as urged by the Group of 77 and LDCs. Nevertheless, the target's indicators emphasize the desire for national governments to attend to the needs of their populations through domestic spending to assist the poor and vulnerable and reduce poverty. Indeed, although the target's language seems to emphasize foreign aid flows,

---

[492] Economic and Social Council forum on financing for development, 'Follow-up and review of the financing for development outcomes and the means of implementation of the 2030 Agenda for Sustainable Development', E/FFDF/2021/L.1 (14 April 2021).

[493] ibid.

[494] DCF, *DCF Survey Study 2020: Toward Effective Development Cooperation in the COVID-19 Period* (United Nations 2020) ix. (<https://www.un.org/development/desa/financing/sites/www.un.org.development.desa.financing/files/2021-05/2020%20DCF%20Survey%20Study.pdf> accessed 24 May 2021).

[495] For example, 2021 High-level Meeting of the Development Cooperation Forum, 6–7 May 2021 (held online) (<https://www.un.org/development/desa/financing/events/2021-high-level-meeting-development-cooperation-forum-dcf> accessed 24 May 2021).

[496] Including, eg, in OWG 11: Lesotho, for the African Group; Argentina, Bolivia and Ecuador; and Indonesia, China, and Kazakhstan, IISD, 32(11) Earth Negotiations Bulletin 4 (May 2014).

[497] In discussions of the MOI within SDG 17 negotiations, the United States, Canada and Israel were proponents of encouraging property rights, stable investment climates, and conducive business environments. See Encyclopedia Groupinica, p 154, footnotes 1712–1715 and accompanying text.

the fact that the first indicator looks at domestic spending is a sign that the stakeholders representing donor interests maintained a strong position within the negotiations.

The other revealing aspect of target 1.a is its acknowledgement of the role of private enterprise in contributing to achieving SDG 1. This is not particularly surprising, as the value of private sector activity in achieving the SDGs has been generally acknowledged and there had been growing attention to non-governmental development assistance donors since the MDG years. Still, the lack of a clear international legal framework for regulating non-governmental actors leaves open room for critics of the privatization of development assistance, particularly when the donors are profit-driven enterprises. Reducing poverty in all its forms, however, is going to require broad participation from both the private and the public sector. With more attention given to ensuring private donors are responding to the real needs of those they aim to help, more benefits can be secured.[498]

Like other targets, progress on target 1.a will require more quality data on governmental expenditures than are currently available. While the data on development assistance in the form of ODA is reliable and of high quality, even the OECD is currently unable to assess the level of expenditures on international public goods. The lack of data is more severe when looking at essential services spending. While 2018 figures for health spending are available, a time lag of three years makes it impossible for policy-makers to have accurate assessments of policy progress or regression when facing urgent decision-making needs (such as were needed in the wake of the COVID-19 pandemic of 2020–21). For education, the data situation is even worse, with the latest figures often at least five years old, and thirty-nine countries not reporting more recently than those for 2011.[499] As data collection improves, the information required for tracking progress should become more readily available.

Better data, however, will not eliminate the fundamental problem with target 1.a: the approach it takes to poverty reduction by assuming that more spending will result in less poverty. This assumption is understandable but overly simplistic. Kharas and McArthur's findings indicate that it will take careful and highly contextualized analyses to draw any real conclusions about the effectiveness of a particular spending programme for poverty reduction, and they warn of the problems attendant on looking at general figures of spending in a certain sector as an indication of real improvements. First, they stress that 'government spending does not guarantee SDG outcomes'.[500] Spending, rather, needs to be carefully tailored to context—meaning that the target 1.a emphasis on overall amounts is to a large degree irrelevant if the ultimate aim is to eradicate the negative effects of multidimensional poverty. Recounting how smaller but better targeted spending may bring about greater improvements in education and health, these authors suggest that the SDG 1 MOI are poor policy prescriptions:

---

[498] See, eg, Independent Evaluation Group, *The Private Sector and Poverty Reduction: Lessons from the Field* (World Bank 2012) (describing the successes and failures of individual private sector projects aimed at reducing poverty).

[499] See <https://data.worldbank.org/indicator/SE.XPD.TOTL.GD.ZS?most_recent_year_desc=false> accessed 24 May 2021.

[500] Kharas and McArthur (n 462) 22.

The fact that annual global SDG spending is already on track to grow by more than $10 trillion over 15 years underscores the problems caused when framing the question of SDG financing as 'how to mobilize trillions of aggregate global dollars for the SDGs.' Instead, the key question is, 'how to ensure the right resources are available in the right places to help solve the relevant problems.'[501]

Finally, the key to effective poverty reduction is going to be the combination of increased resource expenditures with solid institutional frameworks.[502] The development community has struggled with the intertwined effects of corruption and foreign aid for years, with some high-profile arguments claiming that foreign aid should not be offered, due to its usurpation by corrupt regimes.[503] Current majority views are less extreme, but the AAAA framework itself speaks to the need to ensure that governments act to 'deter, detect, prevent and counter corruption and bribery'.[504] This concern has been taken on by the various fora on development cooperation as well as, and in more depth, by the High Level Panel on International Financial Accountability, Transparency and Integrity for Achieving the 2030 Agenda (FACTI), called into being in 2020. The FACTI's 2021 report addresses the need for tackling 'illicit financial flows' (IFFs) in order to ensure that the SDGs can be achieved.[505] Bribery, but also money laundering, stolen assets, and tax avoidance, foster greater inequalities by transferring from the poorest to the richest.[506] The FACTI therefore call for accountability, legitimacy, transparency, and fairness to define the financial framework for sustainable development.[507]

FACTI's work does not cover the full range of the intersection between illicit financial flows and poverty. Nevertheless, it is a good starting point. Further questions, such as those regarding odious debt, are also relevant to the issues surrounding financing SDG 1's implementation. Target 1.a's omission of any reference to improved governance (including but not limited to reduced corruption and enhanced accountability of both donors and recipients, to tax fairness, or to the management of debt) is a lost opportunity to acknowledge the arguments of those who speak out against foreign aid, the involvement of the private sector in poverty-reduction efforts, and the motivations of donors. These topics would need to be explicit parts of SDG 1 if the goal is to ensure that efforts to improve the lives of the most disadvantaged are not wasted.

---

[501] ibid.

[502] ibid 25.

[503] Moyo helped popularize the idea that foreign aid hurt countries more than it helped due to its effects on corruption. D Moyo, *Dead Aid: Why Aid is Not Working and How There is a Better Way for Africa* (Palgrave Macmillan 2009). Easterly also criticizes aid, arguing that it is ineffective at best. W Easterly, *The White Man's Burden: Why the West's Efforts to Aid the Rest Have done so Much Ill and So Little Good* (Penguin 2007). Kalu's more subtle analysis points to the historically based establishment of exploitative governance as the reason for Africa's failure to develop—suggesting that foreign aid itself is not relevant. Kalu (n 147) 193–96. For an overview of the current discussions, see MG Quibria, 'Foreign Aid and Corruption: Anti-Corruption Strategies Need Greater Alignment with the Objective of Aid Effectiveness' (2017) 18(2) Georgetown Journal of International Law 10.

[504] A/RES/69/313, para 25.

[505] FACTI, 'Financial Integrity for Sustainable Development: Report of the High Level Panel on International Financial Accountability, Transparency and Integrity for Achieving the 2030 Agenda' (February 2021).

[506] ibid 4.

[507] ibid 13–26.

G. Target 1.b Create Sound Policy Frameworks at the National, Regional, and International Levels, Based on Pro-Poor and Gender-Sensitive Development Strategies, to Support Accelerated Investment in Poverty Eradication Actions

1. SDG Indicator 1.b.1

a) *Proportion of government recurrent and capital spending to sectors that disproportionately benefit women, the poor and vulnerable groups*

2. Sources of Target

The OWG discussions from the beginning were concerned with ensuring that the most disadvantaged be particularly in the focus of efforts to improve the lives of all, and target 1.b attempts to tie the 'no-one left behind' principle of the SDGs with the call for increased investments to financially support the SDGs. Even if the February 2014 Focus Area document did not explicitly take up the idea of measuring financial flows to marginalized groups within the discussion of poverty eradication, there were calls for creating 'a climate favourable to investment' in Focus Area 8 (Economic growth),[508] for 'promoting differentially high per capita income growth at the bottom of the income distribution' in Focus Area 12 (Promoting equality),[509] and to 'mobilizing additional financial resources from multiple sources' in Focus Area 18 (Means of implementation).[510] Delegate comments recorded in the Encyclopedia Groupinica indicate numerous supporters of the idea of targeted actions to create policies to stimulate poverty-reducing investment. Benin (for the LDCs) mentioned the need for policies to benefit 'the poor and the marginalized groups' of society, as did Trinidad and Tobago (for the Caribbean Community (CARICOM)), who called for 'ensuring equality of economic opportunities for all, including marginalised groups'.[511] Promotion of private sector-friendly policies also received early attention from a broad range of OWG members, many of whom emphasized the importance of supporting small and medium-sized businesses.[512]

The April OWG 10 failed to add much to the discussion of investment contexts aimed particularly at poverty eradication. Most of the delegate comments maintained a focus on equality and inclusive growth rather than on preferential actions to assist the most disadvantaged.[513] France (for Germany and Switzerland) brought in the concept

---

[508] 'Focus Area Document' at 3.

[509] ibid 5.

[510] ibid 7.

[511] Encyclopedia Groupinica 77, footnotes 900 and 903 and accompanying text. See also ibid 82–83, footnotes 970 and 971 and accompanying text (comments by Ireland/Norway/Denmark on the need to focus investment and job creation and support and rural and 'peri-urban' infrastructure to help the poor and marginalized).

[512] For example, ibid 81, footnotes 947–955 and accompanying text (with comments from the Alliance of Small Island States, Australia/Netherlands/United Kingdom, United States/Canada/Israel, Ireland/Norway/Denmark, but also Argentina/Bolivia/Ecuador, Bhutan/Thailand/Vietnam.

[513] See generally IISD, 32(10) Earth Negotiations Bulletin (7 April 2014). But note that Morocco suggested a target on poverty eradication in rural areas. ibid 6.

of 'responsible private' investments,[514] a point echoed by the Third World Network, who called for international standards for investors.[515]

The May and even the June OWG discussions did not exhibit much change in terms of the delegates' comments. The question of whether to have MOIs at all were still being debated, as was the placement of inequality within the goals, and the possibly unfair paucity of economic goals within the overall framework.[516]

It was in the informal sessions of July 2014 that the text of target 1.b appeared. Although reportedly some delegations wanted to remove it to Goal 17, the text remained in Goal 1.[517]

3. Statistical/Empirical Analysis

The custodian agency responsible for providing data on target 1.b is the United Nations International Children's Emergency Fund (UNICEF). The sole original indicator 1.b.1, which asked for disaggregated data on spending targets, is now up for replacement with a more generalized indicator: 'Pro-poor public spending'.[518] This is to look at government spending for education, health, and poverty-directed cash and near-cash transfers.[519]

A 2021 UNICEF report warns that public resource spending on health, education, and social protection is under threat, in particular due to the burdens of debt payments and the financial effects of COVID-19.[520] According to the report:

> [i]n 2019, 25 countries spent more on debt service than on social spending on education, health and social protection combined ... and seven of these 25 countries are amongst those with the highest rates of multidimensional child poverty, with over 60 per cent of children severely deprived of at least one essential social service (namely, education, health, housing, nutrition, water or sanitation).[521]

In South Sudan, for example, the government spends 13.54 per cent of its GDP to service its debt, and only 1.21 per cent on social spending.[522] In Haiti, 21.25 per cent of GDP goes to servicing debt and less than 6 per cent to social spending.[523] Moreover, while health budgets and social protection budgets increased in nearly 100 and eighty countries, respectively, in response to COVID-19, education budgets and child protection budgets fell in some, putting children living in poverty in those countries at

---

[514] ibid 5.
[515] ibid 21.
[516] See IISD, 32(11) Earth Negotiations Bulletin, 18–19.
[517] IISD, 32(13) Earth Negotiations Bulletin, 5.
[518] See proposed replacement indicator <https://unstats.un.org/unsd/statcom/51st-session/documents/2020-2-SDG-IAEG-E.pdf> (Pro-Poor public social spending).
[519] SDG Indicators: Metadata repository (last updated April 2020), p 1 <https://unstats.un.org/sdgs/metadata/files/Metadata-01-0b-01.pdf (viewed 5 June 2021).
[520] UNICEF, *COVID-19 and the Looming Debt Crisis* (April 2021) 15.
[521] ibid.
[522] ibid 16.
[523] ibid.

particular risk.[524] The Outcome Document of the 2021 Financing for Development Conference, too, notes that the participants 'are deeply concerned that the pandemic has widened existing inequalities in children's access to learning.[525]

4. Implementation Efforts at the Domestic and International Levels

The call for public spending to alleviate the disadvantages of poverty is supported by the same range of measures as have been discussed above. With health, education, and social spending as the central measures in target 1.b, the overlap with targets 1.3 and 1.4 is particularly pronounced, as are the efforts taken in the context of SDG 3 (health) and 4 (education).

The most noteworthy efforts being taken to pursue the goals of target 1.b itself are those relating to debt relief. A brief look highlights the latest global action to assist pro-poor spending by reducing the amount debtor countries need to pay their creditors.

Governmental debt is incurred when a government borrows money from another government, an international or regional institution, or a private lender. Loans may be offered to countries either at market rates of interest (non-concessional) or at less-than-market rates (concessional).[526] As market interest rates rise with the risk of payment default, the countries with the least ability to pay often face the highest costs for debt from private lenders. As the ratio of debt servicing to income rises, debt repayment becomes more difficult and governments may need to redirect resources that would otherwise be available for social spending and poverty reduction toward paying creditors.[527] Debt servicing for governments, therefore, can have severely negative impact on those living in poverty in debtor countries.

The problems of debt's relationship to poverty have been discussed for decades and global financial crises have often spurred renewed interest in addressing the topic, as the effects of debt become particularly obvious.[528] Thus, the 2008 financial crisis which left not only low-income countries facing growing indebtedness and increasing costs for servicing existing debt, but also middle- and high-income countries (Argentina, Greece, Ireland, and Spain among them) and the more recent global economic downturn caused by the spread of COVID-19 have led to numerous discussions and initiatives, most aiming to reduce the debt servicing burdens by persuading the lenders to agree to forgive the debt.[529]

---

[524] ibid 18.

[525] E/FFDF/2021/L.1, para 15

[526] Some financing may be available through outright grants, requiring no repayment at all.

[527] C Thomas, 'International Debt Forgiveness and Global Poverty Reduction' (2000) 27 Fordham Urban Law Journal 1711, 1712.

[528] For example, GF Rea, 'Restructuring Sovereign Debt' (1983) 77 American Society of International Law Proceedings 312; GC Abbott, 'Debt Relief for the Poorer Developing Countries' (1987) 19(1) Case Western Journal of International Law 1; D. Logie and M. Rowson, 'Poverty and Health: Debt Relief Could Help Achieve Human Rights Objectives' (1998) 3 Health & Human Rights 82, 86–88; Thomas (n 527); D Tladi, 'International Monetary Fund Conditionality, Debt and Poverty: Toward a Strong Anthropocentric Model of Sustainability' (2004) 16(1) South African Mercantile Law Journal 31.

[529] For example, G-24 and GDP Center Webinar, 'Collective Action Clauses in Motion: Lessons and Challenges for Covid-19 Era Sovereign Debt Restructuring' (August 2020); O Lienau, 'Sovereign Debt, Private Wealth, and Market Failure' (2020) 60(2) Virginia Journal of International Law 299; C. Hofmann, 'Greek Debt Relief' (2017) 37(1) Oxford Journal of Legal Studies 1; SK Park and TR Samples, 'Tribunalizing Sovereign Debt: Argentina's

The IMF and World Bank's Heavily Indebted Poor Countries Initiative (HIPC), started in 1996, and the supplemental Multilateral Debt Relief Initiative of 2005 are two such programmes directly targeting debtor nations' ability to provide social and economic support to their populations. Under the two initiatives, countries commit to establishing 'a track record of reform and sound policies' and implement reforms in exchange for forgiveness of their debts by public and (some) private creditors. The conditions on the forgiveness require that the countries use the moneys that would otherwise go to paying off their debts for social spending (health, education, and social services).[530] The results of multilateral debt relief are not entirely satisfactory, largely due to the lack of agreement on the part of 'non-Paris', or private, lenders to forgive the debt they hold and because not all countries needing debt relief are eligible.

A new attempt to offer financial respite from debt burdens came in the wake of the COVID-19 pandemic, when the G20 countries agreed to suspend debt servicing by the poorest countries for twenty months (May 2020 until December 2021).[531] The Debt Service Suspension Initiative (DSSI) is a programme to benefit International Development Association (IDA)[532] and LDC governments by allowing them to stop making payments on IMF and World Bank debt during the COVID crisis. According to UNICEF, the DSSI has helped nearly fifty countries to keep up their provision of pro-poor expenditures, but this is far from a comprehensive solution.[533] As of May 2021, the G20 extended the suspension of payment of official bilateral credit for the same countries.[534]

The Sustainable Development Finance Policy (SDFP) is another new debt management programme that indirectly should help IDA countries maintain their ability to contribute public funds to pro-poor programming.[535] Generally designed to improve the sustainability of IDA-country borrowing (through the Debt Sustainability Enhancement Program), the SDFP also relies on a 'Program of Creditor Outreach'.[536]

Experience with Investor-State Dispute Settlement' (2017) 50(4) Vanderbilt Journal of Transnational Law 1033; J Rossi, 'Sovereign Debt Restructuring, National Development and Human Rights' (2016) 23 Sur International Journal of Human Rights 185.

[530] See IMF, Factsheet: Debt Relief Under the Heavily Indebted Poor Countries (HIPC) Initiative (23 March 2021) (<https://www.imf.org/en/About/Factsheets/Sheets/2016/08/01/16/11/Debt-Relief-Under-the-Heavily-Indeb ted-Poor-Countries-Initiative> accessed 5 June 2021); S Hughes and others, 'The HIPC Debt Relief Bill: Making Forgiveness Compulsory' (2010) 4 Law and Financial Markets Review 269, 269–70.

[531] World Bank, 'COVID 19: Debt Service Suspension Initiative' (18 June 2021) (<https://www.worldbank.org/en/topic/debt/brief/covid-19-debt-service-suspension-initiative> accessed 5 June 2021).

[532] IDA countries are the fifty-nine countries below a set per capita GNI or which are not sufficiently creditworthy to borrow from the World Bank, and fifteen so-called blend countries. IDA financing is concessional and is tied to assessments of the borrower's implementation of policies that promote economic growth and poverty reduction. See World Bank, 'How Does IDA Work?' (<https://ida.worldbank.org/about/how-does-ida-work> accessed 5 June 2021).

[533] UNICEF, COVID-19 (n 520) 5.

[534] The World Bank and IMF are also supporting the DSSI by providing financing, much of it in the form of grants, to eligible countries in order to help them maintain their public support programmes. World Bank, 'Factsheet: Debt Service Suspension and COVID-19' (19 May 2021) (<https://www.worldbank.org/en/news/factsheet/2020/05/11/debt-relief-and-covid-19-coronavirus>).

[535] IDA, 'Sustainable Development Finance Policy' (<https://ida.worldbank.org/debt/sustainable-developm ent-finance-policy> accessed 6 June 2021).

[536] IDA, 'Sustainable Development Finance Policy: Promoting sustainable borrowing and lending practices in IDA Countries' (<https://ida.worldbank.org/sites/default/files/pdfs/sdfp-at-a-glance-2020-8-14.pdf> accessed 6 June 2021).

The latter will encourage lenders to take on a more active role in ensuring that their offerings are sustainable and transparent.

5. Critique

Indicator 1.b.1 would suggest that the data submissions should measure the 'Proportion of government recurrent and capital spending to sectors that disproportionately benefit women, the poor and vulnerable groups'. As the target's sole indicator, it appeared that target 1.b was intended as the tool to ensure that governments attend to the most vulnerable in their poverty reduction efforts. According to the UN Stats, however, there is a proposal to change the indicator. The proposed new indicator would be: 'Pro-poor social spending'. This highlights the difficulties of target 1.b's implementation as a goal: reliable measurability of what is important to SDG 1.

As a Tier II indicator, availability of data on the status of pro-poor public spending is a problem. According to UNSTAT, in April 2020, the available data for the target included figures from sixty-six countries, or just over half of the world's population.[537] While this included data on 96 per cent of the people living in South Asia and 95 per cent of those in Latin America and the Caribbean, information is available for less than half of the population in Europe and Central Asia (46 per cent) and Sub-Saharan Africa (45 per cent) and only 19 per cent of the population in East Asia and the Pacific.[538]

By adjusting the measure of target 1.b, countries will probably be more able to report on their progress. However, the re-aggregated focus moves away from the 'leave no one behind' principle. It ignores, in particular, the special difficulties faced by particularly vulnerable groups among the poor and limits the indicator to those that are 'poor' (according to national poverty lines) rather than including those who find themselves in a vulnerable group.

Related to the elimination of the reporting on vulnerable groups is the criticism of target 1.3 that points to the singular focus on governmental spending, as opposed to looking at both spending and taxation. Target 1.b's omission of 'fiscal design is problematic'.[539] This term refers to the structures and instruments a government uses for generating as well as distributing financial resources. The omission of resource generation (often taxation) from the target is particularly disturbing, given that it is an area long regarded as important to ensuring economic growth of developing countries.

At the same time, the conventional wisdom on pro-growth fiscal design is being challenged by studies on the effects of common fiscal patterns on the poor and vulnerable. According to research findings from the Tulane University CEQ Institute, government expenditures for health, education, and direct transfers are often financed by taxes that in the end leave low-income households with less resources than they would

---

[537] SDG Indicators: Metadata repository at p 3.

[538] ibid 3–4.

[539] Tax policy, expenditure rules, rules mandating balanced budgets and the incurrence of debt are included in studies on fiscal design. See C Nerlich and WH Reuter, 'The Design of National Fiscal Frameworks and their Budgetary Impact' (September 2013) European Central Bank Working Paper No 1588, 6.

120   SDG 1

have had without the governmental spending in the first place.[540] 'It is not uncommon', writes Lustig,

> that the net effect of all governments taxing and spending is to leave the poor worse off in terms of actual consumption of private goods and services... [D]emand for investments into infrastructure and public services must be balanced against the competing need to protect low-income households that may otherwise be made worse off from misaligned tax and transfer policies.[541]

Lustig and the CEQ's data reveal that even where poverty is reduced by governmental spending policies, fiscal impoverishment often rises.[542] Indeed, the anti-poor effects of poorly coordinated governmental spending and taxing are so severe as to lead the researchers to suggest a separate SDG 1 target—one that would aim 'to ensure that the fiscal system does not reduce the income of the poor'.[543]

Finally, as with many of the other SDG 1 targets, one can be dissatisfied that the target itself does not point out the existing human rights obligations of most of the UN member States to provide for health and education infrastructures, as well as ensuring food and shelter, on a non-discriminatory basis, to all. The failure of the members to refer to the International Covenants and the various specific human rights treaties is a missed opportunity to underline that the basic aims of SDG 1's targets are substantially covered by existing international law—that states are already under a legal obligation to respect, protect, and promote the basic rights to access to the resources required to live a life of adequate living standards, and that such access must be provided on a non-discriminatory basis.

These critiques should not diminish the benefits of emphasizing governments' obligations to undertake concerted efforts to alleviate the particular difficulties facing low-income individuals and households. Target 1.b will need continuous discussion and improvement if poverty is to be eliminated by 2030, but it—like the other SDG 1 targets—is still a good reminder of the ultimate goal of the SDGs.

---

[540] N Lustig, 'Domestic Resource Mobilization and the Poor, Background paper for Expert Group Meeting: "Strategies for Eradicating Poverty to Achieve Sustainable Development for All"' (draft of 27 May 2016) (<https://www.un.org/esa/socdev/egms/docs/2016/Poverty-SDGs/NoraLustig-paper.pdf> accessed 5 June 2021).
[541] ibid 2.
[542] ibid 6.
[543] ibid 7.

SDG 2

'End Hunger, Achieve Food Security and Improved Nutrition and Promote Sustainable Agriculture ("Zero Hunger")'

Elif Askin

I. Introduction

In September 2015, after several years of discussions and debates, the United Nations (UN) General Assembly adopted the seventeen Sustainable Development Goals (SDGs) and their 169 targets by a resolution entitled 'Transforming our World: The 2030 Agenda for Sustainable Development' (Agenda 2030).[1] The historic document constitutes a universal and transformative 'plan for action for people, planet and prosperity'[2] to guide the sustainable development efforts of all countries, including states from the Global North, from 2016 to 2030.[3] The SDGs replace the Millennium Development Goals (MDGs), a set of eight policy goals that were supposed to have been achieved from 2000 to 2015.[4] Based on a call to 'Leave No One Behind',[5] the new goals represent a notable milestone in the international community's approach to sustainable development in times of globalization. The SDGs are not only broader in scope and more aspirational but also more inclusive and universal than their predecessors, which were directed at supporting the 'developing world'.[6]

Agenda 2030 acknowledges that food plays a critical role in enabling sustainable development.[7] The goal that directly addresses food is Sustainable Development Goal 2

---

[1] United Nations General Assembly (UN GA), Transforming Our World: The 2030 Agenda for Sustainable Development (25 September 2015) UN GA Res 70/1 (Agenda 2030). Each SDG consists of a goal, multiple targets, and indicators. For the terminology see this chapter, Section V.

[2] Agenda 2030 (n 1), Preamble.

[3] ibid. For a general overview on the historical evolution of sustainable development, its meaning and normative content, see U Beyerlin, 'Sustainable Development' in *Max Planck Encyclopaedia of International Law* (online edn, October 2013).

[4] The Millennium Development Goals (MDGs) had been established following the Millennium Summit of the UN in 2000 comprising of eight MDGs for fifteen years, between 2000 and 2015 <https://www.un.org/millenniumgoals> accessed 22 January 2022.

[5] UN Sustainable Development Group (UNSDG), Leave No One Behind <https://unsdg.un.org/2030-agenda/universal-values/leave-no-one-behind> accessed 22 January 2022. See also Agenda 2030 (n 1) para 4.

[6] Agenda 2030 (n 1) para 55; T Pogge, 'The Hunger Games' (2016) 1 Food Ethics 9–27, 19. See also, eg, JD Sachs, 'From Millennium Development Goals to Sustainable Development Goals' (2012) 379 The Lancet 2206–11; D French and LJ Kotzé, 'Introduction' in D French and LJ Kotzé (eds), *Sustainable Development Goals. Law, Theory and Implementation* (Edward Elgar Publishing 2018) 1–12, 2.

[7] A Bley-Palmer and L Young, 'Food System Lessons from the SDGs' in S Dalby and others (eds), *Achieving the Sustainable Development Goals. Global Governance Challenges* (Routledge 2019) 19–35, 23. See also Agenda 2030

(SDG 2).[8] It aims to 'end hunger, achieve food security and improved nutrition and promote sustainable agriculture' (Zero Hunger).[9] SDG 2 is operationalized by eight targets and fourteen indicators.[10] Like all SDGs, SDG 2 seeks to embrace the three dimensions of sustainable development, notably economic growth, social inclusion, and environmental sustainability, to achieve 'Zero Hunger'.[11] It strives to eliminate all forms of hunger and malnutrition by 2030 in order to ensure that all people, in particular children, have year-round access to safe, nutritious, and sufficient food.[12]

Sustainable agriculture is *key* to achieving SDG 2.[13] Promisingly, the goal links the eradication of hunger and malnutrition to a *transformation in agriculture and food systems*[14] and, in particular, to the empowerment of small-scale farmers, including women, pastoralists, and fishers, 'as critical agents of change'.[15] Agriculture provides food for a large number of people and is pivotal to many economic activities.[16] Small-scale famers significantly contribute to global food production,[17] but many of them live in rural and poor areas, have limited access to markets and land to grow food crops, and are vulnerable to shocks like extreme weather, conflicts, pandemics, and socio-economic crises.[18] Therefore, strengthening the resilience and adaptability of small-scale farmers is crucial to overcoming hunger and malnutrition worldwide.[19] Against this backdrop, SDG 2 aims to improve the agricultural productivity and income of small-scale food

(n 1) para 24: 'We are ... determined to end hunger and to achieve food security as a *matter of priority* and to end all forms of malnutrition' (emphasis added).

[8] Sustainable Development Goal 2 'Zero Hunger' (SDG 2) <https://www.un.org/sustainabledevelopment/hunger/> accessed 22 January 2022. There are many other SDGs that relate to hunger and malnutrition, especially SDG 3, see this chapter, Section III.

[9] Agenda 2030 (n 1) Goal 2.

[10] See for the targets and indicators of SDG 2 <https://sdgs.un.org/goals/goal2> accessed 22 January 2022. For an analysis of each target of SDG 2 and accompanying indicators, see this chapter, Section V.

[11] Agenda 2030 (n 1) para 2.

[12] SDG 2, targets 2.1 and 2.2.

[13] High-Level Forum on Sustainable Development (HLPF), 2017 HLPF Thematic Review of SDG 2: End Hunger, Achieve Food Security and Improved Nutrition, and Promote Sustainable Agriculture (2017) <https://sdgs.un.org/sites/default/files/documents/14371SDG 2_format.revised_FINAL_28_04.pdf> accessed 22 January 2022, 1, 9 (HLPF, Thematic Review 2017).

[14] The FAO defines food systems as systems that 'encompass the entire range of actors and their interlinked value-adding activities involved in the production, aggregation, processing, distribution, consumption and disposal of food products that originate from agriculture, forestry or fisheries, and parts of the broader economic, societal and natural environments in which they are embedded. The food system is composed of sub-systems (e.g. farming system, waste management system, input supply system, etc.) and interacts with other key systems (e.g. energy system, trade system, health system, etc.). Therefore, a structural change in the food system might originate from a change in another system; for example, a policy promoting more biofuel in the energy system will have a significant impact on the food system.' See FAO, 'Sustainable Food Systems. Concept and Framework' (2018) <https://www.fao.org/3/ca2079en/CA2079EN.pdf> accessed 22 January 2022. See also J Clapp, *Food* (3rd edn, Polity Press 2020) 2.

[15] HLPF, Thematic Review 2017 (n 13) 1.

[16] UN Conference on Trade and Development (UNCTAD), 'Trade and Environment Review 2013, Wake Up before It's Too Late: Make Agriculture Truly Sustainable Now for Food Security in a Changing Climate' (2013) 6 <http://www.srfood.org/images/stories/pdf/otherdocuments/20130918_UNCTAD_en.pdfY> accessed 22 January 2022.

[17] Clapp (n 14) 4.

[18] HLPF, Thematic Review (n 13) 1, 5. See also FAO, *The State of Food and Agriculture. Making Agrifood Systems More Resilient to Shocks and Stresses* (FAO 2021) 1.

[19] UN, 'The Sustainable Development Goals Report 2021' 28 <https://unstats.un.org/sdgs/report/2021/The-Sustainable-Development-Goals-Report-2021.pdf> accessed 22 January 2022.

INTRODUCTION   123

producers, for example by affording them access to land, other productive resources and inputs, knowledge, and markets.[20]

SDG 2 also addresses recent ecological impacts of industrial agriculture on food production, including biodiversity loss, exposure to toxins from pesticide use, genetically modified crops, and rising greenhouse gas emissions.[21] In particular, climate change has drawn attention to the vulnerabilities of the agricultural sector's production capacity, which is increasingly affected by phenomena such as extreme weather and rising temperatures, potentially leading to food shortages in the future.[22] SDG 2 is designed to ensure that states promote sustainable food production which strengthens the capacity to adapt to climate change and other disasters, improve land and soil quality, and conserve biodiversity.[23] Moreover, SDG 2 also fosters the genetic diversity of seeds, plants, and animals in order to ensure ecosystem health and the integrity of food supply.[24]

Even though the global food system produces enough food to feed the entire world population,[25] states and the international community are currently *not* on track to end world hunger and malnutrition in all its forms by 2030.[26] With less than a decade remaining to meet the time horizon set for achieving the SDGs, the number of people suffering from hunger and food insecurity has been increasing gradually since 2014, after decades of steady decline.[27] The Food and Agriculture Organization (FAO) highlights that the state of hunger, food insecurity, and malnutrition all around the world 'is at a critical juncture'.[28] In 2020, between 720 and 811 million people in the world faced hunger, and approximately 2.37 billion people did not have access to safe, nutritious, and sufficient food.[29] Moreover, the FAO reports that the COVID-19 pandemic pushed an additional 83–132 million people into hunger that same year, thus making the objective of ending hunger even more difficult to achieve.[30] The health crisis has also impacted all forms of malnutrition, including child overweight and adult obesity, which are rapidly increasing in all countries of the world.[31] Unsurprisingly, the right to food,

---

[20] SDG 2, target 2.3.

[21] SDG 2, targets 2.4 and 2.5. See also Clapp (n 14) 3–4; JN Pretty, *Regenerating Agriculture: Policies and Practices for Sustainability and Self-Reliance* (Joseph Henry Books 1995) 58–80.

[22] Clapp (n 14) 3–4.

[23] SDG 2, targets 2.4 and 2.5.

[24] SDG 2, target 2.5.

[25] UN Conference on Trade and Development (UNCTAD), 'Trade and Environment Review 2013, Wake Up before It's Too Late: Make Agriculture Truly Sustainable Now for Food Security in a Changing Climate' (2013) 6 <http://www.srfood.org/images/stories/pdf/otherdocuments/20130918_UNCTAD_en.pdfY> accessed 22 January 2022.

[26] See UN, Goal 2: Zero Hunger <https://www.un.org/sustainabledevelopment/hunger/> accessed 22 January 2022.

[27] UN Economic and Social Council (ECOSOC), 'Progress towards the Sustainable Development Goals, Report of the Secretary-General, 30 April 2021' (UN Doc E/2021/58) para 20.

[28] FAO and others, 'The State of Food Security and Nutrition in the World 2021. Transforming Food Systems for Food Security, Improved Nutrition and Affordable Healthy Diets for All, 2021' vi.

[29] FAO, 'State of Food Security Report 2021' (n 28) xv–xvi.

[30] FAO, 'Tracking Progress on Food and Agriculture-related SDG Indicators 2021. A Report on the Indicators Under the FAO custodianship' (2021) 15 <https://www.fao.org/3/cb6872en/cb6872en.pdf> accessed 22 January 2022.

[31] FAO, 'State of Food Security Report 2021' (n 28) xviii.

recognized widely in numerous international human rights treaties and other instruments, remains one of the least realized human rights of contemporary times.[32]

In today's world, hunger and malnutrition have myriad manifestations and compounding causes. Even though this chapter cannot analyse the causes of hunger and malnutrition in depth, it is worth noting, in light of SDG 2, that conflicts, climate variability and extremes, and economic slowdowns and downturns are nowadays considered to be the major drivers that increase hunger and malnutrition, as stated in a recent progress report by the FAO.[33] Armed conflicts destroy agricultural systems, damage crops, and have negative effects on the availability of food as well as food prices. For example, one of the underlying causes of the conflict in the region of Darfur in Sudan was the depleted productivity of lands due to drought and desertification that necessitated moving the Arab herds to lands of the African tribes in southern Darfur.[34] Financial crises, on the other hand, have a detrimental impact on individuals' access to food and the affordability of healthy diets, due to decline in income or unemployment.[35] Notably, poverty and socio-economic inequality (as well as the COVID-19 pandemic) further amplify and exacerbate hunger and malnutrition, especially in middle- and low-income countries of the Global South.[36]

While SDG 2 recognizes that food production, nutrition, and sustainable agriculture are closely linked to the objective of achieving 'Zero Hunger', the current situation indicates that there are many regulatory gaps and practical obstacles that hinder this goal from being achieved and implemented worldwide. In general, the SDGs, including SDG 2, are praised for their ambitious goals but criticized for being conceptually weak and lacking strong enforcement mechanisms to ensure implementation and accountability.[37] Contemporary critiques perceive Agenda 2030 as a framework that prioritizes economic growth over sustainability.[38] Indeed, Agenda 2030 affirms that states 'envisage a world in which every country enjoys sustained, inclusive and sustainable *economic growth* and decent work for all. A world in which consumption and production patterns and use of all natural resources . . . are sustainable.'[39] Therefore, it has been noted that the SDGs reflect neoliberal policies because they 'privilege the up-holding of commercial interests over commitments to universally ensure entitlements to address fundamental life-sustaining needs'[40] and are also undemocratic as they are mainly implemented through gross domestic product (GDP), market liberalization, and free

[32] K Mechlem, 'Food, Right to, International Protection' in *Max Planck Encyclopedia of Public International Law* (online edn, June 2008) para 1.

[33] ibid xviii. See also Global Network against Food Crises and Food Security Information Network, '2021 Global Report on Food Crises' <https://www.fsinplatform.org/sites/default/files/resources/files/GRFC%202021%20050 521%20med.pdf> accessed 22 January 2022, 22.

[34] Y Abouyoub, 'The Forgotten Culprit. The Ecological Dimension of the Darfur Conflict' (2012) 19 Race, Gender & Class 150–76, 152.

[35] FAO, 'State of Food Security Report 2021' (n 28) xvii–xx.

[36] ibid xix.

[37] On SDGs implementation and monitoring, see this chapter, Section V.

[38] S Adelman, 'The Sustainable Development Goals, Anthropocentrism and Neoliberalism' in French and Kotzé (eds), *Sustainable Development Goals* (n 6) 15–40, 33.

[39] Agenda 2030 (n 1) para 9 (emphasis added).

[40] H Weber, 'Politics of "Leaving No One Behind": Contesting the 2030 Sustainable Development Goals Agenda' (2017) 14 Globalizations 339–414, 400.

trade.[41] Of particular importance here is that the economic approaches to the regulation of food issues are also evident in SDG 2, which mainly focuses on agricultural productivity rather than, for example, on land and soil, environmentally friendly production methods, or social inclusion of rural communities.[42]

This contribution analyses SDG 2 through the lens of public international law. In general, the relationship of the SDGs to international law is the subject of heated debate. International legal scholarship has intensively engaged with the SDGs and the question of what status the SDGs have in international law and what (supporting) role international law plays in the implementation of the goals.[43] The SDGs, including SDG 2, do not impose 'hard' legal obligations on states under current international law but rather entail 'soft' policy objectives and procedures for achieving them.[44] In this context, the question arises as to whether the goals comply with or deviate from existing international rights and obligations in various areas of international law, ranging from international human rights law and international environmental law to international trade and investment law.

SDG 2 directly or indirectly touches upon almost all areas of international law.[45] However, international norms that are relevant to SDG 2 are fragmented and found in various subfields of international law.[46] The main field of international law that is closely linked to or even directly addresses hunger and malnutrition is international human rights law. In particular, economic, social, and cultural rights, including the right to food, are supposed to have the most substantial impact on the realization of SDG 2.[47] As this chapter will show, however, the nexus between food security and sustainable agriculture also creates tensions between the different regimes of international law relevant to SDG 2. While international human rights law principally supports SDG 2 and its aim of empowering individuals to ensure the realization of access to food, international trade and investment law in particular might undermine the objectives of SDG 2 and their successful implementation.[48] Against this backdrop, this chapter calls for a human rights-based approach to SDG 2, and for the need to systematically mainstream human rights not only into other subfields of international law but also into policy areas, such as SDG 2.

Against this backdrop, Section II of this chapter focuses on the development and definition of the terms and core issues of SDG 2. Section III analyses the goal's drafting history. Section IV provides an immanent critique of the goal. In applying a human rights approach to SDG 2, the chapter examines to what extent SDG 2 is in alignment

---

[41] A Salleh, 'Climate, Water, and Livelihood Skills: A Post-Development Reading of the SDGs' (2016) 13 Globalizations 952–59, 953. See also Adelman (n 38) 15–40.

[42] CG Gonzalez, 'SDG 2: End Hunger, Achieve Food Security and Improved Nutrition, and Promote Sustainable Agriculture' in J Ebbesson and E Hey (eds), *The Cambridge Handbook of the Sustainable Development Goals and International Law* (CUP 2022) 72–94, 76.

[43] French and Kotzé, *Sustainable Development Goals* (n 6) 3.

[44] ibid 3.

[45] See A Saab, *Narratives of Hunger in International Law. Feeding the World in Times of Climate Change* (CUP 2019) 10; Gonzalez, 'SDG 2: End Hunger' (n 42) 74.

[46] Gonzalez, 'SDG 2: End Hunger' (n 42) 74.

[47] IT Winkler and M de Carvalho Hernandez, 'Social Rights and Sustainable Development Goals' in C Binder and others (eds), *Research Handbook on International Law and Social Rights* (Edward Elgar 2020) 464–79, 466.

[48] Gonzalez, 'SDG 2: End Hunger' (n 42) 74.

126   SDG 2

with states' human rights obligations that arise from the right to food in particular, but also with relevant rules under international trade and investment law. This section also addresses the opportunities and challenges a rights-based approach presents when applied to SDG 2. The last part of the chapter, Section V, provides a thorough analysis of each target of SDG 2 and its accompanying indicators.

II. Framing SDG 2: Development and Definition of Terms and Core Issues

This section focuses on defining the terms and core issues of SDG 2 as they have evolved over time before turning to a detailed analysis of the goal and its targets. The narratives of the core issues that underlie SDG 2 and influenced its formulation—notably hunger, nutrition, food security, and sustainable agriculture—have changed with time.[49] However, the historical understandings of these issues continue to shape the legal and policy responses to hunger, famine, and malnourishment at the national and international level. Exploring the broader contours of SDG 2 will therefore help to understand the current narrative of SDG 2 as well as the role, relevance, and limitations of international law in relation to this goal.[50]

Despite numerous national, regional, and international efforts to end world hunger, there has been little consensus over the last decades on how to achieve this ambitious objective.[51] Admittedly, even though regulatory gaps—to be elaborated in the next sections—still exist, one of SDG 2's core strengths is that it establishes a much stronger *nexus* between hunger and both nutrition and sustainable agriculture than its predecessor, Millennium Development Goal 1 (MDG 1).[52] MDG 1 combined the eradication of extreme poverty and hunger in a single goal ('eradicate extreme poverty and hunger').[53] Its objective was to halve the proportion of people who suffered from hunger between 1990 and 2015.[54]

Unlike MDG 1, SDG 2 integrates different dimensions of food and nutrition, from undernourishment to micronutrient deficiencies. Just as importantly, it combines agricultural productivity, sustainable food systems, conservation, and the sustainable use of biodiversity.[55] A number of reports on SDG 2 published in recent years demonstrate

---

[49] On the development of food security, see L Jarosz, 'Defining World Hunger: Scale and Neoliberal Ideology in International Food Security Policy Discourse' (2011) 14 Food, Culture and Society 117–39.

[50] For an international law analysis of SDG 2, see this chapter Section III.

[51] A Orford, 'Food Security, Free Trade, and the Battle for the State' (2015) 11 Journal of International Law and International Relations 1–67, 10.

[52] Millennium Development Goal 1 (MDG 1) <https://www.un.org/millenniumgoals/poverty.shtml> accessed 22 January 2022.

[53] ibid. See also S Szabo and others, 'A Collaborative Process towards a SDG 2 Accountability Framework', Report of the Global Open Data for Agriculture and Nutrition, March 2017, 1–16, 8; WL Filho and others (eds), *Zero Hunger, Encyclopaedia of the UN Sustainable Development Goals* (online edn, Springer 2020).

[54] Target 1C of MDG 1 reads: 'Halve, between 1990 and 2015, the proportion of people who suffer from hunger' <https://www.un.org/millenniumgoals/poverty.shtml> accessed 22 January 2022.

[55] D Byerlee and J Fanzo, 'The SDG of Zero Hunger 75 Years On: Turning Full Circle on Agriculture and Nutrition' (2019) 21 Global Food Security 52–59, 57.

that the goal adopts a more expansive approach to hunger and malnutrition and thus offers a more *holistic* view of food issues, encompassing not only nutrition and agriculture but also many other important features of food systems as well as the key drivers that impact these systems.[56]

SDG 2's *integrated approach* is inherited from a long history that has structured legal and policy responses to global hunger.[57] Defined by the FAO as 'an uncomfortable or painful physical sensation caused by insufficient consumption of dietary energy',[58] hunger is certainly not a new 'global' phenomenon.[59] Indeed, as historian James Vernon has noted, 'history, it appears, cannot escape hunger'.[60] The colonial legacy in particular has created many conditions and dynamics that impact hunger, malnourishment, and unsustainable agriculture today.[61] During the colonial period, colonial powers and early transnational corporations were directly involved in the production and trade of crops in the colonies to supply the markets of the Global North.[62] New forms of agricultural production introduced by the colonial powers set the stage for globally oriented markets for food and agricultural commodities.[63] Agricultural land was diverted from food production to cash crop production in India, Africa, and the Americas, as the colonies were forced to produce 'cash crops' like sugar, coffee, tobacco, or cotton.[64] In order to facilitate exports, international trade routes were created to import goods from the colonies to the territories of the colonial powers.[65] After the colonies became independent, they were integrated into the global food economy on strict and highly disadvantageous terms under existing legal regimes.[66] This exposed the countries of the Global South to fluctuations in agricultural commodity prices and declining trade in agricultural goods, among other things.[67]

In 1943, the UN Conference on Food and Agriculture made the first global commitment to end world hunger.[68] The Conference declaration is interesting, exhibiting an approach that corresponds to the current framing of SDG 2.[69] Much like SDG 2, this

---

[56] ibid 57.

[57] See generally on the development of food security and international law's role, Orford (n 51) 10.

[58] See FAO <https://www.fao.org/hunger/en/> accessed 22 January 2022. For the purposes of this chapter, the term hunger is used to include chronic and acute hunger. Also, hunger is to be distinguished from famine. For a definition, see also L Young, *World Hunger* (Routledge 1997) 17–19.

[59] Saab, *Narratives of Hunger in International Law* (n 45) 4.

[60] J Vernon, *Hunger: A Modern History* (Harvard University Press 2007) 1.

[61] See comprehensively A Chadwick, *Law and the Political Economy of Hunger* (OUP 2019) 27–31.

[62] Clapp (n 14) 11, 29.

[63] Chadwick (n 61) 27.

[64] CG Gonzalez, 'Trade Liberalization, Food Security, and the Environment: The Neoliberal Threat to Sustainable Rural Development' (2004) 14 Transnational Law and Contemporary Problems 419–99, 423, 437–39. In turn, the colonies had to buy manufactured goods produced in the Global North, see Young (n 58) 41.

[65] Gonzalez, 'Trade Liberalization, Food Security, and the Environment' (n 64) 433–34; Clapp (n 14) 11.

[66] D Kennedy, 'Three Globalizations of Law and Legal Thought', in D Trubeck and A Santos (eds), *The New Law and Economic Development: A Critical Appraisal* (CUP 2006) 19–73, 57–58. On the role of international law during colonialism, see A Anghie and others (eds), *The Third World and International Order: Law, Politics and Globalization* (Brill 2013).

[67] Young (n 58) 41–42; Gonzalez, 'SDG 2: End Hunger' (n 42) 76–77.

[68] UN Conference on Food and Agriculture, Final Act and Section Reports, Hot Springs, Virginia, 18 May–3 June 1943 <https://collections.nlm.nih.gov/ext/dw/25110080R/PDF/25110080R.pdf> accessed 22 January 2022; Byerlee and Fanzo (n 55) 52.

[69] Byerlee and Franzo (n 55) 54.

declaration emphasized the need to eradicate world hunger by means of an integrated approach to food, nutrition, and agriculture.[70] It stated that increasing food production was essential to fighting hunger but defined a successful outcome primarily by a safe and adequate food supply.[71] While the declaration understood food in terms of calories, it also emphasized the importance of a diversity of nutrients.[72] Following the understanding of sustainable agriculture prevalent at the time, the declaration referred to 'sustainable' food production, which required agricultural and farming practices balanced with conservation methods and ensured the preservation of natural resources for future generations.[73] Furthermore, reflecting the concept of food systems and value chains at the time, the declaration also called for the efficiency of food systems to be improved, and the nutritional value of food to be preserved and enhanced.[74] Finally, the Conference also addressed access to food. Poverty was presented as the main cause of hunger and malnutrition, thus requiring not only a fair distribution of food but also social policy measures to protect the most vulnerable groups in society.[75]

In the post-war period, however, the unprecedented rapid growth of the world population led to a significant shift from an integrated approach to food, nutrition, and sustainable agriculture towards policies that mainly focused on the *supply* of food to eradicate hunger.[76] This change in perspective was based on the widely held perception that hunger was caused by population growth, that this growth was proceeding faster than food production, and that more people would suffer from hunger if population growth was not reduced.[77] Accordingly, in order to keep pace with a growing population, potential regulatory approaches began to focus on the *availability* of rather than *access* to food.[78] This decades-old perception of hunger, which continues to dominate relevant debates, stems from Thomas Malthus and his 1798 *Essay on the Principle of Population*.[79] In this book, Malthus assumed that a growing population in conjunction with an inadequate food supply would naturally lead to hunger. However, he did not take into account that an uneven distribution of food is not merely an issue of food *availability* but also raises legal, political, and social issues related to people's *access* to food.[80]

---

[70] ibid 54.

[71] ibid 53.

[72] ibid 53.

[73] ibid 53.

[74] ibid 53.

[75] ibid 53–54.

[76] ibid 54.

[77] ibid 54; Young (n 58) 3.

[78] Saab, *Narratives of Hunger in International Law* (n 45) 5; Byerlee and Fanzo (n 55) 54.

[79] TR Malthus, *An Essay on the Principle of Population as it Affects the Future Improvement of Society: with Remarks of the Speculations of Mr Godwin, M Condorcet, and Other Writers* (OUP 1993) first published 1798. See also Young (n 58) 3.

[80] Orford (n 51) 11; Saab, *Narratives of Hunger in International Law* (n 45) 5. For a general criticism on the Malthusian understanding of hunger see, eg, C Williams, 'Are There Too Many People? Population, Hunger, and Environmental Degradation' (2010) 68 International Socialist Review <https://isreview.org/issue/68/are-there-too-many-people/> accessed 30 November 2022.

After the Second World War, many Northern states, particularly the United States and Western European countries, sought to ensure *food supply* by supporting their agricultural sectors, providing subsidies to their own producers, and imposing high tariffs and other non-tariff measures, such as import restrictions, in order to ensure demand for domestic agricultural goods.[81] As of the mid-1950s, the General Agreement on Tariffs and Trade (GATT) exempted agricultural products almost entirely from market access requirements[82] so that both the United States and the European states continued the practice of subsidizing agriculture to increase their own production.[83] Food that was overproduced in the Global North due to these subsidies was shipped to the Global South, thus allowing traders from developed countries not only to gain a presence in countries of the Global South but also to sell food at lower prices, ultimately depressing the food prices in these markets.[84] This destroyed the livelihoods in developing countries of many small-scale farmers who largely depended on selling their agricultural products.[85]

The 1960s and 1970s became known as the *fighting hunger* decades, reflected in the FAO's 'Freedom from Hunger' Campaign, the Rockefeller Foundation's Campaign Against Hunger, and the United States War Against Hunger.[86] Although food was imported by developing countries, hunger and malnourishment still persisted in these countries.[87] Responding to the concern that food shortages would incite communism, food exports to developing countries were intended to improve those states' own production.[88] Western states, mainly the United States, exported industrialized agriculture production methods—including high-yield genetically modified grains, pesticides, synthetic fertilizers, and irrigation infrastructure—to developing countries to help them boost crop yields and thus reduce hunger.[89] The imposition of the industrial agriculture model on developing countries in order to increase crop yields, also known as the 'Green Revolution', played a crucial role in transforming agriculture in the Global South.[90] Even though the industrialization of agriculture did increase global food production in the wake of the Green Revolution, it had detrimental socio-economic impacts on small-scale farmers in particular, and exacerbated and entrenched rural inequality in the countries of the Global South.[91] By promoting industrialized agricultural

---

[81] MA Aksoy, 'Global Agricultural Trade Policies' in MA Aksoy and JC Beghin (eds), *Global Agricultural Trade and Developing Countries* (World Bank 2005) 37; Gonzalez, 'SDG 2: End Hunger' (n 42) 77.

[82] General Agreement on Tariffs and Trade (GATT) of 30 October 1947, 55 UNTS 187.

[83] CG Gonzalez, 'Institutionalizing Inequality: The WTO, Agriculture and Developing Countries' (2002) 27 Columbia Journal of Environmental Law 431–87, 438.

[84] Clapp (n 14) 29–39; Gonzalez, 'SDG 2: End Hunger' (n 42) 77.

[85] Gonzalez, 'Institutionalizing Inequality' (n 83) 438.

[86] Byerlee and Fanzo (n 55) 54.

[87] Clapp (n 14) 39.

[88] ibid 39.

[89] Clapp (n 14) 16–17; Gonzalez, 'SDG 2: End Hunger' (n 42) 77; Orford (n 51) 6.

[90] CG Gonzalez, 'The Global Food Crisis: Law, Policy, and the Elusive Quest for Justice' (2002) 13 Yale Human Rights and Development Law Journal, 462–79, 467; Chadwick (n 61) 33–34. See also JH Perkins, *Geopolitics and the Green Revolution* (OUP 1997).

[91] Gonzalez, 'SDG H2: End Hunger' (n 42) 77–78. See in detail Gonzalez, 'Institutionalizing Inequality' (n 83) 431–87; V Shiva, *The Violence of the Green Revolution: Third World Agriculture, Ecology and Politics* (Zed Books 1991).

production, the Green Revolution further converted production land into land for cash crops, displaced local communities, destroyed sustainable agricultural practices and ecosystems, and lowered food prices for small-scale farmers.[92] It also amplified developing countries' dependence on multinational agrifood companies, which were becoming increasingly powerful in transnational settings at that time.[93]

The 1980s and 1990s witnessed significant progress towards defining the terms and objectives that would become central to SDG 2.[94] During these years, the regulatory approaches on how to deal with hunger increasingly shifted from the issue of food supply to *access* to food.[95] In 1981 economist Amartya Sen published his book, *Poverty and Famines: An Essay on Entitlement and Deprivation*.[96] Sen famously argues that 'starvation is the characteristic of some people not *having* enough food to eat. It is not the characteristic of there *being* not enough food to eat.'[97] Furthermore, he points out that hunger is not only a question of availability and distribution of food but rather a political and legal question of 'what determines distribution of food between different sections of community.'[98] The ability to access food thus depends on the ability 'to establish entitlement to enough food'[99] and, ultimately, on rules relating to access to food.[100]

Based on Sen's entitlement approach and on people's ability to access food, the concept of 'food security' became central to the international debates on world hunger in the mid-1980s.[101] In fact, the term 'hunger' became equated with 'food security'.[102] Initially, the term 'food security' referred to the policies of countries to secure access to sufficient supplies of food.[103] In 1986, the World Bank departed from earlier understandings, maintaining that 'food security does not necessarily come from achieving food self-sufficiency in a country, nor from a rapid increase in food production'.[104] It stated that '[f]ood security has to do with *access by all people* at all times to enough food for an active and healthy life'.[105] Correspondingly, food insecurity was defined as a lack of individuals' ability to purchase the food they needed and not as a question of food supply.[106] Recently, international organizations have widely adopted the definition of food security agreed upon at the World Summit in Rome in 1996 and reaffirmed in the Declaration of the World Summit on Food Security in 2009. The Declaration states that '[f]ood security exists when all people, at all times, have physical, social and economic

---

[92] Chadwick (n 61) 34.
[93] Clapp (n 14) 48–49; S George, *How the Other Half Dies: The Real Reasons for World Hunger* (Rowman & Littlefield Publishers 1989), 97; Chadwick (n 61) 34.
[94] Byerlee and Fanzo (n 55) 55.
[95] ibid 55.
[96] A Sen, *Poverty and Famines: An Essay on Entitlement and Deprivation* (OUP 1981).
[97] ibid 1.
[98] ibid 7; Orford (n 51) 12.
[99] Sen (n 96) 8.
[100] ibid 1; Orford (n 51) 12.
[101] Orford (n 51) 6.
[102] Jarosz (n 49) 117.
[103] Chadwick (n 61) 22.
[104] World Bank, 'Poverty and Hunger: Issues and Options for Food Security in Developing Countries' (World Bank 1986) <https://documents1.worldbank.org/curated/en/166331467990005748/pdf/multi-page.pdf> accessed 22 January 2022, 10.
[105] ibid 1 (emphasis added).
[106] ibid 1; Jarosz (n 49) 125.

access to sufficient, safe and nutritious food to meet their dietary needs and food preferences for an active and healthy life'.[107]

While the 1980s and 1990s were an important period for the development of the concept of food security, hunger was still understood in terms of food calories, without taking into account other dimensions of *nutrition*.[108] Correspondingly, it was wrongly assumed that the eradication of hunger, particularly in Africa, would also solve issues of malnutrition and that caloric consumption would increase the consumption of other micronutrients, such as vitamins and minerals.[109] However, hunger and malnutrition are not be understood synonymously.[110] It was not until 1992 that the first UN International Conference on Nutrition stressed the importance of diet quality.[111] In the years that followed, the definition of food and nutrition was expanded to also include micronutrients.[112]

At the beginning of the Millennium, the adoption of the MDGs marked a new era. As already mentioned, MDG 1 set a goal of both halving poverty and hunger.[113] It featured two indicators of hunger: the proportion of underweight children under the age of five and the proportion of the population that is undernourished when measured by calorie intake.[114] MDG 1 was criticized in various respects. First, critics maintained that in deploying a narrow narrative of hunger that largely focused on the number of undernourished people measured in terms of calories, MDG 1 did not capture, for example, the various dimensions of malnutrition, such as stunting, wasting, overweight, and obesity.[115] Second, critics challenged the FAO's definition of 'undernourishment' because of its focus on dietary energy in assessing hunger, which did not include various proteins, vitamins, minerals, and other micronutrients necessary for adequate nourishment, although deficiencies in such nutrients are widespread among poor people in developing countries.[116] Third, MDG 1's indicator for underweight children was considered to be imprecise because it could not be easily transformed into measures to adequately address chronic and acute malnutrition.[117] Fourth, MDG 1 did not cover undernourished individuals in the developed world, as the MDGs were confined to developing countries.[118] Finally, little effort was made to integrate sustainable agriculture into the MDG 1 framework.[119] In general, even though the MDG 1 target of halving

---

[107] World Summit on Food Security, Declaration of the World Summit on Food Security, Rome, 16–18 November 2009, World Summit on Food Security (Rome, 16–18 November 2009), para 2 (footnote 1): 'The four pillars of food security are availability, access, utilization and stability. The nutritional dimension is integral to the concept of food security.'

[108] Byerlee and Fanzo (n 55) 55.

[109] E Kennedy and L Haddad, 'Food Security and Nutrition, 1971–91. Lessons Learned and Future Priorities' (1992) 17 Food Policy 2–6, 3–4.

[110] ibid 3. For a concise definition of malnutrition, see Young (n 58) 19–26.

[111] Byerlee and Fanzo (n 55) 55.

[112] ibid 55. For a current definition of malnutrition, see WHO, 'Malnutrition' <https://www.who.int/newsroom/fact-sheets/detail/malnutrition> accessed 22 January 2022.

[113] See MDG 1 (n 52).

[114] See <https://www.un.org/millenniumgoals/poverty.shtml> accessed 22 January 2022.

[115] Byerlee and Fanzo (n 55) 55–56.

[116] Pogge (n 6) 10–11.

[117] Byerlee and Fanzo (n 55) 55.

[118] Pogge (n 6) 19.

[119] Byerlee and Fanzo (n 55) 56.

132   SDG 2

undernutrition was successful at the global level, progress remained uneven.[120] In Sub-Saharan Africa, for example, hunger rates declined but the number of undernourished people increased due to population growth at the time.[121]

Concomitantly, important steps were taken internationally to set the course for SDG 2.[122] Nutrition became a major issue on the international development agenda.[123] The international community increasingly began to acknowledge that hunger, nutrition, and agriculture needed to be thought of together to address hunger, food insecurity, and malnutrition.[124] While there was progress in this regard, the global food economy faced a global food price crisis from 2006 to 2008 and again in 2010.[125] At the time, the drastic rise in food prices and food shortages led to significantly more undernourished people as many of those affected by the crisis could not produce or purchase enough food to meet their needs.[126] The food crisis also caused political instability and led to several food riots, for example in Egypt, Bangladesh, and Mozambique, where bread prices increased up to 30 per cent.[127] In a report released in 2013, the UN Conference on Trade and Development (UNCTAD) called upon states to 'wake up before it is too late', stating that high and volatile food prices were partly triggered by global warming and that the direct link between fuel and food prices was one of the underlying reasons for the global food crisis.[128] Importantly, the report also noted that food security required a *multi-functional approach* to reflect the major impact of climate change on agricultural productivity, while also acknowledging agricultural productivity—and its production of greenhouse gas emissions—as a key driver of climate change.[129] Consequently, UNCTAD concluded that MDG 1 would not be realized, in particular because 'agriculture has not received the attention it deserves for achieving food security and as an engine of sustainable economic, social and environmental development in developing countries'.[130]

As acknowledged today, food crises present a global problem that demands international responses to the underlying problems of the global food system.[131] This has prompted the international community to intensify its efforts to eradicate hunger and malnutrition in their broader context.[132] Numerous actions at the international level

[120] ibid.
[121] ibid.
[122] ibid.
[123] ibid.
[124] ibid.
[125] Orford (n 5) 2–3.
[126] ibid 2.
[127] ibid 2–3. See generally on food riots, eg, W Bello, *The Food Wars* (Verso 2009). On the food riots in Mozambique, see R Patel, 'Mozambique's Food Riots—The True Face of Global Warming' *The Guardian* (5 September 2010) <https://www.theguardian.com/commentisfree/2010/sep/05/mozambique-food-riots-patel> accessed 22 January 2022.
[128] UN Conference on Trade and Development (UNCTAD), 'Trade and Environment Review 2013: Wake Up Before It Is Too Late' (UNCTAD 2013), iii.
[129] ibid i.
[130] ibid iii.
[131] TA Wise and S Murphy, *Resolving the Food Crisis: Assessing Global Policy Reforms Since 2007* (Institute for Agriculture and Trade Policy (IATP) and Global Development and Environment Institute 2012) 4; Orford (n 51) 4.
[132] Chadwick (n 61) 23. On rising food prices that led to a global food crisis, see, eg, A Mittal, 'The 2008 Food Price Crisis: Rethinking Food Security Policies' UNCTAD Report: G24 Discussion Paper Series 56 (2009).

have also sought to make food security and nutrition a priority issue on the international development agenda.[133] In 2008, the World Bank shifted its focus to *agriculture* and has since financed initiatives for market-oriented agricultural reforms, among other things.[134] In the same year, addressing issues of food security, the UN Secretary-General established a High-Level Task Force on the Global Food Security Crisis, and the FAO reformed its Committee on Food Security.[135] At that time, the work of the former UN Special Rapporteur on the Right to Food, Olivier De Schutter, who has since published several reports on the right to food, drew attention to a *human-rights approach* to hunger.[136] Many of the initiatives at the international level emphasize the importance of agricultural development and food production in developing countries, the pivotal role of smallholder farmers and vulnerable groups, the challenge of limited resources in an era of climate change, and the critical role of public investment.[137] Beyond this, these initiatives also demonstrate that effective international policies require inclusive and intergovernmental platforms—which, like that of SDG 2, include all relevant stakeholders—in order to find effective solutions to hunger, food insecurity, and malnourishment.[138]

III. *Travaux Préparatoires*

With the MDGs due to expire in 2015, preparatory processes for a regulatory framework for the SDGs began at the UN Conference on Sustainable Development (Rio + 20), held in Rio de Janeiro in June 2012.[139] The summit's outcome document, entitled 'The Future We Want',[140] called for the establishment of an intergovernmental Open Working Group (OWG), which was tasked with developing a proposal for the SDGs.[141] This document did not formulate specific goals but rather established a framework for further action, based on thematic areas and cross-sectoral issues that would guide the development of each SDG.[142] It was agreed that the goals 'should be action oriented, concise and easy to communicate, limited in number, *aspirational*, *global* in nature

---

[133] Wise and Murphy (n 131) 4; Orford (n 51) 7.

[134] World Bank, *World Development Report 2008: Agriculture for Development* (World Bank 2007); Orford (n 51) 7.

[135] UN High Level Task Force on the Global Food Security Crisis, 'Comprehensive Framework for Action' (2008), see also UN High Level Task Force on the Global Food Security Crisis, 'Updated Comprehensive Framework for Action' (2008); FAO, Committee on World Food Security, 35th Session, 'Reform of the Committee on World Food Security' (CFS: 2009/2Rev.1), October 2009.

[136] For official reports published by the former Special Rapporteur on the Right to Food, see <http://www.srfood.org/en/official-reports> accessed 22 January 2022; see also Orford (n 51) 7.

[137] Wise and Murphy (n 131) 6.

[138] See UN High Level Task Force on the Global Food Security Crisis, 'Comprehensive Framework for Action' (2008); see also UN High Level Task Force on the Global Food Security Crisis, 'Updated Comprehensive Framework for Action' (2008).

[139] 'UN Report of the Conference on Sustainable Development' (20–22 June 2012), UN Doc A/CONF.216/16.

[140] UNGA, 66/288 'The Future We Want', Resolution adopted by the General Assembly on 27 July 2012 (11 September 2012), UN Doc A/RES/66/288.

[141] ibid para 248.

[142] UN, 'Open Working Group on Sustainable Development Goals (OWG)' <https://sustainabledevelopment.un.org/owg.html> accessed 22 January 2022.

134   SDG 2

and *universally* applicable to all countries while taking into account different *national realities*, capacities and levels of development and respecting national policies and priorities'.[143] The SDGs were thus intended to incorporate the social, economic, and environmental dimensions of sustainable development.[144]

As outlined in the Rio + 20 outcome document, the task was to 'establish an inclusive and transparent *intergovernmental process* on sustainable development goals that is *open to all stakeholders*'.[145] The OWG was established in January 2013 by decision of the UN General Assembly.[146] Composed of thirty members of the five UN regional groups, the OWG's thirty seats were shared among sixty-nine UN Member States, with five seats allocated to each of the African and Asian regional country groups, six seats to countries of the Latin American and Caribbean Group, and five seats to states of the Western European and Others Group (WEOG) and the Eastern Europe regional groups.[147] The OWG could decide on its own methods of working, including ways to involve relevant actors from the UN, civil society, business and scientific community, and academic institutions.[148]

The SDGs resulted from intensive public consultation with states, civil society, and other stakeholders that lasted about two years.[149] The process of developing the SDGs was primarily led by states and was therefore intergovernmental in nature, albeit with broad participation by so-called 'Major Groups' and other civil society actors. In this regard, the SDG negotiations were unprecedented compared to the MDGs, which had been criticized for being top-down, technocratic, and lacking input from civil society.[150] The negotiations on the SDGs moved away from the narrow top-down approach and a wide range of actors worldwide participated in the negotiations, offering their input in many forms.[151]

The intergovernmental negotiations on SDG 2 were conducted in two phases: first by the OWG ('stocktaking phase') and then, from January 2015 until August 2015, in

---

[143] 'The Future We Want' (n 140) para 247 (emphasis added).

[144] UN, 'Open Working Group on Sustainable Development Goals' (n 142).

[145] 'The Future We Want' (n 140) para 248 (emphasis added).

[146] UNGA, 'Open Working Group of the General Assembly on Sustainable Development Goals' (15 January 2013), UN Doc A/67/L.48/Rev.1.

[147] ibid: According to the document's annex, six seats are held by single states: Benin, Congo, Ghana, Hungary, Kenya, and Tanzania. Nine seats are held by pairs of states: Bahamas/Barbados; Belarus/Serbia; Brazil/Nicaragua; Bulgaria/Croatia; Colombia/Guatemala; Mexico/Peru; Montenegro/Slovenia; Poland/Romania; and Zambia/Zimbabwe. Fourteen seats are held by trios of countries: Argentina/Bolivia/Ecuador; Australia/Netherlands/United Kingdom; Bangladesh/Republic of Korea/Saudi Arabia; Bhutan/Thailand/Vietnam; Canada/Israel/United States; Denmark/Ireland/Norway; France/Germany/Switzerland; Italy/Spain/Turkey; China/Indonesia/Kazakhstan; Cyprus/Singapore/United Arab Emirates; Guyana/Haiti/Trinidad and Tobago; India/Pakistan/Sri Lanka; Iran/Japan/Nepal; and Nauru/Palau/Papua New Guinea. One seat is shared by four states, namely Algeria/Egypt/Morocco/Tunisia. On the membership, see also M Farrell, 'Group Politics in Global Development Policy: From the Millennium Development Goals to the Post-2015 Development Agenda' (2017) 12 The Hague Journal of Diplomacy 221–48, 235.

[148] UN, 'Open Working Group on Sustainable Development Goals' (n 142).

[149] Agenda 2030 (n 1) para 6.

[150] M Farrell, 'Negotiating the Sustainable Development Goals' in KE Smith and KV Laatikainen (eds), *Group Politics in UN Multilateralism* (Brill Nijhoff 2020) 241–66, 241. See also S Fukuda-Parr, 'Should Global Goal Setting Continue, and How, in the Post-2015 Era?' (2012) UNDESA Working Paper No 117 5.

[151] Farrell, 'Negotiating the Sustainable Development Goals' (n 150) 249–50.

intergovernmental negotiations ('negotiation phase') involving all 193 UN Member States.

A. OWG: Stocktaking Phase

The stocktaking working sessions were grouped around different thematic areas and cross-sectoral issues identified in the outcome document of Rio + 20.[152] The 3rd session of the OWG (OWG-3), which took place in May 2013, was dedicated to discussions of a cluster of issues on food security, nutrition, and sustainable agriculture.[153] From the very beginning of the stocktaking phase (OWG-3), food security, nutrition, and sustainable agriculture were among the most pressing concerns of the post-2015 development agenda.[154] Against this backdrop, the conceptualization phase on the development of a new SDG focused on a number of *key issues* related to these concerns.[155] However, in general, no consensus could be reached on whether food security, nutrition, and sustainable agriculture should each be the subject of an individual SDG or included in a joint SDG.[156]

The multidimensional nature of food security and nutrition, as well as sustainable agriculture called for a holistic and ecosystem-centred approach to food issues.[157] Such an approach would be able to address the close interlinkages between food, agriculture, land and water, energy, health, biodiversity, and climate change. Accordingly, delegates to OWG-3 agreed that it was vital to consider the interlinkages between food and other areas of sustainable development, but disagreed about how these interlinkages could be transformed into specific goals and targets under the SDGs.[158] Furthermore, OWG-3 served to highlight the importance of a rights-based approach to food.[159] By including food security and nutrition in to the SDG framework, these issues would also be recognized as 'human rights' issues.[160]

The inter-agency Technical Support Team (TST) provided further insights into the key issues discussed during OWG-3. Although food, nutrition, and sustainable agriculture are closely interlinked, the TST issued two separate briefings: one on food security and nutrition and another on sustainable agriculture.[161]

---

[152] See UN GA Res 66/288 (11 September 2012) UN Doc A/Res/66/288.

[153] The other cluster was desertification, land degradation and drought as well as water and sanitation, see OWG3, 'Co-Chair's Summary', Draft 13 June <https://sustainabledevelopment.un.org/content/documents/18590 WG3%20Draft%20Summary%20rev2DOC_1306%20clean.pdf> accessed 22 January 2022.

[154] The Technical Support Team (TST) Issues Brief: Food Security and Nutrition, 1.

[155] OWG-3, Concluding Remarks of Co-Chairs, 24 May 2013, 1.

[156] OWG-3, 'Co-Chair's Summary', Draft 13 June, 6 <https://sustainabledevelopment.un.org/content/docume nts/18590OWG3%20Draft%20Summary%20rev2DOC_1306%20clean.pdf> accessed 22 January 2022.

[157] ibid 6.

[158] ibid 6.

[159] OWG3, 'Co-Chair's Summary', Draft 13 June, 3.

[160] ibid 3.

[161] TST Issues Brief: Food Security and Nutrition; TST Issues Brief: Sustainable Agriculture.

1. Food Security and Nutrition

The development of a SDG on food security and nutrition occurred at a time of significant new challenges—relating to the causes of food insecurity and malnutrition in particular—that deviated significantly from the past.[162] As shown above, this included setbacks caused by food price increases, conflicts, and other shocks.[163] Apart from the well-known challenges of hunger and undernourishment, overweight and obesity became an actual problem in many—mainly Western—countries.[164] Climate-related constraints, degradation of ecosystems, globalization, and market integration had impacted food production, in particular of small-scale farmers.[165] A future goal had to consider these new challenges in order to be effectively achieved.

SDG 2 was mainly developed in comparison to MDG 1.[166] MDG 1 recognized the close link between poverty and food, in particular between income poverty and access to food.[167] However, many agree that the experience with MDG 1 has revealed that poverty and food are not per se correlated and that progress in reducing income poverty does not necessarily lead to a corresponding reduction of caloric intake deficiencies.[168] The debates of OWG-3 thus drew particular attention to agriculture-led growth, which was presented as generally one of the most effective measure in reducing food insecurity and malnutrition.[169] However, growth driven by agriculture could only lead to improved food security if based on more productive, sustainable, resilient, and inclusive farming systems.[170] Accordingly, the rural sector was considered to be especially important, as food insecurity mainly affects poor farmers and rural communities.[171] Furthermore, as discussed above, MDG 1 also did not effectively address malnutrition.[172] It also did not include the specific determinants of food in security, such as gender inequality and social exclusion, nor did it take into account the unequal nutritional outcomes among different groups within societies.[173]

During the discussions, the delegates of OWG-3 mainly agreed that the missing dimensions in MDG 1 should receive particular attention when developing a new goal on food security and nutrition. Many speakers called for the development of policies to improve addressing malnutrition and under- and over-nutrition.[174] These should also include promoting nutrition in the first 1,000 days of life to support children's healthy development as well as objectives on wasting and anaemia.[175] Over-nutrition, which

---

[162] TST Issues Brief: Food Security and Nutrition, 1–2; OWG-3, 'Co-Chair's Summary', Draft 13 June, 2.
[163] TST Issues Brief: Food Security and Nutrition, 1.
[164] ibid 1.
[165] ibid 1.
[166] ibid 2.
[167] ibid 2.
[168] ibid 2; OWG-3, 'Co-Chair's Summary', Draft 13 June, 2.
[169] TST Issues Brief: Food Security and Nutrition, 2.
[170] ibid 2.
[171] ibid 2.
[172] ibid 2.
[173] ibid 2–3.
[174] ibid 4.
[175] ibid 4.

has become an ever-pressing issue mainly in states of the Global North, should be considered in connection with non-communicable diseases.[176]

Against this backdrop, the TST instituted strategies to support the agenda of the stocktaking process that was intended to help develop a goal for food security and nutrition. First, according to the TST, strategies were needed to promote *inclusive growth*, particularly in the *rural sector* and with a focus on *smallholder farmers*.[177] Inclusive growth should also be 'nutritive sensitive' that 'involves and reaches people living in poverty, especially through increased employment and other income earning opportunities.'[178] Second, there was also a strong emphasis on social protection measures to reduce malnutrition.[179] Strategies promoting human capital development, and inclusion, with a particular focus on gender, needed to be included in the agenda on food security and nutrition.[180] In particular, developing countries needed to reduce food losses and wastes in food production, storage, and transport through improvements in technology and infrastructure.[181]

Against this backdrop, the TST formulated several proposals.[182] One of its key recommendations for a potential SDG on food and nutrition (compared to MDG 1) was to revise and strengthen the *nutrition* dimension, broadening it beyond an exclusively caloric intake to include other important nutrients.[183] It also suggested that food security and nutrition needed to be more closely linked to access to safe and clean water.[184] Moreover, the TST emphasized the importance of recognizing the broader issues that impact food security and nutrition, in particular the interdependence between environmental sustainability on the one hand and the resilience of food security and nutrition systems on the other.[185]

Considering the above, the integration of food security and nutrition into the SDG framework was conceived to be achievable in several ways: as a goal on poverty, food security, and nutrition that would build on the approach of MDG 1 and recognize the interrelationship between food security, nutrition, and poverty, or as a goal on food security and nutrition, or as a combination of both goals.[186] Regardless of how food security and nutrition would be integrated into the SDG framework, discussions during the conceptualization phase, as well as the TST issues brief on food security and nutrition, made it clear that achieving sustainable development depended primarily on a variety of (nutrition-related) aspects that needed to be improved, including the underlying causes of food insecurity and malnutrition.

---

[176] ibid 4.
[177] TST Issues Brief: Food Security and Nutrition</IBT>, 3.
[178] ibid 2.
[179] ibid 3.
[180] ibid 3.
[181] OWG-3, 'Co-Chair's Summary', Draft 13 June, 4.
[182] TST Issues Brief: Food Security and Nutrition, 4–5.
[183] ibid 4.
[184] ibid 4.
[185] ibid 4.
[186] ibid 6–7.

2. Sustainable Agriculture

Throughout history, sustainable agriculture has been gradually incorporated into global food governance.[187] An important entry point for the conceptualization phase of SDG 2 was the widely accepted assumption that economic growth, and agricultural growth in particular, would play an important role in alleviating and reducing hunger, food insecurity, and malnutrition.[188] Food production would increase the ability of people and households to purchase and produce more food, which is seen as one of the key factors for reducing poverty.[189] However, as mentioned above, MDG 1 did not capture the nexus between food and nutrition and agriculture.[190]

The outcome document of the Rio + 20 conference highlighted the importance of productive capacity and sustainable agriculture as one of the sets of issues to be included in the post-2015 development agenda.[191] At the conceptualization phase (OWG-3), there was an early recognition that a potential goal should reflect an integrated approach to food security, nutrition, and sustainable agriculture. There appears to have been discussions about how to turn the link between food security, nutrition, and sustainable agriculture into a policy goal (or goals) and what sustainable practices should be included in a potential goal capable of addressing the challenges of hunger and malnutrition in the world.[192] Many speakers emphasized that historical experience had shown that the 'Green Revolution' had lost its usefulness, so there was a call for new agricultural models that would better accommodate sustainable agriculture to counter hunger and malnutrition worldwide.[193]

The TST provided important recommendations on the link between food and sustainable agriculture, and suggested a number of issues to consider in the stocktaking phase. Notably, it pointed out that agriculture, which is understood broadly and includes 'crop and livestock production, fisheries, and forestry', provides income, food, and other essential goods and services, especially for poor people,[194] is 'multifunctional', and operates within complex social, economic, and environmental systems.[195] Accordingly, a potential goal needed to reflect the multiple roles and functions of agriculture in relation to food security and nutrition, which includes not only food

---

[187] See Section II of this chapter.

[188] S Fan and J Brzesk, 'The Nexus between Agriculture and Nutrition: Do Growth Patterns and Conditional Factors Matter?' in S Fan and R Pandya-Lorch (eds), Reshaping Agriculture for Nutrition and Health (International Food Policy Research Institute 2012) 31–38 (32).

[189] ibid 32, 37.

[190] See this chapter, Section II.

[191] 'The Future We Want' (n 140) para 23: 'We reaffirm the importance of supporting developing countries in their efforts to eradicate poverty and promote empowerment of the poor and people in vulnerable situations, including removing barriers to opportunity, enhancing *productive capacity*, developing *sustainable agriculture* and promoting full and productive employment and decent work for all, complemented by effective social policies, including social protection floors, with a view to achieving the internationally agreed development goals, including the Millennium Development Goals' (emphasis added).

[192] See OWG-3, Concluding Remarks of Co-Chairs, 24 May 2013, 4–5.

[193] OWG-3, Concluding Remarks of Co-Chairs, 24 May 2013, 4. For the 'Green Revolution', see this chapter, Section II.

[194] TST Issues Brief: Sustainable Agriculture, 1.

[195] International Assessment of Agricultural Knowledge, Science and Technology for Development (IAASTD), 'International Assessment of Agricultural Knowledge, Science and Technology for Development: Global Report', 2009, 2.

production systems but also social issues, such as access to land, resource distribution, and rural development.[196]

Regarding *sustainable* agriculture, its relevance was raised in the context of two global challenges: the high levels of hunger and malnutrition, particularly in developing countries, and the unsustainable and increasing burden of human activities on the environment.[197] From the exchange of views during OWG-3, one key point raised was that *food production* needed to *increase* in order to meet the demand for food in the face of a growing world population.[198] Likewise, natural resources should be used efficiently, especially in light of the changing food patterns among wealthier populations.[199] However, delegates at OWG-3 agreed that the increase in food production simultaneously has significant impacts on natural resources, resulting in environmental degradation and biodiversity loss, which must be carefully balanced against agricultural productivity.[200]

Accordingly, there was also broad agreement that these challenges posed by food production required a more comprehensive view regarding agricultural and food *systems* to be considered when designing a future goal.[201] Notably, many delegates of OWG-3 and the TST emphasized the need for agricultural and food systems to become more resilient, productive and less wasteful, not only from an economic but also from an environmental and social perspective.[202] Particular attention was given to agricultural and food systems that relied more heavily on ecological principles to improve food production, while reducing the negative environmental and social impacts of agriculture, particularly for smallholders, such as women or indigenous people.[203]

Hence, a consensus seemed to emerge on the dimensions of sustainable agriculture in the context of food security and nutrition during the conceptualization phase.[204] According to the TST, agricultural systems needed to be 'based on ecosystem approaches that conserve, manage and enhance natural resources and take advantage of the natural biological inputs and processes'.[205] This approach would be able to reduce the negative impact of agriculture on the environment and help increase the resilience not only of food production systems but also of other issues underlying these systems.[206] Furthermore, attention was also paid to biodiversity and its ability to provide crop varieties and breeding stock that enable farmers to adopt to changing production and climate conditions.[207] In this respect, the integration of sustainable technologies

---

[196] TST Issues Brief: Sustainable Agriculture</IBT>, 1.

[197] ibid 1.

[198] ibid 1; OWG-3, Concluding Remarks of Co-Chairs, 24 May 2013, 4.

[199] OWG-3, Concluding Remarks of Co-Chairs, 24 May 2013, 4. See also N Alexandratos and J Bruinsma, 'World Agriculture towards 2030/2050: the 2012 Revision' (June 2012) ESA Working Paper No 12-03 <https://www.fao.org/3/ap106e/ap106e.pdf> accessed 22 January 2022.

[200] See TST Issues Brief: Sustainable Agriculture, 1.

[201] See ibid 2–3.

[202] ibid 2–3; OWG-3, Concluding Remarks of Co-Chairs, 24 May 2013, 5.

[203] TST Issues Brief: Sustainable Agriculture, 3; OWG-3, Concluding Remarks of Co-Chairs, 24 May 2013, 5.

[204] TST Issues Brief: Sustainable Agriculture, 4.

[205] ibid 3.

[206] ibid 3.

[207] ibid 3.

140   SDG 2

and practices, including local knowledge, into agricultural production, supported by financial assistance and strong institutional capacities, was seen as vital.[208] Importantly, to be effective, sustainable practices needed also to promote a range of social aspects, particularly better access to land and other resources for the poor and rural populations, and capacity building for smallholder farmers that could enable them to increase their food productivity and resilience to climate change.[209] In fact, most of these sustainable agriculture issues were later integrated in one way or another into SDG 2.

The TST made several proposals on how to achieve these objectives for sustainable agriculture. These proposals focused on sustainable food systems, as mentioned above, but also on food waste and losses, and smallholder productivity and income.[210] In particular, the TST proposed to link the eradication of hunger, food insecurity, and malnutrition with sustainable agriculture, food systems, and agricultural value chains in a *single goal* that should also include access to food and other social issues, such as rural poverty, income, and social protection.[211] Another recommendation concerned the *interlinkages* between the different thematic clusters of the development agenda.[212] Strong emphasis was put on the linkages between food, climate, land, energy, and water.[213] Moreover, sustainable agriculture also needed to cover issues concerning child mortality and maternal health, and gender issues.[214] Finally, a potential goal should be universal but should also take into account different domestic conditions, capacities, and levels of development, which was considered to be particularly crucial for the agricultural sector.[215]

The stocktaking phase on food security, nutrition, and sustainable agriculture ended with OWG-3. The next phase was the intergovernmental negotiations.

B. OWG: Negotiations and Drafting of the Proposed Sustainable Development Goal 2

Following the stocktaking phase, deliberations entered the final phase of the intergovernmental negotiations (OWG-9–13), held from March to June 2014.[216] A 'Focus Area' document based on the first eight sessions of the OWG was released in February 2014 to guide the intergovernmental negotiations of OWG-9.[217] The document was

---

[208] ibid 3.

[209] ibid 3.

[210] ibid 5.

[211] ibid 5.

[212] ibid 6.

[213] ibid 5. See also OWG-3, Concluding Remarks of Co-Chairs, 24 May 2013, 3.

[214] ibid 6.

[215] ibid 6.

[216] See Farrell, 'Negotiating the Sustainable Development Goals' (n 150) 257. For a timeline, see S Hollander and C Panday 'Lessons Learned from the MDGs: The Process of Defining a Post-2015 Agenda' *The Broker* (7 May 2013) <https://www.thebrokeronline.eu/lessons-learned-from-the-mdgs-d38/> accessed 22 January 2022.

[217] OWG-9, 'SDGs Focus Areas' (24 February 2014) <https://sustainabledevelopment.un.org/content/docume nts/3276focusareas.pdf> accessed 22 January 2022.

intended to guide the process of narrowing down the potential SDGs and their accompanying targets.[218]

The document included 'food security and nutrition' in Focus Area 2 to be considered in OWG-9.[219] In their statements on the various Focus Areas, the Major Groups articulated a criticism that has become pivotal to the contemporary understanding of SDG 2. They argued that the areas generally did not follow a 'rights-based approach' to sustainable development but instead focused on 'growth', despite this emphasis having detrimental effects on sustainable development.[220] The Focus Area on food security and nutrition indeed stressed the need to increase sustainable agricultural productivity, improve food systems for 'economic well-being', and ensure food security and nutrition.[221] Accordingly, the Focus Area contained many elements that address sustainable agriculture and food systems, including those that were ultimately included in SDG 2, such as improving access to land ownership for small-scale farmers, but also elements that were either shifted to the targets of other goals or omitted altogether. For instance, an issue that was incorporated into the Focus Area but later became target 12.3 was reducing food waste, an objective closely linked to the achievement of SDG 2.[222]

The deliberations continued with OWG-10 and a 'slightly tweaked'[223] document on Focus Areas that provided more detail on the potential goals and targets compared to the first draft of the document discussed at OWG-9.[224] With the inclusion

---

[218] IISD, 'Summary of the 9th Session of the UN GA OWG on Sustainable SDGs' (3–5 March 2014), vol 39(2), 8 March 2014, 2 <https://enb.iisd.org/events/9th-session-un-general-assemblys-unga-owg-sdgs/summary-report-3-5-march-2014> accessed 12 September 2022.

[219] ibid.

[220] OWG-9, 'Compilation Major Groups Statements and Focus Areas Responses' <https://sustainabledevelopm ent.un.org/content/documents/3362Compilation%20Major%20Groups%20Statements%20and%20Focus%20Ar eas%20Responses_March%2025_final.pdf> accessed 22 January 2022.

[221] OWG-9, 'SDGs Focus Areas' (24 February 2014), Focus Area 2. See also OWG-9, 'Compilation Major Groups Statements and Focus Areas Responses' <https://sustainabledevelopment.un.org/content/documents/ 3362Compilation%20Major%20Groups%20Statements%20and%20Focus%20Areas%20Responses_March%202 5_final.pdf> accessed 22 January 2022.

[222] OWG-9, SDGs Focus Areas (24 February 2014). Target 12.3 reads as follows: 'By 2030, halve per capita global food waste at the retail and consumer levels and reduce food losses along production and supply chains, including post-harvest losses.'

[223] IISD, 'Summary of the 9th Session of the UN GA OWG on Sustainable SDGs' (n 218) 13.

[224] OWG-10, 'Focus Area Document' (19 March 2014) <https://sustainabledevelopment.un.org/content/ documents/3402Focus%20areas_20140319.pdf> accessed 22 January 2022. Focus Area 2 on sustainable agriculture, food security, and nutrition reads as follows: 'Increasing the productivity of agriculture sustainably and improving food systems are important for economic well-being as well as for ensuring food security and nutrition, realization of the right to adequate food and eradication of hunger. Some areas that could be considered include: a) ensuring year-round access by all to affordable, adequate, safe and nutritious food; b) ending child malnutrition and stunting; c) increasing agricultural productivity, including through adequate irrigation, seeds and fertilisers, while in parallel halting and reversing land degradation, drought and desertification; d) improving efficiency of water use in agriculture; e) eliminating use of toxic chemicals; f) enhancing all forms of agricultural biodiversity; g) promoting indigenous and sustainable farming and fishing practices; h) strengthening resilience of farming systems and food supplies to climate change; i) enhancing adherence to internationally recognized guidelines on the responsible governance of tenure of land, fisheries and forests, including full consultation with local communities; j) improved access to credit and other financial services, land tenure, and agricultural extension services, for all, including smallholders, women, indigenous peoples and local communities; k) increased investment and support to research and development on sustainable agricultural technologies; l) reducing post-harvest crop losses and food waste along food supply chains; m) addressing harmful agricultural subsidies; n) addressing price volatility, including through market information and oversight on commodity markets; and o) appropriate means of implementation.'

of sustainable agriculture in the heading of Focus Area 2, the revised document now represented a much stronger nexus between food security and nutrition, and sustainable agriculture.[225] The growth-based approach was balanced against a *rights-based approach*, since the document explicitly stated in its 'chapeau' that agricultural productivity was vital to economic well-being, food security, and nutrition but also to the realization of the right to adequate food and the eradication of hunger.[226] Interestingly, the objective of ending hunger was included neither in the heading of the initial draft nor in the revisited document on the Focus Areas. It was also not suggested as a specific area to be considered under a potential goal.[227]

The deliberations on the consolidation of the Focus Areas partly mirrored the political approaches to sustainable development and food, and agricultural issues more specifically. For example, Bolivia, speaking on behalf of the G77 and China, stressed that governance of fisheries, forests, and land included in the Focus Area was subject to voluntary guidelines and could only be regulated under the jurisdiction of national governments.[228] China suggested naming the agriculture Focus Area 'agricultural development, food security, and nutrition', concentrating on eradicating hunger and ensuring year-round access by all individuals to safe and adequate food.[229] Benin, speaking on behalf of the Least Developed Countries (LDCs), called for 'rural development' to be integrated into the Focus Area, with accompanying targets on 'investment in rural infrastructure, humanitarian food emergencies, and price volatility'.[230] Brazil highlighted the need to end agricultural protectionism and suggested improving open and non-discriminatory market access in developing countries and multilateral trading systems.[231]

During OWG-10, stakeholders and Major Groups also added further proposals to the Focus Area.[232] They suggested that access to appropriate food for all should also include *culturally* appropriate food.[233] Furthermore, they proposed a target on the implementation of productive, resilient, and diverse sustainable agriculture and food systems that would be able to address the negative impacts of climate change.[234] The Major Groups also emphasized an issue already addressed in the initial document, namely the importance of setting a target to halve the global rate of food production losses and waste along food supply chains.[235] Finally, another objective was to ensure that

---

[225] ibid.

[226] ibid.

[227] ibid.

[228] IISD, 'Summary of the 10th Session of the UN GA OWG on Sustainable SDGs' (31 March–4 April 2014) vol. 32 (10), 7 April 2014, 8 <https://enb.iisd.org/events/10th-session-un-general-assemblys-unga-owg-sdgs/summary-report-31-march-4-april-2014> accessed 22 January 2022.

[229] ibid 8.

[230] ibid 8.

[231] ibid 9.

[232] OWG-10, 'Major Groups and other Stakeholders Dialogue with the CO-Chairs on SDGs' (2 April 2014) <https://sustainabledevelopment.un.org/content/documents/3674Compilation%20Document%20on%20Goals%20and%20Targets_April%2011-%20final.pdf> accessed 22 January 2022.

[233] OWG-10, 'Major Groups Compilation Summary', 4 (cluster 3) <https://sustainabledevelopment.un.org/content/documents/3678Compilation%20Summary-%20April%2011-%20final.pdf> accessed 22 January 2022.

[234] ibid 4.

[235] ibid 4.

well-functioning markets were accessible to all and trade policies were reshaped, and that food price volatility was mitigated.[236]

The next negotiation round was OWG-11.[237] A prepared 'working document' contained a list of 16 Focus Areas and approximately 150 targets.[238] This negotiation round was seen as a 'critical juncture' because a set of potential SDGs were formulated for the first time (but still referred to as Focus Areas).[239] Accordingly, compared to OWG-9 and OWG-10, delegates had a clearer understanding of the goals and associated targets.[240] Focus Area 2 of the working document read as follows: 'End hunger and improve nutrition for all through sustainable agriculture and improved food systems.'[241] It included eight targets:

a) all people have access to adequate (safe, affordable, diverse and nutritious) food all year round

b) end malnutrition in all its forms, notably stunting and wasting in children under five years of age

c) by 2030 ensure sustainable food production systems with high yields, and reduce intensity of use of water by at least x per cent, chemicals by at least y per cent, and energy by at least z per cent

d) by 2030 achieve access to adequate inputs, knowledge, productive resources, financial services and markets for small farmers and fishers, with a particular focus on women and indigenous peoples

e) reduce the global rate of loss and waste along the food supply chain by 50 per cent by 2030

f) all countries have in place sustainable land-use policies by 2020, and all drought-prone countries develop and implement drought preparedness policies by 2020

g) achieve climate-smart agriculture that is resilient and adaptable to extreme weather including drought, climate change and natural disasters

h) achieve by 2030 protection of agricultural biodiversity, including through use of the practices and local knowledge related to agro-biodiversity and diversity of food.[242]

As in the previous sessions, Member States and stakeholders had the opportunity to deliberate on the proposal.[243] Importantly, the reference to food security was now

---

[236] ibid 4.

[237] See <https://sustainabledevelopment.un.org/owg11.html> accessed 22 January 2022.

[238] OWG-11, 'Working Document for 5–9 May Session of OWG' (informal document, 17 April 2014) <https://sustainabledevelopment.un.org/content/documents/3686WorkingDoc_0205_additionalsupporters.pdf> accessed 22 January 2022.

[239] IISD, 'Summary of the 11th Session of the UN GA on SDGs: 5–9 May 2014', vol 32 (11), 12 May 2014, 1 <https://enb.iisd.org/events/11th-session-un-general-assemblys-unga-owg-sdgs/summary-report-5-9-may-2014> accessed 22 January 2022. See also, eg, the statement by the G77, 30 April 2014 <https://sustainabledevelopment.un.org/content/documents/8846group77.pdf> accessed 22 January 2022.

[240] See OWG-11, 'Working Document for 5–9 May Session of OWG' (n 238).

[241] ibid.

[242] ibid 1–2.

[243] For the views of the governments on Focus Area 2 based on working document OWG-11, see IISD, 'Summary of the 11th Session of the UN GA on SDGs' (n 239) 5–6.

removed from the heading of the Focus Area. Hence, Lesotho, on behalf of the African Group, suggested a new title for the goal that would again include food security.[244] Furthermore, the revised version added all forms of malnutrition to its scope but did not, for instance, include obesity. Some developed states, such as Switzerland, France, and Germany, therefore proposed to incorporate a target on over-nutrition and obesity into the goal.[245] Others raised concerns about the meaning of the term 'climate-smart agriculture' and suggested replacing it with 'sustainable agriculture'.[246] Finally, based on past experiences with the global food price crisis, some states drew attention once again to the problem of food price volatility, which had been removed from the Focus Area.[247] Along the same lines, Non-Governmental Organizations (NGOs) also suggested a specific target on price volatility.[248]

The next phase of the negotiations was OWG-12, accompanied by a first 'zero draft' of seventeen goals and 212 targets.[249] Proposed goal 2 read as follows: 'End hunger, achieve food security and adequate nutrition for all, and promote sustainable agriculture.'[250] It contained eleven targets:

2.1 end hunger and ensure that all people have access to adequate, safe, affordable, and nutritious food all year round by 2030

2.2 end malnutrition in all its forms, including undernutrition, micronutrient deficiencies and obesity and overweight, with special attention to reducing stunting by 40 per cent and wasting to less than 5 per cent in children less than 5 years of age by 2025, and address the nutritional needs of pregnant and lactating women

2.3 by 2030, substantially increase small-scale food producers' incomes and productivity, including small family farmers, pastoralists and fishers, with a particular focus on women

2.4 by 2030 achieve access to adequate inputs, knowledge and productive resources, financial services and markets, especially for small and family farmers, pastoralists, and fishers, with a particular focus on women

2.5 by 2030, develop food systems that are more productive, sustainable, resilient and efficient, and minimize adverse human and environmental impacts without compromising food and nutrition security

2.6 by 2030 reduce by 50 per cent global food waste at retail and consumer level

2.7 by 2030 reduce by 50 per cent production and post-harvest food losses and those along food supply chains

---

[244] ibid 5.

[245] ibid 6.

[246] ibid 5–6 (China, Kazakhstan, Bangladesh, and Sweden).

[247] ibid 5, see also statements by China, Kazakhstan, and India.

[248] OWG-11, 'NGO Major Group', 5 May 2014 <https://sustainabledevelopment.un.org/content/documents/9798civicus.pdf> accessed 22 January 2022.

[249] OWG-12, 'Introduction and Proposed Goals and Targets on Sustainable Development for the Post2015 Development Agenda' (2 June 2014) <https://sustainabledevelopment.un.org/content/documents/4528zerodraft12OWG.pdf> accessed 22 January 2022.

[250] ibid 4–5.

2.8 by 2030, fully implement agricultural practices that strengthen resilience and adaptation to extreme weather, drought, climate change and natural disasters, in particular for small-scale farmers

2.9 achieve by 2030 protection and sustainable use of agricultural biodiversity, including through enhanced use and application of indigenous practices and local and traditional knowledge, and through agricultural research and development related to agro-biodiversity and diversity of food

2.10 improve effectiveness of addressing humanitarian food emergencies, including as appropriate through stockholding

2.11 by 2030 fully implement measures that curb excessive food price volatility and ensure proper functioning of markets.[251]

Deliberations on the targets of goal 2 continued in various informal meetings.[252] Recommendations primarily concerned the targets' substance.[253] As obesity (target 2.2) was now included in the goal, some participants suggested moving this form of malnutrition to goal 3, which dealt with health.[254] Other proposals aimed at combining some targets, for example small-scale food producers with access to adequate inputs, knowledge, and productive resources, financial services and markets (target 2.3 and target 2.4); food productivity with food systems (target 2.3 and target 2.5); or sustainable food systems with agricultural practices that are resilient against climate change (target 2.5 and target 2.8).[255] Some also argued that targets 2.10 and 2.11 on food price volatility would function better as indicators rather than targets under proposed goal 2.[256]

OWG-13 was the final round of negotiations. Ahead of the deliberations, a revised zero draft of the future SDGs was prepared.[257] Goal 2, entitled 'End hunger, improve nutrition, and promote sustainable agriculture', now comprised nine targets:

2.1 by 2030 end hunger and ensure that all people have access to adequate, safe, affordable, and nutritious food all year round

2.2 by 2030 end all forms of malnutrition, with special attention to stunting and wasting in children under five years of age, and address the nutritional needs of pregnant and lactating women

2.3 by 2030 substantially increase small-scale food producers' productivity and incomes, particularly of women, family farmers and pastoralists through secure access for all to productive resources and inputs, knowledge, financial services and markets

---

[251] ibid 4–5.

[252] IISD, 'Summary of the 12th Session of the UN GA PPWG on SDGs: 16–20 June 2014' (23 June 2014) 32(12) Earth Negotiations Bulletin 3.

[253] ibid 3.

[254] ibid 3.

[255] ibid 3.

[256] ibid 3.

[257] OWG-13, 'Introduction and Proposed Goals and Targets on Sustainable Development for the Post2015 Development Agenda' (Revised Zero Draft, 30 June 2014), 4–5.

146 SDG 2

2.4 by 2030 implement sustainable and resilient agricultural practices including for adaptation to climate change, extreme weather, drought and disasters, and progressively enhance soil quality

2.5 by 2020 maintain genetic diversity of seeds, cultivated plants, farmed and domesticated animals and their wild relatives, and ensure access to and fair and equitable sharing of benefits arising from the utilization of genetic resources and associated traditional knowledge as internationally agreed

2.a increase investment in rural infrastructure, agricultural research, technology development, and capable institutions, particularly in countries that are net food importers

2.b phase out all forms of agricultural export subsidies

2.c end extreme food price volatility including through improved functioning and regulation of food commodity markets and improved market information

2.d create and diversify seed and plant banks, including with traditional varieties, at national, regional and international levels, to safeguard seed and genetic plant diversity.[258]

During the three readings of goal 2, delegations were allowed to make final propositions.[259] In particular, they addressed food security, food loss and waste, different dimensions of malnutrition, types of smallholders, and sustainability in increasing agricultural productivity.[260] Food security was still not included in the goal's heading, but numerous delegates called to reinstate it.[261] Moreover, although participants had requested since the stocktaking process that food loss and waste to be included in goal 2 as a stand-alone target, the final outcome of the negotiation phase incorporated these issues as a target into goal 12.[262] Member States seemed to reach a compromise on the issue of hunger (target 2.1), except on the question of whether to refer to 'vulnerable people' or 'people in vulnerable situations'. The final version then slightly modified this description to include poor people as well ('the poor and people in vulnerable situations').[263] Moreover, delegates wanted to incorporate a list of different forms of malnutrition (target 2.2) in the goal, particularly obesity and overweight, which the target in question ultimately did not include.[264] There was also special emphasis on the nutritional needs of women, adolescent girls, older persons, and women of reproductive age, an objective that was then incorporated into the

---

[258] ibid 4–5.

[259] IISD, 'Summary of the 13th Session of the UN GA OWG on SDGs: 14–19 July 2014' (2014) 32(13) Earth Negotiations Bulletin 5 <https://enb.iisd.org/events/13th-session-un-general-assemblys-unga-owg-sdgs/summary-report-14-19-july-2014> accessed 22 January 2022. Stakeholders and Major Groups also had the opportunity to propose changes to the goals in the revised zero draft, see OWG-13, 'Final Compilation of Amendments to Goals and Targets by Major Groups and other Stakeholders including Citizen's Responses to MY World 6 Priorities', 14–18 July 2014, 6–7 (amendments to proposed goal 2) <https://sustainabledevelopment.un.org/content/documents/4438mgscompilationowg13.pdf> accessed 22 January 2022.

[260] IISD, 'Summary of the 13th Session of the UN GA OWG on SDGs' (n 259) 5.

[261] ibid 5.

[262] ibid 5.

[263] ibid 5.

[264] ibid 5–6.

final wording of target 2.2.[265] Regarding target 2.3 on smallholders, delegates supported including fishers, foresters, and youth in target 2.3.[266] Furthermore, the issues that were discussed extensively were agricultural productivity (target 2.3) as well as food production systems and resilient practices (target 2.4). Participants pointed out that both targets needed to establish that such an increase would have to be achieved in a sustainable manner.[267] Some countries also questioned the appropriateness of incorporating genetic diversity into target 2.5 and called for its deletion, while others highlighted its importance for the proposed goal—successfully so, as the final proposal for SDG 2 refers to the genetic diversity of seeds, cultivated plants, and farmed and domesticated animals.[268] The participants preferred to leave some aspects of target 2.b to the World Trade Organization (WTO) negotiations. With this target in mind, governments also debated the formulation of export subsidies, domestic support, and market access.[269] They argued that target 2.a should refer to developing countries rather than to 'net importers of food.[270]

The final wording of the proposed goal 2 ('End hunger, achieve food security and improved nutrition and promote sustainable agriculture') reads as follows:

2.1 by 2030 end hunger and ensure access by all people, in particular the poor and people in vulnerable situations including infants, to safe, nutritious and sufficient food all year round

2.2 by 2030 end all forms of malnutrition, including achieving by 2025 the internationally agreed targets on stunting and wasting in children under five years of age, and address the nutritional needs of adolescent girls, pregnant and lactating women, and older persons

2.3 by 2030 double the agricultural productivity and the incomes of small-scale food producers, particularly women, indigenous peoples, family farmers, pastoralists and fishers, including through secure and equal access to land, other productive resources and inputs, knowledge, financial services, markets, and opportunities for value addition and non-farm employment

2.4 by 2030 ensure sustainable food production systems and implement resilient agricultural practices that increase productivity and production, that help maintain ecosystems, that strengthen capacity for adaptation to climate change, extreme weather, drought, flooding and other disasters, and that progressively improve land and soil quality

2.5 by 2020 maintain genetic diversity of seeds, cultivated plants, farmed and domesticated animals and their related wild species, including through soundly managed and diversified seed and plant banks at national, regional and

---

[265] ibid 5–6.
[266] ibid 6.
[267] ibid 6.
[268] ibid 6.
[269] ibid 6.
[270] ibid 6.

international levels, and ensure access to and fair and equitable sharing of benefits arising from the utilization of genetic resources and associated traditional knowledge as internationally agreed

2.a increase investment, including through enhanced international cooperation, in rural infrastructure, agricultural research and extension services, technology development, and plant and livestock gene banks to enhance agricultural productive capacity in developing countries, in particular in least developed countries

2.b correct and prevent trade restrictions and distortions in world agricultural markets including by the parallel elimination of all forms of agricultural export subsidies and all export measures with equivalent effect, in accordance with the mandate of the Doha Development Round

2.c adopt measures to ensure the proper functioning of food commodity markets and their derivatives, and facilitate timely access to market information, including on food reserves, in order to help limit extreme food price volatility.[271]

The OWG's mandate ended on 19 July 2014 with the adoption of the final proposal on the SDGs to be approved by the UN General Assembly.[272] In September 2015, the UN General Assembly unanimously adopted the SDGs at its 70th session.[273]

IV. Commentary on SDG 2

A. Interlinkages with Other SDGs

Before considering the relationship between SDG 2 and international law and the question to what extent international law—particularly international human rights law and international trade and investment law—contribute to achieving SDG 2, this part discusses the interlinkages between SDG 2 and the other goals. Compared to the MDGs, which were considered to be fragmented and disjointed, Agenda 2030 states that the SDGs are 'integrated and indivisible'.[274] However, as the following analysis will show, the SDGs do in fact suffer from a lack of integration as the goals are treated as separate areas ('silo approach') and are partially isolated from or in conflict with each other.[275]

---

[271] OWG-13, 'Outcome Document—Introduction to the Proposal of the OWG for SDGs' (19 July 2014) 6–7 <https://sustainabledevelopment.un.org/content/documents/4518SDGs_FINAL_Proposal%20of%20OWG_19%20July%20at%201320hrsver3.pdf> accessed 22 January 2022.

[272] ibid. See also UNGA, 'Report of the OWG of the GA on SDGs (12 August 2014)', UN Doc A/68/970.

[273] Agenda 2030 (n 1).

[274] ibid para 18.

[275] International Council for Science (ICSU) and International Social Science Council (ISSC), 'Review of Targets for the Sustainable Development Goals: The Science Perspective' (International Council for Science 2015) 9. See also RE Kim, 'The Nexus between International Law and the Sustainable Development Goals' (2016) 25 Review of European, Comparative and International Environmental Law 15–26, 15.

COMMENTARY ON SDG 2   149

As highlighted during the negotiations, SDG 2 is not only of paramount importance in itself but has also strong implications for all SDGs and, ultimately, for the achievement of sustainable development.[276] SDG 2 is a multidimensional goal.[277] As reflected in the strong linkages within and between SDG 2 and the other goals, achieving this goal is a complex challenge because it 'couples natural biophysical processes with social and economic processes.'[278] For example, sustainable food production is not the only factor vital to achieving SDG 2. Ensuring safe drinking water and sanitation as well as decreasing inequality are also crucial factors, yet they are not explicitly included in the goal.[279]

Synergies between the SDGs are manifold.[280] In general, SDG 2 is closely linked with almost all other goals, for example with SDG 1 ('No Poverty'), SDG 5 ('Gender Equality'), SDG 8 ('Decent Work and Economic Growth'), SDG 10 ('Reduced Inequalities'), and SDG 12 ('Responsible Consumption and Production').[281] There are further interlinkages with the so-called 'green goals', namely SDG 13 ('Climate Action'), SDG 14 ('Life Below Water'), and SDG 15 ('Life on Land').[282] Importantly, SDG 2 is closely linked to SDG 1 on poverty, and alleviating and reducing poverty in all its dimensions is connected to all aspects of SDG 2.[283] As food security also depends on poverty,[284] the process of ensuring access to food and decreasing food insecurity as part of SDG 2 needs to specifically address marginalization and exclusion, including child poverty, the fight against which is guaranteed in SDG 1.[285]

Furthermore, food production is relevant for the ability to provide people with enough food. At the same time, food production requires a *healthy and clean environment*, so that the realization of SDG 2 also depends heavily on action to tackle climate change, as ensured by SDG 13.[286] Moreover, sustainable food systems require the protection of marine and terrestrial ecosystems, and the sustainable use and conservation of natural resources (SDG 14 and SDG 15), which need to be secured to achieve SDG 2, for example by means of well-functioning institutions or the adoption of environmental laws.[287]

The link between SDG 2 and SDG 5 ('Gender Equality') is especially critical to the achievement of SDG 2.[288] SDG 5 expands on an element that is vital to SDG 2

---

[276] ICSU and ISSC, 'Review of Targets for the Sustainable Development Goals' (n 275) 21.

[277] ibid 19.

[278] ibid 19.

[279] ibid 19.

[280] Gonzalez, 'SDG 2: End Hunger' (n 42) 74. See also French and Kotzé (eds), *Sustainable Development Goals* (n 6) 2.

[281] See ICSU and ISSC, 'Review of Targets for the Sustainable Development Goals' (n 275) 21.

[282] ibid 21. See also French and Kotzé (eds), *Sustainable Development Goals* (n 6) 2.

[283] See target 1.4 of SDG 1: 'By 2030, ensure that all men and women, in particular the poor and the vulnerable, have equal rights to economic resources, as well as access to basic services, ownership and control over land and other forms of property, inheritance, natural resources, appropriate new technology and financial services, including microfinance.' See also ICSU and ISSC, 'Review of Targets for the Sustainable Development Goals' (n 275) 21.

[284] Gonzalez, 'SDG 2: End Hunger' (n 42) 74.

[285] Bley-Palmer and Young (n 7) 26.

[286] Gonzalez, 'SDG 2: End Hunger' (n 42) 74; Bley-Palmer and Young (n 7) 26.

[287] ICSU and ISSC, 'Review of Targets for the Sustainable Development Goals' (n 275) 21; Gonzalez, 'SDG 2: End Hunger' (n 42) 74; Bley-Palmer and Young (n 7) 26.

[288] Bley-Palmer and Young (n 7) 28.

by addressing gender inequality and unequal power relations in the areas of food security, nutrition, agricultural productivity, trade restrictions, and access to markets and land.[289] For instance, target 2.3 requires states to double the agricultural productivity and incomes of small-scale farmers, including women farmers.[290] As Hilal Elver, the former Special Rapporteur on the right to food, noted, gender equality is key because women are responsible for 50 per cent of the world's food production and play a crucial role in achieving food security and healthy nutrition.[291] Women in rural areas are most affected by poverty and malnutrition, as the number of female-headed households continues to increase, yet they own only a very small portion of agricultural land, have limited access to agricultural resources and little say in decision-making processes concerning land use.[292] Also, target 2.4, which promotes sustainable food production systems and resilient agricultural practices, requires a gender approach because women are especially vulnerable to climate change.[293] Target 2.5, which aims to maintain genetic diversity of seeds, is also closely linked to the protection of women who work as small-scale farmers and, based on traditional knowledge, save seeds to feed themselves and their families.[294]

Many individuals in developing countries depend on agricultural activities to provide food for their families. SDG 10 ('Reducing Inequalities') therefore plays a special role for states' progress towards SDG 2.[295] Moreover, agricultural production does not only entail food production but also provides employment opportunities.[296] SDG 2 is therefore also closely associated with SDG 8 on decent work and economic growth.[297] Finally, SDG 16 ('Peace, Justice and Strong Institutions') and SDG 17 ('Partnerships for the Goals') are necessary conditions for the fulfilment of SDG 2 as they promote rule of law and respect for human rights.[298]

Nevertheless, while many synergies exist between SDG 2 and the other goals, there are also many unresolved conflicting issues between them.[299] They arise especially from the integration of the three—economic, social, and environmental—dimensions of sustainable development into the SDG framework.[300] For instance, the objective of providing food for all people will likely lead to an increased demand for fertilizers, which in turn will result in increased pollution of the environment or terrestrial and

---

[289] ibid 28.

[290] Target 2.3, see in detail below Section V.

[291] UNGA, 'Interim Report of the Special Rapporteur on the Right to Food, Hilal Enver, 5 August 2015' (UN Doc A/70/287), para 35. See also I Rae, *Women and the Right to Food. International Law and State Practice* (FAO 2008) 8.

[292] UNGA, 'Interim Report of the Special Rapporteur on the Right to Food, Hilal Enver, 5 August 2015' (n 291) paras 35–36.

[293] ibid para 35; Bley-Palmer and Young (n 7) 28.

[294] Bley-Palmer and Young (n 7) 28. See also C Wichterich, 'Contesting Green Growth, Connecting Care, Commons and Enough' in W Harcourt and IL Nelson (eds), *Practising Feminist Political Ecologies: Moving Beyond the 'Green Economy'* (Zed Books 2015) 67–100.

[295] UNGA, 'Interim Report of the Special Rapporteur on the Right to Food, Hilal Enver, 5 August 2015' (n 291) paras 29–40.

[296] ibid 31.

[297] ibid 31.

[298] Bley-Palmer and Young (n 7) 28.

[299] French and Kotzé, *Sustainable Development Goals* (n 6) 2; Gonzalez, SDG 2: End Hunger' (n 42) 75.

[300] Kim (n 275) 19.

marine ecosystems, thus conflicting with SDG 14 and SDG 15.[301] Furthermore, as mentioned above, measures that arise from target 2.4 and seek to promote sustainable food production systems and resilient agricultural practices might impact not only food security but also the environment.[302] Yet, from an economical point of view, these measures to be taken under target 2.4 might not necessarily be the most efficient ones.[303] Likewise, targets that facilitate free trade, such as target 2.b, might be economical but not environmentally friendly.[304]

The 'water–food–energy' nexus, which was developed to analyse the use and management of resources in light of competing interests and goals, serves as a basis of discussion for the interlinkages between SDG 2 and SDG 6 ('Clean Water and Sanitation') as well as between SDG 2 and SDG 7 ('Affordable and Clean Energy').[305] As the UN has emphasized, the demand for water, food, and energy is increasing, mainly due to population growth, rapid urbanization, and economic growth.[306] Yet agriculture is the world's largest consumer of water resources and energy to produce and supply food.[307] Therefore, increasing food production requires an adequate management of water use to safeguard other ecosystem outputs.[308]

Finally, there is also an important discrepancy between SDG 2 and SDG 8 ('Decent Work and Economic Growth').[309] As stated in Section I of this chapter, 'the SDGs hold fast to neoliberalism and thus fail to reconcile the contradiction between growth and sustainability at the core of sustainable development'.[310] In fact, Agenda 2030 stresses that states 'are committed to developing broader measures of progress to complement gross domestic product'.[311] Many of the SDGs embody this *growth-oriented* approach.[312] For example, target 8.1 aims to '[s]ustain per capita economic growth in accordance with national circumstances and, in particular, at least 7 per cent gross domestic product growth per annum in the least developed countries'.[313] But the target does not refer to the obvious corollary that growth in countries of the Global North needs to slow down in order to tackle climate change.[314] Similarly, Agenda 2030 further states that '[i]nternational trade is an engine for inclusive economic growth and poverty reduction, and contributes to the promotion of sustainable development'.[315]

---

[301] ibid 19.
[302] ibid 19.
[303] ibid 19.
[304] ibid 22.
[305] FAO, 'The Water–Energy–Food Nexus. A New Approach in Support of Food Security and Sustainable Agriculture' (2014) <https://www.fao.org/3/bl496e/bl496e.pdf> accessed 22 January 2022; see also UN, 'Water, Water, Food and Energy' (2018) <https://www.unwater.org/app/uploads/2018/10/WaterFacts_water_food_and_energy_sep2018.pdf> accessed 22 January 2022.
[306] UN, 'Water, Water, Food and Energy' (n 305) 2.
[307] ibid 2.
[308] Kim (n 275) 23.
[309] Gonzalez, 'SDG 2: End Hunger' (n 42) 4.
[310] Adelman (n 38) 34.
[311] Agenda 2030 (n 1) para 48.
[312] See in detail Adelman (n 38) 35–39.
[313] Target 8.1 of SDG 8.
[314] Adelman (n 38) 35–36; Gonzalez, 'SDG 2: End Hunger' (n 42) 75.
[315] Agenda 2030 (n 1) para 68.

152   SDG 2

However, it does not refer to the fact that trade liberalization is also responsible for the dark sides of globalization and persisting inequalities within and across societies.[316]

As regards SDG 2, the goal also includes growth-oriented policies, notably in targets 2.3 and 2.4, both of which address agricultural productivity.[317] But increasing production also poses the risk of unsustainable agriculture, which may in turn have detrimental effects on the achievement of SDG 2.[318] Moreover, a growth-based approach to SDG 2 also shows that the goal links food insecurity to scarcity of food, without considering the fact that social inclusion is necessary to achieve food security as part of SDG 2.[319]

To conclude, integration and coherence between the goals are key to achieving SDG 2. Even though there are many synergies between SDG 2 and other goals, there are also several contradictions that hinder the effective realization of SDG 2.[320] The next section will address the nexus between SDG 2 and international law and the question whether and to what extent international law—especially international human rights law—may help achieve SDG 2 in an integrated manner.

B. The Nexus between SDG 2 and International Law

The SDGs are broadly grounded in international law, which recognizes the objective of sustainable development.[321] Agenda 2030 states that the goals are 'to be implemented in a manner that is consistent with the rights and obligations of states under international law'.[322] The document explicitly refers to a number of international legal instruments, such as the Charter of the United Nations (UN Charter),[323] the Universal Declaration of Human Rights (UDHR)[324], and 'international human rights treaties'.[325] Agenda 2030 also mentions other international instruments, for instance the Declaration on the Right to Development or the Rio Declaration on Environment and Development (Rio Declaration).[326] As such, many the targets of the particular goals can be traced back

---

[316] Adelman (n 38) 36.

[317] Gonzalez, 'SDG 2: End Hunger' (n 42) 76.

[318] ibid 76.

[319] ibid 76.

[320] See Kim (n 275) 25–26.

[321] ibid 15.

[322] Agenda 2030 (n 1) para 18. See also 'The Future We Want' (n 140) para 58(a).

[323] Agenda 2030 (n 1) para 10; Charter of the United Nations of 26 June 1945, in force since 24 October 1945 (UN Charter).

[324] Agenda 2030 (n 1) para 10; Universal Declaration of Human Rights, adopted by General Assembly resolution 217 A(III) of 10 December 1948 (UDHR).

[325] Agenda 2030 (n 1) para 10. Agenda 2030 states in para 19: 'We reaffirm the importance of the Universal Declaration of Human Rights, as well as other international instruments relating to human rights and international law. We emphasize the responsibilities of all States, in conformity with the Charter of the United Nations, to respect, protect and promote human rights and fundamental freedoms for all, without distinction of any kind as to race, colour, sex, language, religion, political or other opinion, national or social origin, property, birth, disability or other status.'

[326] ibid para 10; Declaration on the Right to Development, adopted by General Assembly resolution 41/128 of 4 December 1986; Rio Declaration on Environment and Development (Rio Declaration), 'Report of the UN Conference on Environment and Development, Rio de Janeiro, 3–14 June 1992' (12 August 1992) A/CONF.151/26 (Vol I).

to the wording of the provisions in international treaties.[327] For instance, target 2.1 of SDG 2, which aims to end hunger and ensure food security, is linked to the right to food enshrined in article 11 of the International Covenant on Economic, Social and Cultural Rights (ICESCR).[328]

References to international legal instruments prove that the SDGs do not operate in a 'normative vacuum'.[329] International law serves as a normative framework within which the SDGs and targets can be effectively realized.[330] In practice, however, there are many tensions between the SDGs, which require a set of different policy measures, and the operationalization of various fields of international law that impact the particular goals.[331] Moreover, as noted above, many SDGs, including SDG 2, are even not compatible with existing international obligations (eg international human rights obligations). Indeed, several standards set by the goals fall below those established in international law.[332] In turn, international legal norms can also make it more difficult to achieve the SDGs, a fact exacerbated by the fragmentation of international law.[333]

This section will take a closer look at the subfields of international law that are particularly relevant to SDG 2 in terms of the nexus between hunger and nutrition, and sustainable agriculture. The analysis will focus on the international legal regimes most relevant to the goal, notably international human rights law as well as international trade and investment law. First, the section discusses how these regimes are linked to the goal and its targets. Second, it critically examines the regimes' problematic aspects by highlighting how their impact on the achievement and implementation of SDG 2 may run counter to what was expected.

1. SDG 2 and International Human Rights Law, in particular the Right to Food

Agenda 2030 is based on a strong link between human rights and sustainable development. Unlike the MDGs, it emphasizes the importance of human rights, which implies that Agenda 2030 endorses a human rights approach to the realization of the SDGs.[334] The Agenda's Preamble explicitly states that the SDGs 'seek to realise the human rights of all'.[335] It calls for 'a world of universal respect for human rights and human dignity ... in which the needs of the most vulnerable are met'.[336] Nevertheless,

---

[327] See OWG-10, 'Compendium of Existing Goals and Targets under the 19 Focus Areas being Considered by the Open Working Group' <https://sustainabledevelopment.un.org/content/documents/3507Existing%20targets_1_April_version.xlsx> accessed 22 January 2022.

[328] International Covenant on Economic, Social and Cultural Rights of 16 December 1966, 993 UNTS 3. For an analysis of target 2.1, see this chapter, Section V.

[329] Kim (n 275) 15.

[330] ibid 17.

[331] For human rights law, see LM Collins, 'Sustainable Development Goals and Human Rights: Challenges and Opportunities' in French and Kotzé (eds), *Sustainable Development Goals* (n 6) 66–90.

[332] See French and Kotzé (eds), *Sustainable Development Goals* (n 6) 5.

[333] Kim (n 275) 17.

[334] Collins (n 331) 68. See also Agenda 2030 (n 1), especially para 19. On the MDGs and human rights in general, see P Alston, 'Ships Passing in the Night: The Current State of the Human Rights and Development Debate Seen Through the Lens of the Millennium Development Goals' (2005) 27 Human Rights Quarterly 755–829; M Langford and others (eds), *The Millennium Development Goals and Human Rights: Past, Present and Future* (CUP 2013).

[335] Agenda 2030 (n 1) Preamble.

[336] ibid para 8.

the particular goals are not formulated in the specific language of human rights but are connected to international human rights norms.[337] Accordingly, 'the Human Rights Guide to the Sustainable Development Goals' of the Danish Institute on Human Rights shows that 92 per cent of the 169 targets of the SDGs are linked to international human rights treaties and other instruments.[338] Similarly, the UN Human Rights Office of the High Commissioner (OHCHR) concludes that each goal embraces international human rights norms or certain dimensions thereof.[339]

The SDGs do not impose legally binding obligations on states. This raises the question whether the SDGs' policy commitments comply with states' current human rights obligations that arise from their ratified human rights treaties.[340] Some of the SDGs' commitments may indeed reinforce the objectives of human rights norms. At the same time, however, many of these commitments have a much weaker design than states' human rights obligations, and many of the goals' targets fall short of existing human rights standards.[341] Furthermore, in terms of accountability, Agenda 2030 refers to the 'responsibilities of all States ... to respect, protect and promote human rights'.[342] In this regard, 'responsibility' for human rights in the SDG framework is not equivalent to the law of international responsibility. Instead, the term here indicates softened standards with a political rather than a legal basis in international human rights treaties.[343]

In particular, economic, social, and cultural rights are crucial to the goals and are reflected in them as they are strongly associated with the social dimension of sustainable development outlined in Agenda 2030.[344] In fact, the SDGs seek to tackle global problems, such as poverty, hunger, and inequalities, that hinder the realization of economic, social, and cultural rights worldwide.[345] SDG 2 and in particular target 2.1 on ending hunger and ensuring food security as well as target 2.2 on ending malnutrition are strongly linked to the human right to food.[346] At the international level, the right to food is recognized in legally binding and non-binding instruments.[347] Article 25 of

---

[337] Winkler and Hernandez, 'Social Rights and Sustainable Development Goals' (n 47) 469.

[338] Danish Institute for Human Rights, 'The Human Rights Guide to the Sustainable Development Goals' <https://sdg.humanrights.dk/en/targets2?goal[]=71> accessed 22 January 2022.

[339] OHCHR, 'Summary Table on the Linkages between the SDGs and Relevant International Human Rights Instruments' <https://www.ohchr.org/Documents/Issues/MDGs/Post2015/SDG_HR_Table.pdf> accessed 22 January 2022.

[340] See, eg, OHCHR and Center for Economic and Social Rights (CESCR), 'Who Will Be Accountable? Human Rights and the Post-2015 Development Agenda' (2013) <https://www.ohchr.org/Documents/Publications/WhoWillBeAccountable.pdf> accessed 22 January 2022. See also Winkler and Hernandez, 'Social Rights and Sustainable Development Goals' (n 47) 476.

[341] Collins (n 331) 68.

[342] Agenda 2030 (n 1) para 19. See also Collins (n 331) 69.

[343] See A Peters, 'Global Constitutionalism: The Social Dimension' in T Suami and others (eds), *Global Constitutionalism from European and East Asian Perspectives* (CUP 2018) 277–350, 313, with respect to the Guiding Principles on Business and Human Rights (Ruggie Principles), which also refers to the term 'responsibility' like Agenda 2030.

[344] Winkler and Hernandez, 'Social Rights and Sustainable Development Goals' (n 47) 466.

[345] ibid 466.

[346] On the right to food in general, see, eg, P Alston and K Tomaševski (eds), *The Right to Food* (Martinus Nijhoff 1984).

[347] K Mechlem, 'Food, Right to, International Protection' in *Max Planck Encyclopedia of Public International Law* (OUP online, June 2008) para 9.

the UDHR recognizes the right to food by stating that '[everyone] has the right to a standard of living adequate for the health and well-being of himself and his family, including food'.[348] The central norm on the right to food is contained in article 11 of the ICESCR, which includes two interrelated human rights.[349] Article 11(1) of the ICESCR 'recognize[s] the right of everyone to an adequate standard of living ... including adequate food'[350] and article 11(2) of the ICESCR affirms 'the fundamental right of everyone to be free from hunger'.[351] Furthermore, the right to food is also enshrined in international human rights treaties with regard to specific groups, including women, children, peasants, and rural workers.[352] Specifically, several UN declarations promote the realization of the right to food by recognizing the rights of indigenous peoples and small-scale agricultural producers to lands, natural resources, and the environment.[353]

The UN Committee on Economic, Social and Cultural Rights (CESCR), which monitors the implementation of the ICESCR, has elaborated on the right to food and the corresponding human rights obligations of states in General Comment No 12.[354] The CESCR states that 'the right to adequate food is realized when every man, woman and child, alone or in community with others, has physical and economic access at all times to adequate food or means for its procurement'.[355] This implies, first, '[t]he availability of food in a quantity and quality sufficient to satisfy the dietary needs of individuals, free from adverse substances, and acceptable within a given culture',[356] and, second, '[t]he accessibility of such food in ways that are sustainable and that do not interfere with the enjoyment of other human rights'.[357] Importantly, the right to food should 'not be interpreted in a narrow or restrictive sense which equates it with a minimum package of calories, proteins and other specific nutrients'.[358] The CESCR's definition of access to food is coherent with Amartya Sen's capability approach, which holds that access to food requires a comprehensive understanding of an individual's nourishment that goes beyond merely receiving a minimum number of calories.[359]

The CESCR acknowledges that states not only act as food providers but can also impede individuals' ability to grow or purchase food.[360] In this regard, the right to food

---

[348] UDHR, art 25.

[349] ICESCR, art 11.

[350] ibid art 11(1).

[351] ibid art 11(2).

[352] See also Gonzalez, 'SDG 2: End Hunger' (n 42) 79.

[353] UN Declaration on the Rights of Indigenous Peoples, adopted by the UN GA on 13 September 2007 (UN Doc A/RES/61/295), arts 26–29. UN Declaration on the Rights of Peasants and Other People Working in Rural Areas, adopted by the UNGA on 17 December 2018, arts 5, 17, 18. See also Gonzalez, 'SDG 2: End Hunger' (n 42) 79.

[354] Committee on Economic, Social and Cultural Rights (CESCR), 'General Comment No 12: The Right to Adequate Food' (12 May 1999) UN Doc E/C.12/1999/5 (CESCR, General Comment No 12).

[355] ibid para 6.

[356] ibid para 6.

[357] ibid para 6.

[358] ibid para 6.

[359] M Cohen, 'Right to Food' in Max Planck Encyclopedia of Comparative Constitutional Law (OUP online, August 2016) para 10. On Amartya Sen's capability approach, see also this chapter, Section II.

[360] NCS Lambek, 'Respecting and Protecting the Right to Food: When States Must Get Out of the Kitchen' in NCS Lambek and others (eds), Rethinking Food Systems: Structural Challenges, New Strategies, and the Law (Springer 2014) 101–22, 102.

imposes a threefold typology of human rights obligations on states, notably the duty to respect, to protect, and to fulfil, which are crucial to the achievement of the objectives of SDG 2.[361] First, states are obliged to respect the right to food by abstaining from taking any measure that results in preventing access to food.[362] They must take into account the impact of laws, regulations, and policies on individuals' right of access to food and refrain from actions that impede individuals from accessing food.[363] Moreover, states should also abstain from interfering in the access to land, water, markets, and income of individuals who procure food through purchase or agriculture.[364] Second, the duty to protect the right to food 'requires measures by [states] to ensure that enterprises or private actors do not deprive individuals of their access to adequate food'.[365] In this respect, the former Special Rapporteur on the Right to Food, Jean Ziegler, has noted that 'if the Government does not intervene when a powerful individual evicts people from their land, then the Government violates the obligation to protect the right to food. The Government would also fail to protect the right to food if it took no action if a company polluted a community's water supply'.[366] For instance, states need to adopt environmental regulations to protect access to resources that are necessary for food production.[367] Finally, the duty to fulfil obliges states to 'pro-actively engage in activities intended to strengthen people's access to and utilization of resources and means to ensure their livelihood, including food security'.[368] In order to abide by the duty to fulfil, states particularly need to address the *systemic and structural issues* of food insecurity. They must directly distribute food to individuals who are not able to acquire food themselves.[369]

While states are traditionally responsible for realizing their own population's right to food, the CESCR also emphasizes the transnational dimension of that right (and other ICESCR rights) by imposing on states a duty to cooperate.[370] Article 2(1) of the ICESCR establishes that States Parties need 'to take steps, individually and through international assistance and co-operation, especially economic and technical, to the maximum of its available resources, with a view to achieving progressively the full realization of the rights ... by all appropriate means'.[371] Moreover, where the right to food is concerned, the CESCR explicitly recognizes states' extraterritorial obligations towards individuals abroad.[372] States should take steps to respect the enjoyment of the right to food in other countries and facilitate access to food and provide necessary aid when

---

[361] See CESCR, General Comment No 12 (n 354) para 15. See also art 2 (1) of the ICESCR.

[362] CESCR, General Comment No 12 (n 354), para 15.

[363] Lambek (n 360) 108. See also Gonzalez, 'SDG 2: End Hunger' (n 42) 79.

[364] Lambek (n 360) 108.

[365] CESCR, General Comment No 12 (n 354) para 15.

[366] UN Special Rapporteur on the Right to Food, Jean Ziegler, Note to the Secretary-General, 2001, UN Doc A/56/201, para 28.

[367] Lambek (n 360) 110.

[368] CESCR, General Comment No 12 (n 354) para 15.

[369] ibid para 15; Lambek (n 360) 107.

[370] ICESCR, art 2(1).

[371] ibid.

[372] CESCR, General Comment No 12 (n 354) paras 36–39. See generally on extraterritorial obligations in the area of economic, social, and cultural rights, E Askin, 'Economic and Social Rights, Extraterritorial Application' in *Max Planck Encyclopedia of Public International Law* (OUP online, January 2019).

needed.[373] Article 11(2)(b) of the ICESCR even refers to the distributive dimension of extraterritorial obligations, namely to ensure 'equitable distribution of world food supplies'.[374] While these obligations are 'an obligation of all States', they are 'particularly incumbent upon those States which are in a *position to assist* others in this regard', thus affirming the extraterritorial obligation of wealthy states in particular.[375]

Comparing the right to food with SDG 2 shows that the latter contains two *human rights-related* dimensions of objectives to be achieved: the 'individual' and the 'structural' dimension, both of which embrace diverging human rights standards. The 'individual' dimension of SDG 2, notably target 2.1 on ending hunger and ensuring food security, and target 2.2 on ending malnourishment, reinforces the objectives of the right to food as a means of empowering individuals to realize their basic rights.[376] Yet this does not mean that these targets of SDG 2 cover all elements of the right to food but rather that they support and complement each other.[377] The 'structural' dimension of SDG 2, which is mainly reflected in targets 2.3 and 2.4 on increasing food production and is based on a growth-based economic approach, appears to be in tension with the right to food.[378] In this respect, Hilal Enver argues that '[a] human rights-based approach to food security is contrary to the conventional, economist view that is primarily preoccupied by increasing food production'.[379] Such an approach 'focuses on interventions and services to meet human needs and often regards beneficiaries as passive recipients of acts of generosity or charity'.[380] However, as discussed above, the right to food also requires states to provide an enabling environment in which individuals can purchase or produce food for themselves.[381] Carmen Gonzalez therefore emphasizes that an economic approach focused on increasing food production, often by unsustainable methods, is based on the misguided assumption that hunger and food insecurity are problems of food scarcity rather than problems of food access and food distribution.[382] While targets 2.1 and 2.2 of SDG 2 are generally in line with the right to food by incorporating a human rights approach in to their objectives, targets 2.3 and 2.4, which aim to increase food production, might not contribute to the realization of the right to food.[383] This might be further compounded by international law, notably international trade and investment law.[384]

---

[373] CESCR, General Comment No 12 (n 354) para 36.

[374] ICESCR, art 11(2)(b).

[375] CESCR, 'General Comment No 3 on the Nature of States Parties' Obligations' (14 December 1990) UN Doc E/1991/23), para 14 (emphasis added).

[376] See also Gonzalez, 'SDG 2: End Hunger' (n 42) 80.

[377] See Winkler and Hernandez, 'Social Rights and Sustainable Development Goals' (n 47) 470; See also Gonzalez, 'SDG 2: End Hunger' (n 42) 80.

[378] Gonzalez, 'SDG 2: End Hunger' (n 42) 80.

[379] H Elver, 'Human Rights Based Approach to Sustainable Agricultural Policies and Food Security' in H Ginsky and others (eds), *International Yearbook of Soil Law and Policy 2018* (Springer 2019) 347–72, 363. See also Gonzalez, 'SDG 2: End Hunger' (n 42) 80–81.

[380] Elver (n 379) 363.

[381] ibid 363.

[382] Gonzalez, 'SDG 2: End Hunger' (n 42) 80–81.

[383] ibid 80–81.

[384] ibid 81.

2. SDG 2 and International Economic Law, in particular Trade and Investment Law

International economic law and international trade and investment law in particular might have a detrimental impact on efforts to realize SDG 2.[385] Unlike international human rights law, international trade and investment regimes pose serious challenges to the achievement of the goal and its targets, which are further exacerbated by the growth-based economic model embedded in the structural dimension of SDG 2.[386] These fields of international law support a global food system that remains unable to alleviate the adverse effects of industrial agriculture on individuals' right to food and other human rights, including the rights of small-scale farmers and rural populations, in countries of the Global South.[387] 'After all, international law no longer allows the older forms of colonial power to operate,'[388] argues Anne Orford, '[y]et other forms of colonial power, organised around free trade and constraints on local administrators, perhaps do continue to hold sway.'[389] In other words, '[s]omething in the routine operation of international economic life, organised around global value chains, free trade, and open markets, produces a system of compulsion such that food is exported to foreign lands while the people who grow it are undernourished.'[390]

International trade and investment law continues to shape the distributional features of the global food economy and patterns of hunger and food insecurity, especially in the Global South.[391] International trade treaties like the GATT and the WTO Agreement on Agriculture (AoA)[392] have diminished Southern states' ability to 'join the club'[393] on equal terms, as noted earlier.[394] After the Second World War, the GATT regime established a new economic order, which further exacerbated hunger and food insecurity in developing countries.[395] While the GATT promoted trade liberalization, agricultural trade was in principle excepted from GATT obligations.[396] The United States and European nations continued to subsidize agricultural commodities for export and dumped food surpluses on the local markets of developing countries.[397] This practice had far-reaching impacts on small-scale agriculture and food production in the Global South.[398] The situation was further aggravated in the wake of the debt crisis in the 1980s, when international financial organizations, such as the International Monetary Fund (IMF) and the World Bank, imposed loan conditionalities on developing countries, requiring them to adopt structural adjustment programs that led to 'protectionism in wealthy developed countries' and 'trade liberalization in poor

---

[385] ibid, 81, 85.

[386] ibid 81, 85.

[387] ibid 81; Chadwick (n 61) 48.

[388] Orford (n 51) 16.

[389] ibid.

[390] ibid.

[391] ibid.

[392] Agreement on Agriculture of the World Trade Organization (WTO) of 1 January 1995.

[393] S Humphreys, *Theatre of the Rule of Law: Transnational Legal Intervention in Theory and Practice* (CUP 2012) 213.

[394] Chadwick (n 61) 36. See also this chapter, Section II.

[395] Orford (n 51) 51–53; Gonzalez, 'SDG 2: End Hunger' (n 42) 81.

[396] Gonzalez, 'SDG 2: End Hunger' (n 42) 81.

[397] Orford (n 51) 53; Gonzalez, 'SDG 2: End Hunger' (n 42) 82.

[398] Gonzalez, 'SDG 2: End Hunger' (n 42) 82–83.

developing countries'.[399] For instance, the borrower states had to eliminate non-tariff import barriers or reduce government subsidies to the agricultural sectors.[400] These programmes have since further impacted international agricultural trade, particularly small-scale farmers in rural areas of the Global South, and have exacerbated food insecurity in developing countries.[401]

The AoA, adopted in 1995, aimed to overcome the GATT's double standards and their adverse effects on developing countries and to 'establish a basis for initiating a process of reform of trade in agriculture'[402] and 'a fair and market-oriented agricultural trading system'.[403] The objective of the AoA is to 'provide for substantial progressive reductions in agricultural support and protection sustained over an agreed period of time, resulting in correcting and preventing restrictions and distortions in world agricultural markets'.[404] Despite these aspirations, however, the AoA has expanded international agricultural trade to benefit food producers in developed countries.[405] Many countries of the Global South have not been able to challenge either the inequities that arise when Northern states deploy agricultural subsidies or their cross-border effects, which amplify hunger and food insecurity and infringe upon individuals' human rights in developing countries.[406]

Against this backdrop, a closer look at target 2.b of SDG 2, which aims to eliminate trade restrictions and distortions in agricultural markets, reveals that the target does not effectively address the problems of hunger and food insecurity.[407] To achieve this goal globally, countries need to abandon agricultural subsidies and other trade restrictions that adversely impact the livelihoods of small-scale farmers in developing countries.[408] But target 2.b also needs to focus on the 'systemic' issues that arise from the agricultural sector. Ways of tackling such systemic issues would include the modification of trade agreements and loan conditionalities, and debt cancellation.[409] This needs to be prioritized over policies, proposed in target 17.4, which calls for 'debt financing, debt relief, and debt restructuring' rather than debt cancellation at its core.[410] Finally, SDG 2 also needs to address global supply chains and the responsibilities of multinational corporations.[411]

---

[399] CG Gonzalez, 'Markets, Monoculture, and Malnutrition: Agricultural Trade Policy through an Environmental Justice Lens' (2006) 14 Michigan State Journal of International Law 364; CG Gonzalez, 'Trade Liberalization, Food Security and the Environment: The Neoliberal Threat to Sustainable Rural Development' (2004) 14 Transnational Law and Contemporary Problems 419–98, 458.

[400] Gonzalez, 'Markets, Monoculture, and Malnutrition' (n 399) 364; M Chossudovsky, The Globalisation of Poverty: Impacts of the IMF and World Bank Reforms (Zed Books 1997) 62–63.

[401] Gonzalez, 'Markets, Monoculture, and Malnutrition' (n 399) 362–68; Gonzalez, 'Trade Liberalization, Food Security and the Environment' (n 399) 465.

[402] Agreement on Agriculture (AoA), Preamble.

[403] ibid; Gonzalez, 'Institutionalizing Inequality' (n 83) 450–56.

[404] Agreement on Agriculture (AoA), Preamble; see also Orford (n 51) 54.

[405] Gonzalez, 'Institutionalizing Inequality' (n 83) 450–59; Gonzalez, 'SDG 2: End Hunger' (n 42) 83–84.

[406] Gonzalez, 'SDG 2: End Hunger' (n 42) 85.

[407] ibid 84.

[408] ibid 85. On recent developments in the WTO, see this chapter, Section V.B.7 (target 2.b).

[409] ibid 85.

[410] ibid 85.

[411] See LJL Veldhuizen and others, 'The Missing Middle: Connected Action on Agriculture and Nutrition Across Global, National and Local Levels to Achieve Sustainable Development Goal 2' (2020) 24 Global Food Security 1–6.

Similar to international trade law, international investment law also creates obstacles to the achievement of SDG 2.[412] In many developing countries, foreign investors, notably transnational corporations, lease or purchase agricultural land, for instance for investments in industrial agriculture.[413] Foreign (land) investments might create negative effects on small-scale farmers and rural communities in these countries, such as eviction, environmental pollution, and loss of natural resources, which affect rural land use and food production.[414] One of the major challenges in the context of foreign investments is 'land grabbing' by foreign investors in developing countries.[415] Even though international investment law has recently begun to address the human rights obligations of (foreign) investors and environmental protection,[416] current (international) investment norms still facilitate land grabbing in developing countries by providing foreign investors with legal protection, securing their investments to the detriment of rural communities.[417]

Generally, foreign investors are granted privileges that are usually not assured to the local population affected by the foreign investment, such as land and water rights, tax benefits, and the right to export the agricultural goods investors produce.[418] These investor rights are protected by various legal instruments, namely contracts between foreign investors and host states, Bilateral Investment Treaties (BITs) between investors' host and home states, and free trade agreements.[419] In particular, international investment treaties include minimum standards of protection, such as fair and equitable treatment or the prohibition against expropriation, designed to safeguard investors, for example against the revocation of licences due to environmental pollution or against export restrictions on agricultural commodities.[420] In general, however, host states of foreign investors might be reluctant to protect the rights of rural communities, not only for economic reasons but also due to potential compensation claims that an investor could bring before an arbitral tribunal.[421]

To sum up, international investment law enhances foreign investors' rights to agricultural land to the detriment of poor and rural communities suffering from hunger and food insecurity.[422] Hence, international trade and investment regimes pose important

---

[412] Gonzalez, 'SDG 2: End Hunger' (n 42) 85.

[413] ibid 85–86; A Spieldoch and S Murphy, 'Agricultural Land Acquisitions: Implications for Food Security and Poverty Alleviation' in Michael Kugelman and Susan L. Levenstein (eds), *Land Grab? The Race for the World's Farmland* (Woodrow Wilson International Center for Scholars 2009) 46.

[414] Spieldoch and Murphy (n 413) 43–48. See also Gonzalez, 'SDG 2: End Hunger' (n 42) 86.

[415] See Spieldoch and Murphy (n 413) 41–42.

[416] See, eg, ICSID Award of 8 Dec 2016, *Urbaser S.A. and Consorcio de Aguas Bilbao Bizkaia, Bilbao Biskaia Ur Partzuergoa v The Argentine Republic*, ICSID Case No ARB/07/26; Reciprocal Investment Promotion and Protection Agreement between the Government of the Kingdom of Morocco and the Government of the Federal Republic of Nigeria (Morocco–Nigeria) of 3 December 2016, still not in force, art 18(2).

[417] Gonzalez, 'SDG 2: End Hunger' (n 42) 87–88.

[418] ibid 87; see also C Smaller and H Mann, *A Thirst for Distant Lands: Foreign Investment in Agricultural Land and Water* (International Institute for Sustainable Development 2009) 14.

[419] Department of Economic and Social Affairs, 'Foreign Land Purchases for Agriculture: What Impact on Sustainable Development?' Sustainable Development Innovation Briefs, Issue 8, January 2010, 4; Gonzalez, 'SDG 2: End Hunger' (n 42) 87–88.

[420] See for the international investment standards, M Bungenberg and others (eds), *International Investment Law. A Handbook* (C.H. Beck/Hart/Nomos 2015), ch 7.

[421] Gonzalez, 'SDG 2: End Hunger' (n 42) 88.

[422] ibid 88.

challenges to the achievement of SDG 2, and both legal regimes are also in conflict with international human rights law since they infringe upon the right to food.[423]

C. The Importance of a Rights-Based Approach to SDG 2: Human Rights Mainstreaming

The growth-based economic approach in SDG 2, which is underpinned by international law and by international trade and investment law in particular, generally fails to limit the harmful effects that unsustainable food production, trade liberalization, and unequal land distribution have on individuals' rights and on the environment.[424] As mentioned above, this hinders the effective achievement of the goal. Against this backdrop, this chapter argues that the realization of SDG 2 and its targets should be guided by a *human rights-based approach* in all subfields of international law relevant to the goal, and, importantly, by the policy of 'human rights mainstreaming'[425] within the entire framework of the SDGs.

Human rights, including economic, social, and cultural rights, impact all subfields of international law.[426] Since the beginning of the Millennium, human rights have increasingly permeated various areas of international law, such as international development law,[427] international trade law,[428] and international investment law,[429] all of which have a bearing on the achievement of SDG 2.[430] It has been acknowledged that these (and other) regimes of international law must be interpreted and applied in the light of human rights, taking individuals' rights and basic needs into account.[431] Human rights may act as a counterpoint to legal rules and regimes that interfere with individuals' rights.[432] For instance, human rights can limit the legal protection of foreign investors in situations where an investor's activity results in infringements of the right to food and other human rights of the domestic population.[433]

The call for human rights to be aligned with other international legal regimes was first raised in the context of international development law.[434] In a speech before the World Bank in 2001, the then Human Rights Commissioner Mary Robinson advocated

---

[423] ibid 85.

[424] Gonzalez, 'SDG 2: End Hunger' (n 42) 94.

[425] On human rights mainstreaming within the UN, see G Oberleitner, 'A Decade of Mainstreaming Human Rights in the UN: Achievements, Failures, Challenges' (2008) 26 Netherlands Quarterly of Human Rights 359–90.

[426] Peters, 'Global Constitutionalism' (n 343) 298–99.

[427] See P Alston and M Robinson (eds), *Human Rights and Development: Towards Mutual Reinforcement* (OUP 2005).

[428] See T Cottier and others (eds), *Human Rights and International Trade* (OUP 2005); L Bartels, 'Trade and Human Rights' in F Lachenmann and others (eds), *International Economic Law* (OUP 2015) 816–25.

[429] See P-M Dupuy and others (eds), *Human Rights in International Investment Law and Arbitration* (OUP 2009).

[430] See Peters, 'Global Constitutionalism' (n 343) 298–99.

[431] A Peters, 'The Importance of Having Rights' (2021) 81 Zeitschrift für ausländisches öffentliches Recht (ZaöRV)/Heidelberg Journal of International Law 7–22, 12.

[432] ibid 12.

[433] ibid 12.

[434] ibid 12.

a human rights approach to promote development.[435] In Robinson's words, '[a] rights-based approach is a conceptual framework for the purpose of human development that is normatively based on international human rights standards and operationally directed to promoting and protecting human rights. The rights-based approach integrates the norms, standards and principles of the international human rights system into the plans, policies, and processes of development.'[436] Accordingly, international human rights function here as *benchmarks*, notably as universally recognized legal standards against which development policies can be assessed.[437]

Furthermore, international human rights law provides the procedural tools to operationalize a human rights approach, including human rights impact assessments that help (mostly *ex ante*) to assess whether states' activities adhere to their existing human rights obligations.[438] International human rights bodies have recognized the significance of human rights impact assessments mainly with respect to treaty-making. For instance, in 2011, the former Special Rapporteur on the Right to Food, Olivier De Schutter, released the Guiding Principles on Human Rights Impact Assessments of Trade and Investment Agreements.[439] Basically, these principles seek to guide states in ensuring that their trade and investment agreements are in compliance with their human rights obligations (arising, eg, from the right to food).[440] Principle 1 states that '[a]ll States should prepare human rights impact assessments prior to the conclusion of trade and investment agreements.'[441] However, unlike environmental impact assessments required by general international law,[442] human rights impact assessments are not mandatory under international human rights law.[443]

Human rights can also be directly incorporated into policy areas. An important tool is the policy of 'mainstreaming human rights', which is also relevant for the post-2015 development agenda of the UN.[444] The UN began to mainstream human rights

---

[435] M Robinson, 'Bridging the Gap between Human Rights and Development: From Normative Principle to Operational Relevance', World Bank Presidential Lecture, Washington DC, 3 December 2001, printed in M Robinson, *A Voice for Human Rights* (University of Pennsylvania Press 2006) 299–307. See also Peters, 'The Importance of Having Rights' (n 431) 12.

[436] Robinson (n 435) 303.

[437] M Robinson, 'What Rights Can Add to Good Development Practice' in Alston and Robinson (eds) (n 427) 25–41; Peters, 'The Importance of Having Rights' (n 431) 12.

[438] Peters, 'Global Constitutionalism' (n 343) 298–99. See also G de Beco, 'Human Rights Impact Assessments' (2012) 27 Netherlands Quarterly of Human Rights 139–66.

[439] UN Human Rights Council, 'Guiding Principles on Human Rights Impact Assessments of Trade and Investment Agreements' (19 December 2011) UN Doc A/HRC/19/59/Add.5. See also, eg, CESCR, 'General Comment No 24 on State Obligations under the International Covenant on Economic, Social and Cultural Rights in the Context of Business Activities' (23 June 2017) UN Doc E/C.12/GC/24, para 13: 'The conclusion of such treaties should ... be preceded by human rights impact assessments, taking into account both the positive and negative human rights impacts of trade and investment treaties, including their realization to the right to development.'

[440] UN Human Rights Council, 'Guiding Principles on Human Rights Impact Assessments of Trade and Investment Agreements' (19 December 2011) UN Doc A/HRC/19/59/Add.5, para 1. On trade agreements, see S Walker, *The Future of Human Rights Impact Assessments of Trade Agreements* (Intersentia 2009).

[441] UN Human Rights Council, 'Guiding Principles on Human Rights Impact Assessments of Trade and Investment Agreements' (19 December 2011) UN Doc A/HRC/19/59/Add.5, principle 1.

[442] See International Court of Justice (ICJ), Case Concerning Pulp Mills on the River Uruguay (*Argentina v Uruguay*), judgment of 20 April 2010, para 204.

[443] Peters, 'Global Constitutionalism' (n 343) 323.

[444] Oberleitner (n 425) 359–90; Peters, 'The Importance of Having Rights' (n 431) 13.

COMMENTARY ON SDG 2   163

in its activities when it released a report by the UN Secretary-General on proposed reforms in 1997.[445] Without using the term 'mainstreaming', the report instructed the UN 'to enhance its human rights programme and fully integrate it into the broad range of the organization's activities'.[446] In recent years, the UN has affirmed the validity of this policy in several reports.[447] Human rights mainstreaming now belongs to the core work of the UN development system.[448]

Human rights mainstreaming (sometimes used interchangeably with a 'rights-based approach') is defined as a process of internalizing and operationalizing human rights in an organization's policies and programmes.[449] This means that 'an organization bases its programmes, policies and activities on international human rights law, that is internationally agreed human rights norms, standards and principles, and that it operates in a way which fosters these norms, standards and principles'.[450] In fact, Agenda 2030 has also adopted the policy of human rights mainstreaming. Already in the preparatory phase of the SDGs, several mandate-holders of the Human Rights Council stressed the link between human rights and development policy.[451] They emphasized that '[h]uman rights norms and standards provide concrete guidance as to how goals and targets for the post-2015 development agenda should be framed. Governments have already committed to uphold human rights in numerous international treaties. Grounding development priorities in human rights is not only a legal and moral imperative but can also enhance effectiveness and accountability'.[452] Given that Agenda 2030 includes many references to human rights, the SDG framework can reasonably be said to incorporate a human-rights approach.[453]

In this context, the FAO plays a pivotal role in implementing SDG 2, as it is tasked with monitoring several indicators of the goal.[454] In terms of human rights, the organization's objective and work are closely connected to the right to food.[455] The FAO seeks to raise levels of nutrition and standards of living and aims to contribute to an expanding world economy to ensure freedom from hunger worldwide.[456] According to the FAO's constitution, one of its main tasks is to collect, analyse, interpret, and disseminate information relating to nutrition, food, and agriculture. Another is to promote

---

[445] UNGA, 'Report of the UN Secretary General on Renewing the United Nations: A Programme for Reform' (14 July 1997) UN Doc A/51/950). See also Oberleitner (n 425) 359.

[446] UNGA, 'Report of the UN Secretary General on Renewing the United Nations: A Programme for Reform' (14 July 1997) UN Do. A/51/950), para 79.

[447] Oberleitner (n 425) 361. See, eg, UN, 'In Larger Freedom, Report of the UN Secretary-General' (2 December 2004) UN Doc A/59/565.

[448] A UN Development Group Human Rights Mainstreaming Mechanism was established in 2009. See UN Development Group, 'Mainstreaming Human Rights in Development' (UN 2013).

[449] Oberleitner (n 425) 363.

[450] ibid 363.

[451] M Kaltenborn and others, *Sustainable Development Goals* (Springer 2020) 3.

[452] OHCHR, 'Statement by 17 Special Procedures Mandate-holders of the Human Rights Council on the Post-2015 Development Agenda', Grounding development priorities in human rights: Incentives to improve equality, social security and accountability, 21 May 2013, <https://www.ohchr.org/en/statements/2013/05/statement-17-special-procedures-mandate-holders-human-rights-council-post-2015> accessed 22 January 2022.

[453] See also Collins (n 331) 68.

[454] See below Section V.

[455] Oberleitner (n 425) 376.

[456] FAO Constitution of 16 October 1945</IBT>, Preamble.

164 SDG 2

both scientific, technological, social, and economic research relating to nutrition, food, and agriculture and the processing, marketing, and distribution of food and agricultural products.[457]

Even though the FAO's tasks in combating hunger and food insecurity are mostly 'technical', in nature the organization was instrumental in drafting the right to food in article 11 of the ICESCR.[458] Nevertheless, until the World Food Summit in 1996, the FAO remained reluctant to align its work with the right to food.[459] The outcome document of the World Food Summit, the Rome Declaration on World Food Security and the Summit Plan of Action of 1996, reaffirmed 'the right of everyone to have access to safe and nutritious food, consistent with the right to adequate food and the fundamental right of everyone to be free from hunger' and provided the basis for a human rights-based approach to hunger and food insecurity.[460] In recent years, a 'right to food' approach has been increasingly integrated into the FAO's activities.[461] In 2004, the FAO adopted a set of Voluntary Guidelines to support the progressive realization of the right to food in the context of food security, which marked an important step towards a human rights-based approach and human rights mainstreaming in the FAO.[462]

The alignment of various international legal regimes with human rights and the mainstreaming of human rights into policies, such as the SDGs, have been criticized as inadequate or as a distraction from the structural causes of hunger, food insecurity, or underdevelopment in general.[463] The main challenges arise from the fact that international human rights norms must guide all of an organization's activities, requiring the organization to undergo transformations internally, and to internalize and operationalize international legal rules, especially international human rights law, in its decision-making and bureaucratic processes.[464] This means that right-holders and duty-bearers must be identified and, more importantly, that the organization's activities must comply with human rights.[465] It is therefore not surprising that several (legal) questions regarding the policy of human rights mainstreaming remain disputed.[466]

Nevertheless, a human rights-based approach, and human rights mainstreaming in particular, can have far-reaching benefits that should not be underestimated.[467] While human rights place limits on rules, principles, and policies that adversely affect

[457] ibid art 1.

[458] G Moore, 'FAO: Towards a Right to Food Approach?' in M Windfuhr (ed), Beyond the Nation State. Human Rights in Times of Globalization (Global Publications Foundation 2005) 139–154, 140.

[459] ibid 142. See also Oberleitner (n 425) 378.

[460] Declaration on World Food Security and the Summit Plan of Action, Rome, 13–17 November 1996, para 1; Oberleitner (n 425) 378.

[461] ibid 376–79. See also FAO, The Right to Food <https://www.fao.org/right-to-food/areas-of-work/en/> accessed 22 January 2022.

[462] Voluntary Guidelines to support the progressive realization of the right to adequate food in the context of national food security, adopted by the 127th Session of the FAO Council November 2004 <https://www.fao.org/3/y7937e/y7937e.pdf> accessed 22 January 2022. See also Oberleitner (n 425) 379.

[463] Peters, 'Global Constitutionalism' (n 343) 301. For criticism, see also M Koskenniemi, 'Human Rights Mainstreaming as a Human Rights Mainstreaming as a Strategy for Institutional Power' (2010) 1 Humanity 47–58.

[464] Oberleitner (n 425) 386, 388.

[465] ibid 386.

[466] ibid 386.

[467] ibid 388.

individuals' rights, they also contribute to a more 'coherent multilateralism'.[468] This allows global problems like hunger and food insecurity to be addressed more comprehensively.[469] Human rights mainstreaming does justice to the multidimensional nature of SDG 2 as it is based on the premise that global problems cannot be solved by mere 'technical' or 'economic' solutions to, for example, food insecurity, since all these problems are (also) inevitably linked to human rights issues.[470] Finally, human rights mainstreaming also generates benefits for the international human rights system and helps further develop the understanding and interpretation of human rights. It does so especially with regard to the systemic issues and root causes of global problems that pose challenges given the current architecture of human rights.[471]

V. Commentary on the Targets

A. General Remarks

Since the adoption of the SDGs in 2015, the international community has gradually moved away from debating the goals and begun to focus on their implementation.[472] During the deliberations on the SDGs, states discussed their implementation, especially at the national level, but did not regulate it in detail.[473] However, it was agreed that states have the *primary responsibility* to implement the SDGs at the national level.[474] Implementation now depends on the particular states and national contexts.[475] While states are the key actors in this regard, implementation of the SDGs also requires wider coordination of various sectors and societies.[476] This represents a novel form of governance that differs from top-down approaches and focuses on bottom-up implementation processes based on partnerships between governments stakeholders and international organizations.[477]

As the goals are not legally binding, the mechanisms to enforce compliance and monitor states' progress towards achieving the SDGs are relatively weak.[478] Hence,

---

[468] V Leary, 'International Institutions: Towards Coherent Multilateralism' in L Boisson de Chazournes and V Gowlland-Debbas (eds), *The International Legal System in Quest of Equity and Universality. Liber Amicorum Georges Abi-Saab* (Nijhoff 2001) 823–29; Oberleitner (n 425) 388.

[469] Oberleitner (n 425) 388.

[470] ibid 388.

[471] See also ibid 387–88; see S Marks, 'Human Rights and Root Causes' (2011) 74 The Modern Law Review 57–78.

[472] Sustainable Development Solutions Network (SDSN), 'A Global Initiative for the United Nations, Indicators and a Monitoring Framework for the SDGs—Launching a Data Revolution for the SDGs, A Report to the Secretary-General of the United Nations by the Leadership Council of the SDSN' (12 June 2015) <https://irp-cdn.multiscr eensite.com/be6d1d56/files/uploaded/150612-FINAL-SDSN-Indicator-Report1.pdf> accessed 22 January 2022, 5. See also A Persson and others, 'Follow-up and Review of the Sustainable Development Goals: Alignment vs. Internalization' (2016) 25 Review of European Comparative & International Environmental Law 59–68, 59.

[473] Persson and others, 'Follow-up and Review of the Sustainable Development Goals' (n 472) 59.

[474] ibid 59. See also Agenda 2030 (n 1) para 63.

[475] S Dalby and others, 'Global Governance Challenges in Achieving the Sustainable Development Goals. Introduction' in Dalby and others (eds) (n 7) 1–18, 1.

[476] ibid 1.

[477] ibid 7.

[478] ibid 7.

monitoring is based on voluntary implementation procedures at the national level.[479] In addition, the SDGs are formulated in a flexible manner that allows for *country- and context-specific* implementation, enabling states to prioritize which goals they pursue and how they implement them.[480] Accordingly, each country sets its own national targets and decides how these targets should be incorporated into national policies and strategies for sustainable development.[481]

Given the lack of overarching authority, enforcement and compliance mechanisms, and 'hard' legal obligations,[482] the focus is on the process of monitoring states' performance in implementing the goals.[483] Accordingly, *measuring* progress is considered crucial for the effective implementation of the SDGs.[484] In this context, the UN Statistical Commission established the Inter-Agency and Expert Group on SDG Indicators (IAEG-SDGs) in 2015.[485] The IAEG-SDGs, composed of Member States as well as regional and international agencies acting as observers, was tasked with developing a set of global-level indicators to monitor Member States' progress towards the SDGs and their targets.[486] Subsequently, the 'Global Indicator Framework for the SDGs' was agreed upon at the 48th session of the Statistical Commission in March 2017 and adopted by the UN General Assembly in April 2017.[487]

The main regulatory tools are *targets* and *indicators* that assess and enforce compliance with the SDGs and transform them into practical outcomes.[488] For the purpose of this chapter, a 'goal' is defined as 'an ambitious, but specific 'commitment'.[489] Targets are 'quantified sub-components that will contribute in a major way to achievement of goal' in terms of an outcome variable.[490] Indicators, on the other hand, reflect a 'precise metric from identified databases to assess if target is being met'.[491] To benchmark states' progress towards the SDGs, many expert groups have highlighted the strong potential

---

[479] ibid 7.

[480] ibid 7; JDB Gil and others, 'Sustainable Development Goal 2: Improved Targets and Indicators for Agriculture and Food Security 48 (2019) Ambio 685–98, 686.

[481] Agenda 2030 (n 1) para 55.

[482] Dalby and others (n 475) 1.

[483] Persson and others, 'Follow-up and Review of the Sustainable Development Goals' (n 472) 60. See also Agenda 2030 (n 1) paras 72–73.

[484] Dalby and others (n 475) 7.

[485] See ECOSOC, 'Report of the Inter-agency and Expert Group on Sustainable Development Goal Indicators (UN Statistical Commission, 47th Session)' (8–11 March 2016), UN Doc E/CN.3/2016/2/Rev.1 (19 February 2016). See also Agenda 2030 (n 1) para 75. For more information on the IAEG-SDGs, see <https://unstats.un.org/sdgs/iaeg-sdgs/> accessed 22 January 2022.

[486] Persson and others, 'Follow-up and Review of the Sustainable Development Goals: Alignment vs. Internalization' (n 472) 61.

[487] ECOSOC, 'Report of the Inter-agency and Expert Group on Sustainable Development Goal Indicators (UN Statistical Commission, 48th Session)' (7–10 March 2017) UN Doc E/CN.3/2017/2 (15 December 2016). The UNGA adopted the 'Global indicator framework for the Sustainable Development Goals and targets of the 2030 Agenda for Sustainable Development' by Resolution 71/313 on 6 July 2017, UN Doc A/RES/71/313 (10 July 2017).

[488] Report of the High-Level Panel of Eminent Persons on the Post-2015 Development Agenda, 'A New Global Partnership: Eradicate Poverty and Transform Economies Through Sustainable Development' (2013) 57 <https://www.un.org/development/desa/pd/sites/www.un.org.development.desa.pd/files/unpd-cm13-201502-a_new_global_partnership_eradicate_powerty.pdf> accessed 19 March 2023.

[489] ibid 57.

[490] ibid 57. See also Gil and others (n 480) 686.

[491] ibid 57. See also F Astleithner and others, 'Institutions and Indicators—The Discourse about Indicators in the Context of Sustainability' (2004) 19 Journal of Housing and the Built Environment 7–24, 9.

of a 'data revolution' for the goals.[492] In particular, *indicators* have gradually become the 'backbone of monitoring progress towards the SDGs at the global, national, regional and local levels'.[493] In practice, however, the application of indicators faces several challenges, including the fact that they are operationalized inconsistently and data may be unavailable.[494] To support the implementation of the indicators, the IAEG-SDGs has developed a tier system that classifies them into three tiers according to their level of methodological development and the availability of data at the global level.[495]

SDG 2 comprises eight targets and fourteen indicators.[496] Each target and its associated indicators are intended to achieve a specific dimension of the goal by dates ranging from 2025 to 2030.[497] Targets 2.1–2.5 are directly linked to food security and agricultural sustainability.[498] In addition, targets 2.4 and 2.5 are also linked to the environment.[499] Targets 2a–2c are market-based measures intended to increase agricultural investment and reduce market constraints, distortions, and volatility.[500] Some of the SDG 2 indicators represent *objectives*, while others include *means* to achieve them.[501] The SDG 2 indicators were developed under the auspices of several international institutions: nine were developed by the FAO, two by the WHO, one by the IMF and the World Bank, and two by the Organisation for Economic Cooperation and Development (OECD).[502] The FAO, UNICEF, WHO, OECD, and WTO oversee the monitoring process for the SDG 2 indicators.[503]

In general, as discussed below with respect to each target, a comparison of the SDG 2 targets developed in 2014 and their accompanying indicators added as part of the follow-up process reveals that the scope of SDG 2 has become narrower over time.[504] The indicators are generally based on quantitative factors whose measurability is

---

[492] SDSN, 'A Global Initiative for the United Nations, Indicators and a Monitoring Framework for the SDGs' (n 472).

[493] ibid 7.

[494] AE Cheo and KA Tapiwa, *SDG 2—Zero Hunger: Food Security, Improved Nutrition and Sustainable Agriculture* (Emerald Publishing 2021) 15–41, 31; R Zinkernagel and others, 'Applying the SDGs to Cities: Business as Usual or a New Dawn?' (2018) 10 Sustainability 1–18, 2.

[495] UN, IAEG-SDGs, Tier Classification for Global SDG Indicators, available <https://unstats.un.org/sdgs/iaeg-sdgs/tier-classification/> accessed 22 January 2022. For the current tier classification in 2021, see Tier Classification for Global SDG Indicators as of 29 March 2021 <https://unstats.un.org/sdgs/files/Tier%20Classification%20of%20SDG%20Indicators_29%20Mar%202021_web.pdf> accessed 22 January 2022.

[496] UN Sustainable Development, SDG 2, Targets and Indicators <https://sdgs.un.org/goals/goal2> accessed 22 January 2022. See also UN SDGs, SDG Indicators <https://unstats.un.org/sdgs/indicators/indicators-list/> accessed 22 January 2022. The global indicator framework contains in total 248 indicators for all SDGs. Two hundred and thirty-one indicators are so-called unique indicators and thirteen indicators repeat under the different targets.

[497] Cheo and Tapiwa (n 494) 23. See also Bley-Palmer and Young (n 7) 23.

[498] Gil and others (n 480) 686.

[499] See UN Environment Programme (UNEP), 'Goal 2: Zero Hunger' <https://www.unep.org/explore-topics/sustainable-development-goals/why-do-sustainable-development-goals-matter/goal-2> accessed 22 January 2022.

[500] Gil and others (n 480) 686.

[501] ibid 686.

[502] Szabo and others (n 53) 9.

[503] On the custodian agencies with respect to each SDG 2 indicator, see UN, 'SDG Indicators, Data Collection Information and Focal Points' <https://unstats.un.org/sdgs/dataContacts/?selectIndicator=2.c.1+Indicator+of+food+price+anomalies&selectAgency=> accessed 22 January 2022. On the special role of the custodian agencies, see also ECOSOC, 'Report of the Inter-agency and Expert Group on Sustainable Development Goal Indicators' (15 December 2016) UN Doc E/CN.3/2017/2, para 28.

[504] Bley-Palmer and Young (n 7) 23.

difficult to operationalize.[505] Therefore, even though Agenda 2030 features an inclusive and holistic understanding of sustainable development, the SDG 2 indicators limit this to some extent.[506] Furthermore, a thorough review of the SDG 2 targets and indicators reveals several inconsistencies not only between SDG 2 and other SDGs, as discussed above, but also within SDG 2. While some SDG 2 indicators are relatively well established (eg those for food security and nutrition), others (eg indicators for smallholder income and productivity or for sustainable agriculture) are considered to be imprecise, resulting in vague outcomes in the reporting and monitoring processes of SDG 2.[507] Finally, while the SDG 2 indicators have been formulated quantitatively to measure states' progress, in some cases they are not quantifiable because they consist of unclear concepts.[508]

Against this backdrop, this section analyses each of the SDG 2 targets and their associated indicators. In particular, for each target, the sources, empirical data and domestic and international efforts, and criticisms are discussed, including an assessment of whether the targets are consistent with existing international rights and obligations, especially the obligations of states under international human rights law.

B. SDG 2 Targets and Indicators

1. Target 2.1 By 2030, End hunger and ensure access by all people, in particular the poor and people in vulnerable situations, including infants, to safe, nutritious and sufficient food all year round

a) Source of target

Target 2.1 aims to end hunger and achieve universal access to safe and nutritious food. Individuals are considered to be food insecure 'when they lack regular access to enough safe and nutritious food for growth and development as well as an active and healthy life'.[509] Target 2.1 goes beyond the objective of ending hunger by also recognizing the importance of access to safe, nutritious, and sufficient food for all people worldwide.[510] It is closely linked to the human right to food and reinforces the human rights obligations of states as enshrined in article 11(1) of the ICESCR.[511] As with target 2.1, General Comment No 12 on the right to food refers to vulnerable groups, stating that the right is realized when everyone, including women and children, have physical and economic access to adequate food at all times or the means to procure it.[512] Likewise, other international human rights treaties that are relevant

---

[505] ibid 23.
[506] ibid 23.
[507] Gil and others (n 480) 686; HLPF, '2017 HLPF Thematic Review of SDG 2: End Hunger, Achieve Food Security and Improved Nutrition, and Promote Sustainable Agriculture' 4.
[508] Gil and others (n 480) 686.
[509] See FAO, 'Hunger and Food Insecurity' <https://www.fao.org/hunger/en/> accessed 22 January 2022.
[510] See FAO, 'Tracking Progress on Food and Agriculture-related SDG Indicators 2021' (n 30).
[511] Kaltenborn and others (n 451) 3.
[512] CESCR, General Comment No 12 (n 354) para 6.

to target 2.1 affirm the human right to food of specific groups of persons, including access to food, such as article 24(2)(c) of the Convention on the Rights of the Child (CRC).[513]

At the policy level, target 2.1 can be traced back to the World Food Summit Plan of Action (1996) and the Rome Declaration on World Food Security (1996). Both declarations refer to the right to food in confirming 'the right of everyone to have access to safe and nutritious food, consistent with the right to adequate food and the fundamental right of everyone to be free from hunger'.[514]

b) Empirical analysis: domestic and international efforts of implementation

Target 2.1 of SDG 2 measures *hunger* by using indicator 2.1.1, namely, the 'prevalence of undernourishment' (PoU).[515] Undernourishment exists when a person is not able to purchase enough food to meet the daily minimum dietary energy requirements over a period of one year.[516] Indicator 2.1.1 serves to estimate the proportion of the population whose habitual food consumption does not provide the dietary energy levels needed to maintain a normal active and healthy life.[517]

For decades, the FAO has defined hunger as undernourishment and used the PoU indicator to estimate the extent of hunger in the world.[518] The FAO's recent reports on '[t]he State of Food Security and Nutrition in the World' reveal that the global decline in hunger (PoU) has ended.[519] Empirical data show that between 720 and 811 million people in the world (8.9 per cent of the world population) are estimated to be undernourished in 2020.[520] Approximately 118 million more people faced hunger in 2020 than in 2019.[521] The number of people affected by hunger throughout the world continues to increase—a trend that began in 2014 and continues to this day.[522] Hunger increased in every region of the world from 2015 to 2020 except in eastern and southeastern Asia, with sharp increases in Sub-Saharan Africa, Latin America, and the Caribbean from 2019 to 2020.[523] For example, the PoU in Sub-Saharan Africa was estimated to be 24.1 per cent of the population in 2020 (nearly 264 million people), the highest among all regions.[524]

---

[513] Convention on the Rights of the Child (CRC) of 20 November 1989, 1557 UNTS 3, art 24(2)(c); See also, eg, art 28 of the Convention on the Rights of Persons with Disabilities (CRPD).

[514] World Food Summit Plan of Action, 13–17 November 1996; Rome Declaration on World Food Security, 13–17 November 1996. See also 'The Future We Want' (n 140) para 8: 'We also reaffirm the importance of freedom, peace and security, respect for all human rights, including the right to development and the right to an adequate standard of living, including the right to food, the rule of law, gender equality, the empowerment of women and the overall commitment to just and democratic societies for development.'

[515] See UN SDGs, 'SDG Indicators' <https://unstats.un.org/sdgs/metadata/?Text=&Goal=2&Target> accessed 22 January 2022.

[516] FAO, Factsheets on the 21 SDG Indicators under FAO Custodianship (Rome 2020) 9.

[517] UNSTATS, 'SDG Indicator Metadata' <https://unstats.un.org/sdgs/metadata/files/Metadata-02-01-01.pdf> accessed 22 January 2022.

[518] FAO, 'Hunger and Food Insecurity' <https://www.fao.org/hunger/en/> accessed 22 January 2022.

[519] FAO, 'State of Food Security Report 2021' (n 28).

[520] ibid 8.

[521] ibid 8.

[522] ibid 8.

[523] FAO, 'Tracking Progress on Food and Agriculture-related SDG Indicators 2021' (n 30) 17.

[524] ibid 17.

Target 2.1 of SDG 2 includes not only a target to end hunger but also one to ensure *access* to nutritious and sufficient food for all. Indicator 2.1.2—'prevalence of moderate or severe food insecurity in the population, based on the Food Insecurity Experience Scale (FIES)'—is used to monitor progress towards ensuring access to adequate food for all.[525] The Food Insecurity Experience Scale (FIES) produces a measure of the severity of food insecurity experienced by individuals or households, based on direct interviews.[526] According to recent reports, nearly one in three people in the world did not have access to adequate food in 2020, which is an increase of 320 million people in one year, from 2.05 to 2.37 billion.[527] In the same year, two-thirds of all people experiencing moderate or severe food insecurity worldwide resided in Central Asia and South Asia or in Sub-Saharan Africa.[528] In Latin America and the Caribbean, food insecurity is increasing the fastest.[529] While there was a gradual decrease in the prevalence of food insecurity from 2015 to 2020 in northern America and Europe, the trend changed in 2020.[530] Additionally, at the global level, the gender gap in the prevalence of moderate or severe food insecurity has increased mainly due to the COVID-19 pandemic.[531] In general, the FAO has concluded that data based on indicator 2.1.2 shows that target 2.1 remains far from being realized.[532]

In recent years, there have been numerous efforts at the national and international level to achieve target 2.1. Many countries have been impacted by the COVID-19 pandemic.[533] For example, the 2020 Voluntary National Reviews (VNRs) found that many states were requesting that food security and nutrition issues be placed at the centre of emergency response efforts to address the public health crisis.[534] Recent VNRs provide insights into the various national measures to achieve target 2.1.[535] Countries like Angola, Azerbaijan, Bhutan, Bolivia, Colombia, Egypt, Sierra Leone, and Zimbabwe have prioritized the development of structural programmes, especially for smallholder farmers, to ensure food security.[536] States have also focused on domestic policies that address the distribution of food, such as the establishment of distribution networks for poor and rural communities.[537] For instance, Azerbaijan's State Committee for Affairs

---

[525] ibid 20.

[526] FAO, SDG 2, Indicator 2.1.2 <https://www.fao.org/sustainable-development-goals/indicators/212/en/> accessed 22 January 2022.

[527] FAO, 'Tracking Progress on Food and Agriculture-related SDG Indicators 2021' (n 30) 17.

[528] ibid 22.

[529] ibid 22.

[530] ibid 20–21.

[531] ibid 22.

[532] ibid 20.

[533] HLPF, 'Voluntary National Reviews at the 2021 High-level political forum on sustainable development, Secretariat Background Note' (2021) <https://sustainabledevelopment.un.org/content/documents/28677BN_HLPF_2021_VNR_Main_Messages.pdf> accessed 22 January 2022.

[534] HLPF, 'Voluntary National Reviews (VNRs)' <https://sustainabledevelopment.un.org/vnrs/> accessed 22 January 2022. As part of its review mechanisms, Agenda 2030 calls states to conduct regular reviews of progress at the national and sub-national levels (Voluntary National Reviews), see <https://sustainabledevelopment.un.org/vnrs/> accessed 22 January 2022.

[535] See for the VNRs of states <https://sustainabledevelopment.un.org/vnrs/> accessed 22 January 2022.

[536] HLFP, '2021 Voluntary National Reviews Synthesis Report' (2021) 42 <https://sustainabledevelopment.un.org/content/documents/294382021_VNR_Synthesis_Report.pdf> accessed 22 January 2022.

[537] ibid 42.

of Refugees and Internally Displaced Persons (IDPs), which is a governmental agency, has provided food aid to low-income families with the support of local and international organizations.[538] Similarly, the Bahamas have established the National Food Distribution Taskforce, which includes a public–private social care initiative that delivers emergency food assistance to vulnerable populations.[539] Several other countries, such as Bolivia, Cabo Verde, Cuba, Iraq, Japan, and Namibia, have also implemented similar plans.[540] Finally, from a North–South perspective, many developed countries have reaffirmed their commitment to support the Global South in achieving 'Zero Hunger'.[541] For instance, Norway released an Action Plan for Sustainable Food Systems, designed to help low-income countries provide food for their own population.[542]

c) Critique

Target 2.1 is linked to the right to food and is generally—as discussed above—aligned with international human rights standards.[543] Nevertheless, empirical studies reveal that an implementation gap exists between the standards set in article 11 of the ICESCR and the current situation of hunger and food insecurity in many parts of the world.[544] Eradicating hunger and food insecurity is therefore not only a question of access to food. Instead, it also concerns *structural* and *systemic* problems of global economy, issues that need to be addressed in the implementation of the target.[545]

Criticism is mainly directed at indicator PoU (indicator 2.1.1).[546] PoU is based on the FAO's definition of undernourishment.[547] The indicator focuses on the measurement of dietary energy intake but does not include proteins, vitamins, minerals, and other micronutrients, all of which individuals need for adequate nutrition.[548] For example, a lack of these nutrients is common among poor people in industrialized countries.[549] Moreover, the indicator does not consider health issues that might affect dietary intake and the outcome of the PoU.[550] For example, many individuals in poor regions suffer from diseases that hinder the absorption of nutrients.[551] Also, the indicator measures undernourishment by year and excludes therefore millions of individuals who might be undernourished for a shorter period of time.[552] Scholars have asserted that the current definition of PoU actually excludes millions of undernourished people from its scope.[553] Furthermore, the monitoring of target 2.1 reveals that there are limited data

---

[538] ibid 42.
[539] ibid 42.
[540] HLFP, '2021 Voluntary National Reviews Synthesis Report' (2021) 42.
[541] ibid 43.
[542] ibid 43.
[543] See Section IV.B.1 of this chapter.
[544] See also CESCR, General Comment No 12 (n 354) para 5.
[545] See, eg, Chadwick (n 61).
[546] Pogge (n 6) 11.
[547] ibid 11.
[548] ibid 12.
[549] ibid 11.
[550] ibid 11.
[551] ibid 11.
[552] ibid 12.
[553] ibid 13.

172   SDG 2

on specific groups included in the target, namely the poor, the vulnerable, and children, as data are not yet available for all countries.[554] Finally, even though target 2.1 is congruent with the right to food, indicator 2.1.1 does not effectively monitor the current status of hunger and food insecurity.

2. Target 2.2 By 2030, End all forms of malnutrition, including achieving, by 2025, the internationally agreed targets on stunting and wasting in children under 5 years of age, and address the nutritional needs of adolescent girls, pregnant and lactating women and older persons

a) Source of target

Target 2.2 constitutes the global nutrition target of SDG 2. As with target 2.1, target 2.2 is also based on international human rights law and is linked to article 11(1) and (2) of the ICESCR.[555] The target explicitly refers to the nutrition needs of specific groups. Where children's rights are concerned, target 2.2 is associated with article 24(1) and (2)(c) of the CRC, which imposes human rights obligations on states to combat the malnutrition of children.[556] The target also addresses the nutritional needs of pregnant and lactating women. Against this backdrop, article 12(2) of the Convention on the Elimination of All Forms of Discrimination Against Women (CEDAW) requires states to ensure that women receive appropriate services in connection with pregnancy, confinement, and the post-natal period, as well as adequate nutrition during pregnancy and lactation.[557] Furthermore, the Protocol to the African Charter on Human and Peoples' Rights on the Rights of Women in Africa (Maputo Protocol) also includes extensive obligations on women's right to adequate food, including their nutritional needs during pregnancy and lactation.[558]

b) Empirical analysis: domestic and international efforts of implementation

Target 2.2 contains three indicators that measure states' progress. Two of the indicators address the nutrition of *children under 5 years of age*, and one indicator concerns the nutrition of *women aged 15 to 49 years*. Indicator 2.2.1 measures the 'prevalence of stunting' among children under the age of five (height-for-age <-2 standard deviation from the median of the WHO Child Growth Standards).[559] Children are considered to be stunted, or chronically malnourished, when they are too short for their age.[560] The

---

[554] Gil and others (n 480) 689.

[555] ICESCR, art 11(1) and (2).

[556] CRC, arts 24(1) and 24(2)(c).

[557] Convention on the Elimination of All Forms of Discrimination Against Women (CEDAW) of 18 December 1979, 1249 UNTS 13, art 12(2).

[558] Protocol to the African Charter on Human and Peoples' Rights on the Rights of Women in Africa of 11 July 2003 (Maputo Protocol), adopted by the Meeting of Ministers, Addis Ababa, Ethiopia on 28 March 2003, and the Assembly of the African Union at the second summit of the African Union in Maputo, Mozambique, 21 July 2003, art 14 (2) reads as follows: 'States Parties shall take all appropriate measures to: ... b) establish and strengthen existing pre-natal, delivery and post-natal health and nutritional services for women during pregnancy and while they are breast-feeding'; art 15 'a) provide women with access to clean drinking water, sources of domestic fuel, land, and the means of producing nutritious food; b) establish adequate systems of supply and storage to ensure food security.'

[559] UN SDGS, 'SDG 2 Indicators' (2022) <https://unstats.un.org/sdgs/metadata/?Text=&Goal=2&Target> accessed 22 January 2022.

[560] SDG Report 2021, 29.

recent progress report on the SDGs demonstrates that in 2020, 22 per cent of children under the age of five worldwide (149.2 million) suffered from stunting.[561] Even though these numbers have declined from previous years, the actual number of children affected by stunting is likely to be higher because of the continued difficulties in achieving this target due to the COVID-19 pandemic.[562] The three regions with the highest numbers are Oceania,[563] Sub-Saharan Africa, and Central and Southern Asia, where nearly three-quarters of the world's stunted children live.[564]

Indicator 2.2.2 concerns both the 'prevalence of malnutrition' among children under five years of age and the type of malnutrition, notably wasting and overweight (weight for height >+2 or <−2 standard deviation from the median of the WHO Child Growth Standards).[565] Wasting is defined as a life-threatening form of malnourishment, measured by low weight for height.[566] In 2020, wasting affected approximately 45.4 million children, and overweight affected 38.9 million children.[567] Nevertheless, as noted by the recent report on the SDGs, more children than estimated may have suffered from wasting in recent years, for instance due to disruptions caused by the COVID-19 pandemic.[568] In many countries, the number of overweight children has increased.[569]

Indicator 2.2.3 measures the 'prevalence of anaemia in women aged 15 to 49 years, by pregnancy status'.[570] Anaemia is a condition in which haemoglobin concentration is insufficient to meet the body's physiological needs.[571] Empirical studies illustrate that there has been little progress made over the last years and that nearly one in three women of reproductive age is still affected by anaemia.[572] There is no region in the world that has shown a significant decline in the prevalence of anaemia among women of reproductive age.[573] Africa, and Western Africa in particular, is the region most affected by anaemia.[574]

Recent VNRs regarding target 2.2 reveal that many countries have established surveillance and technical assistance programs to achieve the target, which monitor and ensure the adequate nutrition of children and women, especially in poor communities.[575] For example, Colombia, Malaysia, and Paraguay have adopted national programmes that provide medical check-ups and nutritional diagnostics to children under the age of five and pregnant women who live in poverty.[576] At the international level, UNICEF has established various programmes that help to tackle malnourishment of children.

---

[561] ibid 29.
[562] UNICEF, 'Malnutrition' <https://data.unicef.org/topic/nutrition/malnutrition/> accessed 22 January 2022.
[563] Excluding Australia and New Zealand, see SDG Report 2021, 29.
[564] SDG Report 2021, 29.
[565] UN SDGS, 'SDG 2 Indicators' (n 559).
[566] SDG Report 2021, 29.
[567] ibid 29.
[568] ibid 29.
[569] ibid 29.
[570] UN SDGS, 'SDG 2 Indicators' (n 559).
[571] SDG Report 2021, 29.
[572] FAO, 'State of Food Security Report 2021' (n 28) 33.
[573] ibid 33.
[574] SDG Report 2021, 29.
[575] HLFP, '2021 Voluntary National Reviews Synthesis Report' (2021) 43.
[576] ibid 43.

174   SDG 2

For instance, the Innocenti Framework on Food Systems for Children and Adolescents comprises recommendations for actions on how food systems can be shaped in the light of SDG 2 in order to improve the nutrition of children and adolescents.[577]

c) Critique

Target 2.2 concerns food consumption and aims to end all forms of malnutrition worldwide. As discussed earlier, the target aligns in principle with the right to food and the standards set in article 11 of the ICESCR.[578] The WHO defines malnutrition as undernutrition, micronutrient-related malnutrition (such as a lack of important vitamins and minerals), overweight and obesity, and diet-related non-communicable diseases.[579] Scholars and practitioners have criticized target 2.2 for not adequately covering the different dimensions of the 'quality' of food, which are relevant to ending malnutrition in its various forms.[580] The CESCR also acknowledges this issue with respect to the realization of the right to food. It emphasizes that available food also needs to be of sufficient quality and contain all forms of nutrients.[581] While target 2.2 addresses micro- and macronutrient deficiencies, it indeed does not address all conditions of malnutrition, namely overconsumption (especially in wealthier states) or the consumption of food high in fat or sugars.[582] The target also does not refer to health problems triggered by malnutrition, such as diabetes and cardiovascular diseases.[583] It has been therefore suggested adding new indicators to the target that explicitly address obesity—a concern in developing and developed states—and focus on the health–malnutrition nexus more comprehensively.[584]

Furthermore, target 2.2 refers to specific groups of vulnerable people, namely children, girls, women, and older persons. Hence, the target does not consider the special nutritional needs of *other* vulnerable people, such as poor persons or people suffering from certain diseases. The target thus seems to have a narrower scope, unlike the right to food, which applies to all individuals. Furthermore, there are several reports noting the discriminatory challenges that children from ethnic minorities or children in rural areas face in the context of food and nutrition.[585] Therefore, target 2.2 calls for human rights mainstreaming of the fundamental norms of equality and non-discrimination. Consequently, state authorities should take these human rights standards into account when adopting or implementing policies to address malnutrition of children or other vulnerable groups.

---

[577] UNICEF, 'Food Systems for Children and Adolescents. Working Together to Secure Nutritious Diets', Interim Summary Report, 5–7 November 2018 <https://www.unicef.org/media/94086/file/Food-systems-brochure.pdf> accessed 22 January 2022.
[578] See above Section IV.B.1.
[579] WHO, 'Malnutrition' <https://www.who.int/news-room/fact-sheets/detail/malnutrition> accessed 22 January 2022.
[580] Veldhuizen and others, 'The Missing Middle' (n 411) 1.
[581] CESCR, General Comment No 12 (n 354) paras 8–9.
[582] Veldhuizen and others, 'The Missing Middle' (n 411) 1; Gil and others (n 480) 689.
[583] Veldhuizen and others, 'The Missing Middle' (n 411) 1.
[584] Gil and others (n 480) 689.
[585] Cheo and Tapiwa (n 494) 27.

COMMENTARY ON THE TARGETS 175

Finally, the implementation of target 2.2 creates problems, as it is often challenging, especially in developing countries, to measure complex nutrition levels. In many of these countries, there are serious problems in monitoring especially vulnerable populations.[586] The lack of expertise in these countries' health sectors also hinders the effective implementation of the target.[587]

3. Target 2.3 By 2030, Double the agricultural productivity and incomes of small-scale food producers, in particular women, indigenous peoples, family farmers, pastoralists and fishers, including through secure and equal access to land, other productive resources and inputs, knowledge, financial services, markets and opportunities for value addition and non-farm employment

a) Source

Target 2.3 requires states to double the agricultural productivity and income of small-scale food producers. The target's relationship with international human rights law can be traced back to the right to food enshrined in article 11(2)(a) of the ICESCR, which requires states 'to improve methods of production, conservation and distribution of food by making full use of technical and scientific knowledge, by disseminating knowledge of the principles of nutrition and by developing or reforming agrarian systems in such a way as to achieve the most efficient development and utilization of natural resources'.[588] Furthermore, the Declaration on the Rights of Indigenous Peoples is also relevant to target 2.3 as it includes rights to lands, territories, and the resources of indigenous people.[589] Similarly, the American Declaration on the Rights and Duties of Man states that 'every person has a right to own such private property as meets the essential needs of decent living and helps to maintain the dignity of the individual and of the home'.[590]

b) Empirical analysis: domestic and international efforts of implementation

Target 2.3 consists of two indicators. Indicator 2.3.1 on 'volume of production per labour unit by classes of farming, pastoral and forestry enterprise size' measures the average labour productivity of small-scale food producers.[591] As the FAO points out, small-scale producers in developing countries have a lower productivity than larger-scale producers.[592] In these countries, gender-related data on the productivity of small-scale food producers shows that the productivity of women small-scale producers often exceeds the productivity of men producers.[593]

Indicator 2.3.2 measures the 'average income of small-scale food producers, by sex and indigenous status'.[594] The FAO notes that small-scale food producers have lower

---

[586] ibid 27.
[587] ibid 27.
[588] ICESCR, art 11(2)(a).
[589] UN Declaration on the Rights of Indigenous Peoples, 2 October 2007, adopted by the UNGA, 2 October 2007, A/RES/61/295, art 26(1) and (2).
[590] American Declaration on the Rights and Duties of Man, adopted by the Ninth International Conference of American States, Bogotá, Colombia on 2 May 1948, art XXII.
[591] FAO, 'Tracking Progress on Food and Agriculture-related SDG Indicators 2021' (n 30) 25.
[592] ibid 25.
[593] ibid 26.
[594] ibid 32.

incomes than larger food producers, whereas the incomes of women small-scale food producers are lower than those of men.[595] In many countries for which data are available, male-headed households have higher annual incomes than female-headed households, although the productivity of female small-scale producers is often higher than that of male small-scale producers.[596] In general, measuring states' progress towards target 2.3 poses significant challenges. The indicators require valid information, for example on labour input and revenues for the same production unit. However, available national agricultural surveys rarely collect these data.[597] Against this backdrop, a number of FAO Member States, international institutions, and private sector organizations have developed the 'AGRISurvey' programme to collect data on SDG 2, including target 2.3.[598]

c) Critique

Target 2.3 is important because it calls for doubling agricultural productivity and income for small-scale farmers. Nevertheless, the target and its indicators have been criticized at various levels. As discussed above, the main criticism relates to the *growth-based economic approach* that is inherent in the target and underpinned by international trade and investment law, which does not consider the negative effects of food production on individuals' rights and the environment.[599]

Furthermore, target 2.3 refers to 'small-scale food producers', but the definition of the term remains disputed. Depending on the context, it is used in different ways.[600] Accordingly, some studies have suggested that small-scale food producers should be defined based on land endowment, while others have favoured a definition that directly relates to the producers themselves (eg producers' income or labour productivity).[601] In this regard, the question is whether an absolute or relative definition of small-scale food producers is useful for measuring target 2.3 globally.[602] In 2018, the FAO agreed on a definition of small-scale food producers. According to the organization, small-scale food producers are those who 'fall in the bottom 40 per cent of the distribution of land size and livestock heads and total revenues'.[603]

Target 2.3 only focuses on the *incomes of small-scale producers* and overlooks that large-scale producers can also earn relatively low incomes from farming.[604] Furthermore, target 2.3 also refers to secure and equal access to land, resources, inputs,

---

[595] ibid 31.
[596] ibid 31.
[597] FAO, Indicator 2.3.1 <https://www.fao.org/sustainable-development-goals/indicators/231/en/> accessed 22 January 2022.
[598] FAO, 'The Agricultural Integrated Surveys Programme' <https://www.fao.org/food-agriculture-statistics/capacity-development/agrisurvey/en/> accessed 22 January 2022.
[599] See above Section IV.B.2.
[600] FAO, 'Defining Small-scale Food Producers to Monitor Target 2.3 of the 2030 Agenda for Sustainable Development' (June 2017) <https://www.fao.org/3/i6858e/i6858e.pdf> accessed 22 January 2022.
[601] ibid.
[602] ibid.
[603] FAO, Factsheets on the 21 SDG indicators under FAO custodianship. A highlight of the main indicators with the greatest gaps in country reporting, 2020 <https://www.fao.org/3/ca8958en/CA8958EN.pdf> accessed 22 January 2022, 13.
[604] Veldhuizen and others, 'The Missing Middle' (n 411) 1.

and knowledge. However, it remains unclear by which standards 'access' needs be measured here. As with the previous SDG 2 targets, it is important to interpret access in light of human rights standards and other instruments that deal with access to land, resources, or knowledge, for example with regard to indigenous people.

4. Target 2.4 By 2030, Ensure sustainable food production systems and implement resilient agricultural practices that increase productivity and production, that help maintain ecosystems, that strengthen capacity for adaptation to climate change, extreme weather, drought, flooding and other disasters and that progressively improve land and soil quality

a) Source of target

Target 2.4 focuses on issues related to sustainable agriculture. It aims to ensure sustainable food production systems and establish resilient agricultural practices that increase production but also strengthen the capacity to adapt to climate change and other disasters.[605] Several international treaties and other instruments are relevant to target 2.4, including article 11(2)(a) of the ICESCR and article 24 of the African Charter on Human and Peoples' Rights (Banjul Charter).[606] Article 11(2)(a) of the ICESCR requires states to take measures to 'improve methods of production, conservation and distribution of food ... by developing or reforming agrarian systems in such a way as to achieve the most efficient development and utilization of natural resources'.[607] Article 24 of the Banjul Charter states that '[a]ll peoples shall have the right to a general satisfactory environment favourable to their development'.[608] Furthermore, target 2.4 can also be traced back to legal and policy instruments in the field of international environmental law. For instance, the Paris Agreement recognizes in article 7(2) that climate change 'is a global challenge faced by all with local, subnational, national, regional and international dimensions, and that it is a key component of ... the long-term global response to climate change to protect people, livelihoods and ecosystems'.[609]

b) Empirical analysis: domestic and international efforts of implementation

Indicator 2.4.1 measures the 'proportion of agricultural area under productive and sustainable agriculture'.[610] The indicator is dedicated to the assessment of sustainable agriculture and includes the different dimensions of sustainable development, namely economic, environmental, and social.[611] It applies to agricultural land area of the farm holding, that is, land used to grow crops and raise livestock.[612] The indicator also encompasses, in particular, intensive and extensive production systems, subsistence

---

[605] SDG 2, target 2.4.

[606] African Charter on Human and Peoples' Rights (Banjul Charter), adopted on 27 June 1981, OAU Doc CAB/LEG/67/3 rev. 5, 21 ILM 58 (1982), entered into force 21 October 1986.

[607] ICESCR, art 11(2)(a).

[608] Banjul Charter, art 24.

[609] Paris Agreement of 12 December 2015, UNTS 3156, art 7(2).

[610] UN SDGS, 'SDG 2 Indicators' (n 559).

[611] FAO, 'SDG Indicator 2.4.1' <https://www.fao.org/3/ca5157en/ca5157en.pdf> accessed 22 January 2022.

[612] UNSTATS, 'SDG Indicator Metadata (indicator 2.4.1)' (2021) <https://unstats.un.org/sdgs/metadata/files/Metadata-02-04-01.pdf> accessed 22 January 2022.

agriculture, food and non-food crops and livestock products, agro-forestry, and aquaculture, but not, for example, nomadic pastoralism.[613]

The FAO identifies several key principles of action for achieving sustainable agriculture. Target 2.4 calls for increasing productivity, protecting natural resources, and promoting economic growth.[614] According to the FAO, '[a]griculture and food systems are unsustainable if they fail to benefit those whose livelihoods depend on it, if these systems rely on outdated approaches and technologies, if access to resources, inputs and markets is limited, and if there are no decent job opportunities'.[615]

Food and agricultural production systems are severely impacted by conflict, climate change, and economic crises.[616] Against this backdrop, various efforts have been made at the national and international levels, particularly by the FAO and other international organizations, to help developing countries to ensure sustainable food and agricultural systems, strengthen their resilience, and adapt to climate change.[617] For instance, the FAO's Multidisciplinary Fund has supported agro-ecological transitions by introducing climate-resilient approaches in Senegal.[618] Similarly, the FAO has partnered with other international funds (eg the Adaptation Fund or the Climate Green Fund) to improve the resilience of small-scale farmers to changing environmental conditions, for example in Ethiopia, Kenya, and Uganda.[619]

In 2021, UN Secretary-General António Guterres convened the first-ever Food Systems Summit to improve implementation of the SDGs, including SDG 2.[620] The Summit's purpose was to take new action to make progress on the SDGs, each of which depends to some extent on healthy, sustainable, and equitable food systems.[621] States and other actors issued a call for action at all levels. They recognized the need to adapt food systems to new challenges in a way that is consistent with Agenda 2030, which in turn would help meet the objectives of international agreements like the Paris Agreement.[622] The Summit focused on how to feed a growing population in a way that restores and protects nature, is climate neutral and adapts to national conditions, and enables an inclusive economy.[623]

---

[613] FAO, 'SDG Indicator 2.4.1' <https://www.fao.org/3/ca5157en/ca5157en.pdf> accessed 22 January 2022.
[614] See FAO, 'Sustainable Food and Agriculture' <https://www.fao.org/sustainability/background/en/?key=1> accessed 22 January 2022.
[615] ibid.
[616] FAO, 'State of Food Security Report 2021' (n 28) xviii.
[617] For current projects, see <https://www.fao.org/sustainability/success-stories/en/> accessed 22 January 2022.
[618] FAO, 'Supporting Sustainable Agriculture Transitions in Senegal' <https://www.fao.org/sustainability/success-stories/detail/en/c/1298161/> accessed 22 January 2022.
[619] FAO, 'FAO Partners with the Adaptation Fund to Help Vulnerable Countries Fight the Impact of Climate Change' <https://www.fao.org/news/story/en/item/1296620/icode/> accessed 22 January 2022.
[620] UN, 'Food Systems Summit' (23 September 2021) <https://www.un.org/en/food-systems-summit> accessed 22 January 2022.
[621] UN, 'About the Summit' <https://www.un.org/en/food-systems-summit/about> accessed 22 January 2022.
[622] UN, 'Secretary-General's Chair Summary and Statement of Action on the UN Food Systems Summit, Statement' (23 September 2021) <https://www.un.org/en/food-systems-summit/news/making-food-systems-work-people-planet-and-prosperity> accessed 22 January 2022.
[623] ibid.

c) Critique

Target 2.4 calls for sustainable agriculture, which plays an essential role in achieving SDG 2.[624] The *multidimensional* nature of the target recognizes that eradicating hunger and food insecurity requires a shift in food systems towards more sustainable agriculture.[625] Target 2.4 therefore calls for a radical *transformation* of food and agricultural systems to meet the food needs of a growing population worldwide.[626] Structural changes in food systems, however, impact their foundations, such as food production, global supply chains, transportation networks, and households.[627] Against this backdrop, the FAO emphasizes that '[i]n an ideal world, agrifood systems would be resilient, inclusive and sustainable, producing sufficient, safe and nutritious food for all, and generating livelihoods that guarantee people's economic access to that food'.[628] Compared to other economic sectors, however, agriculture is particularly vulnerable to shocks and crises, such as economic crises, environmental disasters, armed conflicts, or pandemics.[629] The crises have a particular impact on poor and vulnerable people, their income, and ability to grow or purchase food to meet their basic needs.[630] Food and agricultural systems also face environmental challenges like greenhouse gas emissions, land conversion, or biodiversity loss.[631]

The High-Level Panel of Experts on Food Security and Nutrition (HLPE) identifies three elements that characterize food systems, namely food supply chains, food environments (so-called food entry points to acquire, prepare, and consume food), and consumer behaviour.[632] Against this backdrop, target 2.4 has been criticized at various levels related to these characteristics of food systems.[633] A main point of criticism is that the target does not sufficiently address (global) value chains in food and agricultural systems.[634] Value chains are relevant because they link food consumption (targets 2.1 and 2.2) to agricultural production (targets 2.3 and 2.4), and the local to the international level.[635] For example, the transition from grain monocultures to more diverse production systems does not necessarily improve food security and nutrition, as food is often lost along value chains.[636] Moreover, value chains also affect quality of food, food waste,

---

[624] Veldhuizen and others, 'The Missing Middle' (n 411) 1.

[625] Elver (n 379) 350. See also UN, The right to food and a sustainable global food system, contribution of Mr O De Schutter, Special Rapporteur on the Right to Food, 17th session of the UN Commission on Sustainable Development (CSD-17) (4–15 May 2009).

[626] FAO, 'Transforming Food and Agriculture to Achieve the SDGs' (2018) 9 <https://www.fao.org/3/I9900EN/i9900en.pdf> accessed 22 January 2022. See also P Alexander, 'Losses, Inefficiencies and Waste in the Global Food System' (2017) 153 Agricultural Systems 190–200, 190.

[627] FAO, 'The State of Food and Agriculture 2021' xv. According to the HLPE, '[a] food system gathers all the elements (environment, people, inputs, processes, infrastructures, institutions, etc.) and activities that relate to the production, processing, distribution, preparation and consumption of food, and the outputs of these activities, including socio-economic and environmental outcomes'. See HLPE, 'Nutrition and Food Systems. A Report by the High Level Panel of Experts on Food Security and Nutrition' (September 2012) 11.

[628] ibid xvi.

[629] ibid xv, xvii.

[630] ibid xv.

[631] High-Level Panel of Experts (HLPE), 'Nutrition and Food Systems. A Report by the High Level Panel of Experts on Food Security and Nutrition' (September 2012) 14.

[632] ibid 11.

[633] On the criticism concerning the growth-based economic approach, see Section IV.B.2.

[634] Veldhuizen and others, 'The Missing Middle' (n 411) 1.

[635] ibid 2.

[636] ibid 2. See also Alexander (n 626) 192.

and access to food.[637] They generate adverse impacts on individuals' human rights, the environment, and the economy that must be considered when applying a food systems approach (target 2.4) to SDG 2.[638] Therefore, target 2.4 requires coordinated action that focuses on value chains encompassing both food consumption and production.[639]

Furthermore, target 2.4 fails to adequately address the link between sustainable agriculture and nutrition.[640] It remains unclear how agricultural interventions in food systems can address the various forms of malnutrition (target 2.2).[641] Similarly, target 2.4 includes the terms 'sustainable' and 'resilient', the relationship of which is unclear due to the vagueness of the terms, which can lead to different interpretations of these concepts.[642] Accordingly, many terms in target 2.4 would need to be defined more precisely to ensure effective implementation of the target.[643]

5. Target 2.5 By 2020, Maintain the genetic diversity of seeds, cultivated plants and farmed and domesticated animals and their related wild species, including through soundly managed and diversified seed and plant banks at the national, regional and international levels, and promote access to and fair and equitable sharing of benefits arising from the utilization of genetic resources and associated traditional knowledge, as internationally agreed

a) Source of target

Target 2.5 focuses on maintaining genetic diversity of seeds, cultivated plants, and farmed and domesticated animals and their related wild species in food production. From a legal perspective, target 2.5 is linked to the Convention on Biological Diversity.[644] The convention contains, in particular, provisions on the conservation of biological diversity, the sustainable use of its components, and the fair and equitable sharing of the benefits arising from genetic resources.[645] Furthermore, the International Treaty on Plant Genetic Resources for Food and Agriculture also aims to ensure food security and sustainable agriculture through 'the conservation and sustainable use of plant genetic resources for food and agriculture and the fair and equitable sharing of the benefits arising out of their use, in harmony with the Convention on Biological Diversity'.[646] As regards indigenous peoples in particular, the UN Declaration on the Rights of Indigenous Peoples requires states to ensure that indigenous peoples have the right to maintain, protect, and develop their technologies and cultures, including human and genetic resources and seeds, which are also relevant to SDG 2.[647]

---

[637] Veldhuizen and others, 'The Missing Middle' (n 411) 3.

[638] ibid 2.

[639] ibid 3.

[640] See Gil and others (n 480) 695.

[641] ibid 695.

[642] ibid 686.

[643] ibid 686.

[644] Convention on Biological Diversity of 29 December 1993, 1760 UNTS 79.

[645] ibid. See arts 6, 7, 8, 9, 10, 15 of the convention.

[646] International Treaty on Plant Genetic Resources for Food and Agriculture of 3 November 2001 (in force since 29 June 2004), art 1.1.

[647] UN Declaration on the Rights of Indigenous Peoples, art 31.1.

b) Empirical analysis: domestic and international efforts of implementation

Target 2.5 contains two indicators. Indicator 2.5.1 measures the 'number of (a) plant and (b) animal genetic resources for food and agriculture secured in either medium- or long-term conservation facilities'.[648] Indicator 2.5.2 assesses the 'proportion of local breeds classified as being at risk of extinction'.[649] In general, plant and animal genetic resources are under increasing pressure in the agricultural sector due to climate change, although they are relevant to food security and nutrition.[650] Against this backdrop, the growth rate of global stocks of *plant* genetic resources has slowed and is at its lowest level, largely as a result of the COVID-19 pandemic.[651] *Animal* genetic resources are still far from meeting target 2.5, which requires countries to halt the loss of these resources for food and agriculture.[652]

An important development at the international level is the adoption of the International Treaty on Plant Genetic Resources for Food and Agriculture, which might support the achievement of target 2.5.[653] The treaty provides for the realization of farmer's rights,[654] the sustainable use of plant genetic resources for food and agriculture,[655] a funding strategy for the implementation of the treaty's provisions,[656] and the establishment of a global information system to facilitate the exchange of information on plant genetic resources for food and agriculture.[657] The Benefit-Sharing Fund, established under the treaty, provides small-scale farmers with access to a wide range of plant genetic resources.[658]

c) Critique

Plant and animal genetic resources are crucial for the achievement of food security and nutrition.[659] While plant genetic resources form the biological basis of food security, animal genetics are a key element of livestock development.[660] In agriculture, however, a very small proportion of plant species are used, including mainly wheat, rice, and maize.[661] This has in fact resulted in significant genetic erosion and loss of biodiversity.[662] Therefore, target 2.5 calls on states to maintain the genetic diversity of plants and animals, which is also important for the resilience of food and agricultural

---

[648] UN SDGS, 'SDG 2 Indicators' (n 559).

[649] ibid.

[650] FAO, 'Tracking Progress on Food and Agriculture-related SDG Indicators 2021' (n 30) 34.

[651] ibid 34.

[652] ibid 38.

[653] International Treaty on Plant Genetic Resources for Food and Agriculture of 3 November 2001. The treaty currently has 148 Contracting Parties, including one member organization.

[654] International Treaty on Plant Genetic Resources for Food and Agriculture, art 9.

[655] ibid art 6.

[656] ibid art 18.

[657] ibid art 17.

[658] FAO, 'Sharing the Benefits of Plant Genetic Diversity: The Benefit-sharing Fund' <https://www.fao.org/3/ca7158en/CA7158EN.pdf> accessed 22 January 2022.

[659] See <https://www.fao.org/wiews/en/> accessed 22 January 2022.

[660] ibid. See also <https://www.fao.org/animal-genetics/background/why-is-ag-important/en/> accessed 22 January 2022.

[661] Gil and others (n 480) 690.

[662] ibid 690.

systems, and the conservation of biodiversity, among other things.[663] The lack of data to monitor the indicators, however, often hinders the effective implementation of this target.[664]

6. Target 2.a Increase investment, including through enhanced international cooperation, in rural infrastructure, agricultural research and extension services, technology development and plant and livestock gene banks in order to enhance agricultural productive capacity in developing countries, in particular least developed countries

a) Source of target

Target 2.a of SDG 2 aims to increase investment trough *cooperation* in rural infra-structure, agricultural research, and technology, and gene banks. It requires states to cooperate to promote agricultural production in developing countries.[665] Target 2.a is linked to the ICESCR. Article 11 (1) of the ICESCR requires states to cooperate to realize the right to food.[666] States are obliged to cooperate to 'improve methods of production, conservation and distribution of food by making full use of technical and scientific knowledge, by disseminating knowledge of the principles of nutri-tion'.[667] Furthermore, article 15(1)(b) of the ICESCR stipulates the right of everyone 'to enjoy the benefits of scientific progress and its applications'.[668] At the regional level, the Regional Agreement on Access to Information, Public Participation and Justice in Environmental Matters in Latin America and the Caribbean also contains a duty to cooperate in order to strengthen states' national capacities in environmental mat-ters.[669] In this respect, states 'shall give particular consideration to least developed countries, landlocked developing countries and small island developing States from Latin America and the Caribbean'.[670]

b) Empirical analysis: domestic and international efforts of implementation

Target 2.a contains two indicators: indicator 2.a.1 on 'the agriculture orientation index for government expenditures', and indicator 2.a.2 on 'total official flows (official de-velopment assistance (ODA) plus other official flows) to the agricultural sector'.[671] Government expenditures data offer the opportunity to improve food security and nutrition, but also to reduce inequalities and promote inclusive growth.[672] The FAO, which monitors indicator 2.a.1, reports that the agricultural orientation index, which 'compares government expenditure for agriculture, fishing and forestry and the sector's

---

[663] ibid 690.
[664] ibid 690.
[665] Target 2.b of SDG 2.
[666] ICESCR, art 11. See also art 2(1) ICESCR.
[667] ibid art 11(2)(a).
[668] ibid art 15(1)(b).
[669] Regional Agreement on Access to Information, Public Participation and Justice in Environmental Matters in Latin America and the Caribbean (Escazú Agreement), 4 March 2018, art 11(1).
[670] Escazú Agreement, especially art 11(2).
[671] FAO <https://www.fao.org/sustainable-development-goals/indicators/2.a.1/en/> accessed 22 January 2022.
[672] ibid.

contribution to GDP',[673] has increased only slightly worldwide since 2001.[674] However, there are regional differences, revealing progress in Asia and declines in several other regions, for example in Sub-Saharan Africa.[675]

Indicator 2.a.2 is monitored by the OECD and measures the total official flows to the agricultural sector.[676] Empirical studies demonstrate that development assistance has increased since 2000.[677] ODA is an important source of development funding.[678] For example, the G7 countries have contributed 75 per cent of total global ODA.[679] However, only three G7 countries have significantly increased their ODA allocations since 2000, namely the United States, Germany, and the United Kingdom.[680]

c) Critique

Investments in agriculture play an essential role in the achievement and implementation of SDG 2, especially in developing countries.[681] Target 2.a emphasizes in this regard the importance of cooperation among states. The commitment to cooperation is grounded in article 2(1) of the ICESCR.[682] It requires states to cooperate, based on available resources, to progressively realize the rights enshrined in the ICESCR, including the right to food (article 11 ICESCR).[683] The target explicitly addresses wealthier countries, which is also reflected in the practice of the CESCR. The CESCR specifically emphasizes that states are obliged to cooperate if they are 'in a position to assist'.[684] However, in implementing target 2.a, the question arises as to which (developed) countries are obliged to cooperate and with which means investments need to be promoted in developing countries. Target 2.a limits the means of promoting investment in these countries by focusing on government spending and ODA in particular, but not on other possible means and assistance that could achieve this target.

---

[673] ibid.

[674] FAO, 'Tracking Progress on Food and Agriculture-related SDG Indicators 2021' (n 30) 42.

[675] ibid 42.

[676] FAO, 'SDG Indicators, Data Collection Information & Focal Points' <https://unstats.un.org/sdgs/dataContacts/> accessed 22 January 2022.

[677] Center for Development Research (ZEF) of the University of Bonn in cooperation with the Food and Agriculture Organization of the United Nations (FAO), 'Investment Costs and Policy Action Opportunities for Reaching a World Without Hunger (SDG 2)' (October 2020) 20.

[678] OECD, 'The Sustainable Development Goals: An Overview of Relevant OECD Analysis, Tools and Approaches', 6 <https://www.oecd.org/dac/The%20Sustainable%20Development%20Goals%20An%20overview%20of%20relevant%20OECD%20analysis.pdf> accessed 22 January 2022.

[679] ZEF and FAO, 'Investment Costs and Policy Action Opportunities for Reaching a World Without Hunger (SDG 2)' (n 677) 20.

[680] ibid 20. See also OECD, 'COVID-19 spending helped to lift foreign aid to an all-time high in 2020 but more effort needed' (13 April 2021) <https://www.oecd.org/newsroom/covid-19-spending-helped-to-lift-foreign-aid-to-an-all-time-high-in-2020-but-more-effort-needed.htm> accessed 22 January 2022.

[681] FAO <https://www.fao.org/sustainable-development-goals/indicators/2.a.1/en/> accessed 22 January 2022.

[682] ICESCR, art 2 (1) reads as follows: 'Each State Party to the present Covenant undertakes to take steps, individually and through international assistance and co-operation, especially economic and technical, to the maximum of its available resources, with a view to achieving progressively the full realization of the rights recognized in the present Covenant by all appropriate means, including particularly the adoption of legislative measures.'

[683] ibid art 2(1).

[684] CESCR, General Comment No 3 (n 375) para 14. See also this chapter, Section IV.B.1.

184   SDG 2

Although ODA and other official flows are important for the implementation of SDG 2, it remains disputed whether they alone can actually contribute to the achievement of the goal.[685] Most importantly, development cooperation projects that rely on ODA and other official flows might have impacts that extend beyond the specific purpose of the aid.[686] For example, quantitative studies illustrate that aid impacts growth only in the very long-term, but not over a shorter period of time.[687] ODA might also distort (food) prices and thus conflict with target 2.c.[688] Furthermore, aid might increase the dependence of developing countries on countries of the Global North.[689] To sum up, target 2.a does not take into account the negative impact of investments, particularly foreign investments, on the human rights of individuals and local communities in developing countries. A human rights-based approach is therefore essential to limit the adverse impacts of the target.[690]

7. Target 2.b Correct and prevent trade restrictions and distortions in world agricultural markets, including through the parallel elimination of all forms of agricultural export subsidies and all export measures with equivalent effect, in accordance with the mandate of the Doha Development Round

a) Source of target

Target 2.b aims to prevent trade restrictions, market distortions and agricultural export subsidies.[691] From a human rights perspective, target 2.b is linked to article 11(2)(b) of the ICESCR, which obliges states to '[take] into account the problems of both food-importing and food-exporting countries, to ensure an equitable distribution of world food supplies in relation to need'.[692] Additionally, as discussed above, international trade and investment treaties also have implications for target 2.b, particularly the GATT and the AoA as well as bilateral investment treaties and other instruments.[693] Target 2.b should be implemented in accordance with the Doha Development Round, the latest round of trade negotiations among WTO Member States.[694]

b) Empirical analysis: domestic and international efforts of implementation

Target 2.b consists of indicator 2.b.1, which measures 'agricultural export subsidies'.[695] Export subsidies are defined as a form of financial aid or support given to a specific

---

[685] On a general discussion of ODA in the context of the international law of development, see P Dann, *The Law of Development Cooperation. A Comparative Analysis of the World Bank, the EU and Germany* (CUP 2013).

[686] ZEF and FAO, 'Investment Costs and Policy Action Opportunities for Reaching a World Without Hunger (SDG 2)' (n 677) 20.

[687] ibid 23.

[688] ibid 23.

[689] ibid 24.

[690] See also this chapter Section IV.

[691] SDG 2, Target 2.b.

[692] ICESCR, art 11(2)(b).

[693] See above Section IV.B.2.

[694] See WTO, 'The Doha Round' <https://www.wto.org/english/tratop_e/dda_e/dda_e.htm> accessed 22 January 2022.

[695] UN SDGS, 'SDG 2 Indicators' (n 559).

sector.[696] Indicator 2.b.1 seeks to provide information on export subsidies paid annually.[697] The target is monitored by the WTO.[698]

c) Critique

Trade can improve food availability and access to food, for example by creating jobs and increasing incomes, but it can also have negative impacts on them.[699] As such, target 2.b recognizes that trade restrictions in international agricultural markets can have adverse effects on food security. It therefore calls on states to correct and prevent trade restrictions in accordance with the Doha Development Round.

In recent years, negotiations in the WTO have focused on agricultural trade policy reforms that are crucial to improving food security.[700] These negotiations were initiated in the early 2000s under the mandate of the AoA.[701] The Doha Development Round took place in 2001 and introduced reforms to the world trading system by reducing trade barriers and revising trade rules.[702] The Doha Round was initially aimed at correcting the negative effects of the AoA on developing countries.[703] However, no agreement could be reached between developing and developed countries.[704]

An important step was taken at the 2015 Ministerial Conference in Nairobi, where countries agreed to put an *end* to agricultural export subsidies.[705] According to the decision taken at the conference, developed countries commit themselves to immediately phasing out agricultural export subsidies.[706] This is certainly an important development in achieving target 2.b, but as previously discussed, the implementation of the target also needs to focus on measures that address systemic issues impacting food security and agriculture, such as changing unequal trade agreements or debt cancellation for developing countries.[707]

---

[696] UNSTATS, 'SDG Indicator Metadata' <https://unstats.un.org/sdgs/metadata/files/Metadata-02-0B-01.pdf> accessed 22 January 2022.

[697] UNSTATS, 'SDG Indicator Metadata (Indicator 2.b)' <https://unstats.un.org/sdgs/metadata/files/Metadata-02-0B-01.pdf> accessed 22 January 2022.

[698] FAO, 'SDG Indicators, Data Collection Information & Focal Points (Indicator 2.b.1)' <https://unstats.un.org/sdgs/dataContacts/?selectIndicator=2.b.1+Agricultural+export+subsidies&selectAgency=> accessed 22 January 2022.

[699] WTO, 'Food Security' <https://www.wto.org/english/tratop_e/agric_e/food_security_e.htm> accessed 22 January 2022.

[700] See WTO, 'Agriculture Negotiations' <https://www.wto.org/english/tratop_e/agric_e/negoti_e.htm> accessed 22 January 2022.

[701] WTO, 'Food Security' <https://www.wto.org/english/tratop_e/agric_e/food_security_e.htm> accessed 22 January 2022.

[702] See WTO, 'The Doha Round' <https://www.wto.org/english/tratop_e/dda_e/dda_e.htm> accessed 22 January 2022.

[703] Clapp (n 14) 18.

[704] ibid 18.

[705] WTO, 'Agriculture Negotiations' <https://www.wto.org/english/tratop_e/agric_e/negoti_e.htm> accessed 22 January 2022.

[706] WTO, Ministerial Decision of 19 December 2015, WT/MIN(15)/45—WT/L/980, para 6.

[707] See this chapter, Section IV.

186 SDG 2

8. Target 2.c Adopt measures to ensure the proper functioning of food commodity markets and their derivatives and facilitate timely access to market information, including on food reserves, in order to help limit extreme food price volatility

a) Source of target

Target 2.c requires states to take measures to ensure functioning food markets and access to information to limit extreme food price volatility.[708] The target is linked to article 11(2)(b) of the ICESCR. The provision obliges states to ensure an equitable distribution of the world's food supply and to take into account the problems of food-importing and food-exporting countries.[709] Similarly, the Additional Protocol to the American Convention on Human Rights in the Area of Economic, Social and Cultural Rights (Protocol of San Salvador) requires states to improve methods of production, supply, and distribution of food in order to eradicate malnourishment.[710]

b) Empirical analysis: domestic and international efforts of implementation

Target 2.c consists of indicator 2.c.1 on 'food price anomalies'.[711] The indicator measures 'the number of price anomalies that occur on a given food commodity price series over a given period of time'.[712] After years of relative stability, the proportion of countries affected by high food prices increased from 2019 to 2020, mainly due to new developments (eg COVID-19 pandemic) in international markets.[713] In 2020, the proportion of countries confronted with high food prices was highest in Central and South Asia and lowest in East and South-East Asia.[714] More than a third of countries in Western Asia and North Africa continue to be affected by high food prices.[715]

c) Critique

Identifying current and future trends in international food markets is critical to avoiding potential crises that affect food security and nutrition.[716] The target therefore aims to support the achievement of SDG 2, as it also requires states to provide market information to limit food price volatility.[717]

Food price volatility is often related to asymmetries in food production between developed and developing countries.[718] Furthermore, the expansion of international trade over the years and the growing power of transnational corporations in particular in shaping the global food economy have further contributed to making food and agricultural systems more vulnerable to abrupt and uneven changes, including food

---

[708] SDG 2, target 2.c.

[709] ICESCR, art 11(2)(b).

[710] Additional Protocol to the American Convention on Human Rights in the Area of Economic, Social and Cultural rights (Protocol of San Salvador), adopted in San Salvador on 17 November 1988, art 12.2.

[711] UN SDGS, 'SDG 2 Indicators' (n 559).

[712] FAO, 'SDG 2, Indicator 2.c.1' <https://www.fao.org/sustainable-development-goals/indicators/2c1/en/> accessed 22 January 2022.

[713] FAO, 'Tracking Progress on Food and Agriculture-related SDG Indicators 2021' (n 30) 45.

[714] ibid 45.

[715] FAO, 'SDG 2, Indicator 2.c.1' <https://www.fao.org/sustainable-development-goals/indicators/2c1/en/> accessed 22 January 2022.

[716] ibid.

[717] SDG 2, target 2.c.

[718] Clapp (n 14) 24.

prices.[719] Limiting food price volatility therefore requires regulatory changes that respond to the inequalities in the current global food economy.[720] Target 2.b needs therefore to be implemented in an integrated approach with other targets, especially targets related to food production, to achieve SDG 2.

VI. Conclusion

The core strength of SDG 2 is its *strong nexus* between hunger, food security, nutrition, and sustainable agriculture. SDG 2 is innovative compared to MDG 1 because it combines the 'individual' dimension of hunger and food insecurity with the 'structural' dimension of the goal's objectives. SDG 2 calls for the *empowerment of individuals*, especially small-scale farmers, including women, pastoralists, and fishers, but also requires *transformative changes to food and agricultural systems*.

SDG 2 touches upon various areas of international law. This chapter addressed the fields of international law that directly impact the goal's achievement. Like many SDGs of the post-2015 development agenda, the goal is strongly linked to international human rights law. It is also connected to international economic law, notably international trade and investment law. In general, SDG 2 enhances international human rights standards, particularly of the right to food, and supports the individual dimension of the goal, which seeks to empower individuals to achieve food security. Unlike international human rights law, however, international trade and investment law run counter to the goal's objectives and their effective realization.[721] International trade and investment regimes pose serious challenges to the achievement of the 'structural' dimension of SDG 2 and its targets. These challenges are reinforced by a growth-based economic approach to the objectives of SDG 2 (and to Agenda 2030 in general) that focuses on agricultural productivity.[722] While agricultural productivity certainly contributes to the achievement of SDG 2, it can also have an adverse impact on individuals' human rights and the environment. The specific targets do not adequately address this risk. Furthermore, some of the targets are also vaguely formulated, and their associated indicators are not sufficiently measurable.

From an international law perspective, this chapter therefore calls for humanizing SDG 2. The goal can only be effectively achieved when it is (also) guided by a *human rights-based approach* in all subfields of international law relevant to the goal, and, importantly, by the policy of 'human rights mainstreaming' in the entire Agenda 2030. *Mainstreaming human rights* in SDG 2 will contribute to a more 'coherent multilateralism'[723] and allow obstacles arising from the multidimensional approach of the goal to be effectively addressed in light of individuals' human rights and basic needs.

---

[719] ibid 25.
[720] ibid 25.
[721] Gonzalez, 'SDG 2: End Hunger' (n 42) 89.
[722] ibid.
[723] Leary (n 468) 823–29.

SDG 3

'Good Health and Well-Being—Ensure Healthy Lives and Promote Well-Being for All at All Ages'

Jane A Hofbauer and Christina Binder

I. Introduction

The goal of good health and well-being (SDG 3) is central amongst the SDG framework and constitutes one of the centrepieces of the overall objective of sustainable development[1] and development policies more generally. From the start, and throughout its four development decades, the United Nations (UN) had progressively moved towards strengthening the social pillar of development, highlighting among others the connection of human dignity—the core focus of development—and health.[2] In the 1987 Brundtland Report, several passages emphasized the link between health and economic policies, and underscored the dependence of health on a healthy environment.[3] A prime objective of the report, *inter alia*, was to establish focus points for private and public investments and provide for the creation of an institutional framework aimed at ensuring a 'good life' for present and future generations. Based on this, the UN eventually proclaimed sustainable development as its development paradigm,[4] and turned to setting normative goals as a framework for implementing its sustainable development policy.

At the Rio Summit,[5] states had agreed to drafting national sustainable development strategies, which were soon to be complemented by an integrated set of seven objectives/goals that donor countries (principally in form of the Development Assistance Committee (DAC)) agreed upon within the framework of the Organization for Economic Cooperation and Development (OECD). The selected goals were vaguely based on previous UN conferences concerned with development. As listed by the

---

[1] JD Sachs, *The Age of Sustainable Development* (Columbia University Press 2015) 275.

[2] See, eg, United Nations 'International Development Strategy for the 3rd United Nations Development Decade' (5 December 1980) UN Doc A/RES/35/56.

[3] UNGA, 'Report of the World Commission on Environment and Development' (4 August 1987) UN Doc A/42/427.

[4] UN, 'International Development Strategy for the Fourth United Nations Development Decade' (21 December 1990) UN Doc A/RES/45/199, para 14: 'A development process that is responsive to social needs, seeks a significant reduction in extreme poverty, promotes the development and utilization of human resources and skills and is environmentally sound and sustainable.'

[5] Agenda 21 (Preamble, ch 8) 'Rio Declaration on Environment and Development' UN Conference on Environment and Development (Rio de Janeiro, 3–14 June 1992) (14 June 1992) UN Doc A/CONF.151/26/Rev.1 (vol I).

190   SDG 3

report, they are 'education (Jomtien, 1990), children (New York, 1990), the environment (Rio de Janeiro, 1992), human rights (Vienna, 1993), population (Cairo, 1994), social development (Copenhagen, 1995), and women (Beijing, 1995)'.[6] Among the goals on social development, the DAC included the objective of reducing the death rate for infants and children in developing countries by two-thirds of the 1990 level by 2015 (now SDG 3.2), the reduction of the rate of maternal mortality by three-quarters (now SDG 3.1), and the improvement of access through primary health-care systems to reproductive health services (now SDG 3.7), evidencing the importance of health targets which amounted to three of the seven set goals.

The prominence of health-related goals was also carried over into the eight development goals (Millennium Development Goals (MDGs)) adopted by the United Nations. Three of eight MDGs are directly concerned with health issues (Goal 4: reduction of child mortality; Goal 5: improvement of maternal health; and Goal 6: combating of HIV/AIDS, malaria, and other diseases). Additionally, health-related aspects also played a role in a number of the remaining goals, partly as outcome determinants, and partly in the formulation of objectives (particularly Goal 1: eradication of extreme poverty and hunger;[7] Goal 2: achieving universal primary education;[8] Goal 3: promotion of gender equality and empowerment of women;[9] and Goal 7: ensuring environmental sustainability[10]).[11] The health and health-related targets saw significant success rates throughout the 15 years that they informed international development efforts[12] and profited from the tripling of global health assistance.[13] However, major points of criticism related to the MDGs' focus on certain subpopulations (eg women, children) or particular health outcome targets rather than on overcoming systemic deficiencies, that is improving the healthcare system in general.[14] As observed by several authors in the context of the MDG health targets, its simple numerical targets often meant that improvements first and foremost 'typically reach[ed] better-off groups

---

[6] Development Assistance Committee, *Shaping the 21st Century: The Contribution of Development Co-Operation* (OECD 1996) 9. As the report continues, '[t]hese conferences have identified a number of targets to measure the progress of development in particular fields. They reflect broad agreement in the international community, arrived at with the active participation of the developing countries' 9. For details on the process leading up to *Shaping the 21st Century* see D Hulme and J Scott, 'The Political Economy of the MDGs: Retrospect and Prospect for the World's Biggest Promise' (2010) 15(2) New Political Economy 293.

[7] Target 1.c. Halve, between 1990 and 2015, the proportion of people who suffer from hunger.

[8] Target 2.a. Ensure that, by 2015, children everywhere, boys and girls alike, will be able to complete a full course of primary schooling.

[9] Target 3.a. Eliminate gender disparity in primary and secondary education, preferably by 2005, and in all levels of education no later than 2015.

[10] Target 7.c. Halve, by 2015, the proportion of the population without sustainable access to safe drinking water and basic sanitation.

[11] Sachs (n 1) 277.

[12] As highlighted in United Nations, *The Millennium Development Goals Report* (United Nations 2015) 5–6, the global under-five mortality rate declined by more than half (Goal 4), the maternal mortality ratio declined by 45 per cent worldwide (Goal 5), new HIV infections fell by approximately 40 per cent, while the antiretroviral treatment increased from 800,000 to 13.6 million people, and malaria and tuberculosis deaths dropped significantly (Goal 6).

[13] Institute for Health Metrics and Evaluation, *Financing Global Health 2014: Shifts in Funding as the MDG Era Closes* (University of Washington 2015) 17.

[14] M Fehling and others, 'Limitations of the Millennium Development Goals' (2013) 8(10) Global Public Health 1109, 1115–16; WHO, *Health in 2015—From MDGs, Millennium Development Goals to SDGs, Sustainable Development Goals* (World Health Organization 2015) 7.

INTRODUCTION   191

before disadvantaged ones'.[15] In the initial stages of drafting the SDGs, it was therefore emphasized that

138. We recognize that health is a precondition for and an outcome and indicator of all three dimensions of sustainable development. We understand the goals of sustainable development can only be achieved in the absence of a high prevalence of debilitating communicable and non-communicable diseases, and where populations can reach a state of physical, mental and social well-being. We are convinced that action on the social and environmental determinants of health, both for the poor and the vulnerable and for the entire population, is important to create inclusive, equitable, economically productive and healthy societies. We call for the full realization of the right to the enjoyment of the highest attainable standard of physical and mental health.[16]

With such a broad ambit for health-related targets and objectives in mind, that not only underlies all three dimensions of sustainable development but also expressly shift the focus on improving access to health for the poor and vulnerable, the 2030 Agenda for Sustainable Development eventually defined the overall objective of health in the following manner:

26. To promote physical and mental health and well-being, and to extend life expectancy for all, we must achieve universal health coverage and access to quality health care. No one must be left behind. We commit to accelerating the progress made to date in reducing newborn, child and maternal mortality by ending all such preventable deaths before 2030. We are committed to ensuring universal access to sexual and reproductive health-care services, including for family planning, information and education. We will equally accelerate the pace of progress made in fighting malaria, HIV/AIDS, tuberculosis, hepatitis, Ebola and other communicable diseases and epidemics, including by addressing growing anti-microbial resistance and the problem of unattended diseases affecting developing countries. We are committed to the prevention and treatment of non-communicable diseases, including behavioural, developmental and neurological disorders, which constitute a major challenge for sustainable development.[17]

With this as the point of departure, SDG 3 is formulated in a comprehensive and overarching manner, and can often be viewed as the basis for and an inherent part of other SDGs. For example, SDG 1 (end poverty in all its forms everywhere) calls for

---

[15] DR Gwatkin, 'How Much Would Poor People Gain from Faster Progress Towards the Millennium Development Goals for Health?' (2005) 365(9641) Lancet 813; DD Reidpath, and others, 'The Millennium Development Goals Fail Poor Children: The Case for Equity-Adjusted Measures' (2009) 6(4) PLoS Medicine <https://journals.plos.org/plosmedicine/article?id=10.1371/journal.pmed.1000062> accessed 10 October 2021.

[16] UNGA Res 66/288 (11 September 2012) 'The Future We Want' UN Doc A/RES/66/288.

[17] UNGA Res 70/1 (25 September 2015) 'Transforming Our World: The 2030 Agenda for Sustainable Development' UN Doc A/RES/70/1, para 26.

the implementation of social protection systems and measures, which includes health-care.[18] Ending hunger and ensuring access for all to safe, nutritious, and sufficient food (SDG 2, target 2.1), safe drinking water (SDG 6, target 6.1), safe work environments (SDG 8, target 8.8), ensuring access for all to adequate, safe, and affordable housing (SDG 11, target 11.1), reduction of pollution (eg SDG 14, target 14.1) or the promotion of peaceful and inclusive societies (SDG 16) all play a role in achieving good health and well-being, constituting social and environmental determinants of health (which aside from minimal linkages to environmental hazards are not directly addressed in SDG 3). Overall, in addition to the thirteen targets listed in SDG 3 itself, it has been shown that almost every other goal contains targets which might be considered health-related or conducive to health.[19]

The more comprehensive approach is further evident in SDG 3, specifically designated 'Good health and well-being. Ensure healthy lives and promote well-being for all at all ages.' Thus, in contrast to the MDGs, SDG 3 is now aimed at achieving overall health of the general population ('for all').[20] This is also in line with the universalist approach towards sustainable development opted for in the SDGs, that is, several targets have shifted from specific numeric 'halving' targets to apply to all states[21] (eg SDG 3.5: 'strengthening the prevention'; SDG 3.8: 'achieve universal health coverage'; SDG 3.9: 'substantially reducing').

Despite—or in light of—the more universalist approach towards the objective of good health chosen by the drafters of the SDGs, there have been concerns that the lack of quantitative thresholds in a number of the health-related targets might result in the fact that political actors will not invest equally consistent attention to achieving these goals as was the case with the health-related MDGs with clear numerical targets.[22] Initially the fear was expressed that the multiplication of targets within SDG 3 could overwhelm governments in their choices what to prioritize and implement.[23] Notably, there is also no prioritization among the SDG's thirteen targets, even though some seem more far-reaching and essential (eg SDG 3.8 on achieving UHC) and thus more complicated to reach than clear numerical targets (eg SDG 3.6 on halving the number of global deaths and injuries from road traffic accidents).[24] On the other hand, critics have expressed

---

[18] Target 1.3: 'Implement nationally appropriate social protection systems and measures for all, including floors, and by 2030 achieve substantive coverage of the poor and the vulnerable.'

[19] P Howden-Chapman and others, 'SDG 3—Ensure Healthy Lives and Promote Well-Being for All Ages' in International Council for Science (ed), *A Guide to SDG Interactions: From Science to Implementation* (ICSU 2017) 81.

[20] See also M Kaltenborn, 'The Human Rights Framework for Establishing Social Protection Floors and Achieving Universal Health Coverage' in M Kaltenborn and others (eds), *Sustainable Development Goals and Human Rights* (Springer 2020) 29, 43, noting the close link between 3.8 (universal health coverage (UHC)) and SDG 1.3 on social protection systems.

[21] See also M Langford, 'Lost in Transformation? The Politics of the Sustainable Development Goals' (2016) 30(2) Ethics and International Affairs 167.

[22] CJL Murray, 'Shifting to Sustainable Development Goals—Implications for Global Health' (2015) 373 New England Journal of Medicine 1390, 1392.

[23] JD Sachs, 'Goal-Based Development and the SDGs: Implications for Development Finance' (2015) 31 Oxford Review of Economic Policy 268, 274; K Buse and S Hawkes, 'Health in the Sustainable Development Goals: Ready for a Paradigm Shift?' (2015) 11(13) Globalization and Health 1, 5.

[24] Cf AR Chapman, 'Evaluating the Health-Related Targets in the Sustainable Development Goals from a Human Rights Perspective' (2017) 21 International Journal of Human Rights 1098.

concern that overall the 'reduction' to one of the seventeen goals in comparison to the importance that health-related targets had carried among the OECD's development goals or the MDGs might lessen the political attention—and consequently potential funding—on health-related targets.[25] As becomes evident from the mixed progress on SDG 3's targets, some of these fears might not have been unsubstantiated. Yet, it is also clear that the SDG framework is to be seen and implemented as a whole. Only then will the overall transformative objective ('Leave No One Behind') be realized in a fair and equitable fashion.

The following commentary commences with a detailed discussion and analysis of the preparatory proceedings that resulted in SDG 3. This is followed with a section addressing SDG 3 from a comprehensive perspective. This includes an assessment of the role of the World Health Organization (WHO), which serves as the lead agency under SDG 3, as well as a developmental and human rights critique. Finally, each of the thirteen targets and twenty-eight indicators is analysed on their potential to achieving the overall objective of 'Good Health and Well-Being—Ensure Healthy Lives and Promote Well-Being for All at All Ages'.

II. *Travaux Préparatoires*

A. Background

The broad phrasing of SDG 3 on 'Good Health and Well-Being' is the result of multi-year lobbying by WHO, proclaiming as early as 1978 at the Alma-Ata Conference on Primary Health Care the objective of 'the attainment by all peoples of the world by the year 2000 of a level of health that will permit them to lead a socially and economically productive life'.[26] With this, primary healthcare—and its 'removal of the obstacles to health'[27]—was placed at the forefront of WHO's agenda under the slogan 'Health for All',[28] with the Declaration further emphasizing that '[p]rimary health care is the key to attaining this target as part of development in the spirit of social justice'.[29] This constituted a departure from the long-prevailing focus on specific disease-oriented measures

---

[25] Murray (n 22) 1390–91; AL Frey, 'Introduction: Positioning Universal Health Coverage in the Post-2015 Development Agenda' (2015) 24 Washington International Law Journal 419, 423.

[26] 1978 Alma Ata Declaration adopted by the International Conference on Primary Health Care; and the Vienna Declaration and Programme of Action, adopted World Conference on Human Rights (25 June 1993) UN Doc A/CONF.157/23.

[27] H Mahler, 'The Meaning of "Health for All by the Year 2000"' (1981) 2(1) World Health Forum 5.

[28] As adopted by Resolution WHA30.43 'Technical Cooperation' (19 May 1977).

[29] VI: 'Primary health care is essential health care based on practical, scientifically sound and socially acceptable methods and technology made universally accessible to individuals and families in the community through their full participation and a cost the community and country can afford to maintain every stage of their development in the spirit of self-reliance and self-determination. It forms an integral part both of the country's health system, of which it is the central function and main focus, and of the overall social and economic development of the community. It is the first level of contact of individuals, the family and community with the national health system bringing health care as close as possible to where people live and work, and constitutes the first element of a continuing health care process.' See also Frey (n 25) 428.

(such as eradication of malaria) through concerted technological means in global health policy, with little associated social reform.[30] The change was, among others, owed to the shifting political context in which WHO operated following the period of decolonization and a strengthening of the Non-Aligned Movement.[31] Proponents of the New International Economic Order had succeeded in bringing 'together inter-disciplinary public health and development actors from around the world,'[32] with the Declaration adopted at the Conference emphasizing that the 'gross inequality in the health status of the people particularly between developed and developing countries as well as within countries is politically, socially and economically unacceptable and is, therefore, of common concern to all countries.'[33]

Yet despite its initially successful campaign for directing attention at primary health-care and UHC, WHO struggled to sustain a concerted effort among states and other development actors such as the World Bank to close the gap of inequalities by furthering access to primary healthcare.[34] In contrast, several international actors and donors—often heavily influenced by US policies—found that such an ambitious social approach towards healthcare would be unattainable and preferred more easily manageable and small-scale interventions, often—led by the World Bank—in concert with a greater focus on private-sector healthcare providers.[35]

It was not until after a series of reforms within WHO in the 1990s, following the appointment of Gro Harlem Brundtland as Director General in 1998, that the tides shifted. Through a series of tactical steps, for example the establishment of a Commission on Macroeconomics and Health,[36] she succeeded in slowly reclaiming WHO's position as the key player in international health policies. When WHO pushed for UHC as a core objective of health-related development policies[37] during the SDG drafting phase, it proved successful, this time also convincing other important development actors,

---

[30] TM Brown and others, 'The World Health Organization and the Transition from "International" to "Global" Public Health' (2006) 96 American Journal of Public Health 62, 65.

[31] ibid 66.

[32] LO Gostin and BM Meier, 'The Origins of Human Rights in Global Health' in BM Meier and LO Gostin (eds), Human Rights in Global Health: Rights-Based Governance for a Globalizing World (OUP 2018) 21, 35.

[33] 1978 Alma Ata Declaration adopted by the International Conference on Primary Health Care; and the Vienna Declaration and Programme of Action, adopted World Conference on Human Rights (25 June 1993) UN Doc A/CONF.157/23, II.

[34] See also AL Taylor, 'Making the World Health Organization Work: A Legal Framework for Universal Access to the Conditions for Health' (1992) 18 American Journal of Law & Medicine 301, 302.

[35] Brown (n 30) 67–68, also describing how this 'parallel' structure of policies and programmes could be maintained as part of the extrabudgetary funds of WHO (ie funding received from multilateral organizations or donor states rather than from Member States' contributions).

[36] The Commission worked under the chairmanship of Jeffrey Sachs and included a number of former finance officers from the World Bank, International Monetary Fund and other international organizations. In 2001, the Commission published a report on the place of health in global economic development, highlighting as a key recommendation that 'the world's low- and middle-income countries, in partnership with high-income countries, should scale up the access of the world's poor to essential health services, including a focus on specific interventions'. Report of the Commissions on Macroeconomics and Health, 'Macroeconomics and Health: Investing in Health for Economic Development' (2001) 4.

[37] In the early years of MDG implementation, WHO had to pursue this objective in parallel to the MDG framework, see WHA58/33, 'Sustainable Health Financing, Universal Coverage and Social Health Insurance' (25 May 2005).

particularly the World Bank.[38] Hence, in 'The Future We Want', UHC was taken up as a core element of the global health agenda:

> We also recognize the importance of universal health coverage to enhancing health, social cohesion and sustainable human and economic development. We pledge to strengthen health systems towards the provision of equitable universal coverage. We call for the involvement of all relevant actors for coordinated multisectoral action to address urgently the health needs of the world's population.[39]

The change in leadership on 'health in development'—or rather, the reclaiming of leadership from the World Bank—becomes particularly apparent in the years following the Millennium Declaration. While the framework and content of the Declaration built on previous UN development conferences and was negotiated by diplomats,[40] the MDGs and its targets and indicators were developed by technocrats from international financial institutions (particularly the World Bank and the Organisation for the Economic Co-Operation and Development (OECD)) and the United Nations (particularly the UN Development Programme (UNDP))[41] in an attempt to reach a compromise between the DAC's earlier international development goals and the Millennium Declaration.[42] The accompanying monitoring and supervisory framework—which included also other specialized agencies by the UN such as WHO—however was largely developed after the MDGs had been adopted.[43]

In 2002, WHO affirmed its general commitment to the Millennium Declaration, though it only vaguely expressed the intention to 'promote reporting on progress towards internationally agreed goals and targets in the area of reproductive health as part of WHO's contribution'[44] (as the issue of reproductive health had been largely left out in the MDGs). While the MDGs remained on its agenda, WHO remained critical of the relevance of many of the suggested indicators, and continued working on developing and identifying more suitable indicators, also addressing areas which had not

---

[38] Frey (n 25) 428; World Bank Group President Jim Yong Kim's Speech World Health Assembly, 'Poverty, Health and the Human Future' (21 May 2013); WHO/World Bank, 'Tracking Universal Health Coverage—First Global Monitoring Report' (2015); as formulated by the Director-General of WHO, Dr Margaret Chan in 2012: 'UHC is the single most powerful concept that public health has to offer ... the umbrella concept that demands solutions to the biggest problems facing health systems ... the anchor for WHO.'

[39] 'The Future We Want' (n 16) para 139.

[40] With regard to health, the 1994 International Conference on Population and Development (Cairo) and the 1995 World Summit for Social Development (Copenhagen) proved particularly important.

[41] S Fukuda-Parr, *Millennium Development Goals—Ideas, Interests and Influence* (Routledge 2017) 133–34, noting that the dominant representatives were development economists rather than statisticians. A consequence was choosing indicators where data were available and reflected a certain simplicity, which prompted some criticism as 'it did not reflect adequate consultation with the UN statistical networks and the knowledge and experience of specialized agencies in areas such as education and health'.

[42] Hulme and Scott (n 6) 297.

[43] United Nations Development Group, *Indicators for Monitoring the Millennium Development Goals—Definitions, Rationale, Concepts, and Sources* (2003) ST/ESA/STAT/SER.F/95.

[44] WHO Executive Board, 'WHO's contribution to achievement of the development goals of the United Nations Millennium Declaration' EB109.R3 (16 January 2002).

been adequately reflected in the MDGs.[45] In 2004, it was therefore still the World Bank which published an extensive report on the health-related MDGs.[46]

This role, however, slowly began to change over the second half of the MDGs' implementation time frame. Having realized that large parts of the MDG targets related to health, the World Bank—following a meeting between development agencies and developing states hosted by the Canadian International Development Agency (CIDA) and the UK's Department for International Development (DfID)—decided to establish a High-Level Forum on Health MDGs, jointly convened by the World Bank and WHO. At the first meeting (in 2004), it was observed that implementation of the MDGs had been too slow, that higher levels of financial resources for health were needed, as were health information systems in need of strengthening, particularly when it came to monitoring.[47] Following a WHO interregional meeting later that year, the World Health Assembly (WHA) eventually passed Resolution WHA58.30, with the decision placing emphasis on implementation of the MDGs and scheduled its next General Programme of Work (2006–2015) to run in parallel to the time frame for achieving the MDGs.[48]

Both in 2005, at the first comprehensive review of progress on the MDGs,[49] and in 2008, at a High-Level Event on the MDGs by the UN Secretary-General and President of the General Assembly (GA) (marking the halfway point),[50] there were concerns on progress made with regard to the MDGs more generally, but also on several health targets. As addressed in more detail below (Section III.A), around the same time, the WHA decided to become more involved in monitoring the achievement of the health-related MDGs.[51] This moved WHO even more into the role of spearheading the global health agenda. Thus, in 2010, following the High-Level Plenary Meeting of the GA on the MDGs[52] and the launching of the Global Strategy for Women's and Children's Health, the UN Secretary-General requested WHO to 'chair a process to determine the most effective international institutional arrangements for global reporting, oversight and accountability on women's and children's health'[53] which the WHA embraced fully.[54]

---

[45] WHO, *Millennium Development Goals—The Health Indicators: Scope, Definitions and Measurement Methods* (Geneva 2003, WHO/EIP/HFS/03.2) 3.

[46] A Wagstaff and M Claeson, *The Millennium Development Goals for Health—Rising to the Challenges* (The International Bank for Reconstruction and Development/The World Bank 2004).

[47] High-Level Forum on the Health MDGs (Geneva, 8–9 January 2004) <http://www.who.int/hdp/en/summary.pdf> accessed 20 October 2021.

[48] WHA58.30 'Accelerating Achievement of the Internationally Agreed Health-Related Development Goals, including those Contained in the Millennium Declaration' (25 May 2005).

[49] UNGA 60/1 '2005 World Summit Outcome' (16 September 2005) UN Doc A/RES/60/1, paras 17ff, 57, 57(g), and 58(c).

[50] UN, 'High-Level Event on the Millennium Development Goals—Committing to Action: Achieving the Millennium Development Goals. Background note by the Secretary-General' (25 July 2008).

[51] WHA61.18, 'Monitoring of the Achievement of the Health-Related Millennium Development Goals' (24 May 2008).

[52] UNGA Res 65/1, 'Keeping the Promise: United to Achieve the Millennium Development Goals' (22 September 2010) UN Doc A/RES/65/1. In this Resolution, the GA generally requested the Secretary-General to make recommendations 'for further steps to advance the United Nations development agenda beyond 2015' (para 81).

[53] UN Secretary-General Ban Ki-moon, 'Global Strategy for Women's and Children's Health' (UN 2010) 15.

[54] WHO, 'WHO's Role in the Follow-Up to the United Nations High-Level Plenary Meeting of the General Assembly on the Millennium Development Goals (New York, September 2010)' (24 May 2011) WHA64.12, preambular para 5.

By the time the preparations for the Rio + 20 Conference (United Nations Conference on Sustainable Development) had commenced, agreement had been reached among states to develop successor goals to the MDGs. In their assessment of the MDGs, the early criticism of how they had been drafted made it clear that a large process including all stakeholders would be initiated. This was, among others, also channelled by and reflected in a report drawn up by the UN System Task Team on the Post-2015 UN Development Agenda (co-chaired by the Department of Economic and Social Affairs (DESA) and the UNDP).[55]

In response to this criticism, the Rio + 20 Summit Declaration eventually agreed to

> establish an inclusive and transparent intergovernmental process on sustainable development goals that is open to all stakeholders, with a view to developing global sustainable development goals to be agreed by the General Assembly. An open working group shall be constituted ... and shall comprise thirty representatives, nominated by Member States from the five United Nations regional groups.[56]

The Open Working Group (OWG)—a key innovative feature of the drafting process—was tasked to draw up a draft to be discussed by the UN General Assembly by September 2014,[57] while also developing 'modalities to ensure the full involvement of relevant stakeholders and expertise from civil society, the scientific community and the United Nations system'.[58] Even though it was envisioned to comprise only thirty (state) members, given the eagerness of states to participate, agreement was in the end reached to allow for several states to share one spot (leading up to approximately seventy participating states).[59] The set-up of the OWG and the practice of shared membership to the OWG in the form of troikas led to distinct dynamics in comparison to the setting of other international negotiations. Thus, the departure from the traditional voting blocs has been said to have contributed to a 'more democratic, substantive conversation'[60] on the different themes.

---

[55] UN System Task Team on the Post-2015 UN Development Agenda, 'Review of the Contributions of the MDG Agenda to Foster Development: Lessons for the Post-2015 UN Development Agenda' (March 2012). The UN System Task Team had been established by the Secretary-General in 2011, beginning its work in 2012. It comprised more than sixty UN entities, including WHO.

[56] 'The Future We Want' (n 16) para 248. Initially some states/regions (particularly the EU) would have preferred to delegate the task to a technical working group composed of scientists and experts selected by the Secretary-General. See F Dodds and others, *Negotiating the Sustainable Development Goals—A Transformational Agenda for an Insecure World* (Routledge 2017) 19.

[57] Note that this was not the only process within the UN system debating the follow-up/aftermath of the MDGs. Alongside the OWG, the below mentioned High-Level Panel of Eminent Persons on the Post-2015 Development Agenda, UN Global Compact, UN Regional Commissions and a newly appointed Special Adviser on Post-2015 Development Planning (Amina Mohammed) also were tasked with working on any potential future development plan. After a special event held in September 2013 on progress towards the MDGs, it however became clear that 'a process of intergovernmental negotiations' would be launched following the OWG's completion of work. See UNGA 'Outcome Document of the Special Event to Follow up Efforts Made towards Achieving the Millennium Development Goals' (1 October 2013) UN Doc A/68/L.4, paras 20–21.

[58] 'The Future We Want' (n 16) para 248.

[59] Dodds and others (n 56) 31.

[60] M Kamau and others, *Transforming Multilateral Diplomacy—The Inside Story of the Sustainable Development Goals* (Routledge 2018) 128–29.

The OWG was chaired by Hungary and Kenya, one developed and one developing state, which had been appointed by the President of the General Assembly. Its work was guided by the 'rules of procedure, relevant rules and practices of the Committees of the General Assembly, unless decided otherwise by the open working group'.[61]

In addition, the Secretary-General had initiated a series of additional processes which aimed at ensuring wide participation. First, the process was accompanied by input of particularly two additional bodies that were set up to support the Secretary-General in the post-2015 agenda setting, the High-Level Panel of Eminent Persons on the Post-2015 Development Agenda and the Sustainable Development Solutions Network (SDSN).[62] Second, there were a series of national consultations[63] as well as eleven thematic consultations, including one specifically dedicated to health. The latter were organized by the United Nations Development Group (UNDG) and—as the OWG itself—usually chaired by one developing and one developed state, operating with relevant UN agencies and programs. Hence, the Task Team for the Global Thematic Consultation on Health in the Post-2015 Agenda was chaired by Sweden and Botswana, together with WHO and the United Nations International Children's Emergency Fund (UNICEF).[64] The outcome of these thematic consultations were taken up by the High-Level Panel and the Secretary-General's Synthesis Report. The output also was reflected in the issue briefs presented by the UN Technical Support Team (TST) to the OWG (see below).[65]

The OWG sessions were structured in a way to accommodate the wide participatory circle envisioned.[66] Thus, sessions were accompanied by keynote speeches, presentations of the issue briefs, panel discussions, exchanges of views with major groups and other stakeholders, and national statements.

Within this process, the TST functioned as the interagency forum of communication, established to support the UN System Task Team.[67] The channelling of input by the UN system through one forum prevented too intense lobbying by one agency over another. This also was seen as a response to the criticism which had

---

[61] General Assembly Open Working on Sustainable Development Goals—Methods of Work (13 March 2013) <https://sustainabledevelopment.un.org/content/documents/1692OWG_methods_work_adopted_1403.pdf> accessed 16 October 2021.

[62] The High-Level Panel of Eminent Persons on the Post-2015 Development Agenda was set up in July 2012, co-chaired by the Presidents of Indonesia and Liberia as well as the Prime Minister of the United Kingdom. The representatives assembled in the Panel were composed of members of civil society and the private sector, academia, and local and national governments. Their work—and the Secretary-General in general—was supported by the SDSN, established in August 2012 to combine and offer global scientific and technological expertise on the sustainable development framework. See also J Müller (ed), *Reforming the United Nations—A Chronology* (Brill Nijhoff 2016) 73–74.

[63] These took place in about 100 countries, though there is no clear evidence on whether this process was successful in terms of informing the outcome document.

[64] WHO, UNICEF, the Government of Sweden and the Government of Botswana, 'Health in the Post-2015 Agenda—Report of the Global Thematic Consultation on Health' (April 2013) <http://www.post2020hlp.org/wp-content/uploads/docs/health-in-the-post-2015-agenda_LR.pdf> accessed 16 October 2021.

[65] Dodds and others (n 56) 48f.

[66] As noted in the Methods of Work, the 'group's work shall be guided by the principles of openness, transparency, inclusiveness and consensus', General Assembly Open Working on Sustainable Development Goals (n 61).

[67] Established on the basis of UNGA Res 66/288 (11 September 2012) 'The Future We Want' UN Doc A/RES/66/288, para 249. It comprised more than forty bodies, including WHO.

accompanied the drafting of the MDGs, where little involvement aside from agency technocrats had occurred.[68] Representatives of the specialized agencies and related organizations were, however, also allowed to participate as observers in the OWG meetings.[69]

B. The OWG Sessions and the Adoption Phase

1. The Stocktaking Phase—OWG-4 (17–19 June 2013)

The stocktaking phase commenced in March 2013, with a summary of previous work and reports by the Secretary-General[70] and the UN System Task Team.[71] From the start, health remained a priority area of the post-2015 Agenda. This was not too surprising given that there was common agreement among all stakeholders that the MDGs' 'unfinished business' would remain part of the development agenda.[72] With regard to 'health', this also became clear in the report submitted by the High-Level Panel of Eminent Persons on the Post-2015 Development Agenda where—as one of twelve goals—Goal 4 'Ensure Healthy Lives' featured prominently, albeit not extending far beyond the MDGs.[73] Additionally, the thematic discussion led by the Task Team for the Global Thematic Consultation on Health in the Post-2015 Agenda emphasized that health should either be considered a key contributor to an overarching objective of sustainable well-being for all, or that 'maximizing healthy lives' should feature prominently as a stand-alone goal.[74]

Aside from the first session of the OWG, each session was dedicated to one or two specific clusters which were identified broadly along the headings of 'The Future We Want'. The topic 'Health and population'[75]—redrafted to 'Health, population dynamics'—was part of the fourth session (17–19 June 2013) and scheduled for 1.5 days. That the topic featured among the earlier sessions was not only owed to

---

[68] Kamau and others (n 60) 109.

[69] General Assembly Open Working on Sustainable Development Goals (n 61).

[70] UNGA 'Initial Input of the Secretary-General to the Open Working Group on Sustainable Development Goals' (17 December 2012) UN Doc A/67/634; that the initial input should be provided by the Secretary-General was foreseen in UNGA Res 66/288 (11 September 2012) 'The Future We Want' UN Doc A/RES/66/288, para 249.

[71] UN System Task Team on the Post-2015 UN Development Agenda, 'Realizing the Future We Want for All—Report to the Secretary-General' (June 2012).

[72] See also results of the questionnaire among Member States presented by the Secretary-General in UNGA, 'Initial Input of the Secretary-General to the Open Working Group on Sustainable Development Goals' (17 December 2012) UN Doc A/67/634, paras 16–17.

[73] 'A New Global Partnership: Eradicate Poverty and Transform Economies through Sustainable Development—The Report of the High-Level Panel of Eminent Persons on the Post-2015 Development Agenda' (United Nations, 30 May 2013), focusing on five targets: (i) end preventable infant and under-five deaths; (ii) increase by x per cent the proportion of children, adolescents, at-risk adults, and older people that are fully vaccinated; (iii) decrease the maternal mortality ratio to no more than x per 100,000; (iv) ensure universal sexual and reproductive health and rights; (v) reduce the burden of disease from HIV/AIDS, tuberculosis, malaria, neglected tropical diseases, and priority non-communicable diseases (NCDs).

[74] Alongside efforts to accelerate progress on the health MDG agenda, reducing the burden of major NCDs, working towards universal health coverage and access, and taking action on social and environmental determinants of health. See WHO, UNICEF, the Government of Sweden and the Government of Botswana, 'Health in the Post-2015 Agenda' (n 64).

[75] 'The Future We Want' (n 16) paras 138ff.

the remaining objectives to be reached from the MDGs but also had symbolic value and was directed to 'many developing countries, philanthropic organizations, and the United Nations Development Group heads'[76] to alleviate their fear of overlooking these priorities.

Every session opened on the basis of an issue brief which had been prepared by the TST (in total twenty-nine). The sessions were accompanied by expert panellists such as, for example, Anarfi Asamoa-Baah, the Deputy Director-General of WHO, who spoke during the fourth session[77] and a number of targeted side events.[78]

When it came to the stocktaking process regarding health, it quickly became clear that a broader approach than under the MDGs would be chosen. In fact, the 'Future We Want' Declaration had already widened the previous MDG health-related agenda. After emphasizing that 'health is a precondition for and an outcome and indicator of all three dimensions of sustainable development',[79] the declaration called for the 'full realization of the right to the enjoyment of the highest attainable standard of physical and mental health'. For this purpose, the following objectives were listed: UHC (see above fn 39); the fight against communicable diseases such as HIV/AIDS, malaria etc (MDG 6); NCDs (such as cancer, cardiovascular diseases); access to affordable essential medicines and vaccines (in accordance with the Doha Declaration on the TRIPS Agreement and Public Health); the strengthening of health systems through health financing and the recruitment, development, training, and retention of the health workforce; implementation of the right to sexual and reproductive health; and the reduction of maternal and child mortality (MDG 5 and MDG 4).[80]

Additionally, the TST Issue brief on 'Health and Sustainable Development' which was prepared by WHO,[81] the United Nations Population Fund (UNFPA), the Joint United Nations Programme on HIV/AIDS (UNAIDS), UN Women, UNICEF, the World Meteorological Organization (WMO), UNDP, the International Labour Organization (ILO), the Peacebuilding Support Office (PBSO) and the Convention on Biological Diversity (CBD),[82] similar to 'The Future We Want', emphasized at the

---

[76] Kamau and others (n 60) 114.

[77] See reporting by IISD Earth Negotiations Bulletins, 18 June 2013 <https://enb.iisd.org/sdgs/owg4/18jun.html> accessed 23 October 2021.

[78] For example, the report by the Sustainable Development Solutions Network was introduced the opening of the session. See SDSN, 'An Action Agenda for Sustainable Development—Report for the UN Secretary-General' (6 June 2013) <https://unstats.un.org/unsd/broaderprogress/pdf/130613-SDSN-An-Action-Agenda-for-Sustainable-Development-FINAL.pdf> accessed 23 October 2021. The report had been available as a draft for public consultation prior to its final submission to the Secretary-General. Among the twelve thematic groups discussed, Thematic Group 5 was termed 'Achieved Health and Wellbeing at All Ages'. Thereunder, it emphasized the way forward: '[b]y 2030, every country should be well positioned to ensure universal health coverage for all citizens at every stage of life, with particular emphasis on the provision of comprehensive and affordable primary health services delivered through a well--resourced health system', ibid 15. Additionally, the report highlighted the interconnectedness of health with other sectors, the necessity to continue the MDGs targets that had not been reached, and the aim of encouraging healthy life choices by individuals (eg by reducing alcohol and tobacco use).

[79] 'The Future We Want' (n 16) para 138.

[80] ibid, paras 138–146.

[81] WHO also worked on the issue brief relating to water and sanitation, energy, climate change and disaster risk reduction, and sustainable cities and human settlements. For an overview see Kamau and others (n 60) 350ff.

[82] UN System Technical Support Team, 'TST Issues Brief on Health and Sustainable Development' <https://sustainabledevelopment.un.org/owg.html> accessed 16 October 2021.

outset the right to health as enshrined in the ICESCR, and—drawing on the earlier thematic consultations on health—stressed the central role of health in the concept of sustainable development.[83] Given that health had already featured prominently in the MDG framework, the brief contained a number of lessons. Among others, it pointed out the 'unfinished health MDGs' and that this particularly concerned overcoming 'persistent inequities, within and among countries, in access to health information and services.'[84] In order to reach these MDGs, sustained and accelerated efforts were to be made, which linked particularly with the need to strengthen health systems and financial protection. Among the emerging challenges, the brief highlighted 'shifting epidemiological, demographic, and a wide range of environmental and social risk factors. Health financing strategies are needed to ensure equal access for all, and to provide protection against catastrophic health expenditures by individuals and ruinous costs to national economies.'[85] As a point of departure, the principles of *universal relevance* (tied to a focus on disadvantaged in every country and the protection of human rights) and *equity, equality, and non-discrimination* (with special emphasis on *gender equality*) were identified as essential in the definition of new goals, targets and indicators in relation to health. As the brief explained, many of the suggestions on framing the health goal and targets that had been made by the Task Team for the Global Thematic Consultation on Health in the Post-2015 Agenda (March 2013)[86] and the High-level Panel of Eminent Persons on the Post-2015 Development Agenda matched or reflected each other. The significant difference related to the targets for UHC, risks of NCDs, or underlying health determinants, which the report by the High-level Panel of Eminent Persons did not address.[87] These areas, however, had 'found significant support in the health consultation process.'[88]

During the meeting with the major groups (taking place every morning before the OWG session was opened), speakers were heard from the Framework Convention Alliance for Tobacco Control,[89] HelpAge International,[90] the International Federal of Medical Students' Association (IFMSA),[91] Non-Governmental Organization (NGO)

---

[83] ibid 1. See also United Nations Statistical Division (in collaboration with the Friends of the Chair group on broader measures of progress), 'Compendium of Statistical Notes for the Open Working Group on Sustainable Development Goals' (March 2014) Statistical note 10.3 <https://sustainabledevelopment.un.org/content/docume nts/3647Compendium%20of%20statistical%20notes.pdf> accessed 23 October 2021.

[84] UN System Technical Support Team, 'TST Issues Brief on Health and Sustainable Development' (n 82)2.

[85] ibid 4.

[86] WHO, UNICEF, the Government of Sweden and the Government of Botswana, 'Health in the Post-2015 Agenda' (n 64).

[87] As was explained, this was omitted since they chose targets that focused on *health outcomes*, whereas they perceived UHC as an instrument which was essential for reaching such outcomes. This was also noted by the statement made to the OWG by Canada, Israel, and the United States during the 4th session <https://sustainabledeve lopment.un.org/content/documents/7542us7.pdf> accessed 23 October 2021.

[88] UN System Technical Support Team, 'TST Issues Brief on Health and Sustainable Development' (n 82) 7.

[89] Suggesting a target of reducing 'preventable deaths from NCDs by 25% or to reduce tobacco use by 30% by the year 2025' <https://sustainabledevelopment.un.org/content/documents/3695fca.pdf> accessed 23 October 2021.

[90] Urging for a closer link to human rights, as well as the inclusion of (old) age in the target and indicator tools <https://sustainabledevelopment.un.org/content/documents/3674helpage1.pdf> accessed 23 October 2021.

[91] Calling for the integration of health in all sectors, the greater use of disaggregated data and a system's transformation towards UHC <https://sustainabledevelopment.un.org/content/documents/3722ifmsa3.pdf> accessed 23 October 2021.

Major Group Health Cluster,[92] the Women's Major Group,[93] the IFMSA and Major Group of Children & Youth,[94] and the Sustainable World Initiative.[95] Many of their points reflected concerns that had been raised during the Rio Conference. Overall, the input by major groups and other stakeholders was just one, albeit an essential, point of differentiation to the previously closed drafting of the MDGs. Even though their precise impact is difficult to measure, studies have attributed success on issues such as sexual and reproductive health and rights to their involvement.[96] Moreover, many of the interlinkages of particular topics in many of the final goals are said to be owed in part to the concerted mobilization efforts undertaken by specific groups.[97]

The Co-Chairs of the OWG had compiled four guiding questions which were considered as leading themes for the OWG debate on health:

1. What further efforts are needed to continue working on the unfinished health MDGs and what approaches are most likely to yield positive and significant health outcomes, especially for the poor, in the post 2015 period?
2. What are countries' experiences and views in regard to the best strategies to reduce inequality and inequity in health coverage and access, particularly regarding the need to reach disadvantaged groups such as women, adolescents, indigenous people, migrants, and other vulnerable populations?
3. How to balance policy priorities and investments to deal with the unfinished health agenda and at the same time to address the shifting epidemiological profiles such as the emergence of non-communicable diseases globally?
4. What is needed in order to implement a possible goal and/or target(s) relating to health?[98]

The statements delivered by states and observers[99] demonstrated almost unequivocally that health was to remain a central and stand-alone goal in the post-2015 Agenda.[100] It

[92] Reiterating many of the previous commitments made by the international community at Rio or other international conferences <https://sustainabledevelopment.un.org/content/documents/3700ngos.pdf> accessed 23 October 2021.

[93] Speaking on the necessity to ensure more equitable access for all, particularly the disadvantaged, to high-quality health services, in consideration of their different health needs. This should also include, in particular, information on sexual and reproductive health, a matter that was largely disregarded in the MDGs <https://sustainabledevelopment.un.org/content/documents/3702wmg.pdf> accessed 23 October 2021.

[94] Pushing for a 'health-in-all-policies approach', alongside better data systems and UHC <https://sustainabledevelopment.un.org/content/documents/3701ifmsa2.pdf> accessed 23 October 2021.

[95] Highlighting the interlinkages between sexual and reproductive health and rights, population dynamics, economics, and natural resources <https://sustainabledevelopment.un.org/content/documents/3698swi.pdf > accessed 23 October 2021.

[96] AE Yamin, 'Power, Politics and Knowledge Claims: Sexual and Reproductive Health and Rights and in the SDG Era' (2019) 10 (Supplement 1) Global Policy 52; G Sen, 'Gender Equality and Women's Empowerment: Feminist Mobilization for the SDGs' (2019) 10 Global Policy 28.

[97] S Fukuda-Parr and D McNeill, 'Knowledge and Politics in Setting and Measuring the SDGs: Introduction to Special Issue' (2019) 10 Global Policy 5, 11–12.

[98] <https://sustainabledevelopment.un.org/content/documents/1838Guiding%20questions_OWG4.pdf> accessed 23 October 2021.

[99] All together, seventy statements by states and observers were made.

[100] Approximately one month before the stocktaking phase on health took place, the WHA passed Resolution WHA66.11, 'Health in the Post-2015 UN Development Agenda' (27 May 2013), urging member states to ensure precisely that.

brought further agreement on a broad understanding of health (not simply absence of disease but broad well-being), and stressed health not only as a 'contributor to development and ... as an indicator of development'[101] but also as a fundamental human right.

As for the first question, all statements emphasized that work on the 'unfinished health MDGs' would prove crucial for the post-2015 Agenda. However, this was to be complemented by additional targets, in particular UHC (including 'equitable access to quality basic health services; health promotion, prevention, treatment, and financial risk protection'). As the key additional target to be introduced in the post-2015 agenda in relation to health, the debate was accompanied by a presentation by Jeanette Vega of the Rockefeller Foundation on 'Universal Health Coverage, Sustainable Development and the Post-2015 Agenda',[102] underscoring the interrelationship between health and (economic) development as well as the central role of UHC on this issue. There were some statements indicating that this could even be used as the overarching goal ('clear and measurable sustainable development goal for health') given that there were sufficient indicators by WHO or the World Bank that could be used for this purpose (eg out-of-pocket payments for health, skilled-birth attendance, availability of quality essential medicines),[103] and a similar proposal had been made by WHO before the consultation process began.[104] The particular benefit of UHC—underscored in several statements—was its suitability of also constituting a means of reducing inequalities and inequities (thus also a strategy in response to the second question).[105]

There was also a consensus on including NCDs in the new health goal, with several statements emphasizing how this increasingly affected all countries and that this was a growing question given also the future demographic development.[106] A particular focus was placed by several states on the topic of sexual and reproductive health (rights),[107] given that this had previously slipped through the MDGs,[108] as well as the interlinkages of health with several other goals and themes such as environmental pollution, poverty, social protection systems.

[101] See, for many, statement by the Troika (Italy, Spain, and Turkey) <https://sustainabledevelopment.un.org/content/documents/3673spain.pdf> accessed 23 October 2021.

[102] <https://sustainabledevelopment.un.org/content/documents/1861OWG_UHC_RF_Presentation%20June13%20Final.pdf> accessed 23 October 2021.

[103] There were some statements indicating that this could even be used as the overarching goal ('clear and measurable sustainable development goal for health') given that there were sufficient indicators by WHO or the World Bank that could be used for this purpose (eg out-of-pocket payments for health, skilled-birth attendance, availability of quality essential medicines), see Statement by France, Germany, and Switzerland <https://sustainabledevelopment.un.org/content/documents/6560france3.pdf> accessed 23 October 2021.

[104] WHO 'Discussion Paper—Positioning Health in the Post-2015 Development Agenda' (October 2012) <http://www.who.int/topics/millennium_development_goals/post2015/WHOdiscussionpaper_October2012.pdf accessed 22 October 2021.

[105] See, eg, Statement by South Africa <https://sustainabledevelopment.un.org/content/documents/3668southafrica.pdf>; Statement by Troika (Denmark, Norway, and Ireland) <https://sustainabledevelopment.un.org/content/documents/3715norway.pdf> accessed 23 October 2021.

[106] Co-Chairs' Summary bullet point from OWG-4 on 'Health, Population Dynamics' <https://sustainabledevelopment.un.org/content/documents/1871cochairssummary.pdf> accessed 23 October 2021.

[107] See, eg, Statement by Montenegro and Slovenia <https://sustainabledevelopment.un.org/content/documents/5980slovenia9.pdf> accessed 23 October 2021.

[108] See this chapter, Section IV.B.7, target 3.7.

204   SDG 3

When it came to setting targets, the OWG took into account a number of initiatives and targets, which had been set in the years leading to the SDG drafting process. For example, only a month earlier, the WHA had adopted 'a 25% relative reduction in the overall mortality from cardiovascular diseases, cancers, diabetes, or chronic respiratory diseases' by 2025 as a voluntary global target.[109] In addition, the definition and scope of UHC was borrowed from WHO.[110]

The OWG also began the debate on existing and new indicators with regard to health. As for the question how to monitor progress on the overall goal (still understood as 'maximizing health at all stages of life'),[111] it was suggested that 'life expectancy' might constitute the most easily understood and feasible indicator, whereas *healthy* life expectancy could constitute a broader development indicator.[112] While there was agreement on the monitoring of specific target-related mortality rates, UHC indicators should include coverage of interventions and financial risk protection. Additionally, the underlying social and environmental determinants of health should also be included among the indicators.[113]

The session closed with the Co-Chairs emphasizing the key messages of the debate. While there was broad agreement on the scope of the goal, as well as on targets to include, the precise wording and formulation remained open ('Maximize Healthy Lives' or 'Universal Health Coverage for All Citizens at All Stages of Life').[114] This was also taken up in the first progress report by the Co-Chairs of the OWG, to be sent to the President of the General Assembly, drafted immediately after closure of the fourth session.[115]

2. The Negotiation Phase—OWGs-9-13 (March–July 2014)

After eight OWG sessions had been held (until February 2014), the OWG's work moved on to begin preparing a report to submit to the 68th session of the General Assembly. When it came to the negotiation phase, a key challenge was to remain on track and focused in order to finish the work by July 2014. With the help of the UN Secretariat, the Co-Chairs had condensed the previous work on the nineteen Focus Areas which had

---

[109] WHA66.10, 'Follow-up to the Political Declaration of the High-level Meeting of the General Assembly on the Prevention and Control of Non-Communicable Diseases' (27 May 2013).

[110] United Nations Statistical Division (in collaboration with the Friends of the Chair group on broader measures of progress), 'Compendium of Statistical Notes for the Open Working Group on Sustainable Development Goals' (March 2014) Statistical note 10.5 <https://sustainabledevelopment.un.org/content/documents/3647Compendium%20of%20statistical%20notes.pdf> accessed 23 October 2021.

[111] See, eg, Statement by Troika (Denmark, Norway, and Ireland) <https://sustainabledevelopment.un.org/content/documents/3715norway.pdf> accessed 23 October 2021.

[112] United Nations Statistical Division (in collaboration with the Friends of the Chair group on broader measures of progress), 'Compendium of Statistical Notes for the Open Working Group on Sustainable Development Goals' (March 2014) Statistical note 10.13 <https://sustainabledevelopment.un.org/content/documents/3647Compendium%20of%20statistical%20notes.pdf> accessed 23 October 2021.

[113] United Nations Statistical Division (in collaboration with the Friends of the Chair group on broader measures of progress), 'Compendium of Statistical Notes for the Open Working Group on Sustainable Development Goals' (March 2014) Statistical note 10.24 <https://sustainabledevelopment.un.org/content/documents/3647Compendium%20of%20statistical%20notes.pdf> accessed 23 October 2021.

[114] See 'Concluding Remarks of Co-Chairs' <https://sustainabledevelopment.un.org/content/documents/3693cochairsconcluding.pdf> accessed 23 October 2021.

[115] UNGA 'Letter dated 19 July 2013 from the Co-Chairs of the Open Working Group of the General Assembly on Sustainable Development Goals addressed to the President of the General Assembly' (23 July 2013) UN Doc A/67/941.

been discussed, purposefully avoiding terming it 'zero draft' in order to prevent rejection by the OWG members.[116] The starting point on health was summarized in the following manner:

> Healthy populations are important assets for sustainable development. Improving healthy life expectancy is a widely shared endeavor. Therefore ensuring adequate, affordable and accessible health services for all should be progressively realized. Some areas that could be considered include: strengthening health systems, dissemination of medical and public health knowledge and modern technologies; universal health coverage; elimination of preventable child and maternal deaths; preventing and treating communicable diseases, including malaria, HIV/AIDS, tuberculosis, and neglected tropical diseases; eliminating harmful practices; ensuring affordable essential medicines and vaccines for all; promoting healthy diets and lifestyles; addressing non-communicable diseases (NCDs); tackling environmental causes of disease, such as exposure to harmful pollutants and substances; providing for the health needs of persons with disabilities and ageing populations; access to sexual and reproductive health; improved indoor and outdoor air quality; and reducing road accidents. Interlinkages with other focus areas include: food security and nutrition, water and sanitation, economic growth, sustainable consumption and production, climate change, promoting equality, and gender equality.[117]

The opening comments by delegates on this proposal show that it reflected the stocktaking phase well, however many wished for clearer reflection of interlinkages to other Focus Areas. In addition, it became clear that the topic of 'sexual and reproductive health and rights' would become crucial when pushing for agreement.[118]

Following the comments by delegates during the ninth OWG session, the Co-Chairs drafted a revised Focus Area document (19 March 2014), providing some guidance on what the debate had shown could be identified as a potential goal and sub-topics for consideration as targets[119] and a compendium of existing goals and targets relating to the nineteen Focus Areas. With regard to the Focus Area on health, these were drawn

---

[116] Kamau and others (n 60) 171.

[117] Focus Area Document (21 February 2014) <https://sustainabledevelopment.un.org/content/documents/3276focusareas.pdf> accessed 23 October 2021.

[118] See, eg, Statement by Denmark, Ireland, and Norway <https://sustainabledevelopment.un.org/content/documents/7172norway.pdf>; Statement by Saudi Arabia <https://sustainabledevelopment.un.org/content/documents/7202saudiarabia.pdf> accessed 23 October 2021.

[119] 'Realizing the right to the highest attainable standard of mental and physical health and improving healthy life expectancy is a widely shared endeavour. Some areas that could be considered include: a) universal health coverage; b) strengthening health systems, including through increased health financing, development and training of the health workforce, and access to safe, affordable, effective and quality medicines, vaccines and medical technologies; c) ensuring affordable essential medicines and vaccines for all; d) dissemination of medical and public health knowledge, including traditional knowledge; e) elimination of preventable child and maternal deaths; f) significant reduction of child morbidity; g) End the HIV/AIDS epidemic; h) preventing and treating communicable diseases, including malaria, tuberculosis, and neglected tropical diseases; i) addressing non-communicable diseases (NCDs) inter alia through promoting healthy diets and lifestyles, including for youth; j) tackling environmental causes of disease; k) access to sexual and reproductive health, including modern methods of family planning; l) providing for the health needs of persons with disabilities, youth, migrants, and ageing populations; m) eliminating harmful practices; n) reducing road accidents; and o) appropriate means of

from previous practice, for example the MDGs or targets set by the WHA,[120] but also from UN Resolutions (such as the 'Future We Want' Declaration, but also UNGA Res 65/277 'Political Declaration on HIV/AIDS') and Summit Conferences (eg the International Conference on Population and Development and the Beijing Platform for Action).[121] In addition, an Annex on interlinkages was added.[122]

This process of refining and revising targets continued throughout the next OWG sessions. By OWG-11, the Co-Chairs had narrowed down the list to sixteen focus areas, and a suggestion of 148 targets in total (from previously more than 200), eight dedicated to Focus Area 3 ('Healthy life at all ages for all'), highlighting who had supported or suggested a similar target in their statements (whether states or stakeholders).[123] The appropriate means of implementation still remained part of the unfinished business. In principle, the eight targets[124]—though some were adjusted (after an assessment of their feasibility through experts and TST),[125] split up or restructured—reflected the finally agreed targets of SDG 3.

For OWG-12, a 'zero draft' was submitted by the Co-Chairs to the Member States. OWG-12 took place in two parts, a first 'informal-informal' part, which was dedicated particularly to Goals 1–6, those goals which contained the 'unfinished MDGs'.[126] In the aftermath of the meeting on health some few delegations had put forward a suggestion to 'add "well-being to this goal heading to express a meaning of health and well-being beyond physical fitness'.[127] Beyond that, the debate primarily revolved around whether and how to include the point of sexual and reproductive health (rights).[128]

---

implementation.' <https://sustainabledevelopment.un.org/content/documents/3402Focus%20areas_20140319. pdf> accessed 23 October 2021.

[120] Particularly WHA66.10 on non-communicable diseases; WHA65.6 on maternal, infant, and young child nutrition; WHA59/19 on prevention and control of sexually transmitted infections; WHA65/17 on a global vaccine plan.

[121] <https://sustainabledevelopment.un.org/content/documents/3507Existing%20targets_1_April_version. xlsx> accessed 23 October 2021.

[122] On health and population dynamics the following interlinkages were identified: 'sustainable agriculture, food security and nutrition, gender equality and women's empowerment, water and sanitation, economic growth, promote equality, promote sustainable consumption and production, and climate' <https://sustainabledevelopm ent.un.org/content/documents/3387Annex_interlinkages_1903.pdf> accessed 23 October 2021.

[123] 'Working Document for the Eleventh Session of the Open Working Group on SDGs' <https://sustainable development.un.org/content/documents/3686WorkingDoc_0205_additionalsupporters.pdf> accessed 23 October 2021.

[124] 'Healthy life at all ages for all. a) by 2030 reduce the maternal mortality ratio to less than 40 per 100,000 live births, end preventable new-born and child deaths and reduce by x% child and maternal morbidity b) by 2030 end the epidemics of HIV/AIDS, tuberculosis, malaria and neglected tropical diseases c) reduce by x% the risk of premature mortality from non-communicable diseases (NCDs), injuries and promote mental health with strong focus on prevention d) achieve universal health coverage (UHC), including financial risk protection, with particular attention to the most marginalized e) by 2030 ensure universal access to affordable essential medicines and vaccines for all, f) ensure universal access to comprehensive sexual and reproductive health for all, including modern methods of family planning g) decrease by x% the number of deaths and illnesses from indoor and outdoor air pollution and other forms of environmental degradation h) Eliminate narcotic drug and substance abuse' (footnotes linking to the supporting statements omitted).

[125] Kamau and others (n 60) 181–82.

[126] Earth Negotiations Bulletin, 'A Summary of the Twelfth Session of the UN General Assembly Open Working Group on Sustainable Development Goals: 16–20 June 2014' (23 June 2014) <https://enb.iisd.org/events/12th-session-un-general-assemblys-unga-owg-sdgs/summary-report-16-20-june-2014> accessed 14 March 2023.

[127] ibid 16.

[128] This can also be seen from the fact that the revised zero draft contained no mention of this target <https://sus tainabledevelopment.un.org/content/documents/4523zerodraft.pdf> accessed 23 October 2021.

Only after a final marathon session and the help of a specially designated contact group could an agreement be struck to include it as a target, however omitting any reference to rights.[129]

Following the completion of the thirteen OWG sessions, the Co-Chairs presented the final report of the OWG to the UN General Assembly in August 2014.[130] The report which contained the proposal on seventeen SDGs, including their 169 targets, had been adopted by consensus.[131] This included Goal 3, 'Ensure healthy lives and promote well-being for all at all ages', and thirteen targets, of which twelve remained unchanged in comparison to the final SDG outcome. Only target 3.2 was later refined.

In total, economic issues had become more prominent in the final OWG proposal than in the early drafts of the Focus Area Document.[132] Also the goal on health had been slightly narrowed down (from fifteen to thirteen targets), in the end merging or redefining some of the targets into one, while adding/specifying the means of implementation.

3. The Intergovernmental Negotiations—Fine-Tuning and Adoption (January–August 2015)

The report was welcomed by the UN General Assembly, which decided that it 'shall be the main basis for integrating sustainable development goals into the post-2015 development agenda, while recognizing that other inputs will also be considered, in the intergovernmental negotiation process at the sixty-ninth session of the General Assembly'.[133] The formulation reflects the divided approach by the international community—with some (particularly the G77)[134] wanting to proceed on the basis of the already agreed upon goals and targets, whereas others wished to revisit parts of the document. Following the Secretary-General's synthesis report in December 2014,[135] which summarized the ongoing processes, the Intergovernmental Negotiating Committee on SDGs (consisting of all 193 Member States) began its work.

Throughout these eight rounds of intergovernmental negotiations, agreement was reached to leave the OWG proposal largely untouched, aside from some 'technical proofing' of the goals and targets.[136] As the same time, the UN Statistical Commission

---

[129] Kamau and others (n 60) 194–95, 212.

[130] UNGA 'Report of the Open Working Group of the General Assembly on Sustainable Development Goals' (12 August 2014) UN Doc A/68/970.

[131] General Assembly Open Working on Sustainable Development Goals (n 61).

[132] For a content analysis see D Bhattacharya and others, 'A Commentary on the Final Outcome Document of the Open Working Group on SDGs' (2014) 34(2) The SAIS Review of International Affairs 165, 170.

[133] UNGA Res 68/309 'Report of the Open Working Group on Sustainable Development Goals Established pursuant to General Resolution 66/288' (10 September 2014) UN Doc A/RES/68/309.

[134] Repeatedly stressing the 'sanctity of the OWG outcome', as reported in Dodds and others (n 56) 72.

[135] UNGA 'The Road to Dignity by 2030: Ending Poverty, Transforming All Lives and Protecting the Planet—Synthesis Report of the Secretary-General on the Post-2015 Sustainable Development Goals' (4 December 2014) UN Doc A/69/700.

[136] Summary of Stock taking meeting of Intergovernmental Negotiations on the Post-2015 Development Agenda—Remarks delivered by Ambassador David Donoghue, Permanent Representative of Ireland to the UN (and Co-Facilitator of the negotiations) (21 January 2015) <https://sustainabledevelopment.un.org/content/documents/5913Summary%20of%20IGN%20Stock%20Taking%20Mtg%2019_21%20Jan%202015.pdf>

208 SDG 3

had already begun drafting indicators, with the understanding that input by the individual agencies was needed (through the TST). This means that the TST was asked to 'review each target to check that it was fit for purpose (in the sense of specific, action-oriented and measurable) and that all relevant international agreements had been taken into account in formulating it'.[137] Beginning in January 2015, the TST therefore conducted a technical review of the targets, in the end—through the Secretariat—suggesting changes to nineteen targets (of which seventeen were in the end incorporated despite initial resistance by the G77).[138] Three of the suggested adaptations concerned targets contained in SDG 3 (targets 3.2, 3.6, and 3.b), of which—as mentioned above—only target 3.2 ('By 2030, end preventable deaths of newborns and children under 5 years of age') was adapted ('By 2030, end preventable deaths of newborns and children under 5 years of age, with all countries aiming to reduce neonatal mortality to at least as low as 12 per 1,000 live births and under-5 mortality to at least as low as 25 per 1000 live births'). As explained by the TST, this change was owed to *specificity*: 'Numerical targets proposed to specify what "ending preventable deaths" means by 2030 for these age groups. Such numerical targets have been endorsed through UNICEF's and WHO's "A Promise Renewed Initiative" and in the "Every Newborn Action Plan".'[139] The suggested changes to target 3.6 (to bring it in line with targets set in the Decade of Action on Road Safety) and target 3.b (to reflect that the 2011 Doha Declaration does not limit the use of available TRIPS Agreement flexibility to just *essential* medicines) were not made.[140]

In the end, the intergovernmental negotiations produced the final outcome document, which was accepted by the General Assembly in September 2015.[141]

---

accessed 20 October 2021. Most agreed that the number of goals was suitable, but there was some discussion on the targets, with several having been drafted by the OWG under time pressure, and some still containing '*x*' references. See also Dodds and others (n 56) 80–82, noting the revised indicators were to be 'confined to populating the '*x*' values and ensuring consistency with international agreements'.

[137] Dodds and others (n 56) 81.

[138] Kamau and others (n 60) 302.

[139] Targets in the proposed SDGs framework <https://sustainabledevelopment.un.org/content/documents/6769Targets%20document__March.pdf> accessed 25 October 2021.

[140] For an overview of the debate see IISD, Earth Negotiations Bulletin, 'Summary of the Seventh and Eighth Sessions of Intergovernmental Negotiations on the Post-2015 Development Agenda: 20 July–2 August 2015' (5 August 2015, IISD Reporting Services Vol 32(20)) <https://s3.us-west-2.amazonaws.com/enb.iisd.org/archive/download/pdf/enb3220e.pdf?X-Amz-Content-Sha256=UNSIGNED-PAYLOAD&X-Amz-Algorithm=AWS4-HMAC-SHA256&X-Amz-Credential=AKIA6QW3Y WTJ6YORWEEL%2F20211025%2Fus-west-2%2Fs3%2Faws4_request&X-Amz-Date=20211025T150234Z&X-Amz-SignedHeaders=host&X-Amz-Expires=60&X-Amz-Signature=d8bec03076054edeed1b5ae4054f054dc4e63fdd043b1620cfd47eec9179db22> accessed 23 October 2021.

[141] UNGA Res 70/1 (25 September 2015) 'Transforming Our World: The 2030 Agenda for Sustainable Development' UN Doc A/RES/70/1.

III. 'Good Health and Well-Being' in SDG 3

A. The Role of the World Health Organization as the Lead Agency in the Achievement of 'Good Health and Well-Being'

WHO, which was formally established in 1948[142] as one of the now seventeen specialized agencies of the UN,[143] functions as the lead agency concerning SDG 3. The Preamble of WHO's Constitution emphasizes that the 'enjoyment of the highest attainable standard of health is one of the fundamental rights of every human being without distinction of race, religion, political belief, economic or social condition' as well as that '[u]nequal development in different countries in the promotion of health and control of disease, especially communicable disease, is a common danger'.[144] WHO's Constitution thus is the first international treaty to define a human right to health.

The roots of the WHO framework and operation can be found in the work of the earlier international sanitary conferences, several regional sanitary councils, and predecessor intergovernmental organizations such as the 1902 Pan American Sanitary Bureau or the 1907 *Office International d'Hygiene Public* (OIHP). On the one hand, this has led to a broad mandate to work towards 'the attainment by all peoples of the highest possible level of health' (article 1 WHO Constitution). To achieve this objective, WHO's mandate includes 'to act as the directing and coordinating authority on international health work' (article 2(a) WHO Constitution); 'to assist Governments, upon request, in strengthening health services' (article 2(c)); and 'to establish or maintain such administrative and technical services as may be required, including epidemiological and statistical services' (article 2(f)). Its functions range from the strengthening of national health services, over a more operational role (when it comes to controlling or fighting certain diseases or epidemics), to an information-based role (eg through the gathering of statistical data).[145] On the other hand, WHO has been built on the pre-existing regionalized structure(s).[146] Thus, while the WHA (194 members) functions as the decision-making body at the global level[147]—passing resolutions determining

---

[142] Constitution of the World Health Organization (adopted 22 July 1946, entered into force 7 April 1948) 14 UNTS 185.

[143] Agreement between the United Nations and the World Health Organization, approved by the General Assembly of the United Nations on 15 November 1947 and by the World Health Assembly on 10 July 1948, and Protocol concerning the entry into force of the said Agreement (adopted 12 November 1948, approved and entered into force on 10 July 1948 (Article XXII)) 19 UNTS 193.

[144] Preamble, Constitution of the World Health Organization (adopted 22 July 1946, entered into force 7 April 1948) 14 UNTS 185.

[145] For a more detailed overview see Y Beigbeder, *The World Health Organization—Achievements and Failures* (Routledge 2018) 4ff.

[146] Y Beigbeder, *The World Health Organization* (Nijhoff Publishers 1998) ch 1.

[147] The WHA meets annually in Geneva, though it may also convene for special sessions (art 13 WHO Constitution) to, among others, determine WHO's policies, review and approve reports and activities of the Executive Board and the Director-General, name the member states which are entitled to designate a person to serve on the Executive Board, and appoint the Director-General (art 18 WHO Constitution).

steps needed for the implementation of the 2030 Agenda[148]—and the Executive Board (thirty-four persons)[149] with the Secretariat (under the lead of the Director-General)[150] serving in an executive role, wide autonomy is granted to WHO's regional organizations.[151] Owed to insistence by the United States that the Pan American Sanitary Bureau could continue its work under WHO's framework, the six regions have developed considerable authority over setting their own regional policies, staff appointments, and implementing WHO policies, at times even challenging WHO's global leadership.[152]

Even though WHO was not directly among the institutions or bodies involved in drafting the MDGs, they quickly became involved in the monitoring of several targets. In the early stages, monitoring of the MDGs was coordinated by the United Nations Statistics Divisions. WHO participated in the Inter-Agency and Expert Group on MDG Indicators (IAEG-MDG), and prepared a series of annual reports on the basis of these statistics.[153] WHO shared the lead agency responsibility with UNICEF on the majority of health-related targets (child mortality, maternal health, childhood nutritional status, malaria-prevention measures, and access to clean water), and they jointly collaborated with UNAIDS on HIV-related targets. Moreover, through its strong regional representation and country teams, WHO became the lead authority for health-related content within the UN Country Teams.[154] Initially, a lack of data plagued progress on reporting. Hence, in a 2008 report by the Secretariat, WHO presented its plans to 'strengthen its core function of monitoring the health situation and trends in the world by establishing a global health observatory'[155] in order to 'monitor progress towards attaining the health-related Goals.'[156] Since 2008, WHO has therefore played a pivotal role throughout the monitoring process of the health-related MDGs.[157]

As discussed in more detail above, WHO remained closely involved during the SDG drafting phase through the UN System Task Team, the TST, and as one of the lead

[148] See, eg, WHA68.11 (28 May 2016), 'Health in the 2030 Agenda for Sustainable Development', urging Member States to take a series of steps to achieve the Goals and targets of the 2030 Agenda, and requesting the Director-General to works towards the implementation of the SDGs. This constitutes the basis for regular reporting to WHO on progress made towards health-related SDGs, targets, and indicators (see, eg, 'Report by the Director-General on Implementation of the 2030 Agenda for Sustainable Development' A72/11 Rev.1 (16 May 2019)).

[149] These are 'designated by as many Members' (art 24 WHO Constitution), rotating, taking into account a geographical distribution. They shall be 'technically qualified in the field of health'. They are elected for renewable three-year terms (art 25). They meet least twice a year. The Executive Board's functions are listed in art 28 WHO Constitution.

[150] The Director-General is the chief technical and administrative officer of WHO, supported by the Secretariat (arts 30ff).

[151] Beigbeder, *The World Health Organization* (n 145) 7.

[152] Arts 44ff WHO Constitution; for a historical overview see E Fee and others, 'At the Roots of the World Health Organization's Challenges: Politics and Regionalization' (2015) 106(11) American Journal of Public Health 1912; also highlighting the opposing ideological views on public health especially during the early years of the Cold War.

[153] WHO, *Millennium Development Goals* (n 45) 2. Since 2005, these are published in the World Health Statistics series, although initially not all MDG health-related indicators were included for lack of reliable data.

[154] ibid 5.

[155] WHO, 'Monitoring Achievement of the Health-Related Millennium Development Goals—Report by the Secretariat' (10 April 2008) A61/15, para 17.

[156] ibid para 18.

[157] Resolution WHA61.18 (24 May 2008), 'Monitoring of the achievement of the health-related Millennium Development Goals'.

agencies involved in the Task Team for the Global Thematic Consultation on Health in the Post-2015 Agenda (chaired by Sweden and Botswana, with the involvement of UNICEF).[158]

For reporting on progress in relation to SDG 3, WHO depends on close collaboration with other agencies, including UNICEF, UNFPA, the United Nations Office on Drugs and Crime (UNODC), UNAIDS, and the World Bank.[159] Many of the targets agreed upon corresponded or were aligned with already existing targets adopted by the WHA, for example, in relation to non-communicable diseases. As WHO noted shortly after the adoption of the SDGs, '[a]lmost all targets can be linked to strategies and global action plans that have been adopted by the World Health Assembly in recent years or are under development'.[160] This corresponds with the objective of the international community to avoid multiple parallel development agendas competing for leadership, as at times had been the case throughout the MDGs period. In line with this, WHO has also initiated the Global Action Plan for Healthy Lives and Well-being for All (2019), together with twelve other international agencies,[161] directed at enhancing collaboration on health and health-related targets.

Also with regard to monitoring SDG 3 'at the goal level'—that is, ensuring healthy lives and promoting well-being for all at all ages—WHO assumes a particular role. In this regard, an indicator of 'healthy life expectancy' had been suggested, as it was hoped that it could take mortality, morbidity, and disability into account.[162] This was still met with challenges concerning the availability of data,[163] and several experts had therefore pushed for replacing this with the simpler indicator of 'life expectancy'.[164] In part, this was resolved with the adoption of WHO's Thirteenth General Programme of Work (13th GPW 2019–2023), 2023 marking the half-way point towards 2030. The 13th GPW was based on an evaluation process (2011–2017) which focused on WHO's work and position in the international health governance framework. Throughout the evaluation, emphasis was placed, among others, on how WHO could contribute stronger to the transformative SDG framework.[165] Data had showed that while significant global health gains had been achieved, many threats to health persisted, ranging from immediate health concerns to risks stemming from underlying health determinants (such

---

[158] WHO, UNICEF, the Government of Sweden and the Government of Botswana, 'Health in the Post-2015 Agenda' (n 64).

[159] This can also be seen in the Secretariat's document on who will survey data regarding SDG 3's indicators <http://unstats.un.org/sdgs/files/meetings/iaeg-sdgs-meeting-03/Provisional-Proposed-Tiers-for-SDG-Indicators-24-03-16.pdf> accessed 23 October 2021.

[160] WHO, *Health in 2015* (n 14) 195.

[161] The twelve other agencies are: Gavi, the Vaccine Alliance; the Global Financing Facility for Women, Children and Adolescents (GFF); the ILO; The Global Fund to Fight AIDS, Tuberculosis and Malaria (The Global Fund); UNAIDS; UNDP; UNFPA; UNICEF; Unitaid; United Nations Entity for Gender Equality and the Empowerment of Women (UN Women); the World Bank Group; and the World Food Programme (WFP).

[162] WHO, UNICEF, the Government of Sweden and the Government of Botswana, 'Health in the Post-2015 Agenda' (n 64) 54.

[163] WHO, *Health in 2015* (n 14) 10.

[164] ibid 55.

[165] WHO, 'Thirteenth General Programme of Work 2019–2023—Promote Health, Keep the World Safe, Serve the Vulnerable' (WHO 2019) WHO/PRP/18.1.

as conflict or climate change). In response to this, the 13th GPW was based on the SDGs, however it complemented them with a focus on three strategic priorities, termed the 'Triple Billion targets'.[166] If these targets are not achieved by 2023, then it is unlikely the 2030 SDG health targets will be achieved.[167] For this framework, WHO began measuring the overall SDG 3 objective by using healthy life expectancy, meaning the '[a]verage remaining number of years that a person can expect to live in "full health" at a certain age by taking into account years lived in less than full health due to disease and/or injury'.[168]

With regard to the state of 'well-being', a reliable monitoring methodology is still under development[169] and will moreover depend on the understanding of the role well-being plays in the overall global health and development framework. On the one hand, the exact relation between 'well-being' and quality of life has remained unanswered by the SDG framework. By the late 1990s WHO had developed a measurement instrument that was directed at the latter (World Health Organization Quality of Life (WHOQOL)) which assessed 'individuals' perceptions of their position in life in the context of the culture and value systems in which they live and in relation to their goals, expectations, standards and concerns'.[170] However, WHO has emphasized that this cannot be equated with 'well-being' but is rather more multidimensional.[171] As of yet, there is however no specially developed indicator for well-being used by WHO. On the other hand, (human) well-being constitutes an overarching theme of the entire SDG framework. Most recently, Jan-Emmanuel De Neve and Jeffrey Sachs have explored the feasibility of combining a leverage of the SDG Index[172] with the Gallup World Poll (which explores, among others, how individuals evaluate their quality of life, in other words their subjective well-being (SWB)). Six variables are used to measure SWB: GDP per capita, social support, healthy life expectancy/health, freedom to make life choices, values/generosity, and trust in government/freedom from corruption. While progress on SDG 3's targets obviously plays an important role in this assessment, similarly strong relations are identified to progress on a number of other goals. For example, social support links strongly with SDGs 1, 5, and 10.[173]

---

[166] The three specific strategic priorities are: achieving UHC (1 billion more people benefitting from UHC); addressing health emergencies (1 billion more people better protected from health emergencies (UHC); and promoting health populations (1 billion more people enjoying better health and well-being).

[167] WHO, 'Thirteenth General Programme of Work 2019–2023' (n 165) 11.

[168] Health Adjusted Life Expectancy (HALE) <https://portal.who.int/triplebillions/PowerBIDashboards/Indicators?indicatorBookMark=Bookmarkb01917e2cd9b2edd6cbc> accessed 25 October 2021.

[169] WHO, *Health in 2015* (n 14) 11, explaining that self-reported well-being still poses many problems for reliable data gathering, particularly in light of often diverging understandings of 'well-being' and its relation to health.

[170] WHO, *The World Health Organization Quality of Life (WHOQOL)* (1 March 2012) WHO/HIS/HSI Rev.2012.03 (11).

[171] ibid.

[172] The SDG Index is an assessment of states' performance on the seventeen SDGs. It is compiled by teams of independent experts at the Sustainable Development Solutions Network (SDSN) and the Bertelsmann Stiftung and published in the annual Sustainable Development Report.

[173] J-E De Neve and J Sachs, 'Sustainable Development and Human Well-Being' in JF Helliwell and others (eds), *World Happiness Report 2020* (Sustainable Development Solutions Network 2020) 113.

B. Global Health—A Development Perspective and Human Rights Critique

Following the end of the Second World War, WHO's approach towards public health governance departed from the earlier understanding of addressing health in a purely medical fashion. Thus, WHO's mandate (and global health policy) is aimed not only at combatting the spread of (infectious) diseases (as had previously been the case in the International Sanitary Conventions adopted at international sanitary conferences beginning in 1851) but also at improving public health by focusing on the underlying determinants of health.[174] However, initially the development agenda did not pursue an integral approach; instead it was primarily focused on economic growth. It was not until the 1970s that the tides shifted, and a growing recognition of the link between the objective of 'development' and conditions which serve 'the realisation of the potential of human personality'[175] can be found. In this time period, health was soon recognized as part of the development agenda and within it as an essential component for the achievement of other development objectives such as economic development or education.[176] As one realization of this, following the Alma Ata Declaration, the UN General Assembly adopted Resolution 34/58, placing health 'as an integral part of development'.[177]

There remains some debate on whether health is an integral part of the wider development process or whether development results in better health. The interrelationship has been described as complex, though not necessarily correlating. Thus, a higher level of economic development does not necessarily mean a better health status and vice versa.[178] Within the debate, the understanding of *well-being* is particularly interesting. Scholars have struggled coming to terms with its precise meaning and content, or how to attempt measuring it.[179] At the same time, as a multidimensional concept, it has been positioned between health, development and human rights:

---

[174] Gostin and Meier, 'The Origins of Human Rights in Global Health' (n 32) 28; DP Fidler, 'From International Sanitary Conventions to Global Health Security: The New International Health Regulations' (2005) 4 Chinese Journal of International Law 325.

[175] D Seers, *The Meaning of Development* (Institute of Development Studies 1969) 3.

[176] V Adams, 'A History of International Health Encounters: Diplomacy in Transition' in TE Novotny and others (eds), *21st Century Global Health Diplomacy* (World Scientific 2013) 41, 52.

[177] UNGA Res 34/58 (29 November 1979) UN Doc A/RES/34/58.

[178] DR Phillips and Y Verhasselt, 'Introduction: Health and Development' in DR Phillips and Y Verhasselt (eds), *Health and Development* (Routledge 1994) 3, 5, summarizing already early on that '[i]t has long been acknowledged that the health status of the population in any particular place or country influences development. It can be a limiting factor, as generally poor individual health can lower work capacity and productivity; in aggregate in a population, this can severely restrict the growth of economies. On the other hand, economic development can make it possible to finance good environmental health, sanitation and public health campaigns—education, immunization, screening and health promotion—and to provide broader-based social care for needy groups.... there are examples in which economic development, infrastructure expansion and agricultural intensification do not always coincide with improved human well-being. There is, in fact, growing realization that macroeconomic changes may not always filter down to benefit all of the population, and many perhaps soundly based policies in economic terms—notably structural adjustment policies—can have devastating human effects in increasing poverty and maldistribution of resources. In the face of these policies, the health sector alone cannot overcome concomitant health and welfare problems.'

[179] For a good overview of the debate see J Page-Reeves (ed), *Well-Being as a Multidimensional Concept: Understanding Connections among Culture, Community and Health* (Lexington Books 2019).

From the development perspective, well-being means economic processes that allocate resources to improve people's material and social conditions; from the health perspective, it means improving physical, mental, and social dimensions of human existence; and from the human rights perspective, it means ensuring human dignity and the elimination of repressive and oppressive processes. Thus, development introduces the dimension of resource allocation as crucial to realizing human rights in global health. Health advocates can advance their goals by applying a human rights-based approach to development and a right to development, achieving positive outcomes for public health.[180]

Hence, at times it has been asserted that well-being indeed might be classified as part of the 'overarching development goal', emphasizing that this would address 'the need for action on the underlying determinants of health and well-being, including the root causes of ill health, poverty, gender inequality, violence etc'.[181] The mutual interlinkages between these fields are consistently underscored within the SDG framework.

It has increasingly also been argued that the (collective) right to development should be used as a complementary means to the (human) rights to health, an avenue often pursued by health advocates.[182] As highlighted by the former Co-Chair of the High-Level Task Force established to provide a framework of operationalization for the right to development, the shift in emphasis as regards public health policy relates particularly to international (development) cooperation, yet the SDG framework does not adequately enshrine such a human-rights based approach to development, which is generally largely absent from development finance discourse.[183] Much debate has therefore rather investigated the more tangible link between SDG 3 and human rights which 'offer international legal foundations for social justice in public health'.[184]

At the international level, the protection of the right to health—actually 'a right to the highest attainable standard of health'[185]—has been a core objective since its articulation in the 1946 Constitution of the World Health Organization,[186] the adoption of the 1948 American Declaration on the Rights and Duties of Man (article XI),[187] and the

---

[180] SP Marks and A Han, 'Health and Human Rights through Development—The Right to Development, Rights-Based Approach to Development, and Sustainable Development Goals' in LO Gostin and BM Meier (eds), *Foundations of Global Health and Human Rights* (OUP 2020) 329, 329.

[181] WHO, UNICEF, the Government of Sweden and the Government of Botswana, 'Health in the Post-2015 Agenda' (n 64) 53.

[182] BM Meier and AM Fox, 'Development as Health: Employing the Collective Right to Development to Achieve the Goals of the Individual Right to Health' (2008) 30 Human Rights Quarterly 259.

[183] Marks and Han (n 180) 338, 345.

[184] LO and others, 'Global Health Law—Legal Foundations for Social Justice in Public Health' in Gostin and Meier (eds) (n 180) 45.

[185] A Eide, 'Adequate Standard of Living' in D Moeckli and others (eds), *International Human Rights Law* (OUP 2014) 195, 205; see also CESCR 'General Comment No 14: The Right to the Highest Attainable Standard of Health' (11 August 2000) UN Doc E/C.12/2000/4, para 1.

[186] Constitution of the World Health Organization (adopted 22 July 1946, entered into force 7 April 1948) 14 UNTS 185.

[187] 'Every person has the right to the preservation of his health through sanitary and social measures relating to food, clothing, housing and medical care'. American Declaration on the Rights and Duties of Man (1948).

'GOOD HEALTH AND WELL-BEING' IN SDG 3   215

1948 Universal Declaration of Human Rights (UDHR) which in its article 25 contained the interlinked rights to health and to an adequate standard of living.[188]

From the outset of modern international law, following the end of the Second World War, a link between 'global health' and the 'right to health' has permeated the international framework. Through the lens of social medicine, that is viewing 'medicine as an interdisciplinary social science necessary to example how social inequalities shape the experience of disease,'[189] the status of health was increasingly linked to social and environmental conditions, and thus dependent on economic development. 'Public health' was understood to describe structural interventions into the underlying health determinants, with human rights constituting the basis for the public health framework established under international law.[190]

The right to health has since then become firmly anchored in a number of binding international and regional human rights instruments—particularly the International Covenant on Economic, Social and Cultural Rights (article 12 ICESCR)[191]—international soft law instruments,[192] and more than 115 domestic constitutions.[193] Owed to the interlinkage of the right to health with several other human rights,[194] it is also implicitly protected by a number of civil and political rights such as the right to life[195] or the right

[188] UNGA Res 217 (III), International Bill of Human Rights, A Universal Declaration of Human Rights (10 December 1948) UN Doc A/RES/217.
[189] Gostin and Meier, 'The Origins of Human Rights in Global Health' (n 32) 22.
[190] ibid 22–23.
[191] International Covenant on Economic, Social and Cultural Rights (adopted 16 December 1966, entered into force 3 January 1976) 993 UNTS 3; see also arts 10, 11(1)(f), art 12(1), art 14(2)(b)) Convention on the Elimination of All Forms of Discrimination against Women (CEDAW) (adopted 18 December 1979, entered into force 3 September 1981) 1249 UNTS 13; art 24 Convention on the Rights of the Child (adopted 20 November 1989, entered into force 2 September 1990) 1577 UNTS 3; art 25 Convention on the Rights of Persons with Disabilities (adopted 13 December 2006, entered into force 3 May 2008) 2515 UNTS 3; arts 28, 43, 45 International Convention on the Protection of the Rights of All Migrant Workers and Members of their Families (adopted 18 December 1990, entered into force 1 July 2003) 2220 UNTS 3; arts 11, 13 European Social Charter (adopted 18 October 1961, entered into force 26 February 1965) ETS No 163; Art 35 Charter of Fundamental Rights of the European Union (signed and proclaimed 7 December 2000, revised 12 December 2007, entered into force 1 December 2009) [2012] OJ C326/391; art 10 Additional Protocol to the American Convention on Human Rights in the Area of Economic, Social and Cultural Rights (Protocol of San Salvador) (adopted 17 November 1988, entered into force 16 November 1999) OAS Treaty Series No 69; art 19 Inter-American Convention on Protecting the Human Rights of Older Persons (adopted 15 June 2015, entered into force 11 January 2017) 55 ILM 985; art 16 African Charter on Human and Peoples' Rights (adopted 27 June 1981, entered into force 28 December 1988) 1520 UNTS 217; art 14 Protocol to the African Charter on Human and Peoples' Rights on the Rights of Women in Africa (adopted 11 July 2003, entered into force 25 November 2005) OAU Doc CAB/LEG/66.6; art 14 African Charter on the Rights and Welfare of the Child (adopted 11 July 1990, entered into force 29 November 1999) CAB/LEG/24.9/49 (1990); art 39 Arab Charter on Human Rights (adopted 22 May 2004, entered into force 15 March 2008) UN Doc [ST/HR/]CHR/NONE/2004/40/Rev.1.
[192] Inter alia in the 1978 Alma Ata Declaration adopted by the International Conference on Primary Health Care and the Vienna Declaration and Programme of Action, adopted World Conference on Human Rights (25 June 1993) UN Doc A/CONF.157/23.
[193] OHCHR and WHO, 'The Right to Health—Fact Sheet No 31' (Geneva 2008) 10.
[194] C Binder and others, 'Introduction to the Research Handbook on International Law and Social Rights' in C Binder and others (eds), Research Handbook on International Law and Social Rights (Edward Elgar, 2020) xix, xxi.
[195] For example, as recognized by the Human Rights Committee in its General Comment on the right to life, the right to life encompasses inter alia the obligation of states to 'provide safe, legal and effective access to abortion where the life and health of the pregnant women or girl is at risk' (para 8) as well as the duty to take 'appropriate measures to address the general conditions in society that may give rise to direct threats to life or prevent individuals from enjoying their right to life with dignity' (para 26). In this General Comment, obvious health dimensions are covered by the right to life. Human Rights Committee, 'General Committee No 36 on the Right to Life' (30 October 2018) CCPR/C/GC/36.

216   SDG 3

to privacy. Additionally, several other fields of international law, for example intellectual property law, environmental law, and investment law, also contain state obligations which are relevant in matters of public health concern, safety, or access to healthcare.[196] The right to health has been authoritatively interpreted by the Committee on Economic, Social and Cultural Rights in its General Comment No 14, emphasizing that the

> realization of the right to health may be pursued through numerous, complementary approaches, such as the formulation of health policies, or the implementation of health programmes developed by the World Health Organization (WHO), or the adoption of specific legal instruments. Moreover, the right to health includes certain components which are legally enforceable [for example, the principle of non-discrimination in relation to health facilities, goods and services is legally enforceable in numerous national jurisdictions].[197]

In particular, the right to health contains both freedoms—such as sexual and reproductive freedom—and entitlements such as access to a healthcare system.[198] The elements of Availability, Accessibility, Acceptability, and Quality (AAAQ) inform the interpretation and operationalization of the right to health.[199]

Given the inherent link between the (human) right to health and global health policy, it is not surprising that several targets in SDG 3 show parallels to human rights content as developed and interpreted by the Committee on Economic, Social and Cultural Rights (CESCR) (see Table 3.1). In General Comment No 14, the CESCR had already placed focus on aligning the two fields by emphasizing that the right to health included 'a wide range of socio-economic factors that promote conditions in which people can lead a healthy life, and extends to the underlying determinant of health such as food and nutrition, housing, access to safe and potable water and adequate sanitation, safe and healthy working conditions, and a healthy environment'.[200]

For example, SDG target 3.2 on the reduction of child mortality corresponds to the obligation of State Parties of the ICESCR to take steps for 'the reduction of the stillbirth-rate and of infant mortality and for the healthy development of the child'.[201] SDG target 3.1 on reduction of global maternal mortality relates not only to the overall obligation of states to respect, protect, and ensure the right to life, but also to the specific obligation enshrined in the Convention on the Elimination of All Forms of Discrimination

---

[196] S Negri, 'Health, Right to' in C Binder and others (eds), *Encyclopedia of Human Rights* (Edward Elgar 2022) para 6.

[197] CESCR 'General Comment No 14: The Right to the Highest Attainable Standard of Health' (11 August 2000) UN Doc E/C.12/2000/4.

[198] ibid para 8.

[199] ibid para 12. Availability speaks to the existence and sufficient quantity of health and healthcare facilities, goods, and services (also in relation to the underlying determinants of health). Accessibility relates to the physical, economic, and information accessibility for everyone without discrimination. Acceptability concerns the question of medical ethics and cultural appropriateness. Quality refers to the fact that health facilities, goods, and services must be scientifically and medically appropriate and of good quality.

[200] ibid para 4.

[201] Art 12(2)(a) ICESCR.

'GOOD HEALTH AND WELL-BEING' IN SDG 3   217

Table 3.1 Correlation between SDG 3 targets and human rights obligations

SDG 3 overall	• Right to life (UDHR art 3; ICCPR art 6), particularly of women (CEDAW art 12) and children (CRC art 6) • Right to health (UDHR art 25; ICESCR art 12; ICERD art 5(e)(iv)), particularly of women (CEDAW art 12); and children (CRC art 24) • Special protection for mothers and children (ICESCR art 10) • Right to enjoy the benefits of scientific progress and its application (UDHR art 27; ICESCR art 15(1)(b)) • International cooperation (UDHR art 28, Declaration on the Right to Development arts 3–4], particularly in relation to the right to health and children's rights (ICESCR art 2(1); CRC art 4)[a]
3.1 Reduce global maternal mortality	Right to life (UDHR art 3; ICCPR art 6; CEDAW art 12)
3.2 Reduce child mortality	Reduction of infant mortality (ICESCR art 12(2)(a)), right to life (UDHR art 3; ICCPR art 6; CRC art 6), diminish infant and child mortality (CRC art 24(2)(a))
3.3 End epidemics and combat diseases	Prevention, treatment, and control of epidemic, endemic, occupational, and other diseases (ICESCR art 12(2)(c)); Medical service and medical attention (ICESCR art 12(2)(d))
3.4 Reduce premature mortality from non-communicable diseases through prevention and treatment and promote mental health and well-being	Improvement of environmental and industrial hygiene (ICESCR art 12(2)(b); Prevention, treatment, and control of epidemic, endemic, occupational, and other diseases (ICESCR art 12(2)(c)); Medical service and medical attention (ICESCR art 12(2)(d), CRPD art 25)
3.7 Ensure universal access to sexual and reproductive healthcare services	Right of women to health services, including family planning (CEDAW arts 10(h), 11, 12(1))
3.8 Achieve universal health coverage	Medical service and medical attention (ICESCR art 12(2)(d))
3.9 Reduce the number of deaths and illnesses from hazardous chemicals and air, water and soil pollution and contamination	Improvement of environmental and industrial hygiene (ICESCR art 12(2)(b))

[a]OHCHR, 'Summary Table on the Linkages between the SDGs and Relevant International Human Rights Instruments' available at <http://www.ohchr.org/en/issues/SDGS/pages/the2030agenda.aspx> accessed 10 November 2021

against Women (CEDAW) to 'take all appropriate measures to eliminate discrimination against women in the field of health care in order to ensure, on a basis of equality of men and women, access to health care services, including those related to family planning'.[202]

---

[202] Art 12 CEDAW.

218   SDG 3

Additionally, already during the drafting process of the SDGs some—most notably WHO—placed effort on asserting that UHC (target 3.8) would constitute the *practical expression of the right to health*,[203] and overcome the criticism relating to the MDGs that they were 'duplicative' or constituted 'competing alternatives' to international human rights law.[204] While this side-lines the issue of underlying health determinants that—as stated above—are considered key elements of the right to health, UHC reflects a comprehensive approach towards health (care), reflecting certain imperatives of combatting inequalities at the domestic level as mandated also by human rights principles.[205] The four elements—AAAQ—identified as core to the implementation of the right to health at least in part are thus also reflected in the target's formulation ('Achieve universal health coverage, including financial risk protection, access to quality essential health-care services and access to safe, effective, quality and affordable essential medicines and vaccines for all')—availability (achieve UHC), accessibility (in terms of non-discrimination ('for all'), physical, economic ('financial risk protection', 'affordable'), and information accessibility), acceptability and quality, though the target fails to 'confer priority to providing access to health services to poor and disadvantaged communities'[206] as dictated by human rights.

Notwithstanding this partly stark correlation between SDG 3 and international human rights law, at the outset it appears that SDG 3 is formulated in a broader manner than enshrined in (binding) international human rights practice. In part, this is owed to the already wider understanding of health by the WHO Constitution which defines among its basic principles human health as 'a state of complete physical, mental and social well-being and not merely the absence of disease or infirmity'.[207] By resorting to the concept of well-being, WHO 'detached itself from a *purely* biomedical understanding ... of health as being the freedom from physical and mental illnesses and impairments',[208] a notion which as stated above, continues to raise questions.[209] In comparison, article 12(1) ICESCR defines the right to health as the 'right of everyone to the enjoyment of the highest attainable standard of physical and mental health'. The divergence in scope can be understood against the background of international public health policy and WHO's broader health policy mandate which is aimed at improving public health by focusing on the underlying determinants of health.[210] In early human rights terms, this was circumscribed in Article 25 of the Universal Declaration of Human Rights:

---

[203] WHO 'Discussion Paper—Positioning Health in the Post-2015 Development Agenda' (n 104).

[204] For a thorough investigation of this claims, see P Alston, 'Ships Passing in the Night: The Current State of the Human Rights and Development Debate seen through the Lens of the Millennium Development Goals' (2005) 27(3) Human Rights Quarterly 755, 759ff.

[205] G Ooms and others, 'Is Universal Health Coverage the Practical Expression of the Right to Health Care?' (2014) 14 BMC International Health and Human Rights (Article No 3).

[206] See also Chapman (n 24) 1105.

[207] Preamble, Constitution of the World Health Organization (adopted 22 July 1946, entered into force 7 April 1948) 14 UNTS 185.

[208] M Krennerich, 'The Human Right to Health—Fundamentals of a Complex Rights' in S Klotz and others (eds), *Healthcare as a Human Rights Issue—Normative Profile, Conflicts and Implementation* (Bielefeld [transcript] Verlag 2017) 23, 24 (emphasis in original).

[209] R Dodge and others, 'The Challenge of Defining Wellbeing' (2012) 2(3) Journal of Wellbeing 222, pointing to the necessity to clarify the concept given the increased interest in the measurement of well-being.

[210] See also (n 174).

Article 25

1. Everyone has the right to a standard of living adequate for the health and well-being of himself and of his family, including food, clothing, housing and medical care and necessary social services, and the right to security in the event of unemployment, sickness, disability, widowhood, old age or other lack of livelihood in circumstances beyond his control.

2. Motherhood and childhood are entitled to special care and assistance. All children, whether born in or out of wedlock, shall enjoy the same social protection.

In translating such broad definition into the International Covenant on Economic, Social and Cultural Rights, however, WHO's intervention was met with the ideological divide of the Cold War, preventing its expansive definition and interpretation of the right to health—as enshrined in its Constitution—from being adopted. Instead, article 12 ICESCR constitutes a compromise between US and Soviet proposals: a vague pronouncement on the 'right of everyone to the enjoyment of the highest standard of physical and mental health' and an exemplary listing of specific obligations of medical care.[211] The majority of states felt that the inclusion of the notion of 'social well-being' or any definition of 'health' was either unnecessary or subject to too many uncertainties.[212] A too broad definition would also risk lacking 'clear content and is less likely to have a meaningful effect'.[213] In the case of the SDGs, the broader scope can therefore also be attributed to their nature—the SDGs constitute 'a statement of aspirations: a voluntary agreement rather than a binding treaty'.[214]

As for the more explicit link to human rights, the Resolution accompanying the adoption of the SDGs speaks of a set of 'universal and transformative Goals and targets',[215] emphasizing in several passages the link between the SDGs and achieving 'universal respect for human rights and human dignity',[216] with the Agenda being grounded, among others, in the UDHR and international human rights treaties.[217] The seventeen SDGs are directly enshrined in the Agenda, making their connection with the underlying (human rights) framework more explicit than was the case with regard

---

[211] For a summary of the debate see also Gostin and Meier, 'The Origins of Human Rights in Global Health' (n 32) 32–33.

[212] J Tobin, *The Right to Health in International Law* (OUP 2012) 125; note that also other commentators feel that the notion of 'well-being' as enshrined in WHO's definition of health in its vagueness and broadness constitutes 'an unreasonable standard for human rights, policy and law' (J Ruger, 'Toward a Theory of a Right to Health: Capability and Incompletely Theorized Agreements' (2006) 18 Yale Journal of Law & the Humanities 273, 312).

[213] LO Gostin, 'The Human Right to Health: A Right to the "Highest Attainable Standard of Health' (2001) 31 Hastings Center Report 29, 29.

[214] T Pogge and M Sengupta, 'Assessing the Sustainable Development Goals from a Human Rights Perspective' (2016) 32(2) Journal of International and Comparative Social Policy 83, 83.

[215] UNGA Res 70/1 (25 September 2015) 'Transforming Our World: The 2030 Agenda for Sustainable Development' UN Doc A/RES/70/1, para 2. See, however, E Eckermann, 'SDG 3: A Missed Opportunity to Transform Understanding and Monitoring of Health, Well-Being and Development?' (2018) 13 Applied Research Quality Life 261, arguing that the specific targets contained in SDG 3 do not live up to this aspirational nature. See (n 243).

[216] UNGA Res 70/1 (25 September 2015) 'Transforming Our World: The 2030 Agenda for Sustainable Development' UN Doc A/RES/70/1, para 8.

[217] ibid para 10. See also paras 19 and 20 on the importance of human rights for the achievement of the SDGs.

220 SDG 3

to the Millennium Declaration[218] and the Millennium Development Goals. The latter, notably, were only specified a year after the Millennium Declaration had passed in an attempt to structure development aid flows, and—in contrast to the Declaration—thus lack any reference to human rights.[219]

Notwithstanding this closer link, SDG 3 (as the other goals) is not formulated in a rights-based manner. In fact, of the health-related targets, only target 5.6 ('ensure universal access to sexual and reproductive health and reproductive rights as agreed in accordance with the Programme of Action of the International Conference on Population and Development and the Beijing Platform for Action and the outcome documents of their review conferences') speaks expressly about rights. None of the targets or indicators are framed in human rights language or speak of participatory rights when it comes to introducing or changing policies.[220] For example, target 3.7 ('ensure universal access to sexual and reproductive health-care services, including for family planning, information and education, and the integration of reproductive health into national strategies and programmes') aligns with certain entitlements contained in the right to sexual and reproductive health, particularly when it comes to the element of *accessibility*,[221] but fails to turn beneficiaries/recipients into claim holders.[222] Critical voices have noted that this might be the result of a 'deep tension between presenting moral ambition in the language of (human) rights and presenting them in the language of (development) goals',[223] given that their underlying premise differs—one to be achieved immediately, the other incrementally. However, this also impacts questions of legal enforceability of the standards contained therein as well as the identification of accountable actors.[224] Progress towards the SDGs—and thus also SDG 3—is monitored and reviewed, however this alone does not suffice to 'hold states accountable for their human rights obligations relating to the SDGs'.[225] Hence, this also stands in contrast to the growing role of social rights protection in international human rights law, as well as the increasing justiciability thereof.[226] Moreover, the lack of reflection of explicit human rights language in SDG 3 bears the risk of diluting responsibilities and creating

---

[218] UNGA Res 55/2 (8 September 2000) 'United Nations Millennium Declaration' UN Doc A/RES/55/2 (2000).

[219] Annex to UNGA, 'Road Map towards the Implementation of the United Nations Millennium Declaration—Report of the Secretary-General' (6 September 2001) UN Doc A/56/326. See also Hulme and Scott (n 6) 296ff, explaining how the 'process of creating the MDGs was not premediated or consciously planned—it followed an iterative course across a number of agencies and with no clear start or end'.

[220] See also Chapman (n 24) 1099, 1102.

[221] CESCR 'General Comment No 22: The Right to Sexual and Reproductive Health (2 May 2016) UN Doc E/C.12/GC/22, paras 5, 15 (note that the General Comment was published following the adoption of the SDGs, which it therefore makes references to in para 19).

[222] CE Brolan and others, 'Did the Right to Health Get Across the Line? Examining the United Nations Resolution on the Sustainable Development Goals' (2017) BMJ Global Health 1; see also AE Yamin 'Beyond Compassion: The Central Role of Accountability in Applying a Human Rights Framework to Health' (2008) 10 Health and Human Rights Journal 1.

[223] Pogge and Sengupta (n 215) 84.

[224] See, eg, Buse and Hawkes (n 23) 6.

[225] C Williams and P Hunt, 'Neglecting Human Rights: Accountability, Data and Sustainable Development Goal 3' (2017) 21(8) The International Journal of Human Rights 1114, 1116.

[226] See C Binder and others, 'Introduction to the Research Handbook on International Law and Social Rights' (n 194) xixff; see also Kaltenborn (n 20) 31; see also CESCR 'General Comment No 14: The Right to the Highest Attainable Standard of Health' (11 August 2000) UN Doc E/C.12/2000/4, para 59ff.

a parallel universe of global human health policies. In light of this, scholars warn that governments will place their focus on working towards their quantitative targets which they must report progress on rather than achieving the human rights connection outlined in the preambular paragraphs of the Declaration.[227]

However, despite the lack of explicit human rights language, it has been pointed out that a 'right to health minimalist would argue that so long as UHC is incorporated in SDG metrics ... the right to health is *implicitly* preserved via the inclusion of UHC.'[228] From this viewpoint, given that UHC is reflected in the targets and indicators, and that SDG 3 generally correlates with the content of the right to health as defined by the CESCR in General Comment No 14, SDG 3 is considered to align with and safeguard the right to health.[229] Additionally, target 3.8 (on UHC), as well as targets 3.2, 3.3, and 3.7, have been lauded as among those which strive for full realization or eradication of certain objectives, rather than 'reduction', thereby reflecting the object and purpose of universal human rights more directly.[230] Whether this correlates to a 'shared vision [of the fields of global health and human rights] of global health justice'[231] is, however, subject to debate. Given the varying viewpoints on the true impact and relationship between SDG 3 and the right to health under human rights law, efforts have focused on overcoming the earlier gaps in communication[232] between the MDG process and human rights bodies. For example, the Danish Institute for Human Rights has initiated a data mining project (SDG—Human Rights Data Explorer) that 'links monitoring information from the international human rights system to the Goals and targets of the 2030 Agenda for Sustainable Development',[233] noting that approximately 60 per cent of human rights bodies' recommendations and observations in some way link to SDG targets. In a total of 192,131 recommendations analysed by late 2021, most link to SDG 16 (peace, justice, and strong institutions—57,812), SDG 5 (gender equality—29,797), SDG 10 (inequalities—19,966) and SDG 4 (education—14,938). SDG 3 ranks fifth in this list, with 12,237 links.[234]

Finally, a shortcoming which has not been remedied relates to the largely quantitative indicators implemented within the SDG framework applicable to SDG 3. While the monitoring of some targets has been expanded in practice through the implementation of global agendas or strategies, these only in few circumstances include specific human rights indicators. Nevertheless, the Office of the High Commissioner for Human Rights

---

[227] Brolan and others (n 223) 6.

[228] ibid 3 (emphasis in original), relying on Yamin's maximalist/minimalist framing of the right to health and global public health policy introduced in the 1990s.

[229] According to the supplementary file available in the online version of the article by Brolan and others (n 223) sixty-six SDG targets (40 per cent of the overall targets included in the SDG framework) in fact can be synthesized with the right to health and underlying health determinants (UHDs). This number is significantly larger than other calculations as it includes all aspects related to UHDs as well.

[230] cf Pogge and Sengupta (n 215) 89.

[231] Gostin and Meier, 'The Origins of Human Rights in Global Health' (n 32) 38.

[232] On this, see Alston (n 205) 760ff, noting that neither MDG reports consider human rights aside from fleeting references, nor did human rights bodies pay much attention to the MDGs.

[233] Danish Institute for Human Rights, 'SDG—Human Rights Data Explorer' <https://sdgdata.humanrights.dk/en/what-is-the-upr-sdg-data-explorerA> accessed 18 October 2021.

[234] ibid.

222 SDG 3

(OHCHR) has updated its list of human rights indicators to attempt further alignment with the global indicators contained in the SDG framework.[235]

C. Assessment and General Critique

SDG 3 is recognized as one of the core objectives of Agenda 2030. Having been essential to sustainable development policies for decades, its thirteen targets reflect an ambitious and comprehensive approach to global health policy.

Initially, some stakeholders and states expressed concerns that the limiting of health to one of the seventeen SDGs might weaken the position of health as a priority objective in the post-2015 development agenda.[236] This does not seem to align with observations on a conceptual level. First, the different set-up and purpose of the SDGs certainly justifies health remaining concentrated in one goal. The SDGs are to be seen as a cross-cutting framework, building on interlinkages. Health-related aspects are thus addressed in far more goals than SDG 3 only.[237] And second, SDG 3 is frequently considered as central to ensuring human well-being (alongside SDGs 1, 4, 5, 10, and 16), and is supported by other goals which aim to deliver the well-being goals.[238] Yet, despite such a comprehensive approach, there are still gaps among the targets contained in SDG 3, for example, regarding issues such as anti-microbial resistance (until 2020)[239] or lesbian, gay, bisexual, transgender, intersex, and queer or questioning (LGBTIQ) rights. While the former at least was contained in the Declaration,[240] the latter remains entirely unmentioned. Also, immunization coverage is only covered implicitly through other targets.[241] Finally, what might seem surprising is that even though SDG 3 was negotiated in the context of population dynamics, age is missing among SDG 3's targets. In particular, there is no explicit mention of old age.

On the opposite end, criticism has been raised that there is a gap between the innovative heading of SDG 3 which expressly takes up 'well-being' as a priority, and the agreed upon targets, which fail to live up to this expectation.[242] That is, in comparison to other targets, the majority of health-specific targets contained in SDG 3 'rely on traditional indicators of disease and ill-health rather than promoting positive

---

[235] Divided into structural, process, and outcome indicators, see <http://www.ohchr.org/Documents/Issues/HRIndicators/SDG_Indicators_Tables.pdf> accessed 18 October 2021.

[236] Murray (n 22) 1390–91; Frey (n 25) 423.

[237] RM Fernandez, 'SDG3 Good Health and Well-Being: Integration and Connection with Other SDGs' in WL Filho and others (eds), *Good Health and Well-Being. Encyclopedia of the UN Sustainable Development Goals* (Springer 2019). See also WHO, *Health in 2015* (n 14) 195.

[238] J Waage and Others, 'Governing the UN Sustainable Development Goals: Interactions, Infrastructures, and Institutions' (2015) 3(5) The Lancet Global Health e251.

[239] See below, this chapter, Section IV.B.13, target 3.d.

[240] UNGA Res 70/1 (25 September 2015) 'Transforming Our World: The 2030 Agenda for Sustainable Development' UN Doc A/RES/70/1, para 26.

[241] WHO, *Health in 2015* (n 14) 195.

[242] Eckermann (n 216) 262, who discusses how the aspirational concept might however be located in other SDG targets (in relation to gender or equality).

conceptions of well-being'.[243] Only targets 3.7 (on universal access to sexual and reproductive healthcare services) and 3.8 (on UHC) depart from such traditional conception (as do two of the means of implementation). However, even these two targets do not pursue a 'multi-sectorial and contextual understanding of the promotion of health'.[244] At the same time, scholars have noted that the overall objective of SDG 3 to achieve good health and well-being *for all* remains aspirational and vague, difficult to implement in practice, and does not direct attention to those most in need. This point of inequity is also prevalent in the approach pursued with regard to some targets to move away from percentage-decline targets to absolute thresholds (eg to bring the child mortality rate below twenty-five deaths per 1,000 children), which does not afford adequate consideration to differences between states.[245] This concern is demonstrated in the debate surrounding financing for development. Even though there had been a rapid increase in development assistance for health which was supported with financial and technical means of donor organizations, philanthropic organizations, and partner countries for several years, these numbers have stagnated since 2014,[246] with the 2030 Agenda for Sustainable Development emphasizing that 'each country has primary responsibility for its own economic and social development'.[247] Hence, the 2015 Financing for Development Summit did not contain any specific new financing commitments, even less with regard to health.[248] Several calls have been made for reforms to the health landscape which is subject to numerous overlapping, sometimes however conflicting, policy and financing initiatives, suffering from a lack of coordination and effectiveness.[249]

As discussed below, progress on most health targets has been steady, albeit not sufficient to reach the set targets by 2030. A particular challenge has arisen through the COVID-19 pandemic, which has slowed progress or at times even reversed success. As compiled by the High-Level Political Forum (HLPF), several disruptions to essential health services continue more than a year into the pandemic, especially 'those for mental, neurological and substance use disorders; neglected tropical diseases; tuberculosis; HIV and hepatitis B and C; cancer screening; services for other non-communicable diseases, including hypertension and diabetes; family planning and contraception; urgent dental care; malnutrition; immunization; and malaria'.[250]

---

[243] ibid 262.

[244] ibid 263.

[245] Murray (n 22) 1392; S Rushton, 'Health Rights and Realization—Comments on "Rights Language in the Sustainable Development Agenda: Has Right to Health Discourse and Norms Shaped Health Goals?"' (2016) 5(5) International Journal of Health Policy Management 341, 343.

[246] WHO, *Global Spending on Health 2020: Weathering the Storm* (World Health Organization 2020) 12, showing that external aid in 2018 was down to $16.2 billion from $19.3 billion in 2014.

[247] UNGA Res 70/1 (25 September 2015) 'Transforming Our World: The 2030 Agenda for Sustainable Development' UN Doc A/RES/70/1, para 41.

[248] S Moon and O Omole, 'Development Assistance for Health: Critiques, Proposals and Prospects for Change' (2017) 12 Health Economics, Policy and Law 207, 216; UNGA Res 69/313 (27 July 2015) 'Addis Ababa Action Agenda of the Third International Conference on Financing for Development (Addis Ababa Action Agenda)' UN Doc A/RES/69/313, para 77.

[249] For an excellent overview see Moon and Omole (n 249).

[250] High-Level Political Forum on Sustainable Development (ECOSOC) 'Progress towards the Sustainable Development Goals – Report of the Secretary-General' (30 April 2021) UN Doc E/2021/58, paras 32ff.

224 SDG 3

These disruptions are most likely to persist in the years to come, and as of 2021, reaching the 2030 targets seems unlikely in many instances without significant policy changes.

IV. Targets and Indicators of Goal 3

A. Overview

SDG 3 consists of nine outcome targets and four 'means of implementation'[251] targets. Considering the strong emphasis of the MDGs on health-related goals, SDG 3 consists both of targets which already existed in the MDGs and new targets. The order in which the targets are listed follows no obvious systematic structure, and there is no hierarchy among the targets. As suggested by WHO,[252] it is however possible to divide the targets into one overarching objective (target 3.8 Universal health coverage) and three pillars: Pillar 1 consisting of targets which were already contained in the MDGs (targets 3.1–3.3, 3.7); Pillar 2 consisting of new targets (targets 3.4–3.6, 3.9); and Pillar 3 consisting of the suggested means of implementation (targets 3.a–3.d). Hence, with regard to SDG 3, two levels of targets can be distinguished: the overarching objective of achieving good health for all as transformed most specifically in target 3.8, and specific targets. The special role of UHC can also be seen in the Declaration accompanying the SDGs, where paragraph 26, spelling out the commitments in relation to health, opens with UHC, underscoring that it is essential for the objective of leaving no one behind:

> To promote physical and mental health and well-being, and to extend life expectancy for all, we must achieve universal health coverage and access to quality health care. No one must be left behind.[253]

Additionally, owing to the cross-cutting nature of health, health-related targets stemming from all other SDGs, including SDG 17 ('Revitalize the global partnership for sustainable development') regarding implementation must be considered as well. While the SDG framework is drafted with the full intention of benefitting from such interlinkages, studies show that this is particularly pronounced in the case of SDG 3.[254]

---

[251] Means of implementation are defined by Department of Economic and Social Affairs and the United Nations Development Programme as 'the interdependent mix of financial resources, technology development and transfer, capacity building, inclusive and equitable globalisation and trade, regional integration, as well as the creation of a national enabling environment required to implement the new sustainable development agenda'. UN System Technical Support Team, 'TST Issues Brief on Health and Sustainable Development' (n 82).

[252] WHO, *Health in 2015* (n 14) 196.

[253] UNGA Res 70/1 (25 September 2015) 'Transforming Our World: The 2030 Agenda for Sustainable Development' UN Doc A/RES/70/1, para 26.

[254] For an extensive overview on mapping such interlinkages and previously undertaken studies see LM Fonseca and others, 'Mapping the Sustainable Development Goals Relationships' (2020) 12(8) Sustainability 3359.

The most notable interlinkages, among others, are targets in SDG 1 (eg target 1.1, 'By 2030, eradicate extreme poverty for all people everywhere, currently measured as people living on less than $1.25 a day'), SDG 2 (eg target 2.2, 'By 2030, end all forms of malnutrition, including achieving, by 2025, the internationally agreed targets on stunting and wasting in children under 5 years of age, and address the nutritional needs of adolescent girls, pregnant and lactating women and older person'), SDG 4 (target 4.2, 'By 2030, ensure that all girls and boys have access to quality early childhood development, care and pre-primary education so that they are ready for primary education'), SDG 5 (eg target 5.6, 'Ensure universal access to sexual and reproductive health and reproductive rights as agreed in accordance with the Programme of Action of the International Conference on Population and Development and the Beijing Platform for Action and the outcome documents of their review conference'), and SDG 6 ('By 2030, achieve access to adequate and equitable sanitation and hygiene for all and end open defecation, paying special attention to the needs of women and girls and those in vulnerable situations'). SDG 7 (on energy), SDG 8 (on economic growth and decent work), SDG 9 (on infrastructure, industrialization, and innovation), SDG 11 (on cities and human settlements), SDG 13 (on climate change), and SDG 16 (on peaceful and inclusive societies) also contain relevant targets, relating especially to underlying health determinants.

With regard to the inherited targets from the MDGs, generally significant progress had already been made by 2015. Nevertheless, as also highlighted during the drafting debate in the OWG and later bolstered by data in the MDG Report 2015,[255] often particularly the most vulnerable segments of society had been left behind, including the poorest and those disadvantaged due to their sex, age, disability, ethnicity, or geographic location. Thus, it quickly became clear that the MDGs' unfinished business on health would be carried on beyond 2015.[256]

The four new targets extend the health goal beyond its MDG content. The new targets were owed to the broadening of the scope of attention to other health-related issues such as non-communicable diseases, which were estimated to be the cause of approximately 52 per cent of all deaths under the age of seventy,[257] a proportion expected to grow in coming years due to demographic changes. Additionally, even if adolescents were only mentioned expressly in the context of sexual and reproductive health, the focus on road traffic accidents, prevention and treatment of substance abuse, and mental health are key elements in realizing the right to health for this age group.[258]

[255] UN, 'The Millennium Development Goals Report' (n 12) 8–9, noting in relation to the health-related goals that '[a]bout 16,000 children die each day before celebrating their fifth birthday, mostly from preventable causes. The maternal mortality ratio in the developing regions is 14 times higher than in the developed regions. Just half of pregnant women in the developing regions receive the recommended minimum of four antenatal care visits. Only an estimated 36 per cent of the 31.5 million people living with HIV in the developing regions were receiving ART in 2013.'

[256] WHO, *Health in 2015* (n 14) 73.

[257] ibid 143.

[258] See also UNGA 'Report of the Special Rapporteur on the right of everyone to the enjoyment of the highest attainable standard of physical and mental health' (4 April 2016) UN Doc A/HRC/32/32, focusing on adolescents.

226   SDG 3

The four means of implementation contain suggestions for structural reform and include calls for increased health financing and more research and development to address the major health priorities and challenges of our time.[259] With four means of implementation targets, SDG 3 has more targets of this kind than any other goal (aside from SDG 17 which is wholly dedicated to implementation).

Overall, these targets amount to one of the most specific goals of the SDGs, particularly also due the strong roots stemming from the MDGs' focus on health. What remains open is, for example, how to incorporate health outcomes firmly in non-health-related sectors, as would be necessary for targets on the reduction of traffic accidents or pollution.[260] Additionally, the focus of some targets on global reduction goals—for example, targets 3.1 (reduce the global maternal mortality ratio to less than seventy per 100,000 live births), 3.4 (reduce by one-third premature mortality from NCDs through prevention and treatment and promote mental health and well-being), 3.6 (halve the number of global deaths and injuries from road traffic accidents)—will require considerable adaptation at the national level.[261]

Of the 231 indicators adopted by the United Nations Statistical Commission's Interagency and Expert Group on SDG Indicators (IAEG-SDGs) as of 2021, twenty-eight are directly linked to SDG 3.[262] This is by far the largest number of indicators per goal. The selected indicators have the purpose to monitor progress in the implementation of the SDG's targets. In theory, they are designed to function as management tools for states to develop policies in the respective areas and highlight where more efforts are still needed. However, the selection of indicators was subject to heated discussion. Originally forty-eight global and national indicator candidates had been proposed to monitor the health-related targets.[263] Though this was narrowed down, their suitability was initially partly contested, particularly for failing sufficiently to encourage the use of disaggregated data or explicitly incorporating equity data.[264] Moreover, as was the case with regard to the MDGs, initially a number of the selected health-related indicators were not functional as they lacked sound methodology and significant country coverage. Overall, only half of the proposed indicators in SDG 3 were based on a fully established methodology and sufficient data.[265] This left some targets of SDG 3 without

---

[259] See this chapter, Sections IV.B.10–IV.B.13 on targets 3.a–3.d.

[260] Buse and Hawkes (n 23) 5.

[261] A Scott and P Lucci, 'Universality and Ambition in the Post-2015 Development Agenda: A Comparison of Global and National Targets' (2015) 27 Journal of International Development 752, 753.

[262] The Global Indicator Framework was adopted by the General Assembly in A/RES/71/131 (Annex) but is refined annually. In 2020, a comprehensive review took place (as will happen again in 2026). The most current list can therefore be found online <https://unstats.un.org/sdgs/indicators/indicators-list/> accessed 25 October 2021.

[263] Leadership Council of the Sustainable Development Solutions Network, *Indicators and a Monitoring Framework for the Sustainable Development Goals—Launching a Data Revolution for the SDGs* (12 June 2015) 124ff.

[264] AR Chapman, 'The Problems with the Proposed Indicators for Monitoring Universal Health Coverage in the Sustainable Development Goals' Health and Human Rights Journal (17 March 2016) <https://www.hhrjournal.org/2016/03/the-problems-with-the-proposed-indicators-for-monitoring-universal-health-coverage-in-the-sustainable-development-goals/>.

[265] This is based on the 2016 document compiled by the Secretariat regarding the classification of the SDG indicators into three tiers <http://unstats.un.org/sdgs/files/meetings/iaeg-sdgs-meeting-03/Provisional-Proposed-Tiers-for-SDG-Indicators-24-03-16.pdf> accessed 26 October 2021.

any functioning indicators. For example, with regard to target 3.8 (UHC), the two indicators proposed[266] either had an untested or no methodology or lacked sufficient datasets. Similarly, also target 3.4's indicators[267]—aiming at the reduction of mortality with regard to NCDs and the promotion of mental health—lacked sufficient data for regions outside Europe.[268] The suitability of some indicators to function simultaneously as human rights indicators was and still is strongly contested,[269] though efforts such as the abovementioned SDG—Human Rights Data Explorer convincingly show how to align these two fields.

Thus, as can be seen from Table 3.2, the overwhelming majority (twenty-five of twenty-eight) of these indicators are now classified as Tier I indicators.[270] Indicator 3.d.2—one of the three tier II indicators—was only added in March 2020 to close the important gap concerning antimicrobial resistance (see below, Section IV.B.13, target 3.d).

This set of indicators is complemented by at least twenty-five additional health-related indicators. While there is no official list in this regard, WHO has updated its Global Reference List of 100 Core Health Indicators with a particular emphasis on health-related SDGs, specifying their interlinkages with health. These range from data on disaster-related deaths, the prevalence of under-nourishment or malnutrition, the proportion of women subjected to sexual violence, the proportion of girls and women who have undergone female genital mutilation, the proportion of urban population living in slums, informal settlements, or inadequate housing to data on conflict-related deaths.[271]

A frequent point of criticism with regard to the lack of progress on several MDGs related to the failure to improve the overall performance of health systems. WHO and other organizations such as the World Bank or Gavi (the Vaccine Alliance) have therefore begun focusing on health systems strengthening (HSS), which will be a necessary component in achieving SDG 3 as well.[272]

---

[266] Target 3.8.1. 'Coverage of essential health services'; target 3.8.2. 'Number of people covered by health insurance or a public health system per 1,000 population'.

[267] Target 3.4.1. 'Mortality rate attributed to cardiovascular disease, cancer, diabetes or chronic respiratory disease'; target 3.4.2. 'Suicide mortality rate'.

[268] Provisional Proposed Tiers for Global SDG Indicators (24 March 2016) <http://unstats.un.org/sdgs/files/meetings/iaeg-sdgs-meeting-03/Provisional-Proposed-Tiers-for-SDG-Indicators-24-03-16.pdf> accessed 26 October 2021.

[269] See, eg, the selected indicator on mental health (suicide rates) and the discussion in Section IV.B.4 of this chapter on target 3.4. In the context of sexual and reproductive health rights, see Yamin, 'Power, Politics and Knowledge Claims' (n 96); more generally with regard to SDG 3, see Williams and Hunt (n 226) 1114.

[270] UN Statistical Commission, 'Tier Classification for Global SDG Indicators' (as of March 2021) <https://unstats.un.org/sdgs/files/Tier%20Classification%20of%20SDG%20Indicators_29%20Mar%202021_web.pdf> accessed 20 October 2021 2: 'Tier I: Indicator is conceptually clear, has an internationally established methodology and standards are available, and data are regularly produced by countries for at least 50 per cent of countries and of the population in every region where the indicator is relevant. Tier II: Indicator is conceptually clear, has an internationally established methodology and standards are available, but data are not regularly produced by countries'.

[271] WHO, *Global Reference List of 100 Core Health Indicators (Plus Health-Related SDGs)* (2nd edn, World Health Organization 2018) WHO/HIS/IER/GPM/2018.1 (Annex I).

[272] G Seidman, 'Does SDG 3 Have an Adequate Theory of Change for Improving Health Systems Performance?' (2017) 8 Journal of Global Health 2.

228   SDG 3

Table 3.2 SDG 3 Targets and indicators, classification

Goal 3. Ensure healthy lives and promote well-being for all at all ages

3.1 By 2030, reduce the global maternal mortality ratio to less than 70 per 100,000 live births	3.1.1 Maternal mortality ratio	Tier I
	3.1.2 Proportion of births attended by skilled health personnel	Tier I
3.2 By 2030, end preventable deaths of newborns and children under 5 years of age, with all countries aiming to reduce neonatal mortality to at least as low as 12 per 1,000 live births and under-5 mortality to at least as low as 25 per 1,000 live births	3.2.1 Under-5 mortality rate	Tier I
	3.2.2 Neonatal mortality rate	Tier I
3.3 By 2030, end the epidemics of AIDS, tuberculosis, malaria, and neglected tropical diseases and combat hepatitis, water-borne diseases, and other communicable diseases	3.3.1 Number of new HIV infections per 1,000 uninfected population, by sex, age, and key populations	Tier I
	3.3.2 Tuberculosis incidence per 100,000 population	Tier I
	3.3.3 Malaria incidence per 1,000 population	Tier I
	3.3.4 Hepatitis B incidence per 100,000 population	Tier I
	3.3.5 Number of people requiring interventions against neglected tropical diseases	Tier I
3.4 By 2030, reduce by one third premature mortality from non-communicable diseases through prevention and treatment and promote mental health and well-being	3.4.1 Mortality rate attributed to cardiovascular disease, cancer, diabetes, or chronic respiratory disease	Tier I
	3.4.2 Suicide mortality rate	Tier I
3.5 Strengthen the prevention and treatment of substance abuse, including narcotic drug abuse and harmful use of alcohol	3.5.1 Coverage of treatment interventions (pharmacological, psychosocial and rehabilitation and aftercare services) for substance use disorders	Tier II
	3.5.2 Alcohol per capita consumption (aged 15 years and older) within a calendar year in litres of pure alcohol	Tier I
3.6 By 2020, halve the number of global deaths and injuries from road traffic accidents	3.6.1 Death rate due to road traffic injuries	Tier I
3.7 By 2030, ensure universal access to sexual and reproductive healthcare services, including for family planning, information and education, and the integration of reproductive health into national strategies and programmes	3.7.1 Proportion of women of reproductive age (aged 15–49 years) who have their need for family planning satisfied with modern methods	Tier I
	3.7.2 Adolescent birth rate (aged 10–14 years; aged 15–19 years) per 1,000 women in that age group	Tier I

Table 3.2 Continued

Goal 3. Ensure healthy lives and promote well-being for all at all ages

3.8 Achieve universal health coverage, including financial risk protection, access to quality essential healthcare services and access to safe, effective, quality, and affordable essential medicines and vaccines for all	3.8.1 Coverage of essential health services (updated in April 2018 and then again in March 2020, accepting the 14 tracer indicators mentioned below)	Tier I
	3.8.2 Proportion of population with large household expenditures on health as a share of total household expenditure or income	Tier I
3.9 By 2030, substantially reduce the number of deaths and illnesses from hazardous chemicals and air, water, and soil pollution and contamination	3.9.1 Mortality rate attributed to household and ambient air pollution	Tier I
	3.9.2 Mortality rate attributed to unsafe water, unsafe sanitation and lack of hygiene (exposure to unsafe Water, Sanitation and Hygiene for All (WASH) services)	Tier I
	3.9.3 Mortality rate attributed to unintentional poisoning	Tier I
3.a Strengthen the implementation of the World Health Organization Framework Convention on Tobacco Control in all countries, as appropriate	3.a.1 Age-standardized prevalence of current tobacco use among persons aged 15 years and older	Tier I
3.b Support the research and development of vaccines and medicines for the communicable and non-communicable diseases that primarily affect developing countries, provide access to affordable essential medicines and vaccines, in accordance with the Doha Declaration on the TRIPS Agreement and Public Health, which affirms the right of developing countries to use to the full the provisions in the Agreement on Trade-Related Aspects of Intellectual Property Rights regarding flexibilities to protect public health, and, in particular, provide access to medicines for all	3.b.1 Proportion of the target population covered by all vaccines included in their national programme	Tier I
	3.b.2 Total net official development assistance to medical research and basic health sectors	Tier I
	3.b.3 Proportion of health facilities that have a core set of relevant essential medicines available and affordable on a sustainable basis	Tier II
3.c Substantially increase health financing and the recruitment, development, training, and retention of the health workforce in developing countries, especially in least developed countries and small island developing states	3.c.1 Health worker density and distribution	Tier I
3.d Strengthen the capacity of all countries, in particular developing countries, for early warning, risk reduction and management of national and global health risks	3.d.1 International Health Regulations (IHR) capacity and health emergency preparedness	Tier I
	3.d.2 Percentage of bloodstream infections due to selected antimicrobial-resistant organisms	Tier II

B. Commentary and Critique to Individual Targets

1. Target 3.1 By 2030, reduce the global maternal mortality ratio to less than 70 per 100,000 live births

a) Sources of target

Target 3.1 is one of the targets carried over from the MDGs (Goal 5: Improvement of maternal health, target 5.a: Reduce the maternal mortality ratio by 75 per cent). Even though progress had been made, the ratio on average was brought down by only 44 per cent. The target was, however, formulated in more ambitious terms in the SDG framework, aiming to reduce the global maternal mortality ratio (MMR) down to 70/ 100,000 live births. Translated into practical terms at the country level, this means that '*all* countries should reduce MMR by at least two thirds of their 2010 baseline level'.[273] The supplementary national target is that '*no* country should have an MMR greater than 140/100 000 live births ... by 2030'.[274]

The target of reducing maternal mortality has a long history. Maternal health was already a topic in the League of Nations era when its Health Section identified the issue as a global concern following huge improvements in medical programmes regarding maternal health in Western Europe and the United States. Many of these countries considered possibilities of transfers of the benefits of medical progress to their colonial territories, though in practice this was met with considerable opposition.[275] WHO's Constitution nevertheless included among WHO's functions 'to promote maternal and child health and welfare'.[276]

In 1974, the UN adopted the World Population Plan of Action at its World Population Conference held in Bucharest, defining among the goals: 'to reduce mortality levels, particularly infant and maternal mortality levels, to the maximum extent possible in all regions of the world and to reduce national and sub national differentials therein'.[277] Maternal and child health also became an integral part of WHO's 'Health for All' Strategy (to be implemented by 2000).[278] In terms of implementation and funding, initially maternal mortality initially received less funding than child health interventions.[279] Greater momentum however began building through the United Nations Decade for Women (1976–1985), and the adoption of the 1979 Convention on the

---

[273] WHO, 'Strategies toward Ending Preventable Maternal Mortality (EPMM)' (2015) 6 (emphasis in original).

[274] ibid (emphasis in original).

[275] C AbouZahr, 'Safe Motherhood: A Brief History of the Global Movement 1947–2002' (2003) 67 British Medical Bulletin 13, 14.

[276] Art 2(l) Constitution of the World Health Organization (adopted 22 July 1946, entered into force 7 April 1948) 14 UNTS 185.

[277] United Nations Population Information Network (POPIN), UN Population Division, DESA and UNFPA, 'World Population Plan of Action' (August 1974) UN Doc E_CONF.60_19_Plan, para 22.

[278] A-B Moller and others, 'Monitoring Maternal and Newborn Health Outcomes Globally: A Brief History of Key Events and Initiatives' (2019) 24 Tropical Medicine and International Health 1342, 1348.

[279] A Rosenfeld and D Maine, 'Maternal Mortality—A Neglected Tragedy. Where is the M in MCH?' (1985) 13(2) The Lancet 83.

Elimination of All Forms of Discrimination against Women (CEDAW)[280] which stipulated in Article 12 the obligation of all states to 'take all appropriate measures to eliminate discrimination against women in the field of health care in order to ensure, on a basis of equality of men and women, access to health care services, including those related to family planning'.[281] Shortly thereafter, WHO began systematically to publish data on maternal mortality,[282] followed by the launching of the Safe Motherhood Initiative, which called upon states to reduce maternal mortality by 50 per cent by the year 2000.[283]

With the issue having been placed on the international agenda, it was also re-emphasized at several of the World Summit Conferences in the 1990s,[284] eventually being taken up in the OECD development goals,[285] and then the MDGs, extending the target periods until 2015.

b) Empirical analysis and efforts of international/domestic implementation

In 2010, the Global Strategy for Women's and Children's Health was launched by the UN Secretary-General. It was updated in 2015 to incorporate the SDG framework, now termed Global Strategy for Women's, Children's Health and Adolescents' Health 2016–2030.[286] The strategy pursues a multisectoral approach, and relies on sixteen key indicators (largely aligned with the SDG indicator framework) as well as another forty-four technical indicators, far exceeding health service provision.[287] It has been pointed out that the extensive monitoring can easily bring some states to the limits of their analytical capacity.[288]

The most recent comparative data sets—from 2017—show that an average of 211 maternal deaths per 100,000 live births were recorded. While this considerably lower than in 2000 (342/100,000), as of 2021, projections are sceptical that target 3.1 will be

---

[280] Convention on the Elimination of All Forms of Discrimination against Women (CEDAW) (adopted 18 December 1979, entered into force 3 September 1981) 1249 UNTS 13.

[281] Art 12 CEDAW.

[282] 'Maternal Mortality: Helping Women Off the Road to Death' (1986) 40(5) WHO Chronicle 175.

[283] WHO 'Maternal Mortality: Looking Back and Moving Forward' (WHO, 10 February 2017) <http://www.who.int/reproductivehealth/topics/maternal_perinatal/maternal-mortality-looking-back/en/> accessed 15 October 2021.

[284] Particularly the 1994 International Conference on Population and Development (Cairo) and the 1995 Fourth World Conference on Women (Beijing): 'strengthen and reorient health services, particularly primary health care, in order to ensure universal access to quality health services for women and girls; reduce ill health and maternal morbidity and achieve world wide the agreed-upon goal of reducing maternal mortality by at least 50 per cent of the 1990 levels by the year 2000 and a further one half by the year 2015; ensure that the necessary services are available at each level of the health system and make reproductive health care accessible, through the primary health-care system, to all individuals of appropriate ages as soon as possible and no later than the year 2015'.

[285] DAC, Shaping the 21st Century (n 6).

[286] UN Every Woman, Every Child (UNEWEC), 'The Global Strategy for Women's, Children's and Adolescents' Health (2016–2030)' <http://www.who.int/life-course/partners/global-strategy/globalstrategyreport2016-2030-lowres.pdf?ua=1> accessed 15 October 2021.

[287] UN Every Woman, Every Child (UNEWEC), 'Indicator and Monitoring Framework for the Global Strategy for Women's, Children's and Adolescents' Health (2016–2030)' (2016) <http://www.who.int/life-course/publications/gs-Indicator-and-monitoring-framework.pdf> accessed 15 October 2021 (twenty-six of these indicators are not proposed for the SDG process).

[288] T Boerma and others, 'Reaching all Women, Children, and Adolescents with Essential Health Interventions by 2030: A Marathon that Requires a Concerted Effort' (2020) 368 British Medical Journal 1.

reached,[289] even more so in light of the COVID-19 pandemic.[290] Particularly struggling are the low- to middle-income countries (LMICs), and among them the Sub-Saharan African region (542/100,000), whereas high-income countries average at an MMR of 11/100,000.[291] From all mortality rates, this is the largest disparity between high- and lower-income countries[292] and signifies large inequalities in access to high-quality health services.[293] As reported by several low-income states on maternal, child, and newborn health, challenges persist, particularly given a lack of skilled health personnel, malnutrition, poor economic and social status, low accessibility in rural communities and remote areas, and insufficient or delayed transportation, inadequate public health-care financing, limited access to information on family planning, and traditional or religious barriers.[294] Additional factors such as the unequal status of women and girls, lack of access to knowledge, decision-making, and financial power aggravate these factors.[295] Regional programmes such as the Campaign on Accelerated Reduction of Maternal Mortality in Africa (CARMMA), launched in 2009 by the African Union, have however achieved some success by introducing the reduction of MMR as a high-level policy initiative in states such as Rwanda[296] and Zambia,[297] setting these countries on track to meet the target.

Target 3.1 is measured by two of the indicators (MMR and the proportion of births attended by skilled health personnel) used under the MDG framework for target 5.a.[298] While the indicators have been in use for a long period, data collection has proven challenging, and the monitoring is widely considerd 'one of the most complicated health indicators within global frameworks'.[299] Data on the proportion of births attended by skilled health personnel are managed by UNICEF and WHO jointly.

c) Critique

Alongside the above-mentioned obstacles on monitoring MMR, challenges for reliable data arise given the divergences among standardization of professional titles and

---

[289] WHO, *World Health Statistics 2021—Monitoring Health for the SDGs, Sustainable Development Goals* (World Health Organization 2021) 21.

[290] High-Level Political Forum on Sustainable Development (ECOSOC), 'Progress towards the Sustainable Development Goals—Report of the Secretary-General' (30 April 2021) UN Doc E/2021/58, para 33.

[291] Note, however, also these countries have not reduced their MMR by at least two-thirds of their 2010 baseline level.

[292] Moller and others (n 279) 1343.

[293] WHO 'Maternal Mortality Factsheet' (19 September 2019) <http://www.who.int/news-room/fact-sheets/detail/maternal-mortality> accessed 28 October 2021.

[294] DSD and DESA, '2017 Voluntary National Reviews—Synthesis Report' (UN 2018) 10.

[295] WHO and others, *2017 HLPF Thematic Review of SDG 3: Ensure Healthy Lives and Promote Well-Being for All at All Ages* (WHO 2017) 2–3.

[296] PSR Gurusamy and P Darshene Janagaraj, 'A Success Story: The Burden of Maternal, Neonatal and Childhood Mortality in Rwanda—Critical Appraisal of Interventions and Recommendations for the Future' (2018) 22 African Journal of Reproductive Health 9.

[297] A Evans, 'Amplifying Accountability by Benchmarking Results District and National Levels' (2018) 36 Development Policy Review 221.

[298] United Nations Statistics Division, 'Official List of MDG Indicators (as of 15 January 2008) <https://unstats.un.org/unsd/mdg/Host.aspx?Content=Indicators/OfficialList.htm> accessed 28 October 2021.

[299] WHO, 'Indicator Metadata Registry List—Materan Mortality Ratio (per 100 000 Live Births)' <https://www.who.int/data/gho/indicator-metadata-registry/imr-details/26> accessed 14 March 2023.

functions of healthcare providers.[300] As a response to this challenge, the UN's Maternal Mortality Estimation Inter-Agency Group was established in 2010, composed of WHO, UNICEF, UNFPA, the World Bank Group, and UNPD. The group works towards harmonizing data and improving measurement methods.[301] Examples of success (Rwanda, Zambia) show that accurate data increase accountability, thereby enhancing the effectiveness of implementation measures.

2. Target 3.2 By 2030, end preventable deaths of newborns and children under 5 years of age, with all countries aiming to reduce neonatal mortality to at least as low as 12 per 1,000 live births and under-5 mortality to at least as low as 25 per 1,000 live births

a) Sources of target

As with target 3.1, target 3.2 goes back to the MDG framework (Goal 4: reduction of the under-five mortality rate by two-thirds in the period between 1990 and 2015). By 2015, the mortality rate had dropped by more than half to about forty-three deaths/ 1,000 live births.[302] As mentioned above,[303] target 3.2 was the only target in SDG 3 that was refined throughout the intergovernmental negotiation process as it was originally adopted without any numerical target. UNICEF had suggested using the 'A Promised Renewed'[304] targets, which was eventually followed.

There are many similarities in the historical development and focus on child health to what has just been stated under target 3.1, with global awareness and tracking picking up particularly through the 1970s. In comparison to maternal health, however, child health interventions received funding by international agencies much faster,[305] with UNICEF playing an increasingly prominent role.

Specific goal setting commenced at the 1990 World Summit for Children which proclaimed a series of important targets for the development agenda, among others concerning child survival and child health. Aside from calling for the adoption of the Convention on the Rights of the Child, which has become by far the most ratified international human rights treaty with near universal membership,[306] the Plan of Action set a series of goals to be reached by the year 2000. These included the 'reduction of 1990 under-5 mortality rates by one third to a level of 70 per 1,000 live births, whichever is the greater reduction', supported by a series of actions to reach this.[307] This was later extended by the 1994 International Conference on Population and Development

---

[300] SDG Indicator Metadata (16 February 2021) <https://unstats.un.org/sdgs/metadata/files/Metadata-03-01-02.pdf> accessed 23 October 2021.

[301] WHO and others, *Trends in Maternal Mortality 2000–2017—Estimates by WHO, UNICEF, UNFPA, World Bank Group and the United Nations Population Division* (WHO 2019).

[302] UN, 'The Millennium Development Goals Report' (n 12) 5.

[303] See Section II.B.2, this chapter.

[304] Based on a global partnership initiative aimed at ending preventable child and maternal deaths, under the auspices of UNICEF.

[305] Moller and others (n 279) 1348.

[306] As of October 2021, only the United States has not ratified the treaty. See UN Human Rights Treaty Bodies, 'Ratification Status for CRC' <https://tbinternet.ohchr.org/_layouts/15/TreatyBodyExternal/Treaty.aspx?Treaty= CRC&Lang=en> accessed 25 October 2021.

[307] UNGA 'World Declaration on the Survival, Protection and Development of Children, and Plan of Action for Implementing the World Declaration on the Survival, Protection and Development of Children in the 1990s' (18 October 1990) UN Doc A/45/625.

234   SDG 3

(Cairo) to 2015, by which time states should have achieved an infant mortality rate below thirty-five per 1,000 live births and an under-five mortality rate below forty-five per 1,000.

Despite the abovementioned progress on reduction of under-five mortality, it was undisputed to include child health in the SDG framework. UNICEF had suggested placing a stronger focus on the most vulnerable children and particularly the girl child. However, the OWG did not follow this suggestion, instead simply remaining focused on lowering child mortality.[308] In contrast to target 3.1, there is no distinction between the global ratio and national targets.

In comparison to child health, neonatal mortality did not receive as much immediate attention. Even though WHO had begun raising awareness throughout the 1990s and urging for this area to receive more attention, it was not addressed in the MDG framework.[309] This was considered a 'crucial omission in global health research and policy',[310] prompting renewed emphasis on including the issue among development targets.[311] It has been argued that this was owed first to it not being considered a social justice issue as was the case with regard to maternal survival; secondly, it falling between the two advocacy fractions of 'maternal health' and 'child health'; and thirdly, a widespread (but flawed) assumption that it would in any case already be covered by the other two issues.[312] The lack in focus has, however, slowly been rectified over the years, in part also due to network expansion. During the SDG drafting process, new initiatives such as the 2014 'Every Newborn Action Plan'—which was endorsed by the WHA[313]—could successfully lobby to include the reduction of neonatal mortality into SDG target 3.2.[314] Early estimates (see next section) show that the express inclusion in the SDG framework has increased the speed of decline on neonatal mortality, even though the highest probability of dying still exists for newborns.

b) Empirical analysis and efforts of international/domestic implementation
Target 3.2 is measured by two indicators (the under-five mortality rate and the neonatal mortality rate).[315] Since 2010, the UN Inter-Agency Group for Child Mortality Estimation (UN IGME), which is led by UNICEF and WHO, is responsible for tracking and estimating on these indicators. This is essential given the wide prevalence of incomplete or delayed registration data in many countries. In 2020, they estimated that in 2019 the global under-five mortality rate had fallen to 38/1,000 live births from 76/

---

[308] Chapman (n 24) 1101.

[309] Moller and others (n 279) 1354.

[310] See the Lancet series on 'Neonatal Survival' (5 March 2005).

[311] See also Resolution WHA58.31 'Working Towards Universal Coverage of Maternal, Newborn and Child Health Interventions' (May 2005).

[312] SK Smith and J Shiffman, 'Setting the Global Health Agenda: The Influence of Advocates and Ideas on Political Priority for Maternal and Newborn Survival' (2016) 166 Social Science & Medicine 86.

[313] Endorsed by the Resolution WHA67.10 'Newborn Health Action Plan' (24 May 2014).

[314] Smith and Shiffman (n 313) 91.

[315] MDG 4 had also included the additional indicator of 'proportion of 1 year-old children immunized against measles'. This has been expanded to include also other vaccinations and is now included in the means of implementation target 3.b, particularly indicator 3.b.1.

1,000 in 2000, and the neonatal morality rate to 17/1,000 live births from 30/1,000 in 2000.[316]

There have been consistent calls for improvements to the datasets,[317] and particularly the use of disaggregated data 'on the basis of all grounds of discrimination prohibited by international human rights law',[318] however despite work by the IAEG-SGD to provide support in gathering more disaggregated data, progress on this is slow. For instance, while target 3.2 considers age and (partially) sex, it does not (yet) include categories such as income (wealth), geographical local, ethnicity, and migrant status.[319]

That said, UNICEF has gone to great lengths in aligning the SDGs related to children with obligations contained in the CRC. In relation to SDG 3, it has highlighted interlinkages with the Preamble, articles 1–7, 13, 17, 19, 23–25, 27, 29, 31–33.[320] In particular, article 24 CRC on the right of the child to the enjoyment of the highest attainable standard of health[321] is relevant, but also the Convention's emphasis on well-being, the right to life, a full and decent life, and mental health are pertinent.

Measuring target 3.2 also serves as a good indicator of the overall state of the health system as well as the socio-economic progress of a country.[322]

---

[316] UNICEF, WHO, World Bank Group and United Nations, *Levels & Trends in Child Mortality—Report 2020, Estimates Developed by the UN Inter-Agency Group for Child Mortality Estimation* (United Nations Children's Fund 2020).

[317] See also Moller and others (n 279) 1359–60.

[318] Chapman (n 24) 1101.

[319] See Asian Development Bank, *Practical Guidebook on Data Disaggregation for the Sustainable Development Goals* (ADB May 2021).

[320] M Wernham, *Mapping the Global Goals for Sustainable Development and the Convention on the Rights of the Child* (UNICEF 2019) <http://www.unicef.org/media/60231/file> accessed 28 October 2021 (10f).

[321] Convention on the Rights of the Child (adopted 20 November 1989, entered into force 2 September 1990) 1577 UNTS 3, art 24:

1. States Parties recognize the right of the child to the enjoyment of the highest attainable standard of health and to facilities for the treatment of illness and rehabilitation of health. States Parties shall strive to ensure that no child is deprived of his or her right of access to such health care services.

2. States Parties shall pursue full implementation of this right and, in particular, shall take appropriate measures:

    (a) To diminish infant and child mortality;

    (b) To ensure the provision of necessary medical assistance and health care to all children with emphasis on the development of primary health care;

    (c) To combat disease and malnutrition, including within the framework of primary health care, through, inter alia, the application of readily available technology and through the provision of adequate nutritious foods and clean drinking-water, taking into consideration the dangers and risks of environmental pollution;

    (d) To ensure appropriate pre-natal and post-natal health care for mothers;

    (e) To ensure that all segments of society, in particular parents and children, are informed, have access to education and are supported in the use of basic knowledge of child health and nutrition, the advantages of breastfeeding, hygiene and environmental sanitation and the prevention of accidents;

    (f) To develop preventive health care, guidance for parents and family planning education and services.

3. States Parties shall take all effective and appropriate measures with a view to abolishing traditional practices prejudicial to the health of children.

4. States Parties undertake to promote and encourage international co-operation with a view to achieving progressively the full realization of the right recognized in the present article. In this regard, particular account shall be taken of the needs of developing countries.

[322] Y Sanyang, 'Prevalence of Under-Five Years of Age Mortality by Infectious Diseases in West African Region' (2019) 11 International Journal of Africa Nursing Sciences 1.

236   SDG 3

The 'Every Newborn Action Plan' (ENAP) sets out recommendations for states on how to achieve the set indicators. These are implemented by states in their national action plans. As of 2020, more than ninety states were implementing the ENAP recommendations. To support states, an 'Every Newborn Tracking Tool' was developed which not only monitors progress towards the SDG's target on child health but also tracks the implementation of specific policies and programmes.[323] Almost all countries with the highest burden of newborn mortality have completed and set up such an action plan or strengthened existing components.[324]

c) Critique

A crucial omission relates to the fact that despite efforts, stillbirths have still not been included among the SDG targets and indicators.[325] However, the indicator and monitoring framework for the Global Strategy for Women's, Children's and Adolescents' Health (2016–2030) includes the stillbirth rate (as well as an adolescent rate, which has also not been included). Additionally, in 2020, the first report by the UN Inter-Agency Group for Child Mortality Estimation focusing on stillbirths was published, pointing to the need to overcome challenges towards progress and the disregard by many policy instruments.[326] A stillborn rate of less than ten in 1,000 births by 2035 has been suggested.[327]

3. Target 3.3 By 2030, end the epidemics of AIDS, tuberculosis, malaria and neglected tropical diseases and combat hepatitis, water-borne diseases and other communicable diseases

a) Sources of target

Target 3.3 was the third MDG goal carried over (MDG 6 on combating of HIV/AIDS, malaria, and other diseases: target 6.a, Have halted by 2015 and begun to reverse the spread of AIDS; target 6.b, Achieve, by 2010, universal access to treatment for HIV/ AIDS for all those who need it; target 6.c, Have halted by 2015 and begun to reverse the incidence of malaria and other major diseases) into SDG 3.

MDG 6 had been met,[328] warranting a far more ambitious approach when drafting the SDGs. This it was extended by specifically including tuberculosis (which formally was only mentioned as an indicator), neglected tropical diseases, viral hepatitis, and water-borne diseases (which includes, eg, diarrhoeal diseases). In addition, the approach has changed from 'controlling' to 'ending' communicable diseases/the epidemics.[329] The new global target is owed particularly to the previously agreed targets by

---

[323] WHO and UNICEF, *Ending Preventable Newborn Deaths and Stillbirths by 2030—Moving Faster Towards High-Quality Universal Health Coverage in 2020–2025* (WHO July 2020) 7.

[324] An overview of the details of such initiatives can be found at <http://www.healthynewbornnetwork.org/countries/> accessed 27 December 2021.

[325] Moller and others (n 279) 1355–56.

[326] UNICEF and others, 'A Neglected Tragedy—The Global Burden of Stillbirths. Report of the UN Inter-Agency Group for Child Mortality Estimation, 2020' (United Nations 2020).

[327] For more information see <https://alignmnh.org/issue/global-mnh-targets/> accessed 27 October 2021.

[328] UN, 'The Millennium Development Goals Report' (n 12) 44.

[329] WHO, *Health in 2015* (n 14) 102.

the WHA[330] and the UNAIDS Programme Coordination Board.[331] Target 3.3 reflects the persisting vertical approach previously followed in many health-related development programmes. So far, as pointed out in the context of HIV treatment, there are however no clear paths forward from reaching the 2030 objectives, that is, turning the epidemics into endemics which will require continued intervention measures, and how to integrate this more specifically into UHC.[332]

As mentioned, the first three diseases—AIDS, tuberculosis, and malaria—were part of MDG 6. Ending the epidemic of AIDS by 2030 in practice has been defined by the Fast Track: Ending the AIDS Epidemic by 2030 strategy (now succeeded by the 2025 AIDS TARGETS strategy) to mean 'ending AIDS as a public health threat' by reducing HIV incidence and mortality by 90 per cent by 2030 (from the 2010 baseline).[333] This is monitored by ten targets, particularly the 95–95–95 treatment targets for 2025 (95 per cent of people living with HIV knowing their HIV status, 95 per cent of people who know their status receiving treatment, and 95 per cent of people on HIV treatment having a suppressed viral load so their immune system remains strong and they are no longer infectious).[334] This set of additional targets is essential as the SDG framework simply measures the number of new HIV infections per 1,000 uninfected population, by sex, age, and key populations (indicator 3.3.1). In comparison, MDG 6 had relied on five different indicators.[335]

As regards tuberculosis (TB), the End TB Strategy has translated this into reducing the TB incidence by 80 per cent, TB deaths by 90 per cent, and by eliminating catastrophic costs for TB-affected households by 2030.[336] This acknowledges that TB constitutes primarily a development challenge rather than being simply a public health concern, and thereby increases existing inequalities. Thus, the social and environmental determinants of TB require a multisectoral approach.[337] There are essential links to target 3.8 but also to research and innovation.[338]

Ending the epidemic of malaria similarly relies on the global strategy developed by WHO on combatting malaria by 2030.[339] This defines the global targets of reducing malaria mortality rates and the malaria case incidence by 90 per cent by 2030. Additionally, it sets out to eliminate malaria in at least thirty-five countries in which malaria was transmitted in 2015 and to prevent any re-establishment in countries which are malaria-free.[340]

---

[330] See, eg, in regard to NTDs WHA66.12 'Neglected Tropical Diseases' (27 May 2013).

[331] See, eg, UNAIDS Programme Coordinating Board 'Update on the AIDS response in the post-2015 development agenda' (5 June 2014) UNAIDS/PCB (34)/14.4.

[332] Y Assefa and CF Gils, 'Ending the Epidemic of HIV/AIDS by 2030: Will There be an Endgame to HIV, or an Endemic HIV Requiring an Integrated Health Systems Response in Many Countries?' (2020) 100 International Journal of Infectious Diseases 373.

[333] UNAIDS, 'Fast-Track: Ending the AIDS Epidemic by 2030' (UNAIDS 2014) 6.

[334] UNAIDS, *Prevailing against Pandemics by Putting People the Centre* (UNAIDS 2020).

[335] See (n 360) this chapter.

[336] WHO, 'The End TB Strategy' (WHO 2015).

[337] K Lönnroth and M Raviglione, 'The WHO's New End TB Strategy in the Post-2015 Era of the Sustainable Development Goals' (2016) 110 Transactions of the Royal Society of Tropical Medicine and Hygiene 148.

[338] WHO, 'The End TB Strategy' (n 337) 9–10.

[339] WHO, 'Global Technical Strategy for Malaria 2016–2030' (WHO 2021).

[340] ibid Table 1.

The explicit inclusion of neglected tropical diseases (NTDs)[341] can be seen as directly linked to the overall objective of the SDGs to 'leave no-one behind'. They affect 'the poorest and most marginalized populations'.[342] The term itself was suggested in the early 2000s to encapsulate diseases sharing 'two distinct landscapes: a social landscape (poverty) and a geographical landscape (of burden entrenched in tropical countries)'.[343] Still, their inclusion among the indicators was almost overlooked and it was only late in the process that the IAEG-SDGs added it.[344] As was critically observed by Ayenew Addisu et al, the use of the term 'neglected' comes with a 'negative and disempowering connotation'[345] and reflects the 'low profile and status in public health priorities'[346] of those already among the poorest and most marginalized. Hence, it was not until 2012 that WHO published a first roadmap on the prevention and control of NTDs ('Accelerating Work to Overcome the Global Impact of Neglected Tropical Diseases'). With this marked shift, however, by 2020 600 million fewer people require interventions than in 2012.[347] There is a strong link between NTDs and other SDGs and 'successful interventions against NTDs contribution to meeting other SDGs'[348] (such as SDGs 1, 2, 6, 8, etc).[349] A particular strong relationship exists with UHC (target 3.8) given that NTDs constitute 'important tracers for identifying disparities in progress towards both universal health coverage and equitable access to high-quality health services'.[350]

The objective of combatting (viral) hepatitis was newly added in SDG 3. Estimates calculate that viral hepatitis infections taken together lead to a similar mortality rate as HIV. In light thereof, there was some criticism that target 3.3 merely speaks of 'combatting' and not ending hepatitis, which—unlike HIV—is curable (Hepatitis C virus) or can even be prevented with a vaccine (Hepatitis B virus).[351] However, WHO's 'Global Health Sector Strategy on Viral Hepatitis 2016–2021',[352] building on WHA67.6,[353]

---

[341] The category now encompasses twenty diseases (originally seventeen): Buruli ulcer; Chagas disease; Dengue and chikungunya; Dracunculiasis; Echinococcus; Foodborne trematodiases; Human African trypanosomiasis; Leishmaniasis; leprosy; Lymphatic filariasis; Mycetoma; chromoblastomycosis and other deep mycoses; Onchocerciasis; Rabies; Scabies and other ectoparasitoses; Schistosomiasis; Soil-transmitted helminthiases; Snakebite envenoming; Taeniasis and cysticercosis; Trachoma; Yaws.

[342] C Fitzpatrick and D Engels, 'Leaving No One Behind: A Neglected Tropical Disease Indicator and Tracers for the Sustainable Development Goals' (2016) 8 (Suppl 1) International Health 15.

[343] MN Malecela, 'Reflections on the Decade of the Neglected Tropical Diseases' (2019) 11(5) International Health 338, 338.

[344] Dirk Engels, 'Neglected Tropical Diseases in the Sustainable Development Goals' (2016) 367(10015) Lancet 223.

[345] A Addisu and others, 'Neglected Tropical Diseases and the Sustainable Development Goals: An Urgent Call for Action from the Front Line' (2019) BMJ Global Health 1.

[346] ibid.

[347] WHO, 'Ending the Neglect to Attain the Sustainable Development Goals—A Road Map for Neglected Tropical Diseases 2021–2030' (WHO 2020).

[348] SDG Indicator Metadata (7 February 2021) <https://unstats.un.org/sdgs/metadata/files/Metadata-03-03-05.pdf> accessed 23 October 2021.

[349] On the cross-cutting nature see also M Bangert and others, 'The Cross-Cutting Contribution of the End of Neglected Tropical Diseases to the Sustainable Development Goals' (2017) 6(73) Infectious Diseases of Poverty 1.

[350] WHO, Ending the Neglect to Attain the Sustainable Development Goals (n 348 x.

[351] JV Lazarus, 'Hepatitis and the Sustainable Development Goals: Time for An End Run' (BCM On Health, 28 September 2015) <https://blogs.biomedcentral.com/on-health/2015/09/28/hepatitis-sustainable-development-goals-time-end-run/> accessed 29 October 2021.

[352] WHO, 'Global Health Sector Strategy on Viral Hepatitis 2016–2021—Towards Ending Viral Hepatitis' (WHO 2016), covering all five hepatitis viruses (A, B, C, D, and E).

[353] WHA67.6 'Hepatitis' (24 May 2014).

aims higher at eliminating viral hepatitis as a public health threat.[354] Early 2022, the new WHO's 'Global Health Sector Strategies for HIV, Viral Hepatitis and Sexually Transmitted Infections 2022–2030' was released.

Water-borne diseases are those communicable diseases that are transmitted through contaminated water (eg diarrhoeal diseases, cholera, shigella, typhoid, hepatitis A and E, and poliomyelitis). They are caused by a lack of clean water supply, sanitation, and hygiene (WASH), linking this objective inherently with SDG 6 (MDG 7). Monitoring progress on these issues therefore lies with the WHO/UNICEF Joint Monitoring Programme.[355]

There is no clear list on what classifies as 'other' communicable diseases. However, generally it can be understood to include diseases such as meningitis, sexually transmitted infections (STIs), respiratory infections (pneumonia), and vaccine-preventable diseases such as measles.[356] In part, they are covered by specific global strategies such as the 'Global Health Sector Strategy on Sexually Transmitted Infections 2016–2021' (up for renewal in 2022). In addition, where they amount to 'infectious disease outbreaks'—such as COVID-19—they will also become relevant under target 3.b ('Support the research and development of vaccines and medicines for the communicable and non-communicable diseases that primarily affect developing countries, provide access to affordable essential medicines and vaccines') and target 3.d ('Strengthen the capacity of all countries, in particular developing countries, for early warning, risk reduction and management of national and global health risks').[357]

b) Empirical analysis and efforts of international/domestic implementation
Target 3.3 has five indicators.[358] These are significantly fewer than the ten indictors that had been included under MDG 6.[359]

Although by 2021 progress has been made on a number of indicators contained in target 3.3, major inequalities continue to exist, and some of the diseases remained far off the set global target. For example, as concerns HIV, the rate of new infections remained

---

[354] WHO, 'Global Health Sector Strategy on Viral Hepatitis 2016–2021' (n 353).

[355] For the 2021 progress report see WHO/UNICEF Joint Monitoring Programme for Water Supply, Sanitation and Hygiene, 'Progress on Household Drinking Water, Sanitation and Hygiene 2000–2020: Five Years into the SDGs' (WHO and UNICEF 2021).

[356] WHO, *Health in 2015* (n 14) 102–03.

[357] ibid 103.

[358] Indicator 3.3.1, Number of new HIV infections per 1,000 uninfected population, by sex, age, and key populations; indicator 3.3.2, Tuberculosis incidence per 100,000 population; indicator 3.3.2, Tuberculosis incidence per 100,000 population; indicator 3.3.3, Malaria incidence per 1,000 population; indicator 3.3.4, Hepatitis B incidence per 100,000 population; indicator 3.3.5, Number of people requiring interventions against neglected tropical diseases.

[359] Indicator 6.1, HIV prevalence among population aged 15–24 years; indicator 6.2, Condom use at last high-risk sex; indicator 6.3, Proportion of population aged 15–24 years with comprehensive correct knowledge of HIV/AIDS; indicator 6.4 Ratio of school attendance of orphans to school attendance of non-orphans aged 10–14 years; indicator 6.5, Proportion of population with advanced HIV infection with access to antiretroviral drugs; indicator 6.6, Incidence and death rates associated with malaria; indicator 6.7, Proportion of children under 5 sleeping under insecticide-treated bednets; indicator 6.8, Proportion of children under 5 with fever who are treated with appropriate anti-malarial drugs; indicator 6.9, Incidence, prevalence and death rates associated with tuberculosis; indicator 6.10, Proportion of tuberculosis cases detected and cured under directly observed treatment short course.

240   SDG 3

high at 0.37 per 1,000 uninfected population among adults (15–49 years of age), triple the 2020 targets.[360] The stagnation of financial flows and the little progress made on reducing the rate of new infections has been taken as a potential indicator for the decline of the world's overall commitment on achieving the SDG targets, given that it concerns a sector with targets that are clear and globally aligned, and is based on 'extraordinary global mobilisation'.[361]

Also progress on the reduction of malaria incidence rates has stalled. As with many of target 3.3's indicators, the Sub-Saharan African region remains the most affected, and with rapid population growth, the numbers have not decreased over the past two decades, despite some improvements in access to health services.[362] As observed by the African Leaders Malaria Alliance (ALMA),[363] only five Member States achieved the 2020 targets for malaria incidence or mortality (Ethiopia, Cabo Verde, The Gambia, Ghana, and Mauritania),[364] with further set-backs expected in light of the COVID-19 pandemic,[365] in itself also a communicable disease. In 2018, the 'Zero Malaria Starts with Me' campaign was initiated as a response to Africa now accounting for more than 93 per cent of global malaria cases and 94 per cent of global malaria deaths. It aims not only to maintain a high level of political and community-level engagement but also to unlock additional resources (domestically and through innovative mechanisms) to reach the 2030 targets. As of late 2021, more than twenty African states have adopted national campaigns aligned with this initiative,[366] including the introduction of scorecards for accountability, or the establishment of 'End Malaria Councils' for the mainstreaming of action to fight malaria.[367]

c) Critique

Notably, progress on water-borne diseases or 'other' communicable diseases is not measured by any indicator of the IAEG-SDG list. However, as mentioned above, target 3.3's indicators are further specified and extended in a number of strategies and programmes adopted by WHO and UNAIDS. These include, among others, the above-mentioned UNAIDS' 'Fast Track: Ending the AIDS Epidemic by 2030', WHO's 'End TB Strategy', WHO's 'Global Technical Strategy for Malaria 2016–2030', the above-mentioned 'Road

---

[360] High-Level Political Forum on Sustainable Development (ECOSOC) 'Progress towards the Sustainable Development Goals – Report of the Secretary-General' (30 April 2021) UN Doc E/2021/58, para 37, noting also the plateauing in relation to malaria.

[361] L-G Bekker and others, 'Advancing Global Health and Strengthening the HIV Response in the Era of the Sustainable Development Goals: The International AIDS Society—*Lancet* Commission' (2018) 392(10144) The Lancet Commissions 312, 312.

[362] WHO, 'Global Technical Strategy for Malaria 2016–2030' (n 340) 3.

[363] ALMA constitutes part of the Catalytic Framework to End AIDS, TB, and Eliminate Malaria in Africa by 2030.

[364] ALMA, 'Global Report Shows Stalled Progress across Africa and Need for Sustained Action' (12 December 2021) <https://alma2030.org/news/global-report-shows-stalled-progress-across-africa-and-need-for-sustained-action/> accessed 28 December 2021.

[365] High-Level Political Forum on Sustainable Development (ECOSOC), 'Progress towards the Sustainable Development Goals—Report of the Secretary-General' (30 April 2021) UN Doc E/2021/58, para 37, noting this particularly in relation to available numbers on HIV services.

[366] See <https://zeromalaria.africa/> accessed 28 December 2021.

[367] ALMA, '2020 African Union Malaria Progress Report' (2020) Assembly/AU/13(XXXIII).

Map for Neglected Tropical Diseases' (adopted by WHO), WHO's 'Global Strategy on Water Sanitation and Hygiene for Accelerating and Sustaining Progress on NTDs', and WHO's 'Global Health Sector Strategy on Viral Hepatitis'.[368] With the help of adoption of such global health strategies, WHO strives for alignment of work by all health-related actors, as well as pooling and focus of resources.

4. Target 3.4 By 2030, reduce by one-third premature mortality from non-communicable diseases through prevention and treatment and promote mental health and well-being

a) Sources of target

The absence of non-communicable diseases (chronic diseases) among the MDG targets constituted one of the largest gaps in the global health framework. Thus, in 2019, more than 70 per cent of all deaths were caused by non-communicable diseases.[369] While target 3.4 does not specially define which non-communicable diseases are addressed, the supporting policy framework is clear in outlining that focus is placed on the four main types of non-communicable diseases: cardiovascular diseases, cancers, chronic respiratory diseases, and diabetes. A series of behavioural and metabolic risk factors contribute to these diseases (tobacco use; physical inactivity; the harmful use of alcohol and unhealthy diets; raised blood pressure; overweight/obesity; hyperglycaemia (high blood glucose levels); and hyperlipidaemia (high levels of fat in the blood)). In addition, in 2018 air pollution was added to these monitored risk factors.[370]

The basis for the target of reducing by one-third premature mortality from non-communicable diseases was set at the High-Level Meetings of the UN General Assembly on Non-Communicable Diseases in 2011[371] and 2014.[372] These were the result of a campaign launched by the NCD Alliance in 2009 based on an action plan adopted by WHO in 2008.[373]

Target 3.4 also calls upon states to 'promote mental health and well-being'. A neglected issue in the previous MDG framework, WHO adopted a first 'Mental Health Action Plan 2013–2020' in 2013, which has been extended to 2030 in 2019 and updated in 2021.[374] The action plan defines mental health as 'a state of well-being in which the individual realizes his or her own abilities, can cope with the normal stresses of life, can work productively and fruitfully, and is able to make a contribution

---

[368] For an overview see WHO, *Health in 2015* (n 14) 109.

[369] WHO, 'Noncommunicable Diseases Factsheet' (13 April 2021) <http://www.who.int/news-room/fact-she ets/detail/noncommunicable-diseases> accessed 28 October 2021.

[370] UNGA Res 73/2 (10 October 2018) 'Political Declaration of the Third High-Level Meeting of the General Assembly on the Prevention and Control of Non-Communicable Diseases' UN Doc A/RES/73/2, para 31.

[371] UNGA Res 66/2 (16 September 2011) 'Political Declaration of the High-Level Meeting of the General Assembly on the Prevention and Control of Non-Communicable Diseases' UN Doc A/RES/66/2.

[372] UNGA Res 68/300 (7 July 2014) 'Outcome Document of the High-Level Meeting of the General Assembly on the Comprehensive Review and Assessment of the Progress Achieved in the Prevention and Control of Non-Communicable Diseases' UN Doc A/RES/68/300.

[373] NCD Alliance <https://ncdalliance.org/who-we-are/about-ncd-alliance> accessed 30 October 2021.

[374] WHO, 'Comprehensive Mental Health Action Plan 2013–2030' (WHO 2021).

242   SDG 3

to his or her community'.[375] In 2014, WHO published the first suicide prevention report.[376]

b) Empirical analysis and efforts of international/domestic implementation

WHO developed the monitoring framework accompanying the abovementioned political framework on NCDs by defining nine voluntary targets and twenty-five indicators to measure progress.[377] The framework addresses the reduction of non-communicable diseases by focusing on the contributing risk factors such as a 10 per cent relative reduction in the harmful use of alcohol or a 30 per cent relative reduction in prevalence of current tobacco use. The twenty-five indicators used are far more extensive than the SDG indicator (3.4.1, Mortality rate attributed to cardiovascular disease, cancer, diabetes, or chronic respiratory disease),[378] though target 3.4 in this sense is to be read together—in addition to the overarching target 3.8—with target 3.5 (particularly tobacco and alcohol control), target 3.9 (on hazardous chemicals and air, water and soil pollution and contamination), target 3.a (on the WHO Framework Convention on Tobacco Control), as well as target 3.b (on supporting research and development of vaccines and essential medicines for noncommunicable diseases). That said, it has been critically remarked that the current indicator focusing simply on the reduction of the mortality rate does not pay sufficient regard to interventions that focus on reducing disability.[379]

Further support towards achieving target 3.4 and its related elements is received by the United Nations Inter-Agency Task Force on the Prevention and Control of Non-Communicable Diseases (UNIATF) which in 2013 replaced the previously operating UN Ad Hoc Interagency Task Force on Tobacco Control.[380] In 2018, the third High-Level Meeting took place, emphasizing the need for an increase in progress and the need for extension of WHO's 'Global Action Plan' (expected in early 2022).[381]

---

[375] ibid para 6. A special role is played by dementia, which constitutes a cross-cutting disease. In 2017 the Global Dementia Observatory was launched to track the monitoring of the 'Global Action Plan on the Public Response to Dementia 2017–25'. So far, however, only sixty-one states have submitted data. <http://www.who.int/data/gho/data/themes/theme-details/GHO/global-dementia-observatory-(gdo)> accessed 30 October 2021.

[376] WHO, 'Preventing Suicide: A Global Imperative' (WHO 2014).

[377] WHO, 'Global Action Plan for the Prevention and Control of Noncommunicable Diseases 2013–2020' (WHO 2013).

[378] This is defined as the '[m]ortality rate attributed to cardiovascular disease, cancer, diabetes or chronic respiratory disease. Probability of dying between the ages of 30 and 70 years from cardiovascular diseases, cancer, diabetes or chronic respiratory diseases.' WHO, Indicator 3.4.1. Mortality rate attributed to cardiovascular disease, cancer, diabetes or chronic respiratory disease (March 2021) <https://unstats.un.org/sdgs/metadata/files/Metadata-03-04-01.pdf> accessed 21 October 2021. There has been some criticism for only focusing on 'premature mortality' in connection with NCDs, with some NGOs even noting that this might be ageist. See for more detail L Allen and others, 'Quantifying the Global Distribution of Premature Mortality from Non-Communicable Diseases' (2017) 39 Journal of Public Health 698.

[379] For a discussion see TR Frieden and others, 'Reducing Premature Mortality from Cardiovascular and Other Non-Communicable diseases by One Third: Achieving Sustainable Development Indicator 3.4.1' (2020) 15(1) Global Heart 50, noting that the prevention of death ultimately also correlates with decreased disability.

[380] ECOSOC Res 2013/12 (22 July 2013) 'United Nations Inter-Agency Task Force on the Prevention and Control of Non-Communicable Diseases'.

[381] UNGA Res 73/2 (10 October 2018) 'Political Declaration of the Third High-Level Meeting of the General Assembly on the Prevention and Control of Non-Communicable Diseases' UN Doc A/RES/73/2.

Unlike many other global health strategies, the approach pursued with regard to mental health is strongly tied to human rights,[382] given that persons with mental disorders frequently are subject to human rights violations and discrimination. On the one hand, this is linked with the fact that often certain vulnerable groups may be more likely to experience mental health problems. On the other hand, the treatment of mental health disorders frequently is still tied to stigmatization.[383] Based on this, states are called upon to draft mental health policies, plans and laws in line with international and regional human rights instruments.[384] In 2020, the Special Rapporteur on the Right of Everyone to the Enjoyment of the Highest Attainable Standard of Physical and Mental Health submitted their report to the Human Rights Council on elements that were 'needed to set a rights-based global agenda for advancing the right to mental health',[385] underscoring the interlinkages between global mental health and human rights more generally. Additionally, they advocated for a more inclusive and participatory development of adequate frameworks, and a departure from the still prevailing biomedical model.[386] The difficulty in coming to terms how to implement a human rights-based approach can also be seen in the chosen indicator (3.4.2, Suicide mortality rate), while the global health movement had advocated for inclusion of an indicator on service coverage.[387] Additionally, in 2018, the Lancet Commission on global mental health and sustainable development emphasized that instead of a 'final negative outcome ... robust, long-term, and comprehensive monitoring and accountability mechanisms are needed'.[388]

To achieve target 3.4, it is clear that countries need to pursue a comprehensive approach. However, few countries are on track to meet target 3.4, and in some countries the risk of dying from non-communicable diseases has even increased in recent years.[389] Although several countries have strengthened preventive measures, introduced targeted screening programmes for specific diseases, and encouraged healthy lifestyles[390] (eg more than fifty states have introduced a tax on sugar-sweetened beverages),[391] policies on unhealthy lifestyle choices such as alcohol and tobacco consumption and unhealthy diet were frequently lacking implementation.[392] Moreover,

---

[382] See also the special issue on 'Mental Health and Human Rights' in (2020) 22(1) Health and Human Rights Journal.

[383] WHO, 'Comprehensive Mental Health Action Plan 2013–2030' (n 375) paras 7ff; see also J Wogen and MT Restrepo, 'Human Rights, Stigma, and Substance Use' (2020) 22(1) Health and Human Rights Journal 51.

[384] WHO, 'Comprehensive Mental Health Action Plan 2013–2030' (n 375) Global targets 1.1 and 1.2.

[385] Human Rights Council, 'Mental Health and Human Rights: Setting A Rights-Based Global Agenda, Report of the Special Rapporteur on the right of everyone to the enjoyment of the highest attainable standard of physical and mental health' (15 April 2020) UN Doc A/HRC/44/48.

[386] See also already HRC Res 36/13 (9 October 2017) UN Doc A/HRC/RES/36/13.

[387] KR Cratsley and others, 'Human Rights and Global Mental Health: Reducing the Use of Coercive Measures' in AR Dyer and others (eds), Global Mental Health Ethics (Springer Nature Switzerland 2021) 247, 252.

[388] V Patel and others, 'The Lancet Commission on Global Mental Health and Sustainable Development' (2018) 392 The Lancet Commissions 1553, 1590.

[389] NCD Countdown 2030 collaborators, 'NCD Countdown 2030: Pathways to Achieving Sustainable Development Goal Target 3.4' (2020) 396 The Lancet 918, 921–23.

[390] DSD and DESA, '2017 Voluntary National Reviews Synthesis Report' (n 295) 11.

[391] See <http://www.obesityevidencehub.org.au/collections/prevention/countries-that-have-implemented-taxes-on-sugar-sweetened-beverages-ssbs> accessed 28 December 2021.

[392] LN. Allen and others, 'Implementation of Non-Communicable Disease Policies from 2015 to 2020: A Geopolitical Analysis of 194 Countries' (2021) 9 The Lancet Global Health e1528.

244 SDG 3

although there are increasing data on the effectiveness and success of suicide prevention policies by increasing awareness and reducing stigma,[393] they often remain a low
priority, with only approximately fifty states having national strategies in place.[394]

The COVID-19 pandemic increased difficulties in reaching medical services, delayed treatments, and prevented fast access to health services in many instances. Mental
health stress has significantly increased as well, among others owed to severe restrictions of fundamental rights and freedoms.[395] How deep the impact of this crisis on
target 3.4 will be in actual numbers is yet to be fully estimated.

5. Target 3.5 Strengthen the prevention and treatment of substance abuse, including narcotic drug abuse and harmful use of alcohol

a) Sources of target

Target 3.5 is closely linked to the other health targets, particularly target 3.4 by constituting a risk factor of non-communicable diseases as well as a cause for and symptom of
mental health problems.

The inclusion of the qualification 'harmful use' in target 3.5 relating to the use of alcohol
has prompted some discussion on whether there might be a level of alcohol consumption
which is considered healthy.[396] While this has most recently been denied, 'harmful use'
is defined by WHO as 'drinking that causes detrimental health and social consequences
for the drinker, the people around the drinker and society at large, as well as patterns of
drinking that are associated with increased risk of adverse health consequences'.[397] The
approach is thus intersectoral and also addresses effects on third parties such as through
traffic accidents.[398] The 'European Action Plan to Reduce the Harmful Use of Alcohol
2012–2020' (adopted by WHO Europe, the region with the highest prevalence of alcohol
use disorders) includes ten action areas and calls upon states to, among others, reduce the
availability and affordability and introduce marketing restrictions of alcohol.[399]

The field of international drug control has long been primarily viewed from the perspective of crime prevention and prosecution. However, the inclusion of narcotic drug
abuse into the Agenda 2030 has been seen as an opportunity to integrate human rights
and international health policy into this field. In 2016, the UN General Assembly held
a special session on the World Drug Problem, reaffirming that these objectives should
be understood to be 'complementary and mutually reinforcing'.[400] Despite this shift

---

[393] WHO, 'National Suicide Prevention Strategies—Progress, Examples and Indicators' (WHO 2018).

[394] For an overview see <http://www.mindbank.info/collection/topic/suicide_prevention_> accessed 28 December 2021.

[395] HRC 'Mental Health and Human Rights: Setting a Rights-Based Global Agenda, Report of the Special Rapporteur on the Right of Everyone to the Enjoyment of the Highest Attainable Standard of Physical and Mental Health' (15 April 2020) UN Doc A/HRC/44/48, para 79.

[396] R Burton and N Sheron, 'No Level of Alcohol Consumption Improves Health' (2018) 392(10152) The Lancet 987.

[397] WHO, 'Global Strategy to Reduce the Harmful Use of Alcohol' (WHO 2010).

[398] C Ferreira-Borges and others, 'Alcohol Consumption and Sustainable Development' (WHO Regional Office in Europe 2020).

[399] WHO Europe, 'European Action Plan to Reduce the Harmful Use of Alcohol 2012–2020' (World Health Organization Regional Office in Europe 2012).

[400] UNGA Res S-30/1 (19 April 2016) 'Our Joint Commitment to Effectively Addressing and Countering the World Drug Problem' UN Doc A/RES/S-30/1.

towards better integration, it is primarily UNODC (and not WHO) which functions as the key player regarding narcotic substance abuse. Although it is has worked towards adopting a more human rights friendly approach, for example by emphasizing that detention of drug users does not constitute 'treatment',[401] it has so far not adopted any more specific global agenda implementing target 3.5's objectives on substance abuse.

b) Empirical analysis

Target 3.5 is measured by two indicators (3.5.1, Coverage of treatment interventions (pharmacological, psychosocial and rehabilitation and aftercare services) for substance use disorders; 3.5.2, Alcohol per capita consumption (aged fifteen years and older) within a calendar year in litres of pure alcohol). Indicator 3.5.1 is one of three Tier II indicators under SDG 3. This is particularly owed to the 'limited availability of household surveys on substance use and the under-reporting of use among survey respondents'.[402]

c) Critique and efforts of international/domestic implementation

Generally, not too much global data has become available on target 3.5's indicators. However, as emphasized by the High-Level Political Forum on Sustainable Development in passing, health services for substance use disorders have been among those most heavily affected by COVID-19.[403] In addition, it has been warned that the pandemic increased the level of alcohol consumption, potentially resulting in long-term adverse impacts on physical and mental health.[404]

Partly in response, the WHO Executive Board in 2020 issued its decision requesting the WHO Director-General to develop an action plan (2022–2030) on effectively implementing the Global Strategy to Reduce the Harmful Use of Alcohol.[405] In its second draft published in late 2021, among others, it is pointed out that '[a]lcohol remains the only psychoactive and dependence-producing substance that exerts a significant impact on global population health that is not controlled at the international level by legally binding regulatory instruments'.[406] It is also added that while states have increasingly adopted regional or national alcohol policies (such as the EU Strategy on Reducing Alcohol Related Harm),[407] this is least common amongst low-income countries.[408] Whether the action plan will manage to overcome the identified gaps in data and implementation effectiveness will only become visible in the years to come.

---

[401] UNODC and WHO, 'Treatment and Care for People with Drug Use Disorders in Contact with the Criminal Justice Systems' (2018) <http://www.unodc.org/documents/justice-and-prison-reform/UNODC_WHO_Alternatives_to_Conviction_or_Punishment_2018.pdf> accessed 30 October 2021.

[402] WHO, Indicator 3.5.1. Coverage of treatment interventions (pharmacological, psychosocial and rehabilitation and aftercare services) for substance use disorders (September 2019) <https://unstats.un.org/sdgs/metadata/files/Metadata-03-05-01.pdf> accessed 30 October 2021.

[403] High-Level Political Forum on Sustainable Development (ECOSOC) 'Progress towards the Sustainable Development Goals—Report of the Secretary-General' (30 April 2021) UN Doc E/2021/58, para 32.

[404] UN, 'The Sustainable Development Goals Report 2021' (UN 2021) 32.

[405] WHO EB146(14) 'Accelerating Action to Reduce the Harmful Use of Alcohol' (6 February 2020).

[406] WHO, 'Global Alcohol Action Plan 2022–2030 to Strengthen Implementation of the Global Strategy to Reduce the Harmful Use of Alcohol' (2nd draft, 4 October 2021) para 19.

[407] See <http://www.rarha.eu/Pages/default.aspx> accessed 29 December 2021.

[408] WHO, 'Global Alcohol Action Plan 2022–2030 to Strengthen Implementation of the Global Strategy to Reduce the Harmful Use of Alcohol' (n 407) para 13.

246 SDG 3

6. Target 3.6 By 2020, halve the number of global deaths and injuries from road traffic accidents

a) Sources of target

Road accidents not only kill approximately 1.35 million people a year (amongst them particularly young people are affected) but many of the 50 million non-fatal road traffic injuries lead to life-long disability.[409] By far the majority of road traffic accidents occur in LMICs (93 per cent of global road fatalities, with only 60 per cent of the vehicles being registered there).[410] The majority of these accidents are preventable if the right and effective policies are in place.

Unlike the other targets, target 3.6 was set to be achieved already by 2020. This correlated with the United Nations Decade of Action for Road Safety,[411] which had been the result of a series of UN resolutions on improving global road safety following the turn of the century. As emphasized in UNGA Res 64/255, 'this major public health problem has a broad range of social and economic consequences which, if unaddressed, may affect the sustainable development of countries'.[412] In 2015, the UN Secretary-General appointed a UN Secretary-General's Special Envoy for Road Safety (Jean Todt) which is hosted by the United Nations Economic Commission for Europe (UNECE).

Target 3.6 is closely linked to target 11.2 (by 2030, provide access to safe, affordable, accessible, and sustainable transport systems for all, improving road safety, notably by expanding public transport, with special attention to the needs of those in vulnerable situations, women, children, persons with disabilities, and older persons). The latter's relevance is expected to increase even more over the coming years, with the growth of urban centres, and needs to be considered in urban designs.

b) Empirical analysis

Indicator 3.6.1 measures the death rate due to road traffic injuries. In WHO's most recent 'Global Status Report on Road Safety', it can be seen that while the number of deaths has been increasing, the rate of death per 100,000 has slightly decreased since 2000 (from 18.8 to 18.2/100,000). In fact, as WHO notes '[r]oad traffic injuries are currently the leading cause of death for children and young adults aged 5–29 years'.[413] Overall, however, the 2020 target was not met. Hence, in 2020, the UNGA extended target 3.6 by another decade to reach the set out objective (with the objective to halve road traffic deaths and injuries within this period).[414]

c) Critique and efforts of international/domestic implementation

In addition to the 2020 target not being reached, it became clear that also major policy changes will be needed to reach the 2030 target. Hence, in October 2021, UNECE,

---

[409] UNGA Res 74/299 (31 August 2020) 'Improving Global Road Safety' UN Doc A/RES/74/299.
[410] UNECE and UN Secretary General's Special Envoy for Road Safety, 'Road Safety for All' (December 2020) <https://unece.org/sites/default/files/2020-12/Road_Safety_for_All.pdf> accessed 2 November 2021.
[411] UNGA Res 64/255 (10 May 2010) 'Improving Global Road Safety' UN Doc A/RES/64/255.
[412] ibid preambular para 4.
[413] WHO, 'Global Status Report on Road Safety 2018' (WHO 2018) 3.
[414] UNGA Res 74/299 (31 August 2020) 'Improving Global Road Safety' UN Doc A/RES/74/299.

together with WHO and the other UN regional commissions, published the new 'Global Plan for the Decade of Action (2021–2030)'.[415] Alongside the introduction of several safety polices, countries are encouraged anew to ratify and implement several international road safety conventions such as the 1968 Convention on Road Traffic (eighty-five parties), the 1968 Convention on Road Signs and Signals (sixty-eight parties), or the 1997 Agreement concerning the Adoption of Uniforms Conditions for Periodical Technical Inspections of Wheeled Vehicles and the Reciprocal Recognition of Such Inspections (sixteen parties). The framework also includes twelve voluntary performance targets such as to halve the proportion of vehicles travelling over the posted speed limit, ensure that motorcycle riders use standard helmets, and introduce legislation prohibiting the use of mobile phones while driving. Many of these targets also link to the state's obligation to protect the (human) right to life.[416]

This global action is particularly carried further by regional efforts, among which the EU has taken the lead. Hence, the EU—which has adopted the *Vision Zero* initiative to reach zero fatalities and serious injuries by 2050 on European roads—had adopted the Road Safety Policy Framework 2021–2030 which includes efforts to share its best practices and increase international cooperation with other regions (including its EU neighbours, the African Union, and the Association of Southeast Asian Nations (ASEAN)).[417]

7. Target 3.7 By 2030, ensure universal access to sexual and reproductive health-care services, including for family planning, information and education, and the integration of reproductive health into national strategies and programmes

a) *Sources of target*

Target 3.7 was particularly contentious during the negotiations. Sexual and reproductive health had been one of the biggest gaps that had been left out from the MDGs despite earlier international conferences already including it among the core development issues. Thus, the 1994 International Conference for Population and Development defined sexual and reproductive health in a comprehensive and rights-based manner:

> Reproductive health is a state of complete physical, mental and social well-being and not merely the absence of disease or infirmity, in all matters relating to the reproductive system and to its functions and processes. Reproductive health therefore implies that people are able to have a satisfying and safe sex life and that they have the capability to reproduce and the freedom to decide if, when and how often to do so. Implicit in this last condition are the right of men and women to be informed and to have access to safe, effective, affordable and acceptable methods of family planning of their choice, as well as other methods of their choice for regulation of fertility which

[415] UNECE, 'Global Plan—Decade of Action for Road Safety 2021–2030' (October 2021).
[416] S Casey-Maslen, *The Right to Life under International Law—An Interpretative Manual* (CUP 2021) 382ff.
[417] European Commission, *EU Road Safety Policy Framework 2021–2030: Next Steps Towards 'Vision Zero'* (European Union 2020) 25.

248 SDG 3

are not against the law, and the right of access to appropriate health-care services that will enable women to go safely through pregnancy and childbirth and provide couples with the best chance of having a healthy infant. In line with the above definition of reproductive health, reproductive health care is defined as the constellation of methods, techniques and services that contribute to reproductive health and well-being by preventing and solving reproductive health problems. It also includes sexual health, the purpose of which is the enhancement of life and personal relations, and not merely counselling and care related to reproduction and sexually transmitted diseases.[418]

This was confirmed at the 1995 Beijing Fourth World Conference on Woman.[419] However, following concerted efforts by fundamentalists and conservative groups,[420] sexual and reproductive health rights ultimately were cut from the Millennium Declaration and later reduced to MDG target 5.b ('achieve by 2015, universal access to reproductive health'),[421] the 'depoliticized question of maternal health'.[422]

The debate during the drafting and negotiations on whether to include sexual and reproductive health and in which form was divided between those who had strong reservations to the topic (eg Saudi Arabia, Malta), and those (particularly Western European but also Latin American states) who felt strongly that the topic would be essential for any outcome. In 2013, more than thirty states had agreed that 'the promotion and protection of sexual rights and reproductive rights are essential for the achievement of social justice and the national, regional and global commitments to the three pillars of sustainable development'.[423] Yet as described by the Co-Chair Kamau and others, discussions continued until the final day, without any agreement despite support of negotiations in a specifically dedicated contact group. In the end, the proposal contained target 3.7 on universal access to sexual and productive healthcare services, but omitted any reference to rights.[424] Even though target 5.6 does include a reference to reproductive (but not sexual) rights, the two suggested indicators continue to lack a clear methodology for their measurement and in particular fail to consider the actual implementation of a specific legal framework.[425]

b) Empirical analysis and efforts of international/domestic implementation

Target 3.7 is measured with two indicators: 3.7.1, Proportion of women of reproductive age (aged 15–49 years) who have their need for family planning satisfied with modern

---

[418] International Conference on Population and Development, 'Summary of the Programme of Action' (September 1994) para 7.2.

[419] UN 'Beijing Declaration and Platform for Action' (27 October 1995) UN Doc A/CONF.177/20, para 94.

[420] AE Yamin and KL Falb, 'Counting What We Know; Knowing What to Count' (2012) 30(3) Nordic Journal of Human Rights 350, 365.

[421] MDG 5 relied on four indicators (5.3, Contraceptive prevalence rate; 5.4, Adolescent birth rate; 5.5, Antenatal care coverage (at least one visit and at least four visits); 5.6, Unmet need for family planning). Three of these are used for SDG 3 target 3.7 (adolescent birth rate and proportion of women of reproductive age (aged 15–49 years) who have their need for family planning satisfied with modern methods).

[422] Yamin and Falb, 'Counting What We Know' (n 421) 365, in reference to the overall debate.

[423] UN ECLAC, 'Montevideo Consensus on Population and Development' (August 2013).

[424] Kamau and others (n 60) 212.

[425] Yamin, 'Power, Politics and Knowledge Claims' (n 96) 56.

methods; and 3.7.2, Adolescent birth rate (aged 10–14 years; aged 15–19 years) per 1,000 women in that age group.

Not much progress has been made since 2000 on target 3.7.[426] In its most recent World Health Statistics (2021), WHO estimates that '[t]he proportion of women of reproductive age who have their need for family planning satisfied with modern methods has only moderately increased worldwide between 2000 and 2021 from 73.7% to 76.8%.'[427]

WHO has tracks and compiles national policies gathered through surveys on sexual, reproductive, maternal, newborn, child and adolescent health (SRMNCAH), with the results of its most recent survey being published in 2020, encompassing more than 150 countries. The majority (94 per cent) of countries reporting have submitted that they have a national policy or guideline for reproductive health, 88 per cent on family planning/contraception.[428] This, however, as pointed out below does not speak to the components of such policy. With regard to reproductive healthcare policies, WHO recommends that it should include topics relating to 'family planning/contraception, abortion, infertility/fertility care, preconception care, menopause, cervical cancer and violence against women.'[429] Only 39 per cent of states reporting address all of these topics.[430]

c) Critique

Among others, the limited progress on target 3.7 has been traced to 'limited choice of contraceptive methods; inadequate access to services, particularly among young, poorer and unmarried people; perceptions and experience of contraceptive side-effects; cultural or religious opposition; poor service quality and acceptability; bias against some methods among users as well as providers; and gender-based barriers to accessing services.'[431] Thus, despite sexual and reproductive health constituting a cross-cutting issue within the SDG framework, the lack of progress demonstrates that more comprehensive and concentrated action is necessary to overcome the existing barriers.

Additionally, it has been shown that the use of quantitative indicators on a target which at its core is inherently rights-based obscures differences in terminology in implementation (such as the content of sexuality education or the meaning of domestic violence), and in the end sweeps all contextual issues into a 'yes/no' category.[432] Moreover, the limitation to women and disregard of LGBTQ persons, often the subject of discriminatory health service treatment, is concerning.[433]

---

[426] High-Level Political Forum on Sustainable Development (ECOSOC) 'Progress towards the Sustainable Development Goals—Report of the Secretary-General' (30 April 2021) UN Doc E/2021/58, para 35.

[427] WHO, 'World Health Statistics 2021' (n 290) 48.

[428] WHO, 'Sexual, Reproductive, Maternal, Newborn, Child and Adolescent Health Policy Survey 2018–2019: Report' (WHO 2020) 18.

[429] ibid.

[430] As of late 2021, the data processing of these policies is still ongoing. The documents will be available at <https://platform.who.int/data/maternal-newborn-child-adolescent-ageing/national-policies> accessed 14 March 2023.

[431] WHO, 'World Health Statistics 2021' (n 290) 48.

[432] Yamin, 'Power, Politics and Knowledge Claims' (n 96) 57.

[433] In general, the SDGs lack any reference to LGBTQ persons, and even less their rights, a highly problematic (and intentional) omission. For an overview across all SDG targets see CH Logie, 'Sexual Rights and Sexual

250 SDG 3

8. Target 3.8 Achieve universal health coverage, including financial risk protection, access to quality essential health-care services and access to safe, effective, quality and affordable essential medicines and vaccines for all

a) Sources of target

Even though there is no official hierarchy among the targets in SDG 3, target 3.8 ('Universal health coverage (UHC) *for all*') functions as the *overarching* objective of SDG 3.[434] This complements the vertical approach chosen in the MDGs which focused on specific diseases, and aims at directing efforts towards a system-wide reform, perceived as a more sustainable approach.[435] Primary healthcare is considered the key success factor for UHC[436] and should be scaled up significantly to ensure equitable and early access to essential services and medicines. The financial protection offered by UHC is also understood to be core to realizing the overall objectives of the SDGs 'to end extreme poverty' and 'to ensure that every person achieves a basic standard of wellbeing'.[437]

Particularly WHO worked towards placing UHC as a core objective of global health policy, with its member states in 2005 committing to develop their health financing system in such a way to enable UHC.[438] On might speculate whether WHO's efforts increased following the oversight of the MDGs to include any focus on health systems, instead remaining concentrated on targeted interventions in specific fields.[439] Whatever the specific reason might be, following WHO's new focus other international bodies this time followed suit, ranging from the World Bank[440] to the UNGA[441] to the ILO.[442]

Pleasure: Sustainable Development Goals and the Omitted Dimensions of the *Leave No One Behind* Sexual Health Agenda' (2021) Global Public Health <http://www.tandfonline.com/doi/pdf/10.1080/17441692.2021.1953559> accessed 25 October 2021.

[434] UNGA Res 70/1 (25 September 2015) 'Transforming Our World: The 2030 Agenda for Sustainable Development' UN Doc A/RES/70/1, para 26: 'To promote physical and mental health and well-being, and to extend life expectancy for all, we must achieve universal health coverage and access to quality health care.'

[435] WHO, *Health in 2015* (n 14) 41; Frey (n 25) 419.

[436] WHO, *Primary Health Care on the Road to Universal Health Coverage—2019 Global Monitoring Report* (World Health Organization 2020) 85.

[437] See, eg, A Wagstaff and J Kutzin, 'Health and the SDGs: Out of the Doldrums, Heading for the Rapids' (*World Bank Blogs*, 23 March 2016) <http://blogs.worldbank.org/developmenttalk/health-and-sdgs-out-doldrums-heading-rapids> accessed 30 October 2021.

[438] WHO's efforts go as far back as the Alma-Ata Declaration, but renewed emphasis particularly as of 2005: WHA58/33 'Sustainable Health Financing, Universal Coverage and Social Health Insurance' (25 May 2005): '(1) to ensure that health-financing systems include a method for prepayment of financial contributions for health care, with a view to sharing risk among the population and avoiding catastrophic health-care expenditure and impoverishment of individuals as a result of seeking care; (2) to ensure adequate and equitable distribution of good-quality health care infrastructures and human resources for health so that the insurees will receive equitable and good-quality health services according to the benefits package; [...] (4) to plan the transition to universal coverage of their citizens so as to contribute to meeting the needs of the population for health care and improving its quality, to reducing poverty, and to attaining international agreed development goals, including those contained in the United Nations Millennium Declaration, and to achieving health for all.' See also WHO, *Health Systems Financing—The Path to Universal Coverage* (World Health Organization 2010); and WHA64/9 'Sustainable Health Financing Structures and Universal Coverage' (24 May 2011).

[439] For a debate on the uncertainties surrounding the MDG selection see CE Brolan and PS Hill, 'Universal Health Coverage's Evolving Location in the Post-2015 Development Agenda' (2016) 31(4) Health Policy and Planning 514.

[440] See above on the initial scepticism by the World Bank (n 38).

[441] UNGA Res 67/81 (14 March 2013) 'Global Health and Foreign Policy' UN Doc A/RES/67/81.

[442] ILO Recommendation No 202 on national floors of social protection (2012).

Following the 2012 Rio + 20 Conference, the trajectory for UHC to feature centrally in the SDGs was set.[443] Shortly thereafter, the UNGA adopted Resolution 67/81 on Global Health and Foreign Policy in which it was recommended that 'consideration be given to including universal health coverage in the discussions on the post-2015 development agenda in the context of global health challenges';[444] This was reaffirmed in 2017[445] as well as at a High-Level Meeting on UHC at the UNGA in 2019.[446]

b) Empirical analysis and efforts of international/domestic implementation

Target 3.8 is tracked by two indicators. Indicator 3.8.1 (measuring the coverage of essential health services (service coverage index (SCI)) and indicator 3.8.2 (measuring the proportion of population with large household expenditures on health as a share of total household expenditure or income). Initially, they were conceptualized too broad, failing to speak to information such as 'who is covered, what services are covered, the extent of financial protection, with data disaggregated to measure progress across sectors and groups'.[447] As WHO admits, '[n]o ideal measure of essential health service coverage currently exists, either in capturing the full range of potential health services a given population needs or the percentage of people who receive all services they need'.[448] There is thus significant debate on what might be considered essential health-care services.[449]

However, following a multi-year process, in 2018 the IAEG-SDG accepted the newly developed methods and the fourteen tracer indicators for indicator 3.8.1 as suggested by WHO. Thus, the average coverage of essential services is tracked based on tracer interventions[450] that include reproductive, maternal, newborn, and child health,[451] infectious diseases,[452] NCDs,[453] and service capacity and access,[454] among the general and the most disadvantaged population. Notably absent are, however, essential

---

[443] 'The Future We Want' (n 16) para 139.

[444] UNGA 67/81 (12 December 2012) 'Global Health and Foreign Policy' UN Doc A/RES/67/81, para 25.

[445] UNGA 72/139 (12 December 2017) 'Global Health and Foreign Policy: Addressing the Health of the Most Vulnerable for an Inclusive Society' UN Doc A/RES/72/139, para 6: 'Calls upon Member States to accelerate progress towards the goal of universal health coverage, which implies that all people have equal access, without discrimination of any kind, to nationally determined sets of quality promotive, preventive, curative, rehabilitative and palliative basic health services needed and essential, safe, affordable, effective and quality medicines, while ensuring that the use of such services and medicines does not expose the users to financial hardship, with a specific emphasis on the poor, vulnerable and marginalized segments of the population.'

[446] UNGA, Political Declaration of the High-Level Meeting on Universal Health Coverage 'Universal Health Coverage: Moving Together to Build a Healthier World' (23 September 2019) <http://www.un.org/pga/73/wp-content/uploads/sites/53/2019/07/FINAL-draft-UHC-Political-Declaration.pdf> accessed 4 November 2021.

[447] UNGA 'Right of Everyone to the Enjoyment of the Highest Attainable Standard of Physical and Mental Health' (5 August 2016) UN Doc A/71/304, para 80.

[448] WHO, *Primary Health Care on the Road to Universal Health Coverage* (n 437) 124.

[449] See, eg, A Glassman and others (eds), *What's In, What's Out: Designing Benefits for Universal Health Coverage* (Center for Global Development 2017).

[450] For details see WHO, *Primary Health Care on the Road to Universal Health Coverage* (n 437) 113–23.

[451] The four tracer indicators are: family planning; antenatal care, 4 + visits; child immunization; and care-seeking for suspected pneumonia.

[452] The four tracer indicators are: TB effective treatment; HIV treatment; insecticide-treated nets; at least basic sanitation.

[453] The three tracer indicators are: normal blood pressure; mean fasting plasma glucose; tobacco non-smoking.

[454] The three tracer indicators are: hospital bed density; health worker density; International Health Regulations (IHR) core capacity index.

medicines.[455] Comparative data of states on these tracers are measured on a scale from zero to 100 per cent. Still, despite certain progress on this, WHO has reported that it does not yet have sufficient data 'to compare the UHC service coverage index across key dimensions of inequality'.[456]

Moreover, indicator 3.8.2 has been criticized for relying on 'household' measurement as this constitutes an 'oversimplification and masks "intrahousehold inequality"' given certain 'entrenched patterns of discrimination in society at large'.[457]

For the most recent measuring period (2013–2017), countries on average only had the most recent data available for 40 per cent of the tracer indicators. Estimates are therefore imputed through validation or interpolation models, or 'imputed from countries with similar characteristics'.[458] Though progress has been made on the SCI since 2000 (with the index rising from 45 to 66), particularly with regard to infectious diseases, WHO has warned that progress has slowed since 2010 and needs to accelerate to reach the 2030 target. This is even more so as progress made on service coverage has largely come at an increase of out-of-pocket spending (catastrophic household expenditure).[459] For this reason, WHO adopted the above-mentioned 'Triple Billion targets', including specifically the target to reach 'one billion more people benefitting from universal health coverage' by 2023.[460]

The core importance of target 3.8 among SDG 3 is discernible, among others, from the fact that in their VNRs almost all states make reference to measures taken to 'expand or create universal health coverage'.[461] Challenges persist to increasing financial means, but also ensuring sufficiently trained staff, particularly throughout the COVID-19 pandemic. Closing this gap and ensuring adequate financial protection for those in need constitute important steps in achieving not only SDG 3 but also SDG 1 and SDG 10.[462] In responding to this, Cyprus, for example, introduced a new national healthcare system (General Health System, 2019) which now provides Cypriot residents with 'equal and unhindered access to high quality healthcare',[463] overcoming earlier significant gaps in coverage. The reform included expansion of population entitlement (now linked to residence rather than (EU) citizenship, service coverage (to ensure reduced waiting times), and limitations to user charges.[464]

---

[455] H Nygren-Krug, 'The Right(s) Road to Universal Health Coverage' (2019) 21(2) Health and Human Rights Journal 215, 219.

[456] World Health Organization and International Bank for Reconstruction and Development, 'Tracking Universal Health Coverage: 2017 Global Monitoring Report' (WHO 2017) 6.

[457] Nygren-Krug (n 456) 219–20.

[458] WHO, *Primary Health Care on the Road to Universal Health Coverage* (n 437) 13.

[459] ibid 8ff.

[460] WHO, 'Thirteenth General Programme of Work 2019–2023' (n 165) 12.

[461] United Nations and DESA, '2021 Voluntary National Reviews Synthesis Report' (United Nations 2021) 9, see also 43ff.

[462] WHO (Europe), 'Factsheet—Sustainable Development Goals: Health Targets. Financial Protection and the Sustainable Development Goals' (2020) <www.euro.who.int/__data/assets/pdf_file/0003/465429/Financial-protection-and-SDGs-Factsheet-eng.pdf> accessed 3 January 2022.

[463] Republic of Cyprus, 'Second Voluntary National Review—Sustainable Development Goals (SDGs)' (2021) 49.

[464] A Kontemeniotis and M Theodorou, *Can People Afford to Pay for Health Care? New Evidence on Financial Protection in Cyprus* (World Health Organization 2020).

c) Critique

Understanding the overarching objective of SDG 3 as achieving UHC strives to avoid the vague and broad terminology of achieving 'well-being for all', an aspect which the WHO has previously been criticized for.[465] In particular, as mentioned above, UHC has been approximated closest to the entitlements arising from the right to health, in other words a right to a system of health protection providing equality of opportunity for everyone to enjoy the highest attainable level of physical and mental health.[466] At the same time, it has been pointed out that UHC

> cannot be achieved without meeting the core requirements of availability, accessibility, acceptability and quality under the right to health. Among other things, services must be safely and geographically accessible without discrimination. The right to health requires that essential services include those for populations with specialized needs, such as sexual and reproductive health services adapted to the needs of women, girls, including those with disabilities, and transgender persons. Health services and access to underlying determinants must also be economically accessible. Even where there is widespread access to health services, the right to health demands that they be of sufficient quality, including in good working condition and medically and scientifically appropriate.[467]

Thus, from a human rights perspective, target 3.8 has been criticized by the Special Rapporteur on the Right of Everyone to the Enjoyment of the Highest Attainable Standard of Physical and Mental Health for failing to 'make explicit commitments to confer priority to the poor and marginalized either in the process of expanding coverage or in developing priorities as to which services to provide'.[468]

A key challenge concerns the question how to integrate human rights standards into UHC, and ensure that UHC is available and accessible for all. Although WHO set up a Consultative Group on Equity and Universal Health Coverage, which emphasized the need to focus on the worse off in terms of service coverage and health, expand coverage to everyone (particularly also disadvantaged groups) and reduce out-of-pocket payments,[469] and key actors have affirmed the inherent link between health and human rights, recent reports also show that there has been a significant growth of out-of-pocket spending (see *supra*), with the population impoverished by out-of-pocket health spending increasing. Moreover, the impact of this is aggravated by the failure of being able to monitor sufficiently disaggregated data to unveil further inequities.[470]

---

[465] See, eg, M Ssenyonjo, *Economic, Social and Cultural Rights in International Law* (2nd edn, Hart Publishing 2016) 317, 536.

[466] See, eg, L Forman and others, 'Rights Language in the Sustainable Development Agenda: Has Right to Health Discourse and Norms Shaped Health Goals?' (2015) 4 International Journal of Health Policy Management 799, 802; Frey (n 25) 422.

[467] UNGA 'Right of Everyone to the Enjoyment of the Highest Attainable Standard of Physical and Mental Health' (5 August 2016) UN Doc A/71/304, para 79.

[468] ibid para 76.

[469] WHO Consultative Group on Equity and Universal Health Coverage, 'Making Fair Choices on the Path to Universal Health Coverage' (WHO 2014).

[470] Nygren-Krug (n 456) 219.

254   SDG 3

9. Target 3.9 By 2030, substantially reduce the number of deaths and illnesses
   from hazardous chemicals and air, water and soil pollution and contamination

a) Sources of target

The Lancet Commission on pollution and health recently highlighted that '[p]ollution
is one of the great existential challenges of the Anthropocene epoch ... [endangering]
the health of billions'.[471] Environmental risks are the cause for about 25 per cent of
all deaths and diseases a year.[472] Moreover, as emphasized in the Brundtland Report,
environmental degradation and poverty are deeply intertwined,[473] with recent data
showing that 'pollution and pollution-related disease are concentrated among the poor
and contribute to the intergenerational perpetuation of poverty'.[474] Yet, despite this acknowledgement, there are still many uncertainties prevailing, ranging from lack of data
on pollution levels and pollution-related diseases to lack of or 'poor knowledge of the
toxic effect of many chemicals in common use, especially newer classes of chemicals'.[475]
While environmentally sound management of chemicals and waste and the realization of the harmful effects on health, but also economic growth, has been part of the
international development agenda since the 1990s,[476] it has for a long time remained
secondary (particularly as regards funding) to many other development objectives.[477]
It thus did not feature among the MDGs with the exception of MDG target 7.c that focused on sustainable access to safe drinking water and basic sanitation.

With the inclusion of target 3.9 into SDG 3 it was hoped that this lack of attention
might be remedied. Additionally, the SDG framework reflects the recognition that
pollution affects many aspects of development, with links contained particularly in
SDG 6 but also SDG 2 (with reference to soil quality), SDG 7 (on clean energy), SDG
9 (only clean technologies and industrial processes), SDG 11 (sustainable cities and

---

[471] PJ Landrigan, 'The *Lancet* Commission on Pollution and Health' (2018) 391(10119) The Lancet Commissions 462, 465.

[472] WHO, 'Global Strategy on Health, Environment and Climate Change—The Transformation Needed to improve Lives and Wellbeing Sustainably through Healthy Environments' (WHO 2020) 4: 'Air pollution ... alone
causes seven million preventable deaths per year, with more than 90% of people breathing polluted air and almost
3000 million people still depending on polluting fuels such as solid fuels or kerosene for lighting, cooking and
heating. More than half the world's population is still exposed to unsafely managed water, inadequate sanitation
and poor hygiene, resulting in more than 800 000 preventable deaths each year... More than one million workers
die each year because their workplace is unsafe, and more than one million people die from exposure to chemicals'
(footnotes omitted).

[473] UNGA 'Report of the World Commission on Environment and Development' (4 August 1987) UN Doc A/
42/427.

[474] Landrigan (n 472) 488, pointing out that 'environmental injustice' is 'the inequitable exposure of poor, minority, and disenfranchised populations to toxic chemicals, contaminated air and water, unsafe workplaces and
other forms of pollution, and the consequent disproportionate burden among these populations of pollution-
related disease, often in violation of their human rights. Environmental injustice has been characterised as a form
of structural violence'.

[475] ibid 465.

[476] Thus, in the Agenda 21 action programme adopted by the 1992 the United Nations Conference on
Environmental and Development, 'reducing health risks from environmental pollution and hazards' was
adopted as part of the programme areas for which WHO was responsible in implementation. See United Nations
Conference on Environment & Development (Rio, 3–14 June 1992), Agenda 21, paras 6.39ff. Environmentally
sound management of toxic chemicals (paras 19.1ff) and air, water, and soil pollution (paras 16.11ff) were included in other programme areas as well.

[477] Landrigan (n 472) 466.

communities), SDG 12 (responsible consumption and production), SDG 13 (climate change), SDG 14 (water conservation), and SDG 15 (land conservation).

b) Empirical analysis and efforts of international/domestic implementation

As with many of the environment-related targets, target 3.9 does not have a defined quantitative target to reach.[478] Progress is measured by three indicators (3.9.1, Mortality rate attributed to household and ambient air pollution; 3.9.2, Mortality rate attributed to unsafe water, unsafe sanitation and lack of hygiene (exposure to unsafe WASH services);[479] 3.9.3, Mortality rate attributed to unintentional poisoning). The scope is relatively narrow, that is, none of the three indicators is directly addressed towards environmental improvement (eg less pollution) but only assess the impact attributed to unsafe environmental condition. Moreover, the indicators simply measure mortality but do not capture illnesses.[480] While progress has been made on all three indicators,[481] more concerted action will be needed to significantly reduce the numbers of deaths and illnesses.

One example of this is the Global Alliance to Eliminate Lead Paint which was jointly established by UNEP and WHO in 2011. As part of the initiative, a *Model Law and Guidance on Regulating Lead Paint* was introduced in 2017,[482] hoping to encourage more states to introduce such legislation. As of early 2021, only approximately half of the world's states had such legislation in place, with the absence being particularly prominent in low-income countries (only 10 per cent of all states had enacted lead point laws).[483] However, recently some progress has been made, for example in Ethiopia which introduced new lead paint regulations in 2018 with the technical and financial support by UNEP, the Global Environmental Facility (GEF) and the International Persistent Organic Pollutants Elimination Network (IPEN), now constituting a case study example in the region.[484]

---

[478] See also M Elder and SH Olsen, 'The Design of Environmental Priorities in the SDGs' (2019) 10 (Supplement 1) Global Policy 70, 74.

[479] As noted by Williams and Hunt, this is the only indicator under SDG 3 that makes any reference to quality. See Williams and Hunt (n 226) 1129.

[480] Elder and Olsen (n 479) 75.

[481] Death rates from air pollution have dropped from 115/100,000 in to 65/100,000 in 2017; the mortality rate attributed to unintentional poisoning has on average gone down by 27 per cent between 2000 and 2019. Data available at <https://sdg-tracker.org/good-health> and <https://ourworldindata.org/grapher/death-rate-from-poisonings?tab=table> both accessed 4 November 2021. For the target on WASH, no comparative data is currently available. However, in 2021, the WHO/UNICEF Joint Monitoring Programme for Water Supply and Sanitation shows that progress on access to clean drinking water, sanitation and handwashing facilities is being made <https://ourworldindata.org/explorers/water-and-sanitation?tab=table&facet=none&Resource=Drinking+water&Level+of+Access=Safely+managed&Residence=Total&Relative+to+population=Share+of+population&country=IND~USA~KEN~OWID_WRL~BGD~ZAF~CHN> accessed 4 November 2021.

[482] UNEP, *Model Law and Guidance on Regulating Lead Paint* (United Nations Environment Programme 2017).

[483] See <https://saicmknowledge.org/content/lead-paint-law-map> accessed 4 January 2021.

[484] IISD, 'African Regional Meeting on Eliminating Lead in Paint Recommends 90 ppm Limit' (1 October 2019) <https://sdg.iisd.org/news/african-regional-meeting-on-eliminating-lead-in-paint-recommends-90-ppm-limit/> accessed 4 January 2022.

c) Critique

When it comes particularly to target 3.9, it suffers from a fragmented field: only a few instruments deal with environmental pollution and health in an integral manner, and often different authorities—at the national but also at the international level—are responsible.[485] At the international level, for example, responsibility is dispersed among WHO, the World Bank, UNDP, and UNEP (housing the Strategic Approach to International Chemicals Management (SAICM)). However, several initiatives have been introduced over the past years to overcome this fragmented field. For example, since 2009, InforMEA brings together more than twenty Secretariats of Multinational Environmental Agreements (MEAs)—ranging from CITES over the United Nations Convention of Climate Change (UNFCCC)—providing information on research across their treaty texts, Climate Change Conference (COP) decisions, national strategies and policies as well as related judicial decisions. Among others, they filter relevant provisions of MEAs on target 3.9, enabling quick access to information.[486] The WHA approved the 'Chemical Road Map' in 2016 to tie the health sector closer to the SAICM.[487] And in 2020, WHO published its 'Global Strategy on Health, Environment and Climate Change', attempting to take on a clearer leadership role.[488] Moreover, in October 2021 the UN Human Rights Council for the first time recognized an express human right to 'a clean, healthy and *sustainable* environment'.[489] It is hoped that these efforts lead to a more focused action and quicker reduction of deaths.

10. Target 3.a Strengthen the implementation of the WHO Framework Convention on Tobacco Control in all countries, as appropriate

a) Sources of target

Target 3.a is one of four 'means of implementation' targets linked to SDG 3. As mentioned above, SDG 3 has the most means of implementation targets (aside from SDG 17), signifying the importance of health in the overall SDG framework. Yet, target 3.a is not a 'traditional' means of implementation target as it shows little overlap with the seven categories of means of implementation contained in SDG 17 (finance; technology; capacity-building; trade; policy and institutional coherence; multi-stakeholder partnerships; data, monitoring, and accountability).[490] Thus, it is tracked through one (outcome) indicator—3.a.1 Age-standardized prevalence of current tobacco use among persons aged fifteen years and older—which does not measure implementation but rather the 'intended outcome'[491] of the implementation of the WHO Framework Convention on Tobacco Control (WHO FCTC).

---

[485] WHO, 'Global Strategy on Health, Environment and Climate Change' (n 473) 17.

[486] See <http://www.informea.org/en/goal/target-39> accessed 3 January 2022.

[487] WHA69.4, 'The Role of the Health Sector in the Strategic Approach to International Chemicals Management towards the 2020 Goal and Beyond' (28 May 2016).

[488] WHO, 'Global Strategy on Health, Environment and Climate Change' (n 473).

[489] UNHRC Res 48/13 (8 October 2021) 'The Human Rights to a Clean, Healthy and Sustainable Environment' UN Doc A/HRC/RES/48/13.

[490] M Elder and others, 'An Optimistic Analysis of the Means of Implementation for Sustainable Development Goals: Thinking about Goals as Means' (2016) 8(9) Sustainability 962, 968.

[491] Seidman (n 273) 30.

The WHO FCTC was adopted in 2003 and by 2021 had been ratified by 182 states parties.[492] It is the 'first public health treaty negotiated under the auspices of WHO',[493] reinforcing WHO's approach towards the interlinkage between public health and the right to health.[494]

b) Empirical analysis and efforts of international/domestic implementation

Monitoring target 3.a through its above-mentioned indicator has remained challenging, with WHO noting that data collection and survey results have been lagging for several years.[495] Only about one-third of the VNRs include any reference to target 3.a, and the majority of this third simply mention statistical data rather than a detailed discussion or presentation of tobacco control measures.[496] Moreover, the gap between target and indicator becomes obvious in light of recent studies that suggest that there is 'no evidence to indicate that global progress in reducing cigarette consumption has been accelerated by the FCTC treaty mechanism'.[497] Per capita cigarette consumption has been increasing in LMICs, while it has been decreasing in developed countries since the early 1990s. By 2021, tobacco accounts for more than 7 million deaths/year, with four out of five smokers living in LMICs.[498] It has been estimated that the (development assistance) funding gap 'to scale up tobacco control to FCTC-compliant levels' is more than 95 per cent, with domestic spending also still far off target.[499]

On the basis of the WHO FCTC, in 2008 WHO introduced six MPOWER measures as a technical package to reverse the tobacco epidemic: (i) *Monitoring* tobacco consumption and the effectiveness of preventive measures; (ii) *Protect* people from tobacco smoke; (iii) *Offer* help to quit tobacco use; (iv) *Warn* about the dangers of tobacco; (v) *Enforce* bans on tobacco advertising, promotion and sponsorship; and (vi) *Raise* taxes on tobacco.[500] In 2020, WHO estimated that 69 per cent of the world's population had become covered by at least one of these measures,[501] yet implementation is still uneven.[502]

---

[492] WHO Framework Convention on Tobacco Control (adopted 21 May 2003, entered into force 27 February 2005) 2302 UNTS 166.

[493] WHO, *Health in 2015* (n 14) 133.

[494] WHO Framework Convention on Tobacco Control (adopted 21 May 2003, entered into force 27 February 2005) 2302 UNTS 166, Preamble (referring, among others, to WHO's Preamble, the ICESCR, the Convention on the Elimination of All Forms of Discrimination against Women and the Convention on the Rights of the Child).

[495] WHO, 'WHO Report on the Global Tobacco Epidemic, 2021—Addressing New and Emerging Products' (WHO 2021) 22.

[496] FCTC, 'Guide for WHO FCTC Parties on Including SDG Target 3.a in Voluntary National Reviews' (FCTC 2021) 5.

[497] SJ Hoffman and others, 'Impact of the WHO Framework Convention on Tobacco Control on Global Cigarette Consumption: Quasi-Experimental Evaluations Using Interrupted Time Series Analysis and In-Sample Forecast Event Modelling' (2019) 365 British Medical Journal l2287.

[498] WHO 'Noncommunicable Diseases Factsheet' (n 370); BK Matthes and M Zatoński, 'Tobacco Control and Sustainable Development: Shared Challenges and Future Opportunities' (2019) 5(1) Journal of Health Inequalities 71, 72.

[499] R Forrest and SR Taylor, 'It Is Time to Become Serious about Closing the Global Resource Gap for FCTC Implementation' (2020) 18 Tobacco Induced Diseases 103.

[500] WHO, 'WHO Report on the Global Tobacco Epidemic, 2008—The MPOWER Package' (WHO 2008) 23.

[501] WHO, 'WHO Report on the Global Tobacco Epidemic, 2021' (n 496) 20.

[502] FTCC/COP6(16) (18 October 2014) 'Towards a Stronger Contribution of the Conference of the Parties to Achieving the Noncommunicable Disease Global Target on Reduction of Tobacco Use'.

c) Critique

The link between tobacco control and the development agenda has recently received heightened attention. Initially, the topic was added to the SDG framework by virtue of its ties to the NCDs agenda,[503] as can also be seen by its treatment in the Addis Ababa Action Agenda on development finance which highlights that

> [w]e note the enormous burden that non-communicable diseases place on developed and developing countries. These costs are particularly challenging for small island developing States. We recognize, in particular, that, as part of a comprehensive strategy of prevention and control, price and tax measures on tobacco can be an effective and important means to reduce tobacco consumption and health-care costs and represent a revenue stream for financing for development in many countries.[504]

However, since then tobacco has been identified as 'a deadly threat to global development',[505] with close ties to the poor and most vulnerable. Relevant ties for tobacco control can thus also be found in SDG 1, 5, 8, and 12, 14, and 15.[506]

11. Target 3.b Support the research and development of vaccines and medicines for the communicable and non-communicable diseases that primarily affect developing countries, provide access to affordable essential medicines and vaccines, in accordance with the Doha Declaration on the TRIPS Agreement and Public Health, which affirms the right of developing countries to use to the full the provisions in the agreement on trade related aspects of intellectual property rights regarding flexibilities to protect public health, and, in particular, provide access to medicines for all

a) Sources of target

Target 3.b—alongside targets 3.c and 3.d—reflects the imperative of the international community to cooperate on reaching the health targets and overcoming persisting inequities by providing development assistance. It covers two main aspects: research and development of vaccines and medicines; access to affordable essential medicines and vaccines for all.

International trade law constitutes a well-known impediment to the sharing of access to medicines and vaccines.[507] As acknowledged by the UN Human Rights Council, 'the protection of intellectual property is important for the development of new and

---

[503] On the link see S Zhou and J Liberman, 'The Global Tobacco Epidemic and the WHO Framework Convention on Tobacco Control—The Contributions of the World Health Organization's First Convention to Global Health Law and Governance' in GL Burci and B Toebes (eds), *Research Handbook on Global Health Law* (Edward Elgar 2018) 340.

[504] UNGA Res 69/313 (27 July 2015) 'Addis Ababa Action Agenda of the Third International Conference on Financing for Development (Addis Ababa Action Agenda' UN Doc A/RES/69/313, para 32.

[505] M Chan, as cited in Matthes and Zatoński (n 499) 71.

[506] ibid 72–73.

[507] R Nazar and others, 'Role of Public Health and Trade for Achieving Sustainable Development Goals' (2020) Journal of Public Affairs 1, 3.

innovative medicines and vaccines'.[508] That said, the TRIPS Agreement[509] contains a number of so-called TRIPS flexibilities when it comes to its implementation.[510] This includes not only exemptions for LDCs (article 66(1)), but also the 'manner in which the TRIPS Agreement's provisions are interpreted and implemented'.[511] Thus, in 2001, the 4th Ministerial Conference adopted the Doha Declaration on the TRIPS Agreement and Public Health which highlighted that 'the TRIPS Agreement does not and should not prevent Members from taking measures to protect public health. Accordingly, ... we affirm that the Agreement *can and should be interpreted and implemented in a manner supportive of WTO Members' right to protect public health* and, in particular, to promote access to medicines for all. In this connection, we reaffirm the right of WTO Members to use, to the full, the provisions in the TRIPS Agreement, which provide flexibility for this purpose.' [512] There is no exhaustive list what these flexibilities might encompass, but in regard to public health some examples concern, for example, government use or security exceptions.[513] Nevertheless, the equitable access and distribution of (research and use of) medicines and vaccines—though termed 'global public good'[514]—has remained a source of contention, as has become evident during the COVID-19 pandemic.[515]

b) Empirical analysis

There are three indicators suggested for target 3.b: 3.b.1, Proportion of the target population covered by all vaccines included in their national programme; 3.b.2, Total net official development assistance to medical research and basic health sectors; and 3.b.3, Proportion of health facilities that have a core set of relevant essential medicines available and affordable on a sustainable basis.

Indicator 3.b.1 tracks the coverage of four vaccines: DTP containing vaccine, measles containing vaccine, pneumococcal conjugate vaccine, and HPV vaccine. There is a close link to target 3.2 on child health (which had previously included vaccination monitoring against measles in MDG 4). Despite this expansion, this is quite narrow in comparison to other vaccine monitoring programmes. For example, in 2012, the WHA approved the Global Vaccine Action Plan to work towards delivering universal access to immunization by 2020.[516] Work on the action plan stemmed from a collaboration between WHO, UNICEF, Global Alliance for Vaccines and Immunization (Gavi),

---

[508] HRC Res 41/10 (11 July 2019) UN Doc A/HRC/RES/41/10, para 3.

[509] Agreement on Trade-Related Aspects of Intellectual Property Rights (adopted 15 April 1994, entered into force 1 January 1995) 1869 UNTS 299.

[510] CM Correa, 'Interpreting the Flexibility Under the TRIPS Agreement' in CM Correa and RM Hilty (eds), *Access to Medicines and Vaccines—Implementing Flexibility Under Intellectual Property Law* (Springer 2022) 1, 3.

[511] ibid 4.

[512] Doha WTO Ministerial Declaration (14 November 2001) WT/MIN(01)/DEC/1, para 4 (emphasis added).

[513] For a more detailed list see Correa, 'Interpreting the Flexibility Under the TRIPS Agreement' (n 511) 7–8.

[514] G20 Leaders' Declaration (Riyadh Summit, 21–22 November 2020) <www.ilo.org/wcmsp5/groups/public/---dgreports/---dcomm/documents/meetingdocument/wcms_761761.pdf> accessed 5 November 2021, para 3.

[515] See, eg, HM Haugen, 'Does TRIPS (Agreement on Trade-Related Aspects of Intellectual Property Rights) Prevent COVID-19 Vaccines as a Global Public Good?' (2021) 24 The Journal of World Intellectual Property 195.

[516] WHO, 'Global Vaccine Action Plan—Monitoring, Evaluation & Accountability—Secretariat Annual Report 2020' (World Health Organization 2020).

the US National Institute of Allergy and Infectious Diseases (NIAID), and the Bill & Melinda Gates Foundation. The Action Plan developed a series of targets and indicators to monitor progress on immunization goals which had been set in different fora.[517] The programme is aimed at creating access 'to all available vaccines', as well as tracking the development and introduction of new vaccines.[518] By 2020, progress had been made but the overall objectives have not yet been reached.[519] The successor programme (Immunization Agenda 2030),[520] however, builds on the set targets while hoping to adopt a more country-tailored approach.[521] Moreover, indicator 3.b.1 does not directly track progress on the new development of vaccines (such as against COVID-19), which however nevertheless will regularly be reported by WHO.[522] With regard to COVID-19 vaccinations, WHO has also implemented a specific tool (Access to COVID-19 Accelerator) 'to accelerate development, production, and equitable access to COVID-19 tests, treatments, and vaccines'.[523]

Indicator 3.b.2 measures an input into the health system (net official development assistance (ODA)) on the basis of OECD data, however none of the other indicators in SDG 3 tracks any directly linked output nor how it relates to specific targets. Moreover, viewing ODA in such an isolated fashion might not be comprehensive enough.[524] There is wide agreement that an increase in investments is essential in reaching SDG 3,[525] however indicator 3.b.2 does not consider any alternative source of development finance, particularly leaving out the private sector. It also does not indicate any special target which developed states should reach in their ODA funding for health programmes. However, additional data are compiled by the Global Observatory on Health Research and Development.[526] Thus, in 2012, the WHO Consultative Expert Working Group on Research and Development: Financing and Coordination suggested a 0.01

---

[517] For an overview see IA2030, 'Immunization Agenda 2030—A Global Strategy to Leave No One Behind' (2020) 19–20 <https://cdn.who.int/media/docs/default-source/immunization/strategy/ia2030/ia2030-draft-4-wha_b8850379-1fce-4847-bfd1-5d2c9d9e32f8.pdf?sfvrsn=5389656e_66&download=true> accessed 5 November 2021.

[518] WHO, 'Global Vaccine Action Plan 2011–2020' (World Health Organization 2013) Annex 1.

[519] N MacDonald and others, 'Global Vaccine Action Plan Lessons Learned I: Recommendations for the Next Decade' (2020) 38 Vaccine 5364.

[520] WHA65.17 (26 May 2012); WHA73/7 (6 May 2020) 'Global Vaccine Action Plan—Draft Immunization Vision and Strategy: "Immunization Agenda 2030"'.

[521] See IA2030, 'Immunization Agenda 2030—A Global Strategy to Leave No One Behind' (2020) 18 <https://cdn.who.int/media/docs/default-source/immunization/strategy/ia2030/ia2030-draft-4-wha_b8850379-1fce-4847-bfd1-5d2c9d9e32f8.pdf?sfvrsn=5389656e_66&download=true> accessed 5 November 2021.

[522] SDG Indicator Metadata (March 2020) <https://unstats.un.org/sdgs/metadata/files/Metadata-03-0b-01.pdf> accessed 4 November 2021.

[523] <http://www.who.int/initiatives/act-accelerator/about> accessed 5 November 2021.

[524] As observed critically by Seidman: 'While an increase in ODA may signify increasing expenditure on health, it does not take into account government and out-of-pocket spending on health, and it may also cause or exacerbate issues with donor dependency in low- and middle-income countries (LMICs). Further, given the variation in efficiency of health spending across countries, an increase in total ODA may not necessarily represent any changes to health systems outputs.' Seidman (n 273) 30.

[525] L Sachs and JD Sachs, 'Health Priorities For Sustainable Development' in SP Marks and B Rajagopal (eds), *Critical Issues in Human Rights and Development* (Edward Elgar 2021).

[526] <http://www.who.int/observatories/global-observatory-on-health-research-and-development> accessed 6 November 2021.

per cent GDP target for ODA funding of health research and development programs,[527] a target that hardly any state meets.

Indicator 3.b.3 tracks the proportion of health facilities that have a core set of available and affordable relevant essential medicines. By tracking both aspects in one indicator, the objective is to be able to make an overall assessment on access to (essential) medicines.[528] As of late 2021, however, it remains a tier II indicator, meaning that data are currently not available to a sufficient degree. The characterization of medicines as essential relates to a globally defined core set of '32 tracer of essential medicines for acute and chronic, communicable and non-communicable diseases in the primary health care setting'[529] which are selected from the 2017 WHO Model List of Essential Medicines (which contains approximately 400 medicines). Indicator 3.b.3's Metadata contains a detailed description and reasoning for the selection of these particular thirty-two essential medicines in its Annex.

c) Critique

The field of research, development, and access to vaccines and medicines is at a crucial point of intersection between international human rights law and international trade law. From a human rights perspective, the argument can be made that states owe their obligation to protect and fulfil the right to health, including access to vaccines and medicines,[530] not only within their own jurisdiction but also extraterritorially, including through the transfer of environmentally sound technologies, and the regulation of private actors. Thus, in the context of the COVID-19 pandemic, the Committee of Economic, Social and Cultural Rights recalled that '[g]iven the global nature of the pandemic, States have the obligation to support, to the maximum of their available resources, efforts to make vaccines available globally. Vaccine nationalism breaches the extraterritorial obligations of States to avoid taking decisions that limit the ability of other States to make vaccines available to their populations and thus to implement their human rights obligations relating to the right to health, as it results in a shortage of vaccines for those who are most in need in the least developed countries.'[531] Yet, as the pandemic has also shown, despite the pressing need in achieving a more equitable distribution of vaccines and increasing the level of international finance available to support global healthcare advancements, little progress has been made, in light of not only a lack of resources but particularly political support.

---

[527] WHO 'Consultative Expert Working Group on Research and Development: Financing and Coordination' (20 April 2012) (79), A65/24.

[528] SDG Indicator Metadata (January 2019) <https://unstats.un.org/sdgs/metadata/files/Metadata-03-0B-03.pdf> accessed 4 November 2021.

[529] ibid.

[530] HRC Res 41/10 (11 July 2019) UN Doc A/HRC/RES/41/10, para 1: 'Recognizes that access to medicines and vaccines is one of the fundamental elements for the full realization of the right of everyone to the enjoyment of the highest attainable standard of physical and mental health and the correspondent objectives of universal health coverage and health for all, without discrimination, with special attention to reaching those furthest behind first.'

[531] CESCR 'Statement on Universal Affordable Vaccination against Coronavirus Disease (COVID-19), international Cooperation and Intellectual Property' (23 April 2021) UN Doc E/C.12/2021/1, para 4.

262   SDG 3

12. Target 3.c Substantially increase health financing and the recruitment, development, training and retention of the health workforce in developing countries, especially in least developed countries and small island developing states

a) Sources of target

Target 3.c reflects the SDG's changed approach in comparison to earlier development programmes on health by focusing less on 'the funding of vertical programmes' and instead pursuing a 'more system-wide, cross-cutting support',[532] as envisioned also by UHC. It supports the overall SDG framework and its objective of improving health for all by focusing on finance and capacity-building. As WHO projects for 2030, 'the investment needed for educating and employing sufficient health workers to achieve UHC equates to almost 50 per cent of the cost of achieving SDG 3'.[533]

b) Empirical analysis and efforts of international/domestic implementation

Target 3.c is tracked by one indicator: 3.c.1, Health worker density and distribution, which calculates number of medical doctors, nursing, and midwifery personnel, dentists and pharmacists per 10,000 population in the given national and/or sub-national area.[534] There is, however, no clear indication what 'substantially increase' should mean in quantitative terms.

In 2016, in an attempt to work towards the fulfilment of target 3.c, WHO adopted the Global Strategy on Human Resources for Health: Workforce 2030.[535] This promotes an intersectoral approach between education, health, labour, and finance sectors, and sets specific targets. These include, for example, the establishment of accreditation mechanisms for health training institutions (1.1); making progress on course completion rates in medical, nursing, and allied health professionals training institutions (1.3); reducing the dependency on foreign-trained health professionals (2.1, in line with the 2010 WHO Global Code of Practice on the International Recruitment of Health Personnel),[536] creating and sustainable at least 10 million additional full-time jobs in the health- and social-care sectors (2.3); increasing of health financing (eg through bilateral and multilateral agencies, 2.2); the instalment of regulatory mechanisms to promote patient safety and adequate oversight of the private sector (3.3); and the strengthening of data registries (4.1).[537] Given the intersectoral approach, links to other SDGs are relevant as well, particularly SDGs 4 (education), 5 (gender equality), and 8 (decent work).[538]

---

[532] WHO, *Health in 2015* (n 14) 28.

[533] WHO, 'Thirteenth General Programme of Work 2019–2023' (n 165) 15.

[534] SDG Indicator Metadata (March 2021) <https://unstats.un.org/sdgs/metadata/files/Metadata-03-0C-01.pdf> accessed 4 November 2021.

[535] WHA69.19 (28 May 2016) 'Global Strategy on Human Resources for Health: Workforce 2030'.

[536] This voluntary code was adopted in 2010 by WHO, and is monitoring through regular reporting by national authorities. It is aimed at preventing the uncontrolled outflow of health workers. For an overview see A Siyam and others, 'Monitoring the Implementation of the WHO Global Code of Practice on the International Recruitment of Health Personnel' (2013) 91(11) Bulletin of the World Health Organization 816.

[537] WHO, 'Global Strategy on Human Resources for Health: Workforce 2030' (WHO 2016).

[538] See also WHO 'Human Resources for Health—Global Strategy on Human Resources for Health: Workforce 2030. Report by the Director-General' (25 March 2019) A72/24.

Moreover, with its close link to UHC, achieving target 3.c is inherent in WHO's 'Triple Billion targets', constituting part of WHO's priority programmes.[539]

c) Critique

Despite these efforts, as reported by WHO, there remain stark inequalities in distribution of health workers. For example, in the European region, there is on average one medical doctor per 232 people, whereas in the African region there is only one per 3,619 people.[540]

13. **Target 3.d Strengthen the capacity of all countries, in particular developing countries, for early warning, risk reduction and management of national and global health risks**

a) Sources of target

Target 3.d focuses on capacity building for early warning, risk reduction and management of national and global health risks. It addresses the IHRs and the newly added (in 2020) issue of antimicrobial resistance. Thus, though mentioned in the Declaration accompanying the adoption of the SDGs, initially antimicrobial resistance did not find its way into any of the targets or indicators. This omission was begrudged in scholarly circles, as well as in WHO's Global Action Plan on Antimicrobial Resistance which emphasized that '[a]ntimicrobial resistance threatens the very core of modern medicine and the sustainability of an effective, global public health response to the enduring threat from infectious diseases'.[541] Hence, in 2016, the UN adopted a Political Declaration on antimicrobial resistance which recalled that 'antimicrobial resistance challenges the sustainability and effectiveness of the public health response'.[542] Addressing antimicrobial resistance is therefore seen as essential for achieving many of SDG 3's target such as maternal or child health, but also concerns food/animal production and therefore human's livelihoods (SDGs 1, 2, and 8). Links to SDGs 6, 9, 10, 12, and 17 can also be made. The cross-cutting nature of the issue also led to the establishment of an Ad hoc Inter-Agency Coordination Group on Antimicrobial Resistance which published its report in 2019, containing a series of recommendations.[543] This also highlighted once again the urgency of the topic being included in the SDG monitoring framework.

b) Empirical analysis and efforts of international/domestic implementation

Target 3.d is tracked by two indicators: 3.d.1, IHR capacity and health emergency preparedness; 3.d.2, Percentage of bloodstream infections due to selected antimicrobial-resistant organisms.

---

[539] WHO, 'Thirteenth General Programme of Work 2019–2023' (n 165) 15.

[540] WHO, *World Health Statistics 2021* (n 290) 54.

[541] WHO, 'Global Action Plan on Antimicrobial Resistance' (WHO 2015) vii (as adopted by WHA68/2015/REC/1).

[542] UNGA 71/3 (6 October 2016) 'Political Declaration of the High-Level Meeting of the General Assembly on Antimicrobial Resistance', para 2.

[543] Ad hoc Inter-Agency Coordination Group on Antimicrobial Resistance, 'No Time to Wait: Securing the Future from Drug-Resistant Infections—Report to the Secretary-General of the United Nations' (April 2019) <http://www.who.int/docs/default-source/documents/no-time-to-wait-securing-the-future-from-drug-resistant-infections-en.pdfsfvrsn=5b424d7_6> accessed 9 November 2021.

Indicator 3.d.1 relates to the revised 2005 IHRs which were adopted by the WHA under article 21(1) WHO Constitution.[544] These require member states to develop and maintain minimum core capacities for surveillance and response to matters which might become 'public health risks and public health emergencies of international concern' (article 13 IHR). Under article 54 IHR, states should report on the implementation of the IHR to the WHA in a State Party Self-Assessment Annual Reporting (SPAR). The thirteen core capacities are: (i) Legislation and financing; (ii) IHR Coordination and National IHR Focal Point communications; (iii) Surveillance; (iv) National Health Emergency Framework; (v) Health Service Provision; (vi) Risk communication; (vii) Human resources; (viii) Laboratory; (ix) Points of entry; (x) Zoonotic events and the human–animal interface; (xi) Food safety; (xii) Chemical events; (xiii) Radionuclear emergencies.[545]

Indicator 3.d.2 is focused on antimicrobial resistance. As already mentioned, it has been newly added to the monitoring framework in March 2020 by the UN Statistical Commission (as a tier II indicator). Although newly introduced, indicator 3.d.2 can build on the WHO Global Antimicrobial Resistance and Use Surveillance System (GLASS) as a data source. This platform was launched through the Global Action Plan on Antimicrobial Resistance in 2015 and has since then expanded. As of 2021, approximately 100 states have enrolled in GLASS, reporting on a set of indicators which they have implemented in their national strategies and programs.[546]

c) Critique

While target 3.d is focused on capacity building, the IHR framework has been criticized for its lack of 'detailed strategies for capacity building'.[547] In particular, there is no funding allocated to WHO to assist State Parties.[548] Financial assistance for health security was intended to be pooled through such initiatives as the Global Health Security Agenda[549] which supplements the self-reporting under the IHR framework with an external assessment tool, and which has been endorsed by WHO.[550] Moreover, WHO has specified target 3.d in its 'Triple Billion targets', aiming for '1 billion more people better protected from health emergencies' by 2023.[551] Though this underscores the importance of the target, it also demonstrates the lack of financial assistance so far available. The COVID-19 pandemic has underscored how important capacity building in this area remains, and it is expected that international financial assistance will increase.[552]

---

[544] Art 21(a) WHO Constitution: 'The Health Assembly shall have authority to adopt regulations concerning (a) sanitary and quarantine requirements and other procedures designed to prevent the international spread of disease'; WHA58.3 (23 May 2005) 'Revision of the International Health Regulations'.

[545] <https://extranet.who.int/e-spar> accessed 10 November 2021.

[546] The most recent report is from June 2021: WHO, 'Global Antimicrobial Resistance and Use Surveillance System (GLASS) Report' (WHO 2021).

[547] LO Gostin, *Global Health Law* (Harvard University Press 2014) 188.

[548] ibid.

[549] <https://ghsagenda.org/> accessed 8 November 2021.

[550] MR Boyce and others, 'Financial Assistance for Health Security: Effects of International Financial Assistance on Capacities for Preventing, Detecting, and Responding to Public Health Emergencies' (2021) International Journal of Health Policy and Management 1.

[551] WHO, 'Thirteenth General Programme of Work 2019–2023' (n 165) 22.

[552] Boyce and others (n 551) 2.

V. Conclusion

SDG 3 is central to the overall SDG framework and to development in general. With close ties to the previous MDGs, a number of SDG 3's targets continue part of the 'unfinished business' of the Millennium framework. Previous omissions, particularly NCDs, have now been added as new targets. Still, progress on many targets has slowed, with the COVID-19 pandemic raising new challenges to achieving many aspects of development, and particularly SDG 3.

SDG 4

'Ensure Inclusive and Equitable Quality Education and Promote Lifelong Learning Opportunities for All'

Jane Kotzmann, Morgan Stonebridge, and John R Morss*

I. Introduction

Education is central to enabling citizens to participate in society and contribute to broader societal goals. The provision of education is not only fundamental for enabling the exercise of all other human rights but also enabling learners of all ages to promote principles of inclusivity, gender equality, and sustainability needed to address contemporary global challenges. In this respect, the importance of education that empowers learners to tackle current challenges cannot be overstated. Sustainable Development Goal 4 (SDG 4) acknowledges this need by capturing important themes of lifelong learning, provision of inclusive education for children and adults with differing learning needs, need for equality of access and outcome across genders, sensitivity towards gender identification choices, and sustainability.

This acknowledgement and utilization of the far-reaching power of education comes at a time when education is in a state of change and it faces serious obstacles. The COVID-19 pandemic has had a profound impact on learners and learning. Global lockdowns demanded a rapid shift to digital learning as a consequence of school closures, resulting in a difficult transition for those in a position to take it and exclusion from education for the most vulnerable. Progress towards SDG 4 has been further impacted by the COVID-19 pandemic given the reorientation of funding and priorities towards SDG 3, which is concerned with public health and well-being.[1] The recent collapse of the Afghan government and return of the Taliban signals a critical challenge to education, particularly for girls and women, in that region. It raises concerns, not only regarding access to education but also as to whether the content of education will

---

* The authors are immensely grateful for the feedback and research assistance provided by Bruce Chen, Helen Chimonis, Katerina Psathas, Beth Wilkinson, Eden Stubbings, and numerous staff at the Deakin University Law School. Any remaining errors are, of course, the authors' own.

[1] O Ekwebelem and others, 'Threats of COVID-19 to Achieving United Nations Sustainable Development Goals in Africa' (2021) 104(2) The American Journal of Tropical Medicine and Hygiene 457.

268 SDG 4

promote the principles necessary for the full development of the child as an active and global citizen.

Education has a significant role to play in supporting children and adults in crises such as these. The right to education promotes the full enjoyment of all other human rights. It is, as identified by Katarina Tomaševski, former Special Rapporteur on the right to education, a 'multiplier'.[2] The same can be said of SDG 4. The provision of education in the manner captured by SDG 4 will multiply the ability of states to achieve all other Sustainable Development Goals (SDGs) by equipping learners with the knowledge necessary to live empowered lives that promote the broader 2030 Agenda.[3]

II. *Travaux Préparatoires*

A. Background

The immediate genealogy of SDG 4 can be traced, as with other SDGs, from the era of the development of the Millennium Development Goals (MDGs) in the late 1990s. SDG 4 emerged from the articulation, promulgation, and evaluation of those targets in the first fifteen years of the new Millennium, and the specific preparatory work in 2013–14 that resulted in the formulation of SDG 4 as adopted by the United Nations General Assembly (UNGA) in 2015.[4] In that respect, the experience of focusing on the universal provision of education at the primary level by 2015, as set out in MDG 2, was central to the definition of goals related to education for the period 2015 to 2030.

Further back, the SDG project connects with an 'emerging global sustainable development agenda' which can be traced to such initiatives as the 1987 Brundtland Report on Environmental Protection and Sustainable Development[5] and the 1992 United Nations (UN) Conference on Environment and Development, Agenda 21, held in Rio de Janeiro.[6] That sustainable development agenda did not ignore the role of education;[7] however, the focus was predominantly on encouraging and managing global economic growth, while setting in place checks and balances designed to protect long-term environmental resources and, to some extent, the rights and needs of local communities.[8]

---

[2] UN Economic and Social Council, 'Annual Report of the Special Rapporteur on the Right to Education, Katerina Tomaševski, Submitted in Accordance with Commission on Human Rights Resolution 2000/9' (11 January 2001) UN Doc e/CN.4/2001/52.

[3] UNGA Res 66/288 (11 September 2012) UN Doc A/RES/66/288 para 229.

[4] United Nations General Assembly, 'Draft Outcome Document of the United Nations Summit for the Adoption of the Post-2015 Development Agenda' (15 September 2015) UN Doc A/RES/69/315.

[5] Brundtland Commission, *Report of the World Commission on Environment and Development: Our Common Future* (OUP 1987); K Rudd, 'UN 2030: Rebuilding Order in a Fragmenting World' (Chair's Report, Independent Commission on Multilateralism, ICM/IPI, 15 August 2016) 14.

[6] UNGA, 'Report of the UN Conference on Environment and Development' (Rio de Janeiro, 3–14 June 1992) (12 Aug 1992) UN Doc A/CONF.151/26.

[7] See, eg, ibid (Vol III) ch 36.

[8] A Baldin, 'Agenda 21' in P Robbins (ed), *Encyclopedia of Environment and Society* (1st edn, SAGE Publications 2007) 11.

The integration of education goals into a global sustainability agenda has been a mission of the early twenty-first century.[9] In parallel, the economic development agenda has been increasingly tempered by human rights concerns, both individual and collective, including self-determination rights of peoples.[10]

Development, human rights, and sustainability might all be said to converge on education in its broadest senses. In doing so, global trends in educational policy and planning from the 1970s onwards have contributed in significant ways to the broader world view expressed in SDG 4. These trends embrace inclusiveness in educational provision with respect to both children and adults with a disability or with specific learning needs; gender equality and a sensitivity to gender identification choices in educational provision; and the recognition of lifespan needs in relation to education. Other relevant trends in education more generally include trends in pedagogy and in relation to the measurement of educational achievement and of teacher effectiveness. Other relevant aspects of education policy, also evolving significantly in recent decades, include questions of cultural and religious constraints on educational opportunity, and hence such conceptual challenges as the balance of parental authority versus children's autonomy and the balance of universal versus culturally specific rights and needs, and concrete fiscal dilemmas around state funding of faith-based educational institutions. In terms of economic policy questions, the relative role of public and of private educational providers differs across UN Member States, across levels of educational provision from pre-school education to tertiary education and beyond, and fluctuates with governmental change.

Before turning to the Open Working Group (OWG) process that directly generated SDG 4 and provides a history of the negotiations leading to the final goal and targets, a series of contributions contextual to the operational period of the MDGs should be noted. In an initiative of the United Nations Educational, Scientific and Cultural Organization (UNESCO), which was to remain a very significant actor in relation to SDG 4, the 2000 World Education Forum in Education For All[11] set out six education goals to be reached by 2015. The six Education For All (EFA) goals included meeting the learning needs of young people and adults and improving adult literacy. This EFA framework was running in tandem with the MDGs and was more comprehensive.[12] Two years later in 2002, the Johannesburg Plan[13] observed that it was 'essential to mobilize necessary resources' to ensure education promoting sustainable development.[14]

---

[9] For example, rights to education have been covered in various international instruments from the UDHR in 1948, the ICESCR 1966 (also General Comment on art 13), the CRC 1989, the CEDAW 1979, the CRPD 2006, and the Convention on the Elimination of All Forms of Racial Discrimination 1965.

[10] See generally, UN, 'We Need More Urgency to Achieve the 2020 Agenda's Promise to the World's People, human Rights Council Told' *UN News* (New York, 16 January 2019) <https://www.un.org/development/desa/en/news/sustainable/sdgs-human-rights.html> accessed 22 August 2021.

[11] UNESCO, 'Dakar Framework for Action: Education for All' (May 2000).

[12] United Nations Task Team, 'Education and Skills for Inclusive and Sustainable Development Beyond 2015' 6 (May 2012) <https://www.un.org/millenniumgoals/pdf/Think%20Pieces/4_education.pdf > accessed 22 August 2021.

[13] UN, 'Report of the World Summit on Sustainable Development' (Johannesburg, South Africa 26 August–4 September 2002) UN Doc A/CONF.199/20 para 116.

[14] ibid.

270 SDG 4

Evaluation of the MDGs, including MDG 2, took place throughout this period, overlapping with the key planning decisions for SDGs.[15] The significance of education in the MDGs was emphasized by the 2010 report on the 'Central Role of Education in the Millennium Development Goals'.[16] The need for equality of access to secondary education was stressed.[17] Also in 2010, the Right to Education Project's Reflections on 'Measuring Education as a Human Right'[18] and in a more systematic way, The Lancet Commission's report looking beyond the MDGs all contributed to the overall evaluation of the MDGs and hence in effect constituted planning for a future programme.

At the UN level, a UN System Task Team dedicated to the post-2015 Agenda was formed by instruction of the UN Secretary-General in 2011.[19] During 2012 and early 2013 a series of UN-facilitated thematic consultation meetings focused on education took place under the aegis of UNESCO and the United Nations Children's Fund (UNICEF).[20] Also, two Asia-Pacific regional high-level expert meetings focused on education beyond 2015 took place in Bangkok in May and November of 2012. The November meeting gave rise to the 'Beyond 2015' outcome document.[21] Global thematic consultation on education was brought into focus in Dakar in March 2013 (the 'Global Thematic Consultation on Education in the Post-2015 Development Agenda').[22] In the same month, the OWG held its first meeting. The report from the Dakar meeting, 'The World We Want', recommended a rights based approach and proposed a goal of 'Equitable, Quality Education and Lifelong Learning for All'.[23] These Dakar recommendations influenced the deliberations of the High-Level Panel of Eminent Persons, whose report in May 2013 recommended that the overarching goal for education should be to 'provide quality education and lifelong learning'.[24] Early in 2014, UNESCO submitted a position paper on education post-2015 in which it outlined its experiences with the EFA programme and communicated its recommendations on education beyond 2015.[25]

---

[15] Office of the High Commissioner for Human Rights, 'Human Rights and MDGs in Practice: A Review of Country Strategies and Reporting' (Report 2010) <https://www.ohchr.org/Documents/Issues/MDGs/Human_rights_and_MDGs_in_practice_ML.pdf> accessed 22 August 2021.

[16] UNESCO, 'The Central Role of Education in the Millennium Development Goals' (September 2010) ED.2011/WS/2.

[17] ibid 20.

[18] Right to Education Initiative, 'Beyond Statistics: Measuring Education as a Human Right, Reflections' (9 July 2010).

[19] Interoffice Memorandum No 11-08757 (19 September 2011) para 4; ESCWA, 'Regional and Global Priorities: Progress Achieved in the preparation of the United Nations Development Agenda Beyond 2015' (1 October 2021) UN Doc E/ESCWE/2012/C.7/5 (Part I).

[20] M Sachs-Israel, 'The SDG 4-Education 2030 Agenda and its Framework for Action—The Process of its Development and First Steps in Taking It Forward' (2016) 69(3) Bildung und Erziehung 269, 271.

[21] UNESCO Bangkok 'What Education for the Future? Beyond-2015: Rethinking Learning in a Changing World' (Asia-Pacific Regional High-Level Expert Meeting, Bangkok, Outcome Document, 26–28 November 2012).

[22] Y Sayed, 'Making Education a Priority in the Post-2015 Development Agenda' (Report of the Global Thematic Consultation on Education in the Post-2015 Development Agenda, ED-13/EFA/POST-2015/1, 2013).

[23] UNESCO, 'Dakar Framework for Action' (World Education Forum, Dakar, Senegal, 26–28 April 2000).

[24] High-Level Panel of Eminent Persons on the Post-2015 Development Agenda, 'A New Global Partnership: Eradicate Poverty and Transform Economies through Sustainable Development' (Report 2013).

[25] UNESCO, 'Position Paper on Education Post-2015' (February 2014); Yusuf Sayed, 'Making Education a Priority in the Post-2015 Development Agenda' (Report of the Global Thematic Consultation on Education in the Post-2015 Development Agenda, ED-13/EFA/POST-2015/1, 2013).

Meanwhile, following the delivery of the High-Level Report 'Resilient People, Resilient Planet' in January 2012,[26] the 2012 Rio Conference on Sustainable Development (the 'Earth Summit' or 'Rio +20' Conference) took place in June of that year.[27] General recommendations on the role of education in future goal-setting were endorsed in the outcome document for Rio + 20 in 2012, 'The Future We Want'.[28] This Report included advocacy for the significance of going beyond MDGs in education, for example in terms of access to education services for people with disabilities and for Indigenous peoples.[29] An 'open working group' process was proposed for the formulation of sustainable goals.[30]

The UN System Task Team Report to the Secretary-General of June 2012, 'Realizing the Future We Want for All' referred to the Rio + 20 recommendations for the OWG process toward the articulation of SDGs.[31] 'The Future We Want', including its procedural proposals, was itself endorsed at the 66th session of the UNGA in July 2012.[32]

B. The OWG Sessions

Accordingly, by resolution of 'The Future We Want', the UNGA resolved to establish an OWG to develop a proposal for a set of global sustainable development goals to succeed the MDGs.[33] This would be the first time a working group methodology had been employed to articulate a set of development goals.[34] The OWG was then established in January of 2013 by decision 67/555 of the UNGA,[35] guided by the requirement that it be an 'inclusive and transparent intergovernmental process on sustainable development goals that is open to all stakeholders'.[36]

The OWG was subject to standing rules of procedure of Committees of the UNGA, and observers attended its meetings as representatives of Specialised Agencies and related organizations, or of non-governmental organizations (NGOs) in consultative status with Economic and Social Council.[37] At any one time, the OWG was to comprise

---

[26] UN Secretary General's High-Level Panel on Global Sustainability, 'Resilient People, Resilient Planet: A Future worth Choosing' (Report 2012).

[27] UN, 'United Nations Conference on Sustainable Development, Rio+20' <https://sustainabledevelopment. un.org/rio20> accessed 27 August 2021; UNGA Res 66/288 (11 September 2012) UN Doc A/RES/66/288.

[28] UNGA Res 66/288 (11 September 2012) UN Doc A/RES/66/288.

[29] ibid para 229.

[30] ibid para 248.

[31] UNTT, 'Realising the Future We Want for All' (June 2012) <https://sustainabledevelopment.un.org/content/ documents/614Post_2015_UNTTreport.pdf> accessed 27 August 2021.

[32] UNGA Res 66/288 (11 September 2012) UN Doc A/RES/66/288.

[33] ibid para 248.

[34] D O'Connor and others, *Transforming Multilateral Diplomacy: The Inside Story of the Sustainable Development Goals* (Routledge 2018) ch 3.

[35] UNGA Res 67/555 (22 January 2013) UN Doc A/DEC/67/555; UNGA, 'Open Working Group of the General Assembly on Sustainable Development Goals: Draft Decision' (15 January 2013) UN Doc A/67/L.48/Rev.1.

[36] UNGA Res 66/288 (11 September 2012) UN Doc A/RES/66/288 para 48; UNGA, 'Open Working Group of the General Assembly on Sustainable Development Goals: Draft Decision' (15 January 2013) UN Doc A/67/L.48/ Rev.1.

[37] Open Working Group (OWG), 'General Assembly Open Working Group on Sustainable Development Goals: Methods of Work' <https://sustainabledevelopment.un.org/content/documents/1692OWG_methods_wo rk_adopted_1403.pdf> accessed 27 August 2021.

the representatives of thirty country groups drawn from designated pools from one to four UN members in each case (with the groups of three, or 'troikas', making up around half the thirty). In this way, the OWG was composed of representatives from approximately seventy countries that had expressed interest, sharing the thirty seats between them.[38] One notable entity, neither a UN Member State nor a specialized agency nor NGO, contributed to the OWG process, namely the Holy See.[39] The basis for this preferential involvement of only one of the several global faith movements, while hardly novel in the UN context, is not at all clear.[40]

The OWG convened its first meeting in March 2013 and its final meeting in July 2014. Education featured as a priority early in this process. At the first meeting the OWG received an introduction by the Secretariat of the initial input of the Secretary-General to the SDGs, which included a number of priority areas based on a synthesis of questionnaire responses from sixty-three OWG members.[41] Education was the fourth most frequently mentioned area,[42] and thus took a place of 'prime importance' within the SDGs.[43] This area became a focus of the 4th session of the OWG, held in June 2013.[44] This 4th session was one of eight 'stocktaking sessions' in which the participants were advised and requested by the Co-Chairs to avoid negotiation in favour of creating a 'common knowledge base' on the issues.[45]

To support this mutual learning phase, the OWG received an issues brief from the Technical Support Team (TST), which recommended that the SDG agenda include 'education as a cross-cutting issue across all development goals, as well as an explicit education goal'.[46] This was explicitly endorsed by some participant states, including the troika of Papua New Guinea, Nauru, and Palau, speaking also on behalf of the Pacific Small Island Developing States, which declared support for education as a single stand-alone goal, as well as a cross-cutting issue within all other SDGs.[47] At the same time the

---

[38] ibid; UNGA Res 66/288 (11 September 2012) UN Doc A/RES/66/288 para 248; UNGA, 'Open Working Group of the General Assembly on Sustainable Development Goals: Draft Decision' (15 January 2013) UN Doc A/67/L.48/Rev.1.

[39] Vatican, 'Secretariat of State' (2013) <https://www.vatican.va/roman_curia/secretariat_state/2013/index_en.htm> accessed 27 August 2021; F Chullikatt, Intervention by the Holy See at the 4th session of the OWG (17 June 2013) <https://www.vatican.va/roman_curia/secretariat_state/2013/documents/rc_seg-st_20130617_chullikatt-dinamiche-demografiche_it.html> accessed 27 August 2021.

[40] See generally, J Morss, 'The International Legal Status of the Vatican/Holy See Complex' (2015) 26(4) European Journal of International Law 927; I Cismas, *Religious Actors and International Law* (OUP 2014).

[41] UNGA, 'Initial Input of the Secretary-General to the Open-Working Group on Sustainable Development Goals' (17 December 2012) UN Doc A/67/634 pt II.

[42] ibid 5.

[43] UN Secretary-General, 'Remarks at Opening of Open Working Group on the Sustainable Development Goals' (14 March 2013) <https://www.un.org/sg/en/content/sg/speeches/2013-03-14/remarks-opening-open-working-group-sustainable-development-goals> accessed 28 August 2021.

[44] UN, 'Draft Programme of Work: Fourth Session of the General Assembly Open Working Group on Sustainable Development Goals' (12 June 2013) <https://sustainabledevelopment.un.org/content/documents/1777Draft%20PoW%20for%20session4_1206.pdf> accessed 28 August 2021.

[45] International Institute for Sustainable Development, 'Summary of the Fourth Session of the UN General Assembly Open Working Group on Sustainable Development Goals: 17–19 June 2013' (2013) 32(4) Earth Negotiations Bulletin 1, 12 <https://enb.iisd.org/download/pdf/enb3204e.pdf> accessed 28 August 2021.

[46] Technical Support Team, 'TST Issues Brief: Education and Culture' 4 <https://sustainabledevelopment.un.org/content/documents/18290406tstisuesedcult.pdf> accessed 28 August 2021.

[47] RG Aisi 'Intervention Remarks by H.E. Mr Robert G Aisi Permanent Representative of the Independent States of Papua New Guinea to the United Nations and Chair of PSIDS Permanent Missions to the United Nations at the

need for one integrated agenda was recognized in the issue brief provided by the TST to the OWG's 4th session, which stated that 'the achievement of this vision demands a single harmonized global education framework, informed by the successes and challenges of the MDG and EFA agendas'.[48]

As outlined by some OWG contributors, this extended to a desire to ensure the post-2015 agenda was consistent with existing human rights commitments on education. This includes the references to education in the Universal Declaration of Human Rights (UDHR),[49] the International Covenant on Economic, Social and Cultural Rights (ICESCR),[50] the Convention on the Elimination of Discrimination against Women (CEDAW),[51] and the Convention on the Rights of the Child (CRC).[52] This commitment is represented in a statement to the 8th session of the OWG by the troika of the Netherlands, Australia, and the United Kingdom (UK), which recognized that '[t]he post-2015 framework is not a legally-binding treaty and it should not compete with, replicate, or seek to re-negotiate existing legally binding documents, but it should be aligned with, and be underpinned by, those standards'.[53] As a result, the education agenda of the OWG had an extensive existing framework of state obligations with which to align, as well as a need to ensure harmony with broader post-2015 education agendas.

Key features in the state submissions to the 4th session included such varied issues as universal access to primary, secondary and tertiary education; linkages between education and employment opportunities; improvements in quality and related supportive services; lifelong learning; relevant and measurable learning outcomes; special attention for marginalized groups; the use of ICT; closing the gap between formal and informal systems of education; early learning; and the need to ensure corresponding infrastructure development. These issues were reflected in meetings between the Co-Chairs, participants, and other stakeholders, such as NGOs, who emphasized that there was a need 'to shift focus from the mere access to education to quality education, including adequate facilities [and] qualified teachers'.[54] The progress report issued after the 4th session recognized these issues as a high priority and stated that, '[e]ducation is absolutely central to any sustainable development agenda. It is not only an essential investment but an important basis for human enrichment through lifelong learning.'[55]

Fourth Session of the Open Working Group on Sustainable Development' (17 June 2013) <https://sustainabledevelopment.un.org/content/documents/5113PSIDS4.pdf> 2 accessed 28 August 2021.

[48] Technical Support Team, 'TST Issues Brief' (n 46).

[49] Universal Declaration of Human Rights (adopted 10 December 1948) UNGA Res 217 A(III) (UDHR) art 26.

[50] International Convention on Economic, Social and Cultural Rights, opened for signature 19 December 1966, 993 UNTS 3 (entered into force 3 January 1976) (ICESCR) art 13.

[51] Convention on the Elimination of All Forms of Discrimination against Women, opened for signature 18 December 1979, 1249 UNTS 13 (entered into force 3 September 1981) (CEDAW) art 10.

[52] Convention on the Rights of the Child, opened for signature 20 November 1989, 1577 UNTS 3 (entered into force 2 September 1990) (CRC) art 23(3), 28, 29.

[53] OWG, 'Human Rights, The Right to Development, Global Governance: Statement by Netherlands, Australia and the UK' (December 2013) 2 <https://sustainabledevelopment.un.org/content/documents/5338uk.pdf> accessed 28 August 2021.

[54] ibid.

[55] UNGA, 'Progress Report of the Open Working Group of the General Assembly on Sustainable Development Goals' (23 July 2013) UN Doc A/67/941, 79.

274   SDG 4

At the 6th OWG session in December 2013, the focus turned to means of implementation, the needs of countries in special situations, and human rights, including the right to development. Education also featured here, with the Co-Chairs noting in their concluding remarks that 'certain types of intervention can go a long way. Among the most important is investing in education and skills development.'[56] The OWG received an issues brief on the subject of implementation from the TST, which recognized a need to focus on building national administrative and technical capacities to drive sustainable development. This brief emphasized a need to focus efforts on 'developing human resources through, inter alia, training and strengthening professional development, including technical and vocational education and training, the exchange of experience and expertise, knowledge transfer, and through new and emerging technologies, including via ICTs'.[57] This served to reiterate the centrality of education to the success of an overall sustainable development agenda.

Consistent with the principle of education being interlinked to many other goals, it featured again at the 8th and final stocktaking session. Here, education was a primary point in discussions surrounding gender equality and women's empowerment. OWG members and other stakeholders emphasized that access to quality education was a key means to address inequality. For instance, the Denmark, Norway, and Ireland troika proposed in a joint statement that access for girls to primary, secondary, and tertiary education is one of many 'critical interventions [which] will pave the way for women and girls to enjoy the full expression of their rights'.[58]

At the 10th session of the OWG, the Co-Chairs created an Encyclopedia Groupinica[59] which compiled suggestions as to goals and targets as proposed by delegates during the stocktaking sessions. In this document, education was Focus Area 4.[60] This document lists, amongst other points, universal free primary and secondary education, a focus on the most marginalized, the ability to meet minimum learning standards, and lifelong learning for all women and men.[61] The harder questions of priorities, mechanisms, resources, evaluations, and commitments are not addressed in this 'workshopping' document.

At the 11th session of the OWG, delegates discussed a list of sixteen Focus Areas and corresponding potential targets that featured in a working document. At the conclusion of these discussions, there was a consensus that education, as one of the areas considered

[56] OWG, 'Concluding Remarks of Co-Chairs 6th Session of Open Working Group on Sustainable Development Goals' (13 December 2013) <https://sustainabledevelopment.un.org/content/documents/2863Concluding%20 Remarks%20of%20CoChairs%20OWG6%20long%20Fri%20631%20pm.pdf> accessed 28 August 2021.

[57] Technical Support Team, 'TST Issues Brief: Means of Implementation; Global Partnership for Achieving Sustainable Development' 6 <https://sustainabledevelopment.un.org/content/documents/2079Issues%20Br ief%20Means%20of%20Implementation%20Final_TST_141013.pdf> accessed 28 August 2021.

[58] OWG, 'Elements of an Irish/Danish/Norwegian Intervention on the Topic of "Promoting Equality Including Social Equity, Gender Equality and Women's Empowerment"' (5 February 2014) 4 <https://sustainabledevelopm ent.un.org/content/documents/6155ireland.pdf> accessed 28 August 2021.

[59] OWG, 'Encyclopedia Groupinica: A Complication of Goals and Targets Suggestions from OWG-10' (May 2014) <https://sustainabledevelopment.un.org/content/documents/3698EncyclopediaGroupinica.pdf accessed 28 August 2021; O'Connor and others (n 44) 263.

[60] OWG, 'Encyclopedia Groupinica' (n 59).

[61] ibid.

the 'unfinished business of the MDGs', should be expressly included in the post-2015 framework.[62] This working document articulated Goal 4 to be, '[p]rovide quality education and life-long learning for all'.[63] This was consistent with the recommendation from the High Level Panel of Eminent Persons on the Post-2015 Development Agenda, the report of which the OWG was encouraged by the Secretary-General to utilize in the conceptualization of the post-2015 agenda.[64]

The 12th session of the OWG, held in June 2014, provided a 'zero draft' of the proposed goals for the post-2015 development agenda. Within this draft, Goal 4 had been expanded to '[p]rovide equitable and inclusive quality education and life-long learning opportunities for all'.[65] The addition of the words 'equitable' and 'inclusive' here represents the adoption of a wider perspective of the education agenda, one that extends beyond the narrow focus on the quality of education and effective learning. This endorsement of a wider, more inclusive education agenda can be linked in part to extensive lobbying by stakeholders, such as the Major Groups of Workers and Trade Unions, Children and Youth, and Women, which emphasized that access and equality is represented by more than enrolment numbers.[66]

The civil society groups lobbying for a comprehensive and inclusive education agenda also protested the failure of the zero draft to mention comprehensive sexuality education within the targets of Goal 4.[67] For instance, the statement of the Major Group of Children and Youth at the 12th session noted this absence and emphasized that '[s]ustainable development will only occur when girls and boys alike understand their bodies, know their rights, and have the necessary skills to negotiate on important aspects of their lives'.[68] Major Groups and other 'stakeholders' also made amendments to the proposed goals and targets at the 12th session, recommending that target 4.7 be amended to include a reference to comprehensive sexuality education, and that a further target be added providing for 'access to evidence-based, universally accessible, quality, non-judgmental comprehensive sexuality education

---

[62] International Institute for Sustainable Development, 'Summary of the Twelfth Session of the UN General Assembly Open Working Group on Sustainable Development Goals: 16–20 June 2014' (2014) 32(12) Earth Negotiations Bulletin 1, 2 <https://s3.us-west-2.amazonaws.com/enb.iisd.org/archive/download/pdf/enb3212e.pdf?X-Amz-Content-Sha256=UNSIGNED-PAYLOAD&X-Amz-Algorithm=AWS4-HMAC-SHA256&X-Amz-Credential=AKIA6QW3YWTJ6YORWEEL%2F20210828%2Fus-west-2%2Fs3%2Faws4_request&X-Amz-Date=20210828T064717Z&X-Amz-SignedHeaders=host&X-Amz-Expires=60&X-Amz-Signature=308e55e335 8d377c64326795c5ee3fe875ed3d0f5014c8a2b15a3351116838fa> accessed 28 August 2021.

[63] OWG, 'Working Document for 5–9 May Session of Open Working Group' (2014) <https://sustainable development.un.org/content/documents/3686WorkingDoc_0205_additionalsupporters.pdf> accessed 28 August 2021.

[64] UN Secretary-General, 'Remarks at Opening of Open Working Group on the Sustainable Development Goals' (n 43).

[65] OWG-12, 'Introduction and Proposed Goals and Targets on Sustainable Development for the Post 2015 Development Agenda' (2 June 2014) 8–9 <https://sustainabledevelopment.un.org/content/documents/4528zer odraft12OWG.pdf> accessed 14 December 2020.

[66] See, eg, OWG, 'Joint Response to Focus Area 4 on Education' (*Workers and Trade Unions, Women, Children and Youth, NGOs, and Indigenous Peoples' Major Groups* 2014) <https://sustainabledevelopment.un.org/content/ documents/10212Jointmgresponse.pdf> accessed 28 August 2021.

[67] See, eg, OWG, 'Statement for Monday—16th June 2013' (*Children and Youth Major Group* 2014) 2 <https:// sustainabledevelopment.un.org/content/documents/10344Children%20and%20Youth%20Major%20Group. pdf> accessed 28 August 2021.

[68] ibid.

which promotes human rights'.[69] This recommendation was not adopted. The lack of a reference to sexuality education in the zero draft mirrors the lack of international consensus on this issue.

The 13th and last OWG Session was held in July 2014. Prior to this session, on the 30 June, a revised version of the zero draft was shared.[70] The Co-Chairs described the revision as 'carefully refined' and 'tightened', which was 'facilitated by the in-depth and constructive nature of the Group's discussions during the informal-informals'.[71] In light of the tightening that occurred during informal sessions, goal 4 was presented within the revision of the zero draft as '[p]rovide quality education and life-long learning opportunities for all',[72] notably excluding the references to equality and inclusivity that were present in the initial version. The OWG's records indicate that major groups and other stakeholders, largely NGOs, made amendments to this proposal to inform the 13th session.[73] These groups recommended Goal 4 be altered to include 'inclusive' and to substitute 'provide' for 'ensure'.

These recommendations were accepted and at the conclusion of this final session on 19 July, the OWG's proposal was shaped in final form and again included the words inclusive and equitable, and 'provide' was amended to 'ensure'. The OWG Report was submitted to the General Assembly in the form of a letter from the Co-Chairs, Kőrösi and Kamau, dated 1 August 2014.[74] On 10 September 2014 the UNGA agreed that the OWG proposal would form the main basis for the post-2015 agenda.[75]

III. Commentary on Goal

A. Inclusive and Equitable Education in SDG 4

SDG 4 is expressed as a commitment to 'ensure inclusive and equitable quality education and promote lifelong learning opportunities for all'.[76] This constitutes a more ambitious education plan than was set out in the EFA goals and the MDGs of 2000.[77] The goal requires states to ensure access for children and young people to at least twelve

---

[69] OWG, 'Compilation of Amendments to Goals and Targets' (16–20 June 2014) 15 <https://sustainabledevelopment.un.org/content/documents/4269mgscompilation.pdf> accessed 28 August 2021.

[70] OWG Co-chairs, 'Introduction and Proposed Goals and Targets on Sustainable Development for the Post 2015 Development Agenda' (Revised Zero Draft, 30 June 2014) <https://sustainabledevelopment.un.org/content/documents/4523zerodraft.pdf> accessed 28 August 2021.

[71] OWG Co-chairs, 'Letter from Co-Chairs' (30 June 2014) <https://sustainabledevelopment.un.org/content/documents/4324lettercochairs30june14.pdf> accessed 28 August 2021.

[72] ibid.

[73] OWG, 'Compilation of Amendments to Goals and Targets' (n 69).

[74] UNGA, 'Report of the Open Working Group of the General Assembly on Sustainable Development Goals' (12 August 2014) UN Doc A/68/970.

[75] UNGA, 'Report of the Open Working Group on Sustainable Development Goals Established Pursuant to General Assembly Resolution 66/288' (12 September 2014) UN Doc A/RES/68/309.

[76] UN, 'Transforming our World: The 2030 Agenda for Sustainable Development' (25 September 2015) UN Doc A/RES/70/1, goal 4.

[77] UNESCO 'Incheon Declaration and Framework for Action for the Implementation of Sustainable Development Goal 4' (ED-2016/WS/28, 2015) (Incheon Declaration) 22.

years of publicly funded primary and secondary education, of which nine years should be compulsory.[78] Children and young people who are not in school should also have access to education.[79] Moreover, all people should have access to education to ensure that they achieve functional literacy and numeracy skills and can participate in society.[80] States are also encouraged to provide at least one year of compulsory, publicly funded pre-primary education.[81]

While education forms part of the sustainable development agenda through the explicit commitment in SDG 4, it is central to the entire sustainable development agenda.[82] Education is expressly mentioned in target 3.7,[83] target 5.6,[84] target 8.6,[85] target 12.8,[86] and target 13.3.[87] Further, education is fundamentally related to all the SDGs in some way.

The cornerstone of SDG 4 is a commitment to 'inclusion and equity in and through education.'[88] This means that all people must have access to education, and no-one should be excluded or marginalized in this respect.[89] Further, every student is entitled to feel 'valued and respected, and ... enjoy a clear sense of belonging.'[90] To achieve inclusive education, curricula and pedagogy should be tailored to individual needs and address different forms of discrimination and situations that prevent enjoyment of the right to education. Accordingly, government policies and efforts should be directed towards ensuring that the most disadvantaged people, and in particular people with disabilities, are able to enjoy education.[91] In this respect, *MDAC v Belgium* (2018)[92] and more recently *International Federation for Human Rights (FIDH) and Inclusion Europe v Belgium* (2021)[93] saw decisions handed down by the European Committee of Social Rights concerning organizations in violation of their obligations to uphold the right to inclusive education of learners with disabilities.[94] Inclusion should ensure that gender-based discrimination is addressed.[95] The goal also involves developing stronger and more responsive education systems to meet the needs of learners in conflict-affected areas, including internally displaced persons and refugees.[96]

---

[78] ibid 22.
[79] ibid 29.
[80] ibid 29.
[81] ibid 29.
[82] UNESCO 'Unpacking Sustainable Development Goal 4 Education 2030' (2017).
[83] UN, 'Transforming our World' (n 76).
[84] ibid.
[85] ibid.
[86] ibid.
[87] ibid.
[88] Incheon Declaration (n 77) 7.
[89] ibid.
[90] UNESCO, 'Global Education Monitoring Report 2020: Inclusion and Education: All Means All' (2020) v.
[91] Incheon Declaration (n 77) 7.
[92] *Mental Disability Advocacy Centre (MDAC) v Belgium* (2018) 66 EHRR SE13.
[93] *International Federation for Human Rights (FIDH) and Inclusion Europe v Belgium* (no 141 of 2017) [2021] European Committee of Social Rights.
[94] M Spinoy and K Willems, 'FIDH and Inclusion Europe v. Belgium: Chronicle of a Conviction Foretold' EJIL: Talk! (ejiltalk.org) (*Blog of the European Journal of International Law* 2021).
[95] Incheon Declaration (n 77) 30.
[96] ibid 9.

278 SDG 4

In the context of SDG 4, quality education means that all learners should develop baseline literacy and numeracy skills as well as higher-order skills.[97] Quality education is considered to encourage creativity, assist learners to develop positive values and attitudes, and enable them to contribute as global citizens.[98] In order to provide quality education, it is recognized that 'inputs, processes and evaluation of outcomes and mechanisms to measure progress' require reinforcement.[99] In particular, teaching staff need to be qualified, trained, appropriately remunerated, and supported with resources including technology.[100] Methods for teaching and learning and the content that is taught need to be carefully considered to meet the individual needs of learners.[101] Further, learning environments need to be constructed such that they are 'safe, healthy, gender-responsive, inclusive and adequately resourced'.[102]

The promotion of lifelong learning opportunities means that education should be offered to people at all ages and at all levels of education.[103] In this respect, lifelong learning is a process that includes 'all learning activities undertaken throughout life with the aim of improving knowledge, skills and competencies, within personal, civic, social and employment-related perspectives'.[104] As well as primary and secondary education, this includes technical and vocational education and training as well as higher education and research.[105] Non-formal educational opportunities should also be available as a complement and supplement to formal education.[106] Formal, non-formal, and informal education should be recognized, validated, and accredited.[107]

While the human right to education has both civil and political and economic aspects, it indisputably requires significant resourcing. In this respect, SDG 4 will require states to considerably increase public spending on education.[108] States are encouraged to allocate either at least 4 to 6 per cent of Gross Domestic Product or 15 to 20 per cent of total public expenditure, or both, to education.[109]

B. Sources and Linkages with Human Rights

SDG 4 can be clearly traced to a number of international human rights obligations.[110] As noted in the Incheon Framework, strengthening policies, plans, legislation, and systems to ensure that states fulfil these human rights obligations is an important

---

[97] ibid 8.
[98] ibid 8.
[99] ibid.
[100] ibid 30.
[101] ibid.
[102] ibid.
[103] ibid 8.
[104] UNESCO, 'Global Education Monitoring Report 2016: Education for People and Planet: Creating Sustainable Futures for All' (2nd edn, UNESCO 2016) 8.
[105] Incheon Declaration (n 77) 8.
[106] ibid 30.
[107] ibid 8.
[108] ibid 9.
[109] ibid.
[110] Incheon Declaration (n 77) 28.

step towards achieving SDG 4.[111] The principles that underlie SDG 4 are drawn from international instruments and agreements, namely that '[e]ducation is a fundamental human right and an enabling right', that '[e]ducation is a public good', and that '[g]ender equality is inextricably linked to the right to education for all'.[112] The relevant human rights are set out in the UDHR, international human rights treaties, and other UN official documents.[113]

1. UDHR

Article 26 of the UDHR recognizes the human right to education.[114] In this respect, it clearly embraces the concept of 'inclusive' education in that 'everyone' has the right to education. It also requires education to be 'equitable' to the extent that it must be provided freely, at least at the primary and fundamental stages. In terms of 'quality', the objectives of education set out in article 26(2) ensure that there is a baseline quality level of education. While 'everyone' is entitled to education, article 26 does not expressly recognize a right to lifelong learning opportunities.

In addition to its foundational status in the modern history of international human rights, the UDHR is of interest for its approach to issues that remain salient in relation to rights to education. In particular, tensions between aspirations and obligations, between institutional arrangements and global values, and between rights of children, rights of parents, and rights of states, lie not far below the surface of article 26, and these tensions remain in play in the SDGs as well as in international agreements like the CRC.

The place of education within the UDHR is in a group of aspirations focusing on social and economic rights and united by a theme of the development of the human personality.[115] The latter value is itself understood, throughout the UDHR, in terms of the dignity of the individual versus the state. It was the individualist cast of the UDHR that, more than anything else, gave rise to the abstentions from the USSR and other General Assembly members when it was voted on in 1948.[116] A focus on individual liberty and flourishing was undoubtedly more in line with the ideological cast of the Western liberal democracies, victorious in the very recent war, not least the republican democracies of the United States and France, who spearheaded the UDHR initiative itself.[117] At the same time, the jurist most responsible for the drafting of the UDHR, René Cassin, was himself strongly influenced by the social justice traditions of Roman Catholic thought of the mid-twentieth century.[118] Additionally, the UDHR was understood by its drafters and advocates as a major contribution to the lofty aims of the UN as

[111] ibid 31.

[112] ibid 28; UNESCO 'Unpacking Sustainable Development Goal 4 Education 2030' (2017) 8.

[113] See UN, 'Transforming our World' (n 76) 10.

[114] Emphasis added.

[115] P Kennedy, *The Parliament of Man: The United Nations and the Quest for World Government* (Penguin 2006) 179.

[116] A Clapham, 'The General Assembly' in F Megret and P Alston (eds), *The United Nations and Human Rights: A Critical Approach UN and HRs A Critical Appraisal* (OUP 2020) 107.

[117] D. Otto, 'Lost in Translation: Re-scripting the Sexed Subjects of International Human Rights Law' in A Orford (ed), *International Law and Its Others* (CUP 2006) 335.

[118] Kennedy (n 115) 179.

a whole enterprise. Thus, the development of the human personality was understood in terms of the fostering of anti-fascist and more generally, anti-totalitarian attitudes, almost a kind of 'herd immunization' against the re-emergence of the troubling collective movements of the previous two decades.[119] The exact wording of these components of the UDHR went through various drafts,[120] with the final formulation stressing in an upbeat manner that education must contribute to the aims of the UN (the promotion of understanding and tolerance) rather than expressing more darkly or more politically, the anti-fascism agenda as such.

From this confluence of values and agendas, formulations on a world citizen's right to education emerged. Those rights were therefore defined in a top-down manner. In this sense, it is entirely proper to 'read up' the scope of the rights to education enunciated in the UDHR, for example to read in implications for a lifespan orientation to education rather than a somewhat narrower focus on the school years and on the tertiary sector (article 26(1)). Indeed article 27(1) concerning the right 'freely to participate in the cultural life of the community' would seem to refer clearly to adults as well as to children. The reference to higher education being available 'on the basis of merit' at article 26(1) was clearly thought of as an anti-discriminatory clause, with implied reference to the unfair privileges of wealth, gender, or race, even if 'merit' might with hindsight seem not an entirely satisfactory term for the absence of unfair discrimination.

Yet reading down is also justified. In some respects, this is simply to say that the aspirations of the UDHR were qualified in terms of practicalities. Thus, primary ('elementary') education was picked out for free and compulsory status in a manner that, at least for Cassin, represented a key indication of the duties of parents towards their children.[121] A Catholic morality can be seen at work here even if the position would have been uncontroversial and may even remain so in the twenty-first century to some extent. Further than this, there is a considerable gap between lofty ideals for every citizen, and the implementation of appropriate institutions, services and training within a jurisdiction. From the perspective of the twenty-first century, or rather the last quarter of the twentieth, it certainly cannot be assumed that anything like inclusive or mainstreamed education was understood by the drafters and the electors of the UDHR. Just as access to tertiary education was understood to be properly available on the basis of 'merit'—presumably academic merit, that is to say the perceived capacity to benefit—the term 'appropriate' may be read into the prescribed rights. There is no reason to believe that Cassin, Eleanor Roosevelt, or other advocates were mindful of any effort to redefine 'educability' in the context of the prevailing divide between health authority and educational authority responsibilities in advanced and developing countries alike.[122] It would not be until the 1960s and 1970s that 'special education' would emerge as an attempt to

---

[119] G Norris, *The Developing Idea of the Authoritarian Personality: An Historical Review of the Scholarly Debate, 1950–2011* (Edwin Mellen Press 2012) 11.

[120] See J Morsink, *The Universal Declaration of Human Rights: Origins, Drafting, and Intent* (University of Pennsylvania Press 1999) 215.

[121] ibid.

[122] S Salend and LG Duhaney, 'Historical and Philosophical Changes in the Education of Students with Exceptionalities' in A Rotatori and others (eds), *History of Special Education* (Emerald Publishing 2011) 6.

include a much wider range of children into some institutional framework with aims beyond care and 'training' and later still before inclusive education and mainstreaming would become established practices in many countries. In the 1940s, children with a wide variety of handicapping conditions or perceived deficiencies were identified as the responsibility of health authorities rather than education authorities, for example in the United Kingdom. As well as including children with challenging characteristics in terms of intellectual capacity, many children with physical forms of disability or even social stigma were in effect denied inclusion in the educational domain.[123] Physical access was treated as a natural obstacle in many cases so that the education of a child or young person who contracted polio might simply terminate. Without excessively labouring the point, a term like 'appropriate' or a phrase like 'conditional on the capacity to benefit therefrom' may always be read into education rights articulated in the era of the UDHR.

2. Core International Human Rights Treaties

Core international human rights treaties also recognize, to varying degrees, central components of SDG 4 as human rights. One of the most important provisions in terms of the right to education is article 13 of the ICESCR, which affirms the principle that education is a fundamental right and a public good.[124] It provides that 'everyone' has a right to education, which is to be directed towards expressly stated purposes.[125] In terms of ensuring this right is enjoyed, States Parties are obliged to make primary education both compulsory and free.[126] Article 14 requires States Parties that have not yet achieved compulsory and free primary education to develop a plan of action to reach that goal.[127] Article 13 also requires States Parties to ensure that secondary education is generally available, accessible, and to work towards the progressive introduction of free education.[128] Similarly, higher education is to be made equally accessible and progressively free.[129] Further key provisions supporting the status of education as a fundamental right and public good are found in the CRC.[130] Article 28 affirms the right of the child to education and obliges States Parties to achieve the right progressively.[131] Like article 13 of the ICESCR, article 28 requires States Parties to make primary education compulsory and freely available to all,[132] to make secondary education available and accessible to all,[133] and to make higher education accessible to all on the basis of capacity.[134] Beyond these broad rights protections, the International Convention on the

---

[123] ibid.
[124] ICESCR (n 50) art 13.
[125] ibid art 13(1).
[126] ibid art 13(2)(a).
[127] ibid art 14.
[128] ibid art 13(2)(b).
[129] ibid art 13(2)(c).
[130] CRC (n 52) arts 23(3), 28, 29.
[131] ibid art 28(1).
[132] ibid art 28(1)(a).
[133] ibid art 28(1)(b).
[134] International Convention on the Elimination of All Forms of Racial Discrimination (adopted 7 March 1966, entered into force 4 January 1969) 660 UNTS 195 (ICERD) art 28(1)(c).

282 SDG 4

Elimination of Racial Discrimination (ICERD) obliges States Parties to prohibit and eliminate racial discrimination and guarantee the right of all people without discrimination to education and training.[135]

A number of core international human rights instruments affirm that the right to education is held by specific groups of people. The Convention on the Rights of Persons with Disabilities (CRPD) recognizes the right of persons with disabilities to education, without discrimination, and on the basis of equal opportunity.[136] Similarly, the International Convention on the Protection of the Rights of All Migrant Workers and Members of their Families (ICRMW) affirms that migrant workers should enjoy equal treatment with nationals of the state of employment in relation to access to educational institutions and services.[137] Further, pursuant to article 30, children of migrant workers have the 'basic right of access to education on the basis of equality of treatment with nationals of the State concerned'.[138] The CEDAW reinforces the principle that gender equality is inextricably linked to the right to education. Article 10 of CEDAW requires that States Parties work to eliminate discrimination against women in the field of education,[139] while article 14 obliges States Parties to ensure that rural women enjoy equal treatment in access to training and education.[140]

3. Other Core International Human Rights Instruments

Other international instruments also enshrine the status of education as a fundamental human right, an enabling right and a public good. Perhaps most significantly, UNESCO's Convention against Discrimination in Education (CADE)[141] obliges States Parties to work to eliminate and prevent discrimination in education.[142] Other instruments affirm the right to education for specific groups. The Convention Relating to the Status of Refugees[143] requires States Parties to accord refugees the same treatment as nationals as regards primary education.[144] With regard to education other than primary education, access to studies, recognition of foreign credentials, remission of fees and charges, and scholarships, refugees are to be provided treatment as favourable as possible, and no less favourable than aliens in the same circumstances.[145] This standard seems to fall short of the SDG 4 goal to 'ensure inclusive and equitable quality education and promote lifelong learning opportunities for all', and may, therefore, be superseded by the goal. The UN Declaration on the Rights of Indigenous Peoples recognizes that

---

[135] ibid art 5(v).

[136] Convention on the Rights of Persons with Disabilities (adopted 30 March 2007, entered into force 3 May 2008) 2515 UNTS 3 (CRPD) art 24(1).

[137] International Convention on the Protection of the Rights of All Migrant Workers and Members of Their Families (adopted 18 December 1990, entered into force 1 July 2003) 2220 UNTS 3 (ICRMW) art 43.

[138] ibid art 30.

[139] ibid art 10.

[140] ibid art 14(d).

[141] Convention against Discrimination in Education (adopted 14 December 1960 entered into force 22 May 1962) 429 UNTS 93 (CADE).

[142] ibid arts 3, 4.

[143] Convention Relating to the Status of Refugees (adopted 28 July 1951, entered into force 22 April 1954) 189 UNTS 150 (Refugee Convention).

[144] ibid art 22(1).

[145] ibid art 22(2).

Indigenous people, and particularly children, 'have the right to all levels and forms of education of the State without discrimination'.[146] Further, the UNGA's 'Resolution on the Right to Education in Emergency Situations' encourages the development and implementation of strategies and policies to ensure that the right to education is enjoyed to the greatest extent possible in emergency situations.[147]

C. Development

SDG 4 was developed by Member States, facilitated by UNESCO and other partners, and guided by the Steering Committee.[148] The final expression of the goal finds its roots in significant consultations and meetings that occurred between 2012 and 2015.[149] The Global Thematic Consultation on Education in the Post-2015 Development Agenda was co-led by UNESCO and UNICEF and hosted in Dakar in 2013.[150] The Consultation Report identifies principles for a post-2015 education agenda including a human rights-based approach to education and harmonization,[151] as well as priorities for a post-2015 education agenda including access to education at all levels, quality education, and learning.[152] It also identified inclusion as a cross-cutting issue within the global education context.[153] Clear connections can be made between major points highlighted in the Consultation Report and the final expression of SDG 4. The reference to education being 'for all' echoes the language of international human rights documents. The identification of a need for harmonization found its fruition in SDG 4, which, in contrast to the EFA and MDG frameworks, constitutes a 'unified architecture' for education.[154] The Consultation Report notes calls for a post-2015 education goal to encompass all levels of education and to extend to lifelong learning opportunities,[155] which are expressly included in SDG 4. It also notes a 'widespread consensus' that a post-2015 education framework should prioritize quality and learning, which both manifest in the references to 'quality education' and 'learning' in SDG 4.[156] Finally, inclusion is explicitly adopted in SDG 4 via the reference to ensuring 'inclusive' education. SDG 4 clearly aligns with the '[t]wo main imperatives' of equitable access and equitable quality identified in the Consultation Report.[157]

---

[146] United Nations Declaration on the Rights of Indigenous Peoples (13 September 2007) UN Doc A/RES/61/295 (UNDRIP) art 14(2).
[147] UNGA Resolution on the Right to Education in Emergency Situations (27 July 2010) UN Doc A/RES/64/290, arts 7, 8.
[148] Incheon Declaration (n 77) 22. See generally UNESCO, 'Global Education Monitoring Report 2016' (n 104) 172.
[149] Incheon Declaration (n 77) 22.
[150] Y Sayed, 'Making Education a Priority in the Post-2015 Development Agenda: Report of the Global Thematic Consultation on Education in the Post-2015 Development Agenda' (2013) (Consultation Report).
[151] ibid 15–16, 19.
[152] ibid 21–23.
[153] ibid 30.
[154] ibid 19. See also, UNESCO, 'Global Education Monitoring Report' 2016 (n 104) 172.
[155] Consultation Report (n 150) 21.
[156] ibid 22–23.
[157] ibid 35.

The Global EFA Meeting in Muscat, Oman, from 12 to 13 May 2014 constitutes a significant event in the development of SDG 4.[158] Following the Meeting, the Muscat Agreement was adopted by attendees, which influenced the development of SDG 4 and its related goals and means of implementation.[159] The Muscat Agreement affirms that education is a human right and that the post-2015 education agenda should be rights based.[160] It also asserts that the post-2015 education agenda should reflect a view based on equity and inclusion, and specifically gender equality and the elimination of discrimination in and through education.[161] Parties to the Agreement supported an overarching education goal to '[e]nsure equitable and inclusive quality education and lifelong learning for all by 2030'.[162] The expression of this goal is very close to that finally adopted in SDG 4, with amendments to require promotion of rather than ensuring life-long learning, and removal of the reference to 2030. Thus, the significant influence of the Muscat Agreement on SDG 4 is evident.

The process of developing an overarching post-2015 education goal included con-sultation with NGOs in 2014. The Seventh Meeting of the Collective Consultations of NGOs on EFA was primarily directed towards strategizing on civil society engagement in defining the post-2015 education agenda.[163] The resulting publication titled 'Final Declaration: Realizing the Right to Education Beyond 2015' indicates support for an overarching post-2015 education goal as expressed in the Muscat Agreement.[164]

Five regional ministerial conferences organized by UNESCO in 2014 and 2015, and an E-9 Ministerial Review Meeting held from 27 to 28 November 2014,[165] also in-fluenced the development of SDG 4. The conferences were the Asia-Pacific Regional Education Conference in Bangkok, Thailand, from 6 to 8 August 2014; the EFA in Latin America and the Caribbean: Assessment of Progress and Post-2015 Challenges confer-ence in Lima, Peru, from 30 to 31 October 2014; the Arab States Regional Conference on Education Post-2015 in Sharm El Sheikh, Egypt, from 27 to 29 January 2015; the Sub-Saharan Africa Regional Ministerial Conference on Education Post-2015 in Kigali, Rwanda, from 9 to 11 February 2015; and the Regional Ministerial Conference on Education Post-2015 in Paris, France, from 19 to 20 February 2015. Each of these conferences resulted in publication of a statement detailing the outcomes of the con-ference.[166] In this respect, the Bangkok Statement, the Lima Statement, the Sharm El Sheikh Statement, and the Islamabad Statement endorsed the overarching goal

---

[158] Incheon Declaration (n 77) 22.

[159] ibid.

[160] UNESCO 'Global Education for All Meeting' (Muscat, Oman 12–14 May 2014) (Muscat Agreement) paras 6, 8.

[161] ibid para 8.

[162] ibid para 10.

[163] UNESCO 'Final Declaration on Realising the Right to Education Beyond 2015' (May 2014) 7th Meeting of the Collective Consultation of NGOs on Education for All, 2.

[164] ibid para 20.

[165] The E-9 is a forum comprising the nine most highly populated countries of the South: Bangladesh, Brazil, China, Egypt, India, Indonesia, Mexico, Nigeria, and Pakistan; Framework for Action 23.

[166] Respectively, the Bangkok Statement (2014); Lima Statement (2014); Islamabad Statement (2014); Kigali Statement (2015); Sharm El Sheikh Statement (2015), and Paris Statement (2015): Framework for Action 23.

proposed in the Muscat Agreement.[167] The Kigali Statement and the Paris Statement endorsed the goal of the UNGA OWG for SDGs, which was ultimately adopted as SDG 4. Each Statement also highlighted regional perspectives and priority action areas. For example, the Lima Statement highlighted important perspectives from the region, including the importance of education being directed towards equity and inclusion in order to reduce inequality and poverty and the criticality of ensuring education is of high quality.[168]

While the EFA Steering Committee worked towards these targets, which were widely endorsed via the Muscat Declaration, a concurrent process in the form of the intergovernmental OWG was underway.[169] The OWG, established in January 2013 to propose the SDGs, worked towards the articulation of an education-related goal.[170] Ultimately, the OWG, influenced by the Muscat Declaration amongst other inputs,[171] proposed their final education goal in July 2014 expressed as 'ensure inclusive and equitable quality education and promote lifelong learning opportunities for all'.[172]

D. Empirical Evidence

International institutions have established a reporting framework to monitor progress towards attainment of the SDGs, including SDG 4. This framework includes an annual High-level Political Forum (HLPF) on Sustainable Development held every four years with the guidance of the General Assembly, and in other years under the guidance of the Economic and Social Council;[173] an annual SDG Report prepared by the Secretary-General for which UNESCO reports in relation to SDG 4;[174] thematic progress reviews undertaken by the HPLF;[175] and an independent Global Education Monitoring Report (GEMR) produced by UNESCO.[176] The GEMR is particularly significant as it has a mandate to be 'the mechanism for monitoring and reporting on SDG 4 and on education in the other SDGs'.[177] These sources form the basis for the following discussion regarding the empirical evidence for progress towards achievement of SDG 4.

[167] UNESCO, 'Asia-Pacific Statement on Education Beyond 2015' (Bangkok, Thailand 6–8 August 2014) (Bangkok Statement) para 3; UNESCO 'Education for All in Latin America and the Caribbean: Assessment of progress and post-2015 challenges' (Lima, Peru 30–31 October 2014) (Lima Statement) para 4; UNESCO, 'Arab States Regional Conference on Education Post-2015: Towards Quality Education and Lifelong Learning for All' (Sharm El Sheikh, Egypt 27–29 January 2015) (Sharm el Sheikh Statement) para 3; UNESCO, 'Joint E-9 Statement on Education Beyond 2015' (Islamabad, Pakistan 27–28 November 2014) (Islamabad Statement) para 2.
[168] UNESCO 'Education for All in Latin America and the Caribbean: Assessment of progress and post-2015 challenges' (Lima, Peru 30–31 October 2014) (Lima Statement) paras 6, 7, 14.
[169] UNESCO, 'Global Education Monitoring Report 2016' (n 104) 172.
[170] ibid.
[171] ibid.
[172] ibid.
[173] UNESCO, 'Global Education Monitoring Report 2017/8: Accountability in Education: Meeting our Commitments' (2nd edn, UNESCO 2017) 117.
[174] ibid.
[175] One for education was undertaken in 2019; UNESCO, 'Global Education Monitoring Report 2017/8' (n 173) 117.
[176] ibid.
[177] Incheon Declaration (n 77) 11.

SDG 4 as a goal is not only ambitious but also significantly broader than previous global education goals.[178] Accordingly, it is encouraging that states agreed to its adoption. Unfortunately, however, despite some progress the world is not on track to meet the goal by 2030.[179] Millions of children are out of school,[180] and those students that are in school are not necessarily learning.[181] Globally, more than 55 per cent of children and adolescents are not attaining minimum skills in reading and mathematics.[182] Educational inequalities persist, particularly in terms of gender,[183] geographic and urban/rural location, and wealth.[184] Many of the least developed countries, and particularly countries in Sub-Saharan Africa, lack basic educational infrastructure such as electricity, drinking water, and handwashing facilities.[185] Further, adult illiteracy remains high, with 750 million adults illiterate in 2016, two-thirds of whom were women.[186]

Progress towards SDG 4 varies by geographic region and wealth is a significant factor in a state's performance. For example, in relation to ensuring that all girls and boys complete primary education by 2030,[187] Europe, Northern America, Australia, and New Zealand are broadly on track.[188] While states in Eastern and South-Eastern Asia, Latin America, and the Caribbean have made limited or no progress, they are either close to reaching the target or a moderate distance from the target.[189] States in Central and Southern Asia have made fair progress yet remain far from the target.[190] In Northern Africa and Western Asia, states are far from the target, while Pacific Island countries are very far from the target.[191] In Sub-Saharan Africa, while states have made substantial progress, the region remains very far from the target.[192] This situation is reflective of the reality that it costs money to provide education. However, equity issues extend beyond geographic regions. For example, in all countries with reported data, children from the wealthiest households attain greater reading ability by the end of primary and lower secondary education than children from the poorest households.[193]

---

[178] UNESCO, 'Global Education Monitoring Report 2016' (n 104) 172–73.

[179] UN, 'The Sustainable Development Goals Report 2020' (2020) 32; UNESCO Institute for Statistics and UNESCO Global Education Monitoring Report 2019, 'Meeting Commitments: Are Countries on Track to Achieve SDG 4?' (2019) 12.

[180] Report of the Secretary-General, 'Special Edition: Progress Towards the Sustainable Development Goals' (2019) UN Doc E/2019/68, 10.

[181] UN, 'The Sustainable Development Goals Report 2019' (July 2019) 30.

[182] ibid.

[183] Report of the Secretary-General, 'Progress Towards the Sustainable Development Goals' (2018) UN Doc E/2018/64, 6–7; UN Women and United Nations Department of Economic and Social Affairs 'Progress on the Sustainable Development Goals: The Gender Snapshot' (2019) 9; UN, 'The Sustainable Development Goals Report 2019' (July 2019) 31.

[184] Report of the Secretary-General, 'Progress Towards the Sustainable Development Goals' (2018) UN Doc E/2018/64, 6–7; UN, 'The Sustainable Development Goals Report 2019' (July 2019) 30.

[185] ibid 31.

[186] UN, 'The Sustainable Development Goals Report 2019' (July 2019) 31.

[187] UN 'Global Indicator Framework for the Sustainable Development Goals and Targets of the 2030 Agenda for Sustainable Development' (2020) UN Doc E/CN.3/2020/2, 5 (Indicator 4.1.2).

[188] UN 'Sustainable Development Goals Progress Chart' (2020) 2, 5.

[189] ibid.

[190] ibid.

[191] ibid.

[192] ibid.

[193] Report of the Secretary-General, 'Progress Towards the Sustainable Development Goals' (2017) UN Doc E/2017/66, 7.

Globally there is inadequate investment in education if SDG 4 is to be achieved.[194] The manner in which states could cooperate to ensure that all people can access quality education is said to require 'a revolutionary reimagining of education in the modern world'.[195] The Education 2030 Framework for Action supports two targets for the public financing of education: assigning at least 4 per cent to 6 per cent of GDP to education, and allocating at least 15 per cent to 20 per cent of public expenditure to education.[196] While many states have been able to meet these targets, forty-three out of 148 countries failed to meet either standard.[197] Further, in low- and lower-middle-income countries, approximately $39 billion in additional funds per year is required to fill a funding gap. Wealthy states must fill this gap through provision of international aid to education.[198] Unfortunately, however, aid to education has plateaued since 2010 and the proportion of development aid dedicated to education has declined since that time.[199] The consequences of this funding gap are seen in poorer states. For example, in Sub-Saharan Africa there is a relatively low percentage of trained teachers and most schools lack access to electricity or potable water.[200]

The COVID-19 pandemic will have dire implications for the world's ability to achieve SDG 4 objectives by 2030. The pandemic necessitated global school closures such that approximately 90 per cent of all students—approximately 1.5 billion children and young people—were out of school.[201] For these students, protracted school absence has negative impacts on school retention and graduation rates as well as detrimental impacts on student learning outcomes and the social and behavioural growth of young people.[202] Accordingly, school closures necessitated by the pandemic provide a significant obstacle to the global capacity to achieve SDG 4.

Moreover, the effects of COVID-19 will disproportionately affect already disadvantaged populations, consequently exacerbating educational inequality.[203] In particular, school closures are likely to widen the gender gap in education, leaving over 11 million girls out of school and at risk of not returning.[204] Further, while school closures forced most students out of school in 2020, many students were able to continue their schooling through remote learning.[205] Students without access to computers or the

---

[194] President of the Economic and Social Council, 'Summary by the President of the Economic and Social Council of the High-Level Political Forum on Sustainable Development Convened Under the Auspices of the Council at its 2019 Session' (9 August 2019) UN Doc E/HLPF/2019/8, 5.

[195] ibid.

[196] Incheon Declaration (n 77) 67.

[197] UNESCO Institute for Statistics and UNESCO Global Education Monitoring Report 2019, 'Meeting Commitments: Are Countries on Track to Achieve SDG 4?' (2019) 11.

[198] ibid.

[199] ibid.

[200] Report of the Secretary-General, 'Progress Towards the Sustainable Development Goals' (2017) UN Doc E/2017/66, 7.

[201] UN, 'The Sustainable Development Goals Report 2020' (n 179) 3; Report of the Secretary-General, 'Progress towards the Sustainable Development Goals' (2020) UN Doc E/2020/57, 7.

[202] ibid.

[203] UNESCO, 'Global Education Monitoring Report 2020' (n 90) iii; UN, 'The Sustainable Development Goals Report 2020' (n 179) 2, 32.

[204] UN Women and United Nations Department of Economic and Social Affairs, 'Progress on the Sustainable Development Goals: The Gender Snapshot' (2020) 9.

[205] Report of the Secretary-General, 'Progress Towards the Sustainable Development Goals' (2020) UN Doc E/2020/57, 7.

Internet at home and students without sufficient computer skills, however, were unable to continue their learning in this way.[206] In 2019, approximately 87 per cent of European homes had Internet access at home, in contrast with 18 per cent of African households.[207] Similarly, 78 per cent of European households owned a computer, whereas only 11 per cent of African households did.[208] In approximately 40 countries with available data, less than 50 per cent of the population lacked basic computer skills.[209] Thus, as remote learning was not an option for many students in the poorest countries and communities, the consequences of the pandemic on education will be to increase levels of educational inequality.[210]

Relatedly, the HLPF on Sustainable Development identified that issues concerning equality and inclusiveness constitute significant obstacles to achieving SDG 4.[211] This is particularly the case for girls, who have often been excluded from education, and for children living in areas of conflict.[212] The importance of ensuring that no-one is left behind was the focus of the GEMR 2020, which emphasized that when it comes to inclusion 'all means all'.[213]

While, as outlined above, the available data provide an overall picture of insufficient progress, a significant obstacle to the achievement of SDG 4 is the lack of available state data to track performance.[214] The availability of data vary among countries, by region and by source.[215] The GEMR 2020 identifies three key data gaps.[216] First, there is a lack of data to facilitate a discussion in relation to equity in education. In this respect, four out of ten countries did not have recent household survey data that could be used to disaggregate education data.[217] The problem is most acute in Northern Africa and Western Asia.[218] Without the capacity to disaggregate data, it is difficult to assess progress towards specific SDG 4 indicators and in particular those relating to equity and inclusion. Second, there are insufficient data available in relation to learning outcomes. This is particularly the case in Africa, where just three in ten countries have recently provided data on learning outcomes.[219] Further, only 26 per cent of African countries

---

[206] UN, 'The Sustainable Development Goals Report 2020' (n 179) 33.
[207] ibid.
[208] ibid.
[209] ibid.
[210] Report of the Secretary-General, 'Progress Towards the Sustainable Development Goals' (2020) UN Doc E/2020/57, 7.
[211] President of the Economic and Social Council, 'Summary by the President of the Economic and Social Council of the High-Level Political Forum on Sustainable Development Convened Under the Auspices of the Council at its 2019 Session' (9 August 2019) UN Doc E/HLPF/2019/8, 5.
[212] ibid.
[213] UNESCO, 'Global Education Monitoring Report 2020' (n 90) v.
[214] ibid 198; President of the Economic and Social Council, 'Summary by the President of the Economic and Social Council of the High-Level Political Forum on Sustainable Development Convened Under the Auspices of the Council at its 2019 Session' (9 August 2019) UN Doc E/HLPF/2019/8, 4; UNESCO Institute for Statistics and UNESCO Global Education Monitoring Report 2019, 'Meeting Commitments: Are Countries on Track to Achieve SDG 4?' (2019) 12.
[215] UNESCO, UNESCO Institute for Statistics, 'Meeting Commitments: Are Countries on Track to Achieve SDG 4?' (2019).
[216] UNESCO, 'Global Education Monitoring Report 2020' (n 90) 200.
[217] ibid.
[218] ibid 202.
[219] ibid 203.

have reported data on early years reading competence since 2014.[220] Third, data are also lacking in relation to qualified and trained teachers, making progress difficult to assess.[221] The problem is particularly serious in countries in Sub-Saharan Africa.[222] Finally, inadequate finance remains a significant hurdle to data collection and capacity development mechanisms in low and middle-income countries.[223]

As discussed above, fundamentally SDG 4 represents a rights-based approach to education. Thus, progress towards its achievement can also be measured by the extent to which states have signed and ratified relevant international instruments. By ratifying the ICESCR, CRC, ICERD, CRPD, ICRMW, CEDAW, CADE, and the Refugees Convention, states affirm education as a fundamental right that should be enjoyed without discrimination by all people. Countries that have ratified all of these instruments without reservation to relevant education articles[224] include Argentina,[225] Bosnia and Herzegovina,[226] and Mali.[227] On the other hand, many states have failed to ratify some or most of these instruments, including the Holy See,[228] Malaysia,[229] and the United States (US).[230] This omission by the United States in particular, given its international status and influence, provides a significant obstacle to the global adoption and aspiration towards SDG 4.

[220] ibid 205.

[221] UNESCO, 'Global Education Monitoring Report 2020' (n 90) 205.

[222] ibid.

[223] UNESCO, UNESCO Institute for Statistics 'Meeting Commitments: Are Countries on Track to Achieve SDG 4?' (2019) 13.

[224] ICESCR (n 50) art 13; CRC (n 52) art 28; ICERD (n 134) art 5(v); CRPD (n 136) art 24(1); ICRMW (n 137) arts 30, 43; CEDAW (n 51) arts 10, 14; CADE (n 141); Refugee Convention (n 143) art 22.

[225] United Nations Treaty Collection (UNTC), 'Depository Status of Treaties: International Covenant on Economic, Social and Cultural Rights' (Ch IV (3), UNTC status as at 23 August 2021); UNESCO, 'List of States Parties: Convention against discrimination in education' (*UNESCO*) <https://treaties.un.org/Pages/showDetails.aspx?objid=0800000280134150> accessed 1 March 2021; UNTC, 'Depositary Status of Treaties: Convention on the Rights of the Child' (Ch IV (11), UNTC status as at 23 August 2021); UNTC, 'Depositary Status of Treaties: International Convention on the Elimination of All Forms of Racial Discrimination (Ch IV (2), UNTC status as at 24 August 2021); UNTC, 'Depositary Status of Treaties: Convention on the Rights of Persons with Disabilities' (Ch IV (15), UNTC status as at 24 August 2021); UNTC, 'Depositary Status of Treaties: International Convention on the Protection of the Rights of all Migrant Workers and Members of their Families' (Ch IV (13), UNTC status as at 24 August 2021); UNTC, 'Depositary Status of Treaties: Convention on the Elimination of all Forms of Discrimination against Women' (Ch IV (8), UNTC status as at 24-08-2021); UNTC, 'Depositary Status of Treaties: Convention relating to the Status of Refugees' (Ch V (2), UNTC status as at 23 August 2021).

[226] ibid.

[227] Other relevant states in this category include Albania, Bolivia, Burkina Faso, Guatemala, Guinea, Kyrgyzstan, Morocco, Nicaragua, Niger, Nigeria, Peru, Philippines, Senegal, Seychelles, Togo, and Uruguay: ibid.

[228] UNTC, 'Depositary Status of Treaties: International Covenant on Economic, Social and Cultural Rights' (Ch IV (3), UNTC status as at 23 August 2021); UNESCO, 'List of States Parties: Convention against discrimination in education' (UNESCO) <https://treaties.un.org/Pages/showDetails.aspx?objid=0800000280134150> accessed 1 March 2021; UNTC, 'Depositary Status of Treaties: Convention on the Rights of the Child' (Ch IV (11), UNTC status as at 23 August 2021); UNTC, 'Depositary Status of Treaties: International Convention on the Elimination of All Forms of Racial Discrimination (Ch IV (2), UNTC status as at 24 August 2021); UNTC, 'Depositary Status of Treaties: Convention on the Rights of Persons with Disabilities' (Ch IV (15), UNTC status as at 24 August 2021); UNTC, 'Depositary Status of Treaties: International Convention on the Protection of the Rights of all Migrant Workers and Members of their Families' (Ch IV (13), UNTC status as at 24 August 2021); UNTC, 'Depositary Status of Treaties: Convention on the Elimination of all Forms of Discrimination against Women' (Ch IV (8), UNTC status as at 24 August 2021); UNTC, 'Depositary Status of Treaties: Convention relating to the Status of Refugees' (Ch V (2), UNTC status as at 23 August 2021).

[229] ibid.

[230] Other very poor performing states in this respect include Niue, which has ratified the CRC but taken no action in relation to any of the other relevant instruments; ibid.

E. Best Practices

Defining what constitutes a best practice in the context of the SDGs is not a straightforward proposition. This is due to the availability of data as well as inherent delays in the implementation of policy and their subsequent results. Nevertheless, in terms of SDG 4 best practice may be represented by states that have achieved or are near achieving the goal, as well as by states who have implemented policies that are in alignment with the goal. This analysis will consider state practice in each of these categories.

Wealth has a significant influence on a state's performance measured against SDG 4.[231] Developed countries as a group, comprising countries in Europe, Northern America, Australia, and New Zealand, outperform other regions and have made substantial progress to meet or nearly meet the goal of SDG 4.[232] Within this broad category, Finland and Canada are among those countries notable for their outstanding performance.[233] Finland provides publicly funded, high-quality education from early childhood education and care through to higher education, and has achieved SDG 4.[234] It has achieved the targets for completion of primary and secondary education and has increased access to vocational education training.[235] It has met the targets for literacy and numeracy, is increasing opportunities for lifelong learning, and ensures that sustainable development education is incorporated at all levels of education.[236] Nevertheless, Finland faces challenges in addressing a skills gap between female and male students and the influence that socio-economic status has on student learning outcomes.[237] In Canada, responsibility for education rests with provinces and territories, and primary and secondary education is free.[238] Educational institutions charge tuition fees for post-secondary education but these are heavily subsidized by government.[239] Canada has achieved SDG 4 and in this respect has a net primary enrolment rate and lower secondary completion rate of 100 per cent.[240] Nevertheless, challenges that remain include a high degree of gender segregation in education[241] and obstacles to accessing education for Indigenous students.[242]

---

[231] See J Sachs and others, *The Sustainable Development Goals and COVID-19: Sustainable Development Report 2020* (CUP 2020) 40.

[232] UN 'Sustainable Development Goals Progress Chart' (2020) 2, 5.

[233] Other countries that have achieved SDG 4 include China, Mongolia, Singapore, Sri Lanka, Vietnam, Estonia, Japan, the Republic of Korea, Cyprus, Malta, Tajikistan, Cuba, and the Islamic Republic of Iran; J Sachs and others, *The Sustainable Development Goals and COVID-19* (n 231) 40–45.

[234] Prime Minister's Office Finland, 'Voluntary National Review 2020: Finland: Report on the Implementation of the 2030 Agenda for Sustainable Development' (2020) 61, 141; United Nations Department of Economic and Social Affairs, 'Voluntary National Reviews Synthesis Report' (2020) 051.

[235] Prime Minister's Office Finland, 'Voluntary National Review 2020 (n 234) 112.

[236] ibid.

[237] ibid.

[238] Government of Canada, 'Canada's Implementation of the 2030 Agenda for Sustainable Development: Voluntary National Review' (2018) 38.

[239] ibid.

[240] Sachs and others, *The Sustainable Development Goals and COVID-19* (n 179) 164–65.

[241] Government of Canada, 'Canada's Implementation of the 2030 Agenda for Sustainable Development (n 238) 39.

[242] ibid 40.

In anticipation of the HLPF in 2019, which reviewed progress towards SDG 4, the GEMR team prepared a special publication focusing on best practices in implementation of SDG 4 ('Beyond Commitments Report').[243] While monitoring progress towards SDG 4 focuses primarily on quantitative measures, this qualitative analysis provides states with an understanding of the kinds of policies that might assist a state in progressing towards SDG 4.[244] Although it is difficult to assess the extent to which policies are able to achieve SDG 4 until years after implementation, the Beyond Commitments Report provides a framework of the kinds of national policies that are 'best aligned' with SDG 4.[245] This understanding of effective policy-making may be supplemented by reference to voluntary national reviews submitted as a basis for the HLPF.[246]

Broadly, states should ensure that their education policies align with the requirements of SDG 4 and their education commitments under relevant international treaties. In terms of Focus Areas, the Beyond Commitments Report encourages states to ensure that their education plans and policies are aligned with the SDG 4 principles of equity and inclusion.[247] In this respect, education policies need to define what they mean by equity and inclusion, and ensure that their definitions refer to all learners, not just a single group.[248] For example, Vietnam's 2030 education sector plan aims to improve gender equality and assist vulnerable groups, including ethnic minority groups, individuals with disabilities, remote learners, and people living in poverty.[249] The Vietnamese government has taken action to assist each of these groups. For instance, the National Law on Persons with Disabilities 2012 and the Inclusive Education Guidelines for Persons with Disabilities 2006 operate to support the right to education for people with disabilities.[250] State governments should also ensure that education and social welfare policies are designed together in order to support equity.[251] This is also evident in Vietnam's education policy through tuition fee exemptions for five-year-old children in low socio-economic areas from 2018.[252] Government departments of education should monitor inequality as a means of further developing their education inclusion policies.[253] In Thailand, the Independent Committee for Education Reform established the Equitable Education Fund in 2018, which included the development of a database to identify and track target groups as a means of ensuring accountability.[254]

---

[243] UNESCO, 'Beyond Commitments: How Countries Implement SDG 4' (2019) 1.
[244] ibid.
[245] ibid.
[246] See United Nations Department of Economic and Social Affairs, 'High Level Political Forum on Sustainable Development: Voluntary National Reviews' <https://sustainabledevelopment.un.org/hlpf> accessed 19 August 2021.
[247] UNESCO, *Beyond Commitments* (n 243) 14.
[248] ibid 1, 15.
[249] ibid 20.
[250] Vietnam Department for Science, Education, Natural Resources and Environment, Ministry of Planning and Investment, 'Vietnam's Voluntary National Review on the Implementation of the Sustainable Development Goals' (2018) 37.
[251] UNESCO, 'Beyond Commitments' (n 243) 14.
[252] Vietnam Department for Science, Education, Natural Resources and Environment, Ministry of Planning and Investment, 'Viet Nam's Voluntary National Review on the Implementation of the Sustainable Development Goals' (2018) 36–37.
[253] UNESCO, 'Beyond Commitments' (n 243) 14.
[254] ibid 19.

The second area that states are encouraged to focus on in education policy-making for SDG 4 is ensuring quality education and learning. In this respect, states should develop a national assessment system that is able to provide a sound analysis of trends over time.[255] For example, in the Philippines the Department of Education is preparing a framework for monitoring and evaluating education.[256] States should also consider participating in cross-national assessments to build the capacity and provide a benchmark for their education system.[257] In this respect, many states, including Albania and Bhutan, participate in the Programme for International Student Assessment (PISA).[258] PISA looks at literacy, numeracy, scientific knowledge, and real-life skills in fifteen-year-olds.[259] Education monitoring should also be used to influence the development of education curricula, teacher education, and evaluation of policy.[260] For example, in Norway, outstanding school leaders volunteer to assist in municipalities requiring capacity development.[261]

The Beyond Commitments Report urges states to make sure that their education systems provide education that is fit for sustainable development.[262] This involves ensuring that education is directed towards particular aims, being the promotion of 'sustainable development, human rights, gender equality, a culture of peace and non-violence, global citizenship and cultural diversity'.[263] To ensure a national commitment to and ownership of education, affected stakeholders should be encouraged to participate in the development of educational curricula.[264] For example, in Germany the National Action Plan on Education for Sustainable Development (NAPESD) aims to provide education for sustainable development throughout the education system.[265] NAPESD was developed through a wide-ranging participatory process engaging government ministries, stakeholders from the education sector, and universities amongst other stakeholders.[266] States should ensure that there is an alignment between curricula, assessment, and teacher education.[267] For example, in Germany the NAPESD influences both curricula and teacher training.[268]

SDG 4 requires states to focus on education as a lifelong endeavour, not just education through the school system. In this respect, states need to define what their commitment to 'lifelong learning' means for state policy.[269] The commitment may mean different

---

[255] ibid 1, 22.
[256] ibid 23.
[257] ibid 1, 22.
[258] ibid 23.
[259] Organisation for Economic Co-operation and Development (OECD), 'What is PISA?' (OECD) <https://www.oecd.org/pisa/> accessed 19 August 2021.
[260] UNESCO, 'Beyond Commitments' (n 243) 22.
[261] ibid 23.
[262] ibid 2, 28.
[263] ibid 2, 28.
[264] ibid 2, 28.
[265] UNESCO, 'Beyond Commitments' (n 243) 31; The Federal Government of Germany, 'Report of the German Federal Government to the High-Level Political Forum on Sustainable Development' (2016) 26.
[266] UNESCO, 'Beyond Commitments' (n 243) 31.
[267] ibid 2, 28.
[268] ibid 31.
[269] ibid 2, 34.

things to different states depending on their stage of development. For example, while less developed countries may focus on adult literacy, more developed countries may pursue further study opportunities for adults.[270] For example, Afghanistan's approach to lifelong learning focuses on a national literacy strategy, while the Republic of Korea has implemented a fourth Master Plan for Lifelong Learning, which includes, amongst other aspects, paid leave to assist further learning.[271] States should also employ a range of approaches to connect formal and informal education provision.[272] For example, the Japanese Education for Sustainable Development National Implementation Plan and Promotion for Environmental Education Law urges collaboration between various education bodies to implement initiatives in schools, homes, workplaces, and local communities.[273] States must also tackle the inequitable situation whereby individuals who are more educated are also more likely to obtain additional education opportunities.[274]

The Beyond Commitments Report encourages states to engage in cross-sector cooperation. Thus, government departments of education should collaborate with other sectors, including in relation to education planning and implementation of policy measures.[275] For example, in Lithuania the education sector collaborates with other sectors, government tiers, and citizens, resulting in the production of education action plans.[276] As in Lithuania, collaboration may occur with other government departments; however, it should also encompass partnerships with NGOs and private organizations.[277] In Albania, for example, a national group has been established—including government ministries, independent bodies, and civil society organizations—to coordinate and implement the 2016–2020 National Action Plan for Lesbian, Gay, Bisexual, Transgender and Intersex Persons.[278] Moreover, government departments of education should endeavour to take away any administrative obstacles that may prevent multisector collaboration.[279] This is evidenced in Norway's 2017–2020 strategy for 0–24 Samarbeidet (translated as 0 to 24 Cooperation), which endeavours to build inter-agency collaboration and in this respect works to develop capacity for sectors to work together.[280]

The final area that states are urged to focus on in education policy-making for SDG 4 is regional and global cooperation.[281] According to the Beyond Commitments Report, regional organizations need to ensure that their education agendas are both clear and aligned with SDG 4, and cultivate favourable settings for education policy

---

[270] ibid 2.

[271] ibid 35.

[272] ibid 2, 34.

[273] UNESCO, 'Beyond Commitments' (n 243) 39; Japan, 'Japan's Voluntary National Review: Report on the Implementation of the Sustainable Development Goals' (2017) 23.

[274] UNESCO, 'Beyond Commitments' (n 243) 34.

[275] ibid 2, 40.

[276] ibid 41.

[277] ibid 2, 40.

[278] UNESCO, 'Beyond Commitments' (n 243) 44. See also Republic of Albania, Council of Ministers, 'Albania Voluntary National Review on Sustainable Development Goals' (2018) 19.

[279] UNESCO, 'Beyond Commitments' (n 243) 40.

[280] ibid 45.

[281] ibid 2, 46.

294   SDG 4

discussion.[282] For example, the European Union (EU) is building information networks between member countries on shared education issues.[283] This is evidenced by the Education and Training 2020 strategic framework which sets out strategic objectives and operating methods in education for the region.[284] Similarly, the Organisation for Economic Co-operation and Development (OECD) provides country education data via its Indicators of Education Systems programme, published annually in 'Education at a Glance', which assists in cross-country comparison and learning.[285] Governments should also make use of any opportunities to learn from peer states.[286] The Pacific Islands countries use peer learning to promote, through the Pacific Islands Literacy and Numeracy Assessment, the use of education data in developing education policy.[287] Peer learning networks are international public goods, and accordingly the Beyond Commitments Report urges states to fund the costs of their coordination and communication functions.[288]

As alluded to at the outset of this discussion of best practices, states require significant resources in order to achieve SDG 4 targets. Many states, however, and particularly the poorest and most vulnerable states, lack the domestic resources to meet SDG 4 commitments.[289] Therefore, wealthy states should provide development assistance to supplement domestic resources where required. Accordingly, best practice on the part of wealthy states in this respect will involve states providing a high level of official development assistance (ODA) to education in the least developed countries.[290] OECD states that met or came near to the UN target of 0.7 per cent of gross national income (GNI) ODA in 2020 included the United Kingdom, Germany, Denmark, Luxembourg, Norway, and Sweden.[291] Of these states, those with the highest proportions of aid dedicated to education were Luxembourg and Germany.[292]

F. General Critique

As shown in the discussion above, education has played a central role in human rights formulations since the UDHR at the beginning of the UN era, and indeed it can be

---

[282] ibid 2, 46.
[283] ibid 47.
[284] ibid 48.
[285] ibid 48.
[286] ibid 2, 46.
[287] ibid 49.
[288] ibid 2, 46.
[289] United Nations 'Addis Ababa Action Agenda of the Third International Conference on Financing for Development' (2015) 26.
[290] ibid 26, 36–37.
[291] OECD, 'Official Development Assistance (ODA)' (2020) <https://www.oecd.org/dac/financing-sustainable-development/development-finance-standards/official-development-assistance.htm> accessed 19 August 2021.
[292] Based on 2019 data as the most recent data available at the time of writing. Relevant percentages of aid dedicated to education out of total ODA were: United Kingdom 6.13 per cent; Germany 11.5 per cent; Denmark 5.74 per cent; Luxembourg 13.7 per cent; Norway 9.19 per cent; Sweden 2.3 per cent. See OECD, 'Total Flows by Donor' (25 July 2021, Table 1) <https://stats.oecd.org/Index.aspx?lang=en&DataSetCode=TABLE1> accessed 18 August 2021.

COMMENTARY ON GOAL   295

traced back further. The broad concept of freedom for every individual person to achieve their potential, as affirmed in the UDHR, was in essence the same concept as autonomy or 'self-determination' as applied both to individual persons and to whole peoples, in various proclamations and analyses over the centuries. It was, and remains, a tenet of western liberal thought, exemplified for example in Kant's distinction between heteronomy and autonomy as well as in the 'capabilities' approach of Sen and Nussbaum in our own times.[293] The realization of potential also featured strongly in the religious and philosophical traditions of Western Europe going back to Aristotle and Aquinas, and it is the Judeo-Christian traditions that have dominated global formulations on the human condition down to our own time.

For Kant, writing in the late eighteenth century, and consistent with the Enlightenment world view in general, the passage from heteronomy—the subjection to the will of another—to autonomy characterizes the many forms of progressive change observed in the lifeworld of the human. From this point of view the individual child knows no will other than that of his or her parents, but gradually acquires autonomy. Later contributors to what became known as 'developmental psychology' asserted that a stage of heteronomy comprising peer influence, most significant in adolescence, bridged the gap between parent-focused heteronomy and the autonomy of the adult, thus assisting to break the chains of the former.[294] Similarly, in this world view, national or ethnic communities (peoples) evolve over time towards a state in which they are capable and hence deserving, of control over their own affairs.[295]

If education is defined as the process by which full human potential is enabled or unlocked in each new generation by means of the institutions run by the adults, then education is clearly central to civil rights, to political rights, to shared cultural rights, and to collective rights of whole peoples. Moreover, it is central to empowerment and non-discrimination rights for women, for persons with a disability, and indeed for children in general, as indicated in the CRC.

At this level of generality, the benevolence and social progressivism expressed in human rights instruments and in aspirational programmes such as the SDGs can be leavened with some critical perspectives of an equally general nature. Where education is concerned, the interconnected assumptions underlying such terms as 'potential', 'growth', 'development', 'progress', and 'evolution' can all be subject to scrutiny. Thus, the use of the term 'evolve' in the above, in relation to peoples, is no accident. Gradual progressive change, that is to say change understood to be positive, or in some sense 'climbing upward', is the most general intellectual framework underlying the term 'evolution' as used by the Western professional class if not by post-Darwinian zoologists. The most general meaning of the word 'development' is little different except that a stronger sense of rule-governed and perhaps innately driven change, leading to some

---

[293] M Nussbaum, *Creating Capabilities: The Human Development Approach* (Belknap Press 2011).

[294] JR Morss, *The Biologising of Childhood: Developmental Psychology and the Darwinian Myth* (Erlbaum 1990) 146.

[295] R Wilde, *International Territorial Administration: How Trusteeship and the Civilizing Mission Never Went Away* (OUP 2008) 305.

uniformity across different infants, children, and young people of the same chronological age, is associated with the image. Already it may be observed that the emergence of potential in the individual growing child may be understood as the unfolding of something that was always there (perhaps in the genetic material, as we would now say). There is a tension even at this level of both conceptual and practical generality between the notion of development as being on the one hand, teleological—'pulled' by some end point such as individual autonomy or citizenhood—and on the other as being 'pushed' by innate factors. The role of education would vary as between these alternatives. Not only that but there is a tension between an open-endedness in individual development and therefore in education, and the closed picture of normative uniformity whether constrained by biology or by the dictates of the state.

Such frameworks of assumption are both outdated and current. To treat a child's point of view as irrelevant or even meaningless strikes us as archaic, for example in the era of the CRC with its insistence on taking account of the child's perspective on her life circumstances. Yet societies throughout the world continue to apply minimum ages of responsibility for criminal acts, which presuppose that years of cognitive and moral incapacity precede the (in effect, adult) years of culpability. The phenomenon of child soldiers, some of whom grow up to be adult war criminals, brings these problems into troublesome focus.[296] There is a continuity in the understanding of a direction of change, albeit recalibrated. Similarly, an account of non-Western societies as 'behind' or below Western societies is in the twenty-first century rightly rejected as a camouflaged version of racism. The idea of the inferiority of black races, or indeed of the Jews, was not unknown to Kant. The so-called separate development of majority populations governed by a privileged minority is recognized for what it is in our understanding of the Afrikaans word for 'apart-hood', namely 'apartheid'. Yet self-determination in our current scheme of public international law and human rights, for example in the context of the UN Charter, is still accompanied by the paternalistic framework of 'trusteeship' and 'non-self-governing territories'. In that respect, the UN remains an institution founded by the colonizing victors of the Second World War, and the Charter a document in which key aspects of the high-sounding Preamble ('faith in fundamental human rights') was written by segregationist General Jan Smuts of South Africa.[297]

Education and development therefore go hand in hand in conceptual terms. The 'development' of development economics is also characterized by deep commitments to a valourized sense of 'growth' and of a perceived increase in complexity of economic production and ownership. Clearly there are geopolitical stakes in the articulation of any grand plan relating to global economic regulation whether or not it attempts to accommodate concerns over 'sustainability'. Even moderate forms of cultural relativism, such as a level playing field as between Christianity, Islam, and other world faiths, seems beyond reach. All of these critical perspectives obscure as much as they illuminate and

---

[296] See *The Prosecutor v Dominic Ongwen* (2021) ICC Trial Chamber IX.
[297] M Mazower, *Governing the World. The History of an Idea* (Penguin Press 2012) 255; S Dubow, 'Smuts, the United Nations and the Rhetoric of Race and Rights' (2008) 43(1) Journal of Contemporary History 45, 47.

importantly they have been applied by academic commentators to the MDGs just as much as to the subsequent SDGs.[298] Moreover, as critique they play on the same field as the formulations that they respond to: they likewise exist at the intangible level of discourse. Just like the MDGs, critique is rhetoric, paper-thin at best. The implementation of the MDG Education goal in relation to its targets and the evaluation of the attainment thereof, gives rise to more complex questions and calls for more nuanced answers.

SDG 4 may also be subject to criticism on a number of more practical grounds. At the outset, the goal may be criticized for being overly ambitious.[299] While seeking to ensure all people at all stages of life have access to quality education is broadly unobjectionable, such a goal raises significant issues around how to finance education provision, both within and between states. The broad failure of the global community to achieve the MDG or EFA education goals should, perhaps, have operated as a warning. The global community should not expect a different outcome in relation to SDG 4 unless it is prepared to adopt a different approach.[300] Further, SDG 4 is universal in requiring all states to meet the same goal. This, however, overlooks the reality that states approach the goal from extraordinarily different starting points. Without significant levels of international cooperation, it is simply unrealistic to expect all states to be able to achieve SDG 4 within the same time frame.[301]

IV. Targets and Indicators of Goal 4

A. Background

SDG 4 consists of ten targets, canvassing issues that range from basic assessment of literacy and numeracy outcomes to those as ambitious as education for sustainable development and global citizenship education. Each target within SDG 4 features myriad obstacles that must be overcome in order to ensure its achievement. In order to track progress in this respect, each target is accompanied by a number of global and thematic indicators.[302] The indicators were developed by the Inter-Agency and Expert Group on SDG Indicators (IAEG-SDGs), a group created by the UN Statistical Commission.[303] The global indicator framework was adopted by the UNGA on 6 July 2017.[304]

---

[298] W Harcourt, 'The Millennium Development Goals: A missed opportunity?' (2005) 48(1) Society for International Development 1; A Saith, 'From Universal Values to Millennium Development Goals: Lost in translation' (2006) 37(6) Development and Change 1167; J Vandemoortele, 'Ambition is Golden: Meeting the MDGs' (2005) 48 Development 5.

[299] UNESCO, 'Global Education Monitoring Report 2016' (n 104) 172–73.

[300] See generally, ibid ii.

[301] UNESCO Institute for Statistics and UNESCO Global Education Monitoring Report 2019, 'Meeting Commitments: Are Countries on Track to Achieve SDG 4?' (2019) 12.

[302] UNGA (2017) UN Doc A/RES/71/313.

[303] UN, 'IAEG-SDGs' (*Sustainable Development Goals*) <https://unstats.un.org/sdgs/iaeg-sdgs/> accessed 16 September 2021.

[304] UNGA (2017) UN Doc A/RES/71/313.

298   SDG 4

The indicator development process may be contrasted with the consultative and open process that saw the creation of the targets.[305] Where broader, more inclusive themes surrounding education can be seen in the targets, the 'closed' expert-led creation of the monitoring framework has resulted in a narrower set of indicators that at times do not reflect the values evident in the targets. In part, this can be attributed to a 'closing out' of the groups that had barracked for the principles of inclusivity, equality, and broader notions of 'quality' to be included in the targets.[306] It can also be associated with a desire to align the indicators with available data.[307]

In the following sections, the source of each target will be discussed, as well as progress made towards the realization of the various targets. The progress made towards SDG 4 is primarily monitored by UNESCO, as the custodian agency for SDG 4.[308] Particular national and international efforts towards achieving SDG 4 will be discussed, with a view to highlighting some demonstrable ways in which states can implement programmes and policies to achieve SDG 4. A broader analysis of the targets is also provided, including, where relevant, discussion of the specific targets and indicators that evidence a mismatch of ambition.

B. Analysis and Critique of Each Target

1. Target 4.1 By 2030, ensure that all girls and boys complete free, equitable and quality primary and secondary education leading to relevant and effective learning outcomes

a) Sources of target

The language of target 4.1 is strongly aligned with a rights perspective, the source of which can be found in the UDHR and other international human rights instruments.[309] Key elements of target 4.1 include the requirement to ensure both primary and secondary education are free, the explicit reference to equity in the provision of education, as well as the standard of education being of quality and the output constituting relevant and effective learning outcomes. In relation to the first element, the requirement to ensure free primary education can be linked to article 26 of the UDHR, article 4 of the CADE,[310] article 28 of the CRC,[311] and article 13 of the ICESCR.[312] Each of these instruments emphasize the right of children to free primary education. Whilst reference to secondary education is also made in most of the instruments, such references do not

---

[305] K King, 'Lost in Translation? The Challenge of Translating the Global Education Goal and Targets into Global Indicators' (2017) 47(6) Compare: A Journal of Comparative and International Education 801, 806.

[306] E Unterhalter, 'The Many Meanings of Quality Education: Politics of Targets and Indicators in SDG 4' (2019) 10(1) Global Policy 39, 40.

[307] ibid 46.

[308] UNESCO Institute for Statistics, 'Quick Guide to Education Indicators for SDG 4' (UNESCO, 2018) 9.

[309] See above discussion at Section II.B. See UDHR (n 49).

[310] CADE (n 141).

[311] CRC (n 52).

[312] ICESCR (n 50).

require the immediate provision of free education—rather, availability and accessibility are emphasized.

Target 4.1 draws from an established language of inclusivity and equity found in human rights instruments. Equity is broadly concerned with fairness and impartiality. In this respect, the CADE seeks to prevent discrimination in education and promote equality of opportunity and treatment for all in education.[313] Similarly, target 4.1 emphasizes the need for primary and secondary education for *all* boys and girls. Equity requirements may also be found in the CRC and the CRPD. Art 28 of the CRC requires that the right of education be realized 'on the basis of equal opportunity'.[314] In terms of secondary education, States Parties must 'take appropriate measures such as ... offering financial assistance in case of need'.[315] Article 24 of the CRPD seeks to ensure the inclusion of people with disabilities in education on an equal basis with other members of their community.[316]

The need to ensure quality education that produces relevant and effective learning outcomes is both represented in international human rights instruments and an answer to the shortcomings of the MDGs. In regard to its representation in human rights instruments, a link can be found in article 28(3) of the CRC, which connects international cooperation in education to the purpose of eliminating illiteracy.[317] Target 4.1, through its global indicator, emphasizes proficiency in reading and mathematics and utilizes literacy in this respect as a determinate of the quality of the education. Thus, the explicit reference to eliminating illiteracy in article 28(3) of the CRC is a relevant source. Article 24(2)(d) of the CRPD is also relevant given it brings into play the notion of effective education for people with disabilities, and requires at article 24(1) that learning must be directed to '[t]he full development of human potential'.[318] This is a recurrent phrase in international human rights instruments, also evident in article 29(1) of the CRC and represented in article 13 of the ICESCR as the 'full development of the human personality'.[319] This phrase sets a standard for the quality of education, albeit a broader requirement for quality than is present in target 4.1. Finally, turning to the MDGs, the education goal (MDG 2) focused strongly on the number of children enrolled in school, and some success was achieved in this regard.[320] However, following the era of the MDGs, it became clear that enrolment and attendance are not always commensurate with the attainment of key skills, such as literacy and numeracy.[321] This sheds light on the push for quality within SDG 4, and presents MDG 2 as a further source of target 4.1.

---

[313] CADE (n 141) Preamble.
[314] CRC (n 52) art 28(1).
[315] ibid art 28(1)(b).
[316] CRPD (n 136) art 24.
[317] CRC (n 52) art 28(3).
[318] CRPD (n 136).
[319] ICESCR (n 50) art 13.
[320] UNGA 'United Nations Millennium Declaration' (18 September 2000) UN Doc A/RES/55/2.
[321] See International Bank for Reconstruction and Development/The World Bank, 'World Development Report 2018: Learning to Realize Education's Promise' (World Bank 2018) 3.

300 SDG 4

b) Statistical/empirical analysis

Target 4.1 is accompanied by two global indicators. The first, indicator 4.1.1, tracks the progress of target 4.1 by looking to the 'proportion of children and young people (a) in grades 2/3; (b) at the end of primary; and (c) at the end of lower secondary achieving at least a minimum proficiency level in (i) reading and (ii) mathematics, by sex'.[322] The second, indicator 4.1.2, tracks the completion rate of children in primary, lower secondary, and upper secondary education.[323] Of the key elements to target 4.1 outlined above in Section IV.B.1(a), including, 'free', 'equitable', 'quality', and 'relevant and effective learning', the global indicators for the target fail to address free and equitable.

Both indicators 4.1.1 and 4.1.2 reduce the broad meaning of quality in learning to a narrow agenda of completing schooling with a minimum proficiency. This narrow representation of the target in the indicators is likely to be due to the desirability of framing the indicators around data that are already available for use.[324] Arguably, the data that are readily available do not permit a broader and less output-focused measurement of education.[325] In this approach, however, indicators 4.1.1 and 4.1.2 neglect the majority of elements featured in target 4.1. This includes a failure to address the requirement to provide free primary and secondary education. Free education is instead captured by thematic indicator 4.1.7, which was introduced in the Incheon Declaration. Indicator 4.1.7 measures the '[n]umber of years of (a) free and (b) compulsory primary and secondary education guaranteed in legal frameworks'. However, as a thematic indicator, indicator 4.1.7 is voluntary for states and does not carry the same expectation in reporting as global indicators, resulting in insufficient available data.[326]

The emphasis within target 4.1 on the need to ensure access to free education was strongly supported by civil society groups,[327] and in terms of primary school-aged children, is an international legal obligation for states that have ratified the core human rights treaties outlined above. Thus, the ratification of human rights instruments that oblige States Parties to provide education freely, also represents some further level of commitment to target 4.1. As such, it is worth noting the states that have ratified the CADE, the CRC, and the ICESCR without reservation. Amongst such states are Brazil, Finland, Italy, Kazakhstan, and Senegal.[328] Conversely, the United States is the only state which is not a State Party to any of the aforementioned instruments.[329]

---

[322] UNESCO, 'Official List of SDG4 Indicators' (January 2021).

[323] ibid.

[324] King (n 305) 809.

[325] ibid.

[326] WC Smith, 'One Indicator to Rule Them All: How SDG 4.1.1 Dominates the Conversation and What it Means for the Most Marginalized' in AW Wiseman (ed) *Annual Review of Comparative and International Education* (International Perspectives on Education and Society, vol 27, Emerald Publishing 2018) 29.

[327] Unterhalter (n 306) 42.

[328] See UN Human Rights Office of the High Commissioner, 'Status of Ratification Interactive Dashboard' (*OHCHR*) <https://indicators.ohchr.org/> accessed 16 August 2021; UN Human Rights Treaty Bodies, 'UN Treaty Body Database' (*OHCHR*) <https://tbinternet.ohchr.org/_layouts/15/TreatyBodyExternal/Treaty.aspx?Treaty=CRC&Lang=en> accessed 16 August 2021; UN, 'Treaty Collection: Convention against Discrimination in Education' (*UN Treaty Collection*) <https://treaties.un.org/pages/showDetails.aspx?objid=0800000280134150> accessed 16 August 2021.

[329] See UN Human Rights Office of the High Commissioner, 'Status of Ratification Interactive Dashboard' (*OHCHR*) <https://indicators.ohchr.org/> accessed 16 August 2021; UN Human Rights Treaty Bodies, 'UN

In terms of progress in relation to indicator 4.1.1, as at 2015 globally, 56 per cent of primary and lower secondary school-aged children did not meet the minimum proficiency in numeracy and 58 per cent did not meet the minimum in literacy.[330] At the regional level, 84 per cent of children of the same age within Sub-Saharan Africa lacked minimum proficiency in numeracy, and 88 per cent did not meet the minimum level in literacy.[331] Similarly, within Central and Southern Asia the percentage of children not reaching minimum proficiency is 76 per cent for numeracy and 81 per cent for literacy.[332] Within these regions alone, this accounts for around 443 million children of primary or lower secondary age who are not proficient in reading, and 421 million children of the same age who do not have minimum mathematical proficiency. There is a correlation here, as those undergoing numeracy testing must possess literacy skills to allow them to read and understand the questions.[333]

The data also indicate that lacking minimum proficiency in reading or mathematics is not exclusively a problem for children out of school. Data from the UNESCO Institute for Statistics (UIS) showed that in 2017 across every region, the vast majority of children who were not meeting minimum proficiency levels were in school.[334] Out of the estimated 617 million children of primary and lower secondary school age that cannot read proficiently, around two-thirds will have reached the last grade of primary schooling.[335] Further, by 2019, over half of the children in school were not reaching the minimum proficiency levels in literacy or numeracy.[336] This demonstrates that obstacles in achieving target 4.1 arise not only in accessing schooling but also in the quality of learning.

On the other hand, indicator 4.1.2 highlights the number of school-age children that are out of school, which is a clear contributor to low reading and mathematics proficiency rates. In 2018, 258 million children aged between six and seventeen years old were out of school.[337] Increased access to education and progress in educational participation is required to reduce the one third of children out of school, who contribute to the total 617 million primary and secondary school-age children who do not have proficiency in literacy or numeracy. In 2020 and 2021, global school closures as a result of the COVID-19 pandemic prevented approximately 90 per cent of

---

Treaty Body Database' (*OHCHR*) <https://tbinternet.ohchr.org/_layouts/15/TreatyBodyExternal/Treaty.aspx?Treaty=CRC&Lang=en> accessed 16 August 2021; UN, 'Treaty Collection: Convention against Discrimination in Education' (*UN Treaty Collection*) <https://treaties.un.org/pages/showDetails.aspx?objid=0800000280134150> accessed 16 August 2021.

[330] UN, 'The Sustainable Development Goals Report 2019' (July 2019) 30.

[331] ibid.

[332] ibid.

[333] TS Murray, 'Functional Literacy and Numeracy: Definitions and Options for Measurement of SDG 4.6' (GAML Fifth Meeting 17–18 October 2018, UNESCO 2018) 33.

[334] UNESCO, 'Fact Sheet No 46: More than One- Half of Children and Adolescents are Not learning Worldwide' (UIS/FS/2017/ED/46) 11.

[335] ibid 10; Report of the Secretary-General, 'Progress towards the Sustainable Development Goals' (2018) UN Doc E/2018/64, 7.

[336] Report of the Secretary-General, 'Progress towards the Sustainable Development Goals' (2020) UN Doc E/2020/57, 7.

[337] UN, 'The Sustainable Development Goals Report 2020' (n 179).

302   SDG 4

all students—approximately 1.5 billion children and young people—from going to school.[338] Data are not yet available on the full effects of the coronavirus pandemic on access, completion and quality of education. However, it is clear that the extended period of absence from school, combined with the lack of computer and Internet access within many developing countries that severely inhibits remote learning, is likely to slow progress on target 4.1.[339]

Finally, achieving gender parity in literacy and numeracy proficiency has been a challenge that the pandemic is likely to exacerbate.[340] To monitor progress in this respect, indicator 4.1.1 tracks gender gaps in proficiency levels. As detailed in the 2019 report on SDGs, globally the disparity in literacy proficiency favours girls.[341] Data from 2015 show that for every 100 boys who achieved reading proficiency, there were 105 girls in the primary age bracket and 109 girls in the lower secondary age bracket who had reached minimum proficiency.[342] This trend appears converse to out of school rates, as at primary school level in 2018, around 5.5 million more girls than boys were not in school.[343]

c) Efforts taken at domestic and international level
The efforts of countries towards target 4.1 can be seen through legislative or policy commitments that positively impact the number of children reaching minimum proficiency in literacy and numeracy, as well as the number of children completing primary and secondary schooling.

The first example of regional level efforts is the support of Pacific Island Governments towards the Pacific Islands Literacy and Numeracy Assessment (PILNA), and their commitment to monitor educational outcomes through the PILNA model. PILNA was developed in 2006 by UNESCO and the Secretariat for the Pacific Board of Educational Assessment (now known as the Educational Quality and Assessment Programme), as well as representatives from fifteen Pacific Island countries.[344] It was designed to be a common tool for participating countries to recognize and address challenges faced by Pacific Islander students in literacy and numeracy.[345] PILNA thus features collaboration as a key element in its model, which has facilitated consensus amongst national governments in reporting and dissemination of literacy and numeracy data.[346] The model involves a literacy and numeracy assessment measured on a common scale and undertaken by Pacific Islander students on a regular basis.[347] The most recent

---

[338] ibid 3; Report of the Secretary-General, 'Progress towards the Sustainable Development Goals' (2020) UN Doc E/2020/57, 7.
[339] UN, 'The Sustainable Development Goals Report 2020' (n 179).
[340] UN Women, UN Department of Economic and Social Affairs, 'Progress on the Sustainable Development Goals: The Gender Snapshot 2020' (2020).
[341] UN, 'The Sustainable Development Goals Report 2019' (July 2019).
[342] ibid.
[343] ibid.
[344] M Belisle and others, 'Pacific Islands Literacy and Numeracy Assessment: Collaboration and Innovation in Reporting and Dissemination' (Issue 1, Australian Council for Educational Research; Network on Education Quality Monitoring in the Asia-Pacific; UNESCO December 2016).
[345] ibid.
[346] ibid.
[347] ibid.

administration of PILNA occurred in 2018. The results from the 2018 assessment were released in the PILNA report, which showed that the number of students who had not yet met minimum expected levels in literacy as at years 4 and 6 had declined.[348] For instance, in 2012—the first year of PILNA—43 per cent of year 4 students in the participating countries were in the lowest three proficiency levels, whereas in 2018 this proportion decreased to 34 per cent.[349] PILNA represents a joint effort to understand the learning outcomes of students within the Pacific region, and through this can assist in the development of targeted governmental interventions and policies to better enhance the literacy and numeracy skills of the community.

In regard to country level efforts made towards indicator 4.1.2—that is, completion of both primary and secondary education—Norway has implemented a programme involving seven municipalities that aims to keep children and young people in school. Four respective Norwegian ministries have collaborated in the implementation of the 0–24 Samarbeidet (0 to 24 Cooperation) Strategy, which ran from 2017 to 2020 and was initiated by the Nordic Council of Ministers.[350] All Nordic countries and autonomous islands participated in the 0–24 project. The strategy aimed to increase inter-agency cooperation in order to facilitate improved support for vulnerable youth aged between 0 and 24 years within the Nordic region.[351] In the context of this project, vulnerable is defined as relating to 'coping in school, completing school and later social inclusion in everyday working life'.[352] The 0–24 strategy operates with the awareness that students in situations that make them vulnerable, such as poor living conditions or difficulties in school, may face social exclusion and be more dependent on multiple forms of services in the future.[353] The project notes that school completion and drop-out rates in upper secondary school is a key concern in this context.[354]

An interdisciplinary programme implemented by the Faroe Islands has been utilized as a case study by the 0–24 project and presents a strong example of efforts towards increasing school completion rates. The programme, titled Lopfjølin ('the Springboard'), is targeted at students in grades 7–10 within the municipality of Thorshavn who are at risk of not completing their basic education due to social or mental health problems.[355] Lopfjølin began in 2014 and was designed to address an increase in school drop-out rates.[356] It involves collaboration between departments such as child welfare services, primary schools, and the Ministry of Education, and has been offered to all primary school students in Thorshavn since 2017.[357] The student and their

---

[348] Pacific Community, 'Pacific Islands Literacy and Numeracy Assessment 2018 Regional Report' (Educational Quality and Assessment Division: Pacific Community 2019) 1.

[349] ibid 42.

[350] ILS Hansen and others, 'Mind The Gap: Nordic 0–24 Collaboration on Improved Services to Vulnerable Children and Young People' (Fafo final report from the process evaluation 2020) 5.

[351] ibid.

[352] ibid 25.

[353] ibid 15.

[354] ibid 15.

[355] ILS Hansen and others, 'Second Interim Report: Nordic 0–24 Collaboration on Improved Services to Vulnerable Children and Young People' (Fafo 2019) 31.

[356] ibid.

[357] ibid.

family must be registered with child welfare services, who are responsible for devising an action plan which caters to the individual student.[358] The action plan is a collaborative effort between child welfare services and the student, and resources are provided by the school authorities as it relates to the student's absences.[359] Key measures include extensive individual tutoring, educational support, and family counselling, the last of which is utilized to ensure the whole family is supported.[360] As mentioned above, Lopfjølin has been documented and analysed as part of the 0–24 project, with aims to expand the model to the whole of the Faroe Islands.[361] The inter-disciplinary and collaborative nature of this model and the 0–24 project highlights the complexity of dropout rates and the multi-sectoral approach required to increase school completion.

d) Critique

Quality as presented in target 4.1 is defined by the global indicators to mean the literacy and numeracy outcomes of the educational process. While to some degree this definition is likely to have been tailored to reflect the available data, it effectively operates to erase the complexity behind the notion of quality as it exists within education. The meaning of quality has developed in tandem with the education agenda, becoming broader and based on more transparent and generally accepted values, rather than learning outcomes.[362] This understanding was articulated in the Incheon Declaration, which defined quality education to include 'those skills, values, attitudes and knowledge that enable citizens to lead healthy and fulfilled lives, make informed decisions and respond to local and global challenges'.[363] This definition requires a dynamic understanding of quality that relates to the culture and values of the relevant community. It necessitates a focus on more than literacy and numeracy outputs—inclusive of the educational processes, environments, or approaches that contribute to the full development of the human personality as set out in international human rights instruments.

Quality education is thus conceived as promoting many aspects of individual development. In this respect, there is, as summarized by Therese Ferguson and others, a link between quality education and 'other systems such as family, community and ... society'.[364] This conception of quality is reflected in Lopfjølin as outlined above, which offers whole family support as part of a strategy to reduce drop-out rates. Indeed, many country efforts may be perceived as going beyond the SDG 4 requirements reflected in indicators 4.1.1 and 4.1.2. This raises the question of whether the indicators are sufficiently broad to capture states' progress towards target 4.1. On the other hand, the multifaceted meaning of quality, as requiring the development of each child based on their competencies—the process of which is impacted by their existing knowledge

---

[358] ibid 32.
[359] ibid.
[360] ibid.
[361] ibid 33.
[362] Unterhalter (n 306) 42.
[363] ibid 33.
[364] T Ferguson and others, *SDG 4— Quality Education: Inclusivity, Equity and Lifelong Learning for All* (Emerald Publishing 2019) 40.

and environmental factors—may arguably exceed the bounds of 'measurable out-comes' that are 'universally applicable' and capable of cross-country comparison.[365] This may explain why quality is defined narrowly in indicators 4.1.1 and 4.1.2. Concern regarding overly ambitious measurements is valid here given data in education have at times been used in a manner that exacerbates exclusion.[366] For instance, the colla-tion of data and implementation of policies based on that data may operate to suppress Indigenous approaches and perspectives.[367] The result is a silencing of cultural know-ledge and traditions, and a disadvantage for Indigenous children and youth in meeting the indicators.[368]

Despite this, in order to ensure that education fosters the full development of each child's personality—and to preserve the apparent political balance struck in target 4.1—the indicators should reflect the same discourse. The manner in which the indi-cators reduce the notion of quality to the narrow learning outcomes of literacy and numeracy, signals a focus on standardization as opposed to a recognition of the various processes and approaches within 'quality education' that foster the individual capabil-ities of the child.[369] There is a balance that must be found here to ensure the indicators are reflective of the contexts behind them.[370] This is especially important given that indicator selection may have a 'validating' effect.[371] Thus, the manner in which the indi-cators neglect the process of learning and overlook the diverse capabilities of students' amounts to an oversimplification of target 4.1, such that they fail to truly measure a state's performance against target 4.1.

2. Target 4.2 By 2030, ensure that all girls and boys have access to quality early childhood development, care and pre-primary education so that they are ready for primary education

a) Sources of target

At first glance, target 4.2 appears to commit states to additional obligations beyond those set out in human rights instruments. Article 26 of the UDHR, article 28 of the CRC, articles 13 and 14 of the ICESCR and the CADE make no reference to early child-hood care or education (ECCE). Further, proposals to include obligations regarding ECCE in the text of the CRC were rejected.[372]

---

[365] UNGA, 'Report of the Open Working Group of the General Assembly on Sustainable Development Goals' UNGA 68th Session UN Doc A/68/970 (2014) sect IV, para 18.

[366] See generally, J Raina (ed), *Elementary Education in India: Policy Shifts, Issues and Challenges* (Routledge 2021) 272; Unterhalter (n 306) 49.

[367] RJ Alexander, 'Teaching and Learning for All? The Quality Imperative Revisited' (2015) 40 International Journal of Educational Development 250, 255.

[368] A Rogers, 'PISA, Power and Policy: The Emergence of Global Education Governance' (2014) 60 International Review of Education 591, 594.

[369] Raina (n 366) 33.

[370] Alexander (n 367) 251.

[371] ibid.

[372] UN Economic and Social Council, 'Report of the Working Group on a draft convention on the rights of the child' (1989) UN Doc E/CN.4/1989/48, paras 458–459 in OHCHR, *Legislative History of the Convention on the Rights of the Child* (UN2007) vol II, 648–49. See also K Tomaševski, *Education Denied: Costs and Remedies* (Zed Books 2003) 53; G Van Bueren, *The International Law on the Rights of the Child* (Martinus Nijhoff 1998) 234.

Nevertheless, it is clear that the core human rights instruments are authoritatively interpreted to encompass a right to ECCE. The CRC Committee has interpreted the right to education set out in article 28 as encompassing a right to education during early childhood, in light of the child's right to development in article 6.[373] In this respect, the Committee has called on 'States parties to ensure that all young children receive education in the broadest sense ... which acknowledges ... the contribution of organized programmes of early childhood education provided by the State, the community or civil society institutions.'[374] Further, in its concluding observations the Committee has frequently expressed concern in relation to ECCE and has made recommendations including, amongst others, adoption of a policy, strategy, or standards in relation to ECCE, implementation of ECCE plans and expansion and increased access to ECCE.[375]

Similarly, the ICESCR Committee has interpreted article 13 of the ICESCR as imposing an obligation on states to provide pre-school. Although it has not expressly referred to this obligation in its general comments, it has referred to such in its concluding observations. In this respect, it has expressed concern in relation to—for example—the insufficient availability of pre-school education across municipalities,[376] irregular attendance at pre-school,[377] the exclusion of asylum-seeking children from pre-school,[378] and delay in the increase of pre-school education coverage.[379]

The right to ECCE can also be sourced to many other international and regional agreements. For example, the Committee on the Rights of Persons with Disabilities has urged States Parties to 'ensure access to quality early childhood development, care and pre-primary education'.[380] European regional instruments recognize the right to ECCE.[381] Further, the right to ECCE was affirmed in the Education 2030 Incheon

[373] UN Committee on the Rights of the Child, 'General Comment No 7: Implementing Child Rights in Early Childhood' (2005) UN Doc CRC/C/GC/Rev.1, para 28; C Courtis and J Tobin, 'Article 28: The Right to Education' in J Tobin (ed), *The UN Convention on the Rights of the Child: A Commentary* (OUP 2019) 1065.

[374] UN Committee on the Rights of the Child, 'General Comment No 7: Implementing Child Rights in Early Childhood' (2005) UN Doc CRC/C/GC/Rev.1, para 30.

[375] See UN Committee on the Rights of the Child, 'Concluding Observations on the Second Periodic Report of the Federates States of Micronesia' (2020) UN Doc CRC/C/FSM/CO/2, para 59(e); UN Committee on the Rights of the Child, 'Concluding Observations on the Initial Report of the State of Palestine' (2020) UN Doc CRC/C/PSE/CO/1, para 55(a); UN Committee on the Rights of the Child, 'Concluding Observations on the Combined Fifth and Sixth Periodic Reports of Portugal' (2019) UN Doc CRC/C/PRT/CO/5-6*, para 40(d); UN Committee on the Rights of the Child, 'Concluding Observations on the Combined Fourth and Fifth Periodic Reports of Japan' (2019) UN Doc CRC/C/JPN/CO/4-5, para 40(a); UN Committee on the Rights of the Child, 'Concluding Observations on the Combined Fourth and Fifth Periodic Reports of Italy' (2019) UN Doc CRC/C/ITA/CO/5-6*, para 32(d); UN Committee on the Rights of the Child, 'Concluding Observations on the Combined Fourth and Fifth Periodic Reports of El Salvador' (2018) UN Doc CRC/C/CLV/CO/5-6, para 44.

[376] UN Committee on Economic, Social and Cultural Rights (UN CESCR), 'Concluding Observations on the Second Periodic Report of Latvia' (2021) UN Doc E/C.12/LVA/CO/2.

[377] UN CESCR, 'Concluding Observations on the Fifth Periodic Report of Belgium (2020) UN Doc E/C.12/BEL/CO/5 art 56.

[378] UN CESCR, 'Concluding Observations on the Sixth Periodic Report of Norway (2020) UN Doc E/C.12/NOR/CO/6 art 44.

[379] UN CESCR, 'Concluding Observations on the Fourth Periodic Report of Ecuador' (2019) UN Doc E/C.12/ECU/Co/4 art 55.

[380] UN Committee on the Rights of Persons with Disabilities, 'General Comment No 4 (2016) on the Right to Inclusive Education' (2016) UN Doc CRPD/C/GC/4.

[381] European Charter for Regional or Minority Languages (adopted 5 November 1992, entered into force 1 March 1998) European Treaty Series No 148, art 8(1)(a); A European Pillar of Social Rights [2017] OJ C 242/24 art 11. Council of Europe: Committee of Ministers (Recommendation concerning the education of Roma/Gypsy children in Europe) R (2000) 4 (3 February 2000); Committee of Ministers (Recommendations on the education

Declaration and Framework for Action 2015,[382] the Dakar Framework for Action,[383] and the Jomtien Declaration.[384]

b) Statistical/empirical analysis

Target 4.2 is measured by reference to two global indicators. The first is indicator 4.2.1, which looks at the '[p]roportion of children aged 24–59 months who are developmentally on track in health, learning and psychosocial well-being, by sex'.[385] Indicator 4.2.2, the second indicator, considers the '[p]articipation rate in organized learning (one year before the official primary entry age), by sex'.[386] In 2015, indicator 4.2.1 was classified as tier 3— the lowest classification within the tier system.[387] This means that at the time the indicator was introduced, there were no established or readily available standards or methodology for measuring the indicator.[388] Indicator 4.2.1 was recategorized as tier 2 in 2019, signalling that at that time, 'internationally established methodology and standards' were available, but data in relation to those standards were not consistently produced.[389] The lack of regularly produced country data on indicator 4.2.1 can be attributed to the initial absence of an established methodology or standard. When the SDGs began in 2015, so too did efforts from UNICEF in regards to developing a methodology that identified and captured the appropriate milestones of childhood development for the purposes of target 4.2.[390] This was achieved in 2020 with the Early Childhood Development Index 2030 (ECDI2030).

The ECDI2030 is designed to be implemented via national household surveys and consists of twenty questions to be answered by 'mothers or primary caregivers'.[391] The questions focus on the behaviour of children aged between 24–59 months in the situations they ordinarily encounter, as well as the skills they possess.[392] The ECDI2030 provides a standardized tool to accurately measure progress on target 4.2 and collect data that are comparable across countries.[393] However, in the period between the

---

of Roma and Travellers to Europe) CM/REC (2009) 4 (17 June 2009); Council of Europe: Committee of Ministers (Recommendation on ensuring quality education) CM/REC (2012) 13 (12 December 2012); Recommendation on High-Quality Early Childhood Education and Care Systems (22 May 2019).

[382] UNESCO, 'Incheon Declaration and Framework for Action for the Implementation of Sustainable Development Goal 4' (ED-2016/WS/28, 2015).

[383] UNESCO, 'The Dakar Framework for Action. Education for All: Meeting our Collective Commitments' (ED-2000/WS/27, 2000).

[384] UNESCO, 'World Declaration Education for All and Framework for Action to Meet Basic Learning Needs' (Jomtien, Thailand 1990) art 5.

[385] UN, 'Global Indicator Framework for the Sustainable Development Goals and Targets of the 2030 Agenda for Sustainable Development' (2020) UN Doc E/CN.3/2020/2, 5.

[386] ibid.

[387] UN, 'SDG Indicator Metadata' (March 2021).

[388] UN 'Tier Classification for Global SDG Indicators' (29 March 2021).

[389] ibid.

[390] UNICEF 'Early Childhood Development Index 2030: A New Tool to Measure SDG Indicator 4.2.1' (January 2021) <https://data.unicef.org/resources/early-childhood-development-index-2030-ecdi2030/> accessed 18 August 2021.

[391] ibid.

[392] UN, 'SDG Indicator Metadata' (March 2021) <https://unstats.un.org/sdgs/metadata/files/Metadata-04-02-01.pdf> accessed 18 August 2021.

[393] UNICEF 'Early Childhood Development Index 2030: A New Tool to Measure SDG Indicator 4.2.1' (January 2021) <https://data.unicef.org/resources/early-childhood-development-index-2030-ecdi2030/> accessed 18 August 2021.

beginning of the SDG's in 2015, and the point where there are sufficient data available on this measurement—which at the time of writing is yet to be reached—a proxy indicator is used.[394] The proxy indicator for indicator 4.2.1 utilizes the former ECDI to measure 'children aged 36–59 months who are developmentally on-track in at least three of the following four domains: literacy-numeracy, physical, social-emotional and learning'.[395] Thus, this proxy indicator has been utilized for country reporting on SDG 4.2. Given this, currently available data are largely reflective of this proxy indicator as opposed to the principle indicator.[396] Relevantly, the former ECDI and ECDI2030 do not allow for true comparison given they measure different age groups as well as different areas of development.[397]

Against this backdrop, the most recent comparable data within seventy-four countries shows that approximately 70 per cent of children aged between three and four were developmentally on track in at least three of the four domains specified in the proxy indicator.[398] That is, they were reaching the developmental milestones in three of the 'literacy-numeracy, physical, social-emotional [or] learning' domains.[399] This indicates that there are three out of every ten children aged between three and four that are not on track developmentally. It is relevant to note that the ages children achieve developmental milestones may differ across countries, sexes, and cultures,[400] which could contribute to this number. There are also large discrepancies across countries in their progress towards indicator 4.2.1. For instance, in Bosnia and Herzegovina, 96.4 per cent of children were on track in at least three of the four relevant domains in 2012.[401] In Thailand, in 2016, 91.1 per cent of children were on track,[402] and in Nepal this number was 64.4 per cent in 2014.[403] In Sierra Leone, as at 2017, 51.4 per cent of children were attaining these developmental milestones,[404] while in Chad, as at 2015, 32.6 per cent of children were developmentally on track.[405] Clearly, there is considerable discrepancy in progress between countries.

[394] UN 'SDG Indicator Metadata' (March 2021) 3.
[395] ibid 4.
[396] ibid.
[397] ibid.
[398] Report of the Secretary-General, 'Progress Towards the Sustainable Development Goals' (2020) UN Doc E/2020/57, 7.
[399] UN 'SDG Indicator Metadata' (March 2021) 4.
[400] UNICEF, 'Development Status: The Development Status of Children Varies Widely Among Countries' (August 2021) <https://data.unicef.org/topic/early-childhood-development/development-status/> accessed 20 August 2021; I Ozturk Ertem and others, 'Similarities and Differences in Child Development from Birth to Age 3 Years by Sex and Across Four Countries: A Cross-Sectional, Observational Study' (2018) 6 Lancet Global Health 279.
[401] UN 'SDG Country Profile: Bosnia and Herzegovina' (Goal 4) <https://country-profiles.unstatshub.org/bih#goal-4> accessed 20 August 2021.
[402] UN 'SDG Country Profile: Thailand' (Goal 4) <https://country-profiles.unstatshub.org/tha#goal-4> accessed 20 August 2021.
[403] UN 'SDG Country Profile: Nepal' (Goal 4) <https://country-profiles.unstatshub.org/npl#goal-4 > accessed 20 August 2021.
[404] UN 'SDG Country Profile: Sierra Leone' (Goal 4) <https://country-profiles.unstatshub.org/sle#goal-5> accessed 20 August 2021.
[405] UN 'SDG Country Profile: Chad' (Goal 4) <https://country-profiles.unstatshub.org/tcd#goal-4> accessed 20 August 2021.

Great variation between countries is also present in regards to indicator 4.2.2, which measures the '[p]articipation rate in organized learning (one year before the official primary entry age), by sex'.[406] For example, in France as at 2017, there was a participation rate of 99.8 per cent.[407] In Cuba, in 2018, 99.9 per cent of children participated in organized learning one year prior to reaching primary school entry age. In contrast, in Chad in 2016, there was a participation rate of 10 per cent.[408] This is, however, a considerable increase from 2012, when there was a participation rate of 1.3 per cent.[409] A similarly low participation rate is also evident in Djibouti, where it was 12.1 per cent in 2019.[410] Again, progress towards this indicator is evident given the relevant participation rate in Djibouti was 3.3 per cent in 2012.[411] On a global scale, in 2018, 67 per cent of children participated in organized learning one year before the official primary entry age.[412] This is an increase of 5 per cent since 2010, when the participation rate was 62 per cent.[413]

Progress in relation to target 4.2 can also be measured by ratification of relevant international human rights instruments. In this respect, the CRC has been ratified by more countries than any other international human rights instrument.[414] In 2015, both South Sudan and Somalia ratified the CRC, bringing the total number of States Parties to 196.[415] This represents some degree of progress towards target 4.2 given it signals—to an extent—general agreement with the values embodied by the treaty and acceptance of the related obligations. It should be noted, however, that in the absence of an express obligation in the CRC to provide ECCE, states may have overlooked this implied obligation, or interpreted the treaty in a different manner to the Committee on the Rights of the Child. Nevertheless, ratification imposes an obligation on States Parties to report regularly in relation to the CRC,[416] which enables scrutiny of states' performance in relation to CRC obligations. Given the overlap between CRC and target 4.2 obligations, such reporting also permits scrutiny in relation to state behaviour regarding target 4.2.

---

[406] UN 'Global Indicator Framework for the Sustainable Development Goals and Targets of the 2030 Agenda for Sustainable Development' (2020) UN Doc E/CN.3/2020/2, 5.

[407] UN 'SDG Country Profile: France' (Goal 4) <https://country-profiles.unstatshub.org/fra#goal-4> accessed 20 August 2021.

[408] UN 'SDG Country Profile: Chad' (Goal 4) <https://country-profiles.unstatshub.org/tcd#goal-4> accessed 20 August 2021.

[409] M Roser and others, 'Measuring Progress towards the Sustainable Development Goals' (*SDG Tracker*, 2018) <https://sdg-tracker.org/quality-education> accessed 20 August 2021.

[410] UN 'SDG Country Profile: Djibouti' (Goal 4) <https://country-profiles.unstatshub.org/dji#goal-4> accessed 20 August 2021.

[411] Roser and others (n 409).

[412] Report of the Secretary-General, 'Progress Towards the Sustainable Development Goals' (2020) UN Doc E/2020/57, 7.

[413] ibid.

[414] UNTC, 'Depositary Status of Treaties: Convention on the Rights of the Child' (Ch IV (11), UNTC status as at 23 August 2021).

[415] Note that South Sudan and Somalia's ratification of the CRC leaves the United States as the only non-State Party: ibid.

[416] CRC (n 52) art 44.

310 SDG 4

c) Efforts taken at a domestic and international level

On an international level, varying degrees of effort have been made by countries to achieve the ECCE aspects of SDG 4. In relation to early childhood education, high-income countries have achieved an 83 per cent enrolment rate of children in pre-primary education as opposed to 22 per cent in low-income countries.[417] This suggests an urgent need for low- and lower-middle-income countries to increase efforts to expand access to pre-primary education.[418] While progress has been slow and uneven,[419] some domestic efforts stand out as worthy of discussion.

In Australia, efforts towards target 4.2 are represented in part by the development and implementation of the Early Development Census (AEDC).[420] An initiative of the Australian Government, the AEDC tracks early childhood development by assessing children in their first year of full-time school.[421] The AEDC first took place in 2009, and data have been collected every three years since. Five domains are tracked within the AEDC, including the physical health and well-being of the child, their social competence, emotional maturity, language and cognitive skills (school-based), communication skills, and general knowledge.[422] Unlike the newly developed ECDI2030, data for the AEDC are collected by the child's teacher. A teacher that has known the child for at least one month can complete the AEDC instrument, containing approximately 100 questions related to the five development domains. Notably, teachers who are not Aboriginal or Torres Strait Islander are encouraged to seek support from an Indigenous Cultural Consultant (ICC) when completing the instrument in relation to an Indigenous child.[423] This is designed to ensure teachers consider differences in Aboriginal and Torres Strait Islander cultures that may influence childhood development.

Clear efforts towards meeting target 4.2 can also been seen in India. The Ministry of Education recently approved the National Education Policy 2020,[424] which prominently features ECCE. The policy recognizes that the current education structure largely ignores children aged five and under, as education begins in 'Class 1' at the age of six. In order to promote the development and school readiness of children before they reach Class 1, the Indian government has created a framework to ensure the education of children from the age of three. The policy states, '[u]niversal provisioning of quality early childhood development, care, and education must thus be achieved as soon as possible, and no later than 2030, to ensure that all students entering Grade 1 are school ready'.[425] This focus on ECCE, coupled with a deadline of 2030, demonstrates a clear commitment by the Indian government to meet target 4.2.

---

[417] UNICEF, 'A World Ready to Learn: Prioritizing Quality Early Childhood Education' (Advocacy Brief, UNICEF April 2019) 30.

[418] ibid 33.

[419] UNICEF, 'A World Ready to Learn' (n 417) 26.

[420] UNESCO, 'Global Education Monitoring Report 2020' (n 90) 233.

[421] The Social Research Centre, '2018 Australian Early Development Census (AEDC) Data Collection Technical Report' (December 2019) 12.

[422] Australian Early Development Census (AEDC), 'About the AEDC Data Collection' (May 2015) 1.

[423] ibid 2.

[424] Government of India: Ministry of Human Resource Development, 'National Education Policy 2020' (2020).

[425] ibid 7.

In terms of how this commitment will be implemented, the policy envisions a phased expansion of ECCE across the country. It is recognized that existing early-childhood education facilities must be strengthened in order to deliver ECCE to the 'crores'[426] of children that are currently excluded. This will include the expansion and strengthening of stand-alone Anganwadis ('courtyard centres') and pre-schools, as well as Anganwadis and pre-primary classes (for children aged five to six) located within primary schools.[427] Anganwadis were initially implemented by the Indian government in 1975 to address malnutrition in children, however, they now offer a range of services including non-formal pre-school education for children aged between three and six.[428] The policy outlines that these centres will be 'strengthened with high-quality infrastructure, play equipment, and well-trained Anganwadi workers/teachers'.[429] It is further provided that all teachers, in both Anganwadis and pre-schools, will receive specialty training in ECCE to be able to deliver quality education for children to ensure their readiness for primary school.[430] The policy further envisions the implementation of a 'Balavatika', or 'Preparatory Class', that each child will participate in prior to the age of five. These classes will also feature ECCE-qualified teachers, and the format of learning will be primarily play-based. While it remains to be seen how this policy will be implemented, and with what level of success, the prominence of ECCE within the policy demonstrates a strong commitment from India to meeting target 4.2.

d) Critique

Recent research is clear as to the criticality of early years learning.[431] During the early years of life, the brain develops and the experiences and connections a child has can affect their brain development. Thus, early years learning provides the foundation for a person's future life. It is both understandable and admirable, therefore, that the international community was able to commit to ensuring global access to quality early childhood development, care and pre-primary education as set out in target 4.2.

Nevertheless, historically government provision of education has focused on primary and secondary education.[432] Provision of ECCE has been patchy and diverse,

---

[426] ibid. Crores refers to 10 million.

[427] ibid.

[428] Government of Maharashtra, 'Women and Child Development Department: Anganwadi Functions' <https://womenchild.maharashtra.gov.in/content/innerpage/anganwadi-functions.php> accessed 23 August 2021.

[429] Government of India: Ministry of Human Resource Development, 'National Education Policy 2020' (2020) 7.

[430] ibid.

[431] See, eg, K Sylva and others, 'Introduction: Why EPPE?' in K Sylva and others (eds), *Early Childhood Matters: Evidence from the Effective Pre-School and Primary Education Project* (Routledge 2010) 3; OECD, *Starting Strong: Early Childhood Education and Care* (OECD 2001) 3; UNESCO, 'Education for All ("EFA") Global Monitoring Report 2007: Early Childhood Care and Education' (UNESCO, 2006); JJ Heckman and LK Raut, 'Intergenerational Long Term Effects of Preschool-Structural Estimates from a Discrete Dynamic Programming Model' (2016) 191 Journal of Econometrics 164.

[432] Historically, primary, and secondary education (to a set age) has been compulsory in many states, while pre-primary education has not. For example, see the following information in relation to Australia and Sweden: Australian Government, 'Australian Education System' <https://www.studyinaustralia.gov.au/english/australian-education/education-system> accessed 24 August 2021; Sweden Sverige, 'The Swedish School System' <https://sweden.se/life/society/the-swedish-school-system> accessed 24 August 2021.

312   SDG 4

both between and within states.[433] While states now understand the importance of early years learning, establishing and resourcing a system for ECCE takes time and remains an ongoing process. This is reflected in ECCE participation rates reported by states, which are generally well short of the goal of full participation.[434] Further, while the significance of ECCE is now understood, primary and secondary education is still prioritized in most states, and indeed in the SDG framework itself.[435] In this context, committing to full access to quality early childhood development, care, and pre-primary education by 2030, at the same time as committing to numerous other highly ambitious goals, may arguably be so ambitious as to be unrealistic. Of course, time will tell as to whether states are capable of achieving target 4.2. The progress that states have made in this respect, while positive, suggests that the target is unlikely to be achieved.[436]

Criticism may also be directed more specifically at the methodology used to measure progress towards target 4.2. As discussed, indicator 4.2.1 looks at the proportion of children aged two to five years who are on track in terms of their health, learning and psychosocial wellbeing.[437] The ECDI2030 measures this progress via national household surveys that are administered to the child's mother. It is only if the mother is deceased or not living in the same household as the child that the survey is administered to another primary caregiver.[438] It is unclear why the mother is prioritized over other primary caregivers in this way. In this respect, the literature indicates that UNICEF undertook testing in six countries in order 'to understand how mothers interpret questions and respond'.[439] Thus, potentially the argument may be that administering the survey to the mother where possible helps to ensure consistency and comparability of results.

Nevertheless, prioritizing mothers over other primary caregivers fails to appreciate contemporary parenting arrangements and assumes that mothers have better knowledge of their children than other primary caregivers. In many societies, it is common for both the mother and father to work and share child-raising responsibilities. In some households, the father or other caregiver assumes the primary role of child-raising while the mother works full-time.[440] In these kinds of circumstances, the primary caregiver, even if that person is not the mother, is likely to be the person with the best knowledge of the child's development because he or she spends more time with the child. Therefore, the primary caregiver—whether that is the mother or not—would be the

[433] See, eg, K. Sylva and Others, 'Introduction: Why EPPE?' and others (n 431) 2.
[434] UNESCO, 'Global Education Monitoring Report 2020' (n 90) 228.
[435] Target 4.1 requires that 'all girls and boys *complete* free, equitable and quality primary and secondary education', whereas target 4.2 requires only that 'all girls and boys have *access* to quality early childhood development, care and pre-primary education': UN, 'Transforming our World' (n 76) goal 4.
[436] UNESCO, 'Global Education Monitoring Report 2020' (n 90) 228; UNESCO Institute for Statistics & UNESCO Global Education Monitoring Report 2019, 'Meeting Commitments: Are Countries on Track to Achieve SDG 4?' (2019) 6.
[437] UN 'Global Indicator Framework for the Sustainable Development Goals and Targets of the 2030 Agenda for Sustainable Development' (2020) UN Doc E/CN.3/2020/2, 5.
[438] UNICEF, 'Early Childhood Development Index 2030: Instructions for Interviewers' (November 2020) 8.
[439] UNESCO, 'Global Education Monitoring Report 2020' (n 90) 232.
[440] See, eg, Pew Research Center, 'Raising Kids and Running a Household: How Working Parents Share the Load' (4 November 2015); J Baxter, 'Stay-at-home Fathers in Australia' (Research Report, Australian Institute of Family Studies 2018).

most appropriate person to undertake the survey. Prioritizing the mother in such circumstances may easily be perceived as sexist and as based on stereotypical, often outdated, gender roles. It may also undermine the validity of the data being collected given that the primary caregiver is likely to have a better knowledge of the child's development than a mother who spends less time with the child.

A second criticism may be made in relation to indicator 4.2.2, which looks at the participation rate in early childhood education.[441] Indicator 4.2.2 does not make a distinction between children undertaking pre-school education one year before the primary school entry age, and children that start primary school early.[442] In this respect, children that start primary school early, for example, starting primary school at age five where the official starting age is seven, are often disadvantaged. Primary school, in this kind of scenario, can be used as a form of free childcare and is not necessarily advantageous to the child as the care and learning provided may not be age appropriate. In this respect, '[e]arly childhood and primary education should be different in purpose, organization and structure'.[443] In particular, early childhood learning is often characterized by play-based pedagogy and holistic learning, while a shift towards more formal academic learning is often evident in primary education.[444] In spite of this, indicator 4.2.2 includes such children as a sign of progress towards increased participation in early childhood education.

3. Target 4.3 By 2030, ensure equal access for all women and men to affordable and quality technical, vocational and tertiary education, including university

a) Sources of target

Target 4.3 reflects a right to higher education that is captured in many international human rights instruments.[445] UNESCO identifies 'higher education' as education that 'builds on secondary education, providing learning activities in specialized fields of education', which can include, 'academic education' or 'advanced vocational or professional education'.[446] While higher education attracts less focus than its primary and secondary counterparts, the right to higher education is clearly expressed in the UDHR, the ICESCR,[447] the CRC,[448] the CADE,[449] as well as many treaties that protect the rights of specific groups, including, for instance, the CEDAW.[450]

The right to higher education as set out in the ICESCR is the strongest and most comprehensive expression of the right.[451] Article 13(2)(c) of the ICESCR requires

---

[441] UN 'Global Indicator Framework for the Sustainable Development Goals and Targets of the 2030 Agenda for Sustainable Development' (2020) UN Doc E/CN.3/2020/2, 5.

[442] UNESCO, 'Global Education Monitoring Report 2020' (n 90) 234.

[443] ibid 228.

[444] UNICEF, 'A World Ready to Learn' (n 417) 86.

[445] See generally, J Kotzmann, *The Human Rights-Based Approach to Higher Education* (OUP 2018) ch 1.

[446] UNESCO, 'International Standard Classification of Education' (UNESCO 2011) 84; also see generally Kotzmann (n 445) ch 1.

[447] ICESCR (n 50) art 13(2)(c).

[448] CRC (n 52) art 41.

[449] CADE (n 141) art 4(a).

[450] CEDAW (n 51) art 10.

[451] Kotzmann (n 445) 22.

States Parties to make higher education 'equally accessible to all, on the basis of capacity, by every appropriate means, and in particular by the progressive introduction of free education'.[452] Comparatively, article 26 of the UDHR provides that 'technical and professional education shall be made generally available and higher education shall be equally accessible to all on the basis of merit'.[453] As expressed in the ICESCR, the right goes further than article 26 of the UDHR by obliging States Parties progressively to introduce free higher education. Further, article 13(2)(e) of the ICESCR establishes that States Parties must provide an adequate fellowship system until the introduction of free education.[454]

The obligation within target 4.3 to ensure 'equal access' clearly draws on a requirement to provide access to higher education for those without means to pay for it, such as that expressed in article 13(2)(e) of the ICESCR. However, in only requiring states to ensure access to 'affordable' education, target 4.3 does not go as far as the ICESCR. It does, however, draw on key elements of the right to higher education as set out in many international instruments, including access without discrimination and the provision of good quality education.[455] The 'equal access' requirement is also clearly directed towards ensuring education provision 'without discrimination under any grounds',[456] and the reference to 'women and men' indicates a particular focus on ensuring non-discrimination regarding sex. These requirements are echoed in international instruments, including article 26 of the UDHR, '[e]veryone has the right to education' and article 13(1) of the ICESCR, '[t]he States parties to the present Covenant recognize the right of everyone to education'.

b) Statistical/empirical analysis

The progress of target 4.3 is gauged against global indicator 4.3.1, which measures the 'participation rate of youth and adults in formal and non-formal education and training in the previous 12 months, by sex'.[457] This indicator is broad, measuring both youth and adults, formal and non-formal education, training undertaken for work, and training undertaken for non-work purposes, and is also sex-disaggregated.[458] However, unlike targets relating to primary and fundamental learning, target 4.3 does not seek to measure skills gained, nor do either of the thematic indicators.[459] Instead, skills to be gained from higher education are captured somewhat by target 4.4, which is closely linked to target 4.3.[460]

---

[452] ICESCR (n 50) art 13(2)(c).

[453] UDHR (n 49) art 26.

[454] ICESCR (n 50) art 13(2)(e).

[455] UN Committee on Economic, Social and Cultural Rights (CESCR), 'General Comment No 13: The Right to Education (Article 13 of the Covenant)' (1999) UN Doc E/C.12/1999/10, para 6, 7.

[456] A Reis Monteiro, 'The Right of the Child to Education: What Right to What Education?' (2010) 9 Procedia Social and Behavioural Sciences 1988, 1989; C de la Vega, 'The Equal Right to Equal Education: Merely a Guiding Principle or Customary International Legal Right?' (1994) 11 Harvard Black Letter Journal 37, 38.

[457] UNESCO, 'Global Education Monitoring Report: Migration, Displacement and Education: Building Bridges, Not Walls' (2nd edn, 2018) 144.

[458] ibid.

[459] UNESCO, 'Official List of SDG 4 Indicators' (January 2021) indicators 4.3.2, 4.3.3.

[460] For a full discussion on target 4.4, see below.

Indicator 4.3.1 is classified as tier 2, meaning that while it is 'conceptually clear' and has an 'internationally established methodology', country-produced data are not regularly available.[461] As such, discussion on progress is limited by the availability of data, which are imperfect.[462] An increase in available internationally comparable information is required to monitor and make progress towards lifelong learning—an essential tenet within SDG 4.

Available data on adult education and training in formal and non-formal settings within Europe indicate that trends in participation vary by around 10 per cent to 11 per cent between countries.[463] According to the Eurostat Adult Education Survey, the European average for participation in formal or non-formal education and training for adults aged from 25 to 64 years was 44.4 per cent as of 2016.[464] This is an increase of around 11 percentage points since 2007.[465] In the Netherlands, 64.1 per cent of adults aged between 25 and 64 participated in formal or non-formal education,[466] in France 51.3 per cent,[467] and in Italy, 41.5 per cent.[468] Comparatively, Greece had a participation rate of 16.7 per cent,[469] and Romania recorded a participation rate of 7 per cent.[470] While Greece saw a slight increase of 2.2 percentage points since 2007,[471] Romania regressed from 7.4 per cent in 2007.[472] Some variation here can be attributed to the extent countries were impacted by the financial crisis.[473]

The availability of comparable data outside of Europe is limited. Within Africa, there is great variation between countries in terms of the year the latest data became available, which makes comparison difficult. Generally, however, there is still much work to be done regarding indicator 4.3.1 in most countries with data within Africa. For instance, in Malawi, the participation rate in formal or non-formal education was 0.8 per cent in 2017.[474] In Ghana and Rwanda in the same year, the participation rate was 1.8 per cent and 2.5 per cent respectively.[475] In 2018, 7.2 per cent of adults participated

---

[461] UN 'Tier Classification for Global SDG Indicators' (29 March 2021).

[462] UNESCO, 'Global Education Monitoring Report' (n 457) 144.

[463] ibid 145.

[464] Eurostat European Commission, 'Adult Learning Statistics—Characteristics of Education and Training' (June 2021) <https://ec.europa.eu/eurostat/statistics-explained/index.php?title=Adult_learning_statistics_-_characteristics_of_education_and_training&oldid=486940#Formal_and_non-formal_adult_education_and_training> accessed 31 August 2021.

[465] ibid.

[466] ibid.

[467] ibid.

[468] ibid.

[469] ibid.

[470] ibid.

[471] UN 'SDG Country Profile: Greece' (Goal 4) <https://country-profiles.unstatshub.org/grc#goal-4> accessed 31 August 2021.

[472] UN 'SDG Country Profile: Romania' (Goal 4) <https://country-profiles.unstatshub.org/rou#goal-4 > accessed 31 August 2021.

[473] UNESCO, 'Global Education Monitoring Report' (n 457) 145.

[474] UN 'SDG Country Profile: Malawi (Goal 4) <https://country-profiles.unstatshub.org/mwi#goal-4 > accessed 31 August 2021.

[475] UN 'SDG Country Profile: Ghana (Goal 4) <https://country-profiles.unstatshub.org/gha#goal-4> accessed 31 August 2021; UN 'SDG Country Profile: Rwanda (Goal 4) <https://country-profiles.unstatshub.org/rwa#goal-4> accessed 31 August 2021.

in formal or non-formal education or training within Namibia,[476] and 2.5 per cent in South Africa.[477] For South Africa, this was a decrease of almost 1 percentage point since the year 2000.[478] Comparatively, the participation rate in Angola increased from 9.7 per cent in 2004 to 13.8 per cent in 2011.[479]

Further progress is also needed in Asia. In Vietnam in 2015, 0.2 per cent of adults participated in formal or non-formal education.[480] Thailand had a participation rate of 0.5 per cent in 2016,[481] and Myanmar recorded a participation rate of 0.4 per cent in 2017.[482] Similarly, participation in Sri Lanka was at 0.8 per cent in 2016.[483] Singapore and Japan have significantly higher participation rates in formal and non-formal learning, with Singapore at 56.6 per cent in 2015,[484] and Japan at 41.8 per cent in 2012.[485]

Evidently, progress towards indicator 4.3.1 is more advanced in high and upper-middle-income countries. Globally, this is also true in relation to tertiary education. The average enrolment rate in tertiary education reached 38 per cent in 2017 globally, while enrolment was more than 50 per cent in upper-middle-income countries in 2016.[486] This is due in part to the fact that affordability is a key barrier to higher education.[487] Accordingly, while not tracked by the indicators for target 4.3, available data show that higher education is least affordable in Sub-Saharan Africa.[488] For instance, the 2019 GEMR outlines that '[t]he net private cost per student exceeds 60 per cent of the average national income in most countries with data in Sub-Saharan Africa.'[489] Within Guinea and Uganda, it reaches 300 per cent of the average national income.[490] Within Asia, the net private cost per student sits at around 30 per cent of the average national income in Japan and Vietnam.[491] Conversely, tertiary education is generally the most affordable within Europe.[492]

---

[476] UN 'SDG Country Profile: Namibia (Goal 4) <https://country-profiles.unstatshub.org/nam#goal-4> accessed 31 August 2021.

[477] UN 'SDG Country Profile: South Africa (Goal 4) <https://country-profiles.unstatshub.org/zaf#goal-4> accessed 31 August 2021.

[478] ibid.

[479] UN 'SDG Country Profile: Angola (Goal 4) <https://country-profiles.unstatshub.org/ago#goal-4> accessed 31 August 2021.

[480] UN 'SDG Country Profile: Vietnam' (Goal 4) <https://country-profiles.unstatshub.org/vnm#goal-4 > accessed 31 August 2021.

[481] UN 'SDG Country Profile: Thailand' (Goal 4) <https://country-profiles.unstatshub.org/tha#goal-4 > accessed 31 August 2021.

[482] UN 'SDG Country Profile: Myanmar' (Goal 4) <https://country-profiles.unstatshub.org/mmr > accessed 31 August 2021.

[483] UN 'SDG Country Profile: Sri Lanka' (Goal 4) <https://country-profiles.unstatshub.org/lka > accessed 31 August 2021.

[484] UN 'SDG Country Profile: Singapore' (Goal 4) <https://country-profiles.unstatshub.org/sgp#goal-4> accessed 31 August 2021.

[485] UN 'SDG Country Profile: Japan' (Goal 4) <https://country-profiles.unstatshub.org/jpn#goal-4> accessed 31 August 2021.

[486] UNESCO, 'Global Education Monitoring Report' (n 457) 145.

[487] S Ilie and others, 'Understanding Higher Education Access: Inequalities and Early Learning in Low and Lower-Middle-Income Countries' [2021] British Educational Research Journal <https://bera-journals.onlinelibrary.wiley.com/doi/full/10.1002/berj.3723> accessed 31 August 2021.

[488] UNESCO, 'Global Education Monitoring Report' (n 457) 149.

[489] ibid.

[490] ibid.

[491] ibid.

[492] ibid 145.

TARGETS AND INDICATORS   317

c) Efforts taken at domestic and international level

Efforts made towards target 4.3 at the country level are represented by legislative or policy commitments that serve to increase the number of youth and adults participating in high-quality formal and non-formal education. Country-level efforts can be seen in the protection of higher education as a right within regional legal documents. In Europe, for example, article 2 of Protocol No 1 to the European Convention on Human Rights states that '[n]o person shall be denied the right to education',[493] which includes a right of access to existing higher educational institutions.[494] The right to higher education is also protected by the African Charter on Human and Peoples' Rights through article 17, which provides that '[e]very individual shall have the right to education'.[495] Further, article 11(3)(c) of the African Charter on the Rights and Welfare of the Child obliges States Parties to ensure that higher education is 'accessible to all on the basis of capacity and ability by every appropriate means'.[496] Finally, the American Declaration on the Rights and Duties of Man protects the right to education in article XII,[497] and the Additional Protocol to the American Convention on Human Rights (San Salvador Protocol) provides that '[e]veryone has the right to education' at article 13.[498] Many of these instruments are legally binding for the states that have ratified them, which creates additional obligations for States Parties regarding protecting and ensuring the right to higher education. In turn, this places the standards captured by target 4.3 within a framework of legal obligation. To some extent, this increases a state's commitment to the principles of target 4.3 and contributes to efforts made towards meeting the target.

Efforts towards target 4.3 can also be seen by states that have adopted a rights-based approach towards higher education. Finland, for example, has protected education as a human right in its Constitution and offers higher education to Finnish citizens free of charge.[499] Section 16 of the Finnish Constitution provides that, '[e]veryone has the right to basic education free of charge' and requires public authorities to guarantee everyone 'the opportunity to develop themselves without being prevented by economic hardship'.[500] Section 16 further provides that, '[t]he freedom of science, the arts

---

[493] Convention for the Protection of Human Rights and Fundamental Freedoms (European Convention on Human Rights, as amended) (ECHR).

[494] *Tarantino v Italy* (2013) no 25851/09 ECtHR 43; *Leyla Şahin v Turkey* [2005] no 44774/98 ECtHR 134–42; *Mürsel Eren v Turkey* [2006] no 60856/00 ECtHR 41; Kotzmann (n 445) ch 1.

[495] African Charter on Human and Peoples' Rights (adopted 27 June 1981, entered into force 21 October 1986) (1982) 21 ILM 58 (Banjul Charter).

[496] African Charter on the Rights and Welfare of the Child (adopted 11 July 1990, entered into force 29 November 1999) OAU Doc CAB/LEG/24.9/49 art 11(3)(c).

[497] American Declaration on the Rights and Duties of Man, OAS Res XXX adopted by the Ninth International Conference of American States (1948) reprinted in Basic Documents Pertaining to Human Rights in the Inter-American System OEA/Ser L V/II.82 Doc 6 Rev 1 at 17 (1992) (Bogota Declaration) art 12.

[498] Additional Protocol to the American Convention on Human Rights in the Area of Economic, Social and Cultural Rights (Protocol of San Salvador (opened for signature 17 November 1988, entered into force 16 November 1999) OAS Treaty Series No 69 (1988) reprinted in Basic Documents Pertaining to Human Rights in the Inter-American System OEA/ Ser L V/II.82 Doc 6 Rev 1 at 67 (1992) art 13. .

[499] J Välimaa, 'Why Finland and Norway Still Shun University Tuition Fees—Even for International Students' *The Conversation* (17 February 2015) <http://theconversation.com/why-finland-and-norway-still-shun-university-tuition-fees-even-for-international-students-36922> accessed 31 August 2021; Kotzmann (n 445) ch 4.

[500] *Suomen perustuslaki* (1999) SDK 731/1999 (Ministry of Justice (Finland) unofficial translation, The Constitution of Finland) s 16; Kotzmann (n 445) ch 4.

318   SDG 4

and higher education is guaranteed'.[501] In providing higher education free of tuition fees, Finland ensures that its citizens are not subject to economic discrimination when seeking access to higher education. Finland's efforts towards meeting target 4.3 are further represented by the continued provision of quality higher education. In 2016, the student–teacher ratio within higher education was lower than the OECD average of seventeen.[502] National spending on higher education is also higher than the OECD average—at 1.8 per cent of GDP. In providing high-quality education free of charge, Finland exceeds the obligations outlined in target 4.3. These efforts are significant given that affordability—a key component of target 4.3—is not captured by the relevant indicators.

Efforts towards target 4.3 can also be seen in Canada. The World University Service of Canada has operated the Student Refugee Program (SRP) since 1978.[503] The programme facilitates access to higher education by sponsoring[504] refugees to resettle within Canada as permanent residents and undertake university studies.[505] To be eligible, applicants must have been living in Jordan, Kenya, Lebanon, Malawi, Tanzania, or Uganda for a minimum of three years, be aged between eighteen and twenty-five, have completed secondary school, and be competent in speaking and writing English or French.[506] Participants must also be recognized as refugees in their countries of asylum and fulfil the eligibility requirements for Canada's Private Sponsorship of Refugees Program.[507] There are also specific eligibility requirements depending on the applicant's country of asylum.[508] If an applicant meets the strict eligibility requirements and is accepted into the programme, they will receive reduced or free tuition fees, as well as accommodation, basic financial support to buy necessities, and social support.[509] Since its beginning in 1978, the SRP has placed 2,000 refugee students.[510] A study from 2007 found that 85 per cent of sponsored refugee youth were working in their chosen field following graduation and that 97 per cent had completed, or were completing the programme.[511] In recognition of the gender barriers faced by refugee girls, the SRP has been modified by the WUSC to allow girls admission into the programme with lower academic requirements.[512] In providing refugee youth with an opportunity to pursue quality higher education, and by allowing for flexibility in admission requirements

---

[501] ibid.
[502] OECD, 'Education at a Glance 2016: OECD Indicators' (OECD September 2016) 403; Kotzmann (n 445) ch 4.
[503] UNESCO, 'Global Education Monitoring Report' (n 457) 152; World University Service of Canada (WUSC), 'Student Refugee Program: About' (n 503).
[504] Government of Canada, 'Private Sponsorship of Refugees Program- information for refugees' (*Government of Canada* 2018) <https://www.canada.ca/en/immigration-refugees-citizenship/services/refugees/help-outside-canada/private-sponsorship-program/refugees-information.html> accessed 1 September 2021.
[505] WUSC, 'Student Refugee Program: About' 'Student Refugee Program: About' (n 503).
[506] WUSC, 'Student Refugee Program: Potential Sponsored Students' (*WUSC*) <https://srp.wusc.ca/students/> accessed 1 September 2021.
[507] ibid.
[508] ibid.
[509] ibid.
[510] WUSC, 'Student Refugee Program: About' (n 503).
[511] ibid.
[512] ibid.

for young girls, the SRP embodies the principle of equal access for all as outlined in target 4.3.

d) Critique

Higher education, including technical and vocational education, is integral to achieving sustainable development. This was highlighted in the UN document entitled, 'The Future We Want', which recognized the key contributions of higher education to sustainable development, including through innovative research, the development of skills, and fostering sustainable mindsets and ambitions within future leaders.[513] Further, higher education institutions have a specific and significant role to play in the achievement of many targets within SDG 4.[514] For example, higher education institutions are vital in the supply of trained teachers—a necessary component in making universal primary and secondary education a reality, as recognized by the adoption of target 4.c.[515]

Despite the centrality of higher education to the broader sustainability agenda, it has not previously been the beneficiary of meaningful international attention.[516] Rather, attention is generally directed to primary and basic education.[517] Thus, the requirement within target 4.3 to 'ensure access for all' to 'affordable and quality' higher education is a welcome inclusion in the context of a history of insufficient promotion and recognition,[518] despite the comprehensive expression of the right to higher education in article 13 of the ICESCR.

Target 4.3, however, is a less ambitious goal than that set out in article 13 of the ICESCR. Further, indicator 4.3.1 fails to measure the affordability and quality requirements of the target. While indicator 4.3.1 seems to define affordability narrowly through participation and enrolment rates, this is inadequate and erases the complexity of the concept. This may cause affordability and quality to fall outside the purview of policy-makers, given that progress towards these elements is not monitored as part of target 4.3.[519]

Turning first to affordability, target 4.3 requires states to ensure equal access to 'affordable' education, instead of obliging States to provide 'the progressive introduction of free education' as required by article 13 of the ICESCR. Taken in its entirety, article 13 of the ICESCR obliges States Parties to work towards introducing free higher education in light of the resources available after providing free primary and secondary education.[520] Until states have realized this obligation, access to higher education must

---

[513] UN, 'The Future We Want' (Outcome Document Rio + 20 United Nations Conference on Sustainable Development, UN 20–22 June 2021) para 235, 230.

[514] WL Filho and others, 'Sustainable Development Goals and Sustainability Teaching at Universities: Falling Behind or Getting Ahead of the Pack?' (2019) 232 Journal of Cleaner Production 285, 287.

[515] Report of the Secretary-General 'Progress towards the Sustainable Development Goals' (2016) UN Doc E/2016/75*.

[516] Kotzmann (n 445) ch 1.

[517] ibid.

[518] UN, 'Transforming our World' (n 76) target 4.3.

[519] Unterhalter (n 306) 45–47.

[520] Kotzmann (n 445) 43.

be facilitated by an adequate fellowship system.[521] The requirement within target 4.3 to ensure 'affordable' higher education, presumably with assistance from scholarships and other subsidies for those who cannot afford the fees, may not adequately reduce the potentially discriminatory effect of higher education fees. This is because student fees can still act as a 'disproportionate disincentive to students from low-income backgrounds on account of fear of debt or lack of confidence in the benefits of HE [higher education] study'.[522] This is particularly concerning given the general trend—even within States Parties to the ICESCR—is to provide for-fee higher education with a movement towards increasing fees.[523] Given this, it is unfortunate that target 4.3 does not support the fulfilment of this more progressive international obligation.

Secondly, the indicators for target 4.3 focus on participation and enrolment rates but overlook the concept of quality. As a result, the indicators do not canvass the question of what is to be gained in the provision of higher education. In contrast, target 4.1 and its indicators, while limited, outline that quality primary and secondary education must lead to relevant and effective learning outcomes and monitor progress towards literacy and numeracy accordingly. Similarly, indicator 4.2.1 emphasizes that quality early childhood development, care, and pre-primary education should contribute to children's health, learning, and psychosocial well-being.[524] The failure of indicator 4.3.1 to address quality leaves the definition of quality higher education unclear.

To some degree, the question of what is to be gained from 'quality' higher education could be said to be captured by target 4.4, which focuses on employment. Target 4.4, discussed in the following section, aims to 'substantially increase the number of youth and adults' with skills relevant to 'employment, decent jobs and entrepreneurship'.[525] This appears to constitute the definition of quality higher education as it stands within SDG 4. That is, quality higher education within the SDGs is directed to economic purposes, upskilling learners for employment and 'the production of highly qualified manpower'.[526] This definition, however, disregards the concepts of Education for Sustainable Development and Global Citizenship Education that run through the SDGs. This failure is further exacerbated by the manner in which indicator 4.7.1, which assesses progress towards target 4.7 regarding knowledge and skills to promote sustainable development, omits consideration of higher education curricula.[527] As such, higher education appears to be positioned within SDG 4 as operating primarily for the purpose of employment, despite its critical contributions to sustainable development.

---

[521] ICESCR (n 50) art 13(2)(e).

[522] T McCowan, *Education as a Human Right: Principles for a Universal Entitlement to Learning* (Bloomsbury Academic 2013) 118; Kotzmann (n 445) ch 1.

[523] Kotzmann (n 445) ch 1.

[524] UNESCO, 'Official List of SDG 4 Indicators' (January 2021) indicator 4.2.1.

[525] UN, 'Transforming our World' (n 76) target 4.4.

[526] R Barnett, 'The Idea of Quality: Voicing the Educational' (1992) 46(1) Higher Education Quarterly 3, 5–6.

[527] UN, 'Transforming our World' (n 76) target 4, 7.

4. Target 4.4 By 2030, substantially increase the number of youth and adults who have relevant skills, including technical and vocational skills, for employment, decent jobs and entrepreneurship

a) Sources of target

Target 4.4 is suggestive of a desired outcome of the right to education in that it features employment-based skills as a primary focus. As outlined by UNESCO, 'skills for work are acquired in almost all education programmes and, critically, can be acquired outside education systems'.[528] Thus, target 4.4 has a broad capture. Given the reference to technical and vocational skills, target 4.4 is also closely tied to target 4.3, which requires states to ensure equal access to higher education. As stated above, 'higher education' can be described as education that 'builds on secondary education, providing learning activities in specialized fields of education', which can include, 'academic education' or 'advanced vocational or professional education'.[529] Target 4.4 is also relevant to achieving SDG 8[530] and, in particular, target 8.5,[531] which seek to achieve decent work for all.

Articles within the ICESCR and UDHR provide some foundation for target 4.4. As discussed above, article 13(2)(c) of the ICESCR[532] requires States Parties to make higher education 'equally accessible to all, on the basis of capacity, by every appropriate means, and in particular by the progressive introduction of free education'.[533] Similarly, article 26 of the UDHR provides that 'technical and professional education shall be made generally available and higher education shall be equally accessible to all on the basis of merit'.[534] Increasing access to higher education should operate to increase the number of people with skills relevant for employment.

Article 6 of the ICESCR provides a further important source of law for target 4.4. Article 6 recognizes the right to work,[535] with subsection (2) specifically providing that, '[t]he steps to be taken by a State Party to the present Covenant to achieve the full realization of this right shall include technical and vocational guidance and training programmes'.[536] Assistance in interpreting article 6 can be obtained from the Committee on Economic, Social and Cultural Rights' General Comment No 18, which states that '[w]ork as specified in article 6 of the Covenant must be decent work'.[537] This represents a clear connection to the language in target 4.4, which refers to 'decent jobs', and thus General Comment No 18 can provide some guidance as to the meaning of 'decent' within the target. In this respect, General Comment No 18 defines 'decent work' as that which 'respects the fundamental rights of the human person as well as the rights of

---

[528] UNESCO, 'Global Education Monitoring Report 2016' (n 104) 323.
[529] UNESCO, 'International Standard Classification of Education' (UNESCO 2011) 84; also see generally Kotzmann (n 445) ch 1.
[530] UN, 'Transforming our World' (n 76) goal 8.
[531] ibid target 8.5.
[532] ICESCR (n 50) art 13(2)(c).
[533] ibid art 13(2)(c).
[534] UDHR (n 49) art 26.
[535] ICESCR (n 50) art 6(1).
[536] ibid art 6(2).
[537] UN CESCR, 'General Comment No 18: The Right to Work (Article 6 of the Covenant' (2005) UN Doc E/C.12/GC/18, para 7.

workers in terms of conditions of work safety and remuneration. It also provides an income allowing workers to support themselves and their families.'[538] In this way, article 6 of the ICESCR and General Comment No 18 provide some interpretative guidance in relation to target 4.4.

Finally, target 4.4 also appears to be based in part on the UNESCO Convention on Technical and Vocational Education (CTVE).[539] While the CTVE has not been widely ratified,[540] it does contain a comprehensive expression of the principles captured in target 4.4. For instance, article 3(1)(c) requires States Parties to 'provide and develop technical and vocational education programmes that take account of ... employment opportunities and development prospects at the national, regional and local levels.'[541]

b) Statistical/empirical analysis

Target 4.4 is measured by reference to global indicator 4.4.1, which tracks the 'proportion of youth and adults with information and communications technology (ICT) skills by type of skill'.[542] This indicator is assessed by reference to use of a relevant ICT skill within the last three months, as self-assessed by individuals through household surveys. Global indicator 4.4.1 and its associated categories of skills were originally formulated in a manner that required computer usage, however the indicator was revised in 2020, and data collected from 2020 onwards will no longer exclusively track computer-related skills.[543] For example, prior to 2020, a skills category was, 'transferring files between a computer and other devices'.[544] From 2020 onwards, the skill to be tracked is 'transferring files or applications between devices'.[545] In the framework to be utilized from 2020, there are eleven skill categories, ranging from 'using copy and paste tools' to 'programming or coding in digital environments'.[546] These changes to skill categories are unlikely to be reflected in country-reported data for a few years, and thus data discussed in this section are based upon the previous formulation of the skill categories.

Global indicator 4.4.1 is classified as tier II in that it has an 'internationally established methodology'[547] but lacks regularly produced country data. As indicated above, country-produced data are based on the responses given by interviewees to questions on their use of a number of skill categories within the last three months. While this method makes data relatively easy to collect, it does not directly assess individual skills

---

[538] ibid para 7.

[539] Convention on Technical and Vocational Education (adopted 10 November 1989, entered into force 29 August 1991) UNESCO.

[540] W Benedek, 'The Normative Implications of Education for All (EFA): The Right to Education' in AA Yusuf (ed), *Standard-Setting at UNESCO: Normative Action in Education, Science and Culture* (Vol 1, UNESCO 2007) 295, 297.

[541] Convention on Technical and Vocational Education (adopted 10 November 1989, entered into force 29 August 1991) (Paris, 10 November 1989). UNESCO art 3(1)(c).

[542] UN, 'SDG Indicator Metadata' (Target 4.4, June 2020).

[543] ibid.

[544] ibid.

[545] ibid.

[546] ibid.

[547] UN 'Tier Classification for Global SDG Indicators' (29 March 2021) 2.

and cannot measure the extent to which the individual undertakes the activities in an effective manner.[548]

Global indicator 4.4.1 captures a set of skills that are becoming increasingly necessary within the workforce globally. However, ICT skills are only some of the skills that may lead to 'decent work'. Thematic indicator 4.4.3, which measures 'youth/adult education attainment rates by age group and level of education'[549] broadens analysis beyond digital literacy[550] and ICT skills, however it is still limited in its capture of the 'relevant skills' necessary for obtaining employment, decent jobs, and entrepreneurship.[551] This section will briefly discuss thematic indicator 4.4.3 in order to consider a wider range of skills that lead to decent work.

ICT skills are becoming increasingly important in the current pandemic environment with much of the population relying on computer-related skills to undertake education and work. However, basic computer skills are lacking in around 40 per cent of the eighty-six countries with available data.[552] In those countries, less than half of the participating individuals had carried out a skills category that constitutes a 'basic skill' within the last three months, such as sending an e-mail with an attachment.[553] In only twenty of the eighty-six countries with available data, 60–80 per cent of the population possessed basic ICT skills.[554] Predictably, as the skill difficulty increases the proportion of individuals who possess that skill decreases, with less than half of the population in 70 per cent of reporting countries having undertaken a skill that is considered to be a standard skill, such as creating an electronic presentation.[555] Of the eighty-six countries with available data, only three countries had a population of 60–80 per cent that possessed standard ICT skills.

There are significant differences between countries in terms of ICT skills. For example, in ten lower-middle-income countries, a median of 7 per cent of individuals had used basic arithmetic formulas in a spreadsheet.[556] This increases to a median of 40 per cent of individuals in forty-one high-income countries.[557] Disparity is also evident in terms of who possesses ICT skills within a population. Data from UNICEF'S Multiple Indicator Cluster Surveys indicate that women from lower socio-economic groups are less likely to possess ICT skills. For example, in seven low-and lower-middle-income countries, less than 1 per cent of women in the poorest 60 per cent of the population are likely to be able to use basic arithmetic formulas in a spreadsheet.[558] ICT skills are also more likely to be possessed by those in the richest quantile

---

[548] UN 'SDG Indicator Metadata' (Target 4.4, June 2020).

[549] UNESCO 'Official List of SDG 4 Indicators' (January 2021) indicator 4.4.3.

[550] Indicator 4.4.2 measures digital literacy; see UNESCO 'Official List of SDG 4 Indicators' (January 2021) indicator 4.4.2.

[551] ibid target 4.4.

[552] UN, 'The Sustainable Development Goals Report 2020' (n 179) 33.

[553] International Telecommunication Union, *Measuring Digital Development: Facts and* Figures 2020 (ITU Publications 2020) 12.

[554] ibid.

[555] ibid.

[556] UNESCO, 'Global Education Monitoring Report 2020' (n 90) 248.

[557] ibid.

[558] ibid.

324   SDG 4

in some upper-middle-income countries. This is evident in Mongolia, where 39 per cent of women within the richest quantile were able to use basic arithmetic formulas in a spreadsheet, and only 3 per cent of women in the poorest quantile possessed this skill.[559]

In terms of thematic indicator 4.4.3, which measures 'youth/adult education attainment rates by age group and level of education',[560] data from the EU show an increasing rate of tertiary educational attainment. In 2009, EU countries set a target for 40 per cent of thirty to thirty-four year olds to hold a tertiary degree by 2020.[561] The Education and Training Monitor, an annual publication by the European Commission, stated that this target had been met in 2020, with 40.3 per cent of those aged thirty to thirty-four holding a tertiary degree.[562] There are, however, large gaps in tertiary educational attainment between EU countries. For example, in Romania and Italy, the tertiary educational attainment rate of thirty to thirty-four year olds is under 30 per cent, and in the Netherlands, Sweden, and Lithuania, the rate is over 50 per cent.[563]

Outside of the EU, the UIS tracks the share of the population aged twenty-five years and older by educational attainment. Data from 2018 show that 50 per cent of the population aged twenty-five years and older had attained lower secondary education in lower-middle income countries, 57 per cent in middle-income countries and 64 per cent in higher-middle income countries.[564] Comparatively, available data from 2010 to 2015 show that 43 per cent of the population aged twenty-five years and older had attained lower secondary education in middle-income countries, and 45 per cent in upper-middle income countries. Data from that period are not available for lower-middle-income countries, however, it appears that educational attainment across education levels is rising.

c) Efforts taken at domestic and international level

Digital skills have become a 'near-universal requirement' within the job market.[565] Accordingly, these skills are becoming increasingly emphasized within national policies. A number of countries have devised national plans that prioritize increasing ICT skills and digital literacy. One such country is Estonia, with its 'Digital Agenda 2020'.[566] The Digital Agenda recognizes ICT as 'one of the main tools for raising the competitiveness of every economic sector and walk of life' and commits to ensuring the 'acquisition of higher ICT skills in traditional sectors of the Estonian economy'.[567] Moreover,

---

[559] ibid.

[560] UNESCO, 'Official List of SDG 4 Indicators' (January 2021) thematic indicator 4.4.3.

[561] European Commission, 'Education and Training Monitor 2020' (European Commission November 2020) pt 2, 45.

[562] ibid.

[563] ibid.

[564] UNESCO, 'Global Education Monitoring Report 2020' (n 90) 370.

[565] Department for Digital, Culture, Media and Sport, 'No Longer Optional: Employer Demand for Digital Skills' (Burning Glass Technologies June 2019) 7.

[566] Government of the Republic of Estonia, 'Digital Agenda 2020 for Estonia' (2018).

[567] ibid 1.

the Agenda features a 'sub-objective' to develop higher ICT skills within the entire population.

The value of Estonia's efforts towards prioritizing digital literacy and ICT skills became particularly clear during the coronavirus pandemic, as a rapid transition to telecommuting and remote learning was made globally. For example, in 2015, Estonia set a goal to have all study within schools digital by 2020, including the eventual transition to digital exams.[568] Working towards this goal eased the transition to digital education during the pandemic, as the infrastructure was available and largely familiar to students.[569] Yet while Estonia is one of 'the most digitally advanced societies in the world',[570] it still has more work to do to achieve target 4.4. Data from 2018 show that less than 60 per cent of the Estonian population aged fifteen and above are able to copy and paste within a document, and around 44 per cent are able to use basic formula in a spreadsheet.[571]

While not tied directly to the monitoring framework for target 4.4, key efforts towards increasing skills for employment can be seen in Nicaragua. A case study by Maria José Sosa-Díaz and Maria Rosa Fernández-Sánchez details the development of Massive Online Open Courses (MOOCs) in Nicaragua. MOOCs—offered at universities— 'constitute an open, massive, and free system that offers access to high-level training, without distinction as to border, gender, race, class, or socioeconomic level through the democratization of education'.[572] Sosa-Díaz and Fernández-Sánchez found that while significant challenges remain in terms of 'how to mainstream MOOCs' effectiveness', they offer significant potential in terms of contributing to the SDGs—particularly in regards to creating opportunities for inclusive education.[573]

Finally, the #eSkills4Girls initiative can be seen as an example of international effort directed at achieving target 4.4. The project was initiated by the G20,[574] and designed to reduce gender gaps in digital skills and increase employment opportunities for women within the digital sectors of developing countries.[575] The project is backed by a number of organizations, including UNESCO and UN Women, and undertakes and disseminates research, highlights positive practices, and provides policy recommendations. The #eSkills4Girls project is a representation of efforts made by the international

[568] A Kerb, 'Minister Ligi: All School Studies Digital by 2020' (Republic of Estonia: Ministry of Education and Research, 24 July 2015) <https://www.hm.ee/en/news/minister-ligi-all-school-studies-digital-2020> accessed 6 September 2021.

[569] P Vihma, 'Covid-19 is Likely to Change the Future of Leaning. In Estonia, This is Old News' (e-estonia, March 2020) <https://e-estonia.com/covid-19-is-likely-to-change-the-future-of-learning-in-estonia-this-is-old-news/> accessed 6 September 2021.

[570] M Roonemaa, 'Global Lessons from Estonia's Tech-savvy Government' in K Markelova and others (eds), *Agenda 2030: Challenges for Us All* (UNESCO Courier April–June 2017) 27; Vihma, 'Covid-19 is Likely to Change the Future of Leaning' (n 569).

[571] UNESCO, 'Global Education Monitoring Report 2020' (n 90) 378.

[572] MJ Sosa-Díaz and MR Fernández-Sánchez, 'Massive Open Online Courses (MOOC) within the Framework of International Developmental Cooperation as a Strategy to Achieve Sustainable Development Goals' (2020) 12 Sustainability 10187, 10202–04.

[573] ibid.

[574] Group of Twenty.

[575] #eSkills4Girls, 'G20 Leaders endorse #eSkills4Girls' (*G20 Germany 2017, Federal Ministry for Economic Cooperation and Development*) <https://www.eskills4girls.org/g20-endorse-eskills4girls/> accessed 6 September 2021.

326 SDG 4

community to increase awareness of digital skills gaps and assist country-level efforts through recommendations backed by research.

d) Critique

Target 4.4 constitutes an ambitious undertaking. It seeks impact across generations and references a vast number of skills globally relevant to entrepreneurship and obtaining decent work. Given the skills relevant to work will depend heavily on available job opportunities, which differ between and within countries, the diversity of relevant skills is potentially wide.[576]

By including both youth and adults, target 4.4 is also representative of the broader goal of lifelong learning captured by SDG 4. However, the formulation of the target implies that the purpose of adult education and continued skills development in the context of SDG 4 is to gain decent employment or pursue entrepreneurship. As outlined in the preceding section on target 4.3, this frames lifelong learning as fundamentally of economic importance, rather than as a human right and a contributor to a broader goal of global citizenship. Further, given that only information relating to primary and secondary education is utilized for the calculation of indicator 4.7.1,[577] which tracks the '[e]xtent to which (i) global citizenship education and (ii) education for sustainable development are mainstreamed in (a) national education policies; (b) curricula; (c) teacher education; and (d) student assessment',[578] lifelong learning could be said to be practically excluded from the target most relating to the themes of global citizenship and education for sustainable development within SDG 4.

This is important given that, in UNESCO's words, 'policies often prioritize economic objectives, placing more emphasis on formal ALE [adult learning and education] and labour market outcomes than on non-formal ALE, which tends to have less tangible community outcomes'.[579] As the SDGs will influence country investment in adult learning, the practical focus on employment and entrepreneurship within SDG 4 does not provide sufficient impetus to policy makers to direct investment to lifelong learning for a social or personal purposes, rather than economic ones. Ultimately, despite the broad wording of target 4.4, the narrow focus on increasing skills for youth and adults '*for* employment, decent jobs and entrepreneurship'[580] fails to explicitly support the global citizenship aspect of lifelong learning in favour of the economic aspect.[581]

Secondly, the indicators that measure target 4.4 further narrow its focus to, almost exclusively, technological skills. As outlined above, global indicator 4.4.1 reduces 'relevant skills' to ICT skills—a significant narrowing of target 4.4. While digital skills are clearly important, the global indicator for target 4.4 disregards the wide range of skills

---

[576] UNESCO, 'Global Education Monitoring Report 2016' (n 104) 248.

[577] UN 'SDG Indicator Metadata' (Target 4.7, 7 May 2021) 4.

[578] UNESCO 'Official List of SDG 4 Indicators' (January 2021) indicator 4.7.1.

[579] UNESCO Institute for Lifelong Learning, '3rd global Report on Adult Learning and Education' (Report 2016) 14.

[580] UN, 'Transforming our World' (n 76) target 4.4 (emphasis added).

[581] M Elfert, 'Lifelong Learning in Sustainable Development Goal 4: What does it mean for UNESCO's Right-based Approach to Adult Learning and Education?' (2019) 65 International Review of Education 537, 540.

necessary for 'employment, decent jobs and entrepreneurship'.[582] This is one example within SDG 4 of an ambition mismatch between the target and its corresponding indicator,[583] and in the case of target 4.4 it means decent employment that requires minimal technological skills, such as physical labour jobs, is ignored.

The methodology associated with indicator 4.4.1 is also problematic. The indicator tracks the use of relevant ICT skills within the last three months as self-assessed by individuals through household surveys.[584] This includes skills such as 'sending messages (e.g. email, messaging service, SMS) with attached files' or 'using basic arithmetic formulae in a spreadsheet'.[585] As identified by Aaron Benavot and Alasdair McWilliam, it could be said that indicator 4.4.1 'better captures that the respondent is employed in a white-collar occupation (where use of ICT technology is part of the job description), rather than an indication the respondent has the skills to access "decent work" more broadly'.[586] The narrow focus of this indicator appears to be part of a broader and unsurprising desire to align the indicators with readily available data.[587] In this case, however, the indicator is unlikely to provide a true measure of target 4.4.

5. Target 4.5 By 2030, eliminate gender disparities in education and ensure equal access to all levels of education and vocational training for the vulnerable, including persons with disabilities, Indigenous peoples and children in vulnerable situations

a) Sources of target

Target 4.5 and its corresponding indicators can be connected to several core international human rights instruments. Article 26 of the UDHR is relevant in relation to the requirement outlined in target 4.5 to 'ensure equal access to all levels of education'.[588] While, as noted elsewhere, the interpretation of the UDHR on this point requires care, a gesture towards inclusive education for all is provided by article 26, which states that the right to education is held by everyone, and requires the provision of free education at the primary level.[589] This concept can also be linked to the ICESCR, which recognizes the right of everyone to education through article 13, and accordingly requires through article 14 that free and compulsory primary education be provided.[590] The CADE and the CRC also clearly promote concepts of equity found in target 4.5. Like article 13 of the ICESCR, article 4 of the CADE and article 28 of the CRC require that primary education be free and compulsory and that secondary education be equally accessible to all.[591] Article 4 of the CADE further provides that training for the

---

[582] UN, 'Transforming our World' (n 76) target 4.
[583] Unterhalter (n 306) 46; King (n 305) 807.
[584] UN, 'SDG Indicator Metadata' (Target 4.4, June 2020) 2.
[585] ibid.
[586] A Benavot and A McWilliam, 'Monitoring Competencies and Skills for life and Work' in DVV International (ed), *Skills and Competencies* (DVV International, 2016) 44, 46.
[587] King (n 305) 808.
[588] UNESCO 'Official List of SDG 4 Indicators' (January 2021) target 4.5.
[589] UDHR (n 49) art 26(1).
[590] ICESCR (n 50) art 13, 14.
[591] CADE (n 141) art 4(a).

328 SDG 4

teaching profession be afforded without discrimination,[592] which links to the gender parity index in relation to teacher qualifications measured as an indicator of target 4.5. Target 4.5 also measures parity outside of enrolment rates, which can be connected to article 28(e) of CRC in its requirement that regular attendance and reduction of drop-out rates be encouraged.[593]

A further source for target 4.5 is article 24 of the CRPD, which affirms the right to education for persons with disabilities and provides for equal access at all levels of education, including vocational training and lifelong learning without discrimination.[594] There is a clear connection here to target 4.5's commitment to ensure parity at all levels of education for individuals with disabilities. Article 14 of the UNDRIP also constitutes a source of international norms relating to target 4.5, given its commitment to ensuring the right of access of Indigenous individuals without discrimination to the educational systems of states.[595] The provision where possible of education for individuals in the language and the culture of the relevant Indigenous people should also be seen as a measure directed to equality in the sense of equality across cultures and language.[596] The empowerment of Indigenous peoples as communities in relation to the design of educational systems and institutions, as provided in article 14(1), consistent with which any reading of articles 14(2) and 14(3) must be carried out, also constitutes an equality provision.[597] The need to ensure equal access to education at all levels for 'Indigenous peoples' is indicated within target 4.5, a term which can be understood to indicate individuals who identify as members of an Indigenous people as well as in some respects, those communities (peoples) as a whole. Parity with regard to receiving education in a child's first or home language is measured as a component of target 4.5.

CEDAW provides perhaps the clearest source of international law for target 4.5 given the focus on gender parity. Article 10 of CEDAW requires equality between men and women in regard to access and drop-out rates for education at all levels, including vocational training and lifelong learning, and equality with regard to the substance of education and the qualifications of teaching staff.[598] Each of these concepts features as a key component of target 4.5. Article 14 of CEDAW also commits to equality between men and women in rural as well as urban areas,[599] a dimension which is included in the measurement of target 4.5.

Finally, outside the international human rights instruments, target 4.5 can be connected to target 3a of MDG 3, which represents a commitment to 'eliminate gender disparity in primary and secondary education preferably by 2005, and at all levels by 2015'.[600] Target 4.5 embraced and extended the focus of MDG target 3a by including

---

[592] ibid art 4(d).
[593] CRC (n 52) art 28(1)(e).
[594] CRPD (n 136) art 24(1).
[595] <IBT<UNDRIP (n 146) art 14(2).
[596] ibid art 14(3).
[597] ibid art 14(1).
[598] CEDAW (n 51) art 10(a), (b), (e), (f).
[599] ibid art 14(1), (2)(d), art 10(a).
[600] UN, 'Millennium Development Goals Report 2015' (UN 2015) goal 3.

parity at all levels of education, including vocational training, and by committing to ensuring parity for Indigenous individuals and persons with disabilities.

b) Statistical/empirical analysis

The IAEG-SDGs proposed a set of global indicators, which were adopted by the UN General Assembly in 2017. The progress of target 4.5 is gauged against indicator 4.5.1, which attempts to measure the level of disparity between groups of interest. Specifically, indicator 4.5.1 looks to '[p]arity indices (female/male, rural/urban, bottom/top wealth quintile and others such as disability status, indigenous peoples and conflict-affected, as data become available) for all education indicators on this list that can be disaggregated'.[601] The education indicators referred to include those within SDG 4, such as completion and participation rates, proficiency in mathematics and literacy, and the proportion of qualified teachers within different education levels. The ability to monitor the progress of target 4.5 is thus limited by the availability of data that is disaggregated according to sex, location, wealth quintile, disability status, and other variables for all indicators able to be disaggregated.

At the global level, gender parity has been achieved in pre-primary, primary, lower secondary, and upper secondary enrolment.[602] At the tertiary level, disparity favours female students globally, with 112 female students enrolled for every 100 males in 2015.[603] Despite the success at primary level globally, only 66 per cent of countries have achieved gender parity at primary level, with this number decreasing as the education level increases.[604] In terms of children of school age not attending school, on a global level disparity favours male students, with 118 girls out of school for every 100 boys.[605] This disparity extends to lifelong learning, with women constituting two-thirds of the adults who were illiterate as at 2018.[606]

In terms of the location and wealth indices, disparity typically favours those living in urban areas, and the wealthier portion of the population.[607] Disparity in location is at the expense of young people living in rural areas, a finding which remains consistent in low-income through to high-income countries.[608] Regarding proficiency at the primary education level, as at 2015 only twelve from sixty-two countries had achieved parity between urban and rural students in reaching minimum proficiency levels in reading or mathematics.[609] Disparity in education by wealth compares the poorest 20 per cent of the population with the richest 20 per cent. Low-income countries feature

---

[601] UNESCO 'Official List of SDG 4 Indicators' (January 2021) indicator 4.5.1.

[602] UNESCO, 'Global Education Monitoring Report 2017/18 Accountability in Education' (n 173) 185; UN, 'Sustainable Development Goals Report 2018' (UN 2018) 40.

[603] <IBT<UNESCO, 'Global Education Monitoring Report 2017/18' (n 173) 185.

[604] ibid.

[605] UN, 'The Sustainable Development Goals Report 2019' (July 2019) 31.

[606] Report of the Secretary-General, 'Progress Towards the Sustainable Development Goals' (2020) UN Doc E/2020/57, 7.

[607] ibid.

[608] UNESCO Institute for Statistics and UNESCO Global Education Monitoring Report 2019 'Meeting Commitments: Are Countries on Track to Achieve SDG 4?' (2019) 8.

[609] Report of the Secretary-General, 'Progress Towards the Sustainable Development Goals' (2018) UN Doc E/2018/64, 7.

the greatest level of disparity in primary school completion rate, with 34.3 per cent of children from the poorest quintile completing primary school, compared to 78.5 per cent of the children from the richest quintile. Parity between these groups was achieved in 25 per cent of countries at primary level.[610] This fraction decreases as the education level increases, with only 1 per cent of countries achieving wealth parity for upper secondary education.[611]

Information on the various groups that are not represented in the data, such as persons with disabilities or persons who identify as Indigenous, is limited. This is the result of various factors, including in the first case, diverse measures of disability which hamper cross-country comparisons.[612] In the second case, information relating to Indigenous peoples as such—that is, Indigenous communities or populations taken as a whole—is itself difficult to ascertain and to evaluate alongside data pertaining to individual persons. Further, while target 4.5 makes explicit reference to children in vulnerable situations, much of the data are provided by household surveys which accordingly serves to exclude those not living in households, such as the homeless, those with travelling lifestyles and those living in institutions.[613]

The progress of target 4.5 can also be gauged by reference to a country's ratification of international human rights treaties which are linked to the right to education. As outlined above, target 4.5 draws into relevance various human rights instruments, including CEDAW, CADE, ICESCR, and CRPD. Through these instruments, Member States have existing legal obligations to eliminate discrimination and promote equality. Among the countries that have ratified all of the aforementioned instruments without reservation are Afghanistan, Armenia, South Africa, Finland, Guatemala, and Mongolia.[614] Absent from having ratified any of the above is the United States. Ratification of these instruments does not directly correspond to a country's progress towards the implementation of the relevant principles. However, SDG 4, and more specifically, target 4.5, is grounded in UN Member States' human rights obligations, and a commitment towards these long-standing obligations represents one part of the framework required to meet target 4.5. In this respect, 22 experts have recently outlined a number of steps the Biden Administration must take in order to make valuable progress towards the SDGs. A key recommendation by Mark Dorosin is to '[r]enew the federal government's commitment to eliminating racial segregation in schools'.[615]

---

[610] Report of the Secretary-General, 'Progress Towards the Sustainable Development Goals' (2020) UN Doc E/2020/57, 8.

[611] ibid.

[612] UNESCO, 'Global Education Monitoring Report 2017/18' (n 173) 187.

[613] ibid.

[614] UNESCO, 'Global Education Monitoring Report: Gender Report- Building Bridges for Gender Equality' (2019); UNTC, 'Depositary Status of Treaties: International Covenant on Economic, Social and Cultural Rights' (Ch IV (3), UNTC status as at 8 September 2021); UNESCO, 'List of States Parties: Convention against Discrimination in Education' (*UNESCO*) <https://treaties.un.org/Pages/showDetails.aspx?objid=0800000280134150> accessed 9 September 2021; UNTC, 'Depositary Status of Treaties: Convention on the Rights of Persons with Disabilities' (Ch IV (15), UNTC status as at 8 September 2021); UNTC, 'Depositary Status of Treaties: Convention on the Elimination of all Forms of Discrimination against Women' (Ch IV (8), UNTC status as at 8 September 2021).

[615] JC Dernbach and SE Schang, 'Making American a Better Place for All: Sustainable Development Recommendations for the Biden Administration' [2021] Environmental Law Reporter 10210, 10316.

Dorosin outlines that racial segregation in US public schools has remained largely unchanged over fifty years, resulting in 'less access to necessary educational resources, including highly effective teachers and administrators, rigorous curricular offerings, and technology and other infrastructure'.[616] Insufficient efforts here result in insufficient progress towards target 4.5, and may perhaps be interpreted as a reflection of a lack of commitment to the aforementioned human rights treaties.

c) Efforts taken at domestic and international level

Implementation efforts can be determined by reference to the level that a country's education policies align with their international commitments.[617] In the context of target 4.5, this requires policies that correspond with inclusive education for all, that promote equity and work to monitor disparity.[618] This section will outline several legislative and policy measures taken at country level which reflect the commitments made to target 4.5, and will then discuss international efforts made which facilitate these commitments.

Turning first to efforts taken at the domestic level, implementation of the disability-inclusive education objective featured in target 4.5 can be seen in Australia's National Disability Strategy 2010–2020. This strategy included learning and skills as one of six priority areas of policy action, and the Australian Commonwealth Government's 'Report on the Implementation of the Sustainable Development Goals (Voluntary National Review) 2018' recognized the National Disability Strategy as a means by which it would meet its obligations towards inclusive education.[619] The learning and skills policy area covers all levels of education, including early childhood, vocational, and lifelong learning. In developing this strategy, an inclusive policy dialogue was employed involving extensive consultations within the relevant sectors prior to release.[620] The EU adopted a similar strategy in 2010 in identifying a number of areas for action,[621] including education and training. The principles of target 4.5 in relation to the educational inclusion of children and adolescents with disabilities are also reflected in a number of legislative measures implemented by the Russian Federation. This includes various Federal State Educational Standards which are designed to ensure the right to education for students with disabilities.[622] Within Ireland, several programmes also reflect these principles. For instance, the Leadership for Inclusion (LINC) programme operates to support inclusion of children with disabilities into early year's education and ensure that they receive a high-quality education at this level through the provision

---

[616] ibid.

[617] UNESCO, *Beyond Commitments* (n 243).

[618] ibid.

[619] Australian Government, 'Report on the Implementation of the Sustainable Development Goals' (UN High-Level Political Forum on Sustainable Development 2018) 16.

[620] L Davy and others, 'Review of Implementation of the National Disability Strategy 2010–2020' (Final Report prepared for the Department of Social Services, University NSW August 2018) 15.

[621] European Commission, 'European Disability Strategy 2010–2020: A Renewed Commitment to a Barrier-Free Europe' (Communication from the Commission to the European Parliament, the Council, The European Economic and Social Committee and the Committee of the Regions, Brussels, November 2010) 4.

[622] UNESCO and RUDN University, 'Inclusive Education Policy in the Russian Federation' (Background paper prepared for the 2020 Global Education Monitoring Report, 2020) 6.

332 SDG 4

of professional development training.[623] These strategies represent an effort at country level to ensure that individuals with disabilities can access high-quality education at all stages of learning.

New Zealand's Ka Hikitia and Tau Mai Te Reo strategies align with the objective of target 4.5 to ensure equality in education for individuals who identify as Indigenous. Together, these strategies seek to ensure that educational frameworks at all levels support Māori learners and te reo Māori (the Māori language), with an aim to increase the number of New Zealanders both tangata whenua and pakeha, who view te reo Māori as a key part of national identity.[624] Similarly, in Chile, efforts have been made to ensure equality of access to education for Indigenous students. This can be seen through the incorporation of Indigenous languages into the official curriculum within schools with 50 per cent Indigenous students, a policy that was extended to schools with at least 20 per cent Indigenous students on a voluntary basis.[625]

With regard to efforts made towards promoting gender equity at a domestic level, Bangladesh included gender equality as a key focus in its seventh Five-Year Plan (2016–2020) with an aim to promote female enrolment in technical and vocational education.[626] To contribute to this aim, four additional Polytechnic Institutes that are exclusively for women have been set up with seven women's technical schools and colleges also planned.[627] Vietnam adopted the National Strategy on Gender Equality (2011–2020) in 2012, the development of which was supported by UNESCO.[628] This strategy includes a specific objective to 'gradually ensure equal participation in the education and training between men and women'.[629] In 2015, Vietnam's Ministry of Education and Training also partnered with UNESCO in the implementation of the 'Gender Equality and Girls' Education Initiative in Viet Nam'.[630] The stated purpose of this initiative was to mainstream gender in education planning, curriculum, and teaching practices and to raise awareness on gender quality amongst students, parents and the wider community.[631] Efforts towards gender parity in education are also reflected in Austria's education policies. The Austrian University Act extends to all public universities in Austria and identifies gender equality as a guiding principle[632] and as a

---

[623] Leadership for INClusion in the Early Years (LINC), 'Programme Overview' (LINC) <https://lincprogramme.ie/about/programme-overview> accessed 9 September 2021.

[624] New Zealand Ministry of Education, 'Tau Mai Te Reo: The Maori Language in Education Strategy for all Learners' (June 2021) <https://www.education.govt.nz/our-work/overall-strategies-and-policies/tau-mai-te-reo/> accessed 9 September 2021.

[625] UNESCO, 'Global Education Monitoring Report' (n 457) 26.

[626] Government of the People's Republic of Bangladesh, Genera Economics Division Planning Commission, 'Seventh Five Year Plan: Accelerating Growth, Empowering Citizens' (December 2015).

[627] ibid 551.

[628] C Ross and D Ngoc Nga, 'Gender Equality and Girls' Education Initiative in Viet Nam: Empowering girls and women for a more equal society' (UNESCO Final Evaluation Report, May 2018) 14.

[629] Socialist Republic of Viet Nam, 'National Strategy on Gender Equality for the 2011–2020 period' (*Viet Nam Government Portal*, 2012) <http://www.chinhphu.vn/portal/page/portal/English/strategies/strategiesdetails?categoryId=30&articleId=10050924> accessed 9 September 2021.

[630] C Ross and D Ngoc Nga, 'Gender Equality and Girls' Education Initiative in Viet Nam: Empowering girls and women for a more equal society' (UNESCO Final Evaluation Report, May 2018).

[631] ibid.

[632] University Organisation and Studies Act 2002 (National Council of the Republic of Austria) s 2.

duty for universities.[633] A quota was set for women to make up 50 per cent of collegial bodies at universities,[634] which reflects Austria's commitment towards ensuring that the population of universities is closer to its general population.[635]

Efforts made towards target 4.5 are also represented in policies which seek to reduce disparity between the richest and poorest members of a population. In Ghana, an equity policy was introduced which ensures that 30 per cent of students from public junior high schools have access to the top 55 per cent of senior high schools by reserving places within the elite schools.[636] This policy reflects an effort to ensure parity between wealth quantiles in education, and was highlighted by Ghana as a key government intervention in contributing to SDG 4 within its 2019 Voluntary National Review. In Mozambique, the National School Feeding Programme[637] also reflects this objective and has contributed to a decrease in drop-out rates. This programme has been expanded, and in 2019 reached over 150 schools and 118,000 students.[638] Bolivia's Institutional Strategic Plan for the Ministry of Education and the Sectoral Plan for the integral Development of Education for Living Well 2016–2020 focused on increasing access and educational support for a range of disadvantaged and excluded groups.[639] One programme included within this plan is the Juancito Pinto school voucher, which supports poor children in attending school through the offsetting of transport costs, as well as the costs of books and uniforms.[640]

Regarding efforts towards increasing parity between children from rural and urban areas, this objective is reflected in policies developed in Lithuania. This includes the provision of 700 buses to aid home to school transport and support access to education for children in rural areas.[641] In China, efforts have been made towards improving infrastructure in rural schools through several initiatives, including the Rural Primary and Secondary Schools Dilapidated Building Renovation Project in Central and Western China.[642] Further efforts are evident in the Comprehensive Improvement Programme for the Basic Conditions of School Running for Compulsory Education in Schools in Poor Areas, which was introduced in 2014. This programme is focused on investments towards teaching conditions and settings in underdeveloped schools and will fund learning resources as well as the construction of school buildings in rural areas.[643]

---

[633] ibid s 3.

[634] ibid s 20a.

[635] Republic of Austria, 'Austria and the 2030 Agenda: Voluntary National Review- Report on the Implementation of the Sustainable Development Goals' (Vienna 2020) 66.

[636] Republic of Ghana, 'Ghana: Voluntary National Review Report on the Implementation of the 2030 Agenda for Sustainable Development' (June 2019) 41.

[637] Republic of Mozambique, 'Report: Voluntary National Review of Agenda 2030 for Sustainable Development' (2020) 41.

[638] ibid 35.

[639] UNESCO, 'Beyond Commitments' (n 243) 18.

[640] ibid.

[641] C Shewbridge and others, 'OECD Reviews of School Resources: Lithuania' (OECD 2016) 7.

[642] OECD, 'Education in China: A Snapshot' (OECD 2016).

[643] ibid 17.

Turning to efforts made with international application, the Washington Group has worked towards the attainment of target 4.5 through the development of its Disability Statistics.[644] As mentioned above, diverse measures of disability have limited the availability of comparable data for this group. A set of functionality-based questions developed by the Washington Group provides a global standard that has been integrated into a Vulnerability Assessment Framework by the UNHCR.[645] The questions focus on the difficulties people from the age of five experience in seeing, hearing, walking, cognition, self-care, and communication.[646] A bio-psycho-social model of disability is incorporated, based on the fundamental idea that the 'various types of functioning' are 'influenced by environmental barriers, be they at the micro-, meso-, or macro-level'.[647] This will serve to facilitate comprehensive data collection on disability as a social, rather than medical phenomenon,[648] and provide a better insight into the situations faced by people with disabilities, allowing for policies that improve the support of their educational needs.

d) Critique

The goal of equality in its broadest sense continues to present conceptual challenges especially in the context of programmatic efforts to redress the effects of structural injustice within and across societies.[649] A level playing field of equal opportunity exists only as a philosopher's fantasy so that affirmative action in some form is integral to any institutionalized project aimed at social justice and rights-based distribution of the world's resources.[650] It is not a fatal paradox but it is a considerable challenge that special state-based efforts for certain sectors of the population accompany generic improvements in opportunity. The challenge is not met by such platitudes as 'a rising tide lifts all boats' which is an apology for the persistence of privilege. But it is essential to remember that tensions will inevitably arise both at the policy level and the implementation level between positive discrimination however it is couched, and the equality of treatment for all.

The elimination of gender disparities in education is therefore a moving target for a number of reasons and the same may be said of other elements of this target. Gender roles and definitions are culturally dependent in a myriad of ways and are subject to

---

[644] UNESCO, 'Global Education Monitoring Report' (n 457) 175.

[645] Washington Group, 'An Introduction to the Washington Group on Disability Statistics Question Sets' (10 December 2020) <https://www.washingtongroup-disability.com/fileadmin/uploads/wg/Documents/primer.pdf> 4.

[646] J Biermann and L Pfahl, 'A Global Monitoring Practice in the Making: Disability Measurement for UN Sustainable Development Goal 4 on Inclusive Education' (2020) 31(3) Austrian Journal of Historical Studies 192, 205.

[647] ibid 207, quoting D Mont, 'How are the Washington Group Questions Consistent with the Social Model of Disability?' (2019) <https://www.washingtongroup-disability.com/wg-blog/how-are-the-washington-group-questions-consistent-with-the-social-model-of-disability-65/> accessed 24 September 2021.

[648] ibid 208.

[649] J Waldron, *One Another's Equals: The Basis of Human Equality* (Belknap Press 2017); M Nussbaum, *Frontiers of Justice: Disability, Nationality, Species Membership* (Belknap Press 2006).

[650] T Pogge, 'The Role of International Law in Reproducing Massive Property' in S Besson and J Tasioulas (eds) *The Philosophy of International Law* (OUP 2010) 417; J Beckett, 'Creating Poverty' in A Orford and F Hoffmann (eds) *The Oxford Handbook of The Theory of International Law* (OUP 2016) 985.

secular change in ways that policymakers of past decades have generally underestimated. Gender identity is becoming increasingly fluid and multiple in many societies and increasingly recognized as such in the institutions of the state. This is not solely a phenomenon of relatively wealthy western democracies. Some degree of recognition or respect for trans individuals has been well established in some non-western cultures for a long time. However, the heteronormative assumptions prevalent in most if not all societies at present, give rise to various effects relevant to education including the binary segregation of those who define themselves or are defined as female, from those who define themselves or are defined as male. Segregated educational facilities and segregated ablution facilities (washrooms) in otherwise shared ('co-educational') establishments are in some ways very different forms of segregation but in both cases, the role of societal values is at least as important as any evidence-based rationale. Among the societal values at play are arguments about the redressing of the structural disadvantage of girls and young women, such as in lower or more restricted expectations as to career and employment, through segregation at school.

It is therefore not difficult to articulate critical perspectives on policy targets that focus on a male/female dichotomy as if that dichotomy is itself fixed, a brute fact. Focus on such a dichotomy may seem simplistic and even crude. Yet structural disadvantage is itself crude and simplistic as is structural privilege. Other forms of segregation in education also pose complexities. Self-determined segregation in the form of religious schooling whether Islamic, Catholic, Jewish, or other raises other complexities from the perspective of SDG 4. Brought into focus by Target 4.5, equal access cannot be understood to mean the genuine opportunity to attend either a secular school or a school with a faith adherence of whatever kind, whether co-educational or not, because such decisions or preferences are made not by the child concerned, typically even into the teenage years, but by parents and local communities of faith. State funding policies for faith-based schooling as a 'choice' (for parents)—policies that inevitably impact on the resourcing of secular schools—are also part of the matrix by which certain opportunities are made available to certain populations. Of course, discrimination against particular faiths is another threat to equality in education.

Vulnerability is a key focus of Target 4.5. Even if children, in general, are for some purposes categorized as 'vulnerable'—in effect this is the case under CRC[651]—here the narrower category of 'children in vulnerable situations' is employed. This is in many ways to be welcomed, if only in a pragmatic sense, as focusing on the greatest needs of certain individuals. However, this specification renders even more problematic that persons with disabilities are defined as 'vulnerable', a categorization that demands interrogation. If respect and empowerment are generally recognized aims across many fields of social justice then such a categorization is retrogressive.[652] Even more troubling, the implied categorization of Indigenous *peoples*, that is to say, whole populations (or minorities or nations), as 'vulnerable,' cannot be allowed to pass without comment.

---

[651] CRC (n 52).
[652] Nussbaum, *Frontiers of Justice* (n 649) 98.

336 SDG 4

This point is just as salient if the purportedly vulnerable are thought of not as the groups or populations but as individual persons, as the grammar of the target elsewhere indicates (as in 'persons with disabilities'), that is to say, individuals who are members of Indigenous populations. Indigenous vulnerability whether of the whole or the part needs to be thought of, where it exists, as a structural consequence of numerous social and political processes, a contingent effect that could always have been otherwise. Moreover as with disability, for the wording of the target to imply that Indigenous persons or whole peoples are somehow analytically on a par with 'children in vulnerable situations' is remarkably problematic. In the case of indigeneity, the wording of UNDRIP is surely more appropriate.

Finally, a methodological point about empirical findings should be raised. If the educational opportunities for girls and women are and have been excessively constrained in comparison with those for boys and men, how should we evaluate what appears to be a significant over-representation of females on some measurements? This is at the same time a statistical matter, a scientific matter, a matter of values and a matter of policies. That mixture needs careful and transparent handling.

6. Target 4.6 By 2030, ensure that all youth and a substantial proportion of adults, both men and women, achieve literacy and numeracy

a) Sources of target

The foundation of target 4.6 can be found in various human rights instruments, including the CADE, ICESCR, CRC, and CEDAW. For instance, article 4 of the CADE represents a source of each of the key objectives within target 4.6, including the reference to both youth and adults, as well as men and women, in the achievement of literacy and numeracy. Article 4 of the CADE requires States Parties to implement a national policy that promotes equality of opportunity and treatment in education, makes primary education free and compulsory, and encourages education of persons who have not received any primary education or who have not completed primary education.[653] Similarly, article 13 of the ICESCR supports the main objective of target 4.6 in requiring States Parties to ensure compulsory and freely available primary education for all, as well as encouraging fundamental education for those that have not received or completed primary education.[654] Arguably, primary education in this context would include literacy and numeracy as fundamental elements of basic education.[655] Thus, in both cases, the provision of primary education for both youth and adults, and the direct reference to equality within the CADE, clearly underlies the principles within target 4.6.

In a more limited manner, article 28(3) of the CRC directly supports the literacy goal within target 4.6, with the aim of eliminating 'ignorance and illiteracy' and a requirement to take particular account of the needs of developing countries.[656] Moreover,

---

[653] CADE (n 51) art 4.
[654] ICESCR (n 50) art 13.
[655] See Incheon Declaration (n 77) 30; UN Committee on the on the Rights of the Child, 'General Comment No 1: The Aims of Education (article 29)' (17 April 2001) UN Doc CRC/GC/2001/1 para 9.
[656] CRC (n 52) art 28(3).

articles 10(e) and 14(2)(d) of the CEDAW provide a source for the reference to gender equality within target 4.6, as well as the literacy objective for adults. Article 10(e) supports access to continuing education, with direct reference to adult literacy and reducing any educational gap between men and women.[657] Article 14(2)(d) requires both formal and non-formal functional literacy education, as well as services that increase technical proficiency for rural women.[658] There is a clear connection here to the adult literacy objective within target 4.6, as well as the need to ensure equality between men and women in this regard. Each of these provisions contributes to uniformity within international standards which is built upon by target 4.6 and thus represent the primary sources of the target.

b) Statistical/empirical analysis

The progress of target 4.6 can be tracked by reference to indicator 4.6.1, which measures the 'proportion of population in a given age group achieving at least a fixed level of proficiency in functional (a) literacy and (b) numeracy skills, by sex'.[659] The given age group here is youth (aged fifteen to twenty-four years) and adults (aged over fifteen years).[660] The level of proficiency is further defined as 'the benchmark of basic knowledge in a domain (literacy or numeracy) measured through learning assessments'.[661] The reference to 'level of proficiency' allows for a move away from the binary classification of literate versus illiterate, and towards a scale of proficiency.[662] However, this move is limited by the measurement tools available to countries and thus the traditional classification is still largely relied upon.[663] Indicator 4.6.1 is classified as tier II, which means that it is conceptually clear with an internationally established methodology, but is lacking in regular country-produced data.[664] This indicator is further limited by the lack of internationally validated common standards, as well as the current measurement of adult knowledge through household surveys, which may result in a misrepresentation of skills.[665] Against this measurement, it is clear that progress towards target 4.6 has not been sufficient.

To assess the progress towards achieving target 4.6, this section will first discuss progress towards literacy and numeracy skills for youth, before turning briefly to the progress of adults.[666] In terms of indicator 4.6.1, youth is classified as the portion of the population aged between fifteen and twenty-four years, and adults are those over the

---

[657] CEDAW (n 51) art 10(e).

[658] ibid art 14(2)(d).

[659] UN, 'SDG Indicator Metadata' (Target 4.6, May 2021).

[660] ibid.

[661] ibid.

[662] TS Murray, 'Functional Literacy and Numeracy: Definitions and Options for Measurement of SDG 4.6' (Global Alliance to Monitor Learning, UNESCO 17–18 October 2018) 10; UNESCO Institute for Statistics and UNESCO Global Education Monitoring Report 2019 'Meeting Commitments: Are Countries on Track to Achieve SDG 4?' (2019) 9.

[663] UNESCO Institute for Statistics and UNESCO Global Education Monitoring Report 2019, 'Meeting Commitments: Are Countries on Track to Achieve SDG 4?' (2019) 9.

[664] UN, 'Tier Classification for Global SDG Indicators' (28 December 2020).

[665] UN, 'SDG Indicator Metadata' (Target 4.6, May 2021); UNESCO, 'Global Education Monitoring Report 2020' (n 90) 202.

[666] UN, 'SDG Indicator Metadata' (Target 4.6, May 2021).

age of fifteen.[667] The global youth literacy rate is 91.7 per cent as shown in 2019 data.[668] This means that 102 million people between the ages of fifteen and twenty-four do not possess basic reading skills. However, youth literacy has seen a gradual increase over the years, with the rate rising from 86.5 per cent in the year 2000 according to data from the UIS.[669] This steady increase is expected to continue, with projections showing that youth literacy will reach 94 per cent by the end of the SDGs 2030 target.[670]

Despite this increase, gender parity in literacy and numeracy proficiency remains a challenge in the achievement of target 4.6. To monitor progress in this respect, target 4.6 and its corresponding indicator measure gender gaps in proficiency levels. Data from the UIS show that as of 2019, the global literacy rate for men aged between fifteen and twenty-four was 92.8 per cent, while women of the same age bracket possessed literacy skills at a rate of 90.5 per cent.[671] Important regional challenges in achieving literacy for women and girls are also present, such as in Nepal where women living in poverty are literate at a rate of 30 per cent.[672] This trend remains pervasive within the richest quantile, where 75 per cent of Nepalese women are literate, compared to 93 per cent of men.[673] While around two-thirds of countries have achieved gender parity in youth literacy rates,[674] struggles remain for many countries where parity in literacy greatly favours men. For instance, in Chad, fifty-five women possess literacy skills for every 100 men.[675] The data suggest that regional challenges will continue, with projections showing that only slightly more than 80 per cent of youth living in low-income countries will possess basic literacy skills by 2030, compared to 94 per cent globally.[676] This signals that there is still much work to be done to ensure both men and women achieve literacy and numeracy proficiency by 2030, with particular focus needing to be placed on regional challenges.

Finally, as aforementioned, target 4.6 also highlights adult proficiency—that is, the population aged fifteen years and older. In 2018, around 773 million adults lacked

[667] For a discussion on the literacy and numeracy achievements of children and young people under the age of fifteen, see target 4.1 which measures proficiency in reading and mathematics for primary and lower secondary aged children: UN, 'Transforming our World' (n 76) target 4.1.

[668] UNESCO Institute for Statistics and UNESCO Global Education Monitoring Report 2019, 'Meeting Commitments: Are Countries on Track to Achieve SDG 4?' (2019) 9.

[669] The World Bank, 'Literacy Rate, Youth Total (% of people ages 15–24)' (*UNESCO Institute for Statistics*, data as of September 2020) <https://data.worldbank.org/indicator/SE.ADT.1524.LT.FM.ZS> accessed 10 September 2021.

[670] UNESCO Institute for Statistics and UNESCO Global Education Monitoring Report 2019, 'Meeting Commitments: Are Countries on Track to Achieve SDG 4?' (2019) 9.

[671] The World Bank, 'Literacy Rate, Youth (ages 15–24), Gender Parity Index (GPI)' (*UNESCO Institute for Statistics*, data as of September 2020) <https://data.worldbank.org/indicator/SE.ADT.1524.LT.FM.ZS> accessed 10 September 2021.

[672] UNESCO, '4th Global Report on Adult Learning and Education: Key messages and executive summary' (UNESCO Institute for Lifelong Learning 2019) 125.

[673] ibid.

[674] UNICEF, 'Education—Literacy Data: Youth and Adult Literacy Rates' (*UNICEF*, November 2019) <https://data.unicef.org/resources/dataset/education-literacy-data/#:~:text=Globally%2C%20the%20youth%20literacy%20rate,higher%20among%20males%20than%20females> accessed 10 September 2021.

[675] The World Bank, 'Literacy Rate, Youth (ages 15–24), Gender Parity Index (GPI)' (*UNESCO Institute for Statistics*, data as of September 2020) <https://data.worldbank.org/indicator/SE.ADT.1524.LT.FM.ZS> accessed 10 September 2021.

[676] UNESCO Institute for Statistics and UNESCO Global Education Monitoring Report 2019, 'Meeting Commitments: Are Countries on Track to Achieve SDG 4?' (2019) 9.

proficient reading or writing skills, and the percentage of people over the age of fifteen who had achieved literacy in terms of reading or writing was 86 per cent.[677] Disparity between adult men and women in reaching reading proficiency is also evident within this age group. As at 2018, two-thirds of the 773 million illiterate adults were women.[678] Nevertheless, it is encouraging in terms of future progress that the global youth literacy rate is higher than the adult literacy rate.

Separate to the UN monitoring framework, progress towards target 4.6 can also be seen in a country's ratification of the human rights instruments mentioned in Section IV.B.6(a). For instance, the CADE and ICESCR were highlighted in Section IV.B.6(a) for their strong support of target 4.6. Chile, Finland, and Burkina Faso are amongst the countries that have ratified these instruments without reservations which indicates a further level of support towards the target.[679] Ratification of these instruments is not necessarily indicative of, or in alignment with, a country's progress towards target 4.6; however, it does represent another means by which to advance the principles within target 4.6. Finally, as mentioned in the preceding sections, it is worth noting that the United States is not a State Party to any of the instruments outlined in section (a) as supporting target 4.6.

c) Efforts taken at domestic and international level

Literacy and numeracy skills are central to the meaning of 'quality education' within the context of SDG 4.[680] As such, target 4.6 is vital to the achievement of SDG 4 as a whole.[681] Further, education, and accordingly, literacy and numeracy skills, permeate the overall sustainable development agenda in that it is an 'enabling right',[682] and thus efforts taken at a domestic and international level to ensure its achievement are indispensable. Efforts towards target 4.6 at a country level are represented by legislative or policy commitments that contribute to increasing the proportion of both youth and adults that have achieved, and will retain, minimum levels of literacy or numeracy proficiency.

In Lebanon, the Ministry of Social Affairs has launched a programme targeting the retention of literacy skills for refugees. This has been implemented in Bourj Hammoud, a densely populated city within Lebanon, through social service centres that focus on reaching women and girls.[683] This programme recognizes the specific issue of literacy retention for neo-literate refugees and attempts to secure their literacy skills through

---

[677] Report of the Secretary-General, 'Progress towards the Sustainable Development Goals' (2020) UN Doc E/2020/57, 7.

[678] ibid.

[679] UNESCO, 'List of States Parties: Convention against Discrimination in Education' (UNESCO) <https://treaties.un.org/Pages/showDetails.aspx?objid=0800000280134150> accessed 10 September 2021; United Nations Treaty Collection (UNTC), 'Depositary Status of Treaties: International Covenant on Economic, Social and Cultural Rights' (Ch IV (3), UNTC status as at 9 September 2021).

[680] Incheon Declaration (n 77) 30.

[681] UNESCO 'Unpacking Sustainable Development Goal 4 Education 2030' (2017) 7.

[682] Incheon Declaration (n 77) 28.

[683] UNESCO, '4th Global Report on Adult Learning and Education' (n 672) 136.

the provision of seminars and activities.[684] In doing so, this programme highlights the importance of lifelong learning. A focus on youth literacy can also be seen in Lebanon. The Reaching All Children with Education (RACE) Strategy targets school enrolment for Syrian children, and a five-year RACE II plan, operating over 2017–2021, was also recently adopted.[685] Of the first RACE strategy, Lebanon's Ministry of Education and Higher Education highlighted that more than 42 per cent of refugee children of compulsory schooling age 'received a certified education despite significant documentation barriers'[686] as a result of investments made vis a vis this programme. RACE II seeks to facilitate a substantial increase in student enrolment in formal education as well as an increase in the quality of education services.[687]

Efforts to increase education quality can also be seen in the Republic of Korea. South Korea features high educational attainment levels, with 98 per cent of young adults aged twenty-five to thirty-four years old completing upper secondary education as at 2018.[688] However, there is a large gap in literacy and numeracy skills between younger and older generations,[689] thus lifelong learning is a policy priority.[690] It is worth noting that lifelong learning in Korea is divided into two 'pillars', with the first governed by the Ministry of Education and the second by the Ministry of Employment and Labour.[691] The focus of the first pillar is in providing recreational learning opportunities, such as language or calligraphy.[692] These skills are distinguished from the provision of skills that increase employability, which are the focus of the second pillar.[693] This distinction touches on the importance of a literacy discourse separate to a singular focus on increasing human capital.[694] In terms of the quality of lifelong education in Korea, there have been several enhancement strategies implemented. One such strategy is the Lifelong Learning Educators programme, developed by the National Institute for Lifelong Education.[695] The training within this programme allows participants to become a 'lifelong learning expert' within their department, or a lifelong learning educator.[696] The goal here is to increase the professional expertise of trainers and the quality of lifelong learning.[697]

---

[684] ibid 136; G McPherson, 'Lebanon: Refugee Families Finding Hope This Holiday Season' (Jesuit Refugee Service 21 December 2017) <https://www.jrsusa.org/story/lebanon-refugee-families-finding-hope-this-holiday-season/> accessed 10 September 2021.

[685] UNESCO, Kuwait Foundation for the Advancement of Sciences and UNHCR, 'Syrian Refugee Youth Literacy Assessment Study' (UNESCO 2020) 15.

[686] Ministry of Education and Higher Education, Lebanon, 'Reaching All Children with Education: RACE II (2017–2021)' (Ministry of Education and Higher Education August 2016) 3.

[687] ibid 12–18.

[688] OECD, Education at a Glance 2019: OECD Indicators (Country Note: Korea, OECD 2019) 2.

[689] OECD, Strengthening the Governance of Skills Systems: Lessons from Six OECD Countries (OECD April 2020) ch 4, 84.

[690] ibid 85.

[691] ibid.

[692] ibid.

[693] ibid.

[694] T Atkinson and NS Jackson, 'Beyond Economic Interests: Critical Perspectives on Adult Literacy and Numeracy in a Globalised World' (2016) 24(2) Literacy and Numeracy Studies 64, 69.

[695] OECD, Strengthening the Governance of Skills Systems: Lessons from Six OECD Countries (OECD April 2020) ch 4, 86.

[696] ibid.

[697] UNESCO, '4th Global Report on Adult Learning and Education' (n 672) 70.

Within the international arena, the UNESCO Institute for Lifelong Learning co-chairs taskforce 4.6 with the OECD as part of the Global Alliance to Monitor Learning initiative.[698] Taskforce 4.6 has been making efforts to address the limitations in regards to the measurement of literacy and numeracy skills.[699] This work is done in recognition of the fact that globally comparable data are lacking, given that the standard of proficiency varies between countries, and that traditional measurements do not offer a comprehensive picture of the skills of low-literate youth and adults.[700] Thus, the goal here is to ensure there is global learning data that paint an accurate picture of the literacy and numeracy needs of youth and adults, so as to facilitate effective policies that best address these needs.[701] So far, since its inception in 2016, taskforce 4.6 has conducted a number of expert meetings to analyse and discuss existing instruments for literacy and numeracy measurement, and has recommended that the OECD Programme for the International Assessment of Adult Competencies constitute the basis of a global framework.[702] While challenges remain, the international community has made progress towards the availability of global data that will assist countries in their efforts towards reaching target 4.6.

d) Critique

Literacy and numeracy would in many ways appear as universal and cross-culturally equivalent skills, perhaps thought of as quasi-developmental achievements of children growing up anywhere in the modern world. The sense of children and young people as they grow up, and wherever they grow up, being owed such an education by the state of which they are a national, is a powerful one. It is not the least of the concerns that arise when children are stateless as well as in situations of international warfare or civil strife within a State.

From this point of view adults across the world, not least those in positions of authority, have a responsibility to prepare the new generation for life in the modern world, to thereby provide them with opportunities to flourish and to be able in due course to make life-choices among genuinely available options relating to employment and so on. To neglect so to do would be indeed neglect, and the ideologically based denial of such learning opportunities is widely perceived as a scandal especially when deployed across whole populations. Such considerations in many ways underlie the policy of compulsory education itself.

Of course in different cultural settings the language or languages of instruction and of learning will differ, so that literacy, in particular, will be defined accordingly. Yet the localized learning will generally be understood to indicate an underlying

---

[698] UNESCO 'Global Alliance to Monitor Learning (GAML) Taskforce 4.6: Progress Report 2020' (WG/GAML/13, UNESCO 2020).

[699] ibid 5.

[700] ibid.

[701] UNESCO, '4th Global Report on Adult Learning and Education' (n 672) 107.

[702] UNESCO, 'GAML Taskforce 4.6: Progress Report 2018' (GAML5/REF/4.6.1-12, UNESCO Institute for Lifelong Learning October 2018) 2.

achievement shared with school children across the world. With respect to numeracy, it is even more the case that teaching and testing in a culturally appropriate manner is thought of as a means to an end that is universal, in effect a feature of the child's cognitive development. Arithmetic is treated by educators across the globe as substantially or even absolutely, culturally neutral. To the extent that literacy and numeracy are indeed free of local influence at other than a superficial level, these achievements would be ideal candidates for measurable targets comparable without favour or discrimination across all cultural settings. Such considerations are not to be underestimated since a global project such as the SDGs depends for its validity and credibility in many ways upon the trans-cultural and the trans-political. Without naivety over the meaning of the term 'objective', it is certainly the case that literacy and numeracy lend themselves to measurement and comparison in ways that importantly connote a reassuring sense of objective, factual data, detached from the political and the ideological.

From a critical perspective, however, some compromise must be found between an absolute, universalist framework and a perspective that over-emphasizes cultural diversity in these contexts. For cultural and political factors do influence the meaning of and the acquisition of both literacy and numeracy. For example, the cultural importance of oral traditions of learning and of performance varies significantly, and the status of written language (both in terms of reading and writing) varies accordingly. While oral transmission and expression of culture is widely thought of in the West as a sign of the pre-modern and hence 'backward', perhaps to be treated with nostalgia but not with respect, the ethnocentrism of such a view must be acknowledged. The significance of oral traditions is further complicated by their place in religious teaching and in teaching that takes place in religious settings. Several world religions place great weight on the memorization of devotional materials, for example as a rite of passage, so that the education of children, youth and indeed adults may value oral transmission alongside the practice of written language.

Also challenging is the not uncommon situation of the suppression of certain languages in favour of others. World history is replete with examples of the prohibition of Indigenous languages within school systems, in favour of the language of the majority or of the colonizer (which is sometimes one and the same). If the state measures literacy in terms of an official language then children and youth whose home or otherwise most familiar language is other, will clearly be disadvantaged and from the point of view of indicators, the state's evaluation of its literacy rates will be distorted.

The balance between on the one hand universal expectations and standards, with their risk of ethnocentric and hegemonic bias, and on the other the excessive deference to local practices, is difficult to strike and must be thought of as a task that is never complete. The same dilemmas of course arise with the implementation of human rights agreements. Fairness of services and opportunities between males and females, whether in childhood or beyond, must also navigate the question of neutrality or 'gender blindness' as dominance in disguise, of one perspective mastering the vocabulary.

7. Target 4.7 By 2030, ensure that all learners acquire the knowledge and skills needed to promote sustainable development, including, among others, through education for sustainable development and sustainable lifestyles, human rights, gender equality, promotion of a culture of peace and non-violence, global citizenship and appreciation of cultural diversity and of culture's contribution to sustainable development

a) Sources of target

Target 4.7 is perhaps the strongest representation within SDG 4 of the deviation from a focus on access to education and the acquisition of basic skills within international agendas. Global development initiatives have increasingly recognized a need to ensure education is relevant to contemporary challenges and engages learners in issues of sustainability and global citizenship. Early representations of this trend can be seen in the expansion of 'quality education' within goal six of the Dakar Framework for Action on Education for All.[703] The Dakar Framework saw an early link to Education for Sustainable Development (ESD), including through the connection between quality education and quality of life. An earlier and more substantial link can be made to Agenda 21, the framework agreed upon at the 1992 UN Conference on Environment and Development. Chapter 36 of Agenda 21 called for 'reorienting education towards sustainable development',[704] and emphasized that education is 'critical for ... improving the capacity of the people to address environmental and development issues'.[705]

These connections were later strengthened by a number of international initiatives, including the UN Decade of Sustainable Development.[706] A signal that ESD would be included within the SDG on education was then provided by the Global Education First Initiative (GEFI), launched by UN Secretary General Ban Ki-moon in 2012.[707] The GEFI clearly identified global citizenship as a key priority and indicated that it would continue to be a force in the education agenda.[708] The rationale provided was that, '[e]ducation must be transformative and bring shared values to life ... It must give people the understanding, skills and values they need to cooperate in resolving the interconnected challenges of the 21st century'.[709] Recognition of ESD within international agendas such as those highlighted here has facilitated the inclusion of principles that support sustainability within target 4.7.

---

[703] UNESCO, 'The Dakar Framework for Action' (World Education Forum, Dakar, Senegal, 26–28 April 2000) 17.

[704] UN, 'Agenda 21' (United Nations Conference on Environment & Development, Rio de Janeiro, Brazil, 3–14 June 1992) para 36.2.

[705] ibid para 36.3.

[706] 'UN Decade of ESD' (*UNESCO*) <https://en.unesco.org/themes/education-sustainable-development/what-is-esd/un-decade-of-esd> accessed 11 September 2021.

[707] 'Global Education First Initiative' (*UN*) <https://www.un.org/millenniumgoals/pdf/The%20Global%20Education%20First%20Initiative.pdf> accessed 11 September 2021.

[708] S Gallwey, 'Capturing Transformative Change in Education: The Challenge of Tracking Progress Towards SDG Target 4.7' (2016) 23 Policy & Practice: A Development Education Review 124, 126; A Leicht and others, 'From Agenda 21 to Target 4.7: The Development of Education for Sustainable Development' in A Leicht and others (eds), *Issues and Trends in Education for Sustainable Development* (UNESCO, 2018) ch 1.

[709] UNESCO, 'Priority #3: Foster Global Citizenship' (*Global Education First Initiative*) <http://www.unesco.org/new/en/gefi/priorities/global-citizenship/> accessed 11 September 2021.

344   SDG 4

Target 4.7 can also be linked to Article 26 of the UDHR, article 13 of the ICESCR, article 29 of the CRC, and many other international human rights instruments. For example, article 29 of the CRC outlines that a child's education should develop 'respect for the natural environment'[710] and prepare them 'for responsible life in a free society, in the spirit of understanding, peace, tolerance, equality of sexes, and friendship among all peoples, ethnic, national and religious groups and persons of indigenous origin'.[711] The principles of ESD are captured within article 29 in that it connects education to a respect for the environment, and also recognizes principles such as tolerance, peace and respect for all, which are key in enabling students to live sustainable lives.

b) Statistical/empirical analysis

Global indicator 4.7.1 measures progress made towards this target. The global indicator tracks the 'extent to which (i) global citizenship education and (ii) education for sustainable development are mainstreamed in (a) national education policies; (b) curricula; (c) teacher education; and (d) student assessment'.[712] Data are sourced from self-reported responses by UNESCO Member States on the implementation of the 1974 Recommendation concerning Education for International Understanding, Co-operation and Peace and Education relating to Human Rights and Fundamental Freedoms (1974 Recommendation).[713] UNESCO Member States provide quadrennial responses to the 1974 Recommendation. Responses collected for the period from 2012 to 2016, have enabled UNESCO to shape the methodology and questionnaire for the 7th Consultation, which provides the data necessary for determining progress made towards target 4.7.[714]

The 7th round of reporting took place in 2020 and covers the period from 2017 to 2020.[715] This will be the first period of quadrennial reporting that will provide data for indicator 4.7.1.[716] The questionnaire relates to the four components of indicator 4.7.1—policies, curricula, teacher education, and student assessment. A number of questions are asked to determine the extent to which states have integrated ESD and Global Citizenship Education (GCED) within each of the four components. For instance, in order to assess the curricula component of the indicator, states are expected to indicate which ESD and GCED themes are included within the curriculum.[717] There

---

[710] CRC (n 52) art 29(1)(e).

[711] ibid art 29(1)(d).

[712] UN 'SDG Indicator Metadata' (Target 4.7, 7 May 2021) 1; UNESCO 'Official List of SDG 4 Indicators' (January 2021) indicator 4.7.1.

[713] UN 'SDG Indicator Metadata' (Target 4.7, 7 May 2021) 2.

[714] 'UNESCO's Progress Report on Education for Sustainable Development and Global Citizen Chip Education Highlights Crucial Need for Teacher Training' (*UNESCO*, 11 December 2021) <https://en.unesco.org/news/unescos-progress-report-education-sustainable-development-and-global-citizenship-education> accessed 11 September 2021.

[715] UN, 'SDG Indicator Metadata' (Target 4.7, 7 May 2021) 3; A Azoulay, 'Seventh Consultation on the Implementation of the 1974 Recommendation Concerning Education for International Understanding, Co-operation and Peace, and Education Relating to Human Rights and Fundamental Freedoms' (CL/4329, UNESCO 2020) 1.

[716] UN 'SDG Indicator Metadata' (Target 4.7, 7 May 2021) 3.

[717] A Azoulay, 'Seventh Consultation on the Implementation of the 1974 Recommendation Concerning Education for International Understanding, Co-operation and Peace, and Education Relating to Human Rights and Fundamental Freedoms' (CL/4329, UNESCO 2020) 2.

are eight themes in total, including cultural diversity and tolerance, gender equality, human rights, peace and non-violence, climate change, environmental sustainability, human survival and well-being, and sustainable consumption and production, which allows for eight responses.[718] A score is awarded for each theme that is taught as part of the curriculum from pre-primary to tertiary and non-formal education, however only information relating to primary and secondary education is utilized for the purposes of indicator 4.7.1.[719] The scores are not aggregated across components; rather, the lowest score within each component implies the area most in need of country efforts.

The questionnaire is answered by government officials, who are typically those responsible for education. Progress towards indicator 4.7.1 is therefore measured on the basis of self-reporting by governments, which may be a limitation given the potential effects of subjectivity.[720] However, governments are required to provide supporting evidence for their responses where possible.[721] For example, supporting evidence could take the form of links to the relevant education policies. Further, UNESCO reviews country responses and will compare the information provided with other available information. If there is a conflict, UNESCO will question the relevant respondent. State responses are also publicly available once the reporting cycle has ended, with any changes resulting from the UNESCO review implemented, which enhances credibility and transparency.[722] Given the 7th consultation will provide the first available data for indicator 4.7.1, it is difficult to track country progress since the implementation of the SDG agenda. Further, as the consultation ended in December 2020, country responses to the questionnaire are yet to be made publicly available. However, at the time of writing, the results of the 7th consultation have been reported to the 211th Session of UNESCO Executive Board,[723] which provides some indication as to how progress towards indicator 4.7.1 is tracking globally.

The report of results to the 211th Session of UNESCO Executive Board provides that 71 Member States had reported as of 8 March 2021.[724] Of these seventy-one states, around half indicated that the COVID-19 pandemic had negatively impacted education, with some states connecting this to ESD and GCED themes.[725] For instance, some Member States reported that intolerance was increasing within populations.[726] In terms of the four components of indicator 4.7.1, beginning with the legislation and policy component, 90 per cent of the seventy-one Member States reported that all of

---

[718] UN 'SDG Indicator Metadata' (Target 4.7, 7 May 2021) 4; A Azoulay, 'Seventh Consultation on the Implementation of the 1974 Recommendation Concerning Education for International Understanding, Co-operation and Peace, and Education Relating to Human Rights and Fundamental Freedoms' (CL/4329, UNESCO 2020) 12.

[719] UN 'SDG Indicator Metadata' (Target 4.7, 7 May 2021) 4.

[720] UNESCO, 'Progress on Education for Sustainable Development and Global Citizenship Education' (Findings of the 6th Consultation on the Implementation of the 1974 Recommendation, UNESCO 2018) 3.

[721] UN 'SDG Indicator Metadata' (Target 4.7, 7 May 2021) 3–4.

[722] ibid 4.

[723] UNESCO Executive Board, 'Implementation of Standard-Setting Instruments' (12 March 2021) Doc 211 EX/21.II.

[724] ibid para 4.

[725] ibid para 5.

[726] ibid 1.

the eight aforementioned themes are reflected in national or subnational laws across all levels of education—this extends from pre-primary to tertiary and non-formal education.[727] However, in most Member States, the themes are implicitly reflected within legislation.[728] Overall, 90 per cent of the seventy-one countries reported having mainstreamed ESD themes in their laws and policies.[729]

Turning to the curricula component, an average of 97 per cent of the eight ESD themes were reported to be captured within the curricula across all education levels, from pre-primary to tertiary and non-formal education, within the reporting countries.[730] As a whole, more than 90 per cent of the seventy-one countries reported that ESD and GCED themes had been integrated within their curricula in accordance with indicator 4.7.1.[731] As to the third component of target 4.7.1, Member States reported that the eight themes had been integrated within teacher training to a high level.[732] For instance, across all education levels an average of 92 per cent of the eight themes were captured within teacher education.[733] Further, the eight themes were integrated into teacher training at 96 per cent in primary and secondary education overall, and mainstreaming of ESD and GCED themes in teacher training was reported by 89 per cent of countries.[734] Finally, the fourth component of indicator 4.7.1 measures the level to which ESD and GCED themes are mainstreamed within student assessment. Around 86 per cent of countries reported that this had been achieved, with an average of 36 per cent having extensively mainstreamed all ESD and GCED themes across all levels of education.[735]

On average it appears that progress made towards indicator 4.7.1 is high. However, of the 193 countries that agreed upon the SDGs,[736] only seventy-one Member States submitted reports to the 7th consultation, and thus it is difficult to ascertain the level to which the four components of indicator 4.7.1 are mainstreamed on a global level. Further, the report to the 211th Session of UNESCO Executive Board notes that, 'it is clear from some of the responses that levels of integration of ESD and GCED in education systems are considerably higher in some countries than others'.[737] However, as this report is the only source of the results of the 7th consultation at the time of writing, the progress of individual countries is not available. Finally, further progress of UNESCO Member States towards target 4.7 resulting from implementation efforts will not be evident until the 8th consultation.

---

[727] ibid 2.

[728] ibid para 6.

[729] ibid 2.

[730] ibid.

[731] ibid.

[732] UNESCO Executive Board, 'Implementation of Standard-Setting Instruments' (12 March 2021) Doc 211 EX/21.II para 15.

[733] ibid 2.

[734] ibid.

[735] ibid.

[736] UN, 'Sustainable Development Goals Officially Adopted by 193 Countries' (*United Nations in China*, 27 September 2015) <http://www.un.org.cn/info/6/620.html> accessed 11 September 2021.

[737] UNESCO Executive Board, 'Implementation of Standard-Setting Instruments' (12 March 2021) Doc 211 EX/21.II 4.

c) Efforts taken at domestic and international level

This section will discuss efforts at both a country and international level that contribute towards meeting target 4.7. This includes legislative or policy commitments that demonstrate the ESD and GCED principles reflected in target 4.7, and aims to mainstream these principles within each of the four components captured in indicator 4.7.1—that is, national education policies, curricula, teacher education, and student assessment. Thus, this section will discuss both country and international efforts that advance, or seek to advance, education that promotes sustainability and instils values such as respect for all, empathy, and peace and non-violence in learners.

The first example of these efforts can be seen in Kenya. In 2017, Kenya launched the Education for Sustainable Development Policy—the first ESD policy targeted at the education sector within the country.[738] The ESD policy was preceded by the 2013–2018 National Education Sector Plan (NESP),[739] which established six priority investment areas. One investment area was 'social competencies and values', which included ESD as a sub-theme and identified a need to integrate ESD into education policies and 'support youth in their role as change agents for sustainable development'.[740] Following this, the national ESD policy was developed. The policy interprets ESD to be 'holistic and transformational education that addresses learning content and outcomes, pedagogy and the learning environment to achieve societal transformation'.[741]

The policy identifies a series of existing efforts that affect a re-orientation of educational approaches towards ESD, including non-formal learning activities such as clubs focused on the environment, agriculture, or life skills.[742] The development of the 2017 ESD policy saw extensive stakeholder engagement through twenty-three county-level stakeholder consultations, as well as stakeholder engagement on a national level.[743] The twenty-three county-level consultations identified a number of challenges facing the implementation of ESD. Some of the challenges identified included a lack of understanding surrounding the concept of ESD, insufficient ESD training for educators, and insufficient room within the exam focused curriculum to integrate ESD.[744]

---

[738] UNESCO Office in Nairobi, 'Kenya Launched its first education for Sustainable Development Policy' (*UNESCO.int*, 30 March 2017) <http://www.unesco.org/new/en/member-states/single-view/news/kenya_launched_its_first_education_for_sustainable_developme/> accessed 11 September 2021.

[739] Ministry of Education Science and Technology, 'National Education Sector Plan' (Vol 1, *Republic of Kenya*, March 2014) <https://www.globalpartnership.org/sites/default/files/2014-03-Kenya-Education-Plan-2013-2018_0.pdf> accessed 11 September 2021.

[740] ibid.

[741] Ministry of Education, 'Education for Sustainable Development Policy for the Education Sector' (*Republic of Kenya*, 2017) 2 <https://millenniumedu.org/wp-content/uploads/2017/07/unescopolicyforeducationsector.pdf> accessed 11 September 2021.

[742] ibid.

[743] 'ESD for 2030 Toolbox: Implementation (*UNESCO*) <https://en.unesco.org/themes/education-sustainable-development/toolbox/implementation#esd-impl-41> accessed 11 September 2021; Ministry of Education, 'Education for Sustainable Development Policy for the Education Sector' (*Republic of Kenya*, 2017) 10 <https://millenniumedu.org/wp-content/uploads/2017/07/unescopolicyforeducationsector.pdf> accessed 11 September 2021.

[744] Ministry of Education, 'Education for Sustainable Development Policy for the Education Sector' (*Republic of Kenya*, 2017) 7 <https://millenniumedu.org/wp-content/uploads/2017/07/unescopolicyforeducationsector.pdf> accessed 11 September 2021.

348   SDG 4

Informed by the stakeholder consultations,[745] the 2017 ESD policy outlines a number of guiding principles before turning to policy statements and strategies that apply to all levels of education. The guiding principles include emphasizing human rights in education, empowering the population with values that ensure they can contribute to sustainable development, supporting lifelong learning, and promoting holistic learning that connects the many spheres of sustainable development.[746] Turning to policy statements, a number of key areas are identified, including the promotion of 'whole-institution approaches to ESD at all levels and in all settings'.[747] In terms of strategies for achieving this, the policy calls for the establishment of a process that enables all stakeholders within an institution to develop a plan to implement ESD, as well as the need to strengthen approaches to whole-institutional ESD integration through experience sharing.[748] The policy also includes the integration of ESD within early childhood education, primary and secondary schooling, and higher education.[749] Ultimately, the policy reaffirms a commitment to ESD within Kenya and seeks to enable an integration of ESD within the education sector in line with target 4.7.

A further example of efforts towards mainstreaming ESD within national education policies, curricula, teacher education and student assessment can be seen in Japan.[750] Japanese courses of study (national curriculum standards) were recently updated and introduced into pre-schools in 2018, and primary and secondary schools in 2019.[751] These guides integrate ESD themes at all levels and the Ministry of Education, Culture, Sports, Science and Technology (MEXT) requires that an education provided in accordance with the Basic Act on Education in combination with the national curriculum standards will be 'in alignment with the philosophy of ESD'.[752] The Basic Act on Education was issued in 2006 and features a number of educational objectives.[753] These include the need to provide education in a way that promotes equality, peace, respect for culture, and 'the values of respecting life, caring about nature, and desiring to contribute to the preservation of the environment'.[754] The Act also emphasizes the importance of lifelong learning, another concept intertwined with ESD, as ESD itself is considered to be a 'lifelong learning process'.[755]

---

[745] ibid.

[746] ibid.

[747] ibid.

[748] Ministry of Education, 'Education for Sustainable Development Policy for the Education Sector' (*Republic of Kenya*, 2017) 20 <https://millenniumedu.org/wp-content/uploads/2017/07/unescopolicyforeducationsector.pdf> accessed 11 September 2021.

[749] ibid.

[750] A Ohagi, 'Current Climate of ESD in Japan' (*National Institute for Educational Policy Research*, 6 February, 2019) <https://www.nier.go.jp/English/educationjapan/pdf/20190408-02.pdf> accessed 11 September 2021.

[751] 'Curriculum Guidelines ("Courses of Study") and ESD' (*Ministry of Education, Culture, Sports, Science and Technology*, Japan) <https://www.mext.go.jp/en/unesco/title04/detail04/sdetail04/1375712.htm> accessed 11 September 2021.

[752] ibid.

[753] Basic Act on Education 2006.

[754] ibid art 2(3).

[755] 'What is Education for Sustainable Development?' (*UNESCO*) <https://en.unesco.org/themes/education-sustainable-development/what-is-esd> accessed 11 September 2021.

The prominence of ESD within these frameworks represents the centrality of ESD within the education sector in Japan—that is, it is integrated throughout the entire curriculum and emphasized across subjects as opposed to being limited to independent subjects.[756] In part, this is made possible by 'Periods for Integrated Study' (*sougouteki na gakusyu no jikan*), which were introduced into the curricula for primary and secondary schooling in 2002.[757] Integrated Study is not an independent subject that allows for the addition of ESD within schooling. Rather, it is implemented within each subject. It is designed to increase the autonomy of educators, enhance the relevance of learning content in the context of contemporary challenges, and promote engagement amongst students.[758] Integrated Study allows for ESD and GCED themes to be implemented within traditional subjects through learning activities, which serves to compliment the national curriculum standards.[759] A guide published by MEXT in 2017 provides that, 'at primary and secondary education level across the country, an education that seeks to build a sustainable society is being delivered—in each subject, during periods of integrated study, though moral education, and special activities'.[760] The mainstreaming of ESD across the curriculum in Japan represents a key effort towards implementing ESD as required by indicator 4.7.1.

On an international level, the UNESCO Associated Schools Network (ASPnet) is an example of efforts made towards meeting target 4.7. ASPnet is a UNESCO initiative that began in 1953 with thirty-three schools across fifteen countries.[761] It is now a global network of educational institutions spanning across 182 countries.[762] There are currently around 11,000 educational institutions that are members of the network, ranging from pre-primary to higher education, as well as teacher training institutions and non-formal learning.[763] Each member institution must demonstrate commitment to the values of UNESCO and align educational content to these values.[764] ESD and GCED are captured as two key priorities within the ASPnet Strategy for 2014–2021.[765] As members of ASPnet, schools have a 'moral contract' with UNESCO to uphold the objectives and mission of both ASPnet and UNESCO,[766] and are therefore expected

---

[756] U Fredriksson and others, 'A Comparative Study of Curriculums for Education for Sustainable Development (ESD) in Sweden and Japan' (2020) 12(3) Sustainability 1123, 1124.

[757] Ministry of the Environment, 'UNDESD Japan Report' (*ENV*, Interministerial Meeting on the UN DESD 2009) <https://www.env.go.jp/en/policy/edu/undesd/report.pdf> accessed 11 September 2021.

[758] C Bjork, 'Local Implementation of Japan's Integrated Studies Reform: A Preliminary Analysis of Efforts to Decentralise the Curriculum' (2009) 45(1) Comparative Education 23, 27.

[759] Office of the Director-General for International Affairs and Ministry of Education, Culture, Sports, Science and Technology, 'A Guide to Promoting ESD' (1st edn, Japan National Commission for UNESCO, March 2016) 5–6.

[760] ibid 6.

[761] UNESCO, 'ASPnet Strategy 2014–2021' (*UNESCO Associated Schools*, 2013) 1 <http://www.unesco.org/new/fileadmin/MULTIMEDIA/HQ/ED/ED_new/pdf/ASPnet-Strategy-2014-2021.pdf> accessed 11 September 2021.

[762] 'About the Network' (*UNESCO Associated Schools*) <https://aspnet.unesco.org/en-us/Pages/About_the_network.aspx> accessed 11 September 2021.

[763] UNESCO, 'Membership' (*UNESCO Associated Schools*) <https://aspnet.unesco.org/en-us/Pages/Membership.aspx> accessed 11 September 2021.

[764] ibid.

[765] UNESCO, 'Global Citizenship Education' (*UNESCO Associated Schools*) <https://aspnet.unesco.org/en-us/Pages/Global-Citizenship-Education.aspx> accessed 11 September 2021; UNESCO, 'Education for Sustainable Development' (*UNESC Associated Schools*) <https://aspnet.unesco.org/en-us/Pages/Education%20for%20Sustainable%20Development.aspx> accessed 11 September 2021.

[766] UNESCO, 'UNESCO Associated Schools Network' (UNESCO 2018) 13.

350 SDG 4

to be committed to the integration of ESD and GCED within the institutions. ASPnet schools demonstrate good practice towards the implementation of ESD and GCED within schools, and emphasize the importance of knowledge and experience sharing across the network, as well as with broader society and policy-makers. Thus, ASPnet schools represent a key effort in meeting target 4.7.

d) Critique

Target 4.7 is the figurehead for some of the more transformative discourse surrounding SDG 4. As outlined above, it most encapsulates the themes of ESD and GCED that act as enablers for the broader SDG framework.[767] ESD and GCED have been recognized as critical tools for overcoming a number of current and future challenges, including social and economic inequality, loss of biodiversity, and climate change. In this respect, education must prepare the population for the challenges it will face. The notion that education has the ability to equip learners with the knowledge necessary for combatting global challenges is not novel to the SDGs or to the concepts of ESD and GCED.[768] While the urgency of certain challenges has changed over time, the message that education is central to combatting the crises of the day, and for promoting the enjoyment of all other human rights, has remained relatively unchanged.[769] In the era of the MDGs, it was recognized that education could combat poverty and increase global health.[770] In the era of the SDGs, there is now an urgent call to utilize education to combat the challenges of the twenty-first century, namely the climate crisis. A 2020 UNESCO report depicts this urgency in stating, '[w]hat we know, what we believe in and what we do needs to change. What we have learned so far does not prepare us for the challenge. This cannot go on. And the window of opportunity is closing fast. We must urgently learn to live differently'.[771] ESD and GCED are positioned as fundamental instruments in meeting this challenge.

Target 4.7 creates a vital opportunity to merge both ESD and GCED into the curriculum of schools globally. This broadening of ambition compared to what was captured in the MDGs and the demand for urgent action place a great deal of weight on, or hope in, education. Looking to the UNESCO definitions of ESD and GCED respectively, education must equip 'learners with knowledge, skills, values and attitudes to take informed decisions and make responsible actions for environmental integrity, economic viability and a just society'.[772] It must also empower 'learners of all ages ... to

---

[767] UNESCO, 'Education for Sustainable Development: A Roadmap' (UNESCO 2020) 8; UNGA Res 72/222 (20 December 2017) UN Doc A/RES/72/222 para 2; UN, 'Connection Between Global Citizenship education and the SDGs will be Explored During Forum at UN Headquarters' (*Academic Impact*, 31 October 2018) <https://www.un.org/en/academic-impact/connection-between-global-citizenship-education-and-sdgs-will-be-explored-during> accessed 11 September 2021.

[768] See, eg, F Chung, 'Education: A Key to Power and a Tool for Change—A Practitioner's Perspective' (2002) 2(1) Current Issues in Comparative Education 91.

[769] See, eg, ibid; ICESCR (n 50) art 13(1); CADE (n 141) art 5(1)(a).

[770] UN Secretary-General, 'Road Map towards the Implementation of the United Nations Millennium Declaration' (6 September 2001) UN Doc A/56/326 3, 20.

[771] UNESCO, 'Education for Sustainable Development: A Roadmap' (UNESCO 2020) 6.

[772] 'What is Education for Sustainable Development?' (*UNESCO*) <https://en.unesco.org/themes/education-sustainable-development/what-is-esd> accessed 11 September 2021.

become active promoters of more peaceful, tolerant, inclusive, secure and sustainable societies'.[773] Finally, it must do so urgently.[774] Integrating these concepts into schools is clearly relevant to current issues and crucial for facing them.[775] However, the task of preparing learners to face the challenges of the twenty-first century is compounded by the fact that the challenges of previous centuries were not overcome, and are in fact interwoven.[776] Given that the more modest goals set in the MDGs were not met in their entirety, it may be difficult for some to imagine meaningful progress being made towards the ambitious themes captured in target 4.7.

It is worth noting that the widening of ambition by target 4.7 places increased demand and reliance on education—on top of the existing demand associated with the provision of general education.[777] ESD and GCED are also value-laden concepts, with the end point of success relatively unknown. Given the transformative nature of ESD and GCED, and the call to 'urgently learn to live differently', there may be incongruity between the ambitious content taught to influence change in learners and the reality of the world that meets them outside of the classroom. As Wolff explains, '[c]ontemporary educators have to deal with the hugely important moral conflicts facing human-kind, namely the conflicts between social responsibility and individual freedom'.[778] Navigating these ethical conflicts, empowering learners to make sustainable choices, and instilling values that perhaps are not yet reflected in the wider population is clearly a mammoth task, and one with an uncertain outcome.

Despite this, there is a consensus that change to the predominant mode of living is urgently required and education has a vital role to play. Education has long been seen to have a fundamental role in preparing students to engage with future issues.[779] For example, the 1974 Recommendation identifies one of UNESCO's major guiding principles of educational policy as, ensuring a 'readiness on the part of the individual to participate in solving the problems of his community, his country and the world at large'.[780] Looking also to the ICESCR, the purpose of education in part is to enable community participation, promote 'understanding, tolerance and friendship' and further activities to achieve peace.[781] Thus, education has for many years been seen as a capable tool for

---

[773] 'Global Citizenship Education' (*UNESCO*) <https://en.unesco.org/themes/gced> accessed 11 September 2021.

[774] UNESCO, 'Education for Sustainable Development: A Roadmap' (UNESCO 2020) 6.

[775] AV Agbedahin, 'Sustainable Development, Education for Sustainable Development, and the 2030 Agenda for Sustainable Development: Emergence, Efficacy, Eminence, and Future' (2019) 27(4) *Sustainable Development* 669, 671.

[776] J Agyeman and others (eds), *Just Sustainabilities: Development in an Unequal World* (Earthscan Publications 2003).

[777] L-A Wolff, Nature and Sustainability: An Educational Study with Rousseau and Foucault (PhD Thesis, Lambert Academic Publishing AG & Co 2011) 58.

[778] ibid 98.

[779] J Kotzmann, 'Lifting the Cloak of Conceptual Confusion: Exploring the Meaning of the Human Right to Higher Education' (2015) 21(1) Australian Journal of Human Rights 71, 80.

[780] 1974 Recommendation concerning Education for International Understanding, Co-operation and Peace and Education relating to Human Rights and Fundamental Freedoms (adopted 19 November 1974) UNESCO art 4(g).

[781] ICESCR (n 50) art 13(1); Kotzmann, 'Lifting the Cloak of Conceptual Confusion' (n 779) 80.

352   SDG 4

achieving transformative change. In order to ensure that this 'tool'[782] influences the ambitious change set by target 4.7 and the broader SDG 4, further attention must be paid to how ESD and GCED themes are to be implemented, particularly in regards to ensuring that ESD does not merely varnish the anthropocentric perspectives that have brought current challenges to the foreground.[783]

Finally, in regards to the monitoring framework for target 4.7, as outlined above the global indicator tracks the mainstreaming of GCED and ESD 'in (a) national education policies; (b) curricula; (c) teacher education; and (d) student assessment'.[784] Target 4.7 explicitly relates to 'all learners', extending its scope outside of primary and secondary education. The 1974 Recommendation, which is utilized to measure progress towards the global indicator, collects data for pre-primary to tertiary and non-formal education. However, as identified above, only information relating to primary and secondary education is utilized for the purposes of indicator 4.7.1[785] Respondents are expected to cover all levels of education within their responses to the 1974 Recommendation.[786] It is therefore unclear why pre-primary, tertiary, and non-formal education are not included within the calculation. Limiting global indictor 4.7.1 to include only primary and secondary education in the calculation creates a risk that pre-primary, tertiary, and lifelong learning are neglected by states and NGOs in favour of the education levels that constitute progress towards the indicator.

8. Target 4.a Build and upgrade education facilities that are child, disability and gender sensitive and provide safe, non-violent, inclusive and effective learning environments for all

a) Source of target

The notion of all-encompassing and nurturing learning environments is evident in article 9 of the CRPD, which gives meaning behind 'accessibility', and article 24, which stresses the significance of 'education'.[787] By nature, educational inclusivity is a vast concept and has been at the forefront of many global enterprises. Dating back as far as 1979, the UN has acknowledged discrimination as a contentious theme, as highlighted through the CEDAW. Namely, article 10(b) weighs in on the importance of equal exposure to high teaching standards, curricula, and schooling equipment.[788] In a practical sense, initiatives may be illustrated by UNICEF's 'Child-Friendly Cites'.[789] Here,

---

[782] There is some commentary surrounding the undesirability of considering education as a tool. See, eg, B Jickling, 'Environmental Education and Environmental Advocacy' (2003) 34(2) The Journal of Environmental Education 20, 21–22; L-A. Wolff, Nature and Sustainability (n 777) 59.

[783] H Kopnina, 'Education for the Future? Critical Evaluation of Education for Sustainable Development Goals' (2020) 51(1) The Journal of Environmental Education 280, 285.

[784] UN 'SDG Indicator Metadata' (Target 4.7, 7 May 2021) 1; UNESCO 'Official List of SDG 4 Indicators' (January 2021) indicator 4.7.1.

[785] UN 'SDG Indicator Metadata' (Target 4.7, 7 May 2021) 4.

[786] A Azoulay, 'Seventh Consultation on the Implementation of the 1974 Recommendation Concerning Education for International Understanding, Co-operation and Peace, and Education Relating to Human Rights and Fundamental Freedoms' (CL/4329, UNESCO 2020) 2.

[787] CRPD (n 136) art 9, art 22.

[788] CEDAW (n 51) art 10(b).

[789] UNICEF, 'Child Friendly Cites Initiatives: 2030 Agenda' (*UNICEF* 2021) para 2 <https://childfriendlycities. org/2030-agenda/> accessed 11 September 2021.

there is a focus on cultivating a supportive environment for children so they can fulfil their maximum potential at a global and local level.[790]

The concept of 'education facilities' is not limited to tangible structures. Instead, the target directs a holistic approach that assesses the fundamental components of a supportive learning environment. Seemingly, target 4.a employs the narratives of the CRPD and the CEDAW, with inclusivity and sound education systems being its crux. Article 9 of the CRPD mandates states to educate private stakeholders on accessibility issues that people with disabilities experience.[791] Similarly, article 24 provides that states will 'take appropriate measures to ... train professionals and staff to work on all levels of education'.[792] When juxtaposed with the CEDAW, the ideal of professional competence surrounding gendered exclusion is not expressly detailed. Arguably, target 4.a shares greater parallels to the CRDP, however CEDAW remains a vital reference point for gendered educational inclusivity.

b) Statistical/empirical analysis

Progress towards target 4.a is monitored by global indicator 4.a.1 which measures the 'proportion of schools offering basic services, by type of service'.[793] Basic services include those such as electricity, Internet for pedagogical purposes, basic drinking water, handwashing facilities, and adapted infrastructure.[794] This indicator uses a percentage unit of measure based on the accessibility of essential services for primary, lower secondary and upper secondary education.[795] It is reported that this indicator has a comparatively high level of available data.[796] This is because the indicator is part of the data collected by the UIS Survey of Formal Education.[797] However, states with a decentralized educational system or a heavy reliance on the private sector face continuous challenges in coordinating administrative data. A reported 61 per cent of countries have available data on primary schools with access to electricity and 20 per cent for secondary schools with adapted infrastructure for a student with disabilities.[798]

The available data indicate that access to water, sanitation, and electricity is far from universal.[799] Worldwide, over a fifth of primary schools do not have basic drinking water, and over a third do not have basic handwashing facilities.[800] While it is reported

---

[790] ibid.

[791] CRPD (n 136) art 9.

[792] ibid art 22.

[793] UNESCO, 'Official List of SDG 4 Indicators' (January 2021) <http://tcg.uis.unesco.org/wp-content/uploads/sites/4/2020/09/SDG 4_indicator_list.pdf> accessed 21 September 2021.

[794] UN 'SDG Indicator Metadata' (target 4.a, July 2021) 1–2.

[795] ZY Min, 'Indicator 4.a.1' (*UN Statistics Wiki*, 2021) para 4 <https://unstats.un.org/wiki/display/SDGeHandbook/Indicator+4.a.1> accessed 11 September 2021.

[796] UNESCO, '*SDG 4 Data Digest "How to Produce and Use the Global and Thematic Education Indicators"*' (UNESCO 2019) 38.

[797] ibid 39.

[798] UNESCO Institute for Statistics and UNESCO Global Education Monitoring Report 2019 'Meeting Commitments: Are Countries on Track to Achieve SDG 4?' (2019) 12.

[799] ibid 10.

[800] UNICEF, 'Water, Sanitation and Hygiene (WASH)' (*UNICEF*, 2021) <https://www.unicef.org/wash > accessed 30 September 2021.

354   SDG 4

that sanitation and access to drinking water is universal in high-income countries,[801] just over half (53 per cent) of low-income states and only 84 per cent of middle-income states report access to basic drinking water.[802] Globally, '[s]ome 335 million girls attend schools that lack essential menstrual hygiene management facilities'.[803] Among the least developed countries, over two-thirds of primary schools do not have access to electricity, with a lower rate having access to the Internet or computers.[804] The disparity between low and high-income states is substantial, with 37 per cent of upper-secondary schools in low-income states having access to the Internet, compared to 93 per cent in high-income states.[805]

Adequate infrastructure, including appropriate adaptations to that infrastructure, is vital to fostering an inclusive and effective learning environment for all. This includes both physical and technological infrastructure as well as adaptations for students with disabilities. Available data on adapted infrastructure in schools are low, partly because government organized monitoring is rare and data collated by schools are not subject to independent review.[806] One issue contributing to a scarcity of available data is the lack of an agreed-upon definition of adapted infrastructure.[807] Examples can include handrails, widened doorways, modified toilets, and signage accessible to visually impaired students, however a consistent standard is yet to be implemented.[808] The percentage of schools with adequate adaptations to infrastructure and materials for students with disabilities is relatively low. For example, Samoa, Burundi, and Niger report that no primary or lower secondary schools met this criterion.[809]

Target 4.a is further monitored by thematic indicator 4.a.2, which tracks the 'percentage of students experiencing bullying in the last 12 months'.[810] Global statistics indicate that over 30 per cent of eleven to fifteen year olds had experienced bullying in school during the previous twelve months.[811] However, there is significant variation between countries. For instance, low levels of 10 per cent were reported in Armenia, whereas levels of more than 50 per cent were reported in Lithuania, Nepal, and the Philippines.[812] LGBTQ + children are more likely to experience bullying than their heterosexual peers. For example, in the United States, 4.6 per cent of heterosexual students

---

[801] UNESCO Institute for Statistics and UNESCO Global Education Monitoring Report 2019 'Meeting Commitments: Are Countries on Track to Achieve SDG 4?' (2019) 10.

[802] ibid.

[803] UNESCO, 'Global Education Monitoring Report 2020' (n 90) 282 (quoting UNICEF, *Guidance on Menstrual Health and Hygiene* (1st edn, UNICEF, 2019) 27.

[804] UNESCO, 'Ensure Inclusive and Equitable Quality Education and Promote Lifelong Learning Opportunities for All: Progress and Info' (*UNESCO* 2021) para 5 <https://sdgs.un.org/goals/goal4> accessed 30 September 2021.

[805] UNESCO Institute for Statistics and UNESCO Global Education Monitoring Report 2019 'Meeting Commitments: Are Countries on Track to Achieve SDG 4?' (2019) 10.

[806] UNESCO, 'Global Education Monitoring Report 2020' (n 90) 169.

[807] ibid.

[808] ibid.

[809] ibid 168 (data from 2016 to 2018).

[810] UNESCO, 'Official list of SDG 4 Indicators' (January 2021) <http://tcg.uis.unesco.org/wp-content/uploads/sites/4/2020/09/SDG 4_indicator_list.pdf> accessed 21 September 2021.

[811] UNESCO, 'Global Education Monitoring Report 2020' (n 90) 163.

[812] ibid 165 (quoting UNESCO, 'Behind the Numbers: Ending School Violence and Bullying' (2019 UNESCO).

reported not going to school at least once in the past month due to feeling unsafe. This number rose to 12.5 per cent for students who identified as LGBTQ.[813]

Students with disabilities are also more prone to experiencing bullying. In Uganda it was reported that 84 per cent of children with disabilities 'had experienced violence at the hands of peers or staff in the past week'.[814] This number dropped to 53 per cent for students without disabilities.[815] An Australian study found that 56 per cent of students with disabilities had experienced bullying in the previous twelve months, more than twice the rate of bullying experienced by the general school-aged population.[816]

The types of bullying experienced by children is changing, with the prevalence of cyberbullying increasing. Data from 2010 to 2014 show an increase from 7 per cent to 12 per cent of children aged eleven to sixteen years who had experienced cyberbullying.[817] However, these data are sparse. Generally, data show that girls and immigrant children are more likely to be targeted by cyberbullying than boys and native-born students.[818]

Finally, thematic indicator 4.a.3 measures the safety of learning environments, including children's commutes to and from school. This includes natural hazards, armed violence, sexual harassment, and dangerous traffic that may be encountered by students during their commute.[819] Students in poorer countries are at a higher risk of unsafe commuting.[820] This can be due to living in rural areas far from school, where the inability of families to afford public or private means of transport, or the absence of infrastructure, may result in school students walking for several hours per school day.[821] Traffic accidents rank as one of the most severe dangers for school students. Fatal traffic accidents are significantly higher in developing countries.[822] In low-income countries, despite a much lower density of traffic in terms of vehicle ownership per capita, the rate of fatalities to or from school among five to fourteen year olds is much higher than in wealthy countries.[823]

As well as the dangers of road traffic, in many locations, girls are at a greater risk of danger due to the threat of sexual harassment and rape. In Haiti, it was reported that 27 per cent of women who received money for sex before age eighteen 'listed schools and school neighbourhoods as the most common location for solicitation'.[824] Once arrived in school settings, many school students are subject to corporal punishment by school staff. While a total of 132 states worldwide have banned corporal punishment in schools, half of all school-aged children live in states where corporal punishment is

---

[813] ibid 288.

[814] ibid 164.

[815] ibid.

[816] S Gotlib, 'Action Must Be Taken to Stop Bullying of Students with Disability' (*Australia Probono*, 1 May 2018) <https://probonoaustralia.com.au/news/2018/05/action-must-taken-stop-bullying-students-disability/> accessed 22 September 2021.

[817] Data from Belgium, United Kingdom, Denmark, Italy, Portugal, Romania. UNESCO, 'Global Education Monitoring Report 2020' (n 90) 288.

[818] Quoting UNESCO, 'Behind the Numbers: Ending School Violence and Bullying' (2019 UNESCO) 26, 30.

[819] UNESCO, 'Global Education Monitoring Report 2020' (n 90) 284.

[820] ibid 290.

[821] ibid.

[822] ibid.

[823] ibid.

[824] ibid.

356 SDG 4

still allowed.[825] Community attitudes play an important role in this respect, with research in India suggesting a 90 per cent community approval of corporal punishment in schools.[826] Lastly, children's safety as school students is also threatened by environmental factors, quite possibly affecting their home circumstances as well, such as airborne pollution.[827]

c) Efforts taken at domestic and international level

Infrastructure that fosters an inclusive learning space is necessary to ensure that no one is left behind and forms a crucial part of indictor 4.a.1. Accordingly, some countries have made efforts to address a lack of appropriately adapted infrastructure. For example, in India, the Ministry of Social Justice and Empowerment developed an app that allows citizens to photograph and report inadequate infrastructure. In France, parents of children with disabilities can contact a helpline to make requests for adaptations to infrastructure.[828]

In the context of efforts to ensure appropriate infrastructure, as monitored by indicator 4.a.1, it is important to refer to the principle of accessibility. Accessibility as adjustment presupposes and does not challenge the practice of initial design for the non-disabled. The CRPD adopted the concept of universal design, defined as follows: 'the design of products, environments, programmes, and services to be usable by all people to the greatest extent possible, without the need for adaptation or specialised design'.[829] Universal design 'aims to increase functionality and apply to everyone's needs, regardless of age, size or ability'.[830] It is important to note, however, that universal design approaches to modifications have been said to be 'either non-existent or in a nascent stage for global instruments'.[831]

In regards to thematic indicator 4.a.2, data show that the number of children experiencing cyberbullying is increasing.[832] Cyberbullying poses a particular threat given the increase in online learning due to the COVID-19 pandemic. Country efforts made towards reducing cyberbullying are therefore key to ensuring all students experience a safe learning environment. In this respect, country efforts can be seen in Lebanon and Italy, where teacher training is provided on the prevention and reporting of cyberbullying.[833] In the United States, NGO No Bully has created a campaign to reduce cyberbullying by strengthening the Internet skills of five to eight year olds.[834]

Finally, as discussed above, road traffic hazards pose a particular danger to students during their commute to and from school and are monitored as part of thematic

---

[825] ibid 286 (quoting Global initiative to end all corporal punishment of children, 'Global Report 2019: Progress towards Ending Corporal Punishment of Children' 12).

[826] ibid 287.

[827] ibid 288.

[828] UNESCO, 'Global Education Monitoring Report 2020' (n 90) 170.

[829] CRPD (n 136) art 2.

[830] UNESCO, 'Global Education Monitoring Report 2020' (n 90) 170.

[831] C Johnstone and others, 'Quality Education for All? The Promises and Limitations of the SDG Framework for Inclusive Education and Students with Disabilities' in A Wulff (ed), *Grading Goal Four* (Brill 2020) 115.

[832] UNESCO, 'Behind the Numbers: Ending School Violence and Bullying' (UNESCO 2019).

[833] UNESCO, 'Global Education Monitoring Report 2020' (n 90) 288.

[834] ibid.

indicator 4.a.3. Efforts to reduce these hazards for school students include The Global Initiative for Child Health and Mobility, which campaigns for speed limits, footpaths and cycle lanes to ensure safer journeys for children by 2030.[835] It has been reported that the Republic of Korea reduced child traffic injuries by 95 per cent from 1988 to 2012, using an approach that included the designation of safe school routes, road safety legislation and related education, as well as providing free car seats to families in low-income households.[836]

d) Critique

In terms of measurement, the evaluation of the data relating to target 4.a.1 is hindered by the absence of common standards for parameters such as adaptations or proactive designs for infrastructure. Formulae are called for by which the accommodation to a range of differently-abled school students may be quantified.[837]

Unterhalter suggests the indicators for target 4.a are not necessarily an apt proxy for inclusion or quality. Unterhalter observes that none of the means of implementation is reducible to the forms of physical infrastructure detailed in 4a, such as electricity, sanitation, buildings adapted for disabled students, and access to the Internet. There is, Unterhalter notes, insufficient connection to be made between the provision of such physical services, on the one hand, and safe, child-friendly and gender-sensitive schooling, on the other.[838]

As discussed elsewhere within this chapter, the COVID-19 pandemic accelerated the evolution of distance education mediated by the Internet and by other, more traditional means of transmission and communication. In doing so, the significance of 'bricks and mortar' infrastructure was lessened in ways that are probably not ephemeral; that is to say, educational delivery beyond the pandemic will probably be different than before. Just as personal finance dealings in lower-income countries have rapidly taken up new mobile technologies, there is no reason why countries with poor physical infrastructure for delivering education should not in some way turn to the long-term consolidation of methods adopted out of necessity in the pandemic. Of course, those emergency measures may well have disadvantaged some sectors of the population in haste to construct delivery systems of education for the school student populations thought of as normative. Special learning needs of various kinds may well have been neglected or left to the ingenuity and goodwill of teachers and family members in methods which cannot be sustained. More subtle forms of discrimination may also have occurred. However, it remains important that policy-makers do not treat physical school structures as having more significance than they should have vis-à-vis forms of educational provision that are digital or otherwise delivered at a distance.

Discussing digital communication as a vehicle for learning requires attention to the dangers and risks associated with such technologies. As well as cyberbullying, generally

---

[835] ibid 291.
[836] ibid.
[837] ibid 284.
[838] Unterhalter (n 306) 42.

358   SDG 4

understood as involving the conduct of fellow students whether of the same or different ages, the technology also enables surveillance in various forms. Undoubtedly traditional school buildings and pupils' regular attendance allowed a form of state surveillance mediated by teaching staff, examination systems, and, in some countries, by inspectorate processes. However, school students learning from their home setting itself enables and even requires various forms of surveillance. The technology for learning may frequently be outsourced to private companies if the current tertiary sector trend indicates more significant movements, as is probably the case.

To the extent that physical school buildings remain a crucial component of the state's delivery of education, it needs to be observed that the levels of safety, discrimination and inclusion found within those walls are likely to correspond in large degree to the characteristics of the communities which the buildings and the teachers are located. The extent to which schools as such can defy or at least operate beyond the attitudinal and material constraints of their social and cultural environments clearly depends on myriad factors.

9. Target 4.b By 2020, substantially expand globally the number of scholarships available to developing countries, in particular least developed countries, small island developing States and African countries, for enrolment in higher education, including vocational training and information and communications technology, technical, engineering and scientific programmes, in developed countries and other developing countries

a) Source of target

Target 4.b is one of only two targets that relates explicitly to higher education within SDG 4.[839] In this context, it needs to be emphasized that scholarships and other forms of financial support for secondary and tertiary studies within and across borders have a long history.[840] Many state-run programmes originated in colonial arrangements by which colonial senior school students identified as talented were enabled to travel to the metropole, such as London or Paris, to be provided with tertiary education. In many cases, the rationale was quite openly that future leaders and professional elite of colonized territories would be acculturated into the values and practices of the colonizing power.[841] The 'opinion leader' rationale has continued to be the public rationale for state-sponsored programmes even if the underlying policy processes are more complex.[842] A 'change agent' or 'leader' role for those who receive a scholarship are expressly

[839] S Heleta and T Bagus, 'Sustainable Development Goals and Higher Education: Leaving Many Behind' (2021) 81 Higher Education 163–84.

[840] L Tournes and GS Smith, 'Introduction, A World of Exchanges, Conceptualizing the History of International Scholarship Programs (Nineteenth to Twenty-First Centuries)' in L Tournes and GS Smith (eds), *Global Exchanges: Scholarships and Transnational Circulations in the Modern World* (Berghahn Books 2018) 2.

[841] M Mawer, 'Approaches to Analyzing the Outcomes of International Scholarship Programs for Higher Education' (2017) 21(3) Journal of Studies in International Education 230, 45; A Campbell and M Mawer, 'Clarifying Mixed Messages: International Scholarship Programmes in the Sustainable Development Agenda' (2019) 32(2) Higher Education Policy 167, 169.

[842] I Wilson, 'Ends Changed, Means Retained: Scholarship Programs, Political Influence and Drifting Goals' (2015) 17(1) British Journal of Politics and International Relations 130–51, 144.

indicated in some privately funded programmes, such as the MasterCard Foundation Scholars Program.[843] Therefore there are deep connections, if only historical ones, with colonial and post-colonial relationships. This includes those maintained throughout the British Commonwealth and, more generally, with the structures and processes of aid provided by the First World to developing countries since the major decolonization period of the 1950s and 1960s.[844] Cultural diplomacy and 'soft power' continue to be drivers of scholarship programmes.[845]

There is also a long history of philanthropic, charitable, or religious agencies supporting the education of young people defined as both worthy and, in some sense, disadvantaged through scholarships. This has included domestic and international scholarships, where the latter refers to a young person travelling internationally to take up a scholarship. In the domestic sphere, scholarships based on academic merit as measured by the 11+ examination play(ed) a significant role in the UK's private sector (confusingly referred to as 'public schools'). It is difficult to avoid such pejorative terms as 'tokenism' or even 'charity' concerning such practices of the monied establishment. These histories are likely of more direct relevance as sources of target 4.b than human rights agreements, even if the alleviation of global inequality in educational provision is highly congruent with human rights aspirations. The effectiveness of the scholarships system in addressing global inequality is moot. As suggested above, diverse agencies have established public and private scholarships, religious and secular, governmental and civil. They have been subject to various levels of transparency and accountability over the centuries. Scholarship programmes are undoubtedly subject to more significant state and even inter-state regulation in the twenty-first century than ever before; however, the endless possibility of discrimination based on various parameters is difficult to rule out by the nature of such programmes. A human rights-based audit of scholarship programmes is likely to yield a mixed picture.

Taking an even larger perspective, international scholarship programmes are embedded in the politics of international aid and the UN system itself. They are therefore interconnected with the colonial history of our globe. In recent decades multinational private corporations have played a much more significant role in the scholarship domain. The interconnections of economic policies, trade, and geopolitics cannot be avoided when evaluating this target. Africa, in particular, continues to see brain drain and the loss of trained human capital represented by the non-return of those who go overseas for education.[846] It has been observed that World Bank policy towards the funding of tertiary education in poorer countries has favoured the sending of the few to wealthy countries.[847]

---

[843] Campbell and Mawer (n 841) 178.

[844] Tournes and Smith (n 840) 11.

[845] R Bhandari and others, *International Higher Education: Shifting Mobilities, Policy Challenges and New Initiatives* (UNESCO 2018) 8.

[846] R Bhandari and others, 'International Higher Education: Shifting Mobilities, Policy Challenges, and New Initiatives' (Background Paper, UNESCO Global Education Monitoring Report 2019, Migration, Displacement and Education: Building Bridges Not Walls); Heleta and Bagus (n 839) 163.

[847] Heleta and Bagus (n 839) 163–68.

360 SDG 4

Bringing the analysis back to an individual level, given that scholarship programmes primarily consist of selecting individuals as worthy of financial support, it should be noted that individual merit is somewhat problematic from a human rights perspective. On one hand, it is entirely consistent with human rights norms for every individual to be held worthy of quality education, such that any scholarship offer in a sense contributes to the fulfilment of this aspiration. On the other hand, it seems less satisfactory to pick out specific individuals as more worthy than others. Of course, selective scholarships are often held out to benefit whole communities down the track when a more highly educated individual returns, however, like many other aspects of scholarships programmes, this promissory claim stands in need of evidence.

b) Statistical/empirical analysis

Target 4.b is measured by the 'volume of official development assistance flows for scholarships by sector and type of study'.[848] Target 4.b is one of twenty-one SDGs with a 2020 deadline. This deadline has passed, and while progress has been made, the target has not been achieved.[849] To fit within the criteria for 4.b, and thus to count towards the fulfilment of SDG 4, enrolment must take place in 'developed ... [or] other developing countries',[850] and must be funded by official government scholarships, therefore excluding non-governmental scholarship programmes.[851] International education expert Rajika Bhandari estimates that in 2016, there were some 22,000 students from developing countries receiving government funded scholarship-based tertiary education in developed countries. This number represented just under 1 per cent of the developing world's internationally mobile students (those travelling overseas from developing into developed countries).[852]

In 2017, ODA for scholarships amounted to $1.3 billion.[853] Australia, France, Japan, the United Kingdom, and institutions of the EU accounted for nearly two-thirds of this total.[854] Aid for post-secondary education amounted to $3.1 billion in 2018 (scholarships and imputed student costs);[855] ODA for scholarships amounted to $1.6 billion in 2018.[856] While not counted towards progress for target 4.b, non-state providers offer significant scholarship support.[857] In relation to philanthropy and the private sector, it was estimated that the MasterCard Foundation accounted for four times the volume of scholarship funds as the second-biggest philanthropic programme.[858] Mawer reports

[848] UN, 'SDG Indicator Metadata' (9 July 2017) 1.
[849] UN, 'The Sustainable Development Goals Report 2020' (n 179) 61.
[850] UNESCO 'Official List of SDG 4 Indicators' (January 2021).
[851] UNESCO, 'Global Education Monitoring Report' (n 457) 208.
[852] R Bhandari 'Post-secondary Scholarships for Students from Developing Countries: Establishing a Global Baseline' (2017) 54(2) European Journal of Education 533–45.
[853] Report of the Secretary-General, 'Special Edition: Progress Towards the Sustainable Development Goals' (2019) UN Doc E/2019/68.
[854] ibid.
[855] UNESCO, 'Global Education Monitoring Report 2020' (n 90) 292.
[856] Report of the Secretary-General, 'Progress Towards the Sustainable Development Goals' (2020) UN Doc E/20200/57.
[857] UNESCO, 'Global Education Monitoring Report' (n 457) 208.
[858] UNESCO, 'Global Education Monitoring Report 2020' (n 90) 297.

that the combined contributions of the Ford Foundation and MasterCard program since 2000 were approaching a total of $1 billion by 2015.[859]

While overall the volume of ODA for scholarships was stagnant from 2010 to 2016,[860] opportunities in Sub-Saharan Africa increased from 2015.[861] In Sub-Saharan Africa, the top fifty scholarship aid providers contributed between them 94 per cent of the estimated total number of scholarships targeted to Sub-Saharan African students.[862] These programmes offered 30,000 new scholarships in 2019 for 2020 entry.[863] The largest providers to Sub-Saharan students (via government initiatives) were China, with 12,000 opportunities funded annually, followed by South Africa, Russia, the United Kingdom, Turkey, Egypt, India, Germany, and Japan.[864] China increased total scholarships to Sub-Saharan African students for 2019–22 to 50,000, or 5,000 more scholarships per year.[865] The UK's Chevening programme pledged 100 more scholarships annually.[866] In 2015, India announced 50,000 scholarships over the next five years in a pledge to the African Development Bank.[867] The German Academic Exchange Service increased scholarships to the Sub-Saharan region by 900 between 2014 and 2017.[868]

Generally, larger student populations attract more scholarship aid. However, Small Island Developing States tend to receive some of the highest per capita scholarship flows,[869] as highly specialized tertiary education programmes are frequently unavailable in those countries, necessitating overseas study.

c) Efforts taken at domestic and international level

Numerous programmes provide scholarships for students on bases including need and merit. In terms of ODA, key efforts made by countries towards increasing government funded scholarships have been discussed above. A further example can be seen in Australia, where around 10 per cent of government-funded scholarships are given to students in Pacific developing countries to fund their tertiary study in the Pacific region.[870] Given target 4.b does not cover students studying in their home country, this is not counted towards progress. However, it is an important contribution in the context of concerns regarding international scholarships, as detailed in the below critique.

While non-state scholarships are also not counted towards target 4.b, they require recognition as the availability of non-government funded scholarships may influence allocation of government aid.[871] In terms of non-state scholarship programmes, the

---

[859] M Mawer, 'Approaches to Analyzing the Outcomes of International Scholarship Programs for Higher Education' (2017) 21(3) Journal of Studies in International Education 45, 230.

[860] UNESCO, 'Migration, Displacement & Education: Building Bridges Not Walls' (n 458) 208.

[861] UNESCO, 'Global Education Monitoring Report 2020' (n 90) 297.

[862] ibid 295.

[863] ibid.

[864] ibid 297.

[865] ibid.

[866] ibid.

[867] ibid.

[868] ibid.

[869] ibid 294.

[870] T Wood and others, *Change and Continuity in Australian Aid: What the Aid Flows Show* (Development Policy Centre, 11 January 2021) 28.

[871] UNESCO, 'TCG4: Development of SDG Thematic Indicator 4.b.2' (UNESCO, 16–18 January 2018) 4.

362 SDG 4

Ford Foundation's International Fellowship Program targets future leaders in activism and social change, and in this respect emphasizes the role of women, marginalized ethnic groups, and young people living in poverty or with a disability. In the ten years ending 2014, the Program had provided over 4,000 scholarships to young people from marginalized communities in twenty-two countries, most of which were developing countries.[872] Based in Japan, the Ashinaga Africa Initiative, which works with national governments, local NGOs, international universities, and other community-based officials, has sponsored 184 undergraduates from 44 countries since 2014. The vast majority are first-generation higher education students.[873] The (Pan-African) Regional Universities Forum for Capacity Building in Agriculture offers students from rural communities' postgraduate scholarships at universities in their locality or region. It provides access to degrees closely aligned with agricultural opportunities in students' communities, and has resulted in 75 per cent of graduates finding 'decent work'.[874]

d) Critique

Academic and policy-based commentary has pointed out various points of weakness or inadequacy in the design or the implementation of scholarship programmes. Research conducted by Rajika Bhandari has demonstrated a number of data gaps with respect to the national origins and the socio-economic characteristics of scholarship recipients.[875] Bhandari's research showed that of 111 total scholarship programmes identified internationally, fifty-four programmes were government-funded and met the criteria of target 4.b. For twenty-four programmes, some recipient data were missing.[876] While some programmes may be reluctant to disclose recipient data, many do not have quotas relating to these characteristics and thus the national origins and socio-economic backgrounds of students may not be monitored.[877] This hinders understanding of the extent to which scholarships are reaching the most disadvantaged students. Data on completion rates are tracked by nearly all programme providers, and rates are generally high, especially when compared to general undergraduate completion rates.[878] However, given the lack of data on recipient characteristics, 'high rates may reflect privileged backgrounds'.[879]

Further, current indicators give only a partial picture of the volume and type of scholarships. For example, by stating that scholarships must be 'available *to* developing countries', the target excludes large programmes where developing countries fund their citizens to study abroad'.[880] As enrolment must take place in 'developed ... [or] other

---

[872] Bhandari, 'Post-secondary Scholarships for Students from Developing Countries' (n 852) 543.
[873] UNESCO, 'Global Education Monitoring Report 2020' (n 90) 299.
[874] ibid 298.
[875] Bhandari, 'Post-Secondary Scholarships for Students from Developing Countries (n 852) 538.
[876] ibid 537.
[877] UNESCO, 'Global Education Monitoring Report 2016' (n 104) 323.
[878] UNESCO, 'Global Education Monitoring Report 2020' (n 90) 294.
[879] ibid 29.
[880] GEM Report, 'Target 4b—What Is at Stake for Monitoring Progress on Scholarships?' (*World Education Blog*, 12 October 2016) <https://gemreportunesco.wpcomstaging.com/2016/10/18/target-4-5-what-is-at-stake-for-monitoring-progress-on-equity-in-education/> accessed 28 September 2021.

developing countries,[881] programmes in which citizens of a developing country are funded, from whatever source, to study at home are also excluded. The narrow criteria of target 4.b may result in the diversion of resources to the international programmes recognized as 'counting' toward achieving 4.b, thus undermining domestic efforts.

Information regarding scholarship recipients' movements more than one year after graduation is scarce, however evidence indicates that many scholarship recipients do not return to their home countries.[882] This could suggest that an unintended consequence of scholarship programmes is to support the higher education institutions of richer countries instead of benefiting poorer ones.[883] Sending individuals from poor to rich countries for tertiary study may give rise to dependency and impoverishment, undermining efforts to build up tertiary education in developing countries.[884] Helena and Bagus suggest that 'low-income countries will remain passive consumers of knowledge produced elsewhere instead of having capacity to develop knowledge and solutions for their own settings and challenges'.[885] In the context of target 4.b, this may be exacerbated by poor articulation regarding the processes by which international scholarships will contribute to positive outcomes in the home country.[886]

It has also been pointed out that there is currently no single mechanism in place to monitor the number of scholarships available.[887] As target 4.b tracks only scholarship flows from ODA, private and philanthropic scholarships are excluded. This exclusion accords with the lack of obligation for such funders to 'substantially expand' the number of scholarships they offer.[888] However, as mentioned above, the availability of such scholarships can influence the flow of aid from donor countries.[889] Thus, a single mechanism to monitor the number of scholarships, as well as the characteristics of recipients, is necessary to fully understand contributions to target 4.b.

Further, the public and private mix of funding and administration is significant in evaluating the success and the effects of scholarship programmes. The private sector arguably plays a much more significant role globally. This is particularly evident in the developing world and in the domain of scholarships than in any other initiative connected with SDG 4 implementation. The scholarship landscape involves a mix of state-run programmes and programmes funded or administered by NGOs or private agencies. Some of the private parties involved are multinational corporations and some of those corporations' command larger budgets than small independent states. This includes the small states mentioned in target 4.b. Therefore, the private and the public

---

[881] UNESCO 'Official List of SDG 4 Indicators' (January 2021).

[882] UNESCO, 'Global Education Monitoring Report 2020' (n 90) 298; UNESCO, 'Global Education Monitoring Report 2016' (n 104) 320.

[883] Bhandari and others, *International Higher Education* (n 845); UNESCO, 'Global Education Monitoring Report' (n 457) 17–18.

[884] Heleta and Bagus (n 839) 165.

[885] ibid 163–68, 169.

[886] Campbell and Mawer (n 841) 170.

[887] UNESCO, 'Global Education Monitoring Report 2020' (n 90) 294; Bhandari, 'Post-Secondary Scholarships for Students from Developing Countries' (n 852); GEM Report, 'Target 4b—What Is at Stake for Monitoring Progress on Scholarships?' (n 880).

[888] UNESCO 'Official List of SDG 4 Indicators' (January 2021).

[889] GEM Report, 'Target 4b—What Is at Stake for Monitoring Progress on Scholarships?' (n 880).

interplay goes well beyond the private schooling sector, where communities of faith and secular entities are allowed to establish schools alongside those provided by the state, subject to various state regulations. Of course, the private sector plays a crucial role in the tertiary education sector of some states, including wealthy states such as the United States and the secondary sector of Australia. However, scholarship programmes might be seen as more targeted and precise in their adaptability.

Related to these general points about the role of the private sector, it should be stressed that the international scholarship programmes endorsed under target 4.b are aimed at individuals. Such scholarships are not intended for communities or whole populations, except in a 'trickle-down' fashion. It is, in a sense, an apparatus that responds to and nurtures the entrepreneurial, the gifted or the elite. As Campbell and Mawer observe, but apparently without meaning it as a criticism, '[t]arget 4.b is fundamentally about individuals'.[890] In particular, they assert that a properly educated person 'should have "other-regarding goals"'.[891] They should display an attitude aimed at 'enhanc[ing] human development in the world'.[892] While it may be difficult for those who share these authors' cultural world view to disagree with the spirit of this statement, it is uncomfortable for any academic commentator to presume to identify such a prescriptive, moralistic, universal agenda.

Moreover, in the context of scholarship programmes aimed at developing countries, such a prescription paradoxically reinforces the individualism or even messianism of the scholarship program in defining the recipient as an altruistic leader of their people, educated by benevolent aliens and then returned to their home. Given the global aims of the SDG project and the capacity of local communities to support educational initiatives, despite undoubted complexities and challenges, the attachment of the SDG project to the narrowly conceived and in many ways limited institution of the international scholarship, is disappointing. Target 4.b can only be expected to deliver incredibly mixed results even if achieved. Its inclusion in the SDG project must therefore be questioned.

10. Target 4.c By 2030, substantially increase the supply of qualified teachers, including through international cooperation for teacher training in developing countries, especially least-developed countries and small island developing States

a) Sources of target

The 'sources' of target 4.c are not entirely clear. Nevertheless, as a 'means of implementation', target 4.c focuses on the national supply of teachers at pre-primary, primary, and secondary levels trained to the national standard. National standards of teacher training in principle vary from one country to another, yet manifest various communalities. Decisions regarding the 'correct' way to educate teachers and the 'best' ratios of students per teacher may have been guided by developmental psychology research.

---

[890] Campbell and Mawer (n 841) 182.
[891] ibid 180 quoting M Walker, 'A Capital or Capabilities Education Narrative in a World of Staggering Inequalities?' (2012) 32(3) International Journal of Education Development 384, 389.
[892] Walker (n 891) 389.

Alternatively, they may represent conformity and even deference, a post-colonial adherence to the methods and models previously imposed by colonial rulers. At its worst, such methods may reflect a commitment to the educational structures and practices of a bygone era of colonialism that no longer manifests in those former colonial powers today.

Of course, it is important to remember that the state policies of the colonial powers themselves varied concerning the administration of education in their colonial possessions. Thus, the extreme centralization of education policy and practice, down to timetabling of required subject matter which remains a characteristic of metropolitan France, was imposed on its colonies in the South Pacific and elsewhere. Notably, there was a disregard for local culture and minimal accommodation made for time zones. Therefore, the post-colonial after-effects of the colonial era on education cannot be assumed to be the same across the former colonies of different European powers.

Beyond the question of post-colonial effects, all countries bear the imprint of earlier regimes and educational traditions. Such influences include ways that teachers are selected for training, the extent to which teacher education or training is integrated into the tertiary sector more broadly, and the content of the training. That said, even within the most wealthy countries, teacher education has undergone various changes of style from an 'apprenticeship' model focusing on the student-teacher learning 'on the job' from a practising senior colleague to a more institutionalized model of centralized and specialized education for future teachers, and various combinations of those techniques.

b) Statistical/empirical analysis

Data available on global indicator 4.c.1, which measures the 'proportion of teachers with the minimum required qualifications, by education level',[893] are limited. First, data are not available across all regions.[894] Secondly, the available information is not always comprehensive nor complete. For example, the 2020 report for the Democratic Republic of Congo simply noted that the teacher recruitment system had been reformed and that a quality assurance mechanism has been implemented.[895] Thirdly, some patterns in available data indicate dramatic year on year changes that do not appear to plausibly correspond to facts on the ground. For example, between 2010 and 2012, Cameroon indicated a 21 per cent increase in trained teachers and a decrease of the same percentage in 2015, followed by a rise of 23 per cent in 2017.[896] Such data must be considered unreliable.

The 2020 SDG Report indicates that globally 85 per cent of primary school teachers and 86 per cent of secondary school teachers received the minimum required

---

[893] UNESCO 'Official List of SDG 4 Indicators' (January 2021).

[894] UNESCO Institute for Statistics and UNESCO Global Education Monitoring Report 2019 'Meeting Commitments: Are Countries on Track to Achieve SDG 4?' (2019) 10.

[895] UN Sustainable Development Goals, 'Democratic Republic of Congo—Voluntary National Review 2020' (*UN*, 2020) <https://sustainabledevelopment.un.org/memberstates/drc> accessed 22 September 2021.

[896] UNESCO, 'Global Education Monitoring Report 2020' (n 90) 302.

366   SDG 4

training.[897] Based on the limited regional data available, Central Asia had the highest proportion of trained teachers both at primary and secondary levels.[898] Sub-Saharan Africa manifested the lowest proportion with 49 per cent of pre-primary, 64 per cent of primary, 58 per cent of lower secondary, and 43 per cent of upper secondary school teachers having received 'minimum training according to national standards'.[899]

The percentage of primary school teachers' globally receiving training according to national standards has remained at 85 per cent since 2015.[900] The lowest percentages recorded are 64 per cent in Sub-Saharan Africa and 72 per cent in Southern Asia.[901] Data indicate that pre-primary school teachers are less likely to be trained, even in high-income countries like Iceland, where only 64 per cent of pre-primary staff were trained.[902] It is therefore clear that pre-primary teaching is a 'poor relation' of school-based education globally.

c) Efforts taken at domestic and international level

While the coronavirus pandemic that began in the early months of 2020 had dramatic effects on many aspects of the delivery of education, the focus of target 4.c is particularly appropriate for examining both the difficulties and the occasional opportunities that have unfolded globally.[903] The onset of the coronavirus pandemic in 2020 brought new challenges for teachers, schools, and parents of school-age children worldwide. At various times in 2020, many school teachers and administrators had to switch rapidly, almost overnight, to new tools to deliver lessons, distribute content, correct and return homework, and communicate with students and parents. For the latter, whether teachers or not, to be unexpectedly working from home, alongside fulfilling caring responsibilities owed to other family members, has given rise to various difficulties which are relevant to the broader and the narrower goals of education.

Even among high-income countries, few could afford to upskill teachers at short notice in the manner called for in the 2020 pandemic period. In 2018, ahead of the pandemic, head teachers in the Netherlands reported that only 50 per cent of teachers had the technical and pedagogical skills to integrate digital devices in instruction.[904] In Japan, the figure was only 30 per cent.[905] Moreover, only 43 per cent of teachers in the United States felt prepared to facilitate remote learning, and only 20 per cent reported that school leaders provided adequate guidance.[906] In any case, teachers using

---

[897] UN, 'The Sustainable Development Goals Report 2020' (n 179) 33.

[898] UNESCO Institute for Statistics and UNESCO Global Education Monitoring Report 2019 'Meeting Commitments: Are Countries on Track to Achieve SDG 4?' (2019) 10.

[899] UNESCO, 'Global Education Monitoring Report 2020' (n 90) 302.

[900] Report of the Secretary-General, 'Progress Towards the Sustainable Development Goals' (2020) UN Doc E/20200/57.

[901] ibid.

[902] UNESCO, 'Global Education Monitoring Report 2020' (n 90) 300.

[903] UN, 'The Sustainable Development Goals Report 2020' (n 179) 37–38.

[904] UNESCO, 'Global Education Monitoring Report 2020' (n 90) 59.

[905] A Schleicher, *The Impact of COVID-20 on Education: Insights from Education at a Glance 2020* (General Secretary of the OECD 2020) 17.

[906] D Newton, 'Most Teachers Say They Are 'Not Prepared' To Teach Online' *Forbes* (New York, 26 March 2020) <https://www.forbes.com/sites/dereknewton/2020/03/26/most-teachers-say-they-are-not-prepared-to-teach-online/?sh=4c94a8bf7f2c> accessed 9 September 2021.

online platforms have had to learn much more during the crisis than merely a limited number of technical skills.[907] The kind of preparation and resourcing required for online teaching, the design of programmes and assessment, and the self-management skills of a teacher newly working from their home or other non-school settings were all challenges variously met. The attention possible to the individual learner's needs in a traditional classroom setting is a complex matter; the coronavirus pandemic has significantly reframed learning format by digital or other distance delivery. This has resulted in both negative and, at least in principle, positive effects. For instance, some teachers felt under pressure to deliver adequate educational experiences to most of their students resulting in the possible neglect of special learning requirements. However, others may have been able to exploit the individualization potential in digital delivery.

As Chabbot and Sinclair contend, the COVID-19 pandemic highlighted the weaknesses in relying on classroom-based learning for sustainable learning.[908] To meet SDG 4 commitments, immediate training is required for teachers to 'support home-based learning, including low-tech methods as needed to ensure equity'.[909] Some of what teachers and school administrators have learned, which may have included learning about their students' resilience, will surely provide food for thought concerning the future of educational delivery beyond the pandemic.

As noted above, national training standards vary dramatically, and there are a variety of methodological difficulties in comparing standards internationally. Thus, creating a worthwhile mapping of the minimum training levels for teachers worldwide is itself a challenge. In an attempt to coordinate streamlined data collection, the UIS has created the International Standard Classification for Teacher Training Programmes to develop a framework and a data collection strategy, with the aim of improving the monitoring of international teacher training across borders.[910]

d) Critique

Academic commentary on the 'implementation' indicators of target 4.c suggests that the indicators are narrow and, in some ways, superficial where taken as a measure to assess the quality of education being delivered.[911] Tatto argues that the focus should be shifted from quantitative measures to more 'meaningful and valid indicators' such as teacher qualities and the quality of the teacher's education, which she argues are neglected in SDG 4 targets.[912] For Tatto, the narrow and quantitative approach to the evaluation of education, as exemplified in target 4.c, refers only to the proportion of teachers who have minimum training but does not indicate the quality or focus of that

---

[907] UNESCO, 'Global Education Monitoring Report 2020' (n 90) 59.

[908] C Chabbot and M Sinclair, 'SDG 4 and the COVID-19 Emergency: Textbooks, Tutoring and Teachers' (2020) Prospects 1, 7.

[909] ibid.

[910] UNESCO Institute of Statistics, 'Classification Framework for Trained and Qualified Teachers' (2019) TCG6/REF/6.

[911] MT Tatto, 'Comparative Research on Teachers and Teacher Training Education: Global Perspectives to Inform UNESCO's SDG 4 Agenda' (2021) 47(1) Oxford Review of Education 25.

[912] ibid.

training.[913] Thus, it does not assist in tracking the implementation of processes for inclusion and equity.

The contrast drawn by Tatto between a quantitative versus a qualitative approach is undoubtedly simplistic; however, it touches on important issues, both methodological and ideological. The data underlying the evaluation of progress on the target 4.c indicators are admittedly impoverished in terms of methodology. Whether a teacher is trained or not is in effect reduced to a binary 'yes or no', as is the question of whether she has received 'training in pedagogy'.

Clearly, such minimalist data can give rise to superficial information at best, while the practical and fiscal reasons for such an approach are, of course, understood. In relation to ideology, the distinction drawn by Tatto is again simplistic yet not vacuous. For Tatto, a progressive approach to education stands in sharp contrast to an economic or 'econometric' approach.[914] The latter, she suggests, is characteristic of official policy in the less wealthy countries that are the particular focus of SDG 4. While not explored in Tatto's article, it may be assumed that the phenomenon she points to is a consequence of global policy in bodies such as the World Bank rather than Indigenous or otherwise cultural styles. In other words, the contrast Tatto points to is a dualism within Western or Northern political culture. Still, it remains a story about the imposition of certain Western values on Third World countries. Just as important, it is an account of the imposition of inadequate western values. The 'progressive' values are just as much western and northern (or European broadly understood). They reflect educational opinion as it emerged in the last few decades of the twentieth century in the United Kingdom in particular. It is not enough for academic criticism to call for statistical measures to be progressive or qualitative. Nor can global monitoring of educational provisions, to enhance its quality, adopt a qualitative methodology of rich and intensive data gathering, with all its ethical load and resource costs, as can be devoted to specific short-term research studies. Therefore, the impoverished character of the target 4.c measurements must always be kept front of mind in any consideration of its findings.

Tatto's concerns are echoed in the findings of a study into Ghana's approach to SDG 4. While policies implemented indicate a commitment to the achievement of SDG 4, Nketsia and others note the lack of focus in teacher education programmes.[915] They call for reforms that appeal to the four key concepts of SDG 4: quality, equity, inclusion, and lifelong learning, to promote inclusive education.[916]

Supporting the critical comments of Tatto noted above, it has been observed that the target 4.c indicator refers only to the proportion of teachers who have minimum training and gives no indication of the quality or focus of that training.[917] These relatively superficial data do not adequately assist in tracking the implementation of

---

[913] Unterhalter (n 306) 48.

[914] Tatto (n 911) 1.

[915] W Nketsia and others, '"Teacher Educators" and Teacher Trainees' Perspective on Teacher Training for Sustainable Development' (2020) 22(1) Journal of Teacher Education for Sustainability 49, 63.

[916] ibid.

[917] Unterhalter (n 306) 48.

processes for inclusion and equity.[918] This includes specialist training in cultural diversity, language, and teaching children with disabilities. Teachers ought to be trained on inclusion so that differentiating factors are not dealt with separately but rather become part of the core curriculum. Finally, '[s]uch programmes need to focus on tackling entrenched views of some students as deficient and unable to learn' in order to ensure no-one is left behind.[919]

[918] ibid.
[919] UNESCO, 'Global Education Monitoring Report 2020' (n 90) 136.

SDG 5

'Achieve Gender Equality and Empower All Women and Girls'

Rangita de Silva de Alwis

I. Introduction

The 2030 Agenda for Sustainable Development includes a stand-alone goal (Goal 5) on women's equality and empowerment which encompasses among other things, freedom from violence and gender-equal participation in political decision-making and in care-giving.[1]

Apart from the stand-alone goal, the SDGs require systematic mainstreaming of a gender perspective in the implementation of all the Sustainable Development Goals. Both elements converge in paragraph 20 of UN General Assembly Resolution 70/1:

> Realizing gender equality and the empowerment of women and girls will make a crucial contribution to progress across all the Goals and targets. The achievement of full human potential and of sustainable development is not possible if one half of humanity continues to be denied its full human rights and opportunities. Women and girls must enjoy equal access to quality education, economic resources, and political participation as well as equal opportunities with men and boys for employment, leadership, and decision-making at all levels. We will work for a significant increase in investments to close the gender gap and strengthen support for institutions in relation to gender equality and the empowerment of women at the global, regional, and national levels. All forms of discrimination and violence against women and girls will be eliminated, including through the engagement of men and boys. The systematic mainstreaming of a gender perspective in the implementation of the Agenda is crucial.[2]

The role of gender equality in the SDGs is fundamental to the realization of the goals. Pointed out by the General Assembly: 'Billions of our citizens continue to live in poverty and are denied a life of dignity. There are rising inequalities within and among

---

[1] 'The Sustainable Development Goals Report 2020: Achieve Gender Equality and Empower All Women and Girls' (*Unstats.un.org*, 2020) <https://unstats.un.org/sdgs/report/2020/goal-05/> accessed 26 May 2021.

[2] 'Resolution Adopted by the General Assembly on 25 September 2015: Transforming Our World: The 2030 Agenda for Sustainable Development' (*United Nations*, 2015) <https://www.un.org/en/development/desa/populat ion/migration/generalassembly/docs/globalcompact/A_RES_70_1_E.pdf> accessed 19 March 2023.

countries. There are enormous disparities of opportunity, wealth, and power. Gender inequality remains a key challenge.'[3] Goal 5 is a clear affirmation of gender equality as a fulcrum to the realization of the development goals. Throughout the SDGs we see an important acknowledgment that gender is only one axis of difference. Gender-based discrimination intersects with discrimination based on other grounds, such as race, ethnicity, religion, disability, indigenous group, marital status, or migration background. Finally, SDG implementation too, like human rights treaties must tackle, as a priority, the structural causes of inequality. In the words of the Committee on the Convention on the Elimination of Discrimination against Women (CEDAW): 'Realizing the full enjoyment of human rights by women is at the core of the 'transformative' impact of the Agenda 2030.'[4] At the heart of SDG 5 is the acknowledgment that historically unequal power relations between genders prevent the full advancement of women and stand in the way of sustainable development.

II. *Travaux Préparatoires*

SDG 5 builds on some of the targets that were enshrined in the MDGs, specifically MDG 3.[5] The MDGs were eight goals that UN Member States had agreed to achieve by 2015. Although interconnected to other Goals, MDG 3 interpreted gender equality very narrowly. A review of progress related to MDG 3 shows that progress towards gender equality was uneven over the lifetime of the MDGs. Gender equality and women's empowerment in the development agenda requires a human rights-based approach and requires support for and from the women's movement. The Outcome document of the United Nations Conference on Sustainable Development in Rio de Janeiro from 20 to 22 June 2012, was entitled 'The Future We Want' and it stated: 'We underscore that women have a vital role to play in achieving[6] sustainable development. We recognize the leadership role of women and we resolve to promote gender equality[7] and women's empowerment and to ensure their full and effective participation in sustainable development policies, programmes and decision-making at all levels.'[8]

A thirty-member Open Working Group (OWG) of the General Assembly was tasked with preparing a proposal on the SDGs. The Open Working Group was established on 22 January 2013 by decision 67/555 (see A/67/L.48/rev.1) of the General Assembly.

---

[3] ibid.

[4] 'Convention on the Elimination of All Forms of Discrimination Against Women' (*OHCHR*, 1979) <https://www.ohchr.org/en/professionalinterest/pages/cedaw.aspx> accessed 19 March 2023.

[5] Through the four-year process that led to the adoption of the SDGs, policy-makers, researchers, and civil society activists analysed the gaps in the MDGs in order to build a stronger set of goals. Two main goals emerged: to correctly address the structural barriers to gender equality and to address Goal 5 in alignment with the Beijing Platform and the CEDAW. The SDGs must be aligned with human rights standards, including the CEDAW.

[6] 'Attain' was replaced with 'achieve'.

[7] Gender equality is the full realization of women's and girls' human rights and the empowerment of women and girls everywhere.

[8] By 2030, the goal is to eliminate all harmful practices, especially those relating to children, early and forced marriage, and Female Genital Mutilation (FGM) and Honour Killings.

The Co-Chairs' summary bullet points for OWG-8 states that '[g]ender equality was affirmed as an end in itself and as an essential means for sustainable development and poverty eradication. There can be no sustainable development without gender equality and the full participation of women and girls. Gender inequality is the most pervasive form of inequality in the world.' Rightly did the OWG emphasize the synergies between gender equality and sustainable development given the evidence about gender equality's substantial contribution to the realization of inclusive and progressive human development. As the Technical Support Team (TST) reported,[9] for instance, women's participation in public administration is more likely to lead to better allocation of public resources that promote human development priorities such as children's health, nutrition, and access to employment. Strikingly, a positive correlation is found between women's empowerment, environmental sustainability, and achieving food security when women participate in the governance of natural resources through local institutions and have access to and control over agricultural assets and productive resources. By extension, when gender gaps are eliminated in the administration of economic, social, and environmental fields, the structural transformation of countries not only becomes feasible but yields long-term benefits for the entire society. Gender equality contributes to poverty reduction, economic growth, and democratic governance. To this end, it was important that the Working Group emphasized that gender equality, women's rights, and women's empowerment in the SDGs must be aligned with CEDAW, the Beijing Platform for Action (BPfA), and the International Conference on Population and Development (ICPD). Policy action for gender equality should be founded on the mutually enforcing relationship between the human rights and the sustainable development frameworks.[10]

In the light of the centrality of gender equality for the post-2015 development agenda for all countries, delegates to the OWG supported the proposal for a stand-alone goal on gender equality while others were strongly in favour of a twin-track approach, as agreed in the BPfA—that is mainstreaming gender equality across all other SDGs. Leaving the question of a stand-alone or cross-cutting goal aside for the time being, it was accepted that common denominators of either approach should be the issues of violence against women and girls; their participation in the public and private spheres; their economic empowerment; social protection and access to quality education; and sexual and reproductive health and rights.[11] As dialogue progressed, three core priority areas were proposed for a stand-alone goal: (i) freedom from violence against women and girls; (ii) equality in human capabilities, access to opportunities and resources; and (iii) equality in agency, voice, and participation across the full range of decision-making platforms. Simultaneously, the elimination of gender-based discrimination in the country's developmental strategy as a whole did not lose momentum. A gender mainstreaming strategy was important for integrating gender perspectives

---

[9] OWG 8th Session, 'TST Issues Brief: Gender Equality and Women's Empowerment', 3.
[10] ibid 3, 7.
[11] ibid 5.

374   SDG 5

and realizing women's and girls' rights, as codified in human rights treaties, in subject-specific policy actions be they environmental and climate policies, the regulation of the labour market of macroeconomic policies, to name a few.[12] To be true, though, while SDG Goal 5 is seen to complement the CEDAW and the BPfA, more must be done to interpret these goals according to these standard-setting frameworks.

At the 9th OWG session, gender equality and women's empowerment comprised Focus Area 5 and a clear link was established with the Focus Areas on poverty eradication, food security and nutrition, health and population dynamics, education, water and sanitation, economic growth and employment, inclusive societies, the rule of law, and capable institutions.[13] Negotiations of the exact wording of a Goal under Focus Area 5 and the targets it would include took place at the 10th OWG session. Member States, Major Groups, and other stakeholders submitted their proposed targets that corresponded to the eleven identified focus points on the issue of gender equality and women's empowerment, as reported in Encyclopedia Groupinica.[14] A preliminary version of Goal 5 reads: 'Attain gender equality and women's empowerment everywhere.' The more specific targets included:[15]

1. by 2030 end all forms of discrimination against women of all ages
2. by 2030 end violence against women and girls in all its forms
3. by 2030 ensure equal access to education at all levels
4. by 2030 ensure equal employment opportunities for women and equal pay for equal work
5. by 2030 ensure equal access to, and control of, assets and resources, including natural resources management
6. ensure equal participation and leadership of women in decision-making in public and private institutions
7. by 2030 end child, early and forced marriage
8. by 2030 reduce the burden of unpaid care work
9. by 2030 ensure universal access to sexual and reproductive health and reproductive rights
10. promote the availability of gender disaggregated data to improve gender equality policies, including gender sensitive budgeting

It was at the 12th OWG session where the Goal underwent changes in its wording and where targets were made concrete. Women's groups and others proposed the rewording of the goal to '*Achieve* gender equality, *the full realization of all* women and girls' *human rights and their* empowerment'. The goal now comprised eleven targets,

---

[12] ibid 5–8.
[13] OWG 10th session, Annex 1. Interlinkages, 1.
[14] Enyclopedia Groupinica: A Compilation of Goals and Targets Suggestions from OWG-10 in response to Co-Chairs' Focus Area Document dated 19 March 2014, 48–58.
[15] OWG 11th session, Working Document for 5–9 May Session of the OWG.

the majority of which were time-bound, having 2030 or 2020 as the deadline for their achievement.[16] For instance, target 5.1 read: 'by 2030 end all forms of discrimination against all women and girls of all ages'; target 5.6 (resembling now target 5.4) read: 'by 2030 reduce and redistribute unpaid domestic care and domestic work through shared responsibility by states, private sector, communities, and men and women'; target 5.8 (now 5.5.) read: 'by 2020 endure full, equal and effective participation and leadership of women and girls at all levels of decision-making in the public and private spheres, including in conflict prevention, mediation and resolution'. Nevertheless, stakeholders' individual interests in what should be included in the targets and how it would be phrased was also evident. Controversial points were 'early marriage', which India argued was hard to define. Target 5.4 about unpaid work was compromised with the insertion of the clause 'as nationally appropriate' after objections by Egypt, Iran, Indonesia, and Saudi Arabia to the more ground-breaking wording of the target that would acknowledge the value of unpaid care and domestic work, as well as shared responsibility within the household and the family. Still, sexual and reproductive health and rights were the most controversial. Given that the right to legal and safe abortion and the right to birth control fell within the scope of reproductive rights, states where religious and cultural beliefs forbid them opposed strongly any reference to reproductive and sexual rights. Countries from the Middle East (Saudi Arabia and Qatar) took this approach, arguing further that an agreement on universal access to sexual and reproductive health and rights would never be achieved so the target should be eliminated. Similarly, the Holy See and Nigeria claimed that reproductive rights shouldn't be included in the SDGs since the Rio + 20 document did not refer to them at all. Finally, Southern African and Eastern states suggested using language agreed upon at the ICPD in 1994. In the end, reproductive rights but not sexual rights found their place in target 5.6 despite some countries' continuous opposition to the adoption of the target as whole.[17]

Goal 5 was finally adopted in its current form, including six substantive and three means-of-implementation targets.

III. Commentary on the Goal

A. Comparison with MDG

The predecessor of SDG Goal 5 is the Millennium Development Goal (MDG) Goal 3, which sought to promote gender equality and empower women.[18] MDG 3 included one

---

[16] For complete list of amendments to the Goal, see OWG 12th session (Morning Hearings with Major Groups and other Stakeholders, 16–20 June 2014), 'Compilation of Amendments to Goals and Targets' 17–18.

[17] M Kamau and others, *Transforming Multilateral Diplomacy—The Inside Story of the Sustainable Development Goals* (Routledge 2018) 220–21.

[18] 'United Nations Millennium Development Goals' (*United Nations*, 2021) <https://www.un.org/millenniumgoals/gender.shtml> accessed 2 June 2021.

target, target 3.a, which set out to 'eliminate gender disparity in primary and secondary education, preferably by 2005, and in all levels of education no later than 2015'. The MDG framework employed a cross-cutting approach and had gender-related targets under goals that were devoted to other thematic areas: for instance, target 1.b ('Achieve full and productive employment and decent work for all, including women and young people'), target 2.a ('Ensure that, by 2015, children everywhere, boys and girls alike, will be able to complete a full course of primary schooling'), target 5.a ('Reduce by three quarters, between 1990 and 2015, the maternal mortality ratio'), and target 5.b ('Achieve, by 2015, universal access to reproductive health').[19] Critics have argued that this selection of thematic areas 'focused attention on the developing world' and 'effectively [narrowed] the focus on gender issues'.[20] Prioritizing these specific issues 'arguably incentivized states to focus their efforts and scarce resources on activities that would "count" ' for the purposes of the MDGs—at the expense of a broader approach to addressing gender concerns trained on deeper culture change'.[21]

This flaw has been addressed to a certain extent in the 2030 Agenda, as the range of thematic areas concerning gender in the SDG regime is broader than that of the MDG: while education has been migrated to SDG Goal 4 (the education goal), gender issues including gender discrimination, violence, harmful practices, unpaid care and domestic work, sexual and reproductive health and rights, economic empowerment, political participation, and access to Information and Communication Technologies (ICTs) have been assigned individual targets and indicators under SDG 5. The SDG framework, formulated based on a global development agenda, also represents a shift from focusing on developing world issues to universal gender issues. But, as the discussion below will show, what SDG 5 covers does not constitute an exhaustive list of gender issues that require attention and are indispensable to achieving gender equality, such as women's role in peace-making and conflict situations and the root causes of discrimination and violence against women.

The SDG regime, consistent with the previous MDG regime, also adopts a cross-cutting approach: more than half of the other SDGs have targets that mention women and/or gender (SDG 1 on poverty, SDG 2 on hunger, SDG 4 on education, SDG 6 on clean water and sanitation, SDG 8 on decent work and economic growth, SDG 11 on sustainable cities and communities, SDG 13 on climate action, and SDG 17 on partnerships for the goals). This approach embodies the recognition of the 'overarching, cross-cutting nature of gender and the gendered impacts of environmental, social, and economic concerns'.[22]

A major improvement of the SDG regime is the introduction of legal and regulatory frameworks in place as a measurement of progress. In the previous MDG regime, this

[19] ibid.
[20] K Morrow, 'Gender and the Sustainable Development Goals' (2018) Sustainable Development Goals 149.
[21] ibid.
[22] 'Feminist Critiques of the Sustainable Development Goals Analysis and Bibliography' (*Genderandsecurity.org*, 2017) <https://genderandsecurity.org/projects-resources/annotated-bibliographies/feminist-critiques-sustainable-development-goals> accessed 19 March 2023.

element was glaringly absent. The SDG regime acknowledges the fundamental importance of national legislations in ensuring gender equality and women's empowerment, and has under SDG 5 four indicators that measure the level of legal support in a specific area: indicator 5.1.1 (anti-discrimination laws), indicator 5.6.2 (laws and regulations for sexual and reproductive health and rights), indicator 5.a.2 (land right laws), and indicator 5.c.1 (gender budget and oversight programmes). In this sense, the SDG 5 framework combines both top-down and bottom-up measurements that examine both national efforts (laws, regulations, policies, etc) and the actual experience of women and girls (surveys on violence, early marriages, domestic work, etc).

B. A Goal-based Approach

The 2030 Agenda uses a 'target-based, indicator-driven' model. The advantages of such a model are obvious: indicators can communicate progress achieved and what remains to be worked on clearly, and indicators measurement enables comparisons across different regions and countries, and facilitates the allocation of resources. Yet, this indicator-driven model also has the danger of incentivizing countries, especially those with limited means, to focus resources and efforts on the targets and indicators that are more easily quantified and measurable at the expense of other more qualitative targets and indicators.[23] UN agencies' media publications illustrate this point. In the wake of the COVID-19 pandemic, several agencies issued reports that shed light on how the pandemic affected women and girls. What receive the most attention in these reports are usually those indicators where impact can be readily measured and translated into numbers, such as violence and domestic care.[24]

Another weakness of the indicator-centred approach is that it relies heavily on the quantity and quality of data. As Morrow points out, '[d]ata science has struggled to keep pace with the relatively modest demands of monitoring the MDG targets/indicators set, with data disaggregation, in particular, proving problematic with respect to gender throughout the duration of the MDGs'.[25] According to UN Women, as of December 2020, it has 39 per cent of the gender data needed to monitor the SDGs.[26] Data shortage is also a problem for two-thirds of the indicators for gender equality and women's empowerment, and no region had data available for even half of the gender indicators.[27] As will be discussed in the Targets section in Section IV of this

[23] Morrow (n 20) 159.
[24] 'Goal 5 | Department of Economic and Social Affairs' (*United Nations*, 2021) <https://sdgs.un.org/goals/goal5>; 'UN Women from Insights to Action: Gender Equality in the Wake of COVID-19' (*UN Women*, 2021) <https://www.unwomen.org/sites/default/files/Headquarters/Attachments/Sections/Library/Publications/2020/Gender-equality-in-the-wake-of-COVID-19-References-en.pdf> accessed 19 March 2023.
[25] Morrow (n 20) 160.
[26] J Encarnacion and S Maskey, 'We Now Have More Gender-Related SDG Data Than Ever, but Is It Enough?' (*UN Women Data Hub*, 6 May 2021) <https://data.unwomen.org/features/we-now-have-more-gender-related-sdg-data-ever-it-enough> accessed 19 March 2023.
[27] ibid.

378 SDG 5

chapter, many indicators fail to capture fully the ambitious, rosy picture painted by the Target statement, and using the indicators as the sole measurement increases the risks of reductionism and 'extreme simplification of ... often complex areas of social endeavour'.[28]

C. A Mainstream Growth-oriented Approach Rather than Tackling Structural Challenges

Another frequently discussed flaw of the SDGs is that they abide by the mainstream growth-oriented development model:

> There is no fundamental challenge in the SDGs to the economic model of development pursued over the past forty years, which has focused on resource-intensive economic growth as a pre-condition for progressive (redistributive) policies. Authors point out that the 2030 Agenda does not present a strategy for structural reform to tackle poverty and inequality, nor does it challenge existing trade, tax or financial architectures. In that sense, the Agenda thus fails to provide the right 'enabling environment', as well as the necessary financing, for the realization of women's rights.[29]

> The 2030 Agenda seems to take for granted some key elements of the currently dominant economic agenda, centered on continued growth, trade liberalization, and 'partnerships' with the private sector. Past experience suggests that more of the same is unlikely to provide an enabling environment for gender equality and the realization of women's economic and social rights. The hard won gains and vision of the SDGs will be difficult to realize unless the dominant economic model is revised.[30]

D. Neglect of a Structural Lens

Several feminist critics also lament the SDG framework for failing to acknowledge economic and social structures as contributing to and exacerbating gender imbalance.[31] Many existing systemic economic and social models breed and perpetuate gender inequalities, but the SDGs do not do enough to recognize this as the underlying cause of challenges which will be discussed later.

Relatedly, the SDG regime also neglects the historic power relations that underpin obstacles to women's empowerment. It fails adequately to identify broader and

---

[28] Morrow (n 20) 162.

[29] V Esquivel and C Sweetman, 'Gender and the Sustainable Development Goals' (2016) 24 Gender & Development 1.

[30] S Razavi, 'The 2030 Agenda: Challenges of Implementation to Attain Gender Equality and Women's Rights' (2016) 24 Gender & Development 25.

[31] 'Feminist Critiques of the Sustainable Development Goals Analysis and Bibliography' (n 22) 4.

intersectional 'power relations between the North and the South, between the rich and the poor, and between men and women'.[32] In particular, it is paramount to understand that the unequal power relations between men and women perpetuate gender inequality, and 'a focus only on the immediate problems of individual women and girls will fail if these power relations are not transformed'.[33]

Central to inequality and gender-based violence is the acknowledgment of intersectional identity which sees identity as forming at the intersections of axes such as sex, race, ethnicity, class, and sexuality. The Declaration on the Elimination of Violence against Women (DEVAW) draws the links between violence against women and the systemic structures. The Preamble to DEVAW states categorically that:

> [v]iolence against women is a manifestation of historically unequal power relations between men and women, which have led to domination over and discrimination against women by men and to the prevention of the full advancement of women, and that violence against women is one of the crucial social mechanisms by which women are forced into a subordinate position compared with men.

Likewise, regional human rights treaties such as the Preamble to Belém do Pará acknowledges that 'violence against women ... [is] a manifestation of the historically unequal power relations between women and men'. This acknowledgment recognizes that certain groups of women, such as those from racial or ethnic minorities, or other marginalized groups, may require special protection from violence.[34]

E. Human Rights

Despite the progress in reframing SDGs within a rights-based approach, feminist scholars criticise the SDG regime for failing to truly integrate a rights-based approach. The Women's Major Group (WMG), a network of feminist civil society organizations

---

[32] V Esquivel, 'Power and the Sustainable Development Goals: A Feminist Analysis' (2016) 24 Gender & Development 9.

[33] E Stuart and J Woodroffe, 'Leaving No-One Behind: Can the Sustainable Development Goals Succeed Where the Millennium Development Goals Lacked?' (2016) 24 Gender & Development 69.

[34] The CEDAW Committee has identified intersectionality as a basic concept for the understanding of the scope of States Parties' obligations. General Recommendation 28 of the CEDAW states that intersectionality is a basic concept for understanding the scope of the general obligations of States Parties contained in Article 2. The discrimination against women based on sex and gender is inextricably linked with other factors that affect women. In other words, gender falls under the purview of a prohibited category of discrimination including but not limited to race, marital status, pregnancy, HIV status, sexual orientation, or any other status, attribute, or characteristic. A good practice example of an intersectional equal protection clause is Section 15 of the Canadian Charter which affirms: 'Every individual is equal before the law and under the law and has the right to the equal protection and equal benefit of the law without discrimination and, in particular, without discrimination based on race, national or ethnic origin, colour, religion, sex, age, or mental or physical disability.' More recently, the Egyptian Constitution of 2014 covers gender and persons with disability in its equal protection clause. All citizens are equal before the law. They are equal in rights, freedoms, and general duties, without discrimination based on religion, belief, sex, origin, race, colour, language, disability, social class, political or geographic affiliation, or any other.

focusing on gender equality and female empowerment and an active participant in the SDG negotiation process, observes that the SDG framework failed to adequately address human rights issues:

> The SDGs do not fully aim to protect and fulfil human rights for all which should be at the centre of a socially just and ecologically sustainable development agenda as well as the means for achieving it. The recognition of Women's and Girls' human rights in the title of Goal 5 on gender equality, the human right to food, the right to water and sanitation as a goal, women's rights to decision making on peace and security, the rights of indigenous peoples, and the right for women to control their sexuality free of coercion, discrimination and violence ... amongst others are notably absent.[35]

Critics point to the absence of human rights discourse in the formulation of SDG 5 and its targets. Morrow refers to this as an 'arguable devaluation of gender issues by dissociating them from the recognised realm of human rights'.[36] Kabeer acknowledges the combination of a stand-alone goal dedicated to gender equality/women's empowerment and gender-related targets for other goals, but argues that the current framework is 'a watered-down version of feminist demands since the rights perspective is largely missing'.[37]

IV. Targets and Indicators of Goal 5

A. Overview

SDG 5 encompasses nine targets and fourteen indicators. A wide range of agencies monitor the indicators depending on their areas of competence, including UN Women, World Bank, OECD Development Centre, World Health Organization (WHO), UNICEF, United Nations Population Fund (UNFPA), United Nations Office on Drugs and Crime (UNDOC), UNDP, United Nations Statistics Division (UNSD), ILO (International Labour Organization), FAO (Food and Agriculture Organisation), and ITU (International Telecommunication Union).

---

[35] 'Women's "8 Red Flags" Following the Conclusion of the Open Working Group on Sustainable Development Goals (SDGs)' (*Women's Major Group*, 21 July 2014) <https://www.womensmajorgroup.org/wp-content/uploads/2014/07/Womens-Major-Group_OWG_FINALSTATEMENT_21July.pdf> accessed 19 March 2023.

[36] Morrow (n 20) 170.

[37] N Kabeer, 'Gender Equality, The MDGs and The SDGs: Achievements, Lessons and Concerns—IGC' (*IGC*, 1 October 2015) <https://www.theigc.org/blog/gender-equality-the-mdgs-and-the-sdgs-achievements-lessons-and-concerns/> accessed 19 March 2023.

B. Analysis and Critique of Each Target

1. Target 5.1 End all forms of discrimination against all women and girls everywhere

a) Sources of the target

International human rights law prohibits discrimination on the basis of sex. The Convention on the Elimination of All Forms of Discrimination Against Women (CEDAW) commits states to eliminate discrimination against women, and defines 'discrimination against women' as 'any distinction, exclusion or restriction made on the basis of sex which has the effect or purpose of imparting or nullifying the recognition, enjoyment or exercise by women, irrespective of their marital status, on a basis of equality of men and women, of human rights and fundamental freedoms in the political, economic, social, cultural, civil or any other field'.[38] This definition covers both *de jure* (direct) and *de facto* (indirect) discrimination.

b) Empirical analysis

Around the world, more than 2.5 million women and girls are impacted by discriminatory laws and the lack of legal support.[39] Gender disparity in laws correlate with lower levels of education for girls, fewer female skills workers, fewer women landowners, fewer women accessing financial and health services, and more women threatened with violence.

Indicator 5.1.1 is dedicated to measuring a country's level of anti-discrimination legislations ('whether or not legal frameworks are in place to promote, enforce and monitor equality and non-discrimination on the basis of sex').[40] The legal framework is defined broadly and covers laws mechanisms, polices and plans to 'promote, enforce and monitor' gender equality.[41] Specifically, legal frameworks that promote gender equality are those that 'establish women's equal rights with men and entire non-discrimination on the basis of sex', and legal frameworks that 'enforce and monitor' gender equality are those that those that aim at the 'realisation of equality and non-discrimination and implementation of laws, such as policies/plans, establishment of enforcement and monitoring mechanisms, and allocation of financial resources'.[42]

As discussed below, there are two related indicators which also address legal frameworks and policies at the national level: indicator 5.6.2 and indicator 5.a.2. The former measures the number of countries with laws and regulations that guarantee full and equal access to women and men aged fifteen years and older to sexual and reproductive

---

[38] 'Convention on the Elimination of All Forms of Discrimination Against Women' (n 4) arts 1 and 2.

[39] 'Equality in Law for Women and Girls by 2030' (*UN Women*, January 2019) <https://www.unwomen.org/sites/default/files/Headquarters/Attachments/Sections/Library/Publications/2019/Equality-in%20law-for-women-and-girls-en.pdf> accessed 19 March 2023.

[40] 'SDG Indicator Metadata' (*Unstats.un.org*, 1 April 2021) <https://unstats.un.org/sdgs/metadata/files/Metadata-05-01-01.pdf> accessed 21 November 2020.

[41] ibid.

[42] ibid.

382   SDG 5

healthcare, information, and education, and the latter the proportion of countries where the legal framework guarantees some equal rights to land ownership and/or control. To avoid duplication, indicator 5.1.1 complements these indicators and covers non-discriminatory laws not addressed by these two indicators.

Assessment of the indicator is performed by participating countries, using a questionnaire of forty-five 'yes/no' questions covering four areas of law: (i) overarching legal frameworks and public life; (ii) violence against women; (iii) employment and economic benefits; and (iv) marriage and family.[43] The areas of law and questions are based on international gender equality instruments, in particular the CEDAW and the BPfA.[44] The score (0–100) represents the percentage of achievement of a country in one specific area of law.[45] UN Women, World Bank, and the OECD Development Centre are responsible for the data compiling and global monitoring for this indicator.

The SDG Open Datahub displays the scores of countries with available data. For (i) overarching legal frameworks and public life, four countries (Croatia, El Salvador, Spain, Albania) achieve a full score.[46] More than half countries achieve a score higher than 60 in this area.[47] The lowest score reported, 9.09, comes from United Arab Emirates.[48] For (ii) violence against women, only Australia has a full score.[49] The lowest score obtained in this area of law is 33.33 (Jordan, Madagascar, United Arab Emirates, United Republic of Tanzania).[50] For (iii) employment and economic benefits, thirteen countries achieve full score.[51] More than half countries have a score of 60 or higher.[52] One country (Pakistan) scores 0 on this metric.[53] For (iv) marriage and family, five countries achieve full score (Costa Rica, El Salvador, India, Kenya, Panama).[54] The lowest score is 9.09 from Cameroon.

---

[43] ibid.

[44] ibid.

[45] ibid 6.

[46] 'Indicator 5.1.1: Legal Frameworks That Promote Enforce and Monitor Gender Equality (Percentage of Achievement 0–100)Area 1: Overarching Legal Frameworks and Public Life' (*UNSD*) <https://unstats-undesa.opendata.arcgis.com/datasets/indicator-5-1-1-legal-frameworks-that-promote-enforce-and-monitor-gender-equality-percentage-of-achievement-0-100-area-1-overarching-legal-frameworks-and-public-life-3/explore?location=-39.340926%2C-23.658365%2C8.63&showTable=true> accessed 21 November 2020.

[47] ibid.

[48] ibid.

[49] 'Indicator 5.1.1: Legal Frameworks That Promote Enforce and Monitor Gender Equality (Percentage of Achievement 0–100) Area 2: Violence Against Women' (*UNSD*) <https://unstats-undesa.opendata.arcgis.com/datasets/indicator-5-1-1-legal-frameworks-that-promote-enforce-and-monitor-gender-equality-percentage-of-achievement-0-100-area-2-violence-against-women-3> accessed 21 November 2020.

[50] ibid.

[51] 'Indicator 5.1.1: Legal Frameworks That Promote Enforce and Monitor Gender Equality (Percentage of Achievement 0–100)Area 3: Employment and Economic Benefits'(*UNSD*) <https://unstats-undesa.opendata.arcgis.com/datasets/indicator-5-1-1-legal-frameworks-that-promote-enforce-and-monitor-gender-equality-percentage-of-achievement-0-100-area-3-employment-and-economic-benefits-3> accessed 21 November 2020.

[52] ibid.

[53] ibid.

[54] 'Indicator 5.1.1: Legal Frameworks That Promote Enforce and Monitor Gender Equality (Percentage of Achievement 0–100) Area 4: Marriage and Family' (*UNSD*) <https://unstats-undesa.opendata.arcgis.com/datasets/indicator-5-1-1-legal-frameworks-that-promote-enforce-and-monitor-gender-equality-percentage-of-achievement-0-100-area-4-marriage-and-family-3> accessed 21 November 2020.

TARGETS AND INDICATORS 383

Additional data from UN Women shows that forty-nine countries still lack laws protecting women from domestic violence.[55] In eighteen economies, husbands can legally prevent their wives from working.[56] In thirty-nine countries, daughters and sons do not have equal inheritance rights.[57] Additionally, women cannot perform the following activities in the same way or on an equal basis as men:[58]

- Apply for a passport in thirty-seven countries
- Inherit equally as a spouse in thirty-six countries
- Be head of household or family in thirty-one countries
- Get a job or pursue a trade or profession in eighteen countries
- Travel outside their home in seventeen countries
- Obtain a national ID card in eleven countries
- Register a business in four countries
- Open a bank account in three countries

Though not designated as an official data provider, SDG-tracker, a collaborative initiative between the University of Oxford and Global Change Data Lab, also provides data on anti-discrimination laws around the world, which may be relevant for assessing progress made on this target:

- *Area 1: overarching legal frameworks and public life* Data collected up to 2017 indicate that most countries, except for Saudi Arabia, have granted suffrage to women (there are no data on Greenland).[59] For non-discrimination clause in the constitution, data collected up to 2015 show that the results are mixed, clearly less ideal than the universal suffrage situation.[60] Some countries fall into the clear 'yes' category ('use either the word discrimination or the word nondiscrimination or even when there is a "clawback" provision granting exceptions to the nondiscrimination clause for certain areas of the law, such as inheritance, family and customary law'), while some fall into the no category ('there is no nondiscrimination provision, or the nondiscrimination language is present in the preamble but not in an article of the constitution, or there is a provision that merely stipulates that the sexes are equal, or the sexes have equal rights and obligations').[61] Data collected up to 2015

---

[55] 'Turning Promises into Action: Gender Equality in the 2030 Agenda for Sustainable Development' (*UN Women*, 2021) <https://www.unwomen.org/sites/default/files/Headquarters/Attachments/Sections/Library/Publications/2018/SDG-report-Fact-sheet-Europe-and-Northern-America-en.pdf> accessed 19 March 2023.

[56] ibid.

[57] ibid.

[58] 'Equality in Law for Women and Girls by 2030' (n 39).

[59] 'Universal Suffrage Granted to Women' (*Our World in Data*, 2021) <https://ourworldindata.org/grapher/universal-suffrage-granted-to-women?time=2017> accessed 21 November 2020.

[60] 'Does Nondiscrimination Clause Mention Gender in the Constitution?' (*Our World in Data*, 2021) <https://ourworldindata.org/grapher/nondiscrimination-clause-gender?tab=table&time=earliest.latest> accessed 21 November 2020.

[61] ibid.

384 SDG 5

indicate that in most countries, the law does not differentiate between a woman's and a man's testimony in terms of its evidentiary value.[62] A few African and Middle Eastern countries give less weight to a woman's testimony.[63]

- **Area 2: violence against women** The Tunisian law on violence against women, including domestic violence, passed by the parliament on 26 July 2017, was a landmark step for women's rights.[64] It was a long time coming and was preceded by a decade-long struggle by women to create a normative and legal framework to address violence against women. The law defines violence against women as 'any physical, moral, sexual or economic aggression against women based on discrimination between the two sexes and resulting in damage or physical, sexual, psychological or economic suffering to the woman, including threats of such aggression, pressure or deprivation of rights and freedoms, both in public and private life'. The law also criminalizes sexual harassment in public spaces, and the employment of children as domestic workers. The law includes preventive measures, such as directing the Health Ministry to create programmes to train medical staff on how to detect, evaluate, and prevent violence against women and educators on requirements under Tunisian and international law.

  The law includes assistance to domestic violence survivors, including legal, medical, and mental health support. The restraining orders against their abusers require the suspected offender to vacate the home, stay away from the victim and their children, and refrain from violence, threats, damaging property, or contacting the victim, and are important ways in protect the victim under international law.

  Additionally, the law establishes family violence units within Tunisia's Internal Security Forces to process domestic violence complaints and assigning a public prosecutor in each governorate to handle such complaints. The law also prevents mandatory mediation of cases of domestic violence by providing for criminal liability for any official authority who might coerce a woman to drop her complaint or charge.

- **Area 3: employment and economic benefits** Enacting laws that mandate nondiscrimination based on gender in hiring is not a universal practice. Most African countries lack such law; Canada, Russia, and many Middle-East countries also fail to enact such laws.[65] Data collected between 2013 and 2015 indicate that less than half the countries have laws mandating equal pay.[66] Europe and South America fare better in this metric, while most Asian countries don't have such a

---

[62] 'Does a Woman's Testimony Carry the Same Evidentiary Weight in Court as a Man's?' (*Our World in Data*, 2021) <https://ourworldindata.org/grapher/testimony-weight-gender> accessed 21 November 2020.

[63] ibid.

[64] 'Tunisia Passes Historic Law to End Violence Against Women and Girls' (*UN Women*, 10 August 2017) <http://www.unwomen.org/en/news/stories/2017/8/news-tunisia-law-on-ending-violence-against-women?> accessed 7 August 2021.

[65] 'Does the Law Mandate Nondiscrimination Based on Gender in Hiring?' (*Our World in Data*, 2021) <https://ourworldindata.org/grapher/law-mandate-nondiscrimination-hiring?time=2015> accessed 4 June 2021.

[66] 'Does the Law Mandate Equal Remuneration for Females and Males for Work of Equal Value?' (*Our World in Data*, 2021) <https://ourworldindata.org/grapher/law-mandate-equal-pay> accessed 4 June 2021.

law.[67] Most countries have laws that provide for the equal ownership rights for men and women, except for a few South American and African countries.[68]

- *Area 4: marriage and family life* In every country in the world, family law is a locus of gender discrimination and magnifies the unequal status of women in the economic sphere. The elimination of discrimination against women in areas of citizenship, marriage, divorce, succession, inheritance, travel, and customary law will have major ramifications on women's lives, their communities, and their economies.

Data collected up to 2015 show that not all countries have legislations that explicitly criminalize marital rape.[69] Most African and Asian countries don't have such legal protection against rape in place.[70] Although most countries don't have legal requirements that married women obey their husbands, a few African and Middle Eastern countries still have such provisions in the law requiring a wife's obedience.[71] Data collected up to 2015 show that most countries have laws mandating paid or unpaid maternity leave.[72] The United States, Australia, Suriname, Portugal, and Norway still lack such mandates in their laws.[73]

c) Efforts taken at international and national level

China Between 2015 and 2020, there are several highlights in the promotion of anti-discrimination legislations in China. First, the National Assembly enacted the Anti-Domestic Violence Law in December 2015, which became effective on 1 March 2016.[74] The law 'culminates two decades of intensive lobbying by women's rights groups and the official All China Women's Federation' and 'delivers a range of new legal protection measures', including 'China's first statutory definition of domestic violence by national law covering both physical and emotional abuse', and 'forward-thinking prevention measures such as mandatory reporting of abuse and written police warnings against reoffending'.[75] Second, a 2015 amendment criminalized copulation with girls

---

[67] ibid.

[68] 'Do Married Men and Married Women Have Equal Ownership Rights to Property?' (*Our World in Data*, 2021) <https://ourworldindata.org/grapher/gender-rights-to-property> accessed 4 June 2021.

[69] 'Does Legislation Explicitly Criminalise Marital Rape?' (*Our World in Data*, 2015) <https://ourworldindata.org/grapher/does-legislation-explicitly-criminalise-marital-rape> accessed 4 June 2021.

[70] ibid.

[71] 'Are Married Women Required by Law to Obey Their Husbands?' (*Our World in Data*, 2015) <https://ourworldindata.org/grapher/women-required-to-obey-husband> accessed 4 June 2021.

[72] 'Does Law Mandate Paid or Unpaid Maternity Leave" (*Our World in Data*, 2015) <https://ourworldindata.org/grapher/does-law-mandate-paid-or-unpaid-maternity-leave> accessed 4 June 2021.

[73] ibid.

[74] 'Domestic Violence Law 2015' (*China Law Translate*, 27 December 2015) <https://www.chinalawtranslate.com/%e5%8f%8d%e5%ae%b6%e5%ba%ad%e6%9a%b4%e5%8a%9b%e6%b3%95-2015/?lang=en> accessed 8 August 2021.

[75] SL Han, 'China's New Domestic Violence Law: Keeping Victims Out of Harm's Way?' (*Yale Law School Paul Tsai China Center*, 1 June 2017) <https://law.yale.edu/sites/default/files/area/center/china/document/domesticviolence_finalrev.pdf> accessed 4 June 2021.

under the age of 14 as a crime of rape subject to severe punishment.[76] Third, in 2018, the Department of Civil Affairs issued guidance opinions on practising autonomous regulations and customs in villages and rural communities.[77] The opinions emphasized that village and community regulations and autonomous agreements should enforce gender equality.[78] Fourth, in 2019, the Ministry of Human Resources and Social Security published a Circular on Further Regulating Recruitment Activities to Promote Equal Employment for Women. The Circular prohibits discriminatory, gender-based hiring practice and imposes a fine.[79]

Mexico A labour law reform initiative in 2019 proposed that the government should adopt non-judicial mechanisms to reduce sexual harassment in the workplace.[80] This reform would require employers to implement protocols to address sexual harassment, and establish a 'a pre-judicial state-based conciliation procedure' that allows victims of sexual harassment to seek mediation before making a judicial claim.[81] In October 2019, the southern state of Oaxaca decriminalized abortion, making it the second state to adopt such legislation.[82]

Egypt In 2016, the Egyptian People's Assembly approved the amendment to Article 242 of the Penal Code, which now criminalizes the act of female genital mutilation (FGM).[83] Previously, FGM was a misdemeanour and the state imposed the penalty of imprisonment between three months and two years for its practice. In early January 2021, the Egyptian cabinet approved amendments to the 2016 law, increasing the prison sentence up to twenty years in the case of the victim's death. The amended law sets a minimum of five years in prison for removing, modifying, or mutilating a part of a female's genitals. Moreover, medical personnel carrying out the illegal practice could be sentenced to up to ten years in prison.

At the national level, there are several strategy initiatives that set out aspirational goals aiming to reduce gender discrimination. In 2015, Egypt launched the 'Sustainable Development Strategy: Egypt Vision 2030', a national implementation framework for the SDGs.[84] The strategy sets out a 'Developing the Legal and Governance Framework'

---

[76] 'China's Progress Report on Implementation of the 2030 Agenda for Sustainable Development' (*Ministry of Foreign Affairs of the People's Republic of China*, August 2017) <https://www.fmprc.gov.cn/mfa_eng/topics_665678/2030kcxfzyc/201708/P020210525474841044350.pdf> accessed 4 June 2021.

[77] 'China's Progress Report on Implementation of the 2030 Agenda for Sustainable Development' (*Ministry of Foreign Affairs of the People's Republic of China*, September 2019) <https://www.fmprc.gov.cn/mfa_eng/topics_665678/2030kcxfzyc/201909/P020210525474868189879.pdf> accessed 19 March 2023.

[78] ibid.

[79] L Zhang, 'China: Measures Prohibiting Hiring Discrimination Against Women Issued' (*The Library of Congress*, 15 March 2019) <https://www.loc.gov/law/foreign-news/article/china-measures-prohibiting-hiring-discrimination-against-women-issued/> accessed 4 June 2021.

[80] PM Suárez, 'Workplace Sexual Harassment in Mexico: Towards Gender-Transformative Remedies' (*OpenGlobalRights*, 21 July 2020) <https://www.openglobalrights.org/workplace-sexual-harassment-mexico-gender-transformative-remedies/> accessed 4 June 2021 accessed 4 June 2021.

[81] ibid.

[82] 'Mexico Events of 2019' (*Human Rights Watch*) <https://www.hrw.org/world-report/2020/country-chapters/mexico> accessed 4 June 2021.

[83] 'Amendment Penal Code (Criminalization of Act of Female Genital Mutilation)' (*UN Women*) <https://evaw-global-database.unwomen.org/en/countries/africa/egypt/2016/amendment-penal-code-criminalization-of-act-of-female-genital-mutilation> accessed 22 December 2020.

[84] 'A Past Still Present: Addressing Discrimination and Inequality in Egypt' (*Equal Rights Trust*, December 2018) <https://www.equalrightstrust.org/sites/default/files/ertdocs/Egypt_EN_online.pdf> accessed 4 June 2021.

programme which plans to amend articles of the Egyptian Penal Code 'that relate to all aspects of violence against women'.[85] This is regarded as a positive change, but it still fails to 'announce plans to adopt comprehensive equality legislation' and 'specify clear implementation mechanisms'.[86]

In 2017, the government also launched the National Strategy for the Empowerment of Egyptian Women 2030. This strategy was intended to complement the 2015 Development Strategy with a focus on gender development. This strategy is criticized as being paternalistic and patriarchal as one of its objective statement asserts that women require social support to be able to 'contribute to the development of the nation, without compromising their family duties'.[87]

Since 2010, the World Bank has issued eight 'Women, Business and the Law' reports, which measure global progress towards gender equality under the law. The World Bank's 2020 Women, Law and Business Report shows that: from 2016 to 2018, sixty-five economies have carried out eighty-seven reforms to promote women's economic rights. Despite these reforms, according to the Report, 104 economies still have legal barriers to women's employment due to their gender, nearly sixty economies have no laws on sexual harassment in the workplace. According to the World Bank, 2.7 billion women have restrictions from the same choice of employment in which men are employed.

In eighteen countries across the world, husbands can legally prevent their wives from working. The OECD estimates gender-based discrimination in laws in the Middle East and North Africa (MENA) region costs $575 billion ($779.30 billion) a year. The McKinsey Global Institute report on 'The Power of Parity' examines how a 'best in region' scenario in which all countries match the rate of improvement of the fastest improving country in their region could add as much as $12 trillion, or 11 per cent, in annual 2025 gross domestic product (GDP). In a 'full potential' scenario in which women play an identical role in labour markets to that of men, as much as $28 trillion, or 26 per cent, could be added to global annual GDP by 2025. Gender equality by 2030 calls for the removal of gender discriminatory laws on the books and the elimination of the underlying causes of discrimination that still impede women's rights in the private and public spheres.

Though legal gender parity has improved around the world, major differences persist. Many laws and regulations continue to discriminate against women and impede women's well-being and that of their families. Gender equality by 2030 requires urgent action to eliminate the many root causes of discrimination that still curtail women's rights in private and public spheres. For example, discriminatory laws need to change and legislation adopted to advance equality proactively. Yet forty-nine countries still lack laws protecting women from domestic violence, while thirty-nine bar equal inheritance rights for daughters and sons.

The elimination of discrimination against women in areas of citizenship, marriage, divorce, succession, inheritance, travel, and customary law will have major

[85] ibid.
[86] ibid 89–90.
[87] ibid 91.

388 SDG 5

ramifications on women's lives, their communities, and their economies. In many countries such as Egypt, Jordan, and Libya, women must still get permission from their husbands or fathers to work. Unfair inheritance laws disadvantage women in starting a business or seeking a loan and often impoverish women and their families. Labour laws that restrict women's working hours and the sectors they can work in also segregate women, restrict their economic agency, and reinforce stereotypes and expectations that women are primary care-givers who should shoulder housework and child care, impact women's choice of economic participation and employers' decisions to hire them. Discrimination in marriage and divorce impact a woman's rights to economic participation and reinforces an unequal playing field for women. In terms of economic costs, and just one example of inequality, child marriage costs over $60 billion a year and is an enormous barrier to global development.

i) What more needs to be done: some case studies Despite progress, systemic legal discrimination against women negatively impacts sustainable development. The majority of directly discriminatory laws in force relate to the family, including constraining a woman's right to marry, when to marry, whom to marry, and discriminatory marital practices such as 'wife obedience' and polygamy.

Article 1 of CEDAW provides a definition of discrimination against women on the basis of sex and define discrimination as 'any distinction, exclusion or restriction made on the basis of sex which has the effect or purpose of impairing or nullifying the recognition, enjoyment and exercise by women, irrespective of their marital status, on a basis of equality of men and women, of human rights and fundamental freedoms in the political, economic, social, cultural, civil or any other field'. Article 2 calls upon states who have ratified the Convention 'to take all appropriate measures, including legislation, to modify or abolish existing laws, regulations, customs and practices which constitute discrimination against women'.

Polygamy
In several countries, Polygamy is allowed in law. The Committee on the Elimination of Discrimination against Women in its Concluding Observations and in its General Recommendation 21, paragraph 14, General Recommendation 29 has found that polygamous marriages discriminate against women and recommend their prohibition. Polygamy places women and girls at greater risk of contracting HIV/AIDS. It also risks excluding additional wives from asserting their marital and inheritance rights.

Countries like Algeria, Tanzania, and Gabon still legally permit polygamy. According to Article 8 of the Family Code of Algeria, a male is allowed to contract marriage with more than one wife within the limits of the Sharia if there is a just ground and the conditions and intentions of equity can be fulfilled.[88] Polygamous marriages are recognized

---

[88] 'Algeria, Family Code, Article 8' (*UN Women's Family Law Database*) <https://docs.google.com/spreadsheets/d/1yTWuY9ccOlnZloDmoYr37beCve2clyIky7Gyn5l-lb4/edit#gid=0> accessed 4 June 2021.

in Tanzania too and according to the Marriage Act. Section 10(1), monogamous marriages can also be converted to polygamous unions.[89] In Gabon, article 177 of the Family Law states the spouses make the choice on monogamy or polygamy.[90] Despite this choice in the law, most often given the power differentials it will be men who will make the decisions as to the form of marital relations. Moreover, according to article 178, 'the spouses may, during the marriage, renounce the option of monogamy'.[91] Although this waiver is made by a joint declaration before a notary or a civil registry officer who has previously heard the couple separately, given the social, economic, and political power differentials between men and women, it is unlikely that will be a non-discriminatory renouncement.

Guardianship

The male guardianship system is the most significant impediment to realizing women's rights and it effectively renders adult women legally incompetent minors without agency or decision-making powers. In Algeria, according to article 11 of the Family Code, an adult woman concludes her marriage contract in the presence of her 'wali' who is her father or close male relative or any other male of her choice. It is equally temporarily prohibited. Article 30 of the Family Code also prohibits the marriage of a Muslim woman to a non-Muslim man. Saudi Arabia's guardianship laws legalize discrimination and render women minors in the eyes of the law. A recent Saudi directive to government offices attempted to attenuate some of the most restrictive forms of the current guardianship regime in Saudi Arabia. The directive ruled that women could no longer be denied access to government services if they do not have a male guardian's permission. However, even with the new directives, women still need guardian approval if they wish to travel abroad or get a passport. The directive is limited to the public sector and the permission of the guardianship for work in the private sector are still in place.

Husband obedience

Obedience in return for maintenance finds its source in customary Islamic marriage contracts. Obedience in exchange for financial support allows women to be commodified and gives husband's power and control over their spouses. Several countries still maintain husband obedience provisions in the legal system. According to the Family Code of Algeria, article 39(1), the wife is required to obey her husband and grant him respect as the head of the family. Not only is the wife called upon to obey her husband but she must also according to article 39(3) of the Family Code respect the parents and relatives of her husband. Although Chile does not include a husband obedience

---

[89] 'Tanzania, Marriage Act, Section 10(1)' (*UN Women's Family Law Database*) <https://docs.google.com/spreadsheets/d/1yTWuY9ccOlnZloDmoYr37beCve2clyIky7Gyn5l-lb4/edit#gid=0> accessed 4 June 2021.

[90] 'Gabon, Family Law, Article 177' (*UN Women's Family Law Database*) <https://docs.google.com/spreadsheets/d/1yTWuY9ccOlnZloDmoYr37beCve2clyIky7Gyn5l-lb4/edit#gid=0> accessed 4 June 2021.

[91] 'Gabon, Family Law, Article 178' (*UN Women's Family Law Database*) <https://docs.google.com/spreadsheets/d/1yTWuY9ccOlnZloDmoYr37beCve2clyIky7Gyn5l-lb4/edit#gid=0> accessed 4 June 2021.

390   SDG 5

principle, a similar provision according to Chile's Civil Procedure Code's articles 829–832, provides that married women need their husband's or judge's authorization to litigation.

Bank accounts
In Gabon, women still need the permission of a guardian or husband to open a bank account. According to article 257 of the Civil Code although a woman may, on her own signature, open a special current account to deposit or withdraw funds reserved for the household, the opening of this account must be notified by the custodian to the husband.

Customary laws
Customary law has most impact in the area of personal law in regard to matters such as marriage, inheritance and traditional authority. In Botswana, according to the succession rights of the surviving spouse and inheritance and family provisions, the customary law has precedence over other laws in regulating inheritance.

Even in South Africa, where the Constitution states that customary law must be consistent with the Bill of Rights, Section 17 of the Children's Act states that a Minister or any officer in the public service authorized in writing thereto by him or her, may grant written permission to a person under the age of eighteen years to enter into a customary marriage if the Minister or the said officer considers such marriage desirable and in the interests of the parties in question. Moreover, the South African Children's Act, Section 12(5) disallows virginity testing of children under the age of sixteen. The assumption here is that virginity testing is allowed for women and girls over the age of sixteen.

In 2011, the Lebanese parliament repealed article 562 of the Penal Code, the provision that had reduced the sentence for 'honour' crimes. Mobilized by these revisions, women's groups pressed for other reform. Combating honour crimes laws open up space for reform in other areas, including, the following: (i) in 2009, the Association of Banks in Lebanon decided to allow women, for the first time, to open bank accounts for their underage children, independent of the father's legal consent; (ii) in 2014, parliament enacted Law no 293 on domestic violence; (iii) and in late 2016, a parliamentary subcommittee approved a bill to abolish article 522 of the Penal Code, which allowed the prosecution to drop charges against a rapist if he marries his victim.

Fornication is a term for consensual sexual intercourse between two people who are not married to each other and women are punished for sexual intercourse outside of marriage. For example, in Comoros, according to the Penal Code of Article 331, the fornication resulting from the *flagrante delicto* according to the Koranic law may be punished by a sentence of one month to one year of imprisonment and a fine of 20,000 to 150,000 francs or only one of these two penalties. The unmarried woman, who becomes pregnant because of fornication, is liable to the same penalties.

Nationality laws
Nationality laws in over twenty countries (The Bahamas, Bahrain, Barbados, Brunei, Burundi, Iran, Iraq, Jordan, Kiribati, Kuwait, Lebanon, Liberia, Libya, Malaysia,

Mauritania, Nepal, Oman, Qatar, Saudi Arabia, Somalia, Sudan, Swaziland, Syria, Togo, United Arab Emirates) prevent mothers from passing their nationality to their children on an equal basis with fathers. More than double that number of states disallow women equal rights with men in their ability to acquire, change, and retain their nationality, and to confer nationality to non-national spouses. Nationality laws that discriminate on the basis of gender are in violation of Article 9 of the CEDAW, which calls upon states to guarantee equal nationality rights to women. When a state denies equal nationality rights to women and men, it creates a category of second-class citizens and when children are unable to acquire their parents' nationality, it leads to statelessness. Gender discrimination in nationality laws restrict a child's access to public education and health care. Unequal nationality laws also impede access to driver's licences, bank accounts, and access to social welfare programmes. Gender discrimination in nationality laws can contribute to gender-based violence as women are forced to remain in violent relationships for fear of being rendered stateless. The Sierra Leone Citizenship Act is discriminatory in both sex and race. Under the Citizenship Act 1973, one can be a citizen by birth if his father or grandfather was born in Sierra Leone before 19 April 1961. The revised Act of 2017, however, now guarantees an equal right of citizenship to women but men still confer nationality on children. Currently, twenty-five countries still deny women the equal right to pass their citizenship to their children.

One of the most important law reform initiatives in the recent past was the Canadian Senate approval of legislation in 2017 to amend a 141-year-old law that has prevented Indigenous women and their descendants from obtaining the same rights allotted to Indigenous men, including some tax breaks, the ability to vote for Indigenous governments, access to land on reserves, and expanded healthcare coverage, but most of all to pass citizenship rights to their progeny. Under the Indian Act of 1876, if a female member of the First Nation married a non-Indigenous man, then she would lose her First Nation status as well as the right to pass down that status to her children. Male members of the First Nation, however, were not subject to such limitations. Another recent reformist initiative was seen in Jordan. The Jordanian Nationality Law does not allow Jordanian women married to foreign-born spouses to pass on their nationality to their spouses and children. In 2014, the cabinet directed government ministries to grant special privileges to non-citizen children of Jordanian women, including public education and access to public health services. These privileges are unfortunately restricted and apply to children whose mothers have resided in Jordan for a minimum of five years.

d) Critique

As shown, a close reading of the laws around the world reveal that there is much more to be done in revision of discriminatory laws. Target 5.1 assesses the number of anti-discriminatory laws in place, but does not consider the indirect consequences of gender-neutral laws. Other factors, like social norms and judicial interpretation of the law may also affect the extent to which women can actually benefit from legal reforms.

392 SDG 5

In addition, eliminating *de jure* gender discrimination is only the first step to eradicating 'all forms of discrimination'; *de facto* discrimination still persists in almost all areas of a woman's life, but is glaringly absent in target 5.1. Conceivably, *de facto* discrimination is difficult to define and properly measure, but a qualitative indicator that commits stakeholders to adopt policies and campaigns to end *de facto* discrimination can at least increase the awareness of this problem.

2. Target 5.2 Eliminate all forms of violence against all women and girls in the public and private spheres, including trafficking and sexual and other types of exploitation

a) Sources of the target

Target 5.2 is dedicated to the eradication of violence against women. Violence against women is a human rights issue; it imposes negative consequences on a woman's physical, mental, sexual, and reproductive health, and may increase the risk of contracting HIV in some cases.[92] It is also a social plague, impacting a victim's families and communities and imposing substantial social and economic costs. The global cost of violence against women and girls, taking into account public, private, and social cost, is estimated at $1.5 trillion, about 2 per cent of global GDP.[93]

There are a number of international legal frameworks in place that address gender-based violence. The CEDAW, though not explicit mentioning the term, includes violence against women as a form of discrimination.[94] The 1993 DEVAW is the first international instrument to explicitly address violence against women and provides a framework for international and national actions. The 1995 BPfA lists ending violence as one of the areas for priority actions and identifies specific actions for governments to take.[95]

b) Empirical analysis

Target 5.2 encompasses two indicators, one for intimate partner violence (IPV) (5.2.1) and the other for non-intimate partner violence (5.2.2). Indicator 5.2.1 measures the proportion of ever-partnered women and girls aged fifteen years and older subjected to physical, sexual, or psychological violence by a current or former intimate partner in the previous twelve months.[96] It covers any abuse perpetrated by a current or former

---

[92] 'Violence Against Women' (*World Health Organization*, 9 March 2021) <https://www.who.int/news-room/fact-sheets/detail/violence-against-women> accessed 4 June 2021.

[93] 'COVID-19 and Ending Violence Against Women and Girls' (*UN Women*, 2021) <https://www.unwomen.org/sites/default/files/Headquarters/Attachments/Sections/Library/Publications/2020/Issue-brief-COVID-19-and-ending-violence-against-women-and-girls-en.pdf> accessed 26 May 2021.

[94] 'General Recommendations Adopted by the Committee on the Elimination of Violence Against Women: General Recommendation No 19: Violence Against Women' (*United Nations Human Rights Office of the High Commissioner*, 1992) <https://tbinternet.ohchr.org/Treaties/CEDAW/Shared%20Documents/1_Global/INT_CEDAW_GEC_3731_E.pdf> accessed 4 June 2021. The General Recommendation 35 to the CEDAW, expanded the provisions of General Recommendation 19.

[95] 'Beijing Declaration and Platform for Action' (*UN Women*, 2021) <https://www.unwomen.org/sites/default/files/Headquarters/Attachments/Sections/CSW/PFA_E_Final_WEB.pdf> accessed 4 June 2021.

[96] 'Metadata 05-02-01' (*Unstats.un.org*, 2021) <https://unstats.un.org/sdgs/metadata/files/Metadata-05-02-01.pdf> accessed 4 June 2021.

partner within the context of marriage, cohabitation, or any other formal or informal union.[97] Three different forms of violence are included:

- physical violence: any act that is 'aimed at physically hurting the victim and include, but are not limited to acts like pushing, grabbing, twisting the arm, pulling hair, slapping, kicking, biting or hitting with a fist or object, trying to strangle or suffocate, burning or scalding on purpose, or threatening or attacking with some sort of weapon, gun or knife'.
- sexual violence: 'any sort of harmful or unwanted sexual behaviour that is imposed on someone, whether by use of force, intimidation or coercion. It includes acts of abusive sexual contact, forced engagement in sexual acts, attempted or completed sexual acts without consent, non-contact acts such as being forced to watch or participate in pornography, etc. In intimate partner relationships, sexual violence is commonly defined as: being physically forced to have sexual intercourse, having sexual intercourse out of fear for what the partner might do or through coercion, and/or being forced to do something sexual that the woman considers humiliating or degrading.'
- psychological violence (not reported on, see below critique): 'any act intended to induce fear or emotional distress caused by a person's behaviour or act. It includes a range of behaviours that encompass acts of emotional abuse such as being frequently humiliated in public, intimidated or having things you care for destroyed, etc. These often coexist with acts of physical and sexual violence by intimate partners. In addition, surveys often measure controlling behaviours (e.g., being kept from seeing family or friends, or from seeking health care without permission).'[98]

Data are provided by individual countries, which gather the relevant information through (i) specialised national surveys used for measuring violence against women, (ii) violence against women models that are added to household surveys, and (iii) victimization surveys.[99] Data compilers include UNICEF, UN Women, UNODC, UNFPA, UNSD, and WHO.[100]

Surveys conducted from 2000 to 2018 in 106 countries shows that 18 per cent of women and girls fifteen to forty-nine years of age experienced violence by a current or former partner in the twelve months prior to the survey.[101] This translates to 243 million of women and girls in absolute number. These numbers have not reflected the impact of COVID-19, which has greatly increased the risk of IPV for many women and girls. The pandemic has slowed down or even erased some of the progress already achieved on this target, as many countries have instituted lockdown measures, and many women and girls are thus confined to their homes with abusive partners, leading

[97] ibid.
[98] ibid.
[99] ibid.
[100] ibid.
[101] 'The Sustainable Development Goals Report 2020: Achieve Gender Equality and Empower All Women and Girls' (n 1).

to an increase of domestic violence against women and girls. Social isolation and economic insecurity also contributed to the higher risk of IPV. In France, reports of domestic violence have increased by 30 per cent since the lockdown on 17 March 2020.[102] Cyprus and Singapore reported a 30 per cent and 33 per cent increase in helpline calls, respectively.[103] In Argentina, emergency calls for domestic violence increased by 25 per cent since the lockdown in March 2020.[104] A survey of front-line workers in Australia reveals increased requests for help by survivors, and an increased level of complexity of the cases received.[105] A police station in Jingzhou, China recorded a triple number of domestic violence cases in February 2020 compared to the same period the previous year.[106] In the United Kingdom, during the first week of lockdown, there was a 25 per cent increase in phone calls to the National Domestic Abuse Helpline and a 150 per cent increase in visits to the Helpline website.[107] In the United States, the Seattle Police Department reported a 21 per cent increase in domestic violence in March 2002.[108]

Indicator 5.2.2 measures the proportion of women and girls aged fifteen years and older subjected to sexual violence by persons other than an intimate partner in the previous twelve months.[109] This indicator uses the same definition of sexual violence as used by indicator 5.2.1, but in most of the surveys, sexual violence is limited to 'forcing someone into sexual intercourse when she does not want to, as well as attempting to force someone to perform a sexual act against her will or attempting to force her into sexual intercourse'.[110] Similar to indicator 5.2.1, data are collected from individual countries based on specialized national surveys dedicated to measuring violence against women, and international household surveys that include a module on experiences of violence by women.[111] However, compared with indicator 5.2.1, available data for indicator 5.2.2 are far from adequate: many of the surveys do not assess non-partner sexual violence; data from different countries are not necessarily comparable, and many are not collected on a regular basis.[112] Data compilers are UN Women, UNICEF, UNSD, WHO, and UNFPA.

Comparable data are available for a sample of women and girls aged fifteen to forty-nine for 37 low- or middle-income countries.[113] Vanuatu reported the highest prevalence of non-partner violence in 2009, at 33 per cent.[114] This was followed by Australia

[102] 'COVID-19 and Ending Violence Against Women and Girls' (n 93).
[103] ibid.
[104] ibid.
[105] ibid.
[106] 'Justice for Women Amidst COVID-19' (*UN Women*, 2021) <https://www.unwomen.org/sites/default/files/Headquarters/Attachments/Sections/Library/Publications/2020/Justice-for-women-amidst-COVID-19-en.pdf> accessed 26 May 2021.
[107] ibid 19.
[108] ibid.
[109] 'Metadata 05-02-02' (*Unstats.un.org*, 2021) <https://unstats.un.org/sdgs/metadata/files/Metadata-05-02-02.pdf> accessed 4 June 2021.
[110] ibid.
[111] ibid.
[112] ibid.
[113] 'UN Gender Statistics: Data Availability, Human Rights of Women and Girl Children, Indicator 48' (*Genderstats.un.org*) <https://genderstats.un.org/#!/data-availability> accessed 4 June 2021.
[114] ibid.

in 2007, with a proportion of 27 per cent. Region-wise, Africa had the lowest average of reported non-partner violence.[115] The actual number of women and girls affected is likely to be higher, given the stigma and under-reporting of this type of sexual violence.[116]

Trafficking and Sexual Exploitation   Women and girls are more likely to become victims of trafficking and sexual exploitation. These forms of violence are not assigned official indicators, but there are some available data that illustrate how these issues are affecting women and girls. A UNDOC report shows that in 2018, for every ten trafficking victims detected globally, five are adult women and two are girls (totalling 70 per cent of all human trafficking victims).[117] Women and girls are usually trafficked for the purpose of domestic servitude.[118] Girls accounted for more than three out of every four child trafficking victims.[119] Most cases of trafficking within high-income countries involve sexual exploitation of girls or young women.[120]

To combat human trafficking, the Protocol to Prevent, Suppress and Punish Trafficking in Persons, Especially Women and Children entered into force in 2003. It is 'the first global legally binding instrument with an agreed definition on trafficking in persons' and aims to enhance global cooperation in the investigation and prosecution of human trafficking.[121]

c) Efforts taken at international and national level

China As illustrated in Section IV.B.1 of this chapter, one of the most significant developments for China in combating gender-based violence is the enactment of the first anti-domestic violence law in 2016 (see Section IV.B.1 of this chapter). Despite the enactment, activists critiqued the law for failing to provide support to victims, and criminalize intra-marital rape.[122]

In June 2020, the city of Yiwu, Zhejiang Province became the first city in China to allow people getting married to review whether their partner had a history of domestic violence. The city rolled out a domestic violence database that would 'include information on convicted abusers across China as well as those subjected to restraining orders or detention since 2017'.[123] It would include people charged with

---

[115] ibid.

[116] 'Facts and Figures: Ending Violence Against Women' (*UN Women*, November 2021) <https://www.unwomen.org/en/what-we-do/ending-violence-against-women/facts-and-figures#notes> accessed 28 May 2021.

[117] 'Global Report on Trafficking in Persons 2020' (*UNDOC*, 2021) <https://www.unodc.org/documents/data-and-analysis/tip/2021/GLOTiP_2020_15jan_web.pdf> accessed 26 May 2021.

[118] ibid.

[119] 'Global Report on Trafficking in Persons 2018' (*UNDOC*, 2018) <https://www.unodc.org/documents/data-and-analysis/glotip/2018/GLOTiP_2018_BOOK_web_small.pdf> accessed 4 June 2021.

[120] ibid.

[121] 'United Nations Convention Against Transnational Organized Crime and the Protocols Thereto' (*United Nations: Office on Drugs and Crime*) <https://www.unodc.org/unodc/en/organized-crime/intro/UNTOC.html> accessed 4 June 2021.

[122] 'China: Freedom in The World 2021 Country Report' (*Freedom House*, 2021) <https://freedomhouse.org/country/china/freedom-world/2021> accessed 4 June 2021.

[123] Sui-Lee Wee, 'For Those Getting Married, A Searchable Domestic Violence Database' (*The New York Times*, 25 June 2020) <https://www.nytimes.com/2020/06/25/world/asia/china-domestic-violence-database-marriage.html> accessed 4 June 2021.

domestic violence against their partners, older people, and siblings.[124] This measure was welcomed by the public, yet some have express concerns about the protection of personal privacy.[125]

Human trafficking remains a significant problem in China. One of the major achievements came from the 2015 Ninth Amendment to the Criminal Law. Prior to the Ninth Amendment, a purchaser of an abducted woman or child might be exempt from criminal punishment if the purchaser did not prevent the abductee from returning home, or maltreat the child, or obstruct the child's rescue.[126] The Ninth Amendment removed this exemption, providing that such purchaser is still criminally punishable, but may receive a lighter sentence.[127]

Egypt Gender-based violence remains an acute problem in Egypt. Most progress in this area achieved since 2015 came from the Nation Council Women (NCW), other governmental agencies, and independent women's rights organizations. In 2015, the NCW, in collaboration with other governmental and non-governmental organizations, launched the 2015–2020 National Strategy for Combating Violence Against Women (NSVAW).[128] The NSVAW employs a four-pillar approach to combat violence against women.[129] The four pillars stated in NSVAW are prevention, protection, intervention, and legal procedures.[130] In 2017, then President declared 2017 the year of the Egyptian Women and adopted the National Strategy for the Empowerment of Egyptian Women 2030, which aims to 'eliminate the negative phenomena and harmful practices that threaten the life, safety, and dignity of women'.[131]

From 2015 to 2018, the NCW conducted multiple national campaigns involving local communities, which sought to promote national awareness of the importance of combating and reporting cases of violence against women, and providing victim services.[132] Between March 2017 and March 2018, the door-to-door campaign reached an estimated 2 million women.[133] In 2016, the Central Agency for Public Mobilisation and Statistics published for the first time a national survey of measuring the prevalence of gender-based violence experienced by women and girls aged eighteen to sixty-four

---

[124] ibid.

[125] 'The Introduction of a Domestic Violence History Inquiry Mechanism in a City in China is Welcomed, but it Triggers a Discussion of Privacy Rights' (*BBC News* 中文, 27 June 2020) <https://www.bbc.com/zhongwen/simp/chinese-news-53189383> accessed 4 June 2021.

[126] 'Training Related to Combating Human Trafficking in Selected Countries' (*The Library of Congress*, February 2016) <https://www.loc.gov/item/2016296555/> accessed 4 June 2021.

[127] ibid.

[128] 'The National Strategy for Combating Violence Against Women' (*Learningpartnership.org*, 2015) <https://learningpartnership.org/sites/default/files/resources/pdfs/Egypt-National-Strategy-for-Combating-VAW-2015-English.pdf> accessed 4 June 2021.

[129] ibid.

[130] ibid.

[131] 'Egypt Gender Justice & The Law' (*UN Women*, 2018) <https://www2.unwomen.org/-/media/field%20office%20arab%20states/attachments/publications/2018/gender%20justices%20and%20the%20law%20in%20the%20arab%20region/country%20assessments/egypt%20country%20assessment%20-%20english.pdf?la=en&vs=3438> accessed 4 June 2021.

[132] ibid; 'Safe Cities Free from Violence Against Women and Girls' (*USAID*, 23 September 2021) <https://www.usaid.gov/egypt/democracy-human-rights-and-governance/safe-cities-free-violence-against-women-and-girls> accessed 4 June 2021.

[133] 'Egypt Gender Justice & The Law' (n 131).

years old.[134] In May 2017 and 2018, the NCW and the Public Prosecution Office conducted a training programme for 200 family female assistant prosecutors.[135]

In August 2020, the Egyptian parliament approved amendments to the Criminal Procedural Code, which aimed to provide anonymity and protect the identities of sexual violence victims, and to punish those who disclose such information.[136] In March 2021, the NCW launched a COVID-19 response programme, which would aim to increase the awareness and provide protection and response services to women and girls who experience or are at risk of violence especially within COVID-19 context.[137] In the same month, the NCW and UN Women launched a hackathon on social media platforms, which aimed at encouraging digital solutions to gender-based violence.[138]

Mexico Violence against women and girls remains a prevalent problem in Mexico, despite some progress over the year.

In February 2017, the Ministry of Foreign Affairs hosted an event, focusing on 'the sharing of first-hand knowledge among practitioners towards comprehensive, multi-sectoral and human rights-based approaches to prevent and respond to sexual harassment and other forms of sexual violence against women and girls in public spaces'.[139] By the end of 2018, Mexico City and four states had passed legislations criminalizing the circulation of 'revenge pornography' and sex extortion.[140] Individuals who distribute imitate images, audio, videos, or texts may be prosecuted, and may face imprisonment ranging from six months to four years.[141]

In August 2019, the Supreme Court ruled that rape victims could access abortion services without filing a criminal complaint, and healthcare providers could provide abortion services without having to verify a crime was committed.[142] In the same month, there were a series of large demonstrations in response to reports of rapes committed by Mexico City police officers.[143] In November, the Mexico City's government pledged to increase budget for women's care centres, and the federal government announced an action plan to reduce gender-based violence and promote gender equality.[144]

---

[134] ibid 13.

[135] ibid.

[136] 'Human Rights Watch Submission to the Committee on the Elimination of Discrimination Against Women on Egypt' (*Human Rights Watch*, 13 October 2020) <https://www.hrw.org/news/2020/10/13/human-rights-watch-submission-committee-elimination-discrimination-against-women#_ftn12> accessed 4 June 2021.

[137] 'Egypt's NCW Launches New Program for Women's Financial Empowerment in Countryside' (*Egypt Today*, 10 March 2021) <https://www.egypttoday.com/Article/1/99526/Egypt%E2%80%99s-NCW-launches-new-program-for-women%E2%80%99s-financial-empowerment-in> accessed 19 March 2023.

[138] DA Moneim, 'StartEgypt, NCW, UN Women launch digital hackathon aiming to offer solutions to fight violence against women' (*ahramonline*, 3 March 2021) <https://english.ahram.org.eg/NewsContent/1/64/405248/Egypt/Politics-/StartEgypt,-NCW,-UN-Women-launch-digital-hackathon.aspx> accessed 4 June 2021.

[139] 'Mexico City Hosts Global Forum on Safe Cities for Women and Girls' (*UN Women*, 21 February 2017) <https://lac.unwomen.org/en/noticias-y-eventos/articulos/2017/02/announcer-mexico-city-hosts-global-forum-on-safe-cities> accessed 4 June 2021.

[140] 'Mexico 2019 Human Rights Report' (*United States Department of State*, 2019) <https://www.state.gov/wp-content/uploads/2020/02/MEXICO-2019-HUMAN-RIGHTS-REPORT.pdf> accessed 4 June 2021.

[141] ibid.

[142] 'Mexico Events of 2019' (n 82).

[143] 'Mexico: Freedom in the World 2020 Country Report' (*Freedom House*, 2020) <https://freedomhouse.org/country/mexico/freedom-world/2020> accessed 8 August 2021.

[144] ibid.

398 SDG 5

In April 2020, Mexico joined Bolivia in an effort to combat violence against women in politics.[145] It amended eight national legislations to include provisions to prevent and prosecute violence against women in politics.[146] The government has also created a National Registry of Sanctioned Persons for Violence against Women in Politics and adopted measures such as cancelling candidacies of perpetrators of gender-based violence.[147]

European Union The EU made significant efforts to combat gender-based violence both within Europe and around the world.

In 2017, the EU signed the Council of Europe Convention on preventing and combating violence against women and domestic violence, the 'Istanbul Convention', which is the human rights treaty at the pan-Europe level designed to end violence against women and domestic violence.[148] In the same year, the EU launched the NON. NO.NEIN. campaign to raise awareness of gender-based violence.[149] It made available €15 million to twelve national authorities and thirty-two grassroots projects for the development and implementation of awareness-raising and education activities.[150] It organized an EU-wide conference on violence against women with Malta's EU Presidency in February.[151]

In August 2019 at the G7 Biarritz Summit, the EU announced its support to the Initiative for Survivors of Conflict-Related Sexual Violence and committed to allocating €2 million to support the development of an international reparations system for conflict-related sexual violence.[152] During 2018 and 2019, the EU allocated an estimated €52 million in humanitarian aid to the prevention of and response to sexual violence.[153] In 2019, it contributed €133.7 million to programmes in the Caribbean, Central Asia, and the Sub-Saharan African regions that aimed at the elimination of violence against women and girls.[154]

In March 2020, the European Commission presented the Gender Equality Strategy 2020–2025. The goals of the Strategy include ending gender-based violence, providing support and protection to the victims, and holding perpetrates accountable. Under the Strategy, the Commission pledges to develop and finance measures to tackle forced sterilization and forced abortion, and to provide education and training on violence prevention.

---

[145] 'Mexico Joins Bolivia in Efforts to Stop Violence Against Women in Politics' (*UN Women*, 18 March 2021) <https://www.unwomen.org/en/news/stories/2021/3/feature-mexico-joins-bolivia-in-efforts-to-stop-violence-against-women-in-politics> accessed 4 June 2021.

[146] ibid.

[147] ibid.

[148] 'Ending Gender-Based Violence' (*European Commission*) <https://ec.europa.eu/info/policies/justice-and-fundamental-rights/gender-equality/gender-based-violence/ending-gender-based-violence_en> accessed 4 June 2021.

[149] 'Non.No.Nein. Say No! Stop Violence Against Women!' (*European Commission*) <https://ec.europa.eu/justice/saynostopvaw/eu-actions.html> accessed 4 June 2021.

[150] ibid.

[151] ibid.

[152] 'EU Annual Report on Human Rights and Democracy in the World 2019' (*European Union External Action*, 2019) <https://eeas.europa.eu/sites/default/files/annual_report_e-version.pdf> accessed 8 August 2021.

[153] ibid.

[154] ibid.

To address violence in the workplace, the Commission will encourage Member States to 'ratify the International Labour Organization (ILO) Convention on combating violence and harassment in the world of work implement the existing EU rules on protecting workers from sexual harassment, and raise people's awareness of them'.[155] In light of increasing online violence and bullying against women, the Commission will propose the Digital Services Act to clarify online platforms' responsibilities with regard to user-disseminated content.[156] It will also conduct an EU-wide survey to gather data on the prevalence and dynamics of violence against women and other forms of interpersonal violence.

The EU also announced in the Commission Work Program 2021 that it intends to make a new legislative proposal to prevent gender-based violence and domestic violence.[157] The proposal will aim to ensure a minimum level of protection across the EU and strengthen the actions taken by the Member States.[158]

World Bank The World Bank's contribution to combating gender-based violence is mainly achieved through supporting international development projects.

In March 2015, the World Bank launched a Global Platform on Sexual and Gender Based Violence (SGBV), which sought to 'facilitate South-South knowledge-sharing through workshops and yearly learning tours, foster increased cross practice collaboration at the World Bank, build evidence on what works to prevent SGBV, and provide quality services to women, men and child survivors'.[159] In October 2016, it launched a Global Gender-Based Violence (GGBV) Task Force, which would 'build on existing World Bank and other work to tackle violence against women and girls, advising on strengthened approaches to identifying threats and applying lessons in World Bank projects to prevent and respond to sexual exploitation and abuse'.[160] Building on the Task Force's recommendations, the World Bank released an Action Plan in November 2017, which includes administrative and operational measures being adopted to help prevent and respond appropriately to incidences of sexual exploitation and abuse and other forms of gender-based violence in World Bank supported projects.[161] It also developed a GBV risk assessment tool to assess contextual and project-related risks.[162] In 2017, the World Bank also approved a $40 million equivalent International

---

[155] 'A Union of Equality: Gender Equality Strategy 2020–2025' (*EUR-Lex*, 2020) <https://eur-lex.europa.eu/legal-content/EN/TXT/?uri=CELEX%3A52020DC0152> accessed 4 June 2021.

[156] ibid.

[157] 'Ending Gender-Based Violence' (n 148).

[158] ibid.

[159] 'A South-South Learning Tour Explores How to Put an End to Sexual and Gender Based Violence' (*The World Bank*, 11 August 2015) <https://www.worldbank.org/en/news/feature/2015/08/11/a-south-south-learning-tour-explores-how-to-put-an-end-to-sexual-and-gender-based-violence> accessed 4 June 2021.

[160] 'World Bank Launches Global Task Force to Tackle Gender-Based Violence' (*The World Bank*, 13 October 2016) <https://www.worldbank.org/en/news/press-release/2016/10/13/world-bank-launches-global-task-force-to-tackle-gender-based-violence> accessed 4 June 2021.

[161] 'New Action Plan Addresses Gender-Based Violence in World Bank Operations' (*The World Bank*, 8 November 2017) <https://www.worldbank.org/en/news/press-release/2017/11/08/new-action-plan-addresses-gender-based-violence-in-world-bank-operations> accessed 4 June 2021.

[162] 'Gender-Based Violence (Violence Against Women and Girls)' (*The World Bank*, 25 September 2019) <https://www.worldbank.org/en/topic/socialsustainability/brief/violence-against-women-and-girls> accessed 4 June 2021.

400   SDG 5

Development Association credit to Uganda for the Strengthening Social Risk Management and Gender-Based Violence (GBV) Prevention and Response Project.[163] This project aimed to support the implementation of Uganda's national policy on the elimination of gender-based violence and to help strengthen systems for managing social risk in development projects.[164] It also approved the Santa Cruz Road Corridor Connector Project, which would use a three-pronged approach to address potential gender-based violence, and a Grievance Redress Mechanism that includes a specific mandate to address any kind of gender-based violence.[165] In May 2017, it announced an investment of $3.5 million over five years in innovations designed to prevent and respond to gender-based violence.[166]

In August 2018, it committed $100 million to support a Gender-Based Violence Prevention and Response Project in the Democratic Republic of the Congo, which aimed to provide help to survivors of gender-based violence.[167] In November 2020, the World Bank announced that it would introduce a contractor disqualification mechanism, under which it will disqualify contractors for failing to comply with gender-based violence related obligations.[168] A disqualified contractor will not receive Bank-financed contracts for two years.[169] After this period, the contractor needs to demonstrate that it is able to meet the Bank's requirements for preventing gender-based violence before receiving a new Bank-financed contract.[170]

i) A structural response to gender-based violence: the importance of prevention of violence through education   COVID-19 has revealed the systemic nature of GBV. In a time of crisis, women are more likely to become targets of violence.[171] During a public health crisis that called for lock-down or stay-at-home measures, women were less likely to flee their abusers. The pandemic further blurred the lines between the public and the private and exposed the false construct of the public and the private

[163] ibid.
[164] ibid.
[165] ibid.
[166] 'Preventing Gender-Based Violence will Help Women, Girls and Countries Thrive' (*The World Bank*, 18. May 2017) <https://www.worldbank.org/en/news/feature/2017/05/18/preventing-gender-based-violence-help-women-girls-countries-thrive> accessed 4 June 2021.
[167] 'Gender-Based Violence (Violence Against Women and Girls)' (n 162).
[168] 'World Bank to Introduce Contractor Disqualification to Strengthen Prevention of Gender-Based Violence' (*The World Bank*, 24 November 2020) <https://www.worldbank.org/en/news/press-release/2020/11/24/contractor-disqualification-to-strengthen-prevention-of-gender-based-violence> accessed 4 June 2021.
[169] ibid.
[170] ibid.
[171] According to UN Women in Argentina, emergency calls for domestic violence have increased by 25 per cent since the 20 March 2020 lockdown began. In Cyprus and Singapore, telephone help lines have registered an increase of respectively 30 per cent and 35 per cent. In France, there has been a spike of 30 per cent in cases involving domestic violence against women since the 17 March 2020 lockdown. In South Africa, police statistics indicate that 'they received 460 calls a day to their gender-based violence hotline in the first five days of the lockdown alone, nearly double from the weeks prior'. These statistics prompted Ndileka Mandela, Nelson Mandela's granddaughter, to use social media to let women stuck at home with abusers know that 'they [were] not alone, and to encourage them to call police hotlines for help'.

abodes. Even as COVID-19 made the public–private boundaries shift, GBV at home or outside the home was clearly a state responsibility.

Laws around the world primarily provide provisions criminalizing violence against women. Since this model is premised upon responding to domestic violence concerns after the abuse has already happened, there is a concern that these punitive policies alone are insufficient to address the systemic causes of domestic violence. The traditional criminal law model is a case-by-case approach, paying little attention to structural challenges, which contribute not only to the physical, sexual, and psychological injuries suffered by women but also to the economic, racial, and other harms experienced as part of gender-based violence.

Systemic oppression is a form of oppression that is so ingrained in social structures that it is often unquestioned and is handed down from one generation to the next. This section looks at how the SDGs must call for education to address gender stereotypes, and combat traditional notions of gender that perpetuate patriarchal, sexist, and racist social and economic frameworks. Educational curricular, programmes, and textbooks may not only reflect bias and stereotypes but can also play a role in addressing sexist and racist structures by combating stereotypes and deep-seated biases from being further embedded into social structures.

SDGs must address systemic causes of gender-based violence. Moreover, the United Nations Office of the High Commissioner for Human Rights (OHCHR) found that '[i]t is through education that traditions and beliefs which reinforce inequality between the sexes can be challenged' preventing 'the legacy of discrimination [to be] handed from one generation to the next'.

Education has been demonstrated to be a tool in combating systemic and structural forms on inequities. The OHCHR found that '[i]t is through education that traditions and beliefs which reinforce inequality between the sexes can be challenged' preventing 'the legacy of discrimination [to be] handed from one generation to the next'. Educational curricular and programmes can be a tool to uncover structures and systems that subordinate women and minorities and remake structures based on equity.

Several laws now include education on GBV as part of the academic curriculum both at the secondary and the university level. Education on gender inequality and violence against women is one way of addressing entrenched and intersectional social and cultural practices that contribute to violence against women. Historically, education was designed as a way to provide the tools for a livelihood and to inspire good citizenship. Sexism or racism or practices, prejudices, and ideologies that treat one sex or race as inferior to the other in worth and in status are some of the most pernicious problems affecting humanity.

The CEDAW project is ultimately a project to address systemic and structural forms of gender discrimination, biases, and violence against women. Article 10 of the CEDAW makes it clear that gender biases must be eliminated from education. The elimination of gender stereotypes in the educational system as well as education as a

402   SDG 5

tool to advance equity in education is a way to eliminate discrimination as a whole. Article 10 of CEDAW states:

> State Parties shall take all appropriate measures to eliminate discrimination against women in order to ensure to them equal rights with men in the field of education and in particular to ensure, on a basis of equality of men and women: ... (c)The elimination of any stereotyped concept of the roles of men and women at all levels and in all forms of education by encouraging coeducation and other types of education which will help to achieve this aim and, in particular, by the revision of textbooks and school program[s] and the adaption of teaching methods.[172]

For SDG 5 to be addressed fully it is important for legislative reform to address the power structures that constitute the root causes of gender-based violence. These reformist endeavours call for a specific focus on minority and under-represented communities of intersectional identity and the engagement of men and boys who are important shareholders in the SDG agenda. Education has been acknowledged to be a tool in combating systemic and structural forms of inequities.

The laws below list provisions of the laws that highlight education as a prevention tool in anti-violence against women laws. For convenience, these laws have been organized by their subject into the tables below: Table 5.1: curriculum and textbook reform; Table 5.2: engagement of men and boys; and Table 5.3: intersectional educational reform (with a specific focus on the inclusion of indigenous peoples and minorities).

d) Critique

There are several limitations in Target 5.2's framework and data collection. First, while physical and sexual violence are relatively easy to define and detect, the metadata report indicates that psychological violence 'may be conceptualised differently across cultures and in different contexts'.[173] Therefore, though psychological violence is captured in the

---

[172] 'Article 10 also recognizes that *equality* in *education* is the bedrock foundation for women's empowerment in both the private and public spheres, but it can also play a role in breaking down the legacy of discrimination by challenging beliefs that reinforce *gender* inequality.' Article 10 reflects this method of eliminating *gender* discrimination and provides guidelines for State Parties to follow in order to prevent their *educational* systems from perpetuating those cultural stereotypes. The revision of textbooks and school programmes are an important part of this curriculum reform. The language and meaning of article 10(c) provide a framework for achieving systemic change through curricular reform, training, programming, and awareness-raising at all levels of education from kindergarten to post-graduation. That is, article 10(c) provides a model agenda for eliminating gender stereotypes in education as well as promoting gender equal education.

Section (c) of article 10 begins with the language, '[t]he elimination of any stereotyped concept of the roles of men and women'. Article 10(c) recognizes that the current educational system plays a significant factor in developing and disseminating stereotypes, and, due to their tendency to establish deeply imbedded gender biases, all 'stereotyped concepts of the *roles* of men and women' must be eliminated in order to truly eliminate discrimination.

The next clause of article 10 states, 'and, in particular, by the revision of textbooks and school program[s] and the adaption of teaching methods'. This clause gives the specific example of textbook revision because of the huge impact stereotypes in textbooks can have on gender discrimination. Specifically, 'gender bias in textbooks continues to perpetuate stereotypical attitudes about the roles of men and women in the home, the family and the workplace, ultimately constraining the ability for girls to achieve their full potential and negatively affecting the broader society to benefit from the female voice in all aspects of public and private life'.

[173] 'Metadata 05-02-01' (n 96).

Table 5.1 Curriculum and Textbook Reform

		Curriculum and Textbook Reform
Country	Legislation	Relevant Language
Andorra	Law on the Eradication of Gender Violence and Domestic Violence, 2015—Article 6	'Awareness and Prevention from the Educational Sphere 1. Sensitization and prevention measures from the educational field are all the tools, actions and policies that are carried out in educational centres and universities in order to raise awareness of the causes and consequences of gender violence and domestic violence, in order to prevent them from establishing peaceful and equal models of coexistence and respect.'
Ecuador	Law to Prevent and Eradicate Violence Against Women, 2018—Title II, Chapter III	Article 25—Governing body of Higher Education: Without prejudice to the powers established in the respective regulations in force, it will have the following tasks: b) Develop awareness campaigns to disseminate content that promotes the human rights of women and to prevent and eradicate violence against women; d) Create and update specialized protocols to address cases of violence against women, sexual harassment and violence within the scope of higher education; and, disseminate prevention and response mechanisms in the educational community; e) Implement in all curricula the teaching of women's human rights, with elimination of myths, habits and stereotypes that legitimize violence; Article 31—Governing body of Communication Regulation Without prejudice to the powers established in the respective regulations in force, it will have the following tasks: c) Guarantee educational contents that promote sociocultural changes and the eradication of gender stereotypes that promote violence against women, girls, adolescents, youth, adults and the elderly; d) Develop and implement awareness-raising and continuing education programmes for media personnel, on women's human rights, gender approach.
Portugal	Law for the prevention of domestic violence, protection and the assistance of victims, 2009 - Chapter VI Education for citizenship	Article 77—Education: The State ensures the promotion of domestic violence prevention policies by d) Symbolic violence and its structural and institutional character; e) Power relations that mark the personal interactions, groups and social; f) The relationship between children, adolescents, young people and adults.

(continued)

Table 5.1 Continued

		Curriculum and Textbook Reform
Country	**Legislation**	**Relevant Language**
		Article 78—Awareness and information
		The State ensures the promotion of domestic violence prevention policies by:
		a) Preparation of scripts and educational products for awareness-raising and information in schools, which include the themes of education for gender equality, non-violence and peace, for the emotions, as well for the relationship between gender and multiculturalism and the resolution of conflicts through communication;
		b) Creation and dissemination of informative and pedagogical materials directed to the student population;
		c) Conducting competitions in schools to select best pedagogic materials produced in order to conduct temporary exhibitions;
		d) Dynamization of awareness-raising in schools, in partnership with the remaining actors of the educational community, by the military and agents of the security forces involved in proximity policing, community and victim support programmes;
		e) Development of guidelines and products to raise awareness of families about the need for engage in educational strategies as an alternative to violence;
		f) Awareness-raising for the elimination of all sexist and discriminatory references of school materials;
Spain	Law on Comprehensive Protection Measures against Gender Violence, 2004 Chapter I: In the educational field	Article 6. Promotion of equality: 'In order to guarantee effective equality between men and women, educational administrations will ensure that all educational materials eliminate sexist or discriminatory stereotypes and promote the equal value of men and women.'
Kyrgyz Republic	Law on Safeguarding and Protection from Domestic Violence, 2017	Article 13: 'Responsibilities of educational bodies to safeguard and protect from domestic violence 1. For the purpose of exercise of powers set forth by the Government of the Kyrgyz Republic, the authorized educational body: 1) Organize activity of educational bodies to safeguard and protect from domestic violence; 2) Monitor and analyse activity of educational bodies related to the needs of students who fell victim to domestic violence, in obtaining social services and assistance.'
Guinea Bissau	Domestic Violence Law, 2014, Chapter III (on the obligations of the State)	Article 10. Obligations of the State 'In order to prevent, address and eradicate domestic violence, State institutions … must … a) [p]romote the process of modifying the socio-cultural patterns of conduct of women and men, including the design of formal and non-formal education programs and curricula at all levels of the educational process [and] … b) [d]isseminate the right to a life without violence'.

Benin	Law on the Prevention and Repression of Violence against Women, 2012 TITLE 2 AWARENESS, PREVENTION AND DETECTION MEASURES CHAPTER I EDUCATIONAL FIELD	Article 5—'[T]he principles and teachings of mutual respect between the sexes, learning to live together, rejecting and condemning violence, developing critical thinking skills and analysing violence and all gender inequalities will be taken into account in the teaching curricula. These teachings must provide training in the knowledge of and respect for human rights and fundamental freedoms and in understanding the concrete situations that affect them. Similarly, the education system will include, in its quality principles, the removal of obstacles that make it difficult to achieve full equality between men and women, and especially violence against women. They provide training adapted, in content and methods, to the economic, social and cultural developments of the country.' Article 6—'The school is responsible for transmitting and acquiring knowledge and working methods. It aims at gender diversity and real equality between men and women, girls and boys, young girls and young boys, particularly in terms of guidance, detection of violence suffered by young people and the fight against sexism.'
Laos	Law on Preventing and Combatting Violence against Women and Children, 2014—Part III Prevention of Violence against Women and Children	Article 18. Prevention of Violence against Women and Children 'Prevention of violence against women and children shall proceed as follows: Public awareness-raising on violence against women and children; Promotion of the advancement of women and gender equality; Promotion of children's rights; Strengthening the capacity of concerned organizations; Research and data collection; Responsibility of social organizations; Family members' responsibilities; Women's responsibilities; Men's responsibilities.'
Mexico	General Law on Women's Access to a Life Free of Violence, 2007 CHAPTER II—OF THE COMPREHENSIVE PROGRAM TO PREVENT, PUNISH AND ERADICATE VIOLENCE AGAINST WOMEN	Fifth Section. The Ministry of Public Education Article 45 'The Ministry of Public Education shall: I. Define in educational policies the principles of equality, equity and non-discrimination between women and men and full respect for human rights; II. To develop educational programs, at all levels of schooling, that foster the culture of a life free of violence against women, as well as respect for their dignity.'
Italy	Law No 119/2013 (converting into law, with amendments, Law Decree No 39/2013 containing urgent provisions, inter alia, on the fight against gender-based violence), 2013 Chapter I - PREVENTION AND FIGHT AGAINST GENDER-BASED VIOLENCE	Article 5 ((Extraordinary Action Plan Against Sexual and Gender-based Violence 2. The Plan, which aims to ensure homogeneous actions in the national territory, has the following objectives: 'b) to promote adequate training of school staff on gender relations, and against gender-based violence and discrimination, and to promote, within national guidelines for the national curriculum for nursery school and the first cycle of education, guidelines for high schools, technical and vocational schools, curricular and extra-curricular teaching modules for schools of all levels, awareness-raising, information and training for students in order to prevent violence against women and gender-based discrimination, including through the appropriate enhancement of these topics in textbooks; and support of victims of gender-based violence and stalking, and the experiences of associations providing assistance in the sector.'

(continued)

Table 5.1 Continued

		Curriculum and Textbook Reform
Country	**Legislation**	**Relevant Language**
Bosnia		Bosnia provides an intersectional approach and calls for revision of textbooks.

Bosnia provides an intersectional approach and calls for revision of textbooks.
Education
33. The Committee welcomes the increase in the enrolment of girls and women in scientific fields of study and in higher education. Nevertheless, the Committee is concerned about the low percentage of women and girls who choose non-traditional fields of study and career paths, such as mechanical and electrical engineering. It also notes with concern:
(c) The barriers to access high-quality education at all levels faced by Roma, rural, refugee and asylum-seeking girls, girls with disabilities and girls who are victims of child marriage, gender-based violence and trafficking;
(d) Reports of violence against girls in educational institutions;
34. Recalling its general recommendation No 36 (2017) on the right of girls and women to education, as well as target 4.1 of the Sustainable Development Goals, the Committee recommends that the State party:
(a) Encourage further diversification of the educational choices of girls and boys and revise school textbooks and educational materials at the entity, district and cantonal levels to eliminate gender-stereotyped content from teaching materials at all levels of education

Table 5.2 Engagement of Men and Boys

	Engagement of Men and Boys	
Country	Legislation	Relevant Language
Nicaragua	Integral Law on Violence against Women and to Reform Law No 641 'Penal Code', 2012 TITLE III MEASURES OF ATTENTION, PROTECTION, SANCTION, PRELIMINARY AND PRECAUTIONARY MEASURES Chapter I Measures of attention, protection and sanction	Art. 19. Measures of attention and prevention The measures of attention and prevention that are established are the set of measures and actions to protect victims of violence, as part of the obligation of the State, to guarantee women their safety and the full exercise of their human rights. These models must take into consideration: b) 'Provide integral, specialized and free re-education services to the aggressor, to eradicate violent behaviour, through an education that eliminates the stereotypes of male supremacy and the macho patterns that generated their violence.'
United States	Violence Against Women Act, 1994 (As Amended) Subtitle M—Strengthening America's Families by Preventing Violence Against Women and Children	(3) ENGAGING MEN AS LEADERS AND ROLE MODELS.— 'To develop, maintain or enhance programs that work with men to prevent domestic violence, dating violence, sexual assault, and stalking by helping men to serve as role models and social influencers of other men and youth at the individual, school, community or state-wide levels.'
Peru	Act to Prevent, Punish and Eradicate Violence Against Women and Members of the Family Group, 2015 TITLE III PREVENTION OF VIOLENCE, ATTENTION AND RECOVERY OF VICTIMS AND RE-EDUCATION OF AGGRESSORS CHAPTER I PREVENTION OF VIOLENCE, ATTENTION AND RECOVERY OF VICTIMS	Article 27. Promotion, prevention and recovery services for victims of violence 'It is the State's policy to create care and prevention services against violence. The creation and management of temporary shelter homes, programs aimed at men to prevent violent behaviour and other protection services in favor of victims of violence against women and members of the family group will be in charge of the local and regional governments and the Ministry of Women and Vulnerable Populations.'
Laos	Law on Preventing and Combatting Violence against Women and Children, 2014 Part III Prevention of Violence against Women and Children	Article 27. Responsibilities of Men 'Men have responsibilities and [shall] take ownership in preventing violence against women and children, adapt-change the violence behaviour and stop using violence, have a good attitude, respect the rights of individual women and children, aware of and implement their obligation in realizing the gender equality rights and children's rights. In addition men should not hold customs, traditions or beliefs to justify violence against women and children. Men should take ownership in raising awareness, build knowledge on preventing and combatting violence against women and children.'

(continued)

408 SDG 5

Table 5.2 Continued

Engagement of Men and Boys		
Argentina	Law on the Comprehensive Protection of Women, 2009 CHAPTER III—BASIC GUIDELINES FOR STATE POLICIES	Article 10.—Technical strengthening of jurisdictions. The national State must inter-institutionally promote and strengthen the different jurisdictions for the creation and implementation of comprehensive services to assist women who experience violence and the people who use it, and must guarantee: 7-Re-education programmes aimed at men who use violence.
Italy	Law No 119/2013 (converting into law, with amendments, Law Decree No 39/2013 containing urgent provisions, inter alia, on the fight against gender-based violence), 2013 Chapter I - PREVENTION AND FIGHT AGAINST GENDER-BASED VIOLENCE Art. 5 Extraordinary Action Plan Against Sexual and Gender-based Violence	'The Plan, which aims to ensure homogeneous actions in the national territory, has the following objectives: a) to prevent the phenomenon of violence against women through public information and awareness-raising, as well as by increasing the engagement of men and boys in the process of eliminating violence against women and in resolving interpersonal conflicts ... '

indicator, it is actually not reported on in the surveys that provide the data. Another limitation of indicator 5.2.1 is that it fails to measure IPV experienced by women aged fifty years and above, meaning that the actual proportion of women subjected to IPV in the prior twelve months is potentially higher if women aged fifty were surveyed.[174]

Second, indicator 5.2.2 suffers from a severe lack of data. As explained above, many national surveys on violence against women do not collect information on non-intimate partner violence. Currently, UN Gender Stats only has data from thirty-seven low- or middle-income countries, which does not constitute a representative sample. Many of the data are from the early 2000s and are not regularly updated.

Third, data collected from national surveys may not accurately present the whole picture of the IPV situation because sociocultural barriers or fear of retribution may deter some women from disclosing their IPV experience. A study analysing the Demographic and Health Survey data from twenty-four developing countries shows that 40 per cent of women disclosed their IPV experience, out of which only 7 per cent reported to a formal source.[175] Under-reporting is more pronounced in regions where there is community stigma around reporting domestic violence and domestic violence

---

[174] ibid.

[175] T Palermo and others, 'Tip of the Iceberg: Reporting and Gender-Based Violence in Developing Countries' (2013) 179 American Journal of Epidemiology <https://www.ncbi.nlm.nih.gov/pmc/articles/PMC3927971/> accessed 4 June 2021.

Table 5.3 Intersectional Educational Reform

Country	Legislation	Relevant Language
		Intersectional Education Reform
Bolivia	2016–2020 Sectoral Plan for Comprehensive Development of Education to Live Well	Provides a blueprint on decolonizing and depatriarchalizing, along with an intracultural and intercultural approach to ensure equity in education.
Peru	Act to Prevent, Punish and Eradicate Violence Against Women and Members of the Family Group, 2015	Article 45. Sectoral responsibilities The sectors and institutions involved, and regional and local governments, in addition to adopting mechanisms of training, capacitation and permanent specialization, in accordance with their organic laws and other applicable regulations, are responsible for:
		2. The Ministry of Education
	TITLE IV NATIONAL SYSTEM FOR THE PREVENTION, SANCTION AND ERADICATION OF VIOLENCE AGAINST WOMEN AND MEMBERS OF THE FAMILY GROUP	e) Implement in the educational institutions of the Regular Basic Education (EBR) and the Alternative Basic Education (EBA), contents of the National Curricular Design (DCN) on the respect of the right to a life free of violence, with active methodologies and systems of evaluation that are adapted to the diverse cultural, ethnic and linguistic contexts.
United States	FAMILY VIOLENCE PREVENTION AND SERVICES ACT	SEC. 311. GRANTS FOR STATE DOMESTIC VIOLENCE COALITIONS.
		'4) … conduct public education campaigns regarding domestic violence through the use of public service announcements and informative materials that are designed for print media, bill- boards, public transit advertising, electronic-broadcast media, and other vehicles for information that shall inform the public concerning domestic violence, including information aimed at underserved racial, ethnic or language-minority populations'.
United States	Violence Against Women Reauthorization Act, 2013—An Act To reauthorize the Violence Against Women Act of 1994	'SEC. 1301. GRANTS TO SUPPORT FAMILIES IN THE JUSTICE SYSTEM
		'education and outreach programs to improve community access, including enhanced access for underserved populations'.
	VIOLENCE AGAINST WOMEN ACT OF 1994	TITLE IV—VIOLENCE AGAINST WOMEN
		CHAPTER 9—DATA AND RESEARCH
		'The Attorney General shall request the National Academy of Sciences, through its National Research Council, to enter into a contract to develop a research agenda to increase the understanding and control of violence against women, including rape and domestic violence … In setting the agenda, the Academy shall focus primarily on preventive, educative, social, and legal strategies, including addressing the needs of under-served populations.'

(*continued*)

Table 5.3 Continued

		Intersectional Education Reform
Country	Legislation	Relevant Language
Ecuador	Law to Prevent and Eradicate Violence Against Women, 2018	Article 9—Rights of Women: girls, adolescents, young people, adults and older adults, in all their diversity, have the right to recognition, enjoyment, exercise and protection of all human rights and freedoms contemplated in the Constitution of the Republic, international instruments ratified by the State and in the current regulations, which include, among others, the following: '4. To receive clear, accessible, complete, truthful, timely information, in Spanish or in their own language, appropriate to their age and socio-cultural context, in relation to their rights, including their sexual and reproductive health; to know the protection mechanisms; the place of provision of care, emergency, support and comprehensive recovery services; and other procedures contemplated in this law and other concordant regulations ...'
Mexico	General Law on Women's Access to a Life Free of Violence, 2007 CHAPTER III—OF THE DISTRIBUTION OF COMPETENCES IN MATTERS OF PREVENTION, SANCTION AND ERADICATION OF VIOLENCE AGAINST WOMEN	Article 40. The Federation, the federated entities and the municipalities, will contribute to the fulfilment of the objectives of this law in accordance with the competences foreseen in the present ordinance and other applicable legal instruments. First Section. Of the Federation Article 41. Faculties and obligations of the Federation: 'Educate women on human rights in their mother tongue; VI. Ensure the dissemination and promotion of the rights of indigenous women based on the recognition of the pluricultural composition of the nation; VII. Monitor that the uses and customs of the whole society do not threaten the human rights of women; VIII. Coordinate the creation of re-education and social reintegration programs with a gender perspective for aggressors of women'.
Colombia	Law 1257 (on the Awareness, Prevention and Sanctioning of Discrimination and Violence Against Women), 2008 CHAPTER IV—SENSITIZATION AND PREVENTION MEASURES CHAPTER VI—MEASURES OF CARE	Article 14. Duties of the family. The family will have the duty to promote the rights of women in all their recognized life stages, enshrined in this law and likewise the elimination of all forms of violence and inequality against women. These are family duties for these purposes: 10. Carry out all necessary actions to ensure the exercise of women's rights and eliminate violence and discrimination against them in the family environment. Paragraph. For Indigenous Peoples, Afro-descendant communities and other ethnic groups, the obligations of the family shall be established in accordance with their traditions and cultures, provided they are not contrary to the Constitution and international human rights instruments.'

Article 20. Information

'The municipalities and districts will provide information and advice to women victims of violence appropriate to their personal situation, on the services available, the entities in charge of providing said services, the relevant legal procedures and the existing reparation measures. The existing lines of care in the municipalities and districts will immediately, accurately and completely inform the community and the victim of any form of violence, the mechanisms of protection and attention to it. It will be guaranteed through the necessary means that women victims of violence with disabilities, who cannot read or write, or those who speak a language other than Spanish, have full and adequate access to information about existing rights and resources.'

Peru — Act to Prevent, Punish, and Eradicate Violence Against Women and Members of the Family Group, 2015

TITLE IV NATIONAL SYSTEM FOR THE PREVENTION, SANCTION AND ERADICATION OF VIOLENCE AGAINST WOMEN AND MEMBERS OF THE FAMILY GROUP

Article 41. Base Protocol for Joint Action

'The Base Protocol of Joint Action in prevention, care, protection, early detection and continued intervention, sanction and re-education in the face of violence against women and members of the family group contains the guidelines for intersectoral articulation and procedures to ensure global and integral action of the different administrations and services involved. It constitutes an instrument of obligatory compliance under responsibility. The Protocol must consider in a special way the situation of women who, because of their status as such and crossing other variables, are more exposed to violence or greater difficulties in accessing the services provided for in this Law, such as those belonging to indigenous, Andean and Amazonian populations, people of African descent, those in situations of social exclusion and women with disabilities, among others. A similar consideration should include the protocol regarding members of the family group from the human, generational and intercultural rights approach.'

Bolivia — Comprehensive Law to Guarantee Women a Life Free of Violence, 2013

TITLE III PREVENTION, ATTENTION AND PROTECTION

CHAPTER I PREVENTION OF VIOLENCE TOWARDS WOMEN

Article 17—Prevention Criteria

'For the purposes of application of this Law, the central level of the State and the Autonomous Territorial Entities will create and adopt preventive measures that are necessary to modify the violent individual and social behaviours and those that tolerate, naturalize and reproduce violence, under three criteria of action:

1. Structural Prevention. It includes all those measures of an integral nature aimed at modifying attitudes, practices, reactions, actions and omissions that have as their effect and consequence the violence against women, as well as its replacement by attitudes in the behaviour of individual, couples, families, the community, society and state, through raising awareness and educating within the family, at school and other academic levels, at work, health care centres, indigenous communities (campesinas and Afro-Bolivian), political organizations and trade unions, social organizations, and any other scope of social interaction.

(continued)

Table 5.3 Continued

		Intersectional Education Reform
Country	**Legislation**	**Relevant Language**
		2. Individual Prevention. It refers to measures aimed at strengthening and empowering every woman and promoting her skills to identify any possible manifestation of violence or aggression towards her, facing the violence assertively, with the purpose of anticipating its expression or concretion and preventing it from occurring or continuing.
		3. Collective Prevention. Measures designed to prevent violence and protect women through their organizations, institutions or any community to which they belong by affinity (neighbourhood committees, unions, communities, nations, native indigenous people (campesinos), intercultural and Afro-Bolivian).'
		Article 18—Community Prevention
		'The native indigenous authorities campesinas and Afro-Bolivians, shall adopt in communities in which they exercise their functions, preventive measures that they consider more appropriate under the three criteria of action established to prevent any act of violence against women, with the participation of the communities in the planning, execution and follow-up, respecting their rights. No norms or procedures of the indigenous peoples or nations may violate the rights recognized in the Political Constitution of the State and the constitutionality.'
Panama	Law to Criminalize Femicide and Violence Against Women, 2013 CHAPTER VI PUBLIC POLICIES OF AWARENESS, PREVENTION AND ATTENTION	Article 24. 'The municipalities and the county authorities will have the following attributions, in accordance with the mandates of the international conventions, in addition to those attributed to them by the Law: 1. Include the issue of violence against women and training in international conventions to protect the rights of women that are the Law of the Republic, in training programs and municipal and regional development. These issues must be included in the continuous and permanent training of the personnel working in the offices, the traditional authorities and the persons who serve victims, with a periodicity of not less than one year, as well as in the dissemination and information programs that contribute to eradicate violence against women in all its forms, guarantee respect for the dignity of women and promote equality between men and women. To this end, the modules to be used with CONVIMU will be validated in the different national indigenous languages and communication systems.'

is considered a family issue not to be disclosed or discussed publicly. For example, a study conducted in Tanzania shows that while 44 per cent of women experience IPV during their lifetime, many refrain from revealing this fact, as a result of 'gendered social norms that accept IPV and impose stigma and shame upon survivors'.[176]

Fourth, while the target statement envisions the elimination of 'all forms of violence', the two indicators fail to capture the full range of violence women and girls are subjected to, such as cyber violence or economic violence. In the 2020 Comprehensive Review of the global indicators framework, Eurostate proposed a replacement of both indicators to 'proportion of population subjected to physical, sexual, or psychological violence or harassment in the previous twelve months, by sex, age, disability status of the victim, form of violence or harassment, place of occurrence, age at occurrence, and relationship with the offender'.[177] This proposal includes harassment as a form of violence, and includes disability status as a classifying feature of the victim. Both are recommendable. Harassment is also a form of violence, and women with disabilities are more likely than other women to experience violence.[178]

Fifth, although the target statement mentions trafficking and sexual exploitation, no separate indicator is devised to measure the progress on this front. A related target, target 16.2 under SDG 16, seeks to 'end abuse, exploitation, trafficking and all forms of violence against and torture of children', but its approach is not gender-sensitive and does not address trafficking and exploitation of adult women. As mentioned above, women and girls are more likely to become victims of human trafficking and sexual exploitation, so an indicator dedicated to tracking the progress on eliminating trafficking and sexual exploitation against women and girls seems urgent. In the 2020 Comprehensive Review, Germany BMZ suggested adding an additional indicator on human (women) trafficking to target 5.3, but this proposal was not adopted.[179] Whether assigned to target 5.2 or 5.3, it is important to have designed an indicator to track efforts in this area. If data on victims at the country level is difficult to measure, at least the indicator can measure whether there are legislations, programmes or policies in place that combat human trafficking and sexual exploitation targeted at women.

3. Target 5.3 Eliminate all harmful practices, such as child, early, and forced marriage and female genital mutilation

a) Sources of the target

Target 5.3 seeks to address another two human rights issues: child, early and forced marriage, and FGM. Marriage before the age of eighteen is a fundamental human

---

[176] J McCleary-Sills and others, 'Stigma, Shame and Women's Limited Agency in Help-Seeking for Intimate Partner Violence' (2016) 11 Global Public Health <https://pubmed.ncbi.nlm.nih.gov/26156577/> accessed 4 June 2021.

[177] 'Compilation of 2020 Comprehensive Review Proposals Received' (*UN Stats*, 24 June 2019) <https://unstats.un.org/sdgs/files/2020%20Comprehensive%20Review%20Proposals_web.pdf> accessed 4 June 2021.

[178] 'Facts and Figures: Women and Girls with Disabilities' (*UN Women*) <https://www.unwomen.org/en/what-we-do/women-and-girls-with-disabilities/facts-and-figures> accessed 2 June 2021.

[179] 'Report of the Inter-Agency and Expert Group on Sustainable Development Goal Indicators' (*UN Stats*, 2019) <https://unstats.un.org/unsd/statcom/51st-session/documents/2020-2-SDG-IAEG-Rev-EE.pdf> accessed 4 June 2021; 'Compilation of 2020 Comprehensive Review Proposals Received' (n 177).

414 SDG 5

rights violation and affects disproportionately women and girls.[180] This harmful practice often leads to early pregnancy, social isolation, interruption of education, and increases a girl's risks of experiencing domestic violence.[181] This practice is addressed by a number of international instruments. The UN Convention on Consent to Marriage, Minimum Age for Marriage and Registration of Marriages (1964) calls for State Parties to '[eliminate] completely child marriages and the betrothal of young girls before the age of puberty' and to set a minimum age for marriage.[182] It also requires 'full and free consent' before entering into marriage.[183] The Joint General Recommendation No 31 of CEDAW and General Comment No 18 of the CRC on harmful practices (2014), issued by the Committee on the Elimination of Discrimination against Women and the Committee on the Rights of the Child, offer a holistic framework for tackling this harmful practice.[184]

b) Empirical analysis
Indicator 5.3.1 assesses the proportion of women aged twenty to twenty-four years who were married or in a union before age fifteen and before age eighteen.[185] This indicator covers both formal marriages and informal unions, with informal unions defined as 'those in which a couple lives together as if married but for which there has been no formal civil or religious ceremony (i.e., cohabitation)'.[186] Data are collected from individual countries' household surveys and national censuses. UNICEF is the custodian agency for collecting data for this indicator.

Around 2019, one in five women (20.2 per cent) between the ages of twenty and twenty-four years was married before the age of eighteen, compared with about one in four (23.8 per cent) ten years earlier.[187] There were decreases in both the proportion of women that were married/in union before fifteen years (7.4 per cent to 4.9 per cent), and the promotion of women that were married/in union after fifteen but before eighteen (16.4 per cent to 15.3 per cent).[188] Such progress enabled the aversion of 25 million early marriages, of which 7 million were expected based on prior trends, 18 million were enabled by an acceleration of progress.[189]

---

[180] 'The Sustainable Development Goals Report 2020: Achieve Gender Equality and Empower All Women and Girls' (n 1).
[181] 'Facts And Figures: Ending Violence Against Women' (n 116).
[182] 'Convention on Consent to Marriage, Minimum Age for Marriage and Registration of Marriages' (*OHCHR*, 9 December 1964) <https://www.ohchr.org/en/professionalinterest/pages/minimumageformarriage.aspx> accessed 4 June 2021.
[183] Ibid.
[184] 'Committee on the Elimination of Discrimination Against Women: General Recommendations' (*OHCHR*) <https://www.ohchr.org/en/hrbodies/cedaw/pages/recommendations.aspx> accessed 4 June 2021.
[185] 'Metadata 05-03-01' (*Unstats.un.org*, 2021) <https://unstats.un.org/sdgs/metadata/files/Metadata-05-03-01.pdf> accessed 4 June 2021.
[186] ibid.
[187] 'The Sustainable Development Goals Report 2020: Achieve Gender Equality and Empower All Women and Girls' (n 1).
[188] ibid.
[189] 'The Sustainable Development Goals Report 2020: Achieve Gender Equality and Empower All Women and Girls' (n 1) Progress and Info; 'Harmful Practices and Intimate Partner Violence' (*UNICEF DATA*) <https://data.unicef.org/topic/gender/harmful-practices-and-intimate-partner-violence/> accessed 4 June 2021.

Region-specific data show that Southern Asia saw the greatest decline of child marriage during this period, from nearly 50 per cent to 30 per cent, mainly due to progress achieved in India.[190] Currently, the risk of child marriage is highest in Sub-Saharan Africa, where around four in ten women between the age of twenty and twenty-four were married before eighteen.[191] However, at the current rate, no region is on track to eliminate child marriage by 2030, unless efforts are substantially enhanced and maintained.[192]

Like child marriage, FGM is a violation of human rights. FGM imposes negative physical and mental health consequences on affected women and girls, and continues to impact them for the remainder of their lives.[193] FGM is condemned by multiple international treaties, conventions, and national legislations. Article 25 of the Universal Declaration of Human Rights has been used to support the argument that FGM is a violation of the right to health and bodily integrity, which states that 'everyone has the right to a standard of living adequate for health and well-being'.[194] The 1989 UN Convention on the Rights of the Child also condemns FGM as a form of violence against girls.[195]

Indicator 5.3.2 measures the proportion of girls and women aged fifteen to forty-nine years who have undergone FGM and/or cutting, by age eighteen. Under this indicator, FGM refers to 'all procedures involving partial or total removal of the female external genitalia or other injury to the female genital organs for non-medical reasons'. Data are collected from household surveys such as UNICEF-supported MICS (Multiple Indicator Cluster Survey) and individual countries' national surveys. UNICEF is the custodian agency for this indicator.

Globally, at least 200 million women and girls in thirty-one countries where the practice is concentrated have undergone FGM.[196] The practice is becoming less common over the last thirty years. In the countries with nationally representative data, about one in three girls aged fifteen to nineteen years have been subject to the practice, compared to one in two thirty years ago.[197] Fast decline of the practice has occurred in countries including Egypt, Sierra Leone, Benin, and the Maldives.[198] Nevertheless, the current progress may not be fast enough to reach the goal of elimination by 2030.[199] There are

---

[190] ibid.

[191] ibid.

[192] 'Child, Early and Forced Marriage, Including in Humanitarian Settings' (*OHCHR*) <https://www.ohchr.org/EN/Issues/Women/WRGS/Pages/ChildMarriage.aspx> accessed 4 June 2021.

[193] 'Compendium of International and National Legal Frameworks on Female Genital Mutilation: Fourth Edition' (*Openknowledge World Bank*, February 2020) <https://openknowledge.worldbank.org/bitstream/handle/10986/33281/FGM%20Compendium%20Fourth%20Edition%20February%202020.pdf?sequence=1&isAllowed=y> accessed 4 June 2021.

[194] 'Universal Declaration of Human Rights' (*United Nations*, 10 December 1948) <https://www.un.org/en/about-us/universal-declaration-of-human-rights> accessed 4 June 2021.

[195] 'Convention on the Rights of the Child' (*OHCHR*, 20 November 1989) <https://www.ohchr.org/en/professionalinterest/pages/crc.aspx> accessed 4 June 2021.

[196] 'The Sustainable Development Goals Report 2020: Achieve Gender Equality and Empower All Women and Girls' (n 1).

[197] ibid.

[198] ibid.

[199] 'Progress Towards the Sustainable Development Goals' (*UN Stats*, 28 April 2020) <https://unstats.un.org/sdgs/files/report/2020/secretary-general-sdg-report-2020--EN.pdf> accessed 4 June 2021,

still countries where the practice of FGM is almost universal, where at least nine in ten girls and women aged fifteen to forty-nine years have been cut.[200]

The prevalence of the practice varies greatly across countries, with the practice being almost universal in Somalia, Guinea, and Djibouti, while it affects less than 1 per cent of adolescent girls in Cameroon, the Maldives, and Uganda.[201] There also exist wide variations in terms of the type of FGM performed, circumstances surrounding the practice, and size of the affected population groups.[202]

The COVID-19 pandemic, nevertheless, may slow down or even erase the progress already achieved under this target. On the one hand, up to 10 million additional girls face the risk of child marriage in the next decade due to the pandemic.[203] On the other hand, the pandemic is also interrupting programmes to end FGM, and the closure of schools worsens the situation.[204] According to UNICEF, 2 million additional girls may be subjected to FGM in the next decade, and progress needs to be accelerated to meet the goal of total elimination by 2030.[205]

c) Efforts taken at international and national level

Egypt Egypt has made great strides in ending child marriage. In October 2017, the NCW launched the 'No to Underage Marriage' campaign, the main objective of which is to curtail undocumented marriages of minors.[206] In 2020, the Egyptian government announced a plan to amend the country's marriage laws.[207] The change would set a minimum age for marriage and impose penalties for girls' early marriage, seeking to penalise everyone involved in organising the child marriage.[208] In March, 2021, President Abdul Fattah al-Sisi pledged to accelerate efforts to abolish child marriage in the country.[209]

The FGM front also saw progress. There was an increase in the number of girls and mothers who reported actual or potential cases of FGM, a positive sign that the county's efforts to increase community awareness of the practice are effective: between

---

[200] 'The Sustainable Development Goals Report 2020: Achieve Gender Equality and Empower All Women and Girls' (n 1) Progress and Info,

[201] 'Female Genital Mutilation (FGM) Statistics' (*UNICEF DATA*, August 2021) <https://data.unicef.org/topic/child-protection/female-genital-mutilation/> accessed 4 June 2021.

[202] ibid.

[203] 'The Sustainable Development Goals Report 2020: Achieve Gender Equality and Empower All Women and Girls' (n 1) Progress and Info.

[204] 'The Sustainable Development Goals Report 2020: Achieve Gender Equality and Empower All Women and Girls' (n 1).

[205] '2 million Additional Cases of Female Genital Mutilation Likely to Occur Over Next Decade Due to COVID-19' (*UNICEF*, 5 February 2021) <https://www.unicef.org/press-releases/2-million-additional-cases-female-genital-mutilation-likely-occur-over-next-decade> accessed 4 June 2021.

[206] 'Egypt to Issue Law Criminalizing Child Marriage By 2021' (*EgyptToday*, 30 November 2020) <https://www.egypttoday.com/Article/1/94827/Egypt-to-issue-law-criminalizing-child-marriage-by-2021> accessed 4 June 2021.

[207] 'Egypt Seeks to Criminalize Child Marriage' (*Asharq Al-Awsat*, 23 March 2021) <https://english.aawsat.com/home/article/2876886/egypt-seeks-criminalize-child-marriage> accessed 4 June 2021.

[208] ibid.

[209] ibid.

June 2019 and December 2020, there were 1,618 reports, compared with 240 reports in 2005, when a Child Helpline was first established.[210]

At the government level, in August 2016, the Egyptian parliament approved additional penalties for FGM: new amendments to the Penal Code provide for prison terms of five to seven years for those who perform FGM, and up to fifteen years if the case results in permanent disability or death.[211] Anyone who accompanies a girl to undergo FGM will face one to three years in prison.[212] FGM is classified as a felony, not a misdemeanour.[213] In April 2021, the parliament further increased the penalties for FGM, imposing prisons terms of up to twenty years.[214] Anyone who requested an FGM to be performed will also be subject to imprisonment.

Egypt's National Strategy for the Empowerment of Egyptian Women 2030, adopted in 2017, vows to eliminate FGM under its protection pillar.[215] In May 2019, the National Council for Women (NCW) and the National Council for Childhood and Motherhood launched a National Committee for Eliminating FGM, which includes representatives of all concerned ministries, religious and judicial bodies, civil society, and development partners.[216] In 2019, the NCW, in collaboration with UN Women Egypt, released a feature film, 'Between Two Seas', one of the themes of which is FGM.[217] There were public screenings of the film in different governorates throughout 2020, followed by discussions with the audience.[218]

In 2016, the government launched the National Committee for the Eradication of Female Genital Mutilation, which has raised campaigns aiming at increasing the awareness of the harmfulness of FGM since 2016.[219] In December 2020, the Committee met with representatives from medical councils and organizations to devise a plan to fight against the medicalization of FGM.[220] In the same year, a group of doctors raised the 'White Shirts' campaign, hanging up signs that read 'No to FGM' and 'FGM is a crime' in a Cairo metro station, and handing out pamphlets that explained the risks of FGM.[221]

[210] 'As More Families Report FGM Incidents in Egypt, Advocacy Intensifies, And A New Bill Seeks to Increase Penalties' (*UN Women*, 5 February 2021)<https://www.unwomen.org/en/news/stories/2021/2/feature--families-report-fgm-in-egypt-and-advocacy-intensifies> accessed 4 June 2021.

[211] 'Egypt: New Penalties for Female Genital Mutilation' (*Human Rights Watch*, 9 September 2016) <https://www.hrw.org/news/2016/09/09/egypt-new-penalties-female-genital-mutilation> accessed 4 June 2021.

[212] ibid.

[213] S Amin, 'Egyptian Parliament Approves Tougher Penalties for Female Genital Mutilation' (*Al-Monitor*, 2 April 2021) <https://www.al-monitor.com/originals/2021/04/egyptian-parliament-approves-tougher-penalties-female-genital-mutilation> accessed 4 June 2021.

[214] MA Farouk, 'Egypt toughens penalties for FGM; activists remain sceptical' (*Reuters*, 26 April 2021) <https://www.reuters.com/article/egypt-women-fgm/egypt-toughens-penalties-for-fgm-activists-remain-sceptical-idUSL8N2MJ2HQ> accessed 4 June 2021.

[215] 'As More Families Report FGM Incidents in Egypt, Advocacy Intensifies, and A New Bill Seeks to Increase Penalties' (*UN Women*, 5 February 2021) <https://www.unwomen.org/en/news/stories/2021/2/feature--families-report-fgm-in-egypt-and-advocacy-intensifies> accessed 4 June 2021.

[216] ibid.

[217] ibid.

[218] ibid.

[219] S Shippe, 'Female Genital Mutilation in Egypt' (*The Borgen Project*, 20 January 2021) <https://borgenproject.org/female-genital-mutilation-in-egypt/> accessed 4 June 2021.

[220] ibid.

[221] ibid.

Mexico Beginning in 2015, states in Mexico began to adopt a federal law that set the minimum age of marriage for women and men at eighteen years.[222] By the end of 2018, thirty out of thirty-two Mexican states had adopted the reform.[223] The reform was effective in reducing the rate of formal child marriages.[224] In 2019, the federal government issued a decree, prohibiting marriage for children under eighteen in thirty-one states.[225] The decree annulled some laws that allowed local governments and communities to provide exceptions or consent to child marriages.[226]

In 2017, the Mexican government cosponsored the Human Rights Council resolution on recognising the need to address child, early and forced marriage in humanitarian contexts. In 2019, it co-sponsored the resolution on the consequences of child marriage.[227] In 2018, it co-sponsored the UN General Assembly resolutions on child, early, and forced marriage.[228] During its 2018 Universal Periodic Review, Mexico agreed to review recommendations to work towards ensuring that relevant federal legislation is consistent with the General Act on the Rights of Children and Adolescents in respect of the minimum age for marriage.[229]

At the community level, in 2002, a young Mexican girl, Aleida Ruiz, led the campaign 'Let girls be girls, not wives' which aims at eliminating child marriage and protecting Indigenous girls whose families continue to force them into marriage at a very young age.[230] This campaign was joined by corporations, politicians, and the media, and took the form of ballet classes and conferences at schools in Indigenous communities, which explained the importance of eradicating these forced marriages.[231]

EU The EU has long been involved in fighting against child marriage in third countries. Ending child marriage is considered a priority in the 2015–2019 Action plan on human rights and democracy, the EU Gender action plan for 2016–2020, the EU Strategic engagement to gender equality 2016–2019, the EU Action Plan on Human Rights and Democracy 2020–2024, and the Gender Action Plan 2021–2025.[232] The EU contributed €6 million to the UNFPA-UNICEF Global programme to accelerate action to end child marriage, and allocated €18 million to 'tackle harmful practices such as FGM and child marriage' over the 2014–2020 period.[233] In April 2018, the EU Parliament's Women's Rights and Gender Equality Committee 'adopted an opinion

---

[222] C Bellés-Obrero and M Lombardi, 'Can Minimum-Age-Of-Marriage Laws Eradicate Child Marriage? Evidence From Mexico' (*VoxDev*, 1 August 2021) <https://voxdev.org/topic/health-education/can-minimum-age-marriage-laws-eradicate-child-marriage-evidence-mexico> accessed 4 June 2021.

[223] ibid.

[224] ibid.

[225] 'Decree Bans Marriage for Children Under 18, Eliminates Exceptions' (*Mexico News Daily*, 5 June 2019) <https://mexiconewsdaily.com/news/decree-bans-marriage-for-children-under-18/> accessed 4 June 2021.

[226] ibid.

[227] 'Mexico Map' (*Atlas: Girls Not Brides*) <https://atlas.girlsnotbrides.org/map/mexico/> accessed 4 June 2021.

[228] ibid.

[229] ibid.

[230] B Garcia, 'Aleida Ruiz, The Young Mexican at War with Child Marriage' (*AL DÍA News*, 5 March 2021) <https://aldianews.com/articles/culture/social/aleida-ruiz-young-mexican-war-child-marriage/63186> accessed 19 March 2023.

[231] ibid.

[232] 'Child Marriages: Still Too Many' (*European Parliament*, 2018) <https://www.europarl.europa.eu/RegData/etudes/ATAG/2018/623526/EPRS_ATA(2018)623526_EN.pdf> accessed 4 June 2021.

[233] ibid.

calling for the EU's diplomatic arm to develop a clear strategy and dedicate funds to eradicating child and forced marriage by 2030'.

In February 2020, the Parliament adopted a resolution on an EU strategy to put an end to FGM around the world, seeking to 'ensure that FGM is present in all EU policy documents which are being currently negotiated, ... increase EU budget allocated to this cause both internally and externally and ... review the 2013 Communication in order to step up efforts against the practice worldwide, and tackle the disparities in laws, policies, services and provisions among the Member States'.[234]

From 2015 to 2020, EIGE, the EU-initiated body dedicated exclusively to gender equality, carried out several studies that estimated the risks of FMG in Ireland, Portugal, Sweden, Belgium, Cyprus, France, Greece, Italy, Malta, Denmark, Spain, Luxembourg, and Austria.[235]

World Bank In 2016, the World Bank pledged to invest $2.5 billion over five years in education projects that directly benefit adolescent girls, as part of an effort to keep girls in school and delay child marriages.[236] In 2019, the World Bank Africa Region launched a Human Capital Plan, with an objective to empower women to prevent early marriage and pregnancy for adolescent girls.[237] In 2020, the World Bank Group's Legal Vice Presidency published the Compendium of International and National Legal Frameworks on Domestic Violence, a working document surveying the key international and regional instruments that address FGM.[238]

i) What more needs to be done: some case studies Child marriage
SDG 5.3 acknowledges that eliminating child marriage is both a human right and development priority. The SDG goal is to 'eliminate all harmful practices, such as child, early and forced marriage and female genital mutilation'. UNICEF estimates 12 million girls under eighteen are married each year. Girls who marry before they turn eighteen are less likely to remain in school and more likely to experience domestic violence and live a life of economic impoverishment. Maternal deaths related to pregnancy and childbirth are common for girls aged fifteen to nineteen years worldwide, accounting for 70,000 deaths each year. In several countries unequal age of marriage for women and men is common. For example, in Gabon the age of marriage for man is eighteen and for the woman it is fifteen. Nevertheless, the President of the Republic of the Supreme Court may grant age waivers for serious reasons. These exceptions in the law vitiate

---

[234] 'European Parliament Resolution on an EU Strategy to Put an End to Female Genital Mutilation Around the World' (*European Parliament*, 2020) <https://www.europarl.europa.eu/doceo/document/B-9-2020-0090_EN.html> accessed 4 June 2021.

[235] 'Female Genital Mutilation' (*European Institute for Gender Equality*) <https://eige.europa.eu/gender-based-violence/female-genital-mutilation> accessed 4 June 2021.

[236] 'World Bank Group to Invest $2.5 Billion in Education Projects Benefiting Adolescent Girls' (*The World Bank*, 13 April 2016) <https://www.worldbank.org/en/news/press-release/2016/04/13/world-bank-group-to-invest-25-billion-in-education-projects-benefiting-adolescent-girls> accessed 4 June 2021.

[237] '#Blog4Dev Competition: What will it take to end child marriage in your country?'(*The World Bank*, 2019) <https://www.worldbank.org/en/events/2019/10/19/africa-blog4dev-end-child-marriage> accessed June 04 2021.

[238] 'Compendium of International and National Legal Frameworks on Female Genital Mutilation: Fourth Edition' (n 193).

efforts to raise the age of marriage. For example, Sierra Leone too provides exceptions to the age of marriage, in the Child Rights Act, Section 34 which allows underage marriage under special circumstances. The exceptions include marriage under personal law or customary law or with the consent of at least one of her parents or guardians. In Liberia too, the Domestic Relations Law, Subsection 2.2 allows for exception to minimum age of marriage. Males and females under the age of sixteen could apply for a licence for marriage with the consent of his or her parents.

Namibia too allows for marriages of parties over sixteen years of age by the office of marriage according to the Recognition of Marriages Act, article 10.33. In Venezuela, according to the Civil Code, the minimum age of marriage is waived when the girl is pregnant. Girls in refugee communities are often given in marriage as a way to address financial hardships and fear or sexual abuse. Marriage becomes a way to alleviate the burden of caring for a child.

d) Critique

Both indicators were upgraded from tier II to tier I in 2019 after a data review, suggesting that more available data have been and will be regularly produced for these indicators (the difference between a tier I and II indicator is whether data are regularly produced by countries).[239]

However, to eliminate child marriage, the underlying causes, including unequal power relations between men and women and the lack of strong legal frameworks, need to be addressed.

4. **Target 5.4 Recognise and value unpaid care and domestic work through the provision of public services, infrastructure and social protection policies and the promotion of shared responsibility within the household and the family as nationally appropriate**

a) Sources of the target and empirical analysis

The CEDAW asserts the equal rights and obligations of men and women in regards to parenthood and 'demand[s] fully shared responsibility for child-rearing by both sexes'.[240] It also requires the provision and development of social services, in particular child-care facilities, to improve the enabling of an individual's fulfilment of family and work responsibilities.[241] Target 5.4 embodies this equality principle but has a more ambitious goal that captures the whole gamut of unpaid care and domestic work, not just child raising.

In all regions around the world, women devote more of their time to unpaid care work, as compared with men.[242] This leads to less participation in activities outside

---

[239] 'SDG Indicator changes (15 October 2018 and onward)' (*UN Stats*) <https://unstats.un.org/sdgs/files/List_of_changes_since_15_Oct_2018.pdf> accessed June 2 2021; 'Tier Classification for Global SDG Indicators' (*UNSD*) <https://unstats.un.org/sdgs/iaeg-sdgs/tier-classification/> accessed 2 June 2021.

[240] 'Convention on the Elimination of All Forms of Discrimination Against Women' (n 4) Article 16.

[241] 'Convention on the Elimination of All Forms of Discrimination Against Women' (n 4) Article 11.

[242] 'Enabling Women's Economic Empowerment' (*OECD iLibrary*, 2019) <https://www.oecd-ilibrary.org/sites/4d0229cd-en/index.html?itemId=/content/component/4d0229cd-en#figure-d1e414> accessed 4 June 2021.

the household and in the labour market.[243] Progress on this target is important in and of itself, but is also essential for ensuring success for target 5.5, which aims to enhance women's meaningful participation in the political, economic, and public spheres. Target 5.4 also outlines four policy areas to address unpaid care work: public services, infrastructure, social protection, and shared responsibility within the household.

Under this target, indicator 5.4.1 measures the proportion of time spent on unpaid domestic and care work, by sex, age, and location. Unpaid domestic and care work is defined as 'activities related to the provision of services for own final use by household members or by family members living in other households'.[244] It includes 'food preparation, dishwashing, cleaning and upkeep of the dwelling, laundry, ironing, gardening, caring for pets, shopping, installation, servicing and repair of personal and household goods, childcare, and care of the sick, elderly or disabled household and family members, among others'.[245] Time-use surveys provide the main source of data. UNSD is the agency responsible for this indicator. ILO also has some useful data.

Based on data from ninety-one countries between 2001 and 2019, on average, women spend about 2.5 times as many hours as men on unpaid domestic and care work.[246] In 2018, in Asia and the Pacific, women spent 4.1 times more time on unpaid care and domestic work than men.[247] ILO data also show that women are responsible for 80 per cent of domestic work, limiting their effective labour force participation.[248]

The COVID-19 pandemic and the subsequent lock-down measures have confined people at home, and imposed increased burden of unpaid domestic work disproportionately on men and women. UN Women's data suggest that 60 per cent of women and 54 per cent of men reported an increase in time spent on unpaid domestic work since the pandemic began.[249] Twenty-eight per cent of women, compared with 16 per cent of men, reported increased intensity of domestic work.[250] Among the different types of unpaid care and domestic work, gender balance could be observed in pet care (13 per cent of increase in time for women and 14 per cent for men).[251] For all other types, women were more likely to increase their time: cooking and serving meals (32 per cent for women and 18 per percent for men); cleaning of clothes or household (45 per cent for women and 35 per cent for men); shopping for the family (25 per cent for women and 22 per cent for men); and decoration, repairs, and household management (29 per

[243] ibid.

[244] 'Metadata 05-04-01' (*Unstats.un.org*, 2021) <https://unstats.un.org/sdgs/metadata/files/Metadata-05-04-01.pdf> accessed 4 June 2021.

[245] ibid.

[246] 'The Sustainable Development Goals Report 2020: Achieve Gender Equality and Empower All Women and Girls' (n 1) Progress and Info.

[247] 'ILO: Women Do 4 Times More Unpaid Care Work Than Men in Asia and the Pacific' (*International Labor Organization*, 27 June 2018) <https://www.ilo.org/asia/media-centre/news/WCMS_633284/lang--en/index.htm%3E> accessed 4 June 2021.

[248] 'World Employment and Social Outlook: Trends 2020' (*International Labor Organization*, 2020) <https://www.ilo.org/wcmsp5/groups/public/---dgreports/---dcomm/---publ/documents/publication/wcms_734455.pdf> accessed 4 June 2021.

[249] 'Whose Time to Care: Unpaid Care and Domestic Work During COVID-19' (*UN Women Data*) <https://data.unwomen.org/sites/default/files/inline-files/Whose-time-to-care-brief_0.pdf> accessed 25 May 2021.

[250] ibid.

[251] ibid.

422   SDG 5

cent for women and 24 per cent for men).[252] Men were also more likely to report that they did not usually perform these activities.[253]

This gender imbalance was also reflected among the junior members in the household: 64 per cent of parents noted a higher involvement of daughters, while only 57 per cent of parents noted a higher involvement of sons.[254]

During the pandemic, women also disproportionately performed unpaid care work within the household: 56 per cent of women and 51 per cent of men reported increased time spent on unpaid care work, and 33 per cent of women compared with 26 per cent of men increased time spent ton at least three activities related to unpaid care work.[255] Unsurprisingly, women were also more likely than men to increases time spent on caring for children, teaching, playing with, talking to, and reading to children, and providing affective/emotional support for adult family members.[256] A positive note was that men were slightly more likely than women to increase time spent on assisting elderly, sick, or disabled adults.[257]

b) *Efforts taken at international and domestic level*

China in April 2020, as part of the response to the COVID-19 pandemic, the national government announced a series of policies to support long-term care during the pandemic.[258] Though not explicitly stated as intended to relieving women's home care burden, these measures presumably could reduce the amount and difficulty of such work. In February 2021, a family court in Beijing, China issued a landmark ruling requiring a man to pay his wife for the housework she performed during their marriage. The woman was awarded 50,000 RMB ($7,700) for five years of unpaid care and domestic work.[259] The judge indicated that 'housework constitutes intangible property value'.[260]

i) What more needs to be done: some cases Around the world, special protection for women have sometimes been used to justify excluding women from holding certain jobs based on paternalistic views of employers who see women in their roles as primary caregivers. Discrimination and gender differentials in labour laws have a cause and effect relation to women's status in the family. Many of the gender-based restrictions in labour laws relate to women's assumed care giving roles in the family or their biological differences shaped by women's maternal functions. Nigerian Labor Act in Section 55(1) states that woman cannot be employed on night work in a public or private industrial

---

[252] ibid.
[253] ibid.
[254] ibid.
[255] ibid.
[256] ibid.
[257] ibid.
[258] C Shi and others, 'Report from Mainland China: Policies to Support Long-Term Care During the COVID-19 Outbreak' (*LTC Responses to Covid-19*, 18 April 2020) <https://ltccovid.org/2020/04/18/report-from-mainland-china-policies-to-support-long-term-care-during-the-covid-19-outbreak/> accessed 4 June 2021.
[259] 'China Court Orders Man to Pay Wife for Housework in Landmark Case' (*BBC News*, 24 February 2021) <https://www.bbc.com/news/world-asia-china-56178510> accessed 4 June 2021.
[260] ibid.

undertaking or in any branch, or in any agricultural undertaking. Sierra Leone too restricts women's employment. The Employment Act in Section 47(1) states that women or girls of any age shall be employed or allowed to be for the purpose of employment in any mine below ground. Section 48 states that '[n]o girl or woman of any age or boy who appears to be under eighteen years of age shall be employed during the night in any public or private industrial undertaking, or in any branch thereof, other than an undertaking in which only members of the same family are employed'. These provisions reinforce the stereotype that women are less hardworking, fragile, and unable to take care of themselves. It denies women employment opportunities available to men. A list of work occupations that are prohibited for women in Russia lists 456 occupations and thirty-eight industries that are considered too 'arduous', 'dangerous', or 'harmful' to women's health, in particular to their reproductive health. The list was first adopted in the USSR in 1974 and was confirmed in 2000 by Russian Government Regulation No 162 which allowed for exemptions only if safe working conditions were established by the employer. There is a tension between protecting the special needs of women and achieving equality of employment between men and women. A more dynamic conceptualization of women's roles and gender equality must be shaped by laws that envision women and men's roles in gender neutral terms.

Work/family obligations, traditionally thought to be private sphere activities outside the realm of the law are now becoming the lynchpin of gender equality in employment. Laws that view women only or primarily in their care-giving functions can disadvantage women. What is needed instead is a more dynamic conceptualization of women's roles. This can be achieved through work family reconciliation laws that are gender neutral. Today the most critical determinant of gender equality in the workplace and at home is workplace family reconciliation policies that shape both men and women's opportunities to provide care. The re-examination of the correlation between protective gender laws and gender bias in hiring, firing, and leaving employment must be seen as the first step in re-envisioning a more egalitarian workplace. There is a tension between protecting the special needs of women and achieving equality of employment between men and women. The nexus between gender discrimination in the home and workplace subordination can be combated only by workplace policies that facilitate greater male engagement in family care. Today one of the most critical determinants of gender equality is workplace family reconciliation policies that shape both men's and women's opportunities to provide care. For example, the UK's Equality Act of 2006 requires all public authorities, to have 'due regard' for the promotion of equality between the sexes. The law states that the lack of shared caring responsibilities between women and men is often the single biggest cause of the pay gap. Thus, workplace regulations that support both fathers and mothers in taking more responsibility for caring for children is a key predeterminant of gender equality in the workplace. Women's disproportionate share of family and caretaking responsibilities relates directly to the discrimination they face in the labour market and the subsequent inequalities in their economic progress. Unequal care giving policies undermine the rights of everyone in the family and create the feminization of poverty.

424   SDG 5

Sweden was one of the first countries to transform men's and women's roles in the family. This created a paradigm shift around the world in understanding the dual roles of men and women in work and family. Responding to a UN request to report on the status of women, Sweden argued that '[n]o decisive change in the distribution of functions and status as between the sexes can be achieved if the duties of the male in society are assumed to be unaltered'. Women's disproportionate share of family and care-taking responsibilities relate directly to the discrimination they face in the labour market and subsequent inequalities in their social and economic progress. Gender discrimination in the home and workplace can be combated by workplace policies that facilitate greater male engagement as caregivers in the lives of children. Labour laws that equalize employment opportunities for men and women by redistributing family leave benefits create an environment in which women are neither discriminated against nor stereotyped and men are better able to shoulder family and caregiving responsibilities. Unequal family leave polices impede gender equality both in the family and in public life. For example, in Guatemala, women are entitled to paid maternity leave of thirty days before and fifty-four days after childbirth. On the other hand, men are entitled to two days of leave after childbirth.

c) Critique

Indicator 5.4.1 captures only the initial step to achieving target 5.4; that is, recognizing that women disproportionately devote more time to unpaid care and domestic work. More indicators should be formulated to reflect the full spectrum of the aspirations intended by the target: recognizing unpaid care and domestic chores as 'work', valuing such work, and enhancing international and national efforts to devise corresponding legislations, policies and/or programmes to reduce the burden on women in the division of household work.

Unlike targets 5.1, 5.2, and 5.3, which all have a clearly-defined end goal, target 5.4 does not provide stakeholders with a clear numerical level that needs to be achieved. The allocation of domestic work within a family unit, unlike discrimination or violence, has a less straightforward human rights dimension. From a policy-making perspective, this makes it more difficult to use strong language like those used in the first three targets, and to come up with very clear-cut goals. Varying levels of gender stereotypes and women's social status across the globe also make it unrealistic to adopt a one-size-fits-all approach for all countries when it comes to sharing domestic care and work. Hence the 'as nationally appropriate' language.

As mentioned above, target 5.4 outlines four areas of policy actions. Another area that can potentially supplement the list is education reform. In the UN Secretary-General's High-Level Panel on Women's Economic Empowerment in 2017, the Panel called for the fostering of 'social norms change to redistribute care from women to men and ensure that care is their equal right and responsibility' throughout the education system.[261]

---

[261] ibid.

5. Target 5.5 Ensure women's full and effective participation and equal opportunities for leadership at all levels of decision-making in political, economic and public life

a) Sources of the target

The political aspect of target 5.5 could be traced back to the Convention on the Political Rights of Women, adopted in 1952, which asserts women's right to vote, to be eligible for election, and to hold public office.[262] The subsequent instruments provide more detailed illustrations of what women's political participation should entail. Article 7 of the CEDAW calls on State Parties to commit to the promotion of women's equal political rights and participation in political and public life.[263] The BPfA includes as strategic objectives women's equal access to and full participation in power structures and decision-making, and the increase of women's participation in decision-making and leadership.[264] The UN Economic and Social Council resolution calls on governments, political parties, trade unions, and professional and other representative groups to adopt a 30 per cent minimum proportion of women in leadership positions, with a view to achieving equal representation.[265]

Regarding women's economic empowerment, fundamental issues related to employment are addressed specifically under target 8.5 ('achieve full and productive employment and decent work for all women and men ... and equal pay for work of equal value'), and target 5.5 focuses on women's participation at the leadership and decision-making level.

b) Empirical analysis

Indicator 5.5.1 is a quantitative indicator that measures the proportion of seats held by women in (i) national parliaments and (ii) local governments. Data collected by UN Women show that women serve as heads of state or government in only twenty-two countries, and 119 countries have never had a female leader.[266] It takes 130 years to reach gender parity in this regard at the current rate.[267] In ten countries, a woman serves as head of state, and thirteen countries have a female head of government (6.2 per cent).[268] Women accounted for only 21 per cent of government ministers, and only fourteen countries had 50 per cent or more women cabinets.[269] Women accounted for only a 24.7 per cent of health ministerial positions and 13.2 per cent of financial and

---

[262] 'Convention on the Political Rights of Women' (*United Nations Treaty Collection*, 31 March 1953) <https://treaties.un.org/Pages/ViewDetails.aspx?src=TREATY&mtdsg_no=XVI-1&chapter=16> accessed 4 June 2021.

[263] 'Convention on the Elimination of All Forms of Discrimination Against Women' (n 4).

[264] 'Beijing Declaration and Platform for Action' (n 95).

[265] 'Resolutions And Decisions of The Economic and Social Council' (*United Nations*, 1990) <https://www.un.org/ga/search/view_doc.asp?symbol=E/1990/90> accessed 4 June 2021.

[266] 'Facts and Figures: Women's Leadership and Political Participation' (*UN Women*, 15 January 2021) <https://www.unwomen.org/en/what-we-do/leadership-and-political-participation/facts-and-figures#_edn14> accessed 4 June 2021.

[267] ibid.

[268] ibid; 'COVID-19 and Gender Monitor' (*UN Women Data Hub*, 26 June 2020) <https://data.unwomen.org/resources/covid-19-and-gender-monitor> accessed 4 June 2021.

[269] ibid.

426 SDG 5

budget ministerial positions. At the current rate, gender parity in ministerial positions will not be achieved until 2077.[270]

On average, women account for 25 per cent of national parliament positions, an increase of 11 per cent since 1995 and 2.7 per cent since 2015.[271] Only four countries have 50 per cent or more women in parliament in single or lower houses: Rwanda (61 per cent), Cuba (53 per cent), Bolivia (53 per cent), and the United Arab Emirates (50 per cent). Nineteen countries have 40 per cent or more women in parliament, including nine countries in Europe, five in Latin America and the Caribbean, four in Africa, and one in the Pacific.[272] Most of these countries have gender quotas in place that aim at promoting women's representation in national parliaments.[273] Across the globe, twenty-seven countries have less than 10 per cent of women in parliament in single or lower houses; four of these countries have no women in the single or lower chambers.[274] Further, '[in] Latin America and the Caribbean, … Europe and Northern America, women hold more than 30 per cent of parliamentary seats'.[275] In Northern Africa and Western Asia and Oceania, women occupy less than 17 per cent of national parliament seats. Pacific Island States has the lowest representation rate at 6 per cent.[276]

Regarding women's representation in local governments, data from 133 countries indicate that women account for 2.18 million (36 per cent) elected members in deliberative bodies of local governments.[277] Only two countries have more than 50 per cent of women representation, and eighteen countries with more than 40 per cent.[278] Regional variations can also be observed: Central and Southern Asia, 41 per cent; Europe and Northern America, 35 per cent; Oceania, 32 per cent; Sub-Saharan Africa, 29 per cent; Eastern and South-Eastern Asia, 25 per cent; Latin America and the Caribbean, 25 per cent; Western Asia and Northern Africa, 18 per cent.[279]

Indicator 5.5.2 measures the proportion of females in the total number of person employed in managerial positions.[280] Employment in managerial positions is determined based upon the latest version of the International Standard Classification of Occupations (ISCO-08).[281] Data are collected from labour force surveys or similar types of national household surveys that examine employment.[282] ILO is the responsible agency.

By 2019, women accounted for nearly 39 per cent of global labour force and half of the world's working-age population, but occupied only 28.3 per cent of managerial

---

[270] ibid.
[271] ibid.
[272] ibid.
[273] ibid.
[274] ibid.
[275] ibid.
[276] ibid.
[277] ibid.
[278] ibid.
[279] ibid.
[280] 'Metadata 05-05-02' (*Unstats.un.org*, 2021) <https://unstats.un.org/sdgs/metadata/files/Metadata-05-05-02.pdf> accessed 4 June 2021.
[281] ibid.
[282] ibid.

positions (up from 25 per cent in 2000).[283] This proportion increased by three points since 2000. When women do get a job, they are often excluded from decision-making positions.[284] In 2019, women accounted for 41 per cent of managerial positions in South-Eastern Asia and 40 per cent in Northern America, but only 8 per cent in Northern Africa.[285]

i) COVID-19 impact The pandemic has exacerbated pre-existing gender gaps in the labour sector and women's economic insecurity. In Asia and the Pacific, 50 per cent of women in formal employment reported decreases in working time, compared to 35 per cent of men.[286] In Europe and Central Asia, 25 per cent of self-employed women reported job losses compared to 21 per cent of self-employed men.[287] Of those who work in the informal economy, 740 million women experienced a 60 per cent income drop during the first month of the pandemic (81 per cent in sub-Saharan Africa and Latin America, 70 per cent in Europe and Central Asia, and 22 per cent in Asia and the Pacific.).[288]

Of all employment areas, feminized sectors characterized by low pay and poor working conditions are more likely to be affected negatively by the pandemic.[289] Female employment is 19 per cent more at risk compared to male employment;[290] 72 per cent of domestic workers, 80 per cent of whom are women, have lost their jobs as a result of the pandemic.[291]

Against the backdrop of the pandemic, it is critical to increase women's representation and achieve gender balance in leadership positions in relation to the pandemic. This is essential to ensuring that 'gender dimensions and investments in gender equality are included in response and recovery legislation, economic packages and budgets during and after the pandemic.[292]

c) Critique

i) Political participation Indicator 5.5.1 captures women's parliamentary and local government representation, calculating seats held by women at the national parliaments and local governments. Number of seats is an easily measurable item (and methodologically more reliable), as can be seen from the upgrade of the indicator from a tier II to a tier I indicator.[293] Nonetheless, using this indicator as a measurement of women's level of political participation embodies the idea that simply 'sitting women at the table' would be a

---

[283] 'The Sustainable Development Goals Report 2020: Achieve Gender Equality and Empower All Women and Girls' (n 1).

[284] ibid.

[285] ibid.

[286] G Azcona and others, 'From Insights to Action: Gender Equality in the Wake of COVID-19' (*UN Women*, 2021) <https://www.unwomen.org/en/digital-library/publications/2020/09/gender-equality-in-the-wake-of-covid-19> accessed 4 June 2021.

[287] ibid.

[288] ibid.

[289] ibid.

[290] ibid.

[291] ibid.

[292] ibid.

[293] 'SDG Indicator changes (15 October 2018 and onward)' (n 239).

428   SDG 5

sufficient realization of gender equality. Relying only on this indicator to track women's participation and decision-making power in the political sphere is insufficient as the indicator fails to take into account representation at civil organizations and international bodies. While indicator 5.5.1 only encapsulates representation in the judicial branch, also worth considering is whether the addition of representation in the executive and judicial branch provide a more holistic picture of women's involvement in the political world.

Indicator 5.5.2 is limited in the similar regard in the sense that it fails to identify and acknowledge that the lack of female representation at decision-making and management level is due to structural issues. Combined, these two indicators still subscribe to the flawed idea that more positions occupied by women equates to more effective and empowering participation of women in the public and private sphere.

6. Target 5.6 Ensure universal access to sexual and reproductive health and reproductive rights as agreed in accordance with the Programme of Action of the International Conference on Population and Development and the Beijing Platform for Action and the outcome documents of their review conferences

a) Sources of the target

An individual's reproductive and sexual right is an indispensable component of her human rights, including the right to life, the right to be free from torture, the right to privacy, the right to education, and the right to be free from discrimination.[294] The CEDAW guarantees women's equal rights in deciding 'freely and responsibly on the number and spacing of their children and to have access to the information, education and means to enable them to exercise these rights.'[295] In article 10, it articulates that women's right to education includes 'access to specific educational information to help to ensure the health and well-being of families, including information and advice on family planning.'[296] The BPfA recognizes that 'the human rights of women include their right to have control over and decide freely and responsibly on matters related to their sexuality, including sexual and reproductive health, free of coercion, discrimination and violence.'[297]

The Committee on Economic, Social and Cultural Rights (CESCR) General Comment No 14 explains the International Covenant on Economic, Social and Cultural Rights, and states that Article 12.2(a) of the Covenant requires states to 'improve ... maternal health, sexual and reproductive health services, including access to family planning, pre- and post-natal care, emergency obstetric services and access to information, as well as to resources necessary to act on that information.'[298] General Comment No 22 recommends states 'to repeal or eliminate laws, policies and practices

---

[294] 'Sexual and Reproductive Health and Rights' (*OHCHR*) <https://www.ohchr.org/en/issues/women/wrgs/pages/healthrights.aspx> accessed 4 June 2021.
[295] 'Convention on the Elimination of All Forms of Discrimination Against Women' (n 4).
[296] ibid.
[297] 'Beijing Declaration and Platform for Action' (n 95).
[298] 'Substantive Issues Arising in the Implementation of the International Covenant on Economic, Social and Cultural Rights, General Comment No 14' (*United Nations*, 2000) <https://docstore.ohchr.org/SelfServices/FilesHandler.ashx?enc=4slQ6QSmlBEDzFEovLCuW1AVC1NkPsgUedPlF1vfPMJ2c7ey6PAz2qaojTzDJmC0y%2b9t%2bsAtGDNzdEqA6SuP2r0w/6sVBGTpvTSCbiOr4XVFTqhQY65auTFbQRPWNDxL> accessed 4 June 2021.

TARGETS AND INDICATORS

that criminalise, obstruct or undermine access by individuals or a particular group to sexual and reproductive health facilities, services, goods and information'.[299]

b) Empirical analysis

Indicators 5.6.1 and 5.6.2 measure the legal and regulatory framework for sexual and reproductive health and reproductive rights, as well as women's reproductive decision-making. The two indicators are designed to complement each other and offer a 'complementary examination of whether a country has a positive enabling legal and normative framework, and whether its provisions go the last mile to empower all women and girls'.[300] Indicator 5.6.1 measures the proportion of women aged fifteen to forty-nine years who make their own informed decisions regarding sexual relations, contraceptive use and reproductive healthcare.[301] This indicator reflects whether women, irrespective of the country's legal framework, are able to decide on their sexual and reproductive health and reproductive rights. To be considered autonomous and empowered in one's reproductive rights, women need to confirm that they make their own decisions in all three areas: consensual sexual relations, contraceptive use, and seeking reproductive health care for themselves.

For sexual relations, the respondent needs to answer affirmatively to the question ('can you say no to your husband/partner if you do not want to have sexual intercourse?').[302] For contraceptive use, the respondent needs to select either mainly respondent or joint decision ('who usually makes the decision on whether or not you should use contraception?').[303] For reproductive healthcare, respondent should answer 'you' or 'you and your husband/partner jointly' to the question ('who usually makes decision about healthcare for yourself?').[304] Data are collected from national household surveys administered by individual countries. UNFPA is the custodian agency for this target's indicators.

Data from fifty-seven countries shows that as of early 2020, only 55 per cent of married or in-union women aged fifteen to forty-nine make their own decisions regarding sexual and reproductive health and rights.[305] The proportion varies across regions, with Middle Africa and Western Africa in the lower end (less than 40 per cent) and some countries in Europe, South-eastern Asia, Latin America and the Caribbean in the higher end (nearly 80 per cent).[306] The level of autonomy and empowerment also varies

---

[299] 'General Comment No 22 (2016) On the Right to Sexual and Reproductive Health (Article 12 of the International Covenant on Economic, Social and Cultural Rights)' (*United Nations*, 2 May 2016) <https://docstore.ohchr.org/SelfServices/FilesHandler.ashx?enc=4slQ6QSmlBEDzFEovLCuW1a0Szab0oXTdImnsJZZVQfQejF41Tob4CvIjeTiAP6sGFQktiae1vlbbOAekmaOwDOWsUe7N8TLm%2bP3HJPzxjHySkUoHMavD/pyfcp3Ylzg> accessed 4 June 2021.

[300] 'Tracking Women's Decision-Making for Sexual and Reproductive Health and Reproductive Rights' (*UNFPA*, 2020) <https://www.unfpa.org/sites/default/files/resource-pdf/20-033_SDG561-BrochureA4-v1.21.pdf> accessed 4 June 2021.

[301] ibid.
[302] ibid.
[303] ibid.
[304] ibid.
[305] ibid.
[306] ibid.

across the three sub-indicators: women seem to be most autonomous regarding contraceptive use (global average 91 per cent), but lack autonomy on consensual sex (about 75 per cent).[307]

Indicator 5.6.2 measures the number of countries with laws and regulations that guarantee full and equal access to women and men aged fifteen years and older to sexual and reproductive healthcare, information, and education. It aims to 'provide the first comprehensive global assessment of legal and regulatory frameworks regarding access to [sexual and reproductive health and reproductive rights.[308] The goal of the indicator is to 'increase the number of countries with laws and regulations that guarantee women and men full and equal access to sexual and reproductive health care, information and education, and to compel countries to remove legal barriers that interfere with this full and equal access.[309] The indicator assesses thirteen components in four sectors:

- maternity care (maternity care, life-saving commodities, legal status of abortion, post-abortion care)
- comprehensive sexuality education (CSE) and information (CSE law, CSE curriculum)
- contraception and family planning (contraception, consent for contraceptive services, emergency contraception)
- sexual health and well-being (HIV testing and counselling, HIV treatment and care, confidentiality of health status for men and women living with HIV, HPV vaccine)

Among the seventy-five countries which reported complete data, on average, countries have in place 73 per cent of the laws and regulations needed to guarantee full and equal access to sexual and reproductive health rights.[310] When it comes to HIV, the findings are encouraging: on average, countries have in place 87 per cent of laws and regulations for HIV counselling and test services, 91 per cent for HIV treatment, and 96 per cent for HIV confidentiality.[311] Additionally, countries have on average 79 per cent of laws and regulations in place that mandate full, free, and informed consent for contraceptive services.[312] Achievements in maternity care and life-saving commodities are also encouraging (87 and 88 per cent of laws and regulations in place, respectively).[313]

Countries on average are most lacking in formulating laws and regulations for CSE curriculum (57 per cent).[314] Other components that require improvement include

---

[307] ibid.
[308] 'Legal Commitments for Sexual and Reproductive Health and Reproductive Rights for All' (*UNFPA*) <https://www.unfpa.org/sites/default/files/resource-pdf/UNFPA-SDG562-A4-Brochure-v4.15.pdf> accessed 4 June 2021.
[309] ibid.
[310] ibid.
[311] ibid.
[312] ibid.
[313] ibid.
[314] ibid.

human papilloma virus (HPV) vaccine (45 per cent), legal status of abortion (31 per cent), and emergency contraception (69 per cent).[315]

There are regional divides for this indicator. Northern Africa has only 45 per cent of laws and regulations in place, followed by Southern Asia (60 per cent), and Latin America and the Caribbean (66 per cent). New Zealand has the highest level (94 per cent), followed by Europe (84 per cent), and Eastern Asia (83 per cent). The five countries with the highest overall score are Sweden (100), Uruguay (99), Cambodia (98), Finland (98), and Netherlands (98). The five countries with the lowest overall score are South Sudan (16), Trinidad and Tobago (32), Libya (33), Iraq (39), and Belize (42).

7. Target 5.a Undertake reforms to give women equal rights to economic resources, as well as access to ownership and control over land and other forms of property, financial services, inheritance and natural resources, in accordance with national laws

a) Sources of the target

Women's rights to land and property are essential for the realization for gender equality. Several international human rights instruments reference women's equal rights to the access, use, and control over land. The Universal Declaration of Human Rights recognises women's equal rights to property.[316] The International Covenant on Economic, Social and Cultural Rights calls on States Parties to 'undertake to ensure the equal right of men and women to the enjoyment of all economic, social and cultural rights set forth in the present Covenant' and prohibits discrimination based on sex'.[317]

CEDAW calls on States Parties to end discrimination against women in laws, policies and practices, including through the adoption of temporary special measures.[318] Article 15.2 obliges States to accord women equal legal capacity in civil matters, in particular 'equal rights to conclude contracts and to administer property'.[319] Article 16.1(h) obliges states to ensure 'the same rights for both spouses in respect of the ownership, acquisition, management, administration, enjoyment and disposition of property, whether free of charge or for a valuable consideration'.[320]

b) Empirical analysis

Target 5.a has two indicators under it, for both of which FAO is the custodian agency. Both indicators concern land control and/or ownership, and this focus on land reflects the idea that land is a key economic resource. Indicator 5.A.1 is a quantitative indicator, and it measures (i) the proportion of total agricultural population with ownership or secure rights over agricultural land, by sex; and (ii) share of women among owners or

---

[315] ibid.
[316] 'Universal Declaration of Human Rights' (n 194).
[317] ibid.
[318] 'Convention on the Elimination of All Forms of Discrimination Against Women' (n 4).
[319] ibid.
[320] ibid.

rights-bearers of agricultural land, by type of tenure.[321] Part (a) measures how prevalent ownership or secure rights over agricultural land are in the reference population.[322] Part (b) measures the share of women among owners or rights-bearers of agricultural land and can be used to assess the under-representation of women among owners or holders of agricultural land.[323]

A study from 2015 published by the FAO shows that out of the ten countries surveyed, only Ecuador has a higher proportion of female agricultural landowners than male agricultural landowners within the agricultural population.[324] In the other countries surveyed, relatively fewer women than men have ownership and/or secure tenure rights over agricultural land.[325] Globally, women account for only 12.8 per cent of agricultural landholders.[326] In the nine countries surveyed, men own a larger proportion of the land area than women.[327]

The study also shows that out of the ten countries surveyed, there are three where female landowners outnumber men.[328] In Malawi, the relative share of women landowners exceeds 55 per cent.[329] In the few countries with more than one data point, however, there appears a narrowing of the gap between the percentage of men and the percentage of women with ownership and/or secure tenure rights over agricultural land.[330]

Indicator 5.A.2 is a qualitative indicator, which measures the proportion of countries where the legal framework (including customary law) guarantees women's equal rights to land ownership and/or control. It measures the extent of women's disadvantages in ownership of and rights to land, as well as equal legal rights to land ownership.[331] This indicator collects all existing national policy objectives, draft provisions, legal provisions, and implementing legislation that reflect good practices in guaranteeing women's equal rights to land ownership and/or control.[332] The inclusion of this indicator 'acknowledges that greater equality in the ownership and control over land contributes to economic efficiency and has positive multiplier effects for the achievement of a range of other SDGs including poverty reduction (SDG 1), food security (SDG 2), and the welfare of households, communities and countries (SDGs 3, 11, and 16, among others)'.[333]

---

[321] 'The Sustainable Development Goals Report 2020: Achieve Gender Equality and Empower All Women and Girls' (n 1) Targets and Indicators.
[322] 'Sustainable Development Goals 5.A.1' (*FAO*) <https://www.fao.org/sustainable-development-goals/indicators/5a1/en/> accessed 4 June 2021.
[323] ibid.
[324] Ana Paula De La O Campus and others, 'Gender and Land Statistics Recent Developments in FAO'S Gender and Land Rights Database' (*FAO*, 2015) 10 <http://www.fao.org/3/i4862e/i4862e.pdf> accessed 4 June 2021.
[325] ibid 28.
[326] ibid 7.
[327] ibid 14.
[328] 'Sustainable Development Goals 5.A.1' (n 322).
[329] ibid.
[330] ibid.
[331] 'Sustainable Development Goals 5.A.2' (*FAO*) <http://www.fao.org/sustainable-development-goals/indicators/5a2/en/> accessed 4 June 2021.
[332] ibid.
[333] 'Achieving SDG Indicator 5.A.2 in the Western Balkans and Beyond' (*FAO*, 2020) 3 <https://www.fao.org/3/cb0173en/CB0173EN.pdf> accessed 4 June 2021.

FAO suggests that in many countries, '[l]egal frameworks fail to provide enough guarantees for gender equality in ownership and/or control over land', and [s]ubstantial progress is still needed both in law formulation and implementation to realise women's land rights'.[334] Its global assessment of sixteen notational legal frameworks shows that many countries lack legal provisions that provide adequate protection of women's rights to land.[335] The degree to which the legal framework guarantees women's equal rights to land ranges from very low to medium in more than 60 per cent of assessed countries, and only 12 per cent of assessed countries guarantee a very high degree of protection for gender equality in land ownership and/or control.[336] FAO further illustrates that:

> [d]isaggregated data by six key criteria for this type of legal framework suggest that legal provisions that mandate or incentivise joint registration of land in married couples are lacking in most countries. Without the inclusion of women's names and rights on the land registration document, women's property rights remain insecure, particularly for women who separate, divorce, or become abandoned or widowed. In such situations, women may be forced to undertake costly legal action to claim their rights.
>
> In countries in which legal pluralism prevails (where the formal law coexists with customary laws), women land rights are less protected. For instance, in countries where some aspects of customary laws override constitutional provisions, women's land rights are less safeguarded, particularly when it comes to inheritance or matrimonial rights. Likewise, where customary law is recognised, very often the rights of women are not protected if they conflict with the formal law and are more likely to be endangered by entrenched patriarchal norms.[337]

According to the 2021 SDG Progress report, data from thirty-six countries suggest that substantial improvement has been achieved in equal inheritance rights (69 per cent), and to a lesser extent in spousal consent for land transactions (61 per cent). Areas pertaining to land registration, customary law, and women's representation in land governance, among others, are still lagging behind.[338]

In addition to land ownership, target 5.a also aspires to ensure women equal rights' and access to other forms of economic resources, though there are no official indicators measuring '[access to] other forms of property, financial services, inheritance and natural resources'. Regarding women's access to financial services, on the whole, women are less likely to have a bank account than men: a 2017 World Bank report shows that globally, 65 per cent of women have a bank account and 72 per cent of men do.[339] In

---

[334] 'Sustainable Development Goals 5.A.2' (n 331).
[335] ibid.
[336] ibid.
[337] ibid.
[338] 'The Sustainable Development Goals Report 2020: Achieve Gender Equality and Empower All Women and Girls' (n 1) Progress and Info.
[339] 'The Global Findex Database: 1 Account Ownership' (*Global Findex World Bank*, 2017) 23 <https://globalfin dex.worldbank.org/sites/globalfindex/files/chapters/2017%20Findex%20full%20report_chapter1.pdf> accessed 4 June 2021.

developing countries, 67 per cent of men have an account while only 59 per cent of women do.[340] This gender gap has not improved substantially from 2011.[341]

8. Target 5.b Enhance the use of enabling technology, in particular information and communications technology, to promote the empowerment of women

a) Sources of the target

Target 5.b recognizes the increasing importance of information and communications technology (ICT) and aims to harness it as a powerful tool for female empowerment. It is estimated that 90 per cent of future jobs will require knowledge and skills of ICT and other ICT-related fields, including computer, mathematical, architecture, and engineering fields.[342] Mobile phone ownership, in particular, is an important metric that reflects gender equality, since it 'provides women with a degree of independence and autonomy, including for professional purposes'.[343]

b) Empirical analysis

Indicator 5.b.1 measures the proportion of individuals who own a mobile telephone, by sex.[344] An individual owns a mobile phone if 'he/she has a mobile cellular phone device with at least one active SIM card for personal use'.[345] Data are generated based on an annual survey that ITU sends to individual countries.[346]

In the sixty-six countries and territories with data for 2017 to 2019, mobile phone ownership among women was on average 8.5 percentage point lower than for men.[347] In about one-third of the economies surveyed, women's mobile phone ownership is close to parity to that of men.[348] In twelve of these sixty-nine economies, more women own phones than men, while in twenty-six countries, men's mobile ownership is substantially higher than that of women.[349] The gender gap in mobile ownership is most pronounced in South America.[350] Country-specific data show that the mobile phone gender gap is 23 per cent in India, 33 per cent in Bangladesh, and 45 per cent in Pakistan (2018 data).[351] The gender gap ranges from 12 per cent in South Africa to 60 per cent in Rwanda.[352]

---

[340] ibid.
[341] ibid.
[342] P Mlambo-Ngcuka, 'Reshaping the Future: Women, Girls, ICTs and the SDGs' (*ITUNews*, 9 February 2018) <https://news.itu.int/reshaping-future-women-girls-icts/> accessed 4 June 2021.
[343] 'Metadata 05-0B-01' (*Unstats.un.org*, 2021) <https://unstats.un.org/sdgs/metadata/files/Metadata-05-0B-01.pdf> accessed 4 June 2021.
[344] 'The Sustainable Development Goals Report 2020: Achieve Gender Equality and Empower All Women and Girls' (n 1) Targets and Indicators.
[345] 'Metadata 05-0B-01' (n 343).
[346] ibid.
[347] 'The Sustainable Development Goals Report 2020: Achieve Gender Equality and Empower All Women and Girls' (n 1) Progress and Info.
[348] 'Measuring Digital Development Facts and Figures' (*ITU*, 2020) 11 <https://www.itu.int/en/ITU-D/Statistics/Documents/facts/FactsFigures2020.pdf> accessed 4 June 2021.
[349] ibid.
[350] ibid.
[351] 'Women, ICT and Emergency Telecommunications: Opportunities and Constraints' (*ITU*, 2020) 10 <https://www.itu.int/en/ITU-D/Emergency-Telecommunications/Documents/events/2020/Women-ICT-ET/Full-report.pdf> accessed 4 June 2021.
[352] ibid.

Internet usage ITU's 2020 report shows that in 2019, an estimated 55 per cent of the male population was using the Internet, compared with 48 per cent of the female population.[353] The gender gap in Internet usage is higher in developing countries (9 per cent) than developed countries (2 per cent).[354] In developing countries, less than half of the women population use the Internet.[355] Africa has the highest gender gap in Internet usage (17 per cent), followed by Arab states (14 per cent), Asia and the Pacific region (7 per cent).

Between 2013 and 2019, the gender gap approximated zero in the Americas and has been shrinking in Europe.[356] However, the gender gap has been growing in the Arab states, Asia and the Pacific, and Africa, because more of the additional Internet users since 2013 have been men than women.[357]

Regional data Within the EU, 14 per cent of women have never used the Internet, compared with 12 per cent of men.[358] The gender divides are more pronounced in advanced IT skills, tertiary education, employment, and decision-making in the digital sector.[359] Girls and women are less likely to continue studying science and technology beyond the age of fifteen, enter or continue a career in ICT, reach specialist and managerial levels, or start their own tech companies.[360] Men are more likely than women to possess digital skills, use a personal computer on a daily basis, go online through mobile devices, read news online, and make online purchases.[361] In only four EU Member States, the proportion of women who use a computer daily is higher than that of men.[362] In 2016, 4 per cent of women created websites or blogs, compared with 6 per cent of men.[363]

Another 2018 European Parliament report shows that women are underrepresented and make less money than men in the ICT sector.[364] Only 9 per cent of developers and 19 per cent of people in management positions in the ICT sector were women.[365] In 2015, 17.2 per cent of ICT students and 16.7 per cent of employed ICT specialist were women. On average, women earned 18.9 per cent less than men in this

---

[353] 'Measuring Digital Development Facts and Figures' (n 348) 8.
[354] ibid.
[355] ibid.
[356] 'Bridging the Gender Divide' (*ITU*, November 2019) <https://www.itu.int/en/mediacentre/background ers/Pages/bridging-the-gender-divide.aspx#:~:text=Challenges%20and%20solutions-,A%20substantial%20div ide%20persists%20between%20women%20and%20men%20and%20between,gap%20is%2017%20per%20cent> accessed 4 June 2021.
[357] ibid.
[358] 'Gender Equality in the EU'S Digital and Media Sectors' (*European Parliament*, March 2018) 1 <https://www.europarl.europa.eu/cmsdata/139421/EPRS-briefing-614695-Women-and-the-media-FINAL.pdf> accessed 4 June 2021.
[359] ibid.
[360] ibid.
[361] ibid.
[362] ibid.
[363] ibid.
[364] 'More Women in ICT: Empowering Women in the Digital World' (*European Parliament*, 3 August 2018) <https://www.europarl.europa.eu/news/en/headlines/society/20180301STO98927/more-women-in-ict-emp owering-women-in-the-digital-world> accessed 4 June 2021.
[365] ibid.

436   SDG 5

sector.[366] In 2012, across the EU, women occupy less than 30 per cent of ICT sector jobs.[367]

c) Critique

One of the most apparent flaws is that while ICTs capture a wide range of technologies, including Internet, wireless networks, cell phones, computers, and software, there is only one indicator that measures the ownership of cell phones. Ownership does not necessarily equate with informed use, and where data are available, additional indicators should be formulated to measure access (and possibly the skill level) to a computer and the Internet.

9. Target 5.c Adopt and strengthen sound policies and enforceable legislation for the promotion of gender equality and the empowerment of all women and girls at all levels

a) Sources of the target

Target 5.c examines national efforts to promote gender equality from a systemic, procedural perspective. The Beijing Declaration and Platform of Action recognizes the importance of 'the integration of a gender perspective in budgetary decisions on policies and programmes' and 'adequate financing of specific programmes for securing equality between men and women'.[368] The 2030 Agenda for SDG, though not setting a specific target, endeavours to achieve 'a significant increase in investments to close the gender gap and strengthen support for institutions in relation to gender equality and the empowerment of women at the global, regional and national levels'.[369]

b) Empirical analysis

Target 5.c encompasses one indicator, 5.c.1, which measures the percentage of governments with systems to track and make public resource allocations for gender equality.[370] This indicator captures characteristics of a country's fiscal system and aims to encourage national governments to implement budget trading and monitoring systems and endeavour to be transparent about information regarding budget allocations for gender equality and women's empowerment (GEWE).[371] It assesses three criteria: first, if a government has 'programs/policies and resource allocations to foster GEWE'; second, 'if a government has planning and budget tools to track resources for GEWE throughout the public financial management cycle'; and third, if a government has provisions to make allocations for GEWE publicly available.[372] A country would

[366] ibid.
[367] 'Women In ICT' (*European Parliament*, 2012) 6 <https://www.europarl.europa.eu/RegData/etudes/note/join/2012/462469/IPOL-FEMM_NT%282012%29462469_EN.pdf> accessed 4 June 2021.
[368] 'Beijing Declaration and Platform for Action' (n 95) [345]–[346].
[369] 'The Sustainable Development Goals Report 2020: Achieve Gender Equality and Empower All Women and Girls' (n 1).
[370] 'Metadata 05-0C-01' (*Unstats.un.org*, 2021) <https://unstats.un.org/sdgs/metadata/files/Metadata-05-0c-01.pdf> accessed 4 June 2021.
[371] ibid.
[372] ibid.

need to satisfy all three criteria questionnaires with questions assessing these three criteria will be sent to each country's Ministry of Finance or agency in charge of government budget.[373] UN Women, in collaboration with OECD and UNDP, are responsible for the data under this indicator.

In 2018, 81 per cent of sixty-nine countries with data required improvements to track budget allocations for gender equality.[374] This means only thirteen countries have a tracking system in place to monitor gender budget allocations and make them publicly available.

Additional data from UN Women show that progress under this target remains to be achieved. At the national level, resources allocated to promoting gender equality are consistently low.[375] A study on spending shows that in twenty-four countries in the Americas and the Caribbean, budget allocated to the elimination of gender-based violence accounted for less than 1 per cent of the national budget.[376]

c) Critique

Indicator 5.c.1 is not an indicator of quantity or quality of budget allocation.[377] Instead, it looks at whether a country has programmes/policies dedicated to the promotion of GEWE, and whether it also has mechanisms to track budget allocations and that make information publicly available.[378] It is process-oriented and does not provide data on either the sufficiency or quality of the budget.[379] In other words, a country may have well-formulated programmes in place but lack the appropriate resource to implement the programmes.

As mentioned above, the 2030 Agenda commits to the increase in investments, but we are unable to tell this aspect from this indicator and, at least under SDG 5, there is no indicator specifically dedicated to the allocation of resources/budget for GEWE programmes/policies.

Annex/Postscript

The lockdown and quarantine during the COVID-19 emergency spawned different legal measures to address the spike in gender-based violence. France enabled remote protection orders for women survivors of domestic violence through the 'sexual and sexist violence reporting platform'. Specifically, this reporting mechanism allowed women to directly interact with law enforcement officials trained in gender-based/sexual violence

---

[373] ibid.

[374] 'The Sustainable Development Goals Report 2020: Achieve Gender Equality and Empower All Women and Girls' (n 1) Progress and Info,

[375] 'Facts and Figures: Governance and National Planning' (*UN Women*, January 2019) <https://www.unwomen.org/en/what-we-do/governance-and-national-planning/facts-and-figures#notes> accessed 4 June 2021.

[376] ibid.

[377] 'Metadata 05-0C-01' (n 370).

[378] ibid.

[379] ibid.

438 SDG 5

to file claims, during lockdown.[380] South Africa enabled access to courts for women survivors of violence to address, prevent, and combat the spread of COVID-19 in all courts, court precincts, and justice service points. Article 20(b) of the Directions issued by the Minister of Justice provides that applications for interim protection orders, against domestic violence and harassment, could still be heard during the lockdown period.[381] Moreover, South Africa provided other services for women survivors of violence through the development of a strategic plan. South Africa's National Strategic Plan on Gender-Based Violence in the midst of an increase in cases of gender-based violence during the imposition of the COVID-19 lockdown restrictions, amongst other things, broadened the access to justice for survivors of gender-based violence.[382] El Salvador provided access to hotlines for women survivors of violence on 21 April 21 2020 through the establishment of El Centro de Atención Telefónico. A free helpline operated 24/7 and provided assistance for gender-based violence cases.[383] Lebanon too provided for remote protection orders for women survivors of domestic violence through the Attorney General of the Court of Cassation's Public Circular. The Circular provides procedures on obtaining protection orders remotely and instructs public prosecutors specialized in domestic violence to take all possible measures to protect women victims and their children, including not requiring the victim to be present in the judicial police centre for her testimony in case she indicates that she cannot move due to health conditions and allowing the specialized appeal to the General Attorney to hear the victims' testimony via technological means, or by any other means available. Lebanon enabled access to courts for women survivors of violence through the Attorney General of the Court of Cassation's Public Circular. In dealing with cases of domestic violence, the specialized Appeal General Attorney would listen to the victim personally via technological means or by any appropriate means. Egypt promulgated a ministerial decree[384] specifically addressing domestic violence[385] which provided psychological services for women survivors of violence on 6 May 6 2020, through the 'Our Mental Health is a Priority' initiative. This initiative provided psychological assistance to women survivors of violence during the COVID-19 pandemic and raised awareness regarding the availability of psychological and social services available to families in times of crises.[386]

---

[380] Loi No. 2010-769; Code Pénal, arts 132-80, 222-8(4° ter) et 222-24(11°)—Law specifically addressing domestic violence (2022); (WBL 2022 DATA WBL1971-2022 Dataset).

[381] (2020) (WBL2021_COVID19Data_22Feb2021).

[382] ibid.

[383] Ley Contra la Violencia Intrafamiliar; Ley Especial Integral para una Vida Libre de Violencia para las Mujeres, art 8(k) (2020); (WBL 2022 DATA WBL1971-2022 Dataset).

[384] Ministerial Decree No 827/2021, art 1 (2022).

[385] (WBL 2022 DATA WBL1971-2022 Dataset).

[386] (2020) (WBL2021_COVID19Data_22Feb2021).

Law Reform on Women's Economic Participation

Although unrelated to COVID, during the period of 2020–2022, several states removed barriers to equalize opportunities for women to enter the labour market and receive equal wages for equal work. Bahrain, Benin, Burundi, Costa Rica, Montenegro, Saudi Kingdom, and Vietnam prohibited discrimination in employment and legislated equal pay for equal work.[387] Bahrain, Saudi Kingdom, Vietnam, and Costa Rica repealed the prohibition against night work and in jobs that were previously closed to women.[388] Vietnam and the Marshall Islands prohibited discrimination in access to credit, and both Marshall Islands and Montenegro allowed for equal opportunity to register a business.[389] In the Sindh Region, Pakistan, the ban on women night-time employment was repealed; however, the restrictions on registering women owned business remains.[390] During this period, Senegal prohibits discrimination based on gender when calculating health insurance premiums.[391] The UAE made some comprehensive reforms, including equal pay for equal work but also recognized women as heads of household and allowed the equal rights for a woman to choose her place of residence. Moreover, the Central Bank of UAE prohibited gender discrimination in access to credit.[392] In Gabon too, similar measures were taken to equalize both employment opportunities for women and to provide equal access for economic opportunities.[393] Women may choose the place of residence, are recognized as heads of household, have equal access to credit, can open a bank account in their name, and have equal administrative authority over marital assets, including ownership of property.

The legal measures adopted during COVID to increase women's access to justice and economic equity should be seen not as episodic in nature but as part of the state's obligations under the CEDAW. These new legal measures must be sustained as a systemic law reform to address structural inequalities women face.

Legal reforms in Gabon between 2021 and 2022 struck down husband obedience laws and allows women the equal right to decisions regarding residence and to be recognized in law as head of household. Women have equal rights to marital property and access to credit. Women no longer require a husband's permission to get a job. Women also do not need permission of a husband to open a bank account.[394] Despite these reformist programmes during a time of a public health and economic crisis, several countries still retain gender discriminatory laws on the book. On the other hand, Bahrain and Qatar still legally allow a rapist to marry his victim as a way of mitigating the crime

---

[387] (WBL 2022 DATA WBL1971-2022 Dataset).
[388] ibid.
[389] ibid.
[390] ibid.
[391] Loi No 2003-14 du 4 juin 2004 relative aux Mutuelles de santé, art 8 (non-discrimination in access to healthcare).
[392] (WBL 2022 DATA WBL1971-2022 Dataset).
[393] ibid.
[394] See World Bank Women, Business and Law Report 2022.

440   SDG 5

of rape. We also see the rollback of prior gains due to patriarchal politics. For example, the Tunisia's new electoral law—Presidential Decree Law 55—issued in 2022 has eliminated the principle of gender parity in elected assemblies from a previous electoral law. A human rights-based approach to SDG 5 remains critical during this time of a global reckoning on gender equality and an inflection point in the international political economy. The progress towards meeting SDG 5 need to create a radical overhaul of inequitable and patriarchal structures that hold women back.

SDG 6

'Ensure Availability and Sustainable Management of Water and Sanitation for All'

Owen McIntyre

I. Introduction

The Sustainable Development Goals (SDGs) seek to build upon the widely-acknowledged success of the Millennium Development Goals (MDGs),[1] which for the first time established at the global level a set of quantifiable targets for critical elements of the sustainable development paradigm, which were non-binding in character and relied solely upon the political commitment of states and other actors. The SDGs came into effect on 1 January 2016 with the aim of stimulating collective action for the realization of sustainable development and of guiding the developmental decisions of state and other actors over the subsequent fifteen years. Of the seventeen individual goals and 169 targets identified and agreed in the course of an extensive and participative process, SDG 6, which enshrines an unequivocal commitment to '[e]nsure availability and sustainable management of water and sanitation for all', is without question one of the most significant in terms of its potential impact on development outcomes. It is not alone important as a critical developmental goal in its own right but also due to its extensive impact on almost all other sectoral SDGs including, most notably, SDG 1 (eradication of extreme poverty), SDG 2 (eradication of extreme hunger), SDG 3 (improving health and well-being), SDG 4 (inclusive and quality education), SDG 5 (gender equality), SDG 7 (affordable and clean energy), SDG 11 (sustainable cities and communities), SDG 12 (responsible consumption and production), SDG 13 (climate action), SDG 14 (marine and coastal pollution), and SDG 15 (land-based ecosystems). Indeed, several of these SDGs make express mention of water in one or more of their associated targets,[2] indicating that sustainable management of water resources is crucial to their achievement. However, SDG 6 is similarly dependent upon certain other

---

[1] See, eg, JD Sachs, 'From Millennium Development Goals to Sustainable Development Goals' (2012) The Lancet 379, 2206–11.

[2] For example, targets listed under SDG 3 aim to 'end ... water-borne diseases', and 'substantially reduce the number of deaths and illnesses from ... water ... pollution and contamination'; SDG 11 target 4 aims to 'significantly reduce the number of deaths and the number of people affected and substantially decrease the direct economic losses ... caused by ... water-related disasters'; SDG 12 target 4 aims to significantly reduce the release of chemicals and wastes to water; and targets listed under SDG 15 seek to ensure conservation, restoration, and sustainable use of inland freshwater ecosystems, including in particular wetlands, in line with obligations under international agreements.

SDGs. As is the case with many of the other goals, achievement of SDG 6 will be largely dependent upon measures required to advance the non-sectoral, cross-cutting goal set out in SDG 16 (peace, justice, and strong institutions) and the 'good governance' values and arrangements inherent therein.[3] Similarly, it is clear that advances in responsible consumption and production in line with SDG 12 will play a significant role in achieving sustainable water management.

Although the SDGs, like the MDGs which preceded them,[4] are intended to be non-legally binding, they are likely to transform utterly the dynamic of the processes for formation of national, transnational, and international rules for the realization of economic, social, and environmental rights and the promotion of human welfare more generally. It is immediately apparent upon an examination of the specific targets associated with SDG 6[5] that efforts to achieve these targets will need to be supported by formal rules of domestic and international water law, environmental law, and human rights law, which will become increasingly sophisticated and prescriptive in terms of their normative implications.[6] At the same time, it is quite clear that SDG 6 and, more particularly, the specific targets and related indicators set out thereunder, are likely to act as a strong catalyst for the continuing development of international and domestic rules for sustainable water management. The inclusive participatory process employed for the elaboration and adoption of the SDGs, as well as the institutional and administrative mechanisms emerging for their implementation and for monitoring progress, enhance the normative legitimacy of the core values enshrined in socially progressive water-related legal instruments, thereby conferring upon the SDGs the potential to transform the interpretation and continuing development of water law frameworks. For example, the emphasis in SDG target 6.b on ensuring the participation of local communities in water management should do much to promote the, as yet nascent, elaboration of more inclusive and participatory procedural and institutional arrangements for transboundary water cooperation.

SDG 6 can, therefore, impact profoundly on water law in a range of ways which cohere with existing trends in the continuing evolution of water law. For example, it is likely to impact the continuing discourse in national and international law on the human right(s) of access to water and sanitation and, thereby, the normative interpretation and application of the related concept of 'vital human needs' commonly employed in international river basin and water resources agreements.[7] SDG 6 also strongly supports

---

[3] On the intrinsic linkage between such 'good governance' values and realization of the human right(s) to water and sanitation, which in turn corresponds closely with SDG 6, see O McIntyre, 'The Human Right to Water as a Creature of Global Administrative Law' (2012) 37(6) Water International 654–69.

[4] On the progression from the MDGs to the SDGs, see M Orme and others, 'Good Transboundary Water Governance in the 2015 Sustainable Development Goals: A Legal Perspective' (2015) Water International 40(7) 969–83 970–71.

[5] These are available at <https://sdgs.un.org/goals/goal6> accessed 21 November 2022.

[6] On the role of international water law, see O McIntyre, 'International Water Law and Sustainable Development Goal 6: Mutually Reinforcing Paradigms' in D French and LJ Kotze (eds), Sustainable Development Goals: Law, Theory and Implementation (Edward Elgar 2018) 173–201. On the role of domestic normative frameworks in giving effect to the human right to water, see N Cooper and D French, 'SDG17: Partnerships for the Goals – Cooperation within the Framework of a Voluntarist Framework' in ibid 271–304.

[7] Notably, in art 10(2) of the 1997 United Nations Convention on the Law of the Non-Navigational Uses of International Watercourses (1997) 36 ILM 700 (UN Watercourses Convention) and art 5(2) of the 2008

a greater focus on ecosystem-based approaches to water management and regulation and promotes participatory water governance at both the national and international levels. At the purely international level, SDG 6 does much to support and encourage greater transboundary water cooperation among watercourse states. In order to highlight the possible legal implications of the SDGs, this chapter will focus primarily on the multi-faceted, mutually supportive interrelationship between individual targets under SDG 6 and international water law, that is the body of rules and principles applying to the management of international water resources shared between two or more sovereign states.

SDG 6 embodies the solemn commitment of the international community to work towards ensuring, by 2030 at the latest, universal availability of safe and adequate water and sanitation services, along with sustainable management of the water resources on which such services directly depend. As such, it is quite clear that international, transnational and domestic legal frameworks will play a central role in shaping the actions necessary for the realization of SDG 6, despite the latter's non-legally binding character. It is equally apparent, however, that the water and sanitation-related values set out under SDG 6 must inevitably exert significant influence upon the continuing evolution, elaboration, and implementation of legal measures, principles, and approaches related to water and sanitation services provision and to the sustainable management of water resources more generally. This is no less true in respect of international legal frameworks applying to shared transboundary water resources. This chapter aims to illustrate the close, two-way interrelationship between international law and the SDGs by exploring the mutually supportive approaches embodied in international water, environmental and human rights law and in SDG 6. The former bodies of law continue to develop rules and principles intended to promote normatively broad and inclusive rights to water and sanitation and to require environmental protection of shared international water resources and the ecosystems dependent thereon. However, the articulation and solemn adoption of SDG 6 by almost the entire international community of states represents a universal formal political commitment to such values, which can only serve further to legitimize and inform such emerging norms. In addition, the development and agreement of a comprehensive set of targets and indicators related to SDG 6 does much to promote a common understanding of water- and sanitation-related entitlements and duties, and to provide clear benchmarks for the realization of each aspect of the corresponding human right(s) to water and sanitation.

Of course, one could not reasonably expect the targets adopted under SDG 6 and the indicators developed subsequently to be capable of capturing and fully reflecting the complexity and increasing sophistication of the corresponding legal frameworks. For example, the discourse that has been ongoing now for well over twenty years regarding the emerging right(s) to water and sanitation has identified normative elements, both

---

International Law Commission Draft Articles on Transboundary Aquifers, 'Report of the International Law Commission on the Work of Its Sixtieth Session' 11(2) Yearbook of the International Law Commission (2008) (ILC Draft Articles).

444 SDG 6

substantive and procedural,[8] that could not possibly be captured under three indicators.[9] Similarly, the emergence of the so-called ecosystem approach in international water law has given rise to a host of increasingly sophisticated technical standards and methodological tools, such as those relating to environmental flows or to ecosystem services and arrangements for payment, which are not even touched upon by indicator 6.6.1.[10] Therefore, one of the key aims of this chapter is to map the water governance implications of SDG 6 implementation onto the corresponding legal framework for water, particularly that applying at the international level, and to speculate upon the likely influence of each upon the other.

The key Declaration contained in the United Nations General Assembly Resolution by means of which the SDGs were adopted[11] very strongly suggests that the SDGs are to be informed and guided by relevant established and emerging norms of international law. In the case of water access and management in line with SDG 6, these norms will principally be found in the fields of international human rights law, international environmental law, and international water law. The Declaration confirms that '[t]he new Agenda is guided by the purposes and principles of the Charter of the United Nations, including full respect for international law. It is grounded in the Universal Declaration of Human Rights, international human rights treaties' etc.[12] It goes on to explain that key, seminal soft-law instruments have helped to shape the 2030 Agenda, including the 1992 Rio Declaration on Environment and Development.[13] More generally, the Declaration, as well as the targets enumerated under each SDG, are suffused with language which suggests the central relevance of the values underlying international human rights law, environmental law and natural resources law. For example, the Declaration envisages 'a world of universal respect for human rights and human dignity, the rule of law, justice, equality and non-discrimination' and one 'in which consumption and production patterns and use of all natural resources ... are sustainable' and where environmental protection, climate sensitivity, and respect for biodiversity are centrally important.[14] Such language immediately calls to mind the existing international legal frameworks which seek to promote and protect such values. These connotations are even more immediate and direct in respect of SDG 6, where the Declaration sets out a vision of '[a] world where we affirm our commitments regarding

---

[8] UN Committee on Economic, Social and Cultural Rights, 'General Comment No 15 (2002): The right to water (arts 11 and 12 of the International Covenant on Economic, Social and Cultural Rights)', UN Doc E/C.12/2002/11 (20 January 2003) (General Comment No 15) provides a seminal early analysis of the normative and governance implications of the purported emergence of the right to water.

[9] SDG 6.1.1, SDG 6.2.1a, and SDG 6.2.1b.

[10] See, eg, O McIntyre, 'New Approaches for International Water Resources' (2021) 51(1&2) Environmental Policy and Law 43–55; O McIntyre, 'Environmental Protection and the Ecosystem Approach' in SC McCaffrey and others (eds), *Handbook of International Water Law Research* (Edward Elgar 2019) 126–46; O McIntyre, 'Protection and Preservation of Freshwater Ecosystems (Articles 20–23)' in L Boisson de Chazournes and others (eds), *The United Nations Convention on the Law of the Non-Navigational Uses of International Watercourses: A Commentary* (OUP 2018) 193–213.

[11] 'Transforming Our World: The 2030 Agenda for Sustainable Development', UNGA Res. 70/1 (25 September 2015), UN Doc A/RES/70/1.

[12] ibid para 10, 4.

[13] ibid para 11, 4–5.

[14] ibid paras 8 and 9, 4.

the human right(s) to safe drinking water and sanitation and where there is improved hygiene'.[15] This reference to the putative emergence in international human rights law of a human right(s) to water and sanitation, and thus to the associated intense discourse on the legal status and normative implications of such a right(s), is unmistakable.[16]

At the same time, despite its non-binding character, it appears that, in adopting the 2030 Agenda, the international community was aware of the potential legal significance of this solemn universal statement of formal support for emerging, and in some cases contested, rules and principles of international law. For example, the Resolution adopting the 2030 Agenda, which was adopted in the General Assembly without a vote, declared on behalf of the UN Member States that '[w]e reaffirm all the principles of the Rio Declaration on Environment and Development',[17] which includes all of the key principles associated with the field of international environmental law, even though the customary legal status of some of these has not been definitively established.[18] Indeed, where the Declaration states that 'we reaffirm our commitment to international law and emphasize that the Agenda is to be implemented in a manner that is consistent with the rights and obligations of states under international law', it is also careful to 'reaffirm that every State has, and shall freely exercise, full permanent sovereignty over all its wealth, natural resources and economic activity'.[19] The international community appears, therefore, to have been conscious of the possibility that Resolution 70/1 might come to be regarded as sovereign acceptance of certain contested legal paradigms, such as the human right(s) to water and sanitation.[20] This would have clear implications for the 41 states who abstained in the vote on the 2010 UN General Assembly Resolution on the matter of formal international recognition of a human right to water.[21] Even where the 2030 Agenda could not be regarded as tacit state acceptance of emerging international norms for the purposes of identifying applicable rules of customary international law, the targets set out under each SDG, as well as the indicators and the various modalities subsequently developed to assist with implementation, are likely to play a key role in informing the normative content of such emerging norms and in guiding their effective

[15] ibid para 7, 3–4.

[16] For an account of this discourse, see, eg, EB Bluemel, 'The Implications of Formulating a Human Right to Water' (2004) Ecology Law Quarterly 31, 957.

[17] ibid para 12, 5.

[18] Take the example of the so-called precautionary principle approach, codified in Rio Principle 15. Arguing against the principle's customary status, see, eg, D Bodansky, 'Customary (and Not So Customary) International Environmental Law' (1995) Indiana Journal of Global Legal Studies 3(1) 105–19; arguing in favour of its customary status, see, eg, O McIntyre and T Mosedale, 'The Precautionary Principle as a Norm of Customary International Law' (1997) 9 Journal of Environmental Law 221–41.

[19] 'Transforming Our World' (n 11) para 18 6.

[20] Botswana provides an example of a state that had contested the legally binding nature of a human right to water, before losing a 2011 legal battle over the San and Bakgalagadi peoples' access to water in the Central Kalahari Game Reserve. See further, C Morinville and L Rodina, 'Rethinking the Human Right to Water: Water Access and Dispossession in the Botswana's Central Kalahari Game Reserve' (2013) Geoforum 49, 150–59.

[21] 'The human right to water and sanitation', UNGA Resolution 64/292 (28 July 2010), UN Doc A/RES/64/292. States abstaining included Armenia, Australia, Austria, Bosnia and Herzegovina, Botswana, Bulgaria, Canada, Croatia, Cyprus, Czech Republic, Denmark, Estonia, Ethiopia, Greece, Guyana, Iceland, Ireland, Israel, Japan, Kazakhstan, Kenya, Latvia, Lesotho, Lithuania, Luxembourg, Malta, Netherlands, New Zealand, Poland, Republic of Korea, Republic of Moldova, Romania, Slovakia, Sweden, Trinidad and Tobago, Turkey, Ukraine, United Kingdom, United Republic of Tanzania, United States, Zambia.

implementation, regardless of their formal source of legal authority. Consider the targets enumerated under SDG 6, which stress, *inter alia*, the affordability of water services, the protection of vulnerable groups, environmental and ecosystems protection, and public participation rights, thereby highlighting values and objectives which might be expected to guide legal measures adopted in order to realize the human right(s) to water and sanitation. Such measures might derive from international human rights law, international water law, national constitutional law, or national legislation on water services, public health, or environmental protection.

Although the SDGs are clearly guided by, and will operate to pursue the objectives of the international law frameworks relevant to sustainable development,[22] they appear to embody the commitment of the international community to take action beyond the narrow and often restrictive confines of the international law-making process.[23] Therefore, the SDGs represent a novel approach emerging in international policy-making, which began with the MDGs and proceeds on the basis of political commitment rather than binding legal norms.[24] According to one leading authority on the challenge of implementing sustainable development, by packaging social priorities into an easily understandable set of goals, and by establishing measurable and time-bound objectives, these goals 'help to promote global awareness, political accountability, improved metrics, social feedback, and public pressures'.[25] This permits the international community to identity goals and targets which are universal, yet aspirational in nature, and which facilitate, more easily than formal international legal measures, engagement with a range of actors crucial to developmental outcomes, including civil society, the scientific community and the private sector. While the seventeen goals and 169 targets are global in terms of their scope of application, they are also flexible and articulated in such a way as to be capable of taking into account different levels of national capacity and development, while respecting national policies and priorities.[26] However, it would be mistaken to assume that the SDGs are completely divorced from or immune to developments in relevant areas of international law, which are likely both to inform the implementation of measures designed to realize the SDGs and, in turn, to be supported and enhanced by the implementation of such measures.

In order to explore further this complex two-way relationship between SDG 6 and relevant rules of international law, it is necessary to identify in a systematic manner the key values enshrined in each of the targets associated with SDG 6 and to examine how each relates to emerging and established paradigms of international law applying to access to water-related services and to management of water resources. This chapter

---

[22] For example, the Preamble of Resolution 70/1 (n 11) declares that the SDGs 'seek to realize the human rights of all'.

[23] See, eg, in relation to the international environmental law-making process, O McIntyre, 'Changing Patterns of International Environmental Law-Making: Addressing Normative Ineffectiveness' in S Maljean-Dubois (ed), *The Effectiveness of Environmental Law* (Intersentia 2017) 187–220.

[24] Aspects of this approach are evident in the adoption of the 2015 Paris Agreement on Climate Change, UN Doc FCCC/CP/2015/L.9/Rev.1.

[25] Sachs (n 1) 2206.

[26] See United Nations Economic Commission for Europe, *A Healthy Link: The Protocol on Water and Health and the Sustainable Development Goals* (UNECE 2016), UN Doc ECE/INF/NONE/2016/16 3.

will attempt to do so in Section III, following a brief account of the background to the elaboration of SDG 6 provided immediately below in Section II.

II. Background

The problem of access to water was placed firmly on the global political agenda in 2000 by the MDG process, which included a broad goal on 'ensuring environmental sustainability' (MGD 7), which in turn included a more specific target 7.c, which aimed to '[h]alve, by 2015, the proportion of the population without sustainable access to safe drinking water and basic sanitation'.[27] These somewhat narrow targets, focusing exclusively on drinking water supply and sanitation, can be traced back to water-related priorities identified in the context of the International Drinking Water Supply and Sanitation Decade (1981–1990) and enshrined in the New Delhi Statement adopted as a result of the 1990 Global Consultation on Safe Water and Sanitation.[28] The MDG process is generally regarded as having been a success,[29] largely by virtue of the fact that it 'circumvented the lengthy procedures for formal rule-making as a necessary condition for new political attention' and that '[b]y setting clear and measurable targets it helped mobilise resources, commitments and greater coordination'.[30] Despite the clear deficiencies of MDG 7 target 7.c, notably regarding its lack of comprehensiveness in terms of scope and its neglect of universal access, the elaboration of SDG 6 and its related targets was largely shaped by experience gained regarding target 7.c. Therefore, SDG 6 reflects perceived deficiencies in the formulation and implementation of the water-related goals and targets included under MDG 7 as the framers were able 'to capitalise on the insights gained during the implementation of the MDGs'.[31] For example, though the MDG target for drinking water was met,[32] the monitoring approach adopted only measured rates of access to improved water resources without measuring whether such sources were 'safe', as specified in target C. Leading commentators point out that '[i]mproved sources are not always safe [that is, free from contamination], thus if drinking water safety had been monitored alongside access, the MDGs' drinking water target would not have been met'.[33] By any measure, it is beyond argument that the MDG target for extending access to sanitation was missed.[34]

---

[27] See <https://www.un.org/millenniumgoals/environ.shtml> accessed 30 November 2022.

[28] UN Doc A/C.2/45/3 (11 October 1990).

[29] C Pahl-Wostl and others, 'Enhancing Water Security for the Benefits of Humans and Nature—The Role of Governance' (2013) Current Opinion in Environmental Sustainability 5. See also, TST Issues Brief: Water and Sanitation (2013) 1.

[30] C Pahl-Wostl and others, 'Water, Governance and Politics' in JJ Bogardi and others (eds), *Handbook of Water Resources Management: Discourses, Concepts and Examples* (Springer Nature 2021) 253–67, 266.

[31] ibid 267.

[32] The UN reports (<https://www.un.org/millenniumgoals/environ.shtml> accessed 30 November 2022) that:
- The world has met the target of halving the proportion of people without access to improved sources of water, five years ahead of schedule.
- Between 1990 and 2015, 2.6 billion people gained access to improved drinking water sources.

[33] CW Sadoff and others, 'Rethinking Water for SDG 6' (May 2020) 3 Nature Sustainability 346–47 346.

[34] The UN reports (<https://www.un.org/millenniumgoals/environ.shtml> accessed 30 November 2022) that:

448 SDG 6

Generally, the SDGs adopt a more comprehensive approach 'by moving away from a development focus towards a broader sustainability framing', in order that the SDG process might 'become a global process driving transformative change towards sustainability'.[35] More specifically, SDG 6 reflects a significantly more sophisticated understanding of the importance of disparate interrelated aspects of water management, going beyond targets related solely to drinking water supply and sanitation (targets 6.1 and 6.2) to include targets relating to water quality and wastewater discharge and reuse (target 6.3), to water-use efficiency and water scarcity (target 6.4), to implementation of integrated water resources management and transboundary cooperation (target 6.5), and to the protection and restoration of water-related ecosystems (target 6.6). SDG 6 also emphasizes international development cooperation and capacity building in support of developing countries (target 6.a) and the need to support and strengthen the participation of local communities in improving water and sanitation management (target 6.b). The broader framing adopted for SDG 6 also extends the relevance of the dedicated water-related goal beyond the 'developing world', with which MDG 7 target C was primarily concerned, to the entire global community of states and water-users concerned with the global aspiration of sustainable water management. Therefore, SDG 6 demonstrates greater global recognition of the importance of governance in the effective realization of universal equitable access to adequate water and sanitation, as well as the central role of the natural environment in provisioning such access and the broader environmental implications of poor water and sanitation management.[36]

Commentators have sought to map the implications of the experience of implementing the MDGs for the much broader framing of 'sustainable water and sanitation for all' under SDG 6. As regards the focus on governance in SDG 6, for example, Sadoff, Borgomeo, and Uhlenbrook suggest that, by focusing on the provision of capital infrastructure, 'the MDGs' experience demonstrated the limitations of separating water access from equitable, sustainable and efficient water and wastewater management and governance'.[37] Similarly, as regards the inclusion in SDG 6 of robust environment-related targets, the same authors point out that '[t]oday's reality of inequality, climate change and environmental degradation means that governance and water resource constraints are key determinants of our ability to extend and maintain access to water services and achieve sustainable development'.[38] Of course, the inclusion of more comprehensive and ambitious targets presents the challenge of identifying a full suite of appropriate indicators and monitoring methodologies. In the interests of transparency, effective communication, priority setting, and stakeholder mobilization,

- Worldwide 2.1 billion people have gained access to improved sanitation. Despite progress, 2.4 billion are still using unimproved sanitation facilities, including 946 million people who are still practicing open defecation.

[35] Sadoff and others (n 33) 346.
[36] On the complex interrelationship between the SDG 6 targets and the environment, see M Elder and S Høiberg Olsen, 'The Design of Environmental Priorities in the SDGs' (2019) 10(1) Global Policy 70–82 73.
[37] Sadoff and others (n 33) 346.
[38] ibid.

SDG 6 largely employs quantitative indicators, based on numerical measurements and benchmarking, which present a range of practical measurement challenges.[39]

SDG 6 adopts a significantly more sophisticated and inclusive approach to implementation, charging the global scientific community with the task of developing appropriate indicators and monitoring processes, thereby encouraging the broader scientific community 'to become more actively engaged in the global governance process of SDG implementation'.[40] This also allows those sectors, groups, and actors most affected by the implementation process to 'be empowered and encouraged to actively participate in implementation and monitoring'.[41] According to leading commentators in the field, the broader scope of SDG 6, as compared to the MDGs, suggests '[a] renewed and broader view of the costs and benefits of water investments', one which can balance the key imperatives of '[t]he human right to water and sanitation, the critical water needs of the environment and unique cultural characteristics of water'.[42] This is necessary in order to 'support access for all households including the poor and the more vulnerable, and sustain aquatic ecosystems and their environmental services'.[43]

A. *Travaux Préparatoires*

The process of defining the SDGs commenced in 2012 at the Rio + 20 Conference, where the essential topic areas and a set of basic guiding principles for the post-MDG Agenda were established, along with an institutional process for the elaboration of the SDGs.[44] Despite the expansion from eight MDGs to seventeen SDGs, the topic areas ultimately selected largely followed those covered under the MDGs and the priority areas agreed at Rio + 20, though surpassing each in scope and ambition. The guiding principles adopted notably included both a commitment to universality and to the employment of an integrative approach which 'recognizes the fluidity and interconnectedness of the environmental, economic and social aspects of global issues rather than their parallel existence and opens up opportunities for integrative work at multiple levels of governance'.[45] The imperative of universality reflects the increasingly pervasive influence of economic, social, and cultural rights, which have clearly influenced the ambitious targets set out under SDG 6, particularly targets 6.1, 6.2, and 6.b.[46] The adoption of an integrative approach has been promoted since Agenda 21 and is immediately apparent in the inclusion under SDG 6 of developmental, social, environmental

---

[39] ARC Otigara, and others, 'A Review of the SDG 6 Synthesis Report 2018 from an Education, Training and Research Perspective' (2018) 10(10) Water 1353.

[40] A Bhaduri and others, 'Achieving Sustainable Development Goals from a Water Perspective' (2016) 4 Frontiers in Environmental Science 64.

[41] C Pahl-Wostl and others, *Institutional Capacity and Good Governance for Effective Implementation of the SDGs*, Global Water Systems Project Policy Brief (GWSP 2015).

[42] Sadoff and others (n 33) 347.

[43] ibid.

[44] See further, Elder and Høiberg Olsen (n 36) 75.

[45] M Ivanova, 'The Contested Legacy of Rio+20' (2013) 13(4) Global Environmental Politics 1–11.

[46] See General Comment No 15 (n 8).

and economic aspects of water services provision, water resources management and the maintenance of water-related ecosystems and of associated ecosystem services. The institutional arrangements and elaboration process proved particularly important, especially the critically important contribution of the work of the Open Working Group (OWG),[47] which quickly took over the lead role from the UN Secretary-General's High-Level Panel of Eminent Persons on the post-2015 Development Agenda. The OWG avoided the usual North–South and regional divisions that have tended in the past to hamper such global initiatives, with its work culminating in over seventy states sharing thirty seats in 'troikas', sometimes in quite unusual constellations,[48] 'which prevented formation of negotiation blocks and created strong ownership of the project to define the SDGs among participating governments and non-state actors'.[49] The OWG's unique structure and operational modalities, including the assistance provided by its dedicated Technical Support Team (TST) comprising around forty members from across the UN system,[50] also facilitated the critically important role of progressive 'norm entrepreneurs', including certain government and UN officials, as well as members of the scientific community and of civil society.[51] In this way, '[t]he OWG sessions functioned as a capacity building mechanism for all involved'.[52] However, once the OWG had reported and the headline SDGs and targets were agreed,[53] the process for developing the related indicators was quite different from that of the OWG and considerably more technocratic. It was primarily led by the Inter-Agency and Expert Group on the Sustainable Development Goal Indicators (IAEG-SDGs), primarily comprising representatives of national and international statistical agencies, whose members 'were mainly professional statisticians concerned with the cost and feasibility of data gathering rather than the broad objectives of sustainable development' and, in addition, 'were influenced by the development focused legacy of the MDGs'.[54] Thus, some indicators have been criticized by commentators as they 'do not reflect the integrated approach taken by the OWG in formulating goals and targets'.[55]

The third session of the OWG, which convened between 22 and 24 May 2013, deliberated on water and sanitation, alongside food security and nutrition, sustainable agriculture, desertification, land degradation, and drought. A great deal of preparatory work had already been carried out, which clearly informed the work of the OWG on water and sanitation. For example, the policy brief on water security produced to inform the 2012 UN Rio + 20 Conference called for water to 'be given the prominence

---

[47] Established by means of UNGA Decision 67/555, UN Doc A/67/L.48/Rev.1 (15 January 2013).

[48] With one, eg, including Japan, Iran, and Nepal.

[49] Elder and Høiberg Olsen (n 36) 71. See generally, F Dodds and others, *Negotiating the Sustainable Development Goals* (Routledge 2016).

[50] O Kjorven, 'The Unlikely Journey to the 2030 Agenda for Sustainable Development' <https://impakter.com/impakter-essay-unlikely-journey-2030-agenda-sustainable-development/> accessed 30 November 2022.

[51] See Elder and Høiberg Olsen (n 36) who note, eg 77, the critical role of Colombia's chief negotiator, Paula Caballero, who 'supported strengthening the role of the environment in the context of an integrated approach to development'.

[52] ibid.

[53] Report of the Open Working Group on Sustainable Development Goals, UN Doc A/68/970 (12 August 2014).

[54] Elder and Høiberg Olsen (n 36) 79.

[55] ibid at 71 and 80.

it deserves on the global agenda', while advising that '[w]ater security has multiple dimensions, including social, humanitarian, economic and ecological' and, further, that '[h]uman and environmental water needs must be balanced to safeguard biodiversity and ecosystem services'.[56] Similarly, the UN Secretary-General's Advisory Board on Water and Sanitation's call for a post-2015 goal on water highlighted the deep complexity of the water challenge, stressing that '[s]olutions must reach beyond increasing access to water supply and sanitation'.[57] The Board unequivocally recommended 'that the emerging post-2015 agenda includes a dedicated and comprehensive Global Goal on Water that reflects water's comprehensive contribution to development needs'. Advising the OWG directly, the TST recalled the human right to safe drinking water and sanitation, and the commitments made by states in the Johannesburg Plan of Implementation and Millennium Declaration.[58] It notably recounted in full the relevant commitments entered into at Rio + 20, which are immediately recognisable as the precursor to SDG 6,[59] and stressed

[t]he pervasive linkages between water and other priority areas [which] are also reflected in the Rio +20 outcome document, where references to water are made in the following sections: food security and nutrition and sustainable agriculture; sustainable cities and human settlements; health and population; biodiversity; desertification, land degradation and drought; as well as mountains.

While noting the poor progress made in respect of the MDG sanitation target and the pervasive nature of discrimination and inequalities in access to water, sanitation, and hygiene services, the TST clearly favoured a dedicated, stand-alone SDG on water, including sanitation, which would be quite broad in scope. It was influenced in this regard by the positions adopted by the African Ministers Council on Water (AMCOW),[60] the UN Secretary-General's Advisory Board on Water and Sanitation (UNSGAB),[61] the UN Global Compact's CEO Water Mandate,[62] and by the support of several states

[56] Rio + 20 Policy Brief # 1: Water security for a planet under pressure (Rio + 20 UN Conference on Sustainable Development).

[57] UN Secretary-General's Advisory Board on Water and Sanitation, 'Water and Sanitation for All: Securing our Future, Preserving our Planet—UNSGAB's call for a Post-2015 Global Goal on Water' (January 2013).

[58] TST Issues Brief (n 29). Preparation of this Issues Brief was led by UN-Water, with contributions coming from DESA, FAO, ILO, OHCHR, PBSO, UNCBD, UNCCD, UNDP, UNECE, UNECLAC, UNEP, UNESCAP, UNESCO, UNFPA, UNICEF, UNOOSA, UNU, UN-Women, WHO, World Bank, WTO, as well as numerous UN-Water Partners.

[59] The relevant Rio + 20 commitments included the following:
- the progressive realization of access to safe and affordable drinking-water and sanitation for all;
- significantly improve the implementation of integrated water resources management at all levels as appropriate;
- protect and suitably manage ecosystems, as they play a key role in maintaining water quantity and quality;
- address water-related disasters, such as floods and droughts, as well as water scarcity;
- significantly reduce water pollution, increase water quality and significantly improve wastewater treatment;
- improve water efficiency and reduce water losses.

[60] See<http://www.amcow-online.org/images/docs/outcomes_of_the_tunis_post_2015_water_ consultations. pdf> accessed 30 November 2022.

[61] See <www.unsgab.org/content/documents/UNSGABpost2015brief.pdf> accessed 30 November 2022.

[62] See <http://ceowatermandate.org/files/CEOWaterMandateMumbaiPost2015MeetingKey Outputs.pdf> accessed 30 November 2022.

452   SDG 6

identified by means of the Thematic Consultation on Water,[63] to suggest a new agenda that would build upon, but go beyond the MDGs and other existing commitments to

> encourage an integrated approach to water expressed in universally agreed goals which are simple, measurable and able to focus policies, resources and all partners on delivering outcomes that improve people's lives and protect their future and the environment.[64]

Most significantly, perhaps, in their interactions with the OWG Co-Chairs, the key stakeholders consulted emphasized that the goals to be adopted 'should be firmly based in the human right to safe drinking water' and, further, that 'the SDGs should tackle water issues from a wider angle than the MDGs have done and also include water efficiency, wastewater treatment, integrated water management, trans-boundary waters, among others'.[65] As well as proposing specific concrete targets, which are now very largely reflected in SDG 6,[66] the stakeholders prioritized a number of key areas, including universal access to sanitation and menstrual hygiene, which they linked to girls' school attendance. Contributions stressed that water and sanitation should have a stand-alone goal but, consistent with the adoption of an integrative approach, they expressed the hope that 'due to its strong interlinkages with energy, food and agriculture, health, education, among others, it should be reflected in sub-targets for such goals'.[67]

Thus, SDG 6 has its direct antecedents in the MDG and Rio + 20 processes, but its elaboration has been influenced by, and its ultimate form reflects, several of the most important currents in global water law and governance. Most obviously, SDG 6 has been profoundly impacted by the increasingly persuasive discourse on the human right(s) to adequate water and sanitation, which has profoundly influenced almost every aspect of water services and resources management in recent years. Likewise, increasingly sophisticated regulatory approaches to the management of water pollution, water use, and water scarcity are centrally relevant in forming the targets and indicators elaborated under the SDG 6 rubric. SDG 6 also reflects recent legal recognition of the dual significance of water-related ecosystems and the services provided thereby, both in terms of their role in the conservation and provision of water resources and in terms of the role of water in their maintenance. It further recognizes and promotes governance arrangements for the integrated, conjunctive management of water and related resources, including institutional frameworks for transboundary cooperation over shared international water resources. At a purely practical level, SDG 6 highlights

[63] See Global Water Partnership, *National Stakeholder Consultations on Water: Supporting the Post-2015 Development Agenda* (GWP 2013).

[64] TST Issues Brief (n 29) 5–6.

[65] Third session of the OWG (22–24 May), Co-Chairs' meetings with the representatives of Major Groups and other Stakeholders <https://sustainabledevelopment.un.org/topics/sdgs/group3> accessed 30 November 2022.

[66] ibid. Targets proposed included 'universal access to safe water; improved sanitation and hygiene for all; 100 percent wastewater treatment; participatory, democratic water management at the watershed level; decreasing water pollution; increasing water efficiency in different fields; and an end to open defecation'.

[67] ibid.

the importance of meaningful participatory approaches in improving the provision of water and sanitation services and the management of water resources, and of solidarity with developing countries in assisting the adoption and implementation of best practices and appropriate new technologies. By exploring each of the SDG 6 targets in detail, and each of the indicators selected in order to measure progress on their implementation, it is possible to trace the influence of each of these evolving water management paradigms, and to shed further light on the full range of normative implications of SDG 6.

III. Targets and Indicators of Goal 6

A. Overview

One can only discern the precise nature of the values to which the international community has committed in adopting SDG 6, and thus the likely normative implications, both substantive and procedural, of the global water goal's practical implementation, through examination and detailed analysis of each of the specific targets set out thereunder. It is also necessary to take careful account of the indicators developed in respect of each target as these, though developed subsequently and through a different process to the targets, provide important detail of the agreed expectations regarding the practical implementation and normative substance of the latter. Therefore, in analysing each target and its associated indicators it is necessary to map these onto the corresponding legal frameworks, particularly those applying at the international level and thus generally accepted by the international community as relevant for realization of the broad imperative of sustainable development. Of course, as such legal frameworks are dynamic and almost always in a state of flux, with different international norms at different stages of development at any given time, it is important to take account of emerging norms as well as more established legal positions. This is especially so as the implementation of SDG 6 is likely to have a particularly profound impact upon the evolution of emerging legal paradigms, such as the human right(s) to water and sanitation or the ecosystem approach, and vice versa.

B. Analysis and Critique of Each Target

1. Target 6.1 By 2030, achieve universal and equitable access to safe and affordable drinking water for all

The objectives set out under targets 6.1 and 6.2 very closely reflect those encompassed by the human right(s) to water and sanitation originally set out in 2002 by the UN Committee on Economic Social and Cultural Rights (CESCR) on the basis of the Committee's progressive interpretation of the 1966 International Covenant on

454   SDG 6

Economic, Social and Cultural Rights (ICESCR).[68] By emphasizing 'universal and equitable access to safe and affordable drinking water' in target 6.1, the 2030 Agenda appears to mirror the normative content of the right to water identified in General Comment No 15, which focuses on three key factors: availability, quality, and accessibility.[69] In General Comment No 15, 'availability' refers to a supply of water that is 'sufficient and continuous for personal and domestic uses', while 'quality' refers to the safety of the water supply in terms of being 'free from micro-organisms, chemical substances and radiological hazards that constitute a threat to a person's health'. The goal of 'accessibility' as outlined in General Comment No 15 corresponds very closely with the requirements of equitable access and affordability contained in target 6.1, as it comprises four overlapping dimensions: physical accessibility, economic accessibility, non-discrimination, and information accessibility. 'Economic accessibility' requires that '[w]ater and water facilities and services must be affordable to all',[70] while the requirement of 'non-discrimination' dictates that '[w]ater and water facilities and services must be accessible to all, including the most vulnerable or marginalized sections of the population, in law and in fact'. The equitability of access will also depend on 'physical accessibility', meaning that 'adequate water facilities and services must be within safe physical reach for all sections of the population' and, in particular, 'must be accessible within, or in the immediate vicinity of, each household, educational institution and workplace'. Similarly, equitable access will be highly dependent upon the corresponding 'right to seek, receive and impart information concerning water issues'. Therefore, the broad aims set out in target 6.1 have already been elaborated in detail in an authoritative,[71] if contested,[72] interpretation of the normative content of a key instrument of international human rights law, and in certain instruments in the field of international environmental law.[73]

Target 6.1 is also supported by the core values inherent to international water resources law: the body of rules of international law primarily concerned with the utilization and protection of shared international water resources, which is largely

---

[68] General Comment No 15 (n 8). See generally, J Murillo Chavarro, *The Human Right to Water: A Legal Comparative Perspective at the International, Regional and Domestic Level* (Intersentia 2015).

[69] ibid para 12, 4–6.

[70] On requirements regarding the affordability of water-related services, see further, O McIntyre, 'The Emergence of Standards regarding the Right of Access to Water and Sanitation' in S Turner and others (eds), *Environmental Rights: The Development of Standards* (CUP 2019) 147–73 164–66.

[71] See SC McCaffrey, 'The Human Right to Water' in E Brown Weiss and others (eds), *Fresh Water and International Economic Law* (OUP 2005) 93, who explains at 94, that General Comment No 15 constitutes a non-binding but 'highly authoritative interpretation of the Covenant' and of the legal implications which flow from key relevant Covenant provisions. See also M Williams, 'Privatization and the Human Right to Water: Challenges for the New Century' (2007) 28 Michigan Journal of International Law 469 475; Bluemel (n 16) 972.

[72] See McCaffrey (n 71) 103; A Hardberger, 'Life, Liberty and the Pursuit of Water: Evaluating Water as a Human Right and the Duties and Obligations It Creates' (2005) 4(2) Northwestern Journal of International Human Rights 331 361–62.

[73] Notably, the 1999 Protocol on Water and Health to the 1992 UNECE (Helsinki) Convention on the Protection and Use of Transboundary Watercourses and International Lakes, UN Doc MP.WAT/AC.1/1991/1. See further, A Tanzi, 'Reducing the Gap between International Water Law and Human Rights Law: The UNECE Protocol on Water and Health' (2010) 12 International Community Law Review 267; O McIntyre, 'The UNECE Water Convention and the Human Right to Access to Water: The Protocol on Water and Health' in A Tanzi and others (eds), *The UNECE Convention on the Protection and Use of Transboundary Watercourses and International Lakes: Its Contribution to International Water Cooperation* (Brill Nijhoff 2015) 345–66.

codified in, and exemplified by, the 1997 UN Watercourses Convention.[74] The cardinal and overarching rule set out in the Convention is that of equitable and reasonable utilization, under which an equitable allocation between watercourse states of uses or benefits of an international watercourse, or of quantum share of water therefrom, is to be determined having regard to a range of relevant factors which help to characterize each state's economic, social, and environmental dependence upon the shared waters in question.[75] In respect of application of this principle, while the UN Watercourses Convention makes it quite clear that, unless watercourse states have agreed otherwise, 'no use of an international watercourse enjoys inherent priority over other uses',[76] it also provides that '[i]n the event of a conflict between uses of an international watercourse, it shall be resolved ... with special regard being given to the requirements of *vital human needs*'.[77] This long-standing elevation in general international water law of the use of water for meeting vital human needs appears to pre-empt the current discourse in international law on the human right to water and merely reflects long established state and judicial practice confirming that certain basic needs of the population dependent on the waters of a watercourse, in particular the use of water for drinking and other domestic purposes, will be accorded priority.[78] The scope of this prioritized use of shared water resources would appear to correspond closely with target 6.1 and the related human right to water. A Statement of Understanding on article 10(2) was included in the Report of the UN General Assembly Working Group which finalized the drafting of the Convention, providing that, '[i]n determining "vital human needs", special attention is to be paid to providing sufficient water to sustain human life, including both drinking water and water required for production of food in order to prevent starvation'.[79] Leading commentators explain the legal significance and implications of article 10(2) in the following terms:

> [T]he protection of vital human needs entails a 'presumptive' priority over all the other factors listed in Article 6, such presumption being rebuttable only on the basis of the specific circumstances of the individual case. That is to say that watercourse States, in discussing the equitable allocation of shared watercourses, cannot avoid starting

---

[74] United Nations Convention on the Law of the Non-Navigational Uses of International Watercourses (New York, 21 May 1997) 37 International Legal Materials 700, entered into force 17 August 2014 (UNWC).

[75] ibid arts 5 and 6. See also, art V(2) of the International Law Commission's 1966 Helsinki Rules on the Uses of the Waters of International Rivers, ILA Report of the Fifty-Second Conference 484 (Helsinki, 1966). See further, SC McCaffrey, *The Law of International Watercourses* (2nd edn, OUP 2007) 384–405; O McIntyre, *Environmental Protection of International Watercourses under International Law* (Ashgate 2007) 53–86 and 155–90; I Kaya, *Equitable Utilization: The Law of the Non-Navigational Uses of International Watercourses* (Ashgate 2003); McIntyre, 'The UNECE Water Convention and the Principle of Equitable and Reasonable Utilisation' (n 73) 146–60.

[76] Art 10(1).

[77] Art 10(2), emphasis added.

[78] See, eg, J Lipper, 'Equitable Utilization' in AH Garretson and others (eds), *The Law of International Drainage Basins* (Oceana 1967) 60–62.

[79] Oral report of the coordinator of the informal consultations on art 10(2), UN Doc A/C.6/51/SR.57 (1997) 3.

456   SDG 6

negotiations, taking the water supplies needed to support vital human needs as a fixed parameter.[80]

Thus, though article 6(1) of the UN Watercourses Convention also includes among the '[f]actors relevant to equitable and reasonable utilization ... [t]he population dependent on the watercourse in each watercourse State', such dependence, at least to the extent that it relates to vital human needs, appears less a factor to be considered and weighed and more a non-negotiable responsibility to be respected and fulfilled by all watercourse states. As Tanzi and Arcari note, 'this factor is likely to enhance the 'human right dimension' of the use of the waters of international watercourses'.[81] Indirectly emphasizing the priority accorded to such vital human needs by article 10(2), the International Law Commission in its commentary to article 7 (on the duty to prevent significant transboundary harm) of its 1994 Draft Articles, which preceded and provided the basis for the Convention, makes it quite clear that '[a] use that causes significant harm to human health and safety is understood to be inherently inequitable and unreasonable'.[82] Clearly, article 10(2) of the Convention is intended to be consistent with the aim of ensuring to all peoples access to safe and sufficient water supplies, as originally set out in Chapter 18 of Agenda 21,[83] further elaborated in General Comment No 15,[84] and now most notably enshrined in SDG target 6.1. Equally, the universal adoption of SDG 6 might do much to make this presumption of priority accorded to the requirements of vital human needs irrebuttable in any circumstances and their safeguarding even more of a *sine qua non* in international water resources law, quite apart from any corresponding obligation arising under international human rights law.

The pre-existing commitment in international water law to the aims of target 6.1 would only appear to have strengthened in recent years. For example, the International Law Association (ILA) 2004 Berlin Rules on Water Resources Law,[85] intended to update and replace the ILA's seminally important 1966 Helsinki Rules,[86] appear to afford clear and formal priority to vital human needs, defined under that instrument to mean 'waters used for immediate human survival, including drinking, cooking and sanitary needs, as well as water needed for the immediate sustenance of a household'.[87] Article 14 of the Berlin Rules builds upon article 10(2) of the UNWC to accord even greater emphasis and priority to the provision of adequate basic water for all by providing that:

---

[80] A Tanzi and M Arcari, *The United Nations Convention on the Law of International Watercourses* (Kluwer Law International 2001) 141.

[81] ibid 131. See further, SR Tully, 'The Contribution of Human Rights to Freshwater Resource Management' (2003) 14 Yearbook of International Environmental Law 101–37.

[82] International Law Commission, Report of the International Law Commission on the Work of its Forty-Sixth Session, Yearbook of the International Law Commission, 1994, Vol II, Part Two 104, para 14.

[83] UNCED, 'Report of the United Nations Conference on Environment and Development' (Rio de Janeiro, 3–14 June 1992), UN Doc A/CONF.151/26 (vol II) (1992).

[84] General Comment No 15 (n 8).

[85] International Law Association, 'Report of the Seventy-First Conference' (2004) 337.

[86] International Law Association, 'Report of the Fifty-Second Conference' (1966) 484.

[87] Art 3(20).

1. In determining an equitable and reasonable use, states first allocate waters to satisfy vital human needs.
2. No other use or category of uses shall have an inherent preference over any other use or category of uses.

The Berlin Rules further include a distinct Chapter IV on the 'Rights of Persons', including a dedicated article 17 on the 'The Right of Access to Water', which provides, *inter alia*, that '[e]very individual has a right of access to sufficient, safe, acceptable, physically accessible, and affordable water to meet that individual's vital human needs'.[88] Such provisions clearly reflect a growing recognition in general international water law of a human right of access to water, and of the closely related aspirations set out under SDG 6, which are to be pursued in the case of transboundary water resources by prioritization of the need to satisfy vital human needs. Thus, while the universal adoption of SDG 6 serves to enhance the legitimacy and significance of the increasingly firmly established human right to water paradigm in international water law, the primacy long afforded to vital human needs in international water law lends support in state practice to human rights-based approaches and entitlements and, thereby, should assist realization of SDG 6.

As regards the quality of water regarded as 'safe' for the purposes of target 6.1, it is helpful to have regard to any relevant guidance produced by specialized UN agencies. General Comment No 15 notably refers to 1993 World Health Organization (WHO) guidelines[89] that are

> intended to be used as a basis for the development of national standards that, if properly implemented, will ensure the safety of drinking water supplies through the elimination of, or reduction to a minimum concentration of, constituents of water that are known to be hazardous to health.[90]

The current 2017 edition of the WHO guidelines runs to 631 pages and provides a great deal of detail on the microbial, chemical, and radiological aspects of drinking water quality standards, as well as on 'acceptability' aspects regarding taste, odour, and appearance. In addition to specific technical parameters for an extensive list of commonly occurring waterborne pollutants, the guidelines advise on their application in a range of conditions and circumstances, including water scarcity and heavy rainfall, rainwater harvesting, vended water, desalination systems, emergencies and disasters, buildings and healthcare facilities, drinking water for travellers, and aircraft and ships. Further, the guidelines also elaborate on such issues as the respective roles of various actors involved in drinking water supply, water safety plans, and drinking water quality surveillance. Whereas the third step of monitoring for SDG indicator 6.1.1 requires

---

[88] Art 17(1).

[89] WHO, *Guidelines for Drinking Water Quality* (2nd edn, WHO 1993) Vols 1–3.

[90] General Comment No 15 (n 8), para 12(b) 5. WHO is also included among those organizations from whom '[s]tate parties may obtain guidance on appropriate indicators', pursuant to General Comment No 15, para 53 16.

458 SDG 6

'inclusion of water quality testing for faecal contamination and priority chemicals (arsenic and fluoride) by utilities and/or in household survey instruments',[91] it seems reasonable to assume that the results of such testing would be assessed against the values set down in the current WHO guidelines. Such specificity regarding the technical standards to be achieved, as well as regarding the methodologies to be employed to that end, is critically important for establishing the normative character of the human right to water and, thereby, in facilitating practical implementation of target 6.1.

In addition to such standards regarding the safety of water, standards would also appear to be emerging regarding the critical question of economic accessibility of water services. The requirement to ensure affordability[92] with a view to protecting vulnerable people[93] has found its way into the governance frameworks of a range of actors concerned with water services, such as multilateral development banks (MDBs), which are commonly called upon to finance water supply and sanitation system upgrades.[94] Quite typically, paragraph 11 of the 2014 Environmental and Social Policy adopted by the European Bank for Reconstruction and Development (EBRD) stipulates that:

> [t]he EBRD will assess to what extent tariff changes caused by projects may create problems of affordability of basic levels of services for disadvantaged and/or vulnerable groups of the population, and satisfy itself that effective schemes to address this issue are developed and put in place.[95]

Highly specific guidance has been developed by MDBs on the nature of the actions required to ensure economic accessibility of water and sanitation services. For example, since 2010 the African Development Bank (AfDB) has published guidelines distinguishing between cost recovery in respect of urban networked and rural non-networked water supply and sanitation services.[96]

Difficulties in ensuring compliance with the requirement of affordability were highlighted in a 2013 report submitted to the Human Rights Council (HRC) by the former UN Special Rapporteur on the right to safe drinking water and sanitation.[97] The report

[91] UN-Water, *Integrated Monitoring Guide for SDG 6: Targets and Global Indicators* (UN 19 July 2016) 5.

[92] General Comment No 15 (n 8) para 12(c)(ii) 5 provides '*[e]conomic accessibility*: Water, and water facilities and services, must be affordable for all. The direct and indirect costs and charges associated with securing water must be affordable, and must not compromise or threaten the realization of other Covenant rights' (original emphasis).

[93] See ibid para 12(c)(iii) 5.

[94] See, eg, the 2004 World Bank 'Water Resources Sector Strategy', which emphasizes 2, 'poverty-targeted water service interventions (such as water and sanitation and irrigation services for the unserved poor)'. Available at <http://siteresources.worldbank.org/INTINFNETWORK/Resources/water.pdf> accessed 30 November 2022.

[95] EBRD, 'Environmental and Social Policy' (May 2014), para 11 2 <www.ebrd.com/news/publications/polic ies/environmental-and-social-policy.html> accessed 30 November 2022.

[96] See African Development Bank, *Guidelines for User Fees and Cost Recovery for Urban Water and Sanitation* (AfDB 2010) <www.afdb.org/fileadmin/uploads/afdb/Documents/Project-and-Operations/brochure%20c ost%20recouvry%20urban%203_11_2010.pdf> accessed 30 November 2022 and African Development Bank, *Guidelines for User Fees and Cost Recovery for Rural, Non-Networked, Water and Sanitation Delivery* (AfDB 2010) <www.afdb.org/fileadmin/uploads/afdb/Documents/Project-and-Operations/2011_03%20Guidelines%20 for%20User%20Fees%20Cost%20Recovery_Rural.pdf> accessed 30 November 2022..

[97] C de Alburquerque, 'Report of the Special Rapporteur on the Human Right to Safe Drinking Water and Sanitation', UN Doc A/HRC/24/44 (11 July 2013) <www.ohchr.org/EN/HRBodies/HRC/RegularSessions/Sessio n24/Documents/A-HRC-24-44_en.pdf> accessed 30 November 2022. The link between fiscal austerity and states'

focuses on the aggravated risks to realization of the right to water arising in times of economic and financial crisis by virtue of retrogressive austerity measures, and spells out the action necessary to ensure compliance with the non-derogable core obligations arising thereunder. It highlights the problem if 'increased prices and unaffordability-related disconnections'[98] including disconnections in the case of private sector provision,[99] and recommends, *inter alia*, 'a social protection floor, especially for disadvantaged and marginalized groups and individuals'.[100] For the purpose of measuring affordability, the former Special Rapporteur recommended 'comparing per capita incomes against water and sanitation indicators among countries with comparable levels of development [which] provides a more objective benchmark'.[101] Thus, she provides a useful analysis of the affordability benchmarks arising under the framework of the human right(s) to water and sanitation, against which a national regime can be measured in a time of austerity. Clearly, there are lessons here for our understanding of the actions required for effective and meaningful realization of target 6.1 (and target 6.2).

However, the level of affordability which should guide service providers, or public welfare interventions, is essentially a question of policy to be determined by the national authorities charged with water services governance, and the methodologies that such actors might employ to assess affordability continue to evolve. For example, most agencies in the United States have for the past twenty years relied on an influential methodology developed in 1997 by the Environmental Protection Agency (EPA), which compares median household income (MHI) for the utility's service area to the area's average water and sewage bills.[102] As a general rule of thumb, the average sewage bill should not exceed 2 per cent of MHI, while the average drinking water bill should not exceed 2.5 per cent of MHI.[103] However, critics of this methodology point out that it is quite rudimentary and arbitrary. For example, by only looking at average demand across the community, it fails to take account of greater water consumption by rich households, which inflates estimates of essential household needs. Also, by using median income it obscures severe financial pressure on poorer households. Further, the EPA measure ignores the local cost of living, which might exacerbate financial pressure on poor households. Recently, the US Congress has instructed the National Academy of Public Administration (NAPA) to study alternative ways of measuring household water affordability with a view to assisting the EPA in revising its outdated community

---

commitments to economic, social, and cultural rights has also been recognized by civil society organizations in the Vienna + 20 CSO Declaration, adopted on 26 June 2013. See further, O McIntyre, 'The Human Right to Water and Reform of the Irish Water Sector' (2014) 5(1) Journal of Human Rights and the Environment 74–101 75–76.

[98] De Alburquerque (n 97) para 32.

[99] ibid para 44.

[100] ibid paras 15(b) and 73–74.

[101] ibid para 61.

[102] See generally, Environmental Protection Agency, 'Pricing and Affordability of Water Services' (2016) <https://19january2017snapshot.epa.gov/sustainable-water-infrastructure/pricing-and-affordability-water-services_.html> accessed 30 November 2022.

[103] See generally, B Walton, 'When It Comes to Water Service How Expensive Is Too Expensive?' Circle of Blue (24 August 2017) <https://www.circleofblue.org/2017/water-management/comes-water-service-expensive-expensive/> accessed 30 November 2022.

affordability guidelines, with the resulting report presented to Congress in October 2017.[104] US scholars have been busy developing alternative approaches, including one that links water bills to workers' wages by estimating the number of hours at the local minimum wage that a person would need to work in order pay their water bill, and another, called the affordability ratio, which compares a water bill to disposable income for households at the twentieth percentile (lower fifth) of the income distribution.[105] In each case, a monthly water bill would be based on consumption of fifty gallons (roughly 190 litres) per person per day, which is a US estimate of water needed for basic hygiene, drinking, and cooking. Though the issue of affordability is not addressed directly under SDG indicator 6.1.1,[106] or under guidance developed thereunder,[107] the development of relevant methodologies under the global discourse on the right(s) to water and sanitation remains highly relevant, providing normative depth to a key element of target 6.1

In delivering equitable access to adequate water and sanitation services pursuant to SDG targets 6.1 and 6.2, the emergence of performance standards for utilities charged with provision of such services is centrally relevant. Since 2007, International Standards Organization (ISO) Technical Committee 224 has been busy developing a range of service quality standards covering various aspects of the work of water and sanitation services utilities, whether public or private. Standards adopted thus far include those for the quality of water supply and sanitation services provided to users,[108] for the management of wastewater utilities and the assessment of wastewater services,[109] for the management of drinking water utilities and the assessment of drinking water services,[110] for the management of drinking water distribution networks,[111] for crisis management of water utilities,[112] and for benchmarking of water utilities.[113] A host of additional standards impacting the safety of drinking water supply, the adequacy of

[104] National Academy of Public Administration, 'Developing a New Framework for Community Affordability of Clean Water Services' (5 October 2017) <http://www.napawash.org/uploads/Academy_Studies/NAPA_EPA_FINAL_REPORT_110117.pdf> accessed 30 November 2022.

[105] See MP Teodoro, 'Measure Water and Sewer Utility Affordability' (August 2017) Texas A&M University Working Paper <http://mannyteodoro.com/wp-content/uploads/2017/08/mteodoro_affordability-method-working-paper-aug2017.pdf> accessed 30 November 2022.

[106] Indicator 6.1.1 merely measures the '[p]roportion of population using safely managed drinking water services'.

[107] See, eg, UN-Water, 'Step-by-step Methodology for Monitoring Drinking Water and Sanitation (6.1.1)' (UN 27 July 2021) <https://www.unwater.org/publications/step-step-methodology-monitoring-drinking-water-sanitation-6-1-1/> accessed 30 November 2022.

[108] ISO 24510:2007 *Activities related to drinking water and wastewater services—Guidelines for the assessment and for the improvement of the service to users* (2007) <http://www.iso.org/standard/37246.html?browse=tc> accessed 30 November 2022.

[109] ISO 24511:2007 *Activities related to drinking water and wastewater services—Guidelines for the management of wastewater utilities and for the assessment of wastewater services* (2007) <http://www.iso.org/standard/37247.html?browse=tc> accessed 30 November 2022.

[110] ISO 25412:2007 *Activities related to drinking water and wastewater services—Guidelines for the management of drinking water utilities and for the assessment of drinking water services* (2007) <http://www.iso.org/standard/37248.html?browse=tc> accessed 30 November 2022.

[111] ISO 24516-1:2016 *Activities related to drinking water and wastewater services—Guidelines for the management of assets of water supply and wastewater systems—Part 1: Drinking water distribution networks* (2016) <http://www.iso.org/standard/64117.html?browse=tc> accessed 30 November 2022.

[112] ISO 24518: 2015 *Activities related to drinking water and wastewater services—Crisis management of water utilities* (2015) <http://www.iso.org/standard/64118.html?browse=tc> accessed 30 November 2022.

[113] ISO 24523:2017 *Activities related to drinking water and wastewater services—Guidelines for benchmarking of water utilities* (2017) <http://www.iso.org/standard/59814.html?browse=tc> accessed 30 November 2022.

sanitation services or to the efficiency of water use are currently under development relating to, *inter alia*, stormwater management, use of performance indicators, the management of water supply and wastewater system assets, water quality event detection processes, technical specifications for flushable products, and water loss reduction and management projects.[114] The development of such standards by ISO Technical Committee 224 is a truly global exercise, involving thirty-five participating states and seventeen observer states, in liaison with a range of interested international organizations, including the WHO, the World Bank, and the International Water Association, along with leading industry interests.[115] Thus, it provides an almost classic example of the type of global governance activity falling under the rubric of 'global environmental or administrative law', necessitated by ever-increasing 'globalisation'.[116] These standards even attempt to deal with the difficult issue of the 'cost' or 'price' of water services under the rubric of the 'standard of service' to be provided. Clearly the ongoing elaboration and adoption of such globally applicable practice standards, though essentially voluntary, will prove influential in determining an acceptable level of service provision and will help to clarify the nature of due diligence obligations owed by states pursuant to the human right to water and sanitation,[117] whether themselves acting as public service providers or as regulators of public or private-sector service providers.[118] Commentators have cited this elaboration of quasi-normative standards by a body such as the ISO as an example of the 'global administrative law' phenomenon, which describes arrangements comprising 'hybrid blends of public and private actors linked in routines of both formal and informal participation at multiple levels of governance',[119] where the adoption of informal transnational regulatory standards is facilitated by the application of good governance standards reminiscent of national systems of administrative law.[120] The elaboration of such standards must also inform broad normative expectations under SDG 6.

---

[114] See further <http://www.iso.org/committee/299764/x/catalogue/> accessed 30 November 2022.

[115] See further, McIntyre, 'The Human Right to Water as a Creature of Global Administrative Law' (n 3).

[116] See N Walker, *Intimations of Global Law* (CUP 2014) 3–6, describing the phenomenon of 'globalization' in terms of 'a strong trend away from "the local" and the territorially confined, and in particular the state confined, as the main point of reference for many areas of human organisation' and 'the gradual deterritorialisation and disembedding of the basic setting of social organisation'. On the concept of 'global administrative law', see further C Harlow, 'Global Administrative Law: The Quest for Principles and Values' (2006) 17(1) European Journal of International Law 187–214; B Kingsbury, 'Global Environmental Governance as Administration: Implications for International Law' in D Bodansky and others (eds), *Oxford Handbook of International Environmental Law* (OUP 2007) 63–84; B Kingsbury, 'The Concept of "Law" in Global Administrative Law' (2009) 20(1) European Journal of International Law 23–57; B Kingsbury and others, 'Global Governance as Administration: National and Transnational Approaches to Global Administrative Law' (2005) 68(3&4) Law and Contemporary Problems 1–13. On 'global or transnational environmental law', see O McIntyre, 'Transnational Environmental Regulation and the Normativisation of Global Environmental Governance Standards: The Promise of Order from Chaos' (2018) 10(2) Journal of Property, Planning and Environmental Law 92–112.

[117] On the 'due diligence' nature of the key obligations imposed under the human right to water and sanitation, see SC McCaffrey, 'A Human Right to Water: Domestic and International Implications' (1992) 5 Georgetown International Environmental Law Review 1 13; Hardberger (n 72) 336.

[118] For a discussion of the legal significance of the adoption of ISO standards, see B Morgan, 'The Regulatory Face of the Human Right to Water' (2004) 15(5) Water Law 179 182–83.

[119] B Morgan, 'Turning Off the Tap: Urban Water Service Delivery and the Social Construction of Global Administrative Law' (2006) 17(1) European Journal of International Law 215 216 and 224–27.

[120] See further, McIntyre, 'Transnational Environmental Regulation' (n 116).

ISO service standards are also likely to inform the behaviour expected under voluntary codes of corporate conduct[121] where, for instance, water utility companies may refer to SDG 6-related targets alongside human rights-based commitments in their corporate social responsibility policies.[122] Such standards may also prove relevant where they opt to sign up to global codes, such as the UN Global Compact which requires that participating companies should comply with international human rights norms,[123] or the OECD Guidelines for Multinational Enterprises which consist of voluntary principles and standards for responsible business conduct in such areas of relevance to implementation of the right to water and SDG 6 as human rights, environment, information disclosure, the combating of bribery, and consumer interests.[124] It appears, therefore, that a wealth of standards will be available to inform almost any aspect of SDG 6 implementation, notwithstanding the dearth of prescriptive requirements set out under the relevant targets.

2. Target 6.2 By 2030, achieve access to adequate equitable sanitation and hygiene for all and end open defecation, paying special attention to the needs of women and girls and those in vulnerable situations

As regards the legal status of the purported human right to sanitation in international law, the aim set out in target 6.2 may ultimately play a highly formative role. If the formal legal status and justiciability in international law of the human right to water remains in doubt, then even greater uncertainty bedevils the emergence and recognition of the closely related human right of access to sanitation.[125] As a leading commentator could point out in 2010:

> As yet, there is no single resolution of the UN General Assembly on the right to sanitation and no worldwide agreement supporting this right. There is no agreed description of core obligations on sanitation and no definition of the content of the right to sanitation.[126]

---

[121] See further, SD Murphy, 'Taking Multinational Corporate Codes to the Next Level' (2005) 43 Colombia Journal of Transnational Law 388–433.

[122] For example, Suez commits its support to the right to water and sanitation, declaring that 'Suez fully assumes its role in promoting and implementing the right to water and sanitation. Thanks to its expertise, it is able to offer a full range of solutions in response to all issues faced by both developed and developing countries.' See <http://www.suez.com/en/Who-we-are/A-commited-group/Support-the-right-to-water-and-sanitation> accessed 4 February 2022.

[123] UN Global Compact <http://www.unglobalcompact.org/what-is-gc/mission/principles> accessed 30 November 2022. See further, Williams (n 71) 488–91. See also, the Corporate Water Disclosure Guidelines (2014), adopted by the CEO Water Mandate, a network of business leaders established under the auspices of the UN Global Compact, the world's largest corporate sustainability initiative <https://ceowatermandate.org/disclosure/> accessed 30 November 2022.

[124] OECD Guidelines for Multinational Enterprises <http://www.oecd.org/corporate/mne/1922428.pdf> accessed 30 November 2022.

[125] See generally, H Smets (ed), L'accès à L'assainissement, un Droit Fondamental (Edn Johanet 2010).

[126] H Smets, 'The Right to Sanitation: A New Human Right in Developed Countries' (April 2010) 40(2&3) Environmental Policy and Law 112 (at p 3 of online version).

Though the UN General Assembly has since adopted a 2010 Resolution on 'The Human Right to Water *and Sanitation*',[127] Smets' telling observation that states 'in particular have not adopted a General Comment on the Right to Sanitation' remains valid.[128] Thus, by articulating a globally agreed ambition dedicated to universal provision of access to sanitation and hygiene, target 6.2 is likely to have a profound impact on the emergence and realization of an internationally recognized right to sanitation.

Where it does include any express mention of sanitation, General Comment No 15 states that '[e]nsuring that everyone has access to adequate sanitation is not only fundamental for human dignity and privacy, but is one of the principal mechanisms for protecting the quality of drinking water supplies and resources'.[129] This suggests that it focuses primarily on problems of access to safe drinking water rather than the issue of access to sanitation, largely viewing the universal provision of adequate sanitation as necessary for, and ancillary to, provision of safe drinking water.[130] However, it is worth noting that General Comment No 15 does make special mention of 'rural and deprived urban areas' and 'the needs of women and children'—a concern largely reflected in target 6.2, which highlights the need to pay 'special attention to the needs of women and girls and those in vulnerable situations'. Of course, it is immediately clear that realization of the right to sanitation would require very specific guidance on the nature of the obligations imposed and actions involved, which would be quite distinct from those associated with the right to water. For example, methods of cost recovery for sanitation services, and for measuring the affordability of any charging scheme, are likely to be highly specific to different social contexts.[131]

The service or facility of 'sanitation' is defined under the 1999 Protocol on Water and Health to the 1992 UNECE Helsinki Convention[132] as 'the collection, transport, treatment and disposal or reuse of human excreta or domestic wastewater, whether through collective systems or by installations serving a single household or undertaking'.[133] For the specific purpose of articulating a human right to sanitation, the CESCR has more recently adopted the definition employed by the UN Independent Expert on Water and Sanitation, which describes 'sanitation' more generally as 'a system for the collection,

---

[127] UNGA Res 64/294 (26 July 2010), UN Doc A/64/L.63/Rev.1 (emphasis added).

[128] Smets, 'The Rights to Sanitation' (n 126) (at p 3 of online version).

[129] General Comment No 15 (n 8) para 29 10. Similarly, para 1 points out that '[o]ver 1 billion persons lack access to a basic water supply, while several billion do not have access to adequate sanitation, which is the primary cause of water contamination and diseases linked to water'. In addition, when advising that state parties to the Covenant 'should adopt comprehensive and integrated strategies and programmes *to ensure that there is sufficient and safe water*', para 28 suggests that '[s]uch strategies and programmes may include ... reducing and eliminating contamination of watersheds and water related ecosystems by substances such as radiation, harmful chemicals and *human excreta*' (emphasis added).

[130] In a further illustration of this approach, when advising that state parties to the Covenant 'should adopt comprehensive and integrated strategies and programmes *to ensure that there is sufficient and safe water*', para 28 of General Comment No 15 (n 8) suggests that ' [s]uch strategies and programmes may include ... reducing and eliminating contamination of watersheds and water related ecosystems by substances such as radiation, harmful chemicals and *human excreta*' (emphasis added).

[131] See, eg, African Development Bank, *Guidelines for User Fees and Cost Recovery for Urban Water and Sanitation* and *Guidelines for User Fees and Cost Recovery for Rural, Non-Networked, Water and Sanitation Delivery* (n. 96).

[132] McIntyre, 'The UNECE Water Convention and the Principle of Equitable and Reasonable Utilisation' (n 73).

[133] Art 2(8).

464   SDG 6

transport, treatment and disposal or reuse of human excreta and associated hygiene'.[134] Though several legal definitions exist for the concept of 'sanitation', a human right of access to sanitation raises a wide range of questions and optional approaches. Indeed, even such a stalwart supporter of the concept and advocate of its normative status in international law as Henri Smets points out that any law promoting access to sanitation requires policy-makers 'to specify the responsibilities of each person; to define the extent of the undertakings of public authorities; to provide public subsidies; and to specify who will have access to a connection to the sewage networks'.[135] Indeed, it is with a view to identifying best practice in respect of such means of implementation of a putative right to sanitation that the French Water Academy has recently produced an edited volume describing the relevant national legislative frameworks of 16 developed or developing countries.[136]

The CESCR refers on a number of occasions to the imperative of providing access to adequate sanitation in General Comment No 15, its seminal interpretative document on the human right to water.[137] Most notably, paragraph 29 expressly includes among the 'obligations to fulfil' inherent to the right to water the duty of states of '[e]nsuring that everyone has access to adequate sanitation', which it elaborates upon to explain that 'States parties have an obligation to progressively extend safe sanitation services, particularly to rural and deprived urban areas, taking into account the needs of women and children'. Also, in the context of its discussion of water 'availability' as a key factor applying to 'the adequacy of water required for the right to water', paragraph 12(a) states unequivocally that the requirement of sufficient water for 'personal sanitation' applies 'in all circumstances'.[138] In addition, a number of the objectives and values that General Comment No 15 links to the human right to water are strongly suggestive of an associated right to sanitation. For example, both paragraphs 3 and 11 link the human right to water to the concept of human dignity,[139] while paragraphs 6 and 8 refer to the need to ensure 'environmental hygiene' as an aspect of the right to health.[140] Both values strongly imply that access to sanitation is a key element of the right to water. In addition, in its discussion of 'physical accessibility' as another of the factors applying to 'the adequacy of water required for the right to water', paragraph 12(c)(i) emphasizes water facilities being 'culturally appropriate and sensitive to gender, life-cycle and privacy requirement', while paragraph 16(h) stresses '[g]roups facing difficulties with

---

[134] UN Committee on Economic, Social and Cultural Rights, Statement on the Right to Sanitation, UN Doc E/C.12/2010/1, 19 November 2010.

[135] Smets, 'The Right to Sanitation' (n 126) (at p 3 of online version).

[136] See Smets (ed), L'accès à l'assainissement, un droit fondamental (n 125).

[137] General Comment No 15 (n 8).

[138] Para 12(a) provides that '[t]he water supply for each person must be sufficient and continuous for personal and domestic uses. These uses ordinarily include drinking, *personal sanitation*, washing of clothes, food preparation, *personal and household hygiene*' (emphasis added).

[139] Para 3 provides, *inter alia*, that '[t]he right [to water] should also be seen in conjunction with other rights enshrined in the International Bill of Human Rights, foremost among the right to life and human dignity'. Para 11 in turn provides, *inter alia*, that'[t]he elements of the right to water must be *adequate* for human dignity, life and health' (original emphasis).

[140] Para 8 provides, *inter alia*, that '[e]nvironmental hygiene, as an aspect of the right to health under article 12, paragraph 2*(b)*, of the Covenant, encompasses taking steps on a non-discriminatory basis to prevent threats to health from unsafe and toxic water conditions'.

physical access to water, such as older persons, persons with disabilities'. Once again, such concerns immediately evoke problems of adequate access to sanitation. Similarly, both paragraphs 12(c)(i) and 16(b) stress the importance of ensuring the provision of adequate water services to educational institutions, which implies the key role of adequate sanitation facilities in increasing and prolonging the participation of girls in education in many developing countries. Further, paragraph 25 stresses, as an element of the 'obligation to fulfil', the need for states to take steps to ensure that there is appropriate education concerning the hygienic use of water'. This implies the need to promote safe sanitation practices and resonates with the aim under target 6.2 to 'end open defecation' and that under indicator 6.2.1b to provide 'a handwashing facility with soap and water available at home'. Indeed, the latter aim now appears highly prescient having regard to the critical role of handwashing as an effective low-cost measure for addressing COVID-19 transmission.

As noted above, however, it is quite clear from a close examination of the text that General Comment No 15 is primarily concerned with access to safe drinking water and that the CESCR regards the human right to sanitation as ancillary to that primary concern, rather than as an autonomous human right. Indeed, the opening paragraph of General Comment No 15 makes clear the significance of sanitation for realization of the human right to water, and thus the ancillary nature of any right to sanitation, by noting that '[o]ver one billion persons lack access to a basic water supply, while several billion do not have access to adequate sanitation, *which is the primary cause of water contamination and diseases linked to water*'.[141] Also, paragraph 29, cited above as the most important provision in General Comment No 15 supporting the right of access to adequate sanitation, itself provides that such access 'is not only fundamental to human dignity and privacy, but is *one of the principal mechanisms for protecting the quality of drinking water supplies and resources*'.[142] Likewise, paragraph 28 includes among the strategies and programmes required to ensure sufficient and safe water for present and future generations, that of 'reducing and elimination contamination of watersheds and water related ecosystems by substances such as ... *human excreta*'. Similarly, paragraph 8 stresses the significance of 'environmental hygiene' as an aspect of the right to health and advises that this goal 'encompasses taking steps on a non-discriminatory basis *to prevent threats to health from unsafe and toxic water conditions*', requiring that

> For example, States parties should ensure that *natural water resources are protected from contamination by harmful substances and pathogenic microbes*. Likewise, States parties should monitor and combat situations *where aquatic eco-systems serve as a habitat for vectors of disease wherever they pose a risk to human living environments*.[143]

---

[141] General Comment No 15 (n 8) para 1 (emphasis added), referring to figures published by the World Health Organization (WHO) in 2000.
[142] Emphasis added.
[143] General Comment No 15 (n 8) para 8 (emphasis added).

Thus, the focus of General Comment No 15, as a foundational instrument in the discourse on the human right to water, is clearly much more on the continued availability of safe and adequate water than the provision of adequate sanitation per se for the purposes of preserving human dignity. This suggests that the CESCR employs quite a narrow conception of the right to sanitation, requiring only such steps as are necessary to prevent unacceptable risks to human health. Such an approach is, perhaps, to be expected, given the focus of General Comment No 15 and the paucity of instruments of international law giving support to and informing the concept of a human right to sanitation.

Another shortcoming, in terms of the legal status and normative content of the proposed human right to sanitation, is the fact that it has very limited support in the conventional practice of states. While Henri Smets is forced to concede that '[s]ome States have not adopted texts on sanitation prepared by international organizations and in particular have not adopted a General Comment on the Right to Sanitation' nor any 'worldwide agreement supporting this right', he points out that '[r]egional agreements fortunately compensate for such a lack'.[144] According to Smets, the French Water Academy has identified a total of three regional conventional instruments that would appear to support the concept, two human rights agreements and a water resources agreement.[145] The 2004 Arab Charter on Human Rights indeed exhorts States Parties, in pursuit of 'the right of every member of society to the enjoyment of the highest attainable standard of physical and mental health', to take measures for 'providing proper sanitation systems'.[146] More emphatically, the 1999 UNECE Protocol on Water and Health requires that:

> [t]he Parties shall, in particular, take all appropriate measures for the purpose of ensuring ...
> (b) Adequate sanitation of a standard which sufficiently protects human health and the environment. This shall in particular be done through the establishment, improvement and maintenance of collective systems.[147]

However, an explicit right to sanitation is not in fact included in the 1988 Protocol of San Salvador on ESC Rights.[148] Article 11(1) of the Protocol merely provides that '[e]veryone shall have the right to live in a healthy environment and to have access to basic public services', while article 7(d) sets out the state's obligation to guarantee '[s]afety and hygiene at work'. Indeed, article 10 of the 1988 Protocol, which elaborates

---

[144] Smets, 'The Rights to Sanitation' (n 126) p 3 of online version.

[145] ibid at p 3 of online version, referring to Smets (ed), *L'accès à l'assainissement, un droit fondamental* (n 125).

[146] UN Doc CHR/NONE/2004/40/Rev.1 (22 May 2004), art 39(2)(f).

[147] McIntyre, 'The UNECE Water Convention and the Principle of Equitable and Reasonable Utilisation' (n 73); art 4(2)(b).

[148] Additional Protocol to the American Convention on Human Rights in the Area of Economic, Social and Cultural Rights, 'Protocol of San Salvador', OAS Treaty Series No 69 (1988), entered into force 16 November 1999, reprinted in Basic Documents Pertaining to Human Rights in the Inter-American System, OEA/Ser.L.V/II.82 doc.6 rev.1 at 67 (1992).

in some detail on the measures necessary to ensure 'the right to health', fails to include any measures which readily infer a right to sanitation. Other instruments that could be cited in support of a right to sanitation include the 1979 Convention on the Elimination of All Forms of Discrimination Against Women,[149] the 1989 Convention on the Rights of the Child,[150] and the 2003 Protocol to the African Charter on Human and Peoples Rights regarding the Rights of Women.[151]

The generally applicable minimum normative content of any right to sanitation is difficult to identify reliably, as it is likely to be largely relative and dependent on the specific context in which it is applied. There would, for example, need to be a clear distinction made between urban and rural settings. Smets points out that '[t]he content of the right to sanitation is not the same everywhere although the aim is common to all: health and dignity for everyone. Its scope is different in cities and rural areas because in cities a sewage collection system is now a must',[152] though the same author cautions that '[r]ural areas should not be forgotten even if it is necessary to adapt technical requirements and facilitate investment'.[153] Likewise, even though General Comment No 15 doesn't elaborate in any detail on a right to sanitation, the CESCR recognizes that 'States Parties have an obligation to progressively extend safe sanitation services, particularly to rural and deprived urban areas'.[154] In the provision of access to adequate sanitation, and especially services and facilities 'taking into account the needs of women and children',[155] there are likely to arise many other social, cultural and economic factors and variants. Therefore, it is a little disappointing, if also largely understandable, that SDG 6.2 doesn't elaborate beyond the aim of ensuring provision of 'safely managed sanitation services'[156] and 'a handwashing facility with soap and water available at home'.[157] Helpfully, some limited case law exists at national level elaborating on the content of any right to sanitation.[158] In the 2011 *Beja* case,[159] for example, the South African High Court found that the provision by the local authorities of unenclosed toilet facilities in an informal settlement violated a range of constitutional rights, including human dignity (section 10), freedom and security of the

---

[149] 1249 *UNTS* 13 art 14(2) calls on state parties to ensure that women living in rural areas have the right 'to enjoy adequate living conditions, particularly in relation to housing, *sanitation*, electricity and water supply' (emphasis added).

[150] 1577 *UNTS* 3 art 24(2) calls on state parties to combat illness and malnutrition by 'the provision of adequate nutritious foods and clean drinking water, taking into account the *dangers and risks of environmental pollution*' (emphasis added). This suggests that, to the extent that the CRC includes obligations regarding sanitation, these are ancillary to the provision of 'clean drinking water'.

[151] <https://www.ohchr.org/Documents/Issues/Women/WG/ProtocolontheRightsofWomen.pdf> accessed 30 November 2022. Art 18 requires state parties to 'take all appropriate measures ... regulate the management, processing, storage and disposal of domestic waste'. Once again, this provision doesn't focus on sanitation specifically.

[152] Smets, 'The Rights to Sanitation' (n 126) (at p 3 in online version).

[153] ibid (at p 2 in online version).

[154] See General Comment No 15 (n 8) para 29.

[155] ibid.

[156] Indicator 6.2.1a.

[157] Indicator 6.2.1b.

[158] See, eg, the 2009 judgment of the South African Constitutional Court of South Africa in *Nokotyana and Others v Ekurhuleni Metropolitan Municipality and Others* CCT 31/09 [2009] ZACC 33 (19 November 2009), where the South African High Court and Supreme Court engaged in limited deliberation on the number of pit latrines required per household and the need for high-mast security lighting.

[159] *Beja and Others v Premier of the Western Cape and Others* (21332/10) [2011] ZAWCHC 97; [2011] 3 All SA 401 (WCC); 2011 (10) BCLR 1077 (WCC) (29 April 2011).

person (section 12), privacy (section 14), environment (section 24), housing (section 26), and healthcare (section 27). The Court also found that the unenclosed toilets violated the applicable National Standards and Measures to Conserve Water. The decision affirmed that the primary objective of the South African Constitution is the protection of human dignity and reiterated that the requirements of privacy, protection against the elements, and adequate sanitary facilities are central features of the development of adequate housing in South African informal settlements. However, the deliberations of national courts in such matters are of limited guidance only, as they are highly dependent upon the relevant and applicable national constitutional and legislative frameworks.[160] Probably the most comprehensive elaboration of the content of a right to sanitation is that produced by the former Independent Expert on the right to safe drinking water and sanitation, Catarina de Albuquerque, in her 2009 report to the HRC.[161] The report devotes several pages to setting out in some detail '[t]he content of human rights obligations related to sanitation', covering such issues as availability, quality, physical accessibility, affordability and accessibility.[162]

The true value of target 6.2 is that it marks a global consensus and provides a clear and unambiguous focus for action, as well as a formal framework for reporting on and monitoring national progress, on an area that had been hitherto shamefully neglected, the right to sanitation and hygiene. As noted above, General Comment No 15 fails to emphasize the importance of this critical imperative for its own sake and the MDG target for extending access to sanitation was clearly missed,[163] despite the fact that across the world one quarter of the deaths of children under five years of age are attributable to inadequate sanitation.[164] This unsatisfactory situation clearly prompted the HRC's Independent Expert to call for recognition of the right to sanitation as an autonomous human right—one based on the need to protect human dignity and independent of the right to an adequate standard of living, the right to adequate housing, the right to health, and the right to water.[165] That adoption and implementation of an SDG sanitation target can only contribute significantly to the realization of this putative human right, which is so critically important for achieving true sustainable development, is illustrated by the 2021 progress report on implementation of target 6.2, which notes emphatically that '[a]chieving the SDG global target 6.2 by 2030 will require a fourfold increase in the current rate of progress'.[166]

[160] See generally Smets (ed), L'accès à l'assainissement, un droit fondamental (n 125).

[161] Human Rights Council, 'Report of the Independent Expert on the Issue of Human Rights Obligations Related to Access to Safe Drinking Water and Sanitation', UN Doc A/HRC/12/24 (1 July 2009).

[162] ibid at 23–25, paras 69–80.

[163] UN (n 34).

[164] See Human Rights Council (n 161) 4–5, para 5. See further, C Golay, 'Recognition and Definition of the Right to Water and the Right to Sanitation, DPH (November 2009) <http://base.d-p-h.info/fr/fiches/dph/fiche-dph-8111.html> accessed 30 November 2022.

[165] Human Rights Council (n 161) at 18–20, paras 55–59.

[166] UN-Water, 'Summary Progress Update 2021: SDG 6—Water and Sanitation for All' (UN July 2021) 9. More specifically, regarding progress against SDG indicator 6.2.1a (access to safely managed sanitation services), the report notes that '[n]o SDG region is currently on track. 1.7 billion people still lack even basic sanitation services. Among these, 7 out of 10 live in rural areas and 3 out of 10 in least developed countries. 494 million people still practise open defecation and 55 countries still have open defecation rates above 5%.' Regarding progress against SDG indicator 6.2.1b (access to a handwashing facility with soap and water at home), the report notes that '2 out

3. Target 6.3 By 2030, improve water quality by reducing pollution, eliminating dumping and minimizing release of hazardous chemicals and materials, halving the proportion of untreated wastewater and substantially increasing recycling and safe use globally

The environmental pollution-related objectives included under target 6.3 simply reiterate and strengthen the central importance long accorded to environmental values in modern international water law, as reflected in the inclusion of the detailed and imperative pollution provisions contained in Part IV of the UN Watercourses Convention and the even more exacting provisions of the 1992 UNECE Water Convention, which focus on the prevention, control and reduction of 'transboundary impact'.[167] These instruments reflect long-standing concerns among watercourse states regarding the need to protect watercourses as fragile natural resources providing a range of indispensable benefits, including the provision of drinking water and the removal of wastes, which need to be carefully managed in order to achieve balance and sustainability. Pollution control has long been a central concern of international water law,[168] and in an attempt to codify pollution-related measures, article 21(2) of the UN Watercourses Convention now provides that:

Watercourse States shall, individually and, where appropriate, jointly, prevent, reduce and control the pollution of an international watercourse that may cause significant harm to other watercourse States or their environment, including harm to human health or safety, to the use of the waters for any beneficial purpose or to the living resources of the watercourse. Watercourse States shall take steps to harmonize their policies in this connection.

Article 21(3) in turn proceeds to make provision for the holding of consultations amongst states sharing an international watercourse with a view to arriving at mutually agreeable measures and methods to prevent, reduce and control pollution of an international watercourse, such as:

(a) Setting joint water quality objectives and criteria;
(b) Establishing techniques and practices to address pollution from point and non-point sources;
(c) Establishing lists of substances the introduction of which into the waters of an international watercourse is to be prohibited, limited, investigated, or monitored.

---

of 5 people in rural areas and nearly two thirds of the population of least developed countries lack handwashing facilities with soap and water at home. In sub-Saharan Africa 1 out of 3 people have no handwashing facility at all.'

[167] UN Watercourses Convention (n 7) arts 20–23 and UNECE, Convention on the Protection and Use of Transboundary Watercourses and International Lakes (1992) 31 ILM 1312; 1936 UNTS 269; art 3.
[168] For detailed analysis of the emergence of environmental concerns, see generally, McIntyre, *Environmental Protection of International Watercourses* (n 75).

470 SDG 6

Clearly, this article, which codifies related practice and typifies the pollution management provisions contained in almost all international watercourse and water resources agreements, corresponds very closely with the aims set out in target 6.3 and the indicators developed thereunder to increase treatment of household wastewater[169] and industrial wastewater[170] and to improve ambient water quality.[171]

In elaborating upon the significance of article 21, the International Law Commission (ILC), in its detailed commentary to the 1994 Draft Articles which preceded the UN Watercourses Convention, appears to regard the due diligence obligation set out under article 21(2) to prevent, reduce and control pollution as 'applying the general obligation of article 7 to the case of pollution'.[172] Therefore, in order to come within the scope of article 21, the pollution in question must be of a type that 'may cause significant harm to other watercourse states or to their environment', such as the illustrative examples listed under article 21(2), 'harm to human health or safety, to the use of the waters for any beneficial purpose or to the living resources of the watercourse'. International water law's focus upon pollution likely to give rise to such harm further illustrates its direct coherence with the broad aims of target 6.3 and, more indirectly, with those of targets 6.1 and 6.2. The ILC commentary also confirms that 'the principle of precautionary action is applicable, especially in respect of dangerous substances such as those that are toxic, persistent or bio-accumulative',[173] and recognizes that the pollution control framework provided by article 21 is supported by a wealth of 'representative illustrations of international agreements, the work of international organizations, decisions of international courts and tribunals, and other instances of State practice'.[174] Thus the ILC appears expressly to recognize the critical role of the extensive body of developed practice existing in the field of international environmental law in supporting the effective implementation and application of the key pollution control obligation set out in article 21 of the UN Watercourses Convention and, by extension, the aims of target 6.3. Of course, state practice developing in light of the emerging human right to water, consistent with the stipulations of General Comment No 15,[175] as well as practice now developing in light of the efforts of states to implement SDG 6, might also be expected to inform aspects of the due diligence obligation to prevent or reduce environmental pollution arising under international water law.

It is only logical that any water-related goal should encompass entitlements and obligations relating to protection of the natural environment, as this will play a pivotal role in the provision of water-related services. General Comment No 15 similarly declares that the right to water involves both the right of the individual to be free 'from unsafe and toxic water conditions'[176] and from 'contamination of water supplies',[177] and the

---

[169] Indicator 6.3.1 measures the 'Proportion of household wastewater flow safely treated'.
[170] Indicator 6.3.2 measures the 'Proportion of industrial wastewater flow safely treated'.
[171] Indicator 6.3.3 measures the 'Proportion of bodies of water with good ambient water quality'.
[172] ILC (n 82) 122. Art 7 of the UNWC sets out the fundamental obligation of international water law not to cause significant harm to other watercourse states.
[173] ibid.
[174] ibid 123.
[175] General Comment No 15 (n 8) paras 31–35, 11.
[176] ibid para 8, 3.
[177] ibid para 10, 4.

obligation of states to refrain from 'unlawfully diminishing or polluting water'[178] and to adopt legislative and other measures to restrain third parties from polluting water sources.[179] As regards the environmental standards to be applied pursuant to the right to water, General Comment No 15 expressly lists UNEP[180] among the organizations from whom 'States parties may obtain guidance on appropriate indicators',[181] thereby stressing the direct relevance of UN Environment's work on water and freshwater ecosystems. This connection once again highlights the strong interlinkages between the right to water and SDG 6 as UN Environment's Freshwater Strategy 2017–2021 focuses on those SDG targets that relate to water quality and pollution, freshwater ecosystems, integrated water resources management (IWRM), and water-related conflict and disasters.[182]

Official guidance on implementation of SDG 6 emphasizes the use of existing environmental standards set out under relevant multilateral environmental agreements (MEAs), wherever available. For example, UN-Water guidelines relating to target 6.3 on water quality and wastewater,[183] which aim to protect both ecosystem health and human health by eliminating, minimizing, and significantly reducing different streams of pollution into water bodies, advocate doing so in a manner consistent with the Basel Convention on the Control of Transboundary Movements of Hazardous Wastes and their Disposal,[184] the Rotterdam Convention on the Prior Informed Consent Procedure for Certain Hazardous Chemicals and Pesticides in International Trade,[185] and the Stockholm Convention on Persistent Organic Pollutants.[186] Regarding standards stipulated thereunder, the latter Convention has established a Persistent Organic Pollutants Review Committee comprising thirty-one experts nominated by the States Parties, which reviews chemicals nominated for listing and control under the Convention having regard to detailed criteria relating to their persistence, bioaccumulation, potential for long-range environmental transport and toxicity (Annex D), to the likelihood of these chemicals leading to significant adverse effects on human health or the environment (Annex E), and to socio-economic considerations associated with possible control measures (Annex F). The same guidance also refers,[187] to the 1992 UNECE Water Convention[188] and the 1997 UN Watercourses Convention,[189] the former of which is supported by a Secretariat and has been a very important source of technical guidance on all aspects of transboundary water resources management.[190]

---

[178] ibid para 21, 8.
[179] ibid para 23, 9.
[180] Now UN Environment, see <http://ww.unep.org> accessed 30 November 2022.
[181] General Comment No 15 (n 8) para 53, 16.
[182] Specifically, SDG targets 6.3, 6.5, 6.6, 11.5, and 16.1. See UN Environment, 'Freshwater Strategy 2017–2021' (2017) 6.
[183] UN-Water, *Integrated Monitoring Guide for SDG 6: Targets and Global Indicators* (UN July 2016) 8.
[184] 1673 *UNTS* 126; (1989) 28 ILM 657.
[185] 2244 *UNTS* 337; (1999) 38 ILM 1.
[186] 2256 *UNTS* 119; (2001) 40 ILM 532.
[187] UN-Water, *Integrated Monitoring Guide for SDG 6* (n 183) 16–20.
[188] n 167.
[189] n 7.
[190] See further, <https://unece.org/environment-policy/water> accessed 30 November 2022.

472   SDG 6

Therefore, the wealth of standards and practice developed under the auspices of established MEAs assists in informing the requirements of target 6.3, just as it helps to inform the precise normative implications of the human right(s) to water and sanitation.[191] The relatively highly developed domestic legal frameworks for environmental protection of water resources also provide a rich source of environmental standards which function to assist implementation of target 6.3, as they assist realization of the right to water. To take one notable example, the European Union (EU) has long legislated for the management and protection of water resources in the EU Member States and Associated States, prescribing detailed standards such as the limit values introduced for List I substances under the 1976 EU Directive on Pollution Caused by Certain Dangerous Substances Discharged into the Aquatic Environment.[192] Such limit values were not to be exceeded by EU Member States when setting national emission standards for discharges into the aquatic environment. Over time, the EU adopted a comprehensive suite of Directives establishing limit values and water quality objectives relating to all List I substances.[193] The direct and indirect relevance of such a diversity of legal, and even non-legal, environmental standards for understanding the precise requirements of SDG 6 and/or the normative implications of the right(s) to water and sanitation provides an illustration of the phenomenon of growing normative convergence in environmental regulation at all levels commonly referred to as 'global or transnational environmental law'.[194]

4. Target 6.4 By 2030, substantially increase water-use efficiency across all sectors and ensure sustainable withdrawals and supply of freshwater to address water scarcity and substantially reduce the number of people suffering from water scarcity

a) *Water efficiency*

Improving the efficiency of water-use is a complex exercise and indicator 6.4.1[195] is essentially an economic indicator, assessing the extent to which a state's economic growth is dependent upon the use of water resources. In this way, it tracks the change in water-use efficiency over time, measured as the ratio of dollar value added to the volume of water used. It considers water use by all economic activities, with a focus on agriculture, industry, and the service sector. Increasing water-use efficiency over time means decoupling a country's economic growth from its water use, so 'that a given marginal

---

[191] See further, McIntyre, 'The Emergence of Standards' (n 70) 159–62.

[192] Directive 76/464/EEC of 18 May [1976] OJ L129/23.

[193] Including: Directive 82/176/EEC of 27 March 1982 concerning the Discharge of Mercury by the Chlor-Alkali Electrolysis Industry [1982] OJ L81; Directive 84/156/EEC of 17 March 1984 concerning the Discharge of Mercury by the Chlor-Alkali Electrolysis Industry [1984] OJ L74; Directive 83/513/EEC of 24 October 1983 concerning the Discharge of Cadmium [1983] OJ L291/1; Directive 84/491/EEC of 9 October 1984 on Limit Values and Quality Objectives for Discharges of Hexachlorocyclohexane [1984] OJ L274/11; Directive 86/280/EEC of 12 June 1986 on Limit Values and Quality Objectives for Discharges of Certain Dangerous Substances Included in List I of the Annex to Directive 76/464/EEC, including Carbon Tetrachloride, DDT and Pentachlorophenol, [1986] OJ L181/16; Directive 88/347/EEC of 25 June 1988 on Limit Values and Quality Objectives relating to Aldrin, Dieldrin, Endrin, Isodrin, Hexachlorobenzene, Hexachlorobutadine, and Chloroform (1988) OJ L158/35.

[194] See T Yang and R Percival, 'The Emergence of Global Environmental Law' (2009) 36 Ecology Law Quarterly 615–64. See further, McIntyre, 'The Human Right to Water' (n 3); McIntyre, 'Transnational Environmental Regulation and the Normativisation of Global Environmental Governance Standards (n 116).

[195] Indicator 6.4.1 measures 'Change in water-use efficiency over time'.

increase of national income does not correspond to an equivalent or higher marginal increase in water use, *i.e.* economic growth does not imply using more water'.[196] In other words, national economies, and particularly those of water-scarce countries, can continue to grow without needing more water. It is closely linked to indicator 6.4.2,[197] which is essentially an environmental indicator measuring the physical availability of freshwater resources and the impact of water use, as promoting water-use efficiency is particularly important in water-scarce areas. National efforts at increasing water-use efficiency require careful coordination and collaboration between multiple stakeholders and governmental and administrative agencies—a process that can be supported by the IWRM process promoted under target 6.5 and indicator 6.5.1. In turn, data provided under the target 6.4 indicators can inform the IWRM process and measures planned thereunder.

Indicator 6.4.1 demonstrates the long-term ambition and sophistication of the 2030 Agenda, but it has not been without challenges. It employs two key sets of data, which shed light upon the two different dimensions examined—hydrological and economic. These consist of:

- volumes of water used by the different sectors included in the indicator's computation; and
- gross value added (GVA) of the sectors.

As no similar target had been included under the previous MDGs, it was necessary to develop 'an entirely new methodology to monitor the indicator, and to generate and interpret new data computations due to the indicator's lack of previous data'.[198] As one might reasonably expect, this methodology is quite technical in nature:

> The volume of water used by each sector was defined based on the definitions set in the System of Environmental-Economic Accounting for Water (SEEA-Water), which defines water use as the water abstracted by a given economic sector or received from another sector. This definition allows for the use of data collected by AQUASTAT under 'total water withdrawal (TWW)'.
>
> As this indicator focuses on economy, it is calculated by computing individual indicators for each of the main economic sectors, before aggregating them into a single figure. The indicator is defined as the value added per water used (expressed in USD/m^3) over time of a given major economic sector, revealing the trend in water-use efficiency. Economic sectors are designated following the International Standard Industrial Classification of All Economic Activities (ISIC) Revision 4 codes.[199]

---

[196] FAO, 'Progress on Change in Water-Use Efficiency: Global Status and Acceleration Needs for Indicator 6.4.1' (FAO 2021) XIX <file:///C:/Users/omcintyre/Downloads/SDG6_Indicator_Report_641_Progress-on-Water-Use-Efficiency_2021_ENGLISH_pages-1.pdf> accessed 30 November 2022.

[197] Indicator 6.4.2. measures 'Level of water stress: freshwater withdrawal as a proportion of available freshwater resources'.

[198] FAO, 'Progress on Change in Water-Use Efficiency' (n 196) 3. On the indicator 6.4.1 methodology, see further, ibid 11–18.

[199] ibid 3–4.

Engaging effectively with this indicator will clearly require a measure of capacity building, especially among less capacitated developing countries.[200]

The water-use efficiency values articulated in target 6.4 and indicator 6.4.1 have long been reflected in international water law, but are rather limited in terms of their legal significance by the desire to strike an equitable balance between the water-use rights of developed and developing watercourse states, where the former are likely to enjoy greater technical capacity regarding water efficiency. While the UN Watercourses Convention requires that account be taken of the 'conservation, development, protection and economy of use of the water resources of the watercourse and the costs of measures taken to that effect' in determining equitable and reasonable utilization,[201] and the Helsinki Rules refer to 'the avoidance of unnecessary waste in the utilization of the waters of the basin',[202] state and judicial practice suggest that the role of efficient use as a factor in determining an equitable utilization regime for an international watercourse is rather limited.[203] In its commentary to article V of the Helsinki Rules, the ILA took the view that '[a] "beneficial use" need not be the most productive use to which the water may be put, nor need it utilize the most efficient methods known in order to avoid waste and ensure maximum utilization'.[204] It argued that to require otherwise would result in the dislocation of numerous productive uses and would favour more economically and technologically advanced states over less developed states, explaining that 'in its application, the present rule is not designed to foster waste but to hold States to a duty of efficiency which is commensurate with their financial resources'.[205] The position in international law is therefore contextually relative and this approach might be regarded as an early application of the international environmental law principle of 'common but differentiated responsibility', whereby the common environmental obligations of all states are recognized, but some differentiation may be permitted in respect of such obligations on the basis of the different financial and technical capacity of states.[206]

Equally, it is well established that 'no user may be wilfully wasteful or inefficient when it has the means to reduce inefficiency'.[207] The United States Supreme Court set out the nuanced nature of the requirement of efficiency in international water law in its decision in *Colorado v New Mexico*, where the Court stated that it would only protect those rights to water which are 'reasonably required and applied', and continued that

---

[200] See the capacity-building resources to support indicator 6.4.1 listed, ibid 10.

[201] Art 6(1)(f). The ILC commentary (n 7), para 4 101, refers to the avoidance of unnecessary waste of water in the context of 'economy of use'.

[202] n 75, art V(2)(i).

[203] See generally, X Fuentes, 'The Criteria for the Equitable Utilization of International Rivers' (1996) 67 British Yearbook of International Law 337 378 et seq; McIntyre, *Environmental Protection of International Watercourses* (n 75) 173–77.

[204] McIntyre, *Environmental Protection of International Watercourses* (n 75) 487.

[205] ibid. In support of this position, see, eg, 'Report of the Narmada Water Dispute Disputes Tribunal' (Government of India 1979) 1, 112 <http://cwc.gov.in/sites/default/files/Further_report_of_the_narmada_water _disputes_tribunal_1956.pdf> accessed 30 November 2022.

[206] See generally, L Rajamani, *Differential Treatment in International Environmental Law* (OUP 2006); P Cullet, *Differential Treatment in International Environmental Law* (Ashgate 2003); McIntyre (n 75) 260–65.

[207] See Lipper (n 78). See 'Report of the Narmada Water Dispute Disputes Tribunal' * MERGEFORMAT (n 205) 129.

[e]specially ... where water is scarce ... wasteful or inefficient uses will not be protected ... Similarly, concededly senior water rights will be deemed forfeited or substantially diminished where the rights have not been exercised or asserted with reasonable diligence.[208]

The Supreme Court went on to explain that states have 'an affirmative duty to take reasonable steps to conserve and augment the water supply of an interstate stream' and that they have 'a duty to employ "financially and physically feasible" measures "adapted to conserving and equalizing the natural flow".[209] The Court further stated that, in such a situation, '[e]ach of these states [has] a duty to exercise her right reasonably and in a manner calculated to conserve the common supply'.[210]

It is readily apparent, therefore, that international water law has a potentially significant role to play in equitably increasing water-use efficiency, at least as regards shared international water resources, and so can function to assist in realization of target 6.4. However, the elevation of the economic efficiency of water-use to the level of a priority objective through its inclusion in target 6.4, and the universal commitment and practice of states that such inclusion represents, might over time serve to prioritize efficiency as a key factor in determining reasonable and equitable use of international waters. In this respect, the SDGs might once again operate to promote the progressive evolution of international water law in order that it might better address the stark challenges of an increasingly water constrained world.

b) Water scarcity

The objective of addressing water scarcity, as the second element of target 6.4, is measured by means of indicator 6.4.2, which provides an estimate of the pressure exerted by all economic sectors on a country's renewable freshwater resources. It tracks how much freshwater is being withdrawn by all economic activities, compared to the total renewable freshwater resources available. When a territory withdraws 25 per cent or more of its renewable freshwater resources it is said to be 'water-stressed'. At the global level, it is estimated that 18.4 per cent of the total available renewable freshwater resources were being withdrawn in 2018, though this figure hides large regional, national, and subnational variations which make levels of water stress less clear. By facilitating the disaggregation of global, regional, and national data on water stress by river basin and water source (surface—groundwater), indicator 6.4.2 aims 'to provide a finer view of both the causes and effects of water stress, supporting the policy choices of the relevant authorities' regarding mitigation strategies and water distribution options.[211] In addition, by taking account of environmental flow requirements, indicator 6.4.2 seeks

---

[208] 459 US 176 (1982) 184. See further, McCaffrey, *The Law of International Watercourses* (n 75) 333 et seq.
[209] ibid 185.
[210] ibid 185–86.
[211] FAO, 'Progress on Level of Water Stress: Global Status and Acceleration Needs for Indicator 6.4.2' (FAO 2021) XIX <file:///C:/Users/omcintyre/Downloads/SDG6_Indicator_Report_642_Progress-on-Level-of-Water-Stress_2021_ENGLISH_pages-1.pdf> accessed 30 November 2022.

476 SDG 6

to assist in maintaining water-related ecosystem health and resilience. The monitoring of environmental water requirements encourages consideration of ecosystem health when available water resources are being allocated and is therefore closely linked to realization of target 6.6 on the protection and restoration of water-related ecosystems. In essence, indicator 6.4.2 is intended to function as a tool to assist states in water resources planning:

> The indicator shows the extent to which natural freshwater resources are already used and demonstrates the importance of effective supply- and demand-management policies. It indicates the likelihood of increasing competition and conflict between different water uses and users in a situation of increasing water scarcity.[212]

Indicator 6.4.2 was never going to prove as novel and technically challenging as indicator 6.4.1, as the Millennium Development Goals (MDGs) framework had already included a water stress indicator related to target 7.a, which was defined as the 'proportion of total water resources used'.[213] The definition of SDG indicator 6.4.2 is relatively similar to that of the MDG indicator with the exception that it explicitly takes environmental flow requirements (EFR) into consideration. At any rate, these same variables have been monitored by the FAO since 1994 through its global information system on water resources, AQUASTAT. However, the collection of data related to indicator 6.4.2 has proven to be a relatively complex exercise and has suffered from poor reporting on the part of states:

> The process of data collection and analysis remains a major challenge since not all countries report on all the variables necessary to calculate the indicator, and some countries are not reporting with the required frequency for an insightful or accurate monitoring.[214]

The custodian agencies are continuing to take steps to improve the data collection process for indicator 6.4.2 and to assist states in this regard.[215]

Despite the growing prevalence and seriousness of the problem of water scarcity, legal and policy tools for addressing this problem remain, as yet, quite underdeveloped, and so experience gained in implementing indicator 6.4.2 may prove seminally important for the elaboration of formal rules. For example, the regime created under the EU Water Framework Directive (WFD),[216] widely considered to be one of the most highly developed regimes globally for IWRM, fails adequately to address this increasingly urgent problem.

---

[212] ibid 3.
[213] ibid.
[214] ibid XXI and 4.
[215] ibid 4–5.
[216] EU Directive 2000/60/EC, OJ L327/2 (22 December 2000).

The WFD unequivocally lists among its objectives that of 'mitigating the effects of floods and droughts' and recognizes more generally that the quantitative status of a body of water may have an impact on its ecological quality. Annex VII of the WFD sets out the required content of a River Basin Management Plan (RBMP), the key instrument for the coordination of administrative arrangements within river basins and for implementing the substantive objectives set out in the Directive, and stipulates inclusion of an 'estimation of pressures on the quantitative status of water including abstractions' along with a 'list of environmental objectives established ... for surface waters, groundwaters and protected areas' and 'details of the supplementary measures identified as necessary in order to meet the environmental objectives established'. Thus, as the primary legislative instrument for the management and protection of water resources across the entire EU, the WFD is clearly intended to function to address water scarcity and it is reasonable to expect that it should aim to do so in the light of climate change impacts. However, it does not appear that it is operating in practice to meet this objective. A 2007 EU Commission study has found that over 40 per cent of RBMPs don't address the issue of water scarcity and drought at all, while only 12 per cent identify water scarcity and drought pressures by sector, and only 5 per cent include coordinated measures to address this concern, which is increasingly widespread throughout Europe, largely due to impacts associated with climate change.[217] A 2012 Commission review of progress on this issue concluded that trends in respect of water scarcity and drought management in Europe have not been reversed, primarily due to the lack of a dedicated legal instrument which, taking account of climate change risks, might define and implement ecological flow requirements and water efficiency targets, promote economic incentives for water efficiency, and guide land-use practices to respond to water scarcity.[218] While the EU Commission also adopted in 2012 a 'Blueprint to Safeguard Europe's Water Resources',[219] which places considerable emphasis on land-use practices and their impact on the ecological status of water resources and seeks to promote assessment and management of water scarcity and drought specifically in order to mitigate the effects of climate change, it is not at all clear how this can be achieved in the absence of a new legislative framework. The 2012 Blueprint notably calls for the integration of water quantity issues more fully into the overall policy framework, presumably including such fields as the EU nature conservation regime, a requirement that is likely to become ever more urgent as climate change impacts become more fully understood. Therefore, the commitment embodied in target 6.4 and indicators 6.4.1 and 6.4.2, and the policy and practice developed in response, are likely to prove very influential regarding future legislative developments.

---

[217] EU Commission, 'Addressing the challenge of water scarcity and droughts in the European Union', COM (2007)414 final (18 July 2007).

[218] EU Commission, 'Report on the revision of EU policy to combat water scarcity and drought', COM (2012)672 final (14 November 2012).

[219] EU Commission, 'Blueprint to Safeguard Europe's Water Resources', COM (2012)673 final (14 November 2012).

478   SDG 6

5. Target 6.5 By 2030, implement integrated water resources management at all levels, including through transboundary cooperation as appropriate

a) Integrated water resources management

Consistent with the commitment which emerged during elaboration of SDG 6 to the basic principle of adopting an integrative approach, target 6.5 includes an express commitment to promoting full implementation of IWRM at all levels of water governance. Citing a 2012 survey conducted by UNEP,[220] the TST to the OWG noted that

> [r]ecent results from a survey of 130 countries show that there has been widespread approaches to water management worldwide, but significant challenges remain. Since 1992, 80 per cent of countries made some progress in improving the policy, legal, institutional and financial framework for water resources management in response to the 2002 Johannesburg Plan of Implementation which stated that all countries should develop integrated water resources management and water efficiency plans.[221]

However, highlighting continuing gaps and deficiencies, the TST readily conceded that the benefits of improved water governance had only been achieved in some cases and that 'this clearly remains an ongoing process for most countries'.[222] At the practical level, the TST particularly linked progress on integrated approaches to water resources to 'progress on the enabling policy environment', which will positively impact management practices, and to 'improving implementation capacity and stakeholder participation'.[223] Particular constraints in this regard included 'unclear mandates and difficulties in cross-sectoral coordination'.[224]

Since the 1990s, IWRM has provided an overarching governance approach for the sustainable management of water and related resources at the basin-level, both for national and international basins. It is intended to provide an internationally recognized technical water management standard, seeking 'to combine the power of "neutral" technical information with modern public participation norms' and, thereby, 'to correct the environmental and social myopia of previous ... planning and water resources development models as well as introduce greater public involvement and economic discipline into water management and allocation practice'.[225] IWRM is defined by the Global Water Partnership (GWP), its principal promoter, as

---

[220] UNEP, 'The UN-Water Status Report on the Application of Integrated Approaches to Water Resources Management' (UNEP 2012).

[221] TST Issues Brief (n 29) 3.

[222] ibid. More specifically, the TST pointed out that 'fewer countries report advanced implementation for irrigation, rainwater harvesting and investment in natural systems. Evolution towards efficient water use has been uneven across sectors and regions'.

[223] ibid 4.

[224] ibid.

[225] AD Tarlock, 'Four Challenges for International Water Law' (2009) 23/2 Tulane Environmental Law Journal 369–408 405, citing K Conca, *Governing Water: Contentious Transnational Politics and Global Institution Building* (MIT Press 2006) 153–58.

a process which promotes the co-ordinated development and management of water, land and related resources, in order to maximise the resultant economic and social welfare in an equitable manner without compromising the sustainability of vital ecosystems.[226]

While IWRM has long enjoyed widespread support in the declaratory practice of the international community, its legal status remains somewhat unclear. Chapter 18 of Agenda 21, adopted at the UN Conference on Environment and Development (UNCED) in 1992, includes 'integrated water resources development and management' as one of the key programme areas set out thereunder for the freshwater sector with a view to addressing '[t]he fragmentation of responsibilities for water resource development among sectoral agencies'.[227] Agenda 21 proceeds to set out detailed objectives, activities and means of implementation for IWRM,[228] largely based on the core values expressed in the so-called Dublin Principles,[229] agreed as a preparatory text for UNCED. IWRM has been similarly endorsed by the Commission on Sustainable Development (CSD),[230] the UN General Assembly,[231] the Bonn Conference on Freshwater,[232] and the World Summit on Sustainable Development (WSSD).[233] Despite such declarative support, however, the IWRM paradigm only enjoys very limited recognition or support in the formal practice of international water law, earning express mention in only a handful of international conventional instruments,[234] though the 2000 EU Water Framework Directive places a process of integrated river basin management planning

---

[226] Global Water Partnership, 'Integrated Water Resources Management: TAC Background Paper No 4' (GWP 2000).

[227] United Nations Conference on Environment and Development (UNCED), 'Agenda 21: A programme for Action for Sustainable Development, Report of the United Nations Conference on Environment and Development', Annex II, UN Doc A/Conf.151/26/Rev.1 (Vol II) (Rio de Janeiro, 3–14 June 1992), paras 18.5 and 18.6.

[228] ibid paras 18.07–18.22.

[229] International Conference on Water and Environment (ICWE), 'Dublin Statement on Water and Sustainable Development' (Dublin, 26–31 January 1992). The 'Dublin Principles' provide:
   Principle 1: Water is a finite and vulnerable resource:
   Fresh water is a finite and vulnerable resource, essential to sustain life, development, and the environment.
   Principle 2: Participatory approach:
   Water development and management should be based on a participatory approach, involving users, planners, and policy-makers at all levels.
   Principle 3: Role of women:
   Women play a central part in the provision, management and safeguarding of water.
   Principle 4: Social and economic value of water:
   Water is a public good and has a social and economic value in all its competing uses.

[230] Commission on Sustainable Development, 'Report of the Expert Group Meeting on Strategic Approaches to Freshwater Management' (Harare, 27–30 January 1998).

[231] UNGA Res. 55/196, UN Doc A/RES/55196 (1 February 2001).

[232] International Conference on Freshwater, Ministerial Declaration of the International Conference on Freshwater (Bonn, 4 December 2001).

[233] World Summit on Sustainable Development (WSSD), 'Johannesburg Declaration on Sustainable Development' (Johannesburg, 26 August–4 September 2002), UN Doc A/CONF.199/20 (4 September 2002).

[234] For example, art 2 of the 2000 Revised Southern Africa Development Community (SADC) Protocol on Shared Watercourses includes among the instrument's key objectives, 'to … promote a coordinated and integrated environmentally sound development and management of shared watercourses'. Similarly, the Preamble to the Convention on the Sustainable Management of Lake Tanganyika recognizes that 'integrated management of the Lake Basin by the Contracting States is essential to ensure its conservation and the sustainable use of its natural resources and to optimize the benefits derived from it by the Contracting States'.

480 SDG 6

at the very core of European water resources management and protection.[235] Therefore, the precise normative requirements associated with the IWRM paradigm remain rather unclear, despite the best efforts of GWP,[236] which might help to explain the rather broad indicator associated with IWRM.[237]

It is nevertheless quite clear that most aspects of IWRM cohere with key elements of international and domestic water law. In distinguishing between '(good) governance' and 'IWRM', 'terms which are often, but incorrectly, used almost interchangeably', Allan and Rieu-Clarke conclude 'that IWRM is ultimately founded upon two key objectives: equity and sustainability'.[238] Of course, these elusive strategic aims also comprise the two principal objectives of modern international water law. Elsewhere these authors explain that 'IWRM in effect seeks to manage watersheds so that economic, social and environmental concerns are balanced appropriately in decision-making, in such a way as to ensure that the twin aims of *equity* and *sustainability* are achieved'.[239] In the context of a transboundary basin, this account of IWRM might almost define the principle of equitable and reasonable utilization—long acknowledged as the cardinal principle of general international water law. However, these same commentators further note that

> [t]his in effect demands institutional coordination, both vertically and horizontally, across relevant resource management, political and sectoral interests; integrated management, at the basin level, of land, resource exploitation and waters, whether upstream, downstream, ground or surface; and the participation of all relevant stakeholders in decision-making that affects water quality, quantity and flow.[240]

It appears, therefore, that IWRM provides a management framework that can facilitate the complex coordination of multiple interests in water resources at both the domestic and transboundary levels—in effect a bridge between the efficient national management of water resources with a view to sustainably optimizing beneficial water use, as pursued under national legal frameworks, and the inter-state engagement and balancing of interests at the very heart of international water law. This is why GWP's IWRM Toolbox stresses the integration of legal frameworks, requiring in practical terms that

---

[235] Council Directive 2000/60/EC, OJ L327 (22 December 2000). River basin management plans (RBMPs) are to be regularly reviewed by the competent national authorities under arts 5 and 11 of the Directive.

[236] See, eg, M Solanes and F Gonzalez-Villarreal, 'The Dublin Principles for Water as Reflected in a Comparative Assessment for Institutional and Legal Arrangements for Integrated Water Resources Management' (1999) GWP-TAC Background Paper No 3 (GWP).

[237] Indicator 6.5.1 merely relates to 'the degree of integrated water resources management implementation' worldwide, which assesses the status of national development and implementation of Integrated Water Resource Management (IWRM) plans across the world. See <https://sdg-tracker.org/water-and-sanitation> accessed 30 November 2022.

[238] A Allan and A Rieu-Clarke, 'Good Governance and IWRM— A Legal Perspective' (2010) 24 Irrigation and Drainage Systems 239–48 239–40.

[239] ibid at 244.

[240] ibid citing Global Water Partnership (n 226).

the legal, policy and institutional frameworks directly or indirectly affecting water resources management (e.g. forestry, energy, industrial development, municipal water supply, agriculture and environment) should be complementary and regard must be given to the competing needs/requirements of these different sectors in any water plan, policy, legislation or permit to use water.[241]

However, as a water governance paradigm, the utility of the IWRM concept is not without its critics. Yihdego and Gibson, for example, suggest that the approach 'is arguably outdated in the landscape of water governance, pointing out that 'IWRM has come under criticism for its lack of enforcement and its continued water centrism'.[242] Reviewing the experience of putting in place an IWRM regime for the Red River basin in Vietnam, Tarlock suggests that '[i]n short, IWRM proved too clumsy a policy instrument to deal with the scale of problems that the basin faced'.[243] It is generally understood that the widespread support enjoyed by IWRM is in large part due to donor funding and international advocacy. Tarlock, for example, complains that 'it has been adopted by European donor nations as the price for water development aid'.[244] Giordano and Shah caution that the principles underlying IWRM have become overly formalized and prescriptive and that 'the current monopoly of IWRM in global water management discourse is shutting out alternative thinking on pragmatic solutions to existing water problems'.[245] Yihdego and Gibson similarly express concern that '[i]ts inclusion within the SDGs could therefore be viewed as a missed opportunity to develop a more progressive and inclusive approach that measures advancements in a number of ways, rather than on IWRM alone'.[246] Focusing particularly on the practical difficulties of implementing IWRM in developing countries, Agyenim and Gupta conclude that 'developing countries often adopt such paradigm shifts in the management of their water resources primarily as a result of exogenous pressures' and, further, 'that (a) lack of domestic ownership and leadership of the concept, (b) limited resources, and (c) institutional mis-matches, often results in an implementation of the ideas that is limited to implementation in form rather than practice'.[247]

Indicator 6.5.1 provides a metric for the status of national development and implementation of IWRM plans by assessing the four key dimensions of IWRM: enabling environment; institutions and participation; management instruments; and financing.

---

[241] See<https://www.gwp.org/en/learn/iwrm-toolbox/The-Enabling-Environment/Legal-Framework/Integrating_legal_frameworks_for_IWRM/> accessed 30 November 2022.

[242] Z Yihdego and J Gibson, *Implementing International Watercourses Law through the WEF Nexus and SDGs: An Integrated Approach Illustrated in the Zambezi River Basin* (Brill 2020) 27, citing D Benson and others, 'Water Governance in a Comparative Perspective: From IWRM to a "Nexus" Approach?' (2015) 8 Water Alternatives 756–73.

[243] Tarlock (n 225), 407, citing F Molle and C Thai Hoanh, *Implementing Integrated River Basin Management: Lessons from the Red River Basin, Vietnam* (2009) IWMI Research Report No 131.

[244] Tarlock (n 225) 405. See also M Giordano and T Shah, 'From IWRM Back to Integrated Water Resources Management' (2014) 30(3) International Journal of Water Resources Development 364–76.

[245] Giordano and Shah (n 244).

[246] Yihdego and Gibson (n 242) 27.

[247] JB Agyenim and J Gupta, 'IWRM and Developing Countries: Implementation Challenges in Ghana' (2012) 47(48) Physics and Chemistry of the Earth 46–57.

482   SDG 6

However, the latest progress report on indicator 6.5.1 finds a disappointing lack of progress, with 107 states (out of 186 states reporting) considered not to be making sufficient headway.[248] This may reflect some of the difficulties outlined immediately above and the 2021 progress report itself notes the low levels of IWRM implementation among developing countries 'where development challenges are usually significant and capacity may be relatively low'.[249] It further highlights the need to strengthen political will to promote IWRM implementation. IWRM implementation levels are lowest in Latin America and the Caribbean, Oceania, Central and Southern Asia, and Sub-Saharan Africa.[250]

b) Transboundary cooperation

One of the ways in which the values set out in the SDGs cohere most markedly with those central to international water law is through the formers' explicit advocacy of transboundary cooperation in the governance of water resources, arguably the ultimate, defining aim of the latter body of rules.[251] Target 6.5 commits states to, '[by] 2030, implement integrated water resources management at all levels, including through transboundary cooperation as appropriate'. Though IWRM is in essence a technical best practice paradigm of water resources management with little clear legal meaning or significance,[252] a general duty upon states to cooperate over transboundary waters is included in almost all modern water resources conventions and declaratory instruments.[253] In addition to requiring watercourse states to cooperate in good faith 'in order to attain optimal utilization and adequate protection of an international watercourse', article 8 of the UNWC encourages them to 'consider the establishment of joint mechanisms or commissions ... to facilitate cooperation on relevant measures and procedures'. The 1994 ILC commentary on draft article 8 leaves little room for doubt as to the legal status or significance of the duty to cooperate.[254] Concluding that transboundary water cooperation provides an important basis 'in order to fulfil the obligations and attain the objectives set forth in the draft articles', the ILC points out that draft article 8 'refers to the most fundamental principles upon which cooperation between watercourse States is founded', in other words sovereign equality, territorial integrity, mutual benefit, and good faith, before summarizing the very wide range of international conventional instruments, declarations, and resolutions calling for cooperation over the utilization of international watercourses. The duty to cooperate can

---

[248] UN-Water, 'Summary Progress Report 2021—SDG 6—Water and Sanitation for All' (UN July 2021) 25.
[249] ibid 25.
[250] ibid 10.
[251] See, eg, O McIntyre, 'Chapter 15—Water' in E Morgera and K Kulovesi (eds), *Research Handbook on International Law and Natural Resources* (Edward Elgar 2016) 305–26, who describes the 'evolution of modern international water law—from a body of rules primarily concerned with the need to accommodate competing national economic interests based on territorial sovereignty, *to one which is increasingly understood as requiring meaningful inter-State engagement* in pursuit of optimal utilisation of the benefits flowing from shared water resources in a manner that is equitable as well as environmentally and socially sustainable' (emphasis added).
[252] On the legal significance of the IWRM concept, see Allan and Rieu-Clarke (n 238) 239–48.
[253] On the general duty to cooperate in international water law, see generally, C Leb, *Cooperation in the Law of Transboundary Water Resources* (CUP 2013).
[254] ILC (n 82) 105–07.

largely be understood as an 'umbrella' or composite obligation, consisting of a range of procedural requirements, any one or more of which might be applicable in a given situation. These notably include the duty to exchange information relevant to use of the watercourse, the duty to notify co-riparian states of planned projects potentially impacting a shared watercourse and, where necessary, duties to consult and negotiate with such states in a good faith effort to address their concerns.[255]

Beyond the general duty to cooperate over the utilization and protection of shared water resources owed to co-riparian states, General Comment No 15 clearly identifies a duty on states to cooperate in furtherance of realization of the human right to water. It notes that the UNWC

> requires that social and human needs be taken into account in determining the equitable utilization of watercourses, that State parties take measures to prevent significant harm being caused, and [that] special regard must be given to the requirements of vital human needs.[256]

However, General Comment No 15 further notes, in the context of the international obligations imposed upon states by virtue of articles 11 and 12 of the 1966 International Covenant on Economic, Social and Cultural Rights, that

> [t]o comply with their international obligations in relation to the right to water, States parties have to respect the enjoyment of the right in other countries. *International cooperation requires* States parties to refrain from actions that interfere, directly or indirectly, with the enjoyment of the right to water in other countries. Any activities undertaken within the State party's jurisdiction should not deprive another country of the ability to realize the right to water for persons in its jurisdiction.[257]

In fact, the CESCR goes so far as to include the duty to cooperate in realizing the right to water as one of the 'core obligations' of States Parties to the 1966 Covenant.[258] Thus, the international discourse on the human right to water had already begun to alter the focus of the fundamental duty to cooperate under international water law towards pursuit of the availability and sustainable management of water and sanitation for all, an evolutionary transformation supported in no small measure by the successive universal adoption by states of MDG 7 and SDG 6.

It should be noted that General Comment No 15 is emphatic in linking good faith transboundary water cooperation, as required under international water law, to the realization of the human right to water in a number of ways. For example, in listing indicative illustrations of violations of the right to water, it includes the 'failure of a State to take into account its international legal obligations regarding the right to water

---

[255] As exemplified in arts 9 and 11–19 of the UNWC.
[256] General Comment No 15 (n 8) para 31 11.
[257] ibid (emphasis added).
[258] ibid para 38, 13.

when entering into agreements with other States or with international organizations'.[259] Regarding the various norms requiring environmental protection of shared waters, it also advises that

> [v]iolations of the obligation to respect follow from the State party's interference with the right to water. This includes, inter alia: …
> (iii) pollution and diminution of water resources affecting human health.[260]

General Comment No 15 further provides that '[d]epending on the availability of resources, states should facilitate realization of the right to water in other countries, for example through provision of water resources'.[261] Though this provision is couched in soft terms, it could clearly be understood to recognize a requirement that, in utilizing shared water resources, states ensure that adequate water is available for the realization of the human right to water in co-basin states, once again linking human rights requirements to consideration of vital human needs in the practice of inter-state water resources allocation. Likewise, General Comment No 15 generally suggests that

> States parties should ensure that the right to water is given due attention in international agreements and, to that end, should consider the development of further legal instruments. With regard to the conclusion and implementation of other international and regional agreements, States parties should take steps to ensure that these instruments do not adversely impact upon the right to water.

Clearly, this statement suggests that states should only conclude global or regional water resources conventions and river basin treaties that are compatible with full realization of the human right to water in all co-basin states, and should act to further develop and adapt existing treaty regimes to ensure such compatibility. All this suggests that the CESCR envisages a particularly important role for international water law in the realization of the human right to water and, consequently, for effective realization of SDG 6.

Demonstrating the integrated and indivisible nature of the 2030 Agenda, some commentators link target 6.5 to SDG 16, arguing that the former should be analysed in conjunction with the latter, which is concerned with strengthening international cooperation and transboundary good governance.[262] Clearly this aim resonates with the general objectives of the UNWC and of General Comment No 15. For example, these authors refer to the relevance of target 16.3, which seeks to '[p]romote the rule of law at the national and international levels, and ensure equal access to justice for all' which, in addition to promoting adherence to established rules of international water law, 'provides individuals with the ability to react to breaches of both substantive

---

[259] ibid para 44(c)(vii) 14.
[260] ibid para 44(a)(iii) 14.
[261] ibid para 34 11.
[262] See Orme and others (n 4) 978–80.

and procedural obligations in a transboundary water context'.[263] Though international water law has not traditionally concerned itself with the rights of individuals, article 32 of the UNWC on non-discrimination regarding access to legal redress 'for the protection of the interests of persons, natural or juridical, who have suffered or are under a serious threat of suffering significant transboundary harm as a result of activities related to an international watercourse' appears to anticipate a significant role for private recourse by adversely affected legal persons to domestic courts and remedies as a means for establishing effective responsibility for unlawful activities related to international watercourses.[264]

Generally, international water law appears to be developing in a manner consistent with the 'transboundary good governance' values embraced by SDG 16, such as target 16.6, which calls upon states to 'develop effective, accountable and transparent institutions at all levels', target 16.7, which seeks to 'ensure responsive, inclusive, participatory and representative decision-making at all levels', and target 16.10, which aims to 'ensure public access to information and protect fundamental freedoms in accordance with national legislation and international agreements'. Regarding institutions, for example, transboundary water cooperation very often involves the establishment of some form of inter-state institutional machinery to formulate and implement common policies for the management and development of the basin,[265] an approach to managing shared water resources widely endorsed by the international community,[266] and by international bodies concerned with codification of this field of international law.[267]

While the UNECE Water Convention rather unusually imposes a general obligation upon state parties to participate in the establishment of such 'joint bodies',[268] the UNWC merely encourages watercourse states to enter into common management arrangements consistent with the requirements of the principle of equitable and reasonable utilization, the duty to prevent significant transboundary harm, and the general duty to cooperate.[269] Incrementally, such institutions are subjected to requirements of transparency and accountability and to other rapidly evolving constraints of

---

[263] ibid 978.

[264] Similarly, arts 69–71 of the Berlin Rules (n 85) also provide for adversely affected legal individuals to seek recourse before a competent judicial or administrative authority in the state where the harm arises.

[265] See generally, S Schmeier, *Governing International Watercourses: The Contribution of River Basin Organizations to the Effective Governance of Internationally Shared Rivers and Lakes* (Routledge 2013) I. I Dombrowsky, *Conflict, Cooperation and Institutions in International Water Management: An Economic Analysis* (Edward Elgar 2007); O McIntyre, 'The Legal Role and Context of River Basin Organisations' in A Kittikhoun and S Schmeier (eds), *Water Diplomacy and Conflict Management* (Routledge 2021); McIntyre, 'The UNECE Water Convention and the Principle of Equitable and Reasonable Utilisation' (n 73) 28–40.

[266] See McIntyre, 'The UNECE Water Convention and the Principle of Equitable and Reasonable Utilisation' (n 73) 159, who notes that 'well over 100 international river commissions have been established by states'.

[267] Notably, Recommendation 51 of the Stockholm *Action Plan for the Human Environment*, adopted at the 1972 UN Conference on the Human Environment (UNCHE), called for the 'creation of river basin commissions or other appropriate machinery for cooperation between interested states for water resources common to more than one jurisdiction', and set down a number of basic principles by which such commissions should be guided.

[268] 1992 UNECE Convention on the Protection of Transboundary Watercourses and International Lakes (1992) 312 ILM 1312, art 9(2).

[269] Arts 5(2), 8(2), 9, 21, 24, and 33(2). See O McIntyre, 'International Water Law: Concepts, Evolution and Development' in A Earle and others (eds), *Transboundary Water Management: Principles and Practice* (Earthscan 2010) 69–70.

486   SDG 6

administrative good governance. Regarding responsive decision-making and public access to information, the practice of modern international water law has long revolved around processes of prior inter-state notification of planned measures and routine information exchange on the state of shared water resources.[270] However, in recent years such processes have begun to open up in order to facilitate or require broader engagement with the public or, at the very least, key stakeholders.[271] This can be seen in the 2010 judgment of the International Court of Justice (ICJ) in the *Pulp Mills* case, where the Court placed great emphasis on the significance of procedural requirements, and in particular the duty to conduct environmental impact assessment (EIA), in discharging the duty to cooperate over planned projects,[272] while also stressing the role of formal institutional machinery established to facilitate meaningful cooperative engagement.[273] Of course, any credible EIA process will involve significant public and stakeholder disclosure, consultation and engagement. It is clear, therefore, that international water law can and must adapt in order to contribute to realization of the 'transboundary good governance elements' of the SDGs, but equally that the SDGs have a key role in driving further progressive transformation of this body of law.

6. Target 6.6 By 2020, protect and restore water-related ecosystems, including mountains, forests, wetlands, rivers, aquifers and lakes

The inclusion of a dedicated global target and indicator[274] on the protection and restoration of water-related ecosystems reflects the consensus evident in modern international water law regarding the critical importance of maintaining such ecosystems for water resources management, as well as the central role of water in maintaining a range of vital ecosystem services. This consensus is embodied in the ecosystem protection obligation set out in article 20 of the UN Watercourses Convention,[275] in respect of which leading commentators noted in 2001 that

---

[270] Smets, 'The Rights to Sanitation' (n 126).

[271] See, eg, art 16(8) of the 2004 Agreement on the Establishment of the Zambezi Watercourse Commission (ZAMCOM Agreement), which requires, in the context of inter-State notification of '[p]lanned programmes, projects or activities of Member States', that 'Member States shall ensure that the public in an area likely to be affected by a proposed programme, project or activity are informed thereof and are provided with the opportunity for making comments thereon or objections thereto as well as on the transmittal of such comments or objections to the Commission'.

[272] *Pulp Mills on the River Uruguay (Argentina v Uruguay)* (Judgment) [2010] ICJ Rep 14, para 77. See further O McIntyre, 'Procedural Rules of International Water Law and the Imminent Challenges of the Ecosystem Approach' in H Ruiz Fabri and others (eds), *A Bridge over Troubled Waters: Dispute Resolution in the Law of International Watercourses and the Law of the Sea* (Brill Nijhoff 2020) 319–50; O McIntyre, 'The Contribution of Procedural Rules to the Environmental Protection of Transboundary Rivers' in L Boisson de Chazournes and others (eds), *Freshwater and International Law: The Multiple Challenges* (Edward Elgar 2013) 239–65.

[273] *Pulp Mills* (n 272) paras 87–91. See generally, O McIntyre, 'The World Court's Ongoing Contribution to International Water Law: The *Pulp Mills* Case between Argentina and Uruguay' (2011) Water Alternatives 4(2) 124–44.

[274] Indicator 6.6.1 measures the '[p]roportion of river basins showing high surface water extent changes'.

[275] n 7. Art 20 of the UN Watercourses Convention provides that '[w]atercourse States shall, individually and, where appropriate, jointly, protect and preserve the ecosystems of international watercourses'. In addition, art 22 requires watercourse states to prevent the introduction of alien or new species which may be detrimental to the ecosystem of an international watercourse, while art 23 requires watercourse states to take measures to protect and preserve the marine environment, thereby recognizing the problem of marine pollution caused by land-based sources and helping to realize the Targets set out under SDG 14.

progress made in scientific research further shows that the use of watercourses can affect and be affected by processes related to other natural elements, such as soil degradation and desertification, deforestation and climate change [which] has brought water specialists in the last decade to advocate the adoption of less economic-oriented criteria for the management of freshwater resources, following an 'ecosystem approach'.[276]

Such an 'ecosystem approach' has in turn been elaborated upon in an early seminal study of the topic, which advises that

an 'ecosystem approach' requires consideration of the whole system rather than individual components. Living species and their physical environments must be recognized as interconnected, and the focus must be on the interaction between different sub-systems and their responses to stresses resulting from human activity. Not only does interconnectedness imply management approaches that are broad-based in a spatial sense; it requires as well that human interaction with and use of the environment respect the need for maintaining 'ecosystem integrity', in other words, the system's capacity for self-organization.[277]

It is understood, therefore, as a management approach which can inform the application of legal frameworks for water resources utilization, land-use planning, and development control at both the national and transboundary levels. In the specific context of international water law, the concept has been linked to the obligation to protect international watercourses ancillary to the principle of equitable and reasonable utilization,[278] and accordingly to the objective of sustainable development.[279]

This evolution in scientific understanding of river basins as ecosystems has continued and is increasingly reflected in the emergence of sophisticated methodologies which function to inform the normative implications of state obligations to protect watercourse ecosystems,[280] which the 1994 ILC commentary defines as an 'ecological unit consisting of living and non-living components that are interdependent and function as a community'.[281] For example, improved understanding of the technical parameters for analysing environmental flows in a shared watercourse[282] has permitted

[276] Tanzi and Arcari (n 80) 8–9.
[277] J Brunnée and SJ Toope, 'Environmental Security and Freshwater Resources: A Case for International Ecosystem Law' (1994) 5 Yearbook of International Environmental Law 41 55.
[278] According to the ILC's commentary to Draft Article 20 (n 82) 282, the 'obligation to protect the ecosystems of international watercourses is a specific application of the requirement contained in article 5 that watercourse States are to use and develop an international watercourse in a manner that is consistent with adequate protection thereof'.
[279] The ILC commentary further explains that art 20 of the UN Watercourses Convention provides an 'essential basis for sustainable development'. ibid.
[280] See O McIntyre, 'The Protection of Freshwater Ecosystems Revisited: Towards a Common Understanding of the "Ecosystems Approach" to the Protection of Transboundary Water Resources' (2014) Review of European, Comparative and International Environmental Law 23(1) 88.
[281] ILC (n 82) 118.
[282] See J Gooch, *Protecting Ecological Integrity in Transboundary Watercourses: An Integrational Approach towards Implementing Environmental Flows* (Lund University 2016); J Scanlon and A Iza, 'International Legal Foundations for Environmental Flows' (2003) 14 Yearbook of International Environmental Law 81; N LeRoy Poff and others, 'Evolution of Environmental Flows Assessment Science, Principles, and Methodologies' in AC Horne

488   SDG 6

judicial recognition of a corresponding international legal obligation to maintain a minimum environmental flow regime.[283] Similarly, the rapidly evolving ecosystems services concept provides a methodology for the economic and social valuation of natural ecosystems which permits integration of the value of non-marketable benefits into decision-making processes.[284] Of course, lessons learned in the implementation of legal requirements arising under other environmental conventions to protect and preserve associated water-related ecosystems may also inform the environmental and ecosystem obligations set out under Part IV of the UN Watercourses Convention.[285] It is increasingly apparent, for example, that the wealth of detailed technical guidance developed under the auspices of the 1971 Ramsar Convention[286] can play a significant role in informing the ecosystem obligations arising under the UN Watercourses Convention.[287] There exists obvious complementarity between these two instruments with wetlands playing a critical role in the functioning of aquatic ecosystems and in the provision of important ecosystem services, such as flood control, wildlife habitat, groundwater recharge and the 'protection, purification, retention and provision of water resources for water and food supplies ... on which the well-being of people and their livelihoods depend'.[288] Similar complementarity exists regarding other key instruments, such as the 1992 Convention on Biological Diversity (CBD), and the corpus of rules, guidance and practice developed thereunder.[289] The CBD Conference of the Parties (COP) has adopted two successive programmes of work on inland water biodiversity which clarify application of the relevant CBD requirements to watercourse ecosystems,[290] while relevant guidance has been developed under the auspices of the

and others (eds), *Water for the Environment: From Policy and Science to Implementation and Management* (Elsevier 2017); M Dyson and others, *Flow: The Essentials of Environmental Flows* (IUCN 2003); AD Beaton and A Bradford, 'Demonstration of a Methodology for Setting Ecological Flow and Water Level Targets' (2013) 38 Canadian Water Resources Journal 296.

[283] Permanent Court of Arbitration, *Indus Waters Kishenganga Arbitration (Pakistan v India)*, Partial Award, 18 February 2013 para 454.

[284] See Millennium Ecosystem Assessment, *Ecosystems and Human Well-being: Synthesis* (Island Press 2005). See further, A Rieu-Clarke and C Spray, 'Ecosystem Services and International Water Law: Towards a More Effective Determination and Implementation of Equity' (2013) 16(2) Potchefstroom Electronic Law Journal 12.

[285] See further, J Lee, *Preservation of Ecosystems of International Watercourses and the Integration of Relevant Rules* (Brill Nijhoff 2014).

[286] Convention on Wetlands of International Importance especially as Waterfowl Habitat (as amended in 1982 and 1987) (Ramsar, 2 February 1971) (1972) 11 ILM 969. Today the Ramsar Convention has 172 Contracting Parties and applies to 2,472 designated wetland sites covering a total area of 256,240,981 hectares. Many of these wetlands are hydrologically and ecologically connected to international watercourses, in relation to which they constitute critically important components of the watercourse ecosystems.

[287] Such guidance is now consolidated in twenty-one volumes of the Ramsar, *Handbooks for the Wise Use of Wetlands* (4th edn, Ramsar 2010) <https://www.ramsar.org/resources/the-handbooks> accessed 30 November 2022.

[288] Ramsar COP Resolution IX.3 on Engagement of the Ramsar Convention on Wetlands in Ongoing Multilateral Processes Dealing with Water (Kampala, 2005) 1, para 3. In addition, the Preamble to the Convention expressly recognizes the close inter-linkage between wetlands conservation and water resources management by noting 'the fundamental ecological functions of wetlands as regulators of water regimes'.

[289] (Rio de Janeiro, 5 June 1992), 31 ILM (1992) 818. See further S Brels and others, *Transboundary Water Resources Management: The Role of International Watercourse Agreements in Implementation of the CBD* (Secretariat of the CBD 2008).

[290] Programme of Work on Biological Diversity of Inland Water Ecosystems, CBD Decision IV/4 (1998), Annex I; Revised Programme of Work on Inland Water Biological Diversity, CBD Decision VII/4 (2004), Annex.

CBD on a range of issues relevant to protection of watercourse ecosystems, such as invasive alien species.[291] Generally, therefore, effective implementation of the extensive environmental and ecological protection obligations inherent in general international water law is greatly aided by the parallel elaboration of corresponding rules and principles in international environmental law instruments, and their considerable normative specificity and procedural sophistication.

For some time prior to the 1997 adoption of the UN Watercourses Convention, a clear trend was discernible in practice regarding the environmental aspects of international water law of moving away from simple, prescriptive arrangements for the prevention, reduction, or mitigation of water pollution, towards a more ecosystem-oriented approach to the protection and management of shared international basins. Basin agreements, such as the 1978 Great Lakes Water Quality Agreement[292] and the 1995 Mekong Agreement,[293] have long included express ecosystems protection obligations. It has been noted that some of the earliest and most ardent support for the ecosystem approach can be found in regional water resources conventions and basin agreements adopted by developing countries,[294] which may in part be due to the fact that a significantly larger proportion of the populations of such states rely directly upon ecosystems and ecosystem services for their well-being and livelihoods. Thus, water-related ecosystems obligations are entirely consistent with the overarching aims of the 2030 Agenda. This trend has been equally apparent in regional framework agreements concerning shared transboundary basins more generally.[295] Notably, the 1992 UNECE Water Convention, the only other globally applicable framework convention relating to shared international freshwater resources, includes extensive and detailed provisions for the conservation and restoration of the ecosystems of shared basins.[296] This instrument has inspired similar provisions in a number of subsequently adopted European river basin agreements.[297] Seminal early guidelines adopted under the UNECE Water

---

[291] Alien Species that Threaten Ecosystems, Habitats or Species (art 8(h)): Further Consideration of Gaps and Inconsistencies in the International Regulatory Framework, CBD Decision VIII/27 (2006).

[292] (Ottawa, 22 November 1978), 30 UST 1383, TIAS No 9257, arts I and II.

[293] Agreement on Cooperation for Sustainable Development of the Mekong River Basin (Chiang Rai, 5 April 1995), 34 ILM (1995) 864, arts 3 and 7.

[294] O McIntyre, 'The Emergence of an "Ecosystem Approach" to the Protection of International Watercourses under International Law' (2004) Review of European Community and International Environmental Law 13(1) 3–4. See, eg, the 1969 Treaty of the River Plate Basin, Brasilia, 23 April 1969 (1969 8 ILM 905, art 1; the 1975 Statute of the Uruguay River, Salto, 26 February 1975, art 36; 1978 Treaty for Amazonian Cooperation, Brasilia, 3 July 1978, arts I and VII; the 1964 Convention relating to the Statute of the Senegal River, Dakar, 7 February 1964, arts 2 and 4; the 1977 Agreement Creating the Organisation for the Management and Development of the Kagera Basin, Rusumo, 24 August 1977, art 2; the 1978 Convention relating to the Status of the River Gambia, Kaolack, 30 June 1978, art 4; the 1980 Convention Creating the Niger Basin Authority, Faranah, 21 November 1980, art 4(2)(d).

[295] See, eg, the original 1995 Protocol on Shared Watercourse Systems in the Southern African Development Community (SADC), Johannesburg, 28 August 1995, arts 2(3), 2(11), and 2(12), reproduced in Food and Agriculture Organisation, *Treaties Concerning the Non-Navigational Uses of International Watercourses: Africa* (1997) FAO Legislative Study 61 146. However, the 2000 SADC Revised Protocol on Shared Watercourses (Windhoek, 7 August 2000), closely follows the approach taken under the 1997 UNWC, more or less reproducing its provisions on pollution and protection of ecosystems, art 4(2).

[296] n 167; arts 1(2), 2(2)(b), 2(2)(d), and 3(1)(i).

[297] Convention on the Protection of the Rhine, January 22, 1998, arts 2, 3, and 5; Convention on Cooperation for the Protection and Sustainable Use of the Danube River, 29 June 1994, arts 1(c), 2(3), and 2(5); Agreements on the Protection of the Meuse and Scheldt, 26 April 1994, art 3; Framework Agreement on the Sava River Basin, 3 December 2002, 2367 UNTS 688, art 11(a).

490   SDG 6

Convention elaborate upon the meaning and implications of the so-called ecosystem approach.[298]

The somewhat less developed rules of international law relating to the use and protection of shared international groundwater resources would appear to be evolving in a similar vein. The ILC's 2008 Draft Articles on Transboundary Aquifers[299] stress 'the role of the aquifer or aquifer system in the related ecosystem'[300] and, more specifically, call upon states 'to ensure that the quantity and quality of water retained in an aquifer or aquifer system, as well as that discharged through its discharge zones, are sufficient to protect and preserve such ecosystems'.[301] Similarly, the UNECE Model Rules on Transboundary Groundwaters, which were developed under the auspices of the 1992 UNECE Water Convention on the basis of a study of the specific application of the Convention's principles and purport to 'reflect the current state of international water law with regard to transboundary groundwaters',[302] stipulate that '[t]he Parties shall use transboundary groundwaters in a sustainable manner, with a view to maximizing the long-term benefits accruing therefrom and preserving groundwater-dependent ecosystems'.[303]

Indeed, ecosystem obligations have become so centrally important in this field that several river basin agreements which predate this general concern with ecosystem health or integrity have either been amended to incorporate some element of ecosystems protection or have been interpreted creatively by international courts and tribunals as requiring such ecosystem protection. For example, the 1944 Colorado Treaty between the United States and Mexico[304] has recently been amended by Minute 319,[305] which identifies measures intended to 'allow both countries to better assess the long-term opportunities and cooperative measures for water conservation, management and development', including, *inter alia*, 'innovative mechanisms for … restoring environmental flows in the Colorado River down to the Gulf of California'.[306] The established water utilization regime of the Colorado River demonstrates the need for ecosystem protection quite dramatically, with over-allocation of water having led to a reduction of the wetlands in the Colorado Delta, 'once one of the world's great desert river deltas and home to dolphins, fish, birds and other wildlife', to between 5 and 10

---

[298] 'Guidelines on the Ecosystem Approach in Water Management', UN Doc ECE/ENVWA/31 (December 1993).

[299] International Law Commission, 'Report of the International Law Commission on the Work of Its Sixtieth Session' (UN Doc A/63/10, 2008).

[300] Art 5(1)(i).

[301] Art 10.

[302] UNECE Model Rules on Transboundary Groundwaters (UNECE 2014) iii <http://www.unece.org/fileadmin/DAM/env/water/publications/WAT_model_provisions/ece_mp.wat_40_eng.pdf> accessed 30 November 2022.

[303] Provision 2(1).

[304] Treaty between the United States of America and Mexico Respecting Utilization of Waters of the Colorado and Tijuana Rivers and of the Rio Grande (Washington DC, 3 February 1944), 3 UNTS 314.

[305] International Boundary Waters Commission, Minute 319: Interim International Cooperative Measures in the Colorado River Basin Through 2017 and Extension of Minute 318 Cooperative Measures to Address the Continued Effects of the 2010 Earthquake in the Mexicali Valley, Baja California (20 November 2012).

[306] See RM Buono and G Eckstein, 'Minute 319: A Cooperative Approach to Mexico–US Hydro-Relations on the Colorado River' (2014) 39(3) Water International 268–69.

per cent of their historic area of 6,000 km².[307] Where such updating of water resources conventions to include obligations regarding ecosystems protection is neither feasible nor forthcoming, international courts and tribunals may nevertheless take an actively progressive approach to their interpretation so as to take account of prevailing contemporary ecological values and obligations, especially having regard to the subsequent environmental commitments of the states concerned.[308]

Whereas this formal recognition in the UN Watercourses Convention of the normative character and significance of ecosystem protection requirements merely reflects the continuing evolution of international environmental law more generally, notably under the 1992 CBD,[309] the universal adoption of target 6.6 provides a hugely significant endorsement to what is rapidly emerging as a key value in transboundary and domestic water resources management. On the other hand, the increasingly sophisticated legal and technical requirements for ecosystems protection emerging in international water law provide a vital tool for realizing target 6.6, at the level of both national and international basins. It is increasingly clear that continuing elaboration and development of the ecosystem approach to the management of water resources, and of its constitutive normative elements, will be critically important for effective realization of the new overarching imperative of international water law, that is, the optimal and ecologically sustainable use of shared water resources in an era of looming freshwater scarcity. Quite apart from inexorably rising demand for water, food, and energy, and associated large-scale water resources utilization,[310] international water law will have to contend with the very significant ecological challenges posed by climate change and the adaptation measures required to address it.[311] It is noted, for example, as regards the possible impacts of climate change on several of the world's key 'water towers', including the Himalaya-Hindu Kush, the Tibetan Plateau and the Alps, that the accelerated retreat of 31 major glaciers in the past two decades poses a long-term threat to the security of water supplies for billions of people.[312] In terms of the social and economic implications of such climate-related ecological impacts, the Summit outcome document expresses concern that

[307] ibid 266. See also, AD Tarlock, 'Mexico and the United States Assume a Legal Duty to Provide Colorado River Delta Restoration Flows: An Important International Environmental and Water Law Precedent' (2014) 23(1) Review of European, Comparative and International Environmental Law 76.

[308] See, eg, the *Kishenganga Arbitration* (n 284).

[309] n 290, art 1. In addition, art 8(f) obliges state parties to 'rehabilitate and restore degraded ecosystems'.

[310] See, eg, E Brown Weiss, *International Water Law for a Water-Scarce World* (Martinus Nijhoff 2013) 1–7.

[311] See, eg, A Rieu-Clarke and others, *Transboundary Water Governance and Climate Change Adaptation: International Law, Policy Guidelines and Best Practice Application* (UNESCO 2015); JC Sanchez and J Roberts (eds), *Transboundary Water Governance: Adaptation to Climate Change* (IUCN 2014); C MacAlister and N Subramanyam 'Climate Change and Adaptive Water Management: Innovative Solutions from the Global South' (2018) 43 Water International 133; PH Gleick, 'Climate-Proofing Transboundary Water Agreements' (2011) Hydrological Sciences 711.

[312] World Meteorological Organisation, *High Mountain Summit* (WMO, Geneva, 29–31 October 2019) <https://highmountainsummit.wmo.int/en> accessed 30 November 2022, drawing on the findings of the Intergovernmental Panel on Climate Change (IPCC), 'Special Report on the Ocean and Cryosphere in a Changing Climate' (September 2019) <https://www.ipcc.ch/srocc/home/> accessed 30 November 2022.

492   SDG 6

water security is becoming one of the greatest challenges of the world's population, with dwindling availability of freshwater from mountain rivers posing a significant risk factor for local and downstream ecosystems and affecting multiple livelihood sectors, including agriculture and food production, forestry, fisheries, hydropower generation, transportation, tourism, recreation and human health.

Thus, the broad social and environmental objectives of SDG 6, and the practice of states that emerges thereunder, may now inform every aspect of international environmental and natural resources law, which can function to assist attainment of these same objectives. In articulating the cardinal obligation of watercourse states to 'utilize an international watercourse in an equitable and reasonable manner', the UN Watercourses Convention stresses that they shall do so 'with a view to attaining optimal and sustainable utilization thereof and benefits therefrom ... consistent with adequate protection of the watercourse'.[313] The factors identified as relevant to this principle expressly include 'ecological and other factors of a natural character'[314] and '[c]onservation, protection, development and economy of use of the water resources of the watercourse'.[315] The duty to prevent significant transboundary harm remains central to international water law,[316] but might increasingly be expected to include novel forms of ecological disturbance in the light of heightened environmental sensibilities and the wealth of technical guidance on ecological standards and ecosystems management produced under multilateral environmental agreements. The ILC's 1994 commentary hints at the reasoning behind the priority afforded to ecosystems protection, and provides an early water-related articulation of the ecosystem services concept, by explaining that 'protection and preservation of aquatic ecosystems help to ensure their continued viability as life support systems, thus providing an essential basis for sustainable development'.[317]

7. Target 6.a By 2030, expand international cooperation and capacity-building support to developing countries in water- and sanitation-related activities and programmes, including water harvesting, desalination, water efficiency, wastewater treatment, recycling and reuse technologies

Target 6.a recognizes the key role played by international development assistance in efforts to attain all of the targets elaborated under SDG 6, especially in the case of least developed countries, and so indicator 6.a.1 tracks the amount of water and sanitation-related official development assistance (ODA) that is included in a government-coordinated spending plan.[318] For the purposes of indicator 6.a.1, ODA includes both grants and concessional loans with a grant element of at least 25 per cent. A government-coordinated spending plan is defined as a financing plan/budget at the

---

[313] n 7, art 5(1).
[314] Art 6(1)(a).
[315] Art 6(1)(f).
[316] UN Watercourses Convention, art 7. See also art 6(1)(d).
[317] ILC (n 82) 119.
[318] Indicator 6.a.1 measures '[a]mount of water- and sanitation-related official development assistance (ODA) received'.

national or subnational level, clearly assessing the financial resources available and the strategies for financing future requirements.[319] Data are collected on both the amount of ODA committed to the water and sanitation sector and on the amount actually disbursed, and any disparity between these figures may provide important insights. For example, the 2021 progress report shows a growing gap between commitments and disbursements, suggesting that a number of factors might cause this lag in disbursements, including limited capacity in developing countries to disburse or absorb aid funding, procedural complexities for aid disbursements or procurement, and/or delays in the delivery of water or sanitation-related infrastructure.[320] It is worth noting that, while ODA committed to the water and sanitation sector has increased by 9 per cent between 2015 and 2019, disbursements have remained stable at \$8.8 billion.[321] The scope of ODA covered for the purposes of indicator 6.a.1 is broad, and takes account of funds disbursed and committed to a range of water and sanitation-related sectors, 'which include drinking water and sanitation, water resources management (also in agriculture and hydropower), policy and administration and education, as well as waste management'.[322] This is because target 6.a recognizes that 'ODA is a means for implementing all aspects of SDG 6, including through investments in other sectors such as agriculture and energy and education'.[323] Indeed, the latest data demonstrate that concessional lending to utilities represents an ever-larger share of financial transfers:

> The increase in water sector ODA for least developed countries is mainly due to increases in concessional lending, e.g. by 52 per cent from 2015 to 2019, while ODA grants have increased by only 7 per cent during the same time period.[324]

The fact that development assistance has long played a very significant role in supporting the water and sanitation-related activities of developing countries is expressly acknowledged in General Comment No 15, which sets out quite emphatically the role of international assistance in facilitating realization of the human right(s) of access to water and sanitation. In elaborating upon the international obligations incumbent upon states pursuant to the rights to water and sanitation, paragraph 34 states:

> Depending on the availability of resources, States should facilitate realization of the right to water in other countries, for example through provision of water resources, financial and technical assistance, and provide the necessary aid when required. In disaster relief and emergency assistance, including assistance to refugees and displaced persons, priority should be given to Covenant rights, including the provision of adequate water. International assistance should be provided in a manner that is

---

[319] UN-Water, 'Summary Progress Report: SDG 6—Water and Sanitation for All' (UN 2021) 31.
[320] ibid.
[321] UN-Water, 'Summary Progress Update 2021 ' (n 166) 10.
[322] UN-Water, Summary Progress Report: SDG 6—Water and Sanitation for All (UN 2021) 31.
[323] ibid.
[324] UN-Water, 'Summary Progress Update 2021' (n 166) 10.

consistent with the Covenant and other human rights standards, and sustainable and culturally appropriate. The economically developed States parties have a special responsibility and interest to assist the poorer developing States in this regard.[325]

In enumerating the 'core obligations' of state actors, General Comment No 15 stresses the solemn duty under the 1966 Covenant of more economically developed and better capacitated states to assist others in meeting their core duties in respect of the rights to water and sanitation in the following unequivocal terms:

> For the avoidance of any doubt, the Committee wishes to emphasize that it is particularly incumbent on States parties, and other actors in a position to assist, to provide international assistance and cooperation, especially economic and technical which enables developing countries to fulfil their core obligations indicated in paragraph 37 above.[326]

General Comment No 15 further elaborates on this duty to support economic, social, and cultural right(s) through development assistance by calling upon states that are members of international organizations and international financial institutions to 'take steps to ensure that the right to water is taken into account in their lending policies, credit agreements and other international measures'.[327] As a corollary to this aspect of states' duties, and once again stressing the important role of development assistance, it calls upon the UN agencies and other international organizations and development actors engaged in water management issues to do all in their power to support implementation and enjoyment of the right to water.[328] To complete the picture regarding the international duties of states in respect of development assistance, General Comment No 15 makes it quite clear that beneficiary developing states ought to make sure to accept such assistance, especially where this will contribute to preparation and

---

[325] General Comment No 15 (n 8).
[326] ibid para 38 13.
[327] ibid para 36 12.
[328] ibid. Para 60 provides in full:
United Nations agencies and other international organizations concerned with water, such as WHO, FAO, UNICEF, UNEP, UN-Habitat, ILO, UNDP, the International Fund for Agricultural Development (IFAD), as well as international organizations concerned with trade such as the World Trade Organization (WTO), should cooperate effectively with States parties, building on their respective expertise, in relation to the implementation of the right to water at the national level. The international financial institutions, notably the International Monetary Fund and the World Bank, should take into account the right to water in their lending policies, credit agreements, structural adjustment programmes and other development projects (see General Comment No. 2 (1990)), so that the enjoyment of the right to water is promoted. When examining the reports of States parties and their ability to meet the obligations to realize the right to water, the Committee will consider the effects of the assistance provided by all other actors. The incorporation of human rights law and principles in the programmes and policies by international organizations will greatly facilitate implementation of the right to water. The role of the International Federation of the Red Cross and Red Crescent Societies, International Committee of the Red Cross, the Office of the United Nations High Commissioner for Refugees (UNHCR), WHO and UNICEF, as well as non-governmental organizations and other associations, is of particular importance in relation to disaster relief and humanitarian assistance in times of emergencies. Priority in the provision of aid, distribution and management of water and water facilities should be given to the most vulnerable or marginalized groups of the population.

implementation of the relevant national strategy. Paragraph 47 provides that '[w]hen formulating and implementing their right to water national strategies, States parties should avail themselves of technical assistance and cooperation of the United Nations specialized agencies'. Target 6.a, therefore, formalizes the critically important role of ODA in ensuring water and sanitation for all, while indicator 6.a.1 provides a measure of the extent to which donor states, beneficiary states, and international development partners are living up to their respective duties.

This focus on the role of development assistance in support of equitable and efficient water resources management also finds echoes in the field of international water law. For example, article 5 of the UN Watercourses Convention, which articulates the cardinal principle of equitable and reasonable utilization, includes the ancillary principle of 'equitable participation',[329] which suggests that states may be under a duty to assist less capacitated co-basin states to engage effectively in cooperative transboundary initiatives for the sustainable management of shared international freshwater resources.[330] This principle endorses the hugely important role of cooperative institutions, and particularly river basin organizations (RBOs), in the effective management of international watercourses,[331] and one exhaustive study of RBOs confirms their importance for mobilizing development assistance and building capacity amongst less developed riparian states.[332] In addition to serving as a conduit for external development assistance support, RBOs can also provide a mechanism for the equitable and progressive sharing of resources and expertise amongst the riparian states of a single international watercourse, as occurs by means of the International Commission for the Protection of the Danube River (ICPDR).[333] The commitments of states embodied in target 6.a recognize this reality and serve to support further elaboration of such cooperative arrangements.

8. Target 6.b Support and strengthen the participation of local communities in improving water and sanitation management

Recognizing the key significance of meaningful public and community participation in the management and governance of water and sanitation services, and in the protection of water resources and water-related ecosystems, target 6.b seeks to promote national arrangements for facilitating participation. Such participation is understood as a 'mechanism by which individuals and communities can meaningfully contribute to management decisions' and is considered a vital aspect of water management as it 'helps ensure sustainable solutions for all aspects of SDG 6 and contributes to wider reductions in inequality within and among countries'.[334] To that end, indicator 6.b.1 tracks

---

[329] n 7. Art 5(2) provides that '[w]atercourse States shall participate in the use, development and protection of an international watercourse in an equitable and reasonable manner'.

[330] See further, McIntyre, *Environmental Protection of International Watercourses* (n 75) 73.

[331] See generally, Dombrowsky (n 265); McIntyre, 'River Basin Organizations' (n 265).

[332] Schmeier, *Governing International Watercourses* (n 265) 49. She lists, eg, at 305, the various donors engaged in supporting the work of the Mekong River Commission (MRC).

[333] See ibid 202–04.

[334] UN-Water, 'Summary Progress Update 2021' (n 166) 33.

the participation of local communities in water and sanitation management within a country by looking at the existence of procedures in law or policy for participation, as well as at the actual level of participation. As regards procedures for participation, data are gathered in respect of six subsectors: drinking water (rural and urban), sanitation (rural and urban), hygiene promotion, and water resources planning and management. Although two-thirds of 109 countries reporting in 2021 have participation procedures for water and sanitation defined in law, only fourteen countries report high levels of community and user participation for collaborative management and decision-making.[335] This is largely due to a lack of financial or human resources, particularly in rural areas, dedicated to promoting and facilitating meaningful participation.

The meaningful participation of stakeholders and the public, including of course that of local and directly impacted communities, is now universally regarded as a core tenet of good governance and is an increasingly ubiquitous feature of national and international water governance regimes. Drawing on analysis of the practice of the World Bank, Asian Development Bank (ADB) and United Nations Development Programme (UNDP), Allan and Rieu-Clarke, list 'participation', alongside 'accountability' and 'transparency', among the three key elements of 'good governance' in international development policy.[336] These authors define 'participation' in this context as follows:

> The principle that all men and women should have a voice in decision-making, either directly or through legitimate intermediate institutions that represent their interests. Such broad participation is built on freedom of association and speech, as well as capacities to participate constructively (UNDP). Beneficiaries and groups affected by the project should participate so that the government can make informed choices with respect to their needs, and social groups can protect their rights.[337]

Therefore, legal frameworks for water management at all levels should 'establish and maintain the rights of stakeholders, including civil society organisations, and disadvantaged or under-represented groups to participate in decision-making ... *inter alia*, on policy issues, budgetary priorities and development decisions'.[338] As is clear from the above analysis, however, achieving full and meaningful participation by all communities, and particularly those that are disadvantaged or under-represented, requires that authorities actively promote such participation, including by helping to develop their capacity and resources to take part. The scale of this task is borne out by the latest data on indicator 6.b.1 which show that, while '[p]articipatory procedures are increasingly recognized in national policies and laws' and 'while the levels of participation have seen moderate improvement', nevertheless '[a]pproximately 6 out of 10 countries reported that human and financial resources were less than 50 per cent of that needed to support

---

[335] ibid at 33–34.
[336] Allan and Rieu-Clarke (n 238) 242–43.
[337] ibid 243.
[338] ibid 246.

community participation, indicating that increased resources are essential to accelerating progress.[339]

Highlighting the significance of target 6.b, it is clear that any elaboration of the concept of a human right(s) to water and sanitation involves the inclusion of detailed procedural elements regarded as inherent to the concept. In addition to those provisions of global and regional human rights instruments which arguably include or infer this human right, all human rights treaties would now be interpreted and applied so as to require that states facilitate a participative approach in respect of projects or policies that might impact on human rights, by ensuring the adoption of procedures by which interested individuals or communities likely to be affected by such projects or policies can receive and access relevant information, meaningfully participate in decision-making, and, if necessary, have access to some appropriate means of legal recourse.[340] Such a participatory approach to guaranteeing human rights would equally apply to projects or policies which impact on the availability of water resources, and procedural and participative rights are a very significant element of the normative content of the human right to water as put forward in General Comment No 15.[341] Indeed, the requirement for States Parties to the ICESCR to ensure a participatory and transparent process for the adoption and implementation of a national water strategy and plan of action is included among the non-derogable 'core obligations' of states under General Comment No 15.[342] This position has ample support in human rights practice. For example, in the *Ogoni* case the African Commission on Human Rights gave a broad participative reading to article 24 of the African Charter on Human and Peoples' Rights, which acknowledges all peoples' right to a generally satisfactory environment, to include specific procedural guarantees concerning the carrying out of environmental and social impact assessment.[343] Such requirements, which correspond closely with the procedural and informational requirements of the human right to water as set out under General Comment No 15, would equally apply under existing regional human rights instruments to any major project or policy initiative, such as the privatization of a water utility, which threatened the quality or availability of water supply or sanitation services. Similarly, the Inter-American Commission on Human Rights has, in the context of article 11 of the 1988 Additional Protocol to the American Convention on Human Rights in the Area of Economic Social and Cultural Rights,[344] repeatedly recommended the adoption of domestic legislation providing for meaningful and effective participatory mechanisms for Indigenous peoples in the adoption of political, economic, and social decisions that affect their interests.[345]

[339] UN-Water, 'Summary Progress Update 2021' (n 166) 10.
[340] See generally, P Cullet and A Gowlland-Gualtieri, 'Local Communities and Water Investments' in E Brown Weiss and others (eds) (n 71) 303.
[341] See, eg, General Comment No 15 (n 8) paras 12(c)(iv), 16(a), 24, 37(f), 48, 55, and 56.
[342] See ibid para 37(f); para 40 describes the core obligations set out in para 37 as 'non-derogable'.
[343] See Cullet and Gowlland-Gualtieri (n 340) 313–14, citing Communication No 155/96, The Social and Economic Rights Action Center and the Center for Social and Economic Rights v Nigeria, African Commission on Human and Peoples' Rights, 30th Ordinary Session (13–27 October 2001) para 53.
[344] San Salvador (17 November 1988).
[345] See Chapter X to the Second Report on the Situation of Human Rights in Peru, Inter-American Commission on Human Rights; Chapter IX to the Report on the Situation of Human Rights in Ecuador, Inter-American

498 SDG 6

These requirements appear all the more widely accepted and applied when one considers that broad informational and participatory rights are generally also included under regional and global environmental instruments. The concept of participation in international environmental law is exemplified by the 1998 UNECE Aarhus Convention[346] and such participation requirements are also central to the carrying out of an adequate EIA consistent with the standards established under international law.[347] More generally, in the field of sustainable development, all seminal instruments purport to establish participatory standards, which apply not only to states but also to international organizations, including MDBs. Participatory rights are absolutely central to Chapter 18 on freshwater resources of Agenda 21.[348] Therefore, the accumulated practice of regional human rights enforcement bodies strongly suggests that target 6.b reflects the values set out under General Comment No 15 which, in turn, largely involves a codification of existing state obligations under general international human rights law and general international environmental and sustainable development law, rather than an attempt at the progressive development of participatory principles applying to matters of access to water. Likewise, the inclusion of special protections for local and vulnerable communities reflects the position under human rights law. For example, Indigenous peoples are conferred with special participatory rights under General Comment No 15,[349] which might be traced to and justified under ILO Conventions 107 and 169.[350] This focus on meaningful public participation arises from a wide diversity of legal sources, but now finds universal expression in target 6.b.

Target 6.b clearly coheres with current developments and trends in national and international law. Though Rio Principle 10 proclaims a general principle of public participation,[351] which is equally applicable to the management of exclusively national and shared transboundary water resources,[352] and might reasonably be considered to reflect established customary international law,[353] international water agreements

---

Commission on Human Rights, OEA/Ser.L/V/II.96, doc 10 rev. 1 (Recommendations) (24 April 1997); Case 7615 (Brazil), Inter-American Commission on Human Rights, 1984–1985 Annual Report 24, OEA/Ser.L/V/II.66, doc 10, rev. 1 (1985), the *Yanomami* case. See Cullet and Gowlland-Gualtieri (n 340) 314–15. See further, *Awas Tingni Mayagna (Sumo) Indigenous Community v Nicaragua*, Judgment of 31 August 2001, Inter-American Court of Human Rights (Ser. C), No 79 (2001); *Guerra and Others v Italy* (1998) 26 European Human Rights Reports 357; *Zander v Sweden*, 18 European Human Rights Reports 175 (1993).

[346] Convention on Access to Information, Public Participation in Decision-Making and Access to Justice in Environmental Matters (Aarhus, 25 June 1998) 38 ILM 517 (1999).

[347] See, for example, arts 2(2), 2(6), 3(8), and 4(2) of the 1991 UNECE Convention on Environmental Impact Assessment in a Transboundary Context (Espoo, 25 February 1991) 30 ILM 800 (1991). See also, the Protocol on Strategic Environmental Assessment (Kiev, 21 May 2003).

[348] Agenda 21 (Rio de Janeiro, 13 June 1992), UN Doc A/CONF.151/26 (Vols I, II, and III) (1992). See Cullet and Gowlland-Gualtieri (n 340) 305.

[349] See, eg, General Comment No 15 (n 8) paras 16(d), and 37(b), (f), and (h).

[350] Convention concerning the Protection and Integration of Indigenous and Other Tribal and Semi-Tribal Populations in Independent Countries (26 June 1957); Convention concerning Indigenous and Tribal peoples in Independent Countries (27 June 1989), 28 ILM 1382 (1989).

[351] Rio Declaration on Environment and Development (14 June 1992) UN Doc A/CONF.151/26/Rev.1.

[352] See C Bruch, 'Evolution of Public Involvement in International Watercourse Management' in C Bruch and others (eds), *Public Participation in Governance of International Freshwater Resources* (UNU Press 2005) 21–72 28.

[353] J Razzaque, 'Information, Public Participation and Access to Justice In Environmental Matters' in S Alam and others (eds), *Routledge Handbook of International Environmental Law* (Routledge 2012) 137–54 140; J Ebbesson,

which include an express requirement concerning the involvement of stakeholders or the wider public are still relatively rare. In this regard, international water law appears out of step with developments in general international law. For example, article 13 of the ILC 2001 Draft Articles on Prevention of Transboundary Harm from Hazardous Activities includes an obligation to consult affected populations within any process facilitating transboundary EIA, and the commentary thereto makes it quite clear that, in addition to the provision of information to the public, it would require states 'to ascertain the view of the public' likely to be affected, as '[w]ithout that second step, the purpose of the article would be defeated'.[354]

Conventional international water law's focus upon inter-state engagement to the exclusion of meaningful public participation is epitomized by Part III of the UN Watercourses Convention, containing detailed rules on all aspects of inter-state notification of planned measures, reply to such notification, and, where necessary, consultation and negotiation concerning such measures.[355] Similarly, article 9 of the Convention only provides for the regular exchange of data and information at the interstate level, neglecting to say anything about public or stakeholder access. Though the UNECE Water Convention[356] is regarded as 'arguably leading the charge on producing instruments which strengthen joint institutions and stakeholder participation',[357] the Convention itself only requires state Parties to make information relating to the management of transboundary freshwater resources available to the public and says little about public participation.[358] Some European basin agreements inspired by the UNECE Water Convention have tended to take a similarly restrictive approach as regards public or stakeholder participation,[359] whilst others have sought to be more inclusive.[360] There also exists a limited number of basin agreements from other regions, most notably in Africa, which expressly stipulate a requirement of public consultation, such as the 2004 ZAMCOM Agreement[361] and the 2003 Lake Tanganyika Convention.[362]

'Principle 10: Public Participation' in JE Viñuales (ed), *The Rio Declaration on Environment and Development: A Commentary* (OUP 2015) 287.

[354] ILC, 'Report of the International Law Commission on the Work of its 53rd Session', UN Doc A/56/10 165. See further, O McIntyre, 'The Proceduralisation and Growing Maturity of International Water Law' (2011) 22(3) Journal of Environmental Law 475–97 496–97.

[355] n 7, arts 11–19.

[356] n 268.

[357] R Moynihan, 'Inland Water Biodiversity: International Law on Protection oaf Transboundary Freshwater Ecosystems and Biodiversity' in E Morgera and J Razzaque (eds), *Biodiversity and Nature Protection Law* (Edward Elgar 2017) 189–202 200. See further, R Moynihan and BO Magsig, 'The Rising Role of Regional Approaches in International Water Law: Lessons from the UNECE Water Regime and Himalayan Asia for Strengthening Transboundary Water Cooperation' (2014) 23(1) Review of European, Comparative and International Environmental Law 43–58.

[358] n 268, art 16.

[359] Convention on Cooperation for the Protection and Sustainable Use of the Danube River (Sophia, 29 June 1994), art 14.

[360] Art 14 of the Convention on the Protection of the Rhine (Bern, 12 April 1999) provides for NGOs to act as observers, make submissions and enter into consultations with the Commission.

[361] Agreement on the Establishment of the Zambezi Water Commission (Kasane, 13 July 2004), art 16(8).

[362] Convention on Sustainable Management of Lake Tanganyika (Dar es Salaam, 12 June 2003), arts 5(2)(d) and 17.

500   SDG 6

Public participation is clearly recognized as central to effective implementation of the ecosystem approach in the practice guidance developed under CBD. Of the twelve principles identified at CBD COP 5 to guide implementation of the ecosystem approach, Principle 12 recommends the involvement of all sectors of society, while Principle 11 exhorts decision-makers to make use of all forms of information, including Indigenous knowledge.[363] Similarly, Goal 2.5 of the CBD's Revised Programme of Work on Inland Water Biological Diversity recommends broad engagement with '[r]elevant national stakeholders, including representatives of indigenous and local communities'.[364] Likewise, the 2004 guidelines on implementing the ecosystem approach adopted by CBD COP 7 '[r]ecommend that Parties and other Governments facilitate the full and effective participation of indigenous and local communities and other stakeholders'.[365]

It is worth noting, however, that, despite a dearth of treaty provisions expressly providing for public participation in respect of shared international waters, many treaty regimes either require[366] or promote[367] reliance upon EIA of planned projects in order to avoid and minimize adverse impacts and facilitate meaningful inter-state notification, as is now a 'requirement under general international law'[368] irrespective of its inclusion in an applicable conventional instrument, though the International Court of Justice (ICJ) found that 'no legal obligation to consult the affected populations arises for the Parties from the instruments invoked by Argentina'.[369] However, the Court also held that 'it is for each State to determine in its domestic legislation ... the specific content of the environmental impact assessment required in each case'[370] and one would struggle to find a national EIA regime where public or stakeholder participation is not a central element. It is telling that the 1991 UNECE Convention on Transboundary Environmental Impact Assessment, which is intended to inform national development of 'the necessary legal, administrative or other measures' in respect of activities likely to cause significant adverse transboundary impact, requires that '[t]he concerned Parties shall arrange for distribution of the documentation to the authorities and the public of the affected Party in the areas likely to be affected and for the submission of comments to the competent authority of the Party of origin'.[371]

Of course, a significant number of international watercourses have in place permanent institutional structures, which may assist in facilitating structured stakeholder engagement. One commentator suggests that 'practice shows that effective institutional

---

[363] CBD Decision v/6, Ecosystem Approach (22 June 2000), UN Doc UNEP/CBD/COP/5/23.

[364] CBD Decision VII/4 (13 April 2004), Annex 22.

[365] CBD Decision VII/11 (13 April 2004) 2, para 10, UN Doc UNEP/CBD/COP.7/21.

[366] Lake Tanganyika Convention (n 362) art 15.

[367] UN Watercourses Convention (n 362) art 12; ILC Draft Articles on Transboundary Aquifers, art 15(2), Report of the International Law Commission on the Work of Its Sixtieth Session, II(2) Yearbook of the International Law Commission (2008).

[368] Pulp Mills on the River Uruguay (*Argentina v Uruguay*) 2010 ICJ (April 20), para 204.

[369] ibid para 216.

[370] ibid para 205.

[371] Espoo Convention (n 347), where the activities listed in Appendix I to the Convention as requiring EIA include inland waterways and ports, large dams and reservoirs, large-scale groundwater abstraction activities, large-scale pulp and paper manufacturing, major mining operations, and deforestation of large areas—all activities likely to have significant impact upon a watercourse.

management has a degree of flexibility that allows for public input'.[372] A comprehensive 2013 study of water-related institutional cooperation notes that 'RBOs do not act in isolation in their respective river and lake basins', but instead engage a range of external actors, including 'NGOs, civil society groups, knowledge groups and research networks ... as well as other regional institutions either directly dealing with water resources issues ... or implicitly influencing river basin governance through their regional principles, norms, rules and activities'.[373] This is particularly important for effective ecosystems protection, for which

> effective governance requires a bottom-up approach, and one that often sits more easily with non-governmental organisations, working at the interface between state and society. Such "trusted intermediaries" can often work across national or subnational boundaries with a greater flexibility than state bodies, building local consensus around environmental protection and enhancement, and ultimately ecosystem service delivery.[374]

However, if effective public or stakeholder participation is crucial for the protection of watercourse ecosystems, and for addressing the impacts of climate change, it is thus crucial for achieving optimal and sustainable utilization of international watercourses. It follows that it is also critically important for the avoidance or resolution of international water disputes. Therefore, it is quite clear that the prevailing formal paradigm for procedural engagement in international water law, with its almost exclusive focus on inter-state communication, is out of step with target 6.b and therefore, almost by definition, no longer fit for purpose. Discussing the 'Effectiveness of Public Participation in Decision Making' regarding shared international water resources, the chapter contained in the Millennium Ecosystem Assessment on 'Freshwater Ecosystems' provides an indication of the inherent complexity of the participation issues potentially arising:

> It may be limited by factors such as: geographic isolation, common in upper watershed areas; language and educational barriers; access to information that is timely and relevant; whether participation is made possible in the early phases of a process (planning and defining problems); whether the decision process provides an opportunity for deliberation and learning; and legal frameworks that define rights (land tenure, for example) and provide measures of recourse, all of which determine the relative bargaining power of various stakeholders.[375]

---

[372] M Lim, 'Is Water Different from Biodiversity? Governance Criteria for the Effective Management of Transboundary Resources' (2014) 23(1) Review of European, Comparative and International Environmental Law 96–110 104.

[373] Schmeier (n 265) 108.

[374] A Rieu-Clarke and C Spray, 'Ecosystem Services and International Water Law: Towards a More Effective Determination and Implementation of Equity' (2013) 16(2) Potchefstroom Electronic Law Journal 11–65 46.

[375] B Aylward and others, 'Freshwater Ecosystem Services' in B Aylward and others (eds), *Millennium Ecosystem Assessment* (Island Press 2005) 213–55, 227 <https://www.millenniumassessment.org/documents/document.312.aspx.pdf> accessed 30 November 2022.

502   SDG 6

While participatory rights are developing rapidly within the related fields of human rights law[376] and environmental law,[377] it is clear that implementation of the ecosystem approach will demand significant progressive advances in terms of the inclusiveness of the procedural rules employed in international water law.[378]

Thus, target 6.b and indicator 6.b.1 simply reflect a widely recognized core element of good water governance and an increasingly firmly established requirement in national and international law. However, they add significant value to water and sanitation governance by highlighting the benefits of participation, by promoting the sharing of best practice in this regard and by encouraging state actors to engage fully with the practical difficulties and significant costs involved in facilitating truly meaningful participatory governance.

IV. Monitoring and Implementation

Probably the most significant aspect of the Agenda 2030 framework, not least as regards SDG 6, is the highly developed programme for the monitoring of progress against all targets and indicators. This ensures a degree of follow-up on the commitments made by states that can be found in no corresponding formal legal regime or arrangement. The global programme for monitoring implementation of SDG 6 was launched in 2017 following the development, testing, and evaluation of methodologies for monitoring the indicators identified under each target set out thereunder. Based a structured process of periodic national reporting against parameters set out under each indicator, this programme represents a heroic effort, both on the part of national governments, who are expected to make every reasonable effort to generate and submit a comprehensive range of relevant data, and on the part of the international community, where a number of UN agencies act as custodians for the data collected in respect of particular indicators. In addition to promoting the achievement of all eight SDG 6 targets, this monitoring process supports improvement in water management and governance more generally:

> Credible and timely water and sanitation data provide numerous social, economic, and environmental benefits in both public and private sectors, such as stronger political accountability and commitment, as well as public and private investments. It also

---

[376] Rieu-Clarke and Spray (n 374) 48. See further O McIntyre, 'The Role of the Public and the Human Right to Water' in M Tignino and K Sangbana (eds), *Public Participation and Water Resources Management: Where Do We Stand in International Law?* (UNESCO 2015) 139–46.

[377] UNECE Arhus Convention on Accession to Information, Public Participation in Decision-Making and Access to Justice in Environmental Matters (Aarhus, 25 June 1998) 38 ILM 517 (1999); Regional Agreement on Access to Information, Public Participation and Justice in Environmental Matters in Latin America and the Caribbean (Escazú, 4 March 2018), not yet in force.

[378] See further, McIntyre, 'Procedural Rules of International Water Law and the Imminent Challenges of the Ecosystem Approach' (n 272).

enables evidence-based policymaking, regulations, planning and investments at all levels, to ensure the most effective deployment of resources.[379]

Thus, the reporting and monitoring process under SDG 6 encourages the international community to focus upon and address the many challenges facing the water and sanitation sector in a coherent, coordinated, and incremental manner—something which no traditional legal arrangement could ever have achieved. In order to support monitoring regarding progress on SDG 6, the UN-Water Integrated Monitoring Initiative brings together all the UN agencies involved with water and sanitation and mandated to compile data on the SDG 6 indicators,[380] which work together to support countries in monitoring water and sanitation-related targets and in compiling country data to report on global progress towards SDG 6. A significant aspect of this work is the development of standardized methodologies for monitoring the different indicators, in order to ensure that data are comparable across countries and over time.

The importance of monitoring has, however, long been appreciated in the general field of human rights and, more specifically, in relation to the human right(s) of access to water and sanitation. Acutely aware that monitoring compliance with the various facets of the right to water and sanitation is both complex and essential to realization, General Comment No 15 expressly stipulates that the strategy and plan of action to be adopted and implemented by states as a core obligation arising under the right to water 'should include methods, such as right to water indicators and benchmarks, by which progress can be closely monitored'.[381] Accordingly, the former UN Special Rapporteur published detailed guidance on monitoring in 2014.[382] In addition to setting out clearly the international framework for monitoring compliance with human rights, it details the respective roles of state bodies, service providers, and civil society. The guidance advises states on defining structural, process, and outcome indicators of progress towards realization of the right[383] and addresses in detail the monitoring of water and sanitation availability, accessibility, quality, affordability, acceptability, and sustainability. For example, in relation to monitoring the quality of sanitation provision, the guidance explains that 'to safeguard the health benefits of access to sanitation and protect water resources, the full cycle of sanitation provision must be monitored, from collection to transport, treatment and disposal of waste', though it also readily acknowledges that 'at present, there is no agreed global indicator for monitoring this

---

[379] UN-Water, 'Summary Progress Update 2021' (n 166) 4–5.

[380] Including: United Nations Environment Programme (UNEP), United Nations Human Settlements Programme (UN-Habitat), United Nations Children's Fund (UNICEF), Food and Agriculture Organization of the United Nations (FAO), United Nations Economic Commission for Europe (UNECE), United Nations Educational, Scientific and Cultural Organization (UNESCO), World Health Organization (WHO), and World Meteorological Organization (WMO).

[381] General Comment No 15 (n 8) para 37(f). See further paras 47, 53, and 54.

[382] C de Albuqerque, *Monitoring Compliance with the Human Rights to Water and Sanitation* (OHCHR 2014).

[383] ibid at 7, which provides: 'Structural indicators' monitor whether the legislative, policy, and regulatory frameworks of a state or government (at all levels) provide an environment that encourages realization of human rights. 'Process indicators' monitor the action taken to realize human rights; for example, the allocation of resources to services for disadvantaged individuals and groups. 'Outcome indicators' monitor actual access to water and sanitation services; eg, whether households have access to a latrine or whether water is of adequate quality.

504 SDG 6

full provision'.[384] Therefore, though the monitoring requirements under SDG 6 don't meet these exacting standards, they do represent real progress, particularly when one recognizes that monitoring standards for compliance with the right to water and sanitation are as yet at a very early stage in their evolution.[385]

As SDG targets 6.1 and 6.2 closely reflect the core values enshrined in the human right(s) to water and sanitation, the monitoring methodologies developed thereunder are likely to create an incremental template for measuring compliance with and realization of these correlative human rights. Though target 6.1 has a single associated indicator relating to the 'proportion of population using safely managed drinking water services', guidance published by UN-Water elaborates further upon use of this indicator, advising, for example, that 'this indicator can be disaggregated by service level: no service, basic services and safely managed services'.[386] It also includes detailed guidance on the particular testing to occur in household surveys at each of three steps of progressive monitoring of indicator 6.1.1.[387] Similarly, target 6.2 is also measured against a single indicator relating to the 'proportion of population using safely managed sanitation services, including a hand-washing facility with soap and water'. UN-Water guidance on indicator 6.2.1 elaborates on the meaning of 'improved sanitation facilities' and 'handwashing facilities' and advises on disaggregation by service level and on the data to be gleaned from household surveys, and from service providers at each step of progressive monitoring.[388] In the case of both indicators, data received annually from national officials will be compiled by WHO and UNICEF, which are together mandated to act as the responsible custodian.[389] Of course, integrated monitoring for SDG 6 covers the entire range of targets relevant to realization of the right(s) to water and sanitation as set out under General Comment No 15, including water quality and wastewater management, water use and scarcity, water resources management, water-related ecosystems, international cooperation, and stakeholder participation.[390]

Other multilateral organizations, such as the European Union, have also developed sets of indicators for monitoring compliance with and realization of SDG 6, which will similarly inform and assist reporting and monitoring.[391] In addition, in January 2017, the UNESCO International Hydrological Programme (IHP) launched its Water Information Network System (WINS), which aims to provide UNESCO Member States with an open source, open access, web-based information platform to serve as a global reference for decision-makers and stakeholders on water-related issues at all levels.[392] The UNESCO-IHP WINS initiative is a response from the IHP Secretariat to

[384] ibid at 18.
[385] See further, McIntyre, 'The Emergence of Standards' (n 70) 167.
[386] UN-Water, *Integrated Monitoring Guide for SDG 6: Targets and Global Indicators* (UN 2016) 5.
[387] ibid.
[388] ibid.
[389] See WHO/UNICEF JMP, *Progress on Drinking Water, Sanitation and Hygiene: 2017 Update and SDG Baselines* (UN 2017) <https://data.unicef.org/wp-content/uploads/2017/07/JMP-2017-report-launch-version_0.pdf> accessed 30 November 2022.
[390] Respectively, SDG targets 6.3, 6.4, 6.5, 6.6, 6.a, and 6.b.
[391] See EU Eurostat, *EU SDG Indicator Set* (28 April 2017) <http://ec.europa.eu/eurostat/documents/276524/7736915/EU-SDG-indicator-set-with-cover-note-170531.pdf> accessed 30 November 2022.
[392] See further, <http://en.unesco.org/ihp-wins> accessed 30 November 2022.

a request from UNESCO Member States to 'provide support to Member States to build their institutional capacities, human resources and a sound basis in science capacity for the monitoring and implementation of Sustainable Development Goal 6 (SDG 6) and other water-related goals'.[393] Also relevant to monitoring in respect of access to water and sanitation is guidance developed by UNECE and WHO on target setting and reporting under the auspices of the 1999 UNECE Protocol on Water and Health,[394] which imposes obligations upon States Parties in relation to the provision of universal access to adequate supplies of wholesome drinking water.[395] Recognizing that the Protocol 'is a powerful tool to promote and operationalize the achievement of the 2030 Agenda' and that 'the Protocol's provisions and principles fully align with SDG 6', the UNECE/WHO guidance gathers together case studies showcasing good practices and lessons learned in order 'to assist efforts by Parties to the Protocol and other states to effectively shape their target-setting processes'.[396] The guidance showcases best practice in relation to, *inter alia*, institutional arrangements, baseline analysis and prioritization of issues, development of targets and their financial and economic implications, public involvement in target setting, publication and promotion of targets, development of programmes of measures and action plans for implementation, and review and assessment of progress and reporting.

In the course of the second round of reporting on progress in the implementation of SDG 6 carried out in 2021, the custodian agencies have taken the opportunity to highlight examples of national best practice regarding almost all aspects of each target and indicator. For example, in reporting on progress on wastewater treatment pursuant to SDG indicator 6.3.1, the custodian agencies outline Jordan's achievements in reusing treated wastewater in its agricultural sector as a model for other countries with largely agricultural economies operating in water-scarce settings.[397] The report points out that, in order to be in a position to do so, Jordan has put in place advanced safety measures and controls for wastewater reuse including, for example, rigorous effluent quality requirements for three different classifications of agricultural reuse applications based on twelve different environmental parameters (including Biochemical Oxygen Demand, Chemical Oxygen Demand and *Escherichia coli*). The established standards are based on World Health Organization (WHO) guidelines. The entire practice requires careful coordination between farmers, utilities, the Water Authority of Jordan and the Ministry of Water and Irrigation, with farmers requiring a licence from the Ministry of Agriculture detailing the types of crops used and irrigation techniques employed. In

---

[393] UNESCO Press Release (25 January 2017).

[394] UNECE/WHO, *Collection of Good Practices and Lessons Learned on Target Setting and Reporting under the Protocol on Water and Health* (UN 2016). See further, UNECE/WHO, *A Healthy Link: The Protocol on Water and Health and the Sustainable Development Goals* (November 2016), UN Doc ECE/INF/NONE/2016/16 <http://www.unece.org/fileadmin/DAM/env/water/mop4/Informal_doc/1623151_E_FinalWEB_rev.pdf> accessed 30 November 2022.

[395] McIntyre, 'The UNECE Water Convention and the Principle of Equitable and Reasonable Utilisation' (n 73); arts 4(2)(a) and 6(1)(a).

[396] UNECE/WHO, *Collection of Good Practices and Lessons Learned* (n 394) iii.

[397] UN-Water, *Progress on Wastewater Treatment: Global Status and Acceleration Needs for SDG Indicator 6.3.1* (UN 2021) 14.

turn, the Ministry of Health and Jordanian Food and Drug Administration are responsible for monitoring the quality of agricultural produce sold on the market. In relation to dispersed rural households relying upon non-networked domestic wastewater systems employing stand-alone septic tanks, the report highlights the national surveillance programme implemented in Ireland since 2013 to monitor the safety and performance of such wastewater systems.[398] With a legislative requirement to carry out at least 1,000 inspections of domestic wastewater treatment systems each year (representing approximately 0.2 per cent of all systems existing in the country),[399] the programme has routinely found approximately 50 per cent of systems to be non-compliant. Failure results in the issuance of an advisory notice, requiring immediate corrective action which the household must take, though a grant scheme exists to support remediation works among qualifying households. Thus, the inspection programme successfully addresses a serious wastewater treatment deficit commonly experienced in countries with significant widely dispersed rural populations. Similarly, the report on SDG 6.3.2 on ambient water quality reports on a variety of measures successfully adopted by states with a view to engaging more effectively in water quality monitoring, including carefully targeted capacity development in Sierra Leon and citizen biomonitoring in South Africa.[400]

In relation to those areas of water-related activity where the normative commitments of states are more indeterminate and allow a great deal of flexibility in implementation, the SDG monitoring programme plays a particularly important informative role. For example, the 2021 progress report on SDG 6.5.2 on transboundary water cooperation provides the custodian agencies with a valuable opportunity to gather and collate data on the full range of collaborative arrangements and practices engaged in by transboundary watercourse and aquifer states, and to disseminate this to state actors tentatively considering how to frame such initiatives.[401] To this end, using current real-life examples of inter-state cooperative practice, the report comprehensively lists the various benefits to be derived from having in place effective operational arrangements for transboundary water cooperation, including benefits relating to poverty alleviation, food security, health and well-being, clean energy, climate change, terrestrial and marine ecosystem protection, and peace and security.[402]

Thus, the targets set out under SDG 6, and the arrangements necessary for national reporting and for monitoring progress thereon, now lie at the centre of a concerted global effort to understand fully and constructively address the daunting challenges associated with equitable and sustainable global provision of safe and adequate drinking water and sanitation. Perhaps more than any other single aspect of SDG 6, this

---

[398] ibid 15.

[399] Under the 2007 Water Services Act (as amended).

[400] UN-Water, *Progress on Ambient Water Quality: Global Indicator 6.3.2 Updates and Acceleration Needs* (UN 2021) 9 and 14.

[401] See A Rieu-Clarke, 'Can Reporting Enhance Transboundary Water Cooperation? Early Insights from the Water Convention and the Sustainable Development Goals Reporting Exercise' (2020) 29 Review of European, Comparative and International Environmental Law 361–71.

[402] UN-Water, *Progress on Transboundary Water Cooperation: Global Status of SDG Indicator 6.5.2 and Acceleration Needs* (UN 2021) 3.

demonstrates the goal's potential to transform utterly global water management and governance.

V. Conclusion

One should not doubt for a moment that the adoption and progressive implementation of SDG 6 represents an innovative and game-changing paradigm both in terms of the equitable delivery of water and sanitation-related entitlements globally and of the sustainable management of water resources and related ecosystems and services. This is not before time, having regard to the increasingly urgent nature of the problems facing the water sector and the poor results achieved by reliance solely upon traditional governance techniques, including the existing formal legal frameworks. By obtaining the universal voluntary commitment of the international community of states to a set of core water-related values, however aspirational, and presenting these within a structured, coherent, and incremental governance framework, however ambitious, that includes periodic review, annual reporting, and centralized monitoring, however demanding, SDG 6 provides the shared vision to guide global water management and governance for the foreseeable future. From this perspective, SDG 6 represents, by any measure, a truly extraordinary achievement on the part of the institutional machinery of global cooperation.

However, this success is to a significant degree due to the fact that those involved in negotiating and framing SDG 6 did not have to commence the task *de novo*. In addition to the valuable experience gained in implementing MDG 7 target C, they could draw upon the wealth of ongoing progressive developments in the fields of national, international, and transnational human rights law, environmental law and water law, all of which can be associated with the broad objective of sustainable development. The carefully formulated substantive and procedural entitlements included within the rubric of the human right(s) of access to water and sanitation, the established legal frameworks for balancing the social, economic and developmental water needs of competing co-riparian states, the emerging ecosystem-based approach to the management of international water resources and the ecosystem services provided thereby, and the increasingly ubiquitous participation rights granted to water users, other stakeholders, and the general public, will continue to inform implementation of every aspect of SDG 6. In many respects this global goal for water consolidates existing trends in relevant national and international legal frameworks. Such influence runs in both directions, however, and, as the overarching global governance framework for water, the values and methodologies set out under SDG 6 will exert ever-increasing influence over the development of national and international water law frameworks and their application. Drafters of national water-related legislation will need to ensure coherence with the values set out under the full range of SDG 6 targets, while inter-state engagement regarding shared water resources is already being conducted in the light of

508   SDG 6

the requirements of SDG indicator 6.5.2.[403] The influence of SDG 6 as the pre-eminent source of normative guidance as regards water and sanitation governance can only continue to grow. Thus SDG 6 and water-related legal frameworks enjoy a highly synergistic and complementary relationship. SDG 6 provides a formally adopted, yet voluntary global consensus on a comprehensive range of water-related values, along with elaborate compliance monitoring processes, while traditional water law systems provide formal frameworks of notionally binding rules which are often opaque as regard their precise requirements and/or lack practically effective enforcement mechanisms.

---

[403] See UN-Water, *Progress on Transboundary Water Cooperation: Global Status of SDG Indicator 6.5.2 and Acceleration Needs* (UN 2021) <https://www.unwater.org/publications/progress-on-transboundary-water-coop eration-652-2021-update/> accessed 30 November 2022. A currently ongoing Nile Basin Initiative (NBI) project on *Strengthening the Policy Frameworks for Transboundary Water Resources Management in the Nile Basin* includes a component involving a 'report on the status of SDG 6.5.2 (transboundary water governance) in the Nile Basin'.

SDG 7

'Ensure Access to Affordable, Reliable, Sustainable and Modern Energy for All'

Francesco Seatzu and Katerina Akestoridi[*]

I. Introduction

'Energy is the golden thread that connects economic growth, increases social equity, and an environment that allows the world to thrive,'[1] yet for many years energy issues have not been accorded the necessary attention in intergovernmental discourse about development. In light, however, of the acknowledgement that the mainstream growth-led model of development has had detrimental impacts on the environment and has not resulted in the eradication of poverty, the adoption of Agenda 2030 for sustainable development serves as a timely reminder of how important access to affordable, reliable, sustainable, and modern energy services is for human development in an intra- and intergenerational context. On equal footing, the energy crisis the world is currently experiencing as a result of the COVID-19 pandemic and the war in Ukraine has raised energy costs and security of supply to emergency matters. Issues like the aforementioned have been captured by the 'Energy trilemma'.[2] Despite variations in its conceptualization, accessibility, affordability, and sustainability constitute fundamental tenets of the concept. Broadly speaking, all three are relevant to the nexus energy has with society (individuals' needs) and the environment in terms of its positive and negative impacts on them. Sustainable Development Goal (SDG) 7 has the potential to mobilize action towards international policy and law on energy that resolves energy challenges for people while furthering the international community's goals to reverse climate change. Put differently, it can guide stakeholders' efforts to provide energy in a just and equitable manner vis-à-vis people and the natural environment so that 'no-one is left behind' whether now or in the future.

---

[*] The author would like to thank Malik Dahlan, Rosa Lastra, and Gustavo Rochette, editors of *Energy, Law and Ethics* (Edward Elgar Publishing 2022), for giving her access to the book ahead of its publication. Any errors are the author's.

[1] 'Sustainable Energy for All: A Framework for Action- Secretary General's High-Level Group on Sustainable energy for All' (Framework Report) (UN 2012), 4.

[2] World Energy Council, 'World Energy Trilemma Index' <https://www.worldenergy.org/transition-toolkit/world-energy-trilemma-index> accessed 10 April 2022.

510 SDG 7

In the sections that follow, the chapter provides the background to the emergence of SDG 7 (Section II) before commenting on core aspects of the Goal (Section III) and its individual targets (Section IV).

II. *Travaux Préparatoires*

Goal 7 is the first of the three SDGs that expanded the thematic coverage of the post-2015 development agenda beyond the issues addressed by the Millennium Development Goals (MDGs). Agenda 21, which served as the blueprint for the sustainable development agenda, had stressed the essential nature of energy to economic and social development as well as the protection of the environment, demonstrating in its individual chapters how accessible, safe, sound, and efficient energy systems may contribute positively to the improvement of the atmosphere and the promotion of sustainable use of forests and trees for energy supplies, may reduce health risks from energy production, and enhance productivity of human labour and income generation, to name a few examples.[3] Notably, however, energy was left out from the MDGs and only in 2010, at the United Nations General Assembly's (UNGA) High-Level Plenary Meeting, was it admitted that energy was a prerequisite for achieving those goals of the SDGs.

The stocktaking phase provided the opportunity to revert stakeholders' attention to the nexus between energy and other development sectors and bridge the implementation gap in respective integrative policies. Energy was discussed in Open Working Group (OWG)-5 together with economic growth, questions of macroeconomic policy, infrastructure development, and industrialization. The Technical Support Team (TST) brief provided important background information for the discussion on the issue that lasted a day and a half. Energy poverty—that is, lack of (or the absence of sufficient choice in accessing) adequate, affordable, reliable, quality, safe, and environmentally sound energy services to support economic and human development[4]—affected half of the world's population. At the time the TST report was disseminated, almost 3 billion people relied on animal waste, wood, or other solid biomass for heating and cooking;[5] one in five lacked access to electricity with 80 per cent of those living in rural areas and the projection being that electricity access

---

[3] UN Conference on Environment and Development, Rio de Janeiro, Brazil 3–14 June 1992, Agenda 21 <https://sustainabledevelopment.un.org/content/documents/Agenda21.pdf> accessed 4 April 2022, indicatively chs 6E, 7E, 9B(1) and (2), 14K.

[4] Habitat for Humanity, 'What is Energy Poverty?' <https://www.habitat.org/emea/about/what-we-do/residential-energy-efficiency-households/energy-poverty> accessed 1 February 2022; AKN Reddy, 'Energy and Social Issues' in UNDP, *World Energy Assessment: Energy and the Challenge of Sustainability* (UNDP 2000) 44 <https://www.undp.org/sites/g/files/zskgke326/files/publications/World%20Energy%20Assessment-2000.pdf> accessed 6 April 2022.

[5] UN DESA, Compendium of Issue Briefs (2014) 99 (hereafter, Compendium).

rates would not match the pace of population growth.[6] Developing Asia and Sub-Saharan Africa concentrated the majority of countries suffering from the 'energy gap' but simultaneously provided opportunities for accelerated progress towards electricity access. Considering also that investment in infrastructure for universal energy access suffices at only 3 per cent of global investment over the period to 2030, energy poverty could be eliminated rather inexpensively.[7]

Nevertheless, the achievement of this objective was multifaceted and a 'nexus approach' was necessary at the national and international policy levels alike. On the one hand, economic and social development depends largely on energy services and it is estimated that global energy demand will increase by 47 per cent by 2035. On the other, unsustainable energy practices impact negatively on people's socio-economic progress and the environment. For instance, primary energy that is produced from fossil fuels generated more than half of the anthropogenic green-house gas (GHG) emissions according to 2010 estimates. In turn, air pollution is responsible for long-term impediments to human health, the disruption of ecosystems and natural resources, and the worsening of climate change. Moreover, a surge in energy prices such as that following the 2008 financial crisis or the current COVID-19 pandemic increases the cost of food production and purchase. Finally, the TST report stressed the greater burden shared by vulnerable population groups such as women and children in poverty, who are usually those that collect fuel and carry it long distances in order to cover household needs and are thus exposed to health and safety risks and even violence connected with fuel collection.[8]

Due to the systemic imbalances caused by the lack of energy access or untenable practices thereof, it was emphasized at the OWG session that current energy systems should be transformed in order to be responsive to climate change mitigation and adaptation, and promote human development. The importance of energy renewables was highlighted by the Director-General of the International Renewable Energy Agency (IREA) as a promising source for meeting the energy demand but also for a country's economic growth by providing new employment opportunities related to the construction of the appropriate infrastructure and transforming states to exporters of wind or solar energy through large-scale energy plans.[9] In equal measure, the decarbonization and diversification of energy systems drew attention to the matter of cost-effective access and use of energy resources (affordability) and the efficiency of power systems; thus, the development and transfer of new technology whereby access barriers to centralized energy service systems would be overcome (eg Light Emitting Diode (LED) off-grid or hybrid strategies of on- and off-grid coordination), reducing the 'energy

---

[6] WBG, 'SE4ALL Global Tracking Framework' <https://www.worldbank.org/en/topic/energy/publication/Global-Tracking-Framework-Report> accessed I February 2022.

[7] Compendium (n 5) 100.

[8] ibid; World Food Program, 'Handbook on Safe Access to Firewood and Alternative Energy (SAFE)' (2012) <https://documents.wfp.org/stellent/groups/public/documents/newsroom/wfp252989.pdf> accessed 2 February 2022.

[9] OWG-5, Summary, 5 <https://sustainabledevelopment.un.org/owg.html> accessed 2 February 2022.

isolation' some communities are faced with due to economic or geographic reasons;[10] capacity building; access to innovative financing mechanisms; and regulatory reforms were mentioned as drivers of accessible and sustainable energy transition. To this end, an integrated policy framework should address the differentiated needs and diverse development pathways of each country and be built with the participation of beneficiaries and those communities affected negatively by energy projects (eg Indigenous people who are often displaced and locals that see their livelihoods destroyed) in order for energy projects and policies to be just and 'owned' by the implementing country.[11]

A. A Stand-alone or a Cross-cutting Target?

Similar to other goals, the proposals about integrating energy in the new development agenda can be grouped in two categories: energy as a stand-alone goal or a cross-cutting target, which stakeholders negotiated over the course of the last four OWG sessions (OWGs-10–13). During these meetings energy was deliberated under Focus Area 7 and the suggested targets drew upon the themes of (i) universal access to modern energy services; (ii) cleaner energy technologies; (iii) renewable energy and the phasing out of fossil fuels; (iv) energy efficiency in infrastructure, industry, agriculture, and transport; (v) knowledge transfer, regulatory reforms, investments, and partnerships for sustainable energy.[12]

A first stipulation of an autonomous goal on energy came from the UN Secretary General's High Level Panel of Eminent Persons on the Post-2015 Development Agenda (HLP) entitled 'Secure Sustainable Energy'. The goal consisted of four illustrative targets: 7a) to ensure universal access to modern energy services; 7b) double the share of renewable energy in the global energy mix; 7c) double the global rate of improvement in energy efficiency in buildings, industry, agriculture, and transport; and 7d) phase out inefficient fossil fuel subsidies that encourage wasteful consumption.[13] Yet, the UN's partner organization 'Sustainable Energy for All'[14] emphasized universal access to energy in its proposed title for a stand-alone goal on energy and earmarked the deadline for achieving the proposed three objectives (corresponding to the HLP's 7a, 7b, 7c targets) to 2030. Indeed, this proposal reflected better the outcomes of the Global Thematic Consultation on the post-2015 development agenda, which, among others, revealed the gender disparities of energy access and the greater repercussions

[10] ibid, Prof D Kammen (University of California at Berkeley).
[11] ibid 6 (bullet points 3 and 7); OWG-5, 'Co-Chairs Meeting with Major Groups and Other Stakeholders' 2 <https://sustainabledevelopment.un.org/owg.html> accessed 2 February 2022.
[12] OWG, 'Encyclopaedia Groupinica: A Compilation of Goals and Targets Suggestions from OWG 10' (2014) 66–67.
[13] HLP, 'A New Global Partnership: Eradicate Poverty and Transform Economies through Sustainable Development'—Report of the High-Level Panel of Eminent Persons on the Post-2015 Development Agenda (UN Publications 2013) 31.
[14] Initially launched in 2011 by UNSG as an initiative but since 2016 SEforAll operates as a quasi-international organization with a ten-year relationship agreement with the UN <https://f-refresh-seforall.pantheonsite.io/who-we-are/our-relationship-with-the-un> accessed 4 February 2022.

for health, employment, education, etc of women and children.[15] The business world also endorsed the said formulation of the goal during the Global Compact consultations and proposed four targets: (i) universal access to modern energy services; (ii) double the global rate of improvement in energy efficiency in production, distribution, and consumption; (iii) double the share of renewable sources in the energy mix; and (iv) reduce by at least 50 per cent the particulate concentration in urban air without excluding more stringent targets set at the regional level.[16]

Universal access to energy seemed to be a point of agreement among country delegates to the OWG too. For instance, Tanzania framed the goal as 'promote access to affordable and reliable energy for all';[17] representatives of Southern African states supported a goal on 'universal access to clean, reliable and affordable energy';[18] Trinidad and Tobago, representing the Caribbean Community (CARICOM), promoted an energy goal on 'access to sustainable energy for all', and the Russian Federation submitted that a text on energy should definitely refer to access.[19] Equally, universal access to energy was promoted by developed states, which, however, pushed also for the inclusion of technological advancements for the transformation of energy systems and infrastructure towards low-emission through alternative energy sources.[20] In fact, decoupling energy from fossil fuels, and eventually the phase-out of fossil fuels, became a point of heated discussion among country representatives. Saudi Arabia, for instance, opposed specific mention of low-or zero-emission technologies and fossil fuel subsidies despite the country's support for universal access to energy. India as well was cautious about the elimination of subsidies for fossil fuel consumption due to its adverse impact on the energy access of the poor. Iran stressed that the Rio + 20 agreement merely 'invited' nations to give up fossil fuel subsidies and did not contain any explicit commitments to this end.[21] In contrast, Small Island Developing States (SIDS) argued that a shift to renewable energy was crucial for their survival in the light of disasters they suffered as a result of climate change. Henceforth, they were in favour of accelerating investment in green technologies and energy.[22]

While dialogue about the specifics of a separate energy goal continued, other stakeholders praised the advantages of having energy targets included in other clusters of SDGs. Such an option was justified on the basis that it would remedy the silo approach to development policy, which by and large characterized the MDGs. There

---

[15] UNDG, 'The Global Conversation Begins: Emerging views for a New Development Agenda' (2013); also, Major Group of Women, Indigenous People, Partnership on Sustainable, Low Carbon Transport (SLoCat), and IBON International who called for women's participation in decision-making policy about energy with equal access to and control, OWG-10, 'Major Groups and Other Stakeholders Dialogue with the Co-Chairs on SDGs (2 April 2014)—Compilation Document' 14 (OWG-10 MG Dialogue).

[16] UN Global Compact, 'Corporate Sustainability and the UN Post-2015 Development Agenda'—report to the UN SG (17 June 2013) 15.

[17] International Institute for Sustainable Development (IISD), 'Summary of the 10th OWG on SDGs: 31 March–4 April 2014' (2014) 32(10) Earth Negotiations Bulletin 1, 10.

[18] ibid 12.

[19] ibid 11, 12.

[20] ibid 11 (Ireland, Denmark, and Norway).

[21] ibid 12.

[22] PS Chasek and others, *Transforming Multilateral Diplomacy: The Inside Story of the Sustainable Development Goals* (Routledge 2018) 229–30.

514   SDG 7

was also a practical side to this suggestion: the goals could be reduced to a more manageable number that would be easier to communicate to all stakeholders in the international community and mobilize action for their implementation. The Sustainable Development Solutions Network put forward this proposition, associating energy with climate change. Its goal to 'curb human-induced climate change and ensure sustainable energy' promoted sustainable energy for all but evolved around limiting GHG emissions and reducing imminent and emerging risks of climate change. Individual targets included: (a) to decarbonize the energy system, ensure clean energy for all and improve energy efficiency between 2020 and 2050; (b) to reduce non-energy-related greenhouse gases through improved practices in agriculture, forestry, waste management, and industry; and (c) adopt incentives, including pricing GHG emissions, to curb climate change and promote technology transfer to developing countries.[23]

At the OWG-11 the goal was shaped as follows:

Focus area 7.
Energy Ensure access to affordable, sustainable, and reliable modern energy for all

a) by 2030 ensure universal access to sustainable modern energy services
b) double the share of renewable energy in the global energy mix by 2030
c) double the global rate of improvement in energy efficiency, including in buildings, industry, agriculture and transport, by 2030
d) by 2030 increase by x% the share of clean and low- or zero-emission energy technologies, including sustainable biomass and advanced cook stoves
e) by 2030 phase out fossil fuel subsidies that encourage wasteful consumption
Appropriate means of implementation.

The chairs of the OWG welcomed delegates' proposals for elaboration on the targets. The issue of clean and new sources of energy was again a contentious point for government representatives, with some suggesting that references to sustainable modern energy, clean energy, and fossil fuel subsidy phase-out be deleted altogether.[24] Iran called for removing specific percentages in targets while Saudi Arabia withdrew her support for a stand-alone energy goal and communicated her preference that 'cleaner fossil fuel technologies' replaced reference to low- or zero-emission energy technologies.[25] Scepticism was expressed about the definition of 'modern energy' by Major Groups on behalf of Women, IBON, and SLoCat who gave the example of nuclear energy that was considered 'clean' some years ago, yet dangerous. On this account, they proposed to replace 'modern' with 'safe, renewable and environmentally friendly energy'[26] and

---

[23] SDSN, 'An Action Agenda for Sustainable Development: Report for the UN Secretary General' (5 May 2014) xi and 30–31. Note that under the SDSN's classification of SDGs, the goal on energy was Goal 8.
[24] IISD, 'Summary of the 11th Session of the UN General Assembly OWG on SDGs' (2014) 32(11) Earth Negotiations Bulletin 1, 11 (Benin, not relevant for LDCs); 12 (Ecuador, Argentina, Bolivia, Indonesia).
[25] ibid.
[26] OWG-10 MG Dialogue (n 15) 14.

suggested that target e) include the phasing out of fossil fuel and nuclear subsidies by 2020.[27] Support for the replacement of 'modern energy' with 'safe and secure energy' was also expressed by MG Beyond 2015. On the matter of discontinuing the use of fossil fuels, Beyond 2015 suggested that the target be rephrased entirely to provide for the protection of vulnerable groups from the energy transition. Suggested target e) read: 'take immediate steps to phase out and eliminate fossil fuel and nuclear production and consumption subsidies protecting low income and vulnerable populations from negative impacts, shifting this support to provide universal access to energy, renewable energy alternative and energy efficiency.'[28] Similarly, officials from Palau, Papua New Guinea, and Timor-Leste called for the target to be consistent with the polluter-pays principle, the precautionary principle, and the common but differentiated responsibilities principle.[29] Finally the issue of women's empowerment in energy policy was again highlighted by Sweden, Australia, New Zealand, Lichtenstein, and Iceland.[30]

Deliberations at OWG-11, and particularly the insistence of Least Development Countries (LDCs), led to the incorporation of a target specifically addressing access to energy for these disadvantaged states. Target 7.6 read: 'by 2030 expand and upgrade, as appropriate, infrastructure for supply, transmission and distribution of modern and renewable energy services in rural and urban areas, including with a view to doubling primary energy supply per capita for LDCs'. Similarly, former target e), now target 7.5, urged countries to phase out inefficient fossil fuel subsidies with solutions that aim to secure affordable energy for the poorest. Regarding the rest of the targets, they remained with no substantive differences except for proposed target 7.4 (former target d), which did not mention low or zero emissions but clean energy technologies only.

The targets were included in the zero draft document that was disseminated by the Chair of the OWG.[31] However, the content of SDG 7 remained largely unsettled, hence the OWG chairing committee proposed that the 12th formal session of the Group be adjourned to allow for additional input on the substance of the goal on energy by delegations and civil society in informal discussions.[32] Among the suggestions by Major Groups were the necessity to have resilient infrastructure for the supply, transmission and distribution of energy (target 7.6);[33] that improvement of energy intensity (energy/unit GDP) be at least 4.5 per cent every year (target 7.3),[34] and that by 2030 the share of non-fossil energy technologies—especially for women, households, communities,

---

[27] OWG-11 (5–9 May 2014), 'Major Groups and other Stakeholders Morning Hearings: Summary of Statements, 14.

[28] ibid 15.

[29] IISD, 'Summary of the 11th Session' (n 24) 11.

[30] ibid 12.

[31] OWG, 'Introduction and Proposed Goals and Targets on Sustainable Development for the Post-2015 Development Agenda' (2 June 2014), 8.

[32] IISD, 'Summary of the 12th Session of the OWG on the SDGs' (2014) 32(12) Earth Negotiations Bulletin 1, 4.

[33] OWG-12 Morning Hearings with Major Groups and other Stakeholders (16–20 June 2014), 'Compilation of Amendments to Goals and Targets', 21.

[34] OWG-12, Major Group Beyond 2015 'Reaction to the Open Working Group's "Introduction and Proposed Goals and Targets on Sustainable Development for the Post-2015 Development Agenda" (June 2014)', 10.

516   SDG 7

indigenous peoples, farmers, and entrepreneurs—increase by at least ten times globally (target 7.4).[35] At the end of the meetings the heading of SDG 7 read: Ensure access to affordable, sustainable, and reliable energy *services* for all', which was characterized as a narrow reflection of energy concerns that the post-2015 development agenda should address.

OWG-13 marked the end of negotiations of the SDGs. The updated zero draft proposal for SDG 7 was the following:[36]

> Proposed goal 7. Ensure sustainable energy for all
>
> 7.1 by 2030 ensure universal access to affordable, sustainable and reliable energy services
> 7.2 double the share of renewable energy in the global energy mix by 2030
> 7.3 double the global rate of improvement in energy efficiency by 2030
> 7.4 by 2030 phase out fossil fuel production and consumption subsidies that encourage wasteful use, while ensuring secure affordable energy for the poor
> 7.a enhance international cooperation to facilitate access to clean energy technologies, including advanced and cleaner fossil fuel technologies, and promote public and private investment in energy infrastructure and clean energy technologies
> 7.b by 2030 expand infrastructure and upgrade technology for supplying modern and sustainable energy services for all, particularly in LDCs

Commenting on the title of the goal, many delegates found more appropriate the inclusion of a reference to 'affordable and reliable energy', if not the substitution of 'sustainable' with the aforementioned phrase. The meaning of 'modern energy services' continued to worry some delegates alongside the terms 'sustainable energy infrastructure', 'clean energy technologies', and 'renewable energy technologies', prompting a discussion about the appropriateness of such terminology in relation to energy services in developing countries. Another point of disagreement until the last minute concerned the percentage by which the use of renewable energy should be increased. Countries that opposed a cap on renewables prevailed and in the end the phrase 'increase substantially' the share of renewables in the global energy mix was introduced in target 7.2. Finally, the divergent opinions about fossil fuel consumption and production subsidies were resolved through the mediation of a contact group coordinated by Norway.[37] Target 7.4 was eliminated altogether, although the rationalization of inefficient fossil-fuel subsidies was incorporated in Goal 12 as the third Means-of-Implementation

---

[35] OWG-12, 'Comments Prepared by the Women's Major Group on the Zero-Draft Document Prepared by the OWG Co-chairs on 2 June 2014', 11 <https://sustainabledevelopment.un.org/content/documents/10419women.pdf> accessed 8 February 2022.

[36] OWG-13, 'Introduction and Proposed Goals and Targets on Sustainable Development for the Post-2015 Development Agenda' (zero draft rev 1), 7.

[37] IISD, 'Summary of the 13th Session of the UN GA OWG Session on the SDGs (14–19 July 2014)' (2014) 32(13) Earth Negotiations Bulletin 1, 9–10.

(MOI) target (12c).[38] Negotiations closed and SDG 7 was adopted and incorporated in the OWG's final proposal for SDGs to the UN General Assembly as it currently stands.

III. Commentary on the Goal

The point of departure of this commentary is that the political commitments relating to sustainable energy contained in SDG 7 and related targets can add flesh and substance to the otherwise light and abstract skeleton of general international energy law and policy.[39] At the same time, SDG 7 can be upgraded from encompassing merely political commitments to making concrete legally relevant duties when connected to the general principles and norms of international energy law and policy. There is great potential for cross-fertilization between a global sustainable energy policy and a normative legal framework on energy, which in turn can be mutually reinforcing.

More specifically, there are at least three different ways in which this cross-fertilization may be achieved and become successful. SDG 7 may become an instrument to encourage all UN states to: (i) interpret and apply the guiding principles of international energy law and policy in a sustainable manner; (ii) boost the further development of a human rights approach to international energy law and policy; and (iii) use the normative framework of international energy law and policy to achieve energy efficiency at all levels of energy governance.

As this commentary departs from the allegation that SDG 7 and its targets might have an influence on the interpretation and application of international energy law,[40] it is useful to elaborate on the normative status of this goal at the outset. Like the other SDGs, SDG 7 is encapsulated in a legally non-binding resolution of the UNGA. From a purely legal point of view, this means that no international legal duties may be directly predicated on SDG 7 and its related targets. After all, when adopting SDG 7, states did not formally give their consent to be legally bound by this goal and its targets. SDG 7, like all the other SDGs, was adopted as a political aspiration[41] or, in Gupta's words, in the framework of an informal or soft law instrument of global governance.[42] At the same time, if states are influenced by SDG 7 and its related targets when applying international energy law and policy, their conduct constitutes relevant subsequent practice in

---

[38] See SDG 12 in this commentary.

[39] On the general structure and content of 'international energy law', RJ Heffron and others, 'A Treatise for Energy Law' (2018) 11(1) The Journal of World Energy Law & Business 34; K Talus, 'Internationalization of Energy Law' in K Talus (ed), *Research Handbook on International Energy Law* (Edward Elgar Publishing 2014) 3–17; D Nochevnik 'International Energy Charter: The Emergence Of The New Global Energy Governance Architecture' (2015) European Energy Review 3.

[40] A Wawryk, 'International Energy Law as an Academic Discipline' in P Babie and P Leadbeter (eds), *Law as Change: Engaging with the Life and Scholarship of Adrian Bradbrook* (University of Adelaide Press 2014) 223; RJ Zedalis, *International Energy Law Rules Governing Future Exploration, Exploitation and Use of Renewable Resources* (Routledge 2016) 15 ff.

[41] UNGA, 'Transforming Our World: The 2030 Agenda for Sustainable Development' (21 October 2015) UN Doc A/RES/70/1, para 55 (Agenda 2030).

[42] J Gupta, 'Normative Issues in Global Environmental Governance: Connecting Climate Change, Water and Forests' (2015) Journal of Agricultural and Environmental Ethics 413.

the interpretation and application of that branch of international law.[43] SDG 7 can also be used to establish an already evolving customary practice. That legally non-binding UNGA resolutions may produce this effect was already asserted, among others, by the International Court of Justice (ICJ) in its landmark Advisory Opinion on the Legality of the Threat or Use of Nuclear Weapons, when it observed that 'General Assembly resolutions can, in certain circumstances, provide evidence important for establishing the existence of a rule or the emergence of an opinio juris'.[44] It all depends on whether an intention to attribute them legal meaning may be derived from the resolution's content and the conditions of its adoption, but also from the way it influences decision making afterwards. Amongst the good examples of UNGA resolutions that have had such normative influence in the past is the Universal Declaration of Human Rights (UNDHR).[45] Even more significant for our analysis here, is the influence that the MDGs have had on international human rights law. These goals, also adopted through an UNGA resolution, have been recalled by several states as a basis for their own domestic development frameworks, and they have also been used by various international actors such as states, International Governmental Organizations (IGOs), and non-governmental organizations to measure progress.[46] It will be interesting to examine if SDG 7 and its targets has or may exercise a similar influence on international and domestic energy law and policy, and whether it has been or could be used as a tool in the interpretation and application of international energy law and policy in its evolving framework.

A. 'Sustainable' Interpretation and Application of the Guiding Principles of International Energy Law and Policy

How may SDG 7 be used to encourage UN Member States to embrace an interpretation of international energy law and policy conducive to sustainable development? The rest of this section will aim to approach this issue, by demonstrating how SDG 7 and its targets may foster the 'sustainable' interpretation and application of the guiding principles of international energy law by focusing specifically on the human rights approach to energy and by examining the importance of energy efficiency in international law.

In considering how SDG 7 may work as catalyst for a 'sustainable' interpretation and application of international energy laws the first of the principles to look at is the

---

[43] Vienna Convention on the Law of Treaties (adopted 23 May 1969, entered in force 27 January 1980) 1155 UNTS 331.

[44] ICJ 8 July 1996, Advisory Opinion on the Legality of the Threat or Use of Nuclear Weapons [1996] ICJ Rep. 226, para 70.

[45] UN General Assembly, Universal Declaration of Human Rights (adopted 10 December 1948) 217 A (III) (UDHR); about the role of soft law in international sustainable development law and an analysis of the argument that legal statements may be placed in a continuum from weak to strong legal pronunciations, MMTA Brus, 'Soft Law in Public International Law: A Pragmatic or a Principled Choice? Comparing the Sustainable Development Goals and the Paris Agreement' in P Westerman and others (eds), *Legal Validity and Soft Law* (Springer 2018); also, FAC Castaneda, 'A Call for Rethinking the Sourced of International Law: Soft Law and the Other Side of the Coin' (2013) XIII Anuario Mexicano de Derecho Internacional 55.

[46] A Jacob, 'Mind the Gap: Analyzing the Impact of Data Gap in Millennium Development Goals' (MDGs) Indicators on the Progress toward MDGs' (2017) 93 World Development 260.

COMMENTARY ON THE GOAL   519

principle of access to modern energy services, which is acknowledged in the Report of the World Commission on Environment and Development (the 'Brundtland Report').[47] Access to modern energy as well as most of the other guiding principles indicated below may also be found in similarly worded provisions in what is currently the only global normative framework of international energy law and policy, namely the Energy Charter Treaty (ECT)[48] which for this reason is our focus here.

The ECT makes a reference to the principle of access to modern energy services in article 8 in the following terms:

> The signatories underline the importance of access to sustainable, modern, affordable and cleaner energy, in particular in developing countries, which may contribute to energy poverty alleviation.
>
> To this end, the signatories confirm that they will make efforts to strengthen their cooperation and to support initiatives and partnerships at the international level, which are conducive to these goals.

This provision may be interpreted and applied in a rather straightforward sense, namely, as obliging states to do their best—a due diligence duty—to alleviate energy poverty in particular in developing countries. There is another admissible interpretation, according to which a state has a more general obligation to prevent harm caused by energy poverty. Such harm could be felt by a neighbouring country, but it might also be felt by the future generations of the same country in which the harm is caused. Numerous sources, including a 2010 report by the International Energy Agency (IEA)[49] and the Sustainable Energy for All (SE4ALL)[50] initiative suggest either implicitly or explicitly that such a rule would be desirable. But for this to be possible it is necessary to go beyond a mere literal interpretation of the provision. It is indispensable that interpreters use some imagination, and to this end SDG 7 with its associated targets might be a source of inspiration. SDG 7 places the duties generally associated with the no-harm rule in a sustainable development framework. For instance, target 7.1 that urges states to ensure universal access to affordable, reliable, and modern energy services is considered to be a means through which to improve energy accessibility for poverty mitigation in a more general sense. At the same time, it shall be acknowledged that

---

[47] UNGA, UN Conference on Environment and Development (22 December 1989) UN Doc A/RES/44/228.

[48] Energy Charter Treaty (signed 17 December 1994, entered into force 16 April 1998) (1995) 34 ILM 373. On the ECT, see A Konoplyanik and T Wälde, 'Energy Charter Treaty and its Role in International Energy' (2006) 24 Journal of Energy & Natural Resources Law 523; C Bamberger and T Waelde, 'The Energy Charter Treaty' in M Roggenkamp and others (eds), *Energy Law in Europe: National, EU and International Law and Institutions* (OUP 2007) 15 ff; K Hobér, 'The Energy Charter Treaty' (2007) 8 Journal World Investment & Trade 323: AA Konoplyanik, 'Multilateral and Bilateral Energy Investment Treaties: Do We Need a Global Solution? Energy Charter Treaty as Objective Result of Evolution of the International Energy Markets and Instruments of Investment Protection and Stimulation' in K Talus (ed), *Research Handbook on International Energy Law* (n 39) 79–123.

[49] IEA, UNDP, UNIDO, 'Energy Poverty: How to Make Modern Energy Access Universal?' (2015), 7 <http://www.globalbioenergy.org/uploads/media/1009_IEA_-_Energy_poverty.pdf> accessed 9 April 2022.

[50] On the SE4ALL initiative, see T Kaime and R Glicksman, 'An International Legal Framework for SE4ALL: Human Rights and Sustainable Development Imperatives' (2015) 38(5) Fordham International Law Journal 1405, 1409.

there is little support in practice and academic writing for such an expansive interpretation of the energy accessibility rule.

More promising seems to be the interpretation of the second fundamental principle of international energy law, the principle of sovereignty over national resources, which is codified as follows in article 18 of the ECT:

> The Contracting Parties recognise state sovereignty and sovereign rights over energy resources. They reaffirm that these must be exercised in accordance with and subject to the rules of international law.

This principle may be interpreted and applied as referring also to the interests of future generations and the environment itself, therefore moving beyond the inter-state paradigm of the no-harm rule. A crucial question is how the right of states to dispose freely of their natural resources is linked to their obligation to cooperate in energy transition.[51] At first sight, this is an aspect that the ECT has not clarified or resolved in operative terms. This is somewhat surprising given that article 2 ECT declares that the treaty's objective is to 'establish a legal framework in order to promote long-term cooperation in the energy field, based on complementarities and mutual benefits, in accordance with the objectives and principles of the Charter'. Yet, much has been written since about the link between the right of states to dispose of their natural resources and the duty to cooperate in energy matters; most scholars currently defend the view that the latter and the former are not irreconcilable, but some consider the two as separate and even clashing.[52] Against this background, target 7.a—'enhance international cooperation to facilitate access to clean energy research and technology, including renewable energy, energy efficiency and advanced and cleaner fossil-fuel technology, and promote investment in energy infrastructure and clean energy technology'—may be used to link the right of states to dispose freely of their natural resources with the duty to cooperate internationally in sustainable energy.

Moreover, article 19 of the ECT, on the right of each Contracting Party to take precautionary measures to prevent or minimize environmental degradation over energy resources, is phrased as a further elaboration of the no-harm provision. It obliges Contracting states to enforce the polluter-pays principle. Taking a more sustainable approach, this principle might be interpreted and applied as obliging states also to prevent, reduce, and control the pollution from energy production that may produce significant harm to that state's own environment, thus jeopardizing the interests of that state's own future generations. In this regard, article 19(1)(c) of the ECT complements article 18, by clarifying that Contracting Parties in pursuit of sustainable

---

[51] On the subject, N Gunningham, 'Confronting the Challenge of Energy Governance' (2012) 1(1) Transnational Environmental Law 119, 131.

[52] For more information and further references concerning this issue and writings, see J Gilbert, 'The Right to Freely Dispose of Natural Resources: Utopia or Forgotten Right?' (2013) 31 Netherlands Quarterly of Human Rights 314, 341.

development and taking into account their obligations under international agreements concerning the environment shall cooperate in the attainment of the environmental objectives of the Charter and in the field of international environmental standards for the energy cycle. There is no explicit reference to future generations or sustainable development in this provision, but reference to developing and using renewable energy sources for reducing pollution may be interpreted as referring to future uses, that is the utilization of clean energy by future generations.[53] SDG 7's targets, in particular the call for 'ensuring universal access to affordable, reliable and modern energy services' (target 7.1), the call for 'increasing substantially the share of renewable energy in the global energy mix' (target 7.2), and for 'doubling the global rate of improvement in energy efficiency' (target 7.3), may also be used to guide the cooperation envisaged in article 19. SDG 7, with its related indicators and targets, can thus help states to translate the general aim of cooperation into more detailed tasks, that, significantly, may translate a commitment to sustainable energy management and utilization into practice.

Further support for such a sustainable development interpretation and application of energy law's guiding principles can be found in the other environmental provisions of the ECT such as article 24 on the exceptions to the application of the treaty provisions. Pursuant to paragraph 2(i), the Charter provisions do not preclude any Contracting Party from adopting or enforcing any measure necessary to protect human, animal or plant life or health and/or any measure 'designed to benefit investors who are aboriginal people or socially or economically disadvantaged individuals or groups' (article 24, paragraph 2(iii)).

Of equal importance to the first two guiding principles mentioned above is a third and more substantial principle, the principle of energy efficiency. We find this principle being codified in various provisions of the ECT Protocol on energy efficiency and related environmental matters such as article 4 on the division of responsibility and coordination and article 7 on the promotion of energy efficient technology.[54]

This principle to manage energy efficiently surfaced in particular in the OWG debates on SDG 7, where a balance was sought between ensuring energy efficiency and environmental protection.

Lastly, SDG 7 targets could be used by states as a source of inspiration for the modernization of the ECT as well as for elaboration of an international binding Convention on energy management.

---

[53] According to the International Renewable Energy Agency (IRENA), renewable energy resources are all forms of energy produced from renewable sources in a sustainable manner, including bioenergy, geothermal energy, ocean energy, solar energy, and wind energy: IRENA, 'Electricity Storage Technology Brief' (IRENA 2012) <http://www.irena.org/DocumentDownloads/Publications/IRENA-ETSAP%20Tech%20Brief%20E18% 20Electricity-Storage.pdf> accessed 4 April 2022.

[54] S Bruce and S Stephenson, 'SDG 7 on Sustainable Energy for All: Contributions of International Law, Policy and Governance' (2016) <http://dx.doi.org/10.2139/ssrn.2824835> accessed 4 April 2022 recalling that the primary objectives of the ECT's Energy Efficiency Protocol are to promote energy efficiency which encourages environmental benefits through adoption of a list of policy principles which facilitates SDG 7.

B. The Further Development of a Human Rights Approach to International Energy Law and Policy

Energy is an indispensable prerequisite for the realization of human needs for all people in the world.[55] Yet, in the context of human rights law, the promulgation of a universal human right to energy, or a human right to energy services, is hard to find. Article 14 (2)(h) of the Convention on the Elimination of All Forms of Discrimination against Women (CEDAW) is the sole provision in an international human rights instrument that explicitly recognizes a 'right to electricity supply' for women in rural areas as part of the right to adequate standard of living with the purpose of eliminating gender discrimination in the participation and enjoyment of the benefits of rural development.[56] At most, access to energy can be conceptualized as a correlative of a number of socioeconomic rights[57]—the right to an adequate standard of living (article 25 UDHR; article 11 ICESCR); to the highest attainable standard of health (article 12 ICESCR), and crucially the right to development (article 1(1) Declaration on the Right to Development).[58] The nexus between human rights and energy remains underdeveloped even more so in international energy law and practice, including in the recent SE4ALL initiative which is not embedded on a binding international regulatory framework.[59] Could SDG 7 and its targets be used to develop such a nexus?

Although SDG 7 may be narrowly perceived as primarily environmental, it is in fact a critical measure of overall progress of the 2030 Agenda and the seventeen SDGs, which are anchored in human rights.[60] Considered in this way, SDG 7 and its targets may be of help in triggering human development and in bringing a human rights approach to international energy law and policy to prominence. SDG 7 thereby may complement

---

[55] AJ Bradbrook, 'Access to Energy Services in a Human Rights Framework' <https://www.un.org/esa/sustdev/sdissues/energy/op/parliamentarian_forum/bradbrook_hr.pdf> accessed 7 April 2022, 3–6: 'Although energy itself is not a basic human need, it is critical for the fulfilment of all needs. Lack of access to diverse and affordable energy services means that the basic needs of many people are not being met'; A Reddy (n 4); Kaime and Glicksman, 'An International Legal Framework for SE4ALL' (n 50), 1423–30.

[56] Convention on Elimination of All Forms of Discrimination against Women (18 December 1979, entered in force 3 September 1981) 1249 UNTS 13.

[57] J Sing-hang Ngai, 'Energy as a Human Right in Armed Conflict: A Question of Universal Need, Survival, and Human Dignity' (2012) 37(2) Brooklyn Journal of International Law; EB Sacristán, 'Is there a Human Right to Energy' in MR Dahlan and others (eds), *Research Handbook of Energy, Law and Ethics* (Edward Elgar Publishing 2022).

[58] UDHR (n 45); International Covenant on Economic Social Cultural Rights (adopted 16 December 1966, entered into force 3 January 1976) 993 UNTS 3; UNGA, Declaration on the Right to Development (4 December 1986) UN Doc A/RES/41/128; ComICESCR, 'General Comment No 4' (13 December 1991) E/1992/23, para 8(b): 'All beneficiaries of the right to adequate housing should have sustainable access to natural and common resources, safe drinking water, *energy for cooking, heating and lighting*' (emphasis added). Access to electricity is considered an indicator of housing rights according to the Special Rapporteur on The Right to Adequate Housing, Mr Rajindar Sachar, in his final report to the Commission on Human Rights (12 July 1995) UN Doc E/CN.4/Sub.2/1995/12, para 99.

[59] Kaime and Glicksman, 'An International Legal Framework for SE4ALL' (n 50).

[60] Agenda 2030 (n 41) para 10: 'The new Agenda is guided by the purposes and principles of the Charter of the United Nations ... is grounded in the Universal Declaration of Human Rights, international human rights treaties, the Millennium Declaration ....'

the evolving scholarship[61] on the human rights-based approach to the use and management of energy in a similar fashion as the human rights approach has permeated international climate change law and environmental law more generally. In turn, such development will also feed into the approach taken to the transition to cleaner and more sustainable energy sources. Therefore states' human rights obligations and obligations under sustainable development law will also be applicable to energy matters. By way of example, energy infrastructure projects would be designed and implemented on a coherent and principled basis pursuant to states' obligations to conduct environmental impact assessments; to inform, consult, and, where necessary, obtain the consent of individuals, especially vulnerable groups such as women or Indigenous communities, as the beneficiaries of the project; to adhere to the principle of intra- and intergenerational equity and the principle of integration of environmental, human, and economic rights in development—to name a few. Therefore, not only will the basic needs of individuals be met but the latter will be empowered by participating in the formation of energy infrastructure policies and outcomes, the environment will be protected, and development stakeholders (primarily governments but also private actors) can be held accountable against legally binding obligations they bear.[62] Distilling human rights and sustainable development obligations into the more traditional approach to energy governance may alter the latter, which exclusively focuses on the improvement of energy efficiency, renewable energy capacity, and universal access to energy services—defined by numerous legal authors as the three 'pillars' of the current international energy law regime.[63] Possibly, SDG 7 and its targets might become the 'constitutional ingredients' of a whole new normative regime for the management and use of sustainable energies. In this way they can complement the ongoing development of a human rights and sustainable development approach to energy in the contexts of the UN's SE4ALL initiative and the EU treaty.

C. The Increase of Energy-Efficient Technologies in the Management of Clean Energy

The role of energy efficient technologies in national electricity systems is an important aspect to comment on. On this issue, the European Communities (EC) treaty is largely silent with the only exception of article 7 of the Protocol on Energy Efficiency and

---

[61] C-W Shyu, 'A Framework for 'Right to Energy' to meet UN SDG 7: Policy Implications to meet Basic Human Energy Needs, Eradicate Energy Poverty, Enhance Energy Justice, and Uphold Energy Democracy' (2021) 79 Energy Research & Social Science <https://www.sciencedirect.com/science/article/abs/pii/S2214629621002929> accessed 7 April 2022; Sing-hang Ngai (n 57) 615 et seq.

[62] Kaime and Glicksman (n 50) 1434 et seq; SR Tully, 'The Contribution of Human Rights to Universal Energy Access' (2006) 4(3) Northwestern Journal of International Human Rights 518.

[63] On these pillars, see, eg T Kaime, International Energy Policy for Development: Human Rights and Sustainable Development Law Imperatives' in P Cullet (ed) *Research Handbook on Law, Environment and the Global South* (Edward Elgar Publishing 2019) 305–21.

524 SDG 7

Related Environmental Aspects.[64] Article 7 provides that 'Contracting Parties shall encourage commercial trade and cooperation in energy efficient and environmentally sound technologies, energy related services and management practices'.

This provision does not contain a duty of states to use or increase the use of energy efficient technologies in their electricity systems; it only commits Contracting States to encourage and facilitate the use of these technologies.

No-one would question the utility that would arise from an obligation to use energy-efficient technologies under international energy law. The Beijing Declaration on Renewable Energy for Sustainable Development, which was adopted with a very broad majority at the Beijing International Renewable Energy Conference in 2005 (BIREC), indirectly confirms this when it insists on: 'the need for ... resources, both public and private, for investment in ... energy efficiency, including the use of innovative financing mechanisms, such as loan guarantees and the Clean Development Mechanism (CDM), and market-based instruments that can leverage scarce public funds'. It is thus clear that there is a need and also a trend towards the use of efficient technologies to improve energy efficiency.[65]

But is there a duty, under international energy law, to use efficient technologies to improve energy efficiency? It appears that there are no legal sources supporting this conclusion. However, if SDG 7 calls upon all states to double the global rate of improvement in energy efficiency, then this gives us confidence to interpret article 7 of the Energy Protocol—and analogously worded provisions elsewhere—as implicitly recognizing a duty to use efficient technologies to improve energy efficiency at the global, regional, and domestic levels. Again, there is nothing *contra legem* about such interpretation, although a textual reading of article 7 of the Energy Protocol gives little support for it. SDG 7.b, calling upon all states to 'expand infrastructure and upgrade technology for supplying modern and sustainable energy services for all in developing countries, in particular Least Developed Countries, Small Island Developing States, and land-locked developing countries, in accordance with their respective programmes of support', does point us in the right direction. Together with developments elsewhere, as demonstrated in the World Energy Outlook Special Report of 2013 'Redrawing the Energy-Climate Map', SDG 7.3, if implemented at the domestic level, may trigger the development of a new international legal duty requiring states to use efficient technologies to improve energy efficiency.[66] The indicators developed to guide states further in the implementation of target 7.b are also of assistance here.

---

[64] (1995) 34 ILM 446.
[65] Beijing International Renewable Energy Conference 2005, Official Post-Conference Report <https://issuu.com/peterantell/docs/beijing/9> accessed 4 April 2022.
[66] 'WEO-2013 Special Report: Redrawing the Energy Climate Map' (IEA 2013) <https://www.iea.org/reports/redrawing-the-energy-climate-map> accessed 4 April 2022.

IV. Commentary on Targets

A. Target 7.1 By 2030, ensure universal access to affordable, reliable and modern energy for all

1. Sources of the Target

Due to the importance of energy infrastructure and services for economic and human development but also against the background of environmental costs, including the detrimental impact on the climate, the first target of SDG 7 raises access to energy services to a key policy objective of developed and developing states alike. Target 7.1 rests within a number of policy documents that marked the recognition of energy as a fundamental attribute of sustainable development. As briefly mentioned, the Brundtland Report was the first to devote an entire chapter to energy, elaborating on its relationship with development and the environment but it was not until the Energy Charter Treaty[67] and the World Energy Assessment report[68] that *access* to energy gained prominence in the intergovernmental process on sustainable development and the realization of development goals. In the wake of the World Summit on Sustainable Development (WSSD), the *ad hoc* Open-ended Intergovernmental Group of Experts on Energy and Sustainable Development described accessibility of energy as a development challenge and outlined its qualitative characteristics as a means contributing to poverty reduction: 'Improving accessibility of energy implies finding ways and means by which energy services can be delivered reliably, affordably, in an economically viable, socially acceptable and environmentally sound manner.'[69] Similarly, the Water, Energy, Health, Agriculture, and Biodiversity (WEHAB) working group,[70] reporting on energy distinguished three action areas in the context of access to energy and modern energy services which it complemented with indicative targets and proposed activities for implementation:[71]

Action Area 1: Reduce poverty by providing access to modern energy services in rural and peri-urban areas

Action Area 2: Improve health and reduce environmental impacts of traditional fuels and coking devices

Action Area 3: Improve access to affordable and diversified energy sources in Africa

---

[67] See Section III.A, this chapter.

[68] UNDP, *World Energy Assessment* (n 4).

[69] ECOSOC, 'Report of the Ad Hoc Open-ended Intergovernmental Groups of Experts on energy and Sustainable Development' (20 March 2001) E/CN.17/2001/15, para 10 <https://documents-dds-ny.un.org/doc/UNDOC/GEN/N01/294/55/PDF/N0129455.pdf?OpenElement> accessed 4 April 2022 (the report was submitted to the 9th session of the Commission on Sustainable Development (CSD-9)).

[70] An initiative by the then UN Secretary General, Kofi Annan, to study and give impetus to the topics of water, energy, health, agriculture, and biodiversity that had been identified as key focus areas for a coherent approach to the international policy on sustainable development.

[71] WEHAB Working Groups, 'A Framework for Action on Energy' (2022), 16–17 <https://www.gdrc.org/sustdev/un-desd/wehab_energy.pdf> accessed 5 April 2022.

The Johannesburg Plan of Implementation (JPOI) endorsed the above-mentioned areas and elaborated on the actions needed to materialize energy accessibility more broadly, which ranged from energy sector reforms through national energy policies and regulatory reforms to the improvement of rural electrification systems, the use of renewables and modern biomass, and of course international cooperation and public–private partnerships so that access to energy services reaches the poor and improves the living standards of the most marginalized.[72] Indeed, the WSSD was particularly successful in bringing energy issues to the forefront, not least because it explicitly connected the availability and accessibility of energy with the realization of the Millennium Development Goals. However, the fact that no time-bound target for increasing access to energy was set,[73] unlike poverty or access to safe drinking water, was a missed opportunity to embed energy goals in the international development discourse deeper.

The UN Secretary General's SE4All initiative remedied the omission. It set 2030 as the deadline to materialize three interrelated and mutually reinforcing goals, namely: (i) to ensure universal access to modern energy services; (ii) to double the rate of improvement in energy efficiency; and (iii) to double the share of renewable energy in the global energy mix. The identification in the formulation of the objectives with the first three targets ultimately adopted under SDG 7 is noticeable. On the occasion also of the International Year of Energy, as the year 2012 was declared,[74] the initiative aimed at catalysing action-oriented partnerships among governments, the private sector, and civil society for tackling energy issues. To this end, it significantly systematized stakeholder's efforts by launching specific programmes of action (currently twelve)[75] and linking implementation to monitoring through data and reporting platforms.[76] In this respect, accountability and measurement of progress became fundamental pillars of the SE4All's mission. Corroborative to the thrust SE4All gave to international energy policy-making is the reference to it in 'The Future We Want'. Therein states acknowledged the initiative's contribution to the address of energy-related challenges and expressed their determination to cooperate within that framework in order to provide effective solutions in accordance with individual national circumstances, development aspirations, and capacities.[77]

To conclude, the importance of energy access for development was gradually established over the time span of several decades, especially since the late-1980s. The process leading to the incorporation of energy into the development agenda was top-down, as demonstrated by the outcome documents of core UN Summits and UN SG's initiatives.

---

[72] Plan of Implementation of the World Summit on Sustainable Development (2002), paras 9, 20, 21 <https://www.un.org/esa/sustdev/documents/WSSD_POI_PD/English/WSSD_PlanImpl.pdf> accessed 5 April 2022.

[73] Exceptionally a specific target was set for Africa: to ensure access to energy for at least 35 per cent of the population within twenty years; ibid para 56(j)(i).

[74] UNGA, 'International Year of Sustainable energy for All' (16 February 2011) UN Doc A/RES/65/151.

[75] SEforALL, 'Programs' <https://www.seforall.org/impact-areas/programmes> accessed 5 April 2022.

[76] UN, The Secretary General's High-Level Group on Sustainable Energy for All: Report of the Co-Chairs (2012), 13 <https://digitallibrary.un.org/record/785920?ln=en> accessed 5 April 2022.

[77] UNGA (11 September 2012) UN Doc A/RES/66/288, para 127 <https://www.un.org/ga/search/view_doc.asp?symbol=A/RES/66/288&Lang=E> accessed 6 April 2022.

This effort culminated with the adoption of the SDGs, which signify a consensus on priority energy matters despite stakeholders' differentiation on certain aspects expressed during the OWG sessions.

2. Empirical Analysis

Target 7.1 is measured by two indicators, data for which are compiled by the World Bank Group in cooperation with SDG 7 custodian agencies, namely the IEA, the IRENA, and the World Health Organization (WHO).

a) Indicator 7.1.1: Proportion of population with electricity access

A fundamental energy source that contributes to economic and social progress and influences key development indicators such as health, food security, income generation, poverty reduction, etc is electricity. At a basic level, thus, target 7.1.1 focuses on the proportion of population with electricity access, disaggregated by urban and rural access rates per country, regional, and global classifications. For the purposes of monitoring access to electricity only local providers, solar systems, mini-grids, and stand-alone systems are considered as primary sources of lighting. Data are collected from national household surveys and censuses and target the demand side of access rates given that such value captures population's real-life experience in accessing electricity. Nonetheless, both the collection of data and what household surveys capture present limitations. The latter are not conducted on a regular basis while information about rural areas is sometimes inaccurate. Consequently, having a clear picture of access trends becomes difficult. More importantly, though, household surveys do not consider the quality of electricity supply. For a target that aims at universal access to affordable and reliable energy, absence of information about the quality and the cost of energy supply leaves the qualitative attributes of target 7.1 unaddressed.[78] To this end, the World Bank Group's new methodological approach, the Multi-Tier Framework for Measuring Energy Access, aspires to rectify the gap. As the technical report highlights, defining access to energy as being synonymous to household electricity connection or the installation of an electric pole in a village does not take into consideration the quantity and quality of electricity nor questions of affordability and the legality of power connection. Moreover, limiting the source of evidence collection on energy access to household electricity access, leaves outside the scope of measurement access to energy for work facilities or community spaces, which is also important for understanding the relationship between energy supply and socio-economic progress. The report, therefore, emphasizes that monitoring energy access should encompass access to energy supply and services as well as the usability and actual use of energy across households, productive units, and community infrastructure. Accordingly, improvements in the status of energy access should be attested when users experience improvement in

---

[78] UN DESA, Statistics Division, 'SDG Indicators-Metadata Repository' (SDG 7.1 metadata) <https://unstats.un.org/sdgs/metadata/> accessed 10 February 2022.

528   SDG 7

the qualitative attributes of energy supply and not only when they switch from 'not-connected to electricity to connected'.[79]

Until such methodology is fully integrated in the computation method for data on indicator 7.1.1, the empirical analysis of progress on target 7.1 draws upon the databases produced by each custodian agency (eg the World Bank Group's Global Electrification database, the WHO's Global Household Energy Database, IRENA's Public Investment Database, etc). The joint energy progress report of SDG 7 custodian agencies for the year 2021 builds upon the aforementioned databases. Reporting on indicator 7.1.1, the organizations submit that 90 per cent of the global population had access to electricity in 2019, which translates to 759 million people without electricity compared to 1.2 billion nine years ago. However, progress across regions is unequal. It comes to no surprise that Sub-Saharan Africa lags behind most development goals and suffers the largest access deficit, since less than half of the population has electricity access. Positive developments come from Bangladesh, Kenya, and Uganda, which are among the twenty countries with the largest populations lacking electricity access but that have achieved access growth rates of 3 per cent annually since 2010. Looking at disaggregated data between rural and urban areas, disparities are concentrated in the former although access rates in rural areas improved at a much quicker pace than in urban over the two-year period (2017–2019).[80] Statistics from the SG's 2020 SDG progress report corroborates this: only 39 per cent of rural regions in LDCs and 46.2 per cent in landlocked developing countries had electricity access in 2018.[81] In 2019, rural areas counted for 84 per cent of the global population being unserved. With COVID-19 having disrupted the overall development progress, electrification rates should rise from 0.74 to 0.9 percentage points per year if target 7.1 is to be achieved.[82] Africa saw 4 per cent increase in populations without electricity and all countries are financially strained. Access to energy could improve, according to the IEA, through a sustainable recovery plan for the energy sector that would stimulate investment in electricity networks. Indeed, finance for energy has not been managed properly.[83] For example, annual investment of $4.4 billion is necessary to close access gaps in clean cooking by 2030, yet an estimate of 1 per cent has been properly directed to appropriate solutions.[84] Directing appropriate finance to modernizing grids, accelerating the use of renewables, and reducing

---

[79] ESMAP, 'Beyond Connections: Energy Access Redefined' (July 2015), 1–2 <https://openknowledge.worldbank.org/bitstream/handle/10986/24368/Beyond0connect0d000technical0report.pdf?sequence=1&isAllowed=y>; for an explanation of the attributes of electricity access and the tiers, Multi-tier Framework, 'Electricity' <https://mtfenergyaccess.esmap.org/methodology/electricity> websites accessed 13 February 2022.

[80] IEA, IRENA, UNSD, WB, WHO, 'Tracking SDG7: The Energy Progress Report 2021' 4–5 <https://trackingsdg7.esmap.org/data/files/download-documents/2021_tracking_sdg7_report.pdf> accessed 13 February 2020.

[81] ECOSOC, 'Progress towards the Sustainable Development Goals: Report of the Secretary-General—Supplementary Information' (28 April 2020) UN Doc E/2020/57, 79.

[82] 'Energy Progress Report 2021' (n 80) 5.

[83] IEA, 'Energy Access: Achieving Modern Energy for all by 2030 Remains Possible Despite Pandemic-related Delays' <https://www.iea.org/topics/energy-access> accessed 13 February 2022.

[84] SEforAll and Climate Policy Initiative, 'Energising Finance: Understanding the Landscape' (22 October 2019) 26, 75–78 <https://www.seforall.org/system/files/2019-11/EF-2019-UL-SEforALL-w.pdf> accessed 13 February 2022.

disruptions in energy supply are paramount for connecting 100 million people/year to energy sources by 2030.

b) Indicator 7.1.2: Proportion of population with primary reliance on clean fuels and technology

The second indicator of target 7.1 pays more attention to the quality characteristics of energy consumption. As already stressed in the previous section, access to energy should encompass access to services and consider how they improve human development. Target 7.1.2 contributes to this objective by monitoring household energy use in relation to the type of fuel and the technology employed for services such as heating, cooking, and lighting. Truly, the aforementioned services are vital for individual's living and represent a large share of household energy utilization. Energy poverty leads to unsustainable practices such as the combustion of solid fuels (ie wood, charcoal, and biomass) that are particularly polluting and the use of energy inefficient appliances (eg stoves, lamps). Not only are these detrimental for the environment but they also have a negative imprint on human health.[85] Remarkably, high levels of household (indoor) air pollution cause over 4 million deaths annually; more than tuberculosis, HIV, and malaria combined.[86] By measuring thus the adoption of clean fuels and technology for the aforementioned services, indicator 7.1.2 provides evidence for the transition to *modern* energy services of target 7.1 and informs indirectly the health-related target SDG 3.9 that calls for the reduction of deaths and illnesses from hazardous chemicals and air, water, and soil pollution and contamination.[87]

Currently worldwide progress on access to clean cooking is minimal. The most recent data (2019) demonstrate that 2.6 billion people do not have access to clean fuels and technology given that access rates were at 9 per cent only in the last decade (66 per cent compared to 57 per cent in 2010 had access to clean cooking). Comparably, premature deaths due to household air pollution are estimated to 2.5 million. In developing Asia seven times more people lack clean cooking access than electricity. China has marked significant progress in the reduction of biomass and kerosene following the development of natural gas infrastructure, while India has promoted liquefied petroleum gas (LPG) programmes to replace polluting solid fuels. By contrast, the situation in Sub-Saharan Africa remains worrisome in light of the continuous rise of those without access to clean cooking. Almost 500,000 deaths per year are linked to household air pollution, with women and children suffering the most. In parallel, deforestation is an imminent risk as a result of the unsustainable harvesting of fuelwood. Unsurprisingly, the pandemic has affected worldwide progress on this front. Yet, rapid population growth poses another challenge. These two parameters combined suggest that by 2030, 2.4 billion people will remain without access to clean cooking facilities. Pursuant to policy scenarios by the IEA, this is 60 million more compared to 2019 estimates.[88] The

---

[85] WHO, *Guidelines for Indoor Air Quality: Selected Pollutants* (WHO 2010).
[86] UNSD, 'Metadata for Target 7.1.2', 4.a.
[87] See the commentary on SDG 3, Chapter 3 in this book.
[88] IEA, 'SDG7: Data and Projections—Access to Clean Cooking' (*IEA* 2020) <https://www.iea.org/reports/sdg7-data-and-projections/access-to-clean-cooking#abstract> accessed 13 February 2022.

530 SDG 7

consequences of a stagnant recovery from the COVID-19 pandemic and the divide in access to clean cooking that is created by population growth means that achievement of target 7.1 by 2030 is off track.[89]

3. Implementation Efforts at International/Domestic Level

SDG 7 was subjected to close review at the High-Level Political Forum (HLPF) in 2018 and countries were given the opportunity to elaborate on the specific policy measures they have taken to connect more households to the energy grid and provide them with affordable, reliable, less-polluting energy and to facilitate its distribution through technologically upgraded appliances.

Various countries faced issues with the supply of energy which was either unreliable or at risk due to the geographical peculiarities of the country (eg archipelagic states such as the Bahamas) or because of country financial deficits and poor revenue collection, as was the case of Albania. The country's Energy Strategy 2018–2030 focuses on the quality aspects of target 7.1. The government applies a support scheme for poor households by subsidizing increased electricity prices; it has reduced power cuts and has managed to improve the financial consolidation of the energy sector after the unsuccessful privatization of the national distribution operator that led to the accumulation of debt by the company and its administration. Concluding an agreement with the World Bank, the government nationalized the distribution company and inaugurated further investments in the energy sector to extend the country's energy-generating capacity.[90]

Greece has implemented a reduced Social Residential Tariff for electricity to support vulnerable social groups such as the long-term unemployed, families living on low-income, and people with disabilities.[91] In the Latin American region, Uruguay has become the first country to report full access to electricity. Electrification rates reach 99.7 per cent and 98.4 per cent of the population has access to clean technologies and fuels. Nevertheless, access problems remain in rural areas and a proportion of socio-economically vulnerable households in urban areas still need regular and permanent connectivity. The government aspires to solve these issues through programmes such as the rural Electrification Agreement and the Utility Basket.[92] The positive development of access to electricity in social facilities is indicative of the programmes' success. More specifically, all 1,090 schools in rural areas of the country have access to electricity, a goal that has been achieved through investment in solar photovoltaic panels and grid systems.[93]

---

[89] SEforAll, 'SEforAll Analysis of SDG7 Progress–2021' (11 August 2021) <https://www.seforall.org/data-stories/seforall-analysis-of-sdg7-progress-2021> accessed 13 February 2022.

[90] HLPF 2018, VNR Albania, 41–42 <https://sustainabledevelopment.un.org/content/documents/20257ALBANIA_VNR_2018_FINAL2.pdf> accessed 13 February 2022.

[91] HLPF 2018, VNR Greece, 10. <https://sustainabledevelopment.un.org/content/documents/19378Greece_VNR_Greece_2018_pdf_FINAL_140618.pdf> accessed 13 February 2022.

[92] HLPF 2018, VNR Uruguay, 45 <https://sustainabledevelopment.un.org/content/documents/20645OPP_Sintesis_ENG_pagxpag.pdf> accessed 13 February 2022.

[93] HLPF 2018, Synthesis report of VNRs, 42 <https://sustainabledevelopment.un.org/content/documents/210732018_VNRs_Synthesis_compilation_11118_FS_BB_Format_FINAL_cover.pdf> accessed 13 February 2022.

On a regional level finally, the new Regional Electricity Access and Battery-Energy Storage Technologies (BEST) Project approved by the World Bank Group will expand access to grid electricity that will reach over 1 million people, enhance the stability of power supply for another 3.5 million and increase the integration of renewable energy in the West Africa Power Pool for the countries belonging in the Economic Community of West African States (ECOWAS).[94]

4. Critique

Target 7.1 captures the core challenge populations, especially in developing countries and those residing in rural or remote areas, are faced with. Energy, although not a human need itself, is the driver of human progress and an enabler of human well-being.[95] It thus has instrumental value as a means to achieve other goods or, as Amartya Sen would argue, energy is the means to enlarge people's choices, their capabilities, and freedom to lead a life they value.[96] On this account, providing access to energy sources to everyone across regions and within a country can be evaluated from the standpoint of the human development hypothesis and the anthropocentric viewpoint of development. The people-centred nature of Agenda 2030 and its foundation on the principles of universality, equity, and justice justifies this assertion after all. It is against this background that attempts to embed the facilitation of access to energy to states' human rights obligations have emerged. Crucially, access to energy resonates within individual rights of all three generations of rights: as a state's positive obligation in the context of the right to life; to an adequate standard of living; to education; to the right to work; to the right to development, to name a few.[97] A human rights approach to energy access is particularly relevant to developing countries where 'a right to be free from poverty' (in its multidimensional nature)[98] seems more imperative, rendering therefore energy poverty a human rights issue as well. Complementarily, connecting energy access to the objectives of sustainable development, and fundamentally to the concept's normative underpinning—that is, intra- and inter-generational equity; the distribution of the benefits of development within and among present and future generations in a fair and equitable manner (ie distributive justice)—ensuring universal access to energy becomes an aspect of 'energy justice' that facilitates sustainable development, and

[94] WBG, 'WBG Provides $465 Million to Expand energy Access and Renewable Energy Integration in West Africa' (10 June 2021) <https://www.worldbank.org/en/news/press-release/2021/06/10/world-bank-group-provides-465-million-to-expand-energy-access-and-renewable-energy-integration-in-west-africa>; more about the project: <https://projects.worldbank.org/en/projects-operations/project-detail/P167569> accessed 13 February 2022.

[95] L Guruswamy, 'Energy Justice and Sustainable Development' (2010) 21 Colorado Journal of International Environmental Law and Policy 231, 233.

[96] A Sen, *Development as Freedom* (OUP 1991).

[97] A Bradbrook, 'Achieving Access to Modern Energy Services: A Study of Legal Strategies' in Y Omorogbe and AO Ordor (eds) *Ending Africa's Energy Deficit and the Law: Achieving Sustainable Energy for All in Africa* (OUP 2018).

[98] ComICESCR, Poverty and the International Covenant on Economic, Social and Cultural Rights, statement to the Third United Nations Conference on the Least Developed Countries (10 May 2001) E/C.12/2001/10, 8: poverty is 'a human condition characterized by sustained or chronic deprivation of the resources, capabilities, choices, security and power necessary for the enjoyment of an adequate standard of living and other civil, cultural, economic, political and social rights'.

predominantly the needs of the poor.[99] Although there is no single school of thought giving substance to and explaining 'energy justice',[100] thus allowing a uniform application of theory to international energy policy that can capture the needs of everyone everywhere, the concept may nevertheless provide an ethical foundation for sustainable development and a way to address the so-called energy trilemma[101]—accessibility, affordability, and sustainability—in this context.

In light of the above, successful implementation of SDG 7.1 requires pragmatic solutions to energy accessibility guided by ethical considerations and taking into account social and environmental considerations. For a holistic approach to this primary energy challenge, policies ought to go beyond a definition of access to energy that is determined by the proportion of population with access to electricity and primary household reliance on clean energy and technology for cooking, which are currently the two determinants of access to energy based on indicators 7.1 and 7.2. Access should encompass on-grid and off-grid power connections; supply that is regular and absent outages, and is affordable and adequate; improved technologies such as efficient cook stoves and provision for energy stacking. In other words, energy access will have been achieved when an 'end user has the ability to utilise an energy supply that can be used for desired energy services', broadly speaking.[102] Therefore, energy access is interlinked with the benefits of public- and household-level energy services.[103] A broader understanding of energy access based on ethical considerations would also promote accessibility in an equitable and non-discriminatory manner, especially towards women and the youth, as these groups bear the burden of energy poverty the most.[104] Importantly as well, it will not downplay environmental justice. It is on these grounds, namely by mainstreaming the principles of equality, distributive justice, fairness, universality, and environmental sustainability, that individual-centred concerns about access to energy may be integrated and balanced with the objective of environmental protection and the inversion of climate change.

[99] Guruswamy (n 95).

[100] M Dahlan and G Rochette, 'Energy Between Justice and Ethics: A Re-classification of Theoretical Lenses for a Forward Looking Epistemology' in M Dahlan and others (eds), *Research Handbook on Energy, Law and Ethics* (n 57). Commenting on the attributes of the different trends in energy justice theory, the authors find the concept of 'energy ethics' more appropriate to providing the ethical foundation for resolving the energy trilemma or any other challenge in the field of energy.

[101] There are different variations of the trilemma. Interestingly, energy justice is used to describe the energy 'quadrilemma' that adds individuals' participation in the decision-making about energy policies, TM Mose, 'Energy and Climate: The Dilemma, Trilemma, and Quadrilemma' (*ICPAC*, 17 November 2020) <https://icpac. medium.com/energy-and-climate-the-dilemma-trilemma-and-quadrilemma-839a8d657369> accessed 7 April 2022.

[102] SE4All, Global Tracking Framework (vol 3, World Bank 2013) 289. There is no single definition of access to energy. The IEA defines it as access to reliable and affordable access to the energy services necessary to supply the basic needs of daily life (IEA, 'World Energy Outlook Methodology (2019) <www.iea.org/energyaccess/methodol ogy> accessed 8 April 2022.

[103] These are the product of the entire energy system (primary energy sources, energy-related technologies, infrastructure, and labour combined), RJ Heffron and others, 'A Treatise for Energy Law' (n 39) 34.

[104] W Khaemba and A Kingiri, 'Access to Renewable Energy Resources: A Gender and Inclusivity Perspective' in WL Filho and others (eds), *Encyclopedia of the UN Sustainable Development Goals: Affordable and Clean* Energy (Springer 2021) 25.

B. Target 7.2 By 2030, increase substantially the share of renewable energy in the global energy mix

1. Sources of the Target

The discussion about the advantages of renewable energy sources for development and the environment is not new. As early as 1981 participants in the UN Conference of New and Renewable Sources of Energy stressed the importance of advancing new and renewable sources of energy as a means for meeting more effectively demand for economic and social development and called for economy's transition to these resources.[105] The respective Committee that was established purported to monitor implementation of the Nairobi Program of Action, which laid out a framework for research and development (R&D) regarding renewable resources, the transfer, adaptation, and application of mature technologies, the mobilization of financial resources to this end, and institutional cooperation.[106] Lack of political will resulted in the failure of the Commission's mandate. Yet, neither the idea of renewable energy resources as the centrepiece of sustainable development nor the necessity of a monitoring organization was abandoned. The Brundtland Commission acknowledged the contribution of various energy sources to the future energy mix worldwide but cautioned that each comes with its own economic, health, and environmental costs, benefits, and risk-factors that interact with global priorities. As the Commission blatantly put it: 'choosing an energy strategy inevitably means choosing an environmental strategy'.[107]

Even so, scholars are critical of international diplomacy on energy for its failure to promote renewable energy under binding international laws.[108] Bruce has explained the rigid political will for a universally agreed regulatory framework for renewable energy by reference to states' 'anxieties about sovereignty over natural resources and energy security policies'.[109] Correctly, the JPOI was the first soft law instrument to have substantially influenced international energy policy. It proposed specific actions for transition to more sustainable energy sources and contained a goal that resembles in wording SDG 7.2:[110]

---

[105] (17 December 1981) UN Doc A/RES/36/193.

[106] ibid para 6.

[107] Report of the World Commission on Environment and Development: Our Common Future, Chapter 7, para 3 <https://sustainabledevelopment.un.org/content/documents/5987our-common-future.pdf> accessed 17 September 2022.

[108] D Hodas, 'International Law and Sustainable Energy: A Portrait of Failure' in J Benidickson and others, *Environmental Law and Sustainability after Rio* (Edward Elgar Publishing 2011); S Bruce, 'International Law and Renewable Energy: Facilitating Sustainable Energy for All' (2013) 14 Melbourne Journal of International Law; Khaime and Glicksman (n 50) 1413–14.

[109] Bruce (n 108) 5–10. However, the author explains how contemporary understanding of these concepts may actually promote energy cooperation for renewables, especially after large investments by the WBG and the IEA in renewable energy projects.

[110] JPOI (n 72) para 9, 20.

534 SDG 7

§9 ...

b) Improve access to modern biomass technologies and fuelwood sources and supplies and commercialise biomass operations, including the use of agricultural residues, in rural areas and where such practices are sustainable;

c) Promote a sustainable use of biomass and, as appropriate, other renewable energies through improvement of current patterns of use, such as management of resources, more efficient use of fuelwood and new or improved products and technologies;

d) Support the transition to the cleaner use of liquid and gaseous fossil fuels, where considered more environmentally sound, socially acceptable and cost-effective...

§20 ...

c) Develop and disseminate alternative energy technologies with the aim of giving a greater share of the energy mix to renewable energies ...

e) ... substantially increase the global share of renewable energy sources with the objective of increasing its contribution to total energy supply ...

Following the World Summit on Sustainable Development, soft law continued to dominate renewable energy with the World Solar Program[111] and SE4All being the most prominent initiatives for action in the field. Against this background, the absence of renewable energy-based approach to climate change through legally binding provisions in the United Nations Framework Convention of Climate Change (UNFCCC) and the Kyoto Protocol was considered the biggest failure. Apart from the Preamble to the Convention which draws a link between developing countries and energy as a means for their economic growth, a reference to renewable energy in the UNFCCC may be indirectly read in article 4(1)(c) whereby states are called upon to cooperate in the development of technologies that help reduce emissions.[112] Similarly, the Kyoto Protocol only refers to renewable energy in article 2(1)(a) which enumerates (non-exhaustively) policy choices for states in Annex B in their effort to substantiate their obligation to put domestic policies in place for the reduction of GHG emissions. Developments in climate change regulation after the adoption of the Paris Agreement have moved along the same lines, although the agreement has catalytically pushed forward international pledges for reducing emissions until net zero is reached by 2050 and has thus promoted the transition to renewable energy as an imperative if the bet to reverse climate change is to be won.

As inferred from the above, energy issues have emerged on the side-lines of the broader discourse about sustainable development. There has not been a thematic discussion exclusively about energy at the international level under the auspices of the UN. Thereafter, the lack of a multilateral energy treaty or a UNGA declaration on

---

[111] UNGA, Promotion of New and Renewable Sources of Energy, Including the Implementation of the World Solar Programme 1996–2005 (13 March 2006) UN Doc A/RES/60/199.

[112] United Nations Framework Convention on Climate Change 1771 UNTS 107; D Bodansky, 'The United Nations Framework Convention on Climate Change: A Commentary' (1993) 18 Yale Journal of International Law 451, noting that binding obligations for renewable energy were negotiated but eventually abandoned.

energy-related issues might be a consequence of this. Until such time arrives (if ever) when a binding international instrument on Renewable energy is concluded as a result of an intergovernmental process on energy, IRENA is the most competent intergovernmental organization to promote renewable energy in the international agenda and facilitate cooperation.[113] Indeed, the multifaceted activities of the organization and its wide support by states make IRENA ideally placed to drive the energy transition towards sustainable development and climate change mitigation.[114]

2. Empirical Analysis

Indicator 7.2.1: 'Renewable energy share in the total final energy consumption' is the denominator for measuring progress of target 7.2. The indicator considers the amount of renewable energy consumed by the end user rather than the capacity for renewable energy production. Whereas this metric may best serve statistical analysis because it bypasses certain pitfalls associated with the measurement of production, it remains silent about the sustainability of these sources as such, for renewable sources may indicate that their consumption does not jeopardize their availability in the future, yet this does not presuppose that they are environmentally friendly and not harmful to people. An important distinction should be made between modern forms of renewable energy such as wind, solar, hydropower, and bioenergy that is generated from the use of wood, charcoal, or biomass.[115] If actual progress is to be made towards decarbonization, the prevention of deforestation and biodiversity loss and the reduction of premature deaths due to indoor air pollution, emphasis should be laid on modern renewable energy resources. At present the share of renewables in total final energy consumption (TFEC) has not presented significant changes during the last decade and remains steady at approximately 17.1 per cent.[116] However, the share of modern renewables in TFEC has increased since the 2000s, reaching 11 per cent in 2018.[117] The greatest progress is identified in the electricity sector through the contribution of solar PV, hydro, and wind power. New installations of electricity generation capacity were at 7.4 per cent in 2019 and renewable electricity now accounts for 50 per cent of global modern renewable energy consumption.[118] In the sector of heating and transport, modern bioenergy accounts for 50 per cent of TFEC but stronger policy support is needed for phasing out fossil fuel subsidies and minimizing the adverse impacts of the energy transition on the most vulnerable. Overall, renewable energy in the transport sector grew by 7 per cent

---

[113] Conference on the Establishment of the International Renewable Energy Agency, Statute of IRENA (26 January 2009) IRENA/FC/Statute <https://www.irena.org/-/media/Files/IRENA/Agency/About-IRENA/Statute/IRENA_FC_Statute_signed_in_Bonn_26_01_2009_incl_declaration_on_further_authentic_versions.ashx?la=en&hash=FAB3B5AE51B8082B04A7BBB5BDE978065EF67D96&hash=FAB3B5AE51B8082B04A7BBB5BDE978065EF67D96> accessed 8 April 2022.

[114] IRENA <https://www.irena.org/> accessed 8 April 2022; Bruce (n 108) 28–30.

[115] UNSD, 'Metadata Indicator 7.2.1' (15 February 2021). The information sheet lists as renewable resources: hydro, wind, solar, solid biofuels, liquid biofuels, biogas, geothermal, marine, and renewable waste.

[116] Energy Progress Report 2021 (n 80) 8.

[117] IEA (2020), 'SDG7: Data and Projections', IEA, Paris <https://www.iea.org/reports/sdg7-data-and-projections> accessed 8 April 2022.

[118] Energy Progress Report 2021 (n 80) 8.

in 2018 and renewable energy consumption for heating was 9.2 per cent of total heat consumption.[119]

Despite the upward trends in renewable energy consumption, differences among regions show that progress is uneven. By way of example, global renewable energy share in TFEC was 17.32 per cent in 2017 but Western and Central Asia's percentage points were 3.76 and 3.41 respectively.[120] In contrast, Sub-Saharan Africa has the largest share of renewable sources, however 85 per cent refers to traditional use of biomass. When the latter is not taken into account, Latin America and the Caribbean come first due to the extensive use of hydropower for electricity and bioenergy for industrial processes. An interesting figure comes from China, which represents one-fifth of the global modern renewable energy consumption, yet this accounts only for 10 per cent of the country's TFEC. From the developed countries, Germany, Italy, and the United Kingdom have taken the lead in the share of modern renewables in their TFEC.[121]

To conclude, target 7.2 does not call for the increase of renewable energy to reach a specific percentage point. As such, the target is not quantified and estimating what an ideal share of renewable energy would be by 2030 is difficult. To be sure, if the goal for 2050 is net zero emissions, achieving the objective of target 7.2 requires accelerated action. To this end, Energy Compacts that bring together governments, companies, development organizations, and civil society have a great role to play as drivers of public–private partnerships for an equitable and principle-based energy transition.[122]

3. Implementation Efforts at International/Domestic Level

An interesting case study that demonstrates the positive outputs of renewables for access to electricity and environmental protection constitutes the integration of the floating solar photovoltaic plant Cirata into the Java–Bali power system in Indonesia. The country faces important challenges that impact its energy supply and the sustainability of its energy system. Indonesia is the world's fourth most populated state, hence a major energy consumer. In order to meet demand, coal and biofuels production are intense, making the country an important exporter of these energy sources but also a polluter. Moreover, power systems are fragmented in each island group. Despite the economic benefits from this activity, the country needs to modernize its energy system if it wants to continue being a strong player in the energy landscape, achieve domestically universal electricity access in the most efficient way (estimated annual demand at 5 per cent) and, of course minimize the impacts of climate change due to its high fossil fuel emissions. Indeed, about 83 per cent of electricity in Indonesia is generated from fossil fuels. In 2020 the power mix was 63 per cent coal, 18 per cent natural gas, 2 per cent oil, 7 per cent hydroelectric, and 10 per cent geothermal and biofuels. To reverse

[119] ibid 9.
[120] UNSG Progress Report (n 81), Statistical Annex—Target 7.2.
[121] Energy Progress Report 2021 (n 80) 9.
[122] DESA/High-Level Dialogue on Energy, 'Theme Report on Energy Transition: Towards the Achievement of SDG7 and Net-Zero Emissions' (2021) <https://www.un.org/sites/un2.un.org/files/2021-twg_2.pdf> accessed 8 April 2022; UN Energy Compacts <https://www.un.org/en/energycompacts> accessed 13 February 2022.

the situation and achieve the goal of 23 per cent of total electricity production to be generated from renewables by 2025, the government (through its state-owned utility) has partnered with IEA in this project that will upgrade the operating system of the Java–Bali power plant in order to minimize the use of coal and gas, and overcome the shortages in energy production from hydropower when water availability is lower during the dry season.[123]

The example of Nigeria is also indicative of developing countries' potential to grow economically by becoming energy providers but also localize economic benefits from the energy industry and transition to more sustainable energy solutions. The country's Rural Electrification Agency has been collaborating with SEforAll and All On, a Shell-funded impact investment company,[124] to attract private capital for the construction of 5 million new solar energy connections that the government wishes to generate in the framework of its solar energy programme, Solar Power Naija. Investing companies are assigned allotments based on geospatial data analysis on the condition that they provide 20 per cent of their energy connections to their allotted zones. Further opportunities for projects will be informed by geographic, energy, and consumer data that allow the government to identify population groups that remain unserved and assign projects for new connections equitably. So far, it is estimated that 250,000 new jobs have been created and the local solar manufacturing industry has been given a boost.[125] Similarly, since 2018 the Ministry of Power and Renewable Energy in Sri Lanka has been implementing a community-based power generation programme (Soorya Bala Sangramaya), whereby households, commercial and community buildings can have small rooftop power plants installed. Such infrastructure is expected to add 1000 MW of solar electricity to the national grid by 2025, which will contribute to the use of renewables at the level of primary supply. At the time of the report, 44 per cent of total primary energy supply was generated from renewable sources, although fuelwood continued to be widely used in households and industrial estates.[126]

Last but not least, Australia is exemplary for its holistic approach to energy policy with particular focus on augmenting the share of renewable energy in its energy mix. Pursuant to the country's 2018 VNR, 16 per cent of the country's electricity is generated by renewable energy and the country demonstrates significant outputs as a result of its investment in clean energy technology (CET). Remarkably, Australia possessed the seventh place in CET investments and innovation on a global scale. More than 90 per cent of new energy generation comes from wind and solar plants, although coal and gas still dominate energy production. Individual territories such as Tasmania and South Australia have a higher share in renewables, reaching 90 per cent and 50 per cent of electricity demand respectively. Illustrative of the country's innovation in clean energy

---

[123] IEA Scaling up renewables in the Java–Bali power system: A case study (IEA 21 January 2022) <https://www.iea.org/articles/scaling-up-renewables-in-the-java-bali-power-system-a-case-study> accessed 13 February 2022.

[124] (*AllOn*) <https://www.all-on.com/> accessed 13 February 2022.

[125] SEforAll, 'Impact Areas/Country Engagement: Africa' <https://f-refresh-seforall.pantheonsite.io/node/1952> accessed 13 February 2022.

[126] HLPF, Sri Lanka VNR (June 2018), 46–47 <https://sustainabledevelopment.un.org/content/documents/19677FINAL_SriLankaVNR_Report_30Jun2018.pdf> accessed 13 February 2022.

programmes are the solar farms in Lismore (New South Wales), which are funded by the community and operated by the council, as well as the collaboration between the Australian Renewable Energy Agency (ARENA), AGL Energy, and Simply Energy on virtual power plants that will involve 1,000 grid-connected households and businesses with rooftop solar and battery storage in Adelaide.[127]

4. Critique

If target 7.1 had foremost a people-centred character, and thus drew upon the energy-poverty nexus, the second target of SDG 7 places the environment at the heart of the energy discourse. For years the regulation of energy matters had largely neglected environmental sustainability, focusing primarily on regulating utilities, the extraction of national energy resources, the cost of energy supply for consumers, their protection from monopolies, and the efficiency of energy systems. Manifestly, energy was a commodity that served economic objectives of a country (industrialization, trade etc) and secondarily human needs. Renewable energy targets have gained forceful impetus in the light of the climate crisis facing humanity.[128] The ultimate goal of decarbonization and zero emissions by 2050 have accelerated the transition to renewable and cleaner energy. Utility-scale wind, solar, and hydropower infrastructure must dominate the infrastructure for energy production followed by necessary upgrades to the entire energy system for the conversion, delivery, and use of energy and 'complemented by the proliferation of distributed renewables, such as rooftop solar panels, solar water heaters, and community-scale wind and solar projects, further decentralising energy generation and often filling key energy access gaps in developing countries'.[129] SDG 7.2 has the potential to inform global energy transition efforts, and thereafter promote the sustainability dimension of the energy trilemma while emphasizing the quality aspect of access to energy—or otherwise, energy supply—insofar as this is determined by access to 'modern' energy sources (SDG 7.1).

How should states primarily, and the private sector secondarily (eg energy companies), act in order to increase substantially the share renewable energy has in the global energy mix in such way that the three tenets of human development (economic, social, and environmental) can be fulfilled for present and future generations? How can energy transition reconcile the anthropocentric approach to energy with the urgency to restore and safeguard the quality of the environment, upon which human well-being after all depends?

To be sure, energy transition should be just and fair both vis-à-vis human and environmental needs. This means that law and policy for energy transition should be aimed at distributing 'access to the environmental, economic and social benefits associated

---

[127] HLPF, Australia's VNR (2018), 55 <https://sustainabledevelopment.un.org/content/documents/20470VNR_final_approved_version.pdf> accessed 13 February 2022.

[128] TM Mose, 'The Law of Gravitas International: The Energy Transition, Renewable Energy Law and Ethics' in M Dahlan and others (eds) (n 57); Intergovernmental Panel On Climate Change, 'Special Report: Global Warming of 15°—Summary for Policy Makers' (IPCC 2018) <https://www.ipcc.ch/sr15/chapter/spm/> accessed 13 February 2022.

[129] U Outka, 'Ethical Drivers for the Renewable Energy Transition' in Dahlan and others (eds) (n 56).

with the energy sector'[130] as they also rectify the (unequally distributed) environmental harms among regions and communities, in particular those that do not have the means to mitigate and adapt to environmental, including climate, disasters. In this regard energy and environmental justice are complementary in guiding the shift away from fossil fuels. In practice this means that environmental principles and the principles of equity and fairness should be integrated in the decision-making about production, consumption, and distribution of renewable energy and in the actual design of renewable energy infrastructure projects. Indeed, like any other infrastructure project aiming at the realization of development goals that should comply with environmental and social standards,[131] such as environmental impact assessments, the precautionary approach to biodiversity, gender equality, beneficiaries' information and participation in project design and implementation etc, those that promote renewable energy should adhere to the same. Human rights also become relevant given the interplay and mutually reinforcing relationship between development goals and socio-economic and environmental rights. In this way not only will injustices towards the environment and individuals be addressed but they can be avoided in the first place, and importantly the benefits of renewable energy may be justly shared. These objectives constitute the essence of energy and environmental justice, and lie at the core of human rights too.[132]

C. Target 7.3 Double the global rate of improvement in energy efficiency by 2030

1. Sources of Target

While targets 7.a and 7.b have been drafted and formulated as 'means of implementation' targets—in other words as ways to deliver other targets and the goal(s) as a whole—target 7.3, like targets 7.1 and 7.2, was drafted as an 'outcome' target.[133] Yet, target 7.3 may also work as a means of implementation for SDGs 12 (sustainable consumption and production), 13 (combat climate change), and 15 (sustainable use of terrestrial systems).[134]

Energy efficiency is the core content of target 7.3. According to target 7.3, states shall 'double the global rate of improvement in energy efficiency'. Such focus on energy

---

[130] U Outka, 'Fairness in the Low-Carbon Shift: Learning from Environmental Justice' (2017) 82(2) Brooklyn Law Review 789, 790.

[131] For example, the IBRD Environmental and Social Framework (*WBG*) <https://www.worldbank.org/en/projects-operations/environmental-and-social-framework> accessed 8 April 2022; IFC, Environmental and Social Performance Standards <https://www.ifc.org/wps/wcm/connect/Topics_Ext_Content/IFC_External_Corporate_Site/Sustainability-At-IFC/Policies-Standards/Performance-Standards> accessed 8 April 2022.

[132] Mose (n 128); Outka, 'Ethical Drivers for the Renewable Energy Transition' (n 129).

[133] On the distinction between outcome targets and means of implementation targets, see J Bartram and others, 'Policy Review of the Means of Implementation Targets and Indicators for the Sustainable Development Goal for Water and Sanitation' (2018) 1 Clean Water <https://www.nature.com/articles/s41545-018-0003-0#citeas> accessed 4 April 2022.

[134] See accordingly M Loewe and N Rippin, 'The Sustainable Development Goals of the Post-2015 Agenda: Comments on the OWG and SDSN Proposals' (German Development Institute 2015) <http://dx.doi.org/10.2139/ssrn.2567302> accessed 4 April 2022.

efficiency is not difficult to justify. Energy efficiency is one of the strategies to be followed to achieve sustainable and inclusive growth as recalled by the IEA and confirmed by the Energy Efficiency Directive (2017/27/EU), which envisages energy efficiency 'as a top priority of the European Union'.[135] Moreover, energy efficiency is essential to achieve benefits such as the reduction of environment impacts and the boost of energy supply. Furthermore, it is essential to increase market competitiveness.

Seen from this perspective, energy efficiency is intrinsically linked with renewable energy technologies. This link can be understood if one considers that energy technologies such as hydropower, wind energy, and solar energy may achieve more efficiency than any traditional energy source.

2. Empirical Analysis and Implementation Efforts at International/Domestic Level

Target 7.3 is measured by an indicator (the year-on-year percentage change in energy intensity). Since 2010, the IEA and the United Nations Statistics Division (UNSD) are responsible for tracking and estimating this indicator. This is essential given the prevalence of incomplete registration data in several countries.

There have been consistent calls for improvement to the datasets,[136] and particularly the use of disaggregated data 'on the basis of energy statistics programmes that monitor and report comprehensive energy data, and integrate fully with other economic and social national statistical efforts'.[137] However, despite work by the Inter-agency and Expert Group on SDG Indicators (IAEG-SGD) to provide support in gathering more disaggregated data, progress on this is slow. For instance, while target 7.3 considers energy intensity (the energy needed to produce one unit of economic output it does not (yet) include categories such as energy productivity (the ratio of gross domestic product (GDP) to total primary energy supply (TPES)), and the efficiency with which primary energy resources are transformed into useable energy at the point of consumption.

That said, the UN has gone to great lengths to align the SDGs related to energy and climate change with obligations contained in the Paris Agreement. In relation to SDG 7, it has highlighted interlinkages with the Preamble and articles 1–4. Particularly relevant is article 4, para 4 of the Paris Agreement requiring each Party to prepare, communicate, and maintain successive nationally determined contributions (NDCs) that it intends to achieve,[138] but also pertinent is the Agreement's emphasis on long-term low greenhouse gas emission development strategies (LT-LEDS).[139]

---

[135] For further references on this issue, FT Volpon and ECX Junior, 'Access to Modern Energy Services for the Promotion of Sustainable Development' in WL Filho and others (eds), *Affordable and Clean Energy* (Springer 2021) 11 ff.

[136] TAL Aboul-Atta and RH Rashed, 'Analyzing the Relationship between Sustainable Development Indicators and Renewable Energy Consumption' (2021) 45 Journal of Engineering and Applied Science 68 ff.

[137] C Kettner and others, 'Monitoring Sustainable Development: Climate and Energy Policy Indicators' (2020) 2 Journal of Sustainability Research 2020 <https://sustainability.hapres.com/htmls/JSR_1246_Detail.html#sec13> accessed 4 April 2022.

[138] UN, 'Accelerating SDG 7 Achievement: SDG 7 Policy Briefs in Support of the High-Level Political Forum 2019' (2019) <https://sustainabledevelopment.un.org/content/documents/22877UN_FINAL_ONLINE_20190 523.pdf> accessed 4 April 2022.

[139] H Janetschek and others, 'The 2030 Agenda and the Paris Agreement: Voluntary Contributions Towards Thematic Policy Coherence' (2020) 20 Climate Change 430.

Measuring target 7.3 also serves as a good overall indicator of the overall state of the energy system as well as the socio-economic progress of a country.[140]

The Group of Twenty (G20) in its 'Energy Efficiency Action Plan' sets out recommendations for states on how to achieve the set indicators.[141] These are implemented by states in their national action plans. As of 2020, numerous states were implementing the G20 recommendations. To support states in achieving target 7.3, a Renewable Energy Roadmap was developed by IRENA in July 2014.[142]

3. Critique

Calling for improvements in energy efficiency, target 7.3 has been rightly criticized for not being 'sufficiently ambitious to mitigate climate change' and for not reducing the absolute level of emissions from the energy sector.[143] A further criticism that was levelled against the target was that it does not differentiate between high- and low-income countries. Loewe and Rippin have developed this criticism at length, contending that some high-income countries, such as Japan, Germany, and Sweden, have already reached high levels of energy efficiency (even though, of course, more is still possible), whereas other high-income countries—and almost all low- and middle income countries—are still at the beginning stages of implementation. Additional criticisms concern energy efficiency standards at an industry level that have not been included among the target indicators and the inherent uncertainty in 'energy efficiency improvement' in target 7.3.[144]

That having been said, it is also true that target 7.3 has positive values, which demonstrate that it helps in reducing energy consumption.[145]

D. Target 7.a By 2030, enhance international cooperation to facilitate access to clean energy research and technology, including renewable energy, energy efficiency and advanced and cleaner fossil-fuel technology, and promote investments in energy infrastructure and clean energy technology

1. Sources of Target

Target 7.a is an enabling target, supporting the achievement of other targets. It focuses on international public finance flows to developing countries in support of clean and

---

[140] D Firoiu and others, Dynamics of Implementation of SDG 7 Targets in EU Member States 5 Years after the Adoption of the Paris Agreement (2021) 13 Sustainability 8284 ff.

[141] Group of Twenty, 'Energy Efficiency Action Plan: Voluntary Collaboration on Energy Efficiency' (16 November 2014), para 1.2.

[142] IRENA, 'REmap 2030—A Renewable Energy Roadmap' (2014) <https://www.irena.org/publications/2014/Jun/REmap-2030-Full-Report> accessed 4 April 2022. See also M Loewe and others, 'Goal 7: Ensure Access to Affordable, Reliable, Sustainable, And Modern Energy for All' in Loewe and Rippin (eds) (n 134).

[143] Loewe and Rippin (n 134).

[144] Bruce and Stephenson (n 54).

[145] WG Santika and others, 'From Goals to Joules: A Quantitative Approach of Interlinkages between Energy and the Sustainable Development Goals' (2019) 50 Energy Research & Social Science 201 <https://www.sciencedirect.com/science/article/abs/pii/S2214629618308107> accessed 4 April 2022.

renewable energy, and aims at promoting access to research, technology, and investments in clean energy. Like targets 7.2 and 7.b, target 7.a is supported by the IRENA Statute that includes knowledge transfer, capacity building, and promotion of international cooperation among the mandate and objectives of the international organization that it created.

The target is framed in vague and verbose language and appears difficult to be achieved before negotiations on climate finance under the UNFCCC begin to make effective progress.[146]

The target of enhancing international cooperation to facilitate access to energy research and technology has a relatively long history. It dates back to 1960 when the Organisation for Economic Co-operation and Development and the Development and Assistance Committee (OECD/DAC) started collecting data on official and private resource flows at an aggregate level and, since 1973, at an activity level through the Creditor Reporting System (CRS) data.[147] Greater momentum nevertheless was gained with the establishment of IRENA's Public Renewable Energy Investment Database encompassing data on financial flows from a wide range of publicly available sources.

With the issue having been placed on the international agenda, it was also reemphasized at several of the World Energy Council's meetings in the 2000s, being eventually taken up by the OECD development goals, but not by the MDGs that lacked an *ad hoc* objective on energy.

2. Empirical Analysis and Implementation Efforts at the International/ Domestic Level

Although the new non-binding Addis Ababa Action Agenda[148] demonstrates political will and support for target 7.a, only 12 per cent of financial flows in 2017 reached the least-developed countries. It then follows that increased efforts are indispensable to make sure finance reaches the countries most in need.[149]

Target 7.a is measured by a sole indicator (international financial flows to developing countries in support of clean energy research and development and renewable energy production, including in hybrid systems). While the indicator has been in use for a long time, data collection has proven complex and challenging, and estimates on the financial flows in support of clean and renewable energy are frequently updated. The legal and practical complexity surrounding the use of this indicator to measure the progress of target 7.a is further certified by the fact that few contributions in academic writings

---

[146] M Loewe and others, 'Ensure Access to Affordable, Reliable, Sustainable, and Modern Energy for All' in Loewe and Rippin (eds) (n 134).

[147] Sustainable Development Goals, SDG Indicators Metadata repository <https://unstats.un.org/sdgs/metadata/> accessed 4 April 2021.

[148] Addis Ababa Action Agenda of the Third International Conference on Financing for Development: The final text of the outcome document adopted at the Third International Conference on Financing for Development (Addis Ababa, Ethiopia, 13–16 July 2015) and endorsed by the General Assembly in its Resolution 69/313 of 27 July 2015 <https://sustainabledevelopment.un.org/index.php?page=view&type=400&nr=2051&menu=35> accessed 4 April 2022.

[149] Bruce and Stephenson (n 54).

have until now approached this issue and those that have done so have mostly adopted the rather complex indicator developed by the United Nations.[150]

3. Critique

Given the complexity and vagueness of its language and of its indicator, the operationalization of target 7.a is far from easy.

This point may be captured by recalling that, although used by several international intergovernmental organizations such as the IEA and the World Bank, some of the key terms used in target 7.a, such as clean energy and energy efficiency, are undefined both in its text, in the text of other SDG 7 targets, and in international law more generally.

E. Target 7.b By 2030, expand infrastructure and upgrade technology for supplying modern and sustainable energy services for all in developing countries, in particular least developed countries, small island developing States and landlocked developing countries, in accordance with their respective programmes of support

1. Source of Target

Target 7.b aims at 'expanding infrastructure and upgrading technology for supplying modern and sustainable energy services for all in developing countries'. A recent report by the IEA on the 'impediments associated with expansion of infrastructure and the upgrade of technology to supply modern energy services for all in developing countries' shows that this is an objective that is still far from being achieved at least in LDCs.

The most striking peculiarity of the target is that it is the only 'means of implementation' target that was classified as local instead of global.[151] Being classified as such, it is legitimate to argue, as Nicholas Robinson does, that target 7.b may only be achieved through the adoption of new legislation by states. This is also because, as noted again by Robinson, 'currently, regimes deter use of alternative deterrence regimes'.[152]

This said, it remains true that the realization of energy infrastructure policy is also heavily dependent on market forces and financial and geopolitical priorities. Moreover, it is further dependent on the influence exercised by bottom-up initiatives (leaving no-one behind) for their achievement.[153]

---

[150] D McCollum and others, 'SDG7: Ensure Access to Affordable, Reliable, Sustainable and Modern Energy for All' in *International Council for Science, A Guide to SDG Interactions: from Science to Implementation* (ICSU 2017) <https://council.science/wp-content/uploads/2017/05/SDGs-Guide-to-Interactions.pdf> accessed 4 April 2022.

[151] HL van Soesta and others, 'Analysing interactions among Sustainable Development Goals with Integrated Assessment Models' (2019) 1 Global Transitions 210.

[152] N Robinson, 'The UN SDGs and Environmental Law: Cooperative Remedies for Natural Disaster Risks' in J Peel and D Fisher (eds.), *The Role of International Environmental Law in Disaster Risk Reduction* (Martinus Nijhoff 2016) 340 ff.

[153] L Meuleman, *Metagovernance for Sustainability: A Framework for Implementing the Sustainable Development Goals* (Routledge 2018).

544   SDG 7

2. Empirical Analysis and Implementation Efforts at the International/ Domestic Level

Target 7.b is tracked by the following indicator: installed renewable energy-generating capacity in developing countries (in watts per capita).

The indicator relates to the International Recommendations for Energy Statistics which were adopted by the UNSD. These recommendations provide data compilers with an exhaustive set of indications encompassing any aspect of the statistical production process, from key concepts, classifications, and definitions to data sources, data compilation strategies, energy balances, statistical dissemination, and data quality.[154]

3. Critique

Target 7.b has both strengths and weaknesses. Its major strength is that it does not operate in isolation but in conjunction with the technology transfer provisions found in environmental and economic treaty regimes.[155] On the weaknesses front, its major weakness is that it has to be measured according to an indicator that is entirely focused on electricity capacity instead of on more modern technology.

---

[154] The text of the International Recommendations for Energy Statistics is available at <https://unstats.un.org/unsd/energystats/methodology/ires/> accessed 15 April 2022.

[155] AR Harrington, *International Law and Global Governance, Treaty Regimes and Sustainable Development Goals Implementation* (Routledge 2021) 45.

SDG 8

'Promote Sustained, Inclusive and Sustainable Economic Growth, Full and Productive Employment and Decent Work for All'

Francesco Seatzu and Katerina Akestoridi

I. Introduction

Mainstream thinking in international and domestic law considers economic growth,[1] when associated with economic freedom and free trade, a key component of a wider strategy to achieve sustainable development.[2] At the international level, the promotion of economic growth has been a crucial objective in a number of development frameworks since its implicit articulation in the United Nations Conference on the Human Environment (the Stockholm Declaration)[3] and the adoption of the 1992 Rio Declaration on Environment and Development which, in Principle 12, established a precise and direct link between economic growth and sustainable development in all countries.[4] Moreover, the promotion of economic growth has also been a priority in the agendas of the Bretton Woods institutions, namely the World Bank Group and the International Monetary Fund (IMF).[5]

The idea of economic growth as an avenue for achieving sustainable development is, moreover, firmly established in a number of international legal instruments— particularly the Paris Agreement to the United Nations Framework Convention on Climate Change[6]—international soft law instruments like the Addis Ababa Action Agenda of the Third International Conference on Financing for Development[7] and

---

[1] On the meaning of economic growth in the economic literature, see, eg, PN Hess, *Economic Growth and Sustainable Development* (Routledge 2013) 66–33, 99–121.

[2] S Pahuja, *Decolonising International Law: Development, Economic Growth and the Politics of Universality* (CUP 2011) 132 ff; R McCorquodale and S McInerney-Lankford, 'Sustainable Development and International Law' (2020) 114 Proceedings of the ASIL Annual Meeting, 141–43.

[3] UN General Assembly, 'United Nations Conference on the Human Environment' (15 December 1972) UN Doc A/RES/2994 <https://www.refworld.org/docid/3b00f1c840.html> accessed 1 May 2021.

[4] UN Doc A/CONF.151/26 (1992) 31 ILM 874 ff.

[5] On the subject, see, eg,V Dutraive, 'Economic Development and Institutions. Anatomy of the New Institutional Economics' Research Program' (2009) 6 Revue de la regulation <https://journals.openedition.org/regulation/7609> accessed 3 March 2021.

[6] United Nations Framework Convention on Climate Change (9 May 1992) FCCC/CP/2015/10/Add.1 <https://unfccc.int/sites/default/files/english_paris_agreement.pdf> accessed 2 March 2021.

[7] Addis Ababa Action Agenda of the Third International Conference on Financing for Development: (Addis Ababa Action Agenda): the final text of the outcome document adopted at the Third International Conference on

546 SDG 8

international legal decisions such as the leading judgment of the International Court of Justice (ICJ) on the Pulp Mills case.[8] Furthermore, also well-established in numerous, albeit not unanimous, legal writings is the claim that economic growth constitutes an essential component in the holistic concept of the 'human right to development'.[9]

Despite these and other claims and confirmations, the objective of promoting economic growth, along with that of promoting sustainable development in its socio-economic dimension, had not been achieved by the international community by the end of the last century.[10] It is therefore unsurprising that the objective of economic growth constituted an important, though not central topic of the Millennium Development Goals (MDGs), with the first of the eight Goals having been directly concerned with it alongside the other envisaged complementary objective of the eradication of extreme poverty and hunger (Goal 1: Eradicate extreme poverty and hunger).[11] Additionally, growth-related aspects also played a role in some other MDGs, partly as outcomes determinants, and partly in the formulation of different objectives (in particular MDG 3: Promote Gender Equality and Empower Women; MDG 4: Reduce Child Mortality, and MDG 5: Improve Maternal Health).

While the growth-related targets have overall obtained good success rates throughout the fifteen years of application of the MDGs,[12] major points of criticism concern the MDGs' insufficient focus on and scarce attention to the achievement of productive employment and decent work that 'did not expand fast enough to keep up with the growing labour force' according to the Millennium Development Goals Report of 2015.[13] Responding to this, the SDGs reshaped the objective of economic growth in the following more employment-related manner:

> We will seek to build strong economic foundations for all our countries. Sustained, inclusive and sustainable economic growth is essential for prosperity. This will only be possible if wealth is shared and income inequality is addressed. We will work to build dynamic, sustainable, innovative and people-centred economies, promoting youth employment and women's economic empowerment, in particular, and decent

---

Financing for Development: (Addis Ababa, Ethiopia, 13–16 July 2015) and endorsed by the General Assembly in its resolution 69/313 of 27 July 2015 <https://www.loc.gov/item/2019352355/> accessed 1 February 2021.

[8] Pulp Mills on the River Uruguay (*Argentina v Uruguay*), Judgment [2010] ICJ Rep 14.

[9] For further references on this issue, S Kamga and S Heleba, 'Can Economic Growth Translate into Access to Rights? Challenges Faced by Institutions in South Africa in Ensuring that Growth Leads to Better Living Standards' (2012) 9(17) SUR—International Journal of Human Rights 83 <https://sur.conectas.org/wp-content/uploads/2017/11/sur17-eng-serges-kamga-and-siyambonga-heleba.pdf> accessed 23 March 2022.

[10] Pahuja (n 2) 95 ff.

[11] T Pogge, 'Poverty, Hunger and Cosmetic Progress' in M Langford and others (eds), *The Millennium Development Goals and Human Rights: Past, Present and Future* (CUP 2013) 209 ff; P Alston, 'Ships Passing in the Night: The Current State of the Human Rights and Development Debate Seen through the Lens of the Millennium Development Goals' (2005) 7 Human Rights Quarterly 755, 759 ff.

[12] United Nations, 'The Millennium Development Goals Report 2015' (21 September 2015) 5–6 <https://www.un.org/millenniumgoals/2015_MDG_Report/pdf/MDG%202015%20rev%20(July%201).pdf> accessed 24 March 2022.

[13] ibid 17.

work for all.[14] We will eradicate forced labour and human trafficking and end child labour in all its forms. All countries stand to benefit from having a healthy and well-educated workforce with the knowledge and skills needed for productive and fulfilling work and full participation in society. We will strengthen the productive capacities of least-developed countries in all sectors, including through structural transformation. We will adopt policies which increase productive capacities, productivity and productive employment; financial inclusion; sustainable agriculture, pastoralist and fisheries development; sustainable industrial development; universal access to affordable, reliable, sustainable and modern energy services; sustainable transport systems; and quality and resilient infrastructure.[15]

The more employment-related approach is also evident in SDG 8 and related targets and indicators, specifically designed to promote sustained, inclusive, and sustainable economic growth, full and productive employment, and decent work for all.[16] Therefore, in contrast to the MDGs, SDG 8 now also aims at achieving overall productive employment and decent work for all.[17] However, if this is true, it is also true that, in so doing, the SDGs drafters have not adopted the more advanced option suggested by several non-governmental organization (NGO) groups and labour groups of including a stand-alone goal on full employment and decent work in the 2030 Agenda.[18]

Furthermore, the importance of economic growth becomes clear through its explicit formulation as an independent goal (SDG 8) and its overarching character for the achievement of other SDG goals. For instance, SDG 1 (end poverty in all its forms everywhere), like MDG 1, calls for economic growth to eradicate extreme poverty and hunger.[19] Moreover, as 'education directly affects economic growth insofar as it is essential to improve human capital', economic growth is closely tied to SDG 4 (ensure inclusive and equitable quality education). SDG 4's targets therefore stipulate *inter alia* that 'education facilities that are child, disability and gender sensitive and provide safe, non-violent, inclusive and effective learning environments for all should be built and

[14] ILO, '2030 Development Agenda: Major Breakthrough for World of Work' (*ILO*, 4 August 2015) <https://www.ilo.org/global/about-the-ilo/newsroom/news/WCMS_388407/lang--en/index.htm> accessed 24 March 2022, welcoming that decent work is 'now an integral part of the new universal agenda for sustainable development'.
[15] UNGA, 'Transforming our World: Agenda 2030 for Sustainable Development' (21 October 2015) UN Doc A/RES/70/1, para 27.
[16] ibid Goal 8.
[17] 'Guidance Paper: The Post 2015-Development Agenda and its Impact on Business' (IOE 2015) <https://www.ioe-emp.org/fileadmin/ioe_documents/publications/Policy%20Areas/sustainability/EN/_2015-08-26__C-186_The_Post-2015_Development_Agenda_what_does_it_mean_for_business_communication.pdf> accessed 24 March 2022; 'Joint Statement: Human Rights for All Post-2015' (Centre for Economic and Social Rights, 10 May 2013) <http://www.cesr.org/jointstatement-human-rights-all-post-2015> accessed 24 March 2022, further recalling that '[t]he ITUC and human rights NGOs advocated for inclusion a stand-alone goal on full employment and decent work in the 2030 agenda'.
[18] UN Open Working Group, 'Compilation Document Major Groups and other Stakeholders Dialogue with the Co-Chairs on SDGS' (2 April 2014) <https://sustainabledevelopment.un.org/content/documents/3674Compilation%20Document%20on%20Goals%20and%20Targets_April%2011-%20final.pdf> accessed 24 March 2022.
[19] For criticisms of this solution, DF Frey, 'Economic Growth, Full Employment and Decent Work: The Means and Ends in SDG 8' (2017) 21(8) The International Journal of Human Rights 1164, 1177, noting that 'it is unwise to rely on economic growth to eradicate poverty because it is not likely to succeed, and it may obscure other solutions'.

upgraded'. Then again, it has also been stipulated that the objectives of ending the epidemics of AIDS, tuberculosis, malaria, and neglected tropical diseases, and combating hepatitis (SDG 3.3); of recognizing unpaid care and domestic work through the provision of public services, infrastructure, and social protection policies, of promoting shared responsibility within the household and the family as nationally appropriate (SDG 5.4); and of providing access to safe, affordable, accessible, and sustainable transport systems for all, improving road safety, notably by expanding public transport, with special attention to the needs of those in vulnerable situations, women, children, persons with disabilities, and older persons (SDG 11.2) cannot be achieved without promoting economic growth. All in all, there are more than ten targets in other SDGs that are related to economic growth and/or productive employment.

Starting with a detailed presentation of the preparatory proceedings that led to the formulation of SDG 8 as it currently stands (Section II), the commentary discusses each one of the Goal's components separately. Thus, Section III analyses the objective of economic growth and highlights the role of the World Bank Group as the lead development agency for the achievement of economic productivity under SDG 8. In this respect the World Bank's commitments relating to the 2030 Development Agenda are analysed. In turn, Section III.B is devoted to full and productive employment and decent work while the objective of the final part of this piece (Section IV) is to analyse the targets and indicators adopted to monitor progress made towards the achievement of SDG 8 at global, national, regional, and local levels. In so proceeding, the commentary incorporates an exposition and discussion of the main arguments behind the criticisms that have been expressed against SDG 8 as it currently stands and looks in particular at the consequences that arise from the above-mentioned decision to merge the issues of 'economic growth' and 'decent work' under the banner of the same Goal.

II. *Travaux Préparatoires*

A. Background

The regulatory framework of sustainable development emerged from a series of multilateral negotiations at the United Nations that sought to reconcile conflicting views about the relationship between socio-economic development and environmental sustainability. While an early attempt of the international community to align environmental matters with developmental concerns can be traced back to the 1972 UN Conference on the Human Environment,[20] the period between 1992 and 2012 is considered to be the most intense twenty years of consultations on sustainable development. The complexity and the urgency of matters to be discussed led to three seminal UN summits, where Member States sought to develop agreement on and secure decisive

---

[20] (16 June 1972), UN Doc A/Conf48/14/Rev.1. UN Publication Sales No E.73.II.A.14.

support for a framework of action for sustainable development that would be in the interest of humankind: the Rio Conference on Environment and Development;[21] the World Summit for Sustainable Development;[22] and the UN Conference for Sustainable Development (Rio + 20).[23] At the same time, due to the proliferation of actors on the international plane with a vested interest in decision-making for development, parallel multilateral deliberations such as the UN system-wide consultations under the auspices of the UN Task Team (UNTT) for the post-2015 UN Development Agenda,[24] the UN Global Compact consultations,[25] those of the Intergovernmental Committee of Experts on Sustainable Development Finance (ICESDF),[26] and the International Conferences on Financing for Development highlighted additional aspects for a comprehensive post-2015 development agenda.[27]

Sustainable development negotiations were, thus, multidimensional and decisions were embodied into agreements that took various formats, including UN General Assembly Resolutions (eg UN/RES/42/187 (11 Dec 1987) adopting the Report of the World Commission on Environment and Development, 'Our Common Future'), Declarations, conveying high-level political agreement on the topic (eg the Stockholm Declaration[28] and the Rio Declaration on the Environment and Development),[29] Programs of Action such as Agenda 21[30] and the Johannesburg Program of Action,[31] and legally binding treaties such as the Convention on Biodiversity[32] and the UN Framework Convention on Climate Change.[33] Yet, despite their difference in form and normative value, the aforementioned decisions were borne from a rigorous conferencing process where draft texts were discussed with the aim to bridge differences in delegates' proposals and reach common ground on contentious topics. Remarkably, they were adopted by delegates with consensus. Decision-making by consensus has been a distinctive feature of sustainable development negotiations compared to other UN processes where voting takes place. All the same, the decision to form the Sustainable

---

[21] UN <https://www.un.org/en/conferences/environment/rio1992> accessed 14 December 2020.

[22] UN, 'Report of the World Summit on Sustainable Development', Johannesburg, South Africa (26 August–2 September 2002) UN Doc UN/CONF.199/20.

[23] UN, 'Report of the Conference on Sustainable Development' (20–22 June 2012), UN Doc A/CONF.216/16.

[24] UNTT, 'Realising the Future We Want for All' (June 2012) <https://sustainabledevelopment.un.org/content/documents/614Post_2015_UNTTreport.pdf> accessed 14 December 2020.

[25] Report to the UNSG, 'Corporate Sustainability and the UN Post-2015 Development Agenda' (17 June 2013) <https://d306pr3pise04h.cloudfront.net/docs/news_events%2F9.1_news_archives%2F2013_06_18%2FU NGC_Post2015_Report.pdf> accessed 14 December 2020.

[26] ICESDF established by UNGA decision A67/559 <https://sustainabledevelopment.un.org/intergovernmen tal/financecommittee> accessed 14 December 2020.

[27] UN, 'Report of the International Conference on Financing for Development, adopting the Monterey Consensus' (Monterrey, 18–22 March 2002) UN Doc A/CONF.198/11; UN Follow-up International Conference on Financing for Development, 'Doha Declaration on FFD' (Qatar, 29 November–2 December 2008), Un Doc A/CONF.212/L/1/Rev.I. The third ICFF was held in Addis Ababa (n 7).

[28] n 20.

[29] (12 August 1992) UN Doc A/CONF.151/26 (Vol I).

[30] ibid Annex II.

[31] n 22, Annexes.

[32] UN Convention on Biological Diversity (adopted 5 June 1992, in force 29 December 1993) 1760 UNTS 79 and the Cartagena Protocol on Biosafety to the Convention (adopted 29 January 2000, in force 11 September 2003) 2226 UNTS 208.

[33] Adopted 9 May 1992, in force 21 March 1994, 1771 UNTS 107.

Development Goals (SDGs) and their negotiation itself brought radical changes to the way multilateral negotiations on sustainable development are conducted and decisions are made.

The SDGs were proposed in the framework of the preparatory proceedings for the Rio + 20 conference, which was meant to assess progress on the outcomes of previous UN summits on development issues and discuss the institutional framework for sustainable development in order to address emerging challenges more effectively. Their inclusion in the draft outcome document for Rio + 20 did not gain universal support at the beginning. A contested issue was the process whereby the goals would be created. Would that be through a technical working group appointed by the Secretary-General, as was the case with the Millennium Development Goals? Furthermore, whom would the working group comprise and which were the rules of procedure that would guide the discussions?[34] The number and complexity of issues pertaining to development made expert knowledge and evidence-based recommendations necessary. Simultaneously, though, development policy is hardly apolitical to escape oversight from Member States. In light of the eminent risk that negotiations would be stalled by traditional bloc alliances (eg the G77, the EU) or follow the North–South/East–West divide, and of the demand to remedy the pitfalls of the non-inclusive, non-transparent, and purely technocratic MDGs process, States agreed to an 'Open Working Group' (OWG) in which not only them but also stakeholders from the business sector, the epistemic community, civil society (so-called Major Groups), other UN bodies and programmes, and specialized agencies would be represented and actively involved.

Without, thus, deviating from the model of intergovernmental discussions, the opening up to a wider network of participants changed the traditional format of multilateral negotiations. 'Multi' indicated deliberations among different agents, not confined to governments only. Other elements that gave a unique character to multilateral talks this time were the high participation interest of states that led representatives to share the allocated seats to each region, the wide scope of the subject of the OWG deliberations because it covered the entire sustainable development agenda and the end-result of its work, which was the design of goals instead of a draft resolution or a report to be presented to the United Nations General Assembly (UNGA).[35] In addition, the working methods of the OWG differed. The division of the OWG's sessions into two phases was unique: the first eight sessions (March 2013—February 2014) were devoted to '*stocktaking*', namely to gathering information and listening to different views with the purpose to create common understanding and collective knowledge about sustainable development priorities and to establish a uniform conceptualization of sustainability with reference to the five critical areas of importance in the new development agenda: people, planet, prosperity, peace, and partnerships.[36] This phase had catalytic

---

[34] M. Kamau and others (eds), *Transforming Multilateral Diplomacy: The Inside Story of the Sustainable Development Goals* (Routledge 2018) 71–72.

[35] ibid 82–85, 96.

[36] Agenda 2030 (n 15) 3–4.

importance for the design of the SDGs because participants understood that sustainable development issues trespass the interests of particular countries or country groups, therefore negotiations on the SDGs could not be treated as an extension of bilateral or regional political affairs. Moreover, the power dynamics between states, UN technocrats, and civil society were balanced out because an equal footing was given to all contributors in the discussions without states seeing their role as key interlocutors being downsized.[37] Consequently, the SDGs' formation process was depoliticized and democratized, as delegates' participation was set on a level playing field and discussions were not ideologically charged. These attributes gave effect to the principles of openness, inclusiveness, and transparency, and to decision-making by consensus that guided the OWG's mandate.[38] The second phase (five sessions between March 2014 and July 2014) constituted the actual *negotiating* period for the Goals on the basis of the OWG's 'focus area'[39] document that drew on the sessions held thus far. It concluded with the OWG's final proposal[40] for the SDGs, which the Group forwarded to the GA in order to be considered as 'the main basis for integrating the SDGs into the post-2015 development agenda'.[41]

The OWG sessions, therefore, present the drafting history of the SDGs. Similar to the *travaux préparatoires* of treaties that give documentary evidence of the negotiation and drafting of their specific provisions, the meetings constitute an insightful source for understanding (i) the critical conceptual issues that informed the Goals' formulation and how they reflect the normative underpinning of sustainable development, in other words the economic, social, and environmental dimensions in a balanced and integrated manner on the basis of the Rio principles, human rights, equality, sustainability, and existing commitments under international law; (ii) their interlinkages and their coherence with the post-2015 development agenda; (iii) their practical relevance to each country; and (iv) the prospects of their implementation on a national and international level.

In the next section, the OWG sessions are discussed in more detail with the principal focus being on those that informed the content of SDG 8: 'Promote sustained, inclusive and sustainable economic growth, full and productive employment and decent work for all.'

---

[37] Kamau and others (n 34) 103–10; F Dodds and others, 'The OWG: An Unusual Negotiation Process' in F Dodds and others (eds), *Negotiating the Sustainable Development Goals: A Transformational Agenda for an Insecure World* (Routledge 2017), especially 31–34.

[38] GA OWG on SDGs, 'Methods of Work', 6 <https://sustainabledevelopment.un.org/content/documents/1692OWG_methods_work_adopted_1403.pdf> accessed 14 December 2020.

[39] Deliberately called like this to avoid giving the impression that it was a first draft of the Goals that would lead to negotiation of the final text (as in traditional UN negotiations) and ultimately to acceptance or rejection; see further section herein on OWG-9-13.

[40] UN GA, 'Report of the OWG of the GA on SDGs' (12 August 2014) UN Doc A/68/970.

[41] UN GA, 'Resolution Adopted by the GA on 10 September 2014' (12 September 2014) UN Doc A/RES/68/309, para 2.

B. The OWG Sessions

1. The Stocktaking Phase

Stocktaking working sessions were built around thematic clusters from the issues highlighted in the 'Future We Want', the outcome document of Rio + 20.[42] Nonetheless, as from the outset discussions featured interactive dialogue between members of the OWG and other observers, the foundations for the SDGs were shaped by a plurality of sources. Fundamental support was given by expert panels and the inter-agency Technical Support Team (TST),[43] which issued briefs on the topics of each cluster ahead of their discussion in the respective OWG meeting. Amongst other key background documents was the Secretary-General's initial input on the SDGs,[44] communicated to the OWG participants by the UN Department on Economic and Social Affairs (DESA). The document summarized the results of a survey in states regarding development priorities based on national experiences but with an outlook on universally applicable goals, the relevance of the MDGs and their targets to the new goals, as well as challenges to ensure the engagement of all stakeholders. The second was the report by the UNTT, which provided technical inputs to the process for developing the SDGs;[45] the third, the conclusions of the UN Development Group's (UNDG) consultations on the post-2015 development agenda with stakeholders from UN Member States at national and regional level and with individuals. Consultations focused in particular on the thematic areas of the MDGs and imminent challenges such as environmental sustainability and governance, while individuals were engaged through a global online survey in which they could list their preference and provide suggestions for sixteen priority areas for development.[46] Last but not least, the High Level Panel of Eminent Persons (HLPP) gave first-hand recommendations for the design of the SDGs by furnishing the OWG with an illustrative list of twelve universal goals and measurable targets, addressing five areas the Panel perceived as important for a forward-looking, compelling, and integrated sustainable development agenda: (i) to leave no one behind; (ii) to put sustainable development at the core; (iii) to transform economies for jobs and inclusive growth; (iv) to build peace and effective, open, and accountable public institutions; and (v) to forge a new global partnership into national and international politics.[47] Finally, the Sustainable Development Solutions Network (SDSN) became the platform for scientists and academics to bring in their expertise in order to promote practical solutions

---

[42] UNGA Res 66/288 (11 September 2012) UN Doc A/RES/66/288. For information on the clusters under each OWG session (*OWG*) <https://sustainabledevelopment.un.org/owg1.html> accessed 14 December 2020.

[43] UNGA Res 66/288 (n 42) para 249; the TST co-chaired by UN DESA and UNDP and had more than forty entities from the UN system as participating members.

[44] UNGA, 'Initial Input of the Secretary-General to the Open-Working Group on Sustainable Development Goals' (17 December 2012) UN Doc A/67/634.

[45] UNTT (n 24).

[46] UNDG, 'The Global Conversation Begins' (2013) <https://sustainabledevelopment.un.org/content/docume nts/841global-conversation-begins-web.pdf> accessed 14 December 2020.

[47] HLPP, 'A New Global Partnership: Eradicate Poverty and Transform Economies through Sustainable Development' (May 2013), Annex I.

for the implementation of the SDGs. The Network proposed its own set of ten goals that was founded upon the normative concepts of (i) human rights and the right to development, (ii) social inclusion, (iii) the convergence of living standards across countries, and (iv) shared responsibilities and opportunities but relied also on a science-based methodological approach to the creation of the individual targets, thus emphasizing the advancement of metrics systems and the quality of data for monitoring progress towards the Goals' achievement in a reliable way.[48] These reports were meant to inform each other and their content blended into the consultations.

Growth, employment, and decent work were among the issues that topped the list of the most prominent concerns of the international community already from the first session of the OWG that dealt with conceptual aspects of the SDGs. This was not surprising considering the fact that matters addressed by the MDGs continued to preoccupy stakeholders. At the time the OWG convened its sessions, the MDGs were still in force with only two years left until their expiration. Drawing upon the MDGs experience, their success in mobilizing action towards development priorities, but also their shortcomings—their lack of universality and the failure to bring about even outcomes—and the meagre chances that they would be fulfilled by 2015, stakeholders agreed that the SDGs should be elaborated from the foundation of the MDGs in order for them to be in harmony with efforts underway to achieve them and to complete what they didn't.[49]

Under the banner of the MDGs, full and productive employment and decent work for all, including women and young people, constituted target 1.b of MDG 1: Eradicate extreme poverty and hunger. Similarly, growth (measured as gross domestic product (GDP) rate per person employed) was an indicator under this target.[50] Hence, in line with the MDGs, productive employment and inclusive and equitable economic growth were highlighted as priority areas that would contribute to poverty eradication and ensure everyone's access to basic goods and services for a decent life, reducing inequalities and promoting human rights.[51] On this point, however, the UNTT drew attention to the fact that these matters were not adequately addressed by the MDGs, so the SDGs should take a bolder step. To this end, it suggested that a link between growth strategies and employment was indispensable. Employment objectives should be integrated into macroeconomic frameworks and national poverty reduction strategies. Furthermore, it called for key components of inclusive economic development such as the removal of structural barriers to labour markets, better access to financial services, and labour market policies that respect and promote human rights at work.[52]

---

[48] SDSN, 'An Action Agenda for Sustainable Development', Report for the UN Secretary-General (5 May 2014) <https://irp-cdn.multiscreensite.com/be6d1d56/files/uploaded/140505-An-Action-Agenda-for-Sustainable-Development.pdf> accessed 8 December 2020.

[49] Summary of OWG-1 on the SDGs (14–15 March 2013), *Achieving and building on the MDGs*, 2-3; opinions of UN SG's Special Adviser on Post-2015 Development Planning, Amina Mohammed and Executive Vice President's and Managing Director's, World Resources Institute, Manish Bapna, 4 <https://sustainabledevelopment.un.org/content/documents/1700summaryowg.pdf> accessed 14 December 2020.

[50] Millennium Development Goals Indicators (UN official website) <https://unstats.un.org/unsd/mdg/Host.aspx?Content=Indicators/OfficialList.htm> accessed 14 December 2020.

[51] UNGA, 'Initial Input' (n 44) paras 16, 69(b) and (c), 77, 78.

[52] UNTT (n 24) 29.

554   SDG 8

The discussion continued in OWG-2 along the same lines. The conceptualization of the SDGs and poverty eradication were the meeting's focus, yet this time they were analysed in depth in light of the TST's briefs that gave an official input to the meeting.[53] In the interactive exchange of views on the former item of the agenda, it was stressed that poverty eradication in its multidimensional form remained an overarching objective for sustainable development and should be at the core of the SDGs framework.[54] Specifically, it was advised that in a development agenda that seeks to integrated socio-economic and environmental dimensions of development, poverty eradication should be tailored towards access (i) to economic opportunities and productive assets, (ii) to fundamental social goods and services (health, education, and sanitation), and (iii) to natural assets.[55] Correspondingly, in the moderated discussion on the same topic, one speaker noted that attention should also be drawn to issues that youth faces while another said that gender equality is deemed particularly relevant for poverty eradication and should be addressed not only as an 'enabler' of the SDGs but also in its own right.[56] Statements like the above found resonance in the TST's brief on poverty eradication. The TST described employment as a measure to eradicate poverty and reiterated that robust and stable economic growth is also necessary. However, it should not be an end in itself. Instead, growth policies should create decent work and livelihood opportunities for the poor and all groups of society by proactively addressing the specific constraints faced by distinct population groups, including women and youth.[57] Once again, the link between growth and employment was evident since their complementarity could materialize the economic aspect of sustainable development. Their relationship with the social and environmental dimensions was also explicated. For instance, reference was made to decoupling growth from environmental degradation and to the importance of social protection as the backbone for policy measures to ensure employment.[58]

Understandably, the Goal to eradicate poverty encompassed different facets, most of which were also important in their own right. They could stand as separate goals alongside being drivers of poverty eradication. Employment and growth were not exempt. Within this context, the OWG participants observed that there was scope for further refining the goals and targets in order to capture the multiple aspects of poverty and bring together the three dimensions of sustainable development in mutually supportive ways. Hence, they decided to group priority areas into clusters of interlinked issues that would be discussed in the sessions thereafter.[59]

---

[53] TST, 'Issue Brief 1: Conceptual Issues' <https://sustainabledevelopment.un.org/content/documents/1729t stissuesconceptual2.pdf>; 'Issue Brief 2: Poverty Eradication' <https://sustainabledevelopment.un.org/content/documents/1728tstissuespoverty.pdf> both accessed 14 December 2020.

[54] OWG-2, 'Summary', 2 <https://sustainabledevelopment.un.org/content/documents/1813Summary_OWG2_final.pdf> accessed 14 December 2020.

[55] ibid 3–4, 11.

[56] ibid 8, 12.

[57] ibid 10, 13; TST Brief 2: Poverty (n 53) 2–3.

[58] OWG-2 'Summary' (n 54) 14.

[59] ibid, 4, 7, 14, 15; TST Brief 2: Poverty (n 53) 5.

Interestingly, employment and growth were put under different clusters despite the association already drawn between them. They were discussed separately in the fourth and fifth OWG sessions respectively. The following section presents the content of consultations in those meetings.

a) OWG-4 (17–19 June 2013)
Decent work and employment were grouped together with social protection, health, education, and culture. Given that all five topics are fundamental drivers of human development, this cluster purported to shed light purely to the social pillar of sustainable development.

The questions that guided the discussion on employment and decent work were the following three:[60]

1. Which aspects of employment and decent work deserve greater attention in the SDGs framework?
2. Can a stand-alone goal promote coherent and social measures and synergies across economic, social, and environmental dimensions? What is needed in order to implement a possible goal and targets relating to employment and decent work?
3. How can economic growth stimulate employment and what are the constraints for the creation of more and better jobs?

The TST brief on employment and decent work gave valuable insight on the dimensions that ought to be highlighted under this goal since it incorporated the expertise of the International Labor Organization (ILO), the UN Industrial Development Organisation (UNIDO), and UN Women, the entity for gender equality and the empowerment of women.

To begin with, a pointer to how decent work is understood was given for the first time. Albeit being a generic formulation included in the text's footnote, it is mentioned that decent work combines access to full and productive employment with rights at work, social protection, the promotion of social dialogue, and gender equality as cross-cutting issues.[61] Of course, this statement is descriptive and embodies a conceptualization rather than an actual definition of decent work. Moreover, it does not elucidate the relationship between decent work and full and productive employment. It seems that the latter informs the content of the former, yet it is not clear whether they constitute distinct and complementary notions or have a common conceptual core and are used interchangeably. Notwithstanding this limitation, it is discernible that both terms emphasize the quality aspects of employment, which were indeed stressed as a major development challenge. A great number of workers were trapped in informal and

---

[60] OWG-4, 'Guiding Questions' <https://sustainabledevelopment.un.org/content/documents/1838Guiding%20questions_OWG4.pdf> accessed 14 December 2020.
[61] TST Brief 'Employment and Decent Work', 1 <https://sustainabledevelopment.un.org/content/documents/18331106tstissuesemploywork.pdf> (footnote 1) accessed 14 December 2020.

vulnerable jobs with scanty incomes, tentative prospects, and exposure to social, economic, and environmental risks. On the other hand, the brief asserts, opportunities for full-time regular wage employment are scarce compared to temporary and part-time employment opportunities that become increasingly the norm. Variations in pay are yet another element that undermines the quality conditions of work and employment across countries since low or no wage has an adverse impact on access to social protection schemes. Last but not least, labour standards such as freedom of association, collective bargaining, and trade union rights are severely restricted in some cases, having a negative impact on the protection of workers' rights.[62]

Equally, demand for more job opportunities was emphasized as a key priority in all countries. In the aftermath of the global financial crisis, when the OWG took place, high levels of unemployment were an acute problem for people at all ages worldwide. Therefore, the proliferation of employment opportunities was necessary to stimulate the labour market again, yet other parameters such as technological innovation had generated gaps in the labour market, pushing some people out of the workforce because automation gained ground. In addition, demographic trends influence the demand and supply of jobs in contrasting ways. On the one hand, there is the growing number of the world labour force that creates the need for more and new jobs and on the other, the ageing population in developed (and some developing) countries that generates labour and skills shortages, not to mention the pressure on social security systems whose viability depends on a renewable workforce.[63]

Concerns about better employment and for all were particularly juxtaposed against ethnic groups, migrants, people with disabilities, youth, and women. An imbalance in gender dynamics is evident in various employment sectors. Characteristically, in most regions, women are under-represented in wage employment and bear the greatest burden of unpaid care work. Moreover, they comprise a large portion of the unemployed worldwide.[64] Congruently, youth unemployment is alarming in advanced economies where a big group of young people that is neither in employment nor in education or some kind of training is evinced. Analogously, high unemployment rates are noted among the economically active people in the developing world. Reversing the situation by investing in young people's education and technical and vocational training is not only a moral obligation but also an economic and social necessity since they are expected to make productive contributions to society through their job and payable taxes.[65]

Correlations of this kind underscored the complexity of measures required to tackle the challenge of employment within the framework of sustainable development. To say the very least, synergies ought to be materialized with policies that promote education, social protection, the reform of labour institutions, and international strategies on

---

[62] ibid 1–3.
[63] ibid 3–4; TST Brief 'Population Dynamics', 2, 4 <https://sustainabledevelopment.un.org/content/documents/18310406tstissuespopdyn.pdf> accessed 14 December 2020.
[64] TST Brief 'Employment' (n 61) 1, 2;
[65] TST Brief 'Population Dynamics' (n 63) 4.

migration and environmental preservation. Indeed, interrelations of employment with the first two matters were made in this OWG, as social aspects dominated its working agenda. By extension, education was seen as an enabler of employment. In fact, decent work was counted among the interconnected dividends that result from investments in equitable quality education in order for disadvantaged children, youth, and adults to acquire relevant technical/vocational and transferrable skills for decent work. Reaching out to these categories requires innovative interventions through technology and partnerships between education providers, employers, and workers.[66]

The relationship between employment and social protection was rooted in social justice and found legal justification in international human rights and labour law.[67] *Ergo*, the right to social security indivisibly promotes the rights to an adequate standard of living, food, health, education, and the right to work.[68] On this basis, the employment–social protection link was characterized as bidirectional from the viewpoint of policy too.[69] Lack of protection schemes means that the unemployed do not receive benefits that will enable them to overcome the barriers to get back into employment. However, labour market informality and the precariousness of work pose also structural limits to contributory schemes in reaching the most vulnerable (women, youth, migrant workers) since they are not entitled to benefits or guarantees. Social protection can strengthen people's assets and well-being by transferring to people resources, whether monetary (eg income guarantees) or in the form of access to services such as healthcare and education, thus enhancing the productive capacity of populations, increasing their participation in the labour market, and boosting job creation. The latter is especially true for women and migrants' integration into society and the learning of skills that will make them employable. Yet, even the transition to greener economies may be indirectly assisted because of the protective net that can absorb financial distress on affected groups and provide incentives for people to get involved in practices that further environmentally sensitive livelihoods.[70]

---

[66] TST Brief 'Education' 1, 3 <https://sustainabledevelopment.un.org/content/documents/18290406tstisuesedc ult.pdf> accessed 14 December 2020. Education was also discussed as an explicit goal in OWG 4, see Chapter 4 in this book.

[67] TST Brief 'Social Protection' <https://sustainabledevelopment.un.org/content/documents/18320406tsti ssuesocprot.pdf> accessed 14 December 2020, 4. For the purposes of the discussion in OWG 4, social protection referred to a set of public and private policies and programmes aimed at preventing, reducing, and eliminating poverty deprivation and social exclusion, and enhancing resilience and opportunities through promoting human capital and connecting people to decent work and more productive employment. It comprises various types of programmes, including in-kind support and social services, employment guarantees, and unemployment/under-employment support schemes (1 (footnote 2)).

[68] Indicatively: UNGA, Universal Declaration of Human Rights (10 December 1948) UN Doc 217 A (III), art 22; International Covenant on Economic, Social and Cultural Rights (adopted 16 December 1966, entered into force 3 January 1976) UN Res 2200A (XXI), art 9; ICommESCR, General Comment 19, 'The Right to Social Security (Art 9)' (2008) UN Doc E/C.12/GC/19; UN Convention on Elimination of All Forms of Discrimination Against Women (CEDAW) (adopted 18 December 1979, entered into force 3 September 1981) 1249 UNTS 13, art 11(e), art 14(c); ILO, Social Security (Minimum Standards) Convention (adopted 28 June 1952, entered into force 27 April 1955) C102 and ILO, Social Protection Floors Recommendation (adopted 14 June 2012) R202. However the ILO has adopted more standards on social security. For an up-to-date list (*ILO*) <https://www.ilo.org/secsoc/ areas-of-work/legal-advice/WCMS_205339/lang--en/index.htm> accessed 14 December 2020.

[69] Interestingly, a clear target on social protection appears only under SDG 1 (target 1.3) and not under SDG 8, where one can only infer from the descriptive language of some targets (eg 8.5, 8.6) that social protection was a background thought.

[70] TST Brief 'Social Protection' (n 67) especially 3–4.

Finally, a brief note was made on the contribution of culture to employment. In this respect, cultural tourism and creative industries (innovation and entrepreneurship) were mentioned as the means for job creation and economic growth.[71]

In light of the above, the subsequent more elaborate conceptualization of decent work was considered: decent work involves 'opportunities for work that is productive and delivers a fair income, security in the workplace and social protection for families, better prospects for personal development and social integration, freedom for people to express their concerns, organize and participate in the decisions that affect their lives and equality of opportunity and treatment for all women and men'.[72] Notably, the relationship between productive employment and decent work was couched in the same language as in the first formulation without gaining more clarity. It is also interesting that no reference is made to the rights at work this time whereas the elements of social protection and social dialogue that the previous conceptualization skipped are elaborated. Nonetheless, the integration of employment and decent work into the SDGs was conceived achievable under the following two propositions:[73]

a) **A stand-alone goal.** The goal was stipulated in different ways. A group of countries suggested an 'Enhanced Employment and Livelihood Security' goal, which would cover socio-economic and environmental policies for employment generation; entrepreneurship and enterprise development; women and youth participation in labor markets; and social protection. The HLPP on the Post-2015 Development Agenda proposed a candidate Goal 8, entitled 'Create jobs, sustainable livelihoods and equitable growth', with a set of targets and indicators on good and decent jobs and livelihoods; youth employment, education and training; productive capacity and business development through access to finance, better infrastructure and an enabling business environment.[74] Corroborative to the aforementioned proposals was the ILO[75] and the International Trade Union Confederation (ITUC),[76] without proposing a specific wording for the Goal.

b) **As targets that foster an integrated approach to achieving a higher-order goal.** This option considers employment and decent work as an *enabler* for poverty eradication and inclusive economic growth. The proposal came from the World Bank, which viewed job creation as a necessary requirement to ensure that economic growth translates into poverty reduction. On the same note, 'Save the Children' suggested that the goal of 'eradicating extreme income poverty through inclusive growth and decent work' be the first in a set of ten goals aimed at

---

[71] TST Brief 'Education' (n 66) 6–8.

[72] ibid 3–4 footnote 20; Major Group: Local Authorities, Intervention by Aliye Celik <https://sustainabledevelopment.un.org/content/documents/4288authorities2.pdf> accessed 14 December 2020.

[73] TST Brief 'Employment' (n 61) 4–5.

[74] HLPP (n 47) 31, 47–47.

[75] ILO Deputy Director-General Greg Vines, Keynote Address (17 June 2013) <https://sustainabledevelopment.un.org/content/documents/3671ILO.pdf> accessed 14 December 2020.

[76] Major Group Workers & Trade Unions <https://sustainabledevelopment.un.org/content/documents/3652workers.pdf> accessed 14 December 2020.

providing the foundations for human development or, according to another proposal, be a pillar of a goal on 'inclusive economic growth for dignified livelihoods and adequate standards of living' as the basis for human development.

Whatever form the integration of employment and decent work would take within the SDGs framework in the end, it became evident in the discussion that its realization depended on a wider set of structural improvements to the economic system, more sound governance and effectively on a judicious mix of economic and social measures.[77] In this regard, more specific actions were mentioned that could be deemed predecessors of current targets under Goal 8. By way of example, the productive transformation of countries' economies, namely their diversification in line with each countries' resources and needs, so that investment and entrepreneurial opportunities are facilitated and people move into more productive sectors and with better earnings (targets 8.2 and 8.3);[78] commitment to the rule of law, as a consequence of which property rights and human rights, especially the fundamental labour principles and rights at work will be the cornerstone of decent work and will shape improvements in wages, working conditions, social protection schemes and the effective functioning of labour institutions (implicit in targets 8.5, 8.7, and 8.8);[79] the balancing of employment and job availability with environmental sustainability through sustainable modes of consumption and production in order to avoid resource depletion and environmental degradation which have a negative impact on traditional sectors (eg agriculture) and on the most vulnerable groups for whom the environment is a source of income; to adjust industries to more sustainable practices through the use of technology and equip workers with the necessary skills through training to harness new market opportunities that will arise as a result of new sustainable industries (target 8.4);[80] build partnerships with domestic authorities and international organizations that oversee various cross-border sectors such as trade, migration, finance and macroeconomic coordination, education, the environment, gender issues etc, in order to design a comprehensive set of policies that take account of country-specific and international frameworks and regulating processes in these areas with the view to facilitate synergies, complementarities, and overcome bottlenecks that hinder progress.[81]

b) OWG-5 (25–27 November 2013)

The fifth session of the OWG about economic growth, macroeconomic policy, infrastructure development, and industrialization made much more apparent the

---

[77] TST Brief 'Employment' (n 61) 6; P Thomson, Statement on behalf of the G77 and China at the 4th Session of the OWG (17 June 2013) <https://sustainabledevelopment.un.org/content/documents/3667g77.pdf> accessed 14 December 2020.

[78] TST Brief 'Employment' (n 61) point 2, 5.

[79] ibid.

[80] ibid point 3, 6; Franciscan Action Network, The National Partnership for Climate Solutions and Mining Working Group at the UN, 'Jobs v. Jobs in the SDGs' (17 June 2013) <https://sustainabledevelopment.un.org/content/documents/3651jobsvsjobs.pdf > accessed 14 December 2020.

[81] ibid point 5, 7.

cross-cutting nature of development issues and the complexity of their categorization into comprehensive Focus Areas from which single, yet interrelated, goals would emerge. Particularly challenging was the differentiation of Goals from instruments in achieving the SDGs—in other words, the Goals versus the means to their implementation. Besides, targets capturing multiple facets of an issue could be placed under more than one SDG.[82] The perplexity of this matter covered much of the discussion on economic growth. Many delegates/observers to the OWG viewed growth as a means to end poverty and achieve other development goals. Therefore, they viewed economic recommendations as an inextricable component of the post-2015 agenda that should be compiled into an action plan for sustainable development.[83] Concomitantly, though, they could recognize the value of having a growth goal, framed on the additional pillars of environmental sustainability and human development, with equity and human rights at the core, as opposed to pure economic variables (ie economies' GDP).[84] Consequently, considerable thought was given to delineating the underlying causations of growth—the structure of economies, infrastructure, social inclusion, and the economic precariousness of the most vulnerable groups (women and youth), employment, extraction of natural resources, energy efficiency, finance etc. The aforementioned parameters were embodied in the proposal for a goal entitled 'Sustained and Inclusive Economic Growth'. The definition of each attributive element was given as follows:[85]

Inclusive growth is a multidimensional concept, encapsulating income- and non-income related gains that are distributed more equally across society. Poverty reduction is a central axis for assessing prosperity but it is an incomplete indicator if not accompanied by the reduction of inequalities and various forms of discrimination and respect for human rights. Thus, apart from income increase, it generates decent employment opportunities, improvements in workforce education, and realizes the well-being of a country's entire population, including persons with disabilities, women/girls, and minority groups.

Sustained growth indicates economic progress that is 'dynamic, enduring or self-propelling'. It emerges from economies that can generate constantly new activities, which increase productivity rates and the added value to society. Technological innovation, industrial development and investment in infrastructure (for transport, information, and communication, social services such as healthcare etc) are key drivers of good economic outputs. However, growth of this type may be resource-intensive and

---

[82] TST Brief 'Sustained and Inclusive Economic Growth, Infrastructure Development and Industrialisation' (16 October 2013), 6 <https://sustainabledevelopment.un.org/content/documents/2078Draft%20Issue%20Brief_Sustained%20and%20Inclusive%20Economic%20Growth_Final_16Oct.pdf> accessed 14 December 2020.

[83] A Caliari, 'Rethinking Bretton Woods Project' (*Centre of Concern*, 26 November 2013), Preface <https://sustainabledevelopment.un.org/content/documents/4218Caliari.pdf> accessed 14 December 2020.

[84] OWG 5 'Summary', 1–2 <https://sustainabledevelopment.un.org/content/documents/2773Summary%20of%20owg-5_0612.pdf> accessed 14 December 2020, keynote speaker, Prof Bhagwati, emphasized that growth matters and is necessary since it offers opportunities and generated revenues and taxes for a country to be able to afford social spending; Inter-parliamentary Union, Statement by Alessandro Motter (26 November 2013) <https://sustainabledevelopment.un.org/content/documents/4228ipu.pdf> accessed 14 December 2020: 'it would be wrong to posit sustainable growth as a goal. It's at most a means and then only one of several contributors to human well-being.'

[85] TST Brief on Growth (n 82) 1.

damaging to the environment. By contrast, within the new development framework, it should also be *sustainable*.[86] Economic activity should respect environmental limits, reduce carbon emissions and waste in order to reverse the adverse effects on ecosystems and prevent future damages to the climate and the Earth's natural systems. Hence, the promotion of green economy is paramount.

On this account, a number of specific policy steps/targets were put forward for inclusive, sustained, and sustainable economic growth to become meaningful in practice.[87] States should engineer the structural transformation of their economies by providing an enabling environment for the formation and growth of small and medium-size enterprises (SMEs) and giving incentives to businesses to engage in new enterprises. They should also ensure that the benefits of such economic undertakings spread into society. Mechanisms to this end require more strategic interventions by governments, the enforcement of human rights law, and adherence to corporate and social responsibility standards by businesses.[88] Moreover, they may address rural and social infrastructure; redirect tax exemptions towards small and medium-size producers, social solidarity economy initiatives, and correct gender biases implicit in tax policies.[89] Notably, targets on financial policies at a national and international level drew the attention of discussants. Major Groups highlighted that finance should serve the economy and not drive it,[90] hence states should be in a position to frame their finance policies according to the needs of their citizens and national circumstances. Besides, policies should be sound, facilitating access to financial services and affordable financing products (eg loans) that promote the diversification of industry, innovation, and investments in research and development (R&D) through entrepreneurship and start-ups.[91] That said, the restructuring of domestic financial systems was deemed necessary for strengthening domestic financial markets and increasing the quantity of and access to domestic financial resources for all (citizens' economic empowerment). Equally, an open, fair, rule-based, and non-discriminatory international trading system was considered a pillar for growth in each country, especially the least developed. Thus, specific initiatives with a

---

[86] Jeffrey Sachs (SDSN) and Secretary-general of the UNCTAD referred to the importance of continued, ie sustained (economic) development within planetary boundaries, combined with social progress and supported by a new global architecture that effectively mobilizes resources and channel them to achieve maximal development impact, see OWG 5 'Summary' (n 84) 2–3.

[87] Bhagwati (n 84) observed that to a degree the terms 'inclusive and sustainable' have become politically correct catchwords, to which meaning should be given.

[88] UN Human Rights Council, 'Protect, Respect and Remedy: A Framework for Business and Human Rights: Report of the Special Representative of the Secretary-General on the Issue of Human Rights and Transnational Corporations and Other Business Enterprises, John Ruggie' (7 April 2008) UN Doc A/HRC/8/5; UN Principles for Responsible Investment (*UN PRI*) <https://www.unpri.org/> accessed 14 December 2020.

[89] NB Ponte, 'Morning Hearing on Sustained and Inclusive Economic Growth' (Presentation by Women's Major Group, 25 November 2013) <https://sustainabledevelopment.un.org/content/documents/4238women2.pdf> accessed 14 December 2020.

[90] Caliari (n 83).

[91] Major Group Business and Industry, 'Intervention' (26 November 2013), points 3 and 5, where it is highlighted that business is itself one of the most important 'means of implementation' for the SDGs <https://sustainabledevelopment.un.org/content/documents/4338business2.pdf> accessed 14 December 2020.

562   SDG 8

beneficial impact on the latter (such as enhancing the role of aid) were proposed and were elevated to a matter of international coordination and policy coherence.[92]

To conclude, participants in OWG-5 made an effort to balance the sustainability of growth with sustainable human development and seek ways to redistribute resources, promote productive diversification and employment-intensive sectors, and link finance to the necessities of the real economy with the view to fulfil development objectives. Still, they did not express their final view regarding the placement of growth in the SDGs framework until the end of the 'negotiation' phase of OWG meetings.

2. The Negotiation Phase

a) OWGs-9–13 (March–July 2014)

Having concluded the 'stocktaking' sessions, the next stage of deliberations on the SDGs was inaugurated with the presentation of a report summarizing the overarching points of agreement and disagreement on each reviewed thematic cluster.[93] Yet, discussions at OWG-9 proceeded on the basis of the first 'Focus Area' document produced by the OWG Chairs, whereby they aspired to initiate the process of distilling SDGs and accompanying targets.[94] Within the nineteen Focus Areas, economic growth and employment-decent work for all constituted Focus Areas 8 and 11 respectively. The document reiterated the necessity of growth for progress on the social and environmental fronts and stressed that robust economies should provide employment and satisfactory jobs for everyone seeking work. Next, it identified, in the narrative, specific aspects to be considered as targets in pursuit of each one of these fields.[95] Most importantly, however, the document crystallized the other interconnected development priorities to these two subjects as well as the latter's mutually reinforcing character. Thus, poverty eradication, food security, education, industrialization, sustainable consumption and production were common links.

The 10th OWG session continued with a revised draft of Focus Areas, which was more analytical on the potential targets to be included under each Focus Area goal compared to the first draft.[96] An interactive dialogue with stakeholders and Major Groups purported to refine the proposed goals and their potential

---

[92] TST Brief 'Macroeconomic Policy Questions', 5 <https://sustainabledevelopment.un.org/content/docume nts/2076TST%20Issues%20Brief%20-%20Macro%20policy%20questions_Final_11_Oct.pdf> accessed 14 December 2020.

[93] For those related to employment and economic growth, OWG, 'Progress Report', ch III, 11–16, 20 (especially point 136), points 143, 194–95 <https://sustainabledevelopment.un.org/content/documents/3238summaryall owg.pdf> accessed 14 December 2020.

[94] OWG 9, 'SDGs Focus Areas' (24 February 2014) <https://sustainabledevelopment.un.org/content/docume nts/3276focusareas.pdf> accessed 14 December 2020.

[95] Regarding growth, for instance, the document mentioned an open and inclusive trading system, debt sustainability, and shift towards higher productivity sectors. Furthermore, some key enabling factors of growth were mentioned, ranging from conducive regulatory and fiscal systems to better tax administration to a favourable investment climate. Analogously, employment could be facilitated through macroeconomic policy, transition from informal to formal sector employment, decent wages, elimination of gender-based and labour market discrimination, training for those displaced from workforce, implementation and safeguarding of labour laws, ILO norms and standards, to name a few.

[96] OWG-10, 'SDGs Focus Areas' (19 March 2014) <https://sustainabledevelopment.un.org/content/docume nts/3402Focus%20areas_20140319.pdf> accessed 14 December 2020.

targets.[97] With regards to employment and growth, Serbia suggested their consolidation in one Focus Area whereas Tanzania, for the African Group, proposed two stand-alone goals: 'promote sustained, inclusive and equitable economic growth' and 'promote rapid industrialization for employment and decent work'.[98] Other indicative proposals came from Ethiopia, which proposed employment and growth as targets under the Goal to eradicate poverty while Slovenia considered appropriate for some of the employment-related matters such as equal pay for equal work, to be included in gender targets.[99] Pakistan called for evolving education-to-work transition policies by 2020 to increase the employment rate of youth, including from vulnerable categories, as a specific target on employment.[100] Brazil recommended targets to end child and forced labour, human trafficking, and slavery.[101] Trinidad and Tobago classified employment as a target for a goal on sustained and inclusive economic growth; along the same lines was the proposal from Ireland, Denmark, and Norway, which added targets on enabling business environments, job creation, women's participation in the economy, disaster resilience, and resource efficiency. France, Switzerland, and Germany proposed merging growth and infrastructure into one goal and include targets on employment.[102] Last but not least, Workers and Trade Unions said a stand-alone goal on employment is needed and highlighted, *inter alia*, promoting minimum living wages, recognizing the rights of all women, and protecting the rights to social dialogue, union organization, and collective bargaining. Corroborative was the Feminist Task Force's proposition, which suggested that targets should include ensuring decent working conditions, minimum living wage, and reducing the number of the working poor.[103]

By OGW-11, delegates had a clear understanding of the definition of goals and targets. While goals denoted a specific and actionable commitment that is concise and easy to communicate but at the same time remains aspirational, targets constituted specific, time-bound, and measurable objectives that were constructed taking scientific evidence and data into account.[104] The revised 'Focus Area' document contained a list of sixteen development priorities and a first set of emerging Goals was proposed. Infrastructure, employment, and decent work for all were merged into economic growth, comprising the Focus Area of 'economic growth, employment and infrastructure'. The respective goal was formulated as follows: 'Promote sustainable, inclusive,

---

[97] OWG-10, 'Major Groups and Other Stakeholders Dialogue with Co-Chairs on the SDGs (2 April 2014) <https://sustainabledevelopment.un.org/content/documents/3674Compilation%20Document%20on%20Goals%20and%20Targets_April%2011-%20final.pdf> accessed 14 September 2020.

[98] International Institute for Sustainable Development (IISD), 'Summary of the 10th Session of the UN GA Working Groups on the SDGs' (2014) 32(10) Earth Negotiations Bulletin 1, 5 and 10 <https://enb.iisd.org/download/pdf/enb3210e.pdf> accessed 15 December 2020.

[99] ibid 6.

[100] ibid 6.

[101] ibid 7.

[102] ibid 12.

[103] ibid 22.

[104] ibid 3 (Co-Chair Csaba Kőrösi).

564   SDG 8

and sustained economic growth and decent jobs for all', and was complemented by the ten indicative targets below:[105]

a) sustain income growth of the bottom 40% of the income distribution of each country to reduce income inequalities by 2030

b) achieve full and productive employment and decent work for all who seek employment including for marginalized groups by 2030

c) halve the number of youth not in employment, education or training by 2020

d) by 2030 improve by x% the energy and resource productivity of economic activities and reduce by y% their waste and emissions per unit of output

e) create appropriate climate for SMEs, entrepreneurship and innovation by 2020

f) increase the share of high productivity sectors and activities in the economy, and strengthen productive capacities through technological upgrading and greater value addition, with a particular focus on LDCs

g) develop sustainable infrastructure accessible to all, with attention to needs of countries in special situations, and by 2030 provide access for 100% of rural populations to basic infrastructure and services

h) protect the rights of all workers, including migrant workers, in compliance with ILO fundamental rights at work

i) end child labour by 2030

j) encourage formalization of informal sector activities and employment

Interestingly, though, the inclusion of these matters as an actual goal in the SDGs framework was not met with consensus. Together with climate, biodiversity, peace, and the rule of law, employment/decent work and growth were regarded the most 'transformational' goals that expanded the agenda beyond the MDGs and were confronted by the different views on industrialization and economic development between developed and developing countries.[106] For the latter, economic growth was a priority, thus they preferred greater emphasis to be given on it than to employment and infrastructure. In turn, they insisted on a target on a fixed percentage of growth per annum and on a proportion of developing countries upgrading to the next level of economic development with the target period.[107] By contrast, developed countries wanted to see a better balance between growth and environmental sustainability; thereafter, they stressed that targets should highlight the positive economic benefits of greener development (decent green jobs and environmentally sound technologies). Additionally, they underlined the importance of a target on accountable business practices and of capturing social protection in a target in order to achieve strong coherence with poverty eradication

---

[105] OWG-11, 'Working Document for 5–9 May session of OWG' (informal document, 17 April 2014), 4 <https://sustainabledevelopment.un.org/content/documents/3686WorkingDoc_0205_additionalsupporters.pdf> accessed 14 December 2020.

[106] Kamau and others (n 34) 232.

[107] OWG-11, 'Intervention by Vietnam of Behalf of Troika Bhutan/Thailand/Vietnam on Focus Area 7 "Energy" and 8 "Employment, Growth and Infrastructure"' (5–9 May 2014) <https://sustainabledevelopment.un.org/content/documents/9158vietnam5.pdf> accessed 14 December 2020.

(Focus Area 1).[108] Various other combinations were suggested by other countries.[109] As in previous sessions, MGs made their own comments on the goal. These included: a) rewording the goal to 'inclusive economic growth, employment and decent work for all, and resilient infrastructure'[110] or 'Promote sustainable, inclusive, enduring economic growth and employment'[111] and b) amendments to the above-mentioned targets—for example: rephrase target a) as 'sustain *differentially high* income growth'[112] and targets d) and f) to include at the end of the sentence the phrase '*ensure economies operate within safe ecological boundaries*',[113] add targets that officially recognize traditional livelihoods as an economic sector and traditional occupations as forms of employment by 2030,[114] strengthen positive economic and social links between cities and rural areas creating possibilities for decent work,[115] by 2030 extend social security and universal social protection, to those in need, including older persons, people with disabilities, unemployed, children, women, and youth, in particular through the implementation of social protection floors in line with ILO convention 102 and recommendation 202.[116]

With these recommendations in mind, OWG members entered the 12th session in June 2014. Ahead of the meeting, a 'zero draft' of seventeen goals with their targets was compiled, which constituted the basis for the further negotiation of the SDGs. In this document, growth and employment constituted Goal 8, which read: 'Promote strong, inclusive and sustainable economic growth and decent work for all.' The associated targets were sixteen:[117]

8.1. sustain per capita economic growth of at least x% per annum (with x being set at a level appropriate to national circumstances)

8.2. sustain income growth of the bottom 40% of the income distribution of each country of at least y (greater than x)% to reduce income inequalities by 2030

8.3. by 2030 achieve full and productive employment and decent work for all women and men, including for young people and persons with disabilities

8.4. by 2020 halve the number of youth not in employment, education or training

---

[108] OWG-11, 'Comments by Denmark/Ireland and Norway on Economic Growth, Employment and Infrastructure' <https://sustainabledevelopment.un.org/content/documents/9230ireland3.pdf> accessed 14 December 2020.

[109] IISD, 'Summary of the 11th Session of the UN GA OWG on the SDGs' (2014) 32(11) Earth Negotiations Bulletin 1, 12–14 <https://enb.iisd.org/download/pdf/enb3211e.pdf> accessed 14 December 2020.

[110] OWG-11,' Major Groups (MG) and other Stakeholders Morning Hearings: Summary of Statements (FA1-10), MG: Children and Youth, NGOs, Workers and Trade Unions and Committee on Social Development', 15 <https://sustainabledevelopment.un.org/content/documents/3758mgsummary11.pdf> accessed 14 December 2020.

[111] ibid 'MG: Business and Industry', 16.

[112] ibid 15.

[113] ibid 'MG: Beyond 2015', 17.

[114] ibid 16; according to Indigenous Peoples target (j) should read: 'Officially recognise traditional occupations as forms of employment as essential to achieving and sustaining Indigenous Peoples' and other communities' wellbeing and livelihoods.'

[115] ibid 'MG: Local Authorities'.

[116] ibid 15.

[117] OWG-12, 'Introduction and Proposed Goals and Targets on Sustainable Development for the Post-2015 Development Agenda' (2 June 2014), 8–9 <https://sustainabledevelopment.un.org/content/documents/4528zerodraft12OWG.pdf> accessed 14 December 2020.

8.5. create a sound macroeconomic environment with strong fiscal and monetary policies

8.6. create an enabling environment for business with strong national economic institutions and policies that support investment and promote competition

8.7. create incentives for the development of sustainable tourism which takes into account community participation, local culture and local products

8.8. create enabling conditions for increased growth and productivity of micro-, small- and medium-scale enterprises (SMEs), including through policies that promote entrepreneurship, creativity and innovation, and through improved access to markets and financial services

8.9. increase the share of high productivity sectors and activities in the economy, and strengthen productive capacities through technological upgrading, greater value addition and product diversification, with a particular focus on LDCs

8.10. promote greater resource efficiency of economic activities, including through sustainable supply chains, according to national circumstances and capacities

8.11 support the development of quality, reliable, sustainable and resilient infra-structure for transport, energy, water and communications, in particular in developing countries with a focus on access for the rural and urban poor

8.12 improve regional and trans-border infrastructure to promote effective re-gional economic integration and facilitate trade

8.13 end child labour by 2030, protect the rights and ensure safe and secure working environments of all workers, including migrant workers and those in precar-ious employment

8.14. promote formalization of informal sector activities and employment

8.15. by 2030 lower the overall costs in migration processes and minimize transac-tion costs of remittances

8.16. explore the possibility of a broader system of capital accounting looking be-yond GDP and incorporating social, human and environmental capital

Negotiations continued in informal meetings where there was a target-by-target dis-cussion on Goal 8. Once again, proposals referred to amendments to the title of the goal (eg to replace 'sustainable' growth with 'sustained' and 'work' with 'employment') and to the substantive content of the targets. In this regard, they covered the merger of some targets and the allocation of some under other goals (eg target 8.7 to be combined with target 9 of Goal 11; target 8.2 as relevant to Goal 10) or their inclusion into the means of implementation (such as targets 8.6, 8.11, and 8.14)[118] as well as the enrichment of their wording to incorporate more aspects, aiming at comprehensiveness and precision.[119]

---

[118] IISD, 'Summary of 12th Session of the UNGA OWG on the SDGs' (2014) 32(12) Earth Negotiations Bulletin 4–6 <https://enb.iisd.org/download/pdf/enb3212e.pdf> accessed 14 December 2020.

[119] OWG-12, 'Compilation of Amendments to Goals and Targets (morning hearings with MG and Stakeholders, 16–20 June 2014)' 23–26 <https://sustainabledevelopment.un.org/content/documents/4269mgscompilation.pdf> accessed 30 March 2023.

However, even at the end of the meeting, participants were not entirely agreed on the sufficiency with which the economic dimension of development was addressed in the Goal, although there was strong support for the idea to keep Goal 8 separate from Goal 9 (industrialization).[120]

A revised zero draft of the Goals was prepared to inform the final OWG meeting[121] after another set of informal meetings in which stakeholders and MGs presented their last round of proposed amendments to the SDGs.[122] Goal 8 'Promote sustained, inclusive and sustainable economic growth, full and productive employment and decent work for all' comprised now seven targets:

8.1 achieve transformation of economies towards higher levels of productivity through diversification with a focus on high value added sectors

8.2 create a sound macroeconomic environment with employment-friendly policies and an enabling environment at national, regional and international levels for productive investment, creativity and innovation, and formalization and growth of micro-, small- and medium-sized enterprises

8.3 achieve progressively through 2030 global resource efficiency, and endeavour to decouple economic growth from environmental degradation and resource use

8.4 by 2030 achieve full and productive employment and decent work for all women and men, including for young people and persons with disabilities, and equal pay for work of equal value

8.5 take immediate and effective measures to secure the prohibition and elimination of the worst forms of child labour, and by 2020 end child labour in all its forms

8.6 protect the rights and ensure safe and secure working environments of all workers, including migrant workers and those in precarious employment in accordance with ILO norms and standards

8.a improve Aid for Trade support for developing countries, notably through the Enhanced Integrated Framework for LDCs

A second reading of the Goal and its targets allowed for the final propositions to be made by OWG members.[123] During the discussion on the Goal's heading, there were calls in favour of 'sustained' economic growth versus 'sustainable' economic growth. In the end, delegates went with both. Regarding the targets: a target on per

---

[120] IISD, 'Summary of 12th Session' (n 118) 19.

[121] OWG Co-chairs, 'Introduction and Proposed Goals and Targets on Sustainable Development For the Post2015 Development Agenda' (Revised Zero Draft, 30 June 2014) <https://sustainabledevelopment.un.org/content/documents/4523zerodraft.pdf>; Co-Chairs' Letter to OWG members (30 June 2014), in which they emphasized that the zero draft was a testament of the openness and inclusiveness of the OWGs consultations (para 2) <https://sustainabledevelopment.un.org/content/documents/4324lettercochairs30june14.pdf> both accessed 14 December 2020.

[122] OWG-13, 'Final Compilation of Amendments to Goals and Targets by Major Groups and Other Stakeholders, including Citizens' Responses to My World 6 priorities' <https://sustainabledevelopment.un.org/content/documents/4438mgscompilationowg13.pdf> accessed 14 December 2020.

[123] For the entire text that follows, see IISD, 'Summary of the 13th Session of the UN GA OWG on SDGs' (2014) 32(13) Earth Negotiations Bulletin 10–11 <https://enb.iisd.org/download/pdf/enb3213e.pdf> accessed 14 December 2020.

capita economic growth was added after the persistence of some developing countries, which claimed that without a growth rate of 6–8 per cent over a prolonged period of time they wouldn't be able to change their economic status. An agreement was reached on 7 per cent growth rate pursuant to the Istanbul Program of Action. Targets 8.1 and 8.2 were slightly differentiated in the final version of the goal. After the addition of the target on per capita growth, target 8.1 became current target 8.2 and technological innovation was added to its content, thus reading currently: 'achieve higher levels of economic productivity through diversification, technological upgrading and innovation, including through a focus on high-value added and labour-intensive sectors'. Analogously, former target 8.2 became 8.3 and its wording was changed from 'create a sound macroeconomic environment' to 'promote development-oriented policies', while emphasis on an enabling environment for entrepreneurship and SMEs outweighed any reference to fiscal and monetary policies. Moving on, support for resource efficiency under Goal 8 raised some questions since some delegates believed it was a target that fit better under Goal 12. Decoupling of growth from environmental degradation prompted also lengthy discussions, particularly as OWG members questioned the appropriateness of the phrase as an internationally agreed terminology, while developing countries wanted it to be adopted with the qualification 'where appropriate'. A compromise was reached finally, with the wording being '*endeavor* to decouple economic growth from environmental degradation'. Contrariwise, employment and decent work appeared to be the two points able to attract more easily the consent of participants, as they reread the relevant targets. By extension, current target 8.6 on youth unemployment was adopted ('by 2020, substantially reduce the proportion of youth not in employment, education or training') together with the pursuit of a global strategy for youth unemployment and the ILO's Global Jobs Pact as means of implementation (current target 8.b). Moreover, it was agreed to set the time frame for ending child labour to 2025. The matter that seemed to be discussed more was the explicit reference to ILO norms and standards regarding labour rights, which was eventually omitted since not all countries follow them. Ultimately, sustainable tourism was added at the last minute as a target despite the preference of some OWG representatives, who thought it would function better as an indicator.

19 July 2014 marked the end of the OWG's mandate with the adoption of its final proposal on the SDGs for consideration and appropriate action by the UNGA.[124]

---

[124] OWG 13, 'Introduction to the Proposal of the OWG for SDGs' (19 July 2014) <https://sustainabledevelopm ent.un.org/content/documents/4518SDGs_FINAL_Proposal%20of%20OWG_19%20July%20at%201320hrsv er3.pdf> and UNGA, 'Report of the OWG of the GA' (12 August 2014) UN Doc A/68/970.

III. Goal Commentary

A. Inclusive and Sustainable Economic Growth in SDG 8

1. The Neoliberal Connotation of Growth and Its Contradiction with Human Development and Environmental Sustainability

Noteworthy efforts, such as the UN Global Compact's Design for Sustainable Development Goals, have been made to reach a consensus on what 'economic growth' means in the SDGs framework.[125] The 2030 Agenda for Sustainable Development indicates its transformative potential across a wide spectrum of outcomes for the human race, whether to expand the productive capacity of least developed countries (LDCs) or to improve living standards worldwide, referring to it at least ten times.[126] Similarly, International Financial Institutions (IFIs), and in particular the affiliates of the World Bank Group, consider 'sustained, inclusive and sustainable economic growth' as closely linked to global issues such as poverty and environmental protection.[127] In fact, they firmly contend that sustained and sustainable economic growth can be obtained by all countries through a mix of ingredients to be combined by policy-makers and politicians within their own national realities. They often argue that inequality may be approached in a manner that does not compromise economic growth and productivity.[128] In this context, economic growth in Agenda 2030 and SDG 8 is purported to reflect a 'transformative new consensus',[129] namely that its achievement is interrelated with objectives such as reducing inequalities, eliminating extreme poverty and hunger, and protecting the environment. Thus, a more human-centred perception of economic growth is shaped in the new development framework that is associated to human rights, human development, and environmental sustainability.

Nevertheless, there is room to contest the assumption that 'sustained, inclusive and sustainable economic growth' in SDG 8 and related targets expresses an idea different to neoliberal economic growth.[130] The International Trade Union Confederation (ITUC) explicitly adopts this view when it asserts that SDG 8 fails to offer a prudent and feasible alternative to neoliberal growth based on structural transformation. Shirin M

---

[125] United Nations Global Compact, 'Corporate Sustainability and the United Nations Post-2015 Development Agenda: Perspectives from UN Global Compact Participants on Global Priorities and How to Engage Business Towards Sustainable Development Goals, Report to the United Nations Secretary-General' (17 June 2013) <https://d306pr3pise04h.cloudfront.net/docs/news_events%2F9.1_news_archives%2F2013_06_18%2FUNGC_Post2015_Report.pdf> accessed 15 February 2021.

[126] Frey, 'Economic Growth, Full Employment and Decent Work' (n 19) 1176 ff.

[127] Further references are found in World Bank, 'Global Program on Sustainability' <https://www.worldbank.org/en/programs/global-program-on-sustainability> accessed 14 March 2021.

[128] ibid.

[129] Frey, 'Economic Growth, Full Employment and Decent Work' (n 19) 1176 ff.

[130] Neoliberalism is an economic theory and an ideological conviction that maximizes the economic freedom for individuals and requires reducing the amount of state intervention to the bare minimum including labour protections. See WE Murray, 'Neoliberalism and Development', *International Encyclopedia of Human Geography* (Elsevier Science 2009) 120 ff.

570   SDG 8

Rai, Benjamin D Brown, and Kanchana N Ruwanpura would seem to agree with these and other similar considerations when they state that 'dividing 'development' into discrete goals runs counter to recognizing the structural and systematic connections that underpin these goals and aspirations'.[131] And that is not all; even the 'Action Agenda for Sustainable Development' prepared by the Leadership Council of the Sustainable Development Solutions Network (SDSN) seems implicitly to share these views and opinions when omitting to indicate economic growth as a stand-alone goal in the attached proposal of SDGs and targets.[132] Various and decisive reasons may lead to this conclusion: first, multinational corporations (MNCs) and private corporations have deeply influenced the notion of 'sustained, inclusive and sustainable economic growth' in SDG 8. Another (indirect) reason supporting this possible contestation is that there are few explicit linkages between SDG 8, particularly it's growth-related aspect, and human rights,[133] despite the fact that economic growth—especially rapid economic growth[134]—may be contrary to upholding human rights norms, as the example of the human right to water shows.[135] Yet, acknowledging the existence of legally enforceable rights for individuals is indeed of crucial significance for transforming development policy commitments into practice.[136] Thirdly, it is the mere fact that economic growth is formulated as an independent goal, which raised a number of concerns such as that by Frey who states: 'Raising economic growth, even "sustained, sustainable economic growth" as described in SDG 8 to the level of a goal is imprudent' 'because it ... potentially confuses the *ends* and *means* of development' and also because it 'is not likely to succeed while obscuring real challenges and potentially transformative solutions'.[137] Jason Hickel blames SDG 8 for being in contradiction with several other goals, especially SDG 13 on climate action, SDG 14 (Life below water), and SDG 15 (Life on land). According to him, SDG 8, as currently conceived, contradicts the sustainability objectives of the SDGs, in particular because 'even growth at 3% makes it

---

[131] SM Rai and others, 'SDG 8: Decent Work and Economic Growth—A Gendered Analysis' (2019) 113 World Development 368, 377 ff.

[132] SDSN, 'An Action Agenda for Sustainable Development' (n 48).

[133] Advisory Council on International Affairs, 'Sustainable Development Goals and Human Rights: An Indivisible Bond' <https://www.asser.nl/media/5625/advisory-report-110.pdf >accessed 28 March 2022.

[134] SP Huntington, *Political Order in Changing Societies* (Yale University Press 1968) 53 ff.

[135] UNGA, 'The Human Right to Safe Drinking Water and Sanitation' (9 October 2012) UN Doc A/HRC/RES/21/2, para 14. See also WM Cole, 'Too Much of a Good Thing? Economic Growth and Human Rights, 1960 to 2010' (2017) 67 Social Science Research 72, 81, also recalling that '[h]uman rights scores in the world's poorest nations initially improve as their economies grow but then taper off and decline at higher rates of growth'; M Langford, 'Rethinking the Metrics of Progress: The Case of Water and Sanitation' in M Langford and others (eds) (n 11) 461 ff; O Spijkers, 'The Sustainable Human Right to Water as Reflected in the Sustainable Development Goals' (2020) 16 (2) Utrecht Law Review 18.

[136] Incidentally, this is a point that was implicitly understood by the Office of the High Commissioner (OHCHR) when it argued that the SDGs aim at reflecting the content of corresponding human rights provisions. See also SDSN, 'An Action Agenda for Sustainable Development' (n 48) describing the SDGs as complementary to the tools of international law, such as legally binding global conventions and treaties, by providing a shared normative framework that fosters collaboration across eleven countries.

[137] Frey, 'Economic Growth, Full Employment and Decent Work' (n 19) 1175 ff, also observing that '[e]levating "economic growth" to the status of an SDG unnecessarily confuses the well-accepted and long-standing commitment of UN member states to human development and human rights as the ends of development'. And, further, '[r]ather than calling for promotion of economic growth, the UN Charter obligates states "to promote conditions of economic and social progress"'.

impossible to reduce resource use and carbon emissions enough to stay within the 2°C warming limits'.[138] Giorgios Kallis also shared this view and went even further when he claimed that instead of aiming for economic growth, the SDGs should aim at building upon advances in the field of 'sustainable degrowth' which acknowledges the limits of the Earth's systems to cope with continued growth, the inability of technological efficiency to meet growing demands, and the need to 'down-shift' sustainably to reduce society's throughput (or emissions and related use of resources).[139] He also stated that '[a]lthough SDG 8.4 advocates the "decoupling" of growth from production and consumption, it does not convincingly articulate how this would be possible or engage with literature on ecological limits'[140] and recalled that SDG 8 fails to address: 'depletion accrued through social reproduction'.[141]

In similar line of reasoning and thinking Diane Frey and Gillian MacNaughton argue that 'SDG 8 appears to condition the human rights to full employment and decent work upon economic growth'.[142] Equally important are also concerns that the focus of SDG 8 on GDP and per capita growth may result in excluding much of social reproductive work, therefore creating tension between SDG 8 and SDG 5 (Gender equality), the latter calling *inter alia* for the recognition of the value of unpaid care and domestic work. This concern draws upon critiques highlighting the non-linearity of the growth–employment relationship,[143] the gender gaps in SDG 8 targets and indicators,[144] and the low correlations between economic growth and human development (comprising a subset of human rights).[145] It is furthermore linked to more general criticisms about GDP as an appropriate tool for measuring a country's growth and overall development status. Sanjay G Reddy and Ingrid Harvold Kvangraven[146] note that 'the relationship between GDP growth and human development is not always robust, even in low and middle income countries'. Moreover, Mary Nyasimi and Linda Peake claim that income inequality should be included in any measurement of inclusive economic growth and suggest that a new sustainable development index shall be developed to integrate the

[138] J Hickel, 'The Contradiction of the Sustainable Development Goals: Growth Versus Ecology on a Finite Planet' (2019) 27 Sustainable Development 873 ff.

[139] G Kallis and J Hickel, 'Is Green Growth Possible?' (2019) 25 New Political Economy 469. See also World Bank Group, *Poverty and Shared Prosperity 2016: Taking on Inequality* (The World Bank 2016) 2, claiming that 'slower growth may be offset with and even overcome by greater redistribution and narrowing of inequality'.

[140] G Kallis, 'In Defence of Degrowth' (2011) 70 Ecological Economics 873; Hickel (n 138) 876.

[141] Kallis, 'In Defence of Degrowth' (n 140) 873 ff.

[142] DF Frey and G MacNaughton, 'A Human Rights Lens on Full Employment and Decent Work in the 2030 Sustainable Development Agenda' (2016) Journal of Workplace Rights 7 ff <https://journals.sagepub.com/doi/pdf/10.1177/2158244016649580> accessed 27 March 2022.

[143] Frey, 'Economic Growth, Full Employment and Decent Work' (n 19) 1169: 'the relationship between economic growth and employment is not a linear relationship'.

[144] Rai and others (n 131) 81 ff.

[145] Cole (n 135) 72 ff; MML Lim and others, 'Reframing the Sustainable Development Goals to Achieve Sustainable Development in the Anthropocene—A Systems Approach' (2018) (23)(3) Ecology and Society <https://www.ecologyandsociety.org/vol23/iss3/art22/> accessed 27 March 2022.

[146] IH Kvangraven and SG Reddy, 'Global Development Goals: If at All, Why, When and How? (2015) The New School for Social Research—Working Papers 23/2015 <https://www.researchgate.net/publication/282914682_Global_Development_Goals_If_At_All_Why_When_and_How> accessed 28 March 2022.

economic (composite of GDP per capita and income inequality), environmental (CO_2 per capita), and social (expected longevity at birth) dimensions.[147]

Other scholars have also noted that SDG 8's focus on decent work and economic growth is inadequate[148] and that productive employment and decent work for all men and women by 2030 would have requested to take into account the value and costs of social reproduction.[149] Again, it has also been claimed that SDG 8 should have refrained from referring to 'inclusiveness' because it is critical for sustaining economic growth and that SDG 8 has been formulated and contextualized in a manner that gives cause for concern because it is embedded in potentially conflicting visions of development.[150] Diane Frey explained this point clearly when she stated that: '*while* corporate interests represented by the International Organization of Employers (IOE) advanced a market-centered business approach *where* governments are not human rights duty bearers … human rights and labour groups envision a rights-based partnership in which all actors at the global and national level are accountable for their contributions to development and the creation of decent work for all'.[151]

All things considered, the fact that SDG 8 has partially been formulated in a human rights-based language and partially in a business-centred language gives credence to the observation that economic growth was not understood in the SDGs framework in general and in SDG 8 in particular as a means towards the ends of social justice, human dignity, gender equality, and well-being, but rather as a proxy indicator of good governance or fiscal policy.[152] It moreover raises additional questions and issues concerning the enforceability of the selected standards and targets (including means of implementation (MOI) targets) as well as the identification of accountability actors. Thereafter, it puts the link between sustainable development that is genuinely rights-based and economic growth that is not to a hard test.[153]

[147] M Nyasimi and L Peake, 'Review of SDG 5: Achieve Gender Equality and Empower All Women and Girls' in (2015) ICSU, ISSC Review of Targets for the Sustainable Development Goals: The Science Perspective (ICSU 2015) <https://www.researchgate.net/publication/288737370_Review_of_SDG_5_Achieve_gender_equality_and_empower_all_women_and_girls> accessed 28 March 2022.

[148] DF Frey and G MacNaughton, 'Full Employment and Decent Work in the Post 2015 Development Agenda' in N Shawki (ed), *International Norms, Normative Change, and the UN Sustainable Development Goals* (Lexington Books 2016) 185–201, 195–96; Frey, 'Economic Growth, Full Employment and Decent Work' (n 19) 1165, stressing that '[t]he merger of a goal on the human rights to full employment and decent work with a goal one economic growth presents a perplexing combination'.

[149] Rai and others (n 131) 368–80.

[150] Frey, 'Economic Growth, Full Employment and Decent Work' (n 19) 1177: 'Despite the World Bank's efforts, there is legitimate cause to question whether 'sustained, inclusive and sustainable economic growth' in SDG 8 represents a new consensus and whether it is distinguishable from neoliberal growth.'

[151] ibid 1177 ff.

[152] M Darrow, 'Masters or Servants: Development Goals and Human Rights' in M Langford and others (eds) (n 11) 94 ff.

[153] For similar remarks in relation to SDG 3, C Binder and JA Hofbauer, 'Good Health and Well-Being. Ensure Healthy Lives and Promote Well-Being for All at All Ages' in P Duran and others (eds), *International Society and Sustainable Development Goals* (Thomson Reuters Aranzadi 2016) 205, citing K Buse and S Hawkes, 'Health in the Sustainable Development Goals: Ready for a Paradigm Shift?' (2015) 11 Globalization and Health 13 <https://globalizationandhealth.biomedcentral.com/articles/10.1186/s12992-015-0098-8#citeas> accessed 23 March 2022.

B. The Role of the World Bank in the Achievement of SDG 8

The World Bank has proved essential in forming the new economic growth-related targets of the SDGs. This is especially evident with regard to target 8.1 and target 8.2, which have been on the World Bank agenda since the foundation of the International Bank for Reconstruction and Development (IBRD) in 1945 at the Bretton Woods conference. Although international focus on economic growth in low-income countries for a long period remained modest, at least if compared with the focus on official development assistance (ODA) to developing countries, the IBRD remained dedicated to embedding it within international development policy.[154] By 2013, a new World Bank Group Strategy was adopted by the Development Committee of the World Bank to support countries in building economic prosperity in a sustainable manner.[155] This managed to bring on board all important international institutions, including the ILO, IMF, and the EU and contributed to the shift to incorporate economic growth as an overarching goal in the SDGs.

Additionally, the World Bank institutions have been key actors of the monitoring process of the economic growth-related MDGs since 2006. With regard to the SDGs, the relevance of monitoring has received new attention. The Anticipated Impact Measurement and Monitoring (AIMM) framework is a clear confirmation of this.[156] It is therefore not surprising that the World Bank has remained a key cornerstone to this process. Moreover, for reporting on the SDG process, the World Bank depends on strict and regular cooperation with other international development institutions, including the ILO, IMF, and regional/sub-regional development banks.[157]

Lastly, also with regard to monitoring SDG 8 'at the goal level', the World Bank assumes a particular role and responsibility as a 'co-custodian' for twenty indicators.[158] In this regard, an indicator of 'equality and non-discrimination on the basis of sex' has been suggested but not accepted.[159]

Considering the dominant role that the World Bank has in particular during the monitoring process, its role in contributing to an understanding of SDG 8 from a human rights-based perspective may thus not be underestimated.

---

[154] J Masters and A Chatzky, 'The World Bank Group's Role in Global Development' (*Council on Foreign Relations*, 9 April 2019) <https://www.cfr.org/backgrounder/world-bank-groups-role-global-development> accessed 30 March 2023 highlighting that '[i]n recent decades, the Bank's primary focus has shifted from partnering with middle-income nations on growth-related programs and trade liberalization toward an emphasis on global poverty alleviation'.

[155] ibid.

[156] Further information on the Anticipated Impact Measurement and Monitoring <https://www.ifc.org/wps/wcm/connect/topics_ext_content/ifc_external_corporate_site/development+impact/aimm> accessed 23 March 2022.

[157] Masters and Chatzky (n 154).

[158] World Bank, 'WDI and the Sustainable Development Goals' <https://datatopics.worldbank.org/world-development-indicators/wdi-and-the-sustainable-development-goals.html> accessed 20 March 2021.

[159] ibid.

C. Full and Productive Employment and Decent Work for All

There is little disagreement that work is 'a vital ingredient of well-being'.[160] It is a necessity because it enables people to earn a livelihood and become economically secure. Through work, individuals acquire goods that are essential to meet their basic needs such as food and housing and other commodities they consider important for life. Yet, the benefits of work are not confined to consumption goods. Work is 'the path to personal development and fulfillment'[161] because individuals get access to non-material goods such as healthcare, education, and culture, which improve their living standards and enlarge their choices on the social and economic front, thus, creating the circumstances for them to unleash their potential, creativity, and spirit.[162] Work is also important for social cohesion. It confers on individuals a social role from which they derive a feeling of self-esteem and appreciation of others. Work enhances an individual's sense of belonging into society and encourages the formation of social relationships on the basis of mutual respect.[163] It allows people to participate fully in society while affording them a sense of dignity and worth.[164] Consequently, work is not simply an activity that increases the value of a free-market economy; it is not merely an economic transaction and workers are not inputs into a production process. In addition to this, work is the means for individuals to pursue their physical and spiritual development and well-being.

To the extent that upon these very rudiments rests the economic and social advancement of all peoples and the friendly relations among nations, work became a connecting line between social justice and peace and was incorporated in international policy and cooperation on social and economic affairs. Under article 55 of the UN Charter, the international community pledges strongly 'to promote higher standards of living, full employment and conditions of economic progress and development with full respect for and observance of human rights, as a means to international peace'.[165] Analogously, the ILO constitution envisions the establishment of enduring peace through just labour

[160] H Collins, 'Discrimination, Equality and Social Inclusion' (2003) 66(1) Modern Law Review 16, 29.

[161] Pope Francis, 'Laudato Sì: On Care for Our Common Home', para 128: 'Work is a Necessity, Part of the Meaning of Life on This Earth, a Path to Growth, Human Development and Personal Fulfilment' <http://www.vatican.va/content/dam/francesco/pdf/encyclicals/documents/papa-francesco_20150524_enciclica-laudato-si_en.pdf> accessed 20 March 21.

[162] UNDP, 'Human Development Report 2015', 1 and 29 <https://www.undp.org/publications/human-development-report-2015> accessed 23 March 2022.

[163] ibid. V Mantouvalou, 'Introduction' in V Mantouvalou (ed), *The Right to Work: Legal and Philosophical Perspectives* (Hart Publishing 2015); ILO, 'Employment Promotion and Protection against Unemployment Convention (No 168)' (1988), Preamble para 2, retrieved from <https://www.ilo.org/dyn/normlex/en/f?p=NORMLEXPUB:12100:0::NO:12100:P12100_INSTRUMENT_ID:312313:NO> accessed 20 March 21.

[164] Dignity and self-realization have both been considered foundations of the right to work. On the former, G Mundlak, 'The Right to Work—The Value of Work' in D Barak-Erez and A Gross (eds), *Exploring Social Rights: Between Theory and Practice* (Hart Publishing 2007) 341 at 348 ff; and G Mundlak, 'The Right to Work: Linking Human Rights and Employment Policy' (2007) 146 International Labour Review 189, 197; J Elster, 'Is There (or Should There Be) A Right to Work?' in A Gutmann (ed), *Democracy and the Welfare State* (Princeton University Press 1988) 53, 77. On the latter, H Collins, 'Is There a Human Right to Work' in V Mantouvalou (ed), *The Right to Work* (n 163); Collins, 'Discrimination, Equality and Social Inclusion' (n 160) 25.

[165] Charter of the United Nations (signed 26 June 1945, entered in force 24 October 1945) 892 UNTS 119.

conditions, freedom, dignity, and equality of opportunity in the world of work. In this respect, the ILO states that labour is not a commodity and recognizes the following obligations its programmes should fulfil:[166]

(a) full employment and the raising of standards of living; (b) the employment of workers in the occupations in which they can have the satisfaction of giving the fullest measure of their skill and attainments and make their greatest contribution to the common well-being; (c) the provision, as a means to the attainment of this end and under adequate guarantees for all concerned, of facilities for training and the transfer of labour, including migration for employment and settlement; (d) policies in regard to wages and earnings, hours and other conditions of work calculated to ensure a just share of the fruits of progress to all, and a minimum living wage to all employed and in need of such protection; (e) the effective recognition of the right of collective bargaining, the cooperation of management and labour in the continuous improvement of productive efficiency, and the collaboration of workers and employers in the preparation and application of social and economic measures; (f) the extension of social security measures to provide a basic income to all in need of such protection and comprehensive medical care; (g) adequate protection for the life and health of workers in all occupations; (h) provision for child welfare and maternity protection; (i) the provision of adequate nutrition, housing and facilities for recreation and culture; (j) the assurance of equality of educational and vocational opportunity.

Within this context, a combination of normative action—in terms of setting legal and legislative standards for access to employment and the enjoyment of favourable work conditions for all—and institution building for materializing this objective was launched. Efforts ran in parallel under the auspices of the UN and the ILO respectively.

1. The Human Right to Decent Work

Full employment was promoted under the UN pillars of human rights and development. The essence of the objective is reflected in article 23 UDHR, which in paragraph 1 reads: 'everyone has the right to work, to free choice of employment, to just and favorable conditions of work and to protection against unemployment'. The subsequent paragraphs stipulate the right to equal pay for equal work; to just and favourable remuneration and social protection; and the right to form and join trade unions. Furthermore, article 25 establishes the right to social security whereby individuals are entitled to protection in the event of, *inter alia*, unemployment, sickness, and disability that may deprive them of the ability to work and thus impede their and their families' right to adequate standard of living. The connection between article 23 and article 25 that the UDHR establishes demonstrates the inherent link between work and human

---

[166] ILO Constitution, Preamble and the annexed Declaration of Philadelphia concerning the aims and purposes of the ILO, arts I and II retrieved from <https://www.ilo.org/dyn/normlex/en/f?p=1000:62:0::NO:62:P62_LIST_ENTRIE_ID:2453907:NO#A1> accessed 20 March 21.

576   SDG 8

dignity. Importantly, it exhibits the importance of work for realizing other human rights. The latter becomes more apparent in the International Covenant on Economic, Social and Cultural Rights (ICESCR), in which the right to work is addressed more comprehensively and states' obligations are specified. Article 6 ICESCR defines the right to work as 'the right of everyone to the opportunity to gain his living by work freely chosen or accepted'. States shall take appropriate steps to safeguard this right and achieve its full realization. Indicatively, these include technical and vocational guidance and training programmes, policies, and techniques that foster steady economic, social, and cultural development and full and productive employment under conditions upholding fundamental political and economic freedoms (article 6(2)) such as the prohibition of slavery, forced and compulsory labour (article 8(3)(c) International Covenant on Civil and Political Rights (ICCPR)) and freedom of association (article 22 ICCPR). Supplementarily, other human rights treaties reaffirm the right to work as an inalienable right of all human beings as they set forth the legal framework for the protection of specific groups such as women, children, and migrant workers.[167]

In defining the normative content of the right to work, the Committee on CESCR specifies that it is a right to *decent work*, which is conceptualized as 'work that respects the fundamental rights of the human person as well as the right of workers in terms of conditions of work safety and remuneration, respect of their physical and mental integrity in the exercise of their employment and provision of sufficient income to support themselves and their families'.[168] By implication, decent work is freely chosen or accepted and encompasses an array of elements that broaden the notion's scope. Derived correlative rights and duties pertain to the individual as a worker but are placed within the entire frame of rights s/he is entitled to by virtue of being human. Thus, interlinked components of the right to work constitute the enjoyment of just and favourable conditions of work that comprise an individual's fair wage and equal remuneration for work of equal value without discrimination, health and safety standards at work, equal opportunities for promotion, reasonable limitation of working hours, and paid periodic holidays for rest and leisure (article 7 ICESCR). The realization of these rights has a positive horizontal effect on the fulfilment of other rights in the Covenant, including the right to an adequate standard of living (article 11 ICESCR) and to social security (article 9 ICESCR),[169] whose claiming is furthered by the exercise of the collective dimension of work rights as enshrined in the right to form and join trade unions, the

[167] Convention on Elimination of all forms of Discrimination Against Women (adopted 18 December 1979, entered into force 3 September 1981) 1249 UNTS 13, arts 11, 12; Convention on the Rights of the Child (adopted 20 November 1989, entered into force 2 September 1990) 2577 UNTS 3, art 32; International Convention on the Protection of the Rights of All Migrant Workers and Members of their Families (18 December 1990, entered into force 1 July 2003) 2220 UNTS 3, arts 11, 25, 26, 40, 52, 54; International Convention on Elimination of Racial Discrimination (adopted 21 December 1965, entered into force 4 January 1969) 660 UNTS 195, art 5(e)(i) and regional instruments: European Social Charter (adopted 18 October 1961, entered into force 26 February 1965) ETS 35, art 1; African Charter on Human and People's Rights (Banjul Charter) (adopted 27 June 1981, entered into force 21 October 1986) (1982) 21 ILM 58, art 15; Additional Protocol to American Convention on Human Rights in the Area of Economic Social and Cultural Rights (Protocol of San Salvador) (adopted 17 November 1988, entered into force 16 November 1999) A-52, art 6.

[168] CommICESCR, 'General Comment 18' (6 February 2006) E/C.12/GC/18, para 7.

[169] CommICESCR, 'General Comment 19' (4 February 2008) E/C.12/GC/19, especially paras 2, 16, and 17.

latter's free function and the right to strike (article 8 ICESCR). Indeed, the Committee has explicitly stated that trade unionization and the right to strike are 'crucial means of introducing, maintaining and defending just and favourable conditions of work'.[170]

The mutually reinforcing and interdependent nature of the right to work with other human rights cannot be refuted then. However, the right to work is neither absolute nor unconditional. Unlike other human rights that are universal, the classification of someone as a worker depends on citizenship or immigration status, in which case access to the labour market is conditioned upon having a valid visa or work permit. On the face of it, this conditionality seems to contradict the justification of the right to work upon human dignity, which the Committee clearly endorses when stating that the said right 'forms an inseparable and inherent part of human dignity'.[171] By extension, it casts doubt as to the nature of labour rights as human rights. Collins, while engaging in the task to seek possible justifications for labour law in human rights theory,[172] defined human rights as rights bestowed on everyone by virtue of being human. Such rights are 'universal and imperative, with a special moral weight that normally overrides other considerations'.[173] Against this definition, he contended that labour rights do not share the same urgency as human rights and therefore are not a compelling moral imperative. Crucially, labour rights are not universal since they are only accorded to those in a paid employment relationship, and are not timeless fundamental needs. Regarding the non-universalist nature of labour rights, the advisory opinion of the Inter-American Court of Human Rights on the rights of undocumented migrants becomes relevant. According to the Court 'labor rights necessarily arise from the circumstance of being a worker. A person who is engaged in a remunerated activity, immediately becomes a worker and acquires the rights inherent in that condition ....'[174] The fact that a right is conditional upon a particular status does not mean that it is not a human right. Once a person becomes a worker, that person is entitled to all rights and duties attached to his status. In that sense, labour rights are universal.[175] As Mantouvalou also explains, 'universality in international human rights law is a normative concept, i.e. it indicates that everyone *should* enjoy the right to work; not that everyone *actually* enjoys it'.[176] Human rights can sometimes be restricted or be conditional upon a particular status so long as such restriction or conditionality is not arbitrary.[177]

[170] CommICESCR, 'General Comment 23' (27 April 2016) E/C.12/GC/23, para 1.

[171] CommICESCR, 'GC 18' (n 168) para 1. See also F Seatzu, 'Out of the Darkness into Light? CESCR General Comment on the Right to Work' in MK Sinha (ed), *Business and Human Rights* (New Delhi 2013) ch 15.

[172] H Collins, 'Theory of Rights as Justifications for Labour Law' in G Davidov and B Langille (eds), *The Idea of Labour Law* (OUP 2011) 137.

[173] ibid 140.

[174] *Juridical condition and Rights of the Undocumented Migrants*, Advisory Opinion OC-18, Inter-American Court of Human Rights Series A No 18 (17 September 2003) paras 133–a34.

[175] V Mantouvalou, 'Are Labour Rights Human Rights' (2012) 3(3) European Labour Law Journal 151, 166. The author argues that labour rights are timeless entitlements if they are to be understood as human rights with an abstract normative standard. In this event, they will entail abstract principles able to address any situation that occurs without having to be revised. Therefore, irrespective of the specific expression the labour right will gain, at a normative level it will be timeless.

[176] V Mantouvalou, 'The right to non-exploitative work', section II in Mantouvalou (ed), *The Right to Work—Legal and Philosophical Perspectives* (n 163).

[177] ibid; J Tasioulas, 'On the Nature of Human Rights' in G Ernst and J-C Heilinger (eds), *The Philosophy of Human Rights* (De Gruyter 2011) 17, 37.

The right to work constitutes such an example, however it does not mean that as such, the regulatory framework for human rights is inadequate to defend labour rights, a criticism also voiced by those who question the potential of human rights conventions to effectively address violations of labour rights. Opponents of the 'labor rights as human rights'[178] debate found their objections to the conceptual differences[179] between human rights and labour rights and the diverse interests they promote; the 'individualistic' character of human rights as opposed to the 'collective' nature of labour rights.[180] That said, human rights give priority to the individual and his/her interests over society.[181] To the contrary, labour rights advocate for solidarity and unity. As Youngdahl states, 'a rights discourse individualizes the struggle at work. However, the powerless can only progress their work life in concert with each other, not alone.'[182] Yet, the CESCR Committee recognizes an individual and collective dimension to the right to work as noted above. Moreover, in contemporary human rights discourse the dichotomy between individual and collective rights is not so sharp.[183] A glance at the UDHR, which embodies civil and political rights exercised through collective action, such as freedom of association, and individual labour rights such as the right to decent working conditions, the right to work, or the prohibition of slavery and forced labour, evidences that 'atomization'[184] is not an inherent element of the nature of human rights. Supportive to the textual justification of the combined nature of rights is the 'factual' argument that individuals exercise their rights within a broad personal, economic, and cultural environment.[185] As individuals interact within this social framework, the exercise of their individual rights may also have a strong collective dimension, which allows for the conclusion that individual rights and solidarity are mutually reinforcing.[186] Therefore, touching upon both human rights principles and solidarity, workers' rights are promoted more effectively.

In this respect, states should ensure the progressive realization to the exercise of the right to work by making it available, accessible, and acceptable to individuals.[187] At its core,[188] this duty translates into the obligation to ensure the right of access to employment and avoid discriminatory practices and unequal treatment of individuals in the private and public sectors (especially regarding the disadvantaged and marginalized). Enacting legislation is key in this regard. Another means towards the same direction is to implement a national employment strategy and plan of action with inputs from all workers and employers that address concerns holistically and to facilitate and

---

[178] VA Leary, 'The Paradox of Workers 'Rights as Human Rights' in LA Compa and SF Diamond (eds), *Human Rights, Labor Rights and International Trade* (University of Pennsylvania Press 2003) 22.

[179] K Kolben, 'Labor Rights as Human Rights' (2010) 50(2) Virginia Journal of International Law 450, 468.

[180] J Youngdahl, 'Solidarity First, Labor Rights Are Not the Same as Human Rights' (2009) 18(1) New Labour Forum 30, 31.

[181] C Taylor, *Philosophy and the Human Sciences*: Philosophical Papers 2 (CUP 1985) 187.

[182] Youngdahl (n 180) 31–32.

[183] L Compa, 'Solidarity and Human Rights, A Response to Youngdahl' (2009) 18(1) New Labor Forum 38.

[184] <Youngdahl (n 180) 31–32.

[185] ibid.

[186] ibid.

[187] CommICESCR, 'General Comment 18' (n 168) para 12.

[188] ibid para 31. On core obligations, see CommICESCR, 'General Comment 3' (14 December 1990) E/1991/23.

promote the right to work through technical and vocational education plans.[189] These measures alongside those undertaken by the state in relation to its obligation to respect and protect the right contribute to the safeguarding of the right to work in full. Remarkably, states' compliance with human rights law is significant from a developmental perspective as well. States, while designing their national development strategy and engaging in international cooperative policies, should endeavour to promote the right to work of their populations. Therefore, structural adjustment policies, project management agreements with multilateral development banks (MDBs), or multilateral packs for economic and technical assistance to contracting parties should not obstruct its realization. According to the Committee, states' failure to do so, to enforce the above-described measures, and even monitor their implementation by identifying right-to-work indicators and benchmarks, amounts to a violation of the obligation to fulfil the right to work.[190] We would add, it stalls development progress too, given that work is an economic and social development objective. There is, thus, a convergence point between the human rights and development perception of work,[191] which the SDGs can foster if sustainable human well-being is to be achieved.

We will test the reality of our assumption in Section IV of our chapter, where we discuss the targets of SDG 8. Before that, we will consider the developmental impact of standard setting for work and employment from the social justice standpoint as it evolved from the ILO's mandate.

2. The ILO's Decent Work Agenda

Since its foundation at the end of the First World War, the ILO, which is the UN's specialized agency that focuses on work and poverty,[192] has been at the forefront of the defence of workers' fundamental rights and freedoms[193] mainly through the elaboration of 'its unique corpus of social justice'.[194] To this end, a number of conventions

---

[189] CommICESCR, 'General Comment 18' (n 168) para 12.

[190] ibid paras 29–30, 36, 46–47.

[191] On the human rights-based approach to development, BI Hamm, 'A Human Rights Approach to Development' (2001) 23(4) Human Rights Quarterly 1005; P Uvin, 'From the Right to Development to the Rights-Based Approach: How 'Human Rights' Entered Development' (207) 17(4–5) Development in Practice 597; UNSDG, 'The Human Rights-based Approach to Development Cooperation: Towards a Common Understanding Among UN Agencies' (2003) <https://unsdg.un.org/resources/human-rights-based-approach-development-cooperation-towards-common-understanding-among-un> accessed 28 March 2022.

[192] 'Origins and History' (*ILO*) <http://www.ilo.org/global/about-the-ilo/history/lang--en/index.htm> accessed 20 January 2021.

[193] N Valticos, 'International Labour Standards and Human Rights: Approaching the Year 2000' (1998) 137 International Labour Review 135; F Wolf, 'ILO Experience in the Implementation of Human Rights' (1975) 10 Journal of International Law and Economics 599; HGB de la Cruz and others, *The International Labor Organization: The International Standards System and Basic Human Rights* (Westview Press 1996) 33–34; C Di Turi, *Globalizzazione dell'economia e diritti umani fondamentali in materia di lavoro: il ruolo dell'OIL e dell'OMC* (Giuffrè 2007); C Di Turi, Globalizzazione dell'economia e diritti fondamentali in materia di lavoro [2000] Rivista di diritto internazionale 113; Mantouvalou, 'Are Labour Rights Human Rights?' (n 175); JB Pérez, 'The International Labour Organisation (ILO) as an Actor of Global Governance: Sufficiently Involved to Help Overcome the Latest Financial and Economic Crisis?' [2013] Anuario de Acción Humanitaria y Derechos Humanos—Yearbook on Humanitarian Action and Human Rights 109.

[194] See W Jenks, 'Human Rights, Social Justice and Peace—The Broader Significance of the ILO Experience', Norwegian Nobel Institute, Symposium on the international protection of human rights, 25–27 September 1967, 37.

580 SDG 8

and non-binding recommendations purport to regulate the mandated topics by the organization as outlined in its constitution, namely work hours,[195] wages,[196] health and safety,[197] freedom of association,[198] forced and compulsory labour,[199] child labour,[200] vocational training,[201] employment policy,[202] non-discrimination in employment,[203] and social security.[204] Yet, the disruptions caused by accelerated globalization in the 1990s,[205] which enhanced free-market structures but dismantled state social policy through privatization, deregulation, weakening of collective bargaining, and changing the character of the employer–employee relationship in several Western and non-Western countries,[206] led the ILO to readjust its mission in light of the general cry to give a human face to the global economy, make globalization more equitable, contribute to poverty eradication, and foster sustainable development.[207] Stating that the ILO's mission finds resonance in people's preoccupation to find sustained opportunities

[195] ILO, C014, Weekly Rest (Industry) Convention, 1921 (17 November 1921); ILO, C 106, Weekly Rest (Commerce and Offices) Convention, 1957 (26 June 1957); ILO, C175, Part-TimeWork Convention, 1994 (24 June 1994); ILO, C171, Night Work Convention, 1990 (26 June 1990); ILO, P089, Protocol of 1990 to the Night Work (Women) Convention (Revised), 1948 (26 June 1990).

[196] ILO, C094, Labour Clauses (Public Contracts) Convention, 1949 (29 June 1949); ILO, C095, Protection of Wages Convention, 1949 (1 July 1949); ILO, C131, Minimum Wage Fixing Convention, 1970 (22 June 1970); ILO, C173, Protection of Workers' Claims (Employer's Insolvency) Convention, 1992 (23 June 1992).

[197] ILO, C155, Occupational Safety and Health Convention, 1981 (22 June 1981); ILO, P089, Protocol of 2002 to the Occupational Safety and Health Convention, 1981 (20 June 2002); ILO, C161, Occupational Health Services Convention, 1985 (25 June 1985); LO, C187, Promotional Framework for Occupational Safety and Health Convention, 2006 (15 June 2006).

[198] ILO, C087, Freedom of Association and Protection of the Right to Organise Convention, 1948 (9 July 1948); ILO, C098, Right to Organise and Collective Bargaining Convention, 1949 (1 July 1949); ILO, C141, Rural Workers' Organisations Convention, 1975 (23 June 1975).

[199] ILO C029, Forced Labour Convention, 1930 (28 June 1930); ILO C105, Abolition of Forced Labour Convention, 1957 (25 June 1957); ILO, P029, Protocol of 2014 to the Forced Labour Convention, 1930 (11 June 2014).

[200] ILO, C138, Minimum Age Convention, 1973 (26 June 1973); ILO, C182, Worst Forms of Child Labour Convention, 1999 (17 July 1999); ILO, C077 Medical Examination of Young Persons (Industry) Convention, 1946 (9 October 1946); ILO C078, Medical Examination of Young Persons (Non-Industrial Occupations) Convention, 1946 (9 October 1946); ILO, C124, Medical Examination of Young Persons (Underground Work) Convention, 1965 (23 June 1965).

[201] ILO, C140, Paid Educational Leave Convention, 1974 (24 June 1974); ILO, C142, Human Resources Development Convention, 1975 (23 June 1975).

[202] C122, Employment Policy Convention, 1964 (9 July 1964); C159, Vocational Rehabilitation and Employment (Disabled Persons) Convention, 1983 (20 July 1983); C181, Private employment Agencies convention (19 June 1997).

[203] C100, Equal Remuneration Convention, 1951 (29 July 1951); Cl11, Discrimination (Employment and Occupation) Convention, 1958 (25 June 1958); C156, Workers with Family Responsibilities Convention, 1981 (23 June 1981).

[204] ILO, C102, Social Security (Minimum Standards) Convention, 1952 (28 June 1952); ILO, C130, Medical Care and Sickness Benefits Convention, 1969 (25 June 1969); ILO, C128, Invalidity, Old-Age and Survivors' Benefits Convention, 1967 (7 June 1967); ILO, C121, Employment Injury Benefits Convention, 1964 (8 July 1964); ILO, C168, Employment Promotion and Protection against Unemployment Convention, 1988 (21 June 1988); ILO, C118, Equality of Treatment (Social Security) Convention, 1962 (28 June 1962); ILO, C157, Maintenance of Social Security Rights Convention, 1982 (21 June 1982).

[205] D Hulme, 'The Making of the Millennium Development Goals: Human Development Meets Results-based Management in an Imperfect World 15' (2007) Brooks World Poverty Institute, Working Paper No 16, 3–5.

[206] S de Silva, 'The Changing Focus of Industrial Relations and Human Resource Management' (ILO Workshop on Employers' Organisations in Asia-Pacific in the 21st Century, Turin, Italy, 5–13 May 1997) <https://www.acade mia.edu/6573105/INTERNATIONAL_LABOUR_ORGANISATION_The_Changing_Focus_of_Industrial_ Relations_and_Human_Resource_Management_Bureau_For_Employers_Activities_International_Labour_Offi ce_Contents> accessed 20 March 2021; G Rodgers and others, The ILO and the Quest for Social Justice, 1919–2009 (ILO 2009) 33.

[207] Rodgers and others (n 206) 224.

for decent work, its director phrased the institution's goal as 'promoting opportunities for women and men to obtain decent and productive work, in conditions of freedom, equity, security and human dignity'.[208]

Within this context, the ILO's Decent Work Agenda emerged. On the premise that employment has both qualitative and quantitative dimensions irrespective of differences in the type of work provided and the conditions under which it is performed, decent work was defined as 'productive work, which generates adequate income and is backed by an adequate social protection scheme'.[209] It applies not only to workers in the formal economy but also to the self-employed, home workers, and to unregulated wage workers. It refers to sufficient opportunities for work for all, remuneration (in cash and in kind), and embraces healthy working conditions and safety at work.[210] Social security and income security afforded by the state pursuant to its degree of development are also envisaged as fundamental ingredients of the notion of decent work. Furthermore, tripartism and social dialogue are both objectives in their own right, guaranteeing participation and democratic processes, as well as a means of achieving decent work.[211] Fundamentally, the Agenda aims to become the converging focus of the ILO's strategic objectives of full employment, labour rights, social protection, and dialogue that were set out in its constitution and reflected in the four Core Labour Standards that derived from the Declaration on Fundamental Principles and Rights at Work (freedom of association, abolition of forced and child labour, and elimination of discrimination in employment).[212] The said constituents were classified under four pillars, upon which the ILO's decent work policy would be structured: (i) rights at work; (ii) promoting employment; (iii) expansion of social protection, and (iv) the promotion of social dialogue.[213]

Nearly ten years after, the ILO Declaration on Social Justice for a Fair Globalization referred again to the above-named four foundations of decent work and lucidly clarified that they shall be conceived as multi-pronged, 'inseparable, interrelated and mutually supportive'.[214] This has noteworthy ramifications for the successful execution of the strategy as 'failure to promote any one of them would harm progress towards the others'.[215] However, compliance with the soft law standards on full employment and decent work of the ILO's Decent Work Agenda would not only be a milestone towards social justice but would promote efficiently the ILO's constitutional provision and values into programs of integrated development. The ILO itself draws this association with development when recognizing that its strategic objectives illustrate aspects of economic

---

[208] ILO, '1999 Report of the Director-General: Decent Work. International Labour Conference, 87th Session, Geneva', 3 <www.ilo.org/public/english/standards/relm/ilc/ilc87/rep-i.htm> accessed 20 March 21.
[209] ibid 13.
[210] ibid.
[211] ibid 13.
[212] ILO, 'Declaration of Fundamental Principles and Rights at Work' (1998) 37 ILM 1233.
[213] G MacNaughton and D Frey, 'Decent Work, Human Rights and the Sustainable Development Goals' (2016) 47 Georgetown Journal of International Law 607, 622; 'Decent Work Report' (n 208) 4.
[214] ILO, 'Working with the ILO—Decent Work and System Wide Coherence' <http://rconline.undg.org/wp-content/uploads/2011/11/RC_brochure_Final_WEB_Feb111.pdf> accessed 17 September 2022.
[215] ibid.

582   SDG 8

and social development. 'Principles and rights at work provide the ground rules and the framework for development; employment and incomes are the way in which production and output are translated into effective demand and decent standards of living. Social protection ensures human security and civic inclusion, and enables economic reform. Social dialogue links production with distribution, and ensures equity and participation in the development process.'[216] In the ILO's understanding, decent work adheres 'to social norms for income, conditions, security, dignity and rights'.[217] Regarding the latter in particular, the ILO reinstates their importance for the realization of development aims, although it refrains to refer to decent work as a human right and it is true that not all labour rights in the ILO conventions correspond to human rights. Nevertheless, it recognizes that 'respect for them will facilitate development. For instance, guaranteeing rights at work enables people to claim freely a fair share of the wealth they have helped to generate, and to seek more and better work. In this manner economic growth translates into social equity and employment at all stages of the development path.'[218] Such recognition demonstrates the mutual reinforcing link of the human rights and social justice regimes regarding work and raises development as their common point of convergence.

Section IV on the targets of SDG 8 shows the extent to which human rights, social justice, and development merge, in practice, into development policy, leading successfully (or not) to concrete and measurable outcomes on decent work.

IV. Targets and Indicators of Goal 8

A. Overview

The Global Indicator Framework for Sustainable Development Goals (GIF) was developed by the Inter-Agency and Expert Group on SDG Indicators (IAEG-SDGs) and agreed upon at the 48th session of the United Nations Statistical Commission (UNSC) held in March 2017.[219] Among the 230 indicators agreed on, seventeen are directly traceable to SDG 8. Furthermore, given the strong links existing between SDG 8 and other SDGs such as SDG 5, SDG 12, and SDG 13, other indicators are relevant as well. Although there is no official list in this regard, this encompasses roughly another ten indicators contained in SDG 1 (such as the proportion of total adult population with secure tenure rights to land, with legally recognized documentation, and who perceive their rights to land as secure, by sex, and by type of tenure, and the proportion

---

[216] 'Decent Work Report' (n 208) 7–8.
[217] MacNaughton and Frey, 'Decent Work, Human Rights and the Sustainable Development Goals' (n 213) 629.
[218] 'Decent Work Report' (n 208) 7.
[219] ECOSOC, 'Report of the Inter-agency and Expert Group on Sustainable Development Goal Indicators' (UN Statistical Commission, 48th Session) (7–10 March 2017) UN Doc E/CN.3/2017/2 (15 December 2016). The UNGA adopted the GIF by Resolution 71/313 on 6 July 2017 (10 July 2017) UN Doc A/RES/71/313.

of population living in households with access to basic services), SDG 12 (such as the number of countries with sustainable consumption and production (SCP) national action plans or SCP mainstreamed as a priority or a target into national policies), SDG 13 (such as the proportion of local governments that adopt and implement local disaster risk reduction strategies in line with national disaster risk reduction strategies), and SDG 14 (sustainable fisheries as a proportion of GDP in small island developing states, LDCs, and all countries).[220]

The selected indicators pursue the main objective of monitoring progress in the implementation of SDG 8 targets at global, national, regional, and local levels. In doing so, they work as management instruments for states to elaborate sustainable economic growth and employment policies in the respective areas and highlight when additional efforts are still indispensable.[221] SDG 8 comprises ten targets, some of which resemble the respective targets under MDG 1, and two means of implementation (ie increase Aid for Trade support to developing countries (8.a) and implement the ILO Global Jobs Pact and a global strategy for youth employment (8.b)). The order according to which they are presented in the Goal follows no systematic pattern. It is nevertheless possible to group them into one overarching objective and three 'pillars': decoupling economic growth and productivity from environmental degradation, as embodied in target 8.4, as the overarching objective; target 8.5 (former MDG 1, target 2)—'full and productive employment, as well as decent work for all, including young people and women'—as the first pillar; the new targets 8.1–8.3, 8.6, 8.8, and 8.10 as the second pillar and the two MOI as the third pillar.[222]

Nevertheless, even the selection of indicators was the object of lively discussions amongst the SDGs drafters, as indirectly confirmed by a comparison of the actual indicators with the suggested ones.[223] Originally, more than fifty indicator candidates had been proposed to monitor SDG 8's targets.[224] Having been narrowed down, the indicators are now reduced to those that are strictly essential for an effective implementation of the targets or, to use the same terminology as in 'Provisional Proposed Tiers for Global SDG Indicators' by the IAEG-SDG Co-Chairs, to those ones that have been considered as having both a significant country coverage and a sound methodology.[225]

---

[220] Interlinkages Working Group of the Inter-Agency and Expert Group on Sustainable Development Goal Indicators (IAEG-SDGs), Interlinkages of the 2030 Agenda for Sustainable Development, 9 March 2019,<https://unstats.un.org/unsd/statcom/50th-session/documents/BG-Item3a-Interlinkages-2030-Agenda-for-Sustainable-Development-E.pdf and <https://unstats.un.org/unsd/statcom/51st-session/documents/BG-Item3a-Interlinkages-Workstream-E.pdf> accessed 25 March 2021.

[221] Leadership Council of the SDSN, 'Indicators for Sustainable Development Goals' (Draft, February 2014) <https://sustainabledevelopment.un.org/content/documents/3233indicatorreport.pdf> accessed 25 March 2021.

[222] ILO, 'ILO Implementation Plan—2030 Agenda for Sustainable Development' (12 August 2016) <https://www.ilo.org/global/topics/sdg-2030/WCMS_510122/lang--en/index.htm> accessed 28 March 2021.

[223] A Bill-Weilandt and others, 'Monitoring Progress Towards the SDGs: The Proliferation of Quantification in International Development Policy and Practice' (2016) <https://forccast.hypotheses.org/files/2017/06/PSIA-2016-Monitoring_Progress_Towards_the_SDGs.pdf > accessed 28 March 2021.

[224] Leadership Council of the SDSN, 'Indicators and a Monitoring Framework for the Sustainable Development Goals - Launching a Data Revolution for the SDGs' (Draft, March 2015) <https://sustainabledevelopment.un.org/content/documents/2013150612-FINAL-SDSN-Indicator-Report1.pdf> accessed 9 February 2021.

[225] UNSTATS <https://unstats.un.org/sdgs/files/meetings/iaeg-sdgs-meeting-03/Provisional-Proposed-Tiers-for-SDG-Indicators-24-03-16.pdf> accessed 9 February 2020. In reality, not all indicators were backed by a sound methodology. Indicators were classified under three tiers based on their level of methodological development and data availability with tier 3 encompassing indicators for which there was no established methodology/standard

584 SDG 8

This guarantees that in principle all the targets of SDG 8 are complemented by fully functioning indicators. However, SDG 8.b.1 which lacks an indicator supported by an adequate methodology[226] is an exception to this general rule.[227]

The indicators will primarily be monitored by the WB and ILO, which serve as the two lead agencies in SDG 8.[228]

A distinct, though closely related issue is whether the selected indicators may function simultaneously as human rights indicators. As discussed below, this does not appear to be the case, given the little space and direct references that have been assigned so far to human rights in the SDGs framework, including the indicators.[229]

B. Analysis and Critique of Each Target

1. Target 8.1 Sustain per capita economic growth in accordance with national circumstances and, in particular, at least 7 per cent gross domestic product growth per annum in the least developed countries

a) Sources of the target and empirical analysis

This target relates to LDCs. However, it should be remembered that every single country (not to mention every MNC) aims at achieving economic growth.

A quick comparison of this target with others reveals that it is the only quantified target of SDG 8. This is far from being irrelevant in practice as suggested by Mark Elder and Simon Høiberg Olsen, who also recall that 'generally, quantification is in the indicators, not the targets' and that target 8.1 being so framed 'could undermine

---

or they were still being developed/tested. However, the Group's agreement on annual refinements of the initial indicators and a comprehensive review of the framework by the UNSC in 2020 (see E/CN.3/2017/2 (n 219) paras 15, 21–23; the next comprehensive review will be in 2025) has led to the elimination of tier 3 indicators. The tier classification that is currently in effect after the 2020 review can be found here <https://unstats.un.org/sdgs/files/Tier%20Classification%20of%20SDG%20Indicators_28%20Dec%202020_web.pdf> accessed 9 February 2021. For information on annual refinements and the 2020 review, ECOSOC, 'Report of the Inter-Agency and Expert Group on Sustainable Development Goal Indicators' (UNSC 49th Session, 6–9 March 2018) (19 December 2017) UN Doc E/CN.3/2018/2; ECOSOC, 'Report of the Inter-Agency and Expert Group on Sustainable Development Goal Indicators' (UNSC 50th Session, 5–8 March 2019) (19 December 2018) UN Doc E/CN.3/2019/2; ECOSOC, 'Report of the Inter-Agency and Expert Group on Sustainable Development Goal Indicators' (UNSC 51st Session, 3–6 March 2020) (20 December 2019) UN Doc E/CN.3/2020/2, Annex II (comprehensive review), Annex III (annual refinement). The GIF since 2020 can be found at <https://unstats.un.org/sdgs/indicators/Global%20Indicator%20Framework%20after%202020%20review_Eng.pdf> accessed 9 February 2021.

[226] But see the efforts made for the definition of an indicator for SDG 8 1.b by the ILO (ILO, Methodology for SDG indicator 8.b.1 on youth employment, 10–19 October 2018) <https://www.ilo.org/wcmsp5/groups/public/---dgreports/---stat/documents/meetingdocument/wcms_636035.pdf> accessed 9 February 2021.

[227] SDG 8.b.1 only refers to the '[e]xistence of a developed and operationalized national strategy for youth employment, as a distinct strategy or as part of a national employment strategy'.

[228] On the role of custodian agencies, E/CN.3/2017/2 (n 219) para 28. The World Bank and the ILO partner with other agencies such as the OECD, the UNEP, the UNCDF, and the WTO for some of the targets and there are occasions where the latter are the only custodian agencies of a target. See analytically, current tier classification tables (n 225).

[229] S Janoušková and others, 'Global SDGs Assessments: Helping or Confusing Indicators?' (2018) 10 (5) Sustainability, 1 ff <https://www.mdpi.com/2071-1050/10/5/1540> accessed 28 March 2021.

environmental protection if target 8.4 on decoupling (which might not necessarily be achievable or realistic) is not implemented simultaneously'.[230]

There are also other potential effects worth to mention. For instance, the difficulty (if not practical impossibility) of achieving 7 per cent gross domestic product growth per annum in the LDCs through 2030, as SDG 8 (SDG 8.1) requires 'while at the same time upholding the SDGs' commitment to the sustainability objectives, specifically (a) achieving sustainable use of natural resources and (b) reducing greenhouse gas emissions rapidly enough to keep us within the carbon budget for keeping temperature rise at 2 °C'.[231]

b) Implementation efforts at the international/domestic level

World Bank data suggest that only five LDCs achieved over a 7 per cent growth rate in 2017. While the average growth rate for the same period was of only 4.4 per cent in the Asian, African, and Pacific Island LDCs.

c) Critique

Annual growth rate of real GDP per capita, calculated as the percentage change in the real GDP per capita between two consecutive years, is the only indicator to measure the realization of target 1 in SDG 8 agreed by the IAEG-SDGs. This indicator raises obvious problems. The first, in order of importance, is that GDP does not account for the environmental and social costs of production. For instance, growth in real GDP per capita reveals nothing regarding energy and material interactions with the environment.[232] Second, some questions may arise when comparing GDP estimates at global level. As also suggested by the UN Statistics Division (UNSD), the difficulty of these problems should not be underestimated.

2. Target 8.2 Achieve higher levels of economic productivity through diversification, technological upgrading and innovation, including through a focus on high-value added and labour-intensive sectors

a) Sources of the target and its critique

Target 8.2 puts the focus on the centrality of technology and new innovations for economic growth and productivity. This is far from being surprising, because technology and innovation together with science are generally recognized as amongst the main drivers of productivity increases and key long-term levers for economic growth.[233] Some recent references in this sense are given by the Addis Ababa Action Agenda (AAAA) that has identified concrete actions and policies—including science,

---

[230] M Elder and P King, 'Introduction: Raising the Level of Ambition' in M Elder and P King (eds), *Realising the Transformative Potential of the SDGs* (Institute of Global Environmental Strategy 2018) <https://www.greengrow thknowledge.org/sites/default/files/downloads/resource/SDGs per cent20flagship.pdf> accessed 29 March 2021.

[231] J Hickel, 'The Contradiction of the Sustainable Development Goals: Growth Versus Ecology on a Finite Planet' (2019) 27(5) Sustainable Development 873.

[232] Global SDG Indicator Platform, '8.1.1 Annual Growth Rate of Real GDP' <https://sdg.tracking-progress. org/indicator/8-1-1-annual-growth-rate-of-real-gdp-per-capita/> accessed 28 March 2021.

[233] RG Lipsey and others, *Economic Transformation* (OUP 2006) 1 ff.

586   SDG 8

technology, and innovation (STI)—as support for achieving SDGs, and by the negotiations during COP21 in December 2015 that addressed STI issues, proposing a framework for enhanced action on technology development and transfer.[234]

Relevant and recent references to STI are also included in the SDGs. STI features strongly both in Goal 17 as a means of implementation and as a cross-cutting means to meet other Goals and targets such as: SDGs 2.a, 3.b, 6.a, 7.a, 8.2, 14.4, and 14.a.[235] Promoting innovation was envisaged as part of SDG 9 related to resilient infrastructure and inclusive, sustainable industrialization, while target 9.5 upgrades the role of innovation and research policy beyond STI as one of the means of implementation.[236] A Technology Facilitation Mechanism for supporting the policies for SDGs was also foreseen in the 2030 Agenda.[237]

Regrettably, however, target 8.2 only refers to technology and innovation and does not mention science. But this omission cannot be seen as intentional, since it would be meaningless to interpret target 8.2 as only referring to technology and innovation issues. There are in fact several reasons supporting a broad interpretation of target 8.2 and thus also supporting the inclusion of science in it, the most important and visible being the links between target 8.2 and target 9.4.[238] The latter calls for modernizing infrastructure and converting industries to being sustainable, in particular using resources more efficiently and promoting the adoption of technologies by 2030.

Target 8.2 does not only focus on STI issues. It also focuses on labour-intensity issues. This is because, from the neo-liberalistic perspective that implicitly informs the 17 SDGs and their related Targets, including target 8.2, focusing on labour-intensity issues and sectors may be of significance for increasing economic growth rates.[239]

Furthermore, target 8.2 focuses on the diversification of markets that it treated as a sustainable development target in itself. Once again, the reason behind this is not difficult to discern: the potential positive influence that 'diversification' may have on economic growth and productivity, in terms of both GDP and employment, and on the achievement of other SDGs, such as access to education (SDG 4.1, 4.2), healthcare and other basic services (SDG 1.4), child and maternal health (SDG 3.1, 3.2).[240]

---

[234] E Giovannini and others, 'The Role of Science, Technology and Innovation Policies to Foster the Implementation of the SDGs' (2015) (*European Commission*) <http://publications.europa.eu/resource/cellar/23db9ac3-0dcd-11e6-ba9a-01aa75ed71a1.0001.03/DOC_1> accessed 28 March 2021.

[235] ibid.

[236] E Giovannini and F Roure, 'The Inclusion of Science, Technology and Innovation (STI) in the Financing of the 17 Sustainable Development Goals (SDGs)' (2017) 88 Annales des Mines—Responsabilité et environnement, 40–44 <http://www.annales.org/re/2017/re_88_octobre_2017.pdf> accessed 30 March 2022.

[237] For further references on this issue, see PP Walsha and others, 'The Role of Science, Technology and Innovation in the UN 2030 agenda' (2020) 154 Technological Forecasting and Social Change 119957.

[238] P Schroeder and others, 'The Relevance of Circular Economy Practices to the Sustainable Development Goals' (2019) 23 Journal of Industrial Ecology, 77.

[239] F Dahlmann and others, 'Corporate Actors, the UN Sustainable Development Goals and Earth System Governance: A Research Agenda' (2019) 6 The Anthropocene Review 167.

[240] Amplius, see FAO, 'Transforming the Livestock Sector through the Sustainable Development Goals', available at <http://www.fao.org/3/CA1201EN/ca1201en.pdf> accessed 17 September 2022.

TARGETS AND INDICATORS 587

b) Empirical analysis

The only indicator to measure the realization of target 8.2 in Goal 8 agreed by the IAEG-SDGs is the following: annual growth rate of real GDP per employed person. As formulated, the indicator is easy to measure. Moreover, like the majority of the other indicators for SDG 8, it is also supported by an established methodology.[241] However, the fact remains that it is not immune to criticisms, and this is obvious given the references it makes to GDP and per capita GDP.

c) Implementation efforts at the international and domestic level

The 2017 report on the SDGs assessment and Agenda 2063 by the Economic Commission for Africa (ECA) observes that: 'the agricultural value added per worker in Africa (excluding North Africa) at constant dollars is US\$ 1,221, *well* below the world average of US\$ 1,978 and US\$ 1,657 for Asia and the Pacific countries, which continue to search for policy mixes to help accelerate progress on these targets'.

3. Target 8.3 Promote development-oriented policies that support productive activities, decent job creation, entrepreneurship, creativity and innovation, and encourage the formalization and growth of micro-, small- and medium-sized enterprises, including through access to financial services

a) Sources of the target and its critique

A thorough glance at this text reveals that target 8.3 is mainly about encouraging micro-, small-, and medium-sized enterprises (MSMEs) (curiously not defined) in their double role as drivers of the economy and beneficiaries of inclusive development.[242] The rationale behind this focus is not difficult to understand. Globally, MSMEs comprise 95 per cent of all enterprises, account for more than half of all jobs worldwide, and are responsible for generating the majority of new jobs.[243] Moreover, MSMEs are universally perceived as a major target for facilitating the attainment of the SDGs.[244]

There is little to no uncertainty that the Addis Ababa Action Agenda of the Third International Conference on Financing for Development constituted one, and perhaps the most important, source of inspiration for target 8.3. This is especially evident if one looks at paragraphs 35–49 of the Agenda which address actions and considerations related to 'domestic and international private business and finance' (paragraph 35), highlight the crucial influence of foreign direct investment (FDI) on sustainable development (paragraph 36) and call for a human rights-based approach to business development and for the promotion of business good practices that share the common

---

[241] HLPF, 'Discussion on SDG 8—Decent Work and Economic Growth' <https://sustainabledevelopment.un.org/content/documents/23844BN_SDG_8_Decent_work.pdf> accessed 25 March 2021.

[242] DESA, 'Micro, Small and Medium-sized Enterprises (MSMEs) and their Role in Achieving the Sustainable Development' <https://sustainabledevelopment.un.org/content/documents/26073MSMEs_and_SDGs.pdf> accessed 28 March 2021.

[243] 'State of Play Business and the Sustainable Development Goals: Mind the Gap—Challenges for Implementation' (IHRB 2015) <https://www.ihrb.org/pdf/state-of-play/Business-and-the-SDGs.pdf > accessed 28 March 2021.

[244] DESA, 'Micro, Small and Medium-sized Enterprises (MSMEs) and their Role in Achieving the Sustainable Development' (n 242).

vision of sustainable development while looking into the social impact of their operations (paragraph 37).

Although not specified in target 8.3, the ILO Tripartite Declaration of Principles concerning Multinational Enterprises and Social Policy (the MNE Declaration or Tripartite Declaration), an international non-binding document produced by the International Labour Organization (ILO), is the guideline to be used for enhancing the impact of business operations in achieving decent work for all by 2030.[245] The reason is threefold. First, because the MNE Declaration is the only global instrument in the area of MNEs and their relation to social policy. Second, because the Declaration, though not legally binding *per se*, translates general principles derived from international labour rules and standards into operations to be undertaken by MSMEs.[246] Third and lastly, because the Declaration addresses and thus makes publicly accountable governments as well as social partners and urges them to put in place a normative and policy framework able to elicit a positive contribution on the part of the private sector to decent work and socio-economic development.[247]

b) Empirical analysis
The only indicator to measure the realization of target 3 in Goal 8 agreed by IAEG-SDGs confirms the centrality of the above-mentioned object and objective in the target since it refers to the proportion of informal employment in total employment, by sector and sex. Enhancing creativity, youth innovation, and decent job creation are the other objectives pursued, mainly but not exclusively, by target 8.3, as also suggested by its language.

c) Implementation efforts at the international and domestic levels
According to the SDG report of 2020, the income of workers in informal employment has drastically decreased by 60 per cent in the first months of COVID-19 crisis globally.

4. Target 8.4 Improve progressively, through 2030, global resource efficiency
    in consumption and production and endeavour to decouple economic growth
    from environmental degradation, in accordance with the 10-Year Framework
    of Programmes on Sustainable Consumption and Production, with developed
    countries taking the lead
a) Sources of the target and its critique
Target 8.4 functions as the overarching objective of SDG 8.[248] This complements the dual and rigid approach chosen in SDG 8 which focuses on economic development

---

[245] ILO, Tripartite Declaration of Principles concerning MNE and Social Policy as amended (2017) <https://www.ilo.org/wcmsp5/groups/public/---ed_emp/---emp_ent/---multi/documents/publication/wcms_094386.pdf> accessed 15 April 2021.

[246] ibid.

[247] ibid.

[248] A Oliveira and others, 'A Systemic and Contextual Framework to Define a Country's 2030 Agenda from a Foresight Perspective' (2019) 11(22) Sustainability 24 <https://www.mdpi.com/2071-1050/11/22/6360/htm> accessed 28 March 2021, claiming that 'progress in targets 8.4 ("Resource efficiency"), and 9.4 ("Upgraded

and decent work, and aims at decoupling economic growth and productivity from use of natural resources by improving progressively global resource efficiency in consumption and production, perceived as a more sustainable approach.

In order to avoid the risk of being considered vague and unhelpful, target 8.4 provides that the above-mentioned objective should be pursued and accomplished in accordance with the ten-year framework of programmes on sustainable consumption and production (10YFP)[249] and in accordance with the Common but differentiated responsibility (CBDR) principle even though this principle has not been mentioned explicitly, but only indirectly, by claiming that developed countries should take the lead of the 10YFP. The 10YFP is a global commitment, made by member states at the Rio + 20 conference on Sustainable Development in 2012, to accelerate the shift towards sustainable consumption and production in both developing and developed countries.[250]

b) Empirical analysis and implementation efforts at the international and domestic levels

The choice of referring to the 10YFP as a compliance benchmark is neither strange nor hard to understand. It is not strange since target 12.1 specifically calls for the implementation of the 10YFP.[251] It is not difficult to understand because the 10YFP supports capacity building and makes access to financial and technical assistance easier to developing countries for this shift.[252] Moreover, the 10YFP—through its complex organization, which consists of a Secretariat, a UN Interagency Coordination Group, a small Board, National and Stakeholders Focal Points, and a Member State Body to receive the report—develops, replicates, and scales up sustainable consumption and production and resource efficiency initiatives and measures such as green products and green business and waste water and ground water management systems, either at national or regional levels, decoupling environmental degradation and resource utilization from economic growth.[253]

However, the choice of referring to the 10YFP, though significant and praiseworthy, does not avoid the problem that considerations of economic growth overthrow a recognition of environmental depletion in the only measure of socio-economic growth

---

infrastructure") has a great influence on the resultant targets' achievement'; ICSU, ISSC, *Review of Targets for The Sustainable Development Goals: The Science Perspective* (ICSU 2015).

[249] HLPF, 'The 10 Year Framework of Programmes on Sustainable Consumption and Production Patterns (10YFP)' <https://sustainabledevelopment.un.org/content/documents/1444HLPF_10YFP2.pdf> accessed 27 March 2021.

[250] ibid.

[251] Target 12.1 aims to '[i]mplement the 10-Year Framework of Programmes on Sustainable Consumption and Production Patterns, all countries taking action, with developed countries taking the lead, taking into account the development and capabilities of developing countries'.

[252] HLPF, 'The 10 Year Framework of Programmes on Sustainable Consumption and Production Patterns (10YFP)' (n 249).

[253] C Arden Clarke, 'The 10-Year Framework of Programmes on Sustainable Consumption and Production (10YFP)' <https://stg-wedocs.unep.org/bitstream/handle/20.500.11822/13484/Charles_Arden_10YFP_prese ntation_GC_27_150213rev.pdf?sequence=1> accessed 17 September 2022.

indicated in SDG 8, namely GDP.[254] This is precisely why target 8.4 may be criticized and contested as not consistent with the international rule of law.

That is not all, as there are also other reasons for concern, such as, notably, the indicator chosen for target 8.4 that refers to material footprint per unit of GDP. In fact, although reducing the material footprint is an important element in achieving development goals,[255] there are other aspects of decoupling that could have been included, so the indicator chosen must be considered as inadequate and not so SMART (not specific, measurable, achievable, realistic, and time-bound), though this was a key initial concept of the SDGs.[256]

5. Target 8.5 By 2030, achieve full and productive employment and decent work for all women and men, including for young people and persons with disabilities, and equal pay for work of equal value

a) Sources of the target

Target 8.5 constitutes the backbone of Goal 8 on the segment of employment and decent work since it serves as a standard of progress on the core of the right to work and the ILO's four pillars of its Decent Work Agenda, namely access to employment and its quality, in respect of which this target singles out fair and equal remuneration commensurate with the value of work provided. To begin with, the rise of employment and decent work from a target in the MDGs (sub-target 1.b) to a self-standing development goal is significant in its own right. We should recall that employment was neglected in the Millennium Summit and it was not until 2007 that MDG 1B was added[257] in recognition of the fact that full and productive employment are key to poverty reduction.[258] Moreover, the restatement of the goal's content in target 8.5 in language indicating the requirement to achieve full and productive employment rather than simply promote it as the heading of Goal 8 suggests, consolidates the importance of employment and

---

[254] UN SG Report (8 May 2019) UN Doc E/2019/68 <https://unstats.un.org/sdgs/report/2019/The-Sustainable-Development-Goals-Report-2019.pdf> accessed 17 September 2022.

[255] But see Hickel, 'The contradiction of the sustainable development goals: Growth versus ecology on a finite planet' (n 231) 4, observing that '[t]he only way to achieve the GDP growth target while at the same time reducing material footprint is to achieve *absolute* decoupling' and that '[r]egardless of the target we might choose, the objective of reducing material footprint by any amount requires a dramatic reversal of present trends'.

[256] M Elder and SH Olsen, 'The Design of Environmental Priorities in the SDGs' (2019) 10 Global Policy 70 stressing that 'only target 8.1 on economic growth is quantified, which could undermine environmental protection if target 8.4 on decoupling (which might not necessarily be achievable or realistic) is not implemented simultaneously'.

[257] For the background on the MDGs reform and inclusion of decent work as a target, see R Van der Hoevem 'Full Employment Target: What Lessons for a Post-2015 Development Agenda?' (2014) 15(2–3) Journal of Human Development and Capabilities 161; MacNaughton and Frey, 'Decent Work, Human Rights and the Sustainable Development Goals' (n 213) 633–41.

[258] ILO International Labour Conference, 'Report of the Director-General: Working out of Poverty' (2003) <http://www.ilo.org/public/english/standards/relmn/ilc/ilc9l/pdf/rep-i-a.pdf> accessed 17 September 2022; CommICESCR, Substantive Issues Arising in the Implementation of the International Covenant on Economic, Social and Cultural Rights: Poverty and the International Covenant on Economic, Social and Cultural Rights (10 May 2001) UN Doc E/C.12/2001/10: 'The rights to work, an adequate standard of living, housing, food, health and education, which lie at the heart of the Covenant, have a direct and immediate bearing upon the eradication of poverty'; OHCHR, Principles and Guidelines for a Human Rights Approach to Poverty Reduction Strategies (2006) UN Doc HR/PUB/06/12, 108–28; ILO, Decent Work and Poverty Reduction Strategies: A Reference Manual for ILO Staff and Constituents (2005) <http://www.ilo.org/dyn/infoecon/docs/627/F286029509/Decent Work-PRSstext.pdf.> accessed 1 April 2021.

decent work for development. Further, the fifteen-year time frame set to achieve the target is a major improvement from the MDGs where the respective sub-target was not time-bound. To have a clear deadline for achieving the goal is a benchmark for accountability checks against governments in relation to their obligation to uphold their commitments under Goal 8. While predominantly their political accountability will be improved since Agenda 2030 was agreed at a high political level, there is potential for a positive impact on holding them to account for compliance with the ILO regime and their legal responsibility to fulfil the human right to decent work, although target 8.5 is not framed in the language of rights. Still, the corresponding legal frameworks can be easily discerned and measuring progress in achieving the goal could—or should, according to the Chairpersons of the UN Human Rights Treaty Bodies—include an assessment of contribution to the protection of the (underpinned) fundamental rights.[259]

b) Empirical analysis and a critique of the effectiveness of indicators

Target 8.5 would be ideally placed to align indicators for full and productive employment and decent work for all with states' ILO and human rights obligations and the monitoring mechanisms of the treaty bodies. This is because one can read in the target the four pillars of the Decent Work Agenda and it would be possible to blend ILO indicators on work and employment with the human rights indicators designed by the OHCHR. In this regard, decent work elements that are captured under targets 8.6–8.8 would be covered comprehensively. McNoughton and Frey's model indicators of target 8.5 are very illustrative:[260]

> **Indicator 1:** ratification of core human rights treaties, including optional protocols and ILO Conventions on Full Employment and decent Work
> **Indicator 2:** unemployment and underemployment rates by sex, target groups and level of education
> **Indicator 3:** share of informal employment in total employment by sex, target groups and level of education
> **Indicator 4:** collective bargaining coverage rate
> **Indicator 5:** ration of lowest/highest income quintiles

By contrast, target 8.5 encompasses only two indicators, 8.5.1 'average hourly earnings of employees, by sex, age, occupation and persons with disabilities'[261] and 8.5.2 'unemployment rate, by sex, age and persons with disabilities' which may be appropriate to measure progress on some elements of decent work at a macro level (mostly the second pillar of the Decent Work Agenda: fostering employment) but certainly not holistically.

---

[259] OHCHR, Joint Statement on the Post-2015 Development Agenda (18 January 2015) <https://www.ohchr.org/EN/NewsEvents/Pages/DisplayNews.aspx?NewsID=15505&LangID=E> accessed 29 March 21.

[260] MacNoughton and Frey, 'Decent Work, Human Rights and the Sustainable Development Goals' (n 213) 661.

[261] The indicator was refined in the 2020 comprehensive review. Initially, it read: 'Average hourly earnings of *female and male* employees by occupation, age and persons with disabilities', E/CN.3/2020/2 (n 225), 20 (italics added). Target 8.5.1 is a tier 2 indicator, whereas target 8.5.2 is tier 1.

592   SDG 8

Indeed, earnings are a key element of the quality of employment and give an insight into employees' adequacy of income and purchasing power, their living standards, and working conditions given that trends in employees' earnings shed light to the improvement or deterioration of workers' circumstances in a particular employment sector and the economy more generally. Moreover, observation of earnings, disaggregated by sex, disability status, and occupation allows for the equality dimension of employment to be materialized into a measurable unit. Thus, the gender gap and the discrimination of people with disabilities, as a distinct category of workers, is mapped and can be fruitfully utilized for targeted policy-making aimed at eliminating such challenges, which otherwise differentiate working conditions and living standards among population groups engaging into activities (the production of goods or the provision of services) for pay or profit.[262]

Analogously, the ILO deems the unemployment rate a well-suited indicator for assessing the efficiency and effectiveness of an economy to absorb its labour force, in other words its ability to generate enough jobs for all persons of working age actively seeking employment. It reflects in principle the inclusiveness of the labour market and the extent to which the labour supply is (under)utilized. However, there is a caveat to what the unemployment rate indicator demonstrates regarding full and productive employment: it does not convey anything about the living standards and economic resources of the unemployed, their ethnic origin, and education level, nor does it distinguish forms of labour underutilization such as people in time-related underemployment (eg part-time workers), long-term or short-term unemployment, those in informal employment, and the potential labour force (eg those restricted to access the labour market due to various personal, social, and economic barriers).[263]

As a result, comprehensive conclusions about the implementation status of target 8.5 should be drawn from the combined interpretation of its two indicators and other pointers of labour utilization and the quality of employment. In fact, a similar criticism was raised against indicators of target 1.b in the MDGs, especially indicator 1.5 that measured the employment to population ratio and indicator 1.4 measuring productivity growth as GDP rate per employed person. Both were critiqued for not being a direct measure of progress towards the target as they did not capture the quality aspect of employment and work, requiring additional elements for appropriate monitoring.[264]

Indicator limitations such as the one just described reveal that the elaboration of a measurement system for development objectives is highly challenging. The choice and design of an indicator ought to match the goal and its targets, namely reflect its aspirations. Simultaneously, however, it is also driven by a focus on performance and on achieving demonstrable results. Accordingly, emphasis is given on data availability

---

[262] *Decent Work and the Sustainable Development Goals: A Guidebook on SDG Labour Market Indicators, Department of Statistics (STATISTICS)* (ILO 2018), 20–25 (ILO Guidebook); SDG Indicators Metadata Repository, metadata sheet for indicator 8.5.1 <http://www.unstats.un.org> accessed 9 February 2021 (Metadata Repository).

[263] ibid 26–31; Metadata Repository (n 262) sheet for indicator 8.5.2.

[264] MacNaughton and Frey, 'Decent Work, Human Rights and the Sustainable Development Goals' (n 213) 639–41.

and collection, on precision and accuracy pursuant to commonly accepted statistical standards and principles for the thematic category of the goals measured. Often such 'results-based management'[265] approach to development aims, while supporting progress assessment, reporting, and accountability, undermines the complexity of the targets' content and downplays the quantitative nature of development progress overall.[266] Numeric indicators may not be able to capture the multiple facets of a societal problem nor its underlying causes. Target 8.5.2 is a good illustration. Thus, in addition to understanding the key measurable dimensions of a given goal, it is important that the metrics system is not detached from the theoretical framework of sustainable development and its embedded global values that define human well-being. Development is a normative concept and a very contested notion that has acquired different meanings according to the theories and models of development pursued over time. Still, how it is defined and what the practical outcomes are constitute a normative judgment about the most preferable way to settle economic, social, cultural, and environmental challenges.[267] Hence, systems of measurement need to have their conceptual foundation in the political economy in place in order to be relevant and effective tools for the management of developmental affairs and decision-making in the field. That is because in setting standards for the evaluation of progress in global development, indicators serve also 'as the basis for societal actors' conceptualising sustainability and wellbeing'.[268] If, in translating development into tangible outcomes, they decontextualize the latter from their normative frame, indicators become norms in their own right and the endeavours to meet the goals are carried out in silos. Such an effect is far from the intended purpose of measurement in policy and development governance in particular. The aim is not to structure progress evaluation around individual thematic categories (ie those of each goal) but to realize the transformative potential of the SDGs as it occurs from the Goals' interlinkages and the elimination of trade-offs between them in order to realize development priorities without putting other development challenges on the margins. The SDGs themselves and their indicators should bridge the normative realm of 'sustainable human development' with policy implementation.[269] By extension, measurement is not a purely scientific and technical exercise; the methods and instruments employed test in practice 'norms, values and power structures that underline ideas of what is being measured, why and by whom'.[270] It arises then that informed decisions and effective development governance depend equally on sound statistical models and

[265] A Binnebdijk, 'Results-based Management in the Development Cooperation Agencies: A Review of Experience', DAC Working Party on Aid Effectiveness (OECD 2001).

[266] S Fukuda-Parr, 'Global Goals as a Policy Tool: Intended and Unintended Consequences' (2014) 15(2–3) Journal of Human Development and Capabilities 118; J Waage and others, 'The Millennium Development Goals: A Cross-Sectoral Analysis and Principles for Goal Setting after 2015' (2010) 376 The Lancet 991.

[267] R Hanlin and W Brown, International Development in a Changing World (The Open University 2013) <http://www.open.edu/openlearn/society/international-development/understanding-international-developm ent/content-section-2.2> accessed 20 February 2020.

[268] L Pintér and others, 'Measuring Progress in Achieving the Sustainable Development Goals' in N Kanie and F Biermann (eds), Governing through Goals: Sustainable Development Goals as Governance Innovation (MIT Press 2017) 100.

[269] ibid 113.

[270] ibid 100.

594   SDG 8

data as well as on a conceptual framework for measurement. When either is missing or is not robust enough, successful implementation is impeded.

The consequences on the effective monitoring of implementation that derive from the lack of sound statistical information and reporting by each country were noted by the UN Secretary-General in his annual reports on the SDGs submitted to the High-Level Political Forum (HLPF) on sustainable development. For example, there is a clear statement in the 2017 report about the lack of data for some targets.[271] Unsurprisingly, the picture for SDG 8's implementation status is incomplete. In contrast, by the year 2020 its depiction is more detailed.

More specifically, in 2017 the image on the state of target 8.5 globally is configured only by data on the unemployment indicator. The global unemployment rate stood at 5.7 per cent with women more likely to be unemployed than men across all age groups. Tremendous differences are marked in Northern Africa, where the percentage of unemployed women reached 20 per cent compared to 9.7 per cent of men. Youth unemployment worldwide was also three times higher than adult unemployment (12.8 per cent v 4.4 per cent). Again, Northern Africa has the highest rates (28.6 per cent), followed by Western Asia (25.5 per cent).[272] Remarkably, no data exist for the unemployment rate of people with disabilities. Moving on to the year 2018, the situation seems unchanged. Lack of data on target 8.5.1 and incomplete data for target 8.5.2 (eg no information about unemployed people with disabilities) seem to debunk the ILO's anticipation that the revised (in 2017) statistical standards on work, employment, and labour underutilization will provide better data for decent work under the 2030 Agenda.[273] Although there is no statistical table for indicator 8.5.1 annexed to the Secretary General's (SG's) report, it is reported that a survey in forty-five countries showed that the median gender pay gap is 12.5 per cent, favouring men.[274] This is a common characteristic between developing and developed countries, although the size of the wage gap differs. The ILO statistics for 2018, corresponding to eighteen regions and a 105 countries, corroborate this finding.[275] It is interesting to note here that the gender pay gap measures inequality in pay but captures a broader concept than that of 'equal pay for work of equal value', which target 8.5 mentions.[276] Hence, for this specific dimension of the target to be depicted in the metrics, disaggregation by occupation and skills level is required.

[271] ECOSOC, 'Progress towards the Sustainable Development Goals, Report of the Secretary-General' (11 May 2017) UN Doc E/2017/66, para 2.
[272] ibid para 12 and tables for Goal 8 in statistical annex, 69–72 (note: the presented statistics in the report are from 2016).
[273] ECOSOC, 'Report of the International Labour Organization on recent developments in work and employment statistics' (Statistical Commission, 49th session, 6–9 March 2018) (18 December 2017) UN Doc E/CN.3/2018/18; ILOSTAT's indicator description on earnings and labour cost <https://www.ilo.org/ilostat-files/Documents/description_EAR_EN.pdf> and on unemployment <https://www.ilo.org/ilostat-files/Documents/description_UR_EN.pdf> both accessed 9 February 2021.
[274] UN SG's Report (10 May 2018) UN Doc E/2018/64, paras 75 and 76 and annex, 65–67.
[275] ILOSTAT explorer <https://www.ilo.org/shinyapps/bulkexplorer18/?lang=en&segment=indicator&id=SDG_0851_SEX_OCU_NB_A> accessed 9 February 2020.
[276] E Ortiz-Ospina, 'Key Facts about the Gender Pay Gap' (*Our World in Data*, Oxford Martin School, University of Oxford, 19 February 2018) <https://ourworldindata.org/six-facts-pay-gap> accessed 9 February 2020.

The 2019 report incorporates more targeted information about target 8.5. In that year, Goal 8 was also reviewed in depth at the HLPF under the auspices of the ECOSOC in the context of its theme 'Empowering people and ensuring inclusiveness and equality'.[277] Submissions by Major Groups, IGOs, and countries' voluntary reviews complemented the SG's report, leading to a more comprehensive view on Goal 8. Gender inequality, manifested through earning disparities, persisted. Data from sixty-two countries showed that men's median hourly pay was 12 per cent higher than that of women and the gap rose to 20 per cent in managerial and professional occupations, craft, and plant machine operators. Regarding unemployment, the global rate stood at 5 per cent in 2018 with gender disparities at less than 1 per cent but there were great variations among regions. Western Asia and Northern Africa (9.9 per cent) suffered an unemployment rate 2.5 times higher than Central and Southern Asia (3.2 per cent). Youth unemployment was 12 per cent globally compared to 4 per cent of adults.[278] The insufficient effort to provide people with disabilities equal access to decent employment and accessibility in the workplace was highlighted by the Organizations, which urged for the mainstreaming in the implementation and monitoring of the 2030 Agenda of their rights through the development and consistent use of disability-inclusive indicators.[279]

c) Implementation efforts at the international and domestic levels

Notwithstanding the marginalized attention to the aforementioned population group, it is particularly encouraging that several countries have adopted measures to reduce the unemployment rate of persons with disabilities. For instance the Republic of Congo, Croatia, and Kuwait have set quotas on the percentage of employees who must be persons with disabilities. Israel has created aid programmes to facilitate the hiring of groups with low participation in the workforce, including people with disabilities,[280] while Chile pursued a legislative reform that encourages the inclusion of people with disabilities in the workforce.[281] In general, though, all forty-seven countries which presented their reviews have intensified their efforts to increase the number of jobs and the participation of women and youth in the labour force through multifaceted policies that draw upon the linkage between employment and education or social security and technological innovation, combining thus target 8.5 with others of Goal 8 (eg target 8.6) or other goals (eg Goal 4) in their national policy plans.[282]

Nevertheless, with only ten years until the expiry year for the SDGs, the SG reports that the international community is not on track to achieve the Goals and progress is

---

[277] HLPF (9–18 July 2019) <https://sustainabledevelopment.un.org/hlpf/2019> accessed 9 February 2020.

[278] UN SG Report (8 May 2019) UN Doc E/2019/68, para 29 and special edition, 39 <https://unstats.un.org/sdgs/report/2019/> accessed 9 February 2020.

[279] ECOSOC, 'Synthesis of voluntary submissions by functional commission of the ECOSOC and other intergovernmental bodies and forums' (10 May 2019) UN Doc E/HLPF/2019/4, paras 83 and 162.

[280] Israel, National Voluntary Review (2019), 155 <https://sustainabledevelopment.un.org/content/documents/23576ISRAEL_13191_SDGISRAEL.pdf> accessed 9 February 2021.

[281] DESA, 'Voluntary National Reviews Synthesis Report' (2019) 48<https://sustainabledevelopment.un.org/content/documents/252302019_VNR_Synthesis_Report_DESA.pdf> accessed 9 February 2021.

[282] ECOSOC, 'Compilation of Main Messages for the 2019 Voluntary National Reviews' (24 May 2019) UN Doc E/HLPF/2019/5.

uneven. Indeed, according to the 2020 progress chart, progress on target 8.5 has stalled and even deteriorated in regions such as Sub-Saharan Africa, Latin America and the Caribbean, Northern Africa, and Western Asia.[283] Thus, 2020 marked the beginning of the 'Decade of Action' for the SDGs that called for accelerated efforts at global and local levels, and by all stakeholders, including youth, businesses, and civil society, in order to streamline public and private financing for development, the international governance mechanism for development, national development strategies, research, and technology with SDG priorities.[284] Unfortunately, the outbreak of the COVID-19 pandemic has disrupted implementation towards the SDGs given the socio-economic repercussions of a primarily health crisis. With regards to employment and decent work, the ILO estimated a drop in global working hours by 14 per cent in the second quarter of 2020, equivalent to 400 million full-time workers doing a forty-eight-hour working week.[285] Due to the unemployment and underemployment caused, workers in the informal economy, which represent half of the global labour force, were expected to see a 60 per cent decline in their incomes.[286] Women have been severely hit given their over-representation in informal work.[287] Accordingly, the youth didn't seem to fair better since unemployment rates in the group aged fifteen to twenty-four years marked a difference of 18 percentage points from the adult unemployment rate in some regions.[288]

Against this background, almost all UN development agencies and human rights treaty monitoring bodies such as the CESCR, the CEDAW, the OHCHR recommended to the 2020 HLPF the protection of workers through rapid and decisive national and international coordinated policy responses.[289] The same was reiterated in regional forums that reviewed the implementation of Agenda 2030. For instance, the African Regional Forum urged Member States to adopt integrated pro-employment approaches in their macroeconomic and sectoral economic policy frameworks to stimulate labour demand and decent jobs.[290] Similarly, civil society organizations emphasized the implementation of a human rights-based policy and financing framework for development and the SDGs, reporting that citizens in the European region had 'patchy access', among others, to the right to decent work. In turn, they recommended that the Economic Commission for the region of Europe designed urgent economic stimulus

[283] DESA, UN Statistics Division 'Sustainable Development Goals Progress Chart 2020' <https://unstats.un.org/sdgs/report/2020/progress-chart-2020.pdf> accessed 9 February 2021.

[284] A Guterres, Remarks to HLPF on Sustainable Development (24 September 2019) <https://www.un.org/sg/en/content/sg/speeches/2019-09-24/remarks-high-level-political-sustainable-development-forum> accessed 9 February 2021 and UNGA, 'Resolution, adopting political declaration 74/4 of the HLPF on sustainable development under the auspices of the GA' (21 October 2019) UN Doc A/RES/74/4, especially paras 4, 26.

[285] UNSG Report (28 April 2020) UN Doc E/2020/57, para 73 and special edition, 41 <https://unstats.un.org/sdgs/report/2020/> accessed 9 February 2021.

[286] ibid para 76.

[287] ECOSOC, 'Discussion papers on the HLPF, submitted by Major Groups and other Stakeholders' (1 May 2020), UN Doc E/HLPF/2020/2, para 2.

[288] For example, Western Asia and Northern Africa, UNSG Report 2020 (n 285), para 78 and statistical annex, 90.

[289] ECOSOC, 'Synthesis of voluntary submissions by functional commissions of the ECOSOC and other intergovernmental bodies and forums' (4 May 2020) UN Doc E/HLPF/2020/4, 17 point (c).

[290] ECOSOC, 'Input from the Sixth Session of the Africa Regional forum on Sustainable Development' (1 May 2020) UN Doc E/HLPF/2020/3/Add.1, para 50 (b).

plans and social protection measures to safeguard the health and income of workers.[291] Certainly, the pandemic highlighted the socio-economic inequalities among and within states and their differences in capacity and preparedness to deliver effectively on fundamental aspects of human well-being. However, it is important to note that the health emergency only exacerbated the otherwise long-standing structural problems in international and domestic governance frameworks that have underscored the political, social, and economic context of countries, especially developing ones. Moreover, it stressed the importance of policy coherence and partnerships in order to address development challenges. For example, the aforementioned stakeholders' remarks in the context of the 2020 HLPF regarding the promotion of access to employment and the protection of earnings (target 8.5) showcased their intertwined nature with other matters such as health, social protection, and the development of transferable skills for better employability. To be sure, sustainable development requires a new model for development that integrates socio-economic (and environmental) aspects in a reinforcing way.

d) Critique

What is evident from the analysis is that full employment and decent work for all, defined in terms of fair and just remuneration in target 8.5, is not an 'acquis' of everyone. There is a fall in global unemployment but the uneven decline of regional rates indicates that in absolute numbers a great number of people, especially youth, are excluded from the job market. Equally, a clear vision regarding workers' circumstances, that is, living standard and work conditions, is not easy to form because data on hourly earnings do not seem to be systematic or easily comparable between countries even for the same employment sector. Consequently, the deficit of productive employment is not adequately depicted in the projections for the realization of Goal 8. Whereas the problem might often be in the way the indicators have been designed, states' insufficient statistical capacity for monitoring implementation of the 2030 Agenda and supporting informed and evidence-based decision-making is also a problem to effective policy design and analysis. Surely, the SDGs agenda has tailored stakeholders' attention to the most pressing development priorities of our century and has galvanized action towards their achievement. The achievements regarding target 8.5, however incomplete, show that the Goals, in principle, are fit for purpose considering the manner in which they have framed development priorities. Yet, if we agree that the SDGs have a bearing in law and reflect principles and norms of relevant fields in international law, do they actually serve as the driver for embedding the latter in policy and do they reinforce them in the jurisdictions of countries and internationally?

To date there is no evidence strongly suggesting so. Countries' reporting does not make such correlations and it seems that efforts towards employment and decent work

---

[291] ECOSOC, 'Input from the fourth Session of the Regional Forum on Sustainable Development for the Economic Commission for Europe Region' (1 May 2020) UN Doc E/HLPF/2020/3/Add.2, paras 18–19.

598   SDG 8

in development policy are demoted from states' legal obligations under the ILO or the ICESCR.

6. Target 8.6 By 2020, substantially reduce the proportion of youth not in employment, education or training

a) Sources of the target and empirical analysis

Target 8.6 supplements target 8.5 since the rate of youth not in employment, education, or training (youth NEET) provides significant complementary information about labour force participation and unemployment rates. In essence, the target measures the underutilization of labour, as specified in the category of young people aged fifteen to twenty-four years, who could potentially contribute to national development and growth through their work or by advancing their qualifications. In this regard, the respective indicator—proportion of youth NEET—differs from indicator 8.5.2 because it expressly takes into account the *potential* labour force that is not captured by the unemployment indicator. In general, however, the indicator is more complex not only because it comprises two different subgroups (the unemployed youth who are not in education or training and the youth outside the labour force, who are not in education or training) but also due to its link to education, which consists of formal and non-formal and vocational training.[292] Qualitative aspects of the latter may not be actually measured here, yet conclusions around education exclusion could be inferred. As such, information may assist positively further investigation into the causes keeping youth outside the labour force (eg the mismatch of skills learned with the demands of the job market or other social and economic obstacles) and education alike. Inclusiveness, which is a common denominator of Goal 4 and Goal 8, is informed in parallel by data from both; hence, effectuating the interrelationship of those goals.

Such potential is moderated in practice, though. The requirement for reliable information on two elements, the labour market status and youth's participation in education/training, presupposes that national labour force surveys are detailed and return solid information that make comparisons feasible. This is not always achievable given the variations in individual state's capacity to collect data. A glance at the Global SDG Indicators Database that holds records for indicator 8.6.1 since 2000 confirms the scarcity of country data until 2011, when they start becoming more systematic.[293] This intermittent reporting explains the ILO's affirmation that clear global and regional estimates of the youth NEET are unavailable.[294] Nevertheless, the figures from countries that could report on target 8.6 show that in 2017 more than one-tenth of the youth population were neither in employment nor in education with young women more likely than young men to fall into that category in almost 70 per cent of those

---

[292] ILO Guidebook (2018) (n 262), 31–34; ILOSTAT indicator description of the youth NEET rate <http://www.ilo.org/ilostat-files/Documents/description_NEET_EN.pdf> and SDGs Metadata Repository (n 262) metadata sheet for indicator 8.6.1 <unstats.un.org> accessed 11 February 2021.

[293] UN Statistics Division, Global SDG Indicator Database <https://unstats.un.org/sdgs/indicators/database/> accessed 2 March 2021.

[294] ILO Guidebook (2018) (n 262) 34.

countries.[295] The year 2018 marked no noticeable reduction in rates[296] but a reduction to one-fifth of the world's youth NEET was documented in the 2019 report by the SG. Still, young women were twice as likely as young men to be outside the labour force and not in education/training. In Central and Southern Asia the gender difference between young women and men NEET was 36 percentage points (46 per cent young women's NEET compared to 10 per cent of young men's).[297] The 2019 progress chart designed by the UN Statistics Division on the basis of the most available data as of September that year visualizes the SG's remarks: in all regions limited or no progress is made on target 8.6 with Northern Africa, Western, Central and Southern Asia having very high NEET rates. From the developed countries, only Australia and New Zealand have a very low percentage.[298] Currently, young people not in employment or education reach 22 per cent globally. When disaggregated by sex, the youth NEET rate rises up to 31.1 per cent for females compared to 13.9 per cent for males globally. As in the previous years, Central and Southern Asia seem to suffer the highest numbers of youth NEET (30.1 per cent) and are followed by LDCs (20.9 per cent) and Small Island Developing States (SIDS, 24.1 per cent). Unsurprisingly, female NEET rates are higher too—47.9 per cent in Central and Southern Asia, 29.9 per cent in LDCs, and 30.4 per cent in SIDS.[299]

b) Implementation efforts at the international and domestic levels
How major a challenge the exclusion of youth from the job market and from opportunities to develop their skills is for countries across regions becomes particularly evident from a look at their national reviews. Bosnia and Herzegovina, Indonesia, Lesotho, Mauritius, Mongolia, Oman, and Pakistan, to name a few, underscored the lack of harmonization between the education system and the demands of the labour market that causes the skills mismatch.[300] In response, the policies put forward range from offering funding to support students from regional and remote areas to undertake courses in science, technology, engineering, and mathematics (STEM), agriculture, and health, such as the 'Rural and Regional Enterprise Scholarships' by Australia; to the establishment of centres responsible for the labour market placement of students with disabilities and young people, such as Hungary's 'Special Development Centre for the Promotion of Employment in the Labour Market';[301] to programmes for youth training, job search, and employment, such as the 'Youth Guarantee' programme implemented by Poland, Lithuania, Ireland, and other EU Member States[302] or the 'NEET Activation Schemes

---

[295] UNSG SDG Report 2017 (n 271) para 12, bullet point 3. Note that the statistical information used in all reports by the SG refers to the previous year of the report.

[296] UNSG SDG Report 2018 (n 274) para 77. It is interesting also that in both years, 2017 and 2018, there is no statistical table for indicator 8.6.1 annexed to the SG's reports.

[297] UNSG Report 2019 (n 278) para 29, bullet point 6 and UN Statistics Division, SDG Story Map 2019 <https://unstats.un.org/sdgs/report/2019/storymap/> accessed 2 Mar 2021.

[298] DESA, UN Statistics Division 'Sustainable Development Goals Progress Chart 2019' <https://unstats.un.org/sdgs/report/2019/progress-chart.pdf> accessed 2 Mar 2021.

[299] UNSG SDG Report 2020 (n 285) para 79 and annex, 91–92 (first time ever that a statistics table for target 8.6 is incorporated in SG's report).

[300] DESA, 'VNR Synthesis Report' (2019) (n 281) 48.

[301] DESA, 'VNR Synthesis Report' (2018) 28 <https://sustainabledevelopment.un.org/content/documents/210732018_VNRs_Synthesis_compilation_11118_FS_BB_Format_FINAL_cover.pdf> accessed 2 March 2021.

[302] ibid 44.

I & II' by Malta that offers skills training to people who have been out of the workforce for extended periods of time.[303]

c) Critique

Governments' efforts on tackling youth NEET are encouraging but a comparison of the 2020 data with those of 2005 show that no region has managed to reduce *substantially* the proportion of youth NEET by the year 2020, which is the deadline for target 8.6. The decline is 1 per cent globally and on average 2 per cent regionally, as shown by the statistics table for indicator 8.6.1 that is annexed to the Secretary-General's 2020 SDG report. No doubt, more action is needed on this front. A reason for the unsatisfactory outcomes might be the fact that the target calls only for a 'substantial reduction' of youth NEET instead of establishing a specific benchmark of progress (eg total elimination or by a certain percentage). Nonetheless, the target brings again to the forefront the issue of youth unemployment, which was crossed out from the MDGs in 2007 when the target on decent work was added.

7. Target 8.7 Take immediate and effective measures to eradicate forced labour, end modern slavery and human trafficking and secure the prohibition and elimination of the worst forms of child labour, including recruitment and use of child soldiers, and by 2025 end child labour in all its forms

a) Sources of the target

If work is to afford a person a sense of dignity and worth, at a very minimum it has to be non-exploitative. Hardly anyone would disagree that exploitation, defined in general terms as taking unfair advantage of another person, constitutes nowadays a moral wrong, sometimes grave. In the context of labour relations, though, it has not always been described as such. Karl Marx considers exploitation an inherent element of workers' labour in a capitalist society insofar as capitalists appropriate the value produced by workers' labour power. In turn, workers as a class are always forced to work since they do not own property and the means of production for their subsistence. As a result, coercion and oppression seem to be attributes of wage labour, created by the very structure of a class-based society.[304] Even today, the employer–employee relationship is unequal and the latter is subordinated to the former, yet the contemporary understanding of coercion entails severe restriction on an individual's freedom and is largely associated with abuse. In such instances, we speak about extreme forms of exploitation. These are, in particular, condemned under human rights law because they constitute gross violations of human rights. However, there are also more subtle forms of unfair treatment at work that could be classified as exploitation such as when employers take advantage of the employee's personal circumstances in a specific transaction between

---

[303] Malta, Voluntary National Review on the Implementation of the 2030 Agenda (2018), 34 <https://sustainabledevelopment.un.org/content/documents/20203Malta_VNR_Final.pdf> accessed 2 March 2021.

[304] M Zwolinski and A Wertheimer, 'Exploitation', *The Stanford Encyclopedia of Philosophy* (Summer edn, 2017) <https://plato.stanford.edu/archives/sum2017/entries/exploitation/> accessed 31 March 21.

them or of their vulnerability, weakening their bargaining power. Exploitation of this kind may violate rights at work captured under both human rights and labour law but is not always severe (eg unfair wages, unfair dismissal, exclusion from inspections pursuant to health and safety laws etc).[305] Nonetheless, the moral wrong is still great because it is exactly upon this vulnerability that the employer rests to promote his economic interests. Such an attitude conflicts with the respect and dignity human beings should treat one another.[306]

Target 8.7 touches on the worst expression of labour exploitation that is manifested in modern forms of slavery and forced and compulsory labour. Human trafficking is also linked to exploitation in its most severe manifestations, encompassing the aforementioned forms of labour exploitation and others such as the exploitation of workers in the sex industry. From the perspective of human rights law, everyone should be protected from such abusive situations. Yet, some groups of individuals possess characteristics that make them more vulnerable than others and should therefore be given enhanced protection. Children constitute such a category since childhood is entitled to special care and assistance.[307] For this reason child labour is distinguished. While in some cases work experience is beneficial for children's inclusion in society and a positive way to prepare them to lead their adult lives, not all employment of children is desirable or even acceptable. Child labour impacts a child's full and harmonious development because it interferes with the child's education, health, and general welfare in physical, mental, spiritual, moral, and social terms.[308] In addition to the adverse effects on children themselves, child labour is an indicator of a country's low development status and persistence of poverty. Being a moral wrong, child labour is prohibited under both human rights and labour law.

In the light of the above, target 8.7 is probably the most distinguishable for its direct bearing on both fields of law, as it seeks to promote the first pillar of the Decent Work Agenda (Rights at work).

i) Slavery, servitude, forced and compulsory labour as grave forms of exploitation Codification of the right not to be subjected to slavery, servitude, forced and compulsory labour is found in the form of an absolute civil right in the UDHR (article 4) and the ICCPR (article 8). The European Convention on Human Rights (ECHR) that guarantees predominantly civil and political rights contains a similar provision under article 4:

1. No one shall be held in slavery or servitude.
2. No one shall be required to perform forced or compulsory labour

---

[305] V Mantouvalou, 'The Right to Non-exploitative Work' in Mantouvalou (ed), *The Right to Work- Legal and Philosophical Perspectives* (n 163).

[306] UDHR (n 68) art 1; A Wood, 'Exploitation' in K Schaff (ed), *Philosophy and the Problems of Work: A Reader* (Rowman and Littlefield Publishers 2001) 153: 'proper respect for others is violated when we treat their vulnerabilities as opportunities to advance our own interests or projects. It is degrading to have your weaknesses taken advantage of, and dishonourable to use the weaknesses of other for your ends.'

[307] CRC (n 167) Preamble.

[308] CRC (n 167) arts 32, 34–36, 39; ILO Guidebook (n 262) 36.

602 SDG 8

The normative force of the right in all three instruments is the same; states cannot place any restrictions on the right nor derogate from their obligation to guarantee it. Interestingly, the provisions do not name exploitation as being a core element of these forms of ill treatment. On the contrary, the link between exploitation and human trafficking is explicit in the definition of trafficking in article 3 of the Protocol to Prevent, Suppress and Punish Trafficking in persons, especially Women and Children, which supplements the UN Conventions against Transnational Organised Crime. Moreover, the same article gives an unequivocal explanation of the meaning of exploitation.[309]

> Trafficking in persons shall mean the recruitment, transportation, transfer, harbouring or receipt of persons, by means of the threat or use of force or other forms of coercion ... or of a position of vulnerability or of the giving or receiving of payments or benefits to achieve the consent of a person having control over another person, *for the purpose of exploitation*. Exploitation shall include at a minimum, the exploitation of the prostitution of others or other forms of sexual exploitation, forced labour or services, slavery or practices similar to slavery, servitude. ...

The purpose of exploitation comprises the *mens rea* of the offence of trafficking, which states shall criminalize as such in their domestic legal systems.

Under the human rights jurisprudence, slavery, servitude, and forced labour became associated with exploitation apropos the *Siliadin v France*[310] judgment of the European Court of Human Rights (ECtHR). The case concerned a migrant domestic worker, a Tongolese national who had arrived in France on a tourist visa under the agreement that she would provide her host family with short-term housework help until repaying them the cost of her air ticket. In return, they would make the necessary arrangements for the regularization of her immigration status and education. Instead, Siliadin had her passport confiscated and remained in the family's house working as a servant. Later on, a settlement between the family and Siliadin's father found the applicant being 'lent' to a couple with three young children. During her stay with the new host family she worked as a housemaid and child-minder. She was forced to work fifteen hours a day, seven days a week, had to cook, clean the house and her employer's office, receiving no payment for her work. Her living conditions were also degrading since she wore old clothes, slept on a mattress in the children's room, she was rarely allowed to leave the house, and had no privacy. The applicant filed an application before the ECtHR claiming violation of article 4 ECHR on the account that the French law, which criminalizes under article 225 (13)–(14) taking advantage of a person's vulnerability or situation of dependence and obtaining services without pay or subjecting the worker

---

[309] Protocol to Prevent, Supress and Punish Trafficking in Person, Especially Women and Children, supplementing the UN Convention against Transnational Organised Crime (adopted 15 November 2000, entered into force 25 December 2003) 2237 UNTS 319; The same definition of exploitation is endorsed by art 2 Directive 2011/36/EU of the European Parliament and Council (5 April 2011) on preventing and combating trafficking in human beings and protecting victims that replaced Council Framework decision 2002/629/JHA [2011] OJ L101/1.

[310] App no 7331/01 (ECtHR, 26 July 2005).

TARGETS AND INDICATORS   603

to working and living conditions incompatible with human dignity, did not meet the standards set by the Convention regarding states' positive obligations.

The Court engaged in an interpretive task to elucidate the distinct features of each notion. It defined slavery pursuant to the 1926 Slavery Convention[311] as 'the status or condition of a person over whom any or all of the powers attaching to the right of ownership are exercised'.[312] According to the Court's view, a legal right to ownership was constituent of the notion and it sustained that 'the evidence did not suggest that Siliadin was held in slavery in the "proper sense," namely that her employers exercised a genuine legal right of legal ownership over her, thus reducing her to the status of an "object"'.[313] To the extent that the 'right of ownership' is understood in terms of property law perspectives, it is truly difficult to contest the Court's conclusion that Siliadin was not owned. Private law ownership on human beings is nowadays a 'legal impossibility'.[314] Yet, a deeper reflection on the wording of the 1926 Convention reveals that the authoritative definition of slavery is much broader;[315] reference to slavery as a 'status' or 'condition' over whom *powers attaching to the right of ownership are exercised*[316] allows for a conceptualization of the phenomenon that exceeds the boundaries of legal ownership and permits the notion of slavery to obtain contemporary relevance. Indeed, adherence to the criterion of legal ownership has been considered a literal misreading[317] of the provisions of the Slavery Convention that fails to embrace actual circumstances of one person's total subjection to another, as if that person were an object legally owned. By contrast, in enquiring the existence of slavery, one should identify practical analogues of the liberties and entitlements the legal right to ownership echoes and not this right in itself.[318] On this account, the classification of a person's situation as slavery hinges upon a factual element—the *de facto* exercise of the powers attached to the right of ownership that result in the person being controlled in a manner equivalent to *de jure* possession.[319] In fact, the Court itself adopted a more expansive interpretation of slavery in *Rantsev v Cyprus and Russia*,[320] a case of sex trafficking. In order to address the question whether human trafficking for sexual exploitation fell within the ambit of slavery, the Court denoted that 'trafficking, by its very nature and aim of exploitation, treats human beings as commodities to be bought and sold and put to forced labour ... it implies close surveillance of the activities of victims, whose movements are often circumscribed and involves the use of violence and threats against the victims, who work and live under poor conditions; such practices are based "on the exercise of

[311] 1926 Convention to Suppress the Slave Trade and Slavery (entered into force 9 March 1927) 60 LNTS 253.
[312] ibid art 1.
[313] *Siliadin v France* (n 310) para 122.
[314] J Allain and others, 'Property and the Definition of Slavery' (2012) 61(4) International and Comparative Law Quarterly 915, 920.
[315] A Nicholson, 'Reflections on Siliadin v. France: Slavery and Legal Definition' [2010] International Journal of Human Rights 705, 711.
[316] Emphasis added.
[317] NL McGeehan, 'Misunderstood and Neglected: The Marginalization of Slavery in International Law' (2012) 16 International Journal of Human Rights 436, 440.
[318] Allain and others (n 314) 921.
[319] ibid 924.
[320] *Rantsev v Cyprus and Russia*, App no 25965/04 (ECtHR, judgment 10 January 2010).

powers attaching to the right of ownership".[321] In any event, the discussion of slavery again under article 4 ECHR in light of present manifestations of coercion and abuse in labour relations as illustrated by domestic work, trafficked women in the sex industry, and other examples have drawn the attention to what has been classified as 'modern slavery'.[322]

To return to *Siliadin*, the Court denounced the exploitative practices against her as constituting forced labour—at the very least—and servitude. Forced labour was defined in the light of article 2(1) of ILO's Forced Labour Convention, which delineates forced labour as 'all work or service which is exacted from any person under the menace of any penalty and for which the said person has not offered himself voluntarily'.[323] Crucially, two criteria fulfil the notion of forced labour: (i) the threat of penalty of any kind, ranging from physical violence to more subtle forms like psychological or financial penalties[324] and (ii) involuntary commencement of the assignments. On the other hand, servitude is a broader notion and encompasses a serious denial of freedom because it includes the obligation to provide certain services for someone, to live in that person's property and the impossibility of changing this condition.[325] Siliadin fulfilled all three criteria.

Slavery, servitude, and forced/compulsory labour are considered three distinct practices. Yet, drawing the dividing line of differentiation between them is, as a matter of fact, hard to achieve because the three notions share common elements: each one of them builds on coercion and in all three circumstances, exercise of control over a person and that person's inability to alter her situation are somehow present. In most of the cases, an individual's exploitation and abuse could be equally classified under more than one of these concepts. That said, all three constitute severe forms of exploitation that give rise to criminalization. However, there is scope to argue that labour law may complement the criminal law paradigm since workers' exploitation may not always amount to grave violations of their rights—in fact, exploitation should now only be viewed in these narrow terms. This could be done through regulatory provisions that close the legal loopholes that create or exacerbate a worker's vulnerability and weaken his/her bargaining power, as mentioned earlier.[326] In the discussed case of domestic work, the element of vulnerability would be the worker's migration status. Sometimes it is not only employers that take advantage of the employee's personal circumstances but the state also creates the circumstances for such exploitation to take place through law.

---

[321] ibid para 281.

[322] C Griffiths, 'Behind Closed Doors: Exposing Modern Slavery on a Global Scale. An Interview with Kevin Bales' (2010) 29 Equality, Diversity & Inclusion: An International Journal 716; *Chowdury and Others v Greece*, App no 21884/15 (ECtHR, 30 March 2017).

[323] ILO Forced Labour Convention No 29 (entered into force 1 May 1932), art 2(1); *Van der Mussele v Belgium*, App no 8919/80 (ECtHR, 23 November 1983) para 32.

[324] K Bakirci, 'Human Trafficking and Forced Labour: A Criticism of the International Labour Organization' (2009) 16 Journal of Financial Crime 160, 161–62.

[325] *Van Droogenbroeck v Belgium* (Commission's report, 9 July 1980) Series B, No 44, 30 (paras 78–80).

[326] Mantouvalou, 'The Right to Non-exploitative Work' (n 305); V Mantouvalou, 'Legal Construction of Structures of Exploitation' in H Collins and others (eds), *Philosophical Foundations of Labour Law* (OUP 2018).

However, it could be argued, that this manifestation of exploitation is dealt with under target 8.8.

ii) Economic exploitation of children Effective abolition of child labour constitutes one of the Core Labour Standards, introduced as such by the Declaration on Fundamental Principles and Rights at work. The Declaration is a soft law instrument and, like any other international declaration, it is not legally binding. By implication, the abolition of child labour as a standard therein—it could be argued—has a lower normative status, hence it permits a weaker degree of expectation regarding state compliance since soft low standards are applied through voluntary acceptance. Indeed, considering the fact that criteria for distinguishing acceptable and permissible employment of children from exploitation are framed by legally binding conventions,[327] notably the ILO's Minimum Age Convention[328] and the later Convention on Worst forms of Labour,[329] the categorization of child labour as a standard seems to moderate the severity of a practice that denies children their freedom in childhood, deprives them of their dignity, and hinders their development for the future. Such an argument, though, is not true. Soft law instruments in international law have a constructive role in the creation of the normative framework on a given matter together with binding law. That is because they are able to reunite the international community around shared values and influence behaviour in the legal sphere indirectly since they emerge from inclusive deliberations under the auspices of the competent international governing body for the regulating matter, which gives to their content the authority and legitimacy necessary to become the pull towards compliance for stakeholders and a source of their obligations to implement them. The Declaration on Fundamental Principles served exactly this purpose; it classified the rights enshrined in the ILO conventions as fundamental and expanded the normative force to capture stakeholders, in this case Member States of the ILO, that have not signed or ratified them and would not be otherwise bound by the obligations they set in relation to the treatment of children in employment. Moreover, it linked compliance with the prohibition of child labour to ILO membership by virtue of which states are necessarily compelled by its constitution to realize principles concerning fundamental rights. Remarkably, the ILO expanded the applicability and normative impetus of the Declaration and the Conventions on child labour to businesses, workers', and employers' organizations through the launch of the International Programme on the Elimination of Child Labour (IPEC).[330] Pursuance of the programme's objective was premised on capacity building through partnership agreements with actors such as local communities, multilateral institutions (eg UNICEF), and NGOs with the purpose to raise awareness of child labour in the public and fund programmes to promote

---

[327] These Conventions are the most recent, however the ILO has given priority to child labour since its establishment in 1919 with another minimum age convention and a convention on night work for young persons in industry (ILO 2018b).

[328] ILO Convention No 138 (1973).

[329] ILO Convention No 182 (1999).

[330] ILO Decent Work Report (n 208) 16–17.

the implementation and monitoring of compliant legislation at a national and sectoral level, to institute alternatives to child labour, and to produce data for effective action, including measurement of child labour's impact on development.

Child labour has been a core human rights issue at the UN level as well since the institutional framework of the organization's predecessor, the League of Nations. Article 4 of the 1924 Geneva Declaration stated '[t]he child must be put in a position to earn a livelihood, and must be protected against every form of exploitation'.[331] Later on, Principle 9 of the Declaration on the Right of the Child elaborated on the notion of exploitative work for a child, defining it as 'any occupation or employment, which would prejudice his health or education, or interfere with his physical, mental or moral development'.[332] With the adoption and enactment of the Convention on the Rights of the Child (CRC), the aforementioned standards were incorporated into law and are enshrined in article 32 CRC that prohibits the economic exploitation of children. States are urged to take specific measures towards that end (eg minimum age for admission to employment, regulation of hours and conditions of employment, penalties and sanctions) having regard to the relevant provisions of other international instruments. In this way, labour and human rights law on exploitative practices regarding children at work become aligned.

iii) Child labour at the intersection of labour and human rights law Within this context, the framework of international standards on child labour lies at the intersection of labour and human rights law. More specifically, under the ILO's Minimum Age Convention States undertake the responsibility to pursue a national policy designed to ensure the effective abolition of child labour and to raise progressively the minimum age for admission to employment of work to a level consistent with the fullest physical and mental development of young persons. In accordance with this, the minimum age for work is set at the age of fifteen when compulsory education ends so that work doesn't interfere with schooling.[333] The rule being this, light work or jobs that do not have an adverse effect on a child's health, education, and training are permitted from the age of thirteen. In contrast, hazardous work, namely 'employment or work which by its nature or the circumstances in which it is carried out is likely to jeopardize the health, safety or morals of young persons', is prohibited for children entirely.[334] Hazardous work is exemplified further by Recommendation No 190 on the Worst Forms of Child Labour and article 3(d) of ILO Convention No 182, for which the determinant of hazardousness is primarily the specific forms of work and not the child's age vulnerability. Accordingly, the Recommendation's definition of hazardous work refers to:[335]

---

[331] League of Nations Declaration 1924.
[332] UN, Declaration on the Rights of the Child (20 November 1959) UN Doc A/RES/1386 (XIV).
[333] ILO Convention No 138, art 2.
[334] ibid art 3(1).
[335] ILO Worst Forms of Child Labour Recommendation No 190 (1999) <https://www.ilo.org/dyn/normlex/en/f?p=NORMLEXPUB:12100:0::NO::P12100_INSTRUMENT_ID:312528> accessed 28 March 2021.

(a) work which exposes children to physical, psychological or sexual abuse;

(b) work underground, under water, at dangerous heights or in confined spaces;

(c) work with dangerous machinery, equipment and tools, or which involves the manual handling or transport of heavy loads;

(d) work in an unhealthy environment, which may, for example, expose children to hazardous substances, agents or processes, or to temperatures, noise levels, or vibrations damaging to their health;

(e) work under particularly difficult conditions such as work for long hours or during the night or work where the child is unreasonably confined to the premises of the employer.

On the other hand, Convention 182 deals with the worst forms of child labour:

(a) all forms of slavery or practices similar to slavery, such as the sale and trafficking of children, debt bondage and serfdom and forced or compulsory labour, including forced or compulsory recruitment of children for use in armed conflict;

(b) the use, procuring or offering of a child for prostitution, for the production of pornography or for pornographic performances;

(c) the use, procuring or offering of a child for illicit activities, in particular for the production and trafficking of drugs as defined in the relevant international treaties;

(d) work which, by its nature or the circumstances in which it is carried out, is likely to harm the health, safety or morals of children.

The reflection of human rights law on the protection of children from exploitation of any kind is clear in the provisions of this article. First, the wording of paragraph (d) is similar to that of Principle 9 of the Declaration on the Rights of the Child. Secondly, the remaining paragraphs correlate to articles 33–36 CRC that safeguard children's right to be protected from illicit use of narcotic drugs, sexual exploitation, and any other form of abuse prejudicial to any aspect of the child's welfare, including slavery and like practices, servitude, forced and compulsory labour, human trafficking, and children's forced or compulsory recruitment for use in armed conflict. Children soldiers as well as the sale of children, child prostitution and pornography have received particular attention under the CRC. Protection from these manifestations of children's exploitation is not confined to the core provision of article 32 but is regulated in detail in two Optional Protocols (Optional Protocol to the Convention on the Rights of the Child on the Involvement of Children in Armed Conflicts (OPAC) and Optional Protocol to the Convention on the Rights of the Child on the Sale of Children, Child Prostitution and Child Pornography (OPSC)) adopted in 2000. What is interesting is the harmonization of the children's right with the labour rights perspective on child labour by the reference in the Protocols' Preamble of the relevant legal instruments and ILO Convention No 182 in particular. At the same time, protection under human rights is a bit broader.

608   SDG 8

Whereas under the ILO Convention on Worst Forms of Child Labour compulsory recruitment in armed conflict would be banned as a slavery-like practice, under the OPAC voluntary recruitment is also covered. Likewise, 'the OPSC goes beyond ILO Convention No. 182 by providing more detailed definitions of sale of children, child prostitution, and child pornography, requiring the penalization or criminalization of acts that are covered by these definitions as well as complicity, permitting the establishment of extraterritorial jurisdiction over the offenses and pronouncing the offenses linked to these acts as extraditable'.[336]

International standards on child labour are furthermore enumerated in various business and human rights guidelines (BHR) that are voluntary, non-binding principles with which private actors (businesses) and financing institutions that fund development projects comply by incorporating them into their operating frameworks. Three sets of BHR guidelines are relevant here; the ILO Tripartite Declaration of Principles concerning MNEs and Social Policy; the OECD Guidelines for MNEs and the Children's Rights and Business Principles (CRBPs), which resulted from collaboration between UNICEF, the UN Global Compact, and Save the Children. In line also with the United Nations Guiding Principles on Business and Human Rights's (UNGP) 'Protect, Respect, Remedy framework', the OECD Guidelines refer to businesses' duty 'to contribute to the abolition of child labour and take immediate and effective measures to secure the prohibition and elimination of the worst forms of child labour as a matter of urgency'.[337] With similar wording, the ILO Declaration states that 'multinational enterprises, as well as national enterprises, should respect the minimum age for admission to employment or work in order to secure the effective abolition of child labour and should take immediate and effective measures within their competence to secure the prohibition and elimination of the worst forms of child labour as a matter of urgency'.[338] Comparably, the CRBPs, which are the only set of standards that directly focus on children's rights in the context of the human right duties of business', incorporate the elimination of child labour in its ten principles.[339] Last but not least, the International Finance Corporation's Performance Standards[340] and the World Bank's new Environmental and Social Framework on Labour and Working Conditions[341] clearly state that funded partners will not employ children in an economically

---

[336] GE Türkelli and others, 'Eradicating Child Labor: Ending Economic Exploitation of Children as an Objective of Sustainable Development' in WL Filho and others (eds), *Decent Work and Economic Growth* (Springer 2021) 394. On children soldiers, see *ex multis* D Casalin, 'Recruitment and Use of Child Soldiers in International Law: Prohibition and Elimination' in ibid; M Happold, *Child Soldiers In International Law* (Juris Publishing 2005).

[337] OECD, *Guidelines for Multinational Enterprises* (OECD 2011), ch V, art 1(c) <https://www.oecd.org/corporate/mne/48004323.pdf> accessed 1 April 2021.

[338] ILO, 'Tripartite Declaration of Principles concerning MNE and Social Policy' (n 245) para 27.

[339] UNICEF, 'UN Global Compact and Save the Children' (2012) <https://d306pr3pise04h.cloudfront.net/docs/issues_doc%2Fhuman_rights%2FCRBP%2FChildrens_Rights_and_Business_Principles.pdf> accessed 15 April 2021.

[340] 'IFC Performance Standards on Environmental and Social Sustainability' (2012) <https://www.ifc.org/wps/wcm/connect/topics_ext_content/ifc_external_corporate_site/sustainability-at-ifc/publications/publications_handbook_pps> accessed 18 April 2021.

[341] WBG, 'Environmental and Social Standards-ESS2 Labor and Working Conditions' (2018) <https://thedocs.worldbank.org/en/doc/837721522762050108-0290022018/original/ESFFramework.pdf#page=45&zoom=80> accessed 18 April 2021.

exploitative manner nor will they engage them in to hazardous work or work that inter-feres with their development.

Considering the above, it arises that the rules governing child labour are an amal-gamation of minimum age requirements and restrictions based on the type and nature of work performed by children. Among the respective treaties and soft law standards, the ILO Conventions set the benchmarks for the prohibition of child labour and are accepted as such in all other regulatory fields. Yet, despite the comprehensive set of binding and non-binding norms, and of the widely endorsed urgency to tackle the phenomenon, it is difficult to conclude to a definition of child labour due to its many manifestations. From a basic standpoint, child labour can be deemed a subcategory of children in employment, encompassing children below the minimum age who work or those engaged in the worst forms of child labour, while children in hazardous work further specify the notion of child labour, referring to all children in work that has negative impacts on their health, safety and development due to its nature or type.[342] Consequently, child labour could be defined broadly as 'work performed by a child that is harmful to his or her physical and mental development by virtue of being physically, mentally, socially, or morally dangerous or harmful or that interferes with schooling by causing non-attendance, premature school leaving, or combination of school with heavy and long hours of work'.[343]

b) Empirical analysis, countries' implementation efforts, and critique

The many facets of child labour incorporated in the working definition above sug-gest that a policy for its elimination is confronted with complexity. It is not enough to take steps to suppress child labour alone but measures should address the background causes that nurture the phenomenon such as poverty of households, unequal educa-tional opportunities, or poor returns of education, credit, and land market inequalities etc. The SDGs present a fruitful opportunity to tackle the root causes of child labour given the interlinked and interdependent nature of the goals. Ending poverty (SDG 1), hunger (SDG 2), ensuring education for all (SDG 4), and making societies more inclusive (SDG 16) would eliminate the reasons that encourage the practice of child labour. Thereafter, it is important to have comprehensive data on all these aspects in order to measure progress on the elimination of child labour holistically. Indicator 8.7.1 measures only the proportion and number of children aged five to seventeen years en-gaged in child labour, disaggregated by sex and age (five to eleven, twelve to fourteen, and fifteen to seventeen age groups). Nevertheless, it has been designed by a detailed methodology that translates the legal standards governing the concept of child labour into statistical terms so that the incidence and distribution of child labour can be meas-ured effectively. More often than not, though, reported data give information about children's engagement in economic activities and household chores rather than the quality of their working conditions or whether they are forced into some types of the

---

[342] Türkelli and others (n 336) 394.
[343] ILO, 'What is Child Labor' <https://www.ilo.org/ipec/facts/lang--en/index.htm> accessed 18 April 2021.

worst forms of child labour. Consequently, hazardous work and the most abusive labour practices are not captured by the indicator for reporting on SDG 8.[344]

Indeed, reporting on target SDG 8.7 has been inconsistent and there are missing values for individual countries as well as entire regions regarding child labour. According to the SG's 2017 report, child labour remains a serious concern, although figures show a declining trend. Within a ten-year period, from 2000 to 2012, the number of working children declined by 78 million (246 million in 2000 v 168 million in 2012). More than half of child labourers (85 million children) participate in hazardous work and 59 per cent of this work is done in the agricultural sector. Girls have made greater progress than boys, with the number of girls engaged in child labour declining by 40 per cent during the same reference period compared to a decline of 25 per cent for boys.[345] Since 2017, there is no information in the SG's reports. However, the ILO-IPEC's reporting framework fills in the gap. Five- to eleven-year-old children make up nearly half of all children in child labour and nearly a quarter of them in hazardous work. Furthermore, the declining trends of child labour among fifteen to seventeen year olds might not be due to successful policies but due to the diminishing demand for young workers above the minimum age. Supportive of the claim is the fact that child labour decline rates stalled for those in the age group five to eleven years. What is worrying, though, is that progress is not uniform and regional discrepancies abound in decline rates. In fact, Sub-Saharan Africa experienced a 1 per cent increase in child labour prevalence rates between 2012 and 2016.[346]

If numbers remain like this, child labour will not be ended by the year 2025, which is the chronological goal of target 8.7. Accelerated progress is required, meaning that countries' national strategies should be more targeted. National voluntary reviews demonstrate that child labour preoccupies governments, whose efforts are tailored towards the domestication of International conventions on the Elimination of Child Labour (eg Sierra Leone's Decent work Country Program)[347] and the implementation of action plans. The specifics of the programmes vary.[348] They are based on strengthened control measures and preventive communication with the families of the children subjected to labour, and the development of a statistical survey methodology to study the state of child labour in the country (Azerbaijan);[349] others, such as Turkey's 2018 National Program for the Elimination of Child Labour, have established mobile teams of police and social workers to identify child beggars on streets and ensure fast public

[344] UNSC, Metadata sheet on target 8.7.1; ILO Guidebook (n 262) 36–40.
[345] UNSG Report 2017 (n 271) para 12, 10.
[346] ILO, 'Global Estimates of Child Labor: Results and Trends, 2012–2016' (2017) <https://www.ilo.org/global/publications/books/WCMS_575499/lang--en/index.htm> accessed 28 March 2022.
[347] VNR Sierra Leone (2019), 7–8, 29 <https://sustainabledevelopment.un.org/content/documents/23378Sierra_Leone_VNR_FINAL.pdf> accessed 31 March 2021.
[348] DESA, 'VNR Synthesis Report (2019)' (n 281) 48–49 mentioning examples of countries that have reported specific anti-child labour policies such as Cameroon, Algeria, Chile, Guyana, Ghana, Indonesia, Serbia, Tunisia, Turkmenistan, and Iceland.
[349] VNR Azerbaijan (2019), 80 <https://sustainabledevelopment.un.org/content/documents/23411AZERBAIJAN_VNR_Report.pdf> accessed 31 March 2021.

TARGETS AND INDICATORS   611

intervention or are targeted at supporting seasonal agricultural families to avoid using their children for their work by offering the latter schooling where their families migrate and healthcare services (Turkey's project on the Elimination of Worst Forms of Child Labour in Seasonal Agriculture in Hazelnut Harvesting).[350] By contrast, countries do not report anything about their progress to tackle human trafficking and the worst forms of labour exploitation, namely slavery and the similar practices of servitude and forced labour. Strikingly, target 8.7.1 does not capture this dimension of target 8.7. Henceforth, progress monitoring on the entire target is impossible and definitely impedes its achievement—something particularly worrisome given the centrality of non-exploitation in the concept of decent work.

8. Target 8.8 Protect labour rights and promote safe and secure working environments for all workers, including migrant workers, in particular women migrants, and those in precarious employment

a) Sources of the target and empirical analysis
Target 8.8 seems to be in principle another praiseworthy effort to found the employment aspect of SDG 8 on the human rights and ILO social justice regime. It suffices a glance at the target's wording to observe the prominent reference to the protection of labour rights in general and the distinct attention to the promotion of favourable working conditions, in respect of which health and safety are addressed here. Precarious employment is put under the spotlight. Reference is also made to migrant workers and migrant women, possibly in recognition of their important contribution to growth—through the labour they provide in the host country as well as the remittances they send to their homeland, helping their family to escape poverty—but also their vulnerability that leads them to accept precarious jobs or appalling working conditions. However, these very elements that make target 8.8 laudable may hinder its success. The aggregation of labour rights into one target alone renders it an all-encompassing target, which is moreover difficult to monitor because the realization of its constituents demand many diverse indicators—for working conditions, union rights, social security, adequate standard of living etc. There is an imminent risk that target 8.8 means 'all and nothing (or very little)' at the same time.[351]

i) Indicator 8.8.1 That the critique is pragmatic becomes evident by the target's indicators, although one is better placed than the other. Indicator 8.8.1 measures fatal and non-fatal occupational injuries per 100,000 workers, disaggregated by sex and migrant status. At a glance, the indicator is understandable and seems to measure progress directly towards the target's aspect on health and safety at work. Confirmation of the indicator's suitability arises in the authoritative analysis of article 7(b) ICESCR

---

[350] VNR Turkey (2019), 42, 88–89 <https://sustainabledevelopment.un.org/content/documents/23862Turkey_VNR_110719.pdf> accessed 31 March 2021.
[351] MacNaughton and Frey, 'Decent Work, Human Rights and the Sustainable Development Goals' (n 213) 655.

on healthy and safe working conditions by the Committee. In brief, the Committee focuses on occupational accidents and disease as well, stating further that their prevention is as fundamental an aspect of the right to just and favourable conditions of work as it is integral to the realization of the right to the highest attainable level of physical and mental health.[352] Respectively, article 12(2)(b)–(c) ICESCR specify that states should take steps to improve all aspects of environmental and industrial hygiene, and prevent, treat, and control occupational diseases. Towards this aim, national strategies should possess the following qualitative attributes: (i) ensure the participation of all categories of workers, employers and representative organizations in their formulation; (ii) indicate specific actions to be taken by employers for the protection of workers; (iii) have a due process of reporting, and investigation; and (iv) a remedial system, including access to grievance mechanisms, award of compensation, and imposition of penalties to offenders.[353] These elements are clearly infused by the human rights-based approach to public policy, which the ILO standards on occupational safety complement by detailing the policy measures according to occupation and economic activity. Indicator 8.8.1 can be a valuable source of impetus towards this direction, if the numerical figures are put into perspective and are used to evaluate the effectiveness of preventive measures, to estimate social and economic consequences from non-compliance with health and safety standards, and to inform stakeholders.[354] As expected, the ILO guidebook on labour market indicators does not make any connection with the Committee's delineation of national policy.[355] Yet, the latter highlights the importance of reliable data on the fullest possible range of occupational accidents and disease, disaggregated by sex and other grounds, and respecting human rights principles. Indicator 8.8.1 is not anchored in the normative framework of rights, although it would definitely add value to performance monitoring of development programmes.

Nowhere does a human rights-based approach become more relevant than in relation to specific groups of workers such as women and migrant workers. For instance, specific measures might be necessary to protect the safety and health of pregnant workers in relation to travel or night work.[356] Similarly, migrant workers are often victims of exploitation having to work in dangerous and unhealthy conditions. Their vulnerability is recognized in international law in the UN Convention on the Rights of All Migrant Workers and Members of their families (CMW).[357] The Preamble to the Convention refers explicitly to the situation of vulnerability in which migrant workers[358] and their family members find themselves due to their absence from their state of origin and the

---

[352] CommICESCR, GC 23 (2016) (n 170) paras 1, 25.

[353] ibid paras 27–29.

[354] UNSC, metadata on indicators 8.8.1 (March 2020), 1.

[355] ILO Guidebook (n 262) 40–45.

[356] B Aziz and E Parrott, 'Developing Good Policies for the Health of Pregnant Workers' (1996) 92(47) Nursing Times 32.

[357] n 167.

[358] Migrant status is determined according to country of birth (native-born or foreign-born) or country of citizenship (citizen or non-citizen) (UNSC, Metadata on indicator 8.8.1 (January 2021), 2.c.).

difficulties they may encounter in the state of employment.[359] Undocumented migrants are even more vulnerable than documented, hence the several provisions in the CMW targeting this group (eg articles 25(3) and 28).

Data disaggregation that complies with the respective human rights instruments (CEDAW and CMW) would foster target 8.8 substantially, as indirectly suggested by the ILO's Methodology for SDG indicator 8.8.2.[360] In fact, having recalled that *all* violations of freedom of association and collective bargaining (FACB) rights based on migrant status or sex are coded and embodied in the indicator,[361] it states that 'the textual information on which this coding is based will also be made available in a separate document in an effort to highlight such violations'.[362]

Indicator 8.8.1: implementation efforts at the international and domestic levels
In general, countries haven taken occupational risk management seriously but it is difficult to match the qualitative elements of their policies with the Committee's on the International Covenant on Economic, Social and Cultural Rights (CommICESCR or CESCR) proposals—after all, reporting on them is not required in the context of the SDGs given the lack of clear link with human rights standards. The same cannot be said, though, in order to justify another pitfall of the reports, namely the passing reference to women and migrants. For example, Kazakhstan, which has a high number of accidents at workplaces (every year 1,500 workers get injured and 250 people lose their lives), introduced a new programme, involving the establishment of production councils and the hiring of labour protection technical inspectors to perform controls on-site. The government has also promoted the implementation of health and safety standards, having more than 1,700 large enterprises that comply with regulations. Finally, workers employed in sectors with hazardous and dangerous working conditions are compensated through a range of awards.[363] Yet, there is no specification of the challenges faced by women and migrants regarding work conditions. As a second example, Iceland's policy appears to be more comprehensive. Icelandic authorities ensure that workplaces carry out risk assessments and have a plan for health and safety at work, which also includes a dispute resolution mechanism so that issues can be resolved in accordance with applicable law and regulations on-site. Those who have suffered occupational injuries are supported through social security schemes. Similarly,

[359] UNGA, 'Human Rights of Migrants, Report of the Special Rapporteur of the Commission on Human Rights, Gabriela Rodríguez Pizarro' (9 August 2022) UN Doc A/57/292.

[360] On the difficulties of measuring violations of FACB rights, see, eg, M Anner and others, 'Labour Rights Indicators: A New Resource for Better Understanding of Labour Rights in the World' (2017) 274 Global Labour Column <https://www.researchgate.net/publication/317102298_Labour_rights_indicators_a_new_resource_for_better_understanding_of_labour_rights_in_the_world> accessed 30 April 2021.

[361] ILO, Methodology for SDG indicator 8.8.2 on labour rights (10–19 October 2018) <https://www.ilo.org/wcmsp5/groups/public/---dgreports/---stat/documents/meetingdocument/wcms_636033.pdf> accessed 30 March 2021.

[362] The disaggregation by sex and migrant status is, however, not currently available (UNSC, 'Metadata on Indicators 8.8.2' (January 2021)).

[363] VNR Kazakhstan (2019), 68 <https://sustainabledevelopment.un.org/content/documents/23946KAZAKHSTAN_DNO__eng_4.Juli19.pdf> accessed 30 Mar 21.

614   SDG 8

the country's report discusses the unfavourable situation of immigrants only in relation to the lower wages they receive.[364]

Globally, the UN SG's 2019 report on the SDGs mentions that data from fifty-five countries show a median of three deaths and 889 non-fatal injuries occurred per 100,000 employees.[365] This is not a great improvement from the previous year, for which four fatal and 911 non-fatal injuries were reported.[366] Still, the ILO advises to be cautious with global estimates due to underreporting of accidents to national authorities and non-comprehensive, thus comparable, national records.[367]

ii) Indicator 8.8.2 Indicator 8.8.2—level of national compliance with labour rights (freedom of association and collective bargaining) based on ILO textual sources by sex and migrant status—is more problematic. Its wording, namely the determination of labour rights by reference in brackets only to union rights, denotes a discrepancy between what the target aspires to realize and what is actually monitored. Labour rights encompass a broader set of rights, not only freedom of association, which is nevertheless a very important element of decent work since it enables the participation and exercise of agency of social partners in the development policies that seek to promote work and employment. Social dialogue has not been monitored under other targets of Goal 8. Hence, its inclusion under 8.8.2 is indispensable. However, the target is not a direct measure of progress towards target 8.8 as labour rights are defined restrictively.

The described imprecision cannot be remedied, in our view, even if the justification for measuring FACB rests in the proposition that their exercise promotes components of the individual dimension of the right to work. Indeed both the CommICESCR[368] and the ILO regard this group of rights 'enabling rights' for rights at work; they provide an essential foundation for social dialogue between employers, workers, and governments, ensuring that negotiated outcomes for work relations are fair and equitable, labour market governance is effective, and therefore decent work becomes reality.[369] Due to their importance for sustained progress in the regulation of work-related matters, the ILO constitution includes freedom of association among its normative foundations[370] whereas the Declaration of Fundamental Principles and Rights at Work[371] proclaims freedom of association and the effective recognition of the right to collective bargaining as a Core Labour Standard which ILO Members have the constitutional obligation to respect, promote, and realize even if they have not ratified the respective conventions (Convention No 87, Freedom of Association and Protection of the Right to Organise (1948); Convention No 98, Right to Organise and Collective Bargaining

---

[364] Iceland, VNR (2019), 23 and 60 <https://sustainabledevelopment.un.org/content/documents/23408VNR_Iceland_2019_web_final.pdf> accessed 30 Mar 21.
[365] UNSG Report 2019 (n 278) para 29.
[366] UNSG Report 2018 (n 274), para 78.
[367] ILO Guidebook (n 262) 42–44.
[368] Confirmed by the CommICESCR, GC 23 (2016) (n 170) para 1.
[369] UNSC, 'Metadata on Indicator 8.8.2' (October 2020), 1–2.
[370] ILO Constitution and annexed Declaration of Philadelphia (n 166) Preamble and art I(b).
[371] ILO, 'Declaration of Fundamental Principles and Rights at Work' (n 212) para 2(a).

Convention (1949)).[372] Accordingly, the UDHR (article 20), the ICCPR (articles 21, 22), the European Social Charter (articles 5, 6), the Convention on the Protection of all Migrant Workers (article 26) are only some examples of other international treaties that impose obligations on states to uphold these rights.

These documents (the ILO's especially) have constituted the definitional source for indicator 8.8.2. In this regard, the methodology behind the indicator's construction is commendable because it draws directly upon them and the comments of the ILO organs, which supervise their implementation.[373] The richness of the evaluation criteria, which incorporate violations (in law and practice)[374] not only of workers' right to establish/join trade unions or interference with the independence of unions and their members but also infringement of civil rights that prohibit the fulfilment of the former (eg unlawful deprivation of liberty of unionists as a result of trade union activities, interference with the union's property, lack of due process in relevant court proceedings etc), demonstrate the pluralism in the indicator's content and the interdependent and indivisible nature of economic, social, and political liberties for successful development policies in decent work.[375] On a conceptual account, thus, the indicator seems to be comprehensive. Challenges in practice remain, however, as the ILO reports. First, values are missing for countries that have not ratified both ILO conventions on the matter and available data cover the period 2015–2017 until now. Secondly, disaggregation by sex and migration status would necessitate re-coding all violations taking special care of these variables and more time to produce the information.[376] Based on the above, the statistical annex to the SG's 2020 SDG report shows that the worldwide score for the period 2015–2017 is 5.5 on a scale between 0 (high level of compliance with FACB rights) and 10 (low levels of compliance with FACB rights). European countries are the best performers, keeping their score stable at 0.8 in the course of these three years. As with other targets of SDG 8, Northern Africa and Western Asia have low levels of compliance having a combined average score of 6.4 in 2017.[377] By implication, indicator 8.8.2 is not fully operational.

---

[372] ILO <https://www.ilo.org/dyn/normlex/en/f?p=NORMLEXPUB:12100:0::NO:12100:P12100_INSTRU MENT_ID:312232:NO>;<https://www.ilo.org/dyn/normlex/en/f?p=NORMLEXPUB:12100:0::NO:12100:P1210 0_INSTRUMENT_ID:312243:NO> accessed 30 Mar 21.

[373] Digest of Decisions and Principles of the Freedom of Association Committee of the Governing Body of the ILO (ILO 2006) <https://www.ilo.org/global/standards/applying-and-promoting-international-labour-standa rds/committee-on-freedom-of-association/WCMS_090632/lang--en/index.htm>; Freedom of Association and Collective Bargaining: General Survey of the Reports on the Freedom of Association and the Right to Organise Convention (No 87), 1948, and the Right to Organise and Collective Bargaining Convention (No 98) (ILO 1994) <https://www.ilo.org/public/libdoc/ilo/P/09661/09661(1994-81-4B).pdf>; General Survey on the Fundamental Conventions Concerning Rights at Work in Light of the ILO Declaration on Social Justice for a Fair Globalization, 2008 (ILO 2012) <<https://www.ilo.org/wcmsp5/groups/public/---ed_norm/---relconf/docume nts/meetingdocument/wcms_174846.pdf>.

[374] The ILO explains that violations in practice correspond to acts in violation of law that conforms with FACB rights.

[375] Metadata on 8.8.2 (n 369) 3–14. Importantly, the indicator does not compare compliance among ILO member states (ibid 16).

[376] ibid.

[377] SG SDG Report 2020 (n 285) annex, table for target 8.8.

616   SDG 8

b) Critique

In light of the above, it is difficult to assess progress on the elimination of unstable employment if one considers that precarious work goes beyond the form of employment to encompass a range of factors that contribute to a worker's employment instability, lack of legal and union protection, and economic vulnerability and high risks of ill-health. The concept of precariousness embodies several dimensions relating to employment status, form of employment, control over working conditions exercised through collective bargaining and union representation, legal protection, social context (eg occupation industry and geography), and the interaction of social relations based on gender, race, political, and economic conditions such as economic liberalization and the flexibility of the labour market. The indicators of target 8.8 do not cover all these elements and those that they capture, namely aspects of decent working conditions and union rights, are partially telling about workplace challenges of decent work, gender equality, the labour market challenges of migrants, all of which feature in this target.

9. Target 8.9 By 2030, devise and implement policies to promote sustainable tourism that creates jobs and promotes local culture and products

a) Sources of the target

The synergies between tourism and economic growth, human wellbeing and the natural environment have been addressed at international fora, even before the advent of the SDGs. In his report to the Commission on Sustainable Development at its seventh session (19–30 April 1999), the Secretary-General of the UN World Tourism Organization (SG UNWTO) mentioned that the prospect of economic development from tourism was accepted as axiomatic by almost all governments already since its emergence as a global phenomenon.[378] Tourism was considered a driver of GDP growth in numerous ways: by increasing foreign exchange reserves; stimulating investments in infrastructure, human capital, and technology, which would increase competitiveness; promoting industrial development; generating employment, and boosting earnings not only in the tourist industry *per se* but across the entire value chain, including food services, transportation, and merchandise production. Indeed, in 1998 7.9 per cent of the global export value of goods and services came from tourism, which surpassed leading industries at the time (eg automotive products and chemicals).[379] Yet, today's data also prove the continuous development of the sector that has become the largest in international trade services and the main economic activity for many countries. In 2018 international tourist arrivals and tourism exports marked positive value, having risen to $1.4 billion and $1.7 trillion (circa 2 per

---

[378] SG UNWTO, 'Tourism and Sustainable Development' (15 January 1999) UN Doc E/CN.17/1999/5/Add.1.

[379] SG UNWTO, 'Sustainable Development of Tourism' to the Commission on Sustainable Development acting as the preparatory committee for the World Summit on Sustainable development (2 March 2001) UN Doc E/CN.17/2001/PC/21, para 4.

cent of global GDP) respectively.[380] Moreover, tourism contributed $8.9 trillion to the world's GDP in 2019 through 330 million jobs, which translates to one in ten jobs around the world being created by the sector and to a 10.3 per cent representation of global GDP.[381] Without question, tourism has enjoyed sustained growth over the decades.

Nevertheless, the maximization of profit and the expansion of employment opportunities were not followed by analogous returns for the society and the natural environment. While the social output of tourism has been valuable, having spurred poverty alleviation, the preservation of cultural heritage, local customs and values, and having facilitated their dissemination to a wider audience of the current and future generations thanks to travel, it has not necessarily led entirely to improved quality of life for local communities or individuals who work in the sector. For instance, precarious working conditions, child labour, human trafficking for sexual exploitation, and the destruction of Indigenous cultures and lifestyle are some of the setbacks reported for the social sphere.[382] Similarly, nature-based tourism has led sometimes to the utilization of natural resources in a non-damaging manner while providing benefits to locals and improving their quality of life (eg wildlife parks that protect vulnerable ecosystems but are also a source of revenue for locals or scientific tourism for biology research in coastal and coral reef areas).[383] However, the relationship between tourism and the environment has more often been conflicting than harmonious and symbiotic.[384] Tourism's pressure on the environment is multifaceted: land degradation, pollution, overconsumption and waste, depletion of natural resources, excessive use of energy and water resources, loss of biodiversity and climate change are some of the global environmental consequences of tourism.[385] Eventually, tourism-led growth provokes economic, social, cultural, and environmental concerns that need to be balanced and reconciled in a mutually reinforcing way.[386]

---

[380] UNWTO, 'International Tourism Highlights' (2019) 2 <https://www.e-unwto.org/doi/epdf/10.18111/9789284421152> accessed 10 March 2021.

[381] World Travel & Tourism Council, 'Economic Impact Reports' (2019) <https://wttc.org/Research/Economic-Impact> accessed 10 March 21. A downfall in numbers was reported due to the COVID-19 outbreak international travel decreased by 60–80 per cent, SDG Report 2020 special edition (n 285) 41.

[382] SG UNWTO, 'Tourism and Sustainable Development' (n 378) para 2; SG UNWTO, 'Sustainable development of tourism' (n 379) paras 7–8.

[383] For example, the South Luangwa National Park (SLNP) in eastern Zambia, known worldwide for walking and motor safaris. A study by UNDP and the University of Florida found that the park had great economic value for the locals while serving the preservation of wildlife in the area. However, further investment in the protection of biodiversity is needed. Curaçao (Kingdom of the Netherlands) is an example of scientific tourism. See, UNWTO and UNDP, *Tourism and the SDGs—Journey to 2030* (January 2018) 28, 37 <https://www.e-unwto.org/doi/epdf/10.18111/9789284419401> accessed 8 March 2021.

[384] A Williams, 'Reconciling Tourism and the Environment: A Task for International Environmental Law' (2007) 9 Vermont Journal of Environmental Law 23, 26–29.

[385] S Gössling, 'Global Environmental Consequences of Tourism' (2002) 12 Global Environmental Change 283; UNWTO and UNDP, *Tourism and the SDGs—Journey to 2030* (n 383) 30.

[386] Williams (n 384) 25; A Bândoi and others, 'The Relationship between Development of Tourism, Quality of Life and Sustainable Performance in EU Countries' (2020) 12 Sustainability 1628 (provides a good literature review on the topic).

618   SDG 8

The sustainability of tourism got under the spotlight of the UN against the background of discussions about sustainable development and the implementation of the respective plans of action. With the correlation between development and the environment already established by the Stockholm Declaration[387] and reinforced by the Rio Principles (Principles 3 and 4),[388] Agenda 21 was the first document where explicit reference to sustainable tourism is made, although the Rio Declaration did not refer to it at all. By way of example, environmentally sound and culturally sensitive tourism programmes are proposed as a means for the sustainable development of urban and rural settlements and as a way of decentralizing urban development ((paragraph 7.20(e)); the value of ecotourism is highlighted in relation to the efficient utilization of forests, the promotion and management of wildlife (paragraphs 11.20, 11.22(h)) and integrated watershed development as a means of income for dependent populations (paragraph 13.15(b)); finally, there is the general promulgation for countries to promote environmentally sound leisure and tourism following guidelines by the UNWTO and the United Nations Environment Programme (UNEP) (paragraph 36.10(g)). In the same vein, the Johannesburg Declaration categorizes tourism among the activities that ought to manage the natural resource base of economic and social development. It then exemplifies the necessary actions for harnessing the natural and cultural assets of regions without jeopardizing their value, underscoring among others the importance of education in raising awareness on the sustainability of tourism and of international cooperation through capacity building and technical assistance to countries that lack the tools to attract suitable investments and manage tourism activities effectively, such as Small Island Developing Countries (SIDC) and some in Africa.[389] However, the summit with leverage effect on the integration of tourism into the sustainable development agenda was the World Conference on Sustainable Development in 2012. Heads of states explicitly acknowledged sustainable tourism as one of the thematic Focus Areas for sustainable development. Devoting a separate section to it in the outcome document, 'The Future We Want', they drew in detail the close linkages of tourism with all three dimensions of development by explicating the associations with employment, trade, investment, entrepreneurship and the establishment of SMEs, access to finance, and the preservation of human and natural environment as a whole.[390] Crucially, stakeholders

[387] UNGA, Report of the UN Conference on the Human Environment (5–16 June 1972), Declaration of the United Nations Conference on the Human Environment UN Doc A/CONF.48.14.Rev.1: Principle 8 'economic and social development is essential for ensuring a favourable living and working environment for man and for creating conditions on earth that are necessary for the improvement of the quality of life'; Principle 11 'the environmental policies of all States should enhance and not adversely affect the present or future development potential of developing countries, nor should they hamper the attainment of better living conditions for all'; Principle 13 'states should adopt an integrated and co-ordinated approach to their development planning so as to ensure that development is compatible with the need to protect and improve environment for the benefit of their population'.

[388] UNGA, 'Report of the UN Conference on Environment and Development' (Rio de Janeiro, 3–14 June 1992) (12 August 1992) UN Doc A/CONF.151/26 (Vol I): Principle 3 reads: 'The right to development must be fulfilled so as to equitably meet developmental and environmental needs of present and future generations'; Principle 4 reads: 'In order to achieve sustainable development, environmental protection shall constitute an integral part of the development process and cannot be considered in isolation from it'.

[389] UNGA, Report of the World Summit on Sustainable Development (26 August–4 September 2002), UN Doc A/CONF.199/20, paras 43, 58(g), 70.

[390] UNGA, 'The Future We Want' (11 September 2012) A/RES/66/288, paras 130–131.

underlined the importance of setting appropriate guidelines, regulations, and legislation in accordance with national priorities in order to foster sustainable tourism. Such remarks drew attention to the necessity for a regulatory framework of tourism that associates its principles and objectives as a primarily economic activity with those of sustainable development, therefore establishing theoretical and practical coherence with the tenets of the current development model. As such, sustainable tourism was brought not only under the purview of sustainable development policy but also of the law on sustainable development. Foremost, the exact determination of sustainable tourism as a notion was paramount.

In light of the embedded interplay of tourism and development in international public policy talks, terms such as 'responsible tourism', 'ethical tourism', and 'green tourism' were coined in order to embody the applicability of sustainable development's core attribute to the context of tourism development.[391] However, a clear-cut definition has not been possible to agree on, probably because the transposition of sustainable development, which suffers the criticism of being an ill-defined and vague notion itself,[392] bears upon the same deficit.[393] Consequently the paradigm shift towards sustainable tourism development remained in essence tourism-centric, namely it focused on tourism's instrumentality for economic growth and did not give due regard to sustainable development considerations.[394] Other times, the concept evolved in isolation from the evolution of the meaning of sustainable development, which resulted in a very simplistic paradigm for sustainable tourism that was unable to address legitimately the sustainability equation (ie sustainable human development) when applied to different country realities.[395] By contrast, the UNWTO's conceptual definition seems to have harmonized tourism and sustainable development more successfully: '[Sustainable] tourism takes full account of its current and future economic, social and environmental impacts, addressing the needs of visitors, the industry, the environment and host communities.' Furthermore, it is stressed that a suitable balance between the three aforementioned dimensions is vital for the long-term sustainability of tourism itself.[396] The

---

[391] Bândoi and others (n 386).

[392] M Redclift, *Sustainable Development: Exploring the Contradictions* (Routledge 1987); J Lélé, 'Sustainable Development: A critical Review' (1991) 16(6) World Development 607; D Worster, 'The Shaky Ground of Sustainability' in W Sachs (eds), *Global Ecology: A New Arena of Political Conflict* (Zed Books 1993) 132–45. On the multiple definitions of sustainable development, indicatively: A Steer and W Wade-Gery, 'Sustainable Development: Theory and Practice for a Sustainable Future' (1993) 1(3) Sustainable Development 23; J Heinen, 'Emerging, Diverging and Converging Paradigms on Sustainable Development' (1994) 1 International Journal of Sustainable Development and World Ecology 22.

[393] Williams (n 384) 29 citing in footnote 31 the seminal work of J Krippendorf, *The Holiday Makers: Understanding the Impact of Leisure and Travel* (Vera Andrassy trans, Heinemann 1987) and in footnote 32 A Marx, 'Towards Sustainability? The Case of Tourism and the EU' (1997) 6 European Environmental Law Review 181, 181–82; H Müller, 'The Thorny Path to Sustainable tourism Development' in L France (ed), *The Earthscan Reader in Sustainable Tourism* (Routledge 1997) 29–35; K Woodward, 'Loving the Environment to Death: Can Law Protect the Environment from the Leisure Threat?' (1996) 5 European Environmental Law Review 148, 149–50; and PE Murphy, 'Tourism and Sustainable Development' in WF Theobald (ed), *Global Tourism: The Next Decade* (Butterworth-Heinemann 1994) 274–75.

[394] C Hunter, 'On the Need to Re-Conceptualise Sustainable Tourism Development' (1995) 3 Journal of Sustainable Tourism 155.

[395] C Hunter, 'Sustainable Tourism as an adaptive paradigm' (1997) 34(4) Annals of Tourism Research 850.

[396] UNWTO, 'Sustainable Development' <https://www.unwto.org/sustainable-development> accessed 8 March 2021. Another way the UNWTO has envisaged sustainable tourism is: 'leading to management of all resources in

620   SDG 8

organization then elaborates its understanding of the notion in the following three points:

(1) environmental resources, which constitute a key element in tourism development should be used in an optimal manner, maintaining ecological processes and helping to conserve natural heritage and biodiversity;

(2) the socio-cultural authenticity of host communities should be respected, their built and living cultural heritage and traditional values should be conserved with the view to foster cultural understanding and tolerance;

(3) viable, long-term economic operations should be ensured that provide socio-economic benefits to all stakeholders, including stable employment, income/earning opportunities and social services to host communities, which should be distributed fairly aiming at alleviating poverty.[397]

By these stipulations, the UNWTO definitely endorses the substantive element of sustainable development (the consolidation of the concept's economic, social, and environmental dimensions) as well as its theoretical underpinning, namely intra- and intergenerational equity, distributive justice, fairness and universality, given the reference to tourism's current and future impacts on the environment and on all stakeholders, who are, moreover, endowed with informed participation in decision-making. These characteristics allow a direct juxtaposition of sustainable tourism with sustainable development when conceptualized as an integrated economic, social, and environmental *process* that aims at improving the well-being of present and future generations based on stakeholders active and meaningful participation and the fair distribution of benefits, including the sustainable use of natural resources and the protection of the environment. Accordingly, the UNWTO's characterization of sustainable tourism development as 'a continuous *process* that requires constant monitoring' is correct.[398]

In essence, the three points above echo stakeholder rights and duties in existing international agreements, especially in the fields of human rights and environmental law, that potentially provide solid foundations for a framework within which tourism activities for development may be regulated and coordinated efficiently. Indeed, the human dimension of tourism resonates in the International Bill of Rights, particularly articles 13 and 24 UDHR, article 7 ICESC, and article 12(2) ICCPR that guarantee respectively everyone's right to rest and leisure, to reasonable limitation of working hours, periodic holidays with pay and remuneration of public holidays, and one's freedom to leave any country, including his own.[399] Whereas it would be far-reaching to coin a human right

such a way that economic, social and aesthetic needs can be fulfilled while maintaining cultural integrity, essential ecological processes, biological diversity and life support systems', E/CN.17/2001/PC/21 (n 157) para 9.

[397] ibid; UNEP, UNWTO, 'Making Tourism More Sustainable—A Guide for Policy Makers' (2005) 11–12 <https://wedocs.unep.org/bitstream/handle/20.500.11822/8741/-Making%20Tourism%20More%20Sustainable_%20A%20Guide%20for%20Policy%20Makers-2005445.pdf?sequence=3&isAllowed=y> accessed 8 March 21.
[398] UNWTO, 'Sustainable Development' (n 396).
[399] UDHR (n 68), also art 23; ICESCR (adopted 16 December 1966, entered into force 3 January 1976) 993 UNTS 3, also arts 6, 7, 12; ICCPR (adopted 16 December 1966, entered into force 23 March 1976) 999 UNTS 171.

to tourism as such, the latter's correlation with the right to rest and leisure and the right to work cannot be contested. Furthermore, more specific aspects of tourism as a vehicle to promote cultural values and to safeguard the human and natural environment (terrestrial and marine ecosystems) have equally their legal basis on particular articles in the aforementioned human rights treaties (or other human agreements and resolutions) and environmental law—articles 22 and 27 UDHR, article 15 ICESCR, article 24 African Charter on Human and Peoples Rights, UNGA Resolution 45/94 (1990) declaring that all individuals are entitled to live in an environment adequate for their health and well-being, the Biodiversity Convention, the UN Convention on the Law of the Sea (UNCLOS), the UNFCCC etc.[400] It is these very legal sources that informed the content of the Manila Declaration on World Tourism in 1980, ahead of the Brundtland Commission's report. The Declaration acknowledges travel as 'an aspect of the fulfilment of the human being' that can contribute to 'social stability, mutual recognition among individuals and peoples and become a vital force for world peace because it provides the moral and intellectual basis for solidarity, international understanding, interdependence and cooperation.'[401] Participating countries are encouraged to promote and enhance tourism activities, yet it is affirmed that economic returns shall not be the only motive for states to expand the sector. 'The satisfaction of tourism requirement must not be prejudicial to the social and economic interests of the population in destination areas, to the environment and its resources, the preservation of which constitutes fundamental responsibility of State.'[402] Tourism's economic aspects ought to account for the cultural and environmental dimensions as well.

In the following years, the 'Tourist Code and Tourism Bill of Rights'[403] and the 'Hague Declaration on Tourism'[404] reflected the same spirit and created the foundations for international cooperation and rapprochement between peoples based on a set of principles that aim at facilitating tourism as a factor of individual and collective development. Amongst the most notable are Principles II, III, V, and X of the Hague Declaration because they articulate tourism's position in a country's development strategy by indicating specific measures whereby tourism may contribute to sustainable development. In doing so, they may be considered the precursor of the more detailed and comprehensive frame of reference for sustainable tourism as embodied in the Chengdu Declaration on Tourism and the SDGs[405] and fundamentally the Global

---

[400] NKS Dharwmawan, 'Tourism and Environment: Toward Promoting Sustainable Development of Tourism: A Human Rights Perspective' (2012) 2 Indonesian Law Review 23. For the environmental dimension of tourism, Williams (n 384) and SDGs 12, 14, 15 in the commentary.

[401] Manila Declaration (27 September–10 October 1980) paras 13, 14 <https://www.univeur.org/cuebc/downloads/PDF%20carte/65.%20Manila.PDF> accessed 11 March 21.

[402] ibid paras 8, 18.

[403] UNWTO (14 June 1985) A/6/11 <https://www.e-unwto.org/doi/epdf/10.18111/unwtogad.1985.1.hp408 706117j8366> accessed 17 March 21.

[404] Hague Declaration <https://www.univeur.org/cuebc/downloads/PDF%20carte/68.%20The%20Hague.PDF> accessed 12 March 21.

[405] UNWTO (2017) <https://www.e-unwto.org/doi/pdf/10.18111/unwtogad.2017.1.g51w645001604506> accessed 8 March 21; UN GA Res 70/193 'International year of Sustainable tourism for Development, 2017' (9 February 2016) UN Doc A/RES/70/193, wherein a number of other resolutions and declarations on tourism are being invoked.

622   SDG 8

Code of Ethics for Tourism (GCET).[406] The latter comprises ten interdependent principles on the basis of which the aforementioned documents should be interpreted and applied by stakeholders (national, regional, and local administrations, enterprises, workers in the sector, and all entities belonging in the industry). In the GCET UNWTO Member States, representatives of the industry, and NGOs 'state their wish to promote an equitable, responsible and sustainable tourism order with shared benefits for all sectors of society'. To this end, they reaffirm tourism's contribution to personal and collective development and mutual understanding between the peoples as its fundamental aims (articles 1, 2). Tourism itself is pronounced as a universal right that is a corollary of the right to rest and leisure (article 7) and its role as a driver for development is restated (article 3). Within this context, activities should respect gender equality and promote human rights with emphasis on the most vulnerable—children, the elderly, the disabled, ethnic minorities, and Indigenous people; all kinds of human abuse, whether sexual or labour exploitation against women and children, are incompatible with the said purposes and must be combatted in accordance with international law while the fundamental rights of workers should be guaranteed (article 9); cultural rights ought to be upheld and environmental concerns addressed through impact assessments and compliance with the law (article 3). Undeniably, the GCET underscores the human dimension of tourism and the relevance of a human rights-based approach to its development given the centrality of human rights in the principles. The environmental aspect of tourism is equally stressed by reference to core documents such as the Rio and Stockholm declarations. At the same time though, stakeholders' persuasion that tourism's objectives can only be achieved in an economic climate that favours an open and liberalized international economy (paragraphs 5 and 12 Preamble), highlights the trade-offs inherent to the sustainable development paradigm and the latent risk that the social and environmental pillars may be compromised in light of economic growth. To avoid this, it is important that GCET should be interpreted in light of the sustainable development principles—especially the integration principle—enshrined in the Rio and Stockholm Declarations.

b) Empirical analysis and implementation efforts at international and domestic levels
Against this background, Agenda 2030 consolidated sustainable tourism in the process of sustainable development. Apart from target 8.9, sustainable tourism directly influences the achievement of Goals 12 and 14, as analysed in the respective chapters herein. However, its positive contribution to the international community's development objectives is wider. In their NVR for 2016 and 2017, many countries reported that sustainable tourism has triggered innovation and improved infrastructure (SDG 9), strengthened efforts to protect cultural and natural heritage in their territory (SDG 11.4 and 11.a), helped reduce poverty and hunger (SDGs 1 and 2), and created fruitful

---

[406] UNGA (21 December 2001) UN Doc A/RES/56/212 <https://webunwto.s3.eu-west-1.amazonaws.com/imported_images/37802/gcetbrochureglobalcodeen.pdf> accessed 8 March 21.

partnership agreements between countries.[407] With regards to sustainable tourism's contribution to Goal 8, country initiatives sound promising. Indicatively, New Zealand's Tourism Strategy constitutes a partnership between the business sector, local communities, and the government, which has a leading role in tourism, to ensure that growth is inclusive, productive, and sustainable. Tourism businesses have committed to environmental sustainability by 2025 under the New Zealand Tourism Sustainability Commitment.[408] The government established the Tourism Infrastructure Fund that supports small communities receiving large numbers of visitors to fund basic tourism infrastructure while through the international visitor levy, tourists contribute to the conservation of land used on their trips. Finally, the government's investment in tourism is principled since it is decided and executed according to the country's tourism strategy and a developed investment framework for the regions.[409] Malta's initiatives are equally compelling, capturing the country's 'Vision for Tourism 2030'. On the occasion of Malta being the European Capital of Culture in 2018, the Valletta 2018 Foundation was established by the government with the purpose to transform the capital into a creative city, raise awareness about the country's cultural identity and improve well-being though culture.[410] Tourists' expenditure represents 29 per cent of total employment and the government has set up the STAR Awards to honour employees in the tourist industry for their outstanding work. Last but not least, the Maltese government considers very important the existence of qualified employees in the tourism and hospitality sector and lays emphasis on the continuous improvement of their skills, which aspires to achieve through the Recognition of Prior Learning scheme by the Institute of Tourism Studies and the Skills Card (Proficiency Acknowledgement in Tourism).[411] Finally, Greece has inaugurated the Alternative Tourism Initiative (ATI) whose primary objective is to boost the competitiveness of SMEs in tourism and attract investments in order to diversify her tourism product towards alternative forms (eg medical and wellness tourism, gastronomic, cultural, and religious tourism etc).[412]

---

[407] UNWTO, UNDP *Tourism and the SDGs* (n 383) 26–29. Country examples mentioned are: (i) Zimbabwe's Tokwe Mukosi dam that promotes agriculture and tourism (SDG 9); (ii) Portugal, which uses tourism to diversify on-farm activities beneficial for local development and Italy that aims at the preservation of cultural and natural heritage through tourism such as the Rosas mine in Sardinia (R Cannas, 'The Sustainable Tourism Management of Cultural Heritage: the Case of the Rosas Mine in Sardinia' (2016) 14 Alma Tourism 38) [SDG 11]; (iii) Slovenia, partnering with countries in the Western Balkans to support environmental infrastructure projects or Japan's 'African clean cities' project (SDG 17; see also p 64 for more examples regarding this goal). Information about other initiatives that promote tourism's role in the advancement of the SDGs can be found here: UNWTO, 'Tourism for SDGs' <https://tourism4sdgs.org/initiatives/> accessed 10 March 2021 (filter based on region, country, SDG theme, and submission type).

[408] NVR New Zealand, 'He Waka eke Noa-Towards a Better Future, Together' (2019) 87 <https://sustainable development.un.org/content/documents/23333New_Zealand_Voluntary_National_Review_2019_Final.pdf> accessed 10 March 2021.

[409] ibid 65.

[410] VNR Malta (n 303) 59.

[411] ibid 60.

[412] Hellenic Republic, 'VNR on Implementation of the 2030 Agenda for Sustainable Development' (2018), 33 <https://sustainabledevelopment.un.org/content/documents/19378Greece_VNR_Greece_2018_pdf_FINAL_140618.pdf> accessed 10 March 2021. On Tourism and Culture (cultural tourism), see UNWTO <https://www.unwto.org/tourism-and-culture> accessed 10 March 2021.

624   SDG 8

Efforts by developing countries and LDCs are also remarkable despite the greater number of challenges they face. For example, Cameroon's tourism strategy, which has been in place since 2005, was updated in 2017 with a project aiming at the modernization and development of tourism. Among other measures, the government created the platform TERRI-TOURISM and Best Artisans of the World (Meilleurs Artisans du Monde—MAM) which is a registrar of young unemployed graduates of the tourism industry. Moreover, the country founded Offices of Tourism in Europe that are mandated to promote Cameroon as a tourism destination, while domestically authorities implement projects that promote cultural tourism such as that regarding the site of Mbimbia.[413] Palau, an SIDC heavily dependent on tourism, has taken action to promote it in light of other goals apart from SDGs 8, 12, and 14. An illustrative example is the modules on sustainable tourism that are offered as part of a specialized curriculum for development in primary education (SDG 4).[414] In addition, the government's 'Responsible Tourism Policy' aims at changing the profile of Palau's tourism industry from mass-market packaged tours that brought high-volumes of tourists but low revenues and major threats to the country's environmental and socio-cultural attributes, into a high-value model that intends to create a visitor industry which is respectful of Palau's people and its environment while being a strong source of revenue for the economy.[415] Interestingly, however, the country's voluntary review does not mention how sustainable tourism has improved job availability in the country, which is really an omission given the high importance of the industry for Palau's economic growth.

The cases mentioned above are not exhaustive but they constitute a good illustration of the actions taken by local authorities to advance sustainable tourism as an end but also a means to their development in a sustainable way. It is remarkable though that more attention is paid to the value of the economic contribution of tourism whereas the element of job creation deriving from policies that promote sustainable tourism is reported less consistently. Such tactic is indeed surprising given that tourism's importance for employment is underscored often. Recently, the Secretary-General UNWTO apropos the G20 Summit in Saudi Arabia stated 'around the world, in countries at all development levels, many millions of jobs and businesses are dependent on a strong and thriving tourism sector' as it has a 'unique power to transform lives and provide opportunities, including for those who might otherwise be left behind'.[416] Yet, the fact that under the GIF, target 8.9 is monitored only by an indicator that measures 'tourism direct GDP as a proportion of total GDP and in growth rate' makes the reason behind such focus self-explanatory.[417] Target 8.9.2 that was meant to measure the proportion

[413] Republic of Cameroon, 'Examen National Volontaire odd, Cameroon' (June 2019), 51 <https://sustainable development.un.org/content/documents/24180CAMEROON_Rapport_VNR_0507_2019.pdf> accessed 10 March 21.

[414] Palau Voluntary National Review (2019), 17 <https://sustainabledevelopment.un.org/content/documents/23606VNR_FINAL_21June2019_UN_Version.pdf> accessed 10 March 21.

[415] ibid 27, 28 (Pristine Palau Tourism), 30.

[416] Z Pololikashvili, 'Responsible and Inclusive Growth at Heart of Tourism's Recovery' Arab News (8 December 2020) <https://www.arabnews.com/node/1774391> accessed 10 March 2022.

[417] E/CN.3/2020/2 (n 225) 18; UNSC, Metadata for target 8.9' <https://unstats.un.org/sdgs/metadata/files/Metadata-08-09-01.pdf> accessed 10 March 2022. On the measurement of sustainable tourism, see: DESA (Statistics Division), *Tourism Satellite Account: Recommended Methodological Framework 2008* (DESA 2010);

of jobs in sustainable tourism industries out of total tourism jobs was deleted at the 2020 comprehensive review due to the conceptual shortcomings and the methodological challenges it presented since a statistical definition of 'tourism jobs' or 'sustainable tourism industries' was not easy to form.[418] We cannot claim to have the expertise required to express judgment on the statistical methodology behind the said indicator but the choice to remove it seems to be valid from the standpoint of decent work given that what makes jobs in the tourism sector sustainable on this account does not differ from what other indicators under SDG 8 measure (eg compliance with human rights and labour law standards). Notwithstanding this, target 8.9.2 is yet another example of the complexity the quantification of normative concepts entails; not always can numeric indicators simplify and specify a narrative of development planning, let alone the intersecting axioms of sustainable development.

c) Critique

Against this background, the question that arises is to what extent the objectives of sustainable tourism are finally commensurate with those of sustainable development, which is the prevailing development paradigm. It is true that the way in which sustainable tourism is conceptualized embraces the holistic approach to development advocated by sustainable development. The regulatory framework for sustainable tourism, namely the individual declarations on tourism and the GCET, also bear upon the foundational international instruments for sustainable development. It might fall in the realm of soft law but its employment with binding instruments in international economic, human rights, and environmental law can result into the further development of rules and guidelines for tourism activities to become truly sustainable. In practice, however, the efforts to operationalize sustainable tourism as a development tool concentrate on the growth-led hypothesis for development. In this respect, the actions taken to remedy the environmental pressures that derive from tourism activities seem to be motivated by the sustainability of tourism itself, thus the improvement of the tourism product rather than tourism's true developmental contribution.[419] By extension, tourism's relationship with human development for local populations is downplayed. There is not much evidence to prove that benefits of tourism regarding human capital are fairly distributed among stakeholder groups or that the needs of local communities in terms of improved living standards and income generation are met. In fact, the critique holds that it is the degree and measure of human development that promotes tourism[420] because local populations are then empowered to participate in the

---

UNWTO, 'Measuring Sustainable Tourism: A Call for Action—Report of the 6th International Conference on Tourism' (Manila, Philippines, 21–23 June 2017). In the AAAA stakeholders also called on the UN system to develop transparent measurements of progress of sustainable development and implement tools to monitor sustainable development impacts for sustainable tourism, AAAA (n 7) para 129.

[418] J Kester (UNWTO), 'Measuring Sustainable Tourism and the SDGs under Section 'Reviewing Indicators' (6th Meeting IAEG-SDG, Manama, Kingdom of Bahrain).

[419] Williams (n 384).

[420] MA Rivera, 'The Synergies between Human Development, Economic Growth, and Tourism within a Developing Country: An Empirical Model for Ecuador' (2017) 6(3) Journal of Destination Marketing and

626 SDG 8

development process in a sustainable way. Otherwise, poverty encourages unsustainable practices aiming at quick returns from tourism because it is imperative that immediate needs are met. In light of this, tourism may fulfil its role under Goal 8, being a driver of growth, but only partially since its impact on human development cannot be traced easily.

10. Target 8.10 Strengthen the capacity of domestic financial institutions to encourage and expand access to banking, insurance and financial services for all

a) Sources of the target and its critique

Like most SDG targets, target 8.10 speaks to multiple scales of both the problem and solution dimensions.[421]

Concerning its content, target 8.10 incorporates the well-consolidated idea that domestic financial institutions (DFIs) such as central banks, development banks, and sovereign wealth funds are essential in promoting sustainable development.[422] It also incorporates the idea that DFIs must be strengthened in their capacity to access and use financial, banking, and other (national and international) services for the benefit of all.[423] Somewhat surprisingly, however, target 8.10 does not give any space to the equally widespread idea that DFIs more often than not need to be reformed for the purposes of achieving SDG 8, as confirmed by several works and peer-reviewed studies.[424]

The formulation chosen for target 8.10 suggests that it has close links with other SDGs and targets of Agenda 2030, and in particular with those that directly or indirectly deal with domestic resource mobilization (DRM) policies, strategies, and programmes[425] and SDG 17 (Partnership for the goals).[426]

Management 221; Z Liu, 'Sustainable Tourism Development: A Critique' (2003) 11(6) Journal of Sustainable Tourism 459.

[421] HL van Soest and others, 'Analysing Interactions among Sustainable Development Goals with Integrated Assessment Models' (2019) 1 Global Transition 210, 214.

[422] MS Khattak, The Nexus of Government Incentives and Sustainable Development Goals: Is the Management of Resources the Solution to Non-Profit Organisations?' (2020) 26(6) Technological and Economic Development of Economy 1284 <https://journals.vgtu.lt/index.php/TEDE/article/view/13404> accessed 10 March 2022, recalling 'a report issued by Ernst & Young Global Limited (2015) which suggests that the challenge for today's businesses is to address sustainability in a way that meets the current and future needs of their customers, employees, communities and the environment' and argued that 'the financial services industry has a critical role to play in making this happen across both the public and private sectors'.

[423] A Fouejieu and others, 'Unlocking Access to Finance for SMEs: A Cross-Country Analysis' (IMF 2020) <https://www.elibrary.imf.org/view/journals/001/2020/055/article-A001-en.xml> accessed 10 March 2022, stressing amongst other things that access to domestic finance facilitates SMEs to engage in community practice.

[424] V Andreoni and A Miola, Competitiveness and Sustainable Development Goals (Publications Office of the European Union 2016) <https://webcache.googleusercontent.com/search?q=cache:jAP7ZbdoXmQJ:https://publications.jrc.ec.europa.eu/repository/bitstream/JRC103576/lb-na-28316-en-n.pdf+&cd=2&hl=it&ct=clnk&gl=it> accessed 10 March 2022.

[425] F Seatzu, 'Sustainable Financing through Domestic Resource Mobilization (DRM) The Role of International Law' in I Bantekas and C Lumina (eds), Sovereign Debt and Human Rights (OUP 2018) 527; such as SDG 1, target 1.b according to which: 'a significant mobilization of resources from a variety of sources, including through enhanced development cooperation, *shall be achieved* in order to provide adequate and predictable means for developing countries, in particular least developed (LDC) countries, to implement programmes and policies to end poverty in all its dimensions'.

[426] SDG 17 calls on the door community to step up its international support to strengthen DRM, including through international support to developing and less developed countries to improve domestic capacity for tax and other revenue collection.

b) Empirical analysis and implementation efforts at the international and domestic levels

Two indicators have been agreed by the IAEG-SDGs for measuring the realization of target 8.10. The first in order of exposition is the following (8.10.1): (a) number of commercial bank branches per 100,000 adults and (b) number of automated teller machines (ATMs) per 100,000 adults. Having been developed as a quantitative indicator, this first indicator requires little or no comment from a legal point of view. The second selected indicator (8.10.2) is the proportion of adults (fifteen years and older) with an account at a bank or other financial institution or with a mobile-money-service provider. Like the previous one, this is a quantitative indicator that is based on sound theoretical considerations and has been demonstrated to be meaningful and fully applicable in actual practice.

Regrettably, though useful in several noteworthy respects, neither of these two indicators for target 8.10 provides a suitable database paradigm for measuring the effective increase of sustainable financial investments. Perhaps the best solution would be to adopt a third indicator for target 8.10, specifically referring to the number of sustainable financial products and services per 100,000 adults. This suggested solution would be not only feasible and effective, but also in line with the main Outcome document of the Rio + 20 Summit which rightly claims that progress towards the achievement of the Goals shall be assessed and accompanied by targets and indicators while taking into consideration different national circumstances and levels of development.[427]

11. Target 8.a Increase Aid for Trade support for developing countries, in particular least developed countries, including through the Enhanced Integrated Framework for Trade related Technical Assistance to Least Developed Countries

a) Sources of the target, empirical analysis, and critique

Target 8.a deals with the issue of aid for trade for developing countries. Like other SDG targets, this is a goal to be achieved within each state by the members of the United Nations.

Formulated as above, target 8.a is an end in itself and also an essential means of implementation for the SDG 8 targets and for other SDG Goals and targets such as, notably, SDG 17.11. Aid for trade being first of all a political issue, it is a recognition of the political nature of the realization of SDGs.[428] This target about aid for trade support for developing countries is not surprising within a Goal (SDG 8) that is dedicated to economic growth and productive work—at least if one considers that aid for trade initiatives aim at aligning donor and partner countries' strategies in enhancing trade as leverage for poverty reduction.[429]

---

[427] 'The Future We Want' (n 390)

[428] M Loewe and others, 'Promote Sustained, Inclusive and Sustainable Economic Growth, Full and Productive Employment and Decent Work For All' in M Loewe and N Rippin (eds), *The Sustainable Development Goals of the Post-2015 Agenda: Comments on the OWG and SDSN Proposals* (German Development Institute 2015)<https://www.academia.edu/27972176/The_Sustainable_Development_Goals_of_the_Post_2015_Agenda_Comments_on_the_OWG_and_SDSN_Proposals> accessed 10 March 2022.

[429] W Hynes and P Holden, 'What Future for the Global Aid for Trade Initiative? Towards an Assessment of its Achievements and Limitations' (2016) Development Policy Review 593.

628   SDG 8

From this consideration, and from the fact that the idea according to which developing countries should receive affirmative action from the trading system is an enduring contribution of international trade law,[430] it emerges that target 8.a has a well-defined place and a role to play in the post-2015 development agenda. If further evidence is required to corroborate this conclusion, such evidence may indirectly be received from SDG 17.2 calling for 'developed countries to implement fully their official development assistance commitments, including the commitment by many developed countries to achieve the target of 0.7 per cent of ODA/GNI to developing countries and 0.15–0.20 per cent of ODA/GNI to least developed countries'. Moreover, evidence can also be indirectly obtained from SDG 17.4 requesting developed countries to 'assist developing countries in attaining long-term debt sustainability through coordinated policies aimed at fostering debt financing, debt relief and debt restructuring, as appropriate, and address the external debt of highly indebted poor countries to reduce debt distress'. The difficulties that WTO has met so far in implementing its Aid for Trade (AFT) Initiative of 2016 suggest however that the implementation of target 8.a will not be an easy task to accomplish for the members of the United Nations.[431]

The only agreed indicator to measure progress in reaching target 8.a is the following: Aid for Trade commitments and disbursements. Given its formulation, the indicator does not seem to be the most suitable to measure the implementation of target 8.a. This is because it is an indicator that can hardly be enforced in practice, since it is too abstract and cannot be quantified easily. For this it is not difficult to conclude that the IAEG-SDGs would have to be encouraged to replace it with a quantitative and/or more operative indicator to measure the achievement of target 8.a.

12. Target 8.b By 2020, develop and operationalize a global strategy for youth
    employment and implement the Global Jobs Pact of the International
    Labour Organization

a) Sources of the target
Youth unemployment is stated as a major concern of Agenda 2030. Two targets under Goal 8, the general target (8.5) and target 8.6, aspire to reduce substantially the number of youth not in employment, education, or training and achieve full employment and decent work for this social group. Target 8.b complements these targets by prompting states to develop and operationalize a strategy to promote youth employment issues, whether distinct or as part of a national employment strategy, by 2020.

Youth unemployment is differentiated from unemployment in adults due to the risks posed to this group of individuals. First is the issue of access to employment. Given that it facilitates integration into society, its absence favours social exclusion and related

---

[430] According to the WTO Secretariat, 'The WTO Agreements contain special provisions which give developing countries special rights': WTO, 'Special and Differential Treatment Provisions' <https://www.wto.org/english/tratop_e/devel_e/dev_special_differential_provisions_e.htm> accessed 10 March 2022. In addition, these 'special and differential' (S&D) provisions require 'all WTO members to safeguard the trade interests of developing countries" and to "increase trading opportunity for developing countries', ibid.

[431] On these difficulties, see, eg, H-H Lee and others, 'Do Developing-country WTO Members Receive More Aid for Trade (AfT)?' (2015) 38 The World Economy 1462 ff.

problems such as urban violence or the creation of youth NEET, who are wasted human capital and do not contribute to the economic welfare of the society.[432] The quality of employment is the second worrying aspect. In emerging and developing countries, 16.7 per cent of young workers earn incomes below the threshold of extreme poverty ($1.90/day) since they work in the informal economy or are engaged in non-standard employment. What this signifies is the trend that the youth undertake irregular employment, facing most of the times undignified working conditions, no rights at work, and no social protection. Casual, temporary, and part-time employment is also frequent. Employment under these circumstances enhances the economic and social vulnerability of the youth, who sometimes become working poor, as they cannot meet basic needs. Therefore, low levels of productivity and labour poverty are to the detriment of this group's well-being in a way analogous to children's well-being discussed under target 8.7. Of course, there is also a broader social and economic impact of youth unemployment; the inability of social security systems to support the retired population because they lack the contributions from young workers, persistence of poverty and decrease of growth prospects of a country due to lower incomes of its population and lower demand, thus lower GDP. It could be said though that the relation between economic growth and employment rates among youth is bidirectional. At times of economic recession, the risk of young people facing unemployment is greater. Thereafter, micro- and macroeconomic stability boosts access to work for young people.

The ILO has called for vigorous, collective action to address the youth unemployment crisis and has instituted a multi-pronged approach to respond to the crisis. Within the context of the Global Jobs Pact,[433] which was instituted a year after the outbreak of the 2008 economic recession, the ILO presented an integrated portfolio of policies aimed at generating employment, extending social protection, respecting labour standards, promoting social dialogue, and shaping globalization. Guided by the Decent Work Agenda and the ILO Declaration on Social Justice for a fair Globalisation, the Pact embraces a human-centred approach to promoting jobs.[434] In addition, the organization's Call for Action[435] on youth unemployment elaborates on the Pact. Having the same normative foundations, the Call for Action outlines the specific fronts on which governments, employers, and financial institutions should base their time-bound action plans for decent youth employment. They included pro-employment economic policies; labour market policies; boosting employability through education, training, skills, and the school-to-work transition; fostering youth entrepreneurship and self-employment; and a rights-based approach to youth unemployment, ensuring that all components of the right to

---

[432] The creation of 'idle young people' is also linked to exclusion due to persistent youth unemployment, A Goujard and others, 'The Labour Market for Young People' in P Gregg and J Wadswort (eds) *The Labour Market in Winter: the State of Working Britain* (OUP 2011) 39.

[433] ILO <https://www.ilo.org/wcmsp5/groups/public/---ed_norm/---relconf/documents/meetingdocument/wcms_115076.pdf> accessed 7 April 2021.

[434] ILO <https://www.ilo.org/wcmsp5/groups/public/---ed_norm/---relconf/documents/meetingdocument/wcms_115076.pdf> accessed 31 March 2021.

[435] ILO <https://www.ilo.org/wcmsp5/groups/public/---ed_norm/---relconf/documents/meetingdocument/wcms_185950.pdf> accessed 7 April 2021.

630   SDG 8

access work as well as the corollary rights on decent working conditions and collective bargaining are upheld.[436]

b) Empirical analysis and implementation efforts at the international and domestic levels

Indicator 8.b.1—'existence of a developed and operationalized national strategy for youth employment, as a distinct strategy or as part of a national employment strategy'— is intended to measure the degree to which states have taken action to counter youth labour with market strategies in accordance with the framework set by the ILO Jobs Pact and Call for Action. The indicator is binary as it examines if a country has a strategy as well as if it is acting on it or not. For this purpose two terms determine countries' policies: 'developed strategy' indicates an officially adopted document that articulates a set of measures and provisions aimed at promoting youth employment within a time frame, and 'operationalized strategy', which denotes the existence of an action plan with allocated resources and institutional responsibilities clearly defined. The indicator does not, however, assess the impact of this strategy. Moreover, countries that might be operationalizing a strategy to fight youth unemployment but have not adopted it by official processes and cannot present any *de jure* record are also excluded from monitoring.[437] Exclusion of *de facto* policies and the fact that the impact of the policies is not scrutinized challenges the effectiveness of this indicator for monitoring progress implementation on target 8.b. If these features were included, target 8.b would be ideal to assess the interlinkages with targets 8.5–8.7, and the other Goals such as the one on education that is relevant to the youth.

Country reporting on target 8.b in the context of SDG monitoring is not systematic. Data on the Global database for the SDGs appear for the first time in 2019. Indeed, mention of youth unemployment in the SG's reports is made only in the said year. Evidence suggests, however, that youth unemployment is high on the agenda of many governments. As the SG reports, ninety-nine out of 102 countries that provided data had a youth employment strategy or a plan to develop one in the near future.[438] The ILO's youth employment policies database is helpful in this regard as a source of information, despite the fact that it was not designed with the SDGs in mind. Examples from the sixty-five countries covered by the database are the following.[439]

South Africa's National development plan until 2030, a long-term strategy to increase employment and broaden opportunities through education, vocational training, and work experience and public employment programmes, among others; the country's National Skills Development Strategy (2011–2016) aims at linking skills development to career paths, career development, and promoting sustainable employment

---

[436] For the international labour standards relevant to work and young persons, see <https://www.ilo.org/employment/Whatwedo/Publications/WCMS_115993/lang--en/index.htm> accessed 4 December 2022.

[437] UNSC, metadata sheet on target 8.b and ILO Guidebook (n 262) 65.

[438] SG Report 2020 (n 285) para 81.

[439] ILO, YouthPOL <https://www.ilo.org/employment/areas/youth-employment/youth-pol/lang--en/index.htm> and <https://www.ilo.org/dyn/youthpol/en/f?p=30850:1001:0::NO> accessed 7 April 2021.

and in-work progression. Zambia has adopted and operationalized the National Youth Policy 2006, the technical education, vocational, and entrepreneurship training policy and the Sixth National Development Plan, 'Sustained Economic Growth and Poverty Reduction', in order to promote jobs and skills development for the youth. Last but not least, the Russian Federation tackles youth unemployment from the standpoint of education through the Federal targeted Program of Education Development that ran until 2020, general national employment plans such as the National Program on Employment Promotion and more specific such as the Fundamentals of the State Youth Policy of the Russian Federation Action plan that has been in force since 2015 and will end in 2025. A broader outlook is taken by the country's regulatory framework on long-term social and economic development until 2020. These strategies are aimed at structural and technological innovations in all education levels in order to bring the content and structure of professional education in correspondence with the needs of the labour market and create conducive infrastructure for education and training of employees for a modern economy; at creating conditions for successful socialization and effective self-realization of young people so that they develop into their fullest potential and add value to the country's effort for innovative development. Tasks under these policies also involve young people in social practices; support scientific, creative, and entrepreneurial young activities; develop a coherent system for supporting youth with leadership skills, initiative, and talented youth; and promote the formation of legal, cultural, and moral values among young people.

c) *Critique*

It is encouraging that countries include youth unemployment in their national development plans and adopt also distinct strategies. Such combination increases the chances of a holistic approach to the problem. The absence of adequate data, though, does not allow concrete conclusions regarding progress on target 8.b or on any other of the related targets of Goal 8 that refer to the youth. The source of the problem lies in the methodology behind the design of the goal; giving regard to the formal adoption and operationalization of youth unemployment strategies satisfies only the formality of the matter; its essence lies in the impact of these strategies, which is not captured. In light of this, the purpose of target 8.b as means of implementation of Goal 8 targets is moderated.

V. Conclusion

The focus on the achievement of economic growth and productive employment in a single goal has been met with both criticism and praise. SDG 8 is more comprehensive than its predecessor, MDG 1 that concentrated only on growth-related issues. It encompasses new objectives, and most significantly, is conceptualized under the overarching objective of achieving decent work for all. Nevertheless, there are some important gaps in SDG 8, especially with regard to how to link economic growth and human rights, namely how to approach growth-related issues in an integrated human rights manner. Therefore, narrowing down growth and productive work to one single goal could result in scattered attention to individual targets and to a loss of focus. By way of example, the persistence on GDP and per capita growth in the Goal places all the pressure upon satisfying this aim to the detriment of the decent work objective, especially reproductive work and its economic and social importance. From a gender perspective as well, less attention to reproductive work in SDG 8 leads to a tension between the Goal and SDG 5, which calls for the recognition of the value of unpaid care and domestic work. Such trade-offs within SDG 8 point to the lingering influence of neoliberal growth, which purportedly outweighs decent work as an organizing principle for development policy. Still, it should not be forgotten that economic growth and productive work constitute underlying determinants of all three pillars of sustainable human development, namely development that aims at enhancing individual's capabilities now and in the future through a comprehensive strategy that integrates the economic, social, and environmental dimensions of human well-being. It is through this lens that the interplay between economic growth and decent work should be viewed in order for both concepts to find their place in and have the appropriate impact on the formulation of development initiatives whether these are shaped by international institutions or national governments.

SDG 9

'Build Resilient Infrastructure, Promote Inclusive and Sustainable Industrialization, and Foster Innovation'

P Sean Morris

I. Introduction

Part of the legal foundation of Sustainable Development Goal (SDG) 9[1] has already been set in a decision by the International Court of Justice (ICJ) in 1997, the *Gabcikovo-Nagymaros* decision,[2] and partly in the international instrument creating the World Trade Organization (WTO), which also recognized sustainable development.[3] These two means of legal recognition of sustainable development can inform us on the rise of SDG 9 and any perceived relationship SDG 9 may have with law and norms. Yet, this commentary is not about the ICJ *Gabcikovo-Nagymaros* decision nor the WTO, but by pointing out these legal developments a framework on the evolution of SDG 9 and its meta-relationship in the global legal corpus may help us to appreciate some of the challenges and legal complexities of SDG 9.[4]

The embodiment of the corpus of the SDGs[5] could ideally be that of SDG 9, which seeks to 'build resilient infrastructure, promote inclusive and sustainable industrialisation and foster innovation.'[6] This ambitious and expansive goal has been at the epicentre of global development especially as a concern of many countries in the Global South. For these countries, in order to migrate from the status of developing country

---

[1] UNGA Res 70/1 'Transforming Our World: The 2030 Agenda for Sustainable Development' (25 September 2015), UN Doc A/Res/70/1, on other occasions, I will refer to SDG 9 specifically pinpointing to this document or simply 'SDG 9'.

[2] Case Concerning the Gabcikovo-Nagymaros Project (*Hungary v Slovakia*) (Judgment) 25 September 1997 ICJ Reports 7. For a discussion on framing the case along sustainable development see MM Mbengue, 'On Sustainable Development: A Conversation with Judge Weeramantry' in S Forlati and others (eds), *The Gabcikovo-Nagymaros Judgement and Its Contribution to the Development of International Law* (Brill 2020).

[3] Marrakech Agreement Establishing the World Trade Organization, 15 April 1994, 1867 UNTS 3 (1995). The preamble states *inter alia*: '[F]or the optimal use of the world's resources in accordance with the objective of sustainable development, seeking both to protect and preserve the environment and to enhance the means for doing so in a manner consistent with their respective needs and concerns at different levels of economic development.'

[4] I posit in this commentary that a meta-relationship of legal rules will need to take into consideration when the norms of SDG 9 have fully evolved. The meta-relationship is in part how commercial/conflicts of law at the domestic level, along with existing rules of international law and a novel area of global innovation law, collides to meet the requirements of SDG 9.

[5] 'The 2030 Agenda' (n 1).

[6] ibid.

or under-developed countries to that of developed countries, they crave the necessary infrastructure developments that holds the economies of the Global North together.[7]

As, the adage goes, 'if you build, they will come', and infrastructure sits at the heart of how a society can gather steam for industrialization. This could either be through many factors such as technological advancement and the sharing of those technologies through knowledge, the transfer of technology, and inventions that can foster innovation. Yet, the gap between the Global North and the Global South is ever widening and the resilience to overcome this gap, although achievable and admirable, history has shown that the great industrializations over the last two centuries generally occur over a fifty-year period.[8]

For the United Nations (UN), the SDGs are set as the benchmarks for all nations, whether in the Global North or the Global South, to measure and achieve a degree of sustainability which, among other things, by 2030 should reflect the advancement of human society, which can be measured in industry, innovation, and infrastructure. This great expectation is envisioned to transform modern human society to reflect the broader development agenda for a world that is inclusive where the rules and norms of (global) law help to underpin such great expectations.

The integration[9] of the world under the auspices of the SDGs confronts significant challenges including those relating to legal divergences on the two concepts that frame the goals: 'sustainable' and 'development'.[10] As a concept, 'sustainable development', however, has its roots in the 1980 report by the International Union for the Conservation of Nature and Natural Resources (IUCN)[11] and later gained popularity in the Brundtland Report of 1987.[12] While, the operative words in the concept sustainable

---

[7] For a general reading on the division between the global north and the global south from an environmental perspective see S Alam and others (eds), *International Environmental Law and the Global South* (CUP 2015).

[8] The industrialization of Europe in historical context is useful in this regard, as various countries experienced bouts of industrial development at different pace. Moreover, legal regulation and property protection especially in innovation or other forms of rule of law also ensured that European, United States, and later industrialization in 'peripheral' countries became a reality. For some of the general literature on the historical aspects of industrialization, see, eg, B van Leeuwen and others (eds), *An Economic History of Regional Industrialization* (Routledge 2020); T Kemp, *Historical Patterns of Industrialization* (2nd edn, Routledge 2013); P Bairoch, 'International Industrialization Levels from 1750 to 1890' (1982) 11 Journal of European Economic History 269–33; A Grubler, 'Industrialization as a Historical Phenomenon' in R Socolow and others (eds), *Industrial Ecology and Global Change* (CUP, 1995).

[9] I am using the concept of integration here to refer to the process of creating a universal system under the SDGs and as such it a process of forming into a common whole. Moreover, there is also the linkage of the concept of integration to sustainable development, where the International Law Association (ILA) notes that 'integration is pivotal to the promotion of sustainable development. It is the principle of integration that both brings together the many challenges confronting the international community', see, ILA, Committee on International Law on Sustainable Development Seventy-First Report, Berlin Conference 2004, 13.

[10] For discussion on the concepts and meaning of 'sustainable' and 'development', see, eg, VP Nanda, 'Sustainable Development' in L Guruswamy (ed), *International Energy and Poverty: The Emerging Contours* (Routledge 2015) 84–95.

[11] International Union for the Conservation of Nature and Natural Resource, World Conservation Strategy: Living Resource Conservation for Sustainable Development (1980) IV.

[12] Chairman of the World Commission on Environment and Development, 'Report of the World Commission on Environment and Development: Our Common Future', s 1, UN Doc A/42/427, Annex (4 August 1987), para 27, setting out the concept sustainable development: 'humanity has the ability to make development sustainable to ensure that it meets the needs of the present without compromising the ability of future generations to meet their own needs'. See also, World Commission on Environment and Development (WCED), *Our Common Future* (OUP 1987).

development are in part a shift from previous Third World notions of development into the present 'sustainable development' in the SDGs, the repackaging of the concept into that of 'sustainable' comes with its own interpretation and practice.[13]

Arguably, for some countries in the Global South, underdevelopment and traditional approaches to, for example, farming or infrastructures may not necessarily comport with the large-scale industrial practices of the Global North, and in that context, may represent a 'sustainable' approach. At the same time, development as such, may not take the approach as practised elsewhere to include the urbanization of towns. Rather, development may entail simplistic practices that rest on how there are shared resources and communal approaches to urbanization. The point is that there are a number of ways in which the concepts of 'sustainable' and 'development' may be contrasted and also the extent to which they fit the paradigms of the localities in different parts of the world. Thus, it might not necessarily be that integration of the world through 'sustainable development' may lead to the desired outcomes and gaps will remain in which the practices, interpretation, and the concepts are invoked to mean different things.

Yet, the consolidation of 'sustainable' and 'development' is also forging a new world through integration and the need to eliminate the imbalances that exist between nations in the Global North and those in the Global South. Thus, even if sustainability is a proxy for development, it is also an indication that the two concepts can be interpreted in such a way that the goals are achievable and in that way the imbalances would no longer be a concern. This outlook, however, is still dependent on how the different integrating factors of (i) the seventeen SDGs are cross-matched so that the success of one SDG goal can eliminate deficiencies in another SDG goal, and (ii) the degree of legal responses to each SDG goal.

Such legal responses may take a rule of law approach. The rule of law is complex,[14] and the SDGs sit at the legal junction of global law, where public international law, transnational law, global governance, global private law, commercial/conflicts of law, domestic law, and 'legal rights' in general will need to respond to the legality of the goals.[15] For instance, what is the legal nature of each goal, are they local rules covered by national legislations or are they global rules covered by international conventions? The legality question at this moment is complex, and while global law may be more adaptive towards 'sustainability' as such, this may not necessarily be the same for 'development'. This is because of the way the global economic system is structured—law

---

[13] The precise contours or definitions of the concept 'sustainable development' generally takes into account three pillars: economic, social, and environmental factors, when considering best practices for development as such. The origins and history of the concept emerged over a series of events, starting with ideological insights in the 1960s through works such as R Carson, *Silent Spring* (Houghton Mifflin Company 1962). International conferences, such as the 1972 Stockholm Conference, also played a role in the evolution of the concept 'sustainable development', UN Conference on the Human Environment, Report on the United Nations Conference on the Human Environment, A/CONF.48/14/Rev.1, ch 1 (16 June 1972); see also, Nanda (n 10) 84.

[14] My idea of the rule of in this context is broadly within the prism of international law, see WW Bishop, 'The International Rule of Law' (1961) 59 Michigan Law Review 553–74; K Gorobets, 'The International Rule of Law and the Idea of Normative Authority' (2020) 12 Hague Journal on the Rule of Law 227–49.

[15] I attempt to discuss some of these in this commentary but not all can be covered, however for recent readings on SDGs and global governance see A Harrington, *International Law and Global Governance: Treaty Regimes and Sustainable Development Goals Implementation* (Routledge 2021).

636   SDG 9

as such is designed for economic effects of 'sustainability' but not for 'development'. This prognosis also comes back to how the two concepts are interpreted and how legal relations between both concepts are applied and interpreted so that 'economic rights' in sustainability discourse are protected, as a matter of the rule of law, but law is not designed to enable 'a right to development', as it were. Nevertheless, the legalities that will emerge from SDG 9 when international law, commercial law/conflicts of law, and new dimensions of global law are factored in can be seen as creating a meta-relationship so that legal aspects of SDG 9 are better understood than they currently are.

At the normative level, there is an international declaration on the right to development by the United Nations General Assembly (UNGA) of December 1986.[16] However, as a declaration, this document does not carry the force of law as such in the international legal system. The right to development discourse has been around for some time now,[17] and its modern indirect incarnation in the SDGs is to some extent a reflection of an issue that has not been fully resolved. The right to development, as captured in article 1.1 of the UN Declaration states:

> The right to development is an inalienable human right by virtue of which every human person and all peoples are entitled to participate in, contribute to, and enjoy economic, social, cultural and political development, in which all human rights and fundamental freedoms can be fully realized.[18]

This, of course, has a number of factors, ranging from human rights to culture and social issues. However, for the sake of brevity, and to locate the right to development as an economic issue, arguably then the right to development fits into a global construct of great expectations and integration[19] but does not necessarily promote any form of economic development since legal rules exist to extract the economic benefits of the factors that promote economic development. For example, while the invention of the smart phone promotes development as such, the thousands of patents in a single smart device enable the patent owners to invoke their rights in the event there is an infringement.[20]

---

[16] United Nations General Assembly, Declaration on the Right to Development, GA Res. 41/128 (adopted 4 December 1986) (hereinafter 'Right to Development Declaration'). As of 2020, a new twist in the right to development emerges, where steps have been taken for a convention thereby moving from the 'declaration' stage to a more meaningful 'legal' document; see, Right to Development Draft Convention (2020), UN Doc A/HRC/WG.2/21/2/Add.1, 20 January 2020.

[17] For some general readings on the right to development see, eg, A Sengupta, 'Elements of a Theory of the Right to Development' in K Basu and R Kanbur (eds), *Arguments for a Better World: Essays in Honor of Amartya Sen: Volume I: Ethics, Welfare and Measurement* (OUP 2008); B Rajagopal, 'Right to Development and Global Governance: Old and New Challenges Twenty-Five Years On' (2013) 35 Human Rights Quarterly 893–909; ID Bunn, 'The Right to Development: Implications for International Economic Law' (2000) 15 American University International Law Review 1425–67; RN Kiwanuka, 'Developing Rights: The UN Declaration on the Right to Development' (1988) 35 Netherlands International Law Review 257–72; JM Mbaku, 'The Political Economy of Development: An Empirical Analysis of the Effects of the Institutional Framework on Economic Development' (1994) 29 Studies in Comparative International Development 3–21.

[18] See Right to Development Declaration (n 16).

[19] See n 9 for my take on the concept of integration in as much it is essential to sustainable development.

[20] It is estimated that more than a quarter million of patents are in a single smartphone, see the case history and various briefs of *Samsung Electronics Co., Ltd., et al v Apple Inc.*, 137 S. Ct. 429 (2016); Amici Curiae of 50 Intellectual Property Professors in Support of Petitioners, p 7: 'by one estimate, there are 250,000 patents that arguably cover various aspects of a smartphone'. See also in general, T Chid, 'Fighting the Smartphone Patent War with

INTRODUCTION   637

The point of this example is merely to demonstrate that development as such is closely intertwined with the legal rights that reward economic activities.

Firms at the global level that engage in sustainable practices are not expected to promote a right to economic development. Rather, firms seek to maintain market share or expand their market reach while at the same time rely on the rule of law to extract their economic outputs. However, by engaging with 'sustainability' and 'development' firms signal citizenry and acceptable norms. A firm active in design and production of smart phones in different countries can and will embrace the rhetoric of sustainable development while ensuring that the laws of those jurisdictions are consistent with the rule of law as such (and comparable to the same laws in its home jurisdiction) in order to enforce the different legal rights it has in the design and production of smart phones. For example, a firm engaged in designing and producing smart phones may find that that battery parts produced from cobalt may harm the environment. The cobalt, for instance, can only be sourced in an underdeveloped country, where the approach to sustainability and development may be different from the approach in the home jurisdiction of the smart phone manufacture. At the same time, due to the global pressures on cobalt mining, the smart phone manufacturer has embraced the rhetoric of sustainability and development to ensure that ethical practices exist for cobalt mining. The dilemma, however, is that without the cobalt, smart phones are inoperable and without the income generated from cobalt mining, the underdeveloped country may find it difficult to engage in the very act of development or the rhetoric of sustainability. But the more chilling effect has to do with the existence of global laws that are obligatory for the cobalt-mining country. In order to ensure that the patents protecting the smart phone are enforceable in the cobalt-mining country, that country must sign up to the global rules on intellectual property rights currently set out in the Treaty on Trade-Related Aspects of Intellectual Property Rights (TRIPs) Agreement.[21] It is under this circumstance that the rule of law or global rules under the TRIPs Agreement supersede the right to development. In other words, patent protection is afforded to the smart-phone manufacture at the global and local level while there are no global rules for the right to development. Furthermore, engaging with the rhetoric and practice of sustainability ensures that perceived conditions are met but are not legally required. Thus, different conditions for 'sustainability' and 'development' may come into conflict with 'legal

RAND-Encumbered Patents' (2012) 27 Annual Review of Law and Technology 209–40; D Kappos, 'Investing in America's Future Through Innovation: How the Debate over the Smart Phone Patent Wars (Re) Raises Issues at the Foundation of Long-Term Incentive Systems' (2013) 16 Stanford Technology Law Review 485–501; J Contreras and R Lakshane, 'Patents and Mobile Devices in India: An Empirical Survey' (2017) 50 Vanderbilt Journal of Transnational Law 1–44.

[21] Agreement on Trade-Related Aspects of Intellectual Property Rights, 15 April 1994, Marrakesh Agreement Establishing the World Trade Organization, Annex 1C, 1869 UNTS 299 (hereinafter 'TRIPs Agreement'). But see PN Upreti, 'Nepal's First National Intellectual Property Policy—2017: Never too Late' (2017) 12 Journal of Intellectual Property Law & Practice 550, 552 (setting out some of the technological links with international intellectual property protection). A broader implication of this discussion is that it links the narratives with those on developing countries where they must meet international obligations to enforce intellectual property rights but at the same time, they need to strengthen their own internal enforcements which can be a challenge).

638   SDG 9

rights'. Legal rights as such are only there to extract economic benefits, while the right to development rests on a broad construct to include aspects of economic activities.

The SDGs are in part agents of change—to frame the narratives of legal rights and economic benefits in a different paradigm. As change agents in the international system the SDGs through Goal 9 on innovation, infrastructure, and industrialization drive a new imagination of development that is sustainable. The SDGs seek in particular to transform development in a sustainable manner and, equally, SDG 9 on industry, innovation, and infrastructure has the potential to be the main agent of change in relation to the other SDGs. Further, SDG 9 is also about redressing the imbalances of the world economies caused by 'poverty in all its forms and dimensions'[22] as with the other SDGs. While the SDGs expanded the vision of the Millennium Development Goals (MDGs) that ran from around 2000 to 2015[23] a core theme in the SDGs and was also in the MDGs is the right to development. In both the SDGs and the MDGs issues relating to the three pillars of 'economic, social, and environmental'[24] rights largely produce part of the narrative on the right to development. Therefore, SDGs individual goals (which are in themselves a complex network of targets) are connected to how the right to development is reincarnated and refined. That reincarnation is within the parameters of SDG 9: to build resilient infrastructure, promote industrialization, and foster innovation.

The emergence of SDG 9 has been the result of various actors where interests, preferences, and expertise have been crucial to the framing of the goal itself along with its targets and indicators. And while it might be a challenge in realizing SDG 9, its formation and evolution reflect the extent to which the different actors cooperated in order to take action to promote sustainable development that reflects three areas of economic advancement of human society: innovation, infrastructure, and industry. Given that SDG 9 is a combination of how private enterprise has led the charge for its desired preferences to be included in SDG 9 and when combined with the interests of states for economic development through sustainability and resilient infrastructures, it is likely that interests of the state and those of private enterprise will cause conflict.[25]

While there has been collective action by the different parties to ensure that the SDGs were transformed from ideas into concrete policy initiatives, the underlying 'economic' and 'power' framework of SDG 9 is centred on how private economic enterprises can deliver the facets of SDG 9. Another factor is the extent that states are able to accommodate every necessary action of private economic enterprises in order for states to be able to claim the ideals of SDG 9 successfully. Thus, in some ways, SDG 9 is a reflection

---

[22] Preamble, first para, SDGs Declaration, 25 September 2015.

[23] Millennium Declaration, United Nations, 8 September 2000, UN Doc A/RES/55/2; see also, J Vandemoortele, 'The MDG Conundrum: Meeting the Targets Without Missing the Point' (2009) 27 Development Policy Review 355–71 (offering an optimistic assessment of the then MDGs). For a critical assessment and comparison of several goals in both the MDGs and the SDGs see JB Carant, 'Unheard Voices: A Critical Discourse Analysis of the Millennium Development Goals' Evolution into the Sustainable Development Goals' (2016) 38 Third World Quarterly 16–41.

[24] Given the strong linkage of sustainable development to the environment, scholars have also argued that sustainable development as such encapsulate 'the needs of [the] economy, society and environment', see R Libby and S Will, 'History for the Anthropocene' (2007) 5 History Compass 1694–719, 1695.

[25] See, eg, RS Dimitrov, 'Knowledge, Power and Interests in Environmental Regime Formation' (2003) 47 International Studies Quarterly 123–50.

of how on the one hand, 'power' as such is important for the different parties that are involved in SDG 9, and on the other, how 'knowledge' or 'expertise' will be shared among the different actors in order to deliver sustainable development. The rest of this commentary highlights some of these pitfalls and also shows how some of the power and knowledge dynamics during the negotiations for SDG 9 became a form of collective in order to help improve human society. The commentary will also look at some of the international legal regulatory challenges. The commentary will then finally assess the different targets and indicators of SDG 9 and their current status to ascertain whether SDG 9 as it currently stands can effectively deliver the task of sustainable development.

II. Goal Commentary: Framing and Negotiating Industry, Innovation, and Infrastructure

In thinking about how the negotiations for SDG 9 emerged, transfixed and ultimately shaped into norms and common concerns, there are a number of factors to consider. Some of those factors, such as the role of the MDGs, are for example present throughout the various commentaries in this volume, or the role of the different actors ranging from a coalition of civil society to transnational corporate actors are important. Yet, it is also important to distinguish between some of the actors such as international organizations and civil society and their own agendas during the negotiating phases for SDG 9.

One of the important distinctions to be made among these actors is that some, such as international organizations, have a legal personality in the international legal system and others do not.[26] For instance, the coalition of civil society is broad and while there were some transnational non-governmental organizations (NGOs) involved, others were local organizations or individuals who do not have legal capacity in the international legal system. This distinction is important since it set apart how an emerging 'legal personality' of SDG 9 is taking shape and can affect other areas such as intellectual property rights or the role of international organisations in managing the SDGs. Another comment worthy of pointing out at this stage is that the differences in the targets of SDG 9 (later discussed) are on the one hand more attributable to transnational corporations as opposed to civil society, and on the other, between international organizations with legal personality as opposed to transnational corporations. In this context the international organizations that act as custodians for different parts of SDG 9

---

[26] The subject matter of the legal personality of international organizations or the legal personality of individuals and non-state actors is still a perilous matter that often needs to handle with care, but see N White, *The Law of International Organisations* (3rd edn, Manchester University Press 2016); A Kjeldgaard-Pedersen, *The International Legal Personality of the Individual* (OUP 2018); J Klabbers, 'Transforming Institutions: Autonomous International Organisations in Institutional Theory' (2017) 6 Cambridge International Law Journal 105–21; W Worster, 'Relative International Legal Personality of Non-State Actors' (2016) 42 Brooklyn Journal of International Law 207–74. Recently, scholars have promoted the idea of 'trust funds' as having legal personality and this novel argument may well be applied to the SDGs given that they are coordinated by numerous UN agencies, they are norm-making, and the SDGs are all together a collective of international actions. For the arguments on trust funds see I Bantekas, 'The Legal Personality of World Bank Funds under International Law' (2021) 56 Tulsa Law Review 209–54.

640   SDG 9

are relevant, and these include, the World Bank, the International Telecommunications Union (ITU), International Energy Agency (IEA), and the International Civil Aviation Organization (ICAO).

Hence, for these reasons, sustainable development in SDG 9 will tend to have a strong legal character when 'innovation' is invoked and, at the same time, integrate a bottom-up approach due to the involvement of civil society in the negotiating phase. This latter observation in some ways is also applicable to the other SDGs. But the key thing to remember when comparing SDG 9 to the other SDGs is that SDG 9 and its targets are business oriented (innovation and industry) with a strong nexus for the application of legal rules such as intellectual property rights while balancing the role of international organizations (infrastructure) with civil society for a bottom-up approach. Hence, a framing of SDG 9 through its evolution in the MDGs and then the wide array of actors such as transnational corporations, international organizations, and civil society during the negotiating phase can help our understanding of the important role of SDG 9 in sustainable development as part of a mandate that should be successful.

A. Towards a Revitalized Vision of Global Sustainable Development

At the turn of the twenty-first century, the UN accelerated its vision for environmental protection that are linked to development, a process that began with the Stockholm Conference of 1972 and various other initiatives in the 1980s through to the 1990s. Thus, in September 2000, through the UN Millennium Declaration, the world was introduced to a set of targets for poverty eradication.[27] Part of the ideals of the Millennium Declaration was to realize 'an environment—at the national and global levels alike—which is conducive to the development and to the elimination of poverty'.[28] The Millennium Declaration had eight goals and eighteen targets and another forty-eight indicators for a vision of the world in 2015. It was a failed vision, and the MDGs, as they became known, were redesigned with more goals and targets, set for another fifteen years so that by 2030 'the three dimensions of sustainable development: the economic, social and environmental'[29] are achieved in an integrated and indivisible way. But as the MDGs faded into the background, the universal SDGs were designed with transparency, participation, monitoring, and other safeguards to ensure their success.

Unlike the preceding eight SDGs which have had a counterpart in the MDGs, SDG 9 and the subsequent targets do not have an MDG equivalent.[30] Rather, SDG 9 heralds

[27] Millennium Declaration (n 23).
[28] ibid s III, para 12.
[29] SDG 2030 Agenda, preamble; see also, UN General Assembly, 'Report of the Open Working Group of the General Assembly on Sustainable Development Goals', UN Doc A/68/970 (12 August 2014) proposing seventeen SDGs.
[30] For a general comparison see E Haliscelik and MA Soyas, 'Sustainable Development from Millennium 2015 to Sustainable Development Goals 2030' (2019) 27 Sustainable Development 545–72; J Vandemoortele, 'From Simple-Minded MDGs to Muddle-Headed SDGs' (2018) 5 Development Studies Research 83–89.

a new beginning beyond the MDGs and therefore has the potential to see the visions of the SDGs and those previously elaborated in the MDGs become real. The primary focus of the MDGs was the eradication of poverty, with little and few actual indicators. The SDGs, on the other hand, are more comprehensive and take into account the three pillars of economic, social, and environmental approach to development. Unlike the MDGs, which were heavily oriented towards developing countries, the SDGs are universalist in that they apply to all nations. As universal principles, the SDGs also include states, international organizations, transnational corporations, various NGOs (and derivatives) to engage from conception to vision. That is, different actors had a say in the ideas, negotiations, drafting, and continued execution of the SDGs. This wide array of actors broadens the focus of the SDGs to set new and ethical visions of innovation, infrastructure, and industry as the institutional beams of participatory capitalism.[31]

Even though many of the current SDGs are built upon the former MDGs, the range of participation by non-state actors in the SDGs has given them a more inclusive form of achievement in that they embrace a multitude of actors, and they continue to do so. As such, the numerous actors, with various visions of sustainability and development, have in turn transformed the SDGs as part of a global instrument of collective action. This allows a bottom-up approach reflecting changes in the global economy and how those changes are part of the larger corpus of moving beyond the elimination of poverty discourse to a better understanding of utilizing resources in a sustainable way.

Such understanding, therefore, can reduce the costs associated with poverty eradication by utilizing existing resources to create more efficient commodification of resources and ideas. This point of view supports the efforts of sustainable development where the interactions of humans and the resources around them are transformed into instruments that are beneficial for (i) humans, and the general welfare of society; (ii) the ability of states to mitigate demands for additional resources or (infrastructure); and (iii) the market retention of products that can contribute to how firms are further mobilized and how they provide sustainable commodities.

When compared to the MDGs, the SDGs are only part of a continuum that the ways and means of achieving sustainable development shift in 'strategic vision' while the underlying premise remains the same. This, in part, largely rests upon how the processes of transformation will take into account initiatives such as those relating to technology, the market, society, or the state, and are able to overcome challenges that can range from cultural to institutional.[32] One of those challenges relates to culture and the degree of what is considered sustainable in different societies. Naturally, a subsistence farmer in the Global South who grazed and planted seeds for generations on a plot of land using the same methods and traditions handed down for generations may view

---

[31] But see W Streeck, 'Taking Capitalism Seriously: Towards an Institutional Approach to Contemporary Political Economy' (2011) 9 Socio-Economic Review 137–67, 138 (framing capitalism as a 'set of interrelated social institutions'); A Kenis and M Lievens, *The Limits of the Green Economy: From Re-Inventing Capitalism to Re-Politicising the Present* (Routledge 2015).

[32] See I Scoones, 'The Politics of Sustainability and Development' (2016) 41 Annual Review of Environment and Resources 293–319.

those methods as 'sustainable'. This latter practice of sustainable may not comport with what a farmer elsewhere thinks of his farming. For example, a farmer in the Global North who carries out the same operation with mechanized and chemical support may think of finding ways to make his operations 'sustainable'.[33] In this latter example, the difference in farming practices suggests that 'sustainable' approaches are often based on numerous factors.

The above example indicates the extent to which culture influences the notion of sustainable and whether sustainable development can be achieved.[34] The understanding of cultural practices as they relate to sustainable development is linked to how much one can understand the state and stage of development in different societies. However, where the broader initiatives of the SDGs go beyond those of the MDGs, and in particular how facets of SDG 9 overlap with all aspects of economic activities in a society, then the question of comparison in different cultures become minor. This is because the SDGs in their current formulation, or at least the targets and indicators relating to SDG 9, are formulated in such a way to represent global society as opposed to the cultural society. In other words, SDG 9 is universal in the sense that its underlying premise is to create a global and unprecedented transformation of all societies in the world.[35]

The global transformation that SDG 9 aims at is ambitious. This is because they cover such a broad array of activities that will change the lifestyle and well-being of the world's population. They range from the processes that involve how the market creates jobs and sustains affordable pricing for daily commodities (industry); how market actors and the state can coordinate their efforts to put in place the required structural initiatives (infrastructure); how research and development (R&D) along with technological advancement will improve the lives and capacity of individuals and society (innovation); and equally how resilient each mode of transformation can reduce carbon emission and engage in greener or circular form of economic activities (see further Chapter 12 in this book for a detailed explanation of the circular economy, pp xx–xx). It is these types of transformative processes that separate the SDGs from the MDGs and that have the capacity to make sustainable development a reality (but not exactly by the target date of 2030).

Thus, while the MDGs serve as the foundation for the SDGs, the strength of each initiative is in their power to transform global society, and the SDGs have moved beyond the MDGs to promote a form of economic sustainability (at least within the form of SDG 9). In that regard the ideas of the MDGs faded and gave way to a more powerful narrative of transformation and sustainability where technology and innovation, market actors and infrastructural development, and resilient transformations are key

---

[33] For a more refined assessment of similar examples, see D Brockington and S Ponte, 'The Green Economy in the Global South: Experiences, Redistributions and Resistance' (2015) 36 Third World Quarterly 2197–206.

[34] But see A Jamison, *The Making of Green Knowledge: Environmental Politics and Cultural Transformation* (CUP 2001) (suggesting the need for 'cognitive dimensions of social interactions') 39.

[35] For a general reading on the 'ecological' nexus to this transformation see APJ Mol, *Globalization and the Environmental Reform: The Ecological Modernization of the Global Economy* (MIT Press 2001).

GOAL COMMENTARY   643

to the universal application of the facets of SDG 9. It is the universal appeal of the SDGs where they form not only part of the narrative on 'global sustainability' but also are seen as essential to the framework of globalization where states, non-state actors, and private market entrepreneurs collectively frame and cooperate on the basis of the principles of sustainable development as a path to a greener and 'commodified' society.[36]

B. State-led Actors and the Open Working Group (OWG) Sessions

The Open Working Group (OWG), an international body comprising states, led the process that eventually formed the final 'narratives' and form of the SDGs.[37] Mandated by the 2012 UN Conference on Sustainable Development, the OWG was to develop the SDGs through a mixture of factors that took into account environmental, social, and economic concerns. By 19 July 2014 the OWG came up with seventeen goals and 169 targets which were the result of over a dozen rounds of preparatory meetings.[38] The SDG proposals were produced by the OWG in its 'outcome document' that the UNGA would formally endorse in its sixty-ninth session in 2015 as global policy.[39] The drafting of SDG 9 in the outcome document[40] was not substantially different from that of SDG 9 adopted by the UNGA.[41] Moreover, of the thirteen meetings the OWG had,[42] SDG 9 was covered in different 'clusters' during various sessions such as OWG-10.[43]

[36] On the latter, see J Clapp and P Dauvergne, *Paths to a Green World: Political Economy of the Global Environment* (2nd edn, MIT Press 2011).

[37] Open Working Group (OWG) on Sustainable Development Goals, 22 January 2013, established by UNGA decision 67/55, UN Doc A/67/L.48/Rev.1. The OWG was established in part as a response to 'The Future We Want' (UNGA Resolution A/RES/66/288, 11 September 2012, para 248).

[38] The OWG negotiated and drafted the SDGs in thirteen rounds of meetings from March 2013 to July 2014 to produce the blueprint of 2030 development agenda, see 'Report of the Open Working Group of the General Assembly on Sustainable Development Goals' (UN Doc A/68/970, 12 August 2014) (hereinafter 'Report of the OWG' or sometimes 'Outcome document'); see also M Farrell, 'Group Politics in Global Development Policy: From the Millennium Development Goals to the Post-2015 Development Agenda' (2017) 12 The Hague Journal of Diplomacy 221–48.

[39] UNGA 69th Session, Resolution adopted by the General Assembly on 1 September 2015/–69/315—Draft Outcome Document of the United Nations Summit for the Adoption of the post-2015 Development Agenda, UN Doc A/RES/69/315, 15 September 2015; for assessment and general commentaries on the OWG see generally, D Bhattacharya and others, 'A Commentary on the Final Outcome Document of the Open Working Group on SDGs' (2014) 34 The SAIS Review of International Affairs 165–77.

[40] SDG 9 in the outcome document as discussed in Bhattacharya (n 39); see Report of the Open Working Group of the General Assembly on Sustainable Development Goals (UN Doc A/68/970, 12 August 2014).

[41] UNGA Resolution (n 39).

[42] UN General Assembly's (UNGA) OWG on SDGs, Session 1, 14 March 2013–15 March 2013, New York; UN General Assembly's (UNGA) OWG on SDGs, Session 2, 17 April 2013–19 April 2013; UN General Assembly's (UNGA) OWG on SDGs, Session 3, 22 May 2013–24 May 2013; UN General Assembly's (UNGA) OWG on SDGs, Session 4, 17 June 2013–19 June 2013; UN General Assembly's (UNGA) OWG on SDGs, Session 5, 25 November 2013–27 November 2013; UN General Assembly's (UNGA) OWG on SDGs, Session 6, 9 December 2013–13 December 2013; UN General Assembly's (UNGA) OWG on SDGs, Session 7, 6 January 2014–10 January 2014; UN General Assembly's (UNGA) OWG on SDGs, Session 8, 3 February 2014–7 February 2014; UN General Assembly's (UNGA) OWG on SDGs, Session 9, 3 March 2014–5 March 2014; UN General Assembly's (UNGA) OWG on SDGs, Session 10, 31 March–4 April 2014; UN General Assembly's (UNGA) OWG on SDGs, Session 11, 5 May 2014–9 May 2014; UN General Assembly's (UNGA) OWG on SDGs, Session 12, 16 June 2014—20 June 2014; UN General Assembly's (UNGA) OWG on SDGs, Session 13, 14 July–19 July 2014. For the sake of consistency, the primary meeting for the purposes of this chapter is OWG Session 10 and will be referred to as 'OWG-10'.

[43] SDG 9 was not handled as a single goal *per se*, rather, each aspect, target, or indicator had been discussed during different sessions as part of a larger cluster discussion, so for example in OWG-10, Cluster 4 covered infrastructure and industrialization.

644   SDG 9

In this section of the commentary I will look at two aspects to help frame an understanding of how SDG 9 became an important but elusive SDG. I will do this by looking first at the wider political dynamics that link sustainability with economic development as such.[44] Secondly, by looking at how the different facets of SDG 9 were handled or framed will provide a picture of what went on during the different sessions of the OWG. Given that the OWG comprised states with a few non-state actors who participated in the OWG sessions as either observers or representatives of civil society, the question of politics can help with a view of framing the 'power, interests and expertise'[45] of states on the one hand and those of non-state actors on the other during the OWG sessions.[46]

The political dynamics of how states would engage with sustainability was evident in the OWG-1 in March 2013 when the fifty-seven UN Member States that gathered made a variety of statements that were of a general nature and rarely addressed a specific issue 'to include in the goals.'[47] During the general discussions, states were fully aware of the need to build on the MDG principles but also 'the need for universal support when defining the SDGs.'[48] Important, however, was the fact that the efforts of states during OWG-1, their general statements, and interactive discussions had been a form of collective action in order to coordinate, consolidate, and draft the SDGs. The states had set the tone to engage in 'civil' collective action knowing full well that the previous MDGs were unsuccessful and the effort to create the SDGs was a second chance where failure was not an option. Hence, collective action allowed them to engage in interactive and voluntary discussions that would eventually lead to an all-inclusive form of public goods transformation at the global level in the form of the SDGs.

One form of transformation that states had in mind concerned innovation and by the time of OWG-2,[49] states were prepared to embrace the technology and innovation transformation that the SDGs can bring about. The charge on innovation at OWG-2 was curiously led by states that are outside of the margins of 'developed' states. Hence, Nigeria, Zambia, and Slovenia, along with support from the 'Expert Group Meeting on Science and SDGs'[50] and the 'Business and Industry Major Group',[51] pushed for innovation and know-how as part of the SDGs. Zambia, for example, specifically referred to the importance of 'science and technological innovation'[52] and similarly, Slovenia highlighted the urgency of 'innovation and expertise.'[53] It was a narrative that the Expert

---

[44] See, eg, JS Dryzek, *The Politics of the Earth: Environmental Discourses* (OUP 2013); I Scoones and others (eds), *The Politics of Green Transformation* (Routledge 2015); Clapp and Dauvergne (n 36).

[45] But see Dimitrov (n 25); P Haas, 'Policy Knowledge and Epistemic Communities' in NJ Smelser and PB Baltes (eds), *International Encyclopaedia of the Social and Behavioural Sciences* (Elsevier 2001).

[46] See n 42 for the various OWG Sessions.

[47] Final Summary Report of OWG Session 1, p 1.

[48] This view was express by then Secretary General Ban Kai Moon, see Final Summary Report of OWG Session 1, p 3.

[49] UN General Assembly's (UNGA) OWG on SDGs, Session 2, 17 April 2013–19 April 2013 (hereinafter 'Second Session of the OWG').

[50] UN General Assembly's (UNGA) OWG on SDGs, Session 2, 17 April 2013–19 April 2013, Summary of the Second Session of the UN General Assembly Open Working Group on Sustainable Development Goals: 17–19 April 2013 (hereinafter 'Summary of OWG Second Session') p 3.

[51] ibid p 5.

[52] ibid p 4.

[53] ibid p 5.

Group Meeting on Science and SDGs had framed earlier in the discussions as it was of the view that 'developing countries' had the need for 'new forms of governance' that *inter alia* relate to 'innovation.[54] The overall importance of OWG-2 was therefore its emphasis on innovation, science, and technology as evidence by the Expert Group Meeting on Science and SDGs and also the role of the Business and Industry Major Group. In short, they had set in motion at OWG-2 the narrative that would emerge for aspects of SDG 9 that relates to innovation and/or digital technologies.

But perhaps one way of looking at what took place during OWG-2, insofar as the role of the Expert Group Meeting on Science and SDGs and the Business and Industry Major Group are concerned, is that states embraced the narratives framed by these two groups in order to take the lead on promoting and framing aspects of SDG 9. In other words, states saw the need for technological transformation as part of the answer to sustainable development. The need for the transformation of states, especially in the developing world and less-developed regions of middle economies such as Slovenia, is of course an urgent one. The linkage of this transformation to sustainability through the SDGs and in SDG 9 is also seen as part of the broader view of innovation and industrialization where states can play a strong role.

States alone, however, cannot lead technological transformation in developing countries and private actors such as those represented by the Business and Industry Major Group during OWG-2 can also push forward the necessary technological transformation that is based on market and financial investments or R&D to spur innovation. Because of the linkage of technological innovation with sustainability in the context of SDG 9, inevitably, there is also the need of how approaches to climate adaption can be resilient or harness the existing resources in developing nations as part of resilience efforts. The broader picture is however that technological transformation based on innovation and sustainability where the state and private entrepreneurial actors are key players is aimed at achieving part of the sustainable development agenda by effectively shifting the innovation game between the two players, states and market actors, in order to realize the commitments in SDG 9.

As the different facets of SDG 9 began to emerge in the OWG sessions, the summary reports began to show how the dialogues between states and the non-state actors frame the thinking of issues such as infrastructure. Infrastructural development would complement the technological and innovation nexus in SDG 9 and therefore become a focal point of how states can promote sustainability and development. In that regard, in OWG-3,[55] states were more comfortably in linking infrastructure to technology and innovation or investments. For example, Uruguay was explicit on the linkage of infrastructure to innovation and technology as (even to the extent such linkage can eradicate hunger) providing it is 'through investments in technology innovation and

---

[54] ibid p 3.
[55] UN General Assembly's (UNGA) OWG on SDGs, Session 3, 22 May 2013–24 May 2013 (hereinafter 'Third Session of the OWG').

infrastructure.'[56] One of the interesting observations about OWG-3 was the extent to which many of the other SDGs such as those relating to water or food security was linked to infrastructure.[57]

The various linkages of infrastructure as such to other SDGs in OWG-3 suggest that states were either seeking a way to decouple infrastructure away from an evolving SDG 9. Conversely, states were hoping that a linkage of infrastructure across multiple SDGs would generate a more robust approach to development and as such would address the immediate concerns of the various (developing) states that had interactive discussions or made general comments on infrastructure and sustainable development during OWG-3. In a more formal sense, however, the linkage of infrastructure across multiple SDGs during OWG-3 could have been an attempt by states to develop a common foundation with the other actors during the negotiations. This could also be seen as directly ensuring that a common outcome at the policy implementation stage would be relevant to how market actors are essential for infrastructural development.[58]

Thus, states during OWG-3 made an attempt to find effective and sustainable transformation of infrastructure with the hope that the involvement of other SDGs could design or deliver sustainable development on a broader scale without shifting the market relations that private actors have with states. This approach may have been an attempt for states to shape their own vision of the SDGs so that infrastructure emerged as a stand-alone goal and not as a current linkage to SDG 9. Although some concerns about infrastructure were raised in OWG-4,[59] it was not until OWG-5[60] that infrastructure became the actual focus of serious discussion.

Building on the previous statements or views of infrastructure in the previous OWG sessions states were able to develop their ideas more concretely in OWG-5 where, *inter alia*, 'infrastructure development and industrialization' was on the agenda.[61] The different parts that made up SDG 9 were finally taking shape during OWG-5 as infrastructure was now linked with industrialization. The linkage of infrastructure to industrialization was part of a strategy to ensure that both areas are better positioned to evolve as 'key drivers of economic growth'.[62] The strategic significance of tying

[56] UN General Assembly's (UNGA) OWG on SDGs, Session 3, 22 May 2013–24 May 2013, Summary of the Third Session of the UN General Assembly Open Working Group on Sustainable Development Goals: 22–24 May 2013 (hereinafter 'Summary of Third Session') p 7.

[57] Summary of OWG Third Session, p 9, Cape Verde making the link to water quantity; Demark also made a similar link, p 11; Argentina made the link of infrastructure and food security, p 6; Bangladesh, made the link of infrastructure and land quality, p 6.

[58] In terms of similar arguments relating to my conception of common outcome, the use of 'co-production' in the climate change literature is useful, see, eg, C Miller and Ca Wyborn, 'Co-Production in Global Sustainability: Histories and Theories' (2020) 113 Environmental Science & Policy 88–95.

[59] UN General Assembly's (UNGA) OWG on SDGs, Session 4, 17 June 2013–19 June 2013, Summary of the Fourth Session of the UN General Assembly Open Working Group on Sustainable Development Goals: 17–19 June 2013 (hereinafter 'Summary of Fourth Session OWG'), Columbia for instance called for 'the necessary infrastructure and technology' to deliver health and education, p 6; and, similar views shared by Bahamas and the Caribbean Community (CARICOM), p 9.

[60] UN General Assembly's (UNGA) OWG on SDGs, Session 5, 25 November 2013–27 November 2013 (hereinafter 'Fifth Session OWG').

[61] UN General Assembly's (UNGA) OWG on SDGs, Session 5, 25 November 2013–27 November 2013, Summary of the Fifth Session of the UN General Assembly Open Working Group on Sustainable Development Goals: 25–27 November 2013 (hereinafter 'Summary of Fifth Session OWG').

[62] ibid p 1.

infrastructure to industrialization during OWG-5 has been a shift from the multiple linkage of infrastructure and other SDGs in the previous sessions.

The realignment of infrastructure with industrialization would now require addressing some of the challenges involved in framing or designing targets that are both an innovation and technological concern but with the ability to drive economic growth. Hence, states such as Russia would highlight how international institutions such as the United Nations Industrial Development Organization (UNIDO) could assist achieving economic growth through 'industrial development' and 'a science-based approach'.[63] It was a similar sentiment that the Director General of UNIDO mentioned during an address to OWG-5 saying that 'no country in history has achieved economic growth and tackled poverty without significant industrialization'.[64] Through the dialogues between states in OWG-5, a clear pattern emerged where infrastructure, industrialization, and an emphasis on the significance of economic growth is dependent on how the elements of science-based approaches can be incorporated into what was beginning to look like Goal 9 of the SDGs.

Thus, as states expressed various sentiments regarding infrastructure and industrialization at OWG-5,[65] such sentiments, it can be argued, were about a collective vision for the baseline of and conceptual outline of framing and designing SDG 9 as an element of sustainable development. Such collective vision highlights the different role for industrialization or infrastructure to the extent that they can work together to ensure that SDG 9 as a policy tool also contains the right mix of incentives for private actors who will execute the different processes and structures as part of efforts to design sustainable economic development based on the three foundations of SDG 9: innovation, infrastructure, and industry.

The use of 'industrialization' and 'infrastructure' during OWG-5 appeared to have been based on how individual states conceptualized each one as having different purposes. For example, while some states referred to the linkage of the term with investments, energy, or the need for other physical structural development,[66] some states appeared to conflate what was actually meant by the terms with their linkage to issues such as 'human rights'.[67] On other occasions, states were either using the concepts as part of an accepted linguistic pattern in that the terms were only being repeated without any solid form of proposals supporting them, and on other occasions it was evident that some developed states had little interest in promoting a precise meaning of concepts

---

[63] ibid p 5.

[64] ibid p 3. Vietnam concurred and noted that 'industrialization is important for bringing about structural change and infrastructure development should complement this', p 4.

[65] Summary of the Fifth Session OWG, p 3, Gabon on industrialization as a tool of economic transformation; p 4, Turkey on the need for industrialization to be environmentally sound; p 4, Ghana on the need for commodity-based industrialization; p 4, Zimbabwe on 'the importance of industrialization and infrastructure investments'. Because of the coupling of industrialization with infrastructure, states, as in some of the previous sessions, were cognizant of the potential positive effects of linking other areas with infrastructure and industrialization, p 3, Tunisia on infrastructure and 'enhanced agricultural practices'; p 4, Singapore on infrastructure development and 'structure of the economy'; p 4, Romania on infrastructure and human rights'; p 5, Columbia on infrastructure and 'connectivity'; p 5, Cameroon on infrastructure on energy'; while, South Africa pointed to its coordination on regional infrastructure initiatives throughout Africa, p 5.

[66] See generally n 65.

[67] See Romania (n 65).

648   SDG 9

such as 'infrastructure'. This suggests that specific problems of industrialization and infrastructural development are unique to certain states, and for others, the terms were only meant as a form of adaptation for the different proposals or perceptions of the emerging SDG during OWG-5, such as on sustainability. Nonetheless, by the end the Fifth Session of the OWG it was clear that SDG 9 was emerging as an individual SDG policy since two essential components of that goal, infrastructure and industrialization, had been discussed among states and to a certain degree with contributions from individuals or civil society.

An evolving SDG 9 also appeared in OWG-6[68] where, for instance, the interaction of innovation with technology and other incentives for R&D formed part of the discussions.[69] Perhaps this was because of the intervention by Keith Maskus, representing the University of Colorado, who set out in clear terms the necessity and gravity of innovation for an evolving SDG 9.

The following quotation, reporting the views of Maskus, captures most of the parameters on innovation in relation to technology, patents, and R&D:

> [K]ey factors in technology transfer include the economic climate, economic governance, and openness to skilled labor migration. Incentives for R&D and dissemination remain inadequate, and while emerging global networks for innovation and research hold promise for R&D and learning, they do not have high participation of poor countries ... countries with higher science and R&D capacity are better placed to benefit from technology transfer.[70]

The views of Maskus are, in part, the opposite of those of developing states who in previous sessions of the OWG embraced a general language of technology and innovation as needed in the SDGs. From the above quotation, Maskus was clearly making it known that some countries had more to lose from technology transfer, while others had more to gain.

But when one considers the fact that OWG-5 essentially formulated the concepts of 'infrastructure and industrialization' and OWG-6 developed innovation in more specific terms, and its relationship with science and technology, a clear picture of SDG 9 was finally emerging. Innovation, as broad a concept as it is, has traits that are similar to how industrialization progresses in any given society.

Yet, innovation in the context of the OWG sessions must also be seen in terms of its relationship with sustainability and/or how innovation can contribute to greener and cleaner form of technologies. Thus, for OWG-6 to frame innovation properly with the paradigm of SDG 9, one consideration would have been how much innovation is

---

[68] UN General Assembly's (UNGA) OWG on SDGs, Session 6, 9 December 2013–13 December 2013 (hereinafter 'Sixth Session of the OWG').

[69] UN General Assembly's (UNGA) OWG on SDGs, Session 6, 9 December 2013–13 December 2013, Summary of the Sixth Session of the UN General Assembly Open Working Group on Sustainable Development Goals: 9–13 December 2013 (hereinafter 'Summary of Sixth Session'), p 3.

[70] ibid p 3.

related to sustainability and the extent to which innovation can influence infrastructure and industrialization. The trend in the previous sessions of the OWGs suggest that this was the case. What had emerged in the previous six sessions of the OWG was a common theme where innovation was linked to R&D or technologies to reduce carbon emission and eventually contribute to the industrialization of society. It was perhaps no coincidence that during OWG-7,[71] states such as Croatia did not hesitate to invoke innovation as part of the need for 'new business models' to 'move to a more sustainable economy',[72] even if the overall focus of OWG-7 concerned sustainable cities. Nevertheless, one is inclined to think that innovation under the auspices of the SDGs or the way innovation was formulated during the OWG sessions will continue to be a strong mode of commodifying knowledge that relates to sustainability.

While the evidence thus far, up to OWG-7, suggests that the evolving SDG 9 centred mostly on innovation and/or infrastructure as a whole, industry, as part of the formal content of SDG 9, had not been given much attention. However, narratives on industry were occasionally implied in how states alluded to economic development or how the Business and Major Group intervened in some of the discussions. The business mechanisms that create jobs or the underlying features of commodification of innovation are part of the overall framework of what is seen as an industry. There are various industry-related activities that are attached to SDG 9 that form part of an industry. These activities may include mining, energy, manufacturing, or transport. These types of activities are tied to how sustainability or the need to reduce carbon emission promotes economic development while remaining true to the overall project of the SDGs.

Throughout the rest of the OWG sessions, aspects of SDG 9 would only be linked to a particular SDG in as much such a linkage could be seen as contributing to the drivers for economic growth or targets across other goals. However, even if an evolving SDG 9 was not the mainstay of a particular OWG session, non-state actors such as the Business and Industry Group would be present to offer observations. For example, in Session Eight of the OWG,[73] the Group raised the issue of 'the rule of law' as having an 'essential' role 'to ending poverty'.[74] Much of the discussion in the OWG sessions over economic growth and sustainability revolved around whether the specific goal and targets under consideration would promote 'inclusive economic growth'[75] or how the different SDGs can 'focus on an inclusive green economy' to generate a paradigm shift for sustainable development.[76]

---

[71] UN General Assembly's (UNGA) OWG on SDGs, Session 7, 6 January 2014–10 January 2014 (hereinafter 'Seventh Session of the OWG').

[72] UN General Assembly's (UNGA) OWG on SDGs, Session 7, 6 January 2014–10 January 2014, Summary of the Seventh Session of the UN General Assembly Open Working Group on Sustainable Development Goals: 6–10 January 2014 (hereinafter 'Summary of Seventh Session'), p 9.

[73] UN General Assembly's (UNGA) OWG on SDGs, Session 8, 3 February 2014–7 February 2014 (hereinafter 'Session Eight OWG').

[74] UN General Assembly's (UNGA) OWG on SDGs, Session 8, 3 February 2014–7 February 2014, Summary of the Eighth Session of the UN General Assembly Open Working Group on Sustainable Development Goals: 3–7 February 2014 (hereinafter 'Summary Session Eight OWG'), p 15.

[75] For example, such views were raised by the EU, see ibid p 8.

[76] Summary of OWG Second Session, p 5.

650 SDG 9

In some ways, these views and approaches were not surprising but what was striking was the level of commitment states were willing to give during their engagement in the OWG sessions by invoking concepts that were just as evasive as the diplomatic tone the state representatives used during the dialogues in the OWG sessions. The different dialogues by states were not so much in conflict but they appeared to be addressing different issues and different aspirations. However, the core issue that maintained a sense of coherence was the invocation of concepts such as 'sustainability' or 'sustainable development'.

One of the clearest and strongest objection raised by a state on the general direction and formulation of the SDGs (including the evolving SDG 9) came from Benin. That state's intervention at OWG-9[77] came at an appropriate time since the dialogue that occurred in the previous eight sessions were now being narrowed down.[78]

Benin, for the LDCs, said one-size-fits-all treatment of countries in the name of universality is not acceptable. The SDGs must be guided by the principle of Differential and Preferential Treatment for LDCs. [Benin] called for separate goals on: economic growth; industrialization; infrastructure; and employment and decent work for all. [Benin] also stressed the importance of: energy access, renewable energy, and energy efficiency; universal education; reproductive health; water and sanitation; climate change, disaster risk reduction and the need for 'building resilient societies', and means of implementation.[79]

Although Benin's statement eventually aligned with the 'universal dialect' of the OWG sessions, by raising the one-size-fits-all treatment, Benin was also concerned that meeting the targets of SDG 9 was going to be a challenge.

At this stage, dialogues in the OWG sessions were moving beyond talk to reality as the OWG began to shift into a different mode to come up with the draft SDGs (technically nineteen Focus Areas).[80] Perhaps reality had begun to sink in and other countries started to see the gravity of the 'universal approach' that the SDGs would bring about. And yet the previous MDGs certainly had some

---

[77] UN General Assembly's (UNGA) OWG on SDGs, Session 9, 3 March 2014–5 March 2014 (hereinafter 'Session Nine of the OWG').

[78] UN General Assembly's (UNGA) OWG on SDGs, Session 9, 3 March 2014–5 March 2014, Summary of the Ninth Session of the UN General Assembly Open Working Group on Sustainable Development Goals: 3–5 March 2014 (hereinafter 'Summary of Ninth Session OWG'), p 1.

[79] ibid p 3.

[80] The Ninth Session of the OWG discussed nineteen focused areas that eventually formed the seventeen SDGs. The nineteen Focus Areas: (i) poverty eradication; (ii) food security and nutrition; (iii) health and population dynamics; (iv) education; (v) gender equality and women's empowerment; (vi) water and sanitation; (vii) energy; (viii) economic growth; (ix) industrialization; (x) infrastructure; (xi) employment and decent work for all; (xii) promoting equality; (xiii) sustainable cities and human settlements; (xiv) sustainable consumption and production; (xv) climate; (xvi) marine resources, oceans, and seas; (xvii) ecosystems and biodiversity; (xviii) means of implementation; (xix) peaceful and non-violent societies, capable institutions; see Summary of Ninth Session OWG, p 2.

'universal' qualities; perhaps Benin only wanted to put on the record some level of disquiet[81] even though it was fully behind the SDG process.

One could argue that the disquiet that began to emerge as the SDGs were being finalized came about because views and voices by Member States were not adequately addressed during the previous OWG sessions. On the other hand, one could also make the argument that the interests and preferences of states and/or industry were extremely diverse and they had not come to a satisfactory or amicable understanding between them. And then there is the disparity in terms of development, where Member States are classified as 'developed', 'developing', 'Least-developed Countries (LDCs)', and so forth. Even though Member States of the OWGs had an equal voice during the sessions and their votes are equal in the UNGA, their level of economic development differs in the sense that what one state may consider a necessity to promote economic growth another state may see as unnecessary or superfluous. Thus, because states with different levels of development and economic interests had to find a solution to this point in order to make concrete proposals on the SDGs, their disquiet was set aside in the interest of a universal goal of 'sustainable development'.

To understand how Member States of the OWG eventually arrived at the seventeen SDGs, their targets, and indicators, it is useful to recount that the OWG between 2013 and 2014 had a total of thirteen meetings. Of those thirteen meetings, the first eight were essentially dialogues, and the ninth meeting was putting the ideas generated from the dialogues onto paper, the so-called Focus Areas. In OWG-10 [82] the Member States and non-state actors were able to comment on the nineteen 'Focus Areas'[83] and the 'potential targets related to each focus area'.[84] SDG 9 has roots in a major cluster: (i) 'economic growth, industrialization, infrastructure, and energy',[85] and from elements of (ii) two areas: (a & b) 'Focus Areas 9 and 10 (industrialization and infrastructure)',[86] and (c) a collection of ideas about technology and innovation that at different points were discussed in several sessions of the OWG and Focus Area 18 (means of implementation (MOI)).

The cluster of economic growth, industrialization, infrastructure, and energy, promoted by developing countries including China at OWG-10 contained two elements of SDG 9, infrastructure and industrialization.

However, as Focus Areas in OWG-10, forming SDG 9 meant that certain cluster areas would need to shift to targets and indicators and be incorporated in other Focus Areas. Thus, a number of states had different ideas:

---

[81] NGO representatives were thrown out of the 12th session of the OWG as that session was closed to them, see Open Letter to Co-Chairs and all the Member States of the OWG on SDGs, 16 June 2014, 'The Organising Partners of the Major Groups and Stakeholders'.

[82] UN General Assembly's (UNGA) OWG on SDGs, Session 10, 31 March–4 April 2014 (hereinafter 'Tenth Session of the OWG' or 'OWG-10').

[83] Summary of Ninth Session OWG, p 2.

[84] UN General Assembly's (UNGA) OWG on SDGs, Session 10, 31 March–4 April 2014, Summary of OWG-10 of the UN General Assembly Open Working Group on Sustainable Development Goals: 31 March–4 April 2014 (hereinafter 'Summary Tenth Session OWG'), p 1.

[85] ibid p 10.

[86] ibid p 5.

652   SDG 9

Tanzania, for the African Group, proposed three stand-alone goals: 'promote sustained, inclusive, and equitable economic growth'; 'promote rapid industrialization for employment and decent work', and 'promote access to affordable and reliable energy for all.' Proposed targets included focus on investment, infrastructure, and technological capability in developing countries.[87]

The above proposal essentially captured all the elements that would frame SDG 9 in its current form, 'Build resilient infrastructure, promote inclusive and sustainable industrialization and foster innovation', provided that one can interpret technological capability within the realm of innovation. Serbia wanted the consolidation of 'Focus Areas 9 and 10 (industrialization and infrastructure)',[88] and, as we now know, this proposal was taken into account.

While there had been a clear approach to industrialization and infrastructure, what had remained somewhat unclear was the aspect of innovation during OWG-10. The Focus Areas had not developed a concept of innovation and although there had been discussions on the relevance of technology, energy, the means of implementation, and a host of issues that contain aspects of innovation, as a policy tool, its rise and evolution in the OWG, was yet to be unveiled.

In OWG-11[89] it was about reaching a 'zero draft' of the SDGs[90] based on a working document with some sixteen Focus Areas as the main focal points for discussion.[91] The elements of SDG 9 had on this occasion remained in the same order as discussions in OWG-9 and OWG-10, and one could find 'infrastructure' in Focus Area 8[92] and 'industrialization' in Focus Area 9.[93] The major difference between the Eleventh and the two previous meetings were that the goals had been evolving, and what was not clarified earlier was made clear during OWG-11. Thus, fleshing out the evolving SDGs into Focus Areas that were set out in a logical manner was undertaken in this Session.

The few challenges the OWG faced had to do with 'refining the targets'[94] or 'limit[ing] their number to a manageable amount'.[95] The issue of innovation at this point also seemed elusive. At one point the issue of MOI in general for Focus Area 6 on water and sanitation was destined for absorption into the need to foster innovation based on an intervention from Iran: 'MOI could include access to multilateral financial resources for developing countries, and affordable access to *relevant knowledge,*

---

[87] ibid p 10.

[88] ibid p 5. India had similar ideas and 'expressed strong support for stand-alone goals on economic growth, industrialization and infrastructure', see ibid p 12.

[89] UN General Assembly's (UNGA) OWG on SDGs, Session 11, 5 May 2014–9 May 2014 (hereinafter 'Eleventh Session of the OWG').

[90] UN General Assembly's (UNGA) OWG on SDGs, Session 11, 5 May 2014–9 May 2014, Summary of the Eleventh Session of the UN General Assembly Open Working Group on Sustainable Development Goals: 5–9 May 2014 (hereinafter 'Summary of Eleventh OWG'), p 3.

[91] ibid p 1, noting that 'delegates commented on a list of 16 "focus areas" and approximately 150 potential targets related to each focus area'.

[92] ibid p 12.

[93] ibid p 14.

[94] ibid p 3.

[95] ibid p 3.

GOAL COMMENTARY 653

science, technologies and innovations.[96] Such intervention however, also points to the contrasting views of nations in terms of what constitutes innovation as opposed to innovation from the business perspective, as we will later see unfold.

Overall, however, states were seeing the need to further consolidate the Focus Areas and there were calls for the prototype of SDG 9—Focus Areas 8[97] and 9—to merge. 'Switzerland, also for Germany and France, encouraged merging the focus areas on economic growth and industrialization, and incorporating inclusive green growth, innovation, decent work, population and climate change in the focus area.'[98] Similarly, Lesotho, in OWG-11, 'said infrastructure should be incorporated into a goal on industrialization.'[99] The alignment of the industrialized states' views on merging the clusters to form SDG 9 is significant since those states have a potential bigger gain in the economic windfalls of 'innovation' than states who did not enjoy the same degree of industrialization (if one considers the degree of patenting by those states).

There are two observations that are worth mentioning about OWG-11 in relation to the evolving SDG 9. The first is that there was consensus on the need to consolidate elements of Focus Areas 8 and 9 and that view had the support of a number of states. The second observation is that the titles of the Focus Areas were poorly drafted as they had areas that clearly belonged to other Focus Areas. Moreover, the Focus Areas that OWG-11 discussed seemed to have deviated from the views of states during some of the previous sessions. Take, for example, 'Focus Area 9. Industrialization and Promoting Equality Among Nations.'[100] For some states, such as Japan, the wording was clearly not specific enough: 'the issue of equality at all levels is important for the SDGs, but ... the concept should [not] be merged with industrialization.'[101] Focusing on the concepts of infrastructure and industrialization provides greater insights into the building blocks of SDG 9 and how negotiating skills would accelerate the desire for an outcome to satisfy all parties. Some states during OWG-11 tried to separate the specific targets or how specific zero draft goals were framed—especially Focus Areas 8 and 9 which, *inter alia*, concerned infrastructure and industrialization.

The shift from zero draft to full proposal was only evident at OWG-12,[102] where the proposed SDG 9 under the title 'Promote sustainable industrialization'[103] was about to mature into a fully fledged SDG. At this stage, there were seventeen proposed goals, consisting of the familiar issues from the MDGs and newer issues that emanated from the SDG discussions. The latter include industrialization and infrastructure. These two pillars clearly have affinity with what has been seen as 'development' in the MDGs and

---

[96] ibid p 11 (emphasis added).

[97] This carried the title: 'Economic Growth, Employment and Infrastructure', ibid p 12.

[98] ibid p 13.

[99] ibid p 12. See also, Brazil on 'combining infrastructure with industrialization', ibid p 13; Tunisia, on 'infrastructure also could be linked with industrialization', ibid p 13.

[100] ibid p 14.

[101] ibid p 14.

[102] UN General Assembly's (UNGA) OWG on SDGs, Session 12, 16 June 2014–20 June 2014 (hereinafter 'Twelfth Session of the OWG').

[103] UN General Assembly's (UNGA) OWG on SDGs, Session 12, 16 June 2014–20 June 2014, Summary of the Twelfth Session of the UN General Assembly Open Working Group on Sustainable Development Goals: 16–20 June 2014 (hereinafter 'Summary of the Twelfth OWG'), p 6.

654   SDG 9

the concept of 'development' in the SDGs. It was now a matter of integrating 'sustainable' as concept into that evolving SDG 9, and the role of 'innovation' was crucial to complete the three-dimensional Goal 9.[104]

The negotiations and the draft SDG 9 were now in full operational mode. A series of 'informal-informal consultations' during OWG-12 was aimed at 'merging goal areas and views on the 17 goal headings contained in the zero draft'[105] and essentially to refine and create a *tighter* final set of proposals. The make-up of the Proposed SDG 9 during OWG-12, however, still did not impress a number of states.[106]

Interestingly, it was at OWG-12 that the concept of innovation[107] gradually emerged before finally finding a home in the adopted version of SDG 9. One might be inclined to think that a refined concept of innovation or the elements that are associated with innovation such as R&D had had a separate preparatory commission and were injected overnight prior to OWG-12. Furthermore, one could argue that the OWG made a genuine attempt to amalgamate and sharpen a concept of innovation to be linked with 'infrastructure and industrialization'. Regardless of the primary origins of innovation, by OWG-12 it had become a concept, primed to form part of SDG 9 in the SDGs.

The Summary Report made note of the fact that division still permeated the OWG 'on whether SDG 9 should be a stand-alone goal or merged with Goal 8. Some wanted a stronger focus on industrialization'[108] while 'others thought the industrialization targets could be incorporated into Goal 12' including 'a proposal to include the transfer of environmentally sound technologies in the title'.[109] Those developments were not a surprise since they existed throughout the entire OWG sessions, hence what is relevant was that a concrete goal emerged in the form of a 'Proposed SDG 9' and it was almost similar to the current SDG 9.

Given that this chapter relies on the Summary Reports produced in the Earth Negotiations Bulletin for the discussions and what took place during the OWG sessions to make observations, some of them may contain limitations compared to what others may have drawn elsewhere in this book. But it is important to show how the negotiations and counter-negotiations progresses and in Table 9.1, a condensed and redacted version of the Proposed SDG 9—considered at OWG-12 as presented in the Summary Report—is shown.[110] The comment section in the table is my observations.

Table 9.1 represents the 'informal discussions on the zero draft'[111] where the proposal for SDG 9 was part of the newer issues in the SDGs. However, there were other

---

[104] But see infra n 106.

[105] Summary of the Twelfth OWG, p 3.

[106] ibid p 3: 'Germany, also for France and Switzerland, said the goals on sustainable economic growth and industrialization lacked a vision of inclusive and environmentally friendly growth, as each goal must reflect a 'three-dimensional' approach to sustainable development', ibid p 3.

[107] ibid p 6, Proposed Goal 9.8.

[108] ibid p 6.

[109] ibid p 6.

[110] ibid pp 6–7.

[111] ibid p 4.

GOAL COMMENTARY   655

Table 9.1 Showing Proposed SDG 9—considered at OWG-12

Goal #	Target/Indicator	Comment
9.1	'achieve structural transformation of economies towards progressively higher levels of productivity in all sectors and activities'	
9.2	'respect national policy space and national circumstances for industrial development, particularly in developing countries'	
9.3	'ensure a conducive policy environment, including encouragement of industrial entrepreneurship and enterprise formation with inclusion of micro-and SMEs.'	
9.4	'significantly raise industry's share of employment and GDP in line national strategies, including doubling manufacturing's share in LDCs by 2030.'	
9.5	'increase industrial diversification in developing countries, including through enhanced domestic processing of raw materials and commodities and through new product development.'	
9.6	'support the integration of developing country industrial enterprises, particularly in Africa and LDCs, into regional and global value chains.'	
9.7	'create decent industrial sector jobs and promote job-rich industrial development.'	
9.8	'promote industrial research, development and innovation, including raising the ratio of research and development (R&D) workers per one million people by x% and the share of R&D spending in GDP by y%.'	
9.9	'upgrade the technological capabilities of industrial sectors in developing countries, including in middle income countries, and improve industrial resource efficiency by accelerating the development, transfer and adoption of environmentally sound technologies and processes.'	This target specifically addresses 'green innovation' and/ or 'carbon emission' and form part of the notion of 'innovation' in the final version of SDG 9.
9.10	'promote indigenous technology development and the growth of domestic innovation in developing countries.'	
9.11	'by 2030 retrofit x% of existing industries with clean technologies and environmentally sound industrial processes to achieve y% energy and z% resource-efficiency improvement, with all countries taking action, developed countries taking the lead and developing countries following a similar pattern taking into account their development needs and capabilities.'	This target also addresses reducing carbon emission and green technologies and therefore fulfil the idea or notion of 'sustainability'.

(continued)

656 SDG 9

Table 9.1 Continued

Goal #	Target/Indicator	Comment
9.12	'ensure small-scale industrial producers have affordable access to credit and financial services.'	
Further new targets proposed for inclusion in SDG 9	1. 'reduce significantly the levels of contamination of industries in all sectors, while achieving high production levels across productive sectors in all countries, in harmony with nature, in context of the respect, restoration, and regeneration of ecosystems; and 2. by 2030 implement plans and measures to strengthen industrialization in all sectors, in harmony with nature, including environmentally sound technologies.'	

drafts circulating that came out of other 'informal-informal consultations'[112] which some delegates felt betrayed by or did them a 'disservice'.[113]

The informal discussions, however, concerned the consolidation of goals and had reduced the number to fifteen.[114] The informal-informal consultations framed the Proposed SDG 9 to 'promote inclusive and sustainable industrialization',[115] yet it was also a contentious proposal in the sense that states had problems with some of the targets similar to those in the zero draft proposal.

The interesting factor, however, about the informal-informal consultations proposal for SDG 9 was the fact that some delegates were now calling for the addition of 'innovation' to Goal 9.[116] One of the suggestions from the informal-informal consultations was for the title of SDG 9 to read 'Build infrastructure and promote inclusive and sustainable industrialization and innovation'.[117] This was a significant development as we will later see; the proposal helped to change and refine the corpus of SDG 9 with a similar title to the one that came from the informal discussions. But more importantly, it was the first time that the elusive concept of innovation which had dogged the OWG sessions was given full association with infrastructure and industrialization.

Whether or not this was a political-diplomatic game[118] or significant effort during the informal-informal consultations by non-state actors, two things emerged. First, some

---

[112] ibid p 16.
[113] ibid p 16.
[114] ibid p 16.
[115] ibid p 17.
[116] ibid p 17.
[117] ibid p 17.
[118] For general works on game theory for instance in international negotiations see generally, C Bjola, 'Using Momentum Analysis to Explain and Forecast the Outcome of International Negotiations' (2015) 20 International Negotiation 319–49; JK Sebenius, 'Negotiation Arithmetic: Adding and Subtracting Issues and Parties' (1983) 37 International Organization 281–316; RD Putman, 'Diplomacy and Domestic Politics: The Logic of Two-Level Games' (1988) 42 International Organization 427–60.

states were not happy as they felt betrayed (the fact that some discussions and proposals actually took place without their input), and secondly, innovation as such—the nucleus of SDG 9—was injected into a redesigned SDG 9 as part of the newer issues of the SDGs.

The turn to innovation in SDG 9 at that stage as an additional part to complement infrastructure and industrialization was strategic. Although some delegates were surprised at the outcome of the informal-informal consultations, and the now-reduced fifteen proposed Goals, the delegates had to embrace such 'strategic outcomes'. Thus, it was also an opportunity for delegates to make a connection with what had already been addressed in different forms throughout the entire OWG sessions. Thus, such a strategic outcome was the fact that science, technology, R&D, technology transfer, and know-how are all elements that comprise the concept of innovation.

By the summer of 2014, the OWG sessions had reached their zenith and delegates had to produce a document for the UNGA with final proposals for the SDGs. OWG-13 [119] was therefore the last opportunity to deliver on the tasks they were given. By 19 July 2014, the OWG adopted the 'Proposal of the Open Working Group for Sustainable Development Goals' [120] a document containing '17 goals and 169 targets (including 62 targets on means of implementation'. [121] Each of the OWG sessions had in various ways addressed some of the newer issues in the SDGs and each of those sessions had touched upon different aspects of SDG 9, both formally and informally, or indirectly when linking with other issues and goals during the dialogues and negotiations in the OWG sessions.

Yet, of the three major components of SDG 9 'industry, infrastructure, and innovation', the latter was conceptualized formally in OWG-12, and formally polished and presented in OWG-13: 'Proposed SDG 9. Build resilient infrastructure, promote inclusive and sustainable industrialization and foster innovation'. [122] This proposal essentially capitalized on a few factors that were already present in the OWG sessions but also on classic negotiation tactics. There are however two factors worth pointing out.

The first is issue framing; that is, where the relevance of an issue that has universal support and appeals to both Member States and non-state actors is based on existing knowledge and input. This was evident in how the OWG handled matters relating to infrastructure and industrialization in the different sessions. The second factor relates to negotiation tactics where it is possible to frame an issue that is 'difficult' as part of an existing issue with universal support such as infrastructure and industrialization.

Hence, while informal-informal consultations sharpened the notion of innovation and injected the concept in the last-minute dialogues of the OWG, its relevance should be seen in how it was linked to the existing issues with universal support, infrastructure

---

[119] UN General Assembly's (UNGA) OWG on SDGs, Session 13, 14 July–19 July 2014 (hereinafter 'Thirteenth Session of the OWG').

[120] UN General Assembly's (UNGA) OWG on SDGs, Session 13, 14 July–19 July 2014, Summary of the Thirteenth Session of the UN General Assembly Open Working Group on Sustainable Development Goals: 14–19 July 2014 (hereinafter 'Summary of Thirteenth OWG'), p 1.

[121] ibid p 1.

[122] ibid p 11.

658   SDG 9

and industrialization. Such an approach would mitigate the need for further negotiation but also help to provide assurances that the linking of the issue was part of the overall goal on the inclusive and sustainable agenda for economic growth.

Table 9.2, based on the Summary Report of OWG-13, shows the targets of SDG 9 in condensed form.

The above discussion on the role of states in the OWG is based primarily on secondary reporting on the matter, and hence my assessment may have limitations. But such limitations are only to the extent that the secondary reporting are not official summaries produced by UN bodies *per se*. Nonetheless, other commentators who have also examined the OWG outcome document have observed and concluded that, *inter alia*, the proposals produced in the OWG sessions 'largely converges [sic] with many of the reports produced by other UN processes'.[123] This is also a fair assessment based on the examination of other secondary analyses of the OWG outcome document.[124]

The proposal and drafting stage of the SDGs and their eventual formation in the OWG sessions took over a year, and while some of the SDGs were familiar due to their association with the MDGs, others were so-called newer issues. SDG 9 on industry, infrastructure, and innovation has been one of those newer issues. The premise and different clusters of SDG 9 are sound and reasonable, but at the same time, its final negotiation and outcome was a diplomatic *coup d'état*, especially as far as the final cluster of 'innovation' is concerned. This is because despite its evident importance throughout the OWG sessions, 'innovation' as a concept was interpreted in various forms or alluded to without any coherent approach.

It was only in OWG-12 that a coherent formulation of innovation was introduced, even then to the dismay of some Member States. Yet, the most overlooked aspect of the formulation and introduction of innovation to the dialogues and eventually incorporation into SDG 9 is its relationship with private enterprise. In other words, perhaps, innovation was all along the major 'goal' of SDG 9 and its last-minute introduction in a sharpened state was to reflect and avoid any suggestions in that direction.

C. Non-state Actors or 'Major Groups'

Non-state actors in the OWG process at the UN have been and still continue to be referred to by the UN machinery as 'Major Groups'. This commentary on SDG 9 will sometime refer to 'Major Groups'.[125] However, the primary ontological term in this

---

[123] D Bhattacharya and others, 'A Commentary on the Final Outcome Document of the Open Working Group on SDGs' (2014) 34 The SAIS Review of International Affairs 165–77, 175.

[124] See, eg, O Spijkers and A Honniball, 'Developing Global Participation (2): Shaping the Sustainable Development Goals' (2015) 17 International Community Law Review 251–96, 285–87 (discussing the working and outcomes of the OWGs).

[125] The concept of 'Major Groups' as such is in one way synonymous with non-state actors or non-governmental organizations, and hence, the concept arose on a number of occasions in the Open Working Group sessions on the SDGs. The concept, however, has roots in the 1992 Agenda 21 document which, among other things, points out that 'broad public participation in decision-making' where individuals, groups, and organizations can contribute

GOAL COMMENTARY 659

Table 9.2 Proposed SDG 9—considered at OWG-13[†]

Proposed SDG 9. Build resilient infrastructure, promote inclusive and sustainable industrialization and foster innovation

Target #	Proposed targets	*Final Targets*[§]
9.1	'(infrastructure) in the final draft is the result of merging two targets from the zero draft, one on quality, reliable, sustainable and resilient infrastructure and one on regional and trans-border infrastructure.'	'develop quality, reliable, sustainable and resilient infrastructure, including regional and trans-border infrastructure, to support economic development and human well-being, with a focus on affordable and equitable access for all'
9.2	'(sustainable industrialization)'[*]	'promote inclusive and sustainable industrialization, and by 2030 raise significantly industry's share of employment and GDP in line with national circumstances, and double its share in LDCs'
9.3	'(on access to financial services)'	'increase the access of small-scale industrial and other enterprises, particularly in developing countries, to financial services including affordable credit and their integration into value chains and markets'
9.4	'(sustainable industrialization)'	'by 2030 upgrade infrastructure and retrofit industries to make them sustainable, with increased resource use efficiency and greater adoption of clean and environmentally sound technologies and industrial processes, all countries taking action in accordance with their respective capabilities'
9.5	'(upgrading technology)'[♦]	'enhance scientific research, upgrade the technological capabilities of industrial sectors in all countries, particularly developing countries, including by 2030 encouraging innovation and increasing the number of R&D workers per one million people by x% and public and private R&D spending'
9.a (MOI)	'(sustainable infrastructure development in developing countries)'	'facilitate sustainable and resilient infrastructure development in developing countries through enhanced financial, technological and technical support to African countries, LDCs, LLDCs and SIDS'
9.b (MOI)	'(domestic technology development and innovation)'[♠]	'support domestic technology development, research and innovation in developing countries including by ensuring a conducive policy environment for *inter alia*, industrial diversification and value addition to commodities'
9.c (MOI)	'(ICT access)'[♥]	'significantly increase access to ICT and strive to provide universal and affordable access to internet in LDCs by 2020'

† ibid p 11–12.

[*] This target would continue to be contentious with 'many delegations' calling for its removal; see Summary of Thirteenth OWG (n 120) p 11.

[♦] This was one of rare moments where there was a new addition, as this target was not in the 'revised zero draft' discussed in the Twelfth Session of the OWG; see Summary of Thirteenth OWG (n 120) p 12.

[♠] This target was also a late addition and 'was not in the revised draft and was added as "promote indigenous technology development and innovation in developing countries"'; see Summary of Thirteenth OWG (n 120) p 12.

[♥] This was another late addition and 'initially it called for access to telecommunications services and providing 100% access to the internet in LDCs by 2020'; see Summary of Thirteenth OWG (n 120) p 12.

660   SDG 9

section of the commentary is 'non-state actors' and/or on other occasions, a distinction is drawn among three primary non-state actors. Definitional aspects of 'Major Groups' as per the UN machinery, has been detailed earlier,[126] and thus the discussion here points to the three sets of non-state actors that primarily contributed to aspects of SDG 9.

During the development phase of the SDGs, the UN reported that more than 1 million 'voices' contributed to the conceptualization of the goals.[127] The Million Voices Report, in the general scheme of things, represents the input, that is the participation, of the 'peoples' through various forms of outreach, global conversation, and consultation. One key highlight of the Million Voices Report is the fact that the need for technological innovation was essential in order to develop a new framework for the SDGs: 'There was also broad agreement to increase support for R&D to drive technological innovation and support clean energy technologies',[128] the report said. This synthesis by the Million Voices Report, reflecting the voices of ordinary people, indicates the centrality of how innovation as part of the broader goal of industry, infrastructure, and innovation has support from a 'bottom-up' perspective.

The design and execution of the Million Voices Report is a separate matter, however innovation gradually began to emanate within the SDGs. The same bottom-up approach to the other two components of SDG 9, industry and infrastructure, was also reflected in the Million Voices Report. For industry, it was evident from the Million Voices Report that the bulk of the concerns were from developing countries, and concerned areas such as agriculture, manufacturing, and job security.

Additionally, the corporate social responsibility of transnational corporations and the effect of trading agreements were also highlighted. Hence, for African 'peoples' it was, as per the Million Voices Report, the need 'for increased transparency in contractual arrangements with multinational companies in the industry' for natural resources.[129] And, similarly, Indonesian people had concerns over the protection of domestic goods 'with an emphasis on reducing or recalibrating Free Trade Agreements to protect small or traditional industry, particularly farmers and fishermen'.[130] These examples show how the input of the people also reflect certain concerns that are unique to their geographic locales.

But perhaps, the most resonant aspect of the 'voices' of the people had to do with the extractive industry, mining, and the linkages of all three aspects of sustainable

---

to sustainable development; see Agenda 21, ch 23, and further at para 38.42 noting: 'Non-governmental organizations and major groups are important partners in the implementation of Agenda 21. Relevant non-governmental organizations, including the scientific community, the private sector and women's group, should be given opportunities to make their contributions and establish appropriate relationships with the United Nations system.' United Nations Conference on Environment and Development, Rio de Janeiro, Brazil 3–14 June 1992, Agenda 21.

[126] Agenda 21, para 38.42.
[127] 'A Million Voices: The World We Want' (United Nations Development Group, December 2013) (hereinafter 'UN Million Voices Report').
[128] ibid 121.
[129] ibid 57.
[130] ibid 73.

development: the economic, the social, and the environmental. It was a concern for the voices representing countries such as Bangladesh, Tanzania, Mozambique, Uganda, and Malawi for 'clear plans for investing the benefits from extractive industries into national human capital and infrastructure'.[131] The Million Voices Report framed the problems with the extractive industry, as per the voices of the people, as one with 'limited ability' to create jobs,[132] yet painted mining as one of the big potential growth industries for developing countries. 'Nevertheless, the growth of extractive industries can provide opportunities to low-income countries to raise much-needed resources which they can invest in human development.'[133] These stark contrasting views, developing countries' pessimism regarding mining's capability to help the populace and the optimistic framing of the potential of the extractive industries by the authors of the Million Voices Report, show the general division of views regarding sustainable development as a concept. It was also evident that the bulk of the concern of people from developing countries relates to infrastructure development, ranging from education facilities, roads, rail, electricity, telecommunications, energy, and health facilities. And while the infrastructure concerns were universal, they were expressed in greater number by people from Africa.[134]

The Million Voices Report helped to demonstrate how a bottom-up approach or concerns about industry, infrastructure, and innovation had support from the peoples of the world. This helped to establish the SDGs and SDG 9 in particular as universal goals for the benefit of mankind. Although the voices of the people are important, it is also fair to say that the major actors in the conceptualization of the SDGs can be narrowed down to three types: (i) international organizations; (ii) transnational corporations; and (iii) civil society (NGOs). The first session of the OWG would give an insight into how the role of different non-state actors would participate in the drafting and negotiations of the SDGs.

For the different non-state actors who represented different aspects of SDG 9, it was their knowledge and expertise that would help guide how the OWG formulated SDG 9 into a policy tool.[135] Thus, the role of non-state actors during the drafting and

---

[131] ibid 57.

[132] ibid 127.

[133] ibid. The Million Voices Report, however, highlighted the recommendation from the 'people': 'Therefore, participants recommended linking extractive sectors with other sectors; using fiscal revenues from extractive industries to support the development of employment-intensive sectors; and slowing down the extraction of non-renewable mineral resources on both the production and consumption side by using taxes and eliminating consumption benefits', ibid.

[134] ibid 49.

[135] Major Groups would enjoy the privilege of meeting with Co-Chairs of the OWG in sessions prior the opening of each formal session, and in those sessions, Major Groups would often refine and/or made their positions clearer as during formal sessions they did not technically have the floor. For one particular session, when the proposed SDGs were being fine-tuned into 'Focus Areas', the Major Groups essentially contributed to the document the same way as states would, see Major Groups and Other Stakeholders Dialogue with the Co-Chairs on SDGs, 2 April 2014: 3:00–4:30; Conference Room 1, UNHQ, Compilation Document. Major groups relating to Goal 9 as such that were present at this session were, for the cluster of 'Economic Growth', Business & Industry, and NGOs, p 10, promoting, inter alia, 'policies to encourage innovation, including research, development, deployment and diffusion of new technologies', p 11; for the cluster of 'Industrialization', NGOs, especially highlighting the importance of 'technology development and innovation in developing countries by addressing the constraints imposed by intellectual property rights rules in the World Trade Agreement TRIPS Agreement as well as through both Free

negotiations was a show of the power and reach of epistemic forces in the global policy-setting arena. During the preparatory meetings of the OWG and the OWG sessions, the presence of various epistemic forces[136] would help to create a narrative along the three pillars of sustainability in addition to that on 'technological know-how'. For example, in OWG-1,[137] the role of different epistemic communities in the negotiations was acknowledge in the Final Summary Report of OWG Session 1.[138]

The Final Summary Report of Session 1 grouped the different epistemic forces as 'The Business and Industry, Local Authorities and Scientific and Technology Community Major Groups'.[139] These major groupings had a role in as much as how SDG 9 would evolve even if the role of epistemic forces in the OWG Sessions was largely to offer 'advice and support'.[140] Nonetheless, the Final Summary Report of OWG Session 1 notes that the Business and Industry, Local Authorities, and Scientific and Technology Community Major Groups were concerned with, *inter alia*, 'considering technological know-how; and reflecting economic circumstances'.[141] This early consideration of technological know-how and the interrelationship with economic matters would be further stressed during the next OWG Sessions, and by the final OWG Session the notion of innovation and/or harnessing digital technologies would form a concrete part of SDG 9.

The engagement of the different non-state actors in the SDGs shared a collective desire for action that was in part based on how specific epistemic knowledge and expertise would help design a policy goal that can lead to tangible results. From a more formal theoretical perspective, some scholars have referred to such cooperation as a form of 'reconciling supply of scientific information with users' demands'[142] in order to be used by decision-makers.[143] Naturally, this is only one formal view as there are many others that capture the sentiment of cooperation between scientific groups and policy-makers, but by injecting the idea of scientific information with user demands here it is possible to see how the different major groupings (that is, non-state actors) contributed to the negotiations and drafting of SDG 9 which is itself a complex amalgamation of

---

Trade Agreement's and Bilateral Investment Treaties', p 12. Interestingly, out of the same meeting, and as presented in the 'Cluster Statements Summary Document', it was the 'Women and NGOs' that focused on the importance of infrastructure, see Cluster 4: Infrastructure (FA10), Cluster Statement Summary Document, p 3.

[136] I am using the term 'epistemic forces/community' to generally refer to knowledge producers, but for discussion on the term see Haas (n 45).

[137] UN General Assembly's (UNGA) OWG on SDGs, Session 1, 14 March 2013–15 March 2013.

[138] Summary of the First Session of the UN General Assembly Open Working Group on Sustainable Development Goals: 13–15 March 2013 (2013) 32 Earth Negotiations Bulletin 1–9 (hereinafter Final Summary Report of OWG Session 1').

[139] ibid p 6.

[140] My usage of advice and support here is based on a reconstruction of epistemic communities by Haas (n 45).

[141] Final Summary Report of OWG Session 1, p 6.

[142] E McNie, 'Reconciling the Supply of Scientific Information with User Demands: An Analysis of the Problem and Review of the Literature' (2007) 10 Environmental Science & Policy 17–38, 18. See also, L van Kerkhoff and Louis Lebel, 'Linking Knowledge and Action for Sustainable Development' (2006) 31 Annual Review of Environment and Resources 445–77.

[143] McNie (n 143).

interests and preferences of myriad epistemic forces and business networks working in tandem with states.

The complexity of SDG 9 can be garnered from its very design which is an amalgamation of business preferences (industry), business interests (innovation), business desires (infrastructure), and the ideals of businesses (resilience). From this perspective then, user demands are those of businesses—the private generators of wealth creation through economic operations in a given society. On the other hand, one could make the argument that the role of scientific information further strengthens business user demands as scientific information gathered for innovation (R&D), how to reduce carbon emissions (resilient), and reconciling these with sustainability and development poses challenges for states (policy-makers). Yet drafting the SDGs, from conception to (eventual) realization, have been a collective action where participation, integration, learning, and negotiation by the different actors contribute towards their evolution and the idea of sustainable development.[144]

During the drafting and negotiations of the SDGs, different non-state actors or epistemic forces such as those collectively discussed further below (international organizations, transnational corporations, and civil society including NGOs) all contributed their expertise, scientific knowledge, preferences, and interests[145] (including to matters that served as basis for the formation of SDG 9). The entire process which saw the amalgamation of ideas and information to realize the SDGs is in itself a great achievement but the variety of actors and their expertise or preferences also suggest that SDG 9 could potentially gravitate towards wealth maximization for the actors who will actually develop and implement SDG 9 and its targets. In other words, SDG 9 is heavily based on norms and practices of private enterprise and other economic actors in a society. It is private enterprise and their knowledge and expertise that is useful for the policy formation process of SDG 9, in this instance. They supply the knowledge and are the actual users of such knowledge and will in turn be the main economic actors to benefit from SDG 9. So, their vested interested must be fully compatible with how SDG 9 emerges as a global norm through the SDGs.

But it is more useful to consider in greater detail how the different non-state actors engage in the policy formation and knowledge input of the SDGs, in particular SDG 9. It is useful to consider who they were, what their interests and preferences were, how much expertise they contributed, and how their contribution shaped the design of SDG 9. By looking at the three categories of non-state actors during the formation of the SDGs, with particular emphasis on SDG 9, their role and expertise should give further

---

[144] On this latter argument see generally, Kerkhoff and Lebel (n 143).

[145] See M Kamau and others, *Transforming Multilateral Diplomacy: The Inside Story of the Sustainable Development Goals* (Routledge 2018) 161–62 noting that the Co-Chairs of OWG sessions would convene early morning dialogues with Major Groups, which mirrored official negotiations and the same questions presented to states were also answered by Major Groups and 'provided contributions to the same document' that states would negotiate during the formal OWG sessions.

insight into the extent they were able to influence states vis-à-vis the OWG to draft and design the SDGs in a certain way. Furthermore, the relationship that the different non-state actors had with each other should be helpful in understanding whether their efforts were a form of 'collective action' or whether there were tensions between them. This is important since any apparent findings to the contrary would suggest that there were greater competing forces or ideals in SDG 9 and the characteristics of the individual non-state actors were more important as opposed to the common desire for sustainable development.

The overall process on the formulation and eventual proposals for the SDGs involved dozens of non-state actors or 'Major Groups'.[146] For the purposes of the rest of the discussion below, those Major Groups are classified in three types: (i) international organizations; (ii) transnational corporations; and (iii) civil society (NGOs). This classification helps focus on contributions that were related specifically to the evolving Goal 9 in the OWG sessions. The classification into three types in the rest of the discussion here is based on a hierarchical structure where traditional intergovernmental and other lead international organizations are seen as major contributors to global policy-making,[147] followed by transnational corporations (and derivatives) that exercise influence due to their economic power,[148] and civil society (including smaller NGOs) that lend legitimacy and expertise to the system of global policy-making.[149]

1. International Non-governmental Organizations (INGOs) and Intergovernmental Organizations (IGOs)

International organizations[150] are at the beating heart of international relations, and those institutions, whether designed by states, such as international intergovernmental organizations (IGOs), or those designed and evolved by non-state actors such as international non-governmental organizations (INGOs) promoting a specific cause or issue, are often seen as part of the transformation in international governance and relations.[151] Whether or not states delegate or participate in international diplomacy as a formal or informal process through international organizations, the role of international organizations has significantly expanded to the point that some scholars have

---

[146] See also n 136. Formally, the Major Groups related to the SDGs process are: Indigenous Peoples; Local Authorities; NGOs; Workers and Trade; Women; Science and Technology; Business and Industry; Global Task Force; Global Partnership for Sustainable Development Goals; Technology Divides; Human Rights for All Post-2015; Children & Youth. These Major Groups made statements and presentations during the various OWG sessions.

[147] See also Haas (n 45); Kamau and others (n 146).

[148] Here my thoughts are for example on custodian organizations such as the World Bank for parts of SDG 9.

[149] Haas (n 45).

[150] See further below in this commentary where I discuss the 'tier classifications' of custodian agencies.

[151] Formally, these lines of arguments are much proliferated in the academic literature, but see generally, R Cox and HK Jacobson, *The Anatomy of Influence: Decision Making in International Organizations* (Yale University Press 1973); K Abbott and D Snidal, 'Why States Act Through Formal International Organizations' (1998) 42 Journal of Conflict Resolution 3–32.

argued that international organizations are law-makers.[152] This is a significant observation, and that argument, combined with those on 'regime complexity', is a reminder of the norms and governance structures that international organizations help to create at the global level.[153]

Although the SDG processes included a variety of non-state actors, the most visible of these actors were international organizations (IGOs and INGOs). Through their co-ordination and facilitation they helped other actors in the SDG processes to frame and deliver the SDG proposals. The form and process that international organizations took in the SDG process also included acting as advisors or even experts on behalf of some Member States. The role international organizations had at the OWG sessions, for example, suggests that what was at stake in the SDGs was too complex for state actors alone to coordinate and implement, and as such there was the need for international organizations to inject themselves in the mechanisms of global coordination and administration of the negotiating process of the SDGs.

International organizations (both types, IGOs and INGOs) are generally co-ordinators and leaders in multilateral negotiations or issues implementation. On the one hand, IGOs lead or facilitate multilateral negotiations, such as on chemical weapons or international insolvency laws,[154] or they take the lead on multilateral treaty negotiations.[155] On the other, international organizations such as the International Union for Conservation of Nature and Natural Resources (IUCN) facilitate and coordinate specific issues.[156] The SDG process saw a flurry of activities where dozens of different types of international organizations gave statements on the evolving goals.

While the UN and various designated UN Agencies were heavily influential (and continue to lead) on the coordination of the SDGs process, acting as secretariat, there have been other international organizations that actively supported and continue to play supportive role for the SDGs. These international organizations including the Organisation for Economic Co-operation and Development (OECD), the European Union (EU), the international IDEA (Institute for Democracy and Electoral Assistance), the Inter-Parliamentary Union,[157] and others. For example, the UN Secretary General, the UN Development Programme (UNDP), World Bank, International Monetary Fund (IMF), WTO, and other UN Agencies, contributed, *inter alia*, to the 'technical

---

[152] See the classic work of J Alvarez, *International Organizations as Law-Makers* (OUP 2005); a more recent work is spot on in its analysis, see S Block-Lieb and T Halliday, *Global Lawmakers: International Organizations in the Crafting of World Markets* (CUP 2017).

[153] For arguments on regime complexity see generally, K Abbot, 'The Transnational Regime Complex for Climate Change' (2012) 30 Environmental Planning Governance Policy 571–90.

[154] The Organisation for the Prohibition of Chemical Weapons (OPCW) is one such IGO, and for matters discussing insolvency law and law-making at the international level see Block-Lieb and Halliday (n 153).

[155] See Alvarez (n 153).

[156] At the First Session of the OWG, IUCN, highlighted the need for 'a nature-based solutions approach, since nature is critical for access to economic and social development', see Final Summary Report of OWG Session 1 (n 139) p 7.

[157] At the First Session of the OWG, the IPU lent its voice and support for achieving the SDGs, ibid.

666 SDG 9

knowledge to the OWG members as they embarked on the stocktaking process'.[158] Through these efforts and other nodes of administration of the SDG process especially at the OWG sessions international organizations extended their leverage in the global policy-making process.

Such leverage, arguably, is part of how the transformation of sustainable governance has emerged and will continue to play a prominent role in international governance for decades beyond 2030. This growing role in the international system will overlap with those of other non-state actors such as civil society as such or transnational corporations (as discussed in the next two examples 2 and 3) and will have analogies with those of states in the international policy-making arena.[159] This overlap and analogy with states will of course raise a different set of questions as to whether international organizations are accountable or have a legitimate mandate.[160] Such questions are already prevalent in the literature, however it is worth pointing out that international organizations that are currently active in the global system of climate change and environmental politics, especially within the realm of the SDGs, do have a certain amount of legitimacy due to their policy mandates or expertise.

International intergovernmental organizations with some amount of legitimacy due to their policy mandates include those which perform both facilitation, administration, and coordination of climate change polices and other offshoots of environmental protection are good examples. These include the United Nations Framework Convention on Climate Change 1992 (UNFCCC),[161] the UNDP, the United Nations Environment Programme (UNEP), UN Habitat, and the Food and Agricultural Organization (FAO). Their legitimacy, one could argue, stems from their role as coordinators, custodians, and policy experts, and therefore their legitimacy has been strengthened by the expansion of issues in global environmental governance and to the extent that new issues from the SDGs are vital to their function in the international system.

At the same time, INGOs could equally argue that those very same new issues and the need for additional monitoring of IGOs requires them to be more active in the international system. Thus, on both sides of the equation, the SDGs and the multimodal complexities that SDG 9 presents for international environmental governance will always raise the issue of legitimacy. However, given that the clear objective is to achieve sustainable economic growth, it is increasingly clear that international organizations are not merely coordinators, facilitators, or advisers, but rather, international organizations are relevant actors that seek to transform international governance through the SDGs.

The relevance of international organizations to the international system of governance and in particular for sustainable development is formally supported by the relevant provisions in the UN Charter. According to article 71 of the Charter, the Economic

---

[158] Kamau and others, *Transforming Multilateral Diplomacy* (n 146) 159.

[159] For similar arguments in relation to the overlapping functions see J Hadden, *Networks in Contention: The Divisive Politics of Climate Change* (CUP 2015).

[160] See also, S Bernstein, 'Legitimacy in Global Environmental Governance' (2005) 1 Journal of International Law and International Relations 139–66; O Widerberg and P Pattberg, 'Accountability Challenges in the Transnational Regime Complex for Climate change' (2017) 34 Review of Policy Research 68–87.

[161] United Nations Framework Convention on Climate Change 1992, 1771 UNTS 107.

and Social Council (ECOSOC) can 'make suitable arrangements for consultations with non-governmental organizations which are concerned with matters within its competence'.[162] INGOs themselves can be credited for the UN Charter's recognition and validation of their role in the international policy-making and governance system through 'consultations'.[163] Based on article 71 of the UN Charter, ECOSOC can facilitate NGOs to submit written communications and other forms of input in international negotiations.[164] Thus, it is the formal structure of article 71 which gives NGOs a voice at the table of international negotiations, especially those facilitated by the UN System, which makes INGOs analogous entities to states in international negotiations and conferences.[165]

While there are some clear affinities between the two types of international organizations identified in this section, the emergence of the SDGs and the OWG negotiation sessions for their proposal were ultimately led by states, and in that context, states will continue to be at the forefront of how global policy-making is conducted, but will do so with the input, contribution, and advice from international organizations. This parallel track of global policy-making will lead to further transformation of the international governance systems and in principle raise competition for rule-making in other areas at the global level or in the context of the SDGs' 'sustainability standards'.[166] These interactions and competition for rule-making can help the dynamic relationship that currently exists with different non-state actors and the extent to which meta-governance/meta relationships will drive standards or standardization among different actors in the international governance system. One clear implication of meta standards and relationships in the international governance system is that it affects the application and provision of legal rules. In the concluding part of this commentary some views on the meta-relationship of law will be introduced.

2. Transnational Corporations
Transnational corporations are the driving forces behind the speed and development of economic growth. To this end, transnational corporations are business entities that operate in several states in a range of economic activities. At the OWG sessions, arguably, transnational corporations were represented by what the UN machinery referred to as the 'Business Sector' or 'Business and Major Industry Group'. Cognizant of their important role in matters of economic growth and sustainable development, representatives of transnational corporations were rather blunt about their role in and importance for the SDGs and the wider goal of sustainable development: 'without us, to be frank,

---

[162] UN Charter, art 71.

[163] During the negotiations for the UN Charter, NGOs present in San Francisco insisted on such a provision, but the account varies. For a useful discussion on NGOs at San Francisco, see K Kruse and S Tuck, *Fog of War: The Second World War and the Civil Rights Movement* (OUP 2012) especially ch 10.

[164] Sample discussions include, C Alger, 'The Emerging Roles of the NGOs in the UN System: From Article 71 to a People's Millennium Assembly' (2002) 8 Global Governance 93–118.

[165] But see K Raustiala, 'States, NGOs, and International Environmental Institutions' (1997) 41 International Studies Quarterly 719–40.

[166] EF Lambin and T Thorlakson, 'Sustainability Standards: Interactions Between Private Actors, Civil Society, and Governments' (2018) 43 Annual Review of Environment and Resources 369–93.

668 SDG 9

none of these will be able to deliver', the Global Business Alliance explained during the OWG sessions.[167]

Thus, for the most part, transnational corporations in the OWG sessions saw themselves as performing two primary functions: first being participants and promoters of sustainable goals in the evolving SDGs, and second as the key actors that are able to deliver on the majority of the economic aspects of the SDGs including those relating to SDG 9. From these two perspectives, transnational corporations had their own visions for and interests in supporting the SDGs, and were confident of the fact that sustainable development is a matter for economic entrepreneurs, and states can only lay out some guidelines in order to achieve sustainable development.

The positions of transnational corporations during the OWG sessions only diverged to the extent that they needed the support of states and/or other non-economic Major Groups to reach consensus on issues such as infrastructure and innovation.

Transnational corporations in the SDG processes, including those represented by the Business and Industry Major Group, devoted their input on mitigating the impact of implementing specific sustainability targets on their operations. Thus, during the Twelfth OWG Session, an intervention by the Business and Industry Major Group on the Proposed SDG 9, 'Promote Sustainable Industrialization', suggested that the targets should be replaced by an extensive list, which reads similarly to the final targets.[168]

The replacement targets for SDG 9, the Business and Industry Major Group suggested at OWG-12, are:

9.1 by 2030 ensure a conducive policy environment for industrial development, including enabling environments for investment and clear enforced environmental regulations

9.2 by 2030 increase industrial diversity particularly in developing countries, especially LDCs, LLDCs, and SIDS, with a focus on shifting towards higher value-added activities

9.3 by 2030 full implementation of UN trade and transport facilitation tools such as the TIR Convention and the Harmonization Convention

9.4 by 2030 increase investment in and maintain basic and ancillary infrastructure including road and rail; electricity generation and supply, including renewable energy; information and communication technologies; water and wastewater services; and the recovery of resources and use materials

9.5 by [2030] implement national plans and measures systematically encourage the strengthening of the technological capabilities of industrial sectors, including plans to accelerate development, dissemination and adoption of environmentally

---

[167] See, Global Business Alliance (n 189).

[168] Outcome Document, Compilation of Amendments to Goals and Targets by Major Groups During Morning Hearings—OWG 12, Morning Hearings with Major Groups and other Stakeholders, Twelfth Session of the Open Working Group on Sustainable Development Goals, 16–20 June, 2014 (hereinafter 'Compilation of Amendments').

GOAL COMMENTARY 669

sound industrial technologies, processes and management systems, maintaining strong intellectual rights protection

9.6 by 2030 develop sustainable infrastructure accessible to all, with attention to needs of countries in special situations, and provide access for x% of rural population to basic infrastructure and service

9.7 by 2030, expand access by x% to safe, affordable, accessible and sustainable transport.[169]

The above interventions by representatives of transnational corporations in the OWG's penultimate session were well thought out. First, the interventions were structured in such a way that they were 'adoptable' by the OWG (which some, with minor modification, eventually were), and the interventions delivered the key preferences and interests of transnational corporations in as much as it relates to their core economic activities.

Thus, by first acknowledging in intervention 9.1 the need for good environmental regulations—and thereby their support for sustainability—they then showed that they were primarily concerned about rules both internationally and locally. This was evident by the call for harmonization of international rules (9.3) and the need for strong intellectual property rights protection (9.5).[170] Another key interest that the intervention of transnational corporation showed was that relating to core economic activities as set out in intervention 9.4, including those on technology and energy.

The Final Compilations saw additional changes to SDG 9, however those changes included those proposed by other civil society actors,[171] and hence such input was part

---

[169] ibid p 28.

[170] ibid intervention 9.5.

[171] Final Compilation of Amendments to Goals and Targets by Major Groups and other Stakeholders including Citizen's responses to MY World 6 Priorities, To Inform the Thirteenth and last Session of the Open Working Group on Sustainable Development Goals, 14–18 July 2014 (hereinafter 'Final Compilation of Amendments'), pp 15–16. The verbatim proposal for Goal 9 along with bold text is as follows:

Proposed goal 9
Promote sustainable infrastructure and industrialization and foster innovation
With support of the Women's Major Group, the Major Group for Children and Youth, the NGO's Major Group, the Workers and Trade Unions' Major Group, Oxfam, Islamic Relief, Policy International Cooperative Alliance and CEEweb for Biodiversity
Rewording of goal to: Promote ~~sustainable~~ **resilient** infrastructure and **sustainable** ~~industrialization~~ **production** and **service development and** foster innovation **and added value creation**
Amendments to targets:
9.1 support the development of quality, reliable, safe, sustainable and resilient **and gender sensitive** infrastructure **and public services** for energy, water, waste management, transport, ports, **healthcare, education, public buildings** and ICT, with a focus on affordable access for all
9.2 improve regional and trans-border infrastructure to promote regional connectivity and integration and to facilitate trade **under the human rights framework based on socially and environmentally sound criteria**
9.3 create decent industrial jobs and significantly raise industry's share of employment and GDP in line with national circumstances, including doubling manufacturing's share in LDCs by 2030
9.4 ensure that **cooperatives,** small-scale industrial and other enterprises, particularly in LDCs, have affordable access to credit and are integrated into national, regional and global value chains and markets **with a gender equality approach**

of the broader participatory role of non-state actors in SDG 9. Thus, for the time being, the focus here remains on the input of transnational corporations.

While transnational corporations are committed to the SDGs, the targets and indicators of SDG 9 are also a strong reflection of their interests and preferences in terms of maximizing sustainable development for their benefit. Naturally, as the OWG sessions revealed, only 'businesses', as it were, can deliver on sustainable economic development. At the OWG, transnational corporations confirmed that they are not merely informal participants or agents of international bodies. Rather, they were acting in their own capacity as shapers of the formal pillars relating to economic development in the SDGs.

For transnational corporations, the SDGs represent a long-term vision that draws on the backing of states and civil society actors to provide support through values and processes of the mechanisms for industrialization and infrastructure development and the related innovation that are associated with those clusters in Agenda 2030. With the OWG, transnational corporations found support from states and civil society actors alike where they formed a collective approach to identifying the mutual and relevant targets but also ensuring that such targets are tied to aspects of environmental protection through 'green values'.

The interests and preferences of transnational corporations are substantially different from other actors in general, and although at the OWG transnational corporations were able to unite with other actors to ensure that the proposals for the SDGs met the requirements of 'sustainability', transnational corporations are not accountable nor will they be accountable to, say, civil society actors. Thus, for transnational corporations, the SDGs represent in part how to ensure that their economic interests are

9.5 by 2030 upgrade infrastructure and retrofit industries to make them sustainable, with greater adoption of clean technologies and **socially and** environmentally sound industrial processes, with developed countries taking the lead and all countries taking action in accordance with their respective capabilities **with full accordance to human rights framework and gender equality**

9.5 bis by 2030, increase by x% the resource-efficiency, transparency and accountability of industry, reduce by y% harmful chemicals used and waste generated, and decrease by z% the intensity of carbon emissions from the industrial sector

9.5 ter achieve structural transformation of economies towards social and environmental responsible production patterns, in all sectors and activities

9.5 quat introduce a global corporate basic tax floor to promote sustainable development

9.a. facilitate sustainable **socially and environmentally sound** infrastructure development, with emphasis on enhanced **public, transparent and accountable** financial and technical support to LDCs

9.b. ensure a conducive policy environment at all levels for industrial transparent and accountable development, ensuring that no extra territorial practices generate negative social and environmental impacts, promoting entrepreneurship, cooperatives and innovation, for socially and environmentally sustainable solutions, ensuring high risk developments fulfil sustainability criteria, applying the no-data no market principle, with special attention to national circumstances in developing countries

9.c. enhance R&D activities and upgrade technological capabilities, **including indigenous technologies**, including access to environmentally **and socially** sound technologies in all countries

9.d. shorten the supply chain from the production phase to the consumption site in order to reduce the social and environmental impact of transport

9.e. by 2030 retrofit x% of existing industries with clean technologies and environmentally sound industrial processes to achieve y% absolute energy and z% resource-reduction improvement, with all countries taking action, developed countries taking the lead and developing countries following a similar pattern taking into account their development needs and capabilities, also with the help of the internet.

positioned and supported within the context of the SDG processes and the level of influence they can have on the development of international rules that can affect those economic interests.

When one considers the fact that SDG 9 contains issues relating to innovation and industrialization, then transnational corporations are genuinely concerned as to whether their investments and/or intellectual property rights will face problems of enforcement or appropriation.[172] Thus, transnational corporations saw an opportunity during the OWG to influence states and civil society actors to a certain degree so that their support for environmental protection is of a higher standard and meets the requirements of sustainable development.

The long-term effect of such influence can only be ascertained from the degree and enactment of domestic legislations on various aspects of climate change, green technology, innovation, and other areas of SDG 9 where corporate owners would need the force of the law to protect their investments or how stronger enforcement measures for intellectual property rights are required. Given that any such legislations will be of a domestic, transnational/global, or international nature, they will help to inform how the idea of meta-relationships in law as such is important to the overall nature of SDG 9.

3. Civil Society (NGOs)

The third category of actors involved in the dialogues and negotiations of the SDGs that had been active at the OWG level are 'civil society actors'. This section will use the term 'civil society actors' for the purposes of the discussions and as a blanket term to mean non-governmental organizations, social movements, and individuals. The role of civil society actors in the OWG sessions and the ultimate drafting of the proposed goals were essentially to advise and observe, since only states had the formal capacity to draft the SDGs.

In general, the participation of civil society actors in global policy-making or international regulation is not new;[173] however, at the OWG sessions (and the various global initiatives on climate change and the environment), civil society actors had been particularly active. Contemporary literature in general has referred to the participation of civil society actors in international negotiations and policy-making as influential.[174] During the OWG sessions there had been a large input from civil society actors by their umbrella representatives who made statements on most of the proposed goals or in the dialogues leading up to the formation of the goals.

---

[172] The contemporary debates on intellectual property rights and investment are useful in this context; see, eg, PS Morris, 'Chorzow Factory: Intellectual Property and the Continuity of International Law in Investor-State Dispute Settlement' (2020) Queen Mary Journal of Intellectual Property 179; C Geiger (ed), *Research Handbook on Intellectual Property and Investment Law* (Edward Elgar 2020).

[173] See also, RW Mansbach and others, *The Web of World Politics: Nonstate Actors in the Global System* (Prentice Hall 1976).

[174] For example, MM Betsill and E Corell (eds), *NGO Diplomacy: The Influence of Nongovernmental Organizations in International Environmental Negotiations* (MIT Press 2008); H van Asselt, 'The Role of Non-State Actors in Reviewing in Ambition, Implementation, and Compliance in the Paris Agreement' (2016) 6 Climate Law 91–108; K Backstrand and others, 'Non-State Actors in Global Climate Governance: From Copenhagen to Paris and Beyond' (2017) 26 Environmental Politics 561–79.

672   SDG 9

The presence of civil society at the OWG sessions was part of the broader inclusive participatory role of non-state actors, including those discussed earlier. For civil society however, at the OWG sessions, non-state actors were also labelled 'stakeholders' or 'civil society'. This was a practical approach and led to better dialogues on some occasions. One of the advantages that civil society actors had during the OWG sessions was the fact that they brought with them specialized knowledge,[175] but on other occasions, civil society actors at the OWG sessions were merely 'advocating'.[176] At the OWG sessions civil society actors indicated that infrastructure and industrialization were opportunities to transform economic development and inequality.

The 'Major Groups'[177] which raised concerns regarding 'innovation', in relation to SDG 9, at OWG-1, were part of the broad coalition of civil society which made their voice heard on the matter. The 'Major Groups' role at the OWG sessions has been set out in Agenda 21[178] which identified sectors such as non-governmental organizations, business and industry, and the scientific and technological community among the Major Groups.[179] At OWG-1 only 'three civil society representatives delivered statements'[180] and this is likely to have included what the Summary Report of Session 1 referred to as 'Major Groups'[181] such as those representing technological interests.[182] States were, however, the major speakers at OWG-1 and it was an opportunity to set in motion 'great diplomatic skills'[183] that would be required for the following twelve meetings and for producing the outcome document of the SDGs.

Civil society actors on a whole are competent in most of the issue areas they advocate for or through experience gained from their participation in international policy-making. Moreover, civil society actors can engage in international negotiation to the extent that those negotiations fit their overall efforts. However, unlike states which may need to stick to a particular discourse in international negotiation, civil society actors can change course if they so desire. Hence, the freedom that civil society actors enjoy at the international level and/or during multilateral negotiations afford them the ability to be agents of change.

---

[175] See Haas (n 45) on epistemic communities for example, to which I rely on for this formulation; see also, EH Riedel, 'The Development of International Law: Alternatives to Treaty Making? International Organisations and Non State Actors' in R Wolfrum and V Röben (eds), *Developments of International Law in Treaty Making* (Springer 2005).

[176] See also Outcome Document/Resolution (n 39) para 6 highlighting the fact that civil society was listened to.

[177] The Business and Industry, Local Authorities and Scientific and Technology Community Major Groups, in Summary of the First Session of the UN General Assembly Open Working Group on Sustainable Development Goals: 13–15 March 2013, p 6.

[178] Agenda 21 (n 126).

[179] ibid paras 23.1–32.14.

[180] Final Summary Report OWG Session 1, p 1.

[181] ibid p 6.

[182] In addition to the 'The Business and Industry, Local Authorities and Scientific and Technology Community Major Groups', the Summary Report of Session 1 also mentions '[t]he Farmers, NGOs, and Children and Youth Major Groups', ibid p 5, and '[t]he Women, Indigenous Peoples and Trade Unions Major Groups', ibid p 6. Thus, these three 'Major Groups' were representatives of civil society as such during the First Session of the OWG. However, for the purposes of the discussions in relation to SDG 9, 'Technology Community Major Group', ibid p 6 is the immediate concern as that Group had a broad coalition with interests and preferences for Goal 9.

[183] This was the characterization and task given to those present at the First Session by UNGA President Vuk Jeremic during his opening speech, see Final Summary Report OWG Session 1, p 3.

The involvement and willingness of civil society actors in the SDG process and especially to accept the proposals in the OWG sessions are indications that the goals they set out to achieve, to 'contribute and formulate' the SDGs, have been a success. The success is seen in how targets and indicators have reflected the views and preferences of civil society actors such as the Sustainable Development Solutions Network (SDSN).[184] Their participation and proximity to the policy-making level in the UN system on sustainable development have generated norms and certain 'green values' to help achieve economic growth and sustainable development.

Given that SDG 9 spreads across a spectrum of issue areas, green values and other forms of economic sustainability can only go as far as they are required to achieve specific targets and indicators. There are bound to be clashes of values and norms where the means of implementing other aspects of SDG 9 are concerned. Some civil society actors have been aware of the fact that green values do not comport with realizing economic benefits in other areas that are SDG 9 related. Hence, civil society actors during the OWG sessions were often motivated by their own interests for a desired outcome; that is, to make a proposal, as opposed to no proposal at all.[185]

Finally, it is important to consider the fact that civil society actors in the OWG sessions and in the overall SDG process form part of a wider 'global political process', where the highest form of influence and political engagement is at the UN system level. Thus, if states coordinate and manage world peace and security as political actors at the UN level, then civil society actors in the broadest sense, including non-state actors, are the informal analogies to states in that civil society and non-state actors engage and contribute to world peace, security, and sustainable development.

The evidence from the OWG sessions also suggests that civil society actors acted according to the policy needs and desires of states. Hence civil society actors that gained a seat at the negotiating and discussion table were able to contribute to various global political issues via the UN coordinating systems. Thus, while states are able to contribute to world peace, security, and sustainable development at the UNGA or the UN Security Council, in a similar way, civil society actors other non-state actors had gained their own state-like credentials through the support of the UN Secretary General and the 2nd Committee of the UNGA[186] to participate in the global process of the SDGs.

4. Actors and Narratives—An Assessment

The role and impact of three categories of actors in the evolution of the SDGs and in particular their relations with the forming of SDG 9 requires a broader assessment in what I will refer to as 'actors and narratives'. This is crucial as it can help us to understand the role of the three categories from a variety of lenses and their thought processes, that

---

[184] See M Loewe and N Rippin, 'The Sustainable Development Goals of the Post-2015 Agenda: Comments on the OWG and SDSN Proposal (2015) <https://papers.ssrn.com/sol3/papers.cfm?abstract_id=2567302> accessed 18 September 2022.

[185] ibid.

[186] See R Krapp, 'Sustainable Development in the Second Committee' (2016) 46 Environmental Policy and Law 10–13.

is, how they shaped the narratives on sustainability and the 'agendas' they espoused during the accession of SDG 9. Although theoretical research has shown that non-state actors have historically mobilized or lobbied for the inclusion of 'agendas' in global policy-making and regulatory development,[187] the influence of these non-state actors is often accompanied by 'quiet politics'.[188] The linkage of SDG 9 to quiet politics was as a result of the deep connection that the targets and indicators in SDG 9 have with the business community.

The goals and targets of SDG 9 are mutually dependent on how the business community can deliver on infrastructural development (even with state aid), create or expand the necessary industries for job creation, promote further R&D for innovation, and enhance sustainable industrialization.[189] The nature of agenda-setting in global policy-making is generally an epistemic form of cooperation, but such participation where global civil societies and NGOs, transnational corporations, and international organizations are competing for the same influence over a desired common outcome such as sustainable development and industrialization indicates that their interests and policy preferences are aligned. Through such alignment of preferences and interests the desired common outcome of sustainable industrialization is achievable based on how the targets and goals are seen as part of the quiet politics to mobilize the global community into the marketplace for the three support structures of SDG 9, industry, innovation, and infrastructure.

The argument that actors and narratives influenced the design and policy-making of SDG 9 with strong support structures from the business community has merit when consideration is given to, for example, SDG 9 as representing their interests and preferences. The engagement of the business community in the evolution of SDG 9 as a catalyst to development and the inherent economic incentives that alignment to the sustainability agenda brings suggest that the actions of the business community at the global level are mutually dependent on specific relationships.

The first of these relationships includes viewing *innovation* as a common desired outcome of state actors in the international system. Secondly, the extent to which *infrastructure* forms part of the common desired outcome of state actors in the international system. Thirdly, integrating *industry* as essential to the common desired outcome of state actors in the international system. The net benefit will therefore lead to sustainable industrialization for both the state as an actor in the international system and the business community as a collective actor in the international system.

---

[187] See Haas (n 45) on epistemic communities.

[188] I am using the same term that Culpepper has used to argue that corporate actors for example have long had influence over the political structures of democracies (states) and in the process design the rules that govern corporate activities that favours their interest and policy preferences, see PD Culepepper, *Quiet Politics and Business Power: Corporate Control in Europe and Japan* (CUP 2011).

[189] In fact, during the OWG sessions, the representatives of businesses and major industry were blunt in their language when describing their role and or their views to certain aspects of the evolving SDGs, for instance, in one session, where the evolving SDG on economic growth was taking shape, the Global Business Alliance 'expressed concern with all of the focus areas, since "without us, to be frank, none of these will be able to deliver"', UN General Assembly's (UNGA) OWG on SDGs, Session 10, 31 March–4 April 2014, p 21.

The desired outcomes as just mentioned have also been discussed in aspects of the academic literature, and one reasoning has been that the business community can influence legal, regulatory, and policy-making as either part of agenda-setting that involves quiet politics.[190] In other words, 'agenda-setting'[191] has generally been part of the desired outcomes of non-state actors when taking part in the discussions or negotiations on SDGs. Furthermore, by influencing how legal and regulatory rules evolve also suggests that an internal element is part of how we consider those rules and regulations in the form a relationship—and in later parts of this commentary, some attempt will be made to flesh out the integration of rules whether domestic, transnational/global, or international as a meta-relationship.

The final point to consider from the actors and narrative argument is the actual usage of 'narratives'[192] by the three key actors as outlined above (transnational corporations, civil societies and NGOs, and international organizations) to help frame the acceptance of SDG 9. Given that the likelihood of criticism exists for the role and involvement of the business community through their quiet politics methods, then one conceivable way of mitigating any potential criticisms is to accept and frame the language used in the standard narrative with vague concepts around the *alpha primus* 'sustainability'.[193]

As part of the strategy of global engagement in the sustainable development agenda, narratives are embraced so that the harmony of the agenda-setting is in tune with the interests of those state actors who are the ultimate creators and enablers of sustainable development.[194] The same hymn sheet often comprises melodies that include 'environmental sustainability',[195] 'economic sustainability',[196] 'ecological modernization',[197] 'social sustainability',[198] 'green economy', and other concepts that once repeated become standard language representing the same desired common outcome, to build resilient infrastructure, promote inclusive and sustainable industrialization, and foster innovation. Thus, the more engaged an actor is with the language, key terms and concepts, and other modes of description that are able to send signals of understanding and

---

[190] Culepepper (n 189).

[191] FR Baumgartner and BD Jones, *Agendas and Instability in American Politics* (University of Chicago Press 1993).

[192] The notion of 'narrative' here also refers to the use of different terminologies to describe the goal or niche area of sustainable development in which an actor is involved. In general, the different concepts that are used to describe an area of sustainable development can also be problematic as defining the concept of 'sustainable development' as mentioned earlier in this chapter and elsewhere in this volume, and the reader must bear in mind, that concepts and terms relating to sustainable development in general have changed over the years; on this latter point, see MA Khan, 'Sustainable Development: The Key Concepts, Issues and Implications', Keynote Paper Given at the International Sustainable Development Research Conference, 27–29 March 1995, Manchester, UK, printed in (1995) 3 Sustainable Development 63–69. In general, the literature is plentiful that traces the origins of the concept 'sustainable development' but very few that extrapolate the sub-concepts and devout their discussion on their evolution, for discussions on the former, see JA Du Pisani, 'Sustainable Development: Historical Roots of the Concept' (2006) 3 Environmental Sciences 83–96.

[193] For a legal theoretical discussion see generally, T Endicott, *Vagueness in Law* (OUP 2000).

[194] But see J Tosun and J Leininger, 'Governing the Interlinkages Between the Sustainable Development Goals: Approaches to Attain Policy Integration' (2017) 1 Global Challenges 1, 1 using target 17.14 'to enhance policy coherence' to suggest how crucial it is for competent national authorities to work in tandem with states.

[195] Khan (n 193) 64.

[196] ibid 64.

[197] See n 203.

[198] Khan (n 193) 64.

676   SDG 9

appreciation for innovation, infrastructure, and industry, the more likely they are convinced that the goals and targets will be met.

The repetition of key concepts and terms that form part of the overarching narrative on sustainable development and the specifics of SDG 9 create assurances and familiarity with outcomes and targets and the ways and procedures necessary to promote a successful outcome. But more importantly, narratives also suggest that preferences and interests are translatable into negotiating power so that actions and preferences are realized in any policy-making initiative taken by states at the international level. The OWG sessions and the sub-group which had responsibility for SDG 9 is one example of how narratives, influence, and actions were realized when the sub-groups focused on the concrete issues of industry, innovation, and infrastructure. Through their interactions and mobilization we are able to see the outcome of the common desire to build resilient infrastructure, promote inclusive and sustainable industrialization, and foster innovation.

III. Target Commentary: Targets and Indicators of Industry, Innovation, and Infrastructure

A. Introducing SDG 9: Industry, Innovation, and Infrastructure

Consisting of eight targets and twelve indicators, SDG 9 is ambitious and could transform life on Earth as we know it, should its three pillars—industry, infrastructure, and innovation—be realized. With an ambition to raise the quality of life of humans and create opportunities for 'sustainable and innovative industrialization' into the next millennia, SDG 9 rests on the assumptions that the next revolution in human history will be inclusive. Moreover, SDG 9 emphasizes the role of technology, digital technologies, and the resilience of infrastructure to advance society into an ecological future.[199]

---

[199] For some early theoretical discussions on ecological modernization see, eg, M Hajer, *The Politics of Environmental Discourse: Ecological Modernization and the Policy Process* (OUP 1995); O Langhelle, 'Why Ecological Modernization and Sustainable Development Should Not Be Conflated' (2000) 2 Journal of Environmental Policy and Planning 303–22; S Baker, 'Sustainable Development as Symbolic Commitment: Declaratory Policy and the Seductive Appeal of Ecological Modernisation in the European Union' (2007) 16 Environmental Politics 297–317. Some recent discussions include, J Ewing, 'Hollow Ecology: Ecological Modernization Theory and the Death of Nature' (2017) 23 Journal of World-Systems Research 126–55; M Jänicke, 'Ecological Modernization as Global Industrial Revolution' (2017) 25 Journal of Environmental Policy and Administration 1–32; A Machin, 'Changing the Story? The Discourse of Ecological Modernisation in the European Union' (2019) 28 Environmental Politics 208–27; H Weber and M Weber, 'When Means of Implementation Meet Ecological Modernization Theory: A Critical Frame for Thinking About Sustainable Development Goals Initiative' (2020) 136 World Development 1–11. Some legal related discussion on ecological modernization include: C Lant, 'Natural Resource Sustainability from the Geographical Side of Ecological Economics' (2008) 44 Tulsa Law Review 51–66; J McGee and J Wenta, 'Technology Transfer Institutions in Global Climate Governance: The Tension between Equity Principles and Market Allocation' (2014) 23 Review of European, Comparative & International Environmental Law 367–81; J Hojnik, 'Ecological Modernization through Servitization: EU Regulatory Support for Sustainable Product-Service Systems' (2018) 27 Review of European, Comparative & International Environmental Law 162–75; K Wilkinson Cross, 'Technological Innovations Tackling Biodiversity Loss: Solutions or Misdirection?' (2019) 1 Law, Technology and Humans 100–28; P Barresi, 'China's Ecological Civilization Concept as a Principle of Global Environmental Governance' (2020) 4 Chinese Journal of Environmental Law 235–61.

At the heart of this entangled and interconnecting goal is 'innovation', even if its siblings include 'industry' and 'infrastructure' to mobilize 'industrialization'. The reason why innovation is central to this goal is because R&D, information and communications technology (ICT), and 'resilient' infrastructure for modernization and industrialization are crucial to realize the desired outcome of SDG 9.

In terms of resilient infrastructure, innovation is key when factors such as climate change technologies, efficient buildings, and other forms of industrialization depend on innovations for the modern world. Another relevance of innovation in this framework is its relationship to R&D, technology, and intellectual property rights. This relationship therefore rests on the extent to which certain legal questions involving the protection of private rights such as patented technologies or climate technology will be able to be enforced under a SDG 9 umbrella. Furthermore, the broader role of other forms of legal protections under domestic and international legal rules must also be taken into account. Hence, innovation as a concept under SDG 9 is further linked to various preferences and interests of the business community and the common desired outcome of the entire development agenda of states.

The integration of industry, innovation, and infrastructure in SDG 9 is at best an experiment given that there are diverse factors that relate to this goal and its targets. Yet, it is also an experiment that, upon careful implementation and monitoring of each desired target, can lead to tangible results. The integration of the different facets of SDG 9 also suggests that the targets and indicators of SDG 9 can *per se* generate positive economic effects that will in turn drive economic development and, in the process, fulfil the wishes of the multitude of actors with interests in SDG 9.

Given that SDG 9 is a broad coalition of different frameworks, these frameworks are best summarized as (i) innovation framework; (ii) resilient framework; (iii) physical infrastructure framework; and (iv) industry framework. All four frameworks are interconnected in that they are business oriented, development focused, and environmentally conscious of climate change initiatives. For the innovation framework, the role of the business community at all levels is integral in determining how different aspects of innovation such as (i) technological progress; (ii) R&D with the ability to commercialize all potential new discoveries; and (iii) ensuring that strong intellectual property rules (along with general corporate rules for businesses) can effectively engage in the commercialization of innovation. Furthermore, the extent to which artificial intelligence is adopted and used in different technologies will also be an added incentive toward the new generation of innovation that can spur economic growth.

This new generation of innovation entails, for instance, the reach of automation or solar technologies. At the same time, the innovation framework is crucial to how other sectors of the economy can be resilient. It might be the case that in some areas of the economy, the impact of climate change may be very damaging and cause existing technologies to deteriorate. If this happens, one of the remedies would be to develop and implement more resilient systems that can minimize the impact of Mother Nature (eg hurricanes). Furthermore, if existing systems in countries affected by the impact of climate change can be more resilient, then the cost savings can spur investment in other

678   SDG 9

physical infrastructures. Hence, it is important for the physical infrastructure framework as envisaged in SDG 9 to develop and replace the current age-old technologies and designs still in use in most countries.

The development of physical infrastructures in some regions or countries will require the building of new infrastructures such as roads, rail, telecommunications, and towns. This is the case in most of Africa and parts of Asia and the Pacific region. In other regions, it will require only replacing some of the physical infrastructure which has been in place for more than a century. Therefore, the economic drivers of most societies are the presence and capabilities of basic infrastructure such as roads, modes of transport, modes of energy, modes of telecommunication, and social services including schools, hospitals, and amenities for general well-being.

There are great disparities among regions, for instance between African and some Asian societies. The greatest need for infrastructure investments is in these societies, including Latin America and the Caribbean, and therefore, the infrastructure framework of SDG 9 when compared to the innovation or resilient framework is needed in greater degree in these societies as opposed to European or North American societies. These frameworks in SDG 9 are therefore key to best solving and achieving sustainable development, especially when the peculiarities of the different societies are taken into consideration. Moreover, the different frameworks of SDG 9 mentioned here equate primarily to how the different actors in a society can, through cooperation, relate to the industry framework, as all three frameworks require investment and business activities in order to be realized.

B. A Long-term View of Individual Targets

The targets and indicators[200] of SDG 9 are designed to generate maximum economic effect to spur growth, innovation, and economic development. As business-oriented targets, SDG 9 targets in part aim to respond to how best to maximize economic development and promote sustainability at the same time in a business environment. The targets are designed so to have maximum impact on the various economic activities in their sphere such as infrastructure development (target 9.1); enhancing manufacturing capabilities (target 9.2); harnessing the creativity, innovation, and business acumen of entrepreneurs in small and medium-size enterprises (SMEs) (target 9.3);[201] reducing

---

[200] Although some of the SDGs, at least 1–8 have their origins in the MDGs, as indicated earlier, Goals 9–17 are recent additions to the revised SDGs 2030, and based on earlier literature, 'goals', 'targets', and 'indicators' are about 'making choices'; see TM Parris and RW Kates, 'Characterizing and Measuring Sustainable Development' (2003) 28 Annual Review of Environment and Resources 559–86, 572. They further defined, goals, targets, and indicators in the following way: '*goals* are broad, but specific qualitative statements about objectives chosen from the major categories of what to sustain and what to develop.... *Indicators* are quantitative measures selected to assess progress toward or away from a stated goal.... *Targets* use indicators to make goals specific with endpoints and timetables. ....' ibid 572–73.

[201] To the extent that small firms have a role to play in the broader policies on the environment, see, eg, R Baylis and others, 'Company Size, Environmental Regulation and Ecological Modernization: Further Analysis at the Level of the Firm' (1998) 7 Business Strategy and the Environment 285–96; G Noci and R Verganti, 'Managing

carbon output and promoting more efficient technologies that are sustainable (target 9.4); and ensuring that access to digital technologies and telecommunication capabilities are accessible globally (target 9.c).

The different targets, goals, and indicators of SDG 9 purport in effect to foster convergence so that ecological industrialization can be accelerated at a rate to ensure that by 2030, some of the serious inequalities that currently exist in the world are eliminated. Certainly, SDG 9 as it currently stands, with its three pillars of industry, innovation, and infrastructure, is co-dependent on how states and the business community are able to develop, identify, and subsequently adopt or embrace the different facets of ecological industrialization along with the complementary facets in technological innovations.[202]

While there are analogies of ecological modernization with SDG 9 as such,[203] the notion of ecological industrialization captures better the frame and spirit of SDG 9. This is because all three pillars of SDG 9 essentially lead to a form of industrialization, whether as 'innovation industrialization', 'infrastructure industrialization', or 'industry industrialization'. And, under those circumstances, ecologic sustainability and innovation in terms of digital technologies, R&D, and telecommunication will dictate the outcome of SDG 9. Thus, in one form, it is safe to posit that ecological industrialization from the perspective of SDG 9 aims at transforming the different economic activities that are reliant on innovation.

C. Custodians and Tier Classifications

It is important to point out that the individual targets in SDG 9 are managed by different institutions which officially serve as the custodians. In this regard, several UN agencies perform custodian roles for SDG 9 targets based on the 'tier structure' or classification of SDG 9.[204] The relevant agencies include the World Bank, ICAO, OECD, UNIDO,

---

'Green' Product Innovation in Small Firms' (1999) 29 R&D Management 1–15; K Sloan and others, 'Towards Sustainability: Examining the Drivers and Change Process within SMEs' (2013) 3 Journal of Management and Sustainability 19–30; D Williamson and others, 'Drivers of Environmental Behaviour in Manufacturing SMEs and the Implications for CSR' (2006) 67 Journal of Business Ethics 317–39; M Blakeney and G Mengistie, 'Intellectual Property and Economic Development in Sub-Saharan Africa' (2011) 14 Journal of World Intellectual Property 238–64; R Crossley and others, 'Sustainability and Legitimacy Theory: The Case of Sustainable Social and Environmental Practices of Small and Medium-Sized Enterprises' (2021) 30 Business Strategy and the Environment 3740.

[202] There is growing field that supports and defends the idea of 'industrial ecology' especially in the hard sciences such as engineering; however, my usage of the term 'ecological industrialization' here is purely a coincident as I coined the term as a generic one mostly by drawing parallels with innovation in the legal sense and also by playing on the discussion on 'ecological modernization', but see BR Allenby, 'Industrial Ecology: Governance, Laws and Regulations' in RU Ayres and LW Ayres (eds), *A Handbook of Industrial Ecology* (Edward Elgar 2002) 60–69.

[203] But see Weber and Weber (n 200) arguing that the SDGs in general align with ecological modernization theory.

[204] On tier structure in general see UN Statistics, Tier Classification for Global SDG Indicators as of 29 March 2021, and (hereinafter as 'Tier Classification Sheet'). This document is made available as a result of the Inter-Agency and Expert Group on SDG Indicators (IAEG-SDGs). The SDG indicators are classified into three tiers: 'Tier 1' is deemed 'conceptually clear'; 'Tier 2' with less frequent data; and 'Tier 3' 'with no internally established methodologically or standard' (available up to October 2021) to offer. An overview is available at <https://unstats.un.org/sdgs/iaeg-sdgs/tier-classification/> accessed 23 October 2021. For a general literature on SDG classifications, see,

680 SDG 9

the International Energy Agency (IEA), the United Nations Educational, Scientific and Cultural Organisation (UNESCO), the International Telecommunications Union (ITU), International Transport Forum (ITF), and the UNESCO Institute for Statistics (UIS). In this regard it is always important to link not only the progress (during the implementation and realization aspects of SDG 9) to these agencies but also the relative social and economic themes of SDG 9 targets to wider society.

The different custodians of SDG 9 targets are in a sense coordinating bodies or they seek to monitor and capture the actual progress on the indicators and targets. Moreover, they serve in many capacities where states, other international non-custodian bodies, or the interactions of inter-custodian agencies on the SDG targets are able to develop governance structures. Thus, the role of the custodians of the SDG targets in general are also a form of governance mechanism given that they effectively orchestrate the SDG targets.[205]

Based on the Tier Classification Sheet,[206] SDG 9 targets fall into two tiers, that is 'tier 1' and 'tier 2'. The latter comprise targets 9.1 and 9.3. However, it should be noted that the 'indicators' for target 9.1, which are subdivided into 9.1.1[207] and 9.1.2,[208] indicators are classified as both 'tier 2' and 'tier 1' with tier 1 classification applying to indicator 9.1.2, and tier 2 classification to target 9.3. Similarly, the sub-divided indicators 9.3.1 and 9.3.2 are classified as tier 2 (9.3.1) and tier 1 (9.3.2).

The remaining targets for SDG 9 are all classified as tier 1. Thus target 9.2 (UNIDO and as custodian agency for 9.2.1 with the World Bank as partner agency, and the UNIDO for indicator 9.2.2); target 9.4 (UNIDO and IEA as custodian agencies with UNEP as partner agency); 9.5 (UNESCO-UIS as custodian agencies); 9.a (OECD as custodian agency); 9.b (UNIDO as custodian agency, with partner agency being the OECD); and 9.c (ITU as custodian agency) are tier 1 classifications. The function of these agencies is therefore to orchestrate the different tiers of SDG 9 targets and, in the process, also to act as an authoritative one-stop shop for how SDG 9 targets and indicators are evolving. Furthermore, these agencies, when viewed in the broader spectrum of their role in international society, are to coordinate and collaborate on issues such as industrialization, ecological governance and sustainability, economic development and finance, and other functions that correlate with the visions of SDG 9. Some studies have found that there is a direct correlation between SDG 9 in general and industrialization trends across the world especially when the pace of industrialization is measured in advanced economies.[209]

---

eg, B Fu and others, 'Classification, Coordination, Collaboration: A Systems Approach for Advancing Sustainable Development Goals' (2020) 7 National Science Review 838–40.

[205] See also Abbott and Snidal (n 216), from which I appropriate the term orchestration.

[206] Tier Classification Sheet (n 204).

[207] The World Bank is the Custodian Agency whilst partner agencies are the UNEP, UNECE (United Nations Economic Commission for Europe), and Asian Development Bank (ADB).

[208] The ICAO, ITF-OECD are Custodian Agencies whilst the UPU, UNEP, and UNECE are partner agencies.

[209] See P Kynclova and others, 'Composite Index as a Measure on Achieving Sustainable Development Goal 9 (SDG-9) Industry-Related Targets: The SDG-9 Index' (2020) 265(1) Applied Energy, Article ID: 114755. Using data from 126 countries to develop the industrial development SDG-9 index, the authors claim that 'industrialized economies performed best in all dimensions of the SDG-9 index, including all countries achieved the top normalized scores equal to 1'. See, ibid, Figure 6 and resulting discussions. The study concludes that '[t]he 2030

D. Assessment of Individual Targets

Unlike the goals of SDG 9, the targets of SDG 9 are specific outcomes to be realized under practical circumstances. SDG 9 targets force the key players, especially those in the private sector, to present concrete outcomes. At the same time, states play a key role in SDG 9 targets given that states are guided by the goals in SDG 9. There are five targets and three semi-targets in SDG 9 and all are treated as eight targets in this discussion (although the so-called semi-targets can be seen as sub-goals).[210]

The eight targets of SDG 9 are in most ways economic targets in that they are a set of economic objectives to be realized.[211] Thus, when assessing the individual targets of SDG 9, one must ask what are the economic goals or what objectives does SDG 9 hope to achieve? This does not mean that a different deployment of the individual targets of SDG 9 cannot be raised using a different vocabulary such as a justice or philosophical point of view or even business and human rights.[212] But as things stand at the moment, given that SDG 9 is overarching an economic set of initiatives, it is best to frame the targets from that perspective.

Within economic and public policy circles the term 'target' is often seen as part of a policy formation generally referring to the 'desired values to certain economic variables' and how they are achievable.[213] This understanding also comports with some of the works that attempt to frame the targets of the SDGs in general along the same broader narrative on economic approaches to the SDG targets.[214]

Agenda for Sustainable Development recognizes the importance of encompassing all dimensions of sustainable development to ensure sustainable social and economic progress worldwide.'

[210] For consistency purposes, the reader will see that Agenda 2030 and the overall SDGs generally refer to theses as MOIs—means of implementation targets—and for SDG 9, targets (a–c).

[211] Conceptually, I am also using the term 'target' as part of a wider framework in which different disciplinary approaches may refer to it as either 'nexus' or 'interactions', and as such having a broad appeal to its parent term in this commentary 'sustainability', but for other discussions, see, eg, I Boas and others, 'Cross-Sectoral Strategies in Global Sustainability Governance: Towards a Nexus Approach' (2016) 16 International Environmental Agreements: Politics, Law and Economics 449–64.

[212] On this latter see K Akestoridi, 'The Role of Business in International Development and the Attainment of the Sustainable Development Goals' in I Bantekas and M Stein (eds), The Cambridge Companion to Business and Human Rights Law (CUP 2021), 86, 87 (linking profits to the SDGs); for a general reading see T Parris and R Kates, 'Characterizing and Measuring Sustainable Development' (2003) 28 Annual Review of Environmental Resources 559–86, 572–77 (discussing the formulation of goals and targets in sustainability).

[213] JM Fleming, 'Targets and Instruments' (1968) 15(3) IMF Staff Papers 387–404, 388. In terms of recent economic literature, the focus is similar in that certain objectives are targets based on rationale economic or public policy and are used to inform why 'targets' as such are important, see generally, G-M Angeletos and KA Sastry, 'Managing Expectations: Instruments Versus Targets' (2020) 136(4) The Quarterly Journal of Economics 2467–532 (this is a purely empirical paper and is mentioned here to support some of the rationale economic arguments in this section on assessment of SDG 9 targets), however, for a recent discussion on the overall assessment of the SDGs using economic, empirical, and policy arguments see JA van Zantern and R van Tulder, 'Towards Nexus-Based Governance: Defining Interactions Between Economic Activities and Sustainable Development Goals (SDGs)' (2021) 28 International Journal of Sustainable Development & World Ecology 210–26. This latter study has shown that economic activities are crucial to SDG targets.

[214] See, eg, T Hak and others, 'Sustainable Development Goals: A Need for Relevant Indicators' (2016) 60 Ecological Indicators 565–73. This study in general describes the need for 'appropriate indicators for targets' utilizing new or old sets, and in particular the authors suggest that 'quantitative and qualitative forms of indicators are necessary to assess targets', at 569.

682 SDG 9

The SDG targets are currently (that is, during the development and reporting stage) monitored by the High Level Political Forum (HLPF). The HLPF sits at the top of the hierarchal pyramid and the coordinating agencies referred to in the previous section are merely authoritative one-stop shops for information. Commentators see the HLPF as serving in an 'orchestrating' role for other global bodies and therefore 'help[s] to facilitate a nexus approach' to the SDG targets.[215] In fact, it is this mode of governance by the HLPF that enables states currently to demonstrate the progress they are making with their individual targets. The eight targets of SDG 9 have a nexus or interact[216] with the other SDG targets.[217] However, SDG 9 targets are individual in the sense that they pertain to a specific sets of priorities that have economic goals and how they create a nexus with businesses.[218] Moreover, the fact that SDG 9 targets cut across multiple industries, have specific targets related to innovation and they bridge the relationship between governments and private project developers (eg infrastructure projects) suggests that SDG 9 targets are an important feature of how public–private partnerships operate.

These orchestrating dimensions of SDG 9 targets in one sense relate to how SDG 9 on a general scale is positioned as the driver for innovation and economic prosperity. In another, SDG 9 is intimately connected to how a society perceives 'innovation, industry, and infrastructure' from business and economic objectives where the state only functions as an enabler.[219] In other words, private producers generate innovation which in turn supports how industries are organized and generate economic output through infrastructure and knowledge development.

Hence, one may also refer to these interactions as 'economic complexity'[220] where no single entity is responsible for economic and, in our case, 'sustainable development'.

---

[215] Boas and others (n 212) at 457; van Zantern and van Tulder (n 214). But see K Abbott and D Snidal, 'Strengthening International Law Regulation Through International New Governance: Overcoming the Orchestration Deficit' (2009) 42 Vanderbilt Journal of Transnational Law 501–78 (proposing and discussing the term 'orchestration').

[216] On interaction see Boas and others (n 212) and, A Warchold and others, 'Variations in Sustainable Development Goal Interactions: Population, Regional, and Income Disaggregation' (2021) 29(2) Sustainable Development 285–99 (looking at the interactions of the SDGs across a variety of development spectrums). That study, however, did not find any interactions *per se* with SDG 9 compared to some of the other SDGs and this suggest to me that SDG 9 is still a complex goal due to its market-oriented approach and the existing legal rules that needs to be taken into account when SDG 9 is being discussed. Thus, it is not surprising that it is often difficult to find assessments of SDG 9 in the current (economic/social science literature) that measure SDG 9 accurately or capture its impact.

[217] But see E Barbier and J Burgess, 'Sustainable Development Goal Indicators—Analysing Trade-Offs and Complementaries' (2019) 122 World Development 295–305.

[218] But see C Allen and others, 'Prioritising SDG Targets: Assessing Baselines, GAPS and Interlinkages' (2019) 14 Sustainability Science 421–38, 432 (finding, *inter alia*, that '[t]argets for sustainable infrastructure and industry (9.4) ... scored high in terms of systemic impact, and moderate in terms of urgency and policy gap, which placed them within the top ten targets').

[219] For similar views in relation to climate change see S Chan and W Amling, 'Does Orchestration in the Global Climate Action Agenda Effectively Prioritize and Mobilize Transnational Climate Adaptation Action?' (2019) 19 International Environmental Agreements: Politics, Law and Economics 429–46, 440 (suggesting that non-state actors can better engage with 'shortcomings in state-centred governance through addressing complementary functions'). For similar arguments in relation to intellectual property and innovation see PS Morris, 'The Practices of Private Global Norm Production and Intellectual Property Epistemic Communities' (2020) Syracuse Journal of International Law and Commerce 157.

[220] I am borrowing the term as employed in R Hausmann and others, *The Atlas of Economic Complexity: Mapping Paths to Prosperity* (MIT Press 2014).

Rather, market-based mechanisms along the existing legal frameworks will help to determine the overall success of how the targets in SDG 9 are achieved.[221] Presently, states are responsible for reporting to the HLPF the status and progress of their targets, and below the individual targets in SDG 9 are examined (according to information as at October 2021).

E. The Individual Targets and Their Legal Characteristics

This section provides an update on the individual targets of SDG 9 and a brief commentary in relation to their legal characteristics. I am using the term 'legal characteristics' for a set of relationships as opposed to a formal legal sense, given that the SDGs are 'norms' in a general sense that are in the making and have yet to take any legal form.[222] As such, the legal characteristics of SDG 9 may vary from different regulatory protection that may interact with SDG 9 such as intellectual property, legal aspects of road transport, or investment law. However, those characteristics are not the focus of attention here.

Cleary, the presence of 'innovation' also connotes how different forms of regulation, including those for intellectual property, clean technology, and ICT among others, require individual assessment pertaining to the targets and indicators of SDG 9. Such fully fledged discussion is also not the aim here, rather a link to specific legal relations will suffice to generate some of the broader implications of SDG 9 targets and indicators with current regulatory instruments and other legal characteristics. Thus, this overview, like the commentary in general, can only provide the necessary footpath to the broader legal discussions (for another time and place).

One practical observation that must finally be acknowledged at this stage. Despite the language and framing of the targets of SDG 9, often in cumbersome sentences or what may seem like the inclusion of many targets and goals cobbled into a single target, the reality is that SDG 9 targets are about better infrastructure, promotion of prosperity, and expanding information technology. In other words, SDG 9 targets encompass a host of issues ranging from infrastructure, innovation, the role and use of information technologies, research and innovation, service, and other issues that support their broader objectives. This must be borne in mind when assessing and reading what the targets of SDG 9 are, including those which technically should have been achieved already (by 2020) compared to the realities of writing this commentary in October 2021. Notwithstanding this 'layman' overview of SDG 9, scientifically, the key terms in SDG 9

---

[221] On broader arguments on market-based mechanisms see M Kumar Shrivastava and S Bhaduri, 'Market-Based Mechanism and "Climate Justice": Reframing the Debate for a Way Forward' (2019) 19 International Environmental Agreements: Politics, Law and Economics' 497–513; and for some legal arguments on SDG 9 in general see J Denoncourt, 'Companies and UN 2030 Sustainable Development Goal 9: Industry, Innovation and Infrastructure' (2020) 20 Journal of Corporate Law Studies 199–235.

[222] See also V Barral, 'Sustainable Development in International Law: Nature and Operation of an Evolutive Legal Norm' (2012) 23 European Journal of International Law 377–400.

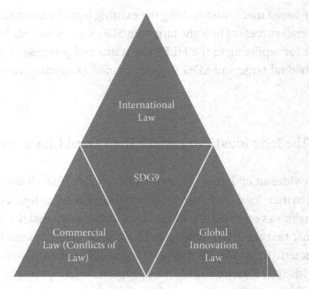

Figure 9.1 Depicting a meta-relationship of SDG9 and legal rules where international law, commercial law, and global innovation law form part of this system.

and targets are 'infrastructure', 'innovation', and 'industry', and the associate derivatives of those terms.

The legal characteristics of SDG 9 traverses all possible legal imaginations and issues that have a substantial legal character.[223] These vary from how states interact with each other and therefore require the use of public international law to the very mundane on contracts and their role in the domestic legal system in relation to clean technology or infrastructure projects, to knowledge creation issues in intellectual property rights. Those legal characteristics are only mentioned in passing here in order to alert the reader to the different substantial issues that would require the invocation of legal rules *per se* on SDG 9.

I would interpret the legal characteristics of SDG 9 as forming a meta-relationship in three broad areas, where all targets and indicators of SDG 9 have an integral role. Schematically, this meta-relationship may take the form (see figure 9.1) where (i) international law for state relationships and treaty obligations are the main concern; (ii) commercial law/conflict of laws where contractual and private international law matters among the different stakeholders form the backbone; and (iii) global innovation

---

[223] Although the SDGs are evolving norms, the notion of sustainable development have found its way in international legal instruments and in this context, the nature of sustainable development goals can also be said to ascertain a legal character. For an example of an international instrument where sustainable development as a concept is used see, Convention for Cooperation in the Sustainable Development of the Marine and Coastal Environment of the Northeast Pacific, 18 February 2002 (hereinafter 'Antigua Convention'). Article 3(1)(a) provides that ' "Sustainable development" means the process of progressive change in the quality of the life of human beings, which place it as the centre and primordial subject of development, by means of economic growth with social equity and the transformation of methods of production and consumption patterns, and which is sustained in the ecological balance and vital support of the region.' See also, Gabcikovo-Nagymaros Project (n 2).

law,[224] where intellectual property rights, licensing/trade secrets, and emerging rules for the protection of knowledge creation and transfer are developed.

These meta-relationships are only played out in the different targets of SDG 9 and may not necessarily apply to other SDGs. However, the emerging consensus is that 'innovation' sits at the very heart of SDG 9 and the legal rules for such innovation are what matters.

In order to frame the current status of the targets in SDG 9, reports available in October 2021 and statistics from the UN division are mostly relied upon. The statistical accounts are gathered mostly from the SDG Dashboard set up for this purpose.[225] However, there are several limitations with the Dashboard in that there are no reports or up-to-date reporting for SDG 9 targets. Moreover, the description across the Dashboard is vague and repetitive, and this often gets picked up by other web portals.

The academic debates have also zoomed in on some of the challenges statistical data represent for the SDGs,[226] and notwithstanding criticisms in the early phase of developing SDG reporting, other international bodies including custodian agencies have produced statistical data of their own. In light of these limitations, this section of the commentary engages in statistical comparison using data from the Dashboard, reports by custodian agencies, the SDG 2021 Report,[227] individual country reports to the HPLF, or other available literature, and offers a general legal comment based on the model of legal characteristics set out earlier as forming a legal meta-relationship.[228]

1. Target 9.1 Develop quality, reliable, sustainable and resilient infrastructure, including regional and trans-border infrastructure, to support economic development and human well-being, with a focus on affordable and equitable access for all

Many natural hazards affect the world on a daily basis. The most frequent and destructive are often tropical hurricanes, cyclones, and earthquakes. These events are usually limited to the Caribbean, parts of Asia and Africa, and sometimes other nations such as the United States, China, or maritime Europe. Continental Europe and North America also face natural hazards including those caused by snow, flooding, and other disasters. Globally, climate change and unequal development have triggered a storm of 'natural poverty' both to infrastructure and the daily livelihoods of people.

The SDGs and in particular target 9.1 seek to alleviate these problems by enabling the development of 'resilient infrastructure' and subsidiary means to 'support economic development'. COVID-19 has also shown the reach of other hazards where epidemics challenge the ability of infrastructure and other capabilities to cope with human

---

[224] This is a novel concept, where the new dynamics of globalization and other emerging legal rules and regulations for intellectual property, technology, and algorithmic *legal data analysis* is forming this new axis of legal imagination as propounded in PS Morris, 'Global Innovation Law' (2021) 41 Northern Illinois Law Review 96.

[225] Available here <https://sdg.tracking-progress.org/dashboard/> accessed 8 September 2022.

[226] E Ordoz, 'The SDG Indicators: A Challenging Task for the International Statistical Community' (2019) 10 Global Policy 141–43 (highlighting some of the early problems with statistical data for the SDGS).

[227] United Nations, 'The Sustainable Development Goals Report 2021' (hereinafter 'SDG 2021 Report').

[228] See figure 9.1 in this commentary for the model on legal characteristics based meta-relationships.

686   SDG 9

well-being and equitable access. Moreover, epidemics have shown that even with modern transport infrastructure such as rail, road, shipping, and air transport, such infrastructure and services can come to halt under *force majeure* of epidemics. It is under these circumstances that target 9.1 seeks to develop resilient infrastructure that also supports economic development and human well-being.

Some of the key economic activities in this target are:

- Quarrying
- Aviation
- Water supply
- Roads, railways, bridges
- Other modes of transport
- Passenger and freight volume
- Telecoms infrastructures
- Wood, metals

The aviation industry (along with ground transport, road, and rail) is essential to target 9.1 yet due to COVID-19, the aviation industry suffered a global plunge in passenger volume in 2020. The ICAO as a custodian institution for parts of target 9.1 reports that in 2020 'the first five months' saw passenger volumes drop to 51 per cent.[229] The significant of this figure is that air transport is a key component of economic development and vital to how target SDG 9.1 can be achieved.

From the few countries in Africa that reported progress on SDG 9 in 2021, Angola was one of them that noted in particular the priority it had been giving SDG 9 'not only to meet its targets, but also as an internal commitment to resume economic growth with social inclusion, towards development'.[230] It was an observation that was in keeping with the general worldwide reporting across different countries that essentially the targets of SDG 9.1 have yet to be fully achieved. Angola, however, remains optimistic that its targets will be met and notes how policy prescriptions have been developed to prioritize SDG 9.[231] The country's National Policy for Technological Science and Innovation policy must be noted, along with the National Strategy for Science Technology and Innovation have been given the force of law through the enactment of 'Decrees 201/11 of July 20th, 196/11 of July 11th, and 224/11 of August 11th' as part of Angola's overall efforts for expanding the government's commitment 'to insert technological science and innovation in the country's development strategy'.[232] This latter legal development, I may posit, falls within the commercial law (including administrative law) nexus of the

---

[229] 'The Sustainable Development Goals Report 2020' (n 228) p 42.

[230] Angola, Voluntary National Review on the Implementation of the 2030 Agenda for Sustainable Development 2021 (hereinafter 'Angola 2021 Report'), p 63.

[231] ibid p 64 highlighting the following policy prescriptions: 'National Science, Technology and Innovation Policy and Strategy; Telecommunications and Information Technology Infrastructure Development Program', and industrial development plan (PDIA 2025), 'Program for the Promotion of Production in the Manufacturing Industry; Transport, Logistics and Distribution Policy'.

[232] ibid.

TARGET COMMENTARY 687

legal meta-relationship paradigm this commentary is advocating as part of the broader legal nexus of understanding how legal rules by governments for regulating private commercial activities are evolving under the SDGs.

2. Target 9.2 Promote inclusive and sustainable industrialization, and by 2030 raise significantly industry's share of employment and GDP in line with national circumstances, and double its share in the LDCs

Thematically, this target covers industrialization, the need for higher employment and, broadly, industry. In addition, the target also links with how the 'global value chain' is connected to 'economic growth'.[233] A key priority of this target is the so-called least-developed countries (LDCs) which are spread geographically throughout Africa, Asia Pacific- and Haiti in the Caribbean.[234]

In February 2021, the UN Committee for Policy Development listed some forty-six countries as LDCs, of which Angola, Bhutan, Sao Tome, and Solomon Islands will 'graduate' from this category by the end of 2024.[235] While LDCs are a major priority of this Goal, this does not mean that other developed or near-industrialized countries will miss out on this target. On the contrary, the target cuts across a number of industries in all countries and how private stakeholders such as businesses and entrepreneurs can contribute to an increase in employment and retool current manufacturing or other means of production using clean technology.[236]

Some of the key economic activities in this target are:

- Mining
- Manufacturing

---

[233] See Weber and Weber (n 200) 7. For a general discussion on global value chains and linkage to sustainability in a legal dimension, see J Salminen and M Rajavuori, 'Transnational Sustainability Laws and the Regulation of Global Value Chains: Comparison and a Framework for Analysis' (2019) 26 Maastricht Journal of European and Comparative Law 602.

[234] The classification is based on UN Country Classifications 2019, World Economic Situation and Prospects, p 173 <https://www.un.org/development/desa/dpad/wp-content/uploads/sites/45/WESP2019_BOOK-ANNEX-en.pdf> accessed 25 October 2021. For discussions on Africa in a broad sense see E Opoku and I Yan, 'Industrialization as Driver for Sustainable Economic Growth in Africa' (2017) 28 The Journal of International Trade and Economic Development 30–56. A drawback of target 9.2 for least developed countries is the fact that they 'often rely on a limited number of commodity exports which makes them extremely vulnerable to shocks [and in 2019 were] off track in relation to the Goal 9 target to double the manufacturing industry's share of GDP by 2030. The shortfall is especially severe in the medium and high-technology sectors. Those sectors represent 47.4 per cent of manufacturing production in North America and Europe, but only 10.4 per cent in the least developed countries', see United Nations, 'The Future is Now—Science for Achieving Sustainable Development—Global Sustainable Development Report 2019', p 15. See also, T Moyo, 'Promoting Inclusive and Sustainable Industrialisation in Africa: A Review of Progress, Challenges and Prospects' (2017) Proceedings of the 2nd Annual International Conference on Public Administration and Development Alternatives, 26–28 July 2017, Gaborone, Botswana, 365–75, 371 (discussing some of the similar challenges due to fluctuation in world market prices).

[235] Bhutan for instance by the end of 2023 will no longer classify as LDC, see General Assembly Resolution A/RES/73/133 adopted on 13 December 2018; the UN Committee for Policy Development list is available here—<https://www.un.org/development/desa/dpad/wp-content/uploads/sites/45/publication/ldc_list.pdf> accessed 25 October 2021. The LDC group is also a powerful voting bloc in SDGs, climate change, and other UN body's initiatives and hence as sovereign states. Economic designations as such should not mean when LDCs vote in the UNGA, they are not exercising sovereign power. See also, S Haug and others, 'The "Global South" in the Study of World Politics: Examining a Meta Category' (2021) 42 Third World Quarterly 1923–44.

[236] For some discussions on the legal aspects of clean technology see Z Liscow and Q Karpilow, 'Innovation Snowballing and Climate Law' (2017) Washington University Law Review 387; J Xiang, 'Cleantech Innovation by Developing Countries' (2020) 18 Boston University International Law Journal 185–239.

688   SDG 9

- Power generation (energy)
- Machinery
- Freight transport and storage

Based on the lexical framing of the target, there are two indicators designed to help achieve target 9.2.[237] The first indicator, 9.2.1, focuses on 'manufacturing value added as a proportion of GDP per capita', and target 9.2.2 focuses on 'manufacturing employment as a proportion of total employment'. Here we can see that 'manufacturing' and the 'employment' that such manufacturing generates will feed into the overall target of reducing unemployment in LDCs along with external spillovers for 'sustainable manufacturing' processes.[238]

While it is expected that LDCs will ultimately gain from an increase in manufacturing activities, higher employment, and, where possible, 'greener manufacturing', the same can also be said for developed nations such as those in Europe who will also benefit from target 9.2 as they seek to 're-industrialize' through clean technology, among other gains.[239] Most of the firms that have been engaged in general manufacturing in LDCs are medium-size enterprises or on occasions an established unit of a larger global conglomerate. The factors that drive firms to develop manufacturing capabilities in LDCs are, on the one hand, the obvious sustainability criteria—environment, economy, and society—and on the other, access to raw materials or lower production costs.

While the issue of 'sustainable manufacturing' has long been a concern for manufacturers, it is also an issue that has significant negative effects. These negative effects may include automation (autonomous robots) of manufacturing, hence replacing a number of human employees, or the rise of new manufacturing processes such as three-dimensional (3D) printing or other additive process.[240] While these types of manufacturing processes can help to industrialize current manufacturing capabilities they also suggest that sustainable industrialization will vary according to LDCs and other countries aiming for a 'fourth industrialization'.

---

[237] The concept of manufacturing value added (MVA) is a ratio between MVA and GDP, and this target has seen positive development in parts of the ASEAN economies. See, ASEAN Sustainable Development Goals Indicators Baseline Report 2020 (ASEAN Secretariat, Jakarta, 2020), pp 90–92.

[238] For an introductory reading to what some of the aspects of sustainable manufacturing entails see C Machado and others, 'Sustainable Manufacturing in Industry 4.0: An Emerging Research Agenda' (2020) 58 International Journal of Production Research 1462–84. See also, A Sartal and others, 'The Sustainable Manufacturing Concept, Evolution and Opportunities within Industry 4.0: A Literature Review' (2020) 12(5) Advances in Mechanical Engineering 1–17.

[239] The narrative here is generally on the 're-industrialization' or 'fourth industrialization' in reference to European states or North America, whilst other countries such as China for example see the positive benefits of achieving target 9.2; see generally, Q Yuan and others, 'Inclusive and Sustainable Industrial Development in China: An Efficiency-Based Analysis for Current Status and Improving Potentials' (2020) 268 Applied Energy, Article 114876. See also E Westkamper, *Towards the Re-Industrialization of Europe: A Concept for Manufacturing for 2030* (Springer 2014); E Sutherland, 'The Fourth Industrial Revolution: The Case of South Africa' (2020) 47 Politikon 233–52.

[240] For discussions on additive manufacturing see D Eyers and others, 'The Impact of Additive Manufacturing on the Product-Process Matrix' (2019) Production Planning and Control, <https://doi.org/10.1080/09537 287.2021.1876940> accessed 18 September 2022; see also T Kurfess and W Cass, 'Rethinking Additive Manufacturing and Intellectual Property Protection' (2014) 57 Research Technology Management 35–42.

Even through a regulatory and legal lens, the huge disparity in relation to legal enforcement and capacity for legal protection of new rights or innovation in green manufacturing is substantial between LDCs and those aiming for a fourth industrialization. While a majority of LDCs in principle have English common law traits[241] and therefore a capacity to respond to new legal problems or other mechanisms to safeguard green manufacturing, this does not mean that those countries will formally enact new provisions for the benefit of new manufacturing capabilities or the associated rights and obligations that may arise from issues relating to property, investment, and innovation for sustainable development.

LDCs are more likely to rely on existing legal provisions or 'common law traits' to provide effective remedy since overhauling their legal systems will require more formal modes of investments and capital injection. Thus, while SDG 9 and target 9.2 are appropriate indicators for broader investments and capital injection, the progress report in 2021 has so far revealed that only general manufacturing has improved globally.

Using data from the SDG tracking and progress web portal in October 2021, a comparison was drawn up between the African nation of Benin and the European nation of Luxembourg on manufacturing employment/proportion of total employment. The figures have only a small degree of difference in terms of value. For Benin, this value represents 7.5 per cent and for Luxembourg the value was 4.6 per cent. These are relative two small nations where manufacturing capacities are low.[242] In this regard, there is room for target 9.2 further to enable employment and subsequently sustainable industrialization in Benin and comparably Luxembourg. Perhaps even more worrying, as this trend reveals, is that the notion of 'sustainable industrialization' that the target promotes has to do with how much access a nation state has to resources in order to use that resource more efficiently or build upon its previous accomplishments (such as employment turnover) in order to generate economic growth along those required for sustainable industrialization.

Nevertheless, some nations in the LDCs such as Angola have been giving priority to aspects of SDG 9 in particular how target 9.2 and manufacturing can drive economic growth. In this regard, countries such as Angola believe that the abundance of natural resources can work in their favour to transform the local economy. Thus, Angola was one of the few LDCs to embrace SDG 9 positively and this points to the need for continued investment in different sectors.[243] Angola points to its non-oil sectors as avenues for growth and in particular in 'Education, Science and Technology; Technology Transfer; Industrial Production, Competitiveness, Employment, Sustainability, and Building Resilient Infrastructure to support development'.[244] These are based on the policies that

---

[241] See also, I Bantekas, 'The Globalization of English Contract Law: Three Salient Illustrations' (2021) 137 Law Quarterly Review 130.

[242] To generate the data, the dashboard function must be utilised and is therefore not a live link, but for illustrative purpose, it can be found here <https://sdg.tracking-progress.org/dashboard/> accessed 18 September 2022. But see, S Asumadu-Sarkodie and P Sastewaa Owusu, 'Carbon Dioxide Emission, Electricity Consumption, Industrialization, and Economic Growth Nexus: The Beninese Case' (2016) 11 Energy Sources 1089–96 (showing how industrialization will increase carbon dioxide emission).

[243] Angola SDG Report 2021, p 63.

[244] ibid p 70.

690   SDG 9

the country has prioritized for 2025.[245] In short, matters relating to contract law and investment law will form two of the main legal issues for target 9.2 in Goal 9.

3. Target 9.3 Increase the access of small-scale industrial and other enterprises, particularly in developing countries, to financial services including affordable credit and their integration into value chains and markets

Overall, the target of SDG 9.3 is defined by share of the value added by small-scale enterprises in the total value added of enterprises. This target is oriented heavily toward developing countries where small-scale enterprises tend to outstrip large-scale enterprises. At the same time, this target relates to professional activities and services derived from that of repair services. Thus, access to financial services and credit can foster greater involvement of SMEs in domestic economies and access to global markets. The SDG Reports for 2020 and 2021 have revealed the uphill battles that countries in the Global South are facing regarding financial services.

Some of the key economic activities in this target are:

- Transportation and storage
- Financial intermediation
- Manufacturing
- Arts and entertainment
- Hospitality
- Construction
- Vehicular repair and maintenance
- Administrative and support services
- Education
- Professional and technical activities

The UN SDG 2020 Report, for example, communicated the following:

Small-scale industrial enterprises are major sources of employment in developing and emerging economies. They are central to income-generation and the alleviation of poverty and will play a crucial role in the recovery of the global economy post-COVID-19. However, they are vulnerable due to their small size and limited resources. They do not have the capacity to deal with unexpected shocks, such as the current crisis, without help from governments. Access to credit is particularly important to small-scale firms for increasing their competitiveness and enabling them to integrate into local and global value chains. In developing countries, 34.7 per cent of small-scale industries (manufacturing and services) benefit from loans or lines of credit. However, only 22.9 per cent of small-scale industries in sub-Saharan Africa received loans or lines of credit, compared with almost half in Latin America and the Caribbean, according to recent data. Providing fiscal stimulus and access to financial

[245] ibid p 64.

services in support of small-and medium-sized enterprises is essential to enabling them to survive and thrive during and after the crisis.[246]

For developing nations, some aspects of boosting SMEs as part of a larger effort on economic growth continue to be a challenge. Indonesia, for example, reported that it has put in place policy mechanisms in an effort to reduce the challenges especially to make 'access to finance for entrepreneurs' a priority.[247]

A developed nation such as Sweden notes that there has been an overall growth trend in lending to non-financial companies and this indicates 'a growing need for capital supply among companies'.[248] In the case of Denmark, the country has fulfilled target 9.3 'as the vast majority of Danish companies are assessed as having good opportunities for financing'.[249] For the Czech Republic, target 9.3 has a good standing when compared to the rest of the EU due to 'the availability of funding for small and medium-sized enterprises'.[250]

These disparities on lending in the developed nations compare to the LDCs will need to close. While it is possible for access to finance by small-scale enterprises in the developed nations can continue to boost their overall economic development, this cannot be said of developing nations where it is still a problem to gain access to loans by small scale enterprises. But the two main legal issues that will surface will be international especially in relation to financial services and the GATS, or road transport issues under international conventions for goods.

4. Target 9.4 By 2030, upgrade infrastructure and retrofit industries to make them sustainable, with increased resource use efficiency and greater adoption of clean and environmentally sound technologies and industrial processes, all countries taking in accordance with their respective capabilities

The reduction of carbon emission and equally greater rise in clean technology and energy are a primary concern of target 9.4. The target aims to capture how best to maximize resource efficiency and the correlation with industrial production on the environment. Here, the concept of innovation is fundamental to achieving this target, but capital investment is also a significant factor, especially when countries in the Global South or the LDCs need to match their counterparts in the developed world. Another aspect of this target is the broader impact of circular economy on how resource efficiency can be maximized.[251]

---

[246] SDG 2020 Report (n 228) p 43.

[247] Indonesia's Voluntary National Review (VNR) 2021 (hereinafter 'Indonesia SDG Report 2021'), p 326: 'Strengthening entrepreneurship, micro small and medium enterprises (MSMEs) and cooperatives through increasing business capacity and access to finance for entrepreneurs and increasing the creation of start-ups and business opportunities.'

[248] Sweden, Report on the Implementation of the 2030 Agenda for Sustainable Development (hereinafter 'Sweden SDG Report 2021'), p 99.

[249] Denmark, Voluntary National Review 2021 (hereinafter 'Denmark SDG Report 2021'), p 110.

[250] Second Voluntary National Review of the 2030 Agenda in the Czech Republic 2021 (hereinafter 'Czech SDG Report 2021'), p 52.

[251] A helpful discussion is also that of D D'Amato, 'Sustainability Narratives as Transformative Solution Pathways: Zooming in on the Circular Economy' (2021) 1 Circular Economy and Sustainability 231–42.

692 SDG 9

The circular economy (see Chapter 12 in this book) is intricately connected to most of the overall targets in SDG 9 given that economic and business activities are essential to both areas. [252] On the other, the use of material and resource and the actual requirement under target 9.4 for environmentally sound approaches are encouraging.[253] The different considerations for the circular economy will also have an impact on how energy is consumed or generated and hence strategies for that economic activity under target 9.4 of the SDGs are important so that actors can 'move forward from an existing state, while promoting a pragmatic view on what to reach'.[254] It will also be crucial to get larger corporate actors involved in how the circular economy take shape, even in the daily activities of human beings which are connected to electronic gadgets such as smart phones which when damaged are not usually recycled but replaced with a new device.[255]

Some of the key economic activities in this target are:

- Reduce and recycle
- Circular economy

A challenge will also include how to reduce CO_2 especially when industrialization is dependent on heavy energy consumption through mining.[256]

North Korea in its progress report for 2021 reported on its efforts to reduce carbon emission, which saw a reduction in 2020 of 0.3 per cent compared to 2015, when respectively carbon emissions per unit of value added was 9.7 and 9.4 per cent.[257] While this is positive figure for the North Koreans' efforts, there are challenges in other areas in meeting this target and the North Korean Progress SDG Report 2021 was brutally honest: 'the emission of carbon dioxide has been increased as compared to 2015, while the consumption of Ozone depleting substances has been/is being reduced by 10.3 per cent annually ... The industrial sector is developed towards balancing demand and production, minimizing pollutants, and protecting resources.'[258] In other nations such as

---

[252] The circular economy, though broad a concept, when viewed strictly from a private business activity involves some form of economic incentives to the business operators, and in that regard, even in simple things such as bottle recycling, where regulation by the state and private norms of individuals are important, 'the policy levers that can be manipulated—bottle deposits and recycling laws—potentially have a powerful effect on recycling rates'; see WK Viscusi and others, 'Promoting Recycling: Private Values, Social Norms, and Economic Incentives' (2011) 101 American Economic Review 65, 70.

[253] See also Denmark SDG Report 2021, p 48: 'The key idea in a circular economy or bioeconomy is to keep materials in circulation for as long as possible to retain or even increase their value and reduce the impact on the environment.'

[254] This quote is based on an argument for setting up targets for the circular economy as such and not necessarily linked to the SDGs, see P Morseletto, 'Targets for a Circular Economy' (2020) 153 Resources, Conservation and Recycling 1–12, 2.

[255] An EU study as far back as 2016 recommended the need to recycle smart phones; see European Commission, 'Closing the Loop: An EU Action Plan for the Circular Economy', COM(2015) 614 final, Brussels 2.12. 2015.

[256] See J Steen, 'Build Resilient Infrastructure, Promote Inclusive and Sustainable Industrialization and Foster Innovation' in C Parra and others (eds), *Mining, Materials, and the Sustainable Development Goals (SDGs): 2030 and Beyond* (CRC Press, Taylor and Francis 2021) 85 (noting that 'mining provides raw materials for infrastructure and industrialization' and that 'the digital economy is thus based upon mined products in the same way that the industrial revolution was').

[257] Democratic People's Republic of Korea, Voluntary National Review on the Implementation of the 2030 Agenda 2021 (hereinafter 'North Korea SDG Progress Report 2021), p 33.

[258] ibid.

those in the developed world, part of the condition for financial grants to companies is that they must demonstrate a low level of emissions.

In Sweden, there has been a downward trend in the level of emissions.[259] Based on this comparative assessment with North Korea and Sweden in terms of meeting target 9.4 on emissions, in some ways both countries have been honest in terms of the deficits they face in reaching this target.

In other emerging economies such as Thailand, the focus has been on government policies to boost and foster aspects of SDG 9, such as the circular economy. Thus, the Thai government reported that it 'has designated the Bio-Circular Green (BCG) Economy Model as a National Agenda in order to escape middle-income trap and drive forward sustainability and inclusive growth.'[260] Since Thailand is one of the few emerging or developing economies to put emphasis on the circular economy in its 2021 SDG Report, it also has parallels with those in the developed world such as Denmark. In fact, Denmark in its 2021 SDG Report highlighted the need for a circular economy both in Denmark and abroad.[261]

The overall trend for target 9.4 is in 2021, most countries have not met the target but are close or have taken positive steps to meet the target. Some of the major developed economies such as Norway have made it clear in their reports.[262] From a methodological point of view, Norway and Denmark were noticeable countries to report the use of both 'government' and 'civil society' assessment for their SDGs. And for target 9.4, the government assessment for Norway indicates there is a long way to go.[263] The government reported that it had not yet met the target for 9.4 but is very close and the steps are positive in terms of reaching this target: 'Norway has a well-regarded set of measures for research and development (R&D) and innovation activities in the business sector. Sustainability issues are high on the agenda.'[264] Although Norway is performing well in other areas of SDG 9, that is, on track to meet those targets, the use of civil society to peer-review the assessment by the government has been an overall positive development. The issue that creates a link to the meta-legal relationships is the need for recycling laws in most countries.

5. Target 9.5 Enhance scientific research, upgrade the technological capabilities
   of industrial sectors in all countries, particularly developing countries, including

---

[259] Sweden SDG Report 2021, p 99: 'From 2010 to 2018, emission intensity (emissions per unit produced in the economy) has shown a downward trend. At the aggregate level, emissions have fallen, while the economy has grown.'

[260] Thailand's Voluntary National Review on the Implementation of the 2030 Agenda for Suitable Development 2021 (hereinafter 'Thai SDG Report 2021'), p 43, and further stating '[t]he development of the BCG economy model will focus on four sectors: (1) agriculture and food; (2) medical services and wellness; (3) bioenergy, biomaterials, and biochemical; and (4) tourism and creative economy'. For other small nations such as those in the Caribbean, tourism investments are also crucial and are tied to how the SDGs can be realized; see generally A Spencer and L McBean, 'Alignment of Tourism Investment to the SDGs in Jamaica: An Exploratory Study' (2020) 12 Worldwide Hospitality and Tourism Themes 261.

[261] Denmark SDG Report 2021.

[262] See, eg, Norway, Voluntary National Review 2021 Norway (hereinafter 'Norway SDG 2021 Report').

[263] The key to this claim is based on the interpretation of the emoji's Norway used to indicate its level of preparedness, and hence the emoji (symbol) representing the government assessment indicates 'Norway has not met the target, but is close', as explained on p 55.

[264] Norway SDG 2021 Report, p 72.

694   SDG 9

by 2030 encouraging innovation and increasing the number of R&D workers per
one million people by x% and public and private R&D spending

This important target of SDG 9 reaches out to public and private actors as it aims to
capture how R&D and other forms of scientific research can be accelerated. This tier 1
target is being monitored by UNESCO. It covers knowledge production and dissemination through R&D investments. To achieve this, states (or private entities) must inject
substantial financial capital in R&D so that knowledge production and its availability
can be shared among 'humankind'. Crucial to this target are 'researchers' who will engage in the 'conception or creation of new knowledge'. Moreover, since government and
private financial backing is crucial to achieve at least 3 per cent of GDP in 2030 for R&D
spending, this might only be possible in countries which have traditionally invested
heavily in R&D.

Some of the key economic activities in this target are:

- Space transport (R&D)
- ICT upgrade

In the EU, for example, private enterprises continue to be the biggest spenders for research
development and innovation.[265] When compared to other countries, especially in the
LDCs or North Korea, then the situation and figures are different.[266]

Developing countries such as Egypt have reported a mild increase on how they are
ranked globally from an innovation perspective.[267] This is also the same for developed
countries such as Japan. Egypt was one of the few developing countries to report that
COVID-19 'impact on various industry, innovation, & infrastructure indicators for
Egypt is considerably minor'.[268] In some other developing countries such as Cabo Verde,
it was a matter of restating that they are committed to improving scientific research and
innovation.[269]

---

[265] Eurostat, SDG 9—Industry, Innovation and Infrastructure (Statistics Explained), May 2021, p 4: 'An analysis
of gross domestic expenditure on R&D by sector of performance shows that the two biggest spenders in 2019 remained the business enterprise sector (66.3% of total R&D expenditure) and the higher education sector (21.6%).
The share of the government sector was about 11.5%, while the private non-profit sector accounted for less than
1.0% of the total R&D expenditure.'

[266] North Korea, for example, reported that in 2020, for target 9.5.1, its R&D expenditure as a proportion of GDP
was 9.6 per cent, North Korea SDG 2021 Report, p 61.

[267] Egypt, Egypt's 2021 Voluntary National Review (hereinafter 'Egypt 2021 SDG Report').

[268] ibid p 52.

[269] Cabo Verde, Voluntary National Review on the Implementation of the 2030 Agenda for Sustainable
Development 2021 (hereinafter 'Cabo Verde SDG Report 2021'), p 100: 'Cabo Verdean authorities recognize that
it is a priority to strengthen scientific research and improve technological capacities, particularly in industrial sectors. Thus, Cabo Verdean authorities will provide the country with a scientific and technological research policy
that builds a knowledge-based society, with standards of quality and efficiency of global reference, based on the
exchange between cultural and scientific capacities at national and international scales and taking advantage of
comparative advantages and promoting innovation and integrated and transversal scientific development. As
such, they are committed to investing in research and development, which is expected to reach nearly 2% of GDP
in 2030.'

TARGET COMMENTARY   695

In its report, Japan chose to highlight how it compares with other industrial nations on the Global Innovation Index and was concerned about a fall in its ranking.[270] Furthermore, for Japan empirical data or the lack of it regarding the progress on SDG is another concern: 'There is inadequate provision of scientifically accurate information and challenges in the interface between science and policy. This is also evident in the COVID-19 measures, highlighting the importance of putting in place proven preventive measures.'[271] Japan, however, was more optimistic that its 'Sixth Science, Technology and Innovation Basic Plan' of 2021 would help it to achieve comprehensive growth in science and technology.[272] Japan's optimism for the Sixth Science Plan is based partly on international collaboration.[273] Moreover, it will seek to promote measures for the implementation of the Sixth Science plan in a systemic manner.[274] In short, Japan plans to use science and diplomacy as a tool for collaboration on SDG 9 based on its strength in the area and to spread science, technology, and innovation to other parts of the world.

Other major economies such as Norway also note that their progress on meeting target 9.5 is close but the target has not yet been met: 'Public research funding has increased in recent years. The challenge is to stimulate a sustainable, innovative and competitive private sector that contributes to the green shift.'[275] While the approach by different developed countries is different, it goes to show what strengths those countries have and how they can use them to benefit other nations or develop them for their own local requirements to meet all SDG 9 targets in full. Further amendments or new laws on intellectual property or innovation will help to generate the requirements for target 9.5.

6. Target 9.a Facilitate sustainable and resilient infrastructure development
   in developing countries through enhanced financial, technological and technical
   support to African countries, LDCs, LLDCs and SIDS

One of the most advanced economies in Europe—Germany—reported in 2021 that the status of SDG 9 is heading in the right direction 'but the target will be missed by

---

[270] Japan, Voluntary National Review 2021, Report on the Implementation of 2030 Agenda: Toward Achieving the SDGs in the Post-COVID-19 Era (hereinafter 'Japan 2021 SDG Report'), p 118: 'Japan has generally shown the ability to rank in the top 10 for the indicators of public institutions, infrastructure, market maturity, business sophistication, and knowledge and technology output. However, the rankings for the indicators of human capital, research, and creative output are generally low.'

[271] ibid p 140.

[272] ibid.

[273] ibid p 62. This states in full: 'Science, technology, and innovation (STI) are fundamental elements of peace and prosperity by supporting economic and social development and playing important roles in ensuring safety and security. For this reason, the Sixth Science and Technology Innovation Basic Plan formulated in March 2021 states that it is important for Japan to be actively involved in international collaboration and cooperation by utilizing STI's potential to solve global-scale issues. In this plan, Japan has set (i) addressing global climate change, and (ii) addressing biodiversity as key policy issues and has decided to focus on research and development of those issues. Japan contributes to the development of STI in Japan and world, the enhancement of relations with other countries, the peace and stability of the international community, and the resolution of global issues through the promotion of 'science and technology diplomacy' by utilizing its outstanding science and technology'.

[274] ibid p 118.

[275] Norway SDG Report 2021, p 72.

696 SDG 9

between 5% and 20%'.[276] According to the German SDG 2021 Report, there is no assessment for the roll-out of broadband as per share of households, and there is a cloudy outlook for private and public expenditure on R&D.[277] But these assessments are not necessarily an indication that Germany hasn't made advancement in these areas.

On the contrary, as developed nation Germany is doing well[278] in these reported areas on SDG 9. However, what is important is the fact that Germany (and a few other nations) highlighted the efforts towards helping developing countries. For example, the German Report notes:

In developing countries, the German Government is funding education and training measures, some specifically for women and girls, the development of innovative digital ecosystems, and support for an African data economy or pan-African e commerce initiative.[279]

These efforts by Germany capture some of the difficulties that African nations and other developing nations face and point to the fact that the ability to meet the targets of SDG 9 also requires external assistance—technical and financial. Some African nations such as Zimbabwe reported that they face a huge deficit in terms of meeting the overall targets but that some areas, such as ICT and industry, present greater challenges than others.[280] In line with a vision for an African data economy, Zimbabwe reports that it has 'successfully commissioned the National Data Centre and launched the Local Authorities Digital System (LADS)' and other initiatives for a data economy.[281] When the vision for global science and technology innovation by Japan are factored into similar visions by Germany, and countries such as Zimbabwe have taken steps towards a global data economy, it appears that such a collaboration may actually reduce the current technology gap in some of the LDCs. Legally, the rise of data laws and regulating the big economy will also play a factor in the link to meta-legal relationship.

[276] Report on the Implementation of the 2030 Agenda for Sustainable Development, German Voluntary National Review to the HLPF 2021 (hereinafter 'German SDG Report 2021'), p 21, on the meaning of the 'cloudy' symbol that represents its assessment scale.

[277] ibid p 74.

[278] The report stated by 2025 broadband coverage will close some gaps and that country's 'High-Tech Strategy takes the objective of strengthening Germany's standing in global competition, pooling resources more effectively and creating fresh stimulus for innovation in business and society', ibid p 76.

[279] ibid p 77.

[280] Zimbabwe's Second Voluntary National Review 2021 (hereinafter 'Zimbabwe SDG Report 2021').

[281] ibid pp 88–89: 'In order to improve efficiency and effectiveness in Government internal operations and administration, Government successfully commissioned the National Data Centre and launched the Local Authorities Digital System (LADS) which is a locally developed Enterprise Resource Planning (ERP) solution expected to be used in 92 local authorities. Other initiatives being undertaken by Government and the private sector include set up of the National ICT Device Factory, implementation of National Data Centre, development of E-Government Enterprise Architecture and Interoperability Framework, upgrade of Government Internet Services Provider (GISP) infrastructure, enhancement and optimization of Government common connectivity infrastructure, expansion Public Finance Management System (PFMS) coverage to all districts, and establishment of Community Information Centers at sub-national levels.' Although these intended actions also match those of target 9.c, their significance in relation to the 'German vision' under 9.a mentioned earlier lie in the fact that a coherent and established government approach is also needed to make a privately driven e-commerce and data economy work.

TARGET COMMENTARY   697

7. Target 9.b Support domestic technology development, research and innovation
   in developing countries including ensuring a conducive policy environment
   for inter alia industrial diversification and value addition to commodities

In most cases, because raw commodities are often specific to a country or geographic region, it is often difficult for a country to diversify into other commodities or manufacturing capabilities. This challenge is recognized by most of the developing countries, which also face simultaneous challenges such as access to finance or technological innovation. Angola, for example, in its 2021 report places the diversification challenge as a 'medium to long-term' one, especially when the country needs to move beyond oil production.[282] This and other challenges prompted Angola to request a delay in its graduation from LDCs to at least 2024.[283]

The lack of access to technology transfer is another significant role that Angola reported as some of the challenges that is slowing economic development:

> Another major challenge for the development of Human Capital has to do with improving the quality of education and professional skills of young people, as well as technology transfer in order to promote a more sustainable and resilient development that contributes to economic diversification.[284]

Here the case of Angola is significant in that industrial diversification affects all parts of the economy (and many other countries). Moreover, key to the strategy of industrial diversification is the extent to which access to technology transfer or how R&D through an educated population can aid such diversification.

Another important highlight from the Angola SDG 2021 Report is the fact that it outlines how regional trade agreements are important to its industrial diversification:

> [I]n order to be competitive in the African Continental Free Trade Area (AfCETA) context, Angola will have to renew its efforts to keep pace among its future competitors through industrial diversification strategy.[285]

On a broader context, the numerous free trade agreements globally such as the Asia Pacific, the Transatlantic, and others under negotiations, suggest that states will face additional legal obligations to ensure that on the one hand, they have policies conducive to investment, and on the other, states reduce their monopoly holds on the production of essential commodities. But as Angola reports on its progress for SDG 9, part of government policy intervention will be the 'establishment of industrial nuclei' to renew

---

[282] Angola SDG Report 2021, p vii: 'Angola has another medium and long-term challenge of accelerating its economic diversification efforts beyond oil and diamond exploration and reducing its structural vulnerability, recognized in the request to postpone its Least Developed Country (LDC) graduation to 2024, approved by the United Nations General Assembly in February 2021.'

[283] ibid.

[284] ibid.

[285] ibid 66.

698   SDG 9

efforts for diversification and promote 'inclusive and sustainable industrialization and fostering innovation'.[286]

It is important to note that in the developed world a number of countries have focused on how medium- and high-tech industry can generate innovation and growth. Thus a number of OECD countries have sought to enhance how exports of high-tech goods from advanced economies to the developing world will have positive spillovers and contribute to SDG 9 in general.[287] The meta-legal relationship will thus involve additional bilateral investment agreements and expansion of trade agreements.

8. Target 9.c Significantly increase access to ICT and strive to provide universal and affordable access to internet in LDCs by 2020

Where access to digital and information technologies has been a key target in SDG 9 and in particular as envisaged in target 9.c, most of the countries have reported significant progress in this area in 2021. Hence, countries in Africa, Europe, and Asia have said that most aspects of digital transformation have been achieved. In the EU, for example, small nations such as Cyprus said significant progress in SDG 9 'moved from a low average of less than 40% in 2017 to 72% in 2020, making the biggest progress made by Cyprus in all SDGs'.[288] Another area in which Cyprus reported positively has been the number of patent applications it made to the European Patent Office (EPO) which increased by 16.6 per cent to 2020. In Cyprus' SDG Report of 2017, the reported patent applications were 46.0 per cent and this increased to 53.7 per cent in 2020.[289] Thus, these positive highlights suggest that Cyprus (and many other EU nations) are performing well on meeting the targets of SDG 9.

Some of the key economic activities in this target are:

- Internet of Things
- Digital transformation
- Science and tech hubs

For non-EU nations, the road to digital transformation and information communication technologies has been one of mixed blessings.[290] ICT is the key aspect of this sub-target and it can be measured by access to the Internet or access to mobile telephony.

---

[286] ibid pp 70–71.
[287] OECD, 'Industrial Policy for Sustainable Development Goals: Increasing the Private Sector's Contribution 2021' (hereinafter 'OECD Private Sector'), p 77: 'The spillovers from medium- and high-tech industries (MHTIs) are usually higher than those of less technologically intensive industries. This is because MHTIs usually provide more opportunities for the upskilling of labour and for innovation in production processes.'
[288] Republic of Cyprus, Second Voluntary National Review Sustainable Development Goals (SDGs), June 2021 (hereinafter Cyprus SDG Report 2021'), p 29.
[289] ibid p 74. Largely, this is part of the Annex to 2021 report by Cyprus as highlighting the progress to meet the other SDGs.
[290] See, eg, Namibia, Second Voluntary National Review Report on the Implementation of the Sustainable Development Goals Towards Agenda 2030 (hereinafter 'Namibia SDG Report 2021'). While Namibia had excellent roll-out of broadband and the entire country has been covered, north of 80 per cent, efforts are still underway 'to address the challenges of rural communities, achieve rural industrialisation, and foster innovation' in hard to reach regions. Namibia SDG Report 2021, p 38.

For mobile telephony, where the ITU is a custodian agency, a key indicator to measure this target include the actual percentage of the population covered by a mobile network. According to the SDG 2020 Report, the world had achieved 'practically universal' mobile connection, and yet 'about half the global population is offline, mostly in LDCs'.[291] Although the 2020 SDG Report did not mention the root cause of this disparity, part of the reason may lie in the fact that in LDCs such as those in Sub-Saharan Africa, access to the Internet is usually via mobile devices as opposed to laptops or desktop computers.[292] There are limitations to the extent to which a mobile device can make individuals productive over the Internet, and it appears that part of the remedy is to ensure that laptops and desktops are also universally available in Sub-Saharan Africa in the same fashion as mobile devices.

Nonetheless, the SDG 2020 Report to support its claim of 'practically universal' mobile connections globally reports:

With COVID-19 forcing many to work, learn, seek health care and socialize from home, digital technologies and internet connectivity have been more a part of our daily lives. To access the internet, mobile connections provide flexibility, particularly in places where fixed-broad service is unavailable or unaffordable. Coverage of mobile access has expanded rapidly. In 2019, almost the entire world population (97 per cent) lived within reach of a mobile cellular signal, and 93 per cent lived within reach of a mobile-broadband signal. Least developed countries have seen significant growth in coverage of mobile-broadband signals, from 51 per cent in 2015 to 79 per cent in 2019. However, just 54 per cent of the global population actually used the Internet. Most of the offline population lives in LDCs, where only 19 per cent use the Internet, compared with 87 per cent in developed countries. Key reasons for this large gap are the cost of using the internet and lack of necessary skills.[293]

From this quotation, the last clause stating 'lack of necessary skills' appears to be an afterthought as opposed to what I think is the root cause, not having access to actual devices—laptops and desktop computers.

Nevertheless, apart from parts of the Pacific Island Countries and Sub-Saharan Africa, this target from SDG 9 had the highest success rate at the end of 2021, especially in relation to increased access to mobile networks. Outside Sub-Saharan Africa, China has pointed out how it plans to use ICT to revolutionize transport as part of its progress report in order to generate an 'industrial transformation'.[294] In this regard, China points to the need for new technological infrastructure such as 6G (sixth-generation)

---

[291] SDG 2020 Report, p 43.
[292] For a general discussion see also, B Mutsvairo and M Ragnedda (eds), *Mapping the Digital Divide in Africa: A Mediated Analysis* (Amsterdam University Press 2019).
[293] SDG 2020 Report, p 43.
[294] China's VNR Report on Implementation of the 2030 Agenda for Sustainable Development (hereinafter 'China SDG Report 2021') p 70.

technologies as part of this transformation.[295] Other developing nations such as Antigua and Barbuda have also pointed to ICT and mobile advances as one of the few bright spots in meeting SDG 9 overall.[296] But the simple fact that some nations are looking forward to the 'fourth industrial revolution' or how '6G' technology' will revolutionize their economic development, whilst other countries are only managing with mobile devices suggests that the tools for productivity in the next 'industrial revolution' needs to be universally accessible. The legal notion of global innovation law, including patent laws and regulating the Internet of things, fits the paradigm of this sub-goal.

9. SDG 9 Legal Relations

The legal characteristics of SDG 9 fall under several areas of legal relations. Classification-wise, the three broad areas are 'international law', 'commercial law', and 'intellectual property law', and these legal classifications can be further broken down into several sub-legal categories. However, it is only prudent to discuss, in brief, the major classifications of SDG 9 and their present status. First, because the SDGs in general interact with other treaties and agreements there is an onus on states to fulfil their pledges and obligations undertaken in those treaties. Secondly, SDG 9 represents a major challenge to global innovation law in that issues of intellectual property rights, technology transfer, and licensing, along with regulatory aspects of clean technology, will bring into direct conflict goals and protected legal rights. Moreover, commercial law issues especially on customs and road transport are significant.

Even if some of these legal obstacles were to be overcome, the policy of technology transfer or licensing is also a political matter in a number of the developed countries. This is because, from a policy point of view, these countries do not support technology transfer or have made vain attempts to support the minimum measures under international agreements.

The civil society assessment of Norway's progress on the SDGs in 2021 was equally cognizant of such a fact:

> Internationally, Norway does not support regulations that facilitate technology transfer in the e-commerce negotiations currently taking place in the WTO. Depriving countries in the global south of the opportunity to transfer knowledge and technology from the multi-national technology companies operating in these countries impedes the development of poor countries' own digital industry.[297]

---

[295] ibid: 'We will speed up large-scale deployment of 5G network and start developing 6G technologies.... There will be an all-out effort to develop the Internet of Things and to allow access by both fixed-line and mobile devices through narrowband as well as broadband. We will accelerate the building of a national integrated big data center system, build a number of national hub nodes and clusters of big data centers, and build exascale and 10× exascale supercomputing centers. Traditional infrastructure such as transportation, energy and municipal services will be digitalized at a faster pace.'

[296] See Antigua and Barbuda, 2021 Voluntary National Review of Antigua and Barbuda (hereinafter 'Antigua and Barbuda SDG Report 2021'), p 74: 'The country's mobile-cellular penetration rates surpass both regional and worldwide levels. The fixed-broadband market has been partially competitive since 2000.'

[297] Norway SDG Report 2021, p 73.

TARGET COMMENTARY 701

There are also other areas of technology transfer and licensing which are proving to be critical to how developing and emerging countries tackle global pandemics, and this was most evident in the TRIPs Waiver discussions for vaccines.[298] Nonetheless, these concerns straddle the meta-relationship of legal rules mentioned earlier where international law, commercial law/conflict of laws, and global innovation law have emerged on the international landscape.

It goes without saying that the SDGs have a nexus with international law. That nexus pertains to the numerous international agreements in the area of environmental protection and climate change, or perhaps when international judicial rulings such as the ICJ 1997 decision in the *Gabcikovo-Nagymaros* case are taken into account.[299]

From a treaty perspective, the Convention on International Trade in Endangered Species of Wild Fauna and Flora (CITES),[300] UNFCCC,[301] the Paris Agreement,[302] and the 2021 United Nations Climate Change Conference (COP26) already link a number of goals with the SDGs. The signs were there after the Paris Agreement that states were still aiming for more ambitious efforts to achieve some of the objectives set out in the Paris Agreement. So, for example, the Heads of State Declaration for Greater Climate Ambition 2018 (HOSDGCLA) had pushed the boundaries further.[303]

The COP26 Conference in Glasgow 2021 in its draft agreement mentions in its preamble the nexus of sustainability with SDG 9: 'the importance of ensuring sustainable, resilient and global inclusive recovery' from COVID-19[304] or technology mechanisms'.[305] Moreover, the burgeoning literature on climate change,[306] sustainability, and green innovation sprung from the various treaties and initiatives has further informed

---

[298] TRIPs Agreement, art 31(b) sets out waiver requirements for intellectual property rights, most notably that 'requirements may be waived by a member in the case of a national emergency or other circumstances of extreme urgency or in cases of public non-commercial use'. The proposal for a TRIPs waiver in light of COVID 19 is the WTO Waiver from Certain Provisions of the TRIPS Agreement for the Prevention, Containment and Treatment of COVID-19, Communication from India and South Africa, WTO Doc IP/C/W/699, 2 October 2020. For the debates on the TRIPs waiver and COVID 19 vaccines, see P Yu, 'A Critical Appraisal of the COVID-19 TRIPS Waiver' in T Pihlajarinne and others (eds), *Intellectual Property Rights in the Post Pandemic World: An Integrated Framework of Sustainability, Innovation and Global Justice* (Edward Elgar forthcoming 2023); B Mercurio, 'WTO Waiver from Intellectual Property Protection for Covid-19 Vaccines and Treatments: A Critical Review' (2021) 62 Virginia Journal of International Law Online 10; HM Haugen, 'Does TRIPS (Agreement on Trade-Related Aspects of Intellectual Property Rights) Prevent COVID-19 Vaccines as a Global Public Good?' (2021) 24 Journal of World Intellectual Property 195–220; A McMahon, 'Patents, Access to Health and COVID-19: The Role of Compulsory and Government-Use Licensing in Ireland' (2020) 71 Northern Ireland Legal Quarterly 667.

[299] Case Concerning the Gabcikovo-Nagymaros Project (*Hungary v Slovakia*) (Judgment) 25 September 1997 ICJ Reports 7.

[300] Convention on International Trade in Endangered Species of Wild Fauna and Flora (3 March 1973).

[301] UN Framework Convention on Climate Change, 1 June 1992, 1771 UNTS 107.

[302] A 2015 Agreement Concluded and adopted in Paris as a Decision of the UNFCCC, see UNFCC Dec. 1/CP.21, UN Doc FCCC/CP/2015/10/Add.1 (29 January 2016).

[303] Heads of State Declaration for Greater Climate Ambition, November 2018.

[304] COP 26 Draft Agreement, Draft Text 1/CMA.2, version 10/11/2021, 05:51.

[305] ibid para 59.

[306] See, eg, C Ryngaert, 'Climate Change Mitigation Techniques and International Law: Assessing the Externalities of Reforestation and Geoengineering' (2016) 30 Ratio Juris 273–89; O Ruppel and others (eds), *Climate Change: International Law and Global Governance—Volume 1—Legal Responsibilities and Global Responsibility* (Nomos 2013); A Brown, *Intellectual Property, Climate Change and Technology: Managing National Legal Intersections, Relationships and Conflicts* (Edward Elgar 2019).

the international legal community and academia on some of the pitfalls that states face or what further needs to be done.[307]

Naturally, the obvious question is why not link the SDGs to those treaties rather than inching toward a new 'sustainability treaty'? The answer to that question cannot be addressed here, but perhaps what the ICJ reminded us of 1997 is worth repeating: 'This need to reconcile economic development with protection of the environment is aptly expressed in the concept of sustainable development.'[308] Thus, with this forward-looking statement, it is perhaps easier to follow that pattern and link SDG 9 with international law and standards as such.

From the above general discussion on the targets in SDG 9, it is difficult to mask the fact that private stakeholders have been present at the negotiations of SDG 9 and will continue to play a greater role in the implementation and adaptability of SDG 9 targets and indicators. Moreover, the role of private stakeholders in the overall SDGs 2030 Agenda is also analogous to similar roles they had in treaty negotiations or the generation of private standards in trade treaties at the multilateral and bilateral level. Thus, SDG 9 and other global sustainability standards and targets in the 2030 Agenda will continue to recognize 'that private stakeholders have a useful role' especially in implementation.[309]

IV. Empirical Results: Sample Study on Vaccines and Technological Innovation: Law, Intellectual Property, and Sustainable Development

In this section I offer a brief discussion on a proxy of innovation in the light of COVID-19.

The following observation from the SDG Report 2021 captures the vaccine revolution in response to COVID-19 as an example of technological revolution:

> Due to tariffs and trade tensions between the world's dominant economies, global manufacturing growth was already in decline before the COVID-19 pandemic. When it struck, the movement of people and goods was restricted, disrupting global value chains, as well as global manufacturing and transport industries. Small-scale industries in particular have been severely affected. The lack of resilient infrastructure, information and communication technologies, and basic services limits a country's

---

[307] See also N Craik and others (eds), *Global Environmental Change and Innovation in International Law* (CUP 2018); C Zhou, *The Legal Barriers to Technology Transfer under the UN Framework Convention on Climate Change: The Example of China* (Springer 2019); K Kulovesi and S Oberthur, 'Assessing the EU's 2030 Climate and Energy Policy Framework: Incremental Change Toward Radical Transformation?' (2020) 29 Review of Economic, Comparative and International Law 151–66; MD Mahatab Uddin, *Climate Change Law, Technology Transfer and Sustainable Development* (Routledge 2021).

[308] Case Concerning the Gabcikovo-Nagymaros Project (*Hungary v Slovakia*) (Judgment) 25 September 1997 ICJ Reports 7, p 75.

[309] This argument is not new and various legal and interdisciplinary literature continues to raise similar concerns on the rising global role of private stakeholders, but for a recent discussion at the EU level and free trade agreements see M Bronckers and G Gruni, 'Retooling the Sustainability Standards in EU Free Trade Agreements' (2021) 24 Journal of International Economic Law 25–51, 33.

ability to perform and adjust to shocks. For the global community to achieve SDG9, industrialization, improvements in infrastructure, and the promotion of technological innovation by increasing investment in research and development are key. *The development and production of vaccines against COVID-19 in record time is one example of the power of technological innovation, which has given the world cause for hope.* (emphasis added)[310]

Identifying vaccine production as an example of technological innovation in the SDG 2021 Report is an important fact.

The previous parts of the quoted paragraph from the SDG 2021 Report capture the targets and indicators of SDG 9. More importantly, referring to the astonishing speed with which vaccines were produced during the pandemic as a sample of technological innovation also speaks volume. This is because SDG 9 aims to capture a multitude of issues, and under the 'innovation' umbrella alone are dozens of sub-issues which also fit the generic label of technological innovation.

Hence, in order to discuss one of these narrower issues, the production of vaccine is a good example, especially in the era of pandemic. But from a more legal and strategic point of view, the production of vaccines is also R&D intensive, requires substantial investment, and comes with a host of legal and regulatory issues including intellectual property rights.[311] Furthermore, if we are to factor in the common concern of the SDGs more broadly, then there are questions of 'access to medicine' or waivers on vaccine patents. The question of a vaccine waiver takes place at the national level after a facilitative or endorsed decision by the WTO.[312]

For three major (Western) vaccine producers for COVID-19,[313] Pfizer-BioNTech,[314] Moderna,[315] and AstraZeneca,[316] those producers registered a considerable number of patents for COVID-19 including previous patents for similar respiratory illnesses.[317] The major patent assignees for coronaviruses are the Academy of Military Medical

---

[310] SDG Report 2021 (n 228) 44.

[311] For a comprehensive discussion on legal and societal issues relating to vaccine production as a result of COVID 19 see JL Contreras, 'The Open COVID Pledge: Design, Implementation and Preliminary Assessment of an Intellectual Property Commons' (2021) 2021 Utah Law Review 833.

[312] See also McMahon (n 299) for a discussion on the situation in Ireland. See also, TRIPs art 31.

[313] For a fruitful discussion on COVID 19 innovation see AS Alshrari and others, 'Innovations and Development of Covid-19 Vaccines: A Patent Review' (2021) Journal of Infection and Public Health, <https://www.sciencedir ect.com/science/article/pii/S1876034121003427> accessed 18 September 2022.

[314] See also, MW Tenforde and others, 'Sustained Effectives of Pfizer-BioNTech and Moderna Vaccines Against COVID-19 Associated Hospitalizations Among Adules—United States, March—July 2021' (2021) 70 Morbidity and Mortality Weekly Report 1156–62.

[315] ibid.

[316] This vaccine has roots at Oxford University where it was developed under a subsidiary of the university (Oxford University Innovation Ltd), which handles all patents and licensing matters relating to Oxford University researchers and those of the university. However, a host of other subsidiaries and independent companies also collaborated including a spin out company Vaccitech Ltd, for a brief on those developments, see, C Garrison, 'How the "Oxford" Covid-19 Vaccine Became the "AtraZeneca" Covid-19 Vaccine' (2020) Medicines Law & Policy 1.

[317] At the global level, data from the WIPO Statistics Data Centre show that in 2020 there were 3,276,700 million patent applications compare 3,226,100 in 2019 representing a growth of 1.6 per cent. China, the United States, Japan, South Korea, and the European Patent Office (EPO) were responsible for the bulk of applications with China alone accounting for 45.7 per cent.

Sciences (China), Fudan University (China), US Department of Health and Human Sciences, AstraZeneca (Sweden), Tsinghua University (China), University of California, Korea Research Institute of Bioscience and Biotechnology (South Korea), Novartis (Switzerland), 3M Company (US), and InterMune(US).[318]

The granting of a patent as a legal right is covered by patent legislations domestically and internationally.[319] The international rules are those under the TRIPs Agreement—specifically, article 27(1) which states that patents are granted for 'inventions' that 'are new, involve an inventive step and are capable of industrial application'.[320] In order to produce a vaccine and obtain subsequent patent protection, vaccines are developed through multiple stages most of which require regulatory approval.[321] Thus, from the initial R&D to human trials, the process often involves some 'legal' questions or the protection of 'proprietary rights'.

Most of the legal questions during the 'innovation' or 'development' process of vaccines are generally settled under the patent rules of the domestic state (and to a lesser extent under international rules). The R&D of vaccines for COVID-19 has been a global effort and the HLPF of the UN SDGs recognized these efforts as part of the technological revolution for the SDGs in general.[322] Other observers saw those efforts as a 'push and pull' system of COVID-19 innovation.[323] At the end of 2021, most of the developed world (Europe and the Americas) surpassed more than 50 per cent of their populations receiving two doses of vaccines and were on the threshold of delivering a third 'booster' dose. On the other hand, the situation has been grim for LDCs and other developing countries where even the first dose of COVID-19 vaccine has not been administered to the general population.

The World Health Organization has been leading an effort to minimize the so-called vaccine inequality[324] and part of the response has been the Covax[325] vaccine—a pooling system where COVID-19 vaccines are made available at a reduced price to least developed and developing countries. There are various manufacturers involved in producing

---

[318] I gathered this list from the paper by K Liu and others, 'Global Landscape of Patents Related to Human Coronaviruses' (2021) 17 International Journal of Biological Science 1588–99, Table 1.

[319] In the United Kingdom, the granting of a patent is under The Patents Act 1977 (as amended), under which a patent may be granted 'only for an invention' that meets the following conditions: (i) the invention is new; (ii) it involves an inventive step; and (iii) it is capable of industrial application.

[320] TRIPs Agreement, art 27(1).

[321] See, eg n 320 above on the legal requirements for patent protection in the United Kingdom. However, for discussions on patents and pandemics see also, Liu and others, 'Global Landscape of Patents Related to Human Coronaviruses' (n 319); see also O Gurgula and J Hull, 'Compulsory Licensing of Trade Secrets: Ensuring Access to COVID-19 Vaccines via Involuntary Technology Transfer' (2021) Journal of Intellectual Property Law and Practice 1241.

[322] UN SDG Report (n 311).

[323] B Sampat and K Shalden, 'The Covid-19 Innovation System' (2021) 40 Health Affairs 400–07, <https://www.healthaffairs.org/doi/full/10.1377/hlthaff.2020.02097> accessed 18 September 2022.

[324] See also LN Sadat, 'Pandemic Nationalism, COVID-19, and International Law' (2021) 20 Washington University Global Studies Law Review 561; N Munung and others, 'Priorities for Global Access to Life-Saving Interventions During Public Health Emergencies: Crisis Nationalism, Solidarity or Charity?' (2021) Global Public Health doi:10.1080/17441692.2021.1977973; K Lee and J Piper, 'The WHO and the COVID-19 Pandemic: Less Reform, More Innovation' (2020) 26 Global Governance 523–33.

[325] The official term is the COVID-19 Vaccine Global Access Facility (COVAX).

Covax and hence, for countries procuring through the Covax-administered mechanism, there are various advantages and disadvantages. Notwithstanding the good intentions of Covax, it is an initiative, along with the proprietary rights for vaccines, that creates concerns for all three prongs of the meta-relationship of SDG 9 described earlier where international law, commercial law/conflicts of law, and global innovation law collide.[326]

This collision, however, does not seem so bad when SDG 9 is invoked along with the overall SDGs whose role is to diffuse how law responds to economic and social needs while at the same time projecting a balancing force for the coordination of international law (including global health regulations) to those on intellectual property rights to ensure that innovation is justly compensated. Perhaps, rather than looking at what SDG 9 tells us about innovation or the apparent praise by the UN SDG Report of 2021 on the global achievement of vaccine innovation, we should revert to the reminder of target 3.8 in SDG 3, that 'access to safe, effective, quality and affordable essential medicines and vaccines for all',[327] is part of the gentle reminder of humanity.[328] In that context, vaccine innovation, intellectual property, and sustainable development in the broader system of the SDGs is one safeguard to balance the competing forces of law, proprietary rights, and sustainable development.

V. Critique, Findings, and Outlook

To sum up the main findings at the end of 2021 on the progress of SDG 9, there is a long way to go for countries to meet the targets. The reports for 2021 also reflect, in some instances, the achievements and developments prior to the start of COVID-19, thereby showing only achievements up to the end of 2019. Most countries reported positive developments or have achieved target 9.c, however the other targets were work in progress. In fact, the achievements of SDG 9 can be captured by the assessment by the EU which in May 2021 has found that from an R&D perspective, progress has been made 'in terms of R&D personnel, patent applications and tertiary educational attainment'.[329] This same trend, especially in patent applications, was evident in a number of other

---

[326] See figure 9.1 on the matter of the meta-relationship of SDG 9.

[327] SDG target 3.8.

[328] Perhaps it is an appropriate time to invoke a topic that has not been discussed in this commentary but still fit the developments, In November 2020 the UN Human Rights Commissioner noted that 'intellectual property rights should not override States' obligations to protect and fulfil the right to health, which entails providing for immunization and treatment against major infectious diseases to all without discrimination'; see Statement by UN Human Rights Expert, 'Universal Access to Vaccines is Essential for Prevention and Containment of COVID-19 Around the World', 9 November 2020, <https://www.ohchr.org/EN/NewsEvents/Pages/DisplayNews.aspx?New sID=26484&LangID=E> accessed 18 September 2022; see also Statement by the Committee on Economic, Social and Cultural Rights, 'Statement on Universal Affordable Vaccination against Coronavirus Disease (COVID-19), International Cooperation and Intellectual Property', UN Doc E/C.12/2021/1/, 23 April 2021.

[329] Eurostat, 'SDG 9—Industry, Innovation and Infrastructure: Statistics Explained', May 2021, p 2.

706 SDG 9

countries including Angola[330] and Cyprus,[331] or efforts to introduce new patent laws such as in Laos.[332]

The interesting thing, however, is that part of the rise in patent applications and innovation relates to significant efforts, including R&D innovation, steered toward vaccines for COVID-19. In other cases, a number of countries were also making efforts to increase their research personnel per population in order to foster innovation. For other areas in SDG 9 such as CO_2 emissions, only a few nations reported their attempts to reduce carbon emissions leading up to the end of 2021. On the other hand, the manufacturing sector was a bright spot for a number of countries, where target 9.2 generally is concerned. The trend in that area has been positive in a number of countries both in the Global South, Asia Pacific, and the EU. In the EU, it was evident that 'indicators on sustainable infrastructure show unfavourable trends for sustainable transport and mobility patterns'.[333] It was a similar story for the more than forty countries that the commentary here examined.[334]

For the countries that reported on their progress on SDG 9 or implemented their individual targets in the review period 2021, the data extracted from reports to the HLFP on the selected countries, or the so-called Voluntary National Review (VNRs),[335] on every occasion warned of the impact of COVID-19. The VNR database (accessed 31 October 2021) forty-two countries filed reports for 2021.[336] For the Bahamas and Guatemala, there were no accessible PDF documents, and for the discussions on the selected countries, only reports filed in English were used.

Some countries in the 2021 VNR reported no progress on SDG 9. This was the case with Azerbaijan[337] and Lao People's Democratic Republic.[338] In most cases, the

[330] Angola SDG Report 2021, p 69. In the case of Angola, the patent statistics were telling two stories: 'Research and innovation remain weak, with a very low level of gross Research and Development (R&D) expenditure of GDP (0.03%) in 2016 and a very limited number of researchers (18.8) per million population ... This results in a limited number of patents applied for (from 117 to 82) but with an increasing number of patents granted nationally (from 22 to 33) between 2019 and 2020.'

[331] Cyprus SDG Report 2021, p 74.

[332] Laos SDG Report 2021, p 64.

[333] Eurostat, 'SDG 9—Industry, Innovation and Infrastructure: Statistics Explained', May 2021, p 2.

[334] See the list of countries at n 337). See also, OECD/UN-Habitat/UNOPS, 'Global State of National Urban Policy 2021: Achieving Sustainable Development Goals and Delivering Climate Action (2021)', where this joint study on urban policy, and by the same extent on the infrastructure aspects of SDG 9 found that there was moderate contribution to SDG 9 and even so only the developed nations saw these moderate achievements: 'The NUP's moderate to extensive contribution to SDG 9 varied across the five regions, with countries in Europe and North America leading at 38%, Africa, Asia and the Pacific and Latin America and the Caribbean at 19% each. Only 5% of NUPs in Arab States were reported as "moderate and extensive", p 120.

[335] See also, HLPF, Handbook for the Preparation of Voluntary National Reviews (The 2022 Edition), <https://sustainabledevelopment.un.org/content/documents/29410VNR_Handbook_2022_English.pdf> accessed 18 September 2022.

[336] These countries are: Afghanistan; Angola; Antigua and Barbuda; Azerbaijan; Bahamas; Bhutan; Bolivia; Cabo Verde; China; Chad; Colombia; Cuba; Cyprus; Czech Republic; Democratic People's Republic of Korea; Denmark; Dominican Republic; Egypt; Germany; Guatemala; Indonesia; Iraq; Japan; Lao People's Democratic Republic; Madagascar; Malaysia; Marshall Islands; Mexico; Namibia; Nicaragua; Niger; Norway; Paraguay; Qatar; San Marino; Sierra Leone; Spain; Sweden; Thailand; Tunisia; Uruguay; and Zimbabwe. The reports were filed in July 2021 at the HLPF. See also ECOSOC, Compilation of Main Messages for the 2021 Voluntary National Reviews: Note by the Secretariat, E/HLPF/2021/5*, 7 May 2021 (HLPF Meeting 6–15 July 2021).

[337] Republic of Azerbaijan, Third Voluntary National Review 2021. Azerbaijan VNR focuses on nine of the seventeen SDGs and SDG 9 was also excluded from the VNR.

[338] Lao People's Democratic Republic, Voluntary National Review: On the Implementation of the 2030 Agenda for Sustainable Development 2021. Lao's report, however, did contain a statistical annex with developments on

recovery from COVID-19 was part of the reason to exclude progress especially on SDG 9.[339] Most of the countries that reported no progress on SDG 9 can be found in the Middle East, Africa, and the Asia Pacific region,[340] with the exception of the Latin American nation of Uruguay.[341] Some reports mentioned specific statistics on each indicators of SDG 9 as achieved up to 2019,[342] and other countries explicitly stated that they are reporting on SDGs that are priorities.[343]

There are a few final observations that can be made about SDG 9. First, SDG 9 is economically oriented in that it is about creating economic development and business opportunities. In that respect, there is no 'human dimension' or a totally 'socially oriented' way of looking at SDG 9. This is what separates SDG 9 from the other sixteen SDGs, even though one is likely to find economic aspects in some of the other SDGs. To understand or achieve the 'social' or 'human' dimensions of SDG 9, one must look at the broader aspects of the SDGs in general and how their spillover effect may impact SDG 9 in that respect.

Secondly, from a legal perspective, there are a few legal characteristics of SDG 9 that might be seen as 'incoherent' where other legal principles are concerned. For example, SDG 9 overall interacts with commercial law and emerging legal areas such as global innovation law or international commercial law on road transport. Thus, where, for example, global innovation law entails the protection of economic activities or protecting rights in technologies that emerge from clean technology or R&D into patented goods, such laws cannot accommodate consumer welfare or the 'social welfare' of the beneficiaries. Rather, the laws are to protect rights and obligations while at the same time ensuring that new technologies and product innovation are compatible with other legal and regulatory standards.

Thirdly, from a matter of the practical aspects of states absorbing the norms of SDG 9, a potential problem lies in how dispute settlements can solve inter-state conflicts regarding

each SDG, and interestingly on SDG 9, for 2019, there were 1,692 full-time researchers, as per target 9.5.2 to encourage and boost innovation, p 132.

[339] This too has been acknowledged by ECOSOC's own assessment, see 'Progress Towards the Sustainable Development Goals: Report of the Secretary General', E/2021/58, 30 April 20121, delivered to the High Level Political Forum on Sustainable Development, convened under the auspices of the Economic and Social Council, 23 July 2020–22 July 2021. Para 106 notes: 'The pandemic affected manufacturing by disrupting global value chains and restricting the movement of people and goods, resulting in a significant drop of 8.4 per cent in manufacturing production in 2020. The global share of manufacturing value added in GDP fell from 16.5 per cent in 2019 to 15.9 in 2020.'

[340] for example, Qatar, Qatar Voluntary National Review 2021: Report on the Implementation of the 2030 Agenda for Sustainable Development; Islamic Republic of Afghanistan Voluntary National Review (VNR) 2021; The Republic of Iraq, The Second National Voluntary Review Report on the Achievement of the Sustainable Development Goals 2021: Iraq ... And the Path Back to the Development, July 2021; Bhutan, Transformations for Sustainable Development in the 21st Century: Bhuthan's Second Voluntary National Report on the Implementation of the 2030 Agenda for Sustainable Development; Government of Sierra Leone, 2021 VNR Report on SDGs in Sierra Leone, June 2021; Malaysia Voluntary National Review (VNR) 2021. The Malaysian Report however had some useful statistics on achievable indicators for SDG 9 up to 2019, p 29; while Bhuthan summarized some of the areas for SDG 9 that needs further action, Bhutan Report, pp 21–22.

[341] Uruguay, Summary—Voluntary National Review: Uruguay 2021.

[342] Malaysia, in this respect.

[343] Republic of the Marshall Islands, Voluntary National Review. In the case of the Marshall Islands, an annex was attached giving indications and progress on the remaining SDGs, and in this annex SDG 9, for example, mentions how cross-border sea transport and other modes of transports are gradually being developed to meet national and international standards, p 66.

breach of international legal obligations under international law on the environment or climate change. This is a more complex matter, and since SDG 9 is yet to evolve into treaty form, it will be a long way before such a conflict of norms matters may arise. Yet, if one takes matters relating to 'industrialization' in SDG 9, even contemporary trade agreements may be seen as obstacles to the 'sustainable industrialization' aspect of SDG 9 when states will have to subsidize the means of industrialization that may be in contravention to global trade rules.

The new visions and standards that SDG 9 and the other SDGs discussed in this book promote are a form of governance and norm-making one from a variety of actors.[344] These various actors have embraced norm-making and norm-sustaining in the international system that, among other things, edges towards 'global sustainability law and governance'. These standards cut across sectors and industries and involve a global compact of nations. Thus, emerging economies,[345] developed economies, and fully industrialized economies are all taking part—promoting their *specific* interests or *all* interests in the SDGs. Never mind that even when all seventeen SDGs are discussed in chronological order by various commentators, it is not surprising often to find that SDG 9 is missing from those discussions.[346] The reason for this exemption is not clear but based on research for this commentary, it is safe to argue that SDG 9 represents an entirely new agenda for Agenda 2030 that is either purely market-driven or has serious legal deficiencies when it comes into contact with legal regulations such as property protection or investment law.[347] One might even dare to ask whether SDG 9 is the ultimate agenda for Agenda 2030.[348] In fact, from an economic perspective, most of the economic activities in the SDGs are in most ways focused on SDG 9—that is its general aim, targets, and sub-targets.

The larger issues of reducing carbon emissions, investment in R&D, promotion and access to information technology and job creation through the manufacturing industry or the financial industry are economic activities that require both private and public capacities. The volume of sustainable industrialization that SDG 9 speaks of is so enormous that even scientific studies that attempted to map the literature on the subject

---

[344] On norm-making by sustainable development as such see generally Barral (n 223).

[345] See, eg, A Negi and others (eds), *Sustainability Standards and Global Governance: Experiences of Emerging Economies* (Springer 2020).

[346] See, eg, S Bragdon, 'Living Links Connecting the United Nations Sustainable Development Goals: Small-Scale Farmers and Agricultural Biodiversity' (2019) 21 San Diego International Law Journal 155 (eg discussing twelve SDGs but not including SDG 9). This does not mean that the general literature that offers different perspectives on the SDGs altogether ignores SDG 9 or any other; on the contrary, the literature generally discuss the seventeen SDGs, albeit from different angles; see, eg, I Franco and others (eds), *Actioning the Global Goals for Local Impact: Towards Sustainability Science, Policy, Education and Practice* (Springer 2020).

[347] On investment law and the SDGs see K Schefer, 'Sustainability in International Investment Law: Building on What Exists by Enhancing the Right to Regulate' (2021) 31 Swiss Review International and European Law 193; see also L Johnson and others, 'Aligning International Investment Agreements with the Sustainable Development Goals' (2019) 58 Columbia Journal of Transnational Law 58–120; M-C Cordonier Segger, Inspiration for Integration: Interpreting International Trade and Investment Accords for Sustainable Development' (2017) 3 Canadian Journal of Comparative and Contemporary Law 159–215.

[348] This is perhaps a question I will have to explore in-depth elsewhere, but no doubt it fuels my own 'conclusions' *per se* on this commentary.

matter have been unable to capture the complete 'nexus governance'. Nevertheless, scholars adequately agree that 'most economic activities are expected to positively impact industrialization, infrastructure, and innovation'.[349]

The major legal achievements in terms of SDG 9 (up to 2021) fall into two categories: (i) patent coverage and (ii) legislations on carbon emissions. Thus, a number of countries have reported an increase in patent applications and this was most notable with EU countries where patent applications to the regional EPO increased. The figures declined in 2020 but those prior to and after it increased significantly. Outside the EU, countries such as Laos and Angola have also made progress on the legislative front—at least in the case of Laos where the country sought to implement new intellectual property rules. For Namibia, the state continued to support and encourage innovation for firms and individuals to seek patent protection. In terms of carbon emission, again the legislative developments point mostly to Europe where rules were introduced to limit carbon emission in new vehicles.[350] Yet, the other interlegalities that I introduced in this commentary on the meta-relationship of SDG 9 in relation to international law, commercial law/conflicts of law and global innovation law also capture how the challenges that aspects of SDG 9 will need to address. One such challenge includes how to enforce private rights under international law when clearly other legalities such as commercial law concerns domestic matters.

At a personnel level, I think the SDGs are akin to a 'Marshall Plan', except that they have lofty ideas that are unrealizable in the time frame to 2030. They are more likely achievable by the middle of the century, that is by 2050.

---

[349] See van Zantern and van Tulder (n 214). A recent encyclopaedic compendium on SDG 9 appears to fall short on the totality of SDG 9 and its targets, and hence, whilst it was available for my consultation nearing completion of this comment, I did not find it useful. However, for reference see WL Filho and others (eds), *Industry, Innovation and Infrastructure* (Springer 2021).

[350] The rules were introduced in Regulation 2019/631, or formally, European Parliament and Council of the European Union (2019), Regulation (EU) 2019/631 of the European Parliament and of the Council of 17 April 2019 setting CO2 Emission Performance Standards for new Passenger Cars and for New Light Commercial Vehicles, and repealing Regulation (EC) No 443/2009 and (EU) No 510/2011, OJL 111.

SDG 10
'Reduce Inequality Within and Among Countries'

Johanna Aleria P Lorenzo

I. Introduction

What are the international legal bases for Sustainable Development Goal 10 (SDG 10) and its targets? In what ways is inequality deemed relevant in different fields of international law, and what legal rights and obligations, if any, arise therefrom? How does public international law support the pursuit of sustainable development in relation to reducing inequalities within and among states? These inquiries motivate the present chapter. The discussion will highlight, among others, some of the tensions between the principle of sovereign equality of states and the duty to cooperate, including the implementation of the latter via the special and differential treatment principle. It will likewise elaborate the central role of international human rights law in this grand effort to close the gaps among peoples and between states.

SDG 10 seeks to capture the overarching objective and clarion call of the 2030 Agenda for Sustainable Development[1] to 'Leave No One Behind'. As envisaged by the United Nations (UN), to leave no-one behind means 'addressing patterns of exclusion, structural constraints and unequal power relations that produce and reproduce inequalities over generations, and moving towards both formal and substantive equality for all groups in society' not only through governments' legal, policy, and institutional measures but also by the 'free, active and meaningful participation of all stakeholders, particularly the most marginalized, in mechanisms for ensuring accountability, recourse and remedies to all'.[2] Reducing inequalities thus goes hand in hand with ensuring inclusion—in labour markets, political leadership, or quality healthcare and education—not only by closing gaps among persons, groups, and states but also lifting the bottom up ('reach the farthest behind') and guaranteeing the equal realization of each individual's human rights.[3]

---

[1] 'Transforming Our World: The 2030 Agenda for Sustainable Development' (25 September 2015) UNGA Res 70/1 (2030 Agenda).

[2] Chief Executives Board for Coordination (CEB), 'Equality and non-discrimination at the heart of sustainable development: a Shared United Nations Framework for Action, Report of the High-level Committee on Programmes at its thirty-second session' (9 November 2016) CEB/2016/6/Add.1 (UN Shared Framework) 20.

[3] See United Nations Department of Economic and Social Affairs (UNDESA) and World Bank Group (WBG), 'Sustainable Development Goal 10—Reduced Inequalities: Progress and Prospects, An Expert Group Meeting in preparation for HLPF 2019: Empowering People and Ensuring Inclusiveness and Equality', Concept Note (2–3

712   SDG 10

Inequality, like the closely related problem of poverty,[4] is multi-faceted.[5] It has myriad manifestations and often compounding causes. Aiming to address, more specifically to reduce, inequalities, thus entails multiple interlinked actions in various fronts by several actors. The complexities are heightened by the conceptual, theoretical, empirical, and normative debates surrounding inequalities and efforts to reduce them. While similar debates confront the other goals, some issues are arguably inherent or peculiar to Goal 10. Those issues are the focus of this chapter. As will be elaborated below, however, the cross-cutting character of inequality makes those other debates relevant to the discussion as well.

The UN Secretary-General understands equality to be a 'foundational principle of development'.[6] In a 2019 report, he lauded the progress made after four years of implementing the SDGs but also lamented that progress is proceeding at a slow pace, with disadvantaged population groups—such as youth, persons with disabilities (PWDs), inhabitants of rural areas—continuing largely to remain excluded from life opportunities and the enjoyment of fundamental human rights.[7] Among the identified 'systemic gaps in the overall response to the 2030 Agenda' that required specific actions were 'placing special focus on the most vulnerable to ensure that as countries progress, they leave no one behind' and 'strengthening institutions and making them more effective and inclusive'.[8]

This imperative has recently become more pressing, as the COVID-19 pandemic highlighted and aggravated pre-existing inequalities within and among states. Various sources confirm that marginalized and vulnerable segments of populations in both rich and poor countries have been disproportionately suffering the adverse health and economic consequences of the persisting crisis. Likewise, efforts to address this global emergency, particularly the proposed waiver of certain intellectual property rights over the vaccines, have highlighted not only the wide disparities in states' resources and capabilities, but more importantly an enduring conflict of interests between industrialized and developing countries that prevents genuine and effective international cooperation. Whatever modest gains have been achieved relative to SDG 10 and its targets in the last five years now stand to be undone, especially if the principles underpinning Goal 10 are ignored in current recovery and transition plans and actions.

April 2019) 3 <https://sustainabledevelopment.un.org/content/documents/21453SDG_10_EGM_2019_conc ept_note_30Jan_consolidated.pdf> accessed 5 November 2021 (UNDESA&WBG).

[4] See UNDESA, *Inequality and the 2030 Agenda for Sustainable Development*, Development Issues No 4 (21 October 2015) 2 <https://www.un.org/en/development/desa/policy/wess/wess_dev_issues/dsp_policy_04.pdf> accessed 5 November 2021 (UNDESA, *Inequality and 2030*).
[5] See Report of the Secretary-General, 'Empowering People and Ensuring Inclusiveness and Equality' (1 May 2019) E/2019/65 (Secretary-General, Empowering People) paras 7 and 63.
[6] ibid para 6.
[7] Report of the Secretary-General, 'Special Edition: Progress Towards the Sustainable Development Goals' (8 May 2019) E/2019/68 (Secretary-General, *Special Edition*) paras 9 and 49.
[8] ibid para 18.

INTRODUCTION 713

A. Cognate Concepts

Reducing inequality means, intuitively, increasing equality. As conceived within the 2030 Agenda, the Goal is more expansive in that it additionally aims to achieve inclusion and empowerment of marginalized and vulnerable groups and to eliminate discrimination against particular persons, thereby implicating established international human rights obligations, as explained below. To improve our understanding of the centrality and complexity of Goal 10, a brief digression into the definition of equality and its cognate concepts—equity, non-discrimination, inclusion, and empowerment—is in order.[9]

Thematically, SDG 10 broaches but hardly tackles the broader notion of fairness, especially at the global scale. Fairness encompasses equity and equality: 'While equity brings a helpful focus on "fairness", the concept of "equality" brings an additional focus on legal protection, particularly for groups that are discriminated against.'[10] In this respect, equality can further be broken down into *formal* or procedural (same/consistent treatment and opportunities for all; likes must be treated alike) and *substantive* aspects. Substantive equality typically entails treatment that depends on a recognition of certain differences, 'structural disadvantage and historical discrimination.'[11] In some situations, substantive equality could require *redistribution* to obtain equality of both opportunities or access and outcomes.

In some domestic legislation, the remedial function of redistribution—in the sense of correcting pre-existing or structural inequalities—converges with the idea of affirmative action or *positive (reverse) discrimination.*[12] International human rights law recognizes equality and non-discrimination to be fundamental principles that are essential to the exercise and enjoyment of all kinds of human rights. Discrimination in this context refers to 'any distinction, exclusion, restriction or preference or other differential treatment that is directly or indirectly based on the prohibited grounds of discrimination and which has the intention or effect of nullifying or impairing the recognition, enjoyment or exercise, on an equal footing, of [human] rights.'[13]

The 2030 Agenda adopts this perspective, one manifestation being the addition of the qualifier 'inclusive' to economic growth. Inclusive growth means that growth should 'not contribute to rising inequalities', implying either that 'the outcomes of growth apply to everyone (i.e., rising living standards)' or 'the opportunities for growth apply to everyone (i.e., greater equality of opportunity or higher levels of employment).'[14] In

---

[9] I add inclusion and empowerment to the UN Shared Framework's list of concepts that are different but closely related to equality.

[10] UN Shared Framework, 21.

[11] ibid 24.

[12] C Barnard and B Hepple, 'Substantive Equality' (2000) 59 The Cambridge Law Journal 562.

[13] Committee on Economic, Social and Cultural Rights (CESCR), 'General Comment No 20: Non-discrimination in Economic, Social and Cultural Rights' (art 2, para 2, of the International Covenant on Economic, Social and Cultural Rights (2 July 2009) E/C.12/GC/20 (GC20) para 7. See also Human Rights Committee (CCPR), 'General Comment No 18: Nondiscrimination' (1989) (GC18' para 7. The ICCPR, ICERD, CEDAW, and CRPD likewise contain this definition.

[14] UNDESA, *Inequality and 2030* (n 4) 1.

turn, achieving inclusion and equality entails empowerment, meaning 'a combination of rules and mechanisms that not only formally ensure the exercise of rights but also guarantee enabling factors that ensure that particularly groups that are typically left behind are effectively able to use those rules and mechanisms'.[15] Understood in this manner, empowerment resonates with the notion of substantive equality.

It bears emphasizing that inequality is both a human rights and a sustainable development concern, meaning several concepts related to equality link Goal 10 to human rights broadly and to the international legal framework therefor more specifically. Principles underlying the so-called rights-based approach to development, for instance, include 'equality and non-discrimination' and 'participation and inclusion'. In parallel, sustainable development principles include 'broad public participation' and 'equity' (both intra- and inter-generational), as expressed in the notion of common but differentiated responsibilities. Given that *participation* appears as a common denominator of these two frameworks, its importance needs further elaboration. As the UN Secretary-General aptly stated, 'participation is not just a fundamental right and a key dimension of social inclusion but also a highly important mechanism for strengthening democracy and transitioning to more egalitarian societies'.[16] Moreover, participation, which presupposes recognition, empowers individuals; creates more transparent and accountable public institutions; and thereby contributes to eliminating marginalization and discrimination—ensuring that no-one is left behind.[17] Accordingly, policy-makers are advised to consider the synergies among '(a) rights and justice; (b) norms and institutions; (c) participation and voice; and (d) resources and capabilities'[18] to include and empower the groups previously marginalized in the decision-making processes. These statements hint at, but do not fully and clearly establish the normative connection between the human rights and the sustainable development frameworks. Here, the debates between Nancy Fraser and Axel Honneth, regarding the value of participation and the different approaches (redistribution, recognition, both) for enabling certain groups to participate, are particularly salient.[19]

Significantly, the Committee on Economic, Social and Cultural Rights (CESCR), the treaty body tasked to monitor implementation of the International Covenant on Economic, Social and Cultural Rights (ICESCR),[20] has underscored the interlinkages among discrimination, human rights, economic growth, and sustainable development, placing discrimination and fulfilment of economic, social, and cultural (ESC) rights in an inverse relationship: 'Economic growth has not, in itself, led to sustainable development, and individuals and groups of individuals continue to face socio-economic inequality, often because of entrenched historical and contemporary forms of discrimination.'[21] The Committee additionally observed that States

---

[15] Secretary-General, 'Empowering People' (n 5) para 14.

[16] ibid para 13.

[17] ibid para 42.

[18] ibid para 46.

[19] N Fraser and A Honneth (eds), *Redistribution or Recognition?: A Political-Philosophical Exchange* (Verso 2003).

[20] International Covenant on Economic, Social and Cultural Rights (adopted 16 December 1966, entered into force 3 January 1976) 993 UNTS 3 (ICESCR).

[21] CESCR GC20, para 1.

Parties' duties relative to discrimination in the context of ESC rights are twofold: to prohibit and, in some instances, to eliminate.[22] It cited as examples of the latter the obligation under International Labour Organization (ILO) Convention No 111 concerning Discrimination in Respect of Employment and Occupation (1958) and the obligation under the United Nations Educational, Scientific and Cultural Organization (UNESCO) Convention against Discrimination in Education.

The discussion above also provides the necessary context for interpreting the other goals, six of them[23] include some of these words—'equitable', 'inclusive'—that relate to equality. Parenthetically, this count excludes those goals, which reaffirm the *universality* of the SDGs by using the phrase 'for all', that are also relevant to meeting SDG 10. Indeed, a textual reading of the goals is inadequate to appreciate Goal 10's interlinkages, especially as this enumeration omits one of the most important—if not *the* most important—goal that SDG 10 is interconnected with, that is Goal 1. From an international human rights law lens, poverty constitutes a socio-economic situation that cannot be a ground for discriminating against persons or groups and could, in limited cases, indicate a systematic human rights violation. As the CESCR explained that 'pervasive discrimination, stigmatization and negative stereotyping' that arise from poverty or homelessness 'can lead to the refusal of, or unequal access to, the same quality of education and health care as others, as well as the denial of or unequal access to public places'.[24]

As a final point, while the foregoing highlights the synergistic elements of the goals of poverty eradication and inequality reduction, it is important at the outset to view this relationship with a healthy scepticism. The predominant approach of treating inequalities as a function of poverty and economic growth, of 'outgrowing' the problem of disparities, is not beyond reproach. Particularly regarding inter-state inequalities, the SDG 10 targets are inadequate because they merely aim to increase the developing countries' incomes without addressing the political, social, economic, and legal structures and practices that perpetuate historical disparities. The current structure of the Goal and targets creates an artificial and specious divide between intra- and inter-state inequalities that, in turn, give the false impression that states individually are to address the disparities among persons and groups within their jurisdiction, and that other states and international organizations bear no responsibility for making those efforts possible.

B. Inequality of Opportunities versus Inequality of Outcomes

Closely related to the distinction between formal and substantive equality, as well as between horizontal and vertical inequality, is the question of what policy-makers and legislators ought to equalize: opportunities or outcomes. Under international human rights law, *formal equality*—availability of the same opportunities for all—is guaranteed

---

[22] ibid para 5.
[23] SDGs 4, 5, 8, 9, 11, 16.
[24] CESCR GC20, para 35.

716   SDG 10

at a minimum. However, as treaty bodies increasingly recognize and a number of scholars argue, formal equality is in reality often insufficient to ensure equal enjoyment of human rights.[25] Accordingly, the concept of *substantive equality* has emerged to 'take ... into account a number of overlapping factors: discrimination is often indirect; inequality can be structural; both unequal outcomes and unequal opportunities must be scrutinised; and different treatment might be required to move towards equality in practice, including temporary measures and affirmative action'.[26] Simply put, substantive equality emphasizes both opportunities and outcomes, takes a broader and deeper view of disparities, and thereby demands more fundamental and institutional reforms. Significantly, inequality of opportunities and of outcomes are inextricably linked. The Special Rapporteur on extreme poverty and human rights, Philip Alston, lamented that '[t]he situation of high inequality in many countries today does not conform to [John Rawls'] idea of "fair equality of opportunity" ' because 'poor people [in many societies] start the "race of life" at a disadvantage and will meet many more hurdles on their way than others'.[27] Alston concluded that respecting the equal rights and dignity of all persons requires addressing extreme inequality, and although perfect economic equality is neither achievable nor desirable, 'every human being is entitled—at the very least—to equal opportunity'.[28]

The Expert Group Meeting—convened to discuss SDG 10's progress and prospects— likewise recommended that policies aimed at reducing inequalities must 'focus on reducing inequality of opportunity by addressing the root causes of vast opportunity gaps between different groups in society', because opportunity inequality can harm human potential and economic growth and is easier to remedy than outcome inequality.[29] This recommendation aligns with existing international human rights standards, which do not call for absolute equality of income or wealth for all but expect states to move 'towards equality in incomes and wealth in situations where inequalities have become extreme enough to threaten stability, undercut democratic processes, and harm the realization of human rights, including the right to an adequate standard of living for all'.[30] Interestingly, too, in the preamble to the Draft Convention on the Right to Development,[31] 'equality of opportunity for development' is deemed 'a prerogative both of nations and of individuals who constitute nations', signifying that unequal distribution of opportunities can occur at the inter- and intra-state levels and that both can have an impact on the improvement of human and planetary well-being.

---

[25] See Report of the Special Rapporteur on extreme poverty and human rights, P Alston, 'Extreme Inequality and Human Rights' (27 May 2015) A/HRC/29/31, para 54.

[26] I Saiz and K Donald, 'Tackling Inequality through the Sustainable Development Goals: Human Rights in Practice' (2017) 21 The International Journal of Human Rights 1029, 1035.

[27] Alston, 'Extreme Inequality and Human Rights' (n 25) para 13.

[28] ibid paras 12 and 48.

[29] WBG and UNDESA, *Expert Group Meeting: Reducing Inequalities—SDG 10 Progress and Prospects*, Outcomes: Key Messages (2–3 April 2019) 3 <https://thedocs.worldbank.org/en/doc/604131558125031287-017 0022019/original/SDG 10EGMOutcomedocument.pdf> accessed 5 November 2021.

[30] UN Shared Framework, 24.

[31] Draft convention on the right to development (17 January 2020) A/HRC/WG.2/21/2 (Draft RTD Convention).

C. Horizontal versus Vertical Inequalities

To simplify, horizontal inequalities refer to group-based disadvantages, which are typically produced by social hierarchies and 'tend to be associated with identities... ascribed from birth such as race, caste and ethnicity [and, in some societies, religion and language]'.[32] Issues of access, equal opportunity, discrimination, and social exclusion—quite familiar to many human rights lawyers—are often analysed under this category.[33] On the other hand, vertical inequalities—which most economists primarily focus on—are concerned with disparities among persons individually, rather than as members of a particular (culturally defined) group, and as such, look into individual income and wealth differentials.[34]

These analytical distinctions are not meant to discount the far more complex reality that there are overlaps between individual and group-based inequalities, and that discrimination can be both a result and a source of both inequalities, as seen in the fact that 'the poorest section of the population [in many countries often] coincides with social and ethnic groups that experience discrimination'.[35] Distinguishing is nonetheless a vital step, at least an initial one, that enables better understanding of the limitations or deficiencies of current analyses and approaches. For instance, some scholars have pointed out that international human rights law, as currently interpreted, does not sufficiently address non-group-based inequalities, even though 'extreme vertical inequalities—in income, wealth and social outcome—are of increasing global concern',[36] especially given emerging evidence suggesting that particularly high levels of vertical inequalities 'can also produce social unrest and can be a key factor in creating economic instability and limiting the sustainability of economic growth'.[37] It is indeed only recently that human rights bodies and scholars have begun paying due attention to vertical economic inequalities by considering the ways that vertical inequalities impact human rights and contribute to 'horizontal inequalities, social disparities and to other human rights deprivations'.[38] MacNaughton noted that 'SDG 10 ... flags this equality gap in the human rights framework' and explained that not all hope is lost as there remain 'multiple paths to addressing vertical inequalities in the International Bill of Human Rights, which holds a rich source of equality provisions that should be distinguished and conceptualised' to 'set limits on the rising gaps between rich and poor'.[39]

---

[32] V Paz Arauco and others, 'Strengthening Social Justice to Address Intersecting Inequalities post-2015' (2014) Overseas Development Institute (ODI) Report, 10 <https://cdn.odi.org/media/documents/9213.pdf> accessed 20 August 2021.

[33] See UNDESA, *Inequality and 2030* (n 3).

[34] UN Shared Framework, 22–23.

[35] Alston, 'Extreme Inequality and Human Rights' (n 25) para 24.

[36] G MacNaughton, 'Vertical Inequalities: Are the SDGs and Human Rights up to the Challenges?' (2017) 21 The International Journal of Human Rights 1050, 1056.

[37] UN Shared Framework, 22.

[38] Center for Economic and Social Rights (CESR), 'From Disparity to Dignity: Tackling Economic Inequality through the Sustainable Development Goals' (2016) Human Rights Policy Brief, 11–12 <https://www.cesr.org/sites/default/files/disparity_to_dignity_SDG 10.pdf> accessed 20 August 2021.

[39] MacNaughton (n 36) 1066.

718   SDG 10

She accordingly offered a restrained commendation of SDG 10, which is a 'great step forward from the MDGs' as it 'introduced inequalities onto the development agenda' and used indicators that are linked to international human rights law, but remains deficient because none of the targets successfully addresses vertical inequalities.[40]

D. Intersecting Dimensions

Further adding to the breadth and depth of Goal 10 is the fact that it seeks to cover not only *income* and economic inequality, but also other types of inequalities, such as those relating to social, cultural, and political factors. Unequal opportunities often intersect with and mutually reinforce economic disparities and disparate outcomes. The notion of 'intersecting inequalities' pertains to 'the "deep exclusion" of groups of people who suffer multiple forms [economic, social, spatial and political] of discrimination and disadvantage'.[41] Such intersections are neither natural nor inevitable, but, as Charles Tilly argued, they are linked to systematic exploitation and opportunity hoarding and institutionalized (through processes he calls 'emulation' and 'adaptation') categorical inequalities.[42] Tilly's account invites greater attention to structural factors perpetuating durable inequality and lends powerful insights into additional courses of action that, I submit, SDG 10 should incorporate. I adopt the view of those advocating that if the level of social justice is to be enhanced, both domestically and globally, it is necessary to scrutinize and remedy disadvantages, not in isolation but in terms of their interactions.[43] I find Fraser's two-pronged approach, encompassing both redistribution and recognition to remedy intersecting 'axes of subordination',[44] apropos of the various dimensions of economic disadvantage and status subordination that SDG 10 seeks to address. A human rights-based approach to development similarly focuses on these intersecting inequalities, meaning analyses and recommendations centre on the interaction among different socio-political-cultural disparities and how they shape or are reinforced by economic inequalities of income and wealth.[45]

The Special Rapporteur on extreme poverty and human rights supports this approach, explaining that apart from income and wealth, human well-being is also impacted by the distribution of 'political power, health, education or housing' in a society, and, given the interactive and reinforcing character of social and economic inequalities,[46] it is

---

[40] ibid 1063.

[41] Arauco and others (n 32) 1.

[42] See C Tilly, *Durable Inequality* (University of California Press 1998). I thank Ingo Venzke for referring me to this classic.

[43] ibid 11.

[44] N Fraser, 'Social Justice in the Age of Identity Politics: Redistribution, Recognition, and Participation' in Fraser and Honneth (eds), *Redistribution or Recognition?* (n 19).

[45] CESR (n 38) 13.

[46] See also UN Climate Change, UN Office on Drugs and Crime, and UN Women, 'Tackling Global Challenges to Equality and Inclusion Through the Gender-Responsive Implementation of the 2030 Agenda for Sustainable Development: Spotlight on SDGs 10, 13 and 16', Expert Group Meeting Report and Recommendations (27–28 February 2019) 7 <https://sustainabledevelopment.un.org/content/documents/23808EGMViennaFin.pdf> accessed 26 November 2021 (Expert Group).

crucial to analyse them together.[47] Relevantly for the SDG targets directed at legislative and administrative measures, the Special Rapporteur stressed: 'Economic inequalities are not only the result of market forces, but equally of political forces that affect laws, regulations and institutions.'[48] On the role of law, including international law, in reducing inequalities, I echo Frances Stewart's expansion of Rousseau's thought—interpreting '[t]he "force of circumstances" that tends to destroy equality' as including factors arising 'from the global and domestic political system, which can prevent the changes needed to bring about a just distribution.'[49]

E. Intrinsic and Instrumental Values

To conclude this introductory section, it is valuable to keep in mind the aforementioned interlinkages[50] that hint at the dual importance of equality: the intrinsic and the instrumental. The former refers to the assertion that equality is inherently valuable and worth pursuing, independent of other possible valuable outcomes that might be achieved in its pursuit. Roughly translated into human rights language, this aspect means that there is a distinct right to equality, although such right may also be interdependent with other rights. The instrumental value of equality, on the other hand, means that equality—or the reduction of inequalities—is important because it secures or helps to obtain other values or essential objectives. This aspect considers the harmful impacts of inequality on economic growth and poverty reduction, social cohesion, political participation, and environmental protection efforts, and resonates with the framing of equality as a sustainable development concern.[51] The introductory paragraph to an earlier version of SDG 10 succinctly illustrates this framing:

> Inequalities within countries can be socially destabilizing and also have negative consequences for economic growth. Inequalities among countries can have negative effects on global solidarity and international cooperation to address shared challenges.[52]

The Technical Support Team (TST) was also slightly critical of the merely implicit attention given by the MDGs to addressing inequalities, stressing that their focus on national averages 'may have led to perverse outcomes whereby already marginalized groups have tended to be "left until last"', thus exacerbating existing inequalities.[53] The TST discussed several features of inequality, including the inherent value of equality: 'Exclusion, discrimination and violence ... [are] intrinsically objectionable

---

[47] Alston, 'Extreme Inequality and Human Rights' (n 25) para 6.
[48] ibid para 17.
[49] Frances Stewart, 'Changing Perspectives on Inequality and Development' (2016) 51 Studies in Comparative International Development 60, 61.
[50] Secretary-General, 'Empowering People' (n 5) para 15.
[51] Secretary-General, 'Special Edition' (n 7) para 16.
[52] OWG10, Focus area 12 (Promote equality).
[53] TST Issues Brief, 'Promoting Equality, including Social Equity' (TST 2014) 1.

on moral grounds, based on common notions of justice and fairness.'[54] Lastly, it briefly acknowledged that these manifestations of inequality—exclusion, discrimination, violence—can, in fact, constitute violations of obligations under international human rights law.

While analytically distinct, the intrinsic and the instrumental importance of equality are in fact intimately connected and not necessarily inconsistent with each other. The human rights and the sustainable development frameworks share an emphasis on 'equality and non-discrimination in access to economic and social opportunities', as well as the 'meaningful participation of [all] individuals in decisions that affect their lives and well-being'.[55] International human rights law is primarily concerned with 'enabling people to claim their entitlements through legal as well as other means',[56] and has had more experience with and more tools available for addressing horizontal inequalities. At the same time, it recognizes that 'inequalities adversely impact on the enjoyment of a full array of civil, political, social, economic and cultural rights', signifying that the framework also considers vertical inequalities and the instrumental value of equality.[57] Some commentators argue, however, that the human rights framework itself needs further refinement to better conceptualize and address vertical inequalities. Conversely, among economic and development thinkers, some have been advocating for increasing consideration and deeper analysis of horizontal inequalities, not only because group-based disparities tend to fuel violent conflict that impairs development prospects but also because they are patently unfair and unjust.[58]

II. *Travaux Préparatoires*

What may be considered the *travaux préparatoires* of the 2030 Agenda and the SDGs consist of the outputs from the Open Working Group (OWG), complemented by a report from the High-Level Panel (HLP) appointed by the UN Secretary-General.[59]

A. OWG: Stocktaking Phase

At the conceptualization phase (OWG-2), there was an early recognition of the interdependence and interlinkages among the SDGs and, indeed, it was emphasized that

---

[54] ibid 3.

[55] S Fukuda-Parr and others, 'The Power of Numbers: A Critical Review of Millennium Development Goal Targets for Human Development and Human Rights' (2014) 15 Journal of Human Development and Capabilities 105, 108.

[56] ibid.

[57] MacNaughton (n 36) 1065.

[58] F Stewart, 'What Horizontal Inequalities Are and Why They Matter' (*The Progressive Post*, 14 June 2015) <https://progressivepost.eu/what-horizontal-inequalities-are-and-why-they-matter/> accessed 2 December 2021.

[59] In the succeeding paragraphs, references to discussions at the OWG, including presentations made by particular individuals or non-governmental organizations (NGOs), are sourced from the summaries and compilations prepared by the Co-Chairs and/or the UN for each session <https://sustainabledevelopment.un.org/owg.html> accessed 16 October 2021.

the crucial role of the Goals is to highlight the integration of the three dimensions—economic, environmental, and social—of sustainable development. There appears to have been some discussion on the goal of reducing inequalities, such as through the acknowledgement that '[w]omen and disadvantaged groups, indigenous peoples and ethnic minorities must be addressed through ambitious and measurable targets and indicators in all relevant goals'. Likewise, in the context of poverty eradication sitting at the core of the SDGs, among the 'critical drivers' of poverty eradication that need to be addressed are the empowerment of women and gender equality and poor people's access to justice. More broadly, a number of participants pointed out the close link between poverty and inequality—'not only in terms of income but in access to education and assets, to vital services and to political voice'—and the need to think about how the goals and targets can reflect this link. In this respect, in inviting the OWG to identify entry points for the SDGs to 'support progress toward eradication of poverty and empower the weakest and most vulnerable', Co-Chair Kamau cited equity as an example. Also included in the cross-cutting, enabling conditions for sustainable development are 'improving income distribution' and 'reducing inequality'.

Regarding inequalities at the international level, its relevance was raised in the context of discussing the importance of means of implementation, with some speakers emphasizing that the international governance system, particularly the international financial institutions (IFIs), requires reform 'so it can respond adequately to the sustainable development agenda and ensure that all countries' voices can be heard'. Many echoed the necessity for 'a just, fair and transparent international trade and financial system' to enable national governments in their poverty eradication efforts. Notably, however, some speakers also stressed that, without waiting for such international institutional reforms to occur, global partnerships need thinking beyond the traditional donor–recipient relationships and should 'innovate to take into account the shifts in global distribution of power'. The imperative for reforms in international economic and financial institutions was raised again during OWG-5, wherein the Brookings Institution presented on Financing for Development and stressed importance of a stable international financial system in 'reallocating global investment towards sustainable development'. During the same session, another presentation highlighted the consistently high and positive growth rate of many developing countries but noted that there remain challenges, such as the lack of inclusiveness of such growth ('many people were left behind'), the increasing inequality within countries, and the structural unemployment of women and youth in both developed and developing countries. As summarized by the Co-Chairs, inclusive growth requires sound domestic macroeconomic policies, supported by an enabling international environment, including a revamped global partnership. These discussions indicate the interlinkages among Goals 10, 8, and 17. At the end of OWG-5, however, the question of how multilateral governance for sustainable development can be strengthened was left unanswered.

Picking up from the previous session, OWG-6's four areas of focus include 'global partnership for achieving sustainable development'. The presentation from the South Centre drew attention to the close link between global partnerships and means of implementation, in that the success of the former depends on 'finance, technology and supportive international regimes, including trade'. Among this NGO's recommendations, accordingly, is the inclusion of means of implementation both as a stand-alone goal and as part of each individual SDG. In the delegations' exchange of views, there emerged a recognition that, despite the increasing importance of external financing sources, 'such as South–South and triangular cooperation, remittances, philanthropy and innovative development finance', they are not a substitute for but a complement to traditional official development assistance (ODA). The Chair of the Organisation for Economic Cooperation and Development, Development Assistance Committee (OECD-DAC) affirmed this fact, especially for small island developing states (SIDS) and least developed countries (LDCs), and reiterated the catalytic function of ODA in leveraging other financing flows. Likewise, the World Bank Group special envoy 'discussed the many diverse needs and situations of the different categories of developing countries' and 'cautioned against neglecting to prioritize the countries "who have been left behind" when developing the post-2015 agenda'. Relatedly, another presenter argued that agreement on the universality of goals requires recognition of the varying development opportunities and structural economic vulnerabilities across countries. These insights from the OECD and the World Bank Group presumably informed the means of implementation targets (10.a–10.c) under Goal 10. From the exchange of views during OWG-6, one key point raised is the 'need to ensure that the human rights of the most vulnerable and marginalized are upheld, including indigenous peoples, to eliminate all forms of discrimination, including against women and girls, and to promote economic and legal empowerment of the poor and of women'. The recurring theme of reforming the international financial and economic architecture was likewise raised.

OWG-8, which is the last session in the stocktaking phase, tackled the topic of promoting equality. Particular attention was given to social equity, gender equality, and women's empowerment. It was during OWG-8 that the components of Goal 10, as presently phrased, were elaborated. Instrumental in this regard was the presentation from Jose Antonio Ocampo, who advocated for a stand-alone goal on reducing inequalities based on data showing the gravity of inequalities both among and within countries. Among his findings: 'Inequality among countries is by far the most important, and roughly 80 per cent of in-country inequalities are associated with inequalities across countries; yet while the differences between developing and developed countries are declining, the differences among developing countries are increasing.' Citing Branko Milanovic, the TST corroborated this fact: 'Income inequality *between countries* is higher than that within a large majority of countries, such that individual incomes are still largely associated with a person's citizenship and location.'[60] States, as well as representatives of international organizations and Major Groups, reacted to this and other presentations by affirming that '[p]ersistent inequalities [along various spheres] perpetuate ... exclusion and marginalization further and in turn affect social cohesion,

---

[60] TST, 'Promoting Equality' (n 53) 1 (italics in the original).

sustainability, economic growth and overall development outcomes'. This apparent consensus, however, did not (as yet) extend to agreement on having a stand-alone goal on inequalities. The alternative under consideration was to integrate the promotion of equality across the entire framework. The exchange of views raised and fleshed out some of the targets that now appear under SDG 10. Also discussed were other items considered important in reducing inequalities, but these targets were eventually included in other closely related SDGs:

- Social protection floors and free or subsidized health care, food and other social services can make an important impact on reducing inequalities.[61]
- Fostering employment opportunities for those traditionally excluded from the labour market, aiming to provide equal pay for equal work in the formal and informal sectors and supporting small and medium enterprises will also be important milestones in ensuring equality.[62]

B. OWG: Negotiations and Drafting of Proposed Sustainable Development Goals

The Co-Chairs consolidated information from Member States and other stakeholders to identify areas where further actions are needed for the international community to 'realize greater impacts of the much sought[-after] transformative change'. With the stocktaking phase concluded, by the time of its ninth session, the OWG already had a draft list of focus areas 'to start the process of building consensus'. In a nutshell, they 'emphasized that eradication of poverty, inequitable development within and among states as well as protection of the environment are among the most pressing sustainable development challenges facing humankind in this century'. The draft contained nineteen focus areas.

Focus Area 12 ('Promoting equality') covers both inequalities within and between countries. These inequalities are considered 'socially destabilizing', harmful to economic growth, and can also 'have negative effects on global solidarity and international cooperation to address shared challenges'. The connection between in-country and inter-state inequalities are not articulated very well in this draft, although the areas that are deemed to further greater equality between countries pertain to pursuing 'high and sustained growth in developing countries' through, among others, 'progress in education, industrialization, infrastructure, energy and means of implementation'. This phrasing, however, still does not pay enough attention to addressing inequalities between countries.

Unlike the other focus areas that enumerate interlinkages to other focus areas, Focus Area 12 does not have such enumeration. Focus Area 1, 'Poverty eradication', also does

---

[61] Target 1.3.
[62] Targets 8.3 and 8.5.

not have a list, but the cited reason is the multidimensionality of poverty that thereby linked it to action in all other focus areas. This draft is vague in its stance on whether reduction of inequalities or promotion of equality is as cross-cutting as poverty eradication. Notably, promoting equality is only expressly mentioned as being interlinked to two other Focus Areas, namely, 'Health and population dynamics' (Focus Area 3) and 'Peaceful and non-violent societies, capable institutions' (Focus Area 19). The latter begins with a statement that '[e]quality within and between countries is a key determinant of peaceful, non-violent and inclusive societies'.

The Major Groups and other Stakeholders (MGoS) 'welcome[d] the inclusion of a focus area on promoting equality', since '[d]evelopment will never be human, sustainable or even efficient if it doesn't make social justice and reducing inequalities between and within countries as its core themes'. In their response to the draft, they stressed that addressing inequalities requires not only 'a conscious decision to direct resources, services and power to those who have most difficulty in accessing them' but also 'focussing [sic] on extreme wealth reduction ... through redistributive justice and progressive taxation policies'. Among the suggested ways 'to ensure that the framework truly promotes equality' is data disaggregation 'by income quintiles, disability, age, gender, ethnic and religious group and many other situations faced by the most at risk and marginalized' so that a state's fulfilment of targets will only be deemed successful when all these groups have been covered. Another suggestion is to enable the most vulnerable and marginalized to participate in the decision-making process, as well as in implementing the framework and monitoring its implementation. The MGoS' statement urged a greater focus on social protection, which, according to them, is more than just a way to reduce vulnerabilities but 'is the best tool to reduce inequalities and level up the playing field for those that experience poverty, marginalization and unequal access to services and natural resources'.[63] Lastly, they pointed out a glaring omission in the draft: the recognition of interlinkages between promoting equality and employment creation (Focus Area 11). In their view, '[a]ny goal on employment ... must address all existing inequalities and marginalization in the labor market, for example [through] laws and policy to protect both formal and informal economy workers, employment policies that target groups with difficulties to access their first job ... and giving visibility to the unpaid care work carried out by women'. Many of these suggestions were eventually incorporated, albeit in Goals besides SDG 10.

As to the linkage between equality promotion and health, the MGoS' statement on the latter focus area elaborated: 'Any goal on health must ... [e]nsure universal health care and coverage that is based on human rights, addresses underlying and structural inequalities, and gives particular attention to women, young people, and marginalized groups (such as young people living with HIV and people of diverse sexual orientations and gender identities).' The Women and Children and Youth Major Groups proposed

---

[63] UNDESA & WBG (n 3) seem to take a similar position as they consider minimum social protection guarantees as helpful in remedying exclusion, but also posit that mere provision cannot necessarily ensure use or access, hence, better understanding of barriers is needed.

having 'a separate focus area on governance, which includes a clear mandate and mechanisms for how civil society and marginalized groups ... can influence government at the national and international levels'.

As the importance of interlinking focus areas grew in prominence, the creation of a separate annex listing these interlinkages became necessary. Concomitantly, when OWG-10 began, the Co-Chairs urged the participants 'to initiate an in-depth consideration of the focus areas with a view to consolidating and clustering them whenever possible, with an eye to formulating goals and targets'. Oddly, the Interlinkages Annex seemed to have singled out Focus Area 12 on promoting inequality, in the sense that it is the only Focus Area that did not specify the other Focus Areas with which it was interlinked. Rather, the paragraph under Focus Area 12 appeared to list targets or action items to realize the goal: 'Some areas that could be considered in furtherance of greater equality within and among countries *through high and sustained growth in developing countries* include progress in education, energy, industrialization, infrastructure, and peaceful and non-violent societies, rule of law and capable institutions.'[64] For comparison, the paragraph under Focus Area 3 read: 'Interlinkages with other areas include: sustainable agriculture, food security and nutrition, gender equality and women's empowerment, water and sanitation, economic growth, promote equality, promote sustainable consumption and production, and climate.' The two other Focus Areas that do not begin with 'Interlinkages with other areas' are Focus Area 1 (Poverty eradication) and Focus Area 18 (Means of implementation/Global partnership for sustainable development).

While this new annex made no additional contribution to understanding how equality promotion relates to other focus areas, the revised draft list of focus areas included some substantial changes. One is a better recognition of the distinctiveness, albeit without ignoring the interrelation, of inequalities within and between countries. This shift can be inferred from the enumeration of actions to further equality among countries, such as 'promoting an open, rules-based, non-discriminatory and equitable multilateral trading system'; 'pursuing policies for planned, well managed and legal migration'; and 'reducing the transaction costs of remittances'. Importantly, these items were later included as targets in the final version of the sustainable development agenda, although not all under SDG 10.

Another crucial change made during OWG-10 is the clustering of focus areas. Cluster 1 combines Focus Area 1 (poverty eradication) and Focus Area 12 (promoting equality). The MGoS' statement on this cluster welcomed the calls, made for both Focus Areas, for data disaggregation to evaluate success in meeting targets. Corroborating the clustering of these two focus areas, the NGO Major Group emphasized that poverty eradication 'can only be achieved if we focus on eliminating inequality and equitably redistribut[ing] wealth—we must not leave anyone behind'. Further, the Stakeholder Group on Ageing pointed out: 'Inequality and poverty later in life are directly related to inequalities of opportunity experienced when young.' This point—the interrelatedness

---

[64] Emphasis added.

726 SDG 10

of equality in outcomes and in opportunities—would become the subject of subsequent discussions, not only within the OWG but also among scholars and commentators. Generally, the MGoS supported having a stand-alone goal on equality promotion, explaining at the same time that it should be 'mainstreamed across all goals in different targets'. Similar to the acknowledgement of the multidimensional character of poverty, this proposed Goal's targets should likewise 'address not only its economic but also its social, cultural and political aspects'. Remarkably, among the four proposed targets, only one makes an attempt at quantification: 'Decrease national income inequality. This can be measured by the ratio of the income of the richest 10% of the population to the bottom 10% of the population. This target also addresses extreme wealth as a means to reduce inequality.'

For OWG-11, two main documents were under consideration: (i) the revised working document listing the focus areas, and (ii) a compilation document containing the goals and targets proposed and elaborated during OWG-10. The latter is entitled, 'Encyclopedia Groupinica: A Compilation of Goals and Targets Suggestions from OWG-10' (Encyclopedia Groupinica). There was also a draft 'chapeau' circulated but it did not appear to have been considered in detail by the Group. The revised working document made two major interrelated changes regarding the goal of promoting equality: first, in-country and inter-state inequalities were separated; second, each was lumped together with other Focus Areas—the former with poverty eradication and the latter with industrialization. Accordingly, the Focus Areas were reduced from nineteen to sixteen, and those relevant to inequality were renamed, thus: Focus Area 1, 'Poverty eradication, building shared prosperity and promoting equality' and Focus Area 9, 'Industrialization and promoting equality among nations'. These revisions were not merely formal or cosmetic. Rather, they substantively and substantially narrowed the targets or actions relating to the reduction of inequalities, specifically those within countries. Most of the targets for reducing inter-state inequalities were transferred to Focus Area 15 'Means of implementation/Global partnership for sustainable development', which now included the following: promoting 'open, rules-based, non-discriminatory and equitable multilateral trading and financial systems';[65] providing 'greater duty-free and quota-free market access to [LDCs] in keeping with [WTO] decisions'; and promoting 'inclusive, participatory decision-making at both national and international levels, including conclusion of reforms for increasing effective participation of developing countries in international financial institutions'. The equality-related targets under revised Focus Area 1 were limited to (i) implementation by 2030 of 'nationally appropriate social protection measures including floors, with focus on coverage of the most marginalized'; (ii) achieving 'full and productive employment for

[65] Whereas the OWG-10 draft explicitly mentioned 'phasing out harmful subsidies', the OWG-11 revised working document only provided a clause 'including complying with the agricultural mandate of the WTO Doha Round' at the end of the target regarding a non-discriminatory and equitable multilateral trading system. According to the footnote to this clause, certain Latin American states proposed that indicators for this target 'could address progress of developed countries towards eliminating all forms of agricultural export subsidies, substantially reducing domestic support and substantially improving market access for developing countries'.

all, including women and young people'; and (iii) ensuring 'equality of economic opportunity for all women and men'.

Other targets previously included in the Focus Area on promoting equality were transferred and scattered to other Focus Areas. Prominently, 'sustain economic growth of the bottom 40% of the income distribution of each country to reduce income inequalities by 2030' was placed in Focus Area 8, 'Economic growth, employment and infrastructure'; while 'mobilize additional financial resources from multiple sources, including reducing the cost of remittances' in Focus Area 15, 'Means of implementation/Global partnership for sustainable development'.

The target that first appeared in the OWG-10 draft—'working towards inclusive societies that respect and promote cultural diversity'—is nowhere to be found in the revised working document. Strangely, although the revised working document had removed the stand-alone focus area on promoting equality, the Encyclopedia Groupinica retained it. The relevant contents of the latter are discussed below, as they pertain mostly to the targets proposed by Member States and MGoS. Suffice to say for now that the OWG-11 documents marked the first time that more definite timelines were identified.

Following the strong opposition by several MGoS against merging the goals on poverty and equality, the stand-alone focus area (goal) on promoting equality re-emerged during OWG-12. The zero draft dated 2 June 2014, which already included a chapeau resembling a preamble, comprising eleven paragraphs—mostly derived from the Rio + 20 Outcome Document, 'The Future We Want'—contained seventeen Focus Areas, with Focus Area 10 entitled 'Reduce inequality within and among countries'.[66] This proposed Goal 10 had a total of twelve targets, seven for reducing inequality among social groups within countries and five 'international actions to reduce inequalities among nations'.

In preparation for OWG-13, the zero draft was revised to 'simplify and harmonize the phrasing of some of the goals' and 'substantially consolidate[e] the number of targets'. The adjustments were, according to the Co-Chairs, for the purpose of 'more closely reflect[ing] areas of agreement and expressed priorities'. Since the Group was nearing the end of its work, changes to the zero draft had become more granular, that is, primarily concerning the targets. Indeed, at the OWG's conclusion, the revised zero draft had been further revised to refine the targets, including their precise wording. The OWG's final proposal—the further revised zero draft—reflects the 2030 Agenda, including the SDGs, as currently worded and adopted by the UN General Assembly.

C. HLP Report

The High-level Panel's recommendations did not include a stand-alone goal on reducing inequalities. Nevertheless, some targets currently appearing under SDG 10 and/or

---

[66] Focus Area 1 became 'End poverty in all its forms everywhere' and Focus Area 9, 'Promote sustainable industrialization'.

728 SDG 10

SDG 17 that pertain to inequalities among countries, are placed under their proposed goal, 'Create a Global Enabling Environment and Catalyse Long-Term Finance':

> 12a. Support an open, fair and development-friendly trading system, substantially reducing trade-distorting measures, including agricultural subsidies, while improving market access of developing country products[67]
>
> 12b. Implement reforms to ensure stability of the global financial system and encourage stable, long-term private investment[68]
>
> 12d. Developed countries that have not done so to make concrete efforts towards the target of 0.7% of gross national product (GNP) as official development assistance to developing countries and 0.15 to 0.20% of GNP of developed countries to least developed countries; other countries should move toward voluntary targets for complementary financial assistance[69]

The Panel discussed, however indirectly, promotion of equality relative to the poverty eradication goal. They viewed 'social discrimination and exclusion' as among the myriad manifestations of poverty. They also related poverty and inequality in their justification for the proposed target on social protection coverage: 'Social assistance programs are another potential game-changer that can directly improve equality ... But social assistance programs vary considerably in quality and perverse incentives can be created if the focus is just on access.'[70] They thus enjoined experts to think about ways to measure all aspects of quality and come up with appropriate standards.

The topic of inequalities seemed to also have figured into the Panel's conceptualization of proposed Goal 8, since it referred to *equitable* growth. Moreover, the Panel explained in the context of proposed Goal 11 that '[j]obs and inclusive growth are linked to peace and stability', because they improve social cohesion and 'deter people from joining criminal networks or armed groups'. However, based on this report at least, it is not very clear how they defined 'broad-based, equitable growth' and 'inclusive and sustainable economic development'—apart from saying that the former 'requires more than raising GDP' and that the latter is linked to labour market conditions and the existence of 'good and decent jobs'. The HLP also understood equitable growth and more 'opportunity for all' as being connected to 'an open, fair and development-friendly trading system', especially considering that the growth of many developing countries in recent years is 'driven by trade more than aid'.[71] They nevertheless did not discount

---

[67] cf target 17.10. This target is one of those identified by the HLP as 'requir[ing] further technical work to find appropriate indicators'.

[68] This target likewise still needs additional technical work to identify proper indicators. This target relates to the same subject matter as target 10.5.

[69] cf targets 10.b and 17.2.

[70] Report of the High-Level Panel of Eminent Persons on the Post-2015 Development Agenda, 'A New Global Partnership: Eradicate Poverty and Transform Economies Through Sustainable Development' (2013) 33 <https://www.un.org/sg/sites/www.un.org.sg/files/files/HLP_P2015_Report.pdf> accessed 16 October 2021 (HLP Report).

[71] ibid 54.

the importance of aid, as '55 cents of every dollar of foreign capital that comes into low-income countries is ODA'.[72]

III. Commentary on the Goal

As inequality takes different shapes and is often the result of more than one factor, SDG 10's shortened title ('reduced inequalities') rightly and more accurately refers to the phenomenon in the plural form. At the same time, however, it is reasonable and appropriate to use the singular form[73] (as the 2030 Agenda does), since appreciating and approaching the problem holistically is equally important. In any event, the inclusion of this goal in the 2030 Agenda is a testament to the fact that inequalities are a sustainable development concern—meaning that inequalities and their remedies have economic, environmental, and social (human rights) dimensions.[74] Moreover, as aptly framed by Goal 10, inequalities occur at both the national and the international levels. As one author correctly noted, globalization has made inequality 'a problem happening within a shared [global] space'.[75] Strikingly, though, SDG 10 does not tackle *global* inequality[76]—the income and wealth disparities among individuals transnationally or across borders[77]—which can be attributed to both intra- and inter-state inequalities. Yet, evidence shows that '[e]ven if we completely eliminated intracountry inequality, we would [still] be left with very high levels of global interpersonal inequality'.[78]

The Goal and its targets can also be criticized for not addressing—or at least not clearly and adequately tackling—*wealth* (*contra* income) inequality[79] and the *environmental* dimensions (eg global distribution of carbon emissions)[80] of inequality. Regarding the latter, emerging evidence indicates that 'people in more equal rich countries consume less, produce less and waste and emit less carbon, on average', so 'the most unequal affluent countries contribute more to climate change via pollution than their more equal counterparts'.[81] Conversely, unintended adverse environmental impacts can result from misguided measures to reduce economic inequalities by simply increasing the lowest quintiles' income levels; some studies show that 'at the individual level,

---

[72] ibid 55.

[73] In the Preamble to the Draft Convention on the Right to Development, 'inequality within and across countries' is among the enumerated serious obstacles, together with poverty and climate change, to the realization of the right to development.

[74] See UN Shared Framework, 9.

[75] FJ Garcia, 'Globalization, Inequality & International Economic Law' (2017) 8 Religions 78, 3.

[76] See A Kaya, 'Global Inequality', Oxford Bibliographies (2011) <https://www.oxfordbibliographies.com/view/document/obo-9780199756223/obo-9780199756223-0025.xml> accessed 5 November 2021; M Roser, 'Global Economic Inequality' (2013) <https://ourworldindata.org/global-economic-inequality> accessed 5 November 2021.

[77] United Nations, 'Inequality – Bridging the Divide' (n.d.) <https://www.un.org/en/un75/inequality-bridging-divide> accessed 29 October 2021.

[78] Stewart (n 49) 75. Citing Lakner and Milanovic (2013).

[79] See T Piketty, *Capital in the Twenty-First Century* (The Belknap Press of Harvard University Press 2014).

[80] Stewart (n 49) 68.

[81] D Dorling, 'Is Inequality Bad for the Environment?' *The Guardian* (4 July 2017) <https://www.theguardian.com/inequality/2017/jul/04/is-inequality-bad-for-the-environment> accessed 4 November 2021.

income is positively linked with carbon emissions' and 'income growth at the bottom end of the distribution ... can lead to higher pollution levels'.[82] The UN Department of Economic and Social Affairs (UNDESA), however, warned states against crafting and implementing climate change mitigation measures that could 'eliminate access or opportunities [for certain population groups] through changes in economic structures or legislation on resource uses'.[83] The TST additionally pointed to how social protection can also further environmental objectives, such as by 'provid[ing] incentives for poor people [and highly food insecure populations residing in degraded environments] to engage in conservation activities ... and to shift to more sustainable practices involving environmental management and sustainable agriculture'.[84]

The UNDESA highlighted that the SDGs do not sufficiently recognize this interrelationship, despite the Intergovernmental Panel on Climate Change's (IPCC) findings that 'the poorest are the most vulnerable to the effects of climate change'.[85] Scholars have only begun examining the vicious interrelationship between inequality and climate change, as illustrated in (i) disadvantaged groups' increased exposure to climate hazards; (ii) their greater susceptibility to damages due to climate hazards; and (iii) how inequality weakens these groups' 'relative ability to cope with and recover from the damages they suffer'.[86] The intersections between economic disadvantages and environmental vulnerabilities manifest at the global level too: '[d]irect economic losses from disasters have increased by more than 150 per cent over the past 20 years, with losses disproportionately borne by vulnerable developing countries', making certain population groups within the latter even more vulnerable and insecure.[87] The extreme environmental and climate vulnerability of many SIDS is worsened by the fact that their economies are usually characterized by less diversification, huge debt burdens, and 'lack of access to concessional finance (due to their middle-income country status)'.[88]

In sum, ecological problems can exacerbate existing economic and social vulnerabilities and disparities. The harmful impacts of climate change disproportionately fall on poor states and marginalized communities within countries. Conversely, solutions to environmental issues can help remedy the marginalization of certain groups. Some of these solutions, however, also require financial assistance, including transfer or redistribution of economic resources across States. SDG 10's omission of the environmental dimension is thus a missed opportunity to enhance sustainable development strategies.

Nevertheless, compared to its predecessor, the SDGs do pay more attention to environment-related concerns, such as climate change, biodiversity, water resources, and the marine environment—as illustrated by the fact that 'the preamble to the

---

[82] L Chancel and others, 'Reducing Inequalities within Countries: Assessing the Potential of the Sustainable Development Goals' (2018) 9 Global Policy 5, 8.

[83] UNDESA, *Inequality and 2030* (n 4) 4.

[84] TST, *Issues Brief: Social Protection* (2013) (TST, Social Protection) 4.

[85] UNDESA, *Inequality and 2030* (n 4) 4.

[86] SN Islam and J Winkel, 'Climate Change and Social Inequality' (2017) DESA Working Paper No 152, 2 <https://www.un.org/esa/desa/papers/2017/wp152_2017.pdf> accessed 26 November 2021.

[87] Secretary-General, 'Special Edition' (n 7) para 14.

[88] ibid para 45.

Agenda for Sustainable Development fully recognizes the seriousness of the environmental challenge' and that there are three (13, 14, 15) interlinked Goals addressing environmental issues. As Alan Boyle rightly observed, '[n]one of this adds anything new to international environmental policy or law, but it does serve to reaffirm existing commitments within the context of a process whose outcomes the UN will review in due course'.[89] Moreover, the inclusion of these environment-related goals in the 2030 Agenda is, I think, a means to introduce, perhaps even improve the integration of, international environmental law and policy to other areas of the international legal order that impact the pursuit of sustainable development. The two most relevant fields, particularly for SDG 10, are international human rights law and international economic law.

SDG 10 is unique and novel in that it does not have a 'predecessor' or a counterpart from the previous list of goals. Its inclusion in the post-2015 development agenda, however, can be seen, in part, as a reaction to the deficiencies in implementation and outcomes of the MDGs, particularly their inadequate reflection of 'some of the key human rights principles, including concern with the most vulnerable and marginalized, removing discrimination and respecting the rights of all, participation, and rights that require universal access to services'.[90] Hence, the catchphrase 'leave no one behind' underpinning Goal 10—and indeed the entire 2030 Agenda—is an important improvement from the much-criticized 'cherry-picking' and 'low-hanging fruit' approach under the MDGs that resulted in uneven or unequal progress for different groups— failing to reach the worst off and most vulnerable and 'leaving the marginalised even further behind more fortunate groups'.[91] A study on how targets and indicators can distort[92] governments' incentives and policy prioritization concluded that across the MDGs 'inequality and discrimination were almost entirely neglected', in that 'important progress in aggregate national outcomes' masked the unevenness of such progress across populations, resulting in the continued marginalization of the poorest.[93] The TST recognized this critical weakness of the MDG agenda and thus proposed as a remedy—to be effected in the post-2015 development agenda—the better use of data disaggregation to monitor progress among vulnerable groups.[94]

Another criticism against the MDGs that the SDGs sought to address pertains to the 'immunity' of developed countries, to whom the MDGs were not made to apply— thereby bringing into starker relief the inequality among states. Unlike the MDGs, 'the SDGs are a global agenda [comprising] universal goals that set targets for all—not just

---

[89] A Boyle, 'Climate Change, Sustainable Development, and Human Rights' in M Kaltenborn and others (eds), *Sustainable Development Goals and Human Rights* (Springer International Publishing 2020) 173–74.

[90] Expert Group (n 46) 12.

[91] E Stuart and J Woodroffe, 'Leaving No-One behind: Can the Sustainable Development Goals Succeed Where the Millennium Development Goals Lacked?' (2016) 24 Gender & Development 69, 71.

[92] See J Briant Carant, 'Unheard Voices: A Critical Discourse Analysis of the Millennium Development Goals' Evolution into the Sustainable Development Goals' (2017) 38 Third World Quarterly 16, 24.

[93] Fukuda-Parr and others (n 55) 110. See also UN System Task Team, 'Review of the contributions of the MDG Agenda to foster development' (2012), 3–4.

[94] UN System Task Team (n 93), 20.

poor—countries, and are as relevant for the USA as for Liberia'.[95] By acknowledging and shedding light on the reality of such disparity, the 2030 Agenda took on a politically sensitive issue and is thus considered an advancement as compared to the Millennium Declaration. In the words of Fukuda-Parr, 'Goal 10 requires a reversal rather than acceleration of current trends in many countries ... [and] it draws international attention to the need for wealthy, ostensibly "developed" countries to address issues which draw the model they have followed into question'.[96] This point highlights a graver defect of the MDGs, that is their failure to 'profoundly question ... power and the current economic model'[97] that, in turn, led to 'an undue and mechanistic association of poverty reduction with economic growth with no reference to the structural causes of poverty and to inequality as a core development challenge'.[98] Relatedly, Wouter Vandenhole argues that the attempt to operationalize the right to development under the MDGs is likewise deficient, because they did not clarify the distributive allocation of development obligations, despite having introduced the notion of an enabling international economic environment.[99] As elaborated below, in terms of challenging deeply held economic theories that link income growth and poverty reduction to inequality, the SDGs do not seem to significantly deviate from the MDGs.

Moreover, equality itself was not accorded similar prominence and priority as poverty eradication, notwithstanding the comments by some Member States and MGoS representatives in the OWG concerning the fundamental and cross-cutting character of the Goal on reducing inequalities. The disparate treatment of these topics can be gleaned from the proposed chapeau or Preamble, where only poverty eradication is considered as 'the greatest challenge facing the world today and an indispensable requirement for sustainable development'.[100] The identified overarching objectives and essential requirements for sustainable development only include, in addition to poverty eradication, 'changing unsustainable and promoting sustainable patterns of consumption and production' and 'protecting and managing the natural resource base of economic and social development'. Reducing inequalities is glaringly conspicuous in its absence, at least in the first few paragraphs of the chapeau. In the OWG-13 revised zero draft, it is not until the fifth paragraph that equity and inclusion are mentioned:

> We recognize that people, of all ages and abilities, are at the centre of sustainable development and, in this regard, we strive for a world that is just, equitable and inclusive, and we commit to work together to promote sustained and inclusive economic growth, social development and environmental protection and thereby to benefit all.

---

[95] S Fukuda-Parr, 'From the Millennium Development Goals to the Sustainable Development Goals: Shifts in Purpose, Concept, and Politics of Global Goal Setting for Development' (2016) 24 Gender & Development 43, 44.

[96] ibid 48.

[97] ibid 50.

[98] UN System Task Team (n 93) 15.

[99] W Vandenhole, 'Towards a Division of Labour for Sustainable Development: Extraterritorial Human Rights Obligations' in Kaltenborn and others (eds), Sustainable Development Goals and Human Rights ((n 89) 225.

[100] Substantially the same wordings in OWG-11 Chapeau, OWG-12 Zero draft, OWG-13 Revised zero draft, OWG-13 Final proposal.

COMMENTARY ON THE GOAL   733

As further revised, the fourth paragraph of the OWG's final proposal read:

> People are at the centre of sustainable development and, in this regard, Rio + 20 prom-
> ised to strive for a world that is just, equitable and inclusive, and committed to work
> together to promote sustained and inclusive economic growth, social development
> and environmental protection and thereby to benefit all, in particular the children of
> the world, youth and future generations of the world without distinction of any kind
> such as age, sex, disability, culture, race, ethnicity, origin, migratory status, religion,
> economic or other status.

The earlier formulation is clearer, more emphatic, and more coherent. The final version seems to have sacrificed clarity and impact for comprehensiveness, by including
an extended list of statuses that cannot be used to unduly distinguish among the beneficiaries of development. The awkward arrangement of this sentence, which was already
long to begin with, leaves much to be desired in terms of effectively conveying its message concerning the pursuit of equality.

In contrast, the final proposal made a substantial clarification to the OWG-13 revised zero draft regarding the paragraph on the relationship between international
cooperation and meeting the persistent challenges peculiar to developing countries.
Accordingly, the sentence 'We reaffirm our commitment to strengthen international
cooperation to address the persistent challenges related to sustainable development for
all, in particular in developing countries' was elaborated thus:

> Rio + 20 reaffirmed the commitment to strengthen international cooperation to ad-
> dress the persistent challenges related to sustainable development for all, in particular
> in developing countries. In this regard, it reaffirmed the need to achieve economic sta-
> bility, sustained economic growth, the promotion of social equity and the protection
> of the environment, while enhancing gender equality, women's empowerment and
> equal employment for all, and the protection, survival and development of children to
> their full potential, including through education.[101]

Views differed about the implications of characterizing a concern as 'cross-cutting' —
whether such character justifies a stand-alone goal, or inclusion in each individual
goal, or both. Goal 10 was subjected to such debate. This situation stands in contrast
to the case of poverty eradication, which from the very beginning was identified as an
overarching objective and as permeating the entire sustainable development agenda.
The same is true for gender equality. Nevertheless, inequality was not the only concern subjected to this debate. 'Sustainable consumption and production' was likewise disputed as a cross-cutting concern during OWG-7. Although climate change
was accepted as a cross-cutting issue, some opined that it can be addressed 'without a
stand-alone goal, while respecting the role of and commitments under the UNFCCC'.

---

[101] Para 11.

A probable explanation for these distinctions is the fact that poverty eradication and gender equality were already part of the MDGs. Moreover, '[g]ender inequality was overwhelmingly recognized [during OWG-8] as the most pervasive form of inequality in the world'. On the other hand, inequality, climate change, and sustainable consumption and production are fairly new topics.

The controversy surrounding whether to include a stand-alone goal on reducing inequalities can also be viewed as among the multiple fault-lines between developing and developed states. One commentator noted that the restoration of the stand-alone goal on inequality in the OWG working draft was upon the strong insistence of developing countries, supported by several civil society organizations, arguing that because 'inequalities between countries have been a major driver of [in-country] inequalities globally and historically', developed countries should also be assigned due responsibilities for meeting targets on 'within country' inequalities.[102]

The TST echoed other proposals and recommended the inclusion of a self-standing goal on reducing inequalities, which 'could include a focus on global and national income inequalities as well as addressing the elimination of discriminatory laws, policies and social practices'.[103] Indeed, it highlighted that, while the post-2015 development agenda should rightly maintain the attention given to the 'social dimension of the MDGs', there need to be 'greater emphasis ... on addressing inequalities both within and among countries [and] to make specific provision for countries lagging behind, as well as for the inclusion of marginalized groups of society in the implementation, monitoring and evaluation of the [sustainable development goals]'.[104] The TST added that, in contrast to the MDGs, which did not explicitly consider how to benefit 'the lowest quintiles and most excluded groups', the new goals should work to the benefit of the latter and reflect the increasingly urgent concern regarding 'social equity and inequalities within countries (intra-national equality and equity)'.[105]

A. Inequality and International Law

The very wording of SDG 10 suggests that its objective and related actions involve, to some extent, the relationship among states. Targets 10.6 and 10.7, as well as the Means of Implementation (MOI) targets, refer to international organizations, migration, and external financial flows. There are express statements in the 2030 Agenda pertaining to its implementation 'in a manner that is consistent with the rights and obligations of States under international law' and in accordance with 'the purposes and principles of the Charter of the United Nations, including full respect for international law'. Further,

---

[102] R Sengupta, 'SDGs: The Disappearing Act of the "Inequality" Goal', Third World Network Info Service on UN Sustainable Development (2014) <https://archive.globalpolicy.org/component/content/article/252-the-millenium-development-goals/52649-sdgs-the-disappearing-act-of-the-inequality-goal.html> accessed 26 October 2021.

[103] TST, Equality Brief (n 53) 8.

[104] TST Issues Brief, 'Conceptual Issues (2013)' 3.

[105] ibid 5.

as the UNDESA and the World Bank Group aptly stated, 'SDG 10 is a space within the 2030 Agenda to address inequalities linked to multilateral decision making, as well as complex global flows of finance, people, technology and other resources'.[106] As these topics concern transboundary interactions, it seems straightforward to assume that international law, as a framework for ordering inter-state relationships and regulating state conduct, would be quite relevant to these matters.

A deeper look into the international legal order, particularly contemporary international economic law, however, reveals that issues of inequality are largely taken for granted and international legal norms addressing such issues are scant. This omission urgently needs correction, because even while recognizing that international law itself needs reform due to its contribution to and perpetuation of present-day inequalities, the question of '[w]hether inequalities are diminished or expanded by globalization will depend on how globalization is managed'.[107] International legal norms and processes have proven to be capable of managing interdependence and realizing shared objectives. In appreciating international law's positive role, I agree with Edward Kwakwa that although international law is not expected to modify nature (that has created some of the present-day inequalities among states), its function is not 'to re-emphasize or exacerbate the inequality already existing'[108] either.

Analysing inequalities from an international legal perspective and in the context of the 2030 Agenda can involve several related inquiries. The first pertains to whether and how international law obliges its subjects to achieve and maintain equality of a particular kind. The second asks how international organizations, tribunals, and/or quasi-judicial bodies treat the factual disparities in states' economic capabilities and political power, given the effects of these inequalities on states' compliance with treaty- or custom-based obligations, including those that require international cooperation and assistance and that relate to sustainable development. The third critiques the very design of international law that has contributed to, and perpetuates, present-day inequalities, 'by distributing value under the guise of maximizing it, and by confining the pursuit of human rights to the enactment of minimal standards of protection rather than structural transformation'.[109] It is beyond the scope of this chapter to delve into each of these questions and to discuss them separately, as they rightfully deserve. Instead, I deliberately limit my analysis here to a brief discussion of special and differential treatment (SDT) in international trade law, expressly mentioned in target 10.a, with some references to related principles of common but differentiated responsibility (CBDR) in international environmental law and of progressive realization in international human rights law.

---

[106] UNDESA & WBG (n 3) 5.

[107] ibid.

[108] E Kwakwa, 'Emerging International Development Law and Traditional International Law—Congruence or Cleavage?' (1987) 17 Georgia Journal of International & Comparative Law 431, 451.

[109] I Venzke, 'The Law of the Global Economy and the Spectre of Inequality' [2021] London Review of International Law 3.

Before proceeding, it bears noting at the outset that, unlike the SDG 10 targets pertaining to intra-country inequalities that are mostly grounded in international human rights law, targets 10.5, 10.6, 10.7, 10.a, 10.b, and 10.c rest on less solid legal bases (particularly from a legal positivist standpoint) and are more susceptible to intense political debates. This difference can be explained by the fact that international law generally overlooks asymmetries in power and wealth among states, upholding instead their formal equality as sovereigns. Also, in terms of addressing inequalities among individuals across jurisdictions, although there are so-called extraterritorial human rights obligations that are arguably *lex ferenda*, human rights law predominantly remains construed as being limited to territorial boundaries. Indeed, commitments to reduce inter-state inequalities, including global income inequality, are mainly found in international soft law instruments, such as the 2030 Agenda itself and the Addis Ababa Action Agenda (AAAA).[110] These commitments are thus subject to the voluntary actions of certain, mostly developed, states. Countries like Denmark, Germany, Norway, Sweden, and the United Kingdom, for instance, report in their Voluntary National Reviews (VNRs)[111] addressing SDG implementation not only domestically but also abroad through foreign and development policies. Leaving aside for now the interesting but immense debate about the status of these cooperative efforts as international *legal* obligations, I submit that such actions are nonetheless subject to these states' obligations under international human rights law to ensure that assistance and cooperation do not prevent fulfilment of human rights. It is here that human rights—and equality—impact assessments could play a vital role.

Moreover, it bears emphasizing that a more equitable international economic system entails giving due attention to actual disparities among States and the special needs of those in the developing world. It also requires an understanding of development that is more sensitive to the greater interdependence of economies and societies. The intersections between Goals 10 and 17 are thus salient. In these overlapping concerns, international law can facilitate or regulate the integration of economic, environmental, and social objectives identified by states and by the international community. Significantly, the aforementioned soft law obligations could still harden over time, especially in the light of ongoing codification efforts regarding the Draft Convention on the Right to Development. I anticipate that the adoption of this treaty would be an important initial step towards the revival or consolidation of 'international development law', which could empower the developing states comprising majority of the international community by 'respond[ing] to the major goal of eliminating existing inequalities in international economic relations'.[112]

---

[110] Addis Ababa Action Agenda of the Third International Conference on Financing for Development (27 July 2015) UNGA Res 69/313 (Addis Ababa Action Agenda).

[111] High-Level Political Forum on Sustainable Development, 'Voluntary National Reviews' <https://sustainable development.un.org/vnrs/> accessed 12 November 2021.

[112] Kwakwa (n 108) 453.

B. Human Rights and Labour Rights

Reasonable grounds exist to argue that inequality is a human rights issue: it 'is both a consequence and a cause of human rights deprivations', that is '[m]any of the key determinants of inequality—from the erosion of labor rights and the weakening of public services, to systemic discrimination and the capture of democratic decision-making by self-serving elites—can be framed as denials of internationally guaranteed human rights'.[113] Given the overall emphasis of the 2030 Agenda on the holistic well-being of all persons, one of the most obvious normative standards with which to analyse the Goals, including SDG 10, is international human rights law. Significantly, the elimination of discrimination and inequalities is among the prevailing and prominent injunctions in this legal field. The right of all human beings, especially individuals belonging to some historically marginalized and/or vulnerable groups, not to be discriminated against is well-established. Indeed, the non-discrimination principle is enshrined in the Universal Declaration of Human Rights[114] and can be found in all the core human rights treaties.[115] As mentioned in the Introduction, however, there is no discrete and explicit 'right to equality'. Instead, most legal provisions relating to disparities are prohibitions against discrimination, meaning, the law enjoins states, as duty-holders, to respect, protect, and fulfil human rights without distinction, exclusion, restriction, or preference of any kind based on status or characteristics attributable to the right-bearers. In any case, international law is relevant and useful to the 2030 Agenda on two aspects: first, provisions under human rights treaties serve as normative standards to evaluate SDG actions and progress; second, international human rights mechanisms allow SDG data, methods, assumptions, and narratives to be questioned by 'bring[ing] an extra procedural layer of accountability' and 'provid[ing] a different [and alternative] type of accountability'.[116]

In the following sections, specific human rights provisions applicable to each target will be identified and briefly discussed. For instance, target 10.4 covers care and family leave policies, as well as labour protections, that correspond to existing human rights guarantees regarding social security and decent work. Target 10.5 on financial regulation involves states' international legal obligation to protect, meaning, their duty to establish rules and mechanisms to hold third parties (eg banks, credit rating agencies, private financial actors) responsible 'for finance-related individual and systemic

---

[113] CESR (n 38) 12.

[114] Universal Declaration of Human Rights (10 December 1948) UNGA Res 217 A(III) (UDHR) art 2.

[115] ICESCR, arts 2(2) and 3; International Covenant on Civil and Political Rights (1966, entered into force 23 March 1976) 999 UNTS 171 (ICCPR) art 2(1); International Convention on the Elimination of All Forms of Racial Discrimination (1965, entered into force 4 January 1969) 660 UNTS 195 (ICERD) art 1(1) in relation to art 2; Convention on the Rights of the Child (1989, entered into force 2 September 1990) 1577 UNTS 3 (CRC) art 2(1); Convention on the Elimination of All Forms of Discrimination against Women (1979, entered into force 3 September 1981) 1249 UNTS 13 (CEDAW) arts 1 and 3; Convention on the Rights of Persons with Disabilities (adopted without vote 24 January 2007) UNGA Res 61/106, Annex I (CRPD) art 4(1); International Convention on the Protection of All Migrant Workers and Members of their Families (1990, entered into force 1 July 2003) UNGA Res 45/158 (ICRMW) art 7.

[116] CESR (n 38) 38.

738   SDG 10

human rights abuses, such as predatory lending or financial speculation in food and housing markets'.[117]

SDG 10's concern about inequalities within and among states can also be a fitting object of extraterritorial human rights obligations, because 'inequalities between countries ... have substantial impact on the realization of human rights as well as the achievement of sustainable development'[118] in domestic settings. Using the notion of extraterritoriality, especially in relation to economic, social, and cultural rights 'can shed useful light on the common but differentiated responsibilities of states to reduce inequality and prevent deepening disparity'[119] and can also foster 'more rigorous monitoring and accountability' for the fulfilment of both Goals 10 and 17.[120]

While there are explicit references to the UDHR and international human rights treaties in the 2030 Agenda, the purportedly human rights-based approach of the SDGs is disputed because the Goals' 'progressive commitments for development' conflict with, and 'do not pay sufficient attention to human rights and the corresponding obligations' that require immediate fulfilment.[121] This critique aligns with the ICESCR, which provides for the progressive realization[122] of certain obligations therein, taking into account the resources available to a state and its concomitant capability to comply, but also requires immediate fulfilment of minimum core obligations.[123]

The other aspect of the appraisal and the recommended solution—that is, adoption of a genuine human rights-based approach by 'specify[ing] responsible global actors, principles of distributing sustainable development commitments among them, means for their implementation, as well as monitoring and accountability mechanisms' to remove sustainability commitments from the complete control of 'self-obliging actors'[124]—is well-taken. Indeed, as affirmed in the Draft RTD Convention, there exist universal principles common to all human rights, namely, 'accountability, empowerment, participation, non-discrimination, equality and equity'.[125] Relevantly, as Margot Salomon stressed, the 'global system that structurally disadvantages half the world population' and causes the prevailing inequality today and certain states' failure to secure the socio-economic rights of so many people are deliberate policy options and practical projects of those who hold power within the international political economy.[126] More critically, another scholar argued that the SDGs 'reflect a highly problematic approach to development', because they treat poverty and inequality as 'stages on the rung of the

---

[117] ibid 18–19.
[118] MacNaughton (n 36) 1051.
[119] CESR (n 38) 29–30.
[120] ibid 39.
[121] E Pribytkova, 'Global Obligations for Sustainable Development: Harmonizing the 2030 Agenda for Sustainable Development and International Human Rights Law' (2019) 41 University of Pennsylvania Journal of International Law 1031, 1048–49.
[122] Art 2(1).
[123] The non-discrimination obligation in art 2(2) is one such obligation requiring immediate fulfilment.
[124] Pribytkova (n 121) 1053.
[125] Draft RTD Convention, art 3(b).
[126] ME Salomon, 'Why Should It Matter That Others Have More? Poverty, Inequality, and the Potential of International Human Rights Law' (2011) 37 Review of International Studies 2137, 2145–46.

(metaphoric) ladder rather than in *relational* terms'.[127] A human rights approach to Goal 10 thus requires states to adopt predistributive and redistributive policies, some of which are addressed by the existing targets.[128]

Also deserving of closer attention is the critical observation about there being a lack of consensus on the implications of the states' 'pledge to avoid exclusion, marginalisation and neglect of the worst-off at the centre of the 2030 Agenda', which from a human rights perspective means addressing not only extreme poverty but also 'discrimination, social exclusion and economic inequality'.[129] As Saiz and Donald argued, ' "leaving no one behind" should entail preventing some from getting too far ahead at the expense of others'.[130] Otherwise stated, a human rights-based approach to development demands not only paying attention to absolute poverty and basic needs but also '[t]ackling inequalities (of opportunity *and outcome*) and the systemic discrimination (direct and indirect) that fuel these disparities'.[131]

I consider this argument to dovetail with the broader call by the Special Rapporteur on extreme poverty and human rights to take ESC rights seriously[132] and to put back 'questions of resources and redistribution' into the human rights equation.[133] This proposition implies, among others, the removal of the artificial separation between international human rights law and international economic law that has restrained human rights forums from tackling notions of distributive equality[134] and issues of the 'availability of resources and equality of access to those resources' and has also enabled IFIs and other international economic organizations to eschew human rights concerns in the context of their policies and programmes. I will further discuss these points below in Subsection III.C. The imperative for international cooperation and for creating a favourable international environment to realize SDG 10 likewise belongs to this theme, insofar as 'human rights norms also set out binding duties on states to cooperate internationally to reduce disparities in their capacity to fulfil human rights, including the right to development, and to ensure their policies and practices do not fuel deprivation and disparities in other countries'.[135]

Despite its clear importance to the goal of reducing inequalities, international human rights law, as it currently stands, can itself be criticized for confining itself to minimum thresholds, particularly as regards socio-economic rights, instead of also devoting attention to systemic and structural issues such as the gap between groups and the distribution of power in a society. As Salomon eloquently stated:

---

[127] H Weber, 'Politics of "Leaving No One Behind": Contesting the 2030 Sustainable Development Goals Agenda' (2017) 14 Globalizations 399, 407–408 (italics in the original).
[128] CESR (n 38) 15.
[129] Saiz and Donald (n 26) 1031.
[130] ibid.
[131] CESR (n 38) 11 (italics in the original).
[132] SR on extreme inequality and human rights (n 25) para 50.
[133] ibid para 56.
[134] ibid para 55.
[135] CESR (n 38) 12.

740   SDG 10

'Minimum' then is the threshold that pertains to the downtrodden, to the deprived, to the victims of human rights violations. *However, by focusing our attention on what is minimally required, the doctrine overlooks the significance of appraising the wider implications of having a minority of people continue to secure a 'maximum' level of rights.* Given the shared dependencies created by globalisation, should concern not be with those who possess not only less than the minimum, but far more than the minimum, insofar as those two conditions are relational? *In order to address the 'massive and systemic breach' of international human rights law that poverty represents, it would seem that international law in this area should be preoccupied not purely with the absolute position of the worse-off members of our global society, but also with the inequality that characterises our contemporary world order.*[136]

This critique bears similar concerns as Ingo Venzke, who found it problematic that human rights discourses had focused on 'poverty, minimal protection and basic needs', thereby neglecting 'the crucial [structural] question of why somebody may be poor or struggle to meet basic needs'.[137] Along similar lines, the CEB acknowledged, albeit in a less critical manner, that intersecting and mutually reinforcing structural drivers and barriers in various domains (economic, social, political, cultural, urban, environmental) deeply entrench inequalities and 'lead to systematic disadvantage and the perpetuation of discrimination, inequality and exclusion from generation to generation'.[138] They concluded that '[a]ddressing inequalities is also … about addressing structural barriers, reversing unequal distributions of power, resources and opportunities and challenging discriminatory laws, policies, social norms and stereotypes'.[139] Significantly, the foregoing reproach of international human rights law, and of international law more broadly, for disregarding structural concerns finds even greater resonance in international economic law, to which the discussion now turns.

C. Trade, Investment, Aid

Apart from being valuable in itself, equality is instrumental to growth, poverty eradication, and other developmental goals. Necessarily, therefore, analysing SDG 10 would benefit from an economic perspective and such analysis would touch upon concerns tackled within international economic (trade, investment, finance) law.

Exemplifying this instrumental perspective on equality, *Realizing the Future We Want for All* explains that, when qualified as 'inclusive', economic development refers not simply to a pro-poor focus but to universality and attention to 'vulnerable populations in precarious livelihoods', since vulnerabilities have many sources apart from poverty. Achieving inclusive economic development thus entails 'an approach that

---

[136] Salomon (n 126) 2144 (citation omitted) (emphasis added).
[137] Venzke (n 109) 8.
[138] UN Shared Framework, 13.
[139] ibid.

aligns the imperatives of macroeconomic stability and financial sustainability with broader structural development policies enabling adequate generation of productive employment and decent work, reduction of poverty and inequalities, low-carbon as well as resource-and waste-efficient economic growth, and welfare protection.[140] It is this 'transformed' outlook on development—which gives due consideration to structural issues such as inequality—that is sought to be achieved through the 2030 Agenda and Goal 10 more specifically. In fact, during the drafting process of the SDGs, there were proposals to include targets on global (apart from national) income inequalities, 'such as reducing the global Palma ratio or that each country reaches at least the next World Bank income category by 2030'.[141] More crucially, there were also suggestions to address global or international inequalities 'through a strengthened set of targets and indicators for a more equitable global system in relation to trade, investment, debt relief, technology transfer and global governance'.[142] These recommendations seemed to be responding to criticisms against the MDGs, and such criticisms arguably echoed the demands—mainly from Third World countries—in previous decades to renew the international economic order, which perpetuated if not aggravated the existing inequalities between rich powerful states in the North and impoverished newly decolonized states in the South.

In the end, however, the suggested targets were not adopted in the 2030 Agenda, which instead opted to focus on enhancing the voice and representation of developing countries (target 10.6), improving the implementation of their special and differential treatment within international trade law (target 10.a), and increasing the aid and capital flows to the developing world (target 10.b). To the extent that these targets do not go so far as to question or challenge the neoliberal underpinnings of the current international economic legal framework and institutions, it can be expected that the SDGs would be criticized for supporting rather than transforming the international economic order that has negligently disregarded 'approaches to economic activity that are more compassionate, or indeed more effective when it comes to poverty reduction and narrowing the gap on inequality, as well as with regard to economic growth in developing countries'.[143]

Existing legal regimes, including the international organizations, concerned with trade, investment, and finance have had their respective clashes with other fields of international law, such as human rights law, when 'non-economic' concerns arise, especially in the course of a dispute before the World Trade Organization (WTO) Dispute Settlement Body or an investor–state arbitral tribunal. It is beyond the scope of this chapter to discuss how these tensions are managed or resolved, depending on the stage of the international lawmaking process in which they occur. In the context of the 2030

---

[140] UN System Task Team on the Post-2015 UN Development Agenda, *Realizing the Future We Want for All* (2012), para 80.

[141] TST, Equality Brief (n 53) 6.

[142] ibid.

[143] ME Salomon, 'Poverty, Privilege and International Law: The Millennium Development Goals and the Guise of Humanitarianism', *German Yearbook of International Law*, vol 51 (2008) 46.

Agenda, it appears that its chosen approach to 'humanize' international economic law, which governs many if not most of the activities needed to meet the Goals, and to make development sustainable, is by fleshing out the embedded human rights norms in the targets and indicators. With respect to SDG 10 particularly, however, this approach might face difficulties, since human rights norms and international legal rules that address inequalities, especially at the global or international level, remain scarce. It therefore becomes more imperative to 'move, seriously and expeditiously, to correct the inequities that have long plagued the international system to the disadvantage of developing countries' and to 'continue to remedy the policy incoherence between current modes of international governance in matters of trade, finance and investment on the one hand, and the norms and standards for labour, environment, human rights, equality and sustainability on the other', as the UN Secretary-General enjoined.[144]

D. Inequality, Interlinkages, and Sustainable Development

The interlinkages of SDG 10 with the other Goals were made clearer by the COVID-19 crisis, which itself is a multidimensional (public health, economic, social, political) phenomenon. In its 2020 SDG Report, the UN emphasized that it is the most vulnerable groups that are being hit hardest by the pandemic.[145] In a background document, 'COVID-19 and the global SDG indicators', presented to the Statistical Commission, the Inter-Agency and Expert Group on Sustainable Development Goal Indicators (IAEG-SDGs) prepared a list of indicators that 'can serve as a starting point for countries to focus their monitoring efforts on the impacts of COVID-19 on the SDGs'. Interestingly, one of the Group's findings concerned how adverse impacts on at least four Goals have, in turn, also adversely affected SDG 10:

o Goal 4 (Quality Education): The closure of schools clearly bears negative effects on this Goal, and it is also becoming clear that 'remote learning [is] less effective and not accessible for some [students]'.

o Goal 5 (Gender Equality): Apart from the fact that '[w]omen account for majority of health and social care workers who are more exposed to COVID-19', the lockdowns and various restrictions on movement have exposed them to increased levels of violence.

o Goal 8 (Decent Work and Economic Growth): The general suspension of economic activities meant 'lower income, less work time, [and] unemployment for certain occupations'.

---

[144] Synthesis report of the Secretary-General on the post-2015 sustainable development agenda, 'The Road to Dignity by 2030: Ending Poverty, Transforming All Lives and Protecting the Planet' (4 December 2014), para 95.
[145] UN, 'The Sustainable Development Goals Report 2020 15' (SDG Report 2020).

o Goal 11 (Sustainable Cities and Communities): 'Population living in slums face higher risk of exposure to COVID-19 due to high population density and poor sanitation conditions'.

Recognizing these interlinkages is valuable in 'build[ing] on synergies among the Goals, enabl[ing] progress on several Goals (enablers of development) and address[ing] trade-offs between targets and policy areas'.[146] It is, however, only the first step in implementing the 2030 Agenda. Another hurdle that needs to be overcome is the fact that 'institutions, governance and skill sets have not yet adapted to translate this nexus of information into effective whole-of-Government and whole-of-society approaches and cross-sectoral action aligned with the 2030 Agenda'.[147] A human rights NGO rightly pointed out that the inclusion of a stand-alone goal on reducing inequalities is one thing, but implementing it and its associated targets is another critical matter altogether, especially considering that 'SDG10 has no obvious thematic body or set of institutions at the national or international level whose mandate is to drive actions and funding to this goal, monitor its achievement and hold decision-makers to account for any lack of progress (unlike other sustainable development goals which have dedicated UN agencies, mechanisms or committees)'.[148] The Special Rapporteur on extreme poverty and human rights likewise highlighted this problematic artificial separation between the mandates of international human rights bodies and international economic organizations. Notably, grappling with the dual nature of equality as both a goal in itself and a means to achieve other goals does not necessarily mean that the choice is between pursuing it through siloed institutions and simply letting circumstances decide which agency is to take charge. It is more advisable to correct the various international institutions' siloed approach, since SDG 10 'require[s] the most profound and lasting changes to the "business-as-usual" economic and development model'.[149]

IV. Commentary on the Targets

SDG 10 comprises ten targets: seven directly aimed at reducing inequalities within and among countries, while three are implementation targets relating to inter-state inequalities.

For the purposes of this section, the following definitions used by the HLP are adopted:[150]

Goal—expresses an ambitious, but specific, commitment. Always starts with a verb/ action.

---

[146] Secretary-General, 'Special Edition' (n 7) para 82.
[147] ibid para 82.
[148] CESR (n 38) 9.
[149] ibid 10.
[150] HLP Report (n 70) 57.

744 SDG 10

Targets—quantified sub-components that will contribute in a major way to achievement of goal. Should be an outcome variable.

Indicators—precise metric from identified databases to assess if target is being met (often multiple indicators are used).

The uncertainty that riddled SDG 10's history—the challenges about its being a stand-alone goal and the separation of its components and merger into other goals—spilled over to its associated targets such that some of the previously proposed targets were entirely omitted from the final version, while others were transferred to the related goals, and other targets were duplicated in more than one goal. There are also a few targets that have been substantially altered relative to the original proposal.

A. Omitted Targets

A controversial omission from the SDG 10 target on income inequality concerns the recognition of the fact that capital and labour have, over time, been receiving considerably disparate or unequal incomes. One proposed target in the OWG-12 zero draft stated: 'work towards revising the decline of the share of labour income in GDP where relevant'. Instead of including this item as a target under Goal 10, 'Labour share of GDP' became indicator 10.4.1.

An even more glaring and contentious omission in the targets for Goal 10 pertains to the lack of a specific target on reducing global inequality. On policy and economic grounds, Anderson found this absence surprising, because 'around two-thirds of income inequality at the global level is due to inequality between countries, as opposed to inequality within countries'[151]—which means, in my view, that meeting such a target would be beyond the competence of any individual state. Conversely, this connection between inequalities at the national and the international levels implies that for many states, particularly those in the developing world, meeting the target to reduce intra-country inequalities would be contingent on the reduction of inter-country inequalities.

B. Duplicated Targets

Demonstrating inequality's cross-cutting character, some SDG 10 targets overlap with targets in other goals, namely, 1, 5, 8, 16, and 17.

ODA targets, for instance, appear in both Goals 10 and 17. The former refers to ODA as among those financial flows that states are encouraged to direct where the need is greatest. The latter provides some quantification of the ODA expected from developed countries. Target 1.a is also relevant, to the extent that it seeks to ensure that developing

---

[151] E Anderson, 'Equality as a Global Goal' (2016) 30 Ethics & International Affairs 189, 197.

countries, particularly LDCs, have adequate and predictable resources, 'including through enhanced development cooperation', for implementing 'programmes and policies to end poverty in all its dimensions'.

Similarly, both Goals have trade-related targets that should be read together to better understand how international trade can address inequality. For example, target 17.12—providing for duty-free and quota-free market access for LDCs, including the use of transparent and simple preferential rules of origin—complements target 10.a, which aims at implementing SDT for developing countries to reduce inequalities among states. Arguably, it would have been equally *apropos* to place target 17.11—'Significantly increase the exports of developing countries, in particular with a view to doubling the least developed countries' share of global exports by 2020'—under SDG 10, because, if implemented (and following the logic of target 10.1 concerning in-country inequality), this target would presumably have the effect of increasing the income of LDCs relative to the rest of the world. In this respect, SDG 8 also contains target 8.a, which refers to '[i]ncreas[ing] Aid for Trade support for developing countries, in particular least developed countries, including through the Enhanced Integrated Framework for Trade-related Technical Assistance to Least Developed Countries'.

Targets 10.6 and 16.8 are essentially the same, in that they both aim to enhance the developing countries' representation and participation in global decision-making processes. However, for target 16.7—'Ensure responsive, inclusive, participatory and representative decision-making at all levels'—there does not appear to be a parallel target for national or local decision-making processes under Goal 10. The most closely related target would be target 5.5, which provides: 'Ensure women's full and effective participation and equal opportunities for leadership at all levels of decision-making in political, economic and public life'.

Goals 10 and 5 are obviously interrelated, since gender inequality is one, perhaps *the* most pervasive, form of inequality. Thus, targets 5.1–5.4, as well as targets 5.a and 5.c, can be read as elaborating target 10.3.

C. Transferred Targets

Since SDG 10 is concerned with addressing the vulnerabilities of certain groups and aiming to narrow the gaps between groups, whether of states or of individuals, it is important to have sufficiently detailed information describing the situation of the groups of concern. For this reason, proposed targets under the predecessors of SDG 10 included disaggregation of data. For instance, target 10.7 in the OWG-12 zero draft stated: 'ensure the availability of high-quality, timely and disaggregated data to ensure monitoring of progress for marginalized groups and people in vulnerable situations'. This target was complemented by another under the Proposed Goal 17 ('Strengthen and enhance the means of implementation and global partnership for sustainable development'). In the same draft, targets under Proposed Goal 17 were divided according to which goals they are intended to implement. Accordingly, target 17.36—'by 2020, substantially strengthen capacities for data collection and statistical analysis relevant to sustainable development with a focus on generating timely and high-quality data disaggregated, as appropriate, by income, gender, age, race, ethnicity, and rural/urban location'—fell under means of implementation for Proposed Goal 10 ('Reduce inequality within and among countries'). By the time of the OWG-13, targets 10.7 and 17.36 have been merged and placed under the goal on means of implementation. Target 17.18 in the Final Proposal thus provided: 'by 2020, enhance capacity building support to developing countries, including LDCs and SIDS, to significantly increase the availability of high-quality, timely and reliable data disaggregated by income, gender, age, race, ethnicity, migratory status, disability, geographic location and other characteristics relevant in national contexts'. Presently, target 17.18 in the 2030 Agenda has the same wording.

Debt sustainability is another target, which was initially included under the goal on promoting equality and eventually ended up under the goal on means of implementation. In the OWG-12 zero draft, target 10.12, which was among the 'international actions to reduce inequalities among nations', read: 'assist developing countries in attaining long term debt sustainability through coordinated policies aimed at fostering debt financing, debt relief and debt restructuring'. This topic, including debt relief, had previously been discussed as part of the goal on economic growth (OWG-9 and 10) and the goal on means of implementation (OWG-11). During OWG-11, some participants[152] even proposed to include a similar target under the Focus Area on poverty eradication. During OWG-13, the target to 'assist developing countries in attaining long term debt sustainability' already appeared under the Finance category of targets under Proposed Goal 17 on strengthening the means of implementation. Target 17.4 in the OWG's Final Proposal was adopted verbatim in the 2030 Agenda. It is curious that, unlike the ODA targets that now appear under both Goals 10 and 17[153], this debt-related target was deemed more appropriate to only be part of the means of implementation.

D. The Current Targets

1. Target 10.1 By 2030, progressively achieve and sustain income growth of the bottom 40% of the population at a rate higher than the national average

a) Source of target

In its earlier iterations, this target focused on the *comparative* income, wealth, and/or growth thereof between the bottom 40 per cent and the top 10 per cent of the population:

- By 2030, half the gap between the income ratios of top 10 per cent and bottom 40 per cent of a country[154]

---

[152] Benin and the Group of 77.
[153] ODA and Debt are both under the 'Finance' category.
[154] Encyclopedia Groupinica, Proposal by Pakistan for inclusion under Focus Area 12. Promote equality.

- Reduce income inequality in all countries such that the post-tax transfer income of the poorest 40 per cent is no less than the post-tax, post-transfer income of the richest 10 per cent[155]
- Decrease national income inequality as measured by the ratio of the income of the richest and bottom 10 per cent of the population[156]

The MGoS also advocated looking more specifically on 'post-tax, post-transfer' incomes:

- 10.1 through 2030 sustain *wealth* growth of the bottom 40 per cent of the population at a rate higher than the national average
- 10.*bis* reduce income inequality in all countries such that the post-tax, post-transfer income of the poorest 40 per cent is no less than the post-tax, post-transfer income of the richest 10 per cent

These proposals are tied to others that pertain to more structural and systemic reforms, such as the adoption of 'progressive taxation systems, redistributive economic and social policies, [and] wage and social protection',[157] on the theory that existing inequalities are largely caused, and can therefore be corrected, by taxes and government-effected transfers. Significantly, in the OWG-12 zero draft, the goal on promoting 'strong, inclusive and sustainable economic growth and decent work for all' also contained a target that read:

8.2 sustain income growth of the bottom 40% of the income distribution of each country of [*sic*] at least y (greater than x)% to reduce income inequalities by 2030

Another interesting aspect of this target's evolution is that it was included under Focus Area 8 on 'Economic growth, employment and infrastructure' in the OWG-11 working document. Indeed, the current language of target 10.1 is copied almost verbatim from the OWG-11 draft: 'sustain income growth of the bottom 40% of the income distribution of each country to reduce income inequalities by 2030'.

Several commentators have since criticized target 10.1 for failing to use the Palma ratio to measure income inequality and disregarding proposals concerned with the income growth not only of the bottom percentage of the population but also of the top percentage. Instead, target 10.1 hewed closely to the proposal under the original Focus Area Document (first circulated during OWG-9), which provided: 'promoting differentially high per capita income growth at the bottom of the income distribution'. Echoing other scholars, Doyle and Stiglitz argued that 'the best indicator for these targets is the Palma ratio, which effectively focuses on extreme inequality—the ratio of

---

[155] Proposed amendment (by several MGoS) to target 10.2 in the OWG-12 zero draft.
[156] Encyclopedia Groupinica, Proposal by Children & Youth, NGOs for inclusion under Focus Area 12.
[157] OWG-13, MGoS Compilation.

748 SDG 10

incomes at the very top to those at the bottom'.[158] All countries' attention should be on extreme inequalities, they posited, because it is such kind that is most harmful to equitable and sustainable economic growth and which 'undermine social and political stability'.[159] CESR expounded that, because intense income and wealth concentration at the top have both economic and political impacts, '"leaving no one behind" should entail preventing some from getting too far ahead at the expense of others'.[160]

The OWG's Final Proposal, which was eventually adopted by the UN General Assembly, also made a substantial change at the last minute by adding a verb to the target and placing a qualifier before it:

> 10.1 by 2030 *progressively achieve* and sustain income growth at the bottom 40% of the population at a rate higher than the national average

This added phrase could be construed as weakening target 10.1's time-bound character. To counter such interpretation, the notion of 'progressive realization' of certain economic, social, and cultural rights should be applied to clarify the meaning of this target. I expound this point in the Critique below.

b) Empirical analysis: domestic and international efforts

In the very first SDG report after the 2030 Agenda was adopted, the UN revealed the status quo, and in some way, set the baseline for monitoring progress on target 10.1: 'In 56 out of 94 [nearly 60 per cent] countries with data for the period 2007–2012, the per capita income of the poorest 40 per cent of households grew more rapidly than the national average.'[161] Strikingly, one reported statistic—'9 out of the 56 countries [where the income of the poorest grew faster than the national average] experienced negative income growth rates'—seems to refute the instrumental view on equality by showing that 'faster growth for the poorest does not necessarily imply greater prosperity' overall.[162] Even assuming that this apparent correlation holds, the same data can be interpreted to justify focusing, as target 10.1 does, on the bottom 40 per cent inasmuch as the latter 'are particularly vulnerable to economic changes'—as shown by the fact that 'in most countries with contractions in per capita income/consumption, the bottom 40 per cent fared worse than the overall population'.[163] According to the UN, these findings suggest that 'sustained income growth overall is necessary to reduce inequality and ensure shared prosperity'.[164]

---

[158] MW Doyle and JE Stiglitz, 'Eliminating Extreme Inequality: A Sustainable Development Goal, 2015–2030' (2014) 28 Ethics & International Affairs 5, 10.

[159] ibid.

[160] CESR (n 38) 10–11.

[161] UN, 'Sustainable Development Goals Report 2016' 8 (SDG Report 2016).

[162] ibid 30.

[163] UN, 'Sustainable Development Goals Report 2017' 38 (SDG Report 2017). Here, the sample size was reduced (from 94 to 83 countries) and the observation period was limited to 2011–2015 (*contra* 2007–2012 in the 2016 report). Despite the adjustment, there does not appear to be much variation from the 'baseline' previously set: '[T]he income and/or consumption of the bottom 40 per cent of the population grew faster than the national average in 49 out of the 83 [59 per cent] countries with data (accounting for three quarters of the world's population).'

[164] ibid 38.

The SDG Reports from 2016 to 2018[165] consistently relayed that the income growth of the poorest 40 per cent has been higher than the national income growth. It was in the 2019 SDG Report, however, that the UN provided a more nuanced interpretation of the data:

In 92 countries with comparable data over the period 2011 to 2016, the results were mixed. In 69 countries [75%], the poorest 40% saw their income grow, but with *large variations across countries*. In 50 out of those 69 countries, income growth in the poorest 40% of the population was faster than the national average. *Notably, however, the bottom 40% still received less than 25% of overall income.* In many countries, an increasing share of income goes to the top 1%.[166]

With regard to the share of income received by the top 1 per cent, an Expert Group, which specifically studied SDGs 10, 13, and 16, reported that 'the national income share of the top 1 per cent [of the American population] has increased substantially, from close to 10 per cent in 1980 to 20 per cent in 2016', while in European countries, although the top 1 per cent was also receiving nearly 10 per cent of the national income in 1980, their income share 'has risen less drastically to 12 per cent in 2016'.[167] The same study found that '[i]n 2018, the wealth of the world's billionaires increased by $2.5 billion a day, while the poorest half of the world (3.8 billion people) saw a decline in 11% in wealth'.[168] Notably, these statistics concern *global* inequality, which, as earlier mentioned, is not specifically addressed by any of the SDG 10 targets.

The fact that the national income share of the wealthiest 1 per cent has been rising (quite sharply in some places) implies that growth is becoming less inclusive in certain areas over the years. According to the World Bank:

Growth has been inclusive for the period circa 2012–2017: out of a total of 91 economies with available data, 74 economies had positive shared prosperity, and 53 had positive shared prosperity premiums. *But the gains are uneven*: shared prosperity and shared prosperity premiums are lower, on average, in conflict-afflicted and fragile and low-income economies than in middle- and high-income economies. These measures for 68 economies can be compared with an estimate of shared prosperity in an earlier period (circa 2010–15), revealing a *downward trend in shared prosperity in half the economies with available data*.[169]

The same World Bank report nonetheless insisted that 'economic growth has benefited those at the bottom of the distribution more than proportionately' since the income of

---

[165] UN, 'Sustainable Development Goals Report 2018', 9 (SDG Report 2018): 'Between 2010 and 2016, in 60 out of 94 [~64 per cent] countries with data, the incomes of the poorest 40 per cent of the population grew faster than those of the entire population.'
[166] UN, 'Sustainable Development Goals Report 2019', 42 (SDG Report 2019) (emphasis added).
[167] Expert Group (n 46) 20.
[168] ibid 8 (citation omitted).
[169] World Bank, *Poverty and Shared Prosperity 2020: Reversals of Fortune* (2020) 81 (emphasis added).

750   SDG 10

the bottom 40 per cent is growing faster than the average population in fifty-three of ninety-one economies.[170]

Different economic theories and growth models (with their respective assumptions and philosophies) offer various recommendations about the measures necessary to achieve target 10.1. This chapter is not the place to evaluate these theories and models. Suffice to say that, among the most prominent tools that countries widely employ to alter income distribution and reduce inequalities are (i) taxation; (ii) social protection programmes, including human capital investment; and (iii) labour market policies. As will be seen below, many of these measures could contribute to multiple targets. The United Kingdom, for instance, reports actions to increase the National Living Wage and to provide disabled people with Access to Work as part of its achievements under target 10.1.[171] One World Bank report provided the example of North Macedonia whose efforts to expand job opportunities—public employment, infrastructure investments, active labour market policies, establishment of special economic zones—benefited the bottom forty per cent.[172] Likewise, the Philippines' bottom forty per cent benefited from the transition of agricultural workers to 'better-paying services sectors jobs' and the higher social spending for the expanded conditional cash transfer programme ('Pantawid Pamilyang Pilipino Program').[173] Indonesia has a similar Family of Hope Program, and its ongoing social protection system reform includes developing an integrated data collection system that would extend the data further than the bottom 40 per cent.[174]

c) Critique

International human rights law does not impose a clear and express obligation for states to increase the income or wealth of certain groups and/or to equalize income across their populations. Rather, what existing legal provisions do require—in recognition of the reality that material assets are needed to access certain goods and services—is for states to take steps or special measures to progressively achieve the full realization of economic, social, and cultural rights,[175] as well as to guarantee that such rights can be exercised without discrimination of any kind.[176] In the case of particular collectivities—children,[177] women,[178] PWDs[179]—states are mandated to expend resources (either their own or obtained through international cooperation) 'to ensure the adequate development and protection of [such] groups or individuals belonging to them, for the purpose of guaranteeing them the full and equal enjoyment of human rights and fundamental freedoms'.[180] Various UN treaty bodies, particularly those created through

---

[170] ibid 85–86.
[171] United Kingdom, VNR 2019.
[172] World Bank (n 169) 87.
[173] ibid. See also Philippines, VNR 2019.
[174] Indonesia, VNR 2021.
[175] ICESCR, art 2(1).
[176] ICESCR, art 2(2).
[177] CRC, art 4.
[178] CEDAW art 3.
[179] CRPD art 28(2).
[180] ICERD art 2(2).

the ICERD and the CEDAW, have elaborated that States Parties' obligations with regard to eliminating discrimination involve both negative and positive duties, with the latter also potentially involving non-identical or special treatment for some groups who have been historically marginalized and/or disadvantaged. As the Human Rights Committee elaborated in the context of the International Covenant on Civil and Political Rights, the principle of equality, which complements non-discrimination, 'sometimes requires States parties to take affirmative action in order to diminish or eliminate conditions which cause or help to perpetuate discrimination prohibited by the Covenant'.[181]

The phrase 'progressively realize' has been at the centre of many discussions among academics and practitioners alike in relation to ICESCR article 2(1). Early on, the CESCR elaborated on the nature of States Parties' obligations under this provision and clarified that, although the Covenant generally acknowledges the reality of resource constraints faced by some states, through the concept of 'progressive realization', a number of obligations imposed by this treaty 'are of immediate effect'—an example of which is the 'undertak[ing] to guarantee the rights' involved 'without discrimination of any kind' that appears in the immediately succeeding paragraph.[182] Therefore, despite the flexibilities permitted by the concept, there remains an obligation 'to move as expeditiously and effectively as possible towards [the] goal', which obligation implies that 'deliberately retrogressive measures' are discouraged and 'would require the most careful consideration and would need to be fully justified ... in the context of the full use of the maximum available resources'.[183]

For target 10.1, it bears stressing that the verb qualified by the term 'progressively', is 'achieve', which is synonymous to 'realize' and refers to a result. Following the CESCR's interpretation,[184] this target should be read as requiring states to take 'deliberate, concrete and targeted steps' towards sustaining the income growth of the bottom 40 per cent 'within a reasonably short time' after the adoption of the 2030 Agenda. This interpretative exercise, however, cannot remedy the inadequacy of the target in addressing other economic inequalities, such as intergenerational wealth gaps, which international human rights law does not specifically address either.

It is not easy at first glance to glean that target 10.1 pertains to income inequality, but as one author explained, this target 'is essentially a matter of accounting' such that it can be rephrased in this way: 'By 2030, progressively achieve and sustain a reduction in income inequality, as measured by the share of the bottom 40 percent of the population in national income, alongside economic growth.'[185] This wording would have indeed been clearer, but it remains insufficient to tackle the concerns that it is not only income inequality that matters but also inequality in wealth, especially as disparities in the latter significantly contribute to the former and are in fact graver. The UNDESA itself pointed

---

[181] CCPR GC18, para 10.
[182] CESCR, 'General Comment No 3: The Nature of States Parties' Obligations' (art 2, para 1 of the Covenant) (14 December 1990) E/1991/23, para 1.
[183] ibid para 9.
[184] ibid para 2.
[185] Anderson (n 151) 193.

out the omission from this target of 'the potential for redistributive policies to ameliorate inequality, particularly related to wealth'.[186]

Crucially, meeting target 10.1 might not actually result to reducing intra-country inequalities, as demonstrated by the experiences of some developed countries, wherein '[e]ven if the bottom 40 per cent were to see their incomes grow at faster than average, income inequality could still be rising if the share of the income at the top is rising faster and the share of the quintiles in the middle is declining'.[187] The case of Nigeria is also revealing, in that its steady and relatively high growth did not reduce inequality, especially as 'the richest 10% earn more than twice as much as the poorest 40%'.[188]

These situations, in both the Global North and the Global South, illustrate that the goals of poverty reduction and of inequality reduction are not always and necessarily aligned.[189] It also bolsters the case for fine-tuning target 10.1 and its associated indicator so that they more directly address the gaps between certain groups in society rather than simply increasing the income of those at the bottom without regard to the income of the top earners. Indeed, the CEB itself recognized that indicator 10.1.1 needs to be supplemented by other measures of income and wealth inequalities, because it 'may not adequately identify the point at which inequalities reach high levels'.[190] Likewise, the Expert Group recommended using both the Palma ratio and the Gini coefficient to build a comprehensive monitoring framework for SDG 10.[191] Here it is important to learn from history: 'Rising top income shares [across different countries] drove inequality dynamics in the past decades'.[192] This concern was likewise reaffirmed four years after the adoption of the 2030 Agenda, as the UN Secretary-General highlighted the worrisome fact that '[i]ncome inequality continues to rise in many parts of the world, even as the bottom 40 per cent of the population in many countries has experienced positive growth rates'.[193]

Remarkably, one scholar posited that because target 10.1 is concerned about poverty, instead of vertical inequality, its achievement 'would be completely consistent with growing income inequality'.[194] Margot Salomon's emphatic explanation of why target 10.1 is deficient deserves a fuller citation:

> One reason why reducing economic inequality matters, and not just reducing poverty, is because poverty is not only unfair, it is needlessly unfair ... World Bank figures indicate that high-income countries that already receive 81 per cent of the global product could

---

[186] UNDESA, *Inequality and 2030* (n 4) 4.

[187] ibid.

[188] ActionAid, 'Not Ready, Still Waiting: Governments Have a Long Way to Go in Preparing to Address Gender Inequality and the SDGs' (2016) 23 <https://actionaid.org/sites/default/files/not_ready_still_waiting.pdf> accessed 20 August 2021.

[189] This proposition is not to discount the genuine need to reduce poverty and increase resources available to the poorest of the poor. In fact, many emerging and developing economies risk are facing formidable development challenges, risking a 'middle-income trap', due to the high and pervasive poverty and inequality levels in their societies. See Secretary-General, 'Special Edition' (n 5) para 47.

[190] UN Shared Framework, 22.

[191] Expert Group (n 46) 20.

[192] Chancel and others (n 82) 10.

[193] Secretary-General, 'Special Edition' (n 7) para 31.

[194] MacNaughton (n 36) 1058.

give up a modest degree of their wealth—0.7 per cent gross national income, which is enough to eradicate poverty—without sacrificing anything of comparable value. In fact one could assume that they would be going some way to fulfilling their treaty obligations by undertaking measures within the 'framework of international cooperation' to the 'maximum extent of their available resources' towards the realisation of these rights.[195]

I will elaborate the very important point regarding international cooperation and assistance, particularly as a matter of international human rights obligation, when I discuss the MOI targets, especially 10.a and 10.b.

Lastly, one way to make target 10.1 an inequality-reducing rather than a poverty-reducing target is to adopt the Palma ratio and reframe it in this wise: 'progressively reduce the ratio of the income share received by the top 10% to the income share of the bottom 40% ... in all countries to less than 1 by 2030'.[196] This suggestion, however, would still not be enough to address the increasing income inequalities among states, exacerbating as well the power disparities between states in the Global North and the Global South. In this regard, one NGO reported two interrelated phenomena: (i) in the period 1998–2008, the bottom 5 per cent of the global income distribution did not make any advancements; (ii) in the same period, 'the top 5% (and indeed the top 1%) ... have done particularly well'—signifying that the gap between the wealthiest and the poorest states is on the rise.[197] Significantly, it bears reiterating that these phenomena would also pose challenges for developing countries to even meet target 10.1. It would therefore be advisable to revisit the possibility of including a separate target under Goal 10 specifically addressing inter-country income inequalities.

2. Target 10.2 By 2030, empower and promote the social, economic and political inclusion of all, irrespective of age, sex, disability, race, ethnicity, origin, religion or economic or other status

a) Source of target

The current wording is a leaner, more streamlined version of various earlier proposals. Two aspects of this target were subjected to exchanges and revisions: (i) types of inclusion and (ii) excluded groups. The time frame 'by 2030' had been inserted as early as OWG-12, upon the MGoS' suggestion. They also proposed adding 'political' to 'social and economic inclusion'. As to the (non-) bases for excluding persons or groups, the MGoS preferred a more detailed and expansive language:

> by 2030 take actions to ensure, empower and promote the social, economic and political inclusion of all irrespective of race, ethnicity, gender, age, sex, disability, *sexual orientation and gender identity, social, legal or economic status, or any other social attribute* that may be a basis for discrimination, marginalization and inequalities.[198]

---

[195] Salomon (n 126) 2144 (citations omitted).
[196] MacNaughton (n 36) 1058 (citations omitted).
[197] Arauco and others (n 32) 5–6.
[198] OWG-13, MGoS Compilation.

754 SDG 10

In other versions of MGoS' proposal, the inclusion is directed at 'the poor, the marginalized and people in vulnerable situations', which phrase is then followed by a list of traditionally/historically excluded groups, such as Indigenous peoples, women, migrants, 'and all other human populations, subgroups, and minorities'.[199]

b) Empirical analysis: domestic and international efforts

The indicator for target 10.2—'Proportion of people living below 50 per cent of median income, by sex, age and persons with disabilities'—looks at relative poverty and inequality. A study of 110 high- and low-income countries showed that '[i]ncome inequality is not strongly correlated with either poverty or affluence', meaning, 'both rich and poor countries have high and low levels of inequality'.[200] The same analysis revealed that in the most unequal country 26 per cent of its population live below 50 per cent of the median income level, while 'the most equal country had 3 per cent'. In this respect, the interrelationship among poverty, vulnerability, and inequality, as well as their multidimensionality, is the premise of Ghana's Livelihood Empowerment Against Poverty (LEAP) interventions, whose aims include increased school enrolments and poor households' improved access to healthcare, insurance, and skills-building.[201] Likewise, South Africa's Broad-Based Black Economic Empowerment (BBBEE), together with its land reform and rural transformation initiatives, takes this approach.[202]

The UN Secretary-General lauded Latin America and the Caribbean for making significant progress regarding social indicators like poverty and inequality reduction but lamented that the commitment to leave no-one behind has been made more particularly challenging by '[g]lobalization in trade and finance, technological change, the restricted role of trade unions and the limited redistributive power of taxes and social policies'.[203] Similarly, Europe's achievement of the target to reduce extreme poverty to 3 per cent is diluted by pressing challenges, including inequality.[204] Based on a 2019 OECD report, the Member States[205] are, on average, 'furthest from their targets on Gender Equality (5) ... and Reducing Inequality (10)'.[206] Indicators for relative income poverty rate (1.2.1 and 10.2.1) are listed as among those where the group is lagging. There are, however, significant variations in the distances from targets across the countries, especially in relation to these two Goals.

Notably, some states (eg the United Kingdom) report under Target 10.2 their inclusion and diversity policies and laws relating to the lesbian, gay, bisexual, and transexual (LGBT) community. Others, including Denmark,[207] Germany,[208] New Zealand,[209] the

---

[199] OWG-12, MGoS Compilation.
[200] SDG Report 2019, 42.
[201] Ghana, VNR 2019.
[202] South Africa, VNR 2019.
[203] Secretary-General, 'Special Edition' (n 7) para 43.
[204] ibid para 44.
[205] Not all OECD member countries are DAC members.
[206] OECD, *Measuring Distance to the SDG Targets 2019: An Assessment of Where OECD Countries Stand* (2019) <https://doi.org/10.1787/a8caf3fa-en> accessed 16 October 2021.
[207] VNR 2021.
[208] ibid.
[209] VNR 2019.

Philippines,[210] and Serbia,[211] also mention in this respect their initiatives to enhance the living conditions of PWDs and vulnerable groups like the aged/senior citizens. In other countries, these actions, particularly legislative efforts, are part of achieving target 10.3.

c) Critique

Target 10.2 broadly captures the 2030 Agenda's 'Leave No One Behind' mantra by focusing on inclusion, a notion that, at least analytically, is intricately related but not entirely similar to non-discrimination. Under international human rights law, discrimination is legally defined to cover exclusion[212] based on certain attributes or characteristics of persons or groups of individuals. The prohibited grounds for discrimination enumerated in target 10.2 parallel those listed under human rights treaties, but indicator 10.2.1 strikingly limits the disaggregation of data to only three of the enumerated grounds: sex, age, and disability. Not only does this omission render uncertain the implementation and monitoring of the target, but it also opens up the possibility for states to act inconsistently with their existing international human rights obligations. While the SDGs were clearly not intended to modify the law or create new international legal obligations, the signatory states to UNGA Resolution have committed to be 'guided by the purposes and principles of the Charter of the United Nations, including full respect for international law'.[213] This statement can be construed to mean that the 2030 Agenda should complement, perhaps even enhance, states' compliance with undertakings they have legally committed to. Accordingly, the goals and their associated targets serve to clarify or elaborate rather than confuse and delimit existing international legal obligations.

Being one of only three SDG 10 time-bound targets, target 10.2 appears at first glance to be concrete enough. It fails, however, to satisfy the criterion that a target should be an outcome variable, since the verb 'promote' more aptly pertains to a process that cannot easily be quantified. This difficulty is further reflected in the chosen indicator. Viewed against the target's evolution and the issues that the drafters and stakeholders deemed important—for example political and not only economic and social inclusion—the chosen indicator is inadequate, if not inaccurate. Apart from simply focusing on the percentage of the population living below 50 per cent of the median income, the disaggregation it requires is only for sex, age, and disabilities, thereby omitting the other statuses—that is, race, ethnicity, origin, religion—that are specifically mentioned in the Goal itself.

Nevertheless, target 10.2's recognition of various forms of inclusion—social, economic, political—crucially draws attention to issues of opportunity and access to services that are important for human capital accumulation, human development, and states' compliance with human rights obligations. For instance, a person's arbitrary

---

[210] ibid.
[211] ibid.
[212] Other discriminatory actions are: distinction, restriction, preference. See ICERD, art 1(1); CEDAW, art 1.
[213] 2030 Agenda, para 10.

exclusion from the exercise of political rights,[214] such as voting, holding public office, or participating in non-governmental organizations,[215] would not only constitute a violation of an international legal obligation on the part of the state but can also harm the excluded person's economic and social prospects. Significantly, such impairment of economic prospects can likewise constitute a human rights violation, since the ICESCR upholds the 'right of everyone to an adequate standard of living ... including adequate food, clothing and housing, and to the continuous improvement of living conditions'.[216] It is also worth noting that ICERD specifically applies the non-discrimination principle to rights enshrined in ILO Conventions,[217] namely, the 'rights to work, to free choice of employment, to just and favourable conditions of work, to protection against unemployment, to equal pay for equal work, to just and favourable enumeration'.[218] Similarly, ICESCR provides for labour-related rights. Among the States Parties' obligations relative to the right of everyone to the enjoyment of just and favourable conditions of work is to ensure '[f]air wages and equal remuneration for work of equal value without distinction of any kind, in particular women being guaranteed conditions of work not inferior to those enjoyed by men, with equal pay for equal work'.[219] To some extent, CEDAW has begun to take a comprehensive view of discrimination and draw the lines connecting different kinds of exclusion by expressly recognizing the value of participation in 'the elaboration and implementation of development planning at all levels',[220] and more expansively, the formulation of government policy, which can cover practically all aspects of life.

Recognizing the interrelationship among social, economic, and political inclusion bridges target 10.2 to target 10.3. In realizing these targets, states are advised to go beyond income redistribution and instead pursue policies that are truly progressive, meaning, 'doing disproportionately more for those groups who are furthest behind' by complementing universal coverage of health and education services with 'targeted programs to overcome the structural and economic barriers faced by disadvantaged groups that prevent them from accessing the full benefits of even universally available services'.[221] To recall, although upholding the principle of non-discrimination, international human rights law allows for disparate or differential treatment of individuals or groups that are not similarly situated to begin with. Another international human rights legal principle enshrined in the ICESCR and particularly salient to the target's timeline, is *non-retrogression*, which requires states to justify any retrogressive step 'by reference to the totality of [ICESCR] rights' and after 'the most careful consideration of all alternatives',[222] to attain continuous progress in living standards, and to ring-fence

---

[214] ICCPR, art 25; ICERD, art 5(c).

[215] CEDAW, art 7(c).

[216] ICESCR, art 11(1).

[217] Protection of Wages Convention (ILO 95); Equal Remuneration Convention (ILO 100); Discrimination (Employment and Occupation) Convention (ILO 111); Minimum Wage Fixing Convention (ILO 131).

[218] ICERD, art 5(e)(i).

[219] ICESCR, art 7(a)(i).

[220] CEDAW, art 14(2)(a).

[221] Expert Group (n 46) 2. See also Secretary-General, 'Empowering People' (n 7) para 37.

[222] CESCR, 'General Comment No 19: The Right to Social Security' (art 9) (4 February 2008) E/C.12/GC19 (GC19), para 42.

resources 'during crises and in periods of economic austerity to protect the existing levels of rights realization, or at the very least ensure that the impacts of policy changes do not disproportionately fall on the poorest and most marginalized'.[223]

3. Target 10.3 Ensure equal opportunity and reduce inequalities of outcome, including by eliminating discriminatory laws, policies and practices and promoting appropriate legislation, policies and actions in this regard

a) Source of target

During OWG-12, target 10.3 consisted of two targets:

10.1 by 2030 eliminate discriminatory laws, policies and practices *and recognize and fulfill the cultural, social, economic, civil, political, and environmental rights for all human populations, subgroups, and minorities*[224]

10.3 by 2030 *eliminate*[225] inequalities of opportunity and *minimize inequalities of outcome among all* social groups, including economic (*income, assets, and access to resources*), social, and environmental inequalities

During OWG-11, Pakistan ('By 2025, affirmative actions in law and policies to reduce ethnic, religious, gender and disability based discrimination') and the Children & Youth NGOs ('Expand adoption of comprehensive legal and educational systems to fight discrimination and stigmatization of the marginalized') proposed related targets.

By OWG-13, these two targets have been combined, such that the main target— reduction of inequalities of opportunity and outcome—subsumed the aims of eliminating discriminatory legislation and policies and of promoting appropriate legislation, policies, and actions. Hence, the repeal and/or amendment of discriminatory laws and the enactment of appropriate legislative or other measures to eliminate discrimination are only some of the ways that inequalities of opportunity and outcome can be reduced. While the MGoS seemed to agree with such merger, they insisted (unsuccessfully) on distinguishing between inequality of opportunity and inequality of outcome—with the former requiring elimination and the latter minimization by 2030.

b) Empirical analysis: domestic and international efforts

Among the SDG 10 targets, target 10.3 is of special interest for legal professionals. Being one of the most explicitly law-oriented, it recognizes the importance of the domestic legal system in addressing inequalities. Target 10.3 prescribes, among others, legislation and law reform to achieve equality. Based on available empirical research, the application of this prescription has largely been limited towards the improvement of gender equality, although some also examine intersecting inequalities.[226]

---

[223] UN Shared Framework, 23.
[224] Zero draft, as revised by MGoS' proposals (in italics).
[225] 'reduce' in the zero draft.
[226] See Secretary-General, 'Special Edition' (n 7) para 26; Expert Group (n 46) 18.

758   SDG 10

Several countries have adopted positive action interventions, with some like India even providing constitutional basis therefor,[227] to reduce inter-group inequalities. Norway reported that the 2014 amendment to its Constitution added a human rights chapter, which established the right to equality under the law and the prohibition of discrimination as constitutional principles.[228] These measures are generally found to be effective in addressing discrimination and backwardness experienced by certain groups, although 'large disparities ... often remain over long periods'.[229] The experiences of countries, such as Bolivia, Brazil, and Ecuador, also show that affirmative action interventions need to be complemented by more universal and inclusive policies.[230] Addressing intersecting inequalities and reaching an 'inclusive political settlement', that is 'one in which social justice is an explicit concern of both politics and policy-making', according to the Overseas Development Institute (ODI), require the following: 'social mobilisation, political change, constitutional reforms, increased political participation in pluri-national states, a combination of universal and targeted or affirmative action especially in the policy field, and further mobilisation around the implementation of rights and guarantees'.[231] Similarly, Saiz and Donald explained that a human rights-based approach to implementing target 10.3 'would include special measures and affirmative action to reach particular groups and would seek to avoid and tackle indirect discrimination, including through carefully disaggregated analysis of outcomes'.[232] The reason for paying attention to vulnerable and disadvantaged groups, as one NGO emphasized, is that ignoring them would 'further marginaliz[e] them from public intervention, and further skew ... the true extent of inequality'.[233]

In the two most recent VNRs (2019, 2021) where SDG 10 was given particular focus, some countries (eg Denmark,[234] Germany,[235] New Zealand,[236] the Philippines,[237] the United Kingdom[238]) highlighted legislative enactments to increase employment opportunities for PWDs and improve their overall living standards. Recent Danish legislation requires municipalities 'to initiate preparations for the transition to adult life when young people with a disability turn 16 years old'.[239] The United Kingdom also mentioned as part of its international efforts concerning target 10.3, the Department for International Development's (DfID) Disability Inclusion Strategy (2018–2023) and the Foreign, Commonwealth & Development Office's (FCDO) UK Aid Connect, which supports tolerance and freedom of religion or belief and promotes LGBT inclusion.

[227] Arauco and others (n 32) 56.
[228] VNR 2021.
[229] Arauco and others (n 32) 59.
[230] ibid 60.
[231] ibid 61.
[232] Saiz and Donald (n 26) 1035.
[233] CESR (n 38) 33.
[234] VNR 2021.
[235] Bundesteilhabegesetz (Federal Participation Act), passed in December 2016.
[236] Disability Action Plan 2019–2023.
[237] Republic Act No 10524, 'An Act Expanding the Positions Reserved for Persons With Disability, Amending for the purpose Republic Act No 7277, as Amended, Otherwise Known as The Magna Carta for Persons With Disability' (2013).
[238] Access to Work programme.
[239] VNR 2021, 141.

c) Critique

Whereas target 10.2 hints at the need to address issues of access and opportunity, target 10.3 more directly tackles structural concerns and even prescribes a specific means to do so, 'by eliminating discriminatory laws, policies and practices'. To recall, states' treaty obligations vis-à-vis the principles of non-discrimination and equality consist of both prohibition and elimination. In addition to prohibiting states from adopting discriminatory laws, international human rights law also obliges them to adopt legislation (and other regulatory or administrative measures) that prevents non-state actors from discriminating against individuals and/or groups of individuals. Under CEDAW article 2, States Parties undertake to, among others, 'adopt appropriate legislative and other measures, including sanctions where appropriate, prohibiting all discrimination against women'. Additionally, ICERD States Parties 'shall take effective measures to review governmental, national and local policies, and to amend, rescind or nullify all laws and regulations which have the effect of creating or perpetuating racial discrimination'.[240] Likewise, ICCPR article 26 mandates equal protection of the law and States Parties' obligation to enact laws that 'shall prohibit any discrimination and guarantee to all persons equal and effective protection against discrimination on any [of the enumerated] ground'. The Human Rights Committee, which monitors ICCPR implementation, interpreted this provision as constituting a right distinct and autonomous from article 2 and as thereby imposing on states the obligation to ensure that the content and application of their legislation are not discriminatory. It highlighted that certain instances of *de facto* discrimination necessitate States Parties' 'affirmative action in order to diminish or eliminate conditions which cause or help to perpetuate discrimination prohibited by the Covenant', such that preferential treatment might be extended to a certain segment of the population whose enjoyment of human rights is being prevented or impaired.[241]

The CESCR similarly construed ICESCR article 2(2) as a guarantee against both formal and substantive discrimination, implying that '[e]liminating discrimination in practice requires paying sufficient attention to groups or individuals which suffer historical or persistent prejudice instead of merely comparing the formal treatment of individuals in similar situations'.[242] This legal guarantee thus runs parallel to target 10.3's concern about equality of both opportunities and outcomes. To attain both, the target seems to heed the CESCR's recommendations, namely, 'States parties must therefore immediately adopt the necessary measures to prevent, diminish and eliminate the conditions and attitudes which cause or perpetuate substantive or de facto discrimination'.[243] Significantly, the CESCR identified standards for the legitimacy of measures undertaken for this purpose. The measures must 'represent *reasonable, objective and proportional* means to redress de facto discrimination and are discontinued when substantive equality has been sustainably achieved'.[244] Applying these standards should

---

[240] ICERD, art 2, para 1 (c).
[241] CCPR, GC18, para 10.
[242] CESCR, GC20, para 8.
[243] ibid.
[244] ibid para 9 (emphasis added).

include an evaluation of the measures' compatibility with the nature of ESC rights; whether they are 'solely for the purpose of promoting the general welfare in a democratic society',[245] and the existence of 'a clear and reasonable relationship of proportionality between the aim sought to be realized and the measures or omissions and their effects'.[246]

The CESCR likewise pays particular attention to the notion of *systemic discrimination*, which refers to 'legal rules, policies, practices or predominant cultural attitudes in either the public or private sector which create relative disadvantages for some groups, and privileges for other groups'.[247] Recognizing that the elimination of systemic discrimination often requires 'devoting greater resources to traditionally neglected groups' and pursuing 'a range of laws, policies and programmes', the CESCR recommended other actions for States Parties to undertake, including 'using incentives to encourage public and private actors to change their attitudes and behaviour in relation to individuals and groups of individuals facing systemic discrimination, or penalize them in case of non-compliance'.[248]

CEDAW provides a longer and more detailed list of states' undertakings to pursue a policy of eliminating discrimination against women. Apart from adopting appropriate legislative and other means to prohibit all discrimination, the enumeration also includes embodying the principle of equality of men and women in national constitutions; ensuring the existence of competent national tribunals and other public institutions to effectively protect women against any act of discrimination; and repealing all national penal provisions that constitute discrimination against women.[249] CRPD similarly obliges States Parties to 'take all appropriate measures, including legislation, to modify or abolish existing laws, regulations, customs and practices that constitute discrimination'.[250] Placed within the 'Respect, Protect, Fulfill' framework, this aspect requires states to protect people, especially certain vulnerable or marginalized persons, against discrimination perpetrated by private entities, such as employers, educational institutions, or even family members. Consistent with this duty to protect is target 10.3's explicit reference to discriminatory 'practices', which together with laws and policies should be eliminated to ensure equal opportunities and reduce inequality of outcomes. It recognizes the reality that discrimination and inclusion result not only from official, public, and formal acts but from private and informal practices as well. Indeed, societal attitudes (eg racism, xenophobia, homophobia) are appropriate objects of legislation under certain circumstances, since particularly vulnerable and marginalized groups 'such as lesbian, gay, bisexual, transsexual and intersex (LGBTI) persons, men who have sex with men, sex workers, people living with HIV/AIDS, people who

---

[245] ICESCR, art 4.
[246] CESCR, 'General Comment No 10: The Role of National Human Rights Institutions in Protection of Economic, Social and Cultural Rights' (14 December 1998) E/C.12/1998/25, para 13.
[247] CESCR, GC20, para 12.
[248] ibid para 39.
[249] CEDAW, art 2.
[250] CRPD, art 4(1)(b).

inject drugs, prisoners or people in detention' are excluded and discriminated against 'because Governments refuse to protect them'.[251]

Indicator 10.3.1 ('Percentage of population reporting having personally felt discriminated against or harassed within the last 12 months on the basis of a ground of discrimination prohibited under international human rights law') is repeated as indicator 16.b.1, since target 16.b pertains to the promotion and enforcement of non-discriminatory laws and policies. Apart from the subjective element of this indicator (personal feelings and opinions), the difficulty in gathering such data casts doubt about its ability to measure progress in achieving target 10.3, which as explained above, entails complex systemic actions. One viable and reasonable way to augment this deficiency is through a separate indicator that monitors and 'explicitly requires an increase in national compliance with international human rights laws as measured by the international human rights treaty bodies'.[252]

4. Target 10.4 Adopt policies, especially fiscal, wage and social protection policies, and progressively achieve greater equality

a) Source of target

The current indicators for target 10.4, especially indicator 10.4.1, make more sense when read in the context of the target's history. In the OWG-12 zero draft, target 10.4 read: 'work towards revising the decline of the share of labour income in GDP where relevant'. The Workers and Trade Unions Major Group proposed this amendment: 'Promote appropriately designed wage policies, including minimum living wages, to address the decline of the share of labour income in GDP where relevant.' More generally, during the same session, the MGoS suggested adding a target stating, 'transition to economic systems, structural approaches, and macroeconomic (fiscal and monetary) policies that generate increasing inequality rather than inequalities'. During OWG-13, the MGoS' proposals were as follows:

> 10.4 progressively adopt policies especially fiscal policies to promote greater equality *of wealth including progressive taxation systems, redistributive economic and social policies, wage and social protection and the adoption of country-by-country reporting standards for all transnational corporations*
>
> 10.4 *bis by 2030 through the promotion of appropriately designed wage policies, including minimum living wages, increase* work towards reversing the decline of the share of labour income in GDP *by x%* where relevant *in line with productivity increases*

These proposals were, however, collapsed or reduced to the present wording of target 10.4, wherein wage and social protection have been added as among the policies—together with fiscal—to be adopted. Target 10.4 uses a conjunction 'and' that, if read

---

[251] UN Shared Framework, 12–13.
[252] MacNaughton (n 36) 1059–60.

762   SDG 10

literally, seemingly signifies that it has two distinct components: (i) the adoption of fiscal, wage, and social protection policies; and (ii) the progressive achievement of greater equality. In its prior iterations, however, the adoption of these policies was seen as serving the purpose of promoting greater equality. The latter interpretation is more coherent and reasonable.

Targets 1.3 and 10.4 can be read in conjunction, since the former refers to implementation of 'nationally appropriate social protection systems and measures for all, including floors, and by 2030 achieve substantial coverage of the poor and the vulnerable', while the latter alludes to the adoption of social protection policies to 'progressively achieve greater equality'. Significantly, the origin of target 1.3 can be traced to one item under Focus Area 1 ('Poverty eradication, building shared prosperity and promoting equality')[253] that provided: 'by 2030 implement nationally appropriate social protection measures including floors, with focus on coverage of the most marginalized'. Remarkably, a footnote to this item stated the need for disaggregated data to track progress, particularly on the focus group, that is most marginalized. In the earlier iteration of this target in the OWG-9 Focus Area Document, social protection is deemed to reduce the vulnerabilities of particular groups, which were more specifically identified as the following: 'the poor, including children, youth, unemployed, persons with disabilities, indigenous peoples and local communities and older persons'. Focus Area 12 on promoting equality also included 'strengthening social protection systems' as one of its action items.

b) Empirical analysis: domestic and international efforts
Target 10.4 and its indicators are closely connected to target 10.1. While the latter focuses on the income growth rate of a particular percentile of the population, target 10.4 mentions the broad classification of policies that can redistribute income and contribute to reduction of inequalities. Significantly, indicator 10.1.1—Labour share of GDP—aligns with earlier discussions, both in the OWG and among scholars, about the remuneration received by workers (and their share of national output) being a key factor in the shape of a country's income distribution. As the Special Rapporteur on extreme poverty and human rights observed, although there is difficulty in definitively establishing the causal relationship between the protection of core labour rights (eg rights to freedom of association and collective bargaining) and the reduction of economic inequalities, 'various studies point to a relationship between the lack of protection of core labour rights and deunionization and between deunionization and growing wage inequality'.[254]

The 2019 SDG Report affirmed that the share of labour in national incomes globally has been decreasing since 2004.[255] There are slight differences between developed and developing regions: in the former, 'labour share of GDP fell almost 58 per cent in 2000

---

[253] OWG-11 Working Document.
[254] Alston, 'Extreme Inequality and Human Rights' (n 25) para 22.
[255] SDG Report 2019, 43.

to just over 55 per cent in 2015', whereas in the latter, workers experienced a negligible improvement—from 54 to 55 per cent—in their share of national output.[256] It is thus crucial for states—as some like Cyprus, Denmark, Germany, and New Zealand are already doing (based on their VNRs)—to implement minimum wage legislation and labour market programmes/policies that specifically target marginalized groups.

Although target 10.4 mentions the adoption of social protection policies as among the means to progressively achieve greater equality, there is currently no corresponding indicator to measure and monitor such action. Yet, many states—Czech Republic, Ghana, Indonesia, Norway, South Africa, and Sweden—report in their VNRs the contribution of such policies (eg social safety nets, unemployment and disability benefits, education subsidies) to their effective efforts to achieve this target.

Studies show positive results from developing countries' investment in social protection programs since the 1990s: for instance in South Africa, 'social protection measures (including the old age pensions, child support grant and disability grant) reduced the Gini coefficient from 0.63 to 0.60 in 2000, with the impact increasing over time', while Brazil's and Argentina's social security and universal health coverage programmes have been lauded for 'contribut[ing] to significant declines in inequality'.[257] Still, the UN and the development community have consistently lamented that more than half (55 per cent), or as many as 4 billion people, of the world's population is not covered by '[s]ocial protection systems [that] help prevent and reduce poverty and provide a safety net for the vulnerable'.[258]

Largely ignored in current state efforts regarding target 10.4 is the redistributive role of taxation, particularly taxes on wealth, property, and inheritance. Yet, there is empirical evidence suggesting that reducing inequalities requires progressive taxation measures, which make the 'well-off contribute a larger proportion of their income than those with fewer resources'.[259] Another study attributed the difference in US and European income-inequality levels to their tax systems' progressivity and to 'educational and wage-setting policies more favorable to low- and middle-income groups'.[260] Notably, even policies that were not originally intended to redistribute income (and/or wealth) can have distributional impacts, as in the case of fiscal and/or monetary policies, such as quantitative easing and austerity, which were found to have deepened inequality in the United States after the 2007/2008 global economic crisis.[261] Hence, the Expert Group could have been more critical of its findings that the tax systems in many countries are becoming more regressive and that '[t]axation of wealth and assets are systematically under-utilized in high, middle- and low-income countries alike'.[262]

---

[256] SDG Report 2016, 31.
[257] Secretary-General, 'Special Edition' (n 7) para 21.
[258] ibid 22 (citations omitted).
[259] CESR (n 38) 27.
[260] Expert Group (n 46) 20 (citations omitted).
[261] See UN Shared Framework, 10–11: 'In the United States, the top one per cent now holds one third of United States total wealth, while low and middle-class households are increasingly indebted.'
[262] Expert Group (n 46) 27.

Significantly, one of the most successful welfare states, Sweden, considers active redistribution through taxes and transfers to be important in strengthening economically disadvantaged households.[263] South Africa[264] and Malaysia[265] also cite progressive taxation as one of their inequality-reducing tools. Moreover, a combination of the abovementioned measures has been shown to be effective in achieving equality. In the Republic of Korea, for example, efforts to reduce inequality include 'increase[d] social spending (including a universal child support grant), increase[d] taxation on the largest corporations and the highest earners, and [drastic increase of] the minimum wage'.[266]

As a final point, it bears stressing that although taxation policy has traditionally been considered a sovereign prerogative and part of a state's exclusive domain, the present interconnectedness of economies, the ease of capital mobility, and the existence of multi- or transnational corporations, make it imperative for states, as human rights duty-bearers, to cooperate with one another and 'creat[e] a fairer international tax system that can help to improve economic inequality within and between countries'.[267] The recent G7 pledge to collectively enact a global minimum corporate tax (of at least 15 per cent)[268] could be a step towards this direction.

c) Critique

Comments and observations above regarding the phrase 'progressively achieve' under target 10.1 are equally relevant to the present target, which directs the term to the aim of 'greater equality'. Despite the fact that wage and social protection policies were added to target 10.4 almost as an afterthought, the first of the two current indicators looks at how such policies impact the labour share of GDP. The rationale behind this choice presumably rests on an envisioned role of economic growth in reducing inequalities and achieving sustainable development—a relationship that operates by tracing the distribution of income across different factors of production (land, labour, capital) and ensuring that increased national income translates to higher incomes for workers and improved living standards.[269] Indeed, the labour market is seen as 'a central and organizing feature linking the economic and social spheres', thus social and labour inclusion policies 'can serve to reverse social inequalities'.[270] Parenthetically, to the extent that Goal 8 concerns decent employment, one of its targets refers to the established and

---

[263] Sweden, VNR 2021.

[264] South Africa, VNR 2021.

[265] Malaysia, VNR 2021.

[266] Expert Group (n 46) 19 (citation omitted).

[267] CESR (n 38) 27 (citation omitted).

[268] 'G7 Finance Ministers & Central Bank Governors Communiqué', London, United Kingdom, 5 June 2021, para 16 <https://assets.publishing.service.gov.uk/government/uploads/system/uploads/attachment_data/file/991 640/FMCBGs_communique_-_5_June.pdf> accessed 1 September 2021. See also 'G7 Finance Ministers Agree Historic Global Tax Agreement' (*G7 UK Presidency 2021*, 5 June 2021) <https://www.g7uk.org/g7-finance-minist ers-agree-historic-global-tax-agreement/>; D Lawder and L Thomas, 'Everything You Need to Know about the G7's Plans for a Global Minimum Tax' (*World Economic Forum*, 7 June 2021) <https://www.weforum.org/agenda/ 2021/06/g7-corperation-tax-global-minimum-wealth-profits-world-taxation/> accessed 1 September 2021.

[269] See SDG Report 2019, 43.

[270] Secretary-General, 'Empowering People' (n 5) para 17.

well-known international labour law standard of 'equal pay for work of equal value', which complements indicator 10.4.1's focus on labour's GDP share.

Regarding social protection policies, the UN's annually published SDG Reports almost consistently highlight their role not only in ending poverty but in reducing intra-State inequalities as well. This excerpt from the 2017 Report is illustrative: 'Benefits for children, mothers with newborns, persons with disabilities, older persons and those who are poor and without jobs ensure that no one is left behind.'[271] On the other hand, the 2018 SDG Report showed the dismal situation that, '[b]ased on 2016 estimates, only 45 per cent of the world's population were effectively covered by at least one social protection cash benefit, leaving 4 billion people behind.'[272]

Amidst the foregoing discussion about the role of social protection policies in 'help[ing] prevent and reduce poverty and inequality at every stage of people's lives,'[273] it bears highlighting that social security is not simply a matter of state discretion or strategy but constitutes an international legal obligation.[274] The TST correctly recognized that apart from '[s]ocial protection [being] based on widely shared principles of justice, and ... grounded in ... [several] human rights instruments, as well as the ILO Conventions and Recommendations on social security and nationally-defined social protection floors', it also 'contributes to the realization of various other human rights, including the right to an adequate standard of living, food, health and education.'[275] Indeed, ICESCR article 9 provides for the 'right of everyone to social security, including social insurance'. CRPD article 28(2) likewise recognizes the 'right of persons with disabilities to social protection and to the enjoyment of that right without discrimination', and among the appropriate measures to implement such right is ensuring 'access by persons with disabilities and their families living in situations of poverty to assistance from the State with disability-related expenses, including adequate training, counselling, financial assistance and respite care'.

It also bears emphasizing that the coverage of social protection policies is and must not arbitrarily exclude non-citizens. ICRMW article 27(1) specifically requires the state of employment to afford migrant workers, in terms of social security the same treatment granted to nationals. This provision is consistent with ILO 118 Equality of Treatment (Social Security) Convention, which requires a signatory ILO Member State to 'grant within its territory to the nationals of any other Member for which the Convention is in force equality of treatment under its legislation with its own nationals, both as regards coverage and as regards the right to benefits, in respect of every branch of social security for which it has accepted the obligations of the Convention.'[276] Significantly, several other international agreements and instruments under the ILO's auspices are relevant to SDG 10, namely, ILO 102 Social Security (Minimum Standards) Convention; ILO

---

[271] SDG Report 2017, 17.
[272] SDG Report 2018, 15.
[273] ibid.
[274] UDHR, art 22; CRC, art 26(1).
[275] TST, Social Protection (n 84) 4.
[276] ILO 118, art 3(1). See also ILO 118, art 4.

157 Maintenance of Social Security Rights Convention; ILO Rec 202 Social Protection Floors Recommendation.

The right to social security is highly relevant to Goal 10 and to the SDGs in general, given the redistributive character of social security and its 'important role in poverty reduction and alleviation, preventing social exclusion and promoting social inclusion'.[277] As the CESCR succinctly put, 'social security should be treated as a social good, and not primarily as a mere instrument of economic or financial policy'.[278] This statement, however, is not to discount the instrumental value of social security, as the Committee itself had raised concerns that denial or lack of access to social security, apart from being a violation of article 9 in and of itself, also undermines the realization of other rights under the ICESCR.[279] Indeed, in the discussion of the elements—availability, adequacy, accessibility—of the right, these inherent and instrumental values have been consistently emphasized. Interestingly, in relation to the first element, the CESCR additionally mentioned the sustainability of the social security system as it pertains to its inter-generational aspect: 'The schemes should also be sustainable, including those concerning the provision of pensions, in order *to ensure that the right can be realized for present and future generations.*'[280] Also of relevance is the prescription to focus the social security system on the most disadvantaged and marginalized groups, including through non-contributory schemes in order to ensure universal coverage.[281] In striking a balance between universal coverage and necessary disparate treatment, states can heed the CESCR's recommendation to 'give special attention to those individuals and groups who traditionally face difficulties in exercising [the] right [to social security]'.[282] Further, the following recommendation echoes the overall theme of the SDGs and Goal 10 to leave no-one behind: 'Low-cost and alternative schemes could be developed to cover immediately those without access to social security, although the aim should be to integrate them into regular social security schemes.'[283]

The second indicator for target 10.4 refers to the redistributive impact of fiscal policy, 'the difference between prefiscal and postfiscal income inequality (as measured by the Gini coefficient)'.[284] This indicator acknowledges and stresses the importance of taxes and transfers as governmental instruments to impact distribution. Importantly, from an international legal perspective, the human rights norm of non-discrimination requires progressivity of a state's tax structure, since the latter 'shapes the allocation of income and assets across the population, and thereby affects levels of inequality and human rights enjoyment'.[285] As Alston succinctly put it, 'tax policy is, in many respects,

---

[277] CESCR, GC19 para 3.

[278] ibid para 10.

[279] ibid para 8.

[280] ibid para 11 (emphasis added).

[281] ibid para 23.

[282] ibid para 31.

[283] ibid para 51.

[284] N Lustig and others, 'The Redistributive Impact of Fiscal Policy Indicator: A New Global Standard for Assessing Government Effectiveness in Tackling Inequality within the SDG Framework' (*World Bank Blogs*, 11 June 2020) <https://blogs.worldbank.org/opendata/redistributive-impact-fiscal-policy-indicator-new-global-standard-assessing-government> accessed 8 June 2021.

[285] Alston, 'Extreme Inequality and Human Rights' (n 25) para 53.

human rights policy'.[286] A UN Expert Group likewise affirmed that '[t]ax is the primary redistributive instrument governments have to reduce inequalities and realize human rights' and cautioned that 'different types of taxes have very different distributional outcomes across lines of race, class and gender'.[287]

Prior to the introduction of indicator 10.4.2 in March 2020, what is striking about target 10.4 is how there appears to be limited attention in the targets and indicators given to the role of taxation and fiscal policies in achieving Goal 10. Indeed, this point has been flagged quite early on, in relation to the concern about target 10.1 failing to reduce inequality even if the income of the bottom 40 per cent does grow faster than the national average: 'the limited discussion of taxation as a fundamental factor in correcting income inequalities means that important issues appear to have been side-stepped'.[288] One commentator criticized target 10.4 for being the 'most vague of the four targets on reducing inequalities within countries' because, instead of providing a measurable objective to achieve, it simply enumerates 'means to achieve equality', and even then 'does not set any parameters for such policies'.[289] On the other hand, the vagueness and overbreadth of target 10.4 can also be seen as its strength, since it can thus cover a wide range of economic and regulatory policies[290]—for example minimum wage laws, legislative safeguards for collective bargaining, social protection of workers—needed to equalize opportunities among different groups. However, lest they unwittingly trade off the achievement of one goal for another, states need to be circumspect in using these instruments, since 'the impact on poverty may differ from the impact on inequality', meaning, although fiscal policy 'always reduces inequality – albeit sometimes very negligibly—that is not true for poverty'.[291]

5. Target 10.5 Improve the regulation and monitoring of global financial markets and institutions and strengthen the implementation of such regulations

a) Source of target

The current language of target 10.5 is practically the same as when it was first proposed during OWG-12. This fact, however, is not indicative of outright and general agreement about the matter. Indeed, some stakeholders made a few attempts to elaborate on this target and make clearer its relevance to the Goal. For instance, during OWG-12, the MGoS proposed:

> 10.10 improve regulation *and accountability* of global financial markets and institutions and strengthen their implementation, *transitioning to structural approaches and macroeconomic (fiscal and monetary) policies that generate increasing equality rather than inequalities among nations*

---

[286] ibid para 53.
[287] Expert Group (n 46) 27.
[288] UNDESA, *Inequality and 2030* (n 4) 4.
[289] MacNaughton (n 36) 1060.
[290] Expert Group (n 46) 2.
[291] Lustig and others (n 284).

768   SDG 10

When the OWG-13 zero draft reverted to the original text, the MGoS again proposed additions:

10.5 improve *strengthen* [*sic*] regulation and monitoring of global financial markets and institutions, *ensuring governance reform in global financial* institutions, *ensuring that all countries participate equally in decision-making and in compliance with international human rights, social, and environmental highest standards,* and strengthen implementation of such regulations *which must allow countries to apply temporary capital restrictions and seek to negotiate agreements on temporary debt standstill between debtors and creditors, with due diligence measures for accountability and transparency*

Although intended to expound on the significance of the target, this proposal is overly long and convoluted. Hence, the Co-Chairs' decision to discard it seems understandable. Moreover, part of the proposal—concerning all countries' equal participation in decision-making—has been transformed into a separate target, namely, target 10.6.

In contrast to other targets, however, apart from these exchanges of proposed wordings, there do not appear to be lengthy and substantial discussions on target 10.5. There is scant explanation as to how this target is intended to achieve the goal of reducing inequalities among states. It can be gleaned from the OWG records that the purpose of effectively regulating and supervising the movement of capital, the architecture facilitating its flows, and the systemically important financial institutions participating in such markets is to 'reduc[e] international financial instability and instability of commodity prices'.[292] This target also seems to have been originally conceptualized as part of the overall MOI goal, since it addresses not only the reduction of inter-state inequalities by facilitating the flows of needed capital developing countries but also the curbing of illicit financial flows that impact on the formation of peaceful societies and institutions founded on the rule of law. As expounded below, this target's purported contribution to reducing inter-state inequalities has been weakened by the selected indicator and is not currently supported by empirical evidence.

b) Empirical analysis: domestic and international efforts
Indicator 10.5.1, The Financial Soundness Indicators (FSI), examines a country's financial system, the stability of which, according to the UN, 'is key to efficiently allocating resources, managing risks, and ensuring that macroeconomic objectives that benefit all are met'.[293] The Secretary-General added that equal access to financial services requires a robust and sound financial system, which is threatened by '[h]igh loan asset impairment, measured by the ratio of non-performing loans to total loans for deposit takers'.[294] The FSI comprises seven sub-indicators, including the non-performing loans

---

[292] OWG-10 Cluster Statements, Submission on behalf of Women, NGOs, Indigenous peoples, and other Stakeholders, 'Means of Implementation/Global partnership for sustainable development (FA 18)'.
[293] SDG Report 2019, 42.
[294] Secretary-General, 'Special Edition' (n 7) para 31.

as a percentage of total gross loans. The 2019 SDG Report showed that in half of the 138 countries studied from 2010–2017, this ratio was less than 5 per cent, but '[i]n 2017, more than one quarter of the countries showed a higher percentage of non-performing loans (10 per cent or more), and four countries showed a proportion of higher than 30 per cent'.[295]

As part of its contribution to the reform of global financial markets, Germany additionally reported its efforts to incentivize private financial actors towards greater sustainable investment. It remains to be seen, however, whether such notion of sustainable investment or finance would include the objective of reducing inequalities. Parenthetically, this initiative could also be considered under target 10.b, if it extends to foreign investors.

c) Critique

The current legal framework to regulate and monitor financial markets—broadly composed of banks, insurance companies, and capital market participants—is still heavily domestic in character, meaning, individual states' laws and regulations primarily govern the activities of these entities. At the same time, as these markets have now become globalized and intricately connected—a fact starkly highlighted by the 2008 financial and economic crisis—a clear and strong argument for cross-border coordination among different regulators and harmonization of national rules can be made. There is, however, no international law (at least in the 'hard' sense, that is treaties, custom, general principles) on financial markets regulation, although multilateral institutions like the International Monetary Fund (IMF) provide relevant policy guidance and conduct country surveillance monitoring the 'exchange rate, monetary, fiscal, … financial policies [and] macro-critical structural reforms'.[296] David Zaring described the 'post-crisis global regulatory architecture' thus:

> The interlocking parts of regulatory governance amount to a form of administration. It represents the 'agencification' of a previously informal and diverse regulatory process, replete with a degree of political oversight, a bureaucratic middle, and a bottom that has adopted many of the trappings of administrative law to get the work done.[297]

Global financial regulation thus necessarily involves both the international, at which level policy formulation occurs, and the domestic, 'where [the policy] is implemented and made into binding legal instruments'.[298] This dualist configuration can be problematic from a welfare perspective, including from a sustainable development standpoint, because despite the imperative for internationally harmonized rules and principles in order to achieve the greatest welfare gains, 'states [still] tend to deviate from this model

---

[295] SDG Report 2019, 42.
[296] International Monetary Fund, 'IMF Surveillance' (2021) <https://www.imf.org/en/About/Factsheets/IMF-Surveillance> accessed 5 November 2021.
[297] D Zaring, *The Globalized Governance of Finance* (CUP 2019) 15.
[298] ibid 124–25.

by pursuing national interests, i.e. acting in a protectionist way' due to internal political pressures.[299] Notably, political oversight of global financial markets mainly comes from the G20, which does not have a legal mandate to perform any international regulatory function—not even a distinct international legal personality as it is not an international organization—but has nonetheless emerged as a vital agenda-setter for post-crisis financial regulation. Briefly, the grouping's work consists of 'regularly consider[ing] risks to the financial system' and assessing 'whether its policy prescriptions have in fact been implemented, and, if so, whether they have a desired effect'——with a focus on global growth and the occasional 'lip service towards making that growth inclusive (in particular, including countries that are not members of the G20)'.[300]

Given that states can have different motivations and objectives to regulate financial markets, the ambiguity and overbreadth of target 10.5 riddle its implementation with difficulties and render its contribution to inequalities reduction and sustainable development uncertain. The target does not sufficiently direct states' attention and action towards a clear and common aim. This vagueness can additionally be detrimental to human rights, especially considering the impact of (fairly) recent austerity policies arising from the 2008 global financial crisis and the accumulation of sovereign debt. Cephas Lumina aptly pointed out that the problem of unsustainable debt burdens and the corresponding need to better regulate global financial markets and institutions are concerns not only of developing countries but of developed ones—for example Greece, Ireland, Portugal, Spain—as well.[301]

Target 10.5 seemingly begins turning the focus to inter-state inequalities (and its link to intra-state inequalities), consistent with what many stakeholders participating in the OWG originally intended. Using the FSI as indicator, however, actually retains the attention and burden on the individual country's financial system and macroeconomic performance. While there are legitimate grounds to monitor financial stability, target 10.5 and its associated indicator also need to account for the reality that the growing global financial instability—and the accompanying inequalities within countries—can partly be attributed to liberalization efforts advocated by the Global North and to the acts of select private actors therein. This relationship manifests through several channels: 'facilitating boom and bust cycles or asset bubbles; undermining the capacity of governments to use several macroeconomic and social policy tools that can help to mitigate or tackle inequality; and making financial systems more prone to requiring government "bail outs" for private financial firms in times of crisis'.[302] Indeed, in today's open and integrated world economy, 'national and global inequality dynamics are closely interrelated, with structural shifts and changing production patterns in the global economy affecting inequalities both within and between countries'[303] and the

---

[299] C Tietje and M Lehmann, 'The Role and Prospects of International Law in Financial Regulation and Supervision' (2010) 13 Journal of International Economic Law 663, 677–78.

[300] Zaring (n 297) 17.

[301] C Lumina, 'Sovereign Debt and Human Rights: Making the Connection' in I Bantekas and C Lumina (eds), *Sovereign Debt and Human Rights* (OUP 2018) 170.

[302] CESR (n 38) 18 (citation omitted).

[303] UN Shared Framework, 14.

operation and regulation of national markets are contingent not only on national laws and regulations but are also structured by international rules particularly within the trade and financial regimes.

In this regard, it would also be worth monitoring whether other developed countries that predominantly comprise the Financial Stability Board (FSB) would follow Germany's suggestion about the importance of 'accommodat[ing] the right of countries in the Global South to help shape policy with a view to ensuring sustainable governance of the financial markets'.[304] It complements the UK's endorsement of the G20 Eminent Persons Group (EPG)[305] recommendations regarding the reform of the global financial system 'to ensure sustainable, inclusive growth and improve financial surveillance'.[306] Notably, target 10.5 was copied almost verbatim in the Draft RTD Convention, particularly in the article elaborating the duty to cooperate. The regulation and monitoring of global financial markets and institutions fall under the States Parties' 'duty to cooperate to create a social and international order conducive to the right to development'.[307]

6. Target 10.6 Ensure enhanced representation and voice for developing countries in decision-making in global international economic and financial institutions in order to deliver more effective, credible, accountable and legitimate institutions

a) Source of target

At some point during its drafting history, target 10.6 was lumped together with the target concerning global financial markets regulation. As early as OWG-11, though, several developing and least developed states had proposed the inclusion of a distinct target calling for reforms in the IFIs' governing bodies by eliminating North-South asymmetries therein. In the OWG-12 zero draft, this target read: 'promote strong international institutions, including through the conclusion of reforms for increasing effective and democratic participation of developing countries in international financial institutions'. The OWG-13 Revised zero draft version added a timeline ('by 2030') and read: 'ensure equitable representation and voice of developing countries in global institutions of governance and development'. The Final Proposal removed the timeline and added a phrase describing the desired characteristics of the reformed international economic and financial institutions: 'effective, credible, accountable and legitimate'.

b) Empirical analysis: domestic and international efforts

The two major IFIs, the IMF and the World Bank (also collectively referred to as the Bretton Woods Institutions), and the regional/multilateral development banks are the main objects of target 10.6, since these are the international organizations that adopt a *weighted voting system*, meaning, a state's vote depends on its capital contribution.

---

[304] Germany, VNR 2021.

[305] Report of the G20 Eminent Persons Group on Global Financial Governance (EPG), 'Making the Global Financial System Work for All' (2018) <https://www.globalfinancialgovernance.org/assets/pdf/G20EPG-Full per cent20Report.pdf> accessed 5 November 2021.

[306] United Kingdom, VNR 2019.

[307] Draft RTD Convention, art 13(4)(c).

772 SDG 10

Put more bluntly, wealthier and more powerful states are better heard and represented in these international institutions, as their votes carry more influence, and sometimes even possess veto power over systemic decisions. The IFIs' peculiar governance structure stands in contrast with that of the other international (economic) organizations like the UNGA and the WTO, which use a 'one member, one vote system' and where developing countries represent over 70 per cent of their membership.

Nonetheless, some reforms have already been, and continue to be, undertaken. From an international legal perspective, these reforms involve amendments to these international organizations' constituent instruments—technically international agreements within the meaning of the Vienna Convention on the Law of Treaties—yet such amendments only required the votes, not directly of states convening at the UN or a separate conference, but of the Board of Governors in a primarily internal process.

At the IMF, the Board Reform Amendment, which took effect on 26 January 2016, together with a broader and earlier package of quota and governance reforms,[308] effectively resulted in two major changes: (i) creation of an all-elected IMF's Executive Board, and (ii) increase of the quota shares of emerging market and developing countries.[309] These changes are labelled 'historic' since it is the first time that 'four emerging market countries (Brazil, China, India, and Russia) will be among the 10 largest members of the IMF', meaning, more than 6 per cent of quota shares will shift to this group and developing countries.[310] At the World Bank, more specifically the International Bank for Reconstruction and Development (IBRD), the major and equally historic reforms occurred in April 2010: 'A 3.13 percentage point increase in the voting power of Developing and Transition countries (DTCs) . . . bring[s] them to 47.19 percent – a total shift to DTCs of 4.59 percentage points since 2008'.[311] The DTCs' voting power likewise increased at the International Finance Corporation (IFC), the World Bank Group's private sector arm. The Secretary-General noted, however, that 'full implementation [of these reforms] will [still] leave developing countries with just over 40 per cent of the voting rights, still short of the 75 per cent they represent in World Bank membership in terms of the number of countries'.[312] In their VNRs, several developed countries[313] mention their support of further enhanced representation within IFIs through reforms in quota shares and voting power, but besides lip-service, one cannot glean any concrete action reported towards this target.

---

[308] IMF, Press Release: IMF Board of Governors Approves Major Quota and Governance Reforms, Press Release 10/477 (16 December 2010) <https://www.imf.org/en/News/Articles/2015/09/14/01/49/pr10477> accessed 5 November 2021.

[309] See IMF, Press Release: Historic Quota and Governance Reforms Become Effective, Press Release No 16/25 (27 January 2016) <https://www.imf.org/en/News/Articles/2015/09/14/01/49/pr1625a> accessed 5 November 2021.

[310] ibid. Other top ten members include the United States, Japan, and the four largest European countries (France, Germany, Italy, and the United Kingdom).

[311] World Bank, Press Release: World Bank Reforms Voting Power, Gets $86 Billion Boost (25 April 2010) <https://www.worldbank.org/en/news/press-release/2010/04/25/world-bank-reforms-voting-power-gets-86-billion-boost> accessed 5 November 2021.

[312] Secretary-General, 'Special Edition' (n 7) para 31.

[313] See, eg, Germany, Norway, Sweden, United Kingdom.

c) Critique

Although there were no express references during the OWG deliberations to the New International Economic Order (NIEO) and the international instruments[314] this movement produced, many proposals—including those related to target 10.6—evoked its ideals, principles, and demands. Indeed, calls for establishing reforms in the international economic and legal order during the 1960s and 1970s were premised on, among others, the desire to 'correct inequalities and redress existing injustices, make it possible to eliminate the widening gap between the developed and the developing countries and ensure steadily accelerating economic and social development and peace and justice for present and future generations'.[315] In a striking resemblance to target 10.6, one of the statements in the NIEO Declaration referred to the necessity for 'active, full and equal participation of the developing countries in the formulation and application of all decisions that concern the international community'—taking into account the paradoxical situation at that time (and indubitably continues to this day) wherein developing countries' roles in all fields of international activity had been growing but they also remained extremely vulnerable to 'external economic impulses'.[316]

Continuing along similar lines, albeit focused on refining the notion of development as a human right, the Draft Convention on the Right to Development (adopting the approach of the 1986 Declaration) includes target 10.6—copied almost verbatim like target 10.5—as among the means by which States Parties can implement their duty to cooperate relative to realizing the right to development.[317] Parenthetically, several other SDG 10 targets are part of the enumeration in this provision regarding the duty to cooperate. This ongoing codification work can crucially remedy my observation that targets relating to inter-state inequalities have a weaker link to international human rights law, in contrast to the targets on intra-state inequalities.

Legal bases for this stronger link are not lacking. The UDHR provides that, '[e]veryone is entitled to a social and international order in which the rights and freedoms set forth in this Declaration can be fully realized'.[318] Moreover, common article 1(1) of the ICCPR and the ICESCR uphold the right of self-determination, which entitles all peoples to 'freely determine their political status and freely pursue their economic, social and cultural development'. The right to self-determination is intimately related to the right to development, such that the two are mutually reinforcing. In the Draft RTD Convention, this relationship is expressed in the core provision, stating, 'Every human person and all peoples have the right to active, free and meaningful participation in development and in the fair distribution of benefits resulting therefrom'.[319] Notably, in its first paragraph, this provision also implicitly recognizes the intimate

---

[314] Programme of Action on the Establishment of a New International Economic Order (1 May 1974) UNGA Res 3202(S-VI).

[315] Declaration on the Establishment of a New International Economic Order (1 May 1974) UNGA Res 3201(S-VI) (NIEO Declaration), Preamble.

[316] ibid para 2.

[317] Draft RTD Convention, art 13(4)(d).

[318] UDHR, art 28.

[319] Art 4.

relationship between equality of opportunity and equality of outcome, as well as the interaction among political, social, and economic inclusion. It is a recognition of these linkages that is similarly needed but somewhat missing in SDG 10's treatment of targets relating to intra-state inequalities, on the one hand, and those on inter-state inequalities, on the other.

The Special Rapporteur on extreme poverty and human rights also echoed the long-standing criticisms against IFIs, specifically the IMF, with regard to their structural adjustment policies' impact of weakening state power, which is essential in ensuring equitable income distribution within a country.[320] In this regard, target 10.6 aims to accord developing countries greater voice in decision-making and representation within international economic and financial organizations, with the expectation that such reforms would thereby constrain IFIs from imposing conditionalities that limit the ability of states, particularly in the developing world, to undertake redistributive laws and policies, including in times of crisis.

Not unlike other targets under SDG 10, target 10.6 and its associated indicator (in common with target 16.8) can be criticized for failing to provide 'benchmarks or deadlines to achieve them', which omission thereby dilutes their potential 'to address inequality of power in the global economic structure'.[321] Indicator 10.6.1 is also deficient for failing to identify the responsible actors and to incentivize them to pursue the specific actions 'such as concrete steps towards voting reform at the IFIs'.[322] Lastly, indicator 10.6.1 seems broader than its target. While target 10.6 speaks of 'international economic and financial institutions', the indicator refers to the 'percentage of members and voting rights of developing countries in *international organizations*'. Strictly speaking, international economic organizations and IFIs are only subsets of international (or intergovernmental) organizations, which also encompass entities, such as the United Nations Educational, Scientific and Cultural Organization (UNESCO) and the World Health Organization (WHO), neither of which is an IFI or an international economic organization. The breadth of this indicator, however, can be justified by the fact that it also repeats as an indicator under target 16.8, which calls for the broadening and strengthening of participation by developing countries in global governance institutions. Significantly, the existence of this common/shared indicator bears some promise of establishing the aforementioned connection that needs to be recognized—between the intra- and inter-state inequalities targets and among the various types of exclusion—and moving towards 'a human-centered framework of analysis and policy construction'[323] that does not mask or deny the impact of political inequalities among states on international economic (trade, investment, finance) and development decisions made by or through various international institutions.

---

[320] Alston, 'Extreme Inequality and Human Rights' (n 25) para 44.
[321] MacNaughton (n 36) 1060.
[322] Saiz and Donald (n 26) 1034.
[323] Salomon (n 143) 60.

COMMENTARY ON THE TARGETS 775

7. Target 10.7 Facilitate orderly, safe, regular and responsible migration and mobility of people, including through the implementation of planned and well-managed migration policies

a) Source of target

In earlier versions of target 10.7, different stakeholders attempted to include the topics of brain drain and migrant workers' rights. During OWG-12, the MGoS proposed an amendment of the zero draft:

> 10.11 facilitate greater international mobility of labour *and ensure workers' rights for migrant workers* while mitigating brain drain

As seen from the current wording of target 10.7, the topic of migrant workers' human and labour rights was excluded. It was incorporated instead into target 8.8 under the goal on economic growth and decent jobs. Subsequent iterations also removed explicit mention of brain drain. However, using the negotiating history, it can reasonably be deemed as read into the notion of the 'orderly, safe, and responsible migration and mobility of people' sought to be achieved through, among others, 'planned and well-managed migration policies'.

One notable proposal relating to target 10.7 was put forward by Pakistan during OWG-11: 'By 2030, increase migration flows by 10% particularly of skilled labour from lower income countries to higher income countries.' The OWG itself proposed another version that would have been one of the MOI targets for the goal on reducing inequalities:

> 17.35 enhance global cooperation to facilitate orderly, safe, responsible migration and mobility of people, including through implementation of planned and managed migration policies that facilitate migrants' contribution to sustainable development

These proposals, however, did not make it into the final version of the OWG's proposed goals and targets.

b) Empirical analysis: domestic and international efforts

Indicator 10.7.2—Number of countries with migration policies that facilitate orderly, safe, regular and responsible migration and mobility of people—is further broken down into (i) the number and (ii) the proportion of countries with such migration policies, by policy domain. There are six policy domains: (i) Migrant rights; (ii) Whole-of-government/Evidence-based policy-making; (iii) Cooperation and partnerships; (iv) Socio-economic well-being; (v) Mobility dimension of crises; and (vi) Safe, orderly and regular migration. This classification is derived from the Migration Governance Framework (MiGOF) conceptualized by the International Organization for Migration (IOM), which, together with the UNDESA, was tasked by the IAEG-SDGs to develop an indicator for target 10.7.

State reporting on indicator 10.7.2 was first made in the 2019 SDG Report, which examined 105 countries and found significant variations across the policy domains. Specifically, according to the Report, over 40 per cent of the countries lacked a comprehensive set of measures in the domains of migrant rights and socio-economic well-being.[324] Two new indicators for target 10.7 were introduced in 2021, namely, 'Number of people who died or disappeared in the process of migration towards an international destination' (indicator 10.7.3) and 'Proportion of the population who are refugees, by country of origin' (indicator 10.7.4). Statistics on these indicators are not yet available, given that they have only been added recently.

Destination states, typically in the Global North, mention support—political, financial, or both[325]—of the UN's 2018 Global Compact for Safe, Orderly and Regular Migration.[326] An interesting legislative effort is Germany's Skilled Immigration Act (2020), which 'expand[s] the ways in which people, especially the vocationally qualified, can immigrate' to the country.[327] Norway also has policies aimed at improving immigrant groups' access to the labour market and increasing their labour force participation.[328] Cyprus likewise reported labour market programmes on vocational training for third-country nationals.[329] Since target 10.7 is 'the most migration-governance-specific SDG target',[330] and considering that different countries expectedly have varying migration laws and policies, depending on, among others, whether they are an origin, transit, or destination state, most surveys of efforts are often limited.

c) Critique

Migrants do not lose their human rights—to life,[331] to liberty and security of person,[332] and to not be subjected to cruel, inhuman or degrading treatment or punishment,[333] among others—when they cross borders to seek and obtain employment abroad. The ICCPR and the ICRMW likewise uphold the rights not to perform forced or compulsory labour[334] and not to be held in slavery.[335] Additionally, the prohibition against slavery is a customary, and arguably a *jus cogens*, norm.[336] Moreover, these human rights attach not only to the migrant worker herself but also to her family members. In this regard, article 10(2) CRC complementarily provides that, in recognition of a child's

---

[324] SDG Report 2019, 43.
[325] Germany, VNR 2021; Sweden, VNR 2021; United Kingdom, VNR 2019.
[326] Intergovernmental Conference to Adopt the Global Compact for Safe, Orderly and Regular Migration, 'Draft outcome document of the Conference' (30 July 2018) A/CONF.231/3 (Global Compact).
[327] Germany, VNR 2021.
[328] Norway, VNR 2021.
[329] Cyprus, VNR 2019.
[330] UNDESA, 'International Migration 2019', Report (2019) 55 <https://www.un.org/en/development/desa/population/migration/publications/migrationreport/docs/InternationalMigration2019_Report.pdf> accessed 29 October 2021.
[331] ICCPR, art 6(1).
[332] ibid art 9(1).
[333] ibid art 7.
[334] ibid art 8(3)(a); ICRMW, art 11(2).
[335] ICCPR, art 8(1) and (2); ICRMW, art 11(1).
[336] D Weissbrodt and Anti-Slavery International, 'Abolishing Slavery and Its Contemporary Forms' (United Nations Office of the High Commissioner for Human Rights 2002) HR/PUB/02/4 para 6.

right to maintain personal relations and direct contacts, on a regular basis, with both parents even when the latter reside in different states, States Parties to the treaty 'shall respect the right of the child and his or her parents to leave any country, including their own, and to enter their own country'.

The broad and vague wording of target 10.7 accommodates the multidimensionality of migration and its politically charged and contentious character. The meaning of 'orderly, safe, regular and responsible migration' could be derived from the international legal framework comprising discrete and sparse treaties, a few customary norms, and soft law instruments. The ICRMW and the ILO Migrant Workers (Supplementary Provisions), 1975 (No 143) are the most *apropos* here. The latter is specifically concerned with prosecuting 'authors of manpower trafficking', that is 'organisers of illicit or clandestine movements of migrants for employment',[337] for which purpose States Parties 'shall take such measures as are necessary, at the national and the international level, for systematic contact and exchange of information on the subject with other States, in consultation with representative organisations of employers and workers'.[338] Relevantly, the Migrant Smuggling Protocol[339] provides that the obligation to criminalize and prosecute the practice shall not extend to the migrants themselves.[340] Its Part II, entitled 'Equality of Opportunity and Treatment', also contains a Member's undertaking 'to declare and pursue a national policy designed to promote and to guarantee ... equality of opportunity and treatment in respect of employment and occupation, of social security, of trade union and cultural rights and of individual and collective freedoms for [migrant workers and their family members]'.[341]

The last portion of target 10.7 referring to 'planned and well-managed migration policies' presumably contemplates the need to balance the facilitation of 'orderly, safe, regular and responsible migration', on the one hand, and the reduction of irregular migration (both its incidence and negative consequences), on the other. For this purpose, the Global Compact presents a 'comprehensive approach [that] is needed to optimize the overall benefits of migration, while addressing the risks and challenges for individuals and communities in countries of origin, transit and destination'.[342] Such comprehensive approach is pertinent to the concerns of SDG 10, such as 'strengthen[ing] the welfare of all members of societies by minimizing disparities, avoiding polarization and increasing public confidence in policies and institutions related to migration, in line with the acknowledgement that fully integrated migrants are better positioned to contribute to prosperity'.[343] Also relevant is Objective 17 to '[e]liminate all forms of discrimination and promoted evidence-based public discourse to shape perceptions of migration', wherein the states committed to 'condemn and counter expressions, acts

---

[337] ILO 143, art 5 in relation to art 3.
[338] ibid art 4.
[339] Protocol Against the Smuggling of Migrants by Land, Sea, and Air, Supplementing the United Nations Convention Against Transnational Organized Crime (not yet in force).
[340] Arts 5 and 6.
[341] Art 10.
[342] Global Compact, para 11.
[343] ibid para 32 (Objective 16: Empower migrants and societies to realize full inclusion and social cohesion).

778   SDG 10

and manifestations of racism, racial discrimination, violence, xenophobia and related intolerance against all migrants in conformity with international human rights law'.[344] This objective, if taken seriously, could potentially contribute to the needed 'rethinking [of] human development not in terms of individual freedom and free markets but around the concept of equality'[345] not only between foreign and domestic workers but also between the countries of origin and the migrant-receiving states.

Significantly, sustainable development is one of the cross-cutting and interdependent principles guiding the Global Compact. Such linkage should not only mean viewing migration in terms of its contribution to 'positive development outcomes'[346] but engaging as well in genuine efforts to address the root causes of migration—one of which is the widening disparity between developed countries (where global capital is concentrated) and labour-rich states in the Global South. It further entails re-evaluating 'the value of labour and its transformative capacity',[347] and recognizing its fundamental importance to wealth generation.

From a legal positivist view, however, the Global Compact is soft law. Its non-legally binding status could be explained by the perceived need to accommodate the unfortunate reality that while international cooperation is imperative in this area, there remains a strong concern to 'uphold ... the sovereignty of States and their obligations under international law',[348] This needless accommodation, however, obscures the point that state sovereignty is no longer a blanket justification for inaction or non-interference, especially given a contemporary and increasingly comprehensive understanding of the obligation of international cooperation and assistance under the UN Charter. Notably, in the Draft RTD Convention, target 10.7 is in fact recognized as vital to the creation of a social and international order conducive to realizing the right to development, and is thus among the several ways that states should implement their duty to cooperate.[349] This counterpart provision in the Draft Convention importantly adds the qualifier 'rights-based' to 'planned and well-managed' migration policies that should be implemented. Notably, the Convention drafters meant for the sub-paragraphs of article 13(4) to be a '*verbatim* reproduction of the consensually agreed text of the 2030 Agenda [to] eliminate ... any scope for controversy or contest', meaning, they simply reaffirm the already existing legal obligations of states under international labour law and international human rights law, including in the ICRMW. In the same vein, target 10.7 should be implemented, especially by States Parties to the relevant treaties, with those background norms in mind. Finally, to the extent that migration is recognized as a tool to reduce inter-state inequalities, its promotion as part of sustainable development cannot dehumanize labour as a productive factor, and should move states towards a

---

[344] ibid para 33.
[345] RD Wise and others, 'Reframing the Debate on Migration, Development and Human Rights' (2013) 19 Population, Space and Place 430, 439.
[346] Global Compact, para 15(e).
[347] Wise and others (n 345) 440.
[348] Global Compact, para 7.
[349] Draft RTD Convention, art 13(4)(h).

rights-based rather than a border-control approach to the admission of persons into their jurisdiction.

8. Target 10.a Implement the principle of special and differential treatment for developing countries, in particular least developed countries, in accordance with World Trade Organization agreements

a) Source of target

In one of its earliest iterations, target 10.a did not refer specifically to the SDT principle. Rather, the then proposed target simply referred to the promotion of 'an open, rules-based, non-discriminatory and equitable multilateral trading system'.[350] This target eventually became target 17.10. At certain points in the drafting history of the post-2015 development agenda, there had been more than one global trade-related targets, but all of them were placed under the MOI goal. One such target focused on the Global South's market access:

> 17.24 improve market access for agricultural, fisheries and industrial exports of developing countries in particular African countries, Least Developed Countries, LLDCs and SIDS with a view to increasing their share of exports in global markets

The SDT principle was first raised during OWG-12 through the MGoS' proposed additional target under the goal on reducing inequalities:

> by 2030, reform trade systems to promote equality among trade partners, recognizing the need for special and differential treatment of developing countries, and more equal distribution of profits along the value chain, by x% over y number of years

The OWG accepted this proposal, hence, the OWG-13 Revised zero draft included target 10.a, stating 'respect the principle of special and differential treatment for least developed countries in relevant international agreements including the WTO'. The MGoS subsequently sought to amend this target by expressly mentioning that SDT is to be accorded not only to LDCs but also, more generally, to developing countries. After further revisions, the OWG's Final Proposal stated:

> 10.a implement the principle of special and differential treatment for developing countries, in particular least developed countries, in accordance with WTO agreements

What is remarkable about this revised wording is the change in the verb from 're-spect' to 'implement'. It is unclear from the records why such change was effected. One possible explanation might lie in the fact that, as elaborated below, the SDT principle is contained in different provisions under several agreements, and some of these provisions require positive actions, whether by the developed WTO Member States or by the

---

[350] OWG-10 Focus Area Document.

780   SDG 10

developing WTO Member States themselves who are meant to benefit from such provisions. The change was therefore appropriate, although it would have also been accurate, perhaps more so, to retain both verbs, since some of the SDT provisions do require implementation (positive act)—for example, providing technical assistance to the developing or least developed country—while others can be complied with by one state respecting (negative act) another Member State's exercise of rights or privileges—for example not expecting reciprocity in compliance with certain treaty obligations or by refraining from suing a developing country who is entitled to delayed implementation of commitments.

b) Empirical analysis: domestic and international efforts

The sole indicator for target 10.a—'Proportion of tariff lines applied to imports from [LDCs] and developing countries with zero-tariff'—is a narrow and limited representation of the SDT principle. Yet, SDG Reports have consistently been measuring and tracking the LDCs' and developing countries' share of imports entering developed countries duty-free. According to the UN, between 2000 and 2014, this indicator increased from 70 to 84 per cent for LDCs, and from 65 to 79 per cent for developing countries.[351] Curiously, when the period of observation is shortened to 2005–2015, the magnitude of increase is less drastic: 'the proportion of tariff lines globally with duty-free treatment for products originating in developing countries increased from 41 per cent to 50 per cent; for products originating in the least developed countries, the proportion rose from 49 per cent to 65 per cent'.[352] The 2018 SDG Report also recorded for the period 2010–2016, a 20 per cent increase in the proportion of products exported to the world markets by LDCs (64.4 per cent) and SIDS (64.1 per cent) that faced zero tariffs.[353] According to the same report, '[d]eveloping countries overall had duty-free market access for about 50 per cent of all products exported in 2016'.[354] Between 2016 and 2017, LDCs' coverage of duty-free treatment increased by 5.5 percentage points, reaching 65.6 per cent of all products exported.[355]

The 2018 SDG Report also included the following data under SDG 17 (specifically target 17.10) that are also relevant to SDG 10: 'For all groups of countries, tariffs on imports levied under preferential trade agreements, which include bilateral and regional free-trade agreements, have been declining over time'.[356] This shared attention towards tariff levels and preferential treatment illustrates the close relationship between Goals 10 and 17. Their common object of observation makes it normal to compare these targets and their respective indicators. Such comparison reveals that they have practically the same shortcomings—those relating to inadequate quantification and specification of deadlines—that thereby weaken their accountability function.[357]

[351] SDG Report 2016, 8.
[352] SDG Report 2017, 39.
[353] SDG Report 2018, 9.
[354] ibid.
[355] SDG Report 2019, 43.
[356] SDG Report 2018, 32.
[357] Anderson (n 151) 198.

States extending tariff or trade preferences to developing countries rarely include such acts under target 10.a. Hence, the UK's report of its Taxation (Cross-Border Trade) Act is singular, especially because such Act 'enshrines into UK law the commitment contained in the Goals to provide duty-free, quota-free trade access for Least Developed Countries'.[358] Similar domestic legislation in more countries could partly augment the weak legal basis and implementation of SDT at the international level.

c) Critique

SDG 10 presupposes that implementing the SDT principle would reduce inequalities among states (and presumably also within countries), and this reduction, in turn, would contribute to sustainable development. Another implicit premise—inferred from target 10.a's express reference to its relevant international legal framework, in other words, international trade law, more specifically WTO covered agreements and jurisprudence—is that SDT would lead to developing countries' economic growth through increased market access. These assumptions are dubious, not least because the target's object of implementation, the SDT principle, is itself ambiguous.

Under WTO law, this principle is expressed or embedded in several provisions under various treaties. Based on the WTO Secretariat's classification, there are a total of 155 SDT provisions in WTO covered agreements as of March 2021.[359] Introduced in 2001, the WTO Secretariat's typology comprises:

(a) Provisions aimed at increasing the trade opportunities of developing country Members;

(b) Provisions under which WTO Members should safeguard the interests of developing country Members;

(c) Flexibility of commitments, of action, and use of policy instruments;

(d) Transitional time-periods;

(e) Technical assistance;

(f) Provisions relating to LDC Members.

Since 2013, a Monitoring Mechanism has been tasked to 'act as a focal point within the WTO to analyse and review the implementation of S&D [special and differential] provisions' and 'review all aspects of implementation of S&D provisions with a view to facilitating integration of developing and least-developed Members into the multilateral trading system'.[360] The Monitoring Mechanism forms part of the WTO Members' earlier reaffirmation that SDT provisions 'are an integral part of the WTO Agreements' and the states' recognition of the need to review such provisions 'with a view to strengthening them and making them more precise, effective and operational'.[361] The creation

---

[358] United Kingdom, VNR 2019, 134.

[359] WTO, *Special and Differential Treatment Provisions in WTO Agreements and Decisions – Note by the Secretariat* (2 March 2021) WT/COMTD/W/258.

[360] WTO Ministerial Decision, *Monitoring Mechanism on Special and Differential Treatment* (11 December 2013) WT/MIN(13)/45, WT/L/920 (Monitoring Mechanism Decision) paras 3 and 4.

[361] *Hong Kong Ministerial Declaration* (18 December 2005) WT/MIN(05)/DEC, para 35.

782   SDG 10

of the mechanism is only one among several outstanding issues that the Committee on Trade and Development (CTD), in Special Session, was instructed to address. Another issue that the Ministerial Decision mentioned is 'the incorporation of S&D treatment into the architecture of WTO rules'.[362]

The Monitoring Mechanism's objective to instil the SDT provisions with greater precision, effectiveness, and operability is herculean yet severely limited at the same time, since in performing its functions, it is barred from 'alter[ing], or in any manner affect[ing], Members' rights and obligations under WTO Agreements, Ministerial or General Council Decisions, or interpret their legal nature'.[363] Such limitation could prevent the mechanism from addressing doubts regarding the normative force and legal significance of many SDT provisions, which are couched in hortatory, vague, or 'best-efforts' language. For instance, the General Agreement on Tariffs and Trade (GATT) article XXXVII, which belongs to Part IV—Trade and Development, enumerates the developed Members' commitments in a non-committal manner: 'The developed contracting parties shall to the fullest extent possible—that is, except when compelling reasons, which may include legal reasons, make it impossible – give effect to the following provisions.' Another sub-paragraph mandates ('shall') developed WTO Member States to 'give active consideration to the adoption of other measures designed to provide greater scope for the development of imports from less-developed contracting parties and collaborate in appropriate international action to this end'.[364]

What 'giv[ing] active consideration' legally entails, however, has not yet been clarified or elaborated in WTO jurisprudence. Indeed, even the most prominent embodiment or manifestation of SDT, the so-called Enabling Clause,[365] has yet to be adequately and clearly interpreted by panels and/or the Appellate Body. In a nutshell, the Enabling Clause makes it legally permissible, among others, for developed Member States to accord preferential or more favourable treatment to developing-country Members, without the need to accord the same treatment to other states and without running afoul of the fundamental most-favoured-nation (MFN) treatment obligation. The landmark *Generalised System of Preferences (GSP) case* affirmed that the Enabling Clause 'is among the "positive efforts" called for in the Preamble to the WTO Agreement to be taken by developed-country Members to enhance the "economic development" of developing-country Members'.[366]

As mentioned, other SDT provisions are simply additional flexibilities that developing countries can avail of and/or extended timelines (with some that have already lapsed) for compliance. A study by Vineet Hegde and Jan Wouters proposed a typology that clarifies the legal status of the SDT provisions, to complement the WTO Secretariat's classification system, which focuses on economic rationales. Based on their

---

[362] ibid para 38.
[363] Monitoring Mechanism Decision, para 5.
[364] General Agreement on Tariffs and Trade (GATT), art XXXVIII, para 3(b).
[365] *Differential and More Favourable Treatment Reciprocity and Fuller Participation of Developing Countries,* Decision of 28 November 1979, L/4903.
[366] *European Communities—Conditions for the Granting of Tariff Preferences to Developing Countries—Appellate Body Report* (7 April 2004) WT/DS246/AB/R, para 92.

typology, among the 227 commitments found in WTO covered agreements and ministerial decisions, 195 are *legal* obligations and thirty-two are non-legal, aspirational/ political commitments.[367] Only 170 of these 195 legal obligations remain alive. Using the obligations of means-result dichotomy, these authors concluded that 'only 21% (47 provisions) of SDT provisions oblige developed Members to provide differential treatment to developing Members' while the remainder does 'not require that treatment in any concrete manner'.[368]

Given the foregoing uncertainties and ambiguities, it is questionable how the HLP can claim that 'implement[ing] the principle of special and differential treatment' can contribute 'in a major way' to achieving the goal of reducing inter-state inequalities. One possibility, I submit, is to establish such link through the duty of international cooperation and assistance under articles 55 and 56 of the UN Charter. Such an approach draws inspiration from the Draft RTD Convention, which considers target 10.a—together with target 17.10—as a means of implementing the 'duty to cooperate to create a social and international order conducive to the realization of the right to development'.[369] Notably, other SDT provisions obligate developed States to consult and collaborate with developing Members. Pertinent indicators to capture the performance of such duties are thus needed. From the perspective of sustainable development, which is an objective expressly mentioned in the Preamble to the Agreement Establishing the WTO, these duties of consultation and collaboration align with the principle of participation,[370] one component of which is inclusiveness in development decision-making processes. This point illustrates a connection with target 10.6 and reinforces the importance of enhancing developing countries' voice and representation in international economic organizations. Significantly, the obligations to consider different conditions in other WTO Members' (especially developing countries) territories and to engage in 'serious, across-the-board negotiations with the objective of concluding bilateral or multilateral agreements' were discussed by the Appellate Body in the *Shrimp/Turtle Case*.[371] The International Court of Justice (ICJ) has similarly recognized the role of procedural obligations, like the duties to negotiate, consult, and cooperate, in operationalizing the concept of sustainable development.[372]

Some critical remarks additionally need to be raised regarding indicator 10.a.1. First, considering the SDT principle's various manifestations in several WTO provisions, having a sole indicator for target 10.a is woefully inadequate. Second, indicator 10.a.1, 'Proportion of tariff lines applied to imports from least developed countries and developing countries with zero tariff', is limited to measuring, imperfectly at that,

[367] V Hegde and J Wouters, 'Special and Differential Treatment Under the World Trade Organization: A Legal Typology' (2021) 24 Journal of International Economic Law 551, 556–57.

[368] ibid 571.

[369] Draft RTD Convention, art 13(4), paras (a) and (b).

[370] Rio Declaration on Environment and Development (12 August 1992) A/CONF.151/26, Principle 10.

[371] *United States—Import Prohibition of Certain Shrimp and Shrimp Products—Appellate Body Report* (12 October 1998) WT/DS58/AB/R, paras 164–166.

[372] See *Gabčíkovo-Nagymaros Project (Hungary v Slovakia)* [1997] ICJ Rep 7; *Pulp Mills on the River Uruguay (Argentina v Uruguay)* [2006] ICJ Rep 113; *Whaling in the Antarctic (Australia v Japan, New Zealand intervening)* [2014] ICJ Rep 226.

the developing states' access to global trade, for which the developed WTO Members' duty is merely one of reviewing—without more—the developing Members' progress.[373] Indicator 10.a.1 seems more suitable for either target 17.11 or 17.12. In fact, the respective indicators for each of these targets overlap with what target 10.a's lone target is presently measuring and monitoring. Yet, it is important to note that, as the Expert Mechanism on the Right to Development rightly observed, measuring worldwide weighted tariff average does not sufficiently match target 17.10's aim of a non-discriminatory and equitable multilateral trading system.[374]

Equating SDT with preferential tariff treatment is gravely erroneous: the former is much broader than the latter. It is seriously doubtful whether target 10.a could genuinely reduce inter-state inequalities, given that, similar to the critique of target 10.1, poverty reduction by raising the bottom—for example through developing countries' higher GDP growth—would not necessarily lead to narrowing disparities, in the absence of concomitant attention to the disproportionate gains at the top.[375] To partly rectify this deficiency, indicators for target 10.a should additionally include measurements relating to *Aid for Trade*, which programme is underpinned by WTO Member States' duty to cooperate. For instance, the OECD's Creditor Reporting System (CRS) database contains proxies for different kinds of aid-for-trade flows that could be adopted as Target 10.a indicators: technical assistance for trade policy and regulations; economic infrastructure; productive capacity building; and trade-related adjustment.[376] Notably, these capacity building initiatives are also fitting opportunities for cooperation among different international organizations, that is the WTO, the IFIs, and other international development agencies. This critique and the concomitant recommendation are, of course, not to refute that zero-tariff access for the Global South's products can help improve these countries' economic situation and, possibly, even help them address inequalities within their jurisdictions. It remains crucial to continue 'remov[ing] the barriers affecting market access for products produced by poor countries [to help] achieve a more even distribution of the gains from trade', but in order for trade laws and policies to reduce inter-state inequalities, as the 2030 Agenda envisions, multilateral efforts should likewise be directed to '[e]liminating supply-side restrictions and developing productive capacity'.[377] Indeed, as in inequality at the domestic level, merely creating opportunity—here, market access—does not guarantee equal, much less equitable, outcomes, since the beneficiaries of such opportunity may not be able to utilize such access to begin with. Otherwise stated, some WTO Members, particularly LDCs, might not even have

---

[373] GATT art XXXVIII:2(a) and (d).

[374] Expert Mechanism on the Right to Development, *Operationalizing the Right to Development in Achieving the Sustainable Development Goals* (6 July 2021) A/HRC/48/63, para 49.

[375] MacNaughton (n 36) 1061.

[376] OECD, 'Aid-for-trade statistical queries' (n.d.) <https://www.oecd.org/dac/aft/aid-for-tradestatisticalqueries.htm> accessed 5 November 2021.

[377] Secretary-General, 'Empowering People' (n 5) para 22.

COMMENTARY ON THE TARGETS   785

adequate productive capacity and legal resources[378] to effectively participate and exercise their rights in the multilateral trading system.

9. Target 10.b Encourage official development assistance and financial flows, including foreign direct investment, to States where the need is greatest, in particular least developed countries, African countries, small island developing States and landlocked developing countries, in accordance with their national plans and programmes

a) Source of target

Like the trade-related targets that were moved from one goal to another throughout the drafting history, target 10.b can trace its origins to proposed MOI targets for the poverty-elimination goal.[379] The OWG-12 zero draft contained the following proposals:

> 17.3 developed countries implement fully ODA commitments to provide 0.7% of GNI in ODA to developing countries of which 0.15–0.20% to least-developed countries on an agreed timeline based on internationally agreed principles
>
> 17.4 direct ODA and encourage financial flows to states where the need is greatest, in particular African countries, LDCs, SIDS, LLDCs, and vulnerable states

Later, target 17.3 became the current target 17.2, while target 17.4 became target 10.b, which the MGoS sought to revise thus:

> 10.b direct *and reconfigure* ODA and encourage financial flows, including foreign direct investment *based on the human rights framework[,] gender equality and sustainability criteria* to states where the need is greatest, in particular, LDCs, African countries, SIDS, and LLDCs

The OWG's Final Proposal did not incorporate these proposed amendments and retained almost the same wording as the OWG-13 Revised zero draft. However, the action word was changed from 'direct' to 'encourage', and the final version also added an important caveat at the end ('in accordance with [recipients'] national plans and programmes'). This phrase dovetails with target 17.15, which enjoins respect each country's policy space and leadership. Notably, during OWG-11, Brazil and Nicaragua proposed a similar target under the goal on promoting equality: 'Protecting "policy space" of developing countries to strengthen ... institutional capacities to address their unique needs and circumstances in the pursuit of sustainable development.'

---

[378] See G Shaffer, *Emerging Powers and the World Trading System: The Past and Future of International Economic Law* (CUP 2021) (developing 'trade law capacity' was crucial to making WTO membership beneficial to the emerging economies).

[379] In the UN's SDG Reports since 2016, ODA data can be found under SDG 17 rather than SDG 10.

786 SDG 10

b) Empirical analysis: domestic and international efforts

The ODA (otherwise known as 'aid') level, particularly from OECD-DAC countries, is one of the most closely monitored and reported statistic among the targets and indicators in SDG 10—a testament to its prevalence and enduring but unjustified acceptance.[380] Most developed states consider aid as a matter of political and/or moral obligation, rather than a legal one, thereby making this resource flow susceptible to their whims or 'charitable' inclinations. A potential game-changer could be if more countries followed the UK's example of legislating[381] the obligation to spend 0.7 per cent of its national income on ODA. Another notable endeavour is that of the Czech Republic, which encourages its entrepreneurs to invest in developing countries by providing subsidy support to map business opportunities in those countries and by guaranteeing loans of private companies, 'under the condition that their investment will have an impact on development (e.g. local employment, or the sustainable use of natural resources)'.[382] Somewhat related is Denmark's advisory service for its businesses to undertake due diligence to ensure protection of human rights and labour rights in global supply chains.[383]

In the same year that the UNGA approved the 2030 Agenda, ODA from OECD-DAC Member States stood at its 'highest level ever reached' in the amount of $131.6 billion, a 6.9 per cent increase in real terms from the previous year (2014).[384] In contrast, private resource flows steeply declined in 2015, causing a contraction of total global resource flows for development to developing countries.[385] Notably, though, this ODA increase was mostly attributable to higher expenditures for refugee costs.[386] In 2017, as donor countries spent less on refugees inside their territories, net ODA dropped (0.6 per cent in real terms) from $158 billion (2016)[387] to $146.6 billion.[388] While OECD-DAC members' bilateral ODA to LDCs has been on the rise since 2016,[389] it fell by 3 per cent in real terms from 2017, such that in 2018, 'less aid went to LDCs and African countries, where it is needed most'.[390] It is also disappointing that '[b]ilateral development partners' respect for country policies declined from 64 per cent in 2016 to 57 per cent in 2018' and 'only around half of result indicators ... for [development projects and programmes] were drawn from country-owned result frameworks'.[391]

Based on a 2019 OECD report measuring distance to the SDG targets, OECD-DAC states have, during the period 1980–2017, collectively never reached half of the 0.7 per

---

[380] See MA Clemens and TJ Moss, 'Ghost of 0.7 per cent: Origins and Relevance of the International Aid Target' (2005) Center for Global Development, Working Paper Number 68 <https://www.cgdev.org/publication/ghost-07-origins-and-relevance-international-aid-target-working-paper-68> accessed 5 November 2021.

[381] United Kingdom, VNR 2019.

[382] Czech Republic, VNR 2021, 55.

[383] Denmark, VNR 2021. The country, however, reports this initiative as part of Goals 12 and 13.

[384] SDG Report 2016, 44. This figure, which constitutes 0.3 per cent of the OECD-DAC countries' gross national income (GNI), is on par with 2014.

[385] SDG Report 2017, 39.

[386] SDG Report 2016, 44.

[387] SDG Report 2018, 9.

[388] ibid 30.

[389] ibid.

[390] SDG Report 2019, 56 (emphasis added).

[391] Secretary-General, 'Special Edition' (n 7) para 38.

cent of GNI target earlier agreed upon at the UNGA—with their ODA 'hover[ing] at around 0.3% of GNI over the past three decades'. Yet, another OECD study claimed that although ODA budgets tend to fall particularly during recessions, 'ODA has by and large remained resilient' amidst the previous economic crises and '[s]ixty years of data ... show that ODA budgets and commitments [have been] driven by a political willingness to respond to human needs and co-ordinate to meet internationally agreed goals'.[392]

c) Critique

Target 10.b broadly concerns global financial flows, of which the two most prominent are ODA and foreign direct investment (FDI). The movement and transfer of each source of capital is governed by different international legal regimes. FDI, predominantly private capital, is regulated by international investment law, while aid, considered as international public finance, is covered by the so-called law of development cooperation. This commentary on target 10.b will thus be divided into two parts, the first dealing with the international legal framework for aid and the second briefly tackling international investment law. At the outset, it bears stressing that this target is deficient, because its lone associated indicator lumps together these resource flows instead of making a salient distinction between the character (public v private) of their sources.

Philipp Dann identifies and describes the *law of development cooperation* as, essentially, 'the law of ODA transfers' that is composed of the 'laws on the basic institutional setup of donors, recipients and rule-making in this area' and thereby 'regulates the procedures, instruments and criteria by which ODA is awarded'.[393] Given its scope and object, the field of law has both domestic and international components, with the latter consisting mostly of soft law or instruments that arguably contain political and moral, instead of legal, commitments. An example of such instrument is the AAAA, which is a key document accompanying the 2030 Agenda as it addresses the matter of financing the implementation of the SDGs and sustainable development more broadly. Regarding target 10.b, among the AAAA's noteworthy parts concern the: (i) complementary role of international public finance vis-à-vis domestic public resources;[394] (ii) call for ODA providers to reaffirm their respective ODA commitments, in the amounts indicated in international instruments;[395] and (iii) strengthening of country systems and promotion of country ownership, to improve the quality, impact, and effectiveness of development cooperation.[396] Significantly, the origins and *raison d'être* of the law of development cooperation rest on an imperative to address the reality of 'massive material inequalities between states and crushing poverty in developing countries'.[397] It remains, however, an under-studied and underdeveloped field.

---

[392] OECD, *Six Decades of ODA: Insights and Outlook in the COVID-19 Crisis*, OECD Development Cooperation Profiles 2020 (2020) (OECD, *Six Decades*) 9.

[393] P Dann, *The Law of Development Cooperation: A Comparative Analysis of the World Bank, the EU and Germany* (CUP 2013) 13–14.

[394] Addis Ababa Action Agenda, Part II (Action areas) C (International development cooperation), para 50.

[395] ibid para 51.

[396] ibid para 58.

[397] Dann (n 393) 219.

788   SDG 10

To recall, the oft-repeated 0.7 per cent of GNI target for ODA was agreed upon at the UN General Assembly as early as 1970:

> Each economically advanced country will progressively increase its official development assistance to the developing countries and will exert its best efforts to reach a minimum net amount of 0.7 per cent of its gross national product at market prices by the middle of the Decade.[398]

The legal status and binding character of the obligation to provide aid, particularly in the minimum amount prescribed by the UNGA Resolution and subsequent international instruments,[399] have been extensively and intensively debated but quite beyond the scope of this chapter. However, I submit that SDG 10's MOI targets and particularly target 10.b involve the duty of international cooperation and assistance. While several developed states continue to dispute the existence of a legal obligation to provide aid, the CESCR reminded states 'in a position to assist others' of their obligation to engage in 'international cooperation for development' grounding its interpretation of the phrase 'maximum of its available resources' on UN Charter articles 55 and 56.[400]

Another ground for challenging the continuing relevance and appropriateness of this target is the fact that it looks at the state of the economy of the donors, particularly their national budgets, rather than the beneficiaries/recipients' financial requirements and development priorities. As Clemens and Moss aptly argued, although 'ODA/GNI ... could be considered a *relative* measure of a country's "generosity" toward international development ... [it] does not tell us anything about the "right" *absolute* size of flows to a particular set of countries'.[401] A donor-centric approach to development cooperation runs counter to the principle of country ownership, which is broadly understood as comprising the aid-receiving states' commitment to '[e]xercise leadership in developing and implementing their national development strategies through broad consultative processes', on the one hand, and the donor states' commitment to '[r]espect partner [beneficiary] country leadership and help strengthen their capacity to exercise it'.[402] The UN Secretary-General pointed out that leaving no-one behind, as the 2030 Agenda enjoins, entails directing international attention and action, specifically development cooperation, towards vulnerable countries and supporting their 'capacity to enact and finance their development strategies and advance poverty eradication and other [SDGs]'.[403]

---

[398] International Development Strategy for the Second United Nations Development Decade, UNGA Res 2626 (XXV) (21 December 76), para 43.

[399] See, eg, Copenhagen Declaration on Social Development, A/CONF.166/9 (1995), Commitment 9, para (l); Johannesburg Declaration on Sustainable Development and Plan of Implementation of the World Summit on Sustainable Development, A/CONF.199/20 (2002), Part X (Means of Implementation), para 85(a); Monterrey Consensus on Financing for Development, A/CONF.198/11 (2002), para 42.

[400] CESCR, GC3, para 14.

[401] Clemens and Moss (n 380) 18 (italics in the original).

[402] OECD, *Paris Declaration on Aid Effectiveness* (2005), Part II (Partnership Commitments), paras 14 and 15.

[403] Secretary-General, 'Special Edition' (n 7) para 79.

COMMENTARY ON THE TARGETS   789

Similar to the earlier discussion on SDT in international trade law, target 10.b is likely to confront implementation and monitoring difficulties, not least because a clear legal obligation has yet to be adequately articulated to complement this political and moral commitment. Such a legal basis might nevertheless be forthcoming, through the Draft RTD Convention, which adopts almost *verbatim* target 10.b in its provision concerning the implementation of states' duty to cooperate for development.[404] This ongoing treaty-making process is perhaps the opportune time to revisit and possibly revise the 0.7 per cent aid target, which, according to Clemens and Moss, was determined arbitrarily 'based on a series of assumptions that no longer are true, and justified by a model that is no longer considered credible'.[405]

Another implicit assumption in target 10.b—that FDI would serve the beneficiary countries' needs—also requires further scrutiny. The academic literature on the relationship between international investment law and sustainable development has grown considerably in the past two or three decades, concurrent with the exponential increase in bilateral investment treaties (BITs) and the consolidation of investment treaty arbitration jurisprudence, which includes disputes involving public policy issues such as environmental and human rights protection vis-à-vis fair and equitable treatment (FET) of investors. Given space constraints, I will focus my comments, first, on the initial debates surrounding the *Salini* test, which deals with whether the existence of a treaty-protected investment depends on demonstrated contribution to the host state's economic development, and second, on the ongoing efforts to draft international investment agreements (IIAs) that recognize and integrate sustainable development concerns in all its three dimensions.

The *Salini* test enumerates criteria for defining an 'investment' and conditions determining whether such investment is entitled to the protections afforded by an IIA: (i) contribution of assets; (ii) certain duration of performance of the contract; (iii) participation in the risks of the transaction; and (iv) contribution to the economic development of the host state.[406] The fourth element is most relevant here, since target 10.b presupposes that global financial flows like FDI would help 'States where the need is greatest' in pursuing their national development plans and programmes. By measuring total resource flows *for* development, indicator 10.b.1 implies that ODA, FDI, and other financial flows should[407] serve development purposes. Remarkably, this last element, which the *Salini* arbitral tribunal itself added, albeit without sufficient explanation, is the one that became controversial.[408] Treatments by subsequent arbitrators[409] agreeing

---

[404] Draft RTD Convention, art 13(4)(e).

[405] Clemens and Moss (n 380) 3.

[406] *Salini et al v Morocco* ICSID Case No ARB/00/4 (23 July 2001) Decision on Jurisdiction, para 52.

[407] Whether such flows *would, in fact,* result to development is an empirical matter to be established rather than a 'given' that is presumed as a matter of law. Ingo Venzke has helpfully highlighted the problem in the latter approach.

[408] See DA Desierto, 'Development as an International Right: Investment in the New Trade-Based IIAs' (2012) 3 Trade, Law and Development 296, 313; A Grabowski, 'The Definition of Investment under the ICSID Convention: A Defense of Salini' (2014) 15 Chicago Journal of International Law 287, 290–91; D Tamada, 'Must Investments Contribute to the Development of the Host State? The Salini Test Scrutinised' in P Szwedo and others (eds), *Law and Development: Balancing Principles and Values* (Springer Nature 2019) 102.

[409] *Joy Mining v Egypt* ICSID Case No. ARB/03/11 (6 August 2004) Award on Jurisdiction; *Helnan International Hotels v Egypt* ICSID Case No. ARB/05/19 (17 October 2006) Decision of the Tribunal on Objection to Jurisdiction.

with the addition of the development criterion posit that it has a textual justification: the Preamble to the International Centre for Settlement of Investment Disputes (ICSID) Convention[410] mentions 'the role of private international investment' in relation to 'the need for international cooperation for development'. Tribunals rejecting the 'development criterion' contend, among others, that it can already be subsumed by[411] or presumed from[412] the three other factors/elements. This divergence remains unresolved.

Another recurring criticism against IIAs is that they impose burdens on host states and grant investors and investments with rights, but without creating any corresponding obligations. This critique becomes amplified when host states assert their *right to regulate*[413]—to prevent or mitigate adverse environmental and/or social impacts of FDI—and end up, in some cases, getting hauled to arbitration proceedings and made to incur financial liabilities, thereby potentially resulting to a regulatory chill.[414]

Nonetheless, efforts moving international investment law towards greater sensitivity to these public interest and sustainable development concerns seem underway. Several authors have closely studied and reported on the rising trend in recent years among trade and investment treaties to include separate chapters and/or express provisions addressing 'non-economic' matters, such as labour rights and natural resources management, and to thereby treat economic, environmental, and social issues in a more integrated manner.[415] Additionally, some of these new trade and investment agreements contain provisions concerning development cooperation rules that could be helpful in legalizing (or hardening) obligations relating to aid, in parallel to reinforcing existing duties concerning market access and investment promotion and protection. For example, the 2012 interim Economic Partnership Agreement between the EU and the Eastern and Southern Africa (ESA) states contain an entire chapter on 'Economic Cooperation and Development' and its last provision states: 'The EC Party shall put at the disposal of ESA financial assistance to contribute to implement the programmes and projects to be developed under the areas of cooperation identified in this Agreement and relevant chapters and under the detailed Development Matrix.'[416]

---

[410] Convention on the Settlement of Investment Disputes between States and Nationals of Other States, 575 UNTS 159 (1965).

[411] *LESI-Dipenta v Algeria* ICSID Case No. ARB/03/8 (10 January 2005) Award.

[412] *Quiborax S.A. et al v Plurinational State of Bolivia* ICSID Case No ARB/06/2 (27 September 2012) Decision on Jurisdiction.

[413] See C Titi, *The Right to Regulate in International Investment Law* (Nomos 2014); Y Levashova, *The Right of States to Regulate in International Investment Law: The Search for Balance between Public Interest and Fair and Equitable Treatment* (Wolters Kluwer 2019).

[414] See A Schram and others, 'Internalisation of International Investment Agreements in Public Policymaking: Developing a Conceptual Framework of Regulatory Chill' (2018) 9 Global Policy 193; K Tienhaara, 'Regulatory Chill in a Warming World: The Threat to Climate Policy Posed by Investor–State Dispute Settlement' (2018) 7 Transnational Environmental Law 229; AM Alenezi, 'Preventing the Regulatory Chill of International Investment Law and Arbitration' (2020) 9 International Law Research 85. But see SW Schill, 'Do Investment Treaties Chill Unilateral State Regulation to Mitigate Climate Change?' (2007) 24 Journal of International Arbitration 469.

[415] See, eg, M-C Cordonier Segger, *Crafting Trade and Investment Accords for Sustainable Development: Athena's Treaties* (OUP 2021); L Johnson and others, 'Aligning International Investment Agreements with the Sustainable Development Goals' (2019) 58 Columbia Journal of Transnational Law 58; H Mann, 'Reconceptualizing International Investment Law: Its Role in Sustainable Development' (2013) 17 Lewis & Clark Law Review 521.

[416] See, eg, Interim Economic Partnership Agreement between the EU and the Eastern and Southern Africa States, art 52, 'Financial undertakings' (2012).

Still, there remains scepticism about the suitability and potency of international human rights law to guide states' conduct relating to ODA and FDI. Part of the reason is that under contemporary international investment law, and international law more generally, foreign investors, even those possessing resources and power greater than several developing countries, are non-state actors, who do not and cannot bear international legal obligations. Moreover, the concepts of redistribution and redistributive equality, which are necessary to realize the SDGs and address the defining challenges of our time (ie poverty, inequality, climate change), 'have remained un- or under-theorised in human rights law',[417] and their links to the duties of international cooperation and assistance have yet to be fully explored and established as well.

10. **Target 10.c By 2030, reduce to less than 3 per cent the transaction costs of migrant remittances and eliminate remittance corridors with costs higher than 5 per cent**

a) Source of target

Target 10.c, like other SDG 10 targets, had been moved from one goal to another during the drafting process. Reducing transaction costs of remittances was an original target under the equality promotion goal. In the OWG-12 zero draft, where it was proposed as an MOI target for the goal on reducing inequalities within and among countries, the version read:

> 17.34 by 2030 reduce to 5% or below the transaction costs of migrants' remittances, including regulatory and administrative costs

During the same session, the MGoS proposed a related target under the goal regarding the promotion of strong, inclusive, and sustainable economic growth and decent work for all. Their proposal was an amendment to the zero draft:

> 8.15 by 2030 reduce the overall costs in migration processes, *guarantee human rights of persons regardless of their geographical condition, regulate the conditions of migration to ensure compliance with decent work provisions,* and minimize transaction costs of remittances

By the time of the OWG-13, the target pertaining to remittances had returned to the goal on reducing inequality within and between countries. The Final Proposal stated:

> 10.c by 2030, reduce to less than 3% the transaction costs of migrant remittances and eliminate remittance corridors with costs higher than 5%

---

[417] Vandenhole (n 99) 235–36.

792 SDG 10

b) Empirical analysis: domestic and international efforts

The volume of personal remittances—which 'tend to be a more reliable, less volatile' income source—has surpassed the combined ODA and FDI amounts, whose growth has stagnated in the past several years.[418] As the UN reported, 'remittances to low- and lower-middle-income countries [in 2016] were more than three times the amount of ODA and were greater than ODA and FDI combined'.[419] Remittances have now indeed become 'the largest source of external financing' in low- and middle-income countries, as '[t]otal global remittances reached $689 billion in 2018, up from $633 billion in 2017'.[420] Remarkably, similar to other types of external finance, remittances data are sometimes reported as part of SDG 17 instead of SDG 10. In the 2017 SDG report, updates on the progress in SDG 17 targets included the fact that developing countries received 75 per cent of the $575 billion total international remittances in 2016, although these figures still represented a drop for a second consecutive year, since remittances to developing countries have been 'declining by 2.4 per cent over 2015'.[421]

The 2018 record-high amount was more than [thrice] the amount of ODA received by this group of countries and 'was significantly larger than [FDI] (if China is excluded)'.[422] This upward trend, however, risks a reversal or a slowdown due to the COVID-19 pandemic: 'Reductions in remittances as well as in tourism and domestic resource mobilisation ... severely curtail the amount of financing available to developing countries to put economic and social support packages in place.'[423] In contrast, ODA is expected to be resilient in 2020 and 2021, and it may even increase during this period.[424]

Problematically, the positive trend of increasing migrant remittances has not been matched by a decrease in remittance costs, which are crucial to maximizing any positive developmental impact of this resource flow. Even though there has been some decline between 2012 and 2015, 'the cost of sending money across international borders remains high', averaging 7.5 per cent of the amount remitted in 2015[425] and around 7.2 per cent in 2017.[426] While this percentage has slightly declined further to 7 per cent in 2019,[427] it remains significantly higher than the 3 per cent that target 10.c aims for. According to the UN:

> On average, post offices and money transfer operators charge over 6 per cent of the amount remitted; commercial banks charge 11 per cent; and the global average cost of transferring money is just over 7 per cent, according to World Bank Remittance Prices

---

[418] SDG Report 2018, 31.
[419] ibid.
[420] SDG Report 2019, 57.
[421] SDG Report 2017, 55.
[422] SDG Report 2019, 57.
[423] OECD, 'Learning from Crises, Building Resilience', Development Co-operation Report 2020 (2020), 24 (citations omitted).
[424] OECD, *Six Decades* (n 392) 13.
[425] SDG Report 2016, 31.
[426] SDG Report 2018, 9.
[427] SDG Report 2019, 57.

COMMENTARY ON THE TARGETS 793

Worldwide. While the cost of sending money has declined gradually since 2008, all three of these remittance services providers charge significantly more than the 3 per cent target. New and improved technologies, such as prepaid cards and mobile operators, charge lower fees for sending money home (between 2 per cent and 4 per cent), but are not yet widely available or used in many remittance corridors.[428]

Some states in the Global North, which typically host migrant workers, have included their support of fintech companies that innovate cost-effective payment solutions as part of meeting target 10.c.[429] Meanwhile, the Swedish Consumer Agency operates 'Money Sweden', an online service that compares remittance costs to enable migrants to send money more easily and help push down market prices through transparency and competition.[430]

c) Critique

By focusing on lowering remittance costs, target 10.c and its related indicator seek to maximize the net amount accruing to migrants and their families. This objective presupposes the valuable contribution of remittances to (i) migrant workers' income growth, (ii) potential reduction of disparities in income distribution within countries, (iii) economic growth of many developing countries that are net senders of migrant workers, and (iv) potential narrowing of the income gap between developed and developing states. These interrelated changes are tackled in Objective 20 of the Global Compact, through which states commit 'to promote faster, safer and cheaper remittances by further developing existing conducive policy and regulatory environments that enable competition, regulation and innovation on the remittance market' and

to optimize the transformative impact of remittances on the well-being of migrant workers and their families, as well as on the sustainable development of countries, while respecting that remittances constitute an important source of private capital and cannot be equated to other international financial flows, such as foreign direct investment, official development assistance or other public sources of financing for development.[431]

The heads of state and government who adopted the AAAA made similar commitments, recognizing that migrants, not least because of their personal remittances to their families, contribute positively to inclusive growth and sustainable development not only in their countries of origin but also in transit and destination countries as well.

ILO instruments constitute the relevant international legal framework for target 10.c. Convention No 97 (Migration for Employment Convention (Revised)), article 9 enjoins States Parties to allow 'the transfer of such part of the earnings and savings

---

[428] SDG Report 2017, 39.
[429] United Kingdom, VNR 2019.
[430] Sweden, VNR 2021, 136.
[431] Global Compact, para 36.

of the migrant for employment as the migrant may desire', although this undertaking is qualified/limited by the clause 'taking into account the limits allowed by national laws and regulations concerning export and import of currency'. To some extent, this obligation's language itself weakens its normative force, as it provides that the ILO Member 'undertakes to permit ... the transfer', which thereby subjects it to similar constraints faced by ICESCR article 2(1). Complementing CO97 is the ILO Multilateral Framework on Labour Migration, which comprises non-binding principles and guidelines for a 'rights-based approach to labour migration'. One guideline to give practical effect to the principle[432]—that migration contributes to the development of both the individual migrant (and her family) and the states (origin and destination alike)—is 'reducing the costs of remittance transfers, including by facilitating accessible financial services, reducing transaction fees, providing tax incentives and promoting greater competition between financial institutions'. Significantly, the ILO-endorsed migrant-centred and rights-based approach to remittances potentially bolsters target 10.c, since this approach considers 'vital to improving migrant workers' incomes and capacity to contribute to development' the abovementioned principles underpinning the goal to reduce inequalities, namely, non-discrimination and equality of treatment.

E. Final Observations on Targets, Indicators, and Data

Indicators 'that are amenable to disaggregation to reveal inter-group disparities and the possible presence of discrimination' are important so that progress on efforts to address 'vulnerability, insecurity, and exclusion' and to ensure 'meaningful participation, voice and accountability' can be appropriately measured and monitored. The TST identified data disaggregation as one of the ways to address inequalities in the post-2015 agenda, because '[s]etting [tailored] targets to reduce gaps [between social and economic groups] (e.g. in health and education outcomes, in incomes and employment) will ensure that the most deprived are not "left until last"'. One NGO supported this view, stating that the value-added of the 'leave no-one behind' principle 'will be in its intermediate application, and in particular the setting of 'stepping stone' equity targets ... with a focus on closing the gaps', such that attention and action are directed 'on the most marginalised from the outset, making it harder to simply focus on the easy wins, leave the difficult work to later or revert to the status quo'.[433]

Measuring and monitoring progress, as well as disaggregating data, do not only serve to ensure achievement of the Goals but they also, more crucially, form part of states' international legal obligations under ICESCR article 2(2). According to the CESCR, because effective monitoring involves evaluating 'both the steps taken and the results achieved' in eliminating discrimination, '[n]ational ... policies and plans should use

---

[432] Principle 15.
[433] Christian Aid, 'Leave No One Behind—From Goals to Implementation' (2015) 12 <https://www.christian aid.org.uk/sites/default/files/2017-08/leave-noone-behind-june-2015.pdf> accessed 20 August 2021.

appropriate indicators and benchmarks, disaggregated on the basis of the prohibited grounds of discrimination'.[434] Indeed, the very absence of sufficient data regarding the inequalities and disadvantages confronting racial minorities, migrants, persons with disabilities, and other vulnerable groups is, in itself, 'an indication of their marginalization'.[435] Making concrete the rhetoric to leave no-one behind will be challenging, as the UN itself acknowledged, 'because disaggregated data tell us that the benefits of development are far from equally shared' and, in order to realize the commitment to reach first those who are furthest behind, 'data and indicators [addressing] specific groups within a population, including the most vulnerable' are vital.[436]

However, it is perhaps also prudent to not excessively rely on metrics, targets, and indicators, given that 'quantification reduces complex and intangible visions—such as development that is inclusive—into concrete measurable objectives' and thereby distorts incentives and behaviours of relevant actors.[437] Underlying Fukuda-Parr's critique is the claim that the SDGs, like the MDGs before them, do not and cannot replace 'a consensus development agenda'[438]—which should presumably be contained in an legally binding international instrument—that would set out more concrete rights (of both individuals and states) and adequately delineate responsibilities of states and non-state actors alike. As I repeatedly discussed in this chapter, the Draft Convention on the Right to Development can become such an instrument, given its provisions that address the reduction of inequalities within and among states, and that are thus important in enhancing SDG 10's international law foundations.

V. Conclusion

The complexity and scope of the issue and sub-issues that SDG 10 seeks to address are both its strength and weakness. In terms of ambitiousness, especially at inception, it aims high, but past and current trends in its implementation do not quite match the ambition. From an international law perspective, the targets dealing with intra-country inequalities find strong bases in multiple human rights treaties and instruments, which enshrine, among others, the right to non-discrimination. In contrast, one finds less solid legal foundations for the targets concerning inter-country inequalities, which have thus far not been governed, or only minimally, by either treaty or customary law—indicative of the broader critique that international law, with its emphasis on the legal fiction of sovereign equality of its subjects, glosses over real-world material disparities among states. The general duty to cooperate arguably underpins the MOI targets, but their grounding in international economic law requires further scrutiny and development.

---

[434] CESCR, GC20, para 41.
[435] TST, Equality Brief (n 53) 1.
[436] SDG Report 2016, 11.
[437] Fukuda-Parr (n 95) 49.
[438] Fukuda-Parr and others (n 55) 115.

796 SDG 10

Although it proclaims to tackle inequalities within and among states, Goal 10 does not genuinely and adequately recognize the intricate link between the two, thereby also failing to address global (*contra* international) inequality. What could bind together these topics, and perhaps enhance the achievement of the targets, is a greater emphasis on states' duties of international cooperation and assistance. Interestingly, progress on codification of development-related rights and obligations has been taking place in international human rights law, rather than the international economic legal order, where parallel efforts largely seem unfruitful thus far. The massive implications of this choice—whether from the perspective of the fragmentation of international law or the formation of 'international sustainable development law'—are beyond the scope of this chapter. I surmise, though, that it could offer better prospects for solidifying the public international law dimensions of SDG 10, particularly the targets on inter-state inequalities and on MOI. The irony is that the 2030 Agenda envisions states' implementation of the SDGs to require an enabling international *economic* environment and strengthened and enhanced *global economic* governance, suggesting that some, if not most, of the actions and reforms needed to achieve sustainable development depend on and are shaped by the international economic order and, necessarily, its underlying legal system.

The notion of an *enabling* international economic environment can be interpreted as necessitating active or positive efforts rather than a mere *laissez-faire* approach. To draw from states' practices, in implementing their inequality-related international human rights obligations at the domestic level, I submit that 'to enable' signifies first, a recognition of material disparities among states and the vulnerabilities of many persons across these states, and second, more crucially, actions on the part of the relatively more capable, to correct the imbalance and empower or capacitate the weaker states to effectively participate in and derive benefits from international economic arrangements. The crystallizing right to development reminds us that the human person stands at the centre of these efforts to improve the capacity of all states to pursue development. Moreover, as the Expert Mechanism emphatically framed one of the key normative principles of the 1986 Declaration on the Right to Development: 'Development is not merely a privilege enjoyed by human beings and peoples, nor are they mere subjects of charity.' Another normative principle, which I think provides legal foundation for enjoining powerful states and international organizations to engage in 'affirmative action', at the international level conceives of the state as agent of all persons under its jurisdiction 'to demand respect for the right to development from other States and international organizations'. The imperfections in the structure of Goal 10 and its targets and indicators could thus still be rectified by the progressive development of international law. In this process, the 2030 Agenda can at least be credited for according a long-overdue attention by the international community to the wicked problem of intersecting inequalities and its impacts on all three dimensions—economic, social, environmental—of sustainable development.

Answering the questions posed at the beginning of this chapter reveals (i) the potency of international human rights law to tackle many, but not (yet) all, facets of inequalities among individuals and groups of persons within a given country; and (ii) the limitation of the existing international legal framework, specifically that which regulates global economic relations, to address contemporary disparities in both outcomes and opportunities, among states, some of which are rooted in historical injustices. These shortcomings should invite legal scholars to revisit and further examine the premises of international law, with the aim of augmenting the discipline's ability to address the still-growing gaps among peoples and states. This appraisal is especially urgent in the face of increasing interdependence among human society, the natural environment, and the global economy. Re-emphasizing and elaborating the duty to cooperate and activating the untapped potential of international organizations in this regard are crucial to this endeavour.

SDG 11

'Make Cities and Human Settlements Inclusive, Safe, Resilient, and Sustainable'

Hannah Birkenkötter

I. Introduction

Amongst the Sustainable Development Goals (SDGs), SDG 11 occupies a special place. It is the only goal that concerns an entity of governance—cities and human settlements—and thereby both an actor and a physical space. While actors at different governance levels are called upon to implement the 2030 Agenda as part of the 'Global Partnership for Sustainable Development' (SDG 17.16), SDG 11 singles out cities and human settlements as entities of particular relevance. Human settlements and city networks have been important at various times throughout history, ranging from antique agorae to medieval city networks and beyond. At the same time, contemporary international law scholarship has until recently largely neglected cities both as an object of international legal regulation as well as in their role as actors on the international plane.[1]

Human settlements have been the object of international regulation at least since the first UN Conference on Human Settlements in 1976, even if regulation of cities and human settlements through international norms and standards can be traced back further. With increased regulation of human settlements, cities as governance entities have also emerged as actors in their own right, claiming agency instead of being reduced to mere objects of regulation. In recent decades, important city networks on specific topics such as climate change or urban crime have emerged as new actors on the international scene.[2] Part of this evolution can be credited to the United Nations'

---

[1] There are few publications that explicitly treat cities from an international law perspective, but their number has increased recently. See HP Aust and J Nijman (eds), *Research Handbook on International Law and Cities* (Edward Elgar 2021); HP Aust, *Das Recht der globalen Stadt. Grenzüberschreitende Dimensionen kommunaler Selbstverwaltung* (Mohr Siebeck 2017); A Beaudouin, *Droit international des villes* (Mare & Martin 2021); S Bouteligier, *Cities, Networks, and Global Environmental Governance. Spaces of Innovation, Places of Leadership* (Routledge 2013). An account of the role of the city in the encounter of international law and development, using the example of Bogotá's transformation, is given by L Eslava, *Local Space, Global Life. The Everyday Operation of International Law and Development* (CUP 2015). An early landmark publication on the role of cities in global governance is S Sassen, *The Global City* (2nd edn, Princeton University Press 2001).

[2] On climate change, see, eg, the C40 network <https://www.c40.org>accessed 30 December 2021; on urban crime see the Global Network on Safer Cities <https://unhabitat.org/network/global-network-on-safer-cit ies>accessed 30 December 2021. On the role of city networks in general see SR Foster and C Swiney, 'City Networks and the Glocalization of Urban Governance' in Aust and Nijman (eds) (n 1) 368–80.

(UN) human settlement agenda. SDG 11 needs to be read in conjunction with the UN's Habitat agenda, notably with the outcome of the Habitat III conference in 2016, the 'New Urban Agenda'.[3] The United Nations Human Settlements Programme (UN-Habitat) is the lead agency within the UN system on human settlements and thus is instrumental in monitoring the implementation of both SDG 11 as well as the New Urban Agenda.

In addition, SDG 11 is intimately connected to several other goals as well as to other fields of international law. The roots of the human settlements agenda can be traced back to the 1972 UN Conference on the Human Environment in Stockholm, and since the 1990s there has been a strong connection between the human settlements agenda and the environmental agenda. In addition, SDG 11 references cultural and natural heritage protection and disaster risk reduction (targets 11.4 and 11.5). The very first target, target 11.1, aims at ensuring access for all to adequate, safe, and affordable housing. The right to adequate housing is an integral part of the right to an adequate standard of living, enshrined in article 11 of the International Covenant on Economic, Social and Cultural Rights (ICESCR), even though this connection has not always been made explicit throughout the history of the UN human settlements agenda.

The COVID-19 pandemic has been a huge setback to achieving SDG 11. In 2020, over 90 per cent of COVID-19 cases were occurring in urban areas,[4] even though only about 55 per cent of the world's population lives in urban areas.[5] The global economy is expected to contract by a total of 3 per cent according to the latest World Cities Report, UN-Habitat's flagship publication.[6] With most economic activity concentrated in cities, this will have both short-term and long-term effects: short-term impacts include increased unemployment, lower wages, increasing poverty, and strained health systems with unequal access, which in turn will exacerbate long-term consequences that might include severe bankruptcies, less integration into the global value chain, and consequently an erosion of productive capacities.[7] At the same time, it might be asked to what extent economic impact ought to outweigh other dimensions of SDG 11. The COVID-19 pandemic has been framed by the UN system, in particular the Secretary-General, as an opportunity to 'build back better'.[8] This applies also to SDG 11.

---

[3] Adopted at the UN Conference on Housing and Sustainable Urban Development (Habitat III) in Quito, Ecuador, on 20 September 2016 and endorsed by the UN General Assembly on 23 December 2016, UN Doc A/Res/71/256. The New Urban Agenda consists of the Quito Declaration and the Quito Implementation Plan for the New Urban Agenda.

[4] UN Secretary-General, Policy Brief: COVID-19 in an Urban World <https://www.un.org/sites/un2.un.org/files/sg_policy_brief_covid_urban_world_july_2020.pdf> accessed 30 December 2021, p 2.

[5] As of 2018, cf UN Department of Economic and Social Affairs, 'World Urbanization Prospects—The 2018 Revision' <https://population.un.org/wup/Publications/Files/WUP2018-KeyFacts.pdf> accessed 30 December 2021.

[6] UN-Habitat, 'World Cities Report 2020: The Value of Sustainable Urbanization' <https://unhabitat.org/sites/default/files/2020/10/wcr_2020_report.pdf> accessed 30 December 2021, ch 1.

[7] ibid p 88.

[8] UN Secretary-General, 'Socio-economic Impact Report 2020' <https://www.un.org/sites/un2.un.org/files/sg_report_socio-economic_impact_of_covid19.pdf> accessed 30 December 2021, p 2; specifically relating to urban settings UN Secretary-General, 'Policy Brief: COVID-19 in an Urban World' (n 4).

This commentary on SDG 11 proceeds as follows. In Section II, the *travaux préparatoires* are examined. Since SDG 11 is tightly linked to the UN human settlements agenda, this includes a brief outline of the Habitat agenda in the UN system. This will be followed by an overall commentary on SDG 11, linking it to pertinent questions and sub-fields of international law, before Section IV provides commentary on each of the targets and their indicators.

II. *Travaux Préparatoires*

In a narrow sense, the *travaux préparatoires* of SDG 11 only concern the years 2012–2014, when the Sustainable Development Goals were negotiated. However, SDG 11 cannot be examined independently of the New Urban Agenda, which was adopted in 2016 and is explicitly understood as 'contribut[ing] to the implementation and localization of the 2030 Agenda'. The New Urban Agenda is thus placed in the context of the 2030 Agenda for Sustainable Development, which had been adopted just one year prior.[9] The New Urban Agenda as the outcome of the Habitat III conference in turn cannot be examined independently of the Habitat Agenda that dates back to at least 1976, when the first UN conference on human settlements took place.[10] Since 1976, two more global Habitat conferences took place in 1996 (Habitat II) and in 2016 (Habitat III), in addition to the regular meetings of the UN-Habitat Assembly (until 2001 the UN Commission on Human Settlements; and between 2001 and 2019 the UN-Habitat Governing Council).[11] Each of the three Habitat conferences were also the impetus for institutional changes within the UN system. This section thus proceeds in two steps. It first provides an overview of the main developments on the UN's human settlement agenda and shows links between UN-Habitat and the UN's sustainability agenda. In

---

[9] New Urban Agenda, Quito Declaration, UN Doc A/Res/71/256, Annex, para 6: 'We take full account of the milestone achievements of the year 2015, in particular the 2030 Agenda for Sustainable Development', and para 9: 'The implementation of the New Urban Agenda contributes to the implementation and localization of the 2030 Agenda on Sustainable Development in an integrated manner, and to the achievement of the Sustainable Development Goals and targets.'

[10] United Nations Conference on Human Settlements, UN Doc A/CONF.70/15. Note that human settlements had been subject to discussion years before the Habitat Conference.

[11] The UN Commission on Human Settlements was established by the General Assembly in 1977, following the 1976 UN Conference on Human Settlements. Resolution 32/162 transformed the previous Committee on Housing, Building and Planning into a Commission on Human Settlements that should report to the General Assembly through the Economic and Social Council and was to be serviced by a newly established Secretariat unit, the United Nations Centre for Human Settlements (Habitat), cf UN Doc A/Res/32/162. The UN Human Settlements institutions were substantially reformed in 2001, following the 1996 Habitat II Conference and the 2001 General Assembly Special Session to Review the Implementation of the Habitat Agenda, cf A/Res/S-25/2 (Declaration on Cities and Other Human Settlements in the New Millennium). The General Assembly replaced the Commission on Human Settlements and its secretariat, the Centre for Human Settlements (Habitat), with a United Nations Human Settlements Programme (UN-Habitat), consisting of a Governing Council replacing the former Commission and a subsidiary organ of the General Assembly, and the Centre for Human Settlements with a Secretariat serving UN-Habitat as a UN programme, cf UN Doc A/Res/56/206. In 2018, the General Assembly dissolved the Governing Council and replaced it with the UN-Habitat Assembly, an inter-governmental body with universal membership, cf UN Docs A/Res/73/239, para 2, and A/73/726 (Report on the work of the Open-ended Working Group established by the Chair of the Committee of Permanent Representatives to the United Nations Human Settlements Programme (UN-Habitat)).

a second step, the negotiations of SDG 11 are traced. The Habitat III conference and the contents of the New Urban Agenda are treated in Section III (Commentary on the Goal), as Habitat III took place *after* the SDGs were adopted and are not counted as part of the *travaux préparatoires* for this reason.

A. The UN-Habitat Agenda: From Vancouver to Istanbul and Beyond

Interest in human settlement policies within the UN system first emerged as early as in the late 1940s, when a small Housing, Building and Planning Branch was established in the UN Division of Social Affairs.[12] Over the next two and a half decades, human settlement policies were discussed and adopted in various organs within the UN system, and consolidated into a UN Long-range International Programme of Concerted Action in the Field of Housing and Related Facilities in 1959.[13] Institutionally, these debates were flanked by the establishment of a UN Group of Experts in 1962, as well as a UN Committee on Housing, Building and Planning as an inter-governmental body.[14] The 1976 UN Conference on Human Settlements thus constitutes both a 'culminating point of a growing international co-operation' on matters of housing and human settlement policies,[15] as well as the foundation for the further institutionalization of human settlements as an international policy field.

The 1970s are of some importance to the UN system as a whole as this decade saw for the first time several global conferences on topics that still are of great influence today. This includes the 1972 UN Conference on the Human Environment, also known as the Stockholm Conference, which is considered foundational for the internationalization of environmental politics and international environmental law.[16] The Stockholm Conference also had an important impact on the UN human settlements agenda. Its Principle 15 proclaimed that '[p]lanning must be applied to human settlements and urbanization with a view to avoiding adverse effects on the environment and obtaining maximum social, economic and environmental benefits for all'.[17] The Stockholm Outcome clearly anticipated that human settlement planning was indispensable to ensure environmental protection and contains several recommendations

---

[12] R Harris and C Giles, 'A Mixed Message: The Agents and Forms of International Housing Policy, 1945–1973' (2003) 27 Habitat International 167–91, at 171. See on this also G Wadlig, 'The International (Un)Making of "Tenure Security"', dissertation, NYU School of Law (2022, on file with author). The first UN entity to provide support and aid in, amongst other things, housing issues was the UN Relief and Rehabilitation Administration (UNRAA), which was terminated in 1947, cf E Weissmann, 'Human Settlements—Struggle for Identity' (1978) 3(3/4) Habitat International 227–41, 228–29.

[13] ibid 231.

[14] ibid 232–33.

[15] ibid 228.

[16] WB Chambers, *Interlinkages and the Effectiveness of Multilateral Environmental Agreements* (Tokyo United Nations University Press 2008) 17–24. Other important conferences from the 1970s include the 1974 World Population Conference, the 1975 First World Conference on Women, and the 1978 Conference on International Human Rights.

[17] Declaration of the United Nations Conference on the Human Environment, Principle 15, UN Doc A/CONF.48/14/Rev.1.

regarding human settlements. These recommendations include, crucially, that various UN programmes should provide technical assistance in the field of urban planning at the request of governments, that resources for human settlement programmes should be mobilized, and that a conference on human settlements should be held under UN auspices.[18] Human settlements and environmental protection were thus linked since the inception of the Habitat agenda at the UN, even if the two policy fields evolved in parallel for several years.

This is so in part because consolidating human settlements as a policy field with its own institutions was subject to a distinct process within the UN, building on previous work in this area. Following a four-year preparatory process, the first UN Conference on Human Settlements took place in 1976 in Vancouver, Canada.[19] Its outcome consists of a declaration and a set of recommendations for national action and international cooperation. The Vancouver Declaration needs to be read in the broader context of newly independent states' attempt to install a New International Economic Order, which is explicitly referenced in the Declaration.[20] Thus far, international human settlements policies had primarily aimed at providing assistance to states, with such policies being viewed as a domestic prerogative. Accordingly, international cooperation in the Vancouver Outcome is seen exclusively as 'support[ing] national action'.[21] At the same time, the Vancouver Outcome explicitly establishes a link to international human rights law, specifically the Universal Declaration of Human Rights,[22] and its Declaration of Principles explicitly links human settlement policies to satisfying basic human needs in a 'frame of freedom, dignity and social justice'.[23] This connection between international human rights and ensuring that basic needs are met in human settlement policies are still guiding principles for today's Habitat agenda, even if the link to the New International Economic Order has waned.[24]

The Vancouver Outcome included a call to strengthen international cooperation to support domestic action on human settlements and provide technical assistance at the request of governments. To comply with this call, several institutional changes followed, most importantly the establishment of a Commission on Human Settlements as a functional commission of the Economic and Social Council, and a United Nations Centre for Human Settlements (Habitat) within the UN Secretariat.[25] The Centre was to assist the Commission on Human Settlements in its work, but it also received a mandate to initiate its own human settlement projects and to coordinate human settlement activities throughout the UN system, as well as to serve as a focal point for information

---

[18] Action Plan for the Human Environment, Recommendations 1(a), 2(2)(b), 17, UN Doc A/CONF.48/14/Rev.1.

[19] Report of Habitat: United Nations Conference on Human Settlements, UN Doc A/CONF.70/15.

[20] 'It is therefore essential to implement urgently the New International Economic Order', cf Vancouver Declaration, UN Doc A/CONF.70/15, p 6, para 14.

[21] cf UN Doc A/Res/32/162, Part I, para (b) (resolution establishing the Commission on Human Settlements).

[22] Recommendations for national action, A/CONF.70/15, p 10, para 3.

[23] Declaration of Principles, contained in A/CONF.70/15, p 4, para 1.

[24] On the fate of the New International Economic Order cf A Anghie, *Imperialism, Sovereignty and the Making of International Law* (CUP 2004) ch 4.

[25] UN Doc A/Res/32/162.

804 SDG 11

collection. It was also charged with managing the funds of the United Nations Habitat and Human Settlements Foundation (UNHHSF) which had been created two years prior and had been nestled under the umbrella of the UN Environment Programme (UNEP).[26] However, the impact of Habitat throughout the first two decades of its existence was stifled, in part due to a lack of financial and human resources and an overall lack of means of implementation in the Vancouver Outcome.[27]

In order to fund projects, Habitat cooperated with the UN Development Programme (UNDP) as well as with the World Bank. The World Bank had formulated its policy approach on urbanization in 1972, the same year in which the Stockholm Conference took place.[28] In this 1972 Sector Working Paper on urbanization, the World Bank committed to directly assist a number of urban centres—Bogota, San José, Klang Valley in Malaysia, and Singapore—and highlighted that it would cooperate with both the UNDP as well as the UN Centre for Housing, Building and Planning, which would be transformed into Habitat following the Vancouver Conference.[29] In turn, a collaboration with the UNEP as foreseen in the Vancouver Outcome did not materialize.[30] The Commission on Human Settlements did meet regularly, but the lack of funding seriously impeded any real policy impact the Commission might have had.

The World Bank urban policy of the 1970s and 1980s was marked by an increasing decentralization and a shift away from national governments as the primary entities responsible for urban development. This is part of a broader shift from interventionist strategies toward a free market-oriented approach that aimed at enabling public administration at the sub-national level to change conditions for private investment, instead of working with national governments.[31] In 1986, the World Bank, UNDP, and Habitat jointly launched an Urban Management Program to raise the profile of urban governance which, while marked by ideological differences between Habitat and the World Bank, ultimately introduced a neoliberal approach to urban governance.[32] All of these developments resulted in raising the profile of cities as actors in their own right throughout the 1980s and 1990s.[33]

The Habitat agenda received new impetus in 1996 with the Second United Nations Conference on Human Settlement (Habitat II).[34] Similar to the Habitat I conference, the Habitat II conference was one of several major world summits that marked the decade and generated several important policy

[26] UN Doc A/Res/32/162, part III, para 3 (c); for the creation of the UNHHSF cf UN Doc A/Res/3327 (XXIX).

[27] UN-Habitat, History and Mandate <https://unhabitat.org/history-mandate-role-in-the-un-system> accessed 30 December 2021; see also Wadlig (n 12).

[28] World Bank, Urbanization Sector Working Paper <https://documents1.worldbank.org/curated/en/9810914 68765865507/pdf/multi-page.pdf> accessed 30 December 2021.

[29] ibid 55–60.

[30] Wadlig (n 12).

[31] MGA Jones and P Ward, 'The World Bank's "New" Urban Management Programme: Paradigm Shift or Policy Continuity?' (1994) 18(3) Habitat International 33–51, especially 33–34.

[32] Wadlig (n 12).

[33] The transformation of the 'developmental state' that still marked the Vancouver Outcome through decentralization, emphasizing the importance of local authorities and thereby internationalizing them is addressed thoroughly by L Eslava, *Local Space, Global Life. The Everyday Operation of International Law and Development* (CUP 2015).

[34] Report of the United Nations Conference on Human Settlements (Habitat II), UN Doc A/CONF.165/14.

agendas.[35] All major world summits of the 1990s consolidated previous policy agendas and at the same time set the foundation for their further development. Habitat II is no exception. It built on the 1994 International Conference on Development and Population and was marked by two main topics: how to provide adequate shelter for all, and how to ensure 'safer, healthier and more livable, equitable, sustainable and productive' human settlements in an age of rapid urbanization.[36] The focus on 'sustainable human settlements' indicates a persistent link with the environmental agenda: sustainability had been the focus of the 1992 UN Conference on Environment and Development, also known as the 'Earth Summit', in Rio de Janeiro. At the same time, Habitat II marks a stark departure from Habitat I. Whereas in 1976, human settlements had not been defined and rural settlement had been prevalent in many parts of the world, a fact also reflected in the Vancouver Outcome, at the time of Habitat II, urbanization had moved to the forefront of human settlement considerations. In 1976, close to 38 per cent of the world's population lived in cities; this number had risen to 45 per cent by 1996 and was expected to (and in fact did) exceed 50 per cent a decade later.[37]

The focus on urban life brought different topics to the fore during Habitat II. For one, cities are the central entity of concern throughout the Istanbul Outcome, which is formally addressed to 'all settlements—large, medium and small',[38] but primarily has in view urban dwellings when focusing, for example, on lack of shelter and homelessness. Another topic that is notably absent from the Vancouver Outcome, but prevalent in the Istanbul Agenda, is safety and urban crime. Again, we can see here a shift to concerns for city dwellers. Following the Habitat II Agenda, cities also became more important actors in UN-Habitat's institutional set-up. While the Istanbul Outcome states that the primary responsibility for implementing the new Habitat Agenda would lie with governments,[39] city networks became more important in the following years. These networks had experienced a renaissance with the end of the Cold War[40] and now became more formalized partners. The most important institutionalization of cities as actors is the World Urban Forum, a merger of the former Urban Environment Forum and the International Forum on Urban Poverty.[41] It started as a 'non-legislative technical

[35] Major world conferences of that decade include the 1990 World Summit for Children and the 1990 World Conference on Education for All, the 1992 Conference on Environment and Development in Rio de Janeiro, the 1994 International Conference on Population and Development, the 1995 Fourth World Conference on Women in Beijing, the World Summit for Social Development in Copenhagen in the same year, and the World Food Summit in Rome in 1996.

[36] UN-Habitat, United Nations Conference on Human Settlements: Habitat II <https://www.un.org/en/conferences/habitat/istanbul1996> accessed 30 December 2021.

[37] The World Bank Data, Urban Population, available at <https://data.worldbank.org/indicator/SP.URB.TOTL.IN.ZS> accessed 30 December 2021.

[38] Report of the United Nations Conference on Human Settlements (Habitat II), UN Doc A/CONF.165/14, Habitat Agenda, para 7.

[39] Report of the United Nations Conference on Human Settlements (Habitat II), UN Doc A/CONF.165/14, Habitat Agenda, para 213.

[40] Aust (n 1) § 2, section IV.

[41] M Wortmann, 'United Nations Human Settlements Programme (UN- HABITAT)' in *Max Planck Encyclopedia of Public International Law* (2007) [online], para 7.

806   SDG 11

forum'[42] for experts and is today 'the premier global conference on sustainable urbanization', bringing together different actors including representatives of national, regional, and local governments, academics, business people, community leaders, and urban planners.[43]

The World Urban Forum was part of a broader restructuring of the human settlement architecture within the UN system in 2001. The main result of this restructuring was the establishment of UN-Habitat as a fully fledged UN programme (United Nations Human Settlements Programme, or UN-Habitat in short). The legal basis for these changes is contained in General Assembly resolution 56/206 of 21 December 2001.[44] This resolution provides for the following:

- Transformation of the Commission on Human Settlements into the Governing Council of UN-Habitat;
- Establishment of UN-Habitat as a subsidiary organ of the General Assembly;
- Transformation of the UN Centre for Human Settlements into the Secretariat of UN-Habitat under the direction of an Executive-Director at the level of UN Under-Secretary-General, elected by the General Assembly upon recommendation of the Secretary-General.

While resolution 56/206 significantly improved UN-Habitat's standing within the UN system institutionally, the budget was still amongst the lowest in the UN system, with only 5 per cent of UN-Habitat's budget as of 2007 coming from the regular UN budget and most of its funds coming from voluntary bilateral and multilateral contributions, from both states and local authorities.[45]

Cities further became the focus of UN activities through the Millennium Declaration and the Millennium Development Goals (MDGs). The MDGs provide an important backdrop for the negotiation of SDG 11, as the SDG process brought together the Rio process and the follow-up process to the MDGs.[46] In the Millennium Declaration, states committed to achieving, by 2020, 'a significant improvement in the lives of at least 100 million slum dwellers as proposed in the "Cities Without Slums" initiative'.[47] This commitment was transformed into target 7.D of the Millennium Development Goals: 'By 2020, to have achieved a significant improvement in the lives of at least 100 million slum dwellers', measured by one single indicator, namely the proportion

---

[42] UN General Assembly, Strengthening the mandate and status of the Commission on Human Settlements and the status, role, and functions of the United Nations Centre for Human Settlements (Habitat), UN Doc A/Res/56/206, Section B para 3.

[43] World Urban Forum <https://wuf.unhabitat.org> accessed 30 December 2021.

[44] UN General Assembly, Strengthening the mandate and status of the Commission on Human Settlements and the status, role and functions of the United Nations Centre for Human Settlements (Habitat), UN Doc A/Res/56/206.

[45] Wortmann (n 41) para 10.

[46] S Fukuda-Parr, 'Sustainable Development Goals' in TG Weiss and S Daws (eds), *The Oxford Handbook on the United Nations* (2 edn, OUP 2018) 764–78, 769.

[47] UN General Assembly, Millennium Declaration, UN Doc A/Res/55/2, para 19.

of urban population living in slums.[48] This single indicator has been criticized as it did not focus holistically on cities or urban governance, or on a rights-based approach, but simply on eliminating slums, with problematic consequences at the local policy level.[49]

B. SDG 11 in the Negotiations of the 2030 Agenda for Sustainable Development

Throughout the negotiation process, there was little disagreement that cities and urbanization were important issues that should be reflected in the 2030 Agenda and the SDGs. The topic of cities and urbanization was present from the very beginning. The SDG process was kicked off with the Rio + 20 Outcome Document, 'The Future We Want', which explicitly calls for SDGs.[50] The Rio + 20 Outcome Document also contains four paragraphs on 'sustainable cities and human settlements'.[51] These are the foundation for the negotiation of SDG 11. 'The Future We Want' focuses on the topics that were prevalent on the Habitat Agenda throughout the 2000s, marked both by the Istanbul Outcome and the Millennium Declaration and the MDGs: slum upgrading and affordable housing, as well as drinking water and sanitation. It also puts a big emphasis on mobility and sustainable transport as well as other infrastructure considerations such as waste management. Note that by 2012, governments were no longer considered the primary entities responsible for the implementation of the Habitat Agenda, as had been the case in 1996. On the contrary, 'The Future We Want' acknowledges 'the important role of municipal governments in setting a vision for sustainable cities' as well as 'partnerships among cities and communities'.[52]

The topics addressed in 'The Future We Want' can be seen as the first input into the SDG negotiation process. While there was no doubt that urban issues ought to be included in the 2030 Agenda, there was a big question mark as to whether this should be done through the means of a stand-alone goal on cities, or whether urban governance issues should be mainstreamed throughout the Agenda, with a number of targets under several other substantive goals addressing urban issues.[53] The report of the High-level Panel of Eminent Persons, issued in 2013 and an important document for the negotiation of the SDGs, contained a list of model goals, none of which were city-specific.[54] Rather, urbanization was considered a cross-cutting issue, to be reflected in different goals. For example, model Goal 6 on achieving universal access to water and sanitation

[48] United Nations, 'Millennium Development Goals Indicators' <https://millenniumindicators.un.org/unsd/mdg/Host.aspx?Content=Indicators/OfficialList.htm> accessed 30 December 2021.

[49] For a study on negative human rights implications of a security-driven approach to 'upgrading slums' in Rio de Janeiro see CM Oliveira, 'Global Goals and Urban Development. The Territorial Effects of Implementing the MDGs in Brazil' in HP Aust and A du Plessis (eds), *The Globalisation of Urban Governance* (Routledge 2019) 173–85.

[50] UN General Assembly, 'The Future We Want', A/Res/66/288, Annex, paras 245 et seq.

[51] ibid paras 134–37.

[52] UN General Assembly, 'The Future We Want' (n 50) paras 136–37.

[53] N Arajärvi, 'Including Cities in the 2030 Agenda—A Review of the Post-2015 Process' in Aust and du Plessis (eds) (n 49) 17–37.

[54] High-level Panel report, UN Doc A/67/890, Annex.

contained a target specifically addressing freshwater supply and water efficiency in urban areas.[55] The Panel acknowledged that '[c]ities are where the battle for sustainable development will be won or lost', but also emphasized that rural areas ought to be taken into account as well, and therefore recommended that the goals should focus on the inclusion of local authorities, rather than explicitly on cities alone.[56]

This question—whether or not there should be a stand-alone goal on cities or whether the issue should be streamlined—remained contentious throughout a number of sessions of the Open Working Group, with the troika composed of the United States, Canada, and Israel explicitly advocating against a stand-alone goal.[57] Similarly, there was no thematic consultation on the topic of cities. UN-Habitat was designated as one of four lead agencies on the topic of population dynamics.[58] This changed in 2014. The Progress Report of the Open Working Group and the Focus Areas Document introduced cities as a focus area in their own right, Focus Area 13.[59] Focus Area 13 suggested eleven 'areas that could be considered', with a number of these areas resembling later targets of SDG 11:

- Area a) addresses eradicating slum conditions, reflected today in target 11.1;
- Area b) addresses access to sustainable transport, reflected today in target 11.2;
- Area d) addresses resilience to climate change and disaster risk reduction, reflected today in target 11.5;
- Area e) addresses safe public spaces, reflected today in target 11.7;
- Area f) addresses capacities for urban planning, reflected today in target 11.3;
- Area g) on links between cities, peri-urban and rural areas is taken up almost verbatim by target 11.a;
- Area j) addresses cultural and natural heritage, reflected today in target 11.4.

Even if the Progress Report recognized disagreement as to whether the issue of cities should be treated as a goal in its own right or as a cross-cutting issue, the Focus Areas document really constitutes the shift towards a stand-alone goal on cities. Afterwards, the question of a stand-alone goal was no longer an issue, and SDG 11 was no longer contentious, including its targets as reflected in the Focus Areas document.[60] The next section will lay out the main contents of SDG 11 and situate it in a broader context of urban governance as well as in international law.

[55] ibid Annex, p 30.
[56] ibid p 17.
[57] Arajärvi (n 53) 21.
[58] Alongside the International Organization for Migration (UNFPA), United Nations Department of Economic and Social Affairs (UNDESA), and the International Organization for Migration (IOM), cf F Dodds and others, *Negotiating the Sustainable Development Goals: A Transformational Agenda for an Insecure World* (Routledge 2017) 49.
[59] <https://sustainabledevelopment.un.org/content/documents/3402Focus%20areas_20140319.pdf>.
[60] Arajärvi (n 53).

III. Commentary on the Goal

SDG 11 occupies a special place amongst the seventeen SDGs. It is the only goal that is directed at a specific public actor—local government ('cities and human settlements')—and one of two stand-alone goals that are actor-centred, rather than issue-centred, along with SDG 5 on gender equality and its focus on women.[61] Both of these goals had initially been conceived not as stand-alone goals but as cross-cutting issues. SDG 11 thus presents several clear intersections with other SDGs. It contains a total of ten targets, seven on specific issues and three on means of implementation (targets 11.a–11.c), out of which one target has not been operationalized, with no suitable indicator found thus far.[62] Several of the targets take up topics that were subjects of the Habitat II Agenda as well as target 7.D of the MDGs aiming at reducing the number of slum dwellers: adequate housing, access to safe public transport and safe public spaces, inclusive and participatory planning, and building up resilience are all topics that are present throughout SDG 11. As a cross-cutting consideration, SDG 11 presents multiple links to other SDGs which are addressed in more detail in Subsection II.A, below.

There are different ways in which we can frame the broad topics addressed by SDG 11. The SDG website, which is managed by UNDESA, presents disaster risk reduction, sustainable transport and sustainable cities, and human settlements as the three large issues that SDG 11 takes into consideration.[63] Another way is to look at SDG 11 through the lens of its custodian agencies. Custodian agencies are those UN agencies, Specialized Agencies, programmes, funds, or Secretariat entities that are responsible for collecting data on specific SDG indicators.[64] UN-Habitat is the most important custodian agency for SDG 11 and is responsible for seven of its fifteen indicators while being a partner agency for an additional five indicators.[65] This means that there are only two indicators and one target in which UN-Habitat is not involved: target 11.4 with indicator 11.4.1 on the protection of the world's cultural and natural heritage, which is monitored and implemented by the United Nations Educational, Scientific and Cultural Organisation (UNESCO) and the International Union for Conservation on Nature, and indicator 11.5.2 on disaster risk reduction, monitored by the United Nations Office for Disaster Risk Reduction (UNDRR).[66]

---

[61] On the specificity of SDG 11 vis-à-vis other goals see HP Aust and A du Plessis, 'The Globalisation of Urban Governance—Legal Perspectives on Sustainable Development Goal 11' in Aust and du Plessis (eds) (n 49) 3–16.

[62] See for more detailed commentary on this target this chapter Section 3, target 11.c.

[63] <https://sdgs.un.org/goals/goal11> accessed 12 October 2021.

[64] cf for a good overview of the different types of UN entities that act as custodian agencies United Nations Economic Commission for Europe, Understanding the system of custodian agencies for Sustainable Development Indicators, UN Doc ECE/CES/2018/39. For an up-to-date overview (as of 2021) of all custodian agencies by indicator see United Nations Statistics Division, Tier Classification for Global SDG Indicators as of 29 March 2021 <https://unstats.un.org/sdgs/files/Tier%20Classification%20of%20SDG%20Indicators_29%20Mar%202021_web.pdf> accessed 30 December 2021.

[65] United Nations Statistics Division, Tier Classification for Global SDG Indicators as of 29 March 2021 <https://unstats.un.org/sdgs/files/Tier%20Classification%20of%20SDG%20Indicators_29%20Mar%202021_web.pdf> accessed 30 December 2021.

[66] UNDRR also monitors indicator 11.5.1, measuring number of deaths. Note that UN-Habitat is a partnering agency here, ibid.

810 SDG 11

UN-Habitat's framing of SDG 11 thus carries considerable weight within the UN system. UN-Habitat's primary role is 'to provide technical assistance to improve planning, policies, legislation and governance as well as support access to land, housing and basic services', according to its own annual report of 2020.[67] Its work, as all work of UN agencies, programmes, and funds, is pre-structured by a multi-year strategic plan. In addition, the realm of urban governance within the UN system is governed across various entities through a System-Wide Strategy on Sustainable Urban Development, which was adopted by the UN Chief Executives Board 'to enhance coherence and coordination across the United Nations System in its efforts to assist Member States in the achievement of the 2030 Agenda and related global agreements through better planned urbanization, drawing upon the Addis Ababa Action Agenda, the Sendai Framework, the Paris Agreement on Climate Change, the Global Compact for Migrants and the New Urban Agenda'.[68] On the basis of these frameworks, UN-Habitat has identified four so-called Domains of Change in which it operates:

- Reduced spatial inequality and poverty in communities across the urban-rural continuum;
- Enhanced shared prosperity of cities and regions;
- Strengthened climate action and improved urban environment; and
- Effective urban crisis prevention and response.[69]

In these four areas, UN-Habitat carries out several projects and initiatives, nurtures networks with multiple partners, including donor agencies, local governments, city networks, non-governmental organizations, and national governments, and engages in documentation, publication, and knowledge sharing.

In a *legal* commentary to the SDGs, it is important to point out that the normative work that UN-Habitat and other UN agencies engage in the realm of urban governance is largely governed by a multitude of standards that would generally be classified as 'soft law'.[70] Where the activities relate to 'hard law' multilateral treaties, this is pointed out in the commentary on the goal as a whole as well as in the individual target commentaries. The 2030 Agenda in and of itself is of course 'soft law', in that it was adopted as a resolution by the General Assembly. Yet, it is a policy document of highest importance and thus exerts a considerable normative pull.[71] Similarly, this commentary operates

---

[67] UN-Habitat, Annual Report 2020 <https://unhabitat.org/sites/default/files/2021/05/annual_progress_report_2020_final.pdf> accessed 30 December 2021, p 3.

[68] UN System Chief Executives Board for Coordination, United Nations System-Wide Strategy on Sustainable Urban Development, UN Doc CEB/2019/1/Add.5, para 27.

[69] UN-Habitat, Annual Report 2020 <https://unhabitat.org/sites/default/files/2021/05/annual_progress_report_2020_final.pdf> accessed 30 December 2021, p 5.

[70] On the notion of soft law see D Thürer, 'Soft Law' in *Max Planck Encyclopedia of Public International Law* (2009); for a critique see J Klabbers, 'The Undesirability of Soft Law' (1998) 67 Nordic Journal of International Law 381–91. On the continued relevance of soft law in today's legal practice see T Broude and Y Shereshevsky, 'Explaining the Practical Purchase of Soft Law: Competing and Complementary Behavior Hypotheses' in HG Cohen and T Meyer (eds), *International Law as Behavior* (CUP 2021) 98–127).

[71] M Goldmann, 'We Need to Cut Off the Head of the King: Past, Present, and Future Approaches to International Soft Law' (2012) 25(2) Leiden Journal of International Law 335–68, has argued that 'soft law' instruments are

on the assumption that operational activities of UN agencies, most of which are norma-tively guided by soft law instruments, have an important normative pull, as UN entities engage directly with local actors and engage in project cooperation.[72] The commentary as a whole and the commentaries on targets in particular focus on instruments that are guiding operational activities by various UN entities, primarily those entities that act as custodian agencies for each individual target. This commentary thus associates itself with scholarship that understands indicators as a governance technique with consider-able normative and practical import.[73]

This general commentary section proceeds as follows. In Subsection II.A, I address some general themes and issues that structure global urban governance today and that are addressed by SDG 11 and the New Urban Agenda. This includes the recent turn to spatiality as a primary concern for global urban governance. This Subsection also briefly touches upon inter-linkages between SDG 11 and other SDGs. It explores where implementation of SDG 11, globally speaking, stands, and looks at the impact of the COVID-19 pandemic in urban spaces. Subsection II.B turns to a contentious question of international law scholarship regarding cities: whether cities are subjects of inter-national law, and whether they ought to be considered thus. Subsections II.C and II.D explore broad interlinkages of SDG 11 with sub-fields of international law, with a main focus on international human rights law.

A. Cities and Urbanization in the 2030 Agenda and the New Urban Agenda and Linkages to Other SDGs

Four buzz words animate SDG 11: inclusivity, safety, resilience, and sustainability. Those are the four attributes that, according to SDG 11, cities and human settlements should strive for. At the core of these four themes sits the question of how space in cities is distributed, how it is built, who can access which spaces—in short, whether public space is inclusive and safe, resilient, and sustainable. Public space is at the core of the New Urban Agenda, which mentions it no less than eleven times throughout the text, in addition to a whole section on managing urban spatial development.[74] In SDG 11 as well as in the New Urban Agenda, spatiality is a social consideration: public spaces are an important factor in cities and human settlements and can have the potential for

---

today often the functional equivalent of multilateral treaties, while ultimately suggesting that the concepts of inter-national law and public authority ought to be dissociated from one another. Of course, the 2030 Agenda alone could not be invoked in front of an international court. But that does not render it insignificant, on the contrary.

[72] I have made this point elsewhere, see H Birkenkötter, 'Ensuring Access to Public Space as a Dimension of "Safe Cities"' in Aust and du Plessis (eds) (n 49) 127–50.
[73] SE Merry and others, *The Quiet Power of Indicators: Measuring Governance, Corruption, and Rule of Law* (CUP 2015); SE Merry, 'Firming Up Soft Law: The Impact of Indicators on Transnational Human Rights Legal Orders' in TC Halliday and G Shaffer (eds), *Transnational Legal Orders* (CUP 2015) 374–99; A Fisher and S Fukuda-Parr, 'Introduction—Data, Knowledge, Politics and Localizing the SDGs' (2019) 20(4) Journal of Human Development and Capabilities 375–85.
[74] New Urban Agenda, Quito Implementation Plan for the New Urban Agenda, UN Doc A/Res/71/256, Annex, paras 93–125.

addressing social inequality. As the New Urban Agenda puts it: 'the spatial organization, accessibility and design of urban space, as well as the infrastructure and the basic services provision, together with development policies, can promote or hinder social cohesion, equality and inclusion'.[75]

This turn to spatiality is a relatively new phenomenon. The Habitat II Declaration and Programme of Action mention spaces in passing but do not dedicate any further explanation to it—despite the Habitat II agenda spanning over 100 pages and 241 paragraphs. Open spaces and green spaces are mentioned in a mere handful of paragraphs and as part of enumerations.[76] The New Urban Agenda and SDG 11, in particular its target 7, put public spaces centre-stage: the New Urban Agenda highlights safe, inclusive, accessible, green, and quality public spaces amongst the visions for cities and human settlements and declares planning to 'optimize the spatial dimension of the urban form' as part of the urban paradigm shift for a New Urban Agenda.[77] The 2020 Global Cities Report describes the New Urban Agenda as 'a spatial framework for how to achieve a number of the goals and targets'.[78]

While SDG 11 mentions cities and other human settlements, which would include rural dwellings, as of equal concern, it is the rapid urbanization and concentration of the world's population in cities that poses the biggest challenge to sustainability and resilience. The 2030 Agenda's Political Declaration thus emphasizes that 'sustainable *urban* development and management are crucial' and specifically mentions the impact of '*cities* on the global climate system'.[79] The Habitat III Agenda is even clearer in its focus on cities and affirms that '[p]opulations, economic activities, social and cultural interactions, as well as environmental and humanitarian impacts, are increasingly concentrated in cities, and this poses massive sustainability challenges'.[80] At the same time, the New Urban Agenda aspires to frame urbanization not only as a challenge but also as an opportunity: 'there is a need to take advantage of the opportunities presented by urbanization as an engine of sustained and inclusive economic growth, social and cultural development, and environmental protection'.[81] The 2030 Agenda and the New Urban Agenda also refer to one another explicitly.[82]

---

[75] ibid para 25.

[76] For example, Istanbul Declaration, para 11: 'We shall promote the conservation, rehabilitation and maintenance of buildings, monuments, open spaces, landscapes and settlement patterns of historical, cultural, architectural, natural, religious and spiritual value', and Habitat Agenda, para 27: 'Equitable human settlements are those in which all people, without discrimination of any kind as to race, colour, sex, language, religion, political or other opinion, national or social origin, property, birth or other status, have equal access to housing, infrastructure, health services, adequate food and water, education and open spaces.'

[77] New Urban Agenda, Quito Declaration, UN Doc A/Res/71/256, Annex, paras 13 (b) and 15 (c) (iii).

[78] UN-Habitat, 'World Cities Report 2020' (n 6) p xvi.

[79] UN Doc A/Res/70/1, para 34, emphasis added.

[80] New Urban Agenda, Quito Declaration, UN Doc A/Res/71/256, Annex, para 2.

[81] ibid para 4.

[82] UN Doc A/Res/70/1, para 34; New Urban Agenda, Quito Declaration, UN Doc A/Res/71/256, Annex, para 6 (referring to the 2030 Agenda, the Addis Ababa Action Agenda and eleven other global agendas), and para 9, stating that '[t]he implementation of the New Urban Agenda contributes to the implementation and localization of the 2030 Agenda for Sustainable Development in an integrated manner, and to the achievement of the Sustainable Development Goals and targets, including Goal 11'.

As mentioned earlier, SDG 11 and the issue of human settlements were originally conceptualized as a cross-cutting issue. It is therefore no surprise that its targets link to several other SDGs. The UN System-Wide Strategy on Sustainable Urban Development identifies links to each of the seventeen goals, with particularly strong links to SDG 1 (end poverty), SDG 3 (ensure healthy lives), SDG 4 (ensure inclusive and equitable quality education), SDG 5 (gender equality), SDG 8 (decent work for all), SDG 10 (reduced inequalities), and SDG 16 (peaceful and inclusive societies).[83]

SDG 11 has been subject to review at the High-Level Political Forum once, in 2018, alongside SDG 6 (water and sanitation for all), SDG 7 (access to energy for all), SDG 12 (sustainable consumption and production patterns), SDG 15 (life on land), and SDG 17 (Global Partnership for Sustainable Development). It is set to be reviewed again at the High-Level Political Foum in 2023. The Ministerial Declaration issued at the 2018 High-Level Political Forum emphasizes amongst other things the challenges cities and local authorities face in providing adequate housing and resilient infrastructure in light of rapid urbanization. The Declaration also points to the rising number of people living in slums, the need to improve waste management and levels of particulate matter in the air, and it emphasizes the necessity of long-term planning and design of urban spaces.[84] As of 2018, 54 per cent of the world's population was living in cities and this number is expected to rise, with possibly two-thirds of the world's population living in cities by 2030.[85]

As early as 2018, the Ministerial Declaration of the High-Level Political Forum stated that '[t]he vulnerability of cities to epidemics, disasters and to the impacts of climate change has increased because of rapid population growth and unplanned urbanization'.[86] This seems like a forecast of the COVID-19 pandemic that dominated 2020 and 2021 and greatly impacted progress in implementing the SDGs. This is especially true for SDG 11: over 90 per cent of confirmed COVID-19 cases were reported from urban areas, rendering cities the epicentres of the pandemic.[87] COVID-19, according to the World Cities Report 2020, 'has exposed and exacerbated underlying inequalities in cities. The poor are the most vulnerable and the most likely to die from the disease'.[88] Existing social and economic inequalities were widened by the pandemic, with a spatial dimension in so far as the most affected areas in urban settings were economically less viable areas and areas of informal settlement with high population density.[89] The COVID-19 pandemic and the challenges it has brought for the urban space shows that

---

[83] See figure I in UN System Chief Executives Board for Coordination, United Nations System-Wide Strategy on Sustainable Urban Development, UN Doc CEB/2019/1/Add.5, para 28.

[84] Ministerial declaration of the 2018 high-level political forum on sustainable development, convened under the auspices of the Economic and Social Council, on the theme 'Transformation towards sustainable and resilient societies', UN Doc E/HLS/2018/1, para 25.

[85] 2018 Review of SDGs implementation: SDG 11—Make cities and human settlements inclusive, safe, resilient and sustainable, Background Note <https://sustainabledevelopment.un.org/content/documents/20063197282018_background_notes_SDG_11_v3.pdf> accessed 30 December 2021, p 1.

[86] Ministerial declaration of the 2018 high-level political forum on sustainable development, convened under the auspices of the Economic and Social Council, on the theme 'Transformation towards sustainable and resilient societies', UN Doc E/HLS/2018/1, para 25.

[87] UN Secretary-General, 'Policy Brief: COVID-19 in an Urban World' (n 4) p 2.

[88] UN-Habitat, 'World Cities Report 2020' (n 6) Executive Director's Introduction, p iv.

[89] UN Secretary-General, 'Policy Brief: COVID-19 in an Urban World' (n 4) pp 9–10.

the city might, after all, not be 'the ideal locus for sustainable development' which it has been thought to be.[90] The current 2021 Sustainable Development Goals Report and its data paint a picture of persisting challenges in implementing SDG 11. According to the 2021 data, no country in the world has yet achieved SDG 11, and in most countries either significant or major challenges remain.[91] At the same time, it is clear that urbanization will continue to unfold despite these challenges. Therefore, it is even more urgent to address implementation challenges in SDG 11. From a legal perspective, one such challenge is the uncertain status of cities and local governments in global governance and international law. The next section addresses this question.

B. Cities as Subjects of International Law and Their Relationship with International Organizations

The *travaux préparatoires* of SDG 11 show that cities and human settlements have been the object of international legal regulation through the United Nations' Habitat agendas for at least the past half century. Negotiated under the auspices of the United Nations, in particular the UN General Assembly, cities and human settlements have thus long been part of international law, especially the secondary law of the United Nations (most importantly the resolutions which established the Centre for Human Settlements and later UN-Habitat as a UN programme). At the same time, international legal scholarship has only recently started to devote attention to cities. This lack of engagement with cities is possibly the result of international law's traditionally more state-centred outlook.[92] With an increasing number of city networks that operate transnationally,[93] the question arises whether cities and human settlements can and ought to be considered at least partial subjects of international law. This section considers this question. It is argued that cities cannot claim legal subjectivity *de lege lata* in current public international law, but that they are legal subjects in today's transnational legal ordering,[94] as they enter into legal relationships with other legal entities, and as they are increasingly viewed not only as objects of global regulation but rather as actors 'which aspire to shape the practice in this field'.[95]

---

[90] The quotation is taken from HP Aust and A Rodiles, 'Cities and Local Governments: International Development from Below?' (2021) KFG Working Paper Series No 50, Berlin 12.

[91] JD Sachs and others, *Sustainable Development Report 2021: The Decade of Action for the Sustainable Development Goals* (CUP 2021) Dashboard <https://dashboards.sdgindex.org/map/goals/SDG11> accessed 30 December 2021, Sustainable cities and communities, overall score.

[92] HP Aust and JE Nijman, 'The Emerging Role of Cities in International Law—Introductory Remarks on Practice' in Aust and Nijman (eds) (n 1) 2, similarly C Swiney, 'The Urbanization of International Law and International Relations: The Rising Soft Power of Cities in Global Governance' (2020) 41 Michigan Journal of International Law 227–78.

[93] Swiney points out that the number of city networks has increased from nine in 2006 to well over 200 today, with an average of four new international city networks emerging every year, ibid 270.

[94] This notion is taken from Halliday and Shaffer (eds) (n 73), who develop transnational legal ordering, or orders, as an analytical frame for the way in which international, regional, and domestic law, as well as different forms of transnational law, intersect.

[95] Aust and Rodiles (n 90) 7.

Legal personality or subjectivity generally describes the capacity to enter legal relationships and the faculty of possessing rights and duties under a given legal regime. The main consequence of legal subjectivity is the capacity to engage in legal relationships with one another. In international law, states have long been considered the original and primary subjects.[96] In addition, it has long been established that international organizations possess international legal personality;[97] the same is also true for individuals.[98] Important consequences of possessing legal personality in international law are, amongst others, the capacity of entering into treaties with one another, responsibility under international law for internationally wrongful acts,[99] and legal standing in front of international courts and tribunals.

Historically, cities do not possess formal status as a subject of international law *de lege lata*, from the perspective of public international law.[100] Neither the UN Charter, nor any multilateral treaty negotiated under UN auspices, nor any decision of the International Court of Justice mention cities, let alone confirm their existence as legal entities in international law.[101] This means that as a general rule, cities cannot obtain legal standing in international courts and tribunals, although there might be exceptional cases in the fields of international investment dispute settlement under the International Centre for Settlement of Investment Disputes as well as under EU law.[102] Similarly, they are not subject to the rules of state responsibility—rather, it is the state that will be responsible for violations of international law committed by cities.[103] Lastly, the Vienna Convention on the Law of Treaties formally does not view treaties to which a municipal entity is a party as a treaty under public international law,[104] even though it has been argued that, for example, loan agreements concluded between the World Bank and city governments ought to be considered international treaties, governed by international law.[105]

This last paragraph has shown that there are some empirical reasons to believe that cities are today subjects of international law. The most evident reason to believe so are

[96] C Walter, 'Subjects of International Law' in *Max Planck Encyclopedia of Public International Law* (2007). For an in-depth treatment of the concept of international legal personality see JE Nijman, *The Concept of International Legal Personality* (T.M.C. Asser Press 2004).

[97] Reparation for Injuries suffered in the service of the United Nations, Advisory Opinion: ICJ Reports 1949, 174, 178.

[98] Individuals possess rights under international human rights law, amongst others, and duties under international criminal law. For a comprehensive treatment of subjective international rights see A Peters, *Beyond Human Rights: The Legal Status of the Individual in International Law*, Cambridge Studies in International and Comparative Law (J Huston, trans, CUP 2016).

[99] See the Articles on the Responsibility of States for Internationally Wrongful Acts, contained in UN Doc A/Res/56/83, Annex, and the Draft Articles on the Responsibility of International Organizations, contained in UN Doc A/66/10, para 87.

[100] Swiney (n 92) 233–34; Aust (n 1) 142.

[101] Y Blank, 'International Legal Personality/Subjectivity of Cities' in Aust and Nijman (eds) (n 1) 103, 106.

[102] M Baumgärtel, 'Dispute Settlement' in Aust and Nijman (eds) (n 1), 147.

[103] cf art 4 Articles on the Responsibility of States for Internationally Wrongful Acts, contained in UN Doc A/Res/56/83, Annex; see also Swiney (n 92) 235; K Creutz, 'Responsibility' in Aust and Nijman (eds) (n 1) 135.

[104] Art 2(1)(a) Vienna Convention on the Law of Treaties: "treaty' means an international agreement concluded between States'; likewise, the 1986 Vienna Convention on the Law of Treaties between States and International Organizations or Between International Organizations does not mention cities at all.

[105] M Riegner, 'International Institutions and the City: Towards a Comparative Law of Glocal Governance' in Aust and Nijman (eds) (n 1) 44–45.

816 SDG 11

the manifold agreements in the field of development cooperation to which city governments are parties, and which often are legal in character.[106] The most important agreements are agreements in the field of development assistance, concluded between donors and recipients, be it with regard to financial or technical assistance. Such agreements are pre-structured by the donor agencies' institutional law and typically involve a variety of actors as well as implementing agreements which are typically governed by domestic law.[107] The World Bank, for example, is legally able and has a preference to conclude loan agreements directly with sub-state entities, in other words, with city governments.[108]

Cities and local governments also use other, non-traditional ways of connecting with one another and with other actors in the international sphere. Christie Swiney identifies six ways in which cities partake in international relations: cities form an increasing number of networks; they ally with international organizations; they gain recognition in international agendas, notably the 2030 Agenda and the New Urban Agenda; they mirror state-based coalitions and structures; they harness the language of international law; and they act to implement norms of international law.[109] Similarly, Helmut Aust identifies different ways in which public international law is increasingly receptive towards cities and local governments as actors in international law, be it through recognition of cities in a number of global political processes that are structured by international law (such as processes on climate change or sustainability), or be it through increasing informal law-making that is driven by cities.[110] City networks are particularly important ways in which cities as entities relate to one another. There are city networks of all sizes and shapes, with currently well over 200 such networks and an average of four networks emerging each year.[111] Some networks that are of particular importance include ICLEI—Local Governments for Sustainability (formerly known as the 'International Council for Local Environment Initiatives'), United Cities and Local Governments (UCLG), and the C40 network of mayors.

Acknowledging legal subjectivity of cities in international law does not mean that states will lose their status as subjects of international law.[112] On the contrary, states are anything but side-lined.[113] But cities are acknowledged as actors in their own right, and not only as objects of regulation. This becomes visible when contrasting language

---

[106] M Riegner, 'Development Cooperation and the City' in Aust and Nijman (eds) (n 1) 251–64. One could of course also argue that these agreements are more akin to private law agreements. International organizations enter into private law agreements with eg corporations (on matters such as procurement, rental contracts etc), and there is no doubt that this does not render corporations subjects of *public* international law. There are, however, good reasons to believe that loan agreements and development cooperation agreements that touch upon governance issues are of a public law character and thus ought to be governed by public international law. This is Riegner's argument in Riegner, 'International Institutions and the City' (n 105).

[107] P Dann and M Riegner, 'Foreign Aid Agreements' in *Max Planck Encyclopedia of Public International Law* (2014).

[108] Riegner, 'Development Cooperation and the City' (n 106) 254.

[109] Swiney (n 92) 243–69.

[110] Aust (n 1) Part II, § 4.

[111] Swiney (n 92).

[112] Blank (n 101) 104: 'This novel worldview in which international legal personality/subjectivity is conceptualized so as to include cities does not do away with the state.'

[113] Aust and Rodiles (n 90) 9.

from the first Habitat Agenda in 1976 with the 2016 New Urban Agenda. The 1976 Vancouver Declaration speaks of a 'responsibility for increased activity of the national Governments'[114] and all actions lie within the responsibility of national governments. In turn, the 2016 New Urban Agenda recognizes 'the leading role of national Governments, *as appropriate* ... and the *equally important contributions* of subnational and local governments' in bringing about the urban paradigm shift the New Urban Agenda proclaims.[115]

In addition to these empirical observations, there are several normative arguments that might support the view that cities ought to be viewed as having legal personality. Yishai Blank argues that cities can constitute an important counterpart to the almighty state in several ways: he suggests that cities are better places for participatory democracy and can serve to combat populism; that they can enhance the voices of minorities who often tend to dwell in cities rather than rural areas, and he cites evidence that the more diverse and pluralistic composition of city populations might serve as drivers for experimentalism and economic growth.[116] Participatory democracy is at least partially taken up in SDG 11, target 3, which calls for enhancing participatory and inclusive human settlement planning and management.[117] From a normative standpoint, the notion of experimentalism can also be understood in a more far-reaching manner. Gráinne De Búrca, Robert Keohane, and Charles Sabel have argued that institutionalized processes of problem-solving are normatively desirable if five factors come together: a broadly shared perception of a common problem; the articulation of a framework with open-ended goals; implementation of these global, open-ended goals in a local context and with local adaptation; feedback from local contexts to the global level; and lastly, periodic and continued re-evaluation and revision where appropriate.[118] It is easy to see how according legal personality to cities and local governments, and thus augmenting their standing in international processes, might facilitate this recurrent cycle of norm shaping and norm evolution.[119]

Some cautious remarks ought to be made at this point. It is not believed that giving legal personality to cities will act as panacea for all current challenges in global governance. Indeed, one practical consequence ought to be borne in mind: the sheer number of local governments that exist worldwide. Yishai Blank has pointed this out and mentions over 30,000 local governments in France alone, and over 250,000 urban and rural localities in India.[120] It is easy to see that participating in global governance processes might then be restricted to those cities and municipalities that are affluent or otherwise

[114] UN Doc A/CONF.10/15, Vancouver Declaration, p 2.

[115] New Urban Agenda, Quito Declaration, UN Doc A/Res/71/256, Annex, para 15 b), emphasis added. This point is also highlighted, with different conclusions drawn, by Swiney (n 92) 253.

[116] Blank (n 101) 114–18.

[117] See commentary on target 11.3 in this chapter.

[118] G De Búrca and others, 'Global Experimentalist Governance' (2014) 44(3) British Journal of Political Science 477–86.

[119] De Búrca and others' theory adds to existing theories of norm cascading and norm cycles, by 'closing the circle', so to speak. For norm cycles in international relations see the foundational contribution by M Finnemore and K Sikkink, 'International Norm Dynamics and Political Change' (1998) 52(04) International Organization 887–917.

[120] Blank (n 101) 118.

powerful, thus contributing to already existing inequalities. Similarly, the normative grounds provided in favour of according legal personality to cities might allow an overly positive image of the 'city as the ideal locus' for sustainable development in all its dimensions to take hold.[121] Yet, the increasing activities of cities and local governments at the global level, their engaging in various forms of agreements, some of which are arguably governed by public international law, and their economic and political power all indicate that they have already acquired the status of legal persons in processes of transnational legal ordering. If legal personality comes not only with rights, but also duties, if according legal personality under international law might also increase accountability of cities, then this is yet another normative argument that would speak in favour of recognizing cities as legal subjects.

C. SDG 11 and International Human Rights

Neither SDG 11, including its targets, nor any of the indicators for SDG 11 mention international human rights law as part, or a measurement of the achievement, of Goal 11, and only one metadata document includes a reference to human rights.[122] This is unlike indicators for other goals: indicator for target 10.3 ('ensure equal opportunity and reduce inequalities of outcome, including by discriminatory laws'), for example, looks at the proportion of a population reporting having felt discriminated against 'on the basis of a ground of discrimination prohibited under international human rights law';[123] the indicator for target 16.a measures the existence of national human rights institutions;[124] and target 4.7 mentions human rights education as part of the goal on education.[125]

The absence of human rights language in many parts of the SDGs generally,[126] and in SDG 11 specifically, bears the risk of a systematic neglect of human rights dimensions. This section attempts to link the contents of SDG 11 to international human rights law. Several of these connections are made through human rights language that is mirrored in several targets. These will be expanded upon in more detail below, in the commentary on each relevant target. This section provides a more general overview, including links with international human rights law that are not explicit in SDG 11 but that could be made. This also includes a brief overview on the increasing number of cities that self-style as 'human rights cities', which includes the adoption of local human rights

---

[121] Aust and Rodiles (n 90) 12.

[122] The metadata document for target 11.1 references art 25 of the Universal Declaration of Human Rights and two General Comments from the CESCR on the right to adequate housing as part of the right to an adequate standard of living, cf United Nations, Metadata 11.1.1 (October 2020) <https://unstats.un.org/sdgs/metadata/files/Metadata-11-01-01.pdf> accessed 30 December 2021.

[123] Indicator 10.3.1, contained in UN Doc A/Res/71/313.

[124] Indicator 16.a.1, contained in ibid.

[125] Target 4.7, contained in UN Doc A/Res/70/1, Annex.

[126] On this see the contributions in the Special Issue by IT Winkler and C Williams, 'The Sustainable Development Goals and Human Rights: A Critical Early Review' (2017) 21(8) The International Journal of Human Rights 1023–28.

COMMENTARY ON THE GOAL 819

agendas and institutions and implementation of international human rights law at the local level, sometimes in open disagreement with federal government.[127]

As mentioned at the outset, SDG 11 is animated by four buzz words, or themes: inclusivity, safety, resilience, and sustainability. All these themes bear links to existing international human rights treaties in different aspects. Inclusivity and safety in SDG 11 are a particular concern for three groups that are also groups specially protected by human rights treaties: children, women, and persons with disabilities. Women's rights are enshrined in the 1979 Convention on the Elimination of Discrimination Against Women (CEDAW); children's rights are the subject of the 1990 UN Convention on the Rights of the Child (CRC); and the rights of persons with disabilities are codified in the 2006 UN Convention on the Rights of Persons with Disabilities. Two indicators call for disaggregated data that covers specifically these three groups: indicator 11.2.1 on access to transport, and indicator 11.7.2 on access to safe public spaces.[128]

In addition to group-specific human rights treaties, SDG 11 is also intimately linked to the International Covenant on Economic, Social and Cultural Rights (ICESCR), in particular to its article 11 enshrining the right to an adequate standard of living. This link is particularly strong in target 11.1 on access for all to adequate, safe, and affordable housing and will be discussed in the commentary on this target. The New Urban Agenda further links the right to adequate housing explicitly to the right to an adequate standard of living, which also includes, amongst other things, access to safe and affordable drinking water and sanitation, which the SDGs address in SDG 6.[129]

Civil and political rights are addressed in two ways: to the extent that civil and political rights are based on the idea of participation, SDG 11 and the New Urban Agenda emphasize participation in human settlement planning (target 11.3). The New Urban Agenda explicitly envisions 'human settlements that ... are participatory, promote civic engagement, engender a sense of belonging and ownership'.[130] Second, the right to life, enshrined in article 6 of the International Covenant on Civil and Political Rights (ICCPR), is concerned where SDG 11 addresses resilience and sustainability, in particular where it links to the Sendai Framework on disaster risk reduction.[131] The treaty monitoring body to the ICCPR, the Human Rights Committee, has made explicit that States Parties to the ICCPR need to develop disaster management plans as part of their duties under article 6 ICCPR and that climate change constitutes a particular danger to the right to life.[132] The right to life also plays a role in terms of safety, understood as physical integrity.[133]

Beyond these explicit textual links that can be made between SDG 11 and existing international human rights law, cities have long played a role in the implementation

---

[127] See on human rights cities the volume by B Oomen and others (eds), *Global Urban Justice: The Rise of Human Rights Cities* (CUP 2016).
[128] On the latter see Birkenkötter (n 72).
[129] New Urban Agenda, Quito Declaration, UN Doc A/Res/71/256, Annex, para 13 a).
[130] ibid para 13 b).
[131] Sendai Framework for Disaster Risk Reduction 2015–2030, contained in UN Doc A/Res/69/283, Annex.
[132] General Comment No 36, The right to life (2019), UN Doc CCPR/C/GC/36, paras 26 and 62.
[133] See on this in more depth commentary below in this chapter on target 11.7.

of international human rights, sometimes in opposition to their central governments. The city ordinances of San Francisco and Los Angeles implementing CEDAW at the local level, despite the well-known objections of the United States federal government to ratifying CEDAW, are perhaps the best-known examples of an international human rights treaty's local implementation against the will of the federal government.[134] In addition to implementing individual instruments, there exists an increasing number of cities that self-identify as 'human rights cities'.[135] Such human rights cities have entered into networks to learn from each other,[136] they are organizing annual fora under the auspices of existing city networks,[137] or they have adopted charters that explicitly recognize a 'right to the city' to guide their action.[138] Three ways in which cities engage with international human rights can thus be discerned: cities sometimes invoke human rights and use them to oppose central government; cities might use international human rights language in order to enter the international sphere and assert themselves as actors; and lastly, individuals living in the city can invoke individual human rights, as well as the broader 'right to the city', against government, both at the local and the national level.[139]

D. SDG 11 and Other International Instruments: UNESCO, Sendai Framework, and Environmental Standards, Including Climate Change

SDG 11 makes explicit reference to a number of specialized international legal fields and various international instruments. These will be addressed in more detail when discussing the individual targets and indicators that invoke specific legal fields. This section serves to provide an overview. Target 11.4 calls for a strengthened effort to 'protect and safeguard the world's cultural and natural heritage', a clear reference to international natural and cultural heritage law under the auspices of UNESCO. UNESCO does not play a big role in monitoring SDG 11, with the exception of target 11.4.[140] At the same time, UNESCO has been active with regard to cities on its own initiative, having launched several city networks. In 2004, UNESCO launched both the International Coalition of Inclusive and Sustainable Cities (ICCAR) and the UNESCO

---

[134] J Resnik, 'Comparative (In)equalities: CEDAW, the Jurisdiction of Gender, and the Heterogeneity of Transnational Law Production' (2012) 10(2) International Journal of Constitutional Law 531–50.

[135] Oomen and others (eds) (n 127).

[136] See the European cities listed on the website of the Human Rights Cities Network <https://humanrightscities.net/human-rights-cities/> accessed 30 December 2021.

[137] This is the case of Gwangju, South Korea, cf <https://www.uclg-cisdp.org/en/news/world-human-rights-cities-forum-whrcf-gwangju> accessed 30 December 2021.

[138] This is the case of eg Mexico City, cf A-M Sánchez Rodríguez, 'The Right to the City in Mexico City' in Oomen and others (eds) (n 127) 220..

[139] Aust (n 1) 364–65.

[140] It is, however, the main custodian agency for almost all targets and indicators of SDG 4, cf United Nations Statistics Division, Tier Classification for Global SDG Indicators as of 29 March 2021 <https://unstats.un.org/sdgs/files/Tier%20Classification%20of%20SDG%20Indicators_29%20Mar%202021_web.pdf> accessed 30 December 2021.

COMMENTARY ON THE GOAL   821

Creative Cities Network (UCCN), acting as an interlocutor and facilitator to both. In addition, it supports half a dozen or so programmes that address different dimensions of sustainable cities through education. These programmes and networks were consolidated into the UNESCO Cities Platform in 2019.[141]

Targets 11.5 and 11.b address disaster risk reduction, with target 11.b explicitly mentioning the Sendai Framework for Disaster Risk Reduction 2015–2030, which was adopted just a few months prior to the 2030 Agenda.[142] The Sendai Framework for Disaster Risk Reduction is the only international agenda that is explicitly mentioned in SDG 11. Disaster Risk Reduction at the UN goes hand in hand with climate change mitigation and adaptation measures and broader environmental concerns, as it addresses hazards. Hazards in turn were defined in the predecessor agenda to the Sendai Framework, the Hyogo Framework for Action, as 'a potentially damaging physical event, phenomenon or human activity that may cause the loss of life or injury, property damage, social and economic disruption or environmental degradation. Hazards can include latent conditions that may represent future threats and can have different origins: natural (geological, hydrometeorological and biological) or induced by human processes (environmental degradation and technological hazards).'[143]

This definition steers disaster risk reduction clearly in the direction of environmental degradation prevention, and the Sendai Framework of Action explicitly names climate change as 'one of the drivers of disaster risk'.[144] In target 11.b, disaster risk reduction and climate change mitigation and adaptation are mentioned next to one another. Cities have been important actors in the field of climate change law for some time now, as they have entered climate diplomacy and claimed spaces hitherto reserved for states.[145] Cities are crucial in combatting climate change as they are amongst its main drivers: according to the UNFCCC Secretariat, they consume more than two-thirds of the world's energy and account for over 70 per cent of global carbon dioxide emissions.[146] Local Authorities have been recognized as a Major Group in the Rio process since 1992.[147] Within the UNFCCC annual Conferences of Parties, local authorities partake through the Local Governments and Municipal Authorities (LGMA) constituency,[148] alongside and in close collaboration with several important city networks accredited with UNFCCC, including the aforementioned ICLEI and C40 networks.[149]

---

[141] UNESCO, UNESCO Cities Platform, Leaflet <https://en.unesco.org/system/files/unesco_cities_leaflet_eng_print_v2.pdf> accessed 30 December 2021.

[142] Sendai Framework for Disaster Risk Reduction 2015–2030 (n 131) Annex.

[143] Hyogo Framework for Action, Preamble, FN 2, contained in UN Doc A/CONF.206/6.

[144] Sendai Framework for Disaster Risk Reduction 2015–2030 (n 131) Annex, para 13.

[145] Bouteligier (n 1).

[146] UNFCCC, Urban Climate Action Is Crucial to Bend the Emissions Curve, 2020 <https://unfccc.int/news/urban-climate-action-is-crucial-to-bend-the-emissions-curve> accessed 30 December 2021.

[147] Agenda 21, Chapter 28 (Local Authorities' Initiatives in Support of Agenda 21), contained in UN Doc A/CONF.151/26/Rev.1 (Vol I).

[148] Local Governments and Municipal Authorities, About the LGMA <https://www.cities-and-regions.org/about-the-lgma/> accessed 30 December 2021.

[149] See the list of UNFCCC accredited organizations at Local Governments and Municipal Authorities, About the LGMA <https://www.cities-and-regions.org/about-the-lgma/> accessed 30 December 2021.

822   SDG 11

Through these networks, city leaders have been vocal at various Conference of Parties (COP) meetings. For example, 200 mayors attended a parallel city summit at the 2009 Conference of Parties to the UN Framework Convention on Climate Change (COP15) in Copenhagen.[150] At the same time, reference to sub-national governance levels is scarce in UNFCCC-related documents. In a move called a 'historic first' by the LGMA,[151] the Paris Agreement recognized in its Preamble the 'importance of the engagements of all levels of government and various actors ... in addressing climate change'.[152] At the same time, it is important to note that such engagement is subject to 'respective national legislations of Parties', a typical qualifier that is often sought by national governments to mitigate friction between local and national governance levels, as outlined, for example, with respect to human rights treaties in the previous section.[153] At the same time, the acknowledgement in the Preamble of the Paris Agreement gives more visibility to cities and local governments in the COP process. At COP26 in Glasgow (the most recent COP at the time of writing), LGMA adopted a four-point action roadmap through which LGMA members proclaim to (i) contribute to nationally determined contributions (NDCs) through locally aligned climate action plans; (ii) support efforts to raise local climate financing initiatives; (iii) integrate climate action with broader social justice concerns, including gender equality and health concerns; and (iv) raise the profile of local governance in international negotiations.[154] The Glasgow Climate Pact recognizes at different points the importance of local communities and local policy and governance levels, crucially in the parts on implementation and collaboration.[155]

Beyond climate change, SDG 11 also presents broader links to international environmental law. Air quality and waste management are explicitly addressed in target 11.6. Air pollution and waste, especially when they cross borders and become transboundary hazards, have long been part of international environmental law and subject of a number of international treaties and other normative regimes.[156] At the same time, and similar to international human rights law, there is no explicit reference made to existing instruments regulating air pollution or waste management. It is therefore questionable whether instruments such as the 1979 United Nations Economic Commission

[150] Swiney (n 92) 256–57.

[151] See Local Governments and Municipal Authorities, LGMA Glasgow Time4MultilevelAction Roadmap, 2020 <https://www.global-taskforce.org/sites/default/files/2021-11/LGMA%20Glasgow%20Time4MultilevelAction%20Roadmap.pdf> accessed 30 December 2021.

[152] Paris Agreement, 2015, Preamble.

[153] The 2030 Agenda also contains similar qualifiers in crucial targets, see, eg, target 5.a on ensuring women's equal rights, which qualifies 'access to ownership and control over land and other forms of property, financial services, inheritance and natural resources, in accordance with national laws'; or target 16.10 protecting 'public access to information and protect fundamental freedoms', but 'in accordance with national legislation', UN Doc A/Res/70/1, Annex.

[154] Local Governments and Municipal Authorities, LGMA Glasgow Time4MultilevelAction Roadmap, 2020 <https://www.global-taskforce.org/sites/default/files/2021-11/LGMA%20Glasgow%20Time4MultilevelAction%20Roadmap.pdf> accessed 30 December 2021.

[155] Glasgow Climate Pact, 2021, chs VII and VIII, Advance Unedited Version <https://unfccc.int/sites/default/files/resource/cop26_auv_2f_cover_decision.pdf> accessed 30 December 2021.

[156] cf the chapters on atmospheric protection and hazardous substances and activities, and waste, respectively, in P Sands and others, *Principles of International Environmental Law* (4th edn, CUP 2018) chs 7 and 12.

for Europe (UNECE)'s Long-Range Transboundary Air Pollution Convention[157] or UNEP's 1987 Cairo Guidelines and Principles for the Environmentally Sound Management of Hazardous Waste,[158] to name but two examples of prominent instruments of varying legal value, play a role in SDG implementation. This is even more so because UNEP does not act as custodian agency for any of SDG 11's targets. It will therefore be up to individual actors to establish links between target 11.6 and international instruments combatting environmental degradation.

IV. Commentaries on Targets and Indicators

SDG 11 comprises a total of ten targets of which three are designed as means of implementation targets, indicated by the fact that they are not numbered but alphabetically listed. Leaving aside the broader question of whether this division makes sense, the status of implementation target can be questioned at least for target 11.b on disaster risk reduction, as this target is both time-bound (2020) and aims at ensuring the implementation of a specific framework, namely the Sendai Framework for Disaster Risk Reduction, rather than SDG 11 as a whole.[159]

Like all targets of the 2030 Agenda, SDG 11's ten targets must be read in conjunction with the Global Indicator Framework, adopted by the General Assembly almost two years after the SDGs and subject to constant refinement. The long delay between the adoption of the goals and the Indicator Framework suggests that indicators, even if supposedly based on expert authority and technical considerations, were subject to political disagreement and contention.[160] This is especially true for the indicators of SDG 11, many of which were new and thus challenging to monitor even for countries with advanced monitoring and statistical capacities.[161] The Global Indicator Framework contains fifteen indicators developed to measure progress on the implementation of SDG 11's ten targets. As will be shown throughout the analysis of each individual target, the indicators impact greatly how the targets are interpreted, even if their sheer number sets them apart from prior global indicator sets and might perhaps decrease their focus.[162]

It has already been mentioned that no indicator or target of SDG 11 contains any explicit reference to human rights instruments, or even a global reference to international

---

[157] Convention on long-range transboundary air pollution, Geneva, 13 November 1979, UNTS vol 1302, p 217.

[158] Decision 14/30 of the UNEP Governing Council, 17 June 1987, UN Doc UNEP/GC.14/17, Annex II.

[159] This is also reflected in indicator 11.b.1, cf UN Doc A/Res/71/313, Annex.

[160] S Fukuda-Parr, 'Sustainable Development Goals' (n 46) 773–74

[161] Policy Brief in Support of the First SDG 11 Review at the UN High-Level Political Forum 2018, p 2.

[162] For such a reading M Riegner, 'The End of Indicators: The World Bank's Doing Business Indicators Are Dead—Long Live Global Data Governance!', *Völkerrechtsblog*, 6 October 2021, doi: 10.17176/20211006-133821-0, but see the reply by A Fisher, 'Indicators 2.0: From Ranks and Reports to Dashboards and Databanks: Governance-by-indicators-by-infrastructure', *Völkerrechtsblog*, 23 November 2021, doi: 10.17176/20211123-204439-0. The normative force of indicators has been seminally treated in Merry and others (eds) (n 73); arguing that the 'collection of numbers' through indicators in the SDG framework still constitutes a powerful regulatory tool A Fisher and S Fukuda-Parr, 'Introduction—Data, Knowledge, Politics and Localizing the SDGs' (2019) 20(4) Journal of Human Development and Capabilities 375–85.

824   SDG 11

human rights law, as is the case in target 10.3 (ensure equal opportunity).[163] However, some of the targets contain human rights language that allows for linkage to international human rights law. The following sections will establish the necessary connections between individual targets and existing human rights instruments as well as other instruments of international law relevant to the targets and indicators.

A. Target 11.1 By 2030, ensure access for all to adequate, safe and affordable housing and basic services and upgrade slums

1. Sources of Target

This target addresses an issue that advanced to the core of the Habitat agenda since at least the Habitat II Conference in 1996: adequate shelter for all.[164] The topic had been put on Habitat's agenda a decade earlier, when the General Assembly tasked Habitat and the Commission on Human Settlement with developing a Global Strategy for Shelter to the Year 2000.[165] The wording of the target 'adequate, safe and affordable housing' is closely related to human rights language, specifically the right to adequate housing. As mentioned earlier, this is the only target in SDG 11 where metadata specifically mentions international human rights law.[166]

The right to adequate housing forms part of the right to an adequate standard of living, enshrined in article 11 ICESCR. The New Urban Agenda—unlike the 2030 Agenda—makes this connection explicit. The Quito Implementation Plan states: 'We commit ourselves to promoting national, subnational and local housing policies that support the progressive realization of the right to adequate housing for all as a component of the right to an adequate standard of living.'[167] The wording in article 11(1) ICESCR builds on article 25(1) of the Universal Declaration of Human Rights. It is also contained in several other core human rights treaties.[168] In 2000, the former Commission on Human Rights further established a mandate for a Special Rapporteur on the right to adequate housing.[169] At the time of writing, Professor Balakrishnan Rajagopal is the mandate holder, focusing in his latest reports on the impact of COVID-19 on the right to housing, on taking stock of twenty years of the mandate,

---

[163] See the indicator for target 10.3: '10.3.1 Proportion of population reporting having personally felt discriminated against or harassed in the previous 12 months on the basis of a ground of discrimination prohibited under international human rights law' in UN Doc A/Res/71/313.

[164] The question of housing dates back much further on the UN agenda, but the language of 'adequate shelter for all' is rooted in the Habitat II Agenda. See this chapter Subsection I.A).

[165] UN Doc A/Res/42/191, paras 3–4.

[166] Subsection II.C this chapter. See United Nations, Metadata 11.1.1 (October 2020) <https://unstats.un.org/sdgs/metadata/files/Metadata-11-01-01.pdf>accessed 30 December 2021.

[167] New Urban Agenda, Quito Implementation Plan for the New Urban Agenda (n 74) Annex, para 31.

[168] Art 5(e)(iii) of the International Convention on the Elimination of All Forms of Racial Discrimination, art 14(2) of the Convention on the Elimination of All Forms of Discrimination against Women, art 27(3) of the Convention on the Rights of the Child.

[169] Commission on Human Rights Resolution 2000/9 of 17 April 2000, available at <https://www.ohchr.org/en/issues/housing/pages/housingindex.aspx> accessed 30 December 2021.

and on discrimination in the context of housing.[170] Throughout the twenty years of the mandate's existence, the various Special Rapporteurs developed several guidelines anchored in human rights law. While these guidelines do not have the status of treaty law, they have made an important contribution to the realization of the human right to adequate housing.[171] Three sets of guidelines exist: the 2008 Basic Principles and Guidelines on Development-Based Evictions and Displacement, the 2014 Guiding Principles on Security of Tenure for the Urban Poor, and the 2020 Guidelines for the Implementation of the Right to Adequate Housing.[172]

The Committee on Economic, Social and Cultural Rights (CESCR) has also contributed to shaping the right to adequate housing, through two General Comments that specify obligations of ICESCR state parties with respect to the right to housing.[173] According to General Comment No 4, the right to housing should not be restricted to mere shelter, but encompasses the right to live somewhere in security, peace, and dignity. Similarly, the Guiding Principles on Security of Tenure for the Urban Poor define security of tenure as 'a set of relationships with respect to housing and land, established through statutory or customary law or informal or hybrid arrangements, that enables one to live in one's home in security, peace and dignity'.[174] This entails a number of components that are crucial to the right to housing: legal security of tenure; availability of services, facilities and infrastructure; affordability; habitability; accessibility (in particular for persons with disabilities); location that allows access to employment options and/or schooling; and cultural adequacy.[175] The right to housing also interacts with a number of other human rights, notably the right not to be subjected to arbitrary or unlawful interference with one's privacy, family, home, or correspondence (article 17 ICCPR).[176] The CESCR has further specified that the obligation to ensure legal security of tenure is incompatible with forced evictions, that evictions ought to be used exclusively as a last resort, and if no other option is feasible, that there need to be legal remedies available for evicted persons, and that certain processual guarantees need to be put into place.[177]

State obligations under the right to adequate housing can be classified into three categories, as is the case for all social and economic rights, namely an obligation to

---

[170] Office of the High Commissioner for Human Rights, Special Rapporteur on the Right to Adequate Housing <https://www.ohchr.org/en/issues/housing/pages/housingindex.aspx> accessed 30 December 2021.

[171] Special Rapporteur on the Right to Adequate Housing, 'Twenty Years of Promoting and Protecting the Right to Adequate Housing: Taking Stock and Moving Forward', UN Doc A/HRC/47/43, para 9.

[172] All available at Office of the High Commissioner for Human Rights, Special Rapporteur on the Right to Adequate Housing <https://www.ohchr.org/en/issues/housing/pages/housingindex.aspx> accessed 30 December 2021.

[173] CESCR, General Comment No 4 (1991), contained in UN Doc E/1992/23, and General Comment No 7 (1997), contained in UN Doc E/1998/22, Annex IV.

[174] Report of the Special Rapporteur on adequate housing as a component of the right to an adequate standard of living, and on the right to non-discrimination in this context, Raquel Rolnik, Guiding principles on security of tenure for the urban poor, UN Doc A/HRC/25/54, p 3.

[175] CESCR, General Comment No 4 (n 173).

[176] ibid.

[177] CESCR, General Comment No 7 (1997), contained in UN Doc E/1998/22, Annex IV.

respect, an obligation to protect, and an obligation to fulfil.[178] Forced evictions carried out by the state are an infringement of a state's obligation to respect, whereas the obligation to protect requires states to ensure that third parties do not unduly interfere with the right to adequate housing. The obligation to fulfil is an obligation of progressive realization that tasks states with, for example, developing national housing plans and preventing homelessness within their national means.[179]

2. Empirical Analysis

Compared to this standard from international human rights law, the relevant indicator for target 11.1 in the Global Indicator Framework is rather limited. Indicator 11.1.1 only measures the proportion of urban population living in slums, informal settlements, or inadequate housing. This indicator is very close to its predecessor, MDG target 7.D, focused on 'improvement in the lives of at least 100 million slum dwellers'.[180] Reducing the target on adequate housing to slum 'upgrading' is problematic for several reasons: first, the indicator does not specify what 'inadequate housing' constitutes; and second, the simple proportion of urban population living in slums does not specify how slums should be transformed or what measures could be undertaken to improve the housing situation for slum dwellers. There have been case studies showing that implementation of the MDGs with the goal to 'improve the lives of slum dwellers' by reducing the number of people living in slums has led to a normalization of violence against people living in slums or informal settlements and has in fact contributed to the kinds of forced eviction that international human rights law prohibits.[181]

UN-Habitat as the lead agency on SDG 11 has developed eight criteria to measure the three dimensions of indicator 11.1.1: access to water; access to sanitation; sufficient living area and no overcrowding; structural quality, durability and location; security of tenure; affordability; accessibility and cultural adequacy.[182] The last three criteria in particular are novel in comparison to the MDGs and are aligned with components of the right to adequate housing. Here, we see a response to criticism regarding the MDG indicator and its lack of accounting for human rights dimensions.

At the time of writing, implementation of target 11.1 is experiencing a reverse trend. 1.6 billion people, or 20 per cent of the world's population, are living in inadequate, crowded, or unsafe housing, according to the 2020 World Cities Report.[183] In cities, numbers tend to be higher than the worldwide average. Whereas urban population living in slums was reduced from 28 per cent in 2000 to 23 per cent in 2014, the trend is now reversing, with an increase to 24 per cent in 2018.[184] Current data show that

---

[178] Office of the High Commissioner for Human Rights/UN-Habitat, 'The Right to Adequate Housing', Factsheet No 21 Rev. 1 <https://www.ohchr.org/documents/publications/fs21_rev_1_housing_en.pdf> accessed 30 December 2021, p 33.

[179] ibid p 33–34.

[180] Millennium Development Goals Target 7.D; first contained in UN Doc A/57/270, p 31.

[181] See Oliveira (n 49) for a case study of Rio de Janeiro, Brazil.

[182] UN-Habitat, Urban SDG Monitoring Series 2019 <https://unhabitat.org/sites/default/files/2020/06/the_urban_sdg_monitoring_series_monitoring_sdg_indicator_11.1.1.pdf> accessed 30 December 2021.

[183] UN-Habitat, 'World Cities Report 2020' (n 6) p 25.

[184] United Nations, 'The Sustainable Development Goals Report 2020' <https://unstats.un.org/sdgs/report/2020/> accessed 30 December 2021, p 46.

the problem of informal settlements and slum dwelling is particularly prevalent on the African continent, in the Middle East, Central and South East Asia, and the Indian subcontinent, as well as parts of Central and South America.[185] Balakrishnan Rajagopal, the current Special Rapporteur on the Right to Adequate Housing, has further pointed out that the COVID-19 pandemic has contributed to increased housing insecurity, as has conflict, disaster, natural hazards, development-induced displacement, and forced evictions, which have all increased in recent years.[186]

3. Implementation Efforts Taken at Domestic and International Level

Despite the reverse trends in implementing SDG 11.1, there are notable efforts aimed at implementing this target. The World Cities Report 2020 highlights, for example, the 2018 Declaration of Cities for Adequate Housing.[187] This declaration was adopted at the 2018 High-Level Political Forum, facilitated by the United Cities and Local Governments Network, one of the many city networks mentioned above.[188] Through this declaration, a growing number of city governments commit to developing more mixed residential solutions and improved urban planning, and call for increased fiscal and legal powers to regulate the real estate market and increased funding for local housing projects.[189] At the time of writing, some thirty-eight city governments and three metropolitan regions had signed this declaration, including important metropolitan centres such as New York, Seoul, London, Mexico City, Medellín, Taipei, and the Greater Paris Area.[190]

For almost two decades, UN-Habitat and the UN Office of the High Commissioner for Human Rights (OHCHR) have operated the UN Housing Rights Programme (UNHRP) in order to assist states, but also local governments, with implementing the right to adequate housing through technical assistance.[191] To date, UN-Habitat has advised forty-two governments on how to analyse the urban housing sector and design a regulatory framework that would respect the right to adequate housing.[192] UN-Habitat also facilitates the Global Land Tool Network, which, according to its own description, is a 'dynamic and multisectoral alliance of international partners committed to increasing access to land and tenure security for all, with a particular focus on the poor, women and youth'.[193] UN Habitat's work in assisting local governments and launching

---

[185] Sachs and Others (n 91) <https://dashboards.sdgindex.org/map/indicators/proportion-of-urban-populat ion-living-in-slums> accessed 30 December 2021, Proportion of population living in slums, overall score.
[186] Special Rapporteur on the Right to Adequate Housing, 'Twenty Years of Promoting and Protecting the Right to Adequate Housing' (n 171).
[187] UN-Habitat, 'World Cities Report 2020' (n 6) p 214.
[188] See Subsection II.B this chapter.
[189] Cities for Adequate Housing, Municipalist Declaration of Local Governments for the Right to Housing and the Right to the City, New York, 16 July 2018 <https://citiesforhousing.org/#section--0> accessed 30 December 2021.
[190] Cities for Adequate Housing, Endorsing cities <https://citiesforhousing.org/cities/> accessed 30 December 2021.
[191] UN-Habitat, United Nations Housing Rights Programme <https://mirror.unhabitat.org/content.asp?ID= 798&catid=282&typeid=24&subMenuId=0> accessed 30 December 2021.
[192] UN-Habitat, Housing Rights <https://unhabitat.org/programme/housing-rights> accessed 30 December 2021.
[193] Global Land Tool Network, About GLTN <https://gltn.net/about-gltn/> accessed 30 December 2021.

828   SDG 11

multi-actor networks are typical examples of how international and domestic implementation interact in today's transnational legal ordering.[194]

In addition to UN Habitat's efforts, the Special Rapporteur on the Right to Adequate Housing also contributes to the implementation of the right to adequate housing. For example, in response to the COVID-19 pandemic, then-Special Rapporteur on the Right to Adequate Housing, Leilani Farha, set up online consultations and developed a set of guidelines to protect the right to adequate housing during the pandemic on the basis of these consultations.[195] These guidance notes address specific aspects of the right to adequate housing, such as the prohibition of evictions, protecting homeless persons, or protecting housing from financialization.[196] The Special Rapporteur's country visits have also ushered in housing law reforms, for example in Portugal, Mexico, New Zealand, Kenya, and Chile.[197] Note that these efforts are not taken exclusively as efforts to implement target 11.1 specifically; rather, they aim at implementing the right to adequate housing more generally.

4. Critique

As mentioned before, a primary criticism of indicator 11.1.1, and its predecessor, MDG target 7.D, was and is its focus on slums and slum dwellers. While target 11.1 and its wording of 'adequate housing' has sought to connect the SDGs more closely with the human right to adequate housing, a disconnect between the SDGs and international human rights law remains.[198] The SDG Report's Dashboard for 2021 only shows the proportion of urban population living in slums and does not portray other dimensions of the right to adequate housing. Since dashboards to some extent regulate and thus implicitly govern our perception of norms,[199] this is an important limitation to target 11.1 and its indicator. At the same time, data even for this limited indicator of proportion of urban population living in slums are unavailable for important countries such as Russia.

A broader criticism relates to the different ways in which adequate housing and the right to housing can be and have been understood. The right to adequate housing has a broader meaning than simply a roof over one's head and includes dimensions of living in dignity and in culturally adequate shelter.[200] Yet, the right to adequate housing and related international instruments have in recent years focused in a rather narrow way on 'security of tenure', understood as a formal legal title to land. This displays a Western,

---

[194] Halliday and Shaffer (eds) (n 73); see also this chapter Subsection II.B.

[195] Special Rapporteur on the Right to Adequate Housing, 'Twenty Years of Promoting and Protecting the Right to Adequate Housing' (n 171) para 14.

[196] See the resources at Office of the High Commissioner for Human Rights, Protecting the right to housing in the context of the COVID-19 outbreak <https://www.ohchr.org/EN/Issues/Housing/Pages/COVID19RightTo Housing.aspx> accessed 30 December 2021.

[197] Special Rapporteur on the Right to Adequate Housing, 'Twenty Years of Promoting and Protecting the Right to Adequate Housing' (n 171) paras 28–29.

[198] For a general critique of this disconnect see Winkler and Williams (n 126) and the further contributions in that Special Issue.

[199] Fisher (n 162).

[200] Special Rapporteur on the Right to Adequate Housing, 'Twenty Years of Promoting and Protecting the Right to Adequate Housing' (n 171) para 56.

capitalist, and individualistic understanding of how people relate to land, thus reducing tenure security to formal ownership and property rights, without taking into account different cultures, traditions and understandings of property as well as understanding tenure security as security of home.[201]

Lastly, despite the many international instruments and efforts undertaken both at the international and the domestic levels, the problem of inadequate shelter persists in many parts of the world. The statistics mentioned above in the section on empirical analysis point to the fact that no easy answer is available in securing adequate housing, and the Special Rapporteur has recently pointed out that spatial discrimination is an increasing problem in ensuring the right to adequate housing.[202] Ensuring the right to adequate housing is thus a multidimensional challenge that goes beyond simply measuring the proportion of urban population living in slums or informal or inadequate housing, as is suggested by indicator 11.1.1.

B. Target 11.2 By 2030, provide access to safe, affordable, accessible and sustainable transport systems for all, improving road safety, notably by expanding public transport, with special attention to the needs of those in vulnerable situations, women, children, persons with disabilities and older persons

1. Sources of Target

Target 11.2 addresses access to transport systems, in particular public transportation. Transport has been an issue on the Habitat Agenda since the Habitat II Conference, even though the focus of the Habitat Agenda was largely on adverse environmental effects of transport systems. Yet, the Habitat Agenda already acknowledged that 'transport in human settlements should be done in a way that promotes good access for all to places of work, social interaction and leisure'.[203] Access to transport as a means of ensuring participation in society has thus been on the radar of the Habitat Agenda for some time. Target 11.2 also intersects with several other goals, notably SDG 9 on infrastructure and specifically target 9.1 on accessible infrastructure for all, which includes access to all-season roads.[204] To the extent that target 11.2 focuses on women as a vulnerable group and safety concerns, it also intersects with SDG 5, specifically with target 5.2 on violence against women, even though this dimension is not visible at all at the indicator level.[205] Related targets within SDG 11 are target 11.3 on sustainable

---

[201] Wadlig (n 12).

[202] Report of the Special Rapporteur on adequate housing as a component of the right to an adequate standard of living, and on the right to non-discrimination in this context, Balakrishnan Rajagopal, Discrimination in the context of housing. UN Doc A/76/408 (Advance Unedited Version).

[203] Report of the United Nations Conference on Human Settlements (Habitat II), UN Doc A/CONF.165/14, Habitat Agenda, para 149.

[204] UN 2030 Agenda on Sustainable Development, UN Doc A/Res/70/1, target 9.1, and indicator 9.1.1, contained in UN Doc A/Res/71/313, Annex.

[205] See this chapter Subsection IV.B.4 on critique of this target.

urbanization, in particular its indicator 11.3.1 on the ratio of land consumption rate to population growth rate, and target 11.7 on access to public space.[206]

Target 11.2 is measured by one sole indicator. Indicator 11.2.1 measures the proportion of population that has convenient access to public transport, by sex, age, and persons with disabilities. Disaggregation of data is based on the wording of the target that specifically targets women, children, older persons, and persons with disabilities. This opens links to provisions of the Convention on the Rights of Persons with Disabilities (CRPD).

The CRPD addresses transportation and mobility for people with disabilities in two articles. Article 20 CRPD ensures the right to personal mobility, whereas article 9 CRPD ensures *inter alia* access to transportation. Article 9 (1) CRPD obliges States Parties explicitly to 'ensure to persons with disabilities access … to transportation'. Article 9 has been an important provision for the work of the CRPD's treaty monitoring body, the Committee on the Rights of Persons with Disabilities.[207] As early as in its second General Comment, the Committee clarified that accessibility as ensured by article 9 CRPD ought to be understood as a precondition to live independently and participate fully in life.[208] This also applies to elderly people. States are under a legal obligation to define domestic accessibility standards and to develop legislation in this regard.[209] Article 20 CRPD in turn ensures personal mobility. Whereas accessibility in article 9 CRPD relates to the broader environment, article 20 focuses on the individual and thus is more specific.[210] Specific obligations under article 20 include measures to facilitate personal mobility, for example through signal indicators.[211] This relates to transportation infrastructure broadly speaking. Note, however, that this connection between the CRPD and target 11.2 is not reflected in the SDG's metadata document, nor is this connection mentioned in any other SDG-related documentation that was reviewed for this commentary, including past SDG reports and the SDG Dashboard.

The New Urban Agenda deepens the scope of target 11.2.[212] It contains several more specific recommendations with regard to transport, including such topics as urban–rural linkages, road safety (with special view to the four vulnerable groups identified in indicator 11.2.1), and transport financing.[213] But similarly to the link to international human rights law, the link between the New Urban Agenda and target 11.2 is not

---

[206] United Nations, Metadata 11.2.1 (September 2021) <https://unstats.un.org/sdgs/metadata/files/Metadata-11-02-01.pdf> accessed 30 December 2021.

[207] A Lawson, 'Art. 9' in I Bantekas and others (eds), *The UN Convention on the Rights of Persons with Disabilities: A Commentary* (OUP 2018) 260.

[208] Committee on the Rights of Persons with Disabilities, General Comment No 2 (2014), UN Doc CRPD/C/GC/2.

[209] ibid.

[210] L Kovudhikulrungsri and A Hendriks, 'Art. 20' in Bantekas and others (eds) (n 207) 561–62, using an example from the delegate of India throughout the *travaux préparatoires*: whereas building a ramp for a person in a wheelchair would fall under art 9 CRPD, the provision of the wheelchair as a measure that concerns the person directly would fall under art 20 CRPD.

[211] ibid 569–70.

[212] UN-Habitat, 'World Cities Report 2020' (n 6) p 10.

[213] New Urban Agenda, Quito Implementation Plan for the New Urban Agenda (n 74) Annex, paras 113–18.

COMMENTARIES ON TARGETS AND INDICATORS 831

reflected in target 11.2's metadata document, and accordingly finds little reflection in SDG reporting.

2. Empirical Analysis

According to the 2020 Sustainable Development Goals Report, only half of the world's urban population has convenient access to public transportation. Convenient access is given when the walking distance to a low-capacity transport system, that is a bus or a tram, is within 500 metres, and a high-capacity transport system (trains, subways, and ferries) is available within 1,000 metres of walking.[214] Informal transportation systems are prevalent in many countries, leading to less regularity and reliability. Moreover, informal transportation systems will generally not have standardized routines to address the needs of people with reduced mobility. Accordingly, only 41.3 per cent of the world's population is satisfied with public transportation.[215] Whilst lower- and upper-middle-income countries have experienced an increase in satisfaction with public transportation, public transportation is particularly bad in low-income countries, and is not improving in high-income countries, according to the 2021 SDG Report.[216]

Limited access to public transportation has adverse effects on other SDGs, and, relatedly, on human rights. The 2018 UN flagship report on disability and development highlighted, for example, that a significantly higher number of people with disabilities did not seek necessary healthcare because there was no transport available or because cost of the transport was too high.[217] The same report also adverted to the fact that students with disabilities often drop out of school because no transport to school is available.[218] This is in line with legal commentary on article 20 CRPD which has highlighted the link between the right to inclusive education and personal mobility.[219] The 2020 World Cities Report has pointed out more generally that a lack of urban transport systems results in less inclusive cities.[220]

3. Implementation Efforts Taken at Domestic and International Level

As evidenced by the previous section, there exists a serious implementation gap with regard to target 11.2, with only half of the world's urban population having convenient access to public transportation and less than half of the world's population being satisfied with public transportation. The COVID-19 pandemic has imposed additional challenges to safety in public transport, especially in big cities where millions of people tend to use public transport on a daily basis.[221] This has in turn led to several cities,

---

[214] United Nations, 'The Sustainable Development Goals Report 2020' (n 184) p 46.

[215] Sachs and others (n 91) <https://dashboards.sdgindex.org/map/indicators/satisfaction-with-public-transport> accessed 30 December 2021, Satisfaction with public transport, overall score.

[216] ibid 499–505.

[217] United Nations, Realization of the Sustainable Development Goals, for and with Persons with Disabilities— UN Flagship Report on Disability and Development, 2018 <https://www.ohchr.org/Documents/HRBodies/CRPD/UN2018FlagshipReportDisability.pdf> accessed 30 December 2021, p 79.

[218] ibid 108–09.

[219] Kovudhikulrungsri and Hendriks (n 210) 567.

[220] UN-Habitat, 'World Cities Report 2020' (n 6) p xxi.

[221] Pointing out the need for additional safety measures due to the pandemic United Nations, 'The Sustainable Development Goals Report 2020' (n 184) p 46.

especially in Europe, implementing or expanding their bicycle lane networks.[222] But cycling lanes are also becoming increasingly popular outside of Europe: according to UN-Habitat, Cairo had installed more than 100 cycle lanes accommodating up to 200 bicycles in three neighbourhoods and UN-Habitat is supporting the city of Ankara, Turkey, in developing a city-wide Bicycle Strategy.[223] Finding solutions that are based on human-powered, non-motorized mobility solutions has an important effect on reducing greenhouse gas emissions; where biking or walking cannot be implemented, for example due to too long distances, expanding public transport systems is the next best thing to reduce greenhouse gas emissions.[224]

Bus rapid transit systems are one example of a successful implementation measure in achieving target 11.2. A bus rapid transit system typically includes specifically designed bus lanes and bus stops that are only accessible to passengers, similar to subway stops, so as to increase security. Bus rapid transit systems are especially successful in Latin American countries, with over 20 million passengers each day in a total of sixty-one cities.[225] Bogotá has long been considered a gold standard with a daily ridership of over 2 million passengers; in Bogotá and elsewhere, bus rapid transit systems have considerably reduced commute time for passengers.[226] Of course, it is important that such systems be designed in such a way as to take into account the rights and safety of those groups that target 11.2 seeks to protect. This is true both for implementing novel and expanding existing public transport systems.

One example of how the rights of persons with disabilities come into play when expanding public transport systems can be found in the individual complaints procedure of *F v Austria*.[227] A blind Austrian citizen who relies on public transport on a daily basis launched a complaint because the city of Linz, where he resides, did not install digital audio information that had been available on all stops of a tram line when expanding the tram line. The complainant therefore had no possibility of accessing information without asking other passers-by. The Committee on the Rights of Persons with Disabilities found that this constituted a violation of the complainant's rights under, amongst others, article 9(2) CRPD, as the audio information system could have been installed at a low cost and with limited additional effort. Thus, the author of the complaint was denied equal access to public transport. Note, however, that this is an implementation practice that does not explicitly relate to target 11.2, but rather seeks to uphold the provisions of the CRPD.

---

[222] L Alderman, '"Corona cycleways" become the new post-confinement commute', *The New York Times*, 12 June 2020 <https://www.nytimes.com/2020/06/12/business/paris-bicycles-commute-coronavirus.html> accessed 30 December 2021.

[223] UN-Habitat, Mobility and Transport <https://unhabitat.org/topic/mobility-and-transport> accessed 30 December 2021.

[224] UN-Habitat, 'World Cities Report 2020' (n 6) p 60.

[225] Global BRT data <https://brtdata.org> accessed 30 December 2021.

[226] UN-Habitat, 'World Cities Report 2020' (n 6) p 106.

[227] Committee on the Rights of Persons with Disabilities, Communication No 21/2014, Views adopted by the Committee at its fourteenth session, UN Doc CRPD/C/14/D/21/2014.

4. Critique

Target 11.2 is an important target in ensuring sustainable human settlements, especially cities. In order to expand its full potential, it ought to be explicitly linked to both other targets within the SDGs as well as international instruments, especially the CRPD. On the basis of the text of target 11.2, there are several intersections with other SDGs that can be forged. For example, to the extent that target 11.2 focuses on women as a vulnerable group and safety concerns, it intersects with SDG 5, specifically with target 5.2 on violence against women. However, this has not translated into measurement of the target. Instead, this dimension is eclipsed by the only indicator measuring target 11.2. Indicator 11.2.1 exclusively measures 'convenient access', but does not measure, for example, harassment. This is to some extent remedied through indicator 11.7.2, addressed below; however, the specific link between public transport systems and safety that is prominent in the target gets lost at the indicator level. This translates into implementation measures: for example, in Latin America and the Caribbean, over half of public transportation users are women, but public transportation systems are often designed without sufficiently accounting for women's safety needs.[228]

Similarly, the link to international human rights law, especially to articles 9 and 20 CRPD, is weak in practice. The metadata document does not mention the CRPD at all.[229] While a case for accessibility as a human right can be made in terms of sources, this has not translated into actual measurement of the target. Additionally, the transportation needs of children and the elderly, while specifically mentioned by target 11.2, are not specially addressed by international law instruments.

Lastly, the target is not uniformly measured. Whereas the indicator initially spoke of 'convenient' access, the latest iteration of the indicator currently measures 'satisfaction' with public transport rather than convenient access.[230] This is at odds with the New Urban Agenda, which places emphasis on the planning dimension of sustainable transport. Amongst other things, the New Urban Agenda explicitly calls for coordinated transport planning and common frameworks to be put into place at the national, subnational, and local levels, and for sustainable national urban transport and mobility policies that extend to procurement and take into account green technologies.[231] This is not reflected in the current texts relating to indicator 11.2.1.

---

[228] UN-Habitat, 'World Cities Report 2020' (n 6) p 63, citing the city of Puebla, Mexico, as an example where many families living in affordable housing need to walk long distances to access public transportation, which leads to women exposing themselves to risks.

[229] United Nations, Metadata 11.2.1 (September 2021) <https://unstats.un.org/sdgs/metadata/files/Metadata-11-02-01.pdf> accessed 30 December 2021.

[230] Sachs and others (n 91).

[231] New Urban Agenda, Quito Implementation Plan for the New Urban Agenda (n 74) Annex, paras 114–116.

C. Target 11.3 By 2030, enhance inclusive and sustainable urbanization and capacity for participatory, integrated and sustainable human settlement planning and management in all countries

1. Sources of Target

This target is concerned with two different things. The first part of target 11.3 is concerned with 'enhanc[ing] inclusive and sustainable urbanization'. The target is time-bound (2030), yet vague ('enhance'), so whether or not it has been achieved is subject to some degree of interpretative leeway. Inclusive and sustainable urbanization is measured as the ratio of land consumption rate to population growth rate.[232] This makes clear that inclusive and sustainable urbanization is primarily understood as how much space is available in urban settings.

The latter part of target 11.3 concerns 'capacity for participatory, integrated and sustainable human settlements planning' and thus more broadly participatory decision-making. Participatory decision-making is an important component of current good governance debates, and the SDGs are no exception. A more general target on participatory decision-making is contained in SDG 16.7 ('responsive, inclusive, participatory and representative decision-making at all levels'). SDG 5 also contains a target on participation of women in decision-making (target 5.5, ensure women's full and effective participation and equal opportunities for leadership at all levels of decision-making in political, economic and public life), and target 10.6 aims at enhanced representation of developing countries in decision-making in global financial institutions.

While target 11.3 itself does not speak of *democratic* decision-making, this is clarified in the indicator. Indicator 11.3.2 measures not only the proportion of cities with a direct participation structure but also the proportion of cities with management that operates regularly and democratically. To what extent democratic governance is rooted in international human rights law is a matter of some debate.[233] Article 21(1) of the Universal Declaration of Human Rights proclaims that '[e]veryone has the right to take part in the government of his country, directly or through freely chosen representatives', but no international human rights treaty contains an explicit right to democracy or democratic government. The 1993 Vienna Declaration of the World Conference on Human Rights proclaimed that '[t]he international community should support the strengthening and promoting of democracy, development and respect for human rights and fundamental freedoms in the entire world',[234] but it leaves open how democracy and

---

[232] Indicator 11.3.1, cf United Nations, Metadata 11.3.1 (March 2021) <https://unstats.un.org/sdgs/metadata/files/Metadata-11-03-01.pdf> accessed 30 December 2021.

[233] See for an overview with an ultimately sceptical view G Fox, 'Democracy, Right to, International Protection' in *Max Planck Encyclopedia of Public International Law* (2008). An early argument in favour of a normative entitlement to democratic government is made by TM Franck, 'The Emerging Right to Democratic Governance' (1992) 86(1) American Journal of International Law 46–91.

[234] Vienna Declaration of the World Conference on Human Rights, 1993, contained in UN Doc A/CONF.157/23, para 8.

human rights intersect.[235] At the same time, it has been argued that article 21 of the Universal Declaration of Human Rights can be seen as a basis for a right to democratic self-government, which should be seen as warranted also from a theoretical point of view.[236] A right to democracy might exist regionally, especially in the Americas, where the Organization of American States' 2001 Inter-American Democratic Charter proclaims that '[t]he peoples of the Americas have a right to democracy and their governments have an obligation to promote and defend it'.[237]

2. Empirical Analysis

With regard to the first part of target 11.3, two data points are necessary: population growth and the land consumption rate. While the former is rather straightforward, measuring the land consumption rate necessitates new technologies and might be challenging for this reason.[238] In the context of indicator 11.3.1, 'land consumption' is understood as 'the uptake of land by urbanized land uses, which often involves conversion of land from non-urban to urban functions'.[239] The 2020 Sustainable Development Report contains data on the amount of built-up area per person and notes an increase: physical expansion of cities according to this data was faster than their rates of population growth, which does not fare well for achieving this particular target. The report also notes that the rapid physical expansion of cities was sometimes the result of unplanned urban sprawl, which has negative consequences, such as more costly service delivery.[240]

An increase of built-up area per capita was noted in all regions except for Sub-Saharan Africa and Eastern and Southern Asia. The World Cities Report 2020 contains data for the ratio of land consumption rate to population growth rate between 2000 and 2015 for select cities. By far the highest ratio of land consumption in this sample is found in Xingping, Shaanxi province in China, and there are several East and South-East Asian cities that have experienced a high rate of land consumption vis-à-vis population growth. Several European cities, such as Nice (France) and Berlin (Germany), also present high ratios of land consumption to population growth.[241]

The second indicator of target 11.3 measures the availability of structures for participation of civil society in urban planning and management.[242] This is a tier 2 indicator,

---

[235] Fox, 'Democracy, Right to, International Protection' (n 233) para 5.

[236] For this view see explicitly S Benhabib, 'Is There a Human Right to Democracy? Beyond Interventionism and Indifference' in C Corradetti (ed), *Philosophical Dimensions of Human Rights* (Springer 2012) 191–213. For the opposing view that a human right to democracy is not warranted from a theoretical point of view see J Cohen, 'Is There a Human Right to Democracy?' in C Sypnowich (ed), *The Egalitarian Conscience: Essays in Honour of G. A. Cohen* (OUP 2006) 226–48.

[237] Organization of American States, Inter-American Democratic Charter, 2001, art 1, available at <https://www.oas.org/charter/docs/resolution1_en_p4.htm> accessed 30 December 2021.

[238] United Nations, Metadata 11.3.1 (March 2021) <https://unstats.un.org/sdgs/metadata/files/Metadata-11-03-01.pdf> accessed 30 December 2021.

[239] ibid.

[240] 'The Sustainable Development Goals Report 2020' (n 184) p 47.

[241] See the data in table C1, UN-Habitat, 'World Cities Report 2020' (n 6) pp 322–34.

[242] United Nations, 'Metadata 11.3.2' (November 2018) <https://unstats.un.org/sdgs/metadata/files/Metadata-11-03-02.pdf> accessed 30 December 2021.

836 SDG 11

which might explain why there are no data on participatory decision-making structures contained in the 2021 SDG Report.[243]

3. Implementation Efforts Taken at Domestic and International Level

While little empirical data are available on participatory decision-making, there appears to be general agreement that it is an important normative demand. As mentioned before,[244] it has been argued that under certain circumstances, cities might be particularly well-suited places for participatory, democratic structures as they instil a sense of community, so as to become 'masters of their own fate'.[245] The importance of participatory planning is thus highlighted as a normative demand in guidelines and reports, for example in UN-Habitat's International Guidelines on Urban and Territorial Planning.[246] UN-Habitat's World Cities Report 2020 lists as one example of participatory structures an initiative by a Dutch civil society organization that provides land mapping in order to recognize and secure land rights.[247]

With regard to indicator 11.3.1, it is especially important that a rise in the ratio of land consumption to population growth not be the result of unplanned urban sprawl. The 2020 Sustainable Development Goals Report thus highlights that 154 countries had some form of national urban plan as of May 2020.[248] One example of how urban planning could be improved and be made more just is a pilot project in the Sanggau district of West-Kalimantan, Borneo, Indonesia which showed that communities' negotiations with companies happen on unequal terms and that mapping communities' land might be a way to remedy this. The World Cities Report concludes that similar examples could help to resolve land conflicts in rapidly growing urban areas.[249]

4. Critique

As mentioned before, target 11.3 contains two dimensions: 'enhanc[ing] inclusive and sustainable urbanization' and the 'capacity for participatory, integrated and sustainable human settlements planning', with distinct indicators. One risk is that the connection between these two dimensions gets lost: as the World Cities Report 2020 points out, the ratio of land consumption to population growth rate is indicative of cities' planning and management capacities, and it is therefore important that both dimensions of target 11.3 be read jointly.[250] This is especially problematic if planning capacities—the second dimension of target 11.3—are measured with a view only to their participatory

---

[243] Tier 1 indicators are indicators that are conceptually clear, have an internationally established methodology for measuring, and are regularly measured (in at least 50 per cent of the countries). Tier 2 indicators are also indicators that are conceptually clear and have an internationally established methodology, but where data is not regularly produced.

[244] See Section III.B this chapter.

[245] Blank (n 101) 114.

[246] UN-Habitat, International Guidelines on Urban and Territorial Planning, 2015 <https://unhabitat.org/international-guidelines-on-urban-and-territorial-planning> accessed 30 December 2021.

[247] UN-Habitat, 'World Cities Report 2020' (n 6) p 116.

[248] 'The Sustainable Development Goals Report 2020' (n 184) p 47.

[249] UN-Habitat, 'World Cities Report 2020' (n 6) p 104.

[250] ibid p 116.

dimension, and not looking at urban planning more generally. Additionally, the target as a whole is formulated in a vague manner ('enhance'), so whether or not it will have been achieved is subject to interpretation to an important degree.

Indicator 11.3.1's focus on the ratio of land consumption rate to population growth rate makes clear that inclusive and sustainable urbanization is primarily understood as how much space is available in urban settings. At the same time, the indicator does not measure *how* built-up area is built up. This includes questions such as materials used, harmony with existing surroundings, invasiveness into grounds and natural habitat, etc. All of these are important dimensions of inclusive and sustainable urbanization.

Indicator 11.3.2 is concerned with democratic decision-making, and thus at face value ought to address the whole of governing structures within a city. However, the metadata document makes clear that democratic participation is understood as participation of civil society organizations.[251] This focus is problematic in two ways. First, it does not address planning beyond participatory structures, and in particular leaves out connections between the use of urban land (indicator 11.3.1) and urban planning. Second, the focus on civil society organizations reveals a limited understanding of democracy and is at odds with rights-based approaches focusing on individual persons.

D. Target 11.4 Strengthen efforts to protect and safeguard the world's cultural and natural heritage

1. Sources of Target

The target on cultural and natural heritage is the only target within SDG 11 for which UN-Habitat acts neither as custodian agency for the indicator, nor as a partner agency. UNESCO is target 11.4's custodian agency whereas the International Union for Conservation of Nature acts as partner agency. Target 11.4's sole indicator, indicator 11.4.1, measures expenditure. Expenditure is measured for several factors: both public and private expenditures per capita spent on the preservation, protection, and conservation of all cultural and natural heritage are measured, and the data are to be disaggregated by type of heritage, level of government, and kind of expenditure/private funding.

The relevant legal instrument with regard to cultural and natural heritage is the World Heritage Convention ('Convention Concerning the Protection of the World Cultural and Natural Heritage'), which has been ratified by some 194 states and is thus close to being universally applicable. The Convention was adopted by the UNESCO General Conference in 1972 and UNESCO acts as depositary of the Convention.[252] Cultural and natural heritage are defined in articles 2 and 3 of the Convention and States Parties to the Convention undertake to identify cultural and natural heritage

---

[251] United Nations, 'Metadata 11.3.2' (November 2018) <https://unstats.un.org/sdgs/metadata/files/Metadata-11-03-02.pdf> accessed 30 December 2021.

[252] UNESCO, The World Heritage Convention <https://whc.unesco.org/en/convention/> accessed 30 December 2021.

838 SDG 11

sites, report them to the World Heritage Committee, and generally undertake measures for the preservation of such sites.[253] With a list of more than 1,000 heritage sites and its holistic approach to heritage as comprising both natural and cultural sites, the Convention is amongst the most successful instruments in the realm of heritage protection. One commentator attributes this success to 'the careful balance struck by the World Heritage Convention between the national interest of the territorial State to give the maximum visibility to its cultural and natural treasures and the general interest of humanity in their preservation'.[254]

2. Empirical Analysis

Natural and cultural heritage protection are exclusively mentioned in SDG 11 and in no other SDG. Natural and cultural heritage protection are thus regarded as a primary concern of cities and local governments. This contrasts with the somewhat older World Heritage Convention, which is explicitly geared towards states. By measuring expenditure for heritage protection at *different* governance levels, target 11.4 arguably carries the potential of highlighting cities' importance in protecting heritage. In addition, by calling for disaggregated data on different types of natural and cultural heritage and making heritage sites listed with the World Heritage Center one of several heritage categories to measure, target 11.4 also addresses a broader range of heritage than the World Heritage Convention.

Data on target 11.4 can be retrieved through UNESCO's statistical branch, the UNESCO Institute for Statistics.[255] Data were first made available in 2021, on the basis of a survey conducted between June 2020 and February 2021 to which sixty-two countries responded.[256] One important result of this survey is that countries are better able to identify public expenditure than private expenditure (only six countries were able to provide data on total public *and* private expenditure, and five of these six countries are EU Member States) and that they are mostly able to do so for the national level, less so at the local level, for which target 11.4 also calls.[257] Expenditure per capita was highest in European countries according to this first survey. Overall, data collection for target 11.4 remains a challenge.[258]

---

[253] See arts 4–6 and 11 of the Convention Concerning the Protection of the World Cultural and Natural Heritage.
[254] F Francioni, 'Cultural Heritage' in *Max Planck Encyclopedia of Public International Law* (2020).
[255] UNESCO Institute for Statistics, Sustainable Development Goal 11.4 <http://uis.unesco.org/en/topic/sustainable-development-goal-11-4> accessed 30 December 2021.
[256] UNESCO Institute for Statistics, 'Tracking investment to safeguard the world's cultural and natural heritage: Results of the 2020 UIS Survey on Expenditure on Cultural and Natural Heritage (SDG indicator 11.4.1)' <http://uis.unesco.org/sites/default/files/documents/uis_culture_and_heritage_report_2021_web.pdf> accessed 30 December 2021, p 4.
[257] UNESCO Institute for Statistics, 'Tracking investment to safeguard the world's cultural and natural heritage' (n 256) pp 5–6.
[258] See also the metadata document for target 11.4, which mentions variation between countries in terms of data availability and lack of availability of private expenditure data, United Nations, 'Metadata 11.4.1' (December 2021) <https://unstats.un.org/sdgs/metadata/files/Metadata-11-04-01.pdf> accessed 30 December 2021.

COMMENTARIES ON TARGETS AND INDICATORS 839

3. Implementation Efforts Taken at Domestic and International Level

As mentioned earlier, target 11.4 is the only target for which UN-Habitat does not act as custodian or partner agency. The responsibility for globally implementing target 11.4 within the UN system therefore lies with UNESCO as custodian agency and the International Union for Conservation of Nature as partner agency. UNESCO's Institute for Statistics is currently planning to develop a strategy to assist countries in data reporting, including a series of webinars and consultations to improve understanding of the data collection challenges countries face.[259]

Beyond target 11.4, UNESCO's work on World Heritage is guided by its ten-year strategic plan, adopted by the World Heritage Committee.[260] Its implementation work is centred around the 'five Cs': credibility, conservation, capacity building, communication, and communities. Credibility refers to the World Heritage List; conservation to World Heritage properties; capacity building is offered to actors at different governance levels to better understand World Heritage Convention instruments and to better implement them; communication is necessary to increase public awareness about World Heritage; and communities' roles in the implementation of the Convention ought to be enhanced.[261] UNESCO has put into place several programmes and projects. One such project, highlighted by the World Cities Report 2020 as a best practice for implementation of target 11.4, is the programme for submerged heritage which provided funding to the Baiheliang archaeological site in Fuling, China: Baiheliang is an archaeological site which was submerged due to the Three Gorges Dam, but it is today accessible through an underwater museum that received support from UNESCO.[262]

Beyond formal programme activity by UNESCO and its cultural heritage protection instruments and assistance activities, cities can also leverage their cultural heritage—irrespective of formal status under the World Heritage Convention—to attract investments and economic activity. One example is the city of Ségou in Mali: this former capital of the ancient Bamara kingdom is characterized by Sudanese terracotta architecture as well as colonial buildings. The city leveraged this cultural heritage with an annual festival to attract visitors, which has proven to be a major catalyst for the global economy, attracting some 30,000 visitors every year.[263]

4. Critique

Target 11.4 is the only target where UN-Habitat is not involved as custodian or partner agency. This bears the risk of isolating efforts at implementing target 11.4 from the other targets of SDG 11. This risk is further enhanced by the fact that the target on cultural and natural heritage is the only target within SDG 11 that is neither time-bound

---

[259] UNESCO Institute for Statistics, 'Tracking investment to safeguard the world's cultural and natural heritage' (n 256) p 4.

[260] UNESCO World Heritage Committee, Strategic Action Plan for the Implementation of the *World Heritage Convention* 2012–2022, contained in UNESCO Doc WHC-11/18.GA/11 <https://whc.unesco.org/archive/2011/whc11-18ga-11-en.pdf> accessed 30 December 2021.

[261] ibid p 4.

[262] UN-Habitat, 'World Cities Report 2020' (n 6) p 116.

[263] ibid p 171.

840 SDG 11

nor does it prescribe a specific outcome. Rather, it is limited to 'strengthening' efforts to protect cultural and natural heritage. To what extent target 11.4 can be regarded as 'achieved' is thus subject to a considerable amount of interpretation. In addition, by placing the target in the context of cities and urban governance, target 11.4 might distract from states' responsibility in protecting cultural and natural heritage as well. At the same time, this focus also bears the potential of highlighting local governments' important role in protecting natural and cultural heritage.

A second major challenge for target 11.4 lies in the SDGs' data-based approach. There are no data in the current SDG report on target 11.4, which points not only to a missing interface between UNESCO and the other custodian agencies, in particular UN-Habitat, but also to a lack of data availability. The UNESCO Statistical Institute's report, mentioned above in the section on empirical analysis, only contains data from twenty-nine countries out of the sixty-two countries that responded to the survey, because only the data from twenty-nine countries were sufficiently complete to calculate the indicator.[264] Challenges remain specifically with regard to private expenditure data, where UNESCO's Statistical Institute expects several years of capacity building and financial investment before data coverage can be raised to an acceptable level.[265]

The Institute has further highlighted that limiting target 11.4 to the financial dimension, that is, expenditure, provides only a partial image of the complex issue of heritage protection, as it does not take into view, for example, the work of countless voluntary workers that are often crucial to heritage conservation.[266] Lastly, the pandemic provides both a challenge with regard to data availability as well as more generally for heritage sites, but has also leveraged creative potential as many sites transitioned to online offers.[267]

E. Target 11.5 By 2030, significantly reduce the number of deaths and the number of people affected and substantially decrease the direct economic losses relative to global gross domestic product caused by disasters, including water-related disasters, with a focus on protecting the poor and people in vulnerable situations

1. Sources of Target
Target 11.5 aims at reducing the number of disaster-related deaths by 2030. While it is time-bound, it does not prescribe a specific result, but simply aims at 'significantly

---

[264] UNESCO Institute for Statistics, 'Tracking investment to safeguard the world's cultural and natural heritage' (n 256) p 4. The method on how to calculate the indicator is contained in United Nations, 'Metadata 11.4.1' (December 2021) <https://unstats.un.org/sdgs/metadata/files/Metadata-11-04-01.pdf> accessed 30 December 2021.

[265] United Nations, Metadata 11.4.1 (December 2021) <https://unstats.un.org/sdgs/metadata/files/Metadata-11-04-01.pdf> accessed 30 December 2021.

[266] UNESCO Institute for Statistics, 'Tracking investment to safeguard the world's cultural and natural heritage' (n 256) p 8.

[267] ibid p 9.

reducing' the number of deaths and economic losses that are caused by disasters. There exists no overarching treaty in international law that addresses disaster risk reduction, even though there are several treaties that regulate different types of disasters such as nuclear accidents or oil pollution as well as a number of regional treaties addressing disaster relief.[268] Disaster risk reduction is addressed in article 9 of the International Law Commission's Draft Articles on the Protection of Persons in the Event of Disasters, which provides that states shall take appropriate measures to reduce the risk of disasters, including risk assessments, dissemination of risk and loss information, and early warning systems.[269] The piecemeal international treaties, the work of the International Law Commission, and soft law instruments together make for an emerging body of an international law of disaster relief.[270] As article 9 of the Draft Articles on the Protection of Persons in the Event of Disasters evidences, disaster relief also comprises disaster risk reduction.

Absent a formally binding international treaty, the most important instrument governing disaster risk reduction is the Sendai Framework for Disaster Risk Reduction, which was adopted just a few months prior to the 2030 Agenda and with the SDGs in mind.[271] As mentioned before, target 11.5 is best read together with target 11.b, which explicitly mentions the Sendai Framework. This Framework spans the same time frame as the SDGs (2015–2030) and is explicitly understood as a contribution to sustainable development. This includes an explicit call to align indicators to measure progress in the implementation of the Sendai Framework with the Inter-Agency and Expert Group on SDG indicators.[272] The Sendai Framework makes concrete target 11.5 as it explicitly aims at lower mortality rates from disasters for the decade 2020–2030 compared with the decade 2005–2015.

Target 11.5 touches on several international human rights, including the right to life (article 6 ICCPR) and the right to health (article 12 ICESCR). The Human Rights Committee, which monitors implementation of the ICCPR, has explicitly stated that environmental degradation and climate change constitute dangers to the right to life.[273] This has also been reiterated by the same body in an individual complaints procedure, where the Committee stated that 'environmental degradation, climate change and unsustainable development constitute some of the most pressing and serious threats to the ability of present and future generations to enjoy the right to life'.[274]

---

[268] S Sivakumaran, 'Techniques in International Law-Making: Extrapolation, Analogy, Form and the Emergence of an International Law of Disaster Relief' (2017) 28(4) European Journal of International Law 1097–132, 1100–101.

[269] International Law Commission, Draft Articles on the Protection of Persons in the Event of Disasters, adopted by the International Law Commission at its sixty-eighth session, in 2016, and submitted to the General Assembly as a part of the Commission's report covering the work of that session (UN Doc A/71/10) para 48.

[270] Sivakumaran (n 268).

[271] Sendai Framework for Disaster Risk Reduction 2015–2030 (n 131) Annex.

[272] ibid Annex, paras 48(c), 50.

[273] Human Rights Committee, General Comment No 36, The right to life (2019), UN Doc CCPR/C/GC/36, para 62.

[274] Views adopted by the Human Rights Committee under art 5(4) of the Optional Protocol, concerning communication No 2728/2016, *Ioane Teitiota v New Zealand*, UN Doc CCPR/C/127/D/2728/2016, para 9.4.

2. Empirical Analysis

Target 11.5 has two indicators. Indicator 11.5.1 measures the number of deaths, missing persons and directly affected persons attributed to disasters per 100,000 population. This is the same indicator as indicator 1.5.1 (measuring target 1.5, 'build the resilience of the poor and those in vulnerable situations and reduce their exposure and vulnerability to ... disasters') and indicator 13.1.1 (measuring target 13.1, 'strengthen resilience and adaptive capacity to climate-related hazards and natural disasters').[275] Indicator 11.5.2 measures direct economic loss in relation to global GDP as well as damage to critical infrastructure and the number of disruptions to basic services that are attributed to disasters. Both indicators are not specific to urban settings but apply universally. They both also measure several things: deaths, missing persons, and directly affected persons as well as economic loss, infrastructure damage, and disruptions. All of these dimensions are mirrored and concretized in the Sendai Framework for Action, and in its indicator framework developed by an Open-ended Intergovernmental Expert Working Group, which was explicitly mandated to develop indicators coherent with the work of the Inter-Agency and Expert Group on Sustainable Development Goal Indicators.[276] The Sendai Monitoring Framework with seven targets (agreed upon in the Sendai Framework)[277] and thirty-eight indicators (developed by the Expert Group) was officially launched in early 2018.[278]

The Sendai Framework Indicators disaggregate indicator 11.5.1 (number of deaths, missing persons, and directly affected persons) into a total of eight individual indicators, specifying that 'being affected by' is understood as injury or illness, damaged dwellings, destroyed dwellings or disrupted or destroyed livelihoods (indicators B2–B5).[279] Similarly, indicator 11.5.2 (direct economic loss, damage to infrastructure, and disruptions to basic services) is split into two targets in the Sendai Framework, and a total of fourteen indicators, which are in part further disaggregated. 'Economic loss' is thus understood to include, amongst other things, agricultural loss, loss of productive assets, and direct economic loss due to cultural heritage damage; 'basic services' include primarily health and educational facilities and services, and disaster-induced disruptions thereto.[280] Given that the Sendai Framework indicators and the indicators for target 11.5 are so tightly interwoven, it seems logical that the custodian agency for target 11.5 is the UNDRR (formerly UN International Strategy for Disaster Reduction Secretariat, UNISDR), a UN Secretariat unit that sits in Geneva.[281] UNEP

---

[275] Further information on the interconnectedness of different SDGs with the Sendai Framework is available at <https://www.preventionweb.net/sendai-framework/Integrated> accessed 30 December 2021, monitoring of the global targets of the Sendai Framework and the Sustainable Development Goals.

[276] cf UN Doc A/Res/69/284, establishing an open-ended intergovernmental expert working group on indicators and terminology relating to disaster risk reduction. The Open-ended Intergovernmental Expert Working Group presented its report in 2016, UN Doc A/71/644, which was endorsed by the General Assembly in UN Doc A/Res/71/276.

[277] Sendai Framework for Disaster Risk Reduction 2015–2030 (n 131) Annex, para 18.

[278] UN Doc A/Res/72/218, para 21.

[279] See all targets and indicators for the Sendai Framework here: <https://www.preventionweb.net/sendai-framework/sendai-framework-indicators> accessed 30 December 2021.

[280] Sendai Framework Indicators, Global targets C and D, indicators C1–C6 and D1–D8.

[281] Ministry of Foreign Affairs and Trade/Manatū Aorere New Zealand, United Nations Handbook 2019–20, pp 228–29.

and UN-Habitat are partner agencies for indicator 11.5.1, and UNEP as well for indicator 11.5.2. This reflects again a strong connection between disaster risk reduction and environmental hazards, in particular climate change. It was already mentioned that the Sendai Framework for Disaster Risk Reduction, and consequently target 11.5, understand hazards in a way that clearly connects them to climate change. This emphasis on climate change has been criticized, as it puts too much emphasis on a single hazard.[282]

Despite the importance of target 11.5, data on monitoring are relatively scarce. According to UNDRR, for target groups B and C, which contain the targets mirroring target 11.5, more than 100 countries have not even started reporting yet in the current cycle.[283] This might be in part due to the fact that the area of disaster-related statistics is relatively new.[284] On the basis of the data that are available, the trends are alarming: the mortality rate due to disasters has increased both when comparing the past decade with the baseline decade (2005–2014) as well as when comparing the data from 2019 with data from 2020 (the latest data available at the time of writing). An increase compared to 2019 can also be observed for people being affected by disasters and damages to critical infrastructure.[285] The timely availability of data is a major challenge and is at the heart of UNDRR's current efforts.[286]

3. Implementation Efforts Taken at Domestic and International Level

At the international level, UNDRR has launched a cross-stakeholder initiative called 'Making Cities Resilient 2030' (MCR2030) on the basis of a prior decade-long campaign on resilient cities. MCR2030 specifically targets cities' resilience and disaster risk reduction efforts, and currently comprises 509 cities covering some 263 million people.[287] The main 'stakeholders' are several city networks (UCLG, C40, the Resilient Cities Network, ICLEI, and the World Council on City Data) and a number of UN entities (UNDRR, UN-Habitat, and the UN Office for Project Services, UNOPS) as well as the Japanese development agency JICA and the World Bank. The initiative operates mainly as a knowledge-sharing venue through which city governments can first become aware of the need for disaster risk reduction and then develop a disaster risk reduction and resilience strategy, which is implemented in a last step.[288] This is a typical project-management approach to multi-stakeholder initiatives. UN-Habitat, in turn, runs several projects and networks in the field of disaster risk reduction. This includes UN-Habitat's Urban Resilience Hub, which contains information on technical

---

[282] I Kelman, 'Climate Change and the Sendai Framework for Disaster Risk Reduction' (2015) 6(2) International Journal of Disaster Risk Science 117–27.

[283] Data for the year 2020, available at <https://sendaimonitor.undrr.org> accessed 30 December 2021.

[284] Policy Brief in Support of the First SDG 11 Review at the UN High-Level Political Forum 2018, p 4.

[285] Analytics for the year 2020, global data, available at <https://sendaimonitor.undrr.org/analytics/global-targets/16> accessed 30 December 2021.

[286] See also this chapter, target 11.b, and Policy Brief in Support of the First SDG 11 Review at the UN High-Level Political Forum 2018, p 4.

[287] UN Office for Disaster Risk Reduction, Making Cities Resilient <https://mcr2030.undrr.org> accessed 30 December 2021.

[288] MCR2030, Policy Brief <https://mcr2030.undrr.org/sites/default/files/2021-04/MCR2030%20in%20English%20ver.2%20%2820210302%29.pdf> accessed 30 December 2021.

assistance projects, a virtual library on resilience and disaster risk reduction, and reports and news on best practices from different places around the world.[289]

Often, disaster risk reduction efforts are tied to broader climate change action plans. One example of best practice that is highlighted in the 2020 World Cities Report is the Peruvian Action Plan on Gender and Climate Change: in its section on risk management, the plan highlights the importance of including traditional knowledge and integrating it with expertise.[290] The COVID-19 pandemic has further highlighted the importance of including disaster risk reduction strategies into urban planning: many city governments and local authorities are revising local urban strategies to be better prepared for the next pandemic, according to the 2020 SDG Report.[291]

4. Critique

The emerging field of international disaster law is primarily focused on disaster relief, not on disaster risk reduction. The ILC's Draft Articles on the Protection of Persons in the Event of Disasters only mention disaster risk reduction in one of its articles, even if it should be highlighted that the ILC's commentaries do mention the various disaster risk reduction soft law instruments.[292] This is despite the fact that disaster risk reduction is arguably a crucial part of any emerging law of disaster relief, given that it is aimed at preventing disasters in the first place, or at least at mitigating their effects. It is therefore advisable to systematically include duties of disaster risk reduction into instruments of disaster relief and to connect risk reduction and relief activities.

F. Target 11.6 By 2030, reduce the adverse per capita environmental impact of cities, including by paying special attention to air quality and municipal and other waste management

1. Sources of Target

Target 11.6 seeks to reduce the adverse environmental impact of cities, with a particular view to air quality and municipal waste management. Similar to target 11.5, this target is time-bound, but is formulated in a vague way, with no specific goal as to how much adverse impact ought to be reduced (eg concrete levels of reduction of fine particulate matter). It has two targets: indicator 11.6.1 focuses on urban waste management whereas indicator 11.6.2 addresses air quality. Both inadequate waste management as well as too high levels of particulate matter constitute threats to health and are therefore relevant to the right to health, article 12 ICESCR; and, as air pollution causes around

---

[289] UN-Habitat, Urban Resilience Hub <https://urbanresiliencehub.org> accessed 30 December 2021.

[290] UN-Habitat, 'World Cities Report 2020' (n 6) p 116.

[291] 'The Sustainable Development Goals Report 2020' (n 184) p 47.

[292] International Law Commission, Draft Articles on the protection of persons in the event of disasters, with commentaries <https://legal.un.org/ilc/texts/instruments/english/commentaries/6_3_2016.pdf> accessed 30 December 2021. Similarly, Sandesh Sivakumaran has provided an excellent and comprehensive analysis of an emerging law of international disaster relief but does not mention the Sendai Framework, or its predecessor, the Hyogo Framework for Action, Sivakumaran (n 268) 1097–132.

3.4 million deaths a year,[293] also to the right to life. In 2012, poor air quality was the reason for 7 million premature deaths worldwide.[294]

Indicator 11.6.1 is a tier 2 indicator in joint custody of UN-Habitat and the UN Statistical Division (UNSD). This means that the indicator is conceptually clear and follows an internationally established methodology, but data are not regularly produced. International and transnational waste management regulation is still relatively piecemeal and fragmented. A particular concern of international environmental law has been the definition of waste,[295] a problem circumvented by indicator 11.6.1, which focuses explicitly on urban solid waste (also known as municipal solid waste, or, more colloquially, household trash). This includes waste from households, commerce/trade and small businesses, bulky waste, and waste from municipal services, but excludes waste from municipal construction and the sewage network.[296] At the same time, there is no global regulation for landfill, even if there are some international treaties that prohibit the disposal of municipal waste into watercourses or the sea.[297] Regulation exists regionally, particularly at the EU level.[298] Target 11.6 and its indicator 11.6.1 therefore rely on soft normative requirements that are mainly pushed forward by UN-Habitat as custodian agency at the global level.

This is very different from indicator 11.6.2. Target 11.6's second indicator builds on a solid foundation of international environmental law. Transboundary air pollution is a well-established sub-field in international environmental law. Indicator 11.6.2 measures annual mean levels of fine particulate matter in cities and is a tier 1 indicator, which means that it follows a well-established methodology and that countries regularly produce data for this indicator. In international environmental law, air pollution is generally understood as defined by the UNECE Convention on Long-range Transboundary Air Pollution, whose article 1 defines air pollution as 'the introduction by man, directly or indirectly, of substances or energy into the air resulting in deleterious effects of such a nature as to endanger human health, harm living resources and ecosystems and material property and impair or interfere with amenities and other legitimate uses of the environment'.[299] If target 11.6 measures levels of fine particulate matter, this is mirroring the definition of 'introduction of substances into the air'. Particulate matter (PM2.5 and PM10) are also at the heart of the World Health Organization's (WHO) global air quality guidelines,[300] which are not formally legally binding, but, in the words of the WHO itself, 'provide WHO Member States with an

---

[293] Policy Brief in Support of the First SDG 11 Review at the UN High-Level Political Forum 2018, p 4.

[294] UN-Habitat, 'World Cities Report 2020' (n 6) p 191.

[295] Sands and others (n 156) ch 12.

[296] United Nations, 'Metadata 11.6.1' (September 2020) <https://unstats.un.org/sdgs/metadata/files/Metadata-11-06-01.pdf> accessed 30 December 2021.

[297] Sands and others (n 156) ch 12.

[298] See for an overview of EU waste law instruments <https://ec.europa.eu/environment/topics/waste-and-recycling/waste-law_en> accessed 30 December 2021.

[299] UNECE Convention on Long-range Transboundary Air Pollution; cf for this definition also Second report on the protection of the atmosphere by Shinya Murase, Special Rapporteur to the International Law Commission, UN Doc A/CN.4/681, paras 12, 17.

[300] WHO, 'Global Air Quality Guidelines' <https://www.who.int/publications/i/item/9789240034228> accessed 30 December 2021.

846 SDG 11

evidence-informed tool that they can use to inform legislation and policy'.[301] It is there-fore natural that the custodian agency for this second indicator is the WHO, with UN-Habitat, UNEP, and the Organisation for Economic Cooperation and Development (OECD) as partner organizations.

2. Empirical Analysis

Huge implementation challenges persist for this target. With regard to indicator 11.6.1, challenges already exist at the level of data collection: according to the metadata docu-ment for this indicator, data especially from low- and middle-income-countries are based on global estimates rather than on actual data collection in these countries, which makes the data rather unreliable.[302] Bearing in mind the problem of data reliability, the 2020 World Cities Report provides some numbers that demonstrate an overall in-crease of municipal solid waste collection comparing numbers from 2001–2010 and 2010–2018. However, waste collection is still only at about just over 50 per cent in Sub-Saharan Africa, and it has declined in several regions of the world, including North America and Europe, North Africa and Western Asia, and in Latin America and the Caribbean.[303] The COVID-19 pandemic has exacerbated the problem, especially with regard to single-use plastic waste.[304]

Air pollution similarly is a persistent problem. According to the UN Secretariat's 2018 High-level Political Forum's Review paper, 91 per cent of the world's urban population were breathing air that did not meet WHO's Air Quality Guidelines, and more than half were exposed to levels that exceeded the recommended safety standard by 2.5 times.[305] Data from the 2021 SDG report show that implementa-tion of indicator 11.6.2 regarding air pollution is very unevenly distributed. Fewer than two dozen countries have achieved this goal, and the vast majority of these are countries from the Western European and Others Group (WEOG), with the excep-tion of only four countries in other parts of the world, namely: Brunei Darussalam, Sri Lanka, the Maldives, and Uruguay. The entire African continent as well as the Middle East and large parts of South East and East Asia, including India and China, are facing significant challenges in making progress towards achieving target 11.6.[306]

3. Implementation Efforts Taken at Domestic and International Level

With regard to indicator 11.6.1, global implementation efforts are aimed primarily at procuring and producing reliable data. It is clear that many cities are increasingly facing

---

[301] ibid Executive Summary, p 2.
[302] United Nations, Metadata 11.6.1 (September 2020) <https://unstats.un.org/sdgs/metadata/files/Metadata-11-06-01.pdf> accessed 30 December 2021.
[303] UN-Habitat, 'World Cities Report 2020' (n 6) p 80.
[304] ibid p xxiv.
[305] 2018 Review of SDG implementation: SDG 11—Make cities and human settlements inclusive, safe, resilient and sustainable, p 5.
[306] Sachs and others (n 91), Annual mean concentration of particulate matter of less than 2.5 microns in diam-eter (PM2.5), overall score.

solid waste management challenges.[307] The decrease of solid waste collection in several regions of the world, as mentioned in the previous section, also points to the fact that the higher the income level of a city, the more waste it produces—economic development is thus an obstacle to the waste problem of the twenty-first century.[308] The UN's Statistical Division and UNEP have been sending out questionnaires on municipal solid waste treatment for about twenty years and to more than 160 countries, but the response rate regularly stagnates at around 50 per cent, in addition to data being incomplete or otherwise unreliable.[309]

In part to respond to these challenges, UN-Habitat launched 'Waste Wise Cities', a programme that is nudging cities to follow a number of principles, so as to call themselves 'waste wise'. These principles include efforts towards collecting the data required for monitoring indicator 11.6.1: as a first step, municipalities are asked to assess the quantity and the type of waste generated, and the principles also ask for regular reviews on waste management.[310] UN-Habitat has also developed a toolkit that guides municipal governments through the steps that are necessary in order to generate data for indicator 11.6.1.[311] Waste Wise Cities is thus yet another network with soft rules. Cities can join by writing a letter of intent, but without incurring any financial or other legal obligation. At the local level, the 2020 World Cities Report highlights a waste-pickers' cooperative in Pune, India, with over 3,000 members, most of whom are Dalit and female. This cooperative provides door-to-door waste pick-up service to over 2.3 million people, including half a million slum dwellers.[312] Similarly, the city governments of Belo Horizonte in Brazil and of Accra, Ghana, have provided informal waste pickers with an opportunity to participate in the city's institutional waste management, which has benefited those cities' waste management systems.[313]

International implementation efforts for indicator 11.6.2 lie primarily with WHO, which acts both as a platform for knowledge exchange as well as a technical assistance partner. It spearheads amongst other things a Working Group on monitoring indicator 11.6.2, which includes the World Meteorological Organization, UNEP, the World Bank, UN-Habitat, and the UNECE. In terms of technical cooperation, it offers advice and technical assistance to countries and local governments that want to reduce their particulate matter concentration.[314] At the local level, city governments increasingly adopt measures to reduce air pollution: Dakar's Territorial Climate Energy Plan, for example, includes measures to promote modern cooking fuels and renewable energy to

[307] United Nations, 'Metadata 11.6.1' (September 2020) <https://unstats.un.org/sdgs/metadata/files/Metadata-11-06-01.pdf> accessed 30 December 2021.

[308] ibid.

[309] ibid.

[310] UN-Habitat, Waste Wise Cities <https://unhabitat.org/waste-wise-cities accessed 30 December 2021.

[311] UN-Habitat, Waste Wise Cities Tool—Step by Step Guide to Assess a City's Municipal Solid Waste Management Performance <https://unhabitat.org/sites/default/files/2021-10/Waste%20wise%20cities%20tool%20-%20EN%2013.pdf> accessed 30 December 2021.

[312] UN-Habitat, 'World Cities Report 2020' (n 6) p 117.

[313] ibid p 136, 211.

[314] See the resources at WHO, 'Air Pollution' <https://www.who.int/health-topics/air-pollution> accessed 30 December 2021.

increase air quality.[315] In Brussels, several residents along with the non-governmental organization ClientEarth sued the Brussels regional government for failing to correctly monitor the level of air pollution in the city; the government was ordered to respect EU law and take immediate action to remedy the breach of EU legal standards for air quality monitoring.[316]

4. Critique

Good waste governance is crucial in order to build sustainable cities in the twenty-first century and remains a key challenge for the decades to come.[317] Experiences from individual cities show that cities' waste management systems can benefit from the integration of informal waste pickers, as they often know challenges of which city administrators might be unaware. This dimension has yet to be integrated systematically into waste management programmes and it is so far not reflected in the indicator. Similarly, the indicator, focusing on waste collection only, does not address creative solutions of recycling or approaches that aim at transforming waste to energy.

Both poor waste management and air pollution constitute considerable challenges to the right to health, and, especially in the case of air pollution, also to the right to life. This human rights dimension is not yet reflected in target 11.6's indicators, nor do many of the programmes aimed at improving waste management and/or air quality explicitly operate with a rights-based approach. As cities move towards incorporating both dimensions of target 11.6 into their urban planning, it is important to integrate informal workers and disadvantaged groups into planning efforts, as the examples of waste pickers from Ghana and Brazil show.

G. Target 11.7 By 2030, provide universal access to safe, inclusive and accessible, green and public spaces, in particular for women and children, older persons and persons with disabilities

1. Sources of Target

The time-bound target 11.7 seeks to provide access to safe, inclusive, and accessible, green and public spaces. It mentions four groups that are deemed to particularly face obstacles in accessing public spaces, and that were already mentioned in target 11.2 (access to public transportation): women, children, older persons, and persons with disabilities. In so far as women, children, and persons with disabilities are concerned, these groups can rely generally on the non-discrimination provisions from the CEDAW, CRC, and CRPD, respectively. While these roots in international human

---

[315] UN-Habitat, 'World Cities Report 2020' (n 6) p 211.

[316] ClientEarth, ClientEarth and Brussels residents win five-year legal battle for clean air, Press Release 29 January 2021 <https://www.clientearth.org/latest/press-office/press/clientearth-and-brussels-residents-win-five-year-legal-battle-for-clean-air/> accessed 30 December 2021.

[317] United Nations, Metadata 11.6.1 (September 2020) <https://unstats.un.org/sdgs/metadata/files/Metadata-11-06-01.pdf> accessed 30 December 2021.

rights law exist, none of these instruments recognizes specifically a right to access public space. The closest to such a norm can be found in article 9 CRPD, which provides for a right of accessibility to their physical environment for persons with disabilities.[318] The Committee on the Rights of Persons with Disabilities has repeatedly recommended that accessibility of green spaces needs to be ensured for persons with disabilities.[319] General Comment No 2 on accessibility clarifies that this includes, for example, access of guide dogs to public spaces; a ban for guide dogs to enter public spaces would constitute a prohibited act of disability-based discrimination.[320]

Target 11.7 contains two indicators. Indicator 11.7.1 measures the average share of the built-up area of cities that is open space for public use for all, disaggregated by sex, age, and persons with disabilities. The custodian agency here is UN-Habitat, which has worked on standardization of methodology for monitoring public spaces. The turn to public spaces and spatial considerations in general is a relatively new development on the Habitat agenda: in 2011, UN-Habitat's Governing Council adopted a resolution on sustainable urban development through access to quality urban public spaces, in which it invited governments and local authorities to implement urban environmental planning and management with a view to enhancing urban public spaces, and crucially also requested that UN-Habitat develop a policy approach on the role of place-making and an implementation plan in this regard.[321] The evolving norm of public space is a good example of how normative change has been steered through operational activities from UN entities, some of which are referenced in the section on implementation below, rather than through top-down policy change initiated by Member States.[322]

Indicator 11.7.2 measures safety of urban spaces and indicates that the most important dimension of safe, inclusive, and accessible green and public spaces is safety. Safety is considered a causal factor that affects accessibility and inclusivity, especially for the four groups that target 11.7 considers.[323] In measuring the proportion of persons victim to physical or sexual harassment, disaggregated by sex, age, disability status, and place of occurrence, indicator 11.7.2 makes clear that safety in target 11.7 is primarily understood as the absence of physical violence and sexual harassment. Sexual harassment is understood as behaviour with a sexual connotation suitable to intimidate their victims, whereas physical harassment means all harassing behaviours that can cause fear for physical integrity and/or emotional distress.[324] Target 11.7 has thus strong links to SDG 5 on gender equality, especially target 5.2 on eliminating violence against women, and SDG 16 on peaceful societies, in particular target 16.1 on

---

[318] See for the relevance of art 9 CRPD for SDG 11 also commentary in this chapter on target 11.2.
[319] Lawson (n 207) 275.
[320] Committee on the Rights of Persons with Disabilities, General Comment No 2 (2014), UN Doc CRPD/C/GC/2, para 29.
[321] UN-Habitat Governing Council, Resolution 23/4 of 15 April 2011, contained in UN Doc A/66/8, pp 13–14.
[322] See on this extensively Birkenkötter (n 72).
[323] Policy Brief in Support of the First SDG 11 Review at the UN High-Level Political Forum 2018, p 5: 'Levels of safety in a city affect the level of accessibility and inclusivity, particularly for the vulnerable urban populations including women and children, older persons and persons with disabilities.'
[324] United Nations, Metadata 11.7.2 (November 2018) <https://unstats.un.org/sdgs/metadata/files/Metadata-11-07-02.pdf> accessed 30 December 2021.

850   SDG 11

reducing all forms of violence. UN Women, the UN's entity on gender equality and custodian agency for most of SDG 5's targets, is thus an important partner organization for indicator 11.7.2. The custodian agency for this indicator is the UN Office on Drugs and Crime, a part of the UN Secretariat established in 1997 based in Vienna.[325] UN-Habitat and UN Women are partner organizations for indicator 11.7.2.

2. Empirical Analysis

As mentioned, indicator 11.7.1 measures the average share of the built-up area of cities that is open space for public use for all, disaggregated by sex, age, and persons with disabilities. The World Cities Report 2020 contains open space indicators for select cities which shows that most cities' share of open public space is well below 10 per cent of its built-up area. Notable exceptions are the cities of Saidpur, Bangladesh; Belgrade, Serbia; London, United Kingdom; and Canberra, Australia.[326]

At the time of writing, no data on indicator 11.7.2 were contained in UNODC's database.[327] The metadata document states that data for target 11.7 ought to be collected as part of UNODC's United Nations Crime Trends Survey.[328] This indicator is a tier 2 indicator, which might explain lack of data.[329]

3. Implementation Efforts Taken at Domestic and International Level

As a result of the UN-Habitat Governing Council's resolution on quality urban spaces, referenced in the section on sources, UN-Habitat launched the Global Public Space Programme in 2012.[330] UN-Habitat's work on public space operates on the assumption that quality public space is a precondition for many of the targets that SDG 11 promotes, and that through 'its multifunctional and multi-disciplinary nature, public space offers a holistic view of the city, such as social inclusion, gender equality, the benefits of nature and green spaces, governance, health, safety, education, climate change, transport, energy and the local urban economy',[331] to use the words of UN-Habitat's chief expert on public space.[332] This programme is listed as a best practice in the 2020 World Cities

[325] United Nations, 'Metadata 11.7.2' (November 2018) <https://unstats.un.org/sdgs/metadata/files/Metadata-11-07-02.pdf> accessed 30 December 2021.
United Nations, 'Metadata 11.6.1' (September 2020) <https://unstats.un.org/sdgs/metadata/files/Metadata-11-06-01.pdf> accessed 30 December 2021.
[326] UN-Habitat, 'World Cities Report 2020' (n 6) pp 335–40.
[327] UN Office of Drugs and Crime, Data (UNODC) <https://dataunodc.un.org/sdgs> accessed 25 December 2021: at this time, data were only available for SDGs 3 and 16.
[328] United Nations, 'Metadata 11.7.2' (November 2018) <https://unstats.un.org/sdgs/metadata/files/Metadata-11-07-02.pdf> accessed 30 December 2021.
[329] United Nations Statistics Division, Tier Classification for Global SDG Indicators as of 29 March 2021 https://unstats.un.org/sdgs/files/Tier%20Classification%20of%20SDG%20Indicators_29%20Mar%202021_web.pdf> accessed 30 December 2021.
[330] UN-Habitat, Global Public Space Programme <https://unhabitat.org/programme/global-public-space-programme> accessed 30 December 2021.
[331] C Andersson, 'Public Space and the New Urban Agenda' (2016) 1(1) The Journal of Public Space 5–10, 7.
[332] Cecilia Andersson is listed as the sole expert on UN-Habitat's Global Public Space Programme's website, cf <https://unhabitat.org/programme/global-public-space-programme> accessed 30 December 2021.

Report, highlighting cooperation of UN-Habitat with the city of Nairobi, Kenya, in launching a city-wide programme to revitalize public space.[333]

Safety and public space have been conceived of jointly in programmes by other entities that are engaging in implementation and monitoring of this target. Chief amongst them has been UN Women's 'Safe cities and safe public spaces' flagship programme.[334] For ten years, UN Women has collaborated through multi-stakeholder partnerships with twenty-seven cities in improving access to safe public spaces for women. The flagship programme works through four steps that are typical for contemporary UN operational activities and their managerial approach to normative change: in a first step, a scoping study is carried out to provide initial data and to ensure an understanding of the amplitude of the safety issues women are facing in a specific place; in a second step, laws and policies aimed at improving the situation are developed, which are then implemented through capacity building and training; this results, thirdly, in allocating adequate economic resources, which ultimately leads to normative change.[335] Examples include, for example, the issuing of an ordinance against catcalling in Quezon City, the Philippines, and an ordinance against public harassment of women in Quito, Ecuador, or the establishment of vendors' associations for markets that include 50 per cent women in executive positions in Port Moresby, Papua New Guinea.[336]

4. Critique

As evidenced above, data collection especially for indicator 11.7.2 is slow. Both indicators for target 11.7 are tier 2 indicators, which might explain lack of comparative and sound data.[337] Beyond this obstacle to sound empirical analysis, one might question the safety focus of indicator 11.7.2. Target 11.7 at face value puts different dimensions of public space on an equal footing: it speaks not only of safe, but also of inclusive and accessible green and public spaces. Green spaces allude to environmental concerns whereas inclusive and accessible spaces look specifically at persons who might experience physical access barriers to public spaces. By focusing on safety alone, indicator 11.7.2 eclipses these arguably equally important dimensions of public space.

---

[333] UN-Habitat, 'World Cities Report 2020' (n 6) p 117.

[334] UN Women, Creating safe and empowering public spaces with women and girls <https://www.unwomen.org/en/what-we-do/ending-violence-against-women/creating-safe-public-spaces> accessed 30 December 2021.

[335] See this framing in UN Women's latest report on the Safe cities and safe public spaces report: UN Women, Safe Cities and Safe Public Spaces Global Results Report, 2017 <https://www.unwomen.org/-/media/headquart ers/attachments/sections/library/publications/2017/safe-cities-and-safe-public-spaces-global-results-report-en.pdf?la=en&vs=45> accessed 30 December 2021, p 3.

[336] Birkenkötter (n 72) 139.

[337] United Nations Statistics Division, Tier Classification for Global SDG Indicators as of 29 March 2021 <https://unstats.un.org/sdgs/files/Tier%20Classification%20of%20SDG%20Indicators_29%20Mar%202 021_web.pdf> accessed 30 December 2021.

852   SDG 11

H. Target 11.a Support positive economic, social and environmental links between urban, peri-urban and rural areas by strengthening national and regional development planning

1. Sources of Target

Target 11.a is designed as a means of implementation target that is neither time-bound nor linked to a specific outcome. It focuses on planning as a crucial, perhaps *the* crucial implementation means to ensure that SDG 11 as a whole is achieved. Linking economic, social, and environmental matters through planning also highlights the cross-cutting nature of SDG 11.

Urban planning is not subject to any international treaty. Perhaps the most important guiding instrument is UN-Habitat's International Guidelines on Urban and Territorial Planning.[338] These guidelines were developed by UN-Habitat at the request of UN-Habitat's Governing Council and approved by the Governing Council in 2015 'as a valuable guide that may be used towards the achievement of sustainable development'.[339] National Urban Policies also feature prominently in the New Urban Agenda, which emphasizes the importance of such policies for interlinking different governance levels and commits states to using national urban policies at the appropriate governance level.[340]

2. Empirical Analysis

Target 11.a's only indicator measures how many people live in cities that actually implement urban and regional development plans. The indicator was initially judged ambitious and hard to measure, but refinement of the indicator has now included several qualifiers: it focuses on *national* urban plans, not on local planning, that need to (I) respond to population dynamics; (II) ensure balanced territorial development; and (III) increase local fiscal space. These modifications have rendered indicator 11.a.1 a tier 1 indicator administered by UN-Habitat, with the UN Population Fund (UNFPA) as partner organization.[341]

UN-Habitat's Policy, Legislation and Governance Section (PLGS) administers the Urban Policy Platform which includes the National Urban Policy Database, in which all relevant data is collected.[342] The data show that out of 194 states for which

---

[338] UN-Habitat, International Guidelines on Urban and Territorial Planning, 2015 <https://unhabitat.org/international-guidelines-on-urban-and-territorial-planning> accessed 30 December 2021.

[339] UN-Habitat Governing Council, Resolution 25/6. International guidelines on urban and territorial planning, adopted 23 April 2015, contained in UN Doc A/70/5, pp 35–37.

[340] New Urban Agenda, UN Doc A/Res/71/256, Annex, paras 15(c)(i), 87, 89.

[341] United Nations Statistics Division, Tier Classification for Global SDG Indicators as of 29 March 2021 <https://unstats.un.org/sdgs/files/Tier%20Classification%20of%20SDG%20Indicators_29%20Mar%202021_web.pdf> accessed 30 December 2021.

[342] UN-Habitat, Urban Policy Platform, NUP map <https://urbanpolicyplatform.org/national-urban-policy-database/#map> accessed 30 December 2021.

data is collected, only some thirty-two countries do not have any form of urban planning. Fifty-six countries are supported by UN-Habitat in their national urban planning processes, with over a third of the countries located on the African continent and only one state in the WEOG receiving UN-Habitat support in their urban planning.[343]

3. Implementation Efforts Taken at Domestic and International Level

Beyond National Urban Policies, city governments' action is crucial in achieving this particular target; and ideally, cities' planning policies should align with their National Urban Policies as well as with international instruments. One best practice example is the city of Seoul, Republic of Korea. Participatory urban planning reaches back to the 1990s in Seoul, and the city has since 2015 aligned its city planning with international agendas. This includes the city's 'Master Plan for Sustainable Development (2016–2035)', as well as the '2030 Seoul Plan for the implementation of the SDGs'.[344] Mexico City brought together members of the government as well as officials and representatives of the city's main institutions and introduced the SDGs as the roadmap for the new planning process that began after the 2018 municipal elections.[345] These are but two examples of cities that have explicitly aligned their urban planning with the SDGs and the 2030 Agenda.[346]

4. Critique

According to the latest Global State of National Urban Policy report of 2021, jointly authored by the OECD, UN-Habitat, and the Cities Alliance, the COVID-19 pandemic has raised the profile of national urban planning as a key component of recovery and as crucial towards building more resilient cities.[347] In coming years, national urban policy planning impacted by international agencies such as UN-Habitat or the OECD is set to become ever more important. Yet, as the data from the National Urban Policy Database shows, global assistance is unevenly given. This might lead to an uneven application of a global standard of urban planning across the globe. Additionally, it is important to not consider urban planning a panacea for the challenges of urbanization. The World Cities Report highlights that the mere existence of public planning instruments does not guarantee that local public goals will be achieved.[348]

---

[343] This state is Sweden. UN-Habitat supports two countries from the Eastern European Block (Serbia and Belarus); all other countries are in the African, Asian, Middle Eastern or Latin American and the Caribbean regional groups. cf UN-Habitat, Urban Policy Platform, NUPs supported by UN-Habitat <https://urbanpolicyplatform.org/national-urban-policy-database/#un-habitat-support> accessed 30 December 2021.

[344] UN-Habitat, 'World Cities Report 2020' (n 6) p 221.

[345] UN-Habitat, 'World Cities Report 2020' (n 6) p 220.

[346] More examples are contained in ibid pp 220–21, and at p 117.

[347] OECD/UN-Habitat/Cities Alliance, Global State of National Urban Policy 2021: Achieving Sustainable Development Goals and Delivering Climate Action, 2021 <https://unhabitat.org/sites/default/files/2021/06/gsnup_2021.pdf> accessed 30 December 2021, p 13 and ch 2.

[348] UN-Habitat, 'World Cities Report 2020' (n 6) p 221.

I. Target 11.b By 2020, substantially increase the number of cities and human settlements adopting and implementing integrated policies and plans towards inclusion, resource efficiency, mitigation and adaptation to climate change, resilience to disasters, and develop and implement, in line with the Sendai Framework for Disaster Risk Reduction 2015–2030, holistic disaster risk management at all levels

1. Sources of Target

Target 11.b is another implementation target and also aims at better planning. Specifically, it aims to ensure that countries as well as local governments adopt disaster risk reduction strategies in line with the Sendai Framework for Disaster Risk Reduction 2015–2030, which is a soft law international instrument.[349] Target 11.b, while serving as a cross-cutting implementation target, has specifically close ties to target 11.5 on reducing the number of affected people and economic losses due to disasters. The same connections between disaster risk reduction and other substantive fields of international law and global governance regulation as for target 11.5 apply here.[350] In so far as disaster risk reduction and planning help to mitigate risks to the right to life, the right to health, and the right to an adequate standard of living, there is a clear human rights connection. The Human Rights Committee considers the development of disaster management plans a state obligation under article 6 ICCPR.[351] In addition, the text of target 11.b explicitly mentions resilience to disaster and mitigation and adaptation to climate change side-by-side. This again raises the question of overemphasizing a single hazard in the context of disaster risk reduction.[352]

Differently from target 11.a, target 11.b not only aims at the national level but also at the local level: indicator 11.b.1 measures how many countries adopt and implement national disaster risk reduction strategies in line with the Sendai Framework for Disaster Risk Reduction 2015–2030, whereas indicator 11.b.2 looks at the proportion of local governments that adopt and implement local disaster risk reduction strategies in line with national disaster risk reduction strategies. The custodian agency for both indicators is the UN Office for Disaster Risk Reduction (UNDRR), with UNEP and UN-Habitat serving as partner agencies. This is the same setup as for indicator 11.5.1.

2. Empirical Analysis

Target 11.b is the only target that was set to be achieved prior to the 2030 deadline, namely by 2020. At the same time, the target had no concrete result in mind, but simply

---

[349] For further detail on the Sendai Framework and more generally on disaster risk reduction and disaster relief in international law see Subsection IV.E.1.

[350] For further detail on the Sendai Framework and more generally on disaster risk reduction and disaster relief in international law see Subsection IV.E.1.

[351] Human Rights Committee, General Comment No. 36, The right to life (2019), UN Doc CCPR/C/GC/36, para 26.

[352] Kelman (n 282).

aimed at a 'substantial increase' in the number of cities and human settlements adopting policies on disaster risk reduction.

The 2020 Sustainable Development Goals Report contained a progress summary for those twenty-one targets in the 2030 Agenda that were set to be achieved by the 2020 deadline. Progress for target 11.b has been judged as 'insufficient to meet the target', even though some progress had been made. As of April 2020, eighty-five countries had reported national disaster risk reduction strategies that were at least to some extent aligned with the Sendai Framework, but only six of these countries reported fully aligned national strategies. Fifty-five countries reported that some of their local governments had local strategies aligned with national strategies.[353] Like target 11.5, target 11.b is mirrored in the Sendai indicators (indicators E1–E3), which are identical to the SDG indicators.[354]

3. Implementation Efforts Taken at Domestic and International Level

One important factor in an effective resilience strategy is the integration of different policy tools and instruments. The Global Assessment Report on Disaster Risk Reduction explicitly calls for a need to overcome 'siloed approaches and duplicative efforts in implementing disaster risk reduction, climate change and sustainable development'.[355] One best practice in this regard is Tonga, which has issued a Joint Action Plan on Climate Change Adaptation and Disaster Risk Management, anchored in the SDGs and other relevant international instruments.[356] Other positive examples are the planning efforts of Egypt and Mozambique, both of which integrate their disaster risk reduction plans with climate change policies and strategies for sustainable development.[357]

4. Critique

Many countries develop disaster risk reduction strategies that are either not aligned with international instruments, or not aligned with related strategies, in particular climate change and sustainable development strategies. Integration, as outlined in the previous section on best practices, is key to successful disaster risk reduction. In addition, the criticism formulated above for target 11.5—namely that an emerging international law of disaster relief is not sufficiently focusing on the prevention dimension which is covered by disaster risk reduction—also applies to this target.

---

[353] 'The Sustainable Development Goals Report 2020' (n 184) p 61.

[354] Sendai Framework Indicators, Global target E and indicators E1–E3 <https://www.preventionweb.net/sendai-framework/sendai-framework-indicators> accessed 30 December 2021.

[355] United Nations Office for Disaster Risk Reduction, Global Assessment Report on Disaster Risk Reduction <https://gar.undrr.org> accessed 30 December 2021, Chapter 11, p 329.

[356] ibid 330.

[357] ibid 331.

856 SDG 11

J. Target 11.c Support least developed countries, including through financial and technical assistance, in building sustainable and resilient buildings utilizing local materials

1. Sources of Target

Target 11.c is situated in the broader context of financing for development and technical assistance. The most important international document on financing for development at the time of writing is the 2015 Addis Ababa Action Agenda, negotiated as part of the 2030 Agenda package, but separate from the SDGs as such.[358] Target 11.c calls for support to least developed countries in building resilient buildings, using local materials. This support can be either financial aid or technical assistance. The Addis Ababa Action Agenda mirrors target 11.c's wording ('We will support cities and local authorities of developing countries, particularly in least developed countries and small island developing States, in implementing ... sustainable and resilient buildings using local materials'), but without providing more detail on how this support is supposed to be operationalized.[359]

2. Empirical Analysis

In practice, target 11.c plays little to no role. The Inter-Agency and Expert Group on SDG Indicators originally proposed measuring the proportion of financial support to the least developed countries that is allocated to the construction and retrofitting of sustainable, resilient, and resource-efficient buildings utilizing local materials. This indicator is currently listed on tier 3, that is, no suitable methodology for measuring the target could be agreed on.

3. Implementation Efforts Taken at Domestic and International Level

Since there does not even exist a commonly agreed understanding as to the meaning of target 11.c, there are no implementation efforts undertaken with a view to this target specifically.

4. Critique

To date, the Expert Group has not agreed on a replacement indicator, but instead 'encouraged the global statistical community to work to develop an indicator that could be used', hoping to be able to include a replacement indicator by 2025, that is a mere five years before the 2030 Agenda is scheduled to be achieved.[360] Similarly, other international documents, such as the Addis Ababa Action Agenda, merely mirror the

---

[358] Addis Ababa Action Agenda of the Third International Conference on Financing for Development, contained in UN Doc A/Res/69/313.

[359] ibid para 34.

[360] Report of the Inter-Agency and Expert Group on Sustainable Development Goal Indicators 2019/20, UN Doc E/CN.3/2020/2, para 23.

wording of target 11.c, without providing further clarification.[361] Implementation of this target is thus dispersed; the 2020 Global Cities Report mentions in an *ad hoc* manner the example of a competition hosted by the C40 network, called 'Reinventing Cities', where urban projects aimed at developing carbon-neutral buildings in sites in decline compete.[362] However, this has little to do with the financial and technical assistance impetus that drives the language of target 11.c. It is unlikely that progress will be made on this specific target, or that explicit links to existing instruments will be established, given that the target has not been operationalized since 2015. The Expert Group simply 'encourages countries, international and regional organizations, and stakeholders to attempt to monitor this target in whatever way they deem relevant to their national, regional or thematic context'.[363] Absent even agreement on what that relevance could be, it seems unlikely that data points will emerge in a way that makes them utilizable for monitoring progress on the target.

[361] Addis Ababa Action Agenda (n 358) Annex, para 34: 'We will support cities and local authorities of developing countries, particularly in least developed countries and small island developing States, in implementing resilient and environmentally sound infrastructure, including ... sustainable and resilient buildings using local materials.'

[362] UN-Habitat, 'World Cities Report 2020' (n 6) p 118. Further information on this specific competition can be found at <https://www.c40reinventingcities.org> accessed 30 December 2021.

[363] Report of the Inter-Agency and Expert Group on Sustainable Development Goal Indicators 2019/20, UN Doc E/CN.3/2020/2, para 23.

SDG 12

'Ensure Sustainable Consumption and Production Patterns'

Kateřina Mitkidis and Adriana Šefčíková

I. Introduction

Unsustainable patterns in consumption and production were recognized as a major driver of environmental degradation by 1992.[1,2] Together with poverty eradication and management of natural resources, shifting towards sustainable consumption and production (SCP) were later labelled as 'the overarching objectives of and essential requirements for sustainable development'.[3] The unsustainability of production and consumption patterns, namely the dissonance between the static reservoirs of resources on the one hand and the rapid global population growth and, thus, growing consumption on the other, have since been used to frame the international sustainability agenda and theories.[4] Yet, as the idea of economic growth pervades the capitalist system in most current democracies, any discourse of direct limitations of production and consumption has largely been silenced.[5] As early as 1987, the Brundtland Report came with the concept of 'sustainable development' (SD),[6] trying to reconcile the objective of environmental protection with that of development. It, thus, did not abandon the idea of economic growth, but argued that economic growth should be limited by ecological possibility.[7] The links to social rights were also made. The Brundtland Report was said to underline 'both the limits of the carrying capacity of Earth and also the need for reducing poverty and equitable development' those within the inter-generational timeline.[8]

---

[1] The chapter is based on data available as of 30 October 2021. References to the later developments of the new EU Corporate Sustainability Reporting Directive and the Proposal for Corporate Sustainability Due Diligence constitute an exception.

[2] United Nations General Assembly (UNGA), 'Report of the UN Conference on Environment and Development' (Rio de Janeiro, 3–14 June 1992), 12 August 1992, UN Doc A/CONF.151/26 (Vol II), ch 4.

[3] UNGA, 'The Future We Want' (11 September 2012) A/RES/66/288, para 4.

[4] J Rockström and others, 'Planetary Boundaries: Exploring the Safe Operating Space for Humanity' (2009) 14(2) Ecology and Society, Resilience Alliance; DH Meadows and others, *The Limits to Growth: A Report for the Club of Rome's Project on the Predicament of Mankind* (Universe Books 1972).

[5] D Gasper and others, 'The Framing of Sustainable Consumption and Production in SDG 12' (2019) 10(S1) Global Policy 83, 90.

[6] Gro Harlem Brundtland, 'Report of the World Commission on Environment and Development: Our Common Future' (4 August 1987) official record of the UNGA, A/42/427, para 54.

[7] ibid para 58.

[8] J Srivastava, 'Sustainable Consumption and Production: Mapping the Conceptual Terrain' in RB Swain and S Sweet (eds), *Sustainable Consumption and Production* (Vol I, Palgrave Macmillan 2021) 23.

860   SDG 12

The concept of economic growth remains present also in the SDGs, most clearly under SDG 8.[9] SDG 8 opens up with target 8.1, clearly stipulating continuous economic growth to be desirable and presenting a clear quantifiable indicator of an annual growth rate of real gross domestic product (GDP) per capita.[10] Target 8.4 then speaks of decoupling of economic growth from environmental degradation, but in an overwhelmingly vague manner, using such words as 'progressively' and 'endeavour'.[11] SDG 8 has been criticized for internal contradiction and contested feasibility.[12]

Notably for our chapter, target 8.4 ties the decoupling of economic growth from environmental degradation to the 10-Year Framework of Programmes on Sustainable Consumption and Production (10YFP).[13] As target 12.1, it extends and follows discussions taken at the 1992 Earth Summit (Rio de Janeiro) and the 2002 World Summit on Sustainable Development (Johannesburg),[14] which called on states to (respectively) discontinue unsustainable production and consumption patterns and to use 10YFP to facilitate the shift to sustainable one.[15]

Under the 10YFP framework, SCP has been defined as '[a] holistic approach to minimizing the negative environmental impacts from consumption and production systems while promoting quality of life for all', in other words 'doing *more and better with less*.'[16] This framing of SCP also permeates SDG 12 aiming to 'ensure sustainable consumption and production patterns'. SCP thus serves as a topic bridging the economic and social and environmental SDGs and is considered a *conditio sine qua non* of SD, and SDG 12 is considered to be an enabler for the achievement of other SDGs.[17]

The bridging character of the SCP topics serves as a starting point to discussions on SDG 12 in this commentary. First and foremost, the chapter's introductory part offers a closer insight into the preparatory works on SDG 12, including the discussion on whether SCP should be a stand-alone goal or incorporated in other SDGs. Moreover, links are made in regard to the role of the common but differentiated responsibilities (CBDR) principle and international law instruments in the development of SDG 12. The introductory section also explains the structure of the goal and a selection of covered topics and difficulties related to their regulation. Finally, the introduction sheds

[9] Chapter 8 on SDG 8, this book.
[10] Chapter 8 on SDG 8, this book.
[11] Chapter 8 on SDG 8, this book.
[12] Chapter 8 on SDG 8, this book.
[13] UN, 'Letter dated 18 June 2012 from the Permanent Representative of Brazil to the United Nations addressed to the Secretary-General of the United Nations Conference on Sustainable Development' (19 June 2012) A/CONF.216/5, annex.
[14] The work on 10YFP started in 2002 in Johannesburg and was further fuelled in 2003 through the establishment of the Marrakesh Process, a global multi-stakeholder process to support the implementation of SCP and to develop a Global Framework for Action on SCP, the so-called 10YFP.
[15] See more under target 12.1.
[16] UNEP, 'Paving the Way for Sustainable Consumption and Production: The Marrakesh Process Progress Report, Towards a 10 Year Framework of Programmes on Sustainable Consumption and Production' (2011) 10 <https://sustainabledevelopment.un.org/content/documents/947Paving_the_way_final.pdf> accessed 26 October 2021.
[17] United Nations Economic Commission for Europe (UNECE), 'Successful approaches to delivering on sustainable consumption and production by 2030' (Regional Forum on Sustainable Development for the UNECE Region, 1–2 March 2018).

light on regional differences between developed and developing countries, followed by an overall critique of the goal. The second part of the commentary is devoted to the analysis of the individual targets. The historical, political, and legal roots of each target are defined, followed by a review of its wording and suitability of its indicator(s). Furthermore, progress on each target is assessed based on the existing statistical information. Finally, initiatives at the national, regional, and international levels are presented to complete the picture.

II. *Travaux Préparatoires*

A. Contested Issues During the Negotiations

1. A Stand-alone versus an Integrated Goal

The UN Millennium Development Goals (MDGs), the SDGs' predecessor, neither specifically referred to SCP within their text nor within the formulation of their targets and indicators. Yet, implicit linkages can be made, namely to MDG 1 (Eradicate extreme poverty and hunger) and MDG 7 (Ensure environmental sustainability). SCP-related topics, however, appeared early on during the stocktaking sessions of the UN's Open Working Group on Sustainable Development Goals (OWG). At OWG-2, multiple presenters put SCP on the negotiation agenda as a separate topic of discussion[18] or as a topic integrated under other issues such as the elimination of hunger.[19] During the following sessions, the various sub-topics of SCP were reiterated as important enablers to the individual proposed goals. The position of SCP on the intersection between economic, social, and environmental interests had become increasingly obvious and the question arose whether SCP should be a stand-alone goal or whether SCP-related targets should be subsumed under other SDGs. Considerable space was devoted to this question at OWG-7 and the session's concluding remarks noted that a strong disagreement on this topic existed among the participating delegations.[20]

During the SDGs' negotiation phase the OWG repeatedly returned to this question. The preferred option largely followed the developed/developing countries axis. Overall, the developed countries were more in favour of spreading SCP-related targets among the relevant SDGs.[21] Developing countries then represented a strong voice for

---

[18] See, eg, European Union and its Member States—Speaking points on 'conceptualizing the SDGs and the SDG process', Meeting of the General Assembly Open Working Group on Sustainable Development Goals United Nations, New York, 17–19 April 2013.

[19] P Caballero, Advisor to Minister María Angela Holguín, Minister of Foreign Affairs of Colombia and Member of the High Level Panel, The SDGs and the Post-2015 Process', 17 April 2013 (OWG 2).

[20] Concluding Remarks of Co-Chairs (OWG-7) 3.

[21] See, eg, Canada, Israel, and United States, OWG-10 ('our commitment to SCP will be much more powerful if it is reflected in concrete targets under relevant goals, like those we have just mentioned, rather than as a standalone goal'); and Poland and Romania, OWG-11 ('We do not support a stand-alone goal on SCP, as we consider SCP as a catalyst for sustainable development, that can bind together the economic, social and environmental dimensions and can be mainstreamed throughout the document').

862 SDG 12

a stand-alone goal.[22] Interestingly, the G77 and China group has never explicitly supported an SCP stand-alone goal.[23] Some countries, notably Finland, maintained that SCP relates strongly to all three aspects of SD and as such should be both a stand-alone goal and integrated within targets of other SDGs.[24] Dodds and colleagues note that '[i]n the OWG negotiations, the goal on sustainable consumption and production became an important test of commitment to a universal agenda'.[25] The authors state that the responsibility in the SCP area tilted clearly to the North,[26] which made it an especially sensitive issue.

At the end, a combined approach was chosen; SCP is a stand-alone Goal 12, while it is also (expressly or implicitly) integrated within targets of other goals.[27,28] For instance, SDG 6 calls for 'sustainable management of water', thus connecting clearly to target 12.2 speaking to 'the sustainable management and efficient use of natural resources'. SDGs 6 and 12 further connect in respect to the management of hazardous chemicals in water (target 6.3) and generally (target 12.4 and its indicators). SDG 7 aims, among others, to 'double the global rate of improvement in energy efficiency' (target 7.3), which clearly delivers also on SDG 12, where increasing resource efficiency is one of the main objectives.[29] Furthermore, SDG 12 is closely connected to the agenda of sustainable cities (SDG 11). Target 11.6 calls for special attention given to waste management, while target 12.5 sets an objective to 'substantially reduce waste generation through prevention, reduction, recycling and reuse'. Other examples could be provided but this would take up too much space, as SDG 12 is overall the Goal that is most interlinked with the rest of SDGs, having connections to fourteen of the sixteen other goals.[30] The combined approach of a stand-alone Goal with simultaneous incorporation of the Goal under other SDGs will optimally deliver on multiple objectives, namely increasing the visibility of the need to shift towards sustainable modes of production and consumption as well as organic integration with the rest of SDGs.[31] But it could also be a source of confusion.[32]

---

[22] For example, Saudi Arabia, OWG-10 ('Sustainable consumption and production deserve to be standalone goals under the SDG'); Iran, OWG-10 ('this is a very important focus area which demands having a standalone goal').

[23] Gasper and others (n 5) 83, 87.

[24] Finland, OWG-10 ('SCP fulfils all the characteristics to feature as an aspirational and 3-dimensional stand-alone goal for sustainable development. But even more importantly, SCP should be incorporated into other focus areas and potential goals.').

[25] F Dodds and others, *Negotiating the Sustainable Development Goals* (Routledge 2017) 34.

[26] ibid.

[27] Thirteen instances, see UNEP and International Institute for Sustainable Development (IISD), 'Sustainable Consumption and Production Indicators for the Future SDGs' (UNEP Discussion Paper, Paris: Division of Technology, Industry and Economics, United Nations Environment Programme 2015).

[28] UNECE, 'Successful approaches to delivering on sustainable consumption and production by 2030' (Regional Forum on Sustainable Development for the UNECE Region, 1–2 March 2018).

[29] UN, Sustainable Development Goals, 'Goal 12: Ensure sustainable consumption and production patterns' <https://www.un.org/sustainabledevelopment/sustainable-consumption-production/> accessed 26 October 2021.

[30] D Le Blanc, 'Towards Integration At Last? The Sustainable Development Goals as a Network of Targets' (2015) 23 Sustainable Development 176, table 1 and figure 3.

[31] L Akenji and M Bengtsson, 'Making Sustainable Consumption and Production the Core of Sustainable Development Goals' (2014) 6(2) Sustainability 513.

[32] ibid.

2. The CBDR Principle

The question of a stand-alone versus integrated SCP goal was closely tied with the discussion on the application of the CBDR principle in the SCP area. Developing countries argued that the CBDR principle should be applied here.[33] The leading argument was that while developing countries must primarily tackle hunger and poverty, developed countries should tackle unsustainable consumption.[34] It might be disputed though who should tackle unsustainable production. Is it the country that produces the specific product or the country that consumes it? A telling example here might be the problem of antimicrobial resistance (AMR), which is a growing global health threat.[35] AMR is connected to antimicrobial (primarily antibiotics) production and use. With improvements in access to medication (which is embedded in SDG 3, target 3.8), the use of antimicrobials increases. Most antimicrobials are produced in India and China[36] where red flags have been raised about the production effluents polluting the local environment with high concentrations of active pharmaceutical ingredients, therefore largely contributing to global AMR. Thus the paradox is, who should tackle (and finance solutions to) this issue; developed countries placing a large demand on deliveries of antimicrobials for their citizens despite the awareness of environmental pollution caused by the production of these, or the countries where the production takes place?

This is just one example from many of the division between the developed and developing countries in respect of SCP, the interrelation between various SDGs, and the calls for differentiation in the responsibilities and required efforts. The application of the CBDR principle within SDGs was opposed by some developed countries, who claimed that the principle is only applicable within the context of international agreements. For example, the troika Australia, the Netherlands, and the United Kingdom stated at OWG-9: 'We take note of the statements on CBDR. We underline that, as defined in Rio principle 7, CBDR applies specifically to global environmental degradation. It is not an overarching principle for the SDGs. We are committed to a universal agenda with shared responsibilities and contributions reflecting countries' evolving capabilities and circumstances.'[37] Other developed countries clearly expressed agreement with the fact that the developed part of the world needs to take the lead in SCP action.[38]

---

[33] See, eg, G77 and China, OWG-11 ('based on the principle of common but differentiated responsibilities, developed countries need to take the lead'); India, OWG 10 ('We do therefore support a standalone goal on sustainable consumption and lifestyles with relevant targets in accordance with the principle of common but differentiated responsibilities') and Brazil and Nicaragua, OWG-11 ('we must reaffirm the undeniable responsibility of developed countries to exercise leadership in promoting a paradigmatic shift in the way their societies produce and consume').

[34] See, eg, Statement by India, Pakistan, and Sri Lanka in OWG Session 7.

[35] World Health Organization, 'Antimicrobial Resistance' (13 October 2020) <https://www.who.int/news-room/fact-sheets/detail/antimicrobial-resistance> accessed 26 October 2021.

[36] China produces 80–90 per cent of antibiotic active pharmaceutical ingredients, India is the world leader in producing finished antibiotics. See SumOfUs (based on research by Changing Markets and Profundo), 'Bad Medicine: How the Pharmaceutical Industry is Contributing to the Global Rise of Antibiotic-Resistant Superbugs' (2015) <https://changingmarket.wpengine.com/wp-content/uploads/2016/12/BAD-MEDICINE-Report-FINAL.pdf> accessed 26 October 2021.

[37] Statements by Australia, Netherlands, and the United Kingdom; Poland, Romania, Japan, and Portugal (all in OWG Session 9).

[38] Sweden, Finland, Germany, France, Switzerland. See Gasper and others (n 5) 88.

864   SDG 12

The negotiations on SDG 12 ended up with a decision to keep the Goal universal, thus avoiding the stipulation of the CBDR principle in Goal 12 and its targets, except for target 12.1.[39]

III. Commentary

A. Content, Structure, and Language of SDG 12

The overall goal of ensuring SCP patterns is to be achieved with the help of eight specific targets (targets 12.1–12.8) plus three targets related to the means of implementation (targets 12.a–12.c). While the formulation of the goal uses the ambitious word 'ensure', the compliance with the individual targets is purely voluntary.[40] There is also no explicit acknowledgment in the wording of the goal and the targets 'of the need for regulatory changes to enforce sustainable practices and to restrict or prohibit unsustainable ones'.[41] As a result, SDG 12 and its targets mainly reiterate what governments have proposed and committed themselves to previously;[42] they do not present any new commitments and stay within the character of aspiration.[43]

The topics covered by the targets do not represent all the areas of SCP, but rather they deal with the topic in a 'fragmented and piecemeal way'.[44] There are topics that did not make it into the text of the SDGs,[45] despite being discussed during the negotiations[46] and/or included in the 10YFP.[47] The language of the targets remains largely vague. Yet, it avoids some earlier proposed terms, such as 'sustainable supply chains',[48] that were opposed by developing countries due to the fear of their ambiguity resulting into trade restrictions and additional obligations to developing countries.[49] Other terms, such as 'sustainable lifestyle' were not included as they were unequally shifting the responsibility for SCP action onto developed countries.[50] During the negotiations, some countries suggested a more quantitative-based wording of the targets. An example can be

---

[39] Gasper and others (n 5) 92.

[40] Srivastava (n 8) 26.

[41] Gasper and others (n 5) 83, 85.

[42] The links between individual targets and international law are discussed below.

[43] UN, 'Transforming Our World: The 2030 Agenda for Sustainable Development' (September 2015) UN Doc A/RES/70/1.

[44] One Planet Network, 'A Platform for Sustainable Development Goal 12' <https://www.oneplanetnetwork.org/platform-sustainable-development-goal-12> accessed 26 October 2021.

[45] A list of considered topics can be found in Open Working Group on Sustainable Development Goals, 'Encyclopedia Groupinica: A Compilation of Goals and Targets Suggestions from OWG 10, In response to Co-Chairs' Focus Area' (19 March 2014) 115 et seq.

[46] Such as sustainability in supply chains (Concluding Remarks of Co-Chairs, OWG-7, 2); improving the access of developing countries to product and technology markets (troika of China, Indonesia, and Kazakhstan, OWG-10); and reduction in per capita energy consumption (India, OWG-10).

[47] Such as sustainable buildings and construction sector.

[48] Concluding Remarks of Co-Chairs (OWG-7) 2.

[49] Gasper and others (n 5) 88.

[50] Brazil and Nicaragua, OWG-9, suggested to include the following wording 'by 2030 implement policies to create a culture of sustainable lifestyles, particular in developed countries'.

a following proposal made by the troika Italy, Spain, and Turkey: 'by 2030, *reduce per capita waste by x per cent* through prevention, reduction, re-use, recycling and other forms of recovery'.[51] Yet, the final formulations stayed largely qualitative and indefinite, maintaining the universality of the goal and leaving the space for further specification through the indicators.

B. SDG 12 and International Law

Looking at customary international law, except for the CBDR principle, SDG 12 is firmly based on the international law principle of no harm. While the no harm principle is further discussed in relation to target 12.2 below, its pedigree can be traced in most of the targets under SDG 12. The no harm principle was formulated as principle 21 of the Stockholm Declaration on Human Environment stating that '[s]tates have, in accordance with the Charter of the United Nations and the principles of international law, the sovereign right to exploit their own resources pursuant to their own environmental policies, and the responsibility to ensure that activities within their jurisdiction or control do not cause damage to the environment of other States or of areas beyond the limits of national jurisdiction'.[52] The link to the production side of SDG 12 is obvious, but there is also a link to consumption. For example, consumption of chemicals in one jurisdiction can harm another or the waste created due to consumption patterns might do the same. While the no harm principle served as a legal source in some high-profile international disputes at international fora, it remains largely ill-defined.[53] However, it certainly provides a moral imperative for activities not only at the state level but also at the industrial and corporate levels.[54] For example, it is a driving force behind the business and human rights agenda, which is based on the cornerstone that businesses should do no harm through their operations, products, and relationships.[55]

Turning to conventional international law, SDG 12, nested in the existing socioeconomic system, links to a vast web of international conventions and regulations. It is thus striking that the only agreements referred to in the text of the Goal and its targets are those on chemicals and hazardous waste.[56] Yet, the lack of explicit connections to international agreements may be logical as SDG 12 rests on the premise of

---

[51] Troika Italy, Spain, and Turkey, OWG-11, p 3; similarly see, eg, Japan, OWG-11 ('by 2030 improve the cyclical use rate by x% through reuse and recycling').

[52] UN General Assembly, United Nations Conference on the Human Environment, 15 December 1972, A/RES/2994 <https://www.refworld.org/docid/3b00f1c840.html> accessed 1 May 2021 (Stockholm Declaration).

[53] For discussion of emblematic cases of the International Court of Justice and arbitration tribunals involving the no harm principle see: M Tignino and C Bréthaut, 'The Role of International Case Law in Implementing the Obligation Not to Cause Significant Harm' (2020) 20 International Environmental Agreements: Politics, Law and Economics 631.

[54] Srivastava (n 8) on the moral imperative, 32–35.

[55] JG Ruggie, 'Global Governance and "New Governance Theory": Lessons from Business and Human Rights' (2014) 20 Global Governance 5, 8.

[56] A Arcuri and E Partiti, 'SDG 12: Ensure Sustainable Consumption and Production Patterns' (TILEC Discussion Paper, DP 2021-007, 2021) 2 <https://papers.ssrn.com/sol3/papers.cfm?abstract_id=3814765> accessed 30 October 2021; see text to target 12.4 below.

866 SDG 12

voluntariness, relying heavily on the soft legal (eg in the case of corporate sustainable reporting) and non-legal tools (eg in the case of education). But even there, a lack of reference to global soft law initiatives, such as the UN Guiding Principles on Business and Human Rights that is based on the no harm principle and uses non-financial reporting (a topic subsumed under target 12.6) as one of its implementation tools,[57] is remarkable and not easily understood. A possible explanation is the focus on universality of the SDGs, their necessarily limited number, and feasibility.

As other SDGs, SDG 12 also has a close connection to human rights.[58] Its bridging (in respect to the three pillars of SD) and enabling character (in respect to other SDGs) links the Goal to a wide variety of human rights.[59] Some of the connections are more evident than others, though. These include the right of all people to freely dispose of their natural wealth and resources.[60] As discussed earlier, this right is not absolute, as it is limited by the no harm principle of international law. The right to health including the right to a safe, clean, healthy, and sustainable environment can be mentioned as another closely connected human right to SDG 12.[61] It connects directly to target 12.4 that aims for sound management of chemicals and all wastes throughout their lifecycle and through it to secure the right to health. The right to adequate food and the right to safe drinking water then clearly connect to targets 12.2 (sustainable management and efficient use of natural resources), 12.3 (food waste and loss), and the already mentioned target 12.4 (chemicals and waste management).[62]

SDG 12 has a very intimate relationship with another field of conventional international law and that is international trade law. It is thus surprising that while the World Trade Organization (WTO) on its own webpage recognizes the links with many SDGs, SDG 12 is missing on the list.[63] In line with the WTO rules, any state can easily regulate SCP aspects of manufacturing processes taking place within their territory. It is more difficult to regulate manufacturing processes in relation to imported products. If a state aims at setting some standards for products manufactured in another jurisdiction, their marketing, or import, scrutiny under the WTO rules is triggered. It is not forbidden *per se* for countries to regulate production processes and methods, including

---

[57] Human Rights Council, 'Guiding Principles on Business and Human Rights: Implementing the United Nations "Protect, Respect and Remedy" Framework' (21 March 2011) A/HRC/17/31.

[58] 'It has been shown that over 90 per cent of SDG targets are embedded in human rights treaties', Human Rights and the SDGs Pursuing Synergies, December 2017 <https://www.universal-rights.org/wp-content/uploads/2017/12/RAPPORT_2017_HUMAN-RIGHTS-SDGS-PURSUING-SYNERGIES_03_12_2017_digital_use-2.pdf> accessed 26 October 2021.

[59] An overview can be found at the Danish Institute for Human Rights, 'The Human Rights Guide to the Sustainable Development Goals' <https://sdg.humanrights.dk/en/targets2?combine_1=xxx&goal=81&target=&instrument=All&title_1=&field_country_tid=All&field_instrument_group_tid=All&combine=> accessed 26 October 2021.

[60] International Covenant on Civil and Political Rights (ICCPR) (adopted 16 December 1966, in force 23 March 1976) 999 UNTS 171, art 1(2); International Covenant on Economic, Social and Cultural Rights (ICESCR) (adopted 19 December 1966, in force 3 January 1976) 993 UNTS 3, art 1(2).

[61] Universal Declaration of Human Rights (adopted 10 December 1948 UNGA Res 217 A(III) (UDHR) art 25(1); ICESCR (n 60) art 12.

[62] UDHR (n 61), art 25(1); ICESCR (n 60) art 11.

[63] WTO, 'The WTO and the Sustainable Development Goals' <https://www.wto.org/english/thewto_e/coher_e/sdgs_e/sdgs_e.htm> accessed 26 October 2021.

COMMENTARY 867

their environmental and social aspects, even if the production takes place abroad.[64] However, the regulation cannot constitute an arbitrary or unjustifiable discrimination, or distort competition among 'like' domestic and imported products. The limits of such regulation of production processes and methods were tested in several disputes decided by the WTO Appellate Body.

Most notably, in the *Shrimp Turtle* case, a group of countries (Malaysia, India, Pakistan, and Thailand) brought a complaint against a ban on import of certain shrimps and shrimp products to the United States.[65] The ban targeted shrimp caught using technology that may have adversely affected certain species of sea turtles listed according to the US Endangered Species Act of 1973 as endangered or threatened. The United States lost the case. The ban was found to cause arbitrary and unjustifiable discrimination. However, the United States in fact did not lose because it tried to protect the environment but rather because it did not impose the ban equally on all other WTO members. It provided technical and financial assistance, and longer transition periods for fishermen to start using turtle-excluder devices only to some countries. Following the decision, the United States amended the application of the ban according to the Appellate Body's recommendation, and in a follow-up dispute initiated by Malaysia the ban was found to be in compliance with the WTO rules.[66]

The SCP production-focused agenda have also started to be carried through free trade agreements. A new generation of agreements in this field include commitments of the parties to protect the environment and social rights. However, such provisions are often vaguely formulated, reflecting the main purpose of the agreements—to facilitate trade—and not to be considered as excessively intrusive.[67]

Also international investment law could potentially be the carrier of SCP standards, particularly to developing countries. Investment treaties in fact often include social and environmental provisions. However, when a dispute arises, those tend to be marginalized.[68] For example, the *Tecmed* case revolved around a dispute between Mexico and a Spanish investor, a company transporting and managing toxic waste, that has continuously breached Mexican laws on hazardous waste.[69] As the breach persisted, the Mexican government decided to replace Tecmed's open licence for the operation of a landfill site with a licence of a limited duration. The company claimed that this violated the provision on fair and equitable treatment in the investment treaty. The award

---

[64] Arcuri and Partiti (n 56) 10.

[65] WTO Appellate Body (AB) Report, US—Import Prohibition of Certain Shrimp and Shrimp Products (US–Shrimp), WT/DS58/AB/R, 12 October 1998 (*US–Shrimp*); similarly Dolphin–Tuna cases (*Tuna–Dolphin I, Tuna–Dolphin II*, and *US–Tuna II (Mexico)*).

[66] *US–Shrimp*, Decision of AB from 21 November 2001 <https://www.wto.org/english/tratop_e/dispu_e/cases_e/ds58_e.htm> accessed 26 October 2021.

[67] K Ellison, 'Rio + 20: How the Tension between Developing and Developed Countries Influenced Sustainable Development Efforts' (2014) 27 Global Business & Development Law Journal 107; R Amos and E Lydgate, 'Trade, Transboundary Impacts the Implementation of SDG 12' (2020) 15 Sustainability Science 1699, 1706.

[68] K Tienhaara, *The Expropriation of Environmental Governance Protecting Foreign Investors at the Expense of Public Policy* (CUP 2009).

[69] *Tecnicas Medioambientales Tecmed S.A. v United Mexican States* (29 May 2003) ICSID Case No ARB(AF)/00/2 (Tecmed).

868   SDG 12

tribunal decided in favour of Tecmed, stating that the Mexican government has acted ambiguously and infringed the legitimate expectations of the investor.[70]

While some decisions of the WTO Appellate body, such as the *Shrimp Turtle* case, bring hope, the whole area of international trade law does not.[71] It remains firmly nested in neoliberalism ideas, where laws and institutions are shaped for the protection of markets.[72] This is mirrored in the asymmetry of the institutional setting in international law 'characterized by strong institutions in the field of international economic law and much weaker ones in the field of international environmental and human rights law'.[73] The following words of John Maynard Keynes, '[t]he difficulty lies not so much in developing new ideas as in escaping from old ones', seem to capture the very core challenge for SDG 12 and SDGs generally. SDG 12 is characterized by a strong presence of private actors in the regulatory sphere, which complicates the situation further.

C. Challenges to Effective Regulation: Variety of Stakeholders and Covered Topics

The negotiations on SDG 12 were strongly influenced by the private sector too;[74] SDG 12 is possibly the goal where the need for cooperation of the public and private sectors is most obvious.[75] Featuring both consumption and production results in involving many types of stakeholders: from individual consumers, through consumer and industrial associations, companies, and markets, to states. This results in a regulatory conundrum where several of the stakeholders perform both the regulator and regulated roles. This is first and foremost true when it comes to states. States serve a dual role of a producer and a consumer as well as of a regulator and a facilitator.[76] But other subjects also wear two hats. For example, multinational enterprises are naturally in the position of regulated objects. However, they have also claimed the regulator's role when, for instance, it comes to securing sustainability in transnational supply chains or sustainability reporting.[77] Industrial and corporate self-regulation presents both advantages and disadvantages. The advantages include a lowering of administrative costs to public budgets, flexibility, specialization, and quick application,[78] and the ability to cross jurisdictional

---

[70] For other similar cases see Arcuri and Partiti (n 56) 15.

[71] D Alessandrini, 'Value-capture, Development and Social Reproduction in International Trade Law' (*Verfassungsblog*, 4 March 2020) <https://verfassungsblog.de/value-capture-development-and-social-reproduction-in-international-trade-law/> accessed 26 October 2021.

[72] Chapter 8 on SDG 8 in this book.

[73] Arcuri and Partiti (n 56) 15.

[74] This was possible due to the multilateral character of the OWG including both states and non-state actors. M Kamau and others (eds), *Transforming Multilateral Diplomacy: the inside Story of the Sustainable Development Goals* (Routledge 2018), ch 3.

[75] S Pizzi and others, 'The Determinants of Business Contribution to the 2030 Agenda: Introducing the SDG Reporting Score' (2021) 30(1) Business Strategy and the Environment (2021) 404, 416.

[76] Srivastava (n 8) 26.

[77] LC Backer, 'Multinational Corporations as Objects and Sources of Transnational Regulation' (2007) 14(2) ILSA Journal of International & Comparative Law 499, 499.

[78] O Gray, 'Well-designed Self and Co-regulation are Essential for Better Regulation' (*Euractiv*, 27 May 2015) <https://www.euractiv.com/section/innovation-industry/opinion/well-designed-self-and-co-regulation-are-essential-for-better-regulation/> accessed 26 October 2021.

borders without the danger of interfering with state sovereignty and, thus, creating so-called transnational private regulation. Disadvantages include doubtful legitimacy, accountability, and enforcement.[79] Transnational private regulation disciplining production processes thus represents two shifts in the legal sphere: a shift from national to global regulation, and a shift from state-made to private regulation.[80] When it comes to vital interests such as environmental and employees' protection, these shifts can be criticized also for their potentially pre-emptive role in the development of adequate public regulation. Basically, the critique claims that by adopting various types of transnational private regulation (such as production standards and codes of conduct), the private sector lulls public regulators into the false belief that the interests in question are taken care of and no new laws are needed.[81] While this motivation can be discussed, possibly more alarming is the fact that transnational private regulation in large relies on consumer pressure as its driving force. The underlying idea is that consumers will punish companies involved in unethical production by not buying their products. This is, however, problematic for several reasons. First, this can only be a potential driver for sustainable behaviour in close-to-consumers sectors.[82] Second, consumers have incomplete information and are not in the position to evaluate the effectiveness of transnational private regulation. Yet, providing constantly increasing amount of information proves to be suboptimal.[83] Third, psychological barriers to consumers' sustainable behaviour, such as the intention-action gap—that is, the fact that consumers who are concerned about the environment do not align their purchasing behaviours to their beliefs—are well-known.[84] However, the solution to them is not.

Overall, it is difficult to regulate production and consumption at the international level as they involve private law relations traditionally regulated through national law. And while some argue that transnational private regulation and self-regulation can help to close this gap,[85] others see it as a delaying tactic of the corporate lobby to prevent any further state-made regulation.[86]

Another issue for regulation in the SCP area is the broad scope of activities that it covers. Which activities will be prioritised in a specific jurisdiction depends on the

---

[79] See, eg, J Black and D Rouch, 'The Development of the Global Markets as Rule-Makers: Engagement and Legitimacy' (2015) 2 Law and Financial Markets Review 218.

[80] F Cafaggi, 'New Foundations of Transnational Private Regulation. Journal of Law and Society' (2011) 38(1) 20, 21.

[81] See, eg, R Reich, 'The Case Against Corporate Social Responsibility' (2008) Goldman School of Public Policy Working Paper No GSPP08-003 <http://dx.doi.org/10.2139/ssrn.1213129> accessed 26 October 2021.

[82] J Haddock-Fraser and I Fraser, 'Assessing Corporate Environmental Reporting Motivations: Differences Between "Close-To-Market" and "Business-To-Business" Companies' (2008) 15(3) Corporate Social Responsibility and Environmental Management 140.

[83] See further discussion on target 12.8, this chapter.

[84] See, eg, M-L Johnstone and LP Tan, 'Exploring the Gap Between Consumers' Green Rhetoric and Purchasing Behaviour' (2015) 132(2) Journal of Business Ethics 311; AR Farias and others, 'The Effects of Temporal Discounting on Perceived Seriousness of Environmental Behavior: Exploring the Moderator Role of Consumer Attitudes Regarding Green Purchasing' (2021) 13(13) Sustainability 7130.

[85] KP Mitkidis, Sustainability Clauses in International Business Contracts (Dovenschmidt Monographs, Vol 3, Eleven International Publishing 2015) 10–11.

[86] See n 81; Gasper and others (n 5) 84.

level of economic and societal development and societal structural settings. Depending then on the focus area, the appropriate governance tools will also differ.[87]

D. Regional Differences

The Western EU Member States have been identified as having the most active approach to SCP in the policy and legal fields.[88] Yet, they struggle to deliver on SDG 12. This is true for most developed countries. From all SDGs, the Organisation for Economic Co-operation and Development (OECD) countries were found to struggle most with SDGs 8, 10, and 12.[89] The reason is '[t]heir inability to fight the growing social divide combined with their overuse of resources'.[90] Developing countries then face challenges particularly in regard to social and environmental SDGs, trying to secure population's essential needs as the wealth in these countries is not adequate to raise red flags in respect to their consumption levels.[91] This is also mirrored in the SDG Progress Chart 2021, where developed countries are considered as substantially progressing/being on track in respect to reduction of domestic material consumption per unit of GDP.[92] However, as the progress towards other SDGs will hopefully be realized, and unless humanity makes radical shifts in the current socio-economic establishment, achieving SDG 12 might gradually become difficult worldwide. In other words, as we move towards achieving the SDGs, eradicating poverty, lifting the living standards of citizens in developing countries, and improving health conditions and raising the average life expectancy, both the global population and thus the consumption levels are likely to increase.[93,94]

The differences in the development levels of UN countries impacted negotiations of SDG 12. As described above, the application of the CBDR principle was discussed, though it was mostly abandoned in the final text of SDG 12 (with target 12.1 as an exception). Transboundary environmental and social harms related to production thus remain under the radar and 'subordinate to the imperative of increasing free trade'.[95]

---

[87] A Tukker and others (eds), *System Innovation for Sustainability 1: Perspectives on Radical Changes to Sustainable Consumption and Production* (Greeenleaf Publishing 2008) 6.

[88] C Wang and others, 'A Literature Review of Sustainable Consumption and Production: A Comparative Analysis in Developed and Developing Economies' (2019) 206 Journal of Cleaner Production 741. Identifying the level of economic development as the decisive factor.

[89] C Kroll with a foreword by K Annan, *Sustainable Development Goals: Are the Rich Countries Ready?* (SGI: Sustainable Governance Indicators, Sustainable Development Solutions Network, Bertelsmann Stiftung 2015) 5.

[90] ibid 5.

[91] More on the developed/developing countries divide, see parts on specific targets, namely Section F.2.

[92] Statistics Division, Department of Economic and Social Affairs, United Nations, 'Sustainable Development Goals Progress Chart 2021' (2021) <https://unstats.un.org/sdgs/report/2021/progress-chart/> accessed 26 October 2021. See more about domestic material consumption under target 12.2.

[93] WHO, 'World Health Statistics 2020: Monitoring Health for the SDGs, Sustainable development goals' (Licence: CC BY-NC-SA 3.0 IGO, Geneva, World Health Organization 2020) 1–5.

[94] See, eg, nn 177, 198, and 356 for impacts of the growing global population on the various targets under SDG 12.

[95] Amos and Lydgate (n 67) 1708; see also earlier discussion on the intersection of SDG 12 with international trade law and target 12.2 text on transboundary harm.

E. Critique

SCP is a necessary precondition to the achievement of SD as envisioned by the UN Agenda 2030. Yet, it remains out of focus of the sustainability discourse and, thus, inadequately funded. According to the finding of the High-Level Political Forum (HLPF), SDG 12 is the 'least resourced' of all the SDGs.[96] This is alarming as funding is necessary not only for the implementation of relevant measures but also for the gathering of data and building of a necessary knowledge base.[97] The question is why there is no adequate regulatory attention and funding provided to SCP.

An answer can be found in 'the gap between intent and implementation'.[98] Similar to the above description of this gap in relation to consumer behaviour, we can also experience this gap at the regulatory level. Intention expressed in SDG 12 requires a reconsideration, restructuring, and re-regulation of the whole socio-economic system our current society is built on. Historically, the leading idea was that we need to decrease consumption. This was replaced with the idea that we need to optimize (also in the word's social and environmental meaning) our production; that we need to do *more and better with less*.[99] Technological advancement is then largely relied on as the tool for such an optimization. The underlying premise is that with innovation in production, consumption will cease to constitute environmental burden, and thus consumption will be allowed to grow. This reliance on technological solutions has, however, been designated to be false as speed in technological innovation does not catch up with the speed of environmental degradation.[100]

The underpinning theories and principles of the current socio-economic and thus also legal systems therefore need to be revisited.[101] In words of Kate Raworth, 'we need to focus on economies that make 'us thrive, whether or not they grow'.[102] This takes us back to the interconnection between SDGs 8 and 12. It also makes one to realize that SCP is still considered an exception, not a norm. Mainstreaming the ethics of sustainability beyond the SDGs will be necessary to facilitate any meaningful regulatory change for SCP[103] as there is regrettably little in the text of SDG 12 that would suggest any alternatives to the currently established economic system as framed through international economic law.[104]

---

[96] High-Level Political Forum on Sustainable Development, '2018 HLPF Review of SDGs implementation: SDG 12—Ensure Sustainable Consumption and Production Patterns' 3 <https://sustainabledevelopment.un.org/content/documents/196532018backgroundnotesSDG12.pdf> accessed 25 October 2021 (HLPF Review 2018).

[97] See, eg, Amos and Lydgate (n 67) 1707 in respect to understanding of transnational.

[98] Srivastava (n 8) 19.

[99] n 16.

[100] M Bengtsson and others, 'Transforming Systems of Consumption and Production for Achieving the Sustainable Development Goals: Moving Beyond Efficiency' (2018) 13 Sustainability Science 1533, 1535.

[101] Arcuri and Partiti (n 56).

[102] K Raworth, *Doughnut Economics, Seven Ways to Think Like a 21st Century Economist* (Penguin 2017).

[103] Srivastava (n 8) 30 et seq.

[104] J Linarelli and others, *The Misery of International Law: Confrontations with Injustice in the Global Economy* (OUP 2018) 266–67.

SDG 12 has, however, not been placed into a normative vacuum. Quite the opposite: there had already been agreed and pursued a global initiative on SCP, the 10YFP. The advantages of synergies and disadvantages of duplication between these two UN initiatives have been largely discussed not only during the SDGs' negotiations but also in academic literature.[105] The success in exploiting the advantages will, among other things, depend on a simultaneous and coordinated implementation, which is currently being pursued by the One Planet Network that established a coordination hub facilitating the sharing of experiences among states globally.[106] The projects' database of the One Planet Network[107] is not only a great source of data and inspiration but it also portrays the fact that SCP implementation measures largely depend on national 'specific interests and priorities, rather than on effective obligations created under SDG 12'.[108]

More specific critique follows in relation to the individual targets.

F. Commentary to Individual Targets

1. Target 12.1 Implement the 10-year framework of programmes on sustainable consumption and production, all countries taking action, with developed countries taking the lead, taking into account the development and capabilities of developing countries

a) Sources of target

Target 12.1 reiterates the already existing international policy consensus on the necessity to shift to SCP patterns, the so-called 10YFP. The 10YFP has been adopted at Rio + 20 Conference to implement the Johannesburg Plan of Implementation, which declared the objective to '[e]ncourage and promote the development of a 10-year framework of programmes in support of regional and national initiatives to accelerate the shift towards sustainable consumption and production'.[109] It is natural that SDG 12 refers to this earlier UN initiative in order to secure continuity and integration, both in the declared commitments and their implementation. And the reference is mutual, as the 10YFP states that it '[s]erves as a tool to support the implementation of global sustainable development commitments'.[110] However, while the hopes are that the two commitments will reinforce each other,[111] some express concerns that this duplication does not add any impetus to the transition to SCP.[112]

---

[105] Akenji and Bengtsson (n 31) table 2.

[106] n 44.

[107] The One Planet Network <https://www.oneplanetnetwork.org/initiatives> accessed 29 October 2021.

[108] Gasper and others (n 5) 88.

[109] UN Report of the World Summit on Sustainable Development (Johannesburg Summit), Johannesburg, South Africa (26 August–2 September 2002) UN Doc UN/CONF.199/20, ch I, resolution 2, annex, para 15 (Johannesburg Plan of Implementation).

[110] UN, A/CONF.216/5 (n 13) annex, para 1c)(x).

[111] Open Working Group of the General Assembly on Sustainable Development Goals (OWG), 'Progress Report' <https://sustainabledevelopment.un.org/content/documents/3238summaryallowg.pdf> accessed 26 October 2020, para 158.

[112] See, eg, Bengtsson (n 100).

The 10YFP encompasses a wide range of activities and areas, among others eradication of poverty, sustainable public procurement, incorporation of the sustainability topic into educational programmes and consumer information, sustainable buildings and construction, and sustainable food systems. Therefore, it touches on and overlaps not only with most of the targets under SDG 12 but also with several other SDGs. Furthermore, it is explicitly mentioned in target 8.4.[113] The main objectives of the 10YFP are to accelerate the shift towards SCP in all countries by supporting regional and national policies and initiatives, capacity building, providing financial and technical assistance to developing countries, and creating an information and knowledge sharing platform on SCP. The 10YFP does not stipulate any measurable goals to be achieved. However, the United Nations Environment Programme (UNEP), the custodian agency for 10YFP and, therefore, also for target 12.1, in 2017 published a document titled Indicators of Success for the 10-Year Framework of Programmes on Sustainable Consumption and Production Patterns: Principles, Process and Methodology.[114] This document introduces and provides the methodology for twenty 10YFP indicators and stipulates their connections to various SDGs and targets.[115] The interconnection between 10YFP and SDGs thus again becomes very clear here.

b) Empirical analysis

Yet, progress towards target 12.1 remains measured by a single indicator (12.1.1) that records the 'number of countries developing, adopting or implementing policy instruments aimed at supporting the shift to sustainable consumption and production'. The indicator thus only counts the number of countries adopting relevant policies and action plans, but it stays short of evaluating the actual progress made towards SCP.[116] This is recognized in the metadata document for target 12.1.1: '[The indicator] does not provide any qualitative information and whether policies were well-designed or if a proper background analysis had been conducted, the quality of implementation, level of enforcement, and its effects.'[117] It is worth noting that the wording of the indicator remained largely the same throughout the OWG discussions; rare suggestions during the negotiations for more precise and stringent formulation of indicator 12.1.1 were not accepted.[118]

Data for target 12.1.1 is provided by the 10YFP National Focal Points and administered by the 10YFP Secretariat (another practical synergy between the two UN initiatives).[119] Countries are asked to report on the adoption of both binding (laws and regulations) and non-binding policy instruments. The rationale behind this broad

---

[113] This book, Chapter 8.
[114] UNEP, 'Indicators of Success for the 10-Year Framework of Programmes on Sustainable Consumption and Production Patterns: Principles, Process and Methodology' (UNEP 2017).
[115] ibid 9–10.
[116] Gasper and others (n 5) 90.
[117] SDG Indicators Metadata Repository, 'Metadata Sheet for Indicator 12.1.1' <https://unstats.un.org/sdgs/metadata/> accessed 25 October 2021 (Metadata 12.1.1).
[118] Gasper and others (n 5) 90.
[119] Metadata 12.1.1 (n 117) data sources.

874   SDG 12

scope of reporting is that binding legislation provides the legal framework of SCP, can be used to enforce appropriate behaviour, and demonstrates governmental support of SCP, while non-binding policy instruments 'ensure institutional engagement, commitment and ownership'.[120] In respect to each instrument, a questionnaire is filled in where information such as the type of instrument, the scope, and connections to other SDGs are indicated.[121]

The UN Report of the Secretary-General from 2021 (SG's Progress Report 2021) shows a positive development towards target 12.1.1, as the number of reported SCP policies and action plans have been steadily growing reaching over 700 throughout eighty-three countries and the European Union in 2020.[122] However, the report also points to the geographical differences between developed and developing countries, where significantly more policies and action plans are reported by developed countries. Compared to the country profiles where developing countries seem to be doing substantially better in delivering towards SDG 12 than developed countries, this questions whether indicator 12.1.1 tells us anything at all about the shift towards SCP patterns. It might, though, also disclose the fact that SDG 12, known as a problematic area in developed countries, is kept in the policy focus.

c) Implementation efforts at domestic/international level

The prevalence of action on target 12.1 by developed countries is in line with the CBDR principle, which is indirectly referred to in the wording of the target calling for 'developed countries taking the lead, taking into account the development and capabilities of developing countries'. First appearing in article 2(2) of the Vienna Convention for the Protection of the Ozone Layer,[123] the CBDR principle was further developed and embodied in article 7 of the Rio Declaration,[124] becoming a well-recognized principle of international environmental law. It aims to reconcile potentially competing interests and calls for global cooperation on addressing environmental challenges: on the one hand, developed states recognize the burden they place on the environment, and their possibilities of action due to the financial and technological resources they possess; on the other hand, developing countries commit themselves to contribute to action within the limits of their reduced capacity to do so and their development needs.[125] Despite being a widely recognized principle, the legal status of the CBDR principle remains controversial.[126] For example, the United States stated that it does not accept the principle to infer 'any international obligations or liabilities' for them or 'any diminution

---

[120] ibid, concepts and definitions.

[121] ibid, methodology.

[122] UN Economic and Social Council (ECOSOC), 'Progress towards the Sustainable Development Goals, Report of the Secretary-General' (30 April 2021) UN Doc E/2021/58, para 133 (SG's Progress Report 2021).

[123] Vienna Convention for the Protection of the Ozone Layer (adopted 22 March 1985, in force 22 September 1988) 1513 UNTS 293 (Vienna Convention).

[124] UNGA, Report of the UN Conference on Environment and Development (Rio de Janeiro, 3–14 June 1992) (12 August 1992) UN Doc A/CONF.151/26 (Vol I) (Rio Declaration).

[125] P-M Dupuy and JE Viñuales, *International Environmental Law* (2nd edn, CUP 2018) 73.

[126] ibid 75; B Mayer, *The International Law on Climate Change* (CUP 2018) 37.

in the responsibilities of developing countries'.[127] As such, the indirect reference to the CBDR principle adds little to target 12.1.

The transition to SCP patterns must happen in all jurisdictional and geographical areas regardless of the countries' individual development levels. Even in countries where consumption is not high now, an increase is expected as the global population and its living standard is expected to grow gradually in line with the progress towards achieving the SDGs.[128] That is why some developed countries and regions help to build the capacities of the developing regions. The SwitchAsia programme,[129] funded by the EU, is an example here.[130] The mission of the programme is '[t]o support the transition of Asian Countries to a low-carbon, resource-efficient and circular economy while promoting sustainable production and consumption patterns within Asia and greener supply chains between Asia and Europe'.[131] It stems from the above that both sides are intended beneficiaries here: Asian countries can directly benefit from the support, while greening international supply chains will help the EU to deliver on other SDGs and targets, such as climate action (SDG 13)[132] or sustainable management and efficient use of natural resources (target 12.2).[133]

The policy and legal development in the SCP area at national level is in line with the 10YFP. The policies therefore cover broad and varied areas of action, such as public education, use of natural resources, and sustainable procurement. For example, in June 2020, Vietnam adopted the National Action Plan on Sustainable Consumption and Production (2021–2030).[134] The plan was developed by the Ministry of Industry and Trade of the Socialist Republic of Vietnam under the supervision of and with the help of funding from the EU's SwitchAsia programme. It covers a wide range of actions and contains quantified goals, both final and intermediate. For example, one of the objectives for the period 2021–2030 is '[a] 5–8% decrease in resources and materials used for production sectors such as textile, steel, plastics, chemical, cement, alcohol and beer, beverage, paper and seafood processing'.[135] The plan works with various activities that should help the country to deliver on the goals with the development of legal frameworks topping the list.[136] Only time will tell how this well-articulated plan will be executed, and whether the goals will be achieved. However, bringing the SCP topics to the

---

[127] Written statement of the United States on principle 7 of the Rio Declaration, in Report of the United Nations Conference on Environment and Development (Rio de Janeiro, 3–14 June 1992) UN, A/CONF.151/26 (Vol. IV) (28 September 1992) para 16.

[128] n 94.

[129] SWITCH-Asia, 'About Us' <https://www.switch-asia.eu/switch-asia/about-us/> accessed 25 October 2021.

[130] The EU has established so-called switch programmes for the Asia Pacific, Africa, and the Mediterranean regions. See HLPF, 'The 10 Year Framework of Programmes on Sustainable Consumption and Production Patterns (10YFP), Interim progress report prepared by the 10YFP Secretariat on behalf of the 10YFP Board for the High-Level Political Forum', p 8.

[131] n 129.

[132] Chapter 13 on SDG 13, this book.

[133] See text on target 12.2 section.

[134] Vietnam, 'National Action Plan on Sustainable Consumption and Production (2021–2030)' <https://www.switch-asia.eu/site/assets/files/2533/national_action_plan_on_scp_vietnam_pdf_pdf.pdf> accessed 25 October 2021.

[135] ibid 3.

[136] ibid 2.

876   SDG 12

front of the policy and legal development in developing countries is undisputedly a step in the right direction.

d) Critique

The implementation of national plans on SCP will arguably depend on an integrated approach to the area, which needs to be supported by carefully coordinated efforts across different governmental branches. Such a coordination may prove difficult to attain, as it was proven by the mid-term report on 10YFP, which stated that 'only 26 of the 71 countries that have reported on their policies on SCP have shared information on national coordination mechanisms. Only a few of these are mandated to coordinate policy implementation across ministries.'[137] Without effective coordination at national level, SCP policies are in danger of fragmentation, mutual negative spill-over effects, and overall zero-sum effect.

Indicator 12.1.1 does not help to close the implementation gap in respect to national plans on SCP. Providing merely a number of countries developing SCP plans, it does not address the quality, feasibility, and enforcement of the plans.[138] In other words, it is based on the implicit assumptions that adoption of a centralized SCP policy will lead to its successful implementation, and that national plans that synthesize multiple SCP objectives are the preferred tools of a societal shift towards SCP.[139] However, adoption does not equal implementation, and an integration of SCP goals into sectoral policy plans and objectives might be more effective.[140]

This discussion is closely connected to the general considerations during the SDGs' negotiation of whether SCP should be a self-standing goal or whether separate SCP topics should be integrated under other relevant SDGs.[141] Basing target 12.1.1 on 10YFP might feel as a natural fit for the first target of SDG 12, a fit that can be backed up by the objective of integration. But it can also be seen as a circular argumentation, as the 10YFP touches on so many other areas encapsulated in SDGs.

A final critical remark goes to the difference between developed and developing states in the SCP context that is further discussed under the subsequent targets. The underlying assumption of 10YFP is that all countries are equal and have shared objectives and, thus, they can work collaboratively on the shift in the consumption and production patterns. However, as production nowadays takes place in complex transnational supply chains allowing corporations to consider and take advantage of different regulatory environments to optimize their production in the desired direction, which is often to minimize costs, the production processes lead to further economic polarization of global society.[142] Target 12.1.1 does not deliver solutions to this polarization.

---

[137] High-Level Political Forum on Sustainable Development, '2018 HLPF Review of SDGs Implementation: SDG 12—Ensure Sustainable Consumption and Production Patterns' 1 <https://sustainabledevelopment.un.org/content/documents/196532018backgroundnotesSDG12.pdf> accessed 25 October 2021 (HLPF Review 2018).

[138] Metadata 12.1.1 (n 117) concepts and definitions.

[139] Bengtsson and others (n 100) 1539.

[140] ibid.

[141] See Introduction to this chapter; Akenji and Bengtsson (n 31) table 2.

[142] J Martens and K Seitz, 'SDG 12 Binding Rules on Business and Human Rights—A Critical Prerequisite to Ensure Sustainable Consumption and Production Patterns' in report by the Civil Society Reflection Group on the

2. Target 12.2 By 2030, achieve the sustainable management and efficient use of natural resources

a) Sources of target

Target 12.2 is the cornerstone of SDG 12. Almost everything humans produce and consume requires input of natural resources, and thus it leaves an environmental (and social) footprint. Target 12.2 aims at reducing the footprint.[143] The twofold focus on 'sustainable management' and 'efficient use' of natural resources, reflecting the double aim of SDG 12 that targets both production and consumption, is a precondition for SD. This can further be qualified as a focus on the extraction of natural resources (primarily in low- and middle-income countries) on the one side, and their use in manufacturing and consumption (primarily in high-income countries) on the other.[144]

The underlying logic is clear from the available numbers. Developed countries had on average more than double the per capita footprints than developing countries for the materials reviewed by the HLPF in 2018.[145] In respect of fossil fuels, the per capita footprints were up to four times higher than in developing countries.[146] This reflects the finding that about two-fifths of raw materials globally are extracted in developing countries for the sole purpose of enabling export of goods and services to developed countries.[147] In other words, developed countries largely outsource their environmentally harmful practices to developing countries.[148] This obscures the understanding of the total and relative global management and use of natural resources, creating a gap that needs to be addressed in the relevant indicators for target 12.2.

The progress toward target 12.2 is to be measured through two indicators: material footprint (MF, indicator 12.2.1) and domestic material consumption (DMC, indicator 12.2.2). Each of the indicators should be calculated in absolute terms, on a per capita basis, and per unit of GDP; in other words each works with three sub-indicators. MF represents the volumes of resources 'needed to support a country's final consumption of goods and services, including the impacts of trade',[149] in other words it takes into account 'materials required across the whole global supply chain to produce a good/service and attributing them to the final demand' in a given country.[150] It is

---

2030 Agenda for Sustainable Development, 'Spotlight on Sustainable Development 2017 Reclaiming Policies for the Public Privatization, Partnerships, Corporate Capture, and Their Impact on Sustainability and Inequality—Assessments and Alternatives' (Global Policy Forum 2017) <https://www.2030spotlight.org/sites/default/files/download/spotlight_170626_final_web.pdf> accessed 18 October 2021 (Spotlight on SD).

[143] MA Gardetti and SS Muthu, *The UN Sustainable Development Goals for the Textile and Fashion Industry* (1st edn, Springer Singapore 2020) 25.

[144] International Resource Panel & UNEP, 'Global Resources Outlook 2019: Natural Resources for the Future We Want' (2019) 24–25 <https://www.resourcepanel.org/reports/global-resources-outlook> accessed 25 October 2021 (Global Resources Outlook 2019).

[145] HLPF Review 2018 (n 137) 2.

[146] ibid.

[147] T Wiedmann and others, 'The Material Footprint of Nations' (2015) 112(20) Proceedings of the National Academy of Sciences 6271, 6272.

[148] Global Resources Outlook 2019 (n 144) 20; Amos and Lydgate (n 67) 1702.

[149] Bengtsson and others (n 100) 1539.

[150] SDG Indicators metadata repository, 'Metadata Sheet for Indicator 12.2.2' <https://unstats.un.org/sdgs/metadata/> accessed 25 October 2021 (Metadata 12.2.2), SDG 12 Hub, 'Indicator 12.2.2' <https://sdg12hub.org/sdg-12-hub/see-progress-on-sdg-12-by-target/122-natural-resources#indicator-item-12.2.2> accessed 25 October 2021.

the consumption-side indicator. DMC represents the amounts of resources extracted and used in each country; it is a territorial, production-side indicator.[151] It can thus happen that a country with a strong extraction industry has high DMC, but low MF as most of the extracted materials are exported.[152] During the negotiations, the originally proposed indicator was criticized for not accounting for transboundary moves, primarily from developing to developed countries as well as for the lack of data for this indicator, especially in developing countries.[153] In order to overcome these challenges, some suggested that 'a resource productivity target could distinguish between absolute decoupling in developed countries and relative decoupling in developing ones'.[154] At the end, the two indicators comprising six measured values (six sub-indicators) should provide a comprehensive understanding of the global management and use of natural resources, including the understanding of inequality among states due to international trade.[155]

Turning to the wording of target 12.2, it refers to 'efficiency' in respect to the use and 'sustainability' in respect to the management of natural resources. This leads to the question of whether the extraction of natural resources can ever be sustainable. When we put non-renewable natural resources into the spotlight, the answer is 'no'. Extraction of non-renewable resources leads directly to unsustainable impacts, not only on the environment (taking the form of primarily, depletion of the resources, and secondarily, for example pollution by manufacturing waste in developing countries)[156] but also on society (such as corruption, poor working conditions, and disruptions of the peace), that SDGs overall aim to rectify.[157] Target 12.2 should thus be read as a call for minimizing the extraction of natural resources and moving away from old production and consumption patterns to more efficient ones.[158] Progressively increased use of renewable resources and simultaneous reconsideration of the linear basis of the current economies should both be a part of the path towards SCP. The circular economy model is a widely discussed and partially implemented alternative being 'an economic system in which both matter and energy circulate, reducing the influence of human activity on the environment'.[159,160]

b) Empirical analysis

Development and deployment of such alternative models is critical for the achievement of SDG 12, as both MF and DMC in absolute terms and per capita have globally been steadily growing.[161] There is a positive trend registered in respect to global MF and

---

[151] SDG Indicators metadata repository, 'Metadata Sheet for Indicator 8.4.2' <https://unstats.un.org/sdgs/metadata/> accessed 25 October 2021 (Metadata 8.4.2).

[152] For quantified data see International Resource Panel & UNEP (n 144) 20–21.

[153] Gasper and others (n 5) 91.

[154] OWG (n 111) para 162.

[155] Bengtsson and others (n 100) 1539.

[156] Wang and others (n 88) 750.

[157] Spotlight on SD (n 142) 121–123.

[158] Gardetti and Muthu (n 143) 25.

[159] ibid 26.

[160] More on circular economy below and under target 12.5.

[161] SDG 12 Hub, 'Target 12.2 Resource Use' <https://sdg12hub.org/sdg-12-hub/see-progress-on-sdg-12-by-target/122-natural-resources#indicator-item-12.2.2> accessed 25 October 2021.

DMC values per unit of GDP, where a decrease has been registered between 2011 and 2017.[162] This shows that less resources are needed to produce one unit of output,[163] and thus points towards a successful decoupling of environmental impacts from economic growth. However, it is misleading to look on the aggregate global numbers here, the same as in respect to many other SDGs and their targets. While the average of per capita MF in G20 countries in 2015 was calculated at 15 tonnes per capita,[164] developed countries have at least double the per capita material footprint than developing countries when it comes to all types of materials and this quadruples when it comes to fossil fuels.[165] For example, while Indonesia registered MF of 6 tonnes per capita in 2015, the United States registered 32 tonnes per capita.[166] Even though resource extraction and processing in developing countries are mainly seen in the negative light, there are some positive economic and social impacts, which are a result of these activities. For example, in 2015, these areas accounted for 70 per cent of all jobs nationally in China and 33 per cent in Mexico.[167] However, negative environmental impacts tilt the scale.

What is clear from the available data is that economically strong countries with a high living standard stand out as over-consumers of natural resources[168] and as having trouble in delivering on SDG 12 in general.[169] The consumption patterns fuelled by the economic resources at the individual level together with pollution and emissions leakage due to strict regulation in developed countries are among the driving forces of the pertaining differences in natural resources management and use globally, and of the inability of developing countries to deliver fully on other SDGs. For example, the EU's demand and consumption of palm oil compromises Indonesia's ability to meet SDG 13 (climate action) and SDG 15 (life on land), as Indonesia drains its peat bogs and sells timber to make space for palm oil production.[170,171]

c) Implementation efforts at domestic/international level
It is, thus, essential that both the production and consumption sides of society are involved in achieving target 12.2. Consumer demand for circularity, especially in developed countries, has the potential to lead to a more sustainable management of natural resources. The EU can be named here as a frontrunner in circular economy policy and law development. In March 2020, the EU adopted A New Circular Economy Action Plan for a Cleaner and More Competitive Europe where it presented its policy plan to

---

[162] Data for 2017 are the latest registered data in the SDG 12 Hub as of the time of writing this chapter.
[163] HLPF Review 2018 (n 137).
[164] International Resource Panel, 'Natural Resource Use in the Group of 20: Status, Trends, and Solutions' (2019) <https://www.resourcepanel.org/reports/natural-resource-use-group-20> accessed 25 October 2021.
[165] HLPF Review 2018 (n 137).
[166] International Resource Panel (n 164).
[167] ibid 15 and 52 respectively.
[168] B Bauer and others (PlanMiljø), 'Sustainable Consumption and Production An Analysis of Nordic Progress towards SDG12, and the Way Ahead' (Nordic Council of Ministers 2018) 7 <http://norden.diva-portal.org/smash/record.jsf?pid=diva2 per cent3A1231011&dswid=190> accessed 28 October 2021 (Nordic Report).
[169] Amos and Lydgate (n 67) 1703.
[170] ibid.
[171] On the EU's DMC values and their interpretation, see also Amos and Lydgate (n 67) 1703 referring to Eurostat 2018, pp 2, 4–5.

decouple 'economic growth from resource use, while ensuring the long-term competitiveness of the EU and leaving no one behind'. To achieve that, the EU 'needs to accelerate the transition towards a regenerative growth model that gives back to the planet more than it takes, advance towards keeping its resource consumption within planetary boundaries, and therefore strive to reduce its consumption footprint and double its circular material use rate in the coming decade'.[172] This ambitious policy presumes changes in different areas of law, not least consumer law. There the EU aims, among others, to provide consumers with comprehensive information about products they buy, including their environmental impacts, and to fight planned early obsolescence.[173]

Consumer awareness of sustainability translated into the demand for recyclability, durability, and local production,[174] and societal changes, such as dietary changes and limiting the generation of food waste,[175] could shake the strategy employed by many corporations 'to reap profits from selling products and lifestyles linked to materialistic desires and a reductionist dream of what life should be'[176] and halt the realization of the predictions that the growing global population will lead to multiplication of the current rates of natural resources' consumption until 2030 and beyond.[177]

While consumer preferences and behaviour are of utmost importance when it comes to driving economies, production, and trade towards a more considerate and sustainable use of natural resources, policies and legal frameworks must support this shift. The International Resource Panel[178] identifies areas of focus for the G20 countries on their way to decoupling of natural resources' use from their economic growth.[179] For example, it states that '[m]aterial efficient urban design is ... critical' for South Africa, where a considerable build-up of infrastructure is expected in the upcoming decades. For South Korea, it then states that '[m]ore renewable energies, a rapid exit from coal, and less natural gas-based power production would decrease the impacts of fossil extraction and metal and mineral processing'.[180] To put these recommendations into operation, not only a clear policy (ie political will) including targets and indicators is needed but also development of implementation tools (eg sustainable finance and unlocking the resistance to changes through education). The legal framework is one of the building blocks for a successful deployment of such tools.

---

[172] Communication from the Commission to the European Parliament, the Council, the European Economic and Social Committee and the Committee of the Regions, A new Circular Economy Action Plan For a cleaner and more competitive Europe COM(2020) 98 final, 11 March 2020 (CEAP).

[173] For a critique of the information-based approach to consumer protection, see section on target 12.8 below.

[174] Engaging Society for Sustainability on Consumer Policy, 'Strengthening the Role of Consumers in the Green Transition: How to Properly Guide Consumers Towards Sustainable Decisions', response to the public consultation of European Commission's proposal 'Consumer Policy—Strengthening the Role of Consumers in the Green Transition' (2021) <https://ec.europa.eu/info/law/better-regulation/have-your-say/initiatives/12467-Consumer-policy-strengthening-the-role-of-consumers-in-the-green-transition/F547557_en> accessed 25 October 2021.

[175] Global Resources Outlook 2019 (n 144) 31.

[176] Spotlight on SD (n 142) 95.

[177] See, eg, Global Resources Outlook 2019 (n 144) 27; Gardetti and Muthu (n 143) 71; OWG (n 111) para 52.

[178] IRP is a scientific panel of experts that aims to help nations use natural resources sustainably without compromising economic growth and human needs. It was established by the United Nations Environment Programme (UNEP) in 2007. UNEP is the custodian agency of target 12.2.

[179] International Resource Panel (n 164).

[180] ibid.

COMMENTARY 881

Legal action at national level must be tuned specifically to the areas that could help balance out the inequalities in natural resource extraction, use, and consumption between high-income countries and low- and middle-income countries. That is hard to achieve, especially in low- and middle-income countries where extraction of natural resources and the related production is a vital means to raise the living standard, overcome poverty, fight lack of food, and solve other social and economic issues. It is thus often left to developed countries to try to influence the behaviour and activities in developing countries through extra-territorial regulation, that is through regulation adopted in one jurisdiction aiming to indirectly regulate in another jurisdiction. The EU's REACH regulation[181] can be mentioned here as an example. REACH prescribes obligations for the importers of chemicals to the EU's internal market, and some chemicals can be fully banned under the regulation based on the environmental and human health risks they pose.[182] By closing the EU's market to harmful chemicals, the EU influences products' composition and production processes outside its borders, as anybody who wants to import (products including) chemicals must comply with the regulation.[183]

Regionally, some efforts are registered in high-income countries aimed at curbing natural resources' use globally. For example, the Nordic countries have expressed an intention 'to prepare a joint Nordic guideline for the development of Green National Accounts and carry out a pilot for all the Nordic countries'.[184]

National extraterritorial laws and regional cooperation aim to close the gap of missing international law. International law is not well-equipped to regulate the use and management of natural resources. That is because any efforts to regulate and control the extraction and use of natural resources across borders could violate the principle of permanent sovereignty of nations over natural resources within their jurisdiction, a well- and long-established customary right, confirmed in various international policy documents, such as Principle 2 of the Rio Declaration.[185,186] The principle of national sovereignty over natural resources is though not limitless. It is restricted by another principle of international (environmental) law, the no harm principle, which is understood as the responsibility of states 'to ensure that activities within their jurisdiction or control do not cause damage to the environment of other States or of areas beyond the limits of national jurisdiction'.[187] The no harm principle is, though, vaguely defined, facing the problems of, for example, defining *de minimis* levels and the adequate level of

---

[181] Regulation (EC) No 1907/2006 of the European Parliament and of the Council of 18 December 2006 concerning the Registration, Evaluation, Authorisation and Restriction of Chemicals (REACH), establishing a European Chemicals Agency, amending Directive 1999/45/EC and repealing Council Regulation (EEC) No 793/93 and Commission Regulation (EC) No 1488/94 as well as Council Directive 76/769/EEC and Commission Directives 91/155/EEC, 93/67/EEC, 93/105/EC and 2000/21/EC [2006] OJ L136/3 (REACH Regulation); on REACH, see further text to target 12.4.

[182] Further on REACH, see text to target 12.4 below.

[183] Further on REACH, see text to target 12.4 below.

[184] Nordic report (n 168) 38.

[185] UNGA, 'Permanent Sovereignty over Natural Resources' (14 December 1962) Resolution 1803 (XVII); Rio Declaration (n 124).

[186] Amos and Lydgate (n 67) 1707.

[187] Rio Declaration (n 124) principle 2; see also Section I, this chapter.

882   SDG 12

preventive action.[188] The Espoo Convention and Kiev Protocol aim to operationalize the right of nations over their natural resources within the limits of the no harm principle by requiring participating states to conduct transboundary impact assessments for certain types of actions and strategic environmental assessment of plans and programmes respectively.[189] However, these obligations are mostly nudging states to consider environmental impacts in their activities, but they do not ensure that they will in fact do so.[190]

d) Critique

It stems from the above that the legal and regulatory landscape for sustainable management and efficient use of natural resources remains full of gaps. It mirrors the complicated rights and interests of states, where high-income countries are dependent on import of both natural resources embedded in products and raw natural resources to sustain their living standards, while extraction of natural resources in middle- and low-income countries represent not only their sovereign right but also the possibility for social and economic development. This interdependency naturally leads to doubts about the achievability of target 12.2, as on the one hand with the increase in the global population and the simultaneous increase in the living standards in middle- and low-countries (SDG 1, no poverty), consumption levels will also grow, and on the other hand the consumption-based economy in high-income countries proves difficult to shift to more sustainable economic models. Overall, it is overly optimistic to rely on technology and process-based improvements, such as deployment of the carbon capture and storage technology, to lead us in the transition to sustainability.[191]

The above is aggravated by the wording of target 12.2, which distinguishes the level of ambition in respect to the management and use of natural resources, these expected to be 'sustainable' and 'efficient' respectively. This is problematic, as the wording suggests that resource extraction and consumption are not directly connected and that they can be treated separately.

Moreover, the target stays at a general level, not prescribing any quantitative objectives,[192] and while it is monitored through two indicators with six sub-indicators, no guidelines exist with regard to which of the measurements should be paid the most attention.[193]

Finally, a major gap in the target is the lack of reference to the use of non-renewable sources, which, as discussed above, can never be sustainable,[194] and the lack of

---

[188] Mayer (n 126) 69.

[189] Convention on Environmental Impact Assessment in a Transboundary Context (adopted in 1991, entered into force on 10 September 1997) 1989 UNTS 309 (Espoo Convention); Protocol on Strategic Environmental Assessment to The Convention on Environmental Impact Assessment in a Transboundary Context (adopted on 21 May 2003, entered into force 11 July 2010) 2685 UNTS 140 (Kiev Protocol).

[190] On limitations of these international law instruments see: Amos and Lydgate (n 67) 1706.

[191] Gasper and others (n 5) 92.

[192] ibid 86.

[193] Bengtsson and others (n 100) 1539.

[194] Spotlight on SD (n 142) 121–23.

COMMENTARY   883

acknowledgment of the international trade-related spill-over effect, which undermines the developing countries' ability to deliver on other SDGs.[195]

3. Target 12.3 By the end of 2030, halve per capita global food waste at the retail and consumer levels and reduce food losses along production and supply chains, including post-harvest losses

a) Sources of target

Humans produce significant amounts of food annually, yet a substantial proportion of the world population starves. The Food and Agriculture Organization of the United Nations (FAO) estimated that in 2020, between 720 and 811 million people were hungry.[196] At the same time, almost one-third of the food produced globally is still being thrown out or lost.[197] The OWG Report informs us that '[f]ood wastage at the retail and consumer end of the value chain ... hampers the capacity of the food system to meet demands from growing populations and changing diets'.[198] As multiple sources suggest, abandoning our current unsustainable practices leading to food waste and food loss (FWL) could help achieve food security worldwide.[199]

Poor logistics, processing, pests, unsustainable marketing, misunderstood labelling, improper storage, and excessive buying are all reasons for the growing FWL around the globe.[200] According to the Rome Declaration of Nutrition of 2014, 'food losses and waste throughout the food chain should be reduced in order to contribute to food security, nutrition, and sustainable development'.[201] If we succeed in preventing food being lost or wasted at various levels of the food supply chain from production to consumption (harvest, wholesale, restaurants, consumers), we could solve the problem of malnutrition and further myriad negative economic, environmental and social effects resulting from FWL.

First, we could prevent economic losses stemming from unwise use of resources in food production and food consumption, amounting to \$936 billion per year.[202] Moreover, the growing pressure on our environment could be alleviated. Rotting food in landfills produce methane, a greenhouse gas (GHG) that contributes to the climate

---

[195] Z Xu and others, 'Impacts of International Trade on Global Sustainable Development' (2020) 3 Nature Sustainability 964, 967–69.

[196] FAO, International Fund for Agricultural Development, UNICEF, World Food Programme, and WHO, 'The State of Food Security and Nutrition in the World 2021. Transforming Food Systems for Food Security, Improved Nutrition and Affordable Healthy Diets for All' (FAO 2021), iv <https://www-fao-org.ez.statsbiblioteket.dk:12048/publications/sofi/2021/en/> accessed 29 October 2021.

[197] One-third as measured by weight. Gustavsson and others, 'Global Food Losses and Food Waste—Extent, Causes and Prevention' (FAO, 2011) <https://www.fao.org/3/i2697e/i2697e.pdf> accessed 15 September 2021.

[198] OWG (n 111) para 51.

[199] FG Santeramo, 'Exploring the Link among Food Loss, Waste and Food Security: What the Research Should Focus On?' (2021) 10(26) Agriculture & Food Security 2.

[200] B Garske and others, 'Challenges of Food Waste Governance: An Assessment of European Legislation on Food Waste and Recommendations for Improvement by Economic Instruments' (2020) 9(7) 231 Land 1, 6; Gustavsson and others (n 197) v.

[201] WHO and FAO, Second International Conference on Nutrition, Conference Outcome Document: Rome Declaration on Nutrition (Rome, 19–21 November 2014) ICN2 2014/2, para 14 n).

[202] Food and Agriculture Organization of the United Nations, 'Food Wastage Footprint & Climate Change' (FAO 2015).

change.[203] The recent studies show that food waste results in 8 per cent of global GHG emissions (1.3 tonnes), which is only 3 per cent lower than the second greatest GHG state emitter, the United States.[204] Furthermore, water used for production of food, which is eventually lost or wasted, amounts to one-quarter of all water used in agriculture annually.[205] What is more, current agriculture practices exploit land and thereby affect biodiversity and lead to loss of natural ecosystems.[206] Finally, by abandoning unsustainable practices, social aspects of food waste, such as food security and malnutrition, could be solved.[207] And so, even though FWL is primarily defined in target 12.3, it has further implications for delivery of other SDGs. For instance, it can influence the food security and agricultural productivity under SDG 2, good health under SDG 3, state of our climate defined in SDG 13, use of land under SDG 15, and water resources SDG 14.[208]

FWL has come to scholarly attention only recently and has generated various definitions, names, and understandings of what food waste and food loss represent.[209] According to the FAO, food loss is an inadvertent decrease in mass or quality of food intended for human consumption.[210] At the same time, food loss refers to food which is spoilt before it reaches retailers and consumers.[211] On the other side of the coin, food waste refers to '[f]ood losses occurring at the end of the supply chain'.[212] Food waste is therefore connected to behaviour of consumers and retailers and it is often intentional.[213] The distribution of FWL along the supply chain differs depending on geographical areas. While developing countries struggle more at the beginning of the supply chain, at the production stage,[214] developed countries are mainly guilty of wasting food later on, at the retail and consumption stages.[215]

Turning to the wording of target 12.3, we notice that it is the only truly quantifiable target within SDG 12. The goal of reducing the food waste by 50 per cent by 2030 is indeed ambitious, nevertheless the same ambition is lacking at the level of production

---

[203] K Flanagan and others, 'Reducing Food Loss and Waste Setting a Global Action Agenda' (World Resources Institute 2019) p 39 <https://www.wri.org/research/reducing-food-loss-and-waste-setting-global-action-agenda> accessed 22 September 2021.

[204] FAO, 'Food Wastage Footprint, Impacts on Natural Resources, Summary Report' (2013) 6.

[205] M Kummu and others, 'Lost Food, Wasted Resources: Global Food Supply Chain Losses and Their Impacts on Freshwater, Cropland, and Fertiliser Use.' (2012) 438 Science of the Total Environment 477, 483.

[206] Intergovernmental Panel on Climate Change (IPCC), 'IPCC report Climate Change and Land: An IPCC Special Report on Climate Change, Desertification, Land Degradation, Sustainable Land Management, Food Security, and Greenhouse Gas Fluxes in Terrestrial Ecosystems' (2019) <https://www.ipcc.ch/site/assets/uploads/2019/11/SRCCL-Full-Report-Compiled-191128.pdf> accessed 28 October 2021.

[207] C Caldeira and others, 'Global Food Waste' in WL Filho and others (eds), *Responsible Consumption and Production. Encyclopedia of the UN Sustainable Development Goals* (Springer 2020) 277.

[208] ibid 270, figure 1.

[209] DMA Roodhuyzen and others, 'Putting Together the Puzzle of Consumer Food Waste: Towards an Integral Perspective' (2017) 68 Trends in Food Science and Technology 37, 41–43.

[210] A Telesetsky, 'Waste Not, Want Not: The Right to Food, Food Waste and the Sustainable Development Goals' (2014) 42(3) Denver Journal of International Law & Policy 479, 480.

[211] Caldeira and others (n 207) 271–72.

[212] Gustavsson and others (n 197) 2.

[213] Caldeira and others (n 207) 272.

[214] Initiative Save FOOD, 'SAVE FOOD INITIATIVE: Our Mission and Objectives' <https://www.save-food.org/en/Save_Food_Initiative/Mission> accessed 10 September 2021.

[215] Garske and others (n 200) 6; FAO, 'Global Food Losses and Food Waste. Extent, Causes and Prevention' (FAO: Rome, Italy, 2011).

and supply chains, so-called food losses, as for those no quantifiable targets were established.

b) Empirical analysis

In order to identify suitable measures and policies, we need to measure not only quantity of the food lost/wasted, but also what kind of food is lost/wasted, and in which parts of the food supply chain the losses appear.[216] Through developing insights into concrete countries' situations, prevention measures and policies put in place might become more effective. To this end, two indicators were developed for measurement of target 12.3. These mirror the FAO's distinction between the food loss and food waste. The first indicator 12.3.1(a), the so-called food loss index (FLI) reflects the losses on the supply side of the industry for key commodities across the supply chain,[217] '[i]t measures the changes in percentage losses for a basket of 10 main commodities by country in comparison with a base period'.[218] FLI's custodian is FAO.

The second indicator 12.3.1(b), the food waste index (FWI), developed later,[219] serves to measure the demand side at the level of retailers and consumers and is under custodianship of UNEP. FWI is then divided into total food waste including waste from home consumption, out of home consumption, retail and manufacture; and food waste per capita, which refers to the total food waste divided by population. In contrast to the FLI, FWI does not centre solely around the waste occurring for key commodities but measures aggregated data for food waste from all kinds of waste streams. Similarly to SDG 12.4 and 12.5, the UNEP Questionnaire on Environment Statistics (Waste Section) is used for collection of data. The indicator is built upon a three-level methodology system.[220] The level 1 aims at states, which have not undertaken their own food waste measurements. This level is therefore based on modelling and extrapolating of data from other countries, which leads to rough estimations about the country's food waste situation. Level 2 is a foundation stone of the methodology as it examines and measures actual data on food waste collected in the specific country. Finally, level 3 provides additional information, such as disaggregation of data by food waste composition and destination. This allows for the development and use of better prevention strategies by policy-makers. Even though the newly adopted indicator 12.3(b) tries to facilitate countries' transition until they develop their own measurement structures and produce, this causes multiple challenges. First, level 1 comprises an imperfect picture of the situation in the country. Secondly, it uses the estimates and therefore cannot

---

[216] K Flanagan and others (of the World Resources Institute), 'SDG Target 12.3 on Food Loss and Waste: 2019 Progress Report, an Annual Update on Behalf of Champions 12.3' (World Resources Institute, Champions 12.3, 2019) 2 <https://champions123.org/sites/default/files/2020-09/champions-12-3-2019-progress-report.pdf> accessed 20 September 2021.

[217] SDG Indicators metadata repository, 'Metadata Sheet for Indicator 12.3.1(b)' <https://unstats.un.org/sdgs/metadata/> accessed 28 October 2021 (Metadata 12.3.1(b)).

[218] FAO, 'Sustainable Development Goals' <https://www.fao.org/sustainable-development-goals/indicators/1231/en/> accessed 29 October 2021.

[219] In 2019, with a first reporting cycle in 2021.

[220] All three levels described in depth in UNEP, 'Food Waste Index Report' (2021) <https://www.unep.org/resources/report/unep-food-waste-index-report-2021> accessed 25 October 2021.

be compared with data produced by countries using level 2 and 3. Finally, currently only seventeen countries have high-quality data on food waste compatible with SDG 12.3.1(b).[221]

The SG's Progress Report 2021 shows that FLI, that is food lost after harvesting, namely during transport, storage, and processing,[222] is currently almost at 14 per cent globally.[223] The differences across regions are striking. While we could expect the most developed countries to be the culprits here, data show that the first place belongs to the Central and Southern Asia region with almost 20.7 per cent. The lowest index was measured in Australia and New Zealand, at 5.8 per cent.

According to the UN Food Waste Index Report, around 121 kilograms of global food is wasted annually per capita.[224] In aggregate, around 569 million tonnes of food waste is produced only at the level of households.[225] The second highest score is food services, followed by retail at the bottom with 118 million tonnes annually.[226] The total number for food waste produced in 2019 in all the above-mentioned sectors amounts to almost 1 billion tonnes.[227]

c) Implementation efforts at domestic/international level
Efforts taken regarding food waste can be noted on multiple levels. While there is a lack of legal international framework dedicated to FWL,[228] several civil society and national legal and non-legal initiatives were established for making the transition from farm to fork less resource-intensive and wasteful.

At the national level, most of the legal initiatives are based on the so-called Target–Measure–Act strategy, which stems from the logic that first we need to set intentions through concrete reduction targets, then measure the actual food waste, and finally set things in motion and act.[229] While the first step of this scenario is widely implemented in national policies and strategies, the latter consisting of unified methodology and actual action are falling behind.[230] There are, however, some noteworthy pieces of legislation across the world's jurisdictions targeting companies and consumers in diverse ways. The first group of laws is based on command-and-control logic. Exemplarily, laws prescribing retailers donating excessive food to food charities are becoming more common. For illustration, the state of New York adopted a top-down approach and

---

[221] ibid 5.

[222] V Kiaya, 'Post-Harvest Losses and Strategies to Reduce Them' (Action Contre la Faim (ACF), Technical Paper, January 2014) <https://www.actioncontrelafaim.org/en/publication/post-harvest-losses-and-strategies-to-reduce-them/> accessed 28 October 2021.

[223] SG's Progress Report 2021 (n 122) para 135.

[224] UNEP (n 220) 70.

[225] ibid.

[226] ibid.

[227] ibid.

[228] Telesetsky (n 210) 481.

[229] B Lipinski (of the World Resources Institute), 'SDG Target 12.3 on Food Loss and Waste: 2020 Progress Report, an Annual Update on Behalf of Champions 12.3' 4 (Champions 12.3, 2020) <https://champions123.org/sites/default/files/2020-09/champions-12-3-2020-progress-report.pdf> accessed 20 September 2021.

[230] ibid 6, figure 2.

legally obliged supermarkets to donate unused food to charities.[231] Further incentives of a similar nature can be found in France, which in 2016 adopted a law that aims at retailers and forbids them to throw out food which was not sold.[232] Instead, the food should be donated. The French retailers with retail space greater than 400 m^2 are therefore obliged to enter into agreements with charities, food banks, or similar and give them edible food which is not sold.[233] A similar approach was adopted also in the Czech Republic,[234] Italy,[235] and Argentina.[236] Scotland provides another example of top-down legislation, which prescribes that businesses that produce more than 5 kilos of food waste have to have all food waste and spoiled items collected for recycling.[237]

Food donation can also be motivated through the use of bottom-up and reflexive legislation (rather than command-and-control legislation), for instance through tax deductions, or removing regulatory barriers such as by not imposing liability on donors. The United States incentivizes food donation on different levels. The first piece of legislation, which aimed at facilitation of donation of excessive food, appeared in 1996 when Bill Emerson Good Samaritan Food Donation Act was adopted.[238] The law states that you are protected from liability if you donate to a non-profit organization and later the donated product causes harm.[239] Moreover, according to federal tax deductions, all businesses may deduct up to 15 per cent of their taxable income for food donations.[240]

An entirely distinct perspective on how to combat FWL was adopted in China's new law (2021), which bans binge-eating videos and competitions, allows restaurants to fine customers who leave excessive amount of leftovers, and punishes marketing practices which makes consumers buy excessive amounts of food by a fine of ¥10,000 ($1,540).[241]

---

[231] NYS Excess Food Act, Senate Bill S4176A, Assembly Bill A4398A <https://www.nysenate.gov/legislation/bills/2019/a4398> accessed 28 October 2021.

[232] Act no 2016-138 on Fight against the Food Waste (Loi n° 2016-138 du 11 février 2016 relative à la lutte contre le gaspillage alimentaire) (11 February 2016) <https://www.legifrance.gouv.fr/jorf/id/JORFTEXT000032036289> accessed 26 October 2021. L Lemos, '4 Ways France is Leading the Food Waste Agenda' (*Winnow Solutions*, 24 July 2019) <https://blog.winnowsolutions.com/4-ways-france-is-leading-the-food-waste-agenda> accessed 10 September 2021.

[233] Act no 2016-138 on Fight against the Food Waste (n 232).

[234] Act no 110/1997 Coll. on Foodstuffs and Tobacco Products and on Amendments to Some Related Acts; see also L Steffen, 'Czech Supermarkets Are Now Required to Give Unsold Food to Charity' (*Intelligent Living*, 7 April 2019) <https://www.intelligentliving.co/czech-unsold-food> accessed 25 October 2021.

[235] Act no 166 Coll. concerning the donation and distribution of food and pharmaceutical products for purposes of social solidarity and for the limitation of waste (Disposizioni concernenti la donazione e la distribuzione di prodotti alimentari e farmaceutici a fini di solidarietà sociale e per la limitazione degli sprechi) (19 August 2016) <https://www.gazzettaufficiale.it/eli/id/2016/08/30/16G00179/sg> accessed 30 October 2021; J Lazell and others, *Routledge Handbook of Food Waste* (Taylor and Francis 2020) 164.

[236] Flanagan and others (n 216) 17; L Lemos, 'How Governments around the World Are Encouraging Food Waste Initiatives' (*Winnow Solutions*, 23 August 2019) <https://blog.winnowsolutions.com/how-governments-around-the-world-are-encouraging-food-waste-initiatives> accessed 25 October 2021.

[237] The Waste (Scotland) Regulations 2012 (asp 148).

[238] Bill Emerson Good Samaritan Food Donation Act, Pub. L. No 104-210, 110 Stat. 3011, 3011 (1996) (codified at 42 USC § 1791 (2011), s 1(c).

[239] ibid.

[240] For general tax deduction requirements see s 170 of Internal Revenue Code (IRC), enhanced tax deduction requirements in s 501(c)(3); See also Harvard Food Law & Policy Clinic and the University of Arkansas School of Law, 'Federal Enhanced Tax Deduction for Food Donation: A Legal Guide' (Food Recovery Project 2016) 4 <http://www.chlpi.org//wp-content/uploads/2013/12/Food-Donation-Fed-Tax-Guide-for-Pub-2.pdf> accessed 26 October 2021.

[241] Anti-food Waste Law of the People's Republic of China, Order No 78 of the President of the People's Republic of China (29 April 2021) <http://en.pkulaw.cn/display.aspx?id=784dd95fb4357d58bdfb&lib=law&SearchKeyword=Food per cent20Waste&SearchCKeyword=> accessed 26 October 2021. According to state-owned media: L

888 SDG 12

Despite the undeniable logic regarding excessive restaurant food waste provision, from the business perspective, it does not seem very feasible that restaurants would fine their own patrons.

Finally, non-profit organizations or voluntary initiatives play a role in prevention of FWL. The success of such partnerships can be seen in the example of the United Kingdom, which managed to reduce food loss by 27 per cent.[242] This means that the United Kingdom is already halfway towards target 12.3, partly thanks to the existence of the Courtauld Commitment between the biggest UK supermarkets, which pledge to cut FWL by 50 per cent by 2030, in line with SDG 12.3.[243] Moreover, ReFED, a national non-profit organization based in the United States, advocates the end of food waste and food loss, contributing towards achievement of SDG 12.3 through analyses of food supply chains inefficiencies, promoting innovation, capital, and stakeholders engagement.[244] Finally, another frontrunner in the field of FWL reduction, Denmark, is home to multiple initiatives, such as the think-tank ONE\THIRD, which targets Danish food producers and retailers through a voluntary agreement.[245] Denmark managed to achieve measurable progress when it reduced its food waste by 14,000 tonnes from 2011 to 2017, although not by these innovative approaches alone.[246]

Partnerships, however, do not blossom only at the level of states. Various governments, businesses, farmers, researchers, and civil society unite their knowledge in projects such as Champions 12.3 platform, which aims to lead by example and share good practices, or a partnership of UNEP and FAO, Think.Eat.Save,[247] which is a part of the Sustainable Food Systems Programme of the 10 Year Framework of Programmes on Sustainable Consumption and Production.[248]

Internationally, there is no legal framework which is strictly devoted to FWL. Nevertheless, environmental aspects of food waste are indirectly addressed in the UN Framework Convention on Climate Change (UNFCCC)[249] and the Convention on Biodiversity (CBD).[250] Those treaties both implicitly mention that it is necessary to develop strategies to stabilize food production in a way which does not threaten climate or biological diversity.[251] When we consider the detrimental impact that FWL has on

Caiyu, 'China Adopts Law against Food Waste; Binge Eating, Excessive Leftovers to Face Fines' *Global Times* (29 April 2021) <https://www.globaltimes.cn/page/202104/1222490.shtml> accessed 26 October 2021;

[242] Lipinski (n 229) 2.
[243] WRAP, 'The Courtauld Commitment 2030' <https://wrap.org.uk/taking-action/food-drink/initiatives/courtauld-commitment> accessed 29 October 2021.
[244] ReFED, 'Our Mission' <https://refed.com/about/who-we-are/#about-us> accessed 29 October 2021.
[245] ONE\THIRD, 'About ONE\THIRD' <https://onethird.dk/about-us/> accessed 25 September 2021.
[246] The Local, 'Danish Consumers Reduced Food Waste by 14,000 Tonnes in Six Years' (18 April 2018) <https://www.thelocal.dk/20180418/danish-consumers-reduced-food-waste-by-14000-tonnes-in-6-years/> accessed 30 October 2021.
[247] Think.Eat.Save, 'About Think.Eat.Save' <https://www.unep.org/thinkeatsave/about-thinkeatsave> accessed 25 September 2021.
[248] See n 16 and further discussion on 10YFP under target 12.1.
[249] UN Framework Convention on Climate Change (adopted 9 May 1992, in force 21 March 1994) 1771 UNTS 107 (UNFCCC).
[250] UN Convention on Biological Diversity (adopted 5 June 1992, in force 29 December 1993), 1760 UNTS 79 (CBD).
[251] See art 2 UNFCCC (n 249) and art 11 CBD (n 250).

our climate, the question arises to what extent are the FWL targets integrated in nationally determined contributions (NDCs) introduced by the Paris Agreement.[252] The answer is that only a marginal number of countries include FWL in their NDCs.[253] For example, Ghana '[p]romotes innovations in post-harvest storage and food processing and forest products in 43 administrative districts [out of 216]'.[254] According to the Reducing Food Loss and Waste Report of the World Resources Institute, more countries should be engaged in this matter.[255]

Apart from the environmental elements to be considered, the social facet of FWL has been increasingly linked to human rights. Multiple resources imply that reduction of food waste should be regarded as an aspect of the right to food.[256] The International Covenant on Economic, Social and Cultural Rights (ICESCR)[257] in article 11.2.a, for example, states that parties to ICESCR shall take steps '[t]o improve methods of production, conservation and distribution of food by making full use of technical and scientific knowledge ... by developing or reforming agrarian systems in such a way as to achieve the most efficient development and utilization of natural resources'.[258] Some scholars interpret the 'conservation ... of food' in article 11.2.a as an obligation to 'protect food resources from waste', even though such an obligation is not mentioned explicitly.[259]

Regionally, the EU addressed food waste in 2016 when the EU Platform on Food Losses and Food Waste was established in order to mobilize selected experts and stakeholders.[260] In addition, in 2019 the EU Council adopted the Directive on Unfair Trading Practices[261] targeting contractual tactics that can lead to food waste at the production stage such as late payments for perishable products and last-minute order cancellations.[262] After the Green Deal in 2019 and the new Circular Economy Action Plan in 2020 were adopted,[263] the EU's Farm to Fork strategy was born.[264] Here the European Commission explained its further steps for achieving reduction of FWL. It aims at setting legally binding targets to reduce food loss across the EU, addressing

---

[252] UN, 'Adoption of the Paris Agreement' (adopted 12 December 2015, entry into force 4 November 2016) FCCC/CP/2015/L.9 (Paris Agreement).

[253] Flanagan and others (n 203) 101.

[254] Links between SDGs and NDCs can be found here: Climate Watch, 'NDC-SDG Linkages' <https://www.climatewatchdata.org/ndcs-sdg?goal=12> accessed 24 September 2021.

[255] Flanagan and others (n 203) 102.

[256] Telesetsky (n 210) 483.

[257] ICESCR (n 60) art 11.2.a.

[258] ibid art 12.2.a.

[259] Telesetsky (n 210) 483.

[260] Section 5.2 of the Communication from the Commission to the European Parliament, the Council, the European Economic and Social Committee and the Committee of the Regions, 'Closing the Loop—An EU Action Plan for the Circular Economy' COM(2015) 614, 2 December 2015.

[261] Directive 2019/633 of the European Parliament and of the Council of 17 April 2019 on unfair trading practices in business-to-business relationships in the agricultural and food supply chain [2019] OJ L 111/59.

[262] ibid.

[263] See further text to target 12.5.

[264] Communication from the Commission to the European Parliament, the Council, the European Economic and Social Committee and The Committee of the Regions, 'A Farm to Fork Strategy for a Fair, Healthy and Environmentally-friendly Food System' COM(2020) 381, 20 May 2020.

confusion related to expiration labels, and finally exploring more ways of preventing food losses at the production stage.[265]

d) Critique

Target 12.3 steps up the FWL reduction ambition only partially. While it defines concrete targets for food waste, food losses are omitted. The food loss part of the target therefore remains ambiguous. Moreover, the target does not address or measure FWL drivers which would enable policy-makers to design the right measures to halt FWL along the whole food supply chain. Additional information of a more behavioural nature answering questions such as why we are throwing out our food are needed for better policy design.

On top of that, despite a growing number of states reporting on the FWL, the measurement of FWL has to overcome multiple obstacles such as the growing number of actors in and the interconnectedness of supply chains, which makes any measurement efforts increasingly challenging and costly.[266] Moreover, data are often concentrated on specific steps in the food supply chains (especially households).[267] Finally, comparability is curbed by the use of different units of measurement, and the fact that estimations are based on different stages of the food supply chain, or commodities, and different understandings of inedible parts of food, etc.[268] Finally, current and future data are not comparable to former FAO data as those used different calculation methods.[269]

Legislation adopted at the national level puts a lot of focus at the end of the supply chain, largely targeting consumers and retailers. Such a solution is piecemeal and more efforts aimed at the production side are necessary. The amount of food lost before it reaches consumers is not negligible and therefore the problem should be addressed, without exemptions, along the whole food supply chain. Moreover, even though multiple campaigns were launched in order to motivate consumers to save food, as mentioned in SDG 12.8, we cannot rely purely on education and access to relevant information to change the way consumers behave and make decisions as this does not necessarily lead to desired, greener decisions.[270]

Finally, many national initiatives build on the reduction of barriers to food donations or ordering supermarkets to donate such surplus food. Nonetheless food charities do not have the capacity to receive such an extensive amount of food and thereby the problem is merely transferred from one actor to another. This approach makes

---

[265] ibid.
[266] Garske and others (n 200) 5; FAO, 'Methodological proposal for Monitoring SDG Target 12.3.1. Sub-indicator 12.3.1.A. The Food Loss Index Design, Data Collection Methods and Challenges' (2019) FAO Statistics Working Paper Series 18–13, pp 3–4 <https://www-fao-org.ez.statsbiblioteket.dk:12048/policy-support/tools-and-publications/resources-details/en/c/1236154/> accessed 28 October 2021.
[267] Garske and others (n 200) 5.
[268] UNEP (n 220) 15.
[269] ibid 72.
[270] See further discussion under target 12.8 below.

food banks a 'dumping ground' and limits retailers' responsibility for their own food waste.[271]

4. Target 12.4 By 2020, achieve the environmentally sound management of chemicals and all wastes throughout their life cycle, in accordance with agreed international frameworks, and significantly reduce their release to air, water and soil in order to minimize their adverse impacts on human health and the environment

a) Sources of target and empirical analysis

Chemicals have become a fundamental part of our lives. Pharmaceuticals, agriculture, textiles are all areas in which chemicals play a pivotal role. While chemicals undeniably facilitate our lives and innovate industrial and agricultural processes, we must consider the growing concerns related to hazards posed by chemicals to human health and the natural environment. Mounting evidence shows that even a low dose of certain chemicals can cause cancer, gene mutation, allergies, or affect our reproductive system.[272] From the environmental perspective, chemicals can negatively affect pollinators, insects, aquatic species, and bird populations, and thereby influence whole ecosystems;[273] furthermore, some of them can become hazardous waste, or lead to ozone layer depletion.[274] Moreover, many of these hazards manifest themselves only after extended exposure. On top of that, a cumulative effect of exposure to multiple chemicals through different routes remains underexplored.[275] In 2018, the European Environment Agency highlighted that 62 per cent of the total volume of chemicals which are consumed in the EU pose a hazard to human health.[276] This number, however, represents only the hazards by chemicals we know, while a large number of chemicals in the world market remain unexplored in regard to their inherent physical, chemical, and biological properties. The statistics show that less than 0.1 per cent of industrial and agricultural chemicals with known intrinsic health hazards are regulated by existing instruments.[277]

The problem of chemicals, which is also the case for most of the environmental issues, is not isolated. Therefore, the SDGs pair the chemicals together with another

---

[271] SD Porter, 'Food Waste in the UK and EU: A Policy and Practice Perspective' in C Reynolds and others (eds), *Routledge Handbook of Food Waste* (1st edn, Routledge 2020) 164.

[272] Milieu Ltd, Ökopol, Risk & Policy Analysts (RPA), and RIVM, 'Study for the Strategy for the Non-Toxic Environment of the 7th Environment Action Programme' (European Commission, 8 September 2017), 29, 80, 123.

[273] Communication from the Commission to the European Parliament, the Council, The European Economic and Social Committee and the Committee of the Regions, Chemicals Strategy for Sustainability Towards a Toxic-Free Environment COM(2020) 667, 14 November 2020, 1; UNEP, 'Global Chemicals Outlook From legacies to Innovative Solutions: Implementing the 2030 Agenda for Sustainable Development' (2019, United Nations Environment Programme) 147 (GCOII).

[274] SAICM, 'Submission from UNEP: Assessment on linkages with other clusters related to chemicals and waste management and options to coordinate and cooperate on areas of common interest' (SAICM/IP.4/INF/3, 5 March 2020) 11–13.

[275] Scientific Committees on Health and Environmental Risks, Scientific Committee on Emerging and Newly Identified Health Risks Scientific Committee on Consumer Safety, 'Toxicity and Assessment of Chemical Mixtures' (European Commission and Directorate-General for Health & Consumers 2011) <https://ec.europa.eu/health/sites/health/files/scientific_committees/environmental_risks/docs/scher_o_155.pdf> accessed 14 October 2021.

[276] European Environment Agency (EEA), 'Environmental Indicator Report 2018 in support of the Monitoring of the Seventh Environment Action Programme' (No 19/2018, EEA 2018) <https://www.eea.europa.eu/airs/2018/environment-and-health/production-of-hazardous-chemicals> accessed 4 July 2021.

[277] UNGA, 'Report of the Special Rapporteur on the implications for human rights of the environmentally sound management and disposal of hazardous substances and wastes' (15 November 2018) A/73/567, para 64.

892   SDG 12

closely related cluster: waste. Contrary to the historical regulation of chemicals and wastes, which treated those two areas separately,[278] today's approach is based on their indivisibility. The underlying reason is that in order to preclude chemicals from being released into the environment, we need, among other things, to prevent the waste containing such chemicals from being improperly handled. It is not exceptional that especially municipal solid waste has one or more hazardous properties. Typical household waste containing among other items batteries, paints, cleaning agents, and nail polish, for example, can be toxic, radioactive, infectious, and/or flammable.[279] If we take into consideration that municipal solid waste amounts to approximately 2.1 billion tonnes per year, and that 33 per cent of this waste is not handled properly, the link between waste and chemicals becomes more urgent.[280] Apart from household consumption, hazardous waste can originate also from other widespread processes of an industrial nature, such as agriculture or construction, or have a non-industrial character, most notably waste related to healthcare and pharmaceuticals.[281] A specific type of hazardous waste, which deserves particular attention, is e-waste consisting of old computers, TVs, and household appliances, such as refrigerators.[282] Such waste contains a variety of chemicals detrimental to human health such as mercury and flame retardants.[283] According to the SG's Progress Report 2021, the amount of e-waste produced globally from 2010 to 2019 almost doubled and yet only 17.5 per cent is recycled.[284] In addition, the current statistics produced by the Global E-Waste Monitor 2020 show that by 2030, the overall amount of e-waste produced could reach an alarming 74.7 million tonnes.[285] What is more, the e-waste issue has more than just environmental connotations; economics can also come into play. As most of e-waste contains some kind of precious metal such as copper, iron, or gold, it is estimated that by means of recycling we would be able to recover $10 million from metals contained in e-waste.[286] Some sources even indicate that almost 7 per cent of the world's gold resources might be contained in e-waste.[287]

b) Implementation efforts at domestic/international level
Internationally, the use of chemicals is regulated by means of different multilateral instruments. Several efforts which facilitate the realization of target 12.4 can be

---

[278] GCOII (n 273) 12.

[279] ibid 108.

[280] S Kaza and others. 'What a Waste 2.0: A Global Snapshot of Solid Waste Management to 2050' (Urban Development Series, Washington, DC, World Bank 2018) p 3, 5 <http://hdl.handle.net/10986/30317> accessed 12 August 2021 (What a Waste).

[281] GCOII (n 273) 93.

[282] V Forti and others, 'The Global E-waste Monitor 2020: Quantities, Flows and the Circular Economy Potential' (United Nations University (UNU)/United Nations Institute for Training and Research (UNITAR)—co-hosted SCYCLE Programme, International Telecommunication Union (ITU), and International Solid Waste Association (ISWA), Bonn/Geneva/Rotterdam, 2020), 19 (Global E-Waste Monitor).

[283] GCOII (n 273) 115; Forti and others (n 282) 19.

[284] SG's Progress Report 2021 (n 122) annex, 153; UN, 'The Sustainable Development Goals Report 2021', 51.

[285] Global E-Waste Monitor (n 282) 13.

[286] ibid 15.

[287] Gregory Micallef Associates, '1,000% More Gold in E-Waste Than Gold-Ore' (23 July 2020) <https://www.gmal.co.uk/more-gold-in-e-waste-than-gold-ore/> accessed 16 September 2021.

COMMENTARY 893

mentioned. Among the most fundamental milestones in the international regulation of chemical substances and processes ranks a range of internationally acknowledged multilateral environmental agreements (MEAs). Those treaties address a diverse portfolio of issues related to chemicals' production, management, and disposal. Exemplarily, the Basel Convention[288] is concerned with the transboundary movement of hazardous wastes, and the Rotterdam Convention[289] introduces the prior informed consent procedure for certain hazardous chemicals and pesticides in international trade, in order to gain better understanding about chemicals' characteristics; the rest of the group of treaties pursue a goal of controlling a certain type of hazardous chemicals, such as mercury (Minamata Convention),[290] persistent organic pollutants (POPs) (Stockholm Convention),[291] and so-called substances depleting the ozone layer (Montreal Protocol).[292] Despite adopting different approaches, the MEAs' main objective remains the same: to protect the environment and human health from potential harm caused by chemicals and wastes respectively.[293] Apart from the multilateral instruments mentioned above, the 2002 Johannesburg World Summit on Sustainable Development took centre stage in the sustainable transition of the chemical industry when it called for concerted action and proclaimed the necessity to '[r]enew the commitment, as advanced in Agenda 21, to sound management of chemicals throughout their life cycle and of hazardous wastes for sustainable development as well as for the protection of human health and the environment'.[294]

While the international law framework constitutes a critical part of the chemical management, voluntary agreements and other initiatives should not be omitted in this overview. In particular, the Strategic Approach to International Chemicals Management (SAICM) plays a cardinal role.[295] It was adopted in 2006 by the first International Conference for Chemicals Management (ICCM1) advocating chemical safety in line with what was pledged at the Johannesburg Implementation Plan[296] and contributing towards the safe chemical management until the sunset date 2020. The Johannesburg Summit provided yet more impetus and gave momentum to the implementation of the Globally Harmonized System of Classification and Labelling of

[288] Basel Convention on the Control of Transboundary Movements of Hazardous Wastes and Their Disposal (adopted 22 March 1989, in force 5 May 1992) 1673 UNTS 57.
[289] Rotterdam Convention on the Prior Informed Consent Procedure for Certain Hazardous Chemicals and Pesticides in International Trade (adopted 10 September 1998, in force 24 February 2004) 2244 UNTS 337 (Rotterdam Convention).
[290] Minamata Convention on Mercury (adopted 10 October 2013, in force 16 August 2017) (Minamata Convention).
[291] Stockholm Convention on Persistent Organic Pollutants (adopted 22 May 2001, in force 17 May 2004), 2256 UNTS 119 (Stockholm Convention).
[292] Montreal Protocol on Substances that Deplete the Ozone Layer (adopted 14–16 September 1987, in force 1 January 1989) 1522 UNTS 3 (Montreal Protocol).
[293] Preamble and art 4(2) of the Basel Convention; art 1 of the Rotterdam Convention; art 1 of the Minamata Convention; art 1 of the Stockholm Convention; preamble of the Montreal Protocol.
[294] Johannesburg Plan of Implementation (n 109) para 23.
[295] UNEP, 'Strategic Approach to International Chemicals Management', SAICM texts and resolutions of the International Conference on Chemicals Management' <http://www.saicm.org/About/Documents/tabid/5460/language/en-US/Default.aspx> accessed 30 October 2021.
[296] Johannesburg Plan of Implementation (n 109).

Chemicals,[297] which helps communicate potential hazards through labelling, thereby aligning different measures at national, regional, and international levels. In the long run, this tool facilitates safe use, transport, and disposal of chemicals.[298] As chemicals are the major cause of health issues of both an acute and a chronic nature, the WHO also stepped into the debate in 2005 and adopted the International Health Regulations providing obligations and recommendations for countries, helping them to prepare for the potential event of a public health concern caused by chemicals.[299] Later, in 2017, WHO launched the Chemicals Road Map in order to work more closely with SAICM towards the 2020 goal.[300] As part of this task, WHO established a Global Chemicals and Health Network designed to provide assistance to national healthcare author- ities.[301] The concerns related to health also led other authorities, such as FAO, to adopt the latest version of the International Code of Conduct on Pesticide Management in 2013—this code of conduct was addressed to both the public actors as well as the indus- tries.[302] As the sunset date for the SAICM is long overdue, the fifth ICCM will decide on further comprehensive steps beyond the 2020 target; until then, SAICM's mandate remains unchanged.[303]

One of the most comprehensive regulations of chemicals' 'screening' can be found in the EU, which in 2006 adopted the REACH Regulation introducing four stages of managing chemicals: registration, evaluation, authorization, and restriction.[304] The fundamental ambition of REACH is both the protection of human health and the en- vironment.[305] It is based on the 'no data, no market'[306] principle, which means that it is an obligation of importers/manufacturers to gather and provide a wide range of information on a substance if the volume of chemical they manufacture/import[307] exceeds 1 tonne per year, and to register those with the European Chemicals Agency

---

[297] ibid para 23(c). UN, Globally Harmonized System of Classification and Labelling of Chemicals (GHS) (2011), ST/SG/AC.10/20/Rev.4, para 10 (foreword).

[298] ibid para 1.1.1.3.

[299] WHO, 'International Health Regulations' (2005) <https://www.who.int/publications/i/item/9789241580 496> accessed 29 October 2021.

[300] WHO, 'WHO Chemicals Road Map' (WHO 2017) <https://www.who.int/publications/i/item/WHO-FWC-PHE-EPE-17.03> accessed 10 August 2021.

[301] The WHO Chemicals Road Map mandated the establishment of the WHO Global Chemicals and Health Network see here: WHO, 'The WHO Chemicals Road Map' <https://www.who.int/teams/environment-climate-change-and-health/chemical-safety-and-health/chemicals-road-map> accessed 26 October 2021.

[302] FAO and WHO, The International Code of Conduct on Pesticide Management (2014) <http://www.fao. org/fileadmin/templates/agphome/documents/Pests_Pesticides/Code/CODE_2014Sep_ENG.pdf> accessed 10 August 2021.

[303] The ICCM5 was postponed due to the COVID-19 outbreak, see here: Chemical Watch, 'Negotiations for UN post-2020 framework indefinitely postponed' (10 February 2021) <https://chemicalwatch.com/214078/negotiati ons-for-un-post-2020-framework-indefinitely-postponed> accessed 27 October 2021; IISD, 'Fifth Meeting of the International Conference on Chemicals Management (ICCM5) (Postponed)' <https://sdg.iisd.org/events/intern ational-conference-on-chemicals-management-iccm5/> accessed 27 October 2021.

[304] REACH (n 181).

[305] ibid art 29.

[306] ibid art 5.

[307] According to art 7 of REACH (n 181), it includes producers and importers of articles 'for any substance con- tained in those articles if the substance is present for any substance contained in those articles, if both the following conditions are met: (a) the substance is present in those articles in quantities totalling over 1 tonne per producer or importer per year; (b) the substance is intended to be released under normal or reasonably foreseeable conditions of use'.

in Helsinki (ECHA),[308] otherwise they will not be allowed to introduce the chemical on the EU market.[309] This stands in contrast to previous legislation, which places the burden of proving the hazardous properties on public authorities.[310] Moreover, certain substances which represent a high risk (so-called Substances of Very High Concern)[311] can require authorization granted only if the risks are adequately controlled, socio-economic benefits of the use outweigh the risks, and no alternatives are available.[312] Restrictions according to REACH require industries to apply for certain uses for substances representing unacceptable risk for human health or the environment.[313] The overall objective of REACH is then to substitute the most hazardous substances with safer alternatives (the so-called substitution principle).[314]

Other initiatives based on REACH have gradually emerged around the world,[315] and the most noteworthy efforts have been made in Japan,[316] South Korea (K-REACH),[317] and Turkey.[318]

While national legislation constitutes a core of the chemical regulation around the world, regional initiatives have gained increasing importance. An example of this is the Association of Southeast Asian Nations (ASEAN), which mobilized resources and endorsed further cooperation among the countries of the region.[319] Its working group notably conducts shared research on chemicals and waste, shares knowledge and experience, and further coordinates national actions.[320]

The measurement of target 12.4 is intimately linked to the global legal framework we introduced above. It is especially true for the first of the two indicators, 12.4.1, which aspires to display a number of parties to MEAs on hazardous waste and other chemicals that meet their commitments and obligations in transmitting information as required by each of the relevant agreements.[321] This indicator is classified as a Tier I indicator; it 'is conceptually clear, has an internationally established methodology and standards are available, and data are regularly produced by countries for at least 50 per cent of

---

[308] REACH (n 181) art 6 (1).

[309] ibid arts 5 and 6.

[310] Previous EU chemicals legislation: Council Directive of 27 July 1976 on the approximation of the laws, regulations and administrative provisions of the Member States relating to restrictions on the marketing and use of certain dangerous substances and preparations (76/769/EEC) [1976] OJ L 262/201.

[311] REACH (n 181) art 55, recitals (69).

[312] ibid title VII, art 60(4).

[313] ibid title VIII, art 68.

[314] ibid recitals 70.

[315] V Heyvaert, 'Regulating Chemical Risk: REACH in a Global Governance Perspective' in J Eriksson and others (eds), *Regulating Chemical Risks: European and Global Challenges* (Springer 2010) 217.

[316] N Yoshiko, 'Assessing Policy Reach: Japan's Chemical Policy Reform in Response to EU's REACH Regulation' (2010) 22(2) Journal of Environmental Law 171.

[317] GCOII (n 273) 254, S Ha and others, 'Act on the Registration and Evaluation of Chemicals (K-REACH) and Replacement, Reduction or Refinement Best Practices' (2016) 31 Environmental Health and Toxicology, e2016026.

[318] GCOII (n 273) 258; Chemical Watch, 'Turkey Publishes Law Modelled on REACH' (*Chemicals Watch*, 29 June 2017) <https://chemicalwatch. com/57284/turkey-publishes-law-modelled-on-reach> accessed 28 August 2021.

[319] ASEAN Cooperation on Environment, 'ASEAN Cooperation on Chemicals and Waste' <https://environment.asean.org/awgcw/> accessed 18 August 2021.

[320] ibid.

[321] SDG Indicators metadata repository, metadata sheet for indicator 12.4.1 <https://unstats.un.org/sdgs/metadata/> accessed 3 July 2021 (Metadata 12.4.1).

countries and of the population in every region where the indicator is relevant'.[322] The progress of the indicator is measured through a country score, which is determined as an average annual information transmission rate of required information.[323] Reporting takes place in five different periods, and a country can score depending on the amount of information it sends to the respective Convention Secretariat.[324] The main criticism of the indicator relates to the fact that it is mainly process-oriented, focusing on compliance in regard to reporting on transmission of information required by each relevant international agreements (such as the number of country contacts designated, number of national reports, national implementation plans, etc) rather than assessing the quality of the submitted information.[325] Furthermore, as already noted, only 0.1 per cent of global chemicals are covered by the current international regulation.[326] In light of the above, it remains questionable how this indicator can deliver effectively on target 12.4 and significantly reduce the release, and minimize the undesirable impact, of chemicals.[327] According to the SG's Progress Report 2021, there is 99.8 per cent compliance in regard to information provided on the implementation of states' obligations documented solely in the case of the Montreal Protocol and its requirements.[328] The second-best compliance numbers appear in relation to the Rotterdam Convention, which is, nonetheless, significantly reduced to only 75.2 per cent compliance rate.[329] Finally, the Stockholm Convention and the Basel Convention lag behind with 50.3 per cent and 60.7 per cent information transmission rates respectively.[330]

States soon came to the conclusion that indicator 12.4.1 will not sufficiently support the target[331] so they agreed on indicator 12.4.2. This indicator aims to capture (i) hazardous waste generated per capita, and (ii) proportion of hazardous waste treated, by type of treatment. The agencies collect national data through the UNSD/UNEP Questionnaire on Environment statistics (waste section) with the first SDG reporting cycle being 2020.[332] According to the SDG metadata indicator, the hazardous waste generated includes the total quantity of hazardous waste collected, hazardous waste given by generator to treatment or disposal facilities, and an estimation of unaccounted hazardous waste.[333] The proportion of hazardous waste treated represents a quantity of hazardous waste treated, for example by means of recycling, incineration, landfilling, and/or other, during a reporting year, divided by a quantity of hazardous

---

[322] Provision Proposed Tiers for Global SDG Indicators (as of 24 March 2016) <https://unstats.un.org/sdgs/files/meetings/iaeg-sdgs-meeting-03/Provisional-Proposed-Tiers-for-SDG-Indicators-24-03-16.pdf> accessed 10 July 2021; IAEG-SDGs, 'Tier Classification for Global SDG Indicators' <https://unstats.un.org/sdgs/iaeg-sdgs/tier-classification/> accessed 29 October 2021.

[323] Metadata 12.4.1 (n 321).

[324] ibid.

[325] Gasper and others (n 5) 90.

[326] UNGA (n 277) para 64.

[327] Gasper and others (n 5) 90.

[328] SG's Progress Report 2021 (n 122) annex, p 151.

[329] ibid.

[330] ibid.

[331] Gasper and others (n 5) 90.

[332] SDG Indicators metadata repository, metadata sheet for indicator 12.4.2 <https://unstats.un.org/sdgs/metadata/> accessed 3 July 2021 (Metadata 12.4.2).

[333] ibid.

waste generated multiplied by 100.[334] Under indicator 12.4.1, another indicator, on e-waste, was subsumed.[335] The computation method thus resembles the general hazardous waste indicator.[336] Despite the effort to include a wide range of data under the ambit of indicator 12.4.2, practical and methodological limitations remain. One of the key issues concerns countries' under-reporting, which might be a result of insufficient resources or concerns regarding the bad reputation which a country may attract related to being responsible for the generation of large volumes of hazardous waste.[337] Moreover, yet another obstacle of a legal nature is the diverse definitions of what is regarded as waste under different jurisdictions. Even though many countries base their laws on the Basel Convention's terminology, others go further.[338] As long as multiple definitions are in play, this exercise of comparison between the countries remains distorted.[339] Finally, unaccounted waste represents an issue of a specific nature, in particular a way of its measurement.[340] As the SG's Progress Report 2021 documented, only data on a sub-indicator related to e-waste are provided in the statistical annex.[341] The report shows that in 2019 more than 50 million tonnes of e-waste were generated worldwide, which translates to 7.3 kilograms of waste per capita.[342] Nevertheless, only 17.5 per cent of the waste is managed in an environmentally sustainable way.[343] Most e-waste was generated in Asia, while Europe and Northern America rank first in the percentage of collected (0.47 per cent) and recycled (31.8 per cent) e-waste.[344]

c) Critique

Witnessing country tendencies portrayed via statistical analysis above, the contours of a possible human rights' violation appear more visibly than ever. Understanding the severity of the situation as early as 1995, the Commission on Human Rights (today's Human Rights Committee) created a mandate of the Special Rapporteur on toxics and human rights. More recently, in 2006, the Dubai Declaration on International Chemicals Management confirmed that 'respecting human rights and fundamental freedoms, understanding and respecting ecosystem integrity and addressing the gap between the current reality and our ambition to elevate global efforts to achieve the sound

---

[334] ibid.

[335] ibid.

[336] ibid.

[337] Metadata 12.4.2 (n 332) 4.b, comment and limitations.

[338] K Pope, *Global Waste Management: Models for Tackling the International Waste Crisis* (Kogan Page 2020) 200.

[339] National definitions of hazardous waste can be found here: Basel Convention <http://www.basel.int/Countries/NationalDefinitions/NationalDefinitionsofHazardousWastes/tabid/1480/Default.aspx> accessed 30 October 2021.

[340] Environmental SDG Indicators, a course developed by UNEP, UNSIAP, and UNITAR, Module 3. Measuring Waste in the SDGs <https://www.unitar.org/event/full-catalog/environmental-sdg-indicators> accessed 30 October 2021.

[341] SG's Progress Report 2021 (n 122) para 136 and annex, p 152–54; general data on hazardous waste generation in line with indicator 12.4.2 are not available in their complexity and are not a part of the SG's Progress Report.

[342] ibid.

[343] ibid.

[344] ibid.

898   SDG 12

management of chemicals'.[345] The Special Rapporteur on several occasions shared the clear link between human rights and toxics. For illustration, in the report from October 2018 he confirmed that 'exposure to hazardous substances is fundamentally about the right to life, non-discrimination and the right to bodily integrity, and dependent on the realization of everyone's right to information, meaningful participation, freedoms of association and assembly, and the right to an effective remedy, among others'.[346] The Special Rapporteur's investigation particularly stressed the vulnerability of certain groups which are more susceptible than others to hazardous chemicals.[347] The danger posed by these substances disproportionately affects especially children, women, and workers, more often in low- and middle-income countries, the main reason being export of waste from wealthier to poorer countries and insufficient access to information related to the hazardous properties of chemicals.[348] As a result, the Special Rapporteur called for a halt of the 'silent pandemics', where children are born 'pre-polluted', suffer birth defects, diabetes, reduced intelligence, and learning disabilities, and called for compliance with the Convention on the Rights of the Child[349] and the obligation to prevent childhood exposure to pollution and toxic substances contained therein.[350] Apart from children, another extremely vulnerable group exposed to chemicals on a daily basis deserve consideration: workers, agriculture workers being those most often endangered.[351] Workers coming in contact with chemicals, such as pesticides, are often treated for asthma, contact dermatitis, pulmonary diseases, or cancer.[352] In 2017, 2.78 million workers died of the aftermath of the consequences of their working conditions,[353] and the International Labour Organization (ILO) estimates 160 million cases of occupational diseases reported annually.[354] In 2018, the Korean company Samsung failed at arbitration and was obliged to reimburse employees suffering from the work-related illness as a result of chemical exposure in its manufacturing plants.[355] Occupational Safety and Health therefore should be, and rightly has been, at the top of the priority list of the ILO's agenda. For this reason, the ILO in the 1990s adopted

---

[345] International Conference on Chemicals Management, 'Dubai Declaration on International Chemicals Management' (4–6 February 2006).

[346] UNGA, 'Report of the Special Rapporteur on the implications for human rights of the environmentally sound management and disposal of hazardous substances and wastes' (15 November 2018) A/73/567, para 8; see also UNGA, 'Report of the Special Rapporteur on the implications for human rights of the environmentally sound management and disposal of hazardous substances and wastes' (20 July 2017) UN Doc. A/HRC/36/41.

[347] ibid para 32.

[348] ibid para 25.

[349] Convention on the Rights of the Child (adopted 20 November 1989, in force 2 September 1990) 1577 UNTS 3.

[350] UNGA, A/73/567 (n 346) paras 26–28.

[351] ibid paras 15–18.

[352] ibid para 5.

[353] P Hämäläinen and others, 'Global Estimates of Occupational Accidents and Workrelated Illnesses 2017' (Workplace Safety and Health Institute 2017).

[354] UNGA, 'Implications for Human Rights of the Environmentally Sound Management and Disposal of Hazardous Substances And Wastes' (5 August 2020) UN Doc A/75/290, para 24; see also ILO Statistics: <https://www.ilo.org/moscow/areas-of-work/occupational-safety-and-health/WCMS_249278/lang--en/index.htm.> accessed 28 October 2021.

[355] Reuters Staff, 'Samsung Electronics to Compensate Ill Workers at Plants after Mediator's Proposal' (Reuters, 1 November 2018) <https://www.reuters.com/article/us-samsung-elec-workers-idUSKCN1N64NQ> accessed 30 June 2021.

the ILO Chemical Convention (No 170) related to the protection of workers, the ILO Prevention of Major Industrial Accidents Convention (No 174), the ILO Safety and Health in Agriculture Convention, 2001 (No 184), and other hazard specific conventions, such as the ILO Asbestos Convention, 1986 (No 162).

Equally to other SDG 12 targets, target 12.4 aims at achieving a very ambitious goal. Despite its significance, the design of its indicators does not mirror the urgency notable from the wording of the goal. In case of the first indicator, it remains arguable to what extent is assessment of the formal compliance with informational obligations fit for the purpose of accomplishing sustainable chemicals management. In particular, when the data acquired are limited by the scope of the selected MEAs, which cover only a small proportion of the worldwide-produced chemicals, and when the qualitative aspects, which could provide actual insights into the achievement of the target, are not considered. Regarding the second indicator, the comparability of data is limited not only due to insufficient reporting of states and companies but also due to a multitude of definitions of (hazardous) waste across jurisdictions, and thus the statistical outcomes generated from the questionnaires may not genuinely depict the current status. Moreover, under-reporting remains a substantial hindrance which contributes to the fact that the data provided do not reflect the reality.

5. Target 12.5 By 2030, substantially reduce waste generation through prevention, reduction, recycling and reuse

a) Sources of target

The world population is growing, and as the number of people around the world rises exponentially, the urban solid waste follows this trend.[356] Two billion tonnes of urban waste annually is the number published by the World Bank, and the predictions made in this regard are even more worrying: some project that the amount of waste will increase by 70 per cent (from 2016 levels) by 2050, reaching a total of almost 3.41 billion tonnes annually.[357] Taking into consideration the hazardous qualities of certain types of waste, such as e-waste,[358] the problem escalates to a different level when not only the quantity but also the quality of waste is critical. In light of these events, it has become of utmost importance to stop the 'throw away culture', especially when, according to the UN Human Settlements Programme, '99 percent of purchased items are discarded within six months'.[359]

While the problem of waste around the world intensifies, waste management, especially in developing countries, falls behind. Paragraph 167 of the progress report of the OWG of the General Assembly on SDGs states that 'many developing countries,

---

[356] RU Pandey and others, 'Exploring Linkages between Sustainable Consumption and Prevailing Green Practices in Reuse and Recycling of Household Waste: Case of Bhopal City in India.' (2018) 173 Journal of Cleaner Production 49.

[357] World Bank, 'Brief Solid Waste Management' (23 September 2019) <https://www.worldbank.org/en/topic/urbandevelopment/brief/solid-waste-management> accessed 4 September 2021.

[358] See text to target 12.4 above.

[359] IISD, 'UN Urges Tackling Waste Management on World Habitat Day' (9 October 2018) <https://sdg.iisd.org/news/un-urges-tackling-waste-management-on-world-habitat-day/> accessed 3 September 2021.

900   SDG 12

including LDCs [Least Developed Countries] and SIDS [Small Island Developing States], need capacity building and technology transfer to manage ... waste sustainably. The illegal waste trade such as dumping of e-waste has to be halted.'[360] According to the World Bank, 33 per cent of globally produced waste is openly dumped.[361] The inappropriate handling of waste then triggers a variety of both environmental and social effects. To name a few, waste contributes to an increased emission of GHGs, the exploitation of natural resources, spreading of disease, flooding, and environmental pollution.[362]

Environmentally sound management of solid waste has been included in chapter 21 of Agenda 21 in 1992 as a reaction to the aggravating quantitative waste problem.[363] Agenda 21 established the necessity to manage waste through the application of the so-called 3Rs principle (reduce, reuse, and recycle),[364] to increase recovery from waste, and it called for concrete action based on policies, strategies, laws, and regulations.[365] In 2002, the World Summit on Sustainable Development in Johannesburg confirmed the priority of solid waste management and called for prevention and minimalization of waste through maximization of re-use, recycling, and the use of environmentally friendly alternative materials, with the participation of government authorities and all stakeholders.[366]

As noted above, the waste hierarchy based on 3Rs has its irreplaceable position in waste management and is embedded in policies across the jurisdictions.[367] The principle is based on the assumption that when handling waste, we should proceed in multiple hierarchical steps which are ranked according to their environmental soundness. First, we should aim at reducing the volumes of wastes produced altogether. This preventive action can be applied through the whole lifecycle of a product.[368] If reduction of waste is out of the question, waste managers should prioritize re-use as a second option. Re-use refers to a repetitive use of products which still have characteristics allowing others their continuous use. Only if both these strategies fail does recycling come into play.[369] This waste management hierarchy is in different ways and degrees embedded in many policies at national, regional, and international levels,[370] and target

[360] OWG (n 111) para 167.

[361] What a Waste (n 280) 5.

[362] L Rodić and DC Wilson, 'Resolving Governance Issues to Achieve Priority Sustainable Development Goals Related to Solid Waste Management in Developing Countries' (2017) 9(3) 404 Sustainability 1, 1–2.

[363] UNGA, 'Report of the UN Conference on Environment and Development' (Rio de Janeiro, 3–14 June 1992) (12 Aug 1992) UN Doc A/CONF.151/26 (Vol II) (Agenda 21).

[364] Agenda 21 (n 363) ch 21.

[365] ibid 21.5.

[366] Johannesburg Plan of Implementation (n 109) para 22.

[367] CT Marques and BMF Gomes, 'Reuse, Reduce, Recycle' in Filho and others (eds) (n 207) 627.

[368] UNEP and International Solid Waste Association, 'Global Waste Management Outlook' (2015) p 30–31 <https://www.unep.org/resources/report/global-waste-management-outlook> accessed 30 October 2021.

[369] Marques and others (n 367).

[370] EU waste hierarchy embedded in Directive 2008/98/EC of the European Parliament and of the Council of 19 November 2008 on waste and repealing certain Directives OJ L 312/3, art 4 (2008) (Waste Framework Directive).

12.5 indirectly refers to it when it requires that we 'substantially reduce waste generation through prevention, reduction, recycling and reuse'.

Increasing material and resource consumption and the generation of immense amounts of waste have led mankind to propose a new systematic approach—the circular economy model (CE)—which would enable us to operate within safe planetary boundaries.[371] The CE has surfaced as an alternative to linear consumption based on the 'take–make–dispose' model which emerged at the end of the Industrial Revolution.[372] While the linear model is not sustainable in the long run, the CE is a restorative concept 'where the value of products, materials and resources is maintained in the economy for as long as possible, and the generation of waste is minimised'.[373] To put it simply, in CE, materials are used over again, never leaving the imaginary cycle, and thus the amount of used materials and produced waste is significantly reduced. Unlike traditional waste management concepts, CE aims at covering the whole lifecycle of a product, targeting both the production and consumption sides of that cycle. Consequently, it simultaneously ensures economic growth without jeopardizing future resources, understanding that uncontrolled consumption of natural resources is not the only way to achieve economic prosperity. A by-product of the CE concept is the promotion of innovation and the creation of employment.[374]

The transition towards CE is connected to several concepts, which are slowly becoming implanted in policies around the world. Circular product design, circular public procurement, and circular business models based on sharing and post-ownership can be used as examples.[375] Paragraph 165 of the Progress report of the Open Working Group of the General Assembly on SDGs confirms that the transition towards circular models is desired, noting that 'sustainability of products and services should start at the design phase using a life-cycle approach. Then products can be designed to end not as waste but as material for recovery, recycling and reuse'.[376] Target 12.7 oriented at sustainable public procurement practices can partially support achievement of target 12.5, for example by procuring used products.[377] When searching for best CE practices around the world, the Ellen McArthur Foundation, a promoter of CE, administers a database on its website, categorized by topics such as fashion, food, plastics, and cities.[378]

---

[371] Rockström and others (n 4).

[372] Marques and others (n 367) 627–28.

[373] Communication from the Commission to the European Parliament, the Council, the European Economic and Social Committee and The Committee of the Regions Closing the Loop—An EU Action Plan for the Circular Economy COM(2015) 614 final, 2 December 2015.

[374] J Horbach and C Rammer, 'Circular Economy Innovations, Growth and Employment at the Firm Level: Empirical Evidence from Germany' (2020) 24 Journal of Industrial Ecology 615.

[375] F Zoll, 'From a Product-Based Economy to Services? Legal Aspects of an Economy in Transition' in B Keirsbilck and E Terryn (eds), *Consumer Protection in a Circular Economy* (1st edn, Intersentia 2019).

[376] OWG (n 111) para 165.

[377] More about sustainable public procurement can be found in the text to target 12.7section; M Fabian and others '9 Principles for a Circular Economy' (German Environment Agency 2020) <http://www.umweltbundes amt.de/publikationen> accessed 15 September 2021.

[378] Ellen McArthur Foundation <https://ellenmacarthurfoundation.org/> accessed 28 October 2021.

902 SDG 12

b) Empirical analysis

Indicator 12.5.1 measuring the achievement of target 12.5 is the national recycling rate (NRR) and tonnes of material recycled.[379] According to the definition, the NRR represents the quantity of material recycled in a country plus quantities exported for recycling out of total waste generated in the country, minus material imported intended for recycling.[380] The chosen custodian agencies are UNEP and Sustainable Cycles (SCYCLE) Programme (UNU/UNITAR)[381] (for e-waste sub-indicator). Because the first reporting cycle took place in 2020, the SG's Progress Report 2021 does not contain relevant information in this regard. As of the date of writing this chapter, the only available data are from 2014 and 2015 municipal waste statistics of OECD countries and sub-indicator data on e-waste which are identical to the sub-indicator 12.4.2.[382] Nevertheless, the World Bank's Report from 2016 provides a partial picture of how much waste is recycled worldwide by regions with North America (33 per cent) and Europe and Central Asia (20 per cent) being at the top, and Latin America and the Caribbean (4.5 per cent) and South Asia (5 per cent) occupying the bottom.[383] Overall, the report shows that only 13.5 per cent of global waste is recycled.[384] Apart from target 12.5, complementary waste indicator 11.6.1 illustrates the situation in the concrete waste stream, urban solid waste, when it measures municipal solid waste collection.[385]

A quick glance at the wording of the target suffices to unveil its vagueness. The final version of target 12.5 refers to mere 'substantial' reduction. Looking at the objectives of target 12.5, we notice discrepancies between what is measured and what is aimed for in the target's wording.[386] While target 12.5's objective is to 'substantially reduce waste generation through prevention, reduction, recycling and reuse', which points towards the CE concept based on the premise that waste should not be generated in the first place, the indicator associated with target 12.5 focuses only on one of these waste strategies, recycling. Recycling being in the spotlight, according to some sources limits the achievement of substantial results, which the target requests.[387] Several countries realized this during the SDGs negotiations, and some of them even suggested changing the

---

[379] SDG Indicators metadata repository, metadata sheet for indicator 12.5.1 <https://unstats.un.org/sdgs/metadata> accessed 3 July 2021 (Metadata 12.5.1).

[380] ibid.

[381] Focus of SCYCLES is on developing SCP, management and disposal patterns of electrical and electronic equipment.

[382] According to the SG's Progress Report 2021 (n 122), the amount of e-waste produced globally almost doubled from 2010 to 2019, and yet only 17.5 per cent is recycled. In addition, the current statistic produced by the Global E-Waste Monitor (n 282) shows that by 2030, the overall amount of e-waste produced could reach alarming 74.7 million tonnes.

[383] What a Waste (n 280) 35, figure 2.13.

[384] What a Waste (n 280) 34.

[385] See this book, Chapter 11 on SDG 11.

[386] S Guevara and IP Julián, 'Sustainable Consumption and Production: A Crucial Goal for Sustainable Development—Reflections on the Spanish SDG Implementation Report' (2019) 1 Journal of Sustainability Research 1, 10–11.

[387] H Hettiarachchi, 'Going Full Circle: Why Recycling Isn't Enough' (*Our World*, 28 October 2018) <https://ourworld.unu.edu/en/going-full-circle-why-recycling-isnt-enough> accessed 29 October 2021.

indicator, or adopting more indicators, in order to mend this shortcoming.[388] However, ultimately, indicator 12.5.1 remained alone.

c) Implementation efforts at domestic/international level

Except for a distinctive issue of transboundary movement of hazardous waste, the question of waste management remains mainly in the hands of the national policy-makers and is not legislated for at the global level.[389] However, several exceptions at the global and regional levels can be named. An example at the global level is a prominent collaboration between the CE frontrunner, the EU, and UNEP. This partnership focuses on sectors most intensively producing waste, such as food, textiles, electronics, construction, and plastics, introducing initiatives such as digital product passport, which enables consumers to learn about the repairability or recyclability of products.[390]

Regionally, the best practices in waste management and CE can also be illustrated by the example of the EU. In 2019, the EU presented its Green Deal, a part of which became in 2020 the New Circular Economy Action Plan (CEAP).[391] The CEAP among other things aims at developing a sustainable product policy as a 'key to making progress on waste prevention'[392] and aims to develop concrete waste reduction targets in selected areas.[393] In addition, its objective is also the empowerment of consumers through, exemplarily a 'right to repair', which would indirectly lead to a decrease in the generation of waste. Furthermore, the CEAP mentions a crucial focus on the implementation and enforcement of existing waste policies within the EU legal framework. Primary legal framework for scaling down waste and pollution can be found in the EU Waste Framework Directive (WFD).[394] The WFD's contribution lies in the introduction of a comprehensive waste hierarchy (pyramid) building upon the 3Rs principle and it fortifies the concept with the inclusion of the energy recovery step before the disposal. The WFD further promotes extended producer responsibility, the polluter-pays principle, and supports development of CE technologies.[395] Apart from the general framework, the EU's waste legislation centres around key waste streams such as batteries and accumulators, waste from electric and electronic equipment, end-of-life vehicles, mining, packaging, polychlorinated biphenyl/terphenyls, sewage sludge, ships, titanium dioxide, and waste oils.[396]

---

[388] IAEG 2nd meeting 26–28 October 2015, Bangkok, 'Results of Questionnaire on Summary of Comments by IAEG Members (updated 22 October 2015)' statements by Germany, Denmark, Colombia, Canada <https://unstats.un.org/sdgs/meetings/iaeg-sdgs-meeting-02/> accessed 28 October 2021.

[389] A Pires and others, *Sustainable Solid Waste Collection and Management* (1st edn, Springer International Publishing 2019) ch 5.

[390] UNEP, 'European Commission and UNEP will foster the circular economy globally' (4 June 2021) <https://www.unep.org/news-and-stories/story/european-commission-and-unep-will-foster-circular-economy-globally> accessed 20 August 2021.

[391] CEAP (n 172).

[392] ibid 4.1.

[393] ibid 4.1.

[394] Waste Framework Directive (n 370).

[395] ibid arts 8, 14, 16.

[396] For example, European Parliament and Council Directive 94/62/EC of 20 December 1994 on packaging and packaging waste [1994] OJ L 365/10; Council Directive 1999/31/EC of 26 April 1999 on the landfill of waste [1999] OJ L 182/1; Directive 2000/53/EC of the European Parliament and of the Council of 18 September 2000 on end-of

904 SDG 12

At the national level, several legislative frameworks evolved in order to facilitate the transition to CE. According to the OECD's Report, Japan is one of the countries with a comprehensive legislative framework for circular economy.[397] Its Fundamental Law for Establishing a Sound Material-Cycle Society[398] and the Law for Promotion of Effective Utilisation of Resources[399] (integrating 3Rs principle) confirm this. Currently the newest initiative in Japan is the Bill for the Act on Promotion of Resource Circulation for Plastics,[400] which was adopted in March 2021. As the WB's Report shows, plastic accounts for around 17 per cent of the world's waste, which represents the second largest figure after the food waste (44 per cent).[401] The Japanese Minister of Environment, Shinjiro Koizumi, explained that the rationale of the bill is therefore 'creating a society that produces no new plastic waste by 2050'.[402] In order to achieve this ambitious target and avoid plastic litter in the ocean, the new law promotes more stringent recycling practices of plastics, and reduction of the use of plastics in general.[403] Other bold initiatives can be found, for example, in Ireland, whose government adopted the Circular Economy Bill 2021,[404] which aims at the reduction of the consumption of single-use plastic products and at the implementation of better and more functional waste management.[405] Successful stories are also heard from Taiwan, formerly nicknamed the 'Garbage Island'.[406] Taiwan considerably improved its policies, and in 2018 accomplished production of only 0.4 kilograms of waste per person per day.[407] On the other side of the world, Brazil's compelling project established by the government shall not be omitted. The Belo Horizonte's Computer Reconditioning Centre not only contributes to SDG 12, as it reduces electronic waste, but also to SDG 8 because at the same time it

---

life vehicles—Commission Statements [2000] OJ L 269/34; Directive 2006/66/EC of the European Parliament and of the Council of 6 September 2006 on batteries and accumulators and waste batteries and accumulators and repealing Directive 91/157/EEC (Text with EEA relevance) [2006] OJ L 266/1; Directive 2012/19/EU of the European Parliament and of the Council of 4 July 2012 on waste electrical and electronic equipment (WEEE) Text with EEA relevance [2012] OJ L 197/38.

[397] OECD, 'OECD Environmental Performance Reviews: Japan 2010' (2010) pt II, ch 6 <https://read.oecd-ilibrary.org/environment/oecd-environmental-performance-reviews-japan-2010/waste-management-and-the-3rs-reduce-reuse-recycle_9789264087873-7-en#page3> accessed 29 October 2021.

[398] The Basic Act for Establishing a Sound Material-Cycle Society (Act No 110 of 2000) <https://www.env.go.jp/en/laws/recycle/12.pdf> accessed 30 August 2021.

[399] Law for Promotion of Effective Utilisation of Resources <https://www.env.go.jp/en/laws/recycle/06.pdf> accessed 30 August 2021.

[400] Bill for the Act on Promotion of Resource Circulation for Plastics <https://www.meti.go.jp/english/press/2021/0309_001.html.> accessed 30 October 2021.

[401] What a Waste (n 280) 29; see text on target 12.3 above.

[402] Nippon.com, 'Japan Govt Adopts Bill to Promote Plastic Recycling' (2021) <https://www.nippon.com/en/news/yjj2021030900305/> accessed 1 September 2021; A Sheng and X Geng, 'The circular economy grows up' *The Japan Times* (3 August 2021) <https://www.japantimes.co.jp/opinion/2021/08/03/commentary/world-commentary/circular-economy/> accessed 28 October 2021.

[403] ibid.

[404] Government of Ireland, 'General Scheme of the Circular Economy Bill 2021' <https://www.gov.ie/en/publication/89838-circular-economy-bill-2021/> accessed 1 September 2021.

[405] ibid.

[406] C Middlehurst, 'How The Country Once Nicknamed 'Garbage Island' Cut Waste By 30%' *Huffpost* (29 May 2019) <https://www.huffpost.com/entry/taiwan-recycling-garbage-waste_n_5ce6bb1ae4b0547bd133ceba> accessed 27 October 2021.

[407] According to the World Bank's report (n 280), the waste per capita varies from 0.46 kg in Sub-Saharan Africa to 1.18 kg in Europe and Central Asia, all the way up to 2.2 kg in North America.

COMMENTARY 905

tackles youth unemployment.[408] The project, which employs citizens from low-income communities to restore information technology (IT) equipment, markedly scaled up the circularity as '15,000 kilograms of post-use electronics have been diverted from landfill to consumer goods every year on average, since 2008'.[409] Moreover, '10,446 citizens have been trained in basic technological skills, environmental education, and computer remanufacturing' this all promoting SDG 8.[410]

d) Critique

While we see intense action on waste at the national level, the question remains of how much the formulation of target 12.5 and the respective indicator meaningfully contribute to that. Together with target 12.2, target 12.5 is the backbone of SDG 12, yet the measurement through its indicator 12.5.1 does not suffice its needs. While the target outlines several hierarchical steps of how to treat the waste in line with the globally acknowledged waste hierarchy, the indicator only monitors the least preferred option of the waste management, before actual disposal, that is, recycling. If we truly want to achieve target 12.5, measuring the recycling rate will decelerate further progress. Despite the fact that recycling practices should be supported, there is a reason why recycling only occupies third place in the 3Rs principle. Recycling can lead to loss of material and unnecessary energy consumption, and in addition, from an economic perspective it is a costly solution.[411]

Furthermore, the target does not provide a measurable goal, which implementation agents could use as a benchmark. The 'substantial' reduction of generation of waste can therefore produce a myriad of interpretations across jurisdictions, depending on local conditions, which can prevent actual progress towards accomplishing target 12.5.

6. Target 12.6 Encourage companies, especially large and transnational companies, to adopt sustainable practices and to integrate sustainability information into their reporting cycle

a) Sources of target

As discussed earlier, production and consumption take mainly place within private settings. It is thus mostly national private law that is applicable on relevant business-to-business (B2B) and business-to-consumer (B2C) relationships. Public law then comes into play, for example, when regulating certain parts of production, such as health, safety, and environmental standards. However, these laws will primarily be applied at national level; the principle of sovereignty does not allow for cross-border regulation of private actions. International law traditionally binds states, thus it is not the right tool for regulation of private relationships.[412] That is the reason why regulators must

---

[408] Ellen MacArthur Foundation, 'Tackling Electronic Waste and Digital Poverty in Brazil: Belo Horizonte' <https://ellenmacarthurfoundation.org/circular-examples/tackling-electronic-waste> accessed 25 October 2021; see also this book, Chapter 8 on SDG 8.

[409] ibid.

[410] ibid.

[411] Guevara and Julián (n 386) 10–11; Hettiarachchi (n 387).

[412] Although there are some exceptions, eg Convention for International Sale of Goods (adopted 11 April 1980, entered into force 1 January 1988) 1489 UNTS 3.

906   SDG 12

reach for alternative regulatory tools, such as self-regulation or reflexive law, for example through requiring corporate reporting on non-financial aspects of their business and activities.[413]

Buyers can exercise (smaller or bigger) influence both up the supply chain, over their suppliers, and down the supply chain, over their customers and consumers. Looking at persisting unsustainable modes of production and consumption combined with the inability of states to regulate transnationally, it is important that this influence is exploited to achieve the SDG 12. Furthermore, as internationally buying corporations are often economically strong entities,[414] especially in some industries such as oil production, textiles, and food production, they are called on to take responsibility for 'their part' and to use their influence not only to make profit for their shareholders but more importantly to contribute to the general good, namely to sustainability efforts.[415] The legality of pursuing other than financial objectives by companies is widely discussed in legal literature with the general finding that it is not illegal for companies to pursue social and environmental goals so far as it does not undermine their purpose.[416] The extent to which they are allowed to do that will depend on their jurisdictions and not least their type; that is why revision of current national company laws is warranted.[417]

To motivate corporate engagement with social and environmental spheres, regulators in some jurisdictions adopted legislation mandating the largest corporations to report on their non-financial performance. The number of mandatory non-financial reporting requirements has been growing exponentially since 2006, with approximately a 30 per cent increase between 2016 and 2021.[418] This is true for all continents, with Europe leading the pack.[419] Similarly, we have also seen a surge in voluntary non-financial reporting guidelines, whose numbers almost doubled between 2016 and 2021, that is, since the adoption of UN SDGs.[420] Both mandatory and some voluntary non-financial reporting regulations take inspiration from applicable voluntary non-financial guidelines and practices that are widely spread across the world. These include the UN Global Compact Communication on Progress,[421] the Global Reporting Initiative (GRI) Sustainability Reporting Standards,[422] the UN Guiding Principles

---

[413] K Buhmann, 'The Danish CSR Reporting Requirement as Reflexive Law: Employing CSR as a Modality to Promote Public Policy Objectives through Law' (2013) 24(2) European Business Law Review 187.

[414] S Anderson and J Cavanagh, 'Top 200: The Rise of Corporate Global Power' (Institute for Policy Studies, 4 December 2000).

[415] See, eg <https://www.unglobalcompact.org/sdgs/about> accessed 25 October 2021.

[416] See, eg B Sjåfjell and BJ Richardson (eds), *Company Law and Sustainability: Legal Barriers and Opportunities* (CUP 2015).

[417] ibid.

[418] C van der Lugt and others, 'Carrots & Sticks 2020—Sustainability Reporting Policy: Global Trends in Disclosure as the ESG Agenda Goes Mainstream' (Global Reporting Initiative (GRI) and the University of Stellenbosch Business School (USB), July 2020) 17.

[419] ibid 18.

[420] ibid 17.

[421] United Nations Global Compact, 'Basic Guide, Communication on Progress' (2019) <https://d306pr3pise 04h.cloudfront.net/docs/communication_on_progress%2FTools_and_Publications%2FCOP_Basic_Guide.pdf> accessed 25 October 2021.

[422] Global Reporting Initiative, 'GRI Sustainability Reporting Standards' <https://www.globalreporting.org/how-to-use-the-gri-standards/gri-standards-english-language/> accessed 25 October 2021.

Reporting Framework (focused on human rights),[423] and the International Integrated Reporting Framework (providing guidelines for the integration of financial and non-financial reporting).[424]

The existing reporting laws are often founded on the so-called comply or explain principle.[425] This principle is a gleaming example of reflexive law, in other words law which, rather than requiring concrete action, aims to motivate self-regulation.[426] Using reflexive law makes sense in this area, where (i) it is expected that companies reach throughout their sphere of influence regardless of national, and thus jurisdictional borders; (ii) individual companies have a better knowledge of their abilities, practical conditions (such as financial conditions and power structure of their supply chain), and industrial realities, and thus can take as an ambitious and targeted action as necessary. This said, the comply or explain principle may also be too weak a motivation for companies, leading to the opposite and inducing only minimal compliance, sometimes referred to as a box-ticking exercise.[427] Still, adopting new non-financial reporting laws (in other words, increased legalization of the area), although based on the comply or explain principle, may tap into and increase the internal motivation of companies to engage with sustainability.

The effect of different motivations on companies' non-financial reporting has been widely studied, yet research does not agree on whether external or internal factors are decisive, therefore the conclusion is that both categories are significant.[428] Both mandatory and voluntary regulations pertain to the external factors category. SDG 12 follows the voluntary path, expecting that companies are merely encouraged to adopt and report on sustainability practices. This presents some questions regarding effectiveness that are discussed further below.

At the time of the SDGs' adoption, corporate non-financial reporting was a known tool of corporate social responsibility, which at that time was already legislated for in some jurisdictions[429] and has blossomed within the international soft law area.[430] In that sense, target 12.6 largely repeats what has been agreed and accepted by large corporations and governments at other fora, while staying at the level of encouragement.

The aim of target 12.6 can be seen in driving not only changes in the companies in developed countries but through the increasing attention within non-financial reports

---

[423] UN Guiding Principles Reporting Framework <https://www.ungpreporting.org> accessed 25 October 2021.

[424] The International Framework (January 2021) <https://integratedreporting.org/wp-content/uploads/2021/01/InternationalIntegratedReportingFramework.pdf> accessed 25 October 2021.

[425] Van der Lugt and others (n 418) 19; S Pizzi and others, 'The "Comply-or-Explain" Principle in Directive 95/2014/EU. A Rhetorical Analysis of Italian PIEs' (2021) 12(1) Sustainability Accounting, Management and Policy Journal 30.

[426] MM Rahim, 'Meta-Regulation Approach of Law: A Potential Legal Strategy to Develop Socially Responsible Business Self-Regulation in Least Developed Common Law Countries' (2011) 40(2) Common Law World Review 174.

[427] J Quinn and B Connolly, 'The Non-Financial Information Directive: An Assessment of Its Impact on Corporate Social Responsibility' (2017) 14(1) European Company Law 15, 19.

[428] For example, X Liu and V Anbumozhi, 'Determinant Factors of Corporate Environmental Information Disclosure: An Empirical Study of Chinese Listed Companies' (2009) 17 Journal of Cleaner Production 593.

[429] For example, in France: Article 116 of Law No 2001-420 dated 15 May 2001, on New Economic Regulations and Denmark: Danish Financial Statements Act, Section 99a, as amended by Law No 1403 of 27 December 2008.

[430] Particularly UN Global Compact <https://www.unglobalcompact.org> accessed 25 October 2021.

908   SDG 12

paid to supply chain initiatives, also to influence international supply chains and thus extend the level of protection within environmental and social standards to developing countries.

b) Empirical analysis

The progress towards target 12.6 is measured using one indicator 12.6.1. The indicator for target 12.6 has, just like the entire SDG 12, been developed in cooperation between states and UN agencies, but with especially strong presence of non-state actors. When it comes to indicator 12.6.1, it was developed primarily by the UN Conference on Trade and Development (UNCTAD) in consultations with such expertise organizations, as the GRI, Sustainable Stock Exchanges Initiative, and member governments of the Group of Friends of Paragraph 47 (GoF47).[431] The indicator provides one value: number of companies publishing sustainability reports. The UNCTAD and the UNEP serve as the custodian agencies for indicator 12.6.1.

Regarding indicator 12.6.1, the Global SDG Indicators Database provides numbers of companies issuing sustainability reports in individual countries and continents (data reference 2020). However, the registered numbers seem quite low. For example, the database lists that 1,213 European companies issue sustainability reports of the minimum requirement level, and 612 European companies issue sustainability reports of the advanced requirement levels.[432] This seems strikingly low, as more than 11,500 large companies and corporate groups across the EU are obliged to prepare a non-financial statement according to article 19a of Directive 2013/34/EU.[433] The reason might be that in order to count against fulfilment of target 12.6, the reports must cover a relatively extensive list of topics (inspired heavily by the voluntary GRI Sustainability Reporting Standards), which differs from the known regulations, such as Directive 2013/34/EU or the UN Global Compact.[434] Indicator 12.6.1 can therefore be seen as stricter and more concrete in respect of the requirements regarding the content of corporate sustainability reporting. It is though rather flexible when it comes to the form of reporting. Not only are stand-alone sustainability reports counted against the target but indicator 12.6.1 focuses on sustainability information published by a company regardless of its form, thus encompassing, for example, sustainability-related information integrated

---

[431] UN Statistics Division (2017), 'Work Plans for Tier III Indicators (as of 3 March 2017)' (Statistical Commission 48th Session, 7–10 March 2017) p 135 <https://unstats.un.org/sdgs/tierIII-indicators/> accessed 30 October 2021.

[432] UN, SDG Indicators Database <https://unstats.un.org/sdgs/indicators/database/> accessed 25 October 2021; though, the progress report notes that 'a pilot review conducted in 2020 on a random sample of about 4,000 companies in the United Nations Global Compact database and the Sustainability Disclosure database of the Global Reporting Initiative indicates that 85 per cent of companies reported on minimum requirements for sustainability issues and 40 per cent on advanced requirements for such issues'.

[433] Directive 2013/34/EU of the European Parliament and of the Council of 26 June 2013 on the annual financial statements, consolidated financial statements and related reports of certain types of undertakings, amending Directive 2006/43/EC of the European Parliament and of the Council and repealing Council Directives 78/660/EEC and 83/349/EEC [2013] OJ L 182/19, as amended by Directive 2014/95/EU.

[434] SDG Indicators metadata repository, metadata sheet for indicator 12.6.1 <https://unstats.un.org/sdgs/metadata> accessed 3 July 2021 (Metadata 12.6.1), update March 2021, other methodological considerations, method of computation.

into the company's annual report and information provided on its website.[435] Gathering the numbers of reporting companies is thus a daunting task, where relying on existing public and private databases of sustainability reports is necessary.[436] The large variety of databases, regulations of sustainability reporting, and reporting practices then make the assessment of the quality and comparability of the reports extremely difficult, if possible at all.[437]

As non-financial reporting existed before the SDGs were adopted, what new do SDGs bring to the field, and how are SDGs reflected in corporate reporting? A report by KPMG (2017) showed an increasing tendency in the number of non-financial reporting after SDGs' adoption but pointed also to the fact that only 39 per cent of the sample companies make a clear connection between their corporate responsibility activities and the SDGs.[438] The lack of formal disclosure does not, however, mean that the sample companies do not undertake activities and measures towards fulfilment of the SDGs, rather it is a proof of missing standards and guidance on how to report on corporate contributions to the SDGs[439] that would be globally accepted and followed.

c) Implementation efforts at domestic/international level

Considering the various levels of economic and environmental development and the contrasting positions of developed and developing countries toward SDG 12,[440] regulatory efforts within corporate sustainability reporting have developed at the national rather than the international level. While the former is dominated by public laws and regulations adopted by governmental agencies,[441] the latter is characterized by soft law standards and guidelines adopted mainly by non-state actors.

Governments play a central role in incentivising companies' move toward more sustainable business practices.[442] Law is then a crucial tool in their hands. The EU has one of the most developed regulations. In 2014, the EU adopted Directive 2014/95/EU that introduced article 19a to Directive 2013/34/EU, making it mandatory for large enterprises to accompany their annual reports with non-financial statements.[443] The Directive obliges companies with more than 500 employees to report, as a minimum, on environmental matters, social matters and treatment of employees, respect for

[435] ibid, other methodological considerations, rationale.
[436] ibid annex II.
[437] Van der Lugt and others (n 418).
[438] KPMG, 'The Road Ahead. The KPMG Survey of Corporate Responsibility Reporting' (2017) p 39 <https://www.integratedreporting.org/wp-content/uploads/2017/10/kpmg-survey-of-corporate-responsibility-reporting-2017.pdf> accessed 25 October 2021. The sample companies consist of 4,900 companies comprising the top 100 companies by revenue in each of the forty-nine countries covered by the report. Similar findings are to be found in PWC, 'SDG Reporting Challenge. From Promise to Reality: Does Business Really Care about the SDGs? And What Needs to Happen to Turn Words into Action' (2018) <https://www.pwc.com/gx/en/sustainability/SDG/sdg-reporting-2018.pdf> accessed 25 October 2021.
[439] Pizzi and others (n 75) 405.
[440] See Introduction to this chapter.
[441] Van der Lugt and others (n 418) 14.
[442] R Scheyvens and others, 'The Private Sector and the SDGs: The Need to Move Beyond "Business as Usual"' (2016) 24 Sustainable Development 371.
[443] Directive 2014/95/EU amending Directive 2013/34/EU as regards disclosure of non-financial and diversity information by certain large undertakings and groups [2014] OJ L 330/1.

human rights, anti-corruption and bribery, and diversity on company boards, and this should be done to the extent necessary to understand companies' development, performance, position, and impact of their activity. If a company does not pursue policies in relation to one or more of those topics, the report should include a clear and reasoned explanation why (the comply or explain principle). Moreover, it is not just the policies that should be reported on but also their outcomes and relevant non-financial key performance indicators (KPIs), a brief description of the company's business model, and the principal risks to those matters that can be ascribed to the company's operations, business relationships, products, or services.[444]

National and regional non-financial reporting laws though do not necessarily refer to or align with the SDGs (especially considering the above-mentioned minimum content of sustainability reports required for inclusion under indicator 12.6.1). To remedy this, the EU has recently adopted a new Corporate Sustainability Reporting Directive (CSRD) replacing the currently applicable rules gradually from 2024.[445] The new directive presents an exciting development, extending the applicability of the requirement to prepare an annual non-financial statement to all large companies and all companies listed on regulated markets, requiring not only assurance of the existence of a sustainability report but also of its content, and introducing more detailed reporting requirements. The Preamble of the directive expressly refers to the SDGs and can be seen as an example of increased legalization of sustainability reporting.

On the global level, multiple efforts are taken to consolidate existing regulations, experience, and practice of non-financial reporting in order to measure the progress toward SDG 12 and to establish a meaningful framework to report on corporate contributions to the SDGs in general. One of the leading efforts is the SDG Compass developed in cooperation with the Global Reporting Initiative, UN, and World Business Council for Sustainable Development (2017).[446] The objective is 'to support companies in aligning their strategies with the SDGs and in measuring and managing their contribution.'[447] The SDG Compass is based on a five-step process encompassing: (i) understanding the SDGs, (ii) defining priorities, (iii) setting goals, (iv) integrating, and (v) reporting and communicating. In 2017, the Agreed Conclusions of the thirty-fourth session of the Intergovernmental Working Group of Experts on International Standards of Accounting and Reporting (ISAR) requested UNCTAD to develop a guiding document. This resulted in publication of the UNCTAD Core Indicators for company reporting on the contribution towards the attainment of the SDGs.[448] The Core Indicators provide companies with 'detailed definitions and data sources for the

---

[444] Directive 2013/34/EU (n 433) art 19a.

[445] Directive (EU) 2022/2464 of the European Parliament and of the Council of 14 December 2022 amending Regulation (EU) No 537/2014, Directive 2004/109/EC, Directive 2006/43/EC, and Directive 2013/34/EU, as regards corporate sustainability reporting [2022] OJ L 322/15.

[446] World Business Council for Sustainable Development, 'CEO guide to the SDGs' (2017) <https://sdghub.com/ceo-guide/> accessed 25 October 2021.

[447] SDG Compass <https://sdgcompass.org> accessed 25 October 2021.

[448] Guidance on core indicators for entity reporting on contribution towards implementation of the Sustainable Development Goals <https://unctad.org/webflyer/guidance-core-indicators-entity-reporting-contribution-towards-implementation-sustainable> accessed 25 October 2021.

core indicators in the company accounts to assist the entities in the reporting'.[449] The Core Indicators also serve as inspiration in the continuous works on the specification of the 12.6.1 indicator. The indicator's metadata document also states that '[t]he purpose is not to create a new reporting standard or framework, but to ensure that the minimum requirement for Indicator 12.6.1 is aligned with existing global frameworks currently used by companies, so that they may continue to use these frameworks and be counted towards the indicator'.[450]

d) Critique

It is clear that without the involvement of businesses, SDG 12 cannot be achieved. Thus, appropriate motivation of companies to embody sustainable practices is crucial. The use of reflexive regulation, such as non-financial reporting requirements has for long been seen as a more favourable alternative to hard, jurisdiction-limited laws. Yet, the experience of incomparable sustainability reports of widely varying scope and quality questions whether voluntary reporting is adequate for achieving the SDGs. It has thus been met with scepticism when target 12.6 was formulated to only 'encourage' companies to adopt sustainable practices and sustainability reporting, reducing the initial suggestions to establish a specific percentage increase in corporate sustainability reporting.[451]

As indicator 12.6.1 suggests, target 12.6 relies on sustainability reporting requirements as the tool to encourage companies to shift towards sustainable practices. This could be questioned, as it has been argued, on the one hand, that even mandatory reporting requirements do not necessarily lead to change in behaviour.[452] On the other hand, some research pointed to situations of 'positive relationship between nonfinancial reporting regulation and the adoption of sustainable practices by companies without any substantial changes in terms of sustainability reporting quality'.[453] Thus, it cannot be concluded that sustainability reporting is a genuine mirror of the adoption of sustainable practices by companies; it can be both under- and over-estimating the made progress. It follows that the indicator is merely a 'publication count', rather than a realistic measurement of the achievement of target 12.6.

Finally, target 12.6 follows the idea that we can decouple production from environmental degradation,[454] which supports the view that if we secure green production, we do not need to lower consumption. This is a dangerous approach in the current world, where the global population, and thus the consumer base, continue to increase.[455]

---

[449] Metadata 12.6.1 (n 434).
[450] ibid.
[451] Gasper and others (n 5) 88.
[452] G Jackson and others, 'Mandatory Non-financial Disclosure and its Influence on CSR: An International Comparison' (2019) 162 Journal of Business Ethics 323.
[453] Pizzi and others (n 75) 406, referring to J-N Chauvey and others, 'The Normativity and Legitimacy of CSR Disclosure: Evidence from France' (2015) 130(4) Journal of Business Ethics 789.
[454] Gasper and others (n 5) 85.
[455] See nn 93 and 94 and the accompanying text.

912 SDG 12

Overall, the contribution of target 12.6 to a further deployment of non-financial reporting practices seems quite limited so far, as it requires only encouragement of corporate sustainable practices and sustainability reporting, while many companies have in fact had experience in non-financial reporting on a voluntary or mandatory basis before. Also, while the indicator proclaims that it focuses both on increasing the quantity and quality of corporate sustainability reporting,[456] achieving the latter, which is a better indication of the actual shift towards sustainable modes of production, seems so far an unsurmountable task due to the jungle of existing practices and mostly voluntary-based regulations.

7. Target 12.7 Promote public procurement practices that are sustainable, in accordance with national policies and priorities

a) Sources of target

Public procurement (PP) 'is the buying and contracting by public actors of the goods, services and works they need to fulfil their functions'.[457] Public authorities, being one of the biggest consumers worldwide, play a vital role in SCP as they have an immense purchasing power over goods and services, notably up to 12 per cent of GDP in the OECD countries and around 30 per cent in developing countries.[458] Because of this, an appreciable proportion of GDP is generated as a result of purchases made by the public sector. Due to the immense volume of investments from the public buyers, PP can assist in promoting a range of objectives not related to the economics and delivery of goods and services itself, but linked to other values, such as environmental protection, social inclusion, diversity, equality, ethical considerations and last, but not least, human rights protection.[459] This trend, which is emblematic for the past several decades, is referred to as sustainable public procurement (SPP). The European Commission defines SPP as 'a process by which public authorities seek to achieve an appropriate balance between the three pillars of sustainable development—economic, social and environmental— when procuring goods, services or works at all stages of the project'.[460] SPP is sometimes divided into two main categories: (i) green public procurement (GPP), focusing on environmental issues, such as energy conservation, and (ii) socially responsible public procurement, focusing on socio-economic issues, such as diversity or equality.

The standard purpose of PP is to achieve the best value for money; however, a transformation towards sustainability is increasingly visible, as public authorities use PP more strategically for promotion of further societal goals.[461] In this way, SPP has

---

[456] S Pizzi and others, 'Achieving Sustainable Development Goals through Non-financial Regulation. First Insights from the Transposition of Directive 95/2014/EU in Italy' in S Garzella (ed), *Corporate Social Responsibility, Theoretical Analysis and Practical Implications* (Franco Angeli 2020) 15.

[457] S Arrowsmith and P Kunzlik, *Social and Environmental Policies in EU Procurement Law: New Directives and New Directions* (CUP 2009) 9.

[458] United Nations Environment Programme, 'Sustainable Procurement' (United Nations Environment programme, undated) <http://web.unep.org/resourceefficiency/ what-we-do/sustainable-lifestyles/sustainable-procurement> accessed 28 September 2021.

[459] B Sjåfjell and A Wiesbrock, *Sustainable Public Procurement Under EU Law: New Perspectives on the State as Stakeholder* (CUP 2016) ch 1.

[460] European Commission, 'Green and Sustainable Public Procurement' available at <https://ec.europa.eu/environment/gpp/versus_en.htm> accessed 26 October 2021.

[461] Sjåfjell and Wiesbrock (n 459) ch 1.

a potential to indirectly influence states' performance on other SDGs, such as SDG 8 (decent work and economic growth), SDG 9 (sustainable industrialization and innovation), SDG 11 (sustainable cities and communities), and SDG 13 (climate change). Moreover, states' procurement practices can further motivate other market players to adopt a more sustainable approach and directly prompt the contractors and subcontractors in supply chains to act responsibly.[462] Some scholars and international organizations therefore argue that it is desirable that PP rules are designed in a way which supports and promotes such objectives, especially in cases, where a government is one of the main purchasers of the product or service, for example in the healthcare sector, which represents around 9 per cent of GDP expenditure in OECD countries.[463]

By the end of nineteenth century, social aspects of PP were discussed in politics.[464] Environmental protection followed a century later, when the link between environmental protection and SPP was established.[465] The past couple of decades have seen a rapid development in SPP policy-making, especially in the GPP area. One of the first times the concept was mentioned at the international level can be traced back to Agenda 21,[466] which encouraged national governments to adopt more environmentally friendly PP practices.[467] After that call, Norway,[468] Korea,[469] and Japan became some of the pioneers in the area, introducing the first GPP instruments in the 1990s.[470] The Johannesburg World Summit on Sustainable Development in 2002 provided another nudge towards SPP.[471] The Johannesburg Summit led to the Marrakech Process focused on the implementation of Sustainable Consumption and Production and in 2003 to the establishment of Marrakech Task Force (MTF) on Sustainable Public Procurement which provided training, mentoring, and other support to public authorities, especially in developing countries, in order to achieve smooth adoption of more SPP worldwide.[472]

According to the United Nations Guiding Principles on Business and Human Rights (UNGPs), states and governments have a duty to protect human rights where the respective state functions as a commercial actor, that is, where public authorities procure

---

[462] So-called sustainable strategic public procurement.

[463] OECD, 'Health and Public Procurement' <<https://www.oecd.org/gov/public-procurement/health/ > accessed 12 August 2021.

[464] C McCrudden, 'Using public procurement to achieve social outcomes' (2004) 28(4) Natural Resources Forum 257, 258.

[465] UNEP, 'Global Review of Sustainable Public Procurement 2017' (2017) p 12 <https://www.unep.org/resources/report/2017-global-review-sustainable-public-procurement> accessed 26 October 2021.

[466] Agenda 21 (n 363).

[467] ibid ch 4.

[468] 'Norway was one of the first countries to embark on the green procurement journey, with the establishment of GRIP the Norwegian Foundation for Sustainable Consumption and Production, by the Ministry of Environment in 1993.' See in O Perera and others, 'State of Play in Sustainable Public Procurement' (IISD, The Energy and Resources Institute (TERA), November 2007) p 31 <https://www.iisd.org/system/files/publications/state_procurement.pdf> accessed 30 October 2021.

[469] Public authorities recommended to buy Korea eco label products<https://www.oneplanetnetwork.org/initiative/green-public-procurement-republic-korea.

[470] A Adell and others, 'Green Public Procurement in the Republic of Korea: A Decade of Progress and Lessons Learned' (UNEP and KEITI, 2019) <https://wedocs.unep.org/handle/20.500.11822/32535> accessed 30 October 2021 (Korea Report).

[471] Johannesburg Plan of Implementation (n 109) III, para 19.

[472] See nn 14 and 16.

914   SDG 12

products and services.[473] While environmental considerations have been strongly embedded in PP of many jurisdictions,[474] societal considerations and human rights stayed central only in a handful of states, such as South Africa or Kenya.[475] And yet, social issues connected to public purchases, especially those outsourced to developing countries, have become increasingly alarming.[476] The recent COVID-19 crisis, for instance, manifestly illuminated the link between public purchases and the dangers of human rights abuses via supply chains. Poor labour conditions, forced and child labour, among other things, made it to the front pages of global media as the world's governments procured personal protective equipment such as face masks and gloves without engaging with further investigation of the labour conditions of people producing them.[477] Supply chains were exposed to the public eye, and human rights violations became a centre of discussion in relation to PP practices, sending a clear message that trying to achieve the best value for money without any consideration of other objectives of PP might lead to detrimental consequences for workers throughout supply chains.

Similarly to other SDG 12 targets, the wording of target 12.7 is characterized by weak language directing us towards 'promoting' SPP rather than towards a better measurable goal. Even though Denmark, Estonia, and Brazil suggested an indictor which would reflect a share of SPP in the country in question, this approach was not followed.[478] In addition, the former proposition of the goal which aspired to 'substantially increase' the volume of SPP was abandoned.[479]

b) Empirical analysis

In order to measure the achievements of target 12.7, UNEP embarked on a journey of developing a suitable methodology with the help of the One Planet Sustainable Public Procurement Programme.[480] The first version of the methodology dates back to 2016 and was authored by the Technical Expert Group of the One Planet Sustainable Public Procurement Programme, in further cooperation with the ICLEI-Local Governments for Sustainability,[481] the Korea Environmental Industry and Technology Committee

---

[473] Human Rights Council (n 57) principles 4, 5, 6.

[474] Martin-Ortega and O'Brien (2019).

[475] M Andhov and others, 'Sustainability through Public Procurement: The Way Forward—Reform Proposals' (2020) <https://dx.doi.org/10.2139/ssrn.3559393> accessed 5 September 2021, see also Public Procurement and Human Rights: A Survey of Twenty Jurisdictions (July 2016) <http://www.hrprocurementlab.org/wp-content/uploads/2016/06/Public-Procurement-and-Human-Rights-A-Survey-of-Twenty-Jurisdictions-Final.pdf.

[476] O Martin-Ortega, 'Modern Slavery and Human Rights Risks in Global Supply Chains: The Role of Public Buyers' (2017) 8(4) Global Policy 512.

[477] See, eg, H Ellis-Petersen, 'NHS Rubber Gloves Made in Malaysian Factories Linked with Forced Labour' The Guardian (London, 9 Dec 2018); E Szeto and others, 'Hidden Camera Reveals "Appalling" Conditions in Overseas PPE Factory Supplying Canadian Hospitals, Expert Says' CBC News (15 January 2021) British Medical Association and others, 'Healthier procurement: Improvements for working conditions for surgical instruments manufacture in Pakistan' (2015) <https://www.bma.org.uk/media/1095/po-healthierprocurement_bma-10-04-2015-1.pdf> accessed 26 October 2021.

[478] Gasper and others (n 5) 90.

[479] ibid.

[480] One Planet Network, 'Sustainable Public Procurement' <https://www.oneplanetnetwork.org/sustainable-public-procurement> accessed 29 August 2021.

[481] ICLEI—Local Governments for Sustainability <www.iclei.org> accessed 12 September 2021.

(KEITI),[482] Ecoinstitut,[483] and Industrial Economics (IEc).[484] In 2017, UNEP launched a second edition of the Global Review of Sustainable Public Procurement[485] assessing policies from fifty-five countries, which contributed to defining indicator 12.7.1 and clarified the possibilities of its measurement and data collection. After that, the methodology underwent two pilot testings, one in 2019, and one in 2020.[486] 2020 also marks the year when the indicator was reclassified from a Tier III indicator, meaning that '[n]o internationally established methodology or standards are yet available for the indicator, but methodology/standards are being (or will be) developed or tested', to a Tier II indicator, which means that '[i]ndicator is conceptually clear, has an internationally established methodology and standards are available, but data are not regularly produced by countries'.[487]

The methodology is addressed to national governments, guiding policy-makers and practitioners for the purpose of reporting on SDG 12.7 and thereby measures progress achieved in SPP. Indicator 12.7.1 counts the number of countries implementing SPP policies and action plans. The two overarching goals are to assess whether the countries have developed SPP policies and action plans, and whether they are implementing them.[488] The methodology evaluates the existence of SPP action, efforts of the countries and their results, and quantifies it in line with six designated parameters, which constitute a final score. Those parameters include information on:

- **Existence of a SPP action plan/policy**, and/or SPP regulatory requirements. This includes any supporting evidence or reference to a precise instrument, such as concrete laws and policies;
- **Public procurement regulatory framework conducive to SPP**. This parameter assesses whether specific legal provisions facilitate or mandate the use of SPP. For instance, whether the sustainability requirements are included in contracts in a form of technical specifications, eco or social labels, or standards. Moreover, it assesses the selection and exclusion of suppliers based on sustainability criteria. Sustainability requirements are also assessed for award criteria and contract performance clauses;
- **Practical support delivered to procurement practitioners** in the implementation of SPP. This includes various types of guidelines, a catalogue of eco-labelled

[482] Korea Environmental Industry and Technology Committee <http://www.keiti.re.kr/site/eng/01/10101010 000002018121305.jsp> accessed 12 September 2021.

[483] Ecoinstitut SCCL (sustainability consulting firm) <http://www.ecoinstitut.coop/en/index.html> accessed 28 October 2021.

[484] Industrial Economics, Inc. (economic and environmental consulting firm), Industrial Economics <http://www.indecon.com> accessed 28 October 2021.

[485] UNEP, 'Global Review of Sustainable Public Procurement 2017' (2017) <https://www.unep.org/resources/report/2017-global-review-sustainable-public-procurement> accessed 26 October 2021.

[486] UNEP and One Planet Network, 'SDG Indicator 12.7.1, SPP Index Calculation Methodology & Guidelines' (updated 18 June 2021, 2021).

[487] IAEG-SDGs, 'Tier Classification for Global SDG Indicators' <https://unstats.un.org/sdgs/iaeg-sdgs/tier-classification/> accessed 29 October 2021; The Tier classification that is currently in effect after the 2020 review can be found here <https://unstats.un.org/sdgs/files/Tier%20Classification%20of%20SDG%20Indicators_28%20 Dec%202020_web.pdf> accessed 28 October 2021.

[488] UNEP & One Planet Network (n 486) 3.

products communication channels, training sessions, and best practice case studies;

- **SPP purchasing criteria/buying standards/requirements** are available for specific categories of products or services;[489]
- **Existence of a SPP monitoring system;**
- **Percentage of sustainable purchase of priority products/services.**[490]

The data collection started in 2020, therefore the SG's Progress Report 2021 provides only a brief note stating that forty countries' reports on SPP policies and that action plans are available,[491] but no detail is provided regarding the content of such policies or their further qualitative assessment.

SPP is not monitored and measured only under the SDGs framework. OECD's Methodology for Assessing Procurement Systems (OECD-MAPS) inspects the national PP systems from the viewpoint of sustainability.[492] It introduces for instance indicator 3(a) which analyses whether (i) the country in question had adopted a policy and an implementation plan to implement SPP in support of national policy objectives, (ii) whether the legal and regulatory framework includes provisions on the inclusion of sustainability criteria in PP, and (iii) whether those provisions are balanced against primary objectives of PP and ensure value for money.[493]

c) Implementation efforts at domestic/international level

SPP is primarily an issue of national and local policy and is therefore rarely implemented on an international scale. Despite this fact, accelerating efforts from the international organizations and an array of partnerships were established for further cooperation among public authorities.[494] These initiatives constitute an irreplaceable component on the journey to achieve sustainable procurement practices worldwide. These mostly soft law instruments proved to be a non-invasive way to encourage national governments and PP practitioners towards more sustainable actions.[495] Providing guidelines, information, and standards on how to integrate sustainability, share good practices, and technical support are only a small portion of actions offered at the international and regional levels.[496] Globally, the first steps were taken by the UN, which for example published the UN Guide to Environmental Labels for Procurement Practitioners of the United Nations Systems,[497] Buying for a Better World: A Guide

---

[489] For example, EU GPP criteria for various groups of products available here: European Commission, 'EU GPP criteria' <https://ec.europa.eu/environment/gpp/eu_gpp_criteria_en.htm> accessed 15 October 2021.

[490] More information on each of the parameters can be found in UNEP and One planet Network (n 486).

[491] SG's Progress Report 2021 (n 122) para 138.

[492] OECD, 'Methodology for Assessing Procurement Systems (MAPS)' (2018) <https://www.mapsinitiative.org/methodology/MAPS-Methodology-ENG.pdf> accessed 28 October 2021.

[493] ibid indicator 3(a).

[494] R Caranta, 'Helping Public Procurement go Green: The Role of International Organisations' (2013) 8(1) European Procurement & Public Private Partnership Law Review 49.

[495] ibid 50.

[496] ibid.

[497] United Nations Office for Project Services, 'A Guide to Environmental Labels—for Procurement Practitioners of the United Nations Systems' (2009).

for Sustainable Procurement for the UN System,[498] and UNEP's Sustainable Public Procurement Implementation Guideline.[499] Later on, UNEP embarked on a journey of monitoring SPP actions, which in 2013 resulted in the Global Review of Sustainable Public Procurement,[500] followed in 2017 by new updated data.[501] Further global efforts can be illustrated by the work of the Sustainable Public Procurement Programme of the One Planet Network under the auspices of the UNEP whose objective is coordination of governmental, non-governmental, public and private parties, and providing not only funding but also experience, which facilitates SPP implementation.[502] Regionally, the Procura + Network,[503] and Procurement Forum[504] connects European public authorities and experts, while the Asian Pacific Green Public Procurement Network focuses on Asia and the Pacific area.[505] Cities as separate entities also play a significant role in SPP and contribute to achieving target 12.7 by adopting more sustainable practices. Therefore, the Global Lead City Network on Sustainable Procurement works with their member cities and supports them in achieving individually set targets.[506] Exemplarily, the South African city, Tshwane, encourages procurers to adopt minimum sustainability requirements.[507] Apart from the wide range of platforms, networks, guidelines and other elements, the International Organization for Standardization (ISO) navigates organizations how to incorporate sustainability into public procurement through its standard ISO 20400:2017.[508] Despite not being legally binding, it can be seen as a useful starting point based on wide consensus and unified terminology, which allows organizations to improve their understanding of how to integrate sustainability into their practices.

Depending on the volume of purchases or the subject matter of the contract, rules on PP might be to a certain degree harmonized at global or regional levels.[509] For example, WTO's Agreement on Governmental Procurement (GPA), UNCITRAL Model Law on

---

[498] UNEP, United Nations Office for Project Services (UNOPS), the ILO, and the ILO's International Training Center, 'Buying for a Better World A Guide for Sustainable Procurement for the UN System' (2011).

[499] UNEP, 'Sustainable Public Procurement Implementation Guidelines' (2012).

[500] A O'Rourke and others, 'Sustainable Public Procurement: A Global Review' (UNEP 2013).

[501] UNEP, 'Global Review of Sustainable Public Procurement 2017' (n 485).

[502] See n 480; Directive 2014/25/EU of the European Parliament and of the Council of 26 February 2014 on procurement by entities operating in the water, energy, transport and postal services sectors and repealing Directive 2004/17/EC [2014] OJ L 94/243; Directive 2009/81/EC of the European Parliament and of the Council of 13 July 2009 on the coordination of procedures for the award of certain works contracts, supply contracts and service contracts by contracting authorities or entities in the fields of defence and security, and amending Directives 2004/17/EC and 2004/18/EC [2009] OJ L 216/76.

[503] Procura + Network <https://procuraplus.org/home/> accessed 9 September 2021.

[504] Procurement Forum <https://procurement-forum.eu> accessed 10 September 2021.

[505] UNEP, 'Asia Pacific Green Public Procurement (GPP) Network' <https://www.unep.org/explore-topics/resource-efficiency/what-we-do/sustainable-public-procurement/asia-pacific-green> accessed 19 September 2021.

[506] Global Lead City Network on Sustainable Procurement <https://glcn-on-sp.org/home/> accessed 21 September 2021.

[507] One Planet Network, 'City of Tshwane—Using Procurement to Become a Liveable, Resilient and Inclusive City' (23 March 2021) <https://www.oneplanetnetwork.org/city-tshwane-using-procurement-become-liveable-resilient-and-inclusive-city> accessed 12 September 2021.

[508] International Organization for Standardization, ISO 20400:2017 Sustainable procurement—Guidance <https://www.iso.org/standard/63026.html> accessed 8 September 2021.

[509] R Caranta and C Cravero, 'Sustainability and Public Procurement' in A La Chimia and P Trepte (eds), *Public Procurement and Aid Effectiveness: A Roadmap under Construction* (Bloomsbury Publishing Plc. 2019).

918   SDG 12

Public Procurement,[510] and the EU's Public Procurement Directives[511] provide such unified sets of rules. While in some cases harmonization leads to a strengthening of the SPP's position, in other cases, the wording of the instrument remains very traditional, protecting primary (economic) objectives of the public procurement. The example of the latter is the WTO's GPA,[512] which despite having a working group for SPP does not assign the same importance to it as to the traditional objectives of the public procurement. In turn, the EU is a frontrunner in SPP. In 2014, it adopted Directive 2014/24/EU (the Public Procurement Directive),[513] which facilitated (but did not mandate) the possibility of inclusion of sustainability criteria in public contracts. According to the Directive and scholarly literature, environmental and social criteria can be imposed at all levels of the procurement process,[514] as long as there is a link to the subject matter (L2SM) of the contract.[515] In this way, public authorities can only set sustainability criteria which are relevant for the concrete contract, and all other businesses outside the contractual relationship should not be taken into consideration. Effective use of SPP depends on dismantling the connection between PP and the lowest price; therefore, the EU promotes abandonment of the lowest price criterion and advocates for adoption of the Most Economically Advantageous Tenders (MEAT).[516] Lifecycle costing and ecolabels, which are explicitly mentioned in the Public Procurement Directive, are two of the tools which can enable such a transition. Although the EU has done a great portion of work on simplifying the SPP processes for public authorities, through for example providing exemplary criteria, the proportion of tenders awarded based on MEAT continues to be low.[517] Therefore, the New Circular Economy Action Plan adopted in 2020 shifted the existing approach, when it indicated that 'the Commission will propose minimum *mandatory* green public procurement (GPP) criteria and targets in sectoral legislation'.[518]

After a long history of ambitious advancement of the GPP, the EU now turns to social considerations related to the SPP. In 2021, it published the second edition of Buying Social—A Guide to Taking Account of Social Considerations in Public Procurement,[519] which guides public procurers on the way to more socially responsible PP.[520] Moreover,

[510] United Nations Commission on International Trade Law, 'UNCITRAL Model Law on Public Procurement' [2011] (United Nations Publications 2014).

[511] See n 513.

[512] WTO, 'WTO Agreement on Government Procurement (GPA)' (revised version) (adopted March 2012, in force 6 April 2014).

[513] Directive 2014/24/EU of The European Parliament and of The Council of 26 February 2014 on public procurement and repealing Directive 2004/18/EC [2014] OJ L 94/65 (Public Procurement Directive).

[514] M Andrecka and KP Mitkidis, 'Sustainability Requirements in EU Public and Private Procurement—A Right or an Obligation?' (2017) 1 Nordic Journal of Commercial Law 55, 69.

[515] A Semple, 'The Link Tothe Subject Matter: A Glass Ceiling for Sustainable Public Contracts?' in B Sjåfjell and A Wiesbrock (eds), *Sustainable Public Procurement under EU Law: New Perspectives on the State as Stakeholder* (CUP 2015).

[516] Art 67 of Public Procurement Directive (n 513).

[517] Andhov and others (n 475) 6.

[518] CEAP (n 172) 2.2, emphasis added.

[519] European Commission, 'Buying Social—A Guide to Taking Account of Social Considerations in Public Procurement (2nd edition)' C(2021) 3573, 26 May 2021.

[520] ibid.

the European Commission has in line with UNGPs adopted a proposal for a Directive on Corporate Sustainability Due Diligence, whose objective is to, among others, address the problem of human rights' violations in supply chains.[521] This Directive will require that EU Member States and the undertakings owned by them only procure from undertakings which 'prove they have not been sanctioned for due diligence breaches'.[522]

Nationally, the approaches towards SPP vary. The Nordic region is most often used as the best practice example. Indicatively, Norway's legislation contains mandatory provisions on inclusion of clauses on wages and decent working conditions by the public authorities when purchasing certain types of products and services.[523] Sweden, in turn, adopted a common code of conduct for suppliers, suppliers questionnaires, and factory audits which prevent further human right violations which could be traced back to the purchases of public authorities.[524] Finally, Finland's partnership, KEINO, increases the awareness of public authorities regarding SPP.[525] Apart from the Nordic countries, Scotland's sustainable procurement duty stands out. According to the Scottish legislation, contracting authorities are required to think about how the product/service they are buying can improve the social, environmental, and economic well-being of the area in which it operates, focusing on inequality.[526] Furthermore, it promotes involvement of small and medium-size enterprises (SMEs) and innovation.[527] Also, countries outside the European continent have developed praiseworthy efforts. Argentina, for illustration, has a well-developed e-tendering portal called Argentina Compra accompanied by the so-called Sistema de Identificación de Bienes y Servicios (SIByS). SIByS includes criteria for different types of products and information about their sustainability. Due to close cooperation of these two systems, Argentina Compra can determine a number of public purchases.[528,529] Finally, an OECD Report from 2017 uses Korea as one of the best examples of GPP.[530] Korean GPP dates back to 1990s when the public authorities were encouraged to use the Korean eco-label when procuring products and services, but it was the Korean Act on Promotion of Purchase of Green

---

[521] Proposal for a Directive of the European Parliament and of the Council on Corporate Sustainability Due Diligence and amending Directive (EU) 2019/1937 (COM/2022/71 final); European Commission, 'Sustainable Corporate Governance' <https://ec.europa.eu/info/law/better-regulation/have-your-say/initiatives/12548-Sustainable-corporate-governance_en> accessed 29 October 2021.

[522] European Coalition for Corporate Justice, 'Dangerous gaps undermine EU Commission's new legislation on sustainable supply chains' <https://corporatejustice.org/news/dangerous-gaps-undermine-eu-commissions-new-legislation-on-sustainable-supply-chains/> accessed 21 March 2023, compare: Public Procurement Directive: art 18—sanctions—exclusion from the public procurement, art 69(3) of the Public Procurement Directive requires the contracting public authorities to 'reject the tender, where they have established that the tender is abnormally law because it does not comply with applicable obligations referred to in Art. 18(2)'.

[523] Norwegian Act on Public Procurement of 17 June 2016, No 73 (LOV-2016-06-17-73) paras 5–6 <https://lovdata.no/dokument/NL/lov/2016-06-17-73> accessed 26 October 2021.

[524] Andhov and others (n 475) 26.

[525] KEINO, 'About KEINO' <https://www.hankintakeino.fi/en/about-keino> accessed 5 September 2021.

[526] Procurement Reform (Scotland) Act 2014 (asp 12), s 9.

[527] ibid.

[528] In 2015, 14 per cent of products and services in Argentina were sustainable; UNEP, 'Global Review of Sustainable Public Procurement 2017' (n 485) 27.

[529] ibid 26–27; Argentina Compra <http://www.argentinacompra.gov.ar> accessed 28 October 2021.

[530] OECD, 'OECD Environmental Performance Reviews: Korea 2017' (OECD Publishing, 2017).

920   SDG 12

Products (KAPPGP) from 2005, which sparked the interest of foreign academics.[531] The KAPPGP requires public procurers to set a voluntary target and an implementation plan and submit this to the Ministry of Environment.[532] In addition, once a year all the green purchases undertaken in the past year must be reported to the ministry.[533] The Korean Online E-Procurement System (KONEPS) together with KEITI's Green Procurement Information System (GPIS) then facilitate monitoring of the amount of green products procured, due to classification, and tracking of products.[534] Moreover, public authorities are also motivated financially to procure in a sustainable way by the way of obtaining larger budgets.[535]

d) Critique

Using public procurement as a strategic instrument which promotes sustainability is a truly challenging task. This mission requires functional processes, human resources, and a knowledge base as a starting point. The complexity of the problem, contradictory interests of the three pillars of SD, and insufficient knowledge are all factors that can have a discouraging effect on public authorities when adopting SPP actions. Moreover, the weak language of the target itself, referring to mere promotion of SPP, may undermine its relevance in the eyes of states which might not assign it the highest priority.

The methodology of indicator 12.7.1 entails a detailed list of SPP parameters and is well-developed in terms of providing a picture of the *existence* of the sustainable public procurement policies, legislation, support, and monitoring in the selected country. Yet, it does not include sufficient qualitative data and evidence on how well these are integrated in the system. Even though the indicator informs us about the fact whether the SPP was implemented, we do not learn about the practical effects of this implementation. An exception is the monitoring of a percentage of the sustainable purchase of priority products/services. This number, though, might not be a direct result of the legislation adopted. The effects of measures which were set in place would deserve more attention to develop a complete picture of the state of the SPP. We should be particularly cautious so that the reporting on indicator 12.7.1 does not become a mere manual ticking box exercise and that the public authorities also abide by their own sustainability strategies, deliver on their promises, and measure and check what was achieved. The effects of measures which were set in place would deserve more attention to develop a complete picture of the state of the SPP.

Even though some regional frameworks have advanced SPP policies, there are persistent barriers. As an example, the EU introduced through the Court of Justice of the

---

[531] Korean Act on Promotion of Purchase of Green Products (KAPPGP) <https://www.oneplanetnetwork.org/sites/default/files/korea_act_on_promotion_of_purchase_of_green_products.pdf> accessed 19 October 2021, see also: UNEP, 'Green Public Procurement in the Republic of Korea: A Decade of Progress and Lessons Learned' (2019) 10.

[532] KAPPGP (n 531) art 8.

[533] ibid art 9.

[534] Korean Online E-Procurement System: KONEPS <https://www.dgovkorea.go.kr/service1/g2c_07/koneps> accessed 28 October 2021; KEITI's Green Procurement Information System: GPIS <www.greenproduct.go.kr> accessed 28 October 2021.

[535] KAPPGP (n 531) art 15.

European Union the L2SM, in order to prevent sustainability clauses being used in a discriminatory manner.[536] This on the one hand allowed for limited used of sustainability criteria in PP around the EU, on the other hand, the notion of the L2SM remains ill-defined and its effect in practice questionable.[537] The question remains, whether introduction of minimum mandatory criteria could lift the big cloud hanging over the concept of L2SM.

Success in using SPP also depends on the buyers' market power, therefore pooling the efforts in SPP might increase its effect. Illustratively, the Big Buyers Initiative unites some of the EU contracting authorities, in order to introduce sustainability in selected areas, such as electric vehicles, or circular constructions.[538]

8. Target 12.8 By 2030, ensure that people everywhere have the relevant information and awareness for sustainable development and lifestyles in harmony with nature

a) Sources of target

The UN SDGs formulate a global vision for a sustainable future of human existence on the Earth. It has long been understood that a profound transformation in human thinking and behaviour is a precondition for the SDGs' success. This transformation can be facilitated through efforts to secure public access to relevant information, to increase awareness of SD, and to secure the proliferation of sustainability topics throughout education at all levels. As Irina Bokova, former Director-General of UNESCO stated in 2012, '[e]ducation is the most powerful path to sustainability. Economic and technological solutions, political regulations or financial incentives are not enough. We need a fundamental change in the way we think and act.'[539] In other words, success of the SDGs will largely depend on the understanding, support, and action of individuals; individuals must become 'sustainability change-makers'.[540] The focus on the importance of SD) permeates the SDGs, and is expressly noted in targets 4.7,[541] 12.8, and 13.3.[542] In respect to SDG 12, the relevance is obvious. Consumption patterns depend on individuals' behaviour, and it is this behaviour that needs to be influenced. In that context, consumer law becomes relevant as a possible tool for steering consumer behaviour through securing adequate information and providing other incentives.

The main roots of target 12.8 can be found in Agenda 21—Chapter 36, 'Promoting education, public awareness and training'.[543] Agenda 21 set forth a reorientation of education towards SD as it recognized the critical role of education for 'promoting sustainable development and improving the capacity of the people to address environment and

---

[536] Case C-513/99 *Concordia Bus* [2002] ECR I-7213; Case C-448/01 *EVN and Wienstrom* [2003] ECR I-14527; Case C-368/10 *Commission v Kingdom of the Netherlands* [2012] ECR I-284.

[537] Andhov and others (n 475) 38.

[538] Big Buyers for Climate and Environment <https://bigbuyers.eu/> accessed 29 October 2021.

[539] UNESCO, 'Shaping the Future We Want, UN Decade of Education for Sustainable Development' (2005–2014) final report 16 <https://sustainabledevelopment.un.org/index.php?page=view&type=400&nr=1682&menu=35>.

[540] Nordic report (n 168) 30.

[541] Chapter 4 on SDG 4, this book.

[542] Chapter 13 on SDG 13, this book.

[543] Agenda 21 (n 363) ch 36.

922   SDG 12

development issues'.[544] The overarching idea is to influence peoples' environmental and ethical awareness, values, attitudes, skills, and behaviour through education, awareness, and training, and to motivate public participation in decision-making.[545] This was also reflected in all three conventions adopted in 1992 in Rio: the UNFCCC,[546] the UN CBD,[547] and the UN Convention to Combat Desertification.[548]

Following Agenda 21, the UN declared the period between 2005 and 2014 as the United Nations Decade of Education for Sustainable Development (DESD) and designated UNESCO as the agency leading the policy area.[549] During the DESD many efforts and events aimed at:

1. Improving access and retention in quality basic education.
2. Reorienting existing educational programmes to address sustainability.
3. Increasing public understanding and awareness of sustainability.
4. Providing training to advance sustainability across all sectors.[550]

After completing the DESD,[551] UNESCO moved on to the implementation of the Global Action Programme (GAP) on ESD (2015–2019), aimed at scaling-up already initiated ESD efforts.[552] The GAP has been followed by the Education for Sustainable Development: Towards achieving the SDGs (ESD for 2030) framework.[553] The ESD for 2030 continues with five GAP Priority Action Areas: (i) advancing policy, (ii) transforming learning and training environments, (iii) building capacities of educators and trainers, (iv) mobilizing youth, and (v) accelerating sustainable solutions at local level.[554]

SDG 12 does not figure centrally in the ESD for 2030. The framework is most closely connected to SDG 4 (Education).[555,556] It is of course a natural connection, but it is well recognized that education, awareness, and access to information as subsumed under target 12.8 are 'enabler[s] for the successful achievement of other SDG targets'.[557] However, it is also recognized that tools highlighted in target 12.8 will need to

---

[544] ibid para 36.3.

[545] ibid para 36.3.

[546] UNFCCC (n 249) art 6.

[547] CBD (n 250) art 13.

[548] United Nations Convention to Combat Desertification in those Countries Experiencing Serious Drought and/or Desertification, Particularly in Africa (adopted 17 June 1994, in force 26 December 1996) 1954 UNTS 3, arts 19 and 8.

[549] UNGA, 'United Nations Decade of Education for Sustainable Development' (20 December 2002) A/RES/57/254.

[550] UNESCO, 'United Nations Decade of Education for Sustainable Development (2005–2014): International Implementation Scheme' (2005) ED/DESD/2005/PI/01.

[551] UNESCO, 'Shaping the Future We Want' (n 539).

[552] UNESCO, 'Integrated Comprehensive Strategy for Category 2 Institutes and Centres Under the Auspices of UNESCO' (November 2013) 37 C/Resolution 93.

[553] UNESCO, 'Framework for the Implementation of Education for Sustainable Development (ESD) Beyond 2019' (3 September 2019) 40 C/23.

[554] ibid annex II, para 5.10.

[555] ibid annex I, para 6.

[556] Chapter 4 on SDG 4, this book.

[557] Gardetti and Muthu (n 143) 4.

be combined with other tools, such as appropriate pricing and adequate regulation to facilitate a change in current consumption patterns.[558]

As for the wording of target 12.8, it presents an exception within SDG 12 to an otherwise prevalent trend of diluting originally proposed wording of the targets throughout negotiations. While other targets became vaguer during the negotiation process, target 12.8 stepped up the ambition, and finally the target seeks to 'ensure' access to information and awareness rather than 'redouble efforts' in these areas as was earlier proposed.[559]

While target 12.8 (together with target 4.7) is sometimes understood as particularly aimed at younger generations,[560] it should not be limited to this target group. The target aims at increasing access to information and awareness for SD broadly across the general public, as it is important that a shift towards sustainable consumption and generally sustainable behaviour at individual level is initiated as soon as possible, not awaiting the time when the current youth sit in the decision-making chairs.

It is also important to acknowledge other objectives within target 12.8 besides education. Particularly, it is important to secure a broad access to information, as it helps to overcome inequalities and creates a basis for fortification of the support to the sustainability agenda.[561]

b) Empirical analysis

Using such broad concepts as 'relevant information' and 'lifestyles in harmony with nature' in the wording of the target makes it difficult to measure progress towards target 12.8. There is one associated indicator (12.8.1), which is classified is a Tier II indicator and is a common indicator measuring progress towards targets 4.7, 12.8, and 13.3. The indicator reads as follows: 'Extent to which (i) global citizenship education and (ii) education for sustainable development are mainstreamed in (a) national education policies; (b) curricula; (c) teacher education; and (d) student assessment.'[562] The focus is clear—to monitor whether and to what extent ESD and global citizenship education (GCED) are integrated in all aspects of countries' education systems.[563] Data are gathered through the use of the questionnaire for the monitoring of the implementation of the 1974 Recommendation concerning Education for International Understanding, Co-operation and Peace and Education relating to Human Rights and Fundamental Freedoms.[564] This Recommendation naturally does not include a direct reference to UN SDGs as it was adopted long before the SDGs' inception, but is used because it

---

[558] OWG (n 111) para 163.

[559] Gasper and others (n 5) 8.

[560] Nordic report (n 168) 30.

[561] Independent Group of Scientists appointed by the Secretary-General, 'Global Sustainable Development Report 2019: The Future is Now—Science for Achieving Sustainable Development' (United Nations 2019) p. 97 <https://sustainabledevelopment.un.org/content/documents/24797GSDR_report_2019.pdf> accessed 29 October 2021.

[562] SDG Indicators metadata repository, 'Metadata Sheet for Indicator 12.8.1' <https://unstats.un.org/sdgs/metadata/> accessed 25 October 2021 (Metadata 12.8.1).

[563] ibid section 4.a.

[564] UNESCO, 'Records of the General Conference' (18th session, Paris, 17 October to 23 November 1974), volume 1: Resolutions.

924 SDG 12

covers most of the topics seen in targets 4.7, 18.8, and 13.3, and works with a well-established formal mechanism of quadrennial reporting. UNESCO, that administers the Recommendation, then also serves as the custodian of target 12.8. The basis for calculation of the score for indicator 12.8.1 is based on self-reporting by national governments, which is provided every four years. Data for 2017–2020 are yet to be published,[565] although some countries, such as Germany, already have provided the data, detailed methodological considerations, and score.[566] UNESCO will review country responses for consistency and credibility.[567]

The first question in the questionnaire relates directly to law, as it reads: 'Please indicate which GCED and ESD themes are covered in national or sub-national laws, legislation or legal frameworks on education.'[568] The eight themes, which permeate the whole questionnaire, are cultural diversity and tolerance, gender equality, human rights, peace and non-violence, climate change, environmental sustainability, human survival and well-being, and SCP. Evidently, it is the last theme that is especially relevant to SDG 12. However, it is also an extremely broad theme, and thus a positive answer here will not lead to an adequate understanding of whether and to what extent SCP are included in legal frameworks on education. For example, California states in respect of indicator 12.8.1:

> To receive a high school diploma, the State-mandated graduation course requirements include three years of social science education, including world history, culture, and geography. The State Board of Education adopted the History-Social Science Framework for public education. The grade ten curriculum on 'World History, Culture, and Geography: The Modern World' includes a standard that students 'should be able to identify a range of issues—including sustainable development—that could be described as 'transnational' in scope.'[569]

While this is certainly a step in the right direction, this statement does not ensure that target 12.8 is in fact achieved in the state.

Moreover, not only is indicator 12.8.1 based on self-reporting, but data are also scarce. During the last reporting period (2020–2021), seventy-four countries provided reports on the implementation of the 1974 Recommendation concerning Education for International Understanding, Co-operation and Peace and Education relating to Human Rights and Fundamental Freedoms. These seventy-four countries included thirty-two countries from Europe and Northern America.[570] Developing countries and regions are thus under-represented and data are missing.

Moreover, while it is essential that structural changes in national educational programs are made in order to educate students in ESD and GCED, it seems that the

---

[565] The next reporting cycle covers the period 2021–2024.
[566] Statistiches Bundesamt, 'Indicator 12.8.1' <https://sdg-indikatoren.de/en/12-8-1/> accessed 25 October 2021.
[567] Metadata 12.8.1 (n 562) section 4.j.
[568] Metadata 12.8.1 (n 562).
[569] Los Angeles SDGs, 'Indicator 12.8.1' <https://sdgdata.lamayor.org/12-8-1/> accessed 25 October 2021.
[570] Metadata 12.8.1 (n 562) section 5.

indicator is too narrow and does not capture other educational streams (eg provided by cultural or industrial institutions), awareness-raising efforts, and the level of access to relevant information.

c) Implementation efforts at domestic/international level

Despite the troubles with measuring the progress towards target 12.8, implementation efforts are blossoming in many jurisdictions and across various levels of regulation yet it is not always certain that the efforts are effective.[571]

At the international law level, we see that provisions on cooperation on ESD and GCED are implemented in most international conventions in the area of environmental law. For example, article 12 of the Paris Agreement states: 'Parties shall cooperate in taking measures, as appropriate, to enhance climate change education, training, public awareness, public participation and public access to information, recognizing the importance of these steps with respect to enhancing actions under this Agreement.' In some conventions, the provision is more detailed;[572] in others, focus is more on one part, such as access to information.[573] These conventions enjoy wide participation, several of them even global participation. Access to environmental information is also prominently covered in the Aarhus Convention adopted by the United Nations Economic Commission for Europe and the associated Kyiv Protocol.[574] While the scope of the Aarhus Convention is geographically limited, the decisions of its compliance committee[575] can serve as a reference point and inspiration to other nations in respect to the implementation of the SDG targets on access to information, public participation, and access to justice in environmental decision-making.[576]

The international regulatory level delivers on target 12.8 not only through binding international conventions but there is also a plenty of voluntary initiatives. The United Nations-supported initiative Principles for Responsible Management Education (PRME) can be mentioned as an example. The initiative, founded in 2007, engages business and management schools 'to ensure they provide future leaders with the skills needed to balance economic and sustainability goals'.[577] Nowadays, PRME promotes SDGs and uses them as a framework for their work.[578]

---

[571] UNESCO (n 553) annex II, para 4.9.

[572] For example, UNFCCC (n 249) art 6.

[573] For example, Rotterdam Convention (n 289) art 15(2); Stockholm Convention (n 291) art 10(2).

[574] Convention on Access to Information, Public Participation in Decision-making and Access to Justice in Environmental Matters (adopted 25 June 1998, in force 30 October 2001) 2161 UNTS, p 447 (Aarhus Convention); Kyiv Protocol (n 189).

[575] A Andrusevych and S Kern (eds), *Case Law of the Aarhus Convention Compliance Committee (2004– 2014)* (3rd edn, RACSE 2016).

[576] M Gehring and others, 'SDG 12 on Ensuring Sustainable Consumption and Production Patterns: Contributions of International Law, Policy and Governance' (UNEP and Centre for International Sustainable Development Law, Issue Brief 2016) p 6 <https://www.researchgate.net/publication/333610516_SDG_12_on_Ensuring_Sustainable_Consumption_and_Production_Patterns_Contributions_of_International_Law_Policy_and_Governance> accessed 29 October 2021.

[577] Principles for Responsible Management Education, 'What is PRME?' <https://www.unprme.org/about> accessed 25 October 2021.

[578] Principles for Responsible Management Education, 'The SDGs' <https://www.unprme.org/the-sdgs> accessed 25 October 2021.

926   SDG 12

Possibly more closely connected with the topic of SCP are different initiatives promoting companies' SDG reporting, product labelling, and awareness-raising events and activities. Companies' SDG reporting, as discussed under target 12.6, promotes transparency, data collection, and public access to sustainability related information. In this sense target 12.6 can be seen as an enabler of target 12.8, while target 12.8 can be seen as an enabler of the whole SDG 12 as well as other SDGs.

Social and environmental product labelling is a powerful tool in shifting production and consumption towards sustainability. There is an abundance of product labels globally.[579] The amount of product labelling schemes, ranging from international to local, and from publicly to privately driven, may help consumers to make more responsible choices, but may also create confusion and distrust.[580] Some organizations aim to assist consumers in understanding the labelling industry.[581] It is important to note, however, that product labelling does not only target consumers but also influences the production side of products' lifecycle, especially when standards and regulations connected to a particular label are strict and enforced. Production is also influenced positively by an increased focus on transparency and traceability,[582] which provides the relevant information to the consumers so that they can adjust their lifestyles in order to be in harmony with nature.[583] Standards for transparency and traceability have been developed at all levels, but especially by the industry.[584]

Cooperation among states aiming at achieving target 12.8, coordinating efforts, and sharing experience, thrives at regional level. For example, the European Nordic countries stipulate the intention to 'prepare a Nordic guideline on how to mainstream education for SCP/sustainable development goals into national education policies and curricula, based on good international and Nordic practices'.[585]

Last but not least, target 12.8 resonates strongly with cultural institutions globally. Many of them are active ambassadors of SDGs in general and target 12.8 (and targets 4.7 and 13.3) in particular. The initiative 'Adapting Our Culture: A Toolkit for Cultural Organisations Planning for a Climate Changed Future' or chapter 13 of the 'Sustainable Development Guide' prepared by the Canadian Museums Association can be named as examples here.[586] The latter providing concrete guidance for museums on selecting the

---

[579] OECD, 'Environmental labelling and information schemes Policy Perspectives' (May 2016) <https://www.oecd.org/env/labelling-and-information-schemes.htm> accessed 25 October 2021.

[580] Jason Czarnezki and others, 'Creating Order Amidst Food Eco-Label Chaos' (2015) 25 Duke Environmental Law & Policy Forum 281.

[581] Green Choices <https://www.greenerchoices.org> accessed 25 October 2021.

[582] V Kumar and others, 'Developing a Framework for Traceability Implementation in the Textile Supply Chain' (2017) 5(2) Systems.

[583] NP Carrone, 'Traceability and Transparency: A Way Forward for SDG 12 in the Textile and Clothing Industry' in Gardetti and Muthu (n 143) 4.

[584] On the interconnection between traceability and product labelling see, eg, United Nations, 'UNDP Goodwill Ambassador Michelle Yeoh follows the sustainable fashion trail' (UN, 6 August 2018) <https://www.un.org/sustainabledevelopment/blog/2018/08/undp-goodwill-ambassador-michelle-yeoh-follows-the-sustainable-fashion-trail/> accessed 25 October 2021.

[585] Nordic report (n 168) 39.

[586] C Patterson and others, 'Adapting Our Culture: A Toolkit for Cultural Organisations Planning for a Climate Changed Future. Cultural Adaptations' (Cultural Adaptations 2021) <https://www.culturaladaptations.com/news/adapting-our-culture-toolkit-launched/> accessed 25 October 2021; Canadian Museums Association, 'Sustainable Development Guide' (2015) <https://www.museums.ca/client/document/documents.html?categoryId=361> accessed 25 October 2021.

best communication strategy for effective and integrated communication towards the public about SD.[587] However, other institutions, such as zoos, concert halls, sport clubs etc can also effectively convey the messages of the SDGs to the public.[588]

d) Critique

While education and access to relevant information are necessary steps in facilitating the shift in individuals' consumption patterns towards more sustainable ones, it might be naïve and overly optimistic to rely only on these two tools. While education certainly moulds individual choices,[589] other tools and incentives are needed to make this shift happen. Next to providing information, there is specifically a need to redirect consumers' preferences towards recyclability, durability, and local production from their current focus on price, convenience, and ease of use.[590]

To make such a transition, both behavioural and regulatory changes are required. A standard approach to behavioural change is to provide information; people are rational and they can make the right decisions, and when they do not make the right decisions they need information that will help them decide better.[591] But research in behavioural economics has shown that this is not the correct approach.[592] Yet, governments and institutions have acted on the same assumption of the information paradigm for years, and the SDGs follow this path. This is obvious for example in the EU consumer law field, which is largely based on the information policy, presuming that an average consumer is 'reasonably well-informed and reasonably observant and circumspect'.[593] Providing comprehensive information is considered a sufficient basis for making a rational decision by consumers, especially if consumers are given the time to process it.[594] Although this information basis of EU consumer law has long been criticized by legal scholars,[595] providing still more information to consumers forms the centrepiece of the latest consumer policy.[596] Yet, glimpses of change in the approach of governments, institutions, and law have started to appear.[597] Major changes in consumer law will be necessary to ensure achievement of SDG 12. These include a thorough rethinking of the

---

[587] Canadian Museums Association, 'Sustainable Development Guide' (2015), ch 13 <https://www.museums.ca/document/1153/Chapter_13.pdf> accessed 25 October 2021.

[588] See, eg Zoo de Granby, 'The Zoo and Sustainable Development' <https://zoodegranby.com/en/sustainable-development> accessed 25 October 2021.

[589] Spotlight on SD (n 142) 97.

[590] n 174.

[591] GS Becker, *The Economic Approach to Human Behavior* (University of Chicago Press 1976).

[592] D Ariely, *Predictably Irrational: The Hidden Forces That Shape Our Decisions* (HarperCollins 2008).

[593] Case C–216/96 *Gut Springenheide GmbH v Oberkreisdirektor des Kreises Steinfurt* [1998] ECR I–4657.

[594] C Twigg-Flesner and others, 'Protecting Rational Choice: Information and the Right of Withdrawal' in Gt Howells and others (eds), *Handbook of Research on International Consumer Law* (2nd edn, Edward Elgar Publishing 2018).

[595] For example, G Howells, 'The Potential and Limits of Consumer Empowerment through Information' (2005) 32(3) Journal of Law and Society 349; O Ben-Shahar, 'The Myth of the "Opportunity to Read" in Contract Law' (2009) 5(1) European Review of Contract Law 1; GG Howells, and others, *Rethinking EU Consumer Law* (Routledge 2018).

[596] Communication from the Commission to the European Parliament and the Council, New Consumer Agenda, 'Strengthening Consumer Resilience for Sustainable Recovery' COM(2020) 696, 13 November 2020.

[597] For example, LE Europe, VVA Europe, Ipsos, ConPolicy, Trinomics, 'Behavioural Study on Consumers' Engagement in the Circular Economy Final Report' (European Commission Directorate-General for Justice and

928   SDG 12

long-established central concepts, such as that of the 'average consumer' in the EU, and making deliberate use of other than information tools, such as pricing policy, repair guarantees, and regulatory interventions to prevent early obsolescence. This work has already started[598] but much remains to be done.

Therefore, while securing access to relevant information and awareness of sustainability development to all are definitely focal enablers of SDGs, it might have been better to leave this to target 4.7 and place more focus on production and consumption in target 12.8. The choices made in target 12.8 and especially in indicator 12.8.1 capture only a fraction of the changes needed as well as the already initiated efforts. Overall, it can be said that indicator 12.8.1 measures intentions rather than results.

Finally, it should be noted that the content of curricula, information provided to public, and awareness-raising campaigns will need to stay flexible, rather than rigidly legislated for, to account for the dynamic changes in the world and our knowledge about it. In other words, '[w]hat is considered as sustainable production and consumption behaviour today might not be sustainable tomorrow'.[599] Sustainability is characterized by complexity and scientific uncertainty, and this should be reflected in education and information provided to the citizens.

9. Target 12.a Support developing countries to strengthen their scientific and technological capacity to move towards more sustainable patterns of consumption and production

a) Sources of target

Target 12.a deals with the support for developing countries to strengthen their scientific and technological capacity to move towards more SCP patterns. While being a target on its own, target 12.a constitutes, with targets 12.b and 12.c, a trio of targets which establish means of implementation for other SDGs.[600]

The understanding and measurement of target 12.a has evolved since the adoption of SDGs. One of the explanations of how to understand the target is from the research and development standpoint, encouraging developed countries to provide help to developing countries in accessing technological solutions with an added value to environment, that is, technologies which are polluting less, using resources in a more

---

Consumers October 2018) <https://ec.europa.eu/info/sites/default/files/ec_circular_economy_final_report_0.pdf> accessed 29 October 2021; M Hallsworth and others, 'Behavioural Government Using Behavioural Science to Improve How Governments Make Decisions' (The Behavioural Insights Team 2018).

[598] For example, H Schebesta and K Purnhagen, 'The Behaviour of the Average Consumer: A Little Less Normativity and a Little More Reality in the Court's Case Law? Reflections on Teekanne' (2016) 41(4) European Law Review 590; P Siciliani and others, *Consumer Theories of Harm: An Economic Approach to Consumer Law Enforcement and Policy Making* (Bloomsbury Publishing 2019).
[599] Nordic report (n 168) 30.
[600] Guevara and Julián (n 386) 12.

sustainable manner, recycle more, etc.[601] Such technologies are commonly referred to as environmentally sound technologies (ESTs).[602]

The Rio Summit in 1992 emphasized the need for ESTs.[603] Agenda 21 stressed the importance of distribution of ESTs and scientific knowledge across the borders, accentuating the significance of disseminating knowledge to developing countries. In its chapter 34 it states that '[n]ew and efficient technologies will be essential to increase the capabilities, in particular of developing countries, to achieve sustainable development, sustain the world's economy, protect the environment, and alleviate poverty and human suffering'.[604] The majority of global expenditure on research and development is still in hands of countries such as the United States, China, Japan, Germany, South Korea, France, and United Kingdom.[605] While in 2020 the United States spent 3.45 per cent of its GDP on research and development, Mexico spent on research and development only around 0.3 per cent of its GDP.[606] A considerable barrier for developing countries to join this 'elite club' are then especially existing intellectual property rights in a form of patents and trademarks.[607] This further exacerbates the technological divide between developed and developing countries.

While developed countries are at the front of the technological and scientific development, the ICESCR in its article 15(1)(b) recognizes the right of everyone to 'enjoy the benefits of science progress and its applications'.[608] Delving deeper into the wording of the target, we can observe that it tries to reduce existing inequalities. It centres around the idea of 'leapfrogging', which suggests that developed countries should help developing countries skip over often 'dirty' intermediate phases of development (such as the use of unsustainable fossil fuels) through sharing of scientific knowledge and technology.[609] In this way, developing countries can enjoy the progress sooner and use it for ensuring more sustainable processes. What kind of help, whether of monetary or another nature, is not further specified, yet the experience made it clear that a sole access to technological development does not always close the gap between developed and developing countries. The underlying reason is that apart from the necessary technologic

---

[601] See para 34.1 Agenda 21 (n 363) 21.5.

[602] R Kumar and others, 'Environmentally Sound Technologies for Sustainability and Climate Change' in Filho and others (eds) (n 207) 414.

[603] Agenda 21 (n 363) ch 34 (Transfer of Environmentally Sound Technology, Cooperation and Capacity-Building).

[604] Agenda 21 (n 363).

[605] Congressional Research Service, 'Global Research and Development Expenditures: Fact Sheet' (R44283, updated 27 September 2021) <https://sgp.fas.org/crs/misc/R44283.pdf > accessed 27 October 2021; UNESCO Institute for Statistics (UIS), 'How much does you country invest in R&D?' <http://uis.unesco.org/apps/visualisati ons/research-and-development-spending/> accessed 27 October 2021.

[606] OECD, 'Gross domestic spending on R&D' <https://data.oecd.org/rd/gross-domestic-spending-on-r-d.htm> accessed 28 November 2022.

[607] R Kumar and others, 'Environmentally Sound Technologies for Sustainability and Climate Change' in Filho and others (eds) (n 207) 416–17. For more about barriers to technology transfer see K Bouwer, 'Insights for Climate Technology Transfer from International Environmental and Human Rights Law' (2018) 23 (1) Journal of Intellectual Property Rights 7, 8–9.

[608] ICESCR (n 60) art 15.1.b.

[609] UN, 'World Economic and Social Survey 2018 Frontier Technologies for Sustainable Development' (UN Department of Economic and Social Affairs, 2018) E/2018/50/Rev.1 ST/ESA/370, p 4.

infrastructure, technological transfer in most cases requires highly educated human resources, with a couple of exceptions, such as transfer of solar energy.[610]

SDGs are addressed to all countries in the world, regardless of their developmental position. Yet target 12.a, together with target 12.1, place developing countries in the limelight, as their wording indirectly refers to the CBDR principle.[611] Target 12.a then promotes support towards developing countries, but does not mention an overall need of the worldwide implementation of the ESTs.[612] CBDR has a long history going back to the Vienna Convention for the Protection of the Ozone Layer,[613] and the Rio Declaration,[614] and is widely known for its former use in the Kyoto Protocol.[615] The objective of the CBDR principle reflects a very different situation of developed and developing countries. The developed countries' historical responsibility obliges them to provide technological assistance to developing states, the developing countries then pledge to be part of the climate mitigation/adaptation within their reduced capacities.[616]

Building upon the CBDR principle, technological transfer has played a great role in the advancement of mitigation and adaptation efforts in the field of climate change. Technology transfer has become a core instrument as early as during negotiations of the UNFCCC where, in line with the CBDR principle, parties affirmed that developed countries should assist developing countries in innovating and transferring ESTs. UNFCCC in its article 4 stated that states should '[p]romote and cooperate in the development, application and diffusion, including transfer, of technologies, practices and processes that control, reduce or prevent anthropogenic emissions of greenhouse gases'.[617] Building on this framework, PA in its article 10, paragraph 4 establishes technology framework facilitating technology transfer.[618]

b) Empirical analysis

As the below described history of development of indicator 12.a.1 shows, it is extremely difficult to measure how much support is given to developing countries to strengthen their scientific and technological capacity. Indicator 12.a.1 has changed its focus twice to date. The first indicator's objective was to provide a 'number of green patent applications'.[619] This was soon criticized by a number of countries. Some, such as Mexico or the United States, commented on the lack of methodology and definition of the 'green

---

[610] ibid.

[611] See above text to target 12.1.

[612] SDG Indicators metadata repository, 'Metadata Sheet for Indicator 12.a.1' <https://unstats.un.org/sdgs/metadata/> accessed 3 July 2021 (Metadata 12.a.1).

[613] Vienna Convention (n 123) Preamble, para 3.

[614] Rio Declaration (n 124) principle 7.

[615] Kyoto Protocol to the United Nations Framework Convention on Climate Change (adopted 11 December 1997, in force 15 February 2005) 2303 UNTS 162 (Kyoto Protocol), art 3(1).

[616] Dupuy and Viñuales (n 125) 83 et seq.; See more about the CBDR principle in the Introduction to this chapter and the text on target 12.2.

[617] UNFCCC (n 249) art 4.

[618] The Paris Agreement (252) art 10(4).

[619] Metadata compilation from October 2015: <https://unstats.un.org/sdgs/files/Metadata%20Compilation%20for%20SDG%20Indicators%2023%20October%202015%20Update.pdf> accessed 28 October 2021.

patent'.[620] Others, for instance Ecuador, pointed at the fact that there is no relationship between the indicator and the target, and proposed eliminating the indicator.[621] Overall, countries proposed multiple versions of how the target could be measured. For example, Canada's proposal was 'total research and development expenditures' and Colombia suggested 'resources or number of technical cooperation projects to developing countries'.[622] Finally, after a flood of critique, the Inter-agency and Expert Group on SDG Indicators (IAEG-SDG) agreed on the second version of the indicator: '[a]mount of support to developing countries on research and development for sustainable consumption and production and environmentally sound technologies'.[623] However, this version did not have time to settle down and was replaced by the current and latest version.

Indicator 12.a.1, as it stands now, requires measurement of '[i]nstalled renewable energy-generating capacity in developing countries (in watts per capita)'[624] and is guarded by the custodianship of the International Renewable Energy Agency (IRENA). Instead of building upon the second version of the indicator through providing deeper understanding of the terminology and explaining what 'amount of support' means, the indicator took an unexpected step back instead. As a result, this indicator measures only a narrow fragment of what should be achieved by target 12.a. and does not sufficiently cover the wide range of possible types of support developing countries can be given. As a result, it narrow-mindedly fixes its attention to projects related to production of energy in a sustainable way. The substance and goal of target 12.a is therefore reduced to a core minimum.

We learnt in the introductory remarks that historical circumstances of SDG 12 adoption revolved around whether it should be a separate goal or embedded within other SDGs.[625] We have already expressed our concerns related to the repetitive character of some of the SDG 12 targets and circular argumentation in the sub-chapter on SDG 12.1.[626] In case of SDG 12.a, we have to point at a strong resemblance to target 17.7 which intends to '[p]romote the development, transfer, dissemination and diffusion of environmentally sound technologies to developing countries on favourable terms, including on concessional and preferential terms, as mutually agreed'.[627] Reading thoroughly through 17.7, speculations about the necessity of the 12.a target might arise. What is even more astounding, the current 12.a.1 indicator is identical to indicator 7.1.b. Target 7.1 aims to '[b]y 2030, expand infrastructure and upgrade technology for supplying modern and

---

[620] IAEG 2nd meeting 26 – 28 October 2015 Bangkok, 'Results of Questionnaire on Summary of Comments by IAEG Members (updated 22 Oct 2015)' <https://unstats.un.org/sdgs/meetings/iaeg-sdgs-meeting-02/> accessed 28 October 2021.

[621] ibid.

[622] ibid.

[623] Metadata compilation from March 2016 <https://unstats.un.org/sdgs/files/metadata-compilation/Metadata-Goal-12.pdf> accessed 28 October 2021.

[624] Metadata 12.a.1 (n 612).

[625] See Introduction to this chapter.

[626] See more in part on target 12.1.

[627] SDG Indicators metadata repository, 'Metadata Sheet for Indicator 17.7.1' <https://unstats.un.org/sdgs/metadata/> accessed 9 February 2021.

932   SDG 12

sustainable energy services for all in developing countries, in particular least developed countries, small island developing States and landlocked developing countries, in accordance with their respective programmes of support'. A glance reveals that indicator 7.1.b is a better fit for target 7.1 than indicator 12.a.1 is for target 12.a. Looking at the indicator 12.a.1 through critical lenses, the adoption of the same indicator for targets 12.a.1 and 7.1.b seems like a compromise, which resulted in measuring something that does not comprehensibly mirror the orientation of target 12.a. The importance of switching developing countries towards renewable energies is incontestable, but it remains questionable how strong is the relationship between the target and the current indicator.

c) Implementation efforts at domestic/international level

One of the projects oriented at supporting the renewable technologies in developing countries operates under the patronage of IRENA and Abu Dhabi Fund for Development (ADFD), providing low-cost loans to developing countries, in order to advance renewable energy.[628] Yet countries have not settled for projects oriented only at renewable energy. Even though the trajectory of the target has changed, countries still go beyond what is currently measured, that is, installed renewable energy-generating capacity in developing countries (in watts per capita). Denmark, for example, provided support for the Global Green Growth Forum, which is a sustainable resource management in Bolivia.[629] This shows countries' proactivity, as they gather momentum and act beyond what is required in the complex web of SDGs.

d) Critique

Even though the alignment of target 12.a and its indicator is arguable, SDG Report 2021 shows some improvement in the field of electricity capacity installations. In 2018 the number of new renewable electricity capacities installed in developing countries boomed,[630] and 2020 reported even further progress.[631] Nevertheless, as Bengtsson and colleagues pinpoint, even with technological progress, improvement of the state of the environment might not follow.[632] As an example, we can take developed countries, who often have capacities and access to the best ESTs, yet their delivery upon target SDG 12 is one of the worst in the world.[633] Renewable energies are then connected with a number of negative impacts, such as generation of waste. IRENA's data show, for instance, that 'the amount of solar panel waste alone is projected to be 78 million metric tons in 30 years'.[634]

---

[628] IRENA and ADFD, 'Advancing Renewables in Developing Countries Progress of Projects Supported through the IRENA/ADFD Project Facility' (January 2019) <https://www.irena.org/-/media/Files/IRENA/Agency/Publication/2019/Jan/IRENA_ADFD_Advancing_renewables_2019.pdf> accessed 27 October 2021.

[629] Nordic report (n 168) 32; Ministry of Foreign Affairs of Denmark, 'Global Green Growth Forum (3GF)' <https://um.dk/en/foreign-policy/global-green-growth-forum/> accessed 28 October 2021.

[630] UN, 'The Sustainable Development Goals Report 2021' (2021) 51.

[631] ibid.

[632] Bengtsson and others (n 100) 1541.

[633] Bengtsson and others (n 100) 1540–41.

[634] IRENA, 'End-of-life Management Solar Photovoltaic Panels' (June 2016) 12 <https://www.irena.org/-/media/Files/IRENA/Agency/Publication/2016/IRENA_IEAPVPS_End-of-Life_Solar_PV_Panels_2016.pdf> accessed 27 October 2021.

10. Target 12.b Develop and implement tools to monitor sustainable development impacts for sustainable tourism that creates jobs and promotes local culture and products

a) Sources of target

In 2019, tourism contributed to global GDP by 10.4 per cent.[635] The COVID-19 crisis significantly affected tourism industry, which in 2020 accounted for only 5.5 per cent of global GDP.[636] Despite these extreme losses, the position of global tourism is projected to rebound in terms of the number of international arrivals within two-and-a-half to four years.[637] Pre-COVID-19 estimations talked about international tourist arrivals rising up to 1.8 billion annually by 2030.[638] Overall, travel and tourism currently accounts for 8.9 per cent of global employment, making many especially small and developing countries dependant on it.[639] Therefore, addressing the damaging effects of tourism on global environment and communities remains a number one priority.

With active tourism, the economy is thriving and certain positive aspects are reported with regards to conservation and development. For instance, in a nature-based tourism model some of the income from the tourism industry is used for management of natural resources in the area.[640] Nevertheless, the tourism industry is in the majority of cases impacting the environment and local communities in an undesirable way. First of all, the boom of mass tourism takes its toll in the form of biodiversity loss, waste generation, high energy use, overall depletion of natural resources, and noise pollution.[641] Moreover, thanks to the raising number of international travels, the transport-related carbon footprint of global tourism is estimated to be around 5 per cent of the global GHG emissions, endangering especially coastal areas vulnerable to climate change.[642] What is more, the ever-growing number of visitors in the most attractive destinations can lead to their overuse. Local areas damaged as a result of over-tourism make the global headlines.[643] This can be illustrated on the case of the Thailand's Maya Bay beach, which was closed in 2018, in order to ensure its natural conservation.[644] Thailand's

---

[635] World Travel & Tourism Council, 'Economic Impact 2021 Global Economic Impact & Trends 2021' (2021) 4 <https://wttc.org/Research/Economic-Impact> accessed 28 October 2021.

[636] ibid; see more on the problem of waste in text on targets 12.4 and 12.5.

[637] UNTWO, 'Impact Assessment of the Covid-19 Outbreak on International Tourism' <https://www.unwto.org/impact-assessment-of-the-covid-19-outbreak-on-international-tourism> accessed 26 November 2021.

[638] UNWTO, 'International Tourists to Hit 1.8 Billion by 2030' <https://www.unwto.org/archive/global/press-release/2011-10-11/international-tourists-hit-18-billion-2030> accessed 28 October 2021.

[639] World Travel & Tourism Council (n 635) 5.

[640] Such an approach is a principle of a so-called *ecotourism*, see more here: M Wood, 'Ecotourism: Principles, Practices and Policies for Sustainability' (1st edn, United Nations Environment Programme 2002); C Burgoyne and K Mearns, 'Sustainable Tourism/Ecotourism' in Filho and others (eds) (n 207) 818.

[641] S Gössling, 'Global Environmental Consequences of Tourism' (2002) 12 Global Environmental Change 283; UNWTO and UNDP, *Tourism and the SDGs—Journey to 2030* (December 2017) 30.

[642] UNWTO, International Transport Forum, 'Transport-related CO2 Emissions of the Tourism Sector Modelling Results' (UNWTO, December 2019) <https://www.e-unwto.org/doi/epdf/10.18111/9789284416660> accessed 28 October 2021.

[643] S Brewin, 'Tourist Trap: Is Tourism's Explosive Growth Hurting Countries?' (*IISD*, 30 July 2018) <https://www.iisd.org/articles/tourist-trap> accessed 26 October 2021.

[644] H Ellis-Petersen, 'Thailand Bay Made Famous by The Beach Closed Indefinitely', *The Guardian* (Bangkok, 3 October 2018) <https://www.theguardian.com/world/2018/oct/03/thailand-bay-made-famous-by-the-beach-closed-indefinitely> accessed 27 October 2021.

934   SDG 12

example is not the only one, Philippines, Rwanda, and Palau all had to adopt measures to protect their natural and/or cultural heritage.[645] Secondly, tourists' desire to access other cultures and experience them from close heavily influences local inhabitants, and can lead to an array of negative externalities, such as child labour, human trafficking, destruction of local cultures, sexual exploitation, and local over-dependence on tourism.[646]

This ambivalent position of the global tourism led to growing concerns among the scholarly public, and eventually to a development of a definition of sustainable tourism, one that would not lead to negative side-effects on local communities and natural environment.[647] United Nations World Tourism Organisation (UNWTO) interprets sustainable tourism as 'tourism that takes full account of its current and future economic, social and environmental impacts whilst addressing the needs of visitors, the industry, the environment and host communities ... It is a continuous process and requires constant monitoring of impacts.'[648]

As the tourism industry expanded in the twentieth century, international society had to deal with consequences of mass travel. In 1975, the UNWTO was founded. Its position changed over time and sustainable tourism became one of the points on its agenda. In the first five years of its existence, UNWTO adopted the Manila Declaration on World Tourism, which acknowledged that 'the great majority of them [states] have entrusted the World Tourism Organization with the task of ensuring the harmonious and sustained development of tourism.'[649] Just a couple of years later, in 1985, the Hague Declaration and the Tourism Bill of Rights and Tourist Code came to life, suggesting that '[i]n view of this intrinsic inter-relationship between tourism and environment, effective measures should be taken to ... b) [p]romote the integrated planning of tourism development on the basis of the concept of "sustainable development".'[650] In 1995, the first document dedicated solely to sustainable tourism, the Charter for Sustainable Tourism, came to life and proclaimed that '[t]ourism development shall be based on criteria of sustainability, which means that it must be ecologically bearable in the long term, as well as economically viable, and ethically and socially equitable for local communities.'[651] In 1999, the Global Code of Ethics for Tourism (GCET)[652] was drafted.

---

[645] S Brewin (n 643).

[646] See more on sustainable tourism in Chapter 8 of this book, on SDG 8. For more on social impacts on tourism, see G Wall and A Mathieson, *Tourism: Changes, Impacts, And Opportunities* (Pearson Education Limited 2006) ch 6.

[647] Burgoyne and Mearns (n 640) 818.

[648] UNWTO and UNEP, 'Making Tourism More Sustainable—A guide for policy makers' (2005) <https://www.e-unwto.org/doi/epdf/10.18111/9789284408214> accessed 26 October 2021.

[649] UNWTO, 'Manila Declaration on World Tourism' (27 September–10 October 1980) para 3 <https://www.univeur.org/cuebc/downloads/PDF%20carte/65.%20Manila.PDF> accessed 26 October 2021.

[650] UNWTO, 'Hague Declaration and the Tourism Bill of Rights and Tourist Code' (14 June 1985) A/6/11, principle III <https://www.e-unwto.org/doi/epdf/10.18111/unwtogad.1985.1.hp408706117j8366> accessed 26 October 2021.

[651] UNWTO, 'Charter for Sustainable Tourism' (27–28 April 1995) <https://www.e-unwto.org/doi/pdf/10.18111/unwtodeclarations.1995.05.04> accessed 26 October 2021.

[652] UNGA, 'Global Code of Ethics for Tourism' (21 December 2001) UN Doc A/RES/56/212 <https://webunwto.s3.eu-west-1.amazonaws.com/imported_images/37802/gcetbrochureglobalcodeen.pdf> accessed 26 October 2021.

GCET aims at providing guidance to the key players in the tourism industry, referring to human rights aspects of the tourism industry, among others a 'right to tourism'.[653] In light of ongoing SDGs negotiations, the Charter for Sustainable Tourism was reformulated in 2015 at the World Summit on Sustainable Tourism held in Vitoria-Gasteiz, so that it corroborates the development suggested by the UN.[654] After the adoption of SDGs, the 22nd General Assembly of the UNWTO in 2017 published the Chengdu Declaration on Tourism and the Sustainable Development Goals according to which '[n]ational governments together with local authorities and other relevant stakeholders should ensure the necessary changes in policies, business practices and behaviour in order to maximize the contribution of tourism to sustainable and inclusive development, in accordance with national laws and regulations'.[655] Overall, 2017 has become a noteworthy year as it was proclaimed International Year for Sustainable Tourism for Development,[656] which aims at supporting the change of policies and business practices, while UNWTO suggests that we can 'mak[e] tourism a catalyst for positive change'.[657] As the majority of above-mentioned documents were of a soft law nature, in 2019 the UNWTO General Assembly at its 23rd session in St Petersburg adopted the Framework Convention on Tourism and Ethics, the first binding instrument which addresses sexual exploitation of children in the context of tourism.[658] Nonetheless, its practical significance is currently questionable as to date only Indonesia has ratified the Convention.[659]

Agenda 21 was the first UN document explicitly referring to the concept of sustainable tourism. Building on this reference,[660] the 2002 World Summit on Sustainable Development held in Johannesburg required more space for sustainable tourism and eco-tourism.[661] Finally, the topic resonated most clearly through the 2012 World Conference on Sustainable Development. Its outcome document, 'The Future We Want', states that sustainable tourism contributes 'to the three dimensions of sustainable development, has close linkages to other sectors, and can create decent jobs and generate trade opportunities'[662] while underlying 'the importance of establishing,

---

[653] ibid art 7.

[654] UNTWO, 'World Charter for Sustainable Tourism +20' (Vitoria-Gasteiz, 26–27 November 2015) <https://www.oneplanetnetwork.org/sites/default/files/world_charter_for_sustainable_tourism_20.pdf> accessed 26 October 2021.

[655] UNWTO, 'Chengdu Declaration on Tourism and the Sustainable Development Goals' (13 September 2017) <https://www.e-unwto.org/doi/pdf/10.18111/unwtogad.2017.1.g51w645001604506> accessed 26 October 2021.

[656] UNGA, 'International year of Sustainable tourism for Development, 2017) (9 February 2016) UN Doc A/RES/70/193 UNWTO <https://www.unwto.org/tourism4development2017> accessed 30 October 2021.

[657] ibid.

[658] UNWTO GA, 'UNWTO Framework Convention on Tourism and Ethics' (San Petersburg, September 2019) A/RES/722(XXIII) <https://www.e-unwto.org/doi/pdf/10.18111/9789284421671> accessed 26 October 2021.

[659] UNWTO, 'Depositary of the Framework Convention on Tourism Ethic' <https://www.unwto.org/unwto-framework-convention-on-tourism-ethics> accessed 26 October 2021.

[660] Agenda 21 (n 363) paras 13.15 (b) (sustainable tourism), 7.20(e) (environmentally sound and culturally sensitive tourism), 11.20 (eco-tourism), 11.22(h) (eco-tourism).

[661] Johannesburg Plan of Implementation (n 109) ch IV, para 43.

[662] 'The Future We Want' (n 3) paras 130.

936 SDG 12

where necessary, appropriate guidelines and regulations in accordance with national priorities and legislation for promoting and supporting sustainable tourism'.[663]

It stems from the above that sustainable tourism penetrates multiple SDGs topics. While the focus here will be primarily on target 12.b, SDG 8.9 (promotion of sustainable tourism), SDG 13 (climate action), 11.4 (protection and safeguarding world's cultural and natural heritage), and SDG 14 (life below water) can be critically influenced by the good practices in the field of sustainable tourism. Its overarching character becomes clear through SDG 12.1 aiming at implementing 10YFP, where sustainable tourism represents one of the six areas of interest.[664]

The wording of the implementation of target 12.b requires states to '[d]evelop and implement tools to monitor sustainable development impacts for sustainable tourism that creates jobs and promotes local culture and products'.[665] As the Chengdu Declaration highlights: '[t]imely and systematic measurement of the economic, environmental and social impacts of tourism on destinations is of the essence in order to support evidence-based decision making and the effective use of the gathered information in designing informed policy decisions at all levels'.[666]

b) Empirical analysis

To deliver on target 12.b and the Chengdu Declaration, indicator 12.b.1 measures the 'implementation of standard accounting tools to monitor the economic and environmental aspects of tourism sustainability'.[667] To this end, it tracks the degree of implementation of two standard accounting tools, the Tourism Satellite Account (TSA) and the System of Environmental-Economic Accounting (SEEA).[668] These two tools allow for the understanding of tourism's impact from the economic and environmental perspectives. States report through a questionnaire sent by UNWTO on number of variables they were able to compile information for—see the list of variables organized in tables identified below. The score of the state varies from 0 (zero compliance) to 11 (full compliance).

TSA and SEEA tables:

- TSA Table 1 on inbound tourism expenditure
- TSA Table 2 on domestic tourism expenditure
- TSA Table 3 on outbound tourism expenditure

---

[663] ibid 131.

[664] UNEP, 'Paving the Way for Sustainable Consumption and Production: The Marrakesh Process Progress Report, Towards a 10 Year Framework of Programmes on Sustainable Consumption and Production' (2011) <https://sustainabledevelopment.un.org/content/documents/947Paving_the_way_final.pdf> accessed 26 October 2021.

[665] SDG Indicators metadata repository, 'Metadata Sheet for Indicator 12.b.1' <https://unstats.un.org/sdgs/metadata> accessed 3 July 2021 (Metadata 12.b.1), update March 2021.

[666] Chengdu Declaration (n 655) para 2.

[667] Metadata 12.b.1 (n 665).

[668] Metadata 12.b.1 (n 665); UN, Commission of the European Communities, Eurostat, UNWTO, OECD, 'Tourism Satellite Account: Recommended Methodological Framework 2008' (2010) ST/ESA/STAT/SER.F/80/Rev.1.; UN, E, FAO, IMF, OECD and WB, 'System of Environmental-Economic Accounting 2012— Central Framework' (2014) ST/ESA/STAT/Ser.F/109.

COMMENTARY   937

- TSA Table 4 on internal tourism expenditure
- TSA Table 5 on production accounts of tourism industries
- TSA Table 6 domestic supply and internal tourism consumption
- TSA Table 7 on employment in tourism industries
- SEEA table water flows
- SEEA table energy flows
- SEEA table GHG emissions
- SEEA table solid waste

The indicator described above was not the first version. The initial indicator focused on a '[n]umber of sustainable tourism strategies or policies and implemented action plans with agreed monitoring and evaluation tools'.[669] Soon after its adoption, the former indicator became criticized for, among other things, the lack of statistical infrastructure and vagueness of the terms used in its wording.[670]

Data on indicator 12.1.b are currently available for over 150 countries. The statistics show that, for instance, Australia and Mexico provided ten out of eleven tables in 2019. Canada provided seven tables and Netherlands six in the same year,[671] yet most states tables' value stands at 0.[672] The reason behind this might be a different level of implementation of TSA and SEEA across world regions, with low implementation especially reported in developing countries.[673]

Notably, the TSA and SEEA tables do not include any social considerations. This will hopefully be changed through the Measuring the Sustainability of Tourism (MST) programme, formulated by UNWTO together with United Nations Statistics Division, which aims to 'develop statistical framework for measuring tourism's role in sustainable development, including economic, environmental and social dimensions'.[674] MTS should become an international standard on tourism and include data of a social character such as health outcomes, education, community, and decent work.

c) Implementation efforts at domestic/international level

Despite the fact that the existing international treaty, which promotes sustainable tourism, is not widely ratified and accepted,[675] a number of international initiatives and partnerships were formed over the past couple of years in order to leverage progress

---

[669] Former indicators are available here: Metadata compilation from March 2016: <https://unstats.un.org/sdgs/files/metadata-compilation/Metadata-Goal-12.pdf> accessed 28 October 2021; Metadata compilation from October 2015: <https://unstats.un.org/sdgs/files/Metadata%20Compilation%20for%20SDG%20Indicators%2023%20October%202015%20Update.pdf> accessed 27 October 2021.

[670] The proposal for it replacement was presented at: IAEG 10th meeting 21 – 24 October 2019 Addis Ababa, 'Replacement Proposal of 12.b.1' <https://unstats.un.org/sdgs/meetings/iaeg-sdgs-meeting-10/> accessed 28 October 2021.

[671] See data for 2019: SDG Tracker, 'Sustainable Development Goal 12' <https://sdg-tracker.org/sustainable-consumption-production> accessed 27 October 2021.

[672] ibid; eg United Kingdom, United States, and Russia.

[673] Metadata 12.b.1 (n 665) section on limitations.

[674] UNWTO, 'Measuring the Sustainability of Tourism' <https://www.unwto.org/standards/measuring-sustainability-tourism> accessed 26 October 2021.

[675] See UNWTO, 'Depository of the Framework Convention on Tourism Ethic' <https://www.unwto.org/unwto-framework-convention-on-tourism-ethics> accessed 26 October 2021.

938   SDG 12

on SDG 12.b. One of them is the Global Tourism Plastics Initiative (GTPI).[676] Even though this project targets only a needle in a haystack of other issues caused by the global tourists' movement, it holds a significant importance. The recent reports show worrying facts that '[m]arine litter increases in the Mediterranean up to 40 per cent in the peak tourist season.'[677] GTPI's action plan therefore consists of three steps on the agenda: first, eliminate plastic waste; second, innovate the current practices; and lastly, circulate the plastics stemming from tourism.[678] The GTPI further shares information about plastic pollution, fosters procurement practices, and promotes innovation and communication between different actors.[679] Another noteworthy movement is a co-operation of Germany and the International Union for Conservation of Nature (IUCN) on tourism recovery after the COVID-19 crisis.[680] The partnership's focal point is to ensure that such transition is made in a sustainable manner. The partners believe that sustainable tourism can be used as a tool to ensure sustainable development in selected developing and emerging countries. Peru and Vietnam were chosen to participate in the pilot stage of this project, which later expected to scale up globally.[681] While the programme aims at strengthening the social position of locals dependant on tourism, it simultaneously intends to enhance the state of the environment in the area. This can be achieved by ensuring jobs for local people, contributing to environmental objectives, such as collection of marine plastic.[682] Further initiatives focusing on different aspects and areas can be found on Tourism4SDGs website, containing a database of action at all levels of governance.[683]

Similarly to the global action on sustainable tourism, regional efforts are also slowly developing different types of action plans centring on sustainable tourism. Regionally, the Nordic Tourism Cooperation Plan 2019–23, which aims at ensuring sustain-ability in the Nordic tourist industry in line with the UN SDGs can be mentioned.[684] Furthermore, the EU, for instance, in its EU Strategy for Sustainable Tourism calls for the establishment of the European Agency for Tourism, which would provide both the EU and its Member States with a 'factual overview and data for policymakers, en-abling them to devise informed strategies based on collected and analysed tourism data, including on the possible social, economic and environmental impact of these',

---

[676] One Planet Network, 'Global Tourism Plastics Initiative' <https://www.oneplanetnetwork.org/sustainable-tourism/global-tourism-plastics-initiative> accessed 26 October 2021.

[677] Global Tourism Plastics Initiative, 'Tourism's Plastic Pollution Problem' <https://www.oneplanetnetwork.org/sites/default/files/gtpi_brochure_9_october_2020_-_copy_2.pdf> accessed 28 October 2021.

[678] One Planet Network, 'Global Tourism Plastics Initiative' <https://www.oneplanetnetwork.org/sustainable-tourism/global-tourism-plastics-initiative> accessed 26 October 2021.

[679] ibid.

[680] IUCN, 'IUCN and German Government Support Post-COVID Recovery through Sustainable Tourism Initiative' (5 September 2021) <https://www.iucn.org/news/protected-areas/202109/iucn-and-german-government-support-post-covid-recovery-through-sustainable-tourism-initiative> accessed 26 October 2021.

[681] ibid.

[682] ibid.

[683] Tourism for SDGs (platform developed by the UNWTO) <https://tourism4sdgs.org/> accessed 26 October 2021.

[684] Nordic Council of Ministers, 'Plan for Nordic Tourism Co-operation 2019–2023' (2019) <https://norden.diva-portal.org/smash/get/diva2:1330360/FULLTEXT02.pdf> accessed 28 October 2021.

and furthermore it would 'share good practices to make informed decisions about improving tourism policies'.[685]

Looking at the national level we can notice that tourism is embedded in a wide range of different legal areas, from environmental law, administrative law, transportation law, consumer law, to tax law.[686] Yet the sustainability theme has not come to the forefront of the legislation and is mainly included in national tourism policies and strategic documentation.[687] For example, Iceland published in 2019 the Tourism Policy Framework 2020–30.[688] This policy introduced a new Tourism Impact Assessment, considering environmental impacts, infrastructure, society, and economy.[689] Another example of a national programme is the 2018 Tourism Reform Programme from Egypt.[690] This policy refers to SDGs and aims at reforming institutions and legislation, and thereby aligning with sustainability requirements. Even though the current sustainability vision of states from these policy instruments is clear, its actual implementation will be a decisive factor. Only time will tell how these strategic documents translate into action.

While countries struggle promoting the action that would apply globally or even nationally, certain local regional laws emerged. A shining example is the Lombardy Regional Law from 2015.[691] Its article 75(2) states that

[t]he Regional Council shall regulate the forms of contribution and facilitation ... in favor of tourism enterprises and territorial attractiveness, for the interventions directed to implement: ... actions enabling undertakings to reduce water and energy consumption and to reduce or eliminate waste, atmospheric emissions and noise pollution; interventions to achieve a level of environmental protection higher than that established by national and Community standards; measures enabling the generation of energy through processes that rely mainly on renewable energy sources; actions to achieve environmental certification under Community and national rules....[692]

---

[685] European Parliament, 'EU strategy for sustainable tourism European Parliament resolution of 25 March 2021 on establishing an EU strategy for sustainable tourism' 2020/2038(INI), P9_TA(2021)0109, 25 March 2021 <https://www.europarl.europa.eu/doceo/document/TA-9-2021-0109_EN.html> accessed 28 October 2021.

[686] V Franceschelli, 'From Tourism to Sustainable Tourism An Italian Perspective' in V Franceschelli and others (eds), *Sustainable Tourism Law* (Portugal ESHTE Lisboa, Portugal INATEL Foundation 2019) 93.

[687] OECD, 'OECD Tourism Trends and Policies 2020' (OECD Publishing 2020) 96 <https://www.oecd-ilibrary.org/sites/2fde1a1d-en/index.html?itemId=/content/component/2fde1a1d-en#section-d1e47244> accessed 26 October 2021; UNEP and UNWTO, 'Baseline Report on the Integration of Sustainable Consumption and Production Patterns into Tourism Policies' (UNWTO, Madrid, 2019) 46–47<https://www.e-unwto.org/doi/book/10.18111/9789284420605 accessed 30 October 2021.

[688] OECD, 'OECD Tourism Trends and Policies 2020' (n 687) 192.

[689] ibid.

[690] OECD, 'OECD Tourism Trends and Policies 2020' (n 687) 36.

[691] Translation available in Franceschelli (n 686) 95–96. Lombardy Regional Law, Act n. 27 (Legge Regionale 1 ottobre 2015, No 27 Politiche regionali in materia di turismo e attrattività del territorio lombardo (October 2015) <http://normelombardia.consiglio.regione.lombardia.it/normelombardia/Accessibile/main.aspx?iddoc=lr002015100100027&view=showdoc> accessed 30 October 2021.

[692] ibid.

d) Critique

Sustainable tourism transpired in the recent times as a movement of positive action. Despite claims that the connection of words 'sustainable' 'tourism' constitutes an oxymoron, the UNWTO believes that tourism can be an SD driver.[693] Also, the OECD Report on tourism practices from 2020 suggests that it might be partly true.[694] The insufficiencies in indicator 12.b, however, imply that such a role of tourism for now remains in a long-term vision. Even though states have become increasingly aware of the mass tourism issue and promote more sustainable strategies in their policy-making, the outcomes of such strategies are difficult to measure. Moreover, these strategies are very fragmented and relevant at a relatively small scale, which can both bring advantages as those strategies react to local policies and disadvantages as they have a narrow focus although the important sustainability issues are of national or global importance (eg climate change). Overall, the indicator designed for measurement of target 12.b seems like a compromise on several fronts. First, even though it is suggested that it involves sustainability aspects, the TSA ad SEEA tables do not contain social elements, which should be part of the sustainable tourism transition. Moreover, the limitations of the target are mirrored in insufficient tracking of the chosen standard tools, primarily by the developing countries.

11. Target 12.c Rationalize inefficient fossil-fuel subsidies that encourage wasteful consumption by removing market distortions, in accordance with national circumstances, including by restructuring taxation and phasing out those harmful subsidies, where they exist, to reflect their environmental impacts, taking fully into account the specific needs and conditions of developing countries and minimizing the possible adverse impacts on their development in a manner that protects the poor and the affected communities

a) Sources of target

There is a long history of states supporting either production or consumption of fossil fuels.[695] The underlying rationale varies from making energy affordable to all members of the society, through fighting the poverty and fuelling industrialization to ensuring energy security.[696] Today, it is clear that fossil fuel subsidies (FFS) do not represent a way forward, but rather a radical step back on our journey towards achieving a sustainable future. As Antonio Guterres, UN Secretary-General contends: '[g]overnments need to be courageous and smart—that means ending billions of dollars in subsidies for fossil fuels. It means establishing a fair price for carbon. It means stopping investments

---

[693] UNWTO, 'UNWTO Report Links Sustainable Tourism to 17 SDGs' (14 June 2018) <https://sdg.iisd.org/news/unwto-report-links-sustainable-tourism-to-17-sdgs/> accessed 26 October 2021.

[694] OECD, 'OECD Tourism Trends and Policies 2020' (n 687) ch 3.

[695] UNEP, IISD, GSI, and OECD, 'Measuring Fossil Fuel Subsidies in the Context of Sustainable Development Goals' (2019) VII <https://www.unep.org/resources/report/measuring-fossil-fuel-subsidies-context-sustainable-development-goals> accessed 28 October 2021 (Measuring FFS).

[696] SDG Indicators metadata repository, 'Metadata Sheet for Indicator 12.c.1' <https://unstats.un.org/sdgs/metadata> accessed 3 July 2021 (Metadata 12.c.1), update March 2021, rationale.

in unsustainable infrastructure that will lock in bad practices for decades to come. Our future is at stake. Nothing is immune—climate change affects everything.'[697]

In the most simplified way, FFS can be seen as a type of financial benefit provided by states to end-users or producers of energy.[698] In broad terms, we can distinguish two strands of FFS. First, we talk about the so-called consumer subsidies.[699] These subsidies aim at final consumers and allow them to obtain the fossil fuels below the market price.[700] Such a form of FFS is currently used mostly in developing countries.[701] Secondly, there are producer subsidies.[702] These include a high variety of different treatments such as grants, direct payments, taxation, and low-interest loans, and are distinctive to developed countries and countries that are the biggest producers of fossil fuels.[703]

Both types of FFS are connected to a range of negative externalities. First, FFS symbolize a burden placed upon public budgets, when in 2020, $5.9 trillion was spent globally on subsidizing energy with no clean future.[704] Some estimates claim that reforming the FFS and taxes can raise $553 billion annually,[705] other resources argue that we can 'generate USD 1 billion worldwide per day by a tax of 12.5 cents per litre of gasoline and diesel'.[706] Such a significant portion of states' budgets could be used on financing strategic investments in other critical areas including health, education, and sustainable energy.[707] Secondly, environmental consequences are observed as a direct result of subsidising fossil fuels. Apart from driving climate change, air pollution, and land degradation,[708] FFS lead to overconsumption and create a disincentive to the market, leading to less innovation on renewable energy.[709] According to the current research, FFS reform could help reducing carbon emission by 1–4 per cent by 2030.[710]

[697] New Zealand Foreign Affairs, 'Fossil Fuel Subsidy Reform (FFSR)' <https://www.mfat.govt.nz/en/environment/fossil-fuel-subsidy-reform-ffsr/> accessed 28 October 2021.

[698] Fossil Fuel Subsidy Tracker, 'About—What Are Fossil Fuel Subsidies?' <https://fossilfuelsubsidytracker.org/about/> accessed 26 October 2021.

[699] J Skovgaard, *The Economisation of Climate Change: How the G20, the OECD and the IMF Address Fossil Fuel Subsidies and Climate Finance* (CUP 2021) 75, pt III, 75.

[700] ibid 76.

[701] Measuring FFS (n 695) 6.

[702] Skovgaard (n 699) 76.

[703] Measuring FFS (n 695) annex 3.

[704] I Parry and others, 'IMF Working Paper Still Not Getting Energy Prices Right: A Global and Country Update of Fossil Fuel Subsidies' (2021) IMF Working Paper WP/21/236, IMF September 2021, 2 <https://www.imf.org/en/Publications/WP/Issues/2021/09/23/Still-Not-Getting-Energy-Prices-Right-A-Global-and-Country-Update-of-Fossil-Fuel-Subsidies-466004> accessed 27 October 2021.

[705] J Kuehl and others, 'Cutting Emissions Through Fossil Fuel Subsidy Reform and Taxation GSI REPORT' (IISD, July 2021) <https://www.iisd.org/system/files/2021-07/cutting-emissions-fossil-fuel-subsidies-taxation.pdf> accessed 26 October 2021.

[706] P Wooders and T Moerenhout, 'How to Raise an Easy $1 Billion per Day for the COVID-19 Recovery' (IISD, 27 May 2020) <https://www.iisd.org/gsi/subsidy-watch-blog/fuel-tax-covid-19-recovery> accessed 27 October 2021.

[707] J Skovgaard-Petersen and H van Asselt. *The Politics of Fossil Fuel Subsidies and Their Reform* (online edition, CUP 2018) 51.

[708] Kuehl and others (n 705).

[709] J Rentschler and M Bazilian, 'Reforming Fossil Fuel Subsidies: Drivers, Barriers and the State of Progress' (2017) 17(7) Climate Policy 891, 896.

[710] L Merrill and others, 'Fossil Fuel Subsidy Reform Research Suggests Emission Reductions Equivalent to at Least a Quarter of the Commitments Countries Made at Paris' (GSI 8 February 2018) <https://www.iisd.org/gsi/subsidy-watch-blog/fossil-fuel-subsidy-reform-research-suggests-emission-reductions-equivalent> accessed 30 October 2021.

942 SDG 12

Simultaneously, the number of deaths caused by air pollution could be cut by 63 per cent.[711] Finally, FFS result in social consequences, leading to more poverty, gender discrimination, and creating dependency on fossil fuels.[712] In addition, data show that the richer part of the population profits from the FFS to a much higher extent than the poor, to whom the FFS are usually addressed.[713]

It stems from the above that by removing this roadblock represented by the FFS, advancement in other SDGs could be expected. Exemplarily, lowering the FFS could impact SDG 1 (no poverty), SDG 3 (good health and well-being), SDG 7 (affordable and clean energy), and SDG 13 (climate action).[714]

Agenda 21 encouraged states to '[r]emove or reduce those subsidies that do not conform with sustainable development objectives.'[715] 'The Future We Want', a result of the Rio + 20 goes further and in its paragraph 225 calls on '[c]ountries reaffirm the commitments they have made to phase out harmful and inefficient fossil fuel subsidies that encourage wasteful consumption and undermine sustainable development ... to consider rationalizing inefficient fossil fuel subsidies by removing market distortions, including restructuring taxation and phasing out harmful subsidies, where they exist, to reflect their environmental impacts, with such policies taking fully into account the specific needs and conditions of developing countries, with the aim of minimizing the possible adverse impacts on their development and in a manner that protects the poor and the affected communities.'[716]

Looking at the wording of the target 12.c, its language is weak and lacks focus. The choice of words such as 'rationalize', combined with a lack of quantified or chronological targets similar to the one in SDG 14.5 (fisheries subsidies), cause the target to remain vague.[717] Further, the language of the target focuses mainly on 'inefficient' FFS. Taking into consideration that we have not reached a global consensus on what exactly inefficient FFS entail,[718] this is an unfortunate choice of words.

b) Empirical analysis

In order to understand what kind of measures need to be embraced by policy-makers, it is essential to first gain insight into the severity of the FFS problem.[719] Starting by

---

[711] L Merril and others, 'Making the Switch from Fossil Fuel Subsidies to Sustainable Energy' (Nordic Council of Ministers 2017) 22 <https://norden.diva-portal.org/smash/get/diva2:1094676/FULLTEXT02.pdf> accessed 30 October 2021; K Vohra and others, 'Global Mortality from Outdoor Fine Particle Pollution Generated by Fossil Fuel Combustion: Results from GEOS-Chem.' (2021) 195 Environmental Research.

[712] Nordic report (n 168) 36.

[713] The basic objective of most fossil fuel subsidies is support of the poor so that they can afford energy, other motivations can, for example, be ensuring domestic energy supply and reducing dependence on other countries (production subsidies); For more information see: A Bárány and D Grigonytė, 'Measuring Fossil Fuel Subsidies' (ECFIN Economic Brief European Commission, Issue 40, March 2015) 2 <https://ec.europa.eu/economy_fina nce/publications/economic_briefs/2015/pdf/eb40_en.pdf> accessed 30 October 2021; D Coady and others, 'The Unequal Benefits of Fuel Subsidies Revisited: Evidence for Developing Countries' (2015) IMF Working Paper WP/15/250, 4.

[714] Measuring FFS (n 695) 4.

[715] Agenda 21 (n 363) para 8.32 b.

[716] 'The Future We Want' (n 3) para 225.

[717] See Chapter 14 on SDG 14, this book.

[718] Measuring FFS (n 695) 52.

[719] Fossil Fuel Subsidy Tracker, 'About—Why Is It Important to Track Fossil-Fuel Subsidies Transparently?' <https://fossilfuelsubsidytracker.org/about/ > accessed 26 October 2021.

tracking the FFS at the national level, we obtain a full picture of the current situation, which enables us to enact policies fitting the national realities and needs from the social, economic, and environmental perspective.

Notwithstanding the usefulness of national data to national policy-making, their comparability at international and regional levels is confined due to multiple factors.[720] The data differ in scope, ambition, understanding of fossil fuels, and what FFS comprise.[721] This is connected to a persistent shortcoming in the international arena, which to date lacks widely agreed terminology accompanying FFS. Definitions adopted/used by the WTO[722] or International Energy Agency (IEA)[723] are examples of definitions acknowledged by the greatest number of states. The WTO's Agreement on Subsidies and Countervailing Measures (ASCM),[724] is the only legally binding definition of fossil fuels applicable to WTO members. The IEA's definition of fossil fuels asserts that '[f]ossil fuels are taken from natural resources which were formed from biomass in the geological past. By extension, the term fossil is also applied to any secondary fuel manufactured from a fossil fuel.'[725] If we were to be compliant with this definition, secondary commodities such as heat and electricity should the included in the aggregated number relevant to FFS. Until the world agrees on what FFS entail, the translation of national data into a global perspective and their comparability will be a daunting task for all actors involved.[726]

The indicator developed for measurement of target 12.c under the custodianship of UNEP monitors the 'amount of fossil-fuel subsidies (production and consumption) per unit of GDP and as proportion of total national expenditure on fossil fuels.'[727] The FFS shall be measured on global, regional, and national levels.[728] According to the methodology, countries' focus in reporting should be on three sub-indicators: (i) direct transfer of government funds; (ii) induced transfers (price support); and as an optional

---

[720] Measuring FFS (n 695) 24, 28.

[721] Measuring FFS (n 695) 28; Rentschler and Bazilian (n 709) 894–95.

[722] WTO, 'Agreement on Subsidies and Countervailing Measures' (adopted 15 April 1994, in force 1 January 1995) 1869 UNTS 14 (ASCM).

[723] IEA, 'Energy Statistics–Manual. International Energy Agency' (IEA 2005) <https://doi.org/10.1787/978926 4033986-en> accessed 27 November 2021.

[724] Art 1 of ASCM (n 722): 'Definition of a Subsidy: 1.1 For the purpose of this Agreement, a subsidy shall be deemed to exist if: (a) (1) there is a financial contribution by a government or any public body within the territory of a Member (referred to in this Agreement as "government"), i.e. where: (i) a government practice involves a direct transfer of funds (e.g. grants, loans, and equity infusion), potential direct transfers of funds or liabilities (e.g. loan guarantees); (ii) government revenue that is otherwise due is foregone or not collected (e.g. fiscal incentives such as tax credits) (1); (iii) government provides goods or services other than general infrastructure, or purchases goods; (iv) a government makes payments to a funding mechanism, or entrusts or directs a private body to carry out one or more of the type of functions illustrated in (i) to (iii) above which would normally be vested in the government and the practice, in no real sense, differs from practices normally followed by governments; or (a) (2) there is any form of income or price support in the sense of Article XVI of GATT 1994; and (b) a benefit is thereby conferred.'

[725] IEA, 'Energy Statistics–Manual. International Energy Agency' (Paris, 2005) <https://doi.org/10.1787/ 9789264033986-en> accessed 27 November 2021.

[726] Measuring FFS (n 695) 53.

[727] Metadata 12.c.1 (n 696).

[728] SDG 12 Hub, 'Target 12.c Fossil Fuel Subsidies' <https://sdg12hub.org/sdg-12-hub/see-progress-on-sdg-12-by-target/12c-fossil-fuel-subsidies> accessed 25 October 2021.

944   SDG 12

sub-indicator (iii) tax expenditure, other revenue foregone, and under-pricing of goods and services, including risk.[729]

As described above, quantifying global FFS can be challenging. Therefore, in 2019 UNEP published methodological guidance on measurement of the FFS and providing their national estimates titled Measuring Fossil Fuel Subsidies in the Context of the Sustainable Development Goals.[730] As per this methodology, FFS are to be defined in line with the IEA Statistical Manual and the ASCM.[731] Fossil fuels are defined in line with the IEA's interpretation stated above.

A glance at the architecture of indicator 12.c.1 suffices to uncover that the indicator primarily measures the aggregated volume of all types of FFS, not distinguishing between those which are 'inefficient', 'harmful', or which 'encourage wasteful consumption' as described in the wording of the target 12.c.[732] Due to this, the potential of the indicator to improve policy-making remains questionable.

SG's Progress Report 2021 demonstrates where FFS stand.[733] The report illustrates that 2019 marks a year when FFS dropped to $432 billion as opposed to the growing numbers for 2017 and 2018.[734] Notably, the region of Northern Africa supported fossil fuels with 4.24 per cent of GDP as opposed to aggregated number 0.51 per cent worldwide.[735]

Apart from the SDG's indicator, an initiative of the OECD and International Institute for Sustainable Development (IISD), named the Fossil Fuel Subsidies Tracker (FFST),[736] provides further insights into FFS which are problematic.[737] FFST combines data from OECD, IEA, the International Monetary Fund, the UN, and the World Bank. For better orientation, FFST can estimate which fossil fuels are subsidized and which subsidy mechanism is most often used. This way we learn, for example, that induced transfers (governments regulating prices of fuels for consumers) constitute around 54 per cent of the global FFS or that the petroleum products represent 56 per cent of overall FFS.[738]

c) Implementation efforts at domestic/international level

Internationally, FFS received a heightened attention in 2009 by the Group of 20 (G20) which pledged to 'phase out and rationalize over the medium term inefficient fossil fuel subsidies'.[739] A series of further commitments followed from the Asia Pacific Economic Cooperation in November 2009 and G7.[740] FFS finally came into the spotlight,

---

[729] Metadata 12.c.1 (n 696).
[730] Measuring FFS (n 695) (draws on existing methods from the OECD, IEA and the IMF for quantifying and tracking fossil fuel subsidies).
[731] ASCM (n 722).
[732] Gasper and others (n 5) 90.
[733] SG's Progress Report 2021 (n 122) annex, 157–158.
[734] ibid para 139.
[735] ibid annex, 157.
[736] Fossil Fuel Subsidy Tracker <https://fossilfuelsubsidytracker.org/> accessed 26 October 2021.
[737] ibid.
[738] ibid.
[739] G20 Leaders' Statement: The Pittsburgh Summit (24–25 September 2009) <http://www.g20.utoronto.ca/2009/2009communique0925.html#energy> accessed 27 October 2021.
[740] Skovgaard (n 699).

however, with no hard law obligations in sight. Currently, there is no concerted action at the international level and FFS are addressed by different frameworks, such as international climate change regime, international trade regime, regional economic regimes, international economic and energy cooperation, and NGOs.[741] The elimination of FFS is an important step towards the mitigation of climate change, yet neither the UNFCC[742] nor the Kyoto Protocol[743] nor the Paris Agreement[744] contain any mention about the phasing out of FFS. The Paris Agreement, however, demands in its article 2(c) '[m]aking finance flows consistent with a pathway towards low greenhouse gas emissions and climate-resilient development'. NDCs should in the light of this provision encompass certain type of commitment towards reduction of FFS. Still, as of 2019, only fourteen NDCs, representing 8 per cent of the countries introduced such a pledge.[745] Yet, Conference of Parties (COP) meetings reflect the raising interest into this issue. The adoption of a reference to fossil fuel reforms was within the reach at COP21,[746] and has finally found its way into the COP26 outcome document. Specifically, the Glasgow Climate Pact in its paragraph 21 calls on the Parties to (among other things) 'phase-out ... inefficient fossil fuel subsidies, while providing targeted support to the poorest and most vulnerable in line with national circumstances and recognizing the need for support towards a just transition'.[747]

Apart from international organizations and NGOs, a group of countries united in 2010 under the name Friends of Fossil Fuel Subsidy Reform (FFFSR). FFFSR represents a steering force in promotion of FFS reduction.[748] These countries, including Costa Rica, Denmark, Ethiopia, Finland, New Zealand, Norway, Sweden, Switzerland, and Uruguay, 'promote political consensus' on FFS issue and made an appearance for instance at COP21 of the UNFCCC, where they presented a Communiqué on Fossil Fuel Subsidy Reform.[749]

In the past, national FFS reforms appeared mainly for economic reasons.[750] Nowadays, an increasing number of states endorse reformation for the sake of the environment. According to data provided by the IISD, at least fifty-three countries implemented some kind of fossil fuel consumer subsidy or increased taxes reform within the period 2015–2020.[751] COVID-19 crisis is considered one of the triggers of FFS reforms

---

[741] Skovgaard-Petersen (n 707) pt III.

[742] UNFCCC (n 249).

[743] Kyoto Protocol (n 615).

[744] The Paris Agreement (n 252).

[745] IISD and GSI, 'Raising Ambition through Fossil Fuel Subsidy Reform: Greenhouse Gas Emissions Modelling Results from 26 Countries' (June 2019) <https://www.iisd.org/publications/raising-ambition-through-fossil-fuel-subsidy-reform> accessed 26 October 2021.

[746] H van Asselt and K Kulovesi, 'Seizing the Opportunity: Tackling Fossil Fuel Subsidies under the UNFCCC' (2017) 17 International Environmental Agreements: Politics, Law and Economics 357, 360.

[747] UNFCCC, Decision-/CP.26, Glasgow Climate Pact, Advance unedited version <https://unfccc.int/sites/defaul/files/resource/cop26_auv_2f_cover_decision.pdf> accessed 3 December 2021.

[748] Friends of Fossil Fuel Subsidy Reform, 'What is the Friends of Fossil Fuel Subsidy Reform?' <http://fffsr.org/> accessed 26 October 2021.

[749] Friends of Fossil Fuel Subsidy Reform, 'The Communiqué' <http://fffsr.org/communique/> accessed 26 October 2021.

[750] Skovgaard (n 699) 75.

[751] L Sanchez and others, '53 Ways to Reform Fossil Fuel Consumer Subsidies and Pricing' (IISD, 18 August 2020) <https://www.iisd.org/articles/53-ways-reform-fossil-fuel-consumer-subsidies-and-pricing> accessed 27 October 2021.

as it partially led to a decline of fuel demand and thereby to a decrease in the prices of fossil fuels on the global market.[752] The low prices of fossil fuels encouraged many countries to introduce reforms in the field of FFS. However, the OECD already at the beginning of 2021 suggested that the former amount of FSS will probably come back as the energy prices rocket again.[753] Consumer subsidies reforms are generally more visible in middle-income developing countries such as Egypt, India, Indonesia, and Philippines.[754] On the other side of the coin, production subsidies reforms are adopted in developed countries, exemplarily Germany or Spain.[755]

The FFS reforms entail a broad range of different measures. As an example, Zambia and Morocco adopted a swap approach, where instead of subsidizing black energy, they encourage investment into renewable resources.[756] Successful FFS reforms have several common denominators.[757] First, countries which approach the reforms gradually in phases, do not rush the reform but carefully plan the transition, stand out.[758] The necessity to divide the FFS elimination into phases stems from the fact that people from the poorer segments of the society might become exposed to negative economic aftermath of such measures. The metadata on target 12.c inform us that 'there is a need to ensure that poor households that are particularly vulnerable to price increases obtain or retain access to energy'.[759] If this precondition is not fulfilled this can lead to riots similar to those France experienced in 2018 conducted by the 'yellow vests',[760] and Ecuador, when the FFS phasing out was designed in a way that was too hasty and radical.[761] Another sign common to successful stories are compensation packages provided to the economically disadvantaged. For example, the Philippines protected its inhabitants through cash transfer programmes, and Ghana developed a livelihood program to support families.[762,763]

d) Critique
The commitment to phase out FFS mainly through 'rationalization' is designed with precaution. Such stance can be attributed to the highly political nature of the FFS. The

---

[752] OECD and IEA, 'Update on Recent Progress in Reform of Inefficient Fossil-Fuel Subsidies that Encourage Wasteful Consumption' (2021) 10 <www.oecd.org/fossil-fuels/publicationsandfurtherreading/OECD-IEA-G20-Fossil-Fuel-Subsidies-Reform-Update-2021.pdf> accessed 27 October 2021.

[753] ibid 17.

[754] T Van De Graaf and M Blondeel, 'Fossil Fuel Subsidy Reform: An International Norm Perspective' in Skovgaard-Petersen and van Asselt (eds) (n 707) 89.

[755] I Gençsü and others, 'Phase-Out 2020: Monitoring Europe's Fossil Fuel Subsidies' (Overseas Development Institute and Climate Action Network Europe 2017) 23 <https://cdn.odi.org/media/documents/11762.pdf> accessed 27 October 2021.

[756] Richard Bridle and others, 'Fossil Fuel to Clean Energy Subsidy Swaps: How to Pay for an Energy Revolution' (IISD and GSI, June 2019) subchapter 3.4 (Zambia), 3.5 (Morocco).

[757] Principles of designing effective subsidy reforms in: Rentschler and Bazilian (n 709) 904–06.

[758] Sanchez and others (n 751).

[759] Metadata 12.c.1 (n 696).

[760] AJ Rubin and S Sengupta, '"Yellow Vest" Protests Shake France. Here's the Lesson for Climate Change' (*The New York Times*, 6 December 2018) <https://www.nytimes.com/2018/12/06/world/europe/france-fuel-carbon-tax.html> accessed 27 October 2021.

[761] IISD, 'How Reforming Fossil Fuel Subsidies Can Go Wrong: A lesson from Ecuador' (24 October 2019) <https://www.iisd.org/articles/lesson-ecuador-fossil-fuel-subsidies> accessed 27 October 2021.

[762] Sanchez and others (n 751).

[763] More on how to approach FFS reforms in Rentschler and Bazilian (n 709).

Cambridge Dictionary defines the word rationalize as 'to try to find reasons to explain your behaviour, decisions, etc.' which as a first step might be a promising start; nevertheless, it should not end there.[764]

Turning to the indicator 12.c.1, we can notice several insufficiencies. First, the indicator is lacking commitment in respect to time, that is, when should the FFS be phased out the latest. In comparison, a sunset date 2020, appears in target SDG 14.5 on fisheries subsidies.[765] FFS were thus not assigned the same treatment, even though a clear timeframe would provide impetus for policy-makers and legislators to act now. Further, the indicator does not contain separate quantification of FFS which are 'harmful', 'inefficient', or 'encouraging wasteful consumption'. On the one hand, this would of course be a challenging task for reporting states as no definitions of these terms are agreed on internationally, on the other hand, clearer understanding of these terms would allow us to obtain detailed comprehensive data, which could scale up FFS reforms and allow for monitoring particularly FFS which are the main cause of negative externalities.

Finally, the indicator does not inform us about the quality of the reforms around the world but provides just a mathematical exercise when it counts the FFS proportion in relation to the countries' GDP. Yet the target calls for 'taking fully into account the specific needs and conditions of developing countries and minimizing the possible adverse impacts on their development in a manner that protects the poor and the affected communities'.[766] Such requirement does not translate into what is measured by the target as the indicator 12.c.1 does not assess the quality of reforms and further social realities.

---

[764] 'Rationalize', *Cambridge Dictionary* <https://dictionary.cambridge.org/dictionary/english/rationalize> accessed 27 October 2021.

[765] Skovgaard (n 699) 102–03; see also Chapter 14 on SGD 14, this book.

[766] Metadata 12.c.1 (n 696).

SDG 13

'Take Urgent Action to Combat Climate Change and Its Impacts'

Francesca Romanin Jacur

I. Introduction

Climate change is one of the greatest and urgent common concerns of human kind.

Climate change is a highly complex, cross-cutting, and very controversial policy and legal challenge of our time. The international community has been, and still is, struggling with climate change since the late 1980s. Despite the many initiatives at the international level and the universal participation to the multilateral climate change regime, responses to mitigation of the sources of climate change, notably the reduction of greenhouse gas (GHG) emissions, on the one hand, and to its adaptation dimension, including the negative impacts caused by extreme weather events, remain inadequate.

SDG 13 expresses in a very concise form the need to '[t]ake urgent action to combat climate change and its impacts', thereby highlighting three main dimensions of climate change policies: urgency, mitigation action to address the causes of climate change, and adaptation to its negative impacts. A footnote to SDG 13 makes a *renvoi* to the United Nations Framework Convention on Climate Change (UNFCCC) and acknowledges its role as the 'primary international, intergovernmental forum for negotiating the global response to climate change'.

Following the common format of this handbook, this chapter starts by describing the preliminary phases and the *travaux* that led to the adoption of SDG 13. The second part examines SDG 13 and contextualizes it against the backdrop of relevant general principles of international law, as well as its relations with other areas of international law, including human rights, trade, and investment.

The third part examines closely the five targets of SDG 13 with the aim to provide an overview of the climate change legal and policy responses at the international, regional, and national level. Furthermore, it considers the seven indicators relating to the abovementioned targets that provide for measurable criteria to assess progress with regard to the climate change challenge.

II. *Travaux Préparatoires*

A. Background

The process to develop a set of sustainable development goals (SDGs) 'limited in number, aspirational and easy to communicate' has been launched by Member States during the United Nations Conference on Sustainable Development (Rio + 20), held in Rio de Janeiro in June 2012. Although the Rio + 20 outcome document 'The Future We Want' did not elaborate specific goals, it provides that the goals should address in a balanced way all three dimensions of sustainable development and be coherent with and integrated into the UN development agenda beyond 2015. The inclusive and transparent intergovernmental process was led by an Open Working Group (OWG) of thirty members established by the UN General Assembly.[1]

With regard to climate change, in Rio, states 'acknowledge that climate change is a cross-cutting and persistent crisis, and express our concern that the scale and gravity of the negative impacts of climate change affect all countries and undermine the ability of all countries, in particular, developing countries, to achieve sustainable development and the Millennium Development Goals, and threaten the viability and survival of nations. Therefore, we underscore that combating climate change requires urgent and ambitious action, in accordance with the principles and provisions of the United Nations Framework Convention on Climate Change.'[2]

The final document of Rio + 20 reflects the main normative pillars of the international climate change regime and anticipates, in particular with regard to climate finance, some of its innovative developments.

With regard to mitigation, states 'reaffirm that climate change is one of the greatest challenges of our time' and 'express profound alarm that emissions of GHGs continue to rise globally'.[3] States also 'note with grave concern the significant gap between the aggregate effect of mitigation pledges by parties in terms of global annual emissions of GHGs by 2020 and aggregate emission pathways consistent with having a likely chance of holding the increase in global average temperature below 2° C, or 1.5° C above pre-industrial levels'. At the same time, they emphasize that 'adaptation to climate change represents an immediate and urgent global priority', being deeply worried 'that all countries, particularly developing countries, are vulnerable to the adverse impacts of

---

[1] General Assembly, Resolution adopted by the General Assembly on 27 July 2012, The Future We Want, A/RES/66/288* (11 September 2012) ('The Future We Want') para 247 and ff. The OWG was established on 22 January 2013 (see Doc A/67/L.48/rev.1). The OWG decided on its methods of work, including developing modalities to ensure the full involvement of relevant stakeholders and expertise from civil society, the scientific community, and the United Nations system in its work, in order to provide a diversity of perspectives and experience ('The Future We Want' para 248). For detailed information regarding the institutional aspects and the various steps of the intergovernmental process that led to the adoption of the SDGs, visit the website <https://sustainabledevelopment.un.org/owg.html> accessed 21 November 2022.

[2] ibid paras 17 and 25.

[3] ibid paras 190 and ff.

climate change and are already experiencing increased impacts, including persistent drought and extreme weather events, sea-level rise, coastal erosion and ocean acidification, further threatening food security and efforts to eradicate poverty and achieve sustainable development.'[4]

Highlighting the central role of financing the transition to a low-carbon economy, states 'recognize the importance of mobilizing funding from a variety of sources, public and private, bilateral and multilateral, including innovative sources of finance, to support nationally appropriate mitigation actions, adaptation measures, technology development and transfer and capacity building in developing countries. In this regard, we welcome the launching of the Green Climate Fund, and call for its prompt operationalization so as to have an early and adequate replenishment process.'[5]

The Rio + 20 outcome document, 'The Future We Want', recalls and reaffirms the Stockholm and Rio Declarations, and their principles with the express mention of the principles of common but differentiated responsibilities (Rio, principle 7) and of intra- and inter-generational equity.[6] Furthermore, it recognized the need to tackle climate change by endorsing the UN Climate Change regime, in particular mentioning the UNFCCC and the Kyoto Protocol, and praises the progress achieved within this context while urging States Parties to fully implement their commitments under these treaties.[7]

B. OWG-7

At its seventh session, held between 6 and 10 January 2014, the OWG considered climate change and disaster risk reduction, together with other topics, namely 'Sustainable cities and human settlements, sustainable transport', and 'Sustainable consumption and production (including chemicals and waste)'.

Co-Chairs Ambassador Csaba Kőrösi of Hungary and Ambassador Macharia Kamau of Kenya introduced a bullet point document, highlighting some of the major issues for discussions during the OWG-7.[8] In particular, they stressed the urgency of climate change action and the strict linkages existing with disaster risk reduction, while acknowledging that for a number of countries climate change represents an existential threat. Strong actions on climate change mitigation and adaptation are thus among the most effective means of reducing disaster risks. Without such actions, the frequency and intensity of, and the vulnerability to, disasters will only intensify in coming years and decades.

---

[4] ibid.
[5] ibid para 191.
[6] ibid para 191.
[7] ibid para 192.
[8] <https://sustainabledevelopment.un.org/content/documents/2958co-chairs%20summary%20bullet%20poin ts_owg7%2020%20Jan.pdf> accessed 21 November 2022.

952   SDG 13

Another crucial topic on the agenda was the relationship between climate change and sustainable development, with particular regard to the threats deriving from climate change for food security, the intensification of water scarcity and flooding as well as the worsening of sea-level rise. The exposure of the poorest states, namely Small Islands Developing States (SIDS) and Least Developed Countries (LDCs)—including those in Africa—to the impacts of climate change was highlighted.

At this early stage, there was wide support for addressing climate change as a cross-cutting issue framed in terms of sustainable development, rather than as a stand-alone goal. Consideration was given also to the role of and commitments under the UNFCCC, including its principles, and in particular equity and common but differentiated responsibilities and respective capabilities (CBDR-RC) and their evolutionary character.

With regard to the targets which should reflect the challenges of climate change, support was expressed in favour of several issues, including building resilient infrastructure and human settlements, protecting forests, sustainable energy, food security, water management, and promoting low-carbon and climate-resilient development paths. As for the provision for a quantified mitigation target to keep the global temperature increase below 2°C, no uniform position emerged as concerns were raised regarding the fact that such an indication could not be expressed without reference to the UNFCCC context.

During this meeting, many delegations stressed the importance of means of implementation. Discussions about disaster losses highlighted their major impact but also the available tools to address them. As for risk prevention, three main channels were identified: first, the development of pathways that minimize risk generation; second, the reduction of risk; and third, the strengthening of resilience by improving the ability to deal with shocks of all kinds. Some developing countries delegations offered valuable experience in this fields. Among the proposed targets and indicators addressing disaster risk reduction, reference was made to measurement of loss of lives and economic losses. It was noted that disaster risk reduction often focuses only on technical infrastructure questions even though addressing the root causes of risks such as climate change and building resilience through holistic disaster risk planning, land-use planning, communication and educational programmes, good local governance, and social security nets would provide more sustainable results.

During OWG-7, significant contribution to the discussion came from keynote addresses, notes by the UN Technical Support Team, panel discussions, and interactive exchanges of views and national statements. Meetings also involved Major Groups and other Stakeholders.[9] Several speakers noted that climate change is one of the biggest threats to sustainability, and that specifically hampers the progress made to implement the MDGs and similarly to effectively achieve the SDGs. Ongoing discussions

---

[9] Seventh Session of the General Assembly Open Working Group on Sustainable Development Goals, 6–10 January 2014, Trusteeship Council (Conference Building) Co-Chair's meetings with the Major Groups and other Stakeholders.

concerned whether to include climate change in the SDGs as a stand-alone goal or in the targets. This latter solution entails including climate change under other goals such as, for example, on energy, food, water, cities, growth and jobs, and resilience.

In this inclusive session, the relationship with the UN climate change regime was also addressed. While underscoring the fundamental role of reaching a binding commitment to the 2°C target in the multilateral treaty regime, it was stressed how a climate change SDG could provide for a precious complementary and transitional role in the period between 2015 and 2020 when the final agreement was expected to be reached under the UNFCCC negotiations.

Shifting attention to the local dimension of climate change, the OWG mentioned and praised the positive climate mitigation and adaptation initiatives at sub-national level, in particular by cities. In this regard a strong goal on sustainable cities was called for. This theme was at the centre of the Chair's Special Side Event on 'Future Cities We Want'. The key messages emerged from the roundtable discussion include the need to integrate climate change resilience and disaster risk reduction measures into urban planning. Furthermore, it was stressed that for coastal cities with a high-population density that are vulnerable to climate change, the inherent risks associated with natural disasters significantly increase.[10]

The discussions in the OWG could benefit from the input of statistical background information on climate change provided by the Technical Support Team (TST).[11] While statistical notes do not intend to recommend individual or particular sets of goals, targets, or indicators, they aim at providing a comprehensive and neutral picture of the statistical possibilities of measuring and monitoring the main issues. More specifically, the statistical notes provide the OWG with statistical background information on what data are or could be available to monitor possible goals and targets, describing methodologies, data availability, data sources, challenges, and limitations. The statistical notes also raise awareness for the need to consider statistical aspects in the design of the SDGs and the post-2015 development framework.

While a well-established reporting process, guided by the UNFCCC, exists for GHG emissions, comparable statistics on other issues related to climate change are not easily available.

---

[10] On 6 January 2014, the Permanent Mission of Japan and France to the United Nations, and Japan International Cooperation Agency (JICA) in collaboration with Organisation for Economic Co-operation and Development (OECD), United Nations Centre for Regional Development (UNCRD), United Nations Department of Economic and Social Affairs (UNDESA), United Nations Development Programme (UNDP), United Nations Environment Programme (UNEP), UNHABITAT, United Nations Industrial Development Organisation (UNIDO), and UN Sustainable Development Solution Network (UNSDSN) hosted a roundtable meeting on the occasion of the 7th OWG on Sustainable Development Goals (SDGs). The objective of the event was to seek a practical and realistic vision for Sustainable Future Cities, which can enrich the discussions on SDGs/Post-2015 Development Agenda through gathering practical views from various stakeholders in developing and developed countries and international agencies, and identifying practical challenges and opportunities to achieve this vision. See Chair's Summary Special Side Event at the 7th OWG on Sustainable Development Goals Sustainable Future Cities We Want, 6 January 2014.

[11] The TST, under the umbrella of the UN System Task Team (UNTT), which supports the post-2015 development agenda and consists of over sixty UN entities and agencies and international organizations, has been preparing an issue brief providing information on the measurement aspects for each of the twenty-nine issues discussed by the OWG during its first eight sessions.

C. OWG-10

To facilitate the intergovernmental process, the Co-Chairs made available a synthetic guidance document on the scope, purpose, and design of SDGs and of targets.[12] The auspices of the Co-Chairs were that SDGs should integrate and advance the work left incomplete by the MDGs, and follow the Rio + 20 indications regarding the priority areas for the achievement of sustainable development. To function as a driver for implementation and mainstreaming of sustainable development in the UN system as a whole, SDGs should address and incorporate in a balanced way all three dimensions of sustainable development and their interlinkages.

With regard to the design of SDGs, the Co-Chairs suggested that Goals express an ambitious, specific, and actionable commitment. Furthermore, they should be expressed in a concise way and be easy to communicate, aspirational, transformational, limited in number, global in nature, and universally applicable to all countries while taking into account different national realities, capacities, and levels of development and respecting national policies and priorities.

During this meeting, the OWG acknowledged how climate change is closely interconnected with many other concepts and sustainable development challenges, including sustainable agriculture, food security and nutrition, health and population dynamics, education, gender equality and women's empowerment, water and sanitation, energy, sustainable consumption and production, sustainable cities and human settlements, conservation and sustainable use of marine resources, oceans and seas, ecosystems and biodiversity.[13]

The Co-Chairs proposed that during the tenth session of the OWG, the focus areas be considered in a series of different clusters. Climate change was part of Cluster 5, together with 'Sustainable cities and human settlements' and 'Promote Sustainable Consumption and Production'. The recourse of clustering of focal areas is intended to help capture the many synergies existing among different fundamental aspects of sustainable development.

Among the various statements of the states' delegations, different views continued to be expressed regarding to whether climate change should be addressed by one specific devoted target or instead be reflected in targets under other related goals, as a 'pervasive cross cutting issue that shapes all human endeavours'.[14]

---

[12] Co-Chairs of OWG 10th Session, A definitional note on goals and targets https://sustainabledevelopment. un.org/content/documents/7417presentation.pdf accessed 21 November 2022.

[13] Open Working Group on Sustainable Development Goals Annex 1. Interlinkages <https://sustainabledeve lopment.un.org/content/documents/3387Annex_interlinkages_1903.pdf> accessed 21 November 2022.

[14] Statement by Italy–Spain–Turkey <https://sustainabledevelopment.un.org/content/documents/7792italy5. pdf> accessed 21 November 2022. Preference for this latter opinion emerges, for instance, in the Statement by Troika of China, Indonesia, and Kazakhstan on Cluster 4 of focus areas on 10th Session of SDGs OWG. <https:// sustainabledevelopment.un.org/content/documents/7762china5.pdf> accessed 21 November 2022 and in the Remarks by Ambassador Michael Grant of Canada, for the Canada/Israel/US team, 10th Session of the SDG Open Working Group, on Sustainable cities and human settlements and promotion of sustainable consumption and production <https://sustainabledevelopment.un.org/content/documents/8477us21.pdf> accessed 21 November 2022.

TRAVAUX PRÉPARATOIRES 955

D. OWG-11

The Co-Chairs drafted a Focus Area Document stressing that climate change poses a grave threat to sustainable development and poverty eradication and recommends that the principles of the UNFCCC, in particular CBDR-RC, are taken into account, and that there is support for greater ambition in the multilateral negotiations towards a strong and effective agreement in 2015.[15] The Focus Area Document identified the following specific relevant areas to take into consideration: (i) reaffirming and reinforcing existing international commitments, such as limiting the increase in global average temperature through equitable reductions in GHG emissions; (ii) building resilience and adaptive capacity in all vulnerable countries; (iii) introducing, *inter alia*, economic incentives for investments in low-carbon solutions in infrastructure and industry; (iv) developing low-carbon, climate-resilient development strategies and plans; (v) reducing the damage caused by climate-induced and other natural hazards through disaster risk reduction; (vi) improving education and awareness-raising on climate change; and (vii) appropriate means of implementation. These suggestions and proposals triggered in response different positions by Member States, Major Groups, and Other Stakeholders regarding how the Goals and targets should be framed.[16]

E. OWG-13

The Proposed SDG 13 was presented at the Thirteenth Session of the Open Working Group in the following version:

> Promote actions at all levels to address climate change / Build a climate change goal based on the outcome of COP21 of the UNFCCC

> 13.1 hold the increase in global average temperature below a x°C rise in accordance with international agreements
> 13.2 build resilience and adaptive capacity to climate induced hazards in all vulnerable countries 13.3 by 20xx integrate climate change adaptation and mitigation strategies into development plans and poverty reduction strategies
> 13.4 by 20xx introduce instruments and incentives for investments in low-carbon solutions in all relevant sectors

---

[15] Focus Area Document, Focus Area 15. Climate.

[16] For a detailed list of the various positions presented by the representatives, see Open Working Group on Sustainable Development Goals, Encyclopedia Groupinica: A Compilation of Goals and Targets Suggestions from OWG-10.

<https://sustainabledevelopment.un.org/content/documents/3698EncyclopediaGroupinica.pdf> accessed 21 November 2022. This document is a background document of the 11th Meeting of the OWG.

956 SDG 13

13.5 improve education, awareness raising and human and institutional capacity on climate change impact reduction and early warning.[17]

To inform the Thirteenth and last Session of the Open Working Group on Sustainable Development Goals, Major Groups and other stakeholders proposed a series of amendments to the proposed SDG 13 on climate change.

Proposals envisaging a more focused and more ambitious goal with quantified targets of 1.5/2°C and specific deadlines with regards to mitigation, adaptation, and transfer of climate finance were advanced, but were not retained in the final version.[18] In fact, the final version includes only one quantified target related to climate finance: the $100 billion annual commitment by developed countries.

The zero draft document, which closely resembles to the final proposal, reads:

Proposed goal 13. Tackle climate change and its impacts * (* The targets under a Climate Change goal may be part of and complementary to possible targets to be agreed within the framework of the UNFCCC negotiations.)

13.1 strengthen resilience and adaptive capacity to climate induced hazards and natural disasters in all countries

13.2 integrate climate change adaptation and mitigation into national strategies and plans

13.3 improve education, awareness raising and human and institutional capacity on climate change mitigation, impact reduction, and early warning

[17] Introduction and Proposed Goals and Targets on Sustainable Development for the Post-2015 Development Agenda (2 June 2014) <https://sustainabledevelopment.un.org/content/documents/4528zerodraft12OWG.pdf> accessed 21 November 2022.

[18] Noteworthy are the amendments proposed by NGO's Mayor Group, the Women's Major Group, the Major Group for Children and Youth, Beyond 2015, Climate Action Network, and International-Lawyers.org which included the following wording:

13.1 hold the increase in global average temperature below a 1.5/2°C rise in accordance with international agreements; 13.2 integrate climate change adaptation and mitigation into national strategies and plans (add) global annual emissions have declined to less than 40 $GtCO_2e$/yr by 2020, and less than 24 $GtCO_2e$ per year by 2030.... 13.4 (add) by 2020 develop plans that ensure a just transition to climate resilient development and which integrates climate change adaptation and mitigation into all relevant national regional and local strategies and plans; 13.5 (add) By 2020, ensure climate planning and action at all levels is rights-based, participatory and gender equitable.

13.6 (add) by 2020 improve education, awareness raising and human and institutional capacity on climate change mitigation, impact reduction, and early warning [ADD: especially at grassroots level]

13.a ensure the fulfilment of the commitment undertaken by developed country Parties to a goal of mobilizing jointly adequate finance of at least USD100 billion annually by 2020 and rapidly scaling up beyond that from all sources to address the needs of developing countries in the context of meaningful mitigation actions and transparency on implementation

13.b as agreed at least 50 per cent of these funds should be allocated to the Green Climate Fund ensuring the equal funding of adaptation and mitigation needs

13.c introduce instruments and incentives to rapidly reduce investment in fossil fuel and increase public financing, transfer of and domestic support for socially and ecologically sound technology and investments in low-carbon solutions infrastructure, industry, and other sectors

13.d ensure full respect for the principles of CBDR and equity to ensure adequate capacity building, technology transfer and financing for all developing countries.

13.a ensure the fulfilment of the commitment undertaken by developed country Parties to a goal of mobilizing jointly USD100 billion annually by 2020 from all sources to address the needs of developing countries in the context of meaningful mitigation actions and transparency on implementation.[19]

Although it was finally drafted as a stand-alone Goal, SDG 13 maintains close relationships with many other SDGs. A few examples are SDG 1, 'End poverty in all its forms everywhere', as also reflected in its target 1.5, aiming at '[b]y 2030, build(ing) the resilience of the poor and those in vulnerable situations and reduce their exposure and vulnerability to climate-related extreme events and other economic, social and environmental shocks and disasters'. Furthermore, strictly inherent to climate change is also Goal 2, 'End hunger, achieve food security and improved nutrition and promote sustainable agriculture' and its target 2.4, '[b]y 2030, ensure sustainable food production systems and implement resilient agricultural practices that increase productivity and production, that help maintain ecosystems, that strengthen capacity for adaptation to climate change, extreme weather, drought, flooding and other disasters and that progressively improve land and soil quality'.

As will be further examined, with regard to initiatives at the subnational level and with regard to resilience to climate change impacts, of particular relevance is Goal 11, 'Make cities and human settlements inclusive, safe, resilient and sustainable', and its target 11.b, '[b]y 2020, increase by [x] per cent the number of cities and human settlements adopting and implementing integrated policies and plans towards inclusion, resource efficiency, mitigation and adaptation to climate change, resilience to disasters, develop and implement, in line with the forthcoming Hyogo Framework, holistic disaster risk management at all levels'.

The proposal contains seventeen goals with 169 targets covering a broad range of sustainable development issues, including ending poverty and hunger, improving health and education, making cities more sustainable, combating climate change, and protecting oceans and forests. The proposal has been welcomed and praised by UN representatives. The Secretary-General addressed the General Assembly and welcomed the SDGs with the following words:

The 17 Sustainable Development Goals and associated 169 targets put forward by the Group as a clear expression of the vision of the Member States and their wish to have an agenda that can end poverty, achieve shared prosperity and peace, protect the planet and leave no one behind. In the coming months, you will negotiate the final parameters of the Post-2015 Sustainable Development Agenda. The new agenda should include a

---

[19] Introduction and Proposed Goals and Targets on Sustainable Development for the Post-2015 Development Agenda, Final Compilation of Amendments to Goals and Targets <https://sustainabledevelopment.un.org/content/documents/4523zerodraft.pdf> accessed 21 November 2022. For the final proposal, see Introduction to the Proposal of the Open Working Group for Sustainable Development Goals (19 July) <https://sustainabledevelopment.un.org/content/documents/4518SDGs_FINAL_Proposal%20of%20OWG_19%20July%20at%201320hrsver3.pdf> accessed 21 November 2022.

compelling and principled narrative, based on human rights and human dignity. It will require serious commitments for financing and other means of implementation. And it should include strong, inclusive public mechanisms at all levels for reporting, monitoring progress, learning lessons, and ensuring shared responsibility.[20]

III. Principles of International Law and Climate Change

The most important principles that should guide states and other actors in tackling climate change are strictly related to sustainable development, and aim at combining in a balanced way the relationship between the environmental, social, and economic dimension of development. The UNFCCC recognizes the importance of the principle of sustainable development, which should inform and guide the states' actions in tackling climate change in its article 3 entitled 'Principles':

4. The Parties have a right to, and should, promote sustainable development. Policies and measures to protect the climate system against human-induced change should be appropriate for the specific conditions of each Party and should be integrated with national development programmes, taking into account that economic development is essential for adopting measures to address climate change.

5. The Parties should cooperate to promote a supportive and open international economic system that would lead to sustainable economic growth and development in all Parties, particularly developing country Parties, thus enabling them better to address the problems of climate change. Measures taken to combat climate change, including unilateral ones, should not constitute a means of arbitrary or unjustifiable discrimination or a disguised restriction on international trade.[21]

Among the relevant concepts that should inform climate change action there is certainly the precautionary principle, in consideration of the inherent scientific uncertainties linked to the future evolution of the earth climate. The UNFCCC, article 3 with regard to the precautionary 'approach' states that

---

[20] Synthesis Report on the Post-2015 Agenda <https://sustainabledevelopment.un.org/content/docume nts/12120United%20Nations%20Secretary-General%20Ban%20Ki-moons%20Statements.pdf> accessed 21 November 2022. See also the statement of the UN Under-Secretary-General Wu Hongbo: 'The proposal of the Open Working Group brings together a breadth of economic, social and environmental issues in a single set of goals like never before. All those involved in crafting these 17 goals can be proud of themselves. Member States have shown a determination and willingness to work together for people and planet that bodes well for the General Assembly's negotiations on the post-2015 development agenda.' In commenting on the outcome, UNDESA's Assistant Secretary-General Thomas Gass hailed it as a milestone, highlighting the key role played by the Co-Chairs, Ambassador Csaba Kőrösi of Hungary and Ambassador Macharia Kamau of Kenya, the high-level engagement of Member States, and the active involvement of civil society. cf Press Release, UN General Assembly's Open Working Group proposes sustainable development goals <https://sustainabledevelopment.un.org/content/documents/4538pressowg13.pdf> accessed 21 November 2022.

[21] UNFCCC art 3.4 and 3.5.

[t]he Parties should take precautionary measures to anticipate, prevent or minimize the causes of climate change and mitigate its adverse effects. Where there are threats of serious or irreversible damage, lack of full scientific certainty should not be used as a reason for postponing such measures, taking into account that policies and measures to deal with climate change should be cost-effective so as to ensure global benefits at the lowest possible cost. To achieve this, such policies and measures should take into account different socio-economic contexts, be comprehensive, cover all relevant sources, sinks and reservoirs of greenhouse gases and adaptation, and comprise all economic sectors. Efforts to address climate change may be carried out cooperatively by interested Parties.

In fact, despite the Intergovernmental Panel on Climate Change (IPCC) Assessment Reports are progressively precise and reached a high degree of certainty with regard to the anthropogenic contribution to climate change and to the expected scenarios, a certain degree of uncertainty cannot be avoided.[22]

The climate change challenge is universally accepted to be a 'common concern of humankind' and as such requires the international community of states to act and cooperate for the benefit of present and future generations.[23]

In consideration of its crucial importance in the design and implementation of climate change obligations, the principle of CBDR will be further examined in its various dimensions, complexities, and manifestations as well as with regard to its still highly controversial aspects.

A. Equity and Differentiation: The Principle of Common but Differentiated Responsibilities and Respective Capabilities (CBDR-RC)

Equity has been one of the core principles inspiring the climate change regime from its early days.[24] Intra-generational equity is the general principle from which the CBDR principle and its legal obligations derive as they aim at addressing the real imbalances and disparities existing among states by setting differentiated standards of treatment and obligations. This ethical dimension endows differentiation with a particular authority and legitimacy, if it is perceived as well calibrated, which in turn favours the endorsement of the treaty by a great number of Parties by encouraging a sense of community and ownership.[25] The climate change challenge in its global dimension requires

---

[22] The Sixth Report of the IPCC is expected in 2022, but in the meantime an advanced contribution has been taken into account by the Glasgow Climate Pact, adopted by COP26. Climate Change 2021: The Physical Science Basis. Contribution of Working Group I to the Sixth Assessment Report of the Intergovernmental Panel on Climate Change <https://www.ipcc.ch/report/ar6/wg1/> accessed 21 November 2022.

[23] UN General Assembly, Resolution 43/53.

[24] See UNFCCC, Preamble (third para) and art 3.1.

[25] L Rajamani, *Differential Treatment in International Environmental Law* (OUP 2006) 6: 'Differential treatment, in so far as it furthers equality rather than entrenches inequality, has the potential to counterbalance some of the inequities inherent in globalization, and since decisions of the community of sovereign states are increasingly

a response from the international community as a whole. The shared responsibilities that states have with regard to the climate change challenge are generally recognized to be differentiated depending on the respective contributions to the problem, as well as according to the respective capacities to tackle its mitigation and adaptation dimensions in light of different domestic circumstances. This latter complex concept is reflected by the principle of CBDR-RC, which is the cornerstone principle of international climate change law and in particular of the climate change regime.

However, since the very beginning of multilateral climate negotiations, the need to differentiate among countries emerged as an unavoidable legal and policy challenge. Differentiation appeared necessary to adequately reflect states' contributions in terms of emissions of GHGs, as well as to take into account their different capacities to respond to the climate challenges of mitigation and adaptation.

The CBDR principle later evolved into the CBDR-RC and, despite being the cornerstone of the Climate Change regime, at the same time, today it remains its more contentious dimension. These uncertainties surrounding core elements of the principle are reflected in the reluctance of scholars to take a clear-cut position on its legal status.[26]

And indeed, the CBDR-RC principle reflects in its 'constructive ambiguity' many, also conflicting, conceptions of how the burden to address climate change should be equitably shared among states. The principle builds upon two dimensions: responsibilities and capabilities. The former element—responsibilities—is characterized as 'common', in as much as climate change is a global challenge for the international community as a whole and requires action by all states. However, this action may be 'differentiated' across states, in light of several criteria.[27] Hence, responsibilities of states are common and, in this context, they are 'akin to a moral duty', *but* differentiated in that they derive 'from causal agency in creating the problem'.[28]

As for the second parameter, if considering differentiation from the perspective of the 'respective capabilities' dimension, other indicators are relevant, such as vulnerability, economic development, and the specific needs of developing countries. This perspective is certainly more centred on equity and solidarity, considering the importance of the expected support that these countries should receive to be better empowered to face climate change impacts.

If—when interpreting the principle—major consideration is given to the differentiated responsibilities aspect, intended *strictu sensu*, as pointing to a legal duty to act

---

tested against the touchstone of civil society opinion, those decisions based on differential treatment may well be more equitable and therefore defensible in certain situations.'

[26] On the uncertain legal nature of the CDRRC principle, see L Rajamani, *Innovation and Experimentation in the International Climate Change Regime, The Hague Academy of International Law* (Brill/Nijhoff 2020) 195 and reference therein. As candidly recognized by authoritative scholars: 'Although there is universal support for the principle of CBDRRC, there is very little agreement on its rationale, core content, and application in particular situations'; cf D Bodansky and others, *International Climate Change Law* (OUP 2017) 27).

[27] With regard to states' contribution to climate change, relevant criteria are, for instance, historical GHG emissions, pro capita GHG emissions, or GHG emissions linked to national GDP; carbon footprint of the national energy mix.

[28] For a word-by-word analysis of the principle of common but differentiated responsibilities, see Rajamani, *Innovation and Experimentation in the International Climate Change Regime* (n 26) 182.

due to the objective contribution to climate change, the principle can be interpreted as creating legal obligations upon developed countries, which may vary in intensity depending on the different national circumstances, but which nonetheless requires them to act. The Urgenda case provides, as we will see later on, for an illuminating case in this direction.

The CBDR-RC principle is reflected first and foremost in SDG 13.a, which reaffirms the goal of transferring $100 billion each year to developing countries by 2020 to meet their mitigation and adaptation needs. Also SDG 13.b envisages a CBDR-RC-related goal in building capacity in LDCs and taking into consideration the special vulnerability of women, youth, and marginalized communities.

IV. The Multilateral Climate Change Regime

A. The UN Framework Convention on Climate Change (UNFCCC)

Negotiations of the UNFCCC have taken place under the aegis of the UN General Assembly due to the political pressure of developing countries which considered that this forum would have well represented their interests and the framework convention was then adopted at the Rio Conference in 1992. Parties agreed to general obligations and set an institutional structure and decision-making procedures as a basis for their future cooperation in tackling climate change.

The UNFCCC, as its title suggests, is an example of a framework treaty. Starting from the 1980s, this type of treaties is very often used to address environmental challenges at the international level. Indeed, Multilateral Environmental Agreements (MEAs) have boomed and represent the most common source of conventional international law. With these treaties that are 'constitutive, rather than regulatory',[29] states establish a process for the subsequent development of substantive obligations, rather than an immediate set of specific substantive rules. This approach to treaty making favours the greater participation of states because it leaves them a certain *marge de manoeuvre* by not requiring them to undertake stringent commitments straightaway. This aspect is clearly reflected by the generic wording in which the majority of the provisions are phrased and in an emphasis on institutional and procedural rather than substantive matters.[30]

The Conference of the Parties (COP) is the plenary organ governing the treaty, in charge of further developing, monitoring, and implementing treaty provisions.[31] In

---

[29] J Brunnée and S Toope, *Legitimacy and Legality in International Law. An Interactional Account* (CUP 2010) 48.

[30] FR Jacur, *The Dynamics of Multilateral Environmental Agreements. Institutional Architectures and Law-Making Processes* (Editoriale Scientifica 2013).

[31] Under the climate change regime there are three operating plenary meetings of the Parties, each in charge of the implementation of the underlying treaty: the Conference of the Parties to the UNFCCC (COP); the Conference of the Parties serving as the meeting of the Parties to the Kyoto Protocol (CMP), and the Conference of the Parties serving as the meeting of the Parties to the Paris Agreement (CMA). Despite over three decades of operation of the treaties, Parties under the UNFCCC have been unable to agree on the voting Rule, as the several attempts by

962   SDG 13

carrying out its mandate, the COP meets regularly every year and is assisted by the Secretariat providing administrative support and technical expertise. At a lower level in the institutional structure, subsidiary organs, notably the Subsidiary Body for Implementation (SBI) and the Subsidiary Body for Scientific and Technical Advice (SBSTA), assist the COP by providing technical expertise and carrying out other functions assigned to them. They meet periodically when the COP is not convened and keep an ongoing dialogue on the agenda. Open-ended working groups and scientific and technical bodies contribute to disentangle complex issues and facilitate reaching an agreement in the plenary. Furthermore, at the national level administrative bodies participate in the implementation of the treaty and, in a broad sense, they are also part of this institutional 'network'.

The UNFCCC establishes a long-term, evolutionary process to address climate change, which still today constitutes the fundamental legal context of international climate change law. From the normative perspective, the main bricks on which the regime still rests today are the already examined guiding principles, namely equity, sustainable development, precaution, CBDR, and the ultimate objective to 'achieve ... stabilization of greenhouse gas concentrations in the atmosphere at a level that would prevent dangerous anthropogenic interference with the climate system. Such a level should be achieved within a time frame sufficient to allow ecosystems to adapt naturally to climate change, to ensure that food production is not threatened and to enable economic development to proceed in a sustainable manner.'[32]

The UNFCCC sets the long-lasting classification of Parties into Annex I, Annex II, and non-Annex I, according to its article 4. This provision extensively sets the commitments required by each of these groups with regard to *inter alia* mitigation, adaptation, financial and technological assistance, and capacity building.

It establishes an infrastructure of institutions and decision-making mechanisms.[33] It promotes the systematic collection, review, and reporting of data.[34]

B. The Kyoto Protocol

After exhausting and never-ending negotiations, the Kyoto Protocol initially signed in 1997 has eventually entered into force in 2005. While under the parent convention, Parties commit to stabilize their GHG emissions, the Kyoto Protocol strengthens these commitments and requires its Parties to reduce, 'individually or jointly', their respective emissions according to quantified targets 'with a view to reducing their overall emissions of such gases by at least 5 per cent below 1990 levels' within 2012. The Kyoto

the Presidents of the various COPs to bring the Parties to an agreement, and the definitive decision on the majority requirements remains outstanding. In the meantime, decisions are adopted by consensus.

[32] UNFCCC, art 2.
[33] UNFCCC, arts 7, 8, 9, 10, and 11.
[34] UNFCCC, arts 4, 5, and 12.

Protocol further deepened the clear-cut differentiation approach between developed and developing countries. First and foremost, under the Protocol first commitment period (2008–2012), only Annex I countries 'shall, individually or jointly, ensure that their aggregate anthropogenic carbon dioxide emissions' do not exceed quantified limits and must reduce their overall emissions by at least 5 per cent.[35] Hence, according to the Protocol, Annex I Parties have quantified and legally binding mitigation commitments, while other countries may undertake voluntary mitigation actions.[36]

The Kyoto Protocol also sketches a regime of joint responsibility of 'Annex I Parties' in reaching the 5 per cent global reductions of GHGs.[37] For instance, changes in the number of participating states shall not affect the joint commitment undertaken. Most notably, it also expressly envisages that in the event of non-compliance with the overall shared target, each Party shall be responsible for its own level of emissions. Thus, even if states can act jointly, they remain individually responsible in case of failure to achieve the common target. The provisions of the Kyoto Protocol are without prejudice to other arrangements or obligations that may apply pursuant to other agreements between the Parties, for instance, deriving from EU law.

To facilitate Parties in the achievement of their GHG reductions, the Protocol allows them to act jointly and creates the so-called flexibility mechanisms. Through these tools, industrialized states can achieve reductions not only at home, namely on their territories, but also abroad, namely in developing countries and economies in transition, in order to lower the costs of achieving these targets. These innovative financial instruments create an unforeseen implementation scenario, characterized by partnerships between developed and developing states, with the participation of private actors and the establishment of a market where a new environmental commodity is traded. This unique system was adopted under the Kyoto Protocol with the aim of allowing industrialized states to achieve compliance with their obligations to reduce GHG emissions in an effective and economically efficient manner. The system is composed of two project-based mechanisms, the Clean Development Mechanism (CDM)[38] and the Joint Implementation (JI),[39] and a market-based one called the International Emissions Trading scheme (IET).[40] The first two mechanisms rely on the assumption that reductions of GHG emissions are beneficial for the global climate wherever they are achieved. Industrialized countries are encouraged to invest in 'green' projects located in developing countries or in countries with economies in transition where the costs of these reductions are comparatively lower. When the projects respect all the requirements set by the Kyoto Protocol and by the relevant COP decisions, industrialized countries

---

[35] Kyoto Protocol, art 3.1.

[36] An element that considerably softens the rigour of these mitigation commitments is the fact that they are not based on objective assessments of each country's contribution to climate change but reflect in great part a political compromise. This solution proved unavoidable during negotiations, but it weakens the legitimacy and equity of the differentiation among Annex I countries. Bodansky and others, *International Climate Change Law* (n 26) 160.

[37] Kyoto Protocol, art 4.

[38] The CDM is established by art 12 of the Kyoto Protocol.

[39] Kyoto Protocol, art 6.

[40] Kyoto Protocol, art 17 and subsequent implementing decisions.

can offset an equivalent quantity of the reduced emissions from the targets assigned to them by the Protocol.

The three main objectives of the CDM are to contribute to the sustainable development of the host state; to facilitate the achievement of compliance with quantified emission reduction commitments of industrialized states; and to contribute to the ultimate objective of reducing GHG emissions overall. Through the CDM, private investors of industrialized countries parties to the Kyoto Protocol finance GHG emission reduction projects in developing countries parties to the Protocol. The former receive Certified Emissions Credits (CERs) that can be used to offset their commitments or can be sold in the carbon market, and the latter should benefit of low-carbon technology transfer and financial flows that contribute to their sustainable development. The CDM is a hybrid model that combines top-down regulation coming from the treaty bodies of the Kyoto Protocol and bottom-up sustainable development strategies of developing countries hosting the projects.[41] The CDM is based on the principle of common but differentiated responsibilities and in observance of this principle, it differentiates countries according to their historical contribution to GHG emissions and their stage of economic development. The CDM provides for an interesting precedent on the interaction between private investment and climate change and shows a culture clash between the UN 'public interest' negotiating process and the private sector stakeholders operating within the process.[42]

Beside these project-based mechanisms the Kyoto Protocol establishes a market-based mechanism according to which industrialized countries may exchange and trade their entitlements to emit GHGs. These mechanisms introduce innovative elements such as flexibility and the involvement of private subjects, and the combination of these two elements attracts new means and sources of funding, as can be seen by the great development that the carbon market has experienced. To manage this system the COP has created an unprecedented apparatus of institutions and procedural rules so as to facilitate the achievement of real emission reductions.

The flexibility mechanisms facilitate compliance for developed countries with regard to their legally binding emission reductions obligations, by allowing them to ease their burden, by achieving GHG emission reductions in cost-effective ways. For this reason, the flexibility mechanisms were defined and reflect the same clear-cut differentiation: developed countries are the only protagonists of the carbon market, and under the CDM only developed country can obtain credits from the implementation of low-carbon projects in developing countries.

Another dimension of the Kyoto Protocol which is strongly inspired by differentiation among countries is its compliance mechanism. With regard to its institutional

---

[41] Acting through their respective Designated National Authority (DNA), host countries determine autonomously the sustainable development criteria that CDM projects should meet in order to be authorized on their territory.

[42] The CDM faced many challenges because of the sharp instability of its market and criticisms regarding its institutional and procedural features, such as the slow and complex approval process of the projects, the composition of the CDM Executive Board, and the latter being understaffed and underfunded to carry out its mandate.

dimension, the mechanism is divided into an Enforcement Branch, in charge of ensuring compliance of developed countries, and a Facilitative Branch, which is entrusted with assisting developing countries facing compliance issues. Noteworthy is the institutional design and the composition of the Enforcement Branch: even though its mandate is limited to ensure 'Annex I Parties' compliance, it is composed by individuals serving in their personal capacities who are nominated also by developing countries.[43] This independent and balanced composition strengthens the obligations upon 'Annex I Parties', which besides being legally binding also undergo an effective and unbiased compliance control. These institutional characters show that the CBDR principle translates not only into quantified legally binding, but also enforceable, obligations on behalf of 'Annex I Parties' in the pursuit of the global goal of mitigating climate change. Also when looking at the procedures and at the tools at the disposal of the two Branches, a clear-cut differentiation emerges between 'sticks' that are available to the Enforcement Branch, and the 'carrots' to be applied by the Facilitative Branch.[44]

Already during the negotiations of the Kyoto Protocol, the binary differentiation between developing and industrialized countries was criticized for its rigidity. There were no in-built adjustments systems that could allow the treaty to account for the steep increase of GHG emissions in emerging economies, which remained 'labelled' as developing countries under the Protocol's system. This lack of elasticity in adapting to major changing circumstances raised crucial competitiveness concerns of some industrialized countries, notably the United States, and signed the mark that would lead to the lengthy decline (and later death) of the Kyoto Protocol and of its top-down, strongly differentiated approach to climate change mitigation.

The Protocol should be praised for its straightforward ambition, even though this ambition and its rigidity were also major reasons why the Kyoto Protocol failed to gain the support of some crucial players, such as the United States and later Canada, Japan, and Russia. Furthermore, in the long-term it posed a great obstacle to the normative process under the climate change regime, because it has proven extremely difficult to reform it in a way that better combines the often-conflicting demands of all countries.[45]

The overall assessment of the Kyoto Protocol and of its approach to differentiation tells a story of mix success: on the bright side, the treaty obligations have scored a high level of compliance, both with regard to emissions reduction commitments and reporting obligations. The far less successful achievement relates to the effectiveness of

---

[43] Both Branches are composed of one member from each of the five regional groups of the United Nations; one member from the small island developing States, two members from 'Annex I Parties', and two members from 'non-Annex I Parties'.

[44] For a more detailed description of the institutional and procedural aspects of the compliance mechanism of the Kyoto Protocol, and on the practice relating to the cases of non-compliance, see F Romanin Jacur, 'The Kyoto Protocol's Compliance Mechanism, Elgar Encyclopaedia of Environmental Law' in DA Farber and M Peeters (eds), *Climate Change Law* (Edward Elgar Publishing 2016) 239–50.

[45] The lack of support for the Doha Amendment and the fragmentation of international climate governance can be read in this sense. H van Asselt and others, 'Global Climate Change and the Fragmentation of International Law' (2008) 30 Law & Policy 423. In front of the plain inability of the climate change regime to provide for the much-needed effective responses to the continued climate change problem, a variety of different initiatives have been developing starting from the early 2000s. For instance, climate change litigation is growing at the domestic, regional, and international level.

966   SDG 13

the climate change regime as a whole to solve the climate change problem: by weakening the legitimacy and crippling the law-making process almost a decade has passed without meaningful advancements in addressing climate change.

C. The Paris Agreement

From this divisive legacy and in a climate of political mistrust across states who found themselves free but also lost, no longer being grouped into the clear though obsolete categories of the Kyoto Protocol, here the Paris Agreement finds its origins. After lengthy and cumbersome negotiations lasted more than two decades under the aegis of the United Nations, the Paris Agreement is a delicate balance between the many and often conflicting interests and priorities of all the countries of the world. The agreement is the long-awaited and desired outcome that takes the scene away from the binary and highly contested North–South approach of the Kyoto Protocol, proposing instead a new picture, which reflects a different shade of colour for every state.[46] The Agreement sets the foundations for a long-term strengthened international cooperation which combines on the one hand, the flexibility necessary to accommodate the great variety of different national circumstances with, on the other, the necessity to rely on uniform and commonly accepted rules.

In Paris, states clearly wanted to distance themselves from the previous narrative and to build a new 'contract' which has its foundations in a renewed conception of CDBR that should strengthen the multilateral effort and provide for an effective, just, and long-term response to one of the greatest challenges of our time.[47]

In order to rebuild a globally shared path towards a low-carbon future, the Paris Agreement distances itself from the Protocol approach in many—maybe even all possible—ways.

The core pillars of the agreement cover national mitigation measures and international cooperation on mitigation, adaptation, and transfer of finance and technology.

The Paris Agreement consists of a Preamble and twenty-nine articles and is found in an Annex to a Decision of the Conference of the Parties (CMA) that provides for interpretative and complementary guidelines on its application. As regards its legal nature, the Agreement is an international treaty which has been open for signature by states on 22 April 2016 and entered into force upon ratification by fifty-five States representing 55 per cent of global GHG emissions production on 4 November 2016.

The treaty pursues a climate target that is scientifically based and represents the threshold that cannot be passed if the international community is not to face

---

[46] The turn from the 'top-down' approach of the Kyoto Protocol to the 'bottom-up' model of the Paris Agreement can be traced back to the Copenhagen Accord in 2009. On the (re)evolutions of climate negotiations, see Rajamani, *Innovation and Experimentation* (n 26) 94.

[47] Art 2.2 of the Paris Agreement reads: 'This Agreement will be implemented to reflect equity and the principle of common but differentiated responsibilities and respective capabilities, *in the light of different national circumstances*' (emphasis added).

catastrophic adverse climate impacts. The 1.5–2°C, is expressly recognized as the ultimate long-term objective that Parties must meet.[48] Parties agreed to periodically revise every five years and scale up their mitigation commitments.[49]

The Paris Agreement aims at holding the increase in the global average temperature 'well below' the 2°C above pre-industrial levels, possibly within 1.5°C. To achieve this goal, Parties should peak their emissions as soon as possible and adopt urgent reductions of GHGs according to the best available science.[50]

States committed to adopt at the national level mitigation measures according to their respective priorities and capacities. Thanks to this bottom-up approach which leaves discretion to states in deciding the kind of climate measures that suits them better, 190 states, representing 99 per cent of global GHG emissions production communicated their pledges. Although today the aggregate amount of these measures is far from what is scientifically required to keep the temperature rise within the 2°C or 1.5°C limit, Parties agreed to periodically revise every five years and scale up their mitigation commitments.[51] In order to enhance the credibility and transparency of these measures, states shall also communicate complementary technical and scientifically based information on their climate-related measures. Another crucial element of the Paris Agreement is the concept of 'ambition' that must also be read in the perspective of the CBDR principle, as evidenced by article 4.3, which reads: 'Each Party's successive nationally determined contribution will represent a progression beyond the Party's then current nationally determined contribution and reflect its highest possible ambition, reflecting its common but differentiated responsibilities and respective capabilities, in the light of different national circumstances.'

We find here a core compromise of the Paris Agreement which was necessary to ensure the participation of China and the United States, two countries which always stood against legally binding emission reductions commitments: on the one hand, substantive emission reduction objectives and commitments are voluntary and hence not legally binding, at least at the international level (article 4.2, second sentence: 'Parties shall pursue domestic mitigation measures, *with the aim of achieving the objective of such contributions*'); on the other hand, there are legally binding international obligations to periodically prepare, communicate and adjourn the NDCs (article 4.2, first sentence: 'Each Party *shall prepare, communicate and maintain* successive nationally determined contributions that it intends to achieve').

The Paris Agreement envisages reinforced financial commitments of developed countries for mitigation and adaptation initiatives to promote the transition to low-carbon economies in developing states and emerging countries (article 9.3) and encourages the participation of the private sector.[52]

---

[48] Paris Agreement, art 2.1(a).
[49] Paris Agreement, art 4.3 and art 4.9.
[50] Paris Agreement, art 2.1(a) and art 4.
[51] Paris Agreement, art 4.3 and art 4.9.
[52] Paris Agreement, art 9.9.

968   SDG 13

Furthermore, in order to enhance the transparency and the comparability of the action taken, besides communicating every five years on their mitigation measures, developed States Parties shall provide on a biennial basis qualitative and quantitative information on the financial resources transferred. Information provided by states on the mitigation, adaptation, and financial measures they undertake both at the domestic and international level shall be clear and scientifically based. The COP will review the effective implementation of these commitments every five years starting from 2023 in order to evaluate the progress made in the achievement of the assigned objectives.[53]

The main achievements of the Paris Agreement are of a procedural nature in that it envisages duties to periodically communicate the climate-related activities adopted at the national and international level, their revision, and their evaluation according to common standards decided at the international level on a scientific basis.

In view of the urgency of climate change challenges, it is essential that the Paris Agreement becomes operational and that its commitments are effectively implemented as soon as possible, even though subsequent delays threatened its effective implementation, due to the impasse of negotiations in the Madrid COP and to the interruption caused by the COVID-19 pandemic.

D. The Implementation of the Paris Agreement by the Subsequent Conferences of the Parties: From Katowice to Glasgow

The 'package deal' reached in Paris has not exhausted the tireless efforts needed to provide for an effective response to climate change. Just like its forerunners, the UNFCCC and the Kyoto Protocol, the Paris Agreement requires further law-making by its Conference of the Parties, the so-called CMA, to ensure that the promised actions, pledges, and the ambition of States Parties translates into concrete mitigation and adaptation policies.

Steps forward in clarifying the central principles and commitments of the Paris Agreement have been taken by COP 24 held in Katowice, where the so-called Paris Rulebook was adopted. This set of CMA Decisions provides for the much awaited and necessary specifications and details regarding crucial aspects of the Paris Agreement, such as the rules on mitigation, the transparency framework, the compliance mechanism, and the global stocktake.[54]

During the last COP 26 (CMA-3) held in Glasgow, the CMA stressed 'the urgency of enhancing ambition and action in relation to mitigation, adaptation and finance in this critical decade to address the gaps in the implementation of the goals of the Paris Agreement'.[55]

---

[53] Paris Agreement, art 14.
[54] L Rajamani and D Bodansky, 'The Paris Rulebook: Balancing International Prescriptiveness with National Discretion' (2019) 68 International and Comparative Law Quarterly 1023–40.
[55] Glasgow Climate Pact, para 5.

The Glasgow Climate Pact '[n]otes with serious concern' that, according to the latest official UN data that take into account the most recent and updated NDCs submission, the aggregate GHG emission level is estimated to be 13.7 per cent above the 2010 level in 2030.[56] As of December 2021, assuming that every country achieves its NDCs as promised, the global temperature will increase of about 2.7°C by the end of this century. This increase could be reduced to 2.4°C or even 1.8°C, taking into account other zero commitments promised by the European Union and the United States by 2050, China by 2060, and India by 2070, as well as the contribution of the private sector. Although the achievement of this objective does not constitute an absolute success in terms of a definitive response to climate change, it certainly represents a significant progress compared to the precedent scenarios.[57] Against this background, with regard to the temperature goal, the Glasgow Climate Pact reaffirms the need to meet the 1.5°C target to avoid severe climate change impacts. To reach this objective, the Pact indicates the necessary action by setting a quantified mitigation target linked with a precise deadline: 'rapid, deep and sustained reductions in global GHG emissions, including reducing global carbon dioxide emissions by 45 per cent by 2030 relative to the 2010 level and to net zero around mid-century, as well as deep reductions in other greenhouse gases'.[58]

Another major issue traditionally at the centre of climate change negotiations is climate finance. Also with regard to this target, the pledges of the Parties, notably developed states, are below what was pledged in previous COPs, since the meeting in Copenhagen in 2009, and what is expressly provided also by SDG 13.a.1.[59] With regard to adaptation finance, during the recent COP26 in Glasgow it was noted with concern that 'current provision of climate finance for adaptation remains insufficient to respond to worsening climate change impacts in developing country Parties'.[60] To cope with the shortages in the transfer of finance for adaptation, developed Parties should 'at least double their collective provision of climate finance for adaptation to developing country Parties from 2019 levels by 2025'.[61]

Nonetheless, ambition could have been greater and more pragmatic action could have been taken and, according to authoritative observers, 'the can (of heightened ambition) was kicked down the road, with the request that the Parties to the Paris Agreement revisit their NDCs next year'[62] at COP 27. One major issue that has been

---

[56] See Document FCCC/PA/CMA/2021/8/Rev.1 and Nationally determined contribution synthesis report (4 November 2021) at <https://unfccc.int/sites/default/files/resource/message _to_parties_and_observers_on_ndc_ numbers.pdf> accessed 21 November 2022.

[57] Of this view, R Stavins, 'What Happened in Glasgow at COP26?, An Economic View of the Environment' <http://www.robertstavinsblog.org/2021/11/14/what-happened-in-glasgow-at-cop26/> accessed 21 November 2022.

[58] Glasgow Climate Pact, para 22.

[59] ibid para 44-4, the CMA '*Notes with deep regret* that the goal of developed country Parties to mobilize jointly USD 100 billion per year by 2020 in the context of meaningful mitigation actions and transparency on implementation has not yet been met ... ; *Urges* developed country Parties to fully deliver on the USD 100 billion goal urgently and through to 2025 and *emphasizes* the importance of transparency in the implementation of their pledges.' On climate finance, see ibid para on target 13.a.

[60] ibid para 14.

[61] ibid para 18.

[62] cf Stavins, 'What Happened in Glasgow at COP 26?' (n 57).

970   SDG 13

discussed but fell short of being agreed to in Glasgow, and during the preparatory G20 Meeting held in Rome just before the COP, is the undertaking of a clear-cut commitment to phase out the extraction and use of coal and other fossil fuels. The Glasgow Climate Pact contains a rather watered-down provision in this regard, which '[c]alls *upon* Parties to accelerate the development, deployment and dissemination of technologies, and the adoption of policies, to transition towards low-emission energy systems, including by rapidly scaling up the deployment of clean power generation and energy efficiency measures, including accelerating efforts towards the phasedown of unabated coal power and phase-out of inefficient fossil fuel subsidies'.[63]

V. Tackling Climate Change Across Other Fields of International Law

A. Climate Change and Human Rights

Beyond its merely environmental dimension, and in view of the deep interdependence between humankind and nature, climate change entails considerable negative impacts on the enjoyment of fundamental human rights. The disastrous impacts of climate change phenomena, such as cyclones, hurricanes, and wildfires have manifested themselves in various areas of the world and have inflicted incredible suffering on individuals and communities: from the Cyclone Idai in the African and Caribbean Regions, to bushfires increasingly devastating areas in Australia, North America, and Europe, to the radical change in the Arctic ecosystems due to the increased temperatures and melting of the ice. These devastating events threaten and often irreparably hamper the right to a healthy environment, the right to life, to food, and to water. As recognized by the United Nations High Commissioner for Human Rights on the relationship between climate change and human rights: '(ii) climate change has a wide range of implications for the effective enjoyment of human rights, including the rights to life, health, food, water, housing and self-determination, and (iii) environmental degradation, desertification and global climate change are exacerbating destitution and desperation, causing a negative impact on the realization of the right to food, in particular in developing countries'.[64]

The multiple and deep interconnections between human rights and climate change have traditionally been kept outside the intergovernmental framework of the climate change regime. In time, this undeniable normative loophole has been attempted to be compensated in different ways. On the one hand, at the international level, the UN[65]

---

[63] Glasgow Climate Pact (n 58) para 36.

[64] Human Rights Council, Report of the Office of the United Nations High Commissioner for Human Rights on the relationship between climate change and human rights, 15 January 2009, UN Doc A/HRC/10/61, para 56.

[65] See Human Rights Council, Resolution 35, entitled 'Human rights and climate change,' adopted on 19 June 2017, UN Doc A/HRC/35/L.32; Human Rights Council, Report of the Special Rapporteur on the issue of human rights obligations relating to the enjoyment of a safe, clean, healthy and sustainable environment, 1 February 2016, UN Doc A/HRC/31/52, paras 9 and 23; Human Rights Council, Report of the Office of the United Nations High

and regional bodies, like the African Commission on Human and Peoples' Rights,[66] the Organization of American States (OAS), and the Council of Europe have undertaken various climate change-related initiatives. Recently, the Independent Expert on human rights and international solidarity, Obiora Chinedu Okafor, has engaged in examining the enjoyment, or lack thereof, of the human rights-based international solidarity in the context of climate change.[67] On the other hand, moving from the intergovernmental stage to judicial and quasi-judicial courtrooms, climate change-related cases have been brought before human rights judicial and quasi-judicial bodies, and before domestic and European Union courts.[68] These initiatives should be seen as complementary to the treaty-based endeavours and aiming at aligned objectives.

1. The Inter-American Court of Human Rights

The Inter-American Court of Human Rights issued an advisory opinion finding that the right to a healthy environment is a human right.[69] Echoing a Resolution of the OAS General Assembly,[70] the opinion recognizes the 'undeniable' relationship between the protection of the environment and human rights and specifically emphasizes that 'the adverse effects of climate change affect the real enjoyment of human rights'.[71] When called to exercise its advisory function, the Court may interpret relevant international obligations of OAS Member States, including climate change treaties, to assist states in implementing effectively their public policies to protect human rights.[72] The opinion further discussed the responsibility of governments for significant environmental damage that they cause within and beyond their borders. The Court's advisory opinion enables all states who recognize the jurisdiction of the Court—and the citizens of those countries—to file claims regarding environmental harms that impact their human rights. In these cases, the Court assesses whether the respondent state met three types of obligations: first, obligations to prevent environmental damages;[73] second,

---

Commissioner for Human Rights on the relationship between climate change and human rights, 15 January 2009, UN Doc A/HRC/10/61, paras 18 and 24, and Human Rights Council, Analytical study of the relationship between human rights and the environment, Report of the United Nations High Commissioner for Human Rights Report of the United Nations High Commissioner for Human Rights, 16 December 2001, UN Doc. A/HRC/19/34, para 7.

[66] African Commission on Human and Peoples' Rights, Resolution 153 on climate change and human rights and the need to study its impact in Africa, 25 November 2009.

[67] Human Rights Council, Report of the Independent Expert on human rights and international solidarity, A/HRC/44/44 (1 April 2020).

[68] cf *Armando Ferrão Carvalho and Others v The European Parliament and the Council*. In this case the plaintiffs asked the Court of Justice of the European Union to declare three EU legal acts as void for failing to set adequate GHG emissions targets. Full documentation is available at <http://www.peoplesclimatecase.caneurope.org> accessed 21 November 2022.

[69] Advisory Opinion OC-23/17 of 15 November 2017 Requested by the Republic of Colombia, 'A Request for an Advisory Opinion from the Inter-American Court of Human Rights Concerning the Interpretation of Article 1(1), 4(1) and 5(1) of the American Convention on Human Rights'.

[70] OAS General Assembly, Resolution 'Human Rights and Climate Change in the Americas', adopted at the fourth plenary session held on 3 June 2008, AG/RES. 2429 (XXXVIIIO/08).

[71] Advisory Opinion OC-23/17, para 47.

[72] ibid para 24.

[73] To meet this obligation, states must, for example, implement the following actions: (i) issue regulations to prevent damages, (ii) establish contingency plans to minimize the possibility of major environmental accidents, (iii) mitigate significant damage that has already occurred, and (iv) carry out environmental impact studies under the

972   SDG 13

obligations to cooperate;[74] and third, obligations to provide information, justice, and public participation.[75] In this landmark opinion, the Court confirmed that states have duties to prevent that activities within their jurisdictions cause environmental damage and hence negatively affect human rights of people in other states. With regard to climate change, this ruling is of great importance for its implications in the difficult configuration of the extraterritorial reach of climate change damages in that it recognizes the transboundary nature of climate change and its related side effects, and links them with the duty of prevention by expressly envisaging a duty on behalf of states and their corresponding responsibility to avoid extraterritorial human rights violations, which originated from activities under their jurisdictions.

B. International Trade Law and Climate Change:
Conflicts and Synergies

Climate change and trade law pursue different objectives, namely mitigation of GHG emissions and trade liberalization, and have developed following separate paths under the aegis of their respective international regimes, the Climate Change Regime and the World Trade Organization. Recently, however, the economic expansion and the opening of the markets in emerging economies brought a growing demand for energy resources and consequently lead to increases in GHG emissions. On the other side, recently adopted climate change policies entail significant economic effects. Therefore, nowadays these two fields are getting closer and becoming interrelated under their economic, political, social, technical, and legal aspects and increasingly share common objectives. The necessity of coordination between trade and climate change was one of the most important issues addressed during the negotiations of the Doha Round where the difficulties of balancing economic interests and environmental values emerged. For the first time in the history of the World Trade Organization (WTO), negotiations under the Doha Round, which started in 2001, covered also environmental matters, in particular the adoption of specific rules on the relationship between WTO and MEAs and the elimination of barriers to trade in environmental goods and services.[76]

conditions indicated by the Court. The Court requires environmental impact studies to address cumulative impacts, allow the participation of interested persons, and respect the traditions and culture of Indigenous peoples. These studies must also be conducted by independent entities and occur prior to the activities that they evaluate.

[74] To meet this obligation, states must, for example, implement the following actions: (i) cooperate in good faith with states and individuals potentially affected by environmental damage, (ii) notify potentially affected states that a planned activity under their jurisdiction could generate a risk of significant transboundary damages and of environmental emergencies, and (iii) negotiate in good faith with States potentially affected by significant transboundary harm.

[75] To meet this obligation, states must, for example, implement the following actions: (i) access to information related to possible effects on the environment, (ii) the opportunity for citizens to publicly participate in making decisions and policies that may affect the environment, and (iii) access to justice through national courts in regard to their environmental obligations. The Court clarified that persons potentially affected by transboundary damages must have access to justice without discrimination based on their nationality, residence, or the location of the environmental damage.

[76] In particular, para 31 (iii) of the Doha Ministerial Declaration (WT/MIN(01)/Dec/1) calls for 'the reduction, or as appropriate, elimination of tariff and non-tariff barriers on environmental goods and services'.

For decades, and still today, negotiations under the climate change regime to shape future international agreement are engaging with the conflicting economic interests of industrialized countries, especially the United States, and emerging economies, such as China and India. The key concerns that emerge from these negotiating positions are, on one side, to defend the competitiveness of the national industrial sectors and, on the other, to guarantee the utmost priority of the right to economic development.[77] An international agreement that finds some fine-tuning between effective emission reduction policies and related competitive concerns would be the best solution for effective global regulation of trade and climate matters. However, in the absence of consensus on the specific aspects of how these interlinkages should be designed, states have adopted, unilaterally or jointly—but not globally—climate measures to cut carbon emissions coupled with trade measures that should cover the competitiveness concerns and the risk of climate-related 'leakage'.[78]

Many states are considering or have already adopted policies to control climate change and, particularly with regard to the European Union, are taking domestic action to achieve substantial reductions in their emissions. This action is characterized, in particular, by the use of market-based instruments—such as taxation, targeted subsidies, or tradable emission rights—for promoting environmental sustainability, reducing dependence on external resources, and ensuring the competitiveness of different economies. Serious risks of conflicts exist between these measures and WTO law.

The WTO system is based on the economic theory according to which liberalization of international trade helps to increase global prosperity and the individual wealth of states, postulating that an international trade order, composed by rules accepted by all States Members, reduces the risk of trade wars and promotes the maintenance of stability and peace in the international community. For the realization of the aforesaid aims, the WTO system is founded on some fundamental principle and rules: the principle of non-discrimination, the prohibition of quantitative restrictions, and the tariff concessions.

This section will consider the requirements that certain trade-related climate change measures that are in the course of being, or have already been adopted at the national, regional, and international level shall meet to be compatible with trade law, in particular with the General Agreement on Tariffs and Trade (GATT) rules.[79] In particular, the analysis will focus on market-based instruments, such as tradable emission rights,

---

[77] While the United States advocates for emission reduction commitments for all states, and transfer of financial and technical assistance to developing countries in need, most of the emerging economies were willing to maintain the 'Kyoto Protocol approach', ie differentiated commitments in magnitude and legal nature on behalf of developing countries, in accordance with the principle of common but differentiated responsibilities.

[78] This expression refers to the relocation of industries in countries, mainly developing ones, with weak or no carbon reduction programs, to lower their production costs. This practice undermines the effectiveness of climate change regulations by shifting GHG emissions to permissive countries without achieving real global reductions. Moreover, countries with emission reduction policies in place suffer competitiveness damage, in particular for sensible energy-intensive sectors.

[79] Other WTO agreements such as the General Agreement on Trade in Services (GATS), Agreement on Subsidies and Countervailing Measures (ASCM), and Agreement on Technical Barriers to Trade (TBT) are relevant but will not be taken into account in this chapter.

974   SDG 13

and fiscal measures, such as carbon taxes. These policies are not mutually exclusive and could be used together in a comprehensive climate change policy.

This type of measures, allegedly adopted with the main aim of ensuring the effectiveness of the climate measures by preventing 'carbon leakage', are either domestic measures that water down emission reduction commitments for certain productive sectors or border measures, so-called Border Tax Adjustments (BTAs), targeting imports (as well as exports) in order to level the playing field. The design and implementation of these two types of measures pose controversial problems in light of trade law.

WTO members have a large degree of autonomy in determining their own policies in environmental matters and can adopt trade-related measures to protect the environment, as long as such measures comply with WTO rules or fall under one of the exceptions to these rules. A fundamental principle that sets the requirements to be met by trade-related climate measures if they want to pass the 'compatibility test' with WTO law is the principle of non-discrimination, as required by GATT article I (the most favoured nation treatment principle)[80] and article III (principle of national treatment).[81]

A climate change-related measure, be it a tax or a regulation, violating these non-discrimination provisions may still be legitimate under WTO law if it qualifies as an exception under GATT article XX.[82] In order to verify whether a measure qualifies as an exception under article XX, a two-tiered test has to be carried out. First, the measure must come within the scope of one of the specific exceptions and then its content should be analysed in light of the *chapeau*. With regard to climate change measures, they could fall both under paras (b) and (g) of article XX. While para (b) requires the measure to be 'necessary', it could be lighter to pass the test pursuant to para (g) that sets a lower requirement, by providing that the measure should 'relate' to the conservation of exhaustible resources, assuming that climate change can be considered as an 'exhaustible natural resource'.[83]

---

[80] The MFN principle requires that any advantage accorded to an imported product, should be accorded to like products imported from other WTO Members. Article I.1 reads: 'any advantage, favour, privilege or immunity granted by any contracting party to any product originating in or destined for any other country shall be accorded immediately and unconditionally to the *like products* originating in or destined for the territories of all other contracting parties'.

[81] According to the NT principle, an imported product should be treated no less favourably than a like domestic product. Art III, para 4 provides that '[t]he products of the territory of any contracting party imported into the territory of any other contracting party shall be accorded treatment no less favourable than that accorded to like products of national origin'.

[82] Pursuant to GATT, art XX. 'Subject to the requirement that such measures are not applied in a manner which would constitute a means of arbitrary or unjustifiable discrimination between countries where the same conditions prevail, or a disguised restriction on international trade, nothing in this Agreement shall be construed to prevent the adoption or enforcement by any contracting party of measures: ... b) necessary to protect human, animal or plant life or health; ... g) relating to the conservation of exhaustible natural resources if such measures are made effective in conjunction with restrictions on domestic production or consumption....'

[83] Support for this position may be found in the WTO case *United States–Gasoline*, where the panel ruled that clean air was a resource, was natural and could be depleted. Panel Report, United States—Standards for Reformulated and Conventional Gasoline, WT/DS2/R, adopted on 20 May 1996, para 6.37. See also GC Hufbauer and others, *Global Warming and World Trading System* (Peterson Institute for International Economics 2009), recognizing that '[f]or a future panel to refuse to apply this precedent to climate change seems highly unlikely'. Other arguments in favour of this interpretation may be found in the fact that the interpretation of the concept of 'natural resources' is not static but 'evolutionary' and should be made in the light of the actual environmental concerns of the international community.

Once positively ascertained that a climate measure falls within the scope of para (g), WTO jurisprudence clarified that in order to verify that the measure is related to the conservation of exhaustible resources, a 'substantial relation' should exist between the measure and the objective pursued. According to the Appellate Body, this 'nexus' exists when the 'general structure and design' of the measure, that is, the means foreseen, are appropriate to reach the declared environmental aim.[84] Another substantive requirement set by para (g) is that 'restrictions on domestic production and consumption' should be adopted in conjunction with the said measure. The next step will be the consistency with the requirements of the *chapeau*: the measure should pass the test of not being an 'arbitrary or unjustifiable discrimination' and should not consist in a 'disguised restriction on international trade'. The interpretation of the requirements of the *chapeau* entails delicate issues that have been repeatedly addressed by WTO dispute settlement bodies. The main elements that can be outlined and that are relevant for the future analysis of trade-related climate measures are the way the measure is applied, its procedural and substantive aspects, and whether the discrimination it creates has a legitimate cause.

The non-discrimination obligations apply to products (and services) that are 'like' or similar to each other, while products that are not 'like' may be treated differently. WTO jurisprudence interpreted the meaning of 'like' products according to the various provisions of WTO Agreements and generally took a broad interpretation of this notion in order to expand its applicability, and consequently avoid discrimination.[85] Although no definitive interpretation of this concept may be given, some guidelines for the interpretation of 'likeness' may be found in decisions of the WTO dispute settlement bodies.

The Appellate Body maintained that the concept of 'likeness' is linked to the competitive relation between products and has identified four criteria to determine comparability between two products: physical characteristics of the products, end use, consumer tastes and habits, and tariff classification.[86] The Appellate Body also stressed that in interpreting the notion of 'likeness' a case-by-case approach and a discretionary evaluation are unavoidable.

A further aspect, related to the concept of 'likeness', that is of fundamental importance in the exam of climate measures is the issue of the process and production methods of goods (PPMs). The crucial issue in this regard is whether goods, which differ only in the way they have been produced, should be considered 'like': for example, is steel, produced using fossil-sourced energy such as coal, 'like' steel produced with natural gas, renewable energy, or according to energy efficiency productive processes? If they are considered as 'like' products, they shall receive the same treatment, while, on the contrary, if they are different their treatment may take into account their different carbon footprint.

---

[84] *United States–Shrimps*, paras 133 and ff.

[85] The more products are considered 'like', the more discrimination will be avoided. Vice versa, when interpreting 'likeness' in exception provisions, the concept will be interpreted narrowly.

[86] Appellate Body Report on EC-Measures Affecting Asbestos an Asbestos-Containing Products (WT/DS135/AB/R, 12 March 2001), para 101.

976   SDG 13

The majority of authors and WTO case law consider that physically similar goods that differ only in the way they have been produced should be considered as 'like' and that, as a consequence, measures that treat differently these 'like' products on the basis of their production methods violate the principle of non-discrimination of articles I and III. However, new trends are emerging and, in more recent decisions, the Appellate Body has shown to be keen in taking into account PPMs when applying the exceptions under GATT article XX. While in previous cases it was considered that PPMs measures related to the conservation of resources outside the jurisdiction of the country adopting the discriminatory measure could not be covered by the exceptions of article XX, in more recent decisions, such as *Tuna–Dolphin II* and the *Shrimps–Turtle* case, the Panel considered legitimate the trade measures based on PPMs under article XX.[87]

The following sections will briefly describe the fundamental aspects, in the first place, of cap and trade schemes and carbon taxes, as regulatory means to cut carbon emissions and assess their compatibility with the GATT Agreement. Secondly, other type of measures targeting imported products will be considered. These latter, be they BTAs or obligations to purchase a certain amount of carbon credits, are trade measures that may be adopted as an extension of climate policies with the aim of establishing a level playing field between burdens charged on national and imported products.

1. Cap and Trade Schemes

In cap and trade schemes, Parties involved, be they states or private entities, agree to reduce their emissions of GHGs during a given period and set an overall cap to be respected. The cap amount is subdivided into allowances that are distributed to individual emitters and can be traded among participants to the scheme at a price determined by the market.

Emission trading schemes have developed at the international, regional, and national level. At the international level, the Kyoto Protocol scheme is the main market of emission credits, where the participants are the Annex I Parties to the Protocol and private entities that they authorize to trade in emission credits under their supervision and responsibility.[88] Taking advantage of the possibility set by the Kyoto Protocol to fulfil their reduction commitments jointly,[89] European states concluded a burden sharing agreement that creates an emission trading scheme at the European level. This scheme has been the first GHG emission trading scheme to become operative in 2005.

---

[87] The *Tuna–Dolphin* cases (*United State–Tuna/Dolphin I*, GATT DS21/R; *United States–Tuna/Dolphin II*, GATT DS29/R) show the evolution of the WTO jurisprudence on this matter. While in the first case, the Panel held that a measure that protected resources outside the jurisdiction of the State was not covered by art XX, the second Panel considered that measures linked to the production processes in foreign countries were not, per se, outside the scope of art XX.

[88] The international emission trading scheme (IET) is established by art 17 of the Kyoto Protocol. Its concrete functioning has been developed by the COP. See, in particular, Decision 2/CMP.1 Modalities, rules and guidelines for emissions trading under Article 17 of the Kyoto Protocol (FCCC/KP/CMP/2005/8/Add.1), Annex, para 5. The Kyoto units exchanged on this market are in part derived from the cap set by the Kyoto Protocol (the Assigned Amount Units), and in part other Kyoto units (Certified Emission Reductions (CERs), Emission Reduction Units (ERUs)) created by the project-based flexibility mechanisms of the Protocol, the Clean Development Mechanism, and the Joint Implementation. This market started operating in 2008.

[89] Kyoto Protocol, art 4.

At the national level, many countries established emission trading schemes and similar initiatives are currently under review in New Zealand, Australia, and the United States.

Before dealing with the issue of the compatibility of these measures with WTO law, a preliminary matter to be addressed relates to the legal nature of the emissions units that are produced and traded under these schemes in order to determine whether they fall within the scope of WTO Agreements.[90] Many commentators consider that emissions allowances would neither be classifiable as 'products' nor as 'services' and therefore would not be covered by WTO law.[91] Other authors consider these measures as equivalent to taxes or, under certain circumstances, as subsidies in terms of WTO law.[92]

For present purposes, this study considers emissions units to be intangible assets that entitle their owner to emit a certain amount (1 tonne) of GHG emissions. On this assumption, it recognizes that these emissions have a hybrid nature, since they embody an authorization to emit a certain substance and, at the same time, a right that can be sold and transferred.[93] In consideration of their double nature, these credits may be seen both as a state measure (licence, tax, subsidy) and as a good or service. According to this definition, in both cases they are covered by WTO law, because their allocation and trading may alter the competitive conditions of emissions trading markets and of markets where energy and energy-related goods and services are traded.

With regard to potential discriminations within the emissions trading market, a first problem may arise because trading schemes are generally created as a supplemental mean to domestic actions through which emissions reductions can be achieved.[94] Each state is free to determine what it intends as 'supplemental' and accordingly set a limit in trading of credits that are not the result of domestic reductions, being created abroad. This 'origin-based' discrimination could constitute a violation of GATT article III, but could be still justified under GATT article XX. It may be argued that supplementarity, albeit entailing a discrimination, is a necessary element of the scheme that guarantees the environmental integrity of the system, by ensuring that part of the reductions is obtained at home. Therefore, this discrimination between national and foreign emission credits could be justified under GATT article XX if there is sufficient evidence that supplementarity provisions do not constitute arbitrary discrimination or a disguised restriction to trade.

---

[90] In other words, it should be made clear if they can be considered as 'goods', 'services', 'taxes', or even 'subsidies' under WTO law. At present very different positions exist on the matter because no definition exists either of 'allowances' and 'credits' under relevant environmental instruments or of 'goods' and 'services' under the WTO Agreements. A definition of 'allowance' is found in art 3 of the Directive 2003/87/EC establishing a scheme for GHG emission allowance trading within the Community, that defines 'allowance' as: 'an allowance to emit 1 tonne of carbon dioxide equivalent during a specified period valid only for the purposes of meeting the requirements of the Directive and which is transferable in accordance with the provisions of this Directive'.

[91] Of this view J Werksman, 'Greenhouse Gas Emissions Trading and the WTO' (1999) 8(3) Review of European Community and International Environmental Law 2.

[92] In support of this thesis, see J Pawelyn, 'U.S. Federal Climate Policy and Competitiveness Concerns: The Limits and Options of International Trade Law' (Nicholas Institute for Environmental Policy Solutions, Duke University April 2007) 21.

[93] For a similar position, see E Vranes, 'Climate Change and the WTO: EU Emission Treading and the WTO Disciplines on Trade in Goods, Services and Investment Protection' (2009) 43(4) Journal of World Trade 707, 717.

[94] Kyoto Protocol, art 17: 'Any such trading shall be supplemental to domestic actions for the purpose of meeting quantified emission limitation and reduction commitments ....' See also art 30(3) of the ETS Directive.

978 SDG 13

Other potential challenges to the consistency of cap and trade schemes with WTO law may arise with regard to how the following elements are designed and effectively implemented: the stringency of the cap, the way allowances are distributed, the type and extent of the exceptions granted to certain industries, and qualitative restrictions for certain type of offset activities. As for the way of allocating emissions credits on the market, the main methods are the allocation free of charge from the governments to industries covered by the scheme, and auctioning, or a mix of the two methods. Distribution free of charge is generally adopted in the early phases of cap and trade schemes because it 'softens' the impact on competitiveness.[95] However, this method, being 'climate-neutral', is not far-reaching in terms of cutting emissions and may be considered as a subsidy to certain productive sectors and therefore violate the Agreement on Subsidies and Countervailing Measures (ASCM) Agreement. On the other side, when credits are distributed by auctioning and hence have a certain price, industries' competitiveness suffers a stronger impact. This latter solution is more ambitious in terms of climate change mitigation, albeit politically difficult to be approved.

The European experience provides us with a telling example of these situations. The first phase of operation (2005–2007) of the scheme was characterized by a too generous cap, inconsistencies in setting the reduction targets, that is, too many allowances were distributed to the market participants, and free distribution of allowances. This phase ended with a fall in the price of allowances and a general ineffectiveness of the scheme. These shortcomings have been addressed and the subsequent phases have been implemented with new rules setting stricter and more consistent commitments, and the auctioning of a high percentage of allowances.[96] Today, 'the EU ETS is a cornerstone of the Union's climate policy and constitutes its key tool for reducing GHG emissions in a cost-effective way'.[97]

Other potential WTO violations may arise because there are certain activities that are not eligible to create emission credits. Under existing schemes, for example, while trade of carbon credits generated by forestry activities are currently accepted, albeit in a very limited quantity, other activities such as nuclear projects, or carbon capture and storage cannot generate credits. These qualitative restrictions, when not strongly based on environmental arguments, may be challenged and found illegitimate in WTO terms, in that they have a discriminatory impact.[98]

---

[95] Free allocation of credits poses problems when dealing with the possibility of adjustment at the border. In fact, it could be argued that no real cost is imposed on domestic products and therefore no border tax adjustment should be adopted.

[96] Directive 2009/29/EC of the European Parliament and of the Council of 23 April 2009 amending Directive 2003/87/EC so as to improve and extend the greenhouse gas emission allowance trading scheme of the Community, Official Journal of the European Union, L 140/63, 5 June 2009.

[97] Regulation (EU) 2021/1119 of the European Parliament and of the Council of 30 June 2021 establishing the framework for achieving climate neutrality and amending Regulations (EC) No 401/2009 and (EU) 2018/1999 (European Climate Law), Preamble, para 13.

[98] In similar situations the discriminatory effect would relate to the PPMs of carbon credits, ie would affect the project activities through which these credits have been created. In such cases, while a violation of art III may be justified because these qualitative restrictions apply also to domestic credits, a violation of art I could more probably be envisaged and would need to be justified according to art XX. In order to pass the two-tiered test of art XX, provisions that discriminate between carbon credits according to their PPMs would need, in particular, to demonstrate that they are based on legitimate environmental reasons and that they are applied in consistent manner that does not lead to unjustifiable discrimination.

Furthermore, WTO law may be violated by cap and trade schemes that are closed to states that do not have in place a comparable programme of emission reductions. A dispute could be brought to the WTO bodies by a state to which access to the cap and trade scheme is denied, which challenges these conditions as discriminatory. To avoid these barriers which would also hamper the smooth functioning of the carbon market it is essential to design effective linkages among different schemes. These concerns have been taken into account during the latest Glasgow COP26.[99]

WTO jurisprudence identified key elements to be used to assess the legitimacy of a measure, in this case the linking provision, with regard to article XX. The foreign programmes need not be the same but should be 'comparable in effectiveness'.[100] The measure should be designed in a flexible way that allows it to take into account specific conditions of the other countries. Moreover, the state adopting the measure should have a cooperative approach with regard to other countries and should allow them with the opportunity to defend themselves against the specific measure or with the possibility to apply and to demonstrate that they are eligible to participate in the programme.[101]

2. Carbon Taxes

With reference to fiscal measures, states are exempted from constraints in the exercise of their taxation policies. In fact, GATT article III is not a rule finalized for the fiscal harmonization of goods and services but, on the contrary, aims at removing trade barriers between different markets. In this way, the taxes and other forms of fiscal measures must not target the imported products coming from other WTO Member States, causing trade distortions between domestic and imported 'like' products.

For these reasons, WTO law looks in a more favourable way at price-based measures such as taxes because they are more transparent and economically more efficient compared to other regulatory measures. Taxes on certain energy-intensive products and on energy itself may be effective tools to shift consumers and production towards low-emission patterns and clean energy: taxes may be imposed on foreign and domestic goods that have already arrived in the internal market and target the carbon emissions released by national and imported products that take place on the national territory and not abroad. These taxes, as long as they are not discriminatory between domestic and imported products are easily justifiable under GATT law.

A different type of taxation targeting carbon emissions taking place during the production of the goods is more difficult to justify under GATT law because when applied to imported products, these taxes target carbon emissions taking place outside the

---

[99] Draft decision entitled 'Guidance on cooperative approaches referred to in Article 6, paragraph 2, of the Paris Agreement' (Decision-/CMA.3).

[100] *United States–Shrimps*, para 144.

[101] For example, the provision contained in the European scheme that allows mutual recognition only of emission credits coming from countries that have ratified the Kyoto Protocol seems too inflexible in that it does not consider that comparable GHG reductions may take place also beside the present climate change regime. Another example is the linking clause of the proposed US climate change bill. Here again the provision appears inflexible, in my view, as it sets 2005 as the base year for the start of operation of the comparable emission reduction program. This too precise indication may lead to unfair discrimination between schemes that may have started operating later but may nonetheless be comparable in terms of effectiveness in the achievement of emission reductions.

jurisdiction of the importing state. With regard to this kind of taxation, practical problems emerge because it is difficult to ascertain with a sufficient degree of precision those production methods that do not leave any trace in the final product. In particular, the critical point is whether domestic PPMs taxes can be adjusted at the border with regard to imported products. In case of a positive answer, a further issue is how will importers demonstrate that they are entitled to receive a certain rate because they produced electricity according to an environmentally sound process?[102]

While there are internal measures that, as shown, can address the carbon leakage concerns, the main answer to these concerns are border measures that impose the same burden that the climate policy imposes on the national products, on imported products. Depending on the domestic policy in place, these measures may be shaped, as obligations on importers to hold a certain amount of emission credits when a corresponding cap and trade scheme exists, or as taxes, so-called BTAs.[103] The possible adoption of border adjustment measures has provoked a strong negative reaction of emerging economies (in particular, the BRIC Group: Brazil, Russia, India, and China), because they see these measures as forms of protectionism which do not take into account these nations' limited financial and technological capacities.

And indeed, despite the many studies carried out with regard to BTAs, several controversial aspects still exist. These are, for example, whether, in the first place, it is possible to adjust the internal climate measure, tax, or regulation.[104] Once answered positively to this first matter, it remains to be seen if such a tax or regulation meets the substantive requirements of GATT articles I and III, or eventually can be justified as an exception under article XX. More controversial is the admissibility of border adjustments based on the carbon footprint of the imported good during its production process. In particular, assuming that products with different carbon footprints are 'like' products, otherwise the BTAs wouldn't be admissible, it must be verified that imported products are not treated less favourably than domestic like products.[105] Under

---

[102] Instructive experience in this regard may be drawn from certification systems under the WTO, such as the Kimberly Process Certification Scheme, adopted for rough diamonds. The adoption of similar measures could be considered with regard to the certification of through a 'carbon passport' that tracks the GHG emissions released during the productive process of certain products.

[103] According to the GATT Working Group on Border Tax Adjustments, BTAs may be defined as: 'fiscal measures that enable exported products to be relieved of some or all of the tax charged in the exporting country with respect to similar domestic products and that enable imported products sold to consumers to be charged with some or all of the tax charged in the importing country with respect to similar domestic products' (Working Party report, 'Border Tax Adjustments', BISD 18S/97, adopted on 2 December 1970, para 4).

[104] In fact, while price-based measures and taxes imposed on products can easily be adjusted by imposing the same burden to imports, on the other side, the precise individuation of the burden imposed on a national product by a cap-and-trade scheme or taxes targeting PPMs, ie on inputs that are not physically incorporated in the final product, are far more controversial. Hufbauer and others, *Global Warming and World Trading System* (n 83) 39: 'the potential adjustability of environmental taxes levied on the producer of a product—for example, a tax on energy used or the pollution emitted—remains an uncertain and debated issue in trade law'.

[105] An interesting precedent that may be applied *mutatis mutandis* to a carbon tax, is a US tax on ozone-depleting chemicals that has been applied both to domestic and imported products containing or produced with such chemicals, ie based on PPMs, which has never been challenged as a violation of GATT law. Moreover, according to the Appellate Body, a regulatory measure or a tax that treats low and high carbon products differently would not necessarily violate GATT art III, if it could be demonstrated that the 'detrimental effect on a given imported product' is justified by 'factors or circumstances unrelated to the foreign origin of the product'. Appellate Body Report, Dominican Republic—Cigarettes, para 96, WT/DS302/AB/R (adopted 19 May 2005).

WTO law, the concept of 'likeness' has been interpreted in the context of alleged discriminatory measures in an expansive way, leading to considering as 'like products' goods with different carbon footprints; in other words, without taking into account their process and production methods. Recent developments show an opening towards multilateral agreements on carbon border measures, notably with regard to goods produced according to carbon-intensive processes, such as steel and aluminium.[106] From this perspective, in a future dispute regarding a trade-related climate measure discriminating because of the carbon footprint of two otherwise like goods, the environmental argument may constitute a legitimate basis to justify such a measure.

Although at present, a conflict of norms in strict legal terms between international climate change and trade agreements may not be envisaged, there are many potential conflicts that may arise in the concrete implementation of trade-related climate measures.[107] These conflicts, however, could often be solved by using interpretative criteria deriving from the underlying treaties and from the WTO jurisprudence developed with regard to the non-discrimination obligations and their exceptions. It is interesting to observe that, notwithstanding the different objectives pursued by the trade and climate change regimes, the *chapeau* of GATT article XX and article 3.5 of the Framework Convention on Climate Change, that are key interpretative provisions, express exactly the same mutually supportive principle stating that measures, in particular unilateral climate measures, should not be 'applied in a manner which would constitute a means of arbitrary or unjustifiable discrimination between countries or a disguised restriction on international trade'. These provisions send an important message to dispute settlement bodies of the two treaties as well as to negotiators in charge of their normative developments regarding the interpretation of relevant climate and trade commitments.

In conclusion, although no definitive answer to the legitimacy of these instruments can be given, the majority of commentators considers that only taxes on products can be adjusted at the border. Future WTO dispute settlement or international law-making may clarify the matter.[108] In this direction, interesting normative developments are taking place with the European Union where a proposed Regulation establishing a carbon border adjustment mechanism is currently being discussed.[109] This overview of the main features of cap and trade schemes and fiscal measures suggests that these

[106] In occasion of the G20 meeting in Rome in November 2021, it was announced that the EU and US are starting the discussions on a new Global Arrangement on Sustainable Steel and Aluminium (see <https://ec.europa.eu/commission/presscorner/detail/en/ip_21_5721> accessed 21 November 2022).

[107] The climate regime establishes flexible mechanisms not as an obligation but rather as an opportunity that State Parties may use, at their discretion, to lower compliance costs of their reduction obligations and does not contain any reference, as far as carbon taxes are concerned. On these themes, see E Vranes, *Trade and the Environment. Fundamental Issues in International Law. WTO Law, and Legal Theory* (OUP 2009); G Marceau, 'Conflicts of Norms and Conflicts of Jurisdictions: The Relationship Between the WTO Agreement and MEAs and Other Treaties' (2001) 35 Journal of World Trade 1081.

[108] R Vanden Brink, Competitiveness Border Adjustments in U.S. Climate Change Proposals Violate GATT: Suggestions to Utilize GATT's Environmental Exceptions (2010) 21 Colorado Journal of International Environmental Law 85. Hufbauer and others, *Global Warming and World Trading System* (n 83) 66: 'Whether taxes on energy consumed in making a product (sometimes called "embedded energy" or "carbon footprint" taxes) are border-adjustable on an import has not been considered in WTO dispute settlement.'

[109] Proposal for a Regulation of the European Parliament and of the Council establishing a carbon border Adjustment mechanism, COM(2021) 564 final.

regulatory systems could be considered legitimate from a WTO perspective if their structure and design meet certain requirements and if their concrete implementation is carried out in good faith and does not entail disguised protectionist effects.

C. International Investment Law and Climate Change: Towards Convergence

International investment law interacts in more than one way with climate change. The interplay between climate change and international investment law is twofold. On one side, the international community, persuaded by scientific evidence of the dangerous impact of climate change, is intensifying private low-carbon investments. On the other side, similarly to other environmental regulations, climate policies require flexibility to incorporate and respond to political, technological, and scientific evolutions, while investors, especially when involved in long-term and capital-intensive projects, look for the opposite requirement of stability. These characters reflect the classic conflict between host countries' need to adopt environmental regulations in the public interest and foreign investors' rights not to be negatively impacted by them. The purpose of this section is to explore whether climate and investment law can, through an integrated approach, answer the investors' quest for stable and predictable rules governing their activities and thereby contribute more effectively to reach SDG 13.a.

International investment law stems from a fragmented network of bilateral investment treaties (BITs), and investment chapters included in plurilateral agreements, the Free Trade and investment Agreements (FTAs).[110]

The main objective of these treaties is to provide foreign investors with effective protection under international law from potential discriminatory treatments in the countries where the investments are implemented. Furthermore, the enforcement of these rights is ensured by the right of foreign investors to take the host government to arbitration.[111] Under these treaties, Parties reciprocally recognize certain guarantees and standards of treatment for investors of the nationality of the counterparty: the right to be treated not less favourably compared to domestic (National Treatment) and other foreign investors (Most Favoured Nation Treatment); the right to expropriate a foreign investors' property only for public purposes, in a non-discriminatory basis and respecting due process. When these conditions are met, the expropriation will be considered legitimate, and the investor will receive compensation. Expropriation is not limited *stricto sensu* to the deprivation of the title but includes also situations of 'indirect expropriation' where the assets, although remaining in the possession of the investor, are tangibly reduced in their value. Another guarantee for investors is the

---

[110] The origin of the current legal framework governing international investment lies in the failure of a global multilateral agreement on investment protection.

[111] Disputes can be referred by the investor to a number of fora, generally including the International Centre for the Settlement of Investment Disputes (ICSID), the Permanent Court of Arbitration (PCA), according to the arbitration rules of the United Nations Commission on International Trade Law (UNCITRAL) arbitration rules.

standard of fair and equitable treatment, which due to its abstract nature has received controversial interpretations by arbitral tribunals and is experiencing less endorsement by recently negotiated investment agreements.

Criticism of the international investment regime come from many sources—developing countries, civil society, and investors—and concern, more broadly, substantive, procedural, and institutional aspects.[112] Among the major concerns, inherent in the present chapter, are the 'race to the bottom' effect of investment law on public interest policies of host countries, lack of adequate transparency and participation in arbitration procedures, and the fragmented arbitral governance that produces inconsistent and unpredictable awards.

A noteworthy proactive step towards sustainable development values occurred when FTAs recognized that their overall objective is not merely to increase trade flows blindly but rather to ensure that the liberalization of international trade goes hand in hand with sustainable development goals. Embracing this approach based on positive obligations, recent FTAs include substantive provisions that require states to promote human and labour rights and environmental protection within their trade policies and practices, at the domestic and international level. The endorsement of non-trade values by FTAs has taken different paths, for instance through the adoption of regulatory approaches used in other trade agreements, such as the WTO, and being influenced by parallel international legal and policy developments in the areas of environmental protection and climate change. The EU–Japan FTA, endorses the threats deriving from climate change and states the correspondent commitment of the Parties to 'promote the positive contribution of trade to the transition to low greenhouse gas emissions and climate-resilient development'.[113]

States introduce stricter standards on certain industries and may even ban or limit the production or consumption of certain products or services to reduce GHG emissions.[114] The affected industries will bear additional costs to comply with these measures, or in extreme cases might even be forced to close down their business if they are no longer profitable. When the owner of these activities is a foreign investor, and if there is an investment treaty between his country and the host country, he can challenge the regulatory measures for violation of rights and standards under investment law and bring the host government to arbitration.

While unilateral policies autonomously adopted in the exercise of the state regulatory power are more likely to be challenged as protectionist in favour of domestic industries

---

[112] On the backlash against investment agreements and investor-state dispute settlement (ISDS) and its impact on recently negotiated FTAs, see DD Caron and E Shirlow, 'Dissecting Backlash: The Unarticulated Causes of Backlash and its Unintended Consequences' in G Ulfstein and A Føllesdal (eds), *The Judicialization of International Law—A Mixed Blessing?* (OUP 2018) 159.

[113] EU-Japan FTA, Trade and Sustainable Development Chapter, art 4.4.

[114] An example of this kind of measure is the Australian legislation setting a fixed carbon tax starting in July 2012 that later became an emissions trading scheme in 2015. Similarly, California has adopted legislation to establish a comprehensive regulatory scheme, which includes a cap-and-trade mechanism, aiming at reducing its GHG emissions to 1990 levels by 2020. See DM Firger and MB Gerrard, 'Harmonizing Climate Change Policy and International Investment Law: Threats, Challenges, and Opportunities' in KP Sauvant (ed), Yearbook on International Investment Law & Policy 2010–2011 (OUP 2012) 517–65, 536.

984   SDG 13

and therefore discriminatory towards foreign investors, multilaterally agreed rules and standards or regulatory measures adopted to comply with a supranational obligation may have at least *prima facie* a favourable presumption of being in good faith.

Further, with regard to climate measures, it can be convincingly argued that their 'legitimate' purpose is inferred being based on scientific findings as recognized by the great majority of the scientific community and by authoritative international institutions.[115] Energy efficiency standards with a 'multilateral matrix' would derive from criteria mutually agreed by international standards-setting organizations, by treaty, or established by codes of industry or other private associations. The 'outsourcing' and internationalization of responsibility for stricter climate measures has beneficial outcomes in terms of stability and predictability because it links the climate measure to rule-making entities or processes that are not directly dependent on and under the control of the host country.[116]

Environmental treaties, and in particular for present purposes the UNFCCC, the Kyoto Protocol, and the Paris Agreement could be taken into account in investment disputes, provided that the host country and the state of nationality of the investor are parties to them. According to article 31.3(c) of the Vienna Convention on the Law of Treaties, the tribunal in adjudicating a case relating to an alleged discriminatory climate measure shall also take into account 'any relevant rules of international law applicable in the relations between the parties'.[117]

Several countries have created, or are in the process of establishing, incentives for the promotion of renewable energy and of energy efficiency. These policies, as shown by the European experience, entail investment opportunities but also significant regulatory risks for investors.[118] The profitability of clean energy projects is often dependent on governmental subsidies and feed-in tariffs and consequently requires that those be kept stable during the lifecycle of the investment. In this regard, the fair and equitable treatment is a relevant standard that states should respect. As already highlighted, this standard calls for consideration of the legitimate expectations of investors and requires balancing the state interest to introduce regulatory changes with the investors' expectations. Moreover, these changes should be informed by due process principles, such as transparency, reasonableness, and proportionality.[119] This has not always been the case

[115] Legal scholarship has engaged on these matters, see MA Orellana, 'The Role of Science in Investment Arbitrations Concerning Public Health and the Environment, Yearbook of International Environmental Law' (2006) 17 48–72. See T Waelde and A Kolo, 'Environmental Regulation, Investment Protection and 'Regulatory taking' in International Law' (2001) 50 International and Comparative Law Quarterly 811, 846: 'It is unlikely that courts or arbitrators will find a compensable expropriation in cases where governments issue environmental regulation for legitimate purposes, in accordance with the state of scientific knowledge and accepted international guidelines.'

[116] Also, carbon taxes could have a multilateral origin, such as the tax on GHG emission from aviation that European states implemented in 2012 in accordance with the European Emission Trading Directive. cf Directive 2009/29/EC of the European Parliament and of the Council of 23 April 2009 amending Directive 2003/87/EC so as to improve and extend the GHG emission allowance trading scheme of the Community.

[117] Art 31 'General rule of interpretation': '3. There shall be taken into account, together with the context: ... (c) any relevant rules of international law applicable in the relations between the parties.'

[118] A Boute, 'The Potential Contribution of International Investment Protection Law to Combat Climate Change' (2009) 27(3) Journal of Energy & Natural Resources Law 333–76, 342.

[119] SW Schill, 'Do Investment Treaties Chill Unilateral State Regulation to Mitigate Climate Change?' (2007) 24(5) Journal of International Arbitration 469–77.

and unexpected changes in the incentives have occurred and are currently being challenged under the Energy Charter Treaty and other investment agreements.

The Energy Charter Treaty (ECT) is a multilateral treaty that could play a major role in facilitating low-carbon investment. Although it is a treaty that follows the traditional pattern of investment treaties, with the peculiarity of focusing on energy investment, it is the first treaty of this kind that contains an express reference in its Preamble to the climate change regime:[120]

> Recognizing the necessity for the most efficient exploration, production, conversion, storage, transport, distribution and use of energy; Recalling the United Nations Framework Convention on Climate Change, ... and other international environmental agreements with energy-related aspects; and Recognizing the increasingly urgent need for measures to protect the environment, including the decommissioning of energy installations and waste disposal, and for internationally-agreed objectives and criteria for these purposes....

The ECT is complemented by the Energy Charter Protocol on Energy Efficiency and Related Environmental Aspects (PEEREA) that was signed together with the ECT in 1994. The Protocol requires its participating states to formulate clear policies to improve energy efficiency and reduce the energy cycle's negative environmental impact.[121]

The ECT regime of investment protection provides an interesting model that shifts from the purely procedural content of classical investment treaties towards a hybrid model that also considers substantive aspects of the relevant sector in which investments are to be enhanced and protected.

Cases may be categorized under three groupings. A first group are cases in which investors challenge state regulatory measures taken for environmental, thus in particular climate change purposes, that allegedly breach their investment protection guarantees, be they non-discrimination, indirect expropriation, or fair and equitable treatment. An example, in this regard, is the North American Free Trade Agreement (NAFTA) case *Westmoreland v Canada*.[122] In November 2018, the Mining Company Westmoreland Coal Company claimed that it was unlawfully excluded from a scheme developed to compensate investors for losses associated with the Alberta government's Climate Leadership Plan, which accelerated the deadline for the phasing out of coal power to 2030 and the transition to natural gas. The company argued that as the only US investor in Alberta's coal industry, it was excluded from the compensation scheme

---

[120] E Sussman, 'The Energy Charter Treaty's Investor Protection Provisions: Potential to Foster Solutions to Global Warming and Promote Sustainable Development' (2008) 14(2) International Law Students Association Journal of International & Comparative Law 391–404 <https://ssrn.com/abstract=1090261> accessed 21 November 2022.

[121] Through the implementation of PEEREA, the ECT provides transition economies with good practices and a forum in which to share experiences and policy advice on energy efficiency issues. Within this forum, particular attention is paid to such aspects of national energy efficiency strategies, as taxation, pricing policy in the energy sector, environmentally related subsidies, and other mechanisms for financing energy efficiency objectives.

[122] *Westmoreland v Canada*, 2019, ICSID Case No UNCT/20/3, Pending, North American Free Trade Agreement, ch 11.

while Canadian companies were able to benefit from it: this would amount to a violation of article 1102 and article 1105 of NAFTA, which guarantee investors domiciled in Member States national treatment and fair and equitable treatment. The company acknowledged the government's need to 'enact regulations for the public good' but argued that they must also behave fairly towards foreign investors.[123]

Another recent interesting case under the Energy Charter Treaty is *Rockhopper v Italy* concerning the alleged violations of investors' rights due to the reintroduction of a ban on oil and gas exploration within twelve miles of the Italian coastline on behalf of the Italian Parliament.[124]

A second category of cases relates more specifically to renewable energy regulations, which in many jurisdictions—after an initial generous start, coupled with subsidies and incentives to participate in their schemes—have withdrawn some of these benefits, thereby reducing—often in a conspicuous way—the expected profits of investors. A recent case of this kind has been brought against Germany by the Austrian company Strabag, active in the offshore wind energy production, which claims that the way the German government administration managed its renewable energy regime has caused the claimants to abandon their offshore wind projects.[125]

A third category, the most recent one, sees the investors challenging state climate change mitigation targets under the climate change regime as being in breach of investors' rights.

A recent case of this kind is *Uniper v Netherlands*, under the ECT, brought by the German energy company Uniper against the government of the Netherlands alleging that the government's plan to phase out coal by 2030 violates the ECT.[126] It will be interesting to see whether investment arbitration tribunals will be influenced in their reasoning by the similar proceedings and judgment of the Supreme Court regarding the Netherlands climate commitments under the UN Climate Change Regime in the Urgenda case.[127]

The climate and the investment regime story starts with two independent bodies of law pursuing different objectives, combating climate change and protecting foreign investors' assets in host countries, with opposing rationales: the former being a common

[123] *Westmoreland Coal Company v Government of Canada,* Notice of Arbitration and Statement of Claim, 18 November 2019, para 12 <http://climatecasechart.com/climate-change-litigation/wp-content/uploads/sites/16/non-us-case-documents/2018/20181119_ICSID-Case-No.-UNCT203_complaint.pdf> accessed 21 November 2022.

[124] *Rockhopper v Italy*, ECT, ICSID Case No ARB/17/14, Pending. The ban had previously been introduced in 2010 but revoked in 2012. In 2017, UK company Rockhopper Exploration Plc, along with its Italian subsidiary, filed a claim for compensation alleging violations of the investor protection provisions of the Energy Charter Treaty. The claim concerned its interests in the Ombrina Mare oil rig, for which it was hoping to obtain a production concession from the Italian government prior to the introduction of the ban. The company is claiming compensation both for funds spent and for anticipated profits, which may run to $200–300 million.

[125] *Strabag and others v Germany*, Energy Charter Treaty, 2019, ICSID Case No ARB/19/29, Pending. The legal proceedings are proliferating across European states, notably in Spain and Italy. See also, *9REN Holding v Spain*, concerning claims arising out of a series of energy reforms undertaken by the government affecting the renewables sector, including reduction in subsidies for renewable energy producers; *Eskosol v Italy*, concerning a series of governmental decrees to cut tariff incentives for some solar power projects.

[126] ECT, *Uniper v Netherlands*, 2021, ICSID Case No ARB/21/22, Pending. Only this basic information is known, since no public documents are available at the time of writing.

[127] This case will be extensively analysed below.

concern of the international community, the latter a purely private economic concern. Their assumptions are also radically different: while the climate regime struggles to achieve mutual trust among developing and developed countries and private actors, the investment regime is built on the lack of trust towards the legal systems of host countries, and indeed provides for recourse to international arbitration.

Possibly the only aspect common to both regimes was the fact that they had to deal, albeit in different ways, with challenge of the North versus South issue and probably the very fact that this divide is now blurring has brought these two regimes closer to one another.

Looking at the recent evolution of the climate and investment regimes, some common elements emerge: both regimes may be said to have now at least a partially overlapping common goal which is to create a stable and predictable legal regime governing sustainable investments around the world.

Moreover, both regimes are realizing that the way to achieve this goal is by creating solid institutions and reliable procedures in host countries, able to decide effectively on their own economic priorities, moving towards a sustainable development path.

Past experience shows that foreign investments alone do not bring real economic growth in developing countries if they are not coupled with an improvement of the domestic economic, legal, and institutional framework.[128] From a bottom-up perspective, it is crucial therefore to intervene with reforms in key sectors and to strengthen institutions and procedures at the domestic level. These improvements would permit developing, emerging, as well as industrialized countries to create a stable and trustworthy investment environment, to identify their climate priorities, and to engage in significant national strategies.[129]

The need to allow greater flexibility for states to mitigate climate change on their own terms is the very similar and important lesson learned from the experience of the climate change regime: developing and developed countries are reluctant to assume legal obligations if these are not in line with their respective national interests and necessities, which may greatly vary from country to country, depending on their economy, their development stage, their geographic location, and many other factors. The recent trend of investment law goes in the same direction of allowing more flexibility and discretion to national policy-makers in the implementation of their environmental policies.[130]

---

[128] R Sarkar, 'A "Re-Visioned" Foreign Direct Investment Approach from an Emerging Country Perspective: Moving from a Vicious Circle to a Virtuous Cycle' (2010–2011) 17 International Law Students Association Journal of International & Comparative Law 379–92, 386: 'If systemic problems in the underlying economic and legal framework are not addressed by the host country, it may continue to be vulnerable to boom and bust cycles, thus making sustainable economic development all the more illusory.' On the recent trend of recent megaregional agreements requiring their States Parties to improve their domestic regulatory practices see below.

[129] Developing countries, in particular, have a huge potential to achieve relatively cheap GHG emissions, as they often have high energy intensity productions and obsolete energy infrastructures. On the other side, however, their weak institutional and administrative capacity often combined with corruption, unpredictable regulatory changes, nationalizations constitute relevant obstacles to foreign capitals.

[130] The relevance of a host country-centred perspective has been underlined also by UNCTAD in one of its report on 'The Role of International Investment Agreements in Attracting Foreign Direct Investment to Developing Countries'. Also, investor associations are engaged in building capacities in host countries. For example, the UNEP Financial Initiative, a global public–private partnership with over 200 signatories, is focusing on the link between

988 SDG 13

The UNFCCC contributes significantly to build capacities in climate change matters through reporting obligations. Since its entry into force, it has gathered valuable information on domestic climate policies of developed and developing countries. In this way, the UNFCCC plays a highly complementary role with regard to investment regimes. Indeed, traditionally, as already pointed out, these regimes provide for standards and procedures to 'rescue' the investor from the complexities of the host countries, rather than dealing with their economic and institutional development situation. The engagement of developing countries in climate change action is at an early stage and many problematic aspects still need to be addressed in order for NDCs to represent a credible and coherent body of rules on which investors can rely upon, but a constructive way is certainly being pathed. Information on national climate strategies and the relevant commitments, although often general and voluntary, improve transparency and predictability of domestic climate-related regulatory policies, and thereby reduce risks of unexpected changes.

Their effective contribution to create a stable and predictable level playing field for climate-related investments will, however, be conditioned by the way NDCs are monitored, verified, and reviewed. In a credible and robust bottom-up approach, host countries should design their own climate strategies and sustainable development priorities, declare them, and be held accountable for their implementation.[131]

D. Climate Change in the Jurisprudence of International and National Courts

1. The International Court of Justice

The International Court of Justice (ICJ) has not (yet) specifically addressed a climate change-related dispute, although climate policies and related matters have been dealt with in passing. For instance, in the case regarding Certain Activities Carried Out by Nicaragua in the Border Area (*Costa Rica v Nicaragua*), the Court was asked to decide whether Costa Rica was entitled to receive compensation for the loss of environmental goods and services suffered due to Nicaragua's excavation of canals on its territory. Among the services for which Costa Rica sought compensation was the impaired ability of the excavated area to provide 'gas regulation and air quality services, such as carbon sequestration'. Deciding in favour of Costa Rica, the ICJ considered that Nicaragua's dredging activities significantly undermined the capacity of the impacted territory to provide environmental goods and services and ruled that Nicaragua must compensate Costa Rica to the tune of $120,000. With specific regard to the climate change-related policies, the ICJ did 'not consider that the impairment or loss' of carbon sequestration

financial performance and Sustainable Development and has built regional task forces in Africa, Latin America, Asia, and India over the last ten years.

[131] J Werksman and K Herbertson, 'The Legal Character of National Actions and Commitments in a Copenhagen Agreement: Options and Implications', WRI Working Paper, November 2009, 4.

services could be valued as a one-time loss. This was the first case where the ICJ adjudicated a claim for compensation for environmental damage.

2. The East African Court of Justice

In the *Center for Food and Adequate Living Rights et al. v Tanzania and Uganda*, on 6 November 2020, four civil society organizations[132] filed a suit against the governments of Tanzania and Uganda in the East African Court of Justice seeking an injunction to stop the East African Crude Oil Pipeline. Plaintiffs allege that the governments, without objection from the Secretary General of the East African Community, who is responsible for oversight of the East African Community Treaty, signed agreements to build the pipeline without proper environmental, social, human rights, and climate impact assessments. The project allegedly will cause several environmental negative impacts in terms of loss of land, and interferences with ecosystems and wildlife, and will deprive Indigenous communities of their lands.[133] According to the applicants: 'The project is environmentally untenable and will traverse protected areas in East Africa with undue regard to livelihoods, gender, food security, public health, biodiversity and climate change impacts.'[134] Furthermore, they maintain that the 'commissioning, signing and implementation' of the project is in breach of East African Community Law, which includes *inter alia* the UN Framework Convention on Climate Change, and hence 'is illegal, against environmental law protected internationally and regionally, against the rule of law and good governance'. The claims arise under Ugandan national law and the East African Community Treaty and its protocols.[135]

VI. Targets and Indicators of Goal 13

A. Overview

The OWG provided a series of guidelines that the design of targets associated with SDGs should respect.[136] With regard to their content, targets should be specific, science-based, strictly related to their associated goal, and able to contribute to its achievement. Furthermore, guidelines required that targets be measurable; they should

---

[132] The civil society organizations are the Center for Food and Adequate Living Rights, the Africa Institute for Energy Governance, Natural Justice, and the Center for Strategic Litigation in Tanzania.

[133] Application, para 37: 'The EACOP Project contravenes the EAC Treaty and UN Declaration on the Rights of Peasants and Other People Working in Rural Areas in so far as it distorts the peasant and other people working in rural areas conserving and improving biodiversity rights, which constitute the basis for food and agricultural productions, and their contribution in ensuring the right to adequate food and food security, which are fundamental to attaining the internationally agreed developments goals, including the 2030 Agenda for Sustainable Development.' <http://climatecasechart.com/climate-change-litigation/wp-content/uploads/sites/16/non-us-case-documents/2020/20201106_12737_application.pdf> accessed 21 November 2022.

[134] See the Application, para 24.

[135] Application, para 44.

[136] Co-Chairs of OWG 10th Session, A definitional note on goals and targets <https://sustainabledevelopment.un.org/content/documents/7417presentation.pdf> accessed 21 November 2022.

990   SDG 13

be aspirational yet attainable and be flexible in order to change and become more ambitious, when possible. They should be inclusive and 'speak to all relevant stakeholders'.

B. Target 13.1 Strengthen resilience and adaptive capacity to climate-related hazards and natural disasters in all countries

1. Sources of the Target
SDG 13.1 takes into account the expectations of the Rio + 20 mandate entrusted to OWG expressly recognizing

> the importance of stronger interlinkages among disaster risk reduction, recovery and long-term development planning, and call for more coordinated and comprehensive strategies that integrate disaster risk reduction and climate change adaptation considerations into public and private investment, decision-making and the planning of humanitarian and development actions, in order to reduce risk, increase resilience and provide a smoother transition between relief, recovery and development. In this regard, we recognize the need to integrate a gender perspective into the design and implementation of all phases of disaster risk management.[137]

Reversing the order that generally sees mitigation as the first action and adaptation as the second, the first target addresses the impacts of climate change.

In particular, the effects of climate change may result in saltwater flooding, desertification, hurricanes, erosion, and landslides, leading to scarcity of water supplies and affecting food production from agriculture and fishing, as well as destroying land and housing.[138] These aspects have been historically neglected or underestimated by the intergovernmental process but have gained momentum in the last decade.[139]

The need to engage in the management of climate-related disasters is of utmost importance in order to respect the right to life effectively, as recognized by several human rights instruments.[140]

---

[137] 'The Future We Want', para 188.

[138] See, inter alia, United Nations General Assembly, Development and International Cooperation: Environment, Report of the World Commission on Environment and Development, 4 August 1987, UN Doc A/42/427, pp 47, 148, and 204; United Nations General Assembly, Resolution 44/206, 'Possible adverse effects of sea-level rise on islands and coastal areas, particularly low-lying coastal areas', 22 December 1989, UN Doc A/RES/44/206; United Nations General Assembly, Resolution 64/255, Report of the Special Rapporteur on adequate housing as a component of the right to an adequate standard of living, and on the right to non-discrimination in this context, 6 August 2009, UN Doc A/64/255, paras 30–34; United Nations General Assembly, Resolution 66/288, 'The Future We Want', 27 July 2012, UN Doc A/RES/66/288, paras 158, 165, 166, 175, 178, and 190.

[139] United Nations Framework Convention on Climate Change, entered into force on 21 March 1994, Preamble and art 4.8.

[140] Universal Declaration of Human Rights, art 3; International Covenant on Civil and Political Rights (ICCPR), art 6.1; Convention on the Rights of the Child (CRC), art 6.1; American Convention on Human Rights (ACHR), art 4.1; Protocol of San Salvador Additional Protocol to the American Convention on Human Rights in the Area of Economic, Social and Cultural Rights (Protocol of San Salvador), 11.1 Everyone shall have the right to live in a healthy environment and to have access to basic public services. 11.2 The States Parties shall promote the protection, preservation, and improvement of the environment; African Charter on Human and Peoples' Rights (ACHPR), art 4 Human beings are inviolable. Every human being shall be entitled to respect for his life and the

A remarkable example is found in article 22 of the Social Charter of the Americas, which establishes that

> [n]atural and man-made disasters affect populations, economies, and the environment. Reducing the vulnerabilities of countries to these disasters, with particular attention to the most vulnerable regions and communities, including the poorest segments of society, is essential to ensuring nations' progress and the pursuit of a better quality of life. Member states commit to improving regional cooperation and to strengthening their national, technical, and institutional capacity for disaster prevention, preparedness and response, rehabilitation, resilience, risk reduction, impact mitigation, and evaluation. Member states also commit to face the impact of climate variability, including the *El Niño* and *La Niña* phenomena, and the adverse effects of climate change that represent a risk increase in all countries of the Hemisphere, particularly for developing countries.[141]

Other relevant connections exist, for instance, with regard to the multilateral framework convention entrusted to combat desertification: the UN Convention to Combat Desertification (UNCCD), whose article 10.2.a requires States Parties to 'incorporate long-term strategies to combat desertification and mitigate the effects of drought, emphasize implementation and be integrated with national policies for sustainable development'.[142]

The Representative of the Secretary-General on the human rights of internally displaced persons underlined five situations related to climate change and environmental degradation that triggered displacement: (i) increased hydro-meteorological disasters such as hurricanes, flooding, or mudslides; (ii) gradual environmental degradation and slow onset disasters, such as desertification, sinking of coastal zones, or increased salinization of groundwater and soil; (iii) the 'sinking' of small island states; (iv) forced relocation of people from high-risk zones; and (v) violence and armed conflict triggered by the increasing scarcity of necessary resources such as water or inhabitable land.[143]

2. Implementation Efforts and Critique

All regions of the world are undertaking important efforts to tackle climate change. Voluntary National Reviews (VNRs) of implementation of the 2030 Agenda for Sustainable Development at the High-level Political Forum on Sustainable

---

integrity of his person. No one may be arbitrarily deprived of this right. Art 24 All peoples shall have the right to a general satisfactory environment favourable to their development.

[141] Social Charter of the Americas, adopted by the OAS General Assembly on 4 June 2012, OAS Doc AG/doc.5242/12 rev 2.

[142] Convention to Combat Desertification in those Countries Experiencing Serious Drought and/or Desertification, particularly in Africa (UNCCD), Paris, 17 June 1994.

[143] cf Human Rights Council, Report of the Representative of the Secretary-General on the human rights of internally displaced persons, Walter Kälin, 9 February 2009, UN Doc A/HRC/10/13, para 22, and Human Rights Council, Report of the Office of the United Nations High Commissioner for Human Rights on the relationship between climate change and human rights, 15 January 2009, UN Doc A/HRC/10/61, paras 51 and 56.

992 SDG 13

Development (HLPF) are the cornerstone of the follow-up and review framework of the 2030 Agenda.[144]

The latest round of review after the COVID-19 pandemic shows that progress has been slowed down due to the economic downturn with respect to many challenges, including climate change and natural disasters.[145] Nonetheless, important initiatives are being undertaken such as the adoption of national or local disaster risk reduction strategies by an increased number of countries compared to previous periods.[146] Furthermore, as of March 2021, 125 of 154 developing countries are carrying out measures for national adaptation plans.[147]

The African Commission in this regard strongly appealed to the African Union Chairperson, President Cyril Ramaphosa and the African Union (AU) Assembly to declare 2021 the African Union Year on collective action for effective preparedness for addressing the destructive effects of climate change in Africa in accordance with Resolution 417 of the African Commission adopted at its 64th session held in Sharm el Sheikh in Egypt, May 2019.

3. Empirical Analysis

The indicators relating to the SDG 13.1 target are the following:

13.1.1 Number of deaths, missing persons and directly affected persons attributed to disasters per 100,000 population

13.1.2 Number of countries with national and local disaster risk reduction strategies in line with the Sendai Framework for Disaster Risk Reduction 2015-2030.

13.1.3 Proportion of local governments that adopt and implement local disaster risk reduction strategies in line with national disaster risk reduction strategies

Indicators on the impact of climate change and disasters have been produced by the relevant international agencies, and also within countries.

Regarding the disaster risk, the United Nations International Strategy for Disaster Reduction Secretariat (UNISDR) has developed a Global Risk Model for a series of Global Assessment Reports (GARs). It measures annual average loss (AAL) and probable maximum loss (PML) based on probabilistic modelling. Currently the dataset includes AAL and PML for earthquake, cyclones, and floods under the return period of 250 years.[148]

---

[144] Reflecting the principles of sustainable development of countries' ownership, these reports are voluntary and country-led, and will take into account different national realities, capacities and levels of development and priorities. Furthermore, they should be inclusive, participatory, transparent, and thorough review process at the national and sub-national levels, when they are evidence-based and produce tangible lessons and solutions. They were initially prepared by the Secretary-General in December 2015 and common reporting guidelines have been drawn to ensure coherency and comparability of actions.

[145] Report of the Secretary-General, Progress towards the Sustainable Development Goals, 30 April 202, Doc E/2021/58, para 4.

[146] Progress towards the Sustainable Development Goals, para 141.

[147] ibid para 143.

[148] The data are publicly accessible via UNISDR's website.

At the global level, the Creditor Reporting System (CRED) and its Emergency Database provides a series of methodological and conceptual tools for international reference, including the criteria needed to qualify an event as a disaster, the definition of disasters, their classification, and other elements that are useful tools to harmonize the statistical work in this field. Additionally, CRED undertakes data compilation, validation, and analysis. It provides open access to its data through its website. In addition to providing information on the human impact of disasters, such as the number of people killed, injured, or affected, this database provides disaster-related economic damage estimates and disaster-specific international aid contributions.[149]

There is a demand for reliable statistics that can support the measurement and analysis of the drivers and the social and economic consequences of climate change and the related mitigation (and adaptation) measures. Given the complexity of climate change and disaster risk reduction, producing statistics to inform about them requires the collection of a wide range of statistical information regarding scientific, economic, and social data that are produced by different national and international institutions. As recognized by the UN Economic Commission for Europe (UNECE) Task Force on Climate Change Related Statistics, the most important frameworks used for statistics information are the United Nations System of Environmental-Economic Accounting (SEEA) Central Framework,[150] the Framework for the Development of Environmental Statistics (FDES),[151] and the IPCC Schematic Framework (Climate Process Drivers, Climate Change Evidence, Impacts and Vulnerability, Mitigation and Adaptation).

Systematic collection and analysis of these data can provide key information to governments and agencies in charge of disaster risk management activities including relief and recovery activities. It also aids the incorporation of health issues into development and poverty alleviation programmes.[152] However, there is a lack of international consensus regarding best practices for collecting these data. Together with the complexity

---

[149] For more detailed information on these databases, see the Compendium on statistical notes (n 149) para 23.22ff <https://sustainabledevelopment.un.org/content/documents/3647Compendium%20of%20statistical%20notes.pdf> accessed 21 November 2022.

[150] The SEEA Central Framework was created in 2012 by the UN Statistical Commission as an international statistical standard. It provides value added in analysing mitigation and adaptation strategies and their trade-offs and provides an integration framework for the derivation of climate change indicators. As a statistical system the SEEA Central Framework is comprehensive in that it encompasses all known aspects of the environment-economy interaction and uses concepts and classifications consistent with System of National Accounts. For further information on the SEEA's mandate see Compendium on statistical notes (n 149) para 23.7 <https://sustainabledevelopment.un.org/content/documents/3647Compendium%20of%20statistical%20notes.pdf> accessed 21 November 2022.

[151] The FDES provides a structure for a set of basic and core climate change- and disaster-related statistics that can guide statistical and indicator work. It was established by the UN Statistical Commission as the framework for strengthening national environment statistics programmes identifies a basic and a core set of statistics related to climate change and disasters and provides an organizing structure that links them together with all other related fields of environment statistics.

[152] A noteworthy regional initiative is the United Nations Economic Commission for Latin America and the Caribbean (UNECLAC) which developed a handbook which may serve as model also for other regions, 'UNECLAC: Handbook for Estimating the Socio-economic and Environmental Effects of Disasters'. It evaluates the overall impact of disasters associated with natural events and includes a methodology for evaluating this impact. This analysis of disaster impact in terms of damage and losses makes it possible to estimate the impact of disasters on economic growth, on the population's living conditions and on environmental conditions in the region.

994   SDG 13

of collecting reliable information, there remains huge variability in definitions, methodologies, tools, and data sourcing.

Existing indicators of relevance to climate change and disaster risk reduction include those used or implicit in the UNFCCC and IPCC reporting systems (eg national and sectorial GHG emissions, national adaptation and mitigation plans and actions and flows of finance and technology); the UNECE Protocol on Pollutant Release and Transfer Registers (PRTR) with geo-referenced data on industrial pollutants, including GHG emissions; the Hyogo Framework for Action indicators of progress; and the Aichi biodiversity targets. MDG indicators that are most relevant include MDG 7, indicator 7.2 CO_2 emissions, total, per capita and per \$1 GDP (PPP). Several other MDG indicators are closely related to the crosscutting issue of climate change and disaster risk reduction.

C. Target 13.2 Integrate climate change measures into national policies, strategies and planning

1. Sources of the Target and Implementation Efforts
a) Environmental and climate impact assessment
Considering that many human and industrial activities produce large amounts of GHGs, in order to reduce these emissions, it is necessary that states consider their impact across all the relevant industrial, economic, and human activities. The regulatory instrument to perform this evaluation is the environment impact assessment (EIA) procedure, which should ensure that states and other interested stakeholders as well as the public are informed in due time of the impact of a certain project or regulatory measure. Environmental impact assessment has been defined by the International Association for Impact Assessment (IAIA) as 'the process of identifying, predicting, evaluating and mitigating the bio-physical, social and other relevant effects of development proposals prior to major decisions being taken and commitments made'.[153]

These procedural norms, at the crossroads between environmental and human rights, have been broadly recognized and adopted in international fora and are increasingly used as benchmarks to assess performance also in the implementation of energy projects. Their main aims are to link government accountability and environmental protection, involve stakeholders in an early stage of authorization procedures, enhance transparency, and strengthen the environmental integrity of projects.

Recourse to these procedural mechanisms contributes to establish more inclusive consultation platforms and to strengthen dialogue among the population potentially affected, investors, and government representatives. In the framework of these procedures, the state should notify if relevant regulations are being considered and in so doing

---

[153] IAIA, October 2009 <http://www.iaia.org/uploads/pdf/What_is_IA_web.pdf> accessed 21 November 2022.

would allow the investor to calculate in advance the impact on his business and better absorb the impact of regulatory changes and facilitate a pacific adaptation to them.

In 1991, states adopted a dedicated treaty on EIAs in a transboundary context under the framework of the UNECE: the Espoo Convention on Environmental Impact Assessment in a Transboundary Context.[154] According to the Convention, the 'Party of origin' of certain projects must notify the 'affected Party' if the project is likely to cause a significant adverse transboundary impact, leaving to the latter the option to participate in an EIA procedure that the former must conduct before authorizing the project. The obligation to carry out an EIA with regard to transboundary activities that may entail negative environmental impacts has been recognized as an obligation of customary international law.[155] A distinction has been made between project-based EIA, and 'Strategic Environmental Assessment' (SEA) conducted in relation to policies, plans, and programmes well before particular projects are developed.[156] With regard to these latter initiatives, the relevant international agreement is the 'Kiev' Protocol on Strategic Environmental Assessment to the Espoo Convention.[157]

While EIA evaluates potential environmental impacts both for domestic and transboundary activities, such as air, water, and soil pollution, the assessment of the climate change-related effects, in terms of mitigation or adaptation, of a proposed activity were not been adequately taken into consideration, at least until recently. The UNFCCC only defines a very general commitment for Parties to '[t]ake climate change considerations into account, to the extent feasible, in their relevant social, economic and environmental policies and actions'.[158]

It is in the 2010s that state legislation and judicial bodies expressly require that relevant EIA procedures and documents also cover the climate change dimension. Manifestation of this trend at the EU level is reflected in the SEA procedure and the revision of the EIA directive with the requirement that these procedures take into account 'the impact of the project on climate (for example the nature and magnitude of greenhouse gas emissions)'.[159]

[154] Convention on Environmental Impact Assessment in a Transboundary Context (adopted 25 February 1991, entered into force 10 September 1997) 1989 UNTS 309. The UNECE comprises fifty-six states located in Europe, Northern America, and Central Asia.

[155] International Court of Justice, *Pulp Mills on the River Uruguay (Argentina v Uruguay)*, 2010 ICJ Report 14, paras 203–210; Certain Activities Carried Out by Nicaragua in the Border Area (*Costa Rica v Nicaragua*) and Construction of a Road in Costa Rica along the San Juan River (*Nicaragua v Costa Rica*), merits, 2015 ICJ Rep 665, paras 101–105 and 142–162. See also Responsibilities and obligations of States with respect to activities in the Area, Case No 17, Advisory Opinion (ITLOS Seabed Disputes Chamber, 1 February 2011) 50 ILM 458 (2011), paras 141–150.

[156] In the EU, for instance, SEA procedure is established under a different directive, while China's EIA Law establishes EIA and SEA procedures in two different chapters.

[157] 'Kiev' Protocol on Strategic Environmental Assessment to the convention on Environmental Impact Assessment in a Transboundary context (adopted 21 May 2003, entered into force 11 July 2010) 2685 UNTS 140.

[158] UNFCCC, art 4.1(f).

[159] See EU Commission, Guidance on Integrating Climate Change and Biodiversity into Environmental Impact Assessment (2013) <http://ec.europa.eu/environment/EIA/pdf/EIA% 20Guidance.pdf>; and Guidance on Integrating Climate Change and Biodiversity into Strategic Environmental Assessment (2013) <http://ec.eur opa.eu/environment/EIA/pdf/SEA%20Guidance. Pdf> accessed 21 November 2022. Parliament and Council Directive 2014/52, 2014 OJ L124/1, Annex IV para 5(c).

996 SDG 13

Furthermore, for example, the Austrian Federal Administrative Court quashed the approval of the construction of an airport because the EIA documentation failed to consider its climate change impacts.[160]

It is still debatable whether the obligation to perform a climate change impact assessment constitutes an obligation under international customary law.[161] Steps in this direction are shown by the International Law Commission (ILC) in its Draft Guidelines on the Protection of the Atmosphere, where it is stated that '[s]tates have the obligation to ensure that an environmental impact assessment is undertaken of proposed activities under their jurisdiction or control which are likely to cause significant adverse impact on the atmosphere in terms of ... atmospheric degradation ... such as climate change'.[162]

A parallel trend can be seen in the practice of international financial institutions, such as the World Bank, the Asian Development Bank, and the Asian Infrastructure Investment Bank, which have integrated climate change in their safeguard policies and require an assessment of GHG emissions in the context of their environmental and social assessment of projects eligible for their funding.[163] Furthermore, corporations and industries too must progressively introduce the consideration of the climate change impact of their activities.[164]

While the inclusion of climate change risk assessment is certainly a trend finding more and more favour across states and other actors, challenges are still egregious regarding its effective implementation by developing countries,[165] and by financial institutions.[166] With regard to this latter context, a noteworthy example is the transition of Chinese development finance towards low-carbon investment policy, particularly with regard to energy projects under the Belt and Road Initiative (BRI). While the official documents regarding 'Vision and Actions on Jointly Building the Silk Road Economic Belt and 21st-Century Maritime Silk Road'[167] envisage low-carbon investments as an objective of cooperation, carbon externalities linked to the financing of projects by the

---

[160] Bundesverwaltungsgericht (W109 2000179-1/291E) (2 February). This decision was overturned by the Constitutional Court (Verfassungsgerichtshof), E 875/2017 and E 886/2017 (2 August 2017).

[161] Arguing in favour of an emerging norm of customary international law, B Mayer, 'Climate Assessment as an Emerging Obligation under Customary International Law' (2019) 68 International and Comparative Law Quarterly 271–308.

[162] ILC, 'Draft Guidelines on the Protection of the Atmosphere' in ILC Report at Its Seventieth Session, UN Doc A/73/10 (2018) guidelines 4 and 1(c).

[163] World Bank, 'Environmental and Social Framework Setting Environmental and Social Standards for Investment Project Financing' (2016) 61, para 16; ADB, Safeguard Policy Statement (June 2009) 16, para 2; AIIB, 'Environmental and Social Framework' (February 2016) 28.

[164] The Equator Principles: A Financial Industry Benchmark for Determining, Assessing and Managing Environmental and Social Risks in Projects' (June 2013) <http://equator-principles. com/wp-content/uploads/2017/03/equator_principles_III.pdf> accessed 21 November 2022.

[165] cf Mayer, 'Climate Assessment' (n 161) 287, suggesting that '[t]he absence of CA in these and other jurisdictions has more to do with political inertia, hesitancy or, at most, reluctance, than with a deliberate exclusion'.

[166] An example of integrated approach is the management of the climate-related financial risk in the investment decisions of pensions funds and other institutional investors. See E Colombo, 'From Bushfires to Misfires: Climate-related Financial Risk after McVeigh v. Retail Employees Superannuation Trust' (2021) 11(1) Transnational Environmental Law 1–27.

[167] For a critical analysis on the China's energy investments in Central Asia, see H Zhang, 'The Carbon Externality of Investments Financed by China's Development Banks: The Case of Energy Investments in Central Asia' (2019) 20 Journal of World Investment and Trade 335–54.

China Development Bank and the Export-Import Bank of China (EXIM Bank) remain of primary concern.

As already happened in the past, the European Union has embarked in ambitious climate legislation backed up by innovative financial measures to achieve a real and just transition to a carbon-neutral economy. In April 2021, the European Commission (EC) adopted a comprehensive package of measures to facilitate the flow of investments towards sustainable activities, which include the EU Taxonomy Climate Delegated Act, a proposal for a Corporate Sustainability Reporting Directive (CSRD), and the amendment of delegated acts on sustainability preferences, rules on fiduciary duties, and product governance. In Japan, the Basic Guidelines on Climate Transition Finance were published in May 2021 and the Expert Panel on Sustainable Finance delivered its Report, laying out recommendations for policy actions needed to promote sustainable activities in Japan. On a similar wavelength, in the Asia-Pacific region the Pacific Island Forum issued a statement declaring its intention to phase out subsidies for fossil fuels.[168]

Although, as already highlighted, domestic initiatives fall short of achieving the expected global reduction target, many countries, including developing ones, announced in 2019 their intention to reach net-zero emissions by 2050.[169]

A virtuous example is set by New Zealand, where legislation was passed that aims at a net-zero target by 2050. Among the significant actions adopted there are the ending of fossil fuel exploration permits, the planting of 1 billion trees, the pledge to devote NZD 840 million to global climate finance, half of which is to be donated to developing countries in the Pacific.[170]

Moving further towards the local dimension, since it is expected that by 2050 more than 70 per cent of the world population will live in urban areas, cities are crucial areas where climate change mitigation and adaptation actions should be implemented.[171] Subnational authorities create transboundary cooperation networks[172] and cities are often comparatively more ambitious than their central governments in cutting their emissions.[173]

Noteworthy is the action undertaken by the Congress of Local and Regional Authorities of the Council of Europe which has adopted several recommendations encouraging the involvement of citizens, especially youth, in environmental decision-making at the local level,[174] and has underscored the need to endow local and regional

[168] Kainaki II Declaration for Urgent Climate Change Action Now (2019).

[169] See, for instance, <http://www.sdg.iisd.org>.

[170] For more in-depth information on these legislations, see the New Zealand Climate Change Response (Zero Carbon) Amendment Bill (Royal Assent, November 2019) and the Framework for climate change policy and key upcoming decisions, 2018.

[171] See, for instance, OECD, 'Cities and Climate Change: National Governments Enabling Local Action: Policy Perspectives', 2014.

[172] See, for instance, Cities Climate Leadership Group and the Global Covenant of Mayors for Climate and Energy.

[173] J van der Heijden, 'Cities and Subnational Governance: High Ambitious, Innovative Instruments and Polycentric Collaborations?' in A Jordan and others (eds), *Governing Climate Change: Polycentric Action?* (CUP 2018).

[174] REC 276(2009) and RES 292 (2009)—Improving indoor air quality: a new challenge for local authorities.

998   SDG 13

authorities with the necessary resources to implement their climate protection strategies according to an integrated approach, covering energy issues, public transport, spatial planning, architecture and town planning, water and waste management.

Furthermore, with regard to adaptation policies, the Congress urges national policies to take into account the experience matured in the Council of Europe EUR-OPA Major Hazards Agreement, and limit the urban expansion on sea fronts, while at the same time, setting up flood warning systems.[175]

b) Good regulatory practices

States deal with environmental protection matters at home by adopting fairly diverse regulatory approaches. The most striking example is climate change: the EU has taken the lead in climate change negotiations at the international level and is adopting comprehensive climate change regulations. On the other side of the Atlantic, the US has no comprehensive climate change legislation in place, with the Climate Action Plan, enacted during the Obama administration, being fairly diluted during the Trump administration. In response to the government's failure to tackle climate change effectively, there has been a rising number—more than 800—of climate change-related cases brought to domestic courts to raise awareness and influence regulation. Improving regulatory practices and strengthening cooperation on these matters both play a crucial role in effectively combining the promotion of economic interests, namely trade and investments, and the state's ability to pursue its public interest objectives, including climate change.

The crucial importance of establishing good regulatory practices at home and effective regulatory cooperation with other states is a novel area of cooperation in recently negotiated 'mega-regional' FTAs, such as CETA and USMCA.[176] Recent mega-regional FTAs include provisions setting guidelines for the adoption of regulatory measures within the parties and set obligations to strengthen reciprocal cooperation in this area. Good regulatory practices aim at ensuring that the domestic processes are conducted in a transparent framework that allows interested persons—including nationals of other parties—to participate at an early stage in the decision-making process.[177] These practices promote regulatory quality by enhancing objective analysis on the basis of the best available information, accountability, and predictability from early planning to the adoption and review of regulations. In designing regulations, states must explain the objectives and how the planned regulatory act achieves them, as well as any major

---

[175] On adaptation, see REC 231 (2008) and RES 248 (2008)—Climate Change: building adaptive capacity of local and regional authorities. Tackling more specifically climate-related events deriving from sea level rise, see REC 298(2010) and RES 317 (2010), Coastal towns and cities tackling threats from the sea.

[176] According to USMCA, art 28.1: 'regulatory cooperation means an effort between two or more Parties to prevent, reduce, or eliminate unnecessary regulatory differences to facilitate trade and promote economic growth, while maintaining or enhancing standards of public health and safety and environmental protection'; see also CETA at art 21.3 which identifies as the main objectives of regulatory cooperation its contribution 'to the protection of human life, health or safety, animal or plant life or health and the environment', together with building trust, deepening mutual understanding of regulatory governance and facilitating bilateral trade and investment in a way that 'reduces unnecessary differences in regulation'.

[177] See, for example, CETA, art 4.4; USMCA, art 11.7.

alternatives. Although it is not a mandatory requirement, parties are encouraged to carry out a regulatory impact assessment to evaluate the need for and the potential impacts of the proposed regulations and minimize unnecessary divergences. Once finalized, the regulation will be published and kept under periodic review in order to consider whether adjustments are required due to changes in the respective circumstances.[178] Deadlines and time frames may be defined throughout the whole process to ensure that the interested parties are able to submit comments and the regulatory authority can respond.

These good regulatory practices and cooperation provisions represent a promising approach in reducing the divergences between the different regulatory approaches adopted by the parties.[179] If domestic public interest regulatory measures respect common procedural requirements, the likelihood of disputes challenging their adoption and implementation for negatively affecting trade or foreign investments is greatly reduced, if not eliminated altogether. In fact, if these measures are to be effectively enforced, they could ease the inherent tension between domestic public policy space and the protection of investors' rights by requiring states to declare in advance what kind of initiatives they are adopting, provide for the possibility to participate in the decision-making process, strengthen cooperation at an early stage, and increase transparency and accessibility of information. All these elements should prevent protectionist challenges because potential conflicts or critical aspects should emerge and be dealt with in a preventive way without resorting to *ex post* dispute settlement.

2. Empirical Analysis

The first indicator for the present 13.2 target requires to measure the following data: '13.2.1: Number of countries with nationally determined contributions, long-term strategies, national adaptation plans and adaptation communications, as reported to the secretariat of the United Nations Framework Convention on Climate Change.' A second indicator requires to measure '13.2.2 Total greenhouse gas emissions per year'.

With regard to the first indicator, emissions by sector of activity are important (ie globally, two-thirds of GHGs are emitted by the energy sector while 20–30 per cent by agriculture, forestry and other land uses). Most key indicators can be disaggregated to discriminate between the respective contribution by economic activity or by the sector receiving the impact of the extreme event and disasters. A number of other statistics, indicators, and thematic areas are currently being used by the IPCC and UNFCCC, as well as other global, regional, and national institutions.

With regard to the second indicator, and in particular the concentrations of CO_2, NASA and NOAA (National Oceanic and Atmospheric Administration) produce and disseminate long series on carbon dioxide concentrations in the global atmosphere,

---

[178] See CETA, art 21.4; USMCA, arts 28.11.2, 28.13.

[179] Concerns have been raised relating to the fact that the 'export' of 'Western-style' regulatory models could impose too demanding standards on developing countries and undermine their autonomy in choosing their own procedures. See F Ortino and E Lydgate, 'Addressing Domestic Regulation Affecting Trade in Services in CETA, CPTPP, and USMCA: Revolution or Timid Steps?' (2019) 20 Journal of World Investment & Trade 680–704, 697.

1000 SDG 13

based on their basic research on current global concentrations by direct measurement with a global monitoring station network and back thousands of years indirectly from CO_2 contained in ice cores from the past.[180] These science-based indicators and statistics are further disseminated in numerous international and national websites. Furthermore, statistics on the emissions of GHGs to the atmosphere can be found in countries reporting to UNFCCC.[181] GHG emissions, emission reduction and mitigation actions are communicated by parties to the UNFCCC regularly through National Communications (NC). National communications to the UNFCCC require reporting also of other information, including data on socio-economic developments, national circumstances, impact of policies and measures on emissions, basic data used for emission projections, data on vulnerability, financial resources and assistance, transfer of technology, education, training, and public awareness. A robust national GHG inventory, including projected emissions in coming decades, is the basis for parties to UNFCCC to plan efficient national and sub-national action, and document mitigation activities against business-as-usual reference emission levels. Yearly National Inventory Reports (NIRs) from Annex I countries are available since 1990, while only incomplete data are available for developing non-Annex I parties.

3. Critique

The availability of data varies a great deal across countries, in particular developing countries (Non-Annex I parties under the UNFCCC) have significant capacity gaps that limit their ability to report regularly. Nevertheless, the general issues covered by national communications include impacts of climate change on key economic sectors (eg, tourism) and social issues; mitigation, and more specifically costs and effects of policies and measures across sectors, financial resources for mitigation, technology transfer; adaptation, in particular measures taken to minimize adverse impacts of climate change and extreme events, vulnerability assessment (eg, of the health sector and biodiversity), financial resources for adaptation and investment.

D. Target 13.3 Improve education, awareness-raising and human and institutional capacity on climate change mitigation, adaptation, impact reduction and early warning

1. Sources of the Target and Implementation Efforts

The need to strengthen human and institutional capacities of states on climate change-related matters has been one of the main fields of intervention since the early days of the UNFCCC. In light of the CBDR principle it is of paramount importance to

---

[180] <http://climate.nasa.gov/key_indicators> accessed 21 November 2022.

[181] All parties to UNFCCC report biennially, starting at the end of 2014. Such reporting, which includes GHG National Inventories and planned Mitigation actions, including Nationally Appropriate Mitigation Actions (NAMAs) and Reducing Emissions from Deforestation and Degradation (REDD+) activities, are called Biennial Update Reports (BURs).

assist all states in setting up their institutional, technical, and legal framework relating to climate change.[182]

The UNFCCC devoted a specific article to education, training, and public awareness, which provides that parties to the Convention shall:

(a) Promote and facilitate at the national and, as appropriate, subregional and regional levels, and in accordance with national laws and regulations, and within their respective capacities: (i) the development and implementation of educational and public awareness programmes on climate change and its effects; (ii) public access to information on climate change and its effects; (iii) public participation in addressing climate change and its effects and developing adequate responses; and (iv) training of scientific, technical and managerial personnel; (b) Cooperate in and promote, at the international level, and, where appropriate, using existing bodies: (i) the development and exchange of educational and public awareness material on climate change and its effects; and (ii) the development and implementation of education and training programmes, including the strengthening of national institutions and the exchange or secondment of personnel to train experts in this field, in particular for developing countries.[183]

To strengthen awareness of individuals, as well as the larger public more broadly, and provide the persons potentially affected by climate change impacts, particularly useful tools are international treaties at the cross-roads between environmental protection and human rights, which envisage the right of individuals to be informed, to participate in environmental decision-making, and to have recourse to justice in case these first two sets of rights are not being respected by the state. The main treaty in this regard is the Aarhus Convention on Access to Information, Public Participation in Decision-making and Access to Information and Access to Justice in Environmental matters adopted under the auspices of UNECE on 15 June 1998.[184] By promoting these procedural and participatory rights related to sustainable development, the Aarhus Convention contributes effectively to the realization of target 13.3. The implementation of the Aarhus Convention can count on an additional instrument that ensures its effective application by the States Parties. In fact, through the Compliance mechanism established under the Convention, individuals, members of the public, and NGOs can raise questions of compliance before the Implementation Committee, a subsidiary

[182] UNFCCC, art 5: 'The developed country Parties and other developed Parties included in Annex II shall take all practicable steps to promote, facilitate and finance, as appropriate, the transfer of, or access to, environmentally sound technologies and know-how to other Parties, particularly developing country Parties, to enable them to implement the provisions of the Convention. In this process, the developed country Parties shall support the development and enhancement of endogenous capacities and technologies of developing country Parties.'

[183] UNFCCC, art 6.

[184] Convention on Access to Information, Public Participation in Decision-making and Access to Justice in Environmental Matters (Aarhus, Denmark, 25 June 1998), ILM 38 (1999) 517, entered into force on 30 October 2001.

1002   SDG 13

body in charge of controlling the effective implementation of the three pillars of the Convention.[185]

A similar regional treaty is the Escazú Agreement on Access to Information, Public Participation and Justice in Environmental Matters in Latin America and the Caribbean. Re-proposing many of the main features of the Aarhus Convention, this treaty expressly provides that:

> [e]ach Party shall guarantee, to the extent possible within available resources, that the competent authorities generate, collect, publicize and disseminate environmental information relevant to their functions in a systematic, proactive, timely, regular, accessible and comprehensible manner, and periodically update this information and encourage the disaggregation and decentralization of environmental information at the subnational and local levels. Each Party shall strengthen coordination between the different authorities of the State.[186]

Furthermore, with a direct link to the achievement of the target under consideration, the Escazu Agreement expressly contributes to climate change awareness, by requiring that '[e]ach Party shall have in place one or more up-to-date environmental information systems, which may include, inter alia: ... climate change sources aimed at building national capacities'.[187]

Other relevant instruments that aim at strengthening the awareness of citizens with regard to their rights to a healthy environment, and therefore may indirectly contribute to strengthen awareness on climate change-related matters, are found in treaties for the protection of human rights.[188]

a) Climate litigation before domestic courts

There are two pathways generally followed to bring climate change-related litigation before domestic courts: tort-based claims brought against major carbon emitters, and administrative claims against the governments challenging inadequate environmental legislation and pushing towards more ambitious regulatory measures. A noteworthy example of climate 'strategic litigation' that is certainly contributing—in line with SDG 13.3—to raise awareness and strengthen human and institutional capacities on climate change matters is the Urgenda case.

---

[185] See the Compliance Mechanism established under the Aarhus Convention (Decision I/7 on Review of Compliance (23 October 2002), doc ECE/MP.PP/2/Add.8, art 15) and the extensive practice of individuals and NGOs bringing cases to the Committee. PITEA, 'The Non-compliance Procedure of the Aarhus Convention: Between Environmental and Human Rights Control Mechanisms' in D Shelton (ed), *Human Rights and the Environment* (Edward Elgar Publishing 2011) 532.

[186] Escazú Agreement on Access to Information, Public Participation and Justice in Environmental Matters in Latin America and the Caribbean, art 6.1.

[187] Escazú Agreement, 6.3.g.

[188] A noteworthy example is the African Charter on Human and Peoples' Rights (ACHPR), whose art 25 provides that 'States parties to the present Charter shall have the duty to promote and ensure through teaching, education and publication, the respect of the rights and freedoms contained in the present Charter and to see to it that these freedoms and rights as well as corresponding obligations and duties are understood'.

According to the claimant, the Urgenda Foundation, the Netherlands had a specific legal obligation to reduce GHG emissions by 25 per cent in 2020, compared to 1990 levels. This ground-breaking claim raises many questions relating to the evaluation of the ambition of states in their climate policies: what criteria should be used in determining whether NDCs are sufficiently ambitious? Should ambition be measured in light of the specific situation of the state? In other words, is the due diligence standard applicable to be measured in light of the CBDR-RC principle? According to the Court, states have to do what is necessary to fight climate change according to intergenerational equity, CBDR, and the precautionary principle. But then again, how do we determine what is necessary? According to which criteria or standard?

The Supreme Court found that on the basis of articles 2 and 8 of the European Convention on Human Rights (ECHR), the Netherlands has a positive obligation to take measures for the prevention of climate change and to reduce its GHG emissions at least by 25 per cent by the end of 2020, compared to 1990 levels.[189]

The Court reasoning is based on the combined reading of the UN climate change regime treaty provisions, decisions of the COP, and reports of the IPCC, with the human rights obligations to protect the right to life under the ECHR. First, the Court, relying on a precautionary approach, considers that risks caused by climate change are sufficiently real and immediate to bring them within the scope of articles 2 and 8.[190] Once this connection is established, the Court engages in determining the standard of due diligence and in translating the NDC into a quantitative target of emissions reductions. Considering the seriousness and urgency of the threat, the Court held that the Netherlands should undertake necessary actions. To determine what these are in practice, the Court relies on the UN climate change regime standards, considering them as generally accepted both at the international and at the European level. The Court calculated the individual target applicable to the Netherlands by deriving it from the global collective target of developed countries: considering that the Netherlands has one of the highest per capita GHG emissions in the world, the Court found that the 25 per cent collective target of developed countries applies.[191] This far-fetched step of the Court's reasoning expresses an innovative interpretation of the relationship between CBDR and states' individual obligations. This latter qualification constitutes a powerful upgrade in terms of strengthening the legal nature and effectiveness of NDCs: looking at the *Urgenda* case from the perspective of the principle of CBDR, it is noteworthy that the Court did not hesitate to determine the specific target of its Country, relying on the three dimensions of the CBDR principle: responsibilities, capabilities, and special vulnerabilities. Accordingly, the Court reasoning took into account respectively the actual contribution to climate change of the Netherlands as one of the highest per capita emitter of GHGs, its developed

---

[189] Judgment of 20 December 2019.
[190] The fact that these risks would only become apparent in a few decades does not preclude arts 2 and 8 ECHR to offer protection against this threat (§5.6.2).
[191] Judgment of 20 December 2019, §7.3.4.

1004 SDG 13

country status, and, presumably, its special circumstances of being a low-lying state. The Court interpreted the principle of CBDR under the climate regime, *iuncto* with articles 2 and 8 ECHR, as creating partial obligations, which in turn originate partial responsibility to fight global climate change.[192]

Indeed, while under the Paris Agreement, states—'tainted' by the necessities of political compromise—are not legally bound to achieve their NDCs (and supranational bodies or other states would hardly dear to question this approach), conversely, in the Urgenda case the Supreme Court, as the higher domestic jurisdiction, uses these same provisions—still of a non-legally binding character—to interpret due diligence obligations that states owe to their citizens pursuant to human rights treaties. Using its broader discretionary powers, and not being bound by the constraints of international negotiations, the Court can be more demanding of its own state in terms of the ambition and due diligence standard required in climate change mitigation actions.[193] By so doing, the Court stresses the responsibility aspects related to CBDR, and takes a bold stand in interpreting internationally agreed rules and standards of behaviour. This attitude picks up the suggestion of the International Court of Justice in the context of sustainable development that 'new norms and standards ... set forth in a great number of instruments ... have to be taken into consideration and such standards given proper weight'.[194]

This apparent contrast between the architecture of the Paris Agreement and the Supreme Court judgment may lead to constructive and progressive developments. Even though clearly the two interpretations are not aligned, they are the outcome of different contexts and might end up being complementary.[195] Furthermore, they might well contribute to the much-needed effectiveness of the Paris Agreement implementation at the domestic level.

Following the lead provided by the Urgenda case, other strategic litigation cases have been brought and are pending before French, Italian, and the European Union jurisdictions.

---

[192] The Court emphasizes that each state bears an individual responsibility which depends from its contribution to climate change as a whole: 'The State is therefore obliged to reduce greenhouse gas emissions from its territory in proportion to its share of the responsibility.' The extent of responsibility for the inadequate fulfilment of their obligation of conduct to undertake ambitious mitigation policies is measured against the due diligence standard as indicated in the climate regime's rules adopted on the basis of the scientific inputs of the IPCC, and therefore vested with authority and legitimacy.

[193] The *Urgenda* judgment shows that how non-legally binding instruments when read in combination positive obligation of the ECHR, can transform into binding law. On the risks of this 'mutation', see A Nollkaemper and L Burgers, 'A New Classic in Climate Change Litigation: The Dutch Supreme Court Decision in the Urgenda Case', EJIL:TALK! (6 January 2020) <https://www.ejiltalk.org/a-new-classic-in-climate-change-litigation-the-dutch-supreme-court-decision-in-the-urgenda-case/> accessed 21 November 2022.

[194] ICJ, *Gabčikovo Nagymaros Project (Hungaria v Slovakia)*, Judgment, ICJ Reports 1997, p 7, at p 78, para 140.

[195] While welcoming the boldness of this interpretation, it must be acknowledged that according to the rules on treaty interpretation, the provisions of a treaty should be read in the light of their legal order. This would require interpreting NDCs in light of the Paris Agreement, and hence, providing them with legally binding force would arguably go beyond mere interpretation and constitute an exercise of 'proactive law-making' by the Supreme Court.

2. Empirical Analysis

The indicator for this target addresses specifically the education system: '13.3.1, Extent to which (i) global citizenship education and (ii) education for sustainable development are mainstreamed in (a) national education policies; (b) curricula; (c) teacher education; and (d) student assessment.'

Unfortunately, monitoring and reporting on this indicator has not attracted appropriate attention by stakeholders. The 2020 UN SG SDGs report does not provide any relevant information, not to mention the absence of data in the report's statistical annex. Therefore, it is difficult to form a comprehensive view about the extent to which sustainable development and climate change awareness have been incorporated to the purposes of education in national education plans. Notwithstanding this, government's VNRs submitted to the 2019 HLPF demonstrate an encouraging trend in increasing education and awareness of climate change as a policy priority. For instance, Chile, Kazakhstan, and Palau have made climate change a mandatory curriculum subject, while Serbia has introduced extra-curricular activities on environmental education as part of its Strategy for Education Development.[196] Similarly, Guyana's School Outreach Program under the auspices of the Office of Climate Change aspires to institutionalize climate change awareness and education at all levels of education across the country, already benefitting 5,000 students.[197] Finally, Algeria has partnered with civil society, encouraging community members to participate in environmental policy initiatives through the production of mini-films and audiovisual media.[198]

3. Critique

Despite the long-lasting commitment in reinforcing national technical capacities, due also to the complexity of climate change matters, the need for underlying data and regular statistics to inform the policy aspects of climate change and disaster risk reduction remains a pressing requirement and a great challenge for developing countries. Developing and least developed countries and SIDS, among others, still encounter important challenges when producing statistics about the impact of the disasters and other long-term effects of climate change. Statistics and indicators about mitigation and adaptation of climate change and also about disaster risk reduction are less developed and require worldwide investment in statistical capacities for producing them and making them available for monitoring and decision making.

---

[196] Voluntary National Review of the Republic of Serbia on the Implementation of the 2030 Agenda for Sustainable Development (2019) 64 <https://sustainabledevelopment.un.org/content/documents/23471Serbia_VNR_Report_2019_final.pdf> accessed 21 November 2022.

[197] Guyana, 'First Voluntary National Review—HLPF on Sustainable Development (July 2019) 64 <https://sustainabledevelopment.un.org/content/documents/24297Guyana_VNR2019_FINAL_REPORT_070819.pdf> accessed 21 November 2022.

[198] UN DESA, '2019 Voluntary National Reviews Synthesis Report' (HLPF 2019) 58–59 <https://sustainabledevelopment.un.org/content/documents/252302019_VNR_Synthesis_Report_DESA.pdf> accessed 21 November 2022.

E. Target 13.a Implement the commitment undertaken by developed-country parties to the United Nations Framework Convention on Climate Change to a goal of mobilizing jointly $100 billion annually by 2020 from all sources to address the needs of developing countries in the context of meaningful mitigation actions and transparency on implementation and fully operationalize the Green Climate Fund through its capitalization as soon as possible

1. Sources of the Target and Implementation Efforts

While finance for climate action has increased substantially in the last few years, investments in climate activities across the different sectors must reach a much greater scale to achieve a low-carbon, climate-resilient transition. Furthermore, investments in fossil fuels in the energy sector are still very significant.[199]

With regard to its objective, climate finance can be roughly divided in two types: finance delivered to support adaptation projects and funds that support mitigation projects in developing countries. Adaptation activities focus on projects that increase resilience to the adverse impacts of climate change, while mitigation projects deal with the reduction of GHG emissions, for example in the areas of renewable energy or sustainable transport. Despite the pressing need for adaptation programmes and projects, which are particularly necessary for those countries that are most vulnerable to the impacts of climate change, developed countries' investments have so far been devoted for the largest part to climate change mitigation activities.[200] The need to balance the allocation of funds in these two areas is a crucial element of the ongoing negotiations, especially with respect to actions taken by the Green Climate Fund. The provision of financial assistance to developing countries involves different types of actors. When looking at the source of the funds, one of the main public sources for developing countries is Official Development Assistance (ODA) provided through bilateral and multilateral channels. Financial aid may also be provided through specific financing mechanisms and private sector investments.

The legal basis of the obligation to transfer financial resources from developed countries to developing countries is found in UNFCCC, article 4.3, which operationalizes the CBDR-RC principle in this context, by providing that

[t]he developed country Parties and other developed Parties included in Annex II shall provide new and additional financial resources to meet the agreed full costs incurred by developing country Parties in complying with their obligations under Article 12, paragraph 1. They shall also provide such financial resources, including for the transfer of technology, needed by the developing country Parties to meet the

---

[199] In 2016 investments in fossil fuels totalled $781 billion, while the low-carbon ones amounted to $681 billion.
[200] Climate financing provided by developed countries to developing ones increased by 14 per cent in 2016 reaching nearly $38 billion. Climate mitigation investments amounted to roughly $24.3 billion, while climate adaptation reached $5.6 billion and cross-cutting issues amounted to $5.1 billion.

agreed full incremental costs of implementing measures that are covered by paragraph 1 of this Article and that are agreed between a developing country Party and the international entity or entities referred to in Article 11, in accordance with that Article. The implementation of these commitments shall take into account the need for adequacy and predictability in the flow of funds and the importance of appropriate burden sharing among the developed country Parties.

Further, the following provision takes into account climate adaptation finance and need of the most vulnerable states: 'The developed country Parties and other developed Parties included in Annex II shall also assist the developing country Parties that are particularly vulnerable to the adverse effects of climate change in meeting costs of adaptation to those adverse effects.'[201]

The financial mechanism of the climate change regime has been operated since its adoption by the Global Environmental Facility (GEF). This international financial institution was established on a provisional basis by a resolution of the World Bank in 1991 and later restructured in 1994 in order to strengthen the participation of developing countries in its governance and ensure more transparency of its procedures.[202] The 'new' GEF is a multipurpose fund managed by the World Bank and implemented by agencies of the United Nations, which represents an unforeseen institutional body. The GEF finances projects in the areas of biodiversity, climate change, ozone depletion, persistent organic pollutants, and land degradation following the guidelines provided by the COP of each convention. The GEF is a good example of clustering resources in financing sustainable development as it creates synergies among MEAs and favours an integrated approach, avoiding inconsistencies in the disbursement of funding. For instance, GEF projects in climate change mitigation do not include sequestration projects that have been criticized for negatively affecting biodiversity. Smaller funds exist under the Climate Change regime: the Special Climate Change Fund, the Least Developed Countries Fund, and the Adaptation Fund. The GEF is governed by a Council of thirty-two members, of which eighteen represent beneficiary countries and fourteen represent donor countries. The Council meets generally every two years and evaluates the effective functioning of the financial resources allocation. The institutional structure is completed by an independent Secretariat, administered by the World Bank, which responds directly to the GEF Council

---

[201] UNFCCC, art 4.4.

[202] See World Bank, Resolution No 91–5 (October 1991), Annex C, adopted by the Executive Directors of the World Bank and supplemented by tripartite procedural arrangements with the United Nations Development Programme (UNDP) and the United Nations Environment Programme (UNEP). The main objective of this restructuring process, as recognized by the Preamble to the Constituent Instrument of the GEF (ILM 33 (1994), 1283, hereinafter GEF Instrument) is to 'ensure a governance that is transparent and democratic in nature and to promote universality in its participation'. On the GEF, see: L Boisson De Chazournes, 'The Global Environment Facility (GEF): A Unique and Crucial Institution' (2005) 14 Review of European Community and International Environmental Law 193; L Boisson De Chazournes, 'The Global Environment Facility Galaxy: On Linkages among Institutions', in *Max Planck Yearbook of UN Law* (1999) 243; P Sand, 'The Potential Impact of the Global Environment Facility of the World Bank, UNDP and UNEP' in R Wolfrum (ed), *Enforcing Environmental Standards: Economic Mechanisms as Viable Means* (Springer Berlin 1996) 479; J Werksman, 'Consolidating Global Environmental Governance: New Lessons from the GEF?', Paper presented at the Yale Center for Environmental Law and Policy, New Haven, 25 October 2003.

1008 SDG 13

and by the Assembly gathering all representatives of States Parties every three years. At the institutional level, the GEF's governing structure is an interesting experiment of pragmatic reconciliation of the ideals of universality, democracy, and transparency on the one hand, and a small and efficient decision-making body on the other.

The Green Climate Fund (GCF) has been established under the climate convention 'to make a significant and ambitious contribution to the global efforts towards attaining the goals set by the international community to combat climate change'.[203] This objective is to be reached in the context of sustainable development by promoting a 'paradigm shift towards low-emission and climate-resilient development pathways' in developing countries.[204] One of the innovative features of the GCF is that it 'will catalyse climate finance, both public and private, and at the international and national levels'.[205] The guiding principles for the operation of the GCF are transparency, accountability, efficiency and effectiveness, flexibility, and country ownership. In the pursuit of complementarity and coherence, the GCF will conclude appropriate arrangements with other financial institutions within and outside the climate regime to increase the overall contribution of climate finance. Private actors participate in the Board governing the GCF with two representatives, one from a developed and one from a developing country. The private sector, moreover, may contribute to the Fund's replenishment. The GCF will have a 'facility' specifically devoted to financing private initiatives in climate mitigation and adaptation.[206] This facility is expected to promote the involvement of the business sector located in developing countries, SIDS, and LDCs, in particular local, small- and medium-size enterprises and financial intermediaries. Learning from previous experiences, the procedures governing the disbursement of funds are simplified and oriented to achieve broad access to funding. To this aim, a wide range of financial instruments and simultaneous modalities of access are envisaged, including direct access. Traditionally, implementing agencies serve as intermediaries between the funds and the beneficiaries and their task is to oversee that the disbursement process takes place in accordance with their environmental, social, and financial standards. For these purposes, they ensure the monitoring of the financed activities and supervise their implementation. Direct access to the GCF by the beneficiaries bypasses the role of implementing agencies and entrusts public and private institutions of the country hosting the investment with dealing directly with the GCF. In this model the organizations are directly responsible for spending the funds and will thus need to demonstrate that they have adequate accountability systems in place, such as financial, environmental, and social safeguards. Supporters of the 'direct access' approach stress that it ensures greater

---

[203] Governing Instrument for the Green Climate Fund, para 1 (Annex to Decision 3/CP.17, FCCC/CP/2011/9/Add.1).

[204] ibid para 2.

[205] ibid para 3.

[206] The design of the GCF has been a rather short but very intensive process where the contribution of the private sector has been substantial, as demonstrated by the numerous and detailed recommendations from private sector associations to the Transitional Committee in charge of designing the GCF.

country ownership, more streamlined procedures, and lower transaction costs.[207] The operations of the GCF operations shall meet appropriate environmental and social safeguards with performance indicators that will be reviewed periodically to ensure that the sustainable development integrity targets are met and will undergo periodical independent assessments of its financial integrity. Moreover, the whole chain of lending, including the GCF implementing agencies, the trustees, and all organizations involved in the disbursement of funds shall be in compliance with fiduciary standards. The GCF governance combines flexibility with specific requirements that should ensure the reliable and efficient functioning that is essential to gain the credibility and trust of public and private investors. There are innovative elements in its design that are encouraging signs of steps forward in the 'integration process' of private actors in the mandate for sustainable development. Moreover, in many ways the GCF acknowledges the importance of pursuing a country-driven approach and thereby connects global sustainable development goals not only with private investors but also with local actors, thus strengthening coherence between international, national, and local sustainable development policies.

Further encouraging elements for its sound and effective operation are accountability mechanisms, such as the establishment of an independent integrity unit in charge of investigating potential allegations of fraud and corruption, and the creation of a redress mechanism for complaints regarding the functioning of the Fund. These review systems should target the wrongdoings of international organizations and of private investors participating in the financing activities. These investors should also have adequate complaint mechanisms to redress alleged breaches of their agreements with the GCF. This kind of claim generally remains outside the mandate of most accountability mechanisms of international finance institutions (IFIs), which only deal with the private complaints of 'affected people', namely local communities that do not have a contractual relationship with the IFI.

With regard to financial and technology transfer, the Paris Agreement envisages reinforced financial commitments of developed countries for mitigation and adaptation initiatives to promote the transition to low-carbon economies in developing states and emerging countries.[208] In order to enhance the transparency and the comparability of the action taken, besides communicating every five years on their mitigation measures, developed States Parties shall provide qualitative and quantitative information on the financial resources transferred on a biennial basis.[209] Information provided by states on the mitigation, adaptation, and financial measures they undertake both at the domestic and international level shall be clear and scientifically based.

---

[207] The direct access model has already shown positive experiences, such as in the case of a two USD billion loan approved by the World Bank for the Brazilian National Bank for Development. World Resources Institute, *Power, Responsibility and Accountability. Re-Thinking the legitimacy of institutions for Climate Finance* (World Resources Institute 2010) 6 and 45.

[208] Paris Agreement, art 9.3 and 9.9.

[209] Paris Agreement, art 13.9.

1010   SDG 13

2. Empirical Analysis

a) 13.a.1 Amounts provided and mobilized in United States dollars per year in relation to the continued existing collective mobilization goal of the $100 billion commitment through to 2025

The GCF, through its Readiness and Preparatory Support Programme and the Least Developed Countries Fund, has been instrumental in providing funding to ensure the submission of National Adaptation Plans (NAPs) under the Paris Agreement. In 2019, 120 out of 153 developing countries, including five LDCs and four SIDS, had undertaken the process of formulation and implementation of their respective NAPs. As of December 2019, eighty-one countries, of which twenty-nine were LDCs, had submitted eighty-three proposals totalling $203.8 million in requested support from the GCF. Forty proposals have been approved (fourteen from LDCs).

Total climate finance reported by States Parties included in Annex I to the Framework Convention on Climate Change continues to increase, reaching an annual average of $48.7 billion in the period 2017–2018. This represents an increase of 10 per cent compared to the 2015–2016 period. While more than half of all climate-specific financial support in the 2017 and 2018 was targeted at mitigation action, the share of adaptation support is growing, and many countries and territories are prioritizing adaptation in their financial support provision.[210]

3. Critique

The pledges of the Parties, notably developed states, are below what was promised in previous COPs since Copenhagen in 2009, and what is expressly provided also by SDG 13.a.1.[211] With regard to adaptation finance, during the recent COP26 in Glasgow it was noted with concern that 'current provision of climate finance for adaptation remains insufficient to respond to worsening climate change impacts in developing country Parties'.[212] To cope with the shortages in the transfer of finance for adaptation, developed Parties should 'at least double their collective provision of climate finance for adaptation to developing country Parties from 2019 levels by 2025'.[213]

---

[210] Report of the Secretary-General, Progress towards the Sustainable Development Goals, 30 April 202, Doc E/2021/58, para 145.

[211] Glasgow Climate Pact, para 44-4, the CMA 'Notes with deep regret that the goal of developed country Parties to mobilize jointly USD 100 billion per year by 2020 in the context of meaningful mitigation actions and transparency on implementation has not yet been met ...; Urges developed country Parties to fully deliver on the USD 100 billion goal urgently and through to 2025 and emphasizes the importance of transparency in the implementation of their pledges.' On climate finance, see below para on target 13.a.

[212] Glasgow Climate Pact, para 14.

[213] ibid para 18.

F. Target 13.b Promote mechanisms for raising capacity for effective climate change-related planning and management in least developed countries and small island developing States, including focusing on women, youth and local and marginalized communities

1. Sources of the Target and Implementation Efforts

The importance to take into special consideration the situation of SIDS clearly emerges from the Rio + 20 outcome:

> We reaffirm that small island developing States remain a special case for sustainable development in view of their unique and particular vulnerabilities, including their small size, remoteness, narrow resource and export base, and exposure to global environmental challenges and external economic shocks, including to a large range of impacts from climate change and potentially more frequent and intense natural disasters. We note with concern that the outcome of the five-year review of the Mauritius Strategy concluded that small island developing States have made less progress than most other groupings, or even regressed, in economic terms, especially in terms of poverty reduction and debt sustainability. Sea-level rise and other adverse impacts of climate change continue to pose a significant risk to small island developing States and their efforts to achieve sustainable development and, for many, represent the gravest of threats to their survival and viability, including for some through the loss of territory. We also remain concerned that, while small island developing States have progressed in the areas of gender, health, education and the environment, their overall progress towards achieving the Millennium Development Goals has been uneven.[214]

SDG 13.b picks up the legacy mandated by the concerns raised at the Rio + 20 summit and provides for a clear recognition of the special circumstances that affect LDCs, on the one hand, and of the most marginalized and vulnerable categories of people, on the other.

Besides its geographical dimension related to LDCs, this target is deeply intertwined with the human rights realm, and in particular with treaties dealing with the protection of vulnerable categories. Relevant in this context are, for instance, the Convention on the Rights of Persons with Disabilities (CRPD), article 11: 'States Parties shall take, in accordance with their obligations under international law, including international humanitarian law and international human rights law, all necessary measures to ensure the protection and safety of persons with disabilities in situations of risk, including situations of armed conflict, humanitarian emergencies and the occurrence of natural disasters.' And with regard to indigenous people, the United Nations Declaration on the Rights of Indigenous Peoples (UNDRIP), article 18: 'Indigenous peoples have the right to participate in decision-making in matters which would affect their rights, through

---

[214] 'The Future We Want', para 178.

representatives chosen by themselves in accordance with their own procedures, as well as to maintain and develop their own indigenous decision-making institutions.'

Children of today are among the most vulnerable categories, insofar as they are currently excluded from the decision-making and normative process and at the same time, they will be the most affected by climate change impacts in the near future. In the last few years, youth movements have been recognized the status of constituency in international climate negotiations.[215] The role of youth and future generations are gaining momentum with regard to the fight against climate change. While there are several treaties recognizing the rights of children, such as, for example the African Charter on the Rights and Welfare of the Child (ACRWC),[216] in parallel with these developments, a group of young people from different countries has filed a communication with the Committee on the Rights of the Child alleging that five largest polluters are endangering the lives and welfare of youth worldwide.[217]

This case highlights the inter-generational dimension of climate change and offers a great opportunity to take into account the positions and rights of youth and of future generations.

As for the African continent, the African Commission on Human and Peoples' Rights (the African Commission), and the African Committee of Experts on the Rights and Welfare of the Child (ACERWC), two of the three African Union's bodies for the promotion and protection of human and peoples' rights and the rights and welfare of the child, noting that

> Africa has witnessed with increasing ferocity and frequency the recurrence of destructive weather conditions affecting many parts of the continent leading to deaths, destruction of property and livelihoods and displacement. The situation is creating not only the vulnerabilities of individuals and communities in all affected parts of the continent but also poses the most serious threat to the human and peoples' rights and survival of the peoples of the continent. As in the case with all crisis, children are in the most vulnerable situation to bear the brunt of the impacts of climate change.[218]

Although the connections between urban planning, poverty, location of human settlements in risk areas, social and environmental vulnerability, and disasters impact is in general well understood, constructing statistics to inform these relations, capturing the complexity of the phenomena, is fairly difficult and requires significant investment in capacity building and statistical development in the affected countries.

---

[215] See <http://www.youthclimatemovement.wordpress.com>.

[216] ACRWC, '5.1 Every child has an inherent right to life. This right shall be protected by law. 5.2 State Parties to the present Charter shall ensure, to the maximum extent possible, the survival, protection and development of the child.'

[217] See *Communication Sacchi and others, v Argentina et al.*, hearthjustice.org; Communication No 107/2019 (23 Sep 2019) and CRC Decision CRC/C/88/D/107/2019 (8 October 2021).

[218] Press Statement on the occasion of the 33rd Assembly of the Heads of State and Government of the African Union <https://www.achpr.org/pressrelease/detail?id=476> accessed 21 November 2022.

2. Empirical Analysis

Indicator 13.b.1: 'Number of least developed countries and small island developing States with nationally determined contributions, long-term strategies, national adaptation plans and adaptation communications, as reported to the secretariat of the United Nations Framework Convention on Climate Change.' The indicator was reformulated after the comprehensive review of the global indicator framework that took place in 2020. It previously read: 'Number of least developed countries and small island developing States that are receiving specialized support, and amount of support, including finance, technology and capacity-building, for mechanisms for raising capacities for effective climate change-related planning and management, including focusing on women, youth and local and marginalized communities.' Clearly, the rewording of the target draws upon the regulatory framework of the UNFCCC, and in particular the Paris Agreement, that obliges State Parties to report and communicate their mitigation and adaptation strategies pursuant to their national development priorities and circumstances.

Relevant data are largely missing whether one looks at statistics under the previous wording or the current iteration. If fact, the Global SDGs database reports for the year 2021 only on the number of LDCs and SIDS with NDCs, adaptation plans, and communications, and long-term climate change strategies.[219] According to the 2021 SDGs progress report by the UN SG, 125 of 154 developing countries were in the process of formulating and implementing national adaptation plans as of May 2021, twenty-two of which had submitted them to the UNFCCC Secretariat.[220] Still, it is not made explicit how these plans address the concerns of women, the youth and marginalised communities.

Undoubtedly, effective monitoring of target 13.b is far from being a reality but there are signs that all countries' increasing emphasis on climate change-related planning.

3. Critique

During the elaboration of SDG 13, several shortcomings and weaknesses were identified concerning the difficulties to calculate indicators on climate change adaptation and mitigation and disseminate them regularly because of considerable data gaps, particularly in developing countries.

VII. Final Remarks

Progress on SDG13 is falling short of what is needed to meet the targets of the global agenda by 2030. According to the World Meteorological Organization, 2018 was the fourth warmest year on record, with the past four years (2015, 2016, 2017, 2018) being

---

[219] UN DESA (Statistics Division), 'SDGs Global Database' <https://unstats.un.org/sdgs/UNSDG/IndDatabasePage> accessed 21 November 2022.

[220] UN, 'The Sustainable Development Goals Report 2021' 52 <https://www.un-ilibrary.org/content/books/9789210056083/read> accessed 21 November 2022.

1014   SDG 13

the four warmest years on record. The world continues to experience rising sea levels, extreme weather conditions, and increasing concentrations of GHGs. Climate change is a cross-cutting and immediate threat to the achievement of the SDGs, and to the survival and well-being of island nations and coastal communities. This calls for urgent and accelerated action by countries as they implement the 2030 Agenda for Sustainable Development and their commitments to the Paris Agreement on Climate Change. Climate action requires efforts on mitigation, adaptation and means of implementation—climate finance, technology, and capacity building.

Behind the political impasse of reaching a comprehensive agreement to curb GHG emission, fears of losing competitiveness and protection for carbon-intensive industry should be taken into consideration, and in the meantime private investment in climate-related initiatives is increasingly developing. Other relevant actors are international and domestic financial institutions that are fundamental drivers in the transition to a carbon-neutral economy, considering their crucial role in providing finance that boosts innovative technologies and green investments. Furthermore, beside institutional actors, companies and corporate actors are undergoing a process of reformation process that requires them to account for their climate change footprint, among other environmental and social requirements.

While the international negotiations proceed at a very slow path, seeking to build trust among all the various subjects involved, climate change continues apace so other climate initiatives are being undertaken at the international level in the framework of other international organizations, such as International Maritime Organization (IMO), International Civil Aviation Organization (ICAO), and ILO, by trade and investment agreements, as well as at the domestic and regional level.

Despite the steps made towards the progressive transition to a low-carbon or carbon-neutral economy and livelihoods, there is still a deep chasm between states' behaviours and their pledges and what it is realistically and scientifically required to tackle climate change effectively and prevent its grave dangerous impacts.

SDG 14

'Conserve and Sustainably Use the Oceans, Seas, and Marine Resources for Sustainable Development'

Eirini-Erasmia Fasia and Christos Kypraios

I. Introduction

Sustainable Development Goal (SDG) 14 calls for the conservation and sustainable use of oceans, seas, and marine resources. The ocean covers approximately 72 per cent of the Earth's surface and is inextricably linked with life and habitation on it.[1] The seas regulate the climate and weather patterns, while marine ecosystems and resources support the livelihood of billions of people and can contribute to poverty eradication. Additionally, oceans play a key role in human health and well-being, producing oxygen and holding huge reservoirs of biodiversity.[2] It is thus widely accepted that marine environment's destruction is an urgent problem that affects all states across the planet, developing and developed. The United Nations (UN) 1st Global Ocean Assessment in 2015 stated that the oceans' capacity to withstand anthropogenic impacts was deemed near or at its limit.[3] Marine pollution, increased CO_2 emissions, over-fishing, climate change, and ocean acidification are among the current most serious marine challenges. Scientists estimate that there are already hundreds of dead zones in the planet's oceans, whole sections where there is insufficient oxygen to sustain marine flora and fauna.[4] Habitat destruction is the result, among other things, of damaging fishing and agricultural practices, mining, dredging, anchoring, and over-tourism.[5] The majority of fisheries appear to be in a critical state, approaching their depletion due to over-fishing and lack of effective regulation and policing.[6] Currently, it is estimated that 30 per cent of

---

[1] UN, 'Factsheet: People and Oceans' (The Ocean Conference, United Nations, 5–9 June 2017) <https://www.un.org/sustainabledevelopment/wp-content/uploads/2017/05/Ocean-fact-sheet-package.pdf> accessed 13 August 2021.

[2] Anon, 'Un-Gendering the Ocean: Why Women Matter in Ocean Governance for Sustainability—Data on Sustainability Research Reported by E Gissi' (2018) Ecology, Environment & Conservation 95.

[3] UN, 'Summary of the First Global Integrated Marine Assessment', 8, 16, 19 <https://www.un.org/depts/los/global_reporting/WOA_RPROC/Summary.pdf> accessed 19 November 2021.

[4] CL Dybas, 'Dead Zones Spreading in World Oceans' (2005) 7 BioScience 55.

[5] OECD, *Marine Protected Areas: Economics, Management and Effective Policy Mixes* (OECD 2017).

[6] G Schmidt-Traub and others, 'National Baselines for the Sustainable Development Goals Assessed in the SDG Index and Dashboards (2017) 8(10) Nature Geoscience 547–55.

1016   SDG 14

global fisheries are near the point of complete depletion and beyond repair, while 80 per cent of the world's fish stocks are reported as fully exploited or overexploited.[7] Numbers are especially worrying considering population growth and the consequent rise of demand in the next decades.[8] Concerning climate change, its negative effects include sea-level rise, threatening the survival of Small Island Developing States (SIDS) and other coastal communities, as well as intensification of extreme weather phenomena.[9] This extremely alarming situation underlines the necessity of urgent international action 'to protect the world's oceans from the many pressures they face'.[10] The 2012 UN Report on Evaluation of Oceans by the Joint Inspection Unit remarked that although oceans constitute 'a major part of the planet that supports life, drives the climate and ... provides vital resources', ocean and coastal issues have unfortunately received low visibility and priority.[11] Entering the third decade of the twenty-first century, states are expected to step up in order to protect the ocean and its resources. Hence, the inclusion of a specific goal, the SDG 14, as part of the 2030 UN Agenda was without question a major step in highlighting the ocean environment's importance as a general indicator of the planet's health.

The idea of environmental sustainability is traced back to the first UN Conference on Environment and Development in 1972 (UNCED), which was a turning point in the development of international environmental politics as up until then environmental problems were not considered a major issue.[12] In 2010 the concept of environmental sustainable development was endorsed by the International Court of Justice (ICJ) in its seminal *Pulp Mills* case.[13] The predecessors of the SDGs, the 2000 UN Millennium Development Goals (MDGs), included one overarching goal that referred generally to environmental sustainability (MDG 7).[14] That was an all-encompassing goal referring to the sustainable management of natural resources and ecosystems and to climate change and food security. The targets of MDG 7 called for (i) integration of sustainable

[7] UN, 'Resumed Review Conference on the Agreement Relating to the Conservation and Management of Straddling Fish Stocks and Highly Migratory Fish Stocks' <https://www.un.org/depts/los/convention_agreements/reviewconf/FishStocks_EN_A.pdf> accessed 7 July 2021.; UN FAO, 'General Situation of World Fish Stocks' <https://www.fao.org/Newsroom/common/ecg/1000505/en/stocks.pdf> accessed 10 July 2021; M Kituyi and P Thomson, 'Fisheries Subsidies Must Stop' <https://unctad.org/news/90-fish-stocks-are-used-fisheries-subsidies-must-stop> accessed 8 July 2021.

[8] SJ Barkin and ER DeSombre, *Saving Global Fisheries: Reducing Fishing Capacity to Promote Sustainability* (MIT Press 2013) 145–52.

[9] K Cooper and others, 'Can the Benefits of Physical Seabed Restoration Justify the Costs? An Assessment of a Disused Aggregate Extraction Site off the Thames Estuary, UK' (2013) 75 Marine Pollution 33–45; UNDESA, *How Oceans- and Seas-Related Measures Contribute to the Economic, Social and Environmental Dimensions of Sustainable Development: Local and Regional Experiences'* (UNDESA 2014).

[10] Foreword by the Secretary-General of the United Nations, Ban Ki-moon <https://www.un.org/Depts/los/global_reporting/WOA_RPROC/Foreword.pdf> accessed 21 August 2021.

[11] M Munir Jahran and T Inomata, 'Evaluation of Un-Oceans' JIU/REP/2012/3, para 67 <https://www.unjiu.org/sites/www.unjiu.org/files/jiu_document_files/products/en/reports-notes/JIU%20Products/JIU_REP_2012_3_English.pdf> accessed 13 May 2021.

[12] 'United Nations Conference on the Human Environment', UN Environment Conference (Stockholm, 5–16 June 1972) UN Doc A/Conf 48/14/Rev. 1 PC pp 13 and 17.

[13] *Pulp Mills on the River Uruguay (Argentina v. Uruguay)* (Merits, Judgment) 20 April 2010, ICJ Rep 2010, 14, 48–49. The Court stated that the essence of sustainable development lies in the balance between economic development and environmental protection.

[14] UN, *Millennium Development Goals: Progress Report* (UN Dept. of Economic and Social Affairs 2004) MDG 7 '[e]nsure environmental sustainability'.

development principles into country policies, (ii) the reduction of biodiversity loss, (iii) the reduction of the proportion of the population without sustainable access to safe drinking water and basic sanitation, and (iv) a significant improvement in the lives of slum dwellers. It is striking that the MDGs did not include any special reference to the oceans and the marine environment, either as a separate goal or as part of the targets of MDG 7.

Ocean sustainability has only recently become a top priority on the international agenda. Up until the 1960s it was commonplace that states had discretion to pollute the oceans, which were subject only to few regulations. It was the 1967 *Torrey Canyon* oil spill in the Seven Stones Reef that raised awareness of the risk of marine pollution. Since then, major steps have been made towards the development of legal and policy mechanisms promoting ocean protection and sustainability. Ocean sustainability refers to ocean management that aims to improve its environmental status and stop the degradation of the marine ecosystems. States' responsibilities for marine sustainability are reflected in soft law and policy texts[15] and, more importantly, in legally binding instruments and international judgments and awards.[16] SDG 14 forms part of this broad framework.

The SDGs were created in 2015 as a response to the limited success of the MDGs.[17] The UN General Assembly set up seventeen Goals that are intended to be achieved by the year 2030 (UN Agenda 2030).[18] The SDGs are not legally binding upon states. States commit to deliver the SDGs on a voluntary basis and are encouraged to report on their progress. The SDGs focus on sustainability and integrate the three dimensions of sustainable development: biosphere, society, and economy.[19] Seven separate goals along with their targets are dedicated or closely connected to the environment and

[15] *Inter alia*, UN Agenda 21 (1992), ch 17; United Nations. 2004. United Nations world ocean assessment. Regular process for global reporting and assessment of the state of the marine environment, including socio-economic aspects. United Nations Division for Ocean Affaires and Law of the Sea, New York; EU/EC, 2007. Communication from the Commission to the European Parliament, the Council, the European Economic and Social Committee and the Committee of the Regions. An integrated maritime policy for the European Union, COM (2007) 0575 final. Brussels; HELCOM. The Bremen declaration. HELCOM Ministerial Declaration. Helsinki: Helsinki Commission 2003.

[16] *Inter alia*, 2000 Convention on the Conservation and Management of Highly Migratory Fish Stocks in the Western and Central Pacific Ocean; 2001 FAO International Plan of Action to Prevent, Deter and Eliminate Illegal, Unreported and Unregulated Fishing; 1992 Convention on the Protection of the Marine Environment of the North-East Atlantic (OSPAR Convention); 1993 FAO Agreement to Promote Compliance with International Conservation and Management Measures by Fishing Vessels on the High Seas; 1995 FAO Code of Conduct for Responsible Fisheries; 'Responsibilities and Obligations of States Sponsoring Persons and Entities with Respect to Activities in the Area', Advisory Opinion, International Treaty on the Law of the Seas (ITLOS) Case No 17, [2011] ITLOS Rep 10. For commentary see D Freestone, 'Responsibilities and Obligations of States Sponsoring Persons and Entities with Respect to Activities in the Area' (2011) 105 American Journal of International Law 755–61. Request for an Advisory Opinion Submitted by the Sub-regional Fisheries Commission (SRFC), ITLOS Case No 21, 2 April 2015.

[17] JD Sachs, 'From Millennium Development Goals to Sustainable Development Goals' (2012) 379 Lancet, 2206–11.

[18] 'Transforming Our World: the 2030 Agenda for Sustainable Development', UNGA A/Res/70/1 <http://unctad.org/meetings/en/SessionalDocuments/ares70d1_en.pdf> accessed 25 September 2015. See also K Houghton, 'A Sustainable Development Goal for the Ocean: Moving from Goal Framing towards Targets and Indicators for Implementation' (Potsdam Ocean Governance Workshop 2014) Background Document 1; United Nations Environment Programme (UNEP), 'Understanding the State of the Ocean: A Global Manual on Measuring SDG 14.1.1, SDG 14.2.1 and SDG 14.5.1', Nairobi (2021), at 7.

[19] UNEP (n 18).

1018   SDG 14

environmental sustainability. These are SDGs 3 (good health and well-being), 6 (clean water and sanitation), 7 (affordable and clean energy), 12 (responsible consumption and production), 13 (climate action), 14 (life below water), and 15 (life on land). This comes as no surprise considering the pronouncements of the Agenda 2030 with respect to environmental sustainability:

> We recognize that social and economic development depends on the sustainable management of our planet's natural resources. We are therefore determined to conserve and sustainably use oceans and seas, freshwater resources, as well as forests, mountains and drylands and to protect biodiversity, ecosystems and wildlife. We are also determined to promote sustainable tourism, to tackle water scarcity and water pollution to strengthen cooperation on desertification, dust storms, land degradation and drought and to promote resilience and disaster risk reduction. In this regard, we look forward to the thirteenth meeting of the Conference of the Parties to the Convention on Biological Diversity to be held in Mexico.[20]

SDG 14 is exclusively dedicated to the sustainability of marine uses and resources. It includes ten targets calling among others for reduction of marine pollution, restoration of ecosystems, minimization of ocean acidification, and regulation of extraction of marine resources. Further, since ocean sustainability is so fundamental for the planet, SDG 14 is closely connected to other SDGs. In particular, oceans can contribute to end poverty and hunger (SDGs 1 and 2), to advance health and well-being for all (SDG 3), to ensure available water and sanitation (SDG 6), to make cities and human settlement sustainable (SDG 11). SDG 14 is also related to SDG 13 (climate action). In fact, climate action is considered to be integrated into all the SDGs and into SDG 14 specifically. Oceans can moderate the effects of climate change, while conversely climate change has detrimental impacts on the health of marine ecosystems. Finally, SDG 7 (affordable and clean energy) and SDG 15 (ecosystems and biodiversity) are also closely related to the oceans and SDG 14.

The present commentary offers a detailed overview and in-depth analysis of SDG 14. Section II summarizes the *travaux préparatoires* of SDG 14 revealing the process and the deliberations according to which the goal and the targets were created. Section III provides an overview of the two main objectives of SDG 14: conservation and sustainable use; outlines the current legal and policy framework governing the oceans; addresses the main challenges of that framework; and analyses the key notion of cooperation, which can facilitate the advancement of SDG 14. Finally, Section IV examines and evaluates the targets and indicators employed to enable and monitor the implementation of SDG 14.

---

[20] Agenda 2030, para 33.

II. *Travaux Préparatoires*

A. Background

The proposal for the SDGs was developed at the 40th anniversary of the Stockholm Declaration (1st UNCED) during the proceedings of the 9th UNCED in June 2012 at the Rio + 20 conference. One-hundred and ninety-three states agreed to negotiate a wide-ranging agenda with the purpose to strengthen international coordination on key issues in the post-2015 period.

The proceedings whereby the goals would be created was a highly debated and challenging issue. The MDGs had been created through a technical working group appointed by the Secretary-General. One of the criticisms advanced for the MDGs negotiating process is that public debate was almost non-existent.[21] Taking such criticisms on board, eventually, states agreed to an open working group (OWG) process, which involved UN Organizations, civil society, businesses, other stakeholders, and states themselves.[22] These multi-stakeholder negotiations guaranteed a highly participatory grassroots process, remarkably different from the way the MDGs were created.[23]

The OWG was established upon the decision adopted at the Rio + 20 forum in 2012. The sessions of the OWG were held from 2013 to 2014. The first eight OWG sessions, called 'stocktaking', collected information and opinions by experts and stakeholders in order to build a common working ground for the debated issues. The result of this learning process was the 'Focus Area' Document, based on which the actual negotiations took place during the last five sessions (consensus-building stage).[24] The sessions were concluded with the OWG's zero draft submitted and adopted by the UN General Assembly (UNGA) in September 2014.[25] Following the adoption by the GA, intergovernmental negotiations commenced on the Post-2015 Development Agenda which led to eight sessions in the first months of 2015. In January 2015 the GA decided that the OWG proposal would be the main basis for integrating the SDGs into the post-2015 development agenda.[26] The outcome document from the post-2015 negotiations was devoted to implementation and follow-up arrangements for the SDGs.[27] The final document was agreed on 2 August 2015 at the UN Sustainable

---

[21] S Fukuda-Parr, 'Sustainable Development Goals' in TG Weiss and S Daws (eds), *The Oxford Handbook of the United Nations* (OUP 2018) 769–70.

[22] UNGA Decision A/67/L.48/Rev.1, 15 January 2013.

[23] PS Chasek and others, 'Getting to 2030: Negotiating the Post-2015 Sustainable Development Agenda' (2016) 1(25) Review of European Community and International Environmental Law 5–19.

[24] RR Bhandary and others, 'Summary of the UN Sustainable Development Summit: 25–27 September 2015' (2015) 32(24) Earth Negotiations Bulletin 15.

[25] 'Report of the Open Working Group of the General Assembly on Sustainable Development Goals' (12 August 2014) UN Doc A/68/970.

[26] Modalities for the Process of Intergovernmental Negotiations on the Post-2015 Development Agenda (22 December 2014) UN Doc A/69/L.46, at para 2(d).

[27] P Chasek and others, 'Summary of the Sixth Session of Intergovernmental Negotiations on the Post-2015 Development Agenda: 22–25 June 2015' (2015) 32 Earth Negotiations Bulletin 19.

1020   SDG 14

Development Summit.[28] The new agenda, titled 'Transforming Our World: The 2030 Agenda for Sustainable Development', as UN Secretary-General Ban Ki-moon stated, 'speaks to all people in all countries, and calls for action from everyone everywhere. It aims to inspire and create genuine partnerships among all countries and actors.'[29] The High-Level Political Forum (HLPF) was decided to be the primary forum for review of implementation of the goals. Another mechanism that was decided to support the implementation of the SDGs by helping states access the technologies they need to develop sustainably is the Technology Facilitation Mechanism (TFM). The TFM was created as part of the Addis Ababa Action Agenda, which was adopted at the 3rd International Conference on Financing for Development in July 2015 and was also included as part of the 2030 Agenda.[30]

The records of the meetings of the OWG reflect the drafting history of the SDGs and thus they are a valuable source for interpreting and understanding the content of the goals, their underpinnings, and the ways for their practical implementation. The next section discusses the OWG sessions especially those that formed SDG 14: 'Conserve and sustainably use the oceans, seas, and marine resources for sustainable development.'

B. The Open Working Group Sessions (OWG)

1. The Stocktaking Phase (March 2013–February 2014)

The first eight sessions of the OWG were dedicated to stocktaking, that is, to listening, understanding, and collecting information. Stocktaking was organized in thematic clusters from the issues outlined in 'The Future We Want', the outcome document of Rio + 20.[31] The final outcome however was created by a variety of sources reflecting the pluralism of the OWG process. Fundamental to the works of the OWG was the input of the inter-agency Technical Support Team (TST), which provided technical inputs to the process for developing the SDGs. Among the inputs to the SGD negotiations were also the 2012 report of the UN System task Team on the Post-2015 UN Development Agenda, 'Realizing the Future We Want for All' and the report of the

---

[28] A-M Lebada and others, 'Summary of the Seventh and Eighth Sessions of Intergovernmental Negotiations on the Post-2015 Development Agenda: 20 July–2 August 2015' (2015) 32 Earth Negotiations Bulletin 20 at 23.

[29] Secretary-General's Remarks at the General Assembly Plenary Meeting to Adopt the Draft Resolution to Transmit the Agenda 2030 Outcome Document' (1 September 2015). See also PS Chasek and others, 'Getting to 2030: Negotiating the Post-2015 Sustainable Development Agenda' (2016) 25(1) Review of European Community and International Environmental Law 5–14.

[30] United Nations, 'Addis Ababa Action Agenda' (United Nations 2015) at para 123. The Mechanism has as its objectives the support of the achievement of the SDGs; a multi-stakeholder collaboration to achieve SDGs; the strengthening of coherence and synergies among science and technology initiatives within the UN system. The TFM has three main components which include a UN Interagency Task Team on Science, Technology and Innovation for the SDGs (IATT), including the ten-Member Group of representatives from civil society, the private sector, and the scientific community (UN Environment and United Nations Department of Economic and Social Affairs are coordinators); a collaborative Multi-stakeholder Forum on Science, Technology and Innovation for the SDGs (STI Forum); and an online platform as a gateway for information on existing STI initiatives, mechanisms, and programmes.

[31] UNGA Res 66/288 (11 September 2012) UN Doc A/RES/66/288. For information on the clusters see under each OWG session on the OWG's website <https://sustainabledevelopment.un.org/owg1.html> accessed 14 December 2020.

High-level Panel of the Secretary-General on Global Sustainability (A/66/700). The UNGA also prepared another report, synthesizing the input received to a questionnaire sent to Member States and was presented as an input to the work of the Open Working Group on Sustainable Development Goals.[32] The latter report is important as it contains a synthesis of sixty-three Member State responses (including the EU), thus representing one-third of the UN membership. An analysis of responses to the questionnaire revealed that the sustainable management of natural resources was high on the priority list of many respondents.[33] Specifically, oceans and seas ranked tenth out of seventeen priority areas mentioned by Member States (relative frequency of responses).[34]

Scientists and academics were able to contribute to the discussions on SDGs through the Sustainable Development Solutions Network (SDSN), which proposed a set of sustainable goals.[35] In addition, the High-Level Panel of Eminent Persons (HLPP) contributed with recommendations for the design of the SDGs. According to the HLPP the new sustainable development agenda should (i) leave no-one behind; (ii) put sustainable development at the core; (iii) transform economies for jobs and inclusive growth; (iv) build peace and effective, open, and accountable public institutions; and (v) forge a new global partnership in national and international politics.[36]

The first meeting of the OWG took place in March 2012. The OWG discussed the issue of coherence of the process leading to the SDGs with the processes considering the post-2015 development agenda. The OWG framed the questions to be taken into account when formulating the SDGs.[37] The work of the OWG was guided by the rules of procedure, relevant rules and practices of the Committees of the General Assembly, as well as by the principles of openness, transparency, inclusiveness, and consensus.

The 1st session of the OWG (14–15 March 2013) commenced with opening statements by the 67th General Assembly session President Vuk Jeremic and Secretary-General Ban Ki-moon, who stressed the urgency of the OWG's task. Specifically, the Secretary-General highlighted that 'the sustainable development goals must go further to integrate more comprehensively environmental sustainability, because humanity is pressing hard against the planet's ecological boundaries'.

---

[32] UNGA, 'Initial Input of the Secretary-General to the Open-Working Group on Sustainable Development Goals' (17 December 2012) UN Doc A/67/634.
[33] UNGA A/67/634 (17 December 2012), para 13.
[34] ibid, para 16.
[35] SDSN, 'An Action Agenda for Sustainable Development', Report for the UN Secretary-General (5 May 2014) <https://irp-cdn.multiscreensite.com/be6d1d56/files/uploaded/140505-An-Action-Agenda-for-Sustainable-Development.pdf> accessed 8 December 2020.
[36] HLPP, *A New Global Partnership: Eradicate Poverty and Transform Economies through Sustainable Development* (United Nations 2013) Annex I.
[37] 1st Meeting of the Open Working Group on Sustainable Development Goals, Concept Note - Interactive Discussion on the SDGs, GA Hall (14 March 2012). Questions: 1. What specific steps can be taken to ensure that the SDGs are coherent with and integrated into the UN development agenda beyond 2015? 2. How can the SDGs take forward the unfinished business of the MDGs? 3. How might the SDGs strive to balance the economic, social and environmental dimensions of sustainable development? Should the balance be achieved within each goal or in the overall composition of the set of goals? 4. How can the SDGs be at the same time universal in nature but take into account different national realities of the Member States? 5. How can the multiple challenges of sustainable development be distilled and compressed into a short set of aspirational goals?

1022   SDG 14

The discussions during the 1st session mainly revolved around the goal to balance the economic, social, and environmental dimensions of sustainable development and the need to include all stakeholders in the process with a view to enhanced cooperation (see, eg, civil society and private sector). Statements were made that current models for development are unsustainable and that the SDGs should respect the physical constraints of the planet. It is noteworthy that many delegations linked the reduction of environmental degradation with the promotion of social justice and the elimination of inequalities. The protection and conservation of the ocean was among the issues intensively discussed during the first sessions of the OWG. Environmental sustainability in general was part of the MDGs, which at that time were still ongoing and set to expire in 2015. Stakeholders agreed that the SDGs should be elaborated from the foundation of the MDGs.[38] The MDGs were considered a point of departure, but new thinking and innovation were more than welcomed in the works of the OWG.

The stocktaking phase continued in the next sessions, and it was decided that the SDGs were going to be embedded in a broader narrative, which would include, among others, the protection of the planet and the goal to live in harmony with nature. The OWG identified three possible types of goals: (i) human development related goals with little environmental impact associated with their attainment (eg, education); (ii) human development-related goals with important environmental dimensions (eg, water, food, energy); (iii) goals related to common management of global resources. The purpose of the 2nd session was to conduct discussions on conceptualizing the SDGs. Co-Chair Kamau invited the OWG to discuss how the SDGs could build on the MDGs and other existing goals.

A wide range of social, economic, and environmental priority areas were mentioned, including the protection and conservation of the oceans. Some delegations also outlined enabling conditions that are cross-cutting in nature, such as access to markets and technology, education, community well-being and culture, financial development, trade, global governance, economic growth, improving income distribution, and reducing inequality. During the 3rd OWG session it was recognized that there is a need for a holistic approach to objectives that are closely interdependent, such as food, land, and water, as well as between energy, health, biodiversity, and climate change. The Co-Chairs instituted the practice of meetings with representatives of Major Groups and other stakeholders that provided a platform for them to express their views and share their experiences.

During the stocktaking phase the following areas were covered: (i) means of implementation (science and technology, knowledge sharing, and capacity building); (ii) global partnership for achieving sustainable development; (iii) needs of countries in special situations, least developed countries (LDCs) and SIDS. Delegates discussed the means of the implementation for the SDGs along the lines of political will, financing

---

[38] Summary of OWG-1 on the SDGs (14–15 March 2013), *Achieving and building on the MDGs*, 2–3; opinions of UM SG's Special Adviser on Post-2015 Development Planning, Amina Mohammed and Executive Vice President's and Managing Director's, World Resources Institute, Manish Bapna, 4 <https://sustainabledevelopment.un.org/content/documents/1700summaryowg.pdf> accessed 3 April 2021.

technology, capacity building, and partnerships, policies, and institutions.[39] The implementation of the SDGs was decided to be dependent on a robust Global Partnership, characterized by equality, inclusivity, and a fair sharing of responsibilities. Further, the delegations took note of the worsening threats posted by climate change, land degradation, and ocean acidification, among others. Special consideration was given to countries in special situations, such as African countries, Least Developed Countries (LDCs), Landlocked Developing Countries (LLDCs), SIDS, and Middle-income Countries (MICs). For example, it was highlighted that SIDS are disadvantaged by their small size and remoteness from markets, and high exposure to environmental risks. International action to tackle climate change and the sustainable management and use of oceans is priority for SIDS.[40] The TST Issue Brief thoroughly analysed the situation in SIDS in terms of their environment and development. The Brief pointed out that for SIDS, the ocean and coastal environment is of strategic importance and constitutes a valuable development resource. Indeed, for many SIDS the ocean and its vast resources is the firm basis upon which jobs and economic growth depend. Among others, seabed mining activities provide opportunities for their economic growth but at the same time pose several challenges to protecting SIDS marine environment from degradation.

2. The Negotiation Phase (March 2014–July 2014)

Having concluded the 'stocktaking' sessions, the next stage of deliberations on the SDGs was inaugurated with the presentation of a report summarizing the overarching points of agreement and disagreement on each reviewed thematic cluster.[41] During this second phase, the OWG prepared a report for the 68th session of the GA containing a proposal for SDGs.

The role of oceans and seas as Earth's life-support system was widely recognized. Some delegations proposed a comprehensive goal to enhance the benefits of ecosystems and biodiversity for all which could adopt an integrated approach and address vital aspects in the sustainable management and use of natural resources, including oceans and seas, forests, desertification, and land degradation, and biodiversity. Others advocated stand-alone goals on oceans and seas, and biodiversity. It was also mentioned that given the dependence of other areas on the health of these ecosystems, relevant targets and indicators could be integrated into other goal areas such as food security and nutrition, water, and sustainable livelihoods.[42]

The OWG identified the main threats to the oceans and classified them into five broad categories: (i) Unsustainable extraction of marine living resources, including

[39] Concluding Remarks of Co-Chairs 6th Session of Open Working Group on Sustainable Development Goals (13 December 2013).

[40] TST Issues Brief: Needs of Countries in Special Situations—African countries, Least Developed Countries (LDCs), Landlocked Developing Countries (LLDCs), Small Island Developing States (SIDS), and Middle-income Countries (MICs).

[41] UN, 'Progress Report of the Open Working Group of the General Assembly on Sustainable Development Goals', UN Doc A/67/941 <https://sustainabledevelopment.un.org/content/documents/3238summaryallowg.pdf> accessed 6 May 2021.

[42] Progress report of the OWG after the stocktaking phase (25 August 2015) UN Doc A/68/970/Add.2, para 179.

1024   SDG 14

for example overfishing, illegal, unreported, and unregulated (IUU) fishing, and destructive fishing practices as well as the usage of harmful subsidies that contribute to IUU fishing and overcapacity. The unsustainable extraction of marine non-living resources (eg deep sea mining; offshore oil and gas drilling) was also considered a cause for concern. (ii) Ocean acidification and climate change impacts which are caused by increasing atmospheric greenhouse gas concentrations. Negative effects of climate change include increased frequency and intensity of weather and climate extremes, ocean warming, sea-level rise, as well as changes in ocean circulation and salinity. Ocean acidification may have potentially devastating impacts on marine ecosystems, including loss of shellfish, coral reefs (eg through coral bleaching) and calcareous plankton. (iii) Marine pollution from a number of marine and land-based sources, including solid and plastic waste, heavy metals, persistent organic pollutants (POPs), pesticides, nutrients (nitrogen and phosphorus), oil, hazardous substances, radioactive materials, and anthropogenic underwater noise. It was noted that more than 80 per cent of marine pollution is derived from land-based sources. (iv) Alien invasive species that may threaten complex regional ecosystem relationships and marine infrastructure. And (v) physical alteration and destruction of marine habitat which are caused by unsustainable coastal area development (eg direct construction on reef platforms), submarine infrastructure (eg submarine cables), unsustainable tourism, fishing operations in fragile or vulnerable marine areas (eg seagrass beds, coral reefs), and physical damage from ship groundings and anchors.[43]

The OWG further identified the conceptual and methodological tools for the collection of data for oceans and seas. Such data are collected by an array of institutions, such as governments and non-governmental organizations (NGOs). Remarkably however, there is currently no international framework that outlines methodologies, best practices, or common frameworks or standards for management and exchange of data relating to oceans and seas.[44] The collection of data for oceans and seas can be rather costly and challenging due to the vast area of the ocean and the complexity of the ecosystems. It is worth noting that the MDG 7's indicators for oceans and seas were the proportion of fish stocks within safe biological limits (7.4) and the proportion of terrestrial and marine areas protected (7.6). Another related indicator was the proportion of species threatened with extinction (7.7).

The Rio + 20 outcome document had called for Member States to work more closely with Major Groups and other stakeholders, and encourage active participation in processes that contribute to decision-making, planning, and implementation of policies and programmes for sustainable development. Such engagement has been facilitated by UN DESA Division for Sustainable Development Major Groups programme in coordination with the Organizing Partners for each major group. Major groups were

---

[43] Compendium of statistical notes for the OWG on SDGs. Prepared by UN Statistics Division, in collaboration with the Friends of the chair group broader measures of progress (March 2014).

[44] ibid. cf Intergovernmental Oceanographic Commission of UNESCO (2013), Ocean Data Standards, Vol 3: Recommendation for a Quality Flag Scheme for the Exchange of Oceanographic and Marine Meteorological Data (Vol 3, IOC Manuals and Guides, 54).

organized by constituency and thematic areas. Focus Areas 15 and 16 concerned the climate, marine resources, oceans, and seas. In OWG-9 the Major Groups of women, indigenous peoples, youth, and NGOs affirmed the need for restoration, conservation, and sustainable use of oceanic and marine resources, due to provision of economic, social benefits, and ecosystem services to humankind. They stressed the need for explicit focus on restoration and repair of severely damaged areas of marine ecosystems. They recalled that oceans and seas are not only specifically important to SIDS, many LDCs, and coastal states but they affect all states.

Among the focus areas formulated during the negotiation phase, focus area 16 was dedicated to marine resources, oceans, and seas. Sub-areas considered included reducing marine pollution and debris; halting destruction of marine habitat including ocean acidification; promoting sustainable exploitation of marine resources; regulating harvesting of straddling fish stocks; addressing IUU fishing, and destructive fishing practices; eliminating harmful subsidies; ensuring full implementation of regional and international regimes governing oceans and seas and establishing Marine Protected Areas.

The 10th OWG session revised the focus areas, and an interactive dialogue with stakeholders and Major Groups purported to refine the proposed goals and targets.[45] The Co-Chairs proposed that the focus areas be considered in eight clusters. Cluster 6 was decided to be about conservation and sustainable use of marine resources, oceans and seas, ecosystems, and biodiversity. The content of cluster 6 comprised the following objectives: ensuring that all fish stocks are being fished sustainably and rebuilt to healthy levels; protecting vulnerable marine areas and restoring damaged habitats; establishing ecologically representative networks of marine protected areas to increase oceans health and resilience; reducing biodiversity loss and establishing and implementing integrated ocean use plans to prevent conflict; eliminating illegal, unreported and unregulated fishing; reducing land-based pollution, including plastic debris.

Subsequently, the revised 'Focus Area' document proposed a first set of Goals. Revised Focus Area 13 referred to the conservation and sustainable use of marine resources, oceans, and seas. The proposed targets were formulated as following: (i) By 2020, prevent, control and reduce by (X) per cent marine pollution, debris, and marine disposal of waste and tailings, including from land-based activities; (ii) (combined with target (F)); (iii) By 2020, conserve at least 10 per cent of coastal and marine areas, especially areas of particular importance for biodiversity and ecosystem services, through effectively and equitably managed, ecologically representative, and well-connected systems of protected areas and other effective area-based conservation measures within and beyond areas of national jurisdiction, and restore and protect marine ecosystems from significant adverse impacts, especially areas of particular importance for biodiversity and ecosystem services, including by halting and preventing ocean acidification;

---

[45] OWG-10, 'Major Groups and other Stakeholders Dialogue with Co-Chairs on the SDGs' (2 April 2014) <https://sustainabledevelopment.un.org/content/documents/3674Compilation%20Document%20on%20Goals%20and%20Targets_April%2011-%20final.pdf> accessed 14 September 2020.

1026   SDG 14

(iv) Take immediate action to restore and then maintain fish stocks to levels above those that can support maximum sustainable yield, and to end overfishing where it is occurring through management plans based on the precautionary principle and ecosystem approach by 2020; (v) Take immediate action to end IUU fishing. It was further considered that the following target should be added: Educate the public about civic responsibility to emphasize the importance of conservation of marine resources, oceans, and seas, and support educational programmes at all levels, specifically to encourage youth to enter this field. The proposed targets were amended several times before their final stipulation.

A revised zero draft of the Goals was prepared for the final OWG meeting.[46] On 19 July 2014 the OWG's mandate was concluded with the adoption of the final proposal on the SDGs for consideration by the GA.[47]

III. Goal Commentary

A. Conservation and Sustainable Use in SDG 14

Combining the goals of conservation and sustainable use, SDG 14 is among the most complex goals of the 2030 Agenda. On the one hand, SDG 14 encapsulates the deep concern of the UN about the impacts of oceans degradation on global environmental stability and food security and, on the other hand, attempts to assuage states' fears about the repercussion that more radical environmental protection policies may have on economic growth. The success of SDG 14 will thus depend on the fine balancing between these two seemingly contradictory objectives. Further SDG 14 builds upon the already complex and broad legal and policy framework that governs the oceans. Goal 14's targets are thus informed by the already existing obligations, institutions, and mechanisms that are crucial for the attainment of the Goal. Finally, given the multidimensionality and complexity of the problems associated with the oceans, the success of SDG 14 is also overly dependent on international coordination and cooperation. Drawing on these aspects, Subsection III.B addresses the two objectives of SDG 14 and explores the elements for their balancing. Subsection III.C.1 outlines the legal framework that governs the seas; Subsection III.C.2 explore the functional approach and the obligation of states to cooperate in ocean governance. Subsections III.C.3 and III.C.4 analyse specifically the legal framework that governs the conservation and management of the

---

[46] OWG Co-chairs, 'Introduction and Proposed Goals and Targets on Sustainable Development For the Post2015 Development Agenda' (Revised Zero Draft, 30 June 2014) <https://sustainabledevelopment.un.org/content/documents/4523zerodraft.pdf>; Co-Chairs' Letter to OWG members (30 June 2014), in which they emphasized that the zero draft was a testament of the openness and inclusiveness of the OWGs' consultations (para 2) <https://sustainabledevelopment.un.org/content/documents/4324lettercochairs30june14.pdf> both accessed 14 December 2020.

[47] Report of the Open Working Group of the General Assembly on Sustainable Development Goals (12 August 2014) UN Doc A/68/970.

living resources especially on the high seas and the protection and preservation of the marine environment; and, finally, Subsection III.C.5 discusses the monitoring and enforcement challenges with respect to measures promoting ocean sustainability.

B. Balancing between Conservation and Use

Balancing between environmental conservation and sustainable use of resources is a complex issue, as neither objective should be prioritized. This delicate balancing act becomes challenging by the fact that these two goals traditionally do not support one another. The concept of 'sustainable use' may be interpreted by states and industries as a justification for further utilization of marine resources due to, for example, exhaustion of land-based resources. However, such an interpretation might be in direct conflict with the aim of marine preservation and conservation. The debate between conservation and use is not a low-key one. It is rather a pressing issue, especially for the developing states whose economies are still heavily based on the primary sector, as are their efforts to reduce poverty and improve living conditions for their citizens. Imposing a framework that would stall their development could be considered on their part as unjust and immoral.[48]

Agenda 2030 and the seventeen SDGs form a framework around which states are expected to develop policies that will reduce poverty and improve food security on a global level. And while the language used by the UN in its official statements and reports emphasizes the categories of environmental protection and sustainable growth, the Agenda's predominant aim seems to be that of economic growth and eradication of poverty.[49] In the case of SDG 14 in particular, every economic activity taking place under its rubric may be (directly or indirectly) linked with resource exploitation. Fishing, aquaculture, waterborne transport, seabed mining, and tourism are only some examples of such resource-exploitative and environmentally damaging activities that should be transformed or mitigated in order to achieve SDG 14's call for conservation. However, fishing and seabed mining are profitable activities linked with multibillion industries and, under certain conditions, with the survival and prosperity of local communities. The UN is aware of such conflicts of interest between SDG 14's aims as well as of the difficulties that may arise from imposing strict rules on these activities. For this reason, the UN urges the countries to take ownership of the 2030 Agenda and develop their own sustainable development policies to fit their economies.[50]

Nevertheless, at the same time the marine environment's volatility in general and its current critical state in particular that have a direct result on its resources' availability

---

[48] H Salefmul, 'Report. Institute for Public Policy Research (IPPR)' (2005) <http://www.jstor.org/stable/resrep1605> accessed 6 September 2021.

[49] GA Res. 70/1 (21 October 2015), <https://www.un.org/ga/search/view_doc.asp?symbol=A/RES/70/1&Lang=E> accessed 6 September 2021.

[50] GA Res. 70/1 (21 October 2015), at paras 55 and 63 <https://www.un.org/ga/search/view_doc.asp?symbol=A/RES/70/1&Lang=E> accessed 6 September 2021.

1028 SDG 14

provide the ground for calls to states to adopt a stricter policy relating to marine environment, even if this may have adverse effects on their short-term economic growth. In fact, the utilization of the term 'sustainable development' in many respects should be seen as an attempt to downplay the repercussions that adopting such policies may have, underlining that any loss of economic stimulus will be short-term and a necessary sacrifice to achieve long-term economic growth. Moreover, special provisions are included in the targets for the protection of small island and developing states' (SIDS) financial interests, allowing them to set less ambitious objectives in their environmental policies in order to protect industries vital for their growth. In the issue of fisheries subsidies in particular, the UN recognizes that developing states are allowed a differential treatment due to how essential these activities may be for achieving growth and food security.[51]

Agenda 2030 is a plan of economic growth and alleviation of inequalities, an effort to delineate a path to global development in an era where the prevalent model of production and growth is heavily criticized as unsustainable, and not simply to protect the environment. In this light, the UN's choice to combine in Agenda 2030 the objective of environmental protection with that of sustainable economic growth is better understood. By linking the two objectives, states are encouraged to take stricter environmental measures with the prospect of reaping environmental and economic benefits in the future. Additionally, the choice to devote an SDG specifically for the conservation and sustainable use of the oceans and not to integrate it to other closely related SDG's such as SDG 13 (which calls for action against climate change) or SDG 8 (which is devoted to economic growth in general) demonstrates in a very clear way the major shift in the Organization's focus and attitude towards the protection of the marine environment.

The modern concept of 'sustainable development' or 'sustainable use' focuses on both economic development and environmental protection for future generations.[52] The 1972 Stockholm Declaration of the UN Conference on the Human Environment had endorsed the basic idea of 'sustainable development', although it did not use the term (see principle 13). In 1982 the concept of sustainable development was defined by the Report of the World Commission on Environment and Development (WCED) 'Our Common Future' as 'development that meets the needs of the present without compromising the ability of future generations to meet their own needs'.[53] 'Sustainable use' is defined in the 1992 Convention on Biological Diversity (CBD) as the 'use of components of biological diversity in a way and at a rate that does not lead to the long-term decline of biological diversity, thereby maintaining its potential to meet the needs and aspirations of present and future generations'.[54] The idea of sustainable development

---

[51] See target 14.6.

[52] N Schrijver, *The Evolution of Sustainable Development in International Law: Inception, Meaning and Status* (Martinus Nijhoff 2008) 208–09; A Boyle and C Redgwell, *International Law and the Environment* (OUP 2021); Separate Opinion of Judge Cancado Trinidade in the *Case concerning Pulp Mills on the River Uruguay (Argentina v Uruguay)*, ICJ Reports 2010, 185, para 133.

[53] WCED, *Our Common Future* (OUP 1987), 433. See also ILA, New Delhi Declaration of Principles of International Law Relating to Sustainable Development.

[54] Art 2, CBD; see also T Kuhlman and J Farrington, 'What Is Sustainability?' (2010) 2 Sustainability 11, 3436–48.

GOAL COMMENTARY   1029

has been reverberated by the ICJ in the *Gabcikovo-Nagymaros* case[55] as well as the Arbitral Tribunal in the *Arbitration regarding the Iron Rhine Railway* case of 2005.[56] The concept rests upon the idea that natural resources are finite and not inexhaustible. This idea has been illustrated by Hardin who introduced the concept of the tragedy of the commons, that is, the situation in which individuals, conglomerates, and states over-exploit natural resources according to their own self-interest without regard to the planet's well-being.[57]

'Sustainable development' is a key concept in the use of natural resources, including marine living resources, aiming to reconcile environmental protection with the need for development.[58] SDG 14 recognizes that marine natural resources are not inexhaustible, and that conserving and sustainably using them requires action from everyone. All relevant actors need to slow or even abandon whole sectors of economic activities in order to allow oceanic resources like fisheries to recuperate. Without a robust legal framework and detailed policy planning, the ocean as a global common is threatened. As explained in the next section, the Law of the Sea Convention, along with other binding and non-binding instruments, mechanisms, and institutions, aims to create a balance between economic development through the use of the ocean and the need to conserve and manage its resources in a sustainable mode.

C. Framework Governing the Oceans

While the SDGs are not legally binding, the implementation of SDG 14 depends to a great extent on the implementation of legal obligations provided by international law. Of course, this does not disregard the significance of policy initiatives and planning, but it highlights the role of international law in ocean governance.[59] Indeed, target 14.c explicitly refers to the Law of the Sea Convention (LOSC/the Convention) and the legal framework that it provides as the guide that can lead to the successful implementation of SDG 14. In addition, the introduction to chapter 17 of Agenda 21 of 1992 specifically confirms that the LOSC sets forth the rights and obligations of states and provides the international basis upon which to pursue the protection and sustainable development of the marine and coastal environment and its resources.[60] The protection

---

[55] ICJ Reports 1997, p 78, para 140.

[56] *Iron Rhine Arbitration* (Belgium/Netherlands), 27 *RIAA*, pp 28–29, para 59.

[57] G Hardin, 'The Tragedy of the Commons' (1968) 162 Science 3859, 1243–48.

[58] See Philippe Sands,' International Law in the Field of Sustainable Development' (1994) 65 British Yearbook of International Law, 303–81; N Schrijver, *The Evolution of Sustainable Development in International Law: Inception, Meaning and Status* (Brill/Nijhoff 2008); D French 'Sustainable Development' in M Fitzmaurice and others (eds), *Research Handbook on International Environmental Law* (Edward Elgar 2010), 51–68.

[59] A Jordan and T O'Riordan, 'Sustainable Development: The Political and Institutional Challenge' in J Kirkby and others (eds), *The Earthscan Reader in Sustainable Development* (Routledge 1995) 287–89; AG Siswandi, 'Marine Genetic Resources beyond National Jurisdiction and Sustainable Development Goals: The Perspective of Developing Countries' in M Nordquist and others (eds), *The Marine Environment and United Nations Sustainable Development Goal 14: Life below Water* (Brill 2018) 220.

[60] 'Agenda 21', United Nations Conference on Environment & Development Rio de Janeiro, Brazil, 3–14 June 1992 (Agenda 21) <https://sustainabledevelopment.un.org/content/documents/Agenda21.pdf> accessed 15

1030 SDG 14

of community interests (common ocean approach) is central and has become increasingly important in the law of the sea. The present section provides a general overview of the legal framework governing the ocean and explores how sustainability fits in that framework. The analysis facilitates understanding how SDG 14 and its associated targets can be realistically implemented through the existing legal, institutional, and policy framework.

1. Law of the Sea and Sustainability: An Overview

The international law of the sea is one of the oldest branches of international law and it has been evolving for hundreds of years through custom.[61] The ocean has always been fundamental to human life and activity and thus, international rules governing the use of the oceans have been developing since ancient times. Codification of the law started in early twentieth century and culminated with the landmark event of the conclusion of the LOSC in 1982.[62] Two implementation agreements followed the adoption of the LOSC, one essentially modifying the Convention's regime on the deep seabed beyond national jurisdiction and the other elaborating provisions concerning the conservation and management of straddling fish stocks.[63] A third implementation agreement on biodiversity beyond national jurisdiction is possibly under way.[64] The LOSC has been ratified by 168 parties, which include 167 states and the European Union. However, most of the Convention's provisions reflect customary international law and, thus, bind all states. States are bound by the Convention's obligations and shall comply with them, *inter alia*, by harmonizing their national legislations with the Convention and related agreements.

The Law of the Sea Convention sets the overarching framework for almost all sea-related issues. The most widely used portrayal of the Convention is its characterization as a 'Constitution' of the oceans, owed to the wide range of topics that it covers.[65] These are, *inter alia*, the limits and legal regime of the various maritime zones; issues

---

April 2021. See also the Johannesburg Plan of Implementation, adopted at the 2002 World Summit on Sustainable Development, invited States to ratify and implement both the LOSC and its implementing agreements.

[61] D O'Connell, 'The History of International Law is the History of the Law of the Sea and Vice Versa' in IA Shearer (ed), *The International Law of the Sea*, Vol 1 (Clarendon Press 1982) 29; T Treves, 'Historical Development of the Law of the Sea' in D Rothwell and others (eds), *The Oxford Handbook of the Law of the Sea* (OUP 2015); JN Moore, 'Introduction' in MH Nordquist (ed), *United Nations Convention on the Law of the Sea 1982, A Commentary*, Vol 1 (Martinus Nijhoff 1985).

[62] T Treves, 'Historical Development of the Law of the Sea' in D Rothwell and others (eds), *The Oxford Handbook of the Law of the Sea* (n 61): '[UNCLOS III] fundamental event in the history of the law of the sea'.

[63] 1994 Agreement Relating to the Implementation of Part XI of the United Nations Convention on the Law of the Sea of 10 December 1982; 1995 Agreement for the Implementation of the Provisions of the United Nations Convention on the Law of the Sea of 10 December 1982 relating to the Conservation and Management of Straddling Fish Stocks and Highly Migratory Fish Stocks (hereinafter FSA).

[64] See UNGA Res 68/70 (2013).

[65] TB Koh, 'A Constitution of the Oceans' in UN, *The Law of the Sea: Official Text of the United Nations Convention on the Law of the Sea with Annexes and Index* (UN 1983) xxxiii; A Proelss, *United Nations Convention on the Law of the Sea; A Commentary* (C.H. Beck/Hart/Nomos 2017), foreword: 'Quite rightly, the Convention is therefore being called a "Constitution of the oceans"'; preface: 'The UNCLOS, which has convincingly been labelled the "constitution of the oceans"'; see also T Treves, 'Law of the Sea' in *Max Planck Encyclopedia of Public International Law* (2011) <https://opil.ouplaw.com/view/10.1093/law:epil/9780199231690/law-9780199231690-e1186> accessed 13 June 2021.

of marine security; conservation and management of living marine resources; protection and preservation of the marine environment; marine scientific research; development and transfer of marine technology; and activities on the seabed beyond the limits of national jurisdiction. Despite this auspicious cliché, the LOSC is not a constitution, among of the reasons being that it has not been adopted by a constitutional assembly, it does not impose a system of governance within a state and does not create a normative hierarchy between rules.[66] It is, nonetheless, a framework treaty characterized by great flexibility in providing a foundation for any law of the sea question, even if it does not always provide specific answers. A means of doing that is by referring to external rules in its provisions (eg 'generally accepted international rules and standards'). Especially in some parts, for example Part XII that is dedicated to the protection of the marine environment, the Convention contains several such 'rules of reference'.[67] Numerous treaties have been concluded on specialized marine issues at the global and regional level.[68] Article 311 LOSC expressly foresees that States Parties will continue to regulate their relations through subsequent treaties. The provisions of the LOSC must be interpreted with regard to those rules, while law of the sea instruments must be compatible with the Convention. In the same vein, Article 237 highlights the complementary relationship between the LOSC and other conventions on the protection and preservation of the marine environment, anticipating and encouraging an ongoing reconciliation between the LOSC and other relevant conventions.[69]

The LOSC is 'incomplete' by design. Including detailed rules on every use would have made the treaty completely unwieldy and liable to become quickly out of date.[70] Especially on issues of conservation and management of marine resources and the protection and preservation of the environment, the LOSC does not contain comprehensive and detailed rules but rather sets out the legal framework within which detailed norms may be developed and applied.[71] It establishes the obligation of states to cooperate and negotiate appropriate measures for the fulfilment of their duties instead of specifying the precise content of their substantive obligations.[72]

Further, interpretations by international courts and tribunals have contributed to the development of the law of the sea, notably in the field of maritime boundary delimitation but also in marine environmental matters.[73] Non-binding sources of law of the

[66] R Lagoni, 'Preamble', mn 27 in Proelss, *United Nations Convention on the Law of the Sea* (n 65).
[67] *Inter alia*, arts 208(3), 210(6), 211(2).
[68] Indicatively, 1992 Convention for the Protection of the Marine Environment of the North-East Atlantic (OSPAR Convention); 2000 Convention on the Conservation and Management of Highly Migratory Fish Stocks in the Western and Central Pacific Ocean; 2001 Convention on the Protection of the Underwater Cultural Heritage; 2005 Convention for the Suppression of Unlawful Acts against the Safety of Maritime Navigation.
[69] R Warner, 'Conserving Marine Biodiversity in Areas Beyond National Jurisdiction: Co-Evolution and Interaction with the Law of the Sea' in Rothwell and others (eds), *The Oxford Handbook of the Law of the Sea* (n 61) 753.
[70] R Churchill, 'The 1982 United Nations Convention on the Law of the Sea' in Rothwell and others (eds), *The Oxford Handbook of the Law of the Sea* (n 61) 30.
[71] ibid.
[72] See art 118, 63–65 LOSC and analysis above in Section II(1)(b) analysis on conservation and management of the living resources of the high seas under Part VII, Section 2 LOSC.
[73] *Inter alia, Arbitration between Barbados and Trinidad and Tobago* (2006) XXVII RIAA 147; Delimitation of the Maritime Boundary in the Bay of Bengal (Bangladesh/Myanmar) (Judgment) [2012] ITLOS Rep 4; see also the

1032   SDG 14

sea also provide useful guidance on interpretation and application of the law or lead to the formation of new rules. Such sources may have the form of resolutions, guidelines, standards, and declarations.

SDG 14 belongs to this category of non-binding policy instruments and reflects the emergence of the concept of community interests in modern international law.[74] The protection of community interests at sea includes the objectives of SDG 14, that is, the sustainable use of marine resources and marine environmental protection.

The law of the sea and specifically the LOSC does set forth a legal framework for the sustainable use of the ocean. The Convention's Preamble refers to economic, environmental, and social considerations, suggesting a sustainable development approach to the uses of the ocean. The Preamble is not binding upon states but it signifies the intentions of the State Parties to the treaty. Specifically, the Preamble states:

> *Recognizing* the desirability of establishing through this Convention, with due regard for the sovereignty of all States, a legal order for the seas and oceans which will facilitate international communication, and will promote the peaceful uses of the seas and oceans, the equitable and efficient utilization of their resources, the conservation of their living resources, and the study, protection and preservation of the marine environment; *Bearing* in mind that the achievement of these goals will contribute to the realization of a just and equitable international economic order which takes into account the interests and needs of mankind as a whole and, in particular, the special interests and needs of developing countries, whether coastal or land-locked.

Sustainable development or use is further incorporated into treaties and non-binding agreements relating to the conservation of marine living resources. For instance, the concept of sustainable development is expressly mentioned in the UN Fish Stocks Agreement, one of the two implementation agreements of the LOSC.[75] Article 2 stipulates: 'The objective of this Agreement is to ensure the long-term conservation and sustainable use of straddling fish stocks and highly migratory fish stocks through effective implementation of the relevant provisions of the Convention.' Article 5(a) requires coastal states and states fishing on the high seas to 'adopt measures to ensure long-term sustainability of straddling fish stocks and highly migratory fish stocks and promote the objective of their optimum utilization'. Article 5(h) further imposes upon

---

ITLOS *Southern Bluefin Tuna* cases where ITLOS regarded the conservation of the living resources of the sea as an element in the protection and preservation of the marine environment and referred to the precautionary principle.

[74] G Gaja, 'The Protection of General Interests in the International Community: General Course on Public International Law' in *Collected Courses of the Hague Academy of International Law*, Vol 364 (Brill 2011) 8–186; also B Simma, 'From Bilateralism to Community Interests' in *Collected Courses of the Hague Academy of International Law* (Brill 1994) 234: 'arising awareness of the common interests of the international community, a community that comprises not only States, but in the last instance all human beings, has begun to change the nature of international law profoundly'.

[75] Agreement for the Implementation of the Provisions of the United Nations Convention on the Law of the Sea of 10 December 1982 relating to the Conservation and Management of Straddling Fish Stocks and Highly Migratory Fish Stocks, New York, 4 August 1995, art 2.

coastal states and states fishing on the high seas the duty to 'take measures to prevent or eliminate over-fishing and excess fishing capacity and to ensure that levels of fishing effort do not exceed those commensurate with the sustainable use of fishery resources'.

Beyond the LOSC, a range of instruments of variable normative content, binding and non-binding, touch upon marine sustainability and supplement ocean governance at global and regional level.[76] The concept of sustainable development or sustainable use can be seen in Chapter 17 of Agenda 21 of 1992,[77] the 1995 Code of Conduct for Responsible Fisheries (FAO Code of Conduct),[78] the 1999 Rome Declaration on the Implementation of the Code of Conduct for Responsible Fisheries,[79] and the 2001 Reykjavik Declaration on Responsible Fisheries in the Marine Ecosystem.[80] Furthermore, at the 2012 UN Conference on Sustainable Development (Rio + 20) states committed themselves 'to address, on an urgent basis ... the issue of the conservation and sustainable use of marine biological diversity of areas beyond national jurisdiction, including by taking a decision on the development of an international instrument under the United Nations Convention on the Law of the Sea'. Following a two-year Preparatory Committee process, the UNGA adopted Resolution 72/249 to convene an intergovernmental conference (IGC) to develop an international legally binding instrument on marine biodiversity in areas beyond national jurisdiction (BBNJ).

The sustainable development concept is key for the conservation of marine living resources and the protection of marine environment. In legal terms, however, sustainability is not an obligation with a specific content. Sustainability is more of a rubric that refers to various international environmental law obligations.[81] The concept per se does not impose a specific course of action upon states but rather incentivizes the taking of measures on the national and international level with the aim of sustainable development.[82] Judge Weeramantry in his separate opinion for the *Gabcikovo-Nagymaros project* case argued that sustainable development, that is, the need to reconcile economic development with the protection of the environment, is not a concept but a principle with normative value in the light of its wide and general acceptance by the global community. However, Lowe claims that it is unsustainable to argue that sustainable development is a binding norm of international law, however there is a sense in which the

---

[76] The 1993 Convention on Biological Diversity (CBD) is a multilateral treaty that provides a detailed conservation regime that expands on the resource conservation guidelines outlined in the LOSC. The UN Framework Convention on Climate Change (UNFCCC) sets nonbinding limits on greenhouse gas emissions for States. The Global Program of Action for the Protection of the Marine Environment from Land-Based Activities, and the 1994 Barbados Program of Action for Small Island Developing States (SIDS) were also resulted from the 1992 UNCED. Additional international agreements include nonbinding programs that emerged from subsequent sustainable development meetings: the 2002 World Summit on Sustainable Development (WSSD), and the 2012 United Nations Conference on Sustainable Development (UNCSD).

[77] Agenda 21, para 17.46; para 17.75.

[78] Art 7.2.1.

[79] Para 12(n).

[80] Preamble and para 2.

[81] Y Tanaka, *A Dual Approach to Ocean Governance: The Cases of Zonal and Integrated Management in International Law of the Sea* (Routledge 2016) 71–75; V Lowe, 'Sustainable Development and Unsustainable Arguments' in A Boyle and D Freestone (eds), *International Law and Sustainable Development: Past Achievements and Future Challenges* (OUP 1999) 26.

[82] WCED, *Our Common Future* (n 53) 46.

1034   SDG 14

concept of sustainable development exemplifies another species of normativity which is of great potential value in the handling of concepts of international environmental law. According to Lowe 'sustainable development' cannot have the status of a primary rule of international law because it lacks a 'fundamentally norm creating character'. It does not follow, however, that it has no normative status whatsoever. There are other aspects of normativity, rather than a norm that demands a state to conduct in compliance with it.[83] Sustainable development can thus claim a normative status as an element of the process of judicial reasoning. It is a meta-principle, acting upon other legal rules and principles—a legal concept exercising a kind of interstitial normativity, pushing and pulling the boundaries of primary norms when they threaten to overlap or conflict with each other.

The possibility of this kind of normative status arises from the fact that all legal systems are indeterminate. All legal systems contain rules and principles that overlap or conflict in relation to the areas to which they might plausibly be applied. Judge Weeramantry identifies one such pair of rules or principles: the 'right to development' and 'environmental protection', in their normative manifestations, are potentially in conflict. Norms of this kind do have a vitality beyond any specific primary rule. They are free agents, which may in principle be combined with any other rule, modifying that rule. These interstitial/modifying norms do not seek to regulate the conduct of legal persons directly, and they are not addressed to those persons. There is no injunction to 'be reasonable' or to 'balance interests' independent of the primary norms to which the modifying norm is applied: it is the primary norm that carries the prescriptive charge. Modifying norms establish the relationships between other, primary norms. In conclusion, sustainable development performs an interstitial function to adjust overlapping or conflicting rules. Sustainable development is not an independent rule that can for example be applied in adjudication. However, as a concept it facilitates the interpretation and application of LOSC rules governing, for instance, the management of marine living resources.[84]

2. Functional Approach and Cooperation in Ocean Governance

Traditionally, law of the sea's main function is the zonal distribution of jurisdiction of states. The law divides the ocean into marine zones, that is, internal waters, the territorial sea, the contiguous zone, the exclusive economic zone (EEZ), archipelagic waters, the continental shelf, the high seas, and the international seabed area (the Area). These zones are organized into three main areas, areas of sovereignty, areas of sovereign rights and areas beyond national jurisdiction (ABNJ). In zones of sovereignty, such as the territorial sea, the coastal state exercises full legislative and enforcement jurisdiction. Sovereignty is exclusive in the sense that only the state in question may exercise

---

[83] Lowe (n 81).

[84] In this regard, Sofia Guiding Statements explicitly state: 'Treaties and rules of customary international law should be interpreted in the light of principles of sustainable development', ILA, Conference Resolution Sofia 2012, '2012 Sofia Guiding Statements on the Judicial Elaboration of the 2002 New Delhi Declaration of Principles of International Law Relating to Sustainable Development' para 2.

GOAL COMMENTARY 1035

jurisdiction over its territory. In zones like the EEZ, the coastal state enjoys sovereign rights limited to the matters defined by international law, such as management and exploitation of natural resources. Finally, in ABNJ, no state is allowed to make territorial claims. The high seas are governed by the principle of freedom, which aims to ensure the freedom of various uses of the oceans, such as navigation, overflight, laying submarine cables and pipelines, construction of artificial islands, fishing, and marine scientific research. The Area is governed by the principle of the Common Heritage of Humankind (Part XI LOSC), which seeks to promote the common interest of humankind as a whole in present and future generations.

Despite the above neat organization of the states' rights and obligations in jurisdictional zones, the problems that the ocean faces require a more holistic management of the seas and international cooperation. The jurisdictional zones are artificial and manmade and do not correspond to the structure of marine ecosystems. The ocean is one and united and the fish do not confine themselves into delimitation lines. Thus, the traditional law of the sea zonal approach is far from ideal for conservation of marine living resources and biological diversity.

An alternative approach is the functional approach, that is, the law of the common ocean which rests on the international community that shares common interests.[85] This approach provides a framework to ensure international cooperation in marine sectors, such as maritime security, conservation of marine living resources, conservation of marine biological diversity, climate change, and the protection of the marine environment.[86] International cooperation is crucial for sectors such as conservation of marine living resources and biological diversity, as well as marine pollution. To illustrate that, pollution like fisheries is not contained within maritime boundaries, thus coordination and cooperation between states is a prerequisite. The law of the sea provides a legal framework for ensuring international cooperation in marine affairs, thereby safeguarding the common interests of the international community as a whole.[87] Cooperation is an ever-growing goal of the international community in general.[88] The term 'international law of cooperation' that has recently emerged means the cooperation among states 'for the purposes of development to increase the social welfare of the world community'.[89] That spirit of cooperation is also reflected in the LOSC's

---

[85] Tanaka (n 81) 5.

[86] Conservation of fisheries is explicitly addressed in the LOSC. Rights over fisheries are either exclusive to coastal states, shared across states' EEZs, straddling the high seas and EEZs, or highly migratory. The approach adopted is mostly species-specific, eg marine mammals, anadromous, and catadromous stocks. Pollution is also addresses in the LOSC and is mostly source-specific, eg land-based or vessel-source marine pollution, dumping at sea, pollution from seabed activities. Many other treaties deal with marine pollution in the ocean, focusing on harmful substances and waste. The International Convention for the Prevention of Pollution from Ships (MARPOL) for example is the primary instrument for regulating pollution from ships. Climate change is not explicitly addressed in the LOSC. The 2030 Agenda rightly has pointed out that 'climate change is one of the greatest challenges of our time' (para 14). Regarding the impacts of climate change on the ocean, these include ocean acidification, coastal erosion, sea-level rise, and shifting species distribution.

[87] Simma, 'From Bilateralism to Community Interests in International Law' (n 74) 235–43.

[88] <IBT<R Wolfrum, 'International Law of Cooperation' in *Max Planck Encyclopedia of Public International Law* (2010) 2 <https://opil.ouplaw.com/view/10.1093/law:epil/9780199231690/law-9780199231690-e1186> accessed 22 June 2021: Cooperation in itself does not have an innate value as it does not denote the nature of the aim to be achieved (it could denote the mitigation of the climate crisis effects, but also the military cooperation for war).

[89] ibid.

1036   SDG 14

Preamble: '[p]rompted by the desire to settle, in a spirit of mutual understanding and cooperation, all issues relating to the law of the sea'.[90] Indeed, the problems of the oceans are closely interrelated and need to be dealt with in a holistic way.[91] SDG 14 and its targets can be achieved through cooperation at international and most importantly at regional and local levels.

International cooperation requires international institutions, which are of particular importance for protecting community interests at sea. A wide range of international organizations include ocean-related issues within their mandate. The International Maritime Organization (IMO) is the United Nations' specialized agency with responsibility for the safety and security of shipping and the prevention of marine and atmospheric pollution by ships. IMO supports the UN SDGs and is actively working towards the 2030 Agenda.[92] The UN Environment Programme (UNEP) is an international authority that sets the global environmental agenda and promotes the implementation of the environmental dimension of sustainable development within the UN system. UNEP promotes conservation and sustainable use of ocean resources and has created the Regional Seas Programme, which is an action-oriented programme that implements region-specific activities by bringing together various stakeholders like governments, scientific communities, and civil societies for conservation of the marine and coastal environment.[93] The UN Development Programme is also critical for sustainable development, dedicating part of its action plan to ocean governance through SDG 14. The Food and Agriculture Organization (FAO) leads efforts to achieve food security, being particularly active in the fisheries sector. Notably, the FAO envisions a world in which responsible and sustainable use of fisheries makes a contribution to human well-being, food security, and poverty alleviation.[94] The FAO has also a prime role in the conservation and management of fisheries, including review of world fisheries and assistance to developing countries. The United Nations Educational, Scientific and Cultural Organization (UNESCO) promotes scientific research and houses the Intergovernmental Oceanographic Commission (IOC) which is the UN body responsible for supporting ocean science, working to protect the health of the ocean. Recent UN efforts to integrate ocean concerns include the Ocean Conferences and the declaration of the Decade of Ocean Science for Sustainable Development (2021–2030).[95] Intergovernmental organizations also influence ocean management and knowledge generation. Regional Fisheries Management Organizations facilitate fisheries management by establishing and enforcing rules for specific species or advising members within a defined region. Additional examples include the International Whaling

---

[90] Lagoni 'Preamble' in mn 16 Proelss, *United Nations Convention on the Law of the Sea* (n 65).

[91] LOSC Preamble 'the problems of ocean space are closely interrelated and need to be considered as a whole', Recital 3.

[92] IMO, 'IMO and the Sustainable Development Goals' (2015) <https://www.imo.org/en/MediaCentre/HotTopics/Pages/SustainableDevelopmentGoals.aspx> accessed 4 May 2021.

[93] UNEP, 'Regional Seas Programme' <https://www.unep.org/explore-topics/oceans-seas/what-we-do/regional-seas-programme> accessed 5 May 2021.

[94] UN FAO, 'Fisheries and Aquaculture' <https://www.fao.org/fishery/about/en> accessed 3 May 2021.

[95] United Nations Decade of Ocean Science for Sustainable Development (2021–2030) <https://www.ioc.unesco.org/ocean-decade> accessed 4 May 2021.

Commission, charged with the conservation of whales and management of whaling activities worldwide, and the Ramsar Convention for the conservation and sustainable use of wetlands.[96]

The obligation to cooperate has also been explicitly included in certain provisions of the LOSC.[97] Both of the LOSC Implementation Agreements reflect the need of the international community to cooperate. In the 2001 MOX Plant case, the International Tribunal for the Law of the Sea (ITLOS) highlighted the importance of international cooperation, stating that 'the duty to cooperate is a fundamental principle in the prevention of pollution of the marine environment under Part XII of the Convention and general international law'.[98] Indeed, the protection of the marine environment cannot be achieved by a single state. In that regard, Article 197 LOSC stipulates that states shall cooperate 'on a global basis and, as appropriate, on a regional basis, directly or through competent international organizations, in formulating and elaborating international rules, standards and recommended practices and procedures consistent with this Convention, for the protection and preservation of the marine environment, taking into account characteristic regional features'.[99] Article 198 further provides that 'when a State becomes aware of cases in which the marine environment is in imminent danger of being damaged or has been damaged by pollution, it shall immediately notify other States it deems likely to be affected by such damage, as well as the competent international organizations'. Where imminent danger exists, the state in the area affected as well as the competent international organization shall 'cooperate, to the extent possible, in eliminating the effects of pollution and preventing or minimizing the damage' and shall 'jointly develop and promote contingency plans for responding to pollution incidents in the marine environment'.[100] The obligation to cooperate is particularly important in the environmental protection of enclosed or semi enclosed seas (article 123) and in provisions concerning land-based pollution (article 207(4)), pollution from seabed activities subject to national jurisdiction (article 208(5)), pollution from dumping (article 210(4)), pollution from vessels (article 211(1)), and pollution from or through the atmosphere (article 212(3)).

The obligation to cooperate has also been read multiple times into the Convention's provisions by jurisprudence. Both in the *Land Reclamation*[101] and the *MOX/Plant Case*,[102] the ITLOS had imposed cooperative measures on the parties in the disputes on the basis of a general duty of cooperation in relation to the protection and preservation of the marine environment (Part XII LOSC). According to the Court, the duty

---

[96] See Tanaka (n 81) 43.

[97] *Inter alia*, art 43, cooperation between user states and states bordering a strait; art 118, cooperation of states in the conservation and management of living resources; art 123, cooperation of states bordering enclosed or semi-enclosed seas.

[98] The *MOX Plant* case (Request for provisional measures), ITLOS Reports 2002, 110, para 82.

[99] The OSPAR Convention states in its preamble that Article 197 reflects customary international law.

[100] LOSC, article 199.

[101] *Land Reclamation Case by Singapore In and Around the Straits of Johor (Malaysia v Singapore)* (Provisional Measures), Order of 8 October 2003, International Tribunal for the Law of the Sea (ITLOS), <http://www.itlos.org/fileadmin/itlos/documents/cases/case no 12/Order.08.10.03.E.pdf> accessed 12 April 2021.

[102] *MOX Plant* case (*Ireland v United Kingdom*) (Provisional Measures), Order of 3 December 2001 (2002) 41 ILM 405.

1038 SDG 14

of cooperation entails meaningful negotiations and exchange of information between states.[103] Further, international cooperation is enhanced by awareness-raising and the increase of scientific knowledge, as well as by enhancing financing and developing capacity. Awareness-raising may refer to marine scientific research, to information and data with regard to the state of the marine environment as well as of the existing legal commitments and policies. Capacity building may refer to the improvement of funding and resources for ocean-related initiatives, especially with regards to SIDS and LDCs.[104] Finally, cooperation benefits regional governance, which typically suffers from systematic fragmentation and regulatory complexity.

3. Conservation and Management of Marine Living Resources

a) Territorial Sea and EEZ

As mentioned above, the territorial sea and internal waters are under territorial sovereignty and the coastal state can exercise its exclusive jurisdiction over marine resources. Coastal states thus have jurisdiction with respect to conservation and management of fisheries and the LOSC does not contain any explicit obligation for those spaces. The LOSC, however, does pose explicit obligations upon states to conserve marine living resources in the EEZ, where coastal states enjoy sovereign rights for the purpose of exploring and exploiting natural resources. Conservation in the EEZ is critical as most commercially exploitable stocks are located within 200 nautical miles from the shore.

Article 61(1) LOSC requires coastal states to ensure that the maintenance of the EEZ living resources is not endangered by overexploitation. According to the same provision, states need to determine the allowable catch of fish stocks in the EEZ. Further, article 62(2) stipulates that the coastal state must determine its capacity to harvest the EEZ living resources. Other states have access to the surplus of the allowable catch, where the coastal state does not have the capacity to harvest the allowable catch. Article 61(3) establishes the concept of 'maximum sustainable yield'. Maximum sustainable yield aims to maintain oceans productivity by allowing the taking of the number of fish from a stock that is replaced by the annual rate of new recruits entering the stock.[105]

The above framework does not come without practical difficulties. The determination of the 'total allowable catch' is a complex exercise, and the Convention does not contain any guidance for its calculation. Developing states often lack the capacity and the scientific knowledge needed for the determination of the total allowable catch, while the Convention allows broad discretion to states for that determination. Similarly, the 'maximum sustainable yield' concept has been criticized for failing to take into account the ecological interactions of species, the qualitative status of the habitat, and the limits of an area's biomass.[106]

---

[103] MOX Plant case, para 84; Land Reclamation case, para 99; see also Guyana v Suriname, para 478, on art 83(3) LOSC.

[104] K Grip, 'International Marine Environmental Governance: A Review' (2017) 46 Ambio 413–27.

[105] P Birnie and others, International Law and the Environment (3rd edn, OUP 2009) 591.

[106] ibid.

b) High seas

On the high seas all states enjoy the freedom of fishing.[107] As indicated in article 87 LOSC, however, that freedom is not absolute. Article 116 LOSC aims to further concretize the scope of the 'conditional freedom' to fish,[108] by adding certain specific limitations in addition to the general limitations on the exercise of high seas freedoms.[109] This provision expressly stipulates that a state's right to fish in the high seas is subject to its treaty obligations, the rights and duties as well as the interests of coastal states, and the rest of the provisions of the same section ('Conservation and Management of the Living Resources of the High Seas', articles 117–120 LOSC).

Article 117 LOSC requires states 'to take, or to cooperate with other states in taking, such measures for their respective nationals as may be necessary for the conservation of the living resources of the high seas'. This directly establishes the duty of *all* states to ensure the conservation of living resources and control the activities of their nationals, and can be seen as the *quid pro quo* for the right to fish on the high seas.[110] The obligation to 'take' measures, as affirmed by the ICJ in the *Fisheries Jurisdiction (Spain v Canada)* case, includes not only the adoption of laws and regulations but also the enforcement of such measures.[111] Article 117 LOSC establishes a strict and general obligation for *all* states (fishing and non-fishing, coastal with EEZs adjacent to the high seas, port states, states with nationals engaging with activities of fishing vessels, land-locked). Naturally, though, the duty to take measures falls primarily on flag states. Under this article, states are granted a wide margin of appreciation in determining what measures to take in respect of their nationals, while the wording of the provision suggests that although cooperation is encouraged, states remain free to adopt any measures unilaterally.[112]

Article 118 LOSC enshrines in its first sentence the overarching principle of high seas fisheries, that is, that all states have a duty to cooperate in the 'conservation and management of living resources in the areas of the high seas'.[113] The provision does not specify the precise manner of its implementation. However, it has a mandatory character as it becomes evident from the language of the article ('shall cooperate'). The second and third sentences of article 118 LOSC establish more specific duties, that is, that 'States whose nationals exploit identical living resources, or different living resources in the same area, shall enter into negotiations with a view to taking the measures necessary for the conservation of the living resources concerned' while, further, that '[t]hey shall, as appropriate, cooperate to establish sub-regional or regional fisheries organisations

---

[107] FO Vicuña 'The International Law of High Seas Fisheries: From Freedom of Fishing to Sustainable Use' in OS Stokke (ed), *Governing High Seas Fisheries: The Interplay of Global and Regional Regimes* (OUP 2001) 29, where he opines that the fact that LOSC approaches the right to fish within the realm of *conservation and management* of living resources is important as it points towards the importance of sustainability.

[108] R Reyfuse, 'Article 116' in A Proelss and others (eds), *United Nations Convention on the Law of the Sea: A Commentary* (CH Beck/Hart/Nomos 2017) 792.

[109] Arts 87 and 88 LOSC.

[110] Reyfuse, 'Article 116' (n 108) 805.

[111] *Fisheries Jurisdiction (Spain v Canada)* (Jurisdiction of the Court) [1998] ICJ Rep 432 [84].

[112] Reyfuse, 'Article 116' (n 108) 813. See also at 814 the discussion on how to resolve potential conflict between unilateral measures and measures adopted by international cooperation.

[113] The ICJ recognized the existence of such duty in *Fisheries Jurisdiction (United Kingdom v Iceland)* (Merits) [1974] ICJ Rep 3 [72].

1040   SDG 14

to this end'. Despite its mandatory language, the second sentence of article 118 LOSC only establishes an obligation of conduct ('to enter into negotiations') and not an obligation of result.[114] The duty to cooperate under article 118 LOSC is a natural corollary of the duty to conserve a shared natural resource and arises from the duty to have due regard to the interests of other states.[115] It should be read in conjunction with articles 63–65 LOSC, which also establish cooperative obligations in relation to transboundary, shared, straddling,[116] highly migratory stocks,[117] and associated and dependent species, as well as marine mammals. The provision has contributed to the creation of some regional fisheries management organizations (RFMOs) and other regional fisheries management arrangements (RFMAs), as well as to the adoption of additional fisheries regulations under their auspices.

Article 119 LOSC further specifies the duties of states in establishing conservation measures. In determining the allowable catch and establishing other conservation measures for the living resources of the high seas, states are to take into account, among other things, 'the best scientific evidence available' and 'any generally recommended international minimum standards, whether subregional, regional or global'. This provision contemplates the further development of fisheries regulations through the establishment of relevant standards on a regional or global level and provides a textual foothold for taking into consideration external rules of international law for the determination of the obligations of states under the LOSC. The reliance on external standards, even in a non-mandatory manner ('shall take into consideration'), is consistent with the characterization of the LOSC as a 'framework' Convention.[118]

At this point it should be mentioned that the regulation of fishing rights was one of the most controversial issues raised during the negotiations phase for the conclusion of the LOSC. Although the parties managed to reach agreement on the previously problematic issue of the extent of a coastal state's fishing rights, some issues remained unresolved. One of these issues was that of fish stocks that straddled the jurisdictional zones recognized under the LOSC, and the balancing of conflicting interests over such stocks. Due to the absence of concrete agreement, the LOSC simply stresses in articles 63 and 64 the need for cooperation in the management and conservation of highly migratory and straddling fish stocks without setting down any more detailed procedural or substantive obligations on how such cooperation is to be achieved.[119] In the years

---

[114] Reyfuse, 'Article 116' (n 108) 826. In the absence of any articulation in the LOSC, it remains unclear what happens if negotiations fail.

[115] R Reyfuse, 'Regional Fisheries Management Organizations' in Rothwell and others (eds), *The Oxford Handbook of the Law of the Sea* (n 61) 441.

[116] Transboundary stocks consist generally of those stocks which move across a boundary and those which occur on both sides of a boundary at the same time in random movements or in 'dynamic pool' mixing. 'Shared stocks' are stocks that 'straddle' (migrate through or occur in) two or more EEZs, whereas 'straddling stocks' are those that straddle or move across the boundary between an EEZ and the high seas. See M Hayashi 'The Management of Transboundary Fish Stocks under the LOS Convention' (1993) 8(2) International Journal of Marine and Coastal Law 245.

[117] 'Highly migratory' are fish species which undertake ocean migrations and have wide geographic distributions.

[118] C Redgwell, 'Mind the Gap in the GAIRS: The Role of Other Instruments in LOSC Regime Implementation in the Offshore Energy Sector' (2014) 29 The International Journal of Marine and Coastal Law 600, 606.

[119] J Harrison, *Making the Law of the Sea: A Study in the Development of International Law* (CUP 2011) 100.

following the conclusion of the LOSC, it became evident that these provisions were not adequate in order to prevent overfishing of straddling and highly migratory fish stocks, and that further development of international fisheries law might be necessary to face this challenge.

In 1992, the General Assembly convened the UN Conference on Environment and Development (UNCED) in Rio de Janeiro. The protection of the marine environment and the conservation of marine living resources was one of the issues placed on the agenda of the conference. The conference adopted, among others, a comprehensive plan of action to be taken globally, nationally and locally by organizations of the UN system, governments, and major groups in every area in which human impacts on the environment, called 'Agenda 21'. Chapter 17 of Agenda 21 refers to the protection of the oceans, all kinds of seas, and coastal areas, and the protection, rational use, and development of their living resources. It confirms the continuing relevance of LOSC provisions as 'a basis upon which to pursue the protection and sustainable development of the marine and coastal environment and its resources', but it also acknowledges that the 'management of high seas fisheries, including the adoption, monitoring and enforcement of effective conservation measures, is inadequate in many areas and some resources are overutilized' and recognizes the need for further clarification and development. Agenda 21 is a soft law instrument with no legally binding force, but it prompted subsequent conferences and the elaboration of further international instruments regulating high seas fisheries. Specifically, Chapter 17 of Agenda 21 called states to convene, as soon as possible, an intergovernmental conference under the auspices of the UN 'with a view to promoting the effective implementation of the provisions of the LOSC on straddling fish stocks and highly migratory fish stocks'. Following up on this 'commitment', the UNGA decided to convene the Fish Stocks Conference for the conclusion of the UN Fish Stocks Agreement (UNFSA).[120] The purpose of the conference was to fill in the gaps left by the ambiguous settlement achieved in 1982 which was reflected in articles 63 and 64 LOSC by specifying precisely what principles should govern the management and conservation of straddling and highly migratory fish stocks.[121] In other words, as evidenced by its name, the UNFSA is an agreement that buttresses the implementation of the relevant provisions of the LOSC.[122]

4. Protection and Preservation of the Marine Environment

Part XII LOSC is the environmental part of the Convention describing the obligations of states with respect to the protection and preservation of the marine environment. Article 192 LOSC enshrines the general obligation of states to protect and preserve the marine environment and is underpinned by more detailed and stringent provisions in

---

[120] United Nations Conference on Straddling Fish Stocks and Highly Migratory Fish Stocks (22 December 1992) UNGA Res 47/192.

[121] UNGA Res 47/192 (22 December 1992) [3]; Harrison, *Making the Law of the Sea* (n 119) 102.

[122] Not only arts 63 and 64 but also arts 118 and 197. See, eg, Harrison, *Making the Law of the Sea* (n 119) 85; R Warner, 'Conserving Marine Biodiversity in Areas Beyond National Jurisdiction: Co-Evolution and Interaction with the Law of the Sea' in Rothwell and other (eds), *The Oxford Handbook of the Law of the Sea* (n 61) 755.

1042 SDG 14

the rest of the part.[123] In its *Southern Bluefin Tuna* cases, the ITLOS observed that 'the conservation of the living resources of the sea is an element in the protection and preservation of the marine environment'.[124] This has been reaffirmed more recently in the 2015 ITLOS Advisory Opinion[125] as well as in the *South China Sea Arbitration*.[126]

The obligation to protect and preserve the environment includes, among others, a duty to take measures necessary to protect and preserve fragile ecosystems as well as the habitat of depleted, threatened, or endangered species and other forms of marine life.[127] Moreover, similarly, to Part VII LOSC, the second section of Part XII LOSC establishes the framework for 'Global and Region Cooperation' in the protection and preservation of the marine environment. Article 197 LOSC requires that states 'cooperate on a global basis and, as appropriate, on a regional basis, directly or through competent international organisations, in formulating and elaborating international rules, standards and recommended practices and procedures ... for the protection and preservation of the marine environment, taking into account characteristic regional features'. This provision is yet another foothold for states to elaborate on fisheries regulations on a regional level through further cooperative efforts, while it incorporates by reference internationally agreed rules and standards and recommended practices to the LOSC.[128]

5. Monitoring and Enforcement Challenges

Despite the rich legal and policy framework and the great number of actors involved in ocean governance, the implementation of the applicable laws remains challenging. This is because monitoring and enforcement of rules at sea present considerable practical hurdles but also because the density of the legal and policy framework creates regulatory complexity that complicates rather than facilitates implementation.

The term 'monitoring' is used to describe a continuous management activity that uses the systematic collection of data on selected indicators[129] to provide states and other stakeholders with indications of the extent of progress toward the achievement of goals and objectives.[130] The term 'enforcement' refers to the set of actions that states take to achieve compliance with regulations in order to correct or stop situations that endanger the environment.[131] Naturally, data collected in the process of monitoring can also prove useful for the purposes of enforcement, and vice versa.

---

[123] D Czybulka, 'Article 192' in Proelss and others (eds), *United Nations Convention on the Law of the Sea* (n 108) 1278.

[124] *Southern Bluefin Tuna (New Zealand v Japan; Australia v Japan)* (Order for Provisional Measures) [1999] ITLOS Rep 280 [70].

[125] ITLOS Advisory Opinion 2015 [120].

[126] *The South China Sea Arbitration (The Republic of the Philippines v the People's Republic of China)* PCA Case No 2013-19 (Award) 12 July 2016 [956].

[127] Art 194 (5) LOSC.

[128] Czybulka (n 123) 1329.

[129] A measure, quantitative or qualitative, of how close we are to achieving what we set out to achieve, ie our objectives or outcomes.

[130] UNESCO 2009 at 86.

[131] UNESCO 2009 at 85.

The effective monitoring and enforcement of law of the sea rules is an essential basis for the achievement of SDG 14. Although the legal framework is extensive and encompasses provisions relevant to almost all matters related to the use and protection of the seas, enforcement of the framework presents significant obstacles. This partly explains why despite the robust network of legal instruments, serious problems concerning the oceans are ever-present. This subsection presents the enforcement framework governing law of the sea obligations and explains why enforcement can be proved particularly challenging especially on the high seas.

Enforcement in zones of coastal state jurisdiction requires states to have the physical capacity to patrol their waters. Thus, less developed states often struggle with the policing and regulation of the waters under their jurisdiction. Much more challenging, however, is the monitoring and enforcement in the high seas. On high seas enforcement depends on the capacity of the flag states to monitor and enforce the law on the vessels flying their flags. It is apparent that very few states in the world, if any, actually have the capacity to monitor their fleet on the vast areas that the high seas cover, while this is practically impossible for the world's largest open registries, like Panama or Liberia.

In more detail, article 94 LOSC establishes the duty of the flag state to 'effectively exercise its jurisdiction and control in administrative, technical and social matters over ships flying its flag'. This provision complements the principle of exclusive jurisdiction of the flag state over vessels of its nationality on the high seas, enshrined in article 92(1) LOSC.[132] For example, under article 94 LOSC the flag state must adopt the necessary administrative measures to ensure that fishing vessels flying its flag are not involved in activities which will undermine the flag state's responsibilities under the Convention in respect of the conservation and management of marine living resources.[133] If such violations occur other states may report the fact to the flag state under article 94(6) LOSC and the flag state is obliged to investigate and, if appropriate, take any action necessary to remedy the situation.[134] The duty of flag states (among others) to take measures necessary for the conservation and management of the living resources of the high seas is also enshrined in article 117 LOSC. Although article 117 LOSC does not specifically refer to flag states, by virtue of article 92 LOSC the duty falls primarily on the flag states of vessels fishing on the high seas. Moreover, the flag state responsibilities are elaborated in a number of international legal instruments such as the 1993 Agreement to Promote Compliance with International Conservation and Management Measures by Fishing Vessels on the High Seas (FAO Compliance Agreement),[135] the 1995 UNFSA,[136] and various regulations adopted by RFMOs and other RFMAs.

---

[132] Y Tanaka, *The International Law of the Sea* (CUP 2019) 189; D Guilfoyle, 'Article 94' in Proelss and others (eds), *United Nations Convention on the Law of the Sea* (n 108) 709.

[133] ibid.

[134] ibid.

[135] UN FAO Agreement to Promote Compliance with Conservation Measures on the High Seas (adopted 24 November 1993, entered into force 24 April 2003) 2221 UNTS 91 (UN FAO Compliance Agreement).

[136] Agreement for the Implementation of the Provisions of the United Nations Convention on the Law of the Sea of 10 December 1982 relating to the Conservation and Management of Straddling Fish Stocks and Highly Migratory Fish Stocks (adopted 4 August 1995, entered into force 11 December 2001) 2167 UNTS 3 (UNFSA).

1044   SDG 14

The nationality of vessels is the key 'ordering principle' of the high seas regime,[137] and along with its corollary, the exercise of exclusive flag state jurisdiction by the state of nationality, it plays an important role in the regulation of marine activities. Thus, ensuring adequate flag state control over vessels on the high seas and their activities is essential to maintaining order and effectively enforcing the relevant measures. Nonetheless, flag states are not always willing or able to fulfil their obligation to exercise effective jurisdiction and control.[138] Article 91 LOSC requires that 'there must exist a genuine link' between the flag state and a vessel granted its nationality. This latter requirement has been controversial, as the convention does not specify the consequences flowing from the absence of such link. In the case of *M/V Saiga (No 2)*, the ITLOS attempted to shed light on this requirement and held that the purpose of the provision is, essentially, to secure more effective implementation of the duties of the flag state under the LOSC, and not to establish further criteria for the validity of the registration of ships in a flag state.[139] The ITLOS reiterated this view in the *M/V Virginia G* case, adding that the requirement for the existence of a 'genuine link' requires that the flag state 'exercise effective jurisdiction and control over that ship in order to ensure that it operates in accordance with generally accepted international regulations, procedures and practices'.[140] According to this finding, the requirement of genuine link is yet another reiteration of the flag states' duties under the LOSC; it has no independent content and its absence brings about no additional consequences.[141]

The evident problem with such a loose approach to the genuine link requirement is that it fails to address the concerns arising out of the so-called flags of convenience. Many states have developed open registers, which enable vessels to claim nationality of the state with which the vessel has few or no connections.[142] The incentive for both open registry states and shipowners registering their vessels under flags of convenience is primarily economic. Nonetheless, in such cases there is often a lack of substantive regulatory capacity as well as lack of any interest by the flag states in fulfilling their duties as described in the LOSC, as well as other international agreements. Moreover, easy access to the register facilitates the registration of substandard ships, not complying with international safety, and environmental protection and conservation standards.[143]

---

[137] Tanaka (n 132) 193–97; Guilfoyle (n 132) 214. See also a recent affirmation of the importance of the principle of exclusive flag state jurisdiction in the *M/V 'Norstar' Case (Panama v Italy)* (Judgment) [2019] [214–218].

[138] LOSC, art 91. D König, 'Flag of Ships' in *Max Planck Encyclopedia of International Law* (2009); D Guilfoyle, 'Article 91' in Proelss and others (eds), *United Nations Convention on the Law of the Sea* (n 108) 693–95.

[139] M/V 'Saiga' (No 2) *(Saint Vincent and the Grenadines v Guinea)* (Judgment) [1999] ITLOS Rep 10 [83].

[140] M/V 'Virginia G' *(Panama/Guinea-Bissau)* (Judgment) [2014] ITLOS Rep 4 [113]. See also Guilfoyle, 'Article 94' (n 132) 711.

[141] Note that in an effort to strengthen the control of flag states over vessels of their nationality and discourage the use of open registries, UNCTAD organized a diplomatic conference that resulted in the adoption of the 1986 United Nations Convention on Conditions for Registration of Ships (adopted 7 February 1986, not in force). The conference concentrated on the requirement for genuine link and the convention included relevant references, but ultimately it failed to clarify the necessary elements for the registration of vessels in a national registry and reinforced the status quo of open registries. The Convention has never entered into force. See G Kasoulides, 'The 1986 United Nations Convention on the Conditions for Registration of Vessels and the Question of Open Registry' (1989) 20(6) Ocean Development and International Law 543.

[142] A Syrigos, 'Developments on the Interdiction of Vessels on the High Seas' in A Strati and others (eds), *Unresolved Issues and New Challenges to the Law of the Sea* (Martinus Nijhoff 2006) 152.

[143] D König, 'Flags of Convenience' in *Max Planck Encyclopedia of International Law* (2008).

Vessels flying flags of convenience are often involved in illegal, unreported, and unregulated (IUU) fishing.[144] A Statement from the proceedings of the Seventh Session of the UN Commission on Sustainable Development describes the problem very eloquently: 'When fishing companies based in countries that have signed fisheries agreements and conventions ... design arrangements that allow ships under their control to go to sea and ignore those agreements under [the] cover of the flag of a non-signatory they make a mockery of the agreement.'[145]

Beyond the traditional monitoring methods of aerial patrols, on-board observers, and logbooks and records, remote sensing technology has been employed by states and fisheries bodies with the purpose of gathering data, addressing IUU fishing and limiting bycatch impact. Remote sensing, or Earth Observation, is 'the science of extracting information from an object through the analysis of data acquired by a sensor that is not in direct contact with the area.'[146] The most widely used type for surveillance through such technological means is the vessel monitoring system (VMS). VMS provides data to fisheries authorities on the location, course, and speed of vessels through electronic devices that are installed on board vessels. Conventional types of VMSs rely on reports by radio, land-based radar, or sea-based sonar. However, nowadays satellite-based VMSs and also the use of satellite sensor technologies are among the existing tools for fisheries monitoring worldwide.

In general, satellite monitoring is a way to get information over very large areas and detect far more offences than conventional monitoring methods do.[147] Especially when a fishery operates over a large remote area, satellite surveillance systems are particularly useful. In addition, satellites can operate constantly and without interruption and they provide near real-time data.[148] Unlike aircraft, their operation is not dependent upon atmospheric weather conditions that can ground airplanes, or the availability of flight crews. Neither their range nor their operational duration is dictated by fuel capacity or crew endurance.[149]

A final note on implementation challenges has to do with the issue of framework complexity, which can also pose hurdles in the implementation of the legal framework

---

[144] See, eg, R Reyfuse, 'Article 117' in Proelss and others (eds), *United Nations Convention on the Law of the Sea* (n 108) 805. For a definition of IUU fishing see the International Plan of Action to Prevent, Deter and Eliminate Illegal, Unreported and Unregulated Fishing IPOA-IUU) (adopted by UN FAO in 2001).

[145] Simon Upton, Chair, Second London Oceans Workshop, December 1998, as quoted by J Swan, 'Fishing Vessels Operating under Open Registers and the Exercise of Flag State Responsibilities. Information and Options' (2002) UN FAO Fisheries Circular 980, 3.

[146] AC Nunez M, 'Admissibility of Remote Sensing Evidence before International and Regional Tribunals', Innovations in Human Rights Monitoring Working Paper (August 2012) <https://www.amnestyusa.org/pdfs/RemoteSensingAsEvidencePaper.pdf> accessed 7 May 2021.

[147] cf aerial photography which is considered too expensive to obtain land cover information over physically large areas. Satellite monitoring to cover wide and/or remote areas has been estimated by EMSA to be up to ten times cheaper than aerial surveillance (EMSA, Pollution Preparedness and Response Activities, October 2010).

[148] NT Hintzen and others, 'VMS Tools: Open-source Software for the Processing, Analysis and Visualisation of Fisheries Logbook and VMS data' (2012) Fisheries Research 115, 31–34; see also R Enguehard and others, 'Comparing Interactive and Automated Mapping Systems for Supporting Fisheries Enforcement Activities—A Case Study on VMS' (2013) 1(17) Journal of Coastal Conservation 105–19.

[149] K Dighe and others, 'The Use of Satellite Imagery in Environmental Crimes Prosecutions in the US: A Developing Area' in R Purdy and D Leung (eds), *Evidence from Earth Observation Satellites: Emerging Legal Issues* (Martinus Nijhof 2012) 67.

permeating the oceans and may delay the attainment of SDG 14 and its targets. In general, an 'overcrowding of the international ocean management scene'[150] or a 'treaty congestion'[151] can be observed in the field. The abundance of legal instruments may have a negative effect and result in lack of coordination and, even worse, in overlapping and conflicting obligations and responsibilities. It becomes apparent that the interconnection of the issues and the interrelatedness of marine ecosystems call for enhanced cooperation and coordination at the national, regional, and international level with the purpose to promote integration and sustainable management of the oceans.

IV. Human Rights and Goal 14

Any modern discourse on sustainability necessarily includes a human rights dimension. Agenda 2030 is not an exception to that as it is 'an agenda for the people, by the people and with the people'.[152] Under this perspective, human rights provisions in international instruments inform the content of Agenda 2030 and the SDGs and their targets.[153]

The discussion about human rights at sea is a relatively new one. The LOSC contains no explicit reference to human rights. The Convention and other law of the sea instruments are designed for states and not individuals, thus making the law of the sea a state-centred area of law.[154] Yet, the recent discussion of human rights at sea mainly refers to issues related to refugee, migration, and labour law, stemming from incidents like working conditions on board fishing vessels, IUU fishing, and piracy.

However, the environmental aspect of the oceans is related to rights that are more closely connected to SDG 14. These are, among others, the right to a clean environment, the right to food, and the right to natural resources. For example, marine pollution damages marine environment and marine resources that support livelihoods, local communities and economies, and, thus, infringes on the relevant human rights. Indeed, in 1972 the UN Conference on the Human Environment declared that '[m]an has the fundamental right to freedom, equality and adequate conditions of life, in an environment of a quality that permits a life of dignity and well-being, and he bears a solemn responsibility to protect and improve the environment for present and future generations'.[155] According to Boyle, this statement has 'provided the basis for subsequent elaboration of a human right to environmental quality'. However, 'its real-world impact

[150] J Hyvarinen and others, 'The United Nations and Fisheries in 1998' (1998) 4(29) Ocean Development and International Law 323–38.

[151] D Al-Abdulrazzak and others, 'Opportunities for Improving Global Marine Conservation through Multilateral Treaties' (2017) 86 Marine Policy 247–52.

[152] M Robinson, 'Foreword' in F Dodds and others (eds), *Negotiating the Sustainable Development Goals: A Transformational Agenda for an Insecure World* (Routledge 2017) xv.

[153] See I Khan, 'Pathways to Justice: Rule of Law, Human Rights, Sustainable Development and Human Security', Background paper for Human Development Report 2016 (United Nations Development Programme, Human Development Report Office 2016).

[154] I Papanicolopulu, 'The Law of the Sea Convention: No Place for Persons?' (2012) 4 International Journal of Marine and Coastal Law 27.

[155] 1972, UN Conference on the Human Environment, Principle 1.

has been noticeably modest.[156] The right to a quality environment was not repeated in the 1992 Rio Declaration on Environment and Development (Rio Declaration), which merely referred to humans being 'entitled to a healthy and productive life in harmony with nature'.[157]

In general, it can be said that SDG 14 is closely related to a number of rights, such as the right to health, the right to adequate food and drinking water, and the right of all peoples to freely dispose of their natural wealth and resources. The right to health includes the right to safe, clean, healthy, and sustainable environment and is enshrined *inter alia* in article 25(1) of the Universal Declaration of Human Rights (UDHR),[158] Article 12 of the International Covenant on Economic, Social and Cultural Rights (ICESCR),[159] article 24 of the Convention on the Rights of the Child (CRC),[160] article 12 of the Convention on the Elimination of All Forms of Discrimination against Women (CEDAW),[161] and article 28 of the Convention on the Protection of the Rights of All Migrant Workers and Members of Their Families (CMW).[162] The right to adequate food and right to safe drinking water is enshrined *inter alia* in article 25(1) of the UDHR and Article 11 of the ICESCR.[163] The right of all peoples to freely dispose of their natural wealth and resources is enshrined in the common article 1(2) of the ICCPR and the ICESCR.[164] Other relevant human rights instruments to SDG 14 are the Escazu Agreement, a regional agreement on access to information, public participation, and

[156] A Boyle, 'Environment and Human Rights' in *Max Planck Encyclopedia of Public International Law* (April 2009) <https://opil.ouplaw.com/view/10.1093/law:epil/9780199231690/law-9780199231690-e1948> accessed 9 May 2021.

[157] UNGA, A/CONF.151/26 (Vol I) (12 August 1992), Principle 1.

[158] 1. Everyone has the right to a standard of living adequate for the health and well-being of himself and of his family, including food, clothing, housing and medical care and necessary social services, and the right to security in the event of unemployment, sickness, disability, widowhood, old age or other lack of livelihood in circumstances beyond his control.

[159] The States Parties to the present Covenant recognize the right of everyone to the enjoyment of the highest attainable standard of physical and mental health. 2. The steps to be taken by the States Parties to the present Covenant to achieve the full realization of this right shall include those necessary for: (a) The provision for the reduction of the stillbirth-rate and of infant mortality and for the healthy development of the child; (b) The improvement of all aspects of environmental and industrial hygiene; (c) The prevention, treatment and control of epidemic, endemic, occupational and other diseases; (d) The creation of conditions which would assure to all medical service and medical attention in the event of sickness.

[160] 1. States Parties recognize the right of the child to the enjoyment of the highest attainable standard of health and to facilities for the treatment of illness and rehabilitation of health. States Parties shall strive to ensure that no child is deprived of his or her right of access to such health care services.

[161] 1. States Parties shall take all appropriate measures to eliminate discrimination against women in the field of health care in order to ensure, on a basis of equality of men and women, access to health care services, including those related to family planning.

[162] Migrant workers and members of their families shall have the right to receive any medical care that is urgently required for the preservation of their life or the avoidance of irreparable harm to their health on the basis of equality of treatment with nationals of the State concerned. Such emergency medical care shall not be refused them by reason of any irregularity with regard to stay or employment.

[163] 1. The States Parties to the present Covenant recognize the right of everyone to an adequate standard of living for himself and his family, including adequate food, clothing and housing, and to the continuous improvement of living conditions. The States Parties will take appropriate steps to ensure the realization of this right, recognizing to this effect the essential importance of international cooperation based on free consent. 2. The States Parties to the present Covenant, recognizing the fundamental right of everyone to be free from hunger, shall take, individually and through international co-operation, the measures, including specific programmes, which are needed ....

[164] 2. All peoples may, for their own ends, freely dispose of their natural wealth and resources without prejudice to any obligations arising out of international economic co-operation, based upon the principle of mutual benefit, and international law. In no case may a people be deprived of its own means of subsistence.

1048   SDG 14

justice in environmental matters in Latin America and the Caribbean (articles 1, 4–7, 9); the American Declaration on the Rights and Duties of Man (article XI); the Protocol of San Salvador—Additional Protocol to the American Convention on HR in the Area of Economic, Social and Cultural Rights (article 11); the African Charter on Human and People's Rights (articles 16, 24); the Maputo Protocol, Protocol to the African Charter on Human and People's Rights on the Rights of Women in Africa (article 18); and the Convention on Biological Diversity (articles 3, 6, 10, 14).

V. Targets and Indicators of Goal 14

A. Overview

For each goal of the SDGs, a number of specific targets has been agreed. SDG 14 includes ten targets. The last three targets (14.a, 14.b, 14.c) are means of implementation targets, in other words guidelines for developing programmes and policies for the implementation of SDG 14. Most of the targets are specific and they require the implementation of concrete measures to be achieved by a set timeline. This is in contrast to SDG 13 (climate change) for example which presents a high level of abstraction, and the related targets are not clear-cut. According to the OECD for targets to be successful they need to be SMART, that is, Specific, Measurable, Attainable, Relevant—for all countries—and Time-bound.[165] We observe that targets 14.1–14.3, 14.7, and 14.b are stipulated in general terms and are not sufficiently precise. Moreover, most SDG 14 targets are not quantifiable, with the exception of target 14.5 and targets 14.1, 14.3, and 14.7 that can be partly measured in quantitative terms.[166] As a last criticism, we may refer to the fact that certain climate change-related impacts such as sea level rise, ocean warming, and changes in ocean circulation and salinity are not addressed in the SDG 14 targets. Further, it must be noted that, as analysed in Subsection II.A, the two objectives of SDG 14 need to be balanced. The same applies to the separate targets, which sometimes can contradict each other.[167] For instance, there are potential trade-offs between targets 14.7 and 14.b that promote economic activities, and targets 14.2, 14.4, and 14.6 that seek to conserve marine ecosystems.[168]

The implementation and monitoring of the progress of the SDGs and their targets are facilitated through performance indicators and periodical reporting.[169] These

[165] OECD, 'Policy Coherence for Sustainable Development in the SDG Framework: Shaping Targets and Monitoring Progress' (OECD 2015).

[166] ibid; M Loewe and N Rippin (eds), *The Sustainable Development Goals of the Post-2015 Agenda. Comments on the OWG and SDSN Proposals* (German Development Institute 2015).

[167] S Unger and others, 'Achieving the Sustainable Development Goal for the Oceans' (2017) IASS Policy Brief 1.

[168] D Le Blanc and others, 'Mapping the Linkages between Oceans and Other Sustainable Development Goals: A Preliminary Exploration' (2017) DESA Working Paper 149.

[169] *Transforming Our World*, para 75; UN, Report of the Inter-agency and Expert Group on Sustainable Development Goal Indicators. Document E/CN.3/2017/2, Annexe III, IV and V (UN 2017a); UN, Report of the Inter-Agency and Expert Group on Sustainable Development Goal Indicators. Document E/CN.3/2016/2/Rev.1, Annex IV (UN 2016a).

are necessary tools for measuring and verifying whether the goals and targets are on track or have been reached.[170] The global indicator framework for SDGs was developed by the Inter-agency and Expert Group on SDGs Indicators (IAEG-SDGs) and agreed upon at the 48th session of the UN Statistical Commission. The global indicator framework was later adopted by the General Assembly (GA) and is contained in the GA Resolution on Work of the Statistical Commission pertaining to the 2030 Agenda for Sustainable Development.[171] The Statistical Commission has further agreed that the indicator framework will include annual refinements and two revisions in 2020 and 2025.[172] Among the 230 indicators of the framework 10 are directly connected to SDG 14.[173] States are encouraged to develop more specific indicators at the national or regional level.[174] International monitoring is based on national data that States report to the international statistical system.[175] The UN has been criticized for wasting more time and money in creating the list of indicators to be used to measure the progress for each SDG goal than to implement policies that will help to achieve them.[176]

Each SDG indicator falls under the responsibility of an international agency, which operates as a custodian agency for the indicator responsible for facilitating the data and information flow from the national to the global level. The custodian agencies also have the responsibility to standardize SDG indicator methodologies and to support States in strengthening national statistical capacity and reporting mechanisms. The UNEP, for example, is the custodian agency for indicators 14.1.1a, 14.1.1b, 14.2.1, and 14.5.1, and has provided a manual (Global Manual on Ocean Statistics) to guide governments and national institutions in supporting the country-level implementation of the above indicators.[177] The FAO is the custodian agency for another four indicators, 14.4.1, 14.6.1, 14.7.1, and 14.b.[178] The role of technology is crucial for the attainment of most SDG 14 targets, which are in need of data related to marine pollution, ocean acidification, IUU fishing, and other threats to the ecosystems and biodiversity. For instance, remote sensing and satellite observation technology can be relevant for targets 14.1–14.4, 14.6, 14.7, and 14.a, and for indicators 14.3, 14.5, and 14.6.[179]

---

[170] PS Chasek, 'Getting to 2030: Negotiating the Post-2015 Sustainable Development Agenda (Decision 46/101)' in United Nations Statistical Commission, Report on the Forty-Sixth Session (2015) UN Doc. E/2015/24-E/CN.3/2015/40,), 11–12.

[171] (A/RES/71/313), Annex, <https://unstats.un.org/sdgs/indicators/indicators-list/> accessed 8 April 2021.

[172] UNSC, 'Work of the UN Statistical Commission pertaining to the 2030 Agenda for Sustainable Development. Statistical Commission', 48th Session Draft Resolution as of 10 March 2017 (UNSC 2017a).

[173] UNEP, 'Understanding the State of the Ocean' (n 18) 'Executive Summary'.

[174] UNSC, 'Work of the UN Statistical Commission pertaining to the 2030 Agenda for Sustainable Development. Statistical Commission', 48th Session Draft Resolution as of 10 March 2017 (UNSC 2017a).

[175] UN, 'Report of the Inter-agency and Expert Group on Sustainable Development Goal Indicators'. Doc E/CN.3/2017/2, Annexe III, IV and V (UN 2017a).

[176] W Byanyima, 'Why Oxfam Won't Compromise on SDGs' (Greenbiz, 30 November 2016) <https://www.greenbiz.com/article/why-oxfam-wont-compromise-sdgs> accessed 18 July 2021.

[177] UNEP, 'Understanding the State of the Ocean' (n 18).

[178] UN FAO, 'Working for SDG 14. Healthy Oceans for Food Security, Nutrition and Resilient Communities' (UN FAO 2017).

[179] GEO, 'Earth Observations and Geospatial Information: Supporting Official Statistics in Monitoring and Achieving the 2030 Agenda' (GEO 2017); A Anand, 'The Big Data Revolution for Sustainable Development. Independent Evaluation Office' (Global Environmental Facility. XI Meeting of the Latin America and the Caribbean monitoring and evaluation network. Santiago de Chile, 28–30 June 2016).

1050 SDG 14

The following section reviews the targets of SDG 14 separately and analyses the steps that have been or ought to be taken for their attainment. Each target's subsection (a) refers to the sources of the target; (b) provides an empirical/statistical analysis of the target; (c) informs on implementation efforts at domestic and international level, where available; and (d) provides critique on the performance of the target thus far.

B. Analysis and Critique of Each Target

1. Target 14.1 By 2025, prevent and significantly reduce marine pollution of all kinds, in particular from land-based activities, including marine debris and nutrient pollution

a) Source of target

Oceans gravely suffer from pollution and target 14.1 aims to reduce its impacts. The majority of pollution in the oceans results from land-based sources, which explains the specific focus of target 14.1.[180] The target specifically refers to marine debris and nutrient pollution. Marine debris is essentially marine litter, that is, human-created waste that has accidentally or deliberately been released in the ocean. It is estimated that up to 80 per cent of all litter in the seas is made of plastic.[181] Nutrient pollution refers to contamination by excessive inputs of nutrients in the oceans. Such pollution is a primary cause of eutrophication of surface waters, in which excess nutrients (eg nutrient run-off from agriculture or domestic wastewater discharge), usually nitrogen or phosphorus, stimulate algal growth. Pollution and eutrophication are anticipated to increase by 2050.[182]

Other types of marine pollution include atmospheric pollution, pollution from vessels, and deep seabed mining pollution. The silence of target 14.1 about the dangers to the marine environment's health caused by other sources of pollution has been criticized.[183] Similarly, criticism has been expressed for the lack of mention to global warming and sea-level rise phenomena. Global warming is the result of land-based air pollution also known as blanket pollution that traps heat around the earth, and its impact knows no boundaries, affecting equally developed polluter nations and non-polluting developing or small island states. Sea-level rise is caused because of global warming, due to the added water from melting ice sheets and glaciers and the expansion of seawater as it warms. Such phenomena equally affect states, especially small

---

[180] RJ Diaz and R Rosenberg, 'Spreading Dead Zones and Consequences for Marine Ecosystems' (2012) 5891(321) Sciences 169–88; V Tunnicliffe, 'The Nature and Origin of the Modern Hydrothermal Vent Fauna' (1992) 7(4) Palaios 338–50.

[181] UNEP and GRID-Arendal, Marine Litter Vital Graphics, UNEP and GRID-Arendal, Nairobi and Arendal, 2016.

[182] SDG Report 2017, note 12, 10.

[183] S Gilman, 'Underwater Debris is Clouding Hopes for Sustainable Deep-Sea Mining' (27 April 2017) Horizon: The EU Research & Innovation Magazine <https://ec.europa.eu/research-and-innovation/en/horizon-magazine/underwater-debris-clouding-hopes-sustainable-deep-sea-mining> accessed 26 July 2021.

island states and developing states, and endanger the overarching goal of Agenda 2030 which is to limit poverty and improve food security. Despite the specific reference to land-based activities, it is clear that target 14.1 calls for the prevention and reduction of all kinds of marine pollution.

Agenda 2030 has set a tight deadline for the fulfilment of target 14.1. Even though 2025 might be criticized as being an over-ambitious and over-optimistic deadline, it is better to be seen as a serious indication of the critical state in which the ocean is.

b) Empirical analysis

Target 14.1 has been assigned two indicators: indicator 14.1.1.a, an index of coastal eutrophication; and indicator 14.1.1.b plastic debris density.[184] Indicator 14.1.1a aims to measure the state and contribution of countries to coastal eutrophication, which is one of the largest pressures on coastal environments. Coastal eutrophication can lead to serious damage to marine ecosystems and vital sea habitats and can cause the spread of harmful algal blooms. Eutrophication caused by the flow of phosphorus and nitrogen to erodible soil and aquatic ecosystems is a clear indication that forbidden point-source discharges and non-point loadings of fertilizers and nutrients take place in them.[185]

Indicator 14.1.1b concerns plastic debris density. Marine litter is an increasing threat to marine ecosystems and biodiversity, while it also has an impact on tourism, public health, and aquaculture. Plastics specifically pose an increasing threat to marine environments with an estimated 5–13 million tonnes of plastic from land-based sources ending up in marine environments.[186] How much plastic waste ends up in the ocean depends to a great extent to wastewater systems and solid waste management. According to the internationally agreed Group of Experts on the Scientific Aspects of Marine Environmental Protection (GESAMP) guidelines and the existing national data collections, it is recommended that the SDG reporting includes sub-indicators related to beach litter, floating plastic and plastic in the sea column, plastic on the sea floor, and additional optional indicators. Indicators on micro-litter may also be considered as optional.[187] States should aim to report all data related to Indicator 14.1.1, however, not all states have the capacity to do so.[188] UNEP has published a Global Manual on SDG Indicators. Regarding indicator 14.1.1.b it noted:

> There is a need to use existing data from remote sensing, citizen science and in situ monitoring to better understand marine plastics and microplastics; however, much of the research in this field is at an initial stage and in many regions only data related

[184] United Nations, 'Global Indicator Framework' <https://unstats.un.org/sdgs/indicators/Global%20Indicator%20Framework%20after%202021%20refinement_Eng.pdf> accessed 17 June 2021.

[185] Definition of eutrophication. Eutrophication: excess nutrient loading into coastal environments from anthropogenic sources, resulting in excessive growth of aquatic plants, algae, and phytoplankton. See UNEP, 'Global Manual on Oceans Statistics' <https://uneplive.unep.org/media/docs/statistics/egm/global_manual_on_ocean_statistics_towards_a_definition_of_indicator_methodologies.pdf> 11, accessed 16 July 2021.

[186] ibid.

[187] GESAMP, 'Guidelines 2019' <http://www.gesamp.org/publications/guidelines-for-the-monitoring-and-assessment-of-plastic-litter-in-the-ocean> accessed 14 May 2021.

[188] UNEP, 'Global Manual on Ocean Statistics' (n 185).

1052   SDG 14

to beach litter is available. In the marine environment, as it relates to 14.1.1b, there are four fates for marine plastics and microplastics: 1. Washed onto beaches or shore-lines (beach litter) 2. Floating on the water or in the water column 3. Deposited on the seafloor/seabed 4. Ingested by biota (e.g., sea birds). The methodology for SDG 14.1.1b includes potential measurement of these four accumulation types; however, it is also important to note the importance of monitoring information on waste management and the sources of plastic pollution for understanding plastic pollution.[189]

c) Implementation efforts at domestic/international level

According to the 2017 High-Level Political Forum implementation of target 14.1 is hampered by the 'difficulty in negotiating change across the full pathway of the problem and a lack of resources and capacity for delivery in developing countries'.[190] However, global and domestic initiatives have been taken, such as the UN Clean Seas Campaign[191] or international initiatives to make fishing gears compliant with international standards. The HLPF has further recommended the creation of novel approaches for some forms of plastics, for example micro-plastics, and cross-sectorial interventions.[192]

d) Critique

Since target 14.1 focuses on land-based marine pollution, it is worth reviewing the challenges linked to its prevention and reduction. The LOSC provides general duties to prevent land-based pollution. Article 194(2) LOSC imposes an obligation upon states to take all measures necessary to ensure that activities under their jurisdiction or control are so conducted as not to cause damage by pollution to other states and their environment, and that pollution arising from incidents or activities under their jurisdiction or control does not spread beyond the areas where they exercise sovereign rights in accordance with the LOSC. Article 194(3)(a) LOSC stipulates that measures taken shall include, *inter alia*, those designed to minimize to the fullest possible extent 'the release of toxic, harmful, noxious substances, especially those which are persistent, from land-based sources, from or through the atmosphere or by dumping'. More specifically, the LOSC provides prescriptive and enforcement jurisdiction with regard to the regulation of land-based pollution (articles 207(1)(2) and 231 LOSC). It is apparent that these obligations are quite broad. States have adopted additional instruments to tackle marine pollution from land-based sources, but these instruments are of a voluntary nature and, thus, regulation at the international level remains rather weak.[193]

---

[189] UNEP, 'Understanding the State of the Ocean' (n 18).

[190] 2017 HLPF on Sustainable Development, 'Thematic Review of SDG 14' <https://sustainabledevelopment.un.org/content/documents/14375SDG14format-revOD.pdf> accessed December 2021.

[191] <https://www.cleanseas.org/> accessed December 2021.

[192] 2017 HLPF (n 190).

[193] See, eg, the 1985 Montreal Guidelines for the Protection of the Marine Environment against Pollution from Land-Based Sources; the Washington Declaration on the Protection of the Marine Environment from Land-Based Activities and the 1995 Global Programme of Action for the Protection of the Marine Environment from Land-based activities. The 2002 Montreal Declaration on the Protection of the Marine Environment from Land-Based Activities and the 2012 Manila Declaration on Furthering the Implementation of the Global Programme Action

In contrast with other sources of pollution, the regulation of land-based pollution is extremely complicated. Land-based pollution sources vary greatly and each source needs differentiated treatment and measures.[194] Further, a variety of actors and activities are involved in pollution from land-based activities, in contrast, for example, with pollution stemming from vessels.[195] Moreover, states are reluctant to enter into legally binding instruments regulating land-based pollution due to the economic cost of related measures. Land-based pollution activities take place within the territorial sovereignty of states, and hence are closely connected to their economy and development.[196] Therefore, despite the urgent need to adopt regulatory and policy measures, such measures would prove completely ineffectual without the establishment of policing authorities that will guarantee that these regulations will be respected by local communities and industries. There is a real concern about the social and economic impact of these measures, especially by developing states. Imposing measures can have adverse effects on local industries and consequently on local employment. Subsidies, investment packages, fiscal incentives, and retraining schemes for coastal communities that will have to deal with the closure of polluting industries are the most frequently suggested solutions.[197]

Perhaps the most valid argument that justifies the short-term negative impact that these measures may have is that in the long run, measures will benefit communities and the employment rate in them due to the adoption of sustainable growth practices. What is more, insufficient protection of the marine environment from land-based pollution is also closely linked to widespread poverty in developing countries. Marine degradation generates poverty and vice versa.[198] Hence, target 14.1 is closely related to SDG 3 that concerns human welfare and health and the regulation of marine pollution can contribute to combating poverty.[199]

2. Target 14.2 By 2020, sustainably manage and protect marine and coastal ecosystems to avoid significant adverse impacts, including by strengthening their resilience, and take action for their restoration in order to achieve healthy and productive oceans

a) Source of target

Marine and coastal ecosystems suffer from serious degradation. It is estimated that some 20 per cent of coral reefs, 19 per cent of mangroves, and 29 per cent of seagrass

---

for the Protection of the Marine Environment from Land-based Activities (UNEP/GPA/IGR.3/CRP.1/Rev.1, 26 January 2012).

[194] AL Dahl, 'Land-based Pollution and Integrated Coastal Management' (1993) 17 Marine Policy 567.

[195] M Quing-Nan, *Land-Based Marine Pollution: International Law Development* (Springer 1987) 16.

[196] Tanaka (n 132) 336.

[197] V Zanten and others, 'Towards Nexus-Based Governance: Defining Interactions between Economic Activities and Sustainable Development Goals (SDGs)' (2021) 28(3) International Journal of Sustainable Development and World Ecology 210–26.

[198] Tanaka (n 132) 338.

[199] R Long and MR Chaves, 'Bridging the Ocean, Water and Climate Action Goals' in Nordquist and others (eds), *The Marine Environment and United Nations Sustainable Development Goal 14* (n 59) 101.

1054 SDG 14

habitat have been lost over about the last hundred years.[200] Sustainable management of marine areas and coastal habitats is critical for preservation and conservation. Sustainable management of marine and coastal ecosystems includes ecosystem-based approaches using conservation and management measures like spatial management measures (eg marine spatial planning). Such measures can improve the condition of marine ecosystems and the local management of fisheries.

Spatial management measures (SMM) are a type of conservation and management measures (CMM) which specify where in the ocean human activities can occur. CMM more generally are all types of measures introduced to regulate where, when, and how human activities in the ocean can take place. Such measures aim to balance the competing interests of sustainable use of the oceans, on the one hand, and nature conservation and environmental protection on the other. CMM form part of a process that is called Marine Spatial Planning (MSP).[201] Although MSP is not a term of art and no single official definition exists,[202] it can be defined as an integrated, policy-based approach, or a public process aiming at regulating, managing, and protecting the marine environment and addressing the multiple, cumulative, and potentially conflicting uses of the sea.[203] MSP is based on the allocation of marine space in order to achieve sustainable development, including the protection of marine biodiversity and the conservation of marine resources, along with social and economic objectives that have been specified through a political process.[204]

The conservation and management measures can take various forms. First, there are measures that specify the inputs to human activities in a marine management area (input measures), such as limitations on fishing activity and capacity, number of vessels allowed to fish, or shipping vessel size. Second, there are measures that specify the nature of the production process of human activities (process measures), for example, specification of fishing gear type, use of 'best available technology' or 'best environmental practice', and level of waste treatment technology. Third, there are measures that specify the outputs of human activities in a marine management area (output measures), for example, limitations of the amount of pollutants discharged to a marine area, and the allowable catch and/or by-catch.[205] Lastly, there are measures that specify

---

[200] United Nations, 'Ocean Action Hub' <https://www.oceanactionhub.org/sdg-14-targets-context-and-indicators> accessed 9 July 2021.

[201] See 'Maritime Spatial Planning' <https://ec.europa.eu/oceans-and-fisheries/ocean/blue-economy/maritime-spatial-planning_en> accessed 15 May 2021 for the terminology used by the European Commission.

[202] United Nations Environment Programme/Mediterranean Action Plan (UNEP/MAP), 'Marine Spatial Planning and the Protection of Biodiversity beyond National Jurisdiction (BBNJ) in the Mediterranean Sea', Progress Report 17 February 2017.

[203] Several definitions have been elaborated by international organizations, working groups and expert bodies, including under the UN umbrella. See, eg, UK Marine Spatial Planning Pilot Consortium Report (2006) <http://www.abpmer.net/mspp/docs/finals/MSPFinal_report.pdf> accessed 2 August 2021. The MSPP Consortium has been created to research options for developing, implementing, and managing MSP in UK coastal and offshore waters.

[204] C Ehler and F Douvere, Marine Spatial Planning: A Step-by-step Approach toward Ecosystem-based Management', Intergovernmental Oceanographic Commission and Man and the Biosphere Programme (UNESCO 2009).

[205] See KL Cochrane and SM Garcia (eds), A Fishery Manager's Guidebook—Management Measures and their Application (Wiley-Blackwell 2002).

where and when human activities can occur (spatial and temporal measures), such as specification of areas closed to fishing or other human activities, designation of precautionary areas or security zones, designation of marine protected areas, zoning of areas for specific uses, and close of fishing seasons.[206]

The effectiveness of conservation and management measures is today limited by the capacity of states for monitoring and enforcement. This is why the use of technology, in particular satellite data, can prove to be rather beneficial as a means of addressing these limitations and of improving states' capacity to monitor and enforce marine management measures.

Notably, the strictest deadline in the whole Agenda 2030 was set for target 14.2. The failure to reach the deadline may be unsurprising, but it is also a telling example of the difficulty to create global oceans governance and improve monitoring and policing of marine ecosystems.

b) Empirical analysis

The target is assessed by one indicator (14.2.1), namely the 'number of countries using ecosystem-based approaches to managing marine areas'. Essentially what indicator 14.2.1 is calling for is a continuous quantitative analysis of the number of states using ecosystem-based approaches to manage the marine ecosystems in their jurisdiction.[207] Using as an indicator the proportion of national sustainable management measures may offer an accurate picture for assessment. However, an obstacle for the fulfilment of target 14.2 is the lack of willingness by states to impose strict measures in the context of ecosystem-based approaches. Sustainable management activities in the marine environment, and in particular in the EEZs of coastal states can have a negative impact on local communities' traditional way of life and their development.

c) Critique

One important issue that needs special attention with respect to target 14.2 is that of deep seabed mining.[208] It is somehow paradoxical that at the very moment that exhaustion of the planet's natural resources causes such concern for the viability of Earth's growth model, simultaneously we observe for the very same reasons unprecedented demands for earth minerals that can be found in abundance in the ocean floor. The rising prices for these minerals due to the demands of the electronics industry, as well as the fact that metal resources are non-renewable, upgrade the ocean floor to one of the most lucrative areas for exploitation on the planet.

The exploration and exploitation of the mineral resources of the deep seabed (the Area) can only be obtained with the authorization of the International Seabed

---

[206] UNESCO 2009 at 23, Box 6.

[207] United Nations, 'Global Indicator Framework for the Sustainable Development Goals and Targets of the 2030 Agenda for Sustainable Development' (2021) <https://unstats.un.org/sdgs/indicators/Global%20Indica tor%20Framework%20afterr%202021%20refinement_Eng.pdf> accessed 12 September 2021.

[208] World Bank, 'Precautionary Management of Deep Sea Mining Potential in Pacific Island Countries. Washington. D.C.' (Pacific Possible series) (2016) <http://pubdocs.worldbank.org/en/125321460949939983/Paci fic-Possible-Deep-Sea-Mining.pdf> accessed 3 August 2021.

1056 SDG 14

Authority (ISA) pursuant to the LOSC's and the 1994 Implementation Agreement's provisions. The ISA is the international organization that exercises control over activities in the Area[209] and has to guarantee that those activities are carried out for the benefit of humankind as a whole (article 140(1) LOSC). Mining at such depths has not started yet but the technology exists, and the ISA has already granted licences. It is estimated that 1.3 million square kilometres of the ocean floor is covered under ISA licences for deep seabed mining. Equally worrying with this number is the concentration of these licences in one area, that is, the Pacific Ocean and the Clarion–Clipperton Zone in particular.[210]

Proponents of deep seabed drilling claim that seabed sources are extremely rich and concentrated in smaller areas than land-based ones, hence the environmental damage which will be caused by seabed drilling will be less in comparison to its land equivalent, as well as that the financial benefits will outweigh any damage caused to the local ecosystems.[211] Taking advantage of our limited scientific knowledge about deep seabed ecosystems, industry experts downplay seabed mining's impact on them, while they highlight the economic importance of the rare minerals for the transition to a green/blue economy.

The ISA's task relating to the marine environment is to set the regulatory conditions under which deep seabed mining can proceed without causing serious harm to the marine environment. Deep seabed mining may impact fish stocks that are significant for the economies of states.[212] Stocks like tuna or squid live in the water column above mining areas (according to the contracts concluded by the ISA) and they feed on plankton.[213] Deep seabed mining is likely to affect the pelagic biota and possibly lead to smaller standing stocks and loss of biodiversity of benthopelagic fauna.[214] Oceanic ecosystems are already burdened with problems like over-exploitation and climate change. The impacts of seabed mining on fisheries remain unknown and need to be thoroughly studied, especially in the light of ISA's mandate to regulate the exploitation of the Area in such a way that it is a benefit to humankind as a whole.[215] It will thus be critical to monitor the impacts of mining on the ecology, environment, and fishing industry when extraction begins.

---

[209] LOSC 153(2)(3)(4).

[210] Characteristically from the thirty licences that ISA had awarded for mineral exploration in depths greater than 3 kilometres until 2021, twenty-two of them are for areas of the Pacific Ocean and sixteen for the Clarion–Clipperton Zone. M Lodge and others, 'Seabed Mining: International Seabed Authority Environmental Management Plan for the Clarion–Clipperton Zone. A Partnership Approach' (2014) 49 Marine Policy 66–72. F Hauquier and others, 'Distribution of Free-Living Marine Nematodes in the Clarion–Clipperton Zone: Implications for Future Deep-Sea Mining Scenarios' (2019) 16(18) Biogeosciences 3475–89.

[211] BBC News, 'The Secret of the Ocean Floor' <https://www.bbc.co.uk/news/resources/idt-sh/deep_sea_mining> accessed 20 August 2021.

[212] CW Armstrong and others, 'Services from the Deep: Steps Towards Valuation of Deep Sea Goods and Services' (2012) 2 Ecosystem Services 2–13.

[213] UN FAO, 'Marine Policy; UN FAO, The State of World Fisheries and Aquaculture' (Rome 2016).

[214] B Christiansen and others, 'Potential Effects of Deep Sea Bed Mining on Pelagic and Benthopelagic Biota' (2020) April Marine Policy 114.

[215] JA Ardron, 'Transparency in the Operations of the ISA: An Initial Assessment' (2018) 95 Marine Policy 324–31; M Bourrel and others, 'The Common of Heritage of Mankind as a Means to Assess and Advance Equity in Deep Sea Mining' (2018) 95 Marine Policy 311–16.

The ISA has enforcement and legislative jurisdiction with respect to activities in the Area.[216] It has the power to adopt rules and regulations and it has indeed issued three regulations to date, which form the—informally called—deep seabed mining code.[217] The code is an attempt to strike a balance between a precautionary approach to activities in each area and an incremental approach to regulation, with an emphasis on gathering sufficient data to establish an environmental baseline during the exploration phase, in order to assess the range of potential environmental impacts. It is obvious that environmental considerations will need to be far more stringent during the exploitation phase, while the feedback of local communities and island nations that already have to deal with the results of mining close to their shores should be taken seriously into account. It follows that the ISA has an important role to play in the attainment of target 14.2, but also arguably of targets 14.5 and 14.7.

3. Target 14.3 Minimize and address the impacts of ocean acidification, including through enhanced scientific cooperation at all levels.

a) Source of target

Ocean acidification is directly linked with climate change and the rising levels of CO_2 levels in atmosphere.[218] Specifically, ocean acidification is the term that refers to the lowering of ocean pH from increased levels of carbon dioxide coming from the atmosphere and has considerably adverse effects on marine organisms and ecosystems.[219] Shellfish, in particular, have been singled out as the part of the ecosystem most vulnerable to acidification due to the rise in water pH preventing the formation of their shells and reproduction. In turn, this disrupts the feeding cycle of the marine ecosystems and the prey–predator response in them, leading initially to the collapse of their biodiversity and, if the rise of pH continues to their complete ruination.[220]

b) Empirical analysis

Ocean acidification and global warming together pose significant risks on ocean and coastal ecosystems.[221] Thus, target 14.3 is very closely connected to SDG 13 (climate change). The direct link of ocean acidification with climate change is also reflected at the

---

[216] LOSC Annex III, art 17(1).

[217] ISA Regulations on polymetallic nodules, polymetallic sulphides, and cobalt-rich crusts. ISA, Regulations on Prospecting and Exploration for Polymetallic Nodules in the Area (13 July 2000); Regulations on Prospecting and Exploration for Polymetallic Nodules in the Area, Doc No ISBA/19/C/17 (22 July 2013); Regulations on Prospecting and Exploration for Polymetallic Sulphides in the Area, Doc No ISBA/16/A/12/Rev.1 (7 May 2010); Regulations on Prospecting and Exploration for Cobalt-rich Ferromanganese Crusts in the Area, Doc No ISBA/18/A/11 (27 July 2012). See also, JW Moses and AM Brigham, 'Whose Benefit? A Comparative Perspective for the ISA' (2021) 131 Marine Policy 104550.

[218] K Scott, 'Ocean Acidification and Sustainable Development Goal 14: A Goal but no Target?' in Nordquist and others (eds), *The Marine Environment and United Nations Sustainable Development Goal 14* (n 59) 323.

[219] See S Dupont and H Pörner, 'A Snapshot of Ocean Acidification Research' (2013) 160 Marine Biology 1765–71; A Frommel and others, 'Ocean Acidification has Lethal and Sub-Lethal Effects on Larval Development of Yellowfin Tuna, *Thunnus albacares*' (2016) 482 Journal of Experimental Marine Biology and Ecology 18–24.

[220] D Shi and others, 'The Physiological Response of Marine Diatoms to Ocean Acidification: Differential Roles of Seawater CO2 and pH' (2019) 3(5) Journal of Phycology 521–33.

[221] J Talberth and E Niemi, 'Ocean Acidification and Warming: The Economic Toll and Implications for the Social Cost of Carbon' (2019) <https://sustainable-economy.org/wp-content/uploads/2017/02/Talberth-and-Niemi-Revised-11-30-clean.pdf> accessed 17 April 2021.

1058 SDG 14

indicator of target 14.3, namely the level of 'average marine acidity (pH) measured at agreed suite of representative sampling stations'.[222] Carbon dioxide is absorbed by the ocean and dissolves to form carbonic acid. The result is that the ocean becomes more acidic.[223]

Additionally, target 14.3 refers to enhanced scientific cooperation at all levels and thus is directly related to target 14.a that aims to 'increase scientific knowledge, develop research capacity and transfer marine technology, taking into account the Intergovernmental Oceanographic Commission Criteria and Guidelines on the Transfer of Marine Technology, in order to improve ocean health and to enhance the contribution of marine biodiversity to the development of developing countries, in particular small island developing States and least developed countries'.

As presented elsewhere in this chapter, the LOSC contains a general obligation for the protection of the marine environment, while it also establishes obligations with respect to pollution arising from various sources, for example, land-based sources and the atmosphere (articles 207, 212) offshore activities (208, 209), dumping (201), and vessels (2011). These obligations are specified in other legal instruments such as the 1979/83 MARPOL[224] and the 1972 London Convention[225] and its 1996 Protocol.[226] No instrument, however, has as a principal objective the mitigation of ocean acidification. This is despite the fact that ocean acidification is one of the most serious transboundary threats to the oceans.[227]

c) Implementation efforts at international/domestic level

The 2017 HLPF observed that the data for climate changes and their impact on the oceans are quite uncertain, especially at local scales.[228] Therefore, the functioning of marine ecosystems should be further researched in order to facilitate management and decision making related to climate change. According to predictions, ocean acidification may reach a further 100–250 per cent decrease in the upcoming years, causing changes in plankton and oxygen and affecting ecosystems in complex ways. States need to meet their obligations under the UNFCCC Paris Agreement, if not exceed them.

d) Critique

Ocean acidification is not simply a consequence of climate change, it is a major problem alongside climate change. Therefore, the separate target 14.3 responds to the need to separately focus on the matter, instead of dealing solely with climate change. Target 14.3 brings to the fore a problem that has largely remained on the periphery of climate change negotiations.

---

[222] UN SDSN, 'Indicators and a Monitoring Framework' (2012) <https://indicators.report/targets/14-3/> accessed 5 May 2021.

[223] DF Johansen and RA Vestvik, 'The Cost of Saving Our Ocean—Estimating the Funding Gap of Sustainable Development Goal 14' (2020) 112 Marine Policy 103783.

[224] International Convention for the Prevention of Pollution from Ships as Modified by the Protocol of 1978 relating thereto 1340 UNTS 62, entered into force 2 October 1983 (MARPOL 73/78).

[225] 1972 Convention for the Prevention of Marine Pollution by Dumping from Ships and Aircraft, 11 ILM (1972), 262 (London Convention) (in force 30 August 1975).

[226] 1996 Protocol to the London Convention on the Prevention of Marine Pollution by Dumping of Wastes and Other Matter (1997), 35 ILM 1 (in force 8 November 2006).

[227] Johansen and Vestvik, 'The Cost of Saving Our Ocean' (n 220).

[228] 2017 HLPF (n 190).

TARGETS AND INDICATORS

4. Target 14.4 By 2020, effectively regulate harvesting and end overfishing, illegal, unreported and unregulated fishing and destructive fishing practices and implement science-based management plans, in order to restore fish stocks in the shortest time feasible, at least to levels that can produce maximum sustainable yield as determined by their biological characteristics

a) Sources of target

Target 14.4 touches upon the highly concerning issue of overfishing, and illegal, unreported, and unregulated fishing (IUU fishing). States must adopt measures and policies to stop IUU fishing.[229] There is a close relationship between targets 14.2 and 14.4 since there is a need to have an ecosystem approach to fisheries to integrate exploitation and conservation. The target had imposed the tight deadline of 2020, highlighting the critical state at which fisheries are.

b) Empirical analysis

Target's 14.4 indicator (14.4.1) is the 'proportion of fish stocks within biologically sustainable levels'. The indicator is by necessity global, since fish migrate across marine areas of national and beyond national jurisdiction. Stock assessment through collection of relevant data is of course a difficult and technically demanding task. The collection of data on fisheries is a cornerstone of fish stock assessment.[230] Despite the challenges in the assessment of the indicator, the content of target 14.4 is straightforward.

c) Implementation efforts at domestic/international level

Sustainable fisheries management requires scientific knowledge, effective decision-making, and an effective monitoring and enforcement framework and capacity. It is worth reviewing here the fisheries management framework of the high seas and identifying the challenges in the attainment of target 14.4.

As outlined in Section III of this chapter, cooperation is central in fisheries conservation. The duty to cooperate with other states, especially through regional arrangements, is a legal requirement twinned with the enjoyment of the freedom to access high seas living marine resources. The LOSC, the UNFSA, the 1995 FAO Code of Conduct, and the IPOA-IUU all encourage states to cooperate through regional organizations and other arrangements for the conservation and management of marine resources and the protection of the marine environment. States are, thus, expected to participate through regional arrangements in the development and adoption of CMM for high seas fisheries as well as their effective enforcement by vessels, whether flying the flags of participating states or not.

The mechanism through which states typically work together towards the conservation, development and management of fisheries are the Regional Fisheries Bodies (RFBs). According to FAO, the mandates of RFBs vary. Some RFBs have an advisory

---

[229] UN FAO, 'FAO Review of the State of World Marine Fishery Resources', FAO Fisheries and Aquaculture Technical Paper 569, FAO, Rome, 2011.
[230] Johansen and Vestvik, 'The Cost of Saving Our Ocean' (n 220).

1060 SDG 14

mandate, while others that are called RFMOs 'have the mandate to establish fisheries conservation and management measures that are binding on their members'.[231]

RFMOs cover the world's marine and inland regions and have diverse scope of coverage both geographically and materially; some regulate activities with respect to specific species of marine living resources wherever they are found in the oceans (eg tuna and salmon), others are concerned with all the marine living resources of a certain region (sea or ocean), and several others have a quite restricted scope both geographically and materially.[232] RFMOs exhibit considerable diversity and varying rates of progress in their approaches to incorporating environmental protection principles and biodiversity conservation objectives into their management regimes. In general, the ecosystem-based approach to fisheries management and the application of the precautionary principle are considered fundamental for the attainment of high long-term benefits and the minimization of the risk of irreversible change to marine ecosystems.[233] These approaches are informed by scientific knowledge (stock assessment; understanding of the aquatic environment; impacts of fishing and non-fishing related activities) and the key elements of the UNFSA and the FAO Code of Conduct.

The measures and practices of the RFMOs also vary. RFMOs may take input measures in order to restrict the intensity of the fishing effort.[234] Quantitative input measures limit the entry to a fishery, by constraining the number, the type, or the size of vessels used in a particular fishery or the number of gear units allowed to operate (fishing capacity controls), or the amount of fishing time allowed (vessel usage controls). Qualitative input measures include requirements for the mesh or hook size or for the type of fishing gear. Moreover, output measures aim to directly limit catch or qualitative characteristics of the catch, hence significantly protecting recreational fisheries. Quantitative restrictions include total allowable catches (TACs), quotas, trip limits, or bag limits. Qualitative aspects of output measures include size, sex, or maturity level limits.[235] Limiting by-catch, through excluder devices, acoustic deterrents, or mesh requirements, is also considered as output control.[236]

---

[231] See UN FAO, 'What are Regional Fishery Bodies (RFBs)?' <http://www.fao.org/fishery/topic/16800/en> accessed 21 September 2021.

[232] See indicatively, species-specific: North Atlantic Salmon Conservation Organisation (NASCO), North Pacific Anadromous Fish Commission (NPAFC), Convention on the Conservation and Management of Pollock Resources in the Central Bering Sea (CCBSP), North Atlantic Marine Mammal Commission (NAMMCO); region-specific: Commission for the Conservation of Antarctic Marine Living Resources (CCAMLR), General Fisheries Commission for the Mediterranean (GFCM), North-East Atlantic Fisheries Commission (NEAFC), North Pacific Fisheries Commission (NPFC), Northwest Atlantic Fisheries Organisation (NAFO), South East Atlantic Fisheries Organisation (SEAFO), Southern Indian Ocean Fisheries Agreement (SIOFA), South Pacific Regional Fisheries Management Organisation (SPRFMO); species-region-specific: Commission for the Conservation of the Southern Bluefin Tuna (CCSBT), Indian Ocean Tuna Commission (IOTC), Inter-American Tropical Tuna Commission (IATTC), International Commission for the Conservation of Atlantic Tunas (ICCAT), Western and Central Pacific Fisheries Commission (WCPFC).

[233] R Warner, 'Conserving Marine Biodiversity in Areas Beyond National Jurisdiction: Co-Evolution and Interaction with the Law of the Sea' in Rothwell and others (eds), *The Oxford Handbook of the Law of the Sea* (n 61) 759.

[234] J Pope, 'Input and Output Controls' in KL Cochrane (ed), *A Fishery Manager's Guidebook—Management Measures and Their Application* (FAO 2002).

[235] AK Morison, 'Input and Output Controls in Fisheries Management: A Plea for more Consistency in Terminology' (2004) 11 Fisheries Management and Ecology 411, 412.

[236] Pope (n 144).

Further, area and seasonal fishing restrictions are a common practice among RFMOs. Area restrictions limit the geographic region within which harvesting is allowed. They are usually temporary, lasting during spawning or as long as juveniles grow to a full size or during the rebuilding phase of a fishery if needed.[237] Area or time restrictions are essentially a form of input control, but because of their extended use and significance for various objectives, they can be addressed separately.[238] Marine protected areas (MPAs) is the most commonly used restriction of this type including closed seasons, no-take zones, marine sanctuaries, or marine reserves.

d) Critique

From the above analysis, it follows that RFMOs are essentially the organizations responsible for the management of fisheries and the impact of fishing activities on marine ecosystems. However, and in spite of having quite extensive powers, most RFMOs have faced significant challenges in managing the fish stocks for which they are responsible on various levels. The operation of RFMOs has been brought under scrutiny and there have been increasing calls for better performance by stakeholders and international organizations.[239]

As far as the challenges that the RFMOs are facing are concerned, first, managing fish stocks is quite complex from a scientific point of view. The resources are invisible and do not respect maritime boundaries or jurisdictional areas, while the impact of fishing or non-fishing-related activities is not always discernible. Inadequacy of relevant scientific knowledge in combination with inevitable policy considerations of the various stakeholders (such as allocation of fishing opportunities) may bring disagreements in the RFMOs decision-making processes regarding the adoption of CMM. Also, the measures taken by an RFMO might be undermined as a result of fishing by vessels flying the flag of non-Member States (which are often flags of convenience or non-compliance), sometimes operated by nationals of Member States of the RFMO who have re-registered their vessels under such flags specifically to avoid being bound by the RFMO's measures. More importantly, routine monitoring and enforcement of CMM and especially SMM requires large capacity and incurs high costs on states. Thus, the adoption of measures might look good on paper but the potential inability or unwillingness of RFMO members to monitor and take enforcement action render them pointless.[240] Technology may be proved rather helpful in that respect. For example, initiatives like Google's Global Fishing Watch and Pew Charitable Trusts' Project Eyes on

---

[237] See *inter alia* the 'blue ling closed area' of NEAFC <https://www.neafc.org/closures/blueling> accessed 18 September 2021.

[238] S Hall, 'The Use of Technical Measures in Responsible Fisheries' in Cochrane (ed), *A Fishery Manager's Guidebook* (n 234).

[239] *Inter alia* 2016 UN Fish Stocks Review Conference (19 December 2019). A/CONF.210/2016/5; UN GA A/RES/74/18.

[240] KL Dhanjal-Adams and others 'Optimizing Disturbance Management for Wildlife Protection: The Enforcement Allocation Problem' (2016) 53(4) Journal of Applied Ecology 1215.

1062   SDG 14

the Seas use real-time data from vessel transponders and satellite imagery to spot IUU fishing.[241]

5. **Target 14.5 By 2020, conserve at least 10 per cent of coastal and marine areas, consistent with national and international law and based on the best available scientific information**

a) Sources of target

Target 14.5 requires the conservation of at least 10 per cent of coastal and marine areas by 2020. This deadline was overly ambitious. According to the 2017 SDG Report, protected areas covered 13.2 per cent of areas under national jurisdiction and only 0.25 per cent of areas beyond national jurisdiction.[242] The protection of marine areas is essential for protecting the oceans biodiversity and natural resources.

b) Empirical analysis

The agreed indicator for target 14.5 is 'coverage of protected areas in relation to marine areas' (14.5.1). In other words, indicator 14.5.1 measures the MPAs and the marine areas they cover on a global scale. The data for the indicator are nationally and internationally available as they are regularly reported by national authorities to international databases like the World Database on Protected Areas (WDPA), which is curated by UNEP-WCMC, with support from International Union for Conservation of Nature (IUCN).[243] The indicator is valuable although it could be more beneficial if it was further nuanced; for instance, if it was complemented with information on the biodiversity value of the protected areas or the rate of threat the areas face. Finally, as outlined elsewhere in this chapter, management effectiveness is one of the most important problems of area-based management tools and specifically MPAs. This is due to the scarce resources for enforcement, the regulatory complexity in the field and the competition between activities and actors.

c) Implementation efforts at domestic/international level

Environmental management plans can contribute to the implementation of this Target.[244] In that regard, the ISA has adopted regional environmental management plans for the Area, specifically for the Clarion–Clipperton Zone.[245] Regional environmental management plans (REMPs) are developed to (i) provide the relevant organs of ISA, as well as contractors and their sponsoring states, with proactive area-based

[241] A Maaroof, 'Big Data and the 2030 Agenda for Sustainable Development', Final draft report. UNESCAP meeting session 4 (14–15 December, Bangkok, Thailand, 2015).

[242] SDG Report 2017, at 10.

[243] IUCN, 'World Database on Protected Areas' (2018) <https://www.iucn.org/theme/protected-areas/our-work/world-database-protected-areas> accessed 5 August 2021.

[244] D Diz and others, 'Mainstreaming Marine Biodiversity into the SDGs: The Role of Other Effective Area-Based Conservation Measures (SDG 14.5)' (2018) 93 Marine Policy 251–61.

[245] The first REMP for the Clarion–Clipperton Zone was adopted by the Council in 2012 (ISBA/18/C/22), on the basis of the recommendation of the Legal and Technical Commission (LTC) (ISBA/17/LTC/7). This included the designation of a network of nine 'Areas of Particular Environmental Interest' (APEIs). Such APEIs are protected from future exploitation of mineral resources in the Area.

and other management tools to support informed decision-making that balances resource development with conservation; and (ii) provide ISA with a clear and consistent mechanism to identify particular areas thought to be representative of the full range of habitats and biodiversity and ecosystem structures and functions within the relevant management area. The ISA has explicitly stated that REMPs help ISA to 'meet globally agreed goals and targets, such as Sustainable Development Goal 14'.[246]

d) Critique

For the target to be effective, a clearer understanding of the status of marine ecosystems is needed. As 2017 HLPF observes 'determining the objectives of initiatives and measuring effectiveness still needs greater investment and focus'.[247] Further, the development and conclusion of the new agreement for Biodiversity Protection Beyond National Jurisdiction will facilitate and enhance the conservation and management frameworks.

6. Target 14.6 By 2020, prohibit certain forms of fisheries subsidies which contribute to overcapacity and overfishing, eliminate subsidies that contribute to illegal, unreported and unregulated fishing and refrain from introducing new such subsidies, recognizing that appropriate and effective special and differential treatment for developing and least developed countries should be an integral part of the World Trade Organization fisheries subsidies negotiation

a) Sources of target

Target 14.6 is linked with a rather complex issue relating to fishery management, that is, the direct or indirect payments by states to the fishing industry, be it small-scale fishermen, or global marine fishing fleets. Thus, it is perhaps necessary to distinguish between different types of subsidies based on their recipients. Subsidies to artisanal fishers may be beneficial for local communities' economy and culture. Similarly beneficial are subsidies towards fisheries management related scientific research. Most developing and least developed countries and SIDS lack the capacity to conduct relevant research and foster data collection and sustainable marine management policies. Indeed, target 14.4 explicitly recognizes the need for special and differential treatment for developing and least developed states in that respect.

In general, however, subsidies are detrimental and responsible for the overexploitation and depletion of fish stocks. International fleets are heavily subsidized and are responsible for illegal and unreported fishing with an estimated value of several billions of dollars. Harmful fisheries subsidies are estimated to total more than $20 billion a year.[248] Prohibiting and eliminating fisheries subsidies will release important resources that can be redirected to the development of sustainable

---

[246] ISA, 'Environmental Management Plan' (2019) <https://www.isa.org.jm/minerals/environmental-management-plan-clarion-clipperton-zone>, accessed 8 September 2021.
[247] 2017 HLPF (n 190).
[248] M Kituyi, '90 Per Cent of Fish Stocks Are Used Up—Fisheries Subsidies Must Stop' (13 July 2018) <https://unctad.org/news/90-fish-stocks-are-used-fisheries-subsidies-must-stop> accessed 4 August 2021.

1064   SDG 14

marine policies, collection of data and scientific research, as well as to monitoring and enforcement of rules combating IUU fishing. Further, enforcement and sanctions must be directed predominantly against international fishing fleets and not local communities.[249]

b) Empirical analysis

Indicator 14.6.1 refers to the degree of implementation of international instruments aiming to combat illegal, unreported, and unregulated fishing. In that regard, we may briefly refer to the FAO Compliance Agreement, the UNFSA, the 1995 FAO Code of Conduct for Responsible Fisheries (1995 FAO Code),[250] the 2001 International Plan of Action to prevent, deter, and eliminate IUU fishing (IPOA-IUU),[251] the Agreement on Port State Measures (PSMA),[252] and the Voluntary Guidelines for Flag State Performance.[253]

c) Implementation efforts at domestic/international level

The FAO Compliance Agreement aims to enhance the role of flag states and safeguard that a state strengthens its control over its vessels to ensure compliance with international conservation and management measures. One of the principal reasons for embarking on the negotiation of what became the FAO Compliance Agreement was to tackle the problem of 'reflagging'.[254] The agreement notes the special responsibility of flag states to ensure that all their vessels fishing on the high seas are authorized. Moreover, states shall only authorize a vessel to fish if it is satisfied that 'it is able, taking into account the links that exist between it and the fishing vessel concerned, to exercise effectively its responsibilities under this Agreement in respect of that fishing vessel'.[255] This provision seeks to prevent the 'reflagging' of vessels fishing on the high seas under the flags of states that are unable or unwilling to enforce international fisheries conservation and management measures (what has been described above as 'flags of non-compliance'). Moreover, states shall not authorize any vessel previously registered in another state that has undermined the effectiveness of international conservation and management measures.[256] This is intended to limit the ability of vessels with a bad compliance record to shop around for a new flag.[257] Each state shall also maintain

---

[249] D Diz and others, 'Marine Policy Special Issue: SDG Synergies for Sustainable Fisheries and Poverty Alleviation' (2019) Marine Policy 110, 110.

[250] The Code of Conduct for Responsible Fisheries (FAO Res 4/95) (31 October 1995) available at <http://www.fao.org/3/v9878e/V9878E.pdf> (1995 FAO Code).

[251] 2001 International Plan of Action to prevent, deter and eliminate IUU fishing (2 March 2001) <http://www.fao.org/3/a-y1224e.pdf> (IPOA-IUU).

[252] Agreement on Port State Measures to Prevent, Deter and Eliminate Illegal, Unreported and Unregulated Fishing (adopted 22 November 2009, entered into force 5 June 2016) 55 ILM 1157 (2016) (PSMA).

[253] FAO, 'Voluntary Guidelines on Flag State Performance' (13 June 2014) <http://www.fao.org/3/a-i4577t.pdf> accessed 22 August 2021.

[254] R Churchill, 'The International Framework of Fisheries Management' in R Churchill and D Owen (eds), The EC Common Fisheries Policy (Oxford European Union Law Library 2010) 105.

[255] Art III(3) FAO Compliance Agreement.

[256] With limited exceptions, see art III(5) FAO Compliance Agreement.

[257] Churchill (n 254) 105.

a complete record of fishing vessels entitled to fly its flag and authorized to be used for fishing on the high seas.[258]

Enforcement and international cooperation are also covered extensively by the provisions of the FAO Compliance Agreement. Flag states must enforce the Agreement in respect of their vessels and provide sanctions of sufficient gravity to be effective in securing compliance and depriving offenders of the benefits of their illegal activities.[259] Other parties shall assist the flag state in exercising its enforcement responsibilities through the exchange of information and the provision of evidentiary material. Such assistance includes, for the first time in a multilateral fisheries agreement, a degree of port state control.[260] Where a party to the Agreement reasonably believes that a fishing vessel in one of its ports has been used for an activity that undermines the effectiveness of international conservation and management measures, it shall promptly notify the flag state.[261]

The UNFSA aims to ensure the long-term conservation and sustainable use of straddling fish stocks and highly migratory fish stocks, while its provisions apply to areas beyond national jurisdiction.[262] The FSA requires states to apply the precautionary approach widely to conservation, management and exploitation of straddling fish stocks and highly migratory fish stocks and introduces detailed procedures for putting this approach into practice.[263] These detailed guidelines are one of the distinctive features of the Agreement. The general principles underlying the measures which states are required to take include assessment of impact; the adoption of conservation and management measures for species belonging to the same ecosystem or associated with the target stocks; and minimizing pollution, waste, and discards.[264]

Part III UNFSA deals with the mechanisms for international cooperation. One of the central concepts underlying the Agreement is the development of fisheries management through regional organizations. Article 8 UNFSA encourages states to create sub-regional or regional fisheries organizations to ensure the effective conservation of straddling and highly migratory fish stocks. Under this provision, access to the fish stocks is limited to flag states which are members of the relevant fisheries organization or which agree to apply the conservation and management measures established by the organization.[265] In other words, it restricts participation in high seas fisheries to 'those who play by the rules'.[266]

The UNFSA retains the centrality of the principle of flag state jurisdiction but it spells out in greater detail what is expected from States in the exercise of that jurisdiction.[267]

[258] Art IV FAO Compliance Agreement.
[259] Art III(8) FAO Compliance Agreement.
[260] Churchill (n 254) 105.
[261] Art V(2) FAO Compliance Agreement.
[262] Art 2 and 3 UNFSA. Note, however, that some of its provisions also apply to the EEZ of State Parties, see R Barston, 'The Law of the Sea and Regional Fisheries Organizations' (1999) 14(3) International Journal of Marine and Coastal Law 333–36.
[263] Art 6 UNFSA.
[264] See N Matz-Lück and J Fuchs, 'Marine Living Resources' in Rothwell and others (eds), *The Oxford Handbook of the Law of the Sea* (n 61) 491ff.
[265] Art 8(4) UNFSA.
[266] Reyfuse, 'Regional Fisheries Management Organizations' (n 110) 810.
[267] ibid. Part V, art 18 UNFSA.

1066   SDG 14

Article 18 UNFSA provides a detailed, though non-exhaustive list of measures that are to be taken by flag states to 'effectively control' their vessels.[268] The general duty is described in the first paragraph of the article which provides that every state 'whose vessels fish on the high seas shall take such measures as may be necessary to ensure that vessels flying its flag comply with sub-regional and regional conservation and management measures and that such vessels do not engage in any activity which undermines the effectiveness of such measures'. The duty of flag states to exercise control under article 18 includes licensing, regulations, prohibition of unauthorized fishing, establishment of national record of authorized fishing vessels, requirements for markings as well as recording and reporting position, catch, and other fisheries data. The UNFSA further includes provisions on the duty of states to monitor, control, and surveil vessels flying their flags as well as their fishing operations and related activities. The list of proposed measures for States Parties to discharge this duty includes inspection schemes and observers programme (either national or sub-regional and regional) as well as VMS. This is only an indicative list of measures, as seen by the use of the term 'inter alia' in the relevant provision.[269]

Importantly, Part VI UNFSA contains compliance and enforcement provisions. The agreement puts, once more, emphasis on the role of the flag state which shall ensure compliance by vessels flying its flag with sub-regional and regional conservation and management measures for straddling fish stocks and highly migratory fish stocks and shall enforce such measures irrespective of where violations occur.[270] Article 20 UNFSA establishes the obligation of states to cooperate, either directly or through sub-regional or regional arrangements, to ensure compliance with conservation measures. A very interesting feature of the agreement is article 21, which complements article 20 and the obligation to cooperate. Article 21 strengthens the enforcement of regional conservation and management measures by providing for a broad boarding and inspection scheme. This scheme not only extends beyond the confines of flag state enforcement but also extends to vessels of states parties to the UNFSA which do not participate to the regional arrangement that has established the conservation and management measures in question:

> In any high seas area covered by a sub-regional or regional fisheries management organization or arrangement, a State Party which is a member of such organization or a participant in such arrangement may, through its duly authorized inspectors, board and inspect, ... fishing vessels flying the flag of another State Party to this Agreement, *whether or not such State Party is also a member of the organization or a participant in the arrangement*, for the purpose of ensuring compliance with conservation and management measures for straddling fish stocks and highly migratory fish stocks established by that organization or arrangement.[271]

---

[268] Reyfuse, 'Regional Fisheries Management Organizations' (n 110) 810–11.
[269] See art 18(g) UNFSA.
[270] Art 19 UNFSA.
[271] Art 21(1) UNFSA (emphasis added). The following paragraphs of the provision provide further details for the establishment of the boarding and inspection scheme.

The intention of these detailed provisions of the UNFSA is to deter the reflagging of vessels and eliminate the aforementioned problem of flags of convenience and flags of non-compliance by obliging states to take their duty to take conservatory measures under article 117 LOSC seriously.[272] It gives precise content to the duty and ends 'free and unlimited access [to high seas fisheries] ... as this is now tied to and limited by the conditions imposed by collective action'[273] through regional fisheries bodies. It thus provides a strong legal basis for the effective enforcement of regional conservation measures on the high seas.

The 1995 FAO Code is a non-binding instrument[274] with a particularly broad, all-embracing scope, both personal and material. First of all, it refers not only to fisheries management—within both national jurisdiction and the high seas—but also to aquaculture development, integration of fisheries into coastal area management, post-harvest practices and trade, and fisheries research.[275] Moreover it is addressed not only to states but also to 'fishing entities',[276] governmental and non-governmental organizations, and every other actor involved in fisheries. The Code describes principles and management practices which states have agreed should be applicable whenever and wherever fishing takes place. The aim of the Code is to '[set] out principles and international standards of behaviour for responsible practices with a view to ensuring the effective conservation, management and development of living aquatic resources, with due respect for the ecosystem and biodiversity'.[277]

To provide further guidance to states on implementing the 1995 FAO Code, the FAO has led further negotiations on supplementary International Plans of Action, which are non-binding. In 2001 FAO adopted the Plan of Action to prevent, deter, and eliminate IUU fishing. The objective of the IPOA is to 'prevent, deter and eliminate IUU fishing by providing all States with comprehensive, effective and transparent measures by which to act, including through appropriate' RFBs.[278] Although applying to both areas within national jurisdiction and the high seas, the IPOA is primarily aimed at high seas fishing. It covers flag state (registration, authorization, and maintenance of records of their vessels), port state (inspection and prohibition of the landing of catches), coastal state (authorization, effective monitoring), and market state (prevent trade in fish caught in IUU fishing) responsibilities, while it envisages broad participation and coordination among states, as well as representatives from industry, fishing communities, and non-governmental organizations, and the use of a comprehensive and integrated approach, so as to address all impacts of IUU fishing. According to the Plan, all states should, among others, take all possible steps to discourage their nationals from

---

[272] ibid.

[273] L Juda, 'The 1995 Nations Agreement on Straddling Fish Stocks and Highly Migratory Fish Stocks: A Critique' (1997) 2(28) Ocean Development & International Law 147–55.

[274] Art 1.1 1995 FAO Code: This Code is voluntary.

[275] Churchill (n 254) 107.

[276] This is probably a reference to Taiwan. See ibid.

[277] Introduction, 1995 FAO Code.

[278] FAO, 'Report of the Twenty-Fourth Session of the Committee on Fisheries—Rome' (2001) <https://www.fao.org/3/Y2161E/y2161e0p.htm> para 8, accessed 7 August 2021.

1068   SDG 14

engaging in IUU fishing. Paragraph 18 of the Plan provides that 'without prejudice to the primary responsibility of the flag State on the high seas, each State should, to the greatest extent possible, take measures or cooperate to ensure that nationals subject to their jurisdiction do not support or engage in IUU fishing. All States should co-operate to identify those nationals who are the operators or beneficial owners of vessels involved in IUU fishing.' This guideline goes beyond the traditional requirement of control over vessels and extends to 'control over nationals'. Recognizing that fishing activities are carried out by individuals, not by vessels, making citizens abroad liable to domestic sanctions for IUU fishing is a powerful disincentive that is considered an effective tool for the enforcement of fisheries regulations in the high seas.[279] This is an elaboration on articles 116 and 117 LOSC which establish the right for the nationals of all states to engage in fishing on the high seas subject to the states' treaty obligations as well as the duty of all states 'to take, or to cooperate with other States in taking, such measures for their respective nationals as may be necessary for the conservation of the living resources of the high seas'.

The PSMA is the first binding international agreement to specifically target IUU fishing. Its main objective is to prevent, deter, and eliminate IUU fishing by preventing vessels engaged in IUU fishing from using ports and landing their catches. The basic premise of the agreement is that under international law, foreign vessels do not enjoy an automatic right to enter port. This is because ports are within a state's internal waters and thus within its exclusive territorial jurisdiction.[280] Accordingly, coastal states have the right to set conditions regarding the admission of foreign vessels to their ports and can take measures to prevent the breach of such conditions.[281] Hence, they are in a position to enforce international regulations effectively as a condition of access to their ports, having been hailed as a 'powerful and cost-effective means' of combating IUU fishing.[282]

Although there are provisions regarding port state measures for the enforcement of fisheries regulations in previous agreements,[283] the role of the port state is significantly fortified throughout the PSMA in key innovative areas. The Agreement requires the denial of use of ports at three separate points of time: prior to entry into port, upon entry

---

[279] See Ministerially led OECD High Seas Task Force Report, 'Closing the Net: Stopping Illegal Fishing on the High Seas' (Governments of Australia, Canada, Chile, Namibia, New Zealand, and the United Kingdom, WWF, IUCN and the Earth Institute at Columbia University 2006) 34–35 <https://d2ouvy59p0dg6k.cloudfront.net/downloads/high_seas_task_force_report.pdf> accessed 10 September 2021.

[280] See arts 2 and 8 LOSC on internal waters. Art 2 refers to states' sovereignty over internal waters and the territorial sea. Para 3 stipulates that sovereignty over the territorial sea must be exercised subject to the LOSC but places no limitations on sovereignty over internal waters. See further the definition of innocent passage at art 18, LOSC where it becomes clear that the right of innocent passage through the territorial sea does not include a right to enter the internal waters of a state or call at a port facility.

[281] Art 25(2) LOSC on the rights of protection of coastal states further specifies that '[i]n the case of ships proceeding to internal waters or a call at a port facility outside internal waters, the coastal State also has the right to take the necessary steps to prevent any breach of the conditions to which admission of those ships to internal waters or such a call is subject'. An exception to this rule can be found for cases of *force majeure* or distress—see, eg, International Convention for the Safety of Life at Sea (SOLAS) (adopted 1 November 1974, entered into force 25 May 1980) 1184 UNTS 2, arts IV and V and PSMA arts 10 and 11(2).

[282] See Preamble to PSMA.

[283] See, eg, art 23 UNFSA and IPOA-IUU [52–64].

into port, and after inspection. In the first occasion, the port state shall require specific information to be submitted by the vessel before granting entry to a vessel to its port[284] in order to determine in advance whether the vessel requesting entry into its port has engaged in IUU fishing or fishing related activities. If there is sufficient proof of such illegal activities, the port state must deny access to port and communicate this decision to the flag state as well as to any relevant coastal states and appropriate RFMOs.[285] Alternatively, it may grant access to port for the purposes of inspecting the vessel and taking appropriate actions in conformity with international law which are at least as effective as denial of port entry in preventing, deterring, and eliminating IUU fishing.[286]

Once a vessel has entered the ports of a state, PSMA provides the obligation of states to deny the use of its ports for landing, transshipping, packaging, and processing of fish that have not been previously landed as well as other port services including refuelling and resupplying, maintenance, and dry docking, in the following cases: when the vessel cannot present a valid and applicable authorization to fish as required by its flag state or by a coastal state in respect of areas under the national jurisdiction of that state; when the port state receives clear evidence that the fish on board was taken in contravention of applicable requirements of a coastal state in respect of areas under the national jurisdiction of that state; when the flag state does not confirm within a reasonable time that the fish on board was taken in accordance with applicable requirements of a relevant regional fisheries management organization; when the port state has reasonable grounds to believe that the vessel was otherwise engaged in IUU fishing or fishing-related activities unless the vessel can establish otherwise.[287]

States Parties to the PSMA also undertake the obligation to inspect a certain number of vessels in their ports, sufficient to achieve the objective of PSMA.[288] The annual level of inspections is agreed among parties through appropriate RFMOs, FAO or otherwise. In such inspections priority must be given to vessels suspected to have engaged in illegal activities or that have been previously denied access to port as well as vessels with respect to which the port state has received requests or evidence by other states. The port state must complete an inspection report and communicate the report to all relevant actors (flag state, coastal states, states of nationality of the master of the vessel, RFMOs, FAO, and other international organizations).[289] Where, following an inspection, there are clear grounds for believing that a vessel has engaged in IUU fishing or fishing related activities in support of such fishing, the inspecting Party shall not only notify the above but also deny the vessel access to port facilities and services.[290]

The Agreement further specifies the duties of the flag states and their interaction with the duties of port states. Part 5 of the Agreement requires states parties in their

---

[284] The minimum information to be requested is listed in Annex A of the Agreement and includes information on the vessel's and master's ID, fishing, and transhipment authorizations and total catch onboard.

[285] Art 9 PSMA.

[286] Art 9(5) PSMA.

[287] Art 11 PSMA.

[288] Art 12 PSMA.

[289] Art 15 PSMA.

[290] Art 18 PSMA.

1070   SDG 14

capacity as flag states to cooperate with port states, request inspections where their vessels are suspected to have engaged in IUU fishing, encourage their vessels to use ports of states that act consistently with the PSMA, investigate upon receipt of a port state inspection report, and report back on actions taken in this respect.[291] Lastly, an important aspect of the Agreement is that it provides a framework for assistance to developing State Parties, recognizing their special requirements in implementing the duties described in the Agreement.[292] The aim of the agreement is to reduce the incentive of vessels engaging in IUU fishing to continue to operate by blocking fishery products derived from IUU fishing from reaching national and international markets. The effective implementation of the Agreement ultimately contributes to the long-term conservation and sustainable use of living marine resources and marine ecosystems.

Lastly, the Voluntary Guidelines for Flag State Performance provide guidance to strengthen and monitor compliance by flag states with their international duties and obligations regarding the flagging and control of fishing vessels. They cover the relevant responsibilities of flag states on the basis of elements contained in international law, including binding and non-binding international fisheries instruments. Fisheries management, registration and records of vessels, authorizations, monitoring, control, surveillance (MCS), and cooperation between flag states and coastal states are among the central components of the Guidelines. The Guidelines spell out a range of actions that countries can take to ensure that vessels registered under their flags do not conduct IUU fishing, including MCS activities, such as VMS and observers. They promote information exchange and cooperation among countries so that flag states are in a position to refuse to register vessels that are 'flag-hopping' by attempting to register with another flag state or to refuse vessels that have been reported for IUU fishing. The Guidelines also include recommendations on how states can encourage compliance and take action against non-compliance by vessels, as well as on how to enhance international cooperation to assist developing states to fulfil their flag state responsibilities.

d) Critique

As the 2017 HLPF notes, international consensus to discipline subsidies is hampered by their technical complexity, political sensitivities, and the limited transparency of the nature of support measures.[293] However, the above-described framework and the separate target 14.6 facilitate the mitigation of overcapacity and overfishing in the oceans, while taking into consideration the needs of developing countries, including SIDS and LDCs.

---

[291] Art 20 PSMA.
[292] Art 21 PSMA.
[293] 2017 HLPF (n 190).

TARGETS AND INDICATORS 1071

7. Target 14.7 By 2030, increase the economic benefits to Small Island developing States and least developed countries from the sustainable use of marine resources, including through sustainable management of fisheries, aquaculture and tourism

a) Sources of target

Target 14.7 addresses the concern that time and again has been pointed out in this chapter, that is, that sustainable management measures may have adverse impacts on the economies of SIDS and LDCs. Hence, economic incentives and benefits must be given to such states to encourage the sustainable use of marine resources, including through sustainable management of fisheries, aquaculture, and tourism. This practice would bring a balance in the dilemma between exploitation/utilization of resources and conserving/preserving them.

b) Empirical analysis

Small-scale artisanal fisheries accounts for a large percentage of work in developing states.[294] The issue of small-scale fisheries and their opportunities for trade has attracted greater attention the recent years. Target's 14.7 indicator (14.7.1) refers to sustainable fisheries as a proportion of GDP in SIDS, LDCs, and all countries.

c) Implementation efforts at domestic/international level

There are a number of actions that can be taken for the fulfilment of target 14.7. Tourism is among the most frequently cited means through which SIDS would benefit from the transition to a sustainable use of marine resources. However, these provisions require checks and balances that will ensure that any financial benefits from these activities will be directed back to the local communities. In the case of tourism, entry fees, taxes on cruise ships, or a specially designed value-added tax (VAT) could be established and the benefits from them to be transferred directly to the local communities. Further, the 2015 FAO Voluntary Guidelines for Securing Sustainable Small-Scale Fisheries in the Context of Food Security and Poverty Eradication represent a global consensus on principles and guidance for small-scale fisheries governance and development.[295]

d) Critique

It is important for Agenda 2030 to ensure that SIDS can achieve their development goals. Market access is key in that respect. However, the legal and institutional framework that facilitates such access needs further development and support.

---

[294] 2017 HLPF (n 190).
[295] Available at <https://www.fao.org/documents/card/en/c/I4356EN/> accessed December 2021.

1072   SDG 14

8. Target 14.a Increase scientific knowledge, develop research capacity and transfer marine technology, taking into account the Intergovernmental Oceanographic Commission Criteria and Guidelines on the Transfer of Marine Technology, in order to improve ocean health and to enhance the contribution of marine biodiversity to the development of developing countries, in particular small island developing States and least developed countries

a) Sources of target

Target 14.a brings together marine biodiversity, marine technology, and developing states. It calls on states to invest in marine science in order to improve knowledge of marine ecosystems and environments and enhance the contribution of marine biodiversity. The abundance and richness of marine biodiversity is crucial for societies and economies as it can provide food, medicine, and building materials, among other things. The utilization of marine genetic resources for commercial purposes is called marine bioprospecting.[296] Naturally, states with more advanced technology (biotechnology) and greater resources have more opportunities for bioprospecting.

b) Empirical analysis

Scientific research and ocean observations are key to deal with the challenges related to marine ecosystems and investment in research infrastructure at national and international level will contribute to that. Thus, the indicator for target 14.1 (14.a.1) is the proportion of total research budget allocated to research in the field of marine technology.

c) Implementation efforts at domestic/international level

In relation to marine scientific research, article 257 LOSC provides that all states, irrespective of their geographical location, and competent international organizations are entitled to conduct marine scientific research in the water column beyond the limits of the EEZ. Furthermore, under article 256, all states and competent international organizations have the right to conduct marine scientific research in the Area. Marine scientific research must be conducted exclusively for peaceful purposes and with appropriate scientific methods and means compatible with the LOSC. Also, marine scientific research must not unjustifiably interfere with other legitimate uses of the sea compatible with the LOSC and must be conducted in compliance with all relevant regulations adopted in conformity with the Convention, including those for the protection and preservation of the marine environment. Furthermore, under articles 243 and 244, states and competent international organizations are obliged to cooperate in creating favourable conditions for the conduct of marine scientific research and, accordingly, to make available publication and dissemination of information and knowledge resulting from marine scientific research through appropriate channels.

Moreover, there is a number of provisions in the LOSC that touch upon the issue of equality between states in enjoying the benefits resulting from the advancement of marine technology. Article 266 paragraphs 2 and 3 read:

---

[296]   D Farrier and L Tucker, 'Access to Marine Bioresources: Hitching the Conservation Cart to the Bioprospecting Horse' (2001) 3(32) Ocean Development and International Law 214.

TARGETS AND INDICATORS 1073

2. States shall promote the development of the marine scientific and technological capacity of States which may need and request technical assistance in this field, particularly developing States, including land-locked and geographically disadvantaged States, with regard to the exploration, exploitation, conservation and management of marine resources, the protection and preservation of the marine environment, marine scientific research and other activities in the marine environment compatible with the Convention, with a view to accelerating the social and economic development of the developing States. 3. States shall endeavor to foster favorable economic and legal conditions for the transfer of marine technology for the benefit of all parties concerned on an equitable basis.

d) Critique

Target 14.a underscores the relationship between technology, biodiversity, and developing states. Developing states are confronted with an array of problems connected to the oceans, such as pollution, sea-level rise, exhaustion of resources, and coastal poverty.[297] Target 14.a can facilitate the development of developing states through the contribution of marine biodiversity.

However, the existing implementation framework does not adequately address the issue of marine genetic resources.[298] It is not clear whether marine biodiversity research or marine bioprospecting activities are considered as marine scientific research under the Convention.[299] Arguably the LOSC regime as well as the provisions of the Convention on Biological Diversity and the Nagoya Protocol are relevant to marine biodiversity research and bioprospecting activities.[300]

9. Target 14.b Provide access for small-scale artisanal fishers to marine resources and markets

a) Sources of target

Small-scale and artisanal fishers are usually part of the local communities using traditional fishing techniques and tools. Such fishers are usually at a disadvantage when it comes to market and trade access.

---

[297] J Campbell and others, 'Responding to Coastal Poverty: Should We Be Doing Things Differently or Doing Different Things?' in CT Hoanh and others (eds), *Environment and Livelihoods in Tropical Coastal Zones: Managing Agriculture-Fishery-Aquaculture Conflicts* (Cabi International 2006) 274–92.

[298] A Broggiato, 'Marine Genetic Resources beyond National Jurisdiction—Coordination and Harmonization of Governance Regimes' (2011) 1 Environmental Policy and Law 41, 35–42; D Leary, 'Moving the Marine Genetic Resources Debate Forward: Some Reflections' (2012) 2(27) International Journal of Marine and Coastal Law 435–48.

[299] P Birnie, 'Law of the Sea and Ocean Resources: Implications for Marine Scientific Research' (1995) 10(2) International Journal of Marine and Coastal Law 242 and A Soons, 'Marine Scientific Research Provisions in the Convention on the Law of the Sea: Issues of Interpretation' in ED Brown and R Churchill (eds), *The UN Convention on the Law of the Sea: Impact and Implementation* (The Law of the Sea Institute-William S. Richardson 1987).

[300] Siswandi, 'Marine Genetic Resources beyond National Jurisdiction and Sustainable Development Goals' (n 59) 205–07.

1074   SDG 14

b) Empirical analysis

Target's 14.b indicator (14.b.1) is the degree of application of a legal, regulatory, policy, and institutional framework which recognizes and protects access rights for small-scale fisheries.

c) Critique

Even though providing access to marine resources and markets for small-scale artisanal fisheries is beneficial for local economies, attention must be given to limiting the number of small-scale fishers to a certain area at any moment in order to avoid overfishing due to the sheer numbers of vessels that would concentrate in it. In any case, adopting locality as its guiding principle 14.b could have major benefits for local communities and developing nation and thus could easily be used by UN to enlist their support for the 2030 Agenda. Indeed, widening access to artisanal fishers to marine resources and assisting them to forge ties with markets could also be a major step in achieving food security for them and the communities they belong and to improve environmental sustainability.

10. Target 14.c Enhance the conservation and sustainable use of oceans and their resources by implementing international law as reflected in UNCLOS, which provides the legal framework for the conservation and sustainable use of oceans and their resources, as recalled in paragraph 158 of The Future We Want

a) Sources of target

This target explicitly refers to the Law of the Sea Convention and the legal framework that it provides. As illustrated in Section III.C, the LOSC is indeed considered the most authoritative instrument to be taken into account towards the realization of SDG 14.

b) Empirical analysis

The indicator 14.c.1 refers to the number of states making progress in ratifying, accepting and implementing through legal, policy, and institutional frameworks, ocean-related instruments that implement international law, as reflected in the LOSC, for the conservation and sustainable use of the oceans and their resources.

c) Critique

SDG 14 expands on LOSC themes such as marine pollution, fisheries, and conservation to include climate change, ocean acidification, and safeguarding economic benefits for SIDS and other developing states. Also, the future instrument for the conservation and sustainable use of marine biodiversity in areas beyond national jurisdiction will form part of the law of the sea legal framework.[301] The instrument

---

[301] *Development of an International Legally Binding Instrument under the United Nations Convention on the Law of the Sea on the Conservation and Sustainable Use of Marine Biological Diversity of Areas Beyond National Jurisdiction* (6 July 2015) UN Doc GA Res. 69/292 Agenda item 74 (*a*); UNGA, A/72/L.7, 15 November 2017.

will be designed to address matters related to marine genetic resources beyond national jurisdiction, including questions on the sharing of benefits; measures such as area-based management tools, including MPAs, environmental impact assessments, capacity building, and the transfer of marine technology.[302]

---

[302] 28 March–8 April 2016, 9–10 <http://www.iisd.ca/oceans/bbnj/prepcom1/>.

SDG 15

'Protect, Restore and Promote Sustainable Use of Terrestrial Ecosystems, Sustainably Manage Forests, Combat Desertification, and Halt and Reverse Land Degradation and Halt Biodiversity Loss'

Frederic Perron-Welch, Jorge Cabrera Medaglia, Dario Piselli, Alexandra Goodman, and Aleksandra Spasevski

I. *Travaux Préparatoires*

Sustainable Development Goal (SDG) 15[1] addresses life on land through four ambitions: (i) protecting, restoring, and promoting sustainable use of terrestrial biodiversity; (ii) sustainably managing forests; (iii) combatting desertification while halting and reversing land degradation; and (iv) halting biodiversity loss. SDG 15 builds on Millennium Development Goal (MDG) 7 of the 2000 *United Nations Millennium Declaration*[2] (Millennium Declaration), which was not well integrated across the MDGs as it was added as something of an afterthought.[3]

A. The OECD International Development Targets

The MDGs drew on the results of a mid-1990s political initiative spearheaded by the Organisation for Economic Co-operation and Development (OECD) Development Assistance Committee (DAC) in its 1995 policy statement *Development Partnerships in the New Global Context*.[4] This was followed by a set of proposed 'International Development Targets' (IDT) in 1996[5] in the 'landmark'[6] report *Shaping the 21st*

---

[1] Transforming Our World: the 2030 Agenda for Sustainable Development, UN Doc A/RES/70/1, 24.
[2] *United Nations Millennium Declaration*, UN Doc A/RES/55/2 (Millennium Declaration).
[3] BF de Souza Dias and K Garforth, 'Historical Perspectives on the Challenge of Biodiversity Conservation' in E Morgera and J Razzaque (eds), *Biodiversity and Nature Protection* (Edward Elgar 2017) 28.
[4] OECD DAC, *Shaping the 21st Century: The Contribution of Development Cooperation* (OECD 1996) Annex.
[5] S Maxwell, 'International Targets for Poverty Reduction and Food Security: A Mildly Sceptical but Resolutely Pragmatic View with a Call for Greater Subsidiarity' (1999) 30 IDS Bulletin 92, 92–93.
[6] J-P Thérien and C Lloyd, 'Development Assistance on the Brink' (2000) 21 Third World Quarterly 21, 5.

1078   SDG 15

Century: The Contribution of Development Cooperation.[7] The IDTs were principally intended to improve the impact of Official Development Assistance (ODA) on recipient countries' economic well-being[8] and social development.[9] The IDTs did include one high-level target on 'environmental sustainability and regeneration', where a 'current national strategy for sustainable development [NSSD] should be in the process of implementation in every country by 2005, to ensure that current trends in the loss of environmental resources are effectively reversed at both global and national levels by 2015'.[10]

Shaping the 21st Century clarifies the intent behind this target, indicating that there 'should be a current [NSSD] in the process of implementation, in every country by 2005, so as to ensure that current trends in the loss of environmental resources—forests, fisheries, fresh water, climate, soils, biodiversity, stratospheric ozone, the accumulation of hazardous substances and other major indicators are effectively reversed at both global and national levels by 2015'.[11] The OECD DAC described the target as being 'derived from the 1992 Rio Conference on the Environment and Development', and its intent to use NSSDs to ensure socially responsible economic development while protecting resource bases and the environment for the benefit of future generations, and supplementing other global targets established through international processes.[12]

B. The UN Millennium Declaration, Millennium Development Goals, and 2010 Biodiversity Target

The Millennium Declaration incorporated the NSSD IDT as a general goal on environmental stewardship and regeneration,[13] reaffirming support for the principles of sustainable development and a commitment to adopting a new ethic of conservation and stewardship in all environmental actions, including by: (i) ensuring the entry into force of the *Kyoto Protocol*[14] and undertaking its required greenhouse gas (GHG) emissions reductions; (ii) strengthening joint efforts for the management, conservation and sustainable development of all types of forests; (iii) pressing for the full implementation of the *Convention on Biological Diversity*[15] (CBD) and the *United Nations Convention to Combat Desertification*[16] (UNCCD); and (iv) stopping unsustainable exploitation of water resources by developing water management strategies at the regional, national

[7] OECD DAC (n 4).
[8] ibid 9–10.
[9] ibid 10.
[10] ibid 2.
[11] ibid 10.
[12] ibid 11.
[13] P Ladd, *Comments on a Post-2015 Development Framework: Goals for People and Planet?* (UNDP 2011) 2.
[14] *Kyoto Protocol to the United Nations Framework Convention on Climate Change*, 11 December 1997 (in force 16 February 2005) 2303 UNTS 162.
[15] *Convention on Biological Diversity* (in force 29 December 1993) 1760 UNTS 79.
[16] *United Nations Convention to Combat Desertification in those Countries Experiencing Serious Drought and/or Desertification, Particularly in Africa*, 14 October 1994 (in force 26 December 1996) 1954 UNTS 3.

and local levels that promoted equitable access and adequate supplies.[17] Following its adoption, the Millennium Declaration was repackaged by UN policy experts as the MDGs, which included a detailed reworking of MDG 7, and was included in UN Secretary-General Kofi Annan's 2001 'Road Map for implementing the Millennium Declaration'.[18]

Shortly thereafter, but before MDG 7 was formally adopted,[19] the 6th CBD Conference of the Parties (COP) in 2002 adopted a Biodiversity Target for 2010[20] in its *Strategic Plan for the Convention on Biological Diversity.*[21] Therein, Parties committed 'to a more effective and coherent implementation of the three objectives of the Convention, to achieve by 2010 a significant reduction of the current rate of biodiversity loss at the global, regional and national level as a contribution to poverty alleviation and to the benefit of all life on earth'.[22] The 2010 Biodiversity Target was affirmed by the 2002 Johannesburg Plan of Implementation (JPOI) of the World Summit on Sustainable Development (WSSD),[23] which also proposed 20 separate actions on biodiversity to undertake at all levels.[24]

C. The 2005 UN World Summit

High-level government representatives grudgingly accepted the UN-developed MDGs[25] in the 2005 *World Summit Outcome Document,*[26] and agreed to pursue detailed commitments under the heading of 'sustainable development: managing and protecting our common environment'.[27] Among these commitments, states pledged to support and strengthen the implementation of the UNCCD to address the causes of desertification and land degradation, and the poverty resulting therefrom. Means for better UNCCD implementation included the mobilization of adequate and predictable financial resources, technology transfer, and multi-scale capacity building.[28] Beyond UNCCD, CBD Parties were called on to support implementation of other biodiversity-related agreements, as well as uphold the Johannesburg commitment to

---

[17] Millennium Declaration paras 22–23.

[18] UN Secretary-General, *Road Map Towards the Implementation of the UN Millennium Declaration*, UN Doc A/56/326; PS Chasek and others, 'Getting to 2030: Negotiating the Post-2015 Sustainable Development Agenda Special Issue: The SDGs and International Environmental Law' (2016) 25 Review of European Comparative & International Environmental Law 5, 7.

[19] Ladd (n 13) 2: 'As late as 2005, in the build up to the World Summit, the government of the United States argued for removing the references to the MDGs in the draft Summit Outcome Document, with the rationale that they had never been agreed as such ....'

[20] A Balmford and others, 'The Convention on Biological Diversity's 2010 Target' (2005) 307 Science 212.

[21] CBD COP Decision VI/26, *Strategic Plan for the Convention on Biological Diversity.*

[22] ibid para 11.

[23] *Johannesburg Declaration and Plan of Implementation of the World Summit for Sustainable Development*, UN Doc A/CONF.199/L.6/Rev.2, para 44.

[24] ibid para 44(a)–(t).

[25] UN Secretary-General, *In Larger Freedom: Towards Development, Security and Human Rights for All*, UN Doc A/59/2005.

[26] *World Summit Outcome Document*, UN Doc A/RES/60/1, para 17; Ladd (n 13) 3.

[27] *World Summit Outcome Document*, 11.

[28] ibid para 56(b).

1080   SDG 15

significantly reduce the rate of biodiversity loss by 2010 and agreeing to fulfil these commitments[29] and to 'strengthen the conservation, sustainable management and development of all types of forests'.[30] In the same paragraph, Member States also expressed that they 'looked forward to' discussions at the 6th United Nations Forum on Forests (UNFF).

D. The Global Objectives on Forests and Non-Legally Binding Instrument on All Types of Forests

In 2006 UNFF's 6th Session set forth shared global objectives on forests (GOF) 'with a view to achieving the main objective of the international arrangement on forests and enhancing the contribution of forests to the achievement of the internationally agreed development goals, including the [MDGs], in particular with respect to poverty eradication and environmental sustainability, and emphasizing in this regard the importance of political commitment and action at all levels for effective implementation of the sustainable management of all types of forests ... [and agreeing] to work globally and nationally to achieve progress towards their achievement by 2015'.[31] These four global objectives were to: (i) reverse forest cover loss worldwide through sustainable forest management (SFM), including protection, restoration, afforestation and reforestation, while increasing efforts to prevent forest degradation; (ii) enhance forest-based economic, social, and environmental benefits, including improving livelihoods of forest-dependent peoples; (iii) significantly increase protected areas of forests worldwide and other areas of sustainably managed forests, as well as increase the proportion of forest products from sustainably managed forests; and (iv) reverse the decline in ODA for SFM while mobilizing new and varied financial resources for SFM.[32] Following UNFF 6, the UN Economic and Social Council (ECOSOC) requested UNFF 7 to conclude a Non-Legally Binding Instrument (NLBI) on all types of forests. UNFF adopted this NLBI in 2007 and it was affirmed by the UN General Assembly (UNGA) shortly thereafter.[33]

---

[29] ibid para 56(c).

[30] ibid para 56(j), 'strengthen the conservation, sustainable management and development of all types of forests for the benefit of current and future generations, including through enhanced international cooperation, so that trees and forests may contribute fully to the achievement of the internationally agreed development goals, including those contained in the Millennium Declaration, taking full account of the linkages between the forest sector and other sectors'.

[31] *United Nations Forum on Forests: Report of the Sixth Session* (27 May 2005 and 13–24 February 2006), ECOSOC Official Records, 2006 Supplement No 22, para 3.

[32] ibid.

[33] *Non-legally Binding Instrument on All Types of Forests*, UN Doc A/RES/62/98.

E. The Strategic Plan for Biodiversity 2011–2020 and UN Decade on Biodiversity

By late 2010, only some of the JPOI's twenty actions on biodiversity were successfully implemented and the 2010 Biodiversity Target was well off course.[34] At CBD COP 10 in Nagoya, Japan, a more detailed blueprint was agreed to in the *Strategic Plan for Biodiversity 2011–2020* (Strategic Plan 2011–2020) including novel approaches from the new 20 Aichi Biodiversity targets.[35] With a view to enhancing implementation, UNGA declared 2011–2020 as the UN Decade on Biological Diversity,[36] reinforcing its proclamation of 2010 as the International Year of Biodiversity.[37] Thus the UN Secretary-General was tasked with leading coordination of UN System activities for the UN Decade, with support from the CBD Secretariat, the secretariats of other biodiversity-related conventions (BRC), and relevant UN funds, programmes, and agencies.[38]

F. The UN Conference on Sustainable Development (Rio + 20) and Group of 20 (G20) Los Cabos Summit

In 2009, a UNGA resolution agreed to hold a new sustainable development conference in 2012, on the twentieth anniversary of the UN Conference on Environment and Development.[39] The 2012 conference was intended to 'secure renewed political commitment for sustainable development, assess the progress to date and the remaining gaps in the implementation of the outcomes of the major summits on sustainable development, and address new and emerging challenges'.[40]

Relevant to the present SDG Goal 15, the distinguishing theme of the 2012 United Nations Conference on Sustainable Development (Rio + 20) was the green economy in the context of sustainable development and poverty eradication.[41] More specifically, an essential question was how states can achieve 'green growth'.[42] Although many ideas and policies were introduced and endorsed at Rio + 20, no new or binding international commitments resulted.[43] The Rio + 20 Outcome Document, 'The Future We Want',[44] largely reaffirmed states' existing commitments to sustainable development, as

[34] R Adam, 'Missing the 2010 Biodiversity Target: A Wake-up Call for the Convention on Biodiversity' (2010) 21 Colorado Journal of International Environmental Law and Policy 123.

[35] *The Strategic Plan for Biodiversity 2011–2020 and the Aichi Biodiversity Targets*, UN Doc UNEP/CBD/COP/DEC/X/2.

[36] 'Convention on Biological Diversity', UN Doc A/RES/65/161, para 19.

[37] *International Year of Biodiversity, 2010*, UN Doc A/RES/61/203.

[38] ibid para 19.

[39] *Implementation of Agenda 21, the Programme for the Further Implementation of Agenda 21 and the outcomes of the World Summit on Sustainable Development*, UN Doc A/RES/64/236.

[40] M Kamau and others, *Transforming Multilateral Diplomacy: The Inside Story of the Sustainable Development Goals* (Routledge 2018) 31.

[41] ibid.

[42] ibid.

[43] EB Barbier, 'The Green Economy Post Rio+20' (2012) 338 Science 887, 887.

[44] 'The Future We Want', UN Doc A/RES/66/288, Annex.

1082 SDG 15

'[s]tates remain[ed] hesitant to adopt ... concepts that could impose hidden (or not so hidden) limitations or obligations on State conduct ... [as witnessed at Rio + 20] where delegations were enthusiastic about the opportunities presented by the green economy, but hesitant to commit to a rigid formulation of the concept'.[45]

In contrast to other UN conference outcome documents, the Rio + 20 Outcome Document was expressed in language that is decidedly non-obligatory. Rather than declaring principles, the Rio + 20 Document 'uses', 'encourages', 'recognizes', 'acknowledges', and 'stresses' as its core active words. While it endorsed the green economy as an 'important tool available for achieving sustainable development', it declined to provide a definition of green economy or draft a road map for its implementation. Further, no agreement was reached on whether the green economy should be the preferred 'means to achieve sustainable development' or just a 'decision-making framework to foster integrated consideration of the three pillars of sustainable development'.[46] Yet, states did set a high ambition at Rio + 20 when agreeing to negotiate a 'broad agenda that could enhance international coordination on all aspects of human and planetary well-being in the post-2015 period'.[47] These negotiations gave rise to UNGA's 2015 adoption of the 2030 Agenda for Sustainable Development and thus the seventeen SDGs.[48]

Concurrently with Rio + 20, a G20 meeting in Los Cabos, Mexico was underway, and its urgent focus on the ongoing post-2008 global economic crisis diminished G20 political support for 'green growth'.[49] At G20, the topic of 'Inclusive Green Growth' (IGG) was discussed in the Development Working Group (DWG) where IGG was identified as a first key challenge to development.[50] The DWG's ideas for transitioning to IGG focused on socio-economic factors[51] and assisting developing countries' economic recovery from the 2008 financial crisis.[52] Further, the Los Cabos *Leader's Declaration* only requested G20 members to recall IGG as part of their common agenda, 'in light of agreements reached at Rio + 20' and by UNFCCC.[53] Because the G20 Los Cabos meeting failed to recommend concrete actions or policies for IGG, the means to achieving MDG 7 remained a slightly modified status quo.[54]

---

[45] C Brighton, 'Unlikely Bedfellows: The Evolution of the Relationship Between Environment and Development' (2017) 66 International and Comparative Law Quarterly 209, 232.

[46] ibid 229.

[47] Chasek and others, 'Getting to 2030' (n 18) 5.

[48] 'The Future We Want', para 248.

[49] Barbier (n 43) 887.

[50] G20 Development Working Group, '2012 Progress Report' (G20 2012) paras 5–15.

[51] ibid para 8.

[52] See, eg, G20, 'Incorporating Green Growth and Sustainable Development Policies into Structural Reform Agendas: A Report by the OECD, World Bank and United Nations Prepared for the G20 Summit (Los Cabos, 18–19 June 2012)' (G20 2012). Only one page is dedicated to environmental aspects (page 60).

[53] G20, *Los Cabos Leaders Declaration* (G20 2012).

[54] H Baer and others, 'Green Economy Discourses in the Run-Up to Rio 2012' [2012] SSRN Scholarly Paper ID 2023052; Barbier (n 43).

G. Development of the Post-2015 UN Development Framework

Before Rio + 20, the 'green growth' concept was also criticized where its overtly economic focus was seen as developed countries' skewed perspective on sustainable development.[55] During the lead-up to Rio + 20, Colombia and Guatemala strongly advocated for combining the MDGs' poverty-alleviation agenda with sustainability so ecological concerns were commensurable with economic and social issues.[56] Following the political initiative and dialogues underpinning 'The Future We Want',[57] states altered the orientation of the UN development agenda by shifting the focus from developing countries to *all* states. Pursuant to the mandate in 'The Future We Want',[58] UNGA established an Open Working Group (OWG) on Sustainable Development Goals,[59] encouraged CBD Parties 'and all stakeholders, institutions and organizations concerned to give appropriate consideration to biodiversity issues in the elaboration of the post-2015 development agenda, keeping in mind the [Strategic Plan 2011–2020 and Aichi targets] and taking into account the three dimensions of sustainable development'.[60]

Given the complexity of the issues and the need to build trust, the OWG Co-Chairs initiated a 'stocktaking phase' aimed at creating a scientifically based common space to enable all stakeholders access to the same terms of reference to understand the concept of sustainability and its real applications for people, ecosystems, global prosperity, and human security.[61] To achieve this, the OWG created programme of work built around the main topics in 'The Future We Want', placing easier issues first, followed by the more challenging and contested ones.[62]

H. Negotiation of SDG Goal 15

Assisted by the UN Department of Economic and Social Affairs' 'Division for Sustainable Development' (DESA) and the OWG's Technical Support Team (TST),[63] the OWG negotiated SDG Goal 15 while also endeavouring to mainstream biodiversity across all seventeen SDGs. The OWG discussed the content of SDG Goal 15 at

---

[55] B Unmüßig and others, *Critique of the Green Economy: Toward Social and Environmental Equity* (Heinrich Böll Foundation 2012); CL Spash, 'Green Economy, Red Herring' (2012) 21 Environmental Values 95; O Bina, 'The Green Economy and Sustainable Development: An Uneasy Balance?' (2013) 31 Environment and Planning C: Government and Policy 1023; P Ferguson, 'The Green Economy Agenda: Business as Usual or Transformational Discourse?' (2015) 24 Environmental Politics 17; Kamau and others (n 40) 35.

[56] Chasek and others, 'Getting to 2030' (n 18) 8; Kamau and others (n 40) 40–43; JS Dryzek, 'Discourses' in L Rajamani and J Peel (eds), *The Oxford Handbook of International Environmental Law* (OUP 2021) 44.

[57] 'The Future We Want', UN Doc A/RES/66/288, Annex.

[58] ibid para 248.

[59] *The Open Working Group of the General Assembly on Sustainable Development Goals*, UN Doc A/RES/67/555, para (a); Kamau and others (n 40) 47–54.

[60] *Implementation of the Convention on Biological Diversity and its Contribution to Sustainable Development*, UN Doc A/RES/68/214, para 15.

[61] Kamau and others (n 40) 71.

[62] ibid.

[63] Kamau and others (n 40) 78, 86.

1084   SDG 15

its Eighth Session in February 2014 under the agenda item 'Oceans and seas, forests, biodiversity'.[64]

The TST prepared twenty-nine briefs outlining conceptual issues including social, environmental, and economic sustainability challenges. Briefs 25 and 26 were the most formative for SDG Goal 15. Brief 25 highlighted that global forests are an ecosystem of significant import to all sustainability challenges, being defined in diverse ways and playing an important role in economies. It also noted the need for the SDGs to take an integrative approach in protecting global forests. Brief 26 asserted that biodiversity is essential to supporting human well-being and serves as the foundation for many of the planet's life support systems. Brief 26 was greatly influenced and informed by the Strategic Plan 2011–2020 and the Aichi targets, which explains why Goal 15 targets 15.1, 15.2, 15.5, 15.8, and 15.9 aim for full implementation by 2020 rather than 2030.[65] Brief 5 was also influential for Goal 15 and informed targets 15.3 and 15.5. Brief 5 identified desertification, land degradation, and drought as crucial points affecting other development goals and highlighted the link between land degradation and its impact on human populations. The 'stocktaking phase' and TST briefs thus 'allowed all participants to think much more critically because they were faced with concrete information about what they wanted to do and how they would have to do it ... [this] built a common intellectual platform from which the negotiations could commence'.[66]

In July 2014, the OWG finalized and sent its proposed SDGs to UNGA, including Goal 15's text that was later adopted.[67] UNGA responded by stressing 'the importance of continued consideration of the issue of biodiversity, and encourages Member States and all stakeholders to give due consideration to this issue in the elaboration of the post-2015 development agenda'.[68] Soon after, formal intergovernmental negotiations took up the task of agreeing on the final SDG goals. Goal 15's targets were modified slightly in the March negotiations and the July session that produced the Outcome Document.[69]

At the 2015 UN Summit on Sustainable Development, where Agenda 2030 and the SDGs were adopted,[70] Goal 15 was addressed at a high-level interactive dialogue on 'Protecting our Planet and Combatting Climate Change', co-chaired by Presidents Hollande (France) and Humala (Peru). This dialogue determined that '[i]ntegrated actions are needed ... [to achieve] sustainable biodiversity management and use of natural resources, forests, land, mountains, oceans, and seas. This is the only way to meet the growing demand for food, water and energy. It is essential to ensure that women, indigenous peoples and other vulnerable groups have equitable access to land, forests

[64] Report of the Open Working Group of the General Assembly on Sustainable Development Goals, UN Doc A/RES/68/970, para 10(g)(i).
[65] Kamau and others (n 40) 198–99. The Kunming-Montreal Global Biodiversity Framework (GBF) and its 2030 targets provide an update.
[66] ibid 262.
[67] UN, *Open Working Group Proposal for Sustainable Development Goals* (UN 2014).
[68] *Implementation of the Convention on Biological Diversity and its Contribution to Sustainable Development*, UN Doc A/RES/69/222, para 17.
[69] Transforming Our World (n 1).
[70] Kamau and others (n 40) 241–46.

and fisheries.'[71] In response, UNGA updated its statement on integrating biodiversity and development, now stressing 'the importance of mainstreaming biodiversity in the implementation of [Agenda 2030] as part of national implementation plans for the [SDGs] in particular all biodiversity-related Goals and targets'.[72]

The OWG's dedication to mainstreaming biodiversity through all of its proposed SDGs thereby succeeded in biodiversity becoming an essential and recognized component bringing together the SDGs' diverse subject matter, including Goal 15.

II. Commentary on Goal 15

A. Sources

Goal 15 forms one of the main environmental components of Agenda 2030 and responds directly to our sense of urgency over how environmental degradation and climate change will affect the habitability of the land we live on.[73] Goal 15 aims to ensure that life on land can continue; through the protection, restoration, and sustainable use of terrestrial ecosystems, the sustainable management of forests, combating desertification, slowing and reversing land degradation, and halting biodiversity loss. Goal 15's historical significance comes from it being the first globally agreed targets for terrestrial biodiversity and ecosystems.[74] As part of the SDGs, Goal 15 provides a common framework for all UN Member States to better synchronize simultaneous implementation of Multilateral Environmental Agreements (MEAs) and related international priorities. Goal 15 and its targets are underlain by treaties and international instruments including MEAs like the CBD,[75] UNCCD, and the *United Nations Framework Convention on Climate Change*[76] (UNFCCC). To achieve real impact, Goal 15, its targets, and all related international instruments need complementary national implementation in Member States' legislation, policies, and judicial decisions.[77]

Goal 15's subject matter has engaged international debates in law and policy for over a century.[78] Early multilateral treaties like the 1900 London Convention[79] and the 1902

---

[71] UN, *United Nations Summit on Sustainable Development 2015: Informal Summary* (UN 2015) 8.

[72] *Implementation of the Convention on Biological Diversity and its Contribution to Sustainable Development*, UN Doc A/RES/70/207, para 18.

[73] L Niklasson, *Improving the Sustainable Development Goals* (Routledge 2019) 8.

[74] The United States is a non-Party to the CBD, making the distinction between Parties and UN Member States important.

[75] *Convention on Biological Diversity* (n 15).

[76] *United Nations Framework Convention on Climate Change* (adopted 9 May 1992, entered into force 21 March 1994) 1771 UNTS 107.

[77] JC Medaglia and others, *SDG 15 on Terrestrial Ecosystems and Biodiversity: Contributions of International Law, Policy and Governance* (Centre for International Sustainable Development Law and United Nations Environment Programme 2015).

[78] PH Sand, 'A Century of Green Lessons: The Contribution of Nature Conservation Regimes to Global Governance' (2001) 1 International Environmental Agreements: Politics, Law and Economics 33; Dias and Garforth (n 3) 15.

[79] *Convention Designed to Ensure the Conservation of Various Species of Wild Animals in Africa, Which Are Useful to Man or Inoffensive*, 19 May 1900 (not in force), 30 Nouveau Recueil General de Traites et Autres Actes Relatifs

1086   SDG 15

Paris Convention[80] were concerned with natural resource management and protecting wild species and habitats of flora and fauna, setting the tone for future international treaties and instruments.[81] These Conventions 'established bare intergovernmental cooperation for the prevention and the punishment of offences concerning forestry, hunting and fishing'.[82] At that time these concerns sought human utility, where 'the species which are useful were protected; the inoffensive species were mostly ignored; [and] harmful species were to be reduced in number'.[83] Licensing was viewed as the best regulatory approach, conceived of as a way of conserving wildlife stock by limiting their taking through permits, while authorizing the unlicensed killing of 'harmful' species like many large felines, wild canines, dangerous snakes, crocodiles, baboons, and 'other harmful monkeys'.[84] Although rudimentary, these measures provided the germ for modern approaches to 'permitting' wildlife use. The CBD has somewhat altered this anthropocentric focus through its emphasis on the need for conserving and sustainably using all genes, species, and ecosystems, not just those which are high value or charismatic.

The 1933 London Convention reinforced international measures for species conservation and habitat protection. Unlike its predecessor, the 1933 Convention adopted the German imperial approach to nature conservation[85] where 'separating the areas where protection measures are to be enforced and human activities prohibited from those areas where human activities may develop irrespective of environmental considerations'.[86] This approach created an inherent conflict between measures protecting nature or policies to advance socio-economic development. Because most Parties were European states, they leaned toward protecting exemplary species and nature in their imperial possessions while excluding and relocating local peoples when they were seen as an interference with this objective.[87] The 1940 Pan-American Convention[88] followed

---

aux Rapports de Droit International (2d ser, F Stoerk, ed) 430. See SS Hayden, *The International Protection of Wildlife: An Examination of Treaties and Other Agreements for the Preservation of Birds and Mammals* (Colombia University Press 1942) 37–42; MC Maffei, 'Evolving Trends in the International Protection of Species' (1993) 36 German Yearbook of International Law 131, 134–36; M Cioc, *The Game of Conservation: International Treaties to Protect the World's Migratory Animals* (Ohio University Press 2009) 34; M Bowman and others, *Lyster's International Wildlife Law* (CUP 2010) 5, 262–63.

[80] *Convention for the Protection of Birds Useful to Agriculture* 19 March 1902 (in force 12 December 1905) 4 IPE 1615; Maffei (n 79) 135–36. See further Hayden (n 79) 94–98; N Schrijver, *Development without Destruction: The UN and Global Resource Management* (Indiana University Press 2010) 21; Bowman and others (n 79) 5, 200–01.

[81] Cioc (n 79) 39–40; JM Takang, 'From Algiers to Maputo: The Role of the African Convention on the Conservation of Nature and Natural Resources in the Harmonization of Conservation Policy in Africa' (2014) 17 Journal of International Wildlife Law & Policy 165, 168; Schrijver, *Development without Destruction* (n 80) 17, 21–22.

[82] Maffei (n 79) 133.

[83] ibid.

[84] See Schedule 5 to the 1900 Convention.

[85] Hayden (n 79) 36.

[86] Maffei (n 79) 136–37.

[87] See, eg, M Rangarajan, 'Parks, Politics and History: Conservation Dilemmas in Africa' (2003) 1 Conservation and Society 77.

[88] *Convention on Nature Protection and Wild Life Preservation in the Western Hemisphere,* 12 October 1940 (in force 1 May 1942), 161 UNTS 193, 3 Bevans 630. See further Hayden (n 79); S Lyster, *International Wildlife Law: An Analysis of International Treaties Concerned with the Conservation of Wildlife* (Grotius Publications Ltd

COMMENTARY ON GOAL 15 1087

a similar approach in prioritizing the protection of natural sites, wildlife, and habitats, this time through Inter-American cooperation.[89]

A more comprehensive approach to nature conservation began to emerge after the Second World War as science increasingly demonstrated the interconnectedness of nature and the need for humanity to abandon its strictly utilitarian approach to the natural environment to ensure the continuity of life on Earth.[90] This period saw greater efforts on developing methods for both the conservation and 'wise', 'intelligent', 'scientific', 'sustained', or 'optimal' use of living natural resources, reflected in international law and policy measures seeking to balance environmental protection while supporting economic development. Also in this period, earlier environmental protection treaties were revised, for example the 1933 London Convention was replaced by the 1968 Algiers Convention[91] and the 1902 Birds Convention was replaced by the 1950 Birds Convention nominally adopted under the aegis of the UN.[92]

A series of global conservation agreements emerged in the 1970s following a rise of global awareness on the need to balance economic development and environmental protection.[93] These new agreements expanded and detailed what should be conserved and protected, such as threatened habitats of international importance (1971 Ramsar Convention),[94] globally significant natural heritage sites (1972 World Heritage Convention),[95] the conservation and sustainable use of rare species (1973 Convention on International Trade in Endangered Species (CITES)),[96] and the conservation of migratory species (1979 Convention on Migratory Species (CMS)).[97] The 1972 Stockholm Declaration and Plan of Action[98] mapped out important actions for

---

1985); Bowman and others (n 79) 241–61; S Maljean-Dubois, *Le Droit International de La Biodiversité*, vol 407 (Receuils des cours de l'Académie de la Haye, Hague Academy of International Law 2020) para 48.

[89] K Lewis, 'Negotiating for Nature: Conservation Diplomacy and the Convention on Nature Protection and Wildlife Preservation in the Western Hemisphere, 1929–1976' (Doctoral Dissertation, University of New Hampshire 2008) 223–25; Bowman and others (n 79) 252.

[90] See, eg, J Madera, 'The Birth of an Island: Rachel Carson's "The Sea Around Us"' (2017) 45 Women's Studies Quarterly 292; T Robertson, 'Total War and the Total Environment: Fairfield Osborn, William Vogt, and the Birth of Global Ecology' (2012) 17 Environmental History 336.

[91] African Convention on the Conservation of Nature and Natural Resources, 15 September 1968 (in force 16 June 1969) 1001 UNTS 3. See further Bowman and others (n 79) 264–66; Takang (n 81); Maljean-Dubois (n 88) para 47.

[92] International Convention for the Protection of Birds, 18 October 1950 (in force 17 January 1963) in *UNEP Register of Treaties and Other Agreements in the Field of the Environment*, UN Doc UNEP/Env.Law/2005/3, 18. See further Bowman and others (n 79) 201–03; Maljean-Dubois (n 88) para 47.

[93] S Maljean-Dubois and L Rajamani, *La Mise En Oevure Du Droit International de L'Environnement/ Implementation of International Environmental Law* (Hague Academy of International Law 2011) 8.

[94] Convention on Wetlands of International Importance Especially as Waterfowl Habitat, 2 February 1971 (in force 21 December 1975) 996 UNTS 245. See further Bowman and others (n 79) 403–50; Maljean-Dubois (n 88) para 53.

[95] Convention for the Protection of the World Cultural and Natural Heritage, 16 November 1972 (in force 17 December 1975) 11 ILM 1358. See also Bowman and others (n 79) 451–82; Dias and Garforth (n 3) 17; Maljean-Dubois (n 88) para 54; RL Meyer, 'Travaux Preparatoires for the UNESCO World Heritage Convention' (1976) 2 Earth Law Journal 45.

[96] Convention on International Trade in Endangered Species of Wild Fauna and Flora, 3 March 1973 (in force 1 July 1975) 993 UNTS 243. See further Bowman and others (n 79) 483–534; Maljean-Dubois (n 88) para 55.

[97] Convention on the Conservation of Migratory Species of Wild Animals, 23 June 1979 (in force 1 November 1983) 1651 UNTS 333. See further A Kiss and J-P Beurier, *Droit International de L'Environnement* (3rd edn, Pedone 2004) 300–03; Bowman and others (n 79) 535–84; Maljean-Dubois (n 88) para 56.

[98] *Action Plan for the Human Environment*, UN Doc A/CONF.48/14, ch II.

1088 SDG 15

the future conservation of life on land, founded on balancing competing claims of economic development and environmental protection.[99] The Stockholm Declaration significantly influenced the 1980 World Conservation Strategy[100] and the 1982 World Charter for Nature.[101]

Efforts in 1980's international law to safeguard biodiversity and terrestrial ecosystems as an aspect of sustainable development strengthened with the UN General Assembly's adoption of a resolution to initiate the process of developing a global environmental perspective.[102] This culminated in the 1987 report *Our Common Future* submitted by the World Commission on Environment and Development (Brundtland Commission).[103] This ground-breaking report included a set of legal principles for sustainable development proposed by the Brundtland Commission's Legal Experts' Group.[104] The Brundtland Commission was followed by the 1989 Hague Declaration[105] and a 1990 UNGA resolution that convened the United Nations Conference on Environment and Development in 1992.[106] Several significant regional nature conservation agreements were also drafted and agreed in this period, including the 1976 Apia Convention,[107] the 1979 Bern Convention,[108] the 1985 ASEAN Convention,[109] and the 1991 Alpine Convention.[110]

The period between the release of *Our Common Future* in 1987 and the 2015 UN Summit on Sustainable Development witnessed a flourishing of international and regional law and policy instruments that underlie SDG Goal 15. This prolific period for environmental governance brought forth key instruments such as the 1992 CBD,[111]

---

[99] Maljean-Dubois and Rajamani (n 93) 110–11.

[100] *World Conservation Strategy: Living Resource Conservation for Sustainable Development* (IUCN, UNEP Stockholm, WWF 1980). See further LJ Carter, 'Marriage of Conservation and Development' (1980) 207 Science 1328; J McCormick, 'The Origins of the World Conservation Strategy' (1986) 10 Environmental Review 177; S Macekura, 'Conservation for Development: The World Conservation Strategy and the Rise of Sustainable Development Planning' in *Of Limits and Growth: The Rise of Global Sustainable Development in the Twentieth Century* (CUP 2015).

[101] *World Charter for Nature*, UN Doc A/RES/37/7. See also P Jackson, 'A World Charter for Nature' (1983) 12 Ambio 133; HW Wood Jr, 'The United Nations World Charter for Nature: The Developing Nations' Initiative to Establish Protections for the Environment' (1985) 12 Ecology Law Quarterly 977; WE Burhenne and WA Irwin, *The World Charter for Nature/La Charte Mondiale de La Nature* (2nd edn, Erich Schmidt Verlag 1986).

[102] *Process of Preparation of the Environmental Perspective to the Year 2000 and Beyond*, UNGA Doc A/RES/38/161.

[103] World Commission on Environment and Development, *Our Common Future* (OUP 1987). See further HC Bugge, '1987–2007: "Our Common Future" Revisited' in HC Bugge and C Voigt (eds), *Sustainable Development in International and National Law* (Europa Law Publishing 2008).

[104] RD Munro and JG Lammers, *Environmental Protection and Sustainable Development: Legal Principles and Recommendations* (Graham & Trotman Ltd 1987).

[105] 'Hague Declaration on the Environment' (1989) 28 International Legal Materials 1308.

[106] *UN Conference on Environment and Development*, UN Doc A/RES/44/228.

[107] Convention on Conservation of Nature in the South Pacific, 12 June 1976 (in force 28 June 1990) IEL 976:45. See further Kiss and Beurier (n 97) 320–21; Bowman and others (n 79) 383–86; Maljean-Dubois (n 88) para 57.

[108] Convention on the Conservation of European Wildlife and Natural Habitats, 19 September 1979 (in force 1 June 1982) ETS No 104. See further Kiss and Beurier (n 97) 315–20; Bowman and others (n 79) 297–345; Maljean-Dubois (n 88) para 57.

[109] *Association of South-East Asian Nations Agreement on the Conservation of Nature and Natural Resources*, 8 December 1985 (not in force), 15 Environmental Policy & Law 64. See further Kiss and Beurier (n 97) 321–24; Bowman and others (n 79) 376–83; Maljean-Dubois (n 88) para 57.

[110] Convention Concerning the Protection of the Alps, 7 November 1991 (in force 6 March 1995) in *UNEP Register of Treaties and Other Agreements in the Field of the Environment*, UN Doc UNEP/Env.Law/2005/3, 448. See further Kiss and Beurier (n 97) 326–28; Bowman and others (n 79) 639–47; Maljean-Dubois (n 88) para 57.

[111] CBD, supra; See further L Glowka and others, *A Guide to the Convention on Biological Diversity* (IUCN 1994); M Bowman and C Redgwell (eds), *International Law and the Conservation of Biological Diversity* (Kluwer

COMMENTARY ON GOAL 15   1089

Agenda 21,[112] the Rio Forest Principles,[113] 1994's UNCCD, the 2002 Johannesburg Declaration and Plan of Implementation,[114] 2003's Maputo Convention,[115] the 2003 Carpathian Convention,[116] and the 2007 NLBI on all types of forests. Even if non-binding, Rio + 20's 'The Future We Want' outcome document was deeply influential for the creation of the SDGs.[117] Even though SDG Goal 15 has a 'non-legally binding' status, it is built out of a historical and reinforced foundation in international law and policy. This foundation gives SDG Goal 15 and its targets real authority and tangible guidance for international cooperation and national implementation.[118]

B. Developmental Analysis

As outlined through legal history above, Goal 15's merits have roots going back to the colonial era. Historical concerns reflected in Goal 15 included landscape management, the protection of selected animals, plants, and areas, and questions on how to balance economic development with the protection of nature.[119] During and after the imperialist era, Western practices and priorities on these questions dominated the legal and terrestrial landscape of much of the world. Even as terrestrial biodiversity, biological resources, and ecosystems declined dramatically from colonial resource over-exploitation, Western approaches to natural resource management were exported globally. At first this took place within empires, like the British Empire's establishment of an enormous forest conservancy system in India in the 1860s and 1870s, which the British then applied throughout their Empire for financial, industrial, and environmental purposes.[120] This involved the forced resettlement of local peoples[121] and new

Law International 1996); PG Le Prestre (ed), *Governing Global Biodiversity: The Evolution and Implementation of the Convention on Biological Diversity* (Routledge 2002); JC Medaglia, F Perron-Welch, and A Goodman (eds), *Legal Aspects of Implementing the Convention on Biological Diversity* (CUP 2023).

[112] *Agenda 21: Programme of Action for Sustainable Development*, UN Doc A/CONF.151/26 (Vol III).
[113] *Non-legally Binding Authoritative Statement of Principles for a Global Consensus on the Management, Conservation and Sustainable Development of All Types of Forests*, UN Doc A/CONF.151/26 (Volume III) Annex III. See further Kiss and Beurier (n 97) 169; A Savaresi, 'Forest Biodiversity Law' in E Morgera and J Razzaque (eds), *Biodiversity and Nature Protection Law* (Edward Elgar 2017) 204–05.
[114] *Johannesburg Declaration and Plan of Implementation of the World Summit for Sustainable Development*, UN Doc A/CONF.199/L.6/Rev.2.
[115] *African Convention on the Conservation of Nature and Natural Resources (Revised Version)*, 11 July 2003 (in force 7 March 2017) IUCN Doc TRE-001395.
[116] *Framework Convention on the Protection and Sustainable Development of the Carpathians*, 22 May 2003 (in force 4 January 2006). IUCN Doc TRE-001374.
[117] 'The Future We Want', UN Doc A/RES/66/288, Annex.
[118] See JC Medaglia and others, *SDG 15 on Terrestrial Ecosystems and Biodiversity: Contributions of International Law, Policy and Governance* (n 77).
[119] Y Larabi and P Anglade, *Raoul de Clermont: un pionnier de la protection de la nature* (Publibook 2018).
[120] NA Rao, 'Evolution of Forest Policy and Forest Acts of 1865 and 1878' in *Forest Ecology in India: Colonial Maharashtra, 1850–1950* (Foundation Books 2007); RH Grove, Green Imperialism: Colonial Expansion, Tropical Island Edens and the Origins of Environmentalism, 1600–1860 (CUP 1996); G Barton, 'Empire Forestry and the Origins of Environmentalism' (2001) 27 Journal of Historical Geography 529.
[121] D Coghlan and M Brydon-Miller (eds), 'Subalternity', *The SAGE Encyclopedia of Action Research* (SAGE Publications 2022): 'marginalized individuals or groups who are disenfranchised because they are not part of the hegemonic power structure of a society or colony'.

1090 SDG 15

methods of social control that contributed to the emergence of the century's nationalist movements. The imposition and exportation of Western approaches to conversation versus exploitation of nature is a continued hurdle to Indigenous peoples and local communities (IPLC) establishing legal rights to access and manage their traditional territories.[122]

As such, Goal 15's focus on land and natural resource management has historically been associated with imperial oppression and preference for Western values. For example, the London Conventions of 1900 and 1933's prohibitions on harvesting wildlife have 'a long history that is deeply intertwined with social dimensions such as unequal access to land and its resources often related with aspects of power imbalances, inequities and race'.[123] Colonial priorities justified interventionist measures such as forcibly displacing communities and criminalizing local livelihoods and traditions in order to protect game animals and their habitats.[124] In the present day, we continue to be challenged on how to weigh a balance between the inarguable need to ensure life on land continues against the constant drive for socio-economic development. For the overwhelming majority of the global population, this challenge is echoed in the 1972 Stockholm Declaration's observation that under-development causes environmental degradation and that 'developing countries must direct their efforts to development, bearing in mind their priorities and the need to safeguard and improve the environment'.[125] In 1973, the UN Environment Programme (UNEP) energized its focus to respond to the needs of developing countries. The first UNEP Governing Council (GC) agreed to prioritize links between environment and development through enabling 'a more efficient integration of developmental and environmental concerns'[126] through the concept of 'ecologically sound socio-economic development' or 'eco-development' that would improve the support and understanding of rural people's experience and improve utilization of natural resources for development.[127]

The following year, the *Cocoyoc Declaration*[128] became one of 'the first systematic attempts to state, under [UN] auspices, the connections between environmental

---

[122] See generally G Holmes, 'Protection, Politics and Protest: Understanding Resistance to Conservation' (2007) 5 Conservation and Society 184; AP Kinzig and TO McShane, 'Conservation in Africa: Exploring the Impact of Social, Economic and Political Drivers on Conservation Outcomes' (2015) 10 Environmental Research Letters 090201.

[123] C Fuerst and M Gutmann, 'SDG 15—Caretaking, Conservation, and Exploitation in the Evolving Relationship between Humans and Life on Land' in M Gutmann and D Gorman (eds), *Before the UN Sustainable Development Goals: A Historical Companion* (OUP 2022) 450.

[124] Cioc (n 79) ch 1: 'Africa's Apartheid Parks'. See also C Morel, 'Conservation and Indigenous Peoples' Rights: Must One Necessarily Come at the Expense of the Other?' in H Shrumm (ed), *IUCN-CEESP: Policy Matters*, vol 17 (IUCN 2010); R De Bont, '"Primitives" and Protected Areas: International Conservation and the "Naturalization" of Indigenous People, ca. 1910–1975' (2015) 76 Journal of the History of Ideas 215; V Tauli-Corpuz and others, *Cornered by Protected Areas: Replacing 'Fortress' Conservation with Rights-Based Approaches Helps Bring Justice for Indigenous Peoples and Local Communities, Reduces Conflict and Enables Cost-Effective Conservation and Climate Action* (Rights and Resources Initiative 2018).

[125] Stockholm Declaration, para 4.

[126] UNEP GC Decision 1(I), para 4(d).

[127] AS Timoshenko, 'From Stockholm to Rio: The Institutionalization of Sustainable Development' in W Lang (ed), *Sustainable Development and International Law* (Graham & Trotman Ltd 1995) 145.

[128] Adopted by participants at the UNCTAD and UNEP symposium on 'Patterns of Resource Use, Environment and Development Strategies' in Cocoyoc, Mexico in October 1974, see UNEP, *In Defence of the Earth: The Basic Texts on Environment: Founex—Stockholm—Cocoyoc* (UNEP 1981) 107.

COMMENTARY ON GOAL 15   1091

protection and the redistribution of global economic and social resources'.[129] The Cocoyoc Declaration proposed various 'changes in the conduct of economic policy, in the direction of development and in planetary conservation, which appear to us to be essential components of the new system'.[130] Further, it called on 'political leaders, Governments, international organizations and the scientific community to elaborate and start implementing programmes aimed at satisfying the basic needs of the poorest peoples all over the world ... [which] should be designed in such a way to ensure adequate conservation of resources and protection of the environment'.[131]

UNEP GC 3 expanded the scope of eco-development by acknowledging the need to integrate an environmental dimension when analysing the concept of development.[132] UNEP GC 4 introduced an intergenerational aspect to 'environmentally sound development' and presented a new conceptual approach of 'eco-development' which recognizes that 'the preservation of a sound environment is an essential element of development conceived as a global improvement of the quality of human life'.[133] This novel idea that quality of development affects quality of life was a change in perspective from development viewed solely as material progress.[134] This new perspective guided a logical transition to introducing the concept of sustainable development as seen in the 1980 *World Conservation Strategy*,[135] then in *Our Common Future*,[136] and later in the Rio Declaration on Environment and Development.

Goal 15 is backed by decades of modern international consensus that sustainable development requires the survival of life on land as a matter of priority beyond the continued balancing of conversation, economic, and social factors. As states acknowledged in the 1982 *World Charter for Nature*, humanity 'is a part of nature and life depends on the uninterrupted functioning of natural systems ... [and that] [l]asting benefits from nature depend upon the maintenance of essential ecological processes and life support systems, and upon the diversity of life forms, which are jeopardized through excessive exploitation and habitat destruction ...'.[137] Goal 15 aims to strike a balance between the imperative of maintaining the planet's life support systems while ensuring global human development. The main question is therefore how to improve human well-being—and help achieve all SDGs—through protecting life on land. Achieving it will be critical to realizing all SDGs and the objectives of Agenda 2030 more broadly, as socio-economic development must be done within planetary boundaries to ensure our common survival.[138] This is not a straightforward proposition, as the status quo relies

[129] Anonymous, 'The Cocoyoc Declaration' (1975) 29 International Organization 893, 893.
[130] UNEP (n 128) 112.
[131] ibid 116.
[132] UNEP GC Decision 21(III); Timoshenko (n 127) 145.
[133] UNEP GC Decision 79(IV).
[134] Timoshenko (n 127) 146.
[135] IUCN, UNEP, WWF, FAO, and UNESCO, *World Conservation Strategy: Living Resource Conservation for Sustainable Development* (IUCN 1980); V Koester, 'From Stockholm to Brundtland' (1990) 20 Environmental Policy and Law 14.
[136] World Commission on Environment and Development (n 103).
[137] World Charter for Nature, UN Doc A/RES/37/7, Annex, Preamble.
[138] See further J Rockström and others, 'Planetary Boundaries: Exploring the Safe Operating Space for Humanity' (2009) 14 Ecology and Society; C Folke, 'Respecting Planetary Boundaries and Reconnecting to the Biosphere' in Worldwatch Institute (ed), *State of the World 2013: Is Sustainability Still Possible?* (Island Press/Center

1092 SDG 15

on the over-exploitation of nature and a steadily growing environmental footprint.[139] If sustainable development can only be achieved—at minimum—consistently with Goal 15, the international community is far from developing sustainably. Strengthening and closely monitoring implementation will be critical to ensuring global sustainable development and achieving Agenda 2030.

C. Best Practices

Best practices in implementing Goal 15 are founded in international law instruments and international environmental principles that support environmental protection and sustainable development. Many approaches to implementing Goal 15 rely on enforcing regulatory measures and implementing social policies, some of which are well established while others are still episodic and require broader application. Well-established practices for nature conservation include the creation of parks and wilderness reserves and regulating the harvest of select fauna and flora. Whether these constitute 'best practice' depends on whether they are implemented in alignment with environmental science while respecting human rights, particularly those rights expressed in the UN Declarations on the Rights (i) to Development,[140] (ii) on Indigenous Peoples,[141] and (iii) on Peasants and Other People Working in Rural Areas.[142]

Other existing and emerging international and national concepts, principles, practices, and objectives that could constitute, support, or lead to 'best practices' for achieving Goal 15 include: (i) access to environmental information,[143] (ii) access to environmental justice,[144] (iii) benefit-sharing,[145] (iv) common but differentiated responsibilities,[146] (v) conservation and sustainable use of natural

for Resource Economics 2013); W Steffen and others, 'Planetary Boundaries: Guiding Human Development on a Changing Planet' (2015) 347 Science 1259855; J Rockström and others, *Big World, Small Planet: Abundance within Planetary Boundaries* (Yale University Press 2015).

[139] M Wackernagel and W Rees, *Our Ecological Footprint: Reducing Human Impact on the Earth* (New Society 1998).

[140] *United Nations Declaration on the Right to Development*, UNGA Doc A/RES/41/128; N Singh, 'Right to Environment and Sustainable Development as a Principle of International Law' (1987) 29 Journal of the Indian Law Institute 289; Brighton (n 45); D French, '"From Seoul with Love"—The Continuing Relevance of the 1986 Seoul ILA Declaration on Progressive Development of Principles of Public International Law Relating to a New International Economic Order' (2008) 55 Netherlands International Law Review 3.

[141] *United Nations Declaration on the Rights of Indigenous Peoples*, UN Doc A/RES/61/295.

[142] *United Nations Declaration on the Rights of Peasants and Other People Working in Rural Areas*, UN Doc A/RES/73/165.

[143] Rio Declaration, Principle 10. See also S Whittaker, *The Right of Access to Environmental Information* (CUP 2021).

[144] Rio Declaration, Principle 10. See also J Ebbesson, 'Principle 10' in JE Viñuales (ed), *The Rio Declaration on Environment and Development: A Commentary* (OUP 2015).

[145] JC Medaglia and F Perron-Welch, 'The Benefit-Sharing Principle in International Law' (2019) 14 Journal of Intellectual Property Law & Practice 62; JC Medaglia and F Perron-Welch, 'Rules and Practices of International Law on Benefit-Sharing for Sustainable Development' in V Mauerhofer and others (eds), *Sustainability and Law: General and Specific Aspects* (Springer 2020).

[146] Rio Declaration, Principle 7. See also L Rajamani, *Differential Treatment in International Environmental Law* (OUP 2006); S Atapattu, *Emerging Principles of International Environmental Law* (Transnational Publishers 2006) 379–436; L Rajamani, 'The Changing Fortunes of Differential Treatment in the Evolution of International Environmental Law' (2012) 88 International Affairs 605; P Cullet, *Differential Treatment in International*

COMMENTARY ON GOAL 15   1093

resources,[147] (vi) corporate environmental disclosures,[148] (vii) ecological civilization,[149] (viii) ecological law,[150] (ix) economic valuation of biodiversity and ecosystem
services (ecosystem services),[151] (x) the ecosystem approach,[152] (xi) ecosystem restoration,[153] (xii) environmental impact assessment (EIA),[154] (xiii) the environmental rule
of law,[155] (xiv) equity,[156] (xv) good governance,[157] (xvi) Indigenous and community
conserved areas (ICCA),[158] (xvii) integration and interrelationship,[159] (xviii) the landscape approach,[160] (xix) natural infrastructure,[161] (xx) nature-based solutions,[162] (xxi)

Environmental Law (Routledge 2016); P Cullet, 'Differential Treatment in Environmental Law: Addressing
Critiques and Conceptualizing the Next Steps' (2016) 5 Transnational Environmental Law 305.

[147] See N Schrijver, *Sovereignty over Natural Resources: Balancing Rights and Duties* (CUP 1997) 324–35;
AE Boyle and C Redgwell, *Birnie, Boyle, and Redgwell's International Law and the Environment* (4th edn, OUP
2021) 129–41; International Law Association, Resolution 4/2020 *Guidelines on Sustainable Natural Resource
Management for Development.*
[148] See, eg, H Finlay and others, *Disclosing Nature's Potential: Corporate Responses and the Need for Greater
Ambition* (IUCN and CDP 2021) and the work of the Taskforce on Nature-related Financial Disclosures, underlain
by seven principles: market usability, science-based, nature-related risks, purpose-driven, integrated and adaptive,
climate-nature nexus, and globally inclusive. TNFD, 'The TNFD Principles' <https://tnfd.global/the-tnfd-princip
les/> accessed 29 March 2022.
[149] Z Guangyao, 'Ecological Civilization' (2017) 2016 Our Planet 26; B Jiang and others, 'China's Ecological
Civilization Program–Implementing Ecological Redline Policy' (2019) 81 Land Use Policy 111; NA Robinson,
'Ecological Civilization and Legal Norms for Resilient Environmental Governance' (2020) 4 Chinese Journal of
Environmental Law 131.
[150] See, eg, K Anker and others (eds), *From Environmental to Ecological Law* (Routledge 2020); C Sbert, *The Lens
of Ecological Law: A Look at Mining* (Edward Elgar Publishing 2020).
[151] See Millennium Ecosystem Assessment, *Ecosystems and Human Well-being: Synthesis* (Island Press 2005); P
Kumar, *The Economics of Ecosystems and Biodiversity: Ecological and Economic Foundations* (Routledge 2012).
[152] V De Lucia, *The 'Ecosystem Approach' in International Environmental Law: Genealogy and Biopolitics*
(Routledge 2019); D Piselli, 'Operationalizing the Notion of Ecosystem Approach in International Law: A
Quest for Adaptive Legal Systems in the Age of Planetary Boundaries' (Graduate Institute of International and
Development Studies 2022).
[153] *United Nations Decade on Ecosystem Restoration (2021–2030),* UN Doc A/RES/73/284.
[154] *Certain Activities Carried Out by Nicaragua in the Border Area (Costa Rica v. Nicaragua)* and *Construction
of a Road in Costa Rica along the San Juan River (Nicaragua v Costa Rica),* Judgment, ICJ Rep 2015, para 104; J
Harrison, 'Significant International Environmental Law Cases: 2015–16' (2016) 28 Journal of Environmental Law
533, 534–35.
[155] See, eg, IV Nemesio, 'Strengthening Environmental Rule of Law: Enforcement, Combatting Corruption, and
Encouraging Citizen Suits' (2014) 27 Georgetown International Environmental Law Review 321; J Scott, 'From
Environmental Rights to Environmental Rule of Law: A Proposal for Better Environmental Outcomes' (2016) 6
Michigan Journal of Environmental and Administrative Law 203; A Kreilhuber and A Kariuki, 'Environmental
Rule of Law in the Context of Sustainable Development' (2019) 32 Georgetown International Environmental Law
Review 591; S Kumar and others, *Environmental Rule of Law: First Global Report* (UNEP 2019).
[156] Atapattu (n 146) 113–19; E Brown Weiss, *In Fairness to Future Generations: International Law, Common
Patrimony, and Intergenerational Equity* (United Nations University 2006); W Scholtz, 'Equity' in Rajamani and
Peel (eds), *The Oxford Handbook of International Environmental Law* (n 56).
[157] H Addink, 'Good Governance: A Principle of International Law' in C Ryngaert and others (eds), *What's
Wrong with International Law?* (Brill Nijhoff 2015); D Dam-de Jong, *International Law and Governance of Natural
Resources in Conflict and Post-Conflict Situations* (CUP 2015) 22.
[158] Morel (n 124); HC Jonas, 'Indigenous Peoples' and Community Conserved Territories and Areas
(ICCAs): Evolution in International Biodiversity Law' in E Morgera and J Razzaque (eds), *Biodiversity and Nature
Protection Law* (Edward Elgar Publishing 2017).
[159] Stockholm Declaration, Principle 13; Rio Declaration, Principle 4; N Schrijver, *The Evolution of Sustainable
Development in International Law: Inception, Meaning and Status* (Nijhoff 2008) 204; C Voigt, 'The Principle
of Sustainable Development: Integration and Ecological Integrity' in C Voigt (ed), *Rule of Law for Nature: New
Dimensions and Ideas in Environmental Law* (CUP 2013).
[160] J Sayer and others, 'Ten Principles for a Landscape Approach to Reconciling Agriculture, Conservation, and
Other Competing Land Uses' (2013) 110 Proceedings of the National Academy of Sciences 8349; B Arts and others,
'Landscape Approaches: A State-of-the-Art Review' (2017) 42 Annual Review of Environment and Resources 439.
[161] RI McDonald, *Conservation for Cities: How to Plan & Build Natural Infrastructure* (Island Press 2015).
[162] *Ministerial Declaration of the United Nations Environment Assembly at its Fifth Session,* UN Doc UNEP/
EA.5/HLS.1, para 17; *Nature-based Solutions for Supporting Sustainable Development,* UN Doc UNEP/EA5/L9/

1094 SDG 15

payments for ecosystem services (PES),[163] (xxii) planetary trust,[164] (xxiii) the polluter-pays principle,[165] (xxiv) principle of prevention,[166] (xxv) principle of precaution,[167] (xxvi) public participation,[168] (xxvii) public trust,[169] (xxviii) resilience,[170] (xxix) sustainable consumption and production,[171] (xxix) sustainable development,[172] (xxx) sustainable natural resource management,[173] and (xxxi) SFM.[174]

D. Critique

Human survival and development are intrinsically linked to the state of life on land. The scope for human progress and quality of life under Goal 15 is considerable—as

REV.1; *Defining Nature-based Solutions*, IUCN Doc WCC-2016-Res-069-EN; E Cohen-Shacham and others (eds), *Nature-Based Solutions to Address Global Societal Challenges* (IUCN 2016); IUCN, *IUCN Global Standard for Nature-Based Solutions: A User-Friendly Framework for the Verification, Design and Scaling up of NbS* (1st edn, IUCN 2020).

[163] UNECE and others, *The Value of Forests: Payments for Ecosystem Services in a Green Economy* (Geneva Timber and Forest Study Paper 34, United Nations 2014); J Salzman and others, 'The Global Status and Trends of Payments for Ecosystem Services' (2018) 1 Nature Sustainability 136.

[164] E Brown Weiss, 'The Planetary Trust: Conservation and Intergenerational Equity' (1984) 11 Ecology Law Quarterly 495; E Brown Weiss, 'The Future of the Planetary Trust in a Kaleidoscopic World' (2020) 50 Environmental Policy and Law 449.

[165] Rio Declaration, Principle 16. See also Atapattu (n 146) 437–84; Boyle and Redgwell (n 147) 341–45.

[166] See L-A Duvic-Paoli, *The Prevention Principle in International Environmental Law* (CUP 2018); J Brunnée, 'Harm Prevention' in Rajamani and Peel (eds), *The Oxford Handbook of International Environmental Law* (n 56).

[167] Rio Declaration, Principle 15; *Responsibilities and Obligations of States sponsoring Persons and Entities with respect to Activities in the Area*, Case No. 17, ITLOS (Seabed Dispute Chamber), Advisory Opinion of 1 February 2011, para 135. See also DL VanderZwaag, 'The ICJ, ITLOS and the Precautionary Approach: Paltry Progressions, Jurisprudential Jousting' (2013) 35 University of Hawaii Law Review 617; AAC Trindade, 'Principle 15' in Jorge E Viñuales (ed), *The Rio Declaration on Environment and Development: A Commentary* (OUP 2015); C Tollefson, 'A Precautionary Tale: Trials and Tribulations of the Precautionary Principle' in A Ingelson (ed), *Environment in the Courtroom* (University of Calgary Press 2019).

[168] Rio Declaration, Principle 10. See also Atapattu (n 146) 353–76; J Ebbesson, 'Public Participation' in Rajamani and Peel (eds), *The Oxford Handbook of International Environmental Law* (n 56) 351.

[169] See RD Sagarin and M Turnipseed, 'The Public Trust Doctrine: Where Ecology Meets Natural Resources Management' (2012) 37 Annual Review of Environment and Resources 473; PH Sand, 'The Concept of Public Trusteeship in the Transboundary Governance of Biodiversity' in LJ Kotzé and T Marauhn (eds), *Transboundary Governance of Biodiversity* (Brill Nijhoff 2014); A Richardson Oakes, 'Judicial Resources and the Public Trust Doctrine: A Powerful Tool of Environmental Protection?' (2018) 7 Transnational Environmental Law 469.

[170] See BM Hutter, *Risk, Resilience, Inequality and Environmental Law* (Edward Elgar 2017).

[171] See UNEP, *Sustainable Consumption and Production: A Handbook for Policymakers* (UNEP 2016) 10; D Gasper and others, 'The Framing of Sustainable Consumption and Production in SDG 12' (2019) 10 Global Policy 83. See also SDG 12 chapter in this volume.

[172] See International Law Association, 'New Delhi Declaration of Principles of International Law Relating to Sustainable Development' (2002); N Schrijver, 'The New Delhi Declaration of Principles of International Law Relating to Sustainable Development: Commentary' in M-C Cordonier Segger and CG Weermantry (eds), *Sustainable Justice: Reconciling Economic, Social and Environmental Law* (Martinus Nijhoff 2005).

[173] See International Law Association, *ILA Guidelines on the Role of International Law in Sustainable Natural Resources Management for Development*, ILA Resolution No. 4/2020.

[174] *Non-legally Binding Authoritative Statement of Principles for a Global Consensus on the Management, Conservation and Sustainable Development of All Types of Forests* (1992) UN Doc A/CONF.151/26 (Volume III) Annex III; *Non-legally binding instrument on all types of forests*, UN Doc A/RES/62/98. See also K Kunzmann, 'The Non-Legally Binding Instrument on Sustainable Management of All Types of Forests—Towards a Legal Regime for Sustainable Forest Management?' (2008) 9 German Law Journal 981; R Maguire, *The Sustainable Governance of Forest Resources: Legal Concepts and Policy Trends* (Edward Elgar Publishing 2013); JP Sheppard and others, 'Sustainable Forest Management Beyond the Timber-Oriented Status Quo: Transitioning to Co-Production of Timber and Non-Wood Forest Products—a Global Perspective' (2020) 6 Current Forestry Reports 26.

COMMENTARY ON GOAL 15   1095

are its interconnections with other SDGs.[175] Our relationship with the planet has dramatically changed through our increasingly intense intervention in wild terrestrial ecosystems due to seeking basic material needs and advancing political, cultural, and ideological imperatives.[176] Humanity's uncontested effects on biodiversity, and the exploitation of endangered species and finite natural resources in biodiversity-rich habitats continues.[177] As recognized in the World Economic Forum's (WEF) 2022 Global Risks Report, these pose severe risks to human survival. Noting that societal and economic problems both remain top concerns over the next five years, the Global Risks Report indicates that 'over a 10-year horizon, the health of the planet dominates concerns: environmental risks are perceived to be the five most critical long-term threats to the world as well as the most potentially damaging to people and planet, with "climate action failure", "extreme weather", and "biodiversity loss" ranking as the top three most severe risks'.[178] At first glance, it appears that an urgent and broad response is the only appropriate response to preserve life on land. States have seemingly proposed a plan for this response through SDG Goal 15, with achievable targets that could effectuate necessary changes in human behaviour towards our shared habitat.[179]

Yet, Goal 15 'has a relatively long list of ends but only a few specific means to achieve them'.[180] Policy instruments and resource mobilization are suggested, but binding language is avoided.[181] Meeting the sizable challenge of sustaining life on land means addressing a panoply of drivers of biodiversity loss. With 75 per cent of the planet's land surface already significantly altered by humans, and where most indicators of ecosystems and biodiversity show rapid decline,[182] we are now inhabiting a world where ecosystem services or 'Nature's Contributions to People' (NCP) are in decline, species are at increasing risk of extinction, and genetic diversity is dwindling.[183] Endemic biodiversity is being strongly undermined by the introduction of invasive alien species (IAS), and other human-induced environmental changes are creating uncertainty about the sustainability of species, ecosystem functions, and the delivery of ecosystem services and NCP.[184] The cross-cutting nature of the SDGs means that economic and social goals must contribute to achieving SDG Goal 15.[185] This means that socio-development must be reoriented towards not harming and even proactively benefiting life on earth. Whether the 'controversial assumptions about causal mechanisms, such as the importance of economic development in general, and trade and technological development

---

[175] Fuerst and Gutmann (n 123) 449.

[176] ibid 452.

[177] SCBD, *Global Biodiversity Outlook 5* (SCBD 2020); Intergovernmental Science-Policy Platform on Biodiversity and Ecosystem Services, 'Summary for Policymakers of the Global Assessment of Biodiversity and Ecosystem Services' (2019) UN Doc IPBES/7/3.

[178] World Economic Forum, *Global Risks Report 2022* (17th edn, World Economic Forum 2022).

[179] Niklasson (n 73) 64.

[180] ibid.

[181] ibid 64–65.

[182] IPBES, *The Global Assessment Report on Biodiversity and Ecosystem Services – Summary for Policymakers* (IPBES 2019) xv.

[183] ibid xv–xvi.

[184] ibid xvi.

[185] Niklasson (n 73) 65.

1096   SDG 15

in particular'[186] will result in favourable conditions for terrestrial ecosystems and biodiversity by 2030 remains to be seen. Early results thus far are not promising.[187]

The Intergovernmental Panel on Biodiversity and Ecosystem Services (IPBES) identifies the underlying drivers of biodiversity loss as falling into two categories: direct and indirect drivers. The direct drivers with the greatest impact are: (i) changes in land use, principally agricultural expansion and growth in urban areas and associated infrastructure; (ii) the direct exploitation of animals, plants, and other organisms (harvesting, logging, hunting and fishing); (iii) climate change, which exacerbates the impacts of other drivers on nature and human-well-being; (iv) air, water, and soil pollution; and (v) IAS, which are being introduced and spread at an unprecedented rate.[188]

The indirect drivers of change that propel these direct drivers are underpinned by economic, political, and social factors that include human population dynamics, production and consumption patterns, globalization, and trade.[189] Economic incentives generally favour increasing economic activity (and any associated environmental harm), over the conservation or restoration of nature.[190] Cultural value systems—the way in which nature is conceived of and valued—have also been shown to be a powerful indirect driver of biodiversity loss. Territories managed by IPLC are particularly under pressure and their traditional knowledge on ecosystem management is also being lost alongside biodiversity.[191]

The IPBES determined in 2019 that, due to the rapid decline in biodiversity, ecosystem functions and many NCPs, 'most international societal and environmental goals, such as those embodied in the [Aichi targets and Agenda 2030], will not be achieved based on current trajectories. These declines will also undermine other goals, such as those specified in the Paris Agreement adopted under the [UNFCCC] and the 2050 Vision for Biodiversity.'[192] Negative trends are likely to 'continue or worsen ... in response to indirect drivers such as rapid human population growth, unsustainable production and consumption and associated technological development'.[193]

These warnings clearly demonstrate the need for transformational change to achieve many of Goal 15's aims. Some transformative scenarios and pathways exist that could reverse existing trends, in that 'transformative changes in the production and consumption of energy, food, feed, fibre and water, sustainable use, equitable sharing of the benefits arising from use and nature-friendly climate adaptation and mitigation will better support the achievement of future societal and environmental objectives'.[194] Given the many concurrent challenges humanity faces today—such as the COVID-19 pandemic, organizing a global economic recovery, and the re-emergence of war in

---

[186] ibid 129.
[187] UN DESA, The SDGs Report 2020, 54.
[188] IPBES (n 182) xvi–xvii.
[189] ibid xvii.
[190] ibid xviii.
[191] ibid.
[192] ibid.
[193] IPBES (n 182) XIX.
[194] ibid xix.

COMMENTARY ON GOAL 15   1097

Europe—it seems unlikely that states will be able to simultaneously achieve all of the above, and more, by 2030.

From this perspective, 2020 and 2030 have often been framed in intergovernmental negotiations as intermediate waypoints on the path to mid-century goals and targets (eg global net zero emissions under UNFCCC, or land degradation neutrality under UNCCD). For Goal 15, this mid-century goal was first reflected in the vision of 'Harmony with Nature' in the CBD Strategic Plan 2011–2020, which envisions that 'by 2050, biodiversity is valued, conserved, restored and wisely used, maintaining ecosystem services, sustaining a healthy planet and delivering benefits essential for all people'.[195] Whether this idealistic vision can be achieved by 2050, which greatly impacts the success of Goal 15, will largely depend on whether CBD parties can implement the ambitious Kunming-Montreal Global Biodiversity Framework (GBF) with its clear mission and targets for 2030 driving the transformation needed to bring Goal 15 into reality.

Existing policy instruments and new initiatives must be rapidly and more effectively deployed to enlist individual and collective action. But fundamental and structural change often faces concerted opposition from powerful interests.[196] According to the IPBES Global Assessment Report, if existing barriers can be overcome, 'a commitment to mutually supportive international goals and targets, supporting actions by indigenous peoples and local communities at the local level, new frameworks for private sector investment and innovation, inclusive and adaptive governance approaches and arrangements, multi-sectoral planning, and strategic policy mixes can help to transform the public and private sectors to achieve sustainability at the local, national and global levels'.[197] This means 'advancing and aligning local, national and international sustainability efforts and mainstreaming biodiversity and sustainability across all extractive and productive sectors ... so that together, individual and collective actions result in a reversal of the deterioration of ecosystem services at the global level'.[198]

Given this sizable task, the IPBES identified five 'levers' for transformative change that address indirect drivers of biodiversity loss, including (i) developing incentives and broad capacity for environmental responsibility, and eliminating perverse incentives; (ii) reforming sectoral and fragmented decision-making to promote integration across sectors and jurisdictions; (iii) taking pre-emptive and precautionary actions in regulatory and management institutions and businesses to avoid, mitigate, and remedy nature's deterioration, and monitoring outcomes; (iv) managing for resilient social and ecological systems in light of uncertainty and complexity for robust decision-making in numerous scenarios; and (v) strengthening environmental laws and policies, their implementation, and the rule of law.[199] Using these 'levers' will necessitate significant new financial and non-financial resources (particularly in low-capacity contexts), as well as governance approaches that are integrative, inclusive, informed, and adaptive.[200] It will

[195] CBD, *Strategic Plan 2011–2020* (n 21).
[196] IPBES (n 182) xx.
[197] ibid xx–xxi.
[198] ibid xxi.
[199] ibid.
[200] ibid.

1098   SDG 15

also require 'the evolution of global financial and economic systems to build a global sustainable economy, steering away from the current, limited paradigm of economic growth'.[201]

Objectively, it would be challenging for any state or even all states cooperatively to address all the above in so many intervention points. Yet, we face a situation where all of these must be given full effort simultaneously to ensure the survival of life on land as formalized by SDG Goal 15. The scope of Goal 15 and the magnitude of the convoluted problems do not lead to easy solutions, and a comparative lack of indicators does not make monitoring the task any easier. Large data gaps exist in monitoring the status of life on land, and indicators addressing all relevant areas are even more challenging to identify. This will be discussed in the commentaries on each of Goal 15's targets below.

III. Commentaries on Targets

A. Target 15.1 By 2020, ensure the conservation, restoration and sustainable use of terrestrial and inland freshwater ecosystems and their services, in particular forests, wetlands, mountains and drylands, in line with obligations under international agreements

Target 15.1 calls for states to ensure compliance by 2020 with international agreements regarding the conservation, restoration, and sustainable use of terrestrial and inland freshwater ecosystems and their services, particularly forests, wetlands, mountains, and drylands. Indicator 15.1.1 includes (i) forest area as a proportion of total land area, and (ii) the proportion of important sites for terrestrial and freshwater biodiversity that are covered by protected areas, by ecosystem type. Target 15.1 has one implementing target, 15.a, which outlines the need to mobilize and significantly increase financial resources from all sources to conserve and sustainably use biodiversity and ecosystems. In turn, target 15.a's monitoring indicator is ODA and public expenditures on conservation and sustainable use of biodiversity and ecosystems.

1. Source of Target

Given its broad scope, target 15.1 represents a sort of 'chapeau' which subsumes many—if not all—of the other targets under SDG Goal 15. The target consists of a series of distinct commitments that can also be found across a range of different MEAs and international policy instruments. A commonly shared feature of these agreements is the incorporation of the ecosystem concept, which in recent decades has emerged as a new object of international regulation (alongside more traditional regulatory topics like species, natural areas, or sources of pollution). The Ramsar Convention was one of the earliest endeavours to ensure under international law the conservation and

---

[201] IPBES (n 182) xxii–xxiii.

sustainable ('wise') use of a particular category of ecosystems—wetlands.[202] The *World Conservation Strategy* and *World Charter for Nature* also refer to the need to protect ecosystems and ecological processes, culminating in Principle 7 of the Rio Declaration which calls upon states to 'cooperate, in a spirit of global partnership, to protect and restore the health and integrity of the Earth's ecosystem'.

The CBD defines ecosystems as 'dynamic complex[es] of plant, animal and microorganism communities and their non-living environment interacting as a functional unit'.[203] The ecosystem concept has permeated international, regional, and multilateral environmental agreements, touching all subject areas mentioned in target 15.1; namely terrestrial ecosystems,[204] inland freshwater resources,[205] forests,[206] mountains,[207] and drylands.[208] One key 'obligation under international agreements' associated with target 15.1 is the ecosystem approach developed under the CBD and affirmed by the WSSD.[209]

The CBD, adopted in parallel with the Rio Declaration in 1992, remains the most comprehensive international environmental legal instrument addressing target 15.1's objectives. The CBD's regime forms a broad umbrella that enables mutually supportive implementation across other treaty regimes and governance mechanisms.[210] Many of the CBD's obligations and COP decisions directly address target 15.1's subject matter, specifically the conservation, restoration and sustainable use and services of terrestrial and inland freshwater systems,[211] including forests,[212] wetlands,[213] mountains,[214] and drylands.[215]

The CBD has three high-level objectives: (i) biodiversity conservation, (ii) the sustainable use of biological resources, and (iii) the fair and equitable sharing of the benefits arising from the utilization of genetic resources.[216] These objectives apply at the

---

[202] *Ramsar Convention*, art 3(1).

[203] CBD art 2.

[204] For example, Berne Convention, CBD.

[205] *UNECE Convention on the Protection and Use of Transboundary Watercourses and International Lakes*, 17 March 1992 (entered into force 6 October 1996) 31 ILM 1312; *Convention on the Law of the Non-Navigational Uses of International Watercourses*, 21 May 1997 (in force 17 August 2014), 2999 UNTS 77, 36 ILM 700; *Convention on the Protection of the Rhine*, 12 April 1999 (in force 1 Jan 2003) IUCN Doc TRE-001307; *Protocol for Sustainable Development of Lake Victoria Basin*, 29 November 2003 (in force 1 December 2004), IUCN Doc TRE-159877; *Agreement Between Canada and the United States of America on Great Lakes Water Quality, 2012*, CTS E105342. See also JC Sanchez and J Roberts (eds), *Transboundary Water Governance: Adaptation to Climate Change* (IUCN Environmental Policy and Law Paper 75, IUCN 2014); Boyle and Redgwell (n 147) 592–96; R Moynihan, 'An Ecosystem Approach in International Law Concerning Transboundary Freshwater Ecosystems' in *Transboundary Freshwater Ecosystems in International Law: The Role and Impact of the UNECE Environmental Regime* (CUP 2021).

[206] For example, Rio Forest Principles, UN Forest Instrument.

[207] For example, Alpine Convention; Carpathian Convention.

[208] For example, UNCCD.

[209] A Gillespie, *Conservation, Biodiversity and International Law* (Edward Elgar 2013) 483–84.

[210] The so-called Biodiversity-Related Conventions are the most relevant to Target 15.1, particularly the International Treaty on Plant Genetic Resources for Agriculture (ITPGRFA), Convention on Migratory Species, Ramsar Convention, the World Heritage Convention, and the International Plant Protection Convention (IPPC). See SCBD, 'Biodiversity-related Conventions' <http://www.cbd.int/brc>.

[211] For example, *Programme of Work on Inland Waters Biodiversity*, CBD COP Decision VII/4.

[212] For example, *Expanded Programme of Work on Forest Biological Diversity*, CBD COP Decision VI/22.

[213] For example, *Programme of Work on Marine and Coastal Biodiversity*, CBD COP Decision IV/5.

[214] For example, *Programme of Work on Mountain Biologica Diversity*, CBD COP Decision VII/27.

[215] For example, *Programme of Work on Dry and Sub-humid Lands*, CBD COP Decision V/23.

[216] CBD art 1.

1100   SDG 15

ecosystem, species, and genetic levels.[217] For example, article 8 on *in situ* conservation states that, *inter alia*, 'each Contracting Party shall, as far as possible and as appropriate' promote the protection of ecosystems and rehabilitate and restore degraded ones.[218] A series of CBD thematic programmes of work deal with each ecosystem type covered in target 15.1.

Four of the Aichi targets pertain to the protection of ecosystems, including: (i) Aichi target 5 on halving 'the rate of loss of all natural habitats, including forests' and significantly reducing their degradation and fragmentation; (ii) Aichi target 11 on conserving 'at least 17 per cent of terrestrial and inland water, and 10 per cent of coastal and marine areas, especially areas of particular importance for biodiversity and ecosystem services'; (iii) Aichi target 14 on restoring and safeguarding 'ecosystems that provide essential services, including services related to water, and contribute to health, livelihoods and well-being'; and (iv) Aichi target 15 on restoring 'at least 15 per cent of degraded ecosystems'.

In addition, other MEAs and international instruments also contain relevant duties to protect ecosystems. In some cases, these duties are more explicitly defined than those in the CBD, but their scope of operation is restricted to the specific ecosystem type to which it applies. For example, both article 20 of the Watercourses Convention and article 2(2)(d) of the UNECE Water Convention state a general obligation to protect the ecosystems of international watercourses, but both instruments also lay down additional obligations which implicitly recognize the interconnections between international watercourses and other ecosystems. It has been debated whether similar obligations, which are normally considered to impose a duty of due diligence on the Parties, apply regardless of the existence of a transboundary impact, or risk thereof. By contrast, the commitment enshrined in target 15.1 and the CBD does not make a distinction between shared ecosystems and ecosystems located within national jurisdiction and is thus primarily aimed at promoting the conservation and sustainable use of ecosystem services within national borders, as well as the prevention of extraterritorial harm from activities taking place within or under national jurisdiction.[219]

2. Empirical Analysis

Modern efforts to protect and sustainably use the world's ecosystems have advanced thanks to rapid advances in scientists' ability to model complex ecological relationships,[220] as well as through the elaboration of concepts like ecosystem services and NCP which show the fundamental role of ecosystems in the provision of goods and services on which humanity depends.[221] The work of transnational epistemic communities and

[217] See also FAO, *ABS Elements: Elements to Facilitate Domestic Implementation of Access and Benefit-Sharing for Different Subsectors of Genetic Resources for Food and Agriculture with Explanatory Notes* (FAO 2019).

[218] CBD arts 8(d) and (8(f).

[219] CBD art 4.

[220] For example, RA Neugarten and others, *Tools for Measuring, Modelling, and Valuing Ecosystem Services: Guidance for Key Biodiversity Areas, Natural World Heritage Sites, and Protected Areas*, Best Practice Protected Area Guidelines Series No. 28 (IUCN 2018).

[221] See generally ID Thompson and others, 'Forest Biodiversity and the Delivery of Ecosystem Goods and Services: Translating Science into Policy' (2011) 61 BioScience 972.

COMMENTARIES ON TARGETS   1101

major science policy initiatives, including the *Millennium Ecosystem Assessment*,[222] the initiative on *The Economics of Ecosystems and Biodiversity*,[223] and the more recently established IPBES have been instrumental. These initiatives have clarified the links between ecosystems and human well-being and popularized the scientific construct of ecosystems in environmental policy circles.

The inclusion of target 15.1 as part of SDG Goal 15 sits squarely within this trend. The target focuses specifically on objectives for the conservation, restoration and sustainable use of terrestrial and inland freshwater ecosystems, as coastal and marine ecosystems are covered under SDG 14 and its target 14.2. At least in theory, these objectives seem to be widely endorsed at the multilateral level. With 196 States Parties, the CBD enjoys almost universal ratification (a notable exception being the United States, which signed the Convention in 1993 but never ratified it). A comparable level of ratification also characterizes other MEAs that are broadly applicable in this context, such as the UNCCD (196 Parties) and the Ramsar Convention on Wetlands (172 States Parties). Lastly, although important instruments such as the Watercourses Convention and the UNECE Water Convention have a smaller number of Parties, they contain certain provisions that are considered to be a codification of customary obligations,[224] and their impact on the domestic laws of Contracting Parties (particularly with respect to the UNECE Water Convention) has reportedly been significant.[225]

Despite ecosystems' inclusion in a substantial international legal framework, the extent and condition of ecosystems have continued to deteriorate over the past few decades.[226] Long-standing 'direct' and 'indirect' drivers of ecosystem destruction and degradation, including land-use change and overexploitation, continue to exert immense impacts on ecosystems. Present examples include the expansion of urban and agricultural areas, the transformation of tropical forests, and unsustainable hunting, fishing, and forestry practices. Furthermore, these drivers are now compounded by the rapidly accelerating threats posed by climate change, pollution, and introduction of IAS.[227]

The latest edition of the Global Biodiversity Outlook (GBO 5) suggests that the ecosystem-relevant Aichi Biodiversity targets have not been achieved. For example, degradation and fragmentation of habitats remains high in forests, wetlands, and rivers, especially in the most biodiversity-rich ecosystems in tropical regions.[228] In addition, despite a moderate improvement in the proportion of the total land area covered by

[222] Millennium Ecosystem Assessment, *Ecosystems and Human Well-being: Synthesis* (Island Press 2005).

[223] For example, TEEB, *The Economics of Ecosystems and Biodiversity: Mainstreaming the Economics of Nature: A Synthesis of the Approach, Conclusions and Recommendations of TEEB* (TEEB 2010).

[224] For example, the obligation of an equitable and reasonable utilization of international watercourses, which is contained in art 5 of the Watercourses Convention. See also *Gabčíkovo-Nagymaros Project (Hungary v Slovakia) (Merits)* [1997] ICJ Reports 7, para 47.

[225] UNECE, *Progress on Transboundary Water Cooperation Under the Water Convention. Report on implementation of the Convention on the Protection and Use of Transboundary Watercourses and International Lakes* (UNECE 2018).

[226] GM Mace and others, 'Aiming Higher to Bend the Curve of Biodiversity Loss' (2018) 1 Nature Sustainability 448.

[227] IPBES (n 182) 12.

[228] SCBD, *Global Biodiversity Outlook 5* (n 177) 53–54.

1102 SDG 15

protected areas, progress has been more limited in ensuring that such areas are ecologically representative and integrated into coherent networks, situated in areas that are particularly important for biodiversity, and effectively and equitably managed.[229] For example, although the *World Database on Protected Areas* considers that protected areas now comprise almost 15 per cent of all terrestrial and freshwater ecosystems, it has been calculated that less than half of the world's Key Biodiversity Areas are actually protected.[230] This also means that the formal maintenance of ecosystem extent has often not coincided with a parallel preservation of ecosystem condition, that is, the overall quality of an ecosystem in relation to its characteristics and its capacity to maintain flows of ecosystem services.

According to the 2019 IPBES Global Assessment Report, this ongoing alteration of ecosystem structures, processes, and functions since the 1970s has led to sharp declines in a wide range of material, non-material, and regulating contributions that nature provides to humans.[231] Where indicators suggest positive trends in the flow of certain ecosystem services such as the provision of food and raw materials, this is generally considered to be a temporary benefit deriving from unsustainable rates of resource exploitation that are not likely to continue over the long term.[232] Owing to growing scientific awareness about the interconnections between ecological dynamics across different spatial scales,[233] changes in ecosystem integrity at the local or regional level are also increasingly explored in their wider planetary implications. In particular, a group of experts has started to consider biosphere integrity as one of the two core planetary boundaries (together with climate change)[234] that may by themselves determine the stability of the entire Earth System.

3. Efforts at the International and Domestic Levels

The wording of target 15.1, which calls upon countries to protect ecosystems 'in line with obligations under international agreements' suggests that the implementation of existing commitments in this field remains a challenge. At the same time, the wording also highlights how international environmental law principles and rules applicable to ecosystems constitute a key toolbox for understanding and operationalizing the target.

At the international level, the CBD's COP is widely considered to be the leading body tasked with promoting and coordinating efforts to implement the target. This is consistent with its agenda-setting role within the so-called biodiversity cluster of MEAs. The COP's attention to ecosystems is seen in the very definition of biodiversity contained in

---

[229] See generally A Paterson, 'Protected Areas and Spaces' in Medaglia, Perron-Welch, and Goodman (eds), *Legal Aspects of Implementing the Convention on Biological Diversity* (n 111).

[230] BirdLife International, IUCN, and UNEP-WCMC, 'Protected Area Coverage of Key Biodiversity Areas (*keybiodiversityareas.org*) <www.keybiodiversityareas.org> accessed 13 March 2022.

[231] A Purvis and others, 'Chapter 2.2. Status and Trends—Nature' in ES Brondizio and others (eds) *Global Assessment Report of the Intergovernmental Science-Policy Platform on Biodiversity and Ecosystem Services* (IPBES Secretariat 2019).

[232] E Shepherd and others, 'Status and Trends in Global Ecosystem Services and Natural Capital: Assessing Progress Toward Aichi Biodiversity Target 14' (2016) 9(6) Conservation Letters 429.

[233] L Hein and others, 'Spatial Scales, Stakeholders and the Valuation of Ecosystem Services' (2006) 57 Ecological Economics 209.

[234] Rockström and others, 'Planetary Boundaries' (n 138).

the CBD. However, its understanding of ecosystems significantly expanded over time, in line with the parallel evolution of scientific knowledge in this field and the related technical work of the CBD's Subsidiary Body on Scientific, Technical and Technological Advice (SBSTTA). From this standpoint, the progressive elaboration of the concept of 'ecosystem approach' has been particularly important. The concept was established in 1995 as 'the primary framework for action to be taken under the Convention'.[235] This was a foundational decision by the Parties, establishing their intent to use the ecosystem approach as the main tool for the Convention's interpretation and implementation.[236] Accordingly, the SBSTTA has left 'footprints in numerous other COP decisions, and in particular, decisions relating to the thematic work programme of the COP'.[237]

The CBD COP's references to the ecosystem approach contained in its cross-cutting and thematic activities prior to the adoption of the SDGs, as well as its general influence on the interpretation of the provisions of the Convention, cannot be separated from the efforts undertaken since 2015 to achieve target 15.1. The COP has acted to mainstream ecosystem-oriented considerations in its recommendations to the Parties on issues including ecological restoration, spatial planning, and climate change mitigation and adaptation.[238] Most recently, the COP has sought to incorporate the notion of 'ecosystem integrity'[239] more centrally in its Kunming-Montreal GBF that recently replaced the Strategic Plan 2011–2020 and Aichi targets. These actions respond to multiple calls to do so by scientists[240] and non-governmental organizations (NGOs) including the International Union for the Conservation of Nature (IUCN) and the Wildlife Conservation Society.[241]

The Kunming-Montreal GBF negotiations saw the protection of ecosystems elevated to one of the overarching goals for 2050, with Goal A committing that the integrity, connectivity, and resilience of all ecosystems are maintained, enhanced, or restored, substantially increasing the area of natural ecosystems by 2050. This goal appears to be in direct dialogue with target 15.1, as the GBF also contains a number of 2030 action targets that explicitly refer to the conservation and restoration of terrestrial and freshwater

---

[235] COP Decision II/8 (30 November 1995) UN Doc UNEP/CBD/COP/2/19.

[236] F Burhenne-Guilmin, 'Biodiversity and International Law: Historical Perspectives and Present Challenges: Where Do We Come From, Where Are We Going?' in J Firestone and others (eds), *Biodiversity Conservation, Law and Livelihoods: Bridging the North-South Divide: IUCN Academy of Environmental Law Research Studies* (CUP 2008) 32; V Koester, 'The Convention on Biological Diversity and the Concept of Sustainable Development: The Extent and Manner of the Convention's Application of Components of the Concept' in M Bowman and others (eds), *Research Handbook on Biodiversity and the Law* (Edward Elgar 2016) 283.

[237] V Koester, 'The Convention on Biological Diversity and the Concept of Sustainable Development' (n 236) 283.

[238] For example, COP Decision XII/19 'Ecosystem Conservation and Restoration' (17 October 2014) UN Doc UNEP/CBD/COP/DEC/XII/19, para 4; and 5 COP Decision X/33 'Biodiversity and Climate Change' (29 October 2010) UN Doc UNEP/CBD/COP/DEC/X/33.

[239] The notion of ecosystem integrity refers to the capacity of an ecosystem to maintain structures and functions that are characteristics of its ecoregion, thus preserving its completeness and functionality.

[240] For example, E Nicholson and others, 'Scientific Foundations for an Ecosystem Goal, Milestones and Indicators for the Post-2020 Global Biodiversity Framework' (2021) 5 Nature Ecology and Evolution 1338.

[241] For example, 'Synthesis of Views of Parties and Observers on the Scope and Content of the Post-2020 Global Biodiversity Framework' (23 May 2019) UN Doc CBD/POST2020/PREP/1/INF/2. For some of the IUCN and Wildlife Conservation Society's early inputs to the OEWG process, consult the page CBD Secretariat, 'Notification 2019-075' (*cbd.int*, 6 September 2019) <http://www.cbd.int/conferences/post2020/submissions/2019-075> accessed 31 August 2021.

ecosystems. Actions for this include integrated spatial planning, systems of protected and conservation areas, and reduction of pollution and IAS threats. Moreover, several proposed indicators would also provide the COP with composite models for ecosystem integrity or changes in the extent of selected ecosystems.[242]

Beyond the CBD, a number of other international organizations and institutions are involved in the efforts to achieve target 15.1. The FAO and a collaboration between IUCN, UNEP, and UNEP-WCMC are particularly important owing to their monitoring and supporting role, as they are identified as the custodian agencies for the two indicators of target 15.1 by the UN Statistical Commission. In light of the broader evolution of global environmental governance, it should be noted that transnational partnerships and coalitions have also emerged as particularly important actors in the implementation of target 15.1, for example by providing technical tools to decision-makers, such as geospatial data platforms for monitoring and prioritization purposes,[243] or by channelling forms of blended finance towards the protection of biodiversity that is consistent with target 15.1's objectives.[244]

At the regional and domestic levels, the vision of target 15.1 is reflected by the adoption of policy targets to expand the proportion of ecosystems that are protected or restored. For example, the European Union has set a policy target to protect at least 30 per cent of its terrestrial ecosystems by 2030 and proposed ambitious nature restoration targets as part of the EU Biodiversity Strategy[245] that in the future may be included in the EU-wide SDG monitoring framework. In addition, most of the Parties to the CBD have also submitted at least one National Biodiversity Strategy and Action Plan (NBSAP) under article 6 of the Convention, with 177 of the current NBSAPs having been submitted after 2010 thus taking the Aichi Biodiversity targets into account.[246] The notion of subnational and local biodiversity strategies and action plans has also gained traction in the context of the CBD, expressing the broader trend toward the engagement of cities and local governments in the multi-level governance of biodiversity.[247] At present, however, efforts to implement target 15.1 are widely considered to be insufficient, with limited or no progress reported against the two indicators chosen for the target.[248] The respective Aichi targets have not been met either, even though

[242] Decision 15/5. Monitoring framework for the Kunming-Montreal Global Biodiversity Framework, UN Doc CBD/COP/DEC/15/5, Table 2.

[243] See, eg, the UN Biodiversity Lab, which is convened by the UNEP, the GEF, the UN Development Programme, and the CBD. Technical partners are platform developer MapX, NASA, and the UNEP's Global Resource Information Database, while data providers include a wide range of international institutions, research centres, and private companies.

[244] For example, BJ McFarland, 'The Origins and History of Conservation Finance' in *Conservation of Tropical Rainforests* (Palgrave Macmillan 2018).

[245] European Commission, *Communication From the Commission to the European Parliament, the Council, the European Economic and Social Committee and the Committee of the Regions. EU Biodiversity Strategy for 2030. Bringing Nature Back Into our Lives,* 20 May 2020, COM(2020) 380 final.

[246] See 'National Biodiversity Strategies and Action Plans (NBSAPs)' (*cbd.int*) <http://www.cbd.int/nbsap/?msclkid=a9f1130ab1c111ecaeb5fe45ebc8bb06> accessed 1 April 2022.

[247] 'Plan of Action on Subnational Governments, Cities and Other Local Authorities for Biodiversity' CBD Decision X/2 (29 October 2010) UN Doc UNEP/CBD/COP/DEC/X/22.

[248] 'Progress towards the Sustainable Development Goals. Report of the Secretary-General' (30 April 2021) UN Doc E/2021/58, 22–23.

ecological restoration programmes have been launched in many countries and regions and 50 per cent of CBD Parties have included restoration targets in their NBSAPs.[249] In fact, the majority of the targets and commitments contained in NBSAPs have been found to be less ambitious than the Aichi targets that are most relevant for target 15.1.[250]

Currently, the establishment of protected areas remains the main mechanism used to implement target 15.1 at the domestic level,[251] although progress has been greater for marine ecosystems than for Goal 15-relevant terrestrial ecosystems.[252] Other area-based measures, whose primary purpose might not be conservation, are increasingly seen as potentially contributing to the sustainable use of ecosystems, such as areas managed by Indigenous people and privately managed areas. However, these other measures are not being consistently incorporated in country strategies and action plans.[253] The effectiveness of protected areas in mitigating threats such as deforestation varies greatly—depending on legal status, placement, and enforcement capacity, for instance—and the rate of their creation across different countries is often uneven.[254] More broadly, there is emerging consensus on the necessity to ensure that ecosystems are sustainably used *outside* protected areas. This idea recalls the complexity of ecological interactions and posits that even those ecosystems most affected by human activities, such as agricultural or urban systems, play an important role in the provision of ecosystem services.[255] Evidence on the application of an integrated approach to the management of all types of ecosystems, however, remains scarce. For example, existing research consistently shows that biodiversity continues to decline in 'production landscapes' such as areas under agriculture, aquaculture, or forestry.[256]

4. Critique

Prima facie, the formulation of target 15.1 appears unusually ambitious. It is one of the few SDG targets that sets a 2020 deadline for its achievement. Moreover, it calls for the conservation, restoration, and sustainable use of *all* terrestrial and inland freshwater ecosystems and their services, not just those that are particularly degraded or especially important for preserving biodiversity. Upon closer scrutiny, behind target 15.1's ambition may also lie a series of glaring shortcomings. A first potential criticism sees the

---

[249] SCBD, *Global Biodiversity Outlook 5* (n 177) 100.

[250] Analysis of the Contribution of the Targets Established by Parties and Progress Towards the Aichi Biodiversity Targets' (13 March 2018) UN Doc CBD/SBI/2/2/Add.2.

[251] For example, 'Compilation of Main Messages for the 2018 Voluntary National Reviews. Note by the Secretariat' (31 May 2018) UN Doc E/HLPF/2018/5. See also N Dudley and others, 'Editorial Essay: Protected Areas and the Sustainable Development Goals' (2017) 23(2) Parks 9.

[252] SHM Butchart and others, 'Chapter 3. Assessing Progress Towards Meeting Major International Objectives Related to Nature and Nature's Contributions to People' in ES Brondizio and others (eds) *Global Assessment Report of the Intergovernmental Science-Policy Platform on Biodiversity and Ecosystem Services* (IPBES Secretariat 2019) 416–417.

[253] P Gannon and others, 'Status and Prospects for Achieving Aichi Biodiversity Target 11: Implications of National Commitments and Priority Actions' (2017) 23(2) Parks 13.

[254] For example, P Shah and others, 'What Determines the Effectiveness of National Protected Area Networks?' (2021) 16 Environmental Research Letters 074017.

[255] For example, S Wratten and others (eds) Ecosystem Services in Agricultural and Urban Landscapes (John Wiley and Sons 2013).

[256] Butchart and others, 'Assessing Progress Towards Meeting Major International Objectives' (n 252) 412.

1106   SDG 15

difficulty of translating the target's stated objective into any meaningful measure of success, a problem that is aggravated by the target's vague qualitative language. Questions that are left unanswered by target 15.1 include what level of progress is required to consider the target achieved, the reason for excluding important ecosystems such as agroecosystems from the target's scope, and what exactly are the applicable 'obligations under international agreements'.

A second criticism eyes the 2020 deadline assigned to the target as patently unrealistic, not only in the face of worsening global biodiversity trends but especially when it was already clear in 2015 that the CBD's Aichi Biodiversity targets would not be achieved by the end of the decade.[257] From this perspective, it is telling that the Kunming-Montreal GBF negotiations explicitly set 2030 as the target date to *stabilize* current trends in biodiversity, and envision the following twenty years (up to 2050) as the years in which natural ecosystems begin to recover—thus acknowledging the longer-term perspective that is necessary to address the global drivers of ecosystem destruction and degradation.

A third criticism is suggested by the target's guide to align 'with existing international agreements', which could be seen as the target failing to go beyond anything already included in existing MEAs, soft law instruments and political declarations. In other words, it could be argued that target 15.1 merely operates as a restatement of the need for the international community to adhere to already agreed obligations and policy targets under international biodiversity law. Additionally, this could be seen as keeping the CBD regime as the authoritative body for global biodiversity goals. If so, the target could be criticized for ignoring the well-known weaknesses of the CBD regime, including its lack of effective compliance mechanisms, emphasis on non-binding recommendations, and deference to the principle that states have the sovereign right to exploit biological resources located under their jurisdiction.[258]

Inevitably, the vagueness of target 15.1 percolates into the indicators chosen to monitor implementation. Both indicators are significantly narrower in scope than their target, although they have the advantage of having internationally established methodologies and standards, as well as sufficient conceptual clarity and data availability.[259] For example, by tracking forest area as a proportion of total land area, indicator 15.1.1 can only provide a measure of ecosystem extent as a proxy for an actual evaluation of ecosystem condition and integrity. Moreover, the indicator is only relevant to terrestrial ecosystems, and is not applicable to inland freshwater areas. For its part, indicator 15.1.2 can capture the extent to which key biodiversity areas (KBA) particularly important for the global persistence of biodiversity are covered by protected areas and

---

[257] 'Mid-term Review of Progress in Implementation of the Strategic Plan for Biodiversity 2011–2020 Including the Fourth Edition of the Global Biodiversity Outlook, and Actions to Enhance Implementation' CBD Decision XII/1 (14 October 2014) UN Doc UNEP/CBD/COP/DEC/XII/1.

[258] For example, SR Harrop and DJ Pritchard, 'A Hard Instrument Goes Soft: The Implications of the Convention on Biological Diversity's Current Trajectory' (2011) 21(2) Global Environmental Change 474; and Glowka and others (n 111) 2–6, 476.

[259] In the classification of the Inter-agency and Expert Group on SDG Indicators, both indicators are thus defined as 'Tier 1' indicators.

other effective area-based conservation measures (OECMs). This information, however, cannot reveal whether said areas are effectively and equitably managed as this would require the use of additional mechanisms for the assessment of management effectiveness and conservation outcomes.[260] In addition, although it serves to capture those ecosystems that are most important for the protection of biodiversity, the 15.1.2 indicator does not directly relate to the provision of ecosystem services, as most of the criteria used to identify a KBA are concerned with the presence and conservation status of certain subsets of species rather than on ecological processes per se.[261]

It should be noted that the possibility of adequately monitoring trends in ecosystem condition and integrity is still severely constrained by current capabilities for ecosystem assessment and gaps in data availability.[262] From such a standpoint, the chosen indicators could be considered as necessary, if imperfect, proxies. However, the fact remains that these indicators tend to conflate the concept of ecosystem, which focuses on ecological relationships and processes rather than on specific spatial scales, with that of natural areas. Such an approach could potentially create tensions with the monitoring framework that will be adopted as part of the Kunming-Montreal GBF, which will probably try to incorporate emerging measures of ecosystem integrity and functioning through composite indices.

B. Target 15.a Mobilize and significantly increase financial resources from all sources to conserve and sustainably use biodiversity and ecosystems

Owing to the cross-cutting nature of financing aspects in the 2030 Agenda, target 15.a is effectively relevant to the achievement of Goal 15 as a whole. Target 15.a's wording, however, suggests a particularly close link with target 15.1's overarching ambition for conservation and sustainable use, within which the other Goal 15 targets are nested. For this reason, target 15.a is briefly discussed here.

The 'historical' predecessor and indirect source of target 15.a can be found in article 20 of the CBD. CBD article 20 calls on each Party to provide financial support and incentives, in line with its own capabilities, to national activities aimed at achieving the CBD's objectives. At the same time, article 20 also requires developed country Parties to provide 'new and additional' financial resources to developing countries through bilateral, regional, and multilateral channels, to assist them in meeting the costs of implementing CBD's obligations. A substantial increase in the mobilization of financial resources was included as a dedicated target in the Aichi targets to meet the objectives

---

[260] For example, UNEP-WCMC, *Global Statistics from the Global Database on Protected Areas Management Effectiveness (GDPAME)* (UNEP-WCMC 2018).

[261] For example, MN Foster and others, 'The Identification of Sites of Biodiversity Conservation Significance: Progress with the Application of a Global Standard (2012) 4 Journal of Threatened Taxa 2733.

[262] For example, Z Wurtzebach and C Schultz, 'Measuring Ecological Integrity: History, Practical Applications, and Research Opportunities' (2016) 66(6) BioScience 446; and KE Watermeyer and others, 'Using Decision Science to Evaluate Global Biodiversity Indices' (2020) 35(2) Conservation Biology 492.

1108 SDG 15

of the CBD and its Strategic Plan 2011–2020. Further specifications for finance mobilization were made in subsequent CBD COP decisions, including commitments to double international financial flows to developing countries by 2015 and to mobilize domestic financial resources to reduce resource gaps by 2020.[263]

Achieving target 15.a, however, has seen mixed success. Long before the adoption of 15.a, many developed countries failed to respect their obligation to provide additional financial resources to developing country Parties under CBD article 20(2), which has become a sharp point of contention.[264] As recently as 2018, the CBD COP formally urged developed country Parties to honour their article 20 commitments and strive to implement the resource mobilization targets under the Strategic Plan 2011–2020,[265] which have only partially been achieved.[266]

Notably, international public biodiversity finance is estimated to have doubled over the last decade, with bilateral ODA alone increasing by over 100 per cent if all investments relevant to biodiversity are considered.[267] By contrast, despite funding increases in a subset of CBD Parties, domestic resources have not experienced a similar growth, and may have even declined in some countries. Overall, global biodiversity finance is estimated to be in the order of $78–91 billion per year, with most of the funding (around $68 billion per year) still coming from domestic budgets. This is considered to be largely insufficient where financing to fulfil all needs is estimated anywhere between $103 billion and $895 billion per year.[268] In addition, biodiversity finance resources are eclipsed by public subsidies and civil support for activities that are harmful to ecosystem integrity, such as agricultural expansion and overfishing.[269]

From a critical perspective, it should be noted that target 15.a does not contain any quantitative target to be achieved, thus it fails to rally resource mobilization around a universally understood figure like the $100 billion in funding that was agreed during the climate change negotiations in 2009.[270] The lack of a common understanding on what it would mean to 'significantly increase financial resources from all sources' to conserve and sustainably use biodiversity has already led to concerns around the risk of double counting resources allocated to other objectives (eg climate finance) or resources mobilized by different entities within the same country (eg central and local governments),[271] and created tensions in negotiations for the Kunming-Montreal GBF.

---

[263] 'Resource Mobilization', CBD Decision XII/3 (17 October 2014) UN Doc UNEP/CBD/COP/DEC/XII/3, paras 1(a) and (e).

[264] See, eg, 'In-Depth Review of the Application of the Ecosystem Approach: Review of Information in the Third National Reports. Note by the Executive Secretary' (14 June 2007) UN Doc UNEP/CBD/SBSTTA/12/INF/1.

[265] COP Decision 14/22 (30 November 2018) UN Doc CBD/COP/DEC/14/22, para 5.

[266] SCBD, Global Biodiversity Outlook 5 (n 177) 120.

[267] ibid 121–22.

[268] SCBD, 'Estimation of Resources Needed for Implementing the Post-2020 Global Biodiversity Framework' (18 June 2020) UN Doc CBD/SBI/3/5/Add.2, paras 13–21.

[269] OECD, Biodiversity: Finance and the Economic and Business Case for Action (OECD Secretariat 2019).

[270] 'Copenhagen Accord' UNFCCC Decision 2/CP.15, in 'Report of the Conference of the Parties on its Fifteenth Session (30 March 2010) UN Doc FCCC/CP/2009/11/Add.1, para 8.

[271] OECD, A Comprehensive Overview of Global Biodiversity Finance (OECD Secretariat 2020).

C. Target 15.2 By 2020, promote the implementation of sustainable management of all types of forests, halt deforestation, restore degraded forests and substantially increase afforestation and reforestation globally

This 2020-bound target aspires to promote the implementation of sustainable management of all types of forests, halt deforestation, restore degraded forests, and substantially increase afforestation and reforestation globally. There are five sub-indicators used to measure progress towards SFM.[272] Target 15.b recognizes the need to mobilize significant resources from all sources and at all levels to finance SFM, and to provide adequate incentives to developing countries to advance SFM, including for conservation and reforestation. Indicators 15.2.1 and 15.b.1 monitor ODA and public expenditure on conservation and sustainable use of biodiversity and ecosystems.

1. Sources of Target

Despite over three decades of negotiations, no comprehensive international regime addressing the conservation and sustainable use of all types of forests has been agreed.[273] Instead, forests fall within the scope of over ten legally and non-legally binding international treaties and instruments.[274] Of these, the UN Forest Instrument (Forest Instrument) provides the clearest policy guidance for implementing target 15.2 as it provides high-level guidance on implementing forest-related aspects of the CBD, UNFCCC, UNCCD, CITES, Ramsar Convention, World Heritage Convention, and the International Tropical Timber Agreement, 2006 (ITTA).[275]

The CBD serves as the main legal foundation for target 15.2 as an umbrella agreement addressing the conservation and sustainable use of all terrestrial biodiversity. It is complemented by a Programme of Work on Forest Biodiversity and Aichi targets 5, 7, and 15. Aiming to slow and reverse loss of forest cover and forest carbon loss, the UNFCCC requires its Parties to promote and cooperate on the conservation and enhancement of sinks and reservoirs of carbon and methane, including biomass and forests as well as terrestrial and coastal ecosystems.[276]

UNCCD Parties work to combat desertification and mitigate the effects of drought, both of which necessarily involve concerns over forest degradation and loss, which are

---

[272] 'SDG Indicator Metadata' (n.d.) <https://unstats.un.org/sdgs/metadata/files/Metadata-15-02-01.pdf> accessed 10 April 2022.

[273] Maguire (n 174) 70; A Eikermann, *Forests in International Law: Is There Really a Need for an International Forest Convention?* (Springer 2015); E Tramontana, 'Where Are We Now with Global Forest Regulation and Governance? Insights from a "Global Public Goods" Perspective' (2016) 2 Rivista Quadrimestrale di Diritto Dell'Ambiente 4; A Savaresi, 'Forest Biodiversity Law and Policy' in Medaglia, Perron-Welch, and Goodman (eds), *Legal Aspects of Implementing the Convention on Biological Diversity* (n 111).

[274] See BMGS Ruis, 'No Forest Convention but Ten Tree Treaties' (2001) 52 Unasylva 3; Eikermann (n 273); UN Secretary-General, 'Gaps in International Environmental Law and Environment-Related Instruments: Towards A Global Pact for the Environment' UN Doc A/73/419 paras 41, 104.

[275] *International Tropical Timber Agreement, 2006*, 27 January 2006 (in force 7 December 2011), UN Doc TD/TIMBER.3/12.

[276] UNFCCC art 4(1)(d).

often the first step on the road to desertification in arid and dryland areas, areas which are inherently unstable but resilient due to high levels of endemism.[277] Parties aim to respond by using 'long-term integrated strategies that focus simultaneously, in affected areas, on improved productivity of land, and the rehabilitation, conservation and sustainable management of land and water resources, leading to improved living conditions, in particular at the community level'.[278]

Although dedicating some attention to subjects addressed in target 15.2, the ITTA remains 'effectively little more than a commodity-market adjustment among consumer and producer states, with a commitment to increase international trade in tropical timber from sustainably managed and legally harvested forests'.[279]

2. Empirical Analysis

Target 15.2 calls on states to carry out five actions by 2020: (i) promote the implementation of SFM in all types of forests, (ii) halt deforestation, (iii) restore degraded forests, (iv) substantially increase afforestation globally, and (v) substantially increase reforestation globally. As noted above, a multitude of treaties and instruments underlie it, but the Forest Instrument takes primacy in determining its content. The Forest Instrument has established common agreement on what constitutes SFM and instituted four global goals for all types of forests.

The Forest Instrument defines SFM as 'a dynamic and evolving concept that aims to maintain and enhance the economic, social and environmental values of all types of forests, for the benefit of present and future generations'.[280] The Forest Instrument establishes four global objectives on forests, and asks states 'to work globally, regionally and nationally to achieve progress towards their achievement by 2030'.[281] Yet, legally speaking, the CBD remains the most consequential treaty for forests, with a scope covering the conservation of forest biodiversity, sustainable use of the components of forest biodiversity, and the fair and equitable sharing of the benefits resulting from the utilization of forest genetic resources.[282]

Other global initiatives that complement target 15.2 include the CBD's Aichi targets, which proved very influential on its text. Aichi target 7 calls on Parties to sustainably manage forests used for forestry, and ensure the conservation of biodiversity, while Aichi target 5 seeks to at minimum halve the rate of loss of all natural forest habitats and bring forest loss close to zero where feasible, as well as to significantly reduce forest degradation and forest fragmentation. Further, Aichi target 11 calls on states to conserve terrestrial areas, especially areas of particular importance for biodiversity, through effectively and equitably managed, ecologically representative, well-connected systems, and OECMs that are integrated into wider landscapes.

---

[277] FAO, *Trees, Forests and Land Use in Drylands: The First Global Assessment – Full Report* (FAO 2019) 177.
[278] UNCCD art 2(2).
[279] Boyle and Redgwell (n 147) 677.
[280] UN Forest Instrument art 4.
[281] Ibid art 5.
[282] See Savaresi, 'Forest Biodiversity Law' (n 113); Savaresi, 'Forest Biodiversity Law and Policy' (n 273).

In addition, Aichi target 14 calls for the restoration and safeguarding of ecosystems that provide essential services, including services related to water and contribute to health, livelihoods, and well-being while considering the needs of women, Indigenous and local communities, and vulnerable groups. Finally, Aichi target 15 aims to enhance ecosystem resilience and biodiversity contributions to carbon stocks through conservation and restoration, including restoration of at least 15 per cent of degraded ecosystems, thereby combatting desertification and contributing to climate change mitigation and adaptation.

UNFCCC climate change mitigation and adaptation actions also contribute to achieving target 15.2. Specifically, UNFCCC Parties must quantify emissions from land use, land-use change, and forestry (LULUCF). Parties gradually developed the Reducing Emissions from Deforestation and Degradation (REDD) + mechanism through COP decisions, incorporating it into the 2015 Paris Agreement with the aim of reducing emissions from deforestation and forest degradation, while creating roles for conservation, SFM, and enhancement of carbon stocks. The ITTA 2006 also complements target 15.2 by promoting the expansion and diversification of international trade in tropical timber from sustainably managed and legally harvested forests and boosting sustainable management of tropical timber producing forests.[283]

3. Efforts at the Domestic and International Levels
The most direct impacts of the UN Forest Instrument and its predecessors have been through national forest policies. Efforts under the CBD have been carried out under the aegis of NBSAPs, while states are addressing desertification and land degradation under their national action plans. National actions under the UNFCCC are being carried out within the framework of nationally determined contributions (NDCs). Additional regional goals complement this, helping to enhance cooperation between policy and technical sectors.[284] The 2017–2030 UN Strategic Plan for Forests[285] sets out a global framework for action on conserving and sustainably managing forests, while halting deforestation and forest degradation. This was established to complement forest-related matters in the SDGs and other international MEAs. Additionally, technical data and insights help Member States' monitoring of progress towards officially agreed goals.[286]

4. Critique
Most Member States are not on track to meet target 15.2 and b. While there are many established approaches to safeguarding, sustainably using and restoring forest ecosystems, progress is lacking with many states reporting insufficient funding and lack of

---

[283] ITTA 2006 (n 13) art 1.

[284] See, eg, the Goals for European Forests and the European 2020 Targets for Forests.

[285] *United Nations Strategic Plan for Forests 2017–2030*, UN Doc A/RES/71/285.

[286] P Mondal and others, 'A Reporting Framework for Sustainable Development Goal 15: Multi-Scale Monitoring of Forest Degradation Using MODIS, Landsat and Sentinel Data' (2020) 237 Remote Sensing of Environment 111592.

1112 SDG 15

capacity to realize required activities. The lack of a comprehensive, stand-alone forest treaty may undermine the ready achievement of target 15.2 and b, as this means that forest-related issues are fragmented across international bodies and instruments.[287] Although an umbrella treaty on forests could eliminate inconsistencies and duplications, resolve ambiguities, and ensure a cohesive regulatory framework for global forest governance,[288] the political will does not currently exist for a global forest treaty and Member States must work to synchronize their diverse practices on forests to successfully halt and reverse global forest loss and institute sustainable management.[289] This requires meeting most other SDGs, as deforestation is often a consequence of societal demands for valuable forest resources and lands, as well as the need for land for agriculture and pastoralism to feed a still growing global population. Forest-based livelihoods that reduce poverty and help meet all SDGs must be found and implemented broadly.

Cooperation among states and stakeholders is critical to achieving target 15.2. Various countries have emphasized the importance of working with communities who are directly impacted by forest policy and initiatives as important stakeholders. In the years following the promulgation of the SDGs, over 450 corporations pledged to seek zero deforestation and improve the procurement of sustainable forest commodities.[290] Despite increasing action by a wide number of actors and a dramatic increase in MEAs and international instruments, over the past three decades forests have suffered the largest decrease in land area of any terrestrial land cover type, mostly due to conversion for agriculture.[291] This poses 'high risks for irreversible species loss, especially in areas with highly fragmented habitats, such as the biodiversity hotspots'.[292] Alongside the loss of forested lands, forest carbon loss over the tropics has doubled in the early twenty-first century.[293]

GBO 5 focused on shared actions to support forest-relevant Aichi targets, including establishing protected areas, creating sustainable land management plans, and restoring degraded ecosystems. NBSAPs were an important tool for integrating target 15.2 into national policies. A majority of these NBSAPs directly responded to Aichi target's 4, 5, 7, 11, 14, and 15.[294] However, much of the NBSAPs' text related to sustainable management are vague and do not distinguish different sectors like agriculture or forestry. Additionally, very few targets in NBSAPs discuss aquaculture—a long recognized driver of mangrove tree loss in many countries.[295]

---

[287] Tramontana (n 5) 5.

[288] ibid.

[289] CSG Jefferies and others, 'International Law, Innovation, and Environmental Change in the Anthropocene' in N Craik and others (eds), *Global environmental change and innovation in international law* (CUP 2018) 9–10; Tramontana (n 273); Eikermann (n 273) 58.

[290] I Delabre and others, 'Strategies for Tropical Forest Protection and Sustainable Supply Chains: Challenges and Opportunities for Alignment with the UN Sustainable Development Goals' (2020) 15 Sustainability Science 1637.

[291] X Hu and others, 'Recent Global Land Cover Dynamics and Implications for Soil Erosion and Carbon Losses from Deforestation' (2021) 34(100291) Anthropocene 6, 8.

[292] Ibid 9.

[293] Y Feng and others, 'Doubling of Annual Forest Carbon Loss over the Tropics during the Early Twenty-First Century' [2022] Nature Sustainability <https://doi.org/10.1038/s41893-022-00854-3>.

[294] SCBD, *Global Biodiversity Outlook 5* (n 177).

[295] MJ Phillips and others, *Shrimp Culture and the Environment: Lessons from the World's Most Rapidly Expanding Warmwater Aquaculture Sector* (FAO 1993); FE Dierberg and W Kiattisimkul, 'Issues, Impacts, and Implications

COMMENTARIES ON TARGETS 1113

D. Target 15.b Mobilize significant resources from all sources and at all levels to finance sustainable forest management and provide adequate incentives to developing countries to advance such management, including for conservation and reforestation

Target 15.b's two elements are principally aimed at supporting the implementation of target 15.2. The first element calls for a mobilization of significant resources from all sources and at all levels to finance SFM. The second calls on states to provide adequate incentives for developing countries to advance SFM actions including conservation and reforestation. These aspects mirror the call in the fourth Global Objective on Forests to 'Mobilize Financial Resources: Reverse the decline in [ODA] for SFM and mobilize significantly increased new and additional financial resources from all sources for the implementation of [SFM].'

E. Target 15.3 By 2030, combat desertification, restore degraded land and soil, including land affected by desertification, drought and floods, and strive to achieve a land degradation-neutral world

SDG Goal 15's target 15.3 sets a 2030 deadline to combat desertification, restore degraded land and soil, mitigate effects of drought and floods, and strive to achieve a Land Degradation Neutral (LDN) world. FAO monitors the key indicator 15.3.1 by calculating the 'proportion of land that is degraded over the total land area'.[296]

1. Sources of Target
The UNCCD, CBD, and UNFCCC are the main international law sources underlying target 15.3. These Treaties offer support to the creation of national policies for preventing land degradation and desertification, restoring degraded land and soil, and achieving LDN.[297] Among these, the UNCCD provides the primary source given its specific goal of combatting desertification[298] and land degradation[299] in countries

of Shrimp Aquaculture in Thailand' (1996) 20 Environmental Management 649; S Hamilton, 'Assessing the Role of Commercial Aquaculture in Displacing Mangrove Forest' (2013) 89 Bulletin of Marine Science 585; LS Herbeck and others, 'Decadal Trends in Mangrove and Pond Aquaculture Cover on Hainan (China) since 1966: Mangrove Loss, Fragmentation and Associated Biogeochemical Changes' (2020) 233 Estuarine, Coastal and Shelf Science 106531; FAO, *The State of World Fisheries and Aquaculture 2020: Sustainability in Action* (FAO 2020) 124.

[296] SDG Indicator Metadata (n.d.) <https://unstats.un.org/sdgs/metadata/files/Metadata-15-03-01.pdf> accessed 29 March 2022.
[297] P Chasek and others, 'Land Degradation Neutrality: The Science–Policy Interface from the UNCCD to National Implementation' (2019) 92 Environmental Science & Policy 182.
[298] UNCCD art 1(b): '"combating desertification" includes activities which are part of the integrated development of land in arid, semi-arid and dry sub-humid areas for sustainable development which are aimed at: (i) prevention and/or reduction of land degradation; (ii) rehabilitation of partly degraded land; and (iii) reclamation of desertified land'.
[299] ibid art 1(f): '"land degradation" means reduction or loss, in arid, semi-arid and dry sub-humid areas, of the biological or economic productivity and complexity of rainfed cropland, irrigated cropland, or range, pasture, forest and woodlands resulting from land uses or from a process or combination of processes, including processes

1114   SDG 15

experiencing serious drought[300] or desertification.[301] The concept of LDN was developed under the aegis of the UNCCD before being adopted at Rio + 20[302] and subsequently included in Goal 15's target 15.3.

The UNCCD builds on earlier desertification efforts, such as the *Plan of Action to Combat Desertification*[303] (PACD) adopted after the 1977 UN Conference on Desertification organized by UNEP. The PACD was the first—ultimately unsuccessful—attempt to plan for the prevention and response to the advance of desertification in productive lands, and reclaiming desertified land for productive use. Witnessing the harmful impacts of lengthy droughts on terrestrial ecosystems, biodiversity, and livelihoods, PACD sought to sustain and promote the productivity of arid, semi-arid, sub-humid, and other areas vulnerable to desertification to improve living standards—within ecological limits.[304]

In 1992, Chapter 12 of Agenda 21 on combatting desertification defined the concept of 'desertification' and established a negotiating mandate, leading to the creation of the Intergovernmental Negotiating Committee on Desertification (INCD) as a subsidiary body of the UN General Assembly in 1993.[305] UNCCD was adopted in 1994,[306] with Parties holding COP 1 in 1997. In developing the UNCCD's commitments, Parties considered 'the contribution that combating desertification can make to achieving the objectives of the ... [UNFCCC, CBD,] and other related environmental conventions'.[307] The UNCCD's integration of desertification in other environmental treaties shows again how SDG Goal 15 as well as its target 15.3 fits within the three conventions synergistically. For its part, the UNFCCC's aim to prevent increasing climate change requires Parties to promote the sustainable management and conservation of GHG sinks and reservoirs including biomass, forests, and other terrestrial ecosystems.[308]

As noted above, the commitments adopted by Parties to the CBD involve all forms of terrestrial biodiversity, sustainable use of terrestrial biological resources, and

arising from human activities and habitation patterns, such as: (i) soil erosion caused by wind and/ or water; (ii) deterioration of the physical, chemical and biological or economic properties of soil; and (iii) long-term loss of natural vegetation'.

[300] ibid art 1(c). ' "drought" means the naturally occurring phenomenon that exists when precipitation has been significantly below normal recorded levels, causing serious hydrological imbalances that adversely affect land resource production systems'.

[301] ibid art 1(a). ' "desertification" means land degradation in arid, semi-arid and dry sub-humid areas resulting from various factors, including climatic variations and human activities'.

[302] 'The Future We Want', para 206; P Chasek and others, 'Operationalizing Zero Net Land Degradation: The next Stage in International Efforts to Combat Desertification?' (2015) 112 Journal of Arid Environments 5, 5–6.

[303] United Nations Conference on Desertification, *Round-up, Plan of Action and Resolutions* (United Nations 1978), Part B.

[304] ibid 247, 261. MR Biswas, 'U.N. Conference on Desertification, in Retrospect' (1978) 5 Environmental Conservation 247, 261.

[305] *Establishment of an Intergovernmental Negotiating Committee for the Elaboration of an Intergovernmental Convention to Combat Desertification in Those Countries Experiencing Serious Drought and/or Desertification, Particularly in Africa*, UN Doc A/RES/47/188.

[306] Agenda 21, para 12.40; PS Chasek, 'The Convention to Combat Desertification: Lessons Learned for Sustainable Development' (1997) 6 Journal of Environment and Development 147; P-M Dupuy and JE Viñuales, *International Environmental Law* (2nd edn, CUP 2018) 14.

[307] Dupuy and Viñuales, *International Environmental Law* (n 306).

[308] UNFCCC, arts 2 and 4(1)(d).

sharing the benefits resulting from access to and the utilization of genetic resources. Biodiversity is particularly imperilled in arid, semi-arid and dry sub-humid areas, especially where threatened by land degradation, drought, and desertification, making the CBD especially relevant in tackling target 15.3. Furthermore, halting and reversing climate change will be critical to meet target 15.3, as climate change models predict that arid and semi-arid regions worldwide will experience more frequent droughts and increased temperatures in coming decades. Indeed, were current trends to continue, 'current 1-in-100-year droughts would occur every two to five years for most of Africa, Australia, southern Europe, southern and central United States, Central America, the Caribbean, north-west China, and parts of Southern America'.[309] Although not explicitly mentioned in the target's text, meeting the UNFCCC's aim is a *sine qua non* for achieving target 15.3.

2. Empirical Analysis

SDG Goal 15's target 15.3 commits UN Member States to pursuing three different objectives: (i) combatting desertification; (ii) restoring degraded land and soil, including land affected by desertification, drought, and floods; and (iii) striving for an LDN world.

The first objective is squarely situated within the UNCCD, which aims to halt and reverse desertification by addressing its existing harms and future risks. The UNCCD defines 'combatting desertification' as 'activities which are part of the integrated development of land in arid, semi-arid and dry sub-humid areas for sustainable development which are aimed at: (i) prevention and/or reduction of land degradation, (ii) rehabilitation of partly degraded land, and (iii) reclamation of desertified land'.[310]

Target 15.3's second objective is also situated in the UNCCD framework but also has close links to the UNFCCC and CBD. Here, the language used speaks principally to restorative and revitalizing practices aimed at ameliorating the desertification status quo. The UNCCD's goals do include the rehabilitation, conservation and sustainable management of land and water resources, leading to improved living conditions, especially at the community level.[311] Target 15.3 reflects UNFCCC's call to restore degraded land and soil as critical GHG sinks, and reflects CBD topics of conservation of biodiversity and ecosystems.

The third objective of target 15.3 envisions Land Degradation Neutrality, a concept developed under the aegis of the UNCCD, later adopted at Rio + 20,[312] and also relevant to the UNFCCC. The UNCCD defines LDN as a 'state whereby the amount and quality of land resources, necessary to support ecosystem functions and services and enhance food security, remains stable or increases within specified temporal and spatial scales and ecosystems'.[313] The LDN Conceptual

---

[309] G Naumann and others, 'Global Changes in Drought Conditions Under Different Levels of Warming' (2018) 45 Geophysical Research Letters 3285, 3285.

[310] UNCCD art 1(b).

[311] ibid art 2.

[312] 'The Future We Want', para 206; Chasek and others, 'Operationalizing Zero Net Land Degradation' (n 302) 5–6.

[313] UNCCD, *Land Degradation Neutrality for Sustainable Agriculture and Food Security* (UNCCD 2021).

1116 SDG 15

Framework[314] defines LDN in operational terms, with nineteen guiding principles for implementation.[315] With its inclusion as part of target 15.3, LDN is now intended to be operationalized globally by all UNCCD Parties. Thus, LDN can be seen as another globally relevant ambition offering opportunities for mutually synergistic implementation of environmental Treaties.[316]

3. Efforts at the Domestic and International Levels

The UNCCD calls for national governments, civil society, and local populations to cooperate in combatting desertification and mitigating the effects of drought and dryland degradation,[317] promoting sustainable development as the primary means of implementation,[318] and providing a strategic planning framework to coordinate national action programmes (NAPs) on sustainable development and operationalize the Convention's commitments.[319] Parties' obligations are further detailed in five regional annexes with a primary focus on the African continent as the region most imperilled by desertification.[320]

At the international level, several efforts contribute to achieving target 15.3. The framework for these efforts is the UNCCD 2018–2030 Strategic Framework,[321] while other global initiatives complementing this target include the Aichi targets established by the CBD. Relevant targets include Aichi target 4 (sustainable production and consumption), Aichi target 5 (Habitat loss halved or reduced), and Aichi target 15 (Ecosystem restoration and resilience).[322] GBO 5 highlighted further actions that support SDG 15.3, including establishing protected areas, creating sustainable land management plans, and restoring degraded ecosystems. NBSAPs were also an important tool for integrating target 15.3 into national policies. A majority of these NBSAPs contained activities related to Aichi targets 4, 5, and 15,[323] but language on sustainable management was generally vague and NBSAPs frequently do not specify how these commitments will be instituted in production sectors. Hopefully, the 2021–2030 UN Decade on Ecosystem Restoration will raise awareness and support for target 15.3's goals and the recovery of damaged drylands.[324]

---

[314] UNCCD, *Scientific Conceptual Framework for Land Degradation Neutrality: A Report of the Science-Policy Interface* (UNCCD 2017); AL Cowie and others, 'Land in Balance: The Scientific Conceptual Framework for Land Degradation Neutrality' (2018) 79 Environmental Science & Policy 25.

[315] UNCCD, 'LDN Principles' (n.d.) <https://www.unccd.int/land-and-life/land-degradation-neutrality/ldn-principles>.

[316] Chasek and others, 'Operationalizing Zero Net Land Degradation' (n 302) 7.

[317] ibid art 2.

[318] ibid arts 1(a), 2–3.

[319] ibid art 6.

[320] Medaglia and others, *SDG 15 on Terrestrial Ecosystems and Biodiversity: Contributions of International Law, Policy and Governance* (n 77) 8.

[321] Decision 7/COP.13 *The Future Strategic Framework of the Convention*, UN Doc ICCD/COP(13)/21/Add.1.

[322] SCBD, *Global Biodiversity Outlook 5* (n 177).

[323] ibid 5.

[324] FAO, *Trees, Forests and Land Use in Drylands: The First Global Assessment – Full Report* (n 277).

4. Critique

Despite having the most widespread participation of any MEA, the entry into force of the UNCCD 'has not translated into effective prevention of desertification ... not least because [it] is weak on specific commitments'.[325] Despite being in force for over twenty-five years, political support remains inadequate to drive significant change. Indeed, '[d]espite the great need to combat the problems of desertification and aridity and their socio-economic consequences, the [UNCCD] has failed to engender the urgent and positive action required'.[326] In this regard, it has followed in the footsteps of its predecessor from the late 1970s, the non-legally binding PACD.[327]

A significant challenge in assessing UNCCD's implementation is that national data has not been regularly reported, particularly from developing country Parties that have limited resources and capacity.[328] The first review of national reports only occurred in 2018, and while states reported that target 15.3 provides clear definitions and methodologies for reporting, there is contention on how to interpret the data. This is a result of the complex environmental, social, and policy dynamics involved when implementing national laws and policies on desertification and land degradation.[329]

Capacity issues pose another challenge for UNCCD implementation. Developing countries have expressed their need for continuous support to optimize capacity at different levels of government and to maintain their national policy and legislation. Furthermore, a lack of financial resources, lack of personnel, and lack of knowledge are key barriers.[330] Finally, a lack of knowledge has been highlighted as a sizable barrier, as decision-makers may not necessarily understand how to integrate SDG 15.3 into laws and policies.

Moreover, other barriers that prevent thorough national adaptation of target 15.3 are a lack of coordination between different bodies of government. For example, local authorities may lack knowledge and incentive to enforce, monitor, and evaluate land degradation measures which could prevent effective implementation of national policies.[331] Furthermore, desertification, drought, flash floods, and other extreme weather events[332] are being driven by biodiversity loss (eg loss of soil biodiversity)[333] and

---

[325] Boyle and Redgwell (n 147) 673.

[326] ibid 676.

[327] ibid.

[328] ibid.

[329] NC Sims and others, 'A Land Degradation Interpretation Matrix for Reporting on UN SDG Indicator 15.3.1 and Land Degradation Neutrality' (2020) 114 Environmental Science & Policy 1.

[330] For example, IUCN-CEESP, Exploring right to diversity in conservation law, policy and practice' Policy matters 17 (2010) IUCN, 173–242 <http://www.iucn.org/downloads/policy_matters_17___pg_173_204.pdf> accessed 29 March 2022.

[331] ibid.

[332] See, eg, *Combating Sand and Dust Storms*, UN Doc A/RES/72/225, para 8: '*Reaffirms* that climate change is one of the greatest challenges of our time and, among other factors, is a serious challenge to the sustainable development of all countries, including those affected by sand and dust storms, and emphasizes that, among other factors, climate change is an important potential contributor to future wind erosion and the risk of sand and dust storms, especially the occurrence of more extreme wind events and the movement to drier climates, although reverse effects are possible.'

[333] See, eg, C Robb, 'Soil Biodiversity Law and Policy' in Medaglia, Perron-Welch and Goodman (eds), *Legal Aspects of Implementing the Convention on Biodiversity* (n 111).

1118   SDG 15

climate change,[334] meaning that target 15.3 cannot be met without implementing the remainder of SDG 15, and rapidly increasing the speed of implementing SDG 13.

F. Target 15.4 By 2030, ensure the conservation of mountain ecosystems, including their biodiversity, in order to enhance their capacity to provide benefits that are essential for sustainable development

Goal 15's target 15.4 seeks by 2030 for states to ensure the conservation of mountain ecosystems and their biodiversity and enhance their capacity to provide benefits for sustainable development. There are two indicators for this target: (i) coverage by protected areas of important sites for mountain biodiversity, and (ii) the Mountain Green Cover Index (MGCI), which seeks to measure 'the changes of the green vegetation in mountain areas'.[335]

1. Sources of Target

Currently there is no global treaty or instrument on mountains, and where mountains are treated in MEAs (including the CBD, UNCCD, UNFCCC, and World Heritage Convention),[336] it is limited to narrow, specific concerns linked to the objectives of those treaties.[337] In one leading text on international law and environment, the authors place mountains in the broader context of landscape protection—a topic of national concern dating back to the nineteenth century,[338] and international concern early in the twentieth century.[339] Yet, international legal protection of mountain areas is a relatively recent development.[340]

The language of target 15.4 is most closely linked to the CBD and Aichi target 14 on 'ecosystems that provide essential services'. Yet, Chapter 13 of Agenda 21 on 'Managing Fragile Ecosystems: Sustainable Mountain Development' was the first time that the global community signalled concern for mountains as essential ecosystems that need to be preserved, restored, and sustainably developed. Chapter 13 envisioned the

[334] See PR Shukla and others, *Climate Change and Land: An IPCC Special Report on Climate Change, Desertification, Land Degradation, Sustainable Land Management, Food Security, and Greenhouse Gas Fluxes in Terrestrial Ecosystems* (IPCC 2019). See also SDG 13 chapter in this volume.

[335] 'SDG Indicator Metadata' (*unstats.un.org*, n.d.) <https://unstats.un.org/sdgs/metadata/files/Metadata-15-04-02.pdf> accessed 10 April 2022.

[336] A Villeneuve and others, 'The Legal Framework for Sustainable Mountain Management: An Overview of Mountain-Specific Instruments' (2002) 53 Unasylva 56.

[337] ibid

[338] See, eg, TM Lekan, 'The Nature of Home: Landscape Preservation and Local Identities' in D Blackbourn and J Retallack (eds), *Localism, Landscape, and the Ambiguities of Place: German-Speaking Central Europe, 1860–1930* (University of Toronto Press 2007).

[339] Boyle and Redgwell (n 147) 678–80. See, eg, L De Nussac and others (eds), *Le Premier Congrès International Pour La Protection Des Paysages (Paris, 17–20 Octobre 1909), Compte-Rendu* (Société pour la protection des paysages de France 1910).

[340] Boyle and Redgwell (n 147) 678.See also A Strecker, *Landscape Protection in International Law* (1st edn, OUP 2018).

stimulation of national and international action on mountains and freshwater, biodiversity, forests, and climate change.[341]

'The Future We Want' acknowledged the sizable benefits derived from mountain regions and the fragility of mountain ecosystems due to impacts from 'climate change, deforestation and forest degradation, land use change, land degradation and natural disasters'.[342] At that time, these topics were addressed in the scope of the UNCCD, UNFCCC, NLBI, and the *Hyogo Framework for Action 2005–2015*.[343]

Today, the concepts also tie into the goals of target 15.4 as related to the UNCCD, UNFCCC, and UN Forest Instrument. Further, the matter of natural disasters indicates how mountain management might support implementation of the *Sendai Framework for Disaster Risk Reduction 2015–2030*[344] of the Third UN World Conference on Disaster Risk Reduction (DRR). 'The Future We Want' called for enhanced cooperative action by strengthening existing and creating new arrangements and centres of excellence for sustainable mountain development.[345] Lastly, it called for 'greater efforts towards the conservation of mountain ecosystems, including their biodiversity. These points were taken up in the development of Agenda 2030 and SDG Goal 15's target 15.4.

2. Empirical Analysis

By adopting the MGCI as an indicator, target 15.4 implicitly refers to the definition of mountains used by UNEP-WCMC, which classifies mountains 'according to altitude, slope and elevation range'.[346] Steepness indeed represents the only common feature of all mountains.[347] Different types of mountain ecosystems, however, can be found across several geographical regions and biomes, ranging from montane rainforests in tropical and subtropical areas to forests and woodlands in temperate and boreal biomes, as well as ice-sheets, rocky outcrops, and glaciers in polar regions.[348] These ecosystems tend to have their unique ecological traits, climate, geology, and topography, but they all provide critical ecosystem services to human communities, including those living in downstream and far away areas. These services encompass, among others, the regulation of water flows, air quality, and climate; the supply of freshwater, food, timber, fodder, and genetic resources; the creation and maintenance of habitats that may have a

---

[341] ibid.

[342] 'The Future We Want', para 210.

[343] *Hyogo Framework for Action 2005–2015: Building the Resilience of Nations and Communities to Disasters*, UN Doc A/CONF.206/6, 6.

[344] United Nations Office for Disaster Risk Reduction, *Sendai Framework for Disaster Risk Reduction 2015–2030* (United Nations 2015). See also SW von Dach and others (eds), *Safer Lives and Livelihoods in Mountains: Making the Sendai Framework for Disaster Risk Reduction Work for Sustainable Mountain Development* (Centre for Development and Environment, University of Bern 2017).

[345] 'The Future We Want', para 211.

[346] ibid 2.

[347] C Körner and others, 'A Definition of Mountains and Their Bioclimatic Belts for Global Comparisons of Biodiversity Data' (2011) 121 Alpine Botany 73.

[348] For example, DA Keith and others (eds) *The IUCN Global Ecosystem Typology 2.0: Descriptive Profiles for Biomes and Ecosystem Functional Groups* (IUCN 2020).

1120 SDG 15

high degree of endemism; and the provision of intangible services such as cultural heritage and spiritual values.[349]

Despite their importance, mountain ecosystems are particularly fragile, and highly vulnerable to disturbances from land-use change, climate change, population increase, and the unsustainable use of biodiversity and ecosystem services.[350] In recent years, the combined impacts of these drivers have significantly affected the conservation of mountain regions. According to the IPBES Global Assessment Report, there are already 'indications of higher warming in high mountains, resulting in species range shifts, phenology change and low plant productivity'.[351] Although the average share of mountain areas important for biodiversity that are covered by protected areas has been increasing in parts of Asia, Africa, and Europe since 2015, climate change has continued to transform the ecological structure of mountain ecosystems, opening up habitats for new species while leading to the decline of cold-adapted endemics.[352] For its part, the MGCI, which measures the percentage of mountain environments covered by green areas and gauges these areas capacity to fulfil their ecosystem roles and services, has remained essentially constant. As of 2022, approximately 73 per cent of the world's mountain areas are covered by green vegetation, the MGCI being the lowest in Western Asia and North Africa and the highest in Oceania.[353] Existing analyses of voluntary national reviews (VNRs) also reveal that mountains continue to be seldom mentioned by countries in the context of their SDG implementation efforts, and reported information mostly concern pressures faced by mountain ecosystems rather than actions to protect them.[354]

In addition to their diverse characteristics, mountain ecosystems also have diverse populations and experience diverging population trends, with growing land abandonment and depopulation in Europe against increasing intensification of land use and population growth in developing countries. An estimated 915 million people—90 per cent of which are in developing countries—live in mountain regions. Levels of poverty and vulnerability in mountain communities are generally higher than for people living elsewhere, mostly due to the complex political, socio-economic, and environmental challenges facing these areas.[355] According to a systematic review of trend records as assessed by Indigenous people and local communities, the conservation of high mountain habitats was found to exhibit overwhelmingly negative trends,[356] and in 2012, up to 39 per cent of people living in mountain regions in developing countries were considered to be food insecure.[357] These trends are likely to be exacerbated in the

---

[349] For example, PA Egan and MF Price (eds) *Mountain Ecosystem Services and Climate Change: A Global Overview of Potential Threats and Challenges for Adaptation* (UNESCO 2017) 10–14.

[350] For example, C Körner and others, 'Mountain Systems' in Millennium Ecosystem Assessment (ed), *Ecosystems and Human Well-being: Current State and Trends* (Island Press 2005), 683–712.

[351] Purvis and others, 'Chapter 2.2' (n 231) 259.

[352] For example, R Hock and others, 'High Mountain Areas' in HO Pörtner and others (eds), *IPCC Special Report on the Ocean and Cryosphere in a Changing Climate* (CUP 2019) 133–134.

[353] FAO, *Tracking Progress on Food and Agriculture-related SDG Indicators 2021* (FAO 2021) 95–100.

[354] F Pesce and others, *Integrating Biodiversity into the Sustainable Development Agenda: An Analysis of Voluntary National Reviews* (UNEP-WCMC 2020) 33.

[355] FAO, *Mapping the Vulnerability of Mountain Peoples to Food Insecurity* (FAO 2015) 12.

[356] Purvis and others, 'Chapter 2.2' (n 231) 250.

[357] FAO, *Tracking Progress on Food and Agriculture-related SDG Indicators 2021* (n 353) 29.

future due to accelerating anthropogenic pressures including climate change, which is expected to lead to glaciers' retreat, changes in precipitation patterns, alterations to the hydrological cycle, and increased risk of natural hazards.[358] Impacts on Indigenous people may include shifts in hunting opportunities and the size of grasslands used for pastures, and degrading vegetation and rangeland conditions.[359]

3. Efforts at the Domestic and International Levels

Internationally significant mountain ecosystems are concentrated in comparatively few regions, and concerns over shared transboundary mountain biodiversity and ecosystem services predominate in the states sharing mountain regions. Therefore, regional agreements are important sources for legal obligations to support target 15.4. These include the Alpine Convention[360] and Carpathian Convention.[361] At the level of international environmental law, the obligations contained in MEAs such as the CBD, World Heritage Convention, and the UNFCCC can also address this target. From the perspective of biodiversity conservation, the CBD is particularly significant due to the indirect role that its Aichi targets 11 (protected areas), 14 (ecosystem services), and 15 (ecosystem restoration and resilience),[362] as well as the implementation of the NBSAPs of relevant countries, may have in the protection of mountain ecosystems. In addition, the CBD has a trilateral memorandum of cooperation with the Alpine and Carpathian Conventions, and it has also implemented a long-standing Programme of Work on Mountain Biological Diversity,[363] although no decisions have been adopted on the topic since 2010.

Beyond existing MEAs, one of the first international initiatives on mountain development was the creation of the International Centre for Integrated Mountain Development (ICIMOD) with the support of UNESCO Man and the Biosphere Programme. Beginning as a scientific undertaking, ICIMOD is now a regional intergovernmental learning and knowledge sharing centre made up of eight states in the Hindu Kush/Himalayas region.[364]

In 2002, FAO also established the Mountain Partnership as an international voluntary alliance focused on enhancing the lives of people living in mountains while protecting the environment.[365] It now has over 400 members including governments, intergovernmental organizations, major groups, and subnational authorities.[366] The partnership was reportedly successful in enhancing knowledge and expertise about mountain ecosystems while establishing a community of practice for states and other actors.[367] Moreover, hoping to raise the political profile of mountain conservation and

---

[358] Egan and Price (n 349) 16–18.

[359] Purvis and others, 'Chapter 2.2' (n 231) 259.

[360] *Convention on the Protection of the Alps* (n 110).

[361] *Framework Convention on the Protection and Sustainable Development of the Carpathians* (n 116).

[362] SCBD, *Global Biodiversity Outlook 5* (n 177).

[363] For example, *Programme of Work on Mountain Biodiversity* (n 214).

[364] 'Who We Are' (*icimod.org*) <https://www.icimod.org/who-we-are/> accessed 10 April 2022.

[365] FAO, 'Mountain Partnership' (*FAO*, 2022) <http://www.fao.org/mountain-partnership/about/en/> accessed 17 April 2022.

[366] ibid.

[367] Y Makino and others, 'Accelerating the Movement for Mountain Peoples and Policies' (2019) 365 Science 1084.

sustainable use issues, the UN General Assembly declared 2022 as the International Year on Sustainable Mountain Development[368] as the culmination of a series of related Assembly resolutions.[369] As part of the implementation of the International Year's agenda, it was also agreed that a global initiative shall be promoted for the adoption of an action plan for the development of mountain regions, under the leadership of the Kyrgyz Republic.[370]

At the domestic level, target 15.4 demands different strategies for implementation in law and policy. For developed and developing countries, emphasis has been placed on enhancing resilience of mountain ecosystems in a changing climate and investing in adaptation strategies.[371] This involves establishing and effectively managing protected areas but also adopting a landscape approach to the development of mountain regions, including through sustainable forest and watershed management, land restoration, and efforts to support mountain economies and livelihoods in areas such as family farming, social protection, and sustainable tourism.[372] Both developed and developing countries have also established the importance of working with communities who are directly impacted by policy and initiatives, for example through the creation of national mountain committees.[373]

For states that have already developed policies on the conservation of mountain ecosystems, target 15.4 provides support for strengthening them. According to FAO's monitoring activities, states that have adopted policies include Argentina, Romania, Rwanda, and Cameroon.[374] By contrast, for those states that have not, the target provides the grounds to establish related policies. From such a standpoint, it is important to note that countries have the opportunity of reaping co-benefits through their simultaneous efforts to implement target 6.6, which calls on the international community to 'protect and restore water-related ecosystems, including mountains'.

4. Critique

When one considers the emphasis put by SDG Goal 15 on the importance of implementing existing international agreements, the lack of a binding legal instrument applying to all mountain ecosystems may be considered as a significant obstacle to the achievement of target 15.4. The significant political support thrown by the General Assembly behind the objective of sustainable mountain development since 2015 has been an important means of raising the profile of mountain protection, and it has also facilitated the international dissemination of experiences and best practices. However,

---

[368] 'International Year of Sustainable Mountain Development, 2022' UNGA Resolution 76/129 (28 December 2021) UN Doc A/RES/76/129.

[369] 'United Nations Documents' (*fao.org*, n.d.) <https://www.fao.org/mountain-partnership/publications/un-documents/en/> accessed 17 April 2022.

[370] 'International Year of Sustainable Mountain Development' (*fao.org*, n.d.) <https://www.fao.org/mountain-partnership/internationalyear2022/en/> accessed 17 April 2022.

[371] For example, AR Rizvi and others, *Striving Together Towards Resilience: Ecosystem-based Adaptation in Purchase* (IUCN 2012).

[372] 'Sustainable Mountain Development' Report of the Secretary-General (22 July 2019) UN Doc A/74/209, 8–11.

[373] ibid 13–14, 17–18.

[374] FAO, *Mountain Partnership Secretariat Annual Report 2020* (FAO 2021).

it has so far failed to inspire stronger multilateral action on mountains, with the issue notably absent from recent discussions under the CBD and UNFCCC. Despite intense advocacy efforts undertaken by the Mountain Partnership,[375] references to mountain biodiversity also do not appear in the Kunming-Montreal GBF, although some of its headline indicators may be disaggregated at the level of mountain ecosystems.[376] In other words, it could be argued that while target 15.4 has certainly served to put mountains on the global sustainable development agenda, it lacks clear and target-specific opportunities for implementation. As a result, its objectives are partly absorbed by broader ecosystem protection targets (including target 15.1) and partly pursued through soft policy recommendations and capacity-building initiatives directed at national governments.

A second, significant challenge to the implementation of target 15.4 is represented by monitoring challenges and ongoing lack of knowledge. The first, generally accepted definitions of mountains only emerged at the turn of the century,[377] and global initiatives to monitor trends in mountain biodiversity—such as the Global Mountain Biodiversity Assessment—were launched in the same period.[378] Due to their inaccessibility and remoteness, mountains are hard to monitor through *in situ* observation, and even with the diffusion of Earth Observation satellites, which have significantly increased the availability of data about trends of key variables in mountains, challenges posed by cloud cover and rugged terrains remain.[379] These challenges, in turn, make it more difficult to predict future changes and impacts, especially as mountain ecosystems remain fundamentally heterogeneous and the anthropogenic drivers affecting mountain regions continue to be uniquely complex and multidimensional. The MGCI indicator itself, which has been chosen to monitor the achievement of target 15.4, highlights the difficulty of capturing the various dimensions of environmental degradation in mountains. For example, while an increase in the percentage of green cover in mountains may indicate the success of restoration activities and suggest improved integrity of the mountain ecosystems, it could also be the result of glacier retreat and subsequent encroachment of vegetation at higher altitudes due to warmer temperatures.[380]

Even when information related to mountain ecosystems is available, leaders and decision-makers may not necessarily understand how to effectively support the implementation of target 15.4, particularly given the potential trade-offs that may arise between protecting mountain ecosystems and addressing the significant socio-economic challenges facing mountain communities. Groups like the Mountain Partnership aim to reduce this obstacle, facilitating dialogue between civil society, researchers, and

---

[375] For example, Mountain Partnership, 'Including Mountains in the CBD Post-2020 Global Biodiversity Framework' (May 2021) <https://www.fao.org/fileadmin/user_upload/mountain_partnership/docs/Mountain%20Partnership%20Biodiversity%20Policy%20Note.pdf> accessed 12 April 2022.

[376] Decision 15/5. Monitoring framework for the Kunming-Montreal Global Biodiversity Framework (n 242) Table 2.

[377] For example, Körner and others, 'Mountain Systems' (n 350).

[378] 'History' (*gmba.unibe.ch*, n.d.) <https://www.gmba.unibe.ch/about/history/> accessed 17 April 2022.

[379] Hock and others (n 352) 174.

[380] 'SDG Indicator Metadata' (n 335).

1124   SDG 15

governments, and supporting national policy development.[381] However, the problems affecting mountains remain particularly context-specific, and the long-standing neglect of many Indigenous populations and local communities, many of which represent ethnic minorities in their countries, has so far failed to result in a significant mobilization of resources. For this reason, a 2019 report by the UN Secretary-General identified the need for greater investments in disaster risk reduction and preparedness in mountains, faster access to development projects and funds such as the GEF and the Green Climate Fund, and stronger support to the beneficiary fund of the Mountain Partnership.[382]

G. Target 15.5 Take urgent and significant action to reduce the degradation of natural habitats, halt the loss of biodiversity and, by 2020, protect and prevent the extinction of threatened species

This target calls for urgent and significant action to reduce the degradation of natural habitats, halt the loss of biodiversity, and, by 2020, protect and prevent the extinction of threatened species. Indicator 15.5.1 is the Red List Index, developed by the IUCN to identify overall trends in species extinction risk.[383]

In many ways, the target complements target 15.1 by emphasizing the species level of biodiversity over the ecosystem level, as the main objective of a reduction in natural habitat degradation is by definition, the conservation of those species which depend on such habitats for their reproduction and survival. Like several other targets under Goal 15, this target sets a 2020 deadline for its achievement, thus maintaining consistency with the timeline of the CBD's Strategic Plan 2011–2020.

1. Sources of Target

Although wild species conservation MEAs date back more than a century,[384] the primary sources for this target are the modern CBD and its Aichi targets 5 and 12. The CBD requires parties to protect natural habitats,[385] conserve biodiversity,[386] and protect threatened species.[387] The conservation of biodiversity is one of three overarching objectives of the CBD. Some more specific obligations to achieve this objective under Article 8 for *in situ* biodiversity conservation include protecting natural habitats, as well as adopting protection measures to ensure viable species populations and promoting recovery of threatened ones.

---

[381] M Glushkova and others, 'Ecosystem Services from Mountain Forest Ecosystems: Conceptual Framework, Approach and Challenges. (2020) 21(1) Silva Balcancia 47.
[382] 'Sustainable Mountain Development' (n 372) 17.
[383] IUCN, 'Red List Index' (*IUCN Red List of Threatened Species* 2021) <https://www.iucnredlist.org/en>.
[384] For example, Bowman and others (n 79) ch 1.
[385] CBD art 8(d).
[386] ibid art 1.
[387] For example, ibid art 8(d)–(f) and (k).

Aichi target 5 calls for the rate of loss of all natural habitats, including forests, to be 'at least halved and where feasible brought close to zero' by 2020, while simultaneously reducing degradation and fragmentation. For its part, Aichi target 12 addresses the risk of species extinction and commits countries to improving the conservation status of threatened species, particularly those known to be most in decline.

While they should not necessarily be considered as direct sources of target 15.5, the provisions of several other MEAs are also functionally connected to the target's objectives. Indeed, the emergence and development of modern international biodiversity law overlaps in large part with a growing concern towards the conservation of species.[388] A trend is seen in the progressive move from a narrow emphasis on regulating species exploitation (whether for economic, aesthetic, or strictly environmental reasons) towards a broader interest in the mitigation of other drivers of species extinction and even the protection of biodiversity *as a whole*.[389]

Relevant MEAs include, most prominently, those instruments that are commonly considered as part of a 'biodiversity cluster' together with the CBD. These include the CMS, CITES, the Ramsar Convention, and the World Heritage Convention. Where the focus, geographical scope, and choice of regulatory actions among these instruments may differ, including variable combinations of species and area-based measures, all of these instruments aim at key drivers behind species extinction such as demand coming from international trade, over-exploitation, and habitat degradation.[390] In addition, even MEAs that are traditionally associated with other thematic areas and SDG targets, such the UNFCCC (SDG 13) and UNCCD (target 15.3), should be considered strongly linked to the vision enshrined in target 15.5, given the profoundly harmful effects that phenomena such as desertification, land degradation, and climate change have on species and their habitats.

2. Empirical Analysis

In light of limited international progress on target 15.1, the three main units of analysis under target 15.5—namely, natural habitats, biodiversity, and threatened species—continue to exhibit worsening trends. This is despite significant momentum towards the establishment of biodiversity as an essential and urgent issue for the international agenda. Member States' perception of biodiversity loss as an urgent issue is demonstrated by the declaration of 2011–2020 as the UN Decade on Biological Diversity,[391] the sense of anticipation surrounding the adoption of the Kunming-Montreal GBF,[392] and growing political awareness of the interlinkages between biodiversity loss and

---

[388] See Maffei (n 79).

[389] For example, BF de Souza Dias and K Garforth, 'Historical Perspectives on the Challenge of Biodiversity Conservation' in E Morgera and J Razzaque (eds) *Elgar Encyclopedia of Environmental Law. Volume III: Biodiversity and Nature Protection Law* (Edward Elgar 2017).

[390] For an overview, see MJ Bowman and E Goodwin, 'Threatened Species and their Conservation' in Medaglia, Perron-Welch, and Goodman (eds) *Legal Aspects of Implementing the Convention on Biological Diversity* (n 111).

[391] 'Convention on Biological Diversity' (n 36) para 19.

[392] For example, P Greenfield, 'UN Sets Out Paris-style Plan to Cut Extinction Rate by Factor of 10' (*The Guardian*, 12 July 2021) <https://www.theguardian.com/environment/2021/jul/12/change-is-coming-un-sets-out-paris-style-plan-to-cutextinction-rate-tenfold> accessed 27 September 2021.

1126   SDG 15

issues such as the prevention of zoonotic diseases and the sustainability of the global food system.[393]

With respect to habitats, which are defined in the CBD as 'the place or type of site where an organism or population naturally occurs',[394] Aichi target 5 has not been achieved according to all relevant indicators.[395] This is particularly worrying, as the loss of natural habitats due to agricultural expansion, urbanization, mining, energy extraction, and infrastructure development is estimated to represent the main threat for the vast majority of all species assessed in the IUCN Red List.[396] According to the GBO 5, despite slightly slower global rates of deforestation over the past decade, '[l]oss, degradation and fragmentation of habitats remains high in forest and other biomes, especially in the most biodiversity-rich ecosystems in tropical regions. Wilderness areas and global wetlands continue to decline. Fragmentation of rivers remains a critical threat to freshwater biodiversity'.[397] At the same time, increases have been small for forested areas and the formation of new water bodies, mostly due to timber plantations, recent afforestation, or the creation of artificial water reservoirs not having a high significance for biodiversity conservation.[398]

In regard to species, the IUCN Red List data show that species extinction risk has only worsened and the rate of extinction for species has increased over the past thirty years[399] and has far exceeded background extinction rates.[400] Although there has been some success in preventing critically endangered species from going extinct, this has not prevented several species previously at lower risk from becoming threatened.[401] Moreover, it is important to remember that tools like the Red List only provide a portion of the full story of the status for species across the world due to time lags and difficulty in assessing each species. In this context, the rising proportion of livestock breeds and wild relatives of farmed animals that are threatened with extinction suggests a parallel decline in genetic diversity, thus pushing the international community further away from achieving Aichi target 13.[402]

In addition to extinction rates and assessments of species' conservation status, continuing declines are also suggested by other indices such as the Living Planet Index[403] or the Biodiversity Intactness Index,[404] which measure population trends for vertebrate

---

[393] For example, G20 Italia 2021, 'G20 Environment Communiqué Final' (22 July 2021) <https://www.g20.org/wp-content/uploads/2021/07/2021_07_22_ITG20_ENV_Final.pdf> accessed 27 September 2021; and G7 Cornwall UK 2021, 'G7 2030 Nature Compact' (13 June 2021) <https://www.g7uk.org/wpcontent/uploads/2021/06/G7-2030-Nature-Compact-PDF-120KB-4-pages-2.pdf> accessed 28 September 2021.

[394] CBD art 2.

[395] Butchart and others, 'Assessing Progress Towards Meeting Major International Objectives' (n 252) 402–403.

[396] IUCN 'The IUCN Red List of Threatened Species. Version 2021-3' (*IUCN Red List of Threatened Species* 2021) <https://www.iucnredlist.org/en> accessed 29 March 2022.

[397] SCBD, *Global Biodiversity Outlook 5* (n 177) 52.

[398] Butchart and others, 'Assessing Progress Towards Meeting Major International Objectives' (n 252) 410–11.

[399] ibid 421.

[400] AD Barnosky and others, 'Has the Earth's Sixth Mass Extinction Already Arrived?' (2011) 471 *Nature* 51.

[401] SCBD, *Global Biodiversity Outlook 5* (n 177) 86.

[402] ibid 92.

[403] For example, L McRae and others, 'The Diversity-Weighted Living Planet Index: Controlling for Taxonomic Bias in a Global Biodiversity Indicator' (2017) 12 PloS One 1, DOI:10.1371/journal.pone.0169156.

[404] For example, SLL Hill and others, 'Worldwide Impacts of Past and Projected Future Land-Use Change on Local Species Richness and the Biodiversity Intactness Index' (2018) *BioRxiv* <http://biorxiv.org/content/early/2018/05/01/311787.abstract> accessed 20 March 2022.

species and levels of biotic integrity, respectively. Perhaps most importantly, this on-going loss of genetic and functional diversity is increasingly perceived as a core 'planetary boundary' that is capable, on its own, of pushing the Earth system out of its present Holocene state, owing to the central role that biodiversity plays in other global-level dynamics.[405] Despite the large uncertainty involved, it has been argued that this planetary boundary may have already been transgressed.[406]

3. Efforts at the Domestic and International Levels

Target 15.5 contains three distinct commitments: (i) undertaking urgent and signifi-cant action to reduce the degradation of natural habitats, (ii) undertaking urgent and significant action to halt the loss of biodiversity, and (iii) protecting and preventing the extinction of threatened species by 2020. At the international level, efforts to imple-ment these commitments continue to be generally underlain by the CBD as an umbrella agreement for the broader context of halting biodiversity loss. The balancing of coun-tries' sovereign right to exploit their biological resources with the common concern of humankind in biodiversity loss is well-recognized.[407] However, the protection of spe-cies and habitats is not only left to national policies and priorities but is also supported by the provisions of the Convention relating to international cooperation and assist-ance, as well as by the advice and guidance developed by the COP and the SBSTTA.

As mentioned with respect to the sources of target 15.5, action under a number of other MEAs is also directly relevant to the implementation of the target. For example, despite having evolved over time into a broader, ecosystem-oriented instrument, the Ramsar Convention remains concerned with its original goal of protecting wetlands as habitats for aquatic birds and other species.[408] Similarly, the CMS imposes on states hosting endangered migratory species an obligation to conserve and restore the habi-tats that are 'of importance in removing the[se] species from danger of extinction'.[409] In addition, the CMS also lays out a series of species-based actions (eg prohibitions on the taking of specimens, prevention and reduction of factors that may endanger a species) that states are expected to undertake. These include the concluding bilateral or multi-lateral agreements where international cooperation would greatly benefit the conserva-tion status of migratory species.[410]

Other MEAs that speak to protecting natural terrestrial habitats include the Pan American Convention,[411] World Heritage Convention,[412] Agreement on Conservation of Polar Bears, Apia Convention,[413] Berne Convention,[414] ASEAN Convention,[415]

---

[405] Steffen and others, 'Planetary Boundaries' (n 138) 1259855–68.
[406] ibid, and Rockström and others, 'Planetary Boundaries' (n 138) 32.
[407] Bowman and Goodwin, 'Threatened Species' (n 390).
[408] Ramsar Convention art 4.
[409] CMS art III(4)(a).
[410] CMS arts III(4)(b)(c), III(5), and IV–V.
[411] Pan American Convention Preamble.
[412] World Heritage Convention art 2.
[413] Apia Convention Preamble and 1(b).
[414] Convention on the Conservation of European Wildlife and Natural Habitats Preamble, arts 1(1), 3(1), 3(3), 4(1), 4(4) and 12.
[415] ASEAN Convention arts 3(a), 5(c), 7(b), 10(a), 13, 19, 20(4).

1128　SDG 15

Alpine Convention,[416] and the North American Agreement on Environmental Cooperation.[417] Some of these multilateral instruments have explicitly adopted secondary measures to foster the synergies between their conservation objectives and relevant SDG targets. The COP to the CBD, for example, decided that the GBO 5 should include an assessment of the contribution of progress towards the Aichi targets to the SDGs,[418] while the COP to the CMS adopted a resolution highlighting the inclusion of migratory species conservation to the 2030 Agenda.[419]

At the domestic level, the implementation of existing commitments under the CBD and other relevant MEAs provides a framework of measures that countries should take in order to achieve target 15.5. These include, as also detailed for other targets under SDG 15, the definition and updating of NBSAPs and their policies and initiatives that may be included, such as creation of protected areas and OECMs, integrated spatial planning, application of an ecosystem approach to management, and ecological restoration programmes. For example, in 2020 more than 79 per cent and 86 per cent of NBSAPs contained targets related to achieving Aichi targets 5 and 12, even though the level of ambition for such targets was generally lower.[420] In addition, countries may take species-specific conservation measures for those species which are subject to levels of exploitation which may endanger their survival. These generally include the legal regulation of such exploitation, for example through the setting of quotas, open and closed seasons, restrictions on allowed techniques, and even outright bans, but may also extend to breeding and reintroduction programmes.

Many CBD Parties routinely report challenges in implementing their international commitments relating to the protection of species and habitats due to the lack of funding, resources and capacity.[421] Nevertheless, it has been estimated that the rate of species extinction over the past decade could have been up to four times higher in the absence of conservation action, suggesting the important role that conservation strategies and programmes can play in curbing biodiversity loss.[422] In their National Reports contributing to the GBO 5, several countries provided examples of restoring habitats or species populations,[423] and conservation strategies led by Indigenous Peoples and local communities have been shown as highly effective, as they tend to target areas rather than individual species.[424] Even with success stories, however, UN Member States' conservation efforts and policy implementation lack effectiveness, with nearly one quarter

---

[416] Alpine Convention Preamble and arts 2(2), 2(6), 2(10),

[417] North American Agreement on Environmental Cooperation, arts 10(2)(i) and 45(2)(a)(iii).

[418] CBD COP Decision XIII/29 'Global Biodiversity Outlook and Intergovernmental Science-Policy Platform on Biodiversity and Ecosystem Services' (12 December 2016) UN Doc CBD/COP/DEC/XIII/29, para 1(b)(ii).

[419] CMS Resolution 12.3 'Manila Declaration on Sustainable Development and Migratory Species' (October 2017) UN Doc UNEP/CMS/Resolution 12.3.

[420] SCBD, *Global Biodiversity Outlook 5* (n 177) 57 and 91.

[421] For example, ibid 90.

[422] ibid 86; see also FC Bolam and others, 'How Many Bird and Mammal Extinctions has Recent Conservation action prevented?' (2020) 14 Conservation Letters e12762.

[423] S Cairns and others, *Ecological Restoration for Protected Areas: Principles, Guidelines and Best Practices* (IUCN 2012).

[424] For example, Morel (n 124); and Jonas (n 158).

of taxonomically assessed species remaining threatened unless the drivers of biodiversity loss are drastically reduced.[425]

Importantly, all international and domestic protection efforts are fundamentally reliant on constant development of sound evidence about the status, distribution, and very existence of species of wild flora and fauna, as well as data on the effectiveness of conservation measures. Over the past few decades, subsidiary bodies of MEAs, such as the SBSTTA to the CBD, have played a central role in collating and conveying this information to national governments and COPs.[426] However, the interface between science and conservation policy has progressively been augmented by a growing range of institutions, epistemic networks, and capacity-building programmes.

In the context of target 15.5, relevant examples include foundational initiatives relating to species identification and classification, such as the Global Taxonomy Initiative launched by the CBD in 1998,[427] the production and harmonization of global biodiversity indicators (see the Essential Biodiversity Variables from the Group on Earth Observations' Biodiversity Observation Network (GEO BON)),[428] and the development of risk assessment frameworks such as the IUCN Red List Index used by governments and other stakeholders to track their progress in reducing biodiversity loss and protecting threatened species. With respect to the Red List Index, not only has this tool been chosen as the indicator for target 15.5, it is also currently used by the CMS and CITES to support decision-making,[429] and it could even be adopted as one of the headline indicators for the Kunming-Montreal GBF.[430]

4. Critique

The formulation of target 15.5 creates some potential confusion concerning its relationship with targets 15.1 and 15.6, as halting the loss of biodiversity would also encompass, by necessity, the protection of ecosystems and genetic diversity in addition to species and habitats. This lack of conceptual clarity is indirectly addressed by the specific choice of an indicator, the Red List Index, which suggests that the species level of biodiversity represents the main concern of this target. While such clarification satisfactorily serves to delimit the respective scopes of targets 15.1 and 15.5, it leaves a potential gap on genetic diversity, as target 15.6 only focuses on the access and benefit-sharing dimensions of genetic diversity rather than its conservation. Conserving genetic diversity was a key topic of discussion in negotiations on the Kunming-Montreal GBF.

[425] 'Summary Statistics' (*IUCN Red List of Endangered Species* 2021) <https://www.iucnredlist.org/resources/summary-statistics> accessed 29 March 2022.
[426] For example, D-T Avgerinopoulou, *Science-Based Lawmaking: How to Effectively Integrate Science in International Environmental Law* (Springer Nature 2019) ch 7; and RB Churchill and G Ulfstein, 'Autonomous Institutional Arrangements in Multilateral Environmental Agreements: A Little-Noticed Phenomenon in International Law' (2000) 94(4) American Journal of International Law 623.
[427] SCBD, *Guide to the Global Taxonomy Initiative* (CBD Technical Series No 30).
[428] For example, HM Pereira, 'Essential Biodiversity Variables' (2013) 339(6117) Science 277, 277.
[429] IUCN, *IUCN Red List 2017–2020 Report* (IUCN 2020) 6.
[430] Decision 15/5. Monitoring framework for the Kunming-Montreal Global Biodiversity Framework (n 242) Table 1.

1130 SDG 15

The gap is itself partially filled by target 2.5 under Goal 2, which seeks to maintain the genetic diversity of seeds, cultivated plants, farmed and domesticated animals and their wild relatives. However, the narrow scope of target 2.5 excludes the genetic diversity of other wild species, even though the maintenance of such diversity is also potentially important in the provision of ecosystem services, for example in the context of medicinal research or to ensure the survival of wild species in the face of adverse environmental changes.[431]

As with target 15.1, target 15.5 also suffers from a lack of quantitative measures of success, generically calling on the international community to 'take action' with respect to habitats and to 'protect and prevent the extinction of threatened species'. For comparison, Aichi target 5 was more quantitatively specific, as it committed CBD Parties to halve the rate of loss of natural habitats, and where feasible bring it to zero. Aichi target 12 was also vague with respect to the species extinction objective. Different approaches have recently been suggested during the negotiations of the Kunming-Montreal GBF, focusing on the notion of reducing the *rate* and *risk* of extinction to bring it closer to natural background levels.[432] In addition to the vagueness of the target, the choice of a 2020 deadline *de facto* reduces any realistic possibility of meaningful implementation, particularly when considering that even with substantial efforts it would take several years for current rate increases in extinction to be reversed.[433]

A final, potential source of criticism for target 15.5 relates to its limited mention, beyond habitat degradation, of the drivers of biodiversity loss and species extinction; some drivers which are instead scattered across several other targets under Goal 15. From this standpoint, target 15.5 may be read as an unnecessary duplication of the general formulation of SDG 15, which would merely 'certify' progress attained under other targets but would not, by itself, provide clear directions to states and other relevant actors about which measures to take to effectively halt biodiversity loss and prevent species extinction.

H. Target 15.6 Promote fair and equitable sharing of the benefits arising from the utilization of genetic resources and promote appropriate access to such resources, as internationally agreed

This 2030 target calls on states to 'promote fair and equitable sharing of the benefits arising from the utilization of genetic resources and promote appropriate access to such resources, as internationally agreed'. Indicator 15.6.1 is the 'number of countries that have adopted legislative, administrative and policy frameworks to ensure fair and equitable sharing of benefits'.

---

[431] For example, A Miraldo and others, 'An Anthropocene Map of Genetic Diversity' (2016) 353 Science 1532.
[432] Decision 15/4. Kunming-Montreal Global Biodiversity Framework, UN Doc CBD/COP/15/4, Goal A.
[433] For example, G Mace and others, 'Aiming Higher to Bend the Curve of Biodiversity Loss' (2018) 1 Nature Sustainability 448.

1. Sources of Target

The CBD is the primary source for target 15.6, particularly article 15[434] and the 2010 Nagoya Protocol,[435] which establishes rights and duties on access to and fair and equitable benefit-sharing from genetic resources. Another source is the International Treaty on Plant Genetic Resources for Food and Agriculture (ITPGRFA), which addresses fair and equitable sharing of benefits derived from the use of plant genetic resources for food and agriculture (PGRFA) for sustainable agriculture and food security,[436] in harmony with the objectives of the CBD.

During the CBD negotiations process, access and benefit-sharing (ABS) was conceived as a necessary counterpart to incorporating traditional biodiversity issues like nature protection, conservation, and sustainable use.[437] However, there is widespread recognition—particularly among developing countries—that full implementation of ABS has yet to materialize, or that it has simply not met the expectations established in the negotiations.[438] The CBD envisions domestic regulation of ABS under the principle of permanent sovereignty over natural resources, signalling a fundamental shift in both international law and earlier approaches to genetic resources. Whereas genetic resources—particularly plant genetic resources—had previously been considered a common heritage of humanity,[439] the Convention changed this approach and granted states control over the genetic resources (GR) found within their territories. Enabling state control presumed states could improve the control of access to genetic resources and would allow developing countries to profit from the potential value from these genetic resources, thus creating incentives to conserve and sustainably use the resources themselves and biodiversity more broadly.

Progress on ABS in the past three decades has been complex and time consuming. Increasingly, states are creating systems for regulating ABS, but the complex and cross-cutting nature of the issue makes it no easy task. Obstacles to the legal reforms required exist at both national and international levels. A debate against ABS can be

---

[434] *Bonn Guidelines on Access to Genetic Resources and Fair and Equitable Sharing of the Benefits Arising out of their Utilization*, UN Doc UNEP/CBD/COP/6/24.

[435] *Nagoya Protocol on Access to Genetic Resources and the Fair and Equitable Sharing of Benefits Resulting from their Utilization* (in force 12 October 2014) UN Doc UNEP/CBD/COP/10/27.

[436] See JC Medaglia and others, *The Interface between the Nagoya Protocol on ABS and the ITPGRFA at the International Level: Potential Issues for Consideration in Supporting Mutually Supportive Implementation at the National Level* (FNI Report 1/2013, Fridtjof Nansen Institute 2013); R Pavoni and D Piselli, 'Access to Genetic Resources and Benefit Sharing' in E Morgera and J Razzaque (eds), *Biodiversity and Nature Protection Law* (Edward Elgar 2017); Cabrera Medaglia and Perron-Welch, 'Rules and Practices of International Law on Benefit-Sharing for Sustainable Development' (n 145); TJ Hodges and O Rukundo, 'Access to Genetic Resources and Benefit-Sharing' in Medaglia, Perron-Welch, and Goodman (eds), *Legal Aspects of Implementing the Convention on Biological Diversity* (n 111).

[437] See L Glowka and others, *A Guide to the Convention on Biological Diversity* (IUCN 1994); AA Yusuf, 'International Law and Sustainable Development: The Convention on Biological Diversity' (1994) 2 African Yearbook of International Law 109; V Koester, 'The Biodiversity Convention Negotiation Process and Some Comments on the Outcome' (1997) 27 Environmental Policy and Law 175.

[438] JC Medaglia and CL Silva, *Addressing the Problems of Access: Protecting Sources, While Giving Users Certainty* (IUCN 2006).

[439] See *International Undertaking on Plant Genetic Resources for Food and Agriculture*, UN Doc C/83/REP; C De Klemm, 'Conservation of Species: The Need for a New Approach' (1982) 9 Environmental Policy and Law 118. See also generally I Mgbeoji, *Global Biopiracy: Patents, Plants and Indigenous Knowledge* (University of British Colombia 2006).

1132 SDG 15

traced to efforts by colonial powers to gain control of trade in key commodities such as rubber, tea, and cinchona for their own benefit with little regard to the communities and economies from where these resources originated.[440] Over the course of the twentieth century the scope of intellectual property (IP) protection—including patents and plant breeders' rights—has been extended to cover living organisms and parts thereof, making biodiversity and genes a potentially lucrative resource.

Biodiversity-rich countries, primarily from the Global South, became increasingly frustrated with the flow of GR for research in the North, where it could be patented with no returns to the country of origin.[441] The CBD's solution was to recognize permanent sovereignty over genetic resources in article 3, confirming that states can control access to GR located under their national jurisdiction and negotiate benefit-sharing terms. Indeed, the third objective of the Convention is 'the fair and equitable sharing of the benefits arising out of the utilization of GR, including by appropriate access to genetic resources and by appropriate transfer of relevant technologies, taking into account all rights over these resources and to technologies, and by appropriate funding.'[442] Article 15 of the CBD requires access to take place on mutually agreed terms (MAT) and with the prior informed consent (PIC) of the state providing access.

The conservation of genetic diversity aims at preserving the amount of genetic information of all living organisms, including wild animals as well as cultivated species.[443] Its scope applies to biodiversity in areas of national jurisdiction,[444] and to 'processes and activities, carried out under Parties jurisdiction or control, whether its national jurisdiction or beyond its boundaries',[445] thus arguably encompassing all biodiversity on the planet.[446]

It has been argued that part of the rationale behind benefit-sharing is to avoid the exploitation inherent in many North–South forms of resource extraction, which historically led to the unsustainable use of natural resources.[447] Appropriation from the 1980s onward has been largely done through the use of IP rights in the North.[448] ABS was explicitly incorporated into the CBD due to the fact that many biodiversity hotspots with significant potential are located in the Global South. The scheme on benefit-sharing is firmly based upon the concept of sustainable development, as states must aim to find an equitable balance between the interests of the countries of origin and those of states that have the technical and technological means to use genetic resources, to develop

---

[440] See Mgbeoji (n 439); JC Medaglia, 'Access and Benefit-Sharing: North–South Challenges in Implementing the Convention on Biological Diversity and Its Nagoya Protocol' in CG Gonzalez and others (eds), *International Environmental Law and the Global South* (CUP 2015).

[441] ibid.

[442] CBD art 1.

[443] N Matz-Lück, 'Biological Diversity, International Protection' in *Max Planck Encyclopedia of Public International Law* (OUP 2012) para 1.

[444] CBD art 4(a).

[445] ibid art 4(b).

[446] Matz-Lück (n 443) para 28.

[447] P Stoett, 'Wildlife Conservation: Institutional and Normative Considerations' in N Schrijver and F Weiss, eds, *International Law and Sustainable Development: Principles and Practice* (Martinus Nijoff 2004) 514; Medaglia (n 440) 195.

[448] See Mgbeoji (n 439).

and use technologies stemming therefrom.[449] The resulting approach allows states to control access by setting terms that allow them to profit from the potential value of their genetic resources and biodiversity, which creates an incentive to conserve and sustainably use the resources.[450] ABS creates a new income opportunity for the Global South that can enhance its efforts towards sustainable development.[451]

The objectives of the CBD establish a clear link between the conservation and sustainable use of biodiversity with the sharing of benefits resulting from access. The Nagoya Protocol on ABS affirms this link by encouraging users and providers to direct genetic resource derived benefits towards biodiversity conservation and sustainable use of its components.[452] Significantly, the CBD is one of the only conventions to define 'sustainable use of a resource', as 'the use of components of biodiversity in a way and at a rate that does not lead to its long-term decline, thereby maintaining its potential to meet the needs and aspirations of present and future generations'.[453] To clarify this definition, it also defines biodiversity[454] and biological resources,[455] within which it includes genetic resources. Sustainable use focuses on the active management of biological resources, which provides an incentive for conservation by allowing for benefits from use that do not threaten a species or ecosystem.[456] Including genetic and ecosystem diversity into the definition of biodiversity goes further than earlier treaties, which aimed to protect enumerated species or areas from human threats, destruction, or extinction.[457]

At its core, the CBD makes it clear that biodiversity is not a shared global resource but rather that states have sovereign rights over their own biological resources[458] pursuant to their own environmental policies.[459] This sovereignty precept is reinforced in CBD Article 15 which provides that national governments have the authority to determine access to its genetic resources based on national legislation.[460] This was a novel and consequential acknowledgement, as genetic resources were previously perceived as a common heritage of humanity[461] and most biological resources are found within national jurisdictions.[462]

---

[449] Matz-Lück (n 443) para 35.
[450] Medaglia (n 440) 192.
[451] C Richerzhagen, *Protecting Biological Diversity: The Effectiveness of Access and Benefit-Sharing Regimes* (Routledge 2010) 59.
[452] Nagoya Protocol, arts 1 and 9.
[453] CBD art 2. The language used is reminiscent of the definition of sustainable development of the Brundtland Commission.
[454] ibid: 'Biological diversity' means the variability among living organisms from all sources including, *inter alia*, terrestrial, marine, and other aquatic ecosystems and the ecological complexes of which they are part; this includes diversity within species, between species and of ecosystems.
[455] ibid: 'Biological resources' includes genetic resources, organisms or parts thereof, populations, or any other biotic component of ecosystems with actual or potential use or value for humanity.
[456] Matz-Lück (n 443) para 20.
[457] ibid para 2.
[458] CBD, Preamble.
[459] ibid art 3.
[460] ibid art 15. The Nagoya Protocol on ABS reaffirms the principle of sovereign rights over natural resources and recalls art 15 in its Preamble.
[461] Medaglia (n 440) 192.
[462] Matz-Lück (n 443) para 11.

1134 SDG 15

In less stringent terms, the CBD also provides for an additional form of benefit-sharing when recognizing the value of traditional knowledge, innovations, and practices (TKIP) of Indigenous and local communities (ILC) and seeking to equitably share benefits arising from the use of TKIP.[463] TKIP can illuminate new genetic resources with beneficial properties and can thus be linked to ABS. Therefore, the CBD requires each Party to, 'as far as possible and as appropriate' and 'subject to its national legislation' to (i) respect, preserve, and maintain the TKIP of ILC embodying traditional lifestyles relevant for the conservation and sustainable use of biodiversity; (ii) promote their wider application with the approval and involvement of the holders of the TKIP; and (iii) encourage the equitable sharing of the benefits arising therefrom.[464] The Nagoya Protocol on Access and Benefit-Sharing goes further and states that Parties shall take legislative, administrative, or policy measures so that the benefits arising from the utilization of TK associated with genetic resources are shared in a fair and equitable way with ILC holding such knowledge.[465]

The Bonn Guidelines were adopted as a voluntary recommendation clarifying the CBD's benefit-sharing provisions. They first established the link between CBD articles 8(j) (TKIP), 10(c) (customary sustainable use), 15 (access to genetic resources), 16 (access to and transfer of technology), and 19 (handling of biotechnology and distribution of its benefits).[466] Importantly, they provide guidance on the content of benefit-sharing agreements to assist in the development of MAT that ensure fair and equitable benefit-sharing.[467] They indicate that MAT may cover the conditions, obligations, procedures, types, timing, distribution, and mechanisms of benefits to be shared, which will vary depending on what is regarded as fair and equitable in the circumstances.[468] Near-term, medium-term, and long-term benefits should be considered, including up-front payments, milestone payments, and royalties, with the time frame of benefit-sharing clearly stipulated. The balance among near-, medium-, and long-term benefits should be considered on a case-by-case basis.[469]

Benefits should be shared fairly and equitably with all those who have been identified as having contributed to the resource management, scientific, and/or commercial process. The latter may include governmental, non-governmental, or academic institutions and ILC, and be directed to promote conservation and sustainable use of biodiversity.[470] It is recommended that the mechanism for benefit-sharing varies depending on the benefits, the conditions in the country, and the stakeholders involved; it can be flexible, as it should be determined by the partners involved, and will be decided on a case-by-case basis.[471] Mechanisms should include full cooperation in scientific research and

---

[463] CBD, Preamble.
[464] CBD, art 8(j).
[465] Nagoya Protocol, art 5(5).
[466] Bonn Guidelines, para 1.
[467] ibid para 41.
[468] ibid para 45.
[469] ibid para 47.
[470] ibid para 48.
[471] ibid para 49.

technology development, and those that derive from commercial products including trust funds, joint ventures, and licenses with preferential terms.[472]

The Bonn Guidelines have become a legal obligation for most CBD Parties since the adoption of the Nagoya Protocol. The Protocol provides a transparent legal framework for the effective implementation of the CBD's benefit-sharing obligations, providing greater legal certainty for providers and users of genetic resources. Further, these guidelines help to ensure benefit-sharing when resources leave the providing country[473] and encourage the advancement of research on genetic resources which creates incentives to conserve and sustainably use genetic resources. These effects in turn enhance the contribution of biodiversity conservation to development and human well-being.[474] The Nagoya Protocol's Annex demonstrates the sizable breadth of benefit-sharing, indicating how it can contribute to sustainable natural resource management for development and can assist interpreting benefit-sharing more broadly.[475]

The ITPGRFA has as its objective 'the conservation and sustainable use of plant genetic resources for food and agriculture [PGRFA] and the fair and equitable sharing of the benefits arising out of their use, in harmony with the [CBD], for sustainable agriculture and food security'.[476] The Preamble notes that, by exercising their sovereign rights over PGRFA, states can mutually benefit from creating an effective multilateral system (MLS) for facilitated access to a negotiated selection of resources and for the fair and equitable sharing of the benefits arising from their use. The ITPGRFA 'seeks to promote agricultural sustainability within a global system that recognizes the permanent sovereignty and exclusive control of states over PGRFA within their own jurisdiction'.[477] It also lays a foundation to establish an 'equitable food and agricultural system for future generations, through a broader-based multilateral system of facilitated access and benefit sharing of PGRFA, open to and including various different stakeholders'.[478]

---

[472] ibid para 50.

[473] Medaglia (n 440) 194–95.

[474] Medaglia (n 440) 195.

[475] Examples of non-monetary benefits from the Annex to the Nagoya Protocol include: (i) Sharing of R&D results; (ii) Collaboration, cooperation and contribution in scientific R&D programmes, particularly biotech research activities, where possible in the Party providing GR; (iii) Participation in product development; (iv) Collaboration, cooperation and contribution in education and training; (v) Admittance to *ex situ* facilities of GR and to databases; (vi) Transfer to the provider of the GR of knowledge and technology under fair and most favourable terms, including on concessional and preferential terms where agreed, in particular, knowledge and technology that make use of GR, including biotechnology, or that are relevant to the conservation and sustainable utilization of biodiversity; (vii) Strengthening capacities for technology transfer; (viii) Institutional capacity-building; (ix) Human and material resources to strengthen the capacities for the administration and enforcement of access regulations; (x) Training related to GR with the full participation of countries providing GR, and where possible, in such countries; (xi) Access to scientific information relevant to conservation and sustainable use of biodiversity, including biological inventories and taxonomic studies; (xii) Contributions to the local economy; (xiii) Research directed towards priority needs, such as health and food security, taking into account domestic uses of GR in the Party providing GR; (xiv) Institutional and professional relationships that can arise from an ABS agreement and subsequent collaborative activities; (xv) Food and livelihood security benefits; (xvi) Joint ownership of relevant IPR.

[476] *International Treaty on Plant Genetic Resources for Food and Agriculture* 2001 (entered into force 29 June 2004), art 1(1). [ITPGRFA]

[477] ME Footer, 'Our Agricultural Heritage and Sustainability' in N Schrijver and F Weiss, eds, *International Law and Sustainable Development: Principles and Practice* (Martinus Nijhoff 2004) 436.

[478] ibid.

1136   SDG 15

Article 6 creates duties on Parties for the sustainable use of PGRFA, namely that they develop and maintain appropriate policy and legal measures that promote the sustainable use of PGRFA. Article 10 establishes the MLS, stating that Parties exercise their sovereign rights to establish an MLS that is efficient, effective, and transparent to facilitate access to PGRFA and to equitably share the benefits arising from the utilization of PGRFA, on a complementary and mutually reinforcing basis.[479] Although the ITPGRFA applies to PGRFA broadly, the MLS only covers access to the sixty-four food and forage crops listed in its Annex I, and strictly for the purposes of utilization and conservation for research, breeding and training for food and agriculture (other uses are subject to the CBD/Nagoya Protocol). Unlike the bilateral approach promoted by the CBD, the PGRFA are shared based on a standard material transfer agreement (SMTA) adopted by the Governing Body of the ITPGRFA,[480] which includes the benefit-sharing provisions found in Article 13.

Facilitated access to PGRFA that are included in the MLS is recognized as a major benefit of the MLS, and it is agreed that benefits accruing therefrom shall be shared fairly and equitably through the following mechanisms: exchange of information, access to and transfer of technology, capacity building, and the sharing of the benefits arising from commercialization.[481] This 'seeks to redress some of the more obvious asymmetries between GR rich countries of the Global South and the GR hungry countries of the North, by including provisions relating to the sharing of monetary and other benefits arising from commercialization'.[482] There remain some significant challenges in operationalization of the MLS, especially in terms of increasing non-voluntary monetary contributions.[483]

The ITPGRFA Preamble also recognizes benefit-sharing as a fundamental aspect of Farmers' Rights, affirming that these are inherently based on 'the past, present and future contributions of farmers in all regions of the world, particularly those in centres of origin and diversity, in conserving, improving and making available these [PGRFA]'. It also recognizes farmers' rights to save, use, exchange, and sell farm-saved seed and other propagating material, as well as participate in decision-making on, and in the fair and equitable sharing of the benefits arising from, the use of PGRFA. Additionally, it recognizes farmers' importance in realizing and promoting Farmer's Rights at national and international levels.

Like the protection of the TKIP of ILC in the CBD, the ITPGRFA establishes that Parties should take measures to protect and promote Farmer's Rights, including through protection of traditional knowledge relevant to PGRFA, according to their domestic needs and priorities, interests, and law. It further establishes the right for farmers

---

[479] ITPGRFA, arts 10.1 and 10.2.
[480] ibid, art 12.4.
[481] ibid, art 13.2.
[482] Footer (n 477) 449.
[483] See F Wolff, 'The Nagoya Protocol and the Diffusion of Economic Instruments for Ecosystem Services in International Environmental Governance' in S Oberthür and GK Rosendal (eds) *Global Governance of Genetic Resources: Access and Benefit sharing after the Nagoya Protocol* (Routledge 2014) 141–42.

to equitably participate in sharing benefits arising from the utilization of PGRFA.[484] However, much remains to be settled in domestic implementation of farmers' rights.[485]

A further issue is that

in most of the countries that are currently actively providing PGRFA under the multilateral system, there are no positive legal enactments empowering gene bank managers (or anyone else for that matter) to be providers. It is enough in those countries that the country has ratified the Treaty and there is no law prohibiting gene bank managers from acting … and that of all the PGRFA in the country, the material in the national gene banks is the most obviously included material in the MLS. In those countries the gene bank manager feels confident that she may act, and that no one can or will challenge his/her authority for having decided to provide materials pursuant to the Treaty (i.e. using the SMTA) … Again, the appropriate form and content of those enactments will depend upon the political and legal cultures of the countries concerned: they could range from national legislation to ministerial decrees, regulations or guidelines to simply official statements issued from a high-level political office.[486]

2. Empirical Analysis

The development of NBSAPs under the CBD was used as a tool in countries to integrate Aichi targets and the Nagoya Protocol into national policy and actions. The National Strategies were crucial in establishing actions related to the Aichi targets. Relevant targets include Aichi target 16 (Access to and sharing benefits from genetic resources).[487]

In implementing the Nagoya Protocol, countries have to either develop new or amend existing legislative, administrative and policy measures or regulatory requirements to meet the obligations set out in the Protocol. Countries also have to put in place the required institutional measures to support the implementation of the Nagoya Protocol. There are many potential implications for existing legal frameworks as ABS measures must be mutually supportive with a variety of other laws and policies including those on science and technology (S&T), natural resources management, intellectual property rights and IPLC, to name a few.

Furthermore, the operationalization of ABS laws will necessarily vary from one country to the other as circumstances in each country differ. Countries must choose the best options and approaches to design an effective legal reform process that best

---

[484] ITPGRFA, art 9.2(a)–(b).

[485] See ITPGRFA Governing Body Resolution 7/2017 'Implementation of Article 9, Farmers Rights'.

[486] M Halewood (eds) *Mutually Supportive Implementation of the Plant Treaty and the Nagoya Protocol— A Report on 'The International Treaty and the Nagoya Protocol—A Tandem Workshop for National Focal Points'* (Biodiversity International 2015).

[487] 'Contributions of Biodiversity to SDG 15: Life on Land' (*cbd.int*, n.d.) <https://www.cbd.int/development/sdg15/> accessed 20 March 2022.

responds to the specific national needs and priorities. A sound legal reform process can then inform the process of selecting the most suitable legal and regulatory instruments. Against this background and in keeping with the requirements and principles set out in the Protocol, the following are some general objectives that could be pursued in the legal reform process and subsequently when taking steps towards selecting the types of ABS measures for implementation: (i) providing for legal certainty, clarity and transparency in domestic ABS processes and requirements to foster confidence in users and stakeholders; (ii) setting out a functional permitting system (PIC procedures); (iii) defining a clear division of roles and responsibilities, and collaboration mechanisms, for the various government agencies and stakeholders engaged in developing policy and implementing processes related to ABS; (iv) establishing requirements and guidance for the negotiation of MAT to foster fairness and equity; (v) defining the rights and responsibilities of IPLC, and processes for their participation and engagement in ABS policies and processes; (vi) creating mechanisms to monitor and ensure compliance with the terms of national ABS legislation including mechanisms for inter-agency and inter stakeholder cooperation, and where applicable with the terms stipulated in ABS agreements; (vii) addressing intergovernmental cooperation and potential transboundary issues; (viii) developing 'supportive measures' such as codes of conduct, guidelines, model clauses, capacity-building and awareness-raising strategies; (ix) creating measures and instruments to support compliance with other countries' domestic ABS legislation or requirements; (x) promoting conservation, sustainable use, job creation, empowering IPLCs, promoting innovation based on genetic resources and associated TK.

3. Efforts at the Domestic and International Levels

The Nagoya Protocol was notable for many countries as it established a transparent and predictable legal framework. As of 2023, 139 Parties to the CBD ratified their commitments. Of these countries, eighty-seven have put them into their national action plans relative to national access and benefit-sharing measures. Previous reports have only outlined the ongoing intent to implement the protocol at a national level and efforts to increase capacity and awareness. There has been some progress made by states in placing measures, establishing competent authorities, and designating checkpoints related for ABS.[488] However, more measures are needed as reports have indicated there are inconsistencies for both parties and non-parties in the implementation of access and benefit sharing measures. Less than three quarters of countries who have implemented NBSAPs contain initiatives and actions related to achieving SDG target 15.6 and Aichi target 16. Since the first specific national legislation on ABS—the Philippines Executive Order in 1995—and the first regional framework, Decision 391 of the Andean Community, 'The Common Regime for Access to Genetic Resources'—many studies, seminars, publications, laws, and draft laws have been produced and undertaken on this subject.

[488] See ABS Clearing House <https://absch.cbd.int> accessed 16 November 2022.

Several countries and regions have established provisions on ABS for biological and genetic resources in their laws or administrative structures. Countries that do have national ABS frameworks in place have chosen a wide range of mechanisms to regulate access to biological and genetic resources and benefit sharing at the national level. Some countries have developed new stand-alone laws on ABS and others have amended, revised, or updated existing general biodiversity-related laws to introduce and give effect to ABS components. Yet others have promulgated administrative guidelines as they may still be in the process of considering legislative options.

Nearly three decades on from the entry into force of the CBD, and over a decade after the adoption of the Nagoya Protocol, many CBD Parties continue to face challenges adopting and implementing functional national ABS laws and measures. National and regional experiences in implementing the Protocol—both positive and negative—inform global stakeholders on available legislative and policy frameworks, potential risks and mitigation measures, and practical experiences including contracts and permits. Operationalization of the Protocol will require decisions on whether and how to regulate access to genetic resources, how to implement the fair and equitable sharing of benefits resulting from the utilization of genetic resources and traditional knowledge associated with genetic resources, and what measures to implement to support the legislation of provider countries for the purposes of compliance, among others.

The level of national ABS implementation is low and often incomplete.[489] Countries have reached different levels of implementation and have adopted different approaches to regulation, reflecting their national administrative structures, priorities, cultural, and social realities. Some countries have only adopted one measure, generally legislation, while others have adopted a package of measures such as a national strategy, legislation, or regulations or guidelines. However, the package in many countries is often incomplete due to ongoing legislative or administrative development at different levels of government (eg regional, national/federal, and state/provincial level).[490] This implies that no one-size-fits-all ABS measure exists, rather countries must choose between a range of legal or regulatory options to define a best-fit approach tailored to their specific national needs, context, and objectives.[491]

ABS measures can be divided into two broad categories, as a component of NBSAP or included in environmental legislation. Countries that have integrated ABS as a component of their NBSAPs or as part of broader environmental, biodiversity, forest, wildlife, or protected areas legislation, but have not yet regulated ABS in detail. These measures generally provide for the future development of ABS dedicated measures and

---

[489] The information available indicates that the development of national measures has proven difficult for many countries due to a number of factors including a lack of technical expertise, budgetary constraints, weak government structures, and political support, local social conflict and conflict over ownership of genetic resources, see CBD, *Analysis of Existing National, Regional and International Legal Instruments Relating to Access and Benefit-Sharing and Experience Gained in their Implementation, Including Identification of Gaps.* Note by the Executive Secretary. UNEP/CBD/WG-ABS/3/2, Convention on Biological Diversity, Montreal, 2005.

[490] V Normand, *Level of national Implementation of ABS*, paper presented to the International Expert Workshop on Access to Genetic Resources and Benefit Sharing, Cuernavaca, Mexico, October 2004.

[491] ibid.

1140   SDG 15

include some general elements to be addressed (requirement of PIC and MAT, general measures for TK protection/recognition, etc without providing particular details about how the system will operate in practice). These provisions usually have served as an enabling mechanism to provide the legal basis for the development of more detailed regulations and other legal instruments on ABS. Examples of general/enabling provisions can be found in the environmental legislation of El Salvador, China, Mexico, Cameroon, Tanzania, and Spain, among others.

The second category includes countries that have a biodiversity or environmental law (which also addresses other issues in addition to ABS) with more detailed provisions on ABS (including dedicated chapters) but which do not constitute stand-alone ABS legislation. Examples of this approach exist in the biodiversity laws of Costa Rica, Nicaragua, Bhutan, Vanuatu, and Norway. Furthermore, there are countries which have addressed ABS also in great detail specifically in stand-alone measures (sometimes mixed with other elements but clearly the main or only purpose of the legislation is to regulate ABS). Examples of these countries are India, Ethiopia, South Africa, Australia, Ecuador, Peru, Panama, Uganda, Kenya, and Brazil. Other countries have decided to develop short-term policy measures to guide the implementation of ABS.

In any of the cases and scenarios presented above, other relevant laws and regulations could also include ABS provisions or references, for instance in IPR-related legislation, or in measures pertaining to process for approval of products (medicines, cosmetics, foods), funding of, for instance, public research, etc.

Comprehensive ABS measures in developed and developing countries share some similarities from which lessons can be drawn. For instance, most measures include provisions on the scope of application of the laws and on the legal status of genetic resources and associated traditional knowledge; the determination of whether PIC is required for access; procedures for determining access if PIC is required; rules on MAT, and fair and equitable benefit-sharing; monitoring and compliance mechanisms; and the establishment or designation of appropriate institutions to share ABS-relevant information, grant access, and negotiate and enforce benefit-sharing, as well as monitor and check compliance.[492]

Since the adoption and entry into force of the Protocol, countries continue to face challenges in the adoption and implementation of functional national ABS laws and measures. Around eighty countries have some type of laws, measures, or instruments to regulate access to their genetic resources and the fair and equitable sharing of benefits arising from their utilization.[493] The Nagoya Protocol provides a great degree of flexibility and its operationalization will therefore require that countries make decisions on whether and how to regulate access to genetic resources, how to design measures for the fair and equitable sharing of benefits arising from the utilization of genetic

---

[492] T Greiber and others, *An Explanatory Guide to the Nagoya Protocol on Access and Benefit-Sharing* (IUCN 2012) 279–80.

[493] JC Medaglia and others, *Overview of National and Regional Measures on Access and Benefit Sharing: Challenges and Opportunities in Implementing the Nagoya Protocol* (3rd edn, Centre for International Sustainable Development Law 2014).

resources and associated traditional knowledge, how to choose compliance measures, and finally how to set up institutional structures and arrangements that can best support national implementation. The adoption of the Nagoya Protocol has provided new impetus to the implementation of ABS and numerous national laws have been drafted and adopted since 2010.

An important emerging issue is that of 'digital sequence information' (DSI) or 'gene sequence data' being discussed in the framework of the CBD and the Nagoya Protocol and in other forums[494] such as the World Health Organization, the FAO Commission on Genetic Resources for Food and Agriculture, and the ITPGRFA that have agreed on different processes to elucidate the treatment of the 'digital genetic sequences', terminology on which there is no consensus at this time. These pose challenges to the scope of application of access rules, monitoring the utilization of genetic information and for the fair and equitable sharing of benefits, among others.

Brazilian legislation should be highlighted as it is the most advanced on this topic. For the specific determination of the scope of application, the different definitions contemplated in the Brazilian Law must also be used (article 2). The Brazilian 'Genetic Heritage' includes the genetic information of plants, animals, or microorganisms, including metabolites. This conceptualization would cover not only the tangible or physical component (molecules, genes, or substances) but also the intangible or information taken from samples, which would extend the application of the legal system to the 'genetic information' included in databases, going beyond physical samples. Although there are no guidelines or experience on this point, the regulation to the Law requires registration in Brazil's SisGen when the use of the genetic patrimony is made through access to 'in silico' sources. Possibly, the drafting of ABS frameworks will consider these challenges at the time of their design and to try to build the corresponding capacities to interpret and implement regulatory frameworks that cover DSI.[495]

4. Critique

Domestically, target 15.6 has only been partially achieved, for reasons that include limited resources to operationalize the target, especially related to the commitments made for the Nagoya Protocol, as well as the lack of necessary legislation implemented in countries. Many of the actions reported to be found in NBSAPs were vague and did not make explicit reference to the Nagoya Protocol. Though some progress was made, overall SDG target 15.6 was not achieved.

The adoption of the Nagoya Protocol constituted a milestone to generate capacity-building initiatives that usually include the elaboration or amendment of regulatory frameworks, the building or improvement of capacities of different actors—including non-governmental organizations, research centres and universities, the private sector, and local communities and Indigenous peoples—the promotion of the bio-community

---

[494] The UN negotiating process on a legally binding instrument on biodiversity in areas beyond national jurisdiction has also considered the issue of ABS in the case of digital sequence information.

[495] See further MR Muller, *Genetic Resources as Natural Information: Implications for the Convention on Biological Diversity and Nagoya Protocol* (Routledge 2015).

1142 SDG 15

(often called biocultural) protocols mentioned in the Nagoya Protocol, and eventually support to concrete research and development projects that seek to generate new products and processes derived from the use of genetic resources or associated traditional knowledge.

These have been financed mainly by the Global Environmental Fund (GEF) and the German Cooperation Agency (GiZ) and cover regional projects: for example,[496] the ABS Program in Central America and the Dominican Republic (known as the ABS/ CCAD/GIZ programme), and the Project entitled 'Strengthening of Human Resources, Legal Frameworks and Institutional Capacities for the Implementation of the Nagoya Protocol' (also known as the Global ABS Project) executed by UNDP which includes twenty-four countries. This set of initiatives should contribute significantly to develop and reform ABS regulatory frameworks, one of the critical steps for the effective implementation of the CBD and the Protocol, and consequently target 15.6.

I. Target 15.7 Take urgent action to end poaching and trafficking of protected species of flora and fauna and address both demand and supply of illegal wildlife products

Target 15.7 calls on UN Member States to take urgent action to end poaching and trafficking of protected species of flora and fauna and address both demand and supply of illegal wildlife products. Target 15.7's implementing component, target 15.c, seeks to enhance global support for efforts to combat poaching and trafficking of protected species, including by increasing the capacity of local communities to pursue sustainable livelihood opportunities. The sole indicator for both targets 15.7.1 and 15.c is the proportion of traded wildlife that was poached or illicitly trafficked.[497]

1. Sources of Target
CITES is the principal international law source for target 15.7. This treaty aims to 'control or prohibit international trade in species or their products where those species are in danger of extinction owing to unsustainable demand'.[498] It does not seek to directly protect animal and plant species or habitat but rather to regulate the commercial exploitation and trade in species through a trade-related mechanism.[499] Yet, as it covers both flora and fauna, 'it does play a role in preserving component parts of the habitat of some species and thus to the conservation of biodiversity'.[500]

---

[496] See for the document prepared by the CBD Secretariat, *Overview of capacity-building and development initiatives providing direct support to countries for the implementation of the Nagoya Protocol*, UN Doc UNEP/CBD/NP/COP-MOP/2/INF/6.
[497] *Work of the Statistical Commission pertaining to the 2030 Agenda for Sustainable Development*, UN Doc A/RES/71/313, 20.
[498] Boyle and Redgwell (n 147) 660.
[499] ibid.
[500] ibid 661.

Where transnational criminal law aspects emerge in the poaching and trafficking of protected species, the United Nations Convention against Transnational Organized Crime[501] (UNTOC) and the United Nations Convention against Corruption[502] (UNCAC) also have important roles in providing a legal basis for investigating, prosecuting, and adjudicating crimes pertaining to protected species of wild flora and fauna.[503]

2. Empirical Analysis

Target 15.7 is made up of two aspects: (i) taking urgent action to end poaching and trafficking of protected species of flora and fauna, and (ii) addressing both demand and supply of illegal wildlife products. Target 15.c complements these aspects by looking at both sides of the equation, the necessity of enhancing global support for efforts to combat poaching and trafficking of protected species; and increasing the capacity of local communities to pursue sustainable livelihood activities.

The first aspect of targets 15.7 and 15.c commits states to urgently end criminal activities against protected wild species, namely poaching and trafficking, including through enhancing global support for efforts to combat these crimes. The UNGA has repeatedly recognized the significant international cooperation required for this in resolutions on tackling illicit trafficking in wildlife throughout the past decade, including in its latest resolution on wildlife trafficking, which in 2021 reaffirmed and built upon earlier resolutions.[504] This latest resolution recognizes three treaties as being at the core of the matter—CITES, UNTOC, and UNCAC—while also recognizing the importance of MEAs like the CMS, CBD, the Ramsar Convention, and the World Heritage Convention.[505] Emphasizing the cross-cutting nature of this first aspect of targets 15.7 and 15.c, the UN General Assembly remains seized of the issue and addresses it biennially.[506]

The second aspect of targets 15.7 and 15.c commits states to addressing both demand and supply for poaching and trafficking, including by increasing the capacity of local communities to pursue sustainable livelihood activities. This falls more squarely within the CITES mandate to regulate the supply of protected species, and the balance it seeks to strike between development and the conservation and sustainable use of wild flora and fauna. Reducing consumer demand for illegal wildlife products does not fall squarely within any treaty language but will require very significant domestic efforts by UN Member States to achieve SDG target 15.7.

---

[501] *Convention against Transnational Organized Crime* (adopted 12 December 2001, entered into force 29 September 2003) 2225 UNTS 209.

[502] *Convention against Corruption* (adopted 31 October 2003, entered into force 14 December 2005) 2349 UNTS 41.

[503] United Nations Office on Drugs and Crime, 'Mandates' (n.d.) <http://www.unodc.org/unodc/en/wildlife-and-forest-crime/mandates.html>.

[504] *Tackling illicit trafficking in wildlife*, UN Doc A/75/L.116. See also UNGA Resolutions 69/314 (2015), 70/301 (2016), 71/326 (2017), and 73/343 (2019) on the same subject; and ECOSOC Resolution 2013/40 on *Crime prevention and criminal justice responses to illicit trafficking in protected species of wild fauna and flora*.

[505] *Tackling illicit trafficking in wildlife*, Preamble, paras 3, 6–9, 20, 29.

[506] ibid para 44.

1144 SDG 15

3. Efforts at the Domestic and International Levels

Poaching is largely addressed at the domestic level as it consists of a form of trespass—an unlawful taking of flora and fauna.[507] Illegal wildlife trafficking is both a domestic and international issue as it takes place both on the territory of biodiversity-rich states—from source to domestic traders or markets—and internationally, as traders link to the global marketplace in illegally obtained wildlife and their parts.[508]

CITES establishes an inter-operational set of domestic systems where a national export/import permit system is combined with an institutional system on a global scale.[509] As designed, CITES is principally dependent on national implementation—particularly the establishment of at least one Management Authority and Scientific Authority who are responsible for ensuring that permitting conditions are complied with before species or their parts are exported or imported.[510]

The CBD COP has also adopted a series of relevant decisions, including on sustainable wildlife use, particularly species used for food, or wild meat (also known as bushmeat), monitoring tools and databases, multidisciplinary approaches in sustainable wildlife management including alternative livelihoods, subsistence use of wildlife, and wild meat in the context of food security.[511]

At the international level, several general and species-specific programmes or initiatives have been established with the aim of combatting wildlife poaching and trafficking. Some examples include the CITES Monitoring the Illegal Killing of Elephants (MIKE) Programme, the International Consortium on Combating Wildlife Crime (ICCWC),[512] the Global Initiative to End Wildlife Crime,[513] the *African Strategy on Combating Illegal Exploitation and Illegal Trade in Wild Fauna and Flora in Africa*, and the G20 *High-level Principles on Combating Corruption related to Illegal Trade in Wildlife and Wildlife Products*.

A series of efforts and attempts have been undertaken to augment cooperation between Member States, international governmental organizations, NGOs, and align the activities of UN agencies and other entities on preventing and fighting illicit trafficking in wildlife. These include the Paris Declaration of 2013, the London Declaration of 2014, the Kasane Statement of 2015, the Brazzaville Declaration of 2015, the Hanoi Statement of 2016, the Bishkek Declaration of 2017, the London Declaration of 2018, the Lima Declaration of 2019, the Chiang Mai Statement of 2019, the CMS Gandhinagar Declaration of 2020, and the Leaders Pledge for Nature of 2020.

---

[507] 'Poach, v.2', *OED Online* (Oxford University Press n.d.).

[508] See generally RA Sollund, *The Crimes of Wildlife Trafficking: Issues of Justice, Legality and Morality* (Routledge 2019). See also eg F Douglas, 'Reducing Illegal Wildlife Trafficking: CITES and Caviar' (2012) 42 Environmental Policy and Law 57; T Bell, *Combating Wildlife Trafficking: National Strategy, Implementation Plan and Restrictions on Elephant Ivory Trade* (Nova Science Publishers 2016).

[509] Boyle and Redgwell (n 147) 662.

[510] ibid 664.

[511] SCBD, 'Sustainable Wildlife Management' (19 December 2019) <https://www.cbd.int/wildlife>.

[512] A collaborative effort of the CITES Secretariat, the International Criminal Police Organization (INTERPOL), the United Nations Office on Drugs and Crime (UNODC), the World Bank and the World Customs Organization.

[513] A broad-based coalition aiming for the creation of a new global agreement to combat wildlife crime through the adoption of a fourth Protocol to UNTOC. See End Wildlife Crime, 'UNTOC Wildlife Protocol' (*Global Initiative to End Wildlife Crime*, n.d.) <https://endwildlifecrime.org/untoc-wildlife-protocol/>.

4. Critique

CITES has been critiqued for 'its implicit legitimization of wildlife trade, albeit regulated under the convention'.[514] Many species around the world are in rapid decline 'not only because of loss of habitat but also because of increased exploitation'.[515] Trade in protected species is a major contributor to overexploitation, particularly given the contemporary ease of transport which enables millions of live animals and birds to be transported worldwide for the pet trade, ornamental plants to be sourced from remote locales, and a thriving luxury market for products made from rare plants and animals.[516]

Once a species is listed in Appendix I to CITES, 'for those species international commercial trade between parties has been effectively prohibited. Here the problem is not trade, but poaching, illegal trafficking and the involvement of transnational organised crime.'[517] Although CITES requires Parties to enforce its terms by penalizing illegal trade and possession of illegal specimens,[518] there are large gaps in implementation requiring 'improved national criminal enforcement and international criminal cooperation'.[519] Although initiatives and partnerships have emerged to address the implementation gap, there is no treaty directly aimed at curbing illegal wildlife harvesting and trade. It is worth asking whether the global community is asking too much of CITES, which was adopted with species protection in mind—not to fight wildlife crime.

The African elephant is a case in point. Its poor conservation status has been known of and regulated for well over a century, but it was only moved to CITES Appendix I in 1990 following the severe decline of some populations because of poaching and ivory sales. The Appendix I listing 'prohibited all trade in elephant ivory and led to a dramatic fall in sales, but the adverse socio-economic consequences led to a partial relaxation in an attempt to seek a compromise between wildlife protection and human development'.[520] Some elephant populations reported to be well managed were moved to Appendix II, and several one-off sales of existing ivory stocks were allowed to generate income for further conservation measures.[521]

Yet, it remains impossible to distinguish ivory sourced from Appendix II or Appendix I, and allowing this limited trade has 'not stopped poaching and illegal trafficking of ivory'.[522] Indeed, it is challenging to determine more broadly how great a difference CITES has made to reducing illegal wildlife trade, and views are divided on its effectiveness.[523] By broadly continuing to enable some international trade in endangered species rather than banning it, it supports consumer demand for products which they will then obtain legally or illegally, which undermines correctly tracking the status

---

[514] Boyle and Redgwell (n 147) 661.
[515] ibid.
[516] ibid 662.
[517] ibid.
[518] CITES art VIII(1).
[519] Boyle and Redgwell (n 147) 662.
[520] ibid 666.
[521] ibid.
[522] ibid.
[523] IUCN, *Trade Measures in Multilateral Environmental Agreements* (IUCN and CITES 2000).

1146   SDG 15

of the species and weakens regulatory attempts made under CITES to ensure its sustainable use.

As CITES is not fit for meeting target 15.7, improving law enforcement and international cooperation on illegal wildlife trade remains the most relevant path presently open to UN Member States to move forward on target 15.7. Some of this cooperation will take place under the aegis of CITES, while other aspects will occur within the framework of the CBD, and under the auspices of the UNODC.

Challenges noted by states in achieving target 15.7 include the lack of funding available for implementation in both developed and developing countries, particularly for monitoring and implementation efforts, and a general lack of capacity.[524] Consequently, target 15.7 is not on track toward being achieved, but rather, poaching and illegal wildlife trade has increased since its adoption in 2015.[525] Much greater action must be taken to combat the sizable challenges posed by criminal organizations.[526] There has been an unprecedented increase in the illegal wildlife trade, with poached or illicitly trafficked wildlife considered to be a significant threat to the world's most threatened and vulnerable species.[527] It is estimated that wildlife crime is worth $23 billion, while also being a direct threat to biodiversity and ecosystem functions and threatening the livelihoods, well-being, and security of communities.[528] Laws are not presently adequate to tackle the problem, and the main focus must be on strengthening institutions. Weak governance structures have enabled illegal trade at both local, national and international levels. One effective approach is the empowerment of local communities in sustainably managing their biological resources and ensuring that illegal harvesting is actively combatted.[529]

J. Target 15.8 By 2020, introduce measures to prevent the introduction and significantly reduce the impact of invasive alien species on land and water ecosystems and control or eradicate the priority species

This 2020 target calls on states to introduce measures to prevent the introduction of IAS and significantly reduce their impact on land and water ecosystems, and control or eradicate the priority species. Indicator 15.8.1 looks to the proportion of countries with relevant national legislation and which provide adequate resources.

---

[524] SCBD, *Global Biodiversity Outlook 5* (n 177).
[525] ibid.
[526] UNODC, *World Wildlife Crime Report: Trafficking in Protected Species* (UNODC 2020).
[527] KL Clifton and A Rastogi, *Curbing Illegal Wildlife Trade: The Role of Social Network Analysis* (IUCN 2016).
[528] UNEP, *The Environmental Crime Crisis: Threats to Sustainable Development from Illegal Exploitation and Trade in Wildlife and Forest Resources* (UNEP 2014); UNODC (n 526).
[529] See For example, L Niskanen and others, *Strengthening Local Community Engagement in Combatting Illegal Wildlife Trade: Case Studies from Kenya* (IUCN 2018).

1. Sources of Target

The principal source for target 15.8 is Aichi target 9 on IAS, which calls that 'by 2020, invasive alien species and pathways are identified and prioritized, priority species are controlled or eradicated, and measures are in place to manage pathways to prevent their introduction and establishment'. The CBD underlies this commitment, particularly its article 8(h).[530] It is also buttressed by sanitary treaties and standards including the International Plant Protection Convention,[531] and the Terrestrial Animal Health Code[532] of the World Organisation for Animal Health (OIE). Inland water ecosystems can also be severely affected by introductions of water-borne invasive species,[533] which are in part addressed by the UN Watercourses Convention[534] and the Ballast Water Convention.[535]

2. Empirical Analysis

According to a growing amount of research, IAS now constitute one of the leading causes of biodiversity loss globally, with almost one-fifth of the Earth's surface at risk from animal and plant invasions and a doubling of IAS over the past fifty years.[536] The major drivers behind the emergence and spread of IAS include climate change, habitat degradation, and the expansion of trade and mobility networks; all complex challenges whose impact is predicted to continue.[537]

The GBO 5 has found that progress of the international community on the achievement of Aichi target 9 has been mixed. On the one hand, the development of NBSAPs has helped stimulate countries to develop strategies and regulations on IAS. To achieve target 9, countries have created and implemented legislation on identifying introduction pathways and monitoring, controlling, and eradicating IAS, supported by the increasing availability of information and data about the occurrence of invasions.[538] Measures include rules on import and export, national guidelines for management and control of IAS, and establishing zoosanitary and phytosanitary checkpoints. Moreover, a majority of NBSAPs have incorporated targets relating to Aichi target 9 on IAS. Countries have established national strategies for management and eradication, with

---

[530] CBD art 8: 'Each Contracting Party shall, as far as possible and as appropriate: ... (h) Prevent the introduction of, control or eradicate those alien species which threaten ecosystems, habitats or species;'

[531] Maljean-Dubois (n 88) para 50.

[532] OIE, 'Terrestrial Animal Health Code (2021)' <http://www.oie.int/en/what-we-do/standards/codes-and-manuals/terrestrial-code-online-access/> accessed 29 March 2022.

[533] See, eg, K Dölle and DE Kurzmann, 'The Freshwater Mollusk Dreissena Polymorpha (Zebra Mussel)-a Review: Living, Prospects and Jeopardies' (2020) 13 Asian Journal of Environmental Ecology 1. See also DL VanderZwaag and J Boehner, 'Marine and Coastal Law and Policy: Progressions and Limitations' in Medaglia, Perron-Welch and Goodman (eds), *Legal Aspects of Implementing the Convention on Biodiversity* (n 111).

[534] *Convention on the Law of the Non-Navigational Uses of International Watercourses*, 21 May 1997 (in force 17 August 2014) 2999 UNTS 1, art 22.

[535] *International Convention for the Control and Management of Ship's Ballast Water and Sediments, 2004*, 13 February 2004 (in force 8 September 2017).

[536] P Balvanera and others, 'Chapter 2.1. Status and Trends – Drivers of Change' in in ES Brondizio and others (eds) *Global Assessment Report of the Intergovernmental Science-Policy Platform on Biodiversity and Ecosystem Services* (IPBES Secretariat 2019) 126.

[537] ibid.

[538] SCBD, *Global Biodiversity Outlook 5* (n 177) 74.

1148   SDG 15

examples of programmes that have succeeded in eradicating IAS (especially invasive mammals on islands, with 800 reported eradications and 200 since 2010).[539]

On the other hand, though there has been some success, there are few examples of nations fully eradicating IAS after they are established,[540] with eradication a particularly challenging objective in continental ecosystems.[541] According to the IPBES Global Assessment Report, 'the rate of introduction of new IAS seems higher than ever before and with no signs of slowing',[542] and accelerating globalization has so far outpaced efforts to combat invasions. The IUCN Red List Index shows that the pressure exerted by IAS is increasing the risk of extinction for many species of birds, mammals, and amphibians,[543] with developed countries more affected than developing ones partly owing to their higher exposure to trade networks.[544]

3. Efforts at the Domestic and International Levels

The international regulation of IAS 'has been piecemeal and inconsistent, lacking common definitions and approaches: [IAS] are included in instruments regulating pests and have been addressed in instruments addressed to particular pathways through which IAS may be introduced'.[545] Target 15.8 requires states to undertake three actions in both terrestrial and inland water ecosystems to respond to the threat of IAS. First, states should introduce measures to prevent the introduction of IAS, which is the primary and most effective way to halt biodiversity loss resulting from non-native species. Furthermore, states should significantly reduce the impact of IAS, and also control or eradicate priority IAS.

IAS are a cross-cutting issue under the CBD—the principal international framework on the topic—with the requirement to prevent, control, and eradicate IAS paired with Parties' duties to identify and monitor the components and biodiversity, identify processes and categories of activities which have or are likely to have significant adverse impacts on biodiversity, and to monitor their effects through sampling and other techniques.[546]

States' policies and efforts have therefore focused on preventing the introduction of IAS, which is a more cost-effective approach rather than attempting to eradicate them once they are established and actively harm impact native species and ecosystems.[547] Some international efforts under the CBD COP include Guiding Principles on IAS,[548]

---

[539] ibid.

[540] See examples by CR Veitch and MN Clout (eds), *Turning the Tide: The Eradication of Invasive Species* (IUCN 2002).

[541] SCBD, *Global Biodiversity Outlook 5* (n 177) 75.

[542] Balvanera and others (n 536) 126.

[543] 'Red List Index (Impacts of Invasive Alien Species' (*bipindicators.net*, n.d.) <https://www.bipindicators.net/indicators/red-list-index/red-list-index-impacts-of-invasive-alien-species> accessed 12 April 2022.

[544] For example, H Seebens and others, 'No Saturation in the Accumulation of Alien Species Worldwide' (2017) 8 Nature Communications 14435.

[545] Boyle and Redgwell (n 147) 696.

[546] ibid.

[547] For example, IUCN, *IUCN Guidelines for the Prevention of Biodiversity Loss Caused by Alien Invasive Species* (IUCN 2000).

[548] *Guiding Principles for the Prevention, Introduction and Mitigation of Impacts of Alien Species that Threaten Ecosystems*, UN Doc UNEP/CBD/COP/DEC/VI/23, Annex.

which are to be applied in activities aimed at implementing article 8(h) of the CBD[549]—namely prevention and mitigation measures, including control and eradication that should be based on precautionary and ecosystem approaches.[550]

4. Critique

Target 15.8 has not been achieved and IAS are a growing threat to biodiversity worldwide. They occur in all taxonomic groups, affecting all types of ecosystems, causing harm from (i) competition with, or predation of, native species; (ii) disease transmission and harm to native organisms; and (iii) hybridization of native and alien species.[551] Despite clear knowledge of the environmental harm being caused, and the concomitant economic and developmental impacts, introductions of IAS are increasing globally.[552] International trade has multiplied the pathways for IAS to move between countries and regions, both unintentionally (eg ballast water, raw wood products and packaging materials) and intentional introduction (eg legal and illegal international trade in species as pets or for ornamental reasons that are released into the environment).[553]

Challenges noted by states in achieving target 15.8 include limited resources for taking actions against IAS, and a general lack of capacity and awareness, in addition to the lack of adequate legal frameworks for tackling the many different facets of IAS. International efforts remain lacking in effectiveness, likely to be due to insufficient legal bindingness and inadequate implementation of those few measures that do exist. However, it should be noted that a new multilateral instrument developed under the aegis of the International Maritime Organization, the International Convention for the Control and Management of Ships' Ballast Water and Sediments, has entered into force in 2017.[554] According to the GBO 5, this Convention may help manage the introduction of IAS through ballast waters, even though its impact will only become apparent in the future.[555]

K. Target 15.9 By 2020, integrate ecosystem and biodiversity values into national and local planning, development processes, poverty reduction strategies and accounts

This 2020 target calls on Parties to integrate ecosystem and biodiversity values into national and local planning, development processes, poverty reduction strategies, and accounts. By calling for this integration, the target implicitly refers to the concept of

---

[549] Boyle and Redgwell (n 147) 696.
[550] ibid.
[551] ibid 695.
[552] ibid.
[553] ibid. See, eg, V Greenwood, 'The Green-Feathered Terror That Slaughtered Bats in Spain', *The New York Times* (5 October 2018) <https://www.nytimes.com/2018/05/10/science/parakeets-bats-invasive-species.html> accessed 15 April 2022.
[554] *International Convention for the Control and Management of Ships' Ballast Water and Sediments* (n 535).
[555] SCBD, *Global Biodiversity Outlook 5* (n 177) 74.

1150 SDG 15

biodiversity mainstreaming, which arguably constitutes a biodiversity-specific articulation of the principle of integration enshrined in Principle 4 of the Rio Declaration.[556]

Indicator 15.9.1 has two sub-indicators: (i) the number of countries that have established national targets in accordance with or similar to Aichi target 2 in their NBSAPs and the progress reported towards these targets, and (ii) the integration of biodiversity into national accounting and reporting systems through the implementation of the System of Environmental-Economic Accounting (SEEA).[557]

1. Sources of Target

Although attempts to integrate biodiversity concerns in the development process are not necessarily a new endeavour,[558] the CBD and its Aichi targets constitute the principal source for target 15.9. The CBD contains several provisions that are relevant to concepts of biodiversity mainstreaming and integration. Article 6(b) requires Parties to carry out mainstreaming activities by integrating 'as far as possible and as appropriate, the conservation and sustainable use of biological diversity into relevant sectoral or cross-sectoral plans, programmes and policies'.[559] Article 10(a) then extends this integration requirement to national decision-making processes, while several other provisions of the Convention arguably provide the tools through which such integration is to be carried out, for example by laying down obligations to use impact assessments (article 14) and incentive measures (article 11).

At the same time, target 15.9 refers to one specific aspect, namely the integration of ecosystem and biodiversity *values*, which is not directly addressed by the CBD. The most direct predecessor to target 15.9 could thus be considered to be Aichi target 2, through which CBD Parties committed to, by 2020 at the latest, to integrate biodiversity *values* into national and local development and poverty reduction strategies and planning processes, as well as to begin incorporating such values into national accounting and reporting systems. In addition, Aichi target 2 is closely related to at least two other targets included under the Strategic Goal A of the CBD's Strategic Plan 2011–2020, which call for increased societal awareness of biodiversity values (Aichi target 1) and action to address incentives harmful to biodiversity and create positive ones (Aichi target 3).

In and of itself, the notion of value does not necessarily imply a monetary quantification of the benefits that biodiversity and ecosystem services provide to mankind. The IPBES Global Assessment, for example, has noted that measures of value other than economic ones may be particularly important across different socio-cultural contexts, and that some communities and cultures may conceptualise nature in ways that do not correspond to a 'discreet measurable entity'.[560] It is undeniable, however, that a

[556] Rio Declaration, Principle 4; see also N Schrijver, *The Evolution of Sustainable Development in International Law: Inception, Meaning and Status* (Nijhoff 2008) 204.
[557] For information on SEEA, see UN, 'System of Environmental-Economic Accounting' <https://seea.un.org/>.
[558] IIED, *Biodiversity and Development. A State of Knowledge Review: Discussion Paper* (IIED 2013) 18–20.
[559] CBD art 6(b).
[560] KA Brauman and others, 'Chapter 2.3. Status and Trends—Nature's Contributions to People (NCP)' in ES Brondizio and others (eds) *Global Assessment Report of the Intergovernmental Science-Policy Platform on Biodiversity and Ecosystem Services* (IPBES Secretariat 2019) 334.

key driver for the inclusion of the notion of biodiversity and ecosystem values in target 15.9 and Aichi target 2 has been the progressive emergence of economic valuation techniques aimed at assigning a monetary value to components of biodiversity and/or ecosystem services, as part of broader attempts to mainstream biodiversity into economic thinking and policy-making.[561]

2. Empirical Analysis

The concept of biodiversity mainstreaming and integration is a broad one, whose practical application is not always clarified in the instruments in which it is embedded. Its rationale can be found in the fact that biodiversity has traditionally represented a 'marginal' issue in development policy, with the consequence that other political priorities and market distortions, which often undervalue natural systems and provide perverse incentives and environmentally harmful subsidies, have tended to dominate decision-making.[562] According to common interpretation, the plans, strategies and processes to which target 15.9 refers may therefore include: (i) cross-sectoral plans focusing on poverty reduction, economic development, trade and investment, or climate change; (ii) sector-specific plans in areas such as energy, mining, infrastructure, forestry, and agriculture and fisheries; and (iii) spatial planning processes.[563] In addition, successful biodiversity mainstreaming in these areas can occur at multiple spatial scales, ranging from positive outcomes at the level of governance and law (eg greater levels of public participation of biodiversity-dependent communities, expression of biodiversity concerns in national policies and Constitutions) to increased investments in biodiversity conservation and pro-poor management of ecosystem services.[564]

The empirical assessment of target 15.9's achievement is difficult, as the monitoring of regulatory, financial, and capacity-building initiatives taken to mainstream biodiversity values at the national level cannot necessarily reveal whether these initiatives have been successful in changing behaviours, affecting government decisions, and modifying incentives. Despite the information contained in CBD Parties' sixth national reports, which referred to the development of initiatives, policies, studies, technical tools, and investment funds to mainstream biodiversity, the GBO 5 determined that Aichi target 2 was not met.[565]

Moreover, while over 80 per cent of NBSAPs have adopted targets relating to Aichi target 2,[566] the monitoring of target 15.9's implementation reveals that many countries have yet to adopt such targets in national policy and incorporate biodiversity in poverty reduction strategies. Of those that do, a majority report insufficient or no progress in

---

[561] For example, J Farley, 'Ecosystem Services: The Economics Debate' (2012) 1 Ecosystem Services 40; MJ Koetse and others, 'Economic Valuation Methods for Ecosystem Services' in JA Bouma and PJH van Beukering (eds) Ecosystem Services: From Concepts to Practice (CUP 2015).

[562] For example, B Dalal-Calton and S Bass, The Challenges of Environmental Mainstreaming (IIED 2009).

[563] For example, SCBD, Mainstreaming Biodiversity Workshops on National Strategies and Action Plans (CBD 2008).

[564] IIED and UNEP-WCMC, Biodiversity Mainstreaming: A Rapid Diagnostic Tool (IIED and UNEP-WCMC 2012).

[565] SCBD, Global Biodiversity Outlook 5 (n 177) 40.

[566] ibid 43.

achieving Aichi target 2.[567] Similarly, an analysis of the VNRs for the SDGs argued that while many states evaluated the state of natural ecosystems in their reporting, only half had demonstrated a capacity to successfully mainstream biodiversity.[568] In addition, the GBO 5 has found that biodiversity concerns tend to be incorporated in national strategies, but are rarely explicitly integrated in formal planning, accounting, and reporting processes.[569] This failure to fully mainstream biodiversity and ecosystem values is indirectly echoed by the assessment of global trends in the elimination of harmful incentives and the introduction of positive incentives contained in GBO 5 and the IPBES Global Assessment Report, which reveal poor progress despite some attempts to introduce agri-environmental schemes and other forms of payments for ecosystem services.[570]

According to the Local Biodiversity Outlooks 2 (LBO 2), which was published as a companion to the GBO 5 in 2020, current efforts towards biodiversity mainstreaming are also failing at incorporating different culture value systems and viewpoints, and 'going beyond monetary measures of well-being'.[571] This assessment should also be seen in the wider of context of current poverty reduction strategies at the national level, which existing studies criticize for their continued marginalization of Indigenous people and local communities in decision-making.[572]

3. Efforts at the Domestic and International Levels
Target 15.9 has four aspects on integrating ecosystem and biodiversity values, including mainstreaming biodiversity into national and local development and poverty reduction strategies and planning processes, and accounts. Mainstreaming seeks to address the underlying causes of biodiversity loss by incorporating biodiversity concepts throughout various sectors of society and the economy.[573] Though at times difficult to quantify, the target also looks to integrate concepts related to biodiversity into national and local development plans and reporting systems by 2020.

At the international level, activities under the CBD have remained an important source of efforts towards the joint achievement of target 15.9 and Aichi target 2. Recent CBD COP decisions have affirmed the need to incorporate biodiversity and ecosystem services in all spheres of policy-making, with NBSAPs representing the main planning documents through which the integration of biodiversity and ecosystem values in national policies and actions is expected to be achieved. Parties and other relevant actors have particularly been recommended to use the ecosystem approach in sectors including spatial planning, climate mitigation and adaptation, energy and mining, and

---

[567] ibid.
[568] Pesce and others (n 354) 37.
[569] SCBD, *Global Biodiversity Outlook 5* (n 177) 43.
[570] ibid 44–47; and Butchart and others (n 252) 409–410.
[571] Forest Peoples Programme, *Local Biodiversity Outlooks 2* (Forest Peoples Programme 2020) 58.
[572] For example, KK Sangha and others, 'Mainstreaming Indigenous and Local Communities' Connections with Nature for Policy Decision-making' (2019) 19 Global Ecology and Conservation e00668.
[573] See also OECD, *Mainstreaming Biodiversity for Sustainable Development: Policy Highlights* (OECD 2018).

area-based conservation measures, among others.[574] In addition, the use of economic valuation techniques has been promoted as a key means for designing socio-economic incentives for conservation and sustainable use under article 11 of the CBD.[575] Lastly, the CBD COP has encouraged states to mainstream biodiversity in the context of environmental impact assessment processes with the adoption of a set of Voluntary Guidelines on Biodiversity-Inclusive Impact Assessment.[576]

Outside of the CBD and MEA treaty bodies more generally, the concept of ecosystem services has also started to be explored at the level of international dispute settlement, most notably in *Costa Rica v Nicaragua* (Compensation) before the International Court of Justice (ICJ). In this case, not only did Costa Rica argue in favour of using an 'eco-system services approach' as a methodology for the valuation of environmental damage, but the Court itself recognized the impairment of ecosystem services as part of the no-tion of environmental damage that can be compensated for under international law.[577]

Perhaps most importantly, a key component of international efforts to incorporate biodiversity values into decision-making is the introduction of economic accounting frameworks to monitor changes in stocks' and flows of natural capital, a method known as 'natural capital accounting'. In practice, natural capital accounting entails the use statistical datasets that capture how a country's natural resources contribute to the economy, and how this resource base is impacted by policy decisions. A sig-nificant milestone in this respect was the adoption by the United Nations Statistical Commission (UNSC) of a statistical framework for ecosystem accounting known as SEEA—Ecosystem Accounting (SEEA EA), which aims to support policy and moni-toring processes at different scales, with an emphasis on connecting ecosystem and macro-economic information.[578] The UNSC formally recognizes parts of the SEEA EA as an international statistical standard[579] and while such standards are usually not binding, there is an expectation that countries will implement them as part of inter-national efforts to increase the comparability and accessibility of national datasets. Natural capital accounting and ecosystem services valuation techniques have become increasingly prominent in the private sector as well, with public-private collaborations such as the Natural Capital Coalition now seeking to promote the uptake of natural capital assessments by businesses.[580]

---

[574] Notably, Principle 4 of the so-called Malawi Principles endorsed by the CBD to provide conceptual clarity to the concept of ecosystem approach refers to the need to 'understand and manage the ecosystem in an economic context'. See 'Ecosystem Approach' CBD COP Decision V/6 (22 June 2000) UN Doc UNEP/CBD/COP/5/23, 105.

[575] 'Measures for Implementing the Convention on Biological Diversity' CBD COP Decision IV/10 (15 June 1998) UN Doc UNEP/CBD/COP/4/27, 115, para 1.

[576] 'Impact Assessment: Voluntary Guidelines on Biodiversity-Inclusive Impact Assessment' COP Decision VIII/28 (15 June 2006) UN Doc UNEP/CBD/COP/DEC/VIII/28.

[577] *Certain Activities Carried Out by Nicaragua in the Border Area (Costa Rica v. Nicaragua) (Compensation)* [2018], ICJ Reports 15, para 42.

[578] UNSC, 'System of Environmental–Economic Accounting—Ecosystem Accounting: Final Draft' (Background Document, 5 February 2021) <https://unstats.un.org/unsd/statcom/52nd-session/documents/BG-3f-SEEA-EA_Final_draft-E.pdf> accessed 20 May 2021.

[579] UNSC, 'Report on the Fifty-Second Session (1–3 and 5 March 2021)' (22 March 2021) UN Doc E/2021/24-E/CN.3/2021/30, Decision 52/108, 17–18.

[580] Natural Capital Coalition, 'Natural Capital Protocol' (*capitalscoalition.org*) <https://capitalscoalition.org/wp-content/uploads/2021/01/NCC_Protocol.pdf> accessed 14 March 2022.

1154 SDG 15

At the national level, the sheer diversity of efforts undertaken to integrate biodiversity concerns in development processes have gone beyond the formulation of NBSAPs and the adoption of systems of ecosystem accounting. For example, they have included the introduction of payments for ecosystem services policies, the adoption of integrated land use plans,[581] and the preparation of national ecosystem assessments to help provide the necessary knowledge to support decision-making.[582] Furthermore, with respect to the meaningful involvement of Indigenous Peoples and local communities in biodiversity mainstreaming efforts, a number of case studies have highlighted the variety of forms that participatory biodiversity mainstreaming may take in practice, ranging from community-based management of protected areas[583] to collaborative environmental impact assessment procedures.[584]

4. Critique

A major problem in the achievement of target 15.9 is represented by the difficulty of translating the notion of biodiversity mainstreaming into concrete policies and practices, as well as to ensure that biodiversity and ecosystem values are consistently integrated into the actual decisions taken by government authorities or private companies. As convincingly argued in an International Institute for Environment and Development report on mainstreaming, 'often policies and plans remain as dry documents on a shelf that have little bearing on practice on the ground'.[585] The challenge partly relates to limited capacity and financial resources, but it is also fundamentally affected by a systemic failure to reform economic incentives and update political priorities, as demonstrated by the parallel struggle to achieve progress in Aichi target 3 and transition to sustainable production and consumption systems. Though the GBO 5 and LBO 2 reveal positive examples of biodiversity mainstreaming in domestic efforts and policies, it is clear that more action is needed in states facing challenges in implementing mainstreaming approaches, and in incorporating biodiversity values into economic systems. In addition, it can be argued that while mainstreaming may help internalize the costs of biodiversity loss and the benefits of conservation in decision-making processes, more ambitious actions will be needed to fully address the underlying drivers of environmental degradation, including in situations where the economic case for biodiversity may not be immediately evident.

Inevitably, the ambitious nature of target 15.9 reverberates on, and is influenced by, the capacity of states and international organizations to assess progress. On the one hand, the two indicators chosen to monitor implementation can only offer an incomplete picture of the direction of travel. The assessment of national targets related to Aichi target 2 is affected by the diverging approaches that countries have taken to

---

[581] SCBD, *Global Biodiversity Outlook 5* (n 177) 41.
[582] UNEP-WCMC, *National Ecosystem Assessments to Support Implementation of the Convention on Biological Diversity* (UNEP-WCMC 2021).
[583] SCBD, *Mainstreaming Biodiversity Workshops* (n 563).
[584] Forest Peoples Programme (n 571) 62.
[585] IIED (n 558) 38.

incorporate the Aichi targets in national policy and report against them. In addition, the SEEA EA has only been introduced in 2021, and the extent to which countries will incorporate the standard into their national accounts will also not necessarily reveal how such accounts are used to mainstream biodiversity in decision-making.[586] On the other hand, pre-existing knowledge gaps and the inherent difficulty of monitoring biodiversity mainstreaming on the ground have prevented the introduction of more accurate indicators in the Strategic Plan 2011–2020 and the SDG Indicator Framework. These uncertainties risk fuelling a vicious circle, whereby knowledge gaps may not only impede the timely assessment of progress but also reinforce the use of proxy indicators that can mistakenly suggest success despite a lack of on-the-ground implementation.

---

[586] 'SDG Indicator Metadata' (*unstats.un.org*, July 2021) <https://unstats.un.org/sdgs/metadata/files/Metadata-15-09-01.pdf> accessed 18 April 2022.

SDG 16

'Promote Peaceful and Inclusive Societies for Sustainable Development, Provide Access to Justice for All and Build Effective, Accountable, and Inclusive Institutions at All Levels'

Tom Kabau

I. Introduction

Sustainable Development Goal (SDG) 16 is part of seventeen aspirations that address diverse areas of human rights, governance, and environmental protection at the state and international levels that were conceptualized, and are implemented and evaluated, under the auspices of the United Nations (UN). The SDG 16 targets and indicators focus on measuring and evaluating progress in respect of the practices of states in relation to the thematic concepts of peace, access to justice, and accountable and inclusive institutions for purposes of the progressive realization of sustainable development. The SDGs were adopted by states, under the auspices of the United Nations General Assembly (UNGA), through Resolution 70/1 of 2015.[1] The Resolution articulated the necessity of achieving the thematic concerns of peace, justice, and accountable institutions, as articulated under SDG 16, which is premised on their conceptual and practical interdependence.[2] As is evident in the context of SDG 16, the diverse goals are integrated and interrelated.[3] Further, it is noteworthy that SDG 16 is a vital determinant of the realization of other SDGs.[4] For instance, in a society in which the rule of law is absent, it may be problematic to achieve poverty eradication, gender equality, or even food security.[5]

---

[1] SeeT>United Nations General Assembly (UNGA), 'Transforming our World: The 2030 Agenda for Sustainable Development' UN Doc A/RES/70/1 (21 October 2015).

[2] ibid para 35.

[3] ibid Preamble.

[4] T>International Development Law Organisation, 'Goal 16: Peace, Justice and Strong Institutions' (2020) <https://www.idlo.int/sustainable-development-goals/goal-16-peace-justice-and-strong-institutions>T>accessed 23 September 2021.

[5] ibid.

1158   SDG 16

Despite efforts to achieve sustainable development in the context of the post-2015 agenda, some of the aspirations articulated under SDG 16 remain unrealized. The 2020 SDGs Report by the UN observed that insecurity, restricted access to justice, and weak institutions still remain serious obstacles to sustainable development.[6] The 2020 Report pointed out some indicators of the continued challenge of addressing some of the state and transnational challenges that necessitated the conceptual framework of SDG 16 in addressing societal security and developmental needs. For instance, the Report regretted that people in excess of 79.5 million were at the time fleeing conflict, war, and persecution.[7] According to the Report, for every four children, one continues to be deprived of legal identity due to the lack of birth registration, which has the effect of curtailing such children's enjoyment of rights in other areas.[8]

II. *Travaux Préparatoires*

This section examines some of the themes and issues of discussions during the negotiations the SDGs, under the auspices of relevant organs, particularly the Open Working Group (OWG).

A. An Overview of the Preparatory Initiatives

The UN Conference on Sustainable Development, held in Rio de Janeiro in 2012, formally launched the process of developing a set of SDGs that would build upon the MDGs in conformity with the post 2015 development agenda.[9] The UNGA Resolution 66/288 christened 'The Future We Want', which was an outcome of the 2012 Rio de Janeiro Conference on Sustainable Development. The report acknowledged and affirmed that the MDGs had been a helpful instrument for determining particular development objectives under the auspices of the UN activities, and for orienting national priority-setting and resources towards the identified common goals.[10]

Greater impetus for the conceptualization of the SDGs was consolidated when the United Nations Secretary-General (UNSG) established in July 2012 a twenty-seven-member High Level Panel to advise and provide guidance on the ideal post-2015 development framework, as the MDGs neared the end of their timeline.[11] It is noteworthy that the Panel reflected a deliberate effort by the UNSG to reflect balanced

[6] T>United Nations, *The Sustainable Development Goals Report: 2020* (United Nations 2020) 56.
[7] ibid.
[8] ibid.
[9] Sustainable Development Knowledge Platform, 'United Nations Conference on Sustainable Development, Rio+20' (Rio de Janeiro, 20–22 June 2012) <https://sustainabledevelopment.un.org/rio20> accessed 14 July 2021.
[10] UNGA, 'Resolution adopted by the General Assembly on 27 July 2012: The Future We Want' UN Doc A/RES/66/288* (11 September 2012), para 245.
[11] T>United Nations Secretary-General, 'The Secretary-General's High-Level Panel of Eminent Persons on the Post-2015 Development Agenda' <https://www.un.org/sg/en/management/hlppost2015.shtml>T>accessed 23 July 2021.

representation of the UN members dynamics and interests. It was co-chaired by President Ellen Johnson Sirleaf of Liberia, Prime Minister David Cameron of the United Kingdom, and President Susilo Bambang Yudhoyono of Indonesia, in addition to representation from other states, civil society, and even the private sector.[12]

In conceptualizing the SDGs, the UNGA appreciated that the enunciation of objectives could facilitate 'focused and coherent action on sustainable development'.[13] In that context, the UNGA affirmed the necessity, significance and value 'of a set of sustainable development goals'.[14] Outlining the nature of the envisaged SDGs, the UNGA stated that the goals would be premised 'on Agenda 21 and the Johannesburg Plan of Implementation, which fully respect all the Rio Principles', would be consistent with the international legal regime, and would take into consideration diversity in state capacities and circumstances.[15]

Recognizing the necessity of broad participatory engagement by various state and non-state actors, the UNGA Resolution 66/288 envisioned that governments would propel the realization of the goals with the active engagement of the relevant stakeholders.[16] Most of the work of conceptualizing the thematic concepts of the eventual seventeen SDGs occurred under the auspices of a thirty-member Open Working Group on Sustainable Development Goals (but with additional participation of representatives of states and relevant stakeholders) that undertook its negotiations and discussions from 2013 to 2014. The concepts that informed the goals and targets of SDG 16 were given special evaluation during the Eighth Session of the OWG.

B. Formulating SDG 16 Targets: Conceptual and Thematic Considerations

Considerations were given to the conceptual and thematic content of the SDG 16 targets and indicators. Some of the issues ranged from the concerns in respect to the interlinkages between the concepts of peace, justice, and accountable institutions, to the constituent elements of the stated governance conceptions.

1. Deliberation on the Rule of Law and Interdependent Concepts
The UNGA in Resolution 66/288 emphasized that the rule of law at the state and international sphere, together with the associated concepts of good governance and democracy, were core engines of sustainable development.[17] During the OWG sessions, the

---

[12] ibid.
[13] T>UNGA, 'Resolution adopted by the General Assembly on 27 July 2012' (n 10), para 246.
[14] ibid.
[15] ibid.
[16] ibid para 247.
[17] ibid para 10.

1160 SDG 16

inevitable linkages between the rule of law and conflict prevention and peace building were pointed out.[18]

It is practically impossible to institutionalize the rule of law in societies in which there is no peace, particularly in communities engulfed in conflicts. Nonetheless, the governance of a state on the premise of rule of law is a basis of safeguarding durable peace. In that sense, it can be argued that there are aspects of symbiotic relationship between the maintenance of peace and the institutionalization of the rule law in governance. The OWG generally acknowledged Member States' recognition of the entrenchment of the rule of law and access to justice as being core factors in the prevention and resolution of conflicts, and in durable peace-building.[19]

The OWG also highlighted the concern by many states on the institutionalization of the international rule of law, of which they were of the view that it could be achieved through progressive reforms to international organizations, such as the UN and multilateral institutions, with the objective of entrenching and increasing representations, accountability, legitimacy, and transparency.[20]

Differing proposals were given on how to deal with the essential concept of the rule of law in the SDGs structure: from having 'a stand-alone goal to an overarching driver or enabler'.[21] It is noteworthy that some members of the OWG even called for the concepts of governance, the rule of law, and peace to be expressed in a single collective goal form, while others were of the view that the issues should be addressed in a crosscutting manner, but others argued that there was no need to have specific goals on the stated concepts.[22] The rule of law theme eventually became the focus of target 16.3 and was linked to the concern of promoting access to justice by all.

It is noteworthy that there were sentiments within the OWG that it would be difficult to have targets and indicators that are consensual in the context of evaluating peace and good governance.[23] Nonetheless, there were suggestions that targets and indicators to evaluate and measure the rule of law should be 'tailored to specific national legal systems, local practices and values, regardless of where countries are along the development spectrum'.[24]

---

[18] Sustainable Development Knowledge Platform, 'Eighth Session of the Open Working Group on Sustainable Development Goals: Summary of the Co-Chairs' (New York, February 2014) 9 <https://sustainabledevelopment.un.org/content/documents/3417OWG8%20Summary.pdf> accessed 12 July 2021.

[19] Sustainable Development Knowledge Platform, 'Eighth Session of the Open Working Group on Sustainable Development Goals: TST Issues Brief—Conflict Prevention, Post-conflict Peacebuilding and the Promotion of Durable Peace, Rule of Law and Governance' 5 <https://sustainabledevelopment.un.org/content/documents/263 9Issues%20Brief%20on%20Peace%20etc_FINAL_21_Nov.pdf> accessed 12 July 2021.

[20] Sustainable Development Knowledge Platform, 'Eighth Session of the Open Working Group on Sustainable Development Goals: Co-Chairs' Summary Bullet Points from OWG-8' (New York, February 2014) <https://sustainabledevelopment.un.org/owg8.html> accessed 12 July 2021.

[21] Sustainable Development Knowledge Platform, 'Eighth Session of the Open Working Group on Sustainable Development Goals: Summary of the Co-Chairs' (n 18) 9.

[22] T>Sustainable Development Knowledge Platform, 'Eighth Session of the Open Working Group on Sustainable Development Goals: Co-Chairs' Summary Bullet Points from OWG-8' (n 20).

[23] ibid.

[24] Sustainable Development Knowledge Platform, 'Eighth Session of the Open Working Group on Sustainable Development Goals: Summary of the Co-Chairs' (n 18) 9.

TRAVAUX PRÉPARATOIRES

2. Discussions Regarding the Role of Institutions and their Structuring

The OWG was of the view that institutions that are open and effective were essential, as they would form the foundation for sustainable development. According to the members of the Working Group, such institutions (in the context of governance) would require transparency, which would be characterized by public access to information.[25] The OWG argued that transparency could foster trust in government institutions and could be promoted through increased avenues for the public to access information.[26] In addition, the Working Group was of the view that institutions of local government are crucial in fostering participatory and accountable governance.[27]

Further, the OWG advocated for institutional reform to enhance access to justice by focusing on improving efficiency and integrity, and eliminating bias and discrimination in the relevant institutions such as courts, tribunals, and prosecution agencies.[28] In that sense the OWG gave an illustration of greater involvement of women in the justice and security agencies of the state, which it stated would translate to more inclusive access by women and children.[29] It was pointed out that data from thirty-nine countries demonstrated that an increased number of female police officers, for instance, correlated with an increase in the number of reported sexual assault reports.[30] Nonetheless, progress towards accountability in the context of sexual violence was negated by the fact that the female gender comprised, as of 2014, only 27 per cent of judges and 9 per cent of the police force globally.[31]

3. Perspectives Regarding Conflict Resolution and Post-Conflict Peace-Building

The MDG framework was criticized by some participants in the Working Group for its significant weakness in failing to address peace and security concerns.[32] It was argued that the mutually reinforcing and interlinked concepts of peace, governance and the rule of law required a multifaceted approach that included:

> creating responsive, transparent and inclusive governance, promoting dialogue between the organs of state, civil society and the private sector; guaranteeing citizen's rights to access to public information, free, independent and pluralistic media, inclusive economic governance, growth and development, inclusive local and national institutions for conflict prevention, transformation and resolution, and peace building.[33]

---

[25] Sustainable Development Knowledge Platform, 'Eighth Session of the Open Working Group on Sustainable Development Goals: Co-Chairs' Summary Bullet Points from OWG-8' (n 20).

[26] T>Sustainable Development Knowledge Platform, 'Eighth Session of the Open Working Group on Sustainable Development Goals: Concluding Remarks of Co-Chairs 8th Session of Open Working Group on Sustainable Development Goals' (New York, February 2014) <https://sustainabledevelopment.un.org/owg8.html>T>accessed 12 July 2021.

[27] ibid.

[28] T>Sustainable Development Knowledge Platform, 'Eighth Session of the Open Working Group on Sustainable Development Goals: TST Issues Brief' (n 19) 5.

[29] ibid.

[30] ibid.

[31] ibid.

[32] T>Sustainable Development Knowledge Platform, 'Eighth Session of the Open Working Group on Sustainable Development Goals: Summary of the Co-Chairs' (n 18) 9.

[33] ibid.

1162   SDG 16

As the MDGs were implemented, there was increasing recognition that conflicts and insecurity significantly constrained development.[34] Insecurity and conflict often reverse developmental benefits of a state accrued over many years in addition to generally slowing economic progress of states.[35] It is in that context that Goal 16 was conceptualized to address the implications of insecurity and conflict for development outcomes.[36] It is noteworthy that during the OWG deliberations, there had been suggestions for an independent goal that would solely address the issue of stable and peaceful societies.[37]

Due to concerns regarding the contribution of land and land based resources to conflicts, the International Organization for Migration (IOM), hosted a side event to the Eighth Session of the Open Working Group on SDGs on 7 February 2014 under the theme 'land tenure and property rights as tools for promoting peace building and durable peace'.[38] Among the resolutions reached by the participants in the IOM side event was the view that durable and sustainable peace could not be realized without giving special attention to the issue of access to land, land tenure and property rights, and as such, should be a core aspect of the UN Post-2015 Development Agenda, as espoused under the SDG framework.[39]

It was suggested that there was need to focus more on a mix of top-down and bottom-up approaches to the entrenchment of lasting peace and sustainable development in places such as the Eastern Democratic Republic of Congo region, where it was observed that a largely top-down approach had failed to achieve such objectives in the state despite previous massive international efforts.[40] Using the Eastern DRC region as an illustration, it was argued that a top-down approach failed to appropriately consider and address local causes, which demonstrated the need for a mixture of both top-down and bottom-up approaches.[41]

Gender-based violence was highlighted by the OWG as constituting 'one of the most pervasive violations of human rights in all societies', and as such, being a core obstacle to the realization of sustainable development goals.[42] The OWG criticized the MDGs for lacking appropriate indicators to evaluate their targets accurately, particularly in the context of gender-based violence.[43] It was pointed out that while, for instance, MDGs 2

[34] T>Institute for Economics and Peace, 'Sustainable Development Goal 16' (2016) 6 <https://www.economicsa ndpeace.org/>T>accessed 10 February 2021.

[35] ibid.

[36] ibid.

[37] Sustainable Development Knowledge Platform, 'Eighth Session of the Open Working Group on Sustainable Development Goals: Summary of the Co-Chairs' (n 18) 9.

[38] T>Sustainable Development Knowledge Platform, 'Land Tenure and Property Rights as Tools for Promoting Peacebuilding and Durable Peace' *IOM Side Event to the 8th Session of the Open Working Group (OWG) on Sustainable Development Goals Key Messages* (New York, 7 February 2014) <https://sustainabledevelopment. un.org/content/documents/3347iom.pdf>T>accessed 12 July 2021.

[39] ibid.

[40] T>Sustainable Development Knowledge Platform, 'Peace and Sustainable Development: A Two-Way Relationship' (New York, February 2014) <https://sustainabledevelopment.un.org/content/documents/3210s ummary3.pdf>T>accessed 12 July 2021.

[41] ibid.

[42] T>Sustainable Development Knowledge Platform, 'Submission by Prof Rashida Manjoo UN Special Rapporteur on Violence against Women, Its Causes and Consequences' (New York, February 2014) <https://sus tainabledevelopment.un.org/content/documents/3337RM%20submission%20to%20OWG%20on%20post%202 015%20SDGs.pdf>T>accessed 12 July 2021.

[43] ibid.

and 3 targeted gender equality in education, none of the indicators addressed gender-based violence, which is often the reason that many girls are unable to complete their education.[44] According to the Working Group, gender-based violence was one of the core causes of gender inequality, and as such required accurate evaluation through well conceptualized indicators.[45] The Working Group's observation regarding the inaccurate usage of indicators to measure progress towards targets in the context of gender-based violence was a shortcoming that could be identified in other MDGs as well.[46] It was suggested that the SDG framework should integrate 'goals, targets and indicators necessary to glean a full understanding of the causes of violence against women and its effects on sustainable development'.[47] It is noteworthy that some aspects of gender-based violence were eventually addressed under SDG 5, which is concerned with the entrenchment of gender equality and empowerment of women and girls. In particular, target 5.2 focuses on the elimination of 'all forms of violence against ... women and girls in the public and private spheres'.

4. Discourse on Inclusiveness and Broad Participation for Social Equity

The OWG expressed concern for the promotion of inclusive, participatory, representative, and responsive decision-making within states, and internationally, which eventually transitioned into targets 16.7 and 16.8. According to the OWG, social equity required that all forms of exclusion and discrimination be eliminated, that all vulnerable segments of society be granted equitable access to opportunities and services, and that they participate meaningfully in the social, political, and economic affairs of the state.[48]

It was the OWG's view that participatory governance would contribute to conflict prevention and as such, called upon the involvement of various categories of the population including women, youth, and Indigenous peoples in the management of the affairs of states.[49] The Working Group observed that societies in which particular groups were systematically excluded from the political and economic spheres were often at risk of conflicts, whose effect in turn was the reversion of development.[50]

5. Reflections on Access to Justice

Noting that justice is essential in resolving disputes peacefully; addressing marginalization, inequality and poverty; and in ensuring effective remedies in case of violation of human rights, the OWG regretted that obstacles to accessing justice were 'still widespread especially for women, children, poor and marginalized groups and people living

---

[44] ibid.
[45] ibid.
[46] ibid.
[47] ibid.
[48] T>Sustainable Development Knowledge Platform, 'Eighth Session of the Open Working Group on Sustainable Development Goals: Concluding Remarks of Co-Chairs' (n 26).
[49] ibid.
[50] T>Sustainable Development Knowledge Platform, 'Eighth Session of the Open Working Group on Sustainable Development Goals: TST Issues Brief' (n 19) T>7.

1164　SDG 16

in communities affected by violence and conflict'.[51] The OWG also instructively observed that an independent and impartial judicial system is essential for the institutionalization of the rule of law.[52] The final concept of access to justice under target 16.3 was categorized together with the rule of law theme.

6. Focus on Reduction of Corruption and Bribery

The OWG observed that the police force and the judiciary were among the state institutions most affected by corruption.[53] As such, it advocated for the strengthening of the rule of law and democratic governance in order to eliminate such corruption and enhance development prospects.[54] It is noteworthy that the OWG was of the view that additional sources of revenue, which could promote diverse targets such as inclusive and peaceful communities, could be obtained from the reduction of illicit financial flows (IFFs).[55]

7. Perspectives Regarding Elimination of Violence against Children

The elimination of violence against children was also a noteworthy concern raised during the OWG sessions. The Working Group noted that despite the right of children to live in environments free of violence and in safe and caring family settings, millions of minors were subjected to neglect, exploitation, violence, and abuse.[56] The Working Group opined that besides such incidences leading to the death of children, they could also result in detrimental trans-generational and long-term consequences, such as psychological trauma, lost productivity, and poor quality of life.[57] The sum effect may also be reflected in the context of reduced social and human capital, and slowed economic progression.[58] It is noteworthy that the concern regarding children was eventually expressed in target 16.2.

8. Deliberations on the Conceptual Interlinkages and Interdependence of Thematic Concepts

The OWG participants acknowledged the interdependence and interlinkages between the envisaged goals and targets, for instance, by acknowledging that while the rule of law, peace, and good governance were ends in themselves, they were also crucial for purposes of progress towards sustainable development and poverty eradication.[59] They

[51] ibid 5.
[52] ibid.
[53] ibid.
[54] ibid.
[55] Sustainable Development Knowledge Platform, 'Eighth Session of the Open Working Group on Sustainable Development Goals: Co-Chairs' Summary Bullet Points from OWG-8' (n 20).
[56] T>Sustainable Development Knowledge Platform, 'Side-Event on a World Without Violence against Children: Co-Hosted by the Government of Canada and the Government of Paraguay, Child Fund Alliance, Plan International, Save the Children, SOS Children's Villages International, UNICEF and World Vision International (New York, 5 February 2014) <https://sustainabledevelopment.un.org/content/documents/3218Joint%20Side-event.pdf>T>accessed 12 July 2021.
[57] ibid.
[58] ibid.
[59] Sustainable Development Knowledge Platform, 'Eighth Session of the Open Working Group on Sustainable Development Goals: Co-Chairs' Summary Bullet Points from OWG-8' (n 20).

also opined that the absence of the rule of law, conflicts, violence, weak institutions, and fragile institutions had grossly obstructed progress towards the realization of the MDGs.[60] As such, they observed that the highlighted concerns and issues could not be resolved independently, as had been acknowledged by states in previous resolutions under the auspices of the UN.[61] The Group members particularly emphasized the inter-linkages between the rule of law and development, and pointed out there was need to promote the former at both the national and international levels.[62]

The OWG was of the view that violence and conflicts undermine development, and having noted that the Rio + 20 Outcome Document did not address the issue of peace and security, it proposed that the anticipated SDGs should be guided by the contents of the 'The Future We Want' document on the issue.[63] They were also of the view that durable peace and effective conflict prevention would require resolving the root causes, including by ensuring equitable management of natural resources, entrenching inclusive economic governance, and institutionalizing participatory decision-making.[64] The OWG nonetheless pointed out the need to tackle the concepts of 'violence' and 'conflict' as distinct issues that should not be equated, as they required different remedies and solutions.[65]

Acknowledging the national and international linkages between the rule of law, peace, and democratic governance in the context of sustainable development, the OWG noted that deficits in a particular state would in no doubt impact other countries.[66] The diffusion to other states was likely to be 'through economic and financial linkages, migration, refugees, humanitarian crises, pollution, communicable diseases, violence and armed conflicts, terrorism, piracy, organized crime or trafficking in humans, drugs, arms or natural resources' due to progressive globalization and increasing regional integration, which in turn enhanced the likelihood of these cross-border spill overs.[67]

9. Opinions Regarding Improvements to Indicators in the Post-MDGs Period

The UNGA in Resolution A/RES/66/288 of 2012 affirmed that progress towards the realization of the development goals required evaluation through targets and indicators in a framework that was sensitive to diverse national capacities, circumstances, and levels of development.[68] The OWG observed that while the variables of peaceful societies, governance, and the rule of law were not directly measured by the previous MDG indicators, there was evidence that progress towards the realization of the MDGs

---

[60] T>Sustainable Development Knowledge Platform, 'Eighth Session of the Open Working Group on Sustainable Development Goals: TST Issues Brief' (n 19) 1.

[61] ibid.

[62] T>Sustainable Development Knowledge Platform, 'Eighth Session of the Open Working Group on Sustainable Development Goals: Co-Chairs' Summary Bullet Points from OWG-8' (n 20).

[63] ibid.

[64] ibid.

[65] ibid.

[66] T>Sustainable Development Knowledge Platform, 'Eighth Session of the Open Working Group on Sustainable Development Goals: TST Issues Brief' (n 19) 1.

[67] ibid.

[68] UNGA, 'Resolution adopted by the General Assembly on 27 July 2012' (n 10) para 250.

had been hampered by a fragile rule of law, violence, and inequalities.[69] Consequently, the OWG was of the view that it was essential that indicators relating to the rule of law, peace, and governance be incorporated in the post-2015 development framework.[70] The Working Group opined that such inclusion 'would represent a significant step towards compilation and reporting of data on key conditions and governance structures associated with most development indicators', as learnt from the limitations of the MDG framework.[71]

It was appreciated that states were increasingly relying upon the indicators developed to measure the rule of law, security, and governance in their policy planning, and as such, the resulting experiences could be tapped into while developing the post-2015 SDG framework in the states areas of concern, with further improvements being made to address existing lacunas.[72] For instance, the OWG noted that while there were data on rural land usage, there was need to further develop data collection instruments that would evaluate dimensions such as property rights in such contexts as the percentage of men and women with legally recognized tenure rights to land.[73] It is noteworthy that despite the centrality of sound land management practices and land tenure rights to development and conflict resolution, there are no specific targets or indicators in that respect under SDG 16. The OWG acknowledged that there still remained some hindrances to the collation and gathering 'of reliable and comprehensive data in certain areas, despite their salience to sustainable development, for example on the decisions of informal or customary justice mechanisms'.[74]

The OWG emphasized the utmost significance of national data collection and statistical initiatives and mechanisms, highlighting the necessity of their strengthening.[75] The Working Group also appreciated that indicators and measurement instruments had been established by regional and international organizations in relation to the evaluation of accountability and governance, the rule of law, corruption, conflict, justice for juveniles, violence against children, democratic representation, and human trafficking, among others.[76]

III. Goal Commentary

This section examines the legal foundations of SDG 16, particularly in the context of international law. It also evaluates the significance of the conceptual focus of some of the SDG 16 targets through select themes.

[69] T>United Nations Statistics Division (UNSD), 'Compendium of Statistical Notes for the Open Working Group on Sustainable Development Goals (OWG)' (March 2014) 181 <https://sustainabledevelopment.un.org/content/documents/3647Compendium%20of%20statistical%20notes.pdf>T>accessed 12 July 2021.
[70] ibid.
[71] ibid.
[72] ibid 186.
[73] ibid.
[74] ibid.
[75] ibid.
[76] ibid.

A. Legal Foundations and Some Thematic Concerns

As discussed in this section, the SDG 16 targets are premised on international legal obligations, including the principle of sustainable development and the right to development.

1. International Legal Obligations as the Source for SDG 16 Targets
UNGA Resolution 70/1 affirmed that the SDGs were to be guided by the principles of the Charter of the United Nations and other provisions of international law, including the Universal Declaration of Human Rights, the 2005 World Summit Outcome, the Declaration on the Right to Development, and other transnational legal instruments.[77] As such, SDG 16 is premised upon international legal instruments and is to be implemented by states in a manner that is consistent with their rights and obligations under international law.[78] At the core of SDG 16 is the principle of sustainable development, which is discussed in more detail in the sub-section that follows.

Target 16.10 is oriented towards promotion of access to information and protection of fundamental freedoms. Its indicator, 16.10.2, evaluates the extent to which states adopt and implement constitutional, statutory, and policy guarantees for access to information by the general public. Further, its indicator 16.10.1 measures the extent of violation of human rights of journalists, media personnel, and human rights activists, including through killings, arbitrary detentions, and enforced disappearances. As the UNSG affirms, the right of every person to seek, receive, and impart information through diverse forms of media is enshrined in article 19 of the Universal Declaration of Human Rights and article 19 of the International Covenant on Civil and Political Rights (ICCPR).[79] The UNSG acknowledges that the Human Rights Council, under the auspices of the UN, and the General Assembly have previously affirmed that freedom of expression constitutes an essential foundation for a democratic society and is a core prerequisite for societal progress and development.[80] The UNSG has also reiterated the UNGA's previous affirmation that media freedom fosters access to information and democracy, in addition to promoting intercultural discourse, good governance, and peace.[81]

As a mechanism of institutionalizing social equity, target 16.7 of SDG 16 focuses on the entrenchment of inclusive, participatory, and representative decision-making in governance. Article 25 of the ICCPR affirms the right of all individuals to participate

---

[77] T>UNGA, 'Transforming our World' (n 1),T> para 10.

[78] ibid para 18.

[79] UNGA, 'Promotion and Protection of the Right to Freedom of Opinion and Expression: Note by the Secretary General' UN Doc A/71/373 (6 September 2016) para 5. See Universal Declaration of Human Rights, UNGA Res 217A (III) (10 December 1948); International Covenant on Civil and Political Rights (adopted 16 December 1966, entry into force 23 March 1976) 999 UNTS 171.

[80] T>UNGA, 'Promotion and Protection of the Right to Freedom of Opinion' (n 79) para 5.

[81] ibid. See UNGA, 'Resolution Adopted by the General Assembly on 18 December 2013: The Safety of Journalists and the Issue of Impunity' UN Doc A/RES/68/163 (21 February 2014).

in public affairs of their state, directly or through freely chosen representatives, without any form of discrimination whether on the basis of colour, race, gender, language, political opinion, social origin, religion, property, or birth.[82] Article 7 of the Convention on the Elimination of All Forms of Discrimination against Women (CEDAW) requires that women be granted equal opportunities in public and political spheres.[83] In addition, by virtue of article 8 of CEDAW, State Parties undertake to apply appropriate measures to overcome historical discrimination against women, and obstacles to the participation of the female gender in decision-making processes.[84] The United Nations Convention on the Rights of Persons with Disabilities requires Member States to ensure that persons with disabilities fully and effectively participate in public and political affairs on an equal basis with others, whether directly or through their freely chosen representatives.[85]

The 2020 Report of the Working Group on the Issue of Human Rights and Transnational Corporations acknowledges that grievances have arisen due to business corporations and associated government agencies failing to undertake meaningful consultations with local communities, particularly Indigenous peoples, in addition to the failure to comply with the requirement of free, prior, informed consent in respect to commercial activities on their lands, conduct which is in breach of the obligations espoused under the United Nations Declaration on the Rights of Indigenous Peoples.[86] In that context, the 2020 Report of the Working Group highlighted the exclusion and marginalization of Indigenous peoples that is at times exacerbated by business corporations and government agencies.

Target 16.5 focuses on the elimination of bribery and corruption. The fight against corruption and bribery is a subject of international and regional legal instruments, including the universal United Nations Convention against Corruption.[87] Chapter III of the Convention has a liberal conceptualization of the vice of corruption to encompass bribery, misappropriation, or diversion of property by public officials, trading in influence, embezzlement, illicit enrichment, obstruction of justice, and abuse of functions.[88] In the African continent, regional legal instruments recognize the link between eradication of corruption and the institutionalization of the rule of law and constitutionalism. The Preamble to the African Union Convention on Preventing and Combating Corruption acknowledges that the vice 'undermines accountability and transparency in the management of public affairs as well as socio-economic development'.[89] On

---

[82] International Covenant on Civil and Political Rights (n 79).

[83] IBT>Convention on the Elimination of All Forms of Discrimination against Women (adopted 18 December 1979, entry into force 3 September 1981) 1249 UNTS 13.

[84] ibid.

[85] UNGA, 'Convention on the Rights of Persons with Disabilities' UN Doc A/RES/61/106 (24 January 2007).

[86] UNGA, 'Connecting the Business and Human Rights and the Anti-Corruption Agendas: Report of the Working Group on the Issue of Human Rights and Transnational Corporations and other Business Enterprises' UN Doc A/HRC/44/43 (17 June 2020) para 21. See UNGA, 'United Nations Declaration on the Rights of Indigenous Peoples' UN Doc A/RES/61/295 (13 September 2007).

[87] T>United Nations Convention against Corruption, UNGA Res 58/4 (31 October 2003).

[88] ibid.

[89] T>African Union Convention on Preventing and Combating Corruption (adopted 11 July 2003, entry into force 5 August 2006) (2004) 43 ILM 5.

that basis, article 3(1) of the African Union Convention obliges African states to adhere to the principles of 'the rule of law and good governance'.[90] The Southern African Development Community Protocol against Corruption explicitly recognizes in its Preamble that corruption undermines good governance, particularly through the lack of transparency and accountability.[91] The Preamble to the Economic Community of West African States Protocol on the Fight against Corruption acknowledges that transparency in governance, which implies lack of corruption, strengthens democratic institutions.[92]

The proscription of corruption through international legal instruments is essential for purposes of promoting the institutionalization of accountability and transparency in the administration of states. Widespread incidences of corruption and bribery are an impediment to sustainable development due to its diverse retrogressive effects to the society. Kofi Annan aptly summed up the diverse adverse implications of the vice when he observed that:

> [c]orruption is an insidious plague that has a wide range of corrosive effects on societies. It undermines democracy and the rule of law, leads to violations of human rights, distorts markets, erodes the quality of life, and allows organized crime, terrorism and other threats to human security to flourish.[93]

Target 16.9 is concerned with ensuring the provision of legal identity for all, especially through birth registration. This is in conformity with article 7(1) of the Convention on the Rights of the Child (CRC), which espouses the children's right to registration immediately upon birth, to be given a name and nationality.[94] The UNSD has clarified that the registration of children at birth is essential as it is usually the first stride to ensuring their legal recognition, in addition to enhancing opportunities for the protection and enforcement of other rights.[95]

SDG 16.2 focuses on ending the torture abuse, trafficking, and diverse forms of violence against children. The SDG assists states in focusing on and evaluating their implementation of obligations under the Convention on the Rights of the Child (CRC) and its Optional Protocols, which requires that children be protected from all forms of violence.[96]

---

[90] ibid.

[91] Southern African Development Community Protocol against Corruption (adopted 14 August 2001) *reprinted* in United Nations Office on Drugs and Crime (UNODC), *Compendium of International Legal Instruments on Corruption* (2nd edn, United Nations 2005) 259–69.

[92] Economic Community of West African States Protocol on the Fight against Corruption (adopted 21 December 2001) *reprinted* in UNODC, *Compendium of International Legal Instruments on Corruption* (2nd edn United Nations 2005) 211–23.

[93] K Annan, 'The Secretary-General Statement on the Adoption by the General Assembly of the United Nations Convention against Corruption' (New York, 31 October 2003) <http://www.unodc.org/unodc/en/treaties/CAC/background/secretary-general-speech.html> accessed 29 October 2021.

[94] Convention on the Rights of the Child (adopted 20 November 1989) 1577 UNTS 3.

[95] T>UNSD, 'SDG Indicator Metadata' (March 2021).

[96] ibid. See Convention on the Rights of the Child (n 94).

1170 SDG 16

a) Sustainable development as a legal principle

SDG 16 is conceptually founded, to an extent, upon the legal principle of sustainable development. The principle of sustainable development is contentious, though some conceptual aspects of the principle have over the time become clear.[97] As Kemp and Parto observe, 'there has been much dispute about the meaning and implications of the concept and much criticism of the actual behaviour of bodies that have claimed devotion to it', but over time, its conceptual meaning and implications have become less ambiguous.[98] While the principle of sustainable development may be traced to the twentieth-century environmental activism, it has subsequently been conceptualized 'as a broad term encompassing a wide range of social, economic, environmental and political elements'.[99]

i) Meaning and scope of sustainable development The concept of sustainable development implies progress 'that can be maintained over the long term'.[100] It is premised on the model of socio-economic progress that is sensitive to ecological protection, the equitable allocation of resources, and focuses on the long-term usage of resources in order for them to be replenished and preserved for the future generations.[101] As Barral instructively observes, the notion of sustainable development 'pervades the environmental, social, political, economic, and cultural discourses from the local through to the 'global' level by both the public and private sectors, and has also extensively permeated the legal sphere.[102]

The generally acceptable and widely utilized definition of sustainable development is that postulated by the 1987 World Commission on Environment and Development (Brundtland Commission).[103] In its Report titled 'Our Common Future', the Brundtland Commission postulated sustainable development as constituting 'development that meets the needs of the present without compromising the ability of future generations to meet their own needs'.[104] The Brundtland Commission Report is regarded as having been instrumental in placing the concept of sustainable development firmly at the centre of international development ideals and aspirations.[105] It is

---

[97] T>R Kemp and S Parto, 'Governance for Sustainable Development: Moving From Theory to Practice' (2005) 8(1/2) International Journal of Sustainable Development 12,T> 14.

[98] ibid 14.

[99] IB Franco and E Derbyshire, 'SDG 16 Peace, Justice and Strong Institutions: The Untapped Potential of Women for Sustainable Peace in Resource Regions' in IB Franco and others (eds), *Actioning the Global Goals for Local Impact: Towards Sustainability Science, Policy, Education and Practice* (Springer 2020) 265, 268.

[100] M-CC Segger, 'Sustainable Development in International Law' in D Armstrong (ed), *Routledge Handbook of International Law* (Routledge 2009) 355, 356.

[101] T Klarin, 'The Concept of Sustainable Development: From its Beginning to the Contemporary Issues' (2018) 21(1) Zagreb International Review of Economics and Business 67, 68.

[102] V Barral, 'Sustainable Development in International Law: Nature and Operation of an Evolutive Legal Norm' (2012) 23(2) European Journal of International Law 377, 377.

[103] See World Commission on Environment and Development, 'Report of the World Commission on Environment and Development: Our Common Future' (1987) chapter II, part iv; JA Elliott, *An Introduction to Sustainable Development* (4th edn, Routledge 2013) 8–9; A Ross, 'Modern Interpretations of Sustainable Development' (2009) 36(1) Journal of Law and Society 32, 34; Barral (n 102) 378.

[104] World Commission on Environment and Development (n 103) chapter II, part iv.

[105] Elliott (n 103) 8.

noteworthy that transnational organizations that include the UN and the World Bank have embraced the Brundtland Commission's definition of sustainable development.[106] Further, it is arguable that the SDGs gave rise to the notion of inclusive growth, particularly by being premised on the principle of sustainable development through coordinated economic, social, and environmental protection progress.[107]

ii) Legal aspects of sustainable development The concept of sustainable development, as Segger observes, has been endorsed or espoused by states in diverse agreements relating to various thematic concerns.[108] This is in addition to the concept being affirmed in international courts and tribunals, and being asserted through resolutions and declarations adopted under the auspices of the UN and other intergovernmental organizations.[109] An evaluation of state practice and *opinio juris* indicates that the principle of sustainable development is a legal norm on the basis of customary international law. Affirming the customary law nature of sustainable development, Virginie Barral argues as follows in the context of the relevant practice of states:

> Hence, conduct aimed at achieving sustainable development, even if lacking uniformity, can still form valid precedents constituting evidence of the existence of a general practice of states. Despite clear judicial confirmation, it can thus be concluded that sustainable development, as an objective, already constitutes a principle of customary law, even if this principle is a very general one, with a high degree of abstraction and which requires case-by-case substantiation.[110]

The *opinio juris* aspect of sustainable development may be discerned from the repeated adoption of rules relating to the concept.[111] *Opinio juris* implies a belief by a state that a particular conduct is necessary due to the existence of a legal obligation necessitating the behaviour[112] rather than other factors such as ethics and politics. As Segger argues, the evidence of the *opinio juris* nature of sustainable development may be discerned from expressions of belief of a legal obligation in the 'acts of international organizations and other international meetings; statements made by representatives of states, and the conclusion of treaties and the same sources which provide evidence of state practice'.[113] Thus, the evidence that sustainable development constitutes a binding legal obligation may be discerned from recurrent affirmation of legal obligations arising from the concept in treaty provisions, declarations, resolutions, judicial decisions, and programmes of action.[114]

---

[106] Franco and Derbyshire (n 99) 268.

[107] L Shi and others, 'The Evolution of Sustainable Development Theory: Types, Goals, and Research Prospects' (2019) 11 Sustainability 1, 6.

[108] Segger (n 100) 355.

[109] T>Barral (n 102)T> 378.

[110] ibid 388.

[111] ibid.

[112] See *North Sea Continental Shelf* (*Federal Republic of Germany v Denmark; Federal Republic of Germany v Netherlands*) (Judgment) [1969] ICJ Rep 3 para 77.

[113] Segger (n 100) 364.

[114] Barral (n 102) 388.

1172   SDG 16

b) Relevance of the right to development

The concept of sustainable development goals, including those relating to SDG 16 such as entrenchment and promotion of inclusive societies for meaningful development, enhancement of access to justice, and establishment of accountable institutions, is consistent with the advancement and realization of the right to development in international law. As Sengupta opines, under the right to development 'a process of economic growth must be carried out with equity and justice, in a non-discriminatory and participatory manner and with accountability and transparency, making it rights-based or consistent with human rights standards'.[115] Further, the concept of the right to development is broader than its justification and support for a human rights-based approach to development.[116] This is due to the fact that it also considers 'development as a human right in and of itself'.[117] Thus, when the process of development 'is claimed as a right, it can be the object of the right to development'.[118]

According to Sengupta, the right to development is well established 'as an international human right'.[119] It is noteworthy that despite the uncertainties that may exist in other regions, the right to development is a binding treaty entitlement and obligation in Africa. Article 22(2) of the 1981 African Charter on Human and Peoples' Rights explicitly provides that states 'have the duty, individually or collectively, to ensure the exercise of the right to development'.[120] The right to development was also subsequently asserted in the 1986 United Nations Declaration on the Right to Development, and the 1993 Vienna Declaration and Programme of Action.[121] The African Commission and the African Court have also developed jurisprudence of enforcing the right to development as enshrined under the ACHPR.[122] Since the right to development is a legally binding treaty obligation in the African region, the 'soft law' provisions of the 1986 UN Declaration and the 1993 Vienna Declaration serve the purpose of clarifying the nature, scope, and elements of the right.[123] The phrase 'soft law' is often used to describe diverse 'non-legally binding instruments' that have the objective of regulating the activities of states and international organizations.[124] As Shelton instructively observes,

[115] A Sengupta, 'The Human Right to Development' in BA Andreassen and SP Marks (eds), *Development as a Human Right: Legal, Political and Economic Dimensions* (2nd edn, Intersentia 2010) 13, 25.

[116] T>B Ibhawoh, 'The Right to Development: The Politics and Polemics of Power and Resistance' (2011) 33 Human Rights Quarterly 76, 85.

[117] ibid.

[118] T>Sengupta (n 115)T> 16.

[119] ibid 44.

[120] African Charter on Human and Peoples' Rights (adopted 27 June 1981, entry into force 21 October 1986) OAU Doc CAB/LEG/67/3 rev. 5.

[121] See UNGA, 'Declaration on the Right to Development' UN Doc A/RES/41/128 (4 December 1986); Vienna Declaration and Programme of Action (Adopted by the World Conference on Human Rights in Vienna) UN Doc A/CONF.157/23 (25 June 1993).

[122] For instance, see: *Centre for Minority Rights Development (Kenya) and Minority Rights Group International on Behalf of Endorois Welfare Council v Kenya* [2010] African Commission on Human and Peoples' Rights, Application No 276/2003, paras 269–298; *African Commission on Human and Peoples' Rights v Republic of Kenya* [2017] African Court on Human and Peoples' Rights, Application No 006/2012 (Judgment) paras 202–211.

[123] See UNGA, 'Declaration on the Right to Development' (n 121); Vienna Declaration and Programme of Action (n 121).

[124] S Ali and T Kabau, 'Non-State Actors and the Evolution of Humanitarian Norms: Implications of the Sphere Charter in Health and Nutrition Relief' (2014) 5(1–2) Journal of International Humanitarian Legal Studies 70, 79.

although soft law instruments are not legally binding solely on their own, they are often relied upon in order to interpret or fill lacunas in the law.[125]

In the context of the right to development, the requirement that participation be 'meaningful' is an assertion of popular sovereignty in the development process, in which people have the capacity 'to voice their opinions in institutions that enable the exercise of power, recognizing the citizenry as the origin of and the justification for public authority.[126] In particular, article 7(2) of the Declaration on the Right to Development is clear that states should promote 'popular participation' in the development process.[127] Therefore, participation should be democratic, permitting various forums, and should have special considerations for the capacity of the vulnerable, marginalized, and deprived groups to articulate their views and concerns.[128]

The inception of the concept of the right to development was originally a search for a legitimate and justifiable basis for demands for fairness and equity in economic and investment relations between the Global North and the Global South. In the 1960s, Third World countries began to form a coalition that advocated for radical changes to the global economic order, while at the same time developing concepts in relation to the development process and their role in the international economic structure.[129] The notion of the right to development was conceptualized in the 1960s and 1970s through the ideas of African scholars and practitioners, particularly Kéba M'Baye, a Senegalese, and Mohammed Bedajoui, an Algerian.[130] In the 1970s, Bedajoui had stated that:

> [t]he underdeveloped countries, too long excluded from international relations by an inegalitarian and inequitable system, do not hanker after its converse, which would favour them and make the privileged of the past and the present the outcasts of the future. That would be neither just nor possible, neither desirable nor realistic. The right to development is something, which brings life to countries hitherto excluded from that development.[131]

---

[125] D Shelton, 'International Law and "Relative Normativity"' in MD Evans (ed), *International Law* (4th edn, OUP 2014) 137, 161.

[126] F Piovesan, 'Active, Free and Meaningful Participation in Development' in *Realizing the Right to Development* (Essays in Commemoration of 25 Years of the United Nations Declaration on the Right to Development, United Nations 2013) 103, 105–06.

[127] UNGA, 'Declaration on the Right to Development' (n 121).

[128] Piovesan (n 126) 105. The participation model postulated under the human rights-based approach promotes a shift 'towards a more genuinely inclusive and democratic process of popular involvement in decision-making over the resources and institutions that affect people's lives'. A Cornwall and C Nyamu-Musembi, 'Putting the "Rights-Based Approach" to Development into Perspective' (2004) 25(8) Third World Quarterly 1415, 1424.

[129] A Eide, 'Human Rights-Based Development in the Age of Economic Globalisation: Background and Prospects' in Andreassen and Marks (eds), *Development as a Human Right: Legal, Political and Economic Dimensions* (n 115) 275, 282.

[130] OC Okafor, 'A Regional Perspective: Article 22 of the African Charter on Human and Peoples' Rights' in *Realizing the Right to Development: Essays in Commemoration of 25 Years of the United Nations Declaration on the Right to Development* (United Nations 2013) 373, 373–74. See also: ID Bunn, 'The Right to Development: Implications for International Economic Law' (2000) 15(6) American University International Law Review 1425, 1433; P Uvin, 'From the Right to Development to the Rights-Based Approach: How "Human Rights" Entered Development' (2007) 17 (4/5) Development in Practice 597, 598; Ibhawoh (n 116) 83.

[131] M Bedajoui, *Towards a New International Economic Order* (Holmes and Meier Publishers 1979) 72.

1174 SDG 16

Anghie credits the emergence of the right to development to efforts of the Third World to unambiguously connect international human rights law with development.[132] Bunn points out that 'a consistent theme in the debate on the right to development is reform of the "unjust international economic order" toward one based on obligations for human welfare and social justice'.[133]

2. Thematic Considerations in the Conceptualization of SDG 16

This subsection evaluates concerns and discourses in relation to some of the aspirations that constitute SDG 16. Consequently, the significance of the conceptual focus of some of the SDG 16 targets is demonstrated.

a) Conflict resolution and peace as a sustainable development concern

Armed conflicts and incidences of violence are a serious obstacle to the realization of sustainable development. A concern for the resolution of armed conflicts, diverse forms of violence and the entrenchment of sustainable peace contributed to the formulation of targets 16.1, 16.4, and 16.a. There had been concerns by developing states that the SDG 16 implementation may be watered down by the peace and security agenda of the UN, which, as McDermott and collaborating authors observe, is 'perceived as prioritising securitization while ignoring the links between peace and broader goals such as social equity, climate change mitigation and development'.[134] Consequently, it is probably due to such concerns that contributed to 'the arguably mixed messages' that are entrenched in SDG 16's targets.[135] Thus, the broad approach adopted by SDG 16 may be justified on the need to address the multiple root causes of conflicts, and progressively institutionalize governance practices that are premised on the rule of law and accountable institutions, thus promoting the establishment of sustainable peace. For instance, the Truth and Reconciliation Commission (CVR) of Peru found in its 2003 Report that the underlying causes of conflict included tensions regarding access to land, inequality, and structural racism towards the Indigenous peoples, some of which, regrettably, had not been resolved as of 2019.[136] In Colombia, it has been observed that the broader aspects of peace building approaches have the objective of reducing land related grievances that often cause conflicts and limit access to resources, such as coca, that provide funding to armed groups.[137]

---

[132] A Anghie, *Imperialism, Sovereignty and the Making of International Law* (CUP 2004) 257. See also, D Beetham, 'The Right to Development and its Corresponding Obligations' in Andreassen and Marks (eds), *Development as a Human Right: Legal, Political and Economic Dimensions* (n 115) 101, 102.

[133] Bunn (n 130) 1428.

[134] T>CL McDermott and others, 'SDG 16: Peace, Justice and Strong Institutions—A Political Ecology Perspective' in P Katila and others (eds), *Sustainable Development Goals: Their Impacts on Forests and People* (CUP 2019) 510, 511.

[135] ibid.

[136] ibid 519.

[137] ibid.

b) Corruption and bribery as a sustainable development concern

The prevalence of corruption impedes the realization of various forms of human rights, eliminates accountability in the exercise of state power, and weakens public institutions, thus obstructing progress towards the realization of SDG 16, in addition to the objectives articulated in other SDGs.[138] For instance, corruption significantly hinders the entrenchment of respect for the rule of law, progress towards social equity, and inclusiveness in the development process, among others, which are essential in progress towards the attainment of SDG 16 objectives. Pervasive corruption also undermines the entrenchment of constitutionalism, a concept that requires that the governance of a state be executed without the exercise of arbitrary power or tyranny[139] and be within the confines of the rule of law.[140] Constitutionalism contributes to the establishment of 'effective, accountable and inclusive institutions', and access to justice, as aspired under SDG 16. In that context, robust anti-corruption initiatives are part of the rubric of good governance.[141]

When there is pervasive corruption, those in charge of governance fail to perform their duties with the motivation of acting in the best interest of the society.[142] A consequence of high levels of corruption is the development of a culture of impunity among the governing elite and public officials.[143] In addition, corruption has an impact on the judicial and law enforcement organs of a state, denying the citizens the opportunity of enjoying their right to a fair trial, which seriously erodes the rule of law.[144] Widespread impunity can also contribute to frustrations and anger in the citizenry, especially where there are perceptions of lack of equity in the allocation of state resources, leading to anarchy which in turn contributes to a fundamental collapse of the rule of law, as was the case of Kenya during the 2007–2008 post-election violence.[145]

Based on the impact of the vice of corruption in negating the capacity of states to protect, promote and fulfil various forms of human rights, Kofele-Kale has even proposed that the right to be free from corruption should be recognized.[146] In particular,

---

[138] On the contribution of corruption to the egregious violations of human rights, see, for instance: K Olaniyan, 'The African Union Convention on Preventing and Combating Corruption: A Critical Appraisal' (2004) 4 African Human Rights Law Journal 74, 76; United Nations Human Rights, Office of the High Commissioner, 'The Human Rights Case Against Corruption' 4 <http://www.ohchr.org/Documents/Issues/Development/Goo dGovernance/Corruption/HRCaseAgainstCorruption.pdf> accessed 24 June 2021; JR Boles, 'Criminalizing the Problem of Unexplained Wealth: Illicit Enrichment Offenses and Human Rights Violations' (2014)17 Legislation and Public Policy 835, 841; JT Gathii, 'Defining the Relationship between Human Rights and Corruption' (2009) 31 University of Pennsylvania Journal of International Law 125, 126; T Kabau, 'Constitutional Dilemmas in the Recovery of Corruptly Acquired Assets in Kenya: Strengthening Judicial Assault on Corruption' (2016) 1 Africa Journal of Comparative Constitutional Law 23, 37–40.

[139] L-A Thio, 'Constitutionalism in Illiberal Polities' in M Rosenfeld and A Sajó (eds), *The Oxford Handbook of Comparative Constitutional Law* (OUP 2013) 133, 133.

[140] LC Backer, 'From Constitution to Constitutionalism: Global Framework for Legitimate Public Power Systems' (2009) 113(3) Penn State Law Review 672, 679.

[141] Gathii 'Defining the Relationship' (n 138) 150.

[142] United Nations Human Rights, Office of the High Commissioner (n 138) 4.

[143] Gathii 'Defining the Relationship' (n 138) 170.

[144] Kabau (n 138) 27.

[145] Gathii 'Defining the Relationship' (n 138) 170.

[146] He argues that the 'right to a society free of corruption is inherently a basic human right because life, dignity, and other important human values' are dependent on it. T>N Kofele-Kale, 'The Right to a Corruption-Free Society as an Individual and Collective Human Right: Elevating Official Corruption to a Crime under International Law' (2000) 34(1) International Lawyer 149,T> 163.

1176   SDG 16

Kofele-Kale argues that the 'right to a corruption-free society' also complements the 'collective right to development'.[147] Under the Preamble and article 22(2) of the African Charter on Human and Peoples' Rights (ACHPR), states have the duty of facilitating the realization of the right to development.[148]

It is further noteworthy that corruption involves diverse human activities and transactions in different contexts, making it a multifaceted and complex phenomenon.[149] One of the most widely utilized broad definitions of corruption connotes the notion of abuse of public office or position for private gain.[150] Such a definition has been endorsed by the World Bank and authors as being both simple and sufficiently comprehensive to address most manifestations of corruption.[151] A broad conceptualization of corruption is essential since a public position may be violated even in the absence of the more direct act of bribery, such as through practices of patronage and nepotism, or through the diversion of state resources and assets for private benefits.[152] In addition, abuse of a public position can occur through collusion with individuals or entities in the private sector.[153]

Corruption has a significant impact on access to justice and, thus, impedes the institutionalization of the rule of law in fundamental ways. In states where there is pervasive corruption, 'law enforcement and legal reform are impeded by corrupt judges, lawyers, prosecutors, police officers, investigators and auditors'.[154] Widespread corruption negates the 'right to equality before the law and the right to a fair trial, and especially undermines the access of disadvantaged groups to justice, as they cannot afford bribes and cannot trade influence for favourable judgements'.[155]

The UN system has in particular been sensitive in the manner in which business enterprises, sometimes extremely powerful and exceedingly economically endowed transnational corporations (TNCs), are able to violate human rights of populations in various states with impunity through corrupt activities. Some of the UN efforts in the context of business and human rights has been the establishment, by virtue of UNGA Resolution 17/4 in 2011, of the Working Group on the Issue of Human Rights and

---

[147] ibid 165.

[148] African Charter on Human and Peoples' Rights (n 120).

[149] K Obura, 'Towards a Corruption Free Kenya: Demystifying the Concept of Corruption for the Post-2010 Anti-Corruption Agenda' in MK Mbondenyi and others (eds), *Human Rights and Democratic Governance in Kenya: A Post-2007 Appraisal* (Pretoria University Law Press 2015) 239, 240. See also, World Bank, *Helping Countries Combat Corruption: The Role of the World Bank* (World Bank 1997) 8.

[150] See: World Bank (n 149) 8; JP Ganahl, *Corruption, Good Governance, and the African State: A Critical Analysis of the Political-Economic Foundations of Corruption in Sub-Saharan Africa* (Potsdam University Press 2013) 57; Transparency International, *Anticorruption Conventions in Africa: What Civil Society Can Do to Make Them Work* (Transparency International 2006) 4; JM Mbaku, 'International Law and the Fight Against Bureaucratic Corruption in Africa' (2016) 33(3) Arizona Journal of International and Comparative Law 661, 667.

[151] World Bank (n 149) 9; Obura (n 149) 273.

[152] M Sinjela, 'The African Convention on the Prevention and Combating of Corruption' in AA Yusuf and F Ouguergouz (eds), *The African Union: Legal and Institutional Framework—A Manual on the Pan-African Organization* (Martinus Nijhoff Publishers 2012) 291, 291.

[153] NJ Udombana, 'Fighting Corruption Seriously? Africa's Anti-Corruption Convention' (2003) 7 Singapore Journal of International and Comparative Law 447, 463.

[154] T>United Nations Human Rights, Office of the High Commissioner (n 138) 4.

[155] ibid.

Transnational Corporations and other Business Enterprises under the auspices of the UN Human Rights Council.[156]

The 2020 Report of the Working Group on the Issue of Human Rights and Transnational Corporations and other Business Enterprises demonstrates the multifaceted manifestations of corruption in the commercial and investment sector, and provides proposals for eradicating the vice.[157] Proposals to eradicate corruption include the adoption of a human rights based approach by businesses in their investment activities, reforms to public procurement processes, strengthening of land tenure and property rights, disclosure requirements regarding beneficial owners of corporations, and elimination of corporate capture, among others.[158]

c) The rule of law as a sustainable development concern

From a legal perspective, and in both the national and international contexts, some of the fundamental attributes of the principle of the rule of law are the supremacy of the law rather than the influence of other dynamics, such as politics and power.[159] Equality of all subjects before the law is also a fundamental element of the principle.[160] In addition to the stated two procedural aspects, the substantive element of rule of law requires that the law itself be sound.[161] As such, law should reflect, or exemplify, justice and fairness. It is also noteworthy that the rule of law is an aspect of the democratic ethos of constitutionalism. Constitutionalism requires that the government of a state operates within the confines of the rule of law.[162] More broadly conceptualized, the rule of law has been associated with social equity, equality, inclusion, protection of rights, adherence to established laws, and governance through accountable institutions.[163] There is access to justice in a society that adheres to the rule of law, which enables individuals to claim their rights and resolve conflicts without resorting to violence.[164] Under the rule of law, equality is established and sustained in the legal system, and as such, even the vulnerable are able to achieve justice against the more powerful individuals, and discrimination, corruption, and impunity cannot thrive.[165]

The UNGA Resolution 66/288 pointed out that sustainable development required adherence to the rule of law at the state and international levels, together with the

---

[156] UNGA, 'Resolution adopted by the Human Rights Council: Human Rights and Transnational Corporations and Other Business Enterprises 'UN Doc A/HRC/RES/17/4 (6 July 2011).

[157] T>See UNGA, 'Connecting the Business and Human Rights and the Anti-Corruption Agendas' (n 86) paras 6–72.

[158] ibid.

[159] T>H Owada, 'The Rule of Law in a Globalising World' in F Neate (ed), The Rule of Law: Perspectives from Around the Globe (LexisNexis 2009) 151, 153.

[160] ibid. See also, I Brownlie, Rule of Law in International Affairs: International Law at the Fiftieth Anniversary of the United Nations (Kluwer Law International 1998) 214.

[161] Owada (n 159) 154. Brownlie also opines that the principle of rule of law requires that legal norms exemplify 'certain standards of justice, both substantial and procedural'. Brownlie (n 160) 215.

[162] Backer (n 140) 679. Constitutionalism in that sense implies government, and governance, under the confines of the law. A Peters, 'Compensatory Constitutionalism: The Function and Potential of Fundamental International Norms and Structures' (2006) 19 Leiden Journal of International Law 579, 583.

[163] T>International Development Law Organisation (n 4).

[164] ibid.

[165] ibid.

1178   SDG 16

associated concepts of good governance and democracy.[166] Further, the OWG on SDGs acknowledged the inevitable linkages between the rule of law and conflict prevention and peace building.[167] The inclusion of the rule of law concerns as part of SDG 16 is merited and is consistent with the broader trend to promote legality and legal enforcement in governance at the state and international levels for purposes of sustainability, including in the development process.[168]

d) Inclusivity and broad participation as a sustainable development concern

Governance at both the national and international level is increasingly requiring greater inclusivity and broad participation for purposes of legitimizing the actions taken and the decisions made. Further, the emerging forms of participation require greater decentralization of governance actions, in addition to meaningful involvement of the local communities and non-state participants in the making of decisions.[169] Inclusivity and meaningful participation of a broad array of stakeholders in governance activities entails providing reasonable avenues for the representation of the various sectors of government, local communities, minorities, marginalized groups, women, and civil society organizations, among others, in the design, implementation, and review of projects.

The emerging demand for broad, meaningful, and quality participation of the governed is an aspect of popular sovereignty. The concept of popular sovereignty is premised on the affirmation that the citizens of a state are the foundations and determinants of public authority, and should have the capacity to voice their concerns in the governance process.[170] It is noteworthy that article 7(2) of the Declaration on the Right to Development affirms that states have an obligation to promote popular participation in the development process.[171]

According to the High-Level Political Forum on Sustainable Development (HLPFSD), among the core doctrines of the SDG framework was that the implementation, and the process of progress evaluation, be participatory and inclusive.[172] Participatory and inclusive governance facilitates the realization and entrenchment of the SDG 16 goals of peace, access to justice, and accountable, functional, and responsible institutions. In particular, as the OWG observed, participatory governance and involvement of the core segments of the society in the management of state affairs would significantly contribute to conflict prevention.[173] As such, inclusive and participatory governance has the potential to eradicate conflicts, which are core barriers to the

---

[166] UNGA, 'Resolution adopted by the General Assembly on 27 July 2012' (n 10), para 10.
[167] Sustainable Development Knowledge Platform, 'Eighth Session of the Open Working Group on Sustainable Development Goals: Summary of the Co-Chairs' (n 18) 9.
[168] T>McDermott and others (n 134)T> 520.
[169] ibid 525–26.
[170] See Piovesan (n 126) 105–06.
[171] UNGA, 'Declaration on the Right to Development' (n 121).
[172] High-Level Political Forum on Sustainable Development, *Handbook for the Preparation of Voluntary National Reviews* (Department of Economic and Social Affairs, United Nations 2021) 12.
[173] Sustainable Development Knowledge Platform, 'Eighth Session of the Open Working Group on Sustainable Development Goals: Concluding Remarks of Co-Chairs' (n 26).

realization of SDG 16 goals. As pointed out by the OWG, societies in which particular groups were systematically excluded from the political and economic activities of the state were often at a greater risk of conflicts, which in turn had the effect of reversing development.[174]

According to the HLPFSD, the implementation and evaluation of progress of the realization of the SDG 16 at the country level is expected to embrace inclusivity, through the meaningful participation of, among others, various sectors of government, the private sector, civil society organizations, and interest groups.[175]

Beyond assisting developing states improve on impartial, inclusive, and participatory governances and development process through the use of targets and indicators, SDG 16, particularly target 16.7, also facilitates the eradication of inequality and biases in developed states. This is due to the fact that some minorities and Indigenous peoples in developed states often face institutional marginalization, and have challenges such as obstructed access to education and employment opportunities, higher crime rates, difficulties in access to justice, among others. With regard to Aboriginal and Torres Strait Islander peoples in Australia, Schultz observes that:

> [f]or Aboriginal and Torres Strait Islander Australians and other indigenous peoples globally, the creation of SDGs provided opportunities for their needs to be considered in global development aspirations ... These opportunities included using government commitments to the SDGs to reduce the pervasive disadvantage and inequality faced by indigenous peoples ... In the development of the SDGs, indigenous communities drew attention to the contributions they can make to sustainability through their knowledge of sustainable practices, and their aspirations for development based on indigenous cultural norms and values.[176]

It is in that context of marginalization and inequality that Schultz makes reference to statistics to highlight, for instance, the extraordinarily high rates of imprisonment of Aboriginal and Torres Strait Islander people,[177] an issue that is part of the indicator 16.3.2 evaluation focus. She is concerned that high rates of incarceration of young men from the stated ethnicities have the outcome of the concerned communities losing on economic progress, social stability, and the wholesome bringing up of children.[178]

Australia's voluntary national review (VNR) regarding the realization of SDGs has acknowledged that the Aboriginal and Torres Strait Islander peoples are overrepresented in the criminal system, and that as of 2016 they comprised 27 per cent of all the prisoners, yet they are only 3 per cent of the country's population.[179] It is in that

---

[174] Sustainable Development Knowledge Platform, 'Eighth Session of the Open Working Group on Sustainable Development Goals: TST Issues Brief' (n 19) 7.

[175] High-Level Political Forum on Sustainable Development, *Handbook* (n 172) 12.

[176] T>R Schultz, 'Closing the Gap and the Sustainable Development Goals: Listening to Aboriginal and Torres Strait Islander People' (2020) 44(1) Australian and New Zealand Journal of Public HealthT>11, 11.

[177] ibid 12.

[178] ibid.

[179] Australian Government, *Report on the Implementation of the Sustainable Development Goals* (Department of Foreign Affairs and Trade 2018) 103–04.

1180 SDG 16

sense that Schultz suggests that among other reforms, Australia must significantly reduce the incarceration rates of Aboriginal and Torres Strait Islander people for purposes of progress towards the realization of SDG 16.[180] It is noteworthy that the Australian Law Reform Commission was tasked by the Australian Government in 2016 to conduct an inquiry into the high rates of incarceration among the Aboriginal and Torres Strait Islander peoples.[181] The Commission's Report, which was tabled in Parliament in March 2018, made diverse suggestions to reduce the incarnation rates, and also pointed out that reducing such imprisonment numbers would result in improved economic and social conditions of the Aboriginal and Torres Strait Islander peoples.[182]

Concerns for inclusivity and broad participation under the SDG 16 framework proceed beyond the state level to the relations between states at the international sphere. It is noteworthy that target 16.8 has the objective of widening and solidifying developing states participation in the institutions of global governance. In that context, target 16.8 facilitates in eradicating some of the structural and systemic inequalities and inequities that developing states are confronted with in international relations, some of which have been highlighted by Third World Approaches to International Law (TWAIL) proponents. By deconstructing and demystifying international law, TWAIL exponents are able to demonstrate how the international legal regime and its institutions have historically, and in contemporary times, legitimized the subjugation, exploitation, and marginalization of Third World states and their peoples. It is in that context that TWAIL adherents have been concerned with the manner in which the international legal regime and its institutions can be reformed in order to address the concerns and interests of the Third World states and their people appropriately.[183] It is noteworthy that the UN system has been one of the primary institutional avenues through which the Global South has pushed its agenda and aspirations,[184] including through the SDG framework.

IV. Theoretical Perspectives Relevant to SDG 16

The sustainable development aspirations articulated under SDG 16 targets (conflict resolution and peace building, entrenchment of rule of law, enhancing access to justice, institutionalizing inclusive and participatory governance, enhancing the freedom of expression and access to information, and the establishment of inclusive and accountable institutions), and the institutional structure upon which they are evaluated and promoted may be explained from diverse theoretical perspectives.

---

[180] T>Schultz (n 176)T> 12.
[181] ibid 104.
[182] ibid.
[183] See T> A Anghie and BS Chimni, 'Third World Approaches to International Law and Individual Responsibility in Internal Conflicts' (2003) Chinese Journal of International Law 77, 81.
[184] ibid.

A. Third World Approaches to International Law

TWAIL highlights the context in which international legal norms and transnational institutions subjugate, disadvantage, and exploit the states and people of the Third World. TWAIL proceeds beyond criticism, to offering suggestions on how the international legal and institutional system can be restructured to ensure equity, inclusive participation, and fairness to the states of the Third World and their citizens. The ideas postulated by TWAILers are relevant to the realization of the developmental goals postulated under SDG 16 as they include the establishment of inclusive institutions at all levels, including at the international sphere. Target 16.8 in particular espouses the objective of strengthening and widening the participation of developing states in institutions of global governance.

According to James Gathii, 'TWAIL is a decentralized network of academics who share common commitments in their concern about the third world'.[185] Okafor defines TWAIL as follows:

> On a general level, the TWAIL movement within the discipline of international legal studies is best viewed as a broad dialectic (or large umbrella) of opposition to the generally unequal, unfair, and unjust character of an international legal regime that all-too often (but not always) helps subject the Third World to domination, subordination, and serious disadvantage.[186]

As Anghie and Chimni observe, the experience of colonialism and neo-colonialism made Third World peoples acutely sensitive to power relations among states, including the manner in which transnational rules and institutions affect the distribution of power and opportunities between states and peoples.[187] TWAIL has been critical of the manner in which international law both historically and in the modern times undermines and subjugates the Third World in international political, economic, and social relations. In that context, TWAIL has accused colonical international law of, and criticized it for, legitimizing the suppression and domination of Third World peoples, for instance, by excepting 'non-European states from the realm of sovereignty', through the legalization and endorsement of 'unequal treaties between European powers and non-European power', and conceptualization of the notion that it was 'completely legal to acquire sovereignty over non-European societies by conquest'.[188]

In the post-colonial period, TWAIL has been concerned with the way in which the structures of 'international law could be transformed to take into account the needs

---

[185] JT Gathii, 'TWAIL: A Brief History of its Origins, its Decentralized Network, and a Tentative Bibliography' (2011) 3(1) Trade, Law and Development 26, 27.
[186] OC Okafor, 'Newness, Imperialism, and International Legal Reform in Our Time: A TWAIL Perspective' (2005) 43 Osgoode Hall Law Journal 171, 176.
[187] T>Anghie and Chimni (n 183)T> 78.
[188] ibid 80.

1182 SDG 16

and aspirations of the peoples of the newly independent states'.[189] One of the mechanisms that has largely been utilized by the Third World to achieve those objectives is the UN system.[190] The SDG framework under the auspices of the UN, including SDG 16 with target 16.8 that requires the participation of developing states in global governance institutions be strengthened and broadened, represents a global effort towards such transformation. In addition, developing states have previously sought to achieve a new economic order by pushing for 'structural changes to an international economic system which was perceived to disadvantage developing countries, and, more specifically, to regain control over ... [their] natural resources, and to exercise effective control over foreign investors'.[191]

B. Institutionalism

The theoretical perspectives postulated under institutionalism, which is a subset of international law and international relations theory, are supportive of the notion that states rely upon, and are even willing to shed off some of their sovereign powers, to institutions for purposes of achieving collective objectives. The collective aspirations and action under the SDG 16 framework, undertaken under the auspices of the UN, is consistent with the perspectives of institutionalism. The institutional mechanism of the UN has been instrumental to the conceptualization, continued implementation, and consistent review of the sustainable development goals, including the objectives outlined under SDG 16. A broad definition of institutions incorporates rules, norms, and organizations, such as the UN.[192]

Although there is general consensus that states are the major instruments for global reforms, the institutional approach still recognizes that organs within the institution, and even certain international rules, can change the mode of interaction by states and even promote cooperative behaviour on some issues for desirable outcomes,[193] as is the case in the context of SDGs and the post-2015 development agenda generally. It has been observed that by changing the context of interaction and discourse, institutions can and actually do:

> facilitate the negotiation and implementation of agreements as well as other substantive interactions. For example, institutions can reduce the transaction costs of negotiation, provide unbiased information, create cognitive focal points to coordinate decentralized activities, insert neutral actors into situations of conflict, fill gaps in incomplete contracts, and facilitate the pooling of resources.[194]

---

[189] ibid 81.
[190] ibid.
[191] ibid 82.
[192] T>KW Abbott, 'International Relations Theory, International Law, and the Regime Governing Atrocities in Internal Conflicts' (1999) 93(2) American Journal of International Law 361,T> 365–66.
[193] ibid 376.
[194] ibid 365–66.

The theoretical precepts of institutionalism often clash with those of realism, in particular in the context of the primacy of states and efficiency of institutions in international relations. Realism is premised on the notion that the international sphere is anarchical and chaotic, and as such, states are concerned with their security and power.[195] Its proponents regard states as being the primary actors in international relations.[196] Thus, as aptly summed up by Abbott, realism proponents view states as interacting 'in an environment of anarchy, defined as the absence of any central government able to keep peace or enforce agreements. Security is their overriding goal, and self-help their guiding principle.'[197] On that premise, some realists argue that competition is pervasive in such an environment, and consequently, states fail to cooperate even where they are confronted by similar predicaments, or for purposes of pursuing common aspirations.[198]

Although there is general consensus that states are the major instruments for reforms, the institutional approach correctly affirms that organs within the institution, and even certain international rules, can change the mode of interaction by states, and even promote cooperative behaviour on some issues for desirable outcomes.[199] Thus, the argument by some realists that institutions such as the UN have only marginal effects on interstate relations has been criticized as being logically unsound and inadequate, and seems not to take into account the significant roles and functions of intergovernmental organizations such as the UN.[200] In particular, institutions do have an effect on state behaviour,[201] as they are often established to facilitate realization of particular objectives. In the case of SDG 16, institutions, the foremost being the UN, are instrumental in orienting states' practice to conduct that promotes and enhances the entrenchment of peace, access to justice, and establishes inclusive and accountable institutions.

As Keohane points out, it is thus acceptable even to some realists that 'under conditions of interdependence, institutions are essential if people are to have opportunities to pursue the good life.'[202] Abbott similarly admits that even some realists, despite their highly state-centric approach, acknowledge that there is 'a broad spectrum of interests' such as wealth creation, environmental protection, or even sustainable development in the context of SDGs, which call for cooperation between states through institutional mechanisms and avenues.[203] This is due to the reality that the benefits of cooperation through institutions significantly outweigh unregulated conflict among states.[204] In

---

[195] WJ Aceves, 'Institutionalist Theory and International Legal Scholarship' (1997) 12 (2) American University International Law Review 227, 236.

[196] T>Abbott (n 192) 364.

[197] ibid.

[198] Aceves (n 195) 236.

[199] Abbott (n 192) 376.

[200] T>RO Keohane and LL Martin, 'The Promise of Institutionalist Theory' (1995) 20(1) International Security 39,T> 47–48.

[201] ibid 42.

[202] RO Keohane, 'Governance in a Partially Globalized World' (2001) 95(1) American Political Science Review 1–13, 1.

[203] Abbott (n 192) 365.

[204] Keohane (n 202) 1.

1184   SDG 16

that context, SDG 16 provides a framework of aspirational targets and evaluative indicators as a mechanism towards entrenchment of peace, access to justice, and accountable and inclusive institutions through the auspices of the UN.

Proponents of institutionalism argue that even in the absence of a formal governance system or collective government in the international sphere, institutions are capable of promoting and enabling cooperation.[205] That is the case in the context of sustainable development goals, and in particular SDG 16, which exemplifies collective action of states to entrench peace, enhance access to justice, and make institutions more accountable and inclusive, and are undertaken under the auspices of the UN.

Nonetheless, it should be appreciated that the UN operates in interaction and interdependence with other inter-governmental organizations, even in the context of promoting the SDGs, which may be at the universal or regional level. Keohane and Nye have highlighted the reality that the UN system is not the sole operator in international governance but is part of a complex web of institutions and rules that regulate states' interdependent relationships.[206]

From the perspective of institutionalism, it is also arguable that the necessity and benefits of realizing the sustainable development goals has contributed to states' willingness to cede their sovereign powers and rights to institutions such as the UN that manage and regulate thematic issues and evaluate the progress of countries through the notion of targets and indicators. Thus, despite sovereignty concerns and risk aversion by states, where there are huge benefits to be obtained from an institution, countries will willingly trade off some of their sovereignty for membership,[207] as is the case in respect to the SDGs formulation, implementation, and evaluation framework under the auspices of the UN.

C. John Rawls' Theory of Justice

The concepts of social equity, inclusion, broad stakeholder participation, and non-discrimination in the development process at the state and international level, which are articulated under targets 16.7, 16.8, and 16.b, are consistent with the renowned theory of justice postulated by Rawls.[208] It should be noted, however, that Rawls' theory of justice, as postulated, is purely about distributive justice and social equity, and not corrective and retributive aspects of justice as conceptualized under target 16.3 on equal access to justice for all.

In that context, it is noteworthy that the concept of justice is part of moral ideals that are also related to governance, law, and politics,[209] and as such, may have varied

---

[205] Aceves (n 195) 241.

[206] RO Keohane and JS Nye, 'Two Cheers for Multilateralism' (1985) 60 Foreign Policy 148, 151.

[207] B Koremenos and others, 'The Rational Design of International Institutions' in J Trachtman (ed), *International Law and Politics* (Ashgate Publishing Limited 2008) 439, 460.

[208] See for instance, J Rawls, *A Theory of Justice* (Harvard University Press 1971) 60.

[209] T>B Bix, *Jurisprudence: Theory and Context* (5 edn, Sweet and Maxwell 2009) 107.

contexts. In particular, the concept of justice may be delineated into distributive and corrective justice.[210] According to Bix:

> Corrective justice involves rectification between two parties, where one has taken from another or harmed the other ... Distributive justice involves the appropriate distribution of goods among a group ('giving each person his or her due'). Most of the better-known modern discussions of justice, which usually treat justice primarily as about the proper structuring of government and society, are basically discussions of distributive justice.[211]

Distributive justice through social equity, the core concern of Rawls' concept of justice, is essential in sustaining peace, facilitating the entrenchment of the rule of law, and entrenching sustainable development. Targets 16.7, 16.8, and 16.b under the SDGs that are oriented towards the creation of social equity, broader avenues of participation, inclusiveness, and non-discrimination in the development process actually promote the concept of distributive justice. On the other part, the concept of access to justice under target 16.3 seems to be oriented towards the entrenchment of corrective justice, as it is concerned with aspects such as the broadening of accessibility to, and the strengthening of the effectiveness, fairness, and accountability of, the criminal and civil justice institutions.

Rawls' theory of justice has utility and significance in sustaining inclusive, non-discriminatory, and participatory decision-making, a core prerequisite for the equitable distribution of resources at the state level for purposes of sustainable development, which is a concern for targets 16.7 and 16.b. Since it was postulated, Rawls' theory of justice has elicited immense interest and influence.[212] Rawls' theory establishes novels ways of conceptualizing the social contract.[213] The social contract between the state and the citizens implies that there exists an obligation on those in charge of governance to fulfil some human rights.[214] Revisiting the ideas of the social contract theory, Rawls' theory is about the establishment of more equitable and inclusive governance structures.[215]

According to Rawls, besides *equal* civil and political rights such as the right to life and liberty, people should also have the right to achieve progress with regard to their economic and social status.[216] Offenheiser and Holcombe opine that on the basis of

[210] ibid.

[211] ibid.

[212] A Bloom, 'Justice: John Rawls vs the Tradition of Political Philosophy' (1975) 69(2) American Political Science Review 648, 648. Rawls' theory of justice has been one of the most widely discussed concepts of distributive justice since its postulation. J Lamont and C Favor, 'Distributive Justice' Stanford Encyclopedia of Philosophy (2017) <https://plato.stanford.edu/entries/justice-distributive/> accessed 25 June 2021.

[213] Bloom (n 212) 650.

[214] RC Offenheiser and SH Holcombe, 'Challenges and Opportunities in Implementing a Rights-Based Approach to Development: An Oxfam America Perspective' (2003) 32 Nonprofit and Voluntary Sector Quarterly 268, 277.

[215] He points out that the principles postulated in his theory are concerned with the basic structuring of the society, especially the manner in which rights and duties are to be granted, and the nature of the system that regulates the distribution of economic and social advantage. Rawls (n 208) 61.

[216] T>Offenheiser and Holcombe (n 214) 277.

1186   SDG 16

Rawls' theory, society should not accept inequalities, whether they originate from fortune, nature, or birth.[217] Describing his theory as concerned with distributive justice in governance, Rawls observes that:

> the primary subject of justice is the basic structure of society, or more exactly, the way in which the major social institutions distribute fundamental rights and duties and determine the division of advantages from social cooperation. By major institutions I understand the political constitution and the principal economic and social arrangements ... Taken together as one scheme, the major institutions define men's rights and duties and influence their life prospects, what they can expect to be and how well they can hope to do. The basic structure is the primary subject of justice because its effects are so profound and present from the start.[218]

Rawls' theory of justice comprises two principles. The first is that 'each person is to have an equal right to the most extensive basic liberty compatible with a similar liberty for others'.[219] The first principle is applicable to political and civil rights, such as right to vote, and freedom of assembly and speech, for which no person should have an advantage over others in a just society.[220] The more technical second principle is based on the idea that '[s]ocial and economic *inequalities* are to be arranged so that they are both (a) to the greatest benefit of the least advantaged and (b) attached to offices and positions open to all under conditions of fair equality of opportunity'.[221] The first part of the second principle essentially implies inequality in the allocation of economic and social benefits should be for the most disadvantaged. In addition, in the second part, the principle implies there is no need for such inequality in the allocation of economic and social benefits if members of society are of the same status. The first part of the second principle, often referred to as the *difference* principle,[222] is the focus of this chapter as it is the most relevant and often most controversial. Rawls' theory hypothesises that such an approach to state governance 'will increase the total wealth of the economy and, under the [d]ifference [p]rinciple, the wealth of the least advantaged'.[223] Under the difference principle, opportunities of the least advantaged are improved by those that are more advantaged.[224] Rawls justifies the difference principle on the basis that no person deserves 'a more favorable starting place in society',[225] especially in the context of social institutions such as a state. Rawls further vindicates the difference principle as follows:

---

[217] ibid.
[218] T>Rawls (n 208) 7.
[219] ibid 60.
[220] ibid 61.
[221] ibid 83. Italics added for emphasis.
[222] ibid 76.
[223] Lamont and Favor (n 212).
[224] T>Rawls (n 208)T> 95.
[225] ibid 102.

This is the principle that undeserved inequalities call for redress; and since inequalities of birth and natural endowment are undeserved, these inequalities are to be somehow compensated for ... Thus the principle holds that in order to treat all persons equally, to provide genuine equality of opportunity, society must give more attention to those with fewer native assets and to those born into the less favorable social positions. The idea is to redress the bias of contingencies in the direction of equality.[226]

Rawls' theory is a well-thought out and compelling justification for the special focus on equity, inclusive participation, and economic and social empowerment of the marginalized in societal institutions, as enshrined in the human rights based concepts of the right to development, and in some of the targets of SDG 16.

V. Commentary on SDG 16 Targets

Progress in the realization and implementation of the SDG 16 targets is measured through select indicators. In that sense, this part commences by evaluating the context in which the various indicators evaluate the SDG 16 targets, including by examining discourses relating to the accuracy, credibility, and limitations of such instruments of statistical analysis and measurement. The section then proceeds to discuss the actual evaluation of the various SDG 16 targets by the select indicators, and in that context, examines statistical data and implementation efforts, among other issues.

A. Evaluating SDG 16 Targets through Indicators

The determination of the level of national and international progress towards the realization of the targets of SDG 16 is achieved through the use of indicators. During the inauguration of the SDGs, it was explained that:

[t]he Goals and targets will be followed up and reviewed using a set of global indicators. These will be complemented by indicators at the regional and national levels which will be developed by Member States, in addition to the outcomes of work undertaken for the development of the baselines for those targets where national and global baseline data does not yet exist ... This framework will be simple yet robust, address all Sustainable Development Goals and targets, including for means of implementation, and preserve the political balance, integration and ambition contained therein.[227]

Indicators have become an integral aspect of measuring and evaluating the diverse targets enumerated under SDG 16. Indicators are essentially an assemblage of

---

[226] ibid 100–01.
[227] UNGA, 'Transforming our World' (n 1), para 75.

1188   SDG 16

rank-ordered and processed data that capture and demonstrate a specified element of performance in a simple and comprehensible form.[228] For purposes of enabling the 'implementation of the global indicator framework' the Inter-agency and Expert Group on SDG Indicators (IAEG-SDGs) categorizes the indicators 'into three tiers based on their level of methodological development and the availability of data at the global level'.[229] The first tier comprises indicators that possess conceptual clarity; their methodology and standards is established internationally; and their data are generated by least 50 per cent of the Member States in relation to half of the population in each region where such indicators are applicable.[230] The tier II indicators comprise those for which data are not regularly generated by Member States, despite their conceptual clarity and already possessing internationally established methodology and standards.[231] In respect to the third category, it constitutes those indicators for which there is the absence of internationally established methodology or standards, although there is the expectation that such methodology or standards are in the process of development and testing, or will be established and tested in the future.[232]

The UNSD works in consultation with indicators' custodian agencies to generate public information on their nature, including the data they provide in the context of achievement of the targets of the SDGs.[233] As of March 2020, the global indicator framework no longer contained any tier III indicators.[234] That is commendable progress towards more effective measurement and evaluation of the progress in the realization of most targets of SDG 16. As explained by the United Nations Department of Economic and Social Affairs:

> All indicators are equally important, and the establishment of the tier system is intended solely to assist in the development of global implementation strategies. For tier I and II indicators, the availability of data at the national level may not necessarily align with the global tier classification and countries can create their own tier classification for implementation.[235]

Indicators are instruments that evaluate and measure the extent of adherence with required practices and levels of obligatory compliance in a transnational context, and are thus, core devices of global governance, including those articulated under the various

---

[228] KE Davis and B Kingsbury, 'Indicators as Interventions: Pitfalls and Prospects in Supporting Development Initiatives' (December 2011) ii <http://iilj.org/wp-content/uploads/2016/08/Davis-Kingsbury-Indicators-as-Interventions-Pitfalls-and-Prospects-in-Supporting-Development-Initiatives-Rockefeller-Foundation-2011. pdf> accessed 11 August 2021; KE Davis, 'Data and Decentralization: Measuring the Performance of Legal Institutions in Multilevel Systems of Governance' (2018) Minnesota Law Review 1619, 1624.

[229] T>United Nations Department of Economic and Social Affairs, Statistics Division, 'IAEG-SDGs: Tier Classification for Global SDG Indicators' (2021) <https://unstats.un.org/sdgs/iaeg-sdgs/tier-classificat ion/>T>accessed 24 October 2021.

[230] ibid.

[231] ibid.

[232] ibid.

[233] UNSD, 'E-Handbook on Sustainable Development Goals Indicators' <https://unstats.un.org/wiki/display/ SDGeHandbook/Home> accessed 9 June 2021.

[234] T>UNDESA, Statistics Division, 'IAEG-SDGs' (n 229).

[235] ibid.

targets of SDG 16. Global governance is undertaken through diverse mechanisms by state and non-state actors. Such transnational governance has traditionally largely relied upon legal and regulatory norms and standards, but is increasingly dependent upon indicators. It is in that context that Rottenburg and Merry draw attention to the 'global proliferation' of indicators, which they view as constituting 'a specific technology of numeric knowledge production relevant to governance'.[236] The reliance on a framework of indicators to evaluate the progress in the quality and extent of realization of the diverse objectives espoused under SDG 16 is part of the realities and evolving trends in transnational governance.

Addressing the challenge of how measurement instruments would be formulated, the OWG observed that recent reports had demonstrated that it was possible and necessary to measure concepts such as rule of law and peace.[237] The OWG also noted that there existed standard methodologies and data collection instruments that were already being utilized in relation to the measurement of rule of law and peace.[238] Acknowledging the necessity and significance of data relating to progress to the realization of SDGs, the OWG noted that access to accurate and timely 'statistics is the basis for understanding the social, economic and political circumstances under which people live, inform decision-makers on priorities, improve evidence-based policies and programmes and chart progress made'.[239] Indicators are essential in measuring and regulating compliance with the generated regulatory norms, whether in the form of soft or hard law. More significantly, indicators may be utilized in measuring and regulating broad participation of diverse stakeholders in the making and implementation of the regulatory norms and thus enhance their democratic legitimacy.

The OWG observed that the data that indicators may provide were an essential instrument for facilitating transparency and accountability, and that the realization of development ideals could be hampered by the lack of evaluation data.[240] The use of indicators can alter the 'power dynamics of decision-making', which may be in the context of global governance.[241] It is in that sense that indicators have become powerful advocacy instruments, from highlighting problems afflicting vulnerable populations to exposing incidences of corruption and abuse of power,[242] which are concerns of SDG 16. Indicators have been powerful instruments for pushing particular perspectives and demonstrating outcomes in relation to policy-making and implementation, as they make data accessible and the related governance activities demonstrated by the

---

[236] R Rottenburg and SE Merry, 'A World of Indicators: The Making of Governmental Knowledge Through Quantification' in R Rottenburg and others (eds), *The World of Indicators: The Making of Governmental Knowledge Through Quantification* (CUP 2015) 1, 2.

[237] T>Sustainable Development Knowledge Platform, 'Eighth Session of the Open Working Group on Sustainable Development Goals: TST Issues Brief' (n 19) 12.

[238] ibid.

[239] ibid.

[240] ibid.

[241] SE Merry, 'Measuring the World: Indicators, Human Rights, and Global Governance' *Anthropology and Law and Society* (New York University, 13 May 2009) 5.

[242] Rottenburg and Merry (n 236) 4.

measures comprehensible and convincing.[243] As a consequence, even those who do not agree with the data are put into a severe burden of justifying their contradictory perceptions and views, and for providing credible evidence to the contrary.[244]

1. Nature and Context of SDG 16 Indicators

The SGD 16 targets, despite being global in nature and expecting universal implementation, are nonetheless sensitive to 'different national realities, capacities and levels of development' and consider diversity in state policies and priorities.[245] As such, despite the SDG 16 targets being 'aspirational and global' each state has the opportunity to define its own targets.[246] In defining their SDG 16 targets, states are to be 'guided by the global level of ambition but taking into account national circumstances'.[247] In particular, states are to determine how the 'aspirational and global targets' of SDG 16 are to be entrenched into their national planning processes and policies.[248] This is due to the fact that other ongoing state processes relating to the social, economic, and environmental fields are also important, and should ideally be linked with the concepts articulated under SDG 16.[249] The UNGA has, crucially, acknowledged the diversity of state resources between countries, and as a consequence, recognized that there may be different visions, models, and approaches to the realization of SDGs across the states.[250]

2. Limitations of Indicators in Measuring SDG 16 Targets' Progress

Some limitations and predicaments have nonetheless been highlighted in respect to the use of indicators which may have an implication on their utilization as measures of progress towards the realization of the SDG 16 objectives. For instance, the extent of rationality, objectivity, and accuracy of the indicators utilized to measure SDG 16 targets may be queried. According to Schultz, while statistical indicators create an impression of rationality and objectivity, some of them may nonetheless result in inaccurate simplistic explanations of the complex and diverse circumstances that they seek to quantify.[251] Schultz makes reference to indicators used to measure cases of Aboriginal children attendance to schools in Australia.[252] She argues that measuring education in a population on the basis of the rate of attendance in schools may be reliant on readily available data and likely to be based on an unstated hypothesis that school attendance results in desired educational outcomes.[253] It is in that context that Schultz argues that in the case of Aboriginal children in secluded areas, 'there is conflicting evidence about the association between school attendance and educational outcomes because schooling

---

[243] T>A von Bogdandy and others, 'From Public International to International Public Law: Translating World Public Opinion into International Public Authority' (2017) 28(1) European Journal of International Law 115, 144.
[244] ibid.
[245] T>UNGA, 'Transforming our World' (n 1), para 55.
[246] ibid.
[247] ibid.
[248] ibid.
[249] ibid.
[250] ibid para 59.
[251] T>Schultz (n 176) 11.
[252] ibid.
[253] ibid.

does not consistently contribute to learning and educational success.[254] While Schultz does not explicitly make reference to SDG 16 indicators, her observation is, nonetheless, useful in highlighting and sensitizing concepts under which the SDG 16 indicators should be configured and evaluated, particularly in the context of their rationality, objectivity, and accuracy.

An illustration may be made in reference to indicator 16.7.1, which utilizes a descriptive representation approach in measuring the extent to which the composition of parliament in a state reflects the various socio-demographic categories within its population, which results in problematic questions of who and what should be replicated in the representative body.[255] For instance, if focus is given to measuring social dimensions such as gender, young people, and minorities in the parliamentary representation, the mechanism may still be queried in the context of its lack of focus on the poor, or even the ethnic groups that are not officially recognized.[256]

There are efforts and activities aimed at enhancing the quality of the data, which may have the effect also of improving its rationality, objectivity, accuracy, and credibility. For instance, in order to safeguard and promote quality management of the data collection, analysis, and presentation in respect to indicator 16.2.3 regarding sexual violence on children, the United Nations International Children's Emergency Fund (UNICEF) collaborates with the states' statistical offices and relevant stakeholders through a consultative process.[257] UNICEF also undertakes regular quality assessment of data by evaluating their consistency and undertaking other relevant validations before the data's dissemination.[258]

Schultz has also cautioned that the use of targets and indicators to evaluate whole populations in a state may obscure regional, community, and individual features and realities.[259] It should, nonetheless, be appreciated that during the OWG sessions, it was argued that targets and indicators of SDG 16 should 'be tailored to specific national legal systems, [and] local practices and values, regardless of where countries are along the development spectrum'.[260]

Schultz has further argued that while the SDG targets can facilitate focus by governments and service providers on desirable measurable outcomes, they however present limited perceptions and viewpoints of people's lives within the subject societies.[261] For instance, the UNSD has cautioned that indicator 16.7.1, which evaluates the extent of diversity of representation in parliaments of states through descriptive representation approach, risks rendering highly diverse representation an end in itself.[262] In that context, it advises that effective representation should not end the moment parliament

---

[254] ibid.
[255] T>UNSD, 'SDG Indicator Metadata' (March 2021).
[256] ibid.
[257] ibid.
[258] ibid.
[259] Schultz (n 176) 11.
[260] Sustainable Development Knowledge Platform, 'Eighth Session of the Open Working Group on Sustainable Development Goals: Summary of the Co-Chairs' (n 18) 9.
[261] Schultz (n 176) 11.
[262] T>UNSD, 'SDG Indicator Metadata' (March 2021).

1192   SDG 16

achieves the appropriate diversity of representation for the various socio-demographic categories of the population but should also progress to evaluations of whether the representatives articulate suitable concerns, and whether they are capable of influencing policies and legislative agendas, among others.[263] Further, as UNSD opines, representation in parliament should be accompanied by high-quality and meaningful participation.[264] As the UNSD instructively states, in the absence of opportunities for citizens to meaningfully and qualitatively participate in parliamentary decision-making processes, representation alone cannot have the outcome of 'effective popular control of the government—one of the fundamental principles of democracy'.[265]

Further, some indicators may provide and evaluate data relating to general variables, and thus miss on vital particular, specific and sectoral aspects of a societal problem. For instance, UNSD has explained that indicator 16.4.1 that evaluates the 'total value' of illicit financial flows focuses on 'the overall size of the problem'.[266] As such, the UNSD concedes that a more specific measurement of the IFFs may be helpful in discerning the core sources and channels of the IFFs, and, thus, facilitate more effective interventions.[267] It is also noteworthy that, as Schultz cautions, the choice of indicators may be premised on certain preferred values and ideals, and as such, the numbers utilized as indicators may not be neutral.[268]

The UNSD metadata relating to the various indicators and targets of SDG 16 include commentaries that evaluate the limitations that relate to the collection, analysis, and presentation of particular forms of information, and at times incorporates suggestions for mitigating the shortcomings.[269] Consequently, such information can significantly assist both the national statistical systems and the custodian agencies in relation to anticipating and mitigating limitations relating to particular indicators, thus improving on the rationality and credibility of the data collection, analysis and presentation methodology.

3. Improving the Credibility and Accuracy of Indicators

The UNSG has argued that for purposes of enhancing the credibility and accuracy of the SDG indicators and statistics, the global statistical system should undertake its functions in conformity with the Fundamental Principles of Official Statistics, and the Economic and Social Council (ECOSOC) Resolution 2006/6.[270] The UNGA articulated the Fundamental Principles of Official Statistics in its Resolution 68/261.[271]

---

[263] ibid.

[264] ibid.

[265] ibid.

[266] T>UNSD, 'SDG Indicator Metadata' (1 October 2020).

[267] ibid.

[268] Schultz (n 176) 11.

[269] For instance, in relation to IFFs under indicator 16.4.1, see UNSD, 'SDG Indicator Metadata' (1 October 2020).

[270] United Nations Economic and Social Council (UNESC), 'Report of the Inter-Agency and Expert Group on Sustainable Development Goal Indicators: Note by the Secretary-General' UN Doc E/CN.3/2019/2 (19 December 2018) 11.

[271] See UNGA, 'Resolution adopted by the General Assembly on 29 January 2014: Fundamental Principles of Official Statistics' UN Doc A/RES/68/261 (3 March 2014).

ECOSOC Resolution 2006/6, adopted in the context of MDGs, called upon states to improve and strengthen their national statistical capacities for purposes of generating timely and credible indicators to evaluate their development strategies and policies, and to measure their implementation of national, regional, and international development commitments and aspirations.[272]

The UNSG has affirmed that the primary sources of data for sustainable development goals global reporting system are the national statistical mechanisms, and as such, pointed out that the quality of data and information that countries provide to international agencies will have an impact on the overall quality, credibility, and accuracy of the universal reporting on the SDGs indicators.[273] For instance, data on sexual violence against children, as evaluated by indicator 16.2.3, are obtained from states' line ministries and other incidental government agencies that have previously conducted national surveys on such forms of offences.[274] Data in respect to indicator 16.3.3 that measures access to dispute resolution mechanisms are obtained from country level surveys, such as those conducted through the respective national statistical offices (NSOs).[275] In that context, it is recommended that NSOs operate as the main contacts for the quality assurance and compilation of data relating to indicator 16.3.3, and work in close collaboration with the ministries in charge of justice and relevant state agencies.[276]

The UNSG has also called for support to strengthen the national statistical systems of developing states, and more specifically African countries, landlocked developing countries (LLCs), small island developing states (SIDS), and least developed countries (LDCs).[277] In that context, UNICEF provides technical and financial support to states in order to enhance their capacity to collect and collate data relating to sexual violence against children that is measured by indicator 16.2.3.[278] The United Nations Office on Drugs and Crime (UNODC) and United Nations Conference on Trade and Development (UNCTAD), the respective custodian agencies for indicator 16.4.1 on illicit financial flows, have been supporting capacity-building in states to enhance the measurement of the indicator.[279]

It is noteworthy that the state data regarding a particular indicator may be collected and collated from different national agencies. For instance, in respect to indicator 16.1.1, data regarding intentional homicides are obtained from both the criminal justice institutions and the public health and civil registration systems.[280] This exemplifies unavoidable interdependence in the state institutions and systems with regard to the gathering of data for evaluating progress towards the realization of SDG 16, and

---

[272] UNESC, 'ECOSOC Resolution 2006/6: Strengthening Statistical Capacity' <https://www.un.org/en/ecosoc/docs/2006/resolution%202006-6.pdf> accessed 25 August 2021.

[273] UNESC, 'Report of the Inter-Agency and Expert Group on Sustainable Development Goal Indicators' (n 270) 13.

[274] UNSD, 'SDG Indicator Metadata' (March 2021).

[275] T>UNSD, 'SDG Indicator Metadata' (June 2020).

[276] ibid.

[277] UNESC, 'Report of the Inter-Agency and Expert Group on Sustainable Development Goal Indicators' (n 270) 11–12.

[278] UNSD, 'SDG Indicator Metadata' (March 2021).

[279] UNSD, 'SDG Indicator Metadata' (1 October 2020).

[280] T>UNSD, 'SDG Indicator Metadata' (19 July 2016).

1194   SDG 16

may necessitate quality collaboration and consultation for purposes of avoiding duplicities or burden shifting.

Modalities of addressing gaps and lacunas in the national statistical systems have also been developed and formulated. In respect to indicator 16.1.1, which evaluates the number of intentional homicides, the World Health Organization (WHO) generates estimates for states in which there is a lack of national data relating to homicide from the countries' criminal justice institutions, and public health and civil registration systems.[281] In addition, WHO and the United UNODC are working together to progressively develop common approaches for the production of joint UNODC-WHO homicide data statistics at the state, regional, and global levels.[282] With regard to indicator 16.2.3 that evaluates incidences of sexual violence in children, UNICEF does not publish any state level estimates in cases where data for a country are entirely missing from the national statistical systems.[283] Similarly, the relevant custodian agencies do not estimate national data in respect of indicator 16.3.3 that evaluates access to dispute resolution mechanisms if no surveys have been undertaken at the country level by the respective state agencies.[284] On the other hand, the UNSD notes that where country data relating to total values of IFFs under indicator 16.4.1 is absent, reference may be made to transnational data sources, or other alternative sources of the information being sought.[285] Nonetheless, UNSD advices that in such cases, comprehensive metadata clarifying the circumstances relating to the missing of the data, and explaining the exhaustiveness of the alternative data for the indicator, is essential.[286]

For purposes of increasing the transparency, accuracy, credibility, and reliability for the global reporting systems in the context of the SDGs, including trust in the data, Member States have been called upon to produce data based on international agreed standards and definitions.[287] It is in that context that there have been efforts to espouse definitions of contentious concepts for adoption by states. In that sense, the UNSD acknowledges that there may be discrepancies in the context of the data generated by states in respect to what is regarded as constituting intentional homicide, in the case of indicator 16.1.1.[288] As UNSD points out, the statistics from one country may be premised on its definition of intentional killing, while the information provided by others and the custodian agency, UNODC, may be in accordance to the International Classification of Crime for Statistical Purposes (ICCS) criteria and guidelines.[289] The ICCS operates under the auspices of UNODC, and was in 2015 endorsed by the United Nations Statistical Commission (UNSC), and the Commission on Crime Prevention

---

[281] ibid.
[282] ibid.
[283] UNSD, 'SDG Indicator Metadata' (March 2021).
[284] UNSD, 'SDG Indicator Metadata' (June 2020).
[285] T>UNSD, 'SDG Indicator Metadata' (1 October 2020).
[286] ibid.
[287] UNESC, 'Report of the Inter-Agency and Expert Group on Sustainable Development Goal Indicators' (n 270) 13.
[288] T>UNSD, 'SDG Indicator Metadata' (19 July 2016).
[289] ibid.

and Criminal Justice (CCPCJ), as an international statistical standard for data collection and collation.[290]

Consequently, in its effort to provide a universally harmonized classification of acts that constitute such deliberate killings for purposes of integrity of collected data and generated statistics, the ICCS defines intentional homicide as constituting '[u]nlawful death inflicted upon a person with the intent to cause death or serious injury'.[291] It proceeds to explain the three constituent elements that render such killing be regarded as constituting intentional homicide.[292] First is the objective element of the killing of an individual by another person.[293] Second is the subjective element of the perpetrator of the offence having had the intention to kill or seriously injure the individual. Third is the legal element of the unlawfulness of the killing.[294]

It is arguable that even if some states do not explicitly have specific reference of such intentional killing under the term 'homicide', it nonetheless qualifies for reporting and evaluation under indicator 16.1.1. For instance, the legal terms used in reference to such offences under Kenya's criminal law justice system are either 'murder' or 'manslaughter'. It is in that context that the International Criminal Court (ICC) states that for purposes of data collection and collation, all deaths that satisfy the espoused three criteria should be regarded as constituting intentional homicide, 'irrespective of definitions provided by national legislations and practices'.[295] The ICC also proceeds to provide examples of particular forms of killings that may be included in statistics relating to homicide in a state, such as murder, death resulting from terrorist activities, serious assault resulting in death, infanticide, femicide, honour killing, voluntary manslaughter, deaths relating to dowry, deaths resulting from law enforcement, and extra judicial killings.[296] Further, the ICC provides guidance in respect to the distinguishing acts that constitute intentional killings on one part, and those that are to be categorized as amounting to war crimes, or conflict and war-related killings on the other part.[297] The UNSD also points out that the 'gradual implementation of ICCS by countries should improve quality and consistency of national and international data' in relation to intentional homicides.[298]

With regard to indicator 16.2.3 evaluating the proportion of young men and women who had experienced sexual violence in childhood, the custodian agency, UNICEF, postulates the definition espoused under General Comment No 13 on the CRC.[299] Under the stated indicator, sexual violence is broadly defined as constituting 'any sexual activities imposed by an adult on a child against which the child is entitled to

[290] UNODC, 'International Classification of Crime for Statistical Purposes (ICCS)' <https://www.unodc.org/unodc/en/data-and-analysis/statistics/iccs.html> accessed 24 September 2021.
[291] T>UNSD, 'SDG Indicator Metadata' (19 July 2016).
[292] ibid.
[293] ibid.
[294] ibid.
[295] ibid.
[296] ibid.
[297] ibid.
[298] ibid.
[299] UNSD, 'SDG Indicator Metadata' (March 2021). See United Nations Committee on the Rights of the Child, 'General Comment No 13 (2011): The Right of the Child to Freedom from all Forms of Violence' UN Doc CRC/C/GC/13 (18 April 2011).

1196   SDG 16

protection by criminal law', and the constituent elements constituting the offence are then itemized.[300]

In the case of indicator 16.3.3 that measures access to dispute resolution mechanisms, the collection and collation of data by national statistical systems is premised on four predetermined survey questions.[301] Nonetheless, the UNSD points out that there may be discrepancies in data from the same country, if more than one survey has been undertaken and disseminated, due to differences in: the wording of the questions, sample designs and sizes, survey methods and operations, structure of the questionnaire, among others.[302] The UNSD clarifies that the data from state surveys that are relied upon for the global reporting in relation to indicator 16.3.3 are those that comply with the recommended standards, when available.[303] Further, as a mechanism of providing methodological guidance in the formulation of questionnaires and the conduct of surveys, the Organisation for Economic Co-operation and Development (OECD) in 2019 published the *Legal Needs Surveys and Access to Justice* guide.[304]

Wherever possible, Member States have been requested to provide necessary data and metadata on SDGs thematic issues to the respective custodian agencies in a timely manner and according to quality standards through existing reporting mechanisms and platforms.[305] The UNSG also requests that Member States submit applicable methodological information in cases where the provided statistics do not satisfy international standards, so that international statistical agencies can adjust the statistics appropriately for purposes of safeguarding international coherence and comparability.[306] With regard to indicator 16.4.1 that focuses on the total values of IFFs, the UNSD recommends that where country data are unavailable, transnational data sources, or other alternative sources of the information can be relied upon.[307] If that occurs, the UNSD advises that it is essential that comprehensive metadata clarifying the circumstances relating to the missing of the data be provided, which should also explain the exhaustiveness and reliability of the alternative data.[308]

Information supplied to Member States by custodian agencies should be reviewed and where there are any questionable or arising issues, the concerned national entities should be notified.[309] In that context, UNICEF undertakes annual consultations with states, either in December or January, in order to review the data and process the feedback obtained for purposes of the global reporting on indicator 16.2.3 in respect of

---

[300] T>UNSD, 'SDG Indicator Metadata' (March 2021).
[301] ibid.
[302] ibid.
[303] ibid.
[304] UNSD, 'SDG Indicator Metadata' (June 2020). See Organisation for Economic Cooperation and Development/Open Society Foundations, *Legal Needs Surveys and Access to Justice* (OECD Publishing 2019).
[305] UNESC, 'Report of the Inter-Agency and Expert Group on Sustainable Development Goal Indicators' (n 270) 13.
[306] ibid.
[307] T>UNSD, 'SDG Indicator Metadata' (1 October 2020).
[308] ibid.
[309] UNESC, 'Report of the Inter-Agency and Expert Group on Sustainable Development Goal Indicators' (n 270) 13.

COMMENTARY ON TARGETS 1197

sexual violence against children.[310] In the case of indicator 16.4.1 on IFFs, states are to be provided with questions and suggestions that require clarification for their review.[311]

Where there are disagreements in respect to national data sources and international country estimates in relation to the measurement of SDG targets, dialogue should be considered between the concerned state departments and the custodian agencies.[312] Such dialogue should have the objective of improving adherence to the 'scientific rigour, international comparability, coherence and the implementation of the Fundamental Principles of Official Statistics.'[313] In that regard, the annual consultations between UNICEF and states affords an opportunity for clarifications, harmonization, and consistency in the information provided by countries in respect to indicator 16.2.3.[314] The extensive consultations are in relation to the compiling, assessment and validation of data from state sources, and focuses on aspects that include the agreed definitions, classifications and methodologies.[315] After review, UNICEF provides feedback to the concerned states regarding the data points that are either accepted or rejected.[316] Where there are rejections of particular data points, UNICEF provides justifications and explanations.[317]

With regard to indicator 16.1.1 that measures the number of intentional homicides, it has been acknowledged that there may be discrepancies between the states produced and internationally estimated data due to differences in definitions.[318] This may arise due to the national data being based on the state definition of actions constituting intentional homicide, while the international data as generated by the UNODC are premised on the definition postulated by the ICCS.[319] Nonetheless, it has been argued that the progressive implementation of the ICCS criteria for the definition of intentional homicide by the national statistical agencies may eventually improve on the consistency, uniformity, and quality of both the state and international data.[320]

With respect to international and supranational statistical agencies, the UNSG has called upon such entities to comply with the applicable principles that regulate international statistical activities.[321] Further, the UNSG calls upon international and supranational statistical agencies and states first to rely upon 'concepts, definitions, classifications, sources, methods and procedures that meet professional and meet scientific standards.'[322] Second, the UNSG calls upon states to fully document, in a transparent

[310] UNSD, 'SDG Indicator Metadata' (March 2021).
[311] UNSD, 'SDG Indicator Metadata' (1 October 2020).
[312] T>UNESC, 'Report of the Inter-Agency and Expert Group on Sustainable Development Goal Indicators' (n 270) 13.
[313] ibid.
[314] T>UNSD, 'SDG Indicator Metadata' (March 2021).
[315] ibid.
[316] ibid.
[317] ibid.
[318] T>UNSD, 'SDG Indicator Metadata' (19 July 2016).
[319] ibid.
[320] ibid.
[321] T>UNESC, 'Report of the Inter-Agency and Expert Group on Sustainable Development Goal Indicators' (n 270) 11.
[322] ibid.

1198 SDG 16

manner, and make accessible their sources of data and information, and data collection, estimation, and adjustment methods utilized.[323]

The UNSG has emphasized that the various custodian agencies of the SDG indicators should be accountable for the accuracy and quality of the statistics that they collate and produce.[324] In that context, the custodian agencies have been called upon to sufficiently explain any discrepancies between state and international data in relation to the indicators for the SDGs targets.[325] Concerned custodial agencies are to provide detailed and comprehensive metadata and methodological guidance to national statistical systems in a timely manner, and any changes made to the state data indicated.[326] The involved international and supranational statistical agencies are to undertake data collection and collation in a coordinated manner by creating efficient and proficient data sharing systems amongst them in order to avoid duplication of efforts.[327] There is some progress in this respect in relation to data collection and collation for SDG 16 as such work has been delegated to specific custodian agencies.[328]

The UNSG recommends that international and supranational statistical agencies only address data requests by states regarding a particular SDG indicator if they are the nominated custodian agency.[329] Data are to be collected and collated through common mechanisms, like joint questionnaires in situations where more than one entity is the nominated custodian agency.[330]

The UNSG calls upon custodian agencies to publicly share and release the data that they collect and collate with the UN Statistics Division and other international and supranational statistical agencies that may require the information in a timely manner and at no cost.[331] Mediums for the open access to and sharing of data on SDGs indicators from international and state statistical agencies are to be supported in order to ensure maximized data availability.[332]

B. Realization and Evaluation of SDG 16 Targets

Some states have integrated the SDGs framework into their developmental objectives and policies. For instance, as Kenya stated in its 2020 voluntary national review (VNR), the country's development agenda is aligned with the SDGs through its Vision 2030.[333] According to Kenya's 2020 VNR, at both the national and sub-national

[323] ibid.
[324] ibid 11–12.
[325] ibid 12.
[326] Ibid.
[327] ibid.
[328] ibid.
[329] ibid.
[330] ibid.
[331] ibid 11–12.
[332] ibid.
[333] T>National Treasury and Planning, Republic of Kenya, *Second Voluntary National Review On The Implementation of the Sustainable Development Goals* (National Treasury and Planning, 2020) 1.

levels 'SDGs have been mainstreamed in sector plans, strategic plans and annual performance contracts', through an approach that incorporates stakeholder's participation.[334] According to the South African VNR of 2019, the country's National Development Plan (NDP): Vision 2030 has a 74 per cent convergence with the SDGs.[335]

While there has been some state and transnational efforts to address the challenges to be confronted through the SDG 16 framework, as of 2020, it was still evident that '[c]onflict, insecurity, weak institutions and limited access to justice remain a great threat to sustainable development'.[336] The 2021 Report of the UNSG on SDGs underscored the need for tangible progress towards the realization of the objective of creating 'peaceful, just and inclusive societies', having observed that millions of people still lived in fragile and conflict-affected countries.[337] The UNSG regretted that approximately 79.5 million people had been forcibly displaced globally towards the end of 2019, which was equivalent to 1 per cent of the population of the world.[338] He also highlighted the negative impact of the COVID-19 pandemic, which he lamented that it had weakened, or even destroyed and dismantled 'rights and protection systems' across various states, in addition to aggravating discriminatory practices and inequalities.[339]

It is noteworthy that states have been undertaking VNRs in which they share their strategies, experiences, opportunities, and pitfalls in the realization of the SDGs. For instance, South Africa conducted its inaugural VNR in 2019, which in a sense was a demonstration of the county's focus on integrated and comprehensive implementation of the 2030 SDGs agenda.[340] As was pointed out in the Report, the inaugural review would assist South Africans comprehend and appreciate the impact of programmes and policies in the realization of sustainable development.[341]

1. Target 16.1 Significantly reduce all forms of violence and related death rates everywhere

a) *Indicator 16.1.1 Number of victims of intentional homicide per 100,000 population, by sex and age*

Indicator 16.1.1 evaluates the number of victims of deliberate killings, referred to as 'intentional homicide' in a population of 100,000 including by gender and age. In that

---

[334] ibid.

[335] Sustainable Development Goals Knowledge Platform, '2019 South Africa Voluntary National Review' 5 <https://sustainabledevelopment.un.org/content/documents/23402RSA_Voluntary_National_Review_Report_ _The_Final_24_July_2019.pdf> accessed 21 October 2021.

[336] UNESC, 'Progress towards the Sustainable Development Goals: Report of the Secretary-General' UN Doc E/2020/57 (28 April 2020) para 130.

[337] T>UNESC, 'Progress towards the Sustainable Development Goals: Report of the Secretary-General' UN Doc E/2021/58 (30 April 2021) para 167.

[338] ibid.

[339] ibid.

[340] T>Sustainable Development Goals Knowledge Platform, '2019 South Africa' (n 335) 5.

[341] ibid 6.

1200   SDG 16

context, the 'indicator is defined as the total count of victims of intentional homicide divided by the total population, expressed per 100,000 population.'[342]

i) **Empirical analysis** Indicator 16.1.1 has been justified by the UNSD through the premise that it 'provides a direct indication of lack of security', in addition to being widely utilized at the national and transnational spheres 'to measure the most extreme form of violent crime'.[343] The UNSD has also argued that the indicator has global applicability, which is beneficial as intentional killings occur in all countries of the world.[344] The designated custodial organizations of indicator 16.1.1 are the UNODC, and the WHO.

The UNSG 2021 Progress Report on SDGs observed that an approximated 437,000 people were victims of intentional killings in 2019.[345] The UNSG Report appreciated that there was a gradual but slow decrease in lethal violence, with the rate of victims of intentional homicide decreasing from 6 for every 100,000 people in 2015 to 5.7 in 2019.[346] Thus, despite the above grim statistics, there seems to have been some progress in eliminating violent and crime activities that result in localized deaths in the form of homicide and murder. The UN Secretary General Report of 2020 had earlier on observed that the 'global rate of homicide per 100,000 persons slowly declined, from 6.8 per cent to 5.9 per cent to 5.8 per cent in 2000, 2015 and 2018, respectively, corresponding to approximately 440,000 victims of homicide, 81 per cent of whom were men and 19 per cent of whom were women'.[347]

As a demonstration of the higher burden of deaths from criminal activities among the developing and least developed states, the 2020 Report observes that in the stated period, two-thirds of the victims of homicide globally were from the Caribbean and Latin America at 33 per cent, and Sub-Saharan Africa at 36 per cent.[348]

Despite the global decrease in intentional killings being marginal, it is nonetheless commendable progress as it is an indication of some increase in human security and peaceful coexistence in communities, which are essential for the realization of other SDG 16 targets. States and relevant non-state actors should build up on the progress in order to significantly eradicate violence and conflicts. It is nonetheless regrettable that, as the UNSG Report observed, two-thirds of the cited victims of intentional killings were from Sub-Saharan Africa, the Caribbean, and the Latin America regions.[349] It is also more appalling that the Report pointed out that there were no indications of the numbers of intentional killings decreasing in Sub-Saharan Africa.[350] The 2021 UNSG Report demonstrates the need for more focused international collaboration by both

---

[342] T>UNSD, 'SDG Indicator Metadata' (19 July 2016).
[343] ibid.
[344] ibid.
[345] T>UNESC, UN Doc E/2021/58 (n 337) paras 168–69.
[346] ibid.
[347] T>UNESC, UN Doc E/2020/57 (n 336) para 131.
[348] ibid.
[349] T>UNESC, UN Doc E/2021/58 (n 337) paras 168–169.
[350] ibid.

state and relevant non-state actors in supporting the states of the Caribbean, and the Latin America regions, and more particularly the Sub-Saharan states, to eradicate the menace of intentional killings, which are not only an exemplification of gross human rights violations, but a serious bar to the realization of SDG 16.

ii) Implementation efforts There have been concerted efforts aimed at reducing homicides and crimes among states, such as the case of Ghana.[351] Some of the approaches adopted by Ghana have included improvements of the police–public relations; enhancement of witness protection; reliance on technology; and enhancement of the recruitment processes, professionalism, terms of service, rules of engagement, and ethical standards of the police.[352] Violence in South Africa remains high, including sexual violations, which is attributed, among other factors, to the high levels of usage of drugs.[353] Consequently, it has been suggested that a core focus policy priority for tackling the challenge of crime in South Africa is to address the drug use menace.[354] Nonetheless, there have been cases of progress in reducing violence in South Africa, such as the decrease of home robberies from 1.59 per cent in the 2013–2014 period, to 0.8 per cent in 2017–2018.[355] There has also been some perceptible increase in the reporting of crimes by victims in South Africa, which is partially attributable to increasing confidence in the legal system.[356] Such crime reporting is commendable as it facilitates action that not only punishes the perpetrators but deters future criminal activities. Further, there has been improvement on the proportion of household heads who expressed confidence in walking alone at night, from 29.4 per cent in 2016–2017 to 31.8 per cent in 2017–2018.[357] While there has been some progress in reducing occurrences of violent crime, South Africa acknowledges that it still remains a highly crime-laden state among those not affected by civil war.[358] This demonstrates the necessity for concerted and consistent efforts to reduce crime in the state.

There has been a general decrease in the crime rates in India which may partly be attributed to a sound legal framework for addressing and penalizing diverse forms of violence, and a robust civil society and media that aggressively complement the efforts of the government.[359] With regard to Kenya, it has been estimated that the proportion of victims of intentional homicide was 4 in a population of 100,000 in 2017, before decreasing to 3 in 2018 and then rising to 4 in 2019.[360] Nonetheless, there is great possibility that some incidences of intention homicide in Kenya were not accurately reported in order to be included in the statistics. Further, while the case in Kenya is not as

[351] See T> Republic of Ghana, *Ghana: Voluntary National Review Report on the Implementation of the 2030 Agenda for Sustainable Development* (National Development Planning Commission 2019) 69.
[352] ibid.
[353] T>Sustainable Development Goals Knowledge Platform, '2019 South Africa' (n 335) 101.
[354] ibid.
[355] ibid.
[356] ibid.
[357] ibid.
[358] ibid 100.
[359] Government of India, *India VNR 2020: Decade of Action—Taking SDGs from Global to Local* (National Institution for Transforming India 2020) 129.
[360] National Treasury and Planning, Republic of Kenya (n 333) 72.

1202   SDG 16

dire as in other states, there is nonetheless need for continued crime reduction efforts by the state.

Some of the legislative initiatives that have been undertaken in Jamaica to reduce crime include the adoption of the Deoxyribonucleic Acid (DNA) Evidence Act in 2016 and the Law Reform (Zones of Special Operations) (Special Security and Community Development Measures) Act in 2017, which are to assist in curbing crime that targets vulnerable communities.[361] Policy measures by Jamaica have included the inauguration of the Violence Interruption Programme in 2016, which prevents the escalation of conflict at the community level, and in which over 1,430 youths at risk of engagement in violence have participated.[362] In order to reduce violence and improve security, Uruguay is focusing on innovative fight against crime, through strategic increase in crime prevention and improved 'crime clearance rate'.[363] In that context, the destruction of apprehended, surrendered or found weapons in Uruguay increased by 15 per cent in 2020.[364] Nonetheless, there is still the challenge of eliminating gender-based violence, which is attributed to most of the homicide cases in which women are the victims.[365] The UK has noted that with cases of homicides and violence rising, it will remain a challenge to eliminate all forms of violence in the country.[366] Consequently, the UK is focused on conceptualizing and implementing serious violence strategies that include support for law enforcement, early interventions and deterrence, and multi-agency action.[367]

b) *Indicator 16.1.2 Conflict-related deaths per 100,000 population, by sex,*
   age, and cause

Other indicators for target 16.1 include 16.1.2 that evaluates the number of conflict related deaths by sex, age, and cause for every 100,000 people in the population, and is under the custody of Office of the United Nations High Commissioner for Human Rights (OHCHR). The continued prevalence of war and conflicts both within and across states remains a serious obstacle towards the realization of human rights, particularly the entitlement to life, and progress towards the full attainment of SDG 16.

i) **Empirical analysis** Indicator 16.1.2 has been justified by the UNSD on the premise that it evaluates the prevalence of armed conflicts and their impact on the loss of life.[368] The UNSD nonetheless acknowledges that a limitation of indicator 16.1.2 is the reality

---

[361] T>Planning Institute of Jamaica, *Jamaica Voluntary National Review on the Implementation of the 2030 Agenda for Sustainable Development* (Planning Institute of Jamaica 2018) 95.

[362] ibid.

[363] T>Sustainable Development Goals Knowledge Platform, 'Summary: Voluntary National Review—Uruguay 2021' 98 <https://sustainabledevelopment.un.org/content/documents/293422021_VNR_Report_Uruguay_English.pdf>T>accessed 21 October 2021.

[364] ibid.

[365] ibid.

[366] T>United Kingdom of Great Britain and Northern Ireland, *Voluntary National Review of Progress Towards the Sustainable Development Goals* (United Kingdom of Great Britain and Northern Ireland 2019) 202.

[367] ibid.

[368] T>UNSD, 'SDG Indicator Metadata' (3 December 2018).

that in armed conflict situations, a large number of deaths remain unreported.[369] In addition, in such circumstances, normal death registration systems are heavily impacted upon by the presence of armed conflict, and may not even function.[370] Further, the participants in an armed conflict may have incentives for misreporting, in the context of reducing or bloating the number of casualties for particular motives.[371]

According to the UNSD, approximately 82.4 million people, translating to approximately 1 per cent of the world population, had at the end of 2020 been displaced due to conflicts, violence and persecution.[372] The UNSD also highlighted the dire situation in which hundreds of millions of people live in conflict affected and fragile countries.[373] Armed conflicts persist, with diverse gross outcomes, among them being the egregious breach of human rights and international humanitarian law for all segments of the population, children included.[374] Pointing to the enduring challenges to human security and protection of human rights due to war, the UNSG Report observed that there had been 69,276 deaths of civilians in twelve of the deadliest armed conflicts globally between 2018 and 2020.[375] Further, the Report pointed out that 5 civilians were killed for every 100,000 people, in which 1 for each 7 murdered was either a woman or a child.[376]

The UNSD appreciated that despite the figures of civilian deaths due to armed conflicts globally remaining high, it nonetheless translated to a significant 61 per cent decline in the annual numbers of victims.[377] Even so, the Sub-Saharan Africa region was grimly in an opposite trajectory, with the UNSD noting that civilian deaths due to armed conflicts in the region increased.[378] This points out to a dire need for concerted international and local efforts for the pre-emption and stoppage of war and conflicts, in addition to peace building and the entrenchment of rule of law in the subject states within the Sub-Saharan Africa region.[379] The UNSD attributed the general reduction in civilian deaths worldwide to some of the deadliest wars becoming less fatal, in addition to more concerted efforts to augment the protection of civilians.[380] The UNSD further reports that for civilians that were killed in armed conflicts in 2020, one out of seven victims was either a child or woman.[381] This demonstrates that there is a significant proportion of women and children civilian victims in armed conflict, which requires special and informed responses in peace keeping and peace building efforts.

---

[369] ibid.
[370] ibid.
[371] ibid.
[372] T>UNDESA, Statistics Division, 'Peace, Justice and Strong Institutions' (2021) <https://unstats.un.org/sdgs/report/2021/goal-16/>T>accessed 18 July 2021.
[373] ibid.
[374] ibid.
[375] T>UNESC, UN Doc E/2021/58 (n 337) paras 168–169.
[376] ibid.
[377] T>UNDESA, Statistics Division, 'Peace, Justice and Strong Institutions' (n 372).
[378] ibid.
[379] ibid.
[380] ibid.
[381] ibid.

1204 SDG 16

ii) Implementation efforts In the case of Sub-Saharan states, peace and stability is gradually being entrenched in Sudan after decades of civil conflict in regions such as Darfur, South Kordofan, and the Blue Nile, which inhibited the country's capacity to progress.[382] There has been a gradual decrease of the number of internally displaced persons (IDPs), from 5 million in 2005 to fewer than 2 million in 2018.[383] According to Sudan, the emerging peace and stability trends are establishing an environment for post-conflict restructuring initiatives that will transform the people from being recipients of humanitarian relief to being active actors in sustainable development activities.[384] Among the noticeable contributions in the peace building and reconstruction efforts is the significant role of treating women impacted upon by the war at the Trauma Centre of the Ahfad University.[385] The University of Khartoum has also utilized its Peace Research Institute (PRI) to collaborate with the University of Nayala, and the University of Diling to establish a referential think-thank that brings together experts and intellectuals engaged in peace building discourses and research for the benefit of the country.[386] There has also been the engagement of local communities in peace building, particularly through reliance on customary laws that usually have greater legitimacy and acceptability at the community level.[387]

Some of the post conflict initiatives undertaken by Liberia include the strengthening of the County Peace Committees at district and county levels in order to promote and safeguard peace, reconciliation and social cohesion in communities.[388] The Ministry of Internal Affairs has also established the Liberia Early Warning and Response Network (LERN) Platform, which has included the deployment of reporters across the country, and providing capacity building to County Peace Committees.[389] There has also been progressive improvement in security in Angola since the cessation of the lengthy and destructive civil conflict in 2002.[390] Consequently, up to 65 per cent of the country's population has reported feeling safe walking alone in the areas in which they reside.[391]

iii) Critique The special focus of indicator 16.1.2 on widespread war and armed conflict, which imply cases that deserve intervention in the form of peace-keeping and peace-enforcement as a prerequisite for stopping violence before other peace-building initiatives can be undertaken, is commendable. It may provide essential data to guide peace-keeping and peace-enforcement efforts, and evaluate the appropriateness

---

[382] T>National Population Council, Sudan, *Voluntary National Review 2018: Implementation of Agenda 2030 and the SDGs for Peace and Development in the Sudan* (National Population Council 2018) 34.

[383] ibid.

[384] ibid.

[385] ibid 38.

[386] ibid.

[387] ibid.

[388] T>Sustainable Development Goals Knowledge Platform, 'Liberia: Voluntary National Review on the Implementation Status of the 2030 Agenda for Sustainable Development' (2020) 88 <https://sustainabledevelopment.un.org/content/documents/26288VNR_2020_Liberia_Report.pdf>T>accessed 23 October 2021.

[389] ibid 90.

[390] T>G de Angola, *Voluntary National Review on the Implementation of the 2030 Agenda for Sustainable Development* (Governo de Angola 2021)T>109.

[391] ibid 110.

and progress of such forms of intervention in conflict affected states. In addition, the obtained data may inform peace-building and post-conflict reconstruction efforts.

Peace-keeping is an impartial form of intervention in another state; it is executed with the consent of the parties to the conflict, and military force is only utilized for purposes of self-defence.[392] It is noteworthy that peace-keeping had originally been conceptualized by the UN to fill the lacuna occasioned by failure to undertake enforcement action under Chapter VII of the Charter, particularly in cases of conflict and war that required protection of civilians.[393] On the other part, peace-enforcement, also referred to as 'second generation peace-keeping operations', 'strategic peace-keeping', 'wider peace-keeping', and 'peace support operations', exemplifies the expanded roles for peace-keeping missions due to the changing nature of the post-Cold War conflicts.[394] These are phrases used to exemplify the grant of Chapter VII of the United Nations Charter enforcement powers to forces intervening in other states through a resolution of the UN Security Council.

After the cessation of the fighting, multifaceted approaches can be utilized for the purpose of peace-building and the institutionalization of the rule of law, in order to prevent the recurrence of the war.[395] In such instances, the data obtained through the utilization of indicator 16.1.2 may be helpful in devising the appropriate bottom-up peace-building and post-conflict recovery efforts, which are essential for purposes of creating sustainable peace. In the case of the Eastern part of the Democratic Republic of Congo (DRC), it has been observed that peace building through largely top-down approaches has been futile due to their failure to appropriately consider and resolve local causes. In that context, it has been suggested that a combination of both bottom-up and top-down approaches may have been of greater significance in institutionalizing peace in Eastern DRC, and preventing the occasional recurrence of widespread war.[396]

c) *Indicator 16.1.3 Proportion of population subjected to (a) physical violence,*
    (b) psychological violence and (c) sexual violence in the previous 12 months
Indicator 16.1.3, which is overseen by UNODC, measures the portion of the population, which, in the preceding period of twelve months, had been subjected to sexual, psychological, or physical violence.

i) **Empirical analysis and implementation efforts** The UNSD has justified the indicator on the premise that it assists in evaluating the prevalence of victimization on the basis of sexual, physical, and psychological violence.[397] Further, as the UNSD notes,

---

[392] R Zacklin, 'The Use of Force in Peacekeeping Operations' in N Blokker and N Schrijver (eds), *The Security Council and the Use of Force: Theory and Reality—A Need for Change?* (Martinus Nijhoff Publishers 2005) 91.

[393] E Suy, 'Is the United Nations Security Council Still Relevant? And Was It Ever?' (2004) 12 Tulane Journal of International and Comparative Law 7, 13.

[394] F Olonisakin, *Reinventing Peacekeeping in Africa: Conceptual and Legal Issues in ECOMOG Operations* (Kluwer Law International 2000) 6.

[395] T>Sustainable Development Knowledge Platform, 'Peace and Sustainable Development' (n 40).

[396] ibid.

[397] T>UNSD, 'SDG Indicator Metadata' (3 December 2018).

1206   SDG 16

the indicator has global utility since such forms of violence are a world-wide phenomenon, affecting all states.[398] The UNSD nonetheless cautions that considering most acts of violence remain largely unreported to authorities, there may be need to undertake sample surveys on the population in order to obtain more representative and reliable data.[399]

Exposure to physical violence, including that of a sexual nature continues to be prevalent. In the case of the states of Sub-Saharan Africa, it has been noted that despite safety appearing to have generally improved in Namibia, 15749 individuals encountered physical violence in 2020, with another 1,079 cases of sexual violence related abuse reported within the same period.[400] It is possible that the psychological impact of COVID-19 pandemic may have increased cases of physical and sexual violence in Namibia.[401] In Zambia, domestic violence is one of the most prevalent forms of violence against the female gender.[402] It is estimated that in Zambia, more than 36 per cent of the women aged between fifteen and forty-nine have experienced some form of physical violence since they were fifteen years of age.[403] Consequently, efforts aimed at elimination of physical and psychological violence in Zambia should also significantly focus on deterring gender-based violence.

In the case of Canada, despite having a high human development index (HDI), it has nonetheless been noted that Indigenous women and girls in the country are disproportionately subjected to all forms of violence due to factors that include socio-economic dynamics, such as poverty and homelessness, in addition to historical reasons such as racism and sexism.[404] Consequently, efforts to eliminate physical and psychological violence must significantly focus on eliminating the factors that have continued to contribute to the disproportionate gender-based violence on Indigenous women in Canada.

d) Indicator 16.1.4 Proportion of population that feel safe walking alone around
the area they live

The fraction of the population that feels safe to walk alone in the precincts of their habitats is measured by indicator 16.1.4, which is also under the custody of UNODC. The UNSD justifies the indicator on the premise that high incidences of fear of crime may be an impediment to development due to the likely results of less activities, reduced contact with the public, and reduced trust.[405] Nonetheless, the UNSD clarifies that the fear of crime does not necessarily imply that such incidences of the vice occur, as it is

---

[398] ibid.

[399] ibid.

[400] T>Republic of Namibia, *Namibia's Second Voluntary National Review Report on the Implementation of the Sustainable Development Goals towards Agenda 2030* (National Planning Commission 2021) 63.

[401] ibid.

[402] T>Republic of Zambia, *Zambia Sustainable Development Goals Voluntary National Review 2020* (Ministry of National Development Planning 2020) 72.

[403] ibid.

[404] Government of Canada, *Canada's Implementation of the 2030 Agenda for Sustainable Development* (Global Affairs Canada 2018) 112.

[405] T>UNSD, 'SDG Indicator Metadata' (19 July 2016).

independent of the actual occurrence.[406] Further, the fear may be influenced by factors such as personal circumstances, discussions, and awareness of crime.[407]

i) Empirical analysis and implementation efforts Some states in the Sub-Saharan Africa region have relatively a good rating in terms of safety. In the case of Rwanda, 83 per cent of residents stated in 2018 that they felt safe to walk alone at night in their habitats, and that they had confidence in the local police force, which implied that the country was the second safest in Africa at the time.[408] With regard to Uganda in 2017, there was an increase of the ratio of people who felt safe to walk alone at night to 61 per cent.[409] A 2019 survey in Namibia indicated that more people felt safe to walk alone at night due to the improvement of the level of safety in the country.[410] Namibia attributes that improvement to the expansion of surveillance cameras in the capital city, Windhoek, and the introduction of community policing projects in major towns.[411] The Safe City project was inaugurated in 2017 in Mauritius to sustain and improve safe working and living environments, in which surveillance cameras were installed across the island state.[412] Other interventions to improve safety in Mauritius have included amendments to the Firearms Act thus enabling better monitoring of firearms in the country, and the establishment of the Independent Police Complains Commission (IPCC), coupled with the installing of surveillance cameras in police stations and cells.[413]

According to Malaysia, the perception of feeling safe improved to 66 per cent in 2019, from 45 per cent in 2018 due to various initiatives, including the introduction and continued implementation of the Safe City Programme, illuminating dark spaces and lanes, installation of surveillance cameras, separation of pedestrian walks from motor roads, and the use of software applications by the public to report crime incidences.[414] In Singapore, the proportion of people with a perception of being safe in their neighbourhoods at night was 93 per cent, which is attributable to a highly effective police force that has resulted in extremely low crime rates.[415] Australia's ranking as a highly safe country is attributable to the citizens and residents supporting public safety objectives that include strict regulation of firearms, and stiff penalties for their trafficking.[416]

---

[406] ibid.
[407] ibid.
[408] Republic of Rwanda, *2019 Rwanda Voluntary National Review (VNR) Report* (Republic of Rwanda 2019) 58.
[409] Republic of Uganda, *Voluntary National Review Report on the Implementation of the 2030 Agenda for Sustainable Development* (Office of the Prime Minister 2020) 68.
[410] T>Republic of Namibia (n 400) 63.
[411] ibid.
[412] T>Ministry of Foreign Affairs, Regional Integration and International Trade, Mauritius, *Voluntary National Review Report of Mauritius 2019* (Ministry of Foreign Affairs, Regional Integration and International Trade 2019) 104.
[413] ibid.
[414] Economic Planning Unit, Malaysia, *Malaysia Voluntary National Review (VNR) 2021* (Economic Planning Unit 2021) 107.
[415] Ministry of Foreign Affairs, Singapore, *Towards a Sustainable and Resilient Singapore* (Ministry of Foreign Affairs 2018) 63.
[416] Australian Government (n 179) 103.

1208   SDG 16

ii) Critique of Target 16.1 Indicators There are some discernible concerns regarding the limitations of the target 16.1 indicators. The first concern is whether the generally conceptualized target 16.1 can orient focus on addressing specific causes of violence, such as conflicts generated by the shortcomings on land tenure and access rights to land-based resources. There was need to integrate the evaluation and measurement, within the SDG 16.1 indicators, the core issue of property rights, and particularly access to land and land-based resources, as it is a major factor that causes and sustains conflicts and violence. The issue of land tenure rights as a cause of conflicts was a topical matter that was given special attention during OWG activities that conceptualized the targets and their indicators.[417] It is noteworthy that the IOM hosted a side event during the Eighth Session of the OWG on SDGs under the theme of 'land tenure and property rights as tools for promoting peace building and durable peace' due to concerns in respect to the significant role of land and land based resources in igniting and fuelling conflicts.[418] In particular, the OWG acknowledged that among the resolutions reached in the event was that institutionalization of sustainable peace often required special attention be given to the issue of access to land, land tenure and property rights.[419] Consequently, it was suggested that a core element of the UN Post-2015 Development Agenda, as espoused under the SDG framework, should be in relation to the issue of access to land, land tenure, and property rights.[420]

A second concern relates to gender perspectives of violence. Based on the multifaceted effects of violence against women, there would have been the need for targets and indicators that would have evaluated the impact of gender-based violence on sustainable development with greater particularity and specificity.[421] During the OWG sessions, the UN Special Rapporteur on Violence against Women, Its Causes and Consequences had proposed a framework of targets and indicators that was 'broad enough to incorporate all forms of violence against women that affect sustainable development, but [also] specific enough to articulate clear, concise and measurable standards [that] all states may strive to achieve.'[422]

2. Target 16.2 End abuse, exploitation, trafficking and all forms of violence against and torture of children

The objective of target 16.2 is to end abuse, exploitation, trafficking, and diverse forms of violence against children. The indicators under target 16.2 are interconnected with some of the targets and indicators of SDG 5 which focuses on the empowerment of women and girls, and the entrenchment of gender equality. There is also correlation with target 8.7 of SDG 8, which focuses on the eradication of diverse forms of child labour, human trafficking, and slavery.

---

[417] See T> Sustainable Development Knowledge Platform, 'Land Tenure and Property Rights' (n 38).
[418] ibid.
[419] ibid.
[420] ibid.
[421] T>Sustainable Development Knowledge Platform, 'Submission by Prof Rashida Manjoo' (n 42).
[422] ibid.

a) Indicator 16.2.1 Proportion of children aged 1–17 years who experienced any physical punishment and/or psychological aggression by caregivers in the past month

Indicator 16.2.1, which is administered by UNICEF, evaluates the ratio of children aged one to seventeen years who may have experienced any form of psychological aggression or physical punishment from care givers within the previous month. The UNSD has pointed out that millions of children in the world are still exposed to diverse modes of exploitation, particularly through trafficking and child labour.[423]

i) Empirical analysis In his 2021 Report, the UNSG regretted that even before the outbreak of the COVID-19 pandemic in early 2019 there was the prevalence of violence against children that affected victims without regard to social status.[424] The UNSD cautions that the risk of children to exploitation, abuse and trafficking is increasing as the COVID-19 epidemic ravages on, particularly due to the ensuing economic distress and incidences of occasional closure of schools to curb the pandemic.[425] The Report particularly pointed out that data from seventy-seven states and territories for the period ranging from 2012 to 2020 indicated the dire case of eight in ten children, of ages one to fourteen years, as having been the subject of 'some form of psychological aggression or physical punishment at home in the previous month'.[426] With regard to statistics for 2020 in percentage, Sub-Saharan Africa had the highest number of such incidences at 84.9 per cent, with other regions statistics being respectively 83.7 per cent for Northern Africa, 82.7 per cent for LDCs, 82.5 per cent for Northern Africa and Western Asia, 69.3 per cent for SIDS, and 62.9 per cent for Central Asia.[427]

ii) Implementation efforts In the case of Nigeria, there is the perception that the domestication of the Convention on the Rights of the Child, and the adoption of the Child Rights Act (CRA) significantly contributed to the reduction of incidences of child abuse.[428] The CRA establishes offences and imprisonment sentences for violence against children and the trafficking of persons.[429] Indonesia is still confronted by substantive numbers of cases of children bullying, with 21 per cent of children of ages thirteen to fifteen years have been subjected to bullying within the previous month in 2015.[430] As an intervention and deterrence to children bullying in schools, Indonesia

---

[423] UNDESA, Statistics Division, 'Peace, Justice and Strong Institutions' (n 372).

[424] UNESC, UN Doc E/2021/58 (n 337) para 170.

[425] UNDESA, Statistics Division, 'Peace, Justice and Strong Institutions' (n 372).

[426] UNESC, UN Doc E/2021/58 (n 337) para 170.

[427] The statistics are in a supplementary annexure to UNGA Resolution E/2021/58. See UNESC, UN Doc E/2021/58 (n 337) 'Supplementary Information' 188.

[428] Office of the Senior Special Assistant to the President on SDGs, Nigeria, *Nigeria: Integration of the SDGs into National Development Planning—A Second Voluntary National Review* (Office of the Senior Special Assistant to the President on SDGs 2020) 71. See Convention on the Rights of the Child (n 94).

[429] Office of the Senior Special Assistant to the President on SDGs, Nigeria (n 428) 71.

[430] T>Republic of Indonesia, *Indonesia's Voluntary National Review (VNR) 2021: Sustainable and Resilient Recovery from the COVID-19 Pandemic for the Achievement of the 2030 Agenda* (Republic of Indonesia 2021) T> 325.

1210 SDG 16

has designed and is implementing programmes aimed at building a positive school climate that include student-led activities.[431]

b) *Indicator 16.2.2 Number of victims of human trafficking per 100,000 population, by sex, age and form of exploitation*

The UNODC manages data relating to indicator 16.2.2, which measures the proportion of victims of trafficking for every 100,000 people, with the data segregated to aspects of age, gender, and the form of exploitation that instigated the trafficking of the subject.

i) Empirical analysis According to the UNSD, there have been incidences of human trafficking in every state.[432] Nonetheless, those engaged in the trafficking are more likely to target the improvised and marginalized, including children.[433] According to the UNSD, one in every three victims of trafficking in 2018 was a child, and the low-income states had half of the shares of the global incidences.[434] The 2021 Report of the UNSG projects similar statistics in relation to the percentage of juvenile victims, by observing that approximately one-third of the victims of trafficking were children.[435] The 2021 UNSG Report pointed out that approximately 38 per cent of the victims were trafficked for purposes of forced labour, while another 50 per cent was for purposes of sexual exploitation.[436] While the UNSD points out that the girls were primarily trafficked for purposes of sexual exploitation, with 72 per cent of the victims subjected to such form of abuse, it also noted that boys were largely trafficked for purposes of forced labour, with 66 per cent of such male juvenile victims subjected to such exploitation.[437] The UNSD statistics and UNSG Report indicate the need for efforts that include special focus on the eradication of the causes of children trafficking.

The UNSD observes that the trafficking of children and their exploitation for labour are closely interlinked, with states recording higher levels of juvenile labour also demonstrating a larger share of the trafficking of minors.[438] The UNSD points to a worrying trend of a recent increase in the child labour for the first time in two decades, which may have been fuelled by the impact of COVID-19 pandemic.[439] The 2021 UNSG Report had particularly cautioned that the aggravation of unemployment by COVID-19 pandemic was likely to result in increased incidences of human trafficking.[440] In that context, the UNSD points out that:

---

[431] ibid 325–26.
[432] T>UNDESA, Statistics Division, 'Peace, Justice and Strong Institutions' (n 372).
[433] ibid.
[434] ibid.
[435] T>UNESC, UN Doc E/2021/58 (n 337) para 171.
[436] ibid.
[437] T>UNDESA, Statistics Division, 'Peace, Justice and Strong Institutions' (n 372).
[438] ibid.
[439] ibid.
[440] UNESC, UN Doc E/2021/58 (n 337) para 171.

[a]t the start of 2020, the number of children engaged in child labour (not including its worst forms, such as children in bonded and forced labour or in commercial sexual exploitation) totalled 160 million (63 million girls and 97 million boys). This translates to almost 1 in 10 children worldwide. Nearly half of children in child labour were engaged in hazardous work (79 million).[441]

The UNSD proceeds to caution that an additional 8.9 million children are likely to have been driven into juvenile labour by the end of 2022 due to the impact of the COVID-19 pandemic, as families are compelled to send children to work in response to decreased income and job losses.[442] It is in that context that the UNSD calls for concerted efforts by states and other relevant actors to urgently expand social protection and income support, which may be helpful in offsetting the menace of the rise in child labour.[443]

ii) Implementation efforts The HLPFSD has appreciated the improvement in the detection of the human trafficking victims, which is helpful in curbing the menace.[444] Highlighting the need for more gender-sensitive approaches to addressing the menace of trafficking, the HLPFSD has observed that the female gender comprises the majority of the victims of human trafficking, particularly due to sexual exploitation motives and objectives.[445]

In its voluntary national review of 2018, Sudan pointed out that the presence of illegal immigrants, vulnerable populations and huge populations of refugees in the country makes the state a source, transit point, and destination of human trafficking.[446] It is in the context of eliminating the menace of human trafficking that Sudan adopted the Anti-Trafficking Act in 2014, in addition to creating the National Committee for Combating Human Trafficking.[447] In addition, the Government of Sudan also established the Rapid Emergency Taskforce and Response Unit to address trafficking crimes in the eastern region of the country.[448]

Liberia has acknowledged, in its 2020 VNR, that trafficking of children remains a serious challenge and predicament particularly as legislation proscribing the menace is not adequately implemented.[449] Often, parents in impoverished and vulnerable rural situations are enticed with promises of better education and livelihood of their children, who are then trafficked into the city and are engaged in diverse forms of exploitation, including commercial sexual activities, and selling of merchandise in the streets.[450]

---

[441] T>UNDESA, Statistics Division, 'Peace, Justice and Strong Institutions' (n 372).

[442] ibid.

[443] ibid.

[444] T>HLPFSD, 'Discussion on SDG 16 – Peace, Justice and Strong Institutions: Background Note' (2019) <https://sustainabledevelopment.un.org/content/documents/23621BN_SDG16.pdf> accessed 12 June 2021.

[445] ibid. See also, UNESC, UN Doc E/2021/58 (n 337) para 171.

[446] T>National Population Council, Sudan (n 382) 39.

[447] ibid.

[448] ibid.

[449] T>Sustainable Development Goals Knowledge Platform, 'Liberia' (n 388) 100.

[450] ibid.

1212 SDG 16

With regard to Namibia, though the proportion of human trafficking is generally low, there has nonetheless been some increase in the number of cases in recent years.[451] For instance, there were seven cases of human trafficking recorded in 2020, with five of the cases being related to sexual exploitation, and the other two of the incidences being work-related.[452] Namibia acknowledges that although the occurrence of the menace is still relatively low, 'one life trafficked is [still] far too many', and as such, is still engaged in concerted efforts to curb the vice.[453]

As a mechanism of fighting against the perils of human trafficking, Jamaica in 2015 created the Office of the National Rapporteur on Trafficking in Persons for purposes of coordinating the various agencies involved in governmental action against the menace.[454] One of the notable achievements was the recording in 2015 of the first case of conviction for human trafficking in the state, in addition to further two convictions in 2016.[455] Jamaica has also adopted and implemented the 'Break the Silence' crusade since June 2015 to sensitize and improve the reporting of child abuse cases, which has had the positive impact of increased reporting of incidences.[456] It is also noteworthy that some 3,702 children benefited from Jamaica's Victim Services Division Children in Court programme, which has the objective of reducing the ordeal that children who interact with the justice system are exposed to.[457]

There had been 1,780 trafficking cases, with 9,594 of the victims rescued in Malaysia from 2015 to the time of compiling the state's VNR in 2021 for work related and sexual exploitation purposes.[458] Some of the initiatives by the Government of Malaysia to curb the vice have included the implementation of the Anti-Trafficking in Persons and Anti-Smuggling of Migrants Act of 2007, in which the Council for Anti-Trafficking in Persons and Anti-Smuggling of Migrants was established.[459] The UK has also pointed out that curbing the vices of all forms of violence against children, including trafficking, abuse, and exploitation, remains its core priority, whether locally or abroad.[460] Consequently, the United Kingdom's VNR of 2019 points out that the state has been funding the Child Trafficking Protection Fund to research and implement innovative modes of protecting susceptible children who are at a risk of trafficking, whether in the UK or in foreign states.[461]

---

[451] T>Republic of Namibia (n 400) 64.
[452] ibid.
[453] ibid.
[454] T>Planning Institute of Jamaica (n 361) 95.
[455] ibid.
[456] ibid.
[457] ibid.
[458] T>Economic Planning Unit, Malaysia (n 414) 108.
[459] ibid.
[460] T>United Kingdom of Great Britain and Northern Ireland (n 366) 193.
[461] ibid.

c) Indicator 16.2.3 Proportion of young women and men aged 18–29 years who experienced sexual violence by age 18

The ratio of the young women and men aged eighteen to twenty-nine years who will have experienced sexual violence by the age of eighteen years is the subject of indicator 16.2.3, and is under the auspices of UNICEF. The UNSD explains that sexual violence 'is one of the most unsettling of children's rights violations', with the consequences having an impact even in adulthood, through mental health challenges and adverse behavioural outcomes.[462] According to the UNSD, indicator 16.2.3 documents 'one of the gravest forms of violence against children' for a matter that is universally relevant.[463]

i) Empirical analysis and implementation efforts With regard to 2019 statistics demonstrating the extent of sexual violence in percentage, the Sub-Saharan Africa was leading at 5.4 per cent, with the other groupings being at 4.8 per cent for the LDCs, 4.2 per cent for the LLDCs, and 1.5 per cent for both Southern Asia, and Central and Southern Asia.[464]

With regard to Uganda, approximately 25 per cent of girls and 11 per cent of boys were reported to have been exposed to incidences of sexual violence within the year preceding 2016, which had largely been perpetuated by strangers and neighbours.[465] This high level of prevalence of sexual violence among children in Uganda was regrettably consistent with higher occurrence of such incidences in Sub-Saharan Africa compared to other regions.

As a mechanism of addressing the vice of child trafficking, abuse, and exploitation, India ratified the Convention on the Rights of the Child, in addition to adopting diverse legal and policy measures to address particular categories and age groups of children.[466] India's National Policy for Children enunciates priorities across broad areas, while the laws deal with particular matters in relation to the protection of children, such as proscription of sexual exploitation of children, and their labour and trafficking; provision of care; and access to education, among others.[467]

3. Target 16.3 Promote the rule of law at the national and international levels and ensure equal access to justice for all

Target 16.3 is premised on the idea that there is an interdependent and mutual reinforcement between the entrenchment of the national and international rule of law with access to justice. The target is reasonably premised on the notion that the institutionalization of the principles of the rule of law will enhance access to justice. That conceptualization of target 16.3 is justifiable as access to justice is also, as has been

---

[462] T>UNSD, 'SDG Indicator Metadata' (March 2021).
[463] ibid.
[464] UNESC, UN Doc E/2021/58 (n 337) 'Supplementary Information' 189.
[465] Republic of Uganda (n 409) 69.
[466] T>Government of India (n 359) 129.
[467] ibid.

1214 SDG 16

observed, an essential component of the rule of law.[468] The interdependence with rule of law is evident in its incorporation of 'the right to a fair trial, equal access to and equality before the courts, and the seeking and obtaining of just, enforceable and timely remedies for human rights violations'.[469]

a) Indicator 16.3.2 Unsentenced detainees as a proportion of overall prison population
i) Empirical analysis Demonstrating the continued global gap in the access to justice by a significant part of the population, the 2020 UNSG Report notes that millions of people still live in circumstances in which they are denied access to justice, protection of human rights, and security.[470] As an indication of lack of good progress in respect to access to justice, the 2020 Report indicates that statistics from 2016 to 2018 demonstrate that the proportion of prisoners placed in detention without being sentenced for any crime remains the same as in 2005, at 31 per cent.[471] Such data are premised on indicator 16.3.2, which measures the ratio of sentenced detainees in relation to the overall prison population, and is under the custody of UNODC. The 2021 UNSG Report noted that there have been no changes to the statistics reported in 2020, with 31 per cent of those in detention constituting individuals held before sentencing.[472] The indicator is premised on the rule of law and notion of the right to a fair trial, which imply that individuals awaiting judicial trial should not be held in custody unnecessarily and for unreasonable periods.[473] It is also premised on the right to the fair trial concept of being presumed innocent until proven guilty.[474] It is also noteworthy that, from a developmental perspective, the UNSD has explained that:

> From a development perspective, extensive use of pre-sentence detention when not necessary ... can divert criminal justice system resources, and exert financial and unemployment burdens on the accused and his or her family. Measuring the relative extent to which pre-sentence detention is used can provide the evidence to assist countries in lowering such burdens and ensuring its proportionate use.[475]

The 2019 statistics in respect to the percentage of detainees who were yet to be sentenced by region indicates that Central and Southern Asia were leading at 58 per cent, followed by Sub-Saharan Africa at 40 per cent.[476] The percentage for the other regions and groupings were, respectively, 36 per cent for Latin America and the Caribbean, 30 per cent for both Oceania region and the Eastern and South-Eastern Asia, 28 per cent

---

[468] T>UNGA, 'Right to Access to Justice for Persons with Albinism: Report of the Independent Expert on the Enjoyment of Human Rights by Persons with Albinism' UN Doc A/HRC/40/62 (15 January 2019) para 15.
[469] ibid.
[470] T>UNESC, UN Doc E/2020/57 (n 336) para 130.
[471] ibid para 134.
[472] UNESC, UN Doc E/2021/58 (n 337) para 172.
[473] T>UNSD, 'SDG Indicator Metadata' (19 July 2016).
[474] ibid.
[475] ibid.
[476] T>UNESC, UN Doc E/2021/58 (n 337) 'Supplementary Information' 189.

for Australia and New Zealand, 21 per cent for Europe and Northern America, and 20 per cent for Northern Africa and West Asia.[477]

ii) Implementation efforts Indicating a high level of prevalence of detaining individuals not yet convicted in Kenya, which is consistent with the cited relatively high numbers in the Sub-Saharan Africa, the proportion of detainees already sentenced in the prison population was 55.9 per cent in 2014, and they increased to 60.5 per cent in 2016.[478] That implies that the rest of the prison population within that period comprised detainees who were yet to be sentenced, which was relatively high. While the statistics are relatively old, they nonetheless indicate the necessity to reflect upon and implement prompt and swift trials for those accused of offences in Kenya, and to grant fair bail and bond terms for less serious offences and misdemeanours as a mechanism of promoting access to justice. There was a marginal drop in the proportion of individuals held in detention before sentencing in Ghana, with the ratio dropping to 13.14 per cent of the total prison population in 2018, from 18.24 per cent in 2015.[479] Diverse stakeholders in the criminal justice system are credited with the progressive trend in Ghana through their interventions to protect and safeguard the rights of pre-trial detainees.[480]

Malaysia highlighted, in its 2021 VNR, the predicament occasioned by COVID-19 pandemic, which have further accentuated the dire situation of congestion in its prisons, with detainees not yet sentenced having increased to 27.5 per cent of the total population in 2019, from 26.5 per cent in 2017.[481] Consequently, as a mechanism of further addressing the problem of congestion in prisons and formulating general detention reforms, an All-Party Parliamentary Group Malaysia for the Reform of All Places of Detention was established in 2020.[482]

b) Indicator 16.3.3 Proportion of the population who have experienced a dispute in the past two years and who accessed a formal or informal dispute resolution mechanism, by type of mechanism

Indicator 16.3.3 documents the proportion of individuals in the population who have encountered a dispute within the previous two years and were able to access a formal or informal dispute resolution mechanism. The custodial agencies of indicator 16.3.3 are the UNODC, the United Nations Development Programme (UNDP), and the OECD.

i) Empirical evaluation methodology The indicator provides crucial information on the overall accessibility of justice institutions, existing obstacles to the process, and the reasons for the exclusion of some people from the system.[483] Segregating between

---

[477] ibid.

[478] Ministry of Devolution and Planning, Kenya, *Implementation of the Agenda 2030 for Sustainable Development in Kenya* (Ministry of Devolution and Planning 2017) 44.

[479] T>Republic of Ghana (n 351) 72.

[480] ibid.

[481] Economic Planning Unit, Malaysia (n 414) 109.

[482] ibid.

[483] UNSD, 'SDG Indicator Metadata' (June 2020).

1216   SDG 16

formal and informal dispute resolution systems assists in obtaining data about the channels preferred by individuals in the enforcement and protection of their rights and interests.[484] There are some merits of reliance on indicator 16.3.3 as conceptualized in measuring access to justice. For instance, it evaluates access to justice from the perspective of those that are confronted by justiciable problems, and it is, thus, people-centred.[485] Data relating to the indicator can be produced on the basis of few survey questions, which can easily be amalgamated into ongoing state surveys.[486] Further, it provides a mechanism for the broad evaluation of peoples' approach to the resolution of the problems that confront them both within and outside of the formal justice institutions.[487]

ii) Implementation efforts Based on the history of conflict that affected state institutions in recent decades, Sierra Leone has performed commendably on the issue of improving access to justice.[488] There has been appointment of High Court judges and magistrates across the country, with a special focus on improving the opportunities of accessing justice in the rural regions.[489] In addition, since the 2015 formation of the Legal Aid Board of Sierra Leone, it has provided legal assistance in the form of advice and representation, among others, to more than 400,000 individuals as of 2021.[490]

Legal Aid South Africa also undertakes a significant role in promoting access to justice in South Africa, by providing quality civil and criminal legal representation and advice services. From 2014 to 2019, the entity has handled approximated 274,782 civil matters and 1,902,251 criminal cases, and granted legal advice services to 1,565,890 individuals.[491] It is also noteworthy that the entity has engaged in strategic litigation in the form of undertaking class actions and instituting legal proceedings to determine constitutional and fundamental issues that safeguard the rights and interests of the indigent and vulnerable sections of the population.[492] South Africa has also improved access to justice through collaboration between the formal and community justice institutions.[493]

In the case of Liberia, the justice sector has progressively contributed to access to justice through increased adjunction, effective administration of courts, and reduction of pre-trial detainees, despite a history of decades of vicious civil war that destroyed the country's institutions.[494] The adjudication rate of disputes is progressively increasing, with 63.28 per cent of cases having been resolved between January 2018 and June 2019, which amounted to an improvement of 13.28 per cent.[495] Some of the approaches in

[484] ibid.
[485] ibid.
[486] ibid.
[487] ibid.
[488] Government of Sierra Leone, *2021 VNR Report on SDGs in Sierra Leone* (Ministry of Planning and Economic Development 2021) 30.
[489] ibid.
[490] ibid.
[491] Sustainable Development Goals Knowledge Platform, '2019 South Africa' (n 335) 107.
[492] ibid.
[493] ibid.
[494] Sustainable Development Goals Knowledge Platform, 'Liberia' (n 388) 91.
[495] ibid.

the justice sector that have resulted in increased adjudication rate of criminal and civil disputes include establishment of court inspectorate offices, training of formal and informal justice actors, construction of additional courts, development of guidelines on legal reform and parliamentary oversight, and implementation of the mapping exercise for the security sector.[496] With regard to Rwanda, it focuses on improving access to justice through, among others, modernizing the civil, administrative, criminal, and commercial disputes adjudication systems; speedy execution of judgments; and promoting legal aid, particularly to the poor and vulnerable sections of the population.[497]

India, through the concept of 'together with all, development for all, the trust of all', has made sustained efforts to end discrimination and exclusion of people belonging to different socio-economic strata, including in the context of access to justice.[498] In particular, there has been the adoption of legislation and policies, and establishment of appropriate schemes and programmes for purposes of enhancing protection and enforcement of fundamental rights of Indian citizens.[499] In the case of Jamaica, the 2018 VNR highlights the access to justice initiatives that include the adoption in 2015 of the Justice Reform Implementation Plan, formulated to guide reform initiatives for the period leading to 2020.[500] The court infrastructure system has been upgraded, refurbished, and expanded in order to improve the quality and provision of justice services.[501] There has also been the automating of cases and documents management through the implementation of a case management system.[502] Also noteworthy is the installation of video-link technology to the Supreme Court, some other courts, and in some mobile units in order to facilitate virtual testifying by witnesses unable to physically attend court.[503]

Article 5(3) of the Constitution of Malaysia guarantees the right to justice, including through recourse to legal aid for every individual.[504] Consequently, there has been the provision of legal assistance through both governmental and private entities.[505] For instance, the Legal Aid Department, established in 1970, has provided diverse legal services in the form of litigation and mediation in criminal, civil and *Syariah* matters.[506] Further, the Malaysian Bar Council established in 1982 the Legal Aid Centre, which provides legal representation, intervention, and counsel to the indigent and underprivileged sections of the society.[507] There is also the National Legal Aid Foundation, which was established in 2011 through the model of public–private collaboration for the purposes of granting legal assistance.[508]

---

[496] ibid.
[497] Republic of Rwanda (n 408) 60.
[498] Government of India (n 359) 129.
[499] ibid.
[500] Planning Institute of Jamaica (n 361) 96.
[501] ibid.
[502] ibid.
[503] ibid.
[504] Economic Planning Unit, Malaysia (n 414) 109.
[505] ibid.
[506] ibid.
[507] ibid.
[508] ibid.

1218   SDG 16

Canada's VNR of 2018 points out that as a parliamentary democracy the state is founded upon the principles of good governance, adherence to the rule of law and peaceful coexistence.[509] In addition, the notion that all people are equal before the law is at the core of the Charter of Rights and Freedoms of the state.[510] Consequently, facilitating access to justice for all has been essential in ensuring that the protections afforded to all under the principle of the rule of law also reach the indigent, and vulnerable, in the Canadian society.[511] In that context, a broad evaluation of the criminal justice system is being undertaken by the Canadian government in order to reduce overrepresentation of vulnerable sections of populations.[512] In addition, as of 2018, the government was engaged in consultations with the populace in order to determine appropriate reforms that would not only render justice more accessible, but also fair and relevant.[513]

According to Singapore, its fidelity to the rule of law concept has had the outcome of institutionalizing a sense of justice and security upon its populace.[514] Consequently, confidence has been entrenched among business enterprises, which value and thrive in an environment in which proprietary rights and interests, and contracts, are appreciated, protected, and enforced.[515] For purposes of improving access to justice, *pro bono* (free) legal services are granted to deserving individuals through collaboration between the government, the Law Society of Singapore, and diverse volunteer entities.[516] Singapore's tradition of affording access to justice though its fidelity to the rule of law principles has contributed to its swift economic and social progression.

With regard to the UK, it is working to render its criminal justice system more just and fair, and ensure that it promotes equality.[517] This is partly due to a review undertaken in 2017, which indicated mistrust of the justice system by ethnic minority groups, including Black and Asian, and underscored the necessity of addressing barriers limiting access to justice.[518] Some of the reformation progress as of 2018 included increasing 'the diversity of those working in the criminal justice system', undertaking a pilot project in respect of 'alternatives to prosecution for those who are eligible', and addressing disparate outcomes in criminal system procedures.[519]

---

[509] Government of Canada (n 404) 113.
[510] ibid.
[511] ibid 111.
[512] ibid 113.
[513] ibid.
[514] Ministry of Foreign Affairs, Singapore (n 415) 61.
[515] ibid.
[516] ibid 62.
[517] United Kingdom of Great Britain and Northern Ireland (n 366) 195.
[518] ibid.
[519] ibid.

COMMENTARY ON TARGETS 1219

4. Target 16.4 By 2030, significantly reduce illicit financial and arms flows, strengthen
   the recovery and return of stolen assets and combat all forms of organized crime

Target 16.4 is also connected to bribery and corruption, which are articulated in target 16.5, as they are also a basis of and enabler of illicit financial flows, stealing of public assets, and organized crime.

*a) Indicator 16.4.1 Total value of inward and outward illicit financial flows
   (in current United States dollars)*

Indicator 16.4.1 measures the amount of inward and outward illicit financial flows, and is under the auspices of UNODC and UNCTAD. The UNSD explains that criminal activities and proscribed tax-related practices often contribute to IFFs, with the proscribed monetary gains being laundered between states, and are a significant challenge to sustainable development particularly in the developing states due to their draining of resources.[520] Consequently, as opined by the UNSD, combating illicit financial flows is crucial in facilitating a robust progress towards the realization of the SDG 16 objective of peace, justice, and resilient institutions.[521] It is noteworthy that IFFs involve activities considered criminal, and may be in the context of illicit commercial and tax practices.[522] As such, definitions developed under the auspices of ICCS provide descriptions for relevant offences in the context of IFFs.[523] According to UNSD, the four core activities that result in IFFs are corruption; illicit tax and commercial undertakings; financing of terrorism and crime, and exploitation type activities that entail the forced and illicit transfer of economic resources between two actors; and participation in illegal markets.[524]

i) Empirical statistics and implementation According to the 2021 VNR of Angola, IFFs have been as high as 3.9 per cent of the country's gross domestic product (GDP) in the 2013–2015 period.[525] Nonetheless, Angola views its proportion of IFF's as being lower than the average among African states, which it ranks at 10 per cent.[526] Some of the actions the government of Angola is focused on include strengthening its national institutions and international partnerships for purposes of elimination of IFFs and corruption, and recovery of stolen funds from foreign states.[527]

Nigeria acknowledges the vulnerability of oil exporting states to IFFs, especially through tax evasion, biased granting of tax waivers, failure to invoice sales, and diversion of exports.[528] The IFFs problem in Nigeria is exacerbated by the fact that oil and gas

[520] UNSD, 'SDG Indicator Metadata' (1 October 2020).
[521] ibid.
[522] ibid.
[523] ibid.
[524] ibid.
[525] Governo de Angola (n 390) 110.
[526] ibid.
[527] ibid.
[528] Office of the Senior Special Assistant to the President on SDGs, Nigeria (n 428) 66.

1220   SDG 16

related products accounted for an estimated 92 per cent of the exports as of 2018.[529] The dire burden of illicit financial flows in Nigeria has been demonstrated by the Executive Secretary of the Nigeria Extractive Industries Transparency Initiative, who has approximated that of the estimated $50–60 billion lost by African states to IFFs, Nigeria's contribution is approximately a whopping 30 per cent of the loss.[530] Consequently, the government of Nigeria is taking action to recover and repatriate stolen financial revenue, including funds deposited in foreign states.[531] In that context, Nigeria has in some instances succeeded in repatriation of IFFs, the most noteworthy being the tracing, relocation, and repatriation of $504 million, which is part of the $3 billion stolen by General Sani Abacha, a former head of state.[532] Nonetheless, such recovery of IFF's is problematic, as was demonstrated by the five-year judicial and diplomatic process to trace, recover, and repatriate the stated looted funds.[533]

b) *Indicator 16.4.2 Proportion of seized, found or surrendered arms whose illicit origin or context has been traced or established by a competent authority in line with international instruments*

Indicator 16.4.2 evaluates the proportion of recovered arms whose illicit origin has been determined by a competent authority. The UNSD explains that since it may be practically problematic to evaluate the types and prevalence of illicit arms flows due to the underground and clandestine nature of the activities, the indicator does not focus on measuring such aspects, but rather is oriented towards assessing 'the efficiency with which the international community combats the phenomenon of illicit arms trafficking'.[534]

i) **Empirical analysis and implementation** Kenya has continued in its concerted efforts to recover small arms and light weaponry as a mechanism of safeguarding and improving both the state and regional peace and security. For instance, in 2019 Kenya recovered a total of 988 small arms and light weaponry.[535] In the case of Jamaica, as part of efforts to curb terrorism and organized crime, there was the 2015 merger of the Organised Crime Investigation Division and the Flying Squad by establishing the Counter-Terrorism and Organised Crime Investigation Branch.[536] Some of the positive outcomes have been the recovery of 143 firearms, 3,809 rounds of ammunition, and crime-related money that was confiscated on the basis of the Proceeds of Crime Act in 2016.[537] A strategic review of the Major Organised Crime and Anti-Corruption Agency (MOCA) has also been undertaken for purposes of enabling the entity operate

---

[529] ibid.
[530] ibid.
[531] ibid 66–67.
[532] ibid.
[533] ibid.
[534] UNSD, 'SDG Indicator Metadata' (26 July 2018).
[535] National Treasury and Planning, Republic of Kenya (n 333) 72.
[536] Planning Institute of Jamaica (n 361) 96.
[537] ibid.

independently.[538] MOCA conducted 489 operations between 2015 and 2016, which resulted in the arrest of 367 individuals, of which 300 were prosecuted for various offences, including organized crime, economic criminalities, public sector corruption, and police fraud.[539]

ii) Critique of target 16.4 indicators Given that target 16.4 includes the strengthening of the recovery and return of stolen assets, there is a glaring lack of an indicator to evaluate such aspects, which are nonetheless essential towards the deterrence of corruption and facilitation of sustainable development. Given the highlighted conceptualization of the target, it is arguable that there was need for a further indicator to measure recovery and repatriation of looted assets given that such action can significantly deter pillage of public assets by public officials, in addition to facilitating the return of financially valuable assets for utilization in the developmental processes of the state.

5. Target 16.5 Substantially reduce corruption and bribery in all their forms

The reduction of bribery and corruption in all its manifestations is the concern of target 16.5. The UNSD highlights the stark reality of corruption by pointing out that:

> Corruption is antithetical to sustainable development, aggravating income inequality, reducing domestic and foreign investment, and significantly lowering the quality of public sector services. Yet it is commonplace in many countries to be asked to pay bribes to access essential public services related to health care, education, water, electricity and the justice system. A country's social and economic development is a key factor in corruption risk.[540]

According to the UNSD, there is more than five times a chance of bribery in a low-income state than in a high-income.[541] In the period ranging from 2011 to 2020, the average rate of bribery in the high-income states was 7.2 per cent, compared to 37.6 per cent for the low-income states according to data obtained from 120 countries and territories.[542]

a) Indicator 16.5.1 Proportion of persons who had at least one contact with a public official and who paid a bribe to a public official, or were asked for a bribe by those public officials, during the previous 12 months

Indicator 16.5.1 assesses the ratio of individuals who in the course of the previous twelve months had contact with a public official and were requested a bribe, whether given or not. The indicator is under the custody of UNODC. The UNSD justifies the

---

[538] ibid.
[539] ibid.
[540] UNDESA, Statistics Division, 'Peace, Justice and Strong Institutions' (n 372).
[541] ibid.
[542] ibid. See also, UNESC, UN Doc E/2021/58 (n 337) para 173.

1222 SDG 16

indicator on the basis that by espousing a direct measure of experiences of bribery, the gauge provides an objective yardstick for evaluating progress in the fight against the vice of corruption.[543]

b) Indicator 16.5.2 Proportion of businesses that had at least one contact with a public official and that paid a bribe to a public official, or were asked for a bribe by those public officials during the previous 12 months

Indicator 16.5.2, which is overseen by the World Bank and the UNODC, assesses the rate of businesses that in the course of the previous twelve months had contact with a public official and were requested to pay a bribe, whether they paid it or not.

i) Empirical analysis The 2021 UNSG Report pointed out that surveys carried out between 2006 and 2020 in 145 states and territories indicated that about one in six business enterprises had been subjected to requests for a bribe by a public official.[544] With regard to regional and other groupings' statistics for incidences of such bribery occurrences involving businesses for 2006 to 2020, the Eastern and South-Eastern Asia region had the highest prevalence at 30 per cent, followed by Least Developed Countries category at 27 per cent.[545] The percentage statistics of other regions and categories were 22 per cent for Oceania (excluding Australia and New Zealand), 21 per cent for both Central and Southern Asia, and Sub-Saharan Africa, 15 per cent for Small Island Developing States, 13 per cent for North Africa and Western Asia, and 9 per cent for both Latin America and the Caribbean, and Europe and Northern America regions.[546]

According to the UNSD, indicator 16.5.2 measures and determines whether gifts and illicit payments are solicited from business enterprises when their proprietors and staff meet public officials in relation to diverse state requirements and services.[547] The UNSD acknowledges that a limitation of the indicator is the fact that corruption is a highly sensitive and secretive activity, and as such, some business enterprises may not be keen on reporting incidences of bribery.[548] As such, it points out that although the data are solicited in an environment of confidentiality, businesses may nonetheless decline to provide an affirmative answer with regard to whether bribery had been solicited from them.[549] As such, the UNSD cautions that the actual incidences of bribery requests upon business enterprises may be higher than the values provided by the indicator.[550]

The UNSD regrets that corruption fundamentally impedes equal access to public services, obstructs fair distribution of resources and development of opportunities,

---

[543] UNSD, 'SDG Indicator Metadata' (19 July 2016).
[544] UNESC, UN Doc E/2021/58 (n 337) para 174.
[545] UNESC, UN Doc E/2021/58 (n 337) 'Supplementary Information' 190.
[546] ibid.
[547] UNSD, 'SDG Indicator Metadata' (11 July 2017).
[548] ibid.
[549] ibid.
[550] ibid.

and generally negates the proper functioning of the economy.[551] Further, it erodes the rule of law, impedes the democratic process, hampers access to justice, and eliminates public trust in state authorities.[552]

ii) Indicators 16.5.1 and 16.5.2 implementation efforts The high prevalence of corruption in Kenya continues to inhibit the effective provision of public services and impede the strengthening of state institutions.[553] Kenya's VNR of 2020 stated that a whopping 62.2 per cent of the population had been requested to pay a bribe to a public official in previous 12 months preceding 2017 and the figure increased to 73.1 per cent in 2018.[554] Kenya was in 2020 ranked 124th out of 180 states and territories in respect to the public notion of absence of corruption by the Transparency International's Corruption Perceptions Index.[555] There has been diverse legal, policy, and institutional mechanisms established to fight diverse forms of corruption in Kenya, but effective activation and implementation of the measures has been hampered by lack of political will and conflict of interest, particularly amongst top government officials and governing elite.

There has been some progress in the fight against the vice of corruption in Sierra Leone following the amendment of the Anti-Corruption Act, and the creation of a Special Court within the High Court of Sierra Leone to prosecute corruption offences, with Special Judges appointed for purposes of speedy and efficient trial of such offences.[556] Consequently, there has been a commendable increase in conviction rates, more timely trials, and an increase in reported cases for purposes of prosecution, from 603 in 2019 to 775 in 2020.[557]

According to Nigeria, corruption surveys indicate that there was a marginal decrease in the proportion of individuals who allege to have been requested within the previous twelve months to pay a bribe to a public official (or who actually paid it) in the period ranging from 2016 to 2019, from 32.3 per cent to 30.2 per cent.[558] The marginal but progressive advancement in the fight against corruption may be attributed to the multifaceted efforts to eradicate the vice. For instance, the National Defence College has been researching on the impact of corruption and strategies for eradicating the vice with the purpose to generate data and influencing governance policies.[559] Further, the Department for International Development (DfID) of the UK provides significant technical assistance to the anti-corruption agencies and civil society organizations (CSOs), through its Anti-Corruption in Nigeria (ACORN) programme.[560] In addition,

---

[551] UNSD, 'SDG Indicator Metadata' (19 July 2016).
[552] ibid.
[553] National Treasury and Planning, Republic of Kenya (n 333) 74.
[554] ibid 73.
[555] Transparency International, 'Corruption Perceptions Index' (2021) <https://www.transparency.org/en/cpi/2020/index/nzl> accessed 26 October 2021.
[556] Government of Sierra Leone (n 491) 50.
[557] ibid.
[558] Office of the Senior Special Assistant to the President on SDGs, Nigeria (n 428) 67.
[559] ibid.
[560] ibid.

the 'Independent Corrupt Practices and Other Related Offences Commission' undertakes the diverse functions of investigation and prosecution of corruption cases.[561] It has also incorporated the recovery of cash and assets through the non-conviction based forfeiture of assets bargain initiative. In 2019, it facilitated the recovery of more than $44 million.[562]

The 2002 formation of the Independent Commission against Corruption of Mauritius and its subsequent work of competently investigating corruption and money laundering crimes have contributed to the state's reputation of being among the least corrupt in the African region.[563] Rwanda has also maintained its position as one of the leading African states engaged in tangible and aggressive fight against corruption through the ratification of a new anti-corruption law in 2018.[564] The anticorruption initiatives in Zimbabwe have included: strengthening of public procurement processes; reforming and empowering the Zimbabwe Anti-Corruption Commission, restructuring financial management through the Public Finance Management Act; safeguarding the independence of the Office of the Auditor General; enhancing transparency in the budgeting processes; and working on a biometric authentication process for the validation of the government.[565]

The Tanzanian government has carried on its anticorruption efforts for purposes of ensuring that citizens obtain quality and appropriate public services through, for instance, legislative initiatives and the designation of a special Court under the state's High Court that specifically handles corruption cases.[566] The state has also adopted measures to increase transparency particularly in public procurement and extractive industries, such as through: creation of an e-procurement portal; adoption of a beneficial ownership register; reforms in the extractive sector; and enhancing transparency in contracting.[567] Zambia's anti-corruption initiatives have included the formation of Integrity Committees, the establishment of electronic services and one-stop service centres in transactions and services involving the government.[568]

There has been some discernible progress in the fight against the vice of corruption in Liberia, with the rate of bribery having dropped to 53 per cent in 2019 from 69 per cent in 2015 and the percentage of the population that felt that the government was commendably fighting corruption increasing from 18 per cent in 2015 to 40 per cent in 2019.[569] Some of the anti-corruption initiatives that are bearing premiums in Liberia include: improvements to and promotion of anti-corruption indicators including

---

[561] ibid 67–69.

[562] ibid.

[563] Ministry of Foreign Affairs, Regional Integration and International Trade, Mauritius (n 412) 104–105.

[564] Republic of Rwanda (n 408) 61.

[565] Sustainable Development Goals Knowledge Platform, 'Zimbabwe's Second Voluntary National Review (VNR)' 107 <https://sustainabledevelopment.un.org/content/documents/279562021_VNR_Report_Zimbabwe. pdf> accessed 23 October 2021.

[566] Sustainable Development Goals Knowledge Platform, 'United Republic of Tanzania: Voluntary National Review (VNR) 2019—Empowering People and Ensuring Inclusiveness and Equality' 96 <https://sustainabledeve lopment.un.org/content/documents/23429VNR_Report_Tanzania_2019_FINAL.pdf>accessed 23 October 2021.

[567] ibid.

[568] Republic of Zambia (n 402) 72.

[569] Sustainable Development Goals Knowledge Platform, 'Liberia' (n 388) 97.

freedom of speech and expression; enhancement of media independence; boosting openness in government budgeting; transparency in public procurement; tolerance of political dissents; and promoting open and robust CSOs.[570] Further initiatives to eliminate corruption in the state have included collaborations between the government and strategic collaborators to strengthen and implement anti-corruption instruments such as the National Code of Conduct, and the adoption of the Corrupt Offense and the Whistle-blower Acts.[571]

India has relied upon, among other measures, the strengthening of the legislative and enforcement mechanisms to eradicate corruption and entrench ethical governance.[572] There have been the complementing and strengthening of the Whistle blowers Protection Act, the Prevention of Money Laundering Act, and the Prevention of Corruption Act, in addition to the promulgation of other enabling legislation.[573] In particular, there has been significant increase in tax compliance and transparency in income and assets disclosures, in addition to the deterrence of unlawful acquisition and concealment of public assets and resources through the adoption of the Fugitive Economic Offenders Act of 2018, and the Black Money (Undisclosed Foreign Income and Assets) and Imposition of Tax Act in 2015.[574]

Premised on the continuing predicaments of corruption and bribery in Malaysia, the country's strategies of eradicating the vices have resulted in improvements of the prosecution and conviction rates of those indicted, and the promulgation of the Anti-Bribery Management System (ABMS) MS ISO 37001 certification in all government agencies for purposes of enhancing the effectiveness of provision of public services.[575] In addition, there is the mandatory obligation to develop and implement Organizational Anti-Corruption Plans in all government ministries, agencies, and statutory bodies, and private entities are encouraged to establish and implement their own corporate anti-corruption plans.[576]

Australia has maintained its low incidences of corruption and associated organized crime through robust legal, policy, and institutional systems that detect, deter, and combat money-laundering and terrorism financing.[577] The mechanisms are also oriented to effectively 'collect, analyse and disseminate financial intelligence on suspicious financial transactions and other matters submitted by regulated businesses (such as financial, remittance and gambling services)'.[578] Further, Australia's Fintel Alliance is based on public and private collaboration that effectively fights money laundering activities and terrorism financing.[579] There is also the broad

[570] ibid.
[571] ibid.
[572] See Government of India (n 359) 131.
[573] ibid.
[574] ibid.
[575] Economic Planning Unit, Malaysia (n 414) 111.
[576] ibid.
[577] Australian Government (n 179) 103.
[578] ibid.
[579] ibid.

1226   SDG 16

cross-government collaboration in the detection, disruption, and deterrence of corruption and serious crime.[580]

Canada's low incidences of corruption and bribery have been due to continued work between the government and diverse stakeholders to prevent, investigate, detect, and prosecute corruption and bribery activities.[581] Through its legal framework that has the objective of detection and deterring money laundering and terrorism financing, there is the mandatory obligation for reporting of suspicious financial transactions, which has assisted in the investigation and prosecution of such offences.[582] In the case of Singapore, the remarkable low levels of corruption in the state has been an outcome of consistent and effective anti-corruption initiatives that have included robust laws such as the Corruption, Drug Trafficking and Other Serious Crimes Act, and the Prevention of Corruption Act.[583]

6. Target 16.6 Develop effective, accountable and transparent institutions at all levels

a) Indicator 16.6.1 Primary government expenditures as a proportion of original approved budget, by sector (or by budget codes or similar)

Indicator 16.6.1, for which the World Bank is the custodial agency, measures the primary government expenditure in relation to the originally approved budget, segregated on the basis of sector or budget codes. As such, the indicator evaluates the extent of subsequent deviation in spending by states from the originally approved budget.

The UNSD justifies the use of the indicator on the premise that it facilitates the capture of the reliability, accuracy, and transparency of government budgets.[584] It evaluates whether governments collect what they promise to, and whether their spending practices adhere to what they publicly commit to utilize.[585] The UNSD further rationalizes the indicator on the premise that it is a simple and intuitive measure that is easy to comprehend, and with a rating that is easily verifiable.[586]

i) Empirical analysis With regard to statistics for states' deviations of more than 15 per cent from approved budgets in the context of regions and other categories for the 2018–2019 period, Oceania (excluding Australia and New Zealand) had the highest rates at 66.7 per cent, followed by Sub-Saharan Africa at 35.7 per cent.[587] The percentage statistics for other regions and categories were respectively 25 per cent for Northern Africa and Western Asia, 14.3 per cent for Eastern and South-Eastern Asia, 9.1 per cent for

---

[580] ibid.
[581] Government of Canada (n 404) 113.
[582] ibid.
[583] Ministry of Foreign Affairs, Singapore (n 415) 62.
[584] UNSD, 'SDG Indicator Metadata' (19 July 2016).
[585] ibid.
[586] ibid.
[587] UNESC, UN Doc E/2021/58 (n 337) 'Supplementary Information' 191.

Central and Southern Asia, 8.3 per cent for Latin America and the Caribbean, and 0 per cent in respect to Europe and Northern America.[588]

b) Indicator 16.6.2 Proportion of population satisfied with their last experience of public services

Indicator 16.6.2 evaluates the ratio of the population that is satisfied by their recent experience of public service, and is overseen by the UNDP. The UNSD points out that evaluation of the populace's satisfaction with public services is a core aspect of institutionalizing a citizen-centred approach to public service delivery, and a vital measure of the overall government performance.[589] From a social contract perspective, Governments have obligations to provide diverse services to the citizens, which should ideally satisfy the expectations of the population in the context of quality, reliability, accessibility, and responsiveness.[590]

i) Empirical evaluation methodology The objective of the indicator is to generate data in relation to satisfaction with public services that may be compared globally. Given the extreme diversity of the services provided by governments, the indicator focuses on three areas of priority, namely healthcare; education; and governmental services relating to identification and registration, such as identification documents, and registration of births, marriages, and deaths.[591]

ii) Implementation efforts For purposes of entrenching accountability, efficiency, and transparency in Namibia's institutions, high-ranking public officials are required to sign performance agreements. Such initiatives have significantly reduced embezzlement of public funds, with Namibia attaining a score above 90 per cent in respect to the rate of accurate budget execution.[592] India has worked to establish accountable and transparent institutions through a parliamentary democracy in which the Union (Federal) government is fully answerable to the parliament in addition to having an independent judiciary and quasi-judicial authorities, and an autonomous Comptroller and Auditor General office.[593]

The bedrock of accountable and transparent public institutions in Austria is a governance system that subscribes to the rule of law and the practical separation of powers between the executive, legislative, and judicial branches of government.[594] Singapore's remarkable economic and social progress has also been premised on having accountable, efficient, and transparent public institutions.[595] The basis of Singapore's public

---

[588] ibid.
[589] UNSD, 'SDG Indicator Metadata' (3 February 2020).
[590] ibid.
[591] ibid.
[592] Republic of Namibia (n 400) 65.
[593] Government of India (n 359) 129–31.
[594] Australian Government (n 179) 102.
[595] Ministry of Foreign Affairs, Singapore (n 415) 62.

1228   SDG 16

institutional structure is a constitutional framework premised on the separation of powers between the executive, legislature, and judiciary, and the guarantees of fundamental rights and liberties to all through the concept of equal protection before the law.[596]

7. Target 16.7 Ensure responsive, inclusive, participatory and representative decision-making at all levels

a) Indicator 16.7.1 Proportions of positions in national and local institutions, including (a) the legislatures; (b) the public service; and (c) the judiciary, compared to national distributions, by sex, age, persons with disabilities and population groups

Target 16.7 of SDG 16 is geared towards the institutionalization of social equity. Indicator 16.7.1 measures the ratio of representation, based on age, sex, persons with disabilities, and population groups, in local and state institutions, including in the parliament, judiciary, and public service. The Inter-Parliamentary Union (IPU) is responsible for the collation of information and data relating to the indicator in respect to the composition of the parliamentary chambers of states.[597]

i) Empirical analysis The UNSD has explained that indicator 16.7.1 is premised on 'descriptive representation'.[598] The concept of descriptive representation focuses on evaluating the extent to which the composition of parliament reflects the diverse socio-demographic categories in the state population.[599] In that context, the indicator is based on an assumption that in cases where parliamentary composition reflects the social diversity of the subject state, then there may be greater legitimacy for the parliamentary activities upon the electorate, since the parliamentarians resemble the people that they represent in relation to age, gender, disability, and ethnicity.[600] The UNSD points out that descriptive representation has often resulted in greater levels of trust in public institutions, since the 'people feel closer to elected representatives who resemble them' in addition to perceiving such representatives as engaged in better quality and fairer decision-making, and as being encumbered less undue influence of vested interests in their decision-making.[601]

The UNSG Report pointed out that as of January 2021, 31.1 per cent of Members of Parliament were forty-five years of age or below, which demonstrated positive progress on diversity of representation in the context of age from the proportion in 2018, when they comprised 28.1 per cent.[602] Form a gender perspective, the Report notes that male parliamentarians dominate the leadership positions of committee chairs and speakers of parliament.[603]

---

[596] ibid.
[597] UNSD, 'SDG Indicator Metadata' (March 2021).
[598] ibid.
[599] ibid.
[600] ibid.
[601] ibid.
[602] UNESC, UN Doc E/2021/58 (n 337) para 175.
[603] ibid.

The UNSD further points out that under its target 16.7, states are encouraged to ensure that the public service is representative of the diversity of the people it serves, given that it is the bedrock of government, and constitutes the avenue in which development and implementation of public policies occurs, besides being the sphere in which society interacts most with the government.[604] States are obliged to report data relating to representation and composition of the public service to the custodian agency, the UNDP, once every two years, or on an annual basis where possible.[605] Through the evaluation and postulation of proportional representation of groups that correlates to their composition in the state population, the UNSD vindicates the indicator on the premise that where the public sector reflects the social diversity of the country, there may be greater legitimacy and acceptability of the arising governance decisions.[606] It has been further pointed out that proportional representation in the public service has been linked to greater levels of trust of public institutions, as the decision-making is perceived to be more inclusive, of better quality and fairer, in addition to perceptions of less undue influence by virtue of vested interests in the decision-making officials.[607]

McDermott and collaborating authors are of the view that, as is the case with other themes of SDG 16, the indicators under the 16.7 target imply significantly 'a focus on state institutions and national level reporting'.[608] It is in that context that they contrast the SDG 16 model with developments in 'international discourse on governance', which they opine that it is increasingly incorporating a 'much broader and more far-reaching understanding of participation'.[609] Broader and deeper contexts of participation would ideally include emphasis on diversity of both participatory opportunities and actors at the community and local levels.

ii) Implementation efforts With regard to state practice, it is noteworthy that the Philippines has resulted in more women being active participants in the political process of the state, with larger percentages of women being elected to legislative and local government positions.[610] Whereas both Houses of Congress are still dominated by men, there has been a huge success by women in the context of constituting a whopping 78.8 per cent of the chief executives in cities as of 2016.[611] In the case of Indonesia, the Girls Leadership Programme, which involves collaboration between the Ministry of Finance and Plan International Indonesia, has the objective of encouraging and mentoring

---

[604] UNSD, 'SDG Indicator Metadata' (16 March 2020).
[605] ibid.
[606] ibid.
[607] ibid.
[608] McDermott and others (n 134) 525.
[609] ibid.
[610] Sustainable Development Goals Knowledge Platform, 'The 2019 Voluntary National Review of the Philippines' 37 <https://sustainabledevelopment.un.org/content/documents/23366Voluntary_National_Review_2019_Philippines.pdf>accessed 23 October 2021.
[611] ibid.

1230   SDG 16

teenage girls and young women channel their aspirations towards developmental actions and seek to be equal participants to the male gender in society processes.[612]

b) Indicator 16.7.2 Proportion of population who believe decision-making is inclusive and responsive, by sex, age, disability and population group

Indicator 16.7.2 evaluates the proportion of the population that is of the view that decision-making at the various levels of a state is inclusive and responsive, including by age, gender, and disability.

i) Implementation efforts In the case of India, technology-driven initiatives and platforms have created avenues for citizen-centric projects, which have significantly improved participatory governance.[613] Such online platforms are also being implemented in Liberia, and as of 2020, the government was in the process of building and piloting a Citizen Feedback Mechanism through which the population can share experiences and provide feedback regarding delivery of public services.[614]

Whilst Uganda's institutional framework provides for inclusivity in the design and implementation of projects and policies, there is nonetheless the need to ensure that the population does practically participate meaningfully and qualitatively.[615] According to Uganda's VNR of 2020, only 29 per cent of the population perceives decision-making as being responsive and inclusive, which is significantly low and thus calls for more concerted efforts by the state.[616] The government of the Philippines established the Participatory Governance Cluster in 2017 for purposes of encouraging and improving the rate of citizen participation in governmental processes by creating spaces and opportunities for participatory engagement.[617]

ii) Critique of target 16.7 indicators An apparent limitation of the indicators of target 16.7 is their failure to focus on the engagement and participatory opportunities of non-state actors, which may broadly be referred to as the civil society organizations and have significantly contributed to the institutionalization of good governance and entrenchment of rule of law in various states. Civil society organizations refer to a broad array of entities that function in the arena between the private sector and the state, for purposes of articulating and safeguarding issues of public concern.[618] The engagement and participation of civil society organization in governance decision-making activities has the

---

[612] Republic of Indonesia (n 430) 325.
[613] Government of India (n 359) 131.
[614] Sustainable Development Goals Knowledge Platform, 'Liberia' (n 388) 95.
[615] Republic of Uganda (n 409) 71.
[616] ibid.
[617] Sustainable Development Goals Knowledge Platform, 'The 2019 Voluntary National Review of the Philippines' (n 613) 33.
[618] Julius Court and others, *Policy Engagement: How Civil Society Can be More Effective* (Overseas Development Institute 2006) 5.

potential to result in better quality and more legitimate outcomes given that the input of diverse interest groups will have been considered.

The HLPF has argued that a core founding principle of 2030 Agenda that resulted in the conceptualization of SDGs is the 'requirement for all implementation and follow-up processes to be participatory and inclusive, including all levels and sectors of government, civil society and the private sector, members of parliament [and] national human rights institutions, among others'.[619] Nonetheless, as discussed, an evaluation of the indicators of target 16.7 demonstrates that there is failure in focusing on measuring spaces and legitimation of some core aspects of inclusive and meaningful participation, particularly those involving the engagement of the CSOs in the state development processes. A focused measurement of the effectiveness of participation of core non-state actors such as CSOs would provide valuable feedback information and data for progressively improving the opportunities and avenues of their involvement.

The High-Level Political Forum argues that the 2030 Agenda through its concept of SDGs 'has a revitalized partnership for sustainable development at its core, and stakeholders are recognized as valuable partners in implementing the goals and raising public awareness'.[620] There is the need to orient the ideals and aspirations articulated by the High-Level Political Forum to practical realities and opportunities, particularly in the context of expanding and evaluating the effectiveness of the opportunities for core non-state actors such as CSOs to participate in the development processes of states. The HLPFSD has observed that diverse stakeholders have been actively involved 'throughout the process of design, implementation, monitoring and review of the 2030 Agenda at all levels in many countries around the world'.[621] Based on the foregoing discussed realities, the statement by the HLPFSD seems more of an inspiration than the reality, if the contextualization of the target 16.7 indicators and their impact is evaluated and appraised deeply. As suggested, there is need to practically measure the opportunities, legitimation, limitations, and realities of the participation of core non-state actors such as CSOs in order to progressively improve their vital role in the development process, and particularly in the realization of the aspirations of SDG 16.

Further, McDermott and collaborating authors make reference to the indicators under target 16.7 in the context of the forest sector, in which they recommend that the new forms of participation call for greater decentralization in the management of such natural resources across the diverse levels of government, in addition to active engagement of the local communities and non-state participants in the making of decisions.[622] They also opine that practically, meaningful inclusion of the local communities in the management of forest resources requires that the land tenure and use rights be appropriately enacted in order to facilitate such engagements, and that the local communities have the capacity to utilize such legal, policy, and institutional opportunities.[623]

---

[619] High-Level Political Forum on Sustainable Development, *Handbook* (n 172) 12.
[620] ibid.
[621] ibid.
[622] McDermott and others (n 134) 525–26.
[623] ibid 527.

1232   SDG 16

Making reference to diverse multistate studies on community participation in forests, and the capacity to benefit from the stated resources, they regret that the 'overarching issues' of such rights and modes of local access 'are notably absent from SDG 16 targets and indicators'.[624]

With respect to state practice, Kenya in its inaugural 2017 VNR pointed out that a core lesson from the MDGs implementation was that strong collaboration and partnerships with diverse stakeholders will be critical for the effective implementation of SDGs.[625] It is in that context that Kenya identified the enhancement of the 'multi-stakeholder participation in the SDGs process' as being a core issue that required concerted action.[626] In the case of Liberia, its legal and policy framework is supportive of the formation and operationalization of vibrant CSOs, including those that act as public watchdogs and accountability reviewers.[627]

8. Target 16.8 Broaden and strengthen the participation of developing countries in the institutions of global governance

a) Indicator 16.8.1 Proportion of members and voting rights of developing countries in international organizations

Target 16.8 has the objective of broadening and strengthening developing states participation in the institutions of global governance. It has a single indicator 16.8.1, which measures the ratio of members of developing states in international organizations and the voting rights of such countries. As such, it is noteworthy that despite being a single indicator, it has two dimensions, namely, the number of developing states, and secondly, the weight of their voting rights.[628]

The custodian agency of the indicator is the Financing for Development Office (FFDO) in the Department of Economic and Social Affairs, under the auspices of the UN. The UNSD explains that the indicator is utilized to evaluate 11 institutions independently, which are the UNGA, the United Nations Security Council (UNSC), the International Monetary Fund (IMF), the International Finance Corporation, the International Bank for Reconstruction and Development (IBRD) (a segment of the World Bank), the Asian Development Bank, the World Trade Organization, the Financial Stability Board, the UNESC, the African Development Bank, and the Inter-American Development Bank.[629]

i) Empirical analysis and implementation efforts With regard to the percentage of developing states that have membership in significant international organizations in accordance with 2019 statistics, it was 74.6 per cent at the IBRD, and 50 per cent at the

---

[624] ibid.

[625] Ministry of Devolution and Planning, Kenya (n 478) 4.

[626] Sustainable Development Goals Knowledge Platform, 'Kenya: Voluntary National Review 2017' <https://sustainabledevelopment.un.org/memberstates/kenya> accessed 20 October 2021.

[627] Sustainable Development Goals Knowledge Platform, 'Liberia' (n 388) 104.

[628] UNSD, 'SDG Indicator Metadata' (19 July 2016).

[629] ibid.

Financial Stability Board.[630] The percentage representation in other organizations was 74.5 per cent at the International Finance Corporation, 74.6 per cent at the IMF, 68.5 per cent at the UNESC, 74.1 per cent at the UN General Assembly, 53.3 per cent at the UNSC, and 72 per cent at the WTO.[631]

The UNSD has justified the indicator on the premise that it has the objective of evaluating the extent to which states, particularly developing ones, enjoy equal representation in international organizations, particularly due to the fact that the UN is premised on the cardinal principle of the sovereign equality of all its Member States, as espoused under its Charter.[632] It is, nonetheless, noteworthy that the designation of states as either 'developed' or 'developing' can be problematic and may be open to contestation. It is in that context that it has been clarified, in the cited 2019 statistical data, that there is no established convention for the categorization of states as either developing or developed under the UN system.[633] For purposes of the 2019 categorization, the FFDO, the UN institution that compiled the data explains that in conformity with common practice, Japan, Canada, United States, European states, Israel, Cyprus, Australia, and New Zealand were regarded as developed, and were, thus, excluded from the data.[634]

ii) Critique As argued by the UNSD, comparative institutional evaluation should be cognisant of the diversity and differences in membership between institutions.[635] It should also be taken into account that often, membership and voting rights are agreed upon by the State Parties to an organization. It is noteworthy that institutional arrangements between organizations, or even in the same entity, may reflect greater democratic representation and legitimacy in decision-making, or have elements of domineering and unrepresentative decision-making. In particular, greater representation of developing states in institutions of global governance does not directly translate to such states' power in decision-making, or that the decisions arising from such intergovernmental organizations are premised on democratic legitimacy.

An illustration is the contrast in representation and democratic legitimacy in decision-making between the UNGA and the UNSC. The UNGA is premised on the concept of membership by every state party to the UN, and all countries have equal voting rights. On the other part, the Security Council comprises five permanent members, and an additional ten non-permanent members representing various geographical regions of the globe that are selected on a rotational basis. At any particular time, the African continent is represented in the UNSC on a non-permanent basis by three states. Further, the chairing of the UNSC sessions is undertaken on a rotational basis

---

[630] UNESC, UN Doc E/2021/58 (n 337 'Supplementary Information' 193–94.
[631] ibid.
[632] UNSD, 'SDG Indicator Metadata' (19 July 2016). See also, Art 2(1) of the UN Charter that affirms the principle of sovereign equality of states. United Nations Charter (24 October 1945) 1 UNTS XVI.
[633] UNESC, UN Doc E/2021/58 (n 337) 'Supplementary Information' 194.
[634] ibid.
[635] UNSD, 'SDG Indicator Metadata' (19 July 2016).

1234 SDG 16

between the permanent and non-permanent members. For instance, Kenya assumed the presidency of the UNSC for the month of October 2021.[636]

Despite the above-discussed diversity of membership and leadership, the five permanent members of the UNSC wield extreme global authority by virtue of the veto power on matters relating to peace and security. Article 27(3) of the UN Charter requires that decisions of the Security Council about non-procedural matters be based on concurring votes of the permanent members. This requirement forms the basis of the veto power. One of the shortcomings and limitations of the UN Charter system was that the veto powers 'allowed any of the Five permanent members of the Security Council to block the collective security system at any time' making it 'dependent upon the continuing political agreement of the Five'.[637]

The veto power by the five permanent members of the Security Council is often cited as a barrier to the effectiveness and efficiency of the UN.[638] And since the Security Council is viewed as the most influential aspect of the UN system, some discussions on reform have centred on its membership.[639] However, any proposal to abolish or even modify the Security Council as it is presently constituted requires the endorsement by the five permanent members.[640] This requirement therefore makes reform to the Council extremely difficult, bordering on impossibility.[641] Therefore, on a practical perspective, it is improbable that on the short term, the veto power will substantially be limited or eliminated.[642]

It is noteworthy that TWAIL proponents continue to deconstruct and critique the international legal norms and institutions in order to expose practices and themes of subjugation, subordination, and domination of the states of the Third World. From a historical perspective, the people of the Third World are often concerned with the manner in which international rules and institutions affect the distribution of power between states, particularly due to the experiences of colonialism and neo-colonialism.[643] It is in that context that TWAIL has been concerned with the manner in which international legal norms and institutions can be transformed to address the interests and aspirations of the Third World states, most of which are former colonies.[644] The UN system has become one of the foremost avenues through which the states of the Third World have pushed their agenda and concerns.[645] The conceptualization of SDGs involved and exemplified concerted efforts to ensure diverse representation, participation, and

---

[636] United Nations Security Council, 'Security Council Presidency' <https://www.un.org/securitycouncil/content/presidency> accessed 25 October 2021.

[637] A Cassese, 'Return to Westphalia? Considerations on the Gradual Erosion of the Charter System' in A Cassese (ed), *The Current Legal Regulation of the Use of Force* (Martinus Nijhoff Publishers 1986) 505, 506; C Gray, *International Law and the Use of Force* (3rd edn, OUP 2008) 255.

[638] S Chesterman and others, *Law and Practice of the United Nations* (OUP 2008) 572.

[639] ibid 568.

[640] ibid 572.

[641] It has been acknowledged that attempts to adjust the Security Council mandate amount to utopia. Suy (n 393) 24.

[642] DD Caron, 'The Legitimacy of the Collective Authority of the Security Council (1993) 87 American Journal of International Law 552, 567.

[643] Anghie and Chimni (n 183) 78.

[644] ibid 81.

[645] ibid.

contribution by various states, including the Third World, through the auspices of the more democratic UNGA.

A significant institutional framework that resulted in the conceptualization of the SDGs was the formation of the twenty-seven members High-Level Panel of Eminent Persons on the Post-2015 Development Agenda by the UNSG in July 2012, which reflected concerted efforts to take into account the diversity of UN members and their interests.[646] The OWG on Sustainable Development Goals would subsequently be established for purposes of guiding thematic discussions on the seventeen SDGs, and it was also reflective of inclusive participation of states, including countries of the Third World.

It is also noteworthy that the conceptualization and promotion of the right to development originated from efforts to entrench fairness and equity in investments and economic relations between the developed and the developing countries. Third World states had begun since the 1960s to form coalitions that sought radical changes to the global economic order as they advocated for more equitable relations and participation.[647] It is in that context that the right to development was conceptualized, with original ideas having been derived from African scholars and practitioners, particularly the Senegalese Kéba M'Baye and the Algerian Mohammed Bedajoui.[648]

9. Target 16.9 By 2030, provide legal identity for all, including birth registration
a) *Indicator 16.9.1 Proportion of children under 5 years of age whose births have been registered with a civil authority, by age*
The provision of legal identity for all, particularly through birth registration, is the concern of target 16.9. The target has a sole indicator 16.9.1, which measures the ratio of children below the age of five years whose births have been registered with a state's civil authority on the basis of their age at the time of the evaluation. It is noteworthy that article 7 of the CRC espouses the children's right to a name and nationality.[649] The custodial agency for the indicator is UNICEF, which regularly provides technical and financial assistance to states to support their efforts to gather quality data in respect to the registration of births.[650]

i) Empirical analysis The 2021 UNSG Report states that data collated in the period ranging from 2010 to 2020 indicate that one in four (25 per cent) children under the age of five was not officially recorded.[651] Demonstrating the dire situation in the Sub-Saharan Africa, the Report further notes that only 45 per cent of children under the age of five had their births registered in the period ranging from 2010 to 2020, which

[646] UNSG, 'The Secretary-General's High-Level Panel' (n 11).
[647] Eide (n 129) 282.
[648] Okafor, 'A Regional Perspective' (n 130) 373–74. See also: Bunn (n 130) 1433; Uvin (n 130) 598; Ibhawoh (n 116) 83.
[649] Convention on the Rights of the Child (n 94).
[650] UNSD, 'SDG Indicator Metadata' (March 2021).
[651] UNESC, UN Doc E/2021/58 (n 337) para 176.

1236   SDG 16

was far below the global average.[652] With regard to available statistics for 2020 specifically, and in percentage, the leading regions were Northern America, Europe, Australia and New Zealand where registrations reached 100 per cent, 98.5 per cent for Central Asia, 94.3 per cent for Latin America and the Caribbean, and 92 per cent for Northern Africa.[653] It is regrettable that 2020 registrations for the LDCs, and Sub-Saharan Africa were merely 44.1 per cent and 44.8 per cent, respectively.[654] Some elements of correlation between the level of economic progress of states and regions with the extent of childbirth registrations may be discerned form the cited statistics for 2020, with economically poor countries such as those in Sub-Saharan Africa and LDCs likely to have higher incidences of unregistered children.

ii) Implementation efforts and critique   As the UNSD states in its justification of indicator 16.9.1 the registration of children at birth is vital as it is usually the first step to ensuring their legal recognition in addition to increasing opportunities for the protection and enforcement of their rights.[655] As an emphasis of the significance of registration of children at birth, the UNSD instructively cautions that:

> Children without official identification documents may be denied health care or education. Later in life, the lack of such documentation can mean that a child may enter into marriage or the labour market, or be conscripted into the armed forces, before the legal age. In adulthood, birth certificates may be required to obtain social assistance or a job in the formal sector, to buy or prove the right to inherit property, to vote and to obtain a passport.[656]

A challenge to the accuracy of the indicator, which demonstrates its limitation, is due to the fact that effective recording and registration of births in many states remain a serious predicament.[657] The grim situation in Sub-Saharan Africa has been highlighted, where only 45 per cent of children under the age of five had their births registered.[658] The UNSD has explained that where credible administrative information is lacking, 'household surveys' have become a vital alternative source of data to measure levels and trends in birth registration.[659] In most low- and middle-income states, such as African countries, household surveys often represent the sole source of data.[660]

Whilst Angola is confronted by the predicament of low birth registrations, there has been a marginal increase in the number of registered children under the age of five, from 25 per cent in 2015 to 28.3 per cent in 2019.[661] In the case of Ghana, resort to

---

[652] ibid.
[653] UNESC, UN Doc E/2021/58 (n 337) 'Supplementary Information' 194–95.
[654] ibid.
[655] UNSD, 'SDG Indicator Metadata' (March 2021).
[656] ibid.
[657] ibid.
[658] UNESC, UN Doc E/2021/58 (n 337) para 176.
[659] UNSD, 'SDG Indicator Metadata' (March 2021).
[660] ibid.
[661] Governo de Angola (n 390) 110–11.

information technology platforms to register births have been a key intervention. For instance, the mobile birth system that focuses on documentation of children below twelve months has significantly improved the practice. Consequently, there has been an increase in registrations of children under five years old from 63 per cent in 2011 to approximately 71 per cent in 2017.[662]

Kenya has fared relatively well with regard to registrations given the low level for the Sub-Saharan region, with the proportion of registered children having been 89.1 per cent in 2019 and 94.5 per cent of the births having occurred in a health facility.[663] In the case of mainland Tanzania, registration of children under the age of five was at 38 per cent in 2018, having increased from a low of 12.9 per cent in 2012.[664] The rates of registrations have been higher in Tanzania's island of Zanzibar, where an electronic and modern civil registration system has been implemented since 2010.[665] Some of the initiatives being undertaken to improve registration of children in both mainland Tanzania and Zanzibar include decentralization of documentation to ward level and at health facilities for free.[666] India's concerted efforts to eradicate the lack of legal identity among children has resulted in the level of registrations being at 84.9 per cent at the national level, with twelve states achieving the desirable 100 per cent registrations.[667] With regard to Indonesia, there has been support from UNICEF in the 2017–2019 period for purposes of increasing the number of birth registrations.[668] UNICEF's intervention has included facilitating and supporting collaboration between local governments and CSOs for purposes of enhancing birth registrations in Indonesia.[669]

10. Target 16.10 Ensure public access to information and protect fundamental freedoms, in accordance with national legislation and international agreements

a) Indicator 16.10.1 Number of verified cases of killing, kidnapping, enforced disappearance, arbitrary detention and torture of journalists, associated media personnel, trade unionists and human rights advocates in the previous 12 months

Target 16.10 obliges states to facilitate and promote 'public access to information and protect fundamental freedoms in accordance with national legislation and international agreements'. In that context, indicator 16.10.1 measures the '[n]umber of verified cases of killing, kidnapping, enforced disappearance, arbitrary detention and torture of journalists, associated media personnel, trade unionists and human rights advocates' within the preceding twelve months. The custodian agencies of the indicator

---

[662] Republic of Ghana (n 351) 73.
[663] National Treasury and Planning, Republic of Kenya (n 333) 73.
[664] Sustainable Development Goals Knowledge Platform, 'United Republic of Tanzania' (n 569) 99.
[665] ibid.
[666] ibid.
[667] Government of India (n 359) 131.
[668] Republic of Indonesia (n 430) 323.
[669] ibid.

1238 SDG 16

are the OHCHR, the United Nations Educational, Scientific and Cultural Organization (UNESCO), and the International Labour Organization (ILO).

i) Empirical analysis Statistics form the UNSD indicates that the prevalence of the obnoxious execution of human rights defenders, journalists, and trade unionists remains high.[670] The UNSD points out that since 2015, there have been reports of murder of human rights defenders, journalists, and trade unionists in over one-third of the UN Member States.[671] As an indication of grim regression in the context of human rights defenders, the UNSD points out that in 2020, there was an 18 per cent increase of the number of killings of such activists, which amounted to 331 victims in thirty-two states, and which was in addition to nineteen cases of enforced disappearances in fourteen states.[672] The UNSD points out that Latin America remains the region most affected by incidences of killings of human rights defenders.[673] According to statistics, it is approximated that 290 human rights defenders, journalists, and trade unionists were killed in Latin America in 2020, with the numbers being forty-three for Central and Southern Asia, thirty-one for Eastern and South-Eastern Asia, nineteen for Northern Africa and Western Asia, eight for Sub-Saharan Africa, and two for Europe and Northern America.[674]

From a gender perspective, women human rights defenders comprise 13 per cent victims of execution.[675] The low percentage could be due to marginally fewer members of the female gender engaging in such risky but essential human rights activism.

The UNSD explains that this indicator is distinct from indicator 16.1.1 (in respect of the number of victims of intentional killings per 100,000 people) in the context of the causal factor or impetus.[676] Under indicator 16.10.1, the motivation is to punish the victim for having participated in activities relating to advocacy for human rights.[677]

In the context of journalists, the UNSD states that sixty-two journalists were executed in 2020, which nonetheless point to some progress in human rights protection, as they constituted the lowest annual number in a decade.[678] The UNSD regrets that impunity is a core cause of the executions of journalists, and observes that in some cases even COVID-19 pandemic containment measures have been utilized in order to avoid accountability for execution of journalists.[679] Consequently, the UNSD highlights the dire need for political will in state institutions to prosecute and hold accountable the perpetrators of the executions, as a key deterrence mechanism to such killings.[680] Further, the UNSD calls upon states to develop a political culture of publicly

---

[670] UNDESA, Statistics Division, 'Peace, Justice and Strong Institutions' (n 372).
[671] ibid.
[672] ibid.
[673] ibid.
[674] ibid.
[675] ibid.
[676] UNSD, 'SDG Indicator Metadata' (8 June 2018).
[677] ibid.
[678] UNDESA, Statistics Division, 'Peace, Justice and Strong Institutions' (n 372).
[679] ibid.
[680] ibid.

acknowledging, and applauding, the vital contributions of courageous journalists to the progressive entrenchment of the rule of law and the establishment of more just societies.[681]

b) Indicator 16.10.2 Number of countries that adopt and implement constitutional, statutory and/or policy guarantees for public access to information

Indicator 16.10.2 measures the number of states that enact and implement constitutional, statutory and policy guarantees for access to information by the general public, and is under the custody of UNESCO.

i) Empirical analysis In that context, the UNSG Progress Report towards the SDGs observed that as of February 2021, 127 states and territories had commendably adopted legislation relating to access to information, though there was still need for improvements in the actual implementation of the enacted laws.[682] The UNSG Report noted that the COVID-19 pandemic had regrettably slowed the rate of progress in the enactment of such legislation, as no state adopted such laws in the course of 2020, with some states actually provisionally suspending the application of legal guarantees relating to access to information.[683] The UNSD has justified the indicator, particularly on the aspect of it focusing on evaluating the ratio of implementation of enacted legislation.[684] It points out that the 'rationale for assessing the implementation dimension is to assess the relevance of legal steps to practical information accessibility'.[685] The UNSD further points out that the indicator focuses on a logical linkage of legislation and policies to their practical effect that is relevant to SDGs concerns.[686]

ii) Implementation efforts As part of its implementation of the 2010 Constitution, Kenya has adopted statutory and policy guarantees for access to information by the public.[687] Access to information is also promoted and safeguarded by the establishment of the Kenya National Commission on Human Rights (KNCHR), which is an autonomous national human rights institutions (NHRIs) that espouses the Principles relating to the Status of National Institutions (Paris Principles).[688]

It is noteworthy that indicator 16.a.1 under target 16.a, which is discussed in the subsequent section, measures the extent to which NHRIs, such as Kenya's KNCHR, conform to the Paris Principles. The objective of the Paris Principles is to ensure the establishment of functionally objective and impartial human rights institutions at the state level that are capable of promoting and safeguarding progressive realization of the SDGs, including those relating to SDG 16. Consequently, the Paris Principles

---

[681] ibid.
[682] UNESC, UN Doc E/2021/58 (n 337) para 178.
[683] ibid.
[684] UNSD, 'SDG Indicator Metadata' (16 January 2017).
[685] Ibid.
[686] ibid.
[687] Ministry of Devolution and Planning, Kenya (n 478) 44.
[688] See ibid.

espouse certain requirements for NHRIs to enable such institutions function effectively and meet their objectives. They require, for instance, that NHRIs be established and vested with the competence to protect and promote human rights.[689] They should be granted broad mandate that is premised on the Constitution or legislation.[690] There should also be guarantees of independence of the NHRIs, and pluralist representation in its composition.[691] They should have adequate finances and resources, and should particularly not be subject to financial control by the state, which might affect their independence.[692]

In the case of South Africa, it has been noted that the Government should be more proactive and open in publishing its information and improve the management of state records in order to enhance the quality of information received by the populace.[693] It has also been pointed out that there is need for greater compliance with the Promotion of Access to Information Act in South Africa.[694] India's Right to Information Act of 2005 contributed to greater transparency and accountability in public institutions.[695] The Act is a legal instrument that is often relied upon by the public to seek information from government authorities, and to hold officials to account.[696]

Sierra Leone has also made some consistent progress since the adoption of the Right to Access Information Law in 2013, and the subsequent establishment in 2014 of the Right to Access Information Commission.[697] Consequently, there has been an increase in the number of people applying to be provided with public information, through the concept of 'freedom of information requests'. Remarkably, an overwhelming majority of requests is successful.[698]

11. Target 16.a Strengthen relevant national institutions, including
    through international cooperation, for building capacity at all levels, in particular
    in developing countries, to prevent violence and combat terrorism and crime

The need to empower national institutions, including through transnational cooperation for purposes of capacity building and especially in the context of developing states, in order to prevent crime and violence, and combat terrorist activities is recognized and affirmed as target 16.a. In that context, SDG 16 affirms the significance of institutions and effective decision-making in facilitating the realization of SDGs.[699]

---

[689] UNGA, 'National Institutions for the Promotion and Protection of Human Rights' UN Doc A/RES/48/134 (4 March 1994) annex.
[690] ibid.
[691] ibid.
[692] ibid.
[693] Sustainable Development Goals Knowledge Platform, '2019 South Africa' (n 335) 105.
[694] ibid 106.
[695] ibid.
[696] Government of India (n 359) 131.
[697] Government of Sierra Leone (n 491) 49.
[698] ibid.
[699] HLPFSD, 'Discussion on SDG 16' (n 444).

a) Indicator 16.a.1 Existence of independent national human rights institutions
in compliance with the Paris Principles

Progress and compliance with target 16.a. is measured through the sole indicator 16.a.1, which evaluates the existence of autonomous NHRIs in conformity with the Paris Principles and is under the custody of the OHCHR.[700] NHRIs are autonomous entities within states that are established for purposes of promoting and protecting human rights.[701] The measuring of NHRIs compliance with the Paris Principles was adopted by the General Assembly in Resolution 48/134.[702]

i) Empirical analysis and implementation In Kenya, there have been some noteworthy efforts to strengthen the relevant national institutions for purposes of preventing crime and violence, including by combating terrorist activities, which have previously presented security challenges. Some of the institutional reforms have included: the installation of secure communication and surveillance systems for the police service; drafting of a 'Roadmap Toolkit' to provide guidance in the training of police officers; and the vetting of the police.[703] There has also been the procurement of police trucks and armoured vehicles to enable the police be more effective in their response to security threats, in addition to the hiring of more police officers and reservists.[704]

Malaysia's institutional reforms to prevent violence and combat terrorism threats have included the 2003 establishment of the Southeast Asia Regional Centre for Counter Terrorism (SEARCCT) by the Ministry of Foreign Affairs, which is a regional centre for deterring and countering violent extremism.[705] As of 2021, SEARCCT had conducted 200 training programmes, in which an estimated 10,000 participants from ninety-five states had been beneficiaries.[706] Further, the Centre has engaged over 8,500 local youths in participatory activities aimed at refuting and opposing terrorism narratives.[707]

According to the UNSD, eighty-two states had autonomous NHRIs that complied with international standards in 2020, and that was an improvement of 17 per cent from the situation in 2015.[708] The progress implies that one in three least developed countries has an internationally compliant NHRI as of 2020, as opposed to one in five in 2015.[709] The UNSD nonetheless cautions that the progress is still insufficient to meet the 2030 target, noting that improvement had stalled in most regions where no new autonomous NHRIs had been created or recognized since 2018.[710]

---

[700] UNSD, 'SDG Indicator Metadata' (19 July 2016).
[701] UNDESA, Statistics Division, 'Peace, Justice and Strong Institutions' (n 372).
[702] See UNGA, 'National Institutions' (n 692).
[703] Ministry of Devolution and Planning, Kenya (n 478) 44.
[704] ibid.
[705] Economic Planning Unit, Malaysia (n 414) 112.
[706] ibid.
[707] ibid.
[708] UNDESA, Statistics Division, 'Peace, Justice and Strong Institutions' (n 372).
[709] ibid.
[710] ibid.

1242   SDG 16

The UNSG Progress Report specifically notes that in 2020, the number of autonomous NHRIs in Sub-Saharan Africa and Europe increased by three, while there was lack of progress in Oceania, the Caribbean, and in Eastern, Western, and South Eastern Asia where no new independent NHRI had been created or recognized since 2018.[711] Under these circumstances, given the need to expand human rights protection and enforcement, the UNSD calls for concerted efforts to establish and strengthen NHRIs in all regions.[712]

The UNSD points out that the establishment and strengthening of NHRIs is a demonstration of a state's commitment to the protection and enforcement of human rights.[713] In particular, the UNSD points out that by strengthening the NHRIs to comply with the Paris Principles, the state provides the NHRI with 'a broad mandate, competence and power to investigate, report on the national human rights situation, and publicize human rights through information and education'.[714] The NHRIs are expected to remain autonomous and exemplify a culture of pluralism despite the fact that they are largely state-funded.[715] They are an essential part of the national human rights protection system, and in circumstances in which a state grants them quasi-judicial competence, such institutions address complaints and assist victims in instituting cases in courts to redress violations.[716]

In the case of Malaysia, the Human Rights Commission of Malaysia (SUHAKAM) was created through legislation in 1999 and has exemplified the Paris Principles on independence in its structure and operations.[717] SUHAKAM has been engaged in diverse activities for the promotion and advancement of human rights, including: addressing public complaints; undertaking trainings; making press releases; issuing publications; and promoting adherence with international obligations.[718]

The Independent National Commission on Human Rights (INRC) of Liberia is credited with raising awareness by conducting trainings relating to human rights on security officials, and other public officials charged with responsibilities relating to rule of law matters.[719] The INRC has also been involved in public awareness campaigns and training initiatives that have focused on traditional leaders for purposes of eliminating retrogressive traditional practices.[720]

ii) **Critique** Reliance on the sole indicator is a core limitation of target 16.a. This is due to the fact that institutional efforts in relation to such thematic issues may relate to

---

[711] UNESC, UN Doc E/2021/58 (n 337) para 179.
[712] UNDESA, Statistics Division, 'Peace, Justice and Strong Institutions' (n 372).
[713] UNSD, 'SDG Indicator Metadata' (19 July 2016).
[714] ibid.
[715] ibid.
[716] ibid.
[717] Economic Planning Unit, Malaysia (n 414) 112.
[718] ibid.
[719] Sustainable Development Goals Knowledge Platform, 'Liberia' (n 388) 100.
[720] ibid.

diverse activities, including police reforms, reliance on technology, training on security matters, and countering extremism within the populace.

12. Target 16.b Promote and enforce non-discriminatory laws and policies for sustainable development

Under target 16.b, sustainable development is to be promoted and facilitated though the enforcement of non-discriminatory laws and policies. Discriminatory practices and subjugation of some segments of the population, whether on the basis of gender, age, race, ethnicity, or religion, may be the outcome of societal stereotyping and biases.

a) Indicator 16.b.1 Proportion of population reporting having personally felt discriminated against or harassed in the previous 12 months on the basis of a ground of discrimination prohibited under international human rights law

The sole indicator 16.b.1 of the target is under the auspices of the OHCHR, and measures the ratio of individuals who have in the previous twelve months felt discriminated against or harassed on the basis of a ground that is proscribed under the international human rights legal regime.[721] As such, the indicator focuses on evaluating the prevalence of discriminatory practices on the basis of the experiences reported by individuals.[722] The UNSD justifies the conceptualization and use of the indicator on the basis that it facilitates an evaluation of the effectiveness of non-discriminatory laws, policies, and practices in states in the context of relevant population groups.[723]

i) Empirical evaluation methodology In the context of the data collection methodology, the OHCHR recommends the utilization of the grounds prohibited by the international human rights legal regime, namely sex; age; health or disability status; ethnicity, colour, or language; migration status; socio-economic status; geographic location or place of residence; marital and family status; religion; sexual orientation or gender identity; and political opinion.[724] The OHCHR acknowledges that the suggested grounds are not exhaustive, and thus recommends that other categories to capture grounds that are not explicitly listed should be considered.[725]

Among the limitations of the indicator is the fact that it does not capture incidences of discrimination that the respondents are unwilling to disclose, or the ones that they are not aware of.[726] As such, further efforts beyond the indicator may be necessary to understand patterns in discrimination and harassment, and to evaluate legislative and policy initiatives impact and responses.[727]

---

[721] UNSD, 'SDG Indicator Metadata' (3 December 2018).
[722] ibid.
[723] ibid.
[724] ibid.
[725] ibid.
[726] ibid.
[727] ibid.

1244 SDG 16

ii) Implementation efforts Some of the states' efforts to curb discrimination include Malaysia's initiatives to promote gender equity and equality through: the adoption of the National Women's Policy and Action Plan; aspirations for having at least 30 per cent of women in decision-making positions in both the public and private sectors; the promotion of the female gender participation in the labour force by encouraging the private sector to adopt flexible working terms and conditions.[728] Liberia's National Gender Policy is instrumental in addressing issues relating to discrimination against the female gender.[729] The Independent Human Rights Commission of Liberia has also been instrumental in the promotion and enforcement of the right to non-discrimination.[730]

With regard to Kenya, article 27(3) of the Constitution that was promulgated in 2010 requires that both genders be provided with equal opportunites and treament, which has the objective of remedying a history of gender inequity in governance.[731] Further, article 27(8) of the Constitution obliges the state to 'take legislative and other measures to implement the principle that not more than two-thirds of the members of elective or appointive bodies shall be of the same gender'. In the case of Namibia, the Office of the Ombudsman addresses complaints relating to allegations of discrimination.[732] It has been noted that there has been a general increase of complaints by people alleged to have been discriminated against in Namibia.[733] The increase has been attributed to the greater access to information on human rights, and the engagement of trade unions, among other factors.[734]

VI. Conclusion

The progressive realization of SDG 16 targets is vital, particularly due to the fact that the aspirations enunciated under this SDG are facilitators and expediters of other developmental goals. Effective realization of other SDGs requires conditions of peace, the rule of law, guarantees of justice, and effective and accountable institutions, which comprise some of the core conceptual themes of SDG 16 targets. As demonstrated by the voluntary national reviews of diverse states and the global statistical reviews conducted under the auspices of the UN, SDG 16 targets have been a core determinant of the post-2015 development agenda of countries. It is noteworthy that some states have assimilated the SDGs framework into their mainstream developmental policies and aspirations.

The UNSG in the 2021 Progress Report cautioned that by early 2020, 'the world was not on track to meet the Goals and targets by 2030'.[735] Some of the core factors

---

[728] Economic Planning Unit, Malaysia (n 414) 112.
[729] Sustainable Development Goals Knowledge Platform, 'Liberia' (n 388) 59.
[730] ibid.
[731] Kenya Law, 'Constitution of Kenya' <http://kenyalaw.org/kl/index.php?id=398> accessed 27 October 2021.
[732] Republic of Namibia (n 400) 65.
[733] ibid.
[734] ibid.
[735] UNESC, UN Doc E/2021/58 (n 337) para 2.

contributing to the lack of consistent progress include wars and conflicts in some states, and the continued pervasiveness of corruption and IFFs in many countries that keep diverting essential financial resources from developing and least developed states that would otherwise contribute to the realization of the SDGs. Nonetheless, the post-2015 development agenda through the SDGs framework offers vital guidance to states in their aspirations for sustainable development. The annual review of progress in various regions and groupings toward the realization of SDG 16 targets provides vital information regarding both progress and retrogression. In addition, the regular VNRs by states continue to provide vital self-evaluation and practical checks regarding their progress, in addition to providing essential comparative information for other countries. The targets and indicators formulated under SDG 16 aspirations of peace, access to justice, and effective and accountable institutions, overall do contribute to tangible and discernible progress towards sustainable development among states, despite some inevitable relapses, limitations, and predicaments.

SDG 17

'Strengthen the Means of Implementation and Revitalize the Global Partnership for Sustainable Development'

Andreas Rechkemmer and Damilola Olawuyi

I. Introduction

This chapter discusses the scope and content of SDG 17. It highlights the preparatory works and context for its establishment and inclusion, the opportunities, risks, and barriers related to its implementation, how opportunities can be leveraged, and how challenges may be overcome through innovative governance approaches.

Our point of departure is the general insight and theorem that any present or future global policy framework ought to fit and mirror the realities—real or anticipated—of the challenges for global policy-making for which it is designed. Since such global challenges and realities of concern tend to play out at and affect various scales and levels, not just the global alone, global policy solutions must also address regional, national, and local issues simultaneously insofar as these are linked to the global problems at hand. As we move deeper into the twenty-first century, it becomes clear that problems, challenges, and opportunities that global policies have been and will have to be designed for are increasingly characterized by unprecedented complexity and multi-causality, often paired with a high level of ambiguity and uncertainty.[1] Furthermore, non-linear trajectories or the cascading of unfolding events or developments of note seem to become the rule rather than the exception, as the phenomenology of climate change, biodiversity loss or the COVID-19 pandemic have shown. Thus, the literature speaks of *wicked problems* and *grand challenges* when such phenomenon is described and it is precisely this type of phenomenon for which much of SDG 17 has been designed (and with it, a plethora of subsequent targets and indicators like for no other of the SDGs) to guide global collective action.[2]

---

[1] Parts of this chapter draw from A Rechkemmer, 'Back to the Future: Learning from the Evolution of Global Sustainability Governance' in AB Brik and LA Pal (eds) *The Future of the Policy Science* (Edward Elgar 2021).

See C Yamu, 'It Is Simply Complex(ity)' (2014) 50(4) disP—The Planning Review 43–53; M Chapman and others, '5 Key Challenges and Solutions for Governing Complex Adaptive (Food) Systems' (2017) 9 Sustainability 1594; Z Kovacic and LJ Di Felice, 'Complexity, Uncertainty and Ambiguity: Implications for European Union Energy Governance' (2019) 53 Energy Research & Social Science 159–69.

[2] See BW Head, 'Wicked Problems in Public Policy' (2008) 3(2) Public Policy 101–18; BW Head, 'Forty Years of Wicked Problems Literature: Forging Closer Links to Policy Studies' (2019) 38(2) Policy and Society

1248 SDG 17

To illustrate the above we provide three examples: (i) Anthropogenic climate change, by itself completely unprecedented in the history of humanity and the planet, highly complex and unfolding in a non-linear fashion with many cascading effects—all of which have to be combined coherently and implemented urgently, consistently and simultaneously in an integrated way. Has there ever been a more daunting challenge to international cooperation and global action? (ii) The novel coronavirus Sars-CoV-2 and the COVID-19 pandemic have illustrated how vicious and complex the multi-scalar occurrence of a global policy problem can be and how intersectional and networked global crises in the twenty-first century may look like. At the same time, the pandemic powerfully illustrates the need for and the added value of SDG 17 as no country, region, or even continent alone is in a position to effectively address and tackle this crisis. From targeted, science-based global action and public–private partnerships via questions of trade and finance, to the need for North–South and South–South cooperation in a spirit of solidarity, COVID-19 literally touches upon the entire set of SDGs as a whole and upon SDG 17 in particular. (iii) Threats to peace, security, democracy, and established institutions have become more complex, intricate, and multi-layered in the twenty-first century. Over the past few decades, there has been a steady paradigmatic shift away from the classic type of inter-state wars that the UN Charter was established for in the first place, toward a proliferating range of intrastate wars, conflict, violence, insurgencies, and fragmentation paired with inherent institutional fragility and failing statehood. Moreover, the various types of global challenges are now being seen in direct combination and correlation, as the wars in Sudan and Syria have demonstrated.

These and many other global risks, threats and challenges have recently been called *grand challenges*, and across epistemic communities, academic disciplines, and professional associations,[3] there is an effort to provide data and decision support to intergovernmental organizations and governments. The UN 2030 Agenda and the SDG policy framework were negotiated, established, and endorsed by the international community with the promise of a better and more systemic and rigorous reflection of such complex and multi-layered problems and their interdependencies thus providing institutions and actors of global governance and international cooperation with an up-to-date and state-of-the-art compendium of key interrelated issues and cues to collective action at the same time. SDG 17 indeed is central and critical in this regard as it yields to build a solid bridge—or, rather, a whole web of bridges—from knowledge to action and engagement. To be effective at scale, global policy frameworks must not only be innovative but catalyse and steer policy transfer and diffusion across different regions, cultures, topographies, economies, and socio-political systems. They also must enable

---

180–97; BW Head and J Alford, 'Wicked Problems: Implications for Public Policy and Management' (2015) 47(6) Administration & Society 711–39; BG Peters, 'What Is So Wicked About Wicked Problems? A Conceptual Analysis and a Research Program' (2017) 36(3) Policy and Society 385–96.

[3] For examples of Grand Challenges frameworks, see National Academy of Engineering, *Grand Challenges for Engineering: Imperatives, Prospects, and Priorities: Summary of a Forum* (The National Academies Press 2016); The Bill & Melinda Gates Foundation, *Global Grand Challenges* (2020) <https://gcgh.grandchallenges.org> accessed 7 January 2023.

multi-level and networked interventions across structures and processes of decision-making and a multitude of agents from governmental as well as non-governmental backgrounds.

Since these latter goals and requirements are generally very difficult to meet, many previous attempts at establishing a workable, effective, and sustainable system or framework of international governance for sustainable development either failed or delivered only partially, as was the case with the Millennium Development Goals (MDGs) and, unfortunately, a large number of multilateral environmental agreements (MEAs). Therefore, the architecture of the SDGs reflects multiple lessons learned from previous experiences and failures in international cooperation. The tightly woven web of goals, targets, indicators, metrics, and implementation tools is not only there to ensure the intersectionality and 'holism' of the policy framework to mirror and reflect the—sometimes wicked—intricacies and complexities of the real world in global development and sustainability challenges but also to enable joint, effective, and efficient implementation strategies that cut across numerous policy problems and sectors. Also, this tight web aims to enable the creation or revival of a multiverse of partnerships, financing mechanisms, economic and policy cooperation frameworks, and so forth. This general logic of the SDG architecture ultimately finds its consequence and epitome in SDG 17 (and thereby explains SDG 17's outstandingly comprehensive list of targets and indicators). To some degree, SDG 17 aims to reflect recent and novel theories and concepts of governance of global public goods and commons under twenty-first-century conditions and tries to make a difference in establishing a new and more just and effective basis for collective action. Ultimately, it aims at establishing a punctuated new equilibrium for global sustainable development action, redefining the relationship between and the role allocation within the 'structure versus agency' continuum.

II. *Travaux Préparatoires*

Global governance for sustainable development did not play any significant role on the global policy stage until the early 1970s. At the time of the United Nations' establishment in 1945, international sustainable development law and policy did not matter. The world organization first focused on peace and security, international cooperation, and human rights.[4] As the Worldwatch Institute notes,[5] sustainability issues were not even considered much of a national threat at that time, let alone a pressing global problem that could provoke international conflict and undermine human health, economic well-being, and social stability. Accordingly, the UN Charter does not even mention the words 'environment', 'sustainability', or 'sustainable development'. However, as a result of the rapidly emerging process of de-colonization and the subsequently quickly

---

[4] See A Rechkemmer, 'Lösungsansätze für globale Umweltprobleme—Globalisierung' in Bundeszentrale für politische Bildung (ed), *Informationen zur politischen Bildung* (Bundeszentrale für politische Bildung 2003) 280.

[5] See Worldwatch Institute, *Partnership for the Planet: An Environmental Agenda for the United Nations* (Worldwatch Institute 1995).

1250   SDG 17

growing number of UN Member States, especially in the 1960s, new issues such as global economic development as well as social affairs made it onto the international and intergovernmental agenda. Furthermore, the state of the global environment was eventually recognized as a policy problem to be dealt with by the international community, in particular by the UN and its specialized agencies. In 1968, the United Nations General Assembly (UNGA) formally recognized the need to address global environmental issues. Resolution 23/198 states that greater attention should be given to the human environment as a basis for sustainable economic and social development. Moreover, the UNGA expressed the hope that donors would assist developing countries through the means of enhanced cooperation to find appropriate solutions for their environmental problems. It was the first time that a link had been established between sustainability policy and development policy. The same resolution also called for the organization of the first world conference on sustainability, the United Nations Conference on the Human Environment (UNCHE). UNCHE—a historic breakthrough—took place in 1972 in Stockholm. Its opening day, 5 June, is still celebrated globally as World Environment Day.

Two remarkable results were achieved: (i) the main concluding document, the Declaration on Human Environment (Stockholm Declaration) endorsed a comprehensive listing of all global environmental and sustainability issues known at the time, and (ii) the establishment of the United Nations Environment Program (UNEP). UNCHE was a step forward, in the sense that for the first time ever, global and national policy actors and stakeholders were able to refer to and rely on an international legal document addressing the full range of known sustainability issues of global concern. Also, the Stockholm Declaration established the systemic interaction between the aspects of environment and development as a new field of global policy and international relations, to be called Sustainable Development.[6] UNCHE also resulted in other important steps forward, such as the formal adoption of the principle of international liability and the 'polluter pays principle', the decision to raise the official development assistance (ODA) of OECD countries to 0.7 per cent of their gross national product (GNP), and the foundation of Earthwatch, a global satellite-based monitoring system.

As noted, the establishment of UNEP was a key moment since it soon started to play a much more proactive and creative role in providing leadership and catalytical support to the invocation of new environmental policy frameworks and regimes such as the Washington Convention on International Trade in Endangered Species of Wild Fauna and Flora (CITES) and the MARPOL Convention restricting intentional discharges by ships (both 1973), the Convention on the Law of the Sea (1982), the Vienna Convention (1985) and its Montreal Protocol on Substances that Deplete the Ozone Layer (1987), and the Basel Convention on transboundary movement of hazardous waste (1989). UNEP also co-established the Intergovernmental Panel on Climate Change (IPCC) in 1990, jointly with the World Meteorological Organization (WMO), another important

---

[6] See KF Hünemörder, '"Environment is Our Love"—Rückblick auf die UN-Umweltkonferenz von Stockholm, in G Altner and others (eds), *Jahrbuch Ökologie* (C.H. Beck 2006).

milestone for global sustainable development governance.[7] Also, apart from launching Earthwatch, the GRID/GPS satellite-imaging project was set up, and input to a multitude of international, regional, and national conferences and policy frameworks as well as to path-breaking global environmental assessments was provided.[8]

The next evolutionary step for the global governance of sustainable development occurred in the 1980s. The World Commission on Environment and Development (WCED), the so-called Brundtland Commission, was established in 1984[9] and was mandated to explore the environment–development nexus with its social, economic, and ecological implications. The Commission's report *Our Common Future* (the Brundtland Report) became famous as it finally coined the term sustainable development, whose definition became a new paradigm: 'Humanity has the ability to make development sustainable—to ensure that it meets the needs of the present without compromising the ability of future generations to meet their own needs.'[10] The report further defined sustainable development as 'a process of change in which the exploitation of resources, the direction of investment, the orientation of technological development, and institutional change are made consistent with future as well as present needs'.[11] According to WCED, sustainable development deals with 'two fundamental issues, i.e., inter-generational equity and comprehensive structural adjustment'.[12] Although the WCED did not invent sustainable development for the international community— it was first introduced in 1980 in the World Conservation Strategy published jointly by the World Conservation Union (IUCN), the World Wildlife Fund (WWF) and UNEP[13]—it was the Brundtland Commission that brought it to fame.

The Brundtland Report became influential by creating a strong link between the policy fields, or sectors, of environment and development, highlighting that poverty, under-development, and the depletion of natural resources are intrinsically linked and interdependent. The WCED's concept soon became the paradigm for the global governance of sustainable development. The publication, dissemination, and reception of the Brundtland Report coincided with the end of the Cold War and the ongoing and ensuing political, social, and economic erosion processes in Eastern Europe. It thus benefited from a rare historical momentum, in which states and their governments seemed ready and eager to revive the principles of collective action and multilateralism and therefore supported the establishment of new and innovative intergovernmental agreements under the aegis of the UN system. It was the time of an important series of world conferences, invoking new forms of international cooperation and governance, through which new and genuine collective goals were identified and, for the most

---

[7] See UNU-IAS, *International Sustainable Development Governance* (United Nations University 2002).

[8] See ibid.

[9] The name referred to WCED's chairwoman, former Prime Minister of Norway, Dr Gro Harlem Brundtland.

[10] See World Commission on Environment and Development (WCED), *Our Common Future* (OUP 1987).

[11] See ibid.

[12] See UE Simonis, *How to Lead World Society towards Sustainable Development?* (WZB Berlin 1998).

[13] See IUCN, UNEP & WWF, *World Conservation Strategy—Living Resource Conservation for Sustainable Development* (IUCN 1991); M Pallemaerts, 'Is Multilateralism the Future? Sustainable Development or Globalisation as a Comprehensive Vision of the Future of Humanity' (2003) 5 (January/February) Environment, Development and Sustainability 275–95.

1252   SDG 17

part, binding treaties were signed. Nation-states showed readiness to sacrifice national interests and traditional sovereignty considerations to some extent. Being wrongly perceived as a so-called soft policy area, global sustainability policy benefited from this momentum, given that heads of states and governments perceived it as a preferred testing ground for the newly identified approach. As such, the international treaties and agreements signed during this period and the institutions and structures established ultimately laid the ground for the UN 2030 Agenda and the SDGs. Many of these institutions, processes, treaties, and agreements also anticipated and prepared for some of the targets and indicators under SDG 17.

In this context, the UNGA decided on the organization of the United Nations Conference on Environment and Development (UNCED), to be held in June 1992 in Rio de Janeiro, Brazil. UNCED's mandate was originally to review and take stock of the development made in the respective sectors of environment and development since the Stockholm Conference of 1972, and to identify new strategies for enhanced collective action at both global and regional levels. It was foreseen to further merge the two sectors into the law and policy field of sustainable development. Yet, UNCED became much more influential, taking the global sustainable development discourse to a new level, conceptually and politically. Several key multilateral resolutions and agreements were agreed upon at UNCED, above all the Rio Declaration and Agenda 21. In addition to the hallmark policy frameworks, the UNCED resulted in new institutions as well as other structural and substantive reorientations, among which are the three 'Rio Conventions': United Nations Framework Convention of Climate Change (UNFCCC), United Nations Convention on Biological Diversity (UNCBD), and United Nations Convention to Combat Desertification (UNCCD); the UN Forum on Forests (UNFF); the UN Commission on Sustainable Development (CSD); the so-called Rio process including the Rio + 5 and Rio + 10 conferences; and a new system of world sustainable development conferences and networks.[14]

The CSD has played a crucial role in the field of sustainable development since its inception. It oversees the system of sustainable development governance on behalf of the United Nations Economic and Social Council (ECOSOC). ECOSOC is the central coordinating body in charge of sustainable development law and policy within the entire UN system, also including affiliated agencies such as the World Bank. The CSD also makes recommendations, for example, concerning the internalization of environmental costs, changes to production and consumption patterns, trade issues such as market access for developing countries, or the mainstreaming of sustainable development issues into national law and policies. It also monitors the payment of 0.7 per cent of OECD and other developed countries' gross domestic product (GDP) as Official Development Assistance (ODA), and the work of the Global Environment Facility (GEF), which was originally founded in 1990 as a major credit programme,

---

[14] See PM Haas, 'UN Conferences and Constructivist Governance of the Environment' (2002) 8(1) Global Governance 73–91; T Fues and B Hamm (eds), *Die Weltkonferenzen der 90er Jahre: Baustellen für Global Governance* (Dietz 2001).

administered jointly by the World Bank, UNEP, and UNDP. The GEF funds projects of global importance, for example on biodiversity, climate change, or international waters. It is perceived as an effective mechanism within the global sustainability governance architecture and became an important player in a rather short period of time. Rio also brought up the so-called development goals, being summed up in the paper 'Shaping the 21st Century' by the Organisation for Economic Cooperation and Development's Development Cooperation Directorate (OECD-DAC), naming seven global goals for sustainable development,[15] ultimately a precursor of the Sustainable Development Goals. They were later, at the UN Millennium Summit in 2000, further elaborated and formally adopted as the Millennium Development Goals (MDGs).[16]

As noted, another important outcome of UNCED that built the institutional architecture of global sustainability governance further, were the so-called Rio Conventions: first, the UNFCCC, which entered into force in 1994 and aims to stabilize the climatic effects of anthropogenic greenhouse gas emissions, seconded by the Kyoto Protocol adopted in 1997 and the Paris Agreement of 2015. Second, the Convention on Biological Diversity (CBD), which entered into force in 1993, seconded by the Cartagena Protocol on Biosafety in 2000. The third Rio Convention, the United Nations Convention to Combat Desertification (UNCCD), entered into force in 1996. Furthermore, the Rio Declaration can be understood as a refined and enhanced version of the Stockholm Declaration of 1972.[17] Its goal is a 'new and equitable global partnership'. Sustainable development cannot be met without inclusion of all actors and stakeholders ('states, key sectors of societies and people') and includes 'eradicating poverty' as an essential and 'indispensable requirement' for sustainable development.[18] Also, the goal to 'decrease the disparities in standards of living' and Principle 25 are of note: 'Peace, development and environmental protection are interdependent and indivisible.' All states, especially the developed states, are called upon to reduce and eliminate 'unsustainable patterns of production and consumption' (Principle 8), to share scientific understanding and technologies (Principle 9), and to 'promote the internalization of environmental costs and the use of economic instruments, taking into account the approach that the polluter should, in principle, bear the cost of pollution' (Principle 16).[19] This polluter-pays principle has, for example, been included in the Kyoto Protocol and the Paris Agreement. Also important is Principle 15, stating that a 'lack of full scientific certainty shall not be used as a reason for postponing cost-effective measures to prevent environmental degradation'.[20] As such, the Rio Declaration on

[15] See OECD, *Thematic Study on the Paris Declaration: Aid Effectiveness and Development Effectiveness* (OECD 1996).

[16] See UNGA, *United Nations Millennium Declaration*, General Assembly resolution 55/2 of 8 September 2000 (United Nations 2000).

[17] See United Nations, 'Stockholm Declaration' (1972) <https://wedocs.unep.org/bitstream/handle/20.500.11822/29567/ELGP1StockD.pdf> accessed 7 January 2023.

[18] See United Nations, *Rio Declaration* (1992), <https://www.un.org/en/development/desa/population/migration/generalassembly/docs/globalcompact/A_CONF.151_26_Vol.I_Declaration.pdf> accessed 7 January 2023.

[19] See ibid.

[20] See J Bernstein, 'The Role of Science in Strengthening Global Environmental Governance' in A Rechkemmer (ed), *UNEO—Towards an International Environment Organization. Approaches to a Sustainable Reform of Global Environmental Governance'* (Nomos 2005).

1254   SDG 17

the one hand anticipated much of the spirit of the 2030 Agenda and the SDGs. On the other, it surpassed many of the targets enshrined in SDG 17 in detail and sharpness—a real problem for enforcement.

In hindsight, the UNCED became a platform for launching innovative governance tools, consisting of various types of approaches and actors. Thus, sustainable development governance—by definition dealing with problems that transcendent the scope and abilities of nation-states—became both a laboratory and a driving force for a conceptual shift in international relations, altering the concepts of sovereignty and territoriality as its underlying principles—at least for some time. Traditionally, the state as a spatial unit is seen as the fundamental ordering force in international relations through a central reliance on dominium-based conceptions. Yet, the UNCED stands for the migration from Westphalian concepts to global governance. The Earth Summit centralized cooperative action on environmental and development targets and tried to replace established state-sovereignty-based patterns and procedures with governance-oriented procedures featured in the legally binding Rio Conventions and further treaties. Remarkably, sustainable development became a major subject of international law for the first time. The conceptual shift can be understood as a process of desired structural and institutional change on the basis of a transformed shared understanding of the underlying normative terms of reference, institutional rules, and functional settings of the international community. We may understand Rio as a case of attempted international quasi-state formation, with no formal cession of sovereignty to supra-national institutions; rather relocating individual state actors' *de facto* sovereignty to transnational authorities, the desired result of which is the emergence of a new governing system, which breaks down the spatial coincidence between state-as-actor and state-as-structure.

Counter to positivist perceptions, international law coincides with socio-historical and socio-political, extra-legal patterns that reflect and reshape the political reality. The step to turn scientific research results and political desiderata on global sustainable development into an extensive framework of supranational treaties and agreements of a binding nature, including instruments of monitoring, evaluation, and dispute settlement, reflects another transformative quality vis-à-vis classic legal (and policy) concepts along with a certain degree of readiness to sacrifice the concept of a dominium-like understanding of territoriality for the sake of yielded supremacy of a supranational process of legislation. This is complemented by the constructing role of knowledge in international relations, and its coefficient, the learning capacity of institutions. Knowledge and information are at times rated higher than genuine political will, national interest, or power. This spirit highly influenced Rio and, in fact, the post-Rio process and became again influential during the drafting of the SDGs and the Paris Agreement where the epistemic community had significant influence on the legal and policy outcomes.[21] All of this has been further complemented since the UNCED by a

---

[21] See PM Haas and EB Haas, 'Learning to Learn: Improving International Governance; (1995) 1(3) Global Governance 255–84; A Wendt, 'Identity and Structural Change in International Politics' in J Lapid and F Kratochwil (eds), *The Return of Culture and Identity in IR Theory* (Lynne Rienner 1996); DL Nielson and MJ

growing number of global public policy networks, the involvement of NGOs and other civil society actors, transnational and local corporations, and the scientific community as they found their way into the newly developed cooperation frameworks and treaties. Strategy pieces such as the so-called bottom-up approach, participatory aspects of policy formulation and implementation, a decentralized logic of intervention, monitoring and assessment, and public–private partnerships (PPPs), were meant to replace traditional policy cycle concepts.[22] These phenomena are characteristic not only of the Rio Earth Summit but of a new era of global governance without which there simply would be no 2030 Agenda, no SDGs, and no Paris Agreement.

The post-Rio stocktaking took place at the World Summit on Sustainable Development (WSSD) in 2002 in Johannesburg. Part of its preparatory work was the 2000 UN Millennium Summit, which adopted the Millennium Declaration and the MDGs. In addition, the World Trade Organization (WTO) ministerial conference of Doha, Qatar, in 2001, and the 2002 International Conference on Financing Development in Monterrey, preceded the WSSD, which provided an opportunity for a comprehensive review of the achievements made since Rio.[23] Johannesburg 2002 signalled a renewed emphasis by states on protecting their own national interests and concerns. This ran counter to the 'postmodern' notions of global governance promoted at and after the Rio Earth Summit. Indeed, the events of 9/11 in 2001 took a heavy toll on multilateralism. Although willing to follow the books of the UN Charter at first, the Bush Jr. administration soon decided to marginalize the UN and favour unilateral moves or 'coalitions of the willing'. However, UN Secretary-General Kofi Annan launched a counter-initiative to salvage the spirit and the institutional, legal and policy results from UNCED and, with these, the spirit of collective action. This initiative led to the United Nations World Summit of 2005, held in conjunction with the 60th Session of the UNGA, also called the 'MDG plus 5 Summit'.

Annan commissioned three major reports to be discussed at this Summit, all of which were about sustainable development and ultimately helped prepare Agenda 2030 and the SDGs. The High-level Panel on Threats, Challenges and Change released its report 'A More Secure World: Our Shared Responsibility' in 2004.[24] Six clusters of threats would have to be faced: economic and social threats, including poverty, infectious disease and environmental degradation; inter-state conflict; internal conflict, including civil war, genocide, and other large-scale atrocities; nuclear, radiological, chemical and

---

Tierney, 'Delegation to International Organizations: Agency Theory and World Bank Environmental Reform' (2003) 57(2) International Organization 241–76.

[22] See F Biermann, *Weltumweltpolitik zwischen Nord und Süd. Die neue Verhandlungsmacht der Entwicklungsländer* (Nomos 1998); A Rechkemmer, 'International Cooperation and Environmental Politics after Rio and Johannesburg (2005) 23(1) Sicherheit und Frieden 40–44; Rechkemmer, *UNEO—Towards an International Environment Organization* (n 20).

[23] See JG Speth, 'Perspectives on the Johannesburg Summit' (2003) 45(1) Environment 24–29; A La Vina and others, 'The outcomes of Johannesburg: Assessing the World Summit on Sustainable Development' (2003) XXIII (Winter-Spring) SAIS Review 1.

[24] See High-Level Panel (HLP), *A More Secure World: Our Shared Responsibility (UN-RES-A/59/565)* (United Nations 2004).

1256   SDG 17

biological weapons; terrorism; and transnational organized crime. These threats were perceived as interdependent and therefore would have to be addressed simultaneously in international law and policy. In particular, the Panel identified food insecurity, land degradation, water scarcity, deforestation, natural disasters, large-scale economic losses, environmental refugees, and global warming as global security threats, adding to existing humanitarian and peace concerns.[25] The Panel's report was seconded by the Millennium Ecosystem Assessment (MA), a cross-sectoral study on the status of the Earth's ecosystems. After several years of work, in 2005 the main Synthesis Report was published, supplemented by more specific reports.[26] It was the first comprehensive study to assess the situation of twenty-four different types of ecosystems and their provisioning of essential services. The Synthesis Report established a connection between the degradation of ecosystem services and security issues. In the eyes of the MA, security refers to 'safety of person and possessions, secure access to necessary resources, and security from natural and human-made disasters.'[27] Following that definition, the MA named a number of security threats that are due to environmental damage. Damaging the environment can therefore lead to increasing economic losses and to rising numbers of disaster victims. Also, stable social networks depend on cultural services which deteriorated ecosystems might no longer be able to provide, leading to instabilities in a society. In particular, the poor are threatened because they are more dependent on ecosystems and their services and thus more vulnerable to their degradation.

In addition, Annan tasked economist Jeffrey Sachs with the production of yet another report, 'Investing in development: a practical plan to achieve the Millennium Development Goals.'[28] It mentions several links between the environment and the MDGs beyond Goal 7 (ensuring environmental sustainability) and shows the interdependency between both. Through the nexus between energy, poverty, and the environment, there is a significant link between sustainability and nearly all of the MDGs. After the 2005 World Summit the UN embarked on three key projects to further advance Global Sustainable Development Governance: (i) enhance countries' performance of meeting the MDGs universally; (ii) salvage the global climate change regime by agreeing on a successor to the Kyoto Protocol; and (iii) planning for a 'Rio +20' Summit to come up with a strong, renewed framework that would replace and surpass both UNCED's outcomes and the MDG regime. It is remarkable that all of these developments and provisions made their imprint not only on the SDGs as a whole but particularly on SDG 17.

By the early 2010s, only modest progress had been made toward most of the MDGs and in most world regions. Therefore, considerable effort was put into the planning and preparation of the United Nations Conference on Sustainable Development (UNCSD)

---

[25] See ibid.

[26] See Millennium Ecosystem Assessment (MA), 'Final Report' (UN 2005) <http://www.millennium assessment.org/proxy/document.356.aspx> accessed 7 January 2023.

[27] See ibid.

[28] See UN Millennium Project (UN MP), *Investing in Development. A Practical Plan to Achieve the Millennium Development Goals* (UN 2005).

in June 2012 in Rio de Janeiro. Rio + 20 resulted in an official outcome document called 'The Future We Want'. The agreement to embark on a successor regime to the MDGs, the Sustainable Development Goals (SDGs) for the time after 2015, represented an important milestone. The UN Secretary-General, Ban ki-Moon, set up a High-level Panel on Global Sustainability (GSP) consisting of present and former international leaders. The GSP released its report 'Resilient People, Resilient Planet: A Future Worth Choosing',[29] which laid the groundwork. In the immediate aftermath of Rio + 20, the UNSG appointed another panel, the High-Level Panel on the Post-2015 Development Agenda. The panel released its final report, 'A New Global Partnership: Eradicate Poverty and Transform Economies through Sustainable Development' in 2013.[30] This report, along with the proceedings, negotiation outcomes and recommendations of an 'Open Working Group' (OWG) (ie open to all UN Member States) established by the UNGA in early 2013, finally guided the UN Secretariat and the member states in identifying the SDG framework for the period 2015–2030,[31] adopted by the UNGA in September 2015 along with the 2030 Agenda. Based on the works and outcomes of both the HLP and the OWG, SDG 17 became the comprehensive capstone of the SDG architecture, not merely replacing the old MDG 8 but aiming at exceeding it by far. A new and stronger notion of 'global partnership' was now supposed to cut across all other sixteen SDGs and guide their path to implementation and accountability, hence the intricate and detailed set of targets and indicators.

The 'making of' the Sustainable Development Goals essentially took place during the OWG deliberations. The UN Member States decided for the first time to device a novel approach to representation in a group with a limitation of thirty seats whereby most of the seats in the OWG were shared by several countries. This modus operandi allowed a more equitable and fluid negotiation process, bypassing and transforming the usual 'inter-bloc' process that tends to produce prisoner-dilemma-like situations with little progress on substance. SDG 17 benefitted from this in that it was balanced, comprehensive, and detailed since it carried the handwriting of the G77 and many developing country parties, not just the donor community. Ultimately, the goal–target–indicator–monitoring methodology probably would not have become a signature—and potentially powerful—element of the SDGs without the strong influence of developing countries and civil society groups in the OWG process throughout its conclusion in July 2014. Again, SDG 17 benefited especially from this arrangement via South-led norm setting on partnerships and financial and technological assistance and solidarity.[32]

---

[29] See United Nations High-Level Panel on Global Sustainability, 'Resilient People, Resilient Planet: A Future Worth Choosing' (UN 2012).

[30] See United Nations, 'Rio+20 Declaration' (2013) <http://sustainabledevelopment.un.org/rio20.html> accessed 7 January 2023.

[31] See ibid.

[32] See D Gasper, 'The Road to the Sustainable Development Goals: Building Global Alliances and Norms' (2019) 15(2) Journal of Global Ethics 118–37, DOI: 10.1080/17449626.2019.1639532; M Kamau and others, *Transforming Multilateral Diplomacy: The Inside Story of the SDGs* (Routledge 2018); F Dodds and others, *Negotiating the Sustainable Development Goals* (Routledge 2017).

III. Commentary on SDG 17

A. Background: SDG 17 in the Context of Globalization and Global Governance

The challenges outlined and quantified in the 2030 Agenda for Sustainable Development and the Sustainable Development Goals[33,34] demonstrate the scale, magnitude, and complexity of international law and policy problems waiting to be addressed as we move deeper into the twenty-first century. Clearly, global policy and international organizations, and with them academia and law, will have to get creative and rethink theories, concepts, models, and methods to get a hold of these problems and inform law, policy, and decision-making going forward.

SDG 17 was added to the sixteen substantive goals to define the aims, scope, and modus operandi for the entire framework built to address the Grand Challenges. Even more, the SDGs and their underlying policy document, the 2030 Agenda for Sustainable Development, are part of an even larger UN global policy architecture geared toward achieving global sustainability, development, and disaster resilience by 2030 and beyond. This architecture includes the Sendai Framework for Disaster Risk Reduction, the Addis Ababa Action Agenda on Financing for Development, and the Paris Agreement on Climate Change. Together, they represent the most comprehensive set of global policy goals and guidelines to date and are the result of an intricate and sometimes ambiguous process of inter-governmental consultations and negotiations under the umbrella of the United Nations based on scientific evidence.[35] Hence, SDG 17 was conceived with the aim to catalyse and enable all goals.

While the SDG framework is the largest set of global policy goals ever, there are even more policy problems outside of the core realm of sustainable development issues, even though that realm by now has become very comprehensive and multi-sectoral.[36] It is probably not coincidental that the largest regime complex[37] in international governance, the global climate change regime, is not only about the Earth's atmosphere, its change, and impacts but also about sustainable development more broadly.[38] Since its inception

---

[33] See United Nations, *Global Environmental Outlook: GEO-6—Healthy Planet, Healthy People* (UN 2019); United Nations, *Global Environmental Outlook: GEO-6—Summary for Policymakers* (UN 2019).

[34] See United Nations, Transforming our World: The 2030 Agenda for Sustainable Development (Resolution adopted by the General Assembly on 25 September 2015) (A/RES/70/1)) (UN 2015).

[35] See ibid; J Sachs and others, *Sustainable Development Report 2019* (Bertelsmann Stiftung 2019).

[36] See ibid.

[37] Regime complexes are clusters of single-issue regimes, which are evolving or established institutional and legal frameworks to govern public goods and issues of multilateral concern. For example, the term 'global climate change regime' refers to the set of institutions and treaties that were adopted through intergovernmental agreements to address the global climate crisis. It encompasses UNFCCC, the Kyoto Protocol, and the Paris Agreement along with scientific input from the IPCC (see A Bradford, 'Regime Theory' in *Max Planck Encyclopedia of Public International Law* (2007) <https://scholarship.law.columbia.edu/faculty_scholarship/1970> accessed 7 January 2023.

[38] See N Dasandi and others, 'Post-2015 Development Agenda Setting in Focus' in J Waage and C Yap, *Thinking Beyond Sectors for Sustainable Development* (Ubiquity Press 2015).

in 1968, global sustainable development governance has shown a remarkable level of growth, persistence, and significance in global policy, international law, and international organizations. The history of sustainable development has never been steady or straightforward; it has included major ups and downs, setbacks and backlashes. Sustainable development was repeatedly even pronounced virtually dead. Yet today it is arguably the most prominent and comprehensive policy field globally, with the 2030 Agenda for Sustainable Development, the Paris Agreement and the SDGs as its most visual programmatic pillars, and a stunning web of structures and institutions at its disposal.

The history of global sustainable development governance holds a number of important lessons for the future of international law, global policy, and their science and practice. It has always been the *avant garde* of global governance, at times postmodern and disruptive, never catering to neoliberal or realist ideology. Sustainable development has often played and experimented with novel and innovative tools and models for policy design, instrumentation, and implementation, and tried to solve the structure–agency conundrum in creative ways. Overall, the history of sustainable development is a story about resilience, sometimes resistance, often through adaptive or transformative approaches and processes.

SDG 17 is unique among the SDGs as it addresses the whole governance framework, the architecture, and the modalities of implementing the entire set of goals and targets, the UN 2030 agenda and even global sustainable development as such. If the SDG framework is to be successful and make a real difference, international cooperation must be recalibrated and this has to include legal, policy, and broad socio-economic efforts world-wide. This recalibration can only be accomplished if the international community of nation-states and multilateral organizations is willing and able to adopt an adaptive governance paradigm that builds on social learning, formal, informal, and local knowledge, participation, bottom-up approaches, and social networks. The aims, scope, and content of such an adaptive governance framework to effectively implement the entire set of SDGs have been discussed in-depth in the academic literature on social-ecological systems and resilience but, oddly, are still underrepresented in the discourse on partnerships and institutions for sustainable development. SDG 17 lays out, to a comprehensive extent, pivotal conditions for successfully applying such an adaptive governance approach. Yet, the fundamental precondition for applying an adaptive governance approach to the implementation mechanism of the SDGs in general (including SDG 17 itself) is a sound and reliable knowledge base, as Goal 17 recognizes. The year 2021, with its advances in data, knowledge, and models regarding the COVID-19 pandemic and climate change, for instance, has illustrated that the knowledge base at the heart of global action for sustainable development has never been so solid. 'Lack of data or knowledge' can no longer be credibly used as an excuse.

After more than five decades of intense data collection, research, and analysis, and a multitude of rigorous assessments, commissioned by the UN and other bodies, there is broad consensus regarding the most pressing global sustainable development problems and the dynamics and interactions between them.[39] It is remarkable that most

---

[39] See P Ekins and others (eds), *Global Environment Outlook—GEO-6: Healthy Planet, Healthy People* (UN and CUP 2019).

of today's global sustainable development problems are interrelated with climate change, whether through correlation or causation, making climate change stand out within the set of SDGs (beyond Goal 13) and amidst world's grand challenges more broadly. Furthermore, all of these challenges, and their inherent adverse impacts, may become or already are drivers of even broader socio-ecological, socio-economic, or socio-political disturbance regimes and crises. To date, an enormous body of literature has accumulated on the interplay between economic globalization, governance, and global sustainable development. Even the terms 'globalization' and 'global governance' are relatively new: their use in academic literature, particularly in the social sciences, and in political rhetoric started to become fashionable only in the early 1990s. Moreover, there are close interlinkages between the phenomenon called globalization and the broad phenomena of global change that directly affect the sustainability of our planet, its natural systems, and human livelihoods and thus sustainable development, ultimately affecting the *raison d'être* and the modalities for Goal 17.[40] Markets are commonly believed to promote efficiency through competition and the division of labour. A globalized economy is believed to offer greater opportunity for people and businesses to access more and larger markets around the globe, '[b]ut markets do not necessarily ensure that the benefits of increased efficiency are shared by all.'[41] Thus, globalization cannot be simplified as a mere phenomenon of trade, supply chains, markets, and financial flows. It needs to be understood more systemically as a complex and disruptive economic, financial, political, geopolitical, colonial, social, cultural, and deep socio-ecological process having reorganized and altered the global landscape, bringing about broad advances and benefits while, at the same time, having led and continuing to lead to massive and unprecedent disturbance and destruction.

As a result of hyper-globalization, the ontology, and the modality of the global governance of public and private goods as well as sustainable development as such have experienced significant alterations and shifts since the Rio Earth Summit 1992—let alone since Stockholm 1972. Yet, MDG 8 did not sufficiently account for these developments and disruptions. Therefore, a thorough analysis and evaluation of the utility of the contemporary global sustainable development governance architecture, including the 2030 Agenda, the SDGs, and Goal 17 in particular, is needed. For instance, various agency forces (eg public, private, and civil society actors, and the power dynamics among them), structures (eg legal and policy frameworks, regimes, and institutions), and dynamic processes (eg science communication, markets, intergovernmental negotiations, or social movements) at play in sustainable development governance are not only interdependent but also largely dependent on the reality that has been shaped by economic globalization. Since present-day globalization is essentially a neoliberal construct, the current predominant legal, political, and institutional architecture of global governance is path-dependent in its reliance on ideologies, resources, and power

---

[40] See International Monetary Fund, *Globalization: A Brief Overview* (IMF 2008) <http://www.imf.org/external/np/exr/ib/2008/053008.htm> accessed 7 January 2023.
[41] See ibid.

structures that continue to support mainstream business interests rather than the common good. The irony is that the same matrix out of which globalization was once born, and through which it is perpetuated, has been allowed to dominate the discourse on global governance of the commons. In other words, the forces that were at the helm of the creation of the current global sustainability crisis and global injustice are often being called upon to produce solutions for them.[42] A critical evaluation of the tools and mechanisms for SDG implementation is therefore in order. This is particularly relevant for SDG 17, which is all about these tools and mechanisms along with international co-operation and partnerships.

B. Governance Modes and Modalities for Implementation of SDG 17

Sustainable development problems can be categorized along three scales of appearance. *Local phenomena* are limited to the spatial dimension of states, for example emissions in industrial zones, air pollution in urban areas, or the locally restricted contamination of a river through chemical waste. *Regional phenomena* are of a transboundary, but geographically limited nature, for example toxic pollution of transboundary rivers, or drought periods in Northern Africa. *Global phenomena* affect trans-regional or world-wide shared resources and sinks, as do climate change and global warming, the pollution of the oceans, the loss of biodiversity, or pandemics as the COVID-19 crisis has shown. Local or regional problems may, and often do, culminate to an extent of a global dimension. For example, a regional drought may trigger chain reactions, such as loss of agricultural productivity, famine, poverty, migration, or social unrest affecting other world regions and the international community, and local water stress which may de-stabilize an entire region and a country's relationship with its neighbours. From a systems perspective, conceptual boundaries between scales appear arbitrary given today's highly interdependent and densely coupled environmental, developmental, and socio-ecological challenges.[43] With regard to the interplay between globalization and the environment, there are two distinct types of causal interaction. First, we know of grave environmental problems that are caused or magnified by globalization-related phenomena (eg land degradation caused by unsustainable land-use due to world market pressures and foreign direct investment (FDI) patterns; the global climate crisis due to industrialization processes and 'exported' unsound technologies). Second, there are intermediate consequences, such as the erosion of environmental safety standards due to competition pressure leading to the deforestation of rain forests, or textile production patterns in Asian countries.[44] SDG 17 aims to identify modes and modalities for

---

[42] See NA Ashford and RP Hall, *Technology, Globalization, and Sustainable Development: Transforming the Industrial State* (2nd edn, Routledge 2018).

[43] See OR Young and others, *Institutions and Environmental Change: Principal Findings, Applications, and Research Frontiers* (MIT Press 2008); A Rechkemmer, *Global Environmental Governance: The United Nations Convention to Combat Desertification* (Wissenschaftszentrum Berlin für Sozialforschung 2004).

[44] See E Altvater and B Mahnkopf, *Globalisierung der Unsicherheit* (Westfälisches Dampfboot 2002).

1262 SDG 17

successful implementation of policies, in ways that do justice to today's multi-scalar, multidimensional, and intersectional problems of sustainable development in a highly globalized world.

Governing sustainable development is indeed intricate and complex. Governance pertains to the management and collective steering of public goods and affairs, resting on but also going beyond legal and policy instruments and frameworks (eg the term 'policy' implies government and often nation-states as principal actors). Ivanova writes:

> Two traditional forms of governance have dominated world affairs until recently—national governance through governmental regulation and international governance through collective action facilitated by international organizations and international regimes. However, governing human relations has become a complicated endeavor that has transcended the national and interstate scale and moved to a global level involving multiple actors across national borders and multiple levels of regulatory authority—from subnational to supranational. In this context, institutional arrangements for cooperation are beginning to take shape more systematically and have now been recognized as critical to the effective tackling of any global problem. Public-private partnerships, multi-stakeholder processes, global public policy networks, and issue networks are regarded as important tools for global governance.[45]

Two points are crucial. First, before the Earth Summit the primary focus of more traditional policy had been on the nation state and its law-making, policy-making, and enforcement capacities. However, in the 1990s, the unfolding discourse on sustainable development governance emphasized the global level (international, intergovernmental, multilateral) as the place and means to address sustainability issues, which were addressed through problem formulation, agenda setting, negotiations, 'deals' to bring about regimes, and an iterative process of institutionalization.[46] Second, the Earth Summit deliberately triggered a globalized process of multiple parallel negotiation streams aiming to address a wide array of issues. However, the negotiation streams were poorly interrelated thematically and badly orchestrated institutionally, resulting in an eclectic collection of largely disjointed, partly fragmented and topical legal agreements and policy frameworks.[47] This policy failure created a path dependency in global sustainable development governance that perpetuated itself in the Rio Conventions and ultimately re-emerged in the MDGs. The SDGs, however, were hoped to change and fix this problem of fragmentation and lack of coherence and orchestration. Hence the intersectionality and looping between the actual Goals and their targets

---

[45] See MH Ivanova, 'Partnerships, International, Organizations, and Global Environmental Governance' in JM Witte and others (eds), *Progress or Peril? The Post-Johannesburg Agenda* (Global Public Policy Institute 2003).
[46] See Young and others (n 43).
[47] See A Rechkemmer, 'International Cooperation and Environmental Politics after Rio and Johannesburg: Synchronicity of Realities in a Post-Postmodern World?' (2005) 23 Sicherheit und Frieden—Security and Peace 40–44; Rechkemmer, *UNEO—Towards an International Environment Organization* (n 20).

and also, the comprehensive nature of SDG 17 whose long list of targets and indicators aims to 'pull all the strings together' are supposed to enable intersectional, joint action.

Meanwhile, multilateral cooperation has been redefined. It now incorporates non-state actors, the scientific community, and non-hierarchical and alternative regulatory and networking patterns. International cooperation has become a more complex and non-linear system of structures and agents that govern at multiple levels and through multiple means. This system includes, but is not limited to, formal and inter-governmental negotiation processes under the UN aegis, which are based on or produce legal agreements and regimes on single issues. Nation states are still important as principal actors, among many others. Schellnhuber and Biermann argue that the regulation of sustainability problems cannot be based on decentralized mechanisms alone. Rather, they require effective and efficient international institutions and legislation.[48] Other scholars highlight the role of non-governmental organizations (NGOs) and the need for a more formalized legitimacy model for the same. In their article 'The Role of NGOs and Civil Society in Global Environmental Governance', Gemmill and Bamidele-Izu identify five major roles for civil society to play in sustainability governance: collecting, disseminating, and analysing information; providing input to agenda-setting and policy development processes; performing operational functions; assessing environmental conditions and monitoring compliance with environmental agreements (a so-called watchdog function); and advocating environmental justice.[49]

The common denominator of all sustainable development governance efforts is the goal of reducing risk and building resilience. Leading governance frameworks suggest that changes can and have to take place with regard to reducing vulnerability by limiting or reducing exposure and sensitivity to an array of risks, threats, and impacts, and by increasing adaptive and coping capacity. These are the primary objectives and ultimately the key success criteria for sustainable development governance in the face of global change. Therefore, *adaptability* is a prerequisite and the most indispensable variable of the equation. Adaptive governance is based on the generic governance concept, adding a dynamic dimension and the resilience goal. The state-of-the-art definition of governance at the national level comes from the UNDP: 'The exercise of political, economic and administrative authority in the management of a country's affairs at all levels. It comprises the mechanisms, processes and institutions through which citizens and groups articulate their interests, exercise their legal rights, meet their obligations and mediate their differences.'[50] As UN-HABITAT notes:

> Two aspects of this definition are relevant ... First, governance is not government. Governance as a concept recognizes that power exists inside and outside the formal

---

[48] See H-J Schellnhuber and F Biermann, 'Eine ökologische Weltordnungspolitik' (2000) 55(12) Internationale Politik 9–16.

[49] See B Gemmill and B Bamidele-Izu, 'The Role of NGOs and Civil Society in Global Environmental Governance' in DC Esty and MH Ivanova (eds), *Global Environmental Governance: Options & Opportunities* (Yale University Press 2002).

[50] See UNDP, *Governance for Sustainable Human Development* (UN 1997).

1264   SDG 17

authority and institutions of government ... Governance includes government, the private sector and civil society. Second, governance emphasizes 'process.' It recognizes that decisions are made based on complex relationships between many actors with different priorities.[51]

In addition to these properties, adaptive governance is characterized by the need for reorganization and renewal during crisis and change. Also, adaptive governance must be 'location specific and tailored to local circumstances.'[52] However, even local action is subject to multilevel governance and cross-scale interactions. For example, urban systems are influenced by, and influence other, governance levels (eg national, regional, and supra-national) and scales (both temporal and spatial). Adaptive governance is embedded in a structure and flow of permanent level-scale complexity. 'The real challenge is dealing with systems that are not only cross-scale but also dynamic, whereby the nature of cross-scale influences in the linked social-ecological system changes over time, creating fundamental problems for division of responsibility between centralized and decentralized agents.'[53]

The following are building blocks and tools for adaptive governance that correspond well with the SDGs as a whole and are crucial to enable SDG 17's effective implementation. The buidling blocks offer a flexible and adaptible toolkit to inform policy-making and legislation for SDG 17 and its targets. In fact, they coincide with select targets. These building blocks and tools are essential for the successful implementation not only of SDG 17 but for all of the SDGs. We will assess to what extent SDG 17 and its targets are congruent and supportive of this prerogative.

Harnessing the dynamics of social networks: Today's approaches to adaptive governance rely on the paradigm of social-ecological systems.[54] This means that social and societal dimensions are central for effective approaches to adaptive governance:

Such governance connects individuals, organizations, agencies, and institutions at multiple organizational levels. Key persons provide leadership, trust, vision, meaning, and they help transform management organizations toward a learning environment. Adaptive governance systems often self-organize as social networks with teams and actor groups that draw on various knowledge systems and experiences for the development of a common understanding and policies.[55]

---

[51] See UN-HABITAT, *Tools to Support Participatory Urban Decision Making* (Urban Governance Toolkit Series) (United Nations 2007).

[52] See The World Bank, *Guide to Climate Change Adaptation in Cities—Executive Summary* (World Bank Group 2011) 3–5.

[53] See C Folke and others, 'Adaptive Governance of Social-Ecological Systems' (2005) 30 Annual Review of Environmental Resources 441–73.

[54] See F Berkes and C Folke, *Linking Social-Ecological Systems: Management Practice and Social Mechanisms for Building Resilience* (CUP 2000); F Berkes and others (eds), *Navigating Social-Ecological Systems: Building Resilience for Complexity and Change* (CUP 2002).

[55] See The World Bank, *Guide to Climate Change Adaptation in Cities* (n 52) 19.

It is this aspect of social networks beyond formal authorities, paired with the availability and application of relevant knowledge systems, that make a difference in moving the SDGs to action on the ground as SDG 17 requests. They are also critical for any form of partnership for implementation. Formal structures alone will not be able to effectively manage, or govern, complex systems under conditions of crisis. 'Stakeholders operate at different levels through social networks. This aspect emphasizes the role of multilevel social networks to generate and transfer knowledge and develop social capital as well as legal, political, and financial support to ... management initiatives.'[56]

Coefficients for adaptive governance systems are self-organization and learning. 'A resilient social-ecological system may make use of crisis as an opportunity to transform into a more desired state.'[57] The World Bank sees adaptation not only as a process of preparing for, and adjusting proactively to, negative impacts but also as offering opportunities. Adapting, if placed under the overall umbrella of resilience building, will force us to work harder on the larger sustainability and social development agendas, which may produce economic benefit. The World Bank concludes: 'Building resilience requires not only robust decision making by those in positions of formal authority, but also a strong web of institutional and social relationships that can provide a safety net for vulnerable populations.'[58] A central tool to harness the potential of social networks for adaptive sustainability governance are so-called bridging organizations 'that emerge to bridge local actors and communities with other scales of organizations. Such bridging organizations can serve as filters for external drivers and also provide opportunities by bringing in resources, knowledge, and other incentives.'[59] They carry a central function for inter-organizational collaboration and can serve as platforms for 'building trust, sense making, learning, vertical and/or horizontal collaboration, and conflict resolution. The bridging organization encompasses the function of ... communicating, translating, and mediating scientific knowledge to make it relevant to policy and action.'[60]

Another important tool for enhanced governance in support of SDG 17 is social learning. Given the magnitude and scale of sustainable development problems, large-scale behavioural change is required from the individual to the societal level. Changes arising from new behaviours are multifaceted and need the right institutional arrangements and incentive schemes to become effective and sustainable. Sustainable development is ultimately a deeply societal and behavioural issue, which means that any solution—and any serious attempt to implement Goal 17's targets—will have to fully imbibe factors of social learning and behavioural change, and their relation to livelihoods, settlements, energy, technology, and production and consumption. Research has shown that large-scale behavioural changes can be triggered and catalysed through processes of social learning, a process of learning that occurs within a social context.

---

[56] ibid.
[57] ibid.
[58] ibid 3–5.
[59] See Berkes and others (eds) (n 54).
[60] ibid.

1266 SDG 17

Human beings learn from one another through observational learning, imitation, and modeling.[61]

Building a participatory knowledge base: 'In recent years cooperative and collaborative efforts and participatory approaches have become increasingly popular in ... management and governmental policy. Stakeholder meetings, engaging different actors in workshop settings, have been part of the process.'[62] Through the described dynamics and effects of social network, collective knowledge and understanding of risk factors and change dynamics is built to enhance the performance of governance systems.[63] These include formal as well as informal (local, traditional, Indigenous) knowledge, which need to be fed into management practices.

> Successful management is characterized by continuous testing, monitoring, and re-evaluation to enhance adaptive responses, acknowledging the inherent uncertainty in complex systems. It is increasingly proposed that knowledge generation ... should be explicitly integrated with adaptive management practices rather than striving for optimization based on past records. This aspect emphasizes a learning environment that requires leadership and changes of social norms within management organizations.[64]

Informal and traditional knowledge systems are relevant and can be powerful and effective tools for local adaptation, especially in a developing and transitional country context, or for ecosystem-based approaches. They should be linked with formal systems to inform governance. As adaptation is motivated by the goal of managing risks and building long-term resilience, risk assessment is an indispensable tool for any action of adaptive governance. The World Bank proposes that we have to 'understand its exposure and sensitivity to a given set of impacts and develop responsive policies and investments that address these vulnerabilities.'[65] Such assessments must be integrated into adaptive governance cycles that start with stakeholder-based identification of 'what needs to be governed' and result in participatory and multi-level action, including but not limited to official government and technical agencies. It is essential that these elements are carried out as truly participatory processes involving not only 'stakeholders' but all relevant social groups and networks.

Integrative planning for enhanced institutional capacity: 'Adaptation is ... an ongoing cycle of preparation, response, and revision. It is a dynamic process, and one that should be revised over time based on new information.'[66] Effective adaptive governance has to be structured and organized as a cyclical sequence of assessment, planning, intervention, and learning elements. This requires flexible institutions and multi-level governance systems.

---

[61] See JE Ormrod, *Human Learning* (3rd edn, Merrill Prentice Hall 1999).
[62] See Berkes and others (eds) (n 54).
[63] ibid.
[64] ibid.
[65] See The World Bank, *Guide to Climate Change Adaptation in Cities* (n 52) 3–5.
[66] ibid.

The sharing of management power and responsibility may involve multiple and often polycentric institutional and organizational linkages among user groups or communities, government agencies, and non-governmental organizations, i.e., neither centralization nor decentralization but cross-level inter-actions. Non-resilient ... systems are vulnerable to external change, whereas a resilient system may even make use of disturbances as opportunities to transform into more desired states.[67]

This requires incorporating sustainability aspects into existing plans, policies, and projects. Governments play a catalytic role in the adaptive governance process.

With the catalytical support of leadership teams, governments can develop specific roadmaps for SDG implementation under SDG 17 that entail plans, policies, and actions as well as a blueprint for the SDG and target-related performance indicators and the prioritizing of activities. 'Measurement, reporting, and verification are important steps in evaluating the efficiency and effectiveness of a ... adaptation effort. Demonstrating that an adaptation action or suite of actions has minimized vulnerability, reduced risk, and increased adaptive capacity helps to inform future decisions and satisfy taxpayers and external funders.'[68] Finally, it is important to apply a multilevel governance framework 'to explore linkages between national, regional and local policies and to explore the strengthening of multilevel, regional and urban governance .... [It] calls for the narrowing or closing of the policy "gaps" between levels of government via the adoption of tools for vertical and horizontal cooperation.'[69]

Social resilience, critical sectors, and good governance: Adaptive governance to enable SDG 17 must place emphasis on social development aspects and involve addressing basic poverty reduction and the full spectrum of the UN 2030 Agenda and the entire set of SDGs.[70] Since adaptive governance is rooted in social networks and their dynamics and draws upon processes of social change, a particular emphasis on social development within SDG 17 implementation is a prerequisite. The social development dimension of adaptive governance must be linked with measures for specific sectors:

Adaptation ... requires collaborative problem solving and coordination across sectors ... [such as] land use, housing, transportation, public health, water supply and sanitation, solid waste, food security, and energy. Adaptation efforts in any of these sectors will often involve multiple government agencies, as well as broad partnerships that include other governments, local communities, nonprofit organizations, academic institutions, and the private sector.[71]

---

[67] See Berkes and others (eds) (n 54).
[68] ibid 39.
[69] ibid 7.
[70] See UN General Assembly (UNGA), '*Transforming Our World: The 2030 Agenda for Sustainable Development*', 21 October 2015, UN Doc A/RES/70/1.
[71] See The World Bank, *Guide to Climate Change Adaptation in Cities* (n 52).

1268 SDG 17

Adaptive governance includes principles of good governance, as UN-HABITAT notes: 'Good … governance is characterized by the interdependent principles of sustainability, equity, efficiency, transparency and accountability, security, civic engagement and citizenship.'[72]

Extreme crises such as global climate change, the COVID-19 pandemic, or the erosion of the rule of law and democratic governance in many Western liberal democratic states with the rise of populism and right-wing extremism, demand agile, flexible, and adaptive policy responses. A simple bounce-back or status quo strategy does not seem a general policy option in such contexts. Therefore, SDG 17 implementation must include evidence-based techniques of adaptive governance as outlined in the building blocks above. However, in the UN system, global sustainable development governance over time has become a widely stretched and densely populated institutional framework consisting of a multitude of agencies, structures, and bodies—plus ongoing negotiation processes and conference series. Yet, this highly fragmented architecture of agencies and regimes working in the field of global sustainability reveals a number of organizational problems, such as an ineffective and certainly also inefficient multiplication of efforts due to a multitude of actors involved. Also, the principle of multilateralism at the global level has suffered serious setbacks since the events of 9/11 in 2001 in the US. National security issues have once more been allowed to dominate the global agenda, bringing forth a restoration of power politics based on national interests. This tendency not only challenges international law, but also undermines all efforts undertaken and already established towards the principles of collective action and SDG governance. There has been a withdrawal from global multilateral cooperation, as seen in strategic policy fields. It is precisely in this present vacuum—fragmented and ineffective global institutions on the one hand, and a general lack of interest in multilateralism on the other—that a new approach is necessary and proposed if the SDGs, and with them SDG 17, are to be salvaged. The establishment of public policy networks involving NGOs, community-based organizations (CBOs), and other civil society actors; transnational, regional, and local corporations; and the scientific community are vital in the goal to replace traditional development concepts. As are a bottom-up-approach; participatory aspects of policy formulation and implementation; a decentralized logic of intervention; and partnership agreements per SDG 17. In addition, mainstreaming and integrating the SDGs into already existing legal and policy frameworks and in other sectors would catalyse and amplify adaptive governance for sustainable development.

---

[72] See UN-HABITAT, *Tools to Support Participatory Urban Decision Making* (n 51).

IV. Commentary on Targets and Indicators of Goal 17

A. Overview

The importance of systemic coherence and harmonization in the implementation of all the SDGs cannot be overemphasized. For several decades, concerns and questions have persisted on how the fragmented implementation of different aspects of sustainable development, such as trade, economy, environment, climate change, energy and food security, amongst others, may result in conflicts, misalignment, and trade-offs.[73] Environmental measures and policies can serve as barriers to international trade and economic growth, while trade measures can stifle environmental protection.[74] For example, governments may introduce a variety of environmental measures, such as energy efficiency standards, feed-in tariffs, or eco-labelling requirements, which may have indirect impacts on FDIs and the growth of domestic economies. Such measures may also come in conflict with the bilateral and multilateral investment obligations of countries, in terms of promoting reciprocity and protecting the investors and their investments.[75,76] Moreover, there is the concern in environmental communities that measures, policies and rules aimed at increasing the flow of investments ('investment measures') may result in adverse social, environmental and human rights impacts.[77] For example, a number of water and agricultural investments, particularly large-scale land-based investment, have been linked with complex social exclusions and human rights violations.[78,79] Similarly, countries may weaken their domestic environmental policy in order to incentivize FDIs or shelter international firms. Such domestic measures could accentuate the relocation of pollution intensive industries to countries with

---

[73] See D Olawuyi, 'Harmonizing International Trade and Climate Change Institutions: Legal and Theoretical Basis for Systemic Integration' (2014) 7(2) Law and Development Review 107–29; R Pavoni, 'Mutual Supportiveness as a Principle of International and Law-Making: A Watershed for the "WTO-and-Competing-Regimes" Debate?' (2010) 21 European Journal of International Law 641.

[74] Olawuyi, 'Harmonizing International Trade and Climate Change Institutions' (n 73).

[75] D Bodansky, 'What's So Bad about Unilateral Action to Protect the Environment?' (2000) 11(2) European Journal of International Law 339; S Yamarik and S Ghosh, 'Is Natural Openness or Trade Policy Good for the Environment?' (2011) 16(06) Environment and Development Economics 657–84.

[76] H Mann, 'Foreign Investment in Agriculture: Some Critical Contract Issues' (2012) 17 Uniform Law Review 129, 129–30.

[77] M Richards and Rights & Resources Initiative, 'Social and Environmental Impacts of Agricultural Large-Scale Land Acquisitions in Africa—With a focus on West and Central Africa' (March 2013) 24–27 <https://landmatrix.org/media/uploads/doc_5797.pdf> accessed 8 January 2023; P Liu, 'Trade & Markets Division of FAO, Part One: Introduction' in P Arias and others (eds), *Trends and Impacts of Foreign Investment in Developing Country Agriculture: Evidence from Case Studies* 4 (FAO 2012) <http://www.fao.org/fileadmin/templates/est/INTERNATIONAL-TRADE/FDIs/Trends_publication_12_November_2012.pdf> accessed 8 January 2023.

[78] See D Olawuyi, 'Energy (and Human Rights) for All: Addressing Human Rights Risks in Energy Access Projects' in R Salter, CG Gonzalez, and EK Warner (eds), *Energy Justice: US and International Perspectives* (Edward Elgar 2018) 73–104, discussing how such investments cause serious human rights violations rather than benefit the communities in which they operate.

[79] C Oya, 'The Land Rush and Classic Agrarian Questions of Capital and Labour: A Systematic Scoping Review of the Socioeconomic Impact of Land Grabs in Africa' (2013) October (34) Third World Quarterly 1532, 1533; S Narula, 'The Global Land Rush: Markets, Rights, and the Politics of Food' (2013) 49 Stanford Journal of International Law 101, 110–12.

1270 SDG 17

lax environmental enforcement—the so-called pollution haven hypothesis—which could ultimately result in increased global pollution, carbon intensity, loss of habitats, livelihoods, and vital economic resources in local communities.[80]

Among others, the undercurrent of tensions and human rights violations resulting from water, energy, and food expansion projects have increased calls for multi-stakeholder partnerships and systemic integration of sustainable development policies and institutions, to enable different regulatory stakeholders to come together and tackle common sustainability-related issues in a coherent manner.[81] Considering the intricate connections between trade, environment, and critical infrastructure development and financing amongst others, some degree of normative integration, harmonization, and mutual supportiveness is necessary to prevent overlap and divergence in implementation efforts.[82] In recent years, a lot of progress has been made to clarify the legal interactions between, and reconcile the complementary benefits of the social, environmental, and economic aspects of sustainable development.[83] For example, more than ever, trade and environmental secretariats of relevant international organizations have come together to propose mutually supportive solutions that can help maximize coherence and partnerships between trade and environmental regimes.[84]

Such partnership and harmonization efforts have assumed greater significance and urgency with the adoption of the UNSDGs. SDG 17 specifically underscores the need for enhanced partnerships—globally, regionally, nationally, and locally—as a required step for attaining all of the SDGs, including those on trade and environment issues.[85] SDG 17.14 specifically encourages all stakeholders to enhance cooperation and policy coherence for sustainable development. In recognizing the importance of trade to the attainment of the SDGs, SDG 17.10 encourages countries to promote a 'universal, rules-based, open, non-discriminatory and equitable multilateral trading system under the World Trade Organization, including through the conclusion of negotiations under its Doha Development Agenda'.[86] SDG 17 provides a holistic framework for coordinated economic, social, and environmental initiatives to promote inclusive, harmonized, and equitable implementation of the SDGs across all spheres to enhance multi-stakeholder partnerships.

[80] O De Schutter, 'The Green Rush: The Global Race for Farmland and the Rights of Land Users' (2011) 52 Harvard International Law Journal 503, 516–17.

[81] M Beisheim and N Simon (2016) 'Multistakeholder Partnerships for Implementing the 2030 Agenda: Improving Accountability and Transparency', Analytical paper for the 2016 ECOSOC Partnership Forum 11, March 2016.

[82] See D Olawuyi, 'Sustainable Development and the Water-Energy-Food Nexus: Legal Challenges and Emerging Solutions' (2020) 103(1) Journal of Environmental Science and Policy 1–9.

[83] See WTO, Trade and Climate Change: A Report by the United Nations Environment Programme and the World Trade Organization (WTO/UNEP 2009).

[84] See CITES and the WTO, Enhancing Cooperation for Sustainable Development (WTO Secretariat 2015).

[85] United Nations, 'Transforming Our World: The 2030 Agenda for Sustainable Development', GA Res. 70/1 (25 September 2015) (2030 Sustainable Development Agenda).

[86] World Trade Organization, CITES and the WTO, Enhancing Cooperation for Sustainable Development (WTO Secretariat 2015).

COMMENTARY ON TARGETS AND INDICATORS   1271

Understanding the integration, convergence, and partnership targets in SDG 17 could provide an avenue to package a collection of interrelated economic, social, and environmental targets into one box to enhance holistic and consistent implementation. The targets in SDG 17 provide an avenue to draw upon relevant economic and financial rules to underpin and inform the design and execution of social and environmental goals in a coordinated, coherent, and less fragmented manner in order to ensure that no-one is left behind.[87]

This section discusses the nineteen targets of SDG 17 under four broad headings: economic and financial targets; trade and market-related targets; knowledge, technology transfer and capacity-building-related targets; and policy coherence and governance-related targets. After discussing the nature of partnerships, collaborations, and synergies required for achieving the targets, it examines the law, policy, and institutional barriers to effective realization of these targets. It also discusses legal and policy imperatives for overcoming these barriers to strengthen high-impact collaboration for the SDGs.

B. Analysis and Critique of Each Target

1. Economic and Financial Targets

SDG 17 contains a wide range of targets aimed at mobilizing finances from a wide range of public, private, and mixed-financing sources to promote inclusive and sustainable development. One of the key challenges to accelerating progress in all of the SDGs is the issue of financing.[88] At a minimum, an additional $2 trillion to $3 trillion a year is required in developing countries alone to bridge current SDG financing gaps.[89] Furthermore, about $90 trillion in infrastructure investment is needed globally by 2030 to achieve climate-smart infrastructure, while addressing power infrastructure deficits will require up to $950 billion.[90] Mobilizing adequate finance to build and maintain SDG-related infrastructure and technology will require leveraging both public and private sector capital. To advance sustainable financing for the SDGs, SDG 17 focuses on increased domestic revenue collection, sustained cross-border inflows through overseas development assistance, and increased foreign direct investment.

---

[87] See D Olawuyi, *The Human Rights Based Approach to Carbon Finance* (CUP 2016) 1–25; Pavoni (n 73) 641.

[88] UNCTAD, 2014, World Investment Report 2014, Investing in the Sustainable Development Goals: An Action Plan (United Nations publication, Sales No E.14.II.D.1).

[89] ibid.

[90] J Rydge and others, 'Ensuring New Infrastructure Is Climate-Smart' (2015) Overseas Development Institute, Working and discussion papers, October 2015; also J Meltzer, 'Financing Sustainable Infrastructure' (2016) 1–5 <https://www.brookings.edu/wp-content/uploads/2016/08/global_20160818_financing_sustainable_infrastructure.pdf> accessed 7 January 2023; A Bhattacharya and others, 'Driving Sustainable Development through Better Infrastructure: Key Elements of a Transformation Program' (2015)1–10 <https://www.brookings.edu/research/driving-sustainable-development-through-better-infrastructure-key-elements-of-a-transformation-program/> accessed 7 January 2023.

1272 SDG 17

a) Target 17.1: Strengthen domestic resource mobilization, including through international support to developing countries, to improve domestic capacity for tax and other revenue collection

Target 1 of SDG 17 calls on countries to mobilize resources to improve domestic revenue collection. This, according to the UN, includes improving the domestic capacity for tax and other revenue collection.[91] Four global trends hinder the availability of domestic revenue needed to finance the SDGs: namely, lax legal framework on taxation and revenue collection especially in developing countries; corruption and illicit financial flows; weak legal framework on public-private partnerships; and sharp drop in commodity prices due to global shocks, such as oil price volatility, the COVID-19 pandemic, climate change, or forced displacements of populations.[92] Addressing each of these challenges will require innovative legal and institutional frameworks that increase domestic capacities for revenue mobilization and transparent utilization.

First, with respect to boosting domestic revenue through taxation, a starting point will be to enact comprehensive legal frameworks on taxation and revenue collection, especially in countries where emphasis on domestic revenue collection has been weak over the years. According to a 2019 report of the International Monetary Fund (IMF), raising tax revenue by 5 percent of GDP could finance about $170 billion in new infrastructure, or a third of the total additional needs for low- and lower-middle-income countries.[93] Yet, resource curse studies show that several developing countries, especially rentier countries that receive large revenues from oil and gas, tend to focus less on raising revenue from domestic taxation.[94] As Ezenagu notes, due to prevailing governance models that prioritise the distribution of fiscal incentives, such as competitive tax-free salaries, tax waivers for enterprises owned by citizens, energy subsidies, as well as other financial benefits to citizens, several oil and gas rich Middle East and North African (MENA) countries 'have not been inclined to tax the citizens and residents'.[95] Consequently, while virtually all MENA countries have tax laws, a survey of extant tax laws across the region shows a lack of comprehensiveness and depth needed to achieve the central aims of a functional and effective taxation system, namely fairness (proportional, regressive, progressive), certainty, efficiency, and convenience.[96]

---

[91] United Nations, SDG Tracker <https://sdg-tracker.org/global-partnerships> accessed 7 January 2023.

[92] OECD, Global Outlook on Financing for Sustainable Development 2021, *A New Way to Invest for People and Planet* <https://www.oecd-ilibrary.org/sites/6ea613f4-en/index.html?itemId=/content/component/6ea613f4-en> accessed 7 January 2023.

[93] D Doumbia and ML Lauridsen, 'Closing the SDG Financing Gap—Trends and Data' (October 2019) <https://www.ifc.org/wps/wcm/connect/842b73cc-12b0-4fe2-b058-d3ee75f74d06/EMCompass-Note-73-Closing-SDGs-Fund-Gap.pdf?MOD=AJPERES&CVID=mSHKl4S> accessed 7 January 2023.

[94] JA Fuinhas and AC Marques, 'Rentierism, Energy and Economic Growth: The Case of Algeria and Egypt' (1965–2010) (2013) 62 Energy Policy 1165–71. AM Álvarez, 'Rentierism in the Algerian Economy based on Oil and Natural Gas' (2010) 38 Energy Policy 6338–48.

[95] A Ezenagu, 'Boom or Bust, Extractives are No Longer Saviours: The Need for Robust Tax Regimes in Gulf Countries' (2021) 8(2) Extractive Industries and Society Journal. For example, although Qatar has a corporate income tax at the rate of 10 per cent, entities wholly owned by Qataris and other Gulf nationals are exempt from corporate income tax. Qatar also levies no tax on personal income of residents and citizens. See Qatar Income Tax Law No 24 of 2018.

[96] H Almutairi, 'Competitive Advantage through Taxation in GCC Countries' (2014) 13(4) International Business & Economics Research J.

With the sharp drop in price of oil, the need to increase domestic revenue generation and mobilize private investment for infrastructure renewal, upgrading, and development, has become very pressing for oil- and gas-dependent economies. For example, due to robust windfall revenues from high oil prices, MENA countries have, for much of the past decade, been able to spend hugely on infrastructure projects. However, since 2014, the price of a barrel of oil has fallen more than 70 per cent, wiping out over $360 billion of revenue from GCC countries in 2015 alone.[97] This has to varying extents weakened government income and earnings, making it very difficult for governments across the region to continue and/or complete several ongoing infrastructure projects.[98] Furthermore, following official forecasts by the Organization of Petroleum Exporting Countries (OPEC), that a return to $100 per barrel price of oil may not be until after 2040,[99] MENA countries have to, more than ever, rethink how to finance ongoing and future infrastructure development plans. In addition to general cost-cutting measures and policies that can help sustain infrastructure investments, oil- and gas-dependent economies must do more to boost domestic revenue collection by developing functional and effective tax systems backed by a comprehensive legal framework.[100] As MENA countries increasingly consider the need to diversify government revenue base through taxation in the aftermath of the recent oil shock, there is an urgent need to develop functional and effective tax systems backed by a comprehensive legal framework.

Taxation laws are a very important means of providing legal certainty and clarity to residents and citizens on their emerging taxation obligations. Furthermore, investors will want to have a clear knowledge of the guiding principles and goals of a country's taxation policies and legislation. By specifying and clarifying obligations under a wide range of taxes such as corporate income tax, value-added tax, stamp duty, amongst others, a comprehensive taxation framework can help boost the sources of revenue required for infrastructure development and social services in a country. Similarly, tax laws can be used to redistribute wealth in society by specifying higher taxation for a certain income threshold and a lower rate for those in need of government support, especially low-income residents and citizens.

Taxation laws can also be designed with the aim of influencing behavioural change, for example through levying 'sin taxes' for environmentally damaging technologies or activities in key sectors such as the oil and gas sector. Similarly, a comprehensive legal framework on taxation can help a country to achieve greater fiscal transparency and accountability in the management of revenue from the oil and gas sector. Tax laws

[97] A Ghafar, 'Will the GCC be able to adjust to Lower Oil Prices' (2016), see <https://www.brookings.edu/blog/markaz/2016/02/18/will-the-gcc-be-able-to-adjust-to-lower-oil-prices/> accessed 21 June 2022.

[98] A Husain and others, 'Global Implications of Lower Oil Prices' International Monetary Fund, July 2015 <http://www.imf.org/external/pubs/ft/sdn/2015/sdn1515.pdf> accessed 12 October 2021.

[99] Organization of Petroleum Exporting Countries (OPEC), '2015 World Oil Outlook', see <http://www.opec.org/opec_web/static_files_project/media/downloads/publications/WOO%202015.pdf> accessed 7 January 2023; also 'OPEC: Oil won't be worth $100 a barrel until after 2040', see <https://www.businessinsider.com/opec-oil-wont-be-worth-100-a-barrel-until-after-2040-2015-12> accessed 7 January 2023.

[100] Qatar Financial Center (QFC), 'Public Private Partnerships: A Vehicle of Excellence for the Next Wave of Infrastructure Development in the GCC' (2012), see <http://online.wsj.com/adimg/assetmanagement-related_ppp.pdf> accessed 7 January 2023.

1274   SDG 17

provide important statutory and legislative foundations for the implementation of these and other aims of taxation. The legal framework will also need to specify clear timeframes, procedures and processes for meeting tax obligations, and the penalties for non-compliance. These are practical questions that must be carefully laid out in a legal framework designed to clarify and govern tax obligations.

Secondly, in order to boost domestic revenue collection, it is imperative to address corruption fragilities that result in tax evasion, capital flight and illicit financial flows especially in developing countries. According to the 2020 United Nations Conference on Trade and Development (UNCTAD) Economic Development in Africa Report, every year, an estimated $88.6 billion, equivalent to 3.7 per cent of Africa's GDP, leaves the continent as illicit capital flight, mostly from the natural resource sector.[101] Nigeria alone is responsible for a loss of about $18 billion every year due to illicit financial flows.[102] Other IFFs such as crude oil theft, illegal mining, logging, fishing, and trade in rare plant and animal species continue to stifle progress on all of the SDGs in affected countries.[103] The widespread challenge of IFFs not only strips governments of the revenue and resources needed to finance the SDGs, but also results in widespread impoverishment of individuals and communities that rely on such natural resources for their subsistence.[104]

Addressing IFFs, especially money laundering, tax avoidance and evasion, will require international tax cooperation. A recent report of the United Nations High Level Panel on International Financial Accountability, Transparency and Integrity (FACTI Panel) therefore recognizes the need for a multilateral cooperative approach to create global standards that address IFFs.[105] A cooperative approach will require the creation of global asset registries that provide access to information on real and beneficial owners of corporate entities and assets.[106] Furthermore, the consolidated taxation of multinationals as a single firm will help reduce tax evasion by large multinationals.[107] Similarly, the report identifies the need for a global minimum effective corporate income tax rate as a way of disincentivizing the surge to tax havens.

Addressing IFFs will also require robust law and governance innovations at domestic levels to maximize domestic revenue retention.[108] To enhance domestic revenue

---

[101] UNCTAD, 'Tackling Illicit Financial Flows for Sustainable Development in Africa: Economic Development in Africa Report 2020' (UNCTAD 2020).

[102] ibid.

[103] D Kaufmann, 'Evidence-Based Reflections on Natural Resource Governance and Corruption in Africa' in E Zedillo and others (eds), *Africa at a Fork in the Road: Taking off or Disappointment Once Again?* (Yale Centre for the Study of Globalization 2015).

[104] ibid. See also D Olawuyi, 'Increasing Relevance of Right-Based Approaches to Resource Governance in Africa: Shifting from Regional Aspiration to Local Realization' (2015) 11(2) McGill Int. Journal of Sustainable Development and Policy 113–58

[105] Financial Integrity For Sustainable Development: Report of the High-Level Panel on International Financial Accountability, Transparency And Integrity For Achieving the 2030 Agenda (February 2021) <https://uploads-ssl. webflow.com/5e0bd9edab846816e263d633/602e91032a209d0601ed4a2c_FACTI_Panel_Report.pdf> accessed 8 January 2023.

[106] ibid.

[107] A Ezenagu, 'Global Tax Transformation: Implication for Economic Growth and Development' (9 August 2019) <https://www.afronomicslaw.org/2019/08/09/global-tax-transformation-implication-for-economic-growth-and-development> accessed 7 January 2023.

[108] Natural Resources Governance Institute, '2017 Resource Governance Index' (Natural Resource Governance Institute 2017).

retention in key sectors, governance frameworks must be reinforced to ensure transparency, accountability, and participation (TAP) in resource governance. A TAP governance approach provides a framework for integrating core international human rights norms relating to transparency, accountability, and public participation into decision-making processes on resource production and use.[109] Transparency has been defined as 'the degree to which information is available to outsiders that enables them to have informed voice in decisions and/or to assess the decisions made by insiders'.[110] According to UNCTAD, transparency obligates countries to be ready to subject their transactions to public scrutiny and consideration.[111] Similarly, article 3(3) of the African Union Convention on Preventing and Combating Corruption recognises the need for transparency and accountability as key requirements when it comes to tackling corruption and ensuring proper management of public affairs.[112] Furthermore, in order to promote good governance and reduce natural resource driven conflicts, the African Union Panel of the Wise encourages all African countries to ensure that 'transparency and accountability mechanisms are in place prior to, and during, initiatives to develop and exploit natural resources'.[113] It identifies the need for full reporting on revenues collected from natural resource activities and on how such revenues have been allocated to programmes, governments, and communities. This includes the need to address governance secrecy or information monopolization by advancing public availability, accessibility, and accuracy of information on relevant laws, regulations, and policies.[114]

Accountability on the other hand concerns the obligation to monitor and demonstrate that a project has been conducted in accordance with agreed rules and standards and to report fairly and accurately on performance results vis-à-vis mandated roles and/or plans.[115] The AU Convention on Preventing and Combating Corruption places great emphasis on accountability and transparency as essential tools to promote good governance.[116] An accountable entity or organization reviews and monitors the level at which all human rights, particularly those relating public participation and access to information, are respected and fulfilled in their entire value chain.[117] Participation entails ensuring that all members of the public are able to take part in,

---

[109] I Kolstad and A Wiig, 'Is Transparency the Key to Reducing Corruption in Resource-Rich Countries?' (2009) 37(3) World Development 521.

[110] A Florini, *The Right to Know: Transparency for an Open World* (Columbia University Press 2007).

[111] United Nations Conference on Trade and Development (UNCTAD), 'Transparency: UNCTAD Series on Issues in International Investment Agreements' (United Nations 2004).

[112] African Union, 'African Union Convention on Preventing and Combating Corruption', Maputo, July 2003.

[113] African Union, '"Report of the African Union (2019) Panel of the Wise on Improving the Mediation and Resolution of Natural Resource-Related Conflicts Across Africa: The 5th Thematic Report of the African Union Panel of the Wise', October 2019 <http://wedocs.unep.org/bitstream/handle/20.500.11822/31043/AUP.pdf?sequence=1&isAllowed=y> accessed 12 June 2022.

[114] D Kaufmann and A Bellver, 'Transplarenting Transparency: Initial Empirics and Policy Applications', August 2005 <https://papers.ssrn.com/sol3/papers.cfm?abstract_id=808664> accessed 12 June 2022.

[115] D Olawuyi, 'Corporate Accountability for the Natural Environment and Climate Change' in I Bantekas and MA Stein (eds), *Cambridge Companion to Business and Human Rights* (CUP 2021).

[116] See art 2(5), African Union, 'African Union Convention on Preventing and Combating Corruption,' Maputo, July 2003.

[117] V Williamson and N Eisen, 'The Impact of Open Government: Assessing the Evidence', Centre for Effective Public Management at Brookings, December 2016.

1276   SDG 17

and influence, decision-making processes in order to promote good governance outcomes.[118] The linkage between the TAP elements is well articulated in the 2012 African Union's Resolution on Human Rights-Based Approach to Resource Governance which calls on all African countries to promote transparent, maximum, and effective community participation resource governance, by setting up independent monitoring and accountability mechanisms that ensure that human rights are justiciable and extractive industries and investors legally accountable in all their activities.[119]

Thirdly, mobilizing the required resources needed to finance the SDGs will require increased focus on public–private partnerships (P3) in infrastructure development projects. P3 is simply a contractual arrangement between a public agency (federal, state, or local) and a private sector entity, to jointly develop, finance, implement, and maintain a project.[120] It is a contractual model in which the resources, expertise, skills, and assets of each sector (public and private) are combined and shared in delivering public infrastructure and/or services for the use of the general public.[121] P3 contracts have been increasingly promoted globally as legal and contractual instruments that provide opportunities for governments to partner and collaborate with private sector stakeholders to finance and share the typically high cost of developing large-scale infrastructure projects.[122] According to analysis by Brooking Institution, about half of the additional $3 trillion per annum that will be needed for sustainable infrastructure over the next fifteen years must come from private investment.[123] Already, over 1,000 P3 projects, worth at least $1.5 trillion, have been completed globally during the last twenty-five years.[124] In recent years, annual volume of P3 transactions has averaged around $50–60 billion.[125] P3s establish a long-term contract between a private party and a government entity for providing public infrastructure; allocate risks and management responsibility to the private sector party and link returns to performance.[126] By reducing public sector involvement in the design, financing, and maintenance of public infrastructure, P3s have significantly stimulated private sector investment and participation in the design of large-scale infrastructure in many nations of the world.[127] By

---

[118] Olawuyi (n 87).

[119] African Union, 'Resolution on a Human Rights-Based Approach to Natural Resources Governance—ACHPR/Res.224(LI)2012' <https://www.achpr.org/sessions/resolutions?id=243> accessed 7 January 2023.

[120] D Olawuyi, 'Financing Low-Emission and Climate-Resilient Infrastructure in the Arab Region: Potentials and Limitations of Public-Private Partnership Contracts' in WL Filho and AA Meguid (eds), *Climate Change Adaptation in the Arab Region: Case Studies and Best Practice* (Springer 2017) 533–47.

[121] ibid; see also World Bank, 'Public–Private Partnerships' <http://www.worldbank.org/en/topic/publicprivatepartnerships> accessed 8 January 2023.

[122] ER Yescombe, *Public–Private Partnerships: Principles of Policy and Finance* (Butterworth-Heinemann 2007) 1–20; also O Tolani, 'An Examination of Risk Allocation Preferences in Public-Private Partnerships in Nigeria' (2013) 2(1) Afe Babalola University: Journal of Sustainable Development Law and Policy 206–21

[123] Meltzer, 'Financing Sustainable Infrastructure' (n 90).

[124] D McNichol, 'The United States: The World's Largest Emerging P3 Market: Rebuilding America's Infrastructure' (2013) 1–15 <https://www.danmcnichol.com/wp-content/uploads/2014/03/FINAL-P3-AIG-Whitepaper.pdf> accessed 8 January 2023.

[125] ibid.

[126] World Bank, 'Public–Private Partnerships' (n 121).

[127] For a detailed overview of the adoption of PPPs worldwide, see Qatar Financial Center (QFC), 'Public Private Partnerships: A Vehicle of Excellence for the Next Wave of Infrastructure Development in the GCC' (2012), see <http://online.wsj.com/adimg/assetmanagement-related_ppp.pdf> accessed 21 June 2022.

providing the right law and governance framework and incentives for P3 investments, Gulf Cooperation Council (GCC) countries can unlock private sector capital and financing that can sustain ongoing and future infrastructure projects.

Despite the potential and strengths of the P3 model in financing infrastructure development, its specific viability for financing infrastructure projects remains hindered in many countries due to lack of clear legal and institutional frameworks that underpin P3 design and implementation. The development of P3 projects require clarity on the nature and model of relationship envisaged and created, and how risks are allocated by the parties. In order to attract the significant investment required to develop infrastructure projects through P3 frameworks, innovative governance reforms are required in the way infrastructure projects are designed, approved, financed, and implemented to remove limitations and barriers.

Fourthly, all countries will need to promote disaster risk reduction and resilience (DRRR) in key economic sectors so as to reduce perennial loss from disasters and hazards.[128] Over the last years, progress on various aspects of the SDGs have been impacted by sharp drop in commodity prices due to global shocks. For example, the sharp drop in oil prices since the latter half of 2014, and the ensuing collapse of several industries, factories and institutions in the region, brought to the fore the high vulnerabilities of MENA economies to cyclical swings associated with oil price volatility.[129,130] Consequently, advancing resilience to oil price volatility and cyclical downturns has become high on the legislative and policy agenda in several oil- and gas-dependent countries of the MENA region.[131] The uncertain levels of finance for energy projects during the 'boom or bust' cycles of the oil and gas sector and the resulting disruptions to regional investment, trade, and infrastructure development activities across the region, have accentuated calls for holistic legal and economic reforms to increase the resilience of MENA oil and gas markets to the impacts of oil price volatility.[132]

The paralysing disruptions to oil and gas markets in light of the COVID-19 pandemic have further exacerbated these concerns.[133] Significant declines in demand for oil and gas during the pandemic have resulted in the collapse of oil and gas prices from a peak of $115 a barrel in August 2014 to a record low of $25 at the peak of the coronavirus pandemic.[134] According to World Bank estimates, addressing the impact of

---

[128] D Olawuyi, 'Advancing Resilience to Price Volatility in Oil and Gas Markets: Current Challenges and Ways Forward in the MENA Region' in C Banet and others (eds), *Resilience in Energy, Infrastructure, and Natural Resources Law: Examining Legal Pathways for Sustainability in Times of Disruption* (OUP 2022) 135–49.

[129] ibid.

[130] IMF, 'Global Implications of Lower Oil Prices, International Monetary Fund' (2015) <https://www.imf.org/external/pubs/ft/sdn/2015/sdn1515.pdf> accessed 21 June 2022; also A Ghafar, 'Will the GCC Be Able to Adjust to Lower Oil Prices' (2016) <https://www.brookings.edu/blog/markaz/2016/02/18/will-the-gcc-be-able-to-adjust-to-lower-oil-prices/> accessed 21 June 2022.

[131] Olawuyi (n 128).

[132] See M Al Asoomi, 'Time for Change in Gulf's Energy Policy' Gulf News (22 July 2015) <https://gulfnews.com/business/energy/time-for-change-in-gulfs-energy-policy-1.1553842> accessed 21 June 2022.

[133] See H Keskes, 'How Cheap Oil and The Pandemic Threaten Economies and The Energy Transition in The Middle East and North Africa' (Natural Resource Governance Institute 2020).

[134] L Gurdus, 'Crude Prices Plunge to Lowest Level in History - What Cramer and Others Are Watching' (2020) <https://www.cnbc.com/2020/04/20/crude-prices-plunge-to-record-lows-cramer-others-on-whats-next.html> accessed 16 August 2020.

1278 SDG 17

the sharp drop in the prices of oil due to the COVID-19 pandemic will cost MENA countries approximately $116 billion, almost 4 per cent of the region's combined 2019 GDP.[135] Moreover, there is already evidence of increasing reversal or postponement of energy infrastructure projects in many MENA countries due to the economic downturn resulting from the COVID-19 pandemic.[136] Furthermore, the deployment of low-carbon and renewable energy technologies such as wind turbines, solar panels, and batteries, across the MENA region have faced increased uncertainty due to pandemic-related delays and disruptions.[137]

The COVID-19 pandemic accentuates the need for innovative law and governance approaches to anticipate and manage the short- and long-term impacts of disasters on key economic sectors. DRRR planning requires implementing a wide range of pre-hazard and post-hazard planning measures to enhance resilience to cyclical disruptions and vulnerabilities posed by pandemics, oil price volatility, and other disasters. Pre-hazard measures will include advancing economic diversification to expand the economic and revenue bases at national and local levels, eliminating unsustainable subsidies and fiscal incentives to benefit from additional and diversified revenue base, and diversifying the energy mix to reduce excessive reliance on oil and gas, therefore advancing supply reliability in importing countries and promoting decarbonization objectives. Furthermore, post-hazard measures will include a wide portfolio of wealth management systems (such as sovereign wealth funds and budget stabilization funds) needed to provide timely, effective, and cost-efficient responses that will minimize impacts of future bust cycles and promote a speedy recovery. Such response funds will also need to reflect wider policy objectives such as decarbonization of investment portfolio and assets.[138]

Without mainstreaming DRRR frameworks into resource development and planning, sustaining progress on economic diversification, energy access, and the decarbonization agenda as well as other SDGs will be difficult in times of disasters and shocks.

b) *Target 17.2 Developed Countries to implement fully their official development assistance commitments, including the commitment by many developed countries to achieve the target of 0.7 per cent of gross national income for official development assistance (ODA/GNI) to developing countries and 0.15 to 0.20 per cent of ODA/ GNI to least developed countries; ODA providers are encouraged to consider setting a target to provide at least 0.20 per cent of ODA/GNI to least developed counties*

In addition to domestic revenue mobilization, cross border inflows—through overseas development assistance or grants, multilateral and bilateral loans, remittances,

---

[135] R Arezki and H Nguyen, 'Coping with a Dual Shock: COVID-19 and Oil Prices' <https://www.worldbank. org/en/region/mena/brief/coping-with-a-dual-shock-coronavirus-covid-19-and-oil-prices> accessed 16 August 2020; also 'MENA Economies Face $116 Billion Hit From Virus, Oil Slump: World Bank' <https://www.arabnews. com/node/1656236/business-economy> accessed 7 January 2023.

[136] For example, in April 2020, Algeria announced a 30 per cent cut in public spending, in response to the two shocks—the spread of COVID-19 and the sharp decline in oil prices. This cut is projected to derail Algeria's solar energy project. See International Monetary Fund, 'Policy Responses to Covid-19' <https://www.imf.org/en/top ics/imf-and-covid19/policy-responses-to-covid-19> accessed 22 June 2022; also Keskes (n 133).

[137] Olawuyi (n 128).

[138] ibid.

COMMENTARY ON TARGETS AND INDICATORS   1279

and foreign direct investments—will be required to close the domestic financing gaps that hinder the implementation of SDG-related programmes and infrastructure in developing countries. Target 2 of SDG 17 therefore emphasizes the need for developed countries to sustain official development assistance (ODA) inflows to developing countries in order to meet the 2030 agenda. Specifically, target 17.2 calls on developed countries to 'implement fully their official development assistance commitments'. ODA refers to financial support or government aid from developed countries to advance development in developing countries.[139] ODA recipients are typically countries categorized by the World Bank as low- and middle-income countries based on gross national income (GNI) per capita.[140] Virtually all Sub-Saharan African countries are eligible for ODA grants, and through the inflow of ODA many Sub-Saharan African countries have been able to finance development in key aspects of the SDGs especially climate change, health, education, infrastructure, and government systems. For example, since the adoption of the SDGs in 2015, total cross-border flows to developing countries have increased by more than 32 per cent mostly through ODA grants and remittances.[141] Similarly, COVID-19 has seen a sharp rise of about 3.5 per cent in foreign aid from developed countries to help minimize the impact of the COVID-19 crisis in developing countries.[142] The COVID-19 pandemic has indeed shown the importance of global partnerships in addressing health and other complex development challenges.[143]

However, despite the rise in ODA over the last years, studies indicate that cross-border flows will need to increase by more than 60 per cent (from $234 billion to $358 billion) to close the financing gap in order to meet the SDGs by 2030.[144] The key to closing the financing gap will be for developed countries to increase and sustain their ODA financing commitments to eligible countries. In many Sub-Saharan African countries, governments grapple with prioritizing poverty eradication and providing food and shelter for the poor population. In such context, several of the other SDGs, such as climate change, biodiversity, and education, often take the back seat. The need for cross-border partnership in sustaining progress on all aspects of the SDGs is therefore key. Recent trends that hinder sustained cross-border inflows, as well as their

[139] OECD, Official Development Assistance <https://www.oecd.org/dac/financing-sustainable-development/development-finance-standards/What-is-ODA.pdf> accessed 16 August 2020.
[140] OECD, DAC List of ODA Recipients 2021 <https://www.oecd.org/dac/financing-sustainable-development/development-finance-standards/DAC-List-ODA-Recipients-for-reporting-2021-flows.pdf> accessed 16 August 2020.
[141] V Gaspar and others, *Fiscal Policy and Development: Human, Social, and Physical Investment for the SDGs* (IMF 2019).
[142] OECD, COVID-19 spending helped to lift foreign aid to an all-time high in 2020 but more effort needed; <https://www.oecd.org/newsroom/covid-19-spending-helped-to-lift-foreign-aid-to-an-all-time-high-in-2020-but-more-effort-needed.htm> accessed 16 August 2020.
[143] S Brown, 'The Impact of COVID-19 on Development Assistance' (2021) 76(1) International Journal 42–54. doi:10.1177/0020702020986888
[144] D Doumbia and ML Lauridsen, 'Closing the SDG Financing Gap—Trends and Data' (October 2019) <https://www.ifc.org/wps/wcm/connect/842b73cc-12b0-4fe2-b058-d3ee75f74d06/EMCompass-Note-73-Closing-SDGs-Fund-Gap.pdf?MOD=AJPERES&CVID=mSHKl4S> accessed 14 July 2022. .

1280 SDG 17

accountable utilization, will need to be addressed at international, regional, and domestic levels.

First, the macroeconomic impacts of the oil price volatility have seen a dip in ODA grants to regions with the most need, especially Sub-Saharan Africa. For example, between 2016 and 2017, inflows to the Sub-Saharan Africa region decreased by 27 per cent to $27 billion.[145] The declining levels of ODA assistance leave several low- and middle-income countries with little or no help when it comes to financing the high cost of infrastructure and technology needed to combat climate change and other SDG-related challenges. Several of the SDGs are complex and interrelated and therefore cannot be tackled in isolation. As developed countries recover from the impacts of COVID-19 and the declining commodity prices, economic recovery programmes will need to be underpinned by the SDGs, including a commitment to SDG 17. Therefore, in order to ensure that no country is left behind in SDG implementation, SDG planning in developed countries must be underpinned by a commitment to ODA in key sectors in developing countries.

Secondly, ODA donors will need to implement targeted support programmes aimed at ensuring aid traceability and the transparent utilization of ODA grants in developing countries. For example, for several decades, African countries have been recipients of various forms of ODA and technologies.[146] Despite this, the continent remains one of the least prepared to advance the SDGs. One of the key challenges to SDG financing in several developing countries is the perennial mismanagement of cross-border inflows, including ODA grants. Aid traceability therefore includes tracking ODA funds through open data and aid transparency measures to ensure that ODA funds reach the targets that it was meant for.[147] ODA support programmes can be in the form of training, capacity development, and open data support for ODA recipients so as to ensure country-level transparency and coordination in the utilization of ODA funds. Such efforts can also ensure that ODA programmes are delivered in a citizen-centred manner and that interventions do not only go to a certain segment of the population that are known or favoured by the recipient government.[148] For example, a number of local agencies such as Publish-What You Pay, and Connected Development are increasingly shinning the searchlight on how ODA receipts are utilized by domestic governments in order to ensure accountability and reduce corruption. Such efforts will need to be intensified.[149]

---

[145] ibid; see also United Nations General Assembly, 'Declining Aid, Rising Debt Thwarting World's Ability to Fund Sustainable Development, Speakers Warn at General Assembly High-Level Dialogue' (26 September 2019) <https://www.un.org/press/en/2019/ga12191.doc.htm> 10 April 2022.

[146] D Olawuyi, 'From Technology Transfer to Technology Absorption: Addressing Climate Technology Gaps in Africa' (2018) 36(1) Journal of Energy & Natural Resources Law 61–84.

[147] E-J Quak, 'Donor Agencies' Efforts for Improved Transparency of Delivery Chains for Aid Programmes' (2 April 2020) <https://reliefweb.int/sites/reliefweb.int/files/resources/762_IATI_Transparency_Traceability_Donor_Agencies_Efforts.pdf> accessed 12 June 2022; S Parish and others, *Tracing US Development Flows: Traceability of US Aid to Ghana* (Oxfam International 2018) <https://policy- practice.oxfam.org.uk/publications/tracing-us-development-flows-a-study-of-the-traceability-of- us-aid-to-ghana-620404> accessed 14 November 2021.

[148] S Herring, 'The Business Proposition of Open Aid Data: Why Every US Agency Should Default to Transparency' (*Publish What You Fund*, 30 June 2015).

[149] A Tilley and G Forster, 'Traceability, or Not?' (*Publish What You Fund*, 21 May 2019) <https://www.publishwhatyoufund.org/2019/05/traceability-or-not/> accessed 12 June 2022 ; European Court of Auditors,

COMMENTARY ON TARGETS AND INDICATORS   1281

Thirdly, innovative approaches are required in developing countries to address current excessive dependence on foreign aid.[150] The escalating rise in ODA, without a corresponding rise in social, economic, and environmental development indicates that there is a lacuna in the ODA utilization and diffusion process which has to be urgently addressed. ODA will only provide sustainable development outcomes if recipient countries create the enabling environment to ensure entrepreneurship, job and wealth creation, and technology absorption in key sectors.[151]

c) Targets 17.3 and 17.5 Mobilise additional financial resources for developing countries from multiple sources; Adopt and implement investment promotion regimes for least developed countries

While target 17.2 focuses on cross-border inflows through ODA, targets 17.3 and 17.5 focus on increasing SDG financing through cross-border foreign direct investments. These targets emphasize the importance of international investment as a tool for boosting SDG financing in developing and least developed countries. By increasing FDI inflows to key economic sectors in developing and least developed countries, such countries will be able to mobilize much-needed financing for SDG-related investments. In addition to business-as-usual investments in various sectors of the economy, SDG investment will include tailored and specific investment programmes aimed at boosting the green and low carbon economy, climate action, energy transition, and conservation efforts in accordance with the SDGs. Studies indicate an annual investment gap of $2.5 trillion in developing countries with respect to attaining the SDGs.[152] This raises an urgent need for countries to address all gaps to attracting and retaining FDI inflows.[153]

Over the last decade, international investment law has grown as a body of law that aims to promote and streamline direct investment equity flows, specifically by addressing legal risks and barriers, which may hinder states from attracting more FDIs.[154] Generally, three factors determine the flow of investments to a country, namely the investment potentials or opportunities, the general investment climate, and the legal and institutional capacity of the host country.[155] Investment potential refers to the available investment opportunities in key sectors, such as natural resources, mining, and

---

'Transparency of EU Funds Implemented by NGOs: More Effort Needed', Special Report no 35 (2018) <https://www.eca.europa.eu/Lists/ECADocuments/SR18_35/SR_NGO_FUNDING_EN.pdf> accessed 12 May 2022.

[150] A Kwemo, 'Making Africa Great Again: Reducing Aid Dependency' (20 April 2017) <https://www.brookings.edu/blog/africa-in-focus/2017/04/20/making-africa-great-again-reducing-aid-dependency/> accessed 21 November 2021.

[151] D Olawuyi, 'From Energy Consumers to Energy Citizens: Legal Dimensions of Energy Citizenship' in K Hunter and others (eds), Sustainable Energy Democracy and the Law (Brill 2021) 101–23.

[152] UNCTAD, World Investment Report <https://worldinvestmentreport.unctad.org/world-investment-report-2020/ch5-investing-in-the-sdgs/> accessed 21 November 2021.

[153] JX Zhan and AU Santos-Paulino, 'Investing in the Sustainable Development Goals: Mobilization, Channeling, and Impact' (2021) 4 Journal of International Business Policy 166–83 <https://doi.org/10.1057/s42214-020-00093-3> accessed 7 January 2023.

[154] R Dolzer and C Schreuer, Principles of International Investment Law (2nd edn, OUP 2012) 11.

[155] D Olawuyi, 'Achieving Sustainable Development in Africa through the Clean Development Mechanism: Legal and Institutional Issues Considered' (2009) 17(2) African Journal of International and Comparative Law 270–301.

1282 SDG 17

petroleum sectors. Foreign investors are typically attracted to a country by the availability of profitable and promising investment opportunities. Secondly, a supportive legal and institutional framework that protects investments and allows for the repatriation of profits is essential.[156] The legal and regulatory elements of a supportive entrepreneurial ecosystem include establishing simplified processes for starting or registering a business venture; open, predictable, and business-friendly legislation or policies; tax incentives; flexible entry and exit options for investors; and access to fair and timely dispute resolution mechanisms. Similarly, investors seek adequate legal protection for their innovation and intellectual property; strong public–private partnership regulations, as well as simplified labour and employment laws and processes.[157] Furthermore, there is a need to streamline current process of business registration to address delays, costs of registration, as well as address procedural loopholes that complicate venture registration process.[158] This also includes improving access of small scale business owners and entrepreneurs to financing and venture capital; legal information and education, and/or affordable legal advice and services.

Thirdly, the investment climate entails the level of investment risks associated with investing in a country.[159] Influenced by a wide variety of location-specific factors and sources, including government policies, cultures of public administration, institutional, social, and physical infrastructure, the investment climate determines the level and certainty of returns expected by investors on every investment made by them. The general investment climate of a country can be categorized into the following three main areas:[160]

A. *Macroeconomic and Trade Policy*—This covers the capacity of domestic institutions to reduce the costs of international investment, and to ensure a consistently safe atmosphere for investments (eg fiscal, monetary, trade, and exchange rate policy, administration of customs and ports, security of lives and property, strength of rule of law, and political stability);[161]

B. *Microeconomic Framework*—This focuses on the existence of trade-friendly regulations, predictable government policies and the availability of efficient enforcement agencies, devoid of unnecessary bureaucracy and unwholesome administrative bottlenecks. Thus, a country with flexible and less cumbersome rules on market entry and exit, macro-economic stability, comprehensive legal frameworks on contractual relations, proven enforcement capabilities, availability of

---

[156] G Foster and others, 'Entrepreneurial Ecosystems around the Globe and Company Growth Dynamics'. Paper presented at the World Economic Forum, 2013; Global Entrepreneurship and Development Institute (GEDI) 2018, 'Global Entrepreneurship Index 2018' <http://thegedi.org/2018-global-entrepreneurship-index-data/> accessed 7 January 2023.

[157] Olawuyi, 'From Energy Consumers to Energy Citizens' (n 151).

[158] ibid.

[159] W Smith and M Hallward-Driemeier, 'Understanding the Investment Climate' <https://www.imf.org/external/pubs/ft/fandd/2005/03/pdf/smith.pdf> accessed 8 January 2023.

[160] Olawuyi (n 155).

[161] ibid.

pools of skilled workers and other sources of human capital, will be perceived as an attractive location for SDG investments.

C. *Enabling Infrastructure*—This covers the availability of key public infrastructure necessary for production activities and investments such as electricity, land, efficient security service systems, skilled employees, efficient transportation systems, and the availability of basic infrastructural facilities. Since these basic infrastructures are prerequisites for doing business in a country, developing countries that cannot guarantee them are often considered as unattractive investments locations. Most African countries including Nigeria often score very low when it comes to security issues and investment climate due to the absence of these basic infrastructural facilities and the ineptitude of security agencies in most of these countries.

These three indicators go a long way in shaping the direction of FDI and SDG investments. Thus, developing countries that aim to attract SDG-related investments must make themselves as attractive as possible, by ensuring good performance on each of these indicators. The level of financial and investment risks associated with investing in a country could serve as an incentive or disincentive to attracting SDG investments. There is therefore a direct link between the performance of a nation in terms of FDIs and its suitability for SDG investments. The total FDI in a country typically offers a broader measure that best illustrates the general investment climate in the country. Just like FDIs, SDG investment are very selective and will only flow to countries where strong enabling conditions for investments exist.

Yet, several of the countries in Africa[162] and Latin America, with weak SDG performance also often score very low points in terms of security issues and investment climate and find it difficult to attract and sustain FDI inflows.[163,164] The high risk of insecurity on the ground means that most developed countries often prefer to situate their investment projects in safer and less risky developing states in Asia such as India and China.[165]

In order to sustain progress on all of the SDGs, there is an urgent need for developing countries to address on the ground volatilities and risks that weaken their abilities to attract and sustain FDI inflows.[166] Furthermore, developing countries will need to establish tailored fiscal and financial incentive programmes, such as tax reductions or fast-track registration programmes for green projects, to attract investments in critical sectors.[167] Developed countries also have key roles to play in supporting developing

---

[162] H Coffey, 'World's Most Dangerous Countries for 2021 Revealed' <https://www.independent.co.uk/travel/news-and-advice/most-dangerous-countries-2021-libya-syria-afghanistan-b1765002.html> accessed 21 November 2021.

[163] Olawuyi (n 155).

[164] ibid.

[165] ibid.

[166] ibid.

[167] See JX Zhan and J Karl, 'Investment Incentives for Sustainable Development' in AT Tavares-Lehmann and others (eds), *Rethinking Investment incentives: Trends and policy options* (Columbia University Press 2016).

1284   SDG 17

countries to address insecurity risks, through collaboration in intelligence sharing, training, provision of advanced technologies and equipment needed to address insurgencies and insecurity risks facing developing countries. A partnership approach is required to drive capacity enhancement, surveillance, and innovation in developing countries in order to create more stable environments for FDI inflows. Given that FDIs and SDG investments are beneficial to both the investor and host countries especially in terms of addressing global challenges such as climate change, providing support for developing countries to achieve sustainable and investor-friendly business environments will significantly aid the flow of technology, financing, and technical know-how that are urgently required to address several of the key sustainability challenges facing our current world.

d) Target 17.4 Assist developing countries in attaining long-term debt sustainability through coordinated policies aimed at fostering debt financing, debt relief and debt restructuring, as appropriate and address the external debt of highly indebted poor countries to reduce debt distress

One of the key hindrances to SDG financing in developing countries is the rising levels of sovereign indebtedness.[168] In order to address infrastructure gaps and provide basic necessities to citizens, the last decades have seen an exponential rise in sovereign debts across Africa and Latin America. In the aftermath of the 2008–2009 financial crisis, global interest rates became relatively low which enabled several countries to access sovereign debt on the international capital markets. The severe drop in the price of oil in 2014 also left many oil and gas dependent countries in need of external borrowings in order to meet financing deficits. As a result, more than one-third of Sub-Saharan African countries have been at increased risk of debt distress.[169] The COVID-19 pandemic has further accentuated concerns over rising debt levels in developing countries across Africa and Latin America.[170] Due to economic slowdown and increased health spending associated with the pandemic, debt levels have risen significantly, leaving several developing countries at the brink of debt distress.[171] Without international cooperation and partnership, low-income countries will have to continually choose between financing existing debts, or financing social, health, and infrastructure development programmes.

Target 17.4 calls on developed countries to 'assist developing countries in attaining long-term debt sustainability through coordinated policies aimed at fostering debt financing, debt relief and debt restructuring by 2030'. Debt sustainability refers to the

---

[168] BS Coulibaly, 'Debt Sustainability and Financing for Development: A Key Post-COVID Challenge (9 February 2021) <https://www.brookings.edu/blog/africa-in-focus/2021/02/09/debt-sustainability-and-financing-for-development-a-key-post-covid-challenge/> accessed 21 November 2022.

[169] International Monetary Fund, 'Opening Remarks at Mobilizing with Africa II High-Level Virtual Event' (9 October 2020) <https://www.imf.org/en/News/Articles/2020/10/09/sp100920-opening-remarks-at-mobilizing-with-africa-ii-high-level-virtual> accessed 21 November 2022.

[170] Coulibaly (n 168). See also C Duarte, 'Sustainable Financing for (an Owned) Sustainable Development: Time for Africa to Give the Driver's Seat to Domestic Resource Mobilization' <https://www.un.org/development/desa/en/wp-content/uploads/2020/07/RECOVER_BETTER_0722-1.pdf> accessed 21 November 2022.

[171] International Monetary Fund (n 169).

extent in which a country is able to service its current and future debt obligations (including principal repayments and interests) without default.[172] First, target 17.4 emphasizes the importance of multilateral debt assistance programmes, such as the IMF's Debt Service Suspension Initiatives (DSSIs), debt restructuring, and concessional lending initiatives, all of which are geared towards assisting developing countries to reduce their debt accumulation levels.[173] Debt relief programmes can significantly lower current debt accumulation levels thereby placing low-income countries on the path of debt sustainability. Furthermore, innovative debt-for-nature and climate swaps are urgently required to free up some funds for developing countries to increase or sustain spending on environment, social, health, and infrastructure development programmes thereby accelerating progress on all of the SDGs.

Second, advancing debt sustainability in developing countries will require developed countries, development banks, and other lending agencies to integrate debt sustainability assessments into their lending decisions. The Debt Sustainability Analysis (DSA) Framework, developed by the World Bank and the IMF, provides a practical template and guideline for lending agencies to assess and measure the current debt levels of low-income countries in order to ascertain their abilities to repay without default.[174] By carefully evaluating the risk of external debt distress by a country, lending agencies can assist low-income countries to reassess their borrowing decisions in a manner that does not further exacerbate debt accumulation. Furthermore, lending agencies should ensure that where debt sustainability analyses present adverse impacts and risks of default, such borrowing country must demonstrate clear plans to mitigate such risks through clear and sustainable debt servicing plans. Without a clear mitigation plan, new loan facilities should not be granted. Without such reform to the international debt financing architecture, several developing countries risk accumulating debts without any clear plans for achieving debt sustainability.

Third, debt sustainability can be achieved through technical training and support programmes aimed at building capacity for accountability and public financial management. One of the key drivers of unsustainable debt levels is the lack of transparency, accountability, and good management in public spending, which exacerbate the risk of diversion or misappropriation of sovereign debts that should have been deployed to finance the SDGs. This raises the need for structural governance transformations aimed at ensuring that sovereign debts are transparently utilized for development purposes. Lending agencies and developed countries can establish direct financing arrangements and surveillance programmes aimed at ensuring that debt facilities are paid out directly to contractors and suppliers as a way of reducing the potential for fund diversion or mismanagement.

---

[172] IMF, 'Back to Basics: What is Debt Sustainability' <https://www.imf.org/en/Publications/fandd/issues/2020/09/what-is-debt-sustainability-basics> accessed 19 November 2022.

[173] IMF, 'Questions and Answers on Sovereign Debt Issues' <https://www.imf.org/en/About/FAQ/sovereign-debt> accessed 24 March 2023. See also Marianne Gros, 'COP 27: The IMF Wants More Debt for Nature and Climate Swaps' <https://www.euromoney.com/article/2auxyokl0uzd6etegne9s/esg/cop-27-the-imf-wants-more-debt-for-nature-and-climate-swaps> accessed 24 March 2023.

[174] World Bank, Debt Sustainability Analyses (DSA) <https://www.worldbank.org/en/programs/debt-toolkit/dsa> accessed 19 November 2022.

1286 SDG 17

Furthermore, developed countries can provide assistance to developing countries to implement payment digitalization and surveillance technologies that improve transparency and public access to government records on debt utilization and management. Debt management offices at national levels will require access to state-of-the-art technologies that allow them to track payments, analyse internal and external debt levels, and ensure that debts are actually utilized for development purposes. However, in many cases, such offices function without the required technologies, equipment, tools, and human capacity.[175] Without reform, it would be difficult for low-income countries to develop, implement, and monitor programmes needed to achieve debt sustainability. An essential step therefore will be for developed countries to mobilize technical and capacity development programmes that can improve fiscal responsibility, accountability, and public participation in public financial administration in developing countries.

2. Trade and Market-related Targets

SDG 17 contains a wide range of targets aimed at addressing barriers to free trade and cross border flow of goods and services. Questions about the impact of domestic policies on trade have resulted in some of the most charged debates in international economic law over the last several decades.[176]

Ever since the adoption of the 1944 Bretton Woods Agreement (which resulted in the creation of the WTO, IMF, and the World Bank Group), international economic law has grown rapidly as a distinct and important aspect of modern international law[177] that is designed to eliminate barriers and restrictions to commercial and financial relations amongst countries, while also promoting a cooperative governance framework for monetary relations among sovereign states. While international trade law governs the exchange of goods and services across international borders, the *leitmotif* of international investment law is to promote and streamline the cross-border flow of foreign capital and investment, and to address legal risks and barriers that may hinder the effective implementation of investment agreements.[178] International monetary law has also emerged as an aspect of economic law that governs the flow of payments across international borders and the promotion of global financial stability. By addressing barriers to the cross-border flow of goods, services, and payments, international economic law continues to play key roles in promoting economic integration and sustainable development across the world.

[175] See L Razlog and others, 'State Debt Management in Nigeria: Challenges and Lessons Learned' (2020) World Bank, MTI Discussion Paper No 19.

[176] For an excellent perspective on the history of free trade and environment issues, see D Bodansky and JC Lawrence, 'Trade and Environment' in D Bethlehem and others (eds), *The Oxford Handbook of International Trade Law* (OUP 2009) 506, 513–15.

[177] H Fox, 'The Definition and Sources of International Economic Law' in H Fox (ed), *International Economic Law and Developing States: An Introduction* (The British Institute of International and Comparative Law 1992) 1–23.

[178] See art 1 of Qatar's Law No 13 of 2000 Regulation of the Investment of Non-Qatari Capital in the Economic Activity, which defines foreign investment as foreign capital invested in Qatar in accordance with the provisions of the law. See also R Dolzer and C Schreuer, *Principles of International Investment Law* (2nd edn, OUP 2012) 11.

However, over the last decade concerns have continued to mount on the adverse impacts of restrictive domestic policies on economic integration and global trade co-operation. First is the concern in trade communities that measures, unilateral policies, and rules aimed at protecting the environment from degradation ('environmental measures') might act as barriers to trade.[179] For example, governments might introduce a variety of environmental measures, such as energy efficiency standards or eco-labelling requirements, which might have indirect impacts on international trade and the growth of domestic economies.[180] Such measures may also conflict with the WTO regime, which largely emphasizes the need to prohibit all restrictions on trade other than tariffs.[181]

Secondly, the rise of local content requirements (LCRs) across the world continue to raise questions that such policies might act as barriers to international trade and investment.[182] LCRs are regulatory measures, contractual provisions, and policies that require energy market participants and operators to give priority to nationals, domestic companies, and locally produced materials, in the procurement of goods and services used for energy operations.[183] Although LCRs have been extensively discussed with respect to the oil and gas sector, LCRs have been widely applied in mining, renewable energy, and other energy subsectors.[184] Irrespective of the subsector, LCRs are generally utilized by governments, to generate broader economic benefits for the local economy, beyond fiscal benefits.[185] LCRs can be in form of preferential rates for local industries; mandatory procurement requirements to source goods from local industries; preferential tax and tariff schemes that confer financial benefits on goods or energy produced with local equipment; preference for local goods and services as part of the conditions for approving contracts, permits, or licences; or performance requirements and targets designed to confer benefits on nationals and local industries.[186] Approximately over 90 per cent of resource-rich countries have at least one form of LCR as regards their energy industries, 50 per cent of which impose quantitative performance targets to achieve

---

[179] Bodansky (n 75); S Yamarik and S Ghosh, 'Is Natural Openness or Trade Policy Good for the Environment?' (2011) 16(6) Environment and Development Economics 657–84.

[180] See Bodansky (n 75).

[181] General Agreement on Tariffs and Trade, Marrakesh Agreement Establishing the World Trade Organization, Annex 1A (15 April 1994)1867 UNTS 187, 33 ILM 1153 (hereafter the GATT 1994).

[182] See D Olawuyi, 'Local Content Policies and Their Implications for International Investment Law' in J Chaisse and others (eds), *Handbook of International Investment Law* (Springer 2019) 1–21.

[183] D Olawuyi, *Local Content and Sustainable Development in Global Energy Markets* (CUP 2021) 1–25.

[184] See Organisation for Economic Co-operation and Development (OECD), Working Party of the Trade Committee, 'Local Content Policies in Minerals-Exporting Countries' (OECD 2017); also C Banet, 'Techno-nationalism in the Context of Energy Transition: Regulating Technology Innovation Transfer in Offshore Wind Technologies' in D Zillman and others (eds), *Innovation in Energy Law and Technology: Dynamic Solutions for Energy Transitions* (OUP 2018) 74–98.

[185] D Olawuyi, 'Local Content and Procurement Requirements in Oil and Gas Contracts: Regional Trends in the Middle East and North Africa' (2019) 37(1) Journal of Energy and Natural Resources Law 93–117.

[186] See United Nations Conference on Trade and Development (UNCTAD), 'Foreign Direct Investment and Performance Requirements: New Evidence from Selected Countries', 2003, 2, which defines performance requirements as 'stipulations, imposed on investors, requiring them to meet certain specified goals with respect to their operations in the host country'. In other words, they are measures requiring investors to behave in a particular way or to achieve certain outcomes in the host country. Agreement on Trade-Related Investment Measures, 15 April 1994, Marrakesh Agreement Establishing the World Trade Organization, Annex 1A, 1868 UNTS 186 [TRIMs], Preamble.

1288   SDG 17

certain threshold of local participation and utilization of human and material resources indigenous to that economy.[187] Famous examples include 'Buy American' provisions in the USA, which typically require government contractors to purchase their supplies from American companies even if those supplies are more expensive than the same products purchased from non-American companies.[188] Also, the Feed-in-Tariffs Scheme (FIT Programme) in Ontario, Canada which mandated project operators to procure 'minimum amount of goods and services that come from Ontario' in order to be able to participate in the price guarantees and grid access granted by the FIT.[189] In Australia, Indigenous Land Use Agreements (ILUAs) in the mining sector have stipulated that at least 40 per cent of workforce at the mine will at all times be composed of local Indigenous people.[190] A number of other prominent energy markets, such as Nigeria, Brazil, the UK, Norway, Qatar, and several other countries in Africa and the Middle East have implemented various forms of LCRs in oil, gas, mining, power, and/ or renewable energy sectors.[191] While LCRs are generally designed to unlock the competitiveness of the local economy and workforce, such provisions may conflict with core international treaty provisions on trade and investment, and may stifle progress on the SDGs, especially in countries with unclear and unspecific legal framework on LCRs.[192] For example, the WTO Trade Related Investment Measures (TRIMs) Agreement expressly prohibits measures related to local content, trade balancing, export controls, and certain foreign-exchange restrictions, and certain bilateral treaties limit the use of other performance requirements.[193] Article 2.1 of the TRIMs Agreement requires WTO Members to refrain applying any TRIMs that are inconsistent with the national treatment obligation under article III or XI of the GATT Treaty (1994).[194] Paragraph 1 of the Illustrative List in the Annex of the TRIMs Agreement itemises incompatible TRIMs to include: measures which are 'mandatory or enforceable under domestic law or under administrative rulings'.[195] This specifically includes domestic measures that require an investor to purchase or use products of domestic origin, or from any domestic source.[196] These TRIMs provisions expressly prohibit WTO members from

---

[187]   Olawuyi (n 183).

[188]   T Meyer, 'How Local Discrimination Can Promote Global Public Goods' (2015) 95 Boston University Law Review 1937–2001.

[189]   See, Ontario Ministry of Energy, 'Feed-in Tariff Program Two-Year Review' <https://news.ontario.ca/en/backgrounder/19542/feed-in-tariff-program-two-year-review> accessed 13 January 2023.

[190]   See the Australian Native Title Act 1993 (Cth) see Division 3, Subdivisions B-E. See T Hunter, *Legal Regulatory Frameworks for the sustainable Extraction of Australian Offshore Petroleum Resources: A Critical Functional Analysis* (University of Bergen 2010) ch 4.

[191]   Olawuyi (n 183); see also T Acheampong and others, 'An Assessment of Local Content Policies in Oil and Gas Producing Countries' (2016) 9 Journal of World Energy Law & Business 282; S Tordo and others, 'Local Content Policies in the Oil and Gas Sector' (World Bank 2013); also P Heum, 'Local Content Development—Experiences from Oil and Gas Activities in Norway' (2008) SNF Working Paper No 02/08, Institute for Research in Economics and Business Administration, Bergen;

[192]   Olawuyi (n 183).

[193]   Agreement on Trade-Related Investment Measures, 15 April 1994, Marrakesh Agreement Establishing the World Trade Organization, Annex 1A, 1868 UNTS 186, art 2.1.

[194]   General Agreement on Tariffs and Trade 1994, 15 April 1994, Marrakesh Agreement Establishing the World Trade Organization, Annex 1A, 1867 UNTS 187, 33 ILM 1153 (1994) [GATT].

[195]   TRIMs (n 193).

[196]   ibid, Annex, Illustrative List, para 1.

applying LCRs that mandate investors to make use of domestic goods, raw materials, and products that have a local origin. While there is currently limited case law in this area, lessons from previous WTO decisions, show that overly restrictive LCRs—that is, those that require the use of domestic products over similar imported products or provide mandatory performance targets in order to obtain a governmental advantage—may be found non-permissible and non-compliant with international trade and investment law.[197] Furthermore, mandatory LCRs imposed after an investment is made may breach the host state's commitments and obligations under a bilateral investment treaty (BIT) and under international investment law and could result in complex litigation and/or investor–state arbitration.[198]

SDG 17 therefore emphasizes the need to address and remove all forms of barriers to international trade and investment.

a) Target 17.10 Promote universal, rules-based, open, non-discriminatory and equitable multilateral trading system under the World Trade Organization, including through the conclusion of negotiations under its Doha Development Agenda

Target 17.10 encourages countries to promote a 'universal, rules-based, open, non-discriminatory and equitable multilateral trading system under the World Trade Organization, including through the conclusion of negotiations under its Doha Development Agenda'.[199] This target emphasises the need for harmonized, stable, and equitable economic relations across the world as an essential requirement for advancing the SDGs.

To achieve a universal trading system, there is a need to harmonize and integrate trade and environmental measures to address contentions and overlaps.[200] Recently, the need for a responsible trade and investment approach that integrates environmental protection and sustainable development into economic law and policies have gained rapid ascendancy across the world. This is part of an increasing effort to address the problem of fragmentation and 'regime complex' in international law.[201] For example, there have been efforts amongst some WTO Members to negotiate a plurilateral Environmental Goods Agreement, which aims to eliminate tariffs on a broad range of environmental goods.[202] Reducing tariffs and custom duties on environmental goods is an important idea that could drive down the costs of cleaner technologies and goods,

---

[197] MM Fang, 'Local Content Measures and the WTO Regime: Addressing Contentions and Trade-offs' in Olawuyi (ed), *Local Content and Sustainable Development in Global Energy Markets* (n 183) 41–60.

[198] R Dolzer and C Schreuer, *Principles of International Investment Law* (2nd edn, OUP 2012).

[199] See United Nations, *Transforming Our World: the 2030 Agenda for Sustainable Development*, Resolution adopted by the General Assembly on 25 September 2015, a/res/70/l.

[200] Pavoni (n 73).

[201] K Raustiala and DG Victor, 'The Regime Complex for Plant Genetic Resources' (2004) 58(2) International Organization 277, 279, noting that regime complex alludes to the presence of 'partially overlapping and non-hierarchical institutions governing a particular issue'; UNCTAD, *Phase 2 of IIA reform: Modernizing the Existing Stock of old-generation treaties* (UNCTAD 2017).

[202] See ICTSD Draft Background Paper, 'Environmental Goods and Services at the WTO: Key Issues and State of Play' (1 June 2005). See also M Tothova, 'Liberalization of Trade in Environmentally Preferable Products' (2005) OECD Trade and Environment Working Paper No 2005-06, at 5.

1290   SDG 17

making them more attractive to end-users.[203] However, despite the ambitious intentions of the Environmental Goods Agreement, progress towards its adoption has been very slow, as several key points remain contested.[204] Several of these contentions highlight the growing and increasing geopolitical divisions in international law which makes the process of developing a universal trading system to be increasingly protracted and near difficult under the multilateral trading system.[205] A successful outcome to the ongoing negotiations would be to provide a more inclusive list of environmental goods that encompass the interests and needs of developed and developing countries. For example, considering that natural gas is less polluting than coal, it has been suggested that efficient, lower carbon pollution emitting fuels (natural gas to liquid fuels) and related technologies should come within the category of environmentally preferable products that should attract tariff reductions.[206]

Furthermore, given the growing complexities and slow pace of multilateral negotiations, regional trade agreements, including bilateral and plurilateral trade agreements, may provide less contentious opportunities for countries to integrate and harmonize trade, environment and energy objectives.[207] While there is no consensus on the success or positive impacts of environmental provisions in regional trade agreements, they provide opportunities for two or more like-minded countries to arrive at workable tariff and non-tariff measures, as well as technical cooperation framework on environmental issues, based on shared interests, target areas, and goals.[208] For example, the 2018 Agreement on Environmental Cooperation (AEC) among the Governments of the United States of America, the United Mexican States, and Canada specifically calls on the three countries to facilitate actions 'to remove barriers to trade or investment in environmental goods and services to address global environmental challenges'.[209] While the Agreement does not include a list of environmental goods, it provides a flexible framework for the three countries to mutually introduce measures at the domestic level to eliminate tariffs on those goods from participating countries to the agreement. Furthermore, regional trade agreements can build on existing institutions and governance structures may eliminate concerns over resource, capacity, and epistemic

[203] See ILA, '2018 Report of the Committee on Sustainable Development and the Green Economy in International Trade Law', para 30 <http://www.ila-hq.org/images/ILA/DraftReports/DraftReport_SustainableD ev_GreenEconomy.pdf> accessed June 2019.

[204] See 'Environmental, Business Groups at Odds over Green Goods Initiative' Inside US Trade (23 May 2014); also J Monkelbaan, *Trade Preferences for Environmentally Friendly Goods and Services* (International Centre for Trade and Sustainable Development November 2011) 1–5.

[205] See S Alam and others (eds), *International Environmental Law and the Global South* (CUP 2015) 1–10.

[206] See Submission by the State of Qatar, TN/TE/W/19 (28 January 2003), noting that 'combined-cycle natural gas fired generation systems and advanced gas-turbines systems, known for their energy efficiency and sustainable development potential, be included in the list of environmental goods'.

[207] See I Martínez-Zarzoso, 'Assessing the Effectiveness of Environmental Provisions in Regional Trade Agreements: An Empirical Analysis' (2018) OECD Trade and Environment Working Papers No 2018/02, 9–10.

[208] L Baghdadi and others, 'Are RTA Agreements with Environmental Provisions Reducing Emissions?' (2013) 90(2) Journal of International Economics 378–90; C George and S Yamaguchi, 'Assessing Implementation of Environmental Provisions in Regional Trade Agreements' (2018) OECD Trade and Environment Working Papers, No 2018/01.

[209] Art 10(2)(y). The AEC is a side agreement completed in parallel with the United States–Mexico–Canada Agreement (USMCA) (also referred to as NAFTA 2.0). See K Tienhaara, 'NAFTA 2.0: What Are the Implications for Environmental Governance?' (2019) 1 Earth Systems Governance 100004.

implications of addressing trade barriers to environmental goods. For example, the Commission for Environmental Cooperation that had been originally established under the North American Agreement on Environmental Cooperation (NAAEC) is entrusted with monitoring the implementation of the Environmental Cooperation Agreement (ECA).[210] The AEC Agreement demonstrates a greater potential for countries to build on existing environmental, trade, and social cooperation amongst them to integrate and achieve trade and environmental objectives.[211]

Secondly, achieving a universal trading system will require greater institutional coordination and harmonization between trade and environmental secretariats. Despite the increasing rapprochement between WTO and MEA secretariats, the overarching mandate to supervise treaty implementation in each sector remains under the purview of separate institutions, such as the WTO, UNFCCC, Convention on International Trade in Endangered Species of Wild Fauna and Flora (CITES), amongst others, with distinct mandates, financial and resource allocations, and most times competing and conflicting priorities.[212] Consequently, trade and environmental obligations continue to be implemented and articulated in diverse ways.[213] For example, the Committee on Trade and Environment (CTE) is a mechanism of the WTO and does not include representations from many of the trade relevant MEAs. This makes it complex and difficult to integrate the perspectives of MEA secretariats in the ongoing negotiation processes under the WTO. This problem of institutional coordination and coherence can be addressed through regime interplay management approaches that foster cooperation and minimize duplication.[214] A necessary starting point will be to carefully examine the extent to which the mandates of existing trade and environment institutions are coherent, conflicting, and/or duplicative. Developing a matrix of the respective mandates of the existing institutions, including intersections and opportunities for collaboration, can provide a basis for common and concerted action. Furthermore, it is essential to develop linked platforms and mechanisms to support knowledge and information sharing. For example, trade and environment institutions can leverage their respective expertise, facilities, and best practices by engaging with staff and experts across sectors to assist with reviewing and assessing multisector projects. Through joint initiatives

---

[210] See also art 8 of the Agreement on Environmental Cooperation between Canada and Chile which creates the Canada–Chile Commission for Environmental Cooperation to oversee the implementation of the agreement.

[211] There are now over 121 regional trade agreements with explicit reference to environmental cooperation. See, eg, The Comprehensive Economic and Trade Agreement (CETA), a trade agreement between Canada, the EU, and its Member States. Chapter 24 of CETA focuses on trade and environment. See also The Comprehensive and Progressive Agreement for Trans-Pacific Partnership (CPTPP) between Australia, Malaysia, Mexico, and Peru. The Environment Chapter of the CPTPP aims to promote mutually supportive trade and environmental policies between the countries. See also Japan–Mexico Environmental Cooperation Chapter, Singapore–Korea MOU on CNG Technologies.

[212] CITES and WTO (n 11) 8–11.

[213] ibid.

[214] See H van Asselt, *The Fragmentation of Global Climate Governance Consequences and Management of Regime Interactions* (Edward Elgar 2014) 1–15; S Oberthür and J Pozarowska, 'Managing Institutional Complexity and Fragmentation: The Nagoya Protocol and the Global Governance of Genetic Resources' (2013) 13(3) Global Environmental Politics 100, 102, stating that '[a]s the international legal system becomes more and more complex, the need for interplay management increases'.

1292   SDG 17

and knowledge sharing, inter-agency linkages and partnerships could increase trust and enhance synergic solutions that enhance green economy governance.

Third, target 17.10 emphasizes the need for non-discriminatory trading systems. This raises the need for countries to address the use of LCRs that create unlevel playing ground for international goods and services to compete favourably locally. Blatantly discriminatory and restrictive LCRs may not be able to pass muster in terms of the WTO disciplines.[215] However, the fact that the TRIMs Agreement, as well as many BITs that prohibit LCRs, also include a wide range of exceptions for their use, strongly suggests that when designed and implemented within the frame of permissible limits, LCRs can be compatible and reconciled with the goals of international trade and investment law, and can help countries to substantially increase the economic, social and environmental benefits of FDI.[216] The focus of LCRs on wealth creation, small- and medium-scale entrepreneurship, skill development, social equality, stakeholder engagement, and community empowerment all reinforce the fundamental roles that LCRs can play in advancing the SDGs in global energy markets. Achieving all of the SDGs, especially those relating to poverty eradication (SDG 1), zero hunger (SDG 2), education and lifelong learning (SDG 4), equality and gender justice (SDG 5), energy for all (SDG 7), employment and decent work for all (SDG 8), climate change (SDG 13), stakeholder participation (SDG 16.7), as well as systemic coordination and partnerships (SDG 17) will require local capacity development.[217] It is therefore essential for countries stipulating LCRs to avoid misuse and misalignments that undermine the goals and success of LCRs.[218] The starting point therefore is for national authorities to realign the goals of LCRs to focus mainly on creating high domestic value addition by providing full and fair opportunities for investors, irrespective of the source of the raw materials and goods, nationality of the employees, or storage location of investment data. Relaxing or updating rules on local content could enable developing countries to attract and retain investment in key sectors, most especially in a low oil price economy, when many countries are accelerating economic recovery plans in the aftermath of the global economic downturn resulting from the COVID-19 pandemic.

Target 17.10 requires a systemic and integrated approach that promotes cooperation and inclusiveness, at international, regional, and domestic levels, in the design and implementation of economic instruments. Attracting the required financing to implement the SDGs will require shared and inter-agency understanding on common principles, elements, and standards that can underpin and foster a consistent application of extant trade, environment, and localization policies. As Pavoni rightly argues, the principle of mutual supportiveness in international law implies a duty to negotiate in good faith when necessary to clarify the relationship between competing regimes.[219] For example,

---

[215] MM Fang, 'Local Content Measures and the WTO Regime: Addressing Contentions and Trade-offs' in Olawuyi (ed), *Local Content and Sustainable Development in Global Energy Markets* (n 183) 41–60.

[216] D Olawuyi, 'Advancing Sustainable Development in Local Content Initiatives: Summary for Policy Makers' in Olawuyi (ed), *Local Content and Sustainable Development in Global Energy Markets* (n 183) 413–20.

[217] ibid.

[218] ibid.

[219] R Pavoni, 'Mutual Supportiveness as a Principle of International and Law- Making: A Watershed for the "WTO and Competing Regimes" Debate?' (2010) 21 *European Journal of International Law* 641; also S Oberthür,

coming together to evolve core elements of a green economy approach to trade and environment that are WTO-consistent and compatible with MEAs, can increase the likelihood of synergistic implementation.[220] This approach has been previously adopted with some measure of success under the UN system. For example, to foster a harmonious understanding of human rights rules across the UN system, a common understanding was agreed by all UN agencies in 2003.[221] Despite debates on the scope and success of this document, it has significantly advanced a harmonious understanding and application of human rights norms in various contexts, including trade and environment.[222] It is essential to elaborate mechanisms for combined reporting and stocktaking between trade, environment, and other related institutions in order to ensure coherent implementation of the SDGs.

b) Targets 17.11 and 17.12: Significantly increase the exports of developing countries, in particular with a view to doubling the least developed countries' shares of global exports by 2020; Realise timely implementation of duty-free and quota-free market access on a lasting basis for all least developed countries, consistent with World Trade Organization decisions, including by ensuring that preferential rules of origin applicable to imports from least developed countries are transparent and simple, and contribute to facilitating market access

Considering the intricate connections between economic integration and sustainable development, innovative approaches are required to support low-income countries to export their commodities to global markets. Studies show that if African countries were to achieve only a percentage increase in global exports, this could result in four times the size of the total foreign financial inflow—more than $70 billion of additional income annually—into the continent.[223] Given the importance of export competitiveness to financing the SDGs, SDG 17 identifies both positive and negative actions that can help mobilize financial resources to developing countries from international sources. First is the positive requirement in target 17.11 to 'significantly increase the exports of developing countries, in particular with a view to doubling the least developed countries' share of global exports by 2020.' Export growth and diversification has over the years stimulated innovation, economic growth, and poverty reduction in a number

---

'Interplay Management: Enhancing Environmental Policy Integration Among International Institutions' (2009) 9 International Environmental Agreements: Politics, Law and Economics 371, 376.

[220] S Oberthür, 'Regime Interplay Management' in K Blome and others (eds) *Contested Regime Collisions: Norm Fragmentation in World Society* (CUP 2016) 88, 98–99.

[221] See United Nations, 'The Human Rights Based Approach to Development Cooperation: Towards a Common Understanding among UN Agencies' (2003) <http://www.undg.org/archive_docs/6959-The_Human_Rights_Based_Approach_to_Development_Cooperation_Towards_a_Common_Understanding_among_UN.pdf> accessed 12 October 2018.

[222] E-U Petersmann, 'The "Human Rights Approach" Advocated by the UN High Commissioner for Human Rights and by the ILO: Is it Relevant for WTO Law and Policy?' (2004) 7 Journal of International Economic Law 605–27.

[223] World Bank, World Development Indicators (2020) <https://databank.worldbank.org/source/world-development-indicators> accessed 11 September 2021. See also Office of the United States Trade Representative, 'Trade is Key to Africa's Economic Growth' <https://ustr.gov/about-us/policy-offices/press-office/blog/trade-key-africa's-economic-growth> accessed 24 March 2023.

1294 SDG 17

of developing countries, especially Asian countries such as Bangladesh, China, India, Hong Kong, and Singapore, amongst others.[224] These and other Asian tiger countries have moved from extreme dependence on imports to becoming important exporters of manufactured products.[225] However, in a number of least developing countries, especially in Africa and Latin America, export growth remains hindered by a wide range of complex domestic and international barriers.[226]

First, a key barrier to export competitiveness of developing countries is the prevailing existence of domestic preferences and subsidies to local commodities in developed countries. For example, while a number of developing countries have comparative advantages in fast-moving consumer goods such as sugar, cotton, and groundnuts, the presence of domestic subsidies for these products in Europe and other developed regions hinder the abilities of developing countries to favourably compete in terms of exporting their commodities to these markets.[227] To address this challenge, the Doha Ministerial Declaration calls for 'substantial reductions in trade-distorting domestic support'. Despite this, however, the pace of implementation has been slow. For developing countries to increase exports in such commodities, it is imperative for developed countries to address trade barriers to stifle the abilities of developing countries to access global markets.

A second and related major barrier to developing country exports are the excessive tariffs and taxes on fast moving consumer goods and agricultural products that developing countries mostly want to export.[228] To address this concern, paragraph 31 (iii) of the Doha Ministerial Declaration calls for the 'reduction or, as appropriate, elimination of tariffs and non-tariff barriers on environmental goods and services.'[229] Similarly, the Non-Agricultural Market Access (NAMA) negotiations, based on the Doha Ministerial Declaration of 2001 calls for a reduction or elimination in tariffs, particularly on exportable goods of interest to developing countries. The Framework for Agriculture adopted by the General Council of the WTO in 2004 establishes a tiered formula for reducing tariffs to agricultural products.[230] Despite these efforts however, the pace of implementation has been slow. Target 12.1 therefore calls on countries to 'average tariffs faced by developing countries, least developed countries and small island developing States'. Addressing trade barriers to exports from developing countries can help promote global access to them, which could in turn produce positive environmental, social, and economic benefits.

---

[224] UNCTAD, 'Export Competitiveness and Development in LDCs: Policies, Issues and Priorities for Least Developed Countries for Action During and Beyond UNCTAD XII' (2008) <https://unctad.org/system/files/offic ial-document/aldc20081_en.pdf> accessed 11 September 2021.

[225] ibid.

[226] See G Olasehinde-Williams and AF Oshodi, 'Can Africa Raise Export Competitiveness through Economic Complexity? Evidence from (Non)-Parametric Panel Techniques' (2021) 33(3) African Development Review 426–38.

[227] UNCTAD (n 224).

[228] B Hoekman and others, 'Eliminating Excessive Tariffs on Exports of Least Developed Countries' (2001) World Bank. Policy Research Working Paper No 2604 <https://openknowledge.worldbank.org/handle/10986/ 19658> accessed 7 January 2023.

[229] WTO 'Doha Ministerial Declaration', WT/MIN (01)/DEC/1 (14 November 2001).

[230] Text of the 'July package'—the General Council's post-Cancún decision <https://www.wto.org/english/trato p_e/dda_e/draft_text_gc_dg_31july04_e.htm> accessed 7 January 2023.

A third and related barrier is the stringent and most times protectionist health, safety, and environmental (HSE) requirements, which are often difficult for developing country exports to satisfy. While trade liberalism should not erode HSE requirements, developing countries will need a lot of support to be able to meet the stringent sanitary and HSE requirements that are above and beyond what obtains in the countries of origin of such exports.[231] Some of the HSE requirements, especially those relating to food safety, can be met with better packaging and labelling of products in a manner that complies with HSE requirements in the recipient countries. However, lack of capacity and training often mean that developing countries are unable to accomplish the prescribed upgrades and steps to bring their commodities in line with HSE requirements in developed countries.

International cooperation and partnership are required to address barriers to trade and to support export competitiveness in developing countries. In addition to providing support for upgrading domestic products from developing countries, trade-related training and support can also help developing countries to stimulate holistic trade policy reform that can improve export growth. Without boosting domestic entrepreneurship, economic diversification, growth of non-oil and gas commodities, and development of infrastructure needed to advance manufacturing and processing, export diversification and growth may remain stifled.

3. Knowledge, Technology Transfer, and Capacity-building-related Targets

The years 2020 and 2021 hopefully made many in the international community finally realize that complex, shared global challenges and crises will not go away easily anymore but are likely going to be the norm rather than the exception for humanity throughout this turbulent twenty-first century. First, a full year after the first effective vaccines against COVID-19 were launched and approved by authorities worldwide, global vaccine distribution unfortunately continued to be spotty and a matter of economic and political privilege rather than of equality and fairness. One of the basic laws of responding to pandemics occurring in a highly interdependent transnational environment is that mitigation measures should be taken collectively, simultaneously, and using the same technological and procedural instruments and standards. But this did not occur: too many governments of wealthier nations defied the urgent calls by the UN Secretary-General and the WHO and decided to act according to the principle 'my nation first'. Indeed, the selfishness and Not-In-My-Back-Yard (NIMBY) mentality of some wealthy countries allows new variants to incubate where vaccines are scarce, only to soon boomerang back to privileged nations hoarding doses and patents alike.

Second, around the same time the 6th Assessment Report of the Intergovernmental Panel on Climate Change (IPCC) affirmed that the global climate crisis will certainly further grow and increase, perhaps exponentially, and become even much more

---

[231] ibid; also L Ignacio, 'Implications of standards and technical regulations on export competitiveness' (2007) Draft Framework Paper for the AERC Collaborative Research Project on Export Supply Constraints in Africa. Nairobi.

1296   SDG 17

destructive, disruptive, and deadly than previously projected. However, UNFCCC COP 26 in Glasgow reinforced the widespread fear that it is now increasingly unlikely that the 1.5 ° goal sealed in the Paris Agreement—perhaps even the 2.0 ° fallback position—can still be reached. COP 26, unfortunately, was more of the same: cynical delegations of certain industrialized and carbon-dependent countries as well as ruthless fossil fuel lobbyists coerced poor countries already hit hard by climate change into defensive mode and dictated a watered-down, shallow 'compromise' outcome that is simply far from adequate. Despite some mitigation pundits praising COP 26 for 'keeping the 1.5 ° goal alive', the point is not about what's hypothetically technically feasible but it is very much about: What has been done and continues to be done to this world's poor, marginalized, underdeveloped, disenfranchised, remote people? Much of the COP process carries the ugly handwriting of neoliberalism and neo-colonial rule.

a) Target 17.6 Enhance North–South, South–South and triangular regional and international cooperation on and access to science, technology and innovation and enhance knowledge sharing on mutually agreed terms, including through improved coordination among existing mechanisms, in particular at the United Nations level, and through a global technology; Target 17.7 Promote the development, transfer, dissemination and diffusion of environmentally sound technologies to developing countries on favourable terms, including on concessional and preferential terms, as mutually agreed; Target 17.8 Fully operationalize the technology bank and science, technology and innovation capacity-building mechanism for least developed countries by 2017 and enhance the use of enabling technology, in particular information and communications technology

What COVID-19 responses and the climate policy conundrum as phenomenon of global governance and international cooperation have in common is an observable potentially detrimental mix of short-sightedness, selfishness, and even ruthlessness on the part of some actors with which international solidarity, collective action, and the noble cause of pursuing equality, dignity, and justice in international relations are being hampered or sacrificed for short-term gain, dominance, and privilege. This reality runs counter to the SDGs, SDG 17, and certainly targets 17.6–17.8. Forty years of largely unregulated capitalism, economic globalization, and neoliberal rule have not really furthered the spirit and goals of the Charter of the United Nations. The underlying ideologies have basically ruined our planet, its ecosystems and habitats, and left behind humanity in a state of shock, turmoil, and disintegration—closer to what Hobbes' *Leviathan* described as the State of Nature.[232] Even worse, many of the crises that ought to be tackled collectively and following the rulebook of SDG 17 are now inextricably correlated. For instance, zoonoses and with them epidemics and pandemics are on the rise also because of changing climates, temperatures, precipitation, humidity, biomes, and human habitat. Wars such as in Sudan, Yemen, and Syria are also due to climate change, desertification, water shortage, crop

---

[232] See T Hobbes and JCA Gaskin, *Leviathan* (OUP 1998).

failure, and hunger—as is forced migration as a mass phenomenon. And the list goes on.[233]

The Sars-CoV2 pandemic and climate change powerfully illustrate why targets 17.6–17.8 are critically important. For addressing both crises, access to science, technology and innovation, and enhanced knowledge sharing are key. Furthermore, they have to occur simultaneously and on a shared basis, on mutually agreed terms, and in a spirit of solidarity and assistance. The transfer of power from the Trump administration to the Biden administration in the US set an example in this regard. US President Joe Biden, on his first day in office on 20 January 2021, signed two important executive orders signalling the country's return to the international arena, to global cooperation and multilateralism. The first was for the US to rejoin the 2015 Paris Agreement on climate change, and the other was to re-establish the country's full membership and support to the World Health Organization (WHO).[234]

Both acts were hugely symbolic, especially since they occurred within hours of Biden's inauguration, and set a fundamentally new tone in US foreign policy, but apart from being symbolic, these acts constitute a material and substantial backing of global efforts to address the COVID-19 pandemic and climate change under the aegis of the UN and in the spirit of SDG 17. Clearly, the country hit hardest by the pandemic—both in terms of total infections and deaths—is better off as a member of the very global community that ensures the rapid sharing of research, data, and best practices, coordinates responses in accordance with target 17.6, and comes together to devise evidence-based solutions to the world's most pressing public health issues, be it malaria, tuberculosis, HIV, or COVID-19. But the international community needs the US as well.[235] Since its inception in 1948, the US has been the single largest contributor to the WHO—with a budget of $4.84 billion for the biennium 2020–21, not including COVID-19-related expenses—with a steady share of 22 per cent of the organization's assessed core budget and significant additional voluntary contributions made every single year. Indeed, a great sense of relief was voiced in unison by scientists, senior government officials, and UN leaders alike when the Biden administration applied common sense and restored the US' bond with the WHO on the day of its inception. This step had an immediately relevant and measurable impact on the global response to SARS-CoV-2.[236]

With the unfreezing of previously withheld payments and the allocation of additional, fresh sums of money targeted at global health emergency relief efforts, research and development, and the provision of knowledge, technology, supplies, and teams, the global fight against COVID-19 experienced an important boost. Particularly important was WHO's COVAX initiative, which is a historic and unprecedented fundraising effort

---

[233] See A Rechkemmer, *The Global Climate Crisis Is the New Frontier of Justice*, Op-Ed, Fair Observer (4 January 2022) <https://www.fairobserver.com/more/environment/andreas-rechkemmer-global-climate-crisis-justice-cop26-covid-19-vaccines-omicron-inequality-news-12511/> accessed 7 January 2023.

[234] See A Rechkemmer, 'Why the US Return to the WHO Matters', Op-Ed, Fair Observer (18 March 2021) <https://www.fairobserver.com/region/north_america/andreas-rechkemmer-us-return-who-world-health-organization-coronavirus-covid-pandemic-world-news-98691/> accessed 7 January 2023.

[235] See ibid.

[236] ibid.

to make effective and safe vaccines available to all countries, especially developing ones. Moreover, COVAX entails a proprietary vaccine development programme, including the building of manufacturing capabilities, and provides technical and logistical support to countries in need—a near-perfect illustration of target 17.6 and its call for 'improved coordination among existing mechanisms, in particular at the UN level, and through a global technology facilitation mechanism'. The US quickly became COVAX's largest funder and pledged to donate surplus vaccine stocks in addition to its financial contributions. Biden even endorsed the waiving of intellectual property restriction to open up pertinent patents for developing and least developed countries to more easily produce and distribute the much needed vaccines and medications in the battle against COVID-19. Biden's move was a rare example for a literal implementation of SDG target 17.6 aiming to enable North–South, South–South, and triangular regional and international cooperation.

However, most other OECD member countries opposed the patent waiver and COVAX still has a long way to go. The facility did not meet its goal of buying supply so that 2 billion doses could be fairly and equitably distributed by the end of 2021. The apparent lack of solidarity and tangible support by wealthy nations is disappointing and prompted UN Secretary-General Antonio Guterres to call global vaccine distribution 'wildly uneven and unfair', describing the goal of providing vaccines to all as 'the biggest moral test before the global community'.[237]

In the case of the COVID-19 pandemic with rapidly emerging mutations and variants of the virus, quick, unequivocal, and substantial support—scientific, financial, logistical, and technical—to developing countries and those behind in getting access to effective vaccines is not only a moral obligation for developed countries but also a mere matter of rationality and self-interest since ambitious and aggressive vaccine rollout campaigns in wealthy countries may be in vain as new variants of SARS-CoV-2 can emerge and cause new viral strains at any time. The international community is well advised to support multilateral solutions and collective action in accordance with target 17.6. It is the only reasonable, promising approach to tackling the world's biggest crises in the twenty-first century, thus far.

Likewise, the global climate emergency provides a litmus test for SDG target 17.7 (in addition to targets 17.6 and 17.8, of course).

In a world that is becoming more and more exposed and vulnerable to the effects of global change, combining integrated risk assessment tools with innovative and effective technologies and strategies for both mitigation and adaptation in the face of climate change and other threats is a key prerogative for policy-making. With the focus of both researchers and decision-makers having gradually shifted from observing and assessing the bio-physical aspects of global risks to a more human and society centred understanding of the nature of the problem, the social, behavioural, economic, and technological aspects have entered centre stage of the public discourse. Responses to

---

[237] See 'COVID-19 vaccination "wildly uneven and unfair": UN Secretary-General' (*UN News*, 17 February 2021) <https://news.un.org/en/story/2021/02/1084962> accessed 7 January 2023.

climate change and other risks and challenges have to establish an optimal interplay between mitigation, adaptation, and socio-economic instruments. This is where target 17.7 becomes hugely relevant.[238]

The challenge as we move towards 2030 is to harmonize poverty eradication and all the other SDGs with mitigating the effects of climate change, the pandemic, natural hazards, food security crises, and so forth—all of which require massive public and private investments and the development, transfer, dissemination, and diffusion of environmentally sound technologies to developing countries. Therefore, novel frameworks and approaches such as 'inclusive green growth' or net-zero target informed policies have become influential. But how can these goals be achieved and financed? Obviously, quite fundamental changes have to be introduced that affect both the production and the consumption sectors and allow for real innovation in technologies and energy, in urban mobility, infrastructure, and transportation grids—both in the Global North and the Global South. This topic illustrates the deep social and societal nature of sustainable development strategies, especially in the area of mitigation—it's not just about technology and innovation. Transitions to green and low-carbon economies, whether in OECD countries or in developing countries or LDCs, will have to embed policies, incentive schemes, and economic instruments in a larger societal context of social learning and behavioural change.

Intelligently designed processes of linking state-of-the-art risk assessments with highly effective adaptation and mitigation measures at very large scales will become a key challenge for societies and policy-makers in the years to come, and will require the art of combining integrated risk assessment tools with an advanced approach to adaptive governance and policy-making to implement SDG target 17.7. Martens and Chang[239] presented a conceptual matrix of the vulnerability–adaptation–mitigation nexus and illustrated the predominantly social and societal nature of this set of phenomena and their interaction. Social and societal dynamics constitute the sustainable development conundrum and also hold vulnerability, adaptation, and mitigation together. The IPCC already in its Third Assessment Report (TAR) in 2001[240] defined vulnerability as 'the degree to which a system is susceptible to, or unable to cope with, adverse effects of climate change, including climate variability and extremes'. IPCC lead authors coined our understanding of vulnerability as being composed of exposure, sensitivity, and adaptive capacity. Our societies' policy responses aiming to reduce vulnerability to climate change usually target only one of these three. Martens and Chang write: 'Exposure can be reduced (e.g. by changing the sectoral composition of the economy), sensitivity can be reduced (e.g. by making operational adjustments), and the adaptive capacity can be increased (e.g. by making contingency plans)'.[241]

---

[238] See A Rosemberg, *Embedding Just Transition in Long-term Decarbonization Strategies: Why, What, and How* (WRI 2022) <https://files.wri.org/expert-perspective-rosemberg.pdf> accessed 7 January 2023.

[239] See WJ Martens and CT Chang, *The Social and Behavioural Aspects of Climate Change: Linking Vulnerability, Adaptation and Mitigation* (Greenleaf Publishing 2010).

[240] See Intergovernmental Panel on Climate Change (IPCC), *Climate Change 2001—Synthesis Report* (CUP 2001).

[241] Martens and Chang (n 239).

However, the adaptive capacity of a social-ecological system and sustainable development as such depend on the effective interplay between mitigation and adaptation dynamics mostly expressed by devising such factors as economy, finance, technology, human and social capital, knowledge and learning, and policy and governance tools within partnerships for sustainable development as outlined on SDG 17 and emphasized in targets 17.6–17.8. Therefore, effective policy responses based on SDG 17 always have to strive to achieve a balance and a harmonious interplay between mitigation and adaptation strategies, essentially using a similar approach and toolkit for both. Technological innovation, greening economies and businesses, funding for sustainable development, and, ultimately, the dynamics of inclusive green growth and net-zero policy frameworks are all playing key roles in SDG implementation and form the basis of implementing SDG 17. However, they only effectuate lasting global change and justice in so far as target 17.7 is applied, for they are as good and effective as much as they operate on the system-inherent dynamic of the social and societal sphere of international solidarity, equity, and fairness. Negligence of these societal and global justice roots, whether in terms of action, policy, law, or technology is likely to lead into the wrong direction, that is on to presumably less effective trajectories. Martens and Chang write: 'The willingness and capacity of society to change is critical. Information and awareness-raising can be useful tools to stimulate individual and collective climate action … Mitigation, being an action targeting the long term, means attaching value to the interests of future generations and … can be considered an altruistic response by society'[242]—and this in a North–South context.

Paying due attention to meeting the requirements of targets 17.6–17.8 will be of critical importance when identifying ambitious strategies toward sustainable changes in the technology and energy sectors, low carbon intensity, and green growth, especially in developing as well as rapidly emerging countries. 'Green growth' and 'inclusive growth' are the buzzwords of the day, but are these concepts at all realistic and sustainable? Clearly, there is no simple answer to this question. However, it is obvious that integration is key: integrating policy with risk assessment, mitigation, and adaptation as well as massive support and transfers to developing countries.

The dynamics at play in this context largely build on convergence between law and policy frameworks, economic incentives, financial transfers, technological innovation, and efficiency, all of which have societal and developmental connotations and draw upon the ability of humans and societies to change cultural constructs, attitudes and behaviour through social learning in a just and equitable North–South perspective.

The role of knowledge and technology co-production and dissemination, and the mechanisms and mechanics of social learning require attention, as the foregoing section has shown. Yet this poses some challenges to our governance systems. Our political, legal, and economic institutions have to feature a certain amount of adaptive capacity paired with provisions that foster knowledge production and diffusion and

[242] ibid.

COMMENTARY ON TARGETS AND INDICATORS   1301

technological innovation on the one hand side, and individual and collective learning and behavioural adaptability on the other.

Adequate and progressive approaches to capacity building require a balance between law and policy making, economy and finance, knowledge, technology and innovation, education, and social learning and acceptance as Box 17.1 shows. Goal 17's target 8 exemplifies this and adds a few select details, perhaps not enough though.

A key question in this context is the one on how societies can effectively and fairly link human, economic and social development with environmental sustainability and bold climate change mitigation efforts in an equitable North–South dimension. The

---

Box 17.1 A larger governance context for capacity building

Institutions and global governance

- Changes in institutional and environmental governance frameworks for effective management of ecosystems.

Economics and incentives

- Economic and financial interventions as instruments to regulate the use of ecosystem goods and services.

Knowledge responses

- Effective management of ecosystems is constrained by a lack of knowledge and information.

Technological responses

- Development of technologies designed to increase the efficiency of resource use and reduce impacts of drivers of environmental change.

Social and behavioural responses

- Public education, civil society action, and empowerment of communities can be instrumental in responding to ecosystem degradation.

Source: P Vellinga and N Herb

Note: See P Vellinga and N Herb, *International Human Dimensions Programme (IHDP) on Global Environmental Change: IT Science Plan* (Amsterdam Free University Press 1999).

1302 SDG 17

research agenda of the 'Industrial Transformation Project' of the International Human Dimensions Program on Global Environmental Change (IHDP-IT) produced remarkable work in the fields of energy and material flows, food, cities with focus of water and transportation, information and communication, governance, and transformation processes.[243] IHDP-IT defined the foundation of industrial transformation research as follows:

> Industrial Transformation research starts with the notion that changes in technologies, put differently, changes in the ways in which humans use environmental resources and services, are embedded in the socio-economic realm and modify the natural environment. This embraces processes and products, production and consumption chains and distribution and disposal activities. IT research is also interested in the institutions and incentives that shape these systems (i.e. property, liability, regulations), and how these situate and influence social actors (government, producers, and consumers).[244]

It is critical to understand how these systems might be able to change without producing significant additional greenhouse gas (GHG) emissions, ecosystems failure, injustice, and other adverse effects and collaterals—a key objective of the 2030 Agenda and the SDGs. In other words, the balanced interaction of economy-driven innovation with change processes in provisional systems influenced by law and policy, social change, and global justice is at the heart of these questions.[245]

Industrial transformation and sustainability transitions have been an important focus of the research and policy communities in a number of European countries already for some time, and have included the roles of institutions and behaviour. However, it is important to link the 'Western' discourse on transitions and sustainability to a more in-depth understanding of how social, political, and economic development can occur in other parts of the world, especially in developing countries. Given the transformative changes that are apparent in some rapidly urbanizing and developing countries of Asia, the Middle East, and Africa, this question appears particularly challenging.

> A characteristic feature of much of the current policies and research linked to technology, industry and sustainability relates to product-process innovation and to the question of how to achieve near-term improvements in energy-, resource- and pollution-intensities through the adoption of best available technologies. The achievement of higher-level environmental and sustainability targets—including low-carbon or less resource-intensive development pathways—has attracted less attention.[246]

---

[243] See ibid.
[244] ibid.
[245] See AA Olsthoorn and AJ Wieczorek (eds), *Understanding Industrial Transformation; Views from Different Disciplines* (Springer 2006).
[246] See ibid.

COMMENTARY ON TARGETS AND INDICATORS   1303

The term 'transitions' usually refers to long-term and large-scale changes in human environment-interactions. Transitions touch upon deeply cultural, social, behavioural, and institutional aspects in building upon or bringing about novelty and innovation, especially in the areas of energy, technology, infrastructure, and transport. Their coefficient can be measured in a variety of ways, but in the context of climate change, energy and resource intensity are key. Asia matters because of the sheer scale and rate of urban and industrial growth and 'their profound implications for environmental quality and resources locally, regionally and globally, which make Asia central to sustainable development on a global scale.[247] Can this period of industrial transformation in Asia be useful for sustainable development worldwide? From research in East Asia we know that pro-poor economic growth and technological capacity building have worked if and where the right institutional set-up was provided. 'The relevant institutional conditions range from fundamental starting conditions for industrial-environmental capabilities building (such as political stability, rule of law, and control of corruption), effectiveness of government institutions in carrying out policies, availability of information around technology choices ... to the degree to which development options are structured by international agreements.'[248] Unfortunately, such essential details are missing from targets 17.7 and 17.8.

Taking the sustainability dimension to both consumption and production as well as to both social and technical change must be the overarching goal of every low-carbon development approach. What is needed is a long-term perspective of big change, however, occurring in a relatively short time. The history of technological change and innovation is quite promising in this regard as it shows in a number of cases that even radical and relatively abrupt changes are possible. According to Fred Steward, 'we can look at these examples and can get hold of some patterns such as e.g., the dynamics of transformative innovation and search guidance as to a possible point of intervention. We see that radical change is systemic in nature, takes time, embraces technological and social innovation, involves diversity of actors—on both the production and the consumption side—and disrupts certain social arrangements.'[249] Steward states that the merit of this approach to transitions is that it conceptualizes innovation in relation to a prevailing domain of socio-technical practice in contrast to a more traditional perspective on single technologies or sectors, which is far too narrow a vision. The transitions approach takes note of the complexity of systems and the huge diversity of involved actors. Applying this approach to the question of climate-resilient and inclusive economic growth and innovation is about purposive, not merely emergent change as such change has to be induced.

The transitions approach thus suggests that any technical innovation is embedded in a larger frame of socio-economic conditions and the dynamics of social change. Important in this connection is the concept 'socio-technical regime' which refers to

[247] See UN Environment Programme (UNEP), *Global Environment Outlook 6* (CUP 2019).
[248] See Olsthoorn and Wieczorek (n 246).
[249] See F Steward, 'Transformative Innovation Policy to Meet the Challenge of Climate Change: Sociotechnical Networks Aligned with Consumption and End-Use as New Transition Arenas' (2012) 24(4) Technology Analysis & Strategic Management 331–43.

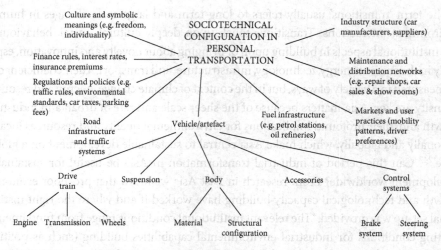

Figure 17.1 Socio-technological regime configuration.
Source: Geels, 2002

a relatively stable configuration of institutions, technologies, rules, practices, and networks of cooperation that determine the evolution and use of technology.[250] In its entirety a socio-technical regime includes production, diffusion, and use of technology. To illustrate how such regimes work, the example of a typical configuration (or 'regime') in the car-manufacturing sector is given Figure 17.1.[251]

Figure 17.1 shows the wider 'landscape' in which the development, production, and diffusion of a car is typically embedded. This scheme can be applied to any (new) technology. The purposive selection and development of new technologies has to take into account and model a variety of non-tech factors, including such things as culture and symbolic meanings, user practices and policies alongside finance rules and markets etc. Such a configuration around an artefact or technology hence is called a socio-technical regime. Regimes tend to be stable and sometimes even 'sticky'. Replacing existing regimes by new ones—in the given case more climate-friendly ones—is essentially like initiating paradigm shifts. To yield real green and low-carbon growth in rapidly emerging countries and developing countries, the wider production-consumption field will have to undergo a number of such paradigm shifts, that is, regime changes. Smith and colleagues write:

> We understand regime change to be a function of two processes: (1.) Shifting selection pressures bearing on the regime; and (2.) The coordination of resources available inside

---

[250] See R Kemp and others, 'Regime Shifts to Sustainability through Processes of Niche Formation: The Approach of Strategic Niche Management' (1998) 10(3) Technology Analysis and Strategic Management 175–95.
[251] See FW Geels, 'Technological Transitions as Evolutionary Reconfiguration Processes: A Multi Level Perspective and a Case Study' (2002) 31 Research Policy 1257–74; FW Geels, 'From Sectoral Systems of Innovation to Sociotechnical Systems. Insights about Dynamics and Change from Sociology and Institutional Theory' (2004) 33 Research Policy 897–920.

and outside the regime to adapt to these pressures. Conventional economic analysis of technical change tends to focus on pressures that operate visibly at the level of the firm (such as pricing, competition, contracts, taxes and charges, regulations, standards, liability, profitability, skills and knowledge). Analysis at the level of the socio-technical regime, on the other hand, includes such factors, but goes beyond them to consider less economically visible pressures emanating from institutional structures and conventions, including changes in broad political economic 'landscapes', or wider socio-cultural attitudes and trends (Geels, 2004). These can be directed at specific regimes, like the activities of the anti-nuclear movement. Or they can be more general, like the ebb and flow of environmental attitudes in society.[252]

Smith and colleagues continue:

All regimes have some capacity and resources to respond to the selection pressures bearing on them. We refer to this feature as the *adaptive capacity of a regime*. In developing Asian economies we observe the rapid growth ... of socio-technical systems ... The specific nature of these socio-technical systems, the technologies they are based on, and the patterns of economic growth and consumption they foster, will have a profound influence on the resources and energy profile of the developing economy.[253]

It is clear from the above that the three targets 6–8 of Goal 17, while providing a sound basis for enabling North–South, South–South, and triangular cooperation on innovation, knowledge and technological transfer and sharing, the agenda is much more intricate. Targets 17.6–17.8 must be augmented and complemented by additional legal, policy, and societal instruments of transformations and transitions to meet the goals of net zero emission, pollution and biodiversity loss based sustainable development worldwide. Target 17.8, which is fairly specific about one aspect of institutional capacity building, was met. The Technology Bank, a newly established body dedicated to the least developed countries was operationalized in September 2017 as requested by target 17.8. It is hosted by the government of Turkey and located in the city of Gebze. As the UN notes, 'the new Bank is expected to improve the utilization of scientific and technological solutions in the world's poorest countries and promote the integration of least developed countries Into the global knowledge-based economy. This will be achieved through improving technology-related policies and facilitating the access to appropriate technologies.'[254] Whether the Bank will make a tangible difference in capacity building for LDCs remains to be seen. So far, no pathbreaking funding streams have been reported.

---

[252] See A Smith and others, 'The Governance of Socio-technical Transitions' (2005) 34 Research Policy 1491–510.
[253] ibid.
[254] United Nations, Technology Bank for Least Developed Countries Operationalized, 22 September 2017 <https://www.un.org/press/en/2017/dev3292.doc.htm> accessed 7 January 2023.

1306   SDG 17

The indicators linked to SDG targets 17.6–17.8 are: 17.6.1 Fixed Internet broadband subscriptions per 100 inhabitants, by speed; 17.7.1 Total amount of approved funding for developing countries to promote the development, transfer, dissemination and diffusion of environmentally sound technologies; 17.8.1 Proportion of individuals using the Internet. Indicators 6.1 and 8.1 are certainly important as access to the Internet is key everywhere, but vital for developing countries. But these indicators are very specific and cover only a tiny fraction of all possibly relevant indicators regarding the transfer of and access to science, knowledge, technology, know-how, intellectual property etc. Given the dramatic need and all intricacies involved as outlined in detail in the foregoing section, having just these two indicators identified is a stunning testimony to the failure of the developed countries and the international donor community to make meaningful commitments. Likewise, indicator 7.1 is so general and broad that it becomes almost meaningless, certainly nothing that the developing world can be satisfied with.[255]

b) Target 17.9 Enhance international support for implementing effective and targeted capacity-building in developing countries to support national plans to implement all the Sustainable Development Goals, including through North-South, South-South and triangular cooperation; Target 17.18 By 2020, enhance capacity-building support to developing countries, including for least developed countries and small island developing States, to increase significantly the availability of high-quality, timely and reliable data disaggregated by income, gender, age, race, ethnicity, migratory status, disability, geographic location and other characteristics relevant in national contexts; Target 17.19 By 2030, build on existing initiatives to develop measurements of progress on sustainable development that complement gross domestic product, and support statistical capacity-building

Target 17.9 stands out among SDG targets, in a negative sense, by remaining oddly generic, and unspecific—certainly the result of tense, sticky political negotiations between developed and developing countries.[256] Developing countries for sure would have preferred a more concrete target with real 'teeth'. The reality is that sustainable development post-2015, and certainly beyond 2030, will require truly disruptive, transformational efforts on the part of both developed and developing countries. Figure 17.2 maps out four types of transitional development trajectories. It appears that only the type 'purposive transition', which requires a high level of coordination between regime members (eg public authorities, technological communities, the finance sector and multilateral development banks (MDBs), consumers in both developed and developing countries),

---

[255] See A Maltais and others, 'SDG 17: Partnerships for the Goals. A Review of Research Needs' (2018) Stockholm Environment Institute. Technical annex to the Formas report *Forskning för Agenda 2030: Översikt av forskningsbehov och vägar framåt*; RS Senise and others, 'Role of Science, Technology, and Innovation Towards SDGS' in WL Filho and others (eds), *Partnerships for the Goals. Encyclopedia of the UN Sustainable Development Goals* (Springer 2021) <https://doi.org/10.1007/978-3-319-95963-4_90> accessed 7 January 2023.
[256] See Maltais and others (n 256).

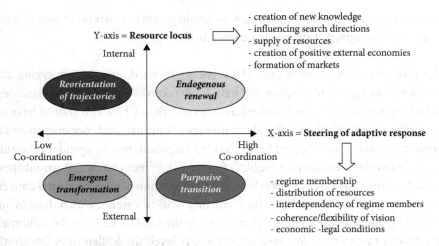

Figure 17.2 Transitional development trajectories.
ªSee Smith and others (n 253).

a relatively high level of external resources (eg through technical, policy and financial aid and loans), and social learning, is appropriate for SDG-based sustainable development in the face of the global Grand Challenges.

It is critical to highlight the transformation dimension within the international development and capacity building discourse. Capacity development as featured in target 17.9 requires a very thoughtful, multi-layered, and strategic approach. In general, the SDGs have constituted a positive step forward to frame and guide enhanced human development cooperation worldwide. However, for the forthcoming years the international community has to embark on a much-increased effort to implement the goals and meet the targets and integrate them with the broader agendas of global environmental change, climate change, and human climate justice in particular, safety and security, and effective risk reduction and disaster management (ie risk governance). SDG target 17.9 is supposed to frame and guide these hugely critical efforts but spectacularly fails to add context, numbers (both financial and temporal) and clear provisions.

An agenda for enhanced SDG implementation through capacity building will have to include, among others, the following objectives:

- Global inequality and its reduction should be given more emphasis: an explicit call for the reduction of inequality should be paired with the objective of economic stability.
- It is a prerogative to stress the importance of cultural diversity and social values, and the principles of accountability and legitimacy for effective capacity building.
- Fragile statehood, political instability, and larger societal uncertainties oftentimes pose risks to capacity building and require the attention of policy-makers.
- The SDG process needs to entail effective tools and standards for risk and safety assessment and integrated risk management in a variety of areas, including those of

1308 SDG 17

natural hazards and extreme events, technology, environmental change, finance, or trade, for capacity building to be sustainable.

As the process of implementing the SDGs moves forward, new and emerging challenges as well as aggravated factors will have to be taken into account and shouldered so as to keep the goals on track and ensure success. Target 17.9 also should have emphasized the aspects of coherence and consistency of international cooperation and development assistance with regard to the existing fragmentation of agendas relevant to sustainable development despite the SDG framework.[257] For instance, it would appear that MEAs almost consistently seem to lack full integration of environmental concerns with poverty alleviation and reducing inequality. This is a trend, which does include the current global climate change regime, notably the UNFCCC. Even the 'epitome' of global development policy formulation at the UN level, the Millennium Declaration (2000), appeared somewhat weak when it comes to intrinsically linking the poverty theme with those of global environmental change, and climate change in particular.[258]

Target 17.9 does not provide nations with concrete examples on how they may go about achieving this. It ignores the links between the impoverished and their environment. Therefore it seems fair to conclude that target 17.9 is insufficient in its present form. At least, it does not have a clear focus.[259] The focus should thus be on monitoring the usage of natural resources and on poverty assessments. If a focus within target 17.9 were placed on capacity building through green growth, other problems may work themselves out, at least to some extent. Thus, target 17.9 missed the chance of prescribing the capacity building model for the future as green, sustainable, carbon neutral, and inclusive.

By comparison, what made the MA[260] so much stronger than the target 17.9? It is probably due to the fact that the MA included concrete analyses of the world's ecosystems. With an assessment of the current state of the environment it is easier for policymakers to see where the problems lie and give more incentive for them to follow the guidelines set forth for capacity building. Whether SDG 17 is ambitious enough can be doubted given the relative weakness of target 17.9. The international community has to embark on an increased effort to integrate the existing set of SDGs with the other agendas of global capacity building, including on climate change, security, and disaster risk reduction. Global inequality and its reduction should be given more emphasis. Fragile statehood, political instability, and larger societal uncertainties oftentimes pose risks to SDG success and global security and require the attention of policy-makers. Target 17.9 does not touch upon these critical questions but remains awfully broad.

---

[257] See Maltais and others (n 256).

[258] See UN General Assembly, *United Nations Millennium Declaration, Resolution Adopted by the General Assembly*, 18 September 2000, A/RES/55/2 <https://www.refworld.org/docid/3b00f4ea3.html> accessed 7 January 2023.

[259] See P Shyamsundar, 'Poverty-Environment Indicators' (2002) The World Bank, Environmental Economics Series Paper No 84.

[260] See UN General Assembly (n 260).

Obviously for political reasons, the negotiating nations were unable to agree on more. However, ultimately, law, policy, and investments at all levels have to seek the resilience of the economic as well as the social and the ecological spheres. In order to enable effective and progressive sustainable development to implement all of the SDGs in line with the whole 2030 Agenda, international law and policy need to ensure that financial and technical support comes from a variety of different sources (eg national governments, international organizations, and the private and investment sectors). Ensuring decent employment (decent wages, sustainable jobs) while building capacity can ensure a more balanced and sustainable socio-economic stability, and assist in alleviating global inequities and local poverty.[261] Still, capacity building in support of target 17.9 will have to include a vision beyond 2030. The post-2030 dimension is helpful in that it allows a reflection of what the SDGs have helped accomplish so far, how successes can be sustained, and what can be done better. Also, the coronavirus crisis has pushed the sustainable development community rethinking the SDG progress and the validity of its indicators.

Climate change, its root causes, impacts, and response options need to be part of the equation for capacity building for the period until 2030 and well beyond. By default, the very case of anthropogenic climate change runs counter to global sustainable development and therefore the SDGs. Climate change results in growing risks and vulnerabilities, particularly in developing countries. It thus severely undermines the achievement of the SDGs 'naturally'. We risk derailment of the SDGs if we fail to mitigate and adapt to climate change effectively and to climate-proof every action done under the guidance of SDG target 17.9. Such capacity building policies can help attain the SDGs in a variety of ways and should be seen as means to implement Goal 17 more effectively.[262]

What SDG 17 should have included, perhaps as an addition to target 17.9, is a focus on connecting climate financing with the rest of sustainable development financing. Climate change financing (for both mitigation and adaptation) can also alleviate poverty. On the mitigation side, carbon funds (national, regional, or global ones) provide ample opportunity for cross-SDG capacity building financing. These include the Clean Development Mechanism (CDM) which was established under the Kyoto Protocol and designed to assist Annex I Parties to comply with emission reduction commitments and to foster sustainable development in developing countries. Microfinance institutions can also help to fill the gap left open by traditional capacity building initiatives, for example by banks and state-run programmes.[263] On adaptation financing (set up at COP 15), multiple possibilities exist through the Nairobi Adaptation Fund, the GEF's Special Climate Change Fund, Least Developed Countries Fund, GEF Trust Fund's Climate Change focal area, the UN-REDD Program, or the World Bank' Pilot Program

---

[261] See I Vij and S Dewan, *Beyond Moral Justification* (Center for American Progress 2010).

[262] See A Rechkemmer, 'Sustaining Climate Change Mitigation—Policy, Technology, and Society' (2010) 4(3) Sustainability 60–73.

[263] See A Hammill and others, 'Microfinance and Climate Change Adaptation' (2008) 39(4) IDS Bulletin 113–22.

1310   SDG 17

for Climate Resilience, Strategic Climate Fund, Forest Carbon Partnership Facility, or Clean Technology Fund.

Poverty eradication, on the other hand, is often financed through the means of microcredits, savings, and other financial services (eg credits and loans). These usually all work together to help alleviate poverty. However, such schemes require adequate governmental policies and laws, a certain momentum in the private sector, and aid (private and government aid).[264] In theory, carbon trading is supposed to help the poor by mandating that wealthier nations buy the right to carbon emissions from poorer nations thus transferring financial flows to such countries. However, this does not change the total amount of emissions and therefore has doubtful relevance for ambitious climate change mitigation efforts. Also, climate change is a root cause for poverty and inequality and addressing these is as a prerequisite for a more just and successful climate policy in and for developing countries. Indeed, there is a complex relationship between poverty, vulnerability, and climate change. Therefore, capacity-building initiatives under target 17.9 must be conceived of and devised in ways that take into account the afore-mentioned interconnections and intricacies and produce inter-sectional efforts.

If capacity building measures are taken to mitigate poverty under the current circumstances, this mitigation is likely to be unsustainable as long as they are not in harmony with the need to address climate change impacts, environmental degradation, and effective risk governance simultaneously. The leading edge of the debate about innovative financing schemes to address capacity building at the poverty–security–environment–climate nexus simultaneously could consist in a mix of public finance from both climate and non-climate sources with private investments. Within the public climate domain, the following tools could be used and merged: phaseout of fossil fuels subsidies, Emission Trading Schemes (ETS) auction proceeds, Assignment Amount Units (AAU) auction proceeds, and pro-poor dedication of carbon taxes on transport and energy. Such tools could be combined with a renewed version of Felix's 'Tobin tax' proposal on major financial transactions, for example:

1. The tax would be applied at a uniform ad valorem rate by, at the least, all the key currency countries. 2. It would be administered and collected by each government on all payments by residents within its jurisdiction that involved a spot currency exchange, including, as in the case of Eurocurrency transactions, exchanges that do not involve the home currency. 3. The proceeds from the tax would be paid into a central fund controlled by the IMF or the World Bank. 4. Subject perhaps to prior IMF consent, countries could form currency areas within which the tax would not apply. That is, small countries that formally tied their currency to a key currency would not be required to levy the tax on intra-area currency exchanges.[265]

---

[264] See ibid.
[265] See D Felix, 'The Tobin Tax Proposal: Background, Issues, and Prospects' (1995) 27(2) Futures 195–208.

The above mixed approach could further be combined with IMF Special Drawing Rights to leverage additional funds.[266]

To sum up, being the only generic target dedicated to capacity development, target 17.9 falls short of details and substance as to *what* capacity development ought to be supported. Its only indicator 'Dollar value of financial and technical assistance (including through North–South, South–South and triangular cooperation) committed to developing countries' (17.9.1) is equally broad and lacks specific orientation on the kind of finance needed to tackle complex needs.

Unlike target 17.9, targets 17.18 and 17.19 are fairly specific and straightforward. They are focused on the aspects of data availability as well as data and statistical capabilities within capacity building needs for developing countries. Indeed, access to high-quality data and information is key for effective SDG implementation. Over recent decades, a large corpus of datasets and literature on sustainable development has accumulated. Among many others, the UN Secretariat, its agencies, and IFIs, have produced or spearheaded the production of a gigantic collection of studies, assessments, and policy guidelines within the domain of sustainable development. However, most of these initiatives have been driven by 'Northern' entities, that is, headquarters and institutions based in OECD countries. Also, most of these endeavours produced or dealt with aggregated data that often lack the resolution and granularity that is needed to assess and guide action locally and on the ground. Therefore, and also with a view to ownership, empowerment, and equity considerations, a genuine capacity to produce and own finely grained, high-resolution, and disaggregated data is vital for developing countries to effectively implement the SDGs.

For instance, the IPCC and its partners have accumulated sufficient data, statistics, models, and knowledge systems to be able to produce decent projections and scenarios. However, there is still a concerning gap in research and data capacity and capabilities in the developing world. That is highly problematic regarding the high resolution which is needed to produce precise local projections whether for adaptation or mitigation. Regarding mitigation efforts of developing countries, many studies at the global level have been carried out since the entry into force of the UNFCCC. The Intergovernmental Panel on Climate Change also draws on such studies. These help the IPCC take a view about the adequacy of commitments in the UNFCCC.

Studies at the country level, however, usually identify the mitigation and adaptation measures available to governments, along with their priority, likely effects, and costs. The studies help governments select measures and negotiate financial assistance. In most cases, one takes as given in country studies certain matters, which global studies treat as issues to be addressed. Sometimes it is too difficult to integrate studies macroeconomically, but one can study sector investment plans and sector policy

---

[266] See International Monetary Fund, *Factsheet: Special Drawing Rights (SDRs)* (IMF 2010) <http://www.imf.org/external/np/exr/facts/sdr.htm> accessed 7 January 2023.

1312　SDG 17

responses. To this effect, local capacity is vital[267]. Moreover, the more data is disaggregated as prescribed by target 17.18—'by income, gender, age, race, ethnicity, migratory status, disability, geographic location and other characteristics relevant in national contexts'—the better policy support can be designed and devised. What applies to disaggregated data also applies to statistical capabilities. Therefore, developing countries—including LDCs and Small Island Developing States (SIDS)– must be equipped with their own nationally appropriate and prioritized statistics capacity to make sense of the data and be in a position to measure progress against meeting the SDG targets along with other sustainable development objectives.[268]

The tracking and mapping of *policy relevant statistics* is by now routine in developed countries but not in developing countries, especially LDCs and SIDS. Statistics are used for annual or periodic indices like the Worldwide Governance Indicators or the Corruption Perceptions Index (to name two of the most prominent). To have such instruments means to be able to register government actions in real-time, in the sequences in which they occur. Over longer periods of time, this can accumulate to a more or less comprehensive 'profile' of sorts on the character, phenomenology, and tilt of a given government's policies in specific policy fields within sustainable development. For example, tight budgets year after year are reasonable evidence of a contractionary fiscal policy stance.[269] The accumulation over time of various policies in health, education, and social protection allows us to classify welfare states into various ideal types.[270] It is vital that developing countries are provided the resources to build and use their proprietary statistical tools to track, map, and analyse policy progress on the SDGs.

Finally, target 17.19 calls for resources to assist developing countries in developing 'measurements of progress on sustainable development that complement gross domestic product'. This aspect follows logically from the discussed calls for capacity building regarding localized disaggregated data and statistical capabilities and tools. Such alternative or complementary measures usually take the form of governance indicators. Governance indicators have grown in large numbers in the last decades,[271] and by now number in the hundreds. Some of the most prominent include the Worldwide Governance Indicators,[272] the Corruption Perceptions Index and related measures,[273]

---

[267] See A Rechkemmer, 'The Poverty–Environment–Climate Nexus in Context of the MDG Review Process and of Financing Tools (strategy paper) (Asian Development Bank 2010).

[268] ibid.

[269] See R Raudla and others, 'The Impact of Fiscal Crisis on Decision-Making Processes in European Governments: Dynamics of a Centralization Cascade' (2015) 75(6) Public Administration Review 842–52.

[270] See K Armingeon and M Beyeler (eds), *The OECD and European Welfare States* (Edward Elgar 2004); G Esping-Andersen, *The Three Worlds of Welfare Capitalism* (Polity Press 1990); W Schelkle, *Collapsing Worlds and Varieties of Welfare Capitalism: In Search of a New Political Economy of Welfare* (2012) London School of Economic, LSE Europe in Question Discussion Paper Series No 54/2012.

[271] See C Arndt and C Oman, *The Politics of Governance Ratings* (2008) Maastricht University, Maastricht Graduate School of Governance, Working Paper MGSoG/2008/WP003; B Buduru and LA Pal, 'The Globalized State: Measuring and Monitoring Governance' (2010) 13(4) European Journal of Cultural Studies 511–30.

[272] See D Kaufmann and others, *The World Wide Governance Indicators: Methodology and Analytical Issues* (The World Bank 2010) <http://papers.ssrn.com/sol3/papers.cfm?abstract_id=1682130> accessed 7 January 2023.

[273] See A Mungiu-Pippidi and M Johnston (eds), *Transitions to Good Governance: Creating Virtuous Circles of Anti-Corruption* (Edward Elgar 2017).

and happiness indexes.[274] This is a well-established field, but with virtually no examples tailored specifically for developing countries. To fill this gap is a key requirement mentioned in target 17.19 and the pertinent indicators.

4. Partnership, Stakeholder, Policy, and Governance-related Targets

a) Target 17.13 Enhance global macroeconomic stability, including through policy coordination and policy coherence; Target 17.14 Enhance policy coherence for sustainable development; Target 17.15 Respect each country's policy space and leadership to establish and implement policies for poverty eradication and sustainable development

One of the most interesting questions in international policy is whether legally binding agreements are more effective than voluntary commitments or consensus-based decisions. For instance, COP 26 finally endorsed a phase down of coal. However, it does not foresee any peak year or any collective target for cutting coal burning annually. As a result, the concept and vision that global sustainable development affairs should be addressed on a collective and truly international basis is still up for debate. It seems unclear whether the approach of consensus driven inter-governmental decision-making without enforceable, legally binding treaties has a meaningful enough effect. Also, the concept and notion of Global Governance could well face a new paradigm shift and gradually be replaced by a 'Club Governance' mode, that is, world politics in smaller, exclusive circles.

At this juncture, the following questions seem prudent, and effective SDG related policies will largely depend on answering them in a satisfying manner: how can threats and adverse impacts still be met and tackled? What are promising strategies well outside the routines and path dependencies of global negotiations? What are the potential and roles for technical and technological solutions and their social and societal acceptance? In the absence of a global breakthrough, additional negotiations in smaller circles, for instance within the G20, or between developed and developing countries, and the formation of so-called coalitions of the willing could lead to partial results and should therefore not be generally dismissed. Especially at regional scale, intense talks between policy-makers and a variety of stakeholders are necessary and have potential to advance solution-oriented efforts worldwide. By the same token, it is important to realize that the global SDG agenda is quite convoluted and has reached a state of almost incomprehensible complexity. It may therefore be fruitful to disentangle some of the most controversial issues and, for instance, yield to strive global agreements on questions of financial subsidies or compensation, on the harmonization of national policies, on technology transfer, or on the creation of new markets.[275]

Also, we will have to 're-marry' the SDG agenda with those on security and human security. Therefore, an integral approach is much needed at the level of global and

---

[274] See JE Stiglitz and others, *Beyond GDP: Measuring What Counts for Economic and Social Performance* (OECD 2018).

[275] See A Rechkemmer, *Is There A Crisis in International Environmental and Development Policy? After the Johannesburg Summit*, SWP Comment 2002/C 03 (SWP 2002).

1314 SDG 17

regional governance systems and collective political action. In the absence of a truly functional global approach to an effective management of the sustainable development crisis, the geographical regions are carrying responsibility, in particular Asia given its unique growth rates and carbon-related dynamics on the one hand side, and rapid development of key technological skills and resources on the other.

To fully implement SDG 17, a global and binding deal implying reliable collective action by all countries would be key. The fact that this deal would have to become effective in less than a decade poses an enormous challenge for policy makers but also society at large. It appears almost self-evident that ambitious targets will most likely not be achieved by governmental and inter-governmental policy-making and regulation alone. Even a very ambitious and legally binding new UN treaty would most likely not lead to the level of changes required without the mobilization of a drastic change in the production–consumption nexus of most countries. Success in this context certainly means to be able to surpass certain societal tipping points to trigger genuine green growth and large-scale behavioural changes.[276]

Also, it will be necessary to develop a variety of different scenarios and trajectories for change, depending on the geographic regions, as it will hardly make sense to simply apply a German or European model to, say, Asian countries and subregions. Martens and Chang conclude: 'The impacts of climate change are felt more immediately by individuals in society and adaptation is typically viewed as obeying the everyday 'self-interests' of individuals. As such, studies on risk perception by individuals, industries and organizations will be critical to understand its influence on the acceptability and ultimate effectiveness of different responses.'[277]

Priority should be given to developing, evaluating, and scaling up interventions designed to build community resilience, address human insecurity, and manage social conflict. Increasingly, cities and counties are recognized as important scales for equity-oriented SDG implementation planning and intervention. Urbanization compounds environmental risks associated with other development challenges and adds additional concerns: increasing density; new security threats; rising social and economic inequality; and strains on infrastructure, service systems, and urban ecologies, including informal settlements in environmentally marginal locations lacking basic services. Marginalized communities are disproportionately harmed by urban and regional environmental inequities. In cities that have suffered significant economic and social disinvestment, low-income communities of colour are particularly vulnerable to new environmental threats because of deteriorated infrastructures, severely reduced social and safety services, and pre-existing environmental inequality.

Rural poverty is another example of human insecurity. It is often associated with land degradation, drought, and desertification (sometimes caused or aggravated by climatic variability and changes, overgrazing, or unsustainable agricultural activities). If the rural poor stay on their land, the degradation pattern will make productivity too low

---

[276] See Rechkemmer, 'Sustaining Climate Change Mitigation' (n 264).
[277] See Martens and Chang (n 239); Rechkemmer, 'Sustaining Climate Change Mitigation' (n 264).

to support the rural inhabitants. Often, they are forced to migrate to other areas where the cycle of degradation will be repeated unless soil conservation education and appropriate incentives appear. On the other hand, the poor may have access to resources that are abundant in their environments, but globally scarce (ie forest cover and biodiversity).[278] Unfortunately, they often lack the resources to make the best use of what they have (soil nutrients, labour, health, etc). For instance, these circumstances can lead the rural poor burning forests to make farmland and providing the nutrients that the soil needs,[279] thereby losing something of even greater value (forests as carbon sinks). Urban poverty, by contrast, is often the result of people migrating from a country to find jobs or basic income. Such jobs are typically in factories or plants that perpetuate dirty industry. 'Particulate pollution from cement mills may only be dangerous in one urban region, acid rain from sulphur emissions may damage forests hundreds of miles from the source, and eutrophication from fertilizer runoff may affect ocean fisheries a thousand miles downstream from the farms that are the source of the problem.'[280]

Therefore, macroeconomic stability, policy coherence, and policy coordination, domestically as well as transnationally, are vital for the SDGs. In order for livelihoods to be sustainable, they must be resilient in the face of stresses and shocks (for agriculture, this could be droughts and floods) without weakening the foundation of resources. If the livelihoods of the poor are not sustainable, coping with the environmental effects of resource overuse could further impoverish them. For instance, as a result of living in a non-sustainable manner, the poor may have to deal with reduced consumption, migration costs, or household depletion. There is no chance for effective, lasting implementation of the SDGs without addressing such compounding and cascading issues coherently and in a coordinated manner. By pursuing the above, donors are called upon to 'respect each country's policy space and leadership to establish and implement policies for poverty eradication and sustainable development', as target 17.15 foresees.

b) *Target 17.16 Enhance the Global Partnership for Sustainable Development, complemented by multi-stakeholder partnerships that mobilize and share knowledge, expertise, technology and financial resources, to support the achievement of the Sustainable Development Goals in all countries, in particular developing countries; Target 17.17 Encourage and promote effective public, public-private and civil society partnerships, building on the experience and resourcing strategies of partnerships*

The interaction between science and policy is as complex as it is vital.[281] Challenges surrounding the interaction between science and policy are especially evident in sustainable development issues, which are typically complex and intricate. Where

---

[278] See EB Barbier, 'The Economic Linkage Between Rural Poverty and Land Degradation: Some Evidence from Africa' (2000) 82 Agriculture, Ecosystems, and Environment 355–72.

[279] See T Reardon and SA Vosti, 'Links Between Rural Poverty and the Environment in Developing Countries: Asset Categories and Investment Poverty' (1995) 23(9) World Development 1495–506.

[280] See S Dasgupta and others, *Poverty/Environment Nexus in Cambodia and Lao People's Republic* (2003) World Bank Group, World Bank Policy Paper No 2960.

[281] The authors wish to acknowledge and thank Deborah Brosnan and James Bohland for their invaluable intellectual input to this section.

policy-makers, the media, and the public demand hard and fast answers, many of the difficult questions faced by science, and thus, the resulting findings, are inherently rife with uncertainty. Additionally, scientific conclusions are often poorly communicated to policy-makers, who then fail to take these conclusions into account. A mutually beneficial dialogue between science and policy requires that research objectives be framed and carried out with policy considerations in mind. At the same time, policy-makers should be aware of the science available and encouraged to take policy-relevant research into account. Areas of high uncertainty must be acknowledged by researchers and policy-makers alike, who, instead of focusing on this uncertainty, should emphasize crucial issues and ranges of possible developments.

An open dialogue between the scientific and political communities is necessary not only for the development of well-guided policies but also for the formation of pertinent research agendas. The SDGs recognize this need, reflected in their objective to promote effective and mutually beneficial communication between scientists, policy-makers, the private sector, and society at large. In general, scientific conclusions must be more effectively communicated. Policy and multi-stakeholder governance in particular necessitate an array of cross-cutting decision support such as on environmental governance, resilience, vulnerability, and adaptation. Knowledge dissemination to those working in the field of global change and sustainable development is a key condition for success with SDG implementation through partnerships and multi-stakeholder arrangements.

And yet, the global COVID-19 pandemic has exposed the unpreparedness and inability of many countries to effectively manage complex risks and ensure community resilience. An important dimension of this dangerous flaw is the sharp divide between those who rely on science to shape policies and actions, and those who undermine or dispel science when inconvenient to their viewpoints and agendas. The divide has manifested itself in myriad ways, through anti-mask protests, arguments that the coronavirus is a hoax, or proclamations about untested or potentially deadly 'treatment regimes'. The divide is fuelled by the rhetoric of politicians and interest groups who use social media to make unscientific claims or attack science in order to promote their political agendas, having little regard for whether the outcome will lead to a resilient, fragile, or collapsing society. These issues, generally defined as science versus ideology, have long been present throughout history. We can point to the recent Ebola crisis as a situation where scientific facts clashed—sometimes disastrously—with cultural values, subjective belief systems, or political ideology. Therefore, the global partnership for the SDGs must emphasize the need for evidence-based policies and adhere to scientific knowledge.

Furthermore, the safety of citizens, the validity of institutions, and the viability of social and economic structures hinge on how we cope with dangerous polarizations. If left unresolved now, these issues will fester and grow as mighty barriers to successfully addressing this and future existential crises such as the next pandemic or climate change. The approach of distancing science from public discourse because it must remain an independent source of expertise, while well-intentioned, does not work.

Certainly, scientific findings must remain untainted and uninfluenced; however, scientists are citizens and part of their communities. Science is a process deliberately designed to reduce uncertainty and identify risk. These are exactly the elements we need to understand in order to manage a pandemic or the threats associated with climate change. Scientific ideas or hypotheses are proposed and repeatedly challenged by testing. Eventually, on an evidential basis, ideas are rejected or accepted and continually refined. It is this dynamic and ever-questioning nature of science that has moved knowledge forward. Today's facts may be disproven and replaced by new facts. By contrast, most scientists see this time as a golden age of rapid breakthroughs in applicable knowledge and technology. We are witnessing an unprecedented global concerted scientific approach to beating the coronavirus, which included the development of vaccines. Reactive policies, even when based on science, are unsustainable whether in a pandemic or managing climate change. Long-term solutions require a commitment to investing in prevention, preparedness, and resilience building. Scientists must be part of multi-stakeholder partnerships and civil society.

At the same time, the COVID-19 pandemic coincides with a worldwide movement toward more authoritarianism and fewer civil liberties. Populism, conspiracy theories, disinformation campaigns, right-wing political extremism, and the rise of autocratic governments are not new phenomena. However, their convolution and combined speed, intensity, and scale are unprecedented and have already led to a significant decline of legitimacy in governance, threatening the very foundation of modern human civilization. In this unfolding drama, COVID-19 has led to a new act, if not a climax— one that appears to catalyse and accelerate the pre-existing tendencies toward undoing the social contract on which liberal democracies and other forms of legitimate governance are based. This raises the important question of whether the social contract that is at the heart of any form of governance is threatened during periods of crises, such as the COVID-19 pandemic or global climate change. As such, the current pandemic may be instructive in revealing whether the tenets of legitimacy and democracy will be under siege when the fallouts from climate change intensify. Therefore, democratic governance remains a key UN value. It is problematic that the targets of SDG 17 do not mention this but rather, speak of countries' entitlement for their own 'policy space' which could be read as a rubber stamp for illegitimate governance.

This distrust in international organizations such as the WHO or international vaccine coalitions has created a globally fragmented response to the coronavirus. Finally, populism encourages an 'us-versus-them' mentality when what is required for a pandemic or any global existential threat is unity of spirit and collaboration based on trust, not transactional benefits. Whether democratic or authoritarian or hybrid systems respond more effectively to global crises such as the COVID-19 pandemic is not simple to say because few 'pure' forms of either are left. Today, the categorization of a regime is not binary, for the delineation between 'democratic' and 'authoritarian' is progressively blurred. Responses to catastrophic events such as the pandemic, Hurricane Katrina or the Californian wildfires do require strong executive leadership, though. This is an important lesson for implementing the SDGs. Also, major global crises pose enormous

1318   SDG 17

risks and challenges to humanity, but they also come with opportunities. The concept of the social contract is foundational to governance. It is also an indispensable condition for partnerships and multi-stakeholder arrangements as envisaged in targets 17.16 and 17.17. Yet it is seen by some as antiquated, not in alignment with contemporary neoliberal ideology where contractual terms are transactional in nature. Still, the relationships between citizens and governments that sustain legitimate and democratic tenets through times of crises require an understanding of the 'glue' that binds us together as nations.

The Centre for European Policy Studies (CEPS) states:

> All public policy seeks to influence behaviour—investment, innovation, consumption—to achieve some socially-desired outcome. If policy is very successful it becomes embedded in social and economic norms and behaviour. But it is also important to remember that policy is always acting in a broader economic and social context. This makes it hard to measure the impact of policy because the phenomenon that policy is seeking to influence ... is also affected by many other factors. A more specific reason why measuring *policy effectiveness* is difficult is our still incomplete knowledge about how policy signals affect the behaviour of economic actors, not only through prices, but through the relative incentives and penalties they generate, and the expectations they shape over the longer term.[282]

It is complicated to measure policy effectiveness especially when novel or innovative policies are analysed. It is even harder to project the impact and effectiveness of future policies, especially in the complex context of sustainable development. Policy analysts usually tend to apply a larger theoretical and analytical framework than economic modellers, to include such variables as power, interest, rules of the game, or normative considerations. It is conceivable that these factors can indeed influence the creation of markets and opportunities, for instance for sustainable investments in new technologies or energy. While projections or predictions regarding the effectiveness of policies are difficult, no one would challenge the fact that pro-active policies to advance the SDGs are a critical component of larger incentivizing schemes and frameworks. Neither policy frameworks nor economic measures alone are likely to create enough potential to trigger significant change in the respective areas of economic, technological, and behavioural patterns, but together can form a strong regime of authoritative forces that indeed influence the behaviour of individuals, markets, and societies, and the emergence and diffusion of powerful development alternatives and green growth, both leading to significant progress in implementing the SDGs.

Given the nature, magnitude, and scale of the sustainable development conundrum, large-scale behavioural change is required from the individual to the societal and supra-societal levels across all geographic regions. In this context it is prerequisite to take into account that changes arising from new behaviours are often multifaceted and

---

[282] See Centre for European Policy Studies (CEPS), *Reaching the 2C Target* (CEPS 2009).

need the right institutional arrangements and incentive schemes to become effective and sustainable. This is the point where both proactive policy-making and good incentives for innovative investments must come in and play out their strength. Integrative approaches, triggered by the right set of policies and economic, financial, and behavioural incentives, can simultaneously address the changes needed. For public policy-makers, entrepreneurs, and investors alike, the key question in this regard is how can we avoid the disruption of the economy and turn the desired and necessary changes into a competitive advantage? If the assumption is correct that the root cause of the present day's sustainability problems lies in the implications of the unsustainable trajectory of industrial revolutions in the nineteenth and twentieth centuries, and therefore in the so-called Western economic paradigm, the SDGs are ultimately a deeply societal and behavioural affair, which means that any solution will have to fully imbibe societal and behavioural factors, and their relation to energy, technology, and production and consumption.

Interdisciplinary research shows that behavioural changes can be catalysed through processes of social learning. Social learning theory focuses on the learning that occurs within a social (or societal) context. It assumes that human beings learn from one another through observational learning, imitation, and modelling. Bandura is considered the leading proponent of this theory. As it comprises attention, memory, and motivation, social learning theory combines both cognitive as well as behavioural frameworks. Social learning theorists say that both awareness on the one side but also expectations of future reinforcements or punishments on the other influence the behaviours that people exhibit.[283] In social learning theory, modelling is a powerful means to generate new behaviour and influence the frequency of previously learned behaviours. People are more likely to engage in new behaviours when they have high self-efficacy, that is when they feel that they will be successful in performing them.

In *Learning to Manage Global Environmental Risks*, the Harvard-based 'Social Learning Group' provided a functional analysis of social responses to climate change, ozone depletion, and acid rain, and analysed a variety of empirical case studies.[284] The authors examined how the interplay of ideas and actions applied to major environmental problems, by means of social learning, laid the foundations for effective global environmental governance and successful risk management. Their study has great potential and significance for the question of how policy innovation and major technological shifts can lead to effective climate change mitigation through social learning. Moreover, Gardner's research suggests that social learning and behavioural change can be achieved through what he calls representational re-descriptions: 'Get the message out in lots and lots of different ways, lots of different symbol systems, lots of different intelligences and lots of different embodiments. The notion that you say it once and it

---

[283] See A Bandura and RH Walters, *Social Learning and Personality Development* (Holt Rinehart and Winston 1963).

[284] See The Social Learning Group, 'earning to Manage Global Environmental Risks: A Functional Analysis of Social Responses to Climate Change, Ozone Depletion, and Acid Rain* (Harvard University Press 2001).

Box 17.2 Health Belief Model (HBM)

(Rosenstock and others, 1994)

- **Perceived Threat:** Consists of two parts: perceived susceptibility and perceived severity of a health condition.
- **Perceived Benefits:** The believed effectiveness of strategies designed to reduce the threat of illness.
- **Perceived Barriers:** The potential negative consequences that may result from taking particular health actions, including physical, psychological, and financial demands.
- **Cues to Action:** Events, either bodily (eg physical symptoms of a health condition) or environmental (eg media publicity) that motivate people to take action.
- **Other Variables:** Diverse demographic, sociopsychological, and structural variables that affect an individual's perceptions and thus indirectly influence health-related behaviour.
- **Self-Efficacy:** The belief in being able to successfully execute the behaviour required to produce the desired outcomes.

gets through is just wrong. You have to be extremely resourceful in finding diverse ways to get the same desired mind-change across.'[285] It is self-evident that social learning and large-scale behavioural changes have to be embedded in specific socio-economic landscapes and the larger societal changes of which they are part. This means that different approaches will have to be identified for poor or extremely poor countries, for emerging economies, and for developed countries, respectively.

A rich body of experience is health where social learning and behavioural change have been studied extensively. The famous Health Belief Model (HBM, see Box 17.2) highlights some of the most important drivers for change and learning.[286] It is fully conceivable that the mechanics at play during such change processes can be of equal or similar value and function for changes that need to occur with regard to climate change mitigation, adaptation and energy efficiency, although long-term studies with similar epistemological value as is the case in the health sector do not yet exist due to the fact that climate change related behavioural change is a relatively recent phenomenon. A 'translation' of the HBM into a climate change context could look as follows.

---

[285] See H Gardner, *Changing Minds* (Harvard University Press 2006).

[286] IM Rosenstock and others, 'The Health Belief Model and HIV Risk Behavior Change' in RJ DiClemente and JL Peterson (eds), *Preventing AIDS. AIDS Prevention and Mental Health* (Springer 1994).

Perceived Threats: This could be developed societies perceiving scrutiny for their lifestyles' contribution to climate change or developing societies that perceive exploitation by affluent nations; could also be the threat felt by more vulnerable nations to the effects of climate change (ie coastal zones).

Perceived Benefits: One potentially all-inclusive benefit of the climate change crisis could be the global governance system, which requires all countries to work together to reach a common goal. Climate conferences can help to set a precedent, making future global discussions and goal setting run more smoothly. Huge potential benefits lie in the development and application of carbon efficient technologies and related economic benefits and return on investments.

Perceived Barriers: Perceived barriers with regards to climate change, as in the health sector, include economic demand. Aside from this, the perceived barriers having to do with climate change are not as easily penetrated as in the HBM model. Climate change problems require a lot more effort and commitment. A great barrier of climate change is that it mandates global citizens not only to recognize the faults of their lifestyles but also the dedication to change.

Cues to Action: Can be physical or social. Physical cues include the consequences of climate change (ie sea-level rise). Since physical cues are not easily observed by all, social cues like the media publicity observed in COPs are necessary to spread awareness.

Other Variables: Another variable could be the fact that many people cannot directly observe the effects of climate change.

Self-Efficacy: 'The belief in being able to successfully execute the behaviour required to produce the desired outcomes.'[287] The SDGs could be an example of this; a plan of action that individuals can depend on and institutions can strive to achieve.

In conclusion, we understand that effective innovation in the area of the SDGs requires social learning and the right governance (or policy) environment in order to become effective and sustainable. Especially the social and behavioural aspect is often neglected or underestimated, which is a mistake. Technological innovation works through imagination, niches and novelties. Societies can develop diverse pathways of technological and economic development and adapt within certain conditions. Social learning plays a key role in this context as it allows establishing and maintaining a collective memory of previous adaptive responses. This often happens through institutions, norms and values, and social traditions. Various social groups have introduced changes and new behavioural patterns to resource use and environmental protection. These actions, by means of social learning processes as described above, have no doubt created a different level of public awareness, which can be replicated in other contexts.

And yet, the pandemic has exposed a severe divide between science and various ideologies. Things have become even more complicated as the pandemic hit a world

---

[287] See VM Mayes and others (eds), *Behaviour Change: Psychological Approaches* (Sage Publications 1989) 128–41.

destabilized by a rapid decline of long-cherished institutions and political values, of legitimacy and good governance, as authoritarianism and extremism continue to rise.

While a new social contract between citizens and their governments is a prerequisite for solving complex global crises, social learning provides the catalyst and process for humanity to change the current divisive and destructive path. Social learning emphasizes the role of the contextual social environment as a driver of behavioural change. It includes rational elements such as cost–benefit calculations and material incentives but focuses more on an iterative learning process that includes observation, imitation and modelling as drivers. Attention and motivation are central to the process, while emotional intelligence, empathy, and compassion were recently added to the cognitive elements of social learning described by Bandura.

Common to the above is an initial approach that builds on a social contract binding all parties as equal citizens in a joint endeavour toward establishing (or re-establishing) a declared common good such that every participant agrees to engage with the community and commits to furthering the common good. This contract must include the participants' empowerment and a clearly shared understanding of essential rules, norms, and values. On that basis, the social learning process can be successful in changing norms, attitudes, and behaviours for the better. Leadership, empowerment, empathy, and the sharing of best practices are important and lead to the co-production of new knowledge and behaviours. In these situations, because scientists participate as citizens and co-learners, the public's fears concerning the implications of scientific findings are mitigated and higher levels of trust are created without disrupting the social fabric of a community. This is the best possible recipe for success in aiming at implementing SDG targets 17.16 and 17.17.

As mentioned, knowledge and understanding are key for effective multi-stakeholder partnerships, participatory development, and public engagement in a spirit of social learning. The responsibility to build public trust in science and knowledge does of course not just lie with scientists alone but with all citizens including policy-makers. As much as it is necessary for scientists to engage with their communities, it is also necessary for non-scientists to engage in a better understanding of science so that the entire citizenry can co-create solutions based on evidence and societal needs and values to advance the SDG agenda. A sense of cautious optimism has emerged that provides the opportunity for societies to engage in social learning. As the world is battling two global crises simultaneously—the COVID-19 pandemic and climate change—it is the time for leaders and citizens to start implementing transformative processes that will lead society forward.

V. Conclusion

Global solidarity and partnerships are required to advance all of the SDGs. SDG 17 provides an in-depth framework through which countries can holistically address deep-seated inequalities and barriers to the financing, technologies, knowledge, and scientific cooperation needed to advance all of the SDGs. Sweeping in its coverage, SDG 17 emphasizes the need for a global partnership approach that addresses the unique vulnerabilities of developing, least developed and small island states to social, economic, and environmental fragilities, which often limit their abilities to make sustained progress in advancing the SDGs. Yet, as demonstrated in this chapter, a confluence of pre-existing legal and structural barriers in the global economic and policy architecture continue to limit progress on the global partnership approaches highlighted in SDG 17. As the COVID-19 pandemic has further shown, without accelerating global solidarity through technology transfer, financial assistance, debt relief, trade support, vaccine equity, and knowledge exchange, global efforts to achieve all of the SDGs by 2030 may be stunted.[288]

To ensure that the goal of global solidarity and partnership in SDG 17 moves from theory to successful policy instrumentation and practical implementation, ideational and logistical challenges that limit the flow of international trade, investment, technologies, and financing must be carefully addressed at all levels. Barriers to the practical implementation of SDG 17 can be holistically addressed by invigorating national sustainable development programmes, policies, and legislation with fiscal and financial incentives needed to attract and sustain SDG investments; putting in place adequate legal and institutional frameworks to mobilize innovative financing and technology innovation from all sources, most especially by promoting public–private partnerships, entrepreneurship and home-grown innovation; and strengthening global and regional cooperation in areas of knowledge transfer, technology support, capacity development, and trade support that will enable goods and services from developing countries to access global markets in a fair and inclusive way. Policy-makers at all levels will also need to increase financial support to research institutions and knowledge networks that can advance North–South–South triangular research and knowledge exchange.[289] Ultimately, the SDG agenda—and with it other agendas of global concern—is a matter of global justice and survival. Measures and instruments must be attuned to yielding the safety and wellbeing of the poor, the marginal, the disenfranchised, and the underserved. The resilience of the weak will determine the fate of the whole. If that is the case, humanity—and with it, other species, ecosystems, and the planet—will benefit as a whole from increased global partnerships and sustained progress on all the SDGs.

---

[288] See Summary by the President of the Economic and Social Council of the High-level Political Forum on Sustainable Development convened under the auspices of the Council at its 2021 session <https://sustainabledeve lopment.un.org/content/documents/29282POEs_summary_of_2021_HLPF.pdf> accessed 7 January 2023.

[289] See, eg, the Association of Environmental Law Lecturers in Middle East and North African Universities (ASSELLMU); Association of Environmental Law Lecturers in African Universities (ASSELLAU), and the European Environmental Law Forum, amongst others.

Index

For the benefit of digital users, indexed terms that span two pages (e.g., 52–53) may, on occasion, appear on only one of those pages.

Tables are indicated by *t* following the page number.

Aarhus Convention 498, 1001–02
  access to environmental information 925
Addis Ababa Action Agenda (AAAA) 111
  corruption, and 114
  energy, and 542
  Financing for Development
      Conference 587–88
    Inter-agency Task Force on Financing for
      Development 111
  goals 107–8
  human rights, and 19–20
  non-communicable diseases, cost of 258
  science, technology and innovation 585–86
  social protection 79, 81–82
    'new social compact' to eliminate poverty
      through 81–82
Addis Ababa Financing for Development (FFD)
    conference 107–8, 116–17
Afghanistan
  education 330–31
    girls 267–68
    lifelong learning 292–93
  health spending 108–9
  land registration 93
  social protection 79
Africa
  African Development Bank 361
    water supply and sanitation services 458
  African Ministers Council on Water
    (AMCOW) 451–52
  droughts 1114–15
  ECA 587
  Economic Commission for Africa (ECA) 587
  Economic Community of West African States
    (ECOWAS) 1168–69
    BEST Project 531
  education 286, 287–89, 315–16
    gender equality 384–85, 429–30
  exports 1293–94
  hunger and malnutrition 131
  infrastructure, need for 678
  loss of trained human capital 359
  malaria 240

North Africa
  accountable and transparent
    institutions 1226–27
  children, violence against 1209
  education 286, 288–89
  gender equality 387
  high food prices 186
  NEET rates 598–99
  SDGs, and 595–96
  sexual and reproductive health rights 431
  unemployment rate 595
  waste collection 846
  women's representation in local
    government 426
  women's unemployment 594
  youth NEET 598–99
  youth unemployment 594
  ODA and foreign direct investment 785–91
  poverty levels 62–63
  sexual violence, non-partner 394–95
  slum dwelling 826–27
  Sub-Saharan Africa *see* Sub-Saharan Africa
  sustainable and resilient infrastructure
    development, facilitating 695–96
African Charter on Human and Peoples' Rights
    (Banjul Charter) 78
  agriculture 177
  development 177
  education 317
  Protocol on Rights of Women in Africa
    (Maputo Protocol) *see under* women
Agenda 21 *see* Rio Declaration on Environment
    and Development and Agenda 21
Agenda 2030 for Sustainable Development 18–
    19, 42, 54, 121–26, 445–46
  AAAA as integral part of 19–20
  cities 807–8
  Declaration in 32
  economic, social, and cultural rights,
    and 154–55
  environmental sustainability 1017–18
  eradicating poverty as greatest global
    challenge 37–38, 43–44

1326 INDEX

Agenda 2030 for Sustainable Development (*cont.*)
food, critical role in sustainable development
of 121–22
full respect for international law 32–33
health, definition of overall objective
of 191–92
human rights
importance of 153–54
'mainstreaming human rights' 163
'responsibility' for human rights in SDG
framework 154
interpretation and application of rules of
international law, influencing 33–34
lasting poverty eradication as overriding
goal 42
multifaceted, all-society approach
needed 54–55
nature and objectives 42
normative status of 33–34
overall objective of health 191
political declaration of intent, as 32
prioritizing economic growth over
sustainability 124–25, 151–52
sustainable tourism 622–23
target-based, indicator-driven' model 377–78
transformative potential 569
youth unemployment 628
Agreement on Port State Measures (PSMA) *see
under* oceans, seas, and marine resources
agriculture
adverse effects of industrial agriculture 158
Agreement on Agriculture (AoA) 158–59
negative effects on developing countries 146
agricultural export subsidies 184–85
agricultural orientation index 182–83
agricultural productivity
focus on 124–25
increasing 175–77
agricultural research, investment in 182–84
armed conflict, and 124
cash crop production 127
climate change, and *see under* climate change
ecosystem health, promoting 123
ensuring food supply by supporting
agricultural sectors 129
environmental challenges 179
environmental consequences of industrial
agriculture on food production 123
eradication of hunger and malnutrition linked
to transformation in 122–23
FAO Commission on Genetic Resources for
Food and Agriculture 1141
first conference on food and
agriculture 127–28

food commodity markets, functioning
of 186–87
genetic diversity of seeds, cultivated plants,
farmed animals 180–82
genetic resources for food and agriculture
see genetic resources
Green Revolution 129–30
historically 127
countries ensuring food supply by
supporting their agricultural sectors 129
industrialization of agriculture 129–30
ITPGRFA *see* genetic resources
market-oriented agricultural reforms 132–33
pivotal to economic activities 122–23
rural infrastructure, investment in 182–84
small-scale farmers/food producers 137,
139–40, 159, 178
agricultural subsidies, and 159
Benefit-Sharing Fund 181
climate-related constraints, and 136, 139–40
definition of 176
developing countries 129, 159, 175
empowerment of 122–23, 187
food insecurity/security 136, 158–59, 170–71
foreign investment, and 160
increasing incomes of small-scale food
producers 175–77
industrialization of agriculture 129–30,
158
land ownership 141
pivotal role of 132–33
women *see under* women
see also food
sustainable agriculture 138–40
key to achieving SDG 2, as 122–23
nexus between hunger, nutrition and
sustainable agriculture 126–27
resilient agricultural practices 177–80
sustainable food production
systems 177–80
trade restrictions and distortions in 184–85
World Bank focus on 132–33
see also SDG 2
air pollution *see* pollution
Albania
education 292, 293
energy 530
gender equality 382
legal frameworks and public life 382
alcohol
harmful use of 241, 242, 243–44
treatment of 244–45
risk factor in non-communicable
diseases 241, 242

INDEX

Algeria
environmental policy 1005
guardianship 389
marriage 389
polygamy 388–89
wife's obedience 389–90
Alma Ata Declaration 213
American Declaration on the Rights and
Duties of Man
environmental protection 1015
right to education 317
right to health 214–15
right to private property 175
Angola
birth registrations 1236–37
education 315–16
energy 697
food security 170–71
IFFs 1219
industrial diversification 697–98
intellectual property 709
LDC status, leaving 687
manufacturing 689–90
patent applications 705–6
SDGs, and 686–87
security 1204
technological science and innovation 686–87,
689–90
technology transfer 697
aquifers 486–92
Argentina
debt 117
domestic violence 393–94
education 289
food waste 886–87
gender equality 393–94
mobilized private funds to 110
mountain ecosystems 1122
social security and universal health
coverage 763
sustainable products 919–20
TOSSD 110
water and sanitation management 500
Asia
agriculture 182–83
Asian Development Bank
poverty 71–72
Central Asia
accountable and transparent
institutions 1226–27
children, violence against 1209
COVID-19, and 427
education 286, 301, 365–66
food insecurity 170

high food prices 186
IWRM implementation 481–82
NEET rates 598–99
pro-poor public spending 119
slum dwelling 826–27
stunted children 172–73
unemployment rate 595
women's representation in local
government 426
youth NEET 598–99
COVID-19, and 71–72, 427
East Asia
accountable and transparent
institutions 1226–27
education 286
high food prices 186
human rights 1242
hunger 169
land consumption 835
pro-poor public spending 119
sexual and reproductive health rights 431
social protection 82
women's representation in local
government 426
education 316
Far East Asia, mobilized private funds to 110
gender equality 384–85, 429–30
hunger 169
infrastructure, need for 678
poverty 60, 71–72
South-Eastern Asia
accountable and transparent
institutions 1226–27
ASEAN 247
education 286
high food prices 186
human rights 1242
hunger 169
slum dwelling 826–27
women's representation in local
government 426
Southern Asia
accountable and transparent
institutions 1226–27
child marriage 415
education 286, 301, 366
food insecurity 170
high food prices 186
IWRM implementation 481–82
land consumption 835
NEET rates 598–99
poverty 65
projects targeting 65
pro-poor public spending 119

1328 INDEX

Asia (*cont.*)
    sexual and reproductive health rights 431
    stunted children 172–73
    unemployment rate 595
    women's representation in local
      government 426
    youth NEET 598–99
  Western Asia
    accountable and transparent
      institutions 1226–27
    children, violence against 1209
    education 286, 288–89
    high food prices 186
    human rights 1242
    NEET rates 598–99
    SDGs, and 595–96
    unemployment rate 595
    waste collection 846
    women's representation in local
      government 426
    youth NEET 598–99
    youth unemployment 594
Australia
  ABS 1140
  Australian Research Council 73–74
  biodiversity 1140
  CBDR 863
  childbirth registrations 1235–36
  climate change 970, 976–77
  corruption and bribery 1222, 1225–26
  desertification 1114–15
  domestic violence 393–94
  droughts 1114–15
  education 273, 286, 290, 310
    bullying 355
    indigenous children 1190–91
    people with disabilities 331–32, 355
    public safety 1207
    scholarships 360–61, 363–64
  emissions trading scheme 976–77
  employment 598–600
  energy 514–15, 537–38
  food loss 886
  gender equality 382, 385, 393–95
  indigenous peoples 1179–80, 1190–91
  justice, access to 1179–80, 1214–15
  natural disasters 98
  open public space in cities 850
  poverty 62, 98
  sexual violence, non-partner 394–95
  sustainable tourism 937
  trade and barriers 1287–89
  women's empowerment 514–15
  youth NEET rates 598–99

Azerbaijan
  child labour 610–11
  food aid 170–71
  food security 170–71
  SDGs, and 706–7
Bahamas
  energy 530
  food security 170–71
  gender equality 390–91
  health spending 108–9
  nationality laws 390–91
Bahrain
  discrimination in employment 439
  nationality laws 390–91
Bangladesh
  exports 1293–94
  extractive industries 660
    energy 528–29
  food riots 132
  gender equality 332–33
  mobile phone ownership 434
  open public space in cities 850
Banjul Charter *see* African Charter on Human
    and Peoples' Rights (Banjul Charter)
banking *see* financial institutions
Barbados
  nationality laws 390–91
Beijing Platform for Action *see* International
    Conference on Population and
    Development and Beijing Platform
    for Action
Belize
  sexual and reproductive health rights 431
Benin
  discrimination in employment 439
  employment 689
  FGM 415–16
  SDGs' scope, and 107, 115, 142, 650–51
Bhutan
  ABS 1140
  biodiversity 1140
  education 292
  food security 170–71
  LDC status, leaving 687
biodiversity
  Biodiversity Target 2010 1078–79
  CBD *see* Convention on Biological
    Diversity (CBD)
  financial resources to conserve and
    sustainably 1107–8
  Global Biodiversity Framework 1097, 1129–30
  halting biodiversity loss, reducing
    degradation of natural habitats 1124–30

INDEX 1329

inland water biodiversity 487–89
integrating biodiversity values in national and
    local planning 1149–55
  natural capital accounting 1153
JPOI 1079, 1081
UN Decade on Biodiversity 1081, 1125–26
VNRs 1151–52
see also SDG 15
Bolivia 107, 142
  education 333
  equal opportunity 758
  food security 170–71
  gender equality 398
    violence against women 398
    women in parliament 426
  health spending 108–9
  sustainable development 932
Botswana
  customary law 390
  gender equality 390
  inheritance 390
Brazil
  agriculture 142
  child and forced labour 562–63
  climate change 980
  education 300
  energy 1287–89
  environment 1140
  genetics 1141
  IMF, and 772
  inequality 758, 785
  social security and universal health
    coverage 763
  waste 847, 848, 904–5
Bretton Woods/Bretton Woods institutions
    45–46, 111, 545, 573, 771–72, 1286
bribery and corruption
  Addis Ababa Action Agenda, and 114
  businesses, and 1222–26
  individuals, and 1221–22
  ODA, and 114
  reduction of corruption and bribery 1164,
    1221–26
  sustainable development concern,
    as 1175–77
Brundtland Commission/Report 21–22,
    194–95, 268–69, 1251–52
  economic growth, need for 45
  education 268–69
  energy 518–19, 525, 533
  environmental degradation and
    poverty 254
  health and economic policies 189
  objective of development 22

sustainable development 634–35, 1088, 1091,
    1170–71
  definition of 22, 23–25, 45, 859, 1028–29,
    1170–71
Brunei
  nationality laws 390–91
  pollution 846
Burundi
  discrimination in employment 439
  education 354
  nationality laws 390–91

Cabo Verde
  food assistance 170–71
  health 240
  scientific research and innovation 694
Cambodia
  sexual and reproductive health rights 431
Cameroon
  education 365
  environmental legislation 1139–40
    conservation of mountain
      ecosystems 1122
  FGM 416
  tourism strategy 624
Canada
  Agreement on Environmental Cooperation
    (AEC) 1290–91
  Canadian International Development Agency
    (CIDA) 196
  Canadian Poverty Reduction Strategy 73
  climate change 965, 985–86
  connecting the poor to markets 87–88
  conservation and management of marine
    living resources 1039
  corruption and bribery 1226
  education 290, 318–19
  gender equality 384–85, 391
  indigenous women
    gender equality 391
    violence against 1206
  justice, access to 1218
  sustainable development 926–27
  sustainable tourism 937
  trade and barriers 1287–89, 1290–91
cap and trade schemes 976–79
carbon taxes 979–82
Caribbean
  accountable and transparent
    institutions 1226–27
  agriculture 182
  CARICOM 115
  childbirth registrations 1235–36
  climate change 970, 1114–15

1330 INDEX

Caribbean (*cont.*)
    corruption and bribery 1222
    droughts 1114–15
    Economic Commission for Latin America
        and the Caribbean (ECLAC) 71
    education 286
    employment 595–96
    energy 513, 536
    Escazú Agreement 1002
    food insecurity 169, 170
    gender equality 398, 426, 429–30, 431, 437
    homicide 1200–1
    human rights 1242
    hunger 169
    infrastructure
        investments 678, 690–91
        need for 678
    IWRM implementation 481–82
    justice, access to 1214–15
    justice in environmental matters, access
        to 1002, 1047–48
    national capacities in environmental
        matters 182
    natural hazards 685
    NHRIs 1242
    poverty 71, 119, 754
    public transportation 833
    SDGs, and 595–96
    sexual and reproductive health rights 431
    sustainable industrialization 687
    waste 846, 902
    women's representation in local
        government 426
Central America
    ABS 1142
    droughts 1114–15
    slum dwelling 826–27
CESCR *see under* International Covenant on
    Economic, Social and Cultural Rights
    (ICESCR)
child marriage 387–88
    causes 420
    COVID-19, and 416
    effects of 419–20
    eliminating 413–20
    human right and development priority,
        as 419–20
    international instruments 413–14
    levels of 414–15, 419–20
children 72–73
    abuse, exploitation, trafficking, violence
        against children, ending 1208–13
    birth registration of children under
        5 years 1235–37

    legal identity including birth
        registration 1235–37
child labour
    business and human rights guidelines
        (BHR) 608–9
    core human rights issue, as 606
    CRC, and 606
    Declaration on the Right of the Child 606
    economic exploitation of children 605–6
    effects of 601
    ending 600–11
    hazardous work 606–7
    ILO, and 605–6, 609
    intersection of labour/human rights law,
        at 606–9
    minimum age for employment of
        children 605–6
    protection of children from
        exploitation 607–8
    tourism, and 617
    worst forms of child labour 605–6, 607–8
child soldiers 296, 607–8
    ending recruitment and use 600–11
cities, and
    green public spaces, safe, inclusive,
        accessible 848–51
    transport systems, safe accessible 833
Convention on the Rights of the Child (CRC)
    child labour 606
    child soldiers 607–8
    child's perspective, taking account of 296
    children categorized as vulnerable 335–36
    education during early childhood 306, 309
    education, right to 273, 281–82, 298–
        99, 327–28
    eliminating 'ignorance and illiteracy' 336–37
    FGM 415
    health 233–34
    respect for natural environment 344
    right to sanitation 466–67
    SDGs, and 235
Declaration on the Rights of the Child 607–8
education *see* education
FGM *see* female genital mutilation (FGM)
Global Strategy for Women's, Children's
    Health and Adolescents' Health
    2016–30 231
health
    Every Newborn Action Plan (ENAP) 236
    Global Initiative for Child Health and
        Mobility 356–57
    healthy development 136–37
    Innocenti Framework on Food Systems for
        Children and Adolescents 173–74

malnutrition/malnourishment 172–74
overweight 173
preventable deaths of newborns and
children under five, ending 233–36
stillbirths 236
stunting 172–73
UN Inter-Agency Group for Child
Mortality Estimation (UN
IGME) 234–35
underweight 131–32
vaccines 259–60
wasting 173
see also SDG 3
marriage *see* child marriage
physical punishment and/or psychological
aggression by caregivers 1209–10
protection of children from
exploitation 607–8
reduction in child mortality (MDG 4) 1–
2, 216–17
right to food 122–23, 154–55, 168–69
sexual exploitation in tourism 934–35
social protection 76–77, 80
UNICEF, and *see* UNICEF
violence against 1209
World Summit for Children 233–34
see also SDG 2
Chile
climate change 1005
education 332, 1005
housing law reforms 828
human rights 339
husband's control over wife 389–90
people with disabilities in workforce 595
China
agriculture 142
antimicrobials 863
climate change 967, 969, 973, 980, 996–97
COVID-19
effects of 63
response to 422
vaccines 703–4
desertification 1114–15
domestic violence 393–94, 395–96
droughts 1114–15
education 333
scholarships 361
energy 529–30, 536
environment 1139–40
exports 1293–94
food waste 887–88
gender equality 385–86, 393–94, 395–96, 422
heritage 839
human trafficking 396

IMF, and 772
infrastructure and industrialization 651, 685,
699–700
investment 1283
land consumption 835
natural hazards 685
ODA 109–10
pollution 846
poverty 69–70
research and development 929
resource extraction 878–79
TOSSD 109–10
unpaid care and domestic work 422
circular economy 642, 691, 692
alternative to linear consumption, as 901
individual countries/regions, and 693, 875,
879–80, 889–90, 903, 904–5, 917–18
nature of 878, 901
cities
adequate, safe, affordable housing, basic
services and upgrade slums 824–29
numbers in inadequate housing 826–27
right to housing 825
State obligations 825–26
UN Housing Rights Programme 827–28
air pollution/quality 844–46, 847–48
climate change, and 821–22, 854–55
country programmes for sustainable urban
development 93–94
COVID-19, and 800, 813–14, 831–32
disaster risk reduction strategies,
importance of 844
national urban planning as key component
of recovery 853
cultural and natural heritage,
protecting 837–40
disasters
disaster-related deaths, reducing number
of 840–44
disaster risk management and resilience to
disasters 854–55
economic activity concentrated in 800
economic, social and environmental links
between areas 852–53
city governments' action, crucial
nature of 853
planning, importance of 852
environmental protection, and 822–23
human rights, and 818–20
human settlement policies historically 799–
800, 802–6, 814
inclusive and sustainable urbanization and
human settlement planning 834–37
democratic governance 834–35, 836

1332 INDEX

cities (*cont.*)
    land consumption 835, 836
    urban planning and management 835–36
  inequalities in 813–14
  International Guidelines on Urban and
    Territorial Planning 825, 852
  international organizations, relationship
    with 814–18
  LDCs building sustainable buildings utilizing
    local materials, support for 856–57
  'Making Cities Resilient 2030' 843–44
  New Urban Agenda 91–93, 800, 801–2, 810,
    811–14, 816–17, 819, 824–25, 830–31,
    833, 852
  public spaces, safe, inclusive, accessible,
    green 848–51
  reducing environmental impact of 844–48
  Sendai Framework for Disaster Risk
    Reduction 821
  spatiality as social consideration 811–12
  subjects of international law, as 814–18
  sustainability, and 812
  transport systems for all, safe, affordable,
    accessible, sustainable 829–33
    bus rapid transit systems 832
    children and the elderly 833
    convenient access to public transportation,
     meaning of 831
    COVID-19, and 831–32
    persons with disabilities 830, 831, 832
    women's safety needs 833
  UN Habitat
    Agenda 802–7
    focus on urban life 804–7
    role of 802–7, 809–11
  UNESCO 820–21
  Urban Management Program 804
  waste management 845, 846–47, 848
  World Cities Report 2020 813–14, 826–27,
    835, 836–37, 839, 850
  World Urban Forum 806
  see also SDG 11
civil society (NGOs) 671–76
  agents of change, as 672
  green values 673
  influential role of 671, 673
  participatory role of non-state actors 672
Clean Development Mechanism (CDM)
    see under Kyoto Protocol
climate change
  agriculture and food production 136,
    178, 179
    vulnerabilities of production capacity 123
  CBDR-RC 959–61

cities 821–22
clean and environmentally sound
  technologies, adopting 691–93
climate-related hazards and natural disasters,
  resilience and adaptive capacity to 990–94
developing countries
  effective climate change-related planning
    and management in 1011–13
  mitigation actions, mobilizing $ 100 billion
    annually for 1006–10
disaster risk, and 98, 105
domestic courts, climate litigation
  before 1002–04
Green Climate Fund, operationalizing 1006–10
human rights, and 970–72
  Inter-American Court of Human
    Rights 971–72
  international trade law and climate
    change 972–82
innovation, and *see* innovation
intergenerational equity, and 1003, 1012
international investment law, and 982–88
international law, and 958–61, 970–89
  equity and
    differentiation: CBDR-RC 959–61
  human rights 970–72
international trade law, and 972–82
  cap and trade schemes 976–79
  carbon taxes 979–82
jurisprudence of international and national
  courts 988–89
  East African Court of Justice 989
  International Court of Justice 988–89
low-carbon technology transfer 964
mitigation and adaptation
  cities and human settlements adopting
    policies for 854–55
  developing countries, mobilizing $100
    billion annually for 1006–10
  education and institutional capacity,
    improving 1000–05
  inadequate response to 949
  technology transfer and 930, 1009
multilateral climate change regime 961–70
  Kyoto Protocol 962–66
  Paris Agreement 966–68
  Paris Agreement, implementation by
    subsequent CoPs 968–70
  UNFCCC 961–62
national policies, strategies and planning,
  climate change measures in 994–1000
  environmental and climate impact
    assessment 994–98
  good regulatory practices 998–99

INDEX 1333

negative impacts caused by extreme weather
events 949
oceans and seas, and *see under* oceans, seas,
and marine resources
Paris Agreement *see* Paris Agreement
poverty, and 43, 66
right to life, climate change as danger to 841
urgent action to combat climate change and
its impacts, need for 949–1014
see also Paris Agreement; Kyoto Protocol;
UN Framework Convention of Climate
Change (UNFCCC); SDG 13
Colombia
food security 170–71
nutrition of children and women 173–74
commentary on SDG 1 43–60
accountability mechanisms, lack of 57
criticisms of targets 55
data, absence of 55
fallacy of intractability 58
human rights in SDGs, failure to take
seriously 57–58
law, place for 55–59
multi-variant nature of poverty reduction and
the law 54–55
poverty reduction as international action
item: history 44–54
Agenda 2030 *see* Agenda 2030
Brundtland Commission 45
'The Future We Want' 44–45
MDG 1, alterations from 50–54
MDG 1 to SDG 1, from 48–49
Millennium Declaration 48
OECD's 'International Development
Goals' 47
post-2015 Agenda, setting 49–54
Rio Declaration 46–47
Rio + 5 meetings 47
Stockholm Declaration 45
UNDP's 'Human Development Report' 46
UN's 'We the Peoples' report 48
World Bank's *Voices of the Poor* project 48
World Bank's 'World Development Report'
(1990) 45–46
World Summit on Social Development
(1995) 47
reaching Goal 1 by 2030 unlikely 59–60
reasons why poverty eradication is primary
SDG 43–44
poverty elimination as overriding
goal 43–44
problems of wealth inequality 43
sustainable development, fight against
poverty as prerequisite 44

requirements for lasting poverty
reduction 58–59
commentary on SDG 1 targets 60–120
target 1.1 eradicate extreme poverty 60–69
COVID-19 effects 63–64
definition 69
indicator 1.1.1 eradicate extreme
poverty 61–69
target 1.2 reduce poverty by at least 50 per
cent 69–76
indicator 1.2.1 halve population below
national poverty line 69
indicator 1.2.2 population in poverty
according to national definitions 69
target 1.3 nationally appropriate social
protection systems and measures 76–86
ILO 80–81
IMF 81
indicator 1.3.1 population covered by social
protection floors/systems 76–77
other actions 82–83
UN Addis Ababa Action Agenda 81–82
target 1.4 equal rights to ownership, basic
services, economic resources 86–96
definition 86
indicator 1.4.1 access to basic services 86
indicator 1.4.2 secure tenure rights to
land 86
target 1.5 build resilience to environmental,
economic, and social disasters 96–105
definition 96
indicator 1.5.1 deaths and affected persons
from natural disasters 96
indicator 1.5.2 direct economic loss from
natural disasters 96
indicator 1.5.3 disaster risk reduction
strategies 97
indicator 1.5.4 local disaster risk
reduction 97
target 1.a mobilization of resources to end
poverty 105–14
definition 105
indicator 1.a.1 domestic resources to
poverty reduction programmes 106
indicator 1.a.2 government spending on
essential services 106
indicator 1.a.3 inflows directly
allocated to poverty reduction
programmes 106
target 1.b pro-poor and gender-sensitive
development strategies 115–20
indicator 1.b.1 spending disproportionately
benefiting women, poor and vulnerable
groups 115

1334 INDEX

commentary on SDG 2 148–87
  interlinkages with other SDGs 148–52
    conflicting issues between goals 150–52
    gender equality 149–50
    SDG 2 as multidimensional goal 149
    sustainable food systems 149
    water–food–energy nexus 151
  nexus between SDG 2 and international
      law 152–61
    importance of rights-based approach to
      SDG 2 161–65
    SDG 2 and international economic
      law 158–61
    SDG 2 and international human rights
      law 153–57
commentary on SDG 2 targets 165–87
  general remarks 165–68
  target 2.1 end hunger and ensure access by all
      to food 168–72
    indicator 2.1.1 prevalence of
      undernourishment (PoU) 169, 171–73
    indicator 2.1.2 prevalence of moderate or
      severe food insecurity 170
  target 2.2 end all forms of
      malnutrition 172–75
    indicator 2.2.1 prevalence of stunting
      among children under five 172–73
    indicator 2.2.2 prevalence of malnutrition
      among children under five 173
    indicator 2.2.3 prevalence of anaemia in
      women 15–49 years 173
  target 2.3 double agricultural productivity
      and incomes of small-scale food
      producers 175–77
    indicator 2.3.1 volume of production per
      labour unit 175
    indicator 2.3.2 average income of small-
      scale food producers 175–76
  target 2.4 sustainable food production
      systems, resilient agricultural
      practices 177–80
    indicator 2.4.1 area under productive and
      sustainable agriculture 177–78
  target 2.5 maintain genetic diversity of
      seeds, cultivated plants, farmed
      animals 180–82
    indicator 2.5.1 plant and animal
      genetic resources for food and
      agriculture 181
    indicator 2.5.2 local breeds classified as
      being at risk of extinction 181
  target 2.a increase investment in
      rural infrastructure, agricultural
      research 182–84

indicator 2.a.1 agriculture orientation index
      for government expenditures 182–83
    indicator 2.a.2 total official flows
      (ODA) 182–83
  target 2.b correct and prevent trade
      restrictions and distortions in
      agriculture 184–85
    indicator 2.b.1 agricultural export
      subsidies 184–85
  target 2.c ensure proper functioning of food
      commodity markets 186–87
    indicator 2.c.1 food price anomalies 186
commentary on SDG 3 targets 224–64
  overview 224–27
    classification of targets and indicators 228t
    indicators 226–27
    inherited targets from MDGs 224, 225
    interlinkages with other SDGs 224–25
    means of implementation 224, 226
    new targets 224, 225
    targets and pillars 224
    UHC as overarching objective 224
  target 3.1 reduce global maternal mortality
      ratio to less than 70 per 100,000 live
      births 230–33
  target 3.2 end preventable deaths of newborns
      and children under five 233–36
  target 3.3 end epidemics of diseases and
      combat communicable diseases 236–39
  target 3.4 reduce by one-third premature
      mortality from non-communicable
      diseases 241–44
  target 3.5 strengthen prevention and
      treatment of substance abuse 244–45
  target 3.6 halve global deaths and injuries
      from road traffic accidents 246–47
  target 3.7 universal access to sexual
      and reproductive health-care
      services 247–49
  target 3.8 achieve universal health
      coverage 250–53
  target 3.9 reduce deaths and illnesses
      from hazardous chemicals and
      pollution 254–56
  target 3.a strengthen implementation of
      WHO Framework Convention on
      Tobacco Control 256–58
  target 3.b support research and development
      of vaccines and medicines 258–61
  target 3.c increase health financing
      and workforce in developing
      countries 262–63
  target 3.d strengthen management of national
      and global health risks 263–64

INDEX 1335

commentary on SDG 4 276–97
  best practices 290–94
    Beyond Commitments Report 291,
      292, 293–94
    developed countries 290
    ensuring quality education and
      learning 292
    lifelong learning, meaning for state policy
      of 292–93
    meaning of 290
    regional and global cooperation 293–94
    wealth, significant influence of 290, 294
  development 283–85
    COVID-19, impact of 267–68, 287–88
    Global Thematic Consultation on
      Education 283
    lack of available state data to track
      performance 288–89
    Muscat Agreement 284, 285
    ratification of relevant international
      instruments 289
    UNESCO ministerial conferences 284–85
  empirical evidence 285–89
    inadequate investment in education 287
    progress varying by geographic region and
      wealth 286
    reporting framework 285
    targets not being met 286
  general critique 294–97
    development, education and 295–97
    education, central role in human rights
      of 294–95
    overly ambitious nature of SDG 4 297
  inclusive and equitable education 276–78
    disadvantaged people 277
    education central to entire sustainable
      development 277
    education for children and young people
      for at least twelve years 276–77
    learners in conflict-affected areas 277, 288
    people with disabilities 277
    promotion of lifelong learning
      opportunities 278
    quality education, nature of 278
    resources for 278
  sources and linkages with human
      rights 278–83
    core international human rights
      treaties 281–82
    education as fundamental human
      right 278–79
    other core international human rights
      instruments 282–83
    UDHR 279–81

commentary on SDG 4 targets 297–369
  background 297–98
    indicators 297, 298
    monitoring framework 298
    UNESCO's monitoring role 298
  target 4.1 all girls and boys having
    complete free, equitable and quality
    education 298–305
  target 4.2 all girls and boys have quality early
    childhood development 305–13
  target 4.3 equal access to affordable and
    quality vocational and tertiary
    education 313–20
  target 4.4 increase youth and adults' decent
    jobs and entrepreneurship 321–27
  target 4.5 eliminate gender disparities
    in education and ensure equal
    access 327–36
  target 4.6 youth and substantial proportion
    of adults to achieve literacy and
    numeracy 336–42
  target 4.7 all learners acquire knowledge
    and skills for sustainable
    development 343–52
  target 4.a education facilities that are child,
    disability and gender sensitive 352–58
  target 4.b expand scholarships for developing/
    least developed countries 358–64
  target 4.c increase supply of qualified teachers
    for developing countries 364–69
commentary on SDG 5 375–80
  comparison with MDG 3 375–77
  goal-based approach 377–78
  human rights 379–80
  mainstream growth-oriented approach 378
  neglect of a structural lens 378–79
commentary on SDG 5 targets 380–437
  overview 380
    organizations with monitoring
      role 380
  target 5.1 end all forms of discrimination
    against all women and girls
    everywhere 381–92
    case law: polygamy 388–89
    case study: customary laws 390
    case study: guardianship 389
    case study: nationality laws 390–91
    case study: wife's obedience 389–90
    employment and economic
      benefits 384–85
    marriage and family life 385
    overarching legal frameworks and public
      life 383–84
    violence against women 384

1336 INDEX

commentary on SDG 5 targets (*cont.*)
  target 5.2 eliminate all forms of violence
    against all women and girls, including
    trafficking and exploitation 392–413
    importance of prevention of violence
      through education 400–2
    trafficking and sexual exploitation 395
  target 5.3 eliminate child, early, and forced
    marriage and FGM 413–20
  target 5.4 recognise and value unpaid care and
    domestic work and promotion of shared
    responsibility within household and
    family as nationally appropriate 420–24
  target 5.5 women's full and effective
    participation and equal opportunities
    for leadership at all levels of decision-
    making in political, economic and public
    life 425–28
    COVID-19 impact 427
  target 5.6 universal access to sexual and
    reproductive health and rights in
    Programme of Action on Population and
    Development and Beijing Platform 428–31
  target 5.a women's equal rights to economic
    resources, property, financial services,
    inheritance, natural resources, in
    accordance with national laws 431–34
  target 5.b use of technology, in particular
    ICT, to promote empowerment of
    women 434–36
    internet usage 435
    regional data 435–36
  target 5.c sound policies and legislation
    to promote gender equality and
    empowerment of all women and
    girls 436–37
commentary on SDG 6 targets 453–502
  overview 453
  target 6.1 universal and equitable access to
    safe and affordable drinking water for
    all 453–62
  target 6.2 adequate equitable sanitation and
    hygiene for all and needs of women and
    girls 462–68
  target 6.3 improve water quality by reducing
    pollution, eliminating dumping and
    minimizing release of hazardous
    chemicals 469–72
  target 6.4 substantially increase water-use
    efficiency and ensure sustainable
    withdrawals and supply of freshwater to
    address water scarcity 472–77
    water efficiency 472–75
    water scarcity 475–77

target 6.5 implement integrated water
    resources management, including
    through transboundary cooperation as
    appropriate 478–86
    integrated water resources
      management 478–82
    transboundary cooperation 482–86
  target 6.6 protect and restore water-related
    ecosystems, including mountains,
    forests, wetlands, rivers, aquifers and
    lakes 486–92
  target 6.a expand international cooperation
    and capacity-building support to
    developing countries in water-and
    sanitation-related activities 492–95
  target 6.b support and strengthen
    participation of local communities
    in improving water and sanitation
    management 495–502
commentary on SDG 7 517–24
  further development of human rights
    approach to energy law and
    policy 522–23
    access to energy as correlative of number of
      socioeconomic rights 522
    human rights approach to use and
      management of energy, SDG 7
      and 522–23
  future effect of SDG 7 517
  increase of energy-efficient technologies in
    management of clean energy 523–24
  normative status of SDG 7 517–18
  political commitments and legal
    duties 517
  'sustainable' interpretation of international
    energy law and policy 518–21
    preventing environmental degradation
      over energy resources 520–21
    principle of access to modern energy
      services 518–20
    principle of energy efficiency 521
    principle of sovereignty over national
      resources 520–21
    socially or economically disadvantaged
      individuals, measures benefiting 521
commentary on SDG 7 targets 525–44
  target 7.1 universal access to affordable,
    reliable and modern energy for
    all 525–32
    indicator 7.1.1 proportion of population
      with electricity access 527–29
    indicator 7.1.2 proportion of population
      with primary reliance on clean fuels and
      technology 529–30

target 7.2 increase substantially share of
  renewable energy in global energy
  mix 533–39
target 7.3 double global rate of improvement
  in energy efficiency by 2030 539–41
target 7.a enhance international cooperation
  to facilitate access to clean energy
  research and technology, and promote
  investments 541–43
target 7.b expand infrastructure and upgrade
  technology for supplying modern and
  sustainable energy services in developing
  countries 543–44
commentary on SDG 8 569–82
  full and productive employment and decent
    work for all 574–82
    human right to decent work 575–79
    ILO's Decent Work Agenda 553
  inclusive and sustainable economic growth in
    SDG 8 569–72
  neoliberal connotation of growth 569–72
  role of World Bank in achievement of
    SDG 8 573
commentary on SDG 8 targets 582–631
  overview 582–84
  target 8.1 sustain per capita economic growth
    and at least 7 per cent GDP growth per
    annum in LDCs 584–85
  target 8.2 higher levels of economic
    productivity through diversification,
    technological upgrading and
    innovation 585–87
  target 8.3 development-oriented policies
    that support productive activities,
    including through access to financial
    services 587–88
  target 8.4 improve global resource efficiency
    in consumption and production and
    decouple economic growth from
    environmental degradation 588–90
    overarching objective of SDG 8,
      as 588–89
    10-Year Framework of
      Programmes 589–90
  target 8.5 full and productive employment
    and decent work for all and equal pay for
    work of equal value 590–98
  target 8.6 substantially reduce proportion of
    youth not in employment, education or
    training 598–600
  target 8.7 eradicate forced labour, end
    modern slavery, human trafficking
    and child labour, and use of child
    soldiers 600–11

child labour at intersection of labour/
  human rights law 606–9
economic exploitation of children 605–6
slavery, servitude, forced/compulsory
  labour as grave exploitation 601–5
target 8.8 protect labour rights, safe working
  for all workers/migrant workers 611–16
  indicator 8.8.1 implementation efforts at
    international/domestic levels 613–14
  indicator 8.8.1 measuring fatal/non-fatal
    occupational injuries 611–12
  indicator 8.8.2 level of national compliance
    with labour rights 614–15
target 8.9 promote sustainable tourism, create
  jobs and promote local culture and
  products 616–26
target 8.10 strengthen domestic financial
  institutions to expand access to banking,
  insurance and financial services for
  all 626–27
target 8.a increase Aid for Trade support
  for developing countries, in particular
  LDCs 627–28
target 8.b operationalize global strategy for
  youth employment and implement
  Global Jobs Pact of ILO 628–31
commentary on SDG 9 639–76
  international organisations, transnational
    corporations and civil society 639–40
    business oriented targets and application of
      legal rules 640
  non-state actors or 'major groups' 658–76
    actors and narrative, assessment of 673–76
    civil society (NGOs) 671–73
    Million Voices Report 658–61
    NGOs and IGOs 664–67
    role of non-state actors in drafting/
      negotiations 661–64
    transnational corporations 667–71
  state-led actors and open working group
    (OWG) sessions 643–58
    condensed/redacted version of proposed
      SDG 9 654–56, 655t
    evolution of SDG 9 653–54
    informal-informal discussions 654–57
    roots of SDG 9 651–52
    targets of SDG 9 in condensed form
      657–58, 659t
  towards revitalized vision of global
    sustainable development 640–43
    cultural practices, understanding 642
    global transformation, aim of 642–43
    utilization of existing resources 641
    wide array of actors participating 640–41

1338   INDEX

commentary on SDG 9 targets 676–702
  assessment of individual targets 681–83
  custodians and tier classifications 679–80
  individual targets and their legal
    characteristics 683–702
  industry, innovation, and
    infrastructure 676–702
  legal relations 700–2
  long-term view of individual targets 678–79
  target 9.1 quality, reliable, sustainable and
    resilient infrastructure, including
    regional and trans-border infrastructure,
    and equitable access for all 685–87
  target 9.2 inclusive and sustainable
    industrialization, raise industry's share
    of employment and GDP in line with
    national circumstances, and double in
    LDCs 687–90
  target 9.3 increase access of small-scale
    enterprises to financial services and
    credit 690–91
  target 9.4 upgrade infrastructure and retrofit
    industries to make sustainable, and clean
    and environmentally sound technologies
    and industrial processes 691–93
  target 9.5 enhance scientific research,
    upgrade the technological capabilities
    of industrial sectors in all countries, and
    encourage innovation and R&D 693–95
  target 9.a sustainable and resilient
    infrastructure development in
    developing countries through enhanced
    support to African countries, LDCs,
    LLDCs and SIDS 641
  target 9.b domestic technology development,
    research and innovation in developing
    countries including ensuring a
    conducive policy environment 697–98
  target 9.c increase access to ICT and universal
    and affordable access to internet in
    LDCs 698–700
commentary on SDG 10 729–43
  environmental dimensions, inequality
    and 729–31
  human rights and labour rights 737–40
  inequality and international law 734–36
  inequality, interlinkages, and sustainable
    development 742–43
  trade, investment, aid 740–42
commentary on SDG 10 targets 60–120
  duplicated targets 744–45
  observations on targets, indicators, and
    data 794–95
  omitted targets 744

target 10.1 achieve income growth of bottom
    40% of population 746–53
target 10.2 promote social, economic and
    political inclusion of all 753–57
target 10.3 ensure equal opportunity
    and reduce inequalities of
    outcome 757–61
target 10.4 adopt policies, especially
    fiscal, wage and social protection
    policies 761–67
target 10.5 improve regulation and
    monitoring of global financial
    markets/institutions and strengthen
    implementation 767–71
target 10.6 enhanced representation
    for developing countries in global
    international economic and financial
    institutions 771–74
target 10.7 orderly, safe, regular and
    responsible migration and mobility of
    people 775–79
target 10.a special and differential treatment
    for developing countries, in particular
    LDCs, in accordance with WTO
    agreements 779–85
target 10.b encourage ODA and financial
    flows, in particular to LDCs, African
    countries, SIDS 785–91
target 10.c reduce to less than 3 per
    cent transaction costs of migrant
    remittances 791–94
transferred targets 745–46
commentary on SDG 11 809–23
  cities and urbanization in 2030 Agenda and
    New Urban Agenda 811–14
  cities as subjects of international law
    and relationship with international
    organizations 814–18
  international human rights, SDG 11
    and 818–20
  UNESCO, Sendai Framework, and
    environmental standards, SDG 11
    and 820–23
  UN Habitat, role of 802–7, 809–11
commentary on SDG 11 targets 823–57
  target 11.1 adequate, safe, affordable
    housing, basic services and upgrade
    slums 824–29
  target 11.2 safe, affordable, accessible,
    sustainable transport systems for
    all 829–33
  target 11.3 inclusive and sustainable
    urbanization and human settlement
    planning 834–37

INDEX 1339

target 11.4 protect and safeguard the world's cultural and natural heritage 837–40

target 11.5 significantly reduce numbers of deaths and people affected by disasters, especially poor and vulnerable 840–44

target 11.6 reduce environmental impact of cities, including by air quality and waste management 844–48

target 11.7 safe, inclusive, accessible, green public spaces, in particular for women and children, older persons and persons with disabilities 848–51

target 11.a positive economic, social and environmental links between urban, peri-urban and rural areas by strengthening planning 852–53

target 11.b implementing mitigation and adaptation to climate change, resilience to disasters, and disaster risk management at all levels 854–55

target 11.c support LDCs, including through assistance, in sustainable buildings utilizing local materials 856–57

commentary on SDG 12 864–947

challenges to effective regulation 868–70

content, structure, and language of SDG 12 864–65

international law, SDG 12 and 865–68

regional differences 870

commentary on SDG 12 targets 872–947

target 12.1 implement 10-year framework on sustainable consumption and production 872–76

target 12.2 sustainable management and efficient use of natural resources 877–83

target 12.3 halve per capita global food waste and reduce food losses 883–91

target 12.4 environmentally sound management of chemicals and all wastes 891–99

target 12.5 reduce waste generation through prevention, reduction, recycling and reuse 899–905

target 12.6 encourage companies to adopt sustainable practices and integrate sustainability information into reporting cycle 905–12

target 12.7 promote sustainable public procurement practices 912–21

target 12.8 ensure everyone has relevant information for sustainable development 921–28

target 12.a support developing countries to strengthen scientific and technological

capacity for more sustainable patterns of consumption and production 928–32

target 12.b develop tools to monitor sustainable development impacts for sustainable tourism that creates jobs and promotes local culture and products 933–40

target 12.c rationalize inefficient fossil-fuel subsidies to reflect environmental impacts, taking into account specific needs and conditions of developing countries 940–47

commentary on SDG 13 targets 989–1013

overview 989–90

target 13.1 strengthen resilience and adaptive capacity to climate-related hazards and natural disasters in all countries 990–94

target 13.2 integrate climate change measures into national policies, strategies and planning 994–1000

target 13.3 improve education and capacity on climate change mitigation, adaptation, impact reduction and early warning 1000–05

target 13.a mobilize $100 billion annually for developing countries' mitigation actions and operationalize Green Climate Fund 1006–10

target 13.b effective climate change-related planning and management in LDCs and SIDS including focusing on women, youth, local, marginalized communities 1011–13

commentary on SDG 14 1026–46

balancing between conservation and use 1027–29

conservation and management of marine living resources 1038–41

conservation and sustainable use in SDG 14 1026–27

framework governing the oceans 1029–46

objectives of SDG 14 1032

commentary on SDG 14 targets 1048–75

overview 1048–50

target 14.1 prevent and significantly reduce marine pollution of all kinds 1050–53

target 14.2 sustainably manage and protect marine and coastal ecosystems 1053–57

target 14.3 minimize and address impacts of ocean acidification, including through enhanced scientific cooperation at all levels 1057–58

1340 INDEX

commentary on SDG 14 (*cont.*)
    target 14.4 end overfishing, illegal,
        unreported and unregulated fishing and
        implement science-based management
        plans 1059–62
    target 14.5 conserve at least 10 per cent of
        coastal and marine areas 1062–63
    target 14.6 prohibit fisheries subsidies which
        contribute to overfishing, eliminate
        subsidies that contribute to illegal,
        unregulated fishing 1063–70
    target 14.7 increase economic benefits to
        SIDS and LDCs from sustainable use of
        marine resources 1071
    target 14.a increase scientific knowledge,
        develop research capacity and transfer
        marine technology 1072–73
    target 14.b access for small-scale artisanal
        fishers to marine resources and
        markets 1073–74
    target 14.c conservation and sustainable
        use of oceans and their resources by
        implementing UNCLOS 1074–75
commentary on SDG 15 1085–98
    best practices 1092–94
    developmental analysis 1089–92
commentary on SDG 15 targets 1098–155
    target 15.1 conservation, restoration and
        sustainable use of terrestrial and
        inland freshwater ecosystems and their
        services 1098–107
    target 15.2 increase financial resources
        to conserve and sustainably use
        biodiversity and ecosystems 1107–8
    target 15.2 promote sustainable management
        of forests, halt deforestation, restore
        degraded forests and increase
        afforestation 1109–12
    target 15.3 combat desertification, restore
        degraded land and soil, and strive
        for a land degradation-neutral
        world 1113–18
    target 15.4 conservation of mountain
        ecosystems, including their
        biodiversity 1118–24
    target 15.5 reduce degradation of
        natural habitats, halt the loss of
        biodiversity and target 15.b mobilize
        resources to finance sustainable forest
        management 1113
    protect and prevent extinction of threatened
        species 1124–30
    target 15.6 fair and equitable sharing of
        benefits of genetic resources 1130–42

    target 15.7 end poaching and trafficking
        of protected species of flora and
        fauna 1142–46
    target 15.8 measures to prevent the
        introduction and significantly reduce the
        impact of invasive alien species on land
        and water ecosystems 1146–49
    target 15.9 integrate ecosystem and
        biodiversity values in planning and
        strategies 1149–55
commentary on SDG 16 1166–80
    legal foundations and thematic
        concerns 1167–80
    international legal obligations as source for
        SDG 16 targets 1167–80
    thematic considerations in
        conceptualization of SDG 16 1174–80
    theoretical perspectives 1111–12
    institutionalism 1182–84
    Rawl's theory of justice 1180–87
    third world approaches to international
        law 1181–82
commentary on SDG 16 targets 1187–244
    critique of target 16.1 indicators 1208
    critique of target 16.4 indicators 1221
    critique of target 16.7 indicators 1230–32
    evaluating SDG 16 targets through
        indicators 1187–98
    improving credibility and accuracy of
        indicators 1192–98
    limitations of indicators in measuring SDG
        16 targets' progress 1190–92
    nature and context of SDG 16
        indicators 1190
    realization and evaluation of SDG 16
        targets 1198–244
    indicator 16.1.1 victims of intentional
        homicide per 100,000 by sex and
        age 1199–202
    indicator 16.1.2 conflict-related deaths
        per 100, 000, by sex, age, and
        cause 1202–5
    indicator 16.1.3 proportion subjected to
        physical, psychological, sexual violence
        in previous 12 months 1205–6
    indicator 16.1.4 proportion feeling safe
        walking alone around their area 1206–8
    indicator 16.2.1 proportion of children who
        experienced physical punishment and/
        or psychological aggression by caregivers
        in past month 1209–10
    indicator 16.2.2 victims of human trafficking
        per 100,000, by sex, age, form of
        exploitation 1210–12

indicator 16.2.3 proportion of women and
men aged 18–29 years who experienced
sexual violence by age 18 1213
indicator 16.3.2 unsentenced
detainees as proportion of prison
population 1214–15
indicator 16.3.3 proportion who accessed formal
or informal dispute resolution mechanism,
by type of mechanism 1215–18
indicator 16.4.1 total value of inward and
outward illicit financial flows 1219–20
indicator 16.4.2 proportion of arms whose
illicit origin or context has been
traced 1220–21
indicator 16.5.1 proportion of persons
who bribed a public official, or were
asked for a bribe during the previous
12 months 1221–22
indicator 16.5.2 proportion of businesses
that bribed a public official, or were
asked for a bribe during the previous
12 months 1222–26
indicator 16.6.1 government expenditures as
proportion of approved budget 1226–27
indicator 16.6.2 proportion satisfied with last
experience of public services 1227–28
indicator 16.7.1 positions in public
institutions, compared to national
distributions, by sex, age, persons
with disabilities and population
groups 1228–30
indicator 16.7.2 proportion who believe
decision-making inclusive and
responsive, by sex, age, disability and
population group 1184
indicator 16.8.1 proportion of members and
voting rights of developing countries in
international organizations 1232–35
indicator 16.9.1 proportion of children
under 5 years with births registered by
age 1235–37
indicator 16.10.1 verified cases of killing,
kidnapping, enforced disappearance,
arbitrary detention and torture of
journalists, trade unionists and
human rights advocates in previous
12 months 1237–39
indicator 16.10.2 number of countries
implementing constitutional, statutory
and/or policy guarantees for public
access to information 1239–40
indicator 16.a.1 independent national human
rights institutions in compliance with
Paris Principles 1241–43

indicator 16.b.1 proportion who
felt discriminated against or
harassed in previous 12 months
on basis of prohibited ground of
discrimination 1243–44
target 16.1 significantly reduce all forms
of violence and related death
rates 1199–208
target 16.2 end abuse, exploitation, trafficking,
violence against children 1208–13
target 16.3 promote rule of law and ensure
equal access to justice for all 1213–18
target 16.4 reduce illicit financial and arms
flows, strengthen recovery and return
of stolen assets and combat organized
crime 1219–21
target 16.5 substantially reduce corruption
and bribery in all forms 1221–26
target 16.6 effective, accountable and transparent
institutions at all levels 1226–28
target 16.7 responsive, inclusive,
participatory and representative
decision-making 1228–32
target 16.8 broaden/strengthen participation
of developing countries in global
governance institutions 1232–35
target 16.9 provide legal identity for all,
including birth registration 1235–37
target 16.10 public access to information and
protect fundamental freedoms 1237–40
target 16.a strengthen national institutions to
prevent violence and combat terrorism
and crime 1240–43
target 16.b promote and enforce non-
discriminatory laws and policies for
sustainable development 1243–44
commentary on SDG 17 1258–68
governance modes and modalities for
implementation of SDG 17 1261–68
SDG 17 in context of globalization and global
governance 1258–61
commentary on SDG 17 targets 1269–322
economic and financial targets 1271–86
knowledge, technology transfer, and capacity-
building-related targets 1295–313
overview 1269–71
partnership, stakeholder, policy, and
governance-related targets 1313–22
target 17.1 improve domestic capacity for tax
and other revenue collection 1272–78
target 17.2 implement ODA commitments,
including 0.7 per cent ODA/GNI to
developing countries and 0.15–0.20 per
cent ODA/ GNI to LDCs 1278–81

1342 INDEX

commentary on SDG 17 targets (*cont.*)
    target 17.3 and target 17.5 additional financial
        resources for developing countries
        and investment promotion regimes for
        LDCs 1281–84
    target 17.4 assist developing countries to
        attain long-term debt sustainability and
        reduce debt distress 1284–86
    target 17.6 cooperation on and access to
        science, technology and innovation and
        enhance knowledge sharing 1296
    target 17.7 promote development and transfer
        of environmentally sound technologies
        to developing countries on favourable
        terms 1296
    target 17.8 operationalize technology bank
        and science, technology and innovation
        capacity-building mechanism for LDCs
        and use of ICT 1296
    target 17.9 support effective and targeted
        capacity-building in developing
        countries 1306
    target 17.10 universal, rules-based, open,
        non-discriminatory and equitable
        multilateral trading system under
        WTO 1289–93
    target 17.11 and target 17.12 increase exports
        of developing countries, and implement
        duty-free and quota-free market
        access 1293–95
    target 17.13 enhance global macroeconomic
        stability 1313–15
    target 17.14 enhance policy coherence for
        sustainable development 1313–15
    target 17.15 respect each country's policy
        space and leadership to implement
        policies for poverty eradication and
        sustainable development 1313–15
    target 17.16 enhance Global Partnership
        for Sustainable Development,
        complemented by multi-stakeholder
        partnerships 1315–22
    target 17.17 promote effective public,
        public-private and civil society
        partnerships 1315–22
    target 17.18 enhance capacity-building
        support to developing countries, and
        increase availability of high-quality,
        timely and reliable data 1306
    target 17.19 develop measurements on
        sustainable development complementing
        gross domestic product, and support
        statistical capacity-building 1306–13
    trade and market-related targets 1286–95

Common but Differentiated Responsibilities
    (CBDR) 863–64
    CDM, and 964
    intra-generational equity as general
        principle 959–60
    Kyoto Protocol, and 930
    SDG 1, and 112–13
    SDG 8, and 589
Common but Differentiated Responsibilities
    and Respective Capabilities (CBDR-RC)
    climate change, and 959–61
conflict resolution and peace
    conflict resolution and post-conflict
        peace-building 1161–63
    sustainable development concern, as 1174
Congo
    education 365
    employment of persons with disabilities 595
    gender-based violence 400
    peace and sustainable
        development 1162, 1205
consumption and production *see* sustainable
    consumption and production
Convention against Discrimination in
    Education (CADE)
    see under education
Convention on Biological Diversity (CBD) 180,
    200–1, 1085–86, 1101, 1102–3
    ABS 1131–37, 1139, 1142
        Bonn Guidelines, and 1134–35
        Nagoya Protocol *see* Nagoya Protocol
    Aichi Biodiversity targets 1106, 1110, 1116,
        1118–19, 1121, 1124–25, 1127–28, 1130,
        1137, 1138, 1147
    biodiversity
        conservation of 1124
        definition of 1133
        loss of 1125–26
        mainstreaming and integration 1150–51,
        1152–53
        not shared global resource 1133
    digital sequence information (DSI) 1141
    ecosystem approach 443–44, 453, 487–90,
        491, 500, 502, 1099, 1102–3
    ecosystems 487–89, 491, 500, 1085–86, 1100,
        1118–19, 1121, 1152–53
        definition of 1099
    food waste 888–89
    forests 1109, 1110
    genetic resources, fair and equitable sharing
        of benefits of 1130–42
    Global Taxonomy Initiative 1129
    habitats, definition of 1126
    inland water biodiversity 487–89, 500

INDEX 1343

invasive alien species (IAS) 487–89, 1147, 1148–49
National Biodiversity Strategy and Action Plans (NBSAP) 1104–5, 1111, 1112, 1116, 1121, 1128, 1137
natural habitats
definition of 1126
loss of 1125, 1126
protection of 1124
objectives 1099–100, 1133
public participation 500
States parties' obligations 1107–8, 1114–15, 1124–25
Strategic Plan 2011–2020 1081, 1097, 1124, 1150
sustainable use, definition of 1028–29, 1133
sustainable wildlife use 1144
terrestrial and inland freshwater systems 1099
threatened species 1124
traditional knowledge and practices 1134, 1136–37
Voluntary Guidelines on Biodiversity-Inclusive Impact Assessment 1153
weaknesses of CBD regime 1106
Convention on International Trade in Endangered Species of Wild Fauna and Flora (CITES) *see under* flora and fauna, protected species of
Convention on the Elimination of All Forms of Discrimination against Women (CEDAW) *see under* women
Convention on the Rights of Persons with Disabilities (CRPD) *see under* disabilities, persons with
Convention on the Rights of the Child (CRC) *see under* children
corruption *see* bribery and corruption
Costa Rica
ABS 1140
biodiversity 1140
discrimination in employment 439
environmental damage 988–89, 1153
fossil fuels 945
marriage and family 382
COVID-19 pandemic
capacity building, importance of 264
child marriage, and 416
cities/urban areas *see under* cities
debt servicing, and 117, 118
domestic/gender-based violence, and 393–94, 400–1, 437–38
education, impact on *see under* education
FGM, and 416

financial effects of 116
food insecurity, gender gap and 170
gendered effects of 63–64, 170, 302
geographically differentiated poverty impact 64
health services, impact on 111–12
hunger, pushing millions into 123–24
inequality, and 712
infectious disease outbreak, as 239
informal employment, effect on 588
infrastructure, impact on 685–86
aviation industry 686
maternal health, effects on 231–32
negative effects on inequality 111–12
poverty, growth of 59, 60, 63–64, 70, 71–72, 83
recovery from 701–2
SDG 3, effects on 223–24
slums, urban dwellers in 89
social protection, and 78–79
unpaid care and domestic work, and 421–22
vaccine 259–60
access to COVID-19 Accelerator 259–60
availability 66, 261
Covax vaccine system 704–5
development and innovation 702–5
vaccine nationalism 261
waste collection, and 846
crime
arms, illicit 1220–21
bribery *see* bribery and corruption
illicit financial flows *see* illicit financial flows
kidnapping, enforced disappearance, arbitrary detention and torture 1237–39
strengthening institutions to combat crime 1240–43
trafficking *see* trafficking and sexual exploitation
violent crime *see* violence and violent crime
Croatia
employment of persons with disabilities 595
gender equality 382
legal frameworks and public life 382
sustainable economy 648–49
Cuba
education 108–9, 309
food security 170–71
gender equality 426
women in parliament 426
cultural and natural heritage, protecting and safeguarding 837–40
primary concern of cities and local governments, as 838
UNESCO's role 839
World Heritage Convention 837–38, 839

1344 INDEX

Cyprus
  domestic violence 393–94
  employment
    minimum wage legislation, need
      for 762–63
    vocational training for third-country
      nationals 776
  gender equality 419
  health 252
  ICT and internet 698
  patent applications 705–6

deaths
  conflict-related deaths 1202–5
  disaster-related deaths 96
  hazardous chemicals and waste, from 254–56
  inadequate sanitation, resulting from 468
  intentional homicide *see under* violence and
    violent crime
  newborns and children under 5 years 233
  reduction of violence and related death
    rates 1199–208
  road traffic accidents, from 246–47
debt relief 117–19
  debt forgiveness 117–18
  Debt Service Suspension Initiative
    (DSSI) 118
  Debt Sustainability Enhancement
    Program 118–19
  G20 suspension of debt 118
  global financial crises, and 117
  governmental debt, nature of 117
  long-term debt sustainability,
    assisting developing countries to
    achieve 1284–86
  negative impact of debt servicing in debtor
    countries 117
  Sustainable Development Finance Policy
    (SDFP) 118–19
Declaration on the Elimination of Violence
    against Women (DEVAW) *see under*
    violence and domestic violence
    against women
Declaration on the Right to Development 32–
    33, 152–53, 522, 636, 796, 1167, 1172–
    73, 1178
Denmark
  circular economy 693
  education 274, 294
  employment 562–63, 758
    minimum wage legislation 762–63
  financing 691
  FMG, risks of 419
  food waste 888

fossil fuels 945
green growth, supporting 932
inclusion and diversity policies 754–
    55, 762–63
ODA 294
SDGs, and 693, 736
desertification
  combating 1113–18
  forest degradation 1109–10
  Plan of Action to Combat Desertification 1114
  UNCCD 1085, 1253–54
    adoption 1114
    ameliorating desertification 1115
    combating desertification 991, 1079–80,
      1109–10, 1113–14, 1115
    combating desertification, definition
      of 1115
    forest-related aspects of 1109
    implementation and assessment of 1079–
      80, 1117–18
    land degradation neutrality 1097, 1113–14,
      1115–16
    land degradation neutrality, definition
      of 1115–16
    Strategic Framework 2018–30 1116
developing countries
  accession to single global economic system 9
  agriculture *see under* agriculture
  aid for economic advancement and political
    stability 10–11
  Aid for Trade 627–28
  capacity-building, effective and targeted 1306
  climate change
    climate-change related planning and
      management 1011–13
    mitigation and adaptation, $100 billion
      annually for 1006–10
  debt relief *see* debt relief
  diseases 239, 258–61
  domestic capacity for tax and other revenue
    collection, supporting 1272–78
  duty-free and quota-free market access,
    implementing 1293–95
  economic growth, threshold of 7 per cent
    GDP per year for 20–21
  education
    qualified teachers *see under* education
    scholarships for higher education
      see under education
    spending on 108–9
  energy services in developing
    countries 543–44
  environmentally sound technologies on
    favourable terms 1296

INDEX 1345

exports, increasing 1293–95
financial institutions, enhanced
 representation in 771–74
financial services 433–34
fishing and marine resources
 artisanal fishers' access to marine resources
  and markets 1073–74
 fishing subsidies 1070
 scientific knowledge, research capacity, and
  transfer of marine technology 1072–73
food exports to 129–30
foreign investment *see* foreign investment/
 foreign direct investment (FDI)
forests, incentives for sustainable
 management of 1113
fossil-fuel subsidies, environmental impacts
 and 940–47
GATT, and 158–59
health financing and health workforce
 in 262–63
income growth for bottom 40% of
 population 746–53
industrialization, sustainable
 industrial diversification 697–98
 promoting inclusive and sustainable
  industrialization 687–90
 small-scale enterprises, financial services
  and 690–91
industrialized agriculture production
 methods exported to 129–30
inequality gap between developed and
 developing countries 2–3
infrastructure
 facilitating sustainable and resilient
  infrastructure development 695–96
 upgrading 691–93
innovation
 domestic technology development,
  research and innovation 697–98
 scientific research and increasing R&D
  workers 693–95
international organizations, proportion of
 members and voting rights in 1232–35
lack of participation in MDG
 framework 14–15
LDCs *see* least developed countries (LDCs)
 and small island developing states (SIDS)
loan conditionalities imposed on 158–59
national planning frameworks for
 development, MDGs and 14–15
ODA and foreign direct investment 109–
 10, 785–91
 0.7 per cent ODA/GNI to developing
  countries 1278–81

additional financial resources for
 developing countries 1281–84
poverty, mobilization of resources to
 end 105–14
 see also poverty
SIDS *see* developed countries (LDCS) and
 small island developing states (SIDS)
special and differential treatment in accordance
 with WTO agreements 779–85
sustainable consumption and production,
 scientific/technological capacity
 for 928–32
technology bank and science,
 operationalizing 1296
unemployment among economically active
 people 556
unfair competition, and 29–30
unfair social constructions beyond minimum
 adequacy, MDGs and 16–17
unsustainable debt stock 29–30
water-and sanitation-related activities,
 expansion of 492–95
youth employment, nature of 628–29
development
 approaches to 7–8
 centrality of human beings in development
  process 22–23
 environmental sustainability, link with 21–22
 finance *see* development finance
 human *see* human development
 purpose of 23–24
 right to *see* right to development (RTD)
 satisfaction of human needs and aspirations
  as objective of 22
 social justice, and 22–23
 sustainable development *see* sustainable
  development
 sustainable human well-being as purpose
  of 23–24
 universalism as guiding ethical value 22–23
Development Cooperation Forum (DCF) 112
development finance *see under* financing
digital skills *see under* education
disabilities, persons with
 cities, and
  green public spaces, safe, inclusive,
   accessible, 848–51
  transport systems, safe, accessible 830,
   831, 832
 Convention on the Rights of Persons with
  Disabilities (CRPD)
  effective education 299
  right of accessibility to their physical
   environment 848–49

1346 INDEX

disabilities, persons with (*cont.*)
    right to education 282, 299, 328
    safe, inclusive, accessible, green public
        spaces 848–51
    education *see under* education
    employment 594, 595
disasters, environmental, economic, and social
    build resilience to environmental, economic,
        and social disasters 96–105
    causal link between disaster preparedness and
        economic development 97, 98
    climate change, and 98, 105
        climate-related hazards and natural
            disasters, resilience to 990–94
    disaster-related deaths 96
        reducing number of 840–44
    economic loss from natural disasters 96
    history 101–4
        adoption of Sendai Framework 104
        Hyogo Framework for Action
            (2005–2015) 103–4
        International Decade for Natural Disaster
            Reduction (1990s) 103
        IRC Conferences 102
        Office for the Coordination of
            Humanitarian Affairs (OCHA) 103
        UNDRO, establishment of 102
        Yokohama Strategy for a Safer World 103
    ILC Draft Articles on protection of
        persons 840–41, 844
    policies for disaster risk management and
        resilience to disasters 854–55
    resilience, meaning of 103–4
    risk reduction strategies 97
        local disaster risk reduction 97
    Sendai Framework *see* Sendai Framework for
        Disaster Risk Reduction (2015–2030)
    UN Office for Disaster Risk Reduction
        (UNDRR) 854
    UN System Task Team's Report 'Disaster Risk
        and Resilience' 97
discrimination
    equality, and *see* equality; inequality
    women, against *see* gender equality
diseases
    communicable diseases
        combating 236–39
        ending 236–37
        examples of 239
        infectious disease outbreaks 239
        premature mortality from,
            reducing 241–44
    confrontation of chronic and infectious
        diseases (MDG 6) 1–2

epidemics/pandemics
    ending 236–39
    impact on infrastructure 685–86
    technology transfer/licensing, and 701
fight against communicable diseases 200
hepatitis, viral 236–37, 238–39, 240–41
HIV/AIDS 236–37, 238–41
malaria 236–37, 240–41
neglected tropical diseases 236–37,
    238, 240–41
non-communicable diseases 241–44
    cost of 258
    main types of 241
    risk factors 241
    UN Inter-Agency Task Force on Prevention
        and Control (UNIATF) 242
STIs 238–39
tuberculosis 236–37, 240–41
water-borne diseases 236–37, 239
WHO Global Health Sector Strategies for
    HIV, Viral Hepatitis and STIs 238–39
see also commentary on SDG 3 targets
dispute resolution mechanisms 1215–18
Djibouti
    education 309
    FGM 416
domestic violence *see* violence and domestic
    violence against women
Dominican Republic
    ABS 1142

early childhood care or education (ECCE)
    see under education
East African Court of Justice 989
economic growth
    avenue for sustainable development,
        as 545–46
    Brundtland Commission/Report 45
    decoupling economic growth from
        environmental degradation 588–90
    economic productivity, increasing 585–87
    financial services, access to 587–88
    global resource efficiency in consumption and
        production, improving 588–90
    LDCs, in 584–85
    MDGs, and 546
    poverty, economic growth to
        eradicate 64–66
        criticism of 20–21, 28–29
    prioritizing economic growth over
        sustainability 124–25, 151–52
    support for productive activities and access to
        financial services 587–88
    see also SDG 8

economic, social, and cultural (ESC) rights
  ICESCR *see* International Covenant on
    Economic, Social and Cultural Rights
    (ICESCR)
ECOSOC
  Financing for Development Forum 111–12
  SDGs, and 666
  supervision of framework of sustainable
    development 25
ecosystems
  CBD, and *see* Convention on Biological
    Diversity (CBD)
  conservation and protection of 1098–107
  destruction of ecosystems 1101–2
  ecosystem concept 1102
  financial resources to conserve and
    sustainably 1107–8
  fundamental role of 1100–1
  integrating ecosystem values in national and
    local planning 1149–55
  sustainably used outside protected areas,
    ensuring 1105
  see also SDG 15
Ecuador
  ABS 1140
  biodiversity 1140
  energy 946
  female agricultural landowners 432
  inequalities, addressing 758
  safety and public space 851
education 116–17
  adult, definition of 337–38
  best practices 290–94
  bullying 354–55
    cyberbullying 356, 357–58
  comprehensive sexuality education
    (CSE) 430–31
  conflict-affected areas, learners in 277, 288
  corporal punishment 355–56
  COVID-19, impact of 267–68, 287–88, 301–
    2, 366–67
    evolution of distance education 357–58
  definition/meaning of 290, 295
  development, and 295–97
  disabilities, persons with 271, 277, 282, 291,
    306–7, 328–29, 330
    accessibility, principle of 356
    adapted infrastructure in schools 354,
      356, 357
    bullying 355
    categorization as vulnerable 335–36
    CRPD 282, 299, 328
    ECCE, right to 306–7
    effective education for 299, 331–32

    equal access 299, 328
    lifelong learning 328
    measures of disability 334
    right to education 277, 282, 299, 306–
      7, 328
    Vulnerability Assessment Framework 334
  disadvantaged people 277
  early childhood care or education
    (ECCE) 305–13
    criticality of early years learning 311
    Early Childhood Development Index 2030
      (ECDI2030) 307–8, 312–13
    patchy and diverse provision 311–12
    right to 306–7
  Education 2030 Framework for Action 287
  education facilities 352–58
    adequate infrastructure 354, 356
    all-encompassing and nurturing learning
      environments 352–53
    basic services 353–54
    characteristics of communities, and 358
    distance education 357–58
    universal design 356
  Education For All (EFA) goals 269, 276–77
  employment, entrepreneurship, and 321–27
    employment-based skills as a primary
      focus 321
  ESD and GCED themes in education 343–52
  faith-based schooling 335
  free, equitable and quality primary and
    secondary education 276–77, 298–305
    free education 298–99, 300
    inclusivity and equity 269, 276–78, 299
    quality education 299, 300, 304–5
  GCED *see* Global Citizenship
    Education (GCED)
  gender equality 274, 282, 287–88, 299, 332–33
    COVID-19, and 302
    gender disparities in education,
      eliminating 327–36
    gender identity, and 334–35
    lifelong learning 329
    literacy and numeracy 336–42
    moving target, as 334–35
    primary level globally 329
    quality between men and women in regard
      to access 328
    segregation in education 335
    teacher training 327–28
    tertiary level 329
  Global Education First Initiative (GEFI) 343
  Global Thematic Consultation on
    Education in Post-2015 Development
    Agenda 270, 283

1348 INDEX

education (*cont.*)
  global trends in educational policy 269
  higher education (tertiary, technical, and
      vocational education) 313–20
    affordability 319–20
    equal access 314
    gender parity, and 329
    higher education, meaning of 313
    quality 319, 320
    right to 313–14
    scholarships 358–64
    sustainable development, and 319, 320
  human rights, and 278–83
    central role of education 294–95
    core international human rights
        treaties 281–82
    education as fundamental human
        right 278–79
    other core international human rights
        instruments 282–83
    UDHR 279–81
  ICESCR, and 273
    compulsory and free primary
        education 281–82, 298–99, 327–28, 336
    education as fundamental right and public
        good 281–82
    higher education 313–14, 321–22
    pre-school education 306
    requirement of free and high-quality
        education 17–18
  ICT/digital skills 322–25, 326–27
    eSkills4Girls initiative 325–26
    online learning 325
  importance of 267, 272
  Incheon Declaration 300, 304, 306–7
  inclusive and equitable
      education 269, 276–78
    resources for 278
  indigenous peoples 282–83, 290, 304–5, 328–
      29, 330, 332
    categorization as vulnerable 335–36
    indigenous languages 342
    school attendance 1190–91
  lifelong learning 19, 315, 340
    economic importance of 326
    gender parity, and 329
    Institute for Lifelong Learning 341
    promotion of opportunities 278
    state policy 292–93
  literacy and numeracy 336–42
    adults 338–39
    cultural and political factors, effects of 342
    lifelong learning, and 340
    refugees 339–40

  universal and cross-culturally equivalent
      skills, as 341–42
  youths 337–38
migrant workers 282
Muscat Agreement 284, 285
OECD Indicators of Education Systems
    programme 293–94
primary education, free 298–99
  gender parity, and 329
  ICESCR 281–82, 298–99
  MDG 2 1–2, 268, 269, 270, 276–77
public financing of 287, 288–89
quality education 292, 299, 300, 304–5
  definition of 304
  literacy and numeracy skills as
      central to 339
  nature of 278
refugees 282–83, 318–19, 339–40
resources and wealth 278, 290, 294
  disparity by wealth 329–30
  inadequate investment in education 287
  progress varying by geographic region and
      wealth 286
right to education 268, 270
  ECCE 306–7
  Right to Education Project 270
  UDHR 279
Rio Conference 2012 271
rural women 282, 328
safe commuting 355–56
  road traffic hazards 356–57
scholarships for higher education 358–64
  developing countries funding citizens to
      study abroad 362–63
  long history of 359
  multinational private corporations,
      and 359, 363–64
  non-state scholarship programmes 361–62
  ODA for scholarships 360–61
  'opinion leader' rationale 358–59
secondary, tertiary, and lifelong learning,
    inclusion of 19
special needs education 280–81, 357, 366–67
spending on education 278
  data on 108, 113
  developing countries, by 108–9
  scholarships for higher education 358–64
sustainable development, and 268–69, 343–52
  Dakar Framework for Action on Education
      for Al 306–7, 343
  GEFI *see* Global Education First
      Initiative (GEFI)
  Education for Sustainable Development
      (ESD) 343–52

INDEX   1349

teachers and teacher training 340
  classroom-based learning for sustainable
    learning, weaknesses of 367
  COVID-19, and 366-67
  ESD and GCED themes 346, 347
  increasing supply of teachers 364-69
  International Standard Classification for
    Teacher Training Programmes 367
  no discrimination in training 327-28
  qualifications 328
  standards/approaches to training
    varying 364-66
  UDHR, and 279-81, 294-95
    aspirations qualified in terms of
      practicalities 280-81
    higher education 313-14, 321
    requirement that education be 'equitable' 279
    right to education 279, 298-99, 313-14,
      327-28
    rights defined in top-down manner 280
  UNESCO, and 269, 270
    Associated Schools Network
      (ASPnet) 349-50
    CADE 282-83, 298-99, 327-28, 336
    Convention on Technical and Vocational
      Education (CTVE) 322
    Global Education Monitoring Report 285
    higher education 313, 322
    Incheon Declaration 300, 304, 306-7
    lifelong learning 341
    ministerial conferences 284-85
    monitoring role 298
    skills for work 321
    UIS statistics 301
  violence against women, preventing
    see violence and domestic violence
    against women
  World Education Forum 269
  youth, definition of 337-38
  see also SDG 4
Egypt
  child marriage 416
  climate change 855
  consumer subsidies reforms 945-46
  COVID-19, and 437-38, 694
  disaster risk reduction plans 855
  FGM 386, 415-17
  food riots 132
  food security 170-71
  gender equality 386-87
    empowerment of women 387
    permission for women to work 387-88
  gender-based violence 386-87, 396-97
    COVID-19, and 437-38

  innovation 694
  scholarships 361
  sustainable tourism 939
  unpaid work 374-75
El Salvador
  environmental legislation 1139-40
  gender-based violence, COVID-19,
    and 437-38
  legal frameworks and public life 382
employment and jobs
  child labour see under children
  culture, and 558
  Decent Work Agenda see under International
    Labour Organization (ILO)
  Declaration of Fundamental Principles and
    Rights at Work 605-6, 614-15
  education, and see under education
  entrepreneurship 321-27
  equal pay for work of equal value 590-98
  exploitation of workers 600-1
  freedom of association and collective
    bargaining 614-15
  full and productive employment and decent
    work for all 574-82, 590-98
    human right to decent work 575-79
    work as connecting line between social
      justice and peace 574-75
    work as vital ingredient of well-being 574
  gender equality, and 384-85, 387
    choice of employment 387
    discrimination in labour laws 387-88,
      422-23
    family obligations, and 423
    median gender pay gap 594, 595
    non-discrimination based on gender in
      hiring 384-85
    permission for women to work 387-88
    prevention of wives from working 387
    sexual harassment in workplace C 387, 394
    women comprising large portion of
      unemployed worldwide 556, 594
    women under-represented in wage
      employment 556
    women's overrepresentation in informal
      work 595-96
    youth NEET 598-99
  human rights and labour rights 737-40
  human trafficking 601
  ICCPR, and see International Covenant on
    Civil and Political Rights (ICCPR)
  ICESCR, and see International Covenant on
    Economic, Social and Cultural Rights
    (ICESCR)
  ICT, and see ICT/digital skills

1350 INDEX

employment and jobs (*cont.*)
  ILO, and *see* International Labour
    Organization (ILO)
  Industry, employment in 687–90
  informal economy, workers in 595–96
    decrease in income following
      COVID-19 588
    women's overrepresentation in informal
      work 595–96
  migrant workers/migrant
    women 611, 612–13
    challenges facing migrant workers 613–14
    UN Convention on the Rights of All
      Migrant Workers 612–13
    vulnerability of 612–13
  national compliance with labour
    rights 614–15
  people with disabilities 594, 595
  precarious employment 611, 616, 617
    concept of precariousness 616
  protection of workers through national/
    international policy responses, need
    for 596–97
  right to work 575–76
    ensuring progressive realization of 578–79
    equality, and 578–79
    individual and collective dimension to 578
    not absolute nor unconditional 577
  safe and secure working environments,
    promoting 611–16
    fatal and non-fatal occupational
      injuries 611–14
    occupational risk management 613–14
  slavery, servitude, forced labour as grave
    exploitation 601–5
    dividing line of differentiation hard to
      achieve 604–5
    forced labour, definition of 604
    slavery, definition of 603–4
  social protection, and 557
  sustainable tourism, 624–25
  UDHR, and 575–76, 578
  unemployment
    drop in global working hours, and 595–96
    economically active people in developing
      world, among 556
    global unemployment rate 595
    indicator about economy, unemployment
      rate as 592, 594
    people with disabilities, no data for 594
    unemployment rates 595
    women comprising large portion of
      unemployed worldwide 556, 594
    youth unemployment 556, 594, 595

  women workers 612–13
    challenges facing women workers 613–14
  youths
    entrepreneurship 321–27
    global strategy for youth employment,
      development of 628–31
    ILO Global Jobs Pact 629–30
    micro-and macroeconomic stability, work
      and 628–29
    not in employment, education or training
      (NEET) 598–600, 628–29
    quality of employment 628–29
    risks from unemployment 628–29
    unemployment 556, 594, 595, 628–29
    youth employment strategies,
      widespread 630–31
  see also SDG 8
energy
  access to affordable, reliable and modern
    energy for all 525–32
  Beijing Declaration on Renewable Energy for
    Sustainable Development 524
  CDM *see under* Kyoto Protocol
  clean energy research and technology,
    facilitating 541–43
  developing countries, sustainable energy
    services in 543–44
  energy
    driver of human progress, as 531–32
    ethical considerations, energy access
      and 532
    fundamental attribute of sustainable
      development 525–27
    three generations of rights, and 531–32
  Energy Charter Treaty 518–21
    access to modern energy, principle of 519–
      20, 525
    energy efficiency, principle of 521
    Energy Protocol 524
    exceptions to application of treaty
      provisions 521
    polluter-pays principle, enforcement
      of 520–21
    precautionary measures on environmental
      degradation of energy resources 520–21
    preventing harm caused by energy
      poverty 519–20
    sovereignty over national resources,
      principle of 520
    States' duty to cooperate in sustainable
      energy 520
  energy efficiency, improving 539–41
    renewable energy, and 540
  fossil-fuel subsidies 940–47

future effect of SDG 7 517
G20 'Energy Efficiency Action Plan' 541
human rights approach to energy law and
policy 522–23
access to energy, and 522
human rights approach to use and
management of energy 522–23
increase of energy-efficient technologies in
management of clean energy 523–24
infrastructure and technology for energy
services in developing countries 543–44
inter-generational equity 509
International Energy Agency (IEA) 519–20,
527, 536–37
energy efficiency 539–40, 543
fossil fuels, definition of 943
impediments to expansion of
infrastructure 543
policy scenarios 529–30
SDGs, and 639–40
Statistical Manual 944
sustainable recovery plan for energy sector,
need for 528–29
intra-generational equity 509
renewable energy, increase proportion in
global energy mix of 533–39
climate change, and 534
energy efficiency, and 540
importance of advancing new and
renewable sources of energy 533
JPOI, and 533–32
renewable energy consumption, uneven
progress in 536
SE4All initiative 526, 534
water–food–energy nexus 151
World Solar Program 534
see also SDG 7
environment
cities, and 822–23
detrimental impact of development
practices on 21
environmental and economic sustainability
crystallizing as urgent 21
environmental degradation
circular nature of poverty and 37–38
decoupling economic growth
from 588–90
poverty, and 254
preventing environmental degradation
over energy resources 520–21
right to life, environmental degradation as
danger to 841
under-development causing 1090
fossil-fuel subsidies, rationalizing 940–47

MDGs, and see MDG 7 environmental
sustainability
physical sustenance and opportunity to
progress, providing 21–22
environment impact assessment (EIA) 994–98
climate change dimension, inclusion
of 995–96
definition of 994
Espoo Convention 995
Strategic Environmental Assessment
(SEA) 995
epidemics see diseases
equality
affirmative action 713
cognate concepts of 713
concern with distribution of goods or
outcomes 16–17
discrimination
meaning of 713
prohibited ground of discrimination, on
basis of 1243–44
ensuring equal opportunity 757–61
equal rights to ownership, basic services,
economic resources 86–96
equality and non-discrimination as
fundamental principles 713
fairness, and 713
fair distribution of income and wealth,
need for 22–23
fairness as aim of equality 16–17
fiscal, wage and social protection policies,
achieving greater equality by 761–67
formal equality 715–16
foundational principle of
development, as 712
fundamental rights, as 21–22
gender equality see gender equality
horizontal versus vertical inequalities 717–18
horizontal inequalities as group-based
disadvantages 717
vertical inequalities as disparities among
persons individually 717
inequality see inequality
instrumental value of 719
intrinsic value of 719
Millennium Declaration, fundamental
concern for equality in 16
nature of 16–17
positions in public institutions 1228–30
redistribution 713
right to equality 719
substantive equality 715–16
UN Charter, and 19–20
universality, and 16–17

1352 INDEX

equity
   equity in context of development 16–17
   equity stemming from idea of 'moral
      equality' 16–17
   exclusion of equity and equality from MDG
      agenda 17–18
   inter-generational equity
      see inter-generational equity
   intragenerational equity
      see intragenerational equity
   Millennium Declaration, fundamental
      concern for equity in 16
   UN Charter, and 19–20
   universality, and 16–17
Estonia
   digital skills 324–25
Ethiopia
   ABS 1140
   biodiversity 1140
   fossil fuels 945
   health 240
   lead paint 255
   small-scale farmers 178
European Convention on Human
      Rights (ECHR)
   slavery and servitude 601, 602
European Union/Europe
   accountable and transparent
      institutions 1226–27
   biodiversity 1104–5
   child marriage 418–19
   circular economy 879–80, 889–90, 903–5
   COVID-19, and 427
   definition of poverty (AROPE) 70–71
   droughts 1114–15
   education 287–88, 290, 293–94, 316, 331–32
      higher education 315, 317, 324
   energy efficiency 523–24, 539–40
   Europe 2020 strategy 72–73
   European Committee of Social Rights
      gender-based discrimination in education,
         addressing 277
      inclusive education of learners with
         disabilities 277
   European Pillar of Social Rights 72–73
   FGM, and 419
   food insecurity 170
   food waste 889–90
   gender equality 384–85
      reproductive and sexual rights 429–30
      violence and domestic violence against
         women 398–99
   harmful chemicals 881, 891, 894–95
   human rights 1242

   non-financial reporting guidelines 906–7,
      908–10
   poverty levels 70–71, 72–73
   poverty reduction 72
   pro-poor public spending 119
   public procurement, sustainable 912,
      916–19, 920–21
   re-industrialization in clean technology 688
   research development and innovation 694
   right to decent work 596–97
   SDG 6, monitoring compliance with 504–5
   SDGs, and 665–66
   sexual and reproductive health rights 431
   Social Protection Systems Programme 82
   sustainable production and
      consumption 875–76, 879
   terrestrial ecosystems 1104–5
   UNECE 246, 596–97, 822–23, 925
      Task Force on Climate Change Related
         Statistics 993
   waste 846, 903
   water resources
      management and protection of 472
      water scarcity 476–77
   women's representation in local
      government 426
   zero commitments 969

Faroe Islands
   education 303–4
female genital mutilation (FGM) 415
   CRC, and 415
   effects of 415
   eliminating 413–20
   levels of 415–16
   UDHR, and 415
   violation of human rights, as 415
finance, development *see* development finance
financial crisis (2008) 117
financial inclusion 88, 90
   microfinance 94
   payment services, right to 94
   potential dangers of financialization 95
   use of financial services 92–91
financial institutions 25
   banking, insurance and financial services for
      all, expanding access to 626–27
   domestic financial institutions,
      strengthening 626–27
   enhanced representation for developing
      countries 771–74
   IMF *see* International Monetary Fund (IMF)
   integrating climate change in safeguard
      policies 996

INDEX 1353

regulation and monitoring of 767–71
sustainable development, and 565
World Bank *see* World Bank/World
    Bank Group
financial services
    financial inclusion *see* financial inclusion
    industrial enterprises' access 690–91
    use of 92–91
financing
    assessment of GHG emissions in projects for
        funding 996–97
    climate change mitigation and
        adaptation 1006–10
    development finance *see under* financing
    foreign aid, rich donor countries'
        support for 9
    human rights, and 19–20
    international organizations' early role
        in 7–12
    single global economic system, developing
        countries' accession to 9
    SMART objectives for donor
        agencies 9, 11
    FDI *see* foreign investment/foreign direct
        investment (FDI)
    Financing for Development
        Conference 19–20
    health, and 222–23
    fossil-fuel subsidies 940–47
Finland
    basic income project 83
    education 290, 300, 317–18, 330–31, 339
    fossil fuels 945
    human rights 330–31, 339
    sexual and reproductive health rights 431
fishing *see* oceans, seas, and marine resources
flora and fauna, protected species of
    CITES 701, 1087–88, 1125
        African elephants 1144, 1145–46
        general and species-specific
            programmes 1144
        illegal trafficking 1145
        inter-operational set of domestic
            systems 1144
        IUCN Red List Index 1129
        objectives 1142–43
        regulating commercial trade in
            species 1142, 1143, 1145–46
        significant international cooperation, need
            for 1143, 1144, 1146
        trade as major contributor to
            overexploitation 1145
    poaching and trafficking, ending 1142–46
    see also SDG 15; species extinction

food
    access to food 130–31
        ensuring access to food 168–72
        regulatory approaches shifting to 130
    agriculture, and *see* agriculture
    climate change, and *see under* climate change
    critical role in sustainable
        development 121–22
    Declaration of the World Summit on Food
        Security (2009) 130–31
    FAO
        Commission on Genetic Resources for
            Food and Agriculture 1141
        food insecurity and malnutrition at critical
            juncture 123–24
        food security 1036–37
        food waste 884, 885
        right to food 163–64
    first conference on food and
        agriculture 127–28
    food commodity markets, functioning
        of 186–87
    food prices 186–87
        food price crises 132–33
    food security/insecurity 123–24, 130–31,
        157, 170
        agricultural trade policy reforms 185
        definition of 130–31
        equitable distribution of world food
            supplies 156–57
        Food Insecurity Experience Scale
            (FIES) 170
        High-Level Task Force 132–33
        nutrition, and 136–37
        Rome Declaration on World Food
            Security 164, 169
        structural adjustment programs,
            and 158–59
    Food Systems Summit 178
    food waste *see* waste management
    genetic resources for food and agriculture *see*
        genetic resources
    global food price crises 132–33
    global food system, adequacy of 123–24
    High-Level Panel of Experts on Food Security
        and Nutrition (HLPE) 179–80
    High-Level Task Force on the Global Food
        Security Crisis 132–33
    hunger *see* hunger
    ITPGRFA *see* genetic resources
    malnutrition *see under* health
    nexus between hunger, nutrition and
        sustainable agriculture 126–27
    Protocol of San Salvador 186

1354 INDEX

food (*cont.*)
    right to food 123–24, 125, 152–53,
        157, 163–64
        CESCR 155–57, 174
        ICESCR 152–53, 154–55, 168–69, 175,
          182, 183
        international human rights law,
          and 153–57
        international trade and investment
          regimes, and 160–61
        UDHR 154–55
    sustainable food systems 149, 177–80
    see also commentary on SDG 2
        targets; hunger
Food and Agriculture Organization (FAO)
    climate change 666
    Committee on Food Security 132–33
    fisheries *see under* oceans, seas, and marine
        pollution
    food *see under* food
    gender equality 380
    hunger *see under* hunger
    hunger 883
        definition of 127, 169
    monitoring SDG 2 163–64
    mountains
        mountain ecosystems 1122
        Mountain Partnership 1121–22
    objectives 163–64
    pesticides 893–94
    SDGs, and 666
    'State of Food Security and Nutrition in the
        World' 169
    sustainable agriculture, principles of action
        for achieving 178
    undernourishment 171–72
    water resources 476
forced labour *see under* employment and jobs
foreign investment/foreign direct investment
    (FDI) 5–6
    agriculture
        agricultural land grabbing in developing
          countries 160
        negative effects of 160–61
        small sale farmers, and 160–61
    Bilateral Investment Treaties (BITs) 160
    human rights obligations of (foreign)
        investors 160
    inequality, addressing 785–91
    international investment treaties 160
    investor rights 160–61
    LDCs 109–10, 721–22, 785–91
    negative impact of investments 184
    small-scale farmers 160

forests
    afforestation and reforestation
        increasing 1109–12
        CBD 1109, 1110
        Programme of Work on Forest
          Biodiversity 1109
    conservation, restoration and sustainable use
        of 1098–107
    deforestation 1109–10, 1111, 1126
        halting 1109–12
        reducing emissions from 1111
    degradation 1111
        reducing emissions from 1111
        restoration of degraded forests 1109–12
    financing sustainable forest management 1113
    global objectives and non-legally binding
        instruments 1080
    habitats, degradation and fragmentation
        of 1101–2
    Paris Agreement 1111
    protecting and restoring 486–92
    sustainable management of 1109–12
    UN Strategic Plan for Forests 1111
    UNFCCC 1109, 1111
    World Heritage Convention 1109
France
    domestic violence 393–94
        COVID-19, and 437–38
    education 309, 315, 356, 360–61, 365
    energy 946
    FMG, risk of 419
    food loss 886–87
    land consumption 835
    local governments 817–18
    migrant workers 602–3
    research and development 929
    UDHR, and 279–80
free trade agreements (FTAs) 29–30, 160, 660,
        697–98, 780, 867, 982–83
    CETA 998–99
    mega-regional FTAs 998–99
    NAFTA 985–86
    USMCA 998–99

Gabon
    child marriage 419–20
    gender equality 439
    guardianship 389–90
    polygamy 388–89
Gambia
    health 240
gender equality
    COVID-19, gendered effects of 63–64,
        170, 302

INDEX 1355

discrimination against women, definition of 381, 388
economic resources, ownership/control of property, financial services 431–34
education *see* education
effects of gender disparity 381, 383
employment and jobs *see* employment and jobs
FGM *see* female genital mutilation (FGM)
food security and hunger 149–50
  food insecurity, gender gap and 170
fundamental role of gender equality 371–74
gender empowerment and empowerment of women (MDG 3) 1–2
gender perspective in implementing all SDGs 371–72
ICT, and *see* ICT/digital skills
inheritance rights *see under* marriage and family life
legal frameworks, and 381–83
  law reform on women's economic participation 439–40
  overarching legal frameworks and public life 383–84
marriage and family life *see* marriage and family life
political, economic and public life, women's participation on 425–28
promoting, sound policies and enforceable legislation 436–37
pro-poor and gender-sensitive development strategies 115–20
stand-alone goal, as 371
suffrage, women's 383–84
technology to promote empowerment of women 434–36
unpaid care and domestic work *see* unpaid care and domestic work
violence, and *see* violence and domestic violence against women
women's economic participation, law reform on 439–40
see also SDG 5
gender-based violence *see* violence and domestic violence against women
General Agreement on Tariffs and Trade (GATT) 129, 158–59, 782, 973–74
agricultural trade excepted from obligations 129, 158–59
cap and trade schemes, and 976–79
carbon taxes, and 979–82
developing countries 158–59
exacerbating hunger and food insecurity in developing countries 158–59

exceptions 974, 976, 977
most favoured nation treatment principle 974
national treatment obligation 1287–89
'origin-based' discrimination 977
Taxes 979
trade barriers between different markets, removing 979
genetic resources
fair and equitable sharing of benefits of 1130–42
FAO Commission on Genetic Resources for Food and Agriculture 1141
plant genetic resources for food and agriculture -ITPGRFA 180, 181
  conservation and sustainable use of 1135
  duties on Parties 1136
  Farmers' Rights, benefit-sharing as fundamental aspect of 1136
  Farmers' Rights, protection and promotion of 1136–37
  mechanisms for sharing 1136, 1137
  objectives 1135
  sharing benefits 1131
state sovereignty, and 1133
see also SDG 15
Germany
education 292, 294, 923–24
  scholarships 361
energy 536, 541, 986
financial markets 771
financing 769
human rights 736
immigration 776
inclusion and diversity 754–55
  employment opportunities 758
  minimum wage legislation, need for 762–63
land consumption 835
ODA 183, 294
production subsidies reforms 945–46
research and development 929
SDGs, and 695–96
sustainable development 292
sustainable investment 769
tourism 937–38
Ghana
birth registrations 1236–37
education 315–16, 333, 368
food loss 888–89
health 240
homicide 1201–2
justice 1215
poverty 754
  livelihood program 946
social protection 763
waste 847, 848

1356 INDEX

Global Alliance for Vaccines and Immunization
    (Gavi) *see* vaccines and medicines
Global Citizenship Education (GCED)
    education 320, 344–47, 349–52
    sustainable consumption and production
        12P160, 335, 923–25
global economic crisis 5
global partnership for development
    (MDG 8) 1–2
Global Partnership for Effective Development
    Cooperation (GPEDC) 111
Global Partnership for Universal Social
    Protection (USP2030) 82
globalization
    artificial construct, as 5–6
    neoliberalism, and 5–7
    wider share of benefits of economic
        globalization, aim of 16
Greece
    debt 117, 770
    education 315
    energy 530
    FGM, risk of 419
    tourism 622–23
gross domestic product (GDP)
    meaning 6–7
guardianship 389
Guatemala
    education 330–31
    maternity leave 424
    SDGs, and 706
Guinea
    education 316
    FGM 416
    safe public spaces 851

hazardous chemicals and waste 254–56, 867–68
    eliminating dumping and minimizing release
        of hazardous chemicals 469–72
    environmentally sound management
        of 891–99
    reducing deaths and illnesses from 254–56
    UNEP's 1987 Cairo Guidelines and
        Principles 822–23
    water quality, and 469–72
health
    alcohol as risk factor in non-communicable
        diseases 241, 242
    anaemia 173
    antimicrobial resistance 263, 264
    children, and *see under* children
    COVID-19 *see* COVID-19
    definition/meaning of 218
    development, as integral part of 213–14

diet quality 131
diseases *see* diseases
financial assistance for health security 264
Global Action Plan for Healthy Lives and
    Well-being for All (2019) 211, 242
Global Thematic Consultation on Health in
    the Post-2015 Agenda 198, 199, 200–
    1, 210–11
hazardous/harmful chemicals *see* hazardous
    chemicals
health financing and health
    workforce 262–63
HIV 430
human rights, and 214–22
    CESCR, and 215–16, 217*t*
    global health, human rights critique
        of 213–22
    health as part of development 213–14
    human rights instruments, and 215–16
    ICESCR, and 200–1, 215–19
    public health framework 215
    right to health 214–22
Lancet Commission 243, 254, 270
malnutrition/malnourishment 123–24, 131
    causes of 124
    children 172–74
    definition of 174
    ending all forms of 172–75
    hunger, and 131
    nutrition, focus on 132–33
    Protocol of San Salvador 186
    see also SDG 2 'Zero Hunger'
maternal health *see under* women
mental health 241–42
    human rights, and 243
    Lancet Commission 243
national and global health risks, management
    of 263–64
nutrition 131, 132–33, 136–37
obesity and overweight 123–24, 136
pollution, and *see* pollution
public health, meaning of 215
resilience to communicable disease 66
right to health
    human rights, and *see under* SDG 3 'Good
        Health and Well-being'
    meaning of 218–19
sexual and reproductive health-care
    services 247–49
spending on health, data on 108, 113
substance abuse, strengthening prevention
    and treatment of 244–45
sustainable development, health as
    precondition for 191

tobacco, and *see* tobacco
UHC *see* universal health coverage (UHC)
undernourishment 169, 171–73
   definition of 171–72
vaccines and medicines, research and
   development of 258–61
water, and *see* water and sanitation
well-being
   meaning of 213–14
   work as vital ingredient of 574
WHO *see* World Health Organization (WHO)
women *see under* women
see also SDG 3
heritage *see* cultural and natural heritage
High-Level Panel of Eminent Persons on the
   Post-2015 Development Agenda
education 270, 274–75
health 199, 200–1
High Level Panel on International Financial
   Accountability, Transparency and
   Integrity for Achieving the 2030 Agenda
   (FACTI) 114
financial framework for sustainable
   development, and 114
need to tackle 'illicit financial flows'
   (IFFs) 114
High-level Political Forum (HLPF) 32
eradicating poverty 66
homicide *see* violence and violent crime
'honour' crimes 390
housing 89–90
   homelessness 89
   inadequate housing 89–90
   slums, urban dwellers in 89
human development
   human development approach 7–8
   human well-being
     measurement of 6–7
     services 19
   IDGs, and *see* International Development
     Goals (IDGs)
   MDGs, and *see* Millennium Development
     Goals (MDGS)
   people at centre of 7–8
   purpose of development 7–8
   rights-based approach 9
   sustainable human well-being as objective of
     development 23–24
human rights
   child labour 606–9
   cities, and *see under* cities
   climate change, and *see under* climate change
   development finance 19–20
   education, and *see under* education

energy law and policy 522–23
FGM 415
foreign investors 160
fundamental freedoms 1237–40
health, and *see under* health
human rights obligations of states 168–69
independent national human rights
   institutions complying with Paris
   Principles 1241–43
inequality, and 714–15, 729
labour rights, and 737–40
MDGs, and 17–18, 219–20
oceans, seas, and marine resources 1046–48
public access to information 1237–40
right to food, and 153–57
SDGs, and 19–21, 57–58, 125, 737–40
   human rights impact assessments 162
   human rights impacting all subfields of
     international law 67
   importance of rights-based approach to
     SDG 2 161–65
   'mainstreaming human rights' 162–63
   'responsibility' for human rights in SDG
     framework 154
   right to food, and 153–57
   SDG 2, and 152–61
   SDGs reinforcing objectives of human
     rights norms 154
Human Rights Council, UN
child, early and forced marriage 418
clean, healthy and sustainable environment,
   right to 256
freedom of expression 1167
human rights
   development policy, and 163
   transnational corporations, and 1176–77
intellectual property 258–59
mental health, right to 243
safe drinking water and sanitation, right
   to 458–59
human trafficking *see* trafficking and sexual
   exploitation
hunger
agriculture, and *see* agriculture
definition of 127
end hunger and ensure access to food 121–
   22, 168–72
FAO 883
   definition of 127, 169
   'Freedom from Hunger' Campaign 129–30
   'fighting hunger' decades of 1960s and
     1970s 129–30
   first global commitment to end world
     hunger 127–28

1358 INDEX

hunger (*cont.*)
  food *see* food
  international law, and 152–61
  malnutrition/malnourishment
    see under health
  see also SDG 2

Iceland
  education 366
  employment 613
  energy 514–15
  poverty levels 70
  sustainable tourism 939
  women's empowerment 514–15
ICT/digital skills
  education, and *see under* education
  employment, and 434
  enhance use of 1296
  gender equality
    careers in ICT 435–36
    internet usage 435
    mobile phone ownership 434
  increase access to ICT 698–700
    key economic activities 698
  use of technology to empower
    women 434–36
illicit financial flows
  recovery and return of stolen assets and
    combat organized crime 1219–21
  UNCTAD 1193, 1219, 1274–75
  UNODC 1193, 1219
  value of 1219–20
  VNRs 1219
inclusivity and broad participation
  green public spaces 848–51
  inclusive and sustainable
    industrialization 687–90
    decision-making, belief in inclusive nature
      of 1230–32
  inclusive education *see* education
  inequality
    inclusive economic growth, and 713–14
    social, economic and political inclusion of
      all, promoting 753–57
    social, economic and political inclusion of
      all 753–57
    social equity, for 1163
    sustainable development concern,
      as 1178–80
  urbanization and human settlement
    planning 834–37
India
  ABS 1140
  antimicrobials 863

childbirth registrations 1237
climate change 969, 973, 980
consumer subsidies reforms 945–46
corruption and bribery 1225
COVID-19, and
  cash transfer scheme 79
CRC 1213
crime 1201–2
disasters 98
education 310–11, 355–56
  scholarships 361
energy 513, 529–30
exports 1293–94
  exports of shrimps 867
forest conservancy 1089–90
gender equality 374–75, 382, 391, 415, 434
IMF, and 772
inequality 758
information, right to 1240
investments 1283
justice, access to 1217
mobile phone ownership 434
mobilized private funds to 110
ODA Pillar I funds to 109–10
parliamentary democracy 1227
participatory governance 1230
pollution 846
poverty 62–63, 66, 70
right to information 1240
slum dwelling 826–27
social protection 79
urban and rural localities 817–18, 826–27
waste 847
indigenous peoples
  access to justice in Australia 1179–80
  access to natural resources 87, 94
  conservation strategies 1128–29
  Declaration on the Rights of Indigenous
    Peoples 175, 180
  education *see under* education
  Energy Charter Treaty, and 521
  gender equality 391
  meaningful and effective participatory
    mechanisms, need for 497
    special participatory rights 498
  tourism, and 617
  traditional knowledge, innovations, and
    practices 1134
Individual Deprivation Measure (IDM) 73–74
Indonesia
  birth registrations 1237
  children bullying 1209–10
  consumer subsidies reforms 945–46
  employment 599–600

INDEX 1359

energy 536–37
financing 691
fossil fuels 878–79
land consumption 836
palm oil production 879
sexual exploitation of children 934–35
social protection 750, 763
unpaid work 374–75
women participating in political
process 1229
industrialization, sustainable 674, 675–76,
677, 679
automation, effects of 688
ecological industrialization 679
heavy energy consumption through
mining 692–93
industrial diversification 697–98
promoting inclusive and sustainable
industrialization 687–90
key economic activities 687–88
small-scale enterprises, financial services
and 690–91
key economic activities 690
see also SDG 9
inequality
cities, in 813–14
COVID-19 highlighting and aggravating 712
domestic legal systems, importance of 757
economic inequality
economic, social, and cultural rights,
realizing 750–51
income growth of bottom 40% of
population, achieving 10S20
inequality reduction and poverty
reduction 752
environmental dimensions, and 729–31
factors perpetuating historical disparities 715
financial markets and institutions
enhanced representation for developing
countries 771–74
regulation and monitoring of 767–71
fiscal, wage and social protection policies,
and 761–67
redistributive impact of fiscal policy 766–67
social protection, importance 765–66
human rights and a sustainable development
concern, as 714–15, 729
human rights and labour rights 737–40
inclusive economic growth, and 713–14
inequality of opportunities vs inequality of
outcomes 715
equal opportunity and reduction
of inequalities of outcome,
ensuring 757–61

interlinkages and sustainable development,
and 742–43
international law, and 734–36
intersecting inequalities 718–19
meaning of 718
issues of inequality taken for granted 735
migration see migration
multi-faceted nature of 712
ODA and foreign direct investment 785–91
social, economic and political inclusion of all,
promoting 753–57
special and differential treatment for
developing countries 779–85
systemic discrimination 760
trade, investment, aid 740–42
wealth inequality 43, 58
see also equality; gender equality;
poverty; SDG 10
information, public access to 1237–40
infrastructure 674, 675–76, 677
developing infrastructure with equitable
access for all 685–87
natural hazards, and 685–86
new infrastructure, need for 678
resilience 677, 685–86
upgrading infrastructure and adopting clean
technology 691–93
circular economy, and see circular economy
key economic activities 692
see also SDG 9
inheritance rights see under marriage and family life
inland freshwater ecosystems
conservation, restoration and sustainable use
of 1098–107
lakes, protecting and restoring 486–92
rivers
degradation and fragmentation of
habitats 1101–2
protect and restore 486–92
innovation 674, 675–76, 677
artificial intelligence 677
central role of 677–78, 685
clean and environmentally sound
technologies 691
climate change, and 677–78
commercialization of 677
'innovation industrialization' 679
intellectual property rights, and
see intellectual property rights
scientific research and increasing R&D
workers 693–95
key economic activities 694
vaccine development 702–5
see also SDG 9

1360 INDEX

Institute for Democracy and Electoral
    Assistance (IDEA)
    SDGs, and 665–66
institutionalism 1182–84
intellectual property rights 677, 700
    consumer welfare, and 707
    LDCs, and 689
    strong rules, ensuring 677
    vaccine development 702–5, 706
Inter-agency and Expert Group on SDG
    Indicators (IAEG-SDGs) 166–67
    education 297, 329
    health 226–27
Inter-agency Task Force on Financing for
    Development 111
Inter-American Court of Human Rights 971–72
inter-generational equity 522–23, 620, 714,
    859, 951
    climate change, and 1003, 1012
    definition of 22–23
    energy supply 509
    environmentally sound development 1091
    normative underpinning of sustainable
        development, as 531–32
    sustainability of social security system,
        and 766
    sustainable development, and 1251
    wealth gaps 751
Intergovernmental Committee of Experts on
    Financing for Sustainable Development
    (ICESDF) 107
International Bill of Human Rights 17–18,
    717–18
International Civil Aviation Organization (ICAO)
    SDG 9, and 639–40
International Conference on Population and
    Development and Beijing Platform for
    Action 205–6, 220–21
    Beijing Platform for Action 373, 436
    universal access to sexual and reproductive
        health and rights 225, 428–31
International Convention on the Elimination of
    Racial Discrimination (ICERD)
    education, and 281–82
    inequality, and 759
International Convention on the Protection
    of the Rights of Migrant Workers
    (ICRMW) *see* migration
International Covenant on Civil and Political
    Rights (ICCPR)
    disaster management plans as state
        obligation 854
    freedom of association 575–76
    inequality 759

prohibition of slavery, forced and compulsory
    labour 575–76, 601, 602
right of self-determination 773–74
slavery *see* slavery and servitude
International Covenant on Economic, Social
    and Cultural Rights (ICESCR) 18
agriculture and production 177
CESCR
    child mortality, reduction of 216–17
    poverty, definition of 49
    right to food 155–57
    right to health 215–16, 217*t*
    state' duty to cooperate 156–57
education *see under* education
equitable distribution of world food
    supplies 156–57
human rights obligations of states 168–69
inequality 759–60
maternal health, sexual and reproductive
    health services 428–29
national water strategy, adoption and
    implementation of 497
right of self-determination 773–74
right to adequate housing 824–25
right to food 152–53, 154–55, 164, 168–69,
    175, 182, 183
right to health 200–1, 215–19
right to work 321–22
sanitation, right to 464–65
social protection 85
states' duty to cooperate 156–57, 182, 183
water, right to 464–65
women's rights to land and property 431
work, right to 575–76
    decent work, nature of 576–77
    individual and collective dimension to 578
    inseparable and inherent part of human
        dignity, as 577
    right to decent work 576–77
    trade unionization 576–77
International Court of Justice 988–89
International Development Association (IDA)
    debt suspension, and 118
International Development Goals (IDGs) 11
    human development crux 11
international economic law *see* legal nature of
    SDGs under international law
International Energy Agency (IEA)
    see under energy
international financial institutions (IFIs)
    see financial institutions
International Institute for Sustainable
    Development (IISD)
    equal rights to economic resources 88–89

INDEX 1361

international investment law
  climate change, and 982–88
  SDG 2, and 158–61
  SDG 12, and 867–68
International Labour Organization (ILO) 200–1
  Convention on Worst forms of Child
    Labour 605–6, 607–8
  data on social spending, collection of 108
  Decent Work Agenda 579–82, 590–92
    definition and scope of decent work 581
    four foundations of decent work 581–
      82, 590–91
  Declaration on Social Justice for a Fair
    Globalization 581–82
  drop in global working hours 595–96
  enduring peace through just labour
    conditions 575
  Forced Labour Convention 604
  foundation of 579–81
  freedom of association and collective
    bargaining 614–15
  gender equality 380
  Global Jobs Pact 629–30
  International Programme on the Elimination
    of Child Labour (IPEC) 605–6
  migrant's remittances 793–94
  Minimum Age Convention 605–6
  obligations of ILO programmes 575
  purposes 579–81
  social protection 80–81
    availability of 78, 79
    Convention (No 102) 80, 85
    fundamental nature of 77
    'Global Flagship Programme:
      Building Social Protection
      Floors for All' 80
    Social Protection Floors Recommendation
      (2012) 80
    World Social Protection Database
      (WSPDB) 81
  Tripartite Declaration/MNE
    Declaration 588, 608–9
  unemployment rate as indicator 592
  youth NEET 598–99
international law
  Agenda 30, and 32–34
  cities as subjects of international law 814–18
    see also cities
  climate change, and see under climate change
  community interests, concept of 1032
  disaster relief, international law of 840–41
  human rights see human rights
  inequality, and 734–36
  institutionalism 1182–84

investment law see international
  investment law
SDGs, and see legal nature of SDGs under
  international law
third world approaches to 1181–82
trade law see international trade law
'zero hunger' (SDG2), and 152–61
  international economic law 158–61
  international human rights law 153–57
International Law Association (ILA)
  Berlin Rules on Water Resources
    Law 456, 457
  Helsinki Rules 456, 474
International Law Commission (ILC) 1134–35
  disaster relief, international law of 840–41
  Draft Articles on Prevention of
    Transboundary Harm 498–99
  Draft Articles on the Protection of Persons in
    the Event of Disasters 840–41, 844
  Draft Articles on Transboundary
    Aquifers 490
  Draft Guidelines on the Protection of the
    Atmosphere 996
  duty to cooperate 482–83
  ecosystems protection 492
  preventing significant transboundary
    harm 456
  water pollution 470
  watercourse ecosystems, definition of 487–89
International Maritime Organization (IMO) see
    under oceans, seas, and marine resources
International Monetary Fund (IMF) 79, 81
  Heavily Indebted Poor Countries Initiative
    (HIPC) 118
  land tenure 91
  loan conditionalities on developing countries,
    imposing 158–59
  Multilateral Debt Relief Initiative
    (2005) 118
  quota and governance reforms 772
  SDGs, and 665–66
  Strategy for IMF Engagement on Social
    Spending 81
  weighted voting system, effects of 771–72
international non-governmental organizations
    (INGOs)
  SDG 9, and 664–67, 673–76
international organizations (IGOs)
  cities, relationship with 814–18
  developing countries, and 1232–35
  early role in development finance 7–12
  need for additional monitoring of 666
  relevant actors, as 666
  SDG 9, and 639–40, 664–67, 673–76

1362 INDEX

International Red Cross (IRC)
  natural disasters 101–2
International Relief Union 101–2
International Telecommunication Union (ITU)
  gender equality 380
  SDG 9, and 639–40
international trade law
  affordable medicines, as impediment to
    sharing access to 258–59
  cap and trade schemes 976–79
  carbon taxes 979–82
  SDG 2, and 158–61
  SDG 12, and 866–68
International Trade Union Confederation
  (ITUC) 558, 569–71
International Treaty on Plant Genetic Resources
  for Food and Agriculture (ITPGRFA)
  see under genetic resources
International Union for the Conservation of
  Nature and Natural Resources (IUCN)
  Red List 1126, 1129, 1148
  SDG 9, and 634–35, 665
International Year for the Eradication of Poverty
  (1996) 47
internet
  provision of universal and affordable access in
    LDCs 698–700
    key economic activities 698
  rights of access to 87–88, 90, 94
  usage 90, 435
  see also ICT/digital skills
Inter-Parliamentary Union 1228
  SDGs, and 665–66
intra-generational equity 522–23, 620, 714, 951
  CBDR principles, and 959–60
  definition of 22–23
  energy supply 509
  normative underpinning of sustainable
    development, as 531–32
invasive alien species on land and water
  ecosystems
  CBD, and 487–89, 1147, 1148–49
  increasing species' risk of extinction 1148
  limited resources for taking actions
    against 1149
  one leading cause of biodiversity loss
    globally 1147
  preventing introduction and reducing impact
    of 1146–49
  ships' ballast water 1149
investment
  capital investment 691
  FDI *see* foreign investment/foreign direct
    investment (FDI)

food production 160–61
inequality, and 740–42
investment climate of a country
  enabling infrastructure 1283
  macroeconomic and trade policy 1282
  Microeconomic Framework 1282–83
investment promotion regimes for
  LDCs 1281–84
ODA *see* Official Development Assistance (ODA)
rural infrastructure, agricultural research,
  in 182–84
Salini test for defining 789–90
trade, aid, and 740–42
transnational corporations 670–71
Iran
  fossil fuels 513, 514–15
  nationality laws 390–91
  unpaid work 374–75
Iraq
  food assistance 170–71
  nationality laws 390–91
  sexual and reproductive health rights 431
Ireland
  circular economy 904–5
  debt servicing 117
  education 274, 331–32
  employment 562–63, 599–600
  financial markets 770
  FMG, risk of 419
  wastewater 505–6
Israel
  employment 595
    people with disabilities 595
  homelessness 89
Italy
  education 300, 315, 324, 356
  energy 536, 986
  food assistance 887
  gender equality 419

Japan
  biodiversity 1081
  circular economy 904–5
  climate change 983, 997
  COVID-19, and 79, 694
  disasters 103–4
  education 292–93, 316, 348, 349, 360–61,
    366–67
    scholarships 361–62
  energy 541
  food assistance 170–71
  green public procurement 913
  Kyoto Protocol, and 965
  REACH 895

research and development 929
science and technology 695, 696
Johannesburg Declaration 33–34, 49, 618–19,
    1088–89
Johannesburg Plan of Implementation (JPOI) 24–
    26, 269, 450–51, 526, 872, 1159
  actions for transition to sustainable energy
      sources 533–32
  Biodiversity Target 1079, 1081
  energy accessibility 526
Joint United Nations Programme on HIV/ AIDS
    (UNAIDS) 200–1, 236–37
  'Fast Track: Ending the AIDS Epidemic by
      2030' 240–41
  WHO, and 210
Jordan
  agricultural produce 505–6
  education 318–19
  gender equality 387–88, 390–91
  nationality laws 390–91
  violence against women 382
  wastewater 505–6
justice
  access to justice 1163–64
    equal access to justice 1213–18
  prisons see prisons
  Rawl's theory of 1200–1
  rule of law see rule of law
  VNRs 1217, 1218
  see also SDG 16

Kazakhstan
  accidents at work 613–14
  climate change 1005
  education 300
Kenya
  ABS 1140
  birth registrations 1237
  corruption 1175, 1223
  crime and violence, preventing 1241
  education 347
    integration of ESD within 348
  energy 528–29
  gender equality 1244
  homicide 1195, 1201–2
  housing law reforms 828
  human rights 913–14, 1239–40
  information, access to 1239
  justice 1215
  marriage and family 382
  peace and security 1220–21
  public space in cities 850–51
  SDGs, and 1198–99, 1232
  small-scale farmers 178

Kiribati
  nationality laws 390–91
knowledge
  cooperation on science, technology,
      innovation and enhance knowledge
      sharing 1296
  environmentally sound technologies to
      developing countries on favourable
      terms 1296
  knowledge economy 87–88
  knowledge, technology transfer, and capacity-
      building-related targets 1295–313
  traditional knowledge and practices 1134,
      1136–37
Kuwait
  employment of persons with
      disabilities 595
  nationality laws 390–91
Kyoto Protocol 944–45, 951, 984, 1078–79
  CBDR, and 930
  Clean Development Mechanism (CDM) 524,
      963–64, 1309–10
    CBDR, and 964
    main objectives 964
  climate change, and 962–66
  compliance mechanism 964–65
  criticisms of 965
  developing and industrialized countries
      differentiation, rigidity of 965
  emission credits 976–77
  FFS, and 944–45
  flexibility mechanisms 963–64
  GHGs, reduction of 963–64
  International Emissions Trading scheme
      (IET) 963–64
  Joint Implementation (JI) 963–64
  North–South approach 966
  obligations under 962–63
  polluter-pays principle 1253–54
  renewable energy 534

lakes see inland freshwater ecosystems
Lancet Commission see under health
land
  access to natural resources 87, 94
  housing see housing
  land consumption 835, 836
  right to own 175
  secure tenure rights to 86
land degradation 1097, 1113–14, 1115–16
  land degradation neutrality 1097, 1113–18
    definition of 1115–16
  restoration of degraded land and
      soil 1113–18

1364 INDEX

Laos
  intellectual property 709
  patent laws 705–6
Latin America
  accountable and transparent
      institutions 1226–27
  birth registrations 1235–36
  bribery 1222
  COVID-19, and 427
  debt 1284
  Economic Commission for Latin America
      and the Caribbean (ECLAC) 71
  education 286
  energy 536
  Escazú Agreement 1002, 1047–48
  exports 1293–94
  food insecurity 170
  gender equality 429–30
  homicide 1200–1, 1238
  human rights 1238
  hunger 169
  infrastructure
      investments 678
      need for 678
  IWRM implementation 481–82
  justice 1214–15
  national capacities in environmental
      matters 182
  poverty levels 71
  pro-poor public spending 119
  public transportation, women's safety
      and 833
  SDGs, and 595–96
  security issues and investment climate 1283
  sexual and reproductive health and
      rights 429–30, 431
  small-scale industries, financing for 690–91
  social indicators 754
  social protection 82
  waste 846, 902
  women's representation in local
      government 426
  women's representation in parliament 426
Law of the Sea Convention (LOSC) 1029–33,
      1034–35, 1074–75
  case law 1031–32, 1033–34, 1037–38,
      1041–42
  conservation and management of marine
      living resources 1038–41
      high seas 1039–41
      territorial sea and EEZ 1038
  cooperation 1037–38, 1072
  framework for almost all sea-related issues,
      as 1030–31

implementation agreements 1032–33
'incomplete' by design 1031
land-based pollution 1052
marine scientific research 1072
  marine technology, equality of states
      and 1072–73
monitoring and enforcement
      challenges 1042–46
  flag state responsibilities 1043–45
  monitoring, meaning of 1042
  remote sensing technology 1045, 1051–52
  satellite monitoring 1045, 1055
nature of 1030–31
overview of international law of the
      sea 1030–34
Preamble 1032
protection and preservation of the marine
      environment 1041–42, 1058
zonal distribution of jurisdiction of
      states 1034–35
least developed countries (LDCs) and small
      island developing states (SIDS)
agriculture 142
Aid for Trade 627–28
birth registration 1235–36
capacity-building, effective and targeted 1306
children, violence against 1209
climate change 100–1, 952, 991, 1011–13,
      1015–16
  climate-change related planning and
      management 1011–13
  mitigation and adaptation, $ 100 billion
      annually for 1006–10
  threatening survival of SIDS 1015–16
debt relief see debt relief
domestic capacity for tax and other revenue
      collection, supporting 1272–78
DSSI, and 118
duty-free and quota-free market access,
      implementing 1293–95
economic growth of 7 per cent GDP per year,
      aim of 20–21, 584–85
energy 513, 524, 543–44
  energy services, expanding infrastructure
      and technology for 543–44
environmental protection 1027–28
  fossil-fuel subsidies, environmental
      impacts and 940–47
environmentally sound technologies on
      favourable terms 1296
exports, increasing 1293–95
financial institutions, enhanced
      representation in 771–74
fishing and marine resources

INDEX   1365

artisanal fisheries 1063, 1071
artisanal fishers' access to marine resources
   and markets 1073–74
economic benefits from sustainable use of
   marine resources, increasing 1071
scientific knowledge, research capacity, and
   transfer of marine technology 1072–73
subsidies 1070
tourism 1033–34
forests, incentives for sustainable
   management of 1113
health financing and health
   workforce 210–11
ICT and internet
   increase access to ICT and universal and
      affordable internet access 698–700
income growth for bottom 40% of
   population 746–53
industrialization, sustainable
   industrial diversification 697–98
   promoting inclusive and sustainable
      industrialization 687–90
   small-scale enterprises, financial services
      and 690–91
infrastructure
   sustainable and resilient infrastructure
      development 695–96
   upgrading 691–93
innovation
   domestic technology development,
      research and innovation 697–98
   innovation and technology capacity-
      building mechanism 1296
   scientific research and increasing R&D
      workers 693–95
international organizations,
   proportion of members and
   voting rights in 1232–35
legal systems 689
marine resources, sustainable
   use of 1071
marine technology, transfer of 1023, 1058
national statistical systems,
   strengthening 1193, 1306, 1311–12
natural disasters, and 100–1
non-communicable diseases, costs of 258
ODA and foreign direct investment 109–10,
   721–22, 785–91
   0.15–0.20 per cent ODA/GNI to
      LDCs 1278–81
   additional financial resources for
      developing countries 1281–84
   investment promotion regimes for
      LDCs 1281–84

poverty
   extreme 68
   mobilization of resources to end
      poverty 105–14
qualified teachers *see under* education
scholarships for higher education
   see under education
special and differential treatment
   in accordance with WTO
   agreements 779–85
sustainable buildings utilizing local
   materials 856–57
sustainable consumption and production,
   scientific and technological capacity
   for 928–32
sustainable fisheries 484
tariffs, and 719–20, 1294
technology bank and science,
   operationalizing 1296
tourism 618–19, 1071
unique vulnerabilities of 1323
waste management 900
water-and sanitation-related activities,
   expansion of 492–95
youth NEET rate 598–99
Lebanon
   education 318–19, 339–40, 356
   gender equality 390–91
   gender-based violence 437–38
   nationality laws 390–91
legal nature of SDGs under international
   law 31–35
   goal-setting and rule-making as means of
      governance, difference between 32
   Goals representing existing international
      commitments 32–33
   human rights/international human
      rights law
      human rights impact assessments 162
      human rights impacting all subfields of
         international law 67
      importance of rights-based approach to
         SDG 2 161–65
      'mainstreaming human
         rights' 162–63
      'responsibility' for human rights in SDG
         framework 154
      right to food, and 153–57
      SDGs and 125
      SDGs reinforcing objectives of human
         rights norms 154
   international investment law
      SDG 2, and 158–61
      SDG 12, and 867–68

1366 INDEX

legal nature of SDGs under international law (*cont.*)
    international trade law
        SDG 2, and 158–61
        SDG 12, and 866–68
    nexus between SDGs and international
        law 32–33, 125, 152–61
    normative consequences of SDGs 34–35
    normative framework, international
        law as 153
    normative status of Agenda 2030 33–34
    political and legal nature of SDGs under
        international law 1–35
    prescriptive norms, Goals as 32–33
    respect for international law 32–33
    SDG 2 and international law, nexus
        between 152–61
      importance of rights-based approach to
        SDG 2 161–65
      SDG 2 and international economic, trade
        and investment law 158–61
      SDG 2 and international human rights
        law 153–57
    SDG 12, international law and 865–68
    stakeholders accountable for their
        conduct 32
    universal acceptance and legitimacy of SDGs,
        effect of 34
Liberia
    child marriage 419–20
    corruption 1224–25
    CSO, and 1232
    flag state, as 1043
    human rights 1242, 1244
    justice 1216–17
    nationality laws 390–91
    peace and security 1204
    public services 1230
    trafficking of children 1211
Libya
    gender equality 387–88, 390–91
    nationality laws 390–91
    sexual and reproductive health
        rights 431
Lichtenstein
    energy 514–15
    women's empowerment 514–15
Lithuania
    education 293, 324, 333, 354–55
    employment 599–600
Luxembourg
    education 294
    employment 689
    gender equality 419
    ODA 294

Malawi
    education 315–16, 318–19
    extractive industries 660
    female agricultural landowners 432
Malaysia
    corruption and bribery 1225
    COVID-19, and 1215
    education 289
    gender equality 390–91, 1244
    human rights 1242
    human trafficking 1212
    justice 1217
    nationality laws 390–91
    nutrition of children and
        women 173–74
    prisons 1215
    progressive taxation 764
    safety in cities 1207
    shrimp exports 867
    violence and terrorism, preventing 1241
Maldives
    FGM 415–16
    pollution 846
malnutrition/malnourishment *see under* health
Malthus, Thomas 40–41
marine resources *see* oceans, seas, and marine
    resources
marriage and family life
    child marriage *see* child marriage
    customary laws 390
    discrimination, definition of 388
    eliminating early and forced
        marriage 413–20
    fornication 390
    gender discrimination, and 385,
        387–92
      effects of discrimination 387–88
      negatively impacting sustainable
        development 388
    guardianship 389
    inheritance rights for women 383, 387–88,
        390, 433
    maternity leave 385
    nationality laws 390–91
    polygamy 388–89
    UN Convention on Consent to
        Marriage, Minimum Age for
        Marriage 413–14
    wife's obedience 385, 388, 389–90
    see also SDG 5
maternal health *see under* women
Mauritania
    health 240
    nationality laws 390–91

MDG 1 eradication of extreme poverty and
hunger 1–2, 39, 50
combining eradication of extreme poverty
and hunger in single goal 126
critical study of 14
defining goal 48–49, 131–32
extreme poverty, focus on 12, 53
SDG 1, and 39
MDG 1 to SDG 1, from 48–49
success of 52
target 1A: halving proportion of people with
income below US$1/ day 14, 17–18
weaknesses of 52–54, 69, 131–32
MDG 1.B employment 590–91
MDG 2 universal primary education 1–2, 268,
269, 276–77
significance of 270
MDG 3 gender equality 372
SDG 3, comparison with 375–77
MDG 7 environmental sustainability 1–2, 451–
52, 1016–17
safe drinking water and basic
sanitation 447, 507–8
MDG 7.D city slum dwellers 806–7
medicines *see* vaccines and medicines
mental health *see under* health
Mexico
abortion 394, 397
Agreement on Environmental Cooperation
(AEC) 1290–91
child marriage 418
environmental legislation 1139–40
gender equality 386
sexual harassment in workplace 394
green patents 930–31
hazardous waste 867–68
housing and planning 827, 828, 853
internet, access to 87–88
research and development 929
resource extraction 878–79
tourism sustainability 937
violence against women 397–98
migration
ICRMW
education 282
slavery 776–77
labour market, immigrants' access to 776
Migrant Smuggling Protocol 777
regular and responsible migration,
facilitating 775–79
safe working for all workers/migrant
workers 611–16
transaction costs of migrant
remittances 791–94

ILO instruments 793–94
importance as external financing 792, 793
Millennium Conference 48
Millennium Declaration 48–49, 195–96,
1078–79
Agenda 2030, and 32–33
aims 2, 13–14, 48, 54, 640
city life 806–7
elements of 640
equity, equality, and
non-discrimination 19–20
fundamental concern for equity and
equality 16
health-related goals 190–91, 224, 225, 226
human impacts of poverty 48
human rights, and 219–20
merger of competing poverty reduction
agendas 12
poverty eradication 640–41
rights language 17–18
WHO, and 195–96
Millennium Development Goals (MDGs) 1–18,
121, 441–42, 447–53, 1078–79
action plan embodying practical
investment 3
adoption by UN 1–2
aims of 2
city life 806–7
delinked from core objectives of Millennium
Declaration 16, 17–18
developed by technocrats from international
financial institutions 195
developing countries
limited nature of involvement in
development 14–15
MGDs heavily oriented towards 640–41
development, right to 638
dynamic nature of 3
economic growth, and 546
health-related goals 190–91, 195–96, 200–1
High-Level Forum on Health MDGs 196
historical and political undercurrents of 3–5
human rights, and 219–20
inconsistency with 17–18
implications of MDGs process for
development paradigm 13–18
individual-oriented approach to
development 2–3
Inter-Agency and Expert Group on MDG
Indicators (IAEG-MDG) 210
International Development Goals as
forerunners 47
international organisations' early role in
development finance 7–12

1368 INDEX

Millennium Development Goals (*cont.*)
minimalistic approach 16–17
narrow understanding of 16
nature of 1–2
neoliberalism, and 5–7
poverty eradication 640–41
results-based management, impact of 13–14
rights language, need for 18
SDGs, and 19, 121
UDHR, drawing upon 2
weaknesses and issues
absence of clear action plan with defined
duties and obligations 15–16
conceptualization, problems with 13–14,
16
exclusion of equity and equality from
agenda 16–18, 732
execution, issues with 14
fragmentation 15–16
human rights standards, neglect of 17–18,
731
'immunity' of developed countries 731–32
ownership of Goals, questions
around 14–16
role of civil and political rights
ignored 17–18
stripped of country-specific
pragmatism 14–15
uneven success in reducing poverty 38
universality absent in formulation
of 16–18
WHO, and 196, 210
WSSD, and 526
Millennium Summit 12, 590–91, 1252–53, 1255
poverty eradication, framework for 11
Million Voices Report 658–61
mobile telephony 699–700
modern slavery *see under* employment and jobs
Montenegro
discrimination in employment 439
poverty eradication 92
Morocco
energy 946
social protection 78
mountain ecosystems
conservation, sustainable use including
biodiversity of 1098–107, 1118–24
disaster risk reduction, and 1119
FAO
mountain ecosystems 1122
Mountain Partnership 1121–24
fragile nature of 1120
Oceania 1120
protecting and restoring 486–92

VNRs 1120–21
World Heritage Convention 1118, 1121
Mozambique
climate change 855
disaster risk management 855
education 333
extractive industries 660–61
food riots 132
Myanmar
education 316

Nagoya Protocol 1073
Access and Benefit-Sharing (ABS) 1131,
1133, 1134, 1138–41
breadth of 1135
capacity-building initiatives 1141–42
States parties' obligations 1137, 1141
Namibia
child marriage 420
education 315–16
food assistance 170–71
gender equality 1244
governance 1244
human trafficking 1212
land tenure 93
patent protection 709
public services 1225
violence and safety 1206, 1207
national developmentalism 3–7
nationality laws 390–91
natural hazards 685
COVID-19 *see* COVID-19
natural heritage *see* cultural and natural heritage
neoliberalism 9, 16
deficiencies in agenda 6
development associated with overall wealth
and growth 6–7, 9, 151–52
development still viewed through 30–31
globalization, and 5–7
growth, neoliberal connotation of 569–72
MDGs, and 5–7
nature of 5–6
privatization, and 5–6
SDGs, and 124–25, 151–52
Nepal
education 308
bullying 354–55
gender equality 338
nationality laws 390–91
poverty 338
Netherlands
CBDR 863
climate change 1003–04
education 273, 315, 324, 366–67

INDEX 1369

emissions trading scheme 976–77
energy 986
SDGs, and 937
sexual and reproductive health rights 431
New International Economic Order 194,
773, 803
New Zealand
accountable and transparent
institutions 1226–27
birth registrations 1235–36
bribery 1222
education 286, 290
emission trading schemes 976–77
energy 514–15
food loss 886
fossil fuels 945
housing law reforms 828
inclusion and diversity policies 754–55
employment opportunities 758
minimum wage legislation, need for 762–63
justice 1214–15
net-zero target 997
sexual and reproductive health rights 431
sustainable tourism 622–23
women's empowerment 514–15
youth NEET rates 598–99
Nicaragua
ABS 1140
biodiversity 1140
education 325
employment 325
environmental protection 988–89
Nigeria
banks and stock exchanges, role of 88
child abuse 1209–10
corruption 1223–24
IFFs 1219–20, 1274
employment, discrimination in 422–23
energy 537, 1287–89
financial inclusion 88
inequality 752
labour laws restricting women 422–23
reproductive rights 374–75
security issues and investment 1283
social protection 78
North Africa *see under* Africa
North America
accountable and transparent
institutions 1226–27
natural hazards 685
bushfires 970
North American Agreement on
Environmental Cooperation 1127–28,
1290–91

North American Free Trade
Agreement 985–86
waste 846, 902
women's representation in local
government 426
Norway
ABS 1140
biodiversity 1140
education 274, 292, 293, 294, 303
employment 919–20
energy 1287–89
environmental protection 913
food systems 170–71
fossil fuels 945
gender equality 385
human rights 736, 758
labour market, immigrants' access to 776
maternity leave 385
ODA 294
SDGs, and 693, 695–96, 700, 736
social protection 763

Oceania
accountable and transparent
institutions 1226–27
bribery 1222
human rights 1242
IWRM implementation 481–82
justice 1214–15
mountain areas 1120
stunted children 172–73
women's representation in local
government 426
women's representation in parliament 426
oceans, seas, and marine resources
climate change
effects of 1015–16
ocean acidification, and 1057–58
coastal and marine areas, conservation
of 1062–63
environmental management plans 1062–63
conservation and use, balancing 1027–29
cooperation
international cooperation 1035–38, 1059
scientific cooperation 1058
UNFSA 1065
destruction of marine environment as urgent
problem 1015–16
FAO 1025, 1049, 1067
Code of Conduct 1033, 1059, 1060, 1064,
1067–68
Compliance Agreement 1043, 1064–65
conservation and management of
fisheries 1036–37

1370 INDEX

oceans, seas, and marine resources (*cont.*)
  food security 1036–37
  Voluntary Guidelines for Flag State
    Performance 1070, 1071
  fishing
    artisanal fishers 1063
    artisanal fishers' access to marine resources
      and markets 1073–74
    ending overfishing, illegal, unreported and
      unregulated fishing 1059–62
    fisheries management framework 1059–61
    fisheries nearing complete
      depletion 1015–16
    marine protected areas 1061
    Regional Fisheries Bodies/
      RFMOs 1059–62
  fishing subsidies
    artisanal fishers, subsidies to 1063
    detrimental subsidies 1063–64
    FAO Code 1067–68
    FAO Compliance Agreement 1064–65
    IPOA 1067–68
    prohibiting and eliminating certain forms
      of 1063–70
    PSMA 1068–70
    'reflagging', addressing 1064–65, 1067
    scientific research subsidies 1063
    UNFSA 1065–67
  framework governing the oceans 1029–46
    conservation and management of marine
      living resources 1038–41
    functional approach and cooperation in
      ocean governance 1034–38
    Law of the Sea Convention *see* Law of the
      Sea Convention (LOSC)
    monitoring and enforcement
      challenges 1042–46
    other instruments on marine sustainability
      or governance 1033
    protection and preservation of the marine
      environment 1041–42
  Intergovernmental Oceanographic
    Commission (IOC) 1036–37
    transfer of marine technology 1072–73
  International Maritime Organization
    (IMO) 1036–37
  International Whaling Commission 1036–37
  marine and coastal ecosystems, sustainably
    managing and protecting 1053–57
    conservation and management measures,
      forms of 1054–55
    degradation of ecosystems 1053–55
    effectiveness of conservation and
      management measures 1055

  Marine Spatial Planning 1054
    spatial management measures 1054
  marine pollution 1015–16, 1017, 1046–47
    deep seabed mining 1050–51, 1055–57
    global warming 1050, 1057–58
    land-based sources, from 1050, 1052–53
    marine debris, nature of 1050
    marine ecosystems and biodiversity, threat
      to 1051
    nutrient pollution 1050
    plastics 1051–52
    preventing and significantly
      reducing 1050–53
    types of 1050–51
  ocean acidification 1057–58
    climate change, and 1057–58
    definition of 1057
    seriousness of 1058
  Ramsar Convention *see* Ramsar Convention
  Regional Fisheries Management
    Organizations (RFMOs) 1036–37,
    1059–62
  scientific knowledge, research capacity, and
    transfer of marine technology 1072–73
  UN Fish Stocks Agreement 1032–33, 1041,
    1059, 1060
    aims of 1065
    compliance and enforcement
      provisions 1066
    flag states' obligations 1065–66
    mechanisms for international
      cooperation 1065
  UNESCO 1036–37
  see also SDG 14
Office for the Coordination of Humanitarian
    Affairs (OCHA) 103
Office of the Disaster Relief Co-ordinator
    (UNDRO) 102, 103
Official Development Assistance (ODA) 107–8
  corruption, and 114
  data on 113
  decline in budgets of 10–11
  importance of 112–13
    important source of development funding,
      ODA as 183
  inequality, addressing 785–91
  LDCs 109–10, 721–22, 785–91
  negative impact of investments 184
  new development agenda, and 10–11
  ODA/GNI contributions to developing
    countries and LDCs 1278–81
  OECD member states, level of ODA
    from 109, 112
  PRSPs, adherence to 68–69

results-oriented public policy reform 10–11
target for ODA funding of health research and
development 260–61
tied aid, emergence of 10–11
total official flows 182–83
see also investment
Oman
employment 599–600
nationality laws 390–91
Open Working Group (OWG)
composition 134, 643
establishment and structure 197–34, 271–72
Focus Areas 650–51, 652–53
OWG-1 644
OWG-2 644–45
OWG-3 645–46
OWG-4 646
OWG-5 646–48
OWG-6 648–49
OWG-7 648–49
OWG-8 649
OWG-9 650, 652
OWG-10 651, 652
OWG-11 652, 653
OWG-12 653–54, 657, 658
OWG-13 657
role 197, 643
SDG 1
centrality of fighting poverty 50, 51–52,
69–70
data on poverty, lack of 52–53
equality 51–52
SDG 2
negotiations and drafting 140–48
stocktaking phase 135–40
SDG 3 197–99
intergovernmental negotiations 207–8
negotiation phase 204–7
OWG sessions and adoption phase 199–208
stocktaking phase 199–204
SDG 4 271–76
SDG 8 552–68
SDG 9 643–58
SDG 10
HLP Report 727–29
negotiations and drafting 723–27
stocktaking phase 720–23
SDG 12 861–64
SDG 13 951–53, 954, 955–58
SDG 14
negotiation phase (March 2014–July
2014) 1023–26
stocktaking phase (March 2013–February
2014) 1020–23

SDGs and targets 26–27, 38–39, 133–34
shaping post-2015 agenda 50–54
Organisation for Economic Co-operation and
Development (OECD)
Children's Rights and Business Principles
(CRBPs) 608–9
definition of 109
Development and Assistance Committee
(DAC) 47, 107, 109, 189–90
best practice guidelines for donors 110–11
monitoring OECD members' foreign
assistance 110
development assistance from member
states 109
education 293–94
expenditures on international public goods,
unable to assess 113
gender equality 380
Guidelines for Multinational
Enterprises 462, 608–9
High-Level Fora on Aid Effectiveness 111
in-country refugee-care expenditures 109
International Development Goals 47,
1077–78
maternal mortality 231
relative poverty 70
SDG 9, and 665–66
social protection 82
statistics on foreign development assistance,
collecting 108
total official support for sustainable
development (TOSSD) 109–10

Pacific Islands/region
education 293–94, 302–3
infrastructure, need for 678
Pakistan
employment 382, 562–63, 599–600
women's employment 439
exports of shrimps 867
mobile phone gender gap 434
Paraguay
nutrition of children and women 173–74
Paris Agreement 822, 1004, 1258–59
ambition, concept of 967
CDBR, and 966, 967
climate change, and 79, 177, 966–68
core pillars of 966
deforestation and forest degradation,
and 1111
economic growth as avenue for sustainable
development 545–46
FFS, and 944–45
financial and technology transfer 1009

1372 INDEX

Paris Agreement (*cont.*)
  implementation by subsequent CoPs 968–70
    Glasgow 968, 1295–96
    Katowice 968
  long-term low greenhouse gas emission
    development strategies 540
  main achievements of 968
  National Adaptation Plans (NAPs) 1010
  nationally determined contributions
    (NDCs) 540, 889
  nature of 966, 967
  objectives 966–67
  polluter-pays principle 1253–54
  renewable energy, and 534
  SDGs, and 177, 540, 701
  States parties' obligations 925, 967, 968, 1004,
    1013, 1058
  US re-joining 1297
Peacebuilding Support Office (PBSO) 200–1
Peru
  ABS 1140
  internet, access to 87–88
  sustainable tourism 937–38
  Truth and Reconciliation Commission 1174
Philippines
  ABS 1138
  agricultural workers 750
  cash transfer programmes 946
  citizen participation in governmental
    processes 1230
  consumer subsidies reforms 945–46
  education 292, 354–55
  inclusion and diversity policies 754–55, 758
  natural and/cultural heritage 933–34
  safety in public spaces 851
  women's participation in political
    process 1229–30
political and legal nature of SDGs under
  international law 1–35
political history of the SDGs 21–27
  Brundtland Commission 22–23
  Conference on the Human Environment
    (1972) 21–22
  genesis in UN summits and consultations 21
  Johannesburg Plan of Implementation
    (JPOI) 24–26, 269
  objective of development, sustainable human
    well-being as 23–24
  UN Conference for Sustainable Development
    (2012) 25–27
  World Summit for Sustainable Development
    2002 (WSSD) 24–26
pollution 256
  air pollution 241, 355–56, 844–46, 847–48

fragmented responsibility for 256
hazardous chemicals, reducing deaths and
    illnesses from 254–56
Lancet Commission 254
marine pollution *see under* oceans, seas, and
    marine resources
reducing deaths and illnesses 254–56
polygamy 388–89
Portugal
  debt 770
  FGM, risk of 419
  gender equality 385
  housing law reforms 828
  maternity leave 385
poverty
  basic income for all 82–83
  causes and effects of 55–56
  circular nature of poverty and environmental
    degradation 37–38
  definition of 49
    moderate poverty (less than $ 2.50/
      day) 20–21
    people living on less than $ 1.90 a day 60
    poverty threshold of $1–a–day 14
  ecological and other crises, and 22
  economic growth to eradicate poverty 64–66
    criticism of 20–21, 28–29
  equal rights to ownership, basic services,
    economic resources 86–96
  eradication of poverty
    Agenda 2030 *see* Agenda 2030
    costs of 641
    freedom from poverty as UN
      imperative 7–8
    JPOI, and 24–25
    MDG 1 *see* MDG 1: eradication of extreme
      poverty and hunger
    Millenium Declaration 12, 640–41
    Millennium Summit framework of poverty
      eradication 11
    multidimensional nature, in 19, 40, 41
    reasons why poverty eradication is primary
      SDG 43–44
    respect for each country's policy
      space 1313–15
  global mechanism on poverty reduction,
    finalization of 12
  hunger *see* hunger
  income-based destitution, narrow conception
    of poverty as 14
  income disparities widening 20–21
  intergenerational perpetuation of 254
  law, and 55–59
  Millennium Declaration, and 12, 640–41

INDEX 1373

mobilization of resources to end
poverty 105–14
multidimensional nature of 8–9, 13,
19, 46–47
multi-sectoral approach to poverty 8–9
natural poverty from natural hazards 685
pro-poor and gender-sensitive development
strategies 115–20
reduction of 69–76
domestic resources 106
history of 44–54
multi-variant nature of poverty reduction
and the law 54–55
relative poverty 19, 40, 41, 60
relief and assistance 58–59
staggering dimensions of poverty
worldwide 7–8
understanding effects of poverty on
individuals, deepening 48
see also inequality; SDG 1
Poverty Reduction Strategy Plans
(PRSPs) 14–15
debt relief, and 68–69
ODA, and 68–69
prisons
unsentenced detainees as proportion of
prison population 1214–15
VNRs 1215
privatization
deprivation and discrimination, and 6
neoliberalism, and 5–6
production, sustainable see sustainable
consumption and production
property ownership
equal rights to ownership, basic services,
economic resources 86–96
right to private property 175
women's ownership and control of land and
property 431–34
see also commentary on SDG 1 targets
public institutions and services
birth registration of children under
5 years 1235–37
bribery of officials see bribery and corruption
decision-making
inclusive and responsive decision-making,
belief in 1230–32
responsive, inclusive, participatory and
representative 1228–32
VNRs 1230
domestic capacity for tax and other revenue
collection, improving 1272–78
effective, accountable and transparent
institutions at all levels 1226–28

fundamental freedoms, protection of 1237–40
global macroeconomic stability,
enhancing 1313–15
government expenditures as proportion of
approved budget 1226–27
independent national human rights
institutions complying with Paris
Principles 1241–43
justice see justice
legal identity including birth registration,
providing 1235–37
non-discriminatory laws/policies
for sustainable development,
promoting 1243–44
partnership, stakeholder, policy, and
governance-related targets 1313–22
procurement see public procurement
public, public-private and civil
society partnerships, promoting
effective 1315–22
public access to information 1237–40
public access to information and protect
fundamental freedoms 1237–40
public institutions, positions by sex, age,
persons with disabilities in 1228–30
satisfaction with public services 1227–28
strengthening institutions to prevent violence/
combat terrorism and crime 1240–43
women's participation in political, economic
and public life 425–28
public procurement
circular public procurement 901
definition 912
green public procurement 912, 917–18
One Planet Sustainable Public Procurement
Programme 914–15, 916–17
purpose 912–14
reforms to public procurement processes 1177
sustainable public procurement 873, 912–21
UNCITRAL Model Law 917–18
UNEP 914–15, 916–17

Qatar
nationality laws 390–91
'quiet politics' 673–74, 675

R&D see innovation
Ramsar Convention see under wetlands
Rawls, John
theory of justice 1184–87
results-based management (RBM) 11
MDGs, and 13–14
over-reliance on precision, accuracy and
relevance of targets 13–14

1374 INDEX

right to development (RTD) 19–20
Rio + 20 see UN Conference on Sustainable
    Development (Rio + 20 Conference)
Rio Conference 1992 46–47
    climate change 961
Rio Conference 2012 201–2, 548–49
    education 271
    gender equality 372
Rio Declaration on Environment and
    Development and Agenda 21 26, 46–47,
    152–53, 197, 444–45
    Agenda 21 as first modern global action plan
        on sustainable development 46–47
    eradication of poverty, call for 46–47
    JPOI as blueprint for 24–25
    lack of progress in improvements under 47
    poverty as complex multidimensional
        problem 46–47
    principle of integration 1149–50
    sustainable tourism 618–19
rivers see inland freshwater ecosystems
road traffic accidents
    commuting to school 356–57
    Global Initiative for Child Health and
        Mobility 356–57
    reducing death and injury from 246–47
Rockefeller Foundation
    Campaign Against Hunger 129–30
Romania
    conservation of mountain ecosystems 1122
    education 315, 324
rule of law
    equal access to justice for all, and 1213–18
    global firms' activities 637–38
    global rules under TRIPS Agreement 637–38
    interdependent concepts, and 1159–60
    justice see justice
    promoting 1213–18
    sustainable development, and 635–36,
        637–38, 1177–78
        rule of law as sustainable development
            concern 1177–78
Russia
    climate change 965, 980
    education 331–32
        scholarships 361
    employment 422–23, 630–31
    energy 513
    gender equality 384–85
        labour laws restricting women 422–23
    human trafficking 603–4
    IMF, and 772
    infrastructure and industrialization 643
    poverty 70

Rwanda
    conservation of mountain ecosystems 1122
    corruption 1224
    education 284–85, 315–16
    justice 1216–17
    maternal mortality 232–33
    mobile phone ownership 434
    natural/cultural heritage 933–34
    safety 1207
    women in parliament 426

sanitation see water and sanitation
Sao Tome
    LDC status, leaving 687
Saudi Arabia
    energy 513, 514–15
    nationality laws 390–91
    sexual and reproductive health 248
    women's rights
        discrimination in employment 439
        guardianship laws 389
        nationality laws 390–91
        unpaid care and domestic work 374–75
        women's suffrage 383–84
SDG 1 'End Poverty in All Its Forms
        Everywhere' 19, 37–120
    background 37–39
    economic growth to eradicate poverty 64–66
    criticism of 20–21, 28–29
    eradication of poverty in its multidimensional
        nature 19, 40, 41
    relative poverty 19, 40, 41, 60
    travaux préparatoires 39–42
        Agenda 2030 42
        lack of unity on implementation
            measures 41–42
        prioritizing poverty 39–42
        UN members' perceived 'priority areas' 39
    see also poverty
SDG 2 'Zero Hunger' 121–87
    aims 121–23
    background 121–26
    development and definition of terms and core
        issues 126–33
        access to food, regulatory approaches
            shifting to 130
        adoption of MDGs 131–32
        countries ensuring food supply by
            supporting their agricultural sectors 129
        'fighting hunger' decades of 1960s and
            1970s 129–30
        first global commitment to end world
            hunger 127–28
        food price crises 132–33

food security 130–31
hunger and malnutrition 131
new focus on supply of food to eradicate hunger 128
nexus between hunger, nutrition and sustainable agriculture 126–27
nutrition, focus on 132–33
ecosystem health, promoting 123
environmental consequences of industrial agriculture on food production 123
focus on agricultural productivity 124–25
obstacles to achieving 124–25
striving to eliminate all forms of hunger and malnutrition by 2030 121–22
sustainable agriculture as key to achieving 122–23
travaux préparatoires 133–48
food security and nutrition 136–37
intergovernmental negotiations on SDG 2 134–35
OWG: negotiations and drafting 140–48
OWG: stocktaking phase 135–40
sustainable agriculture 138–40
SDG 3 'Good Health and Well-being' 189–265
aimed at achieving overall health of general population 192
assessment and critique 192–93, 222–24
COVID-19 pandemic, effects of 223–24
overall objective of SDG 3 remaining aspirational and vague 222–23
progress on health targets 223–24
SDG 3 as core objective of Agenda 222
background 189–93
basis for, and inherent part of, other SDGs, as 191–92
global health, development and human rights critique of 213–22
development, health as part of 213–14
human rights, and 214–22
well-being, meaning of 213–14
lack of quantitative thresholds 192–93
no prioritization among targets 192–93
right to health and human rights 214–22
availability, accessibility, acceptability, and quality (AAAQ), and 216, 218
CESCR, and 215–16, 217t
freedoms and entitlements 216
human rights instruments, in 215–16
ICESCR, and 200–1, 215–19
protection of right to health as core objective 214–15
public health framework 215
right to health, meaning of 218–19

SDG 3 not formulated in rights-based manner 220–22
UHC as practical expression of right to health 218, 221
sustainable development, health as precondition for 191
travaux préparatoires 193–208
background 193–99
intergovernmental negotiations 207–8
negotiation phase 204–7
OWG sessions and adoption phase 199–208
stocktaking phase 199–204
WHO
healthy life expectancy measurement 211–12
lead role in achieving good health and well-being 209–12
reporting on progress in relation to SDG 3 211–12
state of 'well-being, monitoring methodology of 212
wider understanding of health 218
SDG 4 'Inclusive and Equitable Quality Education and Lifelong Learning' 267–369
background 267–68
COVID-19, impact of 267–68
global trends in educational policy 269
importance of education 267, 272
lifelong learning 19
right to education 268
secondary, tertiary, and lifelong learning, inclusion of 19
travaux préparatoires 268–76
background 268–71
OWG sessions 271–76
SDG 5 'Gender Equality and Empower All Women and Girls' 371–440
background 371–72
fundamental role of gender equality 371–74
gender equality as stand-alone goal 371
gender perspective in implementing all SDGs 371–72
law reform on women's economic participation 439–40
travaux préparatoires 372–75
women's economic participation, law reform on 439–40
SDG 6 'Availability and Sustainable Management of Water and Sanitation' 441–508
background 441–53
scope and approach of SDG 6 448–49
travaux préparatoires 449–53

1376 INDEX

SDG 6 'Availability and Sustainable Management of Water and Sanitation' (*cont.*)
  monitoring and implementation 502–7
    challenges of SDG 6 506–7
    examples of national best practice 505–6
    highly developed programme for monitoring of progress 502–3
    importance of monitoring 503–4
    measuring compliance with correlative human rights 504
    UN-Water Integrated Monitoring Initiative 503
  overview 441–47
    aims of SDG 6 443
    ecosystem approach in international water law, emergence of 444–45
    potential impact of SDG 6 442–43
SDG 7 'Access to Affordable, Reliable, Sustainable and Modern Energy' 509–44
  background 509–10
  importance of 509
  travaux préparatoires 510–17
    whether stand-alone or cross-cutting target 512–17
SDG 8 'Sustained, Inclusive and Sustainable Economic Growth and Full Employment' 545–632
  background 545–48
  importance of economic growth as independent goal 547–48
  OWG sessions 552–68
    negotiation phase 562–68
    negotiation phase: OWGs 9–13 (March-July 2014) 562–68
    OWG session 4 (17–19 June 2013) 555–59
    OWG session 5 (25–27 November 2013) 559–62
    stocktaking phase 552–62
  predominant role of economic growth to eradicate poverty, criticism of 20–21, 28–29
  reshaping economic growth in employment-related manner 546–47
  sustained per capita economic growth 20–21
  threshold of 7 per cent of GDP per year for developing countries 20–21
  travaux préparatoires 548–68
    background 548–51
    OWG sessions 552–68
SDG 9 'Resilient Infrastructure, Inclusive and Sustainable Industrialization, and Foster Innovation' 633–709
  aims of global transformation 642–43

  background 633–39
  critique, findings and outlook 705–9
  empirical results: sample study on vaccines and technological innovation 702–5
  Gabcikovo-Nagymaros 633, 701, 1028–29, 1033–34
  global firms' activities, rule of law and 637–38
  imbalances between Global North and Global South 635
  legal divergences on 'sustainable' and 'development' 634–35
  main agent of change in relation to other SDGs, as 638
  origins of 'sustainable development' 634–35
  private economic enterprises, and 638–39
  right to development 636–37, 638
  SDG 9 at epicentre of global development 633–34
SDG 10 'Reduce Inequality Within and Among Countries' 711–97
  aim to 'Leave No One Behind' 711
  background 711–20
  cognate concepts 713–16
  horizontal versus vertical inequalities 717–18
  inequality of opportunities vs inequality of outcomes 715
  intersecting dimensions 718–19
  intrinsic and instrumental values 719–20
  travaux préparatoires 720–29
    HLP Report 727–29
    OWG: negotiations and drafting 723–27
    OWG: stocktaking phase 720–23
SDG 11 'Make Cities and Human Settlements Inclusive, Safe, Resilient, and Sustainable' 799–857
  background 799–801
  travaux préparatoires 801–8
    negotiations of 2030 Agenda, SDG 11 807–8
    UN-Habitat Agenda 802–7
SDG 12 'Sustainable Consumption and Production Patterns' 859–947
  background 859–61
  travaux préparatoires 861–64
    CBDR principle 863–64
    contested issues during negotiations 861–64
    stand-alone versus an integrated goal 861–62
SDG 13 'Urgent Action to Combat Climate Change and Its Impacts' 949–1014
  background 949
  multilateral climate change regime 961–70

Kyoto Protocol 962–66
Paris Agreement 966–68
Paris Agreement, implementation by
    subsequent CoPs 968–70
UNFCCC 961–62
principles of international law and climate
    change 958–61
equity and
    differentiation: CBDR-RC 959–61
tackling climate change across other fields of
    international law 970–89
court jurisprudence, climate change
    in 988–89
human rights and climate change 970–72
international investment law and climate
    change 982–88
international trade law and climate
    change 972–82
travaux préparatoires 950–58
background 950–51
OWG 7 951–53
OWG 10 954
OWG 11 955
OWG 13 955–58
SDG 14 'Conserve and Sustainably Use the
    Oceans, Seas, and Marine Resources'
background 1015–18
human rights, and 1046–48
OWG sessions 1020–26
    negotiation phase (March 2014–July
        2014) 1023–26
    stocktaking phase (March 2013–February
        2014) 1020–23
travaux préparatoires 1019–26
background 1019–20
open working group sessions 1020–26
SDG 15 'Protect, Restore and Promote
    Sustainable Use of Terrestrial
    Ecosystems' 1077–155
travaux préparatoires 1077–85
development of post-2015 UN
    Development Framework 1083
global objectives and non-legally binding
    instrument on forests 1080
negotiation of SDG Goal 15 1083–85
OECD International Development
    Targets 1077–78
Rio + 20 and Group of 20 (G20) Los Cabos
    Summit 1081–82
Strategic Plan for Biodiversity 2011–20 and
    UN Decade on Biodiversity 1081
UN Millennium Declaration, MDGs, and
    2010 Biodiversity Target 1078–79
UN World Summit 2005 1079–80

SDG 16 'Peaceful Sustainable Societies,
    Access to Justice for All and Effective
    Institutions' 1157–245
background 1157–58
formulating SDG 16 targets 1159
    access to justice 1163–64
    conceptual interlinkages and
        interdependence of thematic
        concepts 1164–65
    conflict resolution and post-conflict
        peace-building 1161–63
    elimination of violence against
        children 1164
    improvements to indicators in the post-
        MDGs period 1165–66
    inclusiveness and broad participation for
        social equity 1163
    reduction of corruption and bribery 1164
    role of institutions and their
        structuring 1161
    rule of law and interdependent
        concepts 1159–60
lack of specific measures 28–29
travaux préparatoires
    formulating SDG 16 targets: conceptual
        and thematic considerations 1159–66
    overview of preparatory
        initiatives 1158–59
SDG 17 'Revitalize the Global Partnership for
    Sustainable Development' 1247–323
background 1247–49
travaux préparatoires 1249–57
seas *see* oceans, seas, and marine resources
Sen, Amartya 531–32
    Development as Freedom 49
    *Poverty and Famines: An Essay on Entitlement
        and Deprivation* 130
Sendai Framework for Disaster Risk Reduction
    (2015–2030) 97, 99–101, 841, 854
    adoption and implementation of
        national/local risk reduction
        strategies 101
    cities 821, 843–44
    data requirements 99
    definition of disaster 99n.399, 105
    global disaster mortality 99–100
    indicator framework 842–43
    LDCs 100–1
    reporting, problems with 100–1
    weaknesses 104–5
Senegal
    agro-ecological transitions 178
    education 300
    gender equality 439

1378 INDEX

sexual and reproductive health and
    rights 374–75
    health-care services, universal access
      to 247–49
    indispensable component of human
      rights, as 428
    universal access to 428–31
sexual violence *see* violence and violent crime
Sierra Leone
    child labour 610–11
    child marriage 419–20
    corruption and bribery 1223
    education 108–9, 308
    FGM 415–16
    food security 170–71
    gender equality 390–91, 415–16, 420
    justice, access to 1216
    nationality laws 390–91
    right to information 1240
    water quality monitoring 505–6
Singapore
    corruption 1226
    crime 1207
    domestic violence 393–94
    education 316
    exports 1321
    justice and rule of law 1218
    public institutions 1227–28
slavery and servitude
    definition of slavery 603–4
    ECHR 601, 602
    forced labour *see under* employment and jobs
    ICCPR 575–76, 601, 602, 776–77
    UDHR 601, 602
    see also SDG 8
small island developing states *see* least developed
      countries (LDCs) and small island
      developing
    states (SIDS)
social security/protection systems
    adaptive social protection 83
    availability of social protection varying 78
    basic income for all 82–83
    COVID-19, and 78–79, 83
    employment, and 557
    floors 84
    government spending on essential
      services 106
    inequality, and 765–66
    inter-generational equity, and 766
    nationally appropriate social protection
      systems, poverty and 76–86
    obligations of states 84–86
    poverty reduction, and 86

social assistance 83–84
social insurance 83–84
social security as social good 766
UDHR, and 84–85
universal benefits 83–84
youth unemployment, impact of 628–29
Solomon Islands
    LDC status, leaving 687
Somalia
    education 309
    FGM 416
    nationality laws 390–91
South Africa
    ABS, and 1140
    citizen biomonitoring 505–6
    COVID-19, and 437–38
    education 315–16
      scholarships 361
    employment 630–31
    gender equality 390
    human rights 913–14
    information, right to 1240
    justice 1216
    marriage 390
    mobile phone ownership 434
    National Development Plan, SDGs, and 1198–99
    poverty, combating 754
    sanitation 467–68
    social protection 763, 764
    sustainability in public procurement 916–17
    urban design 880
    violence 1201
      gender-based violence 375–76, 437–38
    water quality monitoring 505–6
South America
    droughts 1114–15
    gender equality 384–85, 434
    informal settlements and slum dwelling 826–27
    mobile phone ownership 434
    poverty 60
    slum dwelling 826–27
South Sudan
    CRC 309
    debt servicing 116–17
    education 309
    gender equality 431
    social spending 116–17
Spain
    debt 117, 770
      debt servicing 117
    environmental legislation 1139–40
    gender equality 419
    legal frameworks and public life 382
    production subsidies reforms 945–46

INDEX 1379

species extinction, preventing 1124–30
  extinction rates 1125–26, 1128–29
  invasive alien species increasing risk of
    extinction 1148
  IUCN Red List 1126, 1129, 1148
  species extinction risk, worsening of 1126
  see also flora and fauna, protected species of
Sri Lanka
  education 316
  energy 537
  pollution 846
Stockholm Conference 46–47, 802–3
Stockholm Declaration 549–50, 624, 865, 1019,
  1028–29
  conservation of life on land 1087–88
  human-centric nature of 45
  sustainable development 45, 545, 621–22,
    1028–29
  under-development causing environmental
    degradation 1090
Sub-Saharan Africa
  agriculture 182–83
  armed conflicts 1203
  birth registration 1235–36, 1237
  bribery 1222
  child labour 610
  child marriage 415
  COVID-19, and 78, 172–73, 427
  debt 1284
  education 286, 288–89, 301, 316, 365–66
    scholarships for higher education 361
  energy 510–11, 528–29
  financial services 91
  food insecurity 170
  gender-based violence 398
  homicide 1200–1
  human rights 1238, 1242
  hunger 131–32, 169
  industrial enterprises 690–91
  Internet access 699
  IWRM implementation 481–82
  justice 1214–15
  land consumption 835
  malaria 240
  maternal mortality 231–32
  mobile money accounts, spread of 91
  mobile networks 699–700
  ODA, and 1278–79, 1280
  peace and stability 1204
  pollution 529–30
  poverty 62–63, 65, 1279–80
    pro-poor public spending 119
    reduction of 65, 68–69
  renewable sources, 536

safety 1207
SDGs, and 595–96
social protection, increase in 78
stunted children 172–73
undernourishment 131–32
violence 1206
  children, against 1209
  sexual violence 1213
waste collection 846
women's representation in local
  government 426
substance abuse
  alcohol *see* alcohol
  health, and *see* health
  strengthening prevention and treatment
    of 244–45
  tobacco *see* tobacco
Sudan
  depleted agriculture of lands, conflict
    and 124
  human trafficking 1211
  nationality laws 390–91
  peace and stability 1204
  refugees 1211
  wars 124, 1204, 1248, 1296–97
sustainable consumption and production
  10-year framework 872–76
  companies, and 905–12
  developing countries' scientific
    and technological capacity,
    supporting 928–32
  effective regulation, challenges to 868–70
  fossil-fuel subsidies, rationalizing 940–47
  international law, and 865–68
  relevant information for sustainable
    development, access to 921–28
  sustainable management and efficient use of
    natural resources 877–83
  sustainable public procurement
    practices 912–21
  sustainable tourism, and 933–40
  waste management *see* waste management
  see also SDG 12
sustainable development
  banking and financial institutions, and 565
  Brundtland Commission *see* Brundtland
    Commission/Report
  concept of
    different concepts/paradigms
      of 635, 641–42
    human development informing content
      of 22–23
    normative status of 1033–34
    sustainability, concept of 1033–34

1380 INDEX

sustainable development (*cont.*)
conflict resolution and peace as sustainable development concern 1174
corruption and bribery as sustainable development concern 1175–77
culture, and 641–42
definition of 22, 23–24, 45, 1170–71
education central to 277
environmental consequences of industrial agriculture on food production 123
food, critical role in sustainable development of 121–22
Global North and Global South, imbalances between 635
goal-setting for sustainable development governance 32
goals *see* Sustainable Development Goals (SDGs)
inclusivity and broad participation as sustainable development concern 1178–80
IUCN, and 634–35
legal divergences on 'sustainable' and 'development' 634–35
legal principle, sustainable development as 1170–71
legal aspects of sustainable development 1171
meaning and scope of sustainable development 1170–71
measurements of progress on sustainable development, developing 1306–13
multi-stakeholder partnerships 1315–22
non-discriminatory laws/policies, promoting 1243–44
objective of 22–24
origins of 'sustainable development' 634–35
policy coherence for sustainable development, enhancing 1313–15
private enterprises, and 638–39
global firms' activities, rule of law and 637–38
state and private enterprise interests, conflict between 638
respect for each country's policy space 1313–15
right to development 636–37, 638
relevance of 1172–74
rules under TRIPS Agreement superseding 637–38
rule of law, and 635–36, 637–38
global rules under TRIPS Agreement 637–38
sustainable development concern, as 1177–78

sustainable tourism, and *see* sustainable tourism
three dimensions of 121–22, 150–51, 640
three pillars of 23–24, 638, 640–41
TOSSD 109–10
UN Conference for Sustainable Development 25–27
UN Decade of Sustainable Development 343
WSSD 24–26, 479–80, 525, 1255
ecosystem approach 1099
JPOI *see* Johannesburg Plan of Implementation (JPOI)
MDGs, and 526
see also SDG 9; SDG 17
Sustainable Development Goals (SGDs)
adoption of 18–19, 441–42
broader framework of development goals 19
change agents, as 638
conflicting issues between goals 150–52
country-and context-specific implementation 165–66
criticisms of 28–31, 124–25
development of 134
development, right to 638
directly enshrined in Agenda 219–20
global instrument of collective action, as 641
holistic approach to development 19
human rights, and 19–21, 737–40
indicators 166–67
interdependence and indivisibility 19–20, 54
legal junction of global law, SDGs sitting at 635–36
legal nature of *see* legal nature of SDGs under international law
mainstream growth-oriented approach 378
MDGs, and *see under* Millennium Development Goals (MDGs)
measuring progress, crucial nature of 166
mechanisms to enforce compliance, weakness of 178
nature of 19, 32, 121, 441–42
neoliberalism, and 124–25, 151–52
new ethical visions of innovation, infrastructure and industry 640–41
non-legally binding 442
non-state actors, participation by 641
political history of *see* political history of the SDGs
respecting national policy space 54–55
restructuring of world's wealth-extracting mechanism not addressed 20–21
right to development, importance of 19–20
rights-based approach 379–80
seeking to realize human rights of all 19–20

set against targets and indicators focused on
measurable outcomes 19, 1017–18
states' primary responsibility to
implement 165
synergies and interlinkages between 148–52
targets and indicators as main regulatory
tools 166–67
transformative action plan 18–19
transformative dimension of
see transformative dimension of SDGs
universalist nature of 641
vague language 20–21
voluntary nature of 1017–18
World Conference on Sustainable
Development 618–19
see also individual SDGs
Sustainable Development Goals Report (2020) 63
Sustainable Development Solutions Network
(SDSN) 198, 513–14, 552–53, 569–71,
673, 1021
sustainable tourism 616–26
Agenda 21 618–19
benefits and disadvantages of tourism 617
development of 618–19
economic development from tourism 616–17
economic, social, and environmental
dimensions 619–20
ecotourism, value of 618–19
employment, and 624–25
job creation and promotion of local culture
and products 933–40
environment, and 617
GDP growth, tourism as driver of 616–17
Global Code of Ethics for Tourism
(GCET) 621–22
Hague Declaration on Tourism 621–22
human rights, and 620–21
impact on quality of life for local
communities 617
nature-based tourism 617
definition of 619–20
UNWTO 619–20
regulatory framework for tourism 618–
19, 625–26
stakeholder rights and duties 620–21
sustainable development objectives,
and 625–26
monitoring sustainable development
impacts for 933–40
Tourist Code and Tourism Bill of
Rights 621–22
UNWTO 616–17
definition of sustainable tourism 619–20
guidelines 618–19

value of ecotourism 618–19
value of international tourism 616–17
see also SDG 8
Swaziland
nationality laws 390–91
Sweden
code of conduct for suppliers 919–20
education 294, 324
emissions 693
energy 514–15, 541
FGM, risk of 419
financing 691
gender equality in work and family 424
human rights 736
migrant workers 793
ODA 294
sexual and reproductive health
rights 431
social protection 79, 763
redistribution through taxes and
transfers 764
women's empowerment 514–15
Syria 1248
nationality laws 390–91
wars 1248, 1296–97

Tanzania
birth registration 1237
corruption 1224
domestic violence 408–13
energy 513
environmental legislation 1139–40
environmental protection 989
extractive industries 660
polygamy 388–89
violence against women 382, 408–13
technology
adopting clean and environmentally sound
technologies 691–93
see also innovation
technology transfer 16–17, 103–4, 544, 697,
740–41, 1000, 1079–80, 1295–313
climate change mitigation and
adaptation 930, 1009
developed countries, and 700
developing countries, and 513–14, 648,
899–900
global pandemics, and 701
low-carbon technology transfer 964
Thailand
circular economy 693
education 291, 308, 316
exports of shrimps 867
sustainable tourism 933–34

1382 INDEX

tobacco
  cigarette consumption 257
  cost of 258
  development agenda, and 258, 259–60
  finance, and 258
  measures to reverse tobacco epidemic 257
  risk factor in non-communicable
    diseases 241, 242
  VNRs, tobacco control measures and 257
  WHO Framework Convention on Tobacco
    Control 256–58
Togo
  nationality laws 390–91
tourism *see* sustainable tourism
trade
  agriculture, trade restrictions and distortions
    in 184–85
  Aid for Trade 583, 627–28, 784–85
  cap and trade schemes 976–79
  carbon taxes 979–82
  developing countries
    implement duty-free and quota-free
      market access 1293–95
    increase exports of 1293–95
  food commodity markets 186–87
  FTAs *see* free trade agreements (FTAs)
  GATT *see* General Agreement on Tariffs and
    Trade (GATT)
  inequality, and 740–42
  international trade law *see* international
    trade law
  investment, aid, and 740–42
  local content requirements (LCRs),
    and 1287–89
  trade and market-related targets 1286–95
  trade liberalization, orthodox positions
    on 29–30
  TRIPS Agreement *see* Treaty on Trade-
    Related Aspects of Intellectual Property
    Rights (TRIPs) Agreement
  WTO *see* World Trade Organization (WTO)
trafficking and sexual exploitation 395, 396,
    413, 603–4
  definition of exploitation 602
  definition of trafficking 602
  employment, trafficking and
    see under employment and jobs
  exploitation as *mens rea* of trafficking 602
  tourism, and 617
  trafficking of children 413, 1211, 1212
  victims per 100, 000, by sex, age, form of
    exploitation 1210–12
transformative dimension of SDGs 27–31
  bold character of new action plan 27–28

  criticisms of 28–31
  development still viewed through
    neoliberalism 30–31
  economic growth to eradicate poverty,
    criticism of 20–21, 28–29
  global well-being, addressing 27–28
  growth representing sole measure of
    progress 30–31
  orthodox positions on trade liberalization,
    prominence of 29–30
  systemic changes to wealth generating
    sources, need for 28–29
  whether development goals founded on
    specific theory of development 30
transnational corporations 667–71
  acting in own capacity as shapers of formal
    pillars on economic development 670
  economic growth, and 667–68, 670–71
  investments and/or intellectual property
    rights 670–71
  maximizing sustainable development for their
    benefit 669–71
Treaty on Trade-Related Aspects of
    Intellectual Property Rights (TRIPs)
    Agreement 637–38
  Doha Declaration on the TRIPS Agreement
    and Public Health 258–61
  global rules under 637–38
  rules under TRIPS superseding right to
    development 637–38
  vaccines, and 701
Trinidad and Tobago
  employment 562–63
  energy 513
  marginalised groups 115
  sexual and reproductive health rights 431
Tunisia
  migration 107
  violence against women 384
Turkey
  biking strategy 831–32
  REACH, and 895
  scholarships 361
  technology 1305
  waste management 864–65

Uganda
  ABS, and 1140
  climate change 989
  education 316, 318–19, 355
  electricity 528–29
  extractive industries 660
  FGM 416
  food and agricultural production 178

gender-based violence 399–400
governmental processes 1230
safety 1207
sexual violence 1213
UN Addis Ababa Action Agenda *see* Addis
        Ababa Action Agenda (AAAA)
UN Charter 53–54, 152–53
    Agenda 2030, and 32–33
    equity, equality, and
        non-discrimination 19–20
    full employment 574–75
    INGOs 666
    international organisations, sustainable
        development and 666
    states' obligations 23–24
    values enshrined in 8–9
UN Conference on Food and Agriculture
        (1943) 127–28
UN Conference on Sustainable Development
        (Rio + 20 Conference and Group of 20
        (G20) Los
    Cabos Summit 25–27, 37, 133–34, 197,
        1081–82
    development of goals for sustainable
        development 26
    'Future We Want' 25–26, 37–39, 133–
        34, 200–1
        focus on poverty reduction 37–38, 44–
            45, 49
        'people-centred' development 87
        state-led process for determining
            goals 38–39
        sustainable development and sustainable
            future 37
    OWG *see* Open Working Group (OWG)
UN Conference on the Human Environment
        (1972) 21, 45, 802–3
UN Conference on Trade and Development
        (UNCTAD) 132
    Core Indicators 910–11
    food prices 132
    illicit financial flows 1193, 1219,
        1274–75
UN Convention of the Law of the Sea *see* Law of
        the Sea Convention (LOSC)
UN Convention to Combat Desertification
        (UNCCD) *see under* desertification
UN Declaration on the Rights of Indigenous
        Peoples 282–83
UN Department of Economic and Social Affairs
        (UNDESA) 111–12, 197
    environmental objectives, and 730
    inequality 734–35
    SDG website 809

UN Development Programme (UNDP) 197,
        200–1, 804
    best practice for aid donors 111
    gender equality 380
    Human Development Report 6–8, 23–24
    SDGs, and 665–66
    spectrum of activities 66
UN Economic and Social Council (ECOSOC)
        see ECOSOC
UN Economic Commission for Europe
        (UNECE) *see under* European Union/
        Europe
UN Educational, Scientific and Cultural
        Organization *see* UNESCO
UN Environment Programme (UNEP) 666,
        1036–37, 1250–51
    developing countries 1090
    disaster reduction 842–43, 854
    fossil fuel subsidies 943–44
    lead paint 255
    public procurement 914–15, 916–17
    SDG Indicators 914–15, 1049, 1051
    sustainable consumption 873
    sustainable development 1036–37, 1091
    sustainable tourism 618–19
    waste 896–97, 902
        food waste 885–86, 888
        hazardous waste 823
UN Fish Stocks Agreement *see under* oceans,
        seas, and marine resources 1032–33
UN Framework Convention of Climate Change
        (UNFCCC) 534, 666, 952, 961–62, 1311
    desertification 1114, 1115, 1125
    education, training, and public
        awareness 1001–02
    food waste 888–89
    forests 1109, 1111
    objectives 1253–54
    'precautionary 'approach 958–59
    reporting requirements 988, 994, 999–1000
    SDGs, and 666, 701, 949
    States' parties' obligations 995, 1111
    sustainable development, principle of 958
    transfer of financial resources 1006–07
UN General Assembly
    declaration on the right to
        development 636–37
    OWG on SDGs *see* Open Working
        Group (OWG)
    UN Decade for the Eradication of
        Poverty 64–65
UNDRO, establishment of 102
UN Global Compact 462, 569, 608–9, 778
    soft law, as 778–79

1384 INDEX

UN Guiding Principles on Business and Human
    Rights 608–9
UN-Habitat
    country programmes for sustainable urban
        development 93–94
    Global Land Tool Network (GLTN) 93
    Habitat Agenda 802–7
    land tenure 91–94
    New Urban Agenda *see under* cities
    SDGs, and 666, 802–7, 809–11
UN Human Rights Office of the High
    Commissioner (OHCHR) 153–54
    human rights indicators 221–22
UN Industrial Development Organization
    (UNIDO) 647
UN International Children's Emergency Fund
    see UNICEF
UN International Conference on Nutrition 131
UN Millennium Campaign
    supporting implementation of MDG 3
UN Millennium Project 3
    supporting implementation of MDG 3
UN Office on Drugs and Crime (UNODC)
    gender equality 380
    human trafficking 395
    illicit financial flows 1193, 1219
    reducing all forms of violence 849–50
    WHO, and 211
UN Population Fund (UNFPA) 200–1
    gender equality 380
    WHO, and 211
UN Scientific Conference on Conservation
    and Utilization of Resources 1949
    (UNSCCUR) 21
UN Special Rapporteur on Extreme Poverty and
    Human Rights
    IMF 81
    Report on the Parlous State of Poverty
        Eradication (2020) 56–57
UN Special Rapporteur on the Right to
    Food 132–33, 156–57
    Guiding Principles on Human Rights Impact
        Assessments 162
UN Statistical Commission 61, 166
    'Global Indicator Framework for the
        SDGs' 166, 582–83
UN Statistics Division (UNSID)
    gender equality 380
UN Watercourses Convention *see under* water
    and sanitation
UN Women *see under* women
UN World Conference on Natural Disaster
    Reduction 103
UN World Population Plan of Action 230–31

UN World Summit 2005 1079–80, 1167, 1256
UN World Summit on Social Development 47
UN World Summit on Sustainable Development
    2002 (WSSD) *see under* sustainable
    development
UN World Tourism Organization (UNWTO)
    see under sustainable tourism
undernourishment *see under* health
UNECE Water Convention *see under* water and
    sanitation
unemployment *see under* employment and jobs
UNESCO
    cities, and 820–21
    cultural and natural heritage 839
    education, and *see under* education
    fisheries 1036–37
    IHP WINS initiative 504–5
    Institute for Statistics (UIS)
        data collection by 108
        education 301, 367
        partners 108
    World Education Forum in Education For
        All 269
UNICEF
    burdens of debt payments 116
    data collection on pro-poor public
        spending 116
    deaths of newborns and children under
        5 years, reducing 233
    DSSI, effects of 118
    gender equality 380
    health 198, 200–1
    malnourishment in children 173–74
    UN Inter-Agency Group for Child Mortality
        Estimation (UN IGME) 234–35
    WHO, and 210
United Arab Emirates
    nationality laws 390–91
    women in parliament 426
United Kingdom
    anti-corruption agencies, assistance
        to 1223–24
    CBDR 863
    child trafficking 1212
    COVID-19, and 393–94
    domestic violence 393–94
    education 273, 280–81, 294, 368
        private schools 359
        scholarships 361
    employment 750
    energy 536, 1287–89
    equality 423, 1218
    financial surveillance 771
    food loss 888

gender equality 423
health MDGs 196
homelessness 89
homicide 1202
human rights 53
inclusion and diversity 754–55
  disability inclusion 758
justice 1218
least-developed countries, taxation and 781
ODA 183, 294, 360–61, 786
public open space in cities 850
research and development 929
violence 1202
  children, against 1212
United States
Agreement on Environmental Cooperation
    (AEC) 1290–91
agriculture
  dumping food surpluses in developing
      countries 158–59
  exporting industrialized agriculture
      production methods 129–30
  food supply, ensuring 129
  subsidizing 129, 158–59
Bill & Melinda Gates Foundation 259–60
CBD, and 1101
CBDR, and 874–75
CEDAW, and 819–20
climate change, and 973
connecting the poor to markets 87–88
COVID-19, and 366–67
domestic violence 393–94
droughts 1114–15
education 108–9, 289, 300, 330–31, 339
  bullying 354–55
  cyberbullying 356
  private sector 363–64
  remote learning 366–67
emission trading schemes 977
fallacy of intractability 58
fiscal and/or monetary policies 763
food donation 887
food supply 129
food waste 883–84
fossil fuels 878–79
gender equality 385
green patent 930–31
homelessness 89
hunger 129–30
  'War against Hunger' campaign 129–30
import of shrimps 867
Kyoto Protocol, and 965
maternal health 230
maternity leave 385

National Institute of Allergy and Infectious
    Diseases (NIAID) 259–60
natural hazards 685
ODA 10–11, 109, 183
Pan American Sanitary Bureau 209–10
Paris Agreement, and 967
poverty levels 70
research and development 929
social protection 78, 79
UDHR, and 279–80
water
  Colorado Treaty 490–91
  cost of water services 459–60
  water conservation 490–91
  water services 459–60, 474
zero commitments 969
Universal Declaration of Human Rights
    (UDHR) 152–53, 773–74
Agenda 2030, and 32–33
dignity of the individual versus the
    state 279–80
education see under education
employment, and see under employment
    and jobs
equity, equality, and
    non-discrimination 19–20
FGM, and 415
forced and compulsory labour 601, 602
government, participation in 834–35
MDGs drawing upon 2
right to adequate standard of living 215
right to food 154–55
right to health 215, 218–19
slavery and servitude 601, 602
social protection 84–85
women's equal rights to property 431
universal health coverage (UHC)
achieving 250–53
practical expression of right to health,
    as 218, 221
universal access to sexual and reproductive
    health and rights 428–31
VNRs 252
WHO, and see under World Health
    Organization (WHO)
see also SDG 3
unpaid care and domestic work 420–24
CEDAW 420
COVID-19, effect of 421–22
definition of 421
less straightforward human rights
    dimension 424
time spent by women on 420–22, 556
urban living see cities

1386 INDEX

Uruguay
crime 1202
energy 530
fossil fuels 945
innovation and technology 645–46
pollution 846
sexual and reproductive health rights 431

vaccines and medicines
affordable essential medicines, access
to 258, 261
international trade law as impediment to
sharing access 258–59
COVID-19, vaccine availability, and 66
Doha Declaration on the TRIPS Agreement
and Public Health 258–61
Gavi 259–60
health systems strengthening (HSS),
focus on 227
Global Vaccine Action Plan 259–60
human rights, and 261
research and development of 239, 258–61
vaccine nationalism 261
vaccines for all 258
WHO Model List of Essential Medicines 261
Vanuatu
ABS 1140
biodiversity 1140
sexual violence, non-partner 394–95
Venezuela
child marriage 420
Vietnam
discrimination in employment 439
education 291, 316, 332–33
IWRM, and 481
sustainable consumption and
production 875–76
sustainable tourism 937–38
violence and domestic violence against women
COVID-19, and 393–94, 400–1, 437–38
DEVAW 379, 392
effects of 392
elimination of 392–413
importance of prevention through
education 400–2
lack of protection from domestic
violence 383, 387
levels of domestic violence 393–94
marital rape 385
sexual violence, non-partner 394–95
statistics 393–95
trafficking see trafficking and sexual
exploitation
types of violence 392–93

physical violence 393, 402–8
psychological violence 393, 402–8
sexual violence 393, 402–8
violence as form of discrimination 392
see also SDG 5
violence and violent crime
children, and see under children
conflict-related deaths 1202–5
feelings of safety walking alone 1206–8
intentional homicide, victims of 1199–202,
1237–39
'honour' crimes 390
kidnapping, enforced disappearance,
arbitrary detention and
torture 1237–39
physical, psychological, and sexual
violence 1205–6
reduction of violence and related death
rates 1199–208
sexual violence 1205–6
experienced by age 18 1213
strengthening institutions to prevent
violence/combat terrorism and
crime 1240–43
trafficking see trafficking and sexual
exploitation
women, and see violence and domestic
violence against women
Voluntary National Reviews (VNRs) 170–71,
736, 991–92, 1198–99, 1244–45
biodiversity 1151–52
bribery 1223
climate change 1005
courts and justice 1217, 1218
decision-making 1230
energy policy 537–38
enhanced representation within
IFIs 772
food security and nutrition issues 170–71
adequate nutrition of children and
women 173–74
foreign and development policies 736
illicit financial flows 1219
impact of COVID-19 706–7
indigenous peoples 1179–80
mountain ecosystems 1120–21
multi-stakeholder participation in the SDGs
process 1232
prisons 1215
SDG implementation domestically 736,
758, 762–63
tobacco control measures 257
trafficking of children 1211, 1212
UHC 252

INDEX   1387

Washington Consensus 5–6
waste management
   cities, in 845, 846–47, 848
   environmentally sound management of
      waste 891–99
   food waste and losses 883–91
   hazardous *see* hazardous chemicals and waste
   LDCs 900
   recycling and reuse 899–905
   waste collection during COVID-19 846
   waste generation, reduction of 899–905
water and sanitation
   access to adequate equitable sanitation and
      hygiene for all 462–68
     definition of sanitation 463–64
     inadequate sanitation, deaths resulting
       from 468
     needs of women and girls and those in
       vulnerable situations 463
     right to sanitation 458–59, 462–68
     States' obligation 464–65
   access to safe and affordable drinking water,
      universal and equitable 453–62, 463
     performance standards for utilities 460–62
     right to water 445–46, 457, 458–59, 462,
      464–65, 466, 483–84
     safety and quality of water 457–58
   affordability of water and sanitation
      services 458–60
     policy determined by national
      authorities 459–60
   African Ministers Council on Water
     (AMCOW) 451–52
   Berlin Rules on Water Resources
     Law 456, 457
   CBD, and *see* Convention for Biological
     Diversity (CBD)
   expanding international cooperation/
     capacity-building for water-related
     activities 492–95
     development assistance 493–95
     duties on States parties 494–95
     ODA 492–93
   Global Consultation on Safe Water and
     Sanitation 447
   Global Water Partnership (GWP) 478
   Helsinki Rules 456, 474
   implementation of integrated water resources
     management 478–86
     integrated water resources
      management 478–82
     transboundary cooperation 482–86
   improvement of water quality by reducing
     pollution 469–72

     environmental standards in multilateral
      agreements 471–72
     prevention, control and reduction of
      pollution 469–70
     protection of the natural
      environment 470–71
   increase of water-use efficiency and
     sustainable withdrawals 472–77
     water efficiency 472–75
     water scarcity 475–77
   integrated water resources
     management 478–82
     constraints 478
     criticisms of 481
     definition of 446–79
     facilitating complex coordination of
      multiple interests 480–81
     institutional coordination, need for 480
     key dimensions of 481–82
     legal status of 479–80
   International Drinking Water Supply and
     Sanitation Decade (1981–1990) 447
   natural water resources, protection from
     contamination of 465
   protection and restoration of water-related
     ecosystems 486–92
     climate change, and 491
     critical importance of maintaining
      ecosystems 486
     ecosystem approach 443–44, 453, 487–90,
      491, 500, 502
     inland water biodiversity 487–89
     river basins as ecosystems 487–89, 490–91
     shared international basins 489–90
     shared international groundwater
      resources 490
     watercourse ecosystems, ILC definition
      of 487–89
     wetlands *see* Ramsar Convention
   supporting local communities in
     improving water and sanitation
     management 495–502
     good governance, and 496
     Indigenous communities 497, 498
     need to actively promote
      participation 496–97
     procedures for participation 495–96
     promoting national arrangements for
      facilitating participation 495–96
     public participation 497–500, 501–2
     stakeholder engagement 500–1
   toilet facilities, unenclosed 467–68
   transboundary cooperation 482–86
     duty to cooperate 482–83

1388 INDEX

water and sanitation (*cont.*)
    inter-state institutional machinery, need
      for 485–86
    recourse for unlawful activities 484–85
    right to water, and 483
    States' obligations 481–84
    UN Global Compact's CEO Water
      Mandate 451–52
    UN Secretary-General
      Advisory Board on Water and
        Sanitation 450–52
      SDGs, and 665–66
    UN Watercourses Convention 471, 489–90
    codification of customary obligations 1101
    ecosystem protection obligations 486,
      487–89, 491, 1100
    equitable and reasonable utilization 454–
      56, 474, 492, 495
    equitable participation 495
    inter-state engagement 499
    pollution provisions 469–70
    water-borne invasive species 1147
    UNECE Protocol on Water and Health 504–5
    UNECE Water Convention 471
    codification of customary obligations 1101
    ecosystem protection and
      conservation 489–90, 1100
    prevention, control and reduction of
      transboundary impact 469–66
    stakeholder participation 499
    State parties' obligations 485–86, 499, 1100
    transboundary groundwaters 490
    water efficiency 472–75
    improving efficiency of water-use as
      complex exercise 472–74
    requirement of efficiency in international
      water law 474
    States' duty to conserve and augment water
      supply 475
    Water Information Network System
      (WINS) 504–5
    water scarcity 475–77
    data collection and analysis 476
    water-stressed renewable freshwater
      resources 475–76
    water security 492
    water-related ecosystems
      protecting and restoring 486–92
    see also SDG 6
'We the Peoples' report 48
wetlands
    conservation, restoration and sustainable use
      of 1098–107
    protecting and restoring 486–92

    Ramsar Convention 1098–99, 1101,
      1125, 1143
    conservation and sustainable use of
      wetlands 1036–37, 1098–99
    threatened habitats of international
      importance 1087–88
    use of wetlands as habitats 1127
women and girls
    CEDAW, and 172, 230–31
    discrimination against women, definition
      of 381, 388
    education 273, 282, 328, 401–2
    eliminating discrimination against
      women 381, 759, 760–61
    eliminating gender biases from
      education 401–2
    nationality laws 390–91
    right to sanitation 466–67
    sexual and reproductive health and
      rights 428
    temporary special measures, adopting 431
    unpaid care and domestic work 420
    violence as form of discrimination 392
    women's equal legal capacity in civil
      matters 431
    women's equal political rights and
      participation in public life 425
    women's health 216–17, 230–31
    women's right to vote and hold public
      office 425
    see also gender equality; SDG 5 'Gender
      Equality and Empower All Women
      and Girls'
changing role of women, effects of 55–56
cities, and
    safe, inclusive, accessible, green public
      spaces 848–51
    transport systems, women's safety needs
      and 833
COVID-19
    effects of 63–64
    labour sector and women's economic
      insecurity, and 427
discrimination against *see* gender equality
economic participation, law reform
    on 439–40
economic resources, access to 431–34
education *see* education
employment and jobs *see* employment
    and jobs
empowerment of small-scale farmers 122–23
farmers 122–23, 149–50, 175–76
    productivity 175
FGM *see* female genital mutilation (FGM)

INDEX 1389

financial services 433–34
gender equality *see* gender equality; SDG
    5 'Gender Equality and Empower All
    Women and Girls'
health
    anaemia in women 15–49 years 173
    discrimination, eliminating 216–17
    Global Strategy for Women's, Children's
        Health and Adolescents' Health
        2016–2030 231
ICT, and *see* ICT/digital skills
inheritance rights *see under* marriage and
    family life
leadership opportunities in public
    life 425–28
local government, women in 426, 427–28
Maputo Protocol 1047–48
    right to food 172
    right to sanitation 466–67
marriage and family life *see* marriage and
    family life
maternal health 8–9, 172
    global concern, issue as 230–31
    improvement of maternal health 1–2
    maternal mortality rates 231–32
    nutritional needs of pregnant and lactating
        women 172
    reduction of global maternal
        mortality 216–17, 230–33
    UN's Maternal Mortality Estimation Inter-
        Agency Group 232–33
    WHO's Safe Motherhood Initiative 230–31
    see also commentary on SDG 3 targets
ownership and control of land, property,
    financial services 431–34
parliament, women in 426, 427–28
political, economic and public life *see* gender
    equality
sexual and reproductive health and rights
    see sexual and reproductive health
    and rights
suffrage 383–84
trafficking *see* trafficking and sexual
    exploitation
UN Decade for Women 230–31
UN Women 555
    access to safe public spaces 849–50, 851
    employment opportunities in digital
        sectors 325
    gender data 377–78
    gender equality/empowerment of
        women 377–78, 380, 383, 393, 394, 397,
        421–22, 425–26, 436–37
    health 200–1

unpaid care and domestic work *see* unpaid
    care and domestic work
violence against *see* violence and domestic
    violence against women
vulnerable group, poverty and 65–66, 71–72
Women's Major Group 201–2, 379–80
World Bank/World Bank Group
    agriculture, focus on 132–33
    BEST Project 531
    child marriage 419
    creation 1286
    data on education expenditures 108
    data on poverty, lack of 52–53
    disasters 101
    Environmental and Social Framework
        on Labour and Working
        Conditions 608–9
    food security 130–31
    gender equality 380
        combating gender-based violence 399–400
        women's economic rights 387
    Global Findex project 91
    global poverty 28
        absolute poverty approach 67
        levels of 61–62
        progress on reducing extreme poverty
            slowing 59
    health systems strengthening (HSS),
        focus on 227
    Heavily Indebted Poor Countries Initiative
        (HIPC) 118
    International Bank for Reconstruction and
        Development (IBRD) 573, 1232
        voting reform 772
    International Finance Corporation
        (IFC) 772, 1232–33
        performance standards 608–9
    land tenure 91
    loan conditionalities on developing countries,
        imposing 158–59
    Multilateral Debt Relief Initiative (2005) 118
    Reversals of Fortune report 63
    SDG 8, and 548, 569, 573
        monitoring role 573
    SDGs, and 639–40, 665–66
    social protection, increase in 78
    tertiary education, funding 359
    urban policy 804
    Voices of the Poor project 48, 49
    weighted voting system, effects of 771–72
    WHO, and 211
    World Bank Group Strategy 573
    World Development Report (1990) 7–8, 45
        purpose of development 7–8

1390 INDEX

World Commission on Environment and
Development (WCED or Brundtland
Commission) *see* Brundtland
Commission/Report
World Data Lab's World Poverty Clock 59–60
World Food Summit (1996) 164
Plan of Action 164, 169
World Health Organization (WHO)
Alma-Ata Conference on Primary Health
Care 193–94
Commission on Macroeconomics and
Health 194–95
COVID-19, and 259–60
development agenda, health as part of 213
'End TB' strategy 240–41
establishment 209
framework and operation, origins of 209–10
gender equality 380
Global Action Plan for Healthy Lives and
Well-being for All (2019) 211, 242
Global Action Plan on Antimicrobial
Resistance 263, 264
Global Health Expenditure Database 108–9
Global Health Sector Strategies for HIV, Viral
Hepatitis and STIs 238–39, 240–41
Global Reference List of 100 Core Health
Indicators 227
Global Strategy on Human Resources for
Health: Workforce 2030 262
Global Strategy on Water Sanitation and
Hygiene 240–41
Global Technical Strategy for Malaria
2016–30 240–41
Health for All strategy 193–94, 230–31
health, meaning of 218
health spending data, collection of 108
health systems strengthening (HSS),
focus on 227
healthy life expectancy measurement 211–12
human right to health, Constitution
defining 209
key player in international health policies,
as 194–95
lead role in achieving good health and
well-being 209–12
mandate 209–10
combating infectious diseases and
improving public health 213
maternal mortality *see under* women
MDGs, and 196, 210
'Mental Health Action Plan' 241–42
Millennium Declaration, and 195–96
Model List of Essential Medicines 261
primary healthcare/'Health for All' 193–94

right to health
meaning of 218
protection of right to health as core
objective 214–15
'Road Map for Neglected Tropical
Diseases' 240–41
sexual and reproductive health-care
services 247–49
spearheading global health agenda 196
structure 209–10
suicide prevention report 241–42
'Triple Billion targets' 263, 264
UN Inter-Agency Group for Child Mortality
Estimation (UN IGME) 234–35
UN Secretary-General's High-Level
Panel on Women's Economic
Empowerment 424
understanding of health 218
universal health coverage as core
objective 192–93, 194–95, 218
core element of the global health
agenda, as 195
vaccine inequality 704–5
water, safety of 457–58
well-being
concept of 218
state of 'well-being, monitoring
methodology of 212
WHO Framework Convention on Tobacco
Control 256–58
World Health Organization Quality of Life
(WHOQOL) 212
see also SDG 3
World Heritage Convention
cities 837–38, 839
forests 1109
mountain ecosystems 1118, 1121
natural heritage sites 1087–88
natural terrestrial habitats 1127–28
species extinction 1125
wild species, protecting 1143
World Meteorological Organization
(WMO) 200–1, 847–48, 1013–14,
1250–51
World Trade Organization (WTO) 25
Agreement on Agriculture
(AoA) 146, 158–59
Aid for Trade 583, 627–28, 784–85
SDG targets on trade pursued under 29–30
SDGs, and 665–66
special and differential treatment (SDT)
agreements
developing countries and LDCs,
for 779–85

Enabling Clause 782
Monitoring Mechanism 781–82
typology of SDT provisions in WTO
    agreements 781–83
sustainable development, and 633
universal, rules-based, equitable multilateral
    trading system 1289–93

Zambia
corruption 1224

employment 630–31
energy 946
gender-based violence 1206
maternal mortality 231–33
Zimbabwe
corruption 1224
food security 170–71
global data economy 696
public procurement 1224
SDGs, and 696